DATE DUE

AP 30			
MAY 0 4 2007			
GAYLORD			PRINTED IN U.S.A.

1980 CATHOLIC ALMANAC

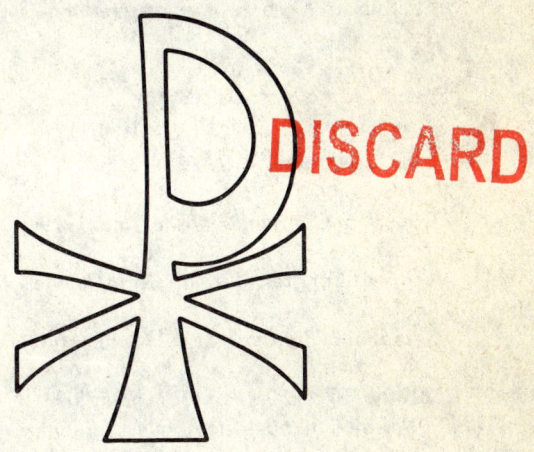

FELICIAN A. FOY, O.F.M.
Editor

Our Sunday Visitor, Inc.
Huntington, Indiana 46750

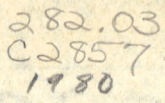
282.03
C2857
1980

Acknowledgments: NC News Service for coverage of news and documentary texts; *The Documents of Vatican II,* Walter M. Abbott, S.J., general editor, Herder and Herder, America Press, New York, 1966, for quotations; *Annuario Pontificio, 1979; The Official Catholic Directory, 1979,* P. J. Kenedy & Sons, New York; The United States Catholic Mission Council, 1302 Eighteenth St. N.W., Washington, D.C. 20036, for U.S. foreign mission compilations and statistics; *Catholic Press Directory, 1979; CCCB 1979 Directory,* copyright © Concacan, Inc., 1979, with permission of the Canadian Conference of Catholic Bishops, 90 Parent Ave., Ottawa, Ont. K1N 7B1, for Canadian Catholic statistics. Other sources are credited in various entries.

Rose M. Avato, Associate Editor

1980 CATHOLIC ALMANAC

©*Copyright Our Sunday Visitor, Inc. 1979*

Library of Congress Catalog Card Number: 73-641001

International Standard Serial Number (ISSN) 0069-1208

ISBN 0-87973-250-4 Paperbound Edition
ISBN 0-87973-260-1 Clothbound Edition

Published with Ecclesiastical Approval

Published, printed and bound in U.S.A. by
Our Sunday Visitor, Inc.
Huntington, Indiana 46750

TABLE OF CONTENTS

Index	4-46
A Journey of Faith	47
Special Reports	48-96
Pope John Paul II	48-49
Papal Pilgrimage to Latin America, Addresses	49-56
Puebla — Keynote Address	53-55
Papal Visit to Poland, Addresses ..	56-61
Papal Visit to Ireland and the United States	62-65
Addresses of John Paul II in Ireland	65-68
Addresses of John Paul II in the United States	68-75
Address to the U.N.	68-70
Redemptor Hominis, Encyclical Letter of John Paul II	75-79
Letter of Pope John Paul II to Priests	79-81
Quand Je Dis Dieu	81
Life after Death	82
Human Sexuality	83-84
Third General Assembly of Latin American Bishops	85-87
Ministry to the Spanish Speaking .	87-89
Black Catholics	89-90
National Catechetical Directory ..	90-91
Abortion Controversy	91-93
Test-Tube Baby	93-94
DNA Research	94
Ministries of the Church	95
Cults	96
News Events	97-154
Dates, Events in Church History	155-65
Ecumenical Councils	166-68
Popes	169-85
20th Century Popes	174-8
Canonizations, Encyclicals	180-8
Hierarchy of the Catholic Church	186-90
Synod of Bishops	188-90
Roman Curia	190-99
Cardinals	199-215
Representatives of the Holy See	215-18
Diplomats at the Vatican	219-20
Vatican City	221-23
Doctrine of the Catholic Church	224-55
Constitution on the Church	224-27
The Pope, Teaching Authority Collegiality	227-29
Constitution on Revelation	229-32
The Bible	233-44
Apostles and Evangelists	245-46
Fathers and Doctors	246-49
Social Doctrine	251-55
Liturgy	256-69
Constitution on the Liturgy	256-58
The Mass	259-61
Liturgical Developments	264-69
Sacraments	270-89
Permanent Diaconate	277-80
Marriage Doctrine	281-83
Pastoral Aspects of Marriage	287-88
Church Calendar	290-304
1980 Calendar	294-99
Saints	305-15
The Mother of Jesus	315-19
Apparitions of Mary	319-20
Eastern Catholic Churches	321-28
Separated Eastern Churches	328-30
Eastern Ecumenism	330-31
Protestant Churches	332-37
Ecumenism	338-48
Ecumenical Dialogues	341-47
Catholic-Jewish Relations	348-50
Judaism	350-51
Islam	351-52
Non-Revealed Religions	352
Glossary	353-95
Biographies	396-418
The Church in Countries throughout the World	419-53
Catholic World Statistics	454-55
Episcopal Conferences	455-58
Catholic International Organizations	458-60
The Catholic Church in Canada	461-72
Biographies of Canadian Bishops .	463-68
Catholic Church Statistics	469-70
History, Chronology of Church in U.S.	473-91
Church-State Supreme Court Decisions, Tax Exemption	491-96
U.S. Hierarchy, Jurisdictions, Statistics	497-521
National Catholic Conferences	521-26
State Catholic Conferences	526-27
Biographies of American Bishops ...	527-67
Religious, Men and Women	568-601
Secular Institutes, Orders	601-04
Missionary Activity of the Church ...	605-09
Catholic Education	610-29
Legal Status, U.S.	610-11
School Aid Decisions	612
Catholic School Statistics	613-17
Catholic Teacher Unions	618
Universities and Colleges in U.S. ..	619-24
Seminaries	624-27
Pontifical Universities, Institutes .	627-29
Pontifical Academy of Sciences	629-30
Social Services	631-48
Facilities for Retired and Aged	631-40
Facilities for Handicapped	640-46
Retreats	649-55
Lay Persons and Their Apostolate ...	656-70
Special Apostolates	657-61
Associations, Movements, Societies	662-70
Communications	671-93
Catholic Periodicals in U.S.	671-81
Catholic Writers' Market	683-86
Radio, Television, Theatre	686-88
Communications Offices	689-93
Honors and Awards	694-703
Deaths	703-04

INDEX

A

Abba, 353
Abbess, 353
Abbey, (Monastery), 380
Abbeys (Abbacies) Nullius, 353
Abbot, 353
Abelard, Peter, 396
Abington v. Schempp (Prayer in Public Schools), 495
Abjuration, 353
Ablution, 353
Aborigines, Australia, Bishops Statement, 115
Abortion (Moral Principles), 73, 353
   French Bishops' Conference, 126
   Italian Bishops' Conference, 106
Abortion, Norway, 135
   Pro-Life Movement, Europe, 112
Abortion Controversy, Developments, U.S. 91-93, 109
   Akron Law, 144
   Anti-Abortion Medical Students, Discrimination, 108, 129
   Conscience Clauses, 94, 124
   Constitutional Convention, 134
   Funding for, 104, 115, 118-19, 128, 134
   In-Hospital Performance, 134
   Lutheran-Church Missouri Synod Resolution, 139
   March for Life, 110
   Medicaid Records, 99
   Notre Dame Conference, 153
   Payment by Private Employers, 134
   Planned Parenthood, 99
   Right to Life Vote, 99
   See also Birthright; Life, Respect for
Abramowicz, Alfred L., Bp., 527
Absolution, 353
   See also Penance (Penitential Celebrations)
Absolution, General, 122, 353
Abstinence, Days of, 292
   Byzantine Rite, 293
Acacius, Patriarch (484), 157
Academy of American Franciscan History, 662
Academy of California Church History, 662
Acadians, see Canada, Church in
Accessory to Sin, 353
Accommodated Senses (Bible), 243
Achillini, Alessandro, 396
Ackerman, Richard, C.S.Sp., Bp., 527
Acolyte, 277
Act of Supremacy (1533), 161
Acta Apostolicae Sedis, 222
Acta Sanctae Sedis, 222
Actors' Guild, Catholic, 687
Acts of the Apostles, 240
Actual Grace, 372
Actual Sin, 390
Ad Gentes (Mission Decree), 168
Ad Limina Visit, 98, 187
Ad Lucem (Internatl. Organization), 458
Ad Purpuratorum Patrum, 199
Adam, Karl, 396
Adenauer, Konrad, 396
Adjutor, St., 305
Adoptionism, 165
Adoration, 354
Adrian, William H., 553
Adultery, 354
Adveniat, German Relief Agency, 105, 131, 146
Advent, 290, 292
Advent, First Sunday, Dates (1980-2004), 300
Advent Wreath, 354
Adventists, 354
Advertising, TV, and Children, 99
Afars and Issas, see Djibouti
Affirmative Action, NCCB-USCC, 139
Afghanistan, 419
Africa
   American Bishops, 507
   Bishops Meeting, 145
   Cardinals, 215
   Catholic Statistics, 454-55

Africa
   Eastern Rite Jurisdictions, 325
   Episcopal Conferences, 145, 457
   Refugees, 121
Africa, Missionary Sisters of Our Lady, 581
African Missions, Society of, 571
Africanus, Sextus, 396
Agape, 354
Agatha, St., 305
Age of Reason, 354
Aged, Eucharistic Fast, 370
Aged, Facilities for, 632-40
Aging, International Year on (UN), 98
Aggiornamento, 354
Agnes, St., 305
Agnes, Sisters of St., 581
Agnosticism, 354
Agnus Dei, 354
Agrarian Reform, World Food Conference, 141
Agreda, Mary of, 396
Agrimissio, 609
Ahern, Patrick V., Bp., 527
Ahr, George William, Bp., 527
Akron, Ohio, Abortion Ordinance, 144
Alabama, 476, 509, 513, 514-15, 518, 614, 632, 643, 646, 649, 689
   Unemployment Tax and Church Schools, 120, 149
Alan of Walsingham, 396
Alarcon, Pedro, 396
Alaska, 476-77, 511, 513, 515, 526, 616, 649, 689
Alb, 261
Albania, 130, 419
Albanian Byzantines, 323
Alberione, Giacomo, 396
Albers, Joseph, 553
Albert (Albrecht), 396
Albert the Great, St., 247
Albertus Magnus Guild, 662
Albigensianism, 165
Albornoz, Gil Alvarez Carillo de, 396
Alcoholics, Social Services, 647
Alcoholism, National Clergy Conference, 667
Alcuin, Albinus, 396
Alemany, Joseph S., O.P., 553
Alencastre, Stephen, SS.CC., 553
Alerding, Herman J., 553
Alexander of Hales, 396
Alexandrian Rite, 322-23
Alexian Brothers, 578
Alfred the Great, 396
Alfrink, Bernard Jan, Card., 200
Algeria, 103, 419
Alhambra, Order of, 668
Aliens, Undocumented, 99, 119, 604
All Saints, 301
All Souls, 301
Alleluia, 354
Allen, Edward P., 553
Allen, Frances, 396
Allende Gossens, Salvator (Chile), 423
Allers, Rudolf, 396
Allin, John M., Bp. (Episcopal), 154
Allocution, 354
Allori, Alessandro, 396
Allori, Cristofano, 396
Allouez, Claude, 415
Alms, 355
Alonso Rodriguez, Bl., 417
Aloysius Gonzaga, St., 305
Alpha and Omega, 355
Alpha Delta Gamma Fraternity, 661
Alphonsus Liguori, St., 247
Altar, 261, 263
   Cloth, 263
   Stone, 261
Altars, New Rites for Dedicating, 268
Alter, Karl J., 553
Altham, John, 415
Althoff, Henry, 553
Amand, St., 305
Amat, Thaddeus, C.M., 553
Ambo (Pulpit), 263

Index

Ambrose, St., 247
Ambrosian Rite, 258
Ambrozic, Aloysius, Bp., 463
Ambry, 264
Amen, 355
America, see United States
American Benedictine Academy, 662
  Catholic Correctional Chaplains Association, 662
  Catholic Historical Association, 662
  Catholic Philosophical Association, 662
  Committee on Italian Migration, 662
  Society of Mature Catholics, 662
American College, Louvain, 185
American Federation of Teachers (AFT), 618
  Catholic Teacher Unions, 618
American Heresy, 475
American Jewish Congress, 133
American Lutheran Church, see Lutheran Churches
Amice, 261
Amin, Idi, Pres., 126
  See also Uganda
Amiot, Jean Marie, 396
Ammen, Daniel, 396
Amnesty International, 111, 120
Amos, 239
Ampere, Andre, 396
Anabaptism, 332
Analogy of Faith, 231
Anaphora (Canons, Eucharistic Prayers), 358
Anathema, 355
Anchieta, Jose, 415
Anchorite, 355
Ancient Order of Hibernians in America, 662
Anderson, Joseph, 553
Anderson, Paul F., Bp., 527
Anderson, William H., 396
Andorra, 419
Andre Bessette, Bro., 464
Andre Grasset de Saint Sauver, Bl., 305
Andreis, Felix, 415
"Andres Bello" Catholic Univ. (Venezuela), 628
Andrew, St. (Apostle), 245
Andrew Corsini, St., 305
Andrew Fournet, St., 305
Angela Merici, St., 305
Angelic Salutation (Hail Mary), 372
Angelic Warfare Confraternity, 660
Angelico, Fra, 396
Angelicum, 629
Angell, Kenneth A., Bp., 527
Angels, 355
Angels, Guardian, 302, 355
Angelus, 355
Anger, 355
Anglican Communion, 333
  Archbishop of Canterbury, 150
  Ecumenical Statements, 116, 346, 347
  General Synod, 101, 116, 140
  See also Episcopal Church, U.S.
Anglican Orders, 355
Anglicans, Canada, Meeting, 131
Anglim, Robert, C.SS.R., 553
Anglin, Margaret, 396
Anglin, Timothy, 396
Angola, 419
Anguilla, 419
Animuccia, Giovanni, 396
Ann (Anne), St., 303
Ann, Sisters of St., 581
Annabring, Joseph, 553
Anne, Sisters of St., 581
Anne de Beaupre, St., Shrine, 471
Anne Mary Javouhey, Bl., 305
Annuario Pontificio, 222
Annulment (Decree of Nullity), 286, 287
Annunciation, 301
Anointing of the Sick, 266, 270, 276
Anselm, St., 247
  Pontifical Athenaeum, 629
Ansgar, St., 305
Ansgar's Scandinavian Catholic League, St., 668
Anthony, St. (Abbot), 305
Anthony, St. (of Padua), 247
Anthony, St., Missionary Servants of St., 581
Anthony Daniel, St., 416
Anthony Mary Claret, St., 305

Anthony Mary Zaccaria, St., 305
Anti-Busing Amendment, 139
Anti-Catholicism and Tax Credit Legislation, 114
Antichrist, 355
Anticlericalism (Clericalism), 362
Antigua, 419
Antilles, Netherlands, 440
Antimension, 327
Antiochene Rite, 323
  in United States, 326
Antiphon, 356
Antipopes, 173-74
Anti-Semitic Language, Liturgical Texts, 101
Anti-Semitism, 348
  Passion Play Text, 139
Antonelli, Ferdinand G., O.F.M., Card., 200
Antonianum, Pontifical Athenaeum, 629
Aparicio, Sebastian, Bl., 415
Apartheid (South Africa), 446
Apocalyptic Book, New Testament (Revelation), 241
Apocrypha, 235
Apollonia, St., 305
Apologetics, 356
Aponte Martinez, Luis, Card., 200
Apostasy (Apostate), 356
Apostles, 245-46
Apostles' Creed, 249
Apostles of Places, 314
Apostleship of Prayer, 662
  Prayer Intentions (1980), 294-99
Apostleship of the Sea, 657
Apostolate, 356
  See also Laity; Lay Apostolate
Apostolate, Sisters Auxiliaries of the, 581
  Sisters of Mary of the Catholic, 594
  Society of the Catholic, see Pallottines
Apostolate for Family Consecration, 662
Apostolate of Christian Action, 662
Apostolate to Aid the Dying, 667
Apostolates, Special, 657-60
Apostolic
  Administrator, 188
  Chamber, 197
  Constitution, 363
  Delegates, 215-18
  Fathers, 246
  Nuncios, 215-18
  Penitentiary, Sacred, 195
  Signatura, 195
Apostolic See (Holy See), 372
Apostolic Succession, 356
Apostolicae Curae, see Anglican Orders
Apostolicam Actuositatem (Lay Apostolate Decree), 168
Apostolos, 293
Appalachia, Catholic Committee, 609
Apparitions of the BVM, 319-20
Apparitions, Disclaimed, Bayside, 124
Appelhans, Stephan A., S.V.D., Bp., 553
Apponyi, Albert, 396
Aquinas, Thomas, St., see Thomas Aquinas, St.
Aquinas Medal, 695
Arab-Israeli Events, see Middle East
Arabian Peninsula, 419
Arabic Studies, Pontifical Institute, 629
Aramburu, Juan Carlos, Card., 200
Archangel, 356
Archangels, Feast, 303
Archbishop, 187
Archbishops
  Canada, 462
  United States, 498-506
  World Statistics, 454
Archconfraternity, see Confraternity
Archconfraternity of Christian Mothers, 662
  Holy Ghost, 662
  Our Lady of Perpetual Help, 662
  Perpetual Adoration, 662
Archdiocese, 356
Archdioceses
  Canada, 462
  United States, 498-506
  World Statistics, 454
Archeology, Pontifical Commission, 196
  Pontifical Institute, 629
Archimandrite, 353
Architecture, see Church Building

Archives, 356
Archives, Ecclesiastical, Italy, Comm., 196
Archives, Vatican II, 197
Archpriest, 356
Argenleiu, Georges Thierry, D', 396
Argentina, 131, 135, 145, 420
　See also Beagle Channel Dispute
Arianism, 165
Aricona, 476- 511, 513, 515, 526, 616, 632, 641, 649, 689
　Voluntary Prayer Unconstitutional, 124
Arkansas, 477, 510, 513, 515, 615, 632, 641, 649, 689
Arkfeld, Leo, S.V.D., Abp., 527
Arliss, Reginald, C.P., Bp., 527
Armenian-Orthodox Church, Dialogue with Catholics, 331
Armenian Rite, 323
　in U.S., 326
Arminianism, 333
Armaments, John Paul II on, 68-9
Arms Exhibition, Chicago, Protest, 115
Arms Industry, Connecticut, 128
Arms Race, 255
　See also SALT II
Armstrong, Robert J., 553
Arnold, Thomas, 396
Arnold, William R., 553
Arns, Paulo E., O.F.M., Card., 200
Arrupe, Pedro, S.J., 148
Art, Byzantine, 327
Art, Liturgical (Sacred), 258, 268
Art, Sacred, Commission, 196
Arzube, Juan, Bp., 527
Ascension (May 15, 1980), 296, 301
　Dates (1980-2004), 300
Asceticism, 356
Ash Wednesday (Feb. 20, 1980), 294, 301
　Dates (1980-2004), 300
Ashes, 356
Asia
　American Bishops, 507
　Cardinals, 214
　Catholic Statistics, 454-55
　Eastern Rite Jurisdictions, 325
Asmara University (Ethiopia), 627
Aspergillum, 357
Aspersion (Baptism), 271
Aspersory, 357
Aspiration, 357
Association
　for Religious and Value Issues in Counseling, 662
　for Social Economics, 662
　for the Sociology of Religion, 662
　of Catholic Trade Unionists, 662
　of Contemplative Sisters, 600
　of Marian Helpers, 662
　of Permanent Diaconate Directors, 119, 280
　of Romanian Catholics, 662
Associations, Catholic, U.S., 662-70
Associations of the Faithful, 603
Assumption, 301
　and Church Teaching on Life after Death, 82
Assumption, Augustinians of, 571
　Little Sisters of, 581
　of Blessed Virgin, Sisters of, 581
　Religious of, 581
Asteriskos, 327
Ateitininkai, 666
Athanasian Creed, 250
Athanasius, St., 247
Atheism, 357
　John Paul II on, 102
　See also Non-Believers, Secretariat
Atkielski, Roman R., 553
Atonement, 357
Atonement, Day of (Yom Kippur), 351
Atonement, Franciscan Friars of, 571
Attila (452), 156
Attributes of God, 357
Attrition, see Contrition
Audet, Lionel, Bp., 463
Audet, Rene, Bp., 463
Audiences, Papal, 222
Augsburg, Peace of (1555), 161
Augustine, Order of St., 571
Augustine, Third Order of St., 604
Augustine of Canterbury, St., 305

Augustine of Hippo, St., 247
Augustinian Recollects, 571
Augustinians, 571
Auschwitz, John Paul II Address, 57, 60-1
Australia, 420
　Aborigines Rights Defended, 115
　Christian-Moslem Dialogue, 151
Austria, 420
Authority
　Encyclicals, 182
　of Councils, 166
　Papal, 227-29
　Religious Superiors, 570
Authority, Teaching, of Church (Magisterium), see Teaching Authority of the Church
Authority in Church, Anglican-Catholic Statement, 347
Autograph (Chirograph), 362
Auxiliaries of Our Lady of the Cenacle, 657
Auxiliary Bishop, 187
Avarice, 357
Ave Maria (Hail Mary), 372
Avery, Martha (Moore), 396
Aviat, Francoise de Sales, Sr., Canonization Cause, 103
Avignon Residency of Papacy, 174
Awards, Catholic, 694-703
Azores, 420

B

Babcock, Allen J., 553
Bacon, David W., 553
Bacon, Roger, 396
Badin, Stephen, 415
Baegert, Johann Jacob, 396
Bafile, Corrado, Card., 200
Baggio, Sebastiano, Card., 200
Bahamas, 420
　John Paul II Visit, 51
Bahrain, 420
Bakhiti, Josephine, Sr., Canonization Cause, 103
Balboa, Vasco Nunez de, 396
Baldachino, 357
Baldwin, Charles Sears, 396
Baldwin, Geoffrey P., 396
Baldwin, Vincent J., Bp., 553, 703
Balearic Islands, 420
Balke, Victor, Bp., 527
Ballestrero, Anastasio Alberto, Card., 201
Baltes, Peter J., 553
Baltimore, Plenary Councils, 474
Balzan Prize, Mother Teresa, 120
Bangladesh, 420
Banim, John and Michael, 396
Banneaux, Apparitions, 319
Banns, Marriage, 284
Baptism, 270, 271-72
　Disciples of Christ — Catholic Agreement, 105
Baptism of the Lord, Feast (Jan. 13, 1980), 294, 301
Baptism of the Spirit, see Charismatic Renewal, Catholic
Baptisms, Catholic, U.S., 514-15
　World, 455
　See also Individual Countries
Baptistery, 264
Baptists, 333
　Churches, U.S., 333-34
　Ecumenical Dialogues, 341-42
Baraga, Frederic, 415
Barbados, 420
Barber, Daniel, 396
Barber, Virgil, 396
Barbieri, Antonio Maria, O.F.M. Cap., Card., 703
Barbour, John, 397
Baring, Maurice, 397
Barnabas, St., 245
Barnabites, 571
Barrera Case, see Wheeler v. Barrera
Barrera Motto, Ernesto, Rev., 101
Barron, Edward, 553
Barry, John, 397
Barry, John (Bp.), 553
Barry, Patrick J., 553
Bartholome, Peter W., Bp., 527
Bartholomeus, Anglicus, 397
Bartholomew, St., 245
Bartlett, Dewey, Sen., 703
Bartolommeo, Fra, 397

Index

Baruch, 238
Basil, St., Congregation of Priests, 571
Basil the Great, St., 247
  Anniversary of Death, 147
Basil the Great, St., Order (Ukrainians), 571
Basil the Great, Srs. of the Order of St., 581
Basilian Fathers, 571
Basilian Salvatorian Fathers, 571
Basilica, 518
  St. John Lateran, 221, 302
  St. Mary Major, 302
  St. Peter, 221
Basilicas, U.S. and Canada, 518-19
Basle, Council of (1431-1449), 160
Basques, 136, 145
Batanian, Ignace, Patriarch, 152
Baudoux, Maurice, Abp., 463
Baum, William W., Card., 125, 138, 201
Baumgartner, Apollinaris, O.F.M. Cap., 553
Bayley, James Roosevelt, 397
Bayma, Joseph, 397
Bayside, N.Y., Visions, 124
Bazin, John S., 553
Bazin, Rene, 397
Bea, Augustin, 397
Beagle Channel Dispute, 108, 123, 148
Beahen, John, Bp., 463
Beardsley, Aubrey V., 397
Beatific Vision, 357
Beatification, 357
  Decrees Approved, 127
Beatifications (1979), 122, 152
  Francisco Coll, 122
  Enrico de Osso y Cervello, 152
  Jacques Desire Laval, 122
Beatitudes, 357-58
Beaton, David, 397
Beauraing, Apparitions, 319
Beauregard, Pierre, 397
Beaven, Thomas D., 553
Beccaria, Giovanni B., 397
Becker, Thomas A., 553
Beckman, Francis J., 553
Becquerel, Antoine Cesar, 397
Becquerel, Antoine Henri, 397
Bede the Venerable, St., 247
Beethoven, Ludwig von, 397
Begin, Floyd L., 553
Begley, Michael J., Bp., 527
Behaim, Martin, 397
Belanger, Valerian, Bp., 464
Belgium, 420-21
Belief, Catholic, see Doctrine, Catholic
Belisle, Giles, Bp., 464
Belize, 421
Bell, Alden, Bp., 527
Bellarmine, St. Robert, 249
Bellarmine Medal, 695
Bellini, Gentile and Giovanni, 397
Belloc, Hilaire, 397
Beltran, Eusebius J., Bp., 527-28
Benedict, St. (of Nursia), 305
Benedict, St., Oblates of, 604
Benedict, St., Order of, 571-72
Benedict XV, Pope, 176
  Canonizations, 180
  Encyclicals, 176, 183
Benedict the Black (il Moro), St., 305
Benedictine Nuns, 581
Benedictine Sisters, 581-82
Benedictines, 571-72
Benedictines, Olivetan, 572
Benedictines, Sylvestrine, 572
Benediction of Blessed Sacrament, 358
Benedictus, 358
Benelli, Giovanni, Card., 201
Benemerenti Medal, 695
Bengsch, Alfred, Card., 201
Benin (Dahomey), 421
Benincasa, Pius A., Bp., 528
Benjamin, Cletus J., 553
Bennett, John G., 553
Benson, Robert Hugh, 397
Benson, William Shepherd, 397
Bentley, John F., 397
Beran, Josef, Abp., see Czechoslovakia

Beras Rojas, Octavio, Card., 201
Berengarian Heresy, 165
Berengario da Carpi, Jacopo, 397
Bergan, Gerald T., 553
Bermuda, 421
Bernadette, St., 305
  Anniversary of Death, 126
  Lourdes Apparitions, 320
Bernanos, Georges, 397
Bernard, Claude, 397
Bernard of Clairvaux, St., 247
Bernard of Menthon, St., 305
Bernardin, Joseph L., Abp., 528
Bernardine of Feltre, Bl., 305
Bernardine of Siena, St., 305
Bernardine Sisters, 587
Bernarding, George, S.V.D., Bp., 528
Bernini, Giovanni, 397
Bertoli, Paolo, Card., 201
Bertran, Louis, St., 415
Bertrand, Louis, 397
Beschi, Costanzo, 397
Besse, Jean, 397
Bethany, Congregation of Oblates, 582
Bethany, Sisters of, 582
Bethlehem Missionaries, Society of, 572
Bethlemita Sisters, 582
Better World Movement, 659
Bhutan, 421
Bhutto, Zulfikar Ali (Pakistan Prime Minister), 122
Biafra, see Nigeria
Bianchini, Francesco, 397
Bible, 233-43
  Authorship, 241
  Canons, 233
  Federation, 234
  First Printed (c. 1456), 160
  Good News Edition, 119
  Inerrancy, 230
  Interpretation, 230, 242-43
  New Testament Text Revision, 99
  Pontifical Commission, 244
  Vatican II Constitution on Revelation, 229-32
  Vulgate Edition, New, 122
  Zaire Lingala Language Edition, 121
  See also Biblical Studies; Tradition
Bible, Mary in, 316
Bible Observance, 100, 145
Bible Reading, Subjective, 106
Bible Reading in Public Schools,
  see Church-State Decisions
Bible Service, 358
Bible Society, Catholic, 663
Bible Study, Fundamentalist Approach, 144
Bible Study, Tennessee, Constitutionality, 144
Biblical Apostolate, World Federation, 234
Biblical Association of America, Catholic, 144, 663
Biblical Commission, Pontifical, 244
Biblical Institute, Pontifical, 629
Biblical Scholarship, 144
Biblical Studies, 232, 243, 244
Bickerstaffe-Drew, Francis, 397
Bidawid, Thomas M., 553
Bielski, Marcin, 397
Bienville, Sieur de, 397
Biggs, Richard Keys, 397
Biglietto, 358
Billuart, Charles, 397
Bilock, John M., Bp., 528
Bination, 261
Binet, Jacques, 397
Binz, Leo, Abp., 528
Bioethics, 94
  In Vitro Fertilization, 93-4, 119
Biographies, 396-18
  Apostles, Evangelists, 245-46
  Bishops, American, 527-67
  Bishops, Canadian, 463-68
  Cardinals, 200-13
  Fathers and Doctors of the Church, 246-49
  John Paul II, 48-9
    See also John Paul II
  Missionaries to the Americas, 415-18
  Popes, Twentieth Century, 174-80
  Saints, 305-11
Biondo, Flavio, 397

Biot, Jean B., 397
Biretta, 358
Birth Control, Catholic Teaching (*Humanae Vitae*), 282-83
　See also Contraception
Birth Control Ad Condemned, 143
Birthright, 648
Bishop, 276
　See also Hierarchy
Bishops, 187
　and Ecumenical Councils, 166
　Collegiality, 75, 107, 228-29, 362
　Conferences, 455-58
　Congregation, 193
　Duties of, John Paul II, 53, 67, 98-9, 128
　First, see Apostles
　Nomination, 187
　Statistics, World, 454
　Synod, 103, 188-90
Bishops, Canadian, 462-68
　Conference, 106, 468
　John Paul II Address, 98
　Social Justice Statement, 135
Bishops, U.S., 498-506, 527-52
　Affirmative Action Employment Policy, 139
　Blood Brothers, 552
　Committees, 522
　Ecumenical Affairs Committee, 100, 340
　John Paul II Meeting (Rome), 98-9
　John Paul II Meeting, Address (Chicago), 73
　Lawsuit against Federal Government, 134
　Meetings, 100, 523-26
　National Conference, 521-22
　of the Past, 553-67
　Retired, 523, 552
　Secretariat, Catholic-Jewish Relations, 348-49
　Serving Overseas, 553
Bishops and Presbyters, Statement, 331
Biskup, George J., Abp., 528
Black Catholics, U.S., 89-90
　Brother Joseph Davis Award, 145
　Conference on Church in Black Community, 120
　Catholic School Enrollment, 617
　Missions, 608
　Sisters Conference, 600
Black Death (1347-1350), 160
Blacks, Rhodesia Election, 126
　See also Rhodesia
Blais, Leo, Bp., 464
Blake, Judith, Dr., 153
Blanc, Anthony, 553
Blanchet, Augustin M., 553
Blanchet, Bertrand, Bp., 464
Blanchet, Francis N., 553
Blanchette, Romeo, Bp., 528
Blase, St., 305
Blasphemy, 358
Blasphemy of the Spirit, 358
Blenk, James, S.M., 554
Blessed Sacrament, see Eucharist, Holy
Blessed Sacrament, Benediction, 358
Blessed Sacrament (Religious)
　and Our Lady, Religious of the Order of, 598
　Congregation of, 572
　Missionary Sisters of Most, 597
　Nuns of Perpetual Adoration, 597
　Oblate Sisters of, 597
　Religious Mercedarians of, 597
　Servants of, 597
　Srs. of, for Indians and Colored People, 598
　Srs. of Incarnate Word, 592
　Srs. Servants of, 598
Blessed Virgin Mary, 315-19
　Annunciation, 301
　Apparitions, 319-20
　Assumption, 301, 318
　Birth, 301
　Feasts, 291
　First Saturday Devotion, 370
　Immaculate Conception, 303, 317
　Immaculate Heart (June 14, 1980), 296, 303
　Joys (Franciscan Crown), 371
　Little Office, 378
　Purification (Presentation of the Lord), 304
　Queenship, 304

Blessed Virgin Mary
　Rosary (Devotion), 387
　Rosary (Feast), 303
　Solemnity, 304
　Sorrows (Feast), 303
　Visitation, 304
　See also Mary
Blessed Virgin Mary (Religious)
　Institute of, 582
　Sisters of Charity, 584
　Sisters of Presentation of, 596
Blessing, 358
Blind, Catholic Facilities for, 646, 648
Blondel, Maurice, 397
Blowick, John, 397
Bloy, Leon, 397
Blue Army, 662
Boardman, John, 554
Boat, 358
"Boat People," 109
Boccaccio, Giovanni, 397
Boccella, John H., T.O.R., Abp., 528
Boeddeker, Alfred, O.F.M. (St. Anthony Dining Room), 647
Boethius, Anicius, 397
Boeynaems, Libert H., SS.CC., 554
Bohachevsky, Constantine, 554
Boileau, George, 554
Boileau-Despreaux, Nicholas, 397
Bokenfohr, John, O.M.I., Bp., 528
Boland, Ernest B., O.P., Bp., 528
Boland, Paschal, O.S.B., 703
Boland, Thomas A., Abp., 554, 703
Bolivarian Pontifical University (Colombia), 627
Bolivia, 145, 421
Bolland, John Van, 397
Bollandists (1643), 161
Bolzano, Bernard, 397
Bon Secours, Sisters of, 582
Bona, Giovanni, 397
Bona, Stanislaus, 554
Bonacum, Thomas, 554
Bonaparte, Charles J., 398
Bonaventure, St., 247
Bonaventure, St., Pontifical Theological Faculty, 629
Boniface, St., 305
Book Clubs, Catholic, 682
Book of Common Prayer (1549), 149, 161
Book of Kells, 158
Books, 682
　Censorship, 360
　Index of Prohibited, 374
　Liturgical, see Lectionary; Sacramentary
　　See also *Human Sexuality*; *Quand Je Dis Dieu*
Books of the Bible, 235-41
Booths, Festival, 350
Borders, William D., Abp., 528
Bordone, Paris, 398
Borecky, Isidore, Bp., 464
Borgess, Caspar H., 554
Borromeo Award, 696
Borrus, Christopher, 398
Bosco, Anthony B., Bp., 528
Bosco, John, St., 308
Boscovich, Ruggiero, 398
Bosio, Antonio, 398
Bossilkoff, Eugene, Bp., see Bulgaria
Bossuet, Jacques, 398
Boston Common, Papal Mass, 63
Botswana, 421
Botticelli, Sandro, 398
Boudreaux, Warren L., Bp., 528
Bourdaloue, Louis, 398
Bourgade, Peter, 554
Bourgeois, Louis, 398
Bourgeoys, Marguerite, Bl., 415
Boy Savior Movement, 660
Boy Scouts, Catholic, 660
Boylan, John J., 554
Boyle, Ellen, Sr., 125
Boyle, Hugh, 554
Boys Town, Charges Unfounded, 100
Bracton, Henry de, 398
Bradley, Denis, 554
Brady, John, 554
Brady, Matthew F., 554

Index

Brady, William O., 554
Braga Rite, 258
Braille, Louis, 398
Bramante, Donato, 398
Brandao Vilela, Avelar, Card., 201
Branly, Edouard, 398
Brazil, 115, 145, 421-22
Bread for the World, 113-14
Brebeuf, John de, St., 415
Breitenbeck, Joseph M., Bp., 528
Brendan, St., 305
Brennan, Andrew J., 554
Brennan, Francis J., 398
Brennan, Peter J. (Catholics in Presidents' Cabinets), 490
Brennan, Thomas F., 554
Brennan, William (Catholics in Supreme Court), 491
Brent Award, 696
Brentano, Klemens, 398
Breuil, Henri, 398
Breviary, 257
Brickner, Balfour, Rabbi, 116
Bridget (Birgitta), St., 305
Bridget (Brigid), St., 305
Bridgettine Sisters, 582
Brief, Apostolic, 358
Briefs, Secretariat of, see Secretariat of State
Brigid, Congregation of St., 582
British Honduras, see Belize
Brizgys, Vincas, Bp., 528
Broadcasters, Religious, Fundamentalist Threat, 99-100, 124
Broadcasters Association, Catholic, see UNDA-USA
Broderick, Bonaventure, 144, 554
Broderick, Edwin B., Bp., 528
Brodeur, Rosario L., Bp., 464
Brondel, John B., 554
Brossart, Ferdinand, 554
Brotherhood Week, National, 115
Brothers, 569
Brothers, U.S., 578-79
 National Assembly, 138, 579-80
Brothers, Statistics, U.S., 508-11, 516
 World, 454
Broun, Heywood Campbell, 398
Brown, Charles A., M.M., Bp., 529
Browne, Charles Farrar, 398
Brownson, Orestes Augustus, 398
Bru, Helen, 105
Bruckner, Anton, 398
Brumidi, Constantini, 398
Brunei, 422
Bruening, Paul, Rev., 703
Brunelleschi, Filippo, 398
Brunetiere, Ferdinand, 398
Brunini, Joseph B., Bp., 529
Brunner, Nola, Sr., 125
Bruno, St., 306
Brust, Leo J., Bp., 529
Brute, Simon G., 554
Brzana, Stanislaus, Bp., 529
Buck, Edward, 398
Buddhists, 352
 Dalai Lama XVI, 150
Buddy, Charles F., 554
Budenz, Louis F., 398
Bueno y Monreal, Jose Maria, Card., 148, 201
Bugnini, Annibale, Abp., 141
Bulgaria, 422
 Foreign Minister's Meeting with Pope, 102
Bulgarian Catholics (Byzantine Rite), 333
Bull, Apostolic, 358
Bull of Demarcation (1493), 160
Bulla, see Bull
Bullarium, see Bull
Bullitt, William C., 398
Burial, Ecclesiastical, 358
 See also Funeral Rites
Burke, Augustin-Emile, Bp., 464
Burke, James C., O.P., Bp., 529
Burke, John, 398
Burke, Joseph A., 554
Burke, Maurice F., 554
Burke, Thomas M., 554
Burke, Thomas N., 398
Burma, 422
Burnand, Sir Francis, 398

Burnett, Peter Hardemann, 398
Burse, 263
Burundi, 422
 Missionaries Expelled, 133
Bus Transportation, Private Schools, Pennsylvania, 134
 See also Church-State Decisions
Busch, Joseph F., 554
Buswell, Charles A., Bp., 529
Butler, Alban, 398
Butler, Pierce, 398
Byelorussians, 323, 326
Byrd, William, 398
Byrne, Andrew, 554
Byrne, Christopher E., 554
Byrne, Edwin V., 554
Byrne, James J., Abp., 529
Byrne, Leo C., 554
Byrne, Patrick, M.M., 554
Byrne, Thomas S., 554
Byzantine Rite (Catholic), 323-24
 Calendar, 292-93
 Catholics, 323-34, 326
 Liturgy Features, 326-28
 Ukrainian Bishops' Meeting, 151
 Vestments, 327

C

Cabana, Georges, Abp., 464
Cabeza de Vaca, Alvar, 398
Cabot, John, 398
Cabral, Pedro Alvares de, 398
Cabrini, Mother (St. Frances Xavier Cabrini), 307
Cabrini Sisters, see Sacred Heart Missionary Sisters
Caedmon, 398
Caesar, Raymond R., Bp., 529
Caggiano, Antonio, Card., 201
Caillouet, L. Abel, Bp., 529
Caius, John, 398
Cajetan, St., 306
Cajetan, Tommaso de Vio, 398
Caldani, Leopold, 398
Calderon de la Barca, Pedro, 398
Calendar, Church, 290-300
 Byzantine, 292-93
 Gregorian (1582), 161
 Revised, 290-92
Califano, Joseph A., 118-19, 129
 See also Catholics in Presidents' Cabinets
California, 115, 139, 477, 511, 513, 515, 518, 526, 616, 624, 632, 640, 641, 643, 649-50, 689
 Conscience Clause for Medical Students, 129
 Missions, 418
 Proposition 13 and Catholic Agencies, 124
Calix Society, 662
Call to Action Workshop, 120
Callan, Josephine McGarry, 703
Callistus I, St., 306
Calumny, 358
Calvary, 358
Calvert, Cecil, 398
Calvert, George, 399
Calvin, John, 332-33
Camaldolese Congregation, 572
Camaldolese Hermits, 572
Cambodia (Kampuchea), 436
 Food for, 153
Camel (Kamel), George, 399
Camerlengo, see Chamberlain
Cameroon, 422
Camillians, 572
Camillus de Lellis, St., 306
Camoes, Luiz Vaz de, 399
Camp David Anniversary, 149
Camp Fire Girls, 660
Campaign for Human Development, 99, 149, 418
Campaign for Surplus Rosaries, 662
Campbell, James, 399
Campinas, University of (Brazil), 627
Campion Award, 696
Campus Ministry, 624
Cana Conferences, 288
Canada, 106, 423, 461-72
 Anglican Meeting, 131
 Basilicas, 518

Canada
  Bishops, Biographies, 463-68
  Bishops' Conference, 106, 468
  Bishops' Statement, Ontario, 120
  Catholic Publications, 471
  Eastern (Byzantine) Rite Catholics, 470
  Latin in Liturgy, 131
  Marriage Guidelines, Parish, 146
  Pontifical Universities, Faculty of, 627, 628
  Refugee Aid, Arrangements, 120, 146
  Separate Schools, 120, 125
  Shrines, 471
  Statistics, 469-71
Canadian Conference of Catholic Bishops, 106, 468
Canal Zone Returned to Panama, 154
Canary Islands, 423
Cancer de Barbastro, Louis, 416
Cancer Homes and Hospitals, 646
Cancer Saint (St. Peregrine), 310
Candle, Paschal, 383
Candlemas Day (Presentation), 304
Candles, 264
Canevin, J.F., Regis, 554
Cano, Melchior, 399
Canon, 358
  of Bible, 233
  of Mass, 260, 265
  See also Liturgical Developments
Canon Law, 358
  Commissions, 196
  Pastoral Nature, 112
  Society of America, 663
Canonization, 358-59
Canonization Causes, 103
Canonizations, from Leo XIII to Present, 180-82
Canons Regular of Holy Cross (Crosier Fathers), 573
Canons Regular of Premontre (Premonstratensians), 576
Canova, Antonio, 399
Canterbury Statement, 346
Canticle, 359
Canticum Laudis (Liturgy of the Hours), 257, 267
Cantwell, John J., 554
Canute (II) the Great, 399
Cap-de-la-Madeleine, Shrine, 471
Cape Verde Islands, 423
Capital Punishment, 135, 359
  Spenkelink Execution, 129
Capital Sins, 359
Cappa Magna, 262
Cappel, Louis, 243
Caprio, Giuseppe, Card., 202
Capucci, Hilarion, Abp., 111, 127
Capuchins, 574
Carberry, John Card., 139, 202
Cardano, Girolamo, 399
Cardijn, Joseph, 399
Cardinal, 199
  Bishops, 199, 213
  Deacons, 199, 214
  in Pectore, 200
  Priests, 199, 213
Cardinal Gibbons Medal, 696
Cardinal Mindszenty Foundation, 663
Cardinal Spellman Award, 696
Cardinal Virtues, 359
Cardinals, 199-215
  American, 215
  Biographies, 200-13
  Categories, 213-14
  Chamberlain, 361
  College, 199-20
  Consistory (1979), 133, 137
  Dean, 199, 365
  Deaths, 98
  Geographical Distribution, 214-15
  John Paul Address to, 102
  Meeting with Pope, 153
  Retirement Age, 199
  Seniority (Categories), 213-14
  Voting Eligibility, 214
  See also Interregnum
Carew, William A., Abp., 464
Carey, M. Cecilia, Sr., 114
Carey, Matthew, 399
Caritas, 603
Caritas Christi, 602

Caritas Internationalis, 143, 458
Carmel, see Mt. Carmel
Carmel Community, 582
Carmelite Brothers of the Eucharist, 578
Carmelite Missionaries of St. Theresa, 582
Carmelite Order, Lay, 604
Carmelite Sisters, 582-83
  for Aged and Infirm, 582
  of Charity, 583
  of Corpus Christi, 582
  of St. Therese of the Infant Jesus, 583
  of the Divine Heart of Jesus, 583
  of the Sacred Heart, 583
Carmelite Third Order (Discalced), 604
Carmelites (Men), 572
Carmelites (Women)
  Calced, 583
  Discalced, 583
Carney, James F., Abp., 464
Carnoy, Jean B., 399
Caroline and Marshall Islands, 423
Carpatho-Russians, 324
Carpini, Giovanni de Piano, 399
Carpino, Francesco, Card., 202
Carrel, Alexis, 399
Carrell, George A., S.J., 554
Carroll, Charles, 399
Carroll, Coleman F., 554
Carroll, Daniel, 399
Carroll, Howard J., 554
Carroll, James J., 554
Carroll, John, 399
Carroll, John P., 554
Carroll, Mark K., Bp., 529
Carroll Center for the Blind, 648
Carson, Caroline A., 110
Carson, Christopher (Kit), 399
Carter, Alexander, Bp., 464
Carter, Gerald Emmett, Card., 202
Carter, Jimmy, Pres., 123-24, 136, 140, 143, 153
  Meeting with John Paul II, White House, 64
Carter, Rosalynn, 128
Carthusians, Order of, 572
Cartier, Jacques, 399
Cartwright, Hubert J., 554
Caruana, George, 554
Caruso, Enrico, 399
Casariego, Mario, C.R.S., Card., 202
Casaroli, Agostino, Card., 202
Casey, James V., Abp., 529
Casey, Lawrence B., 555
Casimir, St., 306
Casimir, Sisters of St., 583
Cassata, John J., Bp., 529
Cassian, St., 306
Cassidy, James E., 555
Cassini, Jean, 399
Cassiodorus, Flavius, 399
Cassock, 262
Castel Gandolfo, 137, 138, 221
Castelli, Benedetto, 399
Castillo, John de, Bl., 416
Catacombs, 359-60
Catafalque, 360
Catala, Magin, 416
Catalonians (Spain), 145
Catechesis, 143, 147
Catechetical Directory, National, 90-1, 118, 523
Catechetics, 190
  Apostolic Exhortation, 91
Catechism, 360
Catechists, Los Angeles, Commissioned, 129
Catechumen, 360
  See also Baptism
Catechumens, Mass, 259
Catechumens, Oil of, 381
Catharism, 165
Cathedra, 360
  See also Ex Cathedra
Cathedral, 516
Cathedrals, U.S., 516-18
Cathedraticum, 360
Catherine Labouré, St., 306
  See also Miraculous Medal
Catherine of Bologna, St., 306
Catherine of Siena, St., 247

Index

Catholic, 360
Action, see Lay Apostolate
Action Medal, 696
Actors' Guild of America, 687
Aid Association, 663
Alliance for Communications, 663
Alumni Clubs International, 663
Apostolate of Radio, TV and Advertising, 663
Associations, 662-70
Audio Visual Educators Assn., 663
Awards, 695-703
Baptisms, U.S., see Baptisms, U.S.
Belief, see Doctrine, Catholic
Bible Society, 663
Biblical Assn. of America, 144, 663
Big Brothers, Inc., 663
Big Sisters, Inc., 663
Business Education Assn., 663
Central Union, 658
Charities, see Charities, Catholic, National Conference
Chronology in U.S., 476-90
Church Extension Society, 609
Colleges, U.S., 619-24
Commission on Intellectual and Cultural Affairs, 663
Committee on Urban Ministry, 663
Communications Foundation, 688
Conference on Ethnic and Neighborhood Affairs, 663
Conferences, State, 526-27
Conferences, U.S., 521-26
Converts, American, see Converts
Daughters of the Americas, 663
Daughters of the Americas, Junior, 661
Dictionary, see Glossary
Doctrine, see Doctrine, Catholic
Eastern Churches, 321-28
Education, see Education, Catholic
Evidence Guild, 663
Family Life, USCC, 657
Family Life Insurance, 663
Family Missionary Alliance, 663
Golden Age, 663
Guardian Society, 663
Health Association, 133, 631
Hierarchy, see Hierarchy
History in the U.S., 473-90
Home Bureau for Dependent Children, 663
Hospitals, see Hospitals, Catholic
Interracial Council of New York, 663
Knights of America, 663
Knights of St. George, 663
Kopling Society, 663
Laity, National Council, 656
Lawyers Guild, 663
League, 663
League for Religious and Civil Rights, 133, 143, 280
Library Association, 663
Medical Mission Board, 658
Men, National Council of, 656
Missions, 605-09
Near East Welfare Association, 664
Negro-American Mission Board, 664
News Agencies, 682
One Parent Organization, 664
Order of Foresters, 664
Organizations, 662-70
Organizations, International, 458-60
Pamphlet Society, 664
Peace Fellowship, 664
Pentecostals, see Charismatic Renewal, Catholic
Periodicals, International, 681-82
Periodicals, U.S., 671-81
Population, see Statistics, Catholic
Press, see Press, Catholic
Press Association, 125, 664
Radio Programs, U.S., 686-87
Relief Services, 131, 144, 148, 153, 656-57
Schools, see Schools, Catholic
Social Doctrine, 251-55
Social Services, 631-48
Societies in U.S., 662-70
Statistics, see Statistics, Catholic
Supreme Court Justices, 491
Television Network, 687-88
Television Programs, U.S., 687
Theatre, U.S., 687
Theological Society of America, 664

Catholic
Traditionalist Movement, 664
Truth Society, 664
Union of the Sick in America, 664
Universities, Pontifical, 627-28
Universities, U.S., 619-24
University of America, 628, 687, 696
War Veterans, 664
Women, National Council of, 656
Worker Movement, 664
Workman, 664
Writers' Guild of America, 664
Writers' Market, 683-86
Youth Organization (CYO), 660
See also Church, Catholic
Catholic-Coptic Orthodox Meeting, 331
Catholic-Jewish Relations, 116, 117, 348-50
Catholic-Moslem Relations, 351
Catholic-Orthodox Dialogues, 345-46
Statements, 104, 330-31
See also Orthodox Churches, Eastern
Catholics
Biographies, 396-418
See also Biographies
Black, 89-90
Eastern Rite, 322-26
in 96th Congress, 100
in Presidents' Cabinets, 490-91
in Statuary Hall, 491
in Supreme Court, 491
Spanish-Speaking, U.S., 87-89
World Statistics, 454-55
Catholics United for the Faith, 664
Catich, Edward, Rev., 703
Cauchy, Augustin, 399
Causality, see Existence of God
Causes of Saints, Congregation, 193-94
Cavalieri, Francesco, 399
Caxton, William, 399
Cayenne, see French Guiana
Cayman Islands, 423
Cé, Marco, Card., 202
Cecilia, St., 306
Cecilia Medal, 697
CELAM, 85-7, 121, 458
See also Latin America; Puebla
Celebes, see Indonesia
Celebret, 360
Celebrezze, Anthony (Catholics in Presidents' Cabinets), 490
Celibacy, 72, 80-1, 360
Cellini, Benvenuto, 399
Cenacle, 360
Cenacle, Congregation of Our Lady of the Retreat in the, 583
Auxiliaries, 657
Cenobitic Life (318), 156
Censer, 360
Censorship of Books, 360-61
Censures, 361
Census, U.S. (1980), 148
Center for Applied Research in the Apostolate, 658
Center for Pastoral Liturgy, 664
Center of Concern, 660
Central African Republic, 423
Central America, 130
American Bishops, 507
Cardinals, 215
Episcopal Conferences, 458
See also Latin America
Central Association of the Miraculous Medal, 664
Central Statistics Office, 197
Ceremonies, Master of, 361
Cerularius, Michael (1043-1059), 158
Cervantes Saavedra, Miguel de, 399
Cesalpino, Andrea, 399
Ceuta, 423
Ceylon, see Sri Lanka
Cezanne, Paul, 399
Chabanel, Noel, St., 416
Chabrat, Guy I., S.S., 555
Chad, 423
Chair of Peter (Feast), 301
Chalcedon, Council of, 167
Chalice, 262
Challoner, Richard, 234, 399
Chamber, Apostolic, 197

Chamberlain, 361
Champlain, Samuel de, 399
Champollion, Jean, 399
Chance, John J., S.S., 555
Chancellor, 361
Chancery, 361
Chancery, Apostolic, see Secretariat of State
Chancery Offices, U.S., 519-21
Chandler, Joseph Ripley, 399
Chant, Gregorian, 258
Chapel, 361
Chapelle, Placide L., 555
Chaplain, 361
Chaplains, National Association of Catholic, 631
Chaplains Aid Association, 664
Chaplains and Legislature, Massachusetts, 144
Chaplet, 361
Chapter, 361
Charbonneau, Paul E., Bp., 464
Charismatic Renewal, Catholic, 135, 150, 472
Charisms, 361-62
Charities, Catholic, National Conference, 109, 631
Charities, Pontifical Council, see Cor Unum
Charity, 362
  Heroic Act, 372
Charity, Brothers of, 578
  Institute of (Rosminians), 577
  Servants of, 572
Charity, Sisters of (List), 583-85
Charity, Works of, 147
Charlemagne, 399
Charles, Missionaries of St., Congr., 575
Charles Borromeo, St., 306
Charles Borromeo, St., Missionary Sisters of, 585
Charles Garnier, St., 416
Charles Lwanga and Comps., Sts. (Uganda Martyrs), 306
Charles Martel, 399
Charles of St. Andrew, Beatification Cause, 127
Charter 77, Czechoslovakia, 130-31, 150-51
Chartrand, Joseph, 555
Chastity, 362
  Religious Life, 570
Chasuble, 261
Chasuble-Alb, 261
Chatard, Francis S., 555
Chateaubriand, Francois Rene de, 399
Chaucer, Geoffrey, 399
Chauliac, Guy de, 399
Chaumonot, Pierre J., 416
Chauve, Constantine, S.M., 105
Chavez, Cesar, UFWA Contract, 144
Chavez, Gilbert, Bp., 529
Cherubim (Angels), 355
Cherbuini, Maria Luigi, 400
Chesterton, Gilbert K., 400
Chesterton Society, Conference, 126
Cheverus, John Lefebvre de, 555
Chevreul, Michel Eugene, 400
Chiasson, Donat, Abp., 464
Child, International Year of, 107, 110, 122, 143, 567
Child Jesus, Sisters of the Poor, 585
Child Labor, Exploitation, 146
Children, Importance, 137
Children, Mass for, 266
Childs, Frederick, 703
Chile, 101, 105, 130, 136, 146, 150, 423
  See also Beagle Channel Dispute
Chimy, Jerome, Bp., 464
China, 423-24
  Religion in, 124, 126, 139, 146
  Settlement of Claims, 119
  U.S. Recognition, 106, 107
Chinese Rites (1704), 162
Chirograph, 363
Chisholm, Shirley, Rep., 110
Choirs of Angels (Angels), 355
Chretienne, Sisters of Ste., 585
Chrism, see Oils, Holy
Christ, 362
  Annunciation, 301
  Ascension, 301
  Baptism, 301
  Circumcision (Solemnity of Mary), 304
  Epiphany (Theophany), 302
  in Gospels, 240
  in History, 59

Christ
  Key to Service, 97
  Kingship, 301
  Mystical Body, 225
  Nativity (Christmas), 301
  Passion, 383
    See Stations of the Cross
  Presentation, 304
  Resurrection (Easter), 302
  Sacred Heart, 304, 387
  Seven Last Words, 389
  Transfiguration, 304
  Virgin Birth, 316
Christ, Redeemer of Man (Encyclical), 75-9
Christ, Society of, 572
Christ, United Church of, 337
Christ Child Society, National, 661
Christ the King (Feast) (Nov. 23, 1980), 301
Christ the King, Rural Parish Workers, 602
Christ the King, Sister Servants, 585
Christ the King, Sisters of St. Francis, 590
Christian, see Christians
Christian Awareness, Mature, 103
Christian Brothers, Congregation of, 578
Christian Charity, Franciscan Sisters of, 588
  Sisters of, 584
Christian Church, U.S. (Disciples of Christ), 337
  Ecumenical Dialogues, 342
Christian Culture Award, 697
Christian Doctrine, Confraternity of, 656
Christian Doctrine, Sisters of Our Lady, 585
Christian Education, Religious of, 585
Christian Family Movement, 658
Christian Initiation, see Baptism
Christian Instruction, Brothers of, 578
Christian Life Communities, 658
Christian Observances, Public Schools, 104
Christian Schools, Brothers, 578
Christian Science, 362
Christian Students, Young, 661
Christian Unity, 125, 130
Christian Unity, Week of Prayer, 107, 395
  See also Ecumenism
Christian Unity Secretariat, 98, 195, 339, 347
Christian Witness, 395
Christianity, 362
Christianity, Political, 100-01
Christianity and Social Progress (Social Doctrine), 251
Christians, 362
Christians, Baptized, Reception, 272
Christie, Alexander, 555
Christmas, 301
  Message, John Paul II, 103-04
Christmastide, 290
Christology, 53
Christopher, St., 306
Christopher Movement, 664
  Awards, 114, 693
  Radio-TV Work, 686, 687
Christos (Christ), 362
Christus Dominus, 168
Chronicles (Books of Bible), 236
Chronology
  Church History, 155-66
  Church in U.S., 476-90
  Ecumenical Councils, 166-68
  Old Testament, 239
  Popes, 169-73
  U.S. Episcopates, 498-506
Chrysostom, John, St., 248
Church, 362
Church (Catholic), 224-27
  and Unity, see Ecumenism
  and World, 251
  and World Council of Churches, 340
  Apostolic Succession, 356
  Art, 258
  Authority, see Magisterium
  Belief, see Doctrine
  Constitution on, 224-27, 227-28, 259, 270-71, 276-77, 315-16, 361, 388
  Creeds, 249-50
  Discipline, Necessity, 98
  Doctrine, 224-55
  Eastern, 321-28
  Freedom Necessary, 58-9

Index

Church (Catholic)
- Hierarchy, 186-88
- History, Dates, 155-66
- in Canada, 461-72
- in Countries of the World, 419-53
  - See also Individual Countries
- in Modern World, Constitution, 251-55, 281-82, 357
- in U.S., 473 ff
- Infallibility, 227-28
- Languages, 377
- Law, see Canon Law
- Liturgy, see Liturgy
- Marriage Doctrine, Laws, see Marriage
- Ministries, 95, 277
- Mystery of, 224-25
- Precepts, 251
- Prophetic Office, 226
- Relations with other Churches, see Ecumenism; Catholic-Jewish Relations
- Rites, 258, 321-25
- Sacraments, 270-77
- Salvation, 388
- Social Doctrine, 251-55
- Statistics, see Statistics
- Treasury, 394
- Year (Calendar), 290-300

Church, Authority in, Anglican-Catholic Statement, 347
Church, Catholic-Orthodox Statement, 330
Church, Purpose of, Anglican-Catholic Statement, 346
Church and State, U.S. (Wall of Separation), 495
- IRS Guidelines, 114
- Relations, 525
- Supreme Court Decisions, 491-95
  - See also Legal Status of Catholic Education
Church in Need, The (Aid Agency), 121
Church Membership, U.S., 133
Church Property, Taxation, 495-96
Churches, Eastern, 321-31
Churches, National Council, 341
Churches, Orthodox, 328-31
Churches, Protestant, in U.S., 333-37
Churches, World Council, see World Council of Churches
Churching, 362
Ciappi, Mario Luigi, O.P., Card., 202
Ciborium, 262
Cimabue, Giovanni, 400
Cimichella, Andre, O.S.M., Bp., 464
Cincture, 261
Circumcision, 362
- Feast, see Solemnity of Mary
Circumincession, 362
Cistercian Nuns, 585
Cistercians, Order of (Men), 572
Cistercians of the Strict Observance (Trappists), 572
Citizens for Educational Freedom, 664
Civardi, Ernesto, Card., 202
Civil Rights, Institutionalized Persons, 129
Civil Rights, USCC and, 109
Civil Rights and Homosexuals, see Homosexuals
Civil Rights League, Catholic, 133, 143, 280
Civiletti, Benjamin (Catholics in Presidents' Cabinets), 491
Clairvaux Abbey (1115), 159
Clancy, William, 555
Clare, St., 306
Clare, St., Order of, see Poor Clare Nuns, Franciscan
Claretians, 572
- Louisiana State University Campus Ministers, 124
Clark, Dick, Sen., 99
Clark, Mark, Gen., 220
Clark, Matthew H., Bp., 529
Claudel, Paul, 400
Claver, Peter, St., 416
Clavius, Christopher, 400
Clement I, St., 306
Clergy, 362
- Congregation, 194
- Immunity, 374
- See also Celibacy
Clergy, Byzantine, 328
Clergy, Chamberlain of Roman, 361
Clergy, Congr. of Our Lady Help of the, 585
Clergy, Servants of Our Lady Queen of, 585
Clerical Communities of Men, 568
Clericalism, 362
Clerics of St. Viator, 577
Clerics Regular, Congregation of (Theatines), 577
Clerics Regular, Ministers of the Sick (Camillians), 572
Clerics Regular Minor, 573
Clerics Regular of St. Paul (Barnabites), 571
Clerke, Agnes Mary, 400
Clinch, Harry A., Bp., 529
Cloister, 362
Clune, Robert B., Bp., 464
Cluny Abbey (910), 158
Coadjutor Bishop, 187
Coady, Moses M., 400
Cobo, Bernabe, 400
Code, 362
- See also Canon Law
Coderre, Gerard M., Bp., 464
Cody, John P., Card., 203
Cody, William, 400
Coggan, Donald, Abp. (Anglican), 111, 150
Cohill, John E., S.V.D., Bp., 529
Coins, Vatican, 108, 222
Colbert, Claudette, 145
Coll, Francisco, Beatification, 122
College of Cardinals, 199-200
- Meeting, 153
Colleges, Catholic, U.S., 619-24
Collegiality, 75, 107, 228-29, 362
- See also Synod of Bishops
Collegian Award, 697
Collettines (Franciscan Poor Clare Nuns), 588
Collins, John J., S.J., 555
Collins, Michael, 400
Collins, Thomas P., M.M., 555
Colombia, 106, 121, 424
Colombo, Giovanni, Card., 203
Colombo, Matteo Realdo, 400
Colorado, 477, 510, 513, 515, 526, 616, 624, 632, 641, 650, 689
Colors, Liturgical, 261-62
Colossians, 241
Colton, Charles H., 555
Columba, St., 306
Columban, St., 306
Columban, St., Missionary Sisters, 585
Columban, St., Society of, 573
Columbian Squires, 660
Columbus, Christopher, 400
Columbus, Knights of, see Knights of Columbus
Comber, John W., M.M., Bp., 529
Comillas, Pontifical Univ. (Spain), 628
Commandments of God, 250
Commissariat of the Holy Land, 363
Commission for Catholic Missions among Colored and Indians, 105, 609
Commissions, Roman Curia, 196-97
Common of Mass, 261
Communicants, First, Papal Mass, 132
Communications, 671-93
Communications Day, 128, 148
Communications Foundation, Catholic, 688
Communications Media, Church Use, 119
- Collection, 130, 134, 523
- Commission, 196
  - See also Press, Catholic
Communications Offices, 689-93
Communion, Holy (Holy Eucharist), 273-75
- Fast before Reception, 370
- First, and First Confession, 273
- in Hand Reception, 617
- Intercommunion, 98, 127, 274, 375
- Intinction, 376
- Ministers, Special, 268
- Reception Outside of Mass, 274
- Reception Twice a Day, 274, 524
- under Forms of Bread and Wine, 274, 524
- Viaticum, 394
- See also Eucharist, Holy
Communion of Mass, 260
Communion of Saints, 363
Communion of the Faithful, 363
Communism, 453-54
- Ostpolitik, 382
"Communist Manifesto" (1848), 162
Community, 253
Comoro Islands, 424
Company of Mary, 594
Company of Mary, Little, 594
Company of St. Paul, 602

Company of St. Ursula, 602
Comunidades de Base (Spanish Speaking), 88
Conaty, Thomas J., 555
Concanen, Richard L., O.P., 555
Concelebration, 363
  Inter-Ritual, 266
Conciliarists, see Florence, Council of
Conclave, see Papal Election
Concord Formula (1577), 161
Concordance, Biblical, 363
Concordat, 363
  of Worms (1122), 159
  Revisions, Italy, 133
  Vatican-Spain, 108
Concupiscence, 363
Condon, William J., 555
Conewego, Chapel (1741), 487
Confalonieri, Carlo, Card., 203
Conference of Major Superiors of Men in U.S., 145, 579
Confession (Penance), 122, 270, 275-76, 363
  Children's, 138
  First, and First Communion, 273
    See also Catechetical Directory
  Frequent, 526
  Revised Rite, 267
  Seal, 389
    See also General Absolution; Penance
Confessional, 264
Confessor, 363
Confirmation, 267, 270, 272-73
  Follow-Up Programs, 525
Confraternity, 363
  of the Immaculate Conception, 664
Confraternity of Christian Doctrine, 656
Confucianism, 352
Congo Republic, 425
Congregationalists, 333
Congregations, Curial, 192-95
Congregations, Religious, 568
Congress, U.S., Religious Affiliations, 100
Congresses, Eucharistic, 368
Connare, William G., Bp., 144, 530
Connecticut, 477-78, 508, 512, 514, 526, 613, 625, 632, 641, 643, 650, 689
  Arms Industry, 128
Connell, Francis J., 400
Connelly, Cornelia, 400
Connelly, James L., Bp., 530
Connolly, John, O.P., 555
Connolly, Matthew, Msgr., 703
Connolly, Thomas A., Abp., 530
Connolly, Thomas J., Bp., 530
Connor, John, 490
Connors, Ronald G., C.SS.R., Bp., 530
Conroy, John J., 555
Conroy, Joseph J., 555
Conscience, 363
  Examination of, 363
Conscience Clauses, 94, 129
Conscientious Objectors, 254
Consecration (Dedication) of Church, 363
Consecration of the Mass, 260
Consistory, 363
Consolata Missionary Sisters, 585
Consolata Society for Foreign Missions, 573
Consortium Perfectae Caritatis, 100, 600
Constance, Council, 167
Constantine the Great, 400
Constantinople, Councils of, 167
Constantinople, Fall of (1453), 160
Constitution, 363
Constitutional Convention, 134
Consubstantiation, 364
Consultation on Church Union, 341
Contardo Ferrini, Bl., 306
Contemplative Institutes (Religious), 142, 568
Contemplative Sisters, Association of, 600
Contraception, 73, 364
  See also *Humanae Vitae*
Contrition, 364
Contumely, 364
Conventuals (Franciscans), 574
Conversion, Progressive, 81
Convert Movement Our Apostolate, 145, 664
Converts (Christian Initiation, Reception of Baptized Christians), 271-72

Converts, U.S., 516
Conwell, Henry, 555
Cook Islands, 425
Cooke, Terence J., Card., 149, 203
Cooray, Thomas B., O.M.I., Card., 203
Cope, 262
Copernicus, Nicolaus, 400
Coppee, Francois, 400
Coptic Orthodox-Catholic Meeting, 133, 331
Copts, Catholic, 323
Cor Unum, 196
Corbett, Timothy, 555
Cordeiro Joseph, Card., 203
Cordi-Marian Missionary Sisters, 585
Cordoba, Francisco Fernandez, 400
Corinthians, 241
Corneille, Pierre, 400
Cornelius, St., 306
Corot, Jean, 400
Corporal, 263
Corporal Works of Mercy, 364
Corporate Responsibility, 109, 143, 149
Corpus Christi (June 8, 1980), 296, 302
  Observances, 132, 135
Correggio, Antonio, 400
Corrigan, Joseph, 555
Corrigan, Michael A., 555
Corrigan, Owen, 555
Corripio Ahumada, Ernesto, Card., 203
Cortez, Hernando, 400
Cory, Herbert Ellsworth, 400
Coscia, Benedict D., O.F.M., Bp., 530
Cosgrove, Henry, 555
Cosgrove, William M., Bp., 530
Cosmas and Damian, Sts., 306
Costa Rica, 425
Costello, Joseph A., 555
Costello, Thomas J., Bp., 530
Cote, Philip, S.J., 555
Cotey, Bernard R., S.D.S., Bp., 530
Cotter, Joseph B., 555
Cotton, Francis R., 555
Couderc, St. Therese, 310
Coulomb, Charles A., 400
Council, Second Vatican, 168
  and Mary, 315
  Excerpts from Documents, 224-27, 227-28, 229-32, 251-55, 256-58, 259, 263, 270-71, 276-77, 281-82, 286, 290, 315-16, 330, 338-39, 348, 351, 357, 361, 366, 370, 371, 393, 451, 569-70, 601
Council of European Bishops, 102, 132, 136, 458
Councils of the Church (Catholic), 364
  Ecumenical, 166-68
  Plenary, 364
  Plenary, Baltimore, 474
  Provincial, 364
Counsels, Evangelical, 364
Counter-Reformation, 364
Countries, Church in, 419-53
Countries, Patrons, 313-14
Countries, Poor, Preferential Treatment, 129
Couperin, Francois, 400
Court, Supreme, see Supreme Court, U.S.
Coury, George, 703
Cousin, Jean, 400
Cousins, William E., Abp., 530
Couture, Jean-Guy, Bp., 464
Couturier, Gerard, Bp., 464
Covenant, 364
Covenant, Old, see Revelation, Constitution
Covenanting, Council for, England, 150
Covetousness (Avarice), 357
Cowley, Leonard P., 555
Crane, Michael J., 555
Crashaw, Richard, 400
Crawford, Francis Marion, 400
Creation, 364
Creator, 364
Creature, 364
Credal Statement, Latin American Bishops, 87
Credi, Lorenz de, 400
Creed of the Mass, 260, 524
  See also Nicene Creed
Creeds of the Church, 249-50
Creighton, Edward, 400
Creighton, John, 400

Index

Cremation, 364-65
Crete, see Greece
Cretin, Joseph, 555
Crib, 365
Crimont, Joseph, 555
Crispin and Crispinian, Sts., 306
Criticism, Biblical, 242
Croatians (Byzantine Rite), 324
   Faithfulness, 123
Cromwell, Oliver (1649), 161
Cronin, Daniel A., Bp., 530
Crosier, 365
Crosier Fathers, 573
Cross
   Pectoral, 383
   Sign of the, 390
   Stations of the, 391-92
   Triumph (Exaltation), 304
Cross, Canons Regular of Holy, 573
   Congregation of Holy (Brothers), 578
   Congregation of Holy (Priests), 573
   Daughters of, 585
   Sisters of the Holy, 585
Cross and Passion, Nuns, 585
   Sisters, 585
Cross and Seven Dolors, Srs. of Holy, 585
"Crossroads," 124, 686
Crowley, Joseph R., Bp., 530
Crowley, Leonard P., Bp., 464
Crowley, Timothy J., 555
Crown, Franciscan, 371
Crowned Shrine, 390
Crucified, Daughters of, 585
Crucifix, 264
Crucifix, Stations (Stations of the Cross), 392
Cruets, 264
Crusade for More Fruitful Preaching, 665
Crusades (1097-1099), 159
Crypt, 365
Cuba, 425
Cult of Saints, 388
Cults, 96, 108
Cum Gravissima, see Cardinals, College
Cummins, John S., Bp., 530
Cunningham, David F., Bp., 555, 703
Cunningham, John F., 555
Cura Animarum, 365
Curacao, see Netherlands Antilles
Curia, 365
Curia, Diocesan, 365
Curia, Roman, 97, 137, 180, 190-99
Curley, Daniel J., 555
Curley, Michael J., 555
Curran, Charles, Rev., 114
Cursillo Movement, 658
Curtis, Alfred A., 555
Curtis, Walter W., Bp., 530
Curtiss, Elden F., Bp., 530
Cusack, Thomas, 555
Cushing, Richard J., 400
Custos, 365
Cyprian, St., 306
Cyprus, 425
Cyril and Methodius, Sts., 306
   See also Czechoslovakia
Cyril and Methodius, Srs. of Sts., 585
Cyril of Alexandria, St., 248
Cyril of Jerusalem, St., 248
Czartoryski, August, S.D.B., Canonization Cause, 103
Czech Catholic Union of Texas, 665
Czech Catholics, National Alliance of, 667
Czechoslovakia, 79, 101, 111, 130-31, 150-51, 425-26
Czestochowa, Our Lady of (Jasna Gora), 395
   John Paul II Visit, 56-7, 59-60
Czestochowa Shrine, Doylestown, Pa., 148

D

Dablon, Claude, 400
Daeger, Albert T., O.F.M., 555
Dahomey, see Benin
Daily, Thomas V., Bp., 530
Daley, Joseph T., Bp., 530
Dalmatic, 261
Daly, Edward C., O.P., 555
Daly, James, Bp., 531
Daly, Mary Tinley, 703

Daly, Thomas A., 400
Damasus I, St., 306
Damian, St. (Sts. Cosmas and Damian.) 306
Damiano, Celestine, 556
Damien, Father (Joseph de Veuster), 400
Damien-Dutton Award, 697
Damien-Dutton Society, 665
Danehy, Thomas J., M.M., 556
Danglmayr, Augustine, Bp., 531
Daniel, 238
Daniel, Anthony, St., 416
Daniel-Rops, Henri, 400
Dante Alighieri, 401
Danzig, 426
D'Antonio, Nicholas, O.F.M., Bp., 531
D'Arcy, John M., Bp., 531
D'Argenlieu, Georges, 396
Dargin, Edward V., Bp., 531
Darmojuwono, Justin, Card., 203
Darwin, Charles (1882), 163
Das Kapital (1867), 163
   See also Communism
Dates, see Chronology
Daughters of Isabella, 665
Daughters of Our Lady of Fatima, 603
Daumer, Georg Friedrich, 401
Davenport, Sir William, 401
David, see Historical Books of Bible
David, John B., S.S., 556
David, St., 306
Davis, James, 565
Davis, James P., Abp., 531
Davis, Joseph M., S.M., Bro. 145
Dawson, Christopher, 401
Day, Dorothy, 120
Day of Atonement, 351
Day of Indiction, 292
DC-10 Crash, Chicago, 129
Deacon, 277
Deaconess, 365
Deacons, First Seven, 277
Deacons, Permanent, 121
Deacons, Permanent, U.S., 105, 119, 277-80
Dead, Resurrection, 82
Dead Sea Scrolls, 235
Deaf, 648
   Facilities for, 640-41, 648
   Foundation for, 144
Dean, 365
Dean of Sacred College, 365
De Araujo Sales, Eugenio, Card., 203
Dearden, John F., Card., 203
Death of God, see Atheism
Death Penalty, see Capital Punishment
Deaths (Oct. 1, 1978 to Oct. 1, 1979), 703-04
Decalogue (Ten Commandments), 250
DeChevrus, John L., 555
Decision, Apostolic, 365
Declaration, 365
Decosse, Aime, Bp., 464
Decree, 365
Decree of Nullity, 286, 287
Decretals, False (847-852), 158
Dedication of a Church, 365
Dedication of Basilica of St. Mary Major, 302
   of Lateran Basilica, 302
De Eggenfelden, Vitricius, Beatification Cause, 127
DeFalco, Lawrence M., Bp., 703
Defensor Pacis (1324), 160
Definitors, 366
De Furstenberg, Maximilien, Card., 204
De Gaulle, Charles, 401
De Goesbriand, Louis, 556
Dei Verbum (Divine Revelation Decree), 168, 229-32, 370, 393
Deism, 366
Deksnys, Antanas L., Bp., 531
Delacroix, Ferdinand, 401
De la Hailandiere, Celestine, 556
Delany, John B., 556
Delaquis, Noel, Bp., 464
Delargey, Reginald John, Card., 703
Delaroche, Paul, 401
Delaware, 478, 508, 512, 514, 613, 632, 641, 650, 689
Delegates, Apostolic, see Apostolic Delegates
Delta Epsilon Sigma, 661

Demers, Modeste, 556
Dempsey, Michael J., O.P., Bp., 531
Dempsey, Michael R., 556
De Neckere, Leo, C.M., 556
Denis, St., 306
Denmark, 426
Denning, Joseph P., Bp., 531
De Osso y Cervello, Enrico, Beatification, 127, 152
De Palma, Joseph A., S.C.J., Bp., 531
De Porres, Martin, St., 417
De Riedmatten, Henri, O.P., 703
DeRoo, Remi, J., Bp., 464
De Rossi, Giovanni, 401
DeSaint Palais, Maurice, 556
DeSales, Francis, St., 248
DeSales Secular Institute, 602
Descartes, Rene, 401
Desegregation, School, Brown Case Anniversary, 129
Desmarais, Joseph A., Bp., 464
De Smet, Pierre, 416
Desmond, Daniel F., 556
De Soto, Hernando, 401
Despair, 366
Despatie, Roger A., Bp., 464
Detachment, 366
Detraction, 366
Deusto, Catholic University (Spain), 628
Deuterocanonical Books, 233
Deutero-Isaiah (Isaiah), 238
Deutero-Zechariah (Zechariah), 239
Deuteronomy, 235
De Valera, Eamon, 401
De Vaux, Roland, 401
Development, Human, see Campaign for Human Development
Development of Peoples, see Social Doctrine
Developmentally Handicapped, Catholic Facilities, 643-46
Devil, 366
Devil's Advocate (Promoter of the Faith), 385
Devlin, Joseph, 401
Devotion, 366
Devotion, Eucharistic, 274
Devotions, 366
Dhanis, Edouard, S.J., 703
Diabolical Obsession, 381
Diabolical Possession, 384
Diaconate, see Deacons, Permanent
Dialogue, Catholic-Moslem, 351
Dialogues, Ecumenical, 341-47
  Evaluation Proposed, 98
Dias, Batholomew, 401
Dictionary, see Glossary
Didache (Second Century), 155
Didymus (Thomas), 246
Dies Irae, 366
Dies Natalis, 291
Dignitatis Humanae (Religious Freedom Declaration), 168, 371
DiJorio, Alberto, Card., 703
Dimmerling, Harold J., Bp., 531
Dimnet, Ernest, 401
Dinand, Joseph N., S.J., 556
Dingman, Maurice J., Bp., 531
Diocesan Laborer Priests, 602
Diocese, 366
Dioceses, Canadian, 462-63
Dioceses, U.S., 490-506
  Chancery Office Addresses, 519-21
  Communications Offices, 689-93
  Eastern Rite, 326
  Permanent Diaconate Programs, 277-80
  with Interstate Lines, 511
Dioceses, World, 454
Diocletian (292, 303), 156
Dionne, Gerard, Bp., 464
Dionysius Exiguus (C. 545), 157
Dior, Christian, 401
Diplomacy, Papal, 118, 215-16
Diplomats, John Paul II Address, 107
Diplomats at Vatican, 219-20
Disarmament, 255
  See also Salt II
Disasters, 98, 103, 113, 129, 148
Discalced, 366
Discalced Carmelites (Nuns), 583
  Carmelites, Order of (Men), 572

Disciple, 366
Disciples of Christ (Christian Church), 337
Disciples of Christ-Catholic Agreement on Baptism, 105
Disciples of the Divine Master, Sister, 586
Disciplina Arcani, 366
Discipline, Church, Preservation Necessary, 98
Discrimination.
  Catholic Military Chaplains, 113
  Harris Poll, 114
  Religious, Bordentown, N.J., Correctional Facility, 114
Diskos, 327
Dismas, St., 306
Dispensation, 366
District of Columbia, 478, 508, 512, 514, 613, 625, 643, 650, 689
Divination, 366
Divine Compassion, Sisters, 586
Divine Love, Oblates to, 586
Divine Office, see Liturgy of the Hours
Divine Positive Law, see Law
Divine Praises, 367
Divine Redeemer, Sisters, 597
Divine Revelation, Constitution, 229-32
Divine Savior, Sisters, 598
Divine Spirit, Congregation, 586
Divine Word, Society of, 573
Divine Worship, Sacraments and, Congregation, 193
Divino Afflante Spiritu (Biblical Studies), 242, 243
Divisch, Wenceslaus (Procopius), 401
Divorce, 73, 285, 288
Divorce Law, Pennsylvania, 125
Divorced and Remarried Catholics, Ministry for, 287-88
  Good Conscience Procedure, 289
  See also Marriage
Divorced Catholics, Judean Society, 666
Djibouti, 427
DNA Research, 95
Dobson, Robert, 556
Docetism, 164
Doctors, Church, 247-49
Doctrinal Statements, 1979
  Life after Death, 82
  Human Sexuality, 83-4
  Quand Je Dis Dieu, 81, 123
Doctrine, Catholic, 224-55
  Development, 230
  Marian, 315-19
  Marriage, 281-83
  Purity and Integrity, 98
  Social, 251-55
Doctrine of the Faith, Congregation, 192
  Statements (1979), 81-4, 123
Dolci, Carlo, 401
Dolinay, Thomas V., Bp., 531
Dolors, see Sorrows of BVM
Domenec, Michael, C.M., 556
Dominations (Angels), 355
Dominic, St., 306
  Sisters of the Third Order of, 586-87
  Third Order Secular, 604
  See also Dominicans
Dominic Savio, St., 307
Dominic Savio Classroom Club, 661
Dominica, 148, 427
Dominican Laity, 604
Dominican Republic, 427
  John Paul II Visit, 49, 51-2
Dominicans (Men), 573
Dominicans (Women), 586-87
Don Bosco Volunteers, 603
Donaghy, Frederick, M.M., Bp., 531
Donahue, Joseph P., 556
Donahue, Patrick J., 556
Donahue, Stephen J., Bp., 531
Donatello, 401
Donation of Pepin (754), 157
Donatism, 165
Donders, Peter, Beatification Cause, 127
Dongon, Thomas, 401
Donizetti, Gaetano, 401
Donnellan, Thomas A., Abp., 531
Donnelly, George J., 556
Donnelly, Henry E., 556
Donnelly, Joseph F., 556
Donohoe, Hugh A., Bp., 531
Donovan, John A., Bp., 532

Index

Donovan, John F., M.M., 703
Donovan, Paul V., Bp., 532
Dooley, Thomas A., 401
Doran, Thomas F., 556
Doria, Andrea, 401
Dornan, Robert, Rep., 99
Dorothy, Institute of Sisters of St., 587
Douay-Rheims Bible, 234
Double Effect Principle, 367
Dougherty, Dennis, 556
Dougherty, John J., Bp., 532
Dougherty, Joseph P., 556
Douville, Arthur, Bp., 464
Dowling, Austin, 556
Doxology, 367
  Mass, 260, 268
Doyle, James L., Bp., 465
Doyle, Wilfrid E., Bp., 465
Doylestown, Pa., Czestochowa Shrine, 148
Dozier, Carroll T., Bp., 532
Draft, 134, 149
Drainville, Gerard, Bp., 465
Drexel, Mary Katherine, 401
Driscoll, Justin A., Bp., 532
Drossaerts, Arthur J., 556
Drum, Hugh A., 401
Drumm, Thomas W., 556
Drury, Thomas, Bp., 149, 532
Dryden, John, 401
Dubois, John, S.S., 556
Dubourg, William L., S.S., 556
Dubuis, Claude M., 556
Duchesne, Rose Philippine, Bl., 416
Dudick, Michael J., Bp., 532
Dudley, Paul, Bp., 532
Dufal, Peter, C.S.C., 556
Duffy, Charles Gavan, 401
Duffy, James A., 556
Duffy, John A., 556
Duggan, James, 556
Duhart, Clarence J., C.SS.R., Bp., 532
Dulia, 367
Dulong, Pierre, 401
Du Maine, Roland Pierre, Bp., 532
Dumas, Jean Baptiste, 401
Dumouchel, Paul, O.M.I., Abp., 465
Dunn, Francis J., Bp., 532
Dunn, John J., 556
Dunne, Edmund M., 556
Dunne, Edward, 556
Dunne, Peter F., 401
Duns Scotus, John, 401
Dunstan, St., 307
Durer, Albrecht, 401
Durick, Joseph A., Bp., 532
Durier, Anthony, 556
Durkin, Martin P., 401
Durning, Dennis, C.S.Sp., Bp., 432
Dutch Church, Synod, 111, 150
Dutch Guiana, see Surinam
Dutton, Ira (Brother Joseph), 401
Duty, 367
Duty, Easter, 367
Duty, Parental, 383
Duval, Leon-Etienne, Card., 204
DuVigneaud, Vincent, Dr., 703
Dwenger, Joseph, C.PP.S., 556
Dwight, Thomas, 401
Dworschak, Leo F., 556
Dwyer, Robert J., 556
Dymphna, St., 307
  National Shrine, 666

E

East Germany, 429-30
Easter, 302
  Controversy, 367
  Date, 300, 367
  Dates (1980-2004), 300
  Duty, 367
  Season, 290-91
  Time, see Easter Duty
  Vigil, 302
  Water, 367
Easter Message, John Paul II, 123
Eastern Churches, Catholic, 321-28
  Celibacy, 360
  Decree (Vatican II), 286, 321-22, 330
  Inter-Ritual Concelebrations, 266
  John Paul II Address, 72
  Jurisdictions, 324-25
  Liturgy, Byzantine Rite, 326-27
  Marriage Laws, 286
  Patriarchs, 321
  Rites, Riches of, 98
  Rites and Faithful, 322-24
  Sacraments, 321
  Sacred Congregation, 192-93
  Statistics, Canada, 470
  Statistics, U.S., 326, 511, 515, 616
  Synods, Assemblies, 325
  Ukrainian Bishops Meeting, Rome, 151
  Worship, 322
  See also Byzantine Rite
Eastern Churches, Separated, 328-30
  Intercommunion, 274
  See also Ecumenism; Orthodox Churches, Eastern; Orthodox Church, Oriental
Eastern Ecumenism, 330-31
Eastern Rite Information Service, 683
Ebacher, Roger, Bp., 465
Ecclesiastes, 237
Ecclesiastical
  Burial, 358
  Calendar, 290-93
  Honors, 694, 695
  Jurisdictions, World (Statistics), 454
  Law, 378
  Provinces, Canada, 462
  Provinces, U.S., 497-98
Ecclesiasticus, see Sirach
Ecclesiology, 367
Eccleston, Samuel, S.S., 556
Eck, Johann, 401
Eckhel, Joseph, 401
Economic Affairs, Prefecture, 197
Ecstasy, 367
Ecthesis (649), 157
Ecuador, 427
  Catholic University, 627
Ecumenical Councils, 166-68
  See also Council, Second Vatican
Ecumenism, 147, 330-31, 338-48, 367-68
  and Intercommunion, 98, 127, 274-75, 375
  and Mary, 319
  and Separated Eastern Christians, 330-31
  Bishops' Committee, 340
  Catholic-Lutheran Committee, New York, 109
  Catholic-Methodist Dialogue, 115
  Catholic-Orthodox Dialogue, Relations, 104, 345-46
  Catholics and British Council of Churches, 121
  Decree on, 338-39
  Dialogues, Evaluation, 98
  Dialogues, U.S., 341-46
  Disciples of Christ — Catholic Agreement, 105
  Eastern, 330-31
  Kentuckiana Community, 139
  National Workshop on Christian Unity, 125
  Participation in Worship, 339
  Reconciliation of Ministries Conference, England, 150
  Statements, 346-47
  Vatican Secretariat, 339
  Week of Prayer for Christian Unity, 107, 395
  World Council of Churches — Vatican, 116, 118
  See also Catholic-Jewish Relations; Catholic-Moslem Relations
Eddy, Mary Baker (Christian Science), 362
Edict of Milan (313), 156
Edith Stein Guild, 665
  Award, 697
Edmund, Society of St., 573
Edmund Campion, St., 307
Education, Catholic, Congregation, 194
Education, Catholic, Gospel Inspiration, 102
Education, Catholic, U.S., 610-27
  Campus Ministry, 624
  Catechetical Directory, 90-1, 118, 523
  Facilities for Handicapped, 640-46
  Legal Status, 610-11
    See also Church-State Decisions
  Report, 617

Education, Catholic
    School Aid Decisions, 612
    Statistics, 613-16, 617
    Supreme Court Decisions (1979), 617
    Teacher Unions, 618
    Unemployment Insurance Tax, 617
    Universities and Colleges, 619-24
    See also Schools, Catholic; Seminaries
Education, Department of, 114, 153, 617
Education, Religious, 656
    Catechetical Directory, 90-1, 118, 523
    Catechetics, Apostolic Exhortation, 91
    Pupils Receiving Instruction, 617
Educational Association, National Catholic, 612
Edwin V. O'Hara Institute, 688
Egan, Michael, O.F.M., 556
Egypt, 427
Egypt-Israeli Peace Agreements, see Middle East Peace Efforts
Eichendorff, Joseph von, 401
Eileton, 327
Eire, see Ireland
Eis, Frederick, 557
Ekandem, Dominic, Card., 204
Elder, William, 557
Elections, Papal, 382-83
    Eligibility of Cardinals, 199, 214
Elections, U.S., and Right-to-Life Vote, 99
Elevation, 368
Elgar, Edward, 401
Elias IV of Antioch, Patriarch (Orthodox), 133
Elijah (Kings), 236
Elisha (Kings), 236
Elizabeth of Hungary, St., 307
Elizabeth of Portugal, St., 307
Elizabeth Seton, St., 307
Elko, Nicholas T., Abp., 532
El Salvador, 427
    New Government, 154
    Persecution, Violence, 101, 111, 121, 131, 141, 151
Elvira Council (306), 156, 360
Elwell, Clarence F., 557
Ember Days, 292
Emblems of Saints, 314-15
Embolism (Prayer for Deliverance), 260
Emmanuel D'Alzon Medal, 697
Emmerich, Anne C., 401
Emmet, Thomas A., S.J., 557
Emotionally Maladjusted, Catholic Facilities, 641-43
Empire, Paul, Rev., 703
"Encuentro," 686
Encuentros, see Spanish-Speaking
Encyclical *Redemptor Hominis*, 75-9, 118
Encyclicals, 182
    Authority, 182
    List, Leo XIII to John Paul II, 182-85
    Social, 251
End Justifies the Means, 368
Endlicher, Stephen, 401
Energy, 232
England, 111, 121, 125, 130, 150, 428
    Anglican Synod, 101, 116, 140
    Catholic Priorities, 125
    Catholic Relief Act (1926), 164
    Martyrs, 181-82
    Popish Plot (1678), 161
    Test Act (1673), 161
    Test Tube Baby, 93-4
England, John, 401
English and Welsh Martyrs, 181-82
Enlightenment, Age, 161
Enrique y Tarancon, Vicente, Card., 204
Enthronement of the Sacred Heart, 665
Environment, 232
Envy, 368
Eparch, 187
Epee, Charles Michel de L', 401
Ephesians, 241
Ephesus, Council, 167
Ephesus, "Robber" Council (449), 156
Ephraem, St., 248
Epikeia, 368
Epimanikia, 327
Epiphany, 302
Episcopal Church, see Anglican Communion
Episcopal Church in U.S., 336

Episcopal Church
    Convention, 149
    Ecumenical Dialogues, 342-43
    See also Ecumenism
Episcopal Conferences, 455-58
Episcopal Vicar, 187
Episcopate, 368
Epistles (Letters), 240-41
Epitrachelion, 327
Equal Rights Amendment (ERA), 570
Equality, 253
Equatorial Guinea, 428
    Government Overthrown, 145
Equivocation, 368
Erasmus, Desiderius, 402
Erasmus, St., 307
Eritrea, see Ethiopia
Escalante, Alonso Manuel, M.M., 557
Eschatology, 368
    Doctrinal Letter on Church Teaching, 82
Escriva de Belaguer, Jose Maria, 402
    See also Opus Dei
Espelage, Bernard, O.F.M., 557
Espelage, Sylvester J., O.F.M., 557
Essenes, see Dead Sea Scrolls
Estaing, Jean Baptiste D', 402
Esther, 237
Etchegaray, Roger, Card., 204
Eternity, 368
    Life after Death, Doctrinal Letter, 82
Ethelbert, St., 307
Ethics, 368
    Situational, 391
Ethiopia, 428
    Food Shortage, 111
Ethiopian Rite Catholics, 323
Ettel, Michael, 130
Etteldorf, Raymond P., Abp., 532
Euangelion (Gospel), 240
Eucharist, Holy, 267, 270, 273-75
    Administration to Non-Catholics, 275
    Devotion Outside of Mass, 274
    Fast, 370
    Hosts, 268
    John Paul II on, 65
    Ministers of, 268
    Ministers of, and Papal Visit, 148
    Reservation of, see Tabernacle
    Sacrifice, see Mass
    See also Communion, Holy; Transubstantiation
Eucharist, Brothers of the Holy, 579
Eucharist, Anglican-Catholic Statement, 346
Eucharist, Lutheran-Catholic Statement, 347
Eucharist, Orthodox Church, 331
Eucharist, Religious of, 587
Eucharistic Congresses, 368
Eucharistic Guard for Nocturnal Adoration, 665
Eucharistic Liturgy, 260
Eucharistic Missionary Sisters, 587
Eucharistic Prayers (Mass), 260, 265-66
    Experimentation, 268-69
Eudes, John, St., 308
Eudists (Congregation of Jesus and Mary), 573
Eugenics, 368-69
Euphrasia Pelletier, St., 307
Europe
    Bishops' Conference, 102, 132, 136, 458
    Cardinals, 214
    Catholic Statistics, 454-55
    Eastern Rite Jurisdictions, 324
    Pro-Life Movement, 112
Eusebius of Vercelli, St., 307
Eustace, Bartholomew J., 557
Eustachius, Bartolommeo, 402
Euthanasia, 369
Euthanasia, England, Survey, 111
Eutychianism, 165
Evangelical Counsels, 364
Evangelion, 293
Evangelists, 245-46
Evangelization, 51-2, 53, 115, 116, 132, 145, 152, 185, 189
    and Liberation, 85
    National Catholic Lay Celebration, 145
Evangelization of Peoples, Congregation of, 194
Evans, George R., Bp., 532
Everson v. Board of Education, 492

Index

Evolution, 369
Ewing J. Franklin, 402
Ewing, Thomas, 402
Ex Cathedra, 228
 See also Infallibility
Exaltation of the Holy Cross, see Triumph of the Cross
Examen, Particular (Examination of Conscience), 363
Exarch, 187
Exceptional Children, see Handicapped, Facilities for
Excommunication, 369
Exegesis, 242
Existentialism, 369
Exner, Adam, O.M.I., Bp., 465
Exodus, 235
Exorcism, 369
Exorcist, 277
Extension Society, 609
External Forum, 370
Extreme Unction, see Anointing of the Sick
Eyck, Hubert Van, 402
Eyck, Jan Van, 402
Eymard League, 665
Ezekiel, 238
Ezra, 236

F

Faber, Frederick, 402
Fabian, St., 307
Fabre, Jean, 402
Fabricius, Hieronymus, 402
Faculties, 370
 of Ecclesiastical Studies, 628-29
Fahey, Leo F., 557
Faith, 370
 Analogy, 231
 Congregation for Doctrine of, 192
 Congregation for Propagation of, 194
 Mysteries, 380
 Necessity, 107
 Privilege of (Petrine Privilege), 285
 Promoter of, 385
 Rule of, 370
 Science and, 118
 Society for Propagation of, 669
  See also Creed, Doctrine
Faithful, Communion of, 363
Faithful, Mass of, 259
Faithful, Prayer of the, 260
Falkland Islands, 428
Fallon, Mary M., 110
Fallopio, Gabriello, 402
False Decretals (847-852), 158
Families for Christ, 665
Family, Committee for, 197
Family, Holy (Feast), 302
Family, White House Conference, 124, 153, 567
Family, Year of, 567
Family and Violence, 129
Family Communion Crusade, 665
Family Life, 136, 147
Family Life, USCC, 657
Family Movement, Christian, 658
Family Rosary Crusade, 665
Family Theater, 687
Farley, James A., 402
Farley, John, 402
Farm, Family, 124, 139
Farm Workers, UFWA Contract, 144
Farmer, Ferdinand, 416
Faroe Islands, 428
Farrelly, John P., 557
Fast, Eucharistic, 370
Fast Days, 292
Fasting, 117
Father, 370
Father McKenna Award, 697
Fathers, Church, 246-49
Fathers of Mercy, 575
Fatima, 320
 Secret, 320
Faye, Herve, 402
Fear, 370
Fearns, John M., 557
Feast Days, 291-92, 301-04
Feast of Weeks, 350
Feasts, Movable, 300

Febronianism (764), 162
Fedders, Edward L., M.M., 557
Federal, Joseph L., Bp., 532
Federal Aid to Education, 611
 See also Church-State Decisions of Supreme Court
Federation of Catholic Physicians Guilds, 668
Federation of Diocesan Liturgical Commissions, 665
Feehan, Daniel F., 557
Feehan, Patrick A., 557
Feeney, Daniel J., 557
Feeney, Thomas J., S.J., 557
Felici, Pericle, Card., 204
Felician Sisters (Sisters of St. Felix), 587
Felicity, St. (Perpetua and Felicity, Sts.), 310
Fellowship of Catholic Scholars, 125, 665
Fenelon, Francois, 402
Fenton, Robert L., 105
Fenwick, Benedict J., S.J., 557
Fenwick, Edward, O.P., 557
Ferdinand III, St., 307
Ferial Days, 292
Fernando Po, see Equatorial Guinea
Ferrari, Ludovico, 402
Ferrario, Joseph A., Bp., 533
Festival of Lights (Hanukkah), 350
Fetus, 91-3
Fiacra, St., 307
Fidelis of Sigmaringen, St., 307
Fides (Mission News Service), 197
Fiji, 428-29
Filipiak, Boleslaw, Card., 704
Filippini, Religious Teachers, 587
Film and Broadcasting, USCC, Office for, 688
Films, Catholic, see Television
Finger Towel, 263
Fink, Francis A., 402
Fink, Michael, O.S.B., 557
Finland, 106, 429
Finnigan, George, C.S.C., 557
Fiorenza, Joseph A., Bp., 533
First Amendment (Wall of Separation), 495
 See also Church-State Decision of Supreme Court
First Catholic Slovak Ladies Association, 665
First Catholic Slovak Union (Jednota), 665
First Friday, 370
First Friday Clubs, 665
First Saturday, 370
Fischer, Max, 402
Fisher, John, St., 308
Fisherman's Ring, 370
Fitzgerald, Edward, 557
Fitzgerald, Edward A., 557
Fitzgerald, Walter, S.J., 557
Fitzgibbon, Catherine, 402
Fitzmaurice, Edmond, 557
Fitzmaurice, John, 557
Fitzpatrick, John B., 557
Fitzpatrick, John J., Bp., 533
Fitzsimon, Laurence J., 557
Fitzsimons, George K., Bp., 533
FitzSimons, Thomas, 402
Fizeau, Armand, 402
Flag, Papal, 221
Flaget, Benedict, 416
Flahiff, George B., C.S.B., Card., 204
Flaherty, J. Louis, 557
Flanagan, Bernard J., Bp., 533
Flanagan, Edwad J., 402
Flannelly, Joseph F., 557
Flasch, Kilian, 557
Flavin, Glennon P., Bp., 533
Fletcher, Albert L., Bp., 533
Floersch, John, 557
Florence, Council, 167-68
Flores, Felixberto, Bp., 533
Flores, Patrick, Abp., 99, 533
Florida, 478, 508, 512, 514, 518, 526, 614, 625, 632, 641, 643, 650, 680
 Capital Punishment, 135
 Haitian Refugees, 144
 Sex Education, 99, 130
Florit, Ermenegildo, Card., 204
Floyd, John P., 402
Foch, Ferdinand, 402
Focolare Movement, 603
Foery, Walter A., 557

Foley, John S., 557
Foley, Maurice, 557
Foley, Thomas, 557
Fontana, Mario, Dr., 704
Food Conference, World, 141
Food for Cambodia, 153
Food Shortage, Ethiopia, 111
Ford, Francis X., 402
Foreign Mission Society of America, Catholic (Maryknoll), 575
Foreign Missions, 605-07
  American Bishops, 507
  U.S. Personnel, 605-06, 607
  See also Missions
Foreign Missions, Consolata Society for, 573
St. Joseph's Society for (Mill Hill Missionaries), 575
Forensic League, Natl. Catholic, 661
Forest, John A., 557
Forest Rangers, 660
Foresters, Catholic Order of, 664
Forgiveness of Sin, 370
  See also Confession; Penance
Form Criticism, 242
Formosa, **see** Taiwan
Forst, Marion F., Bp., 533
Fortier, Jean-Marie, Abp., 465
Fortitude, 370
Fortunatus, Venantius, 402
Fortunatus of Brescia, 402
Fortune Telling, 370
Forty Hours Devotion, 370
Forum, 370-71
Foster, John G., 402
Foster Homes, Children in, 516
Foucauld, Charles Eugene de, 402
Foucault, Jean, 402
Four Books of Sentences (1160), 159
Fowler, Gene, 402
Fox, Joseph J., 557
France, 429
  Bishops' Abortion Statement, 126
  Religious Sanctions (1901), 163
  Revolution (1789), 162
Frances of Rome, St., 307
Frances Xavier Cabrini, St., 307
Francis, Joseph A., S.V.D., Bp., 533
Francis, St., Assisi, 307
  See also Crib; Portiuncula
Francis, St. (Religious)
  Brothers of the Poor, 578
  Little Brothers of, 579
  Secular Order, 604
  Sisters of (List), 587-91
  Third Order Regular (Men), 573
  See also Franciscans; Friars Minor
Francis Borgia, St., 307
Francis de Sales, St., 248
Francis de Sales, St. (Religious)
  Oblate Sisters, 587
  Oblates of, 573
  Society of (Salesians), 577
Francis de Sales, St., Award (CPA), 701
Francis of Paola, St., 307
Francis of Vitoria, 402
Francis Solanus, St., 417
Francis Xavier, St., 307
  Brothers of, 578
  Catholic Mission Sisters, 600
  Medal, 701
Franciscan Apostolate of the Way of the Cross, 665
Franciscan Brothers of Brooklyn, 578
Franciscan Brothers of Christ the King, 578
Franciscan Brothers of the Good News, 579
Franciscan Brothers of the Holy Cross, 579
Franciscan Communications Center, 687
Franciscan Communications Conference, National, 693
Franciscan Crown, 371
Franciscan Friars of the Atonement, 571
Franciscan International Award, 698
Franciscan Missionary Brothers, 579
Franciscan Missions, California, 418
Franciscan Sisters (List), 587-91
Franciscans (Friars Minor), 132, 573
  Capuchins, 574
  Conventuals, 574
  Third Order Regular, 573

Franck, Cesar, 402
Franco, Francisco (1936), 164
Franz, John B., Bp., 533
Frassen, Claudius, 402
Fraternities, 661
Fraunhofer, Joseph von, 402
Frazier, Nancy, 125
Frechette, Louis, 402
Free Will, 371
Freedom, 71, 104
Freedom, Religious, 70, 371
Freeman, James D., Card., 204-05
Freemasons, 371
Freking, Frederick W., Bp., 134, 533
French Guiana, 431
French Revolution (1789), 162
Frenette, Emilien, Bp., 465
Freppel, Charles, 402
Fresnel, Augustine, 403
Frey, Gerard L., Bp., 533
Friar, 371
Friars Minor, Order of (Franciscans), 573-74
  General Chapter, 132
Friars Preachers, Order of (Dominicans), 573
Friend, William B., Bp., 533
Friendship House, 665
Frings, Joseph, Card., 704
Froissart, Jean, 403
Frontenac, Louis, 403
Frontier Apostles, 659
Frosi, Angelo, S.X., Bp., 533
Fruits of the Holy Spirit, 371
Fruits of the Mass, 261
Fu Jen University (Taiwan), 628
Fulcher, George A., Bp., 533
Fulda, Monastery (744), 157
Fulton, Thomas B., Bp. 465
Funeral Mass, Rites, Vestments, 261, 262, 267
Furey, Francis J., Abp., 104, 557, 704
Furlong, Philip J., Bp., 534
Futuna Islands, 452

G

Gabon, 429
Gabriel (Archangel), 303, 356
Gabriel Lalemant, St., 416
Gabriel of the Sorrowful Mother, St., 307
Gabriel Richard Institute, 665
Gabriels, Henry, 557
Gabro, Jaroslav, Bp., 534
Gagarin, Ivan, 403
Gagnon, Edouard, P.S.S., Bp., 465
Galatians, 241
Galberry, Thomas, O.S.A., 557
Galante, Carmine, 139
Galician Ruthenian Catholics, 324
Galilei, Galileo, 403
Gallagher, Michael, 557
Gallagher, Nicholas, 557
Gallagher, Raymond J., Bp., 534
Gallican Declaration (1682), 161
Gallitzin, Demetrius, 416
Galvani, Luigi, 403
Galvin, Edward J., 403
Gama, Vasco de, 403
Gambia, 429
Gambling, 371
Gannon, John M., 558
Ganter, Bernard J., Bp., 534
Gantin, Bernardin, Card., 103, 205
Garcia Diego y Moreno, Francisco, O.F.M., 558
Garcia, Moreno, 403
Garmendia, Francisco, Bp., 534
Garner, Robert F., Bp., 534
Garnier, Charles, St., 416
Garriga, Mariano S., 558
Garrigan, Philip, 558
Garrigou-Lagrange, Reginald, 403
Garrone, Gabriel, Card., 128, 205
Gartland, Francis X., 558
Garvey, Eugene A., 558
Gasquet, Francis, 403
Gassendi, Pierre, 403
Gaston, William, 403
Gaudete Sunday, Vestments, **see** Liturgical Colors
Gaudium et Spes, 168

Index

Gaudium et Spes
   See also Church in Modern World, Constitution
Gaughan, Norbert F., Bp., 534
Gay-Lussac, Joseph, 403
Gay Rights, see Homosexuals
Gehenna (Gehinnom), 371
Gelasian Guild, 665
Gelasius I, St. (494), 157
Gelineau, Louis E., Bp., 534
Gendron, Odore, Bp., 534
General Absolution, 122, 353
Genesis, 235
Genesius, St., 307
Geneva Conference, Refugees, 141
Genevieve, St., 307
Genuflection, 371
Geoffrey of Monmouth, 403
George, St., 307
George M. Cohan Award, 145
Georgetown University, 628
   Radio Station Closed, 110
Georgia, 479, 508, 512, 514, 526, 614, 641, 650, 689
   Church Property Case, 138
Georgian Byzantine Rite, 323
Gerard Majella, St., 307
Gerber, Eugene, Bp., 534
Gerbermann, Hugo, M.M., Bp., 534
Gercke, Daniel J., 558
Gerety, Peter L., Abp., 534
Gerken, Rudolph A., 558
Germany, 429-30
   Adveniat Contributions, 105, 131, 146
   Hitler (1933), 164
   Holocaust Survivors, 116
   Kulturkampf (1871), 163
   Statute of Limitations, War Crimes, 115, 141
Gerow, Richard O., 558
Gerrard, James J., Bp., 534
Gertrude, St., 307
Gethsemani, 371
Ghana, 430
Ghiberti, Lorenzo, 403
Ghirlandjo, Domenico, 403
Gibault, Pierre, 416
Gibbons, Edmund F., 558
Gibbons, Floyd, 403
Gibbons, James, 403
   See also Catholic History of U.S.
Gibraltar, 430
Gibson, Hugh S., 403
Gifts, Preternatural, 385
Gifts of the Holy Spirit, 371
Gigante, Louis, Rev., 153
Gigli, Beniamino, 403
Gilbert, Arthur J., Bp., 465
Gilbert Islands, 430
Gilfillan, Francis, 558
Gill, Eric, 403
Gill, Thomas E., 558
Gillis, James, 403
Gilmore, Joseph, 558
Gilmore, Patrick, 403
Gilmour, Richard, 558
Gintoft, Ethel, 125
Giocondo de Verona, 403
Gioja, Flavio, 403
Giorgione, Giorgio, 403
Giotto de Bondone, 403
Girl Scouts, Catholic, 660
Girouard, Paul J., M.S., 558
Glass, Joseph S., 403
Gleeson, Francis D., S.J., Bp., 534
Glenmary Missioners, 574, 608
   Sisters (Home Mission Sisters of America), 591, 608
   See also Home Missions, U.S.
Glenn, Laurence A., Bp., 534
Glennie, Ignatius, S.J., Bp., 534
Glennon, John, 403
Glorieux, Alphonse J., 558
Glory to God (Mass), 259
Glossary, 353-395
Gluck, Christoph, 403
Gluttony, 371
Gnosticism, 164
Gobban Saer, 403
God, 371-72

God
   Attributes, 357
   Commandments, 250
Godfrey of Bouillon, 403
Godin, Edgar, Bp., 465
Godparents, 271
God-Spell, 240
Goesbriand, Louis J. de, 558
Golden Bull (1338), 160
Golden Spur, Order, 694
Goldstein, David, 403
Gomez Marijuan, Francisco, C.M.F., Bp., 704
Gonzalez Martin, Marcelo, Card., 205
Gonzalez, Roch, Bl., 416
"Good Conscience" Procedures (Marriage), 289
Good Friday (Apr. 4, 1980), 295, 302
   John Paul II Activities, 123
Good News Bible, 119
Good Samaritan Award, 698
Good Shepherd Sisters, 591
Good Shepherd, Society of Brothers, 579
Goodyear, William Henry, 403
Gordon, Andrew, 403
Gorman, Daniel, 558
Gorman, Thomas K., Bp., 534
Gorres, Joseph von, 404
Gospel, 240
Gospel (Mass), see Readings
Gospels, 231, 240
   Authorship, 241
   Synoptic, 240
Gossman, F. Joseph, Bp., 535
Gottwald, George J., Bp., 535
Gounod, Charles, 404
Goupil, Rene, St., 416
Gouyon, Paul, Card., 205
Government, Church, 186-88
   See also Roman Curia
Gower, John, 404
Goya y Lucientes, Francesco, 404
Grace, 372
   at Meals, 372
Grace, Thomas, 558
Grace, Thomas L., O.P., 558
Gracida, Rene H., Bp., 110, 129, 135, 535
Grady, Thomas J., Bp., 535
Graham, John J., Bp., 535
Grail, 659
Granahan, Kathryn O'Hay, 704
Graner, Lawrence, C.S.C., Abp., 535
Granjon, Henry, 558
Grant Park, Chicago, Papal Mass, 74
Grasset de Saint Sauveur, Andre, Bl., 305
Gratian (1160), 159
Gratton, Jean, Bp., 465
Graves, Lawrence P., Bp., 535
Gravier, Jacques, 416
Gravissimum Educationis, 168
Gray, Gordon J., Card., 205
Graymoor Sisters (Franciscan Srs. of the Atonement), 589
Graziano, Lawrence, O.F.M., Bp., 535
Greco, Charles P., Bp., 535
Greco, El, 404
Greece, 143, 431
Greek Byzantine Rite Catholics, 323
Greek Melkites, 323, 326
Green, Francis J., Bp., 535
Green, Joseph, Bp., 535
Greenland, 431
Gregoire, Paul, Abp., 465
Gregorian Calendar (1582), 161
Gregorian Chant, 258
Gregorian Institute of America, 665
Gregorian Masses, 261
Gregorian University, Pontifical, 629
Gregory Nazianzen, St., 248
Gregory of Valencia, 404
Gregory VII, St. (Hildebrand), 307
Gregory the Great, St., 248
Gregory the Great, Order of St., 694
Gregory the Illuminator, St., 307
Grellinger, John B., Bp., 535
Gremial, 262
Grenada, 431
Greschuk, Michael, Bp., 465
Greteman, Frank, Bp., 535

Index

Grey Nuns, see Charity, Sisters of
Grey Nuns of the Sacred Heart, 591
Griffin, James A., 558
Griffin, James A., Bp., 535
Griffin, William A., 558
Griffin, William R., 558
Griffiths, James H., 558
Grijalva, Juan de, 404
Grimaldi, Francesco, 404
Grimes, John, 558
Grimmelsman, Henry J., 558
Gromyko, Andrei, Meeting with John Paul II, 107-08
Gronouski, John (Catholics in Presidents' Cabinets), 490
Gross, William H., C.SS.R., 558
Group Seven, 659
Grutka, Andrew G., Bp., 535
Guadalupe, Brothers of Our Lady of, 579
Guadalupe, Our Lady of, 320
  John Paul II at Shrine, 50
Guadalupe, Sisters of, 591
Guadeloupe, 431
Guam, 431
Guard of Honor of the Immaculate Heart, 665
Guardian Angels, 302, 355
Guardian Angels, Sisters of Holy, 591
Guardini, Romano, 404
Guatemala, 106, 136, 431
Guerri, Sergio, Card., 205
Guertin, George A., 558
Guiana, Dutch, see Surinam
Guiana, French, 431
"Guideline," 686
Guido d'Arezzo, 404
Guild of Catholic Lawyers, 665
  Our Lady of Ransom, 665
  St. Paul, 666
Guilday, Peter, 404
Guilfoyle, George H., Bp., 148, 535
Guilfoyle, Merlin J., Bp., 536
Guilfoyle, Richard T., 558
Guinea, 431
  Archbishop Tchidimbo's Resignation, 142
Guinea, Equatorial, 145, 428
Guinea-Bissau, 431-32
Guiney, Louise Imogen, 404
Gumbleton, Thomas J., Bp., 104, 113-14, 536
Gunn, John E., S.M., 558
Gunpowder Plot (1605), 161
Gurian, Waldemar, 404
Gutenberg, Johann, 404
Guyana, 432
  Jonestown Horror, 101
Guyot, Louis J., Card., 205

H

Haas, Francis J., 558
Habakkuk, 239
Habit, 372
  Religious, 262
Habitual Grace, 372
Hacault, Antoine, Bp., 465
Hacker, Hilary B., Bp., 536
Hackett, John F., Bp., 536
Haenggi, Anton, Bp., 140
Hafey, William, 558
Hagan, John R., 558
Hagarty, Paul, O.S.B., Bp., 536
Haggai, 239
Hagiography, 372
Haid, Leo M., O.S.B., 558
Hail Mary, 372
Hains, Gaston, Bp., 465
Haiti, 154, 432
  Housing for Poor, 144
Haldeman, Samuel Stehman, 404
Hallinan, Paul J., 558
Halpin, Charles A., Abp., 465
Ham, J. Richard, M.M., Bp., 536
Hamelin, Jean-Guy, Bp., 465
Hammes, George A., Bp., 536
Handicapped, Catholic Facilities, 640-46
Handicapped, John Paul II Meeting, 142
Handicapped, "Red Barn" Project, 105
Handicapped, U.S. Bishops Letter, 524
Handmaids of Divine Mercy, 602

Handmaids
  of Mary Immaculate, 591
  of the Precious Blood, 591
Hanifen, Richard C., Bp., 536
Hanna, Edward J., 558
Hannan, Jerome D., 558
Hannan, Philip M., Abp., 536
Hannegan, Robert E., 404
Hanukkah, 350
Hardee, William J., 404
Hare Krishna, 96
Harkins, Matthew, 558
Harland, Henry, 404
Harlem, Papal Visit, 70
Harper, Edward, C.SS.R., Bp., 536
Harrington, Timothy J., Bp., 536
Harris, Joel Chandler, 404
Harris, Vincent M., Bp., 536
Harrison, Francis J., Bp., 536
Hart, Daniel A., Bp., 536
Hart, Joseph, Bp., 536
Hartdegen, Stephen, O.F.M., 134
Hartley, James J., 558
Harty, Jeremiah J., 558
Hassard, John, 404
Hastrich, Jerome J., Bp., 536
Hauy, Rene, 404
Hawaii, 479, 511, 513, 515, 616, 625, 641, 643, 689
  Catholic Protest, 123
  State-Funded Abortions, 115
Hawks, Edward F., 404
Hawthorne, Rose (Lathrop), 406
Haydn, Franz, 404
Hayes, Carlton J. H., 404
Hayes, Helen, 120
Hayes, James M., Abp., 465
Hayes, James T., S.J., Abp., 536
Hayes, Nevin W., O. Carm., Bp., 537
Hayes, Patrick J., 404
Hayes, Ralph L., 558
Head, Edward D., Bp., 537
Health Association, Catholic, 133, 631
Health Care Facilities, 632-40
Health Care Work and Religious, 132
Healy, George, 404
Healy, James A., 558
Heart of Jesus, Institute, 602
Heart of Mary, Daughters of, 594
Heaven, 372
Hebert, Louis, 404
Hebrews (Epistle), 241
Hecht, Abraham, Rabbi, 154
Hecker, Isaac, 404
Hedwig, St., 308
  Shrine, Poland, Papal Visit, 57
Heelan, Edmond, 558
Heffron, Patrick, 558
Hegira (622), 157
Hegumen (Abbot), 353
Hehir, J. Bryan, Rev., 129
Heis, Eduard, 404
Heiss, Michael, 558
Helena, St., 308
Hell, 372
Hellegers, Andre, Dr., 704
Helmont, Jan, 404
Helms, Jesse, Sen., Prayer Amendment, 124
Helmsing, Charles H., Bp., 537
Helpers, Society of, 591
Helpless, Mothers of the, 589
Helsinki Agreements, Anniversary, 143
Hendrick, Thomas A., 559
Hendricken, Thomas F., 559
Hengler, Lawrence, 404
Hennepin, Louis, 404
Hennessy, John, 559
Hennessy, John J., 559
Henni, John J., 559
Henoticon (484), 157
Henry, Harold W., S.S.C., 559
Henry, St., 308
Henry VII, King (1533), 161
Henry the Navigator, 404
Herdtrich, Christian, 404
Heresies, 164-65
Heresy, 164

Index

Heretic, 164
Hermanas Catequistas Guadalupanas, 591
Hermaniuk, Maxim, C.SS.R., Abp., 465
Hermeneutics, 242
Hermit (Anchorite), 355
Heroic Act of Charity, 372
Herrera, Francisco de, 404
Herrmann, Edward J., Bp., 149, 537
Heslin, Thomas, 559
Heston, Edward L., C.S.C., 559
Heterodoxy, 372
Hettinger, Edward G., Bp., 537
Heude, Pierre, 404
Hewit, Augustine Francis, 404
Heywood, John, 404
Hickey, David F., S.J., 559
Hickey, Dennis W., Bp., 537
Hickey, James A., Bp., 149, 537
Hickey, Thomas F., 559
Hickey, William A., 559
Hierarchy, 186
Hierarchy, Canadian, see Bishops, Canadian
Hierarchy, U.S., see Bishops, U.S.
Higgins, George G., Msgr., 109, 150, 525
High Schools, Catholic, see Education, Catholic
Hilary, St., 248
Hildebrand, see Gregory VII
Hill, John Austin (Speakman), 405
Hill, Morton A., S.J., see Morality in Media
Hillinger, Raymond P., 559
Hinduism, 352
Hines, Vincent J., Bp., 537
Hinton, Thomas D., 105
Hippolytus, St., 308
Historical Association, Catholic, 662
   John Gilmary Shea Prize, 699
Historical Books of Bible, 236-37
Historical Sciences, Commission, 196
History
   Catholic, Canada, 461
   Catholic, U.S., 473-90
   Church, Significant Dates, 155-64
Hitler, Adolf (1933), 164
   See also Germany
Hoban, Edward F., 559
Hoban, Michael J., 559
Hoch, Lambert, Bp., 537
Hodapp, Robert, S.J., Bp., 537
Hodges, Joseph J., Bp., 537
Hoeffner, Joseph, Card., 205
Hoey Awards, 698
Hoffman, James R., Bp., 537
Hogan, Eileen, Sr., 110
Hogan, James J., Bp., 537
Hogan, John J., 559
Hogan, Joseph L., Bp., 537
Holbein, Hans, 405
Holenstein, Martin, Rev., 110
Holiness Sects, 337
Holland, John P., 405
Holocaust, Survivors, 116
Holy Child Jesus, Society, 591
Holy Childhood Association, 122, 660
Holy Communion, see Communion, Holy; Eucharist
Holy Days, 292, 301-04
   Byzantine Rite, 293
Holy Eucharist, see Eucharist, Holy
Holy Eucharist, Brothers of, 579
Holy Faith, Sisters of the, 591
Holy Family (Feast), 302
Holy Family (Religious)
   Congregation of Missionaries of, 574
   Congregation of Sisters of, 587
   Little Sisters of, 587
   of Nazareth, Sisters of, 587
   Sisters of, 587
   Sons, 574
Holy Father, see Pope
Holy Ghost, see Holy Spirit
Holy Ghost, Missionaries of, 574
Holy Ghost, Sisters of, 591
Holy Ghost and Mary Immaculate, Sister Servants, 591
Holy Ghost Fathers, 574
Holy Heart of Mary, Servants, 591
Holy Innocents, 302
Holy Land, Commissariat, 363

Holy Land, Shrines, 140
Holy Name, Feast, 291
Holy Name Society (U.S.), 666
Holy Name Society, Natl. Assn., 666
Holy Names of Jesus and Mary, Srs. of, 591
Holy Office, see Doctrine of the Faith Congregation
Holy Oils, 267, 381
Holy Orders, 267, 271, 276-77
Holy Saturday, see Easter Vigil
Holy See, 372
   Publications, 222-23
   Representatives, 215-18, 223
   See also Vatican
Holy Sepulchre, Order of, 694
Holy Spirit, 372
   Blasphemy of, 358
   Fruits of, 371
   Gifts of, 371
   Sins against, 390
Holy Spirit, Baptism of, see Charismatic Renewal, Catholic
Holy Spirit (Religious)
   Daughters of, 591
   Mission Sisters, 591
   Missionary Sisters, Servants, 591
   Sisters of, 591
Holy Spirit of Perpetual Adoration, Sister Servants of, 591
Holy Thursday, 302
   John Paul II, 123
Holy Trinity, 304
Holy Trinity, Missionary Servants of the Most, 577
   Order of Most, 577
   Sisters of Most, 599
Holy Water, 373
Holy Week, 290
   John Paul II Activities, 123
   Liturgy, 267
Holy Week, Byzantine, 293
Holy Year, 373
Home Mission Sisters (Glenmary), 591, 608
Home Missioners of America, 574, 608
Home Missions, U.S., 607-09
   See also Spanish Speaking
Home Visitors of Mary, 592
Homes for Aged and Retired, 632-40
Homily, 260
Homosexuality, 73, 373
   Legislative Bills, 100
   Letter, Cardinal Medeiros, 138
   Ordination, U.S. Episcopal Church, 149
Honduras, 432
   Radio Network, 135
Honduras, British, see Belize
Hong Kong, 432
   Refugee Aid, 151
Honor et Veritas Award, 698
Hope, 373
Hopkins, Gerard, 405
Horner, William Edmonds, 405
Horstmann, Ignatius, 559
Hosanna, 373
Hosea, 238-39
Hospital Association, Catholic (Catholic Health Association), 631
Hospitaller Order of St. John of God, 579
Hospitals, Catholic, U.S., 153, 631
   Association for, 631
   See also Cancer Homes, Hospitals; Health Care Facilities
Host, Sacred, 373
   See also Communion, Holy
Hosts, Guidelines for Making, 268
Houck, William Russell, Bp., 537
Hours, Liturgy of, 143, 257, 267
House of Prayer Experience (HOPE), 655
Howard, Edward, Abp., 537
Howard, Francis W., 559
Howard R. Marraro Prize, 698
Howze, Joseph Lawson, Bp., 537
Hubbard, Bernard, 405
Hubbard, Howard J., Bp., 538
Hubert, Bernard, Bp., 465
Hubert H. Humphrey Civil Rights Award, 109
Hubert, St., 308
Hugh of Cluny, St., 308
Hugh of St. Victor, 405

Hughes, Edward T., Bp., 538
Hughes, John J., 405
Hughes, William A., Bp., 538
Human Development Campaign, 99, 149, 418
Human Life Foundation, 631
Human Rights, 54, 73, 86, 101, 104, 111, 118, 143
Human Rights Declaration, UN, Anniversary, 102, 103
Human Sexuality, Errors Detailed, 83-4
Human Values, Committee for, 120, 525
Humanae Vitae, 73, 282-83
Humani Generis, 182
Hume, George Basil, Card., 111, 130, 136, 205
Humeral Veil, 262
Humility, 373
 John Paul II on, 117
Humility of Mary, Congregation of, 592
 Sisters of, 592
Hungarian Byzantine Catholic Rite, 323
Hungarian Catholic League of America, 666
Hungary, 432-33
 Baptisms, First Communions, 106
 Seminarians, 122
Hunger, World, 106
Hunkeler, Edward, 559
Hunt, Duane G., 559
Hunthausen, Raymond G., Abp., 538
Hunton, George K., 405
Hunyady, Janos, 405
Hurley, Francis T., Abp., 538
Hurley, Joseph P., 559
Hurley, Mark J., Bp., 538
Hus, John, 332
Hussein, King, 103
Huysmans, Joris, 405
Hyde, Henry J., Rep., 99
Hyde Amendment, 118-19
Hyland, Francis E., 559
Hyle, Michael W., 559
Hyperdulia, 373
Hypnosis, 373
Hypostatic Union, 373

I

Iakovos, Abp., Greek Orthodox Primate, 125
Iceland, 433
Iconoclasm, 165
Iconostas, 328
Icons, 373
Idaho, 479, 510, 513, 515, 616, 650, 689
Idolatry, 374
Ignatius of Antioch, St., 308
Ignatius of Loyola, St., 308
IHS, 374
Illig, Alvin A., C.P., 145
Illinois, 479-80, 509, 512, 514, 518, 526, 614, 625, 633, 640, 641, 643-4, 646, 650-51, 689-90
 DC-10 Crash, Chicago, 129
 Papal Visit, Chicago, 64, 73-4
Illinois Club for Catholic Women, 666
Illiteracy, 148
Imesch, Joseph L., Bp., 538
Immaculate Conception, 303, 317
 Anniversary, Definition of Dogma, 139
Immaculate Conception Shrine, 185
 Papal Visit, 74-5
Immaculate Conception (Sisters)
 Little Servant Sisters, 592
 Missionary Sisters, 589
 of BVM, Sisters, 592
 Sisters of, 592
Immaculate Heart of Mary (June 14, 1980), 296, 303
Immaculate Heart of Mary, Brothers, 579
Immaculate Heart of Mary, Brothers of Charity, 579
Immaculate Heart of Mary (Sisters)
 Daughters, 592
 Missionary Sisters, 592
 Sisters, 592
 Sisters, Servants, 592
Immaculate Heart of Mary Mission Society, 574
Immensae Caritatis, 274, 524
 See also Fast, Eucharistic
Immersion, see Baptism
Immigrant Services Offices, New York, 105
Immortality, 374
Immunity of Clergy, 374
Impanation, see Consubstantiation

Impediments, Matrimonial, 285
Imprimatur, 361
Impurity, 374
In Pectore, see Cardinal in Pectore
In Sin, 375
Incardination, 374
Incarnate Word and Blessed Sacrament, Cong., 592
Incarnation, 374
Incense, 374
Incest, 374
Index of Prohibited Books, 374
India, 108, 111, 433
 Adult Catechesis, 126
 Anti-Conversion Bill, 121, 131, 136
Indiana, 480, 509, 512, 514, 518, 526, 614, 625, 633, 641, 644, 651, 690
Indians, American, 608-09
 St. Stephen's Mission Foundation, 145
Indiction, Day of, 292
Indifferentism, 374
Indochina Refugees, 604
Indonesia, 98, 433
Indulgence, 374-75
Indulgence, Portiuncula, 384
Indult, 375
Inerrancy of Bible, 230
Infallibility, 227-28
Infant Formula Peril, Nestle, 106
Infant Jesus, Sisters of the, 592
Infant Jesus of Prague, 375
Information Office, National Catholic, 693
Infused Virtues, 375
Infusion, see Baptism
"In God We Trust," Motto Attacked, 115, 134
Ingres, Jean, 405
Innocent III, Pope, 405
Inquisition, 375
Inquisition, Spanish, 375
INRI, 375
Insemination, Artificial, 375
Insignis Medal, 698-99
Inspiration, Biblical, 230
Institute of Apostolic Oblates, 603
Institute of Blessed Virgin Mary, 582
Institute of Charity (Rosminians), 577
Institute of Secular Missionaries, 602
Institute of the Heart of Jesus, 602
Institute on Religious Life, 666
Institutes, Religious, 568
Institutes, Secular, 601-03
Institutes of Higher Studies, 629
Institutes of the Christian Religion (1536), 161
Institutions, Catholic, see Social Services, Catholic
Institutions, Civil Rights for Residents, 129
Instruction, Apostolic, 375
Intercommunion, 98, 127, 274, 375
Interdict, 375
Inter Mirifica (Communications Document), 168
Internal Forum, 370
Internal Revenue Service Guidelines and Tax Exemption, 114
International
 Catholic Deaf Association, 648
 Catholic Organizations, 137, 458-60
 Commission on English in Liturgy, 101
 "Equipes Notre Dame" (Our Lady's Army), 147
 Eucharistic Congresses (Eucharistic Congresses), 368
 Federation of Catholic Press Agencies, 101
 Institute for Rights of Man, 147
 Institute of the Heart of Jesus, 666
 Liaison, 659
 Organizations, Vatican Representatives, 223
 Theological Commission, 198
 Union of Prayer, 319
 Union of Superiors General, 97, 601
Internuncio, see Representatives, Vatican
Interpretation, Biblical, 230, 242-43
 Teaching Authority of Church, 230
Interracial Council, Catholic, 663
Interracial Justice, National Catholic Conference, 667
Interregnum, 376
Intinction, 274, 376
Introit (Entrance), 259
Investments, 109
In Vitro Fertilization, 93-4, 119
Iona (Island), 116

Index

Iowa, 480, 510, 513, 515, 518, 526, 615, 625, 633, 644, 651, 690
  Papal Visit, 73
Iran, 434
  Appeal for Aid, 141
Iraq, 434
Ireland, 434
  Papal Visit, Addresses, 62-3, 65-8
  Partitioning (1922), 164
  See also North Ireland
Ireland, John, 405
Irenaeus of Lyons, St., 308
Irenicism, 376
Ireton, Peter L., 559
Irish Republican Army, 140-41
Irregularity, 376
Isaac Jogues, St., 416
Isaiah, 238
Iscariot (Judas), 246
Isidore of Seville, St., 248
Isidore the Farmer, St., 308
Islam, 351-52
  Catholic-Moslem Consultation, 143, 351
  Revival, 125
Israel, 434, 524
Israeli-Egyptian Peace, **see** Middle East Peace Efforts
Issenmann, Clarence E., Bp., 538
Italian Catholic Federation of California, 666
Italo-Albanians, 323
Italy, 98, 151, 435
  Abortion, 102-03, 106
  Concordat Revision, Lateran Treaty, 112, 133
  Violence, 107
Itinerarium, 376
Ives, Levi Silliman, 405
Ivory Coast, 435

J

Jablonski, Henryk, Pres. (Poland), 117
Jacopone da Todi, 405
Jadot, Jean, Abp., 405
  Permanent Observer OAS, 113
Jamaica, 435
James the Greater, St., 245
James the Less, St., 245
  Epistle, 241
Jane Frances de Chantal, St., 308
Jansenism, 376
Janssen, John, 559
Janssens, Francis A., 559
Januarius, St., 116, 308
Japan, 435
  Self-Evangelization, 106
Japanese Martyrs, **see** Paul Miki, St.
Jaricot, Pauline, 405
Jasna Gora, Tradition of Shrine, 57, 59-60
Jeanmard, Jules B., 559
Jeanne d'Arc, Sisters of St., 592
Jednota, 144, 665
Jefferson, Mildred, Dr., Pro-Life Crusade, 114
Jehovah's Witnesses, 376-77
Jennings, Edward Q., Bp., 465
Jeremiah, 238
Jerome, St., 248
Jerome Emiliani, St., 308
Jerusalem, 140, 435, 524
Jerusalem Bible, 234
Jerusalem Council (51), 155
Jesuit North American Martyrs, 416
Jesuit Martyrs' Shrine, 471
Jesuit Volunteer Corps, 659
Jesuits, 574
  John Paul II Meeting, 148
  Suppression (1773), 162
Jesus, 377
  See also Christ
Jesus, Congregation of Daughters, 592
  Daughters, 592
  Little Brothers of, 579
  Society of, **see** Jesuits
  Society of Sisters, Faithful Companions, 592
Jesus Caritas Fraternity, 603
Jesus Caritas Priest Fraternities, 603
Jesus Christ, **see** Christ
Jesus Crucified, Congregation of, 592
  and Sorrowful Mother, Poor Sisters, 592
Jesus-Mary, Religious of, 592
Jesus, Mary and Joseph, Missionaries of, 592
Jesus Prayer, 377
Jesus '79, 135
Jesus the Priest, Oblate Sisters of, 592
Jette, Edward, Bp., 465
Jews
  Canon of Scripture, 233
  Christian-Jewish Relations Workshop, 100
  Judaism, 350-51
  Persecution, Germany (1933), 164
  Relations with Catholics, 116, 117, 348-50
  See also Anti-Semitism; Israel
Jiminez, Juan, 405
Joachim, St., 303
Joan Antida, Sisters of Charity of St., 584
Joan of Arc, St., 308
Job, 237
Joel, 239
Jogues, Isaac, St., 416
Johannes, Francis, 559
John, St. (Apostle), 245
  Epistles, 241
  Gospel, 240
John Baptist de la Salle, St., 308
John Berchmans, St., 308
John Bosco, St., 308
John Bosco, Salesians of St., 577
John Capistran, St., 308
John Carroll Society, 666
John Chrysostom, St., 248
John Courtney Murray Award, 699
John Damascene, St., 248
John de Brebeuf, St., 415
John de Castillo, Bl., 416
John de Massias, St., 417
John Eudes, St., 308
John Fisher, St., 308
John Gilmary Shea Prize, 699
John Kanty, St., 308
John LaFarge Memorial Award, 699
John Lalande, St., 416
John Lateran Basilica, 221
  Feast of Dedication, 302
  John Paul II, Possession, 98
John Leonardi, St., 308
John Nepomucene, St., 308
John Neumann, St., 308
John of Austria, 405
John of God, St., 308
John of God, St., Hospitaller Order of, 579
John of the Cross, St., 248
John I, St., 308
John Paul I, Pope, 138, 143
  Biography, 180
John Paul II, Pope, 97-8, 102-03, 106, 107-08, 112-13, 117-18, 122-23, 127-28, 132-33, 137-38, 142-43, 147-48, 152-53
  Biography, 48-9
  Encyclical *Redemptor Hominis*, 75-9
  Ireland Visit, Addresses, 62-3, 65-8
  Latin American Visit and Addresses, 49-56
  Letter to Priests, 79-81
  Parish Visits, Rome, 103, 112
  Poland Visit and Addresses, 56-61
  Puebla Keynote Address, 52-55
  UN Address, 68-70
  United States, Visit, Addresses, 63-5, 68-70
  White House Visit, 64
  Writings, Publication Rights, 98
John the Baptist, St., 303
  Possible Discovery of Remains, 101
John the Baptist, Sisters of St., 593
John XXIII, Pope
  Biography, 179
  Canonizations, 181
  Encyclicals, 185
  Social Encyclicals, 179, 251
  Second Vatican Council, 168, 179
John XXIII Center, 628
John Vianney, St., 308
Johnson, William R., Bp., 538
Joliet, Louis, 405
Jonah, 239
Jones, Inigo, 405
Jones, William A., O.S.A., 559

Jonestown, Guyana, Horror, 101
Jordan, 435
Jordan, Anthony, O.M.I., Abp., 465
Jorgensen, Johannes, 405
Josaphat, St., 308
Joseph, St., 303
Joseph, St. (Religious)
  Congregation of, 574
  Missionary Servants of, 593
  Oblates of, 575
  Poor Sisters of, 593
  Religious Daughters of, 593
  Religious Hospitallers, 593
  Sisters of (List), 593
  Society for Foreign Missions (Mill Hill Missionaries), 575
  Society of the Sacred Heart (Josephite Fathers), 575
Joseph Benedict Cottolengo, St., 308
Joseph Cafasso, St., 309
Joseph Calasanz, St., 309
Joseph of Cupertino, St., 309
Josephinism (1760s), 162
Josephites (Baltimore), 575
Josephites (California), 575
Joseph's Oratory, St., 471
Joshua, 236
Joyce, Robert F., Bp., 538
Joys of the Blessed Virgin Mary (Franciscan Crown), 371
Jubany Arnau, Narciso, Card., 205
Judaism, 350-51
Judaizers, 164
Judas, 246
Jude Thaddeus, St., 245
  Epistle, 241
Judean Society, 666
Judge, Thomas A., 405
Judges, 236
Judgment, Last and Particular, 377
  Rash, 386
Judith, 236
Jugan, Jeanne (Sr. Mary of the Cross), 145, 405
Julian the Apostate (361-363), 156
Juncker, Henry D., 559
Junger, Aegidius, 559
Junior Catholic Daughters of the Americas, 144, 661
Jurisdiction, 377
Jussieu, Bernard de, 405
Justice, 189, 377
Justice and Peace Commission, 97, 196
Justice in Society, 97
Justification, 377
Justin, St., 309
Justinian I, 405

K

Kain, John J., 559
Kampuchea (Cambodia), 436
  Starvation, 153
Kane, Theresa, Sr., 152
Kansas, 480, 510, 513, 515, 526, 615, 625, 634, 644, 651, 690
Kappa Gamma Pi, 661
Karma, see Buddhism
Katholicos, 187
Katona, Stephen, 405
Katzer, Frederick X., 559
Kaye-Smith, Sheila, 405
Keane, James J., 559
Keane, John J., 559
Keane, Patrick J., 559
Kearney, James E., 559
Kearney, Raymond A., 559
Keeler, William H., Bp., 538
Keiley, Benjamin J., 559
Kelleher, Louis J., 560
Kelley, Francis C., 560
Kells, Book of, 158
Kelly, Edward D., 560
Kelly, Edward J., 560
Kelly, Francis M., 560
Kelly, Patrick, 560
Kelly, Thomas, O.P., Bp., 538
Kelly, William, 405
Kenna, John E., 405
Kennally, Vincent, S.J., 560

Kennedy, John F., 405
Kennedy, Joseph, 405
Kennedy, Robert F., 405
Kennedy, Thomas F., 560
Kenny, Michael H., Bp., 538
Kenny, William J., 560
Kenrick, Francis, 560
Kenrick, Peter, 560
Kentuckiana Community, 139
Kentucky, 480, 509, 512, 514, 518, 525, 614, 634, 641, 644, 646, 651, 690
  Interfaith Community, 139
  School Suit, 128
Kenya, 436
Keough, Francis R., 560
Kerygma, 377
Keyes, Edward Lawrence, 405
Keyes, Frances Parkinson, 406
Keyes, Michael, S.M., 560
Keys, Power of, 377
Kiley, Moses E., 560
Killeen, James, Bp., 560
Kilmer, Aline, 406
Kilmer, Joyce, 406
Kim, Stephan Sou Hwan, Card., 206
King, Edward J., Gov., 134
King Award, 699
King James Bible, 234
Kingdom of God, 224
Kingdom of Heaven (God), 372
Kings, Books of, 236
Kingship of Christ, Missionaries, 602
Kinney, John, Bp., 538
Kino, Eusebio, 416
Kir, Felix, 406
Kircher, Athanasius, 406
Klonowski, Henry T., Bp., 560
Klutznik, Philip A., 117
Knights of Columbus, 145, 669-70
Knights (Order) of Malta, 695
Knights of Peter Claver, 144, 666
Knights of St. Gregory, 130, 694
Knights of St. John, 666
  Ladies Auxiliary, 666
Knights of the Immaculata, 666
Knock, Our Lady of, 320
  Shrine, Ireland, Papal Visit, 62, 66-7
Knox, James R., Card., 113, 206
Knox, Ronald A., 406
Knudsen, Boerre, Rev., 135
Kocisko, Stephen, Abp., 539
Kodaly, Zoltan, 406
Koenig, Franz, Card., 206
Koester, Charles R., Bp., 539
Kogy, Lorenz, O.M., 560
Kolbe, Maximilian, Bl., 57, 309
Kolping Society, Catholic, 663
Konarski, Stanislaus, 406
Korea, 436
Kosciusko, Tadeusz, 406
Koudelka, Joseph, 560
Kowalski, Rembert, O.F.M., 560
Kozlowski, Edward, 560
Kraus, Irene, Sr., 110
Krautbauer, Francis X., 560
Krawczak, Arthur H., Bp., 539
Kreisler, Fritz, 406
Krol, John J., Card., 148-49, 206
Kucera, Daniel, O.S.B., Bp., 539
Kucera, Louis B., 560
Ku Klux Klan, 110, 149
Kulturkampf (1871), 163
Kupfer, William, M.M., Bp., 539
Kuwait, 436

L

Labor, see Social Encyclicals
Labor Day Statement, 150
Labrie, Jean-Paul, Bp., 465
La Bruyere, Jean de, 406
Lacey, Michael Pearse, Bp., 465
Lacordaire, Jean, 406
Lacroix, Fernand, C.J.M., Bp., 465
Ladies of Charity in the U.S., 666
Ladislaus, St., 309
Laennec, Rene, 406

Index

Laetare Medal, 699-700
LaFarge, John, 406
LaFarge, John, S.J., 406
  Award, 699
Lafontaine, Jean de, 406
Lafontaine, Jean Marie, Bp., 465
Laicization, 377
Lainez, Diego, 406
Laity, 67-8, 103
  Council for, 196
  Decree, 168
  in Foreign Missions, 606, 607
  National Assembly, Notre Dame, 120
  National Council of Catholic, U.S., 656
  Priesthood of, 385
  Special Ministers (Eucharist), 268
  See also Lay Apostolate; Lay Missionaries
Lalande, John, St., 416
Lalemant, Gabriel, St., 416
Lally, Francis J., Msgr., 114
Lamarck, Jean, 406
Lamb, Hugh, 560
Lamb of God (Mass), 260
Lamb of God, Sisters of, 593
Lambert, Francis, S.M., Bp., 539
Lambert, Rollins, Rev., 145
LaMennais Brothers (Bros. of Christian Instruction), 578
Lamentations, 238
Lamont, Donal, Bp., 135, 140
Lamy, Jean (John) Baptiste, 416
Lance, 327
Land, 138
Landazuri Ricketts, Juan, O.F.M., Card., 206
Landriault, Jacques, Bp., 466
Landrieu, Moon (Catholics in Presidents' Cabinets), 491
Lane, Loras, 560
Lane, Raymond A., M.M., 560
Langevin, Louis-de-Ganzague, Bp., 466
Langton, Stephen, 406
Languages of the Bible, 233
Languages of the Church, 377-78
Laos, 436
Laplace, Pierre, 406
Lapsi (249-251), 156
Lardone, Francesco, Abp., 539
Larkin, W. Thomas, Bp., 539
LaRocque, Eugene, Bp., 466
LaSalette, Missionaries of, 575
LaSalette, Our Lady of, 320
LaSalle, Rene Robert, 406
Las Casas, Bartolome, 416
Las Hermanas, 600
Lasso, Orlando di, 406
Last Judgment, 377
Lateran Agreement, 221
  Fiftieth Anniversary, 112
Lateran Councils, 167, 168
Lateran University, 629
Lathrop, George Parsons, 406
Lathrop, Mother Mary Alphonsa (Rose Hawthorne), 406
Latin America
  Assembly of Religious, 120
  Bishops' Conference (CELAM), 85-87, 113, 458
  Pontifical Commission, 196
  See also Individual Countries
Latin American Bishops' Assembly, Puebla, 85-7
  John Paul II Keynote Address, 52-4
  Pastoral Message to People of Latin America, 86-7
Latin in Liturgy, Canada, 131
Latin Mass, 266
Latin (Roman) Rite, 258
Latreille, Pierre, 406
Latria, see Adoration
Laurier, Sir Wilfrid, 406
Laval, Jacques Desire, Beatification, 122
Laval, John M., 560
Laval University (Canada), 627
Lavialle, Peter, 560
Lavigerie, Charles, 406
Lavoisier, Antoine, 406
Law, 378
  and Moral Values, 148
Law, Bernard F., Bp., 539
Law, Canon, see Canon Law
Law, Civil, 378
Law, Divine, 378

Law, Natural, 378
Lawler, John J., 560
Lawrence, St., 309
Lawrence of Brindisi, St., 248
Lay Apostolate (Organizations), 656-60
Lay Brothers, see Brothers
Law Carmelites, 604
Lay Institutes of Men, 569
Lay Mission-Helpers, 659
Lazarists (Vincentians, Congr. of the Missions), 578
Lazarus Parable, John Paul II on, 70-1
Leadership Conference of Women Religious, 600
League of St. Dymphna, 666
League of Tarcisians of the Sacred Heart, 661
Learning Centers, Catholic, 137
Lebanon, 436, 542
Lebel, Robert, Bp., 466
LeBlanc, Camille A., Bp., 466
Le Blond, Charles, 560
Lectionary, 266
Lector, 378
Ledvina, Emmanuel, 460
Lee, Louis, Rev., 124
Leech, George L., Bp., 539
Lefebvre, Marcel, Archbishop, 98, 106, 136, 140, 146, 151
Lefevere, Peter P., 560
Le Fort, Gertrude von, 406
Legare, Henri, O.M.I., Abp., 466
Legates, Papal, see Representatives, Vatican
Leger, Paul Emile, S.S., Card., 146, 206
Legion of Mary, 659
Legionaries of Christ, 575
Legitimation, 378
Leguerrier, Jules, O.M.I., Bp., 466
Lehar, Ferenc or Franz, 406
Leibold, Paul F., 560
Leipzig, Francis P., Bp., 539
Lekai, Laszlo, Card., 206
Lemaitre, Jules, 406
Lemay, Leo, S.M., Bp., 539
Lemcke, Henry, 406
Lemieux, Marie Joseph, O.P., Abp., 466
L'Enfant, Pierre, 406
Lenihan, Mathias, 560
Lenihan, Thomas M., 560
Lent, 290
  Byzantine Rite, 293
  Papal Messages, 113, 117
Leo I, the Great, St., 248
Leo III, the Isaurian (726), 157
Leo IX, St. (1049-54), 158
Leo XIII, Pope (1878), 163, 174-75
  Archives of Pontificate, 102
  Canonizations, 180
  Document on Anglican Orders, 355
  Encyclicals, 182-83
  Social Teachings, 251
Leonard, Vincent M., Bp., 539
Leonard of Port Maurice, St., 309
Lepanto (1571), 161
Leray, Francis X., 560
Lessard, Raymond W., Bp., 539
Lesotho, 135, 437
Letters (Epistles), 240-41
Letters, Papal, see Encyclicals
Leuken, Veronica, 124
Leven, Stephen A., Bp., 539
Leverrier, Urbain, 406
Levesque, Charles H., Bp., 466
Levesque, Louis, Abp., 466
Leviticus, 235
Ley, Felix, O.F.M. Cap., 560
Liberalism, 378
Liberation Theology, 52-4, 85, 113, 190
Liberia, 437
Liberty, Religious, see Freedom, Religious
Libya, 437
Liechtenstein, 437
Life, Meaning of, 117
Life, Respect, Reverence for, 61, 74-5, 525
Life After Death, 82
Life in Outer Space, 378
Light of Faith, Shades of Sexism, 124
Ligutti, Luigi, Msgr., UN Award, 100
Lille, Catholic University (France), 627
Lillis, Thomas F., 560

Limbo, 378
Linacre, Thomas, 406
Linens, Altar, 263
Lingard, John, 406
Linton, Moses L., 406
Lippi, Fra Filippo, 407
Liszt, Franz von, 407
Litany, 378
Literary Criticism, Bible, 242
Literary Forms of Bible, 230
Lithuania, 451
Lithuanian-American Catholic Services, 666
Lithuanian Catholic Alliance, 666
Lithuanian Catholic Religious Aid, 666
Lithuanian Roman Catholic Federation, 666
Lithuanian Roman Catholic Priests' League, 666
Little Brothers of Jesus, 579
Little Brothers of St. Francis, 579
Little Flower, see Therese of Lisieux, St.
Little Flower Mission League, 666
Little Flower Society, 666
Little Office of Blessed Virgin, 378
Little Sisters of Jesus, 592
Little Sisters of the Poor, 596
Liturgical
  Action, Solemn (Good Friday), 261
  Art, 258, 268
  Colors, 261-62
  Conference, 666
  Developments, 264-69
  Music, 257-58, 267
  Year (Church Calendar), 290-300
Liturgy, 256-69
  Constitution, 256-58, 259, 263, 290, 315, 366
  Developments, 264-69
  Eastern Churches, 326-28
  Eucharistic, 260
  Experimentations, 268-69
  Proposals for Change, Study, 101, 524, 525
  See also Mass
Liturgy of the Hours, 143, 257, 267
Liturgy of the Word, 259-60
Living History Farms, Papal Mass, 73
Living Word, Sisters of, 593
Locke, Jesse A., 407
Lodge, Henry Cabot, 220
Loeven, Paul C., C.M., Rev., 704
Logan Circle, Philadelphia, Papal Mass, 71-2
Lohmuller, Martin J., Bp., 540
Lombard, Peter, 407
Longstreet, James, 407
Lootens, Louis, 560
Loras, Mathias, 560
Lord, Daniel, 407
Lord's Prayer, 260
Loreto, House of, 378
  Papal Pilgrimage, 147
Loretto at the Foot of the Cross, Sisters, 593
Lorraine, Claude de, 407
Lorscheider, Aloisio, O.F.M., Card., 206
L'Osservatore Romano, 222-23
Losten, Basil, Bp., 540
Loughlin, John, 560
Louis, Congregation of Sisters of St., 593
Louis Bertran, St., 415
Louis de Montfort, St., 309
Louis IX of France, St., 309
Louis the Great, 407
Louise de Marillac, St., 309
Louisiana, 114, 481, 510, 513, 515, 518, 526, 615, 625, 634, 640, 641, 644, 651, 690
  Claretians Replaced As Campus Ministers, 124
  Unemployment Tax and Church Schools, 149
Lourdes Apparition, 320
Louvain University, 627
  American College, 185
Loviner, John Forest, 407
Lowney, Denis M., 560
Loyal Christian Benefit Association, 667
Lubachivsky, Myroslav J., Abp., 540
Lublin, Catholic University (Poland), 628
Lucey, Robert E., Abp., 561
Luciani, Albino, Card., see John Paul I, Pope
Lucker, Raymond A., Bp., 540
Lucy, St., 309
Ludden, Patrick A., 561

Luers, John, 561
Lugo, John de, 407
Luke, St., 245
  Gospel, 240
Lumen Gentium, 168
  See also Church, Constitution
Luna (Lunette, Lunula), 262
Lundgren, Danny, Rep., 99
Lussier, Philippe, C.SS.R., Bp., 466
Lust, 378
Luther, Martin, 332
Lutheran-Catholic Dialogue, U.S., 343-44
Lutheran-Catholic Statements, 346, 347
Lutheran Church-Missouri Synod Abortion Resolution, 139
Lutheran Churches, U.S., 334-35
Lutheran-Orthodox Dialogue, 101
Lutheran World Federation, see Lutheran-Catholic Statements
Lutherans, Norway, and Abortion Law, 135
Luxembourg, 437
Lyke, James P., O.F.M., Bp., 540
Lykes Corp. Steel Mill, Youngstown, Ohio, 104, 119
Lynch, George E., Bp., 540
Lynch, Joseph P., 561
Lynch, Patrick N., 561
Lyonnaise Rite, see Rites
Lyons, Catholic Faculties, 627
Lyons, Councils, 167
Lyons, Thomas W., Bp., 540

M

Mabillon, Jean, 407
Macao, 437
McAuliffe, Maurice, 561
McAuliffe, Michael F., Bp., 540
Maccabees, 237
McCafferty, John E., Bp., 540
McCann, Owen, Card., 206
McCarran, Patrick, 407
McCarrick, Theodore E., Bp., 540
McCarthy, Edward A., Abp., 540
McCarthy, John E., 109
McCarthy, John F., Bp., 540
McCarthy, Joseph E., 561
McCarthy, Joseph R., 407
McCarthy, Justin, 561
McCarthy, Raphael, S.J., 704
McCarthy, Thomas J., Bp., 466
McCarty, William T., C.SS.R., 561
McCauley, Vincent, C.S.C., Bp., 540
McClellan, William H., 407
McCloskey, James P., 561
McCloskey, John, 407
McCloskey, William, 561
McCollum v. Board of Education, 493
McCormack, John, 407
McCormick, Anne O'Hare, 407
McCormick, J. Carroll, Bp., 540
McCormick, Patrick J., 561
McCort, John J., 561
McDade, Mary Teresa, Sr., 704
McDevitt, Gerald V., Bp., 540
McDevitt, Philip R., 561
McDonald, Andrew J., Bp., 540
MacDonald, James H., Bp., 466
McDonald, William J., Bp., 541
McDonnell, Charles E., 561
McDonnell, Thomas J., 561
McDonough, Thomas J., Abp., 541
McDowell, John B., Bp., 541
MacEachern, Malcolm A., Bp., 466
Macedonianism, 165
McEleney, John J., S.J., Abp., 541
McEntegart, Bryan, 561
McFadden, James A., 561
MacFarland, Francis P., 561
McFarland, Norman F., Bp., 541
McFaul, James A., 561
McGann, John R., Bp., 126, 541
McGarry, Urban, T.O.R., Bp., 541
McGavick, Alexander J., 561
McGeough, Joseph F., 561
McGill, John, 561
MacGinley, John B., 561
McGivney, Michael J., 407

McGolrick, James, 561
McGovern, Patrick, 561
McGovern, Thomas, 561
McGranery, James P., 407
McGrath, J. Howard, 407
McGrath, Joseph, 561
McGrath, Richard T., Bp., 466
McGucken, Joseph T., Abp., 541
McGuinness, Eugene, 561
McGurkin, Edward A., M.M., Bp., 541
Macharski, Franciszek, Card., 206
McHugh, James T., Msgr., 111, 116
McIntyre, James F., Card., 119, 561, 704
McIntyre, Thomas J., Sen., 99
McKay, Claude, 407
McKenna, Joseph, 407
McKinney, Joseph C., Bp., 150, 525, 541
McLaughlin, Bernard J., Bp., 541
McLaughlin, Charles B., Bp., 561, 704
McLaughlin, Thomas H., 561
McLoughlin, John, 407
McMahon, John J., 561
McMahon, Lawrence, 561
MacMahon, Marie Edme, 407
McManaman, Edward P., 561
McManus, James E., C.SS.R., 561
McManus, William E., Bp., 149, 525, 541
McMullen, John, 561
McNabb, John C., O.S.A., Bp., 541
McNamara, John M., 561
McNamara, Lawrence J., Bp., 541
McNamara, Martin D., 561
McNaughton, William, M.M., Bp., 541
MacNeil, Joseph N., Abp., 466
McNeirny, Francis, 561
McNicholas, John T., O.P., 561
McNicholas, Joseph A., Bp., 541
McNulty, James A., 561
McQuaid, Bernard J., 407
McShea, Joseph M., Bp., 542
McSorley, Francis J., O.M.I., 561
McVinney, Russell J., 561
Machebeuf, Joseph P., 562
Madagascar, 437
Madeira Islands, 437
Madeleva, Sister M., 407
Madonna House Apostolate, 603
Maes, Camillus P., 562
Magazines, Catholic, Canada, 471-72
Magazines, Catholic, International, 681-82
Magazines, Catholic, U.S., 675-81
Magellan, Ferdinand, 407
Magi, 378
Maginn, Edward, Bp., 542
Magisterium (Teaching Authority), 53, 227-28
  and Interpretation of Bible, 230
Magner, Francis, 562
Magnificat, 378
Magsaysay, Ramon, 407
Maguire, John J., Abp., 542
Maguire, Joseph F., Bp., 542
Maher, Leo T., Bp., 542
Mahler, Gustav, 407
Mahoney, Bernard, 562
Mahoney, James, Bp. (Canada), 466
Mahoney, James P., Bp. (U.S.), 542
Mahony, Roger M., Bp., 542
Maine, 481, 508, 512, 514, 613, 634, 646, 651, 690
Mainz Council (848), 158
Major Orders, see Holy Orders
Malabar Rite, see Chaldean Rite
Malachi, 239
Malachy, St., Prophecies, 385
Maladjusted, Catholic Facilities, 641-43
Malagasy Republic, see Madagascar
Malankarese, 323
Malawi, 437
Malaysia, 437
Maldives, 438
Malherbe, Francois, 407
Mali, 438
Mallinckrodt, Hermann von, 407
Mallory, Stephen R., 407
Malone, James W., Bp., 542
Maloney, Charles G., Bp., 542
Maloney, David, Bp., 542

Maloney, Thomas F., 562
Malory, Sir Thomas, 407
Malpighi, Marcello, 408
Malta, 438
Malta, Order of, 695
Malula, Joseph, Card., 207
Malus, Etienne, 408
Man, Dignity, see *Redemptor Hominis*
Manchuria, see China
Mangan, James C., 408
Manichaeism, 165
Manion, Clarence E., 704
Manning Henry E., 408
Manning, Thomas R., O.F.M., Bp., 542
Manning, Timothy, Card., 129, 207
Manogue, Patrick, 416
Mansard, Nicholas, 408
Manucy, Dominic, 562
Manutius, Aldus, 408
Manzoni, Alessandro, 408
Marathonians, 165
Marcellinus and Peter, Sts., 309
March for Life, 110
Marcinkus, Paul C., Bp., 542
Marcionism, 164
Marconi, Dominic A., Bp., 542
Marconi, Guglielmo, 408
Marcos, Ferdinand, Pres., see Philippines
Marcus Aurelius (161-180), 155
Mardaga, Thomas J., Bp., 542
Marechal, Ambrose, S.S., 562
Marella, Paolo, Card., 207
Margaret Clitherow, St., 309
Margaret Mary Alacoque, St., 309
  Promises of Sacred Heart, 387
  See also Sacred Heart
Margaret of Scotland, St., 309
Margil, Antonio, 417
Marguerite Bourgeoys, Bl., 415
Maria Goretti, St., 147, 309
Marialis Cultus, 319
Marian Award, Pius XII, 700
Marian Congress, International, Spain, 148, 152
Marian Devotion, 56, 152
Marian Fathers, 575
Marian Library Medal, 700
Marian Movement of Priests, 667
Marian Sisters of Diocese of Lincoln, 593
Marian Society of Dominican Catechists, 593
Marian Union of Beauraing, 320
Mariana Islands, 438
Mariana Paredes of Jesus, St., 309
Marianist Award, 700
Marianists (Priests), 575
Marianites of the Holy Cross, Sisters, 593
Mariannhill Missionaries, 575
Marianum Theological Faculty, 629
Marie de l'Incarnation, Ven., 417
Marino, Eugene A., S.S.J., Bp., 542
Mariological Society of America, 667
Mariology, see Mary
Mariotte, Edme, 408
Marique, Joseph, S.J., 704
Marist Brothers, 579
Marist Fathers, 575
Marist Sisters, 593
Maritain, Jacques, 408
Maritain, Raissa, 408
Mark, St., 245
  Gospel, 240
Mark Seven Foundation for Deaf, 144
Markham, Thomas F., 562
Markham Prayer Card Apostolate, 667
Marling, Joseph, C.Pp.S., Bp., 542
Maronite Antonine Sisters, 594
Maronites, 323
  in U.S. (Antiochene Rite), 326
Marquette, Jacques, 417
Marriage (Matrimony), 267, 271, 281-89
  Catholic-Orthodox Views, 104
  Doctrine on, 281-83
  Erroneous Opinions, 289
  Guidelines, Parish, Canada, 146
  Laws of the Church, 283-86
  Mixed, 284

Marriage
  Pastoral Aspects, 288
  Permanence, 147
  Procedural Rules in Marriage Cases, 286
  Youth Guidelines, 289
Marriage and Family, 68
Marriage Encounter, 289
Marriages, Invalid, and Sacraments, 287-8
Marshall, John A., Bp., 542
Marsilius of Padua (1324), 160
Martel, Charles, 399
Martens, Wilfried, Prime Minister (Belgium), 138
Martha, St., 309
Martha, Sisters of St., 594
Marthe, Sisters of Sainte, 594
Martin, Albertus, Bp., 466
Martin, Augustus M., 562
Martin, Ralph, 150
Martin de Porres, St., 417
Martin of Tours, St., 309
Martin I, St., 309
Martini, Giambattista, 408
Martinique, 438
Marty, Francois, Card., 207
Marty, Martin, O.S.B., 562
Martyr, 379
Martyrology, 379
Martyrs Shrine, Canada, 471
Marx, Adolph, 572
Marxism, see Communism
Mary, Catholic Teaching, 315-19
  Devotion to, 152
  International Congress, 148, 152
  See also Blessed Virgin Mary
Mary (Religious)
  Company of, 594
  Daughters of Heart of, 594
  Little Company of, 594
  Missionaries of Company (Montfort Fathers), 576
  Missionary Sisters of Society, 594
  Missionary Sons of Immaculate Heart (Claretians), 572
  Servants of, 594
  Sisters of St., 594
  Sisters, Servants of, 594
  Society, 575
  Third Order Secular, 604
Mary, Legion of, 659
Mary and Joseph, Daughters, 594
Mary Help of Christians, Daughters, 594
Mary Immaculate (Religious)
  Daughters, 594
  Oblates of, 575
  Religious, 594
  Sisters, Servants, 594
Mary Magdalene, St., 309
Mary Magdalene de Pazzi, St., 309
Mary Major, Basilica of St., Dedication, 302
Mary of Catholic Apostolate, Sisters, 594
Mary of Immaculate Conception, Daughters, 594
Mary of Namur, Sisters of St., 594
Mary of Providence, Daughters of St., 594
Mary Productions "Airtime," 687
Mary Reparatrix, Society of, 594
Maryheart Crusaders, 667
Maryknoll Fathers, 575
Maryknoll Sisters, 586
Maryland, 481-82, 508, 512, 514, 518, 526, 613, 625, 634, 641, 644, 651, 690
Masaccio, Tommaso, 408
Masons, 371
Masoretic Text, Bible, 233
Mass, The, 259-63
  Byzantine Rite, 326-27
  Canon, see Canon
  Changes, 265-66
  Children's, 266
  Concelebration, 363
  Eucharistic Prayers, 265, 268, 269
  for Non-Catholics, 269
  for People, 379
  Importance of, 137
  Inter-Ritual Concelebration, 266
  Home (Mass for Special Groups), 266
  Hosts, 268
  Latin, 266
  Nuptial, 261

Mass, The
  Places and Altars, 261
  Saturday Evening, 266
  Stipends, 392
  Study, 268, 524, 525
  Tridentine, see Lefebvre, Marcel, Archbishop
  Trination, 266
  Vestments, Vessels, 261-63
Massachusetts, 482, 508, 512, 514, 518, 526, 613, 625, 634-35, 640, 641, 644, 651-52, 690
  Abortion Funding, 128
  Chaplains and Legislature, 144
Massias, John de, St., 417
Massillon, Jean B., 408
Master of Ceremonies, 361
Master of Novices, 379
Mater et Magistra, see Social Doctrine
Mater et Magistra Award, 700
Materialism, 379
  John Paul II on, 62
Matrimony, see Marriage
Matthew, St., 245
  Gospel, 240
Matthias, St., 245
Matthias Corvinus (Hunyady), 408
Matz, Nicholas C., 562
Maundy Thursday, see Holy Thursday
Maurer, Jose Clemente, C.SS.R., Card., 207
Mauriac, Francois, 408
Mauritania, 438
Mauritius, 438
Mauro, Fra, 408
Maximilian Kolbe, Bl., 57, 309
Maximilian I, the Great, 408
May, John L., Bp., 542
May Laws, see Kulturkampf
Maynooth, Papal Visit, 62
Mazarin, Jules, 408
Mazzarella, Bernardino, O.F.M., Bp., 562, 704
Mazzuchelli, Samuel C., 417
Meagher, Thomas, 408
Medal, Miraculous, 320
Medal, Scapular, 389
Medals, Papal, 695
Medals and Awards, Catholic, 695-703
Medeiros, Humberto, Card., 138, 144, 207
Media, see Communications
Media Awards, 670, 693
Medical Mission Sisters, 594
Medical Missionaries of Mary, 594
Meditation, 117, 379
Meek v. Pittenger, 486, 612
Meerschaert, Theophile, 562
Meir, Golda, 704
Mekhitarist Order of Vienna, 575
Melancon, Georges, Bp., 466
Melcher, Joseph, 562
Melilla, 438
Melkite Byzantine Rite, 154, 323
Melkites, U.S., 326
Membre, Zenobius, 417
Men, Conference of Major Superiors, 145, 579
Men, National Council of Catholic, 656
Men, Religious Institutes, Membership, 580-81
Men, Religious Institutes, U.S., 571-80
Men of the Sacred Hearts, 667
Menaion, 293
Mendel, Gregor, 408
Mendel Medal, 700
Mendez, Alfred, C.S.C., Bp., 543
Mendicant Orders (Mendicants), 379
Mennonites, see Anabaptism
Menologion, 293
Mentally Retarded, National Apostolate, 145, 648
Mentally Retarded, Schools for, 643-46
Mercedarian Missionaries of Berriz, 595
Mercedarian Third Order, 604
Mercedarians, 575
Mercier, Desire Joseph, 408
Mercy
  Corporal Works, 364
  Divine, 379
  Spiritual Works, 391
Mercy (Religious)
  Brothers of, 579
  Daughters of Our Lady of, 595

Index

Mercy (Religious)
  Fathers of, 575
  Missionary Sisters of Our Lady of, 595
  Sisters of, 125, 595
  Sisters of, of the Union, 595
Merit, 379
Mersenne, Marin, 408
Merton, Thomas, 104, 408
Messiah, see Christ
Messmer, Sebastian, 562
Mestice, Anthony F., Bp., 543
Mestrovic, Ivan, 408
Metcalfe, Ralph H., Rep., 704
Metempsychosis, 379
Methodist Churches, U.S., 334
  Dialogue, 115, 344-45
  Statement, 347
Methodists, 333
Methodius, St. (Cyril and Methodius, Sts.), 143, 306
  See also Czechoslovakia
Metropolitan, 187
Metternich, Klemans, 408
Metzger, Sidney M., Bp., 543
Mexican Americans, 87-9, 99
  Las Hermanas, 600
  PADRES, 89
Mexicans, Illegal Aliens, 99, 100
Mexico, 438
  Papal Visit, 49-51
  Puebla Meeting, Latin American Bishops, 85-7
Mexico, Twelve Apostles, 417
Meyer, Albert, 562
Meyer, Cyril F., Rev., C.M., 704
Meynell, Alice, 408
Meynell, Wilfrid, 408
Mezzofanti, Giuseppe, 408
Miami, Spanish-Speaking Apostolate, 89
Micah, 239
Michael, Archangel, 303, 356
Michaels, James E., S.S.C., Bp., 543
Michaud, John S., 562
Michel, Robert, Rep., 99
Michelangelo Buonarroti, 408
Michigan, 482-83, 509, 512, 514, 526, 614, 625, 635, 642, 644, 652, 690
Middle East, 124, 524, 525
Middle East Peace Efforts, 106, 118, 149
Miege, John B., S.J., 562
Mieszko (966), 158
Migrants, Pastoral Care, see Spanish-Speaking Ministry
Migration, Pontifical Commission, 117-18
Migration and Refugee Services, USCC, 109
Mihalik, Emil J., Bp., 543
Mikolajczyk, Stanislaus, 408
Milan, Edict (313), 156
Miles, Richard P., 562
Military Chaplains, Catholic, Discrimination, 113
Military Ordinariate (Vicariate), U.S., 506, 511, 515
Military Service, 255
  See also Draft
Militia of Our Lord Jesus Christ, 694
Mill Hill Missionaries, 575
Millennium, 379
Miller, Don, 704
Miller, Nathan L., 408
Millet, Jean, 408
Minder, John, O.S.F.S., Bp., 543
Mindszenty, Jozsef, Card., 408
Minihan, Jeremiah F., 562
Minim, Sisters of Mary Immaculate, 595
Ministries of Church, 95, 277
Minnesota, 483, 509-10, 513, 515, 518, 526, 615, 625, 635, 642, 652, 690
  Medicaid Abortion Records, 99
  University Newspaper, 133
Minor Orders, see Holy Orders
Minorities (U.S.), see Blacks; Indians; Mexican-Americans; Spanish-Speaking
Minton, Sherman, 408
Miracles, 379
Miraculous Meal, 320
Miranda y Gomez, Miguel Dario, Card., 207
Mirari Vos (1832), 162
Misericorde Sisters, 595
Misner, Paul B., C.M., 562
Missal, 379

Missal
  Roman (Sacramentary), 266
Missiology, 380
Mission, 380
Mission, Congregation of (Vincentians), 578
Mission Council, U.S., 606-07
Mission Doctors Association, 459
Mission Helpers of the Sacred Heart, 595
Mission of Our Lady of Bethany, 602
Missionaries, 127, 132
Missionaries, American, 605-09
  Bishops, 507
  in Foreign Countries, 605-06, 607
  in Home Missions, 607-09
Missionaries of Charity, 584
Missionaries of Sacred Heart, 132
Missionaries of St. Charles, 575
Missionaries of the Holy Apostles, 576
Missionary Association of Catholic Women, 667
Missionary Catechists of the Sacred Hearts of Jesus and Mary, 595
Missionary Cenacle Apostolate, 667
Missionary Sisters of the Catholic Apostolate, 595
Missionary Union in the U.S., Pontifical, 668
Missionary Vehicle Association, 667
Missions, 105, 128, 143
  Decree, 168
Missions, Catholic (U.S.), 607-09
  Support Bodies, 105, 128, 143
  See also Spanish Speaking
Missions, Franciscan, of California, 418
Missions, Texas, 104
Mississippi, 483, 509, 513, 515, 614, 635-36, 652, 691
Missouri, 483, 510, 513, 515, 518, 526, 615, 625, 636, 640, 642, 644, 652, 691
Mistral, Gabriela, 408
Mitchell, James P., 409
Mitchell, John, 409
Mitre, 262
Mitty, John J., 562
Mixed Marriages, 284
  Ecumenical Statement, 347
Modalism, 164
Modern World, Constitution (Vatican II), 251-55, 281-82, 357
Modernism, 380
  Syllabus of St. Pius X, 393
Moeller, Henry, 562
Mogrovejo, Turibius de, St., 417
Mohammed (622), 157
Mohler, Johann, 409
Mohr, Josef, 409
Molina, Luis de, 409
Molloy, Thomas E., 562
Molokai, Hawaii, Advisory Commission, 123
Monaco, 438
Monaghan, Francis J., 562
Monaghan, John J., 562
Monarchianism, 164
Monastery, 380
Monasticism (Sixth Century), 157
Mondino dei Luicci, 409
Monge, Gaspard, 409
Mongolian Peoples' Republic, 439
Monica, St., 309
Monk, 380
Monks of the Brotherhood of St. Francis, 576
Monophysite Churches, 329
Monophysitism, 165
Monotheism, 380
Monothelitism, 165
Monsignor (Honorary Prelate), 188
Msgr. John P. Monaghan Social Action Award, 700
Monstrance, 262
Montana, 483-84, 510, 513, 515, 526, 615, 625, 652, 691
Montanism, 165
Montcalm, Marquis, Louis, 409
Monte Cassino (c. 529), 127, 157
Montessori, Maria, 409
Monteux, Pierre, 409
Montfort Fathers, 576
Montgomery, George T., 562
Montserrat, 439
Moon, Parker Thomas, 409
Mooney, Edward, 562
Moore, John, 562

Moore, Thomas, 409
Moore, Thomas Verner, 409
Mora, Francis, 562
Moral Obligations, 250-51
Morality, 380
Morality in Media, Inc., 667
Moran, Neville J., 704
Moran, William J., Bp., 543
Moravian Church, see Hus, John
More, Thomas, St., 310
Moreno, Manuel D., Bp., 543
Morgagni, Giovanni, 409
Morin, Laurent, Bp., 466
Morkovsky, John Louis, Bp., 543
Morley, Sylvanus Griswold, 409
Mormons, 380
Morneau, Robert F., Bp., 543
Morocco, 439
Morris, John, 562
Morrow, Louis, S.D.B., Bp., 543
Mortal Sin, 390
Mortification, 380
Moslems (Muslims), 351-52
　Message to, 143
Mother of God, see Mary, Catholic Teaching
Mother of God, Missionary Sisters, 595
Mother of God, Sisters, Poor Servants, 595
Motherhood, 107
Motta, Carlos Carmelo de Vasconcellos, Card., 207
Motu Proprio, 380
Mount Calvary, Ursuline Sisters of, 599
Mount Carmel, BVM of (July 16), 297
Mount Carmel (Religious)
　Congregation of Our Lady of, 582
　Institute of Our Lady of, 582
　Order of Our Lady, 572
　Third Order of Our Lady (Discalced), 604
　　See also Carmelites
Mountbatten, Lord, 143
Movement for a Better World, 659
Movimiento Familiar Cristiano, 460, 658
Moylan, Stephen, 409
Moynihan, Patrick, Sen., 114
Mozambique, 110, 121, 141, 439
Mozarabic Rite, see Rites
Mozart, J. C. Wolfgang, 409
Mozzoni, Umberto, Card., 207
Mrak, Ignatius, 562
Mueller, Joseph M., Bp., 543
Muench, Aloysius, 409
Mugavero, Francis J., Bp., 543
Mulcahy, John J., Bp., 543
Muldoon, Peter, 562
Mullen, Tobias, 562
Muller, Johann, 409
Muller, Johannes, 409
Mulloy, William T., 562
Mulrooney, Charles R., 543
Mulvee, Robert, Bp., 543
Mundelein, George, 562
Mundo, Michael P., Bp., 543
Munoz Duque, Anibal, Card., 207
Munoz Vega, Pablo, S.J., Card., 106, 208
Muratorian Fragment, 233
Murillo, Bartolome, 409
Murphy, Frank, 409
Murphy, John B., 409
Murphy, Joseph A., 562
Murphy, Michael J., Bp., 543
Murphy, Patrick, S.V.D., 704
Murphy, Philip F., Bp., 544
Murphy, T. Austin, Bp., 544
Murphy, Thomas J., Bp., 544
Murphy, Thomas W., C.SS.R., Bp., 544
Murphy, William F., 562
Murray, John Courtney, 409
Murray, John G., 562
Murray, Philip, 409
Muscat, see Arabian Peninsula
Music, Sacred, 257-58, 267
　Pontifical Institute, 629
Muslims, see Moslems
Mussio, John K., 562
Muzorewa, Abel, Bp. (Methodist), 126, 136, 140
　See also Rhodesia
Mysteries of Faith, 380

Mysteries of Rosary, see Rosary
Mysterium Fidei, see Transubstantiation
Mystery of Church, 224-25
Mystery of Eucharist, see Mass
Mystical Body, 225

N

Nahum, 239
Najmy, Justin, O.S.B.M., 563
Namibia (South West Africa), 439
Napoleon (1789, 1809), 162
Nasalli Rocca di Corneliano, Mario, Card., 208
Nathan, George Jean, 409
National
　Alliance of Czech Catholics, 667
　Apostolate with Mentally Retarded Persons, 145, 648
　Assembly of Religious Brothers, 139, 579
　Assembly of Women Religious, 144, 600
　Association of Boards of Education, 612
　Association of Catholic Chaplains, 631
　Association of Church Personnel Administrators, 667
　Association of Diocesan Ecumenical Officers, 667
　Association of Pastoral Musicians, 667
　Association of Priest Pilots, 667
　Black Sisters Conference, 600
　Catechetical Directory, 90-1, 118, 523
　Catholic Bandmasters' Association, 667
　Catholic Cemetery Conference, 667
　Catholic Conference for Interracial Justice, 104, 667
　Catholic Development Conference, 667
　Catholic Disaster Relief Committee, 667
　Catholic Educational Association, 125, 612
　Catholic Forensic League, 661
　Catholic Offices for Information, 693
　Catholic Pharmacists Guild, 667
　Catholic Rural Life Conference, 656
　Catholic Society of Foresters, 667
　Catholic Stewardship Council, 667
　Catholic Vocation Council, 601
　Catholic Women's Union, 667
　Center for Urban Ethnic Affairs, 667
　Christ Child Society, 661
　Church Goods Association, 667
　Clergy Conference on Alcoholism, 667
　Coalition of American Nuns, 600
　Conference of Catholic Bishops, 100, 521-22
　　See also Bishops (U.S.)
　Conference of Catholic Charities, 109, 631
　Conference of Religious Vocations Directors of Men, 667
　Council of Catholic Laity, 656
　Council of Catholic Men, 656
　Council of Catholic Women, 656
　Council of Churches of Christ, 100, 341
　Federation of Catholic Physicians Guilds, 668
　Federation of Priests' Councils, 100, 119, 628
　Federation of Spiritual Directors, 668
　Forum of Catholic Parent Organizations, 613
　Guild of Catholic Psychiatrists, 668
　Office for Black Catholics, see Black Catholics
　Organization for Continuing Education of Roman Catholic Clergy, 668
　Sisters Vocation Conference, 600
NC News Service, 682
National Labor Relations Board (NLRB), 99, 120, 618
Nativity, Blessed Virgin Mary, 301
Nativity, Christ (Christmas), 301
Nativity, St. John the Baptist, 303
Natural Law, 378
Natural Virtue, see Virtue
Nauru, 439
Navagh, James J., 563
Navarra, Catholic University (Spain), 628
Nazareth, Poor Sisters of, 595
Nazi War Crimes, 115, 141
Neale, Leonard, 563
Nebraska, 484, 510, 513, 515, 526, 615, 636, 642, 644-45, 652, 691
Necedah Shrine, 134
Necromancy, 380
Negroes, see Blacks
Nehemiah, 236
Nelaton, Auguste, 409
Nelson, Knute, O.S.B., 544
Nepal, 439

Index

Neraz, John C., 563
Nereus and Achilleus, Sts., 309
Nerinckx, Charles, 417
Nero (64), 155
Nervi, Pier Luigi, 704
Nestle Infant Formula, Developing Countries, 106
Nestorian Churches, 329
Nestorianism, 165
Netherlands, 111, 116, 128, 150, 439-40
Netherlands Antilles, 440
Network, 668
Neumann, John, St., 308
Nevada, 484, 511, 513, 515, 616, 642, 691
Nevins, John J., Bp., 544
Nevins, Joseph V., Rev., 704
New American Bible, 99, 234
New Caledonia, 440
New English Bible, 234
New Guinea, see Papua New Guinea
New Hampshire, 484, 508, 512, 514, 613, 636, 652, 691
New Hebrides, 440
New Jersey, 114, 484, 508, 512, 514, 526, 613, 625, 636, 640, 642, 645, 646, 652-53, 691
  Church-State Separation and Abortion Ban, 109
  Tax Deduction Law, 129
New Mexico, 484-85, 511, 513, 515, 616, 625, 636, 645, 653, 691
New Testament, 233, 240-41
New York, 100, 124, 133, 485-86, 508, 512, 514, 518, 526, 613, 625, 636-37, 641, 642, 645, 646, 653, 691
  Papal Visit, 63-5
  Right to Life Party, 99
New Zealand, 440
Newell, Hubert M., Bp., 544
Newman, John H., 127, 409
Newman, Thomas A., M.S., 563
News Agencies, Catholic, 682
News Services, U.S., 682-83
News Stories, Top (1978), 105
Newspapers, Catholic, U.S., 671-75
  Awards, 670
Newspapers, Student, Criticized, 133
Neylon, Martin J., S.J., Bp., 544
Ngueme, Francisco Macias, 145
Niagara Univ. (U.S.), 628
Nicaea, Councils, 166, 167
Nicaragua, 106, 116, 131, 141, 147, 151, 440
Nicene Creed, 249-50
Nicholas, St., 309
Nicholas of Lyra, 409
Nicholas of Tolentino, St., 309
Niedergeses, James D., Bp., 544
Niedhammer, Matthew, O.F.M. Cap., 563
Niger, 440
Nigeria, 440
Nihil Obstat (Censorship of Books), 360-61
Nijmegen University (Netherlands), 628
Nilan, John J., 563
Niza, Marcos de, 409
Noa, Thomas L., Bp., 563
Nobel Peace Prize (1979), Mother Teresa, 154
Nobili, Leopoldo, 409
Noble Guards, 221
Nobrega, Manoel, 417
Nocturnal Adoration Society of U.S., 668
Noel, Laurent, Bp., 466
Noel Chabanel, St., 416
Nold, Wendelin J., Bp., 544
Nolker, Bernard C., C.SS.R., Bp., 544
Noll, John F., 409
Nollet, Jean-Antoine, 409
Non-Believers, Secretariat, 196
Non-Christian Religions, Declaration (Vatican II), 168, 348, 351
Non-Christians, Secretariat, 122, 195
Non-Expedit, 380
Non-Revealed Religions, 352
Norbert, St., 309
Norbert, Third Order of St., 604
Norbertines (Premonstratensians), 576
North America, Cardinals, 215
North America, Eastern Rite Jurisdictions, 325
North American College, 630
North American Conference, Separated and Divorced Catholics, 139
North American Martyrs, 416
North Carolina, 486, 508, 512, 514, 613, 637, 645, 653, 691
North Dakota, 486, 510, 513, 515, 526, 615, 626, 637, 642, 653, 691
North Ireland, 65-6, 120, 136, 140, 434
  See also Ireland
Northeast Pastoral Center for Hispanics, 88
Northrop, Henry P., 563
Norway, 135, 440-41
Noser, Adolph, S.V.D., Abp., 544
Nostra Aetate, 168
  See also Catholic-Jewish Relations
Notre Dame (Religious)
  de Namur, Srs. of, 595
  de Sion, Congregation, 596
  des Anges, Missionary Sisters, 596
  School Sisters, 595
  Sisters, 595
  Sisters of Congregation, 595
Notre Dame University, 134, 621
Novak, Alfred, C.SS.R., Bp., 544
Novatianism, 165
Novena, 381
Novice, 381
Novices, Master, 379
Novitiate, see Novice
Noyes, Alfred, 409
Nsubuga, Emmanuel, Card., 208
Nuclear Dangers, 110, 119
Nulla Celebrior, see Patriarchs
Nullity, Decree of (Marriage), 286, 287
Numbers, 235
Nun, 381
Nunc Dimittis, 381
Nuncios, 215-18
Nuptial Mass, 261
Nurses' Schools, Catholic, 515
Nussbaum, Paul J., C.P., 563
Nyerere, Julius, Pres. (Tanzania), 138

O

O Salutaris Hostia, 382
Oath, 381
Oath of Succession (1563), 161
Obadiah, 239
Obedience, 381, 570
Obedience of Faith, 370
Oberammergau Passion Play, 139
Oblate Missionaries of Mary Immaculate, 602
Oblate Sisters of
  Blessed Sacrament, 597
  Providence, 597
  St. Francis de Sales, 587
Oblates of
  Mary Immaculate, 575
  Most Holy Redeemer, 597
  St. Benedict, 604
  St. Francis de Sales, 573
Obligations, Moral, 250-51
O'Boyle, Patrick A., Card., 208
O'Brien, Henry J., 563
O'Brien, Lawrence (Catholics in Presidents' Cabinets), 490
O'Brien, William D., 563
Obsession, Diabolical, 381
O'Byrne, Paul J., Bp., 466
O'Callahan, Joseph, 409
Ocampo, Sebastian, 409
Occasions of Sin, 390
Occultism, 381
Oceania, American Bishops, 507
Oceania, Cardinals, 215
Oceania, Eastern Rite Jurisdictions, 325
O'Connell, Daniel, 410
O'Connell, Denis, 563
O'Connell, Eugene, 563
O'Connell, William, 563
O'Connor, Hubert P., O.M.I., Bp., 466
O'Connor, James, 563
O'Connor, John, 563
O'Connor, John J., Bp., 544
O'Connor, Martin J., Abp., 544
O'Connor, (Mary) Flannery, 410
O'Connor, Michael, 563
O'Connor, William A., Bp., 545
O'Connor, William P., 563
Octave, 381

Index

Octave of Birth of Our Lord (Solemnity of Mary), 304
Oddi, Silvio, Card., 208
O'Dea, Edward J., 563
Odilia, St., 309
Odin, John M., 563
O'Donaghue, Denis, 563
O'Donnell, Cletus F., Bp., 545
O'Donnell, Thomas J., S.J., 120
O'Dowd, James T., 563
O'Dwyer, Joseph, 410
Oertel, Abraham, 410
Of Human Life (Humanae Vitae), 282-83
O'Farrell, Michael J., 563
Offertory, 260
Office, Divine (Liturgy of the Hours), 257, 267
Office of the Blessed Virgin Mary, Little, 378
Offices of the Roman Curia, 197
O'Fiaich, Tomas, Card., 136, 208
O'Flanagan, Dermot, 563
O'Gara, Cuthbert, C.P., 563
O'Gorman, James, O.C.S.O., 563
O'Gorman, Thomas, 563
O'Grady, John F., O.M.I., Bp., 466
O'Hair, Madalyn, 115, 134
O'Hara, Edwin V., 410
O'Hara, Gerald P., 563
O'Hara, John F., 563
O'Hara, Stephen, Bro., 99
O'Hara, William, 563
O'Hara Institute, 688
O'Hare, William F., S.J., 563
O'Hern, John F., 563
O'Higgins, Bernardo, 510
Ohio, 100, 109, 486, 509, 512, 514, 518, 527, 614, 626, 637-38, 641, 642, 645, 653-54, 691
Oil of Catechumens, 381
Oil of the Sick, 381
Oils, Holy, 267, 381
O'Keefe, Gerald, Bp., 545
Oklahoma, 486-87, 510, 513, 515, 615, 638, 654, 692
Oktoechos, 293
Olaf (II) Haraldsson, St., 410
Old Catholics, 381
Old Testament, 231, 233, 235-39
  See also Bible
O'Leary, Edward T., Bp., 545
O'Leary, Thomas, 563
Olga, St. (955), 157
Oliver Plunkett, St., 62, 309
Olivetan Benedictine Sisters, 581
Olwell, Quentin, C.P., 563
O'Malley, Kay and Walter, 704
Oman, 441
O'Mara, John A., Bp., 466
O'Meara, Edward T., Bp., 545
"On This Rock," 686
O'Neill, Arthur J., Bp., 545
O'Neill, Michael C., Abp., 466
O'Neill D'Amour Award, 700
Optatam Totius, 168
Opus Dei, 142
Opus Dei, U.S., 659
Oratorian Fathers, 576
Oratory, 381
Oratory of St. Philip Neri, 576
Order of the Alhambra, 668
Orders, Anglican, see Anglican Orders
Orders, Holy, see Holy Orders
Orders, Religious, 568
Orders of Knighthood, 694
Ordinariate, 381
Ordinary, 381
Ordination, 382
  See also Deacons, Permanent; Holy Orders
Ordination Women, see Women, Ordination
Ordo Paenitentiae, see Penance
O'Regan, Anthony, 563
Oregon, 487, 511, 513, 515, 527, 616, 626, 638, 642-43, 645, 654, 692
  Catholic Conference, 109
O'Reilly, Bernard, 563
O'Reilly, Charles J., 563
O'Reilly, James, 563
O'Reilly, Patrick, 564
O'Reilly, Peter J., 564
O'Reilly, Thomas C., 564

Orellano, Francisco de, 410
Organ Transplants, 382
Organization of American States (OAS), Vatican Observer, 113
Organizations, Catholic, 458-60, 662-70
Oriental Church, 331
Oriental Churches, Sacred Congregation, 192-93
Oriental Studies, Pontifical, Institute, 629
Orientalium Ecclesiarum, 168
  See also Eastern Churches, Catholic
Origen, 410
Original Sin, 382
Orosius, Paul, 410
O'Rourke, Edward W., Bp., 99, 545
Orthodox Churches, Eastern, 328-29
  Agreed Statements on Church, Marriage, 330
  Consultation on Marriage, 104
  Dialogue with Lutherans, 101
  Dialogues, 345
  Easter Date, 300
  Ecumenism, 133, 330
  Guidelines for Ecumenism, 331
  Jurisdictions, 329
Orthodox Churches, Oriental, 331
  Dialogue, 345
Orthodox Roman Catholic Movement, Inc., 119
Ortynsky, Stephen, O.S.B.M., 564
O'Shea, John, C.M., 564
O'Shea, William F., M.M., 564
Ostensorium, 262
Ostpolitik, 382
O'Sullivan, Jeremiah, 564
Ott, Stanley J., Bp., 545
Ottaviani, Alfredo, Card., 142, 704
Ottenweller, Albert H., Bp., 545
Otto I (962), 158
Otunga, Maurice, Card., 208
Ouellet, J. Gilles, P.M.E., 466
Ouellette, Andre, Bp., 467
Our Father (Lord's Prayer), 260
Our Lady, see Apparitions of BVM; Blessed Virgin Mary
Our Lady of Grace, 147
Our Lady of LaSalette, Missionaries, 575
Our Lady of Mercy, Sisters, 596
Our Lady of Sorrows, Sisters, 596
Our Lady of the Garden, Sisters, 596
Our Lady of the Way, Society, 603
Our Lady of Victory Missionary Sisters, 599
Oursler, Fulton, 410
Oxford Movement, 382
Ozanam, Frederic, 410
  See also St. Vincent de Paul Society
Ozanam, Jacques, 410

P

Pacem in Terris, see Social Doctrine
Pachomius (318), 156
Pacioli, Luca, 410
Pactum, Callixtinum (1122), 159
Paderewski, Ignace, 410
Padilla, Juan de, 417
PADRES, 89
Paenitemini, see Penance (Penitence)
Paganism, 382
Pagano, Bernard, Rev., Exonerated, 150
Pakistan, 122, 441
  Islamic Revival, 125
Palaeologus, Michael (1281), 160
Palatine Guard of Honor, 221
Palazzini, Pietro, Card., 208
Palestinian Refugees, 111, 124, 133, 524
  See also Middle East
Palestrina, Giovanni, 410
Pall, 263
Palladio, Andrea, 410
Pallium, 262
Pallottine Sisters, 596
Pallottines, 576
Palm Sunday (Sunday of the Passion), 303
Palmer, Gretta, 410
Palms, 382
Palou, Francisco, 417
Panama, 441
  Canal Zone Control, 154

Index

Pancras, St., 309
Pange Lingua, 382
Pantheism, 382
Papacy, see Pope
Papal
  Addresses, see John Paul II
  Audience, 222
    See also Vatican in News Events
  Election, 382-83
  Flag, 222
  Medals, 695
  Representatives, 215-19, 223
  Secretariat of State, 192
  States (1870), 163
    See also Apostolic; Pontifical; Pope; Vatican
Papini, Giovanni, 410
Pappalardo, Salvatore, Card., 208
Pappin, Bernard F., Bp., 467
Papua New Guinea, 441
Paraclete, 383
Paraclete, Servants of the Holy, 576
Paradis, Wilfrid H., Msgr., 114
Paraguay, 441
Paraliturgical Services, see Devotions
Pardy, James V., M.M., Bp., 545
Pare, Ambroise, 410
Pare, Marius, Bp., 467
Parecattil, Joseph, Card., 208
Paredes of Jesus, St. Mariana, 309
Parent, Charles E., Abp., 467
Parente, Pietro, Card., 208
Parents, Duties, 383
Paris, Bruno, 410
Paris, Catholic Institute, 627
Paris Foreign Mission Society, 576
Pariseau, Mother Joseph, 417
Parish, 383
Parish Visitors of Mary Immaculate, 596
Parker, Matthew, see Anglican Orders
Parochial Schools, see Schools, Catholic
Parousia, 383
Parsch, Pius, 410
Parsons, Wilfrid, 410
Particular Examen, see Conscience, Examination of
Pascal, Blaise, 410
Paschal Baylon, St., 309
Paschal Candle, 383
Paschal Precept, 383
Paschal Season, see Eastertide
Paschal Vigil (Easter Vigil), 302
Paschalis Mysterii, see Calendar, Revised
Paschang, Adolph J., M.M., 564
Paschang, John L., Bp., 545
Passion, Congregation of, 576
Passion of Christ, 383
Passion Play, see Oberammergau
Passion Sunday, 303
Passionist Nuns, 585
Passionist Sisters, 585
Passionists, 576
Passover, 350
Pasteur, Louis, 410
Pastor, 383
Pastor, Ludwig von, 410
Pastor Aeternus (Primacy of Pope), 227
Paten, 262
Pater Noster, 383
Patmore, Coventry, 410
Patriarchates, Catholic, 186-87
Patriarchates, Orthodox, 239
Patriarchs, Catholic, 186-7
  Cardinals, 199
  Synods, 325
Patrick, St., 310
Patrick, St., Brothers of (Patrician Brothers), 575
Patrick's Missionary Society, St., 576
Patrimony of the Holy See, 197
Patripassianism, 164
Patron Saints, 311-14
Patronal Medal, Catholic University, 696
Paul, James F. (Wattson, Lewis Thomas), 415
Paul, John J., Bp., 545
Paul, St. (Apostle), 246
  Epistles, 240-41
  Feast (Peter and Paul), 304
Paul, St. (Religious), Angelic Sisters of, 596

Paul, St. (Religious)
  Daughters of, 596
  for Apostolate of Communications, Society of, 576
  of Chartres, Sisters of, 596
  the Apostle, Missionary Society of, 576
  the First Hermit, Order of, 576
Paul Miki and Companions, Sts., 310
Paul of the Cross, St., 310
Paul VI, Pope, 102, 148
  Biography, 179-80
  Canonizations, 181-82
  Encyclicals, 185, 282-83
Pauline Epistles, 240-41
Pauline Fathers, 576
Pauline Fathers (Doylestown), 148, 576
Pauline Privilege, 285
Paulinus of Nola, St., 310
Paulist Communications Services, 687
Paulist League, 668
Paulist Productions, 687
Paulists, 576
Paupini, Giuseppe, Card., 209
Pax Christi, 460, 659
Pax Christi, USA, 104, 110, 660
Pax Christi (Pious Association), 603
Pax Romana, 460, 660
Pazmany, Peter, 410
Peace
  Commission for, 196
  Efforts, Pleas, 112, 118, 136, 179
  Religion and, World Conference, 149
  World Day for, 108, 142
    See also Middle East Peace Efforts
Peace, Sign of, 383
Peace Award, 700
Peace Plans, Pius XII, 177
Peace Prayer, Mass, 260
Peace Service, Ecumenical, Illinois, 115
Pearce, George H., S.M., Abp., 545
Pechillo, Jerome, T.O.R., Bp., 545
Pectoral Cross, 383
Pednault, Roch, Bp., 467
Peguy, Charles Pierre, 410
Pelagianism, 165
Pellegrino, Michele, Card., 209
Pelletier, Georges, Bp., 467
Pellicer, Anthony, 564
Pelouze, Theophile, 410
Pena, Raymond, Bp., 545
Penalver y Cardenas, Luis, 564
Penance (Penitence), 383
Penance (Sacrament), 270, 275-76
  First, and First Communion, 273
  Penitential Celebrations, 276
    See also General Absolution
Penance and Renewal, 132
Penitential Rite, Mass, 259
Penitentiary, Apostolic, 195
Penney, Alphonsus L., Bp., 467
Pennsylvania, 104, 108, 125, 487-88, 508, 512, 514, 518, 527, 613, 626, 638-39, 641, 645, 646, 654, 692
  Three Mile Incident, 119
Pentateuch, 235-36
Pentecost, 304
  Dates (1980-2004), 300
Pentecost (Jewish Festival), 350
Pentecostal Churches, 337
Pentecostarian, 293
People of God, 225-27
Pepin the Short, 410
  Donation (745), 157
Perche, Napoleon J., 564
Peregrine, St., 310
Perfect Contrition, 364
Perfectae Caritatis, 168
  See also Religious Life
Perfection, Christian Life, 251
Perfectionist Churches, 337
Periodicals, Catholic, 671-82
Perjury, 383
Pernicone, Joseph M., Bp., 545
Perosi, Lorenzo, 410
Perpetua and Felicity, Sts., 310
Perry, Harold R., S.V.D., Bp., 545
Persecution, 383

Persia, see Iran
Persico, Ignatius, O.F.M. Cap., 564
Peru, 441
Perugino, Il, 410
Peschges, John J., 564
Petau (Petavius), Denys, 410
Peter, St. (Apostle), 246
 Epistles, 241
Peter and Paul, Sts., 133, 304
Peter Canisius, St., 249
Peter Chanel, St., 310
Peter Chrysologus, St., 249
Peter Claver, St., 416
Peter Claver, St., Missionary Sisters, 596
Peter Damian, St., 249
Peter Gonzalez, St., 310
Peter Guilday Prize, 700
Peter of Alcantara, St., 310
Peter of Ghent, 417
Peter's Pence, 384
Peterson, John B., 564
Petition, 384
Petrarch, 410
Petrine Privilege, 285
Pews, 263
Phantasiasm, 164
Pharisees, 384
Phelan, Richard, 564
Phelonian, 327
Phi Kappa Theta Fraternity, 661
Philangeli, 668
Philemon, 241
Philip, St. (Apostle), 246
Philip Neri, St., 310
Philip Neri, St., Congregation of Oratory of, 576
 Missionary Teachers, Sisters, 589
Philip of Jesus, St., 310
Philippe, Paul, O.P., Card., 209
Philippians, 241
Philippine Islands, 127, 131, 441
Philosophical Association, American Catholic, 662
Phoebe (Deaconess), 365
Phoenix Park, Dublin, Ireland, Papal Mass, 65
Photius (857), 158
Piarists, 576
Piazzi, Giuseppe, 410
Picachy, Lawrence Trevor, Card., 209
Picard, Jean, 410
Piche, Paul, O.M.I., 467
Picpus Fathers (Sacred Hearts Fathers), 577
Pierce v. Society of Sisters, 492
Pignedoli, Sergio, Card., 209
Pilarczyk, Daniel E., Bp., 545
Pilla, Anthony M., Bp., 546
Pilgrimage, 147
Pilgrimages, Papal, see John Paul II
Pinger, Henry A., O.F.M., Bp., 546
Pinten, Joseph G., 564
Pinturicchio, Bernardino, 410
Pio, Padre, 410
Pious Fund, 384
Pious Schools, Order of, 576
Pious Schools, Sisters of, 596
Pious Union
 of Holy Spirit, 668
 of Prayer, 668
Pire, Dominique Georges, 410
Pironio, Eduardo, Card., 209
Pisa, Council (1409), 160
Pisano, Andrea, 410
 Giovanni, 410
 Nicolo, 410
 Nino, 410
Pitaval, John B., 564
Pitra, Jean, 410
Pittsburgh Catholic, 110
Pius IV, Creed, 250
Pius V, St., 310
Pius VII (1809), 162
Pius IX (1864, 1870), 163
 Order of, 694
 Syllabus, 163, 393
Pius X, St. (1903), 163
 Biography, 175
 Canonizations, 180
 Encyclicals, 183

Pius X (St.)
 Liturgical Movement, 264
 Syllabus, 393
Pius X, St., Brothers of, 579
 Secular Institute of, 603
Pius XI (1922), 164
 Biography, 176-77
 Canonizations, 180
 Encyclicals, 183-84
Pius XII, Pope
 Biography, 177-78
 Canonizations, 181
 Encyclicals, 184
 Liturgical Movement and, 264
 Second Vatican Council, 118
Pius XII Marian Award, 700
Pizarro, Francisco, 411
Plagens, Joseph C., 564
Planned Parenthood, 99, 130, 149
Pledge of Allegiance, Anti-Abortion Version, 99
Plenary Councils, 364
Plenary Councils, Baltimore, 474
Pliny, Rescript to (112), 155
Plourde, Joseph A., Abp., 120, 467
Plumier, Charles, 411
Plunkett, Oliver, St., 62, 309
Pneumatomachists, 165
Pocock, Philip, Abp., 467
Pohier, Jacques, Rev., see *Quand Je Dis Dieu*
Poland, 106, 107, 111, 113, 115, 116, 135, 146, 150, 441-42
 John Paul II Visit, 56-61
Pole, Reginald, 411
Poletti, Ugo, Card., 209
Political Prisoners, see Human Rights
Polo, Marco, 411
Polycarp, St., 310
Polyglot Press, Vatican, 223
Polynesia, French, 442
Polytheism, 384
Poma, Antonio, Card., 209
Pompei and Loreto, Commission for Sanctuaries, 196
Ponce de Leon, 411
Pontian, St., 310
Pontiff, see Pope
Pontifical
 Academy of Sciences, 629-30
 Assn. of the Holy Childhood, 660
 Biblical Commission, 244
 College Josephinum, 629
 Commissions, 196-97
 Faculties of Ecclesiastical Studies, 628-29
 Household, Prefecture, 197
 Institute for Foreign Missions, 576
 Institutes of Higher Studies, 629
 Letters, see Encyclicals
 Mission for Palestine, 668
 Missionary Union, 668
 Orders of Knighthood, 694
 Universities, 627-28
 See also Papal
Poor, Little Sisters of, 596
Poor, Responsibility to, 70-1
Poor Box, 384
Poor Clare Missionary Sisters, 596
Poor Clare Nuns, 588
Poor Clares, 596
Poor Clares of Perpetual Adoration, 589
Poor Handmaids of Jesus Christ, 596
Pope, 186
 Authority, Infallibility, Primacy, 227-29
 Election, 382-83
 See also John Paul II
Pope, Alexander, 411
Pope Joan, 384
Popes (List), 169-73
Popes, Encyclicals (List), 182-85
Popes, False (Antipopes), 173-74
Popes, Twentieth Century, 174-80
"Popish Plot" (1638), 161
Population, Catholic
 Blacks, U.S., 90-1
 Canada, 469-70, 471
 Countries of World, 419-53
 Spanish Speaking, U.S., 88-9
 United States, 130, 508-11
 World Totals, 455

Index

Population, World, 136
Population Commission, UN, 116
Populorum Progressio (Development of Peoples), 179
Populorum Progressio Fund, 121
Porres, Martin de, St., 417
Porter, 277
Portier, Michael, 564
Portiuncula, 384
Portugal, 135, 443
Portuguese Guinea, see Guinea-Bissau
Portuguese Timor, see Timor, Eastern
Possession, Diabolical, 384
Postulant, 384
Poterion, 327
Pouget, Jean, 411
Poulenc, Francis, 411
Poussin, Nicholas, 411
Poverello Medal, 701
Poverty, 384
Povish, Kenneth J., Bp., 546
Power, Cornelius M., Bp., 546
Power, William E., Bp., 467
Power of the Keys, 377
  See also Infallibility; Primacy
Powers (Angels), 355
Pragmatic Sanction (1438), 160
Pragmatism, 384
Prague, Infant Jesus of, 375
Praises, Divine, 367
Prayer, 384
  John Paul II on, 137
Prayer, Houses of, 655
Prayer Amendment, U.S. Senate Vote, 124
Prayer Meetings, see Charismatic Renewal, Catholic
Prayer of the Faithful, 260
Prayer Intentions, Monthly, see Calendar, 1980
Prayer over the Gifts, 260
Precept, Paschal, 383
Precepts, 385
Precepts of the Church, 251
Precious Blood, Feast, see Calendar, Revised
Precious Blood (Religious)
  Daughters of Charity of the Most, 596
  Missionary Sisters, 596
  Sisters Adorers, 596
  Sisters of Most, 596
  Society of, 576
Predestination, see Calvin, John
Preface, 260
Prefect Apostolic, 188
Prefectures Apostolic, World, 454
Prejudice, Pastoral Letter, Richmond, Va., 149
Prelates, 188
Premontre, Order of Canons Regular (Premonstratensians), 576
Prendergast, Edmond, 564
Presbyterian Churches, U.S., 336
Presbyterians, 333
Presbyterians, Reformed, Dialogue, 346
Presbyterium Ordinis, 168
Presence of God, 385
Presentation, 113, 304
  Brothers of Mary, 579
  of Mary, Sisters, 596
  of the BVM, Sisters, 596
  Sisters of St. Mary, 596
Press, Catholic, U.S., 671-86
  Statistics, 671
Press, Freedom, 101
Press, Vatican, 223
Press Association, Catholic, 667
  Awards, 670
Press Office, Vatican, 138, 223
Presumption, 385
Preternatural Gifts, 385
Price, Thomas F., 411
Prie-Dieu, 385
Priest, 276-77
Priesthood, 72-3, 189, 525
Priesthood of the Laity, 385
Priests
  Addresses, Letter of John Paul II, 67, 79-81, 97, 117, 122
  Number Leaving Ministry, 123
  Statistics, World, 454
Priests, U.S. (Statistics), 508-11

Priests, U.S.
  in Foreign Missions, 605-06, 607
  in Home Missions, 607-08
Priests, U.S., Retired, 115
Priests' Councils, National Federation, 628
Priests' Eucharistic League, 668
Primacy of Pope, 227-29
Primary Option, 385
Primate, 187
Primatesta, Raul Francisco, Card., 210
Primeau, Ernest, Bp., 546
Prior, 385
Priscillianism, 165
Privilege, 385
Privilege of Faith (Petrine Privilege), 285
Pro, Miguel, 411
Probabilism, 385
Pro-Cathedral, 385
Pro Comperte Sane, see Roman Curia
Pro Ecclesia et Pontifice Medal, 695
Pro Ecclesia Foundation, 668
Pro-Life Movements, 269
Pro Maria Committee, 668
Prohaszka, Ottokar, 411
Promoter of the Faith, 385
Pro-Nuncio, 215
Pro-Oriente Foundation, 118
Propagation of the Faith, Cong. of, 103, 194
  Society of, 669
Proper of the Mass, 261
Prophecies of St. Malachy, 385
Prophecy, 385-86
Prophets, 238-39
Proposition 13 and Catholic Agencies, 124
Prost, Jude, O.F.M., Bp., 546
Protestant
  Canon of the Bible, 233
  Churches in the U.S., Major, 333-37
  Episcopal Church, U.S., see Episcopal Church, U.S.
  See also Ecumenism
Protestants and Intercommunion, 275
Protocanonical Books, 233
Proulx, Adolph E., Bp., 467
Proulx, Amedee W., Bp., 546
Provancher, Leon, 411
Proverbs, 237
Providence (Sisters)
  Daughters of Divine, 597
  Missionary Catechists, 597
  Oblate Sisters of, 597
  Sisters of, 597
  Sisters of Divine, 597
Providence, Sons of Divine, 576
Providence Association of Ukrainian Catholics, 668
Province, 386
Provinces, Canada, 462
  United States, 497-98
Provincial Councils, 364
Providentissimus Deus, 243
Prudence, 386
Psalms, 237
Pseudoepigrapha, 235
Public Affairs of Church, Council for, 192
Public Schools, 124, 129, 149
  Federal Aid, 611
  Released Time, 610
Publications, Vatican, 222-23
Puccini, Giacomo, 411
Puebla Conference, Latin American Bishops, 52-5, 85-7, 113, 116, 141
Puerto Rico, 140, 146, 444, 518
  Dates in Catholic History, 490
Puerto Rican Catholics in U.S., see Spanish-Speaking
Pugin, Augustus, 411
Pulaski, Casimir, 411
Pulpit, 263
Punishment Due for Sin, 386
Purcell, John B., 564
Purgatory, 386
Purification (Presentation of the Lord), 304
Purificator, 263
Purim, 351
Puritans, 333
Pursley, Leo A., Bp., 546

Puvis de Chavannes, Pierre, 411
Pyx, 263

Q

Qatar, 444
Quadragesimo Anno, see Social Doctrine
Quakers, 333
Quam Singulari, see Communion, First, and First Confession
Quand Je Dis Dieu, Doctrinal Errors, 81, 123
Quanta Cura (1864), 163
Quarter, William, 564
Quartodecimans (Easter Controversy), 367
Quebec Separatism, 125
Queenship of Mary, 304
Quigley, James E., 564
Quinlan, John, 564
Quinlan, Thomas, 411
Quinn, Francis A., Bp., 546
Quinn, John R., Abp., 129, 523, 546
Quinn, William C., C.M., 564
Quinones, Francis, 411
Quintero, Jose Humberto, Card., 210
Quiroga, Vasco de, 417
Qumran Scrolls (Dead Sea Scrolls), 235

R

Racine, Jean, 411
Racism, 386
 Pastoral Letter (Boston, Richmond), 138, 149
Rademacher, Joseph, 564
Radio, Catholic, U.S., 686-87
 Diocesan Communications Directors, 689-93
 Film and Broadcasting Office, 693
Radio, Vatican, 221-22
Radio and TV, Use of, by Evangelicals, 124
Ralph Metcalfe Award, 150
Rameau, Jean Philippe, 411
Randall, Claire, Dr., 153
Randall, James Ryder, 411
Randolph, A. Philip, 704
Raphael, Archangel, 303, 356
Raphael Santi, 411
Rappe, Louis A., 564
Rash Judgment, 386
Raskob Foundation, 668
Rationalism, 386
Ratzinger, Joseph, Card., 210
Rausch, James S., Bp., 546
Ravalli, Antonio, 417
Raya, Joseph M., Abp., 546
Raymbaut, Charles, 417
Raymond Nonnatus, St., 310
Raymond of Penyafort, St., 310
Razafimahatratra, Victor, S.J., Card., 210
Reader (Lector), 277, 378
Readings, Mass, 259
Readings, Office of (Liturgy of Hours), 257
Ready, Michael J., 564
Reason, Age of, 354
Rebaptism Controversy, 165
Recollection, 386
Recollects, Augustinian, 571
Reconciliation, see Penance, Revised Rite
Red Mass, 261
Redditio of Creed, 250
Redeemer, Divine, Sisters of the, 597
Redeemer, Holy (religious)
 Congregation of the Most, 576
 Oblates of the Most, 597
 Order of the Most, 597
 Sisters of the, 597
Redemptor Hominis, 75-81, 118
Redemptorists, 570
Reding, Paul F., Bp., 146, 467
Reed, George E., 114, 139
Reed, Victor J., 564
Reeve, Arthur B., 411
Reformation (1517), 160
 Men, Doctrines, Churches, 332-33
Refuge, Sisters of Our Lady of Charity, 597
Refugees, 102, 109, 120, 121, 131, 146, 151, 604
 Conferences on (Tokyo, Geneva), 136, 141
Regan, Joseph, M.M., Bp., 546
Regimini Ecclesiae Universae (Roman Curia), 190-91
Regina Caeli (Angelus), 355

Regina Medal, 701
Regis College Lay Apostolate, 660
Regnault, Henry, 411
Regular Clergy, 362
Reh, Francis, Bp., 546
Rehring, George J., 564
Reicher, Louis J., Bp., 547
Reiffenstuel, Anaclete, 411
Reilly, Daniel P., Bp., 547
Reilly, Edmond J., 564
Reilly, Thomas R., C.SS.R., Bp., 547
Reinhold, Hans, 411
Reiss, John C., Bp., 547
Relativism, 386
Released Time, 610
 See also Church-State Decisions
Relics, 386
Relief Services, Catholic, 131, 144, 148, 153, 656-57
Religion, 386
Religion and Peace, World Conference, 149
Religions, Non-Revealed, 352
Religious, 568-70
 Congregation for, 194
 Latin America, 120
 Latin American Confederation, 601
 Renewal Guides, John Paul, 97
 Superiors, Organization, International, 601
 Vatican II on, 569-70
 Vicars of, 601
 Women, John Paul II Addresses, 74, 152
Religious, Men, 568-69
 Brothers, National Assembly, 579
 Brothers in World, 454
 Conference of Major Superiors, U.S., 579
 in U.S. (List), 571-80
 in U.S. (Statistics), 508-11
 Priests in the World, 454
 World Membership, 580-81
Religious, Women, U.S., 581-600
 Organizations, 601-02
 Papal Address, 97
 Statistics, 508-11
 Teachers, Catholic Schools, 617
Religious, Women, World, 454
Religious Education, 617
 See also National Catechetical Directory
Religious Freedom, 102, 370
Religious Life, Decree, 168, 569-70
Religious Life, Fundamentals Unchanged, 114
Religious Life, Institute on, 666
Religious News Service, 682-83
Religious Superiors, Non-Catholic, Papal Meeting, 128
Reliquary, 386
Renard, Alexandre, Card., 210
Rene Goupil, St., 416
Reni, Guido, 411
Reparation, 386
 of Congregation of Mary, Sisters of, 597
 Society of the Immaculate Heart of Mary, 668
Repplier, Agnes, 411
Representatives, Vatican, 215-18, 223
Requiem Mass, 261
Rerum Novarum, see Social Doctrine
Rerum Novarum Award, 701
Rescript, 387
Rescript to Pliny (112), 155
Rese, Frederic, 564
Reserved Case, 387
Respect Life Groups, 269
Restitution, 387
Resurrection, see Easter
Resurrection, Priests of Congr., 577
Resurrection, Sisters of, 597
Retarded, Facilities, 643-46
Retired, Facilities for, 632-40
Retreat Houses, U.S., 649-55
Retreats International, 649
Reunion, 444
Revelation, (Dogmatic Constitution), 229-32
 See also Bible
Revelation, Book of, 241
Reverman, Theodore, 564
Revised Standard Version (Bible), 234
Revolution, American, see Catholic History of U.S.
Reymont, Wladislaw, 411
Reynolds, Ignatius A., 564

Rheims, Synod (1148), 159
Rhode, Paul P., 564
Rhode Island, 488, 508, 512, 514, 613, 626, 639, 654, 692
Rhodes, 444
Rhodesia (Zimbabwe), 106, 110, 126, 135, 138, 140, 146, 444
Rhythm, 283
Ribeiro, Antonio, Card., 210
Ribera, Jose, 411
Ricci, Matteo, 411
　See also China
Ricciolo, Giovanni, 411
Rice, Joseph J., 564
Rice, William A., 564
Richard, Gabriel, 417
Richard Reid Memorial Award, 701
Richelieu, Armand, 411
Richter, Henry J., 564
Right to Life Convention, National, 134
Right to Life Crusade, 114
Right to Life Vote and Election Results, 99
　See also Abortion Controversy, Developments; Life, Respect for
Riley, Thomas J., Bp., 564
Ring, 387
　Fisherman's, 370
Rio de Janeiro, University, 627
Rio Grande do Sul, University, 627
Riordan, Patrick W., 564
Rita, St., Sisters of, 597
Rita of Cascia, St., 310
Rites, 258
Rites, Eastern, 322-24
Ritter, Bruce, O.F.M. Conv., 139
Ritter, Joseph, 411
Ritual, 387
Roach, John R., Abp., 547
Robbia, Luca della, 411
Robert Bellarmine, St., 249
Robert Southwell, St., 310
Robichaud, Norbert, Abp., 467
Robidoux, Omer, O.M.I., Bp., 467
Robinson, Pascal, O.F.M., 564
Robinson, William Callyhan, 411
Roborecki, Andrew, 467
Roch, St., 310
Roch Gonzalez, Bl., 416
Rochambeau, Jean, 411
Rochet, 262
Rockne, Knute, 411
Rodimer, Frank J., Bp., 547
Rodriguez, Alonso, Bl., 417
Rodriguez, Miguel, C.SS.R., Bp., 547
Rodzinski, Artur, 411
Rogation Days, 292
Rogito, 387
Rohlman, Henry P., 565
Roman, Agustin, Bp., 547
Roman Catholic Church, see Church
Roman Curia, see Curia, Roman
Roman Martyrology, 379
Roman Missal (Sacramentary), 266
Roman Pontiffs, see Popes
Roman Question, 221
Roman Rite, 258
Romani Pontifici Eligendo, see Interregnum; Papal Election
Romanian Byzantine Rite, 324
Romans, 240-41
Rome, Center of Unity, 137
Romuald, St., 310
Rooker, Frederick Z., 565
Ropert, Gulstan R., SS.CC., 565
Rosales, Julio, Card., 210
Rosary, 387
　Feast, 303
　Franciscan Crown, 371
Rosary, Family, 665
Rosary Altar Society, 668
Rosary League, 668
Rosary, Brothers of the Holy, 579
　Cong. of Our Lady of the Holy, 597
　Missionary Sisters of Our Lady of the Holy, 597
Rosati, Joseph, 417
Rosazza, Peter A., Bp., 547
Rose of Lima, St., 310

Rosecrans, Sylvester, 565
Rosecrans, William Starke, 411
Rosminians (Institute of Charity), 577
Rosh Hashana, 351
Rossi, Agnelo, Card., 210
Rossi, Opilio, Card., 210
Rossini, Gioacchino, 412
Rota, Sacred Roman, 195
Roualt, Georges, 412
Routhier, Henri, O.M.I., Abp., 467
Rouxel, Gustave A., 565
Roy, Maurice, Card., 211
Roy, Raymond, Bp., 467
Rubens, Peter, 412
Rubin, Wladyslaw, Card., 211
Rubrics, Mass, 265
Rubruck, William, 412
Rudin, John J., M.M., Bp., 547
Rugambwa, Laurean, Card., 211
Rule of Faith, 370
Rumania, 444
Rummel, Joseph, 565
Runcie, Robert, Bp., 150
Ruocco, Joseph J., Bp., 547
Rural Development, 124, 138, 141
Rural Life Conference, 656
Rural Life Statement, 139
Rural Parish Workers of Christ the King, 602
Rusnak, Michael, C,SS.R., Bp., 467
Russell, John J., Bp., 547
Russell, William T., 565
Russia, see Union of Soviet Socialist Republics
Russian Byzantine Rite, 324
Ruth, 236
Ruth, George Herman, 412
Ruthenian Byzantine Rite, 324
Ruysbroeck, John, Bl., 412
Rwanda, 444-45
Ryan, Abram J., 412
Ryan, Edward F., 565
Ryan, Gerald, Bp., 547
Ryan, James, 565
Ryan, James C., O.F.M., Bp., 547
Ryan, James H., 565
Ryan, Joseph F., Bp., 467
Ryan, Joseph T., Abp., 113, 547
Ryan, Patrick J., 565
Ryan, Stephen, C.M., 565
Ryan, Vincent J., 565
Ryukyu Islands, 445

S

Sabatini, Lawrence, C.S., Bp., 467
Sabbath, 287
Sabbath (Jewish), 350
Sabellianism, 164
Sacerdotal Fraternity, Congregation of, 577
Sacrament, Blessed, see Blessed Sacrament
Sacrament, Sisters of the Most Holy, 598
Sacramental Forum, see Forum
Sacramental Grace, 372
Sacramentals, 656-57
Sacramentary, 266, 387
Sacramentine Nuns, 598
Sacraments, 270-77
　Congregation, 193
　Eastern Churches, 328
Sacraments, Safeguarding, 98
Sacrarium, 387
Sacred Heart (June 13, 1980), 296, 304
　Enthronement, 387
　Promises, 387
Sacred Heart (Religious)
　Brothers, 579
　Daughters of Our Lady, 598
　Mission Helpers, 595
　Missionaries of, 577
　Missionary Sisters, 598
　Religious of the Apostolate of, 598
　Society Devoted to, 598
　Society of, 598
Sacred Heart Catholic University (Italy), 628
Sacred Heart League, 668
Sacred Heart of Jesus (Religious)
　and of Poor, Servants, 598
　Apostles of, 598

Sacred Heart of Jesus (Religious)
  Congregation of, 577
  for Reparation, Cong. of Handmaids, 598
  Franciscan Missionary Brothers, 579
  Handmaids, 598
  Missionary Sisters of Most, 598
  Oblate Sisters, 598
  Servants of Most, 598
  Sisters of, 598
  Sons (Verona Fathers), 577
Sacred Heart of Mary, Religious, 598
Sacred Heart Program, 687
Sacred Hearts, Fathers of, 577
Sacred Hearts, Religious of Holy Union of, 598
Sacred Hearts and of Perpetual Adoration, Sisters, 598
Sacred Hearts of Jesus and Mary, Missionaries of, 577
  Sisters of, 598
Sacred Scripture, see Bible
Sacrifice of Mass, see Mass
Sacrilege, 387
Sacristy, 388
Sacrosanctum Concilium, 168
  See also Liturgy Constitution
Sacrum Diaconatus Ordinem, see Deacon, Permanent
Sadducees, 388
Sahagun, Bernardino de, 417
Saint
  Anne de Beaupre, Shrine, 471
  Ann's Church, Vatican City, 221
  Ansgar's Scandinavian Catholic League, 668
  Anthony's Guild, 668
  Apollonia Guild, 668
  Christopher (Kitts)-Nevis, 445
  De La Salle Medal, 701
  Francis de Sales Award, 701
  Francis Xavier Medal, 701
  Ignatius Mission, Montana, 153
  Joan's Alliance, 460
  Joseph's Oratory Shrine, 471
  Joseph's University of Beirut, 628
  Jude League, 668
  Lucia, 445
  Margaret of Scotland Guild, 668
  Martin de Porres Guild, 669
  Patrick's Cathedral, Anniversary, 130
  Patrick's College, Maynooth (Ireland), 628
  Paul's University, Ottawa, 627
  Pierre and Miquelon, 445
  Stephen's Indian Mission, 145
  Thomas Aquinas Foundation, 669
  Thomas of Villanueva Univ. (Cuba), 627
  Vincent, 445
  Vincent de Paul Medal, 702
  Vincent de Paul Society, 631
    See also Proper Name of Individual Saints
Saints
  Biographies, 305-11
  Canonization, 358-59
  Canonized since Leo XIII, 180-82
  Communion of, 363
  Congregation for Causes of, 193
  Cult, 388
  Emblems, 314-15
  Patrons, 311-14
  Revised Calendar, 291
  Veneration, 388
    See also Calendar; Feasts
Salamanca, Pontifical Univ. (Spain), 628
Salatka, Charles, Bp., 547
Salazar Lopez, Jose, Card., 211
Salesian Sisters, 594
Salesians of St. John Bosco, 577
Salesianum, Pontifical University, 629
Salpointe, John B., 565
SALT II, 104, 114, 132, 148-49
Salvation, 388
Salvation History, 388
Salvation outside the Church, 388
Salvatorian Fathers, Basilian, 571
Salvatorians, 577
Samoa, 445
Samoa, American, 445
Samore, Antonio, Card., 123, 211
Samuel, 236
San Gallo, Giuliano, 412
San Marino, 445

San Martin, Jose, 412
Sanchez, Robert, Abp., 547-48
Sanctifying Grace, 372
Sanctuary, 263
Sanctuary Lamp, 264
Sands, John D., Rev., 704
Sanschagrin, Albert, O.M.I., 467
Santo Thomas University (Philippine Islands), 628
Santorini, Giovanni, 412
Sao Paulo University (Brazil), 627
Sao Tome and Principe, 445
Sapientia Christiana, 128
Sapiential (Wisdom) Books, 237
Sarbiewski, Mathias, 412
Sarto, Andrea del, 412
Satan, see Devil
Satanism, 388
Satowaki, Joseph Asajiro, Card., 211
Saudi Arabia, 445
Saul, see Historical Books of the Bible
Savage, (Charles) Courtenay, 412
Savaryn, Nile Nicholas, O.S.B.M., Bp., 467
Savior, see Christ
Savior, Company of, 598
  Order of the Most Holy (Bridgettine Sisters), 582
  Sisters of Divine, 598
  Society of Divine, 577
Scandal, 388
Scanderbeg (George Castriota), 412
Scanlan, John J., Bp., 548
Scanlan, Lawrence, 565
Scannel, Richard, 565
Scapular, 388
  Medal, 389
  Promise, 389
Scarletti, Alessandro, 412
Scarpone, Gerald, O.F.M., Bp., 548
Schad, James L., Bp., 548
Scheiner, Christoph, 412
Schenk, Francis, 565
Scher, Philip, 565
Scherer, Alfred Vicente, Card., 211
Scheut Fathers, see Immaculate Heart Missioners
Schexnayder, Maurice, Bp., 548
Schierhoff, Andrew B., Bp., 548
Schinner, Augustine, 565
Schism, Schismatic, 389
Schism, Western, 174
Schladweiler, Alphonse, Bp., 548
Schlaefer, Salvator, O.F.M. Cap., Bp., 548
Schlarman, Joseph H., 565
Schlarman, Stanley G., Bp., 548
Schlegel, Friedrich von, 412
Schlotterback, Edward, O.S.F.S., Bp., 548
Schmid, Christoph von, 412
Schmidt, Firmin M., O.F.M. Cap., Bp., 548
Schmidt, Mathias, O.S. B., Bp., 548
Schmidt, Wilhelm, 412
Schmitt, Adolph C., M.M., Bp., 565
Schmitt, Mark, Bp., 548
Schmondiuk, Joseph, Abp., 565, 704
Schoenherr, Walter J., Bp., 548
Schoenstatt Sisters of Mary, 602
Scholastica, St., 310
Scholasticism, 389
Schools, Catholic (U.S.), 115
  Aid, 610, 611
  Colleges and Universities, 619-24
  for Handicapped, 640-46
  Legal Status, 610
    See also Church-State Decisions of Supreme Court
  NLRB Jurisdiction, 99, 120, 618
  Report, 617
  Right to Collective Bargaining, 150
  Shared Time, 610
  Statistics, 613-16, 617
  Tax Credit Legislation, 114
  Tax Deduction Law, New Jersey, 129
  Teacher Unions, 618
    See also Religious Education; Seminaries
Schools, Desegregation, 129, 149
  Brown Case Anniversary, 129
Schools, Private, 617
  State Regulation, 128, 153
  Unemployment Tax Deduction, 120
Schools, Public, see Public Schools

Index

Schott, Lawrence, 565
Schrembs, Joseph, 565
Schroeffer, Joseph, Card., 211
Schubert, Franz, 412
Schuck, James A., O.F.M., Bp., 548
Schuler, Anthony, S.J., 565
Schulte, Paul C., Abp., 548
Schuman, Robert, 412
Schuster, Eldon, Bp., 548
Schuyler, Philippa, 412
Schwann, Theodor, 412
Schwarz, Berthold, 412
Schwebach, James, 565
Schweiker, Richard, Sen., 108
Schwertner, August J., 565
Science, Faith and, 118
Science and Technology, 143
Sciences, Pontifical Academy, 629-30
Scotland, 116, 126, 445-46
Scotus, John Duns, 401
Scouts, Catholic, 660
Scribes, 389
Scripture, see Bible
Scruple, 389
Scully, William, 565
Sea, Apostleship of, 567
Seal of Confession, 389
Searle, George Mary, 412
Seasons, Church, 290-91
Sebastian, Jerome D., 565
Sebastian, St., 310
Sebastian Aparicio, Bl., 415
Secchi, Angelo, 412
Second Vatican Council, see Council, Second Vatican
Secretariat of State, 192
Secretariats (Roman Curia), 195-96
Secular (Diocesan) Clergy, 362
   Statistics, 454, 508-11
Secular Institutes, 601-03
   Congregation, 194
Secularism, 389
Sede Vacante, see Interregnum
See, 389
Seelos, Francis X., 417
Seghers, Charles J., 417
Segregation and IRS Guidelines, 114
Segura y Saenz, Pedro, 412
Seidenbusch, Rupert, O.S.B., 565
Seidl, Johann Gabriel, 412
Semi-Arians, 165
Seminarians
   Countries of the World, 419-53
   Hungarian, 122
   United States, 627
   World (Summary), 454
Seminaries, Priorities, 117
Seminaries, U.S., 624-26
Seminary, 389
Semi-Pelagianism, 165
Semmelweis, Ignaz, 412
Semmes, Raphael, 412
Senegal, 446
Senses of the Bible, 242-43
Sensi, Giuseppe Maria, Card., 211-12
Senyshyn, Ambrose, O.S.B.M., 565
Separation, Marriage, 285
Seper, Franjo, Card., 212
Septuagint Bible, 234
Seraphim (Angels), 355
Serbs (Byzantine Rite), 324
Sermon on the Mount, 389
Serra, Junipero, 417
Serra Award of the Americas, 702
Serra International, 139, 669
Servants of Mary, Order of Friar (Servites), 577
Servants of Mary, Sisters, 594
Servile Work, 389
Servite Sisters, 594
Servites, 577
Seton, Elizabeth Bayley, St., 307
Seton, Robert J., 565
Seven Holy Founders, 310
Seven Joys of Blessed Virgin Mary, see Franciscan Crown
Seven Last Words of Christ, 389-90
Seventh Day Adventists, 134, 354
Sex Education, 99, 130

Sexist Language, Liturgical Texts, 101
Sexuality, Mistaken Concepts, 83-4
Seychelles Islands, 446
Shahan, Thomas J., 565
Shanahan, Jeremiah, 565
Shanahan, John, 565
Shanley, John, 565
Shanley, Patrick H., O.C.D., 565
Sharing the Light of Faith, see Catechetical Directory
Shaughnessy, Gerald, S.M., 565
Shaw, John W., 565
Shea, Ambrose, 412
Shea, Francis R., Bp., 548
Shea, John D., 412
Sheehan, Daniel E., Abp., 100, 548
Sheehan, Edward T., C.M., 565
Sheehan, Peter, Rev., 153
Sheen, Fulton J., Abp., 110, 549
Shehan, Lawrence J., Card., 212
Sheil, Bernard J., 565
Sheldon, Gilbert I., Bp., 549
Sherbrooke, University of, 627
Sheridan, Philip H., 412
Sherlock, John M., Bp., 467
Shevchenko, Taras, 412
Shields, James, 412
Shinto, 352
Shipman, Andrew Jackson, 413
Shrine, Crowned, 390
Shrine, Immaculate Conception, 185
Shrines, Canada, 471
Shroud of Turin, 390
Shubsda, Thaddeus A., Bp., 549
Siberia, 446
Sick, Anointing of, see Anointing of Sick
Sick, Eucharistic Fast, 370
Sick, Oil of, 381
Sick Calls, 390
Sidarouss, Stephanos I, C.M., Patriarch, Card., 212
Sienkiewicz, Henryk, 412
Sierra Leone, 446
Sign of Contradiction, John Paul II Conferences, 129
Sign of Cross, 390
Signatura, Apostolic, 195
Signs of the Times, 390
Signum Fidei Medal, 702
Sikkim, 446
Silva Henriquez Raul, S.D.B., Card., 212
Simon, Richard (Bible), 243
Simon, St. (Apostle), 246
Simon, William E. (Catholics in Presidents' Cabinets), 490
Simony, 390
Sin, 390
   Accessory to, 353
   Original, 382
   Punishment, 386
Sin, Jamie L., Card., 212
Singapore, 446
Sins
   against Holy Spirit, 390
   Capital, 359
   Forgiveness, 370
   Occasions, 390
   That Cry to Heaven for Vengeance, 391
Sirach, 238
Siri, Giuseppe, Card., 212
Sister, 391
Sisterhood, 391
Sisters, United States, 581-600
   See also Religious, Women
Situation Ethics, 391
Sitwell, Edith, 413
Sixtus II, St., 310
Skinner, Henrietta, 413
Skinner, Patrick J., C.J.M., 468
Skylstad, William, Bp., 549
Slander, 391
Slavic Pope, First, Significance, 59
Slavonic Liturgy, 143
Slipyi or Slipyji, Josyf, Card., 212
Sloth, 391
Slovak Byzantine Catholics, 669
Slovak Catholic Federation of America, 669
Slovak Catholic Sokol, 669
Slovakia, Persecution, 425-26
Smith, Alfred E., 413

Smith, Alphonse, 566
Smith, Eustace J., O.F.M., 566
Smith, Ignatius, 413
Smith, Leo R., 566
Smith, Matthew, 413
Smith, Philip M., O.M.I., 549
Smith, William J., Bp., 468
Smyth, Clement, O.C.S.O., 566
Snyder, John J., Bp., 549
Sobieski, John, 413
Social Communications, Commission, 196
    See also Communications
Social Doctrine of Church, 54, 251-55
Social Justice, Canadian Bishops, 135
Social Security Benefits, 109
Social Service, Sisters of, 598
Social Services, Catholic, U.S., 631-44
Socially Maladjusted, Facilities for, 641-43
Societies, Catholic, in U.S., 662-69
Societies, Religious, see Religious, Men, Women, in U.S.
Society for Propagation of the Faith, 669
Society of St. Peter for Native Clergy, 669
Society of St. Vincent de Paul, 631
Sodality of Our Lady, see Christian Life Communities
SODEPAX (Society for Development and Peace), 116, 340
Soenneker, Henry J., Bp., 549
Solanus, Francis, St., 417
Solemnity of Mary, 304
Sollicitudo Omnium Ecclesiarum (Representatives of Holy
    See), 215
Solomon, see Historical Books of Bible
Solomon Islands, 446
Somalia, 446
Somascan Fathers, 577
Song of Songs, 237
Sophia, Catholic University (Japan), 628
Sorcery, 391
Sorin, Edward F., 417
Sororities, 661
Sorrows (Dolors) of the Blessed Virgin Mary, 303
Soteriological Award, 702
Soteriology, 391
Souls, Holy, see All Souls
South Africa, Republic, 109, 130, 446-47
South America
    Cardinals, 215
    Eastern Rite Jurisdictions, 325
    Episcopal Conferences, 458
    Missionary Bishops, 507
    See also Puebla Assembly of Latin American Bishops
South Bronx, Papal Visit, 70
South Carolina, 488, 508, 512, 514, 614, 639, 654, 692
South Dakota, 104, 488, 510, 513, 515, 615, 626, 639, 654, 692
South West Africa, see Namibia
Southell, Robert, St., 310
Southwest Volunteer Apostolate, 660
Sowada, Alphonse, O.S.C., Bp., 549
Spain, 105, 108, 126, 136, 140, 145, 447
    Civil War (1936), 164
    Inquisition, 375
    Persecution (1931), 164
Spalding, John L., 413
Spalding, Martin, 413
Spallanzani, Lazzaro, 413
Spanish North Africa, 447
Spanish Sahara, see Western Sahara
Spanish Speaking in U.S., 87-9, 99, 119
Spearman, Frank Hamilton, 413
Species, Sacred, 391
Spellman, Francis J., 413
Speltz, George H., Bp., 124, 549
Spence, Francis J., Bp., 467
Spence, John S., 566
Spenkelink, John, Execution, 129
Spiritism, 391
Spiritual Life Institute of America, 669
Spiritual Works of Mercy, 391
Sponsor, see Confirmation
Spoon, 327
Sri Lanka, 447
Stafford, James F., Bp., 549
Stamps, Vatican, 222
Stang, William, 566
Stanislaus, St., 61, 127, 130, 310
Stanton, Martin W., 566

Stariha, John, 566
Starr, Eliza Allen, 413
State and Church, see Church-State
State Catholic Conferences, 526-27
State of Grace, see Grace
Stational Churches, Days, 391
Stations of the Cross, 391-92
Statistics, Catholic
    Canada, 469-70, 471
    Countries of World, 419-53
    Men Religious, 580-81
    U.S., see Statistics, Catholic, U.S.
    World (Summary), 454-55
Statistics, Catholic, U.S.
    Baptisms, 514-15
    Blacks, 90-1
    Converts, 514-15
    Missionary Personnel, 605-07
    Population, 508-11
    Priests, 508-11
    Seminarians, 627
    Schools, 613-16, 617
    Sisters, 508-11
    Summary, 516
Statistics Office, Central, 197
Statuary Hall, U.S., Catholics in, 491
Statues, 264
Statutes, 392
Steck, Leo J., 566
Steiner, Kenneth D., Bp., 549
Stella Maris Medal, 702
Stemper, Alfred M., M.S.C., Bp., 549
Stensen, Niles, 413
Stephen, St. (Deacon), 310
Stephen, St. (King), 310
Stepinac, Aloysius, 413
Stewardship Services, 669
Sticharion, 327
Stigmata, 392
Stigmata, Congregation of Sacred (Stigmatine Frs.), 577
Stipend, Mass, 392
Stock, John, 566
Stoddard, Charles Warren, 413
Stoddard, John Lawson, 413
Stole, 261
Stole Fee, 392
Stone, James K., 413
Storer, Horatio Robinson, 413
Stoss, Veit, 413
Stoup, 392
Stradivari, Antonio, 413
Straling, Philip F., Bp., 549
Strecker, Ignatius, Abp., 549
Stritch, Samuel, 413
Students, Aid, Wisconsin, 108-09
Students, Catholic
    United States, 613-16, 617
    University, College, 619-24
Sturzo, Luigi, 413
Suarez, Francisco, 413
Subdeacon, 277
Subordinationism, 165
Suburban Sees, see Cardinals
Sudan, 447-48
Suenens, Leo J., Card., 154, 212
Suffragan See, 392
Suicide, 392
Sullivan, Bernard, S.J., 566
Sullivan, James S., Bp., 549
Sullivan, John J., Bp., 549
Sullivan, Joseph V., Bp., 114, 124, 549
Sullivan, Walter F., Bp., 100, 149, 549
Sulpice, Society of Priests of St. (Sulpicians), 577
Sunday, 291
Sunday Mass on Saturday, 266
Supererogation, 392
Superiors, Women Religious, Papal Address, 152
Supernatural, 392
Supernatural Virtue, 394
Superstition, 392-93
Supremacy, Act of (1533), 161
Supreme Court, U.S.
    Abortion Rulings, 91-3
    Church-State Decisions, 491-97
    Decisions, 100, 120, 129, 134

Index

Supreme Court, U.S.
  School Decisions, 610, 612
Supreme Court, U.S., Catholics in, 491
Supreme Order of Christ, 694
Surinam, 448
Surplice, 262
Suspension, 393
Sutton, Peter A., O.M.I., Bp., 468
Swanstrom, Edward W., Bp., 550
Swaziland, 448
Swearing, 393
Sweden, 448
Swedenborgianism, 393
Sweeney, James J., 566
Swidler, Leonard, 139
Swint, John J., 566
Swiss Guards, 221
Switzerland, 448
Sword of Loyola Award, 702
Syllabus, 393
Sylvester, Order of St., 694
Sylvester I, St., 310
Sylvestrine Benedictines, 572
Symbols, see Emblems of Saints
Synaxis, 293
Synod, Anglican, 101
Synod, Diocesan, 393
Synod, Dutch, see Dutch Synod
Synod of Bishops, 103, 188-90
Synod of Whitby (664), 157
Synods, Patriarchal, 325
Synoptic Gospels, 240
Syria, 448-49
Syrian Rite Catholics, 323
Syro-Malabar Rite Catholics, 324
Szoka, Edmund C., Bp., 550

T

Tabb, John Banister, 413
Tabernacle, 264
Tabernacles, Festival, 350
Taggart, Marion Ames, 413
Tahiti, see Polynesia, French
Taiwan, 106, 109, 449
Takach, Basil, 566
Takamine, Jokichi, 413
Talbot, Matthew, 413
Tanenbaum, Marc, Rabbi, 139, 154
Taney, Roger Brooke, 413
Tanganyika, see Tanzania
Tanner, Paul F., Bp., 550
Tanzania, 449
Taofinu'u, Pio, S.M., Card., 212
Taoism, 352
Tarcisius, St., 310
Tarpey, Mary Columba, Mother, 704
Tasso, Torquato, 413
Tawil, Joseph, Abp., 550
Tax Credit Legislation, 114, 123
Tax Exemption, Church Property, 114, 495-96
Taylor, John, O.M.I., Bp., 566
Taylor, Myron C., 220
Tchidimbo, Raymond Marie, Abp., 142
Te Deum, 393
Te Deum International, 669
Teachers, Catholic Schools, Lay, 617
  NLRB Jurisdiction, 99, 120
  Right to Collective Bargaining, 120
  Unions, 618
Teachers, Catholic Schools, Religious, 617
Teaching Authority of the Church (Magisterium), 227-29
  and Interpretation of Bible, 230
Teaching Authority and Infallibility, Catholic-Lutheran
  Statement, 347
Teen Encounters, 649
Teilhard de Chardin, Pierre, 413
Tekakwitha, Kateri, 413
Tekakwitha Conference, 144, 609
Television, 687
  Advertising and Children, 99
  Awards, 693
  Diocesan Offices, Directors, 689-93
Television Network, Catholic, 687-88
Temperance, 98, 393
Templeton Foundation Prize (1979), 111

Temporal Punishment, 386
Temptation, 393
Ten Commandments, 250
Tennessee, 488, 509, 513, 514, 614, 639, 643, 646, 654, 692
  Bible Study in Schools, 144
  Unemployment Tax, Church Schools, 120
Teresa, Mother, 116, 120, 146
  Nobel Peace Prize, 154
Teresa (Theresa) of Avila, St., 249
Teresa of Jesus, Society of St., 599
Teresian Institute, 603
Tertullian (206), 155
Tessier, Maxime, Bp., 468
Test-Tube Baby, 93-4, 100
Testament, New and Old, see Bible
Texas, 488-89, 510-513, 515, 527, 615, 626, 637, 643, 646, 654, 692
  Mission Churches, 104
Textbook Loans, see Schools, Catholic, Aid
Thaddeus, Jude, St., 241, 245
Thailand, 141, 449
Thanksgiving, 393
Thayer, John, 413
Theatines, 577
Theatre, Catholic, 687
Theism, 393
Theodosian Code (438), 156
Theological Commission, 198
  Deaconess Statement, 365
  Pastoral Aspects of Marriage, 288
Theological Virtues, 393
Theology, 393
Theophany, see Epiphany
Theresa (Teresa) of Avila, St., 249
Therese Couderc, St., 310
Therese of Lisieux, St., 310
Theresians of America, 669
Thessalonians, 241
Thiandoum, Hyacinthe, Card., 212
Thill, Francis A., 566
Third General Assembly of Latin American Bishops, 85-7, 113, 116, 141
  Keynote Address, John Paul II, 52-5
Third Order Regular of St. Francis, 573
Third Orders (Secular Orders), 604
Thirty-Nine Articles (1563), 161
Thirty Years' War (1648), 161
Thomas, Charles, 413
Thomas, St. (Apostle), 246
  See also India
Thomas a Kempis, 414
Thomas Aquinas, St., 249
  Pontifical University, 629
Thomas Becket, St., 310
Thomas Christians, St., see Syro-Malabar Catholics
Thomas Jefferson Award, 139
Thomas More, St., 310
Thomas More Association Medal, 703
Thomas of Celano, 414
Thomas of Villanova, St., Congregation of Srs., 599
Thompson, Francis, 414
Three Mile Island Nuclear Accident, 119
Thrones, see Angels
Thurible, see Censer
Tibet, 449
Thief, Francis J., 566
Tiefentaller, Joseph, 414
Tierney, Michael, 566
Tihen, J. Henry, 566
Timlin, James C., Bp., 550
Timon, John, C.M., 566
Timor, Eastern, 449
Timothy, St., 311
  Epistle to, 241
Tintoretto, Jacopo, 414
Tiso, Joseph, Msgr., see Czechoslovakia
Tisserant, Eugene, 414
Tithing, 394
Titian, 414
Titular Archbishop, Bishop, 187
Titular Sees, 394
Titus, St., 311
  Epistle, 241
Tobago, 450
Tobin, Maurice J., 414

Tobit, 236
Tocqueville, Alexis Charles de, 414
Todadilla, Anthony de, 417
Toebbe, Augustus M., 566
Togo, 449
Tokelau Islands, 449
Toleration Act, England (1689), 161
Tomasek, Frantisek, Card., 213
Tonga, 449
Tongues, Gift, see Charismatic Renewal
Tonsure, see Holy Orders
Toolen, Thomas J., 566
Topel, Bernard J., Bp., 550
Torricelli, Evangelista, 414
Tortilla Curtain, Undocumented Aliens, 99
Toscanelli, Paolo dal Pozzo, 414
Toscanini, Arturo, 414
Toulouse, Catholic Institute, 627
Tourism, Commission, 196
Tracy, Robert, Bp., 550
Tradition, 229-30
Traditionalist Parish, Minnesota, 119
Transfiguration, 304
Transfinalization, 394
Transignification, 394
Transkei, 450
Translations, Bible, 234
Transplants, Organ, 382
Transubstantiation, 394
  See also Miracles
Trappists, 572
Treacy, John, 566
Treasury of the Church, 394
Treinen, Sylvester, Bp., 550
Trent, Council of, 168
  and Canon of Bible, 243
  and Celibacy, 360
  Doctrine on Mass, 259
Tribunals of Roman Curia, 195
Tridentine Mass, see Lefebvre, Marcel, Archbishop
Triduum, 394
Trination, 261, 266
Trinidad, 450
Trinitarians, 577
Trinity, Blessed, Missionary Servants of Most, 599
Trinity, Holy, 304
  Missionary Servants of Most, 577
  Order of Most, 577
  Sisters of Most, 599
  Third Order Secular of Most, 604
Trin-Nhu-Khue, Joseph Marie, Card., 704
Trin-Van-Can, Joseph, Mary, Card., 213
Triodion, 293
Triumph of the Cross, 304
Trobec, James, 566
Truce of God (1027), 158
Truman, Pres. Harry S., 220
Tschoepe, Thomas, Bp., 550
Tuigg, John, 566
Tulasne, Louis, 414
Tunisia, 450
Tunney, Gene, 704
Turibius de Mogrovejo, St., 417
Turin, Shroud, see Shroud of Turin
Turkey, 450
Turks and Caicos Islands, 450
Turner, William, 566
Tuvalu, see Gilbert Islands
Twelve Apostles of Mexico, 417
Tyler, William, 566
"Type" (648), 157
Typical Sense (Bible), 242

U

Uganda, 112, 113, 126, 131, 151, 450
Uganda Martyrs (Charles Lwanga and Companions, Sts.), 306
Ukrainian Byzantine Rite Catholics, 324
  Bishops' Meeting, Rome, 151
Ukrainians, U.S., 326
  John Paul II Visit, Philadelphia, 64, 72
Una Voce, 131
Unam Sanctam (1302), 160
Unbaptized, 227
UNDA-USA, 688
Under 21 Crisis Center, New York, 139

Undset, Sigrid, 414
Unemployment Tax and Church Schools, 120, 149
Union of Soviet Socialist Republics, 450-51
  German Parishes, 110
  Gromyko Meeting with John Paul II, 107-08
Unions, Teacher, Catholic Schools, 99, 120, 618
Unitarianism, 333
Unitatis Redintegratio, 168
  See also Ecumenism Decree
United Arab Emirates, 451
United Brethren Church, see Hus, John
United Church of Christ, 337
United Farm Workers Union (UFWA), 109, 144
United Methodist Church, 334
  Dialogues, 344
United Nations, 98, 100, 102, 103, 110, 111, 127, 136, 141, 148
  John Paul II Visit, Address, 68-70
    See also Year of Child, International
United Societies of U.S.A., 669
United States
  Apostolic Delegates, 218-19
  Bishops, see Bishops, U.S.
  Catholic Historical Society, 669
  Catholic Population, 508-11
  Eastern Rite Catholics, 326
  History, Catholic, 473-89
  John Paul II Visit, Addresses, 63-5, 68-70
  Jurisdictions, Hierarchy, 497-506
  Liturgical Developments, 264-69
  Missionaries, 605-08
  Pontifical Universities, 628
  Protestant Churches, Major, 333-37
  Recognition of China, 106, 109
  Social Services, Catholic, 631-48
  Statistics, Catholic, see Statistics
  Supreme Court, see Supreme Court
  Universities and Colleges, 619-24
  Vatican Relations, 220
    See also American
United States Catholic Conference, 109, 123, 521-26
  See also Bishops, U.S.
United States Catholic Mission Council, 606-07
United Way and Planned Parenthood, 99, 105, 149
Unity, Christian, see Ecumenism
Universalism, 333
Universities, Pontifical, 152, 627-28
  Norms (*Sapientia Christiana*), 128
Unterkoefler, Ernest L., Bp., 550
Upper Volta, 451
Ursi, Corrado, Card., 213
Ursula, Company of St., 602
Ursula of BVM, Society of Sisters, 599
Ursuline Nuns, 599
Ursuline Sisters, 599
Uruguay, 451
Usury, 394
Utah, 489, 511, 513, 515, 616, 639, 654, 692

V

Vacation and Youth, 137
Vachon, Louis, Bp., 468
Vagnozzi, Egidio, Card., 213
Valdivia, Luis de, 418
Valentine, Basil, 414
Valentine, St., 311
Valois, Charles, Bp., 468
Vaparaiso, Pontifical University (Chile), 627
Van de Velde, James, S.J., 566
Van de Ven, Cornelius, 566
Van de Vyver, Augustine, 566
Vandyke (Van Dyck), Anthony, 414
Van Hoof, Mary, Mrs., 134
Vasari, Giorgio, 414
Vasques de Espinosa, Antonio, 418
Vasquez, Gabriel, 414
Vath, Joseph G., Bp., 550
Vatican City, 221-23
  Commission, 197
  Concordat with Spain, 108
  Diplomatic Relations, 215-18
  Diplomats at, 103, 219-20
  Office for U.S. Visitors, 222
  Press Office, 138, 223
  Representatives, 215-18, 223
  Secretariat of State, 192

Index

Vatican City
  U.S. Relations, 220
Vatican Council, I, 168
Vatican Council II, see Council, Second Vatican
Vaughan, Austin B., Bp., 550
Vaughn, John, O.F.M., Rev., 132
Vega, Lope Felix de, 414
Vehr, Urban, 566
Veigle, Adrian, T.O.R., Bp., 550
Veil, 263
Veil, Humeral, 262
Velasquez, Diego, 414
Veneration Society of Sanctity, 669
Venerini Sisters, 599
Venezuela, 451
Venial Sin, 390
Venice Statement, Authority in Church, 347
Vercelli Medal, 703
Verdaguer, Peter, 566
Verdi, Giuseppe, 414
Vermont, 489, 508, 512, 514, 613, 639, 692
Vernacular Society, 669
Verne, Jules, 414
Vernier, Pierre, 414
Verona, Missionary Sisters of, 599
Verona Fathers, 577
Veronese, Paolo, 414
Veronica, 394
Verot, Augustin, 566
Verrazano, Giovanni da, 414
Verrocchio, Andrea del, 414
Vertin, John, 566
Versalius, Andreas, 414
Vespucci, Amerigo, 414
Vessels, Sacred, 262-63
Vestments, 261-62
  Byzantine, 327
Viaticum, 394
Viator, Clerics of St., 577
Vicar Apostolic, 188
Vicar General, 394
Vicariate of Solidarity, Chile, 101, 105, 121
Vicariates, Apostolic, World, 454
Vico, Francisco de, 414
Victor Emmanuel II (1870), 163
Victory, Missionary Sisters of Our Lady of, 599
Vieira, Antonio, 418
Vienne, Council, 167
Viete, Francois, 414
Vietnam, 451-52
Vigil, Easter, 302
Vignola, Giacomo, 414
Villot, Jean, Card., 108, 118, 704
Vincent, St., 311
Vincent de Paul, St., 311
Vincent de Paul, St. (Religious)
  Daughters of Charity, 584
  Sisters of Charity of, 585
Vincent de Paul, St., Society, 631
Vincent de Paul Medal, St., 702
Vincent Ferrer, St., 311
Vincent of Beauvais, 414
Vincentian Sisters of Charity, 584
Vincentians, 578
Vinci, Leonardo da, 414
Violence, 54, 65-6, 107, 129
  See also Human Rights
Virgin Birth of Christ, 316
Virgin Islands, 452
Virginia, 489, 508, 512, 514, 613, 639, 646, 655
  Test-Tube Baby Clinic, 100
Virginity, 394
Virtue, 394
Virtues (Angels), 355
Virtues, Cardinal, 359
Virtues, Infused, 375
Virtues, Theological, 393
Vischer, Lukas, Dr., 111
Visitation, 304
Visitation Nuns, 599
Visitation Sisters, 599
Vladimir, St., 414
Vocation, 394
Vocation Conference, National Sisters, 600
Vocation Council, National, 601
Vocationist Fathers, 578

Vocationist Sisters, 599
Vocations, John Paul II on, 127
Vogel, Cyril J., Bp., 550
Volk, Hermann, Card., 213
Volpe, John A. (Catholics in Presidents' Cabinets), 490
Volta, Alessandro, 414
Voluntas Dei, 603
Vonesh, Raymond J., Bp., 550
Vorosmarty, Michael, 414
Votive Mass, 261
Vow, 395
Vulgate Bible, 234
  Commission for Revision, 196
  Revised Edition Published, 122

W

Waddill, William, Dr., 135
Wade, Thomas, S.M., 566
Wadhams, Edgar P., 566
Wagner, Robert F., 414
Wagner, Robert F. (Envoy to Pope), 103, 220
Waldensianism, 165
Waldheim, Kurt, 143
Waldschmidt, Paul E., C.S.C., Bp., 550
Waldseemuller, Martin, 414
Walen, Joseph, Msgr., 704
Wales, 452
Walker, Frank, 414
Wall, Leonard J., Bp., 468
Wall of Separation, 495
Wallis and Futuna Islands, 452
Walsh, Emmet, 566
Walsh, James A., M.M., 566
Walsh, James E., M.M., Bp., 551
Walsh, James J., 414
Walsh, Louis S., 566
Walsh, Nicholas E., Bp., 551
Walsh, Thomas J., 566
Walsh, William T., 414
Walters, David, 220
Walworth, Clarence A., 414
Walz v. Tax Commission of New York, 495-96
Wanderer Forum, 139
War, 254-55
Ward, Artemus (Charles Farrar Browne), 398
Ward, Barbara, 120
Ward, John, 567
Ward, John J., Bp., 551
Ward, Maisie, 415
Warren, Leonard, 415
Washington, 489, 511, 513, 515, 527, 616, 626, 639, 643, 655, 692
Water, Baptismal, see Baptism
Water, Easter, 367
Water, Holy, 373
Waters, Vincent J., 567
Watson, Alfred M., Bp., 551
Watters, Loras J., Bp., 119, 551
Watterson, John A., 567
Wattson, Lewis T., 415
Waugh, Evelyn, 415
Way of the Cross, see Stations of the Cross
Wayne, John, 135
Weakland, Rembert, O.S.B., Abp., 525, 551
Weber, Karl, 415
Webster, Benjamin I., Bp., 468
Week of Prayer for Christian Unity, 107, 395
Wehrle, Vincent, 567
Weigel, Gustave, 415
Welch, Thomas A., 567
Weldon, Christopher J., Bp., 551
Welsh, Lawrence H., Bp., 551
Welsh, Thomas J., Bp., 551
Wenceslaus, St., 311
Wesley, John, 333
West, Catholic University of (France), 627
West Virginia, 489, 508, 512, 514, 613, 626, 639, 692
Western Catholic Union, 669
Western Sahara, 452
Western Schism, 174
Westphalia Peace (1648), 161
Whealon, John F., Abp., 119, 551
Wheeler v. Barrera, 494
Whelan, Charles M., S.J., 612
Whelan, James P., O.P., 567

Whelan, Lawrence P., Bp., 468
Whelan, Richard V., 567
Whelan, Robert L., S.J., Bp., 551
Whitby Synod (664), 157
White, Andrew, 418
White, Charles, 567
White, Edward Douglass, 415
White, Helen, 415
White Fathers, 578
White House Conference on Family, 567
White House Visit, John Paul II, 64
White Russian Byzantines, 323
White Sisters, 581
Whitfield, James, 567
Whitsunday, 304
Wigger, Winand, 567
Wilde, Oscar, 415
Wildermuth, Augustine F., S.J., Bp., 551
Wilhelm, Joseph L., Abp., 468
Will, Free, 371
Willebrands, Johannes, Card., 111, 150, 213
Willging, Joseph C., 567
William J. Kerby Foundation, 669
William of Ockham, 415
William the Conqueror, 415
Williams, John J., 567
Williams, Mary Lou, 150
Williams, Michael, 415
Willinger, Aloysius J., C.SS.R., 567
Wimmer, Boniface, 418
Winckelmann, Johann, 415
Windle, Bertram, 415
Windle, Joseph R., Bp., 468
Windsor Statement, 346
Windthorst, Ludwig, 415
Winkelmann, Christian H., 567
Wirz, George O., Bp., 551
Wisconsin, 489-90, 509, 512, 514, 518, 527, 614, 626, 639-40, 641, 643, 646, 655, 692
  Student Aid, 108-09
Wisconsin Council of Women, 669
Wisdom, Daughters of, 599
Wisdom Books, 237
Wiseman, Nicholas, 415
Witness, Christian, 395
Witnesses, Jehovah's, 376-77
Wojtyla, Karol, see John Paul II, Pope
Wolman v. Walter, 495, 612
Women
  Equal Rights Amendment, 570
  Ordination, Anglican Church, 101, 140
Women in Catholic Church
  Appointments, 125
  Archdiocesan Commission, Boston, 144
  National Conference of Catholic Women, 656
  National Women's Ordination Conference, 100, 526
  Ordination, 72, 100, 526
  Religious, Papal Address, 74
  Sexist Language, Liturgical Books, 101
  World Union of Catholic Women's Organizations, 108, 116
Wood, James, 567
Word, Liturgy, 259
Word of God Institute, 669
Work and Workers, Concern, 55, 61, 122, 147
World Catholic Federation of the Biblical Apostolate, 234
World Conference on Law, 148
World Council of Churches, 110, 113, 139, 140
  Working Group with Catholics, 118
World Statistics, Catholic, 454-55
  Men Religious, 580-81
Worldwide Marriage Encounter, 139, 289
Worms, Concordat (1122), 159
Worship, see Adoration
Worship, Divine, Congregation, 193
Worship, Eastern Rite, 322
Worship, Liturgical, see Liturgy
Woznicki, Stephen, 567
Wright, John J., Card., 138, 142, 567, 704
Writers' Market, Catholic, 683-86
Wurm, John, Bp., 551
Wycislo, Aloysius J., Bp., 551
Wycliff, John, 332
Wynne, Robert J., 415
Wyoming, 490, 510, 513, 515, 616, 643, 692
Wyszynski, Stefan, Card., 213

X

Xaverian Brothers, 578
Xaverian Mission Sisters, 600
Xaverian Missionary Fathers, 578
Xaverian Missionary Sisters of Mary, 600
Xavier Society for the Blind, 648
Xavier University, Cincinnati, 109
Ximenes de Cisneros, Francisco, 415

Y

Year, Church (Calendar), 290-300
Year of the Child, International, 107, 110, 122, 143, 146
Yemen, 131, 452
Yemen, Peoples Democratic Republic, 453
Yom Kippur, 351
Yoshida, Shigeru, 415
Young, Andrew, 103
Young, Josue, 567
Young Christian Students, 661
Young Ladies' Institute, 669
Young Men's Institute, 669
Youth, 136, 138
  Papal Counsel, 71, 661
Youth Activities, USCC, 661
Youth Organizations, 660-61
Youville, Marie D', Bl., 418
Yugoslav Byzantines, 324
Yugoslavia, 143, 146, 453
YMCA, 130

Z

Zaire, 121, 453
Zaleski, Alexander M., 567
Zambia, 453
Zanzibar, see Tanzania
Zardetti, Otto, 567
Zayek, Francis, Bp., 551
Zechariah, 239
Zechariah, Canticle (Benedictus), 358
Zephaniah, 239
Zimbabwe Rhodesia, see Rhodesia
Zita, St., 311
Zorach v. Clauson, 493
Zone, 327
Zoungrana, Paul, Card., 213
Zrinyi, Nicholas, 415
Zucchetto, 395
Zumarraga, Juan de, O.F.M., 418
Zurbaran, Francisco de, 415
Zuroweste, Albert R., Bp., 551
Zwingli, Ulrich, 332

Pope John Paul expressed his sympathy Oct. 24 on the death of 90-year-old Argentinian Cardinal Antonio Caggiano. His death reduced the number of Latin American cardinals to 18 and the total number to 129.

PUBLICATION HISTORY

The *Catholic Almanac* originated remotely from *St. Anthony's Almanac*, a 64-page annual with calendar, feature and devotional contents, published by the Franciscans of Holy Name Province from 1904 to 1929.

Completely revised and enlarged, the publication was issued under the title, *The Franciscan Almanac*, by *The Franciscan Magazine* from 1931 to 1933, and by St. Anthony's Guild from 1936 to 1971. From 1940 to 1969, its title was *The National Catholic Almanac*. The present title was adopted in 1969. The 1959 to 1971 editions were produced jointly by St. Anthony's Guild and Doubleday & Co., Inc.

The *Catholic Almanac* was acquired in 1971 by Our Sunday Visitor, Inc., Huntington, Ind. 46750.

A JOURNEY OF FAITH

This was the description Pope John Paul gave of his visit to Ireland and the United States Sept. 29 to Oct. 7, 1979, before a throng of 50,000 persons at a general audience Oct. 10. The text was reported in the Oct. 15 English edition of "L'Osservatore Romano."

"Here I am again back among you, after my pastoral journey to Ireland and to the United States!

"After this event, such a joyful one for me, I feel again the need to thank warmly all those who contributed to its success. I thank those who welcomed me with such kindness: in the first place the President of Ireland Hillery; the Secretary General of the United Nations, Kurt Waldheim; the President of the United States Carter; all the religious, civil and military authorities; and, in the first place, the episcopates. I thank those who transported me and accompanied me with such kind attention. I thank those who provided the service of order and security, and those who transmitted and commented on the various news reports of the various events. Above all, I thank with deep affection the immense crowds, which united around the Vicar of Christ in a brotherly and filial embrace at every stage of my journey. But I want to thank you, too, who certainly prayed for me.

"I always felt the spiritual closeness of millions and millions of persons who, with their prayer, made this journey of faith possible and certainly efficacious.

"It was, in fact, solely a journey of faith, made solely to proclaim the Gospel, to 'strengthen brothers,' to console the afflicted, to bear witness to God's love, to point out to mankind its transcendent destiny.

"Like St. Paul, I preached only Christ, and Christ crucified and risen again for us! (cf. I Cor. 1:23).

"It was a journey of faith; therefore, it was a journey of prayer, centered always on meditation of the Word of God, the celebration of the Eucharist and invocation of the Blessed Virgin.

"It was also an 'itinerant catechesis,' in which it was my intention to stress everywhere, to all classes of persons, the true and ineffaceable patrimony of Catholic doctrine.

"It was also a journey of peace, love and brotherhood, which took me to the headquarters of the United Nations Organization. There, above all, as in all the meetings with the crowds, in the name of Christ and of the Church, I became the spokesman of the peoples eager for justice and peace, on behalf of the poor, the suffering, the oppressed, the humble and children.

"Together let us thank the Lord and Mary most holy for all this!

"God grant that men may become better and better, more and more united and committed to good, forgiveness and brotherly love!

"To thank the Blessed Virgin with all the greater fervor and to implore the grace of conversion and peace, I announce to you now with immense joy that on Sunday, 21 October, I will go on pilgrimage to the Sanctuary of Pompei."

Recollections, Impressions

The Pope recalled a number of highlights and impressions of his trip.

The ruins of the ancient abbey of Clonmacnois in central Ireland, he said, "speak of the life that once pulsed there. It is one of those monasteries in which the Irish monks not only embedded Christianity in the Emerald Isle but from which they carried it to the other countries of Europe. It is difficult to look at that complex of ruins only as a monument to the past. All the generations of Europe owe to it the light of the Gospel and the underpinnings of their culture."

Of the visit to Drogheda and his veneration there of the relics of St. Oliver Plunkett, its one-time bishop who was martyred in 1681, he said: "Only in kneeling before these relics can all the truth of the Irish past and present be expressed. Only there can its wounds be touched with the trust that they will be healed."

Of American Catholics, he said "their Church is very young because their great society is still young."

And: "I confess that I was surprised by such a welcome, by such response" everywhere, observing: "We stuck it out under the rain that fell during the Mass for young people the first evening in Boston. The rain accompanied us on the streets of that city, as it did afterwards on the streets of New York among the skyscrapers. That rain did not stop so many people of good will from persevering in prayer, from waiting for the moment of my arrival, my words, my blessing."

He recounted places where he went and people to whom he spoke — in Harlem and the South Bronx, at Yankee Stadium, Madison Square Garden, Shea Stadium, places in Philadelphia, Iowa, Chicago and Washington, D.C. He singled out for special attention his "historic meeting at the White House" with President Carter.

In a reference to his address before the U.N. General Assembly, he commented: "What else could I have said before that supreme forum of a political nature, if not that which constitutes the core of the Gospel message?"

Observers noted that the Pope's addresses were carefully programmed for appeal to the concerns not only of Catholics but also of persons of other faiths.

Special Reports

POPE JOHN PAUL II

See related entries under John Paul II in Index.

Cardinal-Archbishop Karol Wojtyła of Cracow was elected Bishop of Rome Oct. 16, 1978, on the seventh or eighth ballot cast on the second day of voting at a conclave of 111 cardinals. He chose the name John Paul II and was invested with the pallium, the symbol of his papal office, Oct. 22 in ceremonies attended by more than 250,000 persons in St. Peter's Square.

The 263rd successor of St. Peter as Bishop of Rome and Supreme Pastor of the Universal Church, he is the first non-Italian Pope since Adrian VI (1522-23), the first Polish Pope in the history of the Church, and the youngest at the time of his election since Pius IX (1846-78).

Early Career

Karol Wojtyla was born May 18, 1920, in Wadowice, Poland.

He began higher studies at the age of 18, with major interests in poetry and theater arts. Forced to suspend university courses because of the outbreak of World War II, he went to work in a stone quarry and a chemical plant, thereby earning the later designation of himself as the "Worker Cardinal."

He started studies for the priesthood in 1942 in the underground seminary of Cracow, whose operations had been banned after the Nazi invasion of Poland.

Ordained to the priesthood Nov. 1, 1946, he was immediately sent to Rome for studies at the Angelicum University, where he earned a doctorate in ethics.

Back home in Poland, he worked as an assistant pastor in a village parish and as a chaplain to university students while continuing studies at the Catholic University of Lublin. He was awarded another doctorate there, in moral theology.

He began writing about this time, and eventually produced more than 100 articles and several books on ethical and other themes. Phenomenology was one of his fields of expertise.

University teaching came next, in 1953, with appointment in 1954 to the position of lecturer and later to the chair of ethics at the Catholic University of Lublin, the most prestigious institute of higher learning in Poland.

Bishop and Cardinal

He was ordained Auxiliary Bishop of Cracow Sept. 28, 1958, became vicar capitular in 1962 after the death of Apostolic Administrator Eugeniusz Baziak, and was appointed Archbishop Jan. 13, 1964. He was the first residential head of the see since the death of Cardinal Adam Sapieha in 1951. Between then and 1964 the archdiocese was run by administrators because the Communist government refused to permit the appointment and ministry of a residential bishop.

Archbishop Wojtyla attended all sessions of the Second Vatican Council from 1962 to 1965, and was one of the writers of the *Pastoral Constitution on the Church in the Modern World.* He also contributed input to the *Declaration on Religious Freedom* and the *Decree on the Instruments of Social Communication.*

His efforts to put into effect the directives of the council induced him to write a book, *Foundations of Renewal,* in 1972 and to start that same year an archdiocesan synod he saw concluded as Pope during his visit to Poland in 1979.

He was inducted into the College of Cardinals June 26, 1967, as one of the younger members, and subsequently served actively in the Congregation for the Sacraments and Divine Worship, the Congregation for the Clergy, and the Congregation for Catholic Education.

He also served as a theological consultant to Pope Paul VI.

He attended assemblies of the Synod of Bishops as a representative of the Polish Bishops' Conference and was a member of the synod's permanent council.

From the beginning of his priestly career, and especially during his episcopate, the Cardinal was vigorous in the defense of human and religious rights, the rights of workers, and rights to religious education.

Close to Cardinal Wyszynski and in company with his fellow bishops, he negotiated the tightrope of Catholic survival in a country under Communist control. With them, as their spokesman at times, he was stalwart in resisting efforts of the regime to impose atheism, materialism and secularism on the people and culture of Poland.

The First Year

Since the beginning of his pontificate, John Paul has been active as Bishop of Rome, with frequent visits to parishes and institutions of the diocese for the celebration of Mass and participation in other events. During these visits, as well as others to places of pilgrimage and historic significance in Italy, he has had perhaps more personal contact with the faithful than any other Pope. The number of attendants at weekly general audiences at the Vatican and Castel Gandolfo has been unprecedented.

Key Encyclical

Unprecedented also has been the attention focused on him during his first three pilgrimages of faith in 1979 — to the Dominican Republic and Mexico, Poland, Ireland and the United States — when he celebrated Mass, spoke and moved among millions of people.

The messages he delivered during these trips were the equivalent of doctrinal, pastoral and social encyclical letters on a wide variety of subjects, all related to the key document of the first year of his pontificate. This was the formal encyclical *Redemptor Hominis*, a treatise on Christian anthropology dealing with the divine and human aspects of redemption and the mission of the Church to carry on a dialogue of salvation with all peoples.

Other significant documents issued in 1979 included *Sapientia Christiana*, concerning pontifical institutions of higher learning, a decree in which he promulgated a New Vulgate version of the Bible, and a letter to priests detailing the dignity, fidelity and responsibilities of their calling. Additional statements and addresses, too numerous to mention, covered a wide variety of topics related to Christian life and actual conditions of those to whom they were addressed.

In his relations with the hierarchy in 1979, the Pope met with groups of bishops making required *ad limina* visits to the Vatican, for first-hand reports and admonitions regarding dioceses all over the world. In June, he inducted 14 new cardinals into the Sacred College, raising its membership at that time to 135. He scheduled a particular synod of the Dutch bishops early in 1980, to cope with problems of the troubled Church in their country, and the sixth assembly of the Synod of Bishops later in the year.

PAPAL PILGRIMAGE TO LATIN AMERICA

Following is a log of the principal events of Pope John Paul's "pilgrimage of faith" to Latin America, Jan. 25 to 31, 1979.

During the first trip ever made by a Pope to the Dominican Republic and Mexico, the Holy Father:

• was seen, heard and enthusiastically cheered by perhaps 10 million persons in the two countries;

• mingled and spoke with people of all ranks of society;

• formally opened and keynoted the Third General Assembly of Latin American Bishops at Puebla;

• delivered — in the pastoral manner of his presence and actions, and in the contents of more than 30 addresses — the equivalent of a major social encyclical letter on evangelization and its relationship to authentic human liberation, with special reference to Latin America but with meaning for all regions of the world.

JANUARY 25

Pope John Paul II departed on his "pilgrimage of faith" to Latin America from Rome's Fiumicino Airport at 8:20 a.m., local time, aboard a chartered Alitalia DC-10 bound for the Dominican Republic.

En route, he radioed messages of greeting to President Valery Giscard D'Estaing and President Jimmy Carter while flying over France and Puerto Rico, respectively. He met with journalists aboard for an hour and a quarter, talking and answering questions related to the purpose of his trip, liberation theology, socialism, the possibility of a future visit to the United States, and other subjects.

The DC-10 landed at 1:28 p.m., local time, at Las Americas Airport outside Santo Domingo.

On leaving the plane, the Pope kissed the ground of the "Cradle of Catholicism" in the Western Hemisphere, the Island of Hispaniola where Columbus landed on his second voyage and where the first Mass in the New World was celebrated in 1493. He was greeted with official honors by President Antonio Guzman and members of his cabinet, as well as by church officials and an enthusiastic crowd.

Thousands of people cheered the Pope along the length of an 18-mile motorcade to the Santo Domingo Cathedral, where he met with and spoke to a gathering of bishops, priests, religious and lay persons.

Early in the evening, before a throng of 250,000 persons in Independence Square, he concelebrated Mass with about 100 bishops from the Caribbean area and the United States. The theme of his homily was integral evangelization for religious and human development.

At the end of the officially declared "Day of Joy," the Pope met with members of the diplomatic corps at the residence of the papal nuncio in Santo Domingo, where he spent the night.

JANUARY 26

The Holy Father celebrated an early morning Mass in the Santo Domingo Cathedral before a congregation of priests, men and women religious, and seminarians. He urged them in a homily to base their lives and activities on "the criteria of the Gospel lived with integrity and joy, and with the immense confidence and hope that the cross of Christ contains." He also told them that "men must see in us the dispensers of God's mysteries, the credible witnesses of his presence in the world."

After Mass, the Pope visited the *Los Minas* barrio where he met with school children, the sick and other people in the area of St. Vincent de Paul Parish. While there, he appealed for efforts to help the poor and others in depressed circumstances to improve their conditions of life, "to develop more and more the possibilities of obtaining a situation of greater human and Christian dignity."

He boarded an Aeromexico DC-10 for the flight to Mexico City late in the morning, after spending 21 hours in the Dominican Republic.

The Pope arrived at Mexico City's international airport after a four-hour flight and was greeted by a massed throng of cheering people as he alighted from the plane and kissed the ground. Church dignitaries on hand were headed by Cardinal Jose Salazar, president of the Mexican Bishops' Conference, and Archbishop Ernesto Corripio Ahumada of Mexico City. President Jose Lopez Portillo welcomed him as a distinguished, but not as an official, visitor.

At least a million people lined the route of the Pope's motorcade from the airport to the Mexico City Cathedral. He celebrated Mass there before a congregation of about 5,000 persons and preached a homily on fidelity to the Church. He concluded the liturgy from the cathedral balcony, where he extended his greetings and blessing to the hundreds of thousands of people in the square outside.

Later, the Pope visited President Portillo at his residence. He also met with diplomats and other persons at the apostolic delegation in Mexico City, where he spent his nights while in the country.

JANUARY 27

The Pope started the day at a meeting with Poles living in Mexico City and its environs.

Later in the morning, he was driven through dense and cheering crowds to the Basilica of Our Lady of Guadalupe.

He concelebrated Mass there shortly after noon with 300 bishops, in ceremonies marking the formal opening of the Third General Assembly of Latin American Bishops. In a homily related to the theme of the assembly, "The Present and Future of Evangelization in Latin America," he emphasized the quest for continuing and new approaches to evangelization, church renewal and human development. About 500,000 people were massed outside the basilica during the Mass, which was attended by a congregation of 12,000.

During the afternoon, the Pope addressed a gathering of nuns at the Michelangelo Institute in Mexico City. While telling them that a spirit of fidelity prevailed among most women religious, he also noted the existence among some of confusion about "the essence of consecrated life," and of problems related to prayer, the vows, community life and radical activism. The Church and humanity, he said in conclusion, "await your generous giving of yourselves, the dedication of your free heart that will increase unsuspectingly its potentialities of love in a world that is losing its capacity for altruism, for self-sacrificing and disinterested love."

Afterwards, at a meeting with priests and men religious in the Guadalupe Basilica, he focused remarks on their authentic identity and mission as servants of the faith, the Church and the people they are called to serve. He urged them not to "dilute (their) charism" of true evangelical commitment with "an exaggerated interest in the broad field of temporal problems."

The Holy Father spent the evening in meetings with bishops of Mexico.

JANUARY 28

The Pope was driven to Puebla, 65 miles southeast of Mexico City, in the morning.

In the afternoon, he delivered the keynote address — the longest and most extensive during his visit — at the first working session of the Third General Assembly of Latin American Bishops at the Palafox Seminary.

In the address, he stressed the multiple role of bishops as teachers of the truth concerning Christ, the mission of the Church, and man; as signs and builders of unity in the Church and general society; and as defenders and promoters of human dignity. He called on them to give high priority to consideration and action regarding ministry to the family and young people, and to the development of vocations to the priesthood and religious life.

One of these priorities, ministry to the family, was the theme of a homily delivered by the Holy Father later in the afternoon during a Mass celebrated outside the seminary before a throng of tens of thousands of people.

The Pope ended his time in Puebla in meetings with groups of bishops, and returned by car to Mexico City in the evening.

JANUARY 29

The Holy Father flew to Oaxaca, nearly 300 miles to the southeast, after earlier morning visits to a home for the elderly and children and to a pediatrics hospital in Mexico City.

He flew by helicopter from Oaxaca to Cuilapan where he addressed a gathering of Indians on the plight of the rural poor and was entertained by them.

On the way back to the state capital, he visited the Marian shrine of Our Lady of La Soledad, the patroness of southern Mexico.

During a concelebrated Mass in the cathedral at Oaxaca, the Holy Father conferred the ministries of lector and acolyte on 25 Indians (21 lectors, four acolytes). He also, in a homily, addressed the commitment of lay persons by baptism and confirmation to be witnesses and active participants in the evangelizing mission of the Church. Lay people, he said, "are the closest agents of the renewal of man and of the things which surround him."

On his return to Mexico City in the evening, the Pope met with representatives of national Catholic organizations.

JANUARY 30

The Pope started the day at a gathering of 60,000 elementary school children in Mexico City. While with them at the Michelangelo Institute, he said in a brief address that education is "an inalienable right."

He then flew to Guadalajara, the second largest city in the country, about 300 miles to the northwest. There he toured the Santa Cecilia barrio on the outskirts; addressed 100,000 persons, mostly workers, in the Jalisco Stadium; loudspeakered greetings to inmates of the state prison as he passed by; spoke to contemplative nuns in the cathedral; concelebrated Mass at the Shrine of Our Lady of the Immaculate Conception of Zapopan; and met with students for the priesthood, diocesan and religious, at the Guadalajara Seminary.

In his talk at the stadium, the Pope described the Christian concept of work and called not just for criticism of injustice but, above all, for effective action by workers and others "to create justice."

He told the nuns that their contemplative way of life was greatly esteemed by the Church. He said it was neither irrelevant nor out of date but was, rather, a special call for spreading the kingdom of God in "a specific way."

During Mass in the cathedral, the Pope prayed for the intercession of Mary to help "overcome structures of sin" in society and to obtain for Latin Americans and all peoples the grace of true liberation.

Before boarding the plane for the return flight to Mexico City in the evening, the Holy Father was serenaded by 70,000 youngsters singing "Amigo."

JANUARY 31-FEBRUARY 1

The Pope's last day in Mexico started with a busy morning.

He had a surprise visit from the foreign ministers of five countries — Costa Rica, El Salvador, Guatemala, Honduras and Nicaragua — who asked him to return at a future date for another visit to Latin America.

Afterwards, he addressed 150,000 students of Catholic universities at the Guadalupe Basilica; met with 1,100 members of the working press and other media; and attended an exhibition of horsemanship by Mexican cowboys.

In midafternoon, the Holy Father flew from Mexico City to Monterrey. There, speaking before a large crowd gathered near the San Luisito Bridge, he addressed the problems of migrant workers and called for action to correct injustices affecting them.

The Pope left Monterrey early in the evening on the first leg of the flight to Rome.

En route, he radioed greetings to Fidel Castro as he flew over Cuba. During a refueling stop in The Bahamas, he took part in a postmidnight interfaith prayer service attended by 5,000 persons at the Queen Elizabeth Sports Center in Nassau.

One hundred and 77 hours and 15,500 miles after leaving Rome, the Holy Father returned to Fiumicino Airport early in the afternoon of Feb. 1.

He said on arrival that the Latin American visit was "an unforgettable experience."

LATIN AMERICAN ADDRESSES OF JOHN PAUL II

Following are excerpts and accounts of the substance of several of the more than 30 addresses delivered in Spanish by Pope John Paul II during his Latin American pilgrimage of faith Jan. 25 to 31, 1979.

The excerpts, with some paragraph changes, are from translations circulated by the NC Documentary Service, Origins.

PILGRIM OF PEACE

Homily preached during Mass Jan. 25 in Independence Square, Santo Domingo.

Purpose of the Visit: "I have come to these American lands as a traveler of peace and hope, to participate in an ecclesiastical event of evangelization" (Third General Assembly of Latin American Bishops).

"This present period of the history of humanity requires a new transmission of faith in order to communicate to men today the perennial message of Christ, adapted to the realistic conditions of life."

Evangelization: "This evangelization is a constant and essential requirement of ecclesiastical dynamics."

"Evangelization . . . is . . . above all the announcement of the good word of Christ the Savior."

"The Church . . . wants to continue its mission of faith and defense of human rights. She invites Christians to commit themselves to constructing a more just, humane and habitable world which does not close itself in but, rather, opens itself to God."

Meaning of Justice in the World: "Making this world more just includes, among other things: to make the effort, to strive to have a world in which no more children lack sufficient nutrition, education, instruction; that there be no more children without proper formation; that there be no more poor peasants without land, so that they can live and develop with dignity; that there be no more workers mistreated nor whose rights are lessened; that there be no more systems which permit the exploitation of man by man or by the state; that there be no more corruption; that there be no more of those who have too much while others are lacking everything through no fault of their own; that there not be so many families who are broken, disunited, insufficiently attended; that there be no injustice or inequality in administering justice; that there be no one who is not supported by the law and that the law support everyone equally; that force not prevail over truth and rights, but rather truth and rights over force; and that the economic and political never prevail over the human."

Vertical Orientation of Evangelization: "But do not be content with a more human world. Make an explicitly divine world, more according to God, governed by faith and that which faith inspires — the moral, religious and social progress of man. Do not lose sight of the vertical orientation of evangelization. It can liberate man because it is the revelation of love."

FIDELITY TO THE CHURCH

Homily preached during Mass Jan. 26 in the Mexico City Cathedral.

After recalling the unreserved and persevering fidelity of Mary to the will of God, the Pope said:

"We must be faithful to the Church born once and for all from the plan of God . . . born not of the people or from reason, but from God. She is born today to build among all men a people willing to grow in faith, hope and fraternal love."

"The Pope expects from you a coherence between your own lives and the life of the Church. This coherence implies an awareness of your identity as Catholics, it means giving public witness to it. The Church today needs laymen who will give witness to their faith and share her mission in the world, being the ferment of faith, justice and human dignity, in order to build a more human and fraternal world from which we can look up to God."

"The Pope desires that your coherence in the faith not be short-lived but that it continue and deepen."

PUEBLA — PURPOSE

Pope John Paul II addressed the purpose of the Third General Assembly of Latin American Bishops in a homily delivered during a Mass he concelebrated with them Jan. 27, 1979, at the Basilica of Our Lady of Guadalupe. The Mass marked the formal opening of the assembly. The homily was an introduction to the contents of the address the Pope delivered the following day during the first working session of the assembly at the Palafox Seminary in Puebla.

Continuation of Medellin: "With this meeting of bishops, we wish to link ourselves with the previous conference of the Latin American bishops that took place 10 years ago at Medellin, together with the Eucharistic Congress at Bogota in which Pope Paul VI . . . took part. We have come here not so much to examine again . . . the same problem (of evangelization and human development), but rather to review it in a new way. . . .

"We wish to take as our point of departure what is contained in the documents and resolutions of that conference. And, at the same time, we wish . . . to take a correct and necessary step forward."

Call of Medellin: "The Medellin meeting . . . was meant to be an impulse of spiritual renewal, a new 'spirit' in the face of the future, in full ecclesial fidelity in interpreting the signs of the time in Latin America. The evangelizing intention was quite clear. It is obvious in the 16 themes dealt with, grouped about three great, mutually complementary topics, namely, human advancement, evangelization and growth in faith, and the visible Church and her structures.

"By opting for the man of Latin America seen in his entirety, by showing preferential yet not exclusive love for the poor, and by encouraging integral liberation of individuals and peoples, Medellin . . . was a call of hope toward more Christian and more human goals."

Search for New Ways: "But more than 10 years have passed, and interpretations have been given that have been at times contradictory, not always correct, not always beneficial for the Church. The Church is therefore looking for ways that will enable her to understand more deeply and to fulfill more zealously the mission she has been given by Christ Jesus."

Intentions of the Church: The Church, in imitation of Mary, "wishes in her turn to be a good mother and to care for souls in all their needs, by proclaiming the Gospel, administering the sacraments, safeguarding family life with the sacrament of matrimony, gathering all into the eucharistic community by means of the holy Sacrament of the Altar, and by being lovingly with them from the cradle until they enter eternity."

For Strength of Lay Persons: The Holy Father prayed, through the intercession of Mary, that the faith of the laity might be strengthened so that, in "every field of social, professional, cultural and political life, they may act in accordance with the truth and the law brought by (her) Son to mankind, in order to lead everyone to eternal salvation and, at the same time, to make life on earth more human, more worthy of man."

The Pope pledged to Mary the readiness of the bishops "to serve unreservedly the cause of (her) Son, the cause of the Gospel, and the cause of peace based on justice and love between individuals and peoples."

PUEBLA — KEYNOTE

Keynote address delivered by the Pope Jan. 28 during the first working session of the Third General Assembly of Latin American Bishops at the Palafox Seminary, Puebla.

"This third conference . . . will . . . have to take as its point of departure the conclusions of Medellín, with all the positive elements that they contained, but without ignoring the incorrect interpretations made at times and which call for calm discernment, opportune criticism and clear choices of position."

Bishops Are Teachers: The principal duty of bishops . . . "is to be teachers of the truth . . . that comes from God . . . that brings with it the principle of the authentic liberation of man . . . that truth which is the only one that offers a solid basis for an adequate praxis."

"To be watchful for purity of doctrine . . . is . . . together with the proclamation of the Gospel, the primary and irreplaceable duty of the pastor, of the teacher of faith."

"Careful and zealous transmission of the truth concerning Jesus Christ . . . is at the center of evangelization and constitutes its essential content."

Need for Solid Christology: "Light on so many doctrinal and pastoral themes and questions . . . must come from a solid Christology."

"Today there occur in many places . . . 're-readings' of the Gospel, the result of theoretical speculations rather than authentic meditation on the word of God and a true commitment to the Gospel. They cause confusion by diverging from the central criteria of the faith of the Church, and some people have the effrontery to pass them on under the guise of catechesis to the Christian communities.

False Ideas about Christ: "In some cases either Christ's divinity is passed over in silence, or some people in fact fall into forms of interpretation at variance with the Church's faith. Christ is said to be merely a 'prophet,' one who proclaimed God's kingdom and love, but not the true Son of God, and therefore not the center and object of the very Gospel message."

Christ Not a Political Subversive: "In other cases people claim to show Jesus as politically committed, as one who fought against Roman oppression and the authorities, and also as one involved in the class struggle. This idea of Christ as a political figure, as the subversive Man from Nazareth, does not tally with the Church's catechesis. By confusing the insidious pretexts of Jesus' accusers with the very different attitude of Jesus himself, some people adduce as the cause of his death the outcome of a political conflict, and nothing is said of the Lord's will to deliver himself and of his consciousness of his redemptive mission."

Servant of Yahweh: "The Gospels clearly show that for Jesus anything that would alter his mission as the servant of Yahweh was a temptation. He does not accept the position of those who mixed the things of God with merely political attitudes. He unequivocally rejects recourse to violence. He opens his message of conversion to everybody. . . . The perspective of his mission . . . consists in complete salvation through a transforming, peacemaking, pardoning and reconciling love."

Evangelization Must Affirm Church's Faith in Christ: "Evangelization in the present and future of Latin America cannot cease to affirm the Church's faith: Jesus Christ, the Word and the Son of God, becomes man in order to come close to man and to offer him . . . salvation, the great gift of God."

"Any form of silence, disregard, mutilation or inadequate emphasis regarding the total mystery of Jesus Christ that diverges from the Church's faith, cannot be the valid content of evangelization."

Evangelization and Ecclesiology: "There is no guarantee of serious and vigorous evangelizing activity without a well-founded ecclesiology."

"The first reason is that evangelization is the essential mission, the distinctive vocation and the deepest identity of the Church. . . . A second reason is that 'evangelization is for no one an individual and isolated act; it is one that is deeply ecclesial' (*Evangelii Nuntiandi*, No. 60; Apostolic Exhortation of Paul VI) which is not subject to the discretionary power of individualistic criteria and perspectives but to that of communion with the Church and her pastors."

Respect for the Magisterium: "How could there be authentic evangelizing if there were not ready and sincere reverence for the sacred magisterium, in clear awareness that by submitting to it the people of God are not accepting the word of men but the true word of God? The objective importance of this magisterium must always be kept in mind and also safeguarded, because of the attacks being leveled nowadays in various quarters against certain truths of the Catholic faith."

The Church and the Kingdom of God: "A certain uneasiness is at times noticed with regard to the very interpretation of the nature and mission of the Church. Allusion is made, for instance, to the separation that some set up between the Church and the kingdom of God. The kingdom of God is emptied of its full content and is understood in a rather secularist sense. It is interpreted as being reached not by faith and membership in the Church, but by the mere changing of structures and social and political involvement, and as being present wherever there is a certain type of involvement and activity for justice. This is to forget that 'the Church receives the mission to proclaim and to establish among all peoples the kingdom of Christ and of God. She becomes on earth the seed and beginning of that kingdom' " (*Dogmatic Constitution on the Church,* No. 5; Second Vatican Council).

Secular Liberation Not Identical with Salvation: "Pope John Paul I . . . warned that 'it is wrong to state that political, economic and social liberation coincide with salvation in Jesus Christ, that the kingdom of God is identified with the kingdom of man.' "

Foundation of Social Teaching: "Thanks to the Gospel, the Church has the truth about man . . . found in an anthropology that the Church never ceases to fathom more thoroughly and to communicate to others. The primordial affirmation of this anthropology is that man is God's image and cannot be reduced to a mere portion of nature or a nameless element in the human city."

"The Church has the right and the duty to proclaim the truth about man that she has received from her teacher, Jesus Christ."

"This complete truth about the human being constitutes the foundation of the Church's social teaching and the basis also of true liberation. In the light of this truth, man is not a being subjected to economic or political processes; these processes are, instead, directed to man and are subjected to him."

Service of Unity: The bishops' "pastoral service of truth is completed by a like service of unity" among themselves and between themselves, priests, religious and lay persons.

The Church and Human Rights: Human "dignity is infringed on the individual level when due regard is lacking for values such as freedom, the right to profess one's religion, physical and mental integrity, the right to essential goods and to life. . . . It is infringed on the social and political levels when man cannot exercise his right of participation, or is subjected to unjust and unlawful coercion, or is submitted to physical or mental torture. . . ."

"If the Church makes herself present in the defense or in the advancement of man, she does so in line with her mission which, although it is religious and not social or political, cannot fail to consider man in the entirety of his being."

The Church's " 'evangelizing mission has as an essential part action for justice and the tasks of the advancement of man' " (*Evangelii Nuntiandi,* No. 31).

"The Church's action in earthly matters . . . is always intended to be at the service of man . . . as she sees him in the Christian vision of the anthropology that she adopts."

Evangelical Commitment to Liberation: "She therefore does not need to have recourse to ideological systems in order to love, defend and collaborate in the liberation of man. At the center of the message of which she is the depository and herald, she finds inspiration for acting in favor of brotherhood, justice and peace, against all forms of domination, slavery, discrimination, violence, attacks on religious liberty, aggression against man, and whatever attacks life."

"It is . . . not through opportunism nor thirst for novelty that the Church . . . defends human rights. It is through a true evangelical commitment which . . is a commitment to the most needy. In fidelity to this commitment, the Church wishes to stay free with regard to the competing systems, in order to opt only for man."

Violence Not the Way: "Whatever the miseries or sufferings that afflict man, it is not through violence . . . but through the truth concerning man that he journeys toward a better future."

Private Property and Social Obligation: "The Church's teaching, according to which all private property involves a social obligation, (has) an urgent character," and the Church has a mission to teach and form consciences concerning this obligation. "In this way she will be working in favor of society, within which this Christian and evangelical principle will finally bear the fruit of a more just and equitable distribution of goods, not only within each nation but also in the world in general, ensuring that the stronger countries do not use their power to the detriment of the weaker ones."

Justice the Basis of Peace: "Internal and international peace can only be ensured if a social and economic system based on justice flourishes."

"It is necessary in international life to call upon ethical principles, the demands of justice, the primary commandment of which is that of love. Primacy must be given to what is moral, to what is spiritual, to what springs from the full truth concerning man."

The Pope listed a series of contemporary violations of human rights in national and international situations, and called for evangelization "so that the Lord may transform hearts and humanize political and economic systems, with man's responsible commitment as the starting point."

Integral Liberation: "Pastoral commitments in this field must be encouraged through a correct Christian idea of liberation . . . in its integral and profound meaning, as Jesus proclaimed and realized it.

• "Liberation from everything that oppresses man but which, above all, is liberation from sin and the Evil One, in the joy of knowing God and being known by him.

• "Liberation made up of reconciliation and forgiveness.

• "Liberation springing from the reality of being children of God . . . , a reality which makes us recognize in every man a brother of ours, capable of being transformed in his heart through God's mercy.

- "Liberation that, with the energy of love, urges us toward fellowship, the summit and fullness of which we find in the Lord.
- "Liberation as the overcoming of the various forms of slavery and man-made idols, and as the growth of the new man.
- "Liberation that, in the framework of the Church's proper mission, is not reduced to the simple and narrow economic, political, social or cultural dimension, and is not sacrificed to the demands of any strategy, practice or short-term solution."

"To safeguard the originality of Christian liberation and the energies that it is capable of releasing, one must at all costs avoid any form of curtailment or ambiguity."

Liberation Content and Attitudes: "There are many signs that help to distinguish when the liberation in question is Christian and when, on the other hand, it is based rather on ideologies that rob it of consistency with an evangelical view of man, of things and events. They are signs drawn from the content of what the evangelizers proclaim or from the concrete attitudes that they adopt.

"At the level of content, one must see what is their fidelity to the word of God, to the Church's living tradition and to her magisterium.

"As for attitudes, one must consider what sense of communion they have with the bishops, in the first place, and with the other sectors of the people of God; what contribution they make to the real building up of the community; in what form they lovingly care for the poor, the sick, the dispossessed, the neglected and the oppressed; and in what way they find in them the image of the poor and suffering Jesus, and strive to relieve their need and serve Christ in them."

"Placing responsible confidence in this social doctrine (of the Church) is the guarantee, in a member of the Church, of his commitment in the delicate and demanding social tasks and of his efforts in favor of the liberation or advancement of his brothers and sisters."

Three Priorities: Before concluding his address, the Pope noted that the bishops would "consider many pastoral themes of great significance" during their meeting. He mentioned three of particular importance: ministry to the family, ministry to youth, and the need for developing vocations to the priesthood and religious life.

He ended with a prayer for the intercession of Our Lady of Guadalupe, that she might obtain for the bishops:

"the boldness of prophets and the evangelical prudence of pastors;

"the clearsightedness of teachers and the reliability of guides and directors;

"courage as witnesses, and the calmness, patience and gentleness of fathers."

THE FAMILY

The importance of ministry to families in Latin America, noted by the bishops at their general assembly in 1968 at Medellin, was emphasized by the Pope in a homily preached during a Mass celebrated Jan. 28 outdoors at the Palafox Seminary, Puebla.

He said that such ministry "appears today even more urgent" because of threats to family life posed by divorce legislation, abortion, "depressing rates of disease, poverty and misery, ignorance and illiteracy, inhuman housing conditions, chronic undernourishment, and so many other sorrowful realities."

He stated that "the Church commits herself to give her help" in overcoming these evils, and called on governments and other organizations to make an "intelligent, daring and persevering" family policy a key part of their activities.

"In this, undoubtedly," he said, "is found the future — the hope — of the continent."

RURAL POOR

Address to a throng of Indian peasant farmers Jan. 29, at Cuilapan, State of Oaxaca.

The Pope spoke of the rights of rural workers and people to respect for their dignity, to effective help and "access to development," and the need for measures to protect them from deprivation and the destructiveness of "barriers of exploitation."

He noted the necessity of "bold transformations" and "urgent agricultural reforms." In connection with reforms, he said the Church defends "the legitimate right to private property, but it teaches with no less clarity that, above all, private property carries with it a social obligation, so that material possessions may serve the general goal that God intended. And, if the common good requires it, there must be no doubt about expropriation itself, carried out in the proper manner."

It is "not just, it is not human, it is not Christian for certain clearly unjust situations (of rural life) to continue."

In conclusion, the Pope called on the farmers to "work to improve your human life. But don't stop there. Make yourselves ever more worthy morally and religiously."

WORK AND JUSTICE

Address delivered Jan. 30 at Jalisco Stadium, Guadalajara.

"Work is not a burden but a blessing of God which calls man to subdue the earth and to transform it" for the continuation of "his creative divine work."

"Work should be not just a necessity but a true vocation, the call of God to build a new world in which justice and brotherhood flourish as a foretaste of the kingdom of God in which there are no deprivations or limitations."

"Work should be the means through which all creation is made subject to the dignity of the human person as a son of God."

Referring to justice, the Pope said: "For the Christian, it is not enough to denounce injustice. He must be the witness and agent of justice. The worker has rights which he should defend legally; but he also has duties which he ought to accomplish with generosity. As Christians, you are called to be the builders of justice and true liberty because you are the forgers of social justice."

PAPAL VISIT TO POLAND

Following is a log of the principal events of Pope John Paul's visit to Poland June 2 to 10, 1979, during which he became the first Pope to travel to Eastern Europe, the first to enter a Communist nation, and the first to return to his homeland in more than 600 years.

The occasion for the visit was the celebration of the 900th anniversary of the murder of St. Stanislaus, patron of Poland, by King Boleslaus the Bold in 1079.

The visit was pastoral in intent. In meetings and addresses, the Holy Father emphasized the Catholic heritage and culture of Poland, stressing the significance of faith in the past and present. Political overtones were unavoidable in his numerous references to the right of the Church to carry out its mission and to the responsibility of governments to respect the religious and human rights of citizens. But he made no explicit mention of either Communism or any Communist nation.

The attitude of the Polish government toward the Pope was respectful but reserved. The reception accorded him by the people was overwhelming.

JUNE 2

The Holy Father departed for Poland from Rome's Fiumicino Airport shortly after 8:00 a.m. aboard an Alitalia 727. During the two-hour flight he sent messages of greeting and peace to the heads of state in Italy, Austria, Yugoslavia and Czechoslovakia, and chatted with more than 80 journalists aboard the plane.

On deplaning at Okecie Airport, he knelt to kiss the ground of his native land before receiving the greetings of Cardinal Stefan Wyszynski, primate of Poland, and Henryk Jablonski, president of the Polish Council of State.

At the airport and wherever he went during his nine-day visit, he was cheered with unrestrained enthusiasm by thousands of people.

He was driven in a motorcade to St. John's Cathedral in Warsaw where Cardinal Wyszynski greeted him again, in the name of the bishops and people of Poland. Afterwards he made a brief stop at the shrine of the Merciful Mother of God, patroness of the city.

Early in the afternoon he exchanged greetings at the Belvedere Palace with Edward Gierek, first secretary of the Polish Communist Party, and other government officials.

Shortly before 4:00 p.m. he paused for prayer at the tomb of the Unknown Soldier in Victory Square, and then began the celebration of Mass in the square before a throng of nearly 200,000 persons.

After the conclusion of the Mass at about 7:15, he retired to the cardinal's residence where he spent the night.

JUNE 3

The Pope started the day with a morning Mass celebrated before 25,000 or more young people outside St. Anne's Church in Warsaw's Castle Square.

Later, he went by helicopter to Gniezno, the primatial see of Poland dating from the year 1000, where he celebrated Mass in the cathedral. His homily, one of the most significant of nearly 40 addresses delivered during his visit, stressed the potential implications of his role as a Slavic Pope in East-West relations and in ecumenical relations with the Orthodox.

He ended the day as he had begun, with an address to a large gathering of young people on the religious background, content and genius of Polish culture.

JUNE 4

The Holy Father left Gniezno for Czestochowa and the beginning of a three-day stay there at the Monastery of Jasna Gora and the Shrine of Our Lady of Czestochowa, the centuries-old spiritual center and capital of Poland.

He concelebrated a midday Mass with a large number of bishops at the shrine and focused his homily on the significance of the shrine and Marian devotion in Polish history. He also consecrated the people of Poland and of the entire Church to Mary, in a renewal of the consecration made by Pope Paul VI in 1966 when the nation commemorated the 1000th anniversary of its evangelization.

Late in the afternoon he met with representatives of the Diocese of Czestochowa and spoke to them about the arrival in the city of the replica of the Czestochowa icon in circulation among parishes of the country since 1957.

He addressed a gathering of medical personnel, sick and suffering people in the evening at the Monastery of Jasna Gora.

JUNE 5

The Pope celebrated an early morning Mass for a large assembly of sisters at the Czestochowa shrine. In a homily he recalled previous statements of his concerning the nature of their religious vocation, which he called "a visible sign of the Gospel for all" and a "special treasure of the Church." He urged them to make their convents "centers of prayer, meditation and dialogue" with Christ.

He attended the morning session of the 169th general assembly of Polish bishops and delivered an important address, called delicate but strong, on the role of the hierarchy in Polish history and on the responsibility of the bishops to deal with Church-state relations in the country.

After the meeting, while reciting the Angelus with the bishops and people in commemoration of the incarnation of Jesus, he called the prayer a "constant reminder to one and all of how great is the dignity of man."

During the afternoon he visited the Shrine of St. Hedwig at Trzebnica and celebrated a second Mass of the day at 5:00 p.m. for tens of thousands of people from Silesia. He prayed for unity of the family which, with its origin in the sacrament of matrimony, is "the seat of justice and love." He also prayed for the unity of Poland and for reconciliation between nations.

Late in the evening, at the Czestochowa shrine, he led the people in the "Call of Jasna Gora" prayer which is recited daily at the sanctuary: "Mary, Queen of Poland, I am close to you, I remember you, I watch." He added this comment: "We must be watchful ... and solicitous for the entire well-being of every man, because this is the task incumbent on all of us. We cannot permit the loss of what is human, Polish and Christian on this earth."

Speaking of the family on the same occasion, the Pope said:

"The family is the first and basic human community. It is a sphere of life, it is a sphere of love. The life of every society, nation and state depends on the family, on whether the family is a true sphere of life and love in their midst. Much has to be done. Indeed, everything possible has to be done to give to the family those means that it needs: means for employment, means for housing, means to support itself, care for life which has been conceived, social respect for fatherhood and motherhood, the joy given by children born into the world, the full right to education and at the same time the various types of help needed for education."

JUNE 6

The Holy Father celebrated Mass outdoors at the Pauline Fathers' Monastery of Jasna Gora before a gathering of 500,000 young people, including a large number of students for the priesthood. He reminded them all in a homily of their call to discipleship with Christ.

At an 11 o'clock Mass in Czestochowa's Holy Family Cathedral, he told a congregation of priests and men religious about the importance of their calling in the life of the Church and its members. He also paid tribute to priests who died in concentration camps during World War II.

He ended the Czestochowa phase of his visit with a Mass celebrated at 5:00 o'clock at the shrine for 300,000 workers from Silesia and Zaglebie Dabroskie, the mining and industrial heartland of Poland. They were people he had wanted, but had not been permitted, to visit in their own localities. The nature of work and its relationship to prayer were the principal themes of his homily.

The Pope left Czestochowa after Mass and flew to Cracow, the center of his activity for the balance of his time in Poland. On arrival, he went immediately to the Wawel Cathedral and addressed priests of the archdiocese where he had served as bishop and archbishop for 20 years before being elected to the papacy.

JUNE 7

The Pope went in the morning to Wadowice, where he was born, baptized and spent the first 18 years of his life. He spoke to the townsfolk in the marketplace and met briefly with a priest who had been one of his teachers.

Back in Cracow, he visited the Shrine of Kalwaria Zebrzydowska, where he spoke about the mystery of the union of Jesus and Mary.

He toured the concentration-death camps of Auschwitz I (Oswiecim) and II (Brzezinka, Birkenau), calling attention to the people of many nations, especially Jews and Poles, who died there. He called the camps, where four million people were exterminated during World War II, the "Golgotha of the modern world." He visited the hunger bunker in which Blessed Maximilian Kolbe gave his life to save that of Franciszek Gajowniczek, the father of a family marked for death. Gajowniczek later received Communion from the Pope during the Mass the Pontiff concelebrated at Auschwitz with about 200 death-camp survivors and other priests. The Mass was attended by one of the largest congregations in history.

JUNE 8

The Pope met in the morning with a group of Catholic editors and intellectuals.

Afterwards, he addressed bishops attending the concluding session of the Cracow Archdiocesan Synod which he started seven years earlier. In summarizing its proceedings, he noted its accomplishments in reviewing and renewing church structures, procedures and ministries to meet contemporary conditions and needs.

Also in Cracow, he spoke and met for two

hours with 65,000 university students.

The Holy Father journeyed to Nowy Targ, a mountain town near the southern border, to address a vast gathering and to deliver a major address on the right to work, the right to land, and the family.

JUNE 9

The Pope visited a Cracow cemetery where his parents and brother were buried and prayed quietly at their vault.

At the Shrine of the Cross of Mogila near Nowa Huta, the site of a church he started despite government opposition and which he dedicated in 1977, he addressed the theme of the dignity of human work before a large crowd. The place and occasion, as well as the Holy Father's address, were significant because of their symbolic relation to persistent refusals by the government to permit the building of badly needed new churches.

The Pope also addressed members of the Cracow Theological Faculty, with remarks about the nature and importance of their work in the training of priests.

His final address of the day was to church delegations, mostly of bishops, from about 24 countries.

JUNE 10

The Pope's final Mass in Poland was celebrated outdoors in Cracow with an estimated attendance of two million. It was the last major observance of the St. Stanislaus Jubilee, marking the murder of the Saint by King Boleslaus the Bold in 1079.

The Holy Father met and mingled with many people during his last day in Poland, and also crowned a 15th century painting of Our Lady of Makow in a final gesture of devotion in honor of the Virgin Mary.

He asked journalists who covered his activities "to tell the world, to tell the peoples of all your countries, . . . that the Pope prays for them every day, many times every day, wherever he is, and that he trusts they pray for him."

Before leaving for Rome from the Balice Airport outside Cracow, he said:

"Our times need a witness which expresses openly the will to bring nations and regimes closer to one another, as an indispensable condition for peace in the world. Our times require us not to shut ourselves up in the rigid frontiers of systems, but to seek all that is necessary for the good of man, who must find everywhere the awareness and certainty of his authentic citizenship . . . in whatever system of relationships and forces."

He left the country as he had entered it on June 2, with a kiss of the soil of his homeland.

ADDRESSES OF JOHN PAUL II IN POLAND

Following are excerpts from several of the nearly 40 addresses delivered by Pope John Paul II during his trip to Poland June 2 to 10, 1979.

The excerpts are from translations circulated by the NC Documentary Service, Origins.

PURPOSE OF HIS VISIT

Address on arrival June 2 at Okecie Airport outside Warsaw.

"My visit has been dictated by strictly religious motives. Furthermore, I earnestly hope that my present journey in Poland may serve the great cause of rapproachement and of collaboration among nations; that it may be useful for reciprocal understanding, for reconciliation and for peace in the contemporary world. I desire finally that the fruit of this visit may be the internal unity of my fellow-countrymen and also a further favorable development of the relations between the state and the Church in my beloved motherland."

"May my stay . . . help the great cause of peace, friendship in relations between nations, and social justice."

BASIS OF PEACE

Address during meeting with Polish officials June 2 at the Belvedere Palace, Warsaw.

"Peace and the drawing together of peoples can be achieved only on the principle of respect for the objective rights of the nation, such as the right to existence, to freedom to be a social and political subject, and also to the formation of its own culture and civilization."

Progress and International Order: "The social doctrine of the Church . . . always supports authentic progress and the peaceful development of humanity. Therefore, while all forms of political, economic or cultural colonialism remain in contradition to the exigencies of the international order, it is necessary to esteem all the alliances and pacts which are based on reciprocal respect and on the recognition of the good of every nation and of every state in the system of reciprocal relations. It is important that the nations and the states, uniting themselves for the aim of a voluntary collaboration and one that is in conformity with that goal, find at the same time in this collaboration the increase of their own well-being and their own prosperity. It is precisely this system of international relations and such resolutions among the states that the Apostolic See hopes for in the name of the fundamental premises of justice and peace in the contemporary world."

Church Wants Freedom To Serve: "The Church wishes to serve people . . . in the temporal dimension of their life and existence."

"By establishing a religious relationship

with people, the Church consolidates them in their natural social bonds. The history of the Church in Poland has confirmed in an eminent way that the Church in our motherland has always sought in various ways, to train sons and daughters who are of assistance to the state, good citizens and useful and creative workers in the various spheres of social, professional and cultural life. And this derives from the fundamental mission of the Church, which everywhere and always strives to make people better, more conscious of their dignity, and more devoted in their lives to their family, social, professional and patriotic commitments. It is her mission to make people more confident, more courageous, conscious of their rights and duties, socially responsible, creative and useful."

"For this activity the Church does not desire privileges, but only and exclusively what is essential for the accomplishment of her mission."

CHRIST IN HISTORY

Homily preached during Mass June 2 in Victory Square, Warsaw.

The Holy Father began with a mention of regret that the Polish government had refused to permit Paul VI to visit the country in 1966 for the celebration of the 1000th anniversary of the evangelization of Poland. He also noted that the occasion of his own visit was the commemoration of the 900th anniversary of the murder of St. Stanislaus by King Boleslaus the Bold.

Man Cannot Be Understood without Christ: "Have we not the right — in view of the ... election of a Polish Pope — to think that Poland has become nowadays the land of a particularly responsible witness to the faith?"

"To Poland the Church brought Christ, the key to understanding that great and fundamental reality that is man. For man cannot be fully understood without Christ. Or, rather, man is incapable of understanding himself fully without Christ. He cannot understand who he is, nor what his true dignity is, nor what his vocation is, nor what his final end is. He cannot understand any of this without Christ."

Christ Cannot Be Kept out of History: "Therefore, Christ cannot be kept out of the history of man in any part of the globe. ... The history of the nation is, above all, the history of people. And the history of each person unfolds in Jesus Christ. In him it becomes the history of salvation."

"It is ... impossible without Christ to understand the history of the Polish nation ... If we reject this key to understanding our nation, we lay ourselves open to a substantial misunderstanding. We no longer understand ourselves. It is impossible without Christ to understand this nation with its past, so full of splendor and also of terrible difficulties."

FIRST SLAVIC POPE

Homily preached during Mass June 3 in the cathedral at Gniezno.

The Pope speculated about the unique significance of his role as the first Slavic Pontiff, in the context of the history of the Church and the religious history of Slavic peoples (Poles, Croats, Slovenes, Bulgarians, Moravians, Slovaks, Czechs, Serbs and Lithuanians) who were evangelized between 650 and 1387.

His Role: "Is it not Christ's will, is it not what the Holy Spirit disposes, that this Pope, in whose heart is deeply engraved the history of his own nation from its very beginning and also the history of the brother peoples and the neighboring peoples, should in a special way manifest and confirm in our age the presence of these peoples in the Church and their specific contribution to the history of Christianity?"

"Is it not the design of Providence that he should reveal the developments that have taken place here in this part of Europe. . . .

"Is it not Christ's will, is it not what the Holy Spirit disposes, that this Polish Pope, this Slav Pope, should at this precise moment manifest the spiritual unity of Christian Europe? Although there are two great traditions, that of the West and that of the East, to which it is indebted, through both of them Christian Europe professes 'one faith, one baptism, one God and Father of us all' (Eph. 4:5-6), the Father of our Lord Jesus Christ."

Witness to Christ: "This Pope ... today comes to this place to give witness to Christ, ... who is living in the souls of the nations that have long since accepted him as "the way, and the truth, and life" (Jn. 14:6). He comes here to speak before the whole Church, before Europe and the world, of those often forgotten nations and peoples. . . . He comes here to point out the paths that in one way or another lead back toward the Pentecost upper room, toward the cross and resurrection. He comes here to embrace all these peoples, together with his own nation, and to hold them close to the heart of the Church, to the heart of the Mother of the Church in whom he has unlimited trust."

TRADITION OF JASNA GORA

Homily preached during Mass June 4 at the Shrine of Our Lady of Czestochowa.

The Nation's Shrine: "The image of Jasna Gora expresses a tradition and a language of faith."

"The Virgin of Jasna Gora has revealed her maternal solicitude for every soul; for every family; for every human being living in this land, working here, fighting and falling on the battlefield, condemned to extermination, fighting against himself, winning or losing; for every human being who must leave the soil of his motherland and emigrate; for every human being."

"The Poles are accustomed to link with this place, this shrine, the many happenings of their lives."

"Jasna Gora has shown itself an inward bond in Polish life, a force that touches the depths of our hearts and holds the entire nation in the humble yet strong attitude of fidelity to God, to the Church and to her hierarchy."

"Jasna Gora is, in fact, not only a place of pilgrimage for the Poles of their motherland and of the whole world, but (is) also the nation's shrine. ... If we want to know how (their) history is interpreted by the heart of the Poles, we must come here, we must listen to this shrine, we must hear the echo of the life of the whole nation in the heart of its Mother and Queen. And, if her heart beats with a tone of disquiet, if it echoes with solicitude and the cry for the conversion and strengthening of consciences, this invitation must be accepted. It is an invitation springing from maternal love, which in its own way is shaping the historical processes in the land of wpoland."

Consecration of the Church to Mary: "I entrust to you, Mother of the Church, all the problems of this Church, the whole of her mission and of her service."

"Help us in the great endeavor that we are carrying out to meet in a more and more mature way our brothers in faith, with whom so many things unite us, although there is still something dividing us."

"Allow us in the future to go out to meet all human beings and all peoples who seek God and wish to serve him by means of the different religions. Help us all to proclaim Christ."

"Show us always how we are to serve the individual and humanity in every nation, how we are to lead them along the ways of salvation, how we are to protect justice and peace."

"Grant that the Church may enjoy freedom and peace in fulfilling her saving mission and that, to this end, she may become mature with a new maturity of faith and inner unity."

ADDRESS TO BISHOPS

Address delivered June 5 at the opening meeting of the 169th general assembly of Polish bishops.

The Church in Polish History: "The Church ... is the visible reality of a clearly defined hierarchical order. This order determines the Church as a well defined community and society which, through its own hierarchical order, forms part of the history of humanity, of the history of the individual peoples and nations."

"When national and state structures were lacking (in Poland), society, for the most part Catholic, found support in the hierarchical order of the Church. And this helped society to overcome the times of the partition of the country and the times of occupation; it helped society to maintain, and even to deepen, its understanding and awareness of its own identity."

"The Church in Poland is rooted in its catholicity. ..." "The Church has a meaning for the nation's culture, which is marked not only by the tradition of visible links with Rome, but also possesses the characteristic of universality proper to Catholicism and the characteristic of openness to everything which in the universal exchange of good things becomes the portion of each of those who take part in it."

"The Polish episcopate, in close collaboration with the Apostolic See, especially during the pontificates of John XXIII and Paul VI, did a great deal for (Church-state) normalization."

Bishops To Work for Church-State Normalization: "The Polish episcopate has its own expereinces in this important field. Basing itself on the teaching of Vatican II, it has worked out a series of documents of theory, which are known to the Apostolic See, and at the same time it has worked out a series of pastoral attitudes that confirm readiness for dialogue. They clearly show that authentic dialogue must respect the convictions of believers, ensure all the rights of citizens and also the normal conditions for the activity of the Church as a religious community to which the vast majority of Poles belong. We are aware that this dialogue cannot be easy, because it takes place between two concepts of the world which are diametrically opposed; but it must be possible and effective if the good of individuals and the nation demands it. The Polish episcopate must not cease to undertake with solicitude initiatives which are important for the present-day Church. In addition, in the future there must be clarity in the principles of procedure which in the present situation have been worked out within the ecclesial community, regarding both the attitude of clergy and lay people and the status of individual institutions. Clarity of principles, as also their practical implementation is a source of moral strength and also serves the process of a true normalization."

AT AUSCHWITZ

Homily preached during a Mass June 7 at the site of the Auschwitz concentration camps.

The Holy Father called Auschwitz "a place built on hatred and contempt for man in the name of a crazed ideology. A place built on cruelty ... this Golgotha of the modern world."

"Oswiecim is a testimony of war. War brings with it a disproportionate growth of hatred, destruction and cruelty. It cannot be denied that it also manifests new capabilities of human courage, heroism and patriotism, but the fact remains that it is the reckoning of the losses that prevails. That reckoning prevails more and more, since each day sees an increase in the destructive capacity of the weapons invented by modern technology. Not only those who directly bring wars about are responsible for them, but also those who fail to do all they can to prevent them."

RIGHT TO WORK AND LAND

Address delivered June 8 at Nowy Targ.

"This is the great and fundamental right of man: the right to work and the right to land. Although the development of the economy may take us in another direction, although progress may be evaluated on the basis of industrialization, although today's generation may leave en masse the countryside and the work of the fields, nevertheless the right to land does not cease to constitute the basis of a sound economy and sociology."

"I wish . . . that the personal link with the land may not cease . . . even in our industrialized generation."

Family Vocation: "The Creator gave the earth to man so that he 'might subdue' it — and on this dominion of man over the earth he based the fundamental right of man to life. This right is closely linked to the vocation of man to the family and to procreation. . . . This union in love of two persons — man and woman — becomes fruitful in a new human life. The Creator made this vivifying unity of persons the first sacrament, and the Redeemer confirmed this perennial sacrament of love and of life, giving it a new dignity and impressing upon it the seal of his sanctity. The right of man to life is joined, through the will of the Creator and by virtue of the cross of Christ, to the indissoluble sacrament of matrimony."

Respect for Life: "The family is the fundamental cell of social life. It is the fundamental human community. Such as the family is, so is the nation — because so is man. . . . I always pray for this, that the Polish family may generate life and be faithful to the sacred right to life. If the right of man to life is infringed in the moment in which he begins to be conceived in the maternal womb, a blow is struck at the whole moral order which serves to insure man's inviolable goods. Life occupies the first place among these. The Church defends the right to life, not only out of regard for the majesty of the Creator . . . but also through respect for the essential good of man."

TASK OF THE CHURCH

Address delivered June 9 at a meeting in Cracow with members of church delegations from about 24 nations.

"I desire to wish . . . that this, our common meditation on the events which took place 900 years ago (connected with the murder of St. Stanislaus) may help us to see with even greater clarity the mission of Christianity and of the Church in their relationship to the modern world. Perhaps this has a particular importance for the Europe of today that finds herself at a point of new searching for her distinctive and suitable path."

"The task of Christianity and of the Church cannot be other than a creative participation in these efforts. Only in this way, and in no other, can there be expressed and actuated our solicitude for the preservation and defense of the Christian patrimony of the individual European countries."

DIALOGUE OF SALVATION

Homily preached during Mass June 10 in Cracow.

The Holy Father reviewed salient events and factors in the Catholic history of Poland, and said that the country's Christian tradition "is not a limiting factor (on freedom) but a treasure, a spiritual enrichment" which cannot be cast off because it "has always constituted the basis of our identity."

"You must be strong with the strength of faith, hope and charity, a charity that is aware, mature and responsible, and which helps us to set up the great dialogue with man and the world rooted in the dialogue with God himself, . . . the dialogue of salvation."

"We must work for peace and reconciliation between the people and the nations of the whole world. We must try to come close to one another. We must open the frontiers. When we are strong with the spirit of God, we are also strong with faith in man, strong with faith, hope and charity which are inseparable, and ready to give witness to the cause of man. . . . There is no imperialism in the Church, only service. There is only the death of Christ on Calvary. There is the activity of the Holy Spirit, the fruit of that death, the Holy Spirit who is always with all of us, with the whole of mankind, 'until the end of the world' (Mt. 28:30)."

ST. STANISLAUS

St. Stanislaus, patron of Poland, was born July 26, 1030, at Szczepanow. Well educated and ordained a priest, he became bishop of Cracow in 1072. Before long, he was in conflict with Boleslaus II the Bold (Daring), a ruler known for his cruelty and scandalous personal morals. The saint apparently got involved not only in efforts to influence Boleslaus to change his ways but also in political opposition to the injustices of his regime. His excommunication of the sovereign was the prelude to his death, while celebrating Mass in a chapel dedicated to St. Michael, at the hands of Boleslaus. The saint was canonized in 1253.

PAPAL VISIT TO IRELAND AND THE UNITED STATES

Following is an account of the principal events of Pope John Paul's pastoral visit to Ireland and the United States Sept. 29 to Oct. 8, 1979. The visit was made at the invitation of the respective bishops, United Nations Secretary General Kurt Waldheim, and President Jimmy Carter.

The Holy Father traveled 11,200 air miles during the trip, visited 12 major cities and delivered more than 70 addresses at assemblies for Masses and other occasions. He was warmly greeted and enthusiastically cheered by millions of people who saw him "live" or followed his round of activities in blanket coverage by the print and electronic media.

SEPTEMBER 29

Pope John Paul departed at about 8:00 a.m. from the Leonardo da Vinci Airport at Fiumicino aboard the Aer Lingus 747 "St. Patrick" for the start of his third major pastoral pilgrimage of the year, to Ireland and the United States.

En route, he sent messages of greeting to the presidents of Italy, Switzerland and France, and to Queen Elizabeth II of England.

On alighting from the plane at Dublin's Shannon Airport, he kissed the ground and was warmly greeted by a cheering crowd of 20,000 persons headed by officials of the Irish Republic and the Church. During brief welcoming ceremonies, he said he felt "the need to express my esteem for the Christian traditions of this land, as well as the gratitude of the Catholic Church for the glorious contribution made by Ireland over the centuries to the spreading of the faith."

The Holy Father celebrated Mass early in the afternoon in Dublin's 1,760-acre Phoenix Park before a throng of 1.2 million people. In his homily he proposed Eucharistic devotion in combination with corresponding action in daily life as the antidote to encroaching materialism in Ireland.

Peace, coupled with a passionate plea for an end to violence in Northern Ireland, was the theme of an address he delivered late in the afternoon during a Liturgy of the Word at Drogheda, some 30 miles south of the border of the beleaguered northern counties. The site was within the territory of the primatial See of Armagh established by St. Patrick. Enshrined at the altar from which the Pope spoke to the gaterhing of 250,000 people was a relic of St. Oliver Plunkett, a bishop of Armagh who was martyred for the faith in 1681.

Back in Dublin, the Pope met and spoke with the president of Ireland and members of the government and diplomatic corps. The need for united Christian service in the cause of peace was the theme of his address to a gathering of bishops and other leaders of the Anglican Church of Ireland, the Presbyterian Church, and additional representatives of the Irish Council of Churches. He told journalists about the service potential of their profession. He reminded visiting Catholic bishops of the debt of gratitude they owed Irish missionaries of the past for establishing the Church in their respective countries.

The Pope spent the nights of Sept. 29 and 30 at the residence of the apostolic nuncio in Dublin.

SEPTEMBER 30

The Pope began the day with two meetings — with handicapped persons at Cabra, the Dominican convent in Dublin, and with a group of Poles, mostly from England, at the nunciature.

Later in the morning, he celebrated Mass for a throng of 250,000 young people at the Ballybrit Racecourse in Galway. He said in a homily that he believed in them and saw in them the future of Ireland and the Church. With awareness of the problems and challenges facing them, he urged them to follow Christ in quest of the full measure of their redeemed humanity.

With 200 priests, he concelebrated a second outdoor Mass in the afternoon at the 100-year-old Shrine of Our Lady of Knock, where he consecrated the people of Ireland to Mary after calling on his hearers to follow her advice by doing what her Son wants done in the conduct of everyday life for the accomplishment of his will.

In the evening, he met and dined at the Dominican convent with the bishops of Ireland. He spoke about their duties as pastors, with special reference to their commitment to their priests, the constant proclamation of the word of God, the development of lay participation in evangelization, and their presence with the people in trials and suffering. He urged them to extend every possible effort for peace in Northern Ireland, noting with some regret that he had not got any closer to the troubled area than Drogheda the day before.

OCTOBER 1

The Holy Father flew to Maynooth for a meeting at St. Patrick's College with priests, men and women religious, seminarians and university students. He said in the course of an address: "This is a wonderful time in the history of the Church. This is a wonderful time to be a priest, to be a religious, to be a missionary for Christ."

The dignity and mission of lay persons, with related reverence for marriage and the family, were the subjects of the Pope's homily at a late morning Mass in Limerick, the last stop of the Irish phase of his trip.

During the 50-odd hours of his stay in Ireland, the Pope was seen by about 2.5 million people, more than half of the Irish population, at Masses and in motorcades and other appearances. Millions more throughout the world saw and heard him via television and radio exhort the predominantly Catholic population to firm adherence to their heritage of faith, and to efforts for an end to violence in the North.

"St. Patrick" flew the Pope from Shannon to Logan International Airport, Boston, where he arrived shortly before 3:00 p.m., EDT. He was formally welcomed by Mrs. Rosalynn Carter, on behalf of the President and people of the United States, a number of bishops and an invited assembly of 400 persons. In reply to Mrs. Carter, who greeted him "not as a stranger," the Pope said: "America, America, God shed his grace on thee, And crown thy good with brotherhood from sea to shining sea."

The Holy Father was driven in a motorcade to Boston's Holy Cross Cathedral where he spoke to a welcoming gathering of bishops, priests, religious and lay persons.

He celebrated Mass on the crowded, rain-drenched Boston Common at about 5:00 p.m. and delivered a homily addressed primarily to young people, whom he urged to exercise an "option of love" that will reflect the love of Christ in their lives.

He spent the night at the residence of Cardinal Humberto Medeiros.

OCTOBER 2

Pope John Paul left Boston for New York at about 8:00 a.m. aboard TWA's "Shepherd I" and arrived at 9:15 at LaGuardia Airport where he was greeted by United Nations Secretary General Kurt Waldheim and other officials of the world body.

At U.N. headquarters, he delivered a major address on peace, justice and human rights keyed to the central theme of individual, human dignity.

After the hour-long address, the Pope met and spoke with U.N. delegates and staff members, representatives of non-governmental organizations, diplomats and journalists.

St. Patrick's Cathedral was the next stop, for prayer and an exchange of greetings with Cardinal Terence Cooke before a gathering that included city, state and federal officials, as well as Greek Orthodox Archbishop Iakovos, Dr. Claire Randall, general secretary of the National Council of Churches, and Rabbi Marc Tanenbaum of the American Jewish Committee.

En route to Yankee Stadium by motorcade for an evening Mass, the Pope stopped and spoke briefly at St. Charles Borromeo Church in Harlem and in a Hispanic neighborhood in the South Bronx.

Eighty thousand people greeted him with tremendous enthusiasm at the stadium. He addressed them in a homily which stressed the responsibility of those who have more to provide from their substance for those who have less, and even nothing.

The Pope spent the night at the residence of Cardinal Cooke.

OCTOBER 3

The Holy Father started the day with two quite different meetings.

The first was a reverential, but cheering, prayer service in St. Patrick's Cathedral with priests, religious and seminarians. The significance of the Liturgy of the Hours was the theme of his brief address.

The second meeting was an unabashedly enthusiastic encounter with some 19,000 students of Catholic and public schools in Madison Square Garden. He asked them, between their singing and cheering, to accept their responsibility in the Church to spread the Gospel.

More enthusiasm greeted the Pope as his motorcade made its way through one of downtown Manhattan's greatest ticker-tape parades to Battery Park. There, with the Statue of Liberty and Ellis Island behind him across the bay, he spoke of liberty and appealed "to all who love freedom and justice to give a chance to all in need, to the poor and the powerless."

Leaving the Battery, the Pope's motorcade passed through Brooklyn on the way to Shea Stadium. The only stop en route was at St. James Cathedral where he greeted a waiting group of Polish children and adults.

At Shea Stadium, the last stop on his New York itinerary, the Pope asked 50,000 or more rain-soaked people to give New York a soul by accepting and discharging responsibility for their community.

He left LaGuardia Airport behind schedule and arrived near mid-afternoon in Philadelphia. He was driven through the southern part of the city to a welcoming assembly of people headed by a personal friend, Cardinal John J. Krol, at the Cathedral of Sts. Peter and Paul.

Nearby Logan Square, at a midpoint of the city's picturesque parkway, was the site of a Mass celebrated before a throng of 1.2 million people. The Pope spoke of human-Christian values in his homily, reaffirming traditional, doctrine concerning freedom — in the city with the Liberty Bell — and sexual morality.

At the Archdiocesan Seminary of St. Charles Borromeo late in the evening, he addressed 180 students for the priesthood and others on the subjects of studies, seminary discipline, the fidelity and celibacy of priests.

He spent the night at the cardinal's residence.

OCTOBER 4

The Pope's first visit of the day was to the Church of St. Peter, with its tomb of St. John

Neumann, the fourth bishop of Philadelphia who was canonized in 1977.

Next, he greeted a congregation at the Ukrainian Cathedral of the Immaculate Conception, where he spoke about the unity of the Church and the diversity of its people in rites and customs.

At the Civic Center with 17,000 priests, seminarians and nuns, the Pope concelebrated Mass with representatives of priests' senates and councils from all U.S. dioceses. Essentials of the priesthood were the topics of his homily — their calling, discipline and ministry (as stated in other addresses and summarized in his letter of the previous Holy Thursday to priests throughout the world).

The Holy Father left Philadelphia at 12:25 p.m. on a flight to Des Moines, Iowa, en route to the Irish Settlement in nearby Cumming. He met there with 200 or more parishioners of St. Patrick's Church in the least crowded and simplest of his many encounters in the U.S. One of those who greeted him was Joseph A. Hays, the farmer who had asked him in a handwritten invitation to visit the community during his tour.

Living History Farms, a rural life museum near Des Moines, was the Pope's next stop, for a Mass celebrated before a throng of 350,000 persons. The land and its stewardship were the themes of his homily.

The Pope was in the air again shortly after the Mass, and an hour later completed the third of his major touch-downs of the day at O'Hare International Airport, Chicago. He was cheered by thousands during the drive into the city.

In the evening of the feast of St. Francis of Assisi, he visited the Franciscan community at St. Peter's Friary in The Loop, where he talked about the main features of religious life and the service of religious to the Church.

The last stop of the busy day was at Chicago's Holy Name Cathedral, for brief ceremonial greetings.

The Pope spent this and the next night at the residence of Cardinal John P. Cody.

OCTOBER 5

The Pope made an early morning visit to the Pilsen section of the city where he addressed a large gathering of Hispanics and praised the Campaign for Human Development for its work in assisting self-help projects in the area. Next, he celebrated Mass for members of Chicago's large Polish community at the Church of the Five Holy Martyrs in Brighton Park.

Afterwards, he addressed an extraordinary, closed meeting of the National Conference of Catholic Bishops at Quigley South Seminary. He called attention in a straightforward address to doctrinal and moral positions firmly held by the teaching authority of the Church and stated by the bishops themselves, despite controversy raised about them among some Catholics. He emphasized the primary concern of the Second Vatican Council about the effective safeguarding and teaching of Christian doctrine.

In the afternoon, the Pope concelebrated Mass with more than 300 bishops in crowded Grant Park. The leading idea of his homily was unity in the Church.

He was the guest of honor at an evening concert by the Chicago Symphony Orchestra.

OCTOBER 6

The Holy Father boarded "Shepherd I" at about 8:00 a.m. for a flight to Andrews Air Force Base in Virginia. He was greeted there by Mrs. Carter, Vice President Walter Mondale and Secretary of State Cyrus Vance.

He celebrated Mass at St. Matthew's Cathedral in Washington and urged a congregation of more than 1,400 priests, deacons and members of the Archdiocesan Pastoral Council "to look to Mary as the model of the Church, as the best example of the discipleship of Christ."

In the afternoon, the Holy Father was the guest of honor at two White House lawn receptions tendered by President Center and attended by 7,500 persons, including members of the Cabinet, Congress, the Supreme Court and diplomatic corps. In between, he met privately for an hour with the President in the Oval Office.

The President called the papal visit "a milestone in the long intertwined history of our country and its faith in God." Pope John Paul said he hoped the meeting "would serve the cause of world peace, international understanding and the promotion of full respect for human rights everywhere."

Afterwards, the Pope visited the headquarters of the Organization of American States, where he met with and spoke to 8,000 Hispanic and Anglo representatives of 28 nations in the Western Hemisphere.

Later in the evening, he attended a reception of the diplomatic corps at the apostolic delegation.

OCTOBER 7

The Holy Father began his last day in the United States at a prayer service with 7,000 sisters at the National Shrine of the Immaculate Conception.

Introductory remarks by Sister of Mercy Theresa Kane, president of the Leadership Conference of Women Religious, included the statement: "Our contemplation leads us to state that the Church in its struggle to be faithful to its call for reverence and dignity for all persons must respond by providing the possibility of women as persons being included in all ministries of the Church."

The Pope confined his address to the relation of the nuns to the role of Mary and to their consecrated service in the Church, without calling attention again to the position of the Church, stated by himself only three days before, against the ordination of women to the priesthood.

The Pope addressed subjects related to theology and the nature and character of Catholic education at a gathering at the Catholic University fieldhouse. He also spoke to 200 representatives of other Christian churches at the chapel of Trinity College, where he had his last meeting in the U.S. with a group of handicapped persons.

The last public event of the pastoral tour of the country was a Mass celebrated on the Washington Mall, between the Capitol and the Washington Monument, before a throng of 175,000 persons. In line with the basic human-dignity premise of most of his talks in this country, the thrust of his final homily was respect for life at all stages.

The Holy Father departed from Andrews Air Force Base shortly before 9:00 p.m., with the prayer: "That God will bless America so that she may increasingly become — and truly be — and long remain — 'One nation, under God, with liberty and justice for all.' "

"Shepherd I" touched down Oct. 8 at 9:21 a.m., Rome time, at Fiumicino.

ADDRESSES OF JOHN PAUL II IN IRELAND

Following are excerpts from several of the addresses delivered by Pope John Paul II during his pastoral visit to Ireland Sept. 29 to Oct. 1, 1979.

The excerpts are from texts circulated by the NC Documentary Service, Origins.

EUCHARIST VS MATERIALISM

Homily delivered Sept. 29 during Mass at Phoenix Park, Dublin.

Materialism: "Pervading materialism imposes its dominion on man today in many different forms and with an aggressiveness that spares no one. The most sacred principles, which were the sure guides for the behavior of individuals and society, are being hollowed out by false pretences concerning freedom, the sacredness of life, the indissolubility of marriage, the true sense of human sexuality, the right attitude towards the material goods that progress has to offer. Many people now are tempted to self-indulgence and consumerism, and human identity is often defined by what one owns."

The Eucharist: "And so, it becomes all the more urgent to steep ourselves in the truth that comes from Christ, 'who is the way, the truth and the life' (Jn. 14:6), and in the strength that he himself offers us through his spirit. It is especially in the Eucharist that the power and the love of the Lord are given to us."

"There must always be consistency between what we believe and what we do. We cannot live on the glories of our past Christian history. Our union with Christ in the Eucharist must be expressed in the truth of our lives today — in our actions, in our behavior, in our lifestyle, and in our relationships with others. . . . The truth of our union with Jesus Christ in the Eucharist is tested by whether or not we really love our fellow men and women; it is tested by how we treat others; especially our families: husbands and wives, children and parents, brothers and sisters. It is tested by whether or not we try to be reconciled with our enemies, on whether or not we forgive those who hurt us or offend us. It is tested by whether we practice in life what our faith teaches us. We must always remember what Jesus said: 'You are my friends if you do what I command you' (Jn. 15:14)."

"The Eucharist transforms our lives."

PLEA AGAINST VIOLENCE

Address delivered Sept. 29 during a Liturgy of the Word at Drogheda.

Not a Religious War: "The tragic events taking place in Northern Ireland do not have their source in the fact of belonging to different churches and confessions; that this is not — despite what is so often repeated before world opinion — a religious war, a struggle between Catholics and Protestants. On the contrary, Catholics and Protestants, as people who confess Christ, taking inspiration from their faith and the Gospel, are seeking to draw closer to one another in unity and peace. When they recall the greatest commandment of Christ, the commandment of love, they cannot behave otherwise."

Human Rights Are Primary: "Every human being has inalienable rights that must be respected. Each human community — ethnic, historical, cultural or religious — has rights which must be respected. Peace is threatened every time one of these rights is violated. The moral law, guardian of human rights, protector of the dignity of man, cannot be set aside by any person or group, or by the state itself, for any cause, not even for security or in the interests of law and order. The law of God stands in judgment over all reasons of state. As long as injustices exist in any of the areas that touch upon the dignity of the human person, be it in the political, social or economic field, be it in the cultural or religious sphere, true peace will not exist."

No Peace by Violence: "Violence is unacceptable as a solution to problems . . . violence is unworthy of man. Violence is a lie, for it goes against the truth of our faith, the truth of our humanity. Violence destroys what it claims to defend: the dignity, the life, the freedom of human beings. Violence is a crime against humanity, for it destroys the very fabric of society. I pray with you that the moral sense and Christian conviction of Irish men and women may never become obscured and blunted by the lie of violence, that nobody may ever call murder by any other name than murder, that the spiral of violence may never be given the distinction of unavoidable logic or necessary retaliation."

YOUNG PEOPLE

Homily delivered Sept. 30 during a Mass attended by young people at the Ballybrit Racecourse, Galway.

Anti-Christian Trends and Influence: "You, like other young people of your age in other countries, are affected by what is happening in society around you. Although you still live in an atmosphere where true religious and moral principles are held in honor, you have to realize that your fidelity to these principles will be tested in many ways."

"The lure of pleasure, to be had whenever and wherever it can be found, will be strong and it may be presented to you as part of progress towards greater autonomy and freedom from rules. The desire to be free from external restraints may manifest itself very strongly in the sexual domain, since this is an area that is so closely tied to a human personality. The moral standards that the Church and society have held up to you for so long a time will be presented as obsolete and a hindrance to the full development of your own personality. Mass media, entertainment and literature will present a model for living where all too often it is every man for himself, and where the unrestrained affirmation of self leaves no room for concern for others.

"You will hear people tell you that your religious practices are hopelessly out of date; that they hamper your style and your future; that, with everything that social and scientific progress has to offer, you will be able to organize your own lives, and that God has played out his role. Even many religious persons will adopt such attitudes, breathing them in from the surrounding atmosphere, without attending to the practical atheism that is at their origin."

"Do not close your eyes to the moral sickness that stalks your society today, and from which your youth alone will not protect you. How many young people have already warped their consciences and have substituted the true joy of life with drugs, sex, alcohol, vandalism and the empty pursuit of mere material possessions."

Christ Has the Key: "Something else is needed: something that you will find only in Christ, for he alone is the measure and the scale that you must use to evaluate your own life. In Christ you will discover the true greatness of your own humanity; he will make you understand your own dignity as human beings 'created to the image and likeness of God' (Gn. 1:26). Christ has the answers to your questions and the key to history; he has the power to uplift hearts. He keeps calling you, he keeps inviting you, he who is 'the way, and the truth, and the life' (Jn. 14:6). Yes, Christ calls you, but he calls you in truth. His call is demanding, because he invites you to let yourselves be 'captured' by him completely, so that your whole lives will be seen in a different light. . . . Without heeding the call of Jesus, it will not be possible to realize the fullness of your own humanity."

UNITED CHRISTIAN SERVICE

Address delivered Sept. 29 at Cabra, the Dominican Convent in Dublin, to representatives of other Christian churches in Ireland.

"Ireland . . . has special and urgent need for the united service of Christians. All Irish Christians must stand together to defend spiritual and moral values against the inroads of materialism and moral permissiveness. Christians must unite together to promote justice and defend the rights and dignity of every human person. All Christians in Ireland must join together in opposing all violence and all assaults against the human person — from whatever quarter they come — and in finding Christian answers to the grave problems of Northern Ireland. We must all be ministers of reconciliation. We must by example as well as by word try to move citizens, communities and politicians toward the ways of tolerance, cooperation and love. No fear of criticism, no risk of resentment, must deter us from this task. The charity of Christ compels us."

DO WHAT HE SAYS

Homily delivered during Mass Sept. 30 at the Shrine of Our Lady of Knock.

Moment for Decision: "The present time is an important moment in the history of the universal Church, and, in particular, of the Church in Ireland. So many things have changed. So many valuable new insights have been gained in what it means to be Christian. So many new problems have to be faced by the faithful, either because of the increased pace of change in society or because of the new demands that are made on the people of God — demands to live to the fullest the mission of evangelization. . . . Like so many times before when the Church was faced with a new challenge, we turn to Mary, the Mother of God and the Seat of Wisdom trusting that she will show us again the way to her Son."

"Do Whatever He Tells You": "Mary was truly united with Jesus. Not many of her own words have been preserved in the Gospels, but those that have been recorded refer us again to her Son and to his word. At Cana in Galilee, she turned from her Son to the servants and said 'Do whatever he tells you' (Jn.

2:5). This same message, she still speaks to us today."

"Christ has not left his followers without guidance in the task of understanding and living the Gospel. Before returning to his Father, he promised to send his Holy Spirit to the Church."

"This same spirit guides the successors of the Apostles, your bishops, united with the Bishop of Rome, to whom it was entrusted to preserve the faith and to 'preach the Gospel to the whole creation' (Mk. 16:14). Listen to their voices, for they bring you the word of the Lord."

DUTY OF BISHOPS

Address delivered Sept. 30 to the bishops of Ireland at Cabra, the Dominican Convent in Dublin.

Bishops can perform their duty, to guide and sustain the flock, "in no other way than by suffering with those who suffer and by weeping with those who weep (Cf. Rom. 12:15)."

"Faith and social ethics demand from us respect for the established state authorities. But this respect also finds its expression in individual acts of mediation, in persuasion, in moral influence and, indeed, in firm requests. . . . Precisely because we are defenseless, we have a special right and duty to influence those who wield the sword of authority. For it is well known that, in the field of political action, as elsewhere, not everything can be obtained by means of the sword. There are deeper reasons and stronger laws to which men, nations and peoples are subject. It is for us to discern these reasons and in their light to become, before those in authority, spokesmen for the moral order. This order is superior to force and violence. In this superiority of the moral order is expressed all the dignity of men and nations."

"I earnestly hope that, in a continued effort, you and our brothers (clergy and members of other churches) in the faith will become spokesmen for the just reasons of peace and reconciliation before those who wield the sword and those who perish by the sword."

PRIESTS

Address delivered Oct. 1 to priests, religious and seminarians at St. Patrick's College, Maynooth. (Portions relating to men and women religious are covered under other Almanac entries.)

"What the people expect from you, more than anything else, is faithfulness to the priesthood. This is what speaks to them of the faithfulness of God. This is what strengthens them to be faithful to Christ through all the difficulties of their lives, of their marriages. In a world so marked by instability as our world today, we need more signs and witnesses to God's fidelity to us and to the fidelity we owe to him. This is what causes such great sadness to the Church, such great but often silent anguish among the people of God, when priests fail in their fidelity to their priestly commitment. That countersign, that counter-witness, has been one of the set-backs to the great hopes for renewal aroused throughout the Church by the Second Vatican Council. Yet this has also driven priests, and the whole Church, to more intense and fervent prayer, for it has taught us all that without Christ we can do nothing (Cf. Jn. 15:5). And the fidelity of the immense majority of priests has shone with even greater clarity."

"This is a wonderful time in the history of the Church. This is a wonderful time to be a priest, to be a religious, to be a missionary for Christ. Rejoice in the Lord always. Rejoice in your vocation."

LAITY AND FAMILY

Homily delivered Oct. 1 during Mass in Limerick.

Dignity and Mission of Lay Persons: "St. Peter says that Christians are 'a royal priesthood, a holy nation' (1 Pt. 2:9). All Christians, incorporated into Christ and his Church by baptism, are consecrated to God. They are called to profess the faith which they have received. By the sacrament of confirmation, they are further endowed by the Holy Spirit with special strength to be witnesses of Christ and sharers in his mission of salvation. Every lay Christian is therefore an extraordinary work of God's grace and is called to the heights of holiness. Sometimes, lay men and women do not seem to appreciate to the full the dignity and the vocation that is theirs as lay people. No, there is no such thing as an 'ordinary layman,' for all of you have been called to conversion through the death and resurrection of Jesus Christ. As God's holy people you are called to fulfill your role in the evangelization of the world.

"Yes, the laity are 'a chosen race, a holy priesthood,' (and are) also called to be 'the salt of the earth' and 'the light of the world.'

"It is their specific vocation and mission to express the Gospel in their lives and thereby to insert the Gospel as a leaven into the reality of the world in which they live and work. The great forces which shape the world — politics, the mass media, science, technology, culture, education, industry and work — are precisely the areas where lay people are especially competent to exercise their mission. If these forces are guided by people who are true disciples of Christ and who are, at the same time, fully competent in the relevant secular knowledge and skill, then indeed will the world be transformed from within by Christ's redeeming power."

"To accomplish this you must have . . . consistency between your faith and your daily life. You cannot be a genuine Christian on

Sunday unless you try to be true to Christ's spirit also in your work, your commercial dealings, at your trade union or your employers' or professional meetings."

Marriage and Family: "Revere and protect your family and your family life, for the family is the primary field of Christian action for the Irish laity, the place where your 'royal priesthood' is chiefly exercised. The Christian family has been in the past Ireland's greatest spiritual resource. Modern conditions and social changes have created new patterns and new difficulties for family life and for Christian marriage. I want to say to you: Do not be discouraged, do not follow the trends where a close-knit family is seen as outdated. The Christian family is more important for the Church and for society today than ever before.

"It is true that the stability and sanctity of marriage are being threatened by new ideas and by the aspirations of some. Divorce, for whatever reason it is introduced, inevitably becomes easier and easier to obtain and it gradually comes to be accepted as a normal part of life. The very possibility of divorce in the sphere of civil law makes stable and permanent marriages more difficult for everyone."

"Marriage must include openness to the gift of children. Generous openness to accept children from God as the gift to their love is the mark of the Christian couple. Respect the God-given cycle of life, for this respect is part of our respect for God himself, who created male and female, who created them in his own image, reflecting his own life-giving love in the patterns of their sexual being."

ADDRESSES OF JOHN PAUL II IN THE UNITED STATES

Following are excerpts from several of the addresses delivered by Pope John Paul during his pastoral visit to the U.S. Oct. 1 to 7, 1979.

The excerpts are from texts circulated by the NC Documentary Service, Origins.

ADDRESS TO U.N.

Address delivered Oct. 2 before the 34th General Assembly of the United Nations.

Fundamental Relations of Political Activity: "Each one of you (delegates) . . . represents a particular state, system and political structure; but what you represent, above all, are individual human beings. . . . This relationship is what provides the reason for all political activity, whether national or iternational, for in the final analysis this activity comes from man, is exercised by man and is for man. And, if political activity is cut off from this fundamental relationship and finality, if it becomes in a way its own end, it loses much of its reason to exist. Even more, it can also give rise to a specific alienation; it can become extraneous to man; it can come to contradict humanity itself. In reality, what justifies the existence of any political activity is service to man, concerned and responsible attention to the essential problems and duties of his earthly existence in its social dimension and significance, on which also the good of each person depends."

"I would like to express the wish that, in view of its universal character, the United Nations Organization will never cease to be the forum, the high tribune, from which all man's problems are appraised in truth and justice."

Primacy of Spiritual Values: "The progress of humanity must be measured not only by the progress of science and technology . . . but also and chiefly by the primacy given to spiritual values and by the progress of moral life. In this field is manifested the full dominion of reason, through truth, in the behavior of the individual and of society, and also the control of reason over nature."

"The Universal Declaration of Human Rights . . . must remain the basic value in the United Nations Organization, with which the consciences of the members must be confronted and from which they must draw continual inspiration."

Problems of Peace: "It is my fervent hope that a solution . . . to the Middle East crises may draw nearer. While being prepared to recognize the value of any concrete step or attempt made to settle the conflict, I want to recall that it would have no value if it did not truly represent the first stone of a general overall peace in the area, a peace that, being necessarily based on equitable recognition of the rights of all, cannot fail to include the consideration and just settlement of the Palestinian question. Connected with this question is that of the tranquillity, independence and territorial integrity of Lebanon within the formula that has made it an example of peaceful and mutually fruitful coexistence between distinct communities, a formula that I hope will, in the common interest, be maintained, with the adjustments required by the developments of the situation. I also hope for a special statute that, under international guarantee — as my predecessor Paul VI indicated — would respect the particular nature of Jerusalem, a heritage sacred to the veneration of millions of believers of the three great monotheistic religions, Judaism, Christianity and Islam."

Armaments: "We are troubled also by reports of the development of weaponry exceeding in quality and size the means of war and destruction ever known before. . . . We applaud the decisions and agreements aimed at reducing the arms race. Nevertheless, the life of humanity today is seriously endangered by the threat of destruction and by the risk arising even from accepting certain tranquilizing reports. And the resistance to actual concrete proposals of real disarmament ... shows that, together with the will for peace that all profess and that most desire, there is also in existence ... the contrary and the negation of this will. The continual preparations for war demonstrated by the production of ever more numerous, powerful and sophisticated weapons in various countries show that there is a desire to be ready for war; and, being ready, means being able to start it; it also means taking the risk that sometime, somewhere, somehow, someone can set in motion the terrible mechanism of general destruction.

"It is therefore necessary to make a continuing and even more energetic effort to do away with the very possibility of provoking war, and to make such catastrophes impossible by influencing the attitudes and convictions, the very intentions and aspirations of governments and peoples."

Material and Spiritual Values: "Man lives at the same time both in the world of material values and in that of spiritual values. ... Material and spiritual realities may be viewed separately in order to understand better that, in the concrete human being, they are inseparable, and to see that any threat to human rights, whether in the field of material realities or in that of spiritual realities, is equally dangerous for peace, since in every instance it concerns man in his entirety. ... A constant rule of the history of humanity ... is based on the relationship between spiritual values and material or economic values. In this relationship, it is the spiritual values that are pre-eminent, both on account of the nature of these values and also for reasons concerning the good of man. The pre-eminence of the values of the spirit defines the proper sense of earthly material goods and the way to use them. This pre-eminence is therefore at the basis of a just peace. It is also a contributing factor to ensuring that material development, technical development and the development of civilization are at the service of what constitutes man."

"A critical analysis of our modern civilization shows that in the last 100 years it has contributed as never before to the development of material good, but that it has also given rise, both in theory and still more in practice, to a series of attitudes in which sensitivity to the spiritual dimension of human existence is diminished to a great or less extent, as a result of certain premises which reduce the meaning of human life chiefly to the many different material and economic factors — I mean to the demands of production, the market, consumption, the accumulation of riches, or of the growing bureaucracy with which an attempt is made to regulate these very processes."

Threats against Rights and Peace: "The first ... is linked in an overall sense with the distribution of material goods. This distribution is frequently unjust both within individual societies and on the planet as a whole."

"Various forms of inequality in the possession of material goods, and in the enjoyment of them, can often be explained by different historical and cultural causes and circumstances. But, while these circumstances can diminish the moral responsibility of people today, they do not prevent the situations of inequality from being marked by injustice and social injury."

"There is never any lack of systematic threats and violations of human rights. Disturbing factors are frequently present in the form of the frightful diparities between excessively rich individuals and groups on the one hand, and on the other hand the majority made up of the poor or indeed of the destitute, who lack food and opportunities for work and education and are in great numbers condemned to hunger and disease. And concern is also caused at times by the radical separation of work from property, by man's indifference to the production enterprise to which he is linked only by a work obligation, without feeling that he is working for a good that will be his or for himself. It is no secret that the abyss separating the minority of the excessively rich from the multitude of the destitute is a very grave symptom in the life of any society. This must also be said with even greater insistence with regard to the abyss separating countries and regions of the earth. Surely the only way to overcome this serious disparity between areas of satiety and areas of hunger and depression is through coordinated cooperation by all countries. This requires above all else a unity inspired by an authentic perspective of peace. Everything will depend on whether these differences and contrasts in the sphere of the possession of goods will be systematically reduced through truly effective means, on whether the belts of hunger, malnutrition, destitution, underdevelopment, disease and illiteracy will disappear from the economic map of the earth, and on whether peaceful cooperation will avoid imposing conditions of exploitation and economic or political dependence, which would only be a form of neocolonialism."

"A second systematic threat to man in his inalienable rights in the modern world, a threat which constitutes no less a danger than the first to the cause of peace, (consists of) various forms of injustice in the field of the spirit. ... For centuries the thrust of civilization has been in one direction: that of giving the life of individual political societies a form in which there can be fully safeguarded the objective rights of the spirit, of human conscience and of human creativity, including man's relationship with God. Yet, in spite of this we still see in this field recurring threats and violations, often with no possibility of appealing to a higher authority or of obtaining an effective remedy. Structures . . . often exist in which the practical exercise of these freedoms condemns man, in fact if not formally, to become a second-class or third-class citizen, to see compromised his chances of social advancement, his professional career or his access to certain posts of responsibility, and to lose even the possibility of educating his children freely. It is a question of the highest importance that in internal social life, as well as in international life, all human beings in every nation and country should be able to enjoy effectively their full rights under any political regime or system.

"Only the safeguarding of this real completeness of rights for every human being without discrimination can ensure peace at its very roots."

Religious Freedom: "With regard to religious freedom, which I, as pope, am bound to have particularly at heart, precisely with a view to safeguarding peace, I would like to repeat here, as a contribution to respect for man's spiritual dimension, some principles contained in the Second Vatican Council's *Declaration on Religious Freedom* (No. 2): 'In accordance with their dignity, all human beings, because they are persons, that is, beings endowed with reason and free will and therefore bearing personal responsibility, are both impelled by their nature and bound by a moral obligation to seek the truth, especially religious truth. They are also bound to adhere to the truth once they come to know it and to direct their whole lives in accordance with its demands.'

" 'The practice of religion of its very nature consists primarily of those voluntary and free internal acts by which a human being directly sets his course toward God. No merely human power can either command or prohibit acts of this kind. But man's social nature itself requires that he give external expression to his internal acts of religion, that he communicate with others in religious matters and that he profess his religion in community.' (Ibid., No. 3)."

What Kind of Inheritance for Children?: The United Nations Organization has proclaimed 1979 the Year of the Child."

"In this perspective we must ask ourselves whether there will continue to accumulate over the heads of this new generation of children the threat of common extermination for which the means are in the hands of the modern states, especially the major world powers. Are the children to receive the arms race from us as a necessary inheritance? How are we to explain this unbridled race?"

"Can our age still really believe that the breathtaking spiral of armaments is at the service of world peace? In alleging the threat of a potential enemy, is it really not rather the intention to keep for oneself a means of threat, in order to get the upper hand with the aid of one's own arsenal of destruction? Here too it is the human dimension of peace that tends to vanish in favor of ever new possible forms of imperialism.

"It must be our solemn wish here for our children, for the children of all the nations on earth, that this point will never be reached. And for that reason I do not cease to pray to God each day so that in his mercy he may save us from so terrible a day."

IN HARLEM AND SOUTH BRONX

Brief remarks Oct. 2 during stops at St. Charles Borromeo Parish, Harlem, and a barrio in the South Bronx.

In Harlem: The Pope noted that many people have never known the joy of the good news of the Gospel, and added: "We must go to them, therefore, as messengers of hope. We must bring to them the witness of true joy. We must pledge to them our commitment to work for a just society and city where they feel respected and loved."

In the South Bronx: Speaking in Spanish, the Holy Father said: "I come here because I know of the difficult conditions of your existence, because I know that your lives are marked by pain. . . . Brothers and Sisters and Friends, do not give in to despair, but work together, take the steps possible for you in the task of increasing your dignity, unite your efforts toward the goals of human and moral advancement. And do not forget that God has your lives in his care, goes with you, calls you to better things, calls you to overcome."

LAZARUS AT OUR DOORS

Homily delivered Oct. 2 during Mass at Yankee Stadium.

Sensitivity to Those in Need: "Social thinking and social practice inspired by the Gospel must always be marked by a special sensitivity toward those who are most in distress. . . . There are many poor people of this sort around the world. There are many in your own midst."

"The poor of the United States and of the world are your brothers and sisters in Christ. You must never be content to leave them just the crumbs from the feast. You must take of your substance, and not just of your abundance, in order to help them. And you must treat them like guests at your family table."

Simple Life-Style: "It is principally the task of lay people to put (Christian principles) into practice in concrete projects, to define priorities and to develop models that are suitable for promoting man's real good."

"In order to bring this undertaking to a successful conclusion, fresh spiritual and moral energy drawn from the inexhaustible divine source is needed. This energy does not develop easily. The life-style of many members of our rich and permissive societies is easy, and so is the life-style of increasing groups inside the poorer countries. As I said last year to the plenary assembly of the Pontifical Commission Justice and Peace, 'Christians will want to be in the vanguard in favoring ways of life that decisively break with the frenzy of consumerism, exhausting and joyless' (Nov. 11, 1978). It is not a question of slowing down progress, for there is no human progress when everything conspires to give full reign to the instincts of self-interest, sex and power. We must find a simple way of living. For it is not right that the standard of living of the rich countries should seek to maintain itself by draining off a great part of the reserves of energy and raw materials that are meant to serve the whole of humanity."

Lazarus at Our Doors: "The parable of the rich man and Lazarus must always be present in our memory; it must form our conscience. Christ demands openness from the rich, the affluent, the economically advanced; openness to the poor, the underdeveloped and the disadvantaged. Christ demands an openness that is more than benign attention, more than token actions or half-hearted efforts that leave the poor as destitute as before or even more so.

"All of humanity must think of the parable of the rich man and the beggar. Humanity must translate it into contemporary terms of economy and politics, in terms of all human rights, in terms of relations between the 'First,' 'Second' and 'Third' World. We cannot stand idly by when thousands of human beings are dying of hunger. Nor can we remain indifferent when the rights of the human spirit are trampled upon, when violence is done to the human conscience in matters of truth, religion and cultural creativity.

"We cannot stand idly by, enjoying our own riches and freedom, if, in any place, the Lazarus of the 20th century stands at our doors."

WITNESS TO FAITH

Address to young people Oct. 2 in Madison Square Garden.

"When you wonder about the mystery of yourself, look to Christ who gives you the meaning of life.

"When you wonder what it means to be a mature person, look to Christ who is the fullness of humanity.

"And when you wonder about your role in the future of the world and of the United States, look to Christ. Only in Christ will you fulfill your potential as an American citizen and as a citizen of the world community."

"The church needs you. The world needs you because it needs Christ, and you belong to Christ. And so I ask you to accept your responsibility in the Church, to help by your words, and, above all, by the example of your lives — to spread the Gospel. You do this by praying, and by being just and truthful and pure."

"By a real Christian life, by the practice of your religion, you are called to give witness to your faith. And, because actions speak louder than words, you are called to proclaim, by the conduct of your daily lives, that you really do believe that Jesus Christ is Lord!"

FREEDOM IN THE U.S.

Address delivered Oct. 3 at Battery Park, against the background of the Statue of Liberty and Ellis Island across the bay.

"Every nation has its historical symbols. . . . Such a symbol in the United States is the Statue of Liberty. This is an impressive symbol of what the United States has stood for from the very beginning of its history; this is a symbol of freedom."

"It will always remain one of the glorious achievements of this nation that, when people looked toward America, they received together with freedom also a chance for their own advancement. This tradition must be honored also today. The freedom that was gained must be ratified each day by the firm rejection of whatever wounds, weakens or dishonors human life. And so I appeal to all who love freedom and justice to give a chance to all in need, to the poor and the powerless."

The Pope concluded his brief address with greetings to all who were gathered in the park, especially to leaders of the Jewish community (see separate entry).

FREEDOM

Homily delivered Oct. 3 during Mass at Logan Circle, Philadelphia.

"Freedom can . . . never be construed without relation to the truth as revealed by Jesus Christ and proposed by his Church; nor can it be seen as a pretext for moral anarchy — for every moral order must remain linked to truth."

"This is especially relevant when one considers the domain of human sexuality. Here, as in any other field, there can be no true freedom without respect for the truth regarding the nature of human sexuality and marriage. In today's society, we see so many disturbing tendencies and so much laxity regarding the Christian view on sexuality that have all one thing in common: recourse to the concept of freedom to justify any behavior that is no longer consonant with the true moral order and the teaching of the Church. Moral norms do not militate against the freedom of the person or the couple: on the contrary, they exist precisely for that freedom, since they are given to ensure the right use of freedom. Whoever refuses to accept these norms and to act accordingly, whoever seeks to liberate himself or herself from these norms, is not truly free. Free indeed is the person who models his or her behavior in a responsible way according to the exigencies of the objective good. What I have said here regards the whole of conjugal morality, but it applies as well to priests with regard to the obligations of celibacy. The cohesion of freedom and ethics has also its consequences for the pursuit of the common good in society and for ther national independence which the Liberty Bell announced two centuries ago.

"Divine law is the sole standard of human liberty and is given to us in the Gospel of Christ, the Gospel of redemption."

SEMINARIANS

Address delivered Oct. 3 at St. Charles Borromeo Seminary of the Philadelphia archdiocese.

"Before you can be ordained, you are called by Christ to make a free and irrevocable commitment to be faithful to him and to his Church. Human dignity requires that you maintain this commitment, that you keep your promise to Christ, no matter what difficulties you may encounter and no matter what temptations you may be exposed to."

"Take time to reflect on the serious obligations and the difficulties which are part of the priest's life. Consider whether Christ is calling you to the celibate life. You can make a responsible decision for celibacy only after you have reached the firm conviction that Christ is indeed offering you this gift, which is intended for the good of the Church and for the service of others."

"In the final analysis, perseverance in fidelity is a proof, not of human strength and courage, but of the efficacy of Christ's grace. And so, if we are going to persevere, we shall have to be men of prayer who, through the Eucharist, the Liturgy of the Hours and our personal encounters with Christ, find the courage and grace to be faithful."

UNITY WITH DIVERSITY

Address delivered Oct. 4 in the Ukrainian Cathedral of the Immaculate Conception, Philadelphia.

"The various traditions within the Church give expression to the multitude of ways the Gospel can take root and flower in the lives of God's people. They are living evidence of the richness of the Church. Each one, while united to all the others in the same faith, the same sacraments and the same government, is nevertheless manifested in its own liturgy, ecclesiastical discipline and spiritual patrimony."

"Catholic unity entails a recognition of the successor of St. Peter and his ministry of strengthening and preserving intact the communion of the universal Church, while safeguarding the existence of legitimate individual traditions within it. The Ukrainian Church, as well as the other Eastern Churches, has a right and duty, in accordance with the teaching of the Second Vatican Council, to preserve its own ecclesiastical and spiritual patrimony. It is precisely because these individual traditions are also intended for the enrichment of the universal Church that the Apostolic See of Rome takes great care to protect and foster each one. In turn, the ecclesial communities that follow these traditions are called to adhere with love and respect to certain particular forms of discipline which my predecessors and I, in fulfilling our pastoral responsibility to the universal Church, have judged necessary for the well-being of the whole body of Christ."

PRIESTS

Address to priests delivered Oct. 4 at the Civic Center, Philadelphia.

Characteristics of the Priesthood:
• "Priesthood is forever. We do not return the gift given. It cannot be that God who gave the impulse to say 'yes' now wishes to hear 'no.' "

• "Nor should it surprise the world that the call of God through the Church continues to offer us a celibate ministry of love and service after the example of Our Lord Jesus Christ. God's call has indeed stirred us to the depths of our being. And, after centuries of experience, the Church knows how deeply fitting it is that priests should give this concrete response in their lives to express the totality of the 'yes' they have spoken to the Lord who calls them by name to his service."

• "The fact that there is a personal, individual call to the priesthood given by the Lord to "the men he himself had decided on," is in accord with the prophetic tradition. It should help us, too, to understand that the Church's traditional decision to call men to the priesthood, and not to call women, is not a statement about human rights, nor an exclusion of women from holiness and mission in the Church. Rather, this decision expresses the conviction of the Church about this particular dimension of the gift of priesthood by which God has chosen to shepherd his flock."

Essential Points:
• "Priesthood is mission and service; it is being 'sent out' from Jesus to 'give his flock a shepherd's care.' "

• "The very success of our priesthood depends on our fidelity to the magisterium, through which the Church guards 'the rich deposit of faith with the help of the Holy Spirit who dwells within us' (2 Tm. 1:14)."

• "Priestly ministry is never to be conceived in terms of an acquisition; insofar as it is a gift, it is a gift to be proclaimed and shared with others."

• "Just as Jesus was most perfectly a 'man for others' in giving himself up totally on the cross, so the priest is most of all servant and 'man for others' when he acts in *persona Christi*' in the Eucharist, leading the Church in that celebration in which his sacrifice of the cross is renewed. For, in the Church's daily Eucharistic worship, the 'good news' that the Apostles were sent out to proclaim is preached in its fullness; the work of our redemption is reenacted."

• "All our pastoral endeavors are incomplete until our people are led to full and active participation in the Eucharistic Sacrifice."

• "Unity among priests is not a unity or fraternity that is directed toward itself. It is for the sake of the Gospel, to symbolize, in the living out of the priesthood, the essential direction to which the Gospel calls all people: to the union of love with him (Christ) and one another."

FARMERS

Homily delivered Oct. 4 during Mass at the Living History Farms near Des Moines, Iowa.

"To all of you who are farmers and all who are associated with agricultural production, I want to say this: The Church highly esteems your work. Christ himself showed his esteem for agriculture when he described God his Father as 'the vinedresser' (Jn. 5:1). You cooperate with the Creator, the 'vinedresser,' in sustaining and nurturing life. You fulfill the command of God given at the very beginning: 'Fill the earth and subdue it' (Gn. 1:28). . . . By hard work you have become masters of the earth and you have subdued it. . . . You support the lives of millions who themselves do not work on the land, but who live because of what you produce."

Three Attitudes: "Three attitudes in particular are appropriate for rural life.

• **Gratitude:** "Every day the farmer is reminded of how much he depends on God. From the heavens come the rain, the wind and the sunshine. They occur without the farmer's command or control. The farmer prepares the soil, plants the seed and cultivates the crop. But God makes it grow; he alone is the source of life. Even the natural disasters . . . remind the farmer of his dependence upon God."

• **Stewardship:** "The land must be conserved with care, since it is intended to be fruitful for generation upon generation. . . . You are stewards of some of the most important resources God has given to the world. Therefore, conserve the land well, so that your children's children and generations after them will inherit an even richer land than was entrusted to you. . . . Farming . . . will always be more than an enterprise of profit-making. In farming, you cooperate with the creator in the very sustenance of life on earth."

• **Generosity:** "You . . . are stewards of a gift from God which was intended for the good of all humanity. You are (and have) the potential to provide food for the millions who have nothing to eat and thus help to rid the world of famine."

"Farmers everywhere provide bread for all humanity, but it is Christ alone who is the bread of life. He alone satisfies the deepest hunger of humanity."

BISHOPS

Address delivered Oct. 5 to an extraordinary meeting of the U.S. bishops at Quigley South Seminary, Chicago.

In view of the primary concern of the Second Vatican Council, "that the sacred deposit of Christian doctrine should be more effectively guarded and taught," the Pope stressed several subjects covered by the bishops in their 1976 pastoral letter, "To Live in Christ Jesus."

Human Rights: "You repeatedly proclaim human rights and human dignity and the incomparable worth of people of every racial and ethnic origin."

No Divorce: "You faced the question of the indissolubility of marriage, rightly stating: 'The covenant between a man and a woman joined in Christian marriage is as indissoluble and irrevocable as God's love for his people and Christ's love for his Church.' "

Contraception: "You rightly spoke against both the ideology of contraception and contraceptive acts, as did the encyclical *Humanae Vitae*. And I myself today, with the same conviction of Paul VI, ratify the teaching of this encyclical."

Homosexual Activity: "You also rightly stated: 'Homosexual activity . . . as distinguished from homosexual orientation, is morally wrong.' "

Abortion: "You also gave witness to the truth . . . when . . . you reaffirmed the right to life and the inviolability of every human life, including the life of unborn children. You clearly said: 'To destroy these innocent unborn children is an unspeakable crime. . . . Their right to life must be recognized and fully protected by the law.' "

Euthanasia: "You clearly spoke up for the aged, asserting: 'Euthanasia or mercy killing . . . is a grave moral evil. . . . Such killing is incompatible with respect for human dignity and reverence for life.' "

Respect for Life: "You gave further witness to the fact that all aspects of human life are sacred."

The Pope also noted that "intercommunion between divided Christians is not the answer to Christ's appeal for perfect unity"; called for efforts to safeguard and deepen the sense and practice of the sacrament of reconciliation while observing "the precise limits of general absolution"; and urged recall of the fact that "the validity of all liturgical development and the effectiveness of every liturgical sign presupposes the great principle that the Catholic liturgy is theocentric and that it is, above all, 'the worship of divine majesty.' "

UNITY OF THE CHURCH

Homily delivered Oct. 5 during Mass in Grant Park, Chicago.

"We are all bound together, as the People of God, the body of Christ, in a unity that transcends the diversity of our origin, culture, education and personality — in a unity that does not exclude a rich diversity in ministries and services."

"If . . . the Church . . . is to be a forcefully discernible sign of the Gospel message, all her members must show forth, in the words of Paul VI, that 'harmony and consistency of doctrine, life and worship which marked the first days of her existence' (Apostolic Exhortation, "Reconciliation within the Church," No. 2), when Christians 'devoted themselves to the Apostles' teachings, to the breaking of bread and the prayers' " (Acts 2:42).

"The mission of evangelization that is mine and yours, must be carried out through a constant unselfish witnessing to the unity of love."

"Love is the power that gives rise to dialogue, in which we listen to each other and learn from each other. Love gives rise, above all, to the dialogue of prayer in which we listen to God's word, which is alive in the Holy Bible and alive in the life of the Church. Let love, then, build the bridges across our differences and at times our contrasting positions. Let love for each other and love for the truth be the answer to polarization, when factions are formed because of differing views in matters that relate to faith or to the priorities for action. No one in the ecclesial community should ever feel alienated or unloved, even when tensions arise in the course of the common efforts to bring the fruits of the Gospel to society around us. Our unity as Christians, as Catholics, must always be a unity of love in Jesus Christ Our Lord."

WOMEN RELIGIOUS

Address delivered Oct. 7 to women religious at the National Shrine of the Immaculate Conception, Washington, D.C.

Called by Jesus: "You are called by Jesus himself to verify and manifest in your lives and in your activities your deepened relationship with his Church. This bond of union with the Church must also be shown in the spirit and apostolic endeavors of every religious institute. For faithfulness to Christ, especially in religious life, can never be separated from faithfulness to the Church. This ecclesial dimension of the vocation of religious consecration has many important practical consequences for institutes themselves and for each individual member. It implies, for example, a greater public witness to the Gospel, since you represent, in a special way as women religious, the spousal relationship of the Church to Christ. The ecclesial dimension also requires, on the part of individual members as well as entire institutes, a faithfulness to the original charisms which God has given to his Church, through your founders and foundresses. It means that institutes are called to continue to foster, in dynamic faithfulness, those corporate commitments which were related to the original charism, which were authenticated by the Church and which still fulfill important needs of the People of God."

"Christ remains primary in your life only when he enjoys the first place in your mind and heart. Thus, you must continuously unite yourself to him in prayer. Without prayer, religious life has no meaning. It has lost contact with its source, it has emptied itself of substance, and it no longer can fulfill its goal. Without prayer there can be no joy, no hope, no peace. For prayer is what keeps us in touch with Christ."

Service in the Church: "Your service in the Church is . . . an extension of Christ to whom you have dedicated your life. For it is not yourself that you put forward, but Christ Jesus as Lord. Like John the Baptist, you know that, for Christ to increase, you must decrease. And so your life must be characterized by a complete availablity: a readiness to serve as the needs of the Church require, a readiness to give public witness to the Christ whom we love.

"The need for this public witness becomes a constant call to inner conversion, to justice and holiness of life on the part of each religious. It also becomes an invitation to each institute to reflect on the purity of its corporate ecclesial witness. And it is for this reason that, in my address last November to the International Union of Superiors General, I mentioned that it is not unimportant that your consecration to God should be manifested in the permanent exterior sign of a simple and suitable religious garb. This is not only my personal conviction, but also the desire of the Church, often expressed by so many of the faithful."

"As daughters of the Church — a title cherished by so many of your great saints — you are called to a generous and loving adherence to the authentic magisterium of the Church, which is a solid guarantee of the fruitfulness of all your apostolates and an indispensable condition for the proper interpretations of the 'signs of the times.'

MARRIAGE, FAMILY, VALUE OF LIFE

Homily delivered Oct. 7 during Mass on the Mall, Washington, D.C.

"We will stand up every time that human life is threatened. When the sacredness of life before birth is attacked, we will stand up and proclaim that no one ever has the authority to destroy unborn life. When a child is described as a burden or looked upon only as a means to satisfy an emotional need, we will stand up and insist that every child is a unique and unrepeatable gift of God, with the right to a loving and united family. When the institution of marriage is abandoned to human selfishness or reduced to a temporary, conditional arrangement that can easily be terminated, we will stand up and affirm the indissolubility of the marriage bond. When the value of the family is threatened because of social and economic pressures, we will stand up and reaffirm that the family is necessary not only for the private good of every person, but also for the common good of every society, nation and state. When freedom is used to dominate the weak, to squander natural resources and energy, and to deny basic necessities to people, we will stand up and reaffirm the demands of justice and social love. When the sick, the aged or the dying are abandoned in loneliness, we will stand up and proclaim that they are worthy of love, care and respect."

REDEMPTOR HOMINIS, ENCYCLICAL LETTER OF JOHN PAUL II

Redemptor Hominis ("Redeemer of Man") is the title of the first encyclical letter of Pope John Paul II. It was dated Mar. 4 and published Mar. 15, 1979.

Its four major headings are: Inheritance (received from his predecessors), The Mystery of the Redemption, Redeemed Man and His Situation in the Modern World, The Church's Mission and Man's Destiny.

The following excerpts are from the translation circulated by NC News Service. Lead lines have been added and section numbers indicated.

Incarnation and Redemption: "The Redeemer of Man, Jesus Christ, is the center of the universe and of history."

The "act of redemption marked the high point of the history of man within God's loving plan. God entered the history of humanity and, as a man, became an actor in that history. . . . Through the incarnation, God gave human life the dimensions that he intended man to have from his first beginning; he has granted that dimension definitively" (No. 1).

"There is a link between the first fundamental truth of the incarnation . . . and the ministry that . . . has become my specific duty" in the See of Peter.

I. Inheritance

"I wish . . . to express my love for the unique inheritance left to the Church by Popes John XXIII and Paul VI, and my personal readiness to develop that inheritance with God's help."

"I am linked with the whole tradition of the Apostolic See and with all my predecessors in the expanse of the 20th century and of the preceding centuries. I am connected, through one after another of the various ages back to the most remote, with the line of the mission and ministry that confers on St. Peter's See an altogether special place in the Church" (No. 2).

Dialogue of Salvation: "The Church's consciousness must go with universal openness. . . . Such openness . . . is what gives the Church her apostolic or, in other words, her missionary dynamism, professing and proclaiming in its entirety the whole of the truth transmitted by Christ. At the same time, she must carry on the dialogue that Paul VI . . . called 'the dialogue of salvation' " with all peoples (No. 4).

Collegiality: "The Church is now more united in the fellowship of service and in the awareness of apostolate. This unity springs from the principle of collegiality, mentioned by the Second Vatican Council" — and expressed in the Synod of Bishops and other collegial and collaborative bodies like bishops' conferences, synods, councils of priests and lay persons (No. 5).

Ecumenical Commitment: "What shall I say of all the initiatives that have sprung from the new ecumenical orientation? . . . In the present historical situation of Christianity and the world, the only possibility we see of fulfilling the Church's universal mission, with regard to ecumenical questions, is that of seeking sincerely, perseveringly, humbly and also courageously the ways of drawing closer together and of union. . . . We must, therefore, seek unity without being discouraged at the difficulties that can appear or accumulate along that road; otherwise, we would be unfaithful to the word of Christ, we would fail to accomplish his testament."

"True ecumenical activity means openness, drawing closer, availablility for dialogue, and a shared investigation of the truth in the full evangelical and Christian sense; but in no way does it or can it mean giving up or in any way diminishing the treasures of divine truth that the Church has constantly confessed and taught. To all who, for whatever reason, would wish to dissuade the Church from seeking the universal unity of Christians, the question must once again be put: Have we the right not to do it? Can we fail to have trust . . . in our Lord's grace?"

Non-Christian Religions: "What we have just said must also be applied — although in another way and with due differences — to activity for coming closer together with representatives of the non-Christian religions, an activity expressed through dialogue, contacts, prayer in common, investigation of the treasures of human spirituality in which, as we know, the members of these religions also are not lacking" (No. 6).

II. Mystery of Redemption

Direction toward Christ: "What should we do in order that this new advent of the Church, connected with the approaching end of the second millennium, may bring us closer to him whom Scripture calls "everlasting Father? ... This is the fundamental question that the new Pope must put to himself."

"Our spirit is set in one direction ... toward Christ, the Redeemer of man."

Redemption the Fundamental Concern: "The Church never ceases to relive his death on the cross and his resurrection, which constitute the content of the Church's daily life. ... The Church lives his mystery, draws unwearyingly from it and continually seeks ways of bringing this mystery of her Master and Lord to humanity. ... The Church stays within the mystery of the redemption, which has become the fundamental principle of her life and mission" (No. 7).

"The Redeemer of the world! In him has been revealed in a new and more wonderful way the fundamental truth concerning creation which the Book of Genesis (Chap. 1) gives witness when it repeats several times: 'God saw that it was good.' ... In Jesus Christ the visible world which God created for man ... recovers again its original link with the divine source of wisdom and love."

Citing the *Pastoral Constitution on the Church in the Modern World* (No. 22), the Pope said: Christ " 'is himself the perfect man who has restored in the children of Adam that likeness to God which had been disfigured ever since the first sin. Human nature, by the very fact that it was assumed, not absorbed, in him, has been raised in us also to a dignity beyond comparison. For, by his incarnation, he, the Son of God, in a certain way united himself with each man' " (No. 8).

"Jesus Christ, the Son of the living God, became our reconciliation with the Father" (No. 9).

Christ Reveals Man to Himself: "Christ the Redeemer 'fully reveals man to himself.' ... This is the human dimension of the mystery of the redemption. In this dimension man finds again the greatness, dignity and value that belong to his humanity. in the mystery of the redemption man becomes newly 'expressed' and, in a way, is newly created. ... The man who wishes to understand himself thoroughly ... must 'appropriate' and assimiliate the whole reality of the incarnation and redemption in order to find himself."

"The Church knows with all the certainty of faith that the redemption that took place through the cross has definitively restored his dignity to man and given back meaning to his life in the world, a meaning that was lost to a considerable extent because of sin."

"The Church's fundamental function in every age, and particularly in ours, is to direct man's gaze, to point the awareness and experience of the whole of humanity, toward the mystery of God, to help all men to be familiar with the profundity of the redemption taking place in Christ Jesus" (No. 10).

Mission of Followers of Christ: "All of us who are Christ's followers must ... meet and unite around him. ... We can and must immediately reach and display to the world our unity in proclaiming the mystery of Christ, in revealing the divine dimension and also the human dimension of the redemption, and in struggling with unwearying perseverance for the dignity that each human being has reached and can continually reach in Christ; namely, the dignity of both the grace of divine adoption and the inner truth of humanity, a truth which ... is still clearer in the light of the reality that is Jesus Christ."

"Jesus Christ is the stable principle and fixed center of the mission that God himself has entrusted to man. We must all share in this mission and concentrate all our forces on it, since it is more necessary than ever for modern mankind" (No. 11).

Missionary Attitude: "All Christians must find what already unites them, even before their full communion is achieved. ... Thanks to this unity, we can together come close to the magnificent heritage of the human spirit that has been manifested in all religions. ... The missionary attitude always begins with a feeling of deep esteem for 'what is in man' (Jn. 2:26). ... The mission is never destruction but, instead, a taking up and fresh building" (No. 12).

III. Redeemed Man, His Situation

Fundamental Task of the Church: "The Church sees its fundamental task in enabling that union (of man with Christ) to be brought about and renewed continually. The Church wishes to serve this single end: that each person may be able to find Christ, in order that Christ may walk with each person the path of life, with the power of the truth about man and the world that is contained in the mystery of the incarnation and the redemption, and with the power of the love that is radiated by that truth."

Man the Way for the Church: "Out of regard for Christ and in view of the mystery that constitutes the Church's own life, the Church cannot remain insensible to whatever serves man's true welfare, any more than she can remain indifferent to what threatens it" (No. 13).

"The Church cannot abandon man, for his destiny — that is to say, his election, calling, birth and death, salvation or perdition — is so closely and unbreakably linked with Christ. ... Man is the primary route that the Church must travel in fulfilling her mission. He is the primary and fundamental way for the Church, the way traced out by Christ himself, the way that leads invariably through the mystery of the incarnation and the redemption."

"Since this man (in his concrete circumstances) is the way for the Church, ... the Church of today must be aware in an always new manner of man's 'situation' ... of his possibilities ... of the threats to man and of all that seems to oppose the endeavor 'to make human life ever more human' (*Pastoral Constitution on the Church in the Modern World*, No. 38; Encyclical, *Development of Peoples*, No. 21) and make every element of his life correspond to man's true dignity" (No. 14).

Condition of Contemporary Man: "The man of today seems to be under threat from what he produces; that is to say, from the result of the work of his hands and, even more so, of the work of his intellect and the tendencies of his will.... What this manifold activity of man yields is not only subjected to 'alienation,' in the sense that it is simply taken away from the person who produces it, but rather it turns against man himself, at least in part, through the indirect consequences of its effects returning on himself."

"This state of menace ... shows itself in various directions and various degrees of intensity." It derives from exploitation of the earth and natural resources, from excessive consumerism, and from technological development and progress uncontrolled by rational planning and adequate norms of morality.

Essential Questions: "The essential questions concerning man's situation today and in the future" are:

"Do all the conquests attained until now and those projected for the future of technology accord with man's moral and spiritual progress? In this context, is man, as man, developing and progressing, or is he regressing and being degraded in his humanity? ... Does good prevail over evil? ... Is there a growth of social love, of respect for the rights of others? ... Or, on the contrary, is there an increase of various degrees of selfishness, exaggerated nationalism instead of authentic love of country, and also the propensity to exploit the whole of material progress — and that in the technology of production for the exclusive purpose of dominating others or of favoring this or that imperialism?"

"The Church considers an essential, unbreakably united element of her mission (to be) solicitude for man, for his humanity, for the future of man on earth, and therefore also for the course set for the whole of development and progress" (No. 15).

Priorities: "Man's situation in the modern world seems indeed to be far removed from the objective demands of the moral order, from the requirements of justice and, even more, of social love."

"The essential meaning of kingship and dominion over the visible world, which the Creator himself gave man for his task, consists in the priority of ethics over technology, in the primacy of the person over things, and in the superiority of spirit over matter."

Danger: "There is already a real perceptible danger that, while man's dominion over the world of things is making enormous advances, he might lose the essential threads of his dominion and in various ways let his humanity be subjected to the world and become himself something subject to manipulation in many ways — even if the manipulation is often not perceptible directly — through the whole of the organization of community life, through the production system, and through pressure from the means of social communication. Man cannot relinquish himself or the place in the visible world that belongs to him; he cannot become the slave of things, the slave of economic systems, the slave of production, the slave of his own products."

The phenomenon of the modern world "far removed from the objective demands of the moral order ... brings into question the financial, monetary, production and commercial mechanisms that ... support the world economy. These are proving incapable either of remedying the unjust social conditions inherited from the past or of dealing with the urgent challenges and ethical demands of the present."

Changes Needed: "The principle of solidarity, in a wide sense, must inspire the effective search for appropriate institutions and mechanisms, whether in the sector of trade — where the laws of healthy competition must be allowed to lead the way — or on the level of a wider and more immediate redistribution of riches and of control over them — in order that the economically developing peoples may be able not only to satisfy their essential needs but also to advance gradually and effectively."

"This difficult road of the indispensable transformation of the structures of economic life is one on which it will not be easy to go forward without the intervention of a true conversion of mind and heart."

"Economic development ... must be constantly programmed and realized within a perspective of universal joint development of each individual and people.... Otherwise, the category of 'economic progress' becomes in isolation a superior category subordinating the whole of human existence to its partial demands, suffocating man, breaking up society and ending up by entangling itself in its own tensions and excesses."

"We all know well that the areas of misery and hunger on our globe could have been made fertile in a short time, if the gigantic investments for armaments at the service of war and destruction had been changed into investments for food at the service of life" (No. 16).

Human Rights: "There is no need for the

Church to confirm how closely this problem (of human rights in society) is linked with her mission in the modern world. Indeed, it is at the very basis of social and international peace, as has been declared by John XXIII, the Second Vatican Council and later Paul VI, in detailed documents."

"The Church . . . must continually ask . . . whether the (U.N.) Declaration of Human Rights and the acceptance of their 'letter' mean everywhere the actualization of their 'spirit.' Indeed, well-founded fears arise that very often we are still far from this actualization and that at times the spirit of social and public life is painfully opposed to the declared 'letter' of human rights."

"The Church has always taught the duty to act for the common good and . . . that the fundamental duty of power is solicitude for the common good of society. . . . The rights of power can only be understood on the basis of respect for the objective and inviolable rights of man."

Religious Freedom: "These rights . . . include the right to religious freedom, together with the right to freedom of conscience. . . . The curtailment of the religious freedom of individuals and communities is . . . an attack on man's very dignity, independent of the religion professed or of the concept of the world which these individuals and communities have. The curtailment and violation of religious freedom are in contrast with man's dignity and his objective rights. . . . It is . . . difficult . . . to accept a position that gives only atheism the right of citizenship in public and social life, while believers are, as though by principle, barely tolerated or are treated as second-class citizens or are even . . . entirely deprived of the rights of citizenship."

"I appeal in the name of all believers throughout the world to those on whom the organization of social and political life in some way depends, earnestly requesting them to respect the rights of religion and of the Church's activity. No privilege is asked for, but only respect for an elementary right. Actuation of this right is one of the fundamental tests of man's authentic progress in any regime, in any society, system or milieu" (No. 17).

IV. Church's Mission and Man's Destiny

"If this Mystical Body of Christ (the Church) is God's people . . . this means that in it each man receives within himself the breath of life that comes from Christ. . . . The Church has only one life: that which is given her by her Spouse and Lord. Indeed, precisely because Christ united himself with her in his mystery of redemption, the Church must be strongly united with each man."

"This union of Christ with man is in itself a mystery" (from which) is born 'the new man,' called to become a partaker of God's life (2 Pt. 1:4), and newly created in Christ for the fullness of grace and truth (Eph. 2:10; Jn. 1:14, 16). . . . This life, which the Father has promised and offered to each man in Jesus Christ . . . is the final fulfillment of man's vocation."

Triple Mission: "If . . . man is the way for the Church's daily life, the Church must be always aware of the divine adoption (of man) . . . and of his destination to grace and glory (Rom. 8:15, 30). By reflecting ever anew on all this, and by accepting it with a faith that is more and more firm, the Church also makes herself better fitted for the service to man to which Christ the Lord calls her. . . . The Church performs this ministry by sharing in the 'triple office' belonging to her Master and Redeemer. . . . When we become aware that we share in Christ's triple mission . . . as priest, as prophet and as king (*Dogmatic Constitution on the Church*, Nos. 31 to 36), we also become more aware of what must receive service from the whole of the Church as the society and community of the people of God on earth, and we must likewise understand how each one of us must share in this mission and service" (No. 18).

Responsibility for Truth: "The Church is the subject of social responsibility for divine truth," by professing and teaching it faithfully and by giving witness to it in action.

"We have become sharers in this mission of the prophet Christ." We are responsible for loving divine truth and for "seeking the most exact understanding of it, in order to bring it closer to ourselves and others in all its saving power."

Theologians have a special responsibility as "servants of divine truth." They function correctly "when they seek to serve the official teaching authority of the Church . . . when they place themselves at the service of solicitude in teaching and giving pastoral care." Their work in the study of divine truth may be carried out with different methods, but it "cannot depart from the fundamental unity in the teaching of faith and morals, which is that work's end. . . . Nobody can make of theology, as it were, a simple collection of his own personal ideas, but everybody must be aware of being in close contact with the mission of teaching truth for which the Church is responsible."

All "members of the people of God" — pastors, priests, men and women religious, lay persons — "have their own parts to play in Christ's prophetic mission and service of divine truth" (No. 19).

The Eucharist: "The Church . . . shares . . . in the power of (Christ's) redeeming action . . . in a sacramental form, especially in the Eucharist (*Constitution on the Sacred Liturgy*, No. 10). . . . There is in this sacrament a continual renewing of the mystery of the sacrifice of himself that Christ offered to the Father on the altar of the cross."

"By celebrating and partaking of the Eucharist, we unite ourselves with Christ ... through the redeeming act of his sacrifice.... The Eucharist is the sacrament in which our new being is most completely expressed."

"The Eucharist builds the Church."

"The Eucharist is at one and the same time a sacrifice-sacrament, a communion-sacrament and a presence-sacrament.... It cannot be treated merely as an 'occasion' for manifesting ... (the) brotherhood (of Christ's disciples and confessors). When celebrating the sacrament of the Body and Blood of the Lord, the full magnitude of the divine mystery must be respected, as must the full meaning of this sacramental sign in which Christ is really present and is received.... This is the source of the duty to carry out rigorously the liturgical rules and everything that is a manifestation of community worship."

And Penance: There is a "close link between the Eucharist and penance." They "become in a sense two closely connected dimensions of authentic life in accordance with the spirit of the Gospel, of truly Christian life."

"In recent years much has been done to highlight in the Church's practice ... the community aspect of penance, and especially of the sacrament of penance. We cannot, however, forget that conversion is a particularly profound inward act in which the individual cannot be replaced by others and cannot make the community be a substitute for him.... In faithfully observing the centuries-old practice of the sacrament of penance — of individual confession with a personal act of sorrow and the intention to amend and make satisfaction — the Church is ... defending the human soul's individual right ... to a more personal encounter with the crucified, forgiving Christ ... through the minister of the sacrament of reconciliation."

"In the Church ... there must be a lively felt need for penance, both in its sacramental aspect and in what concerns penance as a virtue" (No. 20).

Mission of Kingship: The Second Vatican Council highlighted the participation of Christians in "Christ's kingly mission.... This dignity, in keeping with the example of Christ, is expressed in readiness to serve others worthily and effectively" in the ways of each one's particular vocation.

"It is precisely the principle of the 'kingly service' that imposes on each one of us ... the duty to demand of himself exactly what we have been called to, what we have personally obliged ourselves to by God's grace, in order to respond to our vocation.... Each member of the people of God has 'his own special gift' (1 Cor. 7:7).... Although this 'gift' is a personal vocation and a form of participation in the Church's saving work, it also serves others, builds the Church and the fraternal communities in the various spheres of human life."

"Mature humanity means full use of the gift of freedom received from the Creator.... Freedom is a great gift only when we know how to use it consciously for everything that is our true good" (No. 21).

Mary: "The Church is a mother," given and giving life from within by the working of the Holy Spirit.

Mary is the Mother of the Church because "she gave human life to the Son of God ... from whom the whole of the people of God receives the grace and dignity of election."

"Nobody else can bring us, as Mary can, into the divine and human dimensions of this mystery" (of redemption) (No. 22).

LETTER OF POPE JOHN PAUL II TO PRIESTS

Following are excerpts from a "Letter of the Supreme Pontiff John Paul II to All Priests of the Church on the Occasion of Holy Thursday, 1979." The letter was dated Apr. 9.

These excerpts, with lead lines added, are from the official Vatican translation circulated by NC News Service.

Chosen from among Men: The priesthood which we share ... remains in explicit relationship with the common priesthood of the faithful ... of all the baptized; but, at the same time, it differs from that priesthood 'essentially and not only in degree' *(Dogmatic Constitution on the Church,* Second Vatican Council; No. 10). In this way the words of the author of the Letter to the Hebrews about the priest, who has been "chosen from among men ... appointed to act on behalf of men" (Heb. 5:1), take on their full meaning.

The common priesthood of the faithful and the ministerial or hierarchical priesthood are nonetheless ordered one to another; each in its own proper way shares in the one priesthood of Christ.

Priesthood Is from Christ, for Service: Our sacramental priesthood ... constitutes a special ... "service," in relation to the community of believers. It does not, however, take its origin from that community, as though it were the community that "called" or "delegated." The sacramental priesthood ... comes from Christ himself, from the fullness of his priesthood. This fullness finds its expression in the fact that Christ ... calls some and enables them to be ministers of his own sacramental sacrifice, the Eucharist — in which all the faithful share.

Our whole priestly existence is and must be deeply imbued with ... service.

Priestly Integrity and Identity: The priesthood calls for a particular integrity of life and service, and precisely such integrity is supremely fitting for our priestly identity.

Since the priesthood is given to us so that we can increasingly serve others, after the example of Christ the Lord, the priesthood cannot be renounced because of the difficulties that we meet and the sacrifices asked of us. Like the Apostles, we have left everything to follow Christ (cf. Mt. 19:27); therefore we must persevere beside him also through the cross.

Pastoral Charge: The special care for the salvation of others, for truth, for the love and holiness of the whole people of God, for the spiritual unity of the Church . . . is exercised in various ways. . . . These ways differ from one another, and it is just impossible to name them all, one by one. . . . Nevertheless, within all these differences, you are always and everywhere the bearers of your particular vocation. You are bearers of the grace of Christ . . . of the charism of the Good Shepherd. And this you can never forget; this you can never renounce.

Strive to be "artists" of pastoral work. There have been many such in the history of the Church. . . . Each of them was different from the others, was himself, was the son of his own time and was "up to date" with respect to his own time. But this "bringing up to date" of each of them was an original response to the Gospel, a response needed precisely for those times. It was the response of holiness and zeal. There is no other rule apart from this for "bringing ourselves up to date." . . . Without any doubt, the various attempts and projects aimed at the "secularization" of the priestly life cannot be considered an adequate "bringing up to date."

Deceptive Call for Secularization: Those who call for the secularization of priestly life and applaud its various manifestations will undoubtedly abandon us when we succumb to temptation. We shall then cease to be necessary and popular. Our time is characterized by different forms of "manipulation" and "exploitation" of man, but we cannot give in to any of these (cf. Discourse of John Paul II to the Clergy of Rome, Nov. 9, 1978). In practical terms, the only priest who will always prove necessary to people is the priest who is conscious of the full meaning of his priesthood.

Our pastoral activity demands that we should be close to people and all their problems . . . "in a priestly way." . . . Our task is to serve truth and justice in the dimensions of human "temporality," but always in a perspective that is the perspective of eternal salvation. . . . Our brethren in the faith, and unbelievers too, expect us always to be able to show them this perspective.

Celibacy: We cannot reason (about celibacy) with categories different from those used by the Second Vatican Council, the Synod of Bishops and the great Pope Paul VI himself (in support of clerical celibacy). We can only seek to understand this question more deeply . . ., freeing ourselves from the various objections that have always . . . been raised against priestly celibacy, and also freeing ourselves from the different interpretations that appeal to criteria alien to the Gospel, to tradition and to the Church's magisterium — criteria, we would add, whose "anthropological" correctness and basis in fact are seen to be very dubious and of relative value.

Tradition of the Latin Chruch: The Latin Church has wished, and continues to wish, . . . that all those who receive the sacrament of orders should embrace this renunciation "for the sake of the kingdom of heaven." This tradition, however, is linked with respect for different traditions of other churches.

None of the reasons whereby people sometimes try to "convince us" of the inopportuneness of celibacy corresponds to the truth . . . that the Church proclaims and seeks to realize in life through the commitment to which priests oblige themselves before ordination.

Why does the Latin Catholic Church link this gift . . . with the vocation to the hierarchical and ministerial priesthood? She does it because celibacy "for the sake of the kingdom" is not only an eschatological sign; it also has a great social meaning . . . for the service of the people of God.

Man for Others: Through his celibacy, the priest becomes the "man for others," in a different way than the man who by binding himself in conjugal union with a woman also becomes, as husband and father, a man "for others," especially in the radius of his own family. . . . The heart of the priest, in order that it may be available for this service (to all people), must be free. Celibacy is a sign of the freedom that exists for the sake of service. According to this sign, the hierarchical or ministerial priesthood is, according to the tradition of our Church, more strictly "ordered" to the common priesthood of the faithful.

Responsibility for Celibacy: The often widespread view that priestly celibacy in the Catholic Church is an institution imposed by law . . . is the result of a misunderstanding, if not of downright bad faith. We all know that it is not so. Every Christian who receives the sacrament of orders commits himself to celibacy with full awareness and freedom. . . . It is obvious that such a decision obliges not only by virtue of a law laid down by the Church but also by virtue of personal responsibility. It is a matter here of keeping one's word to Christ and the Church. Keeping one's word . . . is shown in all its clarity when this keeping of one's promise to Christ . . . encounters difficulties, is put to the test, or is exposed to temptation — all things that do not spare the priest, any more than they spare any other Christian.

At such a moment, the individual must seek support in more fervent prayer. ... Prayer is indeed the source of strength for sustaining what is wavering. ... One must think of all these things especially in moments of crisis, and not have recourse to a dispensation, understood as an "administrative intervention," as though in fact it were not, on the contrary, a matter of a profound question of conscience and a test of humanity. God has a right to test each one of us in this way. ... But God also wishes us all to emerge victorious from such tests, and he gives us adequate help for this.

Married and Celibate Fidelity: One should add at this point that the commitment to married fidelity, which derives from the sacrament of matrimony, creates similar obligations in its own sphere; this married commitment sometimes becomes a source of similar trials and experiences for husbands and wives, who also have a way of proving the value of their love in these "trials by fire." Love, in fact, in all its dimensions, is not only a call but also a duty. Finally, we should add that our brothers and sisters joined by the marriage bond have the right to expect from us, priests and pastors, good example and the witness of fidelity to one's vocation until death, a fidelity to the vocation we choose through the sacrament of orders just as they choose it through the sacrament of matrimony.

Need for Progressive Conversion: We must all be converted anew every day. ... This is a fundamental exigency of the Gospel addressed to everyone (cf. Mt. 4:17; Mk. 1:15), and all the more do we consider it addressed to us. If we have the duty of helping others to be converted, we have to do the same continuously in our own lives. Being converted means returning to the very grace of our vocation. ... continually "giving an account" before the Lord of our hearts about our service, our zeal and our fidelity. ... "giving an account" of our negligences and sins, of our timidity, of our lack of faith and hope, of our thinking only "in a human way" and not "in a divine way" ... seeking again the pardon and strength of God in the sacrament of reconciliation, and thus always beginning anew and every day progressing, overcoming ourselves, making spiritual conquests.

Being converted means "to pray continually and never lose heart" (Lk. 18:1).

Prayer likewise enables us continually to rediscover the dimensions of that kingdom for whose coming we pray every day.

We must link prayer with continuous work upon ourselves (for spiritual and intellectual development, through study and related activities).

We must be converted every day, we must rediscover every day the gift obtained from Christ himself in the sacrament of orders, by penetrating the importance of the salvific mission of the Church and by reflecting on the great meaning of our vocation in the light of that mission.

Mary, Mother of Priests: I desire that all of you, together with me, should find in Mary the Mother of the priesthood which we have received from Christ. I also desire that you should entrust your priesthood to her in a special way.

In our ministerial priesthood there is the wonderful and penetrating dimension of nearness to the Mother of Christ. So, let us try to live in that dimension.

QUAND JE DIS DIEU

Following is an excerpt from a declaration in which the Congregation for the Doctrine of the Faith called attention to doctrinal errors in a book written by French Dominican Father Jacques Pohier, a teacher at the Catholic Institute of Paris. The declaration, dated Apr. 3, 1979, was approved by Pope John Paul. This translation was published in the English edition of "L'Osservatore Romano" Apr. 17, 1979. Subheads have been added.

Evident Errors

1. Among the more evident errors in this book, one should note the denial of these truths: the intention of Christ to give to his Passion a redemptive and sacrificial value; the bodily resurrection of Christ and his continuation as a real subject after the end of his historical existence; life after death, resurrection, and eternal life with God as man's vocation; the presence in sacred Scripture of true teaching which has an objective meaning that faith can perceive and that the magisterium of the Church, assisted by the Holy Spirit, can authentically determine.

Other Statements

2. Added to and mixed in with these errors, one finds many other dangerous statements, so ambiguous and of such a nature as to generate uncertainty in the minds of the faithful about the following important articles of the Catholic faith: the Christian concept of the transcendent God; the real presence of Christ in the Eucharist as taught by the Council of Trent and, more recently, by Pope Paul VI in his encyclical *Mysterium Fidei;* the specific role of the priest in effecting this real presence; and the exercise of infallibility in the Church. With regard to the divinity of Christ, the author expresses himself in such an unusual manner that it cannot be determined whether he still professes this truth in its traditional Catholic meaning.

With this declaration, the Congregation for the Doctrine of the Faith, concerned for the good of the faithful, calls attention to the gravity of the errors here denounced, and to the impossibility of considering them as opinions left to the free discussion of theologians.

LIFE AFTER DEATH

Following is an excerpt from a "Letter on Certain Questions concerning Eschatology" addressed to bishops throughout the world by the Congregation for the Doctrine of the Faith. The letter, dated May 17, 1979, was approved by Pope John Paul. The text was circulated Aug. 2, 1979, by the NC Documentary Service, Origins (Vol. 9, No. 9). Subheads have been added.

Teaching of the Church

The sacred congregation, whose task is to advance and protect the doctrine of the faith, here wishes to recall what the Church teaches in the name of Christ, especially concerning what happens between the death of the Christian and the general resurrection.

• 1. The Church believes (Cf. The Creed) in the resurrection of the dead.

• 2. The Church understands this resurrection as referring to the whole person; for the elect it is nothing other than the extension to human beings of the resurrection of Christ itself.

• 3. The Church affirms that a spiritual element survives and subsists after death, an element endowed with consciousness and will, so that the "human self" subsists. To designate this element, the Church uses the word "soul," the accepted term in the usage of Scripture and tradition. Although not unaware that this term has various meanings in the Bible, the church thinks that there is no valid reason for rejecting it; moreover, she considers that the use of some word as a vehicle is absolutely indispensable in order to support the faith of Christians.

• 4. The Church excludes every way of thinking or speaking that would render meaningless or unintelligible her prayers, her funeral rites and the religious acts offered for the dead. All these are, in their substance, *loci theologici* (points of theology).

• 5. In accordance with the Scriptures, the Church looks for "the glorious manifestation of our Lord, Jesus Christ" (Dogmatic Constitution on Revelation, I, 4), believing it to be distinct and deferred with respect to the situation of people immediately after death.

• 6. In teaching her doctrine about man's destiny after death, the Church excludes any explanation that would deprive the Assumption of the Virgin Mary of its unique meaning; namely, the fact that the bodily glorification of the Virgin is an anticipation of the glorification that is the destiny of all the other elect.

• 7. In fidelity to the New Testament and tradition, the Church believes in the happiness of the just who will one day be with Christ. She believes that there will be eternal punishment for the sinner, who will be deprived of the sight of God, and that this punishment will have a repercussion on the whole being of the sinner. She believes in the possibility of a purification for the elect before they see God, a purification altogether different from the punishment of the damned. This is what the church means when speaking of hell and purgatory.

Caution about Representations

When dealing with man's situation after death, one must especially beware of arbitrary imaginative representations: excess of this kind is a major cause of the difficulties that Christian faith often encounters. Respect must, however, be given to the images employed in the Scriptures. Their profound meaning must be discerned, while avoiding the risk of overattenuating them, since this often empties of substance the realities designated by the images.

Neither Scripture nor theology provides sufficient light for a proper picture of life after death. Christians must firmly hold the two following essential points: On the one hand, they must believe in the fundamental continuity, thanks to the power of the Holy Spirit, between our present life in Christ and the future life (charity is the law of the kingdom of God and our charity on earth will be the measure of our sharing in God's glory in heaven); on the other hand, they must be clearly aware of the radical break between the present life and the future one, due to the fact that the economy of faith will be replaced by the economy of fullness of life: We shall be with Christ and "we shall see God" (Cf. 1 Jn. 3:2), and it is in these promises and marvelous mysteries that our hope essentially consists. Our imagination may be incapable of reaching these heights, but our heart does so instinctively and completely.

Pastoral Responsibility

Having recalled these points of doctrine, we would now like to clarify the principal features of the pastoral responsibility to be exercised in the present circumstances in accordance with Christian prudence.

The difficulties connected with these questions impose serious obligations on theologians, whose function is indispensable. Accordingly they have every right to encouragement from us and to the margin of freedom lawfully demanded by their methodology. We must however unceasingly remind Christians of the Church's teaching, which is the basis both of Christian life and of scholarly research. Efforts must also be made to ensure that theologians share in our pastoral concern, so that their studies and research may not be thoughtlessly set before the faithful, who today more than ever are exposed to dangers to their faith.

HUMAN SEXUALITY

The following critique of "Human Sexuality," a book published in 1977 by a special committee of the Catholic Theological Society of America, was addressed by the Congregation for the Doctrine of the Faith to Archbishop John R. Quinn, president of the National Conference of Catholic Bishops.

The text, made public Aug. 8, was distributed Aug. 30, 1979, by the NC Documentary Service, Origins (Vol. 9, No. 11). Subheads have been added.

The book *Human Sexuality* has already received substantial criticism on the part of theologians, of numerous American bishops and of the doctrinal commission of the American episcopal conference. It would seem clear that the authors of this book, who speak of "encouraging others to join us in the continuing search for more satisfying answers to the mystery of human sexuality" (p. xv), will have to give rigorous reconsideration to the position they have assumed in the light of such criticism. This is all the more important, since the topic of the book — human sexuality — and the attempt to offer "helpful practical guidelines to beleaguered pastors, priests, counselors and teachers," charges the authors with an enormous responsibility for the erroneous conclusions and the potentially harmful impact these ideas can have on the correct formation of the Christian consciences of so many people.

Need for Intervention

This sacred congregation, considering the fact that this book and its opinions have been given wide distribution within the United States, throughout the English-speaking world and elsewhere through various translations, considers it a duty to intervene by calling attention to the errors contained in this book and by inviting the authors to correct these errors. Here we limit our considerations to some of these errors which seem to be the most fundamental and to touch the heart of the matter. This limitation should not lead to the inference that other errors of a historical, scriptural and theological nature are not to be found in this book as well.

Mistaken Concept of Sexuality

1) A most pervasive mistake in this book is the manipulation of the concept or definition of human sexuality. "Sexuality then is the mode or manner by which humans experience and express both the incompleteness of their individualities as well as their relatedness to each other as male and female. . . . This definition broadens the meaning of sexuality beyond the merely genital and generative and is so to be understood in all that follows" (p. 82). This definition refers to what may be called generic sexuality, in which "sex is seen as a force that permeates, influences, and affects every act of a person's being at every moment of existence." In this generic sense the book quotes the Vatican "Declaration on Certain Questions Concerning Sexual Ethics," which acknowledged this basic human differentiation, saying: "It is from sex that the human person receives the characteristics which, on the biological, psychological and spiritual levels, make that person a man or a woman, and thereby largely condition his or her progress toward maturity and insertion into society" (*Persona Humana*, 1).

It is not, however, in this area of generic sexuality that the moral problematic of chastity is engaged. This occurs rather within the more specific field of sexual being and behavior called genital sexuality, which, while existing within the field of generic sexuality, has its specific rules corresponding to its proper structure and finality. These do not simply coincide with those of generic sexuality. Hence, while *Human Sexuality* cites the first paragraph of *Persona Humana*, as noted above, it fails to refer to the rest of the document's teaching on human sexuality, especially Number 5, which clearly states that "the use of the sexual function has its true meaning and moral rectitude only in true marriage."

No Specific Norms

It is equally evident that Vatican II, in Number 51 of *Gaudium et Spes* ("Pastoral Constitution on the Church in the Modern World"), speaks clearly of genital rather than generic sexuality when it indicates that the moral character of sexual conduct "does not depend solely on sincere intentions or on an evaluation of motives. It must be determined by objective standards. These, based on the nature of the human person and his acts, preserve the full sense of mutual self-giving and human procreation in the context of true love. Such a goal cannot be achieved unless the virtue of conjugal chastity is sincerely practiced." While the first part of this quotation is often cited in *Human Sexuality*, the last part is regularly omitted, an omission extended also to the following sentence in *Gaudium et Spes*, Number 51, which states: "Relying on these principles, sons of the Church may not undertake methods of regulating procreation which are found blameworthy by the teaching authority of the Church in its unfolding of divine law." While the book speaks in fact exclusively about genital sexuality, it sets aside the specific norms for genital sexuality and instead attempts to resolve questions by the criteria of generic sexuality (Cf. No. 2, below).

Furthermore, in regard to the teaching of Vatican II, we note here another mistaken notion. This book repeatedly states that the council deliberately refused to retain the traditional hierarchy of primary and secondary ends of marriage, opening "the Church to a new and deeper understanding of the meaning and value of conjugal love" (p. 125 and passim). On the contrary, the (council's) Commission of the Modi declared explicitly, replying to a proposal brought forward by many fathers to put this hierarchical distinction into the text of Number 48: "In a pastoral text which intends to institute a dialogue with the world, juridical elements are not required. . . . In any case, the primordial importance of procreation and education is shown at least 10 times in the text" (Cf. Nos. 48 and 50).

"Creative Growth" Purpose

2) In the view of sexuality described in *Human Sexuality*, the formulation of its purpose undergoes a substantial change with respect to the classical formulation: The traditional "procreative and unitive purpose" of sexuality, consistently developed in all the magisterial documents through Vatican II and *Humanae Vitae*, is substituted by a "creative and integrative purpose," also called "creative growth toward integration," which describes a broad and vague purpose applicable to any generic sexuality (and practically to any human action). Admitting that procreation is only one possible form of creativity, but not essential to sexuality (Cf. p. 38, sq.), is a gratuitous change in the accepted terms without any substantial argument, a change which contradicts the formulation used in Vatican II and assumed in *Persona Humana*. This change of purpose and consequently of the criteria for morality in human sexuality evidently changes all the traditional conclusions about sexual behavior; it even precludes the possibility of fruitful theological discussion by removing the common terminology.

Subjective Criteria

3) The authors of this book try to give more concrete content to the formal criterion, "creative growth toward integration" (p. 92, sq.), but hardly anything in this development seems to refer specifically to genital sexual activity. It is true that they intend to give only some "particularly significant" values (Cf. p. 92); nevertheless, those cited (e.g. honest, joyous, socially responsible) may be postulated equally well of most human activity.

The authors pretend that these are not purely subjective criteria, though in fact they are: The personal judgments about these factors are so different, determined by personal sentiments, feelings, customs, etc., that it would be next to impossible to single out definite criteria of what exactly integrates a particular person or contributes to his or her creative growth in any specific sexual activity.

Thus in Chapter 5, the criteria for discerning "creative growth toward integration," when applied to specific areas of sexual activity, yield no manageable or helpful rules for serious formation in matters of sexuality. In the book, moreover, they are called "guidelines" which can never be regarded as "absolute and universal moral norms" (p. 97).

Church Teaching Contradicted

4) The practical applications proposed in Chapter 5 show clearly the consequences of this theory of human sexuality. These conclusions either dissociate themselves from or directly contradict Catholic teaching as consistently proposed by moral theologians and as taught by the Church's magisterium. The intention expressed in the preface — "The fifth chapter . . . attempts to provide information and assistance for leaders in pastoral ministry to help them form and guide consciences in this area according to the mind of Jesus" — is sadly unfulfilled, indeed, even reversed.

The authors nearly always find a way to allow for integrative growth through the neglect or destruction of some intrinsic element of sexual morality, particularly its procreative ordination. And if some forms of sexual conduct are disapproved, it is only because of the supposed absence, generally expressed in the form of a doubt, of "human integration" (as in swinging, mate-swapping, bestiality), and not becasue these actions are opposed to the nature of human sexuality. When some action is considered completely immoral, it is never for intrinsic reasons, on the basis of objective finality, but only because the authors happen not to see, for their part, any way of making it so for some human integration. This subjection of theological and scientific arguments to evaluation by criteria primarily derived from one's present experience of what is human or less than human gives rise to a relativism in human conduct which recognizes no absolute values. Given these criteria, it is small wonder that this book pays such scant attention to the documents of the Church's magisterium, whose clear teaching and helpful norms of morality in the area of human sexuality it often openly contradicts.

LATIN AMERICAN BACKGROUND

The prelates assembled at Puebla, Mexico, for the Third General Assembly of Latin American Bishops were from countries with many things in common: political control by authoritarian regimes; economic domination by a wealthy upper class and considerable foreign capital; widespread poverty and unemployment; political impotence of the majority; governmental opposition, because of a national security complex, to persons of all kinds seeking social change; various kinds and degrees of repression and violence. One country, Nicaragua, was in the throes of revolution. El Salvador was one step removed from a political coup.

THIRD GENERAL ASSEMBLY OF LATIN AMERICAN BISHOPS

Evangelization was the theme of the Third General Assembly of Latin American Bishops held Jan. 27 to Feb. 13, 1979, at the Palafox Seminary in Puebla, Mexico. It was convened by the Latin American Bishops' Conference (CELAM) for the purpose of formulating guiding theory and practice for church ministry throughout the continent.

The assembly was the third of its kind since 1955 when bishops, together July 25 to Aug. 4 in Rio de Janeiro at an International Eucharistic Congress, decided to form a conference or council as a collegial, continent-wide service and liaison agency. CELAM was approved by Pope Pius XII the following Nov. 2, and central offices were set up in Bogota. The second general assembly, meeting Aug. 24 to Sept. 6, 1968, issued the "Medellin Guidelines" (under the title, *The Church in the Present-Day Transformation of Latin America in the Light of the Council),* which have had a strong influence on the course of church action in the pastoral and social-action fields. The third meeting addressed many of the concerns treated at Medellin, with a view to updating ways and means of getting its principles in effective touch with contemporary conditions of the people of Latin America.

Delegates and Officials

The principal attendants at the assembly were 187 delegates representing episcopal conferences in 22 nations. Also present were nearly 200 advisors and observers. Among the latter were Archbishop John R. Quinn and Bishop Thomas C. Kelly, president and general secretary, respectively, of the National Conference of Catholic Bishops and the U.S. Catholic Conference.

The presiding officers were: Cardinal Sebastiano Baggio, prefect of the Congregation for Bishops and president of the Pontifical Commission for Latin America; Cardinal Aloisio Lorscheider, president of the Brazilian Bishops' Conference, and Archbishop (later Cardinal) Ernesto Corripio Ahumada of Mexico City. The general secretary was Coadjutor Archbishop Alfonso Lopez Trujillo of Medellin.

Preparation and Background

Preparations for the assembly, under the direction of CELAM, took place over a two-year period of extensive consultation among the episcopal conferences of all Latin American countries. Final working papers covering a wide range of subjects reflected factual data, pastoral experience and implications with respect to the mission of the Church, people, and their economic, political, social and cultural institutions.

Additional documentary background for deliberations came from documents of the Second Vatican Council, especially the *Dogmatic Constitution on the Church* and the *Pastoral Constitution on the Church in the Modern World;* the "Medellin Guidelines" of 1968; the statement of the 1974 assembly of the Synod of Bishops on evangelization; and the related apostolic letter of Pope Paul VI, *Evangelii Nuntiandi.*

Pope John Paul II contributed to the agenda with two addresses Jan. 27 and 28 at the formal opening and first working session of the assembly. (See Latin American Addresses of Pope John Paul II.)

FINAL REPORT AND MESSAGE

The Puebla assembly produced a final report of more than 200 pages and a pastoral "Message to the People of Latin America."

The report is a mandate for pastoral action and social change in which the bishops pledged themselves to become the "voice of the voiceless masses." They keynoted the document as follows.

"Since Medellin, the Church . . . has examined the signs of the times and is generously disposed to contribute to the construction of a new society which is more just and fraternal, and which is a crying demand of our peoples.

"In this way tradition and progress . . . are today brought together in the search for a new synthesis which brings together the potential of the future and the energies which come from our common roots."

Liberation and Evangelization

"Total liberation . . . is of the essence for evangelization which aims at the true fulfillment of the human person. . . . There are two inseparable elements in it: liberation from all forms of servitude, from personal and social sin, from all that divides man and society because of selfishness and sin. Liberation is also growth of the person through communion with God and with people."

"Liberation as implemented in history — our own personal history and the history of peoples — embraces the various dimensions of existence: social, political, economic, cultural, as well as their interaction."

"The foundations of liberation are indicated in the truth about Christ, the truth about the Church and truth about man."

"The bishops of Latin America have very grave reason to urgently foster liberating evangelization as redress for social and individual sin because, since Medellin (1968), the condition of the majority was worsened considerably."

"The entire Christian community is responsible for the evangelization, liberation and development of man, in community with its legitimate pastors and guided by them.... Our social teachings must provide an effective answer to the challenges and grave problems of the real world of Latin America. It demands of us consistency, creativity, courage and total generosity."

Papal Approval

Pope John Paul approved the report of the assembly Mar. 23, 1979, in a letter addressed to CELAM officials. He said:

"This document ... offers ... a rich set of pastoral and doctrinal guidelines on questions of supreme importance. It must serve ... as a light and permanent stimulus for evangelization in the present and future of Latin America."

"Your experiences, rules, concerns and aspirations, in faithfulness to the Lord, to his Church and to Peter's See, must become life for the communities which you serve."

"God grant that all ecclesial communities will soon be informed and penetrated by the spirit of Puebla and the directives of this historic conference."

PASTORAL MESSAGE

The bishops at Puebla also issued an 11-page pastoral "Message to the People of Latin America." The following excerpts are from the translation published in the Feb. 26, 1979, English edition of "L'Osservatore Romano." Lead lines have been added.

Living the Gospel: Christianity, which brings with it the originality of love, is not always practiced in its entirety by us Christians (despite the existence of) great hidden heroism, much silent holiness, many marvelous acts of sacrifice.

We wish not only to convert others, but also to convert ourselves together with others in order that our dioceses, parishes, institutions, communities and religious congregations may be not an obstacle but, on the contrary, an incentive to live the Gospel (in Latin America where) the gap between the many who possess little and the few who possess a lot is increasing. The values of our culture are in danger. Fundamental human rights are being violated.

What the Church Has To Offer: What have we to offer before the serious and complex problems of our time?

John Paul II, in the opening address of his pontificate in St. Peter's Square, replies to us in an incisive, stupendous way, presenting Christ as the answer of universal salvation.... "To his saving power open the boundaries of states, economic and political systems, the vast fields of culture, civilization and development."

It seems to us that here lies the potentiality of the seeds of liberation for the Latin American man, our hope to construct, day by day, the reality of our true destiny. Thus, the men of this continent, the object of our pastoral concern, have an essential significance for the Church, since Christ assumed humanity and its actual condition, except sin. And, by so doing, he shared the immanent and transcendent vocation of all men.

Human Rights: (Man's) rights should be recognized, so that his life should not be a kind of abomination; so that nature, the work of God, should not be devastated contrary to his legitimate aspirations. Man demands ... that physical and moral violence, abuse of power, manipulation of money, abuse of sex and, finally, the breaking of the Lord's commandments, should be eliminated; because what is contrary to man's dignity wounds God, in a certain way.

Pastoral Preoccupations: What interests us as pastors is the complete proclamation of the truth about Jesus Christ, the mission of the Church, and the nature, dignity and ultimate purpose of man.

It is moving to perceive in the soul of the people spiritual riches overflowing with faith, hope and love. From this standpoint, Latin America is an example for all the other continents.... The Gospel which we preach is such splendid good news as to convert and transform minds and hearts, since it can communicate the greatness of man's destiny, prefigured in the Risen Christ.

Our pastoral preoccupations for the humblest members of the social body ... do not intend to exclude from our concern and from our hearts the other representatives of the social framework in which we live.

Cause of the Poor: Since we believe that the revision of the religious and moral behavior of men must be reflected in the political and economic spheres in our countries, we call upon all, without distinction of class, to accept and make their own the cause of the poor as though it were a question of accepting and making their own the cause of Christ himself.

Family: We call ... the family of Latin America to take its place in the heart of Christ, transforming itself more and more every day into a privileged place of evangelization, of respect for life, and of community love.

Youth: We call ... on the young to overcome the obstacles that threaten their rights to conscious and responsible participation in the construction of a better world. ... The time of protest, expressed in exotic forms or by means of inopportune exaltation, is now over. ... The time has come for reflection and full acceptance of the challenge to live fully the essential values of true and complete humanism.

Agents of the Apostolate: We greet all those ... who generously exercise the apostolate in our particular churches. Exhorting you to continue your labors in favor of the Gospel, we call upon you to make an increasing effort for the apostolate of vocations. ... The Church needs more diocesan and religious priests. ... She needs laity aware of their mission within the Church and in the construction of the temporal city.

Civilization of Love: We desire to address all men of good will ... engaged in tasks and missions in the most varied fields of culture, science, politics, education, work, the media of social communications, art.

We call on them to be generous constructors of (what Pope Paul VI called) the "civilization of love," inspired by the word, the life and the full donation of Christ, and based on justice, truth and freedom.

The civilization of love:

• Rejects violence, selfishness, waste, exploitation and moral disorders.

• Proposes to all the evangelical riches of national and international reconciliation.

• Condemns absolute divisions and psychological walls which violently separate men, institutions and national communities. Therefore, it defends with ardor the thesis of the integration of Latin America. In unity and in variety there are elements of continental value which deserve to be appreciated and studied far more than national interests. Our countries ... must be reminded of the urgent necessity of preserving and increasing the heritage of continental peace.

• Rejects subjection and dependence, detrimental to the dignity of Latin America. We do not accept being a satellite of any country in the world, far less of its ideologies. We wish to live on brotherly terms with everyone, because we reject narrow and inflexible nationalisms. It is time for Latin America to tell developed nations not to keep us at a standstill, not to hinder our progress, not to exploit us; on the contrary, to help us generously to overcome the barriers of our underdevelopment, respecting our culture, our principles, our sovereignty, our identity, our natural resources.

Appeal to Leaders: We respectfully and confidently call upon all those in charge of the political and social order to dwell on these reflections which have sprung from our experiences.

To work for justice, for truth, for love and for freedom, in the framework of communion and participation, is to work for universal peace.

Credal Statement (in which the bishops repeated a profession of faith voiced by the Second General Assembly of Latin American Bishops in 1968 in Medellin, Colombia): "God is present, alive, in Jesus Christ the liberator, in the heart of Latin America. We believe in the power of the Gospel. We believe in the efficacy of the evangelical value of communion and participation to bring forth creativity and to promote new experiences and new pastoral projects. We believe in the grace and strength of the Lord Jesus who instills life, who pushes us to conversion and solidarity. We believe in the hope which nourishes and strengthens man on his way to God, our Father. We believe in the civilization of love."

MINISTRY TO THE SPANISH-SPEAKING

The U.S. Census Bureau reported the following estimates, as of March, 1978.

Census Figures

• There are 12 million persons in the United States who claimed Spanish origin. About 7.2 million were of Mexican origin, 1.8 million of Puerto Rican origin, 700,000 of Cuban origin, 900,000 of Central or South American origin, and about 1.5 million of other Spanish origin.

• Most families of Spanish origin (85 per cent) live in metropolitan areas, as compared with 65 per cent of families not of Spanish origin.

• About 21 per cent of Spanish-origin families had incomes below the poverty level in 1977, as compared with about 9 per cent of families not of Spanish origin. The median incomes of Spanish-origin men and women were lower than those not of Spanish origin.

• A relatively small proportion (5 per cent) of employed men of Spanish origin were working in farm occupations. About 58 per cent were blue-collar workers, 24 per cent were white-collar workers, and 13 per cent were in service occupations. Of all employed women of Spanish origin (45 per cent), about one-half were white-collar workers, one-fourth were blue-collar workers, and one-fifth were in service occupations.

• The Spanish-origin population included a substantially larger proportion of young persons under the age of 18 (42 per cent) than did the population not of Spanish origin (29 per cent).

• Fifty-seven per cent of 25 to 29-year-old adults of Spanish origin had completed at least a high school education.

Distribution

Various reports indicate that most persons of Spanish origin in the southwestern states are Mexican-American. Large numbers of Mexican Americans are also in the Chicago area, Ohio, northern Indiana and southern Michigan.

Persons of Puerto Rican origin, although concentrated especially in the New York metropolitan area, also have large numbers in Chicago and Philadelphia.

Persons of Cuban origin are most numerous in Florida, particularly in the areas of Miami and Tampa. There are smaller concentrations in New York, northeastern New Jersey, Los Angeles, Long Beach, Calif., Chicago and urban areas of northwestern Indiana.

The vast majority of persons of Spanish origin in the U.S. have been baptized in the Catholic Church and comprise between 20 and 25 per cent of the Catholic population.

In 1979, there were nine Hispanic bishops (three heads of dioceses and six auxiliaries, all named since 1970), approximately 200 Hispanic priests (augmented by others speaking Spanish), 380 Hispanics in U.S. seminaries, more than 450 Hispanic permanent deacons, and a larger number of women religious.

Variable Conditions

Pastoral ministry to the Spanish-speaking in the United States varies, depending on differences among the people and the availability of personnel to carry it out.

The pattern in cities with large numbers of Spanish-speaking is built around special churches, centers or other agencies where pastoral and additional forms of service are provided in a manner suited to the needs, language and culture of the people. Services in some places are extensive and include legal advice, job placement, language instruction, recreational and social assistance, specialized counseling, replacement services. In many places, however, even where there are special ministries, the needs are generally greater than the means required to meet them.

Some of the urban dwellers have been absorbed into established parishes and routines of church life and activity. Many Spanish-speaking communities, especially those with transients, remain in need of special ministries.

An itinerant form of ministry best meets the needs of the thousands of migrant workers who follow the crops in various areas of the country. Some of these ministries are carried out from centers and include other services — health, instruction for children, etc. — in addition to opportunities for attending Mass and receiving the sacraments.

Special ministries for the Spanish-speaking have been in operation for a long time in dioceses of the Southwest. The total number of dioceses with such ministries is more than 75.

Two Encuentros

Pastoral care for the Spanish-speaking was the central concern of the 1972 *Primer Encuentro Nacional Hispano de Pastoral*, a national meeting of diocesan bishops and their delegates sponsored by the U.S. Catholic Conference. Needs pinpointed in deliberations were for: greater participation by the Spanish-speaking in leadership and decision-making at all levels in the Church in the U.S.; the development of programs for Christian leadership formation; the establishment of nationally coordinated regional centers of pastoral research and reflection.

A second National Hispanic Pastoral Encuentro held Aug. 18 to 21, 1977, in Washington, was attended by 500 delegates and 600 observers representative of Hispanic Catholics throughout the country. Among them were eight Hispanic bishops named since 1970, 50 more bishops, about 100 priests, additional religious and a majority number of lay persons.

The business of the meeting concerned the pastoral and social ministry of the Church to the Spanish-speaking. It was handled in six plenary sessions and 36 workshops which turned out some 30 resolutions under the headings of evangelization, ministries, education, political responsibility, human rights, and ethical pluralism in the unity of the Church and general society.

Implementation of recommendations that emanated from the encuentros went forward in 1978 and 1979. Particular emphasis was focused at meetings and in actions on increasing language capability among persons involved in ministry, awareness of Hispanic cultural elements in liturgy and practice, leadership development, and moves for the formation of basic Christian communities (*comunidades de base*). A task force for implementation was chaired by Archbishop Robert F. Sanchez of Santa Fe, N.M.

Agencies and Organizations

Secretariat for the Spanish-Speaking: The national secretariat of the U.S. Catholic Conference, for service in promoting and coordinating pastoral ministry to the Spanish-speaking. Its basic orientation is toward integral evangelization, combining religious ministry with development efforts in programs geared to the culture and needs of Hispanics. Its concerns are urban and migrant Spanish-speaking people; communications and publications in line with secretariat purposes and the service of people; bilingual and bicultural religious and general education; liaison for and representation of Hispanics with church, civic and governmental agencies.

Paul Sedillo, Jr., is director of the national office at 1312 Massachusetts Ave. N.W., Washington, D.C. 20005.

The secretariat has regional offices in California and the Midwest. A Southwest Regional Office for the Spanish-speaking, directed by Ms. Lupe Anguiano, is located at 2114 Commerce St., San Antonio, Tex. 78207.

The secretariat also has working relations with the **Northeast Pastoral Center for Hispanics,** established in 1976 and supported by bishops in 14 states from New England to Virginia. It shares the objectives of the national secretariat in efforts to develop a full array of pastoral programs for the Spanish-speaking.

Mario J. Paredes is executive director of

the center, which is located at 1011 First Ave., New York, N.Y. 10022.

In the Southwest, 55 Mexican-American priests organized **PADRES** in February, 1970, to help the Church identify more closely with the pastoral, social, economic and educational needs of the Spanish-speaking. PADRES is an acronym for the Spanish title, "Padres Asociados para Derechos Religiosos, Educativos y Sociales."

Leadership development of Hispanos is one of the principal concerns of PADRES, a national organization with membership open to priests, brothers, deacons, seminarians and others interested in working with the Hispanic community. Father Luis Olivares, C.M.F., is the national president. Brother Trinidad Sanchez, S.J., is the executive director. Offices are located at 3112 W. Ashby St., San Antonio, Tex. 78228.

An analogous organization of Chicano sisters, **Las Hermanas,** was organized in 1971 (see separate entry).

The **Mexican American Cultural Center:** was founded in February, 1971, with grants from the Texas Catholic Conference and PADRES, the assistance of Las Hermanas, and the use of a facility belonging to the San Antonio archdiocese. It is a pastoral-cultural center with continuing programs in three institutes, on language, pastoral leadership and publications.

Fathers Virgil Elizondo and Ricardo Ramirez are president and executive vice president, respectively, of the center, which is located at 3019 French Pl., P.O. Box 28185, San Antonio, Tex. 78228.

Miami Apostolate

The Spanish-Speaking Apostolate in metropolitan Miami is one of the most extensive in the country. It serves a population of well over 553,174 people: more than 424,000 Cubans who have established residence there since Fidel Castro rose to power Jan. 1, 1959; a permanent Latin population of more than 50,000; and some 100,000 migrant workers. Directly involved in the apostolate are 71 Spanish-speaking priests and 88 religious brothers and sisters. Spanish-speaking priests are assigned to 39 parishes.

Centro Hispano Catolico (Spanish Catholic Center), founded by Archbishop Coleman F. Carroll in October, 1959, provides many forms of assistance to new arrivals from Latin countries, including: pastoral counseling, orientation to life in the U.S., employment services, medicine-food-clothing distribution, day nursery and kindergarten care, programs for senior citizens, and home visits. Located in the center are Archdiocesan Offices for Immigration Services and the Latin American Affairs Office which fosters cultural relations with Latin American countries.

The staff of the center consists of a chaplain, four Sisters of Social Service, and more than a score of lay persons. Sister Suzanne, S.S.S., is supervisor. of the center. The episcopal vicar for Spanish-speaking peoples in the archdiocese is Bishop Agustin Roman. The center is located at 130 N. E. 2nd St., Miami, Fla. 33132.

Officers of the Migration and Refugee Service, U.S. Catholic Conference, in Miami figured largely in the work of receiving and resettling many of the refugees who have come to this country via the Cuban airlift and Spain.

All told, 299,651 persons were resettled between 1961 and the end of 1975. The states with the highest numbers of resettled Cubans were New York (80,997), New Jersey (59,404), California (39,939), and Illinois (22,450).

BLACK CATHOLICS

The National Office for Black Catholics, organized in August, 1970, is a central agency with the general purposes of promoting active and full participation by black Catholics in the Church and of making more effective the apostolate of the Church in the black community.

Walter Hubbard is president of the office's board of directors. Brother Cyprian Lamar Rowe, is executive director. The liaison officer with the National Conference of Catholic Bishops is Auxiliary Bishop Joseph A. McNicholas of St. Louis.

The NOBC office is located at 1234 Massachusetts Ave. N.W., Washington, D.C. 20005. Its publication is entitled *Impact*.

NOBC Affiliates

The NOBC has affiliates in various cities throughout the country. Three of its member bodies are:

• The National Black Catholic Clergy Caucus, formed at a charter meeting in April, 1968, in Detroit. Its president is Brother Booker Ashe, O.F.M. Cap., House of Peace, 1702 W. Walnut St., Milwaukee, Wis. 53205.

• The National Black Sisters' Conference (see separate entry).

• The National Black Catholic Lay Caucus.

Principal support for NOBC operations comes from proceeds of a Black Catholics Concerned collection conducted in parishes annually in October.

Objectives

NOBC operations are in support of the aspirations and calls of black Catholics for a number of significant objectives.

Josephite Center

The Josephite Pastoral Center was established in September, 1968, as an educational and pastoral service agency for the Josephites in their mission work, specifically in the black community. St. Joseph's Society of the Sacred Heart, the sponsoring body, has about 185 priests and 20 brothers in 80 mostly southern parishes in 18 dioceses.

The center's operative functions are in the fields of education, research, planning and consultation, and mission development. Its purpose, as stated in a booklet reporting its first 10 years of operation, is to "provide resources and services (not only to its own men but also to others involved in ministry to black people) fostering positive attitudes and appreciation toward race, particularly blackness. Our goal is to make concrete what Pope Paul VI stated, 'the gift of blackness must enrich the Church.'"

Father Joseph A. Benintende, S.S.J., is the executive director of the center, located at St. Joseph Seminary, 1200 Varnum St. N.E., Washington, D.C. 20017.

One of several actions of the Josephites in 1978 was the publication in February of a paper entitled "Black Institutions — An Expression of Life."

The paper acknowledged the desirability of integration in church and other institutions. Its principal thesis, however, was a defense of the existence of separate black institutions wanted by the black community. Such institutions, the paper said, should not be disbanded, eliminated or absorbed by white institutions because they have an identity and vitality of their own as "valid expressions of black people's culture, talent, industry and determination."

"Black people," declared Father Eugene McManus, vicar general of the Josephites, "define integration not as assimilation but as a pluralism of true equals."

Black Catholic Population in the U.S.

(Sources: *Statistical Profile of Black Catholics*, published by the Josephite Pastoral Center, Washington, D.C., 1975 figures; *Official Catholic Directory, 1976*, total Catholic population figures. Hawaii and Alaska are not included in totals.)

Region	Black Caths.	Total Black Pop.	Perc. Caths. Black Pop.	Cath. Pop.	Perc. Blacks Cath. Pop.
New England	20,675	386,557	5.3	5,673,372	.4
Middle Atlantic	158,882	3,950,356	4.0	12,941,250	1.2
E. North Central	180,689	3,867,653	4.6	10,420,011	1.7
W. North Central	51,286	697,760	7.3	3,245,895	1.6
S. Atlantic	132,904	6,381,843	2.1	2,715,806	4.8
E. South Central	30,234	2,569,625	1.7	634,349	4.7
W. South Central	237,368	3,005,587	7.9	3,631,334	6.5
Mountain	6,607	178,416	3.7	1,562,453	.4
Pacific	98,209	1,512,018	6.4	5,294,512	1.8
TOTALS	916,854	22,549,815	4.0	46,118,982	2.0

Up to 1926, only 10 black American priests were ordained in the U.S. One hundred and 13 were ordained between 1930 and 1960; 83 of them belonged to religious communities.

NATIONAL CATECHETICAL DIRECTORY APPROVED

Following is the text of a letter from the Congregation for the Clergy concerning the National Catechetical Directory, entitled "Sharing the Light of Faith." Dated Oct. 30, 1978, and addressed to Archbishop John R. Quinn, the letter was read at the Nov. 13 to 16 meeting of the National Conference of Catholic Bishops and the United States Catholic Conference. The text was circulated by NC News Service.

This congregation finds *Sharing the Light of Faith* to be a generally faithful application of the *General Catechetical Directory* to the American pastoral scene. It is outstanding for its ecclesial spirit, its clarity of expression, its emphasis on memorization of basic prayers and doctrinal formulations, its solid argument and its flexibility.

Approval and Reservations

The substantial orthodoxy of *Sharing the Light of Faith* should be apparent to anyone who studies the entire work attentively. Doctrinal statements that may seem incomplete at first reading of one section are habitually rounded out in another. On the other hand, there are certain points of importance that should be reworked before the publication of the first edition.

• 1. Pages 39-44: The employment of capital and small letters (Revelation, revelation) to distinguish various meanings of the notion of revelation tends to engender confusion. It would seem to be less open to misunderstanding if the word "revelation" standing alone, without modifiers, quotations or italics, were to signify public, divine revelation in the strict sense, and that other expressions be chosen to indicate other modes by which God manifests himself to men.

• 2. Page 113: Not only should the catechesis for the sacrament of reconciliation precede first holy Communion, but youngsters should normally receive the sacrament of penance before their first holy Communion. (Cf. joint declarations of the Congregations for the Sacraments and Divine Worship and for the Clergy, 1973 and 1977; and also the address of Pope Paul VI to the bishops of New York Province, May 20, 1978.)

• Page 111: This section concerning the administration of general absolution would more faithfully reflect existing norms if it brought out more clearly that general absolution will only be rarely extended, and also that the circumstances indicating its administration must indeed be serious.

• Pages 119-120: The specific nature of the priesthood should be more exactly expressed by placing due emphasis on its sacrificial-eucharistic aspect, as well as on the concept of the configuration of the priest to Christ. In classical theological terminology, the ministerial priest acts not only in the name of Christ but "in the person of Christ" (*Dogmatic Constitution on the Church*, No. 10).

As a corollary of the above, it might be well to distinguish more clearly the character of the priest and bishop from that of the deacon, and also from the common priesthood of the faithful (page 77, lines 25-28) which differs from the ministerial or hierarchical priesthood "essentially and not only in degree" (*Ibid*, No. 10).

Authorization and Future Review

Sharing the Light of Faith is a consoling reflection of the American catechetical reality and it is a source of profound satisfaction to the Holy See that this new national directory enjoys such widespread consensus in a nation so vast and so varied in its cultural and religious traditions.

Having noted that the episcopal conference plans to review the text periodically for updating and improvement, and that "approximately five years after its approval by the Holy See it will be submitted to extensive consultation," this congregation hereby authorizes, without further need for further consultation, the use of *Sharing the Light of Faith* with the above-mentioned revisions. After a period of five years, we shall be happy to review the planned second edition.

APOSTOLIC EXHORTATION

Instruction and formation in the faith was the subject of an apostolic exhortation issued by Pope John Paul Oct. 16, 1979. The document, entitled *Catechesi Tradendae*, was made public Oct. 25. It was written in response to and on the basis of recommendations made by the 1977 assembly of the Synod of Bishops.

The Church "must offer catechesis her best resources in people and energy, without sparing effort, toil or material means," the document stated. It warned against "the tendency in various quarters to minimize" the importance of catechesis and against "the abandonment of serious and orderly study of the message of Christ in the name of a method concentrating on life experience."

"Authentic catechesis is always an orderly and systematic initiation into the revelation that God has given of himself to humanity in Christ Jesus." It must deal with essentials, and not be either "improvised" or theological research or discussion of all disputed questions. Nevertheless, it "must be sufficiently complete" and "be an integral Christian initiation open to all the factors of Christian life."

The document also said, among other things:

• The various creeds, especially the Creed of the People of God issued by Paul VI in 1968, should be used as "a sure point of reference for the content of catechesis."

• The Church has a "sacred duty and an inalienable right" to conduct its catechesis, even though "the right is being violated by many states, even to the point of attaching criminal penalties to it."

• Different methodologies for various cultures, age groups or special circumstances are valid to the extent that they are "inspired by the humble concern to stay closer to a content that must remain intact."

ABORTION CONTROVERSY — CONTINUED

See related entries in News Events, also: Birthright, Right to Life, Human Life Foundation, Conscience Clauses.

Controversy over the abortion issue continued in 1978 and 1979, resulting in some gains for the pro-life movement but not enough to overcome prevailing pro-abortion influences in society and judicial decisions.

Supreme Court Decisions

At the center of the controversy were several principal decisions handed down by the U.S. Supreme Court since 1973.

• In Roe v. Wade and Dole v. Bolton, the Court ruled on Jan. 22, 1973: (1) During the first three months of pregnancy, a woman's right to privacy is paramount. Accordingly, she has an unrestricted right to abortion with the consent and cooperation of a physician. (2) In the second trimester, the principle controlling legislation on abortion procedures is the health or welfare of the mother, understood in the widest possible sense. (3) in the "state subsequent to viability," the controlling principles are the State's "interest in the potentiality of human life" and "the preservation of the life or health of the mother."

The rulings canonized the absolutely private right of a woman to have an abortion and denied to the unborn the right to life.

- In Danforth v. Planned Parenthood, the Court ruled on July 1, 1976, against the constitutionality of state laws requiring spousal (in the case of a married woman) or parental (in the case of a minor) consent for an abortion.
- The Court ruled on June 20, 1977, that the U.S. Constitution does not require states to pay for nontherepeutic (elective) abortions and does not require public hospitals to provide them.

The U.S. Supreme Court did not make any substantial rulings on abortion in 1978. It did, however, agree to accept a case from Pennsylvania (Beal v. Franklin) involving the basic question: Does the right to abortion mean the right to a dead fetus?

At issue was a portion of the 1974 Pennsylvania Abortion Control Act. The key provision of the law, struck down in lower court, provided that abortions, done when "the fetus is viable if there is sufficient reason to believe that the fetus may be viable," should be done in a manner protecting the fetus, unless the life or health of the mother would be adversely affected.

- The Court ruled, 6 to 3, on Jan. 9, 1979, that the Pennsylvania law was unconstitutional, on the ground of its vagueness. The decision had the effect of meaning that a woman exercising a legal right to have an abortion had the right to a dead fetus and that the doctor performing the abortion could not be charged civilly or criminally for the death of the fetus.
- The Court ruled July 2, 1979, against the constitutionality of a Massachusetts law requiring a minor to consult with her parents before having an abortion. In the absence of parental consent (which the Court had already ruled was not required) or parental consultation (not required either), a court could clear the way for the abortion of a minor judged to be mature enough to have one.

Funding Background

Backgrounding abortion developments in 1978 and 1979 was legal action in 1976 and 1977 which blocked enforcement of the Hyde Amendment against the funding of abortions not needed to save the life of the mother.

On June 20, 1977, the Supreme Court ruled that states are not required to pay for elective Medicaid abortions and that public hospitals are not required to perform them. Subsequently, a 10-month injunction against the Hyde Amendment was reversed, and the Department of Health, Education and Welfare ended federal funding for elective abortions early in August.

As the Hyde Amendment died at the end of September, the House of Representatives and the Senate remained deadlocked over an abortion-funding amendment to an appropriations bill for HEW and the Department of Labor. The deadlock was broken in December when the two Houses agreed on language prohibiting abortion funding except when the mother's life would be endangered or she would face severe and long-lasting physical damage if she carried the pregnancy to full term, or if pregnancy resulted from rape or incest.

In 1979, another funding deadlock was broken when the House and Senate agreed on a compromise permitting temporary funding of abortion until Nov. 20 to save the life of a mother and in cases of rape or incest. Originally, the House called for a stricter bill permitting funding only in cases of danger of maternal death. The Senate wanted a less restrictive measure permitting funding in cases when a mother would face severe and long-lasting physical damage if she carried a pregnancy to full term.

The Second Session of the 95th Congress in 1978 provided maternity benefit coverage for pregnant women working for companies with disability programs, and funds to help pregnant teen-agers.

Pro-life advocates were heartened in both years by signs of increasing support in the House of Representatives, where more votes than before were cast for restrictive funding proposals. The Senate, however, still favored abortion funding on a freer basis for "medical reasons" of almost any imaginable kind.

Sixteen states were still paying for elective abortions in 1979.

Court decisions in some states resulted in injunctions against laws restricting funding for elective abortions. Invasion of privacy, denial of equal protection of law, and discrimination against the poor were the usual legal grounds of support for such decisions.

Informed Consent

Court action testing the constitutionality of "informed consent" statutes was underway in 1978 and 1979.

Injunctions were in effect in May, 1979, against such restrictive measures in Akron, O., Tennessee, Oklahoma and Louisiana. More than 25 other states, however, had statutes of the same type under consideration.

The generally required:
- a 24 hour waiting period before performance of an abortion;
- notification of a parent or husband at least 24 hours before performance of an abortion;
- warnings of possible medical dangers from the operation;
- counseling on alternatives to abortion;
- telling the woman that an unborn child "is a human life from the moment of conception."

It was reported in June, 1979, that 15 states had passed resolutions calling for a constitutional convention to act on a pro-life amendment. It seemed unlikely that a move of this kind would eventuate in a convention, or that a convention, if called, would limit itself just to consideration of such an amendment.

Protests of the sit-in type, along with other demonstrations, were staged during 1979 against abortion clinics and other installations in various places. Some of them resulted in arrests, fines, and short jail terms.

Responsible leaders of the pro-life movement disavowed any connection with violence connected with some of the protests.

Charges Against the Church

The Catholic Church is the largest and strongest institutional opponent of abortion, because of its firm teaching and practice on the subject, and also because of the number of its members who are against it.

Because this is so in a cultural climate favoring abortion and moral liberalism, the Church has been accused and charged with:

• dominating the pro-life movement;

• trying to force its views on others who do not share its faith;

• violating a peculiar interpretation of the principle of separation of Church and state.

These accusations have been implicit and explicit in reporting of the abortion controversy ever since it began.

The Church insists, however, on its right to speak and act on moral issues on an equal basis with others who claim rights of conscience and freedom to influence others in a society which is subject not only to the laws of man but, above all, to universal moral law.

New Jersey Superior Court Judge David Furman, while striking down Jan. 10, 1979, a state ban on the funding of elective abortions for women on welfare, rejected the argument that the ban violated the principle of separation of Church and state. He called untenable the plaintiff's contention that the law was rooted in religious beliefs and that the Catholic Church had intervened in the legislative process with undue pressure. He wrote: "Whatever the peril to a democratic society of predominant influence by one religion over the legislative process, such a constitutional attack has not been upheld in any cited federal or state decision. Active support of the opposition to legislating on gambling and alcoholic beverages by various organized religions has been commonplace."

Statistics

Estimates indicate that nearly or more than an average of one million abortions a year, reported and unreported, have been performed in the U.S. since the Supreme Court handed down the decisions of Jan. 22, 1973.

The HEW Center for Disease Control reported in August, 1978, that 988,267 abortions were performed in 1976, an increase of 18 per cent over the total reported for the previous year. Also reported was an increase in the ratio of abortions to live births, from 272 per 1,000 in 1975 to 312 per thousand in 1976.

Secretary of Health, Education and Welfare Joseph Califano told a House of Representatives appropriations subcommittee Mar. 8, 1979, that the Hyde Amendment restricting federal funding of abortions had reduced Medicaid-paid abortions by 99 per cent from a previous level of about 250,000 a year. Between Feb. 14 and Dec. 31, 1978, he said, HEW paid for 2,421 abortions. The larger percentage of abortions was performed on young, white, unmarried women with few or no children.

TEST-TUBE BABY

The first authenticated birth of a child conceived outside of a mother's womb occurred July 25, 1978, in Lancashire, England. The girl, Louise, was the daughter of Gilbert John and Lesley Brown.

Steps in the conception and birth of the child were surgical removal of eggs from the mother, fertiilization by sperm of the father in a laboratory vessel, and subsequent implantation and development of the fetus in the mother's womb.

The doctors who conducted the procedure were Patrick C. Steptoe and Robert G. Edwards.

Praise for the scientific advance represented by the *in vitro* conception was matched with scientific and moral cautions. Pope Pius XII and traditional Catholic moral norms were quoted against the procedure because, among other things, of the divorce between normal marital intercourse and procreation.

Moral Considerations

"*In vitro* fertilization involves externalizing both sperm and ovum," stated Andre E. Hellegers and Father Richard A. McCormick, S.J., in an article published in the Aug. 19, 1978, edition of *America*. They continued: "It is, from the technological point of view, a step beyond artificial insemination that externalizes only the sperm. . . . Thus, at least some of the basic ethical considerations that surround *in vitro* fertilization are already present in the discussion of artifical insemination."

Moral norms relevant to both of these processes were stated by Pope Pius XII on two particular occasions.

Pius XII Statements

In an address to the Fourth International Convention of Catholic Doctors Sept. 29, 1949, he said:

"The practice of artificial insemination, when it is applied to man, cannot be considered exclusively, nor even principally, from the biological and medical viewpoint, while leaving aside the viewpoint of morality and law."

"Artifical insemination outside of marriage is to be condemned purely and simply as immoral."

"Artificial insemination in marriage with the use of an active element from a third person is equally immoral and as such is to be rejected summarily."

"With regard to the lawfulness of artificial insemination in marriage ... the simple fact that the desired result is obtained by this means does not justify the employment of the method itself; nor does the desire of the marriage partners — most legitimate in itself — to have a child, suffice to prove the lawfulness of a recourse to artificial insemination for the fulfillment of that desire."

Speaking again, before the Second World Congress on Fertility and Sterility May 19, 1956, the Pope said:

"With regard to artificial fecundation, not only is there reason to be extremely reserved, but it must be absolutely rejected. In speaking thus, one is not necessarily forbidding the use of certain artificial means destined solely to facilitate the natural act or to achieve the attainment of the natural act normally performed."

"On the subject of the experiments in artificial fecundation *in vitro*, let it suffice for Us to observe that they must be rejected as immoral and absolutely illicit."

Caution

Pressure has been mounting in the U.S. for an end to a four-year moratorium on federal funding for *in vitro* experimentation. The Ethics Advisory Board of the Department of Health, Education and Welfare, in a report issued in March, 1979, concluded that such research is acceptable despite substantial ethical arguments against it.

Several months earlier, researchers of the Eastern Virginia Medical School proposed plans to open a clinic for this type of research. Bishop Walter E. Sullivan of Richmond said in a pastoral letter issued in November, 1978, that the proposal raised "serious moral and ethical implications" that had not been addressed by society. He also denounced the "cultural schizophrenia" existing in Virginia, "where we announce research into making test-tube babies and at the same time, through legal abortion, deny life to 50,000 healthy babies each year."

The clinic had not been established by the time of writing.

DNA RESEARCH

The U.S. Bishops' Committee for Human Values, in a statement released in May, 1977, expressed concern over the balance of risk and benefit involved in gene-splicing made possible by the identification and experimental use of DNA (deoxyribonucleic acid), the chemical basis and agent of heredity.

The transplanting of genetic material from one species of cells to another produces new cells (forms of life) of a higher order which can be beneficial or dangerous, depending on the nature of the recombinants and the manner in which they are handled. Such gene-splicing has yielded a remarkable fund of information about the chemistry and mechanisms of heredity.

Practically all DNA research and experimentation has been carreid on within the limits of federal guidelines designed to minimize hazards to the environment and human health through the controlled use of weak-strain bacteria in escape-proof laboratories. The guidelines — primarily for the direction of federal grantees — were predicated on risk factors now considered too high by some experts but still regarded as relevant by others.

Pertinent questions are being asked about how far to go with experimentation and whether and how to expand it from generally pharmaceutical confines to industrial use in chemistry, agriculture and food production, without harmful results.

The bishops' committee cautioned against doing whatever science can do with DNA just because it can be done. The statement said: "We ought not now to follow slavishly the technological imperative that 'all that can be done, must be done.' ... Our actions ... must reflect the range of human goods in the process" of determining how to proceed toward enlightened public policy, with communication and collaboration between the scientific community and the public.

BIOETHICS

Bioethics is "the systematic study of human conduct in the area of the life sciences and health care, insofar as this conduct is examined in light of moral values and principles" (*Encyclopedia of Bioethics,* Ed. Warren Reich; Free Press-Macmillan).

Subjects include: abortion, *in vitro* fertilization, human experimentation, sterilization, euthanasia, organ transplants, right to health care, therapist-patient relationships, war and science, population ethics, environmental health, informed consent.

CONSCIENCE CLAUSES

Conscience clauses — generally granting civil and criminal immunity to health personnel and institutions (with some exceptions) refusing to cooperate in abortion procedures for moral, ethical or religious reasons — or their equivalent have been adopted in at least 39 states. One clause of this type is the Church Amendment.

MINISTRIES OF THE CHURCH

The ministries of bishops, priests and deacons for sacramental and pastoral service are defined by the terms of their ordination in the sacrament of order. So are the minor ministries of ordained and commissioned acolytes and lectors.

The ministries of religious are defined by the nature and the collective and individual apostolates of their communities.

Less thought of perhaps, but of no less importance for the total good of the Church and the people it is commissioned to serve, are the ministries of lay persons.

Ministry Is for Everyone

Everyone who is baptized is initiated into participation in the threefold mission of Christ, as priest, prophet and head of the kingdom of God. This initiation, carried forward by confirmation and supplemented as the case may be by the sacraments of order and matrimony, is for a life of worship, of witness to Christian belief and love, and of action for building the kingdom of God.

Summarily, these are the objects of all ministry, although in ways that are appropriately different for those who are ordained, for those with religious profession, and for lay persons.

The Second Vatican Council spelled out the ideological background in several key documents, including: the *Dogmatic Constitution on the Church*, the *Decree on the Appropriate Renewal of Religious Life* and the *Decree on the Apostolate of the Laity*.

All the baptized are assigned by that fact to apostolic witness, to ministry, in a way that matches their states in life, their gifts of nature and grace, and their opportunities for service — to, in and through the Church, and for building the kingdom of God through service to people.

Lay persons have the world of secular affairs as their specific sphere of ministry, because it belongs to them more than it does to those with holy orders and those who are religious. For lay persons, life where they are — in work, the professions, marriage, the single state, etc. — is their mission. And the mission is to minister there for the accomplishment of God's designs, to mediate faith, love and grace to people around them.

Ordained men and religious men and women minister to the world as well; but, as noted earlier, they do so in the pattern of assigned service and in response to apostolic opportunities appropriate to them.

The range of ministries of the Church are as extensive as the sacramental, pastoral and human needs of people to be served. Accordingly, the potential for ministry calls for continuous development.

Such development has been taking place in recent years in the ministries of the ordained and religious, expanding in many directions and affecting the nature of their profession and the reach of their various apostolates.

This process will continue, and it will do so in such a way that those immediately engaged will be more active in making and directing the decisions which shape the forms of their lives and works. This development is evidenced in a striking way by the results of renewal efforts of religious communities.

The expansion of ministries is also indicated by the restoration of the permanent diaconate in the Roman Church.

Distinctive Lay Ministry

Lay persons, as well as those with orders and vows, have distinctive ministries of their own. These ministries, while related to the others, are not just imitations of them but have dimensions of their own which derive from the patterns of their lives and their involvement in the secular world.

Lay persons have their own gifts and opportunities for ministry. Yet, many of them do not realize that what they have been doing for years is really ministry. To overcome this lack of awareness, efforts are needed to empower the laity and affirm them in their roles as ministers in various areas.

Lay ministry coordinators have laid stress on the fact that lay ministry has its own forms and models which are different from the ones shaping the ministries of the ordained and religious.

Some coordinators have suggested that lay ministry could be enhanced and made better known and more effective if people were commissioned for it in some kind of formal way for definite periods of time. This view, however, is not shared by everyone.

Archbishop Jean Jadot, apostolic delegate to the U.S., took exception to it in an address at a religious education conference Mar. 1, 1979, in North Carolina. He said he had reservations about the establishment of a formal ministry of catechist because it "would have the effect of making the source of lay ministry the official recognition by the Church, rather than the right and duty flowing from our incorporation into the Church by baptism and later enhanced by confirmation."

Forty-seven signers of a "Chicago Declaration of Christian Concern," issued in December, 1977, expressed a similar view, contending that over-institutionalizing lay ministry was hindering its development and having the effect of relaxing the urgency of lay initiative deriving from the universal vocation of all members of the Church to ministry. Lay initiative was also being stalled, the signers felt, because priests and religious were usurping lay roles and were not active enough in stimulating lay persons to assume ministries that should be theirs.

CULTS

A considerable number of religious and non-religious cults unrelated to main-line Christian denominations have developed in the United States in recent years. They are variously estimated to number from several hundred to several thousand, with a membership of present and past adherents amounting to perhaps three million.

Many cults mushroomed in the anti-establishment 1960s. Observers now are of the opinion that they peaked about four or five years ago, but that some of them are still influential, especially among young people seeking escape from social and personal confusion, truth instead of doubt and uncertainty, community instead of loneliness and alienation, rapture in place of the tedium of ordinary life.

Influential Cults

• The Holy Spirit Association for the Unification of Christianity, better known simply as the Unification Church, is the creation of Sun Myung Moon, a Korean industrialist, who claims he had a meeting with Christ in 1932 and received a commission to prepare for the coming of a new messiah. Its "bible" is Moon's *Divine Principle*. Among its tenets are those stating that: the Bible was written in code, which Moon understands and interprets; Christ is a "failed messiah" and Christianity "a failure"; Jewry has "no reason to exist."

The church, started in 1954 and introduced in the United States in 1959, cannot be considered Christian, according to a study report issued in December, 1976, by an interdenominational commission of scholars under the auspices of the National Council of Churches.

It is estimated that Moon followers worldwide may number as high as 500 million, mostly in Korea and Japan. There may be between 7,000 and 10,000 full-time members in a total of about 37,000 in the U.S. The membership in this country is predominantly white, middle-class and young, ranging in age from 18 to 30 and averaging 24 years of age. Approximately 35 per cent and 15 percent are said to be converts from Catholicism and Judaism, respectively.

• The Hare Krishna sect, with a background and regimen of Hindu ideology and discipline, was introduced in the United States in 1965 by A.C. Bhaktivedanta Swami Prabhupada. Until recently, when its members began to conform more to accepted ways of dress and public conduct, the sect was more publicly theatrical and demonstrative than numerous. Chanting processions of its saffron-robed, shaved-head members were not uncommon on the streets of some large cities.

The International Society of Krishna Consciousness traces its origin to the 16th century in India, as one of many sects worshiping one of the eight incarnations of Vishnu, "The Preserver," one of the gods of the Hindu triad. Members undergo a period of training, adopt Hindu names, seek spiritual enlightenment through chanting and the study of Hindu sacred books, and practice a discipline affecting their entire life-style.

Full-time sectaries, numbering about 5,000 in the U.S., live in communes. The society has about 90 temples in the world. About 18 per cent of the members, most of whom are young, are said to be Catholic by baptism.

• The Way Ministry is critical of established religions and what it regards as their lack of power and influence. It promises a way to "abundant living" through conduct based on what is claimed to be a rediscovery of teaching lost to Christianity since the time of the Apostles.

Cults have several factors in common, such as strong leadership, definite discipline and ritual in religious or quasi-religious conduct, and a sense of community and enthusiasm generated by their ideology and peer pressure.

Objectionable Characteristics

Objectionable characteristics of cults were cited in a statement entitled "The Dangers of Pseudo-Religious Cults," issued by the Pennsylvania Conference on Interchurch Cooperation during the winter of 1979. The statement was released less than two months after the suicide-massacre of more than 900 members of the People's Temple cult on the orders of Jim Jones at Jonestown, Guyana (see November News Events).

"1. Their approach, whether in soliciting funds or in recruiting new members, tends to be misleading."

"2. Their method of recruitment and conversion seeks to incapacitate . . . from the free exercise of . . . will, intellect and emotions. This is what has been called 'brainwashing' or mind control. It is a subtle and enslaving process designed to make a person into a highly profitable and easily controlled servant who is completely subservient to the cult's leader(s)."

"3. This process of mind control involves dramatic alienation from family, traumatic destruction of one's sense of personal identity, often with change of name, elimination of all significant human relationships outside the cult, extremely strong peer pressure, purposeful diet manipulation to starve the brain, and arduous and fatigue-producing daily discipline."

"4. Each cult has a messianic-type leader who claims to have received a new, ultimate and final revelation from God."

"5. Cult members often consider themselves to be the only truly good people and perceive all the rest . . . as evil."

NOVEMBER 1978

VATICAN

Justice in Society — Justice was the principal theme of an address delivered by Pope John Paul II during a general audience Nov. 8. Noting that papal encyclicals and documents of the Second Vatican Council are evidence of the Church's concern with it, he said: "Justice is, in a certain way, greater than man and greater than the dimensions of his earthly life.... Every man lives and dies with a certain sense of insatiability for justice, because the world is not capable of satisfying fully a being created in the image of God. And thus, through this hunger for justice, man is opened to God who 'is justice itself.'"

Curia Appointments — The Pope completed the reappointment for undetermined terms of all heads of Congregations of the Roman Curia with the reinstatement Nov. 9 of Cardinal John Wright as prefect of the Congregation for the Clergy. The earlier appointments had lapsed after the deaths of Paul VI and John Paul I.

Address to Priests — The Pope spoke to the clergy of Rome Nov. 9, with emphasis on the distinctiveness and necessity of their priesthood among the people they serve. He said, among other things:

• The "communion of priests among themselves and with the bishop is the fundamental condition of union among the whole people of God."

• "We are necessary for men; we are immensely necessary and not part-time, not half-time, like 'employees.' We are necessary as those who bear witness and reawaken in others the need to testify."

• "Let us not deceive ourselves that we are serving the Gospel if we try to 'water down' our priestly charism through exaggerated interest in the vast field of temporal problems, if we wish to 'secularize' our ways of living and acting, if we cancel even the external signs of our priestly vocation."

• "We must keep the sense of our singular vocation, and this 'singularity' must be expressed, also in our exterior garb. Let us not be ashamed of it. Yes, we are in the world but are not of the world."

• "Our 'ministerial' priesthood, rooted in the sacrament of holy orders, differs essentially from the universal priesthood of the faithful. And it was constituted in order to enlighten more effectively our brothers and sisters who live in the world — that is, the laity — about the fact that in Jesus Christ we are all a 'kingdom of priests' for the Father. The priest reaches this purpose through the ministry of the word and of the sacraments, which is specifically his, and above all through the Eucharistic Sacrifice, for which he alone is authorized. The priest realizes all this also through a suitable life-style. Therefore, our priesthood must be clear and expressive. And if, in the tradition of our Church, it is closely linked with celibacy, this is due precisely to the clarity and 'evangelical' expressiveness referred to in our Lord's words on celibacy 'for the kingdom of heaven' (Mt. 19:12)."

Christ Is the Key to Service — "The first service that the Church must perform in the cause of justice and peace is to invite men to open themselves to Jesus Christ," Pope John Paul told members of the Pontifical Justice and Peace Commission Nov. 11. In Christ, he said, men "will learn again their essential dignity as sons of God ... endowed with unsuspected possibilities which make them capable of facing up to the tasks of the hour, bound to one another in a brotherhood that is rooted in the fatherhood of God." In Christ, persons "will become free for responsible service."

Women and Men Religious — The renewal of congregations of religious must be guided by "love of God" and an understanding of — but not subservience to — contemporary realities, stated Pope John Paul during a meeting Nov. 16 with 600 nuns belonging to the International Union of Superiors General.

He said: "The treasure of the evangelical counsels and the commitment ... to make them the charter of a Christian existence cannot be relativized by public opinion, even if it were ecclesial. The Church and ... the world itself need more than ever men and women who sacrifice everything to follow Christ in the way of the Apostles." The Holy Father also said: "If your consecration to God is really such a deep reality, it is important to bear permanently its exterior sign which a simple and suitable religious habit constitutes. It is the means to remind yourselves constantly of your commitment which contrasts strongly with the spirit of the world. It is a silent but eloquent testimony. It is a sign that our secularized world needs to find on its way — as many Christians, moreover, desire. I ask you to turn this over carefully in your minds."

In an address to 90 members of the Union of Superiors General of men religious, the Pope said Nov. 24 that prayer "has greater value and spiritual fruit than the most intense activity, even apostolic activity tiself." He added that the vocation of members of religious orders to serve the universal Church is carried out in local churches. "Everything must be done," he stated, "so that 'the consecrated life' be developed in individual local churches, so that it may contribute to building them up spiritually, so that it may be their special strength."

Sacramental Discipline — In an address to 38 Canadian bishops Nov. 17, the Pope reconfirmed the practices of individual confession and of first confession before first Communion, reaffirmed doctrine on the indissolubility of marriage, and emphasized the "altogether exceptional character of general absolution." He also said that, because of the central significance of God's word, the Church is called to give "absolute pastoral priority to the ever-more effective guarding and teaching of the deposit of faith."

No Intercommunion without Doctrinal Agreement — Haste to end "the intolerable scandal of the division of Christians" should not lead Catholics to celebrate the Eucharist with other Christians before doctrinal differences are resolved, declared the Pope during a meeting Nov. 18 with members of the Vatican Secretariat for Promoting Christian Unity. Despite its reservations about intercommunion, the Church "desires, as far as it can and in full docility to the suggestions of the Holy Spirit, to intensify at all levels its contribution to this great movement of all Christians."

Meeting with Archbishop Lefebvre — Pope John Paul met privately Nov. 18 with dissident Archbishop Marcel Lefebvre who was suspended from the exercise of holy orders July 24, 1976, for ordaining priests without appropriate authorization. There was no announcement or official comment about the meeting.

Temperance — In the last of four talks on the cardinal virtues, the Holy Father told persons attending a general audience Nov. 22 that temperance is "indispensable, so that man may be fully man." He said: "The temperate man is the one who is master of himself, the one in whom the passions do not dominate the reason, the will, and even the heart. ... We observe clearly that 'to be a man' means to respect one's own dignity, and therefore, among other things, to let oneself be guided by the virtue of temperance."

Riches of the Eastern Rites — The Catholic Church "would be much poorer" without the riches of the Eastern Rites, declared Pope John Paul Nov. 23 before a group of Eastern-Rite bishops from the United States. He said that the traditions of the Eastern Rites "enshrine many great artistic and cultural values, the loss of which would be sorely felt."

The Pope Also:

• Resumed Nov. 9 the practice of meeting individually with bishops in Rome for required *ad limina* visits and reports on the state of their dioceses.

• Attended a Mass in the Sistine Chapel Nov. 10 for cardinals who had died in the previous 12 months: Cardinals Traglia, Taguchi, Violardo, Yu Pin, Gracias and Filipiak.

• Urged film producers and actors to promote authentic human values, in a message marking the 50th anniversary of the International Catholic Film Organization.

• Took possession of the Basilica of St. John Lateran, his cathedral as Bishop of Rome, Nov. 12, in ceremonies completing the formalities of the beginning of his pontificate.

• Conveyed his sympathy to relatives of 199 victims of a plane crash Nov. 15 in Indonesia.

• Consoled an eight-year-old boy following the death of his father, during an audience with 13,000 Italian youngsters Nov. 15.

• Intervened Nov. 25 for the first time in church-state relations by backing complaints of the Italian bishops that the government was restricting welfare activities of the Church by placing their funding and operations under the authority of regional authorities of government.

• Paid tribute on the solemnity of Christ the King, Nov. 26, to the courage of people suffering persecution because of their faith.

Vatican Briefs:

• Msgr. Ettore di Filippo told a United Nations committee that the Vatican was in support of its proposal to convene a world assembly on the elderly and to proclaim an International Year on Aging.

• Members of the Secretariat for Promoting Christian Unity called Nov. 23 for "an evaluation, in some official way," of documents produced in recent years by bilateral consultations between representatives of the Church and other religious bodies. (See Ecumenical Dialogues.)

• The Vatican publishing house announced late in the month that it had received guardianship of rights of publication of all the writings of John Paul II, including those published before his election to the papacy.

Doctrine and Discipline

The Holy Father told a group of 18 U.S. bishops Nov. 9 of his hopes for renewed emphasis on sound doctrine and discipline in the life of the Church. He said:

"This is my own deepest hope today for the pastors of the Church in America, as well as for all the pastors of the universal Church, that (in the words of John XXIII) 'the sacred deposit of Christian doctrine should be more effectively guarded and taught.' ... To present this deposit of Christian doctrine in all its purity and integrity, with all its exigencies and in all its power, is a holy pastoral responsibility. It is, moreover, the most sublime service we can render.

"And the second hope I would express today is a hope for the preservation of the real discipline of the Church. ..."

"These hopes for the life of the Church... intimately depend on every new generation of priests who, with the generosity of love, continue the Church's commitment to the Gospel.... And it is my ardent desire today that a new emphasis on the importance of doctrine and discipline will be the postconciliar contribution of your seminaries, so that 'the word of the Lord may speed on and triumph' (2 Thes. 3:1)."

NATIONAL

Injunction against the NLRB — Federal District Court Judge R. Dixon Herman issued an injunction Nov. 3 against intervention by the National Labor Relations Board on behalf of lay teachers at a Catholic high school in Wilkes Barre, Pa. He ruled that the NLRB has no jurisdiction over Catholic schools and that the injunction was "necessary to protect the religious freedom of this plaintiff, the Catholic school, and those members of its religious mission; and ... to carry out the fundamental purpose of the First Amendment."

Planned Parenthood Criticized — For the second time in a month, Bishop Edward W. O'Rourke of Peoria criticized Planned Parenthood because of its advocacy of artificial birth control and abortion, and called again on the local United Way agency to stop funding the organization. His objections were directed at the objectives and operations of the organization's current "Five Year Plan."

Sex Education — Five Florida bishops issued a statement in which they objected against public-school programs of sex education that "do not take into account the whole person, reference to ethical-moral order, responsibility to other members of society, or the primary right of parents."

CHD Grant — The Campaign for Human Development reported that a seed-money grant of $50,000 awarded in 1976 to a self-help organization in North Memphis, Tenn., had developed into a $2.8 million project for rehabilitating housing, cutting crime, providing job training for high school dropouts and reducing unemployment.

San Antonio Statement — A "Message to the Hispanic Community and to the Christian People of the United States" was issued by 70 participants in a four-day Ecumenical Hispanic Theological Conference at the Mexican American Cultural Center. Signatories of the statement affirmed their need to unite themselves "to those who are fighting to make democracy a political and economic reality."

Right-to-Life Vote — The right-to-life vote in the Nov. 7 elections was considered a factor in the defeat of Senators Dick Clark of Iowa and Thomas J. McIntyre of New Hampshire, and in the return to office of Representatives Henry J. Hyde and Robert Michel of Illinois and Robert K. Dornan and Danny Lundgren of California. In New York, gubernatorial candidate Mary Jane Tobin gained more than enough votes to assure the Right to Life Party a position above that of the Liberal Party on state ballots for the next four years.

Revision of New Testament Text — Bishop Thomas C. Kelly, general secretary of the National Conference of Catholic Bishops and the U.S. Catholic Conference, announced that members of the Catholic Biblical Association would undertake revision of the New Testament text of the New American Bible in a project scheduled for completion by the end of 1982.

Tortilla Curtain — Plans of the U.S. Immigration and Naturalization Service to build fences along the southern border of the U.S. to stem the flow of undocumented Mexican aliens were called "utterly ridiculous" by Bishop Patrick Flores of El Paso. He said the fences would not deter those who really wanted to get into the country.

Anti-Abortion Pledge of Allegiance — Christian Brother Stephen O'Hara, superintendent of Catholic schools in the Providence diocese, announced he would not interfere with the decision of a principal to use an anti-abortion version of the Pledge of Allegiance at St. James' School, West Warwick, R.I. The version ended with the words, "with liberty and justice for all, born and unborn." U.S. Attorney Paul Murray said the version was "probably not illegal."

TV Advertising and Children — Fifteen priests and nuns joined with representatives of several Protestant denominations in support of a proposed ban on TV advertising aimed at young children. A rule proposed by the Federal Trade Commission would ban advertising to children "too young to understand the selling purpose," and (would) severely restrict the advertisement of sugared food products.

Medicaid Abortion Records Are Public Information — The Minnesota Supreme Court ruled 6 to 3 Nov. 24 that records of the names of doctors and clinics performing Medicaid-funded abortions are public information and that *The Catholic Bulletin* (of the St. Paul-Minneapolis archdiocese) "is authorized to have access to it." Release of the information, which the paper tried to secure over a 17-month period, had been opposed by the Minnesota Medical Association and the Minnesota Civil Liberties Union.

Religious Broadcasting — Paid religious programming by fundamentalist broadcasters and "entrepeneurial types that masquerade under the name of religious broadcasting" threaten access to free time ($10 million worth) for the Catholic Church and other mainline religions. So stated Robert Beusse, secretary for communications, U.S. Catholic Conference, in a talk on proposed revisions in the Federal Communications Act to directors of state Catholic conferences meeting in Washington, D.C. More and more often, he said, "the broadcaster bumps the local religious program or the syndicated religious programming coming from the major denominations or the network religious program . . . and puts on a Save-a-Soul telethon, and that (sponsoring) group moves on to the next town just like the old medicine shows."

Abortion Clinic Ban Upheld — The U.S. Supreme Court let stand a Cleveland ordinance banning abortion clinics in areas zoned for retail business and legal and medical offices. Chief U.S. District Court Judge Frank Battisi had ruled earlier against the clinic, declaring that the ordinance "appears to be consonant" with a 1977 Supreme Court decision, and that it did not unduly burden "either the abortion decision or the physician-patient relationship."

128 Catholics in 96th Congress — *Christianity Today*, in a report on the religious affiliations of members of the 96th Congress, indicated: 128 Catholics (115 Representatives and 13 Senators), 75 United Methodists, 70 members of the Episcopal Church, 60 Presbyterians, 57 Baptists, 30 Jews, 19 Lutherans, 16 members of the United Church of Christ, 12 Unitarians, 10 Mormons, six Disciples of Christ and five Greek Orthodox.

Homosexual Bills — By a vote of 26 to 16, the New York City Council rejected a motion to release from committee a bill requiring employers, landlords and others running places of public accommodation to accept homosexuals on an equal basis with heterosexuals or to be held responsible to the Commission on Human Rights for failing to do so. Officials of the New York archdiocese, along with seven national Jewish organizations, opposed the bill. In New Jersey, the bishops announced their support of a bill against a measure which, they said through spokesman Edward J. Leadem, provided for legislative condoning and approving of homosexual acts.

Test-Tube Baby Clinic — In a pastoral letter to people of the Richmond diocese, Bishop Walter F. Sullivan expressed "grave concern" about announced plans of researchers at the Eastern Virginia Medical School to open a clinic for the study of laboratory fertilization." He said the proposal raised "serious moral and ethical implications" that had not been addressed by society. He also denounced the "cultural schizophrenia" existing in Virginia, "where we announce research into making test-tube babies and at the same time, through legal abortion, deny life to 50,000 healthy babies each year."

National Briefs:
• With the recent appointments of L. Franklin Devine and Sister Kristin McNamara of the Sisters of Loreto, eight Catholics were serving in staff positions with the National Council of Churches.

• The United Nations Food and Agriculture Organization awarded a special medal to Msgr. Luigi Ligutti in commemoration of his 50 years of work on agricultural development and the improvement of rural conditions.

• Six months after withdrawing from the National Federation of Priests' Councils, the priests' senate of the Brooklyn diocese voted for reaffiliation.

• National Bible Week was observed Nov. 19 to 26, with focus on "The Word of God Is Light and Life."

• Archbishop Daniel E. Sheehan, chairman of the Boys Town board of directors, declared that recent *Omaha Sun* articles alleging financial mismanagement at the institution "contain a lot of half-truths and some deliberate misstatements."

• Meetings included those of: Four hundred sisters belonging to *Consortium Perfectae Caritatis* Nov. 10 to 12, in Washington, D.C.; 2,000 participants, two-thirds of them nuns, in the Second National Women's Ordination Conference Nov. 10 to 12 in Baltimore; 250 attendants at the Fourth National Workshop on Christian-Jewish Relations.

NCCB-USCC Meeting

About 250 bishops attended the meeting of the National Conference of Catholic Bishops and the United States Catholic Conference Nov. 13 to 16 in Washington, D.C.

Reports received by the bishops included one from the Vatican approving, with several reservations, the text of a *National Catechetical Directory*. The principal statements issued by the assembly were one on the Middle East and another, a pastoral letter, on the handicapped. Two measures approved at the conclusion of post-meeting mail ballotting concerned a national communications collection and authorization for bishops, at their option, to permit Communion under the forms of bread and wine on Sundays and holy days.

Administrative decisions made before the meeting reversed earlier ones that would have terminated the Secretariat for Human Values and ended the advisory services of Msgr. George Higgins.

(See separate entry.)

INTERNATIONAL

Humane Treatment Wanted — While government officials discussed friction between the U.S. and Mexico, Bishop Arturo Lona of Tehuantepec appealed for "humane treatment" of Mexican migrant workers in the U.S. It was estimated that 800,000 to one million impoverished Mexicans crossed the border annually to seek jobs on farms in the Southwest.

Political Christianity — Christianity is being reinterpreted as a scheme of social and political action because of the current politicization of the clergy, declared the Rev. Edward Norman, an Anglican church historian, in a radio broadcast from London Nov. 1. Clergymen, he said, "have allowed themselves — some eagerly, and many others unwittingly — to define their religious values according to the categories and references provided by the compulsive moralism of contemporary intellectual culture." These political adaptations, he added, "are far too relative to be regarded as central in the definition of Christianity itself."

Remains of St. John the Baptist? — Discovery of an ancient coffin unearthed early in the month at the St. Makarios Monastery 60 miles from Cairo sparked speculation that the remains inside might be those of St. John the Baptist. Old manuscripts were cited in support of the belief that the body was interred at the monastery in the 11th century.

Religious Education in Czechoslovakia — The German Catholic news agency, KNA, reported continuing harassment of religious education efforts in Slovakia by atheistic pressure groups and state school officials.

In another development, a group of Czechoslovakian priests and lay persons appealed to the Vatican "not to give us any more government bishops." The appeal was in the form of a secret letter to Archbishop Agostino Casaroli, secretary of the Council for the Public Affairs of the Church, according to the Italian magazine, *Prospettive nel Mundo*.

Jonestown Horror — Catholic journalists and spokesmen added their voices to the chorus of amazement and incredulity over the mass suicide Nov. 18 of more than 900 members of the Temple of God community at Jonestown, Guyana.

Human Rights — More than 2,000 persons attending a Nov. 25 Symposium on Human Rights sponsored by the Vicariate of Solidarity in Santiago, Chile, committed themselves to continue efforts for implementation of documents on human rights such as the encyclical *Pacem in Terris* and declarations by the United Nations and the Organization of American States. They said: "Today we have lighted in this cathedral these lamps of hope (votive candles) in the midst of a world searching for enlightenment. Every Nov. 25 we will come back to rekindle this light and be united ... in the commitment to continue the struggle for every man and woman to have the right to be a human person." No government officials attended or commented on the symposium.

In a separate action, the bishops of Chile declared in a joint statement that no economic law could justify the enslavement of workers. They made the statement in response to a move by the military government to replace the leadership in 2,400 unions after excluding candidates who were "engaged in political activities" or were "militant in political parties."

Press Freedom — Concern over the free flow of information around the world was a major topic at a Nov. 25 business meeting in Rome of the International Federation of Catholic Press Agencies. Father Marcel Furic, reporting on UN efforts to establish international policies on the flow of information, said there was a basic, unresolved division "between the partisans of freedom of information and the partisans of responsibility."

Priest Killed — Father Ernesto Barrera Motto and two other men were killed by government security personnel Nov. 28 in Ciudad Delgado, a suburb of San Salvador, in another incident of violence in El Salvador.

Lutheran-Orthodox Dialogue — Lutheran and Orthodox representatives meeting in Sweden recommended that contacts between their churches be continued, with joint studies on the nature of the Church, tradition and the priesthood.

International Briefs:

• The International Commission on English in the Liturgy, meeting Nov. 1 to 9 in Edinburgh, announced the beginning of study of ways of eliminating sexist and anti-Semitic language in liturgical texts.

• Rich nations should provide two per cent of their gross national product annually to stimulate Third World economies and world trade, declared British economist Barbara Ward during an International Symposium on Human Development sponsored by St. Francis Xavier University, Antigonish, Nova Scotia.

• Amnesty International reported Nov. 20 that religious believers and political dissidents were being subjected to psychiatric repression, persecution and forced labor in Rumania.

English Anglican Synod

The General Synod of the Anglican Church of England, meeting Nov. 6 to 10 in London, rejected a proposal for the ordination of women to the priesthood by a vote of 272 to 246. The vote of the House of Clergy, 149 to 94 against the measure, was decisive. The House of Bishops and the House of Laity voted for the proposal, 32 to 17 and 120 to 106, respectively.

Women had already been ordained to the priesthood in the Anglican Church in Hong Kong, Canada and New Zealand, and in the Episcopal Church in the United States.

The synod also turned down proposals to include a prayer after abortion in the liturgy and to approve the remarriage in church of divorced persons. The remarriage proposal was to be submitted to the 43 dioceses of the Anglican Church of England for further consideration.

DECEMBER 1978

VATICAN

Marian Observance — Pope John Paul joined thousands of persons in tribute to Mary on the feast of the Immaculate Conception, in devotional ceremonies in the *Piazza di Spagna* — the site of a column and statue erected in Rome by Pope Pius IX to commemorate proclamation of the dogma in 1854.

Intelligence Is Stimulated by the Word of God — So stated the Pope Dec. 8 before an audience of 7,000 Catholic university teachers and students. He said that "a fully satisfactory answer to the basic problems of human existence" cannot be found in pure or applied science or in philosophy, but only in religion."

Appeal for Religious Freedom — The Pope marked the 30th anniversary Dec. 11 of the United Nations Universal Declaration on Human Rights with a solemn appeal "that, in every place and by everyone, religious freedom be respected for every person and for all peoples." Calling religious freedom "the basis of all other freedoms," he attacked efforts by states professing atheism to suppress religion. He also called for an end to "the baneful positions of secularism," especially "the erroneous reduction of the religious element to the purely private sphere." The Pope made his appeal in a special message to UN Secretary General Kurt Waldheim.

Church Needs Vital Space — Pope John Paul told Bulgarian Foreign Minister Petar Mladenov Dec. 13 that the Catholic Church "does not seek to obtain privileges" but needs "vital space" to fulfill its religious mission "and also to be able to work — according to its specific nature and with the means proper to it — for the integral and peaceful development of every man and all men." In addition, he noted the need for church and government officials to work together on common causes.

Paul VI and St. Paul — The Holy Father, speaking Dec. 17 at the dedication of a vocational school started by Paul VI, cited his likeness to the Apostle. He asked rhetorically: "Why did he choose the name of Paul? Certainly because he found a particular affinity with the Apostle of the Gentiles. Besides, did not the pontificate of Paul VI bear witness to how deeply he understood, as St. Paul did, the new call of Christ to the universalism of the Church and of Christianity according to the measure of our times? . . . Did he not hear himself called, like this Apostle, to carry the Gospel even to the ends of the earth?"

Address to Cardinals — The Pope spoke of various subjects during his first pre-Christmas meeting with members of the College of Cardinals Dec. 22. Among them were:

• His succession in the papacy to Paul VI and John Paul I, of whom he spoke with praise.

• Concern for justice, human rights, personal dignity and peace in the world.

• His intention to attend the Jan. 27 to Feb. 12, 1979, meeting of the Latin American Bishops' Council in Puebla, Mexico, and to visit the shrine of Our Lady of Guadalupe.

• His acceptance of a request from government officials of Argentina and Chile to mediate their dispute concerning sovereignty over islands in the Beagle Channel. (Later, he named Cardinal Antonio Samore to act as a mediator on his behalf.)

• Opening of the archives of the pontificate of Leo XIII to scholars.

• Designation of the title, Paul VI Hall, for the structure built for papal audiences during his predecessor's pontificate.

Collegial Action — Pope John Paul encouraged all European bishops' conferences to participate effectively in the Council of Bishops' Conferences of Europe, in an address Dec. 19 to members of the council. Such cooperation, he said "is one of the ways of incarnating collegiality. . . . It is only under these conditions (of collegiality) that the analysis of the essential problems of the Church and society and of Christianity can be complete. . . . Your conference must become in some way the nursery in which is expressed, developed and matured not only the awareness of what Christianity was yesterday but the responsibility for what it must be tomorrow."

Atheism — Atheism "is contrary to the fundamental rights of man" in denying or inhibiting his right to seek God, declared the Pope during a general audience Dec. 27. He said: "Man is the being who seeks God. . . . This is the truth about man. . . . It must be granted to man because it defines him. . . . Atheism is not in accord with this criterion . . . when it denies *a priori* that man is the being who seeks God or when, in various ways, it mutilates that search in social, public and cultural life."

Gospel Inspiration in Education — The Pope told members of the Federation of Institutes of Educational Activity late in the month that Catholic schools should refer constantly to the teaching of Christ. He said: "In an era like ours, it is urgent . . . to preserve the image . . . of a Christian school which, in ever loyal observance of the general norms of educational legislation of the respective country, assumes as its point of departure and its goal the ideal of an integral education — human, moral and religious — according to the Gospel of our Lord."

Abortion — Pope John Paul attacked the "recent and sorrowful event of abortion legislation" in Italy during a meeting with representatives of the Italian Catholic Doctors' Association Dec. 28. He also said: "I want to express my sincere admiration for all those health care workers who, following the dictates of right conscience, are daily resisting flattery, pressure, threats and at times even physical violence for not soiling themselves with actions in every way offensive to that sacred value which is human life." He called the right to life "the primordial presupposition of every other human right.

The Pope referred again to abortion, along with divorce, during a New Year's Eve Mass at the Jesuit Church of the Gesu. He said: "Even while maintaining respect toward all those who think differently, it is most difficult to recognize, from an objective and impartial point of view, that one conducts himself by the measure of true human dignity if he betrays matrimonial fidelity or if he allows life conceived in a mother's womb to be exterminated or destroyed. As a consequence, it cannot be admitted that 'the principle of divorce' and 'the principle of abortion' serve the good of men and contribute to making human life truly most human, truly most worthy of man; that they serve the construction of a better society."

Mature Christian Awareness — The Pope called for "mature Christian awareness" among lay Catholics in an audience Dec. 30 with thousands of members of Italian Catholic Action. "It is necessary, above all," he stated, "to have certainty and clarity about the truth which you must believe and practice. If you are insecure, uncertain, confused, contradictory, you cannot build up. It is particularly necessary today to have an enlightened and convinced faith, if you are going to be able to be enlightening and convincing."

The Pope Also:

• Advanced the canonization causes of three persons Dec. 1 with decrees certifying the practice of heroic virtue by: Polish Salesian Father August Czartoryski (1858-93); French Sister Francoise de Sales Aviat, foundress of the Congregation of the Oblate Sisters of St. Francis de Sales (1844-1914); Sudanese Sister Josephine Bakhiti, born into slavery, who died in 1947.

• Celebrated Mass in a parish church of Rome, St. Francis Xavier, for the first time, Dec. 3.

• Appealed to Christian communities to be sensitive to the needs of migrants, in a letter marking Migrants' Day.

• Pleaded for aid to Vietnamese refugees, Dec. 3.

• Expressed his sympathy to relatives of 108 victims of a plane crash Dec. 23 off the coast of Sicily, and to the head of the Algerian National Assembly on the death of President Houari Boumedienne.

• Received the credentials of new ambassadors to the Vatican: Paul Ndiaye of Senegal; Vecdi Turel of Turkey, Dec. 5; John Molloy of the Irish Republic, Dec. 12; Christophe de Kallay of the Sovereign Military Order of Malta, Dec. 14.

• Had meetings with: Robert F. Wagner, special envoy of President Carter, Dec. 4; Andrew Young, U.S. ambassador to the United Nations, Dec. 5; Archbishop John R. Quinn and Bishop Thomas Kelly, president and general secretary, respectively, of the National Conference of Catholic Bishops and the U.S. Catholic Conference; King Hussein of Jordan, Dec. 15.

Vatican Briefs:

• "The Duties of the Christian Family in the Contemporary World" was announced Dec. 9 as the theme of the 1980 assembly of the Synod of Bishops.

• Cardinal Bernardin Gantin, president of the Pontifical Commission for Justice and Peace, said in a letter marking the 30th anniversary of the UN Universal Declaration on Human Rights that excessive individualism is a serious threat to human rights: "It makes any social restraint an inadmissible attack on freedom. This near anarchic atmosphere endangers any social authority although such authority is, of itself, an irreplaceable service for the ordered and solid development of the freedom of everyone."

• The Pontifical Society for the Propagation of the Faith distributed $59 million for the support of missionary activity in 92 countries in 1978.

Christmas Message

The Holy Father addressed a message "to every human being" at Christmas, which he called "the feast of man." Speaking from the central balcony of St. Peter's Basilica at noon, he said:

"I address . . . all the various communities: the peoples, the nations, the regimes, the political, economic, social and cultural systems, and I say:

"Accept the great truth concerning man.

"Accept the full truth concerning man that was uttered on Christmas night.

"Accept this dimension of man that was opened for all human beings on this holy night.

"Accept the mystery in which every human being lives since Christ was born.

"Respect this mystery.

"Allow this mystery to act in every human being.

"Allow him to develop in the outward conditions of his earthly existence.

"Humanity's power resides in this mystery (of the birth of Christ) — the power that permeates everything that is human. Do not make it hard for that power to exercise its influence. Do not destroy its influence. Everything that is human grows from this power:

without this power it perishes; without this power it falls to ruin."

The Pope extended Christmas greetings in 25 languages to people throughout the world.

Speaking earlier in a homily during Mass at midnight, the Pope said:

"On this night let us ... think of all the human beings who fall victim to man's inhumanity, to cruelty, to the lack of any respect, to contempt for the objective rights of every human being. Let us think of those who are lonely, old, or of the homeless, those suffering from hunger, and those whose misery is the result of the exploitation and injustice of economic systems. Let us also think of those who on this night are not allowed to take part in the liturgy of God's birth and who have no priest to celebrate Mass. And let us give a thought also to those whose souls and consciences are tormented no less than their faith."

NATIONAL

Pax Christi against SALT II — The executive council of Pax Christi, during the organization's Dec. 1 to 3 meeting in New York, announced it would not support the Strategic Arms Limitation Treaty being negotiated by the U.S. and the U.S.S.R. Auxiliary Bishop Thomas J. Gumbleton said in a presidential address that the agreement in its existing form would "legitimate" the nuclear arms race and that, "if we supported it, (we would) offer (it) religious legitimization."

Texas Missions — Confusion was reported in the Archdiocese of San Antonio over the effects of the Missions National Park law on the parish operations of four historical missions — San Juan Capistrano, San Francisco de la Espada, San Jose and Concepcion. President Carter, after signing the law Nov. 10, issued a memorandum Nov. 17 in which he said he would consider plans to put its financial and other provisions into effect only if the missions "cease being used as active parish churches and pass into secular ownership." Archbishop Francis J. Furey said the archdiocese would not relinquish ownership or discontinue operations of the missions, as it had done in the case of the Alamo in 1883.

Mill Won't Reopen — Stockholders in the Lykes Corp. defeated by a narrow margin a resolution calling for support of efforts by the Ecumenical Coalition of the Mahoning Valley to reopen under community ownership a Youngstown steel mill closed by the corporation. More than 4,000 jobs in the area were eliminated by closing of the plant.

Merton Centers — The establishment of a Thomas Merton Center for Religious Studies in New York was announced during the Nov. 27 to Dec. 10 commemoration at Columbia University of the 10th anniversary of the death of the Trappist monk. Commemorative ceremonies were also held at the Thomas Merton Studies Center, Bellarmine College, Louisville, the official U.S. despository of his works.

Human Rights — In a statement relating the celebration of Christmas to the observance of Human Rights Week, Dec. 10 to 17, the National Catholic Conference for Interracial Justice urged U.S. approval of United Nations covenants on genocide, racial discrimination, civil, political, economic, social and cultural rights.

Catholic and Orthodox Views of Marriage — Participants in the Eastern Orthodox-Roman Catholic Consultation issued Dec. 12 a statement of agreement on the sacramental nature of marriage. They also noted differences with respect to divorce (permitted in some cases by the Orthodox) and the liturgical celebration of marriage (the Orthodox recognize only their own celebration as valid for members of their churches). The statement was issued after a meeting Dec. 7 and 8 in Washington, D.C.

Christmas Observances in Public Schools — U.S. District Court Judge Andrew Bogue, while reserving judgment on the merits of the case, refused to issue an injunction against Christmas carols and pageants in the public schools of Sioux Falls, S.D. In other developments, the San Antonio Council of Churches called for an end to religious observances of Christmas in the city's public schools, and the American Jewish Congress was circulating a pamphlet — "Religious Holiday Observances in Public Schools: A Guide for Community Action" — urging the exclusion of Christmas hymns, symbols or services from public school programs.

Abortion Payment Ordered — U.S. District Court Judge Louis C. Bechtle ruled Dec. 21 against a Pennsylvania law restricting Medicaid payment for abortions to cases in which a mother's life was endangered by pregnancy. He ordered state payment for all abortions judged medically necessary for women on welfare. Statutes similar to the Pennsylvania law had been upheld in Virginia and Utah.

Social Action Programs — A partial survey of social action agencies in U.S. dioceses indicated that 47 of them were sponsoring programs with federal funding. Among the programs were those dealing with housing (23), employment (18), food (12), health care (11), and community development (11).

Water and Sewer Tax — New York religious leaders protested against a Board of Estimate proposal to rescind the tax-exempt status of churches, synagogues and non-profit educational organizations. The bill was defeated.

Freedom in the World — Freedom House, a New York-based organization describing itself as devoted to strengthening free societies, reported that 563 million people in 24 countries lived in greater freedom in 1978 than in 1977, while 144 million in eight countries lived in less freedom. It was estimated that only 35 per cent of the world's people were in "free" countries.

National Briefs:
- Ninety-eight dioceses and nine religious groups received grants totaling $3,175,000 in 1978 from the Commission for Catholic Missions among the Colored People and the Indians for the support of evangelizing activities.
- Twenty-two of the 58 permanent deacons ordained for the Archdiocese of Los Angeles were Hispanics.
- United Way in Columbia, S.C., stopped funding the local Planned Parenthood organization because of its sponsorship of an abortion clinic.
- Marist Father Constantine Chauve, one of the oldest priests in the world, celebrated his 100th birthday Dec. 17 in Convent, La.
- A New York archdiocesan office for immigrant services was formally inaugurated to aid migrants and illegal aliens in the metropolitan area.
- The Archdiocese of Denver established a special office for pastoral service to divorced, separated and widowed persons.
- Helen Bru, a member of St. Thomas Parish in Chickasaw, Ala., was named "Citizen of the Year" by the Saraland Civic Forum for her work in starting a "Red Barn" project as a haven for physically and mentally handicapped children.
- Retirements: Linus M. Riordan, associate editor of the *Denver Catholic Register*, after 40 years of service to the paper and the Catholic press; Robert L. Fenton, publisher of *The Catholic Digest* since 1969, effective at the end of 1979; Thomas D. Hinton, after 36 years of service to the National Conference of Catholic Bishops and the U.S. Catholic Conference.

Leading News Stories of 1978

Thirty-eight Catholic editors responding to an NC News poll ranked the following as the 10 top news stories of the year.

1. Papal transition, with the death of Paul VI, the election and death of John Paul I, and the election of John Paul II.
2. Tuition tax credits for parents of students of nonpublic schools, defeated in Congress but still a live issue.
3. Birth of the first test-tube baby in England, with its ethical implications.
4. Church-state entanglement in such matters as: pending decision by the U.S. Supreme Court regarding intervention by the National Labor Relations Board in teacher representation in schools of the Archdiocese of Chicago and the Diocese of Fort Wayne-South Bend; rulings by the Internal Revenue Service on schools and publications; a Labor Department ruling on unemployment compensation payments by nonpublic schools.
5. Violations of human rights in Latin America, with focus on Argentina, Chile, El Salvador and Nicaragua.
6. Statements by Pope John Paul II on intercommunion, first confession before first Communion, and priestly celibacy.
7. Political gains of pro-life advocates in the November elections.
8. Mass suicide in Guyana and the nature and implications of cults.
9. Approval of the Panama Canal treaties, with support from Catholic bishops.
10. Agitation for the ordination of women to the priesthood, evidenced by the November convention of the Catholic Women's Ordination Conference.

Pope John Paul II was rated as the top newsmaker of the year.

INTERNATIONAL

New Constitution in Spain — Eighty-eight per cent of the voters in a national election Dec. 6 approved a new constitution changing the form of government to a constitutional monarchy with a two-house legislature and ending the status of the Catholic Church as the official religion of Spain. It was signed by King Juan Carlos Dec. 27. The constitution had the support of the majority of Spanish bishops; they felt that, with the severing of ties to the government and the relinquishing of historical privileges, the Church would have greater freedom to carry out its pastoral mission.

Chilean Rights Agency Honored — The Vicariate of Solidarity, the human rights agency of the Archdiocese of Santiago, Chile, was one of several organizations honored with the award of a United Nations Human Rights Prize Dec. 11, for its work in providing legal aid to political prisoners and for its efforts to pressure the government of Chile on behalf of an estimated 600 missing persons seized by security forces. Amnesty International and the International Committee of the Red Cross were also recipients of UN awards.

Adveniat Contributions — West German Catholics contributed nearly $48 million in 1977 to Adveniat, their bishops' aid agency for Latin America. It was also reported that since 1961 a total of approximately $300 million had been contributed to and allocated by the agency for pastoral projects approved by local bishops in Latin America.

Some Agreement on Baptism — The International Commission for Dialogue between the Disciples of Christ and the Roman Catholic Church reported it had reached agreement on 12 major points concerning baptism during a meeting Dec. 9 to 14 in Rome. A press release issued at the end of the meeting also said: "A number of issues were also outlined for possible future study. Some of these are the meaning of sacrament, the relationship between the faith of the individual and the faith of the community, and the qualifications and role of the minister."

Israeli-Egyptian Agreements Not Reached — December 17, a deadline set in September, came and went without agreement between the governments of Israel and Egypt on either the "Framework for Peace in the Middle East Agreed at Camp David" or the "Framework for the Conclusion of a Peace Treaty between Egypt and Israel."

Infant Formula Peril — An international group of medical experts meeting in Bogota said that widespread use of infant formulas, spurred by commercial advertising, was causing great damage to children of poor Latin American families. They stated that ignorance regarding preparation of the formulas and unsanitary living conditions were causes of a rise in infant mortality rates. The marketing of formulas by the Nestle firm was under criticism by several Catholic organizations in the U.S.

Subjective Bible Reading — Cardinal Anibal Munoz Vega of Bogota criticized the Protestant student movement Alfa y Omega for preaching religion from a "purely subjective reading of the Bible," and reminded Catholics of their obligation "to give witness of the true faith" and to be obedient to their bishops. About 30 of the 106 non-Catholic groups in Colombia were particularly active among the Indians.

Pope's Letter Censored — The Italian news agency ANSA reported Dec. 20 that a letter from Pope John Paul to the people of his former Archdiocese of Cracow was censored by the Polish government before it was released for publication. The deleted portion read: "Speaking in contemporary parlance, we might see in St. Stanislaus the defender of the most important rights of man and of the nation, on which depend their dignity, their morality, their true freedom." St. Stanislaus, the patron of Poland, was killed by King Boleslaus in 1079.

Jesuit Killed — German Father Gerhard Pieper, the 20th Catholic missionary killed in the Rhodesian guerrilla war, was murdered Dec. 26 at Kangaire.

U.S. Recognition of Red China — The bishops' conference of Taiwan issued a statement Dec. 28 in which they strongly criticized the Dec. 15 announcement by President Carter that the U.S. would establish diplomatic relations with the Peoples Republic of China Jan. 1, 1979, and would sever ties with the Nationalist Chinese government. The statement said: "The United States government, in establishing diplomatic relations with Communist China, has turned its back on truth and honesty, (and has) ignored human rights and the aspirations of millions of Chinese who are struggling for freedom."

Self-Evangelization in Japan — The Japanese bishops' Commission on Missionary and Pastoral Care recommended, on completion of a study, that the Church in that country should make greater efforts at self-evangelization before seeking to improve its relationship to society in general. The study also noted a lack of unity among Christians and a need for greater understanding by Christian leaders of the problems of modern society.

CCCB Concerns in 1978 — Concern for spiritual and economic welfare marked activities of the Canadian Conference of Catholic Bishops in 1978. During the year the bishops: issued major pastoral guidelines for the spiritual renewal of individuals and groups; encouraged the government to develop new approaches to industrial development; continued work on a project called "Growth in Faith, in and through Christian Families," and became involved in efforts for respect of human rights in their own and other countries.

International Briefs:

• The UN Food and Agricultural Organization reported during a meeting Nov. 27 to Dec. 6 in Rome that, despite record cereal production in 1978, the number of people suffering from chronic hunger and malnutrition was increasing.

• The Permanent Council of the Italian Bishops' Conference issued a 6,000-word pastoral instruction on respect for life in which they restated the penalty of excommunication for abortion.

• The Church of Notre Dame in downtown Montreal was seriously damaged by a fire Dec. 7.

• Spanish Father Gaspar Garcia Laviana, fighting with Sandinistas against National Guard forces, was killed in mid-December at Punta Orosi, Nicaragua.

• The government of Finland announced that, as of Jan. 1, 1979, it would prohibit the shipment of Bibles to the Soviet Union.

• Father Carlos Stetter, a German missionary working in a rural area, was expelled from Guatemala Dec. 21 on charges of breaking rules governing resident status.

• *Vigilia*, a Catholic monthly published in Budapest, reported that, although 60 per cent of the children in Hungary are baptized as Catholics, only 33 per cent receive first Communion.

Lefebvre Ordinations

Dissident Archbishop Marcel Lefebvre ordained six men to the priesthood on Christmas Eve in Econe, Switzerland, raising his total of such irregular ordinations to about 50 since June 29, 1976. Despite this repeated act of defiance of church discipline, the archbishop was quoted as saying in an interview published in Paris that he hoped "the ceremony will not be badly interpreted by the Vatican, with which contacts are continuing after the meeting last Nov. 18 with the Pope."

JANUARY 1979

VATICAN

Faith Is the Beginning — "In openness to God, man eternally aspires to the realization of himself; faith is the beginning and condition of this realization." So stated Pope John Paul Jan. 7 in comment upon the significance of the solemnity of the Epiphany. He took issue with the opinion that "religion ... deprives man of what is substantially human," and added: "This accusation is the cause of the great damage done to man in the name of the 'progress' of man."

Mass and Message Radioed to Poland — On Jan. 7, the Pope celebrated the first Mass in a series scheduled for weekly broadcast by Vatican Radio to Poland. Noting in a homily that "the year 1979 is the jubilee year of St. Stanislaus" (martyred 900 years earlier), he said: "I wish ... for the spiritual unity for which St. Stanislaus, first through his sacrifice and later his martyrdom, became the source and the inspiration of our ancestors. Today we have need of the same spiritual unity of our fatherland, after so many trials in the course of its history."

Vocation of Motherhood — "Motherhood is the vocation of the woman ... an eternal vocation and a contemporary vocation as well," declared the Pope at a general audience Jan. 10. He said: "We must stand beside every expectant mother ... we must surround with particular assistance motherhood and the great event united with it, the conception and birth of man." It "is necessary to do everything" to make certain that "the authority of the woman-mother is not diminished in family, social and public life and in all of our civilization; in all of our present-day legislation, in the organization of work, in publications, in the culture of daily life, in education and study; in every field of life."

Address to Diplomats — The Pope told diplomats accredited to the Vatican Jan. 12 that the search for solutions to socio-economic problems and for justice in the world "must not be transformed into a program of struggle to ensure control of the world, whatever the imperialism that lies behind the struggle." While appealing especially for respect for religious freedom, he commented on problem conditions in Lebanon, Iran, the Middle East, Northern Ireland and Southeast Asia. He also said that the Church seeks to contribute by its own means — linked to the primacy of spiritual values — to the establishment of order based on justice and peace.

Year and Rights of the Child — Pope John Paul, speaking to journalists Jan. 13 about the International Year of the Child, stated that the Church considers the child "as a subject of inalienable rights ... having a value in himself, a unique destiny." Among the rights of a child, he said, is the "right to truth, in an education which takes into account fundamental ethical values and which makes possible a spiritual education in conformity with the religious membership of the child, with the orientation legitimately desired by the parents, and with the requirements of well-understood freedom of conscience, for which the young person must be prepared and formed throughout childhood and adolescence."

In a related talk on the family and the Church's opposition to abortion, the Pope said Jan. 3 that the value of each individual is not only in line with the logic of Christian faith but also with "the logic ... of every authentic humanism."

Blame for Violence — The Pope, addressing a group of civil administrators Jan. 20, blamed people who proclaim and teach struggle against others for the violence plaguing Rome and other parts of Italy. He decried the activities of those who "proclaim and inculcate, especially in the consciousness of the young, as an ideal of life, struggle against the other, hatred against the one who thinks or acts differently, violence as the sole means for social and political progress. ... Violence generates violence. Hatred generates hatred. ... We cannot invoke God the Father of all if we refuse to behave as brothers" toward others.

Ecumenical Efforts — The search for Christian unity, the theme of the annual Week of Prayer for Christian Unity Jan. 18 to 25, has implications far beyond the strictly religious reunion of Christians, declared the Pope Jan. 21. The quest is inspired by "respect for man, for his conscience, for his religious convictions, as well as for the spiritual patrimony of the individual churches and Christian communities." It "shows indirectly the ways that lead to rapprochement, to living together, to cooperation and to unity of men."

Collegiality of Bishops — The communion of bishops among themselves and with the Pope was the theme of an address delivered by the Holy Father Jan. 23 to members of the permanent council of the Italian Bishops' Conference. Citing the principle of collegiality stated by the Second Vatican Council, he said he needed the help of the bishops to carry out the Church's mission of "building the Church of God, of announcing the Gospel, of serving the elevation of man to the Dignity of son of God, of spreading all the values of the human spirit closely connected with this elevation."

Meeting with Gromyko — Pope John Paul met with Soviet Foreign Minister Andrei Gromyko for an hour and 45 minutes Jan. 24. Their discussion, according to the Vatican

Press Office, concerned "peace, peaceful coexistence and international cooperation. They also touched on problems related to the life of the Catholic Church in the Soviet Union," whose Catholic population was estimated to be about 8.5 million. The meeting was Gromyko's sixth with a Pope.

Pilgrimage of Faith — The Pope departed from Rome's Fiumicino Airport Jan. 25 at 8:20 a.m., local time, on the first leg of a "pilgrimage of faith" to Latin America. (See Papal Pilgrimage to Latin America, Latin American Addresses of John Paul II.)

The Pope Also:
• Spent Jan. 4 and 5 resting at Castel Gandolfo.
• Called for international cooperation as he received the credentials of Gurbachan Singh, the new ambassador of India to the Vatican.
• Formally accepted the request of the Chilean and Argentinian governments to mediate their Beagle Channel dispute.
• Asked Catholic women to defend justice based on belief in God and to promote the "Christian outlook which . . . can totally banish all forms of discrimination against women," in a letter to participants in the Jan. 29 to Feb. 7 assembly of the World Union of Catholic Women's Organizations in Bangalore, India.
• Visited: More than 500 children at *Bambino Gesu* Hospital in Rome, Jan. 7; a second Roman parish, *Santa Maria Liberatrice al Monte Testaccio,* Jan. 14; offices of *L'Osservatore Romano* and quarters of the Swiss Guard, Jan. 17.

Vatican Briefs:
• The Numismatics Office released the last commemorative coins from the pontificate of Paul VI.
• A new Vatican-Spanish concordat, replacing one in force since 1953, was signed Jan. 3 by Secretary of State Cardinal Jean Villot and Foreign Minister Marcellino Oreja Aguirre.
• Cardinal Jean Villot, in his capacity as chamberlain of the Holy Roman Church, was delegated to handle the ordinary administration of the Roman Curia during the Pope's visit to Latin America.

Peace Message

Pope John Paul II urged statesmen in his first World Day of Peace message, Jan. 1, to "makes gestures of peace, even audacious ones, in order to break free from vicious circles and from the deadweight of passions inherited from history."

"Firm principles" for peace listed in the message included the following:

• "Human affairs must be dealt with humanely, not with violence."
• "Tensions, rivalries and conflicts must be settled by reasonable negotiations and not by force."
• "Opposing ideologies must confront each other in a climate of dialogue and free discussion."
• "The legitimate interests of particular groups must also take into account the legitimate interests of the other groups involved and of the demands of the higher common good."
• "Recourse to arms cannot be considered the right means for settling conflicts."
• "Inalienable human rights must be safeguarded in every circumstance."
• "It is not permissible to kill in order to impose a solution."

The theme of the message, "To Reach Peace, Teach Peace," was chosen by Pope Paul VI, who in 1967 designated New Year's Day as the World Day of Peace.

NATIONAL

Warning about Cults — Catholic and Protestant members of the Pennsylvania Conference on Interchurch Cooperation issued a warning early in the month about pseudo-religious cults which "violate the ethics of the Judaeo-Christian traditions as well as our American concept of individual freedom." The churchmen did not mention the names of any cults but cited features characteristic of many, if not all, of them. The characteristics noted were: a "misleading" approach in soliciting funds and recruiting members; methods of conversion which "seek to incapacitate you from the free exercise of your will, intellect and emotions"; alienation from family and the destruction of personal identity; "messianic-type" leadership; a perception of cult members as good and of all others as evil.

Need To Protect Anti-Abortion Students — A survey by the Department of Health, Education and Welfare, indicating that 40 per cent of the country's medical schools questioned applicants about their stance on abortion, pointed up the need for a law to protect pro-life applicants, according to Senator Richard Schweiker of Pennsylvania. He said he intended to introduce in the Senate a measure that would prohibit medical, nursing and osteopathic schools receiving federal funds from discriminating against prospective students who oppose abortion. The study drew responses from nearly 1,000 of 1,371 medical and nursing schools, including 122 of 126 medical schools. Six schools admitted that an applicant's stance on abortion could affect a decision for or against admission.

Yes and No Student Aid in Wisconsin — The U.S. Commissioner of Education approved a plan resolving a conflict between the State of Wisconsin and its nonpublic schools over a federal aid program providing educational materials and services. The aid, provided for under Title IV-B of the Elementary and

Secondary Education Act, had been denied for two years or more because of an adverse constitutional decision by the state's attorney general. Additional aid provided under Title I of the ESEA was still being denied to disadvantaged students in nonpublic schools in the state.

Plea for Boat People — John E. McCarthy, executive director of Migration and Refugee Services, U.S. Catholic Conference, appealed in a letter to the Carter Administration Jan. 4 for aid to 5,000 Vietnamese refugees stranded aboard two ships off Hong Kong and Manila. He said at a press conference Jan. 5 that the Catholic Church in the U.S., working with other agencies, had helped to resettle more than 90,000 Southeast Asian refugees since April, 1975, and was continuing resettlement work for about 3,000 persons a month. He said that MRS was ready to commit itself to resettle 7,000 persons a month.

China Accord — The "resumption of normal diplomatic arrangements between these two powers (the U.S. and the Chinese People's Republic) can provide structures for communication and cooperation which should further international understanding and the pursuit of peace." So stated Bishop Thomas C. Kelly, general secretary of the U.S. Catholic Conference. He added: "The American people ... will welcome this important step (announced by President Carter the previous Dec. 15) in the development of the United States' relations with China. . . . At the same time, they are and should be concerned to insure that U.S. relations with Taiwan will be conducted so as to give a continuing reality to the welfare of the people of Taiwan."

Church-State Wall Not Breached — While striking down Jan. 10 a state ban on elective abortions for women on welfare, a New Jersey Superior Court decision rejected the argument that the ban violated the principle of separation of church and state. Judge David Furman called "untenable" the plaintiffs' contention that the law was rooted in religious beliefs and that the Catholic Church had intervened in the legislative process with undue pressure. He wrote: "Whatever the peril to a democratic society of predominant influence by one religion over the legislative process, such a constitutional attack has not been upheld in any cited federal or state decision. Active support of the opposition to legislating on gambling and alcoholic beverages by various organized religions has been commonplace."

Prayer for Unity — "Serve One Another to the Glory of God" was the theme of the annual Week of Prayer for Christian Unity, Jan. 18 to 25, which was observed throughout the country with interfaith prayer and related services.

A related development was the formation of a New York-based "initiating committee" of Catholics and Lutherans seeking to heal the breach of the Reformation with a yearlong program, starting Oct. 28, designed "to spark a renewal of grassroots" ecumenism.

No USCC Retrenchment — "Despite rumors to the contrary," the U.S. Catholic Conference has not "retrenched" on its commitment to labor and civil rights movements, declared Msgr. George G. Higgins as he received Jan. 23 the Hubert H. Humphrey Civil Rights Award for "selfless and devoted service in the cause of equality" from the Leadership Conference on Civil Rights. Two days later, it was announced that the secretary for special concerns, U.S. Catholic Conference, had been named a special mediator in the dispute between the United Farm Workers of America and lettuce growers in California's Imperial Valley.

Corporate Responsibility — The Interfaith Center on Corporate Responsibility, an agency related to the National Council of Churches of Christ, reported late in the month that more than 50 Protestant and Catholic institutions had filed shareholder resolutions with 30 U.S. banks and corporations in an effort to influence their investment policies and practices in South Africa. The resolutions charged that U.S. investments "provide significant economic support, international credibility and moral legitimacy to the South African government" and its official policy of rigid racial discrimination. It was also reported that members of the center had filed a total of 80 resolutions with 62 U.S. corporations on a variety of issues.

Earlier in the month, the Archdiocese of Cincinnati issued a policy statement containing a pledge not to invest in companies: "whose activities consist primarily in the manufacture of materials and weapons designed to destroy human life"; "which, by reason of their activities, cause injury to consumers, employees and others by violation of laws established to protect health, safety and human rights, particularly if these violations take the form of discrimination or exploitation of people, the environment or natural resources"; "which manufacture or provide products or services contrary to the moral teachings of the Church."

Social Security Cuts Opposed — The National Conference of Catholic Charities and the U.S. Catholic Conference joined a coalition of more than 115 organizations opposing cuts in Social Security benefits proposed by the Carter Administration. They said the cuts would break a "moral compact" with the American people.

National Briefs:

• Property valued at about $6 million was given to Xavier University, Cincinnati, by the United States Shoe Corporation.

• The Archdiocese of Portland and the Diocese of Baker announced establishment of the Oregon Catholic Conference to coordinate "efforts of the Church in matters of statewide concern."

• The dangers of peacetime and wartime nuclear radiation were subjects of talks and discussions at the national conference of Pax Christi, attended by about 800 persons Jan. 13 in Detroit.

• Mary M. Fallon, an employee of the school for 44 years, was named an honorary alumna of St. Charles Borromeo Seminary of the Philadelphia archdiocese.

• Archbishop Fulton J. Sheen was the principal speaker at the 27th National Prayer Breakfast held in Washington at the opening of the first session of the 96th Congress.

• As the Ku Klux Klan began a recruitment drive in northwest Florida, Bishop Rene H. Gracida of Pensacola-Tallahassee warned Catholics that "membership in the organization is incompatible with the teachings of Jesus Christ and his Church."

• *The Pittsburgh Catholic* called Jan. 19 a local black Catholic organization's decision to honor Rep. Shirley Chisholm of New York a "poor choice" because of her voting record for abortion and against aid to nonpublic schools. Several weeks later, the National Office for Black Catholics supported the choice.

• The controversial WGTB-FM radio station was closed down Jan. 31 by Georgetown University because some of its public-affairs programming was at variance with policies of the school.

• Female Firsts: Sister of Mercy Eileen Hogan, full-time Catholic chaplain at a major correctional institution, Rikers Island facility for women, N.Y.; Caroline A. Carson, president of the First Friday Club of Detroit; Sister Irene Kraus, chairlady-elect of the American Hospital Association.

March for Life

At least 60,000 people from all sections of the country converged on Washington, DC, Jan. 22 for the sixth annual March for Life in protest against the 1973 decisions of the U.S. Supreme Court outlawing anti-abortion statutes and in support of efforts for the adoption of a right-to-life amendment to the U.S. Constitution. Similar demonstrations for the same purposes were held in other cities, including Atlanta, Austin, Boston, Pittsburgh and San Diego.

In one of several counter-demonstrations on Jan. 22, a group of 40 Protestant and Jewish clergy led a march on St. Patrick's Cathedral in New York, protesting the Catholic stance against abortion.

Less than two weeks before the March for Life, the U.S. Supreme Court ruled Jan. 9, 6 to 3, against the constitutionality of a Pennsylvania law requiring a doctor to take measures for saving the life of an aborted but viable fetus. A day later, a judge in New Jersey declared that a state law against funding elective abortions was unconstitutional.

(For related developments, see Abortion.)

INTERNATIONAL

Year of the Child — Agencies in many nations began activities related to purposes of the United Nations-sponsored International Year of the Child. The child-welfare focus of the observance was originally proposed by Father Joseph Moerman, secretary general of the International Catholic Child Bureau, in a letter addressed to the UN general secretary in 1973. During the month: the bishops of Portugal published a pastoral letter on the subject; Archbishop Gilles Ouellet, president of the Canadian Conference of Catholic Bishops, issued a statement calling for efforts to improve the lot of children in Canada and developing nations; Pope John Paul emphasized in an address the need of support for the rights of children "from the moment of conception."

Another Missionary Victim — Swiss Father Martin Holenstein, who disappeared while on his way to celebrate Mass New Year's Day, was found shot to death Jan. 3 at a black reservation in Rhodesia. He was the most recent of more than 20 Catholic missionaries killed in the country's continuing guerrilla war.

Discrimination in Mozambique — Bishops of nine dioceses declared in a letter circulating in Lisbon, Portugal, that the Marxist government was discriminating against believers and violating their human rights. "Christians," they said, "are facing grave difficulties in meeting for religious services, in instructing their children in the basics of their religion. Bishops and priests are likewise having difficulties in their pastoral work, and several missionaries have been expelled from the country."

Parishes in the Soviet Union — KNA, the West German Catholic news agency, reported the existence of parishes founded since the 1960s in the central Asian portion of the Soviet Union by German Catholics expelled from the former Volga Republic after World War II. Most of the parishes of 100 members or so had chapels of their own, were run by lay people, and were served only rarely by priests with work permits. They had some kind of legal recognition but an uncertain future.

Meeting of WCC Central Committee — The policy-making Central Committee of the World Council of Churches, at the end of an 11-day meeting in Kingston, Jamaica, agreed to continue support of an anti-racist program in Rhodesia. Controversy over the program — involving a grant of $85,000 allocated in August, 1978, to the Patriotic Front of Zimbabwe for "humanitarian" purposes — led to the suspension of WCC membership by the Salvation Army, the Presbyterian Church in

Ireland and a small Lutheran church in Germany. The controversy also influenced the committee's action in terminating the services of Dr. Lukas Vischer as director of the Faith and Order Commission.

Only One Mass in El Salvador — Only one Mass, for the funeral of Father Octavio Ortiz, was celebrated Sunday, Jan. 21, in El Salvador. All other Masses were suspended on the order of Archbishop Oscar Arnulfo Romero to protest the shooting of the priest Jan. 19 by state security forces. The archbishop also declared the excommunication of those involved in the incident and accused the government of lying about the circumstance of the murder, the fourth of its kind in two years.

In a related development, the Human Rights Commission of the Organization of American States reported that the government of El Salvador was "systematically persecuting" the Catholic Church.

Archbishop Capucci Addressed Palestinians — The Milan daily *Corriere della Sera* reported Jan. 22 that Archbishop Hilarion Capucci, who was convicted in Israel in 1974 of gunrunning for Palestinians, had spoken to guerrillas in Damascus. Two days later, Vatican Press spokesman Father Romeo Panciroli said that the archbishop had acted without Vatican or papal permission in leaving a South American assignment and going to Syria. The conditions for his release from an Israeli prison in November, 1977, were that he should not return to the Middle East or publicly discuss political issues of the region.

Puebla Assembly of Latin American Bishops — "The Future of Evangelization in Latin America" was the theme of the third general assembly of Latin American bishops which held its first working session Jan. 28 at the Palafox Seminary in Puebla, Mexico. The opening was keynoted by Pope John Paul who emphasized the primary evangelizing ministry of the Church in efforts for the integral liberation of people. The assembly, attended by 187 voting delegates and nearly 200 other representatives from 22 countries, continued until Feb. 13. (See additional entries: Puebla, Latin American Addresses of Pope John Paul II, Liberation.)

Trials in Czechoslovakia — The Institute for Religion and Communism at Keston College, London, reported that trials were underway of Father Vojtech Srna, for conducting a retreat at a summer camp, and of camp director Miloslav Svacek, for permitting him to do so, in violation of laws on government supervision of churches and religious organizations.

Vatican Radio reported that regional authorities had summarily withdrawn the permission of Father Miloslav Vlk to carry out pastoral duties in the southwestern Diocese of Ceske Budejovice.

Amnesty International Report — Amnesty International, reporting Jan. 31 on the period from July 1, 1977, to June 30, 1978, disclosed that "prisoners of conscience are now being held in at least 70 countries, and we are investigating other possible cases in a further 12 countries." The contents of the 321-page report portrayed a "depressing picture of systematic violations of basic human rights," declared Thomas Hammarberg, chairman of the AI executive committee. Violations were reported in countries in Eastern and Western Europe, Latin America, Africa and Asia.

International Briefs:

• Nearly two-thirds of the British population favored voluntary euthanasia, according to a survey commissioned by the Voluntary Euthanasia Society.

• Leaders of England's major Christian churches — headed by Cardinal George Basil Hume and Anglican Archbishop Donald Coggan — held an ecumenical service Jan. 22 marking the start of a National Initiative in Evangelism.

• Five hundred and 69 priests were ordained in 1979 in Poland, reported the press office of the bishops' conference; the figure was 131 higher than the one reported for 1977. Seminary enrollment increased from 5,028 in 1977 to 5,325 in 1978.

• Father Rosario Stroscio was expelled from India Jan. 6 after 40 years of missionary work there among the poor; government officials gave no reason for his ouster.

• Catholic agencies were engaged with government and other organizations in efforts to aid an estimated 3.5 million people affected by a critical food shortage in Ethiopia.

• Nikkyo Niwano, a 73-year-old Japanese Buddhist, was named Jan. 29 the winner of the 1979 Templeton Foundation Prize for progress in religion. Previous winners included Mother Teresa of Calcutta and Cardinal Leo J. Suenens of Malines-Brussels.

• The United Nations was urged Jan. 31 to rule the promotion of abortion and sterilization out of its population policy, by Msgr. James T. McHugh, former director of the U.S. Bishops' Secretariat for Pro-Life Activities.

Controversy in Dutch Church

Cardinal Johannes Willebrands convened a special Jan. 13 meeting of the bishops of the Netherlands for discussion of controversial theological, pastoral and liturgical trends affecting the vitality of the Church in the country. Details of the proceedings were not made public, but it was known that Pope John Paul had already begun personal interviews with Dutch bishops at the Vatican. Roman sources said that concern centered on disagreements among the prelates over policies to be followed to preserve unity in church affairs.

FEBRUARY 1979

VATICAN

Homecoming — Pope John Paul landed early in the afternoon of Feb. 1 at Rome's international airport at the end of his first apostolic trip abroad, to Latin America. On alighting from an Aeromexico DC-10, he said: "I am grateful, above all, to the Lord and to the holy Virgin of Guadalupe for the constant aid with which they sustained me in these days (since Jan. 25), permitting me to happily crown a delicate and important initiative undertaken in fulfillment of the universal mandate which Christ himself entrusted to me, calling me to the responsibility of his vicar in the seat of Peter."

Lateran Treaty and Concordat — The Pope marked the 50th anniversary Feb. 11 of the signing of the Lateran Treaty and Concordat with Italy with praise for their provisions regarding Church-state relations. He also expressed a desire that a "revision of the Concordat (under study for 11 years) may be brought soon to a happy completion, as I hope, and as Paul VI and John Paul I ardently desired."

Canon Law Is Pastoral — The judicial activity of the Church is "by its very nature pastoral," declared the Pope Feb. 17 at a meeting with lawyers and judges of the Roman Rota, the Church's main court of appeals. He said: "Canon law serves a supremely educative function, individual and social, in its aim of creating an ordered and fruitful living together, in which the integral development of the human-Christian person might take root and grow.... The fundamental rights of the baptized are not efficacious and cannot be exercised if anyone ignores the duties connected with them by baptism itself — especially if anyone remains unconvinced that the same rights must be exercised in communion with the Church." The Church must always strive to be "the mirror of justice" because it is "the permanent incarnation of the Prince of Justice." The Holy Father emphasized the Church's commitment to human rights, and said: "Perhaps the 20th century will designate the Church as the chief bulwark of support for the human person in the whole span of his earthly life, right from his conception."

Parish Visit — Concern about the lack of neighborhood social services was expressed by the Pope Feb. 18 during his third visit to a parish church in Rome. From the Gospel, he said, "arises the concrete commitment of charity toward brothers ... on behalf of old people, the sick, the down-and-out.... Jesus Christ is present in the midst of you all, to confirm daily the saving presence of God. Here, undoubtedly, exist immense material, economic and social needs; but, above all, there exists the need for this saving strength which is in God and which Christ alone possesses.... It is this saving strength that frees man from sin and directs him toward the good — so that he may lead a life truly worthy of man; so that married couples may give their children not only life but also education and good example; so that true Christian life may flourish here; so that hatred, destruction, dishonesty and scandal may not prevail; so that the work of fathers and mothers may be respected; so that this work may create the indispensable conditions for maintaining the life of the family; so that the fundamental requirements of social justice may be respected; so that true culture, beginning with the culture of daily life, may be developed."

Uganda Centenary — The Holy Father told a group of Ugandans at a general audience Feb. 21: "Your presence gives me the opportunity to express again my esteem and love for the Church in your land, and to render praise and thanksgiving to God who, through the power of the Holy Spirit, has brought forth abundant fruits of holiness and justice in the lives of generations of Ugandans." The 100th anniversary of the establishment of the first permanent mission in the country was commemorated during the month.

Plea for Peace — The Pope pleaded for peace between China and Vietnam Feb. 25. He said: "Whoever participates in the love of Christ for man cannot but grieve and tremble at the lives sacrificed or in peril, and the sufferings and hardships of the combatants and the populations. ... No geographical distance, not even any ideological difference, can weaken the feeling of brotherhood that unites us with every human being who lives in this world, even if he is not baptized — and especially when one thinks that our brothers in faith are among the military and civilians involved in the war."

Pro-Life Task — "Life will win over death," Pope John Paul told a group of persons following their participation in the European Convention of the Pro-Life Movement held in Milan. He said: "Your task consists, in the first place, of an intelligent and diligent activity to sensitize consciences concerning the inviolability of human life in all its stages — in such a way that the right to it may be effectively recognized in custom and in laws as the fundamental value of every society that wants to be called civil. ... It is expressed, then, in the courageous taking of a position against every form of attack on life, from wherever it comes. It is finally translated into the unselfish and respectful offer of concrete aids to persons who are experiencing difficulties in conforming their own behavior to the precepts of conscience. ... It is a work of great humanity and generous charity which can only win the approval of every person aware of the possibilities and risks that are met in this our society."

Faith a Hallmark of Catholic Universities — The study of man in a Catholic university must be enlightened by faith, declared the Pope during an audience late in the month with board members of the International Federation of Catholic Universities. Regarding the study of man, he said that a Christian "knows that he must go beyond the purely natural perspective. . . . His faith makes him approach anthropology in the perspective of the full vocation and salvation of man. It is the light by which he works, the axis which guides his research." A Catholic university's study of man must be "illumined by faith, coherent with faith — in particular with (doctrine concerning) creation and Christ's redemption." Of theological research, he said that it "cannot exist without seeking its source and regulation in Scripture and tradition, in the experience and decisions of the Church recorded by the magisterium in the course of the centuries."

Message for Lent — "Penance in the sense of the Gospel means 'conversion,' above all," declared the Holy Father on Ash Wednesday. He also declared, in a special message calling for participation in lenten campaigns to aid the less fortunate: "Fasting concerns personal asceticism, which is always necessary; but the Church asks the baptized to mark this liturgical season in yet another way. . . . Lent must mean something; it must show the world that the whole people of God, because it is made up of sinners, is preparing in penance to relive liturgically Christ's passion, death and resurrection. This public, collective witness derives from the spirit of penance of each individual and it also leads us to deepen this inward attitude and to strengthen our motivation for it.

"Going without things does not consist only in giving away what we do not need; sometimes it also consists in giving away what we do need. . . . Going without things is to free oneself from the slaveries of a civilization that is always urging people on to greater comfort and consumption. . . . The vineyard of Christian charity is short of workers; the Church is calling you to it. Do not wait until it is too late to help Christ in prison or without clothing, Christ persecuted or a refugee, Christ who is hungry or without a roof. Help our brothers and sisters who lack the bare necessities to escape from inhuman conditions and to reach true human advancement."

The Pope Also:
• As he blessed candles Feb. 2, the feast of the Presentation of the Lord, said they were a "symbol of the light that is Christ."
• Rested Feb. 4 and 5 at Castel Gandolfo after returning from his busy visit to Mexico.
• Told directors and students of the Defense College of the North Atlantic Treaty Organization Feb. 8 that the international arms race is incompatible with efforts for social development.
• Appointed: Archbishop Jean Jadot, apostolic delegate to the U.S., to be the first permanent observer of the Vatican to the Organization of American States; Cardinal James R. Knox, prefect of the Congregation for the Sacraments and Divine Worship, to be his special envoy at Feb. 11 to 17 celebrations commemorating the centenary of the Church in Uganda.
• Conveyed his sympathy to the families of victims (32 killed, about 70 wounded) of an explosion in a bank in Warsaw.
• Officiated Feb. 25 at the wedding of a Roman couple at the request of the bride, a salesgirl.
• In a letter addressed to a Vatican official attending a meeting with representatives of the World of Churches, said he hoped "ways may be found . . . for growing collaboration in all fields which are possible" with the council.

Puebla and Liberation

The Holy Father, during a general audience Feb. 21, endorsed the work of the third general assembly of Latin American bishops at Puebla, Mexico. In reference to the topic of human liberation, he said:

It "is certainly a reality of faith, one of the fundamental themes of the Bible, inscribed profoundly in the saving mission of Christ, in the work of redemption, in his teaching. This theme has never ceased to constitute the content of the spiritual life of Christians."

NATIONAL

Military Chaplains — Coadjutor Archbishop Joseph T. Ryan of the Military Ordinariate notified bishops and religious superiors that consultations had been held with Pentagon officials regarding "perceived discrimination" against Catholic chaplains in the Army. The complaint about discrimination was made by three chaplains who said: "There are now three Protestant chaplain generals in the Army and there is no Catholic influence or input on that triumvirate of power," and "it has been the policy of the Protestant chaplain generals to eliminate the most competitive and successful Catholic chaplains in a pre-screening procedure." The chaplains urged bishops and religious superiors to ask Cardinal Terence Cooke, head of the ordinariate, to "take positive action with the President to correct this continual discrimination against the Catholic Church at the highest echelons of the U.S. Army chaplaincy."

Bread for the World — There must be "a drastic reform of public policy, especially in the structure of this country's foreign aid program," declared Auxiliary Bishop Thomas Gumbleton of Detroit, president of Bread for the World, at a regional meeting of the organization in Knoxville, Tenn. He added: "We need to separate military aid from humanitarian aid and remove it from the control of the State Department." He also called for "some accountability" for multinational corporations which, by and large, "do not produce goods and services needed by the poorer 60 percent of the world market because human needs such as food and housing do not generate profits."

New Pro-Life Crusade — Dr. Mildred Jefferson, former president of the National Right to Life Committee, announced the formation of a new Right to Life Crusade. She called it an umbrella-type of organization of existing pro-life groups with an estimated membership of 25 to 35 million people.

Tax Credits Defeated by Anti-Catholicism — Senator Patrick Moynihan, addressing the Cathedral Club of Brooklyn early in the month, accused Catholics of tolerating a level of discrimination and prejudice that no other religious or ethnic group would permit. He attributed the defeat of tuition tax credit legislation to a combination of anti-Catholic bigotry and to muted Catholic response amounting to a failure of advocacy.

IRS Guidelines — George Reed, general counsel of the U.S. Catholic Conference, told a House subcommittee Feb. 21 that new guidelines of the Internal Revenue Service were an improvement over those issued Aug. 22, 1978, to end the tax exempt status of "segregation academies." The new regulations, he said, took into account the special character of church-related schools and the faith-orientation of their enrollment policies.

Harris Poll on Discrimination — A Louis Harris Poll of 2,405 persons, conducted under the auspices of the National Conference of Christians and Jews, indicated that:

• Most Americans believe Catholics are not discriminated against because of their faith.

• Non-Catholics view Catholics as very much in the mainstream of U.S. society.

• Catholics encounter much less prejudice than blacks, Hispanics or Jews.

Latent anti-Catholic prejudice, particularly at leadership levels, was also reported.

Christopher Awards — About 70 producers, directors, authors and illustrators of motion pictures, TV specials and books were honored with Christopher Awards Feb. 20 for "their contribution to the portrayal of the highest values of the human spirit through their works in 1978."

Fundamentals Are the Same — Despite changes in institutes of women religious since the Second Vatican Council, the fundamentals of religious life remain the same, declared Sister M. Cecilia Carey, general superior of the Dominican Sisters of the Most Holy Rosary. Interviewed by *The Texas Catholic*, she said: "Prayer is as important today as it always was in the life of a religious and in relation to her ministry." Vows are "the heart of religious life"; without them, ministry can very easily become "social service" and nuns mere "social workers." She added: "We also value community very strongly, because of the support and encouragement it provides for ministry each day."

Parochial Podium Denied Father Curran — Bishop Joseph V. Sullivan of Baton Rouge, in an open letter to the academic community of Louisiana State University, said that he could not permit anyone "to use parochial facilities as a podium on a subject of religion or moral ethics about whose orthodoxy I have serious doubt." The bishop's reference was to Father Charles Curran, professor of moral theology at the Catholic University of America. He said, with illustrative quotations: "Some of Father Curran's theological concepts are not in conformity with Catholic doctrine."

Inmate Rights — Authorities at the Bordentown, N.J., Correctional Facility agreed to demands made by Catholic inmates in a lawsuit which charged the institution with religious discrimination. Under terms of a consent decree, officials agreed to post Mass times and to provide office space for activities of the St. Dismas Holy Name Society. Catholic inmates said their requests had been denied while similar ones had been granted to members of other religious groups.

USCC Positions — Views of the U.S. Catholic Conference reported during the month included the following:

• reaffirmation of "long standing" opposition to Administration proposals for a separate Cabinet-level Department of Education: Msgr. Wilfrid Paradis, secretary for education, argued before a Senate committee that such a department could become dominated by public school interests at the expense of private school interests, and would "further increase federal interference in both public and private education in areas that rightfully belong to parents and the local community."

• qualified support for a Strategic Arms Limitation Treaty between the U.S. and the Soviet Union: Bishop Thomas C. Kelly said in a statement that "the bishops feel SALT II deserves support only if it is understood and functions as a necessary, though admittedly limited, step toward true disarmament."

• support for the rights of institutionalized persons: The bishops "believe that all persons have a right to live under conditions which enhance their human dignity, and that our society shares a responsibility to ensure that right." So stated Msgr. Francis J. Lally, secretary for social development and world peace, in a letter to Rep. Robert Kastenmeier, chairman of a House subcommittee.

National Briefs:
- The U.S. Bishops' Committee on Priestly Life and Ministry published "Fullness in Christ: A Report on a Study of Clergy Retirement"; it called for awareness of the ministerial potential of senior and retired priests.
- U.S. Circuit Court Judge James S. Burns ruled Feb. 6 in Honolulu that the Hawaii Department of Social Services and Housing was correct in using state funds to pay for elective abortions of welfare recipients. In Massachusetts, Attorney General Francis X. Bellotti ordered the state's Group Insurance Commission to stop paying for abortion options in medical insurance policies covering some 75,000 state employees.
- An ecumenical peace service, held Feb. 17 in Park Ridge, Ill., was attended by 1,000 persons protesting against the international arms exhibition, Defense Technology '79, which opened the following day in Chicago.
- About 2,000 persons, half of them members of street gangs, took part in a candlelight procession Feb. 18 through the streets of Pacoima, Calif., in a dramatic demonstration of support for efforts to end terrorism, violence and vandalism in the barrios of San Fernando Valley.
- A U.S. appeals court in New Orleans rejected a suit brought by Madalyn O'Hair and other atheists seeking a ban on use of the words, "In God We Trust," as a national motto.
- Observances: Catholic Schools Week, Feb. 4 to 10, with the theme, "Next to the Family, the Catholic School"; the 46th National Brotherhood Week, Feb. 18 to 24, sponsored by the National Conference of Christians and Jews.

Evangelization Study

Archbishop Francis T. Hurley, chairman of the U.S. Bishops' Committee on Evangelization, announced the start of a study intended "to surface information that will help the national Catholic community design and conduct within parishes and dioceses more effective evangelistic programs for the 12 million inactive American Catholics."

The archbishop said there was "a growing response to evangelization among Catholics in this country, but we are still concerned that many fail to appreciate the full definition of evangelization given by Pope Paul VI, which is essentially 'bringing the Good News into all strata of humanity and, through its influence, transforming humanity from within and making it new.' . . . An understanding of evangelization is a base for enriched . . . ministry in the parish setting."

The study was scheduled for completion by January, 1980.

INTERNATIONAL

Harassment in Brazil — At least 30 Brazilian bishops were harassed or persecuted in the previous 10 years because of their activities aimed at ending poverty, according to a study made by the Ecumenical Center for Documentation and Information in Sao Paolo. The report said that from 1968 through 1978 at least 122 priests and religious and 273 lay persons working in church-related programs were arrested, and that 34 priests were tortured and seven were killed. "The reason for church repression," the study declared, "has its roots in the pastoral goals followed by Christians and priests, together with their bishops, in the face of poverty and misery." The agents of repression were the military government and private groups opposed to social action by people of the Church.

Statute of Limitations — The government of West Germany was asked by a delegation of U.S. religious leaders, including representatives of the National Conference of Catholic Bishops and the National Council of Churches, to extend the statute of limitations for Nazi war crimes. The request — "that the door not be closed on the possibility of bringing to justice those guilty of crimes against humanity" — was presented Feb. 6 to West German Ambassador Berndt von Staden in Washington, D.C.

Faith Survives in Poland — The Catholic faith has survived the adversities of Polish history, declared the bishops in a pastoral letter issued late in January. They said their country's history reveals "a continual struggle for the freedom of the Church, the freedom of human conscience, the freedom to believe in God . . ., not only in private but also publicly, in the life of society and the country. . . . Militant political atheism has done everything it could to turn us into a secularized, godless society. We have suffered right into prison, and still we have succeeded in saving what is the most sacred thing in our nation: our belief in God, in his Son Jesus Christ and his most holy Mother."

Support for Australian Aborigines — The Justice and Peace Commission of the Australian Bishops' Conference declared in a statement that the Church should use its resources "to support the struggle of aboriginal people for land rights, restitution and compensation, self-determination, dignity and identity." The 1979 social justice statement also called for separate legal, educational and health services for the "culturally and racially distinct" aborigines.

Catholic-Methodist Dialogue — The joint Catholic-Methodist Commission said after a meeting Jan. 28 to Feb. 1 in Rome that Catholics and Methodists are more united than divided in their understanding of the Holy Spirit. Participants in the dialogue also said in a statement issued Feb. 12 that the Gospel calls Christians to speak in favor of and to respond to the needs of poor, hungry and suffering people.

Right to Responsible Procreation — The U.N. Population Commission asked government to "respect and ensure the right of persons to determine in a free, informed and responsible manner the number and spacing of their children." The commission also urged countries with high mortality levels to take special measures to cut those figures, particularly through provision of primary health services to all their people by 1985. It was reported that world population had increased by 400 million since the last World Population Conference, held in 1974 in Bucharest.

Msgr. James T. McHugh, a member of the Vatican mission to the commission, said in an address: "Families should not be forced to conform to some demographic idea in reaching responsible decisions concerning parenthood, nor should they be abandoned by society or be denied basic assistance for not doing so. Neither should nations be forced to conform to population targets in order to obtain development assistance from other nations or from international agencies. There is no need or justification for invoking 'lifeboat ethics' in trying to develop programs of international assistance or partnership."

Catholic-Jewish Relations — Catholic-Jewish relations have improved significantly in recent years, according to Rabbi Balfour Brickner, head of the Interreligious Affairs Department of the Union of American Hebrew Congregations. Interviewed in Jerusalem during a Holy Land tour by a group of Jews, Protestants and Catholics from the U.S., he said the principal change was a result of the second Vatican Council's definition of the relation of the Church to Judaism. He cited the increasing willingness of Catholics to consider Judaism in unprejudiced terms.

Anglican Synod Decisions — Agreed statements by the Anglican-Roman Catholic International Commission on the Eucharist, church authority, ministry and ordination were approved Feb. 22 by the General Synod of the Church of England. The statements were called "sufficiently congruent with Anglican teaching to provide a theological basis for further dialogue." Speakers at the synod were said to be generally pleased about the improvement in Anglican-Catholic relations in recent years, but warned that unity was not foreseeable in the immediate future.

Mandate Extended — The Committee on Society, Development and Peace (SODEPAX), the only agency operated jointly by the World Council of Churches and the Vatican, had its mandate extended through 1981, according to an announcement made by its headquarters in Geneva. The committee, a liaison office on social issues, was founded in 1968.

Women's Meeting — Two hundred and 20 women from 34 countries attended the two-week general assembly of the World Union of Catholic Women's Organizations in Bangalore, India. The theme of the meeting was "Encounter for Change — Women, Justice, Evangelization." Topics under discussion included human and religious rights, and support for activities of the 1979 International Year of the Child. Elizabeth Lovatt-Dolan of Ireland was reelected president general of the union.

International Briefs:

• The West German Bishops' Conference said in a statement issued early in the month that reliable estimates indicated that, "of the 950,000 Jews who survived" the Holocaust, "between 70 and 90 per cent owed their lives to Catholic aid."

• In working with the poor, giving love is more important than giving money, declared Mother Teresa of Calcutta in an address at a national Rotary convention in Bombay. "If you do not love, you cannot serve," she said.

• Five young members of a group opposed to the regime of Nicaraguan President Anastasio Somoza were killed by government troops Feb. 15 in a Catholic church in Managua.

• Neapolitans were reported offering special prayers for the intercession of their patron, St. Januarius, to rid the city of the "dark disease" which had killed nearly 100 babies in recent months.

• Trustees for the estate of the late 10th Duke of Argyll placed on sale the island of Iona, the "Cradle of Christianity" of Scotland.

• The Catholic Church in Poland sent 93 more missionaries abroad in 1978, bringing the total to 1,064, according to statistics released by the bishops' conference.

• A new Roman Missal was introduced Feb. 28, Ash Wednesday, in all churches of The Netherlands.

Bishops at Puebla

One hundred and 87 voting delegates representing the episcopal conferences of 22 nations attended the third general assembly of Latin American bishops Jan. 27 to Feb. 13 in Puebla, Mexico. The theme of the assembly was "The Future of Evangelization in Latin America." Its principal products were a 240-page document embodying a mandate for pastoral action and social change, and an 11-page message to the people of Latin America. The bishops pledged that they would be the "voice of the voiceless masses" oppressed by poverty and social injustice. Pope John Paul II attended the formal opening and first working session of the assembly and stressed in keynote addresses the topic of integral human liberation through evangelization. (See Third General Assembly of Latin American Bishops.)

MARCH 1979

VATICAN

Meaning of Life — "Only Jesus Christ is the adequate and final answer to the highest question about the meaning of life and history," declared Pope John Paul during an audience Mar. 1 with more than 10,000 Italian military personnel and Red Cross workers. He said: "The most beautiful and enthusiastic adventure that you can touch upon is the personal encounter with Jesus, who ... has the words of life; indeed, of eternal life."

Visit to Poland — Warsaw Radio announced in the evening of Mar. 2 that the Pope would visit Poland June 2 to 10; the report was confirmed by the Vatican two hours later. The Holy Father subsequently addressed a letter to President Henryk Jablonski in which he expressed his gratitude to Polish officials "for their positive attitude" toward the visit, the first ever by a Pope to a country under Communist rule. The Pope had hoped to make the visit during celebrations in May of the 900th anniversary of the martyrdom of St. Stanislaus, the patron of his native land. The compromise date for the trip, according to observers, was intended to lessen the chances of aggravating tension between the regime and the Church.

Lenten Talks — Basic penitential themes of Lent were covered by the Holy Father in several addresses during the month.

• Speaking to the priests of Rome Mar. 2, he emphasized two "essential" aspects of their life: the need for personal holiness and their mission of "building up the community of the People of God." He urged them to renew the sense of their priestly identity, saying: "We must guard carefully against 'dividing' our personality as priests. We must guard carefully against allowing our priesthood to cease being the 'most essential' thing, the 'unifying' element of everything we are involved in. It can never become something 'secondary' or 'supplementary.' "

• "Bowing one's head before God is a sign of humility ... not weak-heartedness," he told a gathering of 50,000 persons in St. Peter's Square Mar. 4. "Humility is creative submission to the power of truth and love. Humility is a rejection of appearance and superficiality," which cause people to become "one-dimensional, cut off from (their) own depth."

• Lenten practices of prayer, fasting and almsgiving should not be considered "simply as passing practices," he said at a general audience Mar. 14. Rather, they should be part of Christian life throughout the year, linked as they are with conversion and truth in spiritual life."

• The Church recommends meditation, he declared Mar. 18, "so that we may share in liberation ... from sin, ... from the concupiscence of the flesh, from the concupiscence of the eyes, from pride of life, ... from all that restricts man, even if the restrictions permit him to preserve the appearance of autonomy."

• Fasting, said the Pope at three general audiences Mar. 21, "has as a goal to introduce into the existence of man not only necessary balance, but also detachment from what could be defined as the 'consumer attitude' " which is particularly characteristic of Western civilization.

Priority for Seminaries — The first one, the Pope told rectors of English-language seminaries in Rome Mar. 3, "is the teaching of God's word in all its purity, with all its exigencies and in all its power.... The word of God — and the word of God alone — is the basis for all ministry, for all pastoral activity, for all priestly action.... When the word of God is seen as the basis of all seminary life and training, and when the great discipline of the Church is embraced by the seminarians as a service to charity, the seminaries become, in the words of Paul VI, 'houses of deep and authentic Christian asceticism, as well as joyful communities sustained by eucharistic piety.' "

Addressing the rectors of Roman ecclesiastical colleges Mar. 16, the Holy Father said that the common life in their institutions should not be "a mere complex of external relationships" but should be "modelled on the spirit which animated ... the Apostles ... in the Cenacle, where 'all these with one mind continued steadfastly in prayer ... with Mary, the Mother of Jesus.' "

Catholic-Jewish Relations — At a meeting Mar. 12 with members of the International Catholic-Jewish Liaison Committee, the Pope declared: "I believe that both sides must continue their strong efforts to overcome the difficulties of the past, so as to fulfill God's commandment of love and to sustain a truly fruitful and fraternal dialogue that contributes to the good of each of the partners involved and to our better service to humanity." Philip A. Klutznik, president of the World Jewish Congress, said that Catholic advances in understanding Judaism since the Second Vatican Council had resulted in increased friendship, "based on the affirmation of a shared reverence for sacred Scripture, the condemnation of anti-Semitism, and support for religious liberty and joint social action."

Risks and Opportunities for Migrants — Working with immigrants is the "work of the whole local church — priests, religious and lay persons," stated the Holy Father Mar. 14 in an address to persons attending a congress sponsored by the Pontifical Commission for

Migration and Tourism. He called migration "a massive phenomenon of our time" which, for migrants, involves "a serious risk of uprooting, of dehumanization and, in some cases, of de-Christianization. . . . But it also involves an opportunity for human and spiritual enrichment, of openness, of welcoming foreigners and of mutual contact with them. For the Church, it is an invitation to be more missionary, to go and meet the foreign brother, to respect him."

People More Important than Political Interests — The Pope, addressing board members of the International Institute for the Rights of Man Mar. 22, said that church teaching makes it clear that "the human person can never be sacrificed to any national or international political interest." The Church's commitment to the defense and promotion of human rights, he added, "flows from the Gospel, where one finds the most profound expression of the dignity of man and the most urgent motive for efforts to promote his rights."

Puebla Report Approved — The Pope formally approved Mar. 23 the final document of more than 200 pages issued at the conclusion of the Third General Assembly of Latin American Bishops, held Jan. 27 to Feb. 13 in Puebla, Mexico. (See Third General Assembly of Latin American Bishops.)

Egyptian-Israeli Peace Treaty — The Pope appealed Mar. 25 for prayer for the success of the treaty to be signed the following day in Washington. "This event," he said, "is formalizing peace between two countries after decades of war and tension, and is giving a decisive impulse to the peace process in the entire region of the Middle East." His endorsement was regarded as significant by political observers who noted that many European governments had refused to comment on the treaty and that the Arab world had condemned it.

Faith and Science — The Pope reaffirmed Mar. 30 the Second Vatican Council's recognition of the freedom of scientific research, and emphasized the fact there is no opposition between faith and science. He said: "Science in itself is good since it is knowledge of the world which is good, created and looked upon by the Creator with satisfaction, according to the Book of Genesis. . . . Original sin has not completely altered this first goodness. Human knowledge of the world is a way of sharing in the knowledge of the Creator. It constitutes, therefore, a first degree of resemblance of man to God, an act of respect toward him."

The Pope Also:
• Spent the week of Mar. 4 to 10 on retreat.
• Concelebrated Mass Mar. 13 for the funeral of Cardinal Jean Villot, secretary of state and chamberlain of the Holy Roman Church under three popes, who died Mar. 9.

• Praised the work of the Pro Oriente Foundation in promoting dialogue with Eastern Orthodox churches, Mar. 29.
• Condemned the murder Mar. 30 in London of British Conservative Member of Parliament Airey Neave as an "act of cowardly and senseless violence."
• Met with: Students of the Pontifical Ecclesiastical Academy, whom he told that the work of Vatican diplomats is "not without sacrifices, almost always hidden, sometimes not sufficiently appreciated," Mar. 17; Bolivian Ambassador Juan Jose Vidaurre Pinto, Mar. 17; King Baudouin and Queen Fabiola of Belgium, Mar. 19; Egyptian Vice President Hosni Mubarak, Mar. 21; Mobutu Sese Seko, president of Zaire, Mar. 29.
• Held three general audiences on each of the last two Wednesdays of the month to accommodate large crowds; 35,000 persons attended audiences Mar. 28.

Vatican Briefs:
• Pope Pius XII "prepared the groundwork" for the Second Vatican Council, declared Father Robert A. Graham, S.J., in comment on the 40th anniversary of the beginning of his 20-year pontificate.
• A communique reported Mar. 23 that church unity, common witness and cooperation in social action were the subjects of discussion during the Feb. 26 to Mar. 2 meeting in Switzerland of the joint working group of the World Council of Churches and the Catholic Church.

Redemptor Hominis

Pope John Paul II issued the first encyclical letter of his pontificate Mar. 15 under the title, *Redemptor Hominis* (Redeemer of Man). Its keynotes are the divine and human aspects of redemption, and the mission of the Church.

"The mystery of redemption," in which Christ reveals God to man and man to himself, "has become the fundamental principle of her (the Church's) life and mission." Accordingly, the letter said the primary engagement of the Church is to a "dialogue of salvation" with and for all people.

(See separate entry for excerpts.)

NATIONAL

Sharing the Light of Faith — The National Catechetical Directory was published under this title March 6 by the Department of Education, U.S. Catholic Conference. The text, in preparation for more than five years, was approved by the National Conference of Catholic Bishops in 1977 and by the Congregation for the Clergy in 1978.

Medicaid-Paid Abortions Down — Secretary of Health, Education and Welfare Joseph Califano told a House of Representatives appropriations subcommittee March 8 that the Hyde Amendment restricting federal funding of abortions had reduced Medicaid abortions by 99 per cent from a previous level of about 250,000 a year. Between Feb. 14 and Dec. 31, 1978, he said, HEW paid for 2,421 abortions. The Hyde Amendment prohibited the use of federal funds by the Departments of Labor and HEW to pay for abortions except in cases of: danger of maternal death; serious, long-lasting physical health damage; pregnancy resulting from rape or incest reported in an appropriate manner. It was also reported that 18 states were continuing payment for abortions with their own funds, either voluntarily or under court order.

China Settlement — Catholic missionary groups were said to be among American church organizations eligible to receive funds from the Republic of China in a settlement of claims made after the Communist government took over the country more than 30 years ago. China agreed in February to pay $80.5 million over five years to American businesses, churches, non-profit institutions and individuals against claims totalling about $197 million. Under the settlement, eight Catholic missionary orders were entitled to receive about $3.6 million.

In Vitro Fertilization — A federal Ethics Advisory Board issued a report with the conclusion that research on in vitro fertilization is ethically acceptable despite substantial ethical arguments against it. Some of the objections include the unknown risk to a child produced in such a manner, the relationship of the procedure to abortion, and the danger that widespread use of the process could lead to even more dangerous forms of genetic manipulation. One of the prime moral objections is against the substitution of technological fertilization for natural fertilization as a consequence of normal marital intercourse. The board's finding, it was said, could lead to an end to a four-year moratorium on in vitro fertilization and embryo transfer in the U.S.

Aid to Aliens — The immigration service of the Archdiocese of Los Angeles aided 33,890 aliens in 1978, bringing to more than 150,000 the number of undocumented men and women assisted by the archdiocese since Cardinal James McIntyre established the agency in 1971. The total number of persons aided during the year was 49,440, including: 33,890 illegal aliens; 2,735 Southeast Asian refugees who were resettled; 12,552 Southeast Asians assisted in adjusting their status to permanent residency, and 263 refugees from Eastern Europe and other countries.

Traditionalist Parish Not Roman Catholic — Bishop Loras J. Watters of Winona warned people of the diocese that a proposed new parish advertising "traditional Catholic Masses" was not part of the Roman Catholic Church. He issued the warning in the Mar. 16 edition of the diocesan newspaper, in connection with an announcement by the Orthodox Roman Catholic Movement, Inc., that it was going to establish a permanent chapel in Rochester, Minn., under the title of Our Lady of the Rosary Parish.

Three Mile Island Accident — Radiation leaks caused by an accident Mar. 28 at the Three Mile Island nuclear plant near Harrisburg, Pa., fueled demands for improved safety standards in the operation of such plants as well for limitations on the development of nuclear energy sources.

No Loan for Reopening Steel Plant — The refusal of the Carter Administration late in the month to grant $245 million in loan guarantees doomed months-long efforts of the Ecumenical Coalition of the Mahoning Valley to reopen a Youngstown steel mill under worker-community ownership.

Communications Hearings — Members of the Communications Committee of the U.S. Catholic Conference began a study of opinions expressed by more than 140 persons at hearings conducted during the month in Washington, D.C., Chicago, San Francisco and Los Angeles. The purpose of the hearings was to explore ways and means of improving church use of print and electronic media. Witnesses were in general agreement about the need to develop "a national vision or strategy for the Church's work in communications."

Good News Bible — Late in the month, the American Bible Society announced the publication of *The Good News Bible with Deuterocanonicals-Apocrypha*, containing the complete Catholic canon of the Scriptures. This canon includes books called deuterocanonical which the Church regards as inspired like the rest of the books of the Bible. The Protestant canon, which regards these books as edifying and useful but not inspired like the rest of the books, calls them apocrypha. This modern-language edition of the Bible has the *imprimatur* (let it be printed) of Archbishop John F. Whealon of Hartford and is approved "for private use but not for general use in the liturgy of the Mass." (See Bible, Canons.)

Meetings — Meetings during the month included the following.

• Hispanic Seminarians, Mar. 2 to 4 in Irving, Texas; attended by 75 students of 12 seminaries. Evangelization was the theme.

• National Conference of Permanent Diaconate Directors, Mar. 4 to 8 in Dallas; attended by 167 participants from 94 dioceses. Father John Hedderman of the Salt Lake City diocese was installed as president. Resolutions passed included one for permission for permanent deacons to administer the sacrament of anointing of the sick, and another for permission for widowed deacons to remarry.

• National Federation of Priests' Councils, House of Delegates, Mar. 11 to 15 in Boston; attended by nearly 200 representatives of 110 local councils and senates. The principal subjects of discussion were ministry, evangelization and community. Emphasized was the need to analyze the structures of society and dioceses as a prelude to evangelization.

• Conference on the Apostolate of the Church in the Black Community, sponsored by the National Office for Black Catholics, Mar. 13 to 16 in Hendersonville, N.C.; attended by nine bishops and 158 invited delegates. The purpose, according to Walter T. Hubbard, president of the NOBC board of directors, was to develop "a plan of action for the next 10 years for black Catholics, clergy, the black community, and for all of us as people of this country."

• National Assembly of the Laity, Mar. 16 to 18 at the University of Notre Dame; attended by more than 100 persons. Participants issued a statement concerning the development of "new initiatives for the laity" and the establishment of a national network of concerned Christian lay persons.

• Call to Action Workshop, attended by more than 300 representatives from various dioceses, in Washington, D.C. Discussions focused on the results of programs stemming from the Bicentennial Call to Action Conference held in 1976 in Detroit.

National Briefs:

• Father Thomas J. O'Donnell, S.J., was named interim coordinator of the Committee for Human Values, National Conference of Catholic Bishops.

• Mother Teresa of Calcutta, Dorothy Day of *The Catholic Worker,* and economist Barbara Ward were called "living Christian heroes worthy of recognition," by the editors of nine U.S. and Canadian church publications.

• Circuit Court Judge Ferrill D. McRae enjoined the Alabama State Department of Industrial Relations from enforcing any state or federal laws which would require schools operated by 17 Lutheran churches to pay unemployment compensation taxes for their employees. In a similar decision, Hamilton County Chancery Court Judge Wilkes Thrasher ruled that Tennessee could not collect unemployment compensation taxes from church-related schools in the state.

• Actress Helen Hayes was named the 99th recipient of the Laetare Medal by the University of Notre Dame.

NLRB Decision

The U.S. Supreme Court ruled, 5 to 4, Mar. 21 that lay teachers in church-related schools are not covered by the National Labor Relations Act, and that officials of such schools cannot be required by law to bargain with unions of lay faculty members. The ground for the decision, according to the majority opinion by Chief Justice Warren Burger, was the legislative history of the law which showed "no clear expression of an affirmative intention of Congress" to include teachers at church-run schools in its coverage.

With its decision, the Court upheld a 1977 ruling by the Seventh Circuit Court of Appeals in National Labor Relations Board v. Catholic Bishop of Chicago (No. 77-752) and Diocese of Fort Wayne-South Bend. The Circuit Court, however, held that intervention by the NLRB was unconstitutional on First Amendment grounds, on which the Supreme Court did not rule.

INTERNATIONAL

Mother Teresa Honored — Mother Teresa of Calcutta was awarded the Balzan Prize for Humanity, Peace and Brotherhood Mar. 1 in Rome. The prize of $300,000 was given for "the exceptional abnegation with which she has dedicated her whole life in aiding, in India and other countries of the world, the victims of hunger, misery and illness, the abandoned and the dying, transforming into tireless action her love for suffering humanity."

Toronto Schools Praised — Ontario Premier William Davis praised the Catholic Schools of metropolitan Toronto for providing leadership in counteracting racism in Canada's multicultural society. He cited the heavy Catholic enrollment in the provincial government's Heritage Language Program, in which students take classes in the language of their cultural heritage. About 33,000 of the 50,000 students in the program were in Catholic schools.

Appeal for More Aid to Refugees — Archbishop Joseph-Aurele Plourde of Ottawa, just returned from a tour of several refugee camps in Thailand, appealed in Ottawa for concerted effort by "the privileged people" of Canada, the United States, Europe and Australia to accept more refugees into their countries, and to increase aid to Thailand, Malaysia and Indonesia where scores of thousands of people had temporary refuge in "absolutely terrible" conditions.

Latin American Religious — One hundred and fifty delegates from religious communities in Latin America attended the Mar. 6 to 16 seventh assembly of the Confederation of Latin American Religious in Santo Domingo. They issued a set of pastoral guidelines modelled after those stated by the Latin American bishops assembled at Puebla, Mexico, in February.

Safeguards for Irish Prisoners — Amnesty International, which monitors violations of human rights, called during the month for a meeting with Britain's Secretary of State for Northern Ireland, Roy Mason, after a British government inquiry found that physical abuse had been inflicted on prisoners held by Ulster authorities. Amnesty's concerns, as also those of Catholic and other observers, included the isolation of prisoners, rules about the admissibility of confessions elicited in circumstances of maltreatment, and inadequate procedures for handling complaints.

Violence Continuing in El Salvador — Violence continued to convulse El Salvador despite the repeal Feb. 27 of the repressive Public Order Law of November, 1977. Archbishop Oscar Arnulfo Romero of San Salvador, who welcomed repeal of the law, said "it would have to be followed up." Instead, he added, little had changed: "The same arbitrary arrests and killings are taking place as before." Victims of violence since the middle of 1977 included at least four priests killed, 10 expelled, 47 Jesuits threatened with death, and an undisclosed number of catechists and other lay persons arrested, tortured, killed and missing.

Catholics and the British Council of Churches — The Catholic Church of England and Wales moved a step closer to joining the British Council of Churches when representatives of both bodies agreed that public statements on moral issues posed no "serious obstacle" to Catholic membership. The bishops refused to join the BCC in 1974 because of concern that membership might commit them to joint statements with which they could not agree or which might cause confusion among Catholics.

Repression in Mozambique — Intensification of persecution of the Church in Mozambique was reported by the independent Catholic newspaper of the Diocese of Ibadan, Nigeria. People were forbidden to gather for Mass or catechetical instruction in one diocese. The bishop of another diocese, Lichinga, and two of his priests were placed under house arrest. Elsewhere, priests were forbidden to visit parishioners or to leave their mission stations.

Refugees in Africa — The All-African Conference of Churches reported that nearly half of the worldwide refugee population of 8.5 million was on the continent. Nearly four million people were in refuge from racial discrimination in southern Africa, political intolerance in newly independent black-ruled countries, civil wars and other armed conflicts.

Vicariate of Solidarity — Since the beginning of operations in 1975, the Vicariate of Solidarity in Chile reported that it had provided legal aid to about 38,000 persons arrested under security laws or fired from their jobs by the government. The most recent effort of the human rights agency was devoted to finding out the whereabouts of 600 to 1,000 persons missing after being detained by security forces.

CELAM Officers and Objective — Seven cardinals and 50 bishops attending a Mar. 27 to 31 meeting of the Latin American Bishops' Council in Teques, Venezuela, elected new officers of the council: Coadjutor Archbishop Alfonso Lopez Trujillo of Medellin, Colombia, president; Bishop Roman Arrieta of Tilaran, Costa Rica (for Spanish-speaking countries) and Archbishop Luciano Cabral Duarte of Aracaju, Brazil (for Portuguese people), vice presidents; Bishop Antonio Quarracino of Avellaneda, Argentina, general secretary. The meeting was keyed to efforts to put into effect the pastoral-social program developed at the Third General Assembly of Latin American Bishops held in February in Puebla, Mexico.

International Briefs:
- The first volume of an edition of the Old Testament in the Lingala language was published in Zaire.
- The International Center for the Diaconate in Freiburg, West Germany, reported that 3,087 of 4,781 active permanent deacons in the world were in the United States.
- The Church in Need, an international Catholic aid agency headquartered in Koenigstein, West Germany, received more than $33.3 million in 1978 from more than 600,000 donors in 14 countries. The agency assists pastoral programs, church construction and religious education, and also provides aid to Catholics suffering from injustice and for their faith in Third World and Communist countries.
- Eight hundred and 47 Colombian families were reported to be beneficiaries of the 10-year-old Populorum Progressio Fund and land-reform program established by Pope Paul VI after his visit to Colombia in 1968. The fund was named after his encyclical of the same title.

Freedom of Religion Bill

The 29 bishops of Kerala State in Southwest India added their names to a growing list of Christians opposed to passage by Parliament of a national, anti-conversion Freedom of Religion Bill intended, according to its sponsors, to prevent forced conversions by the use of fraud, coercion or any other type of inducement.

Under the pretext of protecting religious freedom, the bishops said, the bill sought "to destroy the freedom guaranteed by the constitution." They stated clearly that the Church does not believe in forced conversions.

Critics said terms of the measure were defined so loosely as to prevent any kind of evangelization, and that its obvious intent was to restrict Christianity, a minority faith in the predominantly Hindu country. Under provisions of the bill, it was noted, Mother Teresa of Calcutta could be sentenced to two years in prison because her charitable works could be construed as "inducement" to conversion.

Anti-conversion laws like the bill before Parliament were already in force in several Indian states.

APRIL 1979

VATICAN

This Life and the Next — Pope John Paul, addressing more than 10,000 university students Apr. 5 during a Mass in St. Peter's Basilica, rejected the Marxist contention that belief in everlasting life distracts man from concern about temporal reality. "Human life is a passage," he said. "This life is not a whole which is enclosed in a definitive way between the date of birth and the date of death. It is open toward ultimate completion in God.... The followers of Marx (say) such a concept of life distracts man from temporal reality, and in a certain way cancels it out. The truth is quite otherwise. Only such a concept of life gives full importance to all the problems of temporal reality. It opens up the possibility of their full positioning in the existence of man. Such a concept of life does not permit closing man in temporal things, it does not permit subordinating him completely to them. It is decisive for his freedom."

Letters to Priests and Bishops — The Holy Father addressed letters of 35 pages and eight pages, respectively, to priests and bishops on the occasion of Holy Thursday, Apr. 12. Priestly identity, fidelity and pastoral service were key themes of the letter to priests (see separate entry for excerpts). He urged bishops to deepen relationships with their priests and with each other, in "the brotherly communion of the whole of the Church's episcopal college."

Plea for Clemency — While not mentioning Iran by name, the Pope had executions and related cruelties there in mind as he denounced Apr. 18 the "rekindling of punitive flames in the wake of recent upheavals." Observers said there was no doubt that his plea for humane treatment of prisoners and "clemency for the vanquished" was prompted by concern over developments in the revolution which forced Shah Mohammed Riza Pahlevi into exile in January.

The Pope also referred explicitly to "the worsening of political and social tensions, of armed fighting, in Rhodesia, Uganda and Nicaragua."

Pastoral Ministry among Workers — The Pope urged priests engaged in pastoral work in labor organizations Apr. 25 to strive so that "the gap between the Church and factory narrows and that the fumes of incense mix with those of industry." He said: "Take care, above all, of all those who still are suffering because of their heavy or unhealthy work, of the lack of job security, of poor housing and of insufficient pay."

General Absolution Norms — Pope John Paul, at a meeting Apr. 26 with a group of bishops from India, emphasized the importance of individual confession and called for careful observance of strict norms concerning general absolution. "In particular," he said in reference to his encyclical letter *Redemptor Hominis*, "I noted the need to guard the sacrament of penance, and I stressed that the faithful observance of the centuries-old 'practice of individual confession, with a personal act of sorrow and the intention to amend and make satisfaction' is an expression of the Church's defense of 'man's right to a more personal encounter with the crucified, forgiving Christ.' "

New Vulgate — Pope John Paul formally promulgated the New Vulgate edition of the Bible in an apostolic constitution entitled *Scripturarum Thesaurus* ("The Treasury of the Scriptures"), dated Apr. 25 and made public Apr. 27.

Non-Christians — "The non-Christian world is indeed constantly before the eyes of the Church and the Pope," and "we are truly committed to serve it generously," the Holy Father told members of the Vatican Secretariat for Non-Christians Apr. 27. "The secretariat," he said, "is the symbol and expression of the Church's will to enter into communication with every person, and in particular with the multitudes of those who seek meaning and guidance for their lives in the non-Christian religious traditions."

Cardinal Sergio Pignedoli, president of the secretariat, indicated that the principal topic of discussion at its annual meeting was a set of guidelines for dialogue among Catholics and non-Christians.

Beatifications — Pope John Paul presided at beatification ceremonies for the first time Apr. 29, for: French Holy Ghost Father Jacques Desire Laval (1803-64), a missionary to the people of Mauritius Island for 23 years; and Spanish Dominican Father Francisco Coll (1812-75), founder of the Congregation of the Annunciation, a community of nuns.

The Pope Also:

• Joined other world leaders in appealing to Pakistani authorities to spare the life of Zulfikar Ali Bhutto, the former prime minister; Bhutto was hanged Apr. 4.

• Encouraged Europeans to vote in June elections for a European Parliament, during a meeting Apr. 5 with officials of the body.

• Announced Apr. 6, the day after he appointed four new Hungarian bishops, that seminarians from Hungary would again study at the 400-year-old German-Hungarian College in Rome.

• Expressed special concern Apr. 20 for the children-to-children missionary apostolate on the occasion of the International Year of the Child, in a letter to Archbishop Simon Lourdusamy, president of the council of the Pontifical Holy Childhood Association.

- Named Cardinal Antonio Samore Apr. 24 as his official mediator in the Beagle Channel dispute between Chile and Argentina.
- Met with 6,000 participants in the 10th National Congress of Italian Domestic Workers Apr. 29.
- Praised the fidelity of Croatians to Christ, the Church and Mary as he welcomed a pilgrimage of 8,000 persons Apr. 30.
- Conveyed his sympathy for victims of earthquakes in Yugoslavia and Albania, of floods in Mississippi, and of civil wars in Nicaragua, Uganda and Rhodesia.
- Had meetings with new ambassadors to the Vatican — Brian Clarence Hill of Australia, Apr. 5, and Joseph Charles Leonard Yvon Beaulne of Canada, Apr. 7 — and two Israeli diplomatic officials, Apr. 23.

Vatican Briefs:
- The Congregation for the Doctrine of the Faith issued a declaration Apr. 3 in which it condemned views expressed by French Dominican Father Jacques Pohier concerning the resurrection of Christ and life after death. The congregation said that opinions in his book, *Quand Je Dis Dieu* (see separate entry), were "manifestly not in conformity with revelation and the teaching authority of the Church."

On the same day the declaration was issued, Pope John Paul told teachers and students of theology schools in Rome that the Church needs "priests who build up and do not tear down when teaching faith and morals."

- *L'Osservatore Romano* reported in its Apr. 27 edition that 2,506 priests left the active ministry in 1977. The total number of priests at the end of the year was 406,717. Five years earlier, the total was 435,848.

Holy Week

Pope John Paul began Holy Week with a Mass celebrated on Palm Sunday in St. Peter's Square before a throng of about 70,000 persons. Salvation through the death of Christ was the theme of his homily.

On Holy Thursday morning he concelebrated the Mass of Chrism in St. Peter's Basilica with 2,500 priests of Rome, whom he urged to fidelity and perseverance in their ministry. In the evening he officiated at the Mass of the Lord's Supper during which, in imitating Christ, he washed the feet of 12 men.

He led the Way of the Cross at the Rome Colosseum in the evening of Good Friday. In a brief address, he said: "We must feel and express an especially profound solidarity with all our brothers in the faith who even in our own time (like martyrs before them) are the object of persecutions and discriminations in various parts of the earth. We think especially of those who are condemned, in a certain sense, to 'civil death' with the refusal of the right to live according to their own faith, their own rite, their own religious convictions."

The Holy Father presided at Easter Vigil ceremonies, during which he baptized and confirmed 11 persons.

He addressed a greeting of peace in 32 languages to people throughout the world during a Mass in St. Peter's Square on Easter Sunday. In a message delivered before more than 150,000 persons, he said: "How necessary is his (Christ's) presence, the victory of his spirit, the order coming from his commandment of love, so that men and women, families, nations and continents may enjoy peace. . . . Peace of consciences and peace of hearts. This peace cannot be had unless each of us has the awareness of doing everything in his or her power so that a life worthy of the children of God will be ensured for all men and women. . . . I am thinking at this moment in particular of all those who are suffering for the lack of what is strictly necessary for existence, and above all of the little children who — in their weakness — are the ones who are especially loved by Christ and to whom is dedicated this year, the International Year of the Child."

NATIONAL

USCC Recommendations — In testimony before separate Congressional committees early in the month, the U.S. Catholic Conference recommended higher funding than that proposed by the Carter Administration for housing programs for the elderly and supported foreign economic aid, but urged that $25 million in military aid be denied to the Philippines because of human rights violations there.

Protest in Hawaii — The Diocese of Honolulu formally protested the lack of official Catholic representation on an advisory commission established to assist the U.S. Interior Department to plan future uses of the Kalaupapa Settlement on Molokai, the site of the life and labors of Father Damien de Veuster. A chancery office statement said: "It was a cause of genuine dismay for the Catholic people of Hawaii to discover that the newly nominated commission did not include a member of the Roman Catholic chancery office or the Sacred Hearts Congregation," to which the leper priest belonged.

Tuition Tax Credits, School Prayer, Palestinians — President Carter sketched his ideas on these subjects at a meeting Apr. 6 with members of the Catholic and general press.

- Tuition Tax Credits: "I have always been concerned about the constitutional prohibition against the mixing of Church and state."
- School Prayer: "I think the government ought to stay out of the prayer business and let it be between a person and God, and not let it be part of a school program under any tangible constraints, either a direct order to a

child to pray or an embarrassing situation where the child would feel constrained to pray."

• Palestinians: While indicating his desire for Palestinian participation in discussions of the Mideast peace treaty, he declared: "As long as the Palestinian Liberation Organization's constitution and commitment are dedicated to the destruction of Israel, we will not negotiate with them."

Claretians Dismissed from LSU — Controversy followed the decision of Bishop Joseph V. Sullivan of Baton Rouge to relieve the Claretian Fathers of their duties as campus ministers at Louisiana State University. The bishop, who did not disclose the reasons for their dismissal, announced that the Holy Cross Fathers would take over the ministry program on Aug. 1.

Prayer Amendment Downed — With a 53-to-40 vote Apr. 9, the Senate removed an amendment to a Department of Education bill which would have blocked the Supreme Court from banning state laws on prayer in public schools, and attached it to a bill which was expected to die. The amendment had been proposed by Sen. Jesse Helms of North Carolina in an attempt to offset the effect of Supreme Court decisions in 1962 and 1963 that outlawed statutes on prayer in public schools.

In a related development, U.S. District Court Judge Carl A. Muecke ruled in Phoenix that voluntary prayers during student assemblies at Chandler High School were unconstitutional.

Family Conference Chairman — Jim Guy Tucker, 35, a former Congressman from Arkansas, was named by President Carter to serve as chairman of the White House Conference on Families. His appointment was made nearly a year after the original chairman resigned in controversy, forcing a delay in the conference from December, 1979, to possibly the spring of 1981.

Apparition Claims Not Credible — Msgr. Anthony J. Bevilacqua, chancellor of the Diocese of Brooklyn, declared that "no credibility" could be given to alleged visions and apparitions of "Our Lady of the Roses" claimed since 1970 by Veronica Leuken, a Bayside, Long Island, housewife. He said that a thorough investigation of the visions made in 1974 led to the conclusion that they were the "products of a fertile imagination. . . . It is the official and firm position of the Diocese of Brooklyn that no credibility can be given the so-called visions of Bayside."

Publication Stopped — The Executive Committee of the U.S. Catholic Conference stopped publication of *Light of Faith, Shades of Sexism*, a book it had commissioned on sexist language and stereotypes in religious education materials. Bishop Thomas Kelly, general secretary, said the action was taken because the book, authored by Marianne Swiacki of the private Liturgical Conference, did not adequately reflect the doctrine of the Church and took positions which the bishops either opposed or had not yet addressed.

Church Wiped Out — "For all practical purposes, organized religion does not exist in China any more; the Catholic Church has been wiped out." So stated Chinese Father Louis Lee of the Archdiocese of Dubuque following a two-month visit to his homeland. He said that only two Christian churches were open to serve foreign visitors and diplomatic personnel, there were very few priests, and that, without some change in conditions there, "there won't be any priest in China at all 20 or 30 years from now." He added: "For years, there has been no church to go to, no Mass to attend, no Holy Communion to receive, no sacraments to heal their souls; but the hunger for God, especially among the elderly, increases as the deprivation of church services continues."

Rural Development Policy — Bishop George H. Speltz of St. Cloud, in testimony before a House subcommittee Apr. 25, declared: "The widespread ownership of productive property, long espoused by the Church, is one of the greatest guarantees of human dignity and of democratic freedoms. The movement toward consolidation in agriculture and toward absentee ownership of land erodes whatever economic power remains in the hands of rural people; and, if carried far enough, would permit the rise in non-metropolitan America of a sort of landed gentry." He said the U.S. Catholic Conference would support passage of the Family Farm Development Act, which would direct federal policy toward support for family farms through provisions for commodity programs, soil conservation, aid to new farmers, direct marketing, agricultural research and tax reform.

Electronic Evangelism — Donald A. Thurston, an official of the National Association of Broadcasters, expressed concern Apr. 29 on the "Crossroads" radio program "about the emergence of new religions, of cultism, of evangelical campaigns supported in large part by solicitation of funds over the air. . . . There is a danger ahead when a group suddenly awakens to the great religious potentiality of radio and television, and determines to take advantage of it as quickly and cheaply as possible. That attitude has resulted in extensive criticism of both religion and the broadcasting industry."

Effect of Proposition 13 — Budget cutbacks resulting from Proposition 13, a sharp rollback of property taxes, were having a "significant impact" on services and clients of Catholic agencies, according to a report prepared by the California Conference of Catholic Charities Directors. The report said that diminished state funding was leading to curtailment of services and possibly to cancellation of contracts with public agencies.

Meetings — Meetings during the month included the following.

• Fellowship of Catholic Scholars, Mar. 30 to Apr. 1 in St. Louis; attended by 120 persons. James Hitchcock of St. Louis University was elected president. The organization offered the services of its 400 members to the U.S. bishops in support of church doctrine.

• Pastoral Musicians' Convention, Apr. 17 to 20 in Chicago; attended by some 3,400 persons.

• 16th National Workshop on Christian Unity, Apr. 23 to 26, in Birmingham; attended by more than 400 persons. Cardinal William Baum of Washington said in an address: "We have come together to honor this cause, to discuss the present situation of the ecumenical effort, to rededicate ourselves . . . to celebrate the progress that has been made and to implore from the Lord the wisdom and strength to continue along the path indicated by the Holy Spirit."

National Briefs:

• Catholic, Protestant and Orthodox leaders attended ceremonies Apr. 1 in New York marking the 20th anniversary of the investiture of Archbishop Iakovos as primate of the Greek Orthodox Church in the Americas.

• Nancy Frazier became the first woman reporter assigned to full-time work in the Rome bureau of NC News Service.

• In two firsts for women in the Diocese of Albany, Bishop Howard Hubbard appointed Mercy Sister Ellen Boyle and Josephite Sister Nola Brunner chancery assistant and co-vicar for religious, respectively.

• The Omaha Province of the Sisters of Mercy set up the Health System of Mercy to coordinate planning and services at 14 hospitals and four long-term health facilities sponsored by the community.

• The Pennsylvania Catholic Conference announced its support for a no-fault divorce law with strong provisions for conciliation efforts. Howard Fetterhoff, executive director, said: "There is a significant difference between opposing divorce and opposing reform of laws which deal inadequately with the reality of broken relationships."

Education, Press Conventions

About 18,000 persons attended sessions of the 75th anniversary convention of the National Catholic Educational Association Apr. 16 to 19 in Philadelphia. The theme and subject of many addresses was "Sharing the Light of Faith," the title of the recently published National Catechetical Directory. Pope John Paul, in a message read Apr. 17, told the conventioneers that Catholic schools "must remain a privileged means of Catholic education in America. . . . As an instrument of the apostolate, they are worthy of the greatest sacrifices."

Ethel Gintoft, associate editor of *The Catholic Herald Citizen*, was installed as the first woman president of the Catholic Press Association at the association's convention Apr. 25 to 28 in Fort Lauderdale. Father Walter Burghardt, S.J., editor-in-chief of *Theological Studies*, was honored with the organization's St. Francis De Sales Award for "outstanding journalism." Numerous speakers addressed subjects related to the nature and function of the Catholic press in the Church and general society. One of them, Bishop Thomas J. Grady of Orlando, said: "If the press is to be a builder of community, harmony and unity are not greatly served either by publications which are monotonously humorless and self-righteously hostile or (those) which are predictably cynical and iconoclastic."

INTERNATIONAL

Warning and Prayer — The bishops of Ontario, in a statement on unity and minority rights published in English and French, issued a "warning" — against a possible backlash over Quebec's drive toward political separation — and a "prayer" — that "all might be one" in Canada.

Priorities — Subjects "most urgently requiring action by Catholics today," according to a poll of 20,000 Catholics in England and Wales, were: Christian unity, youth problems and needs, education, the Third World, international justice and peace, world hunger, foreign aid and racial discrimination (apartheid).

Islamic Revival — The revival of Islam in Pakistan should not be a cause of fear and apprehension among Christians, declared the bishops of the country in a pastoral letter. They said that Moslems and Christians face the same "real enemies," described as "a secular view of life, worship of wealth, corruption and oppression." The revival provides "ample grounds for encouragement," they added, noting that it represents an effort "to bring about economic and political stability, and to combat the forces of materialism and secularism."

KNA, the West German Catholic news agency, reported that the revival of Islam in the Middle East, however, was causing problems for religious minorities, especially Jews and members of Eastern Christian countries.

Catholic Facilities To Remain Separate — Frank Gilhooly, president of the Ontario Separate School Trustees' Association, reported that considerable progress had been made in cooperation between Catholic and public schools, but that Catholics were not ready to share facilities with public schools. He said: "There has been progress, and there needs to be more. But we can't allow the

Catholic nature of our system to be diminished."

Easter Mass in China — The official New China News Agency described an Easter Sunday Mass at Immaculate Conception Cathedral in Beijing (Peking), the only Catholic church believed functioning in China. The Italian daily *La Stampa* noted in a front-page story Apr. 17 that it was the first time in many years that the Communist government agency reported on the Mass or on any other Catholic religious service.

Rhodesian Election — Methodist Bishop Abel Muzorewa was elected the first black prime minister of Rhodesia and his United African National Council party won about 67 per cent of votes cast from Apr. 17 to 21. The election, organized by the white-controlled government of Prime Minister Ian Smith, was strongly criticized by members of the Catholic Justice and Peace Commission. They complained that the election took place while the country was under martial law, that candidacy by members of the Patriotic Front was outlawed, and that there would not be any real transfer of power to the black majority. The commission reported, in addition, that the number of victims of civil war in the country had risen beyond 20,000.

Abortion Is an Act of Death — The Permanent Council of the French Bishops' Conference issued statements Apr. 23 in which they condemned abortion and reviewed the effects of a law in effect since 1975. Abortion, they said, is always "the suppression of a human being, an act of death, a grave sin, an evil for society. . . . Pressures have been exerted on women by public opinion, by the environment, by the family, and by the father himself to suppress the unborn child. . . . We are witnesses of a mental degradation. A grave act becomes trivial and, for public opinion, indifferent. It is a question of a moral repression to which we cannot resign ourselves."

Priests in Municipal Offices — Municipal elections in Spain produced a confrontation between several priests elected to town councils and their bishops, prompting the bishops of Galicia to say that "those elected to the councils do not represent the Church, nor can they discharge roles both in the councils and in the ministry." Before the elections, the bishops warned that "current church discipline goes against priests taking up positions of political representation or leadership." Clergy should be "above party politics, as we are convinced that this norm fosters freedom and unity in the Church, and favors service to all people." News commentators noted that most Catholics preferred that priests keep out of politics.

Catholic Characteristics — The most important characteristics of being a Catholic were indicated in the following percentages by 986 Scottish Catholics polled by the Gallup organization in 1978. Results of the poll were published Apr. 24. The characteristics were: being baptized (95), active concern for others (93), being confirmed (90), getting married in the Catholic Church (83), praying regularly (82), making one's Easter duty (81), giving financial support to the Church (79), attending Sunday Mass (78), condemning abortion (77), frequent reception of Holy Communion (76), obeying church teachings (76), sending children to Catholic school (75), supporting church activities (54), being politically aware and interested (51), opposing artificial birth control (46).

Shift to Adult Education — The National Biblical, Catechetical and Liturgical Center in Bangalore, along with its six regional and 10 catechetical centers throughout India, was reported to be shifting its emphasis from youth to adult education. The objective, stated during the All India Catechetical Meeting held in December, 1978, was to make adult catechesis "the main focus of our future endeavor," for the formation of lay leaders on all levels.

International Briefs:

• Members of about 50 Catholic and Lutheran churches in West Germany, Switzerland, Luxembourg and Austria held special prayer services in mid-April for persecuted Christians in Czechoslovakia.

• A Mass commemorating the 100th anniversary of the death of St. Bernadette of Lourdes was celebrated Apr. 16 at her convent of St. Gildard in Nevers, France.

• More than 300 devotees of author G. K. Chesterton met in Toronto for an international conference on the relevance of his economic and social thought to contemporary problems. The conference, with "Chesterton and the Uses of Wealth" as its theme, marked the fifth anniversary of *The Chesterton Review* and the Chesterton Society.

Priests Killed in Uganda

At least two priests were killed during the month in Uganda, as Tanzanian military personnel and Ugandan guerrillas overthrew the government of President Idi Amin who had ruled the country for eight years with tyranny, repression and caprice. Reports concerning the whereabouts and condition of several hundred missionaries were sketchy, but it was thought that most of them were safe and active in their usual ministries despite the disruptions of civil war.

Father Robert Gay, the Canadian Superior of the White Fathers of Africa and a years-long veteran of missionary work in Uganda, expressed hope that "the Ugandan nightmare should be over." He also said: "Christian Ugandans (about 75 per cent of the total population), if they are now given the chance to act freely in the political field, can provide the vital Christian virtues to give the country a new start."

MAY 1979

VATICAN

No Intercommunion without Unity in Faith — Pope John Paul, during a meeting May 4 with 15 bishops of the Antilles, cautioned against intercommunion with non-Catholics. "Sharing in the Eucharist," he said, "presupposes unity in faith," and "intercommunion between divided Christians is not the answer to Christ's appeal for perfect unity. God has set an hour for the realization of his salvific design for Christian unity. . . . The restoration of Christian unity is, above all, a gift of God's love" still to be given us. "Meanwhile, on the basis of our common baptism and the patrimony of faith that we already share, we must intensify our common witness to the Gospel and our common service to humanity."

Prayer for Vocations — This was the subject of at least four addresses of the Holy Father during the month. On May 1 and 2 he combined praises of the Blessed Virgin Mary with appeals for greater numbers of vocations to the priesthood and religious life. He said on May 1: "There are children and young people waiting for someone to teach them the way of salvation. There are men and women whose daily heavy labor causes them to feel keenly the need of God. There are old people, sick and suffering people, waiting for someone to bend over their tribulations and reveal to them the hope of heaven. . . . It is the duty of the Christian people to ask God, through the intercession of Our Lady, that he send workers to the harvest."

In a special message marking the observance May 6 of the 16th annual World Day of Prayer for Vocations, he urged bishops, priests, religious and lay persons to foster vocations, and young people to respond affirmatively to calls to the priesthood and religious life. He reiterated the same appeal in an address to the Italian Bishops' Conference on May 15.

Capucci Appointment — The Pope announced May 7 the appointment of Archbishop Hilarion Capucci as apostolic visitor to communities of Melkite-Rite Catholics in Western Europe. The archbishop was convicted in 1974 in Israel of gun-running for Palestinians and was sentenced to 12 years in prison; he was released in 1977.

UNCTAD Message — Market forces alone should not determine the price of goods, declared the Pope in a message to 2,000 delegates from 159 nations attending the Fifth United Nations Conference on Trade and Development May 7 to June 3 in Manila. For effective international development, he said, the conference should deal with "fundamental questions of the just price and the just contract." Other things to be considered, he added, were the right of people to use of their goods and to adequate payment for decent work and life.

Delegates of underdeveloped countries made a case in their favor for pledges of more aid from wealthier countries, the elimination of trade barriers and the stabilization of raw material prices. Other delegates were opposed to substantial changes in the free enterprise system.

Beatifications — The Pope approved beatification decrees May 10 for four priests: Enrico de Osso y Cervello (1840-96), founder of the Sisters of St. Teresa of Jesus; Peter Donders (1809-87), a Dutch Redemptorist missionary to lepers in Surinam; Charles of St. Andrew (1821-93), a Dutch Passionist; Victricius de Eggenfelden (1842-1924).

Newman Anniversary — The Holy Father noted the 100th anniversary of the elevation of John Henry Newman to the cardinalate in a letter addressed to Archbishop George P. Dwyer, president of the Bishops' Conference of England and Wales. He called Newman one of the Church's "great sons and witnesses of the faith."

St. Stanislaus — The Pope marked the ninth centenary of the death of St. Stanislaus with an apostolic letter, *Rutilans Agmen,* addressed to the Polish people May 12. He raised the rank of the saint's feast, April 11, to the level of an obligatory memorial in the liturgy of the universal Church. St. Stanislaus, the patron of Poland, was murdered by King Boleslaus the Bold in 1079.

Mass at Monte Cassino — Peace and reconciliation can be achieved only "on the principles of justice and mutual love," stated the Pope in a sermon during a Mass celebrated May 18, the 35th anniversary of the bloody battle of Monte Cassino in World War II. "It is difficult," he said, "to enumerate all the calamities which, with the war, descended on man, manifesting — at its end — even the possibility, by means of the most modern technique of armaments, of an eventual mass annihilation, before which past destructions grow pale." He said that people must seek lessons for the future in the bitter experience of the past.

Missionary Consciousness — "The Church must renew its missionary consciousness," the Pope told a crowd of 60,000 persons at his first evening general audience May 23. While praising religious orders of missionaries, he said: "Their numbers must not diminish but, in fact, must grow to meet the immense necessity of the not distant times in which people will open themselves up to Christ and his Gospel."

In related developments: The Pope told 150 national directors of Pontifical Missionary

Aid Societies May 11 that well-off Catholic communities should not be so concerned with their own economic difficulties that they forget their duty to support the missions. The *Fides* news agency reported that the Congregation for the Evangelization of Peoples distributed more than $58 million for the support of missionary projects throughout the world in 1978.

Dutch Synod — A letter delivered May 25 to Cardinal Johannes Willebrands of Utrecht said that the Pope had decided to convene a particular synod early in 1980 of the bishops of The Netherlands, for the purpose of resolving problems of the Church in Holland. The problems concerned seminary training, lay ministries, liturgical aberrations, interfaith relations and interpretations of official teaching in some areas of doctrine and morality.

Duty of Bishops — The Pope emphasized the duty of bishops to communicate the love of God to all people during ordination ceremonies May 27 for 26 bishops from 12 countries. He said: "May your mission and your ministry lead to a strengthening of mutual love, of communal love, of union with the people of God in the Church of Christ, because it is in love and in union that the face of God is revealed in all its luminous simplicity. . . . What the world needs most . . . is precisely love."

Communications Day — The Holy Father, in a message for the 13th World Communications Day May 27, appealed to broadcasters not to use ratings of audience size as their guide to success, and reminded them and parents of their responsibilities to children. He noted that the theme of the day, "Social Communications for the Protection and Development of Childhood in the Family and in Society," had been chosen by Pope Paul VI in connection with the UN International Year of the Child.

Charity — The justification of charity is rooted in the value of man, the Pope told participants in the general assembly of *Caritas Internationalis* May 28. Charity, he said, "is deepest love brought to each and every man, especially to those in need. Its justification and its dynamism have their root in the value of man, his dignity, his right to accede to a decent life in spite of the material or moral misery which besets him as a result of misfortune, natural disasters, disease, unjust social conditions or other causes."

The Pope Also:
• Supported the appeal of the bishops of Italy to people not to vote for candidates proposing political solutions unacceptable to Christian conscience, May 18.
• Told 6,000 Poles at a Mass May 20 in St. Peter's Basilica that the martyrdom of their patron, St. Stanislaus, revealed the superiority of love over material force.
• Met with a group of superiors of non-Catholic religious orders May 21 and asked them to pray for unity among Christians.
• Met with: President Carter's wife Rosalynn and daughter Amy, May 10; U.N. General Secretary Kurt Waldheim, May 21; U.S. Secretary of State Cyrus Vance, May 29.

Sapientia Christiana

Pope John Paul II issued new norms May 25 for Catholic ecclesiastical universities and faculties in an apostolic constitution entited *Sapientia Christiana*. The document, produced over a 12-year period under the direction of three popes and with the collaboration of concerned institutions, superseded a similar constitution, *Deus Scientiarum Dominus*, issued by Pius XI in 1931. The norms were scheduled to go into effect on the first day of the 1980-81 academic year or at the beginning of the 1981 academic year.

Cardinal Gabriel-Marie Garrone, prefect of the Congregation for Catholic Education, said the constitution concerned institutions "connected directly or indirectly with the nature and mission of the Catholic Church," which teach such subjects as theology, philosophy and canon law. The document affected more than 100 academic centers and about 200 related faculties.

NATIONAL

School Suit — The League of Catholic Parent and Teacher Associations of the Archdiocese of Louisville filed a friend-of-the-court brief May 4 asking the Kentucky Supreme Court to rule in favor of a number of Christian schools in a case involving state regulations. Parents and officials of the schools contended that state requirements on textbooks, teacher certification and accreditation standards violated their constitutional rights. The Catholic associations noted that the "Catholic school system could be persecuted in similar fashion."

Abortion Funding — The U.S. Supreme Court refused May 14 to hear an appeal challenging a lower court ruling, in Baird v. Sharp (No. 78-1298), that a 1978 Massachusetts law restricting state funding of abortion was constitutional. The law, in line with the Hyde Amendment, restricted funding to cases of danger of maternal death, rape or incest.

In a related development, a bill that would have required parental consent for an abortion to be performed on a minor was defeated in Connecticut late in the month.

Moratorium on Arms Industry — A study guide published by the Hartford Archdiocesan Evangelization Office called for a moratorium on arms production in Connecticut, where almost one-third of all employees worked in the industry. The guide, which said the nuclear arms race is "the greatest challenge of our time," urged support of legislation to convert military-related jobs to non-military production.

25 Years of School Desegregation — May 17 was the 25th anniversary of the U.S. Supreme Court's ruling in the Brown case, that separate public schools for black and white students were inherently unequal and therefore unconstitutional. A study conducted by the Institute for Southern Studies at Chapel Hill, N.C., indicated that the public schools of the 11 states of the Old Confederacy were the least segregated in the country. Julian Bond, president of the institute, said that "the biggest failure of school integration has been in the urban centers of the North."

It was also reported that at least 89 of more than 160 U.S. dioceses had policies against the enrollment of students for the purpose of avoiding attendance at desegregated schools.

Catechists Commissioned — Cardinal Timothy Manning commissioned 1,500 catechists for service in the Archdiocese of Los Angeles. He urged them to deepen their affection and loyalty to the teaching authority of the Church, and to develop in young people a sense of reverence for God. Seven hundred of the catechists were Spanish-speaking.

Preferential Treatment for Poor Nations — Father J. Bryan Hehir, U.S. Catholic Conference associate secretary for international justice and peace, urged Congress to approve preferential trade rules that would help poor countries compete "in the markets of industrialized countries." He made the recommendation in letters to the chairmen of Senate and House subcommittees.

Technological Morality — Secretary of Health, Education and Welfare Joseph Califano was one of several national figures awarded honorary degrees by Catholic institutions of higher learning during the month. He urged Notre Dame graduates to "hammer out a technological morality" based on "searching questions about the impact of material inventions on human life and human dignity."

Conscience Clause for Medical Students — Dr. James H. Ford of Downey, Calif., asked the California Medical Association to offer "conscience clause" protection for applicants to medical schools and residency programs who are opposed to abortion. He requested an investigation of charges that some medical schools were "directly and openly excluding from medical training programs those who display the slightest negativism or conscientious objection to elective abortion."

Spenkelink Execution — The restoration of capital punishment is a "shameful and regressive step," declared Bishop Thomas C. Kelly, general secretary of the National Conference of Catholic Bishops. He made the statement shortly after the execution May 25 in Florida of convicted murderer John Spenkelink, the first person executed without his consent in more than 12 years. Gary Gilmore, who refused to appeal his sentence, was executed by a firing squad in January, 1977, in Utah.

Tax Deductions Unlawful — The U.S. Supreme Court ruled, 6 to 3, against the constitutionality of a New Jersey law providing tax deductions for tuition paid by parents of students enrolled in church-related elementary and secondary schools. The deductions would have amounted to between $20 and $25 per child.

DC-10 Crash — "It was the most powerful homily I have ever seen," declared Father William J. Lion, one of several priests who administered last rites May 25 at the site of the crash of a DC-10 while taking off from Chicago's O'Hare Airport. "A scene like that," he said, "makes you ask yourself, 'What is this life all about?' It makes you think about getting your priorities in order."

Episcopal Residence for Sale — Archbishop John R. Quinn of San Francisco reported plans to sell his episcopal residence and move into a recently vacated convent in the city, for economic and pastoral reasons.

Civil Rights for Persons in Institutions — A bill designed to protect the civil rights of about one million institutionalized persons was passed by an overwhelming margin (342 to 62) in the House of Representatives, but appeared to be bogged down in the Senate for the second year in a row. The bill would authorize the U.S. Attorney General to sue state and local governments accused of a "pattern or practice" of denying the civil rights of persons in institutions run by a state or under contract with a state. Covered would be persons in homes for juveniles; jails, prisons and pre-trial facilities; nursing homes and other custodial care facilities and institutions for the mentally ill, disabled, retarded, chronically ill or otherwise handicapped.

The U.S. Catholic Conference announced early in the month the formation of an Advisory Committee on Ministry with Handicapped Persons.

National Briefs:

• The spring meeting of the National Conference of Catholic Bishops and the U.S. Catholic Conference was held May 2 to 5 in Chicago. (See separate entry.)

• *Sign of Contradiction*, a collection of conferences given by Pope John Paul II (then Cardinal Karol Wojtyla) to Pope Paul VI and members of the Roman Curia in 1976, was published by Seabury Press, New York.

• Bishop Rene Gracida of Pensacola-Tallahassee urged the people of his diocese to "help stem violence in America by first looking into your homes, then into your hearts." In a statement on family violence, he said: "Increasingly, violence in America is to be found in our homes, and innocent men, women and children are being battered by otherwise responsible members of the same family."

• The 100th anniversary of St. Patrick's Cathedral, New York, was observed May 13 with a solemn Mass and appropriate ceremonies.

• Two Americans were named Knights of St. Gregory by Pope John Paul II: Protestant theologian and ecumenist Rev. George Huntson Williams, a member of the Unitarian Christian Fellowship; and Michael Ettel, secretary since 1941 of the St. Paul-Minneapolis St. Vincent de Paul Society.

• Archbishop Edward A. McCarthy of Miami, in comment on approval by the school boards of Dade and Broward Counties of sex education programs in public schools, declared that it should not be taught apart from moral values. "The attitude that it is acceptable for children to learn about sex without receiving any moral guidance is a violation of human reason and experience," he said.

• Ninety-two dioceses held the first national communications collection on May 27, World Communications Day.

Catholic Population

The Official Catholic Directory, 1979, with figures as of Jan. 1, reported that 49,602,035 Catholics comprised 22.59 per cent of the U.S. population. A decrease of 234,141 from the 1978 figure was indicated but misleading because of what were probable overestimates reported earlier by the Archdiocese of Detroit. There was no clear explanation of Detroit's report of a 400,000 loss in 1978.

One hundred and four dioceses reported population increases, 55 reported decreases, and 10 reported no change.

Chicago remained the largest archdiocese, with 2,415,354 Catholics, followed by Boston (2,016,272), Los Angeles (1,964,000), New York (1,825,090), Newark (1,400,727), Philadelphia (1,377,258) and Detroit (1,187,382). Brooklyn remained the largest diocese, with 1,458,951 Catholics, followed by Rockville Centre, with 1,038,505.

(See statistical entries.)

INTERNATIONAL

Central American Problems — Twenty-five Central American bishops, according to a delayed report, held a five-day, end-of-April meeting in San Jose, Costa Rica, to consider ways and means of defending human rights, promoting vocations to the priesthood and religious life, developing effective programs for evangelization, and alleviating Church-state tensions in El Salvador, Guatemala and Nicaragua. They agreed on the need to "establish living, functional ecclesial communities with Christians willing and ready to find solutions to the serious social and economic problems" of their nations.

Activists Arrested — Labor Day rallies on May 1 in front of churches and at the Catholic University in Santiago, Chile, ended with the arrest of hundreds of demonstrators, including Father Beltran Villegas, a theologian, and Catholic labor leaders Eduardo Rios and Manuel Bustos. The latter two men were charged with protesting against the economic and labor policies of the military junta led by Gen. Augusto Pinochet.

Model Albania — Twelve years after the regime proclaimed Albania to be the "first atheist state in the world," the Communist Party magazine, *Rruga e Partise,* claimed the elimination of religion was so successful that religionless Albania had become the model for all other Communist nations. Massive anti-religious campaigns mounted in 1967 resulted in the closing of more than 2,100 churches, mosques, monasteries and other religious institutions, and in the abrogation of all constitutional guarantees of religious freedom for Moslems (70 per cent of the population), Orthodox (20 per cent), and Catholics (10 per cent).

Christian Unity — The road to Christian unity requires "total dedication to the relentless pursuit of God's truth," declared Cardinal George Basil Hume of Westminster May 8 in the first address ever given by a cardinal to the general assembly of the United Reformed Church in London. He said: "The realization by the baptized that they have ... baptism in common means they recognize or should recognize that the logical outcome must be full organic unity in faith and worship."

Banned Priest — Father Smangaliso Mkhatshana of Pretoria had the distinction of being the only Catholic priest under ban in South Africa, for alleged engagement in unspecified activities aimed at disturbing public order. He was under a five-year travel ban and a 6:00 p.m. to 6:00 a.m. daily curfew; he was also forbidden to speak in public and to meet with more than one person at a time.

YWCA and Planned Parenthood — Catholic cooperation with the Young Women's Christian Association would be "extremely difficult, if not impossible," to maintain if the YWCA continued to join Planned Parenthood in advocating easier access to abortions. So stated the Ontario Catholic Bishops' Conference at a spring meeting in Toronto. A conference spokesman said the 25 bishops were attempting to "clarify" the nature of arrangements between the YWCA and Planned Parenthood.

St. Stanislaus Anniversary — Less than a month before the arrival of Pope John Paul "in his homeland, tens of thousands of Polish Catholics marked the 900th anniversary of their patron saint's murder in 1079 by King Boleslaus the Bold at the altar of the cathedral in Cracow.

Catholics in Charter 77 — Catholics were

increasing their involvement in Charter 77, a dissident rights group in Czechoslovakia, according to the news service of Keston College, a London-based center for the study of religion and Communism. The service reported that two Catholics had been tried and one of them sentenced to an eight-month penal term for writing and signing a 14-point petition calling for greater freedom of religion in the country.

UNCTAD Protest — Bishop Julio Xavier Labayen of Infanta, a prominent director of social action for human development, denounced the martial-law government of Philippine President Ferdinand E. Marcos for sending policemen against several hundred dissidents who gathered May 13 in Manila to discuss the irrelevance for poor people of the Fifth United Nations Conference on Trade and Development. A government spokesman refused to discuss the incident.

Four Priests Killed in Uganda — Two more priests, making a total of four in a month, were killed by soldiers loyal to deposed President Idi Amin. The latest victims — Fathers Silvio Dalmaso and Antonio Fiorante — were slain May 3 and 4 at the Pakwack Mission on the Nile River in the Diocese of Arua. April victims were Fathers Lorenzo Bono and Giuseppe Santi.

In related developments: *Caritas*, the West German Catholic charities organization, reported it was aiding thousands of Ugandan refugees in Kenya and 400 in West Germany. An official of the Ugandan Bishops' Conference appealed May 26 to charitable organizations throughout the world to assist the bishops in efforts "to restore our people in Uganda to a decent human life, which they have missed over the last eight years."

Missing in Argentina — For the second year in a row, the bishops of Argentina presented the military government with a list of persons missing since arrest by security forces, and requested information on their whereabouts and condition. Human rights organizations and relatives of the missing estimated that the number of missing persons was between 15,000 and 20,000.

Violence in El Salvador — Archbishop Oscar Romero of San Salvador, in a statement issued May 23, offered to mediate between parties to escalating violence of "repression and revenge" in El Salvador. The parties were the government, which had declared a state of siege after the assassination of a government official and an aide; members of the seven-group coalition called the People's Revolutionary Bloc, who occupied eight churches as places of refuge while calling for political and economic reforms and the release of several of their leaders; and an unattached group of guerrillas. Eighty-five persons were killed and 86 seriously wounded in clashes since May 1. The archbishop said: "I call on the heart and conscience of responsible leaders to abandon intransigence and, instead, to seek a prompt end to this chain reaction of bloody events."

International Briefs:

• Ways of achieving visible unity with the Catholic Church and how Anglicans could deal with the advance of Islam and new religious sects were among topics discussed by the Anglican Consultative Council at its annual meeting in London, Ontario.

• More than 20,000 persons marched May 14 in New Delhi in another demonstration against a proposed new law that would practically prohibit conversion from one faith to another in India.

• The executive committee of the Canadian Catholic Bishops' Conference announced that it would consider a request from *Una Voce* calling for an end to the "virtual suppression" of Latin in the liturgy. *Una Voce*, noting that the use of Latin was subject to the decision of local bishops, said there was a widespread and erroneous impression "that the use of Latin is forbidden."

• *Adveniat*, a West German organization, earmarked $7 million for mission-aid projects in Latin America.

• Catholic Relief Services reported that it was providing aid, which would eventually cost about $500,000, to refugees from armed conflict along the border between the (North) Yemen Arab Republic and the People's Republic of (South) Yemen.

Civil War in Nicaragua

The Church is persecuted for denouncing individual and social sin, declared Archbishop Miguel Obando Bravo of Managua early in the month as he tried to intervene as a mediator with parties to the civil war in Nicaragua.

"Our prophetic mission of announcing the Gospel and denouncing sin irks some people," he said, "but the Church has no hate for anyone. It only hates sin which shows beyond the abstract form in such real conditions as imprisonment of the innocent, hatred, excesses and other manifestations of unjust structures." For this, the Church "is being called Communist and subversive," especially by the government.

The archbishop made his statement in an NC News interview as the Sandinista Liberation Front began to mount its strongest attacks in two years on the National Guard of President Anastasio Somoza Debayle, whose family had been in control of the government for more than 40 years.

The Church was in the middle of the conflict, with more apparent sympathy with the aims of the Sandinistas than with the repressive policies and actions of the Somoza regime.

JUNE 1979

VATICAN

Trip to Poland — Pope John Paul, four months after completing a pilgrimage of faith to Mexico, set another precedent June 2 to 10 with a visit to Poland.

(See Pope John Paul II in Poland, Addresses of John Paul II in Poland.)

First Communicants — The Holy Father celebrated Mass June 14 in St. Peter's Basilica for more than 5,000 children, first communicants, of the Diocese of Rome. He told them: "Jesus wants to be your most intimate friend, your street companion. . . . Jesus . . . knows you, one by one, personally. He knows your name. He follows you. He accompanies you. He walks with you each day. He participates in your games and he consoles you in moments of grief and sadness."

Corpus Christi — The Pope presided at the celebration of the feast of Corpus Christi June 17, celebrating an evening Mass in the plaza outside the Basilica of St. John Lateran and carrying the Blessed Sacrament in procession to the Basilica of St. Mary Major. In a brief homily, he called the Eucharist "a sign of the adoration owed to God alone . . . who wants us to embrace him, to love him and to adore him, according to the human dimension of our faith."

SALT II — Pope John Paul praised SALT II on June 17, the day before it was signed in Vienna by President Carter and Soviet Foreign Minister Brezhnev. He said the accord "is not yet a reduction of weaponry or, as could be hoped, a provision for disarmament. But that does not mean that the foreseen measures are not a sign, which we ought to greet with pleasure, of the desire to pursue a dialogue, without which every hope of working effectively for peace would vanish. . . . Believers and men of good will, who feel themselves so impelled by conscience to pledge themselves as 'artisans of peace,' cannot ignore the importance of anything that favors a climate of alleviating tensions. This helps to encourage other indispensable progress on the road to the limitation and reduction of armaments."

Social and Health Programs — The Pope called on religious engaged in social and health care work to give top priority to areas of care not covered by government programs. He made the appeal in an address June 18 to 250 participants in the third Italian congress of the Association of Social-and-Health-Care Religious Institutes. Their work, he said, because of the Gospel motivation that inspires it, "has a particular trait, which consists in seeing in the sick, through the suffering they bear in body and spirit, the Person of Jesus himself." He called the work a form of witness to the fact that "the sick person must constitute a permanent priority, at the center of every activity and care for health." The Pope added that the acceptance of suffering should be regarded not as a fatalistic "resignation" but as a matter of "Christian patience," with the "certainty that in the end life will triumph." Such a view "is accompanied by the will and duty to do everything possible to conquer, reduce or overcome the suffering of one's neighbor."

Refugees — The Pope called June 20 for an international conference "as quickly as possible" to cope with the critical problems of Southeast Asian refugees. He did so a few days after the government of Malaysia shocked the world with the threat to tow out to sea the more than 75,000 refugees in the country. The Pope praised "actions already undertaken" for refugees "by some countries, as well as by international organizations, many private initiatives" and the community of the Church. But, he stated, "the problem is so great that it is no longer possible to let the burden of it rest only on a few."

Evangelization — "The basic realization of the Second Vatican Council is nothing other than a new sense of responsibility for the Gospel, for the word, for the sacrament, for the work of salvation, that all the people of God must assume in a way that is appropriate to them." So declared the Pope in an address June 20 to delegates attending the Symposium of the Council of European Bishops' Conferences. Reflecting on "the problem of evangelization" in Europe, he said: "The Church must always evangelize itself. Catholic and Christian Europe have need of such evangelization. . . . Perhaps in no other place as in our continent are there outlined with such clarity the current of denial of religion, the currents of the 'death of God,' of programmed secularization or organized, militant atheism."

Renewal Starts with Penance — "To bring about any spiritual renewal, it is necessary to begin with penance," the Pope told 160 Franciscans attending a general chapter of the Friars Minor, June 21. Father John Vaughn, O.F.M., of the Santa Barbara Province, Calif., became the first elected American minister general of the order.

Missionaries — They are "in the world, but not of the world," said the Pope during an audience June 23 with delegates to a joint chapter of the Sons of the Sacred Heart and Missionaries of the Sacred Heart. He said missionaries must "give primacy to the interior life, to prayer, to meditation, to the spirit of poverty and of sacrifice, in order not to yield to the subtle temptation to adapt themselves to the world." Some attempt such an adaptation, he added, "under the pretext of knowing (the world) better, but in reality at the risk of becoming entangled in its evils."

Unity with Orthodox — The need, desire and effort for unity were themes of remarks made by the Pope at meetings June 23, with a delegation from the Coptic Orthodox Church of Alexandria, and June 28, with a similar group from the Pan-Orthodox Patriarchate of Constantinople.

Concordat with Italy — The Pope, at a meeting June 25 with the new Italian ambassador to the Vatican, said it was his "most heartfelt prayer" that good Church-state relations established by the Lateran Treaty in 1929 would continue under concordat revisions appropriate to changing times and changes in the Italian constitution. Ambassador Bruno Bottai said the government "attaches particular importance" to its relations with the Vatican.

The Pope Also:
• Encouraged 300 attendants at the 27th International Congress of Women Business Leaders June 1 to give the industrial world the benefit of their feminine qualities.
• Retired for a brief stay at Castel Gandolfo the day after returning from Poland.
• Expressed "profound pain" June 13 on learning of the expulsion of 70 missionaries from Burundi for allegedly inciting to rebellion.
• Discussed the rights of Palestinians and the status of Jerusalem at a meeting June 18 with Egyptian officials.
• Conveyed his sympathy to Greek Orthodox officials on the death June 21 of Patriarch Elias IV of Antioch.
• Ordained 88 priests from 15 countries June 24; nine Americans were among them.
• Asked at a general audience June 27 for prayers that the papal ministry might "find new understanding in the Church of our times."
• Marked the feast of Sts. Peter and Paul, which has special meaning for the papacy, with a solemn Mass in St. Peter's Basilica.

New Cardinals

Pope John Paul presided June 30 over ceremonies for the elevation of 13 archbishops and a bishop to the College of Cardinals, bringing its membership to a total of 135. He concelebrated Mass with them on July 1.

Six of the new cardinals were Italian archbishops: Agostino Casaroli, Giuseppe Caprio, Marco Ce, Egano Righi Lambertini, Ernesto Civardi and Anastasio Alberto Ballestrero.

Two were Polish: Archbishop Franciszek Macharski and Bishop Ladislaw Rubin.

The others were archbishops: G. Emmett Carter (Canadian), Ernesto Corripio Ahumada (Mexican), Roger Etchegaray (French), Tomas O'Fiaich (Irish), Joseph-Marie Trinh Van Can (Vietnamese), Joseph Asajiro Satowaki (Japanese).

The name of a 15th cardinal not formally elevated to membership in the Sacred College was not disclosed by the Pope. It was thought that this cardinal *in pectore* was Archbishop Julijonas Steponivicius, apostolic administrator of Vilna, Lithuania.

(See Biographies of Cardinals.)

NATIONAL

Church Membership — The 1979 *Yearbook of American and Canadian Churches* reported a total 1977 membership of 132,812,470 in 222 religious bodies. Increases over 1976 figures were reported by the Catholic Church, the Southern Baptist Convention (1.24 per cent), the Association of Evangelical Lutheran Churches (12 per cent, due largely to defections from the Lutheran Church-Missouri Synod), the Church of Jesus Christ of Latter Day Saints (3.95 per cent), the Church of God of Cleveland, Tenn. (3.46 per cent), and the Seventh Day Adventists (2.46 per cent). Although a seven-year decline in mainline Protestant membership seemed to be slowing, losses were still reported by the Lutheran Church-Missouri Synod, the Episcopal Church and the United Presbyterian Church. The annual volume was published by the National Council of Churches.

Catholic Health Association — The Catholic Hospital Association changed its name to The Catholic Health Association of the United States at the eighth annual Catholic Health Assembly held June 3 to 7 in San Diego. Approximately 1,200 delegates approved a mission statement declaring: "The association is an ecclesial community dedicated to and faithful to the healing mission of the Church. . . . Its mission is to witness in the power of the Spirit the abiding presence and healing mission of Jesus. This is done by promoting the health of those who are sick or those infirmed by age or disability; by respecting human dignity in the experience of sickness and death; and by fostering the physical, psychological, emotional, spiritual and social well-being of people."

Student Newspapers Criticized — *The Observation Post*, student newspaper of the City College of New York, was sharply criticized for running sacrilegious pictures in its May 4 edition. The pictures were called "deeply offensive to women," "sacrilegious to Roman Catholics" and "an affront to all decent people," by the New York chapters of the American Jewish Committee and the American Jewish Congress. The student body of the college voted, 474 to 445, to end student activity funding of the paper.

A special edition of the University of Minnesota student newspaper featured a "scabrous attack on Christianity," according to the Catholic League for Religious and Civil Rights. The archdiocesan *Catholic Bulletin* of St. Paul called the articles the "worst example of journalistic excrement to belch forth from the bowels" (of the paper's office).

Peacetime Draft — A group of 74 Catholics, Protestants and Jews in Illinois declared their opposition to a peacetime draft in a statement released June 7. They said: "We strongly oppose the renewal of draft registration (recommended by a House committee but not in the Senate) and the draft. Compulsory registration and conscription are incompatible with our commitment to human rights and to international peace and justice."

Media Priorities — The Communications Committee of the U.S. Catholic Conference, meeting June 12 to 14 to discuss how to use proceeds from the national communications collection taken up in May, fixed priorities in six areas of media-related activity: (1) media production, (2) development of an improved "delivery system" for church communication, (3) training, (4) activity in communication law and public policy, (5) stronger effort in media relations, (6) assistance to Catholic communication activity in developing countries.

Bishops Sue Federal Government — The U.S. bishops, in the first lawsuit of its kind, challenged the authority of the government, under the 1978 Pregnancy Discrimination Act, to force private employers to pay for abortions of their employees. The suit was filed June 21 by the National Conference of Catholic Bishops and the U.S. Catholic Conference.

Right to Life — Two thousand delegates from 50 states attended the national convention of the Right-to-Life Movement June 21 to 24 in Fort Mitchell, Ky. Dr. Carolyn Gerster of Phoenix, who was reelected to a one-year term as president of the Right-to-Life Committee, stated that the goal in the next three years would be passage of a constitutional amendment not only to protect the unborn but also to check the problems of euthanasia and infant and human experimentation. The surest way to do that, she said, would be by the election to Congress, and especially to the Senate, of men and women who are consistently pro-life and by "retiring to private life" those whose records are "consistently anti-life."

Abortion Developments — The U.S. Supreme Court refused early in the month to lift a lower court's injunction against enforcement of an Illinois law restricting Medicaid abortion funding to cases of danger to a mother's life.

• A New Jersey appeals court upheld the right of the State Board of Medical Examiners to require in-hospital performance of abortions after the 16th week of pregnancy.

• Nevada became the 15th state to call for a constitutional convention to reverse the 1973 abortion decisions of the U.S. Supreme Court.

• Governor Edward J. King of Massachusetts signed restrictive legislation into law June 12: limiting state funding to welfare cases in which a physician certifies in writing that an abortion is necessary to save the life of a mother; prohibiting the use of state funds to subsidize abortions through group health insurance programs for state, county, city and town employees, unless there is certification that an abortion is necessary to save a mother's life.

• The California Court of Appeals upheld, 2-to-1, a state law restricting Medicaid funding (to cases involving a threat to a mother's life, or pregnancy resulting from rape or incest), and requiring that the parents of a minor contemplating an abortion be notified before the operation is performed.

• The House of Representatives voted, 241-to-180, June 27 to restrict abortion funding to cases in which a mother's life is endangered.

Necedah Shrine — Bishop Frederick W. Freking of La Crosse declared that the dedication May 28 of a shrine to the Queen of the Holy Rosary in Necedah, Wis., meant that Mrs. Mary Van Hoof and her followers were no longer part of the Church. The dedication followed at least three diocesan decisions since 1950 that alleged visions and revelations of Mrs. Van Hoof were not of supernatural origin. The man who dedicated the shrine was reported to be Michael Stehlik, "archbishop and metropolitan of North America, American Catholic Church, Roman Catholic Ultrajectine."

U.S. Supreme Court Rulings — Decisions handed down during the month included those which:

• Supported the claim of a San Diego man that his rights were violated when he was fired because his religious beliefs as a Seventh Day Adventist prevented him from belonging to a union.

• Refused to hear Madalyn Murray O'Hair's appeal of a lower court ruling which dismissed her claim that the use of "In God We Trust" on U.S. coins violates the principle of separation of Church and state.

• Upheld a Pennsylvania law providing busing at public expense for students to private schools up to 10 miles away from the boundary of the public school district in which they live.

National Briefs:

• Father Stephen J. Hartdegen, O.F.M., director of the U.S. Center for the Catholic Biblical Apostolate, was awarded June 8 the Presidential Award of the National Catholic Educational Association for his work in directing the translation of the New American Bible and for popularizing the Bible for use in religious education programs.

• Notre Dame University received an anonymous gift of $7 million, the largest in its history, for its development fund. The gift pushed the fund drive past its goal of $130 million.

• John Wayne, 72, one of moviedom's greatest stars, was received into the Catholic Church June 10, the day before his death.

• Murder charges against Dr. William Waddill, accused of strangling a child who survived an abortion, were dismissed June 11 by a judge who declared a mistrial in Orange County Superior Court, California.

• Bishop Rene Gracida of Pensacola-Tallahassee, in full-page ads in five Florida newspapers, declared his opposition to capital punishment and appealed to Gov. Robert Graham not to sign any more death warrants. One hundred and thirty-four persons were on death row in the state.

Jesus '79 Rallies

Thousands of persons attended nearly 40 charismatic "Jesus '79" rallies June 2, the eve of Pentecost, in the United States, Ireland, England, South Africa and Australia. Two of the largest gatherings, attracting a total of about 70,000, assembled at Giants' Stadium in Rutherford, N.J., and Shea Stadium in Queens, N.Y.

In a related development, Archbishop Jean Jadot, apostolic delegate to the U.S., called charismatic renewal "a prominent and effective movement within the overall action of the Spirit of God in our contemporary world." He added, however, that "we cannot refer to it or think of it as the primary source of renewal." The apostolic delegate spoke June 25 at the Fifth National Conference of Priests and Deacons in the Charismatic Movement, held in Steubenville, Ohio.

INTERNATIONAL

Duty to Transform Society — Participating in the Christian transformation of society to make it more livable and lovable "is integral to the task of proclaiming the Gospel message of liberation and salvation," declared the Commission for Social Affairs of the Canadian Conference of Catholic Bishops. A statement circulated by the commission during the month noted that involvement in struggle for social justice is not an optional activity but should be a vital part of a Christian's life and expression of faith.

Stance of Bishops in Lesotho — The bishops of Lesotho stood firm in opposition to population control policies of the government. They argued against artificial birth control and abortion, stating that such methods could never be justified on moral grounds and could lead to genocide. The welfare of people in the resource-poor country, they said, could be better served, and morally, by the development of improved health, social and economic conditions.

Honduras Radio Network — Church authorities in Honduras successfully negotiated with the military government for the return to the air of *Radio Progreso,* a Jesuit-run broadcasting network devoted to peasant causes. The network had been banned for a month by censors who complained about "its protest songs" and its "fostering of class struggle" in alleged violation of constitutional norms.

Reforms Blocked in Portugal — A group of 30 priests in Oporto charged in a signed statement that structural reforms promised by the socialist revolution in the country were not coping with the problems of the people. "Under the so-called solidification of democratic structures," they said, "great injustices escalate, jeopardizing a revolution that so far appears to be suffocated." They added that some church groups were fostering "a blind anti-Communist posture, thus making a given ideology the scapegoat for all evils and aligning the people on the side of special interests. . . . The great majority of Christians . . . are passive toward society and the Church. They contribute to the survival of an unjust order and block efforts by committed Christians for reform."

Norwegian Abortion Law — The Rev. Boerre Knudsen, a Lutheran minister, stopped performing the civil duties required of his office in protest against an abortion law condemned by bishops of the officially established Lutheran Church. He said he would welcome an attempt by the government to remove him from office because it would provide him with "the opportunity to prove that the law on abortion contradicts the paragraph in the Norwegian Constitution which states that the Lutheran faith is the official religion in the Norwegian state."

Corpus Christi in Cracow — For the first time since World War II, authorities in Cracow allowed the traditional Corpus Christi procession to pass through the center of the city. Permission for the Eucharistic observance, it was thought, was a gesture of good will by the government following the visit to Poland of Pope John Paul II, a former archbishop of Cracow.

Jewish Objections in Argentina — The Delegation of Israeli Associations in Argentina complained that the Catholic religion was being taught in public schools under new compulsory programs for moral and civic education. The delegation said in a statement: "To make it compulsory for a Jewish youth to listen to classes, learn lessons and submit examinations about many of the (Catholic) subjects in the new programs, means violating his or her conscience."

Criticism of Rhodesian Plan — Bishop Donal Lamont of Umtali declared June 17 that the internal political settlement in Zimbabwe Rhodesia "is a totally unsatisfactory arrangement. Although it seems to give the African a place in the administration, it is an illusory place because, as has been pointed out by more qualified authorities than I, real power remains in the hands of the white minority." Methodist Bishop Abel Muzorewa became the country's first black prime minister under an arrangement for black participation in, but not effective control of, the government. Bishop Lamont, expelled from the country in 1977 for failing to report the presence of guerrillas in his diocese, was in Umtali to attend the ordination of an auxiliary bishop.

Population Rate Declining — The 1979 "State of the World Population" report issued by the U.N. Fund for Population Activities indicated that a decline in the rate of world population was "evident beyond all doubt." One critical shift, the report noted, was the rapid aging of the world's population, due to falling birthrates and rising life expectancy. Another shift was toward a doubling of urban population since the middle of the century, which is expected to continue. Eleven nations were reported to have reached zero population growth since 1969: East Germany, West Germany, Luxembourg, Austria, Czechoslovakia, Great Britian, Belgium, Denmark, Hungary, Norway and Sweden.

Basque Terrorism — Bishops of the Basque provinces of northern Spain appealed for "the end of the climate of physical and moral violence" that took a toll of 78 lives during the year in their region, Madrid and other cities. As the bishops issued their call, ETA terrorists, claiming "credit" for 40 assassinations, threatened to kill every official representing the central government.

Guatemalan Bishop's Resignation — The resignation early in the month of Bishop Luis Manresa as head of the Diocese of Quezaltenango was for personal reasons, declared the Guatemalan Bishops' Conference in response to claims by the diocesan council of priests that the resignation was forced by outside pressures. "We are convinced," said the council in a statement, "that his resignation is not because of diocesan or personal reasons. ... In all these years our bishop has accomplished a great deal in the pastoral field with utmost dedication. He has been a prophetic voice, often alone, in Central America, and has also rendered valuable services to the Church in Latin America. We want him to continue at the helm." Father Ramon Alonso, of the diocesan communications office, said that "church conservatives and others were making life difficult for the bishop."

Peace Efforts in Northern Ireland — Cardinal-designate Tomas O'Fiaich of Armagh and Anglican Canon William Arlow, secretary of the Irish Council of Churches, issued a joint statement June 25 in which they pledged that they would work together for peace and reconciliation in Northern Ireland. As a symbol of the pledge, Archbishop O'Fiaich invited the canon to attend his installation in the College of Cardinals June 30.

Refugee Quota To Be Doubled — President Jimmy Carter, in an action commended by U.S. and other religious leaders, announced at a Tokyo summit conference late in the month that the United States would double its admissions quota for Vietnamese refugees to 14,000 a month.

Lefebvre Ordinations — For the fourth time in as many years, dissident Archbishop Marcel Lefebvre ordained a group of 30 priests at Econe, Switzerland, on the feast of Sts. Peter and Paul, an occasion of special significance to the papacy. He did so, again, in spite of his suspension from the exercise of orders since July 24, 1976.

A few days before the illicit ordinations, the archbishop dedicated a church in Redford, Mich., for a parish of 200 or more of his followers.

International Briefs:
• More than 100 priests and nuns began a hunger strike in Santiago, Chile, in support of 12 detained labor leaders and 103 seminarians who were suspended from the Catholic University of Santiago by state authorities when they joined in anti-government demonstrations.

• Priests were not being allowed to go into the northern Indian territory of Arunachal Pradesh to perform religious functions, according to Wanglat Lowangcha, general secretary of the People's Party there.

• Approximately 320 family life specialists from 44 countries attended the June 21 to 24 fourth international ecumenical congress sponsored by the Milan-based International Center for Family Studies. The theme of the congress was "The Family: Natural Environment of the Child."

European Bishops and Youth

Armed with what they called "a more profound understanding of the diversity of youth in individual countries," 70 European bishops concluded a five-day meeting June 21 in Rome and returned home to put the knowledge into effect.

A final communique issued by the Symposium of the Council of European Bishops' Conferences said the bishops emphasized the need "to establish personal contacts with youth" because "the Gospel cannot take root in youth without the active and committed presence of bishops." They said they would rely on "the collaboration of all the Christian community and, above all, its priests and its laity involved in the formation of youth." Young people, they added, "expect that the Church will be, first of all, faithful to the Gospel of Jesus Christ."

Cardinal George Basil Hume of Westminster was elected president of the council, to succeed Cardinal-designate Roger Etchegaray of Marseilles.

JULY 1979

VATICAN

Mass with New Cardinals — "This Church exists everywhere, even in those places where, according to human 'laws,' it does not and cannot exist, and where it is condemned to death." So stated the Holy Father July 1 during a Mass he concelebrated with 14 new cardinals. His words were viewed by observers as a challenge to Communist rulers opposed to the Church.

Rome the Center of Unity — The Pope emphasized the unity of the Church with Rome as its center during a July 4 general audience with 20,000 visitors in St. Peter's Square. "The succession (of the Pope) to this episcopal see has a significance not only for the 'local' church here in Rome," he said. "It also has significance for the universal Church; that is to say, for each of the local churches, which thus come to take part in a universal community." With the recent elevation of 14 new cardinals in mind, he said: Through their worldwide representation and their link to Roman churches, "the College of Cardinals unites in itself, and in itself shows, the constitutive dimensions of the Church, both 'local' and 'universal.' The Church built on Peter is 'Roman' in these two dimensions."

Prayer — Pope John Paul offered his thanks to all people, "known and unknown," who pray for him, during a pre-Angelus talk July 8. He also said that "prayer is an invisible link that unites the community of the faithful. It is a very strong and deep link."

International Catholic Organizations — Such organizations play an important part in bringing the good news of the Gospel "to all levels of humanity," according to a letter sent in the Pope's name to the general assembly of the Conference of International Catholic Organizations which met early in the month in Pallanza, Italy. The letter quoted the Holy Father's reference, in an address to representatives of Catholic organizations in Mexico, to the need for "Christians with a vocation to holiness, firm in their faith, secure in the teaching proposed by the authentic teaching authority of the Church, steady and active in the Church, united in a profound spiritual life, nourished by frequent reception of the sacraments of penance and the Eucharist, persevering in evangelical action and witness, effective in their temporal tasks, constant promoters of peace and justice against every violence and oppression, sharp in critically discerning situations and ideologies in the light of the Church's teaching authority, faithful in their hope in the Lord."

Curia Members — The Pope devoted remarks at a July 11 general audience to members of the Roman Curia, the Vatican's complex of central administrative offices. He likened them to the "numerous helpers and collaborators" of the Apostles "who made possible and facilitated the fulfillment" of the Gospel message.

Find Identity in the Mass — People searching for their identity should look first to the Mass for their answer, the Pope told nearly 1,000 young adults July 15 during an early morning Mass in the Vatican Gardens. He said: "The sacrifice in which we are participating, the sacred Mass, will give us each time the answer to the fundamental question, 'Who are we?' . . . We are redeemed; we are full of the remission of sins and of grace; we are called to union with Christ and, as a result, to unite all in Christ." The Church also, he said, answers the question, "What must we do?" by calling us to exercise our "part in the prophetic mission of Christ" by giving witness to faith in daily life.

Pope at Castel Gandolfo — The Pope left the Vatican early in the evening of July 15 for a stay of several weeks at the summer papal residence at Castel Gandolfo, about 15 miles south of Rome. On arrival, he told a gathering of some 3,000 people: "I am your fellow citizen. I am your fellow parishioner." He later interrupted his vacation several times for appearances at the Vatican and visits to several places outside of Rome.

Catholic Learning Centers — They "must be places in which the Church's evangelization meets with the great universal 'academic process' that bears fruit with all the conquests of modern science," declared Pope John Paul July 18 in an address to a general audience of 30,000 persons in St. Peter's Square. "To preach the Gospel, to teach," he said, "means to come into contact with the living person, with human thought, which continuously and in ever new ways and different fields seeks the truth. . . . At the same time, in these learning centers the Church continually deepens, consolidates and renews its own science, that which it ought to transmit to the men of our times as the message of salvation."

Visits to Ireland and the U.S. — Vatican press spokesman Father Romeo Panciroli announced July 21 that the Pope would leave Rome Sept. 29 for visits to Ireland and the United States. (See separate entries.)

Children — "Christ placed an enormous importance on the child," the Pope told a gathering of visitors July 22 at Castel Gandolfo. "He made him, as it were, the spokesman of the cause which he proclaimed and for which he gave his own life. . . . The value of the child in every society lies in the fact that he is a witness of the innocence intended for man by the Creator and heavenly Father." Children are "the source of hope" for the future of nations and of the Church.

Youth on Vacation — The Pope, at a general audience July 25, pledged his thoughts and prayers to "all young people, especially those who spend their vacations seeking God." Vacation time, he said, provides a good opportunity for "the deepening of spiritual life," which should start with an examination of Scripture and participation in the liturgy.

Concern for Missionaries — The Holy Father expressed "profound anxiety and worry" July 29 over the fate of a group of missionaries believed kidnapped by guerrillas July 18 in Zimbabwe Rhodesia. A Jesuit priest and brother and six nuns were in the group of about 40.

The Pope Also:
• Met July 6 with leaders of the American Jewish and Polish-American Catholic Committee, and encouraged their efforts in support of children's literature.
• Took his first dip July 28 in the just-completed swimming pool at Castel Gandolfo.
• Met with: West German Chancellor Helmut Schmidt, July 9; Belgian Prime Minister Wilfried Martens, July 10; President Leopold Senghor of Senegal, July 11; President Julius Nyerere of Tanzania, July 12.

Vatican Briefs:
• Max Bergerre, a correspondent for Italian and French news agencies, was reelected president of the year-old Association of Correspondents Accredited to the Vatican Press Office.
• The *Libreria Editrice Vaticana* published a 115-page volume containing the official documents issued by Pope John Paul I during his brief pontificate.
• Agreements to establish diplomatic relations with Jamaica and The Bahamas were announced July 20 and 27, respectively.
• The Congregation for the Doctrine of the Faith released a letter July 14 reaffirming traditional doctrine concerning life after death. (See Doctrinal Statements.)

Rural Development

Pope John Paul called for efforts to close the gap between rich and poor people in rural life, to check the flight of youth from agricultural work, and to develop better international cooperation on rural issues, in an address July 14 to about 800 participants in the World Conference on Agrarian Reform and Rural Development sponsored by the United Nations Food and Agriculture Organization. He said:

"It is now clear, on the basis of experience, how necessary it is to correct the one-sided industrialization of a country, and to abandon the utopian expectation that industrialization will certainly and directly lead to economic development and civil progress for everyone. . . .

"Love for the land and for work on the land is not an invitation to a nostalgic return to the past, but an affirmation of agriculture as the basis of a healthy economy in the totality of the development and civil progress of each country and of the whole world." Rural development and agrarian reform are issues of "extreme importance for the destiny of the human family, and of lively interest for the Church."

The Pope expressed "heartfelt appreciation" for UN action to promote agricultural and rural development.

NATIONAL

Racism — Cardinal William Baum of Washington, D.C. issued a pastoral letter attacking "the heresy and the sin of racism" as "one of the most serious violations of justice in our community and even in our Church." He called it "the denial of the truth of the dignity of man as revealed in the incarnation of the eternal Son of God." He promised "an increase in our struggle against racism."

Church Property Cases — The U.S. Supreme Court held that the principle of separation of Church and state does not require states to defer to church authorities in resolving disputes over church property. The decision came on a 5-to-4 vote, with majority and minority justices accusing each other of supporting increased governmental entanglement in church affairs. The case involved property rights of the Presbyterian Church in the United States and the breakaway Vineville Presbyterian Church in Macon, Ga. Litigation was handed back to the Georgia Supreme Court.

Confession for Children — "The plain fact is that private confession is, or should be, a most rich school of individual, personal spiritual direction, and for that reason it cannot begin too soon in the life of a person who has come to know the difference between good and evil." So stated Cardinal John Wright, prefect of the Congregation for the Clergy, in an article published in the August edition of *U.S. Catholic*. He also wrote: "It would be well if we priests were to face frankly the manner in which too frequently we have perhaps neglected this positive aspect of spiritual direction and the use of the sacrament of penance as a means of spiritual growth from the earliest possible deliberate and conscious age of moral activity."

Homosexuality — Cardinal Humberto Medeiros of Boston, in a 16-page letter, repeated the Church's traditional condemnation of homosexual acts and life-styles while also calling on priests to minister "with pastoral love" to homosexuals. They "must be treated with understanding," he said, and emphasized that priests "must adhere to the theological positions which have officially been incorporated into church teaching . . . that homosexual acts are intrinsically disordered and can in no case be approved." He specifically criticized priests and theologians who would condone homosexual acts as "personally enriching" or who would approve of "homosexual marriages."

Kentuckiana Community — Catholics, Protestants, Orthodox and Jewish leaders officially inaugurated the Kentuckiana Interfaith Community, replacing the eight-year-old Louisville Area Interfaith Organization for Service. Its objective is to promote and coordinate interfaith relations and activities.

Rural Life Statement — Reactions to the first draft of a rural land statement prepared for 44 Midwestern bishops were sought at hearings held in three Minnesota communities on the first three Sundays of the month. The statement — entitled "Strangers and Guests: Toward Community in the Heartland" — called for support for the family farm and for limitation on the access of large corporations to land holdings.

Marian Observance — A committee headed by Cardinal John J. Carberry announced plans July 23 for a national observance of the 125th anniversary of the definition of the dogma of the Immaculate Conception. The commemoration, to start Dec. 8, was to be a "call for an era of discernment" of "the need to integrate the Blessed Mother into every level of pastoral ministry."

Anti-Busing Amendment Defeated — The House of Representatives, with a vote of 216 to 209, defeated July 24 a proposed constitutional amendment to ban busing for the desegregation of public schools. The U.S. Catholic Conference had a record of opposition to the amendment.

Pledge of Scientists and Theologians — Scientists and theologians concluded a July 12 to 24 Conference on Faith, Science and the Future with a pledge to continue working together in search of a "new and comprehensive vision of reality." Cardinal Humberto Medeiros said in a welcoming address that Christian faith and science cannot ignore each other. He added: "The technology that disregards or ignores the question of Christian ethics, especially the value it places on humanity, will quickly reduce the earth to a desert, the person to an automaton, brotherly love to planned collectivization, and introduce death where God wished life." The conference, held under the auspices of the World Council of Churches at the Massachusetts Institute of Technology, was attended by about 1,000 persons, including a delegation from the Vatican.

Affirmative Action — The National Conference of Catholic Bishops and the U.S. Catholic Conference adopted affirmative action guidelines designed to guarantee equal opportunity for minorities in their employment practices. The introduction to the guidelines stated: "In our effort to secure the human rights rooted in our tradition, we will be prompted not merely by the demands of civil law, but by the moral imperative inherent in that tradition. It will be the continued policy of NCCB-USCC that there be no discrimination because of race, color, sex, national origin, an individual's handicap or age." The guidelines were sent to the heads of all U.S. dioceses for use as models in developing local affirmative action plans.

Passion Play Script — Controversy continued over whether script changes for the 1980 Oberammergau Passion Play went far enough in eliminating anti-Semitism from the text. Leonard Swidler, a Temple University professor, said that "all of the essential problems" and "trouble spots" had been eliminated in recent revisions of the 1860 Weis-Daisenberger text. Rabbi Marc H. Tanenbaum of the American Jewish Committee said the changes were "cosmetic."

Meetings — Meetings during the month included the following.

• Convention of Worldwide Marriage Encounter, June 29 to July 1, at Kent, Ohio; attended by approximately 15,000 persons.

• Fifteenth annual Wanderer Forum, July 6 to 8, in St. Paul; attended by 250 delegates.

• Convention of Serra International, in Colorado Springs. William B. Cashman of Cleveland was installed as president.

• Eighth annual North American Conference of Separated and Divorced Catholics, July 12 to 15, at the University of Notre Dame; attended by 450 participants.

• Eighth National Assembly of Religious Brothers, in New Orleans. Christian Brother William Mueller, president, said that brothers "are going from a role of service to the internal workings of the Church to a new role of general ministry to those in need."

National Briefs:

• George E. Reed, legal specialist with the U.S. bishops' conferences since 1943, announced his retirement at the end of the year.

• The American Bible Society reported a substantial increase in the number of letters received from listeners to Bible-reading programs beamed to China.

• A resolution calling for a constitutional amendment banning abortion except in cases of danger of maternal death was passed at the biennial convention in St. Louis of the Lutheran Church-Missouri Synod.

• Franciscan Father Bruce Ritter was presented with the Thomas Jefferson Award by the American Institute of Public Service, for his work with sex-exploited young people at the Under 21 crisis center in New York City.

• The New York archdiocese refused July 15 to allow a Mass of Christian burial for reputed underworld figure Carmine Galante, saying it would cause scandal.

• New legislation passed in California permitted students to be excused, on parental request, from public schools on religious holidays.

• A three-judge federal appeals court ruled unanimously in Boston that Puerto Rico's effort to examine Catholic school finances was unconstitutional; it would encroach on First Amendment rights without a show of "compelling state interests."

Crisis of Confidence

President Jimmy Carter's "crisis of confidence" address July 15 was hailed by a cross-section of 39 religious leaders, who regarded it as a call to action to cope with the moral and energy problems facing the whole country.

Comment was varied in the Catholic press. One newspaper, *The Monitor* of the Diocese of Trenton, editorialized:

"President Carter ... put his finger on a problem that is even greater than that of excessive oil imports and their soaring costs.... The American people are suffering, he said, from a crisis of the spirit, from a loss of faith and confidence in themselves and in the future. ... The malaise which now afflicts America, even the President must admit, is due in some measure to conditions over which the people feel they have no control — an ever-rising inflation rate, fuel costs that are going through the roof, fear of the future, ineffective leadership in high places. But it can also be traced to a loss of the traditional religious and moral values which sustained the nation in the past."

INTERNATIONAL

Missionaries May Return — United Press International reported Prime Minister Abel Muzorewa as saying that "missionaries of all denominations who were either deported or declared prohibited immigrants by previous governments can now feel free to come back to Zimbabwe Rhodesia if and when their respective denominations need them." The report also said that the previous white government of Ian Smith had deported at least 12 Catholic missionaries. Exiled Bishop Donal Lamont of Umtali called the Muzorewa move a political ploy.

The 100th anniversary of the arrival of the first missionaries in Rhodesia on Aug. 23, 1879, was the subject of a letter from the bishops made public by the *Fides* news agency during the month. The bishops expressed their hope "that the faith take ever deeper roots in the life, customs and traditions of the local people."

Concerns of Spanish Bishops — Seventy-six members of the Spanish Bishops' Conference, at a week-long meeting early in the month, reassessed church work to deal with the implications of new agreements between Spain and the Vatican affecting education, the family, communications, legislation, preservation of historic monuments, chaplains in the armed forces, charitable activities and finances. Cardinal Vicente Enrique Tarancon, head of the conference, said in an opening address July 2 that the Church-state separation effected by the 1978 constitution did not mean that the Church would "renounce the functions which rightfully belong to her in society as befitting her religious mission."

Anglican Decisions — The General Synod of the Church of England rejected July 4 a motion to substantially increase its financial and manpower commitments to the World Council of Churches. The rejection came during debate on relations between the church and the WCC in connection with a controversial WCC grant of $85,000 to the Patriotic Front, a black guerrilla movement in Zimbabwe Rhodesia.

The synod also defeated a motion July 6 which would have allowed Anglican women priests ordained outside England to officiate as priests in England. In doing so, the synod followed the lead of Anglican churches in Central Africa, the South Pacific and Scotland, which rejected the ordination of women and banned those ordained elsewhere from officiating as priests in their territories. Women had been ordained in Anglican churches in the U.S., Hong Kong, Canada and New Zealand.

Jerusalem Shrines — Mayor Teddy Kollek told a group of U.S. journalists visiting Israel recently that "the unity of the city (Jerusalem) as the capital of Israel is not negotiable," but declared also that the rights of Moslems and Christians to control their holy places should be negotiable and should become part of law. He added: "We have no restrictions. Last year, around 200,000 Arabs visited their holy places."

Archbishop Starting Another Church — Bishop Anton Haenggi of Basel warned the people of his diocese that dissident Archbishop Marcel Lefebvre "is not only creating a new place of worship but is instituting 'another church' " by dedicating a chapel for his followers in Bienne, Switzerland. Asking the people to stay away from the chapel dedication July 14, he said: "Our only response to the provocation of Archbishop Lefebvre will be to beseech the Lord that he will arouse us to commit ourselves more animatedly to our communion, and that he will help those who have lost their way to find the road of unity."

Violence Unjustified in Northern Ireland — Violence by Catholics seeking to unite the whole island of Ireland into a single republic is unjustified, declared Bishop William Philbin of Down and Connor during an interview in Belfast. "The position of the Catholic bishops of Ireland is that the conditions to justify violence by Catholic republicans do not exist," he said. Of the outlawed Provisional

Irish Republican Army, he said: "They have an absolute minimum of (local financial and political) support, but they have guns and money. Much of the money, I'm sorry to say, comes from America. What does not come from America comes from robberies here at home."

Puebla Action Program — Sixty Latin American bishops attending a meeting in Medellin, Colombia, mapped out a four-year action program based on directives issued by the Third General Assembly of Latin American Bishops held in February in Puebla, Mexico. Bishop Antonio Quarracino, general secretary of the Latin American Bishops' Council, said the "Global Plan" meant that "Puebla cannot remain a mere memory. It is, rather, a vigorous push toward the task of evangelization of Latin America, a commitment and a serious challenge."

Agrarian Reform — Agrarian reform calls for a complete transformation of rural life and activities, centering on the eradication of poverty and the improvement of human nutrition, according to a "Declaration of Principles and Programs of Action" produced by delegates to the World Food Conference held July 12 to 20 in Rome. Specifically, the delegates called for action by governments and local groups to ensure that rural people have access to land, water and other natural resources; that they receive adequate education, training and extension services; that rural works programs be developed; that the rights of rural people to realistic involvement in the development process by guaranteed.

Refugee Conference — Delegates from more than 60 nations attended the UN-sponsored conference on refugees July 20 and 21 in Geneva. Pledges made during the meeting, along with others made earlier in Tokyo and Bali, included those of participating nations to resettle within a year 200,000 of the approximately 375,000 refugees in Southeast Asia; of Japan, to pay half the cost of processing and transit camps; of the Philippines, to provide a campsite for 50,000; of the U.S., to increase funding for aid and to double the number of refugee admissions per month to 14,000. Actions by the conferees had the support of the U.S. Catholic Conference and the Vatican.

Persecution Toll in El Salvador — The San Salvador archdiocesan weekly, *Orientacion*, reported the following toll of systematic persecution of the Church since January, 1977: priests — five killed, 26 expelled, nine arrested, 50 theatened with death (including Archbishop Oscar A. Romero), 21 made targets of defamation, four tortured, three marked for murder; nuns — one detained, three expelled, two forced to leave under threat; lay persons — hundreds arrested, tortured, killed, missing. Government agencies linked to persecution included the National Guard, the National Police, military intelligence, migration authorities, the armed forces and the paramilitary squadrons known as Orden and Falange.

Church Hampered in Mozambique — The forced closings of 15 Catholic churches, an Anglican cathedral and three Presbyterian churches during the year were evidence of deteriorating relations between the Church and state, according to a report published in Zaire by the newsletter, "Documentation and Information about Africa."

International Briefs:

• The 10 bishops in Thailand appealed in a letter to bishops throughout the world for efforts to influence public opinion and government action to aid Indochinese refugees.

• Mass attendance in Canada increased from 46 per cent in 1978 to 53 per cent in 1979, according to a recent Gallup poll.

• Archbishop Annibale Bugnini, pro-nuncio in Iran, appealed to the Pontifical Council *Cor Unum* and *Caritas Internationalis* for aid to Christian communities in Iran. He said Christians had been particularly hard hit by economic and political chaos and needed immediate assistance.

• The West German legislature extended the statute of limitations on Nazi war crimes.

War Ends in Nicaragua

Ten months of civil war in Nicaragua ended July 17 with the resignation and flight of President Anastasio Somoza. A new government headed by Francisco Urcuyo took over the following day.

The front-line forces in the war were the 12,000-member National Guard and rebel Sandinistas, but the entire population of 2.5 million was involved in one way or another in the struggle for human rights against more than 40 years of control and repression under successive regimes dominated by the Somoza family.

The costs of the war were staggering: 12,000 to 15,000 dead; 20,000 wounded; 250,000 displaced persons; an estimated $8 billion in material damage.

Church support in the struggle was generally in favor of the anti-Somoza forces, although criticism was strong against excesses of both the Sandinistas and the government. Archbishop Miguel Obando Bravo of Managua was among a large number of priests, religious and lay persons who stood for the rights of the people under threat from the government and its extreme right-wing supporters. Priests and religious, along with hundreds of lay persons, were long regarded as subversive by the government; some of them were killed, arrested, expelled and harassed because of their efforts to bring about economic, social and political changes for the benefit of the poor majority in the country.

AUGUST 1979

VATICAN

Praise for Cardinals Ottaviani and Wright — Pope John Paul expressed his praise and sympathy at the deaths Aug. 3 and 10, respectively, of Cardinal Alfredo Ottaviani, 88, prefect of the Doctrinal Congregation from 1959 to 1968, and Cardinal John Wright, 70, prefect of the Congregation for the Clergy since May 1, 1969. Cardinal Wright was the highest ranking American in the Roman Curia.

Paul VI Anniversary — The Holy Father marked the first anniversary of the death of Paul VI Aug. 6 with a private memorial Mass at Castel Gandolfo. He also spoke publicly of his accomplishments on four occasions during the first two weeks of the month. At a general audience Aug. 1, he called Pope Paul a "teacher and pastor of intellects and human consciences in questions that demanded the decision of his supreme authority." He was "the Pope of the Second Vatican Council." Again, on Aug. 8, he said that Paul VI "dedicated the whole 15 years of his difficult pontificate" to the unprecedented transformation of the Church begun by his predecessor, John XXIII — a transformation "dictated by a profound awareness of the Church and by love for its salvific mission." He added on Aug. 12: "Paul VI speaks to us with the many documents of his pontificate.... He speaks and will speak to us yet for a long time because the teachings contained in these documents touch on questions which are always topical."

1980 Peace Day Theme — "Truth, the Power of Peace," was announced Aug. 13 as the Pope's choice for the theme of the 13th World Day of Peace Jan. 1, 1980. The choice was made, according to a statement, because of the Pontiff's belief "that the outlook of too many people today is opposed to peace because it is against truth." Yet: "Truth is the power of peace because it brings about a return to the objective demands of the moral order, the requirements of justice and social love, and to the primacy of being over having."

Praise for Contemplatives — The Pope warmly praised contemplative nuns during a Mass Aug. 14 at the Poor Clare monastery in Castel Gandolfo. He said: "You have not abandoned the world in order to avoid the worries of the world or so as to not concern yourselves with the problems that torment humanity; not at all. You carry them all in your hearts, and in the suffering scenario of history you accompany humanity with your prayers and with your quest for perfection and salvation."

New Vision of Life — The *Magnificat* and Assumption of the Blessed Virgin Mary provide every Catholic with "a new vision of life," declared the Pope at a Mass Aug. 15. "The words of Mary give us a new vision of life," he said, "a vision of a persevering and coherent faith — faith that is the light of daily faith — faith that is the light of daily life ... faith that ... lights up the darkness of death for each of us." The feast of the Assumption, he added, shows that in Mary "our hope is already realized. ... Who could be better to lead us to Christ than the one who gave him to us?"

Missionaries of Certainty — The Pope urged members of the Secular Institute of the Missionaries of Christ the King to be "missionaries of certainty." Addressing them Aug. 15 on the 50th anniversary of the institute's founding, he said: "In a world tormented by so many doubts and so much anguish, you are the missionaries of certainty — certainty about transcendent values ... certainty about the person of Christ ... certainty about the historical reality and the divine mission of the Church."

Opus Dei — The Pope celebrated Mass Aug. 19 for 300 teachers and students of Opus Dei, an international association of priests and lay persons dedicated to promoting Christian values. He called on them to focus on the Eucharist as the center of their lives and secular ministry. "To receive the Eucharist," he said, "means to be transformed in Christ, to remain in him, to live through him." With the Eucharist as their "program of life," he urged them to be "radiators of life," he urged them to be "radiators of light ... bearers of peace ... sowers of joy" in their homes and professional lives.

Resignation Accepted — Pope John Paul, following a meeting Aug. 12 with Archbishop Raymond Marie Tchidimbo, accepted his resignation Aug. 23 as head of the Archdiocese of Conakry, Guinea. The acceptance came about two weeks after the archbishop was released from eight years of imprisonment for alleged participation in an unsuccessful attempt to overthrow the government of President Sekou Toure. He was arrested Dec. 24, 1970, and sentenced to death, but the sentence was subsequently commuted to life imprisonment and then terminated after eight years had been served.

Meeting with the Handicapped — The Holy Father visited Aug. 25 with 50 severely handicapped persons at Castel Gandolfo. He blessed them all individually and told them: "We must be united in prayer. This link between the suffering and the Pope draws us near to our Redeemer, to his cross, to his work of salvation. ... Your suffering, which is truly a cross, a personal cross, participates in the cross of Christ by which the world is always redeemed. ... When one bears the cross in faith, in the spirit of faith, one can achieve happiness even in suffering. And this is a real miracle. I wish each one of you that interior miracle, the miracle of grace."

Anniversary of John Paul I — The Holy Father marked the first anniversary of the election of John Paul I Aug. 26 with a visit to several sections of his predecessor's home diocese of Belluno. During the day he went by chair lift to the top of Mount Marmolada where he blessed a statue of Our Lady of the Dolomites at a height of 10,560 feet.

Serious Thought and Joy — Addressing a group of French youths Aug. 27, the Pope said that, for a Christian, serious thought is necessary because the Gospel is exacting. So are joy and enthusiasm, he added, because the Gospel is not a gloomy pronouncement but the happy good news of salvation.

Liturgy of the Hours — A letter written in the Pope's name and released Aug. 28 said that the Liturgy of the Hours is a prayer "not only of the clergy or those who have a special mandate for it, but of the whole Church.... It is an ecclesial prayer of adoration and praise to the Father ... an extension and prolongation of the Eucharist ... a consecration of time, of that fundamental element in which our existence turns." The letter was addressed to participants in the 30th Italian National Liturgical Week, Aug. 27 to 31.

Year of the Child and Catechesis — Christ's love for children "could be said to constitute an evangelical program" for the International Year of the Child, declared the Pope at a general audience Aug. 29. Linking the U.N. observance with religious education, he said: "Catechesis of children and youths tends always and everywhere to increase in young souls that which is good, noble and worthy. It becomes the school of a better and more mature sense of humanity, which develops in contact with Christ."

The Pope Also:

• Baptized the infant boy of an English mother at Castel Gandolfo Aug. 11.

• Named Cardinal Franjo Seper as his special envoy for celebrations to be held Sept. 2 in Yugoslavia marking the 1,100th anniversary of an historic exchange of letters between Pope John VIII and Croatian Prince Branislav. St. Methodius, in the year following the exchange, brought about the adoption of the Roman-Slavonic liturgy.

• Celebrated an early morning Mass Aug. 30 at Castel Gandolfo for participants in the Italian National Summer Camp.

Vatican Briefs:

• The State Council of Greece, in an announcement published Aug. 21, rejected as illegal the government's July decree establishing diplomatic ties with the Vatican.

• Moslems were asked to help Christians "maintain spiritual values" and to secure peace and justice in the world, by Cardinal Sergio Pignedoli, president of the Commission for Religious Relations with Islam. His "Message to the Moslem World" was issued at the end of Ramadan, the Islamic holy month.

• Mission and Emergency Aid Funds: *Caritas Internationalis* coordinated $40 million worth of emergency, social assistance and developmental aid in 1978. Also during the year, pontifical mission aid societies received $59 million for the support of missionary work throughout the world.

• The Church supports scientific and technological progress which "truly serves the good of the inhabitants of this earth and does not deprive anyone of the just fruits of its advantages and growth." This was the tenor of a Vatican position paper for the U.N. Conference on Science and Technology held Aug. 20 to 31 in Vienna.

Pastoral Visits Announced

The Vatican Press Office announced Aug. 29 that Pope John Paul would visit Ireland Sept. 29 to Oct. 1, at the invitation of the bishops; the United Nations Oct. 2, at the invitation of Kurt Waldheim, secretary general; and the United States Oct. 1 to 7, at the invitation of the bishops and President Jimmy Carter.

The announcement also said: "With deep regret, due to the dreadful murders of recent days (highlighted by the slaying of Lord Mountbatten a few days earlier), it has been decided not to include a venue in Northern Ireland in the papal itinerary."

NATIONAL

Helsinki Accords — In a statement issued Aug. 1, the fourth anniversary of the Helsinki accords, President Jimmy Carter accused the U.S.S.R., Czechoslovakia and East Germany of violations of human rights.

Birth Control Ad — Michael Schwartz, executive director of the Catholic League for Religious and Civil Rights, strongly condemned an advertisement which appeared July 25 in newspapers in 30 cities seeking to enlist Catholics in a campaign to change the Church's opposition to artificial birth control. He said the ad accused Pope Paul VI and the Church of being the cause of world hunger, and added: "The purpose is to divide the Catholic community and interfere with (the Church's) internal affairs."

Corporate Responsibility — An eight-point statement of principles on human rights, workers' liberties, labor relations and company payments to government officials was published by Castle and Cooke, Inc., as a result of efforts by the Passionist Fathers and other religious groups to have the company formulate a code of management-labor relations.

In a related development, a three-day conference sponsored by the Sisters of Charity of

Nazareth in Louisville studied the social responsibility of corporations and the morality of corporate actions.

Chaplains and the Legislature — The Massachusetts Supreme Court ruled unanimously that employing chaplains to begin sessions of the state Senate and House with prayers does not violate either the state or the U.S. Constitution. "There is no evidence that a great degree of government entanglement with religion is occasioned by the employment of legislative chaplains," declared Justice Francis J. Quirico.

Tekakwitha Conference — Four bishops were among 250 participants in the 40th annual Tekakwitha Conference, held Aug. 6 to 9, in Yankton, S.D. Bishop William Connare, chairman of the Missions Committee, National Conference of Catholic Bishops, said in a keynote address: "We must recognize our responsibility to join our American Indian sisters and brothers in their continuing struggle to secure justice."

Foundation for the Deaf — Father Thomas Coughlin, a deaf priest, reported during the month on the progress of a foundation chartered in New York State in June for fostering identity, encouraging vocations to the priesthood and religious life, and developing leadership skills among the deaf. The foundation was named Mark Seven, in view of the healing of a deaf man recounted in the seventh chapter of St. Mark's Gospel.

CRS Record — Bishop Edwin B. Broderick, executive director of Catholic Relief Services, announced that the agency gave assistance to some 14 million people in 1978 while spending a record $291 million in 86 countries in Africa, Latin America and other parts of the world.

Housing for the Poor in Haiti — At the request of Archbishop Edward A. McCarthy of Miami, a lay movement called *Amor en Accion* was sponsoring a 78-unit housing project for the poor in Port-de-Paix, Haiti.

In a related development, the Catholic Service Bureau of the Miami archdiocese praised the action of a federal judge who issued a temporary injunction reinstating work permits for 2,000 Haitian refugees.

Bible Study Constitutional — A U.S. District Court judge in Chattanooga accepted as constitutional a revised program of Bible study in public schools in Tennessee. Judge Frank Wilson rejected arguments that the curricula — revised since February — had religious overtones; he said that all lessons but one were "capable of being taught for their secular, literary and historic worth without religious emphasis."

Akron Abortion Law — U.S. District Court Judge Leroy Contie, Jr., upheld several key portions of an Akron, O., city ordinance restricting abortion. The sections were those dealing with care for the life of a viable fetus, a 24-hour waiting period before an abortion, a conscience clause for doctors and nurses, and prohibitions on federal experimentation.

UFWA Contract — Nine months after the start of a strike against 28 growers in California and Arizona, the Cesar Chavez-led United Farm Workers of America signed its first major contract with West Coast Farms, Inc., a major lettuce grower in California.

Women's Rights and Biblical Scholarship — Cardinal Humberto Medeiros addressed both subjects during the month.

• He decided against the appointment of a separate archdiocesan commission to deal with women's issues, declaring: "The fact is that injustice toward any human person is wrong, because it violates the right of a human being, whether that human being be a man or a woman. In my judgment, the place to address issues of injustice is our Peace and Justice Commission which has recently been established for this purpose."

• He rejected a fundamentalist approach to biblical scholarship in an address during the Aug. 20 to 23 meeting of the Catholic Biblical Association of America. He said: "Those who are nervous or frightened by the work of serious biblical scholarship betray their failure to grasp that marvelous condescension of the Father who speaks in many ways. Many there are and were who could not accept Jesus as coming from the Father because he was too much like us. They predetermine how God should manifest himself among us; and, when that 'image of the invisible God,' that Word Incarnate, does not fit their preconceived notions, they turn from him. In like manner, they would predetermine how God may speak to us, and look at the effort to determine the literary form and the intention of the author with suspicion. They fail to realize that biblical scholarship is not an attack on the truth but a means to attain it. It does not obscure God's message but sheds light on it, for it respects it (the message) for what it is, the very word of God in the words of men."

Meetings — Meetings during the month included the following:

• Junior Catholic Daughters of the Americas, July 31 to Aug. 4 in Rapid City, S.D. Margaret Foley was elected to a two-year term as national president.

• National Assembly of Women Religious, Aug. 2 to 5 in San Antonio; attended by 300 persons.

• National Marriage Encounter conference, Aug. 2 to 5 in Davenport, Iowa; attended by more than 500 couples.

• Knights of Peter Claver convention, in Los Angeles; attended by about 3,000 persons.

• Jednota convention, in Miami; attended by more than 500 persons of Slavic descent. Joseph Kristofic was elected to a three-year term as president.

- Conference of Major Superiors of Men, Aug. 16 to 20 in Atchison, Kans.; attended by 225 representatives of about 55 religious orders.
- National Black Catholic Clergy Caucus conference, in Milwaukee. Capuchin Brother Booker Ashe was elected president. The Brother Joseph Davis Award was presented to Father Rollins Lambert for outstanding service to the Church in the black community.
- National Apostolate with Mentally Retarded Persons, annual conference in Chicopee, Mass.; attended by 125 participants. The theme was "Parish Awareness: Reaching Out and Receiving."
- Supreme Council of the Knights of Columbus, Aug. 21 to 23 in San Diego.
- Catholic Convert Movement of America, 35th anniversary convention in Detroit. Margaret Lynch Gibson was elected president.

National Briefs:
- Father William A. Finucane, S.J., succeeded fellow Jesuit Father John J. Killoren as executive director of the St. Stephen's Indian Mission Foundation in Wyoming.
- Brother Joseph M. Davis was appointed English-speaking Marianist coordinator for Africa.
- Claudette Colbert was presented with the George M. Cohan Award by the Catholic Actors' Guild.
- Little Sisters of the Poor in the Cincinnati area commemorated the 100th anniversary Aug. 29 of the death of their foundress, Jeanne Jugan, Sister Mary of the Cross.
- The American Bible Society announced Nov. 18 as the date for the 1979 observance of Bible Sunday.

Evangelization

More than 1,400 persons took part Aug. 16 to 18 in the first National Catholic Lay Celebration of Evangelization in Washington, D.C. The celebration was sponsored by the Paulist Office for Evangelization, the Catholic University of America and the National Shrine of the Immaculate Conception.

Paulist Father Alvin A. Illig, in a keynote address, stressed the role of ordinary lay persons in spreading the Gospel. In line with that theme, the Mass which concluded the celebration was coupled with a "commissioning service" reaffirming the role of all Christians as evangelists.

INTERNATIONAL

Coup in Equatorial Guinea — The overthrow of President Macias Nguema of Equatorial Guinea in a military coup was announced Aug. 4. The downfall of the "Madman of Malabo," in power since the country gained independence from France in 1968, ended what was generally regarded as one of the most ruthless governments in Africa. Victims included real and imagined political opponents, with the Church high on the list. He confiscated Catholic schools, closed churches, persecuted church personnel (leaving only one missionary priest and 20 native priests to care for 60 per cent of the population), charged ransom for the release of foreign prisoners (including missionaries), closed three seminaries, prohibited parents from giving Christian names to their children, and sought to have himself deified and recognized as "Equatorial Guinea's only true miracle."

One of the first acts of government under the Revolutionary Council which overthrew Macias was a decree allowing the reopening of Catholic missions.

Meeting of African Bishops — The Association of Member Catholic Conferences in Eastern Africa opened a two-week assembly Aug. 5 in Zomba, Malawi, on the theme of small Christian communities. A report indicated strong consensus on the importance of such communities and the need for their development. The report also warned of dangers, such as the isolation of small communities from the broader societies in which they are located, inadequate perceptions of church life, and the possible confusion of such communities with multiplying small religious sects in Africa.

Basques and Catalonians Get Self-Rule — In an effort to isolate terrorist groups and to forestall continuing violence, the Spanish government granted home rule to the Basques and Catalonians early in the month. The action climaxed a long struggle by the two ethnic groups to maintain their cultures and to have greater control over their own resources.

Mediation in Bolivia — Mediation efforts by Archbishop Jorge Manrique of La Paz to end a deadlock after inconclusive presidential elections were helpful in bringing about a compromise and forestalling political violence. "I was concerned that violence would mar the transition to democracy," the archbishop said in explaining his action. "I found good dispositions among the candidates toward a compromise." The candidates were Hernan Siles Zuazo, Victor Paz Estenssoro and Gen. Hugo Banzer.

Labor Unions and Social Reforms — The Social Action Committee of the Argentine bishops asked the military government to honor the rights of labor unions, but at the same time called on union leaders to stick to labor matters and avoid factional politics. They made their appeal as pressure for social action increased among priests, religious and lay persons favoring social reforms.

Amnesty in Brazil — The Brazilian Congress began debate on a proposal to grant amnesty to political prisoners, "except those (about 200) convicted of crimes of terrorism, assault, kidnapping or attempted assault." The proposal was sponsored by President

Joao Baptista Figueiredo in an effort toward political reconciliation after 15 years of military rule.

Centenary in Zimbabwe Rhodesia — The first of two celebrations of the 100th anniversary of the Church in the country was held Aug. 26. The observance took place during a continuation of seven years of guerrilla warfare in which 19 Catholic missionaries had been killed and the work of the Church seriously crippled in the fields of evangelization, education, health and social services.

Refugee Arrangements in Canada — Bishop Paul F. Reding of Hamilton signed an agreement with the Canadian government allowing diocesan groups, with a minimum of bureaucratic administration, to provide sponsorship and assistance to refugees from Indochina. Similar arrangements were already in effect in the archdioceses of Toronto and Ottawa and in the Saskatchewan province.

Bishop Fined — Bishop Antulio Parrilla-Bonilla was found guilty Aug. 23 of trespassing on federal property, fined $500 and placed on probation for one year. He was arrested May 19 while holding an ecumenical service on Vieques island in protest against Navy use of the site for target practice.

Marriage Guidelines — Parish guidelines, stating that marriage cannot be presumed to be a right simply because of a couple's plan to marry, were approved late in the month by Archbishop Antoine Hacault of St. Boniface, Canada. According to the guidelines for St. Bernadette Parish: "Marriage cannot be presumed to be a 'right' simply because the couple is planning marriage. It is a right and privilege of those who are truly part of the Church." The guidelines also covered programs of preparation for marriage and prescribed that: anyone under the age of 18 must be considered to be lacking adequate maturity for Christian marriage; anyone under 20 must have the approval of the parish community; appropriate counselling is in order if a couple is under 20 or if pregnancy is involved.

Child Labor Exploitation — The U.N. reported that in 1979, the International Year of the Child, there were approximately 52 million children working under often harsh and unpaid conditions, and that 400 million were not getting an education. The International Labor Organization said in a related statement that a preliminary study showed that "no state escapes the exploitation of child labor," and added that 80 per cent of the 52 million were employed mostly in family types of enterprises.

International Briefs:

• Father Alirio Napoleon, slain Aug. 5 by machine-gun fire while celebrating Mass in San Esteban Catarina, was the sixth priest killed in 30 months in El Salvador.

• Mother Teresa of Calcutta established a convent of her Missionary Sisters of Charity for the first time in her native country of Yugoslavia, according to an Aug. 8 Vatican Radio report.

• Cardinal Paul-Emile Leger returned to Montreal Aug. 8 after spending 12 years working with handicapped children and lepers in Cameroun.

• Dissident Archbishop Marcel Lefebvre, without providing any substantiating evidence, claimed in Buenos Aires that he no longer had any problems with the Vatican. His actions since being suspended from the exercise of orders in 1976 were at variance with this claim.

• Sources in Poland reported that police were harassing Catholics trying to construct a church in the Diocese of Przemysl, according to a report in the Aug. 15 edition of *Avvenire*, Italy's national Catholic newspaper.

• *Adveniat*, the West German Catholic aid agency, funded 37 projects of the Church in Chile during the first six months of the year. The funding was part of the $8 million distributed among church groups in Latin America.

• Catholics throughout Poland celebrated a day of prayer and thanksgiving for the June visit of Pope John Paul, on Aug. 26, the feast of Our Lady of Czestochowa.

Religion in China

Speculation about new respect for religion in China was open to question. Several non-Catholic religious leaders from China, in New York late in the month, said that religious freedom was returning. There were also reports that scholars in China were working on new translations of the Bible and the Koran, and were engaged in additional religious research. But in the background was the wipe-out of visible religion in the country since the 1940s. Even so, Pope John Paul expressed hope for new respect in an address on Aug. 19.

Toward the end of July, it was reported that Father Michael Fu Tieshan had been elected bishop of Beijing (Peking) under the auspices of the government-controlled National Association of Patriotic Catholics (which elected 36 bishops between 1957 and 1960). The Vatican, in a statement issued Aug. 10, said that all it knew about the election and ordination was what it had learned from news agency reports. The Vatican also said that the election and ordination (like the earlier ones) were out of order and had not been authorized.

The New China News Agency later reported that the new bishop had celebrated Mass in the Beijing cathedral, and that his election was part of the Patriotic Association's effort to run the Church in China "independently of the Vatican," a condition with which the Pope would never agree.

SEPTEMBER 1979

VATICAN

Tribute and Plea — Pope John Paul paid a visit Sept. 1 to Nettuno in tribute to Our Lady of Grace and St. Maria Goretti, who was killed July 6, 1902, while resisting a rapist. The visit coincided with the 40th anniversary of the outbreak of World War II; and the Pope, while celebrating Mass near the Anzio beachhead, pleaded: "Let us pray that God save us and all of humanity from the scourge of war which, if it happens again, would assume the dimensions of an even more terrible apocalypse."

What a Pilgrimage Does — A pilgrimage to Rome renews the sense of "being church," the Pope told about 3,000 visitors Sept. 5. "Making a visit to Peter in the person of his humble successor, you confirm and reaffirm the principle of ecclesial unity," he said.

Pilgrimage to Loreto — The Pope made a second visit early in the month, traveling Sept. 8 to Loreto, the site of what is believed to be the home of the Holy Family (see Loreto, House of). He called the visit a preparatory pilgrimage for his planned trip to Ireland and the United States.

Ecumenical Sensitivity — "Because you represent (the) Greek monastic tradition, you ought to be distinguished by (the) quality of a special ecumenical sensitivity," the Pope told a community of Byzantine-Rite monks Sept. 9 at their monastery near Rome. "By your position, by your formation," he said, "you can do much in this regard, committing yourselves in dialogue and, above all, in prayer to the goal of promoting the hoped-for unity between Catholics and Orthodox." The occasion of the Pontiff's visit was the 1600th anniversary of the death of St. Basil the Great, the founder of Eastern monasticism.

Aid for Nicaragua — The Holy Father issued a "pressing appeal" Sept. 9 for more international aid to Nicaragua. While addressing about 20,000 persons at Castel Gandolfo, he asked the governments of other countries, international relief organizations and voluntary agencies to "demonstrate their solidarity so as to allow that country to confront its immediate and urgent humanitarian needs and obtain financial help in the vast work of reconstruction," following a destructive civil war.

Man Can't Be Reduced to the World — The biblical account of man's creation contains "the affirmation of the absolute impossibility of reducing man to 'the world,' " stated the Pope Sept. 13 during a general audience. The Genesis texts show the relationship of human beings both to God and to created nature, he said. "Already in the first phrases of the Bible man cannot be contained or explained, even at the bottom, by categories drawn from 'the world,' that is, from the visible complex of bodily things."

The Church Cares for Workers — Workers have a special place in the heart of the Church, the Pope declared in a homily during Mass Sept. 13 in Pomezia. Addressing a gathering of 50,000 people, he said: "Let us not forget that work was made for man, and man was not made for work. Otherwise, man would return to being a slave.. . . The Christian element can bring peace, justice and unity to the work place. The Church cannot look at workers without a sincere sentiment of sympathy."

Sense of Pilgrimage — "In our growing age of tourism, Catholics must make an effort to save or restore the deep sense of pilgrimage, which is an exacting break in normal life, a serious spiritual resource, an experience of Christian joy, a new alliance with Christ the Savior, a renewal of ecclesial responsibility. . . . The cultural trip, which has its place and its value, is one thing. The pilgrimage is another." So stated the Pope Sept. 14.

Family Life — Pope John Paul called for strong family life at a meeting Sept. 17 with representatives of the International *Equipes Notre Dame* ("Our Lady's Army"). He said: "You want to live conjugal love and parental love in the light of the Gospel and the Church's teachings, in a climate that places high value on prayer, on sharing in the home, on deep exchanges between spouses over all human and spiritual problems. . . . It is so necessary to renew, at the base, the cells of the Church and society. And the Pope counts on the contribution of your movement of matrimonial spirituality."

Speaking of marriage again two days later, the Pontiff said that Christ was "clear and unequivocal" in his stand against divorce. When questioned by the Pharisees about his stance on marriage, Christ referred them to the early chapters of Genesis, especially to the statements that God "created them male and female" and directed man to "abandon his father and mother and be joined with his wife, and the two shall be one flesh. . . . The reply of Christ is clear and unequivocal."

Charity Work and Catechesis — Those who engage in charitable work in the service of God must not neglect the opportunity it offers to educate others, said the Pope Sept. 20 before a gathering of 500 participants in the national convention of Italian *Caritas*. He said: "I wish to emphasize, above all, the opportunity for a catechesis which ever more clearly illustrates to the faithful the close connection which exists between the word of God, the liturgical expression of it and its concrete translation into the witness of charity. . . . It will serve . . . to stimulate the Christian community to ask itself about the adequacy of its own Christian presence in relation to the historical evolution of needs and to the emerging questions about new forms of poverty."

Law Should Respect Moral Values — Law cannot set aside human and moral values, which are "at the basis of everything," the Pope said Sept. 24 in an address to 400 participants in the Ninth World Conference on Law. "The whole history of law," he said, "shows that law loses its stability and its moral authority, that it is then tempted to make an increasing appeal to constraint and physical force or, on the other hand, to renounce its responsibility ... whenever it ceases to search for truth concerning man and allows itself to be bought off with some harmful form of relativism."

Beagle Channel Negotiations — The Pope urged representatives of Chile and Argentina to put aside suspicion and fear in efforts to resolve a dispute over the control of three Beagle Channel islands and related maritime rights in the South Atlantic and Antarctica. Among those attending the meeting was Cardinal Antonio Samore whom the Pope, at the request of the concerned governments, appointed to act as a mediator.

Departure for Ireland and the United States — The Holy Father began his third pastoral pilgrimage outside of Italy Sept. 29 aboard an Aer Lingus jet bound for Dublin. (See separate entries.)

The Pope Also:
• Celebrated Mass and visited patients and employees Sept. 3 at Queen of the Apostles Hospital in Albano.
• Selected "The Role of Social Communications and Duties of the Family" as the theme for the 1980 observance of World Communications Day May 18.
• Expressed concern about "the vast and grave scourge of illiteracy in the world," in a letter addressed to Amadou-Mahtar M'Bow, general director of the U.N. Economic, Social and Cultural Organization.
• Was joined by nearly 100 catechists from 25 countries at Mass Sept. 12, three days before he ended his brief summer stay at Castel Gandolfo.
• Gave a special private audience Sept. 13 to 10-year-old Stefania Mosca, who was paralyzed in a car accident.
• Named Cardinal Jose Bueno y Monreal to serve as his legate to the 15th International Marian Congress to be held Oct. 9 to 12 in Saragossa, Spain.
• Expressed his sympathy for victims of: Hurricane David, Sept. 4; an air crash in Sardinia, Sept. 14; an earthquake in West Irian, Sept. 14.

Vatican Briefs:
• U.S. church officials were advised that lay ministers of the Eucharist would not be used for the distribution of Holy Communion at Masses celebrated by the Pope during his pastoral visit, because there would be enough priests and deacons available to do so.
• More than 25,000 people attended a memorial Mass Sept. 16 in St. Peter's Basilica for Pope Paul VI, whom the Holy Father called in his homily " 'the Peter,' the rock on which, in this exceptional period of great change after the Second Vatican Council, the Church was built." He singled out for special praise Pope Paul's encyclicals entitled *Populorum Progressio* and *Humanae Vitae*.

Jesuit Collaboration

Pope John Paul, during an audience Sept. 21 at the Vatican, praised the work of the Society of Jesus and told a group of superiors headed by Father Pedro Arrupe, "I count on your collaboration." He said:

"Certainly I do not ignore the fact that the crises which in recent times have troubled and are troubling religious life have not spared your society, causing disorientation among Christian people and worry to the Church, to the hierarchy, and also personally to the people who speak with you."

"I count on your collaboration and, above all, I heartily wish to urge you to promote with every commitment the good which is done in the society and by the society, and together to procure, with the proper firmness, remedies to the deplorable deficiencies" present int he world.

NATIONAL

Hurricane Relief — Catholic Relief Services allocated $50,000 to start a special emergency relief fund for aid to victims of Hurricane David in Dominica, the Dominican Republic, Haiti and Jamaica.

Reluctance To Help with Census — Officials in several dioceses indicated they were reluctant to have the Church assist the U.S. Census Bureau in registering aliens in 1980 without absolute assurance and guarantees that information so obtained would be kept secret and not used against undocumented persons.

No Cover-Up — Bishop George H. Guilfoyle of Camden, one of two Vatican-appointed investigators in the case, denied allegations of a cover-up of financial dealings and operations by the Pauline Fathers at the Doylestown, Pa., Shrine of Our Lady of Czestochowa. He issued the denial in response to allegations by the Gannett News Service that church officials, including the Pope, had quashed an investigation of the shrine. The Gannett articles, Bishop Guilfoyle said, "now assert as problems matters already resolved, and they do so in a way that unfortunately minimizes the genuine renewal and stability achieved at the shrine through the (apostolic) visitation."

SALT II — Cardinal John Krol, in testimony prepared for delivery Sept. 6 before the Senate Foreign Relations Committee, urged the Senate to ratify the second Strategic Arms Limitation Treaty with the U.S.S.R. as a "decelaration" of the arms race and "the beginning of a continuing and necessary process for obtaining meaningful and progressive reductions" in nuclear stockpiles. The cardinal said his views reflected the majority opinion of the Administrative Board, U.S. Catholic Conference.

Twenty-two religious denominations were reported in favor of SALT II ratification, which was not assured.

United Way and Planned Parenthood — Following the withdrawal of South Texas Planned Parenthood from the local United Way, Bishop Thomas Drury instructed pastors of the Corpus Christi diocese to urge people to contribute to the campaign. Earlier, he had said publicly that United Way participation by Planned Parenthood, which "advocates and supports abortion," was a "defiant invasion on the sensibilities" of Catholics.

Funding by Campaign for Human Development — Father Marvin Mottet, national director, reported Sept. 7 that the U.S. bishops' anti-poverty agency had awarded $6,317,700 to 125 self-help projects this year. An additional $20 million was administered and allocated to other projects at diocesan levels.

Religion and Peace Conference — Three hundred and 50 representatives of major religions from nearly 50 countries attended the third assembly of the World Conference on Religion and Peace Aug. 27 to Sept. 7 at Princeton, N.J. Cardinal Terence Cooke told delegates during a prayer service that prayers for peace must be accompanied by "well planned actions" for peace.

No Draft Registration — The House of Representatives, with a 252-to-163 vote, rejected draft registration for 18-year-olds while leaving intact an amendment calling on the President to make a study of registration needs and methods.

Corporate Responsibility — The corporate-responsibility movement ran into confrontation at a meeting of the Financial Writers' Association in New York. Corporation head D. J. Kirchhoff of Castle and Cooke said the movement had recruited "many well-meaning but tragically misguided people to its cause." Timothy Smith, director of the Interfaith Center on Corporate Responsibility, replied: "We see ourselves as loyal critics." Center membership included 14 Protestant denominations and more than 15 Catholic religious institutes.

Racism and Prejudice — Bishop Walter F. Sullivan of Richmond asked Catholics in a pastoral letter to promote interracial harmony and to end prejudice against blacks, Hispanics and Southeast Asian refugees. He said: "We must recognize that some groups of people are often the target of discrimination in the work place, in education, in the housing market, in health care and in the criminal justice system. We continue to stereotype and to deride whole groups of people in our jokes; we look upon others as primitive, lazy, violent or even subhuman. . . . We must work together for the eradication of discrimination within our church community and guarantee that all people can reach their full potential."

In another anti-discrimination incident, Bishop William E. McManus of Fort Wayne-South Bend led an ecumenical prayer meeting in Waynedale, Ind., in counteraction to a march by local members of the Ku Klux Klan.

School Desegregation — Bishops James A. Hickey of Cleveland and Edward J. Herrmann of Columbus were among religious leaders who helped to make the first days of court-ordered, public school desegregation peaceful in their respective cities.

Church Schools Don't Have To Pay — Judge Robert Roland of the 19th Judicial District Court in Baton Rouge ruled that church-run schools in Louisiana do not have to pay federal or state unemployment security taxes. He said in the ruling: "There is nothing whatsoever in the legislative history of the federal amendment to support" the conclusion of U.S. Secretary of Labor Ray Marshall that such schools are obliged to pay the federal tax. "To the contrary, the legislative history specifically states that the amendment 'excludes services of persons where the employer is a church. . . . The language (of the Louisiana law) is clear and unambiguous, and obviously means that the institutions in question are not subject to the (state) tax."

A ruling similar to Judge Roland's was handed down earlier in Alabama.

Camp David Anniversary — The first anniversary of the Camp David accords for peace in the Middle East came and went Sept. 16 with Palestinian and related problems still unresolved between Israel and Egypt.

Episcopal Convention — The 66th triennial convention of the Episcopal Church, meeting Sept. 8 to 20 in Denver, passed a resolution against the ordination of sexually active homosexuals to the priesthood. The resolution did not have the effect of canon law and was opposed by 21 bishops who said they would not pay any attention to it. Another key resolution left to parishes the option to use either the 1928 version of the Book of Common Prayer or a more recent book of the same type. The House of Deputies reaffirmed the church's stance on abortion, opposing federal or state legislation which would deny an individual's right "to reach informed decisions in the matter of abortion and to act upon them." The convention refused to urge ratification of SALT II and adopted a 1980 budget of $15.8 million.

Charismatic Conference — An estimated 15,000 persons attended the sixth general conference on the Catholic Charismatic Renewal Sept. 21 to 23 at New York's Yankee Stadium; the twin themes were evangelism and social justice. Ralph Martin, one of the lay leaders of the movement, said at a press conference that teaching in some sectors of the Church was departing from fundamental truths of the Gospel: "Some theologians and religious educators are really unclear about what the basic Gospel message is. And there is an atmosphere in many seminaries and religious education programs so that those who remain faithful to the Gospel are too timid to speak out clearly about the distortions." Auxiliary Bishop Joseph McKinney of Grand Rapids, the U.S. bishops' liaison officer with the movement, said that its National Service Committee was studying the conditions described by Martin.

Father Pagano Cleared — Guilty pleas by Ronald Clouser of Brookhaven, Pa., finally cleared Father Bernard T. Pagano Sept. 24 of "gentleman bandit" holdup charges in Delaware and Pennsylvania.

National Briefs:

• Five thousand persons attended a welcoming service in St. Patrick's Cathedral, New York City, for His Holiness the Dalai Lama XIV, the exiled spiritual leader of six million Tibetan Buddhists.

• Jim Castelli, federal reporter for NC News Service since 1974, was named religion editor of *The Washington Star*.

• The Ralph Metcalfe Award for Excellence was presented to Mary Lou Williams, jazz pianist and composer, by the National Office for Black Catholics.

Labor Day Statement

An annual Labor Day statement by Msgr. George G. Higgins reminded church leaders that they must "unequivocally recognize" the right of their employees to organize for the purpose of collective bargaining. He said, in part:

"The immediate challenge facing school administrators in the wake of the Supreme Court's decision (that the National Labor Relations Act does not cover lay teachers of church-operated schools) is to establish, in cooperation with Catholic teachers' unions and with the professional assistance of outside experts, a voluntary substitute for the National Labor Relations Board."

Without such a board, he added, Catholic school teachers would be deprived of a right which "the Church is called upon to defend and honor."

INTERNATIONAL

Dutch Synod — Vatican Radio announced Sept. 5 that the seven bishops of The Netherlands would meet in Rome Jan. 14, 1980, to begin a "particular synodal assembly" concerned about "the pastoral work of the Church to be exercised in The Netherlands in the present situation." The communique said the Pope was calling the synod in response to the requests of many bishops, particularly Cardinal Johannes Willebrands, president of the Dutch Bishops' Conference. The Church in Holland had an international reputation as a center of unauthorized innovations and controversial theological opinions. In November, 1977, Pope Paul VI urged the bishops there to steer away from liturgical abuses and "deep disturbances in the field of faith and morals."

Uphold Rights in Poland — The bishops of Poland, in a pastoral letter read in all churches Sept. 9, called on Catholics to openly oppose government attempts to violate religious rights. They called especially for the right of the unborn to life, the rights of mothers after childbirth and the right of children to religious education. The bishops said it was difficult to take seriously the government's stated desire for better relations with the Church when the authorities "refuse to take into consideration the needs of the Church and the rights of the faithful."

New Anglican Archbishop of Canterbury — Bishop Robert Runcie, 57, was named to succeed Archbishop Donald Coggan, due to retire in January, 1980.

Reconciliation of Ministries — More than 300 British Catholic, Anglican and protestant clergymen met Sept. 11 and 12 for an ecumenical conference on the reconciliation of ministries, a key issue on the agenda of the Churches' Council for Covenanting. The council included the Churches of Christ, the Church of England, the Methodist Church, the Moravian Church and the United Reformed Church. The Catholic Church was not party to covenant proposals for full and mutual recognition of ministries.

Missing Persons in Chile — Cardinal Raul Henriquez Silva of Santiago, his auxiliary bishops and priests held liturgical services early in the month in support of hunger-strikers seeking government disclosure of the whereabouts of 400 missing political prisoners. Thirty-five of the demonstrators were arrested in front of a downtown church and detained for violating security law and "holding a political demonstration without a permit."

Arrests in Czechoslovakia — Four priests were among six persons arrested for undisclosed reasons Sept. 10 in a new government crackdown on dissidents, according to sources in Prague. Two of the priests were signatories of "Charter 77," a 3,000-word petition for respect for human rights in the country.

Reports earlier in the year indicated that

regional administrative authorities were depriving priests of the work permits they needed to carry out their pastoral ministry.

Ukrainian Bishops Meet — Twelve Ukrainian-Rite bishops from the United States, Canada, Australia and countries in Latin America and Europe met in Rome Sept. 19 and 20 at a "synod in exile" headed by Cardinal Josyf Slipyi, exiled major archbishop of Lwow. Pope John Paul addressed the bishops and other Ukrainians at a general audience Sept. 19, saying: "To you who have come to Rome to venerate the tombs of the Apostles on the occasion of the 40th anniversary of the episcopacy of your and our venerable Cardinal Josyf Slipyi . . . a special greeting. My paternal salute is also directed to your families, to your bishops, men and women religious as to all Ukrainians, in their homeland and outside it. May God, with the intercession of the Virgin Mother of God, assist you in your Christian life."

Fear in South Korea — Despite a statement by a government official that the government did not intend to change or pass laws to regulate church activities, religious leaders feared that some measures would be taken in the future to curb the Catholic Farmers' Association, the Protestant Urban Industrial Mission and other religious organizations whose actions might be construed as opposition to government policies.

Refugee Aid in Hong Kong — Caritas-Hong Kong was caring for 6,000 refugees and gearing up for the care of 4,000 or more in the near future. The crown colony already had received about 75,000 boat people from Vietnam.

Archbishop Lefebvre Not Reconciled — Disproving unsubstantiated rumors that he had been reconciled with the Church through Pope John Paul dissident Archbishop Marcel Lefebvre celebrated a Tridentine Mass Sept. 23 in Paris and renewed his attack on reforms of the Second Vatican Council. "The enemies of the Church have infiltrated it," he said, "and their prime objective is to destroy the Catholic Mass." The Mass in the Park of Expositions was attended by about 10,000 persons. The Permanent Council of the French Bishops' Conference called the archbishop's action "a provocation" and "a challenge to the Church united with the Pope." (The Tridentine Mass, so called because its norms derived from the Council of Trent, has been replaced by a new Order of the Mass enacted in accord with decisions of the Second Vatican Council. The archbishop's continuing celebration of the Tridentine Mass is symbolic of his defiance of the council and the authority of the Pope.)

Nicaragua after Somoza — The 300 priests of Nicaragua asked the Government of Reconstruction to heed the people's will which led to victory over the oppressive Somoza dynasty. The national clergy association said in a statement: "The civic and political awareness of the people must be fostered to enable them to discharge their mission in society, to give an example of responsibility in the service of the common good. Above all, our people must be the agent of their own history, as they were the decisive factor during the revolution" (which toppled the Somoza regime in July). As the bishops of the country had done earlier, the priests pledged their "cooperation and good will toward the common good and peace," and said that the victorious revolution must become a political effort that "will place natural resources at the service of every citizen, and thus be the tool of the nation's progress." Two priests were ministers in the new government, Fathers Miguel D'Escoto and Ernesto Cardenal.

International Briefs:

• Msgr. Victor Mukasa Womeraka, the first native Ugandan priest, died at the age of 97 in Kitovu.

• Thousands of Italians gathered in St. Peter's Basilica and Square Sept. 13 to mark the 20th anniversary of the consecration of the nation to the Immaculate Heart of Mary.

• Father Silvio Serri, an Italian missionary, became the seventh priest killed in Uganda in recent months.

• Two hundred people gathered at Monash University in Melbourne to take part in Australia's first dialogue between Christians and Moslems.

Intervention Wanted in El Salvador

The bishops of the nation asked the apostolic nuncio to El Salvador to intervene with military authorities to end a "wave of assassinations of priests" and to bring the killers to justice. They were prodded into action by some 300 priests and religious after Father Alirio Napoleon Macias, the sixth priest to meet violent death in slightly over two years, was gunned down at the altar of his church by unknown assailants.

The priests and religious, declaring to the bishops that their "silence thus far is bringing sorrow to us," said: "We are certain that, if the nuncio and all the bishops had raised earlier a vigorous, unanimous voice of protest, the death of many innocent persons would have been avoided."

They also wrote to Pope John Paul, asking his intervention in defense of the people. They gave a partial description of conditions in the country as follows. "In the first six months of this year, at least 406 persons — most of them Catholics — have been killed only because they were trying to search for ways to build a more just society, a more human society, in our nation. In addition, more than 307 persons have been arrested or kidnapped, never to see a court of justice. Many of them are missing, in violation of all law."

OCTOBER 1979

VATICAN

Well-Deserved Rest — On his return from the United States Oct. 8, Pope John Paul retired to Castel Gandolfo for a brief rest.

Patriarch's Death — The Pope expressed his sympathy to all Armenian-Rite Catholics following the death Oct. 9 of retired Armenian-Rite Patriarch Ignace Batanian of Cilicia.

Advice to Women Superiors — Addressing an audience of Italian superiors and provincials Oct. 10, the Pope said: "Now, I would like only to suggest to you superiors the firmness and delicacy necessary in this moment. Show yourselves to be mothers above all, sensible and illuminated, never irritated or embittered for nothing, but blessedly brave in following the voice of the Vicar of Christ, in order that no sister feels depressed or on the fringes, even if she has erred in something. Also, to you I repeat what I said in Ireland: 'You must be courageous in your apostolic undertakings, not letting difficulties, shortage of personnel, insecurity for the future deter or depress you. Always remember that your first apostolic duty is your own sanctification.' " Neither the Pope nor Vatican sources indicated that these remarks had any reference to the challenge given the Pope by Sister Theresa Kane Oct. 7, regarding the admission of women to all ministries of the Church.

Devotion to Mary — Such devotion, "subordinated to the worship of Christ the Savior and connected with him," is a powerful force for interior renewal, declared the Holy Father in a message addressed to two Marian meetings in Saragossa, Spain. The academically-oriented Mariological Congress, Oct. 3 to 12, was centered on discussion of the Marian cult in the 16th century. Topics of the Oct. 9 to 12 International Marian Congress were: Mary and the mission of women in the Church today, Mary and the Christian duty toward the poor, how to present the mystery of Mary in contemporary catechesis, pastoral renewal of the Church and popular devotion to Mary.

Evangelization — This was one of the principal topics of an address by the Pope to 27 Chilean bishops Oct. 13. In the work of evangelization, he said, "you must constitute neither a symposium of experts nor a parliament of politicians nor a congress of scientists and technicians, but instead you must be pastors of your Church, teachers of truth." The Lord "does not ask that the announcement (of the good news) be directed exclusively to the intelligence, as simply a theoretical doctrine; but, involving all the other faculties, it must be transformed into a witness to life which can be revealed in personal, social and national rapport."

Mass for Seminarians — The Pope celebrated Mass Oct. 13 for seminarians of the Rome diocese. He told them: "You are not like other youths who have before them only the normal goals of a career, social position, marriage and earthly satisfactions, even if with Christian and apostolic goals." Christ "has chosen you, in a mysterious but real way, to be saviors with him and like him — he wants to transform you in him, to entrust to you his own divine powers. You must one day act 'in the person of Christ.' ... In you, Christ is eternally young, and through you he rejuvenates the Church. Do not disappoint him. Do not disappoint the people who are waiting for you to bring Christ to them."

Beatification — The Holy Father presided Oct. 14 at ceremonies for the beatification of Enrico de Osso y Cervello (1840-96), the Spanish priest-founder of the Sisters of the Company of St. Teresa of Jesus. He said in a homily: "Prayer became the soul of his priesthood and his apostolate. From it were born his pastoral activity, his organizational work and his writing. He was a great lover of young people and children — and his love was expressed, above all, in the catechetical ministry."

Build the Church — The Pope urged students and faculty members of Rome's 17 pontifical universities and institutes to "participate in building up the Church, which has its origin in Christ himself." He made the appeal during an evening Mass Oct. 15 at the opening of the 1979-80 academic year.

Anniversary of Election — The Holy Father spent the first anniversary of his election, Oct. 16, in the usual ways of a day of business as usual.

More than two weeks earlier, on Sept. 28, he marked the first anniversary of the death of his predecessor, John Paul I. During a Mass concelebrated with 31 cardinals, he said that the pontificate of John Paul I "will remain and will continue to be a help to us all, for the progress and the joy of our faith."

Thanks to the U.N. — The Pope, in a cablegram dated Oct. 19, expressed his "profound gratitude" for the opportunity to address the United Nations Oct. 2. Ambassador Salim Ahmeb Salim of Tanzania, president of the General Assembly, said in reply that the Holy Father's visit to the U.N. was "truly historic" and his address "most inspiring." The address, at the request of representatives of six nations, was circulated as an official document of the world organization.

Visit to Pompeii and Naples — Festive crowds and pleas for social justice, prayer, devotion to Mary and missionary activity marked the Pope's day-long visit Oct. 21. More than 100,000 people witnessed the first-ever visit by a Pope at the Shrine of Our

Lady, Queen of the Rosary, at Pompeii. In Naples, before a throng of 300,000 persons, the Holy Father pleaded: "How can anyone here in Naples close their eyes to the bitter realities such as uncertain life because of a lack of work and the resulting lack of bread, the danger of sickness, inadequate housing, and a situation of crisis spread through all social levels?" He said he intended "to stimulate those spiritual and moral forces that can, indeed must, set social justice in motion."

Meeting of Cardinals — Father Romeo Panciroli, Vatican press spokesman, told journalists Oct. 18 that the Pope would meet with the College of Cardinals Nov. 5 to 8. The announcement ended speculation about the dates of the meeting but not about its agenda. Father Panciroli only said that the meeting would be "a general examination on themes of realities that are of interest to the life of the Church," and would be in keeping with the Pope's desire "that the cardinals, in a particular way, must participate in the pastoral concerns of the successor of Peter."

NATIONAL

Food for Cambodians — Bishop Edwin Broderick, executive director of Catholic Relief Services, joined seven other heads of church-related relief agencies in an appeal to Secretary of State Cyrus Vance for effective U.S. action for the acquisition and distribution of food to starving people in Cambodia. One report said that all or most children under the age of five in the country had died of starvation and that hundreds more were dying daily.

Priest's Appeal Denied — The U.S. Supreme Court declined to review the contempt-of-court conviction of Father Louis R. Gigante of New York, declaring that the protected secrecy of his talks with a penitent did not extend to conversations about those talks with other persons.

Limits to Regulation of Private Schools — The seven-member Kentucky Supreme Court ruled unanimously that the state cannot: require private schools to hold state accreditation; set standards for the quality of instruction; require certification of private school teachers; force private schools to use state-approved textbooks. The ruling was based on the section of the state constitution declaring that no person may "be compelled to send his child to any school to which he may be conscientiously opposed."

Hospital Patients — The Catholic Health Association of the United States reported that 5,740,102 patients were admitted to 641 Catholic hospitals during 1978, an increase of 147,682 over the 1977 total. The average capacity of Catholic hospitals in 1978 was 259 beds.

Ecumenist Official Resigns — Father J. Peter Sheehan, associate director of the Bishops' Committee on Ecumenical and Interreligious Affairs since 1973, resigned the office for a pastorate in the Birmingham diocese.

Office for Families — President Jimmy Carter announced Oct. 15 the formation of an Office for Families within the Department of Health and Human Services, in an address to 1,000 delegates attending the 65th annual meeting of the National Conference of Catholic Charities in Kansas City, Mo. He urged involvement by the social workers in preparations for the White House Conference on Families scheduled for 1981.

Indian Mission Anniversary — The 125th anniversary of the arrival of Jesuit missionaries in western Montana was observed during the month at St. Ignatius Mission.

Abortion Attitudes — Religious affiliation and church attendance are the "premier" indicators of abortion attitude, declared Dr. Judith Blake, a long-time authority on abortion and popular opinion, at the National Conference on Abortion at the University of Notre Dame. Dr. Blake, professor of population policy at the University of California at Los Angeles, said that church-attending Catholics or fundamentalist Protestants were extremely predictable opponents of abortion. She studied 761 respondents who exhibited polarized views on abortion in 1978. Compared to an earlier study, she said, opponents included a much larger share of Protestants than a 1972 study indicated.

Clothing for Relief — Catholic Relief Services released figures indicating that, since the start of the Bishops' Thanksgiving Clothing Collection in 1950, the U.S. Catholic community had contributed more than 500 million pounds of usable clothing, blankets and footwear for the relief of disaster victims and the poor overseas.

Department of Education — President Carter signed a bill Oct. 17 creating the 13th agency of the Cabinet, a new Department of Education. The education division of the U.S. Catholic Conference, along with the National Federation of Teachers, had opposed the bill separating the U.S. Office of Education from the Department of Health, Education and Welfare. A USCC spokesman said, however, that the conference hoped to work with the new department to gain benefits for nonpublic education.

Reactions to the Papal Visit — Pope John Paul — personally magnetic, profoundly attentive to human dignity, straightforward and secure in doctrinal and moral posture — captivated the attention and heart of the country during his pastoral visits to six major cities Oct. 1 to 7.

There were, however, some mixed reactions.

• Dr. Claire Randall, general secretary of the National Conference of Churches, was critical of his traditional stand against the ordination of women to the priesthood. "This is something that I and many women and men, both Protestant and Catholic, cannot accept," she said.

• Rabbi Marc Tanenbaum, director of interreligious affairs of the American Jewish Committee, said there was a positive response to the Pope for making the tragedy of Auschwitz his point of departure when addressing the United Nations. He felt, however, that the Holy Father paid inadequate respect to the nation's 150 million non-Catholics.

• Another rabbi, Abraham Hecht, president of the Rabbinical Alliance of America, said the Pope's statements upholding morality and family life were "enthusiastically welcomed by religious Jews."

• Bishop John M. Allin, presiding bishop of the Episcopal Church, was impressed with the pastoral concern demonstrated by the Pope.

Reactions on the Catholic side were much more positive.

• There were, however, headline-catching critics of doctrinal and moral positions stated by the Pontiff before the extraordinary meeting with the U.S. bishops Oct. 5 and on other occasions during the visit. They commented, in effect, that the Pope needed some education to bring him into touch with what they called the pluralism and reality of the Church in the United States.

INTERNATIONAL

Panama Gets Canal — In accordance with treaties ratified in 1977, sovereignty of the Canal Zone passed to Panama as provisions went into effect for joint U.S.-Panamanian operation of the canal until it comes under complete Panamanian control in 2000. The bishops' conference there, which had supported the treaties, took the occasion of the transfer to declare in a statement: "There is still the very crucial task which is precisely to start the Panamanians and society in general toward a truly democratic community with justice for all. It must be a society in search of development and full participation by all its members, a society that shows special concern for the poor, for those left out of the mainstream, the defenseless."

Cardinal Suenens Resigns — The resignation of Cardinal Leo J. Suenens of Malines-Brussels was accepted by Pope John Paul. The cardinal, a major figure in proceedings of the Second Vatican Council, had submitted the resignation on reaching the age of 75 in July.

Priest Forced Out of Haiti — Father Francilys Petithomme, pastor of a poor parish in Port-de-Paix, was forced to leave Haiti after being threatened with death by government groups opposed to his work for social change.

Polish Priests Found Guilty — Two Polish priests were recently found guilty of having begun construction work on churches without government permission; both were fined and one of them was sentenced to a year in prison.

Melkite Observance and Plans — The Holy Synod of the Melkite-Rite Patriarchate of Antioch announced plans for the celebration in November of the 1600th anniversary of the death of St. Basil the Great. The synod also announced a number of decisions to:

• forbid the practice of "collective absolution";

• reactivate an ecumenical commission and encourage dialogue with the Greek Orthodox Church of Antioch;

• establish a general fund for clergy support;

• require priests to wear cassocks.

New Government in El Salvador — A few days after a military coup overthrew the repressive government, Archbishop Oscar Romero of San Salvador called on the new regime to deliver on its promises of democracy and justice. He said the coup, after three years of political violence, could be considered legitimate since the conditions for a just rebellion against tyranny were there, but noted: "We want to establish very definitely that this government shall deserve the trust and cooperation of the people only when it shows that its promises are not dead words but a guarantee that a new era has begun for our nation."

Nobel Prize for Mother Teresa — The Norwegian Nobel Committee announced the award of the 1979 Nobel Peace Prize to Mother Teresa of Calcutta, foundress of the Missionaries of Charity devoted especially to the care of the dying poor and lepers. In making the award, the committee said it was expressing "its recognition of Mother Teresa's work in bringing help to suffering humanity." On learning of the award, Mother Teresa said, "Thank God for his gift for the poor."

Mother Teresa was born of Albanian parents in Yugoslavia in 1910. She joined the Loreto Sisters in Ireland at the age of 18 and taught school in India until 1948. A year or two later, she founded the Missionaries of Charity to serve the poorest of the poor. In 1952, she opened the Nirmal Hriday (Pure Heart) Home for Dying Destitutes in a dormitory, formerly a Kali temple hostel, donated by the city of Calcutta. Although some of those taken into the home survived, its primary function was, as one Missionary of Charity explained, to be "a shelter where the dying poor may die in dignity." More than 30,000 persons have been brought to the home since it opened. The Missionaries of Charity began caring for lepers in 1957. The community now has about 1,200 members, thousands of auxiliaries and other supporters, and establishments in 30 cities of India and 20 other countries.

Dates and Events in Church History

First Century

Early 30's: First Christian Pentecost: gathering together of the Christian community, outpouring of the Holy Spirit, preaching of St. Peter to Jews in Jerusalem, baptism and aggregation of some 3,000 persons to the Christian community.

St. Stephen, deacon, was stoned to death at Jerusalem; he is venerated as the first Christian martyr.

34-64/67: St. Paul, formerly Saul the persecutor of Christians, was converted, baptized and joined to the college of Apostles. After three major missionary journeys, he was martyred in 64 or 67 at Rome.

39: The Gentile Cornelius and his family were baptized by St. Peter.

42: Persecution of Christians in Palestine broke out during the rule of Herod Agrippa; St. James the Greater, the first Apostle to die, was beheaded in 44; St. Peter was imprisoned for a short time; many Christians fled to Antioch and elsewhere.

At Antioch, the followers of Christ were first called Christians.

49: Christians at Rome, who were considered members of a Jewish sect, were adversely affected by a decree of Claudius which forbade Jewish worship there.

51: The Council of Jerusalem, in which all the Apostles participated under the presidency of St. Peter, decreed that circumcision, dietary regulations, and various other prescriptions of Mosaic Law were not obligatory for Gentile converts to the Christian community. The decree was issued in opposition to Judaizers who contended that observance of the Mosaic Law in its entirety was necessary for salvation.

64: Persecution under Nero: The emperor, accusing Christians of starting a fire which destroyed half of Rome, inaugurated the era of major Roman persecutions.

64/65: Martyrdom of St. Peter at Rome during the Neronian persecution. He established his see and spent his last years there after preaching in and around Jerusalem, establishing a see at Antioch, and presiding at the Council of Jerusalem.

70: Destruction of Jerusalem by Titus.

88-97: Pontificate of St. Clement I, third successor of St. Peter as bishop of Rome, one of the Apostolic Fathers. The *First Epistle of Clement to the Corinthians,* with which he has been identified, was addressed by the Church of Rome to the Church at Corinth, the scene of irregularities and divisions in the Christian community.

95: Domitian persecuted Christians, principally at Rome.

c. 100: Death of St. John, Apostle and Evangelist, marking the end of the Age of the Apostles and the first generation of the Church.

Second Century

c. 107: St. Ignatius of Antioch was martyred at Rome. He was the first writer to use the expression, "the Catholic Church."

112: Rescript to Pliny. Emperor Trajan instructed Pliny, governor of Bithynia, not to search out Christians but to punish them if they were publicly denounced and refused to do homage to the Roman gods. The rescript set a pattern of discretionary leniency for Roman magistrates in dealing with Christians.

117-138: Persecution under Hadrian. Many *Acts of Martyrs* date from this period.

c. 125: Spread of Gnosticism.

c. 155: St. Polycarp, bishop of Smyrna and disciple of St. John the Evangelist, was martyred.

c. 156: Beginning of Montanism.

161-180: Reign of Marcus Aurelius. His persecution, launched in the wake of natural disasters, was more violent than those of his predecessors.

165: St. Justin, an important early Christian writer, was martyred at Rome.

c. 180: St. Irenaeus, bishop of Lyons and one of the great early theologians, wrote *Adversus Haereses.* He stated that the teaching and tradition of the Roman See was the standard for belief.

196: Easter Controversy.

The *Didache,* written in the second century, was an important record of Christian belief, practice and government in the first century.

Latin was introduced in the West as a liturgical language.

The Catechetical School of Alexandria, founded about the middle of the century, increased in importance.

Third Century

202: Persecution under Septimius Severus, who wanted to establish one common religion in the Empire.

206: Tertullian, a convert since 197 and the first great ecclesiastical writer in Latin, joined the heretical Montanists. He died in 230.

215: Death of Clement of Alexandria, teacher of Origen and a founding father of the School of Alexandria.

217-235: St. Hippolytus, the first antipope. He was reconciled to the Church while in prison during persecution in 235.

232-254: Origen established the School of Caesarea after being deposed in 231 as head of the School of Alexandria; he died in 254. A scholar and voluminous writer, he was one of the founders of systematic theology and exerted wide influence for many years.

c. 242: Manichaeism originated in Persia.

249-251: Persecution under Decius. Many of those who denied the faith *(lapsi)* sought readmission to the Church at the end of the persecution in 251. Pope St. Cornelius had correspondence with St. Cyprian on the subject and ordered that *lapsi* were to be readmitted after suitable penance.

250-300: Neo-Platonism of Plotinus and Porphyry gained followers.

251: Novatian, an antipope, was condemned at Rome.

256: Pope St. Stephen I upheld the validity of baptism administered by heretics, in the Rebaptism Controversy.

257: Persecution under Valerian, who attempted to destroy the Church as a social structure.

258: St. Cyprian, bishop of Carthage, was martyred.

c. 260: St. Lucian founded the exegetical School of Antioch.

Pope St. Dionysius condemned teachings of Sabellius and the Marcionites.

St. Paul of Thebes became a hermit.

261: Gallienus issued an edict of toleration which ended general persecution for nearly 40 years.

c. 266: Sabellianism was condemned and Paul of Samosata deposed.

292: Diocletian divided the Roman Empire into East and West. The division emphasized political, cultural and other differences between the two parts of the Empire and influenced the Church in the East and West. The prestige of Rome began to decline.

Fourth Century

303: Persecution broke out under Diocletian. It ended in the West in 306 but continued for 10 years in the East; it was particularly violent in 304.

305: St. Anthony of Heracles established a foundation for hermits near the Red Sea in Egypt.

c. 306: The first local legislation on clerical celibacy was enacted by a council held at Elvira, Spain; bishops, priests, deacons and other ministers were forbidden to have wives.

310: St. Hilarion established a foundation for hermits in Palestine.

311: An edict of toleration issued by Galerius at the urging of Constantine and Licinius officially ended persecution in the West; some persecution continued in the East.

313: The *Edict of Milan* issued by Constantine and Licinius recognized Christianity as a lawful religion and the legal freedom of all religions in the Roman Empire.

314: The Council of Arles condemned Donatism in Africa and declared that baptism by heretics was valid.

318: St. Pachomius established the first foundation of the cenobitic (common) life, as compared with the solitary life of hermits in Upper Egypt.

325: The Ecumenical Council of Nicaea (I), first of its kind in the history of the Church, condemned Arianism; see separate entry.

326: Discovery of the True Cross on which Christ was crucified.

337: Baptism and death of Constantine.

c. 342: Beginning of a 40-year persecution in Persia.

343-344: A local Council of Sardica reaffirmed doctrine formulated by Nicaea I and declared that bishops had the right of appeal to the pope as the highest authority in the Church.

361-363: Julian the Apostate waged an unsuccessful campaign against the Church in an attempt to restore paganism as the religion of the Empire.

c. 365: Persecution under Valens in the East.

c. 376: Beginning of the barbarian invasion in the West.

379: Death of St. Basil, the Father of Monasticism in the East. His writings contributed greatly to the development of rules for the religious life.

381: The Ecumenical Council of Constantinople (I); see separate entry.

382: The *Decree of Pope St. Damasus* listed the Canon of Sacred Scripture.

382-c. 406: St. Jerome translated the Old and New Testaments into Latin. His work is called the Vulgate Version of the Bible.

396: St. Augustine became bishop of Hippo in North Africa.

397: A local Council of Carthage published the Canon of Sacred Scripture.

Fifth Century

410: Visigoths sacked Rome.

411: Donatism was condemned by a council at Carthage.

430: St. Augustine, bishop of Hippo for 35 years, died. He was a strong defender of orthodox doctrine against Manichaeism, Donatism and Pelagianism. The depth and range of his writings made him a dominant influence in Christian thought for many centuries.

431: The Ecumenical Council of Ephesus; see separate entry.

432: St. Patrick arrived in Ireland. By the time of his death in 461 most of the country had been converted, monasteries founded and the hierarchy established.

438: The *Theodosian Code,* a compilation of decrees for the Empire, was issued by Theodosius II. It had great influence on subsequent civil and ecclesiastical law.

449: The Robber Council of Ephesus, which did not have ecclesiastical sanction, declared itself in favor of the opinions of Eutyches who contended that Christ had only one nature.

451: The Ecumenical Council of Chalcedon; see separate entry.

452: Pope St. Leo the Great persuaded Attila the Hun to spare Rome.

455: Vandals sacked Rome. The decline of

imperial Rome dates approximately from this time.

484: Patriarch Acacius of Constantinople was excommunicated for signing the *Henoticon*, a unity law published by Emperor Zeno in 482 to end the turmoil associated with the Monophysite heresy. The document capitulated to the heresy. The excommunication triggered a 35-year-long schism.

494: Pope St. Gelasius I declared in a letter to Emperor Anastasius that the pope had power and authority over the emperor in spiritual matters.

496: Clovis, King of the Franks, was converted and became the defender of Christianity in the West. The Franks became a Catholic people.

Sixth Century

520 and later: Irish monasteries flourished as centers for spiritual life, missionary training and scholarly activity.

529: The Second Council of Orange condemned Semi-Pelagianism.

c. 529: St. Benedict founded the Monte Cassino Abbey. Some years before his death in 543 he wrote a monastic rule which exercised tremendous influence on the form and style of religious life. He is called the Father of Monasticism in the West.

533: John II became the first pope to change his name. The practice did not become general until the time of Sergius IV (1009).

533-534: Emperor Justinian promulgated the *Corpus Juris Civilis* for the Roman world. Like the *Theodosian Code*, it influenced subsequent civil and ecclesiastical law.

c. 545: Death of Dionysius Exiguus who was the first to date history from the birth of Christ, a practice which resulted in use of the B.C. and A.D. abbreviations. His calculations were at least four years late.

553: The Ecumenical Council of Constantinople (II); see separate entry.

585: St. Columban founded an influential monastic school at Luxeuil. He died in 615.

589: The most important of several councils of Toledo was held. The Visigoths renounced Arianism, and St. Leander began the organization of the Church in Spain.

590-604: Pontificate of Pope St. Gregory I the Great. He set the form and style of the papacy which prevailed throughout the Middle Ages; exerted great influence on doctrine and liturgy; was strong in support of monastic discipline and clerical celibacy; authored writings on many subjects. Gregorian Chant is named in his honor.

596: Pope St. Gregory I the Great sent St. Augustine of Canterbury and 40 monks to do missionary work in England.

597: St. Columba died. He founded an important monastery at Iona, established schools and did notable missionary work in Scotland.

By the end of the century, monasteries of nuns were common; Western monasticism was flourishing; monasticism in the East, under the influence of Monophysitism and other factors, was losing its vigor.

Seventh Century

613: St. Columban established the influential Monastery of Bobbio in northern Italy.

622: The Hegira (flight) of Mohammed from Mecca to Medina signalled the beginning of Islam, which, by the end of the century, claimed almost all of the southern Mediterranean area.

629: Emperor Heraclius recovered the True Cross from the Persians.

649: A Lateran Council condemned two erroneous formulas *(Ecthesis* and *Type)* issued by emperors Heraclius and Constans II as means of reconciling Monophysites with the Church.

664: Actions of the Synod of Whitby advanced the adoption of Roman usages in England, especially regarding the date for the observance of Easter. (See Easter Controversy.)

680-681: The Ecumenical Council of Constantinople (III); see separate entry.

692: Trullan Synod. Eastern-Church discipline on clerical celibacy was settled, permitting marriage before ordination to the diaconate and continuation in marriage afterwards, but prohibiting marriage following the death of the wife thereafter. Anti-Roman canons contributed to East-West alienation.

During the century, the monastic influence of Ireland and England increased in Western Europe; schools and learning declined; regulations regarding clerical celibacy became more strict in the East.

Eighth Century

711: Moslems began the conquest of Spain.

726: Emperor Leo III, the Isaurian, launched a campaign against the veneration of sacred images and relics; called Iconoclasm (image-breaking), it caused turmoil in the East until about 843.

731: Pope Gregory II and a synod at Rome condemned Iconoclasm, with a declaration that the veneration of sacred images was in accord with Catholic tradition.

Venerable Bede issued his *Ecclesiastical History of the English People*.

732: Charles Martel defeated the Moslems at Poitiers, halting farther advance by them in the West.

744: The Monastery of Fulda was established by St. Sturm, a disciple of St. Boniface.

754: A council of more than 300 Byzantine bishops endorsed Iconoclast errors. This council and its actions were condemned by the Lateran Synod of 769.

Stephen II (III) crowned Pepin ruler of the Franks. Pepin twice invaded Italy, in 754 and 756, to defend the pope against the Lombards. His land grants to the papacy, called the Donation of Pepin, were later extended by Charlemagne (773) and formed part of the States of the Church.

c. 755: St. Boniface (Winfrid) was martyred. He was called the Apostle of Germany for his missionary work and organization of the hierarchy there.

781: Alcuin was chosen by Charlemagne to organize a Palace School, which became a center of intellectual leadership.

787: The Ecumenical Council of Nicaea (II); see separate entry.

792: A council at Ratisbon condemned Adoptionism.

The famous *Book of Kells* ("The Great Gospel of Columcille") dates from the early eighth or late seventh century.

Ninth Century

800: Charlemagne was crowned Emperor by Pope Leo III on Christmas Day.

Egbert became king of West Saxons. He unified England and strengthened the See of Canterbury.

813: Emperor Leo V, the Armenian, revived Iconoclasm, which persisted until about 843.

814: Charlemagne died.

843: The Treaty of Verdun split the Frankish kingdom among Charlemagne's three grandsons.

844: A Eucharistic controversy involving the writings of Paschasius Radbertus, Ratramnus and Rabanus Maurus occasioned the development of terminology regarding the doctrine of the Real Presence.

846: The Moslems invaded Italy and attacked Rome.

847-852: Period of composition of the *False Decretals*, a collection of forged documents attributed to popes from St. Clement (88-97) to Gregory II (715-731). The *Decretals*, which strongly supported the autonomy and rights of bishops, were suspect for a long time before being repudiated entirely about 1628.

848: The Council of Mainz condemned Gottschalk for heretical teaching regarding predestination. He was also condemned by the Council of Quierzy in 853.

857: Photius displaced Ignatius as patriarch of Constantinople. This marked the beginning of the Photian Schism, a confused state of East-West relations which has not yet been cleared up by historical research. Photius, a man of exceptional ability, died in 891.

865: St. Ansgar, Apostle of Scandinavia, died.

868: Sts. Cyril (d. 869) and Methodius (d. 885) were consecrated bishops. The Apostles of the Slavs devised an alphabet and translated the Gospels and liturgy into the Slavonic language.

869: The Ecumenical Council of Constantinople (IV); see separate entry.

871-c. 900: Reign of Alfred the Great, the only English king ever anointed by a pope at Rome.

Tenth Century

910: William, Duke of Aquitaine, founded the Benedictine Abbey of Cluny, which became a center of monastic and ecclesiastical reform.

915: Pope John X played a leading role in the expulsion of Saracens from central and southern Italy.

955: St. Olga, of the Russian royal family, was baptized.

962: Otto I, the Great, crowned by Pope John XII, revived Charlemagne's kingdom, which became the Holy Roman Empire.

966: Mieszko, first of a royal line in Poland, was baptized; he brought Latin Christianity to Poland.

989: Vladimir, ruler of Russia, was baptized. Russia was subsequently Christianized by Greek missionaries.

993: John XV was the first pope to decree the official canonization of a saint (Ulrich) for the universal Church.

997: St. Stephen became ruler of Hungary. He assisted in organizing the hierarchy and establishing Latin Christianity in that country.

999-1003: Pontificate of Sylvester II (Gerbert of Aquitaine), a Benedictine monk and the first French pope.

Eleventh Century

1009: Beginning of lasting East-West schism in the Church, marked by dropping of the name of Pope Sergius IV from the Byzantine diptychs (the listing of persons prayed for during the liturgy). The deletion was made by Patriarch Sergius II of Constantinople.

1012: St. Romuald founded the Camaldolese Hermits.

1025: The Council of Arras, and other councils later, condemned the Cathari (Neo-Manichaeans, Albigenses).

1027: The Council of Elne proclaimed the Truce of God as a means of stemming violence. The truce involved armistice periods of varying length, which were later extended.

1038: St. John Gualbert founded the Vallombrosians.

1043-1059: Constantinople patriarchate of Michael Cerularius, the key figure in a controversy concerning the primacy of the papacy. His and the Byzantine synod's refusal to acknowledge this primacy in 1054 widened and hardened the East-West schism in the Church.

1047: Pope Clement II died. He was the only pope ever buried in Germany.

1049-54: Pontificate of St. Leo IX, who inaugurated a movement of papal, diocesan, monastic and clerical reform.

1055: Condemnation of the Eucharistic doctrine of Berengarius.

1059: A Lateran Council issued new legislation regarding papal elections. Voting power was entrusted to the Roman cardinals.

1066: Death of St. Edward the Confessor, King of England from 1042 and restorer of Westminster Abbey.

Defeat, at Hastings, of Harold by William I, who subsequently exerted strong influence on the life style of the Church in England.

1073-1085: Pontificate of St. Gregory VII (Hildebrand). A strong pope, he carried forward programs of clerical and general ecclesiastical reform and struggled against Henry IV and other rulers to end the evils of lay investiture. He introduced the Latin liturgy in Spain and set definite dates for the observance of ember days.

1077: Henry IV, excommunicated and suspended from the exercise of imperial powers by Gregory VII, sought absolution from the Pope at Canossa. Henry later repudiated this action and in 1084 forced Gregory to leave Rome.

1079: The Council of Rome condemned Eucharistic errors of Berengarius, who retracted.

1084: St. Bruno founded the Carthusians.

1097-1099: The first of several Crusades undertaken between this time and 1265. Recovery of the Holy Places and gaining free access to them for Christians were the original purposes, but these were diverted to less worthy objectives in various ways. Results included: a Latin Kingdom of Jerusalem, 1099-1187; a military and political misadventure in the form of a Latin Empire of Constantinople, 1204-1261; acquisition, by treaties, of visiting rights for Christians in the Holy Land. East-West economic and cultural relationships increased during the period. In the religious sphere, actions of the Crusaders had the effect of increasing the alienation of the East from the West.

1098: St. Robert founded the Cistercians.

Twelfth Century

1108: Beginnings of the influential Abbey and School of St. Victor.

1115: St. Bernard established the Abbey of Clairvaux and inaugurated the Cistercian Reform.

1118: Christian forces captured Saragossa, Spain; the beginning of the Moslem decline in that country.

1121: St. Norbert established the original monastery of the Praemonstratensians near Laon, France.

1122: The Concordat of Worms (Pactum Callixtinum) was formulated and approved by Pope Callistus II and Emperor Henry V to settle controversy concerning the investiture of prelates. The concordat provided that the emperor could invest prelates with symbols of temporal authority but had no right to invest them with spiritual authority, which came from the Church alone, and that the emperor was not to interfere in papal elections. This was the first concordat in history.

1123: The Ecumenical Council of the Lateran (I), the first of its kind in the West; see separate entry.

1139: The Ecumenical Council of the Lateran (II); see separate entry.

1140: St. Bernard met Abelard in debate at the Council of Sens. Abelard, whose rationalism in theology was condemned for the first time in 1121, died in 1142 at Cluny.

1148: The Synod of Rheims enacted strict disciplinary decrees for communities of women religious.

1152: The Synod of Kells reorganized the Church in Ireland.

1160: Gratian, whose *Decretum* became a basic text of Canon Law, died.

Peter Lombard, compiler of the *Four Books of Sentences,* a standard theology text for nearly 200 years, died.

1170: St. Thomas Becket, archbishop of Canterbury, who clashed with Henry II over Church-state relations, was murdered in his cathedral.

1171: Pope Alexander III reserved the process of canonization of saints to the Holy See.

1179: The Ecumenical Council of the Lateran (III); see separate entry.

1184: Waldenses and other heretics were excommunicated by Pope Lucius III.

Thirteenth Century

1198-1216: Pontificate of Innocent III, during which the papacy reached its medieval peak of authority, influence and prestige in the Church and in relations with civil rulers.

1208: Innocent III called for a crusade, the first in Christendom itself, against the Albigensians.

1209: Verbal approval was given by Innocent III to a rule of life for the Order of Friars Minor, started by St. Francis of Assisi.

1212: The Second Order of Franciscans, the Poor Clares, was founded.

1215: The Ecumenical Council of the Lateran (IV); see separate entry.

1216: Formal papal approval was given to a rule of life for the Order of Preachers, started by St. Dominic.

The Portiuncula Indulgence was granted by the Holy See at the request of St. Francis of Assisi.

1221: The Third Order of St. Francis for lay persons was founded.

1226: Death of St. Francis of Assisi.

1245: The Ecumenical Council of Lyons (I); see separate entry.

1247: Preliminary approval was given by the Holy See to a Carmelite rule of life.

1270: St. Louis IX, king of France, died.

Beginning of papal decline.

1274: The Ecumenical Council of Lyons (II); see separate entry.

Death of St. Thomas Aquinas, Doctor of the Church, of lasting influence; see separate entry.

1280: Pope Nicholas III, who made the *Breviary* the official prayer book for clergy of the Roman Church, died.

1281: The excommunication of Michael Palaeologus by Pope Martin IV ruptured the union effected with the Eastern Church in 1274.

Fourteenth Century

1302: Pope Boniface VIII issued the bull *Unam Sanctam,* concerning the unity of the Church and the temporal power of princes, against the background of a struggle with Philip IV of France; it was the most famous medieval document on the subject.

1308-1378: For a period of approximately 70 years, seven popes resided at Avignon because of unsettled conditions in Rome and other reasons; see separate entry.

1311-1312: The Ecumenical Council of Vienne; see separate entry.

1321: Dante Alighieri died a year after completing the *Divine Comedy.*

1324: Marsilius of Padua completed *Defensor Pacis*, a work condemned by Pope John XXII as heretical because of its denial of papal primacy and the hierarchical structure of the Church, and for other reasons. It was a charter for conciliarism.

1337-1453: Period of the Hundred Years' War, a dynastic struggle between France and England.

1338: Four years after the death of Pope John XXII, who had opposed Louis IV of Bavaria in a years-long controversy, electoral princes declared at the Diet of Rhense that the emperor did not need papal confirmation of his title and right to rule. Charles IV later (1356) said the same thing in a *Golden Bull,* eliminating papal rights in the election of emperors.

1347-1350: The Black Death swept across Europe, killing perhaps one-fourth to one-third of the total population; an estimated 40 per cent of the clergy succumbed.

1374: Petrarch, poet and humanist, died.

1378: Return of the papacy from Avignon to Rome.

Beginning of the Western Schism; see separate entry.

Fifteenth Century

1409: The Council of Pisa, without canonical authority, tried to end the Western Schism but succeeded only in complicating it by electing a third claimant to the papacy; see Western Schism.

1414-1418: The Ecumenical Council of Constance ended the Western Schism; see separate entry.

1431: St. Joan of Arc was burned at the stake.

1431-1449: The Council of Basle, which began with convocation by Pope Martin V in 1431, turned into an anti-papal forum of conciliarists seeking to subject the primacy and authority of the pope to the overriding authority of an assembly of bishops. It was not an ecumenical council.

1438: The Pragmatic Sanction of Bourges was enacted by Charles VIII and the French parliament to curtail papal authority over the Church in France, in the spirit of conciliarism. It found expression in Gallicanism and had effects lasting at least until the French Revolution.

1438-1443: The Ecumenical Council of Florence affirmed the primacy of the pope in opposition to conciliarism and effected a measure of union with separated Eastern Christians; see separate entry.

1453: The fall of Constantinople to the Turks.

c. 1456: Gutenberg issued the first edition of the Bible printed from movable type, at Mainz, Germany.

1476: Pope Sixtus IV ordered observance of the feast of the Immaculate Conception on Dec. 8 throughout the Church.

1492: Columbus discovered the Americas.

1493: Pope Alexander VI issued a *Bull of Demarcation* which determined spheres of influence for the Spanish and Portuguese in the Americas.

The Renaissance, a humanistic movement which originated in Italy in the 14th century, spread to France, Germany, the Low Countries and England. A transitional period between the medieval world and the modern secular world, it introduced profound changes which affected literature and the other arts, general culture, politics and religion.

Sixteenth Century

1512-1517: The Ecumenical Council of the Lateran (V); see separate entry.

1517: Martin Luther signalled the beginning of the Reformation by posting 95 theses at Wittenberg. Subsequently, he broke completely from doctrinal orthodoxy in discourses and three published works (1519 and 1520); was excommunicated on more than 40 charges of heresy (1521); remained the dominant figure in the Reformation in Germany until his death in 1546.

1519: Zwingli triggered the Reformation in Zurich and became its leading proponent there until his death in combat in 1531.

1524: Luther's encouragement of German princes in putting down the two-year Peasants' Revolt gained political support for his cause.

1528: The Order of Friars Minor Capuchin was approved as an autonomous division of the Franciscan Order; like the Jesuits, the Capuchins became leaders in the Counter-Reformation.

1530: The *Augsburg Confession* of Lutheran faith was issued; it was later supplemented by the *Smalcald Articles* approved in 1537.

1533: Henry VIII divorced Catherine of Aragon, married Anne Boleyn, was excommunicated. In 1534 he decreed the Act of Supremacy, making the sovereign the head of the Church in England, under which Sts. John Fisher and Thomas More were executed in 1535. Despite his rejection of papal primacy and actions against monastic life in England, he generally maintained doctrinal orthodoxy until his death in 1547.

1536: John Calvin, leader of the Reformation in Switzerland until his death in 1564, issued the first edition of *Institutes of the Christian Religion,* which became the classical text of Reformed (non-Lutheran) theology.

1540: The constitutions of the Society of Jesus (Jesuits), founded by St. Ignatius of Loyola, were approved.

1541: Start of the 11-year career of St. Francis Xavier as a missionary to the East Indies and Japan.

1545-1563: The Ecumenical Council of Trent formulated statements of Catholic doctrine under attack by the Reformers and mobilized the Counter-Reformation; see separate entry.

1549: The first *Book of Common Prayer* was issued by Edward VI. Revised editions were published in 1552, 1559 and 1662.

1553: Start of the five-year reign of Mary Tudor who tried to counteract actions of Henry VIII against the Roman Church.

1555: Enactment of the Peace of Augsburg, an arrangement of religious territorialism rather than toleration, which recognized the existence of Catholicism and Lutheranism in the German Empire and provided that citizens should adopt the religion of their respective rulers.

1558: Beginning of the reign of Elizabeth I, during which the Church of England took on its definitive form.

1559: Establishment of the hierarchy of the Church of England, with the consecration of Matthew Parker as archbishop of Canterbury.

1563: The first text of the *39 Articles* of the Church of England was issued. Also enacted were a new Act of Supremacy and Oath of Succession to the English throne.

1570: Elizabeth I was excommunicated. Penal measures against Catholics subsequently became more severe.

1571: Defeat of the Turkish armada at Lepanto staved off the invasion of Eastern Europe.

1577: The *Formula of Concord,* the classical statement of Lutheran faith, was issued; it was, generally, a Lutheran counterpart of the canons of the Council of Trent. In 1580, along with other formulas of doctrine, it was included in the *Book of Concord.*

1582: The Gregorian Calendar, named for Pope Gregory XIII, was put into effect and was eventually adopted in most countries; England delayed adoption until 1752.

Seventeenth Century

1605: The Gunpowder Plot, an attempt by Catholic fanatics to blow up James I of England and the houses of Parliament, resulted in an anti-Catholic Oath of Allegiance; the Oath was condemned by Pope Paul V in 1606.

1610: Death of Matteo Ricci, outstanding Jesuit missionary to China, pioneer in cultural relations between China and Europe.

Founding of the first community of Visitation Nuns by Sts. Francis de Sales and Jane de Chantal.

1611: Founding of the Oratorians.

1613: Catholics were banned from Scandinavia.

1625: Founding of the Congregation of the Mission (Vincentians) by St. Vincent de Paul. He founded the Sisters of Charity in 1633.

1642: Death of Galileo, scientist, who was censured by the Congregation of the Holy Office for supporting the Copernican theory of the sun-centered planetary system.

Founding of the Sulpicians by Jacques Olier.

1643: Start of publication of the Bollandist *Acta Sanctorum,* a critical work on lives of the saints.

1648: Provisions in the Peace of Westphalia, ending the Thirty Years' War, extended terms of the Peace of Augsburg (1555) to Calvinists and gave equality to Catholics and Protestants in the 300 states of the Holy Roman Empire.

1649: Oliver Cromwell invaded Ireland and began a severe persecution of the Church there.

1653: Pope Innocent X condemned five propositions of Jansenism, a complex theory which distorted doctrine concerning the relations between divine grace and human freedom. Jansenism was also a rigoristic movement which seriously disturbed the Church in France, the Low Countries and Italy in this and the 18th century.

1673: The Test Act in England barred from public office Catholics who would not deny the doctrine of transubstantiation and receive Communion in the Church of England.

1678: Many English Catholics suffered death as a consequence of the Popish Plot, a false allegation by Titus Oates that Catholics planned to assassinate Charles I, land a French army in the country, burn London, and turn over the government to the Jesuits.

1682: The four articles of the *Gallican Declaration,* drawn up by Bossuet, asserted political and ecclesiastical immunities of France from papal control. The articles, which rejected the primacy of the pope, were condemned in 1690.

1689: The Toleration Act granted a measure of freedom of worship to other English dissenters but not to Catholics.

This century is called the age of Enlightenment or Reason because of the predominating rational and scientific approach of its leading philosophers, scientists and writers with respect to religion, ethics and natural law. This approach downgraded the fact and significance of revealed religion. Also characteristic of the Enlightenment were subjectivism, secularism and optimism regarding human perfectibility.

Eighteenth Century

1704: Chinese Rites—involving the Christian adaptation of elements of Confucianism, veneration of ancestors and Chinese terminology in religion — were condemned by Clement XI. An earlier ban was issued in 1645; a later one, in 1742.

1720: The Passionists were founded by St. Paul of the Cross.

1724: Persecution in China.

1732: The Redemptorists were founded by St. Alphonsus Liguori.

1738: Freemasonry was condemned by Clement XII and Catholics were forbidden to join, under penalty of excommunication; the prohibition was repeated by Benedict XIV in 1751 and by later popes.

1760's: Josephinism, a theory and system of state control of the Church, was initiated in Austria; it remained in force until about 1850.

1764: Febronianism, an unorthodox theory and practice regarding the constitution of the Church and relations between Church and state, was condemned for the first of several times. Proposed by an auxiliary bishop of Trier using the pseudonym Justinus Febronius, it had the effects of minimizing the office of the pope and supporting national churches under state control.

1773: Clement XIV issued a brief of suppression against the Jesuits, following their expulsion from Portugal in 1759, from France in 1764 and from Spain in 1767. Political intrigue and unsubstantiated accusations were principal factors in these developments. The ban, which crippled the Society, contained no condemnation of the Jesuit constitutions, particular Jesuits or Jesuit teaching. The Society was restored in 1814.

1778: Catholics in England were relieved of some civil disabilities dating back to the time of Henry VIII, by an act which permitted them to acquire, own and inherit property. Additional liberties were restored by the Roman Catholic Relief Act of 1791 and subsequent enactments of Parliament.

1789: Religious freedom in the United States was guaranteed under the First Amendment to the Constitution.

Beginning of the French Revolution which resulted in: the secularization of church property and the Civil Constitution of the Clergy in 1790; the persecution of priests, religious and lay persons loyal to papal authority; invasion of the Papal States by Napoleon in 1796; renewal of persecution from 1797-1799; attempts to dechristianize France and establish a new religion; the occupation of Rome by French troops and the forced removal of Pius VI to France in 1798.

Nineteenth Century

1809: Pius VII was made a captive by Napoleon and deported to France where he remained in exile until 1814. During this time he refused to cooperate with Napoleon who sought to bring the Church in France under his own control.

The turbulence in church-state relations in France at the beginning of the century recurred in connection with the Bourbon Restoration, the July Revolution, the second and third Republics, the Second Empire and the Dreyfus case.

1814: The Society of Jesus, suppressed since 1773, was restored.

1817: Reestablishment of the Congregation for the Propagation of the Faith (Propaganda) by Pius VII was an important factor in increasing missionary activity during the century.

1820: Years-long persecution, during which thousands died for the faith, ended in China. Thereafter, communication with the West remained cut off until about 1834. Vigorous missionary work got underway in 1842.

1822: The Pontifical Society for the Propagation of the Faith, inaugurated in France by Pauline Jaricot for the support of missionary activity, was established.

1829: The Catholic Emancipation Act relieved Catholics in England and Ireland of most of the civil disabilities to which they had been subject from the time of Henry VIII.

1832: Gregory XVI, in the encyclical *Mirari Vos*, condemned indifferentism, one of the many ideologies at odds with Christian doctrine which were proposed during the century.

1833: Start of the Oxford Movement which affected the Church of England and resulted in some notable conversions, including that of John Henry Newman in 1845, to the Catholic Church.

Frederick Ozanam founded the Society of St. Vincent de Paul in France. The society, whose objective was works of charity, became worldwide.

1848: The *Communist Manifesto*, a revolutionary document symptomatic of socio-economic crisis, was issued.

1850: The hierarchy was reestablished in England and Nicholas Wiseman made the first archbishop of Westminster. He was succeeded in 1865 by Henry Manning, an Oxford convert and proponent of the rights of labor.

1853: The Catholic hierarchy was reestablished in Holland.

1854: Pius IX proclaimed the dogma of the Immaculate Conception in the bull *Ineffabilis Deus*.

1858: The Blessed Virgin Mary appeared to

St. Bernadette at Lourdes, France; see separate entry.

1864: Pius IX issued the encyclical *Quanta Cura* and the *Syllabus of Errors* in condemnation of some 80 propositions derived from the scientific mentality and rationalism of the century. The subjects in question had deep ramifications in many areas of thought and human endeavor; in religion, they explicitly and/or implicitly rejected divine revelation and the supernatural order.

1867: The first volume of *Das Kapital* was published. Together with the Communist First International, formed in the same year, it had great influence on the subsequent development of Communism and Socialism.

1869: The Anglican Church was disestablished in Ireland.

1869-1870: The First Vatican Council; see separate entry.

1870-1871: Victor Emmanuel II of Sardinia, crowned king of Italy after defeating Austrian and papal forces, marched into Rome in 1870 and expropriated the Papal States after a plebiscite in which Catholics, at the order of Pius IX, did not vote In 1871, Pius IX refused to accept a Law of Guarantees. Confiscation of church property and hindrance of ecclesiastical administration by the regime followed.

1871: The German Empire, a confederation of 26 states, was formed. Government policy launched a Kulturkampf whose May Laws of 1873 were designed to annul papal jurisdiction in Prussia and other states and to place the Church under imperial control. Resistance to the enactments and the persecution they legalized forced the government to modify its anti-Church policy by 1887.

1878: Beginning of the pontificate of Leo XIII, who was pope until his death in 1903. Leo is best known for the encyclical *Rerum Novarum*, which greatly influenced the course of Christian social thought and the labor movement. His other accomplishments included promotion of a revival of Scholastic philosophy and the impetus he gave to scriptural studies.

1881: The first International Eucharistic Congress was held in Lille, France.

Alexander II of Russia died. His policies of Russification — as well as those of his two predecessors and a successor during the century — caused great suffering to Catholics, Jews and Protestants in Poland, Lithuania, the Ukraine and Bessarabia.

1882: Charles Darwin died. His theory of evolution by natural selection, one of several scientific highlights of the century, had extensive repercussions in the faith-and-science controversy.

1889: The Catholic University of America was founded in Washington, D.C.

1893: The US apostolic delegation was set up in Washington, D.C.

Twentieth Century

1901: Restrictive measures in France forced the Jesuits, Benedictines, Carmelites and other religious orders to leave the country. Subsequently, 14,000 schools were suppressed; religious orders and congregations were expelled; the concordat was renounced in 1905; church property was confiscated in 1906. For some years the Holy See, refusing to comply with government demands for the control of bishops' appointments, left some ecclesiastical offices vacant.

1903: Start of the 11-year pontificate of St. Pius X. He initiated the codification of canon law, 1904; removed the ban against participation by Catholics in Italian national elections, 1905; issued decrees calling upon the faithful to receive Holy Communion frequently and daily, and stating that children should begin receiving the Eucharist at the age of seven, 1905 and 1910, respectively; ordered the establishment of the Confraternity of Christian Doctrine in all parishes throughout the world, 1905; condemned Modernism in the decree *Lamentabili* and the encyclical *Pascendi*, 1907.

1908: The United States and England, long under the jurisdiction of the Congregation for the Propagation of the Faith as mission territories, were removed from its control and placed under the common law of the Church.

1910: Laws of separation were enacted in Portugal, marking a point of departure in church-state relations.

1911: The Catholic Foreign Mission Society of America — Maryknoll, the first US-founded society of its type — was established.

1914: Start of World War I, which lasted until 1918.

Start of the eight-year pontificate of Benedict XV. Much of his pontificate was devoted to seeking ways and means of minimizing the material and spiritual havoc of World War I. In 1917 he offered his services as a mediator to the belligerent nations, but his pleas for settlement of the conflict went unheeded.

1917: The Blessed Virgin Mary appeared to three children at Fatima, Portugal; see separate entry.

A new constitution, embodying repressive laws against the Church, was enacted in Mexico. Its implementation resulted in persecution in the 1920's and 1930's.

Bolsheviks seized power in Russia and set up a Communist dictatorship. The event marked the rise of Communism in Russian and world affairs. One of its immediate, and lasting, results was persecution of the Church, Jews and other segments of the population.

1918: The *Code of Canon Law*, in preparation for more than 10 years, went into effect in the Western Church.

1919: Benedict XV stimulated missionary work through the decree *Maximum Illud*, in which he urged the recruiting and training of native clergy in places where the Church was not firmly established.

1922: Beginning of the 17-year pontificate of Pius XI. He subscribed to the Lateran Treaty, 1929, which settled the Roman Question created by the confiscation of the Papal States in 1871; issued the encyclical *Casti Connubii,* 1930, an authoritative statement on Christian marriage; resisted the efforts of Benito Mussolini to control Catholic Action and the Church, in the encyclical *Non Abbiamo Bisogno,* 1931; opposed various Fascist policies; issued the encyclicals *Quadragesimo Anno,* 1931, developing the social doctrine of Leo XIII's *Rerum Novarum,* and *Divini Redemptoris,* 1937, calling for social justice and condemning atheistic Communism; condemned anti-Semitism, 1937.

Ireland was partitioned. All but two of the predominantly Catholic counties were included in the southern part of the country, which eventually attained the status of an independent republic in 1949.

1926: The Catholic Relief Act repealed virtually all legal disabilities of Catholics in England.

1931: Leftists proclaimed Spain a republic and proceeded to disestablish the Church, confiscate church property, deny salaries to the clergy, expel the Jesuits and ban teaching of the Catholic faith. These actions were preludes to the civil war of 1936-1939.

1933: Emergence of Adolf Hitler to power in Germany. By 1935 two of his aims were clear, the elimination of the Jews and control of a single national church. Persecution decimated the Jews over a period of years. The Church was subject to repressive measures, which Pius XI protested futilely in the encyclical *Mit Brennender Sorge* in 1937.

1936: A three-year civil war broke out in Spain between the leftist Loyalists and forces led by Francisco Franco. The Loyalists were defeated and one-man, one-party rule was established. A number of priests, religious and lay persons fell victims to Loyalist persecution.

1939: Start of World War II, which lasted until 1945.

Start of the 19-year pontificate of Pius XII; see separate entry.

1940: Start of a decade of Communist conquest in more than 13 countries, resulting in conditions of persecution for a minimum of 60 million Catholics as well as members of other faiths; see various countries.

Persecution diminished in Mexico through non-enforcement of anti-religious laws still on record.

1950: Pius XII proclaimed the dogma of the Assumption of the Blessed Virgin Mary.

1954: St. Pius X was canonized.

1957: The Communist regime of China attempted to start a national schismatic church.

1958: Beginning of the five-year pontificate of John XXIII; see separate entry.

1962: The Second Vatican Council began the first of four sessions; see separate entry.

1963: Beginning of 15-year pontificate of Paul VI; see separate entry.

1978: Thirty-four-day pontificate of John Paul I; see separate entry.

Beginning of pontificate of John Paul II; see separate entry.

HERESIES

Heresy is the formal and obstinate denial or doubt by a baptized person, who remains a nominal Christian, of any truth which must be believed as a matter of divine and Catholic faith. Formal heresy involves deliberate resistance to the authority of God who communicates revelation through Scripture and tradition and the teaching authority of the Church. Obstinate refusal to accept the infallible teaching of the Church constitutes the canonical crime of heresy.

Formal heretics automatically incur the penalty of excommunication (Canon 1325 of the Code of Canon Law). Material heretics are those who, in good faith and without formal obstinacy, do not accept articles or matters of divine and Catholic faith.

Heresies have been significant not only as disruptions of unity of faith but also as occasions for the clarification and development of doctrine.

Heresies from the beginning of the Church to the 13th century are listed below.

Judaizers: Early converts who claimed that members of the Church had to observe all the requirements of Mosaic Law as well as the obligations of Christian faith. This view was condemned by the Council of Jerusalem held in 51 under the presidency of St. Peter (Acts 15:28).

Gnosticism: A combination of elements of Platonic philosophy and Eastern mystery religions which claimed that its secret knowledge-principle gave its adherents a deeper insight into Christian doctrine than divine revelation and faith. One Gnostic thesis denied the divinity of Christ; others denied the reality of his humanity, calling it mere appearance (**Docetism, Phantasiasm**).

Modalism: A general term covering propositions (**Monarchianism, Patripassianism, Sabellianism**) that the Father, Son and Holy Spirit are not really distinct divine Persons but are only three different modes of being and self-manifestation of the one God. Various forms of Modalism, which appeared in the East in the second century and spread westward, were all condemned.

Marcionism: A Gnostic creation named for its author, who claimed there was total opposition and no connection at all between the Old Testament and the New Testament, between the God of the Jews and the God of the Christians; and that the canon of Scripture consisted only of portions of Luke's Gospel and 10 Epistles of Paul. Marcion was excommunicated in 144 at Rome, and his tenets were condemned again by a Roman council about 260. The heresy was checked at Rome by 200 but persisted for several centuries in the East and had some adherents as late as the Middle Ages.

Montanism: A form of extremism preached about 170 by Montanus of Phrygia, Asia Minor. Its principal tenets were: an imminent second coming of Christ, denial of the divine nature of the Church and its power to forgive sin, excessively rigorous morality. Condemned by Pope St. Zephyrinus (199-217). Tertullian was one of its victims.

Novatianism: A heresy of excessive rigorism named for its author, a priest of Rome and antipope. Its principal tenet was that persons who fell away from the Church under persecution and/or those guilty of serious sin after baptism could not be absolved and readmitted to communion with the Church. The heresy, condemned by a Roman synod in 251, slowly subsided in the West and died in the East by the end of the seventh century.

Subordinationism, Adoptionism: Christological errors and logical antecedents of Arianism. The key tenet was that Christ, while the most excellent of creatures, was subordinate to God whose Son he was by adoption rather than by nature. First proposed at Rome late in the second century, it was condemned by Pope St. Victor in 190 and again in the following century, in 785 by Pope Adrian I, in 794 by a Council of Frankfurt, and in 1177 by Pope Alexander III.

Arianism: Denial of the divinity of Christ, the most devastating of the early heresies, authored by Arius of Alexandria and condemned by the Council of Nicaea I in 325. Arians and several kinds of **Semi-Arians** propagandized their tenets widely, raised havoc in the Church for several centuries, and established their own hierarchies and churches.

Macedonianism: Denial of the divinity of the Holy Spirit, who was said to be a creature of the Son. Condemned by the Council of Constantinople I in 381. Macedonians were also called **Pneumatomachists,** enemies of the Spirit; and **Marathonians,** after the name of one of their leaders, a bishop of Nicomedia.

Nestorianism: Denial of the real unity of divine and human natures in the single divine Person of Christ, proposed by Nestorius, patriarch of Constantinople. He also held that Mary could not be called the Mother of God *(Theotokos);* that is, of the Second Person of the Trinity made Man. Condemned by the councils of Ephesus in 431 and Chalcedon in 451.

Monophysitism: Denial of Christ's human nature; also called **Eutychianism,** after the name of one of its leading advocates. Condemned by the Council of Chalcedon in 451.

Monothelitism: Denial of the human will of Christ. Severus of Antioch and Sergius, patriarch of Constantinople, were leading advocates of the heresy, which was condemned by the Council of Constantinople III in 681.

Priscillianism: A fourth century amalgamation of elements from various sources — Sabellianism, Arianism, Docetism, Pantheism, belief in the diabolical nature of marriage, corruption of Scripture. Condemned by a Council of Braga in 563 on 17 different counts.

Donatism: A development of the error at the heart of the third century **Rebaptism Controversy** (baptism conferred by heretics is invalid because persons deprived of grace are incapable of being ministers of grace to others). Followers of Donatus the Great asserted throughout the fourth century that sacraments administered by sinners were invalid. Condemnation of the heresy is traced to Pope St. Stephen I (254-257) and the principle that sacraments have their efficacy from Christ, not from their human ministers.

Pelagianism: Denial of the supernatural order of things, proposed by Pelagius (360-420), a Breton monk. Proceeding from the assumption that Adam had a natural right to supernatural life, the theory held that man could attain salvation through the efforts of his own free will and natural powers. The theory involved errors concerning the nature of original sin, the meaning of grace and other matters. St. Augustine opposed the heresy, which was condemned by the Council of Ephesus in 431. **Semi-Pelagianism** was condemned by a Council of Orange in 529.

Iconoclasm: An image-breaking campaign which resulted from an edict issued by Eastern Emperor Leo the Isaurian in 726, that the veneration of images, pictures and relics was idolatrous. The theoretical basis of the heresy was the Monophysite error which denied the humanity of Christ. It was denounced several times before its condemnation by the Council of Nicaea II in 787.

Berengarian Heresy: Denial of the Real Presence of Christ under the appearances of bread and wine, the first clear-cut Eucharistic heresy; proposed by Berengarius of Tours (c. 1000-1088). Condemned by various synods and finally by a council held at Rome in 1079.

Waldensianism: Claimed by Peter Waldo, a merchant of Lyons, to be a return to pure Christianity, the heresy rejected the hierarchical structure of the Church, the sacramental system and other doctrines. Its adherents were excommunicated in 1184 and their tenets were condemned several times thereafter.

Albigensianism, Catharism: Related errors based on the old **Manichaean** assumption that two supreme principles of good and evil were operative in creation and life, and that the supreme objective of human endeavor was liberation from evil (matter). The heresy denied the humanity of Christ, the sacramental system and the authority of the Church (and state), and endorsed a moral code which threatened seriously the fabric of social life in southern France and northern Italy in the 12th and 13th centuries. Condemned by councils of the Lateran III and Lateran IV in 1179 and 1215.

ECUMENICAL COUNCILS

An ecumenical council is an assembly of the college of bishops, with and under the presidency of the pope, which has supreme authority over the Church in matters pertaining to faith, morals, worship and discipline.

The Second Vatican Council stated: "The supreme authority with which this college (of bishops) is empowered over the whole Church is exercised in a solemn way through an ecumenical council. A council is never ecumenical unless it is confirmed or at least accepted as such by the successor of Peter. It is the prerogative of the Roman Pontiff to convoke these councils, to preside over them, and to confirm them" (*Dogmatic Constitution on the Church*, No. 22).

Pope Presides

The pope is the head of an ecumenical council; he presides over it either personally or through legates. Conciliar decrees and other actions have binding force only when confirmed and promulgated by him. If a pope dies during a council, it is suspended until reconvened by another pope. An ecumenical council is not superior to a pope; hence, there is no appeal from a pope to a council.

Collectively, the bishops with the pope represent the whole Church. They do this not as democratic representatives of their faithful in a kind of church parliament, but as the successors of the Apostles with divinely given authority, care and responsibility over the whole Church.

Council participants with a deliberative vote are: cardinals; residential patriarchs, primates, archbishops and bishops, even if they are not yet consecrated; abbots and certain other prelates, an abbot primate, abbot superiors of monastic congregations and heads of exempt clerical religious; titular bishops, on invitation. Experts in theology and canon law may be given a consultative vote. Others, including lay persons, may address a council or observe its actions, but may not vote.

Basic legislation concerning ecumenical councils is contained in Canons 222-229 of the Code of Canon Law. Basic doctrinal considerations were stated by the Second Vatican Council in the *Dogmatic Constitution on the Church*.

Background

Ecumenical councils had their prototype in the Council of Jerusalem in 51, at which the Apostles under the leadership of St. Peter decided that converts to the Christian faith were not obliged to observe all the prescriptions of Old Testament law (Acts 15). As early as the second century, bishops got together in regional meetings, synods or councils to take common action for the doctrinal and pastoral good of their communities of faithful. The expansion of such limited assemblies to ecumenical councils was a logical and historical evolution, given the nature and needs of the Church.

Emperors were active in summoning or convoking the first eight councils, especially the first five and the eighth. Among reasons for intervention of this kind were the facts that the emperors regarded themselves as guardians of the faith; that the settlement of religious controversies, which had repercussions in political and social turmoil, served the cause of peace in the state; and that the emperors had at their disposal ways and means of facilitating gatherings of bishops. Imperial actions, however, did not account for the formally ecumenical nature of the councils.

Some councils were attended by relatively few bishops, and the ecumenical character of several was open to question for a time. However, confirmation and de facto recognition of their actions by popes and subsequent councils established them as ecumenical.

Role in History

The councils have played a highly significant role in the history of the Church by witnessing to and defining truths of revelation, by shaping forms of worship and discipline, and by promoting measures for the ever-necessary reform and renewal of Catholic life. In general, they have represented attempts of the Church to mobilize itself in times of crisis for self-preservation, self-purification and growth.

The first eight ecumenical councils were held in the East; the other 13, in the West. The majority of separated Eastern Churches — e.g., the Orthodox — recognize the ecumenical character of the first seven councils, which formulated a great deal of basic doctrine. Nestorians, however, acknowledge only the first two councils; the Monophysite Armenians, Syrians, and Copts acknowledge the first three.

The 21 Councils

The 21 ecumenical councils in the history of the Church are listed below, with indication of their names or titles (taken from the names of the places where they were held); the dates; the reigning and/or approving popes; the emperors who were instrumental in convoking the first eight councils in the East; the number of bishops who attended, when available; the number of sessions; the most significant actions.

1. Nicaea I, 325: St. Sylvester I (Emperor Constantine I); attended by approximately 300 bishops; sessions held between May 20 or June 19 to near the end of August. Condemned Arianism, which denied the divinity of Christ; contributed to formulation of the Nicene Creed; fixed the date of Easter; passed regulations concerning clerical discipline; adopted the civil division of the Empire as the model for the organization of the Church.

2. Constantinople I, 381: St. Damasus I (Emperor Theodosius I); attended by approximately 150 bishops; sessions held from May to July. Condemned various brands of Arianism, and Macedonianism which denied the divinity of the Holy Spirit; contributed to formulation of the Nicene Creed; approved a canon which made the bishop of Constantinople the ranking prelate in the East, with primacy next to that of the pope. Doubt about the ecumenical character of this council was resolved by the ratification of its acts by popes and the Council of Chalcedon.

3. Ephesus, 431: St. Celestine I (Emperor Theodosius II); attended by 150 to 200 bishops; five sessions held between June 22 and July 17. Condemned Nestorianism, which denied the real unity of the divine and human natures in the Person of Christ; defined *Theotokos* ("Bearer of God") as the title of Mary, Mother of the Son of God made Man; condemned Pelagianism, which reduced the supernatural to the natural order of things.

4. Chalcedon, 451: St. Leo I (Emperor Marcian); attended by approximately 600 bishops; 17 sessions held between Oct. 8 and Nov. 1. Condemned: Monophysitism, also called Eutychianism, which denied the humanity of Christ by holding that he had only one, the divine, nature; and the Monophysite Robber Synod of Ephesus, of 449.

5. Constantinople II, 553: Vigilius (Emperor Justinian I); attended by 165 bishops; eight sessions held between May 5 and June 2. Condemned the *Three Chapters,* Nestorian-tainted writings of Theodore of Mopsuestia, Theodoret of Cyprus and Ibas of Edessa.

6. Constantinople III, 680-681: St. Agatho, St. Leo II (Emperor Constantine IV); attended by approximately 170 bishops; 16 sessions held between Nov. 7, 680, and Sept. 16, 681. Condemned Monothelitism, which held that there was only one will, the divine, in Christ; censured Pope Honorius I for a letter to Sergius, bishop of Constantinople, in which he made an ambiguous but not infallible statement about the unity of will and/or operation in Christ. Constantinople III is also called the Trullan Council because its sessions were held in the domed hall, Trullos, of the imperial palace.

7. Nicaea II, 787: Adrian I (Empress Irene); attended by approximately 300 bishops; eight sessions held between Sept. 24 and Oct. 23. Condemned: Iconoclasm, which held that the use of images was idolatry; and Adoptionism, which claimed that Christ was not the Son of God by nature but only by adoption. This was the last council regarded as ecumenical by Orthodox Churches.

8. Constantinople IV, 869-870: Adrian II (Emperor Basil I); attended by 102 bishops; six sessions held between Oct. 5, 869, and Feb. 28, 870. Condemned Iconoclasm; condemned and deposed Photius as patriarch of Constantinople; restored Ignatius to the patriarchate. This was the last ecumenical council held in the East. It was first called ecumenical by canonists toward the end of the 11th century.

9. Lateran I, 1123: Callistus II; attended by approximately 300 bishops; sessions held between Mar. 18 and Apr. 6. Endorsed provisions of the Concordat of Worms concerning the investiture of prelates: approved reform measures in 25 canons.

10. Lateran II, 1139: Innocent II; attended by 900 to 1,000 bishops and abbots; three sessions held in April. Adopted measures against a schism organized by antipope Anacletus; approved 30 disciplinary measures and canons, one of which stated that holy orders is an invalidating impediment to marriage.

11. Lateran III, 1179: Alexander III; attended by at least 300 bishops; three sessions held between Mar. 5 and 19. Enacted measures against the Waldenses and Albigensians; approved reform decrees in 27 canons; provided that popes be elected by two-thirds vote of the cardinals.

12. Lateran IV, 1215: Innocent III; sessions held between Nov. 11 and 30. Ordered annual confession and Communion; defined and made first official use of the term "transubstantiation"; adopted measures to counteract the Cathari and Albigensians; approved 70 canons.

13. Lyons I, 1245: Innocent IV; attended by approximately 150 bishops; three sessions held between June 28 and July 17. Confirmed the deposition of Emperor Frederick II; approved 22 canons.

14. Lyons II, 1274: Gregory X; attended by approximately 500 bishops; six sessions held between May 7 and July 17. Accomplished a temporary reunion of separated Eastern Churches with the Roman Church; issued regulations concerning conclaves for papal elections; approved 31 canons.

15. Vienne, 1311-1312: Clement V; attended by 132 bishops; three sessions held between Oct. 16, 1311, and May 6, 1312. Suppressed the Knights Templar; enacted a number of reform decrees.

16. Constance, 1414-1418: Gregory XII, Martin V; attended by nearly 200 bishops, plus other prelates and many experts; 45 sessions held between Nov. 5, 1414, and Apr. 22, 1418. Took successful action to end the Western Schism; rejected the teachings of Wycliff; condemned Hūs as a heretic. One decree, passed in the earlier stages of the council, asserted the superiority of an ecumenical council over the pope; this was later rejected.

17. Florence (also called Basel-Ferrara-Florence), 1438-1445: Eugene IV; attended by many Latin-Rite and Eastern-Rite bishops; preliminary sessions were held at Basel and Ferrara before definitive work was accomplished at Florence. Reaffirmed the primacy of the pope against the claims of Conciliarists that an ecumenical council is superior to the pope; formulated and approved decrees of union — with the Greeks, July 6, 1439; with the Armenians, Nov. 22, 1439; with the Jacobites, Feb. 4, 1442. These decrees failed to gain general or lasting acceptance in the East.

18. Lateran V, 1512-1517: Julius II, Leo X; 12 sessions held between May 3, 1512, and Mar. 16, 1517. Stated the relation and position of the pope with respect to an ecumenical council; acted to counteract the Pragmatic Sanction of Bourges and exaggerated claims of liberty by the French Church; condemned erroneous teachings concerning the nature of the human soul; stated doctrine concerning indulgences. The council reflected concern for abuses in the Church and the need for reforms but failed to take decisive action in the years immediately preceding the Reformation.

19. Trent, 1545-1563: Paul III, Julius III, Pius IV; 25 sessions held between Dec. 13, 1545, and Dec. 4, 1563. Issued a great number of decrees concerning doctrinal matters opposed by the Reformers, and mobilized the Counter-Reformation. Definitions covered the rule of faith, the nature of justification, grace, faith, original sin and its effects, the seven sacraments, the sacrificial nature of the Mass, the veneration of saints, use of sacred images, belief in purgatory, the doctrine of indulgences, the jurisdiction of the pope over the whole Church. Initiated many reforms for renewal in the liturgy and general discipline in the Church, the promotion of religious instruction, the education of the clergy through the foundation of seminaries, etc. Trent ranks with Vatican II as the greatest ecumenical council held in the West.

20. Vatican I, 1869-1870: Pius IX; attended by approximately 800 bishops and other prelates; four public sessions and 89 general meetings held between Dec. 8, 1869, and July 7, 1870. Defined papal primacy and infallibility in a dogmatic constitution on the Church; covered natural religion, revelation, faith, and the relations between faith and reason in a dogmatic constitution on the Catholic faith. The council suspended sessions Sept. 1 and was adjourned Oct. 20, 1870.

Vatican II

The Second Vatican Council, which was forecast by Pope John XXIII Jan. 25, 1959, was held in four sessions in St. Peter's Basilica.

Pope John convoked it and opened the first session, which ran from Oct. 11 to Dec. 8, 1962. Following John's death June 3, 1963, Pope Paul VI reconvened the council for the other three sessions which ran from Sept. 29 to Dec. 4, 1963; Sept. 14 to Nov. 21, 1964; Sept. 14 to Dec. 8, 1965.

A total of 2,860 Fathers participated in council proceedings, and attendance at meetings varied between 2,000 and 2,500. For various reasons, including the denial of exit from Communist-dominated countries, 274 Fathers could not attend.

The council formulated and promulgated 16 documents — two dogmatic and two pastoral constitutions, nine decrees and three declarations — all of which reflect its basic pastoral orientation toward renewal and reform in the Church. Given below are the Latin and English titles of the documents and their dates of promulgation.

- *Lumen Gentium* (Dogmatic Constitution on the Church), Nov. 21, 1964.
- *Dei Verbum* (Dogmatic Constitution on Divine Revelation), Nov. 18, 1965.
- *Sacrosanctum Concilium* (Constitution on the Sacred Liturgy), Dec. 4, 1963.
- *Gaudium et Spes* (Pastoral Constitution on the Church in the Modern World), Dec. 7, 1965.
- *Christus Dominus* (Decree on the Bishops' Pastoral Office in the Church), Oct. 28, 1965.
- *Ad Gentes* (Decree on the Church's Missionary Activity), Dec. 7, 1965.
- *Unitatis Redintegratio* (Decree on Ecumenism), Nov. 21, 1964.
- *Orientalium Ecclesiarum* (Decree on Eastern Catholic Churches), Nov. 21, 1964.
- *Presbyterorum Ordinis* (Decree on the Ministry and Life of Priests), Dec. 7, 1965.
- *Optatam Totius* (Decree on Priestly Formation), Oct. 28, 1965.
- *Perfectae Caritatis* (Decree on the Appropriate Renewal of the Religious Life), Oct. 28, 1965.
- *Apostolicam Actuositatem* (Decree on the Apostolate of the Laity), Nov. 18, 1965.
- *Inter Mirifica* (Decree on the Instruments of Social Communication), Dec. 4, 1963.
- *Dignitatis Humanae* (Declaration on Religious Freedom), Dec. 7, 1965.
- *Nostra Aetate* (Declaration on the Relationship of the Church to Non-Christian Religions), Oct. 28, 1965.
- *Gravissimum Educationis* (Declaration on Christian Education), Oct. 28, 1965.

The key documents were the four constitutions, which set the ideological basis for all the others. To date, the documents with the most visible effects are those on the liturgy, the Church, the Church in the world, ecumenism, the renewal of religious life, the life and ministry of priests, the lay apostolate.

The main business of the council was to explore and make explicit dimensions of doctrine and Christian life requiring emphasis for the full development of the Church and the better accomplishment of its mission in the contemporary world.

Popes

LIST OF POPES
(Source: *Annuario Pontificio.*)

Information includes the name of the pope, in many cases his name before becoming pope, his birthplace or country of origin, the date of accession to the papacy, and the date of the end of reign which, in all but a few cases, was the date of death. Double dates indicate times of election and coronation.

St. Peter (Simon Bar-Jona): Bethsaida in Galilee; d. c. 67.
St. Linus: Tuscany; 67-76.
St. Anacletus (Cletus): Rome; 76-88.
St. Clement: Rome; 88-97.
St. Evaristus: Greece; 97-105.
St. Alexander I: Rome; 105-115.
St. Sixtus I: Rome; 115-125.
St. Telesphorus: Greece; 125-136.
St. Hyginus: Greece; 136-140.
St. Pius I: Aquileia; 140-155.
St. Anicetus: Syria; 155-166.
St. Soter: Campania; 166-175.
St. Eleutherius: Nicopolis in Epirus; 175-189.

Up to the time of St. Eleutherius, the years indicated for the beginning and end of pontificates are not absolutely certain. Also, up to the middle of the 11th century, there are some doubts about the exact days and months given in chronological tables.

St. Victor I: Africa; 189-199.
St. Zephyrinus: Rome; 199-217.
St. Callistus I: Rome; 217-222.
St. Urban I: Rome; 222-230.
St. Pontian: Rome; July 21, 230, to Sept. 28, 235.
St. Anterus: Greece; Nov. 21, 235, to Jan. 3, 236.
St. Fabian: Rome; Jan. 10, 236, to Jan. 20, 250.
St. Cornelius: Rome; Mar., 251, to June, 253.
St. Lucius I: Rome; June 25, 253, to Mar. 5, 254.
St. Stephen I: Rome; May 12, 254, to Aug. 2, 257.
St. Sixtus II: Greece; Aug. 30, 257, to Aug. 6, 258.
St. Dionysius: July 22, 259, to Dec. 26, 268.
St. Felix I: Rome; Jan. 5, 269, to Dec. 30, 274.
St. Eutychian: Luni; Jan. 4, 275, to Dec. 7, 283.
St. Caius: Dalmatia; Dec, 17, 283, to Apr. 22, 296.
St. Marcellinus: Rome; June 30, 296, to Oct. 25, 304.
St. Marcellus I: Rome; May 27, 308, or June 26, 308, to Jan. 16, 309.
St. Eusebius: Greece; Apr. 18, 309 or 310, to Aug. 17, 309 or 310.
St. Melchiades (**Miltiades**): Africa; July 2, 311, to Jan. 11, 314.
St. Sylvester I: Rome; Jan. 31, 314, to Dec. 31, 335. (Most of the popes before St. Sylvester I were martyrs.)
St. Marcus: Rome; Jan. 18, 336, to Oct. 7, 336.
St. Julius I: Rome; Feb. 6, 337, to Apr. 12, 352.
Liberius: Rome; May 17, 352, to Sept. 24, 366.
St. Damasus I: Spain; Oct. 1, 366, to Dec. 11, 384.
St. Siricius: Rome; Dec. 15, or 22 or 29, 384, to Nov. 26, 399.
St. Anastasius I: Rome; Nov. 27, 399, to Dec. 19, 401.
St. Innocent I: Albano; Dec. 22, 401, to Mar. 12, 417.
St. Zozimus: Greece; Mar. 18, 417, to Dec. 26, 418.
St. Boniface I: Rome; Dec. 28 or 29, 418, to Sept. 4, 422.
St. Celestine I: Campania; Sept. 10, 422, to July 27, 432.
St. Sixtus III: Rome; July 31, 432, to Aug. 19, 440.
St. Leo I (the Great): Tuscany; Sept. 29, 440, to Nov. 10, 461.
St. Hilary: Sardinia; Nov. 19, 461, to Feb. 29, 468.
St. Simplicius: Tivoli; Mar. 3, 468, to Mar. 10, 483.
St. Felix III (II): Rome; Mar. 13, 483, to Mar. 1, 492.

He should be called Felix II, and his successors of the same name should be numbered accordingly. The discrepancy in the numerical designation of popes named Felix was caused by the erroneous insertion in some lists of the name of St. Felix of Rome, a martyr.

St. Gelasius I: Africa; Mar. 1, 492, to Nov. 21, 496.
Anastasius II: Rome; Nov. 24, 496, to Nov. 19, 498.
St. Symmachus: Sardinia; Nov. 22, 498, to July 19, 514.
St. Hormisdas: Frosinone; July 20, 514, to Aug. 6, 523.
St. John I, Martyr: Tuscany; Aug. 13, 523, to May 18, 526.
St. Felix IV (III): Samnium; July 12, 526, to Sept. 22, 530.
Boniface II: Rome; Sept. 22, 530, to Oct. 17, 532.
John II: Rome; Jan. 2, 533, to May 8, 535.

John II was the first pope to change his name. His given name was Mercury.

St. Agapitus I: Rome; May 13, 535, to Apr. 22, 536.
St. Silverius, Martyr: Campania; June 1 or 8, 536, to Nov. 11, 537 (d. Dec. 2, 537).

St. Silverius was violently deposed in March, 537, and abdicated Nov. 11, 537. His successor, Vigilius, was not recognized as pope by all the Roman clergy until his abdication.

Vigilius: Rome; Mar. 29, 537, to June 7, 555.

Pelagius I: Rome; Apr. 16, 556, to Mar. 4, 561.

John III: Rome; July 17, 561, to July 13, 574.

Benedict I: Rome; June 2, 575, to July 30, 579.

Pelagius II: Rome; Nov. 26, 579, to Feb. 7, 590.

St. Gregory I (the Great): Rome; Sept. 3, 590, to Mar. 12, 604.

Sabinian: Blera in Tuscany; Sept. 13, 604, to Feb. 22, 606.

Boniface III: Rome; Feb. 19, 607, to Nov. 12, 607.

St. Boniface IV: Abruzzi; Aug. 25, 608, to May 8, 615.

St. Deusdedit (Adeodatus I): Rome; Oct. 19, 615, to Nov. 8, 618.

Boniface V: Naples; Dec. 23, 619, to Oct. 25, 625.

Honorius I: Campania; Oct. 27, 625, to Oct. 12, 638.

Severinus: Rome; May 28, 640, to Aug. 2, 640.

John IV: Dalmatia; Dec. 24, 640, to Oct. 12, 642.

Theodore I: Greece; Nov. 24, 642, to May 14, 649.

St. Martin I, Martyr: Todi; July, 649, to Sept. 16, 655 (in exile from June 17, 653).

St. Eugene I: Rome; Aug. 10, 654, to June 2, 657.

St. Eugene I was elected during the exile of St. Martin I, who is believed to have endorsed him as pope.

St. Vitalian: Segni; July 30, 657, to Jan. 27, 672.

Adeodatus II: Rome; Apr. 11, 672, to June 17, 676.

Donus: Rome; Nov. 2, 676, to Apr. 11, 678.

St. Agatho: Sicily; June 27, 678, to Jan. 10, 681.

St. Leo II: Sicily; Aug. 17, 682, to July 3, 683.

St. Benedict II: Rome; June 26, 684, to May 8, 685.

John V: Syria; July 23, 685, to Aug. 2, 686.

Conon: birthplace unknown; Oct. 21, 686, to Sept. 21, 687.

St. Sergius I: Syria; Dec. 15, 687, to Sept. 8, 701.

John VI: Greece; Oct. 30, 701, to Jan. 11, 705.

John VII: Greece; Mar. 1, 705, to Oct. 18, 707.

Sisinnius: Syria; Jan. 15, 708, to Feb. 4, 708.

Constantine: Syria; Mar. 25, 708, to Apr. 9, 715.

St. Gregory II: Rome; May 19, 715, to Feb. 11, 731.

St. Gregory III: Syria; Mar. 18, 731, to Nov., 741.

St. Zachary: Greece; Dec. 10, 741, to Mar. 22, 752.

Stephen II (III): Rome; Mar. 26, 752, to Apr. 26, 757.

After the death of St. Zachary, a Roman priest named Stephen was elected but died (four days later) before his consecration as bishop of Rome, which would have marked the beginning of his pontificate. Another Stephen was elected to succeed Zachary as Stephen II. (The first pope with this name was St. Stephen I, 254-57.) The ordinal III appears in parentheses after the name of Stephen II because the name of the earlier elected but deceased priest was included in some lists. Other Stephens have double numbers.

St. Paul I: Rome; Apr. (May 29), 757, to June 28, 767.

Stephen III (IV): Sicily; Aug. 1 (7), 768, to Jan. 24, 772.

Adrian I: Rome; Feb. 1 (9), 772, to Dec. 25, 795.

St. Leo III: Rome; Dec. 26 (27), 795, to June 12, 816.

Stephen IV (V): Rome; June 22, 816, to Jan. 24, 817.

St. Paschal I: Rome; Jan. 25, 817, to Feb. 11, 824.

Eugene II: Rome; Feb. (May), 824, to Aug., 827.

Valentine: Rome; Aug. 827, to Sept., 827.

Gregory IV: Rome; 827, to Jan., 844.

Sergius II: Rome; Jan., 844 to Jan. 27, 847.

St. Leo IV: Rome; Jan. (Apr. 10), 847, to July 17, 855.

Benedict III: Rome; July (Sept. 29), 855, to Apr. 17, 858.

St. Nicholas I (the Great): Rome; Apr. 24, 858, to Nov. 13, 867.

Adrian II: Rome; Dec. 14, 867, to Dec. 14, 872.

John VIII: Rome; Dec. 14, 872, to Dec. 16, 882.

Marinus I: Gallese; Dec. 16, 882, to May 15, 884.

St. Adrian III: Rome; May 17, 884, to Sept., 885. Cult confirmed June 2, 1891.

Stephen V (VI): Rome; Sept., 885, to Sept. 14, 891.

Formosus: Portus; Oct. 6, 891, to Apr. 4, 896.

Boniface VI: Rome; Apr., 896, to Apr., 896.

Stephen VI (VII): Rome; May, 896, to Aug., 897.

Romanus: Gallese; Aug., 897, to Nov., 897.

Theodore II: Rome; Dec., 897, to Dec., 897.

John IX: Tivoli; Jan., 898, to Jan., 900.

Benedict IV: Rome; Jan. (Feb.), 900, to July, 903.

Leo V: Ardea; July, 903, to Sept., 903.

Sergius III: Rome; Jan. 29, 904, to Apr. 14, 911.

Anastasius III: Rome; Apr., 911, to June, 913.

Landus: Sabina; July, 913, to Feb., 914.

John X: Tossignano (Imola); Mar., 914, to May, 928.

Leo VI: Rome; May, 928, to Dec., 928.

Stephen VII (VIII): Rome; Dec., 928, to Feb., 931.

John XI: Rome; Feb. (Mar.), 931, to Dec., 935.

Leo VII: Rome; Jan. 3, 936, to July 13, 939.

Stephen VIII (IX): Rome; July 14, 939, to Oct., 942.

Marinus II: Rome; Oct. 30, 942, to May, 946.

Agapitus II: Rome; May 10, 946, to Dec., 955.

John XII (Octavius): Tusculum; Dec. 16, 955, to May 14, 964 (date of his death).

Leo VIII: Rome; Dec. 4 (6), 963, to Mar. 1, 965.

Benedict V: Rome; May 22, 964, to July 4, 966.

Confusion exists concerning the legitimacy of claims to the pontificate by Leo VIII and Benedict V. John XII was deposed Dec. 4, 963, by a Roman council. If this deposition was invalid, Leo was an antipope. If the deposition of John was valid, Leo was the legitimate pope and Benedict was an antipope.

John XIII: Rome; Oct. 1, 965, to Sept. 6, 972.

Benedict VI: Rome; Jan. 19, 973, to June, 974.

Benedict VII: Rome; Oct. 974, to July 10, 983.

John XIV (Peter Campenora): Pavia; Dec., 983, to Aug. 20, 984.

John XV: Rome; Aug., 985, to Mar., 996.

Gregory V (Bruno of Carinthia): Saxony; May 3, 996, to Feb. 18, 999.

Sylvester II (Gerbert): Auvergne; Apr. 2, 999, to May 12, 1003.

John XVII (Siccone): Rome; June, 1003, to Dec., 1003.

John XVIII (Phasianus): Rome; Jan., 1004, to July, 1009.

Sergius IV (Peter): Rome; July 31, 1009, to May 12, 1012.

The custom of changing one's name on election to the papacy is generally considered to date from the time of Sergius IV. Before his time, several popes had changed their names. After his time, this became a regular practice, with few exceptions; e.g., Adrian VI and Marcellus II.

Benedict VIII (Theophylactus): Tusculum; May 18, 1012, to Apr. 9, 1024.

John XIX (Romanus): Tusculum; Apr. (May), 1024, to 1032.

Benedict IX (Theophylactus): Tusculum; 1032, to 1044.

Sylvester III (John): Rome; Jan. 20, 1045, to Feb. 10, 1045.

Sylvester III was an antipope if the forcible removal of Benedict IX in 1044 was not legitimate.

Benedict IX (second time): Apr. 10, 1045, to May 1, 1045.

Gregory VI (John Gratian): Rome; May 5, 1045, to Dec. 20, 1046.

Clement II (Suitger, Lord of Morsleben and Hornburg): Saxony; Dec. 24 (25), 1046, to Oct. 9, 1047.

If the resignation of Benedict IX in 1045 and his removal at the December, 1046, synod were not legitimate, Gregory VI and Clement II were antipopes.

Benedict IX (third time): Nov. 8, 1047, to July 17, 1048 (d. c. 1055).

Damasus II (Poppo): Bavaria; July 17, 1048, to Aug. 9, 1048.

St. Leo IX (Bruno): Alsace; Feb. 12, 1049, to Apr. 19, 1054.

Victor II (Gebhard): Swabia; Apr. 16, 1055, to July 28, 1057.

Stephen IX (X) (Frederick): Lorraine; Aug. 3, 1057, to Mar. 29, 1058.

Nicholas II (Gerard): Burgundy; Jan. 24, 1059, to July 27, 1061.

Alexander II (Anselmo da Baggio): Milan; Oct. 1, 1061, to Apr. 21, 1073.

St. Gregory VII (Hildebrand): Tuscany; Apr. 22 (June 30), 1073, to May 25, 1085.

Bl. Victor III (Dauferius; Desiderius): Benevento; May 24, 1086, to Sept. 16, 1087. Cult confirmed July 23, 1887.

Bl. Urban II (Otto di Lagery): France; Mar. 12, 1088, to July 29, 1099. Cult confirmed July 14, 1881.

Paschal II (Raniero): Ravenna; Aug. 13 (14), 1099, to Jan. 21, 1118.

Gelasius II (Giovanni Caetani): Gaeta; Jan. 24 (Mar. 10), 1118, to Jan. 28, 1119.

Callistus II (Guido of Burgundy): Burgundy; Feb. 2 (9), 1119, to Dec. 13, 1124.

Honorius II (Lamberto): Fiagnano (Imola); Dec. 15 (21), 1124, to Feb. 13, 1130.

Innocent II (Gregorio Papareschi): Rome; Feb. 14 (23), 1130, to Sept. 24, 1143.

Celestine II (Guido): Citta di Castello; Sept. 26 (Oct. 3), 1143, to Mar. 8, 1144.

Lucius II (Gerardo Caccianemici): Bologna: Mar. 12, 1144, to Feb. 15, 1145.

Bl. Eugene III (Bernardo Paganelli di Montemagno): Pisa; Feb. 15 (18), 1145, to July 8, 1153. Cult confirmed Oct. 3, 1872.

Anastasius IV (Corrado): Rome; July 12, 1153, to Dec, 3, 1154.

Adrian IV (Nicholas Breakspear): England; Dec. 4 (5), 1154, to Sept. 1, 1159.

Alexander III (Rolando Bandinelli): Siena; Sept. 7 (20), 1159, to Aug. 30, 1181.

Lucius III (Ubaldo Allucingoli): Lucca; Sept. 1 (6), 1181, to Sept. 25, 1185.

Urban III (Uberto Crivelli): Milan; Nov. 25 (Dec. 1), 1185, to Oct. 20, 1187.

Gregory VIII (Alberto de Morra): Benevento; Oct. 21 (25), 1187, to Dec. 17, 1187.

Clement III (Paolo Scolari): Rome; Dec. 19 (20), 1187, to Mar., 1191.

Celestine III (Giacinto Bobone): Rome; Mar. 30 (Apr. 14), 1191, to Jan. 8, 1198.

Innocent III (Lotario dei Conti di Segni); Anagni; Jan. 8 (Feb. 22), 1198, to July 16, 1216.

Honorius III (Cencio Savelli): Rome; July 18 (24), 1216, to Mar. 18, 1227.

Gregory IX (Ugolino, Count of Segni): Anagni; Mar. 19 (21), 1227, to Aug. 22, 1241.

Celestine IV (Goffredo Castiglioni): Milan; Oct. 25 (28), 1241, to Nov. 10, 1241.

Innocent IV (Sinibaldo Fieschi): Genoa; June 25 (28), 1243, to Dec. 7, 1254.

Alexander IV (Rinaldo, Count of Segni): Anagni; Dec. 12 (20), 1254, to May 25, 1261.

Urban IV (Jacques Pantaléon): Troyes; Aug. 29 (Sept. 4), 1261, to Oct. 2, 1264.

Clement IV (Guy Foulques or Guido le Gros): France; Feb. 5 (15), 1265, to Nov. 29, 1268.

Bl. Gregory X (Teobaldo Visconti): Piacenza; Sept. 1, 1271 (Mar. 27, 1272), to Jan. 10, 1276. Cult confirmed Sept. 12, 1713.

Bl. Innocent V (Peter of Tarentaise): Savoy; Jan. 21 (Feb. 22), 1276, to June 22, 1276. Cult confirmed Mar. 13, 1898.

Adrian V (Ottobono Fieschi): Genoa: July 11, 1276, to Aug. 18, 1276.

John XXI (Petrus Juliani or Petrus Hispanus): Portugal; Sept. 8 (20), 1276, to May 20, 1277.

Elimination was made of the name of John XX in an effort to rectify the numerical designation of popes named John. The error dates back to the time of John XV.

Nicholas III (Giovanni Gaetano Orsini): Rome; Nov. 25 (Dec. 26), 1277, to Aug. 22, 1280.

Martin IV (Simon de Brie): France; Feb. 22 (Mar. 23), 1281, to Mar. 28, 1285.

The names of Marinus I (882-84) and Marinus II (942-46) were construed as Martin. In view of these two pontificates and the earlier reign of St. Martin I (649-55), this pope was called Martin IV.

Honorius IV (Giacomo Savelli): Rome; Apr. 2 (May 20), 1285, to Apr. 3, 1287.

Nicholas IV (Girolamo Masci): Ascoli; Feb. 22, 1288, to Apr. 4, 1292.

St. Celestine V (Pietro del Murrone): Isernia; July 5 (Aug. 29), 1294, to Dec. 13, 1294; d. 1296. Canonized May 5, 1313.

Boniface VIII (Benedetto Caetani): Anagni; Dec. 24, 1294 (Jan. 23, 1295), to Oct. 11, 1303.

Bl. Benedict XI (Niccolo Boccasini): Treviso; Oct. 22 (27), 1303, to July 7, 1304. Cult confirmed Apr. 24, 1736.

Clement V (Bertrand de Got): France; June 5 (Nov. 14), 1305, to Apr. 20, 1314. (First of Avignon popes.)

John XXII (Jacques d'Euse): Cahors; Aug. 7 (Sept. 5), 1316, to Dec. 4, 1334.

Benedict XII (Jacques Fournier): France; Dec. 20, 1334 (Jan. 8, 1335), to Apr. 25, 1342.

Clement VI (Pierre Roger): France; May 7 (19), 1342, to Dec. 6, 1352.

Innocent VI (Etienne Aubert): France; Dec. 18 (30), 1352, to Sept. 12, 1362.

Bl. Urban V (Guillaume de Grimoard): France; Sept. 28 (Nov. 6), 1362, to Dec. 19, 1370. Cult confirmed Mar. 10, 1870.

Gregory XI (Pierre Roger de Beaufort): France; Dec. 30, 1370 (Jan. 5, 1371), to Mar. 26, 1378. (Last of Avignon popes.)

Urban VI (Bartolomeo Prignano): Naples; Apr. 8 (18), 1378, to Oct. 15, 1389.

Boniface IX (Pietro Tomacelli): Naples; Nov. 2 (9), 1389, to Oct. 1, 1404.

Innocent VII (Cosma Migliorati): Sulmona; Oct. 17 (Nov. 11), 1404, to Nov. 6, 1406.

Gregory XII (Angelo Correr): Venice; Nov. 30 (Dec. 19), 1406, to July 4, 1415, when he voluntarily resigned from the papacy to permit the election of his successor. He died Oct. 18, 1417. (See The Western Schism.)

Martin V (Oddone Colonna): Rome; Nov. 11 (21), 1417, to Feb. 20, 1431.

Eugene IV (Gabriele Condulmer): Venice; Mar. 3 (11), 1431, to Feb. 23, 1447.

Nicholas V (Tommaso Parentucelli): Sarzana; Mar. 6 (19), 1447, to Mar. 24, 1455.

Callistus III (Alfonso Borgia): Jativa (Valencia); Apr. 8 (20), 1455, to Aug. 6, 1458.

Pius II (Enea Silvio Piccolomini): Siena; Aug. 19 (Sept. 3), 1458, to Aug. 15, 1464.

Paul II (Pietro Barbo): Venice; Aug. 30 (Sept. 16), 1464, to July 26, 1471.

Sixtus IV (Francesco della Rovere): Savona; Aug. 9 (25), 1471, to Aug. 12, 1484.

Innocent VIII (Giovanni Battista Cibo): Genoa; Aug. 29 (Sept. 12), 1484, to July 25, 1492.

Alexander VI (Rodrigo Borgia): Jativa (Valencia); Aug. 11 (26), 1492, to Aug. 18, 1503.

Pius III (Francesco Todeschini-Piccolomini): Siena; Sept. 22 (Oct. 1, 8), 1503, to Oct. 18, 1503.

Julius II (Giuliano della Rovere): Savona; Oct. 31 (Nov. 26), 1503, to Feb. 21, 1513.

Leo X (Giovanni de' Medici): Florence; Mar. 9 (19), 1513, to Dec. 1, 1521.

Adrian VI (Adrian Florensz): Utrecht; Jan. 9 (Aug. 31), 1522, to Sept. 14, 1523.

Clement VII (Giulio de' Medici): Florence; Nov. 19 (26), 1523, to Sept. 25, 1534.

Paul III (Alessandro Farnese): Rome; Oct. 13 (Nov. 3), 1534, to Nov. 10, 1549.

Julius III (Giovanni Maria Ciocchi del Monte): Rome; Feb. 7 (22), 1550, to Mar. 23, 1555.

Marcellus II (Marcello Cervini): Montepulciano; Apr. 9 (10), 1555, to May 1, 1555.

Paul IV (Gian Pietro Carafa): Naples; May 23 (26), 1555, to Aug. 18, 1559.

Pius IV (Giovan Angelo de' Medici): Milan; Dec. 25, 1559 (Jan. 6, 1560), to Dec. 9, 1565.

St. Pius V (Antonio-Michele Ghislieri): Bosco (Alexandria); Jan. 7 (17), 1566, to May 1, 1572. Canonized May 22, 1712.

Gregory XIII (Ugo Buoncompagni): Bologna; May 13 (25), 1572, to Apr. 10, 1585.

Sixtus V (Felice Peretti): Grottammare (Ripatransone); Apr. 24 (May 1), 1585, to Aug. 27, 1590.

Urban VII (Giovanni Battista Castagna): Rome; Sept. 15, 1590, to Sept. 27, 1590.

Gregory XIV (Niccolo Sfondrati): Cremona; Dec. 5 (8), 1590, to Oct. 16, 1591.

Innocent IX (Giovanni Antonio Facchinetti): Bologna; Oct. 29 (Nov. 3), 1591, to Dec. 30, 1591.

Clement VIII (Ippolito Aldobrandini): Florence; Jan. 30 (Feb. 9), 1592, to Mar. 3, 1605.

Leo XI (Alessandro de' Medici): Florence; Apr. 1 (10), 1605, to Apr. 27, 1605.

Paul V (Camillo Borghese): Rome; May 16 (29), 1605, to Jan. 28, 1621.

Gregory XV (Alessandro Ludovisi): Bologna; Feb. 9 (14), 1621, to July 8, 1623.

Urban VIII (Maffeo Barberini): Florence; Aug. 6 (Sept. 29), 1623, to July 29, 1644.

Innocent X (Giovanni Battista Pamfili): Rome; Sept. 15 (Oct. 4), 1644, to Jan. 7, 1655.

List of Popes

Alexander VII (Fabio Chigi): Siena; Apr. 7 (18), 1655, to May 22, 1667.
Clement IX (Giulio Rospigliosi): Pistoia; June 20 (26), 1667, to Dec. 9, 1669.
Clement X (Emilio Altieri): Rome; Apr. 29 (May 11), 1670, to July 22, 1676.
Bl. Innocent XI (Benedetto Odescalchi): Como; Sept. 21 (Oct. 4), 1676, to Aug. 12, 1689.
Alexander VIII (Pietro Ottoboni): Venice; Oct. 6 (16), 1689, to Feb. 1, 1691.
Innocent XII (Antonio Pignatelli): Spinazzola; July 12 (15), 1691, to Sept. 27, 1700.
Clement XI (Giovanni Francesco Albani): Urbino; Nov. 23, 30 (Dec. 8), 1700, to Mar. 19, 1721.
Innocent XIII (Michelangelo dei Conti): Rome; May 8 (18), 1721, to Mar. 7, 1724.
Benedict XIII (Pietro Francesco — Vincenzo Maria — Orsini): Gravina (Bari); May 29 (June 4), 1724, to Feb. 21, 1730.
Clement XII (Lorenzo Corsini): Florence; July 12 (16), 1730, to Feb. 6, 1740.
Benedict XIV (Prospero Lambertini): Bologna; Aug. 17 (22), 1740, to May 3, 1758.
Clement XIII (Carlo Rezzonico): Venice; July 6 (16), 1758, to Feb. 2, 1769.
Clement XIV (Giovanni Vincenzo Antonio — Lorenzo — Ganganelli): Rimini; May 19, 28 (June 4), 1769, to Sept. 22, 1774.
Pius VI (Giovanni Angelo Braschi): Cesena; Feb. 15 (22), 1775, to Aug. 29, 1799.
Pius VII (Barnaba — Gregorio — Chiaramonti): Cesena; Mar. 14 (21), 1800, to Aug. 20, 1823.
Leo XII (Annibale della Genga): Genga (Fabriano); Sept. 28 (Oct. 5), 1823, to Feb. 10, 1829.
Pius VIII (Francesco Saverio Castiglioni): Cingoli; Mar. 31 (Apr. 5), 1829, to Nov. 30, 1830.
Gregory XVI (Bartolomeo Alberto — Mauro — Cappellari): Belluno; Feb. 2 (6), 1831, to June 1, 1846.
Pius IX (Giovanni M. Mastai Ferretti): Senigallia; June 16 (21), 1846, to Feb. 7, 1878.
Leo XIII (Gioacchino Pecci): Carpineto (Anagni); Feb. 20 (Mar. 3), 1878, to July 20, 1903.
St. Pius X (Giuseppe Sarto): Riese (Treviso); Aug. 4 (9), 1903, to Aug. 20, 1914. Canonized May 29, 1954.
Benedict XV (Giacomo della Chiesa): Genoa; Sept. 3 (6), 1914, to Jan. 22, 1922.
Pius XI (Achille Ratti): Desio (Milan); Feb. 6 (12), 1922, to Feb. 10, 1939.
Pius XII (Eugenio Pacelli): Rome; Mar. 2 (12), 1939, to Oct. 9, 1958.
John XXIII (Angelo Giuseppe Roncalli): Sotto il Monte (Bergamo); Oct. 28 (Nov. 4), 1958 to June 3, 1963.
Paul VI (Giovanni Battista Montini): Concessio (Brescia); June 21 (June 30), 1963 to Aug. 6, 1978. (See separate entry.)
John Paul I (Albino Luciani): Forno di Canale (Belluno); Aug. 26 (Sept. 3) to Sept. 28, 1978. (See separate entry.)
John Paul II (Karol Wojtyla): Wadowice, Poland; Oct. 16 (22), 1978. to

ANTIPOPES

(Source: *Annuario Pontificio.*)

This list of men who claimed or exercised the papal office in an uncanonical manner includes names, birthplaces and dates of alleged reigns.
St. Hippolytus: Rome; 217-235; was reconciled before his death.
Novatian: Rome; 251.
Felix II: Rome; 355 to Nov. 22, 365.
Ursinus: 366-367.
Eulalius: Dec. 27 or 29, 418, to 419.
Lawrence: 498; 501-505.
Dioscorus: Alexandria; Sept. 22, 530, to Oct. 14, 530.
Theodore: ended alleged reign, 687.
Paschal: ended alleged reign, 687.
Constantine: Nepi; June 28 (July 5), 767, to 769.
Philip: July 31, 768; retired to his monastery on the same day.
John: ended alleged reign, Jan., 844.
Anastasius: Aug., 855, to Sept., 855; d. 880.
Christopher: Rome; July or Sept., 903, to Jan., 904.
Boniface VII: Rome; June, 974, to July, 974; Aug., 984, to July, 985.
John XVI: Rossano; Apr., 997, to Feb., 998.
Gregory: ended alleged reign, 1012.
Benedict X: Rome; Apr. 5, 1058, to Jan. 24, 1059.
Honorius II: Verona; Oct. 28, 1061, to 1072.
Clement III: Parma; June 25, 1080 (Mar. 24, 1084), to Sept. 8, 1100.
Theodoric: ended alleged reign, 1100; d. 1102.
Albert: ended alleged reign, 1102.
Sylvester IV: Rome; Nov. 18, 1105, to 1111.
Gregory VIII: France; Mar. 8, 1118, to 1121.
Celestine II: Rome; ended alleged reign, Dec., 1124.
Anacletus II: Rome; Feb. 14 (23), 1130, to Jan. 25, 1138.
Victor IV: Mar., 1138, to May 29, 1138; submitted to Pope Innocent II.
Victor IV: Montecelio; Sept. 7 (Oct. 4), 1159, to Apr. 20, 1164; he did not recognize his predecessor (Victor IV, above).
Paschal III: Apr. 22 (26), 1164, to Sept. 20, 1168.
Callistus III: Arezzo; Sept., 1168, to Aug. 29, 1178; submitted to Pope Alexander III.
Innocent III: Sezze; Sept. 29, 1179, to 1180.
Nicholas V: Corvaro (Rieti); May 12 (22), 1328, to Aug. 25, 1330; d. Oct. 16, 1333.
Four antipopes of the Western Schism:
Clement VII: Sept. 20 (Oct. 31), 1378, to Sept. 16, 1394.
Benedict XIII: Aragon; Sept. 28 (Oct. 11), 1394, to May 23, 1423.

Alexander V: Crete; June 26 (July 7), 1409, to May 3, 1410.
John XXIII: Naples; May 17 (25), 1410, to May 29, 1415.
Felix V: Savoy; Nov. 5, 1439 (July 24, 1440), to April 7, 1449; d. 1451.

Avignon Papacy

Avignon was the residence of a series of French popes from Clement V to Gregory XI (1309-77). Prominent in the period were power struggles over the mixed interests of Church and state with the rulers of France (Philip IV, John II), Bavaria (Lewis IV), England (Edward III); factionalism of French and Italian churchmen; political as well as ecclesiastical turmoil in Italy, a factor of significance in prolonging the stay of popes in Avignon. Despite some positive achievements, the Avignon papacy was a prologue to the Western Schism which began in 1378.

Western Schism

The Western Schism was a confused state of affairs which divided Christendom into two and then three papal obediences from 1378 to 1417.

It occurred some 50 years after Marsilius theorized that a general (not ecumenical) council of bishops and other persons was superior to a pope and nearly 30 years before the Council of Florence stated definitively that no kind of council had such authority.

It was a period of disaster preceding the even more disastrous period of the Reformation.

Urban VI, following transfer to Rome of the 70-year papal residence at Avignon, was elected pope Apr. 8, 1378, and reigned until his death in 1389. He was succeeded by Boniface IX (1389-1404), Innocent VII (1404-1406) and Gregory XII (1406-1415). These four are considered the legitimate popes of the period.

Some of the cardinals who chose Urban pope, dissatisfied with his conduct of the office, declared that his election was invalid. They proceeded to elect Clement VII, who claimed the papacy from 1378 to 1394. He was succeeded by Benedict XIII.

Prelates seeking to end the state of divided papal loyalties convoked the Council of Pisa which, without authority, found Gregory XII and Benedict XIII, in absentia, guilty on 30-odd charges of schism and heresy, deposed them, and elected a third claimant to the papacy, Alexander V (1409-1410). He was succeeded by John XXIII (1410-1415).

The schism was ended by the Council of Constance (1414-1418). This council, although originally called into session in an irregular manner, acquired authority after being convoked by Gregory XII in 1415. In its early irregular phase, it deposed John XXIII whose election to the papacy was uncanonical anyway. After being formally convoked, it accepted the abdication of Gregory in 1415 and dismissed the claims of Benedict XIII two years later, thus clearing the way for the election of Martin V on Nov. 11, 1417. The Council of Constance also rejected the theories of John Wycliff and condemned John Hus as a heretic.

20th CENTURY POPES

Leo XIII

Leo XIII (Gioacchino Vincenzo Pecci) was born May 2, 1810, in Carpineto, Italy. Although all but three years of his life and pontificate were of the 19th century, his influence extended well into the 20th century.

He was educated at the Jesuit college in Viterbo, the Roman College, the Academy of Noble Ecclesiastics, and the University of the Sapienza. He was ordained to the priesthood in 1837.

He served as an apostolic delegate to two States of the Church, Benevento from 1838 to 1841 and Perugia in 1841 and 1842. Ordained titular archbishop of Damietta, he was papal nuncio to Belgium from January, 1843, until May, 1846; in the post, he had controversial relations with the government over education issues and acquired his first significant experience of industrialized society.

He was archbishop of Perugia from 1846 to 1878. He became a cardinal in 1853 and chamberlain of the Roman Curia in 1877. He was elected to the papacy Feb. 20, 1878. He died July 20, 1903.

Canonizations: He canonized 18 saints and beatified a group of English martyrs.

Church Administration: He established 300 new dioceses and vicariates; restored the hierarchy in Scotland, set up an English, as contrasted with the Portuguese, hierarchy in India; approved the action of the Congregation for the Propagation of the Faith in reorganizing missions in China.

Encyclicals: He issued 50 encyclicals, on subjects ranging from devotional to social. In the former category were *Annum Sacrum*, on the Sacred Heart, in 1899, and nine letters on Mary and the Rosary.

Interfaith Relations: He was unsuccessful in unity overtures made to Orthodox and Slavic Churches. He declared Anglican orders invalid in the apostolic bull *Apostolicae Curae* Sept. 13, 1896.

International Relations: Leo was frustrated in seeking solutions to the Roman Question arising from the seizure of church lands by the Kingdom of Italy in 1870. He also faced anticlerical situations in Belgium and France and in the Kulturkampf policies of Bismarck in Germany.

Social Questions: Much of Leo's influence stemmed from social doctrine stated in numerous encyclicals, concerning liberalism, liberty, the divine origin of authority; socialism, in *Quod Apostolici Muneris,* 1878; the Christian concept of the family, in *Arcanum,* 1880; socialism and economic liberalism, relations between capital and labor, in *Rerum Novarum,* 1891. Two of his social encyclicals were against the African slave trade.

Studies: In the encyclical *Aeterni Patris* of Aug. 4, 1879, he ordered a renewal of philosophical and theological studies in seminaries along scholastic, and especially Thomistic, lines, to counteract influential trends of liberalism and Modernism. He issued guidelines for biblical exegesis in *Providentissimus Deus* Nov. 18, 1893, and established the Pontifical Biblical Commission in 1902.

In other actions affecting scholarship and study, he opened the Vatican Archives to scholars in 1883 and established the Vatican Observatory.

United States: He authorized establishment of the apostolic delegation in Washington, D.C. Jan. 24, 1893. He refused to issue a condemnation of the Knights of Labor. With a document entitled *Testem Benevolentiae,* he eased resolution of questions concerning what was called an American heresy in 1899.

St. Pius X

St. Pius X (Giuseppe Melchiorre Sarto) was born in 1835 in Riese, Italy.

Educated at the college of Castelfranco and the seminary at Padua, he was ordained to the priesthood Sept. 18, 1858. He served as a curate in Trombolo for nine years before beginning an eight-year pastorate at Salzano. He was chancellor of the Treviso diocese from November, 1875, and bishop of Mantua from 1884 until 1893. He was cardinal-patriarch of Venice from that year until his election to the papacy by the conclave held from July 31 to Aug. 4, 1903.

Aims: Pius' principal objectives as pope were "to restore all things in Christ, in order that Christ may be all and in all," and "to teach (and defend) Christian truth and law."

Canonizations, Encyclicals: He canonized four saints and issued 16 encyclicals. One of the encyclicals was issued in commemoration of the 50th anniversary of the proclamation of the dogma of the Immaculate Conception of Mary.

Catechetics: He introduced a whole new era of religious instruction and formation with the encyclical *Acerbo Nimis* of Apr. 15, 1905, in which he called for vigor in establishing and conducting parochial programs of the Confraternity of Christian Doctrine.

Catholic Action: He outlined the role of official Catholic Action in two encyclicals in 1905 and 1906. Favoring organized action by Catholics themselves, he had serious reservations about interconfessional collaboration.

He stoutly maintained claims to papal rights in the anticlerical climate of Italy. He authorized bishops to relax prohibitions against participation by Catholics in some Italian elections.

Church Administration: With the motu proprio *Arduum Sane* of Mar. 19, 1904, he inaugurated the work which resulted in the Code of Canon Law; the code was completed in 1917 and went into effect in the following year. He reorganized and strengthened the Roman Curia with the apostolic constitution *Sapienti Consilio* of June 29, 1908. While promoting the expansion of missionary work, he removed from the jurisdiction of the Congregation for the Propagation of the Faith the Church in the United States, Canada, Newfoundland, England, Ireland, Holland and Luxembourg.

International Relations: He ended traditional prerogatives of Catholic governments with respect to papal elections, in 1904. He opposed anti-Church and anticlerical actions in several countries: Bolivia in 1905, because of anti-religious legislation; France in 1906, for its 1901 action in annulling its concordat with the Holy See, and for the 1905 Law of Separation by which it decreed separation of Church and state, ordered the confiscation of church property, and blocked religious education and the activities of religious orders; Portugal in 1911, for the separation of Church and state and repressive measures which resulted in persecution later.

In 1912 he called on the bishops of Brazil to work for the improvement of conditions among Indians.

Liturgy: "The Pope of the Eucharist," he strongly recommended the frequent reception of Holy Communion in a decree dated Dec. 20, 1905; in another decree, *Quam Singulari,* of Aug. 8, 1910, he called for the early reception of the sacrament by children. He initiated measures for liturgical reform with new norms for sacred music and the start of work on revision of the *Breviary* for recitation of the Divine Office.

Modernism: Pius was a vigorous opponent of "the synthesis of all heresies," which threatened the integrity of doctrine through its influence in philosophy, theology and biblical exegesis. In opposition, he condemned 65 of its propositions as erroneous in the decree *Lamentabili* July 3, 1907; issued the encyclical *Pascendi* in the same vein Sept. 8, 1907; backed both of these with censures; and published the Oath against Modernism in September, 1910, to be taken by all the clergy. Ecclesiastical studies suffered to some extent from these actions, necessary as they were at the time.

Pius followed the lead of Leo XIII in promoting the study of scholastic philosophy. He established the Pontifical Biblical Institute May 7, 1909.

His death, Aug. 20, 1914, was hastened by the outbreak of World War I. He was beatified in 1951 and canonized May 29, 1954. His feast is observed Aug. 21.

Benedict XV

Benedict XV (Giacomo della Chiesa) was born Nov. 21, 1854, in Pegli, Italy.

He was educated at the Royal University of Genoa and Gregorian University in Rome. He was ordained to the priesthood Dec. 21, 1878.

He served in the papal diplomatic corps from 1882 to 1907; as secretary to the nuncio to Spain from 1882 to 1887, as secretary to the papal secretary of state from 1887, and as undersecretary from 1901.

He was ordained archbishop of Bologna Dec. 22, 1907, and spent four years completing a pastoral visitation there. He was made a cardinal just three months before being elected to the papacy Sept. 3, 1914, He died Jan. 22, 1922. Two key efforts of his pontificate were for peace and the relief of human suffering caused by World War I.

Canonizations: Benedict canonized three saints; one of them was Joan of Arc.

Canon Law: He published the Code of Canon Law, developed by the commission set up by St. Pius X, June 28, 1917; it went into effect the following year.

Curia: He made great changes in the personnel of the Curia. He established the Congregation for the Oriental Churches May 1, 1917, and founded the Pontifical Oriental Institute in Rome later in the year.

Encyclicals: He issued 12 encyclicals. Peace was the theme of three of them. In another, published two years after the cessation of hostilities, he wrote about child victims of the war. He followed the lead of Leo XIII in *Spiritus Paraclitus*, Sept. 15, 1920, on biblical studies.

International Relations: He was largely frustrated on the international level because of the events and attitudes of the war period, but the number of diplomats accredited to the Vatican nearly doubled, from 14 to 26, between the time of his accession to the papacy and his death.

Peace Efforts: Benedict's stance in the war was one of absolute impartiality but not of disinterested neutrality. Because he would not take sides, he was suspected by both sides and the seven-point peace plan he offered to all belligerents Aug. 1, 1917, was turned down. The points of the plan were: recognition of the moral force of right; disarmament; acceptance of arbitration in cases of dispute; guarantee of freedom of the seas; renunciation of war indemnities; evacuation and restoration of occupied territories; examination of territorial claims in dispute.

Relief Efforts: Benedict assumed personal charge of Vatican relief efforts during the war. He set up an international missing persons bureau for contacts between prisoners and their families, but was forced to close it because of the suspicion of warring nations that it was a front for espionage operations. He persuaded the Swiss government to admit into the country military victims of tuberculosis.

Roman Question: Benedict arranged a meeting of Benito Mussolini and the papal secretary of state, which marked the first step toward final settlement of the question in 1929.

Pius XI

Pius XI (Ambrogio Damiano Achille Ratti) was born May 31, 1857, in Desio, Italy.

Educated at seminaries in Seviso and Milan, and at the Lombard College, Gregorian University and Academy of St. Thomas in Rome, he was ordained to the priesthood in 1879.

He taught at the major seminary of Milan from 1882 to 1888. Appointed to the staff of the Ambrosian Library in 1888, he remained there until 1911, acquiring a reputation for publishing works on palaeography and serving as director from 1907 to 1911. He then moved to the Vatican Library, of which he was prefect from 1914 to 1918. In 1919, he was named apostolic visitor to Poland in April, nuncio in June, and was made titular archbishop of Lepanto Oct. 28. He was made archbishop of Milan and cardinal June 13, 1921, before being elected to the papacy Feb. 6, 1922. He died Feb. 10, 1939.

Aim: The objective of his pontificate, as stated in the encyclical *Ubi Arcano,* Dec. 23, 1922, was to establish the reign and peace of Christ in society.

Canonizations: He canonized 34 saints, including the Jesuit Martyrs of North America, and conferred the title of Doctor of the Church on Sts. Peter Canisius, John of the Cross, Robert Bellarmine and Albertus Magnus.

Eastern Churches: He called for better understanding of the Eastern Churches in the encyclical *Rerum Orientalium* of Sept. 8, 1928, and developed facilities for the training of Eastern-Rite priests. He inaugurated steps for the codification of Eastern-Church law in 1929. In 1935 he made Syrian Patriarch Tappouni a cardinal.

Encyclicals: His first encyclical, *Ubi Arcano,* in addition to stating the aims of his pontificate, blueprinted Catholic Action and called for its development throughout the Church. In *Quas Primas,* Dec. 11, 1925, he established the feast of Christ the King for universal observance. Subjects of some of his other encyclicals were: Christian education, in *Divini Illius Magistri,* Dec. 31, 1929; Christian marriage, in *Casti Connubii,* Dec. 30, 1930; social conditions and pressure for social change in line with the teaching in *Rerum Novarum,* in *Quadragesimo Anno,* May 15, 1931; atheistic Communism, in *Divini Redemptoris,* Mar. 19, 1937; the priesthood, in *Ad Catholici Sacerdotii,* Dec. 20, 1935.

Missions: Following the lead of Benedict XV, Pius called for the training of native clergy in the pattern of their own respective cultures, and promoted missionary developments in various ways. He ordained six native bishops for China in 1926, one for Japan in 1927, and others for regions of Asia, China and India in 1933. He placed the first 40 mission dioceses under native bishops, saw the number of native priests increase from about 2,600 to more than 7,000 and the number of Catholics in missionary areas more than double from nine million.

In the apostolic constitution *Deus Scientiarum Dominus* of May 24, 1931, he ordered the introduction of missiology into theology courses.

Interfaith Relations: Pius was negative to the ecumenical movement among Protestants but approved the Malines Conversations, 1921 to 1926, between Anglicans and Catholics.

International Relations: Relations with the Mussolini government deteriorated from 1931 on, as indicated in the encyclical *Non Abbiamo Bisogno*, when the regime took steps to curb liberties and activities of the Church; they turned critical in 1938 with the emergence of racist policies. Relations deteriorated also in Germany from 1933 on, resulting finally in condemnation of the Nazis in the encyclical *Mit Brennender Sorge*, March, 1937. Pius sparked a revival of the Church in France by encouraging Catholics to work within the democratic framework of the Republic rather than foment trouble over restoration of a monarchy. Pius was powerless before the civil war which erupted in Spain in July, 1936; sporadic persecution and repression by the Calles regime in Mexico; and systematic persecution of the Church in the Soviet Union. Many of the 10 concordats and two agreements reached with European countries after World War I became casualties of World War II.

Roman Question: Pius negotiated for two and one-half years with the Italian government to settle the Roman Question by means of the Lateran Agreement of 1929. The agreement provided independent status for the State of Vatican City; made Catholicism the official religion of Italy, with pastoral and educational freedom and state recognition of Catholic marriages, religious orders and societies; and provided a financial payment to the Vatican for expropriation of the former States of the Church.

Pius XII

Pius XII (Eugenio Maria Giovanni Pacelli) was born Mar. 2, 1876, in Rome.

Educated at the Gregorian University and the Lateran University, in Rome, he was ordained to the priesthood Apr. 2, 1899.

He entered the Vatican diplomatic service in 1901, worked on the codification of canon law, and was appointed secretary of the Congregation for Ecclesiastical Affairs in 1914. Three years later he was ordained titular archbishop of Sardis and made apostolic nuncio to Bavaria. He was nuncio to Germany from 1920 to 1929, when he was made a cardinal, and took office as papal secretary of state in the following year. His diplomatic negotiations resulted in concordats between the Vatican and Bavaria (1924), Prussia (1929), Baden (1932), Austria and the German Republic (1933). He took part in negotiations which led to settlement of the Roman Question in 1929.

He was elected to the papacy Mar. 2, 1939. He died Oct. 9, 1958, at Castel Gandolfo after the 12th longest pontificate in history.

Canonizations: He canonized 33 saints, including Mother Frances X. Cabrini, the first US citizen-Saint.

Cardinals: He raised 56 prelates to the rank of cardinal in two consistories held in 1946 and 1953. There were 57 cardinals at the time of his death.

Church Organization and Missions: He increased the number of dioceses from 1,696 to 2,048. He established native hierarchies in China (1946), Burma (1955), and parts of Africa, and extended the native structure of the Church in India. He ordained the first black bishop for Africa.

Communism: In addition to opposing and condemning Communism on numerous occasions, he decreed in 1949 the penalty of excommunication for all Catholics holding formal and willing allegiance to the Communist Party and its policies. During his reign the Church was persecuted in some 15 countries which fell under Communist domination.

Doctrine and Liturgy: He proclaimed the dogma of the Assumption of the Blessed Virgin Mary Nov. 1, 1950 (apostolic constitution, *Munificentissimus Deus*).

In various encyclicals and other enactments, he provided background for the *aggiornamento* introduced by his successor, John XXIII: by his formulations of doctrine and practice regarding the Mystical Body of Christ, the liturgy, sacred music and biblical studies; by the revision of the Rites of Holy Week; by initiation of the work which led to the calendar-missal-breviary reform ordered into effect Jan. 1, 1961; by the first of several modifications of the Eucharistic fast; by extending the time of Mass to the evening. He instituted the feasts of Mary, Queen, and of St. Joseph the Worker, and clarified teaching concerning devotion to the Sacred Heart.

His 41 encyclicals and nearly 1,000 public addresses made Pius one of the greatest teaching popes. His concern in all his communications was to deal with specific points at issue and/or to bring Christian principles to bear on contemporary world problems.

Peace Efforts: Before the start of World War II, he tried unsuccessfully to get the contending nations — Germany and Poland,

France and Italy — to settle their differences peaceably. During the war, he offered his services to mediate the widened conflict, spoke out against the horrors of war and the suffering it caused, mobilized relief work for its victims, proposed a five-point program for peace in Christmas messages from 1939 to 1942, and secured a generally open status for the city of Rome. After the war, he endorsed the principles and intent of the United Nations and continued efforts for peace.

United States: Pius appointed more than 200 of the 265 American bishops resident in the US and abroad in 1958, erected 27 dioceses in this country, and raised seven dioceses to archiepiscopal rank.

John XXIII

John XXIII (Angelo Roncalli) was born Nov. 25, 1881, at Sotte il Monte, Italy.

He was educated at the seminary of the Bergamo diocese and the Pontifical Seminary in Rome, where he was ordained to the priesthood Aug. 10, 1904.

He spent the first nine or 10 years of his priesthood as secretary to the bishop of Bergamo and as an instructor in the seminary there. He served as a medic and chaplain in the Italian army during World War I. Afterwards, he resumed duties in his own diocese until he was called to Rome in 1921 for work with the Society for the Propagation of the Faith.

He began diplomatic service in 1925 as titular archbishop of Areopolis and apostolic visitor to Bulgaria. A succession of offices followed: apostolic delegate to Bulgaria (1931-1935); titular archbishop of Mesembria, apostolic delegate to Turkey and Greece, administrator of the Latin vicariate apostolic of Istanbul (1935-1944); apostolic nuncio to France (1944-1953). On these missions, he was engaged in delicate negotiations involving Roman, Eastern-Rite and Orthodox relations; the needs of people suffering from the consequences of World War II; and unsettling suspicions arising from wartime conditions.

He was made a cardinal Jan. 12, 1953, and three days later was appointed patriarch of Venice, the position he held until his election to the papacy Oct. 28, 1958. He died of stomach cancer June 3, 1963.

John was a strong and vigorous pope whose influence far outmeasured both his age and the shortness of his time in the papacy.

Second Vatican Council: John announced Jan. 25, 1959, his intention of convoking the 21st ecumenical council in history to renew life in the Church, to reform its structures and institutions, and to explore ways and means of promoting unity among Christians. Through the council, which completed its work two and one-half years after his death, he ushered in a new era in the history of the Church.

Canon Law: He established a commission Mar. 28, 1963, for revision of the Code of Canon Law. The work of this commission, still underway, will greatly influence the future course of Catholic life and the conduct of ecclesiastical affairs.

Canonizations: He canonized 10 saints. He also beatified Mother Elizabeth Ann Seton, the first native of the US ever so honored. He named St. Lawrence of Brindisi a Doctor of the Church.

Cardinals: He created 52 cardinals in five consistories, raising membership of the College of Cardinals above the traditional number of 70; at one time in 1962, the membership was 87. He made the college more international in representation than it had ever been, appointing the first cardinals from the Philippines, Japan and Africa. He ordered episcopal ordination for all cardinals. He relieved the suburban bishops of Rome of ordinary jurisdiction over their dioceses so they might devote all their time to business of the Roman Curia.

Eastern Rites: He made all Eastern-Rite patriarchs members of the Congregation for the Oriental Churches.

Ecumenism: He assigned to the Second Vatican Council the task of finding ways and means of promoting unity among Christians. He established the Vatican Secretariat for Promoting Christian Unity June 5, 1960. He showed his desire for more cordial relations with the Orthodox by sending personal representatives to visit Patriarch Athenagoras I June 27, 1961; approved a mission of five delegates to the General Assembly of the World Council of Churches which met in New Delhi, India, in November, 1961; removed a number of pejorative references to Jews in the Roman-Rite liturgy for Good Friday.

Encyclicals: Of the eight encyclicals he issued, the two outstanding ones were *Mater et Magistra* ("Christianity and Social Progress"), in which he recapitulated, updated and extended the social doctrine stated earlier by Leo XIII and Pius XI; and *Pacem in Terris* ("Peace on Earth"), the first encyclical ever addressed to all men of good will as well as to Catholics, on the natural-law principles of peace.

Liturgy: In forwarding liturgical reforms already begun by Pius XII, he ordered a calendar-missal-breviary reform into effect Jan. 1, 1961. He authorized the use of vernacular languages in the administration of the sacraments and approved giving Holy Communion to the sick in afternoon hours. He selected the liturgy as the first topic of major discussion by the Second Vatican Council.

Missions: He issued an encyclical on the missionary activity of the Church; established native hierarchies in Indonesia, Vietnam and Korea; and called on North American superiors of religious institutes to have one-tenth of their members assigned to work in Latin America by 1971.

Peace: John spoke and used his moral influence for peace in 1961 when tension developed over Berlin, in 1962 during the Algerian revolt from France, and later the same year in the Cuban missile crisis. His efforts were singled out for honor by the Balzan Peace Foundation. In 1963, he was posthumously awarded the US Presidential Medal of Freedom.

Paul VI

Paul VI (Giovanni Battista Montini) was born Sept. 26, 1897, at Concesio in northern Italy.

Educated at Brescia, he was ordained to the priesthood May 29, 1920. He pursued additional studies at the Pontifical Academy for Noble Ecclesiastics and the Pontifical Gregorian University. In 1924 he began 30 years of service in the Secretariat of State; as undersecretary from 1937 until 1954, he was closely associated with Pius XII and was heavily engaged in organizing informational and relief services during and after World War II.

He was ordained archbishop of Milan Dec. 12, 1954, and was inducted into the College of Cardinals Dec. 15, 1958. He was elected to the papacy June 21, 1963, two days after the conclave began. He died of a heart attack Aug. 6, 1978.

Second Vatican Council: He reconvened the Second Vatican Council after the death of John XXIII, presided over its second, third and fourth sessions, formally promulgated the 16 documents it produced, and devoted the whole of his pontificate to the task of putting them into effect throughout the Church. The main thrust of his pontificate — in a milieu of cultural and other changes in the Church and the world — was toward institutionalization and control of the authentic trends articulated and set in motion by the council.

Canonizations: He canonized more saints, 84, than any other pope. They included groups of 22 Ugandan martyrs and 40 martyrs of England and Wales, as well as two Americans — Elizabeth Ann Bayley Seton and John Nepomucene Neumann.

Cardinals: He created more cardinals, 137, than any other pope and gave the Sacred College a more international complexion than it ever had before. He limited participation in papal elections to 120 cardinals under the age of 80.

Collegiality: He established the Synod of Bishops in 1965 and called it into session five times. He stimulated the formation and operation of regional conferences of bishops, and of consultative bodies on other levels.

Creed and Holy Year: On June 30, 1968, he issued a Creed of the People of God in conjunction with the celebration of a Year of Faith. He proclaimed and led the observance of a Holy Year from Christmas Eve of 1974 to Christmas Eve of 1975.

Diplomacy: He met with many world leaders, including Soviet President Nikolai Podgorny in 1967, Marshal Tito of Yugoslavia in 1971 and President Nicolas Ceausescu of Rumania in 1973. He worked constantly to reduce tension between the Church and the intransigent regimes of Eastern European countries by means of a detente type of policy called Ostpolitik. He agreed to significant revisions of the Vatican's concordat with Spain and initiated efforts to revise the concordat with Italy. More then 40 countries established diplomatic relations with the Vatican during his pontificate.

Encyclicals: He issued seven encyclicals, three of which are the best known. In *Populorum Progressio* ("Development of Peoples") he appealed to wealthy countries to take "concrete action" to promote human development and to remedy imbalances between richer and poorer nations; this encyclical, coupled with other documents and related actions, launched the Church into a new depth of involvement as a public advocate for human rights and for humanizing social, political and economic policies. In *Sacerdotalis Caelibatus* ("Priestly Celibacy") he reaffirmed the strict observance of priestly celibacy throughout the Western Church. In *Humanae Vitae* ("Of Human Life") he condemned abortion, sterilization and artificial birth control, in line with traditional teaching and in "defense of life, the gift of God, the glory of the family, the strength of the people."

Interfaith Relations: He initiated formal consultation and informal dialogue on international and national levels between Catholics and non-Catholics — Orthodox, Anglicans, Protestants, Jews, Moslems, Buddhists, Hindus, and unbelievers. He and Greek Orthodox Patriarch Athenagoras I of Constantinople nullified in 1965 the mutual excommunications imposed by their respective churches in 1054.

Liturgy: He carried out the most extensive liturgical reform in history, involving a new Order of the Mass effective in 1969, a revised church calendar in 1970, revisions and translations into vernacular languages of all sacramental rites and other liturgical texts.

Ministries: He authorized the restoration of the permanent diaconate in the Roman Rite and the establishment of new ministries of lay persons.

Peace: He instituted the annual observance of a World Day of Peace on New Year's Day as a means of addressing a message of peace to all the world's political leaders and the peoples of all nations. The most dramatic of his many appeals for peace and efforts to ease international tensions was his plea for "No more war!" before the United Nations Oct. 4, 1965.

Pilgrimages: A "Pilgrim Pope," he made pastoral visits to the Holy Land and India in 1964, the United Nations and New York City in 1965, Portugal and Turkey in 1967, Colombia in 1968, Switzerland and Uganda in 1969, and Asia, Pacific islands and Australia in 1970. While in Manila in 1970, he was stabbed by a Bolivian artist who made an attempt on his life.

Roman Curia: He reorganized the central administrative organs of the Church in line with provisions of the apostolic constitution, *Regimini Ecclesiae Universae,* streamlining procedures for more effective service and giving the agencies a more international perspective by drawing officials and consultors from all over the world. He also instituted a number of new commissions and other bodies. Coupled with curial reorganization was a simplification of papal ceremonies.

John Paul I

John Paul I (Albino Luciani) was born Oct. 17, 1912, in Forno di Canale (now Canale d'Agordo) in northern Italy.

Educated at the minor seminary in Feltre and the major seminary of the Diocese of Belluno, he was ordained to the priesthood July 7, 1935. He pursued further studies at the Pontifical Gregorian University in Rome and was awarded a doctorate in theology. From 1937 to 1947 he was vice rector of the Belluno seminary, where he taught dogmatic and moral theology, canon law and sacred art. He was appointed vicar general of his diocese in 1947 and served as director of catechetics.

Ordained bishop of Vittorio Veneto Dec. 27, 1958, he attended all sessions of the second Vatican Council, participated in three assemblies of the Synod of Bishops (1971, 1974 and 1977), and was vice president of the Italian Bishops' Conference from 1972 to 1975.

He was appointed archbishop and patriarch of Venice Dec. 15, 1969, and was inducted into the College of Cardinals Mar. 5, 1973.

He was elected to the papacy Aug. 26, 1978, on the fourth ballot cast by the 111 cardinals participating in the largest and one of the shortest conclaves in history. The quickness of his election was matched by the brevity of his pontificate of 33 days, during which he delivered 19 addresses. He died of a heart attack Sept. 28, 1978.

CANONIZATIONS BY LEO XIII AND HIS SUCCESSORS

Canonization is an infallible declaration by the pope that a person who suffered martyrdom and/or practiced Christian virtue to a heroic degree is in glory with God in heaven and is worthy of public honor by the universal Church and of imitation by the faithful.

Leo XIII
(1878-1903)

1881: Clare of Montefalco, virgin (d. 1308); John Baptist de Rossi, priest (1698-1764); Lawrence of Brindisi, doctor (d. 1619); Benedict J. Labre (1748-1783).
1888: Seven Holy Founders of the Servite Order; Peter Claver, priest (1581-1654); John Berchmans (1599-1621); Alphonsus Rodriguez, lay brother (1531-1617).
1897: Anthony M. Zaccaria, founder of Barnabites (1502-1539); Peter Fourier, cofounder of Augustinian Canonesses of Our Lady (1565-1640).
1900: John Baptist de La Salle, founder of Christian Brothers (1651-1719); Rita of Cascia (1381-1457).

St. Pius X
(1903-1914)

1904: Alexander Sauli, bishop (1534-1593); Gerard Majella, lay brother (1725-1755).
1909: Joseph Oriol, priest (1650-1702); Clement M. Hofbauer, priest (1751-1820).

Benedict XV
(1914-1922)

1920: Gabriel of the Sorrowful Mother (1838-1862); Margaret Mary Alacoque, virgin (1647-1690); Joan of Arc, virgin (1412-1431).

Pius XI
(1922-1939)

1925: Therese of Lisieux, virgin (1873-1897); Peter Canisius, doctor (1521-1597); Mary Magdalen Postel, foundress of Sisterhood of Christian Schools (1756-1846); Mary Magdalen Sophie Barat, foundress of Society of the Sacred Heart (1779-1865); John Eudes, founder of Eudist Fathers (1601-1680); John Baptist Vianney (Curé of Ars), priest (1786-1859).
1930: Lucy Filippini, virgin (1672-1732); Catherine Thomas, virgin (1533-1574); Jesuit North American Martyrs (see Index); Robert Bellarmine, bishop-doctor (1542-1621); Theophilus of Corte, priest (1676-1740).
1931: Albert the Great, bishop-doctor (1206-1280) (equivalent canonization).
1933: Andrew Fournet, priest (1752-1834); Bernadette Soubirous, virgin (1844-1879).
1934: Joan Antida Thouret, foundress of Sisters of Charity of St. Joan Antida (1765-1826); Mary Michaeli, foundress of Institute of Handmaids of the Blessed Sacrament (1809-1865); Louise de Marillac, foundress of Sisters of Charity (1591-1660); Joseph Benedict Cottolengo, priest (1786-1842); Pompilius M. Pirotti, priest (1710-1756); Teresa Margaret Redi, virgin (1747-1770); John Bosco, founder of Salesians (1815-1888); Conrad of Parzham, lay brother (1818-1894).

1935: John Fisher, bishop-martyr (1469-1535); Thomas More, martyr (1478-1535).
1938: Andrew Bobola, martyr (1592-1657); John Leonardi, founder of Clerics Regular of the Mother of God (c. 1550-1609); Salvatore of Horta, lay brother (1520-1567).

Pius XII
(1939-1958)

1940: Gemma Galgani, virgin (1878-1903); Mary Euphrasia Pelletier, foundress of Good Shepherd Sisters (1796-1868).
1943: Margaret of Hungary, virgin (d. 1270) (equivalent canonization).
1946: Frances Xavier Cabrini, foundress of Missionary Sisters of the Sacred Heart (1850-1917).
1947: Nicholas of Flue, hermit (1417-1487); John of Britto, martyr (1647-1693); Bernard Realini, priest (1530-1616); Joseph Cafasso, priest (1811-1860); Michael Garicoits, founder of Auxiliary Priests of the Sacred Heart (1797-1863); Jeanne Elizabeth des Ages, cofoundress of Daughters of the Cross (1773-1838); Louis Marie Grignon de Montfort, founder of Montfort Fathers (1673-1716); Catherine Laboure, virgin (1806-1876).
1949: Jeanne de Lestonnac, foundress of Religious of Notre Dame of Bordeaux (1556-1640); Maria Josepha Rossello, foundress of Daughters of Our Lady of Pity (1811-1880).
1950: Emily de Rodat, foundress of Congregation of the Holy Family of Villefranche (1787-1852); Anthony Mary Claret, bishop, founder of Claretians (1807-1870); Bartolomea Capitanio (1807-1833) and Vincenza Gerosa (1784-1847), foundresses of Sisters of Charity of Lovere; Jeanne de Valois, foundress of Annonciades of Bourges (1461-1504); Vincenzo M. Strambi, bishop (1745-1824); Maria Goretti, virgin-martyr (1890-1902); Mariana Paredes of Jesus, virgin (1618-1645).
1951: Maria Domenica Mazzarello, cofoundress of Daughters of Our Lady Help of Christians (1837-1881); Emilie de Vialar, foundress of Sisters of St. Joseph "of the Apparition" (1797-1856); Anthony M. Gianelli, bishop (1789-1846); Ignatius of Laconi, lay brother (1701-1781); Francis Xavier Bianchi, priest (1743-1815).
1954: Pius X, pope (1835-1914); Dominic Savio (1842-1857); Maria Crocifissa di Rosa, foundress of Handmaids of Charity of Brescia (1813-1855); Peter Chanel, priest-martyr (1803-1841); Gaspar del Bufalo, founder of Missioners of the Most Precious Blood (1786-1837); Joseph M. Pignatelli, priest (1737-1811).
1958: Herman Joseph, O. Praem., priest (1150-1241) (equivalent canonization).

John XXIII
(1958-1963)

1959: Joaquina de Vedruna de Mas, foundress of Carmelite Sisters of Charity (1783-1854); Charles of Sezze, lay brother (1613-1670).
1960: Gregory Barbarigo, bishop (1625-1697) (equivalent canonization); John de Ribera, bishop (1532-1611).
1961: Bertilla Boscardin, virgin (1888-1922).
1962: Martin de Porres, lay brother (1579-1639); Peter Julian Eymard, founder of Blessed Sacrament Fathers (1811-1868); Anthony Pucci, priest (1819-1892); Francis Mary of Camporosso, lay brother (1804-1866).
1963: Vincent Pallotti, founder of Pallottine Fathers (1795-1850).

Paul VI
(1963-1978)

1964: Charles Lwanga and Twenty-One Companions, Martyrs of Uganda.
1967: Benilde, lay brother (1805-1862).
1969: Julia Billiart, foundress of Sisters of Notre Dame de Namur (1751-1816).
1970: Maria Della Dolorato Torres Acosta, foundress of Servants Sisters of Mary (1826-1887); Leonard Murialdo, priest, founder of Congregation of St. Joseph (1828-1900); Therese Couderc, foundress of Congregation of Our Lady of the Cenacle (1805-1885); John of Avila, preacher and spiritual director (1499-1569); Sts. Nicholas Tavelic, Deodatus of Aquitaine, Peter of Narbonne and Stephen of Cuneo, martyrs (d. 1391); Forty English and Welsh Martyrs (d. 16th cent.).
1974: Teresa of Jesus Jornet Ibars, foundress of Little Sisters of Abandoned Aged (1843-1897).
1975: Vicenza Maria Lopez Vicuna, foundress of Institute of Daughters of Mary Immaculate (1847-1890); Elizabeth Bayley Seton, foundress of Sisters of Charity in the U.S. (1774-1821); John de Massias, Dominican brother-missionary (1585-1645); Oliver Plunkett, archbishop-martyr (1629-1681); Justin de Jacobis, missionary bishop (1800-1860); John Baptist of the Conception, founder of Reformed Discalced Brothers of the Order of the Most Holy Trinity (1561-1613).
1976: Beatrice da Silva, foundress of Congregation of the Immaculate Conception of the BVM (1424 or 1426-1490); John Ogilvie, Scottish Jesuit martyr (1579-1615).
1977: Rafaela Maria of the Sacred Heart, foundress of Handmaids of the Sacred Heart (1850-1925); John Nepomucene Neumann, bishop (1811-1860); Sharbel Makhlouf, Maronite rite monk (1828-1898).

English and Welsh Martyrs

Forty Martyrs of England and Wales, victims of persecution from 1535 to 1671, were canonized by Pope Paul Oct. 25, 1970.

The martyrs were prosecuted and executed as traitors for refusal to comply with laws enacted by Henry VIII and Elizabeth I regarding supremacy (the sovereign was proclaimed the highest authority of the Church in England, acknowledgment of papal primacy was forbidden), succession and the prohibition of native-born to study for the priesthood abroad and return to England for practice of the ministry.

John Houghton, prior of the London Charterhouse, was the first of his group to die (1535) for opposing Henry's Acts of Supremacy and Succession. Cuthbert Mayne (d. 1577) was the protomartyr of the English seminary at Douay. Margaret Clitherow (d. 1586) and Swithun Wells (d. 1591) were executed for sheltering priests. Richard Gwyn (d. 1584), poet, was the protomartyr of Wales.

Others in the group were:

John Almond, Edmund Arrowsmith, Ambrose Barlow, John Boste, Alexander Briant, Edmund Campion, Philip Evans, Thomas Garnet, Edmund Gennings;

Philip Howard, John Jones, John Kemble, Luke Kirby, Robert Lawrence, David Lewis, Ann Line, John Lloyd;

Henry Morse, Nicholas Owen, John Paine, Polydore Plasden, John Plessington, Richard Reynolds, John Rigby, John Roberts;

Alban Roe, Ralph Sherwin, Robert Southwell, John Southworth, John Stone, John Wall, Henry Walpole, Margaret Ward, Augustine Webster and Eustace White.

ENCYCLICALS ISSUED BY LEO XIII AND HIS SUCCESSORS

An encyclical letter is a pastoral letter addressed by a pope to the whole Church. In general, it concerns matters of doctrine, morals or discipline. Its formal title consists of the first few words of the official text. A few encyclicals, notably *Pacem in Terris* by John XXIII and *Ecclesiam Suam* by Paul VI, have been addressed to "all men of good will" as well as to bishops and the faithful in communion with the Church.

An encyclical epistle, which is like an encyclical letter in many respects, is addressed to part of the Church, that is, to the bishops and faithful of a particular country or area. Its contents may concern other than doctrinal, moral or disciplinary matters of universal significance; for example, the commemoration of historical events, conditions in a certain country.

The authority of encyclicals was stated by Pius XII in the encyclical *Humani Generis* Aug. 12, 1950.

"Nor must it be thought that what is contained in encyclical letters does not of itself demand assent, on the pretext that the popes do not exercise in them the supreme power of their teaching authority. Rather, such teachings belong to the ordinary magisterium, of which it is true to say: 'He who hears you, hears me' (Lk. 10:16); for the most part, too, what is expounded and inculcated in encyclical letters already appertains to Catholic doctrine for other reasons. But if the supreme pontiffs in their official documents purposely pass judgment on a matter debated until then, it is obvious to all that the matter, according to the mind and will of the same pontiffs, cannot be considered any longer a question open for discussion among theologians."

The following list contains the titles and indicates the subject matter of encyclical letters and epistles. The latter are generally distinguishable by the limited scope of their titles or contents.

Leo XIII
(1878-1903)

1878: Inscrutabili Dei Consilio (Evils of Society), Apr. 21.
Quod Apostolici Muneris (Socialism, Communism, Nihilism), Dec. 28.
1879: Aeterni Patris (Scholastic Philosophy, Especially of Thomas Aquinas), Aug. 4.
1880: Arcanum (Christian Marriage), Feb. 10.
Grande Munus (Sts. Cyril and Methodius), Sept. 30.
Sancta Dei Civitas (Three French Societies), Dec. 3.
1881: Diuturnum (Origin of Civil Power), June 29.
1882: Etsi Nos (Conditions in Italy), Feb. 15.
Auspicato Concessum (Third Order of St. Francis), Sept. 17.
Cum Multa (Conditions in Spain), Dec. 8.
1883: Supremi Apostolatus Officio (The Rosary), Sept. 1.
1884: Nobilissima Gallorum Gens (Religious Question in France), Feb. 8.
Humanum Genus (Freemasonry), Apr. 20.
Superiore Anno (Recitation of the Rosary), Aug. 30.
1885: Immortale Dei (The Christian Constitution of States), Nov. 1.
Quod Auctoritate (Proclamation of Extraordinary Jubilee Year), Dec. 22.
1886: Quod Multum (Liberty of the Church in Hungary), Aug. 22.
Pergrata Nobis (Needs of the Church in Portugal), Sept. 14.
1888: Libertas (Human Liberty), June 20.
Paterna Caritas (Recalling the Dissenting Armenians), July 25.
Quam Aerumnosa (Italian Immigrants in America), Dec. 10.
1889: Quamquam Pluries (Patronage of St. Joseph and the Blessed Virgin Mary), Aug. 15.

Encyclicals

1890: Sapientiae Christianae (Chief Duties of Christian Citizens), Jan. 10.
Ab Apostoli (To the Clergy and People of Italy), Oct. 15.
1891: Rerum Novarum (Condition of the Working Classes), May 15.
Octobri Mense (The Rosary), Sept. 22.
1892: Au Milieu des Sollicitudes (Church and State in France), Feb. 16.
Magnae Dei Matris (The Rosary), Sept. 8.
1893: Ad Extremas (Seminaries in the East Indies), June 24.
Constanti Hungarorum (Conditions of the Church in Hungary), Sept. 2.
Laetitiae Sanctae (The Rosary), Sept. 8.
Providentissimus Deus (Study of Holy Scripture), Nov. 18.
1894: Caritatis (Conditions in Poland), Mar. 19.
Iucunda Semper Expectatione (The Rosary), Sept. 8.
Christi Nomen (Society for the Propagation of the Faith), Dec. 24.
1895: Adiutricem (The Rosary), Sept. 5.
1896: Satis Cognitum (Church Unity), June 29.
Fidentum Piumque Animum (The Rosary), Sept. 20.
1897: Divinum Illud Munus (The Holy Spirit, doctrine and devotion), May 9.
Militantis Ecclesiae (Third Centenary of the Death of St. Peter Canisius), Aug. 1.
Augustissimae Virginis (The Rosary), Sept. 12.
Affari Vos (The Manitoba School Question), Dec. 8.
1898: Caritatis Studium (The Magisterium of the Church in Scotland), July 25.
Spesse Volte (Catholic Action in Italy) Aug. 5.
1899: Annum Sacrum (Consecration of Mankind to the Sacred Heart), May 25.
Depuis le Jour (Ecclesiastical Education in France), Sept. 8.
1900: Tametsi Futura Prospicientibus (Jesus Christ, Our Redeemer), Nov. 1.
1901: Graves de Communi Re (Christian Democracy), Jan. 18.
1902: Mirae Caritatis (The Most Holy Eucharist), May 28.
Fin dal Principio (Education of the Clergy in Italy), Dec. 8.

Saint Pius X
(1903-1914)

1903: E Supremi (Restoration of All Things in Christ), Oct. 4.
1904: Ad Diem Illum Laetissimum (Jubilee of the Immaculate Conception), Feb. 2.
Iucunda Sane (Thirteenth Centenary of the Death of St. Gregory the Great), Mar. 12.
1905: Acerbo Nimis (Teaching of Christian Doctrine), Apr. 15.
Il Fermo Proposito (Catholic Action in Italy), June 11.
1906: Vehementer Nos (French Separation Law), Feb. 11.
Tribus Circiter (Condemnation of the Mariavites), Apr. 5.
Pieni l'Animo (Clergy in Italy), July 28.
Gravissimo Officio Munere (Forbidding Associations Cultuelles), Aug. 10.
1907: Une Fois Encore (Separation of Church and State in France), Jan. 6.
Pascendi Dominici Gregis (Modernism), Sept. 8.
1909: Communium Rerum (Eighth Centenary of the Death of St. Anselm), Apr. 21.
1910: Editae Saepe (Third Centenary of the Death of St. Charles Borromeo), May 26.
1911: Iamdudum (Separation Law in Portugal), May 24.
1912: Lacrimabili Statu (Indians of South America), June 7.
Singulari Quadam (Labor Organizations in Germany), Sept. 24.

Benedict XV
(1914-1922)

1914: Ad Beatissimi Apostolorum (Appeal for Peace), Nov. 1.
1917: Humani Generis Redemptionem (Preaching), June 15.
1918: Quod Iam Diu (Peace Congress, Paris), Dec. 1.
1919: In Hac Tanta (Twelfth Centenary of St. Boniface), May 14.
Paterno Iam Diu (Christian Charity of the Children of Central Europe), Nov. 24.
1920: Pacem, Dei Munus Pulcherrimum (Peace and Christian Reconciliation), May 23.
Spiritus Paraclitus (Holy Scripture), Sept. 15.
Principi Apostolorum Petro (St. Ephrem the Syrian, declared Doctor), Oct. 5.
Annus Iam Plenus (Child War Victims), Dec. 1.
1921: Sacra Propediem (Seventh Centenary of the Third Order of St. Francis), Jan. 6.
In Praeclara Summorum (Sixth Centenary of Dante's Death), Apr. 30.
Fausto Appetente Die (Seventh Centenary of the Death of St. Dominic), June 29.

Pius XI
(1922-1939)

1922: Ubi Arcano Dei Consilio (Peace of Christ in the Kingdom of Christ), Dec. 23.
1923: Rerum Omnium Perturbationem (Third Centenary of the Death of St. Francis de Sales), Jan. 26.
Studiorum Ducem (Sixth Centenary of the Canonization of St. Thomas Aquinas), June 29.
Ecclesiam Dei (Third Centenary of the Death of St. Josaphat, Archbishop of Polotsk), Nov. 12.

1924: Maximam Gravissimamque (French Diocesan Associations), Jan. 18.
1925: Quas Primas (Feast of Christ the King), Dec. 11.
1926: Rerum Ecclesiae (Catholic Missions), Feb. 28.
Rite Expiatis (Seventh Centenary of the Death of St. Francis of Assisi), Apr. 30.
Iniquis Afflictisque (Persecution of the Church in Mexico), Nov. 18.
1928: Mortalium Animos (Promotion of True Religious Unity), Jan. 6.
Miserentissimus Redemptor (Reparation Due the Sacred Heart), May 8.
Rerum Orientalium (Reunion with the Eastern Churches), Sept. 8.
1929: Mens Nostra (Promotion of Spiritual Exercises), Dec. 20.
Quinquagesimo Ante (Sacerdotal Jubilee), Dec. 23.
Divini Illius Magistri (Rappresentanti in Terra) (Christian Education of Youth), Dec. 31.
1930: Ad Salutem (Fifteenth Centenary of the Death of St. Augustine), Apr. 20.
Casti Connubii (Christian Marriage), Dec. 31.
1931: Quadragesimo Anno (Social Reconstruction), May 15.
Non Abbiamo Bisogno (Catholic Action), June 29.
Nova Impendet (Economic Crisis, Unemployment, Armaments), Oct. 2.
Lux Veritatis (Fifteenth Centenary of the Council of Ephesus), Dec. 25.
1932: Caritate Christi Compulsi (Sacred Heart and World Distress), May 3.
Acerba Animi (Persecution of the Church in Mexico), Sept. 29.
1933: Dilectissima Nobis (Conditions in Spain), June 3.
1935: Ad Catholici Sacerdotii (Catholic Priesthood), Dec. 20.
1936: Vigilanti Cura (Clean Motion Pictures), June 29.
1937: Mit Brennender Sorge (Church in Germany), Mar. 14.
Divini Redemptoris (Atheistic Communism), Mar. 19.
Firmissimam Constantiam (Nos Es Muy Conocida) (Conditions in Mexico), Mar. 28.
Ingravescentibus Malis (The Rosary) Sept. 29.

Pius XII
(1939-1958)

1939: Summi Pontificatus (Function of the State in Modern World), Oct. 20.
Sertum Laetitiae (To the Church in the United States), Nov. 1.
1940: Saeculo Exeunte Octavo (Missions), June 13.
1943: Mystici Corporis Christi (Mystical Body), June 29.
Divino Afflante Spiritu (Biblical Studies), Sept. 30.
1944: Orientalis Ecclesiae Decus (Fifteenth Centenary of the Death of St. Cyril of Alexandria), Apr. 9.
1945: Communium Interpretes Dolorum (Appeal for Prayers), Apr. 15.
Orientales Omnes Ecclesias (Anniversary of the Ruthenian Reunion), Dec. 23.
1946: Quemadmodum (Call for Intensified Aid to Youth), Jan. 6.
Deiparae Virginis Mariae (Proposing to the Bishops the Question of the Definition of the Dogma of the Assumption), May 1.
1947: Fulgens Radiatur (Fourteenth Centenary of the Death of St. Benedict), Mar. 21.
Mediator Dei (Sacred Liturgy), Nov. 20.
Optatissima Pax (Peace and Social Disorders), Dec. 18.
1948: Auspicia Quaedam (Prayer to Blessed Virgin Mary for Peace), May 1.
In Multiplicibus Curis (Crisis in Palestine), Oct. 24.
1949: Redemptoris Nostri (Internationalization of Jerusalem), Apr. 15.
1950: Anni Sacri (Holy Year Call for Public Prayer), Mar. 12.
Summi Maeroris (Renewed Holy Year Call for Public Prayer), July 19.
Humani Generis (Warnings against Attempts to Distort Catholic Truths), Aug. 12.
Mirabile Illud (Call for Renewed Crusade of Prayers for Peace), Dec. 6.
1951: Evangelii Praecones (Call for Greater Missionary Effort), June 2.
Sempiternus Rex (Fifteenth Centenary of the Council of Chalcedon), Sept. 8.
Ingruentium Malorum (Recitation of the Rosary), Sept. 15.
1952: Orientales Ecclesias (Communist Persecution of the Church; Call for Prayers for the Persecuted), Dec. 15.
1953: Doctor Mellifluus (Eighth Centenary of Death of St. Bernard), May 24.
Fulgens Corona (Call for Catholics to Observe Marian Year), Sept. 8.
1954: Sacra Virginitas (Preeminence of Evangelical Chastity), Mar. 25.
Ecclesiae Fastos (Commemoration of St. Boniface), June 5.
Ad Sinarum Gentem (The Church in China), Oct. 7.
Ad Caeli Reginam (Feast of Queenship of Mary), Oct. 11.
1955: Musicae Sacrae (Sacred Music), Dec. 25.
1956: Haurietis Aquas (The Sacred Heart), May 15.
Luctuosissimi Eventus (Prayers for Hungary), Oct. 28.
Laetamur Admodum (Middle East Crisis), Nov. 1.

Datis Nuperrime (Prayers for Peace), Nov. 5.

1957: Fidei Donum (Missionary Effort, especially in Africa), Apr. 21.

Invicti Athletae Christi (Third Centenary of Death of St. Andrew Bobola), May 16.

Le Pelerinage de Lourdes (Centenary of Lourdes Apparitions), July 2.

Miranda Prorsus (Radio, TV and Motion Pictures), Sept. 8.

1958: Ad Apostolorum Principis (Critical Situation of the Church in China), June 29.

Meminisse Juvat (Prayers for Peace and the Persecuted Church), July 14.

John XXIII
(1958-1963)

1959: Ad Petri Cathedram (Appeal to Separated Christians to Reunite with Church), June 29.

Sacerdotii Nostri Primordia (Centenary of the Cure of Ars), Aug. 1.

Grata Recordatio (Rosary), Sept. 26.

Princeps Pastorum (Missions), Nov. 28.

1961: Mater et Magistra (Christianity and Social Progress), May 15.

Aeterna Dei Sapientia (Fifteenth Centenary of the Death of St. Leo the Great), Nov. 11.

1962: Paenitentiam Agere (Appeal for Works of Penance for Success of the Second Vatican Council), July 1.

1963: Pacem in Terris (Peace on Earth), Apr. 11.

Paul VI
(1963-1978)

1964: Ecclesiam Suam (Second Vatican Council Themes), Aug. 6.

1965: Mense Maio (Prayer for Success of Vatican II, Peace), Apr. 29.

Mysterium Fidei (The Eucharist), Sept. 3.

1966: Christi Matri Rosarii (The Rosary), Sept. 15.

1967: Populorum Progressio (Development of Peoples), Mar. 26.

Sacerdotalis Caelibatus (Priestly Celibacy), June 24.

1968: Humanae Vitae (Birth Control), July 25.

John Paul II
(1978-   )

1979: Redemptor Hominis (Redeemer of Man), Mar. 4.

AMERICAN COLLEGE, LOUVAIN

The American College was founded by the bishops of the United States in 1857 as a residence and house of formation for U.S. seminarians and graduate students pursuing courses in theology and related subjects at the Catholic Universities of Leuven and Louvain-la-Neuve (dating from 1425) in Belgium.

The college is administered by an American rector and staff, and operates under the auspices of a special committee of the National Conference of Catholic Bishops. Bishop Edward W. O'Rourke of Peoria is chairman of the committee. The present rector, the 10th, is Msgr. William Greytak of Helena, Mont.

The address is: American College, University of Louvain, Naamsestraat 100, B-3000 Leuven, Belgium.

The Catholic Universities of Leuven and Louvain-la-Neuve are among the most prestigious in the world.

The current enrollment of the American College includes students from more than 35 dioceses in the U.S., Canada, the Bahamas, the United Kingdom, the Netherlands, Australia and Indonesia.

EVANGELIZATION

Evangelization was one of many subjects covered extensively in statements by Pope John Paul in 1979.

In the U.S., the Bishops' Committee on Evangelization announced in January the start of a study intended "to surface information that will help the national Catholic community design and conduct within parishes and dioceses more effective evangelistic programs for the 12 million inactive American Catholics."

More than 60 million unchurched Americans, as well as inactive Catholics, were the concerns of the first National Catholic Lay Celebration of Evangelization held Aug. 16 to 18 in Washington under the principal auspices of the Paulist Office for Evangelization.

AMERICAN COLLEGE, LOUVAIN

The American College was founded by the bishops of the United States in 1857 as a residence and house of formation for U.S. seminarians and graduate students pursuing courses in theology and related subjects at the Catholic Universities of Leuven and Louvain-la-Neuve (dating from 1425) in Belgium.

The college is administered by an American rector and staff, and operates under the auspices of a special committee of the National Conference of Catholic Bishops. Bishop Edward W. O'Rourke of Peoria is chairman of the committee. The present rector, the 10th, is Msgr. William Greytak of Helena, Mont.

The address is: American College, University of Louvain, Naamsestraat 100, B-3000 Leuven, Belgium.

The Catholic Universities of Leuven and Louvain-la-Neuve are among the most prestigious in the world.

The current enrollment of the American College includes students from more than 35 dioceses in the U.S., Canada, the Bahamas, the United Kingdom, the Netherlands, Australia and Indonesia.

Hierarchy of the Catholic Church

ORGANIZATION AND GOVERNMENT

As a structured society, the Catholic Church is organized and governed along lines corresponding mainly to the jurisdictions of the pope and bishops.

The pope is the supreme head of the Church. He has primacy of jurisdiction as well as honor over the entire Church.

Bishops, in union with and in subordination to the pope, are the successors of the Apostles for care of the Church and for the continuation of Christ's mission in the world. They serve the people of their own dioceses, or local churches, with ordinary authority and jurisdiction. They also share, with the pope and each other, in common concern and effort for the general welfare of the whole Church.

Bishops of exceptional status are Eastern Rite patriarchs who, subject only to the pope, are heads of the faithful belonging to their rites throughout the world.

Subject to the Holy Father and directly responsible to him for the exercise of their ministry of service to people in various jurisdictions or divisions of the Church throughout the world are: resident archbishops and metropolitans (heads of archdioceses), resident bishops (heads of dioceses), vicars and prefects apostolic (heads of vicariates apostolic and prefectures apostolic), certain abbots and prelates, apostolic administrators. Each of these, within his respective territory and according to the provisions of canon law, has ordinary jurisdiction over pastors (who are responsible for the administration of parishes), priests, religious and lay persons.

Also subject to the Holy Father are titular archbishops and bishops (who have delegated jurisdiction), religious orders and congregations of pontifical right, pontifical institutes and faculties, papal nuncios and apostolic delegates.

Assisting the pope and acting in his name in the central government and administration of the Church are cardinals and other officials of the Roman Curia.

THE HIERARCHY

The ministerial hierarchy is the orderly arrangement of the ranks and orders of the clergy to provide for the spiritual care of the faithful, the government of the Church, and the accomplishment of the Church's total mission in the world. Persons belong to this hierarchy by virtue of ordination and canonical mission.

The term hierarchy is also used to designate an entire body or group of bishops; for example, the hierarchy of the Church, the hierarchy of the United States.

Hierarchy of Order: Consists of the pope, bishops, priests and deacons, by divine law. Their purpose, for which they are ordained to holy orders, is to carry out the sacramental and pastoral ministry of the Church.

Hierarchy of Jurisdiction: Consists of the pope and bishops by divine law, and other church officials by ecclesiastical institution and mandate, who have authority to govern and direct the faithful for spiritual ends.

Prelates: Clerics with the authority of public office in the Church — i. e., the authority of jurisdiction in the external forum. They are: the pope, patriarchs, residential archbishops and bishops, certain abbots and prelates, vicars and prefects apostolic, vicars general, certain superiors in clerical exempt religious communities. Titular archbishops and bishops without ordinary jurisdiction are not prelates in the strict sense of the term; neither are pastors, who have very limited jurisdiction in the external forum.

The Pope

His Holiness the Pope is the Bishop of Rome, the Vicar of Jesus Christ, the successor of St. Peter, Prince of the Apostles, the Supreme Pontiff who has the primacy of jurisdiction and not merely of honor over the universal Church, the Patriarch of the West, the Primate of Italy, the Archbishop and Metropolitan of the Roman Province, the Sovereign of the State of Vatican City, Servant of the Servants of God.

Cardinals
(See Index)

Patriarchs

Patriarch, a term which had its origin in the Eastern Church, is the title of a bishop who, second only to the pope, has the highest rank in the hierarchy of jurisdiction. He is the incumbent of one of the sees listed below. Subject only to the pope, an Eastern-Rite patriarch is the head of the faithful belonging to his rite throughout the world. The patriarchal sees are so called because of their special status and dignity in the history of the Church.

The Council of Nicaea (325) recognized three patriarchs — the bishops of Alexandria and Antioch in the East, and of Rome in the West. The First Council of Constantinople (381) added the bishop of Constantinople to the list of patriarchs and gave him rank second only to that of the pope, the bishop of Rome and patriarch of the West; this action was seconded by the Council of Chalcedon (451) and was given full recognition by the

Fourth Lateran Council (1215). The Council of Chalcedon also acknowledged patriarchal rights of the bishop of Jerusalem.

Eastern Rite patriarchs are as follows: one of Alexandria, for the Copts; three of Antioch, one each for the Syrians, Maronites and Greek Melkites (the latter also has the personal title of Greek Melkite patriarch of Alexandria and of Jerusalem). The patriarch of Babylonia, for the Chaldeans, and the patriarch of Sis, or Cilicia, for the Armenians, should be called, more properly, *Katholikos* — that is, a prelate delegated for a universality of causes. These patriarchs are elected by bishops of their rites; they receive approval and the pallium, symbolic of their office, from the pope.

Latin Rite patriarchates were established for Antioch, Jerusalem, Alexandria and Constantinople during the Crusades; afterwards, they became patriarchates in name only. Jerusalem, however, was reconstituted as a patriarchate by Pius IX, in virtue of the bull *Nulla Celebrior* of July 23, 1847. In 1964, the Latin titular patriarchates of Constantinople, Alexandria and Antioch, long a bone of contention in relations with Eastern Rites, were abolished.

As of Sept. 20, 1979, the patriarchs in the Church were:

The Pope, Bishop of Rome, Patriarch of the West; Cardinal Stephanos I Sidarouss, C.M., of Alexandria, for the Copts; Ignace Antoine II Hayek, of Antioch, for the Syrians; Maximos V Hakim, of Antioch, for the Greek Melkites (he also has the titles of Alexandria and Jerusalem for the Greek Melkites); Antoine Khoraiche, of Antioch, for the Maronites; Giacomo Beltritti, of Jerusalem, for the Latin Rite; Paul II Cheikho, of Babylon, for the Chaldeans; Hemaiagh Pierre XVII Ghedighian, of Cilicia, for the Armenians.

The titular patriarchs (in name only) of the Latin Rite were: Cardinal Antonio Ribeiro, of Lisbon; Cardinal Marco Cé of Venice and Archbishop Raul Nicolau Goncalves of the East Indies (Archbishop of Goa and Daman, India). The patriarchate of the West Indies has been vacant since 1963.

Archbishops, Metropolitans

Archbishop: A bishop with the title of an archdiocese.

Metropolitan Archbishop: Head of the principal see, an archdiocese, in an ecclesiastical province consisting of several dioceses. He has the full powers of bishop in his own archdiocese and limited supervisory jurisdiction and influence over the other (suffragan) dioceses in the province.

Titular Archbishop: Has the title of an archdiocese which formerly existed in fact but now exists in title only. He does not have ordinary jurisdiction over an archdiocese.

Archbishop ad personam: A title of personal honor and distinction granted to some bishops. They do not have ordinary jurisdiction over an archdiocese.

Primate: A title given to the ranking prelate of some countries or regions.

Bishops

Residential Bishop: A bishop in charge of a diocese.

Titular Bishops: Have the titles of dioceses which formerly existed in fact but now exist in title only. They have delegated authority of jurisdiction, by grant in line with their assignments, rather than the ordinary jurisdiction of office which belongs to a residential bishop. An auxiliary bishop (titular) is an assistant to a residential bishop. A coadjutor bishop (titular) is an assistant bishop of higher status; some coadjutors have the right of succession to residential sees.

Episcopal Vicar: An assistant, who may or may not be a bishop, appointed by a residential bishop as his deputy for a certain part of a diocese, a determined type of apostolic work, or the faithful of a certain rite.

Eparch, Exarch: Titles of bishops of Eastern-Rite churches.

Nomination of Bishops: Nominees for episcopal ordination are selected in several ways. Final appointment in all cases is subject to decision by the pope.

In the U.S., bishops periodically submit the names of candidates to the archbishop of their province. The names are then considered at a meeting of the bishops of the province, and those receiving a favorable vote are forwarded to the apostolic delegate for transmission to the Holy See. Bishops are free to seek the counsel of priests, religious and lay persons with respect to nominees.

Eastern-Rite churches have their own procedures and synodal regulations for nominating and making final selection of candidates for episcopal ordination.

In some countries where concordat or other special arrangements are in effect, civil governments have specified privileges to express approval or disapproval of candidates for the episcopacy.

Ad Limina Visit: Residential bishops and military vicars are obliged to make a periodic *ad limina* visit ("to the threshold" of the Apostles) to the tombs of Sts. Peter and Paul, have audience with the Holy Father, consult with appropriate Vatican officials and present a written report on conditions in their jurisdictions. The most recent regulations concerning the formalities and scheduling of visits by bishops from various countries, generally every five years, were issued by the Congregation for Bishops in a decree dated Nov. 27, 1975.

Other Prelates

Some prelates and abbots, formerly called *nullius*, have jurisdiction over territories (abbacies, prefectures, prelatures) not under the authority of diocesan bishops.

Vicar Apostolic: Usually a titular bishop who has ordinary jurisdiction over a mission territory. A vicar apostolic could also serve as the administrator of a vacant diocese or a diocese whose bishop is impeded from the exercise of his office.

Prefect Apostolic: A prelate with ordinary jurisdiction over a mission territory.

Apostolic Administrator: Usually a bishop appointed to administer an ecclesiastical jurisdiction temporarily. Administrators of lesser rank are also appointed for special and more restricted supervisory duties.

Vicar General: A bishop's deputy for the administration of a diocese. Such a vicar does not have to be a bishop.

Honorary Prelates

Honorary prelates belonging to the Pontifical Household are: Apostolic Prothonotaries, Honorary Prelates of His Holiness, and Chaplains of His Holiness. Their title is Reverend Monsignor.

SYNOD OF BISHOPS

The Synod of Bishops was chartered by Pope Paul VI Sept. 15, 1965, in a document he issued on his own initiative under the title, *Apostolica Sollicitudo*. According to the document:

• The purposes of the Synod are: "to encourage close union and valued assistance between the Sovereign Pontiff and the bishops of the entire world; to insure that direct and real information is provided on questions and situations touching upon the internal action of the Church and its necessary activity in the world of today; to facilitate agreement on essential points of doctrine and on methods of procedure in the life of the Church."

• The Synod is a central ecclesiastical institution, permanent by nature.

• The Synod is directly and immediately subject to the Pope, who has authority to assign its agenda, to call it into session, and to give its members deliberative as well as advisory authority.

• In addition to a limited number of ex officio members and a few heads of male religious institutes, the majority of the members are elective by and representative of national or regional episcopal conferences. The Pope reserved the right to appoint the general secretary, special secretaries and no more than 15 per cent of the total membership.

The secretary general is Archbishop Jozef Tomko of Czechoslovakia.

First Meeting, 1967

The Synod met for the first time from Sept. 29 to Oct. 29, 1967, in Vatican City. Its objectives, as stated by Pope Paul, were "the preservation and strengthening of the Catholic faith, its integrity, its force, its development, its doctrinal and historical coherence."

One result of synodal deliberations was a recommendation to the Pope to establish an international commission of theologians to assist the Congregation for the Doctrine of the Faith and to broaden approaches to theological research. The commission was subsequently set up by Pope Paul in 1969.

In other actions, the Synod called for the formulation of a Code of Canon Law more pastoral than the one in force since 1918 and more in touch with the mentality, aspirations and needs of people in contemporary circumstances; favored the view that episcopal conferences should have major control over seminaries in their respective areas; suggested some changes in pastoral procedures with respect to mixed marriages, which were authorized in 1970; gave general approval to the New Order of the Mass which was promulgated and put into effect in 1969.

The first meeting of the Synod had 197 participants.

Extraordinary Session

The second Synod of Bishops, meeting in extraordinary session Oct. 11 to 28, 1969, opened the door to wider participation by the bishops with the Pope and each other in the government of the Church.

The business assigned to the meeting by Pope Paul was to seek and examine ways and means of putting into practice the principle of collegiality which figured largely in declarations of the Second Vatican Council on the Church and the pastoral office of bishops.

Accordingly, proceedings were oriented to three main points: (1) the nature and implications of collegiality; (2) the relationships of bishops and their conferences to the Pope; (3) the relationships of bishops and their conferences to each other. The end results were three proposals approved by the bishops and the Pope, and five times that number approved and placed under advisement by the Pope. All proposals pointed in the direction of more cooperative action by all the bishops with the Pope in the conduct of church affairs.

The three proposals which were approved and moved for action provided for regular meetings of the Synod at two-year intervals (later extended to three years), staff organization and operations of the general secretariat in the interim between meetings, and openness of the synodal agenda to suggestions by bishops.

The second meeting had 146 participants.

Between the second and third meetings of the Synod, an advisory council of 15 members (12 elected, three appointed by the Pope) was formed to provide the secretariat with adequate staff for carrying on liaison with episcopal conferences and for drawing up the agenda of synodal meetings. The council, at its first meeting May 12 to 15, 1970, followed the lead of the second assembly by opening the agenda of the 1971 meeting to the suggestions of bishops from all over the world.

Synod '71

The ministerial priesthood and justice in the world were the principal topics of discussion at the third and longest meeting, the Second General Assembly of the Synod, Sept. 30 to Nov. 6, 1971.

Advisory reports on these subjects, compiled from views expressed by the bishops before and during the synodal sessions, were presented to Pope Paul at the end of the meeting. He authorized publication of the reports and said, in a letter made public Dec. 9, that he accepted conclusions reached by the bishops which "conform to the current norms" of church teaching.

The Priesthood

In its report on the priesthood, the Synod described difficulties experienced by priests, stated traditional doctrinal principles on the priesthood, and drew from these principles a set of guidelines for priestly life and ministry in the mission of Christ and the Church, and in the communion of the Church.

The report emphasized the primary and permanent dedication of priests in the Church to the ministry of word, sacrament and pastoral service as a full-time occupation.

The synodal Fathers — with 168 votes in favor without reservations, 21 votes in favor with reservations, and 10 votes against — supported the existing discipline of clerical celibacy. They favored leaving to the discretion of the Pope decisions regarding the ordination of already married men in special circumstances. They did not consider the question of permitting already ordained priests to marry. The majority voted against permitting priests who had left the ministry to resume priestly duties, although they said such priests could serve the Church in other ways and should be treated in a just and fraternal manner.

Justice in the World

In connection with "The Mission of the People of God To Further Justice in the World," a synodal report reviewed a wide range of existing injustices; cited the social-justice imperatives of the Gospel; called for the practice of justice throughout the Church and for greater efforts in education and ecumenical collaboration for justice; and outlined an eight-point program for international action.

Behind the Synod's recommendations were the convictions:

• "The Church . . . has a proper and specific responsibility which is identified with her mission of giving witness before the world of the need for love and justice contained in the Gospel message, a witness to be carried out in church institutions themselves and in the lives of Christians."

• "Action on behalf of justice and participation in the transformation of the world fully appear to us as a constitutive dimension of the preaching of the Gospel; or, in other words, of the Church's mission for the redemption of the human race and its liberation from every oppressive situation."

• "The present situation of the world, seen in the light of faith, calls us back to the very essence of the Christian message, creating in us a deep awareness of its true meaning and of its urgent demands. The mission of preaching the Gospel dictates at the present time that we should dedicate ourselves to the liberation of man even in his present existence in this world. For, unless the Christian message of love and justice shows its effectiveness through action in the cause of justice in the world, it will only with difficulty gain credibility with the men of our times."

The assembly had 210 participants.

Fourth Assembly

"Evangelization of the Modern World" was the theme of the fourth assembly of the Synod, Sept. 27 to Oct. 26, 1974. Its major product was a general statement on the subject, covering the need for it and its relationship to efforts for total human liberation from personal and social evil.

Evangelization

The statement reconfirmed "that the mandate to evangelize all men constitutes the essential mission of the Church," that "the duty to proclaim the Gospel belongs to the whole people of God," and that "this work demands incessant interior conversion on the part of individual Christians and continual renewal of our communities and institutions."

The bishops noted that evangelization is impeded by atheism, secularism, and the repression of religious liberty in a number of countries.

Communication of the Gospel was called "a dynamic process" which "takes place through word, work and life," and which needs "translation," expression and indigenization in terms of the religious and cultural patterns of people in different places.

The statement cited the need and intention for ecumenical collaboration with other Christians for the purpose of rendering "to the world a much broader common witness to Christ, while at the same time working to obtain full union in the Lord."

And Liberation

Regarding the relationship between evangelization and human liberation, the bishops said:

"Faithful to her evangelizing mission, the Church, as a truly poor, praying and fraternal community, can do much to bring about the integral salvation or the full liberation of men. She can draw from the Gospel the most profound reasons and ever new incentives to promote generous dedication to the service of all men — the poor especially, the weak and the oppressed — and to eliminate the social consequences of sin which are translated into unjust social and political structures.

"The Church does not remain within merely political, social and economic limits (elements which she must certainly take into account) but leads towards freedom under all its forms — liberation from sin, from individual or collective selfishness — and to full communion with God and with men who are like brothers. In this way the Church, in her evangelical way, promotes the true and complete liberation of all men, groups and peoples."

The assembly had 209 participants.

Synod '77

"Catechetics in Our Time, with Special Reference to Children and Young People," was the theme of the fifth assembly, Sept. 30 to Oct. 29, 1977. Its major products were a "Message to the People of God," the first synodal statement issued since inception of the body, and two documents presented to Pope Paul — a set of 34 propositions and some 900 suggestions regarding the substance of the propositions and the message on catechetics.

The propositions covered six general subjects in considerable detail: the importance of catechetical renewal, the theme of authentic catechesis, the mode of authentic catechizing, the necessity of catechesis for all Christians, the community as the context and milieu of catechesis, attitudes and other factors affecting catechesis.

The "Message to the People of God" consisted of three parts, dealing with: the world, young people and catechesis; the manifestation of salvation in Christ; catechesis as the task of all people in the Church.

The fifth assembly had 204 delegates.

Sixth Assembly

The theme of the sixth assembly, to be held in 1980, is "The Role of the Christian Family in the Modern World." A preparatory paper on the subject was circulated during the summer of 1979 among bishops throughout the world, for comment and recommendations to be considered by the secretariat and advisory council in drawing up a workable agenda.

U.S. delegates elected by the National Conference of Catholic Bishops to attend the 1980 Synod are: Archbishops John R. Quinn of San Francisco, Joseph L. Bernardin of Cincinnati, Robert F. Sanchez of Santa Fe, and Auxiliary Bishop J. Francis Stafford of Baltimore. The alternates are Bishops Walter W. Curtis of Bridgeport and Lawrence Welsh of Spokane.

ROMAN CURIA

The Roman Curia consists of the Secretariat of State, the Sacred Council for the Public Affairs of the Church, nine congregations, three tribunals, three secretariats, and a complex of commissions, councils and offices which administer church affairs at the highest level.

Background

The Curia evolved gradually from advisory assemblies or synods of the Roman clergy with whose assistance the popes directed church affairs during the first 11 centuries. Its original office was the Apostolic Chancery, dating from the fourth century. The antecedents of its permanently functioning agencies and offices were special commissions of cardinals and prelates. Its establishment in a form resembling what it is now dates from the second half of the 16th century.

Pope Paul VI gave the following short account of the background of the Curia in the apostolic constitution *Regimini Ecclesiae Universae* ("For the Government of the Universal Church"), dated Aug. 15, 1967.

"The Roman Pontiffs, successors to Blessed Peter, have striven to provide for the government of the Universal Church by making use of experts to advise and assist them.

"In this connection, we should remember both the Presbyterium of the City of Rome and the College of Cardinals of the Holy Roman Church which in the course of centuries evolved from it. Then, little by little, as we know, out of that office (Apostolic Chancery) which was set up in the fourth century to transmit papal documents, many offices developed; to these was added the Auditorium, which was a well-developed tribunal in the 13th century and which was more thoroughly organized by John XXII (1316-1334).

"With an increase in the volume of things to be dealt with, bodies or commissions of cardinals selected to treat of specific questions began to be more efficiently organized in the 16th century, from which eventually arose the congregations of the Roman Curia. It is to the credit of our predecessor Sixtus V that, in the constitution *Immensa Aeterni Dei* of Jan. 22, 1588, he arranged the sacred councils in an orderly manner and wisely described the structure of the Roman Curia.

"With the progress of time, however, it happened that some of them became obsolete, others had to be added, and others had to be restructured. This is the work our predecessor St. Pius X set out to do with the constitution *Sapienti Consilio* of June 29, 1908. Its provisions, a lasting testimony to that wise and ingenious pastor of the Church, were with a few changes incorporated into the Code of Canon Law" (Canons 242-264).

Reorganization

Pope Paul initiated a four-year reorganization study in 1963 which resulted in the constitution *Regimini Ecclesiae Universae*. The document was published Aug. 18, 1967, and went into full effect in March, 1968.

While the study was underway, the Pope took preliminary steps toward curial reorganization by reorienting and changing the title of the Sacred Congregation of the Holy Office (to the Sacred Congregation for the Doctrine of the Faith) and by appointing a number of non-Italians to key curial positions.

The stated purposes of the reorganization were to increase the efficiency of the Curia and to make it more responsive to the needs and concerns of the Universal Church. The pursuit of these objectives involved various modifications.

Curial Departments

• The Office of the Pope, including the Papal Secretariat or Secretariat of State and the Council for the Public Affairs of the Church.

• Nine congregations, instead of twelve as formerly. The functions of the Sacred Congregation of Ceremonies were transferred to the Prefecture of the Pontifical Household; the duties of the Sacred Congregation for Extraordinary Ecclesiastical Affairs were taken over by the Sacred Council for the Public Affairs of the Church; the Sacred Congregation of the Basilica of St. Peter was reduced in rank. In 1969, the Sacred Congregation of Rites was phased out of existence and its functions were assigned to the Sacred Congregation for the Causes of Saints and the Sacred Congregation for Divine Worship. In 1975 the Congregation for the Sacraments and Divine Worship was established to replace the Congregation for the Discipline of the Sacraments and the Congregation for Divine Worship.

• Three secretariats, the Council of the Laity and the Pontifical Commission on Justice and Peace.

• Three tribunals.

• Six offices, including the former Apostolic Chancery (abolished in 1973) and Apostolic Chamber, and the newly constituted Prefecture of Economic Affairs, Prefecture of the Pontifical Household, Administration of the Patrimony of the Apostolic See, and Central Statistics Office. Functions of the former Apostolic Datary and the Secretariats of State, of Briefs to Princes, and of Latin Letters were transferred to the Secretariat of State.

Operational Procedures

• The papal secretary or secretary of state has authority to take initiative in coordinating and expediting business through meetings and other cooperative procedures.

• Officials of departments have five-year terms of office, which may be renewed. Resignation is automatic on the death of a pope. The five-year terms of consultors are renewable.

• Diocesan bishops as well as full-time curial personnel have membership in curial departments, in accordance with provisions of the decree *Pro Comperto Sane* of Aug. 6, 1967. Seven diocesan bishops hold five-year membership in each congregation, with full rights to participation in the more important plenary assemblies scheduled once a year. They are also entitled to take part in routine meetings whenever they are in Rome. Three general superiors of male religious institutes hold similar membership in the Sacred Congregation for Religious and Secular Institutes.

• Lay persons are eligible to serve as consultors to curial departments.

• Close liaison with episcopal conferences is required. They should be given prior notice of forthcoming curial decrees affecting them in any special way.

• In line with customary procedure, matters in which the competence of two or more departments is involved are handled on a cooperative basis, with mutual consultation and decision.

• Although Latin remains the official language of the Curia, communication in any of the widely known modern languages is acceptable.

• Informational and financial services are centralized in the Central Statistics Office and the Prefecture of Economic Affairs, respectively.

• Heads of curial departments are required to notify the pope before conducting any serious or extraordinary business.

• Authority to act and decide on many matters belongs to departmental officials in virtue of delegation from the pope. Some matters, however, have to be referred to the pope for final decision.

Internationalization

As of Sept. 20, 1979, heads or principal officers of departments of the Roman Curia (all cardinals unless indicated otherwise) were from the following countries: Italy (Bafile, Baggio, Caprio, Casaroli, Felici, Paupini, Pignedoli, Opilio Rossi, Vagnozzi); France (Philippe, Garrone); Argentina (Pironio); Australia (Knox); Austria (Koenig); Benin (Gantin); Brazil (Agnelo Rossi); Canada (Bishop Gagnon); Germany (Msgr. Ewers); India (Archbishop Lourdusamy); Netherlands (Willebrands); Yugoslavia (Seper).

The international complexion of personnel in the Roman Curia changed considerably during the decade from 1961 to 1970. The number of non-Italians increased from 570 to more than 1,400, a rise of 145 per cent, while the number of Italians increased from 750 to 850, a rise of only 14 per cent. In 1970, 62 per cent were from other countries, as compared with 44 per cent in 1961.

DEPARTMENTS

Secretariat of State: Provides the pope with the closest possible assistance in the care of the Universal Church and in dealings with all departments of the Curia.

The cardinal secretary is the key coordinator of curial operations. He has authority to call meetings of the prefects of all departments for expediting the conduct of business, for consultation and intercommunication. He handles: any and all matters entrusted to him by the pope, and ordinary matters which are not within the competence of other departments; some relations with bishops; relations with representatives of the Holy See, civil governments and their representatives, without prejudice to the competence of the Council for the Public Affairs of the Church.

The cardinal secretary has been likened to a prime minister or head of government because of the significant role he plays in coordinating curial operations at the highest level.

The secretariat has two offices for preparing and writing letters for the pope (functions formerly performed by the Secretariat of Briefs to Princes and the Secretariat of Latin Letters), and a Central Statistics Office.

It also handles work formerly done by the Apostolic Datary (the dating and countersigning of papal documents, and the management of church benefices), and the Apostolic Chancery, abolished in 1973 (care of the pope's leaden seal and the Fisherman's Ring).

It has supervisory duties over the Commission for the Instruments of Social Communication, two Vatican publications, *Acta Apostolicae Sedis* and *Annuario Pontificio*, and the Vatican Personnel Office.

The Prefecture of Vatican City is answerable to the secretary of state.

OFFICIALS: Cardinal Agostino Casaroli, secretary of state, Most Rev. Eduardo Martinez Somalo, undersecretary and secretary of the Cifra.

Council for the Public Affairs of the Church: Handles diplomatic and other relations with civil governments. With the Secretariat of State, it supervises matters concerning nunciatures and apostolic delegations. It also has supervision of the Pontifical Commission for Russia.

OFFICIALS: Cardinal Agostino Casaroli, prefect, secretary of state; Most Rev. Achille Silvestrini, secretary.

BACKGROUND: Originated by Pius VI in 1793 as the Congregation for Extraordinary Affairs from the Kingdom of the Gauls; given wider scope by Pius VII, July 19, 1814; formerly called the Sacred Congregation for Extraordinary Ecclesiastical Affairs.

CONGREGATIONS

Sacred Congregation for the Doctrine of the Faith: Has responsibility to safeguard the doctrine of faith and morals.

Accordingly, it examines doctrinal questions; promotes studies thereon; evaluates theological opinions and, when necessary and after prior consultation with concerned bishops, reproves those regarded as opposed to principles of the faith; examines books on doctrinal matters and can reprove such works, if the contents so warrant, after giving authors the opportunity to defend themselves.

It examines matters pertaining to the Privilege of Faith (Petrine Privilege) in marriage cases, and safeguards the dignity of the sacrament of penance.

It has working relations with the Pontifical Biblical Commission (see separate entry).

In 1969, Pope Paul set up a Theological Commission (see separate entry) as an adjunct to the congregation, to provide it with the advisory services of additional experts in theology and allied disciplines.

OFFICIALS: Cardinal Franjo Seper, prefect; Most Rev. Jerome Hamer, O.P., secretary.

BACKGROUND: At the beginning of the 13th century, legates of Innocent III were commissioned as the Holy Office of the Inquisition to combat heresy; the same task was entrusted to the Dominican Order by Gregory IX in 1231 and to the Friars Minor by Innocent IV from 1243 to 1254. On July 21, 1542 (apostolic constitution *Licet*), Paul III instituted a permanent congregation of cardinals with supreme and universal competence over matters concerning heretics and those suspected of heresy. Pius IV, St. Pius V and Sixtus V further defined the work of the congregation. St. Pius X changed its name to the Congregation of the Holy Office.

Paul VI, in virtue of the motu proprio *Integrae Servandae* of Dec. 7, 1965, began reorganization of the Curia with this body, to which he gave the new title, Sacred Congregation for the Doctrine of the Faith. Its orientation is not merely negative, in the condemnation of error, but positive, in the promotion of orthodox doctrine. The right of appeal, judicial representation, and the consultation of their proper regional conference of bishops, are assured to persons accused of unorthodox doctrine. The office for the censorship of books and the Roman Index of Prohibited Books were abolished.

Sacred Congregation for the Oriental Churches: Has competence in matters concerning the persons and discipline of Eastern Rite Churches. It has jurisdiction over territories in which the majority of Christians belong to Oriental Rites (i.e., Egypt, the Sinai Peninsula, Eritrea, Northern Ethiopia, Southern Albania, Bulgaria, Cyprus, Greece, Iran, Iraq, Lebanon, Palestine, Syria, Jordan, Turkey, Afghanistan, the part of Thrace subject to Turkey); also, over minority communities of Orientals no matter where they live.

To assure adequate and equal representation, it has as many offices as there are rites of Oriental Churches in communion with the Holy See.

It is under mandate to consult with the Secretariat for Promoting Christian Unity on questions concerning separated Oriental Churches, and with the Secretariat for Non-Christians, especially in relations with Moslems.

It has a special commission on the liturgy and an Oriental Church Information Service.

OFFICIALS: *Cardinal Paul Philippe, O.P., prefect; Most Rev. Mario Brini, secretary.*

Members include all Eastern Rite patriarchs and the president of the Secretariat for Promoting Christian Unity. Consultors include the secretary of the same secretariat.

BACKGROUND: Special congregations for the affairs of the Greek and other Oriental Churches were founded long before this body was created by Pius IX Jan. 6, 1862 (apostolic constitution *Romani Pontifices*), and united with the Sacred Congregation for the Propagation of the Faith. The congregation was made autonomous by Benedict XV May 1, 1917 (motu proprio *Dei Providentis*), and given wider authority by Pius XI Mar. 25, 1938 (motu proprio *Sancta Dei Ecclesia*). John XXIII appointed six patriarchs, five of Eastern Rites and one of the Roman Rite, to the congregation and gave them the same rights as cardinals belonging to the body, in March, 1963. Paul VI named representatives of all Eastern-Rite bodies to serve as consultors of the congregation, in November, 1963.

Sacred Congregation for Bishops, formerly called the Sacred Consistorial Congregation: Has functions related in one way or another to bishops and the jurisdictions in which they serve.

Its concerns are: the establishment and changing of dioceses, provinces, military vicariates and other jurisdictions; providing for the naming of bishops and other prelates; studying things concerning the persons, work and pastoral activity of bishops; providing for the care of bishops when they leave office; receiving and studying reports on the conditions of dioceses; general supervision of the holding and recognition of particular councils and conferences of bishops; publishing and circulating pastoral norms and guidelines through conferences of bishops.

It supervises the Pontifical Commission for Latin America and the Pontifical Commission for Migration and Tourism.

OFFICIAL: *Cardinal Sebastiano Baggio, prefect.*

Ex officio members are the prefects of the Council for the Public Affairs of the Church, and of the Congregations for the Doctrine of the Faith, for the Clergy, and for Catholic Education. The substitute secretaries and undersecretaries of these curial departments are ex officio consultors.

BACKGROUND: Established by Sixtus V Jan. 22, 1588 (apostolic constitution *Immensa*); given an extension of powers by St. Pius X June 20, 1908, and Pius XII Aug. 1, 1952 (apostolic constitution *Exsul Familia*).

Sacred Congregation for the Sacraments and Divine Worship: Established in 1975 to replace the Congregation for the Discipline of the Sacraments and the Congregation for Divine Worship.

The congregation consists of two sections — for the sacraments and for divine worship. The former supervises the discipline of the sacraments without prejudice to the competencies of the Sacred Congregation for the Doctrine of the Faith and other curial departments. The latter has general competence over the ritual and pastoral aspects of divine worship in the Roman and other Latin Rites.

OFFICIALS: *Cardinal James R. Knox, prefect; Most Rev. Antonio Innocenti, secretary.*

BACKGROUND: The congregation was established by Paul VI Aug. 1, 1975 (apostolic constitution, *Constans novis studium,* dated July 11, 1975). Formerly its duties were carried out by the Congregation for the Discipline of the Sacraments (instituted by St. Pius X June 29, 1908) and the Congregation for Divine Worship (established by Paul VI, May 8, 1969, to replace the Congregation of Rites instituted by Sixtus V in 1588).

Sacred Congregation for the Causes of Saints: Handles all matters connected with beatification and canonization procedures, and the preservation of relics. These affairs were formerly under the supervision of the Congregation of Rites.

The congregation carries on its work through three sections or offices.

One section is a juridical office with supervisory responsibility over procedures and examinations conducted to determine the holiness of prospective saints. It includes a medical commission for the study of miracles attributed to the intercession of candidates for sainthood.

A second section, headed by the promoter general of the faith, who is popularly called the "Devil's Advocate," serves the purpose of establishing beyond reasonable doubt the evidence of holiness advanced in support of beatification and canonization causes.

Research and evaluation of documentary evidence figuring in canonization causes are the functions of the historic-hagiographical section.

OFFICIALS: Cardinal Corrado Bafile, prefect; Most Rev. Giuseppe Casoria, secretary.

BACKGROUND: The functions and title of this congregation were determined by Paul VI May 8, 1969 (apostolic constitution *Sacra Rituum Congregatio*). Formerly, its duties were carried out by the Congregation of Rites, which was established by Sixtus V in 1588 and affected by legislation of Pius XI in 1930.

Sacred Congregation for the Clergy, formerly called the Sacred Congregation of the Council: Handles matters concerning the persons, work and pastoral ministry of clerics who exercise their apostolate in a diocese. Such clerics are diocesan deacons and priests, and religious who are engaged in ordinary parochial ministry in a diocese.

It carries on its work through three offices.

One office promotes the spiritual growth and formation as well as the professional competence of priests by encouraging the establishment and operation of pastoral institutes and other study opportunities; oversees the general discipline of the clergy, the establishment and conduct of pastoral councils and senates of priests, and resolves controversies among clerics; has a mandate to draw up a set of general principles to direct a better distribution of priests for pastoral service.

A second office, in view of its primary concern for preaching of the word of God, encourages effective apostolic programs and methods, with special emphasis on catechetical and other forms of religious training and formation for the faithful.

A third office has supervisory responsibility over church property and the temporalities of priestly life; among its functions are efforts to provide for the support of the clergy through suitable salary scales, pensions, security and health insurance programs, and other measures.

OFFICIALS: Cardinal Silvio Oddi, prefect; Most Rev. Maximino Romero de Lema, secretary.

BACKGROUND: Established by Pius IV Aug. 2, 1564 (apostolic constitution *Alias Nos*), under the title, Sacred Congregation of the Cardinals Interpreters of the Council of Trent; affected by legislation of Gregory XIII and Sixtus V.

Sacred Congregation for Religious and Secular Institutes, formerly known as the Sacred Congregation of Religious or for the Affairs of Religious: Has dual competence over institutes of religious, together with societies of the common life without vows, and secular institutes.

One section deals with the affairs of all religious institutes and societies of the common life, and their members. It has authority in matters related to the establishment, general direction and suppression of institutes; general discipline in line with their rules and constitutions; the movement toward renewal and adaptation of institutes in contemporary circumstances; the setting up and encouragement of councils and conferences of major religious superiors for intercommunication and other purposes.

A second section has the same competence over the affairs and members of secular institutes as the first has over religious.

OFFICIALS: Cardinal Eduardo Pironio, prefect; Most. Rev. Augustin Mayer, O.S.B., secretary.

BACKGROUND: Founded by Sixtus V May 27, 1586, with the title, Sacred Congregation for Consultations of Regulars (apostolic constitution *Romanus Pontifex*); confirmed by the apostolic constitution *Immensa* Jan. 22, 1588; made part of the Congregation for Consultations of Bishops and other Prelates in 1601; made autonomous by St. Pius X in 1908.

Sacred Congregation for Catholic Education, formerly known as the Sacred Congregation of Seminaries and Universities: Has supervisory competence over institutions and works of Catholic education.

It carries on its work through three offices.

One office handles matters connected with the direction, discipline and temporal administration of seminaries, and with the education of diocesan clergy, religious and members of secular institutes.

A second office oversees Catholic universities, faculties of study and other institutions of higher learning inasmuch as they depend on the authority of the Church; encourages cooperation and mutual assistance among Catholic institutions, and the establishment of Catholic hospices and centers on campuses of non-Catholic institutions.

A third office is concerned in various ways with all Catholic schools below the college-university level, with general questions concerning education and studies, and with the cooperation of conferences of bishops and civil authorities in educational matters.

The congregation supervises Pontifical Works for Priestly Vocations.

OFFICIALS: Cardinal Gabriel Garrone, prefect; Most Rev. Antonio M. Javierre Ortas, secretary.

BACKGROUND: The title and functions of the congregation were defined by Benedict XV Nov. 4, 1915; Pius XI, in 1931 and 1932, and Pius XII, in 1941 and 1949, extended its functions. Its work had previously been carried on by two other congregations erected by Sixtus V in 1588 and Leo XII in 1824.

Sacred Congregation for the Evangelization of Peoples (for the Propagation of the Faith): Directs and coordinates missionary work throughout the world.

Accordingly, it has competence over those

matters which concern all the missions established for the spread of Christ's kingdom. These include: fostering missionary vocations; providing for the training of missionaries in seminaries; assigning missionaries to fields of work; establishing ecclesiastical jurisdictions and proposing candidates to serve them as bishops and in other capacities; encouraging the recruitment and development of indigenous clergy; mobilizing spiritual and financial support for missionary activity.

In general, the varied competence of the congregation extends to most persons and affairs of the Church in areas classified as mission territories.

To promote missionary cooperation, the congregation has a Supreme Council for the Direction of Pontifical Missionary Works. Subject to this council are the general councils of the Missionary Union of the Clergy, the Society for the Propagation of the Faith, the Society of St. Peter the Apostle for Native Clergy, the Society of the Holy Childhood, and the *Fides* news agency.

OFFICIALS: Cardinal Agnelo Rossi, prefect; Most Rev. D. Simon Lourdusamy, secretary.

The heads of the Secretariats for Promoting Christian Unity, for Non-Christians, and for Non-Believers are ex officio members of the congregation.

BACKGROUND: Originated as a commission of cardinals by Gregory XIII and modified by Clement VIII to promote the reconciliation of separated Eastern Christians; erected as a stable congregation by Gregory XV June 22, 1622 (apostolic constitution *Inscrutabili*).

TRIBUNALS

Sacred Apostolic Penitentiary: Has jurisdiction for the internal forum only (sacramental and non-sacramental). It issues decisions on questions of conscience; grants absolutions, dispensations, commutations, sanations and condonations; has charge of non-doctrinal matters pertaining to indulgences.

OFFICIALS: Cardinal Giuseppe Paupini, major penitentiary; Msgr. Luigi de Magistris, regent.

BACKGROUND: Origin dates back to the 12th century; affected by the legislation of many popes; radically reorganized by St. Pius V in 1569; jurisdiction limited to the internal forum by St. Pius X; Benedict XV annexed the Office of Indulgences to it Mar. 25, 1917.

Apostolic Signatura: The principal concerns of this supreme court of the Church are to resolve questions concerning juridical procedure and to supervise the observance of laws and rights at the highest level. It decides the jurisdictional competence of lower courts and has jurisdiction in cases involving personnel and decisions of the Rota. It is the supreme court of the State of Vatican City.

OFFICIALS: Cardinal Pericle Felici, prefect; Most Rev. Aurelio Sabattani, secretary.

BACKGROUND: A permanent office of the Signatura has existed since the time of Eugene IV in the 15th century; affected by the legislation of many popes; reorganized by St. Pius X in 1908 and made the supreme tribunal of the Church.

Sacred Roman Rota: The ordinary court of appeal for cases appealed to the Holy See. It is best known for its competence and decisions in cases concerning the validity of marriage.

OFFICIAL: Msgr. Heinrich Ewers, dean.

BACKGROUND: Originated in the Apostolic Chancery; affected by the legislation of many popes; reorganized by St. Pius X in 1908 and further revised by Pius XI in 1934.

SECRETARIATS

Secretariat for Promoting Christian Unity: Handles relations with members of other Christian ecclesial communities; deals with the correct interpretation and execution of the principles of ecumenism; initiates or promotes Catholic ecumenical groups and coordinates on national and international levels the efforts of those promoting Christian unity; undertakes dialogue regarding ecumenical questions and activities with churches and ecclesial communities separated from the Apostolic See; sends Catholic observer-representatives to Christian gatherings, and invites to Catholic gatherings observers of other churches; orders into execution conciliar decrees dealing with ecumenical affairs.

The Commission for Catholic-Jewish Relations is attached to the secretariat.

It has two offices, for the West and for the East. Each office is under the immediate direction of a delegate.

The prefects of the Congregation for the Oriental Churches and of the Congregation for the Evangelization of Peoples are ex officio members of the secretariat. Consultors include the secretaries of these two departments.

OFFICIALS: Cardinal Johannes Willebrands, president; Rev. Msgr. Charles Moeller, secretary.

BACKGROUND: Established by John XXIII June 5, 1960, as a preparatory secretariat of the Second Vatican Council; raised to commission status during the first session of the council in the fall of 1962; this status confirmed Jan. 3, 1966.

Secretariat for Non-Christians: Is concerned with persons who are not Christians but profess some kind of religious faith. Its function is to promote studies and dialogue for the purpose of increasing mutual understanding and respect between Christians and non-Christians.

The Commission for Catholic-Moslem Relations is attached to the secretariat.

The prefect of the Congregation for the Evangelization of Peoples is an ex officio member of the secretariat.

OFFICIALS: *Cardinal Sergio Pignedoli, president; Msgr. Pietro Rossano, secretary.*

BACKGROUND: Established by Paul VI May 19, 1964.

Secretariat for Non-Believers: Studies the background and philosophy of atheism, and initiates and carries on dialogue with non-believers.

OFFICIALS: *Cardinal Franz Koenig, president; Rev. Vincenzo Miano, S.D.B., secretary.*

BACKGROUND: Established by Paul VI Apr. 9, 1965.

COUNCILS, COMMISSIONS

Laity, Pontifical Council for: Instituted on an experimental basis by Paul VI Jan. 6, 1967; given permanent status Dec. 10, 1976 (motu proprio *Apostolatus Peragendi*); its competence covers the apostolate of the laity in the Church and the discipline of the laity as such. Members are mostly lay people from different parts of the world and involved in different apostolates. The council is headed by a cardinal. The Committee for the Family is attached to the Council while retaining its own identity. Cardinal Opilio Rossi, president.

Justice and Peace, Pontifical Commission: Instituted by Paul VI Jan. 6, 1967, on an experimental basis; reconstituted and made a permanent body Dec. 10, 1976 (motu proprio *Iustitiam et Pacem*). Holy See's organization for examining and studying (from the point of view of doctrine, pastoral practice and the apostolate) problems connected with justice and peace and awakening the sensitivity of the people of God to their responsibility in these areas. Cardinal Bernardin Gantin, president.

Revision of the Code of Canon Law: Instituted by John XXIII Mar. 28, 1963, to replace a former commission dating from 1917; Cardinal Pericle Felici, president.

Revision of the Code of Oriental Canon Law: Reconstituted by Paul VI in 1972 to replace a former commission dating from July 17, 1935, "to prepare . . . the reform of the Code of Oriental Canon Law, both in the sections already published by . . . four motu proprios'' (1,950 canons concerning marriage; processes; religious, church property and terminology; Eastern Rites and persons), "and in the remaining sections which have been completed but not published" (the balance of a total of 2,666 canons); Cardinal Joseph Parecattil, president.

Interpretation of the Decrees of the Second Vatican Council: Cardinal Pericle Felici, president.

Social Communication: Instituted on an experimental basis by Pius XII in 1948; reorganized three times in the 1950's; made permanent commission by John XXIII Feb. 22, 1959; name changed to present title Apr. 11, 1964; authorized to implement the *Decree on the Instruments of Social Communication* promulgated by the Second Vatican Council; under supervision of the Secretariat of State and the Council for the Public Affairs of the Church; Most Rev. Andrzej-Marie Deskur, president; Most Rev. Martin J. O'Connor, president emeritus.

Latin America: Instituted by Pius XII Apr. 19, 1958; placed under supervision of the Congregation for Bishops July, 1969; Cardinal Sebastiano Baggio, president.

Migration and Tourism: Instituted by Paul VI Mar. 19, 1970, for pastoral assistance to migrants, nomads, tourists, sea and air travelers; placed under the general supervision and direction of the Congregation for Bishops; Cardinal Sebastiano Baggio, president.

Cor Unum: Instituted by Paul VI July 15, 1971, to provide informational and coordinating services for Catholic aid and human development organizations and projects on a worldwide scale; Cardinal Bernard Gantin, president.

Theological Commission: Instituted by Paul VI Apr. 11, 1969, as an advisory adjunct of no more than 30 theologians to the Congregation for the Doctrine of the Faith; Cardinal Franjo Seper, president. (See separate entry.)

Biblical Commission: Instituted by Leo XIII Oct. 30, 1902; completely restructured by Paul VI June 27, 1971; Cardinal Franjo Seper, president. (See separate entry.)

Abbey of St. Jerome for the Revision and Emendation of the Vulgate: Instituted by Pius XI June 15, 1933, to replace an earlier commission established by St. Pius X; Rev. Vincent Truijen, superior.

Revision of the New Vulgate: Instituted by Paul VI in 1965 to augment the work of the Abbey of St. Jerome; Most Rev. Edward Schick, president.

Sacred Archeology: Instituted by Pius IX Jan. 6, 1852; Most Rev. Gennaro Verolino, president.

Historical Sciences: Instituted by Pius XII Apr. 7, 1954, as a continuation of a commission dating from 1883; Msgr. Michele Maccarrone, president.

Ecclesiastical Archives of Italy: Instituted by Pius XII Apr. 5, 1955; Msgr. Martino Giusti, president.

Sacred Art in Italy: Instituted by Pius XI Sept. 1, 1924; Most Rev. Giovanni Fallani, president.

Sanctuaries of Pompei and Loreto: Originated by Leo XIII; under supervision of the Congregation for the Clergy; Cardinal Umberto Mozzoni, president.

Russia: Instituted by Pius XI Apr. 6, 1930, to handle all ecclesiastical affairs of the country; placed under supervision of the Congregation for Extraordinary Ecclesiastical Affairs (now the Council for the Public Affairs of the Church) in 1934, with jurisdiction limited to clergy and faithful of the Roman Rite; under supervision of the Council for the Public Affairs of the Church; Cardinal Agostino Casaroli, president.

State of Vatican City: Cardinal Agostino Casaroli, president.

Protection of the Historical and Artistic Monuments of the Holy See: Instituted by Pius XI in 1923, reorganized by Paul VI in 1963; Most Rev. Giovanni Fallani, president.

Preservation of the Faith, Erection of New Churches in Rome: Instituted by Pius XI Aug. 5, 1930, to replace a commission dating from 1902; Cardinal Ugo Poletti, president.

Works of Religion: Instituted by Pius XII June 27, 1942, to bank and administer funds for works of religion; replaced an earlier administration established by Leo XIII in 1887; Most Rev. Paul C. Marcinkus, president.

Family, Committee for: Instituted by Paul VI Jan. 11, 1973, for pastoral research and supportive effort with respect to the spiritual, moral and social needs of the family; it is attached to the Pontifical Council for the Laity. Cardinal Opilio Rossi, president; Most Rev. Edouard Gagnon, vice-president.

Catholic-Jewish Relations: Instituted by Paul VI, Oct. 22, 1974, to promote and foster relations of a religious nature between Jews and Christians; attached to the Secretariat for Christian Unity; Cardinal Johannes Willebrands, president.

Catholic-Moslem Relations: Instituted by Paul VI, Oct. 22, 1974, to promote, regulate and interpret relations between Catholics and Moslems; attached to the Secretariat for Non-Christians; Cardinal Sergio Pignedoli, president.

OFFICES

Prefecture of the Economic Affairs of the Holy See: A financial office which coordinates and supervises administration of the temporalities of the Holy See.

OFFICIALS: Cardinal Egidio Vagnozzi, president; Msgr. Giovanni Angelo Abbo, secretary.

BACKGROUND: Established by Paul VI Aug. 15, 1967.

Apostolic Chamber: Administers the temporal goods and rights of the Holy See between the death of one pope and the election of another, in accordance with special laws.

OFFICIALS: Cardinal Paolo Bertoli, chamberlain of the Holy Roman Church; Most Rev. Ettore Cunial, vice-chamberlain.

BACKGROUND: Originated in the 11th century; reorganized by Pius XI in 1934.

Administration of the Patrimony of the Apostolic See: Handles the estate of the Apostolic See under the direction of papal delegates acting with ordinary or extraordinary authorization.

OFFICIALS: Cardinal Giuseppe Caprio, president; Most Rev. Lorenzo Antonetti, secretary.

BACKGROUND: Some of its functions date back to 1878; established by Paul VI Aug. 15, 1967.

Prefecture of the Pontifical Household: Oversees the papal chapel — which is at the service of the pope in his capacity as spiritual head of the Church — and the pontifical family — which is at the service of the pope as a sovereign. It arranges papal audiences, has charge of preparing non-liturgical elements of papal ceremonies, makes all necessary arrangements for papal visits and trips outside the Vatican, and settles questions of protocol connected with papal audiences and other formalities.

OFFICIALS: Most Rev. Jacques Martin, prefect; Msgr. Dino Monduzzi, regent.

BACKGROUND: Established by Paul VI Aug. 15, 1967, under the title, Prefecture of the Apostolic Palace; it supplanted the Sacred Congregation for Ceremonies founded by Sixtus V Jan. 22, 1588. The office was updated and reorganized under the present title by Paul VI, Mar. 28, 1968.

Central Statistics Office: Compiles, systematizes and analyzes information on the status and condition of the Church and the needs of its pastoral ministry, from parish to top levels.

The office is one of the organs of the Secretariat of State.

BACKGROUND: Established by Paul VI Aug. 15, 1967.

Aid Office: Distributes alms and aid to the aged, sick, handicapped and other persons in need.

OFFICIAL: Most Rev. Antonio M. Travia, director.

BACKGROUND: The office originated as a charitable office in the time of Bl. Gregory X (1271-1276).

Vatican II Archives: Preserves the acts and other documents of the Second Vatican Council.

OFFICIAL: Cardinal Pericle Felici.

Personnel: Set up by Paul VI May 9, 1971, to handle personnel relations in the offices and other agencies of the Vatican.

OFFICIAL: Msgr. Michele Buro.

FIDES

The International Fides Service is the news agency of the Congregation for the Evangelization of Peoples. On the basis of reports from sources in many countries, it issues a periodic service of news, comment and background information concerning missions and missionary activity, in Italian, French, English, Spanish and German.

The office address is Via di Propaganda, 1 C, 00187, Rome Italy.

THEOLOGICAL COMMISSION

Establishment of a Theological Commission as an adjunct to the Congregation for the Doctrine of the Faith was announced by Pope Paul VI Apr. 28, 1969. The move had been recommended by the Second Vatican Council and was proposed by the Synod of Bishops in 1967.

The purpose of the commission is to provide the Doctrinal Congregation with the consultative and advisory services of theologians and scriptural and liturgical experts representative of various schools of thought. The international membership is restricted to 30, and the ordinary term of membership is five years.

Membership

The commission is headed by Cardinal Franjo Seper, prefect of the Doctrinal Congregation. Msgr. Philippe Delhaye of Belgium is secretary. Terms of the following members, appointed or reappointed by Paul VI Aug. 1, 1974, were due to end Dec. 31, 1979.

Barnabas Ahern, C.P. (U.S.); Juan Alfaro, S.J. (Spain); Catalino Arevalo, S.J. (Philippines); Hans Urs von Balthasar (Switzerland); Walter Burghardt, S.J. (U.S.); Carlo Caffaro (Italy); Raniero Cantalamessa (Italy); Ives Congar, O.P. (France); Wilhelm Ernst (East Germany); Olegario Gonzalez de Cardedal (Spain); Edouard Hamel, S.J. (Canada); Boguslaw Inlender (Poland); Bonaventure Kloppenburg, O.F.M. (Brazil); Marie-Joseph Le Guillou, O.P. (France); Karl Lehmann (Germany); J. F. Lescrauwaet, M.S.C. (Holland); John Mahoney, S.J. (Great Britain); Gustave Martelet, S.J. (France); Jorge Medina Estevez (Chile); Vincent Mulago (Zaire);

Cardinal Joseph Ratzinger (Germany); Most Rev. Georges Abi-Saber, Maronite Monk (Lebanon); Heinz Schurmann (East Germany); Otto Semmelroth, S.J. (Germany); Anton Strle (Yugoslavia); Jean-Marie Tillard, O.P. (Canada); Cipriano Vagaggini, O.S.B. (Italy); Jan Walgrave, O.P. (Belgium).

Meetings

The commission met for the first time Oct. 6 to 8, 1969, for organizational purposes and the assignment of subcommissions to studies on the priesthood, the theology of hope, unity of faith and pluralism in theology, the criteria of moral knowledge, and collegiality.

Week-long general assemblies, for discussion and decision on subjects of individual and group research have been held annually, except in 1978, since 1969.

Twenty-six members attending the second meeting, Oct. 5 to 10, 1970, discussed reports on the priestly ministry and collegiality. Views were exchanged about the question of ordaining married men, but marriage was ruled out for already ordained priests wanting to continue in the ministry. With respect to collegiality, no doubt was raised about the pope's authority to act independently in the Church; the consensus, however, was that he would be prudent to engage in wide consultation before acting.

By early 1971, the commission prepared the basis of a feasible working paper on the priesthood for the Synod of Bishops, which met for the third time in the fall. The ordination of women was one of the subjects covered, but it did not figure significantly in discussion by the commission because the issue was not considered urgent. Agreement was reported on two points: tradition militated against ordination but permitted a form of diaconal ordination with a rite and purpose distinctive and proper to women.

Pluralism in theology — concerning different ways of treating, presenting and expressing in practice the unity of faith — was the main subject under consideration at the fourth general assembly Oct. 5 to 11, 1972. The topic had been under study since the first meeting of the commission in 1969.

The October, 1973, meeting, attended by 21 members, completed work on a statement concerning apostolic succession and ordination to holy orders. The necessary sacramental sign of both, the statement said, is the imposition of hands by successors of the Apostles acting in accord with the intention of the Church.

The results of research on Christian morality were discussed at the 1974 meeting, and several articles on the subject were published in 1975.

The majority of members attending the Sept. 25 to Oct. 1, 1975, meeting approved a number of conclusions concerning the relationship between "the mandate given to the ecclesiastical magisterium (the teaching authority of the Church) to protect divine revelation and the task given to theologians to investigate and explain the doctrine of the faith." These conclusions were published by the U.S. Catholic Conference in April, 1977.

Christian salvation and human progress, centering on the nature of and relationship between evangelization and human liberation, was the subject of the meeting held Oct. 4 to 9, 1976. The subject was connected with earlier consideration of the matter by the Synod of Bishops, and also with the contents and tenor of the *Pastoral Constitution on the Church in the Modern World* issued by the Second Vatican Council.

The meeting of Dec. 1 to 6, 1977, focused attention on pastoral aspects of Christian marriage and agreed on a summary of conclusions which: (1) reaffirmed the indissolubility of marriage and the stance of the Church against divorce; (2) declared that the Church should not witness the marriage of Catholics who have rejected the faith and the sacramental nature of marriage. (See Pastoral Aspects of Marriage.)

The 1978 meeting was cancelled because of the papal transition earlier in the year.

It was expected that subcommittee work on Christology would be completed at the general meeting of the commission scheduled in December, 1979

COLLEGE OF CARDINALS

Cardinals are chosen by the pope to serve as his principal assistants and advisers in the central administration of church affairs. Collectively, they form the Sacred College of Cardinals.

The college evolved gradually from synods of Roman clergy with whose assistance popes directed church affairs in the first 11 centuries. The first cardinals, in about the sixth century, were priests of the leading churches of Rome who were assigned liturgical, advisory and administrative duties with the Holy See, and the regional deacons of Rome.

For all cardinals except Eastern patriarchs, membership in the college involves aggregation to the clergy of Rome. This aggregation is signified by the assignment to each cardinal, except the patriarchs, of a special or titular church in Rome.

History of the College

The Sacred College of Cardinals was constituted in its present form and categories of membership in the 12th century. Before that time the pope had a body of advisers selected from among the bishops of dioceses neighboring Rome, priests and deacons of Rome. The college was given definite form in 1150, and in 1179 the selection of cardinals was reserved exclusively to the pope. Sixtus V fixed the number at 70, in 1586. John XXIII set aside this rule when he increased membership at the 1959 and subsequent consistories. The number of cardinals reached an all-time high of 145 under Paul VI in 1973. The number of cardinals entitled to participate in papal elections was limited to 120.

In 1567 the title of cardinal was reserved to members of the college; previously it had been used by priests attached to parish churches of Rome and by the leading clergy of other notable churches. The Code of Canon Law promulgated in 1918 decreed that all cardinals must be priests. Previously there had been lay cardinals (e.g., Cardinal Giacomo Antonelli, d. 1876, Secretary of State to Pius IX). John XXIII provided in the motu proprio *Cum Gravissima* Apr. 15, 1962, that all cardinals would henceforth be bishops.

Pope Paul VI placed age limits on the functions of cardinals in the apostolic letter *Ingravescentem Aetatem*, dated Nov. 21, 1970, and effective as of Jan. 1, 1971. At 80, they cease to be members of curial departments and offices, and become ineligible to take part in papal elections. They retain membership in the College of Cardinals, however, with relevant rights and privileges.

Three Categories

The three categories of members of the college are cardinal bishops, cardinal priests and cardinal deacons.

Cardinal bishops include the six titular bishops of the suburban sees of Rome and Eastern patriarchs.

First in rank are the titular bishops of the suburban sees, neighboring Rome: Ostia, Palestrina, Porto and Santa Rufina, Albano, Velletri, Frascati, Sabina and Poggio Mirteto. The dean of the college holds the title of the See of Ostia as well as his other suburban see. These cardinal bishops are engaged in full-time service in the central administration of church affairs in departments of the Roman Curia.

Four Eastern patriarchs, three of whom have since died, were made cardinal bishops by Paul VI in virtue of the motu proprio *Ad Purpuratorum Patrum* Feb. 11, 1965. Full recognition was given to their position as the heads of ancient liturgies and of sees of apostolic origin. Because of their patriarchal dignity and titles, which antedated the dignity and titles of cardinals, they were not aggregated to the Roman clergy and were not, like other cardinals, given title to Roman churches. The patriarchs were assigned rank among the cardinals in order of seniority, following the suburban titleholders. Patriarchs, at their request, were not included among cardinals inducted into the college in later consistories.

Cardinal priests, who were formerly in charge of leading churches in Rome, are bishops whose dioceses are outside Rome.

Cardinal deacons, who were formerly chosen according to regional divisions of Rome, are titular bishops assigned to full-time service in the Roman Curia.

The officers of the college are the dean and sub-dean, a chamberlain and a secretary. Pope Paul decreed Feb. 26, 1965, that the dean and sub-dean were to be elected by the cardinal bishops. He set this ruling aside in December, 1977, however, when he appointed Cardinals Carlo Confalonieri and Paolo Marella, respectively, as dean and sub-dean.

Selection and Duties

Cardinals are selected by the pope and are inducted into the college in a three-step process. Their nomination is announced and approved at a meeting (secret consistory) attended only by the pope and cardinals who are already members of the college; word of their election and confirmation is then communicated to the cardinals designate by means of a document called a *biglietto*. In successive and more public ceremonies, they receive the cardinalatial red biretta and ring, and concelebrate Mass with the pope and their fellow cardinals.

Cardinals under the age of 80: elect the pope when the Holy See becomes vacant (see Papal Election); are major administrators of church affairs, serving in one or more departments of the Roman Curia. All cardinals enjoy a number of special rights and privileges. Their title, while symbolic of high honor, does not signify any extension of the powers of holy orders. They are called princes of the Church.

A **cardinal in pectore** is one whose selection has been made by the pope but whose name has not been disclosed; he has no title, rights or duties until such disclosure is made, at which time he takes precedence from the time of the secret selection.

BIOGRAPHIES OF CARDINALS

Biographies of the cardinals, as of Oct. 1, 1979, are given below in alphabetical order. For historical notes, order of seniority and geographical distribution of cardinals, see separate entries.

An asterisk indicates cardinals ineligible to take part in papal elections.

Alfrink, Bernard Jan: b. July 5, 1900, Nijkerk, Netherlands; ord. priest Aug. 15, 1924; professor of Sacred Scripture at Utrecht major seminary, 1933; consultor to Pontifical Biblical Commission, Rome, 1944; professor at Catholic University of Nijmegen, 1945; ord. titular archbishop of Tiana and coadjutor archbishop of Utrecht, July 17, 1951; archbishop of Utrecht, 1955-75; cardinal Mar. 28, 1960; titular church, St. Joachim. Former archbishop of Utrecht, member of:
Commission: Revision of Code of Canon Law.

Antonelli,* Ferdinando Giuseppe, O.F.M.: b. July 14, 1896, Subbiano, Italy; solemnly professed in Order of Friars Minor, Apr. 7, 1914; ord. priest July 25, 1922; taught church history, 1928-32, and Christian archeology, 1932-65, at Antonianum; rector magnificus of Antonianum, 1937-43, 1953-59; definitor general of Friars Minor, 1939-45; held various offices in Roman Curia; secretary of Congregation of Rites, 1965-69, and Congregation for Causes of Saints, 1969-73; ord. titular archbishop of Idicra, Mar. 19, 1966; cardinal Mar. 5, 1973; deacon, San Sebastian (on the Palatine).

Aponte Martinez, Luis: b. Aug. 4, 1922, Lajas, Puerto Rico; ord. priest Apr. 10, 1950; parish priest at Ponce; ord. titular bishop of Lares and auxiliary of Ponce, Oct. 12, 1960; bishop of Ponce, 1963-64; archbishop of San Juan, Nov. 4, 1964; cardinal Mar. 5, 1973; titular church, St. Mary Mother of Providence (in Monteverde). Archbishop of San Juan, president of Puerto Rican Episcopal Conference, member of:
Congregation: Causes of Saints.

Aramburu, Juan Carlos: b. Feb. 11, 1912, Reduccion, Argentina; ord. priest in Rome, Oct. 28, 1934; ord. titular bishop of Plataea and auxiliary of Tucuman, Dec. 15, 1946; bishop, 1953, and first archbishop, 1957, of Tucuman; titular archbishop of Torri di Bizacena and coadjutor archbishop of Buenos Aires, June 14, 1967; archbishop of Buenos Aires, Apr. 22, 1975; cardinal May 24, 1976; titular church, St. John Baptist of the Florentines. Archbishop of Buenos Aires, ordinary for Eastern Rite Catholics in Brazil without ordinaries of their own rites, member of:
Congregations: Oriental Churches, Catholic Education.

Arns, Paulo Evaristo, O.F.M.: b. Sept. 14, 1921, Forquilhinha, Brazil; ord. priest Nov. 30, 1945; held various teaching posts; director of *Sponsa Christi*, monthly review for religious, and of the Franciscan publication center in Brazil; ord. titular bishop of Respetta and auxiliary of Sao Paulo, July 3, 1966; archbishop of Sao Paulo, Oct. 22, 1970; cardinal Mar. 5, 1973; titular church, St. Anthony of Padua (in Via Tuscolana). Archbishop of Sao Paulo, member of:
Congregation: Sacraments and Divine Worship;
Secretariat: Non-Believers.

Bafile, Corrado: b. July 4, 1903, L'Aquila, Italy; practiced law in Rome for six years before beginning studies for priesthood; ord. priest Apr. 11, 1936; served in Vatican secretariat of state, 1939-59; ord. titular archbishop of Antiochia in Pisidia, Mar. 19, 1960; apostolic nuncio to Germany, 1960-75; pro-prefect of Sacred Congregation for Causes of Saints, July 18, 1975; cardinal May 24, 1976; deacon, S. Maria (in Portico). Prefect of Sacred Congregation for Causes of Saints, 1976, member of:
Congregation: Clergy;
Tribunal: Apostolic Signatura;
Commission: Revision of Code of Canon Law.

Baggio, Sebastiano: b. May 16, 1913, Rosa, Italy; ord. priest Dec. 21, 1935; ord. titular archbishop of Ephesus, July 26, 1953; served in Vatican diplomatic corps, 1953-69; nuncio to Chile, apostolic delegate to Canada, nuncio to Brazil; cardinal Apr. 28, 1969; archbishop of Cagliari, 1969-73; entered order of cardinal bishops as titular bishop of Velletri, Dec. 12, 1974. Prefect of Sacred Congregation for Bishops, 1973, member of:
Council for Public Affairs of Church;
Congregations: Doctrine of the Faith, Religious and Secular Institutes, Catholic Education, Evangelization of Peoples;
Commissions: Revision of Code of Canon Law, Latin America (President), Migration and Tourism (President), Sanctuaries of Pom-

pei and Loreto, Interpretation of Decrees of Vatican II;
Office: Patrimony of Holy See.

Ballestrero, Anastasio Alberto, O.C.D.: b. Oct. 3, 1913, Genoa, Italy; professed in Order of Discalced Carmelites, 1929; ord. priest June 6, 1936; provincial, 1942-48, and superior general, 1955-67, of Carmelites; author of many books on Christian life; ord. archbishop of Bari, Feb. 2, 1974; archbishop of Turin, Aug. 1, 1977; cardinal June 30, 1979; titular church, S. Maria (sopra Minerva). Archbishop of Turin, president of the Italian Episcopal Conference, 1979, member of:
Congregation: Religious and Secular Institutes;
Commission: Revision of Code of Canon Law.

Baum, William Wakefield: b. Nov. 21, 1926, Dallas, Tex.; moved to Kansas City, Mo., at an early age; ord. priest May 12, 1951; executive director of U.S. bishops commission for ecumenical and interreligious affairs, 1964-69; attended Second Vatican Council as *peritus* (expert adviser); ord. bishop of Springfield-Cape Girardeau, Mo., Apr. 6, 1970; app. archbishop of Washington, D.C., Mar. 5, 1973; cardinal May 24, 1976; titular church, Holy Cross (on the Via Flaminia). Archbishop of Washington, D.C., member of:
Congregations: Doctrine of the Faith, Catholic Education;
Secretariat: Non-Christians.

Benelli, Giovanni: b. May 12, 1921, Poggiole, Italy; ord. priest Oct. 31, 1943; entered diplomatic service of Holy See August, 1947, as attaché of secretariat of state; served in apostolic nunciatures in Ireland (1950-53), France (1953-60), Brazil (1960-62), Spain (1962-65); observer of Holy See at UNESCO, 1965-66; ord. titular archbishop of Tusurus, Sept. 11, 1966; pro-nuncio in Senegal and apostolic delegate to Western Africa, 1966-67; undersecretary of state 1967-77; app. archbishop of Florence, June 3, 1977; cardinal June 27, 1977; titular church, St. Prisca. Archbishop of Florence, member of:
Congregations: Bishops, Catholic Education.

Bengsch, Alfred: b. Sept. 10, 1921, Berlin, Germany; called for military service while in seminary at Fulda, gravely wounded at Normandy and prisoner of Americans, 1944; resumed his studies after the war; ord. priest Apr. 2, 1950; member of faculty of seminaries at Erfurt and Neuzelle; ord. titular bishop of Tubia and auxiliary bishop of Berlin, June 11, 1959; bishop of Berlin, Aug. 16, 1961; received personal title of archbishop, Jan. 14, 1962; cardinal June 26, 1967; titular church, St. Philip Neri (in Eurosia). Archbishop-Bishop of Berlin, member of:
Congregations: Sacraments and Divine Worship, Catholic Education;
Commission: Revision of Code of Canon Law.

Beras Rojas, Octavio: b. Nov. 16, 1906, Seibo, Dominican Republic; ord. priest Aug. 13, 1933; founded national Catholic youth movement; ord. titular archbishop of Euchaitae and coadjutor archbishop of Santo Domingo, Aug. 12, 1945; archbishop of Santo Domingo, Dec. 10, 1961; cardinal May 24, 1976; titular church, San Sisto. Archbishop of Santo Domingo, military vicar of Dominican Republic, member of:
Congregation: Bishops.

Bertoli, Paolo: b. Feb. 1, 1908, Poggio Garfagnana, Italy; ord. priest Aug. 15, 1930; entered diplomatic service of the Holy See, serving in nunciatures in Yugoslavia, France, Haiti and Switzerland; ord. titular archbishop of Nicomedia, May 11, 1952; apostolic delegate to Turkey (1952-53), nuncio to Colombia (1953-59), Lebanon (1959-60), France (1960-69); cardinal Apr. 28, 1969; prefect of Congregation for Causes of Saints, 1969-73; entered order of cardinal bishops as titular bishop of Frascati, 1979. Chamberlain (Camerlengo) of Holy Roman Church, 1979, member of:
Council for Public Affairs of Church;
Congregations: Bishops, Oriental Churches, Evangelization of Peoples;
Tribunal: Apostolic Signatura;
Commissions: Revision of Code of Canon Law, Latin America, State of Vatican City.

Brandao Vilela, Avelar: b. June 13, 1912, Vicosa, Brazil; ord. priest Oct. 27, 1935; professor and spiritual director at diocesan seminary at Aracaju; ord. bishop of Petrolina, Oct. 27, 1946; archbishop of Teresina, Nov. 5, 1955; established 20 social centers and a radio station; introduced agrarian reform of church properties; erected the Institute of Catechetics: archbishop of Sao Salvador da Bahia, Mar. 25, 1971; president of CELAM, 1967-72; co-president of Medellin Conference, 1968; cardinal Mar. 5, 1973; titular church, Sts. Boniface and Alexius. Archbishop of Sao Salvador da Bahia, member of:
Congregations: Clergy, Causes of Saints, Catholic Education;
Commission: Latin America.

Bueno y Monreal, Jose Maria: b. Sept. 11, 1904, Zaragoza, Spain; ord. priest Mar. 19, 1927; ord. bishop of Jaca, Mar. 19, 1946; bishop of Vitoria, May 13, 1950; titular archbishop of Antioch in Pisidia and coadjutor archbishop of Seville, Oct. 27, 1954; archbishop of Seville, Apr. 8, 1957; cardinal Dec. 15, 1958; titular church, Sts. Vitus, Modestus and Crescentia. Archbishop of Seville.

Caggiano,* Antonio: b. Jan. 30, 1889, Coronda, Argentina; ord. priest Mar. 23, 1912; general ecclesiastical counselor of Argentine Catholic Action, 1931; military vicar, 1933; ord. bishop of Rosario, Mar. 17, 1935; cardinal Feb. 18, 1946; titular church, St.

Lawrence (in Panisperna). Archbishop of Buenos Aires, 1959-75.

Caprio, Giuseppe: b. Nov. 15, 1914, Lapio, Italy; ord. priest Dec. 17, 1938; served in diplomatic missions in China (1947-51, when Vatican diplomats were expelled by communists), Belgium (1951-54), and South Vietnam (1954-56); internuncio in China with residence at Taiwan, 1959-67; ord. titular archbishop of Apollonia, Dec. 17, 1961; pro-nuncio in India, 1967-69; secretary of Administration of Patrimony of Holy See, 1969-77; substitute secretary of state, 1977-79; cardinal June 30, 1979; deacon, St. Mary in Via Tuscolana. President of Administration of Patrimony of Holy See, 1979, member of:

Congregation: Evangelization of Peoples;
Commission: Revision of Code of Canon Law.

Carberry, John J.: b. July 31, 1904, Brooklyn, N.Y.; ord. priest July 28, 1929; ord. titular bishop of Elis and coadjutor bishop of Lafayette, Ind., July 25, 1956; bishop of Lafayette, Nov. 20, 1957; bishop of Columbus, Jan. 16, 1965; archbishop of St. Louis, 1968-79; cardinal Apr. 28, 1969; titular church, St. John the Baptist (de Rossi). Former archbishop of St. Louis, member of:

Congregation: Evangelization of Peoples.

Carpino, Francesco: b. May 18, 1905, Palazzolo Acreide, Italy; ord. priest Aug. 14, 1927; ord. titular archbishop of Nicomedia and coadjutor archbishop of Monreale, Apr. 8, 1951; archbishop of Monreale, 1951-61; titular archbishop of Sardica, Jan. 19, 1961; assessor of Sacred Consistorial Congregation, 1961; pro-prefect of Sacred Congregation of the Council, Apr. 7, 1967; cardinal June 26, 1967; archbishop of Palermo, 1967-70; entered order of cardinal bishops as titular bishop of Albano, Jan. 27, 1978. Former archbishop of Palermo, referendary of the Congregation of Bishops, 1970, and member of:

Council for Public Affairs of the Church;
Congregation: Causes of Saints;
Tribunal: Apostolic Signatura.

Carter, Gerald Emmett: b. Mar. 1, 1912, Montreal, Canada; ord. priest May 22, 1937; engaged in pastoral and teaching ministry in Montreal; founder and president of St. Joseph Teachers' College and co-founder and director of Thomas More Institute for adult education; ord. titular bishop of Altiburo and auxiliary bishop of London, Ont., Feb. 2, 1962; bishop of London, 1964-78; vice president, 1971-73, and president, 1975-77, of Canadian Conference of Catholic Bishops; archbishop of Toronto, Apr. 27, 1978; cardinal June 30, 1979; titular church, St. Mary (in Traspontina). Archbishop of Toronto, member of:

Secretariats: Christian Unity, Non-Christians.

Casariego, Mario, C.R.S.: b. Feb. 13, 1909, Figueras de Castropol, Spain; ord. priest July 19, 1936; ord. titular bishop of Pudenziana and auxiliary bishop of Guatemala, Dec. 27, 1958; titular archbishop of Perge and coadjutor archbishop of Guatemala, Nov. 12, 1963; archbishop of Guatemala, Dec. 12, 1964; cardinal Apr. 28, 1969; titular church, St. Mary in Aquiro. Archbishop of Guatemala, member of:

Congregation: Causes of Saints.

Casaroli, Agostino: b. Nov. 24, 1914, Castel San Giovanni, Italy; ord. priest May 27, 1937; entered service of Vatican secretariat of state, 1940; undersecretary, 1961-67, of the Sacred Congregation for Extraordinary Ecclesiastical Affairs, and secretary, 1967-79, of its successor the Council for Public Affairs of the Church; chief negotiator for the Vatican with East European communist governments; missions included visits to Hungary, Yugoslavia, Poland, Czechoslovakia, Bulgaria; headed Vatican delegations to several UN conferences and the Helsinki Conference (1975); ord. titular archbishop of Cartagina, July 16, 1967; cardinal June 30, 1979; titular church, the Twelve Apostles. Secretary of State, 1979, prefect of Council for Public Affairs of the Church, 1979, president of pontifical commission for Vatican City and member of:

Congregations: Doctrine of the Faith, Bishops.

Cé, Marco: b. July 8, 1925, Izano, Italy; ord. priest Mar. 27, 1948; taught sacred scripture and dogmatic theology at seminary in his home diocese of Cremona; rector of seminary, 1957; presided over diocesan liturgical commission, preached youth retreats; ord. titular bishop of Vulturia, May 17, 1970; auxiliary bishop of Bologna, 1970-76; general ecclesiastical assistant of Italian Catholic Action, 1976-78; patriarch of Venice, Dec. 7, 1978; cardinal June 30, 1979; titular church, St. Mark. Patriarch of Venice, member of:

Congregations: Clergy, Catholic Education.

Ciappi, Mario Luigi, O.P.: b. Oct. 6, 1909, Florence, Italy; ord. priest Mar. 26, 1932; papal theologian from 1955, serving Pius XII, John XXIII and Paul VI; ord. titular bishop of Misenum June 18, 1977; cardinal June 27, 1977; deacon, Our Lady of the Sacred Heart (in Piazza Navona). Pro-theologian of pontifical household, member of:

Congregation: Causes of Saints.

Civardi, Ernesto: b. Oct. 21, 1906, Fossarmato, Italy; ord. priest June 29, 1930; assistant rector of Pontifical Lombard Seminary in Rome; held various curial offices; undersecretary, 1953-67, and secretary, 1967-79, of the Congregation for Bishops (known as the Consistorial Congregation until 1967); ord. titular archbishop of Sardica, July 16, 1967; secretary of College of Cardinals, 1967-79; filled office of secretary at 1978 conclaves which elected Popes John Paul I and John

Paul II; cardinal June 30, 1979; deacon, St. Theodore. Member of:
Congregation: Causes of Saints;
Tribunal: Apostolic Signatura.

Cody, John P.: b. Dec. 24, 1907, St. Louis, Mo.; ord. priest Dec. 8, 1931, Rome, Italy; served in Rome, 1932-38; ord. titular bishop of Apollonia and auxiliary bishop of St. Louis, July 2, 1947; coadjutor bishop of St. Joseph, Mo., Jan. 27, 1954; apostolic administrator of St. Joseph, May 9, 1955; coadjutor bishop of Kansas City-St. Joseph, Aug. 29, 1956; bishop of Kansas City-St. Joseph, 1956-61; titular archbishop of Bostra and coadjutor archbishop of New Orleans, Aug. 10, 1961; apostolic administrator of New Orleans, June 1, 1962; archbishop of New Orleans, Nov. 8, 1964; archbishop of Chicago, June 14, 1965; cardinal June 26, 1967; titular church, St. Cecilia. Archbishop of Chicago, member of:
Congregation: Clergy.

Colombo, Giovanni: b. Dec. 6, 1902, Caronno, Italy; ord. priest May 29, 1926; rector of Milan Seminary, 1953; ord. titular bishop of Filippopoli and auxiliary bishop of Milan, Dec. 7, 1960; archbishop of Milan, Aug. 10, 1963; cardinal Feb. 22, 1965; titular church, Sts. Sylvester and Martin (in Montibus). Archbishop of Milan, member of:
Congregations: Sacraments and Divine Worship, Evangelization of Peoples, Catholic Education;
Commission: Revision of Code of Canon Law.

Confalonieri,* Carlo: b. July 25, 1893, Seveso, Italy; ord. priest Mar. 18, 1916; private secretary to Pius XI for 17 years, to Pius XII for two years; ord. archbishop of L'Aquila, May 4, 1941; transferred to titular archbishopric of Nicopoli al Nesto, Feb. 22, 1950; cardinal Dec. 15, 1958; titular bishop of suburban see of Palestrina, Mar. 14, 1972, when he entered order of cardinal bishops, and Ostia, Dec. 12, 1977, when he was named dean of College of Cardinals; prefect of Sacred Congregation for Bishops, 1967-73; sub-dean of college of cardinals, 1974-77. Archpriest of Patriarchal Liberian Basilica, dean of College of Cardinals, Dec. 12, 1977.

Cooke, Terence J.: b. Mar. 1, 1921, New York, N. Y.; ord. priest Dec. 1, 1945; ord. titular bishop of Summa and auxiliary bishop of New York, Dec. 13, 1965; archbishop of New York, Mar. 2, 1968; military vicar for the U.S.; cardinal Apr. 28, 1969; titular church, Sts. John and Paul. Archbishop of New York, military vicar of U.S., member of:
Congregations: Bishops, Oriental Churches, Evangelization of Peoples;
Commission: Migration and Tourism.

Cooray, Thomas B., O.M.I.: b. Dec. 28, 1901, Periyamulla Negombo, Ceylon (now Sri Lanka); ord. priest June 23, 1929; ord. titular archbishop of Preslavo, Mar. 7, 1946; coadjutor archbishop of Colombo, Sri Lanka, 1946-47; succeeded as archbishop of Colombo, July 26, 1947 (retired 1976); cardinal Feb. 22, 1965; titular church, Sts. Nereus and Achilleus. Former archbishop of Colombo, Sri Lanka, member of:
Commission: Revision of Code of Canon Law.

Cordeiro, Joseph: b. Jan. 19, 1918, Bombay, India; ord. priest Aug. 24, 1946; served in educational and other diocesan posts at Karachi, Pakistan; ord. archbishop of Karachi, Aug. 24, 1958, the first native-born prelate in that see; cardinal Mar. 5, 1973; titular church, St. Andrew Apostle ("de Hortis"). Archbishop of Karachi, member of:
Congregation: Religious and Secular Institutes;
Secretariat: Non-Christians;
Commission: Pontifical Council *Cor Unum*.

Corripio Ahumada, Ernesto: b. June 29, 1919, Tampico, Mexico; ord. priest Oct. 25, 1942, in Rome, where he remained until almost the end of World War II; taught and held various positions in local seminary of Tampico, 1945-50; ord. titular bishop of Zapara and auxiliary bishop of Tampico, Mar. 19, 1953; bishop of Tampico, 1956-67; archbishop of Antequera, 1967-76; archbishop of Pueblo de los Angeles, 1976-77; archbishop of Mexico City and primate of Mexico, July 19, 1977; cardinal June 30, 1979; titular church, Mary Immaculate al Tiburtino. Archbishop of Mexico City, member of:
Congregation: Sacraments and Divine Worship;
Commission: Latin America.

Darmojuwono, Justin: b. Nov. 2, 1914, Godean, Indonesia; ord. priest May 25, 1947; ord. archbishop of Semarang, Apr. 6, 1964; cardinal June 26, 1967; titular church, Most Holy Names of Jesus and Mary. Archbishop of Semarang, military vicar of Indonesia, member of:
Congregation: Sacraments and Divine Worship;
Secretariat: Non-Christians.

De Araujo Sales, Eugenio: b. Nov. 8, 1920, Acari, Brazil; ord. priest Nov. 21, 1943; ord. titular bishop of Tibica and auxiliary bishop of Natal, Aug. 15, 1954; archbishop of Sao Salvador, 1968-71; cardinal Apr. 28, 1969; titular church, St. Gregory VII. Archbishop of Rio de Janeiro (1971), ordinary for Eastern Rite Catholics in Brazil without ordinaries of their own rites, member of:
Congregations: Bishops, Clergy, Evangelization of Peoples;
Commission: Social Communications.

Dearden, John F.: b. Oct. 15, 1907, Valley Falls, R. I.; ord. priest Dec. 8, 1932; ord. titular bishop of Sarepta and coadjutor bishop of Pittsburgh, May 18, 1948; bishop of Pittsburgh, Dec. 22, 1950; archbishop of Detroit,

Dec. 18, 1958; first president of the National Conference of Catholic Bishops and the United States Catholic Conference, 1966-71; cardinal Apr. 28, 1969; titular church, St. Pius X (alla Balduina). Archbishop of Detroit, member of:
Congregation: Sacraments and Divine Worship.

De Furstenberg, Maximilien: b. Oct. 23, 1904, Heerlen, Netherlands; ord. priest Aug. 9, 1931; ord. titular archbishop of Palto and apostolic delegate to Japan, Apr. 25, 1949; internuncio, 1952, when Japan established diplomatic relations with the Vatican; apostolic delegate to Australia, New Zealand and Oceania, Feb. 11, 1960; nuncio to Portugal, 1962-67; cardinal June 26, 1967; titular church, Most Sacred Heart of Jesus (a Castro Pretorio); prefect of the Congregation for the Oriental Churches, 1969-73. Grand Master of Equestrian Order of Holy Sepulchre of Jerusalem, member of:
Council for Public Affairs of Church;
Congregations: Bishops, Religious and Secular Institutes, Evangelization of Peoples;
Tribunal: Apostolic Signatura;
Commissions: Revision of Code of Canon Law, Interpretation of Decrees of Vatican II, State of Vatican City, Institute for Works of Religion.

Duval, Leon-Etienne: b. Nov. 9, 1903, Chenex, France; ord. priest Dec. 18, 1926; ord. bishop of Constantine, Algeria, Feb. 11, 1947; archbishop of Algiers, Feb. 3, 1954; cardinal Feb. 22, 1965; titular church, St. Balbina. Archbishop of Algiers, member of:
Congregation: Evangelization of Peoples;
Secretariat: Non-Christians;
Commission: Revision of Code of Canon Law.

Ekandem, Dominic: b. 1917, Ibiono, Nigeria; ord. priest Dec. 7, 1947; ord. titular bishop of Gerapoli di Isauri and auxiliary bishop of Calabar, Feb. 7, 1954, the first Nigerian to become a bishop; first bishop of Ikot Ekpene, Mar. 1, 1963; cardinal May 24, 1976; titular church, San Marcello. Bishop of Ikot Ekpene, president of the Nigerian Episcopal Conference, member of:
Secretariat: Non-Christians.

Enrique y Tarancon, Vicente: b. May 14, 1907, Burriana, Spain; ord. priest Nov. 1, 1929; ord. bishop of Solsona, Mar. 24, 1946; bishop of Oviedo, Apr. 12, 1964; archbishop of Toledo, 1969-71; cardinal Apr. 28, 1969; titular church, St. John Chrysostom. Archbishop of Madrid, 1971, member of:
Congregation: Bishops;
Commission: Revision of Code of Canon Law.

Etchegaray, Roger: b. Sept. 25, 1922, Espelette, France; ord. priest July 13, 1947; deputy director, 1961-66, and secretary general, 1966-70, of French Episcopal Conference; ord. titular bishop of Gemelle di Numidia and auxiliary bishop of Paris, May 27, 1969; archbishop of Marseilles, Dec. 22, 1970; prelate of Mission de France, Nov. 26, 1975; president of French Episcopal Conference, 1975- ; cardinal June 30, 1979; titular church, St. Leo I. Archbishop of Marseilles, prelate of Mission de France, member of:
Secretariat: Christian Unity;
Commission: Social Communications.

Felici, Pericle: b. Aug. 1, 1911, Segni, Italy; ord. priest Oct. 28, 1933; rector of Pontifical Roman Seminary for Legal Studies, 1938-48; judge of Roman Rota, 1947; served on antepreparatory commissions of the Second Vatican Council; ord. titular archbishop of Samosata, Oct. 28, 1960; secretary-general of the Second Vatican Council; accompanied Pope Paul VI on his trip to the UN, Oct. 4, 1965; cardinal June 26, 1967; titular church, St. Apollinare. Prefect of Apostolic Signatura, 1977, member of:
Council for Public Affairs of Church;
Congregations: Doctrine of Faith, Bishops, Sacraments and Divine Worship, Causes of Saints;
Commissions: Revision of Code of Canon Law (President), Revision of Oriental Code of Canon Law, Interpretation of Decrees of Vatican II (President);
Offices: Administration of Patrimony of Holy See, Vatican II Archives.

Flahiff, George B., C.S.B.: b. Oct. 26, 1905, Paris, Ont., Canada; ord. priest Aug. 17, 1930; professor of medieval history at the University of Toronto and Pontifical Institute of Medieval Studies in Toronto, 1934-54; superior general of Basilian Fathers, 1954; ord. archbishop of Winnipeg, May 31, 1961; president of Canadian Conference of Bishops, 1963-65; cardinal Apr. 28, 1969; titular church, St. Mary della Salute (Primavalle). Archbishop of Winnipeg, member of:
Congregation: Religious and Secular Institutes.

Florit, Ermenegildo: b. July 5, 1901, Fagagna, Italy; ord. priest Apr. 11, 1925; taught Sacred Scripture at Lateran University from 1929; pro-rector of Lateran University and Institute of Civil and Canon Law, 1951-54; ord. titular archbishop of Hieropolis and coadjutor archbishop of Florence, Sept. 12, 1954; archbishop of Florence, 1962-77; cardinal Feb. 22, 1965; titular church, Queen of the Apostles. Former archbishop of Florence, member of:
Congregation: Causes of Saints;
Commission: Revision of Code of Canon Law.

Freeman, James D.: b. Nov. 19, 1907, Sydney, Australia; ord. priest July 13, 1930; ord. titular bishop of Ermopoli minore and auxiliary of Sydney, Jan. 24, 1957; bishop of Armidale, 1968-71; archbishop of Sydney, July 9, 1971; cardinal Mar. 5, 1973; titular church,

St. Mary Queen of Peace. Archbishop of Sydney, member of;
Secretariat: Non-Christians.

Gantin, Bernardin: b. May 8, 1922, Toffo, Dahomey (now Benin); ord. priest Jan. 14, 1951; ord. titular bishop of Tipasa di Mauritania and auxiliary bishop of Cotonou, Feb. 3, 1957; archbishop of Cotonou, 1960-71; associate secretary (1971-73) and secretary (1973-75) of Sacred Congregation for Evangelization of Peoples; vice-president (1975) and president (1976) of Pontifical Commission for Justice and Peace; cardinal June 27, 1977; deacon, Sacred Heart of Christ the King. Former archbishop of Cotonou, president of Pontifical Commission for Justice and Peace and the Pontifical Council *Cor Unum*, member of:
Congregations: Causes of Saints, Evangelization of Peoples, Oriental Churches, Religious and Secular Institutes, Catholic Education;
Secretariat: Non-Believers;
Tribunal: Apostolic Signatura.

Garrone, Gabriel-Marie: b. Oct. 12, 1901, Aix-les-Bains, France; ord. priest Apr. 11, 1925; captain during World War II, cited for bravery, taken prisoner; rector of major seminary of Chambery, 1947; ord. titular archbishop of Lemno and coadjutor of Toulouse, June 24, 1947; archbishop of Toulouse, 1956-66; titular archbishop of Torri di Numidia and pro-prefect of Congregation of Seminaries and Universities, Mar. 24, 1966; cardinal June 26, 1967; titular church, St. Sabina. Prefect of Congregation for Catholic Education, 1968, chamberlain of College of Cardinals, 1977, grand chancellor of the Pontifical Gregorian University, member of:
Council for Public Affairs of Church;
Congregations: Doctrine of Faith, Bishops, Evangelization of Peoples, Causes of Saints, Religious and Secular Institutes;
Commission: Revision of Code of Canon Law.

Gonzalez Martin, Marcelo: b. Jan. 16, 1918, Villanubla, Spain; ord. priest June 29, 1941; taught theology and sociology at Valladolid diocesan seminary; founded organization for construction of houses for poor; ord. bishop of Astorga, Mar. 5, 1961; titular archbishop of Case Mediane and coadjutor of Barcelona, Feb. 21, 1966; archbishop of Barcelona, 1967-71; archbishop of Toledo, Dec. 3, 1971; cardinal Mar. 5, 1973; titular church, Sant'Augustine. Archbishop of Toledo, member of:
Congregation: Evangelization of Peoples.

Gouyon, Paul: b. Oct. 24, 1910, Bordeaux, France; ord. priest Mar. 13, 1937; ord. bishop of Bayonne, Oct. 7, 1957; titular archbishop of Pessinonte and coadjutor archbishop of Rennes, Sept. 6, 1963; archbishop of Rennes, Sept. 4, 1964; cardinal Apr. 28, 1969; titular church, the Nativity (Via Gallia). Archbishop of Rennes, member of:
Secretariat: Non-Believers.

Gray, Gordon J.: b. Aug. 10, 1910, Edinburgh, Scotland; ord. priest June 15, 1935; ord. archbishop of Saint Andrews and Edinburgh, Sept. 21, 1951; chairman of International Committee for English in the Liturgy; cardinal Apr. 28, 1969; titular church, St. Clare. Archbishop of Saint Andrews and Edinburgh, member of:
Congregations: Evangelization of Peoples, Sacraments and Divine Worship;
Commission: Social Communications.

Guerri, Sergio: b. Dec. 25, 1905, Tarquinia, Italy; ord. priest Mar. 30, 1929; ord. titular archbishop of Trevi, Apr. 27, 1969; cardinal Apr. 28, 1969; titular church, Most Holy Name of Mary. Pro-president of Pontifical Commission for State of Vatican City, member of:
Congregations: Oriental Churches, Evangelization of Peoples.

Guyot, Louis Jean: b. July 7, 1905, Bordeaux, France; ord. priest June 29, 1932; held various offices in Bordeaux diocese; ord. titular bishop of Helenopolis and coadjutor of Constance, May 4, 1949; bishop of Constance, 1950-66; archbishop of Toulouse, 1966-78; invested with Legion of Honor by French government; cardinal Mar. 5, 1973; titular church, Saint Agnes Outside the Walls. Former archbishop of Toulouse, member of:
Congregation: Catholic Education.

Hoeffner, Joseph: b. Dec. 24, 1906, Horhausen, Germany; ord. priest Oct. 30, 1932; ord. bishop of Munster, Sept. 14, 1962; titular archbishop of Aquileia and coadjutor archbishop of Cologne, Jan. 6, 1969; archbishop of Cologne, Feb. 23, 1969; cardinal Apr. 28, 1969; titular church, St. Andrew of the Valley. Archbishop of Cologne, member of:
Congregations: Oriental Churches, Religious and Secular Institutes, Evangelization of Peoples, Catholic Education;
Secretariat: Non-Believers;
Office: Prefecture of Economic Affairs.

Hume, George Basil, O.S.B.: b. Mar. 2, 1923, Newcastle-upon-Tyne, England; began monastic studies at Benedictine Abbey of St. Laurence at Ampleforth, 1941; made solemn perpetual vows as Benedictine, 1945; ord. priest July 23, 1950; abbot of Ampleforth, 1963-76; ord archbishop of Westminster, Mar. 25, 1976; cardinal May 24, 1976; titular church, S. Silvestro (in Capite). Archbishop of Westminster, member of:
Congregation: Religious and Secular Institutes;
Secretariat: Christian Unity.

Jubany Arnau, Narciso: b. Aug. 12, 1913, Santa Coloma de Farnes, Spain; ord. priest July 30, 1939; professor of law at Barcelona seminary; served on ecclesiastical tribunal; ord. titular bishop of Ortosia and auxiliary of

Barcelona, Jan. 22, 1956; bishop of Gerona, 1964-71; archbishop of Barcelona, Dec. 3, 1971; cardinal Mar. 5, 1973; titular church, San Lorenzo (in Damaso). Archbishop of Barcelona, member of:
Congregations: Sacraments and Divine Worship, Religious and Secular Institutes;
Secretariat: Non-Christians;
Commission: Revision of Code of Canon Law.

Kim, Stephan Sou Hwan: b. May 8, 1922, Tae Gu, Korea; ord. priest Sept. 15, 1951; ord. bishop of Masan, May 31, 1966; archbishop of Seoul, Apr. 9, 1968; cardinal Apr. 28, 1969; titular church, St. Felix of Cantalice (Centocelle). Archbishop of Seoul, apostolic administrator of Pyeong Yang, member of:
Congregation: Evangelization of Peoples;
Secretariat: Non-Christians.

Knox, James R.: b. Mar. 2, 1914, Bayswater, Australia; ord. priest Dec. 22, 1941, at Rome; forced to remain in Rome because of World War II; chaplain and later vice rector of Pontifical Urban University; secretary of apostolic delegation in Japan; ord. titular archbishop of Melitene, Nov. 8, 1953; apostolic delegate to British Africa, 1953-57; internuncio to India and apostolic delegate to Burma and Ceylon (Sri Lanka), 1957-67; archbishop of Melbourne, Australia, 1967-74; cardinal Mar. 5, 1973; titular church, Santa Maria (in Vallicella). Prefect of Sacred Congregation for Discipline of Sacraments and Divine Worship, 1974, member of:
Council for Public Affairs of Church;
Congregations: Bishops, Oriental Churches, Evangelization of Peoples, Catholic Education;
Commissions: Revision of Code of Canon Law, Interpretation of Decrees of Vatican II, Revision of Oriental Code of Canon Law;
Office: Administration of Patrimony of Holy See.

Koenig, Franz: b. Aug. 3, 1905, Rabenstein, Lower Austria; ord. priest Oct. 28, 1933; ord. titular bishop of Livias and coadjutor bishop of Sankt Poelten, Aug. 31, 1952; archbishop of Vienna, May 10, 1956; cardinal Dec. 15, 1958; titular church, St. Eusebius. Archbishop of Vienna, ordinary for faithful of Byzantine Rite living in Austria, president of Secretariat for Non-Believers, member of:
Congregation: Bishops;
Commission: Revision of Code of Canon Law.

Krol, John J.: b. Oct. 26, 1910, Cleveland, Ohio; ord. priest Feb. 20, 1937; ord. titular bishop of Cadi and auxiliary bishop of Cleveland, Sept. 2, 1953; archbishop of Philadelphia, Feb. 11, 1961, installed Mar. 22, 1961; cardinal June 26, 1967; titular church, St. Mary (della Merced) and St. Adrian Martyr; vice-president, 1966-72, and president, 1972-74, of NCCB/USCC. Archbishop of Philadelphia, member of:
Congregation: Oriental Churches;
Commission: Revision of Code of Canon Law.

Landazuri Ricketts, Juan, O. F. M: b. Dec. 19, 1913, Arequipa, Peru; entered Franciscans, 1933; ord. priest Apr. 16, 1939; ord. titular archbishop of Roina and coadjutor archbishop of Lima, Aug. 24, 1952; archbishop of Lima, May 2, 1955; cardinal Mar. 19, 1962; titular church, St. Mary (in Aracoeli). Archbishop of Lima, member of:
Congregations: Clergy, Religious and Secular Institutes, Catholic Education;
Commission: Revision of Code of Canon Law.

Leger, Paul Emile, S.S.: b. Apr. 26, 1904, Valleyfield, Quebec, Canada; ord. priest May 25, 1929; rector Canadian College, Rome, 1947; ord. archbishop of Montreal, Apr. 26, 1950; cardinal Jan. 12, 1953; titular church, St. Mary (of the Angels); resigned as archbishop of Montreal (Apr. 20, 1968) to become missionary to lepers, retired 1979. Former archbishop of Montreal, member of:
Congregation: Evangelization of Peoples;
Commission: Revision of Code of Canon Law.

Lekai, Laszlo: b. Mar. 12, 1910, Zalalovo, Hungary; ord. priest Oct. 28, 1934; professor of philosophy and dogmatic theology at major seminary at Veszprem; arrested and imprisoned by Nazis during World War II; engaged in pastoral work and held diocesan offices after the war; ord. titular bishop of Girus Tirasii and apostolic administrator of Esztergom, Mar. 16, 1972; archbishop of Esztergom and primate of Hungary, Feb. 12, 1976; cardinal May 24, 1976; titular church, S. Teresa (on the Corso d'Italia). Archbishop of Esztergom, member of:
Congregation: Catholic Education.

Lorscheider, Aloisio, O.F.M.: b. Oct. 8, 1924, Linha Geraldo, Brazil; received in Franciscan Order, Feb. 1, 1942; ord. priest Aug. 22, 1948; professor of theology at the Antonianum, Rome, and director of Franciscan international house of studies; ord. bishop of Santo Angelo, Brazil, May 20, 1962; archbishop of Fortaleza, Mar. 26, 1973; president of CELAM, 1975-79; cardinal May 24, 1976; titular church, S. Pietro (in Montorio). Archbishop of Fortaleza, member of:
Congregation: Religious and Secular Institutes.

McCann, Owen: b. June 29, 1907, Woodstock, South Africa; ord. priest Dec. 21, 1935; ord. titular bishop of Stettorio and vicar apostolic of Cape Town, May 18, 1950; first archbishop of Cape Town, Jan. 11, 1951; opponent of apartheid policy; cardinal Feb. 22, 1965; titular church, St. Praxedes. Archbishop of Cape Town, member of:
Congregation: Evangelization of Peoples.

Macharski, Franciszek: b. May 20, 1927, Cracow, Poland; ord. priest Apr. 2, 1950; engaged in pastoral work, 1950-56; continued theological studies in Fribourg, Switzerland, 1956-60; taught pastoral theology at the Faculty of Theology in Cracow; app. rector of archdiocesan seminary at Cracow, 1970; ord. archbishop of Cracow, Jan. 6, 1979, by Pope John Paul II; cardinal June 30, 1979; titular church, St. John at the Latin Gate. Archbishop of Cracow, member of:

Congregations: Clergy, Catholic Education.

Malula, Joseph: b. Dec. 12, 1917, Kinshasa, Zaire; ord. priest June 9, 1946; ord. titular bishop of Attanaso and auxiliary bishop of Kinshasa, Sept. 20, 1959; archbishop of Kinshasa, July 7, 1964; cardinal Apr. 28, 1969; titular church, Ss. Protomartyrs (Via Aurelia Antica). Archbishop of Kinshasa, member of:

Congregation: Evangelization of Peoples.

Manning, Timothy: b. Nov. 15, 1909, Ballingeary, Ireland; completed studies for the priesthood at St. Patrick's Seminary, Menlo Park, Calif.; ord. priest June 16, 1934; became American citizen, Jan. 14, 1944; ord. titular bishop of Lesvi and auxiliary bishop of Los Angeles, Oct. 15, 1946; first bishop of Fresno, 1967-69; titular archbishop of Capri and coadjutor of Los Angeles, May 26, 1969; archbishop of Los Angeles, Jan. 21, 1970; cardinal Mar. 5, 1973; titular church, Santa Lucia. Archbishop of Los Angeles, member of:

Congregations: Evangelization of Peoples, Religious and Secular Institutes.

Marella,* Paolo: b. Jan. 25, 1895, Rome, Italy; ord. priest Feb. 23, 1918; aide in Congregation for Propagation of the Faith; on staff of apostolic delegation, Washington, D.C., 1923-33; ord. titular archbishop of Doclea, Oct. 29, 1933; apostolic delegate to Japan, 1933-48, to Australia, New Zealand and Oceania, 1948-53; nuncio to France, 1953-59; cardinal Dec. 14, 1959; entered order of cardinal bishops as titular bishop of Porto and Santa Rufina, Mar. 14, 1972; president of Secretariat for Non-Christians, 1967-73. Archpriest of St. Peter's Basilica, sub-dean of College of Cardinals, 1977, member of:

Commission: Sacred Art in Italy (Honorary President).

Marty, Francois: b. May 18, 1904, Pachins, France; ord. priest June 28, 1930; ord. bishop of Saint-Flour, May 1, 1952; titular archbishop of Emesa and coadjutor archbishop of Rheims, Dec. 14, 1959; archbishop of Rheims, May 9, 1960; archbishop of Paris, Mar. 26, 1968; cardinal Apr. 28, 1969; titular church, St. Louis of France. Archbishop of Paris, ordinary for Eastern Rite Catholics in France without ordinaries of their own rites, member of:

Congregations: Oriental Churches, Clergy, Sacraments and Divine Worship;

Commission: Revision of Code of Canon Law.

Maurer, Jose Clemente, C.SS.R.: b. Mar. 13, 1900, Puttlingen, Germany; ord. priest Sept. 19, 1925; assigned to Bolivian missions, 1926; became a Bolivian citizen; ord. titular bishop of Cea and auxiliary bishop of La Paz, Apr. 16, 1950; archbishop of Sucre, Oct. 27, 1951; cardinal June 26, 1967; titular church, Most Holy Redeemer and St. Alphonsus. Archbishop of Sucre.

Medeiros, Humberto: b. Oct. 6, 1915, Arrifes, S. Miguel, Azores; came to U.S. at age of 15; became American citizen, 1940; ord. priest June 15, 1946; ord. bishop of Brownsville, Tex., June 9, 1966; archbishop of Boston, Sept. 8, 1970; cardinal Mar. 5, 1973; titular church, Santa Susanna. Archbishop of Boston, member of:

Congregations: Bishops, Catholic Education.

Miranda y Gomez,* Miguel Dario: b. Dec. 19, 1895, Leon, Mexico; ord. priest Oct. 28, 1918; ord. bishop of Tulancingo, Dec. 8, 1937; titular archbishop of Selimbra and coadjutor archbishop of Mexico City, Dec. 20, 1955; archbishop of Mexico City, May 28, 1956; served as president of the Latin American Bishops' Council (CELAM); cardinal Apr. 28, 1969; titular church, St. Mary of Guadalupe (Montemario). Former archbishop of Mexico City (resigned 1977).

Motta,* Carlos Carmelo de Vasconcellos: b. July 16, 1890, Bom Jesus do Amparo, Brazil; ord. priest June 29, 1918; ord. titular bishop of Algiza and auxiliary bishop of Diamantina, Oct. 30, 1932; archbishop of Sao Luis do Maranhao, Dec. 19, 1935; archbishop of Sao Paulo del Brasile, 1944-64; cardinal Feb. 18, 1946; titular church, St. Pancratius. Archbishop of Aparecida (1964).

Mozzoni, Umberto: b. June 29, 1904, Buenos Aires, Argentina; holds Italian citizenship; ord. priest Aug. 14, 1927; professor of theology and canon law at Macerata seminary, Italy; served on Vatican diplomatic staff in Canada, England and Portugal; ord. titular archbishop of Side, Dec. 9, 1954; nuncio to Bolivia, 1954-58, Argentina, 1958-69, Brazil, 1969-73; cardinal Mar. 5, 1973; deacon, St. Eugene. Member of:

Congregations: Oriental Churches, Clergy, Religious and Secular Institutes, Evangelization of Peoples, Causes of Saints;

Tribunal: Apostolic Signatura;

Commissions: Sanctuaries of Pompei and Loreto (President), Institute for Works of Religion.

Munoz Duque, Anibal: b. Oct. 3, 1908, Santa Rosa de Osos, Colombia; ord. priest Nov. 19, 1933; ord. bishop of Soccoro y San Gil, May 27, 1951; bishop of Bucaramango, 1952-59; bishop of Nueva Pamplona, 1959-68; titular archbishop of Cariana and coadjutor archbishop of Bogota, 1968; archbishop of Bogota, July 29, 1972; cardinal Mar. 5, 1973; titular church, St. Bartholomew. Archbishop of Bogota, military vicar, member of:

Congregation: Sacraments and Divine Worship.

Munoz Vega, Pablo, S. J.: b. May 23, 1903, Mira, Ecuador; ord. priest July 25, 1933; ord. titular bishop of Ceramo and auxiliary bishop of Quito, Mar. 19, 1964; archbishop of Quito, June 23, 1967; cardinal Apr. 28, 1969; titular church, St. Robert Bellarmine. Archbishop of Quito, member of:

Congregation: Religious and Secular Institutes.

Nasalli Rocca di Corneliano, Mario: b. Aug. 12, 1903, Piacenza, Italy; ord. priest Apr. 9, 1927; ord. titular archbishop of Anzio, Apr. 20, 1969; cardinal Apr. 28, 1969; titular church, St. John the Baptist. Member of:

Congregations: Sacraments and Divine Worship, Causes of Saints;
Secretariat: Non-Believers.

Nsubuga, Emmanuel: b. Nov. 5, 1914, Kisule, Uganda; ord. priest Dec. 15, 1946; ord. bishop of Kampala, Oct. 30, 1966; cardinal May 24, 1976; titular church, S. Maria Nuova. Archbishop of Kampala, member of:

Congregation: Evangelization of Peoples.

O'Boyle,* Patrick A.: b. July 18, 1896, Scranton, Pa.; ord. priest May 21, 1921; executive director of War Relief Services, NCWC, 1943; ord. archbishop of Washington, Jan. 14, 1948 (retired, 1973); cardinal June 26, 1967; titular church, St. Nicholas (in Carcere). Former archbishop of Washington.

Oddi, Silvio: b. Nov. 14, 1910, Morfasso, Italy; ord. priest May 21, 1933; ord. titular archbishop of Mesembria, Sept. 27, 1953; served in Vatican diplomatic corps, 1953-69; apostolic delegate to Jerusalem, Palestine, Jordan and Cyprus, internuncio to the United Arab Republic, and nuncio to Belgium and Luxembourg; cardinal Apr. 28, 1969; titular church, St. Agatha of the Goths. Prefect of Sacred Congregation for the Clergy, 1979, member of:

Council for Public Affairs of Church;
Congregations: Bishops, Oriental Churches, Causes of Saints;
Tribunal: Apostolic Signatura;
Commission: State of Vatican City.

O'Fiaich, Tomas: b. Nov. 3, 1923; Crossmaglen, Ireland; ord. priest July 6, 1948; lecturer, 1953, and professor, 1959, of modern history at Maynooth College; vice president, 1970, and president, 1974, of Maynooth; prolific author of scholarly works; recognized authority on early Irish Christianity; ord. archbishop of Armagh and primate of All Ireland, Oct. 2, 1977; pledged to work for the cause of peace in Northern Ireland; outspoken in his condemnation of violence; president of Irish Episcopal Conference, 1977-79; cardinal June 30, 1979; titular church, St. Patrick. Archbishop of Armagh, primate of All Ireland, member of:

Congregation: Clergy;
Secretariat: Christian Unity.

Otunga, Maurice: b. January, 1923, Chebukwa, Kenya; son of pagan tribal chief; baptized 1935, at age of 12; ord. priest Oct. 3, 1950, at Rome; taught at Kisumu major seminary for three years; attaché in apostolic delegation at Mombasa, 1953-56; ord. titular bishop of Tacape and auxiliary of Kisumu, Feb. 25, 1957; bishop of Kisii, 1960-69; titular archbishop of Bomarzo and coadjutor of Nairobi, Nov. 15, 1969; archbishop of Nairobi, Oct. 24, 1971; cardinal Mar. 5, 1973; titular church, St. Gregory Barbarigo. Archbishop of Nairobi, member of:

Congregations: Sacraments and Divine Worship, Religious and Secular Institutes.

Palazzini, Pietro: b. May 19, 1912, Piobbico, Pesaro, Italy; ord. priest Dec. 6, 1934; assistant vice-rector of Pontifical Major Roman Seminary and vice-rector and bursar of Pontifical Roman Seminary for Juridical Studies; professor of moral theology at Lateran University; held various offices in Roman Curia; secretary of Congregation of Council (now Clergy), 1958-73; ord. titular archbishop of Caesarea in Cappadocia, Sept. 21, 1962; author of numerous works on moral theology and law; cardinal Mar. 5, 1973; deacon, St. Jerome. Member of:

Congregations: Oriental Churches, Clergy, Causes of Saints;
Tribunal: Apostolic Signatura;
Commissions: Revision of Code of Canon Law, Interpretation of Decrees of Vatican II.

Pappalardo, Salvatore: b. Sept. 23, 1918, Villafranca Sicula, Sicily; ord. priest Apr. 12, 1941; entered diplomatic service of secretariat of state, 1947; ord. titular archbishop of Miletus, Jan. 16, 1966; pro-nuncio in Indonesia, 1966-69; president of Pontifical Ecclesiastical Academy, 1969-70; archbishop of Palermo, Oct. 17, 1970; cardinal Mar. 5, 1973; titular church, St. Mary Odigitria of the Sicilians. Archbishop of Palermo, member of:

Congregations: Oriental Churches, Clergy.

Parecattil, Joseph: b. Apr. 1, 1912, Kidangoor, India; ord. priest Aug. 24, 1939; ord. titular bishop of Aretusa for Syrians and auxiliary bishop of Ernakulam, Nov. 30, 1953; archbishop of Ernakulam (Chaldean-Malabar Rite), July 20, 1956; vice-president of the Indian Bishops' Conference, 1966; appointed one of seven members of Pope Paul VI's advisory council for Eastern Rite churches, 1968; cardinal Apr. 28, 1969; titular church, Our Lady Queen of Peace. Archbishop of Ernakulam of the Chaldean-Malabar Rite, member of:

Congregation: Oriental Churches;
Secretariat: Non-Christians;
Commissions: Revision of Code of Canon Law, Revision of Oriental Code of Canon Law (President).

Parente,* Pietro: b. Feb. 16, 1891, Casalnuovo, Monterotaro, Italy; ord. priest Mar.

18, 1916; director of Archiepiscopal Seminary at Naples, 1916-26; rector of Pontifical Urban College of Propagation of the Faith, 1934-38; Consultor of the Congregations of the Holy Office, Council, Propagation of the Faith, and Seminaries and Universities; ord. archbishop of Perugia, Oct. 23, 1955; titular archbishop of Tolemaide di Tebaide, Oct. 23, 1959; assessor (1959-65) and secretary (1965-67) of Congregation of Holy Office (now Doctrinal Congregation); cardinal June 26, 1967; titular church, St. Lawrence (in Lucina).

Paupini, Giuseppe: b. Feb. 25, 1907, Mondavio, Italy; ord. priest Mar. 19, 1930; ord. titular archbishop of Sebastopolis in Abasgia, Feb. 26, 1956; served in Vatican diplomatic corps, 1956-69; internuncio to Iran, 1956-57; nuncio to Guatemala and El Salvador, 1957-58; nuncio to Colombia, 1959-69; cardinal Apr. 28, 1969; titular church, All Saints Church. Major penitentiary 1973, member of:
Congregation: Causes of Saints;
Commission: State of Vatican City.

Pellegrino, Michele: b. Apr. 25, 1903, Centallo, Italy; ord. priest Sept. 19, 1925; ord. archbishop of Turin, Oct. 17, 1965 (resigned 1977); cardinal June 26, 1967; titular church, Most Holy Name of Jesus. Former archbishop of Turin, member of:
Congregation: Catholic Education.

Philippe, Paul, O.P.: b. Apr. 16, 1905, Paris, France; entered Dominican Order, 1926; ord. priest July 6, 1932; professor at Angelicum, Rome, from 1935; founded Institute of Spirituality for masters of novices at Angelicum, 1950, and school for mistresses of novices, 1953; apostolic visitor of various religious institutes, 1951-56; commissary of the Holy Office, 1955; consultor of various pontifical commissions and congregations from 1958; secretary of Congregation for Religious, 1959; ord. titular archbishop of Heracleopolis Magna, Sept. 21, 1962; secretary of Congregation for Doctrine of Faith, 1967-73; cardinal Mar. 5, 1973; deacon, St. Pius V. Prefect of Congregation for Oriental Churches, 1973, member of:
Congregations: Religious and Secular Institutes, Evangelization of Peoples;
Secretariat: Christian Unity;
Commissions: Revision of Code of Canon Law, Revision of Oriental Code of Canon Law.

Picachy, Lawrence Trevor, S.J.: b. Aug. 7, 1916, Lebong, India; ord. priest Nov. 21, 1947; dean, 1950-54, and then rector, 1954-60, of St. Francis Xavier University College, Calcutta; ord. bishop of Jamshedpur, Sept. 9, 1962; archbishop of Calcutta, May 29, 1969; cardinal May 24, 1976; titular church, Sacred Heart of Mary. Archbishop of Calcutta, president of Indian Episcopal Conference, 1975, member of:
Congregation: Evangelization of Peoples.

Pignedoli, Sergio: b. June 4, 1910, Felina, Italy; ord. priest Apr. 1, 1933; chaplain in Italian navy during World War II; secretary general for organization of 1950 Holy Year; ord. titular archbishop of Iconium, Feb. 11, 1951; nuncio in Bolivia, 1950-54, and Venezuela, 1954-55; auxiliary to Cardinal Montini (later Pope Paul VI) at Milan, 1955-60; apostolic delegate to Central-West Africa, 1960-64, and Canada, 1964-67; secretary of Congregation for Evangelization of Peoples, 1967-73; sent on special mission to Vietnam, 1966; cardinal Mar. 5, 1973; deacon, San Giorgio. President of Secretariat for Non-Christians, 1973, member of:
Congregations: Catholic Education, Evangelization of Peoples, Sacraments and Divine Worship, Causes of Saints, Oriental Churches;
Secretariat: Christian Unity.

Pironio, Eduardo: b. Dec. 3, 1920, Nueve de Julio, Argentina; ord. priest Dec. 5, 1943; taught theology at Pius XII Seminary of Mercedes diocese, 1944-59; vicar general of diocese 1958-60; attended Second Vatican Council as *peritus*; ord. titular bishop of Caeciri, May 31, 1964; apostolic administrator of diocese of Avellaneda, 1967-72; secretary general 1967-72, and president, 1973-75, of CELAM; bishop of Mar del Plata, 1972-75; titular archbishop of Thiges and pro-prefect of Sacred Congregation for Religious and Secular Institutes, Sept. 20, 1975; cardinal May 24, 1976; deacon, Sts. Cosmas and Damian. Prefect of the Sacred Congregation for Religious and Secular Institutes, 1976, member of:
Council for Public Affairs of the Church.
Congregations: Bishops, Sacraments and Divine Worship, Catholic Education, Oriental Churches;
Commissions: Council for the Laity, Revision of Code of Canon Law, Latin America, Interpretation of Decrees of Vatican II.

Poletti, Ugo: b. Apr. 19, 1914, Omegna, Italy; ord. priest June 29, 1938; served in various diocesan offices at Novara; ord. titular bishop of Medeli and auxiliary of Novaro, Sept. 14, 1958; president of Pontifical Mission Aid Society for Italy, 1964-67; archbishop of Spoleto, 1967-69; titular archbishop of Cittanova, 1969; served as second viceregent of Rome, 1969-72; pro-vicar general of Rome, 1972, following the sudden death of Cardinal Dell'Acqua; cardinal Mar. 5, 1973; titular church, Sts. Ambrose and Charles. Vicar general of Rome, 1973, archpriest of Patriarchal Lateran Basilica, 1973, grand chancellor of Lateran University, member of:
Congregations: Clergy, Sacraments and Divine Worship, Oriental Churches, Religious and Secular Institutes;
Commission: Council for the Laity.

Poma, Antonio: b. June 12, 1910, Villanterio, Italy; ord. priest Apr. 15, 1933; ord. titular bishop of Tagaste and auxiliary bishop of Mantova, Dec. 9, 1951; bishop of Mantova, Sept. 8, 1954; titular archbishop of Gerpiniano and coadjutor archbishop of Bologna, July 16, 1967; archbishop of Bologna, Feb. 12, 1968; cardinal Apr. 28, 1969; titular church, St. Luke (al Prenestino). Archbishop of Bologna, member of:

Congregations: Clergy, Catholic Education.

Primatesta, Raul Francisco: b. Apr. 14, 1919, Capilla del Senor, Argentina; ord. priest Oct. 25, 1942, at Rome; taught at minor and major seminaries of La Plata; contributed to several theology reviews; ord. titular bishop of Tanais and auxiliary of La Plata, Aug. 15, 1957; bishop of San Rafael, 1961-65; archbishop of Cordoba, Feb. 16, 1965; cardinal Mar. 5, 1973; titular church, St. Mary Sorrowful Virgin. Archbishop of Cordoba, Argentina, member of:

Congregations: Bishops, Religious and Secular Institutes, Sacraments and Divine Worship.

Quintero, Jose Humberto: b. Sept. 22, 1902, Mucuchies, Venezuela; ord. priest Aug. 22, 1926; ord. titular archbishop of Acrida and coadjutor archbishop of Merida, Dec. 6, 1953; archbishop of Caracas Aug. 31, 1960; cardinal Jan. 16, 1961; titular church, Sts. Andrew and Gregory (al Monte Celio). Archbishop of Caracas.

Ratzinger, Joseph: b. Apr. 16, 1927, Marktl am Inn, Germany; ord. priest June 29, 1951; professor of dogmatic theology at University of Regensburg, 1969-77; member of International Theological Commission; ord. archbishop of Munich-Freising, May 28, 1977; cardinal June 27, 1977; titular church, St. Mary of Consolation (in Tiburtina). Archbishop of Munich-Freising, member of:

Secretariat: Christian Unity;
Commission: International Theological.

Razafimahatratra, Victor, S.J.: b. Sept. 8, 1921, Ambanitsilena-Ranomasina, Madagascar; entered Society of Jesus, 1945; ord. priest July 28, 1956; rector of Fianarantsoa Minor Seminary, 1960-63; superior of Jesuit residence at Ambositra, 1963-69; rector of Tananarive Major Seminary, 1969-71; ord. bishop of Farafangana, Apr. 18, 1971; archbishop of Tananarive, Apr. 10, 1976; cardinal May 24, 1976; titular church, Holy Cross in Jerusalem. Archbishop of Tananarive, president of Madagascar Episcopal Conference, member of:

Congregation: Evangelization of Peoples.

Renard, Alexandre C.: b. June 7, 1906, Avelin, France; ord. priest July 12, 1931; ord. bishop of Versailles, Oct. 19, 1953; archbishop of Lyons, May 28, 1967; cardinal June 26, 1967; titular church, Most Holy Trinity (at Monte Pincio). Archbishop of Lyons, member of:

Congregations: Religious and Secular Institutes, Evangelization of Peoples.

Ribeiro, Antonio: b. May 21, 1928, Gandarela di Basto, Portugal; ord. priest July 5, 1953; professor of fundamental theology at major seminary at Braga; ord. titular bishop of Tigillava and auxiliary of Braga, Sept. 17, 1967; patriarch of Lisbon, May 10, 1971; cardinal Mar. 5, 1973; titular church, St. Anthony of Padua (in Rome). Patriarch of Lisbon, military vicar, member of:

Congregation: Catholic Education;
Commission: Social Communications.

Righi-Lambertini, Egano: b. Feb. 22, 1906, Casalecchio di Reno, Italy; ord. priest May 25, 1929; entered service of secretariat of state, 1939; served in diplomatic missions in France (1949-54), Costa Rica (1955), England (1955-57); first apostolic delegate to Korea, 1957-60; ord. titular archbishop of Doclea, Oct. 28, 1960; apostolic nuncio in Lebanon, 1960-63, Chile, 1963-67, Italy, 1967-69; France, 1969-79; while nuncio in France he also served as special envoy at the Council of Europe, 1974-79; cardinal June 30, 1979; deacon, St. John Bosco in Via Tuscolana. Member of:

Council for Public Affairs of the Church;
Secretariat: Non-Christians.

Rosales, Julio: b. Sept. 18, 1906, Calbayog, Philippines; ord. priest June 2, 1929; ord. bishop of Tagbilaran, Sept. 21, 1946; archbishop of Cebu, Dec. 17, 1949; cardinal Apr. 28, 1969; titular church, Sacred Heart of Jesus (a Vitinia). Archbishop of Cebu, member of:

Congregation: Clergy;
Commission: Revision of Code of Canon Law.

Rossi, Agnelo: b. May 4, 1913, Joaquim Egidio, Brazil; ord. priest Mar. 27, 1937; ord. bishop of Barra do Pirai, Apr. 15, 1956; archbishop of Ribeirao Preto, 1962-64; archbishop of Sao Paulo, 1964-70; cardinal Feb. 22, 1965; titular church, Mother of God. Prefect of Congregation for Evangelization of Peoples, grand chancellor of Pontifical Urban University, member of:

Council for Public Affairs of Church;
Congregations: Clergy, Doctrine of Faith, Bishops, Oriental Churches, Causes of Saints, Religious and Secular Institutes, Catholic Education;
Secretariats: Christian Unity, Non-Christians;
Commissions: Revision of Code of Canon Law, Revision of Oriental Code of Canon Law, Institute for Works of Religion.

Rossi, Opilio: b. May 14, 1910, New York, N.Y.; holds Italian citizenship; ord. priest for diocese of Piacenza, Italy, Mar. 11, 1933; served in nunciatures in Belgium, The Netherlands and Germany, 1938-53; ord. titular archbishop of Ancyra, Dec. 27, 1953; nuncio in Ecuador, 1953-59, Chile, 1959-61, Austria, 1961-76; cardinal May 24, 1976; deacon, S. Maria Liberatrice (on the Monte Testaccio). Member of:

Council for Public Affairs of the Church;

Congregations: Bishops, Oriental Churches, Sacraments and Divine Worship, Religious and Secular Institutes, Evangelization of Peoples;

Commissions: Council for Laity (President), Committee for Family (President).

Roy, Maurice: b. Jan. 25, 1905, Quebec, Canada; ord. priest June 12, 1927; chief of chaplains of Canadian Armed Forces during World War II; ord. bishop of Trois Rivieres, May 1, 1946; military vicar, June 8, 1946; archbishop of Quebec, June 2, 1947; primate of Canada, Jan. 25, 1956; cardinal Feb. 22, 1965; titular church, Our Lady of the Most Holy Sacrament and the Holy Canadian Martyrs. Archbishop of Quebec, primate of Canada, military vicar of Canada, member of:

Congregations: Clergy, Catholic Education;

Commission: Revision of Code of Canon Law.

Rubin, Wladyslaw: b. Sept. 20, 1917, Toki, Poland; seminary studies interrupted during World War II when he was arrested and deported to labor camp; completed studies at St. Joseph's University in Beirut; ord. priest in Beirut June 30, 1946 and served Polish community there; sent to Rome for further studies, 1949; chaplain for Polish refugees in Italy, 1953-58; rector of Polish College in Rome, 1959-64; ord. titular bishop of Serta, primate of Poland's delegate for emigration and auxiliary of Gniezno, Nov. 29, 1964; established contact with Polish emigrants throughout the world; secretary general of Synod of Bishops, 1967-79; cardinal June 30, 1979; deacon, St. Mary in Via Lata. Member of:

Congregations: Doctrine of the Faith, Causes of Saints.

Rugambwa, Laurean: b. July 12, 1912, Bukongo, Tanzania; ord. priest Dec. 12, 1943; ord. titular bishop of Febiano and vicar apostolic of Lower Kagera, Feb. 10, 1952; bishop of Rutabo, Mar. 25, 1953; cardinal Mar. 28, 1960; titular church, St. Francis (a Ripa); bishop of Bukoba, 1960-68. Archbishop of Dar-es-Salaam, 1968, member of:

Congregation: Causes of Saints;

Commission: Revision of Code of Canon Law.

Salazar Lopez, Jose: b. Jan. 12, 1910, Ameca, Mexico; ord. priest May 26, 1934, in Rome; instrumental in building of new seminary at Guadalajara, the largest in Mexico; vice-rector and later rector of seminary; ord. titular bishop of Prusiade and coadjutor bishop of Zamora, Aug. 20, 1961; bishop of Zamora, 1967-70; archbishop of Guadalajara, Feb. 21, 1970; cardinal Mar. 5, 1973; titular church, Santa Emerentia. Archbishop of Guadalajara, member of:

Congregations: Sacraments and Divine Worship, Clergy.

Samore, Antonio: b. Dec. 4, 1905, Bardi, Italy; ord. priest June 10, 1928; served in apostolic nunciatures at Lithuania and Switzerland; worked in Vatican secretariat of state during World War II; assigned to apostolic delegation in Washington, D.C., 1947; nuncio to Colombia, 1950; ord. titular archbishop of Tirnovo, Apr. 16, 1950; secretary of Congregation of Extraordinary Ecclesiastical Affairs, 1953-67; cardinal June 26, 1967; entered order of cardinal bishops as titular bishop of Sabina and Poggia Mirteto, Dec. 12, 1974; prefect of Congregation for Discipline of Sacraments, 1968-74. Librarian and archivist of Holy Roman Church, 1974, member of:

Council for Public Affairs of Church;

Congregations: Oriental Churches, Bishops, Evangelization of Peoples;

Commission: Revision of Code of Canon Law.

Satowaki, Joseph Asajiro: b. Feb. 1, 1904, Shittsu, Japan; ord. priest Dec. 17, 1932; served in various pastoral capacities in Nagasaki archdiocese after his ordination; apostolic administrator of Taiwan (then a Japanese possession), 1941-45; director of Nagasaki minor seminary, 1945-57; vicar general of Nagasaki, 1945; ord. first bishop of Kagoshima, May 3, 1955; archbishop of Nagasaki, Dec. 19, 1968; president of Japanese Episcopal Conference 1979-   ; cardinal June 30, 1979; titular church, St. Mary of Peace. Archbishop of Nagasaki, member of:

Congregation: Evangelization of Peoples;

Secretariat: Non-Christians.

Scherer, Alfred Vicente: b. Feb. 5, 1903, Bom Principio, Brazil; ord. priest Apr. 3, 1926; ord. archbishop of Porto Alegre, Feb. 23, 1947; cardinal Apr. 28, 1969; titular church, Our Lady of La Salette. Archbishop of Porto Alegre, Brazil.

Schroeffer, Joseph: b. Feb. 20, 1903, Ingolstadt, Germany; ord. priest Oct. 28, 1928; studied at the Gregorian University, Rome, 1922-31; returned to Germany 1931; professor at Higher Institute for Philosophical and Theological Studies at Eichstatt; vicar general of diocese of Eichstatt, 1941-48; ord. bishop of Eichstatt, Sept. 21, 1948; app. titular archbishop of Volturnum and secretary of Sacred Congregation for Catholic Education, 1968; cardinal May 24, 1976; deacon, San Saba. Member of:

Council for Public Affairs of the Church;

Congregations: Doctrine of the Faith, Bishops;

Tribunal: Apostolic Signatura;

Commissions: Council for Laity, Revision of Code of Canon Law;

Office: Administration of Patrimony of Holy See.

Sensi, Giuseppe Maria: b. May 27, 1907, Cosenza, Italy; ord. priest Dec. 21, 1929; entered Vatican diplomatic service; served in nunciatures in Hungary, Switzerland, Belgium and Czechoslovakia, 1934-49; ord. titular archbishop of Sardes, July 24, 1955; apostolic nuncio to Costa Rica, 1955; apostolic delegate to Jerusalem, 1956-62; nuncio to Ireland, 1962-67, and Portugal, 1967-76; cardinal May 24, 1976; deacon, SS. Biagio e Carlo (ai Catinari). Member of:

Congregations: Oriental Churches, Evangelization of Peoples;

Office: Prefecture of Economic Affairs.

Seper, Franjo: b. Oct. 2, 1905, Osijek, Yugoslavia; ord. priest Oct. 26, 1930; secretary of Cardinal Stepinac, 1934-41; rector of Zagreb's major seminary, 1941-51; ord. titular archbishop of Filippopoli and coadjutor archbishop of Zagreb, Sept. 21, 1954; archbishop of Zagreb, 1960-69; cardinal Feb. 22, 1965; titular church, Sts. Peter and Paul (in Via Ostia). Prefect of Congregation for Doctrine of the Faith, 1968, member of:

Council for Public Affairs of Church;

Congregations: Bishops, Sacraments and Divine Worship, Catholic Education;

Commissions: Biblical (President), Theological (President), Revision of Code;

Office: Administration of Patrimony of Holy See.

Shehan,* Lawrence J.: b. Mar. 18, 1898, Baltimore, Md.; ord. priest Dec. 23, 1922; ord. titular bishop of Lidda and auxiliary bishop of Baltimore and Washington, Dec. 12, 1945; bishop of Bridgeport, 1953-61; titular archbishop of Nicopolis ad Nestum and coadjutor archbishop of Baltimore, July 10, 1961; archbishop of Baltimore, 1961-74; cardinal Feb. 22, 1965; titular church, St. Clement. Former archbishop of Baltimore.

Sidarouss, Stephanos I, C.M.: b. Feb. 22, 1904, Cairo, Egypt; ord. priest July 2, 1939; ord. titular bishop of Sais, Jan. 25, 1948; auxiliary to the patriarch of Alexandria for the Copts, 1948-58; patriarch of Alexandria, May 10, 1958; cardinal Feb. 22, 1965. Patriarch of Alexandria for the Copts, member of:

Congregation: Oriental Churches;

Secretariat: Christian Unity;

Commissions: Revision of Code of Canon Law, Revision of Code of Oriental Canon Law.

Silva Henriquez, Raul, S.D.B.: b. Sept. 27, 1907, Talca, Chile; ord. priest July 3, 1938; ord. bishop of Valparaiso, Nov. 29, 1959; archbishop of Santiago de Chile, Mar. 14, 1961; cardinal Mar. 19, 1962; titular church, St. Bernard (alle Terme). Archbishop of Santiago de Chile, member of:

Commission: Revision of Code of Canon Law.

Sin, Jaime L.: b. Aug. 31, 1928, New Washington, Philippines; ord. priest Apr. 3, 1954; diocesan missionary in Capiz, 1954-57; app. first rector of the St. Pius X Seminary, Roxas City, 1957; ord. titular bishop of Obba and auxiliary bishop of Jaro, Mar. 18, 1967; apostolic administrator of archdiocese of Jaro, June 20, 1970; titular archbishop of Massa Lubrense and coadjutor archbishop of Jaro, Jan. 15, 1972; archbishop of Jaro, Oct. 8, 1972; archbishop of Manila, Jan. 21, 1974; cardinal May 24, 1976; titular church, S. Maria (ai Monti). Archbishop of Manila, member of:

Congregations: Evangelization of Peoples, Catholic Education;

Commission: Social Communications.

Siri, Giuseppe: b. May 20, 1906, Genoa, Italy; ord. priest Sept. 22, 1928; ord. titular bishop of Liviade and auxiliary bishop of Genoa, May 7, 1944; archbishop of Genoa, May 14, 1946; cardinal Jan. 12, 1953; titular church, St. Mary (della Vittoria). Archbishop of Genoa, member of:

Congregations: Clergy, Catholic Education;

Commission: Revision of Code of Canon Law.

Slipyi or Slipyj,* Josyf (Kobernyckyj-Dyckowskyj): b. Feb. 17, 1892, Zazdrist in the Ukraine; ord. priest Sept. 30, 1917; ord. titular archbishop of Serre, Dec. 22, 1939; coadjutor archbishop of Lwow for the Ukrainians, 1939-44; archbishop of Lwow, Nov. 1, 1944; imprisoned 1945-63 for unspecified crimes; released by Soviets and allowed to go to Rome in February, 1963; named major archbishop by Paul VI, 1963; cardinal Feb. 22, 1965; titular church, St. Athanasius. Archbishop of Lwow (not permitted to exercise his office; he resides in Vatican City), major archbishop of the Ukraine.

Suenens, Leo Josef: b. July 16, 1904, Brussels, Belgium; ord. priest Sept. 4, 1927; ord. titular bishop of Isinda, Dec. 16, 1945; auxiliary bishop of Mechelen, 1945-61; archbishop of Mechelen-Brussels, 1961-79; cardinal Mar. 19, 1962; titular church, St. Peter in Chains. Former archbishop of Mechelen-Brussels, military vicar for Belgium; member of:

Congregations: Evangelization of Peoples, Causes of Saints;

Commission: Revision of Canon Law.

Taofinu'u, Pio, S.M.: b. Dec. 9, 1923, Falealupo, W. Samoa; ord. priest Dec. 8, 1954; joined Society of Mary, 1955; ord. bishop of Apia (now Samoa and Tokelau), May 29, 1968, the first Polynesian bishop; cardinal Mar. 5, 1973; titular church, Sant' Onofrio (on the Janiculum). Bishop of Samoa and Tokelau, member of:

Congregation: Causes of Saints.

Thiandoum, Hyacinthe: b. Feb. 2, 1921, Poponguine, Senegal; ord. priest Apr. 18, 1949; studied at Gregorian University, Rome, 1951-53; returned to Senegal, 1953; ord. archbishop of Dakar, May 20, 1962; cardinal May 24, 1976; titular church, S. Maria (del Popolo). Archbishop of Dakar, president of Senegal-

Mauretania Episcopal Conference, member of:
Congregation: Religious and Secular Institutes;
Commission: Social Communications.

Tomasek,* Frantisek: b. June 30, 1899, Studenka, Moravia, Czechoslovakia; ord. priest July 5, 1922; professor of pedagogy and catechetics at the theology faculty of Olomouc, 1934-39; resumed academic activity after liberation in 1945; author, *Catechism of the Catholic Religion;* ord. titular bishop of Butus and auxiliary of Olomouc, Oct. 13, 1949; only Czech bishop to attend Second Vatican Council; apostolic administrator of Prague, Feb. 18, 1965; cardinal May 24, 1976 (*in pectore*); solemnly proclaimed at June 27, 1977, consistory; titular church, Sts. Vitalis, Valeria, Gervase and Protase. Archbishop of Prague, 1977, member of:
Congregation: Clergy.

Trin-Van-Can, Joseph Mary: b. Mar. 19, 1921, Trac But, Vietnam; ord. priest Dec. 8, 1949; held various offices in Hanoi archdiocese; ord. titular bishop of Ela (with personal title of archbishop) and coadjutor archbishop of Hanoi, June 2, 1963; archbishop of Hanoi, Nov. 27, 1978; cardinal June 30, 1979; titular church, St. Mary in Via. Archbishop of Hanoi, member of:
Congregation: Evangelization of Peoples.

Ursi, Corrado: b. July 26, 1908, Andria, Italy; ord. priest July 25, 1931; vice-rector and later rector of the Pontifical Regional Seminary of Molfetta, 1931-51; ord. bishop of Nardo, Sept. 30, 1951; archbishop of Acerenza, Nov. 30, 1961; archbishop of Naples, May 23, 1966; cardinal June 26, 1967; titular church, St. Callistus. Archbishop of Naples, member of:
Congregation: Catholic Education.

Vagnozzi, Egidio: b. Feb. 2, 1906, Rome, Italy; ord. priest Dec. 22, 1928; served in U.S. apostolic delegation; ord. titular archbishop of Mira, May 22, 1949; apostolic delegate to the Philippines, 1949; first nuncio to Philippines, 1951; apostolic delegate to the U.S., 1958-67; cardinal June 26, 1967; titular church, St. Joseph. President of Prefecture of Economic Affairs of Holy See, member of:
Congregations: Oriental Churches; Evangelization of Peoples;
Tribunal: Apostolic Signatura.

Volk, Hermann: b. Dec. 27, 1903, Steinheim, Germany; ord. priest Apr. 2, 1927; professor of dogmatic theology at University of Muenster; ord. bishop of Mainz, June 5, 1962; cardinal Mar. 5, 1973; titular church, Saints Fabian and Venanzio (at Villa Fiorelli). Bishop of Mainz, member of:
Secretariat: Christian Unity.

Willebrands, Johannes: b. Sept. 4, 1909, Bovenkarspel, Netherlands; ord. priest May 26, 1934; ord. titular bishop of Mauriana, June 28, 1964; secretary of Secretariat for Christian Unity, 1960-69; cardinal Apr. 28, 1969; titular church, St. Sebastian (alle Catacombe). President of Secretariat for Christian Unity, 1969, Archbishop of Utrecht, 1975, military vicar of Netherlands, member of:
Congregations: Doctrine of Faith, Sacraments and Divine Worship, Oriental Churches, Catholic Education, Evangelization of Peoples;
Commissions: Revision of Code of Canon Law, Revision of Oriental Code of Canon Law..

Wyszynski, Stefan: b. Aug. 3, 1901, Zuzela, Poland; ord. priest Aug. 3, 1924; ord. bishop of Lublin, May 12, 1946; archbishop of Gniezno and Warsaw, Nov. 12, 1948; cardinal Jan. 12, 1953; titular church, St. Mary (in Trastavere). He was "deposed" by Polish government in fall of 1953, recognized, 1956. Archbishop of Gniezno and Warsaw, primate of Poland, member of:
Commission: Revision of Canon Law.

Zoungrana, Paul: b. Sept. 3, 1917, Ouagadougou, Upper Volta; ord. priest May 2, 1942; ord. archbishop of Ouagadougou at St. Peter's Basilica by John XXIII, May 8, 1960; cardinal Feb. 22, 1965; titular church, St. Camillus de Lellis. Archbishop of Ouagadougou, member of:
Congregation: Evangelization of Peoples.

CATEGORIES OF CARDINALS
(As of Sept. 20, 1979.)

Information below includes categories of cardinals and dates of consistories at which they were created. Seniority or precedence usually depends on order of elevation, except in the case of cardinal bishops whose seniority depends on date of appointment to suburban see.

Five of these cardinals were named by Pius XII (consistories of Feb. 18, 1946, and Jan. 12, 1953); 10 by John XXIII (consistories of Dec. 15, 1958, Dec. 14, 1959, Mar. 28, 1960, Jan. 16, 1961, and Mar. 19, 1962); 101 by Paul VI (consistories of Feb. 22, 1965, June 26, 1967, Apr. 28, 1969, Mar. 5, 1973, May 24, 1976, and June 27, 1977); 14 by John Paul II (consistory of June 30, 1979).

Order of Bishops

Titular Bishops of Suburban Sees: Carlo Confalonieri, Dean (Dec. 15, 1958); Paolo Marella (Dec. 14, 1959); Antonio Samore (June 26, 1967); Sebastiano Baggio (Apr. 28, 1969); Francesco Carpino (June 26, 1967); Paolo Bertoli (Apr. 28, 1969).
Eastern Rite Patriarch: Stephanos I Sidarouss, C.M. (Feb. 22, 1965).

Order of Priests

1946 (Feb. 18): Carlos Carmelo de Vasconcellos Motta, Antonio Caggiano.
1953 (Jan. 12): Giuseppe Siri, Stefan Wyszynski, Paul Emile Leger, S.S.

1958 (Dec. 15): Jose M. Bueno y Monreal, Franz Koenig.
1960 (Mar. 28): Bernard Jan Alfrink, Laurean Rugambwa.
1961 (Jan. 16): Jose Humberto Quintero.
1962 (Mar. 19): Juan Landazuri Ricketts, O.F.M., Raul Silva Henriquez, S.D.B., Leo Josef Suenens.
1965 (Feb. 22): Josyf Slipyi, Thomas B. Cooray, Maurice Roy, Owen McCann, Leon-Etienne Duval, Ermenegildo Florit, Franjo Seper, Paul Zoungrana, Lawrence J. Shehan, Agnelo Rossi, Giovanni Colombo.
1967 (June 26): Gabriel Garrone, Patrick O'Boyle, Egidio Vagnozzi, Maximilien de Furstenberg, Jose Clemente Maurer, C.SS.R., Pietro Parente, Pericle Felici, John J. Krol, John P. Cody, Corrado Ursi, Alfred Bengsch, Justin Darmojuwono, Michele Pellegrino, Alexandre Renard.
1969 (Apr. 28): Alfredo Vicente Scherer, Julio Rosales, Gordon J. Gray, Silvio Oddi, Miguel Dario Miranda y Gomez, Giuseppe Paupini, Joseph Parecattil, John F. Dearden, Francois Marty;
George Flahiff, Paul Gouyon, Mario Casariego, Vicente Enrique y Tarancon, Joseph Malula, Pablo Muñoz Vega, S.J., Antonio Poma;
John J. Carberry, Terence J. Cooke, Stephan Sou Hwan Kim, Eugenio de Araujo Sales, Joseph Hoeffner, Johannes Willebrands, Mario Nasalli Rocca di Corneliano, Sergio Guerri.
1973 (Mar. 5): Antonio Ribeiro, James Robert Knox, Avelar Brandao Vilela, Joseph Cordeiro, Anibal Muñoz Duque, Luis Aponte Martinez, Raul Francisco Primatesta, Salvatore Pappalardo, Marcelo Gonzalez Martin, Louis Jean Guyot, Ugo Poletti, Timothy Manning, Maurice Otunga, Jose Salazar Lopez, Humberto S. Medeiros, Paulo Evaristo Arns, James Darcy Freeman, Narciso Jubany Arnau, Hermann Volk, Pio Taofinu'u.
1976 (May 24): Octavio Beras Rojas, Juan Carlos Aramburu, Hyacinthe Thiandoum, Emmanuel Nsubuga, Lawrence Trevor Picachy, Jaime L. Sin, William W. Baum, Aloisio Lorscheider, Laszlo Lekai, George Basil Hume, O.S.B., Victor Razafimahatratra, Frantisek Tomasek, Dominic Ekandem.
1977 (June 27): Giovanni Benelli, Joseph Ratzinger.
1979 (June 30): Agostino Casaroli, Marco Ce, Joseph Mary Trin-Van-Can, Ernesto Corripio Ahumada, Joseph Asajiro Satowaki, Roger Etchegaray, Anastasio Alberto Ballestrero, O.C.D., Tomas O'Fiaich, Gerald Emmett Carter, Franciszek Macharski.

Order of Deacons

1973 (Mar. 5): Sergio Pignedoli, Umberto Mozzoni, Pierre Paul Philippe, Pietro Palazzini, Ferdinando Giuseppe Antonelli.
1976 (May 24): Opilio Rossi, Giuseppe Maria Sensi, Corrado Bafile, Joseph Schroeffer, Eduardo Pironio.
1977 (June 27): Bernardin Gantin, Luigi Ciappi.
1979 (June 30): Giuseppe Caprio, Egano Righi-Lambertini, Ernesto Civardi, Wladyslaw Rubin.

Ineligible To Vote

As of Sept. 20, 1979, 11 of the 130 cardinals were ineligible to take part in a papal election in line with the apostolic letter *Ingravescentem Aetatem* effective Jan. 1, 1971, which limited the functions of cardinals after completion of their 80th year.

Cardinals affected were: Antonelli, Caggiano, Confalonieri, Marella, Miranda y Gomez, Motta, O'Boyle, Parente, Shehan, Slipyi, Tomasek.

In 1980, two more cardinals will become ineligible to vote: Jose Clemente Maurer, C.SS.R., after Mar. 13, and Bernard Jan Alfrink, after July 5.

DISTRIBUTION OF CARDINALS

As of Sept. 20, 1979, there were 130 cardinals from more than 50 countries or areas. Listed below are areas, countries, number and last names.

Europe — 68

Italy (36): Antonelli, Bafile, Baggio, Ballestrero, Benelli, Bertoli, Caprio, Carpino, Casaroli, Ce, Ciappi, Civardi, Colombo, Confalonieri, Felici, Florit, Guerri, Marella, Mozzoni, Nasalli Rocca di Corneliano, Oddi, Palazzini, Pappalardo, Parente, Paupini, Pellegrino, Pignedoli, Poletti, Poma, Righi-Lambertini, Rossi, Samore, Sensi, Siri, Ursi, Vagnozzi.
France (7): Etchegaray, Garrone, Gouyon, Guyot, Marty, Philippe, Renard.
Germany (5): Bengsch, Hoeffner, Ratzinger, Schroeffer, Volk.
Spain (4): Bueno y Monreal, Enrique y Tarancon, Gonzalez Martin, Jubany Arnau.
Netherlands (3): Alfrink, De Furstenberg, Willebrands.
Poland (3): Macharski, Rubin, Wyszynski.
One from each of the following countries: Austria, Koenig; Belgium, Suenens; Czechoslovakia, Tomasek; England, Hume; Hungary, Lekai; Ireland, O'Fiaich; Portugal, Ribeiro; Scotland, Gray; Ukraine (now in USSR), Slipyi; Yugoslavia, Seper.

Asia — 10

India (2): Parecattil, Picachy.
Philippines (2): Rosales, Sin.
One from each of the following countries: Indonesia, Darmojuwono; Japan, Satowaki; Korea, Kim; Pakistan, Cordeiro; Sri Lanka, Cooray; Vietnam, Trin-Van-Can.

Oceania — 3

Australia, (2): Freeman, Knox; Pacific Islands (Samoa), Taofinu'u.

Africa — 12

One from each of the following countries: Algeria, Duval; Benin, Gantin; Egypt, Sidarouss; Kenya, Otunga; Madagascar, Razafimahatratra; Nigeria, Ekandem; Senegal, Thiandoum; South Africa, McCann; Tanzania, Rugambwa; Uganda, Nsubuga; Upper Volta, Zoungrana; Zaire, Malula.

North America — 18

United States (10): Baum, Carberry, Cody, Cooke, Dearden, Krol, Manning, Medeiros, O'Boyle, Shehan.

Canada (4): Carter, Flahiff, Leger, Roy.

Mexico (3): Corripio Ahumada, Miranda y Gomez, Salazar Lopez.

Puerto Rico (1): Aponte Martinez.

Central and South America — 19

Brazil (7): Arns, Brandao Vilela, De Araujo Sales, Lorscheider, Motta, Rossi, Scherer.

Argentina (4): Aramburu, Caggiano, Pironio, Primatesta.

One from each of the following countries: Bolivia, Maurer; Chile, Silva Henriquez; Colombia, Munoz Duque; Dominican Republic, Beras Rojas; Ecuador, Munoz Vega, S.J.; Guatemala, Casariego (b. Spain); Peru, Landazuri Ricketts; Venezuela, Quintero.

Cardinals of U.S.

As of Aug. 10, 1979, U.S. cardinals, years of elevation and sees:

Lawrence J. Shehan, 1965, Baltimore (retired 1974); Patrick A. O'Boyle, 1967, Washington (retired 1973); John J. Krol, 1967, Philadelphia; John P. Cody, 1967, Chicago; John F. Dearden, 1969, Detroit; John J. Carberry, 1969, St. Louis (retired 1979); Terence J. Cooke, 1969, New York; Timothy Manning, 1973, Los Angeles; Humberto S. Medeiros, 1973, Boston; William W. Baum, 1976, Washington, D.C.

Deceased cardinals of the United States. Data: years of elevation, sees, years of birth and death.

John McCloskey, 1875, New York, 1810-1885; James Gibbons, 1886, Baltimore, 1834-1921; John Farley, 1911, New York, 1842-1918; William O'Connell, 1911, Boston, 1859-1944; Dennis Dougherty, 1921, Philadelphia, 1865-1951; Patrick Hayes, 1924, New York, 1867-1938; George Mundelein, 1924, Chicago, 1872-1939; John Glennon, 1946, St. Louis, 1862-1946; Edward Mooney, 1946, Detroit, 1882-1958;

Francis Spellman, 1946, New York, 1889-1967; Samuel Stritch, 1946, Chicago, 1887-1958; John O'Hara, C.S.C., 1958, Philadelphia, 1888-1960; Richard Cushing, 1958, Boston, 1895-1970; Albert Meyer, 1959, Chicago, 1903-1965; Aloysius Muench, 1959, Fargo (and papal nuncio), 1889-1962; Joseph Ritter, 1961, St. Louis, 1892-1967; Francis Brennan, 1967, official of Roman Curia, 1894-1968; James F. McIntyre, 1953, Los Angeles, 1886-1979; John J. Wright, 1969, prefect of Congregation for Clergy, 1909-1970.

REPRESENTATIVES OF THE HOLY SEE

Papal representatives and their functions were the subject of a document entitled *Sollicitudo Omnium Ecclesiarum* which Pope Paul issued on his own initiative under the date of June 24, 1969.

Delegates and Nuncios

Papal representatives "receive from the Roman Pontiff the charge of representing him in a fixed way in the various nations or regions of the world.

"When their legation is only to local churches, they are known as apostolic delegates. When to this legation, of a religious and ecclesial nature, there is added diplomatic legation to states and governments, they receive the title of nuncio, pro-nuncio, and internuncio."

[An apostolic nuncio has the diplomatic rank of ambassador extraordinary and plenipotentiary. Traditionally, because the Vatican diplomatic service has the longest uninterrupted history in the world, a nuncio has precedence among diplomats in the country to which he is accredited and serves as dean of the diplomatic corps on state occasions. Since 1965 pro-nuncios, also of ambassadorial rank, have been assigned to countries in which this prerogative is not recognized.]

(Other representatives, who are covered in the Almanac article, Vatican Representatives to International Organizations, are clerics and lay persons "who form . . . part of a pontifical mission attached to international organizations or take part in conferences and congresses." They are variously called delegates or observers.)

"The primary and specific purpose of the mission of a papal representative is to render ever closer and more operative the ties that bind the Apostolic See and the local churches.

"The ordinary function of a pontifical representative is to keep the Holy See regularly and objectively informed about the conditions of the ecclesial community to which he has been sent, and about what may affect the life of the Church and the good of souls.

"On the one hand, he makes known to the Holy See the thinking of the bishops, clergy, religious and faithful of the territory where he carries out his mandate, and forwards to Rome their proposals and their requests; on the other hand, he makes himself the interpreter, with those concerned, of the acts, documents, information and instructions emanating from the Holy See."

Service and Liaison

Representatives, while carrying out their general and special duties, are bound to respect the autonomy of local churches and bishops. Their service and liaison responsibilities include the following:

- **Nomination of Bishops:** To play a key role in compiling, with the advice of ecclesiastics and lay persons, and submitting lists of names of likely candidates to the Holy See with their own recommendations.
- **Bishops:** To aid and counsel local bishops without interfering in the affairs of their jurisdictions.
- **Episcopal Conferences:** To maintain close relations with them and to assist them in every possible way. (Papal representatives do not belong to these conferences.)
- **Religious Communities of Pontifical Rank:** To advise and assist major superiors for the purpose of promoting and consolidating conferences of men and women religious and to coordinate their apostolic activities.
- **Church-State Relations:** The thrust in this area is toward the development of sound relations with civil governments and collaboration in work for peace and the total good of the whole human family.

The mission of a papal representative begins with appointment and assignment by the pope and continues until termination of his mandate. He acts "under the guidance and according to the instructions of the cardinal secretary of state and prefect of the Council for the Public Affairs of the Church, to whom he is directly responsible for the execution of the mandate entrusted to him by the Supreme Pontiff." Normally, representatives are required to retire at the age of 75.

The Pope said clearly in the document that it was a response to demands made during the Second Vatican Council for clarification of the whole system of papal representation to local churches and governments throughout the world.

At the same time, but without any statement to that effect, the document appeared to be a response to criticism voiced in some quarters about the validity and desirability of this system. It was variously charged that the system interfered with administration in local churches; that it deprived local churches of reasonable independence; that it made the conduct of local church affairs dependent on the opinion of a foreigner in a country; that it violated the principle of subsidiarity; that it reflected an erroneous image of the pope as a would-be political sovereign. Refutation of all these charges was implicit in the broad introduction and specific articles of the document.

The State Council of Greece, in an announcement released Aug. 21, 1979, nullified the government's July decree establishing diplomatic relations with Vatican City.

NUNCIOS AND DELEGATES

(Sources: *Annuario Pontificio, L'Osservatore Romano,* NC News Service.)

Data, as of Sept. 10, 1979, country, rank of legation (corresponding to rank of legate unless otherwise noted), name of legate (archbishop unless otherwise noted) as available.

Delegate for Papal Representatives: Archbishop Domenico Enrici, former apostolic delegate to Great Britain, was appointed in July, 1973, to the newly created post of Delegate for Papal Representatives, to coordinate papal diplomatic efforts throughout the world. The office entails responsibility for "following more closely through timely visits the activities of papal representatives . . . and encouraging their rapport with the central offices" of the Secretariat of State and the Council for the Public Affairs of the Church.

Africa, South (Botswana, Rhodesia, South Africa, Namibia, Swaziland): Pretoria, Apostolic Delegation; Edward Cassidy (also Pro-Nuncio to Lesotho).

Algeria: Algiers, Nunciature; Sante Portalupi, Pro-Nuncio (He is also Pro-Nuncio to Morocco and Tunisia and Apostolic Delegate to Libya.)

Angola: Luanda, Apostolic Delegation; Giovanni De Andrea.

Antilles: Apostolic Delegation; Luigi Conti (resides in Port-au-Prince, Haiti).

Argentina: Buenos Aires, Nunciature; Pio Laghi.

Australia: Canberra, Nunciature; Luigi Barbarito, Pro-Nuncio.

Austria: Vienna, Nunciature; Mario Cagna.

Bahamas: Nunciature.

Bangladesh: Dacca, Nunciature; Luigi Accogli, Pro-Nuncio (also Pro-Nuncio to China-Taiwan and Apostolic Delegate to Burma.)

Barbados: Nunciature.

Belgium: Brussels, Nunciature; Igino Cardinale (also Nuncio to Luxembourg).

Benin (formerly Dahomey): Nunciature; Giuseppe Ferraioli, Pro-Nuncio.

Bolivia: La Paz, Nunciature; Alfio Rapisarda.

Botswana: See Africa, South.

Brazil: Brasilia, Nunciature; Carmine Rocco.

Burma: See Bangladesh.

Burundi: Bujumbura, Nunciature; Donato Squicciarini.

Cameroon: Yaounde, Nunciature; Giuseppe Uhac, Pro-Nuncio (also Pro-Nuncio to Gabon Republic and Apostolic Delegate to Equatorial Guinea).

Canada: Ottawa, Nunciature; Angelo Palmas, Pro-Nuncio.

Cape Verde Islands: Nunciature; Luigi Dossena, Pro-Nuncio (resides in Dakar, Senegal).

Central African Republic: Bangui, Nunciature; Oriano Quilici, Pro-Nuncio (also Pro-Nuncio to Congo and Apostolic Delegate to Chad).
Chad: Apostolic Delegation; Oriano Quilici (resides in Bangui, Central African Republic).
Chile: Santiago, Nunciature; Angelo Sodano.
China: Taipei (Taiwan), Nunciature; Luigi Accogli, Pro-Nuncio (also Pro-Nuncio to Bangladesh).
Colombia: Bogota, Nunciature; Angelo Acerbi.
Congo Republic: Brazzaville, Nunciature; Oriano Quilici, Pro-Nuncio (resides in Bangui, Central African Republic).
Costa Rica: San Jose, Nunciature; Lajos Kada.
Cuba: Havana, Nunciature; Giuseppe Laigueglia, Pro-Nuncio.
Cyprus: Nicosia, Nunciature; William A. Carew, Pro-Nuncio (also Apostolic Delegate to Jerusalem).
Dahomey: See Benin.
Denmark: See Scandinavia.
Djibouti: See Red Sea Region.
Dominican Republic: Santo Domingo, Nunciature; Giovanni Gravelli (also Apostolic Delegate to Puerto Rico).
Ecuador: Quito, Nunciature; Vincenzo Farano.
Egypt: Cairo, Nunciature; Achille Glorieux, Pro-Nuncio.
El Salvador: San Salvador, Nunciature; Emanuele Gerada (also Nuncio to Guatemala).
Equatorial Guinea: Santa Isabel, Apostolic Delegation; Giuseppe Uhac (resides in Yaounde, Cameroon).
Ethiopia: Addis Ababa, Nunciature; Raymond Etteldorf, Pro-Nuncio.
Fiji: Nunciature.
Finland: Helsinki, Nunciature; Josip Zabkar, Pro-Nuncio (resides in Copenhagen).
France: Paris, Nunciature; Angelo Felici.
Gabon Republic: Libreville, Nunciature; Giuseppe Uhac, Pro-Nuncio (resides in Yaounde, Cameroon).
Gambia: Nunciature; Johannes Dyba, Pro-Nuncio.
Germany: Bonn, Nunciature; Guido Del Mestri.
Ghana: Accra, Nunciature; Giuseppe Ferraioli, Pro-Nuncio.
Great Britain: London, Apostolic Delegation; Bruno Heim (also Apostolic Delegate to Gibraltar).
Grenada: Nunciature.
Guatemala: Guatemala City, Nunciature; Emanuele Gerada (also Nuncio to El Salvador).
Guinea: Conakry, Apostolic Delegation; Johannes Dyba.
Guinea-Bissau: Apostolic Delegation; Luigi Dossena (Delegate resides at Dakar, Senegal).
Haiti: Port-au-Prince, Nunciature; Luigi Conti (also Apostolic Delegate to Antilles).
Honduras: Tegucigalpa, Nunciature; Gabriel Montalvo (also Nuncio to Nicaragua).
Iceland: Nunciature; Josip Zabkar, Pro-Nuncio (resides in Copenhagen, Denmark).
India: New Delhi, Nunciature; Luciano Storero, Pro-Nuncio.
Indonesia: Jakarta, Nunciature.
Iran: Teheran, Nunciature; Annibale Bugnini, C.M., Pro-Nuncio.
Iraq: Baghdad, Nunciature; Antonio Del Giudice, Pro-Nuncio (also Pro-Nuncio to Kuwait).
Ireland: Dublin, Nunciature; Gaetano Alibrandi.
Italy: Rome, Nunciature; Romolo Carboni.
Ivory Coast: Abidjan, Nunciature; Justo Mullor Garcia, Nuncio.
Jamaica: Nunciature.
Japan: Tokyo, Nunciature; Mario Pio Gaspari, Pro-Nuncio.
Jerusalem, Palestine, Jordan, Israel: Jerusalem, Apostolic Delegation; William A. Carew (also Pro-Nuncio to Cyprus).
Kenya: Nairobi, Nunciature; Agostino Cacciavillan, Pro-Nuncio (also Apostolic Delegate to Seychelles Is.).
Korea: Seoul, Nunciature; Luciano Angeloni, Pro-Nuncio.
Kuwait: Al Kuwait, Nunciature; Antonio Del Giudice, Pro-Nuncio (resides in Baghdad, Iraq).
Laos, Malaysia and Singapore: Bangkok, Apostolic Delegation; Silvio Luoni (resides in Bangkok, Thailand).
Lebanon: Beirut, Nunciature; Carlo Furno.
Lesotho: Maseru, Nunciature; Edward Cassidy, Pro-Nuncio (resides in Pretoria, S. Africa).
Liberia: Monrovia, Nunciature; Johannes Dyba, Pro-Nuncio.
Libya: Apostolic Delegation; Sante Portalupi (resides in Algiers, Algeria).
Luxembourg: Nunciature; Igino Cardinale (resides in Brussels, Belgium).
Madagascar: Tananarive, Nunciature; Sergio Sebastiani, Pro-Nuncio (also Pro-Nuncio to Mauritius and Apostolic Delegate to Reunion).
Malawi: Lilongwe, Nunciature; Georg Zur, Pro-Nuncio (resides in Zambia).
Mali: Bamako, Apostolic Delegation; Luigi Dossena (resides in Dakar, Senegal).
Malta: La Valletta, Nunciature.
Mauritania: Nouakchott, Apostolic Delegation; Luigi Dossena (resides in Dakar, Senegal).
Mauritius: Port Louis, Nunciature; Sergio Sebastiani, Pro-Nuncio (resides in Tananarive, Madagascar).

Mexico: Mexico City, Apostolic Delegation; Girolamo Prigione.
Morocco: Rabat, Nunciature; Sante Portalupi, Pro-Nuncio (resides in Algiers, Algeria).
Mozambique: Maputo, Apostolic Delegation; Francesco Colasuonno.
Namibia: See Africa, South.
Netherlands: The Hague, Nunciature; Bruno Wustenberg, Pro-Nuncio.
New Zealand: Wellington, Nunciature. (Pro-Nuncio is also Pro-Nuncio to Fiji and Apostolic Delegate to Pacific Islands).
Nicaragua: Managua, Nunciature; Gabriel Montalvo (also Nuncio to Honduras).
Niger: Niamey, Nunciature; Justo Mullor Garcia, Pro-Nuncio.
Nigeria: Lagos, Apostolic Delegation; Carlo Curis, Pro-Nuncio.
Norway: See Scandinavia.
Pacific Islands: See New Zealand.
Pakistan: Islamabad, Nunciature; Giulio Einaudi, Pro-Nuncio.
Panama: Panama, Nunciature; Blasco Francisco Collaco.
Papua New Guinea: Port Moresby; Nunciature; Andrea Cordero Lanza di Montezemolo, Pro-Nuncio. (He is also Apostolic Delegate to western and southern Solomon Islands.)
Paraguay: Asuncion, Nunciature; Joseph Mees.
Peru: Lima, Nunciature; Mario Tagliaferri.
Philippines: Manila, Nunciature; Bruno Torpigliani.
Portugal: Lisbon, Nunciature.
Puerto Rico: See Dominican Republic.
Red Sea Region (Somalia, Djibouti, part of Arabian Peninsula): Apostolic Delegation; Giovanni Moretti (resides in Khartoum, Sudan).
Reunion: See Madagascar.
Rhodesia: See Africa, South.
Rwanda: Kigali, Nunciature; Thomas White.
Scandinavia (Denmark, Sweden, Norway): Copenhagen, Denmark, Apostolic Delegation; Josip Zabkar (also Pro-Nuncio to Finland and Iceland).
Senegal: Dakar, Nunciature; Luigi Dossena, Pro-Nuncio (also Pro-Nuncio to Cape Verde Islands and Apostolic Delegate to Guinea-Bissau, Mali and Mauritania.)
Seychelles Islands: See Kenya.
Sierre Leone: Apostolic Delegation; Johannes Dyba.
Solomon Islands: Apostolic Delegation; Andrea Cordero Lanza di Montezemolo (resides in Port Moresby, Papua New Guinea).
Somalia: See Red Sea Region.
South Africa: See Africa, South.
Spain: Madrid, Nunciature; Luigi Dadaglio.
Sri Lanka: Colombo, Nunciature; Nicola Rotunno, Pro-Nuncio.
Sudan: Khartoum, Nunciature; Giovanni Moretti, Pro-Nuncio (also Apostolic Delegate to Red Sea Region).
Swaziland: See Africa, South.
Sweden: See Scandinavia.
Switzerland: Bern, Nunciature; Ambrogio Marchioni.
Syria (Syrian Arab Republic): Damascus, Nunciature; Angelo Pedroni, Pro-Nuncio.
Tanzania: Dar-es-Salaam, Nunciature; Franco Brambilla, Pro-Nuncio.
Thailand: Bangkok, Nunciature; Silvio Luoni, Pro-Nuncio (also Apostolic Delegate to Laos, Malaysia and Singapore).
Togo: Lome, Apostolic Delegation, Giuseppe Ferraioli.
Trinidad and Tobago: Nunciature (established July, 1978).
Tunisia: Tunis, Nunciature; Sante Portalupi, Pro-Nuncio (resides in Algiers, Algeria).
Turkey: Ankara, Nunciature; Salvatore Asta, Pro-Nuncio.
Uganda: Kampala, Nunciature; Henri Lemaitre, Pro-Nuncio.
United States of America: Washington, D.C., Apostolic Delegation; Jean Jadot.
Upper Volta: Ouagadougou, Nunciature; Justo Mullor Garcia, Pro-Nuncio.
Uruguay: Montevideo, Nunciature; Luigi Bellotti.
Venezuela: Caracas, Nunciature; Ubaldo Calabresi.
Vietnam and Kampuchea: Apostolic Delegation.
Yugoslavia: Belgrade, Nunciature; Michele Cecchini, Pro-Nuncio.
Zaire: Kinshasa, Nunciature; Edoardo Rovida, Pro-Nuncio.
Zambia: Lusaka, Nunciature; Georg Zur, Pro-Nuncio (also Pro-Nuncio to Malawi).

Apostolic Delegate to U.S.

The representative of the Pope to the Catholic Church in the United States is Archbishop Jean Jadot, apostolic delegate. He was born Nov. 23, 1909, in Brussels, Belgium; was ordained to the priesthood Feb. 11, 1934; was appointed titular bishop of Zuri Feb. 23, 1968; received episcopal ordination May 1, 1968; was apostolic delegate for Laos, Malaysia and Singapore (1968-71); held the additional post of pro-nuncio in Thailand (1969-71); was pro-nuncio apostolic in Cameroon and Gabon, and apostolic delegate for Equatorial Guinea (1971-73); was named apostolic delegate to the United States in 1973; is the first non-Italian to hold the post.

The U.S. Apostolic Delegation was established Jan. 21, 1893. It is located at 3339 Massachusetts Ave. N.W., Washington, D.C. 20008.

Archbishop Jadot's predecessors were Archbishops: Francesco Satolli (1893-1896), Sebastiano Martinelli, O.S.A. (1896-1902), Diomede Falconio, O.F.M. (1902-1911), Giovanni Bonzano (1911-1922), Pietro Fumasoni-Biondi (1922-1933), Amleto Cicognani (1933-1958), Egidio Vagnozzi (1958-1967) and Luigi Raimondi (1967-1973).

Amleto Cicognani, for 25 years apostolic delegate to the U.S., became a cardinal in 1958 and served as papal secretary of state from 1961 to 1969.

DIPLOMATS AT VATICAN

(Sources: *Annuario Pontificio, L'Osservatore Romano*, NC News Service. As of Sept. 10, 1979.)

Algeria: Raouf Boudjakdji, Ambassador.
Argentina: Ruben Victor Manuel Blanco, Ambassador.
Australia: Brian Clarence Hill, Ambassador.
Austria: Gordian Gudenus, Ambassador.
Bahamas: Ambassador.
Bangladesh: Mohammed Sultan, Ambassador.
Barbados: Ambassador.
Belgium: Felix Standaert, Ambassador.
Benin (formerly Dahomey): Ambassador.
Bolivia: Juan Vidaurre Pinto, Ambassador.
Brazil: Espedito de Freitas Resende, Ambassador.
Burundi: Lazare Nzorubara, Ambassador.
Cameroon: Henri Djeengue Ndoumbe, Ambassador.
Canada: Joseph Charles Leonard Yvon Beaulne, Ambassador.
Cape Verde Islands: Ambassador.
Central African Republic: Ambassador.
Chile: Hector Riesle Contreras, Ambassador.
China (Taiwan): Chow Shu-Kai, Ambassador.
Colombia: Raimundo Emiliani Roman, Ambassador.
Congo Republic: Ambassador.
Costa Rica: Alvaro Aguilar Peralto, Ambassador.
Cuba: Jose Antonio Portuondo Valdor, Ambassador.
Cyprus: Polys Modinos, Ambassador.
Dominican Republic: Juan M. Contin, Ambassador.
Ecuador: Ernesto Valdivieso Chiriboga, Ambassador.
Egypt: Shaffei Abdel Hamid, Ambassador.
El Salvador: Prudencio Llach Schonenberg, Ambassador.
Ethiopia: Ambassador.
Fiji: Ambassador.
Finland: Seppo Taito Pietinen, Ambassador.
France: Georges Galichon, Ambassador.
Gabon: Marcel Sandoungout, Ambassador.
Gambia: Alhaji Bocar Ousman Semega-Janneh, Ambassador.
Germany: Walter Gehlhoff, Ambassador.
Ghana: Yaw Bamful Turkson, Ambassador.
Great Britain: Geoffrey Allan Crossley, Minister.
Grenada: Ambassador.
Guatemala: Luis Valladares y Aycinena, Ambassador.
Haiti: Pierre Mayard, Ambassador.
Honduras: Manuel Luna Mejia, Ambassador.
Iceland: Niels P. Sigurdsson, Ambassador.
India: Gurbachan Singh, Ambassador.
Indonesia: Sunarso Wongsonegoro, Ambassador.
Iran: Fereydoun Diba, Ambassador.
Iraq: Ambassador.
Ireland: John G. Molloy, Ambassador.
Italy: Dr. Bruno Bottai, Ambassador.
Ivory Coast: Joseph Amichia, Ambassador.
Jamaica: Ambassador.
Japan: Kiyoshi Suganuma, Ambassador.
Kenya: Bethuel A. Kiplagat, Ambassador.
Korea: Hyun Joon Shin, Ambassador.
Kuwait: Essa Ahmad Al-Hamad, Ambassador.
Lebanon: Antoine Fattal, Ambassador.
Lesotho: Vitus Mooki Molapo, Ambassador.
Liberia: Herbert Richard Wright Brewer, Ambassador.
Lithuania: Stasys Lozoraitis, Jr., first secretary.
Luxembourg: Edouard Molitor, Ambassador.
Madagascar: Ambassador.
Malawi: Victor Timothy Likaku, Ambassador.
Malta: Paolo Farrugia, Ambassador.
Mauritius: Leckraz Teelock, Ambassador.
Monaco: Cesar Charles Solamito, Minister.
Morocco: Youssef Ben Abbes, Ambassador.
Netherlands: Joseph Laurentius Hubertus Ceulen, Ambassador.
New Zealand: Vivian Scott, Ambassador.
Nicaragua: Alberto Salinas Munoz, Ambassador.
Niger: Kossomi Bourem, Ambassador.
Nigeria: Ignatius Olisemeka, Ambassador.
Order of Malta: Christophe de Kallay, Minister.
Pakistan: Zulfiqar ali Khan, Ambassador.
Panama: Jose Manuel Watson Diez, Ambassador.
Papua New Guinea: Ambassador.
Paraguay: Juan I. Livieres Argana, Ambassador.
Peru: Jorge Nicholson Sologuren, Ambassador.
Philippines: Antonio C. Delgado, Ambassador.
Portugal: Jose Calvet de Magalhaes, Ambassador.
Rwanda: Callixte Hatungimana, Ambassador.
San Marino: Minister.

Senegal: Paul Ndiaye, Ambassador.
Spain: Angel Sanz Briz, Ambassador.
Sri Lanka: Vernon Lorraine Benjamin Mendis, Ambassador.
Sudan: Bashir Bakri, Ambassador.
Syria (Arab Republic): Dia Allah El-Fattal, Ambassador.
Tanzania: Nicholas J. Merinyo Maro, Ambassador.
Thailand: Varachit Nitibhon, Ambassador.
Trinidad and Tobago: Ambassador.
Tunisia: Taoufik Smida, Ambassador.
Turkey: Veedi Turel, Ambassador.
Uganda: Miss Bernadette Olowo, Ambassador.
Upper Volta: Pierre Ilboudo, Ambassador.
Uruguay: Carlos Maria Romero, Ambassador.
Venezuela: Santiago Ochoa Briceno, Ambassador.
Yugoslavia: Zdenko Svete, Ambassador.
Zaire: Tshimbalanga Shala-Dibwe, Ambassador.
Zambia: Miss Lombe Phyllis Chibesakunda, Ambassador.

U.S. — Vatican Relations

Official relations for trade and diplomatic purposes were maintained by the United States and the Papal States while the latter had the character of and acted like other sovereign powers in the international community.

Consular Relations

Consular relations developed in the wake of an announcement, made by the papal nuncio in Paris to the American mission there Dec. 15, 1784, that the Papal States had agreed to open several Mediterranean ports to U.S. shipping.

U.S. consular representation in the Papal States began with the appointment of John B. Sartori, a native of Rome, in June, 1797. Sartori's successors as consuls were: Felix Cicognani, also a Roman, and Americans George W. Greene, Nicholas Browne, William C. Sanders, Daniel LeRoy, Horatio V. Glentworth, W.J. Stillman, Edwin C. Cushman, David M. Armstrong.

Consular officials of the Papal States who served in the U.S. were: Count Ferdinand Lucchesi, 1826 to 1829, who resided in Washington; John B. Sartori, 1829 to 1841, who resided in Trenton, N.J.; Daniel J. Desmond, 1841 to 1850, who resided in Philadelphia; Louis B. Binsse, 1850 to 1895, who resided in New York.

U.S. recognition of the consul of the Papal States did not cease when the states were absorbed into the Kingdom of Italy in 1871, despite pressure from Baron Blanc, the Italian minister. Binsse held the title until his death Mar. 28, 1895. No one was appointed to succeed him.

Diplomatic Relations

The U.S. Senate approved a recommendation, made by President James K. Polk in December, 1847, for the establishment of a diplomatic post in the Papal States. Jacob L. Martin, the first charge d'affaires, arrived in Rome Aug. 2, 1848, and presented his credentials to Pius IX Aug. 19. Martin, who died within a month, was succeeded by Lewis Cass, Jr. Cass became minister resident in 1854 and served in that capacity until his retirement in 1858.

John P. Stockton, who later became a U.S. Senator from New Jersey, was minister resident from 1858 to 1861. Rufus King was named to succeed him but, instead, accepted a commission as a brigadier general in the Army. Alexander W. Randall of Wisconsin took the appointment. He was succeeded in August, 1862, by Richard M. Blatchford who served until the following year. King was again nominated minister resident and served in that capacity until 1867 when the ministry was ended because of objections from some quarters in the U.S. and failure to appropriate funds for its continuation. J. C. Hooker, a secretary, remained in the Papal States until the end of March, 1868, closing the ministry and performing functions of courtesy.

Personal Envoys

Myron C. Taylor was appointed by President Franklin D. Roosevelt in 1939 to serve as his personal representative to Pope Pius XII and continued serving in that capacity during the presidency of Harry S. Truman until 1951. Henry Cabot Lodge was named to the post by President Richard M. Nixon in 1970, served also during the presidency of Gerald Ford, and represented President Carter at the canonization of St. John Neumann in 1977. Neither Taylor nor Lodge had diplomatic status.

President Harry S. Truman nominated Gen. Mark Clark to be ambassador to the Vatican in 1951, but withdrew the nomination at Clark's request because of controversy over the appointment.

None of Truman's three successors — Dwight D. Eisenhower, John F. Kennedy or Lyndon B. Johnson — had a personal representative to the Pope.

Miami attorney David Walters, a Catholic, served as the personal envoy of President Jimmy Carter to the Pope from July, 1977, until his resignation Aug. 16, 1978. He was succeeded by Robert F. Wagner, former mayor of New York, in October, 1978.

At the time of Walters' designation for the non-diplomatic post, the House of Representatives had under consideration an amendment, already passed by the Senate, that would lift an 1867 prohibition against funding for diplomatic relations with the Vatican.

Any initiative for the establishment of formal diplomatic relations would have to be undertaken by the U.S. government.

VATICAN CITY

The State of Vatican City (Stato della Citta del Vaticano) is the territorial seat of the papacy. The smallest sovereign state in the world, it is situated within the city of Rome, embraces an area of 108.7 acres, and includes within its limits the Vatican Palace, museums, art galleries, gardens, libraries, radio station, post office, bank, astronomical observatory, offices, apartments, service facilities, St. Peter's Basilica, and neighboring buildings between the Basilica and Viale Vaticano.

The extraterritorial rights of Vatican City extend to more than 10 buildings in Rome, including the major basilicas and office buildings of various congregations of the Roman Curia, and to the **Villa of Castel Gandolfo** 15 miles southeast of the City of Rome. Castel Gandolfo is the summer residence of the Holy Father.

The government of Vatican City is in the hands of the reigning pope, who has full executive, legislative and judicial power. The administration of affairs, however, is handled by the Pontifical Commission for the State of Vatican City. The legal system is based on Canon Law; in cases where this code does not obtain, the laws of the City of Rome apply. The City is an absolutely neutral state and enjoys all the rights and privileges of a sovereign power. The Secretariat of State (Papal Secretariat) maintains diplomatic relations with other nations. The citizens of Vatican City, and they alone, owe allegiance to the pope as a temporal head of state.

Cardinals of the Roman Curia residing outside Vatican City enjoy the privileges of extraterritoriality.

The normal population is approximately 1,000. While the greater percentage is made up of priests and religious, there are several hundred lay persons living in Vatican City. They are housed in their own apartments in the City and are engaged in secretarial, domestic, trade and service occupations. About 4,000 persons are employed by the Vatican.

Services of honor and order are performed by the Swiss Guards, who have been charged with responsibility for the personal safety of popes since 1506. Additional police and ceremonial functions are under the supervision of a special office. These functions were formerly handled by the Papal Gendarmes, the Palatine Guard of Honor, and the Guard of Honor of the Pope (Pontifical Noble Guard) which Pope Paul disbanded Sept. 14, 1970.

The **Basilica of St. Peter**, built between 1506 and 1626, is the largest church in Christendom and the site of most papal ceremonies. The pope's own patriarchal basilica, however, is **St. John Lateran**, whose origins date back to 324.

St. Ann's is the parish church of Vatican City.

The vicar general of the pope for Vatican City, which is part of the diocese of Rome, is Most Rev. Peter Canisius Van Lierde, O.S.A., titular bishop of Porfireone.

The **Vatican Library,** one of five in the City, has among its holdings 70,000 manuscripts, 770,000 printed books, and 7,500 incunabula.

The independent temporal power of the pope, which is limited to the confines of Vatican City and small areas outside, was for many centuries more extensive than it is now. As late as the nineteenth century, the pope ruled 16,000 square miles of Papal States across the middle of Italy, with a population of over 3,000,000. In 1870 forces of the Kingdom of Italy occupied these lands which, with the exception of the small areas surrounding the Vatican and Lateran in Rome and the Villa of Castel Gandolfo, became part of the Kingdom by the Italian law of May 13, 1871.

The **Roman Question,** occasioned by this seizure and the voluntary confinement of the pope to the limited papal lands, was finally settled with ratification of the Lateran Agreement on June 7, 1929, by the Italian government and Vatican City and provided a financial indemnity for the former Papal States, which became recognized as part of Italy. The Lateran Agreement became Article 7 of the Italian Constitution on Mar. 26, 1947.

Papal Flag

The papal flag consists of two equal vertical stripes of yellow and white, charged with the insignia of the papacy on the white stripe — a triple crown or tiara over two crossed keys, one of gold and one of silver, tied with a red cord and two tassels. The divisions of the crown represent the teaching, sanctifying and ruling offices of the pope. The keys symbolize his jurisdictional authority.

The papal flag is a national flag inasmuch as it is the standard of the Supreme Pontiff as the sovereign of the state of Vatican City. It is also universally accepted by the faithful as a symbol of the supreme spiritual authority of the Holy Father.

In a Catholic church, the papal flag is displayed on a staff on the left side of the sanctuary (facing the congregation), and the American flag is displayed on the right.

Vatican Radio

The declared purpose of Vatican Radio Station HVJ is "that the voice of the Supreme Pastor may be heard throughout the world by means of the ether waves, for the glory of Christ and the salvation of souls." Designed by Guglielmo Marconi, the inventor of radio, and supervised by him until his death, the station was inaugurated by Pope Pius XI in 1931. The original purpose has been extended to a wide variety of programming.

Vatican Radio operates on international wave lengths, transmits programs in 33 languages, and serves as a channel of communication between the Vatican, church officials and listeners in general in many parts of the world. The station broadcasts about 220 hours a week throughout the world.

The staff of 300 broadcasters and technicians includes 32 Jesuits and is directed by Father Robert Tucci, S.J. Headquarters are located in Vatican City. Studios and offices are at Palazzo Pio, Piazza Pia, 3. The transmitters are situated at Santa Maria di Galeria, a 200-acre site 16 miles from Rome.

1979 Vatican Stamps

The Vatican Philatelic Office scheduled the following issues of stamps for 1979. (Issue date is given where available.)

• Series commemorating the beginning of the pontificate of Pope John Paul II, issued Mar. 22, 1979, in three values (170, 250 and 400 lire) featuring three subjects.

• Series commemorating the ninth centenary of the death of St. Stanislaus, issued May 18, 1979, in four values (120, 150, 250 and 500 lire) featuring four subjects.

• Series commemorating the centenary of the death of the astronomer Fr. Angelo Secchi, S.J. (d. 1878), issued June 25, 1979, in three values (180, 220 and 300 lire) featuring three subjects. Printed in 1978 but not issued.

• Series commemorating the sixteenth centenary of the death of St. Basil the Great, issued June 25, 1979, in two values (150 and 520 lire) featuring different subjects.

• Series commemorating the fiftieth anniversary of the establishment of Vatican City State, issued Oct. 11, 1979, in seven values (50, 70, 120, 150, 170, 250 and 450 lire) featuring seven subjects.

• Series commemorating the International Year of the Child.

• Aerogram celebrating the fiftieth anniversary of the establishment of Vatican City State was issued May 28, 1979.

Vatican Coins

The Vatican Numismatics Office issued the following coins during the year:

• Series for the sixteenth year of the pontificate of Pope Paul VI, bearing the date 1978 and issued Feb. 15, 1979. It was composed of seven coins (5, 10, 20, 50, 100, 200 and 500 lire).

• Coin commemorating pontificate of Pope John Paul I, issued Sept. 20, 1979 (1000 lire).

Papal Audiences

General audiences are scheduled weekly, on Wednesday at noon.

In Vatican City, they are held in the Audience Hall on the south side of St. Peter's Basilica. The hall, which was opened in 1971, has a seating capacity of 6,800 and a total capacity of 12,000.

Audiences are also held during the summer at Castel Gandolfo when the pope is there on a working vacation.

General audiences last from about 60 to 90 minutes, during which the pope gives a talk and his blessing. A résumé of the talk, which is usually in Italian, is given in several languages.

Arrangements for papal audiences are handled by an office of the Prefecture of the Apostolic Household.

American visitors can obtain passes for general audiences by applying to the Bishops' Office for United States Visitors to the Vatican, Casa Santa Maria, Via dell'Umilita, 30, 00187 Rome.

Private and group audiences are reserved for dignitaries of various categories and for special occasions.

Publications

Acta Apostolicae Sedis: The only "official commentary" of the Holy See, was established in 1908 for the publication of activities of the Holy See, laws, decrees and acts of congregations and tribunals of the Roman Curia. The first edition was published in January, 1909.

St. Pius X made *AAS* an official organ in 1908. Laws promulgated for the Church ordinarily take effect three months after the date of their publication in this commentary.

The publication, mostly in Latin and Italian, is printed by the Vatican Polyglot Press.

The immediate predecessor of this organ was *Acta Sanctae Sedis,* founded in 1865 and given official status by the Congregation for the Propagation of the Faith in 1904.

Annuario Pontificio: The yearbook of the Holy See. It is edited by the Vatican Secretariat of State and is printed in Italian, with some portions in other languages, by the Vatican Polyglot Press. It covers the worldwide organization of the Church, lists members of the hierarchy, and includes a wide range of statistical information.

The publication of a statistical yearbook of the Holy See dates back to 1716, when a volume called *Notizie* appeared. Publication under the present title began in 1860, was suspended in 1870, and resumed again in 1872 under the title *Catholic Hierarchy.* This volume was printed privately at first, but has been issued by the Vatican Press since 1885. The title *Annuario Pontificio* was restored in 1912, and the yearbook was called an "official publication" until 1924.

L'Osservatore Romano: The daily newspaper of the Holy See. It began publication July 1, 1861, as an independent enterprise under the ownership and direction of four Catholic laymen headed by Marcantonio Pacelli, vice minister of the interior under Pope Pius IX and a grandfather of the late Pius XII. Leo XIII bought the publication in 1890, making it the "pope's" own newspaper.

The only official material in *L'Osservatore Romano* is that which appears under the heading, "Nostre Informazioni." This includes notices of appointments by the Holy See, the texts of papal encyclicals and addresses by the Holy Father and others, various types of documents, accounts of decisions and rulings of administrative bodies, and similar items. Additional material includes news and comment on developments in the Church and the world. Italian is the language most used.

The editorial board is directed by Valerio Volpini. A staff of about 15 reporters covers Rome news sources. A corps of correspondents provides foreign coverage.

A weekly roundup edition in English was inaugurated in 1968. Other weekly editions are printed in French, Spanish, Portuguese and German.

Vatican Press Office: The establishment of a single Vatican Press Office was announced Feb. 29, 1968, to replace service agencies formerly operated by *L'Osservatore Romano* and an office created for press coverage of the Second Vatican Council. Rev. Romeo Panciroli is the director.

Vatican Polyglot Press: The official printing plant of the Vatican.

The Vatican press was conceived by Marcellus II and Pius IV but was actually founded by Sixtus V on Apr. 27, 1587, to print the Vulgate and the writings of the Fathers of the Church and other authors. A Polyglot Press was established in 1626 by the Congregation for the Propagation of the Faith to serve the needs of the Oriental Church. St. Pius X merged both presses under this title.

The plant has facilities for the printing of a wide variety of material in about 30 languages.

Activities of the Holy See: An annual documentary volume covering the activities of the pope — his daily work, general and special audiences, discourses and messages on special occasions, visits outside the Vatican, missionary and charitable endeavors, meetings with diplomats, heads of state and others — and activities of the congregations, commissions, tribunals and offices of the Roman Curia.

Statistical Yearbook of the Church: Issued by the Central Statistics Office of the Church, it contains principal data concerning the presence and work of the Church in the world. The first issue was published in 1972 under the title *Collection of Statistical Tables, 1969*. It is printed in corresponding columns of Italian and Latin. Some of the introductory material is printed in other languages.

VATICAN REPRESENTATIVES

(Sources: *Annuario Pontificio;* NC News Service.)

The Vatican has representatives to a number of quasi-governmental and international organizations.

Governmental Organizations: United Nations (Abp. Giovanni Cheli, permanent observer); UN Office in Geneva (Abp. Jean Rupp, permanent observer); International Atomic Energy Agency (Dr. Hermann Abs, delegate); UN Organization for Industrial Development (Msgr. Mario Peressin, permanent observer); UN Food and Agriculture Organization (Bp. Agostino Ferrari-Toniolo, permanent observer); UN Educational, Scientific and Cultural Organization (Msgr. Renzo Frana, permanent observer);

Council of Europe (Very Rev. Fortunato Baldelli, special envoy with function of permanent observer); Council for Cultural Cooperation of the Council of Europe (delegate); Organization of American States (Abp. Jean Jadot, permanent observer); International Institute for the Unification of Private Law (Prof. Pio Ciprotti, delegate); International Committee of Medicine and Pharmacy (Msgr. Victor Heylen); World Organization of Tourism (Rev. Giovanni Arrighi, O.P.);

Universal Postal Union; International Telecommunications Union; International Council on Grain; World Organization of Intellectual Property; International Union for the Protection of Literary and Artistic Works; International Union for the Protection of Industrial Property; International Organization of Telecommunication via Satellite (Intelsat); European Conference of Postal and Telecommunication Administration (CEPT).

Non-Governmental Organizations: International Committee of Historical Sciences (Msgr. Michele Maccarrone); International Committee of Paleography (Msgr. Jose Ruysschaert); International Committee of the History of Art (Prof. Carlo Pietrangeli); International Committee of Anthropological and Ethnological Sciences;

International Committee for the Neutrality of Medicine (Rev. Michel Riquet, S.J., permanent observer); International Center of Study for the Preservation and Restoration of Cultural Goods (Prof. Carlo Pietrangeli); International Council of Monuments and Sites (Prof. Carlo Pietrangeli); International Alliance on Tourism; International Astronomical Union; International Institute of Administrative Sciences; International Technical Committee for Prevention and Extinction of Fires; World Medical Association.

Although Vatican City is not a member of the United Nations, Pope John Paul's address before the General Assembly Oct. 2, 1979, was published as an official U.N. document.

Doctrine of the Catholic Church

Following are excerpts from the first two chapters of the *Dogmatic Constitution on the Church* promulgated by the Second Vatican Council. They describe the relation of the Catholic Church to the Kingdom of God, the nature and foundation of the Church, the People of God, the necessity of membership and participation in the Church for salvation.

Additional subjects in the constitution are treated in other Almanac entries.

I. MYSTERY OF THE CHURCH

"... By her relationship with Christ, the Church is a kind of sacrament or sign of intimate union with God, and of the unity of all mankind..." (No. 1).

"... He (the eternal Father) planned to assemble in the holy Church all those who would believe in Christ. Already from the beginning of the world the foreshadowing of the Church took place. She was prepared for in a remarkable way throughout the history of the people of Israel and by means of the Old Covenant. Established in the present era of time, the Church was made manifest by the outpouring of the Spirit. At the end of time she will achieve her glorious fulfillment. Then ... all just men from the time of Adam, 'from Abel, the just one, to the last of the elect,' will be gathered together with the Father in the universal Church" (No. 2).

"When the work which the Father had given the Son to do on earth (cf. Jn. 17:4) was accomplished, the Holy Spirit was sent on the day of Pentecost in order that He might forever sanctify the Church, and thus all believers would have access to the Father through Christ in the one Spirit (cf. Eph. 2:18)....

"The Spirit dwells in the Church and in the hearts of the faithful as in a temple (cf. 1 Cor. 3:16; 6:19).... The Spirit guides the Church into the fullness of truth (cf. Jn. 16:13) and gives her a unity of fellowship and service. He furnishes and directs her with various gifts, both hierarchical and charismatic, and adorns her with the fruits of His grace (cf. Eph. 4:11-12; 1 Cor. 12:4; Gal. 5:22). By the power of the gospel He makes the Church grow, perpetually renews her, and leads her to perfect union with her Spouse...." (No. 4).

Foundation of the Church

"The mystery of the holy Church is manifest in her very foundation, for the Lord Jesus inaugurated her by preaching the good news, that is, the coming of God's Kingdom, which, for centuries, had been promised in the Scriptures.... In Christ's word, in His works, and in His presence this kingdom reveals itself to men....

"The miracles of Jesus also confirm that the kingdom has already arrived on earth....

"Before all things, however, the kingdom is clearly visible in the very person of Christ, Son of God and Son of Man....

"When Jesus rose up again after suffering death on the cross for mankind, He manifested that He had been appointed Lord, Messiah, and Priest forever (cf. Acts 2:36; Hb. 5:6; 7:17-21), and He poured out on His disciples the Spirit promised by the Father (cf. Acts 2:33). The Church, consequently, equipped with the gifts of her Founder and faithfully guarding His precepts ... receives the mission to proclaim and to establish among all peoples the kingdom of Christ and of God. She becomes on earth the initial budding forth of that kingdom. While she slowly grows, the Church strains toward the consummation of the kingdom and, with all her strength, hopes and desires to be united in glory with her King" (No. 5).

Figures of the Church

"In the Old Testament the revelation of the kingdom had often been conveyed by figures of speech. In the same way the inner nature of the Church was now to be made known to us through various images....

"... The Church is a sheepfold ... a flock ... a tract of land to be cultivated, the field of God ... His choice vineyard ... the true Vine is Christ ... the edifice of God ... the house of God ... the holy temple (whose members are)... living stones... this Holy City ... a bride ... 'our Mother' ... the spotless spouse of the spotless Lamb ... an exile..." (No. 6).

"In the human nature which He united to Himself, the Son of God redeemed man and transformed him into a new creation (cf. Gal. 6:15; 2 Cor. 5:17) by overcoming death through His own death and resurrection. By communicating His Spirit to His brothers, called together from all peoples, Christ made them mystically into His own body.

"In that body, the life of Christ is poured into the believers, who, through the sacraments, are united in a hidden and real way to Christ who suffered and was glorified. Through baptism we are formed in the likeness of Christ....

"Truly partaking of the body of the Lord in the breaking of the Eucharistic bread, we are taken up into communion with Him and with one another ..." (No. 7).

One Body in Christ

"As all the members of the human body, though they are many, form one body, so also are the faithful in Christ (cf. 1 Cor. 12:12). Also, in the building up of Christ's body there is a flourishing variety of members and functions. There is only one Spirit who . . . distributes His different gifts for the welfare of the Church (cf. 1 Cor. 12:1-11). Among these gifts stands out the grace given to the apostles. To their authority, the Spirit Himself subjected even those who were endowed with charisms (cf. 1 Cor. 14). . . .

"The head of this body is Christ . . ." (No. 7).

Mystical Body of Christ

"Christ, the one Mediator, established and ceaselessly sustains here on earth His holy Church, the community of faith, hope, and charity, as a visible structure. Through her He communicates truth and grace to all. But the society furnished with hierarchical agencies and the Mystical Body of Christ are not to be considered as two realities, nor are the visible assembly and the spiritual community, nor the earthly Church and the Church enriched with heavenly things. Rather they form one interlocked reality which is comprised of a divine and a human element. For this reason . . . this reality is compared to the mystery of the incarnate Word. Just as the assumed nature inseparably united to the divine Word serves Him as a living instrument of salvation, so, in a similar way, does the communal structure of the Church serve Christ's Spirit, who vivifies it by way of building up the body (cf. Eph. 4:16).

"This is the unique Church of Christ which in the Creed we avow as one, holy, catholic, and apostolic. After His Resurrection our Savior handed her over to Peter to be shepherded (Jn. 21:17), commissioning him and the other apostles to propagate and govern her (cf. Mt. 28:18, ff.). Her He erected for all ages as 'the pillar and mainstay of the truth' (1 Tm. 3:15). This Church, constituted and organized in the world as a society, subsists in the Catholic Church, which is governed by the successor of Peter and by the bishops in union with that successor, although many elements of sanctification and of truth can be found outside of her visible structure. These elements, however, as gifts properly belonging to the Church of Christ, possess an inner dynamism toward Catholic unity.

". . . the Church, embracing sinners in her bosom, is at the same time holy and always in need of being purified, and incessantly pursues the path of penance and renewal.

"The Church, 'like a pilgrim in a foreign land, presses forward . . .' announcing the cross and death of the Lord until He comes (cf. 1 Cor. 11:26) . . ." (No. 8).

II. THE PEOPLE OF GOD

"At all times and among every people, God has given welcome to whosoever fears Him and does what is right (cf. Acts 10:35). It has pleased God, however, to make men holy and save them not merely as individuals without any mutual bonds, but by making them into a single people, a people which acknowledges Him in truth and serves Him in holiness. He therefore chose the race of Israel as a people unto Himself. With it He set up a covenant. Step by step He taught this people by manifesting in its history both Himself and the decree of His will, and by making it holy unto Himself. All these things, however, were done by way of preparation and as a figure of that new and perfect covenant which was to be ratified in Christ. . . .

". . . Christ instituted this new covenant, that is to say, the new testament, in His blood (cf. 1 Cor. 11:25), by calling together a people made up of Jew and Gentile, making them one, not according to the flesh but in the Spirit.

"This was to be the new People of God . . . reborn . . . through the Word of the living God (cf. 1 Pt. 1:23) . . . from water and the Holy Spirit (cf. Jn. 3:5-6) . . . 'a chosen race, a royal priesthood, a holy nation, a purchased people. . . . You who in times past were not a people, but are now the people of God' (1 Pt. 2:9-10).

"That messianic people has for its head Christ. . . . Its law is the new commandment to love as Christ loved us (cf. Jn. 13:34). Its goal is the kingdom of God, which has been begun by God Himself on earth, and which is to be further extended until it is brought to perfection by Him at the end of time. . . .

". . . This messianic people, although it does not actually include all men, and may more than once look like a small flock, is nonetheless a lasting and sure seed of unity, hope, and salvation for the whole human race. Established by Christ as a fellowship of life, charity, and truth, it is also used by Him as an instrument for the redemption of all, and is sent forth into the whole world as the light of the world and the salt of the earth (cf. Mt. 5:13-16).

"Israel according to the flesh . . . was already called the Church of God (2 Ezr. 13:1; cf. Nm. 20:4; Dt. 23:1, ff.). Likewise the new Israel . . . is also called the Church of Christ (cf. Mt. 16:18). For He has bought it for Himself with His blood (cf. Acts 20:28), has filled it with His Spirit, and provided it with those means which befit it as a visible and social unity. God has gathered together as one all those who in faith look upon Jesus as the author of salvation and the source of unity and peace, and has established them as the Church, that for each and all she may be the visible sacrament of this saving unity . . ." (No. 9)

Priesthood

". . . The baptized, by regeneration and the anointing of the Holy Spirit, are consecrated into . . . a holy priesthood. . . ."

(All members of the Church participate in

the priesthood of Christ, through the common priesthood of the faithful. See Priesthood of the Laity.)

"Though they differ from one another in essence and not only in degree, the common priesthood of the faithful and the ministerial or hierarchical priesthood are nonetheless interrelated. Each of them in its own special way is a participation in the one priesthood of Christ..." (No. 10).

"It is through the sacraments and the exercise of the virtues that the sacred nature and organic structure of the priestly community is brought into operation..." (No. 11). See Role of the Sacraments.)

Prophetic Office

"The holy People of God shares also in Christ's prophetic office. It spreads abroad a living witness to Him, especially by means of a life of faith and charity and by offering to God a sacrifice of praise.... The body of the faithful as a whole, anointed as they are by the Holy One (cf. Jn. 2:20, 27), cannot err in matters of belief. Thanks to a supernatural sense of faith which characterizes the People as a whole, it manifests this unerring quality when, 'from the bishops down to the last member of the laity,' it shows universal agreement in matters of faith and morals.

"... God's People accepts not the word of men but the very Word of God (cf. 1 Thes. 2:13). It clings without fail to the faith once delivered to the saints (cf. Jude 3), penetrates it more deeply by accurate insights, and applies it more thoroughly to life. All this it does under the lead of a sacred teaching authority to which it loyally defers.

"It is not only through the sacraments and Church ministries that the same Holy Spirit sanctifies and leads the People of God.... He distributes special graces among the faithful of every rank. By these gifts He makes them fit and ready to undertake the various tasks or offices advantageous for the renewal and upbuilding of the Church.... These charismatic gifts... are to be received with thanksgiving and consolation, for they are exceedingly suitable and useful for the needs of the Church.

"... Judgment as to their genuineness and proper use belongs to those who preside over the Church, and to whose special competence it belongs... to test all things and hold fast to that which is good (cf. 1 Thes. 5:12; 19-21)" (No. 12).

All Are Called

"All men are called to belong to the new People of God. Wherefore this People, while remaining one and unique, is to be spread throughout the whole world and must exist in all ages, so that the purpose of God's will may be fulfilled. In the beginning God made human nature one. After His children were scattered, He decreed that they should at length be united again (cf. Jn. 11:52). It was for this reason that God sent His Son... that He might be Teacher, King, and Priest of all, the Head of the New and universal people of the sons of God. For this God finally sent His Son's Spirit as Lord and Lifegiver. He it is who, on behalf of the whole Church and each and every one of those who believe, is the principle of their coming together and remaining together in the teaching of the apostles and in fellowship, in the breaking of bread and in prayers (cf. Acts 2:42)" (No. 13).

One People of God

"It follows that among all the nations of earth there is but one People of God, which takes its citizens from every race, making them citizens of a kingdom which is of a heavenly and not an earthly nature. For all the faithful scattered throughout the world are in communion with each other in the Holy Spirit...the Church or People of God... foster(s) and take(s) to herself, insofar as they are good, the ability, resources and customs of each people. Taking them to herself she purifies, strengthens, and enobles them.... This characteristic of universality which adorns the People of God is a gift from the Lord Himself. By reason of it, the Catholic Church strives energetically and constantly to bring all humanity with all its riches back to Christ its Head in the unity of His Spirit.

"In virtue of this catholicity each individual part of the Church contributes through its special gifts to the good of the other parts and of the whole Church. Thus through the common sharing of gifts... the whole and each of the parts receive increase....

"All men are called to be part of this catholic unity of the People of God.... And there belong to it or are related to it in various ways, the Catholic faithful as well as all who believe in Christ, and indeed the whole of mankind. For all men are called to salvation by the grace of God" (No. 13).

The Catholic Church

"This sacred Synod turns its attention first to the Catholic faithful. Basing itself upon sacred Scripture and tradition, it teaches that the Church... is necessary for salvation. For Christ, made present to us in His Body, which is the Church, is the one Mediator and the unique Way of salvation. In explicit terms He Himself affirmed the necessity of faith and baptism (cf. Mk. 16:16; Jn. 3:5) and thereby affirmed also the necessity of the Church, for through baptism as through a door men enter the Church. Whosoever, therefore, knowing that the Catholic Church was made necessary by God through Jesus Christ, would refuse to enter her or to remain in her could not be saved.

"They are fully incorporated into the society of the Church who, possessing the Spirit of Christ, accept her entire system and all the means of salvation given to her, and through union with her visible structure are joined to Christ, who rules her through the Supreme Pontiff and the bishops. This joining is effected by the bonds of professed faith, of the sacraments, of ecclesiastical government, and of communion. He is not saved, however, who, though he is part of the body of the Church, does not persevere in charity. He remains indeed in the bosom of the Church, but . . . only in a 'bodily' manner and not 'in his heart.' . . .

"Catechumens who, moved by the Holy Spirit, seek with explicit intention to be incorporated into the Church are by that very intention joined to her. . . . Mother Church already embraces them as her own" (No. 14).

Other Christians, The Unbaptized

"The Church recognizes that in many ways she is linked with those who, being baptized, are honored with the name of Christian, though they do not profess the faith in its entirety or do not preserve unity of communion with the successor of Peter. . . .

" . . . We can say that in some real way they are joined with us in the Holy Spirit, for to them also He gives His gifts and graces, and is thereby operative among them with His sanctifying power . . ." (No. 15).

"Finally, those who have not yet received the gospel are related in various ways to the People of God. In the first place there is the people to whom the covenants and the promises were given and from whom Christ was born according to the flesh (cf. Rom. 9:4-5). On account of their fathers, this people remains most dear to God, for God does not repent of the gifts He makes nor of the calls He issues (cf. Rom. 11:28-29).

"But the plan of salvation also includes those who acknowledge the Creator. In the first place among these are the Moslems. . . . Nor is God Himself far distant from those who in shadows and images seek the unknown God. . . .

"Those also can attain to everlasting salvation who through no fault of their own do not know the gospel of Christ or His Church, yet sincerely seek God and, moved by grace, strive by their deeds to do His will as it is known to them through the dictates of conscience. Nor does divine Providence deny the help necessary for salvation to those who, without blame on their part, have not yet arrived at an explicit knowledge of God, but who strive to live a good life, thanks to His grace. Whatever goodness or truth is found among them is looked upon by the Church as a preparation for the Gospel. She regards such qualities as given by Him who enlightens all men so that they may finally have life . . ." (No. 16).

THE POPE, TEACHING AUTHORITY, COLLEGIALITY

The Roman Pontiff — the successor of St. Peter as the Vicar of Christ and head of the Church on earth — has full and supreme authority over the universal Church in matters pertaining to faith and morals (teaching authority), discipline and government (jurisdictional authority).

The primacy of the pope is real and supreme power. It is not merely a prerogative of honor — that is, of his being regarded as the first among equals. Neither does primacy imply that the pope is just the presiding officer of the collective body of bishops. The pope is the head of the Church.

Catholic belief in the primacy of the pope was stated in detail in the dogmatic constitution on the Church, *Pastor Aeternus,* approved in 1870 by the fourth session of the First Vatican Council. Some elaboration of the doctrine was made in the *Dogmatic Constitution on the Church* which was approved and promulgated by the Second Vatican Council Nov. 21, 1964. The entire body of teaching on the subject is based on Scripture and tradition and the centuries-long experience of the Church.

Infallibility

The essential points of doctrine concerning infallibility in the Church and the infallibility of the pope were stated by the Second Vatican Council in the *Dogmatic Constitution on the Church,* as follows:

"This infallibility with which the divine Redeemer willed his Church to be endowed in defining a doctrine of faith and morals extends as far as extends the deposit of divine revelation, which must be religiously guarded and faithfully expounded. This is the infallibility which the Roman Pontiff, the head of the college of bishops, enjoys in virtue of his office, when, as the supreme shepherd and teacher of all the faithful, who confirms his brethren in their faith (cf. Lk. 22:32), he proclaims by a definitive act some doctrine of faith or morals. Therefore his definitions, of themselves, and not from the consent of the Church, are justly styled irreformable, for they are pronounced with the assistance of the Holy Spirit, an assistance promised to him in blessed Peter. Therefore they need no approval of others, nor do they allow an appeal to any other judgment. For then the Roman Pontiff is not pronouncing judgment as a private person. Rather, as the supreme teacher of the universal Church, as one in whom the charism of the infallibility of the Church herself is individually present, he is expounding or defending a doctrine of Catholic faith.

"The infallibility promised to the Church resides also in the body of bishops when that body exercises supreme teaching authority with the successor of Peter. To the resultant definitions the assent of the Church can never be wanting, on account of the activity of that same Holy Spirit, whereby the whole flock of Christ is preserved and progresses in unity of faith.

"But when either the Roman Pontiff or the body of bishops together with him defines a judgment, they pronounce it in accord with revelation itself. All are obliged to maintain and be ruled by this revelation, which, as written or preserved by tradition, is transmitted in its entirety through the legitimate succession of bishops and especially through the care of the Roman Pontiff himself.

"Under the guiding light of the Spirit of truth, revelation is thus religiously preserved and faithfully expounded in the Church. The Roman Pontiff and the bishops, in view of their office and of the importance of the matter, strive painstakingly and by appropriate means to inquire properly into that revelation and to give apt expression to its contents. But they do not allow that there could be any new public revelation pertaining to the divine deposit of faith" (No. 25).

Authentic Teaching

The pope rarely speaks *ex cathedra* — that is, "from the chair" of St. Peter, for the purpose of making an infallible pronouncement. More often and in various ways he states authentic teaching in line with Scripture, tradition, the living experience of the Church, and the whole analogy of faith. Of such teaching, the Second Vatican Council said in its *Dogmatic Constitution on the Church* (No. 25):

". . . Religious submission of will and of mind must be shown in a special way to the authentic teaching authority of the Roman Pontiff, even when he is not speaking *ex cathedra*. That is, it must be shown in such a way that his supreme magisterium is acknowledged with reverence, the judgments made by him are sincerely adhered to, according to his manifest mind and will. His mind and will in the matter may be known chiefly either from the character of the documents, from his frequent repetition of the same doctrine, or from his manner of speaking."

With respect to bishops, the constitution said: "They are authentic teachers, that is, teachers endowed with the authority of Christ, who preach to the people committed to them the faith they must believe and put into practice. By the light of the Holy Spirit, they make that faith clear, bringing forth from the treasury of revelation new things and old (cf. Mt. 13:52), making faith bear fruit and vigilantly warding off any errors which threaten their flock (cf. Tm. 4:1-4).

"Bishops, teaching in communion with the Roman Pontiff, are to be respected by all as witnesses to divine and Catholic truth. In matters of faith and morals, the bishops speak in the name of Christ and the faithful are to accept their teaching and adhere to it with a religious assent of soul."

Magisterium—Teaching Authority

Responsibility for teaching doctrine and judging orthodoxy belongs to the official teaching authority of the Church.

This authority is personalized in the pope, the successor of St. Peter as head of the Church, and in the bishops together and in union with the pope, as it was originally committed to Peter and to the whole college of Apostles under his leadership. They are the official teachers of the Church.

Others have auxiliary relationships with the magisterium: theologians, in the study and clarification of doctrine; teachers — priests, religious, lay persons — who cooperate with the pope and bishops in spreading knowledge of religious truth; the faithful, who by their sense of faith and personal witness contribute to the development of doctrine and the establishment of its relevance to life in the Church and the world.

The magisterium, Pope Paul noted in an address at a general audience Jan. 11, 1967, "is a subordinate and faithful echo and secure interpreter of the divine word." It does not reveal new truths, "nor is it superior to Sacred Scripture." Its competence extends to the limits of divine revelation manifested in Scripture and tradition and the living experience of the Church, with respect to matters of faith and morals and related subjects.

Official teaching in these areas is infallible when it is formally defined, for belief and acceptance by all members of the Church, by the pope, acting in the capacity of supreme shepherd of the flock of Christg and when doctrine is proposed and taught with moral unanimity of bishops with the pope in a solemn collegial manner as in an ecumenical council, and/or in the ordinary course of events. Even when not infallibly defined, official teaching in the areas of faith and morals is authoritative and requires religious assent.

The teachings of the magisterium have been documented in creeds, formulas of faith, decrees and enactments of ecumenical and particular councils, various kinds of doctrinal statements, and other teaching instruments. They have also been incorporated into the liturgy, with the result that the law of prayer is said to be a law of belief.

Collegiality

The bishops of the Church, in union with the pope, have supreme teaching and pastoral authority over the whole Church in addition to the authority of office they have for their own dioceses.

This collegial authority is exercised in a solemn manner in an ecumenical council and can be exercised in other ways as well, "provided that the head of the college calls them to collegiate action, or at least so approves or freely accepts the united action of the dispersed bishops, that it is made a true collegiate act."

This doctrine is grounded on the fact that: "Just as, by the Lord's will, St. Peter and the other apostles constituted one apostolic college, so in a similar way the Roman Pontiff as the successor of Peter, and the bishops as the successors of the apostles are joined together."

Doctrine on collegiality was stated by the Second Vatican Council in the *Dogmatic Constitution on the Church* (Nos. 22 and 23).

REVELATION

Following are excerpts from the *Constitution on Revelation* promulgated by the Second Vatican Council. They describe the nature and process of divine revelation, inspiration and interpretation of Scripture, the Old and New Testaments, and the role of Scripture in the life of the Church.

I. Revelation Itself

". . . God chose to reveal Himself and to make known to us the hidden purpose of His will (cf. Eph. 1:9) by which through Christ, the Word made flesh, man has access to the Father in the Holy Spirit and comes to share in the divine nature (cf. Eph. 2:18; 2 Pt. 1:4). Through this revelation, therefore, the invisible God (cf. Col. 1:15; 1 Tm. 1:17) . . . speaks to men as friends (cf. Ex. 33:11; Jn. 15:14-15) and lives among them (cf. Bar. 3:38) so that He may invite and take them into fellowship with Himself. This plan of revelation is realized by deeds and words having an inner unity: the deeds wrought by God in the history of salvation manifest and confirm the teaching and realities signified by the words, while the words proclaim the deeds and clarify the mystery contained in them. By this revelation then, the deepest truth about God and the salvation of man is made clear to us in Christ, who is the Mediator and at the same time the fullness of all revelation" (No. 2).

"God . . . from the start manifested Himself to our first parents. Then after their fall His promise of redemption aroused in them the hope of being saved (cf. Gn. 3:15), and from that time on He ceaselessly kept the human race in His care, in order to give eternal life to those who perseveringly do good in search of salvation (cf. Rom. 2:6-7). . . . He called Abraham in order to make of him a great nation (cf. Gn. 12:2). Through the patriarchs, and after them through Moses and the prophets, He taught this nation to acknowledge Himself as the one living and true God . . . and to wait for the Savior promised by Him. In this manner He prepared the way for the gospel down through the centuries" (No. 3).

Revelation in Christ

"Then, after speaking in many places and varied ways through the prophets, God 'last of all in these days has spoken to us by His Son' (Hb. 1:1-2). . . . Jesus perfected revelation by fulfilling it through His whole work of making Himself present and manifesting Himself: through His words and deeds, His signs and wonders, but especially through His death and glorious resurrection from the dead and final sending of the spirit of truth. Moreover, He confirmed with divine testimony what revelation proclaimed: that God is with us to free us from the darkness of sin and death, and to raise us up to life eternal.

"The Christian dispensation, therefore, as the new and definitive covenant, will never pass away, and we now await no further new public revelation before the glorious manifestation of our Lord Jesus Christ (cf. 1 Tm. 6:14; Ti. 2:13)" (No. 4).

II. Transmission of Revelation

". . . God has seen to it that what He had revealed for the salvation of all nations would abide perpetually in its full integrity and be handed on to all generations. Therefore Christ the Lord, in whom the full revelation of the supreme God is brought to completion (cf. 2 Cor. 1:20; 3:16; 4:6), commissioned the apostles to preach to all men that gospel which is the source of all saving truth and moral teaching, and thus to impart to them divine gifts. This gospel had been promised in former times through the prophets, and Christ Himself fulfilled it and promulgated it with His own lips. This commission was faithfully fulfilled by the apostles who, by their oral preaching, by example, and by ordinances, handed on what they had received from . . . Christ . . . or what they had learned through the prompting of the Holy Spirit. The commission was fulfilled, too, by those apostles and apostolic men who under the inspiration of the same Holy Spirit committed the message of salvation to writing" (No. 7).

Tradition

"But in order to keep the gospel forever whole and alive within the Church, the apostles left bishops as their successors, 'handing over their own teaching role' to them. This sacred tradition, therefore, and sacred Scripture of both the Old and the New Testament are like a mirror in which the pilgrim Church on earth looks at God . . ." (No. 7).

". . . The apostolic preaching, which is expressed in a special way in the inspired books, was to be preserved by a continuous succession of preachers until the end of time. Therefore the apostles, handing on what they themselves had received, warn the faithful to hold fast to the traditions which they have learned. . . . Now what was handed on by the apostles includes everything which contributes to the holiness of life, and the increase in faith of the People of God; and so the Church, in her teaching, life, and worship, perpetuates and hands on to all generations all that she herself is, all that she believes" (No. 8).

Development of Doctrine

"This tradition which comes from the apostles develops in the Church with the help of the Holy Spirit. For there is a growth in the understanding of the realities and the words which have been handed down. This happens through the contemplation and study made by believers . . . through the intimate understanding of spiritual things they experience, and through the preaching of those who have received through episcopal succession the sure gift of truth. For, as the centuries succeed one another, the Church constantly moves forward toward the fullness of divine truth until the words of God reach their complete fulfillment in her.

"The words of the holy Fathers witness to the living presence of this tradition, whose wealth is poured into the practice and life of the believing and praying Church. Through the same tradition the Church's full canon of the sacred books is known, and the sacred writings themselves are more profoundly understood and unceasingly made active in her; . . . and the Holy Spirit, through whom the living voice of the gospel resounds in the Church, and through her, in the world, leads unto all truth those who believe and makes the word of Christ dwell abundantly in them (cf. Col. 3:16)" (No. 8).

Tradition and Scripture

"Hence there exist a close connection and communication between sacred tradition and sacred Scripture. For both of them, flowing from the same divine wellspring, in a certain way merge into a unity and tend toward the same end. For sacred Scripture is the word of God inasmuch as it is consigned to writing under the inspiration of the divine Spirit. To the successors of the apostles, sacred tradition hands on in its full purity God's word, which was entrusted to the apostles by Christ the Lord and the Holy Spirit. Thus, led by the light of the Spirit of truth, these successors can in their preaching preserve this word of God faithfully, explain it, and make it more widely known. Consequently, it is not from sacred Scripture alone that the Church draws her certainty about everything which has been revealed. Therefore both sacred tradition and sacred Scripture are to be accepted and venerated with the same sense of devotion and reverence" (No. 9).

"Sacred tradition and sacred Scripture form one sacred deposit of the word of God, which is committed to the Church" (No. 10).

Teaching Authority of Church

"The task of authentically interpreting the word of God, whether written or handed on, has been entrusted exclusively to the living teaching office of the Church, whose authority is exercised in the name of Jesus Christ. This teaching office is not above the word of God, but serves it, teaching only what has been handed on . . . it draws from this one deposit of faith everything which it presents for belief as divinely revealed.

"It is clear, therefore, that sacred tradition, sacred Scripture, and the teaching authority of the Church . . . are so linked and joined together that one cannot stand without the others, and that all together and each in its own way under the action of the one Holy Spirit contribute effectively to the salvation of souls" (No. 10).

III. Inspiration, Interpretation

"Those . . . revealed realities . . . contained and presented in sacred Scripture have been committed to writing under the inspiration of the Holy Spirit. Holy Mother Church, relying on the belief of the apostles, holds that the books of both the Old and New Testament in their entirety, with all their parts, are sacred and canonical because, having been written under the inspiration of the Holy Spirit (cf. Jn. 20:31; 2 Tm. 3:16; 2 Pt. 1:19-21; 3:15-16) they have God as their author and have been handed on as such to the Church herself. In composing the sacred books, God chose men and while employed by Him they made use of their powers and abilities, so that with Him acting in them and through them, they, as true authors, consigned to writing everything and only those things which He wanted" (No. 11).

Inerrancy

"Therefore, since everything asserted by the inspired authors or sacred writers must be held to be asserted by the Holy Spirit, it follows that the books of Scripture must be acknowledged as teaching firmly, faithfully, and without error that truth which God wanted put into the sacred writings for the sake of our salvation. Therefore 'all Scripture is inspired by God and useful for teaching, for reproving, for correcting, for instruction in justice; that the man of God may be perfect, equipped for every good work' (2 Tm. 3:16-17)" (No. 11).

Literary Forms

"However, since God speaks in sacred Scripture through men in human fashion, the interpreter of sacred Scripture, in order to see clearly what God wanted to communicate to us, should carefully investigate what meaning the sacred writers really intended, and what God wanted to mainfest by means of their words.

"... The interpreter must investigate what meaning the sacred writer intended to express and actually expressed in particular circumstances as he used contemporary literary forms in accordance with the situation of his own time and culture. For the correct understanding of what the sacred author wanted to assert, due attention must be paid to the customary and characteristic styles of perceiving, speaking, and narrating which prevailed at the time of the sacred writer, and to the customs men normally followed at that period in their everyday dealings with one another" (No. 12).

Analogy of Faith

"... No less serious attention must be given to the content and unity of the whole of Scripture, if the meaning of the sacred texts is to be correctly brought to light. The living tradition of the whole Church must be taken into account along with the harmony which exists between elements of the faith.... all of what has been said about the way of interpreting Scripture is subject finally to the judgment of the Church, which carries out the divine commission and ministry of guarding and interpreting the word of God" (No. 12).

IV. The Old Testament

"In carefully planning and preparing the salvation of the whole human race, the God of supreme love, by a special dispensation, chose for Himself a people to whom He might entrust His promises. First He entered into a covenant with Abraham (cf. Gn. 15:18) and, through Moses, with the people of Israel (cf. Ex. 24:8). To this people which He had acquired for Himself, He so manifested Himself through words and deeds as the one true and living God that Israel came to know by experience the ways of God with men.... The plan of salvation, foretold by the sacred authors, recounted and explained by them, is found as the true word of God in the books of the Old Testament: these books, therefore, written under divine inspiration, remain permanently valuable..." (No. 14).

Principal Purpose

"The principal purpose to which the plan of the Old Covenant was directed was to prepare for the coming both of Christ, the universal Redeemer, and of the messianic kingdom.... Now the books of the Old Testament, in accordance with the state of mankind before the time of salvation established by Christ, reveal to all men the knowledge of God and of man and the ways in which God ... deals with men. These books ... show us true divine pedagogy ..." (No. 15).

"... The books of the Old Testament with all their parts, caught up into the proclamation of the gospel, acquire and show forth their full meaning in the New Testament (cf. Mt. 5:17; Lk. 24:27; Rom. 16:25-26; 2 Cor. 3:14-16) and in turn shed light on it and explain it" (No. 16).

V. The New Testament

"The word of God ... is set forth and shows its power in a most excellent way in the writings of the New Testament. For when the fullness of time arrived (cf. Gal. 4:4), the Word was made flesh and dwelt among us in the fullness of grace and truth (cf. Jn. 1:14). Christ established the Kingdom of God on earth, manifested His Father and Himself by deeds and words, and completed His work by His death, resurrection, and glorious ascension and by the sending of the Holy Spirit. Having been lifted up from the earth, He draws all men to Himself (cf. Jn. 12:32)....
This mystery had not been manifested to other generations as it was now revealed to His holy apostles and prophets in the Holy Spirit (cf. Eph. 3:4-6), so that they might preach the Gospel, stir up faith in Jesus, Christ and Lord, and gather the Church together. To these realities, the writings of the New Testament stand as a perpetual and divine witness" (No. 17).

The Gospels and Other Writings

"... The Gospels have a special preeminence ... for they are the principal witness of the life and teaching of the incarnate Word, our Savior.

"The Church has always and everywhere held and continues to hold that the four Gospels are of apostolic origin. For what the apostles preached ... afterwards they themselves and apostolic men, under the inspiration of the divine Spirit, handed on to us in writing: the foundation of faith, namely, the fourfold Gospel, according to Matthew, Mark, Luke, and John" (No. 18).

"... The four Gospels, ... whose historical character the Church unhesitatingly asserts, faithfully hand on what Jesus Christ, while living among men, really did and taught for their eternal salvation until the day He was taken up into heaven (see Acts 1:1-2). Indeed, after the ascension of the Lord the apostles handed on to their hearers what He had said and done.... The sacred authors wrote the four Gospels, selecting some things from the many which had been handed on by word of mouth or in writing, reducing some of them to a synthesis, explicating some things in view of the situation of their churches, and preserving the form of proclamation but always in such fashion that they told us the honest truth about Jesus. For their intention in writing was that ... we might know 'the truth' concerning those matters about which we have been instructed (cf. Lk. 1:2-4)" (No. 19).

"Besides the four Gospels, the canon of the New Testament also contains the Epistles of St. Paul and other apostolic writings, composed under the inspiration of the Holy Spirit. In these writings . . . those matters which concern Christ the Lord are confirmed, His true teaching is more and more fully stated, the saving power of the divine work of Christ is preached, the story is told of the beginnings of the Church and her marvelous growth, and her glorious fulfillment is foretold" (No. 20).

VI. Scripture in Church Life

"The Church has always venerated the divine Scriptures just as she venerates the body of the Lord. . . . She has always regarded the Scriptures together with sacred tradition as the supreme rule of faith, and will ever do so. For, inspired by God and committed once and for all to writing, they impart the word of God Himself without change, and make the voice of the Holy Spirit resound in the words of the prophets and apostles. Therefore, like the Christian religion itself, all the preaching of the Church must be nourished and ruled by sacred Scripture . . ." (No. 21).

"Easy access to sacred Scripture should be provided for all the Christian faithful. That is why the Church from the very beginning accepted as her own that very ancient Greek translation of the Old Testament which is named after seventy men (the Septuagint); and she has always given a place of honor to other translations, Eastern and Latin, especially the one known as the Vulgate. But since the word of God should be available at all times, the Church with maternal concern sees to it that suitable and correct translations are made into different languages, especially from the original texts of the sacred books. And if, given the opportunity and the approval of Church authority, these translations are produced in cooperation with the separated brethren as well, all Christians will be able to use them" (No. 22).

Biblical Studies, Theology

The constitution encouraged the development and progress of biblical studies "under the watchful care of the sacred teaching office of the Church." (Such studies have made great progress in recent years.)

It noted also: "Sacred theology rests on the written word of God, together with sacred tradition, as its primary and perpetual foundation," and that "the study of the sacred page is, as it were, the soul of sacred theology" (Nos. 23, 24).

ENERGY, ENVIRONMENT

A number of factors combined during 1979 to raise concern over energy and environmental issues to an unprecedented level. One of them was the nuclear accident which occurred March 28 at the Three Mile Island nuclear plant in Pennsylvania.

Some of the elements of concern were voiced by Bishop Joseph Daley of nearby Harrisburg in a statement released Sept. 7.

"Respect for human life and responsible stewardship require that we call for a postponement of construction of nuclear plants, including those now underway."

The moratorium's purpose "would be to provide time for the scientific community to make a more intense study of the safe use of nuclear energy, including radioactive waste disposal and the physical effects of radiation. It should continue until the responsible government agencies can formulate regulations and policies to ensure the proper construction of plants and adequate training of plant personnel to operate the plants, and to guarantee the safety of the plants by a well regulated and properly enforced system of inspection."

Since there is "no ready substitute" for the energy which would be produced by nuclear plants under construction, a construction moratorium "mandates a simultaneous moratorium on increased energy consumption."

"A moratorium will require that each of us make a concerted effort to conserve energy, that we sacrifice some degree of personal comfort and freedom to which we have become accustomed, that we make more efficient use of the available energy for life's necessities rather than its comforts."

The leak at the Three Mile Island plant would have released lethal amounts of radiation if scientists had not been able to prevent core melt-down.

"The most significant fact underscored by this accident," Bishop Daley said, "is that not enough is known about the risks and benefits of nuclear energy to enable us to make a reasonable choice about continued development."

There are still problems concerning radioactive waste disposal, reactor safety and lack of sufficient information about the dangers of exposure to low-level radiation.

Realism requires acknowledging that shutting down existing nuclear plants "would cause significant energy cutbacks, affecting jobs and the production of food and other necessities, as well as our personal lives."

"Realism also requires that we acknowledge that we have entered into nuclear energy development without adequate knowledge of what its effects on human life are, or will be. . . . Realism requires that we acknowledge that we have acted unwisely in allowing the proliferation of nuclear reactors."

Bishop Daley said three principles should shape public debate on nuclear energy:

• Respect for Life: "We cannot wilfully use the goods of the earth or alter the environment for our own benefit without regard for the effect on our neighbors or on the future of the human race."

• Technology, which should be measured by whether it makes human life more human in every respect.

• Terms of debate should be focused on risks and benefits.

THE BIBLE

The Catholic canon of the Old Testament consists of:

- The Pentateuch, the first five books: Genesis (Gn.), Exodus (Ex.), Leviticus (Lv.), Numbers (Nm.), Deuteronomy (Dt.).
- Historical Books: Joshua (Jos.), Judges (Jgs.), Ruth (Ru.), 1 and 2 Samuel (Sm.), 1 and 2 Kings (Kgs.), 1 and 2 Chronicles (Chr.), Ezra (Ezr.), Nehemiah (Neh.), Tobit (Tb.), Judith (Jdt.), Esther (Est.), 1 and 2 Maccabees (Mc.).
- Wisdom Books: Job (Jb.), Psalms (Ps.), Proverbs (Prv.), Ecclesiastes (Eccl.), Song of Songs (Song), Wisdom (Wis.), Sirach (Sir.).
- The Prophets: Isaiah (Is.), Jeremiah (Jer.), Lamentations (Lam.), Baruch (Bar.), Ezechiel (Ez.), Daniel (Dn.), Hosea (Hos.), Joel (Jl.), Amos (Am.), Obadiah (Ob.), Jonah (Jon.), Micah (Mi.), Nahum (Na.), Habakkùk (Hb.), Zephaniah (Zep.), Haggai (Hg.), Zechariah (Zec.), Malachi (Mal.).

The Catholic canon of the New Testament consists of:

- The Gospels of Matthew (Mt.), Mark (Mk.), Luke (Lk.), John (Jn.)
- The Acts of the Apostles (Acts).
- The Pauline Letters — Romans (Rom.), 1 and 2 Corinthians (Cor.), Galatians (Gal.), Ephesians (Eph.), Philippians (Phil.), Colossians (Col.), 1 and 2 Thessalonians (Thes.), 1 and 2 Timothy (Tm.), Titus (Ti.), Philemon (Phlm.), Hebrews (Heb.); the Catholic Letters — James (Jas.), 1 and 2 Peter (Pt.), 1, 2 and 3 John (Jn.), Jude (Jude).
- Revelation (Rv.).

Catholic and Other Canons

The Catholic canon of the Old Testament was determined by the tradition of the Church. It was firm by the fifth century, despite some questioning by scholars, and was stated by the African councils of Hippo in 393 and Carthage in 397 and 419, by Innocent I in 405, and by the Council of Florence in 1441. It was defined by the Council of Trent in the dogmatic decree *De Canonicis Scripturis,* Apr. 8, 1546.

The Jews, although they generally accepted 22 or 24 books as sacred in the first century A.D., did not have a definite canon of sacred writings until late in the second or early in the third century. This canon was fixed by the consensus of rabbinical schools.

The canon of the Hebrew Masoretic Text, which is accepted by modern Jews, consists of 24 books, as follows:

- The Law: Genesis, Exodus, Leviticus, Numbers, Deuteronomy.
- The Prophets: earlier prophets — Joshua, Judges, Samuel, Kings; later prophets — Isaiah, Jeremiah, Ezekiel, and 12 others in one book (Hosea, Joel, Amos, Obadiah, Jonah, Micah, Nahum, Habakkuk, Zephaniah, Haggai, Zechariah, Malachi).
- The Writings: Psalms, Job, Proverbs, Ruth, Song of Songs, Ecclesiastes, Lamentations, Esther, Daniel, Ezra-Nehemiah, Chronicles.

This canon does not include a number of books in the Alexandrian collection of sacred writings — viz., 1 and 2 Maccabees, Tobit, Judith, Sirach, Wisdom, Baruch, and portions of Esther and Daniel (chapters 13 and 14). These additional books and passages, contained in the Septuagint version of the Old Testament and called deuterocanonical, are in the Catholic canon.

These books and passages, called deuterocanonical in terminology coined by Sixtus of Siena (1520-1569), were under discussion for some time until questions about their canonicity were settled. Books admitted into the canon with little or no debate were called protocanonical. The canonical status of both categories of books is the same in the Catholic Bible.

The Protestant canon, in an arrangement of 39 books, is the same as the Hebrew canon.

The Old Testament canon has not been definitely settled by the Orthodox. Since the time of the Reformation, however, they have given some preference to the Protestant canon.

The New Testament canon was firm by the end of the fourth century. By the end of the second century all of the New Testament books were generally known and most of them were acknowledged as inspired. The Muratorian Fragment, dating from about 200, listed most of the books recognized in later decrees as canonical. Prior to the end of the fourth century, however, there were controversies over the inspired character of several books — viz., the Letter to the Hebrews, James, Jude, 2 Peter, 2 and 3 John, and Revelation. Controversy over these books ended in the fourth century, and the canon stated by the councils of Hippo and Carthage and reaffirmed by Innocent I in 405 was solemnly defined by the Council of Trent (1545-63).

Although Martin Luther eliminated the aforementioned books from his New Testament canon, they were reinstated by his followers by the year 1700. Anglicans and Calvinists always retained them.

The Greek and Russian Orthodox have the same New Testament canon as the Catholic Church. Some variations exist among other separated Eastern churches.

Languages of the Bible

Hebrew, Aramaic and Greek were the original languages of the Bible. Most of the Old Testament books were written in Hebrew. Portions of Daniel, Ezra, Jeremiah, Esther, and probably the books of Tobit and Judith were written in Aramaic. The Book of Wisdom, 2 Maccabees and all the books of the New Testament were written in Greek.

Manuscripts and Versions

The original writings of the inspired authors have been lost. The Bible has been transmitted through ancient copies called manuscripts and through translations or versions.

Authoritative Greek manuscripts include the Sinaitic and Vatican manuscripts of the fourth century and the Alexandrine and Parisian of the fifth century A. D.

The Septuagint and Vulgate translations are in a class by themselves.

The Septuagint version, a Greek translation of the Old Testament, was begun about 250 and completed about 100 B. C. The work of several Jewish translators at Alexandria, it differed from the Hebrew Bible in the arrangement of books and included several, later called deuterocanonical, which were not acknowledged as sacred by the community at Jerusalem.

The Vulgate was a Latin version of the Old and New Testaments produced from the original languages by St. Jerome from about 383 to 404. It became the most widely used Latin text for centuries and was regarded as basic long before the Council of Trent designated it as authentic and suitable for use in public reading, controversy, preaching and teaching. Because of its authoritative character, it became the basis for many translations into other languages. A critical revision, in work since 1965, was completed by a pontifical commission in 1977.

Hebrew and Aramaic manuscripts of great antiquity and value have figured more significantly than before in recent scriptural work by Catholic scholars, especially since their use was strongly encouraged, if not mandated, in 1943 by Pius XII in the encyclical *Divino Afflante Spiritu*.

The English translation of the Bible in general use among Catholics until recent years was the *Douay-Rheims*, so called because of the places where it was prepared and published, the New Testament at Rheims in 1582 and the Old Testament at Douay in 1609. The translation was made from the Vulgate text. As revised and issued by Bishop Richard Challoner in 1749 and 1750, it became the standard Catholic English version for about 200 years.

A revision of the Challoner New Testament, made on the basis of the Vulgate text by scholars of the Catholic Biblical Association of America, was published in 1941 in the United States under the sponsorship of the Episcopal Committee of the Confraternity of Christian Doctrine.

New American Bible

A new translation of the entire Bible, the first ever made directly into English from the original languages under Catholic auspices, was projected in 1944 and completed in the fall of 1970 with publication of the *New American Bible*. The Episcopal Committee of the Confraternity of Christian Doctrine sponsored the NAB. The translators were members of the Catholic Biblical Association of America and several fellow scholars of other faiths. The typical edition was produced by St. Anthony Guild Press, Paterson, N. J.

Old Testament portions of the NAB were published in separate volumes before undergoing final revision and being bound in one cover. Genesis and Psalms were issued in 1948 and 1950; Genesis to Ruth, in 1952; Job to Sirach, in 1955; the Prophets, in 1961; Samuel to the Maccabees, in 1969. The new translation of the New Testament was issued for the first time in 1970.

Versions of the Bible approved for use in the Catholic liturgy are the *Douay-Rheims*, the *New American Bible, A New Translation from the Latin Vulgate* by Ronald A. Knox, the Catholic edition of the *Revised Standard Version*, and the *Jerusalem Bible*.

The *Jerusalem Bible* is an English translation of a French version based on the original languages. It was published by Doubleday & Co., Inc., which is also working toward completion of the *Anchor Bible*.

The Protestant counterpart of the *Douay-Rheims Bible* was the *King James Bible*, called the *Authorized Version* in England. Originally published in 1611, it was in general use for more than three centuries. Its modern revisions include the *English Revised Version*, published between 1881 and 1885; the *American Revised Version*, 1901, and revisions of the New Testament (1946) and the Old Testament (1952) published in 1957 in the United States as the *Revised Standard Version*.

The latest revision, a translation in the language of the present day made from Greek and Hebrew sources, is the *New English Bible*, published Mar. 16, 1970. Its New Testament portion was originally published in 1961.

Biblical Federation

The World Catholic Federation for the Biblical Apostolate, established in 1969, sponsors a program designed to create greater awareness among Catholics of the Bible and its use in everyday life. Mill Hill Father Arnold Jurgens is the general secretary.

The Bible as the source of spiritual development, especially for priests, students for the priesthood and religious, was the theme of the 1978 meeting of the federation held in April in Malta, with an attendance of persons from 45 nations.

The U. S. Center for the Catholic Biblical Apostolate, under the direction of Father Stephen Hartdegen, O.F.M., is related to the Department of Education, U. S. Catholic Conference. Address: 1312 Massachusetts Ave. N. W., Washington, D.C. 20005.

APOCRYPHA

Apocrypha are books which have some resemblance to the canonical books in subject matter and title but which have not been recognized as canonical by the Church. They are characterized by a false claim to divine authority; extravagant accounts of events and miracles alleged to be supplemental revelation; material favoring heresy (especially in "New Testament" apocrypha); minimal, if any, historical value.

Among examples of this type of literature itemized by J. McKenzie, S.J., in *Dictionary of the Bible* are: *the Books of Adam and Eve, Martyrdom of Isaiah, Testament of the Patriarchs, Assumption of Moses, Sibylline Oracles; Gospel of James, Gospel of Thomas, Arabic Gospel of the Infancy, History of Joseph the Carpenter; Acts of John, Acts of Paul, Acts of Peter, Acts of Andrew,* and numerous epistles.

Books of this type are called pseudepigrapha by Protestants. They regard the deuterocanonical books in the Catholic canon of Scripture as apocrypha.

DEAD SEA SCROLLS

The Qumran Scrolls, popularly called the Dead Sea Scrolls, are a collection of manuscripts, all but one of them in Hebrew, found between 1947 and 1956 in caves in the Desert of Juda west of the Dead Sea.

Among the findings were a complete text of Isaiah dating from the second century, B.C., more or less extensive fragments of other Old Testament texts (including the deuterocanonical Tobit), and a commentary on Habakkuk. Until the discovery of these materials, the oldest known Hebrew manuscripts were from the 10th century, A.D.

Also found were messianic and apocalyptic texts, and other writings describing the beliefs and practices of the Essenes, a rigoristic Jewish sect.

The scrolls, dating from about the first century before and after Christ, are important sources of information about Hebrew literature, Jewish history during the period between the Old and New Testaments, and the history of Old Testament texts. They established the fact that the Hebrew text of the Old Testament was fixed before the beginning of the Christian era and have had definite effects in recent critical studies and translations of the Old Testament. Together with other scrolls found at Masada, they are still the subject of intensive study.

A theory was proposed in 1972 by Father Jose O'Callaghan, a Spanish papyrologist, that a scrap of one of the scrolls might be a fragment of St. Mark's Gospel dating from about the year 50. Father Pierre Benoit, O. P., discounted the hypothesis, stating that it was based on an erroneous analysis of a photocopy of the scrap in question.

BOOKS OF THE BIBLE

Old Testament
(Dates are before Christ.)

Pentateuch

The Pentateuch is the collective title of the first five books of the Bible. Substantially, they identify the Israelites as Yahweh's Chosen People, cover their history from Egypt to the threshold of the Promised Land, contain the Mosaic Law and Covenant, and disclose the promise of salvation to come. Principal themes concern the divine promise of salvation, Yahweh's fidelity, and the Covenant. Work on the composition of the Pentateuch was completed in the sixth century.

Genesis: The book of origins, according to its title in the Septuagint. In two parts, covers: religious prehistory, including accounts of the origin of the world and man, the original state of innocence and the fall, the promise of salvation, patriarchs before and after the Deluge, the Tower of Babel narrative, genealogies (first 11 chapters); the covenant with Abraham and patriarchal history from Abraham to Joseph (balance of the 50 chapters). Significant are the themes of Yahweh's universal sovereignty and mercy.

Exodus: Named with the Greek word for departure, is a religious epic which describes the oppression of the 12 tribes in Egypt and their departure, liberation or passover therefrom under the leadership of Moses; Yahweh's establishment of the Covenant with them, making them his Chosen People, through the mediation of Moses at Mt. Sinai; instructions concerning the tabernacle, the sanctuary and Ark of the Covenant; the institution of the priesthood. The book is significant because of its theology of liberation and redemption. In Christian interpretation, the Exodus is a figure of baptism.

Leviticus: Mainly legislative in theme and purpose, contains laws regarding sacrifices, ceremonies of ordination and the priesthood of Aaron, legal purity, the holiness code, atonement, the redemption of offerings, and other subjects. Summarily, Levitical laws provided directives for all aspects of religious observance and for the manner in which the Israelites were to conduct themselves with respect to Yahweh and each other. Leviticus was the liturgical handbook of the priesthood.

Numbers: Taking its name from censuses recounted at the beginning and near the end, is a continuation of Exodus. It combines narrative of the Israelites' desert pilgrimage from Sinai to the border of Canaan with laws related to and expansive of those in Leviticus.

Deuteronomy: The concluding book of the Pentateuch, recapitulates, in the form of a testament of Moses, the Law and much of the desert history of the Israelites: enjoins fidelity to the Law as the key to good or bad fortune for the people; gives an account of the commissioning of Joshua as the successor of Moses. Notable themes concern the election of Israel by Yahweh, observance of the Law, prohibitions against the worship of foreign gods, worship of and confidence in Yahweh, the power of Yahweh in nature. The Deuteronomic Code or motif, embodying all of these elements, was the norm for interpreting Israelite history.

Joshua, Judges, Ruth

Joshua: Records the fulfillment of Yahweh's promise to the Israelites in their conquest, occupation and division of Canaan under the leadership of Joshua. It also contains an account of the return of Transjordanian Israelites and of a renewal of the Covenant. It was redacted in final form probably in the sixth century or later.

Judges: Records the actions of charismatic leaders, called judges, of the tribes of Israel between the death of Joshua and the time of Samuel, and a crisis of idolatry among the people. The basic themes are sin and punishment, repentance and deliverance; its purpose was in line with the Deuteronomic motif, that the fortunes of the Israelites were related to their observance or non-observance of the Law and the Covenant. It was redacted in final form probably in the sixth century.

Ruth: Named for the Gentile (Moabite) woman who, through marriage with Boaz, became an Israelite and an ancestress of David (her son, Obed, became his grandfather). Themes are filial piety, faith and trust in Yahweh, the universality of messianic salvation. Dates ranging from c. 950 to the seventh century have been assigned to the origin of the book, whose author is unknown.

Historical Books

These books, while they contain a great deal of factual material, are unique in their preoccupation with interpreting it, in the Deuteronomic manner, in primary relation to the Covenant on which the nation of Israel was founded and in accordance with which community and personal life were judged.

The books are: Samuel 1 and 2, from the end of Judges (c. 1020) to the end of David's reign (c. 961); Kings 1 and 2, from the last days of David to the start of the Babylonian Exile and the destruction of the Temple (587); Chronicles 1 and 2, from the reign of Saul (c. 1020-1000) to the return of the people from the Exile (538); Ezra and Nehemiah, covering the reorganization of the Jewish community after the Exile (458-397); Maccabees 1 and 2, recounting the struggle against attempted suppression of Judaism (168-142).

Three of the books listed below — Tobit, Judith and Esther — are categorized as religious novels.

Samuel 1 and 2: A single work in concept and contents, containing episodic history of the last two Judges, Eli and Samuel, the establishment and rule of the monarchy under Saul and David, and the political consequences of David's rule. The royal messianic dynasty of David was the subject of Nathan's Oracle in 2 Sm. 7. They were edited in final form probably late in the seventh century or during the Exile.

Kings 1 and 2: Cover the last days of David and the career of Solomon, including the building of the Temple and the history of the kingdom during his reign; stories of the prophets Elija and Elisha; the history of the divided kingdom to the fall of Israel in the North (721) and the fall of Judah in the South (587), the destruction of Jerusalem and the Temple. They reflect the Deuteronomic motif in attributing the downfall of the people to corruption of belief and practice in public and private life. They were completed probably in the sixth century.

Chronicles 1 and 2: A collection of historical traditions interpreted in such a way as to present an ideal picture of one people governed by divine law and united in one Temple worship of the one true God. Contents include genealogical tables from Adam to David, the careers of David and Solomon, coverage of the kingdom of Judah to the Exile, and the decree of Cyrus permitting the return of the people and rebuilding of Jerusalem. Both are related to and were written about 400 by the same author, the Chronicler, who composed Ezra and Nehemiah.

Ezra and Nehemiah: A running account of the return of the people to their homeland after the Exile and of practical efforts, under the leadership of Ezra and Nehemiah, to restore and reorganize the religious and political community on the basis of Israelite traditions, divine worship and observance of the Law. Events of great significance were the building of the second Temple, the building of a wall around Jerusalem, and the proclamation of the Law by Ezra. This restored community was the start of Judaism. Both are related to and were written about 400 by the same author, the Chronicler, who composed Chronicles 1 and 2.

Tobit: Written in the literary form of a novel and having greater resemblance to wisdom than to historical literature, narrates the personal history of Tobit, a devout and charitable Jew in exile, and persons connected with him, viz., his son Tobiah, his kinsman Raguel, and Raguel's daughter Sarah. Its purpose was to teach people how to be good Jews. One of its principal themes is patience under trial, with trust in divine Providence which is symbolized by the presence and action of the angel Raphael. It was written about 200.

Judith: Recounts, in the literary form of a historical novel or romance, the preservation of the Israelites from conquest and ruin through the action of Judith. The essential themes are trust in God for deliverance from danger and emphasis on observance of the Law. It was written probably during the Maccabean period.

Esther: Relates, in the literary form of a historical novel or romance, the manner in which Jews in Persia were saved from annihilation through the central role played by Esther, the Jewish wife of Ahasuerus; a fact commemorated by the Jewish feast of Purim. Like Judith, it has trust in divine Providence as its theme and indicates that God's saving will is sometimes realized by persons acting in unlikely ways. Its origin and date are uncertain; it may have been written about 200 near the beginning of the period of strong Hellenistic influence on the Jews.

Maccabees 1 and 2: While related to some extent because of common subject matter, are quite different from each other.

The first book recounts the background and events of the 40-year (175-135) struggle for religious and political freedom led by Judas Maccabaeus and his brothers against the Hellenist Seleucid kings and some Hellenophiles among the Jews. Victory was symbolized by the rededication of the Temple. Against the background of opposition between Jews and Gentiles, the author equated the survival of belief in the one true God with survival of the Jewish people, thus identifying religion with patriotism. It was written probably by a Palestinian Jew after 104.

The second book supplements the first to some extent, covering and giving a theological interpretation to events from 180 to 162. It explains the feast of the Dedication of the Temple, a key event in the survival of Judaism which is commemorated in the feast of Hanukkah; stresses the primacy of God's action in the struggle for survival; and indicates belief in an afterlife and the resurrection of the body. It was written probably by a Jew of Alexandria after 120.

Wisdom Books

With the exceptions of Psalms and the Song of Songs, the titles listed under this heading are called wisdom books because their purpose was to formulate the fruits of human experience in the context of meditation on sacred Scripture and to present them as an aid toward understanding the problems of life. Hebrew wisdom literature was distinctive from pagan literature of the same type, but it had limitations; these were overcome in the New Testament, which added the dimensions of the New Covenant to those of the Old. Solomon was regarded as the archtype of the wise man.

Job: A dramatic, didactic poem consisting mainly of several dialogues between Job and his friends concerning the mystery involved in the coexistence of the just God, evil, and the suffering of the just. It describes an innocent man's experience of suffering and conveys the truth that faith in and submission to God rather than complete understanding, which is impossible, make the experience bearable; also, that the justice of God cannot be defended by affirming that it is realized in this world. Of uncertain authorship, it was written probably between the fifth and third centuries.

Psalms: A collection of 150 religious songs or lyrics reflecting Israelite belief and piety dating from the time of the monarchy to the post-Exilic period, a span of well over 500 years. The psalms, which are a compendium of Old Testament theology, were used in the temple liturgy and were of several types suitable for the king, hymns, lamentations, expressions of confidence and thanksgiving, prophecy, historical meditation and reflection, and the statement of wisdom. About one-half of them are attributed to David; many, by unknown authors, date from the early post-Exilic period.

Proverbs: The oldest book of the wisdom type in the Bible, consisting of collections of sayings attributed to Solomon and other persons regarding a wide variety of subjects including wisdom and its nature, rules of conduct, duties with respect to one's neighbor, the conduct of daily affairs. It reveals many details of Jewish life. Its nucleus dates from the period before the Exile, but no definite date can be assigned for its final compilation.

Ecclesiastes: A treatise about many subjects whose unifying theme is the vanity of strictly human efforts and accomplishments with respect to the achievement of lasting happiness; the only things which are not vain are fear of the Lord and observance of his commandments. The pessimistic tone of the book is due to the absence of a concept of afterlife. It was written by an unknown author about 250.

Song of Songs: A collection of erotic lyrics reflecting various themes, including the celebration of fidelity and love between man and woman. According to one interpretation, the book is a parable of the love of Yahweh for Israel. It was written by an unknown author after the Exile.

Wisdom: Deals with many subjects including the reward of justice; praise of wisdom, a gift of Yahweh proceeding from belief in him and the practice of his Law; the part played by him in the history of his people, especially in their liberation from Egypt; the folly and shame of idolatry. Its contents are taken from the whole sacred literature of the Jews and represent a distillation of its wisdom based on the law, beliefs and traditions of Israel. Contains the first Old Testament affirmation of an afterlife with God. The last book of the Old Testament to be written, it was probably composed about 50 years before Christ by an unknown author to confirm the faith of the Jewish community in Alexandria.

Sirach: Resembling Proverbs, is a collection of sayings handed on by a grandfather to his grandson. It contains a variety of moral instruction and eulogies of patriarchs and other figures in Israelite history. Its moral maxims apply to individuals, the family and community, relations with God, friendship, education, wealth, the Law, divine worship. Its theme is that true wisdom consists in the Law. (It was formerly called Ecclesiasticus, the Church Book, because of its extensive use by the Church for moral instruction.) It was written in Hebrew between 200 and 175, during a period of strong Hellenistic influence, and was translated into Greek after 132.

The Prophets

These books and the prophecies they contain "express judgments of the people's moral conduct, on the basis of the Mosaic alliance between God and Israel. They teach sublime truths and lofty morals. They contain exhortations, threats, announcements of punishment, promises of deliverance. . . . In the affairs of men, their prime concern is the interests of God, especially in what pertains to the Chosen People through whom the Messiah is to come; hence their denunciations of idolatry and of that externalism in worship which exclude the interior spirit of religion. They are concerned also with the universal nature of the moral law, with personal responsibility, with the person and office of the Messiah, and with the conduct of foreign nations" (*The Holy Bible,* Prophetic Books, CCD Edition, 1961; Preface). There are four major (Isaiah, Jeremiah, Ezekiel, Daniel) and 12 minor prophets (distinguished by the length of books), Lamentations and Baruch. Earlier prophets, mentioned in historical books, include Samuel, Gad, Nathan, Elijah and Elisha.

Before the Exile, prophets were the intermediaries through whom God communicated revelation to the people. Afterwards, prophecy lapsed and the written word of the Law served this purpose.

Isaiah: Named for the greatest of the prophets whose career spanned the reigns of three Hebrew kings from 742 to the beginning of the seventh century, in a period of moral breakdown in Judah and threats of invasion by foreign enemies. It is an anthology of poems and oracles credited to him and a number of followers deeply influenced by him. Of special importance are the prophecies concerning Immanuel (6 to 12), including the prophecy of the virgin birth (7:14). Chapters 40 to 55, called Deutero-Isaiah, are attributed to an anonymous poet toward the end of the Exile; this portion contains the Songs of the Servant. The concluding part of the book (56-66) contains oracles by later disciples. One of many themes in Isaiah concerned the saving mission of the remnant of Israel in the divine plan of salvation. It was edited in its present form by 180.

Jeremiah: Combines history, biography and prophecy in a setting of crisis caused by internal and external factors, viz., idolatry and general infidelity to the Law among the Israelites and external threats from the Assyrians, Egyptians and Babylonians. Jeremiah prophesied the promise of a new covenant as well as the destruction of Jerusalem and the Temple. His career began in 626 and ended some years after the beginning of the Exile. The book, the longest in the Bible, was edited in final form after the Exile.

Lamentations: A collection of five laments or elegies over the fall of Jerusalem and the fate of the people in Exile, written by an unknown eyewitness not long after 587. They convey the message that Yahweh struck the people because of their sins and reflect confidence in his love and power to restore his converted people.

Baruch: Against the background of the already begun Exile, it consists of an introduction and several parts: an exile's prayer of confession and petition for forgiveness and the restoration of Israel; a poem praising wisdom and the Law of Moses; a lament in which Jerusalem, personified, bewails the fate of her people and consoles them with the hope of blessings to come; and a polemic against idolatry. Although ascribed to Baruch, Jeremiah's secretary, it was written by several authors probably in the second century.

Ezekiel: Named for the priest-prophet who prophesied in Babylon from 593 to 571, during the first phase of the Exile. To prepare his fellow early exiles for the impending fall of Jerusalem, he reproached the Israelites for past sins and predicted woes to come upon them. After the destruction of the city, the burden of his message was hope and promise of restoration. Ezekiel had great influence on the religion of Israel after the Exile. The book, which contains the substance of his teaching, had a number of authors and editors.

Daniel: The protagonist is a fictional young Jew, taken early to Babylon where he lived until 537, who figured in a series of edifying stories. The stories, which originated from Israelite tradition, recount the trials and triumphs of Daniel and his three companions, and other episodes including those concerning Susannah, Bel, and the Dragon. The book is more apocalyptic than prophetic: it envisions Israel in glory to come and conveys the message that men of faith can resist temptation and overcome adversity. It states the prophetic themes of right conduct, divine control of men and events, and the final triumph of the kingdom. It was written by an unknown author in the 160's to give moral support to Jews during the persecutions of the Maccabean period.

Hosea: Consists of a prophetic parallel between Hosea's marriage and Yahweh's relations with his people. As the prophet was married to a faithless wife whom he would not give up, Yahweh was bound in Covenant with an idolatrous and unjust Israel whom he would not desert but would chastise for purification. Hosea belonged to the Northern Kingdom of Israel and began his career about the middle of the eighth century. He inaugurated the tradition of describing Yahweh's relation to Israel in terms of marriage.

Joel: Is apocalyptic and eschatological regarding divine judgment, the Day of the Lord, which is symbolized by a ravaging invasion of locusts, the judgment of the nations in the Valley of Josaphat, and the outpouring of the Spirit in the messianic era to come. Its message is that God will vindicate and save Israel, in view of the prayer and repentance of the people, and will punish their enemies. It was composed after the period of Nehemiah.

Amos: Consists of an indictment against foreign enemies of Israel; a strong denunciation of the people of Israel, whose infidelity, idolatry and injustice made them subject to divine judgment and punishment; and a messianic oracle regarding Israel's restoration. Amos prophesied in the Northern Kingdom of Israel, at Bethel, in the first half of the eighth century; chronologically, he was the first of the canonical prophets.

Obadiah: A 21-verse prophecy, the shortest and one of the sternest in the Bible, against the Edomites, invaders of southern Judah and enemies of those returning from the Exile to their homeland. It was redacted in final form no later than the end of the fourth century.

Jonah: A parable of divine mercy with the theme that Yahweh wills the salvation of all, not just a few, men who respond to his call. Its protagonist is a disobedient prophet; forced by circumstances beyond his control to preach penance among Gentiles, he is highly successful in his mission but baffled by the divine concern for those who do not belong to the Chosen People. It was written after the Exile.

Micah: Attacks the injustice and corruption of priests, false prophets, officials and people; announces judgment and punishment to come; foretells the restoration of Israel; refers to the saving remnant of Israel. Micah was a contemporary of Isaiah.

Nahum: Dating from about 613, concerns the destruction of Nineveh in 612 and the overthrow of the Assyrian Empire by the Babylonians.

Habakkuk: Dating from about 605-597, concerns sufferings to be inflicted by oppressors on the people of Judah because of their infidelity to the Lord. It also sounds a note of confidence in the Lord, the Savior, and declares that the just will not perish.

Zephaniah: Exercising his ministry in the second half of the seventh century, during a time of widespread idolatry, superstition and religious degradation, he prophesied impending judgment and punishment for Jerusalem and its people. He prophesied too that a holy remnant of the people (Anawim, mentioned also by Amos) would be spared. Zephaniah was a forerunner of Jeremiah.

Haggai: One of the first prophets after the Exile, Haggai in 520 encouraged the returning exiles to reestablish their community and to complete the second Temple (dedicated in 515), for which he envisioned greater glory, in a messianic sense, than that enjoyed by the original Temple of Solomon.

Zechariah: A contemporary of Haggai, he prophesied in the same vein. A second part of the book, called Deutero-Zechariah and composed by one or more unknown authors, relates a vision of the coming of the Prince of Peace, the Messiah of the Poor.

Malachi: Written by an anonymous author, presents a picture of life in the post-Exilic community between 516 and the initiation of reforms by Ezra and Nehemiah about 432. Blame for the troubles of the community is placed mainly on priests for failure to carry out ritual worship and to instruct the people in the proper manner; other factors were religious indifference and the influence of doubters who were scandalized at the prosperity of the wicked. The vision of a universal sacrifice to be offered to Yahweh (1:11) is interpreted in Christian theology as a prophecy of the sacrifice of the Mass. Malachi was the last of the minor prophets.

OLD TESTAMENT DATES

c. 1800 — c. 1600: Period of the patriarchs (Abraham, Isaac, Jacob).

c. 1600: Israelites in Egypt.

c. 1250: Exodus of Israelites from Egypt.

c. 1210: Entrance of Israelites into Canaan.

c. 1210 — c. 1020: Period of the Judges.

c. 1020 — c. 1000: Reign of Saul, first king.

c. 1000 — c. 961: Reign of David.

c. 961 — 922: Reign of Solomon. Temple built during his reign.

922: Division of the Kingdom into Israel (North) and Judah (South).

721: Conquest of Israel by Assyrians.

587-538: Conquest of Judah by Babylonians. Babylonian Captivity and Exile. Destruction of Jerusalem and the Temple, 587. Captivity ended with the return of exiles, following the decree of Cyrus permitting the rebuilding of Jerusalem.

515: Dedication of the Second Temple.

458-397: Restoration and reform of the Jewish religious and political community; building of the Jerusalem wall, 439. Leaders in the movement were Ezra and Nehemiah.

168-142: Period of the Maccabees; war against Syrians.

142: Independence granted to Jews by Demetrius II of Syria.

135-37: Period of the Hasmonean dynasty.

63: Beginning of Roman rule.

37-4: Period of Herod the Great.

New Testament Books

Gospels

The term Gospel is derived from the Anglo-Saxon *god-spell* and the Greek *euangelion*, meaning good news, good tidings. In Christian use, it means the good news of salvation proclaimed by Christ and the Church, and handed on in written form in the Gospels of Matthew, Mark, Luke and John.

The initial proclamation of the coming of the kingdom of God was made by Jesus in and through his Person, teachings and actions, and especially through his Passion, death and resurrection. This proclamation became the center of Christian faith and the core of the oral Gospel tradition with which the Church spread the good news by apostolic preaching for some 30 years before it was committed to writing by the Evangelists.

According to an Instruction issued by the Pontifical Commission for Biblical Studies Apr. 21, 1964:

• The sacred writers selected from the material at their disposal (the oral Gospel tradition, some written collections of sayings and deeds of Jesus, eyewitness accounts) those things which were particularly suitable to the various conditions (liturgical, catechetical, missionary) of the faithful and the aims they had in mind, and they narrated these things in such a way as to correspond with those circumstances and their aims.

• The life and teaching of Jesus were not simply reported in a biographical manner for the purpose of preserving their memory but were "preached" so as to offer the Church the basis of doctrine concerning faith and morals.

• In their works, the Evangelists presented the true sayings of Jesus and the events of his life in the light of the better understanding they had following their enlightenment by the Holy Spirit. They did not transform Christ into a "mythical" Person, nor did they distort his teaching.

Passion narratives are the core of all the Gospels, covering the suffering, death and resurrection of Jesus as central events in bringing about and establishing the New Covenant. Leading up to them are accounts of the mission of John the Baptizer and the ministry of Jesus, especially in Galilee and finally in Jerusalem before the Passion. The infancy of Jesus is covered by Luke and Matthew with narratives inspired by Old Testament citations appropriate to the birth of the Messiah.

Matthew, Mark and Luke, while different in various respects, have so many similarities that they are called Synoptic; their relationships are the subject of the Synoptic Problem.

Matthew: Written in the 70's or 80's for Jewish Christians, with clear reference to Jewish background and identification of Jesus as the divine Messiah, the fulfillment of the Old Testament. Distinctive are the use of Old Testament citations regarding the Person, activity and teaching of Jesus, and the presentation of doctrine in sermons and discourses. The canonical Matthew was written in Greek, with dependence on Mark.

Mark: The first of the Gospels, dating from about 65. Written for Gentile Christians, it is noted for the realism and wealth of concrete details with which it reveals Jesus as Son of God and Savior more by his actions and miracles than by his discourses. Theologically, it is less refined than the other Gospels.

Luke: Written in the 70's or 80's for Gentile Christians. It is noted for the universality of its address, the insight it provides into the Christian way of life, the place it gives to women, the manner in which it emphasizes Jesus' friendship with sinners and compassion for the suffering.

John: Written sometime in the 90's, is the most sublime and theological of the Gospels, and is different from the Synoptics in plan and treatment. Combining accounts of signs with longer discourses and reflections, it progressively reveals the Person and mission of Jesus — as Word, Way, Truth, Life, Light — in line with the purpose, "to help you believe that Jesus is the Messiah, the Son of God, so that through this faith you may have life in his name" (Jn. 20:31). There are questions about the authorship but no doubt about the Johannine tradition behind the Gospel.

Acts of the Apostles

Acts of the Apostles: Written by Luke in the 70's or 80's as a supplement to his Gospel. It describes the origin and spread of Christian communities through the action of the Holy Spirit from the resurrection of Christ to the time of Paul's first Roman imprisonment in the early 60's.

Letters (Epistles)

These letters, the first documents of the New Testament, were written in response to existential needs of the early Christian communities for doctrinal and moral instruction, disciplinary action, practical advice, and exhortation to true Christian living.

Pauline Letters

These letters, which comprise approximately one-fourth of the New Testament, are primary and monumental sources of the development of Christian theology. Several of them may not have had Paul as their actual author, but evidence of the Pauline tradition behind them is strong. The letters to the Colossians, Philippians, Ephesians and Philemon have been called the "Captivity Letters" because of a tradition that they were written while Paul was under house arrest in Rome from 61 to 63.

Romans: Written in the late 50's from

The Bible

Corinth on the central significance of Christ and faith in him for salvation, and the relationship of Christianity to Judaism; the condition of mankind without Christ; justification and the Christian life; duties of Christians.

Corinthians 1: Written near the beginning of 57 from Ephesus to counteract factionalism and disorders, it covers community dissensions, moral irregularities, marriage and celibacy, conduct at religious gatherings, the Eucharist, spiritual gifts (charisms) and their function in the Church, charity, the resurrection of the body.

Corinthians 2: Written later in the same year as 1 Cor., concerning Paul's defense of his apostolic life and ministry, and an appeal for a collection to aid poor Christians in Jerusalem.

Galatians: Written probably between 54 and 57 (perhaps earlier, according to some scholars) to counteract Judaizing opinions and efforts to undermine his authority, it asserts the divine origin of Paul's authority and doctrine, states that justification is not through Mosaic Law but through faith in Christ, insists on the practice of evangelical virtues, especially charity.

Ephesians: Written probably between 61 and 63, or perhaps in the 70's, mainly on the Church as the Mystical Body of Christ.

Philippians: Written between 61 and 63 primarily to thank the Philippians for their kindness to him while he was under house arrest in Rome.

Colossians: Written while he was under house arrest in Rome from 61 to 63 to counteract the influence of self-appointed teachers who were watering down doctrine concerning Christ. It includes two highly important Christological passages, a warning against false teachers, and an instruction on the ideal Christian life.

Thessalonians 1 and 2: Written within a short time of each other probably in 51 from Corinth, mainly on doctrine concerning the Parousia, the second coming of Christ.

Timothy 1 and 2, Titus: Written between 65 and 67, or perhaps in the 70's, giving pastoral counsels to Timothy and Titus who were in charge of churches in Ephesus and Crete, respectively. 1 Tm. emphasizes pastoral responsibility for preserving unity of doctrine; 2 Tm. describes Paul's imprisonment in Rome.

Philemon: A private letter written between 61 and 63 to a wealthy Colossian concerning a slave, Onesimus, who had escaped from him; Paul appealed for kind treatment of the man.

Hebrews: Dating from some time between the mid-60's and the 80's, a complex theological treatise on Christology, the priesthood and sacrifice of Christ, the New Covenant, and the pattern for Christian living. Critical opinion is divided as to whether it was addressed to Judaeo or Gentile Christians.

Catholic Letters, Revelation

These seven letters have been called "catholic" because it was thought for some time, not altogether correctly, that they were not addressed to particular communities.

James: Written sometime between the mid-60's and the 80's (although datable before 62 according to some scholars) in the spirit of Hebrew wisdom literature and the moralism of Tobit. An exhortation to practical Christian living, it is also noteworthy for the doctrine it states on good works and its citation regarding anointing of the sick.

Peter 1 and 2: The first letter may have been written in the mid-60's; the second dates from 100 to 125. Addressed to Christians in Asia Minor, both are exhortations to perseverance in the life of faith despite trials and difficulties arising from pagan influences, isolation from other Christians, and false teaching.

John 1: Written sometime in the 90's and addressed to Asian churches, its message is that God is made known to us in the Son and that fellowship with the Father is attained by living in the light, justice and love of the Son.

John 2: Written sometime in the 90's and addressed to a church in Asia, it commends the people for standing firm in the faith and urges them to perseverance.

John 3: Written sometime in the 90's, it appears to represent an effort to settle a jurisdictional dispute in one of the churches.

Jude: Written sometime between the 70's and 90's, it is a brief treatise against erroneous teachings and practices opposed to law, authority and true Christian freedom.

Revelation: Written in the 90's along the lines of Johannine thought, it is a symbolic and apocalyptic treatment of things to come combined with warning but hope and assurance to the Church regarding the coming of the Lord in glory.

BIBLICAL AUTHORSHIP

Some books of the Bible were not written by the authors to whom they have been traditionally attributed; New Testament examples are the Gospels of Matthew and John, Hebrews, 1 and 2 Timothy, Titus, James, Jude.

This fact, which has never been the subject of dogmatic definition by the Church, does not militate against the canonicity of the books, since canonicity concerns the theological matter of inspiration rather than the historical question of human authorship.

Questions concerning authorship are explained in various ways: (1) according to an old custom whereby literary works of importance were sometimes attributed to famous persons so they would get a reading; (2) authorship, by a disciple or school of disciples, of works derived from the doctrine of a master; (3) authorship by persons writing in the spirit and tradition of a master.

INTERPRETATION OF THE BIBLE

According to the *Constitution on Revelation* issued by the Second Vatican Council, "the interpreter of Sacred Scripture, in order to see clearly what God wanted to communicate to us, should carefully investigate what meaning the sacred writers really intended, and what God wanted to manifest by means of their words" (No. 12).

Hermeneutics, Exegesis

This careful investigation proceeds in accordance with the rules of hermeneutics, the normative science of biblical interpretation and explanation. Hermeneutics in practice is called exegesis.

The principles of hermeneutics are derived from various disciplines and many factors which have to be considered in explaining the Bible and its parts. These include: the original languages and languages of translation of the sacred texts, through philology and linguistics; the quality of texts, through textual criticism; literary forms and genres, through literary and form criticism; cultural, historical, geographical and other conditions which influenced the writers, through related studies; facts and truths of salvation history; the truths and analogy of faith.

Distinctive to biblical hermeneutics, which differs in important respects from literary interpretation in general, is the premise that the Bible, though written by human authors, is the work of divine inspiration in which God reveals his plan for the salvation of men through historical events and persons, and especially through the Person and mission of Christ.

Textual, Form Criticism

Textual criticism is the study of biblical texts, which have been transmitted in copies several times removed from the original manuscripts, for the purpose of establishing the real state of the original texts. This purpose is served by comparison of existing copies; by application to the texts of the disciplines of philology and linguistics; by examination of related works of antiquity; by study of biblical citations in works of the Fathers of the Church and other authors; and by other means of literary study.

Since about 1920, the sayings of Christ have been a particular object of New Testament study, the purpose being to analyze the forms of expression used by the Evangelists in order to ascertain the words actually spoken by him.

Literary Criticism

Literary criticism aims to determine the origin and kinds of literary composition, called forms or genres, employed by the inspired authors. Such determinations are necessary for decision regarding the nature and purpose and, consequently, the meaning of biblical passages. Underlying these studies is the principle that the manner of writing was conditioned by the intention of the authors, the meaning they wanted to convey, and the then-contemporary literary style, mode or medium best adapted to carry their message — e.g., true history, quasi-historical narrative, poems, prayers, hymns, psalms, aphorisms, allegories, discourses. Understanding these media is necessary for the valid interpretation of their message.

Literal Sense

The key to all valid interpretation is the literal sense of biblical passages. Regarding this matter and the relevance to it of the studies and procedures described above, Pius XII wrote the following in the encyclical *Divino Afflante Spiritu*.

"What the literal sense of a passage is, is not always as obvious in the speeches and writings of ancient authors of the East as it is in the works of our own time. For what they wished to express is not to be determined by the rules of grammar and philology alone nor solely by the context; the interpreter must, as it were, go back wholly in spirit to those remote centuries of the East and with the aid of history, archeology, ethnology, and other sciences accurately determine what modes of writing, so to speak, the authors of that ancient period would be likely to use and in fact did use. . . . In explaining the Sacred Scripture and in demonstrating and proving its immunity from all error (the Catholic interpreter) should make a prudent use of this means, determine to what extent the manner of expression or literary mode adopted by the sacred writer may lead to a correct and genuine interpretation; and let him be convinced that this part of his office cannot be neglected without serious detriment to Catholic exegesis."

The literal sense of the Bible is the meaning in the mind of and intended by the inspired writer of a book or passage of the Bible. This is determined by the application to texts of the rules of hermeneutics. It is not to be confused with word-for-word literalism.

Typical Sense

The typical sense is the meaning which a passage has not only in itself but also in reference to something else of which it is a type or foreshadowing. A clear example is the account of the Exodus of the Israelites: in its literal sense, it narrates the liberation of the Israelites from death and oppression in Egypt; in its typical sense, it foreshadowed the liberation of men from sin through the redemptive death and resurrection of Christ. The typical sense of this and other passages emerged in the working out of God's plan of salvation history. It did not have to be in the mind of the author of the original passage.

Accommodated Senses

Accommodated, allegorical and consequent senses are figurative and adaptive meanings given to books and passages of the Bible for moral and other purposes. Such interpretations involve the danger of stretching the literal sense beyond proper proportions. Hermeneutical principles require that interpretations like these respect the integrity of the literal sense of the passages in question.

In the Catholic view, the final word on questions of biblical interpretation belongs to the teaching authority of the Church. In other views, generally derived from basic principles stated by Martin Luther, John Calvin and other Reformers, the primacy belongs to individual judgment acting in response to the inner testimony of the Holy Spirit, the edifying nature of biblical subject matter, the sublimity and simplicity of the message of salvation, the intensity with which Christ is proclaimed.

Biblical Studies

The first center for biblical studies, in some strict sense of the term, was the School of Alexandria, founded in the latter half of the second century. It was noted for allegorical exegesis. Literal interpretation was a hallmark of the School of Antioch.

St. Jerome, who produced the Vulgate, and St. Augustine, author of numerous commentaries, were the most important figures in biblical studies during the patristic period. By the time of the latter's death, the Old and New Testament canons had been stabilized. For some centuries afterwards, there was little or no progress in scriptural studies, although collections were made of scriptural excerpts from the writings of the Fathers of the Church, and the systematic reading of Scripture became established as a feature of monastic life.

Advances were made in the 12th and 13th centuries with the introduction of new principles and methods of scriptural analysis stemming from renewed interest in Hebraic studies and the application of dialectics.

By the time of the Reformation, the Bible had become the first book set in movable type, and more than 100 vernacular editions were in use throughout Europe.

The Council of Trent

In the wake of the Reformation, the Council of Trent formally defined the Canon of the Bible; it also reasserted the authoritative role of tradition and the teaching authority of the Church as well as Scripture with respect to the rule of faith. In the heated atmosphere of the 16th and 17th centuries, the Bible was turned into a polemical weapon; Protestants used it to defend their doctrines, and Catholics countered with citations in support of the dogmas of the Church. One result of this state of affairs was a lack of substantial progress in biblical studies during the period.

Toward the end of the 17th century, Louis Cappel, a Protestant, introduced a methodology for textual criticism, and Richard Simon, a Catholic, inaugurated modern literary and historical criticism. Their work was poorly regarded, however, and went into eclipse until about the beginning of the 19th century. It was then taken over by men whose work threatened to destroy the credibility of not only the Bible but Christianity itself.

Rationalists, and later Modernists, denied the reality of the supernatural and doctrine concerning inspiration of the Bible, which they generally regarded as a strictly human production expressive of the religious sense and experience of mankind. In their hands, the tools of positive critical research became weapons for biblical subversion. The defensive Catholic reaction to their work had the temporary effect of alienating scholars of the Church from solid advances in archeology, philology, history, textual and literary criticism.

Catholic Developments

Major influences in bringing about a change in Catholic attitude toward use of these disciplines in biblical studies were two papal encyclicals and two institutes of special study, the Ecole Biblique, founded in Jerusalem in 1890, and the Pontifical Biblical Institute established in Rome in 1909. The encyclical *Providentissimus Deus,* issued by Leo XIII in 1893, marked an important breakthrough; in addition to defending the concept of divine inspiration and the formal inspiration of the Scriptures, it encouraged the study of allied and ancillary sciences and techniques for a more fruitful understanding of the sacred writings. The encyclical *Divino Afflante Spiritu,* 50 years later, gave encouragement for the use of various forms of criticism as tools of biblical research. The documents encouraged the work of scholars and stimulated wide communication of the fruits of their study.

Great changes in the climate and direction of biblical studies have occurred in recent years. One of them has been an increase in cooperative effort among Catholic, Protestant, Orthodox and Jewish scholars. Their common investigation of the Dead Sea Scrolls is well known. More recently productive was the collaboration in England of Catholics and Protestants in turning out a Catholic edition of the Revised Standard Version of the Bible.

The development and results of biblical studies in this century have directly and significantly affected all phases of the contemporary renewal movement in the Church. Their influence on theology, liturgy, catechetics, and preaching indicate the importance of their function in the life of the Church.

BIBLICAL COMMISSION

The Pontifical Biblical Commission, which has been instrumental in directing the course of Catholic biblical scholarship, was established by Leo XIII Oct. 30, 1902, with the apostolic letter *Vigilantiae Studiique,* at a time when biblical studies were open to great promise as well as to the serious threat of Modernism.

The commission was ordered to promote biblical studies; to safeguard the correct interpretation of Scripture, in the pattern of the rule of faith and against the background of sound scholarship; to state positions which had to be held by Catholics on biblical questions; to indicate questions requiring further study and/or those which were open to the judgment of competent scholars. The commission was also authorized — by St. Pius X in 1904, Pius XI in 1924 and 1931, and Pius XII in 1942 — to set up standards for biblical studies and to grant degrees in Sacred Scripture.

The commission issued 23 decrees or decisions between 1905 and 1953; letters on the scientific study of the Bible (1941) and the Pentateuch (1948); instructions on teaching Scripture in seminaries (1950), biblical associations (1955), and the historical truth of the Gospels (1964).

Pope St. Pius X stated the authority of decisions of the commission in the letter *Illibatae,* which he issued June 29, 1910, on his own initiative:

"All are bound in conscience to submit to the decisions of the Pontifical Biblical Commission pertaining to doctrine, whether already issued or to be issued in the future, in the same way as to the decrees of the Sacred Congregations (of the Roman Curia) approved by the Pontiff; nor can they avoid the stigma both of disobedience and temerity or be free from grave sin who by any spoken or written words impugn these decisions."

Decisions of the commission regarding points of doctrine are not infallible of themselves. They require religious assent, however, so long as there is no positive evidence that they are wrong. They do not close the door to continuing investigation and study.

The commission was reorganized June 27, 1971, in line with directives issued by Paul VI on his own initiative under the title *Sedula Cura.*

Fifteen new norms changed its structure from a virtually independent office of cardinals aided by lifetime consultors into a group of 20 biblical scholars with five-year terms (renewable) linked with the Congregation for the Doctrine of the Faith. Functionally, however, it remains the same.

The commission:
• receives questions and study topics referred to it by a variety of sources, from the pope to Catholic universities and biblical associations;
• is required to meet in plenary session at least once a year and to submit conclusions reached in such meetings to the pope and the Congregation for the Doctrine of the Faith;
• is under directive to promote relationships with non-Catholic as well as Catholic institutes of biblical studies;
• is to be consulted before any new norms on biblical matters are issued;
• retains its authorization to confer academic degrees in biblical studies.

Membership

Cardinal Franjo Seper, prefect of the Congregation for the Doctrine of the Faith, is president of the commission; Albert Descamps, titular bishop of Tunes, is the secretary. The other members, as reported in the 1979 edition of *Annuario Pontificio,* are as follows.

Jose Alonso-Diaz, S.J.; Jean-Dominique Barthelemy, O.P.; Pierre Benoit, O.P.; Raymond Brown, S.S. (who was succeeded on the expiration of his term in April, 1979, by Jerome D. Quinn of St. Paul, Minn.); Henri Cazelles, S.S.; Alfons Deissler; Ignace de la Potterie, S.J.; Jacques Dupont, O.S.B.; Salvator Garofalo; Joachim Gnilka; Pierre Grelot; Alexander Kerrigan, O.F.M.; Lucien Legrand, M.E.P.; Stanislas Lyonnet, S.J.; Carlo M. Martini, S.J.; Antonio Moreno Casamitjana; Ceslas Spicq, O.P.; Benjamin Wambacq, O.Praem.

1979 Meeting

The commission, meeting at the Vatican Apr. 23 to 27, 1979, initiated a study of acculturation in the Old and New Testaments. It is up to biblical science, Pope John Paul told the members from 13 countries, "to establish the distinction" between what is culturally conditioned (language, manner of expression, historical circumstances) "and what must always retain its value" (truth relating to salvation) in the words and events used to communicate divine revelation in the Bible.

Also during the meeting, the Pope formally promulgated the New Vulgate edition of the Bible, produced over a 13-year period by the Pontifical Commission for the New Vulgate.

Pope John Paul, in an address Oct. 26, 1979, to members of the International Theological Commission, defended the need for theologians to deepen their understanding of the truths of faith and to re-explain them in contemporary language. He said: "The study of theologians is not circumscribed . . . to the mere repetition of dogmatic formulas but must see to it that such study helps the Church to an ever-deepening awareness of the mystery of Christ."

APOSTLES AND EVANGELISTS

The Apostles were the men selected, trained and commissioned by Christ to preach the Gospel, to baptize, to establish, direct and care for his Church as servants of God and stewards of his mysteries. They were the first bishops of the Church.

St. Matthew's Gospel lists the Apostles in this order: Peter, Andrew, James the Greater, John, Philip, Bartholomew, Thomas, Matthew, James the Less, Jude, Simon and Judas Iscariot. Matthias was elected to fill the place of Judas. Paul became an Apostle by a special call from Christ. Barnabas was called an Apostle.

Two of the Evangelists, John and Matthew, were Apostles. The other two, Luke and Mark, were closely associated with the apostolic college.

Andrew: Born in Bethsaida, brother of Peter, disciple of John the Baptist, a fisherman, the first Apostle called; according to legend, preached the Gospel in Northern Greece, Epirus and Scythia, and was martyred at Patras about 70; in art, is represented with an x-shaped cross, called St. Andrew's Cross; feast, Nov. 30; is honored as the patron of Russia and Scotland.

Barnabas: Originally called Joseph but named Barnabas by the Apostles, among whom he is ranked because of his collaboration with Paul; a Jew of the Diaspora, born on Cyprus; a cousin of Mark and member of the Christian community at Jerusalem, influenced the Apostles to accept Paul, with whom he became a pioneer missionary outside Palestine and Syria, to Antioch, Cyprus and southern Asia Minor; legend says he was martyred on Cyprus during the Neronian persecution; feast, June 11.

Bartholomew (Nathaniel): A friend of Philip; according to various traditions, preached the Gospel in Ethiopia, India, Persia, and Armenia where he was martyred by being flayed and beheaded; in art, is depicted holding a knife, an instrument of his death; feast, Aug. 24 in the Roman Rite, Aug. 25 in the Byzantine Rite.

James the Greater: A Galilean, son of Zebedee, brother of John (with whom he was called a "son of thunder"), a fisherman; with Peter and John, witnessed the raising of Jairus' daughter to life, the transfiguration, the agony of Jesus in the Garden of Gethsemani; first of the Apostles to die, by the sword in 44 during the rule of Herod Agrippa; there is doubt about a journey legend says he made to Spain and also about the authenticity of relics said to be his at Santiago de Compostela; in art, is depicted carrying a pilgrim's bell; feast, July 25 in the Roman Rite, Apr. 30 in the Byzantine Rite.

James the Less: Son of Alphaeus, called "Less" because he was younger in age or shorter in stature than James the Greater; one of the "catholic" epistles bears his name; was stoned to death in 62 or thrown from the top of the temple in Jerusalem and clubbed to death in 66; in art, is depicted with a club or heavy staff; feast, May 3 in the Roman Rite, Oct. 9 in the Byzantine Rite.

John: A Galilean, son of Zebedee, brother of James the Greater (with whom he was called a "son of thunder"), a fisherman, probably a disciple of John the Baptist, one of the Evangelists, called the "beloved disciple"; with Peter and James the Greater, witnessed the raising of Jairus' daughter to life, the transfiguration, the agony of Jesus in the Garden of Gethsemani; Mary was commended to his special care by Christ; the fourth Gospel, three "catholic" Epistles and Revelation bear his name; according to various accounts, lived at Ephesus in Asia Minor for some time and died a natural death about 100; in art, is represented by an eagle, symbolic of the sublimity of the contents of his Gospel; feast, Dec. 27 in the Roman Rite, May 8 in the Byzantine Rite.

Jude Thaddeus: One of the "catholic" epistles, the shortest, bears his name; various traditions say he preached the Gospel in Mesopotamia, Persia and elsewhere, and was martyred; in art, is depicted with a halberd, the instrument of his death; feast, Oct. 28 in the Roman Rite, June 19 in the Byzantine Rite.

Luke: A Greek convert to the Christian community, called "our most dear physician" by Paul, of whom he was a missionary companion; author of the third Gospel and Acts of the Apostles; the place — Achaia, Bithynia, Egypt — and circumstances of his death are not certain; in art, is depicted as a man, a writer, or an ox (because his Gospel starts at the scene of Temple sacrifice); feast, Oct. 18.

Mark: A cousin of Barnabas and member of the first Christian community at Jerusalem; a missionary companion of Paul and Barnabas, then of Peter; author of the Gospel which bears his name; according to legend, founded the Church at Alexandria, was bishop there and was martyred in the streets of the city; in art, is depicted with his Gospel and a winged lion, symbolic of the voice of John the Baptist crying in the wilderness, at the beginning of his Gospel; feast, Apr. 25.

Matthew: A Galilean, called Levi by Luke and John and the son of Alphaeus by Mark, a tax collector, one of the Evangelists; according to various accounts, preached the Gospel in Judea, Ethiopia, Persia and Parthia, and was martyred; in art, is depicted with a spear, the instrument of his death, and as a winged man in his role as Evangelist; feast, Sept. 21 in the Roman Rite, Nov. 16 in the Byzantine Rite.

Matthias: A disciple of Jesus whom the faithful 11 Apostles chose to replace Judas before the Resurrection; uncertain traditions report that he preached the Gospel in Palestine, Cappadocia or Ethiopia; in art, is represented with a cross and a halberd, the instruments of his death as a martyr; feast, May 14 in the Roman Rite, Aug. 9 in the Byzantine Rite.

Paul: Born at Tarsus, of the tribe of Benjamin, a Roman citizen; participated in the persecution of Christians until the time of his miraculous conversion on the way to Damascus; called by Christ, who revealed himself to him in a special way; became the Apostle of the Gentiles, among whom he did most of his preaching in the course of three major missionary journeys through areas north of Palestine, Cyprus, Asia Minor and Greece; 14 epistles bear his name; two years of imprisonment at Rome, following initial arrest in Jerusalem and confinement at Caesarea, ended with martyrdom, by beheading, outside the walls of the city in 64 or 67 during the Neronian persecution; in art, is depicted in various ways with St. Peter, with a sword, in the scene of his conversion; feasts, June 29, Jan. 25 (Roman Rite).

Peter: Simon, son of Jona, born in Bethsaida, brother of Andrew, a fisherman; called Cephas or Peter by Christ who made him the chief of the Apostles and head of the Church as his vicar; named first in the listings of Apostles in the Synoptic Gospels and the Acts of the Apostles; with James the Greater and John, witnessed the raising of Jairus' daughter to life, the transfiguration, the agony of Jesus in the Garden of Gethsemani; was the first to preach the Gospel in and around Jerusalem and was the leader of the first Christian community there; established a local Church in Antioch; presided over the Council of Jerusalem in 51; wrote two "catholic" epistles to the Christians in Asia Minor; established his see in Rome where he spent his last years and was martyred by crucifixion in 64 or 65 during the Neronian persecution; in art, is depicted carrying two keys, symbolic of his primacy in the Church; feasts, June 29, Feb. 22 (Roman Rite).

Philip: Born in Bethsaida; according to legend, preached the Gospel in Phrygia where he suffered martyrdom by crucifixion; feast, May 3 in the Roman Rite, Nov. 14 in the Byzantine Rite.

Simon: Called the Cananean or the Zealot; according to legend, preached in various places in the Near East and suffered martyrdom by being sawed in two; in art, is depicted with a saw, the instrument of his death, or a book, symbolic of his zeal for the Law; feast, Oct. 28 in the Roman Rite, May 10 in the Byzantine Rite.

Thomas (Didymus): Notable for his initial incredulity regarding the Resurrection and his subsequent forthright confession of the divinity of Christ risen from the dead; according to legend, preached the Gospel in places from the Caspian Sea to the Persian Gulf and eventually reached India where he was martyred near Madras; Thomas Christians trace their origin to him; in art, is depicted kneeling before the risen Christ, or with a carpenter's rule and square; feast, July 3 in the Roman Rite, Oct. 6 in the Byzantine Rite.

JUDAS

The Gospels record only a few facts about Judas, the Apostle who betrayed Christ.

The only non-Galilean among the Apostles, he was from Carioth, a town in southern Juda. He was keeper of the purse in the apostolic band. He was called a petty thief by John. He voiced dismay at the waste of money, which he said might have been spent for the poor, in connection with the anointing incident at Bethany. He took the initiative in arranging the betrayal of Christ. Afterwards, he confessed that he had betrayed an innocent man and cast into the Temple the money he had received for that action. Of his death, Matthew says that he hanged himself; the Acts of the Apostles states that he swelled up and burst open; both reports deal more with the meaning than the manner of his death — the misery of the death of a sinner.

The consensus of speculation over the reason why Judas acted as he did in betraying Christ focuses on disillusionment and unwillingness to accept the concept of a suffering Messiah and personal suffering of his own as an Apostle.

APOSTOLIC FATHERS, FATHERS, DOCTORS OF THE CHURCH

The writers listed below, were outstanding and authoritative witnesses to authentic Christian belief and practice, and played significant roles in giving them expression.

Apostolic Fathers

The Apostolic Fathers were Christian writers of the first and second centuries who are known or believed to have had personal relations with the Apostles, and whose writings echo genuine apostolic teaching.

Chief in importance are: St. Clement (d.c. 97), bishop of Rome and third successor of St. Peter in the papacy; St. Ignatius (50-c. 107), bishop of Antioch and second successor of St. Peter in that see, reputed to be a disciple of St. John; St. Polycarp (69-155), bishop of Smyrna and a disciple of St. John. The authors of the *Didache* and the *Epistle of Barnabas* are also numbered among the Apostolic Fathers.

Other early ecclesiastical writers included: St. Justin, martyr (100-165), of Asia Minor and Rome, a layman and apologist; St. Irenaeus (130-202), bishop of Lyons, who opposed Gnosticism; and St. Cyprian (210-258), bishop of Carthage, who opposed Novatianism.

Fathers and Doctors

The Fathers of the Church were theologians and writers of the first eight centuries who were outstanding for sanctity and learning. They were such authoritative witnesses to the belief and teaching of the Church that their unanimous acceptance of doctrines as divinely revealed has been regarded as evidence that such doctrines were so received by the Church in line with apostolic tradition and Sacred Scripture. Their unanimous rejection of doctrines branded them as heretical. Their writings, however, were not necessarily free of error in all respects.

The greatest of these Fathers were: Sts. Ambrose, Augustine, Jerome and Gregory the Great in the West; Sts. John Chrysostom, Basil the Great, Gregory of Nazianzen and Athanasius in the East.

The Doctors of the Church were ecclesiastical writers of eminent learning and sanctity who have been given this title because of the great advantage the Church has derived from their work. These writings, however, were not necessarily free of error in all respects.

Albert the Great, St. (c. 1200-1280): Born in Swabia, Germany; Dominican; bishop of Regensburg (1260-1262); wrote extensively on logic, natural sciences, ethics, metaphysics, Scripture, systematic theology; contributed to development of Scholasticism; teacher of St. Thomas Aquinas; canonized and proclaimed doctor, 1931; named patron of natural scientists, 1941; called Doctor Universalis, Doctor Expertus; feast, Nov. 15.

Alphonsus Liguori, St. (1696-1787): Born near Naples, Italy; bishop of Agatha of the Goths (1762-1775); founder of the Redemptorists; in addition to his principal work, *Theologiae Moralis*, wrote on prayer, the spiritual life, and doctrinal subjects in response to controversy; canonized, 1839; proclaimed doctor, 1871; named patron of confessors and moralists, 1950; feast, Aug. 1.

Ambrose, St. (c. 340-397): Born in Treves, Germany; bishop of Milan (374-397); one of the strongest opponents of Arianism in the West; his homilies and other writings — on faith, the Holy Spirit, the Incarnation, the sacraments and other subjects — were pastoral and practical; influenced the development of a liturgy at Milan which was named for him; Father and Doctor of the Church; feast, Dec. 7.

Anselm, St. (1033-1109): Born in Aosta, Piedmont, Italy; Benedictine; archbishop of Canterbury (1093-1109); in addition to his principal work, *Cur Deus Homo*, on the atonement and reconciliation of man with God through Christ, wrote about the existence and attributes of God and defended the *Filioque* explanation of the procession of the Holy Spirit from the Father and the Son; canonized, 1494; proclaimed doctor, 1720; called Father of Scholasticism; feast, Apr. 21.

Anthony of Padua, St. (1195-1231): Born in Lisbon, Portugal; first theologian of the Franciscan Order; preacher; canonized, 1232; proclaimed doctor, 1946; called Evangelical Doctor; feast, June 13.

Athanasius, St. (c. 297-373): Born in Alexandria, Egypt; bishop of Alexandria (328-373); participant in the Council of Nicaea I while still a deacon; dominant opponent of Arians whose errors regarding Christ he refuted in *Apology against the Arians, Discourses against the Arians*, and other works; Father and Doctor of the Church; called Father of Orthodoxy; feast, May 2.

Augustine, St. (354-430): Born in Tagaste, North Africa; bishop of Hippo (395-430) after conversion from Manichaeism; works include the autobiographical and mystical *Confessions, City of God*, treatises on the Trinity, grace, passages of the Bible, and doctrines called into question and denied by Manichaeans, Pelagians and Donatists; had strong and lasting influence on Christian theology and philosophy; Father and Doctor of the Church; called Doctor of Grace; feast, Aug. 28.

Basil the Great, St. (c. 329-379): Born in Caesarea, Cappadocia, Asia Minor; bishop of Caesarea (370-379); wrote three books *Contra Eunomium* in refutation of Arian errors, a treatise on the Holy Spirit, many homilies, and several rules for monastic life, on which he had lasting influence; Father and Doctor of the Church; called Father of Monasticism in the East; feast, Jan. 2.

Bede the Venerable, St. (c. 673-735): Born in Northumberland, England; Benedictine; in addition to his principal work, *Ecclesiastical History of the English Nation* (covering the period 597-731), wrote scriptural commentaries; regarded as probably the most learned man in Western Europe of his time; called Father of English History; feast, May 25.

Bernard of Clairvaux, St. (c. 1090-1153): Born near Dijon, France; abbot; monastic reformer, called the second founder of the Cistercian Order; mystical theologian with great influence on devotional life; opponent of the rationalism brought forward by Abelard and others; canonized, 1174; proclaimed doctor, 1830; called Mellifluous Doctor because of his eloquence; feast, Aug. 20.

Bonaventure, St. (c. 1217-1274): Born near Viterbo, Italy; Franciscan; bishop of Albano (1273-1274); cardinal; wrote *Itinerarium Mentis in Deum, De Reductione Artium ad Theologiam, Breviloquium*, scriptural commentaries, additional mystical works affecting devotional life, and a life of St. Francis of Assisi; canonized, 1482; proclaimed doctor, 1588; called Seraphic Doctor; feast, July 15.

Catherine of Siena, St. (c. 1347-1380): Born in Siena, Italy; member of the Third Order of St. Dominic; mystic; authored a long series of letters, mainly concerning spiritual instruction and encouragement, to associates, and

Dialogue, a spiritual testament in four treatises; was active in support of a crusade against the Turks and efforts to end war between papal forces and the Florentine allies; had great influence in inducing Gregory XI to return himself and the Curia to Rome in 1376, to end the Avignon period of the papacy; canonized, 1461; proclaimed the second woman doctor, Oct. 4, 1970; feast, Apr. 29.

Cyril of Alexandria, St. (c. 376-444): Born in Egypt; bishop of Alexandria (412-444); wrote treatises on the Trinity, the Incarnation and other subjects, mostly in refutation of Nestorian errors; made key contributions to the development of Christology; presided at the Council of Ephesus, 431; proclaimed doctor, 1882; feast, June 27.

Cyril of Jerusalem, St. (c. 315-387): Bishop of Jerusalem (350-387); vigorous opponent of Arianism; principal work, *Catecheses,* a prebaptismal explanation of the creed of Jerusalem; proclaimed doctor, 1882; feast, Mar. 18.

Ephraem, St. (c. 306-373): Born in Nisibis, Mesopotamia; counteracted the spread of Gnostic and Arian errors with poems and hymns of his own composition; wrote also on the Eucharist and Mary; proclaimed doctor, 1920; called Deacon of Edessa and Harp of the Holy Spirit; feast, June 9.

Francis de Sales, St. (1567-1622): Born in Savoy; bishop of Geneva (1602-1622); spiritual writer with strong influence on devotional life through treatises such as *Introduction to a Devout Life,* and *The Love of God;* canonized, 1665; proclaimed doctor, 1877; patron of Catholic writers and the Catholic press; feast, Jan. 24.

Gregory Nazianzen, St. (c. 330-c. 390): Born in Arianzus, Cappadocia, Asia Minor; bishop of Constantinople (381-390); vigorous opponent of Arianism; in addition to five theological discourses on the Nicene Creed and the Trinity for which he is best known, wrote letters and poetry; Father and Doctor of the Church; called the Christian Demosthenes because of his eloquence and, in the Eastern Church, The Theologian; feast, Jan. 2.

Gregory I, the Great, St. (c. 540-604): Born in Rome; pope (590-604): wrote many scriptural commentaries, a compendium of theology in the *Book of Morals* based on Job, *Dialogues* concerning the lives of saints, the immortality of the soul, death, purgatory, heaven and hell, and 14 books of letters; enforced papal supremacy and established the position of the pope vis-a-vis the emperor; worked for clerical and monastic reform and the observance of clerical celibacy; Father and Doctor of the Church; feast, Sept. 3.

Hilary of Poitiers, St. (c. 315-368): Born in Poitiers, France; bishop of Poitiers (c. 353-368); wrote *De Synodis,* with the Arian controversy in mind, and *De Trinitate,* the first lengthy study of the doctrine in Latin; introduced Eastern theology to the West; contributed to the development of hymnology; proclaimed doctor, 1851; called the Athanasius of the West because of his vigorous defense of the divinity of Christ against Arians; feast, Jan. 13.

Isidore of Seville, St. (c. 560-636): Born in Cartagena, Spain; bishop of Seville (c. 600-636); in addition to his principal work, *Etymologiae,* an encyclopedia of the knowledge of his day, wrote on theological and historical subjects; regarded as the most learned man of his time; proclaimed doctor, 1722; feast, Apr. 4.

Jerome, St. (c. 343-420): Born in Stridon, Dalmatia; translated the Old Testament from Hebrew into Latin and revised the existing Latin translation of the New Testament to produce the Vulgate version of the Bible; wrote scriptural commentaries and treatises on matters of controversy; regarded as Father and Doctor of the Church from the eighth century; called Father of Biblical Science; feast, Sept. 30.

John Chrysostom, St. (c. 347-407): Born in Antioch, Asia Minor; archbishop of Constantinople (398-407); wrote homilies, scriptural commentaries and letters of wide influence in addition to a classical treatise on the priesthood; proclaimed doctor by the Council of Chalcedon, 451; called the greatest of the Greek Fathers; named patron of preachers, 1909; called golden-mouthed because of his eloquence; feast, Sept. 13.

John Damascene, St. (c. 675-c. 749): Born in Damascus, Syria; monk; wrote *Fountain of Wisdom,* a three-part work including a history of heresies and an exposition of the Christian faith, three *Discourses against the Iconoclasts,* homilies on Mary, biblical commentaries and treatises on moral subjects; proclaimed doctor, 1890; called Golden Speaker because of his eloquence; feast, Dec. 4.

John of the Cross, St. (1542-1591): Born in Old Castile, Spain; Carmelite; founder of Discalced Carmelites; one of the greatest mystical theologians, wrote *The Ascent of Mt. Carmel — The Dark Night, The Spiritual Canticle, The Living Flame of Love;* canonized, 1726; proclaimed doctor, 1926; called Doctor of Mystical Theology; feast, Dec. 14.

Lawrence of Brindisi, St. (1559-1619): Born in Brindisi, Italy; Franciscan (Capuchin); vigorous preacher of strong influence in the post-Reformation period; 15 tomes of collected works include scriptural commentaries, sermons, homilies and doctrinal writings; canonized, 1881; proclaimed doctor, 1959; feast, July 21.

Leo I, the Great, St. (c. 400-461): Born in Tuscany, Italy; pope (440-461); wrote the *Tome of Leo,* to explain doctrine concerning the two natures and one Person of Christ, against the background of the Nestorian and Monophysite heresies; other works included sermons, letters, and writings against the errors of Manichaeism and Pelagianism; was instrumental in dissuading Attila from sacking Rome in 452; proclaimed doctor, 1574; feast, Nov. 10.

Peter Canisius, St. (1521-1597): Born in Nijmegen, Holland; Jesuit; wrote popular expositions of the Catholic faith in several catechisms which were widely circulated in 20 editions in his lifetime alone; was one of the moving figures in the Counter-Reformation period, especially in southern and western Germany; canonized and proclaimed doctor, 1925; feast, Dec. 21.

Peter Chrysologus, St. (c. 400-450): Born in Imola, Italy; served as archbishop of Ravenna (c. 433-450); his sermons and writings, many of which were designed to counteract Monophysitism, were pastoral and practical; proclaimed doctor, 1729; feast, July 30.

Peter Damian, St. (1007-1072): Born in Ravenna, Italy; Benedictine; cardinal; his writings and sermons, many of which concerned ecclesiastical and clerical reform, were pastoral and practical; proclaimed doctor, 1828; feast, Feb. 21.

Robert Bellarmine, St. (1542-1621): Born in Tuscany, Italy; Jesuit; archbishop of Capua (1602-1605); wrote *Controversies*, a three-volume exposition of doctrine under attack during and after the Reformation, two catechisms and the spiritual work, *The Art of Dying Well*, was an authority on ecclesiology and Church-state relations; canonized, 1930; proclaimed doctor, 1931; feast, Sept. 17.

Theresa of Avila, St. (1515-1582): Born in Avila, Spain; entered the Carmelite Order, 1535; in the early 1560's, initiated a primitive Carmelite, discalced-Alcantarine reform which greatly influenced men and women religious, especially in Spain; wrote extensively on spiritual and mystical subjects; principal works included her *Autobiography, Way of Perfection, The Interior Castle, Meditations on the Canticle, The Foundations, Visitation of the Discalced Nuns;* canonized, 1614; proclaimed first woman doctor, Sept. 27, 1970; feast, Oct. 15.

Thomas Aquinas, St. (1225-1274): Born near Naples, Italy; Dominican; teacher and writer on virtually the whole range of philosophy and theology; principal works were *Summa contra Gentiles*, a manual and systematic defense of Christian doctrine, and *Summa Theologiae*, a new (at that time) exposition of theology on philosophical principles; canonized, 1323; proclaimed doctor, 1567; called Doctor Communis, Doctor Angelicus, the Great Synthesizer because of the way in which he related faith and reason, theology and philosophy (especially that of Aristotle), and systematized the presentation of Christian doctrine; named patron of Catholic schools and education, 1880; feast, Jan. 28.

CREEDS

Creeds are formal and official statements of Christian doctrine. As summaries of the principal truths of faith, they are standards of orthodoxy and are useful for instructional purposes, for actual profession of the faith, and for expression of the faith in the liturgy.

The classical creeds are the Apostles' Creed and the Creed of Nicaea-Constantinople. Two others are the Athanasian Creed and the Creed of Pius IV.

Apostles' Creed

Text: I believe in God, the Father almighty, Creator of heaven and earth.

And in Jesus Christ, his only Son, our Lord; who was conceived by the Holy Spirit, born of the Virgin Mary, suffered under Pontius Pilate, was crucified, died, and was buried. He descended into hell; the third day he arose again from the dead; he ascended into heaven, sits at the right hand of God, the Father almighty; from thence he shall come to judge the living and the dead.

I believe in the Holy Spirit, the holy Catholic Church, the communion of saints, the forgiveness of sins, the resurrection of the body, and life everlasting. Amen.

Background: The Apostles' Creed reflects the teaching of the Apostles but is not of apostolic origin. It probably originated in the second century as a rudimentary formula of faith professed by catechumens before the reception of baptism. Baptismal creeds in fourth-century use at Rome and elsewhere in the West closely resembled the present text, which was quoted in a handbook of Christian doctrine written between 710 and 724. This text was in wide use throughout the West by the ninth century. The Apostles' Creed is common to all Christian confessional churches in the West, but is not used in Eastern Churches.

Nicene Creed

The following translation of the Latin text of the creed was prepared by the International Committee on English in the Liturgy.

Text: We believe in one God, the Father, the Almighty, maker of heaven and earth, of all that is seen and unseen.

We believe in one Lord, Jesus Christ, the only Son of God, eternally begotten of the Father, God from God, Light from Light, true God from true God, begotten, not made, one in Being with the Father. Through him all things were made. For us men and for our salvation he came down from heaven: by the power of the Holy Spirit he was born of the Virgin Mary, and became man. For our sake he was crucified under Pontius Pilate; he suffered, died, and was buried. On the third day he rose again in fulfillment of the Scriptures; he ascended into heaven and is seated at the right hand of the Father. He will come again in glory to judge the living and the dead, and his kingdom will have no end.

We believe in the Holy Spirit, the Lord, the giver of life, who proceeds from the Father and the Son. With the Father and the Son he is worshiped and glorified. He has spoken through the prophets.

We believe in one holy catholic and apostolic Church. We acknowledge one baptism for the forgiveness of sins. We look for the resurrection of the dead, and the life of the world to come. Amen.

Background: The Nicene Creed (Creed of Nicaea-Constantinople) consists of elements of doctrine contained in an early baptismal creed of Jerusalem and enactments of the Council of Nicaea (325) and the Council of Constantinople (381). Its strong trinitarian content reflects the doctrinal errors, especially of Arianism, it served to counteract. Theologically, it is much more sophisticated than the Apostles' Creed. Since late in the fifth century, the Nicene Creed has been the only creed in liturgical use in the Eastern Churches. The Western Church adopted it for liturgical use by the end of the eighth century.

The Athanasian Creed

The Athanasian Creed, which has a unique structure, is a two-part summary of doctrine concerning the Trinity and the Incarnation-Redemption bracketed at the beginning and end with the statement that belief in the cited truths is necessary for salvation; it also contains a number of anathemas or condemnatory clauses regarding doctrinal errors. Although attributed to St. Athanasius, it was probably written after his death, between 381 and 428, and may have been authored by St. Ambrose. It is not accepted in the East; in the West, it has place in the liturgy of some other Christian churches as well as in the Roman-Rite Liturgy of the Hours and for the Solemnity of the Holy Trinity.

Creed of Pius IV

The Creed of Pius IV, also called the Profession of Faith of the Council of Trent, was promulgated in the bull *Injunctum Nobis*, Nov. 13, 1564. It is a summary of doctrine defined by the council concerning: Scripture and tradition, original sin and justification, the Mass and sacraments, veneration of the saints, indulgences, the primacy of the See of Rome. It was slightly modified in 1887 to include doctrinal formulations of the First Vatican Council.

REDDITIO OF CREED

The "giving back," by profession, of a baptismal creed by candidates for baptism to a bishop or his representative was one of the immediate preliminaries to reception of the sacrament at the conclusion of the catechumenate in the early Church.

The interrogation concerning truths of faith in the present baptismal rite is reminiscent of this ancient practice.

MORAL OBLIGATIONS

The basic norm of Christian morality is life in Christ. This involves, among other things, the observance of the Ten Commandments, their fulfillment in the twofold law of love of God and neighbor, the implications of the Sermon on the Mount and the whole New Testament, and membership in the Church established by Christ.

The Ten Commandments

The Ten Commandments, the Decalogue, were given by God through Moses to his Chosen People for the guidance of their moral conduct in accord with the demands of the Covenant he established with them as a divine gift. Their observance was essential to participation in the Covenant and the order of salvation based on it.

In the traditional Catholic enumeration and according to Dt. 5:6-21, the Commandments are:

1. "I, the Lord, am your God ... You shall not have other gods besides me. You shall not carve idols...."
2. "You shall not take the name of the Lord, your God, in vain...."
3. "Take care to keep holy the Sabbath day...."
4. "Honor your father and your mother...."
5. "You shall not kill."
6. "You shall not commit adultery."
7. "You shall not steal."
8. "You shall not bear dishonest witness against your neighbor."
9. "You shall not covet your neighbor's wife."
10. "You shall not desire your neighbor's house or field, nor his male or female slave, nor his ox or ass, nor anything that belongs to him" (summarily, his goods).

Another version of the Commandments, substantially the same, is given in Ex. 20:1-17.

The traditional enumeration of the Commandments in Protestant usage differs from the above. Thus: two commandments are made of the first, as above; the third and fourth are equivalent to the second and third, as above, and so on; and the 10th includes the ninth and 10th, as above.

Love of God and Neighbor

The first three of the commandments deal directly with man's relations with God, viz.: acknowledgment of one true God and the rejection of false gods and idols; honor due to God and his name; observance of the Sabbath as the Lord's day.

The rest cover interpersonal relationships, viz.: the obedience due to parents and, logically, to other persons in authority, and the obligations of parents to children and of persons in authority to those under their care; respect for life and physical integrity; fidelity in marriage, and chastity; justice and rights; truth; internal respect for faithfulness in marriage, chastity, and the goods of others.

Perfection in Christian Life

The moral obligations of the Ten Commandments are complemented by others flowing from the twofold law of love, the whole substance and pattern of Christ's teaching, and everything implied in full and active membership and participation in the community of salvation formed by Christ in his Church. Some of these matters are covered in other sections of the Almanac under appropriate headings.

Precepts of the Church

The precepts of the Church of Roman Rite oblige Catholics to:

1. Assist at Mass on Sundays and holy days of obligation. (Also, to desist from unnecessary servile work on these days.)
2. Fast and abstain on the days appointed. (The fasting obligation binds persons from the 21st until the 59th birthday; the days of fast are Ash Wednesday and Good Friday. The abstinence obligation binds from the 14th birthday on these days, and is obligatory for all Fridays in Lent in the U.S.) These regulations, which have been modified in recent years, are penitential in purpose but do not exhaust obligations of penance. Other ways of doing penance are left to personal option.
3. Confess their sins at least once a year.
4. Receive Holy Communion during the Easter time. (In the U.S., the Easter time extends from the First Sunday of Lent to Trinity Sunday.)
5. Contribute to the support of the Church.
6. Observe the laws of the Church concerning marriage.

SOCIAL DOCTRINE

Since the end of the last century, Catholic social doctrine has been formulated in a progressive manner in a number of authoritative documents. Outstanding examples are the encyclicals: *Rerum Novarum*, issued by Leo XIII in 1891; *Quadragesimo Anno*, by Pius XI in 1931; *Mater et Magistra* ("Christianity and Social Progress") and *Pacem in Terris* ("Peace on Earth"), by John XXIII in 1961 and 1963, respectively; and *Populorum Progressio* ("Development of Peoples"), by Paul VI in 1967. Pius XII, among other accomplishments of ideological importance in the social field, made a distinctive contribution with his formulation of a plan for world peace and order in Christmas messages from 1939 to 1941, and in other documentsm

These documents represent the most serious attempts in modern times to systematize the social implications of the Gospel and the rest of divine revelation as well as the socially relevant writings of the Fathers and Doctors of the Church. Their contents are theological penetrations into social life, with particular reference to human rights, the needs of the poor and those in underdeveloped countries, and humane conditions of life, freedom, justice and peace. In some respects, they read like juridical documents; underneath, however, they are Gospel-oriented and pastoral in intention.

Nature of the Doctrine

Pope John, writing in *Christianity and Social Progress,* made the following statement about the nature and scope of the doctrine stated in the encyclicals in particular and related writings in general.

"What the Catholic Church teaches and declares regarding the social life and relationships of men is beyond question for all time valid.

"The cardinal point of this teaching is that individual men are necessarily the foundation, cause, and end of all social institutions . . . insofar as they are social by nature, and raised to an order of existence that transcends and subdues nature.

"Beginning with this very basic principle whereby the dignity of the human person is affirmed and defended, Holy Church — especially during the last century and with the assistance of learned priests and laymen, specialists in the field — has arrived at clear social teachings whereby the mutual relationships of men are ordered. Taking general norms into account, these principles are in accord with the nature of things and the changed conditions of man's social life, or with the special genius of our day. Moreover, these norms can be approved by all."

The Church in the World

Even more Gospel-oriented and pastoral in a distinctive way is the *Pastoral Constitution on the Church in the Modern World* promulgated by the Second Vatican Council in 1965.

Its purpose was to search out the signs of God's presence and meaning in and through the events of this time in human history. Accordingly, it dealt with the situation of men in present circumstances of profound change, challenge and crisis on all levels of life.

The first part of the constitution developed the theme of the Church and man's calling, and focused attention on the dignity of the human person, the problem of atheism, the community of mankind, man's activity throughout the world, and the serving and saving role of the Church in the world. This portion of the document, it has been said, represents the first presentation by the Church in an official text of an organized Christian view of man and society.

The second part of the document considered several problems of special urgency: fostering the nobility of marriage and the family (see Marriage Doctrine), the proper development of culture, socio-economic life, the life of the political community, the fostering of peace (see Peace and War), and the promotion of a community of nations.

In conclusion, the constitution called for action to implement doctrine regarding the role and work of the Church for the total good of mankind.

Following are a number of key excerpts from the ideological heart of the constitution.

One Human Family and Community: "God, who has fatherly concern for everyone, has willed that all men should constitute one family and treat one another in a spirit of brotherhood....

"For this reason, love for God and neighbor is the first and greatest commandment. Sacred Scripture... teaches us that the love of God cannot be separated from love of neighbor.... To men growing daily more dependent on one another, and to a world becoming more unified every day, this truth proves to be of paramount importance..." (No. 24).

Human Person Is Central: "Man's social nature makes it evident that the progress of the human person and the advance of society itself hinge on each other. For the beginning, the subject and the goal of all social institutions is and must be the human person, which for its part and by its very nature stands completely in need of social life. This social life is not something added on to man. Hence, through his dealings with others, through reciprocal duties, and through fraternal dialogue he develops all his gifts and is able to rise to his destiny."

Influence of Social Circumstances: "But if by this social life the human person is greatly aided in responding to his destiny, even in its religious dimensions, it cannot be denied that men are often diverted from doing good and spurred toward evil by the social circumstances in which they live and are immersed from their birth. To be sure the disturbances which so frequently occur in the social order result in part from the natural tensions of economic, political, and social forms. But at a deeper level they flow from man's pride and selfishness, which contaminate even the social sphere. When the structure of affairs is flawed by the consequences of sin, man, already born with a bent toward evil, finds there new inducements to sin, which cannot be overcome without strenuous efforts and the assistance of grace" (No. 25).

"Every social group must take account of the needs and legitimate aspirations of other groups, and even of the general welfare of the entire human family."

Human Necessities: "At the same time however, there is a growing awareness of the exalted dignity proper to the human person, since he stands above all things, and his rights and duties are universal and inviolable. Therefore, there must be made available to all men everything necessary for leading a life truly human, such as food, clothing, and shelter; the right to choose a state of life freely and to found a family, the right to education, to employment, to a good reputation, to respect, to appropriate information, to activity in accord with the upright norm of one's own conscience, to protection of privacy and to rightful freedom in matters religious too.

"Hence, the social order and its development must unceasingly work to the benefit of the human person if the disposition of affairs is to be subordinate to the personal realm and not contrariwise, as the Lord indicated when He said that the Sabbath was made for man, and not man for the Sabbath."

Improvement of Social Order: "This social order requires constant improvement. It must be founded on truth, built on justice, and animated by love; in freedom it should grow every day toward a more humane balance. An improvement in attitudes and widespread changes in society will have to take place if these objectives are to be gained.

"God's Spirit, who with a marvelous providence directs the unfolding of time and renews the face of the earth, is not absent from this development. The ferment of the gospel, too, has aroused and continues to arouse in man's heart the irresistible requirements of his dignity" (No. 26).

Regard for Neighbor as Another Self: "Coming down to practical and particularly urgent consequences, this Council lays stress on reverence for man; everyone must consider his every neighbor without exception as another self, taking into account first of all his life and the means necessary to living it with dignity....

"In our times a special obligation binds us to make ourselves the neighbor of absolutely every person, and of actively helping him when he comes across our path...."

Inhuman Evils: "... Whatever is opposed to life itself, such as any type of murder, genocide, abortion, euthanasia, or willful self-destruction, whatever violates the integrity of the human person, such as mutilation, torments inflicted on body or mind, attempts to coerce the will itself; whatever insults human dignity, such as subhuman living conditions, arbitrary imprisonment, deportation, slavery, prostitution, the selling of women and children; as well as disgraceful working conditions, where men are treated as mere tools for profit, rather than as free and responsible persons; all these things and others of their like are infamies indeed. They poison human society, but they do more harm to those who practice them than those who suffer from the injury. Moreover, they are a supreme dishonor to the Creator" (No. 27).

Respect for Those Who Are Different: "Respect and love ought to be extended also to those who think or act differently than we do in social, political, and religious matters. In fact, the more deeply we come to understand their ways of thinking through such courtesy and love, the more easily will we be able to enter into dialogue with them."

Distinction between Error and Person in Error: "This love and good will,, to be sure, must in no way render us indifferent to truth and goodness. Indeed love itself impels the disciples of Christ to speak the saving truth to all men. But it is necessary to distinguish between error, which always merits repudiation, and the person in error, who never loses the dignity of being a person, even when he is flawed by false or inadequate religious notions. God alone is the judge and searcher of hearts; for that reason He forbids us to make judgments about the internal guilt of anyone.

"The teaching of Christ even requires that we forgive injuries, and extends the law of love to include every enemy . . ." (No. 28).

Men Are Equal but Different: "Since all men possess a rational soul and are created in God's likeness, since they have the same nature and origin, have been redeemed by Christ, and enjoy the same divine calling and destiny, the basic equality of all must receive increasingly greater recognition.

"True, all men are not alike from the point of view of varying physical power and the diversity of intellectual and moral resources. Nevertheless, with respect to the fundamental rights of the person, every type of discrimination, whether social or cultural, whether based on sex, race, color, social condition, language, or religion, is to be overcome and eradicated as contrary to God's intent. . . ."

Humane Conditions for All: ". . . Although rightful differences exist between men, the equal dignity of persons demands that a more humane and just condition of life be brought about. For excessive economic and social differences between the members of the one human family and population groups cause scandal, and militate against social justice, equity, the dignity of the human person, as well as social and international peace.

"Human institutions, both private and public, must labor to minister to the dignity and purpose of man. At the same time let them put up a stubborn fight against any kind of slavery, whether social or political, and safeguard the basic rights of man under every political system. Indeed human institutions themselves must be accommodated by degrees to the highest of all realities, spiritual ones, even though, meanwhile, a long enough time will be required before they arrive at the desired goal" (No. 29).

"Profound and rapid changes make it particularly urgent that no one, ignoring the trend of events or drugged by laziness, content himself with a merely individualistic morality. It grows increasingly true that the obligations of justice and love are fulfilled only if each person, contributing to the common good, according to his own abilities and the needs of others, also promotes and assists the public and private institutions dedicated to bettering the conditions of human life."

Social Necessities Are Prime Duties: "Let everyone consider it his sacred obligation to count social necessities among the primary duties of modern man, and to pay heed to them. For the more unified the world becomes, the more plainly do the offices of men extend beyond particular groups and spread by degrees to the whole world. But this challenge cannot be met unless individual men and their associations cultivate in themselves the moral and social virtues, and promote them in society. Thus, with the needed help of divine grace, men who are truly new and artisans of a new humanity can be forthcoming" (No. 30).

"In order for individual men to discharge with greater exactness the obligations of their conscience toward themselves and the various groups to which they belong, they must be carefully educated to a higher degree of culture through the use of the immense resources available today to the human race. . . ."

Living Conditions and Freedom: ". . . A man can scarcely arrive at the needed sense of responsibility unless his living conditions allow him to become conscious of his dignity, and to rise to his destiny by spending himself for God and for others. But human freedom is often crippled when a man falls into extreme poverty, just as it withers when he indulges in too many of life's comforts and imprisons himself in a kind of splendid isolation. Freedom acquires new strength, by contrast, when a man consents to the unavoidable requirements of social life, takes on the manifold demands of human partnership, and commits himself to the service of the human community.

"Hence, the will to play one's role in common endeavors should be everywhere encouraged . . ." (No. 31).

Communitarian Character of Life: "God did not create man for life in isolation, but, for the formation of social unity. So also 'it has pleased God to make men holy and save them not merely as individuals, without any mutual bonds, but by making them into a single people, a people which acknowledges Him in truth and serves Him in holiness' *(Dogmatic Constitution on the Church,* No. 9). So from the beginning of salvation history He has chosen men not just as individuals but as members of a certain community. Revealing His mind to them, God called these chosen ones 'His people' (Ex. 3:7-12), and, furthermore, made a covenant with them on Sinai.

"This communitarian character is developed and consummated in the work of Jesus Christ. For the very Word made flesh willed to share in the human fellowship. He was present at the wedding of Cana, visited the house of Zacchaeus, ate with publicans and sinners. He revealed the love of the Father and the sublime vocation of man in terms of the most common of social realities and by making use of the speech and the imagery of plain everyday life. Willingly obeying the laws of His country, He sanctified those human ties, especially family ones, from which social relationships arise. He chose to lead the life proper to an artisan of His time and place.

"In His preaching He clearly taught the sons of God to treat one another as brothers. In His prayers He pleaded that all His disciples might be 'one.' Indeed, as the Redeemer of all, He offered Himself for all even to the point of death. . . . He commanded His apostles to preach to all peoples the gospel message so that the human race might become the Family of God, in which the fullness of the Law would be love."

The Community Founded by Christ: "As the first-born of many brethren and through the gift of His Spirit, He founded after His death and resurrection a new brotherly community composed of all those who receive Him in faith and in love. This he did through His Body, which is the Church. There everyone, as members one of the other, would render mutual service according to the different gifts bestowed on each.

"This solidarity must be constantly increased until that day on which it will be brought to perfection. Then, saved by grace, men will offer flawless glory to God as a family beloved of God and of Christ their Brother" (No. 32).

PEACE AND WAR

The following excerpts, stating principles and objectives of social doctrine concerning peace and war, are from the *Pastoral Constitution on the Church in the Modern World* (Nos. 77 to 82) promulgated by the Second Vatican Council.

Call to Peace: ". . . This Council fervently desires to summon Christians to cooperate with all men in making secure among themselves a peace based on justice and love, and in setting up agencies of peace. This Christians should do with the help of Christ, the Author of peace" (No. 77).

Conditions for Peace: "Peace is not merely the absence of war. Nor can it be reduced solely to the maintenance of a balance of power between enemies. Nor is it brought about by dictatorship. Instead, it is rightly and appropriately called 'an enterprise of justice' (Is. 32:7). Peace results from that harmony built into human society by its divine Founder, and actualized by men as they thirst after ever greater justice.

"The common good of men is in its basic sense determined by the eternal law. Still the concrete demands of this common good are constantly changing as time goes on. Hence peace is never attained once and for all, but must be built up ceaselessly. Moreover, since the human will is unsteady and wounded by sin, the achievement of peace requires that everyone constantly master his passions and that lawful authority keep vigilant.

"But such is not enough. This peace cannot be obtained on earth unless personal values are safeguarded and men freely and trustingly share with one another the riches of their inner spirits and their talents. A firm determination to respect other men and peoples and their dignity, as well as the studied practice of brotherhood, are absolutely necessary for the establishment of peace. Hence peace is likewise the fruit of love, which goes beyond what justice can provide."

Renunciation of Violence: ". . . We cannot fail to praise those who renounce the use of violence in the vindication of their rights and who resort to methods of defense which are otherwise available to weaker parties too, provided that this can be done without injury to the rights and duties of others or of the community itself . . ." (No. 78).

Mass Extermination: ". . . The Council wishes to recall first of all the permanent binding force of universal natural law and its all-embracing principles. Man's conscience itself gives ever more emphatic voice to these principles. Therefore, actions which deliberately conflict with these same principles, as well as orders commanding such actions, are criminal. Blind obedience cannot excuse those who yield to them. Among such must first be counted those actions designed for the methodical extermination of an entire people, nation, or ethnic minority. These actions must be vehemently condemned as horrendous crimes. The courage of those who openly and fearlessly resist men who issue such commands merits supreme commendation."

International Agreements: "On the subject of war, quite a large number of nations have subscribed to various international agreements aimed at making military activity and its consequences less inhuman. Such are conventions concerning the handling of wounded or captured soldiers, and various similar agreements. Agreements of this sort must be honored. They should be improved upon."

Conscientious Objectors: ". . . It seems right that laws make humane provisions for the case of those who for reasons of conscience refuse to bear arms, provided, however, that they accept some other form of service to the human community."

Legitimate Defense: "Certainly, war has not been rooted out of human affairs. As long as the danger of war remains and there is no competent and sufficiently powerful authority at the international level, governments cannot be denied the right to legitimate defense once every means of peaceful settlement has been exhausted. Therefore, government authorities and others who share public responsibility have the duty to protect the welfare of the people entrusted to their care and to conduct such grave matters soberly.

"But it is one thing to undertake military action for the just defense of the people, and something else again to seek the subjugation of other nations. Nor does the possession of war potential make every military or political use of it lawful. Neither does the mere fact that war has unhappily begun mean that all is fair between the warring parties."

Nature of Military Service: "Those who are pledged to the service of their country as members of its armed forces should regard themselves as agents of security and freedom on behalf of their people. As long as they fulfill this role properly, they are making a genuine contribution to the establishment of peace" (No. 79).

Total War Condemned: ". . . This most holy Synod makes its own the condemnations of total war already pronounced by recent Popes, and issues the following declaration:

"Any act of war aimed indiscriminately at the destruction of entire cities or of extensive areas along with their population is a crime against God and man himself. It merits unequivocal and unhesitating condemnation.

"The unique hazard of modern warfare consists in this: it provides those who possess modern scientific weapons with a kind of occasion for perpetrating just such abominations. Moreover, through a certain inexorable chain of events, it can urge men on to the most atrocious decisions. That such in fact may never happen in the future, the bishops of the whole world, in unity assembled, beg all men, especially government officials and military leaders, to give unremitting thought to the awesome responsibility which is theirs before God and the entire human race" (No. 80).

Retaliation and Deterrence: "Scientific weapons, to be sure, are not amassed solely for use in war. The defensive strength of any nation is considered to be dependent upon its capacity for immediate retaliation against an adversary. Hence this accumulation of arms, which increases each year, also serves, in a way heretofore unknown, as a deterrent to possible enemy attack. Many regard this state of affairs as the most effective way by which peace of a sort can be maintained between nations at the present time."

Arms Race: "Whatever be the case with this method of deterrence, men should be convinced that the arms race in which so many countries are engaged is not a safe way to preserve a steady peace. Nor is the so-called balance resulting from this race a sure and authentic peace. Rather than being eliminated thereby, the causes of war threaten to grow gradually stronger.

"While extravagant sums are being spent for the furnishing of ever new weapons, an adequate remedy cannot be provided for the multiple miseries afflicting the whole modern world. Disagreements between nations are not really and radically healed. On the contrary other parts of the world are infected with them. New approaches initiated by reformed attitudes must be adopted to remove this trap and to restore genuine peace by emancipating the world from its crushing anxiety.

"Therefore, it must be said again: the arms race is an utterly treacherous trap for humanity, and one which injures the poor to an intolerable degree. It is much to be feared that, if this race persists, it will eventually spawn all the lethal ruin whose path it is now making ready . . ." (No. 81).

Outlaw War: "It is our clear duty, then, to strain every muscle as we work for the time when all war can be completely outlawed by international consent. This goal undoubtedly requires the establishment of some universal public authority acknowledged as such by all, and endowed with effective power to safeguard, on the behalf of all, security, regard for justice, and respect for rights."

Multilateral and Controlled Disarmament: "But before this hoped-for authority can be set up, the highest existing international centers must devote themselves vigorously to the pursuit of better means for obtaining common security. Peace must be born of mutual trust between nations rather than imposed on them through fear of one another's weapons. Hence everyone must labor to put an end at last to the arms race, and to make a true beginning of disarmament, not indeed a unilateral disarmament, but one proceeding at an equal pace according to agreement, and backed up by authentic and workable safeguards.

"In the meantime, efforts which have already been made and are still under way to eliminate the danger of war are not to be underrated. On the contrary, support should be given to the good will of the very many leaders who work hard to do away with war, which they abominate. . . ."

Public Opinion: ". . . Men should take heed not to entrust themselves only to the efforts of others, while remaining careless about their own attitudes. For government officials, who must simultaneously guarantee the good of their own people and promote the universal good, depend on public opinion and feeling to the greatest possible extent. It does them no good to work at building peace so long as feelings of hostility, contempt, and distrust, as well as racial hatred and unbending ideologies, continue to divide men and place them in opposing camps.

"Hence arises a surpassing need for renewed education of attitudes and for new inspiration in the area of public opinion. Those who are dedicated to the work of education . . . should regard as their most weighty task the effort to instruct all in fresh sentiments of peace" (No. 82).

Liturgy

The nature and purpose of the liturgy, along with norms for its revision, were the subject matter of the *Constitution on the Sacred Liturgy* promulgated by the Second Vatican Council. The principles and guidelines stated in this document, the first issued by the Council, are summarized here and/or are incorporated in other Almanac entries on liturgical subjects.

Nature and Purpose of Liturgy

"It is through the liturgy, especially the divine Eucharistic Sacrifice, that 'the work of our redemption is exercised.' The liturgy is thus the outstanding means by which the faithful can express in their lives, and manifest to others, the mystery of Christ and the real nature of the true Church . . ." (No. 2).

"The liturgy is considered as an exercise of the priestly office of Jesus Christ. In the liturgy the sanctification of man is manifested by signs perceptible to the senses, and is effected in a way which is proper to each of these signs; in the liturgy full public worship is performed by the Mystical Body of Jesus Christ, that is, by the Head and His members.

"From this it follows that every liturgical celebration, because it is an action of Christ the priest and of His Body the Church, is a sacred action surpassing all others. No other action of the Church can match its claim to efficacy, nor equal the degree of it" (No. 7).

"The liturgy is the summit toward which the activity of the Church is directed; at the same time it is the fountain from which all her power flows. For the goal of apostolic works is that all who are made sons of God by faith and baptism should come together to praise God in the midst of His Church, to take part in her sacrifice, and to eat the Lord's Supper.

". . . From the liturgy, therefore, and especially from the Eucharist, as from a fountain, grace is channeled into us; and the sanctification of men in Christ and the glorification of God, to which all other activities of the Church are directed as toward their goal, are most powerfully achieved" (No. 10).

Full Participation

"Mother Church earnestly desires that all the faithful be led to that full, conscious, and active participation in liturgical celebrations which is demanded by the very nature of the liturgy. Such participation by the Christian people as 'a chosen race, a royal priesthood, a holy nation, a purchased people' (1 Pt. 2:9; cf. 2:4-5), is their right and duty by reason of their baptism.

"In the restoration and promotion of the sacred liturgy, this full and active participation by all the people is the aim to be considered before all else; for it is the primary and indispensable source from which the faithful are to derive the true Christian spirit . . ." (No. 14).

"In order that the Christian people may more securely derive an abundance of graces from the sacred liturgy, holy Mother Church desires to undertake with great care a general restoration of the liturgy itself. For the liturgy is made up of unchangeable elements divinely instituted, and elements subject to change. The latter not only may but ought to be changed with the passing of time if features have by chance crept in which are less harmonious with the intimate nature of the liturgy, or if existing elements have grown less functional.

"In this restoration, both texts and rites should be drawn up so that they express more clearly the holy things which they signify. Christian people, as far as possible, should be able to understand them with ease and to take part in them fully, actively, and as befits a community . . ." (No. 21).

Norms

Norms regarding the reforms concern the greater use of Scripture; emphasis on the importance of the sermon or homily on biblical and liturgical subjects; use of vernacular languages for prayers of the Mass and for administration of the sacraments; provision for adaptation of rites to cultural patterns.

Approval for reforms of various kinds — in liturgical texts, rites, etc. — depends on the Holy See, regional conferences of bishops and individual bishops, according to provisions of law. No priest has authority to initiate reforms on his own. Reforms may not be introduced just for the sake of innovation, and any that are introduced in the light of present-day circumstances should embody sound tradition.

To assure the desired effect of liturgical reforms, training and instruction are necessary for the clergy, religious and the laity. The functions of diocesan and regional commissions for liturgy, music and art are to set standards and provide leadership for instruction and practical programs in their respective fields.

Most of the constitution's provisions regarding liturgical reforms have to do with the Roman Rite. The document clearly respects the equal dignity of all rites, leaving to the Eastern Churches control over their ancient liturgies.

(For coverage of the **Mystery of the Eucharist**, see The Mass; **Other Sacraments**, see separate entries.)

Sacramentals

Sacramentals, instituted by the Church, "are sacred signs which bear a resemblance to the sacraments: they signify effects, particularly of a spiritual kind, which are obtained through the Church's intercession. By them men are disposed to receive the chief effect of the sacraments, and various occasions in life are rendered holy" (No. 60).

"Thus, for well-disposed members of the faithful, the liturgy of the sacraments and sacramentals sanctifies almost every event in their lives; they are given access to the stream of divine grace which flows from the paschal mystery of the passion, death, and resurrection of Christ, the fountain from which all sacraments and sacramentals draw their power. There is hardly any proper use of material things which cannot thus be directed toward the sanctification of men and the praise of God" (No. 61).   Some common sacramentals are priestly blessings, blessed palm, candles, holy water, medals, scapulars, prayers and ceremonies of the Roman Ritual.

Liturgy of the Hours

The Liturgy of the Hours (Divine Office) is the public prayer of the Church for praising God and sanctifying the day. Its daily celebration is required as a sacred obligation by men in holy orders and by men and women religious who have professed solemn vows. Its celebration by others is highly commended and is to be encouraged in the communuty of the faithful.

"By tradition going back to early Christian times, the Divine Office is arranged so that the whole course of the day and night is made holy by the praises of God. Therefore, when this wonderful song of praise is worthily rendered by priests and others who are deputed for this purpose by Church ordinance, or by the faithful praying together with the priest in an approved form, then it is truly the voice of the bride addressing her bridegroom; it is the very prayer which Christ Himself, together with His body, addresses to the Father" (No. 84).

"Hence all who perform this service are not only fulfilling a duty of the Church, but also are sharing in the greatest honor accorded to Christ's spouse, for by offering these praises to God they are standing before God's throne in the name of the Church their Mother" (No. 85).

The Latin text of the Liturgy of the Hours, under revision since 1965, was described by Pope Paul in the apostolic constitution *Canticum Laudis,* dated Nov. 1, 1970. Its four complete volumes in authorized English translation have been published since May, 1975.

One-volume, partial editions of the Liturgy of the Hours have been published in approved English translation. Entitled *Christian Prayer,* they contain the Morning and Evening Prayers and other elements. They are intended for use by religious and lay persons who are not bound by obligation to pray the Liturgy of the Hours.

The revised Liturgy of the Hours consists of:

• Office of Readings, for reflection on the word of God. The pruncipal parts are three psalms, biblical and non-biblical readings.

• Morning and Evening Prayer, called the "hinges" of the Liturgy of the Hours. The principal parts are a hymn, two psalms, an Old or New Testament canticle, a brief biblical reading, Zechariah's canticle (the *Benedictus,* morning) or Mary's canticle (the *Magnificat,* evening), responsories, intercessions and a concluding prayer.

• Daytime Prayer. The principal parts are a hymn, three psalms, a brief biblical reading and one of three concluding prayers corresponding to the time at which the prayer is offered (midmorning, midday, midafternoon).

• Night Prayer: The principal parts are one or two psalms, a brief biblical reading, Simeon's canticle *(Nunc Dimittis),* a concluding prayer and an antiphon in honor of Mary.

In the new Office, the hours are shorter than they had been, with greater textual variety, meditation aids, and provision for intervals of silence and meditation. The psalms are distributed over a four-week period instead of a week; some psalms, entirely or in part, are not included. Additional canticles from the Old and New Testaments are assigned for Morning and Evening Prayer. Additional scriptural texts have been added and variously arranged for greater internal unity, correspondence to readings at Mass, and relevance to events and themes of salvation history. Readings include some of the best material from the Fathers of the Church and other authors and improved selections on the lives of saints.

The book used for recitation of the Office is the **Breviary.**

For coverage of the **Liturgical Year,** see Church Calendar.

Sacred Music

"The musical tradition of the universal Church is a treasure of immeasurable value, greater even than that of any other art. The main reason for this pre-eminence is that, as sacred melody united to words, it forms a necessary or integral part of the solemn liturgy.

". . . Sacred music increases in holiness to the degree that it is intimately linked with liturgical action, winningly expresses prayerfulness, promotes solidarity, and enriches sacred rites with heightened solemnity. The Church indeed approves of all forms of true art, and admits them into divine worship when they show appropriate qualities" (No. 112).

The constitution decreed:

- Vernacular languages for the people's parts of the liturgy, as well as Latin, may be used.
- Participation in sacred song by the whole body of the faithful, and not just by choirs, is to be encouraged and brought about.
- Provisions should be made for proper musical training for clergy, religious and lay persons.
- While Gregorian Chant has a unique dignity and relationship to the Latin liturgy, other kinds of music are acceptable.
- Native musical traditions should be used, especially in mission areas.
- Various instruments compatible with the dignity of worship may be used.

Gregorian Chant: A form and style of chant called Gregorian was the basis and most highly regarded standard of liturgical music for centuries. It originated probably during the formative period of the Roman liturgy and developed in conjunction with Gallican and other forms of chant. Gregory the Great's connection with it is not clear, although it is known that he had great concern for and interest in church music. The earliest extant written versions of Gregorian chant date from the ninth century. A thousand years later, the Benedictines of Solesmes, France, initiated a revival of chant which gave impetus to the modern liturgical movement.

Sacred Art and Furnishings

"Very rightly the fine arts are considered to rank among the noblest expressions of human genius. This judgment applies especially to religious art and to its highest achievement, which is sacred art. By their very nature both of the latter are related to God's boundless beauty, for this is the reality which these human efforts are trying to express in some way. To the extent that these works aim exclusively at turning men's thoughts to God persuasively and devoutly, they are dedicated to God and to the cause of His greater honor and glory" (No. 122).

The objective of sacred art is "that all things set apart for use in divine worship should be truly worthy, becoming, and beautiful, signs and symbols of heavenly realities. . . . The Church has . . . always reserved to herself the right to pass judgment upon the arts, deciding which of the works of artists are in accordance with faith, piety, and cherished traditional laws, and thereby suited to sacred purposes.

". . . Sacred furnishings should worthily and beautifully serve the dignity of worship . . ." (No. 122).

According to the constitution:

- Contemporary art, as well as that of the past, shall "be given free scope in the Church, provided that it adorns the sacred buildings and holy rites with due honor and reverence . . ." (No. 123).
- Noble beauty, not sumptuous display, should be sought in art, sacred vestments and ornaments.
- "Let bishops carefully exclude from the house of god and from other sacred places those works of artists which are repugnant to faith, morals, and Christian piety, and which offend true religious sense either by their distortion of forms or by lack of artistic worth, by mediocrity or by pretense.
- "When churches are to be built, let great care be taken that they be suitable for the celebration of liturgical services and for the active participation of the faithful" (No. 124).
- "The practice of placing sacred images in churches so that they may be venerated by the faithful is to be firmly maintained. Nevertheless, their number should be moderate and their relative location should reflect right order. Otherwise they may create confusion among the Christian people and promote a faulty sense of devotion" (No. 125).
- Artists should be trained and inspired in the spirit and for the purposes of the liturgy.
- The norms of sacred art should be revised. "These laws refer especially to the worthy and well-planned construction of sacred buildings, the shape and construction of altars, the nobility, location, and security of the Eucharistic tabernacle, the suitability and dignity of the baptistery, the proper use of sacred images, embellishments, and vestments . . ." (No. 128).

RITES

A rite is the manner in which liturgical worship is carried out. It includes the forms and ceremonial observances of liturgical worship.

Different rites have evolved in the course of Church history, giving to liturgical worship forms and usages peculiar and proper to the nature of worship itself and to the culture of the faithful in various circumstances of time and place. Thus, there has been development since apostolic times in prayers and ceremonies of the Mass, the administration of the sacraments, requirements for celebration of the Divine Office. Practices within the patriarchates of Antioch, Rome, Alexandria and Constantinople were the principal sources of the rites in present use.

Eastern Rites, described elsewhere in the Almanac, are proper to Eastern Catholic Churches.

The **Roman** or **Latin Rite,** described in this section, prevails in the Western Church. It was derived from Roman practices and the use of Latin as an official language from the third century onward. Other rites in limited use in the Western Church have been the Ambrosian, the Mozarabic, the Lyonnais, the Braga, and rites peculiar to some religious orders like the Dominicans, Carmelites and Carthusians.

MASS, EUCHARISTIC SACRIFICE AND BANQUET

Declarations of Vatican II

The Second Vatican Council made the following declarations, among others, with respect to the Mass.

"At the Last Supper, on the night when He was betrayed, our Savior instituted the Eucharistic Sacrifice of His Body and Blood. He did this in order to perpetuate the sacrifice of the Cross throughout the centuries until He should come again, and so to entrust to His beloved spouse, the Church, a memorial of His death and resurrection: a sacrament of love, a sign of unity, a bond of charity, a paschal banquet in which Christ is consumed, the mind is filled with grace, and a pledge of future glory is given to us" (*Constitution on the Sacred Liturgy*, No. 47).

". . . As often as the sacrifice of the cross in which 'Christ, our passover, has been sacrificed' (1 Cor. 5:7) is celebrated on an altar, the work of our redemption is carried on. At the same time, in the sacrament of the Eucharistic bread the unity of all believers who form one body in Christ (cf. 1 Cor. 10:17) is both expressed and brought about. All men are called to this union with Christ . . ." (*Dogmatic Constitution on the Church*. No. 3).

". . . The ministerial priest, by the sacred power he enjoys, molds and rules the priestly people. Acting in the person of Christ, he brings about the Eucharistic Sacrifice, and offers it to God in the name of all the people. For their part, the faithful join in the offering of the Eucharist by virtue of their royal priesthood . . ." (*Ibid.*, No. 10).

Declarations of Trent

Among its decrees on the Holy Eucharist, the Council of Trent stated the following points of doctrine on the Mass.

1. There is in the Catholic Church a true Sacrifice, the Mass instituted by Jesus Christ. It is the Sacrifice of His Body and Blood, Soul and Divinity, Himself, under the appearances of bread and wine.

2. This Sacrifice is identical with the Sacrifice of the Cross, inasmuch as Christ is the Priest and Victim in both. A difference lies in the manner of offering, which was bloody upon the Cross and is bloodless on the altar.

3. The Mass is a propitiatory Sacrifice, atoning for sins of the living and dead for whom it is offered.

4. The efficacy of the Mass is derived from the Sacrifice of the Cross, whose super-abundant merits it applies to men.

5. Although the Mass is offered to God alone, it may be celebrated in honor and memory of the saints.

6. Christ instituted the Mass at the Last Supper.

7. Christ ordained the Apostles priests, giving them power and the command to consecrate His Body and Blood to perpetuate and renew the Sacrifice.

ORDER OF MASS

The Mass consists of two principal divisions called the **Liturgy of the Word**, which features the proclamation of the Word of God, and the **Eucharistic Liturgy**, which focuses on the central act of sacrifice in the Consecration and on the Eucharistic Banquet in Holy Communion. (Formerly, these divisions were called, respectively, the **Mass of the Catechumens** and the **Mass of the Faithful**.) In addition to these principal divisions, there are ancillary introductory and concluding rites.

The following description covers the Mass as celebrated with participation by the people. This Order of the Mass was approved by Pope Paul VI in the apostolic constitution *Missale Romanum* dated Apr. 3, 1969, and promulgated in a decree issued Apr. 6, 1969, by the Congregation for Divine Worship. The assigned effective date was Nov. 30, 1969.

Introductory Rites

Entrance: The introductory rites begin with the singing or recitation of an entrance song while the priest approaches the altar, kisses it, and goes to the place where he will be seated. The song consists of one or more scriptural verses stating the theme of the mystery, season or feast commemorated in the Mass.

Greeting: The priest and people make the Sign of the Cross together. The priest then greets them in one of several alternative ways and they reply in a corresponding manner.

Introductory Remarks: At this point, the priest or another of the ministers may introduce the theme of the Mass.

Penitential Rite: The priest and people together acknowledge their sins as a preliminary step toward worthy celebration of the sacred mysteries. This rite includes a brief examination of conscience, a general confession of sin and plea for divine mercy in one of several ways, and a prayer of absolution by the priest. The *Kyrie, eleison* ("Lord, have mercy") is then said if it was not included in one of the foregoing pleas for divine mercy.

Glory to God: A doxology, a hymn of praise to God, sung or said on festive occasions.

Opening Prayer: A prayer of petition offered by the priest on behalf of the worshipping community.

I. Liturgy of the Word

Readings: The featured elements of this liturgy are several readings of passages from the Bible. If three readings are in order, the first is usually from the Old Testament, the second from the New Testament (Epistles, Acts, Revelation), and the third from one of the Gospels; the final reading is always a selection from a Gospel. The first reading(s) is concluded with the formula, "This is the Word of the Lord," to which the people respond, "Thanks be to God." The Gospel reading is concluded with the formula, "This is the Gospel of the Lord," to which the people respond, "Praise to you, Lord Jesus Christ," Between the readings, psalm verses and a Gospel acclamation are sung or said.

Homily: Sermon on a scriptural or liturgical subject; ideally, it should be related to the liturgical service in progress.

Creed: The Nicene profession of faith, by priest and people, on certain occasions.

Prayer of the Faithful: Litany-type prayers of petition, with participation by the people. Called general intercessions, they concern needs of the Church, the salvation of the world, public authorities, persons in need, the local community.

II. Eucharistic Liturgy

Offertory Song: Scriptural verses related to the theme of the Mass, or a suitable hymn, sung or said while things are prepared at the altar for the Eucharistic Liturgy and while the offerings of bread and wine are brought to the altar.

Offertory Procession: Presentation to the priest of the gifts of bread and wine, principally, by participating members of the congregation.

Offering of the Gifts: Consists of the prayers and ceremonies with which the priest offers bread and wine as the elements of the sacrifice to take place during the Eucharistic Prayer and of the Lord's Supper to be shared in Holy Communion. If singing takes place during the offering, the priest can say the prayers and carry out the action silently; if there is no singing, he says the prayers aloud and the people, after each offering, respond with the words, "Blessed be God forever."

Washing of Hands: After offering the bread and wine, the priest cleanses his fingers with water in a brief ceremony of purification.

Pray, Brethren: Prayer that the sacrifice to take place will be acceptable to God. The first part of the prayer is said by the priest; the second, by the people.

Prayer over the Gifts: A prayer of petition offered by the priest on behalf of the worshipping community.

Eucharistic Prayer

Preface: A hymn of praise, introducing the Eucharistic Prayer or Canon, sung or said by the priest following responses by the people. The Order of the Mass contains a variety of prefaces, for use on different occasions.

Holy, Holy, Holy; Blessed Is He: Divine praises sung or said by the priest and people.

Canon: The Eucharistic Prayer of the Mass whose central portion is the Consecration, when the essential act of sacrificial offering takes place with the changing of bread and wine into the Body and Blood of Christ. The prayers of the Canon, which are said by the celebrant only, commemorate principal mysteries of salvation history and include petitions for the Church, the living and dead, and remembrances of saints. There are four Eucharistic Prayers, for use on various occasions and at the option of the priest. (Additional Canons for Masses with children and for reconciliation were approved in 1975.)

Doxology: A formula of divine praise sung or said by the priest while he holds aloft the chalice containing the consecrated wine in one hand and the paten containing the consecrated host in the other.

Communion Rite

Lord's Prayer: Sung or said by the priest and people.

Prayer for Deliverance from evil: Called an **embolism** because it is a development of the final petition of the Lord's Prayer; said by the priest. It concludes with a memorial of the return of the Lord to which the people respond, "For the kingdom, the power, and the glory are yours, now and forever."

Prayer for Peace: Said by the priest, with corresponding responses by the people. The priest can, in accord with local custom, bid the people to exchange a greeting of peace with each other.

Lamb of God: A prayer for divine mercy sung or said while the priest breaks the consecrated host and places a piece of it into the consecrated wine in the chalice.

Communion: The priest, after saying a preparatory prayer, administers Holy Communion to himself and then to the people, thus completing the sacrifice-banquet of the Mass. (This completion is realized even if the celebrant alone receives the Eucharist.) On giving the Eucharist to the people, the priest says, "The Body of Christ," to each recipient; the customary response is "Amen." If the Eucharist is administered under the forms of bread and wine, the priest says, "The Body and Blood of Christ."

Communion Song: Scriptural verses or a suitable hymn sung or said during the distribution of Holy Communion. After Holy Communion is received, some moments may be spent in silent meditation or in the chanting of a psalm or hymn of praise.

Prayer after Communion: A prayer of petition offered by the priest on behalf of the worshipping community.

Concluding Rite

Announcements: Brief announcements to the people are in order at this time.

Dismissal: Consists of a final greeting by the priest, a blessing, and a formula of dismissal. This rite is omitted if another liturgical action immediately follows the Mass; e.g., a procession, the blessing of the body during a funeral rite.

Some parts of the Mass are changeable with the liturgical season or feast, and are called the **proper** of the Mass. Other parts are said to be **common** because they always remain the same.

Additional Mass Notes

Catholics are seriously obliged to attend Mass in a worthy manner on Sundays and holy days of obligation. Failure to do so without a proportionately serious reason is gravely wrong.

It is the custom for priests to celebrate Mass daily whenever possible. To satisfy the needs of the faithful on Sundays and holy days of obligation, they are authorized to say Mass twice (**bination**) or even three times (**trination**). Bination is also permissible on weekdays. On Christmas and All Souls' Day every priest may say three Masses. Mass may be celebrated in the morning, afternoon or evening.

The **fruits of the Mass,** which in itself is of infinite value, are: **general,** for all the faithful; **special (ministerial),** for the intentions or persons specifically intended by the celebrant; **most special (personal),** for the celebrant himself. On Sundays and certain other days pastors are obliged to offer Mass for their parishioners. If a priest accepts a stipend or offering for a Mass, he is obliged in justice to apply the Mass for the designated intention. Mass may be applied for the living and the dead, or for any good intention.

Mass can be celebrated in several ways: e.g., with people present, without their presence (privately), with two or more priests as co-celebrants (concelebration), with greater or less solemnity.

Some of the various types of Masses are: **for the dead** (Funeral Mass or Mass of Christian Burial, Mass for the Dead — formerly called Requiem Mass); **nuptial,** for married couples, with or after the wedding ceremony; **votive,** to honor a Person of the Trinity, a saint, or for some special intention. A **red Mass** is a Votive Mass of the Holy Spirit, celebrated for members of the legal profession that they might exercise prudence and equity in their official capacities. **Gregorian Masses** are a series of 30 Masses celebrated on 30 consecutive days for a deceased person.

The only day of the year on which Mass is not celebrated is Good Friday. In its place, there is a **Solemn Liturgical Action.**

Places, Altars for Mass

The ordinary place for celebrating the Eucharist is a church or other sacred place, at a permanent or movable altar.

Outside of a sacred place, Mass may be celebrated in an appropriate place at a suitable table covered with a linen cloth and corporal.

An **altar stone** containing the relics of saints, which was formerly prescribed, is not required by regulations in effect since the promulgation Apr. 6, 1969, of *Institutio Generalis Missalis Romani.*

A **permanent altar** should have a table of stone, be consecrated, and have enclosed within it relics of some saints.

A **movable altar** may be made of any solid and suitable material. If made of stone and consecrated, it should have enclosed within it relics of some saints; if blessed rather than consecrated, the enclosure of relics is not required.

LITURGICAL VESTMENTS

In the early years of the Church, vestments worn by the ministers at liturgical functions were the same as the garments in ordinary popular use. They became distinctive when their form was not altered to correspond with later variations in popular style. Liturgical vestments are symbolic of the sacred ministry and add appropriate decorum to divine worship.

Mass Vestments

Alb: A body-length tunic of white fabric; a vestment common to all ministers of divine worship.

Amice: A rectangular piece of white cloth worn about the neck, tucked into the collar and falling over the shoulders; worn under the alb.

Chasuble: Originally, a large mantle or cloak covering the body, it is the outer vestment of a priest celebrating Mass or carrying out other sacred actions connected with the Mass.

Cincture: A cord which serves the purpose of a belt, holding the alb close to the body.

Dalmatic: The outer vestment worn by a deacon in place of a chasuble.

Stole: A long, band-like vestment worn about the neck and falling to about the knees. (A stole is used for other functions also.)

The material, form and ornamentation of the aforementioned and other vestments are subject to variation and adaptation, according to norms and decisions of the Holy See and concerned conferences of bishops. The overriding norm is that they should be appropriate for use in divine worship. The customary ornamented vestments are the chasuble, dalmatic and stole.

The minimal vestments required for a priest celebrating Mass are the alb, stole and chasuble.

Chasuble-Alb: A vestment combining the features of the chasuble and alb; for use with a stole by concelebrants and, by way of exception, by celebrants in certain circumstances.

Liturgical Colors

The colors of outer vestments vary with liturgical seasons, feasts and other circumstances. The colors and their use are:

Green: For the season of the year; symbolic of hope and the vitality of the life of faith.

Purple: For Advent and Lent; may also be used in Masses for the dead; symbolic of penance.

Red: For the Sunday of the Passion, the Wednesday of Holy Week, Good Friday, Pentecost; feasts of the Passion of Our Lord, the Apostles and Evangelists, martyrs; symbolic of the supreme sacrifice of life for the love of God.

Rose: May be used in place of purple on the Third Sunday of Advent (Gaudete Sunday) and the Fourth Sunday of Lent (Laetare Sunday); symbolic of anticipatory joy during a time of penance.

White: For Christmastide and Eastertide; feasts and commemorations of Our Lord, except those of the Passion; feasts and commemorations of the Blessed Virgin Mary, angels, saints who are not martyrs, All Saints (Nov. 1), St. John the Baptist (June 24), St. John the Evangelist (Dec. 27), the Chair of St. Peter (Feb. 22), the Conversion of St. Paul (Jan. 25). White, symbolic of purity and integrity of the life of faith, may generally be substituted for other colors, and can be used for funeral and other Masses for the dead.

Options are provided regarding the color of vestments used in offices and Masses for the dead. The newsletter of the U.S. Bishops' Committee on the Liturgy, in line with No. 308 of the "General Instruction of the Roman Missal," announced in July, 1970: "In the dioceses of the United States, white vestments may be used, in addition to violet (**purple**) and **black**, in offices and Masses for the dead."

On more solemn occasions, better than ordinary vestments may be used, even though their color (e.g., gold) does not match the requirements of the day.

Considerable freedom is permitted in the choice of colors of vestments worn for votive Masses.

Other Vestments

Cappa Magna: Flowing vestment with a train, worn by bishops and cardinals.

Cassock: A full-length, close-fitting robe worn by priests and other clerics under liturgical vestments and in ordinary use; usually black for priests, purple for bishops and other prelates, red for cardinals, white for the pope. In place of a cassock, priests belonging to religious institutes wear the habit proper to their institute.

Cope: A mantle-like vestment open in front and fastened across the chest; worn by sacred ministers in processions and other ceremonies, as prescribed by appropriate directives.

Gremial: A rectangular veil of silk or linen placed over the knees of a bishop when he is seated during various episcopal ceremonies.

Habit: The ordinary garb of members of religious institutes, analogous to the cassock of diocesan priests; the form of habits varies from institute to institute.

Humeral Veil: A rectangular vestment worn about the shoulders by a deacon. or priest in Eucharistic processions and for other prescribed liturgical ceremonies.

Mitre: A headdress worn at some liturgical functions by bishops, abbots and, in certain cases, other ecclesiastics.

Pallium: A circular band of white wool about two inches wide, with front and back pendants, marked with six crosses, worn about the neck. It is a symbol of the fullness of the episcopal office. Pope Paul VI, in a document issued July 20, 1978, on his own initiative and entitled *Inter Eximia Episcopalis,* restricted its use to the pope and archbishops of metropolitan sees. The pallium is made from the wool of lambs blessed by the pope on the feast of St. Agnes (Jan. 21).

Rochet: A knee-length, white linen-lace garment of prelates worn under outer vestments.

Surplice: A loose, flowing vestment of white fabric with wide sleeves. For some functions, it is interchangeable with an alb.

Zucchetto: A skullcap worn by bishops and other prelates.

SACRED VESSELS, LINENS

Vessels

Chalice and Paten: The principal sacred vessels required for the celebration of Mass are the **chalice** (cup) and **paten** (plate) in which wine and bread, respectively, are offered, consecrated and consumed. Both should be made of solid and noble material which is not easily breakable or corruptible. Gold coating is required of the interior parts of sacred vessels subject to rust. The cup of a chalice should be made of non-absorbent material.

Vessels for containing consecrated hosts (see below) can be made of material other than solid and noble metal — e. g., ivory, more durable woods — provided the substitute material is locally regarded as noble or rather precious and is suitable for sacred use.

Sacred vessels should be blessed or consecrated, according to prescribed requirements.

Vessels, in addition to the paten, for containing consecrated hosts are:

Ciborium: Used to hold hosts for distribution to the faithful and for reservation in the tabernacle.

Luna, Lunula, Lunette: A small receptacle which holds the sacred host in an upright position in the monstrance.

Monstrance, Ostensorium: A portable receptacle so made that the sacred host, when enclosed therein, may be clearly seen, as at

Benediction or during extended exposition of the Blessed Sacrament.

Pyx: A watch-shaped vessel used in carrying the Eucharist to the sick.

Linens

Altar Cloth: A white cloth, usually of linen, covering the table of an altar. One cloth is sufficient. Three were used according to former requirements.

Burse: A square, stiff flat case, open at one end, in which the folded corporal is placed; the outside is covered with material of the same kind and color as the outer vestments of the celebrant.

Corporal: A square piece of white linen spread on the altar cloth, on which rest the vessels holding the Sacred Species — the consecrated host(s) and wine — during the Eucharistic Liturgy. The corporal is similarly used whenever the Blessed Sacrament is removed from the tabernacle; e. g., during Benediction the vessel containing the Blessed Sacrament rests on a corporal.

Finger Towel: A white rectangular napkin used by the priest to dry his fingers after cleansing them following the offering of gifts at Mass.

Pall: A square piece of stiff material, usually covered with linen, used to cover the chalice at Mass.

Purificator: A white rectangular napkin used for cleansing sacred vessels after the reception of Communion at Mass.

Veil: The chalice intended for use at Mass is covered with a veil made of the same material as the outer vestments of the celebrant.

THE CHURCH BUILDING

A church is a building set aside and dedicated for purposes of divine worship, the place of assembly for a worshiping community.

A Catholic church is the ordinary place in which the faithful assemble for participation in the Eucharistic Liturgy and other forms of divine worship.

In the early years of Christianity, the first places of assembly for the Eucharistic Liturgy were private homes (Acts 2:46; Rom. 16:5; 1 Cor. 16:5; Col. 4:15) and, sometimes, catacombs. Church building began in the latter half of the second century during lulls in persecution and became widespread after enactment of the Edict of Milan in 313, when it finally became possible for the Church to emerge completely from the underground. The oldest and basic norms regarding church buildings date from about that time.

The essential principle underlying all norms for church building was reformulated by the Second Vatican Council, as follows: "When churches are to be built, let great care be taken that they be suitable for the celebration of liturgical services and for the active participation of the faithful" *(Constitution on the Sacred Liturgy,* No. 124).

This principle was subsequently elaborated in detail by the Congregation for Divine Worship in a document entitled *Institutio Generalis Missalis Romani,* which was approved by Paul VI Apr. 3 and promulgated by a decree of the congregation dated Apr. 6, 1969. Coverage of the following items reflects the norms stated in Chapter V of this document.

Sanctuary: The part of the church where the altar of sacrifice is located, the place where the ministers of the liturgy lead the people in prayer, proclaim the word of God and celebrate the Eucharist. It is set off from the body of the church by a distinctive structural feature — e. g., elevation above the main floor — or by ornamentation. (The traditional **communion rail,** which has been removed in recent years in many churches, served this purpose of demarcation.) The customary location of the sanctuary is at the front of the church; it may, however, be centrally located.

Altar: The main altar of sacrifice and table of the Lord is the focal feature of the sanctuary and entire church. It stands by itself, so that the ministers can move about it freely, and is so situated that they face the people during the liturgical action. In addition to this main altar, there may also be others; in new churches, these are situated in side chapels or alcoves removed to some degree from the body of the church.

Adornment of the Altar: The altar table is covered with a suitable linen cloth. Required candelabra and a cross are placed upon or near the altar in plain sight of the people and are so arranged that they do not obscure their view of the liturgical action.

Seats of the Ministers: The seat of the celebrant, corresponding with his role as the presiding minister of the assembly, is best located behind the altar and facing the people; it is raised a bit above the level of the altar but must not have the appearance of a throne. The seats of other ministers are also located in the sanctuary.

Ambo, Pulpit: The stand at which scriptural lessons and psalm responses are read, the word of God preached, and the prayer of the faithful offered. It is so placed that the ministers can be easily seen and heard by the people.

Places for the People: Seats and kneeling benches (**pews**) and other accommodations for the people are so arranged that they can participate in the most appropriate way in the liturgical action and have freedom of movement for the reception of Holy Communion. Reserved seats are out of order.

Place for the Choir: Where it is located depends on the most suitable arrangement for maintaining the unity of the choir with the congregation and for providing its members maximum opportunity for carrying out their proper function and participating fully in the Mass.

Tabernacle: The best place for reserving the Blessed Sacrament is in a chapel suitable for the private devotion of the people. If this is not possible, reservation should be at a side altar or other appropriately adorned place. In either case, the Blessed Sacrament should be kept in a tabernacle, i.e., a safe-like, secure receptacle.

Statues: Images of the Lord, the Blessed Virgin Mary and the saints are legitimately proposed for the veneration of the faithful in churches. Their number and arrangement, however, should be ordered in such a way that they do not distract the people from the central celebration of the Eucharistic Liturgy. There should be only one statue of one and the same saint in a church.

General Adornment and Arrangement of Churches: Churches should be so adorned and fitted out that they serve the direct requirements of divine worship and the needs and reasonable convenience of the people.

Other Items

Ambry: A box containing the holy oils, attached to the wall of the sanctuary in some churches.

Baptistery: The place for administering baptism. Some churches have baptisteries adjoining or near the entrance, a position symbolizing the fact that persons are initiated in the Church and incorporated in Christ through this sacrament. Contemporary liturgical practice favors placement of the baptistery near the sanctuary and altar, or the use of a portable font in the same position, to emphasize the relationship of baptism to the Eucharist, the celebration in sacrifice and banquet of the death and resurrection of Christ.

Candles: Used more for symbolical than illuminative purposes, they represent Christ, the light and life of grace, at liturgical functions. They are made of beeswax.

Confessional: A booth-like structure for the hearing of confessions, with separate compartments for the priest and penitents and a grating or screen between them. The use of confessionals became general in the Roman Rite after the Council of Trent.

Crucifix: A cross bearing the figure of the body of Christ, representative of the Sacrifice of the Cross.

Cruets: Vessels containing the wine and water used at Mass. They are placed on a credence table in the sanctuary.

Holy Water Fonts: Receptacles containing holy water, usually at church entrances, for the use of the faithful.

Sanctuary Lamp: A lamp which is kept burning continuously before a tabernacle in which the Blessed Sacrament is reserved, as a sign of the Real Presence of Christ.

LITURGICAL DEVELOPMENTS

The principal developments covered in this article are enactments of the Holy See and actions related to their implementation in the United States.

Modern Movement

Origins of the modern movement for renewal in the liturgy date back to the 19th century. The key contributing factor was a revival of liturgical and scriptural studies. Of special significance was the work of the Benedictine monks of Solesmes, France, who aroused great interest in the liturgy through the restoration of Gregorian Chant. St. Pius X approved their work in a motu proprio of 1903 and gave additional encouragement to liturgical study and development.

St. Pius X did more than any other single pope to promote early first Communion and the practice of frequent Communion, started the research behind a revised breviary, and appointed a group to investigate possible revisions in the Mass.

The movement attracted some attention in the 1920's and 30's but made little progress.

Significant pioneering developments in the US during the 20's, however, were the establishment of the Liturgical Press, the beginning of publication of *Orate Fratres* (now *Worship*), and the inauguration of the League of the Divine Office by the Benedictines at St. John's Abbey, Collegeville, Minn. Later events of influence were the establishment of the Pius X School of Liturgical Music at Manhattanville College of the Sacred Heart and the organization of a summer school of liturgical music at Mary Manse College by the Gregorian Institute of America. The turning point toward real renewal was reached during and after World War II.

Pius XII gave it impetus and direction, principally through the background teaching in his encyclicals on the *Mystical Body* (1943), *Sacred Liturgy* (1947), and the *Discipline of Sacred Music* (1955), and by means of specific measures affecting the liturgy itself. His work was continued during the pontificates of John XXIII and Paul VI. The Second Vatican Council, in virtue of its *Constitution on the Sacred Liturgy,* inaugurated changes of the greatest significance.

Before and After Vatican II

The most significant liturgical changes made in the years immediately preceding the Second Vatican Council were the following:

(1) Revision of the Rites of Holy Week, for universal observance from 1956.

(2) Modification of the Eucharistic fast and permission for afternoon and evening Mass, in effect from 1953 and extended in 1957.

(3) The Dialogue Mass, introduced in 1958.

(4) Use of popular languages in administration of the sacraments.

(5) Calendar-missal-breviary reform, in effect from Jan. 1, 1961.

(6) Seven-step administration of baptism for adults, approved in 1962.

The *Constitution on the Sacred Liturgy* approved (2,174 to 4) and promulgated by the Second Vatican Council Dec. 4, 1963, marked the beginning of a profound renewal in the Church's corporate worship. Implementation of some of its measures was ordered by Paul VI Jan. 25, 1964, in the motu proprio *Sacram Liturgiam*. On Feb. 29, a special commission, the Consilium for Implementing the Constitution on the Sacred Liturgy, was formed to supervise the execution of the entire program of liturgical reform. Implementation of the program on local and regional levels was left to bishops acting through their own liturgical commissions and in concert with their fellow bishops in national conferences.

Liturgical reform in the United States has been carried out under the direction of the Liturgy Committee, National Conference of Catholic Bishops. Its secretariat, established early in 1965, is located at 1312 Massachusetts Ave. N.W., Washington, D.C. 20005.

Stages of Development

Liturgical development after the Second Vatican Council proceeded in several stages. It started with the formulation of guidelines and directives, and with the translation into vernacular languages of virtually unchanged Latin ritual texts. Then came structural changes in the Mass, the sacraments, the calendar, the Divine Office and other phases of the liturgy. These revisions were just about completed with the publication of a new order for the sacrament of penance in February, 1974. A continuing phase of development, in progress from the beginning, involves efforts to deepen the liturgical sense of the faithful, to increase their participation in worship and to relate it to full Christian life.

Texts and Translations

The master texts of all documents on liturgical reform were in Latin. Effective dates of their implementation depended on the completion and approval of appropriate translations into vernacular languages. English translations were made by the International Committee for English in the Liturgy.

The principal features of liturgical changes and the effective dates of their introduction in the United States are covered below under topical headings. (For expanded coverage of various items, especially the sacraments, see additional entries.)

The Mass

A new Order of the Mass, supplanting the one authorized by the Council of Trent in the 16th century, was introduced in the U.S. Mar. 22, 1970. It had been approved by Paul VI in the apostolic constitution *Missale Romanum*, dated Apr. 3, 1969.

Preliminary and related to it were the following developments.

Mass in English: Introduced Nov. 29, 1964. In the same year, Psalm 42 was eliminated from the prayers at the foot of the altar.

Incidental Changes: The last Gospel (prologue of John) and vernacular prayers following Mass were eliminated Mar. 7, 1965. At the same time, provision was made for the celebrant to say aloud some prayers formerly said silently.

Rubrics: An instruction entitled *Tres Abhinc Annos*, dated May 4 and effective June 29, 1967, simplified directives for the celebration of Mass, approved the practice of saying the canon aloud, altered the Communion and dismissal rites, permitted purple instead of black vestments in Masses for the dead, discontinued wearing of the maniple, and approved in principle the use of vernacular languages for the canon, ordination rites, and lessons of the Divine Office when read in choir.

Canons or Eucharistic Prayers: Three additional Eucharistic prayers authorized May 23, 1968, were approved for use in vernacular translation the following Aug. 15. They have the same basic structure as the traditional Roman Canon, whose use in English was introduced Oct. 22, 1967.

The customary Roman Canon, which dates at least from the beginning of the fifth century and has remained substantially unchanged since the seventh century, is the first in the order of listing of the Eucharistic prayers. It can be used at any time, but is the one of choice for most Sundays, some special feasts like Easter and Pentecost, and for feasts of the Apostles and other saints who are commemorated in the canon. Any preface can be used with it.

The second Eucharistic prayer, the shortest and simplest of all, is best suited for use on weekdays and various special circumstances. It has a preface of its own, but others may be used with it. This canon bears a close resemblance to the one framed by St. Hippolytus about 215.

The third Eucharistic prayer is suitable for use on Sundays and feasts as an alternative to the Roman Canon. It can be used with any preface and has a special formula for remembrance of the dead.

The fourth Eucharistic prayer, the most sophisticated of them all, presents a broad synthesis of salvation history. Based on the Eastern tradition of Antioch, it is best suited for use at Masses attended by persons versed in Sacred Scripture. It has an unchangeable preface.

English translations of three new canons for Masses with children and two for Masses of reconciliation were approved by the Congregation for Divine Worship June 5, 1975, for an experimental period to end with 1977, later extended to the end of 1980. The choice of one each of the canons was left to the judgment of the National Conference of Catholic Bishops.

Lectionary: A new compilation of scriptural readings and psalm responsories for Mass was introduced Mar. 22, 1970. The *Lectionary* contains a three-year cycle of readings for Sundays and solemn feasts, a two-year weekday cycle, and a one-year cycle for the feasts of saints, in addition to readings for a great variety of Masses, ritual Masses and Masses for various needs. There are also responsorial psalms to follow the first readings, and gospel or alleluia versicles to follow the second readings.

Sacramentary (Missal): The Vatican Polyglot Press began distribution in June, 1970, of the Latin text of a new *Roman Missal*, the first revision published in 400 years. The English translation was authorized for optional use beginning July 1, 1974; the mandatory date for use was Dec. 1, 1974.

The missal is the celebrant's book of prayers and sacramental formulas and does not include the readings of the Mass, such as the Gospel and the Epistle. It contains the texts of entrance songs, prefaces and other prayers of the Mass. The number of prefaces is four times greater than it had been. There are 10 commons (or sets of Mass prayers) of martyrs, two of doctors of the Church, and a dozen for saints or groups of saints of various kinds, such as religious, educators and mothers of families. There are Masses during which certain sacraments are administered and others for religious profession, the Church, the pope, priests, Christian unity, the evangelization of nations, persecuted Christians, and other intentions.

Mass for Special Groups: Reasons and norms for the celebration of Mass at special gatherings of the faithful were the subject of an instruction issued May 15, 1969. Two years earlier, the U.S. Bishops' Liturgy Committee went on record in support of the celebration of Mass in private homes.

Sunday Mass on Saturday: The Congregation for the Clergy, under date of Jan. 10, 1970, granted the request that the faithful, where bishops consider it pastorally necessary or useful, may satisfy the precept of participating in Mass in the late afternoon or evening hours of Saturdays and the days before holy days of obligation.

This permission was subsequently renewed for five-year periods Dec. 14, 1974, and June 13, 1979.

Trination: The Congregation for the Sacraments, under date of Jan. 20, 1970, granted to all U.S. bishops the authority to permit priests to celebrate Mass three times on Saturdays and days preceding holy days of obligation, on condition that the first and second Masses are celebrated for weddings and/or funerals and the third Mass is celebrated in the evening so that the precept (of participating in Mass) will be satisfied by the faithful.

Mass in Latin: According to notices issued by the Congregation for Divine Worship June 1, 1971, and Oct. 28, 1974: (1) Bishops may permit the celebration of Mass in Latin for mixed-language groups. (2) Bishops may permit the celebration of one or two Masses in Latin on weekdays or Sundays in any church, irrespective of mixed-language groups involved (1971). (3) Priests may celebrate Mass in Latin when people are not present. (4) The approved revised Order of the Mass is to be used in Latin as well as vernacular languages. (5) By way of exception, bishops may permit older and handicapped priests to use the Council of Trent's Order of the Mass in private celebration of the holy Sacrifice.

Inter-Ritual Concelebration: The Apostolic Delegation in Washington, D.C., announced in June, 1971, that it had received authorization to permit priests of Roman and Eastern rites to celebrate Mass together in the rite of the host church. It was understood that the inter-ritual concelebrations would always be "a manifestation of the unity of the Church and of communion among particular churches."

Ordo of the Sung Mass: In a decree dated June 24 and made public Aug. 24, 1972, the Congregation for Divine Worship issued a new *Ordo of the Sung Mass* — containing Gregorian chants in Latin — to replace the *Graduale Romanum*.

Mass for Children: Late in 1973, the Congregation for Divine Worship issued special guidelines for children's Masses, providing accommodations to the mentality and spiritual growth of pre-adolescents while retaining the principal parts and structures of the Mass. The *Directory for Masses with Children* was approved by Paul VI Oct. 22 and was dated Nov. 1, 1973. English versions of three canons for Masses with children were approved by the congregation June 5, 1975, for an experimental period to end with 1977. Cardinal John Knox, prefect of the congregation, announced Dec. 10, 1977, that experimental use of Masses with children and the Mass of Reconciliation had been extended to the end of 1980.

Sacraments

The general use of English in administration of the sacraments was approved for the U.S. Sept. 14, 1964. Structural changes of the rites were subsequently made and introduced in the U.S. as follows.

Anointing of the Sick: Revised rites, covering also administration of the Eucharist to sick persons, were approved Nov. 30,. 1972, and published Jan. 18, 1973. The effective date for use of the provisional English prayer formula was Dec. 1, 1974.

Baptism: New rites for the baptism of infants, approved Mar. 19, 1969, were introduced June 1, 1970.

Christian Initiation of Adults: Revised rites were issued Jan. 6, 1972, for the Christian initiation of adults — affecting preparation for and reception of baptism, the Eucharist and confirmation; also, the reception of already baptized adults into the Church. These rites, which were introduced in the U.S. on the completion of English translation, nullified a seven-step baptismal process approved in 1962.

Confirmation: Revised rites, issued Aug. 15, 1971, became mandatory in the U.S. Jan. 1, 1973.

Eucharist: Several enactments concerning the Eucharist have been issued since 1966 when permission was given for the superiors of convents to administer Holy Communion in the absence of priests. Paul VI issued an instruction on *Worship of the Eucharistic Mystery* May 25, 1967, and another on the manner of administering Holy Communion May 20, 1969. Limited permission for lay persons to serve as extraordinary ministers of the Eucharist was given in 1971 and extended in 1972. Also in 1972, instructions were issued regarding administration of the Eucharist to other Christians, and in particular circumstances.

Holy Orders: Revised ordination rites for deacons, priests and bishops, validated by prior experimental use, were approved in 1970. The sacrament of holy orders underwent further revision in 1972 with the elimination of the Church-instituted orders of porter, reader, exorcist, acolyte and subdeacon, and of the tonsure ceremony symbolic' of entrance into the clerical state. The former minor orders of reader and acolyte were changed from orders to ministries.

Matrimony: New rites, issued Mar. 19, 1969, were introduced June 1, 1970. Minor revisions had been made in 1964 in conjunction with a directive for imparting the nuptial blessing at all weddings.

Penance: Ritual revision of the sacraments was completed with the approval by Paul VI Dec. 2, 1973, of new directives for the sacrament of penance or reconciliation. The U.S. Bishops' Committee on the Liturgy set Feb. 27, 1977, as the mandatory date for use of the new rite. The committee also declared that it could be used from Mar. 7, 1976, after adequate preparation of priests and people. Earlier, authorization was given by the Holy See in 1968 for the omission of any reference to excommunication or other censures in the formula of absolution unless there was some indication that a censure had actually been incurred by a penitent.

Additional Developments

Calendar: A revised liturgical calendar, approved by Paul VI Feb. 14 and made public May 9, 1969, went into effect in the U.S. in 1972.

Funeral Rites: Revised rites oriented to the resurrection theme went into effect Nov. 1, 1971.

Holy Week: The English version of revised Holy Week rites went into effect in 1971. They introduced concelebration of Mass, placed new emphasis on commemorating the institution of the priesthood on Holy Thursday, and modified Good Friday prayers for other Christians, Jews and other non-Christians.

Liturgy of the Hours: The background, contents, scope and purposes of the revised Divine Office, called the Liturgy of the Hours, were described by Paul VI in the apostolic constitution *Canticum Laudis,* dated Nov. 1, 1970. A provisional English version, incorporating basic features of the master Latin text, was published in 1971. The four complete volumes of the Hours in English have been published since May, 1975. One-volume, partial editions, intended for use by religious and lay persons not bound to pray the Liturgy of the Hours, have also been published in approved form. Nov. 27, 1977, was set by the Congregation for Divine Worship and the National Conference of Catholic Bishops as the effective date for exclusive use in liturgical worship of the translation of the Latin text of the Office approved by the International Committee on English in the Liturgy.

Music: An *Instruction on Music in the Liturgy*,dated Mar. 5 and effective May 14, 1967, encouraged congregational singing during liturgical celebrations and attempted to clarify the role of choirs and trained singers. More significantly, the instruction indicated that a major development underway in the liturgy was a gradual erasure of the distinctive lines traditionally drawn between the sung liturgy and the spoken liturgy, between what had been called the high Mass and the low Mass.

In the same year, the U.S. Bishops' Liturgy Committee approved the use of contemporary music, as well as guitars and other suitable instruments, in the liturgy. The Holy See authorized in 1968 the use of musical instruments other than the organ in liturgical services, "provided they are played in a manner suitable to worship."

Oils: The Congregation for Divine Worship issued a directive in 1971 permitting the use of other oils — from plants, seeds or coconuts — instead of the traditional olive oil in administering some of the sacraments. The directive also provided that oils could be blessed at other times than at the usual Mass of Chrism on Holy Thursday, and authorized bishops' conferences to permit priests to bless oils in cases of necessity.

Eucharistic Prayers: A three-year extension, through 1980, was granted by the Congregation for Divine Worship for continuing experimental use of approved Eucharistic Prayers in Masses for children and Masses of reconciliation.

Environment and Art in Catholic Worship: A booklet with this title was issued by the U.S. Bishops' Committee on the Liturgy in March, 1978.

Eucharistic Ministers: Approval by the Congregation for Divine Worship was reported in August, 1978, of a provisional translation of a "Rite of Commissioning Special Ministers of Holy Communion." Note was made of the fact that such ministers should be called "special" instead of "extraordinary."

Doxology: The bishops' committee called attention in August, 1978, to the directive that the Doxology concluding the Eucharistic Prayer is said or sung by the celebrant (concelebrants) alone, to which the people respond, "Amen."

Churches, Altars, Chalices: The *Newsletter* of the U.S. Bishops' Committee on the Liturgy reported in November, 1978, that the Congregation for Divine Worship had given provisional approval of a new English translation for the rite of dedicating churches and altars, and of a new form for the blessing of chalices.

Study of the Mass: The Bishops' Committee on the Liturgy, following approval of the project by the National Conference of Catholic Bishops in May, 1979, began a three-year study of the function and position of some elements of the Mass, including the Gloria, the sign of peace, the penitential rite and the readings; some changes might be made on completion of the study.

Eucharistic Hosts: Father Thomas Krosnicki, secretary of the Bishops' Committee on the Liturgy, reported in July, 1979, that the committee was preparing new guidelines on the preparation of hosts, in compliance with a request from the Congregation for the Doctrine of the Faith. He said the congregation had "questioned the contents of some of the recipes" used in this country. Cardinal Franjo Seper, prefect of the congregation, stressed the importance of carefully observing traditional theological principles relating to the making of hosts — which should be of wheat, unleavened, with the appearance of food, and capable of being broken and distributed to communicants.

Progress and Problems

Progress toward full implementation of the liturgical renewal envisioned and projected by the Second Vatican Council after 400 years of relatively little liturgical movement has been steady and, on balance, good but not altogether smooth. It has been hindered less by outright opposition than by inadequate pastoral programs of instruction and preparation, foot-dragging and extremes in experimentation. Such factors occasioned a number of official statements intended to counteract their negative effects.

Meaning of Experimentation

Liturgical experimentation, as well as the reluctance of some parties to put into effect the directives of the Second Vatican Council, was one of the subjects covered in a *Pastoral Statement on Liturgical Renewal* issued in May, 1967, by the National Conference of Catholic Bishops. The statement declared:

"Liturgical experimentation has acquired several meanings.... If it means ... privately initiated innovations, it must be disapproved. The Fathers of the council (Vatican II) had no intention whatever of encouraging experiments contrary to liturgical usage and discipline.... Unauthorized liturgical innovations are not genuine experiments at all.... They divert us from the educational work of renewal and from realizing the full potential of the present liturgy. Furthermore, this kind of unauthorized initiative is divisive of the Christian community."

The bishops' statement called for widened liturgical education and greater involvement by congregations in liturgical celebrations.

Norms

A "Third Instruction on the Correct Application of the Constitution on the Sacred Liturgy" was issued by the Congregation for Divine Worship Sept. 3, 1970, to assist bishops in putting liturgical norms — especially those concerning the Mass — into full effect. The document said:

"Liturgical reform is not at all synonymous with so-called desacralization and is not intended as an occasion for what is called secularization. Thus, the liturgy must keep a dignified and sacred character.

"The effectiveness of liturgical actions does not consist in the continual search for newer rites or simpler forms, but in an ever deeper insight into the word of God and the mystery which is celebrated. The priest will assure the presence of God and His mystery in the celebration by following the rites of the Church rather than his own preferences."

The instruction, among other things: stated that no readings of any kind may be substituted for scriptural readings, and that official formulas of the Mass may not be altered; said that the Eucharistic prayer or canon is to be said by the priest alone; noted the Latin-Rite requirement of unleavened wheat bread for the host; provided that women, although they may not serve at the altar, may read scriptural lessons except the Gospel, say prayers of the faithful, make announcements and commentary, be musicians and leaders of song, and act as ushers at Mass; cautioned that experimentation, when necessary and useful, should be carried out in line with prescribed norms.

Eucharistic Prayers

The Congregation for Divine Worship, in an Apr. 27, 1973, letter to the presidents of national conferences of bishops, coupled strong warnings against unauthorized texts with encouragement to employ permissible elements of variety and diversity in the celebration of Mass.

The May *Newsletter* of the U.S. Bishops' Committee on the Liturgy said in comment: "While reserving the decision on additional Eucharistic prayers (only four were approved) strictly to itself, the Holy See . . . 'will not refuse to consider legitimate requests, within the unity of the Roman Rite, and will weigh the petitions presented by episcopal conferences for the preparation and liturgical use of a new Eucharistic prayer in special circumstances; it will propose norms for individual cases.' . . . While the general faculty to permit new Eucharistic prayers is withheld from the episcopal conferences, the possible development for special cases is left open."

Two basic reasons were given against the use of unauthorized texts. "The first is that such a practice weakens Eucharistic and ecclesiastical communion; it is a challenge to both church unity and authority. The second reason, and often the more serious reason, is that many such Eucharistic prayers of private origin are poorly prepared without any sense of the liturgical tradition. Such texts are frequently deficient in the elements of praise and thanksgiving to God . . . just those elements which the liturgical reform has attempted to restore to the Roman liturgy."

MASS FOR NON-CATHOLICS

The Congregation for the Doctrine of the Faith released a decree June 11, 1976, authorizing the celebration of public Masses for deceased non-Catholic Christians under certain conditions.

The decree noted requests for the celebration of "Mass for deceased persons baptized in other churches or ecclesial communities, particularly when the departed showed special devotion and honor for the Catholic religion or held public office at the service of the whole civil community."

It declared: "There is, of course, no difficulty about the celebration of private Masses for these deceased persons."

"However, the present discipline lays down that they shall not be celebrated (publicly) for those who have died outside of full communion with the Catholic Church."

"In view of the present change in the religious and social situation that gave rise to the above-mentioned discipline, the Sacred Congregation for the Doctrine of the Faith has received inquiries from various quarters to ask if, in certain cases, even public Masses can be said for these deceased persons."

In reply, the congregation decreed:

"I. The present discipline regarding he celebration of public Masses for other Christians who have died shall continue to be the general rule. One reason for this is the consideration due to the conscience of these deceased persons, who did not profess the Catholic faith to the full."

"II. Exceptions can be allowed to this general rule, until the new code (of canon law) is promulgated, whenever both the following conditions are verified:

• "1. The public celebration of the Masses must be explicitly requested by the relatives, friends or subjects of the deceased person for a genuine religious motive.

• "2. In the Ordinary's judgment, there must be no scandal for the faithful.

"III. In these cases public Mass may be celebrated, provided, however, that the name of the deceased is not mentioned in the Eucharistic Prayer, since that mention presupposes full communion with the Catholic Church."

The decree was approved by Pope Paul.

RIGHT TO LIFE GROUPS

Representative organizations with members of all religious and philosophical convictions who are concerned with the right-to-life of the unborn and related issues include the following: the National Right-to-Life Committee, the National Committee for a Human Life Amendment, the Ad Hoc Committee in Defense of Life, National Nurses for Life, the Committee of Ten Million, the American Association of Pro-Life Obstetricians and Gynecologists, Alternatives to Abortion, Americans against Abortion, Lawyers for Life, the National Youth Pro-Life Coalition, and various groups with Concerned for Life and Right-to-Life titles.

Despite the opinion in some quarters that right-to-life advocates might just as well have fallen over dead after the Supreme Court decisions of 1973, pro-life organizations have shown remarkable vigor.

In the process, however, they have been subject to strong counter-campaigns which have labeled them fanatical, criticized them for sensationalism, scored them as hostile to "rights" of women and privacy, and charged them with attempts to subvert the U.S. Constitution.

One of the least credible of the charges is that they are all Catholic inspired and dominated. Such is not the case Catholic visibility is high in some sectors of the movement, but it is nowhere nearly as sominant as detractors claim.

Sacraments

The sacraments are actions of Christ and his Church which signify grace, cause it in the act of signifying it, and confer it upon persons properly disposed to receive it. They perpetuate the redemptive activity of Christ, making it present and effective. They infallibly communicate the fruit of that activity — namely grace — to responsive persons with faith. Sacramental actions consist of the union of sensible signs (matter of the sacraments) with the words of the minister (form of the sacraments).

Christ himself immediately instituted the seven sacraments of the New Law by determining their essence and the efficacy of their signs to produce the grace they signify.

Christ is the principal priest or minister of every sacrament; human agents — an ordained priest, baptized persons contracting marriage with each other, any person conferring emergency baptism in a proper manner — are secondary ministers. Sacraments have efficacy from Christ, not from the personal dispositions of their human ministers.

Each sacrament confers sanctifying grace for the special purpose of the sacrament; this is, accordingly, called sacramental grace. It involves a right to actual graces corresponding to the purposes of the respective sacraments.

While sacraments infallibly produce the grace they signify, recipients benefit from them in proportion to their personal dispositions. One of these is the intention to receive sacraments as sacred signs of God's saving and grace-giving action. The state of grace is also necessary for fruitful reception of the Holy Eucharist, confirmation, matrimony, holy orders and anointing of the sick. Baptism is the sacrament in which grace is given in the first instance and original sin is remitted. Penance is the secondary sacrament of reconciliation, in which persons guilty of serious sin after baptism are reconciled with God and the Church, and in which persons already in the state of grace are strengthened in that state.

Role of Sacraments

The Second Vatican Council prefaced a description of the role of the sacraments with the following statement concerning participation by all the faithful in the priesthood of Christ and the exercise of that priesthood by receiving the sacraments (*Dogmatic Constitution on the Church,* Nos. 10 and 11).

"... The baptized by regeneration and the anointing of the Holy Spirit are consecrated into a spiritual house and a holy priesthood. Thus through all those works befitting Christian men they can offer spiritual sacrifice and proclaim the power of Him who has called them out of darkness into His marvelous light (cf. 1 Pt. 2:4-10). . . ."

"Though they differ from one another in essence and not only in degree, the common priesthood of the faithful and the ministerial or hierarchical priesthood (of those ordained to holy orders) are nonetheless interrelated. Each of them in its own special way is a participation in the one priesthood of Christ. The ministerial priest, by the sacred power he enjoys, molds and rules the priestly people. Acting in the person of Christ, he brings about the Eucharistic Sacrifice, and offers it to God in the name of all the people. For their part, the faithful join in the offering of the Eucharist by virtue of their royal priesthood. They likewise exercise that priesthood by receiving the sacraments, by prayer and thanksgiving, by the witness of a holy life, and by self-denial and active charity."

"It is through the sacraments and the exercise of the virtues that the sacred nature and organic structure of the priestly community is brought into operation."

Baptism: "Incorporated into the Church through baptism, the faithful are consecrated by the baptismal character to the exercise of the cult of the Christian religion. Reborn as sons of God, they must confess before men the faith which they have received from God through the Church."

Confirmation: "Bound more intimately to the Church by the sacrament of confirmation, they are endowed by the Holy Spirit with special strength. Hence they are more strictly obliged to spread and defend the faith both by word and by deed as true witnesses of Christ."

Eucharist: "Taking part in the Eucharistic Sacrifice, which is the fount and apex of the whole Christian life, they offer the divine Victim to God, and offer themselves along with It. Thus, both by the act of oblation and through holy Communion, all perform their proper part in this liturgical service, not, indeed, all in the same way but each in that way which is appropriate to himself. Strengthened anew at the holy table by the Body of Christ, they manifest in a practical way that unity of God's People which is suitably signified and wondrously brought about by this most awesome sacrament."

Penance: "Those who approach the sacrament of penance obtain pardon from the mercy of God for offenses committed against Him. They are at the same time reconciled with the Church, which they have wounded by their sins, and which by charity, example, and prayer seeks their conversion."

Anointing of the Sick: "By the sacred anointing of the sick and the prayer of her priests, the whole Church commends those who are ill to the suffering and glorified Lord, asking that He may lighten their suffering and save them (cf. Jas. 5:14-16). She exhorts them, moreover, to contribute to the welfare of the whole People of God by associating themselves freely with the passion and death of Christ (cf. Rom. 8:17; Col. 1:24; 2 Tm. 2:11-12; 1 Pt. 4:13)."

Holy Orders: "Those of the faithful who are consecrated by holy orders are appointed to feed the Church in Christ's name with the Word and the grace of God."

Matrimony: "Christian spouses, in virtue of the sacrament of matrimony, signify and partake of the mystery of that unity and fruitful love which exists between Christ and His Church (cf. Eph. 5:32). The spouses thereby help each other to attain to holiness in their married life and by the rearing and education of their children. And so, in their state and way of life, they have their own special gift among the People of God (cf. 1 Cor. 7:7).

"For from the wedlock of Christians there comes the family, in which new citizens of human society are born. By the grace of the Holy Spirit received in baptism these are made children of God, thus perpetuating the People of God through the centuries. The family is, so to speak, the domestic Church. In it parents should, by their word and example, be the first preachers of the faith to their children. They should encourage them in the vocation which is proper to each of them, fostering with special care any religious vocation.

"Fortified by so many and such powerful means of salvation, all the faithful, whatever their condition or state, are called by the Lord, each in his own way, to that perfect holiness whereby the Father Himself is perfect."

Baptism

Baptism is the sacrament of spiritual regeneration by which a person is incorporated in Christ and made a member of His Mystical Body, given grace, and cleansed of original sin. Actual sins and the punishment due for them are remitted also if the person baptized was guilty of such sins (e.g., in the case of a person baptized after reaching the age of reason). The theological virtues of faith, hope and charity are given with grace. The sacrament confers a character on the soul and can be received only once. Baptism has been called a sacrament of the dead because its purpose is to confer sanctifying grace on persons who do not have it.

The matter is the pouring of water. The form is: "I baptize you in the name of the Father and of the Son and of the Holy Spirit."

The minister of solemn baptism is a priest or deacon, but in case of emergency anyone, including a non-Catholic, can validly baptize. The minister pours water on the forehead of the person being baptized and says the words of the form while the water is flowing. The water used in solemn baptism is blessed during the rite.

The Church recognizes as valid baptism by **immersion, aspersion** (sprinkling of the water), or **infusion** (pouring of the water). In the Western Church, i.e., Roman Rite, the method of infusion is prescribed. The Church recognizes as valid baptisms properly performed by non-Catholic ministers. The baptism of infants has always been considered valid and the general practice of infant baptism was well established by the fifth century. Baptism is conferred conditionally when there is doubt about the validity of a previous baptism or the dispositions of the person.

Baptism is necessary for salvation. If a person cannot receive the baptism of water described above, this can be supplied by baptism of blood (martyrdom suffered for the Catholic faith or some Christian virtue) or by baptism of desire (perfect contrition joined with at least the implicit intention of doing whatever God wills that men should do for salvation).

A sponsor is required for the person being baptized. (See Godparents, below).

A person must be validly baptized before he can receive any of the other sacraments.

Christian Initiation of Infants: Infants should be solemnly baptized as soon after birth as conveniently possible. In danger of death, anyone may baptize an infant. If the child survives, the ceremonies of solemn baptism should be supplied.

The sacrament is ordinarily conferred by a priest or deacon of the parents' parish.

Only Catholics, in their 14th year or older, may be **godparents** or sponsors. Only one is required. Two, one of each sex, are permitted. A non-Catholic Christian cannot be a godparent for a Catholic child, but may serve as a witness to the baptism. A Catholic may not be a godparent for a child baptized in a non-Catholic religion, but may be a witness.

The role of godparents in baptismal ceremonies is secondary to the role of the parents. They serve as representatives of the community of faith and with the parents request baptism for the child and perform other ritual functions. Their function after baptism is to serve as proxies for the parents if the parents should be unable or fail to provide for the religious training of the child.

At baptism every child should be given a name with Christian significance, usually the name of a saint, to symbolize newness of life in Christ.

Christian Initiation of Adults: According to the *Ordo Initiationis Christianae Adultorum* ("Rite of the Christian Initiation of Adults") issued by the Congregation for Divine Worship under date of Jan. 6, 1972, adults are prepared for baptism and reception into the Church in several stages:

• An initial period of inquiry, instruction and evangelization.

- The catechumenate, a period of formal instruction and progressive formation in and familiarity with Christian life. It starts with a statement of purpose and includes a rite in which the catechumen is signed with the cross, blessings, exorcisms, and introduction into church for celebration of the word of God.
- Immediate preparation, called a period of purification and enlightenment, from the beginning of Lent to reception of the sacraments of initiation — baptism, confirmation, Holy Eucharist — at Easter. The period is marked by scrutinies, formal giving of the creed and the Lord's Prayer, the choice of a Christian name, and a final statement of intention.
- A final phase whose objective is greater familiarity with Christian life in the Church through observances of the Easter season and association with the community of the faithful.

The priest who baptizes a catechumen can also administer the sacrament of confirmation.

A sponsor is required for the person being baptized.

The *Ordo* also provides a simple rite of initiation for adults in danger of death and for cases in which all stages of the initiation process are not necessary, and guidelines for: (1) the preparation of adults for the sacraments of confirmation and Holy Eucharist in cases where they have been baptized but have not received further formation in the Christian life; (2) for the formation and initiation of children of catechetical age.

The Church recognizes the right of anyone over the age of seven to request baptism and to receive the sacrament after completing a course of instruction and giving evidence of good will. Practically, in the case of minors in a non-Catholic family or environment, the Church accepts them when other circumstances favor their ability to practice the faith — e.g., well-disposed family situation, the presence of another or several Catholics in the family. Those who are not in such favorable circumstances are prudently advised to defer reception of the sacrament until they attain the maturity necessary for independent practice of the faith.

Reception of Baptized Christians: Procedure for the reception of already baptized Christians into full communion with the Catholic Church is distinguished from the catechumenate, since they have received some Christian formation. Instruction and formation are provided as necessary, however; and conditional baptism is administered if there is reasonable doubt about the validity of the person's previous baptism.

In the rite of reception, the person is invited to join the community of the Church in professing the Nicene Creed and is asked to state: "I believe and profess all that the holy Catholic Church believes, teaches, and proclaims as revealed by God." The priest places his hand on the head of the person, states the formula of admission to full communion, confirms (in the absence of a bishop), gives a sign of peace, and administers Holy Communion during a Eucharistic Liturgy.

Confirmation

Confirmation is the sacrament by which a baptized person, through anointing with chrism and the imposition of hands, is endowed with the gifts and special strength of the Holy Spirit for mature Christian living. The sacrament, which completes the Christian initiation begun wth baptism, confers a character on the soul and can be received only once.

According to the apostolic constitution *Divinae Consortium Naturae* dated Aug. 15, 1971, in conjunction with the *Ordo Confirmationis* ("Rite of Confirmation"): "The sacrament of confirmation is conferred through the anointing with chrism on the forehead, which is done by the imposition of the hand (matter of the sacrament), and through the words: 'N . . . . , receive the seal of the Holy Spirit, the Gift of the Father' " (form of the sacrament). On May 5, 1975, bishops' conferences in English-speaking countries were informed by the Congregation for Divine Worship that Pope Paul had approved this English version of the form of the sacrament: "Be sealed with the gift of the Holy Spirit."

The ordinary minister of confirmation in the Roman Rite is a bishop. Priests may be delegated for the purpose. A pastor can confirm a parishioner in danger of death, and a priest can confirm in ceremonies of Christian initiation.

Ideally, the sacrament is conferred during the Eucharistic Liturgy. Elements of the rite include renewal of the promises of baptism, which confirmation ratifies and completes, and the laying on of hands — by symbolic elevation over the heads of those being confirmed — by the confirming bishop and priests participating in the ceremony.

"The entire rite," according to the *Ordo;* "has a twofold meaning. The laying of hands upon the candidates, done by the bishop and the concelebrating priests, expresses the biblical gesture by which the gift of the Holy Spirit is invoked. . . . The anointing with chrism and the accompanying words clearly signify the effect of the Holy Spirit. Signed with the perfumed oil by the bishop's hand, the baptized person receives the indelible character, the seal of the Lord, together with the Spirit who is given and who conforms the person more perfectly to Christ and gives him the grace of spreading the Lord's presence among men."

A sponsor is required for the person being

confirmed. This can be one of the baptismal sponsors or another person. Parents can serve as sponsors for their own children.

In the Roman Rite, it has been customary for children to receive confirmation within a reasonable time after first Communion and confession. There is a developing trend, however, to defer confirmation until later when its significance for mature Christian living becomes more evident. In the Eastern Rites, confirmation is administered at the same time as baptism.

The Holy Eucharist

The Holy Eucharist is a sacrifice (see The Mass) and the sacrament in which Christ is present and is received under the appearances of bread and wine.

The matter is bread of wheat, unleavened in the Roman Rite and leavened in the Eastern Rites, and wine of grape. The form consists of the words of consecration said by the priest at Mass: "This is my body. . . . This is the cup of my blood" (according to the traditional usage of the Roman Rite).

Only a priest can consecrate bread and wine so they become the body and blood of Christ. After consecration, however, the Eucharist can be administered by deacons and, for various reasons, by religious and lay persons.

Priests celebrating Mass receive the Eucharist under the appearances of bread and wine. In the Roman Rite, others usually receive under the appearances of bread only, i.e., the consecrated host; in some circumstances, however, they may receive under the appearances of both bread and wine. In Eastern-Rite practice, the faithful generally receive a piece of consecrated leavened bread which has been dipped into consecrated wine (i.e., by intinction).

Conditions for receiving the Eucharist, commonly called **Holy Communion,** are the state of grace, the right intention, and observance of the Eucharistic fast.

The faithful of Roman Rite are required by a precept of the Church to receive the Eucharist at least once a year, during the Easter time (in the U.S., from the First Sunday of Lent to Trinity Sunday, inclusive).

(See Eucharistic Fast, Mass, Transubstantiation, Viaticum.)

First Communion and Confession: Children are to be prepared for and given opportunity for receiving both sacraments on reaching the age of discretion, at which time they become subject to general norms concerning confession and Communion. This, together with a stated preference for first confession before first Communion, was the central theme of a document entitled *Sanctus Pontifex* and published May 24, 1973, by the Congregation for the Discipline of the Sacraments and the Congregation for the Clergy, with the approval of Pope Paul VI.

What the document prescribed was the observance of practices ordered by St. Pius X in the decree *Quam Singulari* of Aug. 8, 1910. Its purpose was to counteract pastoral and catechetical experiments virtually denying children the opportunity of receiving both sacraments at the same time. Termination of such experiments was ordered by the end of the 1972-73 school year.

At the time the document was issued, two- or three-year experiments of this kind — routinely deferring reception of the sacrament of penance until after the first reception of Holy Communion — were in effect in more than half of the dioceses of the U.S. They have remained in effect in many places, despite the advisory from the Vatican.

One reason stated in support of such experiments is the view that children are not capable of serious sin at the age of seven or eight, when Communion is generally received for the first time, and therefore prior reception of the sacrament of penance is not necessary. Another reason is the purpose of making the distinctive nature of the two sacraments clearer to children.

The Vatican view reflected convictions that the principle and practice of devotional reception of penance are as valid for children as they are for adults, and that sound catechetical programs can avoid misconceptions about the two sacraments.

A second letter on the same subject and in the same vein was released May 19, 1977, by the aforementioned congregations. It was issued in response to the question:

" 'Whether it is allowed after the declaration of May 24, 1973, to continue to have, as a general rule, the reception of first Communion precede the reception of the sacrament of penance in those parishes in which this practice developed in the past few years.'

"The Sacred Congregations for the Sacraments and Divine Worship and for the Clergy, with the approval of the Supreme Pontiff, reply: Negative, and according to the mind of the declaration.

"The mind of the declaration is that one year after the promulgation of the same declaration, all experiments of receiving first Communion without the sacrament of penance should cease so that the discipline of the Church might be restored, in the spirit of the decree, *Quam Singulari*."

The two letters from the Vatican congregations have not produced uniformity of practice in this country. Simultaneous preparation for both sacraments is provided in some dioceses where a child has the option of receiving either sacrament first, with the counsel of parents, priests and teachers. Programs in other dioceses are geared first to reception of Communion and later to reception of the sacrament of reconciliation.

Commentators on the letters note that: they are disciplinary rather than doctrinal in content; they are subject to pastoral interpretation by bishops; they cannot be interpreted to mean that a person who is not guilty of serious sin must be required to receive the sacrament of penance before (even first) Communion.

Holy Communion under the Forms of Bread and Wine (by separate taking of the consecrated bread and wine or by intinction, the reception of the host dipped in the wine): Such reception is permitted under conditions stated in instructions issued by the Congregation for Divine Worship (May 25, 1967; June 29, 1970), the *General Instruction on the Roman Missal* (No. 242), and directives of bishops' conferences and individual bishops.

Accordingly, Communion can be administered in this way to: persons being baptized, received into communion with the Church, confirmed, receiving anointing of the sick; couples at their wedding or jubilee; religious at profession or renewal of profession; lay persons receiving an ecclesiastical assignment (e.g., lay missionaries); participants at concelebrated Masses, retreats, pastoral commission meetings, daily Masses and on other occasions.

Holy Communion Twice a Day: The reception of Holy Communion at Mass a second time on the same day is permitted in accord with provisions of the "Instruction on Facilitating Communion in Particular Circumstances" *(Immensae Caritatis)* approved by Pope Paul VI Jan. 20 and published by the Congregation for Divine Worship Mar. 29, 1973.

The occasions are: Sunday Mass on Saturday evening or a holy day Mass the previous evening; a second Mass on Christmas or Easter, following reception at midnight Mass or the Mass of the Easter Vigil; the evening Mass of Holy Thursday, following reception at the earlier Mass of Chrism; Masses in which baptism, confirmation, holy orders, matrimony, anointing of the sick, first Communion, Viaticum are administered; some Masses for the dead (e.g., of Christian burial, first anniversary); special occasions — consecration of a church or altar, religious profession, conferring an ecclesiastical assignment (e.g., to lay missionaries), feast of Corpus Christi, parochial visitation, canonical visitation or special meetings of religious, Eucharistic and other congresses, pilgrimages, preaching missions; other occasions designated by the local bishop.

Holy Communion and Eucharistic Devotion outside of Mass: These were the subjects of an instruction *(De Sacra Communione et de Cultu Mysterii Eucharistici extra Missam)* dated June 21 and made public Oct. 18, 1973, by the Congregation for Divine Worship.

Holy Communion can be given outside of Mass to persons unable for a reasonable cause to receive it during Mass on a given day. The ceremonial rite is modeled on the structure of the Mass, consisting of a penitential act, a scriptural reading, the Lord's Prayer, a sign or gesture of peace, giving of the Eucharist, prayer and final blessing. Viaticum and Communion to the sick can be given by extraordinary ministers (authorized lay persons) with appropriate rites.

Forms of devotion outside of Mass are exposition of the Blessed Sacrament (by men or women religious, especially, or lay persons in the absence of a priest; but only a priest can give the blessing), processions and congresses with appropriate rites.

Intercommunion: Church policy on intercommunion was stated in an "Instruction on the Admission of Other Christians to the Eucharist," dated June 1 and made public July 8, 1972, against the background of the *Decree on Ecumenism* approved by the Second Vatican Council, and the *Directory on Ecumenism* issued by the Secretariat for Promoting Christian Unity in 1967.

Basic principles related to intercommunion are:

• "There is an indissoluble link between the mystery of the Church and the mystery of the Eucharist, or between ecclesial and Eucharistic communion; the celebration of the Eucharist of itself signifies the fullness of profession of faith and ecclesial communion" (1972 Instruction).

• "Eucharistic communion practiced by those who are not in full ecclesial communion with each other cannot be the expression of that full unity which the Eucharist of its nature signifies and which in this case does not exist; for this reason such communion cannot be regarded as a means to be used to lead to full ecclesial communion" (1972 Instruction).

• The question of reciprocity "arises only with those churches which have preserved the substance of the Eucharist, the sacrament of orders and apostolic succession" (1967 Directory).

• "A Catholic cannot ask for the Eucharist except from a minister who has been validly ordained" (1967 Directory).

The policy distinguishes between separated Eastern Christians and other Christians.

With Separated Eastern Christians (e.g., Orthodox): These may be given the Eucharist (as well as penance and anointing of the sick) at their request. Catholics may receive these same sacraments from priests of separated Eastern churches if they experience genuine spiritual necessity, seek spiritual benefit, and access to a Catholic priest is morally or physically impossible. This policy (of reciprocity) derives from the facts that the separated Eastern churches have apostolic succession through their bishops, valid priests, and sacramental beliefs and practices in accord with those of the Catholic Church.

With Other Christians (e.g., members of Reformation-related churches, others): Admission to the Eucharist in the Catholic Church, according to the *Directory on Ecumenism,* "is confined to particular cases of those Christians who have a faith in the sacrament in conformity with that of the Church, who experience a serious spiritual need for the Eucharistic sustenance, who for a prolonged period are unable to have recourse to a minister of their own community and who ask for the sacrament of their own accord; all this provided that they have proper dispositions and lead lives worthy of a Christian." The spiritual need is defined as "a need for an increase in spiritual life and a need for a deeper involvement in the mystery of the Church and of its unity."

Circumstances under which Communion may be given to other properly disposed Christians are danger of death, imprisonment, persecution, grave spiritual necessity coupled with no chance of recourse to a minister of their own community. Judgment regarding these and other special circumstances rests with the local bishop.

Catholics cannot ask for the Eucharist from ministers of other Christian churches who have not been validly ordained to the priesthood.

Penance

Penance is the sacrament by which sins committed after baptism are forgiven and a person is reconciled with God and the Church.

A revised ritual for the sacrament — *Ordo Paenitentiae,* published by the Congregation of Divine Worship Feb. 7, 1974 — reiterates standard doctrine concerning the sacrament; emphasizes the social (communal and ecclesial) aspects of sin and conversion, with due regard for personal aspects and individual reception of the sacrament; prescribes three forms for celebration of the sacrament; and presents models for community penitential services.

The U.S. Bishops' Committee on the Liturgy recommended that adequate preparation of priests and people should precede introduction in this country of the revised ritual in English. Recommended dates for its use, after due preparation, were the first Sunday of Lent, 1976 (optional), and the first Sunday of Lent, 1977 (mandatory).

The basic elements of the sacrament are sorrow for sin because of a supernatural motive, confession (of previously unconfessed mortal or grave sins, required; of venial sins also, but not of necessity), and reparation (by means of prayer or other act enjoined by the confessor), all of which comprise the matter of the sacrament; and absolution, which is the form of the sacrament.

The traditional words of absolution — "I absolve you from your sins in the name of the Father, and of the Son, and of the Holy Spirit" — remain unchanged at the conclusion of a petition in the new rite that God may grant pardon and peace through the ministry of the Church.

The minister of the sacrament is an authorized priest — i.e., one who, besides having the power of orders to forgive sins, also has faculties of jurisdiction granted by an ecclesiastical superior and/or by canon law.

The sacrament can be celebrated in three ways.

• For individuals: The traditional manner remains acceptable but is enriched with additional elements including: reception of the penitent and making of the Sign of the Cross; an exhortation by the confessor to trust in God; a possible reading from Scripture; confession of sins; manifestation of repentance; petition for God's forgiveness through the ministry of the Church and the absolution of the priest; praise of God's mercy, and dismissal in peace. Some of these elements are optional.

• For several penitents, in the course of a community celebration including a liturgy of the Word of God and prayers, individual confession and absolution, and an act of thanksgiving.

• For several penitents, in the course of a community celebration, with general confession and general absolution. This method is reserved for special circumstances in which it is morally or physically impossible for persons to confess and be absolved individually, and in view of their need for reconciliation and reception of the Eucharist. Penitents are required to confess at their next individual confession any grave sins absolved in such a general celebration of the sacrament. Judgment regarding circumstances that warrant general confession and absolution belongs principally to the bishop of the place.

Communal celebrations of the sacrament are not held in connection with Mass.

The place of individual confession, as determined by episcopal conferences in accordance with given norms, can be the traditional confessional or another appropriate setting.

The sacrament is necessary, by the institution of Christ, for the reconciliation of persons guilty of grave sins committed after baptism.

A precept of the Church obliges the faithful guilty of grave sin to confess at least once a year.

The Church favors more frequent reception of the sacrament not only for the reconciliation of persons guilty of serious sins but also for reasons of devotion. Devotional confession — in which venial sins or previously forgiven sins are confessed — serves the purpose of confirming persons in penance and conversion.

Penitential Celebrations: Communal penitential celebrations are designed to emphasize the social dimensions of Christian life — the community aspects and significance of penance and reconciliation.

Elements of such celebrations are community prayer, hymns and songs, scriptural and other readings, examination of conscience, general confession and expression of sorrow for sin, acts of penance and reconciliation, and a form of non-sacramental absolution resembling the one in the penitential rite of the Mass.

If the sacrament is celebrated during the service, there must be individual confession and absolution of sin.

(See Absolution, Confession, Confessional, Confessor, Contrition, Faculties, Forgiveness of Sin, Power of the Keys, Seal of Confession, Sin.)

Anointing of the Sick

This sacrament, promulgated by St. James the Apostle (Jas. 5:13-15), is administered to persons who are seriously ill. By the anointing with blessed oil and the prayer of a priest, the sacrament confers on the person comforting grace; the remission of venial sins and inculpably unconfessed mortal sins, together with at least some of the temporal punishment due for sins; and, sometimes, results in an improved state of health.

The matter of this sacrament is the anointing with blessed oil (of the sick — olive oil, or vegetable oil if necessary) of the forehead and hands; in cases of necessity, a single anointing of another portion of the body suffices. The form is: "Through this holy anointing and his most loving mercy, may the Lord assist you by the grace of the Holy Spirit so that, when you have been freed from your sins, he may save you and in his goodness raise you up."

Anointing of the sick, formerly called extreme unction, may be received more than once, e.g., in new or continuing stages of serious illness. Ideally, the sacrament should be administered while the recipient is conscious and in conjunction with the sacraments of penance and the Eucharist. It may be administered conditionally even after apparent death.

The sacrament can be administered during a communal celebration in some circumstances, as in a home for the aged.

Holy Orders

Holy orders is the sacrament by which spiritual power and grace are given to enable an ordained minister to consecrate the Eucharist, forgive sins, perform other pastoral and ecclesiastical functions, and form the community of the People of God. Holy orders confers a character on the soul and can be received only once. The minister of the sacrament is a bishop.

Holy orders, like matrimony but in a different way, is a social sacrament. As the Second Vatican Council declared in the *Dogmatic Constitution on the Church:*

"For the nurturing and constant growth of the People of God, Christ the Lord instituted in His Church a variety of ministries, which work for the good of the whole body. For those ministers who are endowed with sacred power are servants of their brethren, so that all who are of the People of God, and therefore enjoy a true Christian dignity, can work toward a common goal freely and in an orderly way, and arrive at salvation" (No. 18).

"With their helpers, the priests and deacons, bishops have . . . taken up the service of the community, presiding in place of God over the flock whose shepherds they are, as teachers of doctrine, priests of sacred worship, and officers of good order" (No. 20).

The fullness of the priesthood belongs to those who have received the order of **bishop.** Bishops, in hierarchical union with the pope and their fellow bishops, are the successors of the apostles as pastors of the Church: they have individual responsibility for the care of the local churches they serve and collegial responsibility for the care of the universal Church (see Collegiality). In the ordination or consecration of bishops, the essential form is the imposition of hands by the consecrator(s) and the assigned prayer in the preface of the rite of ordination.

A **priest** is an ordained minister with the power to celebrate Mass, administer the sacraments, preach and teach the word of God, impart blessings, and perform additional pastoral functions, according to the mandate of his ecclesiastical superior.

Concerning priests, the Second Vatican Council stated in the *Dogmatic Constitution on the Church* (No. 28):

". . . The divinely established ecclesiastical ministry is exercised on different levels by those who from antiquity have been called bishops, priests, and deacons. Although priests do not possess the highest degree of the priesthood, and although they are dependent on the bishops in the exercise of their power, they are nevertheless united with the bishops in sacerdotal dignity. By the power of the sacrament of orders, and in the image of Christ the eternal High Priest (Hb. 5:1-10; 7:24; 9:11-28), they are consecrated to preach the gospel, shepherd the faithful, and celebrate divine worship as true priests of the New Testament. . . .

"Priests, prudent cooperators with the episcopal order as well as its aides and instruments, are called to serve the People of God. They constitute one priesthood with their bishop, although that priesthood is comprised of different functions. . . ."

In the ordination of a priest of Roman Rite, the essential matter is the imposition of hands on the heads of those being ordained by the ordaining bishop. The essential form is the accompanying prayer in the preface of the ordination ceremony. Other elements in the rite are the presentation of the implements of sacrifice — the chalice containing wine and the paten containing a host — with accompanying prayers.

Regarding the order of **deacon**, the *Dogmatic Constitution on the Church* (No. 29) stated:

"At a lower level of the hierarchy are deacons, upon whom hands are imposed 'not unto the priesthood, but unto a ministry of service.' For strengthened by sacramental grace, in communion with the bishop and his group of priests, they serve the People of God in the ministry of the liturgy, of the word, and of charity. It is the duty of the deacon, to the extent that he has been authorized by competent authority, to administer baptism solemnly, to be custodian and dispenser of the Eucharist, to assist at and bless marriages in the name of the Church, to bring Viaticum to the dying, to read the sacred Scripture to the faithful, to instruct and exhort the people, to preside at the worship and prayer of the faithful, to administer sacramentals, and to officiate at funeral and burial services. (Deacons are) dedicated to duties of charity and administration. . . ."

". . . The diaconate can in the future be restored as a proper and permanent rank of the hierarchy. It pertains to the competent territorial bodies of bishops, of one kind or another, to decide, with the approval of the Supreme Pontiff, whether and where it is opportune for such deacons to be appointed for the care of souls. With the consent of the Roman Pontiff, this diaconate will be able to be conferred upon men of more mature age, even upon those living in the married state. It may also be conferred upon suitable young men. For them, however, the law of celibacy must remain intact" (No. 29).

The Apostles ordained the first seven deacons (Acts 6:1-6): Stephen, Philip, Prochorus, Nicanor, Timon, Parmenas, Nicholas.

Other Ministries: The Church later assigned ministerial duties to men in several other orders, as:

Subdeacon, with specific duties in liturgical worship, especially at Mass. The order, whose first extant mention dates from about the middle of the third century, was regarded as minor until the 13th century; afterwards, it was called a major order in the West but not in the East.

Acolyte, to serve in minor capacities in liturgical worship; a function now performed by Mass servers.

Exorcist, to perform services of exorcism for expelling evil spirits; a function which came to be reserved to specially delegated priests.

Lector, to read scriptural and other passages during liturgical worship; a function now generally performed by lay persons.

Porter, to guard the entrance to an assembly of Christians and to ward off undesirables who tried to gain admittance; an order of early origin and utility but of present insignificance.

Long after it became evident that these positions and functions had fallen into general disuse or did not require clerical ordination, the Holy See started a revision of the orders in 1971. By an indult of Oct. 5, the bishops of the United States were permitted to omit ordaining porters and exorcists. Another indult, dated three days later, permitted the use of revised rites for ordaining acolytes and lectors, and authorized the use of a service celebrating admission to the clerical state in place of the ceremony of tonsure which had previously served this purpose.

To complete the revision, Pope Paul VI abolished Sept. 14, 1972, the orders of porter, exorcist and subdeacon; decreed that laymen, as well as candidates for the diaconate and priesthood, can be installed (rather than ordained) in the ministries (rather than orders) of acolyte and lector; reconfirmed the suppression of tonsure and its replacement with a service of dedication to God and the Church; and stated that a man enters the clerical state on ordination to the diaconate.

There were no doctrinal obstacles to the Pope's action, because the abolished orders had been instituted by the Church for functional purposes and were not considered to be parts of the sacrament of holy orders.

PERMANENT DIACONATE

Authorization for restoration of the permanent diaconate in the Roman Rite — making it possible for men to become deacons permanently, without going on to the priesthood — was promulgated by Pope Paul VI June 18, 1967, in a document entitled *Sacrum Diaconatus Ordinem* ("Sacred Order of the Diaconate").

The Pope's action implemented the desire expressed by the Second Vatican Council for reestablishment of the diaconate as an independent order in its own right not only to supply ministers for carrying on the work of the Church but also to complete the hierarchical structure of the Church of Roman Rite.

Permanent deacons have been traditional in the Eastern Church. The Western Church, however, since the fourth or fifth century, generally followed the practice of conferring the diaconate only as a sacred order preliminary to the priesthood, and of restricting the ministry of deacons to liturgical functions.

The Pope's document, issued on his own initiative, provided:

• Qualified unmarried men 25 years of age or older may be ordained permanent deacons. They cannot marry after ordination.

• Qualified married men 35 years of age or older may be ordained permanent deacons. The consent of the wife of a prospective deacon is required. A married deacon cannot remarry after the death of his wife.

• Preparation for the diaconate includes a course of study and formation over a period of at least three years.

• Candidates who are not religious must be affiliated with a diocese. Reestablishment of the permanent diaconate among religious is reserved to the Holy See.

• Deacons will practice their ministry under the direction of a bishop and with the priests with whom they will be associated. (For functions, see the description of deacon, under Holy Orders.)

Restoration of the permanent diaconate in the United States was approved by the Holy See in October, 1968. Shortly afterwards the U.S. bishops established a committee of the same name, which is chaired by Auxiliary Bishop Eugene A. Marino, S.S.J., of Washington, D.C. The committee operates through a secretariat, of which Msgr. Ernest J. Fiedler is executive director. Its offices are located at 1312 Massachusetts Ave. N. W., Washington, D.C. 20005.

Present Status

The bishops' secretariat reported in October, 1978, that 3,151 permanent deacons had been ordained in the U.S.; that 125 dioceses either had approved programs of formation or were in the process of preparing formation programs; that a total of 2,466 candidates were in training.

Functions

Deacons have various functions, depending on the nature of their assignments. Liturgically, they can officiate at baptisms, weddings, wake services and funerals, can preach and distribute Holy Communion. Some are engaged in religious education work. All are intended to carry out works of charity and pastoral service of one kind or another.

The majority of permanent deacons, 93 per cent of whom are married, continue in their secular work. Their ministry of service is developing in three dimensions: of liturgy, of the word, and of charity. Depending on the individual deacon's abilities and preference, he is assigned by his bishop to either a parochial ministry or to one particular field of service. The latter is the most challenging ministry to develop. Deacons are now active in a variety of ministries including those to prison inmates and their families, the sick in hospitals, nursing homes and homes for the aged, alienated youth, the elderly and the poor, and in various areas of legal service to the indigent, of education and campus ministry. A few have been assigned as quasi-pastors of multi-county, rural parishes. The unlimited possibilities for diaconal ministry are under realistic assessment, diocese by diocese.

Training Programs

There were 125 training centers for deacons as of April, 1979. The first four were established in 1969. One center may serve two or more dioceses in the formation of diaconal candidates.

Continuing efforts are made to recruit Spanish-speaking, black and other minority candidates in training programs. Of the permanent deacons ordained up to October, 1978, five per cent were black, and 15 per cent were Hispanic.

Training programs of spiritual, doctrinal and pastoral formation are generally based on *Permanent Deacons in the United States: Guidelines on Their Formation and Ministry*, published by the Bishops' Committee on the Permanent Diaconate in September, 1971.

Permanent diaconate training centers, diocese by diocese, were as follows, as of April, 1979.

Agana: P.O. Box 1335, Agana, Guam 96910.

Albany: 40 N. Main Ave., Albany, N.Y. 12203.

Alexandria-Shreveport: P.O. Box 13, Natchitoches, La. 71457.

Allentown: 824 N. Graham St., Allentown, Pa. 18103.

Altoona-Johnstown: Chancery Office, Logan Blvd., Box 126, Hollidaysburg, Pa. 16648.

Amarillo: P.O. Box 5644, Amarillo, Tex. 79107.

Arlington: 200 N. Glebe Rd., Suite 704, Arlington, Va. 22203.

Atlanta: St. Mary's Church, Route 5, Rothell Rd., Toccoa, Ga. 30577.

Baltimore: 711 Maiden Choice Lane, Baltimore, Md. 21204.

Baton Rouge: 445 Marquette Ave., Baton Rouge, La. 70806.

Beaumont: P.O. Box 3948, Beaumont, Tex. 77704.

Belleville: 771 Vogel Pl., East St. Louis, Ill. 62205.

Biloxi: P.O. Box 2194, Sacred Heart Church, 3902 Quinn Dr., Pascagoula, Miss. 39576.

Birmingham: P.O. Box 2086, Birmingham, Ala. 35201.

Bismarck: Apt. 206, Mary College, Bismarck, N. Dak. 58501.

Boise: St. Augustine's Center, University of Idaho, Box 3426, Moscow, Ida. 83843.

Boston: 17 Grove St., Lynnfield, Mass. 01940.

Bridgeport: 223 W. Mountain Rd., Ridgefield, Conn. 06877.
Brooklyn: P.O. Box C, Brooklyn, N.Y. 11202.
Brownsville: P.O. Box 670, Mission, Tex. 78572.
Buffalo: Renewal Center, 6969 Strickler Rd., Clarence Center, N.Y. 14032.
Burlington: St. Michael's College, Winooski, Vt. 05404.
Camden: 1845 Haddon Ave., Camden, N.J. 08101.
Caroline and Marshall Islands: P.O. Box 250, U.S. Trust Territory, Pacific 96942.
Charleston: 119 Broad St., Charleston, S.C. 29401.
Cheyenne: Box 70, Pinedale, Wyo. 82941.
Chicago: 155 E. Superior St., Chicago, Ill. 60611; 1845 S. 9th Ave., Maywood, Ill. 60153.
Cincinnati: 5440 Moeller Ave., Cincinnati, O. 45212.
Cleveland: 1031 Superior Ave., Cleveland, O. 44114.
Columbus: 197 E. Gay St., Columbus, O. 43215.
Corpus Christi: 2930 S. Alameda, Corpus Christi, Tex. 78404.
Dallas: P.O. Box 19507, Dallas, Tex. 75219.
Davenport: 705 E. 7th St., Muscatine, Iowa 52761.
Denver: 200 Josephine St., Denver, Colo. 80206.
Des Moines: St. Joseph Educational Center, 1400 Buffalo Rd., West Des Moines, Ia. 50265.
Detroit: Sacred Heart Seminary, 2701 Chicago Blvd., Detroit, Mich. 48206 (pre-ordination); 1234 Washington Blvd., Detroit, Mich. 48226 (post-ordination).
Dodge City: Sacred Heart Church, 332 N. Oak St., Pratt, Kans. 67124.
Dubuque: 106 Chapel Lane, Charles City, Ia. 50616.
Duluth: 215 W. 4th St., Duluth, Minn. 55806.
El Paso: P.O. Box 17548, El Paso, Tex. 79917.
Evansville: P.O. Box 4169, Evansville, Ind. 47711.
Fairbanks: 1500 Birchwood Rd., Anchorage, Alaska 99504.
Fall River: 410 Highland Ave., P.O. Box 7, Fall River, Mass. 02722.
Fargo: 100 35th Ave. N.E., Fargo, N.D. 58102.
Fort Wayne-South Bend: 1020 Capitol, Ft. Wayne, Ind. 46806; 19704 Johnson Rd., South Bend, Ind. 46614.
Fort Worth: P.O. Box 496, Burleson, Tex. 76028.
Fresno: Box 2087, Merced, Calif. 95340.
Gallup: St. William Church, Navajo Star Route "2," Box 64, West Gallup, N.M. 87301.
Galveston-Houston: 824 S. Main St., Box 1277, Pasadena, Tex. 77501.
Gary: P.O. Box 1769, Gary, Ind. 46408.
Grand Rapids: 2001 Robinson Rd. S.E., Grand Rapids, Mich. 49507.
Great Falls: College of Great Falls, Great Falls, Mont. 59405.
Green Bay: 1910 S. Webster, Box 66, Green Bay, Wis. 54305.
Harrisburg: 4800 Union Deposit Rd., P.O. Box 3557, Harrisburg, Pa. 17105.
Hartford: 467 Bloomfield Ave., Bloomfield, Conn. 06002.
Helena: P.O. Box 1729, Helena, Mont. 59601.
Houma-Thibodaux; P.O. Box 9077, Houma, La. 70361.
Indianapolis: 1375 S. Mickley Ave., Indianapolis, Ind. 46241.
Jackson: P.O. Box 427, Magee, Miss. 39111.
Jefferson City: P.O. Box 417, Jefferson City, Mo. 65101.
Joliet: 18 N. Woodlawn Ave., Joliet, Ill. 60435.
Juneau: Cathedral of the Nativity, 329 5th St., Juneau, Alaska 99801.
Kalamazoo: 215 N. Westnedge Ave., Kalamazoo, Mich. 49005.
Kansas City-St. Joseph: Box 1037, Kansas City, Mo. 64141.
Lafayette: 1408-C Carmel Ave., Lafayette, La. 70501.
Lansing: 300 W. Ottawa St., Lansing, Mich. 48933.
Little Rock: 2415 N. Tyler St., Little Rock, Ark. 72207.
Los Angeles: Catholic Information Center, 809 S. Flower St., Los Angeles, Calif. 90017.
Louisville: 3940 Poplar Level Rd., Louisville, Ky. 40213.
Manchester: P.O. Box 157, Manchester, N.H. 03105.
Memphis: 1325 Jefferson Ave., Memphis, Tenn. 38104.
Miami: St. Augustine's Church, 1400 Miller Rd., Coral Gables, Fla. 33146.
Military Ordinariate: 1011 First Ave., New York, N.Y. 10022.
Milwaukee: 3257 S. Lake Dr., Milwaukee, Wis. 53207.
Mobile: 2605 Spring Hill Ave., Mobile, Ala. 36607.
Monterey: 1140 Preston St., Castroville, Calif. 95012.
Nashville: 2400 21st Ave. S., Nashville, Tenn. 37212.
Newark: 221 W. Market St., Newark, N.J. 07103.
New Orleans: 7887 Walmsley Ave., New Orleans, La. 70125.
New York: St. Joseph's Seminary, Dunwoodie, Yonkers, N.Y. 10704.
Norwich: St. Bernard High School, 1593

Norwich-New London Tpke., Uncasville, Conn. 06382.
Oakland: 3840 E. Castro Valley Blvd., Castro Valley, Calif. 94546.
Ogdensburg: St. Lawrence Parish, North Lawrence, N.Y. 12967.
Oklahoma City: P.O. Box 510, Edmond, Okla. 73034.
Omaha: 5316 N. 14th Ave., Omaha, Neb. 68110.
Orange: 440 S. Batavia St., Orange, Calif. 92668.
Orlando: P.O. Box 1800, Orlando, Fla. 32804.
Paterson: Pastoral Ministry Center, 597 Valley Rd., Clifton, N.J. 07013.
Pensacola-Tallahassee: P.O. Box 2528, Panama City, Fla. 32401.
Peoria: 2822 W. Heading Ave., Peoria, Ill. 61604.
Philadelphia: 222 N. 17th St., Philadelphia, Pa. 19103 (Spanish-speaking); 4625 Springfield Ave., Philadelphia, Pa. 19143 (English-speaking).
Phoenix: 400 E. Monroe St., Phoenix, Ariz. 85004.
Pittsburgh: St. Gabriel Church, One St. Gabriel Circle, Pittsburgh, Pa. 15212.
Providence: 900 Warwick Neck Ave., Warwick, R.I. 02889.
Raleigh: 215 Cardinal Gibbons Dr., Raleigh, N.C. 27606.
Rapid City: Plainview, S.D. 57777.
Richmond: 16 N. Laurel St., Richmond, Va. 23220.
Rochester: 2260 Lake Ave., Rochester, N.Y. 14612.
Rockford: R.R. 2, Box 214-A, Rockford, Ill. 61102.
Rockville Centre: 50 N. Park Ave., Rockville Centre, N.Y. 11570.
Sacramento: St. John Vianney, 10497 Coloma Rd., Rancho Cordova, Calif. 95670.
Saginaw: 5800 Weiss, Saginaw, Mich. 48603.
St. Cloud: St. Michael's Rectory, Route 2, St. Cloud, Minn. 56301.
St. Louis: 4445 Lindell Blvd., St. Louis, Mo. 63108.
St. Paul-Minneapolis: 2260 Summit Ave., St. Paul, Minn. 55105.
St. Thomas, Virgin Islands: P.O. Box 1825, St. Thomas, Virgin Is. 00801.
Salt Lake City: 333 E. South Temple St., Salt Lake City, Utah 84111.
San Angelo: P.O. Box 1829, San Angelo, Tex. 76902.
San Antonio: P.O. Box 28240, San Antonio, Tex. 78284.
San Bernardino: Holy Rosary Cathedral, 2525 Arrowhead Ave., San Bernardino, Calif. 92405.
San Diego: 1667 Santa Paula Dr., San Diego, Calif. 92111.
San Francisco: P.O. Box 455, Colma Sta., Daly City, Calif. 94014.
Santa Fe: St. Alice Church, P.O. Box 206, Mountainair, N. Mex. 87036.
Savannah: P.O. Drawer AC, Warner Robbins, Ga. 31093.
Seattle: 907 Terry Ave., Seattle, Wash. 98104.
Sioux City: 1821 Jackson St., P.O. Box 3105, Sioux City, Iowa 51102.
Spokane: 429 E. Sharp, Spokane, Wash. 99202.
Springfield, Mass.: 76 Elliot St., P.O. Box 1730, Springfield, Mass. 01101.
Stockton: P.O. Box 617, Lodi, Calif. 95240.
Superior: 1201 Hughitt St., Superior, Wis. 54880.
Syracuse: 240 Onondaga St., Syracuse, N.Y. 13202.
Toledo: 1933 Spielbusch Ave., Toledo, O. 43624.
Trenton: One Centre St., Trenton, N.J. 08611.
Tucson: 8800 E. 22nd St., P.O. Box 17119, Tucson, Ariz. 85731.
Tulsa: P.O. Box 751, Jenks, Okla. 74037.
Washington: 1200 Varnum St. N.E., Washington, D.C. 20017.
Wheeling-Charleston: P.O. Box 230, 1300 Byron St., Wheeling, W. Va. 26003.
Wilmington: 1925 Delaware Ave., Box K, Wilmington, Del. 19805.
Worcester: Barlin Acres — 284 School St., Boyleston, Mass. 01505.
Yakima: P.O. Box 340, Royal City, Wash. 99357.
Youngstown: 144 W. Wood St., Youngstown, O. 44503.

Association of Permanent Diaconate Directors: Established in 1977 to promote effective communication and facilitate the exchange of information and resources of members; to develop professional expertise and promote research, training and self evaluation; to foster accountability and seek ways to promote means of implementing solutions to problems. Rev. John Hedderman is president. Address: 333 E. South Temple, Salt Lake City, Utah 84111.

CATHOLIC RIGHTS LEAGUE

A membership organization founded in 1973, the Catholic League for Religious and Civil Rights seeks to defend the Church and the Catholic community from defamation and violations of religious and civil rights.

The league, which has no official connection with the Church, has a membership of 28,000 and 11 local U.S. chapters. Father Virgil Blum, S.J. is president.

National headquarters is located at 1100 W. Wells St., Milwaukee, Wis. 53233.

MARRIAGE DOCTRINE

The following excerpts, stating key points of doctrine on marriage, are from the *Pastoral Constitution on the Church in the Modern World* (Nos. 48 to 51) promulgated by the Second Vatican Council.

Conjugal Covenant

"The intimate partnership of married life and love has been established by the Creator and qualified by His laws. It is rooted in the conjugal covenant of irrevocable personal consent....

"... God Himself is the author of matrimony, endowed as it is with various benefits and purposes. All of these have a very decisive bearing on the continuation of the human race, on the personal development and eternal destiny of the individual members of a family, and on the dignity, stability, peace, and prosperity of the family itself and of human society as a whole. By their very nature, the institution of matrimony itself and conjugal love are ordained for the procreation and education of children, and find in them their ultimate crown.

"Thus a man and a woman ... render mutual help and service to each other through an intimate union of their persons and of their actions. Through this union they experience the meaning of their oneness and attain to it with growing perfection day by day. As a mutual gift of two persons, this intimate union, as well as the good of the children, imposes total fidelity on the spouses and argues for an unbreakable oneness between them" (No. 48).

Sacrament of Matrimony

"Christ the Lord abundantly blessed this many-faceted love. ... The Savior of men and the Spouse of the Church comes into the lives of married Christians through the sacrament of matrimony. He abides with them thereafter so that, just as He loved the Church and handed Himself over on her behalf, the spouses may love each other with perpetual fidelity through mutual self-bestowal.

"... Graced with the dignity and office of fatherhood and motherhood, parents will energetically acquit themselves of a duty which devolves primarily on them, namely education, and especially religious education.

"... The Christian family, which springs from marriage as a reflection of the loving covenant uniting Christ with the Church, and as a participation in that covenant, will manifest to all men the Savior's living presence in the world, and the genuine nature of the Church ..." (No. 48).

Conjugal Love

"The biblical Word of God several times urges the betrothed and the married to nourish and develop their wedlock by pure conjugal love and undivided affection. . . .

"This love is an eminently human one since it is directed from one person to another through an affection of the will. It involves the good of the whole person. Therefore it can enrich the expressions of body and mind with a unique dignity, ennobling these expressions as special ingredients and signs of the friendship distinctive of marriage. This love the Lord has judged worthy of special gifts, healing, perfecting, and exalting gifts of grace and of charity.

"Such love, merging the human with the divine, leads the spouses to a free and mutual gift of themselves, a gift proving itself by gentle affection and by deed. Such love pervades the whole of their lives. Indeed, by its generous activity it grows better and grows greater. Therefore it far excels mere erotic inclination, which, selfishly pursued, soon enough fades wretchedly away.

"This love is uniquely expressed and perfected through the marital act. The actions within marriage by which the couple are united intimately and chastely are noble and worthy ones. Expressed in a manner which is truly human, these actions signify and promote that mutual self-giving by which spouses enrich each other with a joyful and a thankful will.

"Sealed by mutual faithfulness and hallowed above all by Christ's sacrament, this love remains steadfastly true in body and in mind, in bright days or dark. It will never be profaned by adultery or divorce. Firmly established by the Lord, the unity of marriage will radiate from the equal personal dignity of wife and husband, a dignity acknowledged by mutual and total love.

"The steady fulfillment of the duties of this Christian vocation demands notable virtue. For this reason, strengthened by grace for holiness of life, the couple will painstakingly cultivate and pray for constancy of love, largeheartedness, and the spirit of sacrifice ..." (No. 49).

Fruitfulness of Marriage

"Marriage and conjugal love are by their nature ordained toward the begetting and educating of children. Children are really the supreme gift of marriage and contribute very substantially to the welfare of their parents. ... God Himself ... wished to share with man a certain special participation in His own creative work. Thus He blessed male and female, saying: 'Increase and multiply' (Gn. 1:28).

"Hence, while not making the other purposes of matrimony of less account, the true practice of conjugal love, and the whole meaning of the family life which results from it, have this aim: that the couple be ready with stout hearts to cooperate with the love of the

Creator and the Savior, who through them will enlarge and enrich His own family day by day.

"Parents should regard as their proper mission the task of transmitting human life and educating those to whom it has been transmitted. They should realize that they are thereby cooperators with the love of God the Creator, and are, so to speak, the interpreters of that love. Thus they will fulfill their task with human and Christian responsibility . . ." (No. 50).

Norms of Judgment

"They will thoughtfully take into account both their own welfare and that of their children, those already born and those which may be foreseen. For this accounting they will reckon with both the material and the spiritual conditions of the times as well as of their state in life. Finally, they will consult the interests of the family group, of temporal society, and of the Church herself.

"The parents themselves should ultimately make this judgment in the sight of God. But in their manner of acting, spouses should be aware that they cannot proceed arbitrarily. They must always be governed according to a conscience dutifully conformed to the divine law itself, and should be submissive toward the Church's teaching office, which authentically interprets that law in the light of the gospel. That divine law reveals and protects the integral meaning of conjugal love, and impels it toward a truly human fulfillment. . . .

"Marriage to be sure is not instituted solely for procreation. Rather, its very nature as an unbreakable compact between persons, and the welfare of the children, both demand that the mutual love of the spouses, too, be embodied in a rightly ordered manner, that it grow and ripen. Therefore, marriage persists as a whole manner and communion of life, and maintains its value and indissolubility, even when offspring are lacking — despite, rather often, the very intense desire of the couple" (No. 50).

Love and Life

"This Council realizes that certain modern conditions often keep couples from arranging their married lives harmoniously, and that they find themselves in circumstances where at least temporarily the size of their families should not be increased. As a result, the faithful exercise of love and the full intimacy of their lives are hard to maintain. But where the intimacy of married life is broken off, it is not rare for its faithfulness to be imperiled and its quality of fruitfulness ruined. For then the upbringing of the children and the courage to accept new ones are both endangered.

"To these problems there are those who presume to offer dishonorable solutions. Indeed, they do not recoil from the taking of life. But the Church issues the reminder that a true contradiction cannot exist between the divine laws pertaining to the transmission of life and those pertaining to the fostering of authentic conjugal love.

"For God, the Lord of Life, has conferred on men the surpassing ministry of safeguarding life — a ministry which must be fulfilled in a manner which is worthy of men. Therefore from the moment of its conception life must be guarded with the greatest care, while abortion and infanticide are unspeakable crimes. The sexual characteristics of man and the human faculty of reproduction wonderfully exceed the dispositions of lower forms of life. Hence the acts themselves which are proper to conjugal love and which are exercised in accord with genuine human dignity must be honored with great reverence" (No. 51).

Church Teaching

"Therefore when there is question of harmonizing conjugal love with the responsible transmission of life, the moral aspect of any procedure does not depend solely on the sincere intentions or on an evaluation of motives. It must be determined by objective standards. These, based on the nature of the human person and his acts, preserve the full sense of mutual self-giving and human procreation in the context of true love. Such a goal cannot be achieved unless the virtue of conjugal chastity is sincerely practiced. Relying on these principles, sons of the Church may not undertake methods of regulating procreation which are found blameworthy by the teaching authority of the Church in its unfolding of the divine law.

"Everyone should be persuaded that human life and the task of transmitting it are not realities bound up with this world alone. Hence they cannot be measured or perceived only in terms of it, but always have a bearing on the eternal destiny of men" (No. 51).

HUMANAE VITAE

Marriage doctrine and morality were the subjects of the encyclical *Humanae Vitae* ("Of Human Life") issued by Pope Paul July 29, 1968. Following are a number of key excerpts from the document, which was framed in the pattern of traditional teaching and statements by the Second Vatican Council.

". . . each and every marriage act ('quilibet matrimonii usus') must remain open to the transmission of life" (No. 11).

"Indeed, by its intimate structure, the conjugal act, while most closely uniting husband and wife, capacitates them for the generation of new lives, according to laws inscribed in the very being of man and of woman. By safeguarding both these essential aspects, the unitive and the procreative, the conjugal act preserves in its fullness the sense of true mutual love and its ordination toward man's most high calling to parenthood" (No. 12).

"It is, in fact, justly observed that a conjugal act imposed upon one's partner without regard for his or her condition and lawful desires is not a true act of love, and therefore denies an exigency of right moral order in the relationships between husband and wife. Hence, one who reflects well must also recognize that a reciprocal act of love which jeopardizes the responsibility to transmit life — which God the Creator, according to particular laws, inserted therein — is in contradiction with the design constitutive of marriage and with the will of the Author of life. To use this divine gift, destroying, even if only partially, its meaning and its purpose, is to contradict the nature both of man and of woman and of their most intimate relationship, and therefore it is to contradict also the plan of God and His will" (No. 13).

Forbidden Actions: ". . . the direct interruption of the generative process already begun, and, above all, directly willed and procured abortion, even if for therapeutic reasons, are to be absolutely excluded as licit means of regulating birth.

"Equally to be excluded . . . is direct sterilization, whether perpetual or temporary, whether of the man or of the woman. Similarly excluded is every action which, either in anticipation of the conjugal act, or in its accomplishment, or in the development of its natural consequences, proposes, whether as an end or as a means, to render procreation impossible.

Inadmissible Principles: "To justify conjugal acts made intentionally infecund, one cannot invoke as valid reasons the lesser evil, or the fact that such acts would constitute a whole together with the fecund acts already performed or to follow later and hence would share in one and the same moral goodness. In truth, if it is sometimes licit to tolerate a lesser evil in order to avoid a greater evil or to promote a greater good, it is not licit, even for the gravest reasons, to do evil so that good may follow therefrom; that is, to make into the object of a positive act of the will something which is intrinsically disorder, and hence unworthy of the human person, even when the intention is to safeguard or promote individual, family or social well-being.

"Consequently, it is an error to think that a conjugal act which is deliberately made infecund, and so is intrinsically dishonest, could be made honest and right by the ensemble of a fecund conjugal life" (No. 14).

Rhythm: "If, then, there are serious motives to space out births, which derive from the physical or psychological conditions of husband and wife, or from external conditions, the Church teaches that it is then licit to take into account the natural rhythms immanent in the generative functions, for the use of marriage in the infecund periods only, and in this way to regulate birth without offending" earlier stated principles (No. 16).

Authoritative Teaching: Pope Paul called the foregoing teaching authoritative, although not infallible. He left it open for further study. As a practical norm to be followed, however, he said it involved the binding force of religious assent.

With pastoral concern, the Pope said: "We do not at all intend to hide the sometimes serious difficulties inherent in the life of Christian married persons; for them, as for everyone else, 'the gate is narrow and the way is hard that leads to life.' But the hope of that life must illuminate their way, as with courage they strive to live with wisdom, justice and piety in this present time, knowing that the figure of this world passes away.

"Let married couples, then, face up to the efforts needed, supported by the faith and hope which 'do not disappoint . . . because God's love has been poured into our hearts through the Holy Spirit, who has been given to us.' Let them implore divine assistance by persevering prayer; above all, let them draw from the source of grace and charity in the Eucharist. And, if sin should still keep its hold over them, let them not be discouraged but rather have recourse with humble perseverance to the mercy of God, which is poured forth in the sacrament of penance" (No. 25).

Reactions: Exception was taken to the binding force of the encyclical — notably by the bishops of Belgium, Austria and France, and many theologians — for several reasons: rights of conscience; questions concerning the natural-law concept underlying the encyclical; the thesis of totality; the proposition that contraception may in some cases be the lesser of two evils. All agreed, however, that conscientious objection to the encyclical could not be taken without serious reasons and reflection.

MARRIAGE LAWS

The Catholic Church, in line with the belief that it was established and commissioned by Christ to provide and administer the means of salvation to men, claims jurisdiction over its members in matters pertaining to marriage, which is a sacrament. The purpose of its laws in this area, consisting of 132 canons, is to safeguard the validity and lawfulness of marriage.

Catholics are bound by all marriage laws of the Church. Non-Catholics, whether baptized or not, are not considered bound by these ecclesiastical laws except in cases of marriage with a Catholic. Certain natural laws, in the Catholic view, bind all men and women, irrespective of their religious beliefs; accordingly, marriage is prohibited before the time of puberty, without knowledge and free mutual consent, in the case of an already existing valid marriage bond, in the case of antecedent and perpetual impotence.

Formalities

These include, in addition to arrangements for the time and place of the marriage ceremony, doctrinal and moral instruction concerning marriage and the recording of data which verifies in documentary form the eligibility and freedom of the persons to marry. Records of this kind, which are confidential, are preserved in the archives of the church where the marriage takes place.

Premarital instructions are the subject matter of Pre-Cana Conferences.

Mixed Marriages

"Mixed Marriages" (*Matrimonia Mixta*) was the subject of: (1) a letter issued under this title by Pope Paul VI Mar. 31, 1970, and (2) a statement, *Implementation of the Apostolic Letter on Mixed Marriages,* approved by the National Conference of Catholic Bishops Nov. 16, 1970.

One of the key points in the bishops' statement referred to the need for mutual pastoral care by ministers of different faiths for the sacredness of marriage and for appropriate preparation and continuing support of parties to a mixed marriage.

Pastoral experience, which the Catholic Church shares with other religious bodies, confirms the fact that marriages of persons of different beliefs involve special problems related to the continuing religious practice of the concerned persons and to the religious education and formation of their children.

Pastoral measures to minimize these problems include instruction of a non-Catholic party in essentials of the Catholic faith for purposes of understanding. Desirably, some instruction should also be given the Catholic party regarding his or her partner's beliefs.

The Catholic party to a mixed marriage is required to declare his (her) intention of continuing practice of the Catholic faith and to promise to do all in his power to share his faith with children born of the marriage by having them baptized and raised as Catholics. No declarations or promises are required of the non-Catholic party, but he (she) must be informed of the declaration and promise made by the Catholic.

Notice of the Catholic's declaration and promise is an essential part of the application made to a bishop for dispensation from the impediment of mixed religion or disparity of worship (see below).

A mixed marriage can take place with a Nuptial Mass. (The bishops' statement added this caution: "To the extent that Eucharistic sharing is not permitted by the general discipline of the Church, this is to be considered when plans are being made to have the mixed marriage at Mass or not.")

The ordinary minister at a mixed marriage is an authorized priest, and the ordinary place is the parish church of the Catholic party. A non-Catholic minister may not only attend the marriage ceremony but may also address, pray with and bless the couple.

For appropriate pastoral reasons, a bishop can grant a dispensation from the Catholic form of marriage and can permit the marriage to take place in a non-Catholic Church with a non-Catholic minister as the officiating minister. A priest may not only attend such a ceremony but may also address, pray with and bless the couple.

"It is not permitted," however, the bishops statement declared, "to have two religious services or to have a single service in which both the Catholic marriage ritual and a non-Catholic marriage ritual are celebrated jointly or successively."

Banns

The banns are public announcements made in their parish churches, usually on three successive Sundays, of the names of persons who intend to marry. Persons who know of reasons in church law why a proposed marriage should not take place, are obliged to make them known to the pastor.

Marital Consent

The exchange of consent to the marriage contract, which is essential for valid marriage, must be rational, free, true and mutual.

Matrimonial consent can be invalidated by an essential defect, substantial error, the strong influence of force and fear, the presence of a condition or intention against the nature of marriage.

Form of Marriage

A Catholic is required, for validity and lawfulness, to contract marriage — with another Catholic or with a non-Catholic — in the presence of a competent priest or deacon and two witnesses.

There are two exceptions to this law. A Roman Rite Catholic (since Mar. 25, 1967) or an Eastern Rite Catholic (since Nov. 21, 1964) can contract marriage validly in the presence of a priest of a separated Eastern Rite Church, provided other requirements of law are complied with. With permission of the competent Roman-Rite or Eastern-Rite bishop, this form of marriage is lawful, as well as valid. (See Eastern Rite Laws, below.)

With these two exceptions, and aside from cases covered by special permission, the Church does not regard as valid any marriages involving Catholics which take place before non-Catholic ministers of religion or civil officials. (See Mixed Marriage Guidelines.)

An excommunication formerly in force against Catholics who celebrated marriage before a non-Catholic minister was abrogated in a decree issued by the Sacred Congregation for the Doctrine of the Faith on Mar. 18, 1966.

The ordinary place of marriage is the parish of the bride, of the Catholic party in case of a mixed marriage, or of an Eastern Rite groom.

Church law regarding the form of marriage does not affect non-Catholics in marriages among themselves. The Church recognizes as valid the marriages of non-Catholics before ministers of religion and civil officials, unless they are rendered null and void on other grounds.

Impediments

Impediments to marriage are factors which render a marriage unlawful or invalid.

Prohibitory Impediments, which make a marriage unlawful but do not affect validity:

• simple vows of virginity, perpetual chastity, celibacy, to enter a religious order or to receive sacred orders;

• difference of religion, which obtains when one party is a Catholic and the other is a baptized non-Catholic.

The impediment of legal relationship is not in force in the US.

Diriment Impediments, which make a marriage invalid as well as unlawful:

• age, which obtains before completion of the 14th year for a woman and the 16th year for a man;

• impotency, if it is antecedent to the marriage and permanent (this differs from sterility, which is not an impediment);

• the bond of an existing valid marriage;

• disparity of worship, which obtains when one party is a Catholic and the other party is unbaptized;

• sacred orders;

• religious profession of the solemn vow of chastity;

• abduction, which impedes the freedom of the person abducted;

• crime, variously involving elements of adultery, promise or attempt to marry, conspiracy to murder a husband or wife;

• blood relationship in the direct line (father-daughter, mother-son, etc.) and within the third degree of the collateral line (brother-sister, first and second cousins);

• affinity, or relationship resulting from a valid marriage, in any degree of the direct line and within the second degree of the collateral line;

• spiritual relationship arising through baptism — between a godchild and godparent, between the person baptized and the one who performed the baptism;

• public honesty, arising from an invalid marriage or from public or notorious concubinage; it renders either party incapable of marrying relatives of the other in the first and second degrees of the direct line.

Dispensations from Impediments: Persons hindered by impediments either may not or cannot marry unless they are dispensed therefrom in view of reasons recognized in canon law. Local bishops can dispense from the impediments most often encountered (e.g., difference of religion, disparity of worship) as well as others.

Decision regarding some dispensations is reserved to the Holy See.

Separation

A valid and consummated marriage of baptized persons cannot be dissolved by any human authority or any cause other than the death of one of the persons.

In other circumstances:

• 1. A valid but unconsummated marriage of baptized persons, or of a baptized and an unbaptized person, can be dissolved:

a. by the solemn religious profession of one of the persons, made with permission of the pope. In such a case, the bond is dissolved at the time of profession, and the other person is free to marry again;

b. by dispensation from the pope, requested for a grave reason by one or both of the persons. If the dispensation is granted, both persons are free to marry again.

Dispensations in these cases are granted for reasons connected with the spiritual welfare of the concerned persons.

• 2. A legitimate marriage, even consummated, of unbaptized persons can be dissolved in favor of one of them who subsequently receives the sacrament of baptism. This is the Pauline Privilege, so called because it was promulgated by St. Paul (1 Cor. 7:12-15) as a means of protecting the faith of converts. Requisites for granting the privilege are:

a. marriage prior to the baptism of either person;

b. reception of baptism by one person;

c. refusal of the unbaptized person to live in peace with the baptized person and without interfering with his or her freedom to practice the Christian faith. The privilege does not apply if the unbaptized person agrees to these conditions.

• 3. A legitimate and consummated marriage of a baptized and an unbaptized person can be dissolved by the pope in virtue of the Privilege of Faith, also called the Petrine Privilege.

Civil Divorce: Because of the unity and the indissolubility of marriage, the Church denies that civil divorce can break the bond of a valid marriage, whether the marriage involves two Catholics, a Catholic and a non-Catholic, or non-Catholics with each other.

In view of serious circumstances of marital distress, the Church permits an innocent and aggrieved party, whether wife or husband, to seek and obtain a civil divorce for the purpose of acquiring title and right to the civil effects of divorce, such as separate habitation and maintenance, and the custody of children. Permission for this kind of action should be obtained from proper church authority. The divorce, if obtained, does not break the bond of a valid marriage.

Under other circumstances — as would obtain if a marriage was invalid (see Decree of Nullity, below) — civil divorce is permitted for civil effects and as a civil ratification of the fact that the marriage bond really does not exist.

No longer in effect is a decree enacted by the Third Plenary Council of Baltimore, declaring automatic excommunication in the U.S. of persons attempting to contract marriage after having obtained a divorce from a valid marriage.

Decree of Nullity, sometimes improperly called an annulment. This is a decision by a competent church authority — e.g., a bishop, a diocesan marriage tribunal, the Sacred Roman Rota — that an apparently valid marriage was actually invalid from the beginning because of the unknown or concealed existence, from the beginning, of a diriment impediment, an essential defect in consent, radical incapability for marriage, or a condition placed by one or both of the parties against the very nature of marriage.

Eastern Rite Laws

Marriage laws of the Eastern Church differ in several respects from the legislation of the Roman Rite. The regulations in effect since May 2, 1949, were contained in the motu proprio *Crebre Allatae* issued by Pius XII the previous February.

According to both the Roman Code of Canon Law and the Oriental Code, marriages between Roman Rite Catholics and Eastern Rite Catholics ordinarily take place in the rite of the groom and have canonical effects in that rite.

Regarding the form for the celebration of marriages between Eastern Catholics and baptized Eastern non-Catholics, the Second Vatican Council declared:

"By way of preventing invalid marriages between Eastern Catholics and baptized Eastern non-Catholics, and in the interests of the permanence and sanctity of marriage and of domestic harmony, this sacred Synod decrees that the canonical 'form' for the celebration of such marriages obliges only for lawfulness. For their validity, the presence of a sacred minister suffices, as long as the other requirements of law are honored" *(Decree on Eastern Catholic Churches,* No. 18).

Marriages taking place in this manner are lawful, as well as valid, with permission of a competent Eastern Rite bishop.

The Rota

The Sacred Roman Rota is the ordinary court of appeal for marriage, and some other cases, which are appealed to the Holy See from lower church courts. Appeals are made to the Rota if decisions by diocesan and archdiocesan courts fail to settle the matter in dispute.

PROCEDURAL RULES

Pope Paul VI promulgated, June 11, 1971, a set of 13 rules designed to speed up the handling of cases in which the validity of marriage is questioned. Norms given in the document, which was issued by the Pope on his own initiative and became effective Oct.31, concern "the constitution of ecclesiastical tribunals and . . . the judicial process which will expedite the matrimonial process itself."

The norms do not affect the reasons for the validity or invalidity of marriages, but only the way in which cases of this kind are handled in church courts.

Pope Paul told judges of the Roman Rota Jan. 30, 1975, that national conferences of bishops seemed "unanimously satisfied" with the procedures authorized in 1971. He also said: "We strongly hope that, with the promulgation of the new code of procedures, unnecessary differences among various ecclesiastical regions will be removed."

U. S. Norms

Twenty-three experimental norms — drawn up by the Canon Law Society of America, approved by the National Conference of Catholic Bishops and the Holy See, and in effect since July, 1970 — were broader in some respects than those decreed by Pope Paul. Among other things, they provided for: one-priest tribunals for specific periods of time instead of just for individual cases; dispensation by the NCCB from the need for review of first decisions regarding the validity or invalidity of a marriage; circumstances affecting the competence of tribunals. Continuing use of the experimental procedural norms was authorized by Paul VI in a letter dated May 22 and announced June 8, 1974 — "until the new order of matrimonial court procedure is promulgated for the Latin Church" in connection with the on-going revision of the Code of Canon Law. Termination of their use had been scheduled for June 30, 1974, following an original authorization for one year and an extension for three more years.

Cases of Non-Consummation

Pope Paul VI promulgated May 31, 1972, norms designed to speed up the handling of cases involving questions about the validity of marriages entered legally but never consummated sexually. The regulations which went into effect July 1, granted local bishops powers previously reserved to the Holy See.

Accordingly local bishops can initiate procedures in cases of this type; testimony and documents are acceptable in any modern language and on tape; physical proof of non-consummation can be omitted if the bishop is satisfied with the statements of the parties and/or witnesses; the number of witnesses is left to the discretion of the bishop.

PASTORAL MINISTRY FOR DIVORCED AND REMARRIED

Ministry to divorced and remarried Catholics is a difficult field of pastoral endeavor, situated as it is in circumstances tantamount to the horns of a dilemma.

At Issue

On the one side is firm church teaching on the permanence of marriage and norms against reception of the Eucharist and full participation in the life of the Church by Catholics in irregular unions.

On the other side are men and women with broken unions followed by second and perhaps happier attempts at marriage which the Church does not recognize as valid and which may not be capable of being validated because of the existence of an earlier marriage bond.

The forces at work in these circumstances are those of the Church, upholding its doctrine and practice regarding the permanence of marriage, and those of many men and women in irregular second marriages who desire full participation in the life of the Church.

Sacramental participation is not possible for those whose first marriage was valid, although there is no bar to their attendance at Mass, to sharing in other activities of the Church, or to their efforts to have children baptized and raised in the Catholic faith.

An exception to this rule is the condition of a divorced and remarried couple living in a brother-sister relationship.

There is no ban against sacramental participation by separated or divorced persons who have not attempted a second marriage.

Unverified estimates of the number of U.S. Catholics who are divorced and remarried vary between three and five million.

Tribunal Action

What can the Church do for them and with them in pastoral ministry, is an old question charged with new urgency because of the rising number of divorced and remarried Catholics.

One way to help is through the agency of marriage tribunals charged with responsibility for investigating and settling questions concerning the validity or invalidity of a prior marriage. There are reasons in canon law justifying the Church in declaring a particular marriage null and void from the beginning, despite the short- or long-term existence of an apparently valid union.

Decrees of nullity are not new in the history of the Church. If such a decree is issued, a man or woman is free to validate a second marriage and live in complete union with the Church.

Canonist L. Mason Knox, writing in the Oct. 16, 1976, edition of *America*, reported that 442 formal decisions, of which 338 were declarations of nullity, were issued by U.S. tribunals in 1968. Following adoption of the American Procedural Norms (see Procedural Rules) in 1970, the number of formal decisions rose in 1974 to 9,293, of which about 80 to 90 per cent were declarations of nullity. Similar decisions were rendered the same year in other canonical processes on grounds of: defect of form (15,722), papal dispensation for non-consummation (120), Pauline Privilege (691), Privilege of Faith (1,761), summary procedure (1,331).

The increase in the number of declarations of nullity is a result not just of new procedures but also, and more significantly, of tribunal judgments regarding the radical incapability of persons to contract valid marriage in the first place.

Reasons behind Decrees

Pastoral experience reveals that some married persons, a short or long time after contracting an apparently valid marriage, exhibit signs that point back to the existence, at the time of marriage, of latent and serious personal deficiencies which made them incapable of valid consent and sacramental commitment.

Such deficiencies might include gross immaturity and those affecting in a serious way the capacity to love, to have a true interpersonal and conjugal relationship, to fulfill marital obligations, to accept the faith aspect of marriage.

Psychological and behavioral factors like these have been given greater attention by tribunals in recent years and have provided grounds for numerous decrees of nullity.

Decisions of this type do not indicate any softening of the Church's attitude regarding the permanence of marriage. They affirm, rather, that some persons who have married were really not capable of doing so.

Serious deficiencies in the capacity for real interpersonal relationship in marriage were the reasons behind a landmark decree of nullity issued in 1973 by the Roman Rota, the Vatican high court of appeals in marriage cases.

Decree Not Always Possible

The tribunal way to a decree of nullity regarding a previous marriage is not open to many persons in second marriages — because grounds are either lacking or, if present, cannot be verified in tribunal process.

Many men and women in this second category are aligned and in sympathy with aims of the North American Conference of Separated and Divorced Catholics, which has several hundred support groups in various parts of the United States and Canada. Formed early in 1972, the conference seeks a special pastoral ministry for divorced Catholics in second irregular unions.

This purpose is shared by the Judeans (founded in 1952) and by official ministries in many U.S. dioceses, by other church agencies and by hosts of priests.

The principal problem involved in such ministry is the degree of sacramental participation open to persons in irregular unions.

Unacceptable Solution

The Congregation for the Doctrine of the Faith advised bishops throughout the world in August, 1973, against one solution of the problem called "good conscience procedure." This involves administration of the sacraments of penance and the Eucharist to divorced and remarried Catholics unable to obtain a decree of nullity for a first marriage who are living in a subsequent marriage "in good faith."

This procedure, despite the fact that it has no standing or recognition in church law, is being advocated and practiced by some priests and remarried Catholics.

(See also Pastoral Aspects of Marriage, below.)

PASTORAL ASPECTS OF MARRIAGE

Pastoral aspects of Christian marriage were the principal subjects of discussion during the Dec. 1 to 6, 1977, meeting of the International Theological Commission. Following is a summary of conclusions developed by a preparatory subcommittee and approved in substance by the commission. The summary — presented in a Vatican radio broadcast by Msgr. Philippe Delhaye, secretary of the commission — appeared in the English edition of "L'Osservatore Romano" Jan. 12, 1978.

Sacramental Institution

Marriage is an institution that the couple, man and woman, do not invent themselves, even if, under the influence of the originality of their love, they think they do. The couple, in fact, is called to enter God's plan. This applies all the more to the Christina couple, since Jesus inserts the love of man and woman in the love between himself and the Church.

There exists, therefore, an institutional aspect of marriage. Institutions, however, are created for man's good; above all, to help him in the presence of possible difficulties. The sacrament of marriage is the source of grace that Christ offers to all Christian spouses who, because of their faith, cannot choose another type of marriage, purely civil or informal. The Church intervenes in this field, in various forms, not as a usurper but in her capacity as a living witness of Christ's concrete presence.

The Christian conception of marriage does not, of course, invalidate the legitimacy of marriage contracted between non-Christian persons, since their marriage has a solidity of its own and, even if they do not know it, bears the stamp of God the Creator and Savior.

In some countries, precisely in those where ideological pluralism exists, the state organizes a purely civil ceremony to regulate the effects of marriage. It must not be considered, however, as a form replacing sacramental marriage. The Church can allow it, however, as happened in the time of Napoleon.

The case was studied of young baptized Christians who have lost the faith or who have never had it. Is it possible for them to contract sacramental marriage, or at least for their union to be blessed?

It seems that two categories must be distinguished.

Some of these young people still have an implicit faith that can be revived and educated. It will therefore be possible, with adequate preparation, to bring them to clear awareness of their intention to wish to do what the Church does in the sacramental act.

In other cases, on the contrary, the lack of faith is complete and obstinate. It is therefore contradictory to wish to make the Church intervene in their marriage pact. If they do so (wish), it is in order to please this or that parent, or in a worldly spirit. In this case the Church must not be a witness of their marriage. These young people, in view of their lack of faith, do not intend to contract a union in Christ, indissoluble and geared to procreation. It seems opportune, therefore, to avoid paraliturgies that may give illusions and cause a scandal.

No Divorce

The sacramentality of Christian marriage strengthens its indissolubility, both internally and externally. That is why the Church does not recognize herself as having the right to dissolve marriages which are contracted voluntarily and are consummated. The grace of Christ, given in the act of sacramental marriage, is the means that makes it possible to overcome the difficulties of married life and to practice mutual faithfulness.

The commission agreed unanimously on the necessity of reaffirming forcefully, in the context of the present erotic civilization, the indissolubility of Christian marriage. There exists in this connection a break between the Church and the world, similar to the one that took place between Christ and the Pharisees who at that time admitted divorce.

Cana Conferences, named for the marriage-miracle passage in St. John's Gospel, are for married couples, with formats covering the multiple aspects of marriage. Pre-Cana Conferences are for engaged persons.

MARRIAGE ENCOUNTER

Marriage Encounter originated in Spain through the efforts of Father Gabriel Calvo who worked out its principal features between 1958 and 1962 with the collaboration of Diego and Fina Bartoneo and other parties interested in ministry to married couples.

The first encounter was held with 28 couples in 1962 in Barcelona. Five years later the first encounter in the U.S. was conducted in conjunction with a convention of the Christian Family Movement at Notre Dame University. ME caught on from this beginning and went nationwide in 1969.

Rapid Development

Along with charismatic renewal, ME has been called one of the fastest growing contemporary developments in the Church.

Indicative of ME development is the number of married couples, more than 500,000, who have experienced weekends with Worldwide ME since 1969. The couples included many Americans and also others in 24 or more countries in Latin America, Europe and the Far East, where ME was first introduced in Japan in 1972. Worldwide ME has a central office at 3711 Long Beach Blvd., Long Beach, Calif. 90807.

National ME groups conduct encounter weekends for nearly 40,000 couples a year. Approximately 4,000 U.S. priests engaged in the movement have experienced an encounter. Paul and Marge Tepper of Norristown, Pa., and Msgr. Korby Thielen of Columbus, O., are members of the executive team. Father Charles Gallagher, associated with the movement since 1968, is on the staff of the Marriage Encounter Resource Community, Valley Stream, N.Y.

The Encounter

ME brings couples together for a 44-hour weekend directed by an already encountered team of several couples and a priest, for the purpose of developing their abilities to communicate with each other in their life together as husband and wife. This purpose is served by direction in techniques given by the team and by private dialogue of each couple. Subjects of the dialogue extend to the whole range of personal and marital concerns. The anticipated result is the enrichment of all personal-marital relationships.

This real communication and sharing by husband and wife, spurred by the encounter and open to development by subsequent daily dialogue between them, is the positive substance of the movement.

The composition of ME groups for the encounter varies; some of them are exclusively Catholic while others have participants of different religious, professional or other special-interest affiliations.

Commentators insist that ME is not for troubled marriages and is not an exercise in group dynamics. Neither is it a retreat, although it has potential for spiritual development.

The identifying logo or emblem of ME consists of wedding bands intertwining a cross and surmounted by a red heart.

Engaged Encounter: A development from ME, designed to facilitate and deepen the communication potential of couples intending to marry. With appropriate modifications, it follows the pattern of the ME weekend and subsequent practice of dialogue.

YOUNG MARRIAGE GUIDELINES

In an effort to forestall the break-up of marriages, a number of dioceses in the U.S. have formulated and put into effect in recent years special guidelines to be followed with respect to prospective marriages, particularly those of persons under ages ranging from 18 to 21.

The general purpose of the guidelines is to determine and develop the maturity and capabilities of the parties to make the full and permanent commitment of marriage. Specific items cover: advance arrangement for marriage; a period of waiting, to avoid hasty and ill-considered unions; consultation with a priest for discussion and understanding of the doctrine and practice of the Church regarding marriage; participation in Pre-Cana conferences and/or other marriage preparation courses.

ERRONEOUS OPINIONS

The Congregation for the Doctrine of the Faith advised bishops throughout the world in August, 1973, that erroneous opinions concerning the indissolubility of marriage were being circulated "in books, Catholic newspapers, and even in seminaries and Catholic schools; and also, in practice, in some ecclesiastical tribunals."

"These opinions," the letter said, "are being used . . . to justify abuses . . . countrary to the present discipline governing the admission to the sacraments of persons who live in irregular (matrimonial) unions."

Among the abuses was a "good conscience procedure" reported from several quarters — i.e., the administration of the sacraments to divorced and remarried Catholics who were unable to obtain a decree of nullity from the Church for their first marriage and were living in a subsequent civil marriage "in good faith."

Accepted norms in force state that the sacraments may be administered to separated or divorced persons who have not remarried; to those who have received a declaration of nullity of a previous marriage and to those who, although remarried, are living in a brother-sister relationship of sexual continence.

The Church Calendar

The calendar of the Roman Church consists of an arrangement throughout the year of a series of liturgical seasons and feasts of saints for purposes of divine worship.

The purposes of this calendar were outlined in the *Constitution on the Sacred Liturgy* (Nos. 102-105) promulgated by the Second Vatican Council.

"Within the cycle of a year ... (the Church) unfolds the whole mystery of Christ, not only from His incarnation and birth until His ascension, but also as reflected in the day of Pentecost, and the expectation of a blessed, hoped-for return of the Lord.

"Recalling thus the mysteries of redemption, the Church opens to the faithful the riches of her Lord's powers and merits, so that these are in some way made present at all times, and the faithful are enabled to lay hold of them and become filled with saving grace" (No. 102).

"In celebrating this annual cycle of Christ's mysteries, holy Church honors with special love the Blessed Mary, Mother of God..." (No. 103).

"The Church has also included in the annual cycle days devoted to the memory of the martyrs and the other saints.... (who) sing God's perfect praise in heaven and offer prayers for us. By celebrating the passage of these saints from earth to heaven the Church proclaims the paschal mystery as achieved in the saints who have suffered and been glorified with Christ; she proposes them to the faithful as examples who draw all to the Father through Christ, and through their merits she pleads for God's favors" (No. 104).

"... In the various seasons of the year and according to her traditional discipline, the Church completes the formation of the faithful by means of pious practices for soul and body, by instruction, prayer, and works of penance and mercy..." (No. 105).

THE REVISED CALENDAR

Pope Paul announced May 9, 1969, his approval of a reorganization of the liturgical year and calendar for the Roman Rite, in implementation of a directive from the Second Vatican Council in 1964. He made the announcement in a document issued on his own initiative and entitled *Paschalis Mysterii*.

The purpose of the action, the Pope said, was "no other ... than to permit the faithful to communicate in a more intense way, through faith, hope and love, in 'the whole mystery of Christ which ... unfolds within the cycle of a year.'"

The motu proprio was dated Feb. 14, 1969. The new calendar was promulgated a month later by a decree of the Congregation for Divine Worship and went into effect Jan. 1, 1970, with provisional modifications. Full implementation of all its parts was delayed in 1970 and 1971, pending the completion of work on related liturgical texts. The U.S. bishops ordered the whole new calendar into effect for 1972.

The revised calendar, whose principal architect was Father Pierre Jounel, professor of liturgy at the Catholic University of Paris, involved some restructuring of the liturgical cycles and changes affecting the feasts of saints.

The Seasons

Advent: The liturgical year begins with the First Sunday of Advent, which introduces a season of four weeks or slightly less duration with the theme of expectation of the coming of Christ. During the first two weeks, the final coming of Christ as Lord and Judge at the end of the world is the focus of attention. From Dec. 17 to 24, the emphasis shifts to anticipation of the celebration of his Nativity on the feast of Christmas.

Advent has four Sundays. Since the 10th century, the first Sunday has marked the beginning of the liturgical year in the Western Church. In the Middle Ages, a kind of pre-Christmas fast was in vogue during the season.

Christmastide: Christmastide opens with the feast of the Nativity, Dec. 25, and lasts until the Sunday after Epiphany. The Holy Family is commemorated on the Sunday within the Christmas octave. Jan. 1 — formerly called the Octave Day of the Nativity and, before that, the feast of the Circumcision of Jesus — has the title of Solemnity of Mary the Mother of God. The Epiphany, scheduled for Jan. 6 in the universal calendar, is celebrated in the U.S. on the Sunday between Jan. 2 and 8. The Baptism of the Lord, observed on the Sunday following Epiphany, marks the end of Christmastide.

The period between the end of Christmastide and the beginning of Lent belongs to the Ordinary Time of the year. Of variable length, the pre-Lenten phase of this season includes what were formerly called the Sundays after Epiphany and the suppressed Sundays of Septuagesima, Sexagesima and Quinquagesima.

Lent: The penitential season of Lent begins on Ash Wednesday, which occurs between Feb. 4 and Mar. 11, depending on the date of Easter, and lasts until Easter. It has six Sundays and 40 weekdays. The climactic last week is called Holy Week. The last three days (Holy Thursday, Good Friday and Holy Saturday) are called the Paschal Triduum.

The origin of Lenten observances dates back to the fourth century or earlier.

Eastertide: Eastertide, whose theme is resurrection from sin to the life of grace, lasts for

50 days, from Easter to Pentecost. Easter, the first Sunday following the vernal equinox, occurs between Mar. 22 and Apr. 25. The terminal phase of Eastertide, between the feast of the Ascension of the Lord and Pentecost, stresses anticipation of the coming and action of the Holy Spirit.

Ordinary Time: The season of Ordinary Time of the year includes not only the period between the end of Christmastide and the beginning of Lent, as noted above, but also all Sundays after Pentecost to the last Sunday of the liturgical year, which is celebrated as the feast of Christ the King. The number of Sundays before Lent and after Pentecost varies, depending on the date of the key feast of Easter. The overall purpose of the season is to elaborate the themes of salvation history.

The various liturgical seasons are characterized in part by the scriptural readings and Mass prayers assigned to each of them. During Advent, for example, the readings are messianic; during Eastertide, from the Acts of the Apostles, chronicling the Resurrection and the original proclamation of Christ by the Apostles, and from the Gospel of John; during Lent, baptismal and penitential passages. Mass prayers reflect the meaning and purpose of the various seasons.

Feasts of Saints

The feasts of saints are celebrated concurrently with the liturgical seasons and feasts of our Lord. Their purpose always has been to illustrate the paschal mysteries as reflected in the lives of saints, to honor them as heroes of holiness, and to appeal for their intercession. For various reasons, however, the number and variety of feasts distracted attention to some degree from the central mysteries of redemption and the universality of holiness in the Church. To remedy these defects, Pope Paul ordered a number of significant changes affecting the feasts of saints.

In line with revised regulations, some feasts were either abolished or relegated to observance in particular places by local option for one of two reasons: (1) lack of sufficient historical evidence for observance of the feasts; (2) lack of universal significance. More than 40 feasts were eliminated; 92 were made optional for particular places, e.g., the diocese or country in which a saint was martyred; more than 60 were ordered for observance throughout the Roman Rite.

Commenting on the elimination of some feasts, *L'Osservatore Della Domenica,* the Vatican City weekly, said: "Generally, the removal of a name from the calendar does not mean passing judgment on the nonexistence (of a saint) or lack of holiness. Many (saints) have been removed (from the calendar) because all that remains certain about them is their name, and this would say too little to the faithful in comparison with many others. Other feasts were removed because they lacked universal significance."

Traditional feasts of our Lord have been retained, except for those of the Holy Name and the Precious Blood which were suppressed.

Most feasts of Blessed Mary the Virgin have been retained. Universal observance obtains for the feasts of the Assumption, Immaculate Conception, Birth, Annunciation (of Our Lord), Presentation of the Lord, Visitation, Our Lady of Sorrows, Our Lady of the Rosary, Presentation, Queenship. Local option governs celebration of the memorials of Our Lady of Lourdes, Our Lady of Mt. Carmel, Dedication of (the Basilica of) St. Mary Major, the Immaculate Heart.

St. Joseph, Husband of Mary, is honored universally on Mar. 19 and by local option on another date (feast of St. Joseph the Worker, which may be observed May 1).

The archangels — Michael, Raphael and Gabriel — are honored with a common feast, Sept. 29, instead of with three separate feasts as before. The feast of the Guardian Angels, Oct. 2, stands.

The traditional feasts of the Apostles and Evangelists have been retained, with several date changes. Sts. Peter and Paul, who are honored with a common feast June 29, each has an additional feast on Feb. 22 (Chair of St. Peter) and Jan. 25 (Conversion of St. Paul).

Other saints, as noted above, are honored on universal and optional feasts throughout the year.

The universality of holiness in the Church is reflected in the distribution of feasts among saints of different periods and locations. Sixty-four saints are of the first 10 centuries, 79 of the last 10 centuries. Most represented are the fourth century (25 saints), the 12th (12), the 16th (17), and the 17th (17). Geographically, there are 126 feasts of European saints, 14 of Asians, eight of Africans, four of Americans, and one of a saint of Oceania.

The feast of a saint, as a general rule, is observed on the day of his death *(dies natalis,* day of birth to glory with God in heaven). Exceptions to this rule include the feasts of St. John the Baptist, who is honored on the day of his birth; Sts. Basil the Great and Gregory Nazianzen, and the brother Saints, Cyril and Methodius, who are commemorated in joint feasts.

Application of this general rule in the revised calendar resulted in date changes of some feasts.

Sundays and Feast Days

Sunday is the original Christian feast day because of the unusually significant events of salvation history which took place and are commemorated on the first day of the week — viz., the Resurrection of Christ, the key event of his life and the fundamental fact of

Christianity; and the descent of the Holy Spirit upon the Apostles on Pentecost, the birthday of the Church. The transfer of observance of the Lord's Day from the Sabbath to Sunday was made in apostolic times. The Mass and Liturgy of the Hours (Divine Office) of each Sunday reflect the themes and set the tones of the various liturgical seasons.

Categories of feasts according to dignity and manner of observance are: solemnity (highest, corresponding to former first-class feasts); feast (corresponding to former second-class feasts); memorial (corresponding to former third-class feasts); optional memorial (observable by local choice). Feasts of the first three categories are observed universally in the Roman Rite.

Fixed feasts are those which are regularly celebrated on the same calendar day each year.

Movable feasts are those which are not observed on the same calendar day each year. Examples of these are Easter (the first Sunday after the first full moon following the vernal equinox), Ascension (40 days after Easter), Pentecost (50 days after Easter), Trinity Sunday (first after Pentecost), Christ the King (last Sunday of the liturgical year).

Holy Days of Obligation

Holy days of obligation are special feasts on which Catholics who have reached the age of reason are seriously obliged, as on Sundays, to assist at Mass and to avoid unnecessary servile work. Serious reasons excuse from the observance of either or both of these obligations.

By enactment of the Third Plenary Council of Baltimore, and with the approval of the Holy See, the holy days of obligation observed in the United States are: Christmas, the Nativity of Jesus, Dec. 25; Solemnity of Mary the Mother of God, Jan. 1; Ascension of the Lord; Assumption of Blessed Mary the Virgin, Aug. 15; All Saints' Day, Nov. 1; Immaculate Conception of Blessed Mary the Virgin, Dec. 8.

In addition to these, there are four other holy days of obligation prescribed in the general law of the Church which are not so observed in the U.S.: Epiphany; St. Joseph, Mar. 19; Corpus Christi; Sts. Peter and Paul, June 29.

Ferial Days, Days of Prayer

Ferial days are weekdays on which no proper feast or vigil is celebrated in the Mass or Liturgy of the Hours (Divine Office). On such days, the Mass may be that of the preceding Sunday, which expresses the liturgical spirit of the season, an optional memorial, a votive Mass, or a Mass for the dead. Ferial days of Advent and Lent are in a special category of their own.

Aside from feast-day considerations, Monday through Friday are called ferial days, and are consecutively numbered from two to six. The first day of the week is Sunday or the Lord's Day, and the seventh is called the Sabbath.

Days of prayer: Dioceses, at times to be designated by local bishops, should observe "days or periods of prayer for the fruits of the earth, prayer for human rights and equality, prayer for world justice and peace, and penitential observance outside of Lent." So states the *Instruction on Particular Calendars* (No. 331) issued by the Congregation for the Sacraments and Divine Worship June 24, 1970.

These days are contemporary equivalents of what were formerly called ember and rogation days.

Ember days originated at Rome about the fifth century, probably as Christian replacements for seasonal festivals of agrarian cults. They were observances of penance, thanksgiving, and petition for divine blessing on the various seasons; they also were occasions of special prayer for clergy to be ordained. These days were observed four times a year.

Rogation days originated in France about the fifth century. They were penitential in character and also occasions of prayer for a bountiful harvest and protection against evil.

Days of Abstinence and Fast

The apostolic constitution *Paenitemini*, in effect since Feb. 23, 1966, authorized the substitution of other works of penance for the customary and common observances of abstinence and fast on various days of the year.

In this country, in line with provisions of the constitution and a 1974 decision of the National Conference of Catholic Bishops, Ash Wednesday and Good Friday are days of fast and abstinence, and all Fridays of Lent are days of abstinence.

The obligation to abstain from meat binds Catholics 14 years of age and older. The obligation to fast, limiting oneself to one full meal and two lighter meals in the course of a day, binds Catholics from the ages of 21 to 59.

BYZANTINE CALENDAR

The Byzantine-Rite calendar has many distinctive features of its own, although it shares common elements with the Roman-Rite calendar—e.g., general purpose, commemoration of the mysteries of faith and of the saints, identical dates for some feasts. Among the distinctive things are the following.

The liturgical year begins on Sept. 1, the **Day of Indiction**, in contrast with the Latin or Roman start on the First Sunday of Advent late in November or early in December. The Advent season begins on Dec. 10.

Cycles of the Year

As in the Roman usage, the dating of feasts follows the Gregorian Calendar. Formerly, until well into this century, the Julian Calendar was used. (The Julian Calendar, which is now about 13 days late, is still used by some Eastern-Rite Churches.)

The year has several cycles, which include proper seasons, the feasts of saints, and series of New Testament readings. All of these elements of worship are contained in liturgical books of the rite.

The ecclesiastical calendar, called the **Menologion,** explains the nature of feasts, other observances and matters pertaining to the liturgy for each day of the year. In some cases, its contents include the lives of saints and the history and meaning of feasts.

The Divine Liturgy (Mass) and Divine Office for the proper of the saints, fixed feasts, and the Christmas season are contained in the **Menaion.** The **Triodion** covers the pre-Lenten season of preparation for Easter; Lent begins two days before the Ash Wednesday observance of the Roman Rite. The **Pentecostarion** contains the liturgical services from Easter to the Sunday of All Saints, the first after Pentecost. The **Evangelion** and **Apostolos** are books in which the Gospels, and Acts of the Apostles and the Epistles, respectively, are arranged according to the order of their reading in the Divine Liturgy and Divine Office throughout the year.

The cyclic progression of liturgical music throughout the year, in successive and repetitive periods of eight weeks, is governed by the **Oktoechos,** the Book of Eight Tones.

Sunday Names

Many Sundays are named after the subject of the Gospel read in the Mass of the day or after the name of a feast falling on the day — e.g., Sunday of the Publican and Pharisee, of the Prodigal Son, of the Samaritan Woman, of St. Thomas the Apostle, of the Fore-Fathers (Old Testament Patriarchs). Other Sundays are named in the same manner as in the Roman calendar — e.g., numbered Sundays of Lent and after Pentecost.

Holy Days, Abstinence, Fast

The calendar lists about 28 holy days. Many of the major holy days coincide with those of the Roman calendar, but the feast of the Immaculate Conception is observed on Dec. 9 instead of Dec. 8, and the feast of All Saints falls on the Sunday after Pentecost rather than on Nov. 1. Instead of a single All Souls' Day, there are five All Souls' Saturdays.

According to regulations in effect in the Byzantine-Rite (Ruthenian) Archeparchy of Pittsburgh and its suffragan sees of Passaic and Parma, holy days are obligatory, solemn and simple, and attendance at the Divine Liturgy is required on five obligatory days — the feasts of the Epiphany, the Ascension, Sts. Peter and Paul, the Assumption of the Blessed Virgin Mary, and Christmas. Although attendance at the liturgy is not obligatory on 15 solemn and seven simple holy days, it is recommended.

In the Byzantine-Rite (Ukrainian) Archeparchy of Philadelphia and its suffragan sees of St. Nicholas (Chicago) and Stamford, the obligatory feasts are the Circumcision, Epiphany, Annunciation, Easter, Ascension, Pentecost, Dormition (Assumption of Mary), Immaculate Conception and Christmas.

Lent

The first day of Lent — the Monday before Ash Wednesday of the Roman Rite — and Good Friday are days of strict abstinence for persons between the ages of 21 and 59. No meat, eggs, or dairy products may be eaten on these days.

All persons over the age of 14 must abstain from meat on Fridays during Lent, Holy Saturday, and the vigils of the feasts of Christmas and Epiphany; abstinence is urged, but is not obligatory, on Wednesdays of Lent. The abstinence obligation is not in force on certain "free" or "privileged" Fridays.

Synaxis

An observance without a counterpart in the Roman calendar is the synaxis. This is a commemoration, on the day following a feast, of persons involved with the occasion for the feast — e.g., Sept. 9, the day following the feast of the Nativity of the Blessed Virgin Mary, is the Synaxis of Joachim and Anna, her parents.

Holy Week

In the Byzantine Rite, Lent is liturgically concluded with the Saturday of Lazarus, the day before Palm Sunday, which commemorates the raising of Lazarus from the dead.

On the following Monday, Tuesday and Wednesday, the Liturgy of the Presanctified is prescribed.

On Holy Thursday, the Liturgy of St. Basil the Great is celebrated together with Vespers.

Good Friday, except when the feast of the Annunciation coincides with it, is the only day of the year on which the Divine Liturgy is not celebrated.

On Holy Saturday, the Liturgy of St. Basil the Great is celebrated along with Vespers.

CALENDAR NOTES

Scriptural Readings

The texts of scriptural readings for Mass on Sundays, holy days and some other days are indicated under the respective dates. The second cycle of readings in the Lectionary is prescribed for the 1979 liturgical year; the third cycle is prescribed for the 1980 liturgical year which begins with the first Sunday of Advent, Dec. 2, 1979.

Weekday cycles of readings are the first and second, respectively, for liturgical years 1979 and 1980.

JANUARY 1980

1—Tues. **Solemnity of Mary, Mother of God. Holy day of obligation.** (Nm. 6:22-27; Gal. 4:4-7; Lk. 2:16-21.)
2—Wed. Sts. Basil the Great and Gregory Nazianzen, bishops-doctors; memorial.
3—Thurs. Weekday.
4—Fri. St. Elizabeth Ann Seton; memorial (in U.S.).
5—Sat. St. John Neumann, bishop; memorial (in U.S.).
6—**Sun. Epiphany of the Lord; solemnity.** (Is. 60:1-6; Eph. 3:2-3a, 5-6; Mt. 2:1-12.)
7—Mon. St. Raymond of Penyafort, priest; optional memorial.
8—Tues. Weekday.
9—Wed. Weekday.
10—Thurs. Weekday.
11—Fri. Weekday.
12—Sat. Weekday.
13—**Sun. Baptism of the Lord; feast.** (Is. 42:1-4, 6-7; Acts. 10:34-38; Lk. 3:15-16, 21-22.) [St. Hilary, bishop-doctor; optional memorial.]
14—Mon. Weekday. (First Week of the Year.)
15—Tues. Weekday.
16—Wed. Weekday.
17—Thurs. St. Anthony, abbot; memorial.
18—Fri. Weekday.
19—Sat. Weekday.
20—**Second Sunday of the Year.** (Is. 62:1-5; 1 Cor. 12:4-11; Jn. 2:1-12.) [St. Fabian, pope-martyr, or St. Sebastian, martyr; optional memorials.]
21—Mon. St. Agnes, virgin-martyr; memorial.
22—Tues. Weekday. St. Vincent, deacon-martyr; optional memorial.
23—Wed. Weekday.
24—Thurs. St. Francis de Sales, bishop-doctor; memorial.
25—Fri. Conversion of St. Paul, apostle; feast.
26—Sat. Sts. Timothy and Titus, bishops; memorial.
27—**Third Sunday of the Year.** (Neh. 8:1-4a, 5-6, 8-10; 1 Cor. 12:12-30; Lk. 1:1-4; 4:14-21.) [St. Angela Merici, virgin; optional memorial.]
28—Mon. St. Thomas Aquinas, priest-doctor; memorial.
29—Tues. Weekday.
30—Wed. Weekday.
31—Thurs. St. John Bosco, priest; memorial.

GENERAL PRAYER INTENTION: That the union of Christians be perceived as the way and instrument of evangelization.

MISSION PRAYER INTENTION: That the internal unity of the Church become so well established that it will attract and lead non-Christians to the Church.

FEBRUARY 1980

1—Fri. Weekday.
2—Sat. Presentation of the Lord; feast.
3—**Fourth Sunday of the Year.** (Jer. 1:4-5, 17-19; 1 Cor. 12:31 to 13:13; Lk. 4:21-30.) [St. Blase, bishop-martyr, or St. Ansgar, bishop; optional memorials.]
4—Mon. Weekday.
5—Tues. St. Agatha, virgin-martyr; memorial.
6—Wed. Sts. Paul Miki and Companions, martyrs; memorial.
7—Thurs. Weekday.
8—Fri. Weekday. St. Jerome Emiliani; optional memorial.
9—Sat. Weekday.
10—**Fifth Sunday of the Year.** (Is. 6:1-2a, 3-8; 1 Cor. 15:1-11; Lk. 5:1-11.) [St. Scholastica, virgin; memorial.]
11—Mon. Weekday. Our Lady of Lourdes; optional memorial.
12—Tues. Weekday.
13—Wed. Weekday.
14—Thurs. Sts. Cyril, monk, and Methodius, bishop; memorial.
15—Fri. Weekday.
16—Sat. Weekday.
17—**Sixth Sunday of the Year.** (Jer. 17: 5-8; 1 Cor. 15:12, 16-20; Lk. 6:17, 20-26.) [Seven Holy Founders of the Servite Order; optional memorial.]
18—Mon. Weekday.
19—Tues. Weekday.
20—Ash Wednesday. Beginning of Lent. *Fast and abstinence.* Ashes are blessed this day and imposed on the forehead of the faithful to remind them of their obligation to do penance for sin and to seek spiritual renewal by means of prayer, fasting, good works, and by bearing with patience and for God's purposes the trials and difficulties of everyday life.
21—Thurs. Weekday of Lent. [St. Peter Damian, bishop-doctor; optional memorial.]
22—Fri. Chair of Peter, apostle; feast. Weekday of Lent. *Abstinence.*
23—Sat. Weekday of Lent. [St. Polycarp, bishop-martyr; memorial.]
24—**First Sunday of Lent.** (Dt. 26:4-10; Rom. 10:8-13; Lk. 4:1-13.)
25—Mon. Weekday of Lent.
26—Tues. Weekday of Lent.
27—Wed. Weekday of Lent.
28—Thurs. Weekday of Lent.
29—Fri. Weekday of Lent. *Abstinence.*

GENERAL PRAYER INTENTION: That Christians work together to foster closer unity of the entire human family.

MISSION PRAYER INTENTION: That missionaries everywhere accept changes in their work (especially those required for effective evangelization in all kinds of cultural and social circumstances).

MARCH 1980

1—Sat. Weekday of Lent.
2—**Second Sunday of Lent.** (Gn. 15:5-12, 17-18; Phil. 3:17 to 4:1; Lk. 9:28b-36.)
3—Mon. Weekday of Lent.
4—Tues. Weekday of Lent. [St. Casimir; optional memorial.]
5—Wed. Weekday of Lent.
6—Thurs. Weekday of Lent.
7—Fri. Weekday of Lent. *Abstinence.* [Sts. Perpetua and Felicity, martyrs; memorial.]
8—Sat. Weekday of Lent. [St. John of God, religious; optional memorial.]
9—**Third Sunday of Lent.** (Ex. 3:1-8a, 13-15; 1 Cor. 10:1-6, 10-12; Lk. 13:1-9.) [St. Frances of Rome, religious; optional memorial.]
10—Mon. Weekday of Lent.
11—Tues. Weekday of Lent.
12—Wed. Weekday of Lent.
13—Thurs. Weekday of Lent.
14—Fri. Weekday of Lent. *Abstinence.*
15—Sat. Weekday of Lent.
16—**Fourth Sunday of Lent.** (Jos. 5:9a, 10-12; 2 Cor. 5:17-21; Lk. 15:1-3, 11-32.)
17—Mon. Weekday of Lent. [St. Patrick, bishop; optional memorial.]
18—Tues. Weekday of Lent. [St. Cyril of Jerusalem, bishop-doctor; optional memorial.]
19—Wed. St. Joseph; solemnity. Weekday of Lent.
20—Thurs. Weekday of Lent.
21—Fri. Weekday of Lent. *Abstinence.*
22—Sat. Weekday of Lent.
23—**Fifth Sunday of Lent.** (Is. 43;16-21; Phil. 3:8-14; Jn. 8:1-11.) [St. Turibius, bishop; optional memorial.]
24—Mon. Weekday of Lent.
25—Tues. Annunciation; solemnity. Weekday of Lent.
26—Wed. Weekday of Lent.
27—Thurs. Weekday of Lent.
28—Fri. Weekday of Lent. *Abstinence.*
29—Sat. Weekday of Lent.
30—**Sunday of the Passion (Palm Sunday).** (Procession — Lk. 19:28-40; Mass — Is. 50:4-7; Phil. 2:6-11; Lk. 22:14 to 23:56.)
31—Monday of Holy Week.

GENERAL PRAYER INTENTION: That the Mass be appreciated as the source of Christian life and love. (Pope John Paul II told an audience of young adults July 15, 1979, to look to the Mass for their identity. He said: "The sacred Mass will give us each time the answer to the fundamental question, 'Who are we?' ... We are redeemed; we are full of the remission of sins and of grace.")

MISSION PRAYER INTENTION: That missionary vocations continue to flourish in the Philippine Islands.

APRIL 1980

1—Tuesday of Holy Week.
2—Wednesday of Holy Week. [St. Francis of Paola, hermit; optional memorial.]
3—Thursday of Holy Week. Holy Thursday. The Paschal Triduum begins with the evening Mass of the Supper of the Lord.
4—Friday of the Passion of the Lord. Good Friday. *Fast and abstinence.* [St. Isidore of Seville, bishop-doctor; optional memorial.]
5—Holy Saturday. The Easter Vigil. [St. Vincent Ferrer, priest; optional memorial.]
6—**Easter Sunday; solemnity.** (Acts 10:34a, 37-43; Col. 3:1-4 or 1 Cor. 5:6b-8; Jn. 20:1-9 or Lk. 24:1-12 or (Evening) Lk. 24:13-35.)
7—Monday of Easter Octave. [St. John Baptist de la Salle, priest; memorial.]
8—Tuesday of Easter Octave.
9—Wednesday of Easter Octave.
10—Thursday of Easter Octave.
11—Friday of Easter Octave. [St. Stanislaus, bishop-martyr; memorial.]
12—Saturday of Easter Octave.
13—**Second Sunday of Easter.** (Acts 5:12-16; Rv. 1:9-11a, 12-13, 17-19; Jn. 20:19-31.) [St. Martin I, pope-martyr; optional memorial.]
14—Mon. Weekday.
15—Tues. Weekday.
16—Wed. Weekday.
17—Thurs. Weekday.
18—Fri. Weekday.
19—Sat. Weekday.
20—**Third Sunday of Easter.** (Acts 5:27b-32, 40b-41; Rv. 5:11-14; Jn. 21:1-19.)
21—Mon. Weekday. St. Anselm, bishop-doctor; optional memorial.
22—Tues. Weekday.
23—Wed. Weekday. St. George, martyr; optional memorial.
24—Thurs. Weekday. St. Fidelis of Sigmaringen, priest-martyr; optional memorial.
25—Fri. Weekday. St. Mark, evangelist; feast.
26—Sat. Weekday.
27—**Fourth Sunday of Easter.** (Acts. 13:14, 43-52; Rv. 7:9, 14b-17; Jn. 10:27-30.)
28—Mon. Weekday. St. Peter Chanel, priest-martyr; optional memorial.
29—Tues. Weekday. St. Catherine of Siena, virgin-doctor; memorial.
30—Wed. Weekday. St. Pius V, pope; optional memorial.

GENERAL PRAYER INTENTION: For an increase of vocations for the Church's mission of evangelization.

MISSION PRAYER INTENTION: That Christian desires for the spread of God's kingdom be communicated to others.

MAY 1980

1—Thurs. Weekday. St. Joseph the Worker; optional memorial.
2—Fri. St. Athanasius, bishop-doctor; memorial.
3—Sat. Sts. Philip and James, apostles; feast.
4—**Fifth Sunday of Easter.** (Acts 14:21-27; Rv. 21:1-5a; Jn. 13:31-33a, 34-35.)
5—Mon. Weekday.
6—Tues. Weekday.
7—Wed. Weekday.
8—Thurs. Weekday.
9—Fri. Weekday.
10—Sat. Weekday.
11—**Sixth Sunday of Easter.** (Acts 15:1-2, 22-29; Rv. 21:10-14, 22-23; Jn. 14:23-29.)
12—Mon. Weekday. Sts Nereus and Achilleus, martyrs, or St. Pancras, martyr; optional memorials.
13—Tues. Weekday.
14—Wed. St. Matthias, apostle; feast.
15—**Thurs. Ascension of the Lord; solemnity. Holy day of obligation.** (Acts 1:1-11; Eph. 1:17-23; Lk. 24:46-53.) [St. Isidore the Farmer; optional memorial in U.S.]
16—Fri. Weekday.
17—Sat. Weekday.
18—**Seventh Sunday of Easter.** (Acts 7:55-60; Rv. 22:12-14, 16-17, 20; Jn. 17:20-26.) [St. John I, pope-martyr; optional memorial.]
19—Mon. Weekday.
20—Tues. Weekday. St. Bernardine of Siena, priest; optional memorial.
21—Wed. Weekday.
22—Thurs. Weekday.
23—Fri. Weekday.
24—Sat. Weekday.
25—**Sun. Pentecost; solemnity.** (Acts 2:1-11; 1 Cor. 12:3b-7, 12-13; Jn. 20:19-23.) [St. Bede the Venerable, priest-doctor, or St. Gregory VII, pope, or St. Mary Magdalene de Pazzi, virgin; optional memorials.]
26—Mon. St. Philip Neri, priest; memorial. (Eighth Week of the Year.)
27—Tues. Weekday. St. Augustine of Canterbury, bishop; optional memorial.
28—Wed. Weekday.
29—Thurs. Weekday.
30—Fri. Weekday.
31—Sat. Visitation of Blessed Mary the Virgin; feast.

GENERAL PRAYER INTENTION: That the decrees of the Second Vatican Council be put into effect in order to increase the growth and development of the Church.

MISSION PRAYER INTENTION: That persecuted Africans offer an example of faith to non-Christians. (Catholics have been persecuted in several African countries.)

JUNE 1980

1—**Trinity Sunday; solemnity.** (Prv. 8:22-31; Rom. 5:1-5; Jn. 16:12-15.) [St. Justin, martyr; memorial.]
2—Mon. Weekday. Sts. Marcellinus and Peter, martyrs; optional memorial. (Ninth Week of the Year.)
3—Tues. Sts. Charles Lwanga and Companions, martyrs; memorial.
4—Wed. Weekday.
5—Thurs. St. Boniface, bishop-martyr; memorial.
6—Fri. Weekday. St. Norbert, bishop; optional memorial.
7—Sat. Weekday.
8—**Sun. Corpus Christi (in U.S.); solemnity.** (Gn. 14:18-20; 1 Cor. 11:23-26; Lk. 9:11b-17.)
9—Mon. Weekday. St. Ephraem, deacon-doctor; optional memorial. (Tenth Week of the Year.)
10—Tues. Weekday.
11—Wed. St. Barnabas, apostle; memorial.
12—Thurs. Weekday.
13—Fri. **Sacred Heart of Jesus; solemnity.** [St. Anthony of Padua, priest-doctor; memorial.]
14—Sat. Weekday. Immaculate Heart of Mary; optional memorial.
15—**Eleventh Sunday of the Year.** (2 Sm. 12:7-10, 13; Gal. 2:16, 19-21; Lk. 7:36 to 8:3.)
16—Mon. Weekday.
17—Tues. Weekday.
18—Wed. Weekday.
19—Thurs. Weekday. St. Romuald, abbot; optional memorial.
20—Fri. Weekday.
21—Sat. St. Aloysius Gonzaga, religious; memorial.
22—**Twelfth Sunday of the Year.** (Zec. 12:10-11; Gal. 3:26-29; Lk. 9:18-24.) [St. Paulinus of Nola, bishop, or Sts. John Fisher, bishop-martyr, and Thomas More, martyr; optional memorials.]
23—Mon. Weekday.
24—Tues. **Birth of St. John the Baptist; solemnity.**
25—Wed. Weekday.
26—Thurs. Weekday.
27—Fri. Weekday. St. Cyril of Alexandria, bishop-doctor; optional memorial.
28—Sat. St. Irenaeus, bishop-martyr; memorial.
29—**Sun. Sts. Peter and Paul, apostles; solemnity.** (Acts 12:1-11; 2 Tm. 4:6-8, 17-18; Mt. 16:13-19.)
30—Mon. Weekday. First Martyrs of the Roman Church; optional memorial. (Thirteenth Week of the Year.)

GENERAL AND MISSION PRAYER INTENTIONS: That young people be successful in creating a civilization of love. That Asians deepen their Gospel awareness by prayer.

JULY 1980

1—Tues. Weekday.
2—Wed. Weekday.
3—Thurs. St. Thomas, apostle; feast.
4—Fri. Weekday. St. Elizabeth of Portugal; optional memorial. Independence Day Votive Mass (in U.S.).
5—Sat. Weekday. St. Anthony Zaccaria, priest; optional memorial.
6—**Fourteenth Sunday of the Year.** (Is. 66:10-14c; Gal 6:14-18; Lk 10:1-12, 17-20.) [St. Maria Goretti, virgin-martyr; optional memorial.]
7—Mon. Weekday.
8—Tues. Weekday
9—Wed. Weekday.
10—Thurs. Weekday.
11—Fri. St. Benedict, abbot; memorial.
12—Sat. Weekday.
13—**Fifteenth Sunday of the Year.** (Dt. 30:10-14; Col 1:15-20; Lk. 10:25-37.) [St. Henry; optional memorial.]
14—Mon. Weekday. St. Camillus de Lellis, priest; optional memorial.
15—Tues. St. Bonaventure, bishop-doctor; memorial.
16—Wed. Weekday. Our Lady of Mt. Carmel; optional memorial.
17—Thurs. Weekday.
18—Fri. Weekday.
19—Sat. Weekday.
20—**Sixteenth Sunday of the Year.** (Gn. 18:1-10a; Col. 1:24-28; Lk. 10:38-42.)
21—Mon. Weekday. St. Lawrence of Brindisi, priest-doctor; optional memorial.
22—Tues. St. Mary Magdalene; memorial.
23—Wed. Weekday. St. Bridget, religious; optional memorial.
24—Thurs. Weekday.
25—Fri. St. James, apostle; feast.
26—Sat. Sts. Joachim and Anne, parents of Mary; memorial.
27—**Seventeenth Sunday of the Year.** (Gn. 18:20-32; Col. 2:12-14; Lk. 11:1-13.)
28—Mon. Weekday.
29—Tues. St. Martha; memorial.
30—Wed. Weekday. St. Peter Chrysologus, bishop-doctor; optional memorial.
31—Thurs. St. Ignatius of Loyola, priest; memorial.

GENERAL PRAYER INTENTION: That social ills be solved in accordance with the teachings of the Church. (The social teachings of the Church, emanating from the Gospel, have been formulated in numerous papal documents since the time of Leo XIII and in the writings of many bishops and Catholic social theorists. Pope John Paul II contributed to the development of this body of teaching during the past year.)

MISSION PRAYER INTENTION: For greater commitment to missionary work by elderly people.

AUGUST 1980

1—Fri. St. Alphonsus Liguori, bishop-doctor; memorial.
2—Sat. Weekday. St. Eusebius of Vercelli, bishop; optional memorial.
3—**Eighteenth Sunday of the Year.** (Eccl. 1:2 and 2:21-23; Col. 3:1-5, 9-11; Lk. 12:13-21.)
4—Mon. St. John Vianney, priest; memorial.
5—Tues. Weekday. Dedication of St. Mary Major Basilica; optional memorial.
6—Wed. Transfiguration of the Lord; feast.
7—Thurs. Weekday. Sts. Sixtus II, pope, and Companions, martyrs, or St. Cajetan, priest; optional memorials.
8—Fri. St. Dominic, priest; memorial.
9—Sat. Weekday.
10—**Nineteenth Sunday of the Year.** (Wis. 18:6-9; Heb. 11:1-2, 8-19; Lk. 12:32-48.) [St. Lawrence, deacon-martyr; feast.]
11—Mon. St. Clare, virgin; memorial.
12—Tues. Weekday.
13—Wed. Weekday. Sts. Pontian, pope, and Hippolytus, priest, martyrs; optional memorial.
14—Thurs. Weekday.
15—**Fri. Assumption of Blessed Mary the Virgin; solemnity. Holy day of obligation.** (Rv. 11:19a and 12:1-6a, 10ab; 1 Cor. 15:20-26; Lk. 1:39-56.)
16—Sat. Weekday. St. Stephen of Hungary; optional memorial.
17—**Twentieth Sunday of the Year.** (Jer. 38:4-6, 8-10; Heb. 12:1-4; Lk. 12:49-53.)
18—Mon. Weekday.
19—Tues. Weekday. St. John Eudes, priest; optional memorial.
20—Wed. St. Bernard of Clairvaux, abbot-doctor; memorial.
21—Thurs. St. Pius X, pope; memorial.
22—Fri. Queenship of Mary; memorial.
23—Sat. Weekday. St. Rose of Lima, virgin; optional memorial.
24—**Twenty-First Sunday of the Year.** (Is. 66:18-21; Heb. 12:5-7, 11-13; Lk. 13:22-30.) [St. Bartholomew, apostle; feast.]
25—Mon. Weekday. St. Louis, or St. Joseph Calasanz, priest; optional memorials.
26—Tues. Weekday.
27—Wed. St. Monica; memorial.
28—Thurs. St. Augustine, bishop-doctor; memorial.
29—Fri. Beheading of St. John the Baptist; memorial.
30—Sat. Weekday.
31—**Twenty-Second Sunday of the Year.** (Sir. 3:17-18, 20, 28-29; Heb. 12:18-19, 22-24a; Lk. 14:1, 7-14.)

GENERAL PRAYER INTENTION: That family problems be studied in the light of the teaching of Christ.

MISSION PRAYER INTENTION: For increased family commitment to the missionary spirit.

SEPTEMBER 1980

1—Mon. Weekday.
2—Tues. Weekday.
3—Wed. St. Gregory the Great, pope-doctor; memorial.
4—Thurs. Weekday.
5—Fri. Weekday.
6—Sat. Weekday.
7—**Twenty-Third Sunday of the Year.** (Wis. 9:13-18b; Phlm. 9b-10, 12-17; Lk. 14:25-33.)
8—Mon. Birth of Mary; feast.
9—Tues. St. Peter Claver, priest; memorial (in U.S.). Weekday.
10—Wed. Weekday.
11—Thurs. Weekday.
12—Fri. Weekday.
13—Sat. St. John Chrysostom, bishop-doctor; memorial.
14—**Sun. Triumph of the Cross; feast.** (Nm. 21:4-9; Phil. 2:6-11; Jn. 3:13-17.)
15—Mon. Our Lady of Sorrows; memorial. (Twenty-Fourth Week of the Year.)
16—Tues. Sts. Cornelius, pope, and Cyprian, bishop, martyrs; memorial.
17—Wed. Weekday. St. Robert Bellarmine, bishop-doctor; optional memorial.
18—Thurs. Weekday.
19—Fri. Weekday. St. Januarius, bishop-martyr; optional memorial.
20—Sat. Weekday.
21—**Twenty-Fifth Sunday of the Year.** (Am. 8:4-7; 1 Tm. 2:1-8; Lk. 16:1-13.) [St. Matthew, apostle-evangelist; feast.]
22—Mon. Weekday.
23—Tues. Weekday.
24—Wed. Weekday.
25—Thurs. Weekday.
26—Fri. Weekday. Sts. Cosmas and Damian, martyrs; optional memorial.
27—Sat. St. Vincent de Paul, priest; memorial.
28—**Twenty-Sixth Sunday of the Year.** (Am. 6:1a, 4-7; 1 Tm. 6:11-16; Lk. 16:19-31.) [St. Wenceslaus, martyr; optional memorial.]
29—Mon. Sts. Michael, Gabriel and Raphael, archangels; feast.
30—Tues. St. Jerome, priest-doctor; memorial.

GENERAL PRAYER INTENTION: That doctors and nurses be tender and kind to the sick. (Pope John Paul told religious engaged in health work June 18 that their work, because of the Gospel motivation that inspires it, "has a particular trait which consists in seeing in the sick ... the Person of Jesus himself." He said the work witnesses to the fact that "the sick person must constitute a permanent priority.")

MISSION PRAYER INTENTION: That all Christians share the Holy Father's concern for evangelization.

OCTOBER 1980

1—Wed. St. Therese of the Child Jesus, virgin; memorial.
2—Thurs. Guardian Angels; memorial.
3—Fri. Weekday.
4—Sat. St. Francis of Assisi; memorial.
5—**Twenty-Seventh Sunday of the Year.** (Hb. 1:2-3 and 2:2-4; 2 Tm 1:6-8, 13-14; Lk. 17:5-10.)
6—Mon. Weekday. St. Bruno, priest; optional memorial.
7—Tues. Our Lady of the Rosary; memorial.
8—Wed. Weekday.
9—Thurs. Weekday. Sts. Denis, bishop, and Companions, martyrs, or St. John Leonard, priest; optional memorials.
10—Fri. Weekday.
11—Sat. Weekday.
12—**Twenty-Eighth Sunday of the Year.** (2 Kgs. 5:14-17; 2 Tm. 2:8-13; Lk. 17:11-19.)
13—Mon. Weekday.
14—Tues. Weekday. St. Callistus I, pope-martyr; optional memorial.
15—Wed. St. Teresa of Avila, virgin-doctor; memorial.
16—Thurs. Weekday. St. Hedwig, religious, or St. Margaret Mary Alacoque, virgin; optional memorials.
17—Fri. St. Ignatius of Antioch, bishop-martyr; memorial.
18—Sat. St. Luke, evangelist; feast.
19—**Twenty-Ninth Sunday of the Year.** (Ex. 17:8-13; 2 Tm. 3:14 to 4:2; Lk. 18:1-8.) [Sts. Isaac Jogues, John de Brebeuf, priests, and Companions, martyrs; memorial (in U.S.). St. Paul of the Cross; optional memorial.]
20—Mon. Weekday.
21—Tues. Weekday.
22—Wed. Weekday.
23—Thurs. Weekday. St. John of Capistrano, priest; optional memorial.
24—Fri. Weekday. St. Anthony Mary Claret, bishop; optional memorial.
25—Sat. Weekday.
26—**Thirtieth Sunday of the Year.** (Sir. 35:12-14, 16-18; 2 Tm. 4:6-8, 16-18; Lk. 18:9-14.)
27—Mon. Weekday.
28—Tues. Sts. Simon and Jude, apostles; feast.
29—Wed. Weekday.
30—Thurs. Weekday.
31—Fri. Weekday.

GENERAL PRAYER INTENTION: That scientific research be used in accordance with moral norms engraved in the human heart.

MISSION PRAYER INTENTION: That the Church adapt itself to all cultures without harm to its unity.

NOVEMBER 1980

1—Sat. All Saints; solemnity. Holy day of obligation. (Rv. 7:2-4, 9-14; 1 Jn. 3:1-3; Mt. 5:1-12a.)
2—Sun. Commemoration of All the Faithful Departed (All Souls' Day). Three Masses proper.
3—Mon. Weekday. St. Martin de Porres, religious; optional memorial. (Thirty-First Week of the Year.)
4—Tues. St. Charles Borromeo, bishop; memorial.
5—Wed. Weekday.
6—Thurs. Weekday.
7—Fri. Weekday.
8—Sat. Weekday.
9—Sun. Dedication of St. John Lateran (Archbasilica of Most Holy Savior); feast.
10—Mon. St. Leo the Great, pope-doctor; memorial. (Thirty-Second Week of the Year.)
11—Tues. St. Martin of Tours, bishop; memorial.
12—Wed. St. Josaphat, bishop-martyr; memorial.
13—Thurs. St. Frances Xavier Cabrini, virgin; memorial (in U.S.).
14—Fri. Weekday.
15—Sat. Weekday. St. Albert the Great, bishop-doctor; optional memorial.
16—Thirty-Third Sunday of the Year. (Mal. 3:19-20a; 2 Thes. 3:7-12; Lk. 21:5-19.) [St. Margaret of Scotland, or St. Gertrude, virgin; optional memorials.]
17—Mon. St. Elizabeth of Hungary, religious; memorial.
18—Tues. Weekday. Dedication of Basilicas of Sts. Peter and Paul, apostles; optional memorial.
19—Wed. Weekday.
20—Thurs. Weekday.
21—Fri. Presentation of Mary; memorial.
22—Sat. St. Cecilia, virgin-martyr; memorial.
23—Sun. Christ the King; solemnity. (2 Sm. 5:1-3; Col. 1:12-20; Lk. 23:35-43.) [St. Clement I, pope-martyr, or St. Columban, abbot; optional memorials.]
24—Mon. Weekday. (Thirty-Fourth (Last) Week of the Year.)
25—Tues. Weekday.
26—Wed. Weekday.
27—Thurs. Thanksgiving Day Votive Mass (in U.S.) Weekday.
28—Fri. Weekday.
29—Sat. Weekday.
30—First Sunday of Advent. (Is. 2:1-5; Rom. 13:11-14; Mt. 24:37-44). [St. Andrew, apostle; feast.]

GENERAL AND MISSION PRAYER INTENTIONS: That journalists use the media to serve truth and love. That religious give effective witness to the vow of poverty.

DECEMBER 1980

1—Mon. Weekday of Advent.
2—Tues. Weekday of Advent.
3—Wed. St. Francis Xavier, priest; memorial.
4—Thurs. Weekday of Advent. St. John Damascene, priest-doctor; optional memorial.
5—Fri. Weekday of Advent.
6—Sat. Weekday of Advent. St. Nicholas, bishop; optional memorial.
7—Second Sunday of Advent. (Is. 11:1-10; Rom. 15:4-9; Mt. 3:1-12.) [St. Ambrose, bishop-doctor; memorial.]
8—Mon. Immaculate Conception of Blessed Mary the Virgin; solemnity. Holy day of obligation. (Gn. 3:9-15, 20; Eph. 1:3-6, 11-12; Lk. 1:26-38.)
9—Tues. Weekday of Advent.
10—Wed. Weekday of Advent.
11—Thurs. Weekday of Advent. St. Damasus. I, pope; optional memorial.
12—Fri. Our Lady of Guadalupe; memorial (in U.S.). Weekday of Advent. St. Jane Frances de Chantal, religious; optional memorial.
13—Sat. St. Lucy, virgin-martyr; memorial.
14—Third Sunday of Advent. (Is. 35:1-6a, 10; Jas. 5:7-10; Mt. 11:2-11.) [St. John of the Cross, priest-doctor; memorial.]
15—Mon. Weekday of Advent.
16—Tues. Weekday of Advent.
17—Wed. Weekday of Advent.
18—Thurs. Weekday of Advent.
19—Fri. Weekday of Advent.
20—Sat. Weekday of Advent.
21—Fourth Sunday of Advent. (Is. 7:10-14; Rom. 1:1-7; Mt. 1:18-24.) [St. Peter Canisius, priest-doctor; optional memorial.]
22—Mon. Weekday of Advent.
23—Tues. Weekday of Advent. [St. John of Kanty, priest; optional memorial.]
24—Wed. Weekday of Advent.
25—Thurs. Christmas. Birth of the Lord; solemnity. Holy day of obligation. (Midnight—Is. 9:1-6; Ti. 2:11-14; Lk. 2:1-14. Dawn—Is. 62:11-12; Ti. 3:4-7; Lk. 2:15-20. During the Day—Is. 52:7-10; Heb. 1:1-6; Jn. 1:1-18.)
26—Fri. St. Stephen, first martyr; feast.
27—Sat. St. John, apostle-evangelist; feast.
28—Sun. Holy Family; feast. (Sir. 3:2-6, 12-14; Col. 3:12-21; Mt. 2:13-15, 19-23.) [Holy Innocents, martyrs; feast.]
29—Mon. Fifth Day of Christmas Octave. St. Thomas Becket, bishop-martyr; optional memorial.
30—Tues. Sixth Day of Christmas Octave.
31—Wed. Seventh Day of Christmas Octave. St. Sylvester I, pope; optional memorial.

GENERAL PRAYER INTENTION: That motorists drive responsibly.
MISSION PRAYER INTENTION: That the sick offer suffering for spread of the Gospel.

TABLE OF MOVABLE FEASTS

Year	Ash Wednesday	Easter	Ascension	Pentecost	Weeks of Ordinary Time				First Sunday of Advent
					Before Lent		After Pent.		
					Week	Ends	Week	Begins	
1980	Feb. 20	Apr. 6	May 15	May 25	6	Feb. 19	8	May 26	Nov. 30
1981	Mar. 4	Apr. 19	May 28	June 7	8	Mar. 3	10	June 8	Nov. 29
1982	Feb. 24	Apr. 11	May 20	May 30	7	Feb. 23	9	May 31	Nov. 28
1983	Feb. 16	Apr. 3	May 12	May 22	6	Feb. 15	8	May 23	Nov. 27
1984	Mar. 7	Apr. 22	May 31	June 10	9	Mar. 6	10	June 11	Dec. 2
1985	Feb. 20	Apr. 7	May 16	May 26	6	Feb. 19	8	May 27	Dec. 1
1986	Feb. 12	Mar. 30	May 8	May 18	5	Feb. 11	7	May 19	Nov. 30
1987	Mar. 4	Apr. 19	May 28	June 7	9	Mar. 3	10	June 8	Nov. 29
1988	Feb. 17	Apr. 3	May 12	May 22	6	Feb. 16	8	May 23	Nov. 27
1989	Feb. 8	Mar. 26	May 4	May 14	5	Feb. 7	6	May 15	Dec. 3
1990	Feb. 28	Apr. 15	May 24	June 3	8	Feb. 27	9	June 4	Dec. 2
1991	Feb. 13	Mar. 31	May 9	May 19	5	Feb. 12	7	May 20	Dec. 1
1992	Mar. 4	Apr. 19	May 28	June 7	9	Mar. 3	10	June 8	Nov. 29
1993	Feb. 24	Apr. 11	May 20	May 30	7	Feb. 23	9	May 31	Nov. 28
1994	Feb. 16	Apr. 3	May 12	May 22	6	Feb. 15	8	May 23	Nov. 27
1995	Mar. 1	Apr. 16	May 25	June 4	8	Feb. 28	9	June 5	Dec. 3
1996	Feb. 21	Apr. 7	May 16	May 26	7	Feb. 20	8	May 27	Dec. 1
1997	Feb. 12	Mar. 30	May 8	May 18	5	Feb. 11	7	May 19	Nov. 30
1998	Feb. 25	Apr. 12	May 21	May 31	7	Feb. 24	9	June 1	Nov. 29
1999	Feb. 17	Apr. 4	May 13	May 23	6	Feb. 16	8	May 24	Nov. 28
2000	Mar. 8	Apr. 23	June 1	June 11	9	Mar. 7	10	June 12	Dec. 3
2001	Feb. 28	Apr. 15	May 24	June 3	7	Feb. 27	9	June 4	Dec. 2
2002	Feb. 13	Mar. 31	May 9	May 19	5	Feb. 12	7	May 20	Dec. 1
2003	Mar. 5	Apr. 20	May 29	June 8	8	Mar. 4	10	June 9	Nov. 30
2004	Feb. 25	Apr. 11	May 20	May 30	7	Feb. 24	9	May 31	Nov. 28

Season of Ordinary Time

Weeks between the end of Christmastide and the beginning of Lent, and from the day after Pentecost to the last Sunday of the liturgical year, belong to the season of Ordinary Time. The table indicates the number and terminal date of the week ending the first part, and the number and starting date of the week beginning the second part, of this season. In some years, a week of this season is eliminated because of calendar conditions.

Date of Easter

The Second Vatican Council's *Constitution on the Sacred Liturgy* said there would be no objection "if the feast of Easter were assigned to a particular Sunday of the Gregorian calendar, provided that those whom it may concern, especially the brethren who are not in communion with the Apostolic See, give their assent."

If calendar and related cultural differences between the Roman Catholic and Orthodox Churches were resolved, they could both celebrate Easter on the same day. Demetrios I, Orthodox Ecumenical Patriarch, and Pope Paul expressed in their 1975 Easter greetings the desire that eventually the Catholic and Orthodox Churches would celebrate the feast at the same time.

Holiday Masses

Liturgical experiments in recent years have led to the development of votive Masses for national holidays, like those introduced in the U.S. for Thanksgiving Day in 1969 and July 4 in 1972. This development is in line with a custom whereby "from the earliest times the Church has crowned many non-Christian feasts with Christian fulfillment by instituting its own liturgical festivals" to coincide with them.

Labor Day, in lieu of a special votive Mass, may be observed with celebration of the Mass of St. Joseph the Worker.

HOLY DAYS AND OTHER FEASTS

The following list includes the six holy days of obligation observed in the United States and additional observances of devotional and historical significance. The dignity or rank of observances is indicated by the terms: **solemnity** (highest in rank, the equivalent of former first class feasts); **feast** (equivalent to former second class feasts); **memorial** (equivalent to former third class feasts, for universal observance); **optional memorial** (for celebration by choice).

All Saints, Nov. 1, holy day of obligation, solemnity. Commemorates all the blessed in heaven, and is intended particularly to honor the blessed who have no special feasts. The background of the feast dates to the fourth century when groups of martyrs, and later other saints, were honored on a common day in various places. In 609 or 610, the Pantheon, a pagan temple at Rome, was consecrated as a Christian church for the honor of Our Lady and the martyrs (later all saints). In 835, Gregory IV fixed Nov. 1 as the date of observance.

All Souls, Commemoration of the Faithful Departed, Nov. 2 (transferable to Nov. 3). The dead were prayed for from the earliest days of Christianity. By the sixth century it was customary in Benedictine monasteries to hold a commemoration of deceased members of the order at Pentecost. A common commemoration of all the faithful departed on the day after All Saints was instituted in 998 by St. Odilo, of the Abbey of Cluny, and an observance of this kind was generally adopted throughout the Church. In 1915, Benedict XV granted priests throughout the world permission to celebrate three Masses for this commemoration. He also granted a special indulgence for the occasion.

Annunciation of the Lord (formerly, Annunciation of the Blessed Virgin Mary), Mar. 25, solemnity. A feast of the Incarnation which commemorates the announcement by the Archangel Gabriel to the Virgin Mary that she was to become the Mother of Christ (Lk. 1:26-38), and the miraculous conception of Christ by her. The feast was instituted about 430 in the East. The Roman observance dates from the seventh century, when celebration was said to be universal.

Ascension of the Lord, movable observance held 40 days after Easter, holy day of obligation, solemnity. Commemorates the Ascension of Christ into heaven 40 days after his Resurrection from the dead (Mk. 16:19; Lk. 24:51; Acts 1:2). The feast recalls the completion of Christ's mission on earth for the salvation of men and his entry into heaven with glorified human nature. The Ascension is a pledge of the final glorification of all who achieve salvation. Documentary evidence of the feast dates from early in the fifth century, but it was observed long before that time in connection with Pentecost and Easter.

Ash Wednesday, movable observance, six and one-half weeks before Easter. It was set as the first day of Lent by St. Gregory the Great (590-604) with the extension of an earlier and shorter penitential season to a total period including 40 weekdays of fasting before Easter. Ashes, symbolic of penance, are blessed and distributed among the faithful during the day. They are used to mark the forehead with the Sign of the Cross, with the reminder: "Remember, man, that you are dust, and unto dust you shall return," or: "Repent, and believe the Good News."

Assumption Aug. 15, holy day of obligation, solemnity. Commemorates the taking into heaven of Mary, soul and body, at the end of her life on earth, a truth of faith that was proclaimed a dogma by Pius XII on Nov. 1, 1950. One of the oldest and most solemn feasts of Mary, it has a history dating back to at least the seventh century when its celebration was already established at Jerusalem and Rome.

Baptism of the Lord, movable, celebrated on the Sunday after Epiphany, feast. Recalls the baptism of Christ by John the Baptist (Mk. 1:9-11), an event associated with the liturgy of the Epiphany. This baptism was the occasion for Christ's manifestation of Himself at the beginning of his public life.

Birth of Mary, Sept. 8, feast. This is a very old feast which originated in the East and found place in the Roman liturgy in the seventh century.

Candlemas Day, Feb. 2. See Presentation of the Lord.

Chair of Peter, Feb. 22, feast. Commemorates establishment of the see of Antioch by Peter. The feast, which has been in the Roman calendar since 336, is a liturgical expression of belief in the episcopacy and hierarchy of the Church.

Christmas, Birth of Our Lord Jesus Christ, Dec. 25, holy day of obligation, solemnity. Commemorates the birth of Christ (Lk. 2:1-20). This event was originally commemorated in the East on the feast of Epiphany or Theophany. The Christmas feast itself originated in the West; by 354 it was certainly kept on Dec. 25. This date may have been set for the observance to offset pagan ceremonies held at about the same time to commemorate the birth of the sun at the winter solstice. Priests may celebrate three Masses on Christmas Day. Christmastide begins with this feast and continues until the Sunday after Epiphany.

Christ the King, movable, celebrated on the last Sunday of the liturgical year, solemnity. Commemorates the royal prerogatives of Christ and is equivalent to a declaration of his rights to the homage, service and fidelity of men in all phases of individual and social life. Pius XI instituted the feast Dec. 11, 1925.

Corpus Christi, movable observance held in the US on the Sunday following Trinity Sunday, solemnity. Commemorates the institution of the Holy Eucharist (Mt. 26:26-28). The feast originated at Liege in 1246 and was extended throughout the Church in the West by Urban IV in 1264. St. Thomas Aquinas composed the Office for the feast.

Dedication of St. John Lateran, Nov. 9, feast. Commemorates the first public consecration of a church, that of the Basilica of the Most Holy Savior by Pope St. Sylvester Nov. 9, 324. The church, as well as the Lateran Palace, was the gift of Emperor Constantine. Since the 12th century it has been known as St. John Lateran, in honor of John the Baptist after whom the adjoining baptistery was named. It was rebuilt by Innocent X (1644-55), reconsecrated by Benedict XIII in 1726, and enlarged by Leo XIII (1878-1903). This basilica is regarded as the church of highest dignity in Rome and throughout the Roman Rite.

Dedication of St. Mary Major, Aug. 5, optional memorial. Commemorates the rebuilding and dedication by Sixtus III (432-40) of a church in honor of Blessed Mary the Virgin. This is the Basilica of St. Mary Major on the Esquiline Hill in Rome. An earlier building was erected during the pontificate of Liberius (352-66); according to legend, it was located on a site covered by a miraculous fall of snow seen by a nobleman favored with a vision of Mary.

Easter, movable celebration held on the first Sunday after the full moon following the vernal equinox (between Mar. 22 and Apr. 25), solemnity with an octave. Commemorates the Resurrection of Christ from the dead (Mk. 16:1-7). The observance of this mystery, kept since the first days of the Church, extends throughout the Easter season which lasts until the feast of Pentecost, a period of 50 days. Every Sunday in the year is regarded as a "little" Easter. The date of Easter determines the dates of movable feasts, such as Ascension and Pentecost, and the number of Sundays after Epiphany and Pentecost.

Easter Vigil (Holy Saturday), day before Easter. Ceremonies are all related to the Resurrection and renewal-in-grace theme of Easter: blessing of the new fire and Paschal Candle, reading of prophecies, blessing of water and the baptismal font, the baptism of converts and renewal of baptismal vows by the faithful, the Litany of the Saints, and the celebration of Mass. The vigil ceremonies are held after sundown, preferably at a time that makes possible the celebration of Mass at midnight.

Epiphany of Our Lord, Jan. 6 or (in the US) a Sunday between Jan. 2 and 8, solemnity. Commemorates the manifestations of the divinity of Christ. It is one of the oldest Christian feasts, with an Eastern origin traceable to the beginning of the third century and antedating the Western feast of Christmas. Originally, it commemorated the manifestations of Christ's divinity — or Theophany — in his birth, the homage of the Magi, and baptism by John the Baptist. Later, the first two of these commemorations were transferred to Christmas when the Eastern Church adopted that feast between 380 and 430. The central feature of the Eastern observance now is the manifestation or declaration of Christ's divinity in his baptism and at the beginning of his public life. The Epiphany was adopted by the Western Church during the same period in which the Eastern Church accepted Christmas. In the Roman Rite, commemoration is made in the Mass of the homage of the wise men from the East (Mt. 2:1-12).

Good Friday, the Friday before Easter, privileged feria of Holy Week. Liturgical elements of the observance are commemoration of the Passion and Death of Christ in the reading of the Passion (according to John), special prayers for the Church and people of all ranks, the veneration of the Cross, and a Communion service. The Solemn Liturgical Action takes place between noon and 9 p.m. This is the only day in the year on which the Eucharistic Liturgy is not celebrated in the Roman Rite.

Guardian Angels, Oct. 2, memorial. Commemorates the angels who protect men from spiritual and physical dangers and assist them in doing good. A feast in their honor celebrated in Spain in the 16th century was extended to the whole Church by Paul V in 1608. In 1670, Clement X set Oct. 2 as the date of observance. Earlier, guardian angels were honored liturgically in conjunction with the feast of St. Michael.

Holy Family, movable observance on the Sunday after Christmas, feast. Commemorates the Holy Family of Jesus, Mary and Joseph as the model of domestic society, holiness and virtue. The devotional background of the feast was very strong in the 17th century. In the 18th century, in prayers composed for a special Mass, a Canadian bishop likened the Christian family to the Holy Family. Leo XIII consecrated families to the Holy Family. In 1921, Benedict XV extended the Divine Office and Mass of the feast to the whole Church.

Holy Innocents, Dec. 28, feast. Commemorates the infants who suffered death at the hands of Herod's soldiers seeking to kill the child Jesus (Mt. 2:13-18). A feast in their honor has been observed since the fifth century.

Holy Thursday, the Thursday before Easter, privileged feria of Holy Week. Commemorates the institution of the Holy Eucharist (which is later celebrated on the special feast of Corpus Christi) and other events of the Last Supper. Ceremonies include the celebration of a principal Mass between 4 and

9 p.m., the washing of feet in imitation of the act of Christ who washed the feet of the Apostles at the Last Supper, the stripping of the altar at the conclusion of Mass. There is also a procession of the Blessed Sacrament to a special place of reposition where It is reserved for veneration by the faithful until the Solemn Liturgical Action on Good Friday. At a special Mass of Chrism, bishops bless oils (of catechumens, chrism, of the sick) for use during the year.

Immaculate Conception, Dec. 8, holy day of obligation, solemnity. Commemorates the fact that Mary, in view of her calling to be the Mother of Christ and in virtue of his merits, was preserved from the first moment of her conception from original sin and was filled with grace from the very beginning of her life. She was the only person so preserved from original sin. The present form of the feast dates from Dec. 8, 1854, when Pius IX defined the dogma of the Immaculate Conception. An earlier feast of the Conception, which testified to long-existing belief in this truth, was observed in the East by the eighth century, in Ireland in the ninth, and subsequently in European countries. In 1846, Mary was proclaimed patroness of the US under this title.

Immaculate Heart of Mary, Saturday following the second Sunday after Pentecost, optional memorial. On May 4, 1944, Pius XII ordered this feast observed throughout the Church in order to obtain Mary's intercession for "peace among nations, freedom for the Church, the conversion of sinners, the love of purity and the practice of virtue." Two years earlier, he consecrated the entire human race to Mary under this title. Devotion to Mary under the title of her Most Pure Heart originated during the Middle Ages. It was given great impetus in the 17th century by the preaching of St. John Eudes, who was the first to celebrate a Mass and Divine Office of Mary under this title. A feast, celebrated in various places and on different dates, was authorized in 1799.

Joachim and Ann, July 26, memorial. Commemorates the parents of Mary. A joint feast, celebrated Sept. 9, originated in the East near the end of the sixth century. Devotion to Ann, introduced in the eighth century at Rome, became widespread in Europe in the 14th century; her feast was extended throughout the Latin Church in 1584. A feast of Joachim was introduced in the West in the 15th century.

John the Baptist, Birth, June 24, solemnity. The precursor of Christ, whose cousin he was, was commemorated universally in the liturgy by the fourth century. He is the only saint, except the Blessed Virgin Mary, whose birthday is observed as a feast. Another feast, on Aug. 29, commemorates his passion and death at the order of Herod (Mk. 6:14-29).

Joseph, Mar. 19, solemnity. Joseph is honored as the husband of the Blessed Virgin Mary, the patron and protector of the universal Church and workman. Devotion to him already existed in the eighth century in the East, and in the 11th in the West. Various feasts were celebrated before the 15th century when Mar. 19 was fixed for his commemoration; this feast was extended to the whole Church in 1621 by Gregory XV. In 1955, Pius XII instituted the feast of St. Joseph the Workman for observance May 1; this feast, which may be celebrated by local option, supplanted the Solemnity or Patronage of St. Joseph formerly observed on the third Wednesday after Easter. St. Joseph was proclaimed protector and patron of the universal Church in 1870 by Pius IX.

Michael, Gabriel and Raphael, Archangels, Sept. 29, feast. A feast bearing the title of Dedication of St. Michael the Archangel formerly commemorated on this date the consecration in 530 of a church near Rome in honor of Michael, the first angel given a liturgical feast. For a while, this feast was combined with a commemoration of the Guardian Angels. The separate feasts of Gabriel (Mar. 24) and Raphael (Oct. 24) were suppressed by the calendar reform of 1969 and this joint feast of the three archangels was instituted.

Octave of Christmas, Jan. 1. See Solemnity of Mary, Mother of God.

Our Lady of Sorrows, Sept. 15, memorial. Recalls the sorrows experienced by Mary in her association with Christ: the prophecy of Simeon (Lk. 2:34-35), the flight into Egypt (Mt. 2:13-21), the three-day separation from Jesus (Lk. 2:41-50), and four incidents connected with the Passion: her meeting with Christ on the way to Calvary, the crucifixion, the removal of Christ's body from the cross, and his burial (Mt. 27:31-61; Mk. 15:20-47; Lk. 23:26-56; Jn. 19:17-42). A Mass and Divine Office of the feast were celebrated by the Servites, especially, in the 17th century, and in 1817 Pius VII extended the observance to the whole Church.

Our Lady of the Rosary, Oct. 7, memorial. Commemorates the Virgin Mary through recall of the mysteries of the Rosary which recapitulate events in her life and the life of Christ. The feast was instituted to commemorate a Christian victory over invading Mohammedan forces at Lepanto on Oct. 7, 1571, and was extended throughout the Church by Clement XI in 1716.

Passion (Palm) Sunday, the Sunday before Easter. Recalls the triumphal entry of Christ into Jerusalem at the beginning of the last week of his life (Mt. 21:1-9). A procession and other ceremonies commemorating this event were held in Jerusalem from very early Christian times and were adopted in Rome by the ninth century, when the blessing of palm for the occasion was introduced. Full liturgical observance includes the blessing of palm and a procession before the principal Mass of the day. The Passion, by Matthew, Mark or Luke, is read during the Mass.

Pentecost, also called **Whitsunday,** movable celebration held 50 days after Easter, solemnity. Commemorates the descent of the Holy Spirit upon the Apostles, the preaching of Peter and the other Apostles to Jews in Jerusalem, the baptism and aggregation of some 3,000 persons to the Christian community (Acts 2:1-41). It is regarded as the birthday of the Catholic Church. The original observance of the feast antedated the earliest extant documentary evidence from the third century.

Peter and Paul, June 29, solemnity. Commemorates the dual martyrdom of Peter by crucifixion and Paul by beheading during the Neronian persecution. This joint commemoration of the two greatest Apostles dates at least from 258 at Rome.

Presentation of the Lord (formerly called Purification of the Blessed Virgin Mary, also Candlemas), Feb. 2, feast. Commemorates the presentation of Jesus in the Temple — according to prescriptions of Mosaic Law (Lv. 12:2-8; Ex. 13:2; Lk. 2:22-32) — and the purification of Mary 40 days after his birth. In the East, where the feast antedated fourth century testimony regarding its existence, it was observed primarily as a feast of Our Lord; in the West, where it was adopted later, it was regarded more as a feast of Mary until the calendar reform of 1969. Its date was set for Feb. 2 after the celebration of Christmas was fixed for Dec. 25, late in the fourth century. The blessing of candles, probably in commemoration of Christ who was the Light to enlighten the Gentiles, became common about the 11th century and gave the feast the secondary name of Candlemas.

Queenship of Mary, Aug. 22, memorial. Commemorates the high dignity of Mary as Queen of heaven, angels and men. Universal observance of the memorial was ordered by Pius XII in the encyclical *Ad Caeli Reginam* Oct. 11, 1954, near the close of a Marian Year observed in connection with the centenary of the proclamation of the dogma of the Immaculate Conception and four years after the proclamation of the dogma of the Assumption. The original date of the memorial was May 31.

Resurrection. See Easter.

Sacred Heart of Jesus, movable observance held on the Friday after Corpus Christi, solemnity. The object of the devotion is the divine Person of Christ, whose heart is the symbol of his love for men — for whom he accomplished the work of Redemption. The Mass and Office now used on the feast were prescribed by Pius XI in 1929. Devotion to the Sacred Heart was introduced into the liturgy in the 17th century through the efforts of St. John Eudes who composed an Office and Mass for the feast. It was furthered as the result of the revelations of St. Margaret Mary Alacoque after 1675 and by the work of Claude de la Colombiere, S.J. In 1765, Clement XIII approved a Mass and Office for the feast, and in 1856 Pius IX extended the observance throughout the Roman Rite.

Solemnity of Mary, Mother of God, Jan. 1, holy day of obligation, solemnity. The calendar reform of 1969, in accord with Eastern tradition, reinstated the Marian character of this commemoration on the octave day of Christmas. The former feast of the Circumcision, dating at least from the first half of the sixth century, marked the initiation of Jesus (Lk. 2:21) in Judaism and by analogy focused attention on the initiation of persons in the Christian religion and their incorporation in Christ through baptism. The feast of the Solemnity supplants the former feast of the Maternity of Mary observed on Oct. 11.

Transfiguration of the Lord, Aug. 6, feast. Commemorates the revelation of his divinity by Christ to Peter, James and John on Mt. Tabor (Mt. 17:1-9). The feast, which is very old, was extended throughout the universal Church in 1457 by Callistus III.

Trinity, Most Holy, movable observance held on the Sunday after Pentecost, solemnity. Commemorates the most sublime mystery of the Christian faith, i.e., that there are Three Divine Persons — Father, Son and Holy Spirit — in one God (Mt. 28:18-20). A votive Mass of the Most Holy Trinity dates from the seventh century; an Office was composed in the 10th century; in 1334, John XXII extended the feast to the universal Church.

Triumph of the Cross, Sept. 14, feast. Commemorates the finding of the cross on which Christ was crucified, in 326 through the efforts of St. Helena, mother of Constantine; the consecration of the Basilica of the Holy Sepulchre nearly 10 years later: and the recovery in 628 or 629 by Emperor Heraclius of a major portion of the cross which had been removed by the Persians from its place of veneration at Jerusalem. The feast originated in Jerusalem and spread through the East before being adopted in the West. General adoption followed the building at Rome of the Basilica of the Holy Cross "in Jerusalem," so called because it was the place of enshrinement of a major portion of the cross of crucifixion.

Visitation, May 31, feast. Commemorates Mary's visit to her cousin Elizabeth after the Annunciation and before the birth of John the Baptist, the precursor of Christ (Lk. 1:39-47). The feast had a medieval origin and was observed in the Franciscan Order before being extended throughout the Church by Urban VI in 1389. It is one of the feasts of the Incarnation and is notable for its recall of the Magnificat, one of the few New Testament canticles, which acknowledges the unique gifts of God to Mary because of her role in the redemptive work of Christ. The canticle is recited at Vespers in the Liturgy of the Hours.

SAINTS

Biographical sketches of additional saints are under other Almanac titles. See Index.

An asterisk with a feast date indicates that a memorial or feast is observed according to the revised Roman-Rite calendar.

Adjutor, St. (d. 1131): Norman knight; fought in First Crusade; monk-recluse after his return; legendary accounts of incidents on journey to Crusade probably account for his patronage of yachtsmen; Apr. 30.

Agatha, St. (d. c. 250): Sicilian virgin-martyr; her intercession credited in Sicily with stopping eruptions of Mt. Etna; patron of nurses; Feb. 5*.

Agnes, St. (d. c. 304): Roman virgin-martyr; martyred at age of 10 or 12; patron of young girls; Jan. 21*.

Aloysius Gonzaga, St. (1568-1591): Italian Jesuit; died while nursing plague-stricken; canonized 1726; patron of youth; June 21*.

Amand, St. (d. c. 676): Apostle of Belgium; b. France; established monasteries throughout Belgium; Feb. 6.

Andre Grasset de Saint Sauveur, Bl. (1758-1792): Canadian priest; martyred in France, Sept. 2, 1792, during the Revolution; one of a group called the Martyrs of Paris who were beatified in 1926.

Andrew Corsini, St. (1302-1373): Italian Carmelite; bishop of Fiesoli; mediator between quarrelsome Italian states; canonized 1629; Feb. 4.

Andrew Fournet, St. (1752-1834): French priest; co-founder with St. Jeanne Elizabeth des Anges of the Congregation of Daughters of the Cross; canonized 1933; May 13.

Angela Merici, St. (1474-1540): Italian nun; foundress of Institute of St. Ursula, 1535, the first teaching order of nuns in the Church; canonized 1807; Jan. 27*.

Anne Mary Javouhey, Bl. (1779-1851): French virgin; foundress of Institute of St. Joseph of Cluny, 1812; beatified 1950; July 15.

Ansgar, St. (801-865): Bishop, Benedictine monk; b. near Amiens; missionary in Denmark, Sweden, Norway and Northern Germany; apostle of Denmark; Feb. 3*.

Anthony Abbot, St. (c. 251-c. 354): Egyptian hermit; patriarch of all monks; established communities for hermits which became models for monastic life, especially in the East; friend and supporter of St. Athanasius in the latter's struggle with the Arians; Jan. 17*.

Anthony Mary Claret, St. (1807-1870): Spanish priest; founder of Missionary Sons of the Immaculate Heart of Mary (Claretians), 1849; archbishop of Santiago, Cuba, 1851-57; canonized 1950; Oct. 24*.

Anthony Mary Zaccaria, St. (1502-1539): Italian priest; founder of Barnabites (Clerks Regular of St. Paul), 1530; canonized 1897; July 5*.

Apollonia, St. (d. 249): Deaconess of Alexandria; martyred during persecution of Decius; her patronage of dentists probably rests on tradition that her teeth were broken by pincers by her persecutors; Feb. 9.

Augustine of Canterbury, St. (d. 604 or 605): Italian missionary; apostle of the English; sent by Pope Gregory I with 40 monks to evangelize England; arrived there 597; first archbishop of Canterbury; May 27*.

Benedict of Nursia, St. (c. 480-547): Abbot; founder of monasticism in Western Europe; established monastery at Monte Cassino; proclaimed patron of Europe by Paul VI in 1964; July 11*.

Benedict the Black (il Moro), St. (1526-1589): Sicilian Franciscan; born a slave; joined Franciscans as lay brother; appointed guardian and novice master; canonized 1807; Apr. 4.

Bernadette Soubirous, St. (1844-1879): French peasant girl favored with series of visions of Blessed Virgin Mary at Lourdes (see Lourdes Apparitions); joined Institute of Sisters of Notre Dame at Nevers, 1866; canonized 1933; Apr. 16.

Bernard of Menthon, St. (d. 1081): Italian priest; founded Alpine hospices near the two passes named for him; patron of mountaineers; May 28.

Bernardine of Feltre, Bl. (1439-1494): Italian Franciscan preacher; a founder of montes pietatis.

Bernardine of Siena, St. (1380-1444): Italian Franciscan; noted preacher and missioner; spread of devotion to Holy Name is attributed to him; represented in art holding to his breast the monogram IHS; canonized 1450; May 20*.

Blase, St. (d. c. 316): Armenian bishop; martyr; the blessing of throats on his feast day derives from tradition that he miraculously saved the life of a boy who had half-swallowed a fish bone; Feb. 3*.

Boniface (Winfrid), St. (d. 754): English Benedictine; bishop, martyr; apostle of Germany; established monastery at Fulda which became center of German missionary work; archbishop of Mainz; martyred near Dukkum in Holland; June 5*.

Brendan, St. (c. 489-583): Irish abbot; founded monasteries; his patronage of sailors probably rests on tradition that he made a seven-year voyage in search of a fabled paradise; called Brendan the Navigator; May 16.

Bridget (Brigid), St. (c. 450-525): Irish nun; founded nunnery at Kildare, the first erected on Irish soil; patron, with Sts. Patrick and Columba, of Ireland; Feb. 1.

Bridget (Birgitta), St. (c. 1303-1373): Swedish mystic; widow; foundress of Order of Our Savior (Brigittines); canonized 1391; wrote *Revelationes*, accounts of her visions; patroness of Sweden; July 23*.

Bruno, St. (1030-1101): German monk; founded Carthusians, 1084, in France; Oct. 6*.

Cabrini, Mother: See Index.

Cajetan of Thiene, St. (1480-1547): Italian lawyer; religious reformer; a founder of Oratory of Divine Love, forerunner of the Theatines; canonized 1671; Aug. 7*.

Callistus I, St. (d. 222): Pope, 217-222; martyr; condemned Sabellianism and other heresies; advocated a policy of mercy toward repentant sinners; Oct. 14*.

Camillus de Lellis, St. (1550-1614): Italian priest; founder of Camillians (Ministers of the Sick); canonized 1746; patron of the sick and of nurses; July 14*.

Casimir, St. (1458-1484): Polish prince; grand duke of Lithuania; noted for his piety; buried at cathedral in Vilna, Lithuania; canonized 1521; patron of Poland and Lithuania; Mar. 4*.

Cassian, St. (d. 298): Roman martyr; an official court stenographer who declared himself a Christian; patron of stenographers; Dec. 3.

Catherine Laboure, St. (1806-1876): French nun; favored with series of visions; first Miraculous Medal (see Index) struck as the result of one of the visions; canonized 1947; Dec. 31.

Catherine of Bologna, St. (1413-1463): Italian Poor Clare; mystic, writer, artist; canonized 1712; patron of artists; Mar. 9.

Cecilia, St. (2nd-3rd century): Roman virgin-martyr; traditional patron of musicians; Nov. 22*.

Charles Borromeo, St. (1538-1584): Italian cardinal; nephew of Pope Pius IV; cardinal bishop of Milan; influential figure in Church reform in Italy; promoted education of clergy; canonized 1610; Nov. 4*.

Charles Lwanga and Companions, Sts. (d. 1886 and 1887): Martyrs of Uganda; pages of King Mwanga of Uganda; Charles Lwanga and 12 companions were martyred near Rubaga, June 3, 1886; the other nine were martyred between May 26, 1886, and Jan. 27, 1887; canonized 1964; first martyrs of black Africa; June 3*.

Christopher, St. (3rd cent.): Early Christian martyr inscribed in Roman calendar about 1550; feast relegated to particular calendars because of legendary nature of accounts of his life; traditional patron of travelers; July 25.

Clare, St. (1194-1253): Foundress of Poor Clares; b. at Assisi; later joined in religious life by her sisters Agnes and Beatrice, and her mother Ortolana; canonized 1255; patroness of television; Aug. 11*.

Clement I, St. (d. c. 100): Pope, 88-97; third successor of St. Peter; wrote important letter to Church in Corinth settling disputes there; venerated as a martyr; Nov. 23*.

Columba, St. (521-597): Irish monk; founded monasteries in Ireland; missionary in Scotland; established monastery at Iona which became the center for conversion of Picts, Scots, and Northern English; Scotland's most famous saint; June 9.

Columban, St. (545-615): Irish monk; scholar; founded monasteries in England and Brittany (famous abbey of Luxeuil), forced into exile because of his criticism of Frankish court; spent last years in northern Italy where he founded abbey at Bobbio; Nov. 23*.

Contardo Ferrini, Bl. (1859-1902): Italian Franciscan tertiary; model of the Catholic professor; beatified 1947; patron of universities; Oct. 17.

Cornelius, St. (d. 253): Pope, 251-253; promoted a policy of mercy with respect to readmission of repentant Christians who had fallen away during the persecution of Decius *(lapsi);* banished from Rome during persecution of Gallus; regarded as a martyr; Sept. 16 (with Cyprian)*.

Cosmas and Damian, Sts. (d. c. 303): Arabian twin brothers; physicians who were martyred during Diocletian persecution; patrons of physicians; Sept. 26*.

Crispin and Crispinian, Sts. (3rd cent.): Early Christian martyrs; said to have met their deaths in Gaul; patrons of shoemakers, a trade they pursued; Oct. 25.

Cyprian, St. (d. 258): Early ecclesiastical writer; b. Africa; bishop of Carthage, 249-258; supported Pope St. Cornelius concerning the readmission of Christians who had apostasized in time of persecution; erred in his teaching that baptism administered by heretics and schismatics was invalid; wrote *De Unitate;* Sept. 16 (with St. Cornelius).*

Cyril and Methodius, Sts.: Greek missionaries; brothers venerated as apostles of the Slavs; Cyril (d. 869) and Methodius (d. 885) began their missionary work in Moravia in 863; developed a Slavonic alphabet; eventually their use of the vernacular in the liturgy was approved; Feb. 14*.

Damasus I, St. (d. 384): Pope, 366-384; opposed Arians and Apollinarians; commissioned St. Jerome to work on Bible translation; developed Roman liturgy; Dec. 11*.

Damian, St.: See Cosmas and Damian, Sts.

David, St. (5th-6th cent.): Welsh monk; founded monastery at Menevia; patron saint of Wales; Mar. 1.

Denis and Companions, Sts. (d. 3rd cent.): Denis, bishop of Paris, and two companions identified by early writers as Rusticus, a priest, and Eleutherius, a deacon; martyred near Paris; Denis is popularly regarded as apostle of France; Oct. 9*.

Dismas, St. (1st cent.): Name given to repentant thief (Good Thief) to whom Jesus promised salvation; regarded as patron of prisoners; Mar. 25.

Dominic, St. (Dominic de Guzman) (1170-1221): Spanish priest; founder of Dominican Order (Friars Preachers), 1215; preached against the Albigensian heresy; a contemporary of St. Francis of Assisi; canonized 1234; Aug. 8*.

Dominic Savio, St. (1842-1857): Italian youth; pupil of St. John Bosco; died before his 15th birthday; canonized 1954; patron of choir boys; Mar. 9.

Dunstan, St. (c. 910-988): English monk; archbishop of Canterbury; initiated reforms in religious life; royal counselor to several kings; considered one of greatest Anglo-Saxon saints; patron of armorers, goldsmiths, locksmiths, jewelers; May 17.

Dymphna, St. (dates uncertain): Nothing certain known of her life; presumably she was an Irish maiden whose relics were discovered at Gheel near Antwerp, Belgium, in the 13th century; since that time many cases of mental illness and epilepsy have been cured at her shrine; patron of those suffering from mental illness; May 15.

Edmund Campion, St. (1540-1581): English Jesuit; convert 1573; martyred at Tyburn; canonized 1970, one of the Forty English and Welsh Martyrs; Dec. 1.

Elizabeth Bayley Seton, St. (1774-1821): American foundress; convert, 1905; founded Sisters of Charity in the U.S.; beatified 1963; canonized Sept. 14, 1975; the first American-born saint; Jan. 4 (U.S.)*.

Elizabeth of Hungary, St. (1207-1231): Queen; became Franciscan tertiary after death of her husband in 1227; devoted life to poor and destitute; a patron of the Third Order of St. Francis; Nov. 17*.

Elizabeth of Portugal, St. (1271-1336): Queen of Portugal; b. Spain; retired to Poor Clare convent as a tertiary after the death of her husband; July 4*.

Erasmus, St. (d. 303): Life surrounded by legend; martyred during Diocletian persecution; patron of sailors; June 2.

Ethelbert, St.(552-676): King of Kent; baptized by St. Augustine 597; issued legal code; furthered spread of Christianity; Feb. 24.

Euphrasia Pelletier, St. (1796-1868): French nun; founded Sisters of the Good Shepherd at Angers, 1829; canonized 1940; Apr. 24.

Eusebius of Vercelli, St. (283-370): Italian bishop; exiled from his see for a time because of his opposition to Arianism; considered a martyr because of sufferings he endured; Aug. 2*.

Fabian, St. (d. 250): Pope, 236-250; martyred under Decius; Jan. 20*.

Felicity, St.: See Perpetua and Felicity, Sts.

Ferdinand III, St. (1198-1252): King of Castile and Leon; waged successful crusade against Mohammedans in Spain; founded university at Salamanca; canonized 1671; May 30.

Fiacre, St. (d. c. 670): Irish hermit; patron of gardeners; Aug. 30.

Fidelis of Sigmaringen, St. (Mark Rey) (1577-1622): German Capuchin; lawyer before he joined the Capuchins; missionary to Swiss Protestants; stabbed to death by peasants who were told he was agent of Austrian emperor; Apr. 24*.

Frances of Rome, St. (1384-1440): Italian model for housewives and widows; happily married for 40 years; after death of her husband in 1436 joined community of Benedictine Oblates she had founded; canonized 1608; patron of motorists; Mar. 9*.

Frances Xavier Cabrini, St. (Mother Cabrini) (1850-1917): American foundress; b. Italy; foundress of Missionary Sisters of the Sacred Heart, 1877; settled in the U.S. 1889; became an American citizen at Seattle 1909; worked among Italian immigrants; canonized 1946, the first American citizen so honored; Nov. 13 (U.S.)*.

Francis Borgia, St. (1510-1572): Spanish Jesuit; joined Jesuits after death of his wife in 1546; became general of the Order, 1565; Oct. 10.

Francis of Assisi, St. (Giovanni di Bernardone) (1182-1226): Founder of the Franciscans, 1209; received stigmata 1224; canonized 1228; one of best known and best loved saints; patron of Catholic Action and of Italy; Oct. 4*.

Francis of Paola, St. (1416-1507): Italian hermit: founder of Minim Friars; Apr. 2*.

Francis Xavier, St. (1506-1552): Spanish Jesuit; missionary to Far East; canonized 1602; patron of foreign missions; considered one of greatest Christian missionaries; Dec. 3*.

Gabriel of the Sorrowful Mother, St. (Francis Possenti) (1838-1862): Italian Passionist; died while a scholastic; canonized 1920; Feb. 27.

Genesius, St. (d. c. 300): Roman actor; according to legend, was converted while performing a burlesque of Christian baptism and was subsequently martyred; patron of actors.

Genevieve, St. (422-500): French nun; a patroness and protectress of Paris; events of her life not authenticated; Jan. 3.

George, St. (d. c. 300): Martyr, probably during Diocletian persecution in Palestine; all other incidents of his life, including story of the dragon, are legendary; patron of England; Apr. 23*.

Gerard Majella, St. (1725-1755): Italian Redemptorist lay brother; noted for supernatural occurrences in his life including bilocation and reading of consciences; canonized 1904; patron of mothers; Oct. 16.

Gertrude, St. (1256-1302): German mystic; writer; helped spread devotion to the Sacred Heart; Nov. 16*.

Gregory VII (Hildebrand), St. (1020?-1085): Pope, 1075-1085; Benedictine monk; adviser to several popes; as pope, strengthened interior life of Church and fought against lay investiture; driven from Rome by Henry IV; died in exile; May 25*.

Gregory the Illuminator, St. (257-332): Martyr; bishop; apostle and patron saint of

Armenia; helped free Armenia from the Persians; Sept. 30.

Hedwig, St. (1174-1243): Moravian noblewoman; married duke of Silesia, head of Polish royal family; fostered religious life in country; canonized 1266; Oct. 16*.

Helena, St. (250-330): Empress; mother of Constantine the Great; associated with discovery of the True Cross; Aug. 18.

Henry, St. (972-1024): Bavarian emperor; cooperated with Benedictine abbeys in restoration of ecclesiastical and social discipline; canonized 1146; July 13*.

Hippolytus, St. (d. c. 236): Roman priest; opposed Pope St. Callistus I in his teaching about the readmission of Christians who had apostasized during time of persecution; elected antipope; reconciled before his martyrdom; important ecclesiastical writer; Aug. 13*.

Hubert, St. (d. 727): Bishop; his patronage of hunters is based on legend that he was converted while hunting; Nov. 3.

Hugh of Cluny (the Great), St. (1024-1109): Abbot of Benedictine foundation at Cluny; supported popes in efforts to reform ecclesiastical abuses; canonized 1120; Apr. 29.

Ignatius of Antioch, St. (d. c. 107): Early ecclesiastical writer; martyr; bishop of Antioch in Syria for 40 years; Oct. 17*.

Ignatius of Loyola, St. (1491-1556): Spanish soldier; renounced military career after recovering from wounds received at siege of Pampeluna (Pamplona) in 1521; founded Society of Jesus (Jesuits), 1534, at Paris; canonized 1622; author *The Book of Spiritual Exercises;* July 31*.

Irenaeus of Lyons, St. (130-202): Early ecclesiastical writer; opposed Gnosticism; bishop of Lyons; traditionally regarded as a martyr; June 28*.

Isidore the Farmer, St. (d. 1170): Spanish layman; farmer; canonized 1622; patron of farmers; May 15 (US)*.

Jane Frances de Chantal, St. (1572-1641): French widow; foundress, under guidance of St. Francis de Sales, of Order of the Visitation; canonized 1767; Dec. 12*.

Januarius (Gennaro), St. (d. 304): Bishop of Benevento; martyred during Diocletian persecution; fame rests on liquefaction of some of his blood preserved in a phial at Naples, an unexplained phenomenon which has occurred regularly about 18 times each year for over 400 years; Sept. 19*.

Jerome Emiliani, St. (1481-1537): Venetian priest; founded Somascan Fathers, 1532, for care of orphans; canonized 1767; patron of orphans and abandoned children; Feb. 8*.

Joan of Arc, St. (1412-1431): French heroine, called The Maid of Orleans, La Pucelle; led French army against English invaders; captured by Burgundians, turned over to ecclesiastical court on charge of heresy, found guilt and burned at the stake; her innocence was declared in 1456; canonized 1920; patroness of France; May 30.

John I, St. (d. 526): Pope, 523-526; martyr; May 18*.

John Baptist de la Salle, St. (1651-1719): French priest; founder of Brothers of the Christian Schools, 1680; canonized 1900; Apr. 7*.

John Berchmans, St. (1599-1621): Belgian Jesuit scholastic; patron of Mass servers; canonized 1888; Aug. 13.

John Bosco, St. (1815-1888): Italian priest; founded Salesians, 1859, for education of boys and cofounded the Daughters of Mary Help of Christians for education of girls; canonized 1934; Jan. 31*.

John Capistran, St. (1386-1456): Italian Franciscan; preacher; papal diplomat; canonized 1690; Oct. 23*.

John Eudes, St. (1601-1680): French priest; founder of Sisters of Our Lady of Charity of Refuge, 1642, and Congregation of Jesus-Mary (Eudists), 1643; canonized 1925; Aug. 19*.

John Fisher, St. (1469-1535): English prelate; theologian; martyr; bishop of Rochester, cardinal; refused to recognize validity of Henry VIII's marriage to Anne Boleyn; upheld supremacy of the pope; beheaded for refusing to acknowledge Henry as head of the Church; canonized 1935; June 22 (with St. Thomas More)*.

John Kanty (Cantius), St. (1395-1473): Polish theologian; canonized 1767; Dec. 23*.

John Leonardi, St. (1550-1609): Italian priest; worked among prisoners and the sick; founded Clerics Regular of the Mother of God; canonized 1938; Oct. 9*.

John Nepomucene, St. (1345-1393): Bohemian priest; regarded as a martyr; canonized 1729; patron of Czechoslovakia; May 16.

John Nepomucene Neumann, St. (1811-1860): American prelate; b. Bohemia; ordained in New York 1836; missionary among Germans near Niagara Falls before joining Redemptorists, 1840; bishop of Philadelphia, 1852; first bishop in U.S. to prescribe Forty Hours devotion in his diocese; beatified 1963; canonized June 19, 1977; Jan. 5 (U.S.)*.

John of God, St. (1495-1550): Portuguese founder; his work among the sick poor led to foundation of Brothers Hospitallers of St. John of God, 1540, in Spain; canonized 1690; patron of sick, hospitals, nurses; Mar. 8*.

John Vianney (Cure of Ars), St. (1786-1859): French parish priest; noted confessor, spent 16 to 18 hours a day in confessional; canonized 1925; patron of parish priests; Aug. 4*.

Josaphat Kuncevyc, St. (1584-1623): Basilian monk; b. Poland; archbishop of Polotsk, Lithuania; worked for reunion of separated Easterners; martyred by mob of schismatics; canonized 1867; Nov. 12*.

Joseph Benedict Cottolengo, St. (1786-1842): Italian priest; established Little Houses of Divine Providence (Piccolo Casa) for care of orphans and the sick; canonized 1934; Apr. 30.

Joseph Cafasso, St. (1811-1860): Italian priest; renowned confessor; promoted devotion to Blessed Sacrament; canonized 1947; June 22.

Joseph Calasanz, St. (1556-1648): Spanish priest; founder of Piarists (Order of Pious Schools); canonized 1767; Aug. 25*.

Joseph of Cupertino, St. (1603-1663): Italian Franciscan; noted for remarkable incidents of levitation; canonized 1767; Sept. 18.

Justin Martyr, St. (100-165): Early ecclesiastical writer; *Apologies for the Christian Religion, Dialog with the Jew Tryphon;* martyred at Rome; June 1*.

Ladislaus, Saint (1040-1095): King of Hungary; supported Pope Gregory VII against Henry IV; canonized 1192; June 27.

Lawrence, St. (d. 258): Widely venerated martyr who suffered death, according to a long-standing but unverifiable legend, by being roasted alive on a gridiron; Aug. 10*.

Leonard of Port Maurice, St. (1676-1751): Italian Franciscan; ascetical writer; preached missions throughout Italy; canonized 1867; patron of parish missions; Nov. 26.

Louis IX, St. (1215-1270): King of France, 1226-1270; participated in Sixth Crusade; patron of Third Order of St. Francis; canonized 1297; Aug. 25*.

Louis de Montfort, St. (1673-1716): French priest; founder of Sisters of Divine Wisdom, 1703, and Missionaries of Company of Mary, 1715; wrote *True Devotion to the Blessed Virgin;* canonized 1947; Apr. 28.

Louise de Marillac, St. (1591-1660): French foundress, with St. Vincent de Paul, of the Sisters of Charity; canonized 1934; Mar. 15.

Lucy, St. (d. 304): Sicilian maiden; martyred during Diocletian persecution; one of most widely venerated early virgin-martyrs; patron of Syracuse, Sicily; invoked by those suffering from eye diseases; Dec. 13*.

Marcellinus and Peter, Sts. (d.c. 304): Early Roman martyrs; June 2*.

Margaret Clitherow, St. (1556-1586): English martyr; convert shortly after her marriage; one of Forty Martyrs of England and Wales; canonized 1970.

Margaret Mary Alacoque, St. (1647-1690): French nun; spread devotion to Sacred Heart in accordance with revelations made to her in 1675 (see Sacred Heart); canonized 1920; Oct. 16*.

Margaret of Scotland, St. (1050-1093): Queen of Scotland; noted for solicitude for the poor and promotion of justice; canonized 1251; Nov. 16*.

Maria Goretti, St. (1890-1902): Italian virgin-martyr; a model of purity; canonized 1950; July 6*.

Mariana Paredes of Jesus, St. (1618-1645): South American recluse; Lily of Quito; canonized, 1950; May 26.

Martha, St. (1st cent.): Sister of Lazarus and Mary of Bethany; Gospel accounts record her concern for homely details; patron of cooks; July 29*.

Martin I, St. (d. 655): Pope, 649; banished from Rome by emperor because of his condemnation of Monothelites; considered a martyr; Apr. 13*.

Martin of Tours, St. (316-397): Bishop of Tours; opposed Arianism and Priscillianism; pioneer of Western monasticism, before St. Benedict; Nov. 11*.

Mary Magdalene, St. (1st cent.): Gospels record her as devoted follower of Christ to whom he appeared after the Resurrection; her identification with Mary of Bethany (sister of Martha and Lazarus) and the woman sinner (Lk 7:36-50) has been questioned; July 22*.

Mary Magdalene de Pazzi, St. (1566-1607): Italian Carmelite nun; recipient of mystical experiences; canonized 1669; May 25*.

Maximilian Kolbe, Bl. (1894-1941): Polish Conventual Franciscan; prisoner at Auschwitz who heroically offered his life in place of a fellow prisoner; beatified 1971.

Methodius, St.: See Index.

Monica, St. (332-387): Mother of St. Augustine; model of a patient mother; her feast is observed in the Roman calendar the day before her son's; Aug. 27*.

Nereus and Achilleus, Sts. (d. c. 100): Early Christian martyrs; soldiers who, according to legend, were baptized by St. Peter; May 12*.

Nicholas of Myra, St. (4th cent.): Bishop of Myra in Asia Minor; one of most popular saints in both East and West; most of the incidents of his life are based on legend; patron of Russia; Dec. 6*.

Nicholas of Tolentino, St. (1245-1365): Italian hermit; famed preacher; canonized 1446; Sept. 10.

Norbert, St. (1080-1134): German bishop; founder of Norbertines or Premonstratensians, 1120; promoted reform of the clergy, devotion to Blessed Sacrament; canonized 1582; June 6*.

Odilia, St. (d. c. 720): Benedictine abbess; according to legend she was born blind, abandoned by her family and adopted by a convent where her sight was miraculously restored; patron of blind; Dec. 13.

Oliver Plunkett, St. (1629-1681): Irish martyr; theologian; archbishop of Armagh and primate of Ireland; beatified 1920; canonized, 1975.

Pancras, St. (d. c. 304): Roman martyr; May 12*.

Paschal Baylon, St. (1540-1592): Spanish Franciscan lay brother; spent life as doorkeeper in various Franciscan friaries; defended doctrine of Real Presence in Blessed Sacrament; canonized 1690; patron of all Eucharistic confraternities and congresses, 1897; May 17.

Patrick, St. (389-461): Famous missionary of Ireland; began missionary work in Ireland about 432; organized the Church there and established it on a lasting foundation; patron of Ireland, with Sts. Bridget and Columba; Mar. 17*.

Paul Miki and Companions, Sts. (d. 1597): Martyrs of Japan; Paul Miki, Jesuit, and twenty-five other priests and laymen were martyred at Nagasaki; canonized 1862, the first canonized martyrs of the Far East; Feb. 6*.

Paul of the Cross, St. (1694-1775): Italian religious; founder of the Passionists; canonized 1867; Oct. 19*.

Paulinus of Nola, St. (d. 451): Bishop of Nola (Spain); writer; June 22*.

Peregrine, St. (1260-1347): Italian Servite; invoked against cancer (he was miraculously cured of cancer of the foot after a vision); canonized 1726; May 1.

Perpetua and Felicity, Sts. (d. 203): Martyrs; Mar. 7*.

Peter Chanel, St. (1803-1841): French Marist; missionary to Oceania, where he was martyred; canonized 1954; Apr. 28*.

Peter Gonzalez, St. (1190-1246): Spanish Dominican; worked among sailors; court chaplain and confessor of King St. Ferdinand of Castile; patron of sailors; Apr. 14.

Peter of Alcantara, St. (1499-1562): Spanish Franciscan; mystic; initiated Franciscan reform; confessor of St. Teresa of Avila; canonized 1669; Oct. 19.

Philip Neri, St. (1515-1595): Italian religious; founded Congregation of the Oratory; considered a second apostle of Rome because of his mission activities there; canonized 1622; May 26*.

Philip of Jesus, St. (1571-1597): Mexican Franciscan; martyred at Nagasaki, Japan; canonized 1862; patron of Mexico City; Feb. 6*.

Pius V, St. (1504-1572): Pope, 1566-1572; enforced decrees of Council of Trent; organized expedition against Turks resulting in victory at Lepanto; canonized 1712; Apr. 30*.

Polycarp, St. (2nd cent.): Bishop of Smyrna; ecclesiastical writer; martyr; Feb. 23*.

Pontian, St. (d. c. 235): Pope, 230-235; exiled to Sardinia by the emperor; regarded as a martyr; Aug. 13 (with Hippolytus)*.

Raymond Nonnatus, St. (d. 1240): Spanish Mercedarian; cardinal; devoted his life to ransoming captives from the Moors; Aug. 31.

Raymond of Penyafort, St. (1175-1275): Spanish Dominican; confessor of Gregory IX; systematized and codified canon law, in effect until 1917; master general of Dominicans, 1238; canonized 1601; Jan. 7*.

Rita of Cascia, St. (1381-1457): Widow; cloistered Augustinian religious of Umbria; invoked in impossible and desperate cases; May 22.

Robert Southwell, St. (1561-1595): English Jesuit; poet; martyred at Tyburn; canonized 1970, one of the Forty English and Welsh Martyrs.

Roch, St. (1350-1379): French layman; pilgrim; devoted life to care of plague-stricken; widely venerated; invoked against pestilence; Aug. 17.

Romuald, St. (951-1027): Italian monk; founded Camaldolese Benedictines; June 19*.

Rose of Lima, St. (1586-1617): Peruvian Dominican tertiary; first native-born saint of the New World; canonized 1671; Aug. 23*.

Scholastica, St. (d. c. 559): Sister of St. Benedict; regarded as first nun of the Benedictine Order; Feb. 10*.

Sebastian, St. (3rd cent.): Roman martyr; traditionally pictured as a handsome youth; martyred by being pierced with arrows; patron of athletes; Jan. 20*.

Seven Holy Founders of the Servants of Mary (Buonfiglio Monaldo, Alexis Falconieri, Benedict dell'Antello, Bartholomew Amidei, Ricovero Uguccione, Gerardino Sostegni, John Buonagiunta Monetti): Florentine youths who founded Servites, 1233, in obedience to a vision; canonized 1888; Feb. 17*.

Sixtus II and Companions, Sts. (d. 258): Sixtus, pope 257-258, and four deacons, martyrs; Aug. 7*.

Stanislaus, St. (1030-1079): Polish bishop; martyr; canonized 1253; Apr. 11*.

Stephen, St. (d. c. 33): First Christian martyr; chosen by the Apostles as the first of the seven deacons; stoned to death; Dec. 26*.

Stephen, St. (975-1038): King; apostle of Hungary; welded Magyars into national unity; canonized 1087; Aug. 16*.

Sylvester I, St. (d. 335): Pope 314-335; first ecumenical council held at Nicaea during his pontificate; Dec. 31*.

Tarcisius, St. (d. 3rd cent.): Early martyr; according to tradition, was martyred while carrying the Blessed Sacrament to some Christians in prison; patron of first communicants; Aug. 15.

Therese Couderc, St. (1805-1885): French religious; foundress of the Religious of Our Lady of the Retreat in the Cenacle, 1827; canonized 1970; Sept. 26.

Therese of Lisieux, St. (1873-1897): French Carmelite nun; b. Therese Martin; allowed to enter Carmel at 15, died nine years later of tuberculosis; her "little way" of spiritual perfection became widely known through her spiritual autobiography; despite her obscure life, became one of the most popular saints; canonized 1925; patron of foreign missions; Oct. 1*.

Thomas Becket, St. (1118-1170): English martyr; archbishop of Canterbury; chancellor under Henry II; murdered for upholding rights of the Church; canonized 1173; Dec. 29*.

Thomas More, St. (1478-1535): English martyr; statesman, chancellor under Henry VIII; author of *Utopia;* opposed Henry's divorce; refused to renounce authority of the papacy; beheaded; canonized 1935; June 22 (with St. John Fisher)*.

Timothy, St. (d. c. 97): Bishop of Ephesus; disciple and companion of St. Paul; martyr; Jan. 26*.

Titus, St. (d. c. 96): Bishop; companion of St. Paul; recipient of one of Paul's epistles; Jan. 26*.

Valentine, St. (d. 269): Priest, physician; martyred at Rome; legendary patron of lovers; Feb. 14.

Vincent, St. (d. 304): Spanish deacon; martyr; Jan. 22*.

Vincent de Paul, St. (1581?-1660): French priest; founder of Congregation of the Mission (Vincentians, Lazarists) and co-founder of Sisters of Charity; declared patron of all charitable organizations and works by Leo XIII; canonized 1737; Sept. 27*.

Vincent Ferrer, St. (1350-1418): Spanish Dominican; famed preacher; Apr. 5*.

Wenceslaus, St. (d. 935): Duke of Bohemia; martyr; patron of Bohemia; Sept. 28*.

Zita, St. (1218-1278): Italian maid; noted for charity to poor; patron of domestics.

SAINTS—PATRONS AND INTERCESSORS

A patron is a saint who is venerated as a special intercessor before God. Most patrons have been so designated as the result of popular devotion and long-standing custom. In many cases, the fact of existing patronal devotion is clear despite historical obscurity regarding its origin. The Church has made official designation of relatively few patrons; in such cases, the dates of designation are given in the list below. The theological background of the patronage of saints includes the dogmas of the Mystical Body of Christ and the Communion of Saints.

Listed below are patron saints of occupations and professions, and saints whose intercession is sought for special needs.

Accountants: St. Matthew.
Actors: St. Genesius.
Advertisers: St. Bernardine of Siena (May 20, 1960).
Alpinists: St. Bernard of Menthon (Aug. 20, 1923).
Altar boys: St. John Berchmans.
Anesthetists: St. Rene Goupil.
Archers: St. Sebastian.
Architects: St. Thomas, Apostle.
Armorers: St. Dunstan.
Art: St. Catherine of Bologna.
Artists: St. Luke, St. Catherine of Bologna.
Astronomers: St. Dominic.
Athletes: St. Sebastian.
Authors: St. Francis de Sales.
Aviators: Our Lady of Loreto (1920), St. Therese of Lisieux, St. Joseph of Cupertino.
Bakers: St. Elizabeth of Hungary, St. Nicholas.
Bankers: St. Matthew.
Barbers: Sts. Cosmas and Damian, St. Louis.
Barren women: St. Anthony of Padua, St. Felicity.
Basket-makers: St. Anthony, Abbot.
Blacksmiths: St. Dunstan.
Blind: St. Odilia, St. Raphael.
Blood banks: St. Januarius.
Bodily ills: Our Lady of Lourdes.
Bookbinders: St. Peter Celestine.
Bookkeepers: St. Matthew.
Booksellers: St. John of God.
Boy Scouts: St. George.
Brewers: St. Augustine of Hippo, St. Luke, St. Nicholas of Myra.
Bricklayers: St. Stephen.
Brides: St. Nicholas of Myra.
Brush makers: St. Anthony, Abbot.
Builders: St. Vincent Ferrer.
Butchers: St. Anthony, Abbot, St. Luke.
Cab drivers: St. Fiacre.
Cabinetmakers: St. Anne.
Cancer patients: St. Peregrine.
Canonists: St. Raymond of Penyafort.
Carpenters: St. Joseph.
Catechists: St. Viator, St. Charles Borromeo, St. Robert Bellarmine.
Catholic Action: St. Francis of Assisi (1916).
Chandlers: St. Ambrose, St. Bernard of Clairvaux.
Charitable societies: St. Vincent de Paul (May 12, 1885).
Children: St. Nicholas of Myra.
Children of Mary: St. Agnes, St. Maria Goretti.
Choir boys: St. Dominic Savio (June 8, 1956), Holy Innocents.
Church: St. Joseph (Dec. 8, 1870).
Clerics: St. Gabriel of the Sorrowful Mother.
Comedians: St. Vitus.
Communications personnel: St. Bernardine.
Confessors: St. Alphonsus Liguori (Apr. 26, 1950), St. John Nepomucene.
Convulsive children: St. Scholastica.
Cooks: St. Lawrence, St. Martha.
Coopers: St. Nicholas of Myra.
Coppersmiths: St. Maurus.
Dairy workers: St. Brigid.
Deaf: St. Francis de Sales.
Dentists: St. Apollonia.
Desperate situations: St. Gregory of Neocaesarea, St. Jude Thaddeus, St. Rita of Cascia.
Dietitians (in hospitals): St. Martha.
Dyers: Sts. Maurice and Lydia.
Dying: St. Joseph.
Ecologists: St. Francis of Assisi.
Editors: St. John Bosco.
Emigrants: St. Frances Xavier Cabrini (Sept. 8, 1950).
Epilepsy: St. Vitus.
Engineers: St. Ferdinand III.

Eucharistic congresses and societies: St. Paschal Baylon (Nov. 28, 1897).
Expectant mothers: St. Raymund Nonnatus, St. Gerard Majella.
Eye diseases: St. Lucy.
Falsely accused: St. Raymund Nonnatus.
Farmers: St. George, St. Isidore.
Farriers: St. John Baptist.
Firemen: St. Florian.
Fire prevention: St. Catherine of Siena.
First communicants: St. Tarcisius.
Fishermen: St. Andrew.
Florists: St. Therese of Lisieux.
Forest workers: St. John Gualbert.
Foundlings: Holy Innocents.
Fullers: St. Anastasius the Fuller, St. James the Less.
Funeral directors: St. Joseph of Arimathea, St. Dismas.
Gardeners: St. Adelard, St. Tryphon, St. Fiacre, St. Phocas.
Glassworkers: St. Luke.
Goldsmiths: St. Dunstan, St. Anastasius.
Gravediggers: St. Anthony, Abbot.
Greetings: St. Valentine.
Grocers: St. Michael.
Hairdressers: St. Martin de Porres.
Happy meetings: St. Raphael.
Hatters: St. Severus of Ravenna, St. James the Less.
Haymakers: Sts. Gervase and Protase.
Headache sufferers: St. Teresa of Avila.
Heart patients: St. John of God.
Hospital administrators: St. Basil the Great, St. Frances X. Cabrini.
Hospitals: St. Camillus de Lellis and St. John of God (June 22, 1886), St. Jude Thaddeus.
Housewives: St. Anne.
Hunters: St. Hubert, St. Eustachius.
Infantrymen: St. Maurice.
Innkeepers: St. Amand, St. Martha.
Invalids: St. Roch.
Jewelers: St. Eligius, St. Dunstan.
Journalists: St. Francis de Sales (Apr. 26, 1923).
Jurists: St. John Capistran.
Laborers: St. Isidore, St. James, St. John Bosco.
Lawyers: St. Ivo, St. Genesius, St. Thomas More.
Learning: St. Ambrose.
Librarians: St. Jerome.
Lighthouse keepers: St. Venerius.
Locksmiths: St. Dunstan.
Maids: St. Zita.
Marble workers: St. Clement I.
Mariners: St. Michael, St. Nicholas of Tolentino.
Medical record librarians: St. Raymond of Penyafort.
Medical social workers: St. John Regis.
Medical technicians: St. Albert the Great.
Mentally ill: St. Dymphna.
Merchants: St. Francis of Assisi, St. Nicholas of Myra.
Messengers: St. Gabriel.
Metal workers: St. Eligius.
Millers: St. Arnulph, St. Victor.
Missions, Foreign: St. Francis Xavier (Mar. 25, 1904), St. Therese of Lisieux (Dec. 14, 1927).
Missions, Negro: St. Peter Claver (1896, Leo XIII), St. Benedict the Black.
Missions, Parish: St. Leonard of Port Maurice (Mar. 17, 1023).
Mothers: St. Monica.
Motorcyclists: Our Lady of Grace.
Motorists: St. Christopher, St. Frances of Rome.
Mountaineers: St. Bernard of Menthon.
Musicians: St. Gregory the Great, St. Cecilia, St. Dunstan.
Nail makers: St. Cloud.
Notaries: St. Luke, St. Mark.
Nurses: St. Camillus de Lellis and St. John of God (1930, Pius XI), St. Agatha, St. Raphael.
Nursing and nursing service: St. Elizabeth of Hungary, St. Catherine of Siena.
Orators: St. John Chrysostom (July 8, 1908).
Organ builders: St. Cecilia.
Orphans: St. Jerome Emiliani.
Painters: St. Luke.
Paratroopers: St. Michael.
Pawnbrokers: St. Nicholas.
Pharmacists: Sts. Cosmas and Damian, St. James the Greater.
Pharmacists (in hospitals): St. Gemma Galgani.
Philosophers: St. Justin.
Physicians: St. Pantaleon, Sts. Cosmas and Damian, St. Luke, St. Raphael.
Pilgrims: St. James.
Plasterers: St. Bartholomew.
Poets: St. David, St. Cecilia.
Poison sufferers: St. Benedict.
Policemen: St. Michael.
Poor: St. Lawrence, St. Anthony of Padua.
Poor souls: St. Nicholas of Tolentino.
Porters: St. Christopher.
Possessed: St. Bruno, St. Denis.
Postal employees: St. Gabriel.
Priests: St. Jean-Baptiste Vianney (Apr. 23, 1929).
Printers: St. John of God, St. Augustine of Hippo, St. Genesius.
Prisoners: St. Dismas, St. Joseph Cafasso
Protector of crops: St. Ansovinus.
Public relations: St. Bernardine of Siena (May 20, 1960).
Public relations (of hospitals): St. Paul, Apostle.
Radiologists: St. Michael (Jan. 15, 1941).
Radio workers: St. Gabriel.
Retreats: St. Ignatius Loyola (July 25, 1922).
Rheumatism: St. James the Greater.
Saddlers: Sts. Crispin and Crispinian.
Sailors: St. Cuthbert, St. Brendan, St. Eulalia, St. Christopher, St. Peter Gonzales, St Erasmus, St. Nicholas.

Scholars: St. Brigid.
Schools, Catholic: St. Thomas Aquinas (Aug. 4, 1880), St. Joseph Calasanz (Aug. 13, 1948).
Scientists: St. Albert (Aug. 13, 1948).
Sculptors: St. Claude.
Seamen: St. Francis of Paola.
Searchers for lost articles: St. Anthony of Padua.
Secretaries: St. Genesius.
Seminarians: St. Charles Borromeo.
Servants: St. Martha, St. Zita.
Shoemakers: Sts. Crispin and Crispinian.
Sick: St. Michael, St. John of God and St. Camillus de Lellis (June 22, 1886).
Silversmiths: St. Andronicus.
Singers: St. Gregory, St. Cecilia.
Skaters: St. Lidwina.
Skiers: St. Bernard.
Social workers: St. Louise de Marillac (Feb. 12, 1960).
Soldiers: St. Hadrian, St. George, St. Ignatius, St. Sebastian, St. Martin of Tours, St. Joan of Arc.
Speleologists: St. Benedict.
Stenographers: St. Genesius, St. Cassian.
Stonecutters: St. Clement.
Stonemasons: St. Stephen.
Students: St. Thomas Aquinas.
Surgeons: Sts. Cosmas and Damian, St. Luke.
Swordsmiths: St. Maurice.
Tailors: St. Homobonus.
Tanners: Sts. Crispin and Crispinian, St. Simon.
Tax collectors: St. Matthew.
Teachers: St. Gregory the Great, St. John Baptist de la Salle (May 15, 1950).
Telecommunications workers: St. Gabriel (Jan. 12, 1951).
Telegraph/telephone workers: St. Gabriel.
Television: St. Clare of Assisi (Feb. 14, 1958).
Television workers: St. Gabriel.
Tertiaries (Franciscan): St. Louis of France, St. Elizabeth of Hungary.
Theologians: St. Augustine, St. Alphonsus Liguori.
Throat sufferers: St. Blase.
Travelers: St. Anthony of Padua, St. Nicholas of Myra, St. Christopher, St. Raphael.
Travel hostesses: St. Bona (Mar. 2, 1962).
Universities: Blessed Contardo Ferrini.
Vocations: St. Alphonsus.
Watchmen: St. Peter of Alcantara.
Weavers: St. Paul the Hermit, St. Anastasius the Fuller, St. Anastasia.
Wine merchants: St. Amand.
Women in labor: St. Anne.
Women's Army Corps: St. Genevieve.
Workingmen: St. Joseph.
Writers: St. Francis de Sales (Apr. 26, 1923), St. Lucy.
Yachtsmen: St. Adjutor.
Young girls: St. Agnes.
Youth: St. Aloysius Gonzaga (1729, Benedict XIII; 1926, Pius XI), St. John Berchmans, St. Gabriel of the Sorrowful Mother.

Patrons of Places

Alsace: St. Odile.
Americas: Our Lady of Guadalupe; St. Rose of Lima.
Argentina: Our Lady of Lujan.
Armenia: St. Gregory Illuminator.
Asia Minor: St. John, Evangelist.
Australia: Our Lady Help of Christians.
Belgium: St. Joseph.
Bohemia: Sts. Wenceslaus, Ludmilla.
Borneo: St. Francis Xavier.
Brazil: Nossa Senhora de Aparecida, Immaculate Conception; St. Peter of Alcantara.
Canada: St. Joseph; St. Anne.
Ceylon (Sri Lanka): St. Lawrence.
Chile: St. James; Our Lady of Mt. Carmel.
China: St. Joseph.
Colombia: St. Peter Claver; St. Louis Bertran.
Corsica: Immaculate Conception.
Czechoslovakia: St. Wenceslaus; St. John Nepomucene; St. Procopius.
Denmark: St. Ansgar; St. Canute.
Dominican Republic: Our Lady of High Grace; St. Dominic.
East Indies: St. Thomas, Apostle.
Ecuador: Sacred Heart.
England: St. George.
Europe: St. Benedict.
Finland: St. Henry.
France: Our Lady of the Assumption; St. Joan of Arc; St. Therese.
Germany: Sts. Boniface, Michael.
Greece: St. Nicholas; St. Andrew.
Holland: St. Willibrord.
Hungary: Blessed Virgin, "Great Lady of Hungary"; St. Stephen, King.
India: Our Lady of Assumption.
Ireland: Sts. Patrick, Brigid and Columba.
Italy: St. Francis of Assisi; St. Catherine of Siena.
Japan: St. Peter Baptist.
Lesotho: Immaculate Heart of Mary.
Lithuania: St. Casimir, Bl. Cunegunda.
Malta: St. Paul; Our Lady of the Assumption.
Mexico: Our Lady of Guadalupe.
Monaco: St. Devota.
Moravia: Sts. Cyril and Methodius.
New Zealand: Our Lady Help of Christians.
Norway: St. Olaf.
Paraguay: Our Lady of Assumption.
Peru: St. Joseph.
Philippines: Sacred Heart of Mary.
Poland: St. Casimir; Bl. Cunegunda; St. Stanislaus of Cracow; Our Lady of Czestochowa.
Portugal: Immaculate Conception; St. Francis Borgia; St. Anthony of Padua; St. Vincent; St. George.
Republic of South Africa: Our Lady of Assumption.

Russia: St. Andrew; St. Nicholas of Myra; St. Therese of Lisieux.
Scandinavia: St. Ansgar.
Scotland: St. Andrew; St. Columba.
Silesia: St. Hedwig.
Slovakia: Our Lady of Sorrows.
South America: St. Rose of Lima.
Spain: St. James; St. Teresa.
Sweden: St. Bridget; St. Eric.
United States: Immaculate Conception.
Uruguay: Our Lady of Lujan.
Wales: St. David.
West Indies: St. Gertrude.

Apostles of Places, Peoples

Alps: St. Bernard of Menthon.
Andalusia (Spain): St. John of Avila.
Antioch: St. Barnabas.
Armenia: St. Gregory the Illuminator; St. Bartholomew.
Austria: St. Severine.
Bavaria: St. Killian.
Brazil: Jose Anchieta.
California: Junipero Serra.
Carinthia (Yugoslavia): St. Virgil.
Colombia: St. Louis Bertran.
Corsica: St. Alexander Sauli.
Crete: St. Titus.
Cyprus: St. Barnabas.
Denmark: St. Ansgar.
England: St. Augustine of Canterbury; St. Gregory the Great.
Ethiopia: St. Frumentius.
Finland: St. Henry.
Florence: St. Andrew Corsini.
France: St. Remigius; St. Martin of Tours; St. Denis.
Friesland (Germany): St. Suitbert; St. Willibrord.
Gaul: St. Irenaeus.
Gentiles: St. Paul.
Georgia (Russia): St. Nino.
Germany: St. Boniface; St. Peter Canisius.
Gothland (Sweden): St. Sigfrid.
Guelderland (Holland): St. Plechelm.
Highlanders (Scotland): St. Columba.
Hungarians (Magyars): St. Stephen, King; St. Gerard; Bl. Astricus.
India: St. Thomas, Apostle.
Indies: St. Francis Xavier.
Ireland: St. Patrick.
Iroquois: Francois Picquit.
Italy: St. Bernardine of Siena.
Japan: St. Francis Xavier.
Malta: St. Paul.
Mexico: The twelve Apostles of Mexico (Franciscans), headed by Fra. Martin de Valencia.
Negro Slaves: St. Peter Claver.
Netherlands: St. Willibrord.
Northumbria (Britain): St. Aidan.
Norway: St. Olaf.
Ottawas (Indians): Fr. Claude Allouez.
Persia: St. Maruthas.
Poland: St. Hyacinth.
Portugal: St. Christian.
Prussia (Slavs): St. Adalbert; St. Bruno of Querfurt.
Rome: St. Philip Neri.
Rumania: St. Nicetas.
Ruthenia: St. Bruno.
Sardinia: St. Ephesus.
Saxony: St. Willihad.
Scandinavia (North): St. Ansgar.
Scotland: St. Palladius.
Slavs: Sts. Cyril and Methodius, St. Adalbert.
Spain: St. James; Sts. Euphrasius and Felix.
Sweden: St. Ansgar.
Switzerland: St. Andeol.
Tournai (Belgium): St. Eligius, St. Piaton.

Emblems of Saints

St. Agatha: Tongs, veil.
St. Agnes: Lamb.
St. Ambrose: Bees, dove, ox, pen.
St. Andrew: Transverse cross.
St. Anne, Mother of the Blessed Virgin: A door.
St. Anthony, Abbot: Bell, hog.
St. Anthony of Padua: Infant Jesus, bread, book, lily.
St. Augustine of Hippo: Dove, child, shell, pen.
St. Barnabas: Stones, ax, lance.
St. Bartholomew: Knife, flayed and holding his skin.
St. Benedict: Broken cup, raven, bell, crosier, bush.
St. Bernard of Clairvaux: Pen, bees, instruments of Passion.
St. Bernardine of Siena: Tablet or sun inscribed with IHS.
St. Blase: Wax, taper, iron comb.
St. Bonaventure: Communion, ciborium, cardinal's hat.
St. Boniface: Oak, ax, book, fox, scourge, fountain, raven, sword.
St. Bridget of Sweden: Book, pilgrim's staff.
St. Bridget of Kildare: Cross, flame over her head, candle.
St. Catherine of Ricci: Ring, crown, crucifix.
St. Catherine of Siena: Stigmata, cross, ring, lily.
St. Cecilia: Organ.
St. Charles Borromeo: Communion, coat of arms with word *Humilitas*.
St. Christopher: Giant, torrent, tree, Child Jesus on his shoulders.
St. Clare of Assisi: Monstrance.
Sts. Cosmas and Damian: A phial, box of ointment.
St. Cyril of Alexandria: Blessed Virgin holding the Child Jesus, pen.
St. Cyril of Jerusalem: Purse, book.
St. Dominic: Rosary, star.
St. Edmund the Martyr: Arrow, sword.
St. Elizabeth of Hungary: Alms, flowers, bread, the poor, a pitcher.
St. Francis of Assisi: Deer, wolf, birds, fish, skull, the Stigmata.

St. Francis Xavier: Crucifix, bell, vessel, Negro.
St. Genevieve: Bread, keys, herd, candle.
St. George: Dragon.
St. Gertrude: Crown, taper, lily.
Sts. Gervase and Protase: Scourge, club, sword.
St. Gregory I (the Great): Tiara, crosier, dove.
St. Helena: Cross.
St. Hilary: Stick, pen, child.
St. Ignatius Loyola: Communion, chasuble, book, apparition of Our Lord.
St. Isidore: Bees, pen.
St. James the Greater: Pilgrim's staff, shell, key, sword.
St. James the Less: Square rule, halberd, club.
St. Jerome: Lion.
St. John Berchmans: Rule of St. Ignatius, cross, rosary.
St. John Chrysostom: Bees, dove, pen.
St. John of God: Alms, a heart, crown of thorns.
St. John the Baptist: Lamb, head cut off on platter, skin of an animal.
St. John the Evangelist: Eagle, chalice, kettle, armor.
St. Josaphat Kuncevyc: Chalice, crown, winged deacon.
St. Joseph, Spouse of the Blessed Virgin: Infant Jesus, lily, rod, plane, carpenter's square.
St. Jude: Sword, square rule, club.
St. Justin Martyr: Ax, sword.
St. Lawrence: Cross, book of the Gospels, gridiron.
St. Leander of Seville: A pen.
St. Liborius: Pebbles, peacock.
St. Longinus: In arms at foot of the cross.
St. Louis IX of France: Crown of thorns, nails.

St. Lucy: Cord, eyes.
St. Luke: Ox, book, brush, palette.
St. Mark: Lion, book.
St. Martha: Holy water sprinkler, dragon.
St. Mary Magdalene: Alabaster box of ointment.
St. Matilda: Purse, alms.
St. Matthew: Winged man, purse, lance.
St. Matthias: Lance.
St. Maurus: Scales, spade, crutch.
St. Meinrad: Two ravens.
St. Michael: Scales, banner, sword, dragon.
St. Monica: Girdle, tears.
St. Nicholas: Three purses or balls, anchor or boat, child.
St. Patrick: Cross, harp, serpent, baptismal font, demons, shamrock.
St. Paul: Sword, book or scroll.
St. Peter: Keys, boat, cock.
St. Philip, Apostle: Column.
St. Philip Neri: Altar, chasuble, vial.
St. Rita of Cascia: Rose, crucifix, thorn.
St. Roch: Angel, dog, bread.
St. Rose of Lima: Crown of thorns, anchor, city.
St. Sebastian: Arrows, crown.
Sts. Sergius and Bacchus: Military garb, palm.
St. Simon: Saw, cross.
St. Simon Stock: Scapular.
St. Teresa of Avila: Heart, arrow, book.
St. Therese of Lisieux: Roses entwining a crucifix.
St. Thomas, Apostle: Lance, ax.
St. Thomas Aquinas: Chalice, monstrance, dove, ox, person trampled under foot.
St. Vincent: Gridiron, boat.
St. Vincent de Paul: Children.
St. Vincent Ferrer: Pulpit, cardinal's hat, trumpet, captives.

THE MOTHER OF JESUS IN CATHOLIC UNDERSTANDING

This article was written by the Rev. Eamon R. Carroll, O. Carm., professor in the Department of Theology, School of Religious Studies, Catholic University of America; author of "Understanding the Mother of Jesus" (published by M. Glazier, Wilmington, Del.; 1979).

Documents of the Second Vatican Council have provided the charter for current Catholic understanding of the Virgin Mary, Mother of Jesus. This conciliar teaching was expanded and applied in the pastoral letter, "Behold Your Mother: Woman of Faith," issued by the U.S. bishops Nov. 21, 1973. Pope Paul VI added guidelines for devotion, in the revised liturgy and with respect to the Rosary, in the letter *Marialis Cultus* ("To Honor Mary"), dated Feb. 2, 1974.

Conciliar Documents

The first conciliar document, the *Constitution on the Sacred Liturgy*, linked Mary with the life, death and exaltation of Jesus, stating:

"In celebrating this annual cycle of Christ's mysteries, holy Church honors with special love blessed Mary, Mother of God, who is joined by an inseparable bond to the saving work of her Son. In her the Church holds up and admires the most excellent fruit of the redemption, and joyfully contemplates, as in a faultless manner, that which she herself wholly desires and hopes to be" (No. 103).

The eighth and final chapter of the *Dogmatic Constitution on the Church* is entitled "The Blessed Virgin Mary, Mother of God, in the Mystery of Christ and the Church." The seventh chapter deals with the communion of saints, the bond between the pilgrim Church on earth and the blessed joined to the risen Christ — what John deSatgé, an English Anglican, describes as the "mutual sharing and caring in Christ for one another." At the Eucharist, above all, "in union with the whole Church we honor Mary, the ever-Virgin Mother of Jesus Christ our Lord and God"

(First Eucharistic Prayer; cf. *Constitution on the Church*, No. 50).

What Catholics believe about the Mother of Jesus is the basis for her place in their prayer life, both in the liturgy and particularly the Eucharist, and in other forms of piety, especially the Rosary. The Church's growth in insight about the Blessed Virgin comes about as Christians ponder the meaning of Mary in prayer as well as in study. The Church has come to know Mary's role by experience and by contemplation of her hidden holiness (*Constitution on the Church*, No. 64). The tradition about Mary has been transmitted by doctrinal teaching and also by life and worship, even as in her own life Mary treasured in her heart God's words and deeds (*Dogmatic Constitution on Divine Revelation*, No. 8).

Mary in the Bible

The possibility of consensus on the Virgin Mary in the Bible was the theme of a book published in 1978, entitled *Mary in the New Testament* (edited by R. E. Brown, J. A. Fitzmyer, J. Reumann and K. P. Donfried). Limiting their study to the New Testament and using critical techniques of interpretation, a team of 12 authors — Catholics, Lutherans, Anglicans and others — agreed on a biblical portrait of Mary the Virgin as the great gospel model of faith commitment.

One valuable insight centers on the "true kinsmen" incident (Mk. 3:31-35; Mt. 12:46-50; Lk. 8:19-21). One day while Jesus was preaching, word was sent to him that his "mother and brethren" wished to see him. In St. Mark, the oldest account, there is a sharp distinction between the circle of the hearers of Jesus, who were "inside" and counted as his "true family," and the relatives "outside," who failed to understand him. St. Mark does not clearly place Mary among the outsiders, but neither does he carefully distinguish her from the other relatives who did not esteem Jesus. St. Luke shifts the focus completely, placing the relatives, especially the Mother of Jesus, among the true followers, as he does also in the Acts of the Apostles by mentioning them in the Upper Room before Pentecost.

St. Luke is fond of speaking of the "word of God." At the Annunciation, Mary consented with the statement, "Be it done to me according to your word" (Lk. 1:26-38), and "the Word was made flesh" (Jn. 1:14). Jesus said in reply to the message about his visitors, "My mother and my brothers are those who hear the word of God and do it" (Lk. 8:21). St. Luke relates this event just after the parables of the sower and the seed and the lamp on the lampstand. Consistent with his high praise of the Virgin Mary in the infancy chapters, he regards Mary as the rich soil — she heard the word and brought forth fruit in abundance, the Holy One who is the Son of God. She is the pure light, rekindled by the coming of the Redeemer; she is the "woman clothed with the sun" (Rv. 12:1), for Jesus is the "sun of justice."

St. Luke alone saved one other mention of Mary during the public ministry of Jesus, in the story of the "enthusiastic woman" (Lk. 11:27-28). One day while Jesus was preaching, a woman cried out, "Blessed is the womb that bore you and the breasts that nursed you." He replied, "Still more blessed are those who hear the word of God and keep it." The obedient Mary, handmaid of the Lord, brought together opposed beatitudes — the anonymous woman's praise of her motherhood and Jesus' tribute to her faith.

In the opening chapter of St. Luke, Elizabeth did the same when, filled with the Holy Spirit, she returned Mary's greeting with the loud cry, "Of all women you are the most blessed, and blessed is the fruit of your womb." Continuing in praise of her young cousin's faith, she added: "Yes, blessed is she who has believed, for the things promised her by the Lord will be fulfilled" (Lk. 1:39-45).

Mary the Virgin

Both St. Luke and St. Matthew, whose infancy narratives differ so much otherwise, agree that Mary conceived Jesus virginally, that her Son had no human father. The Creed affirms that Jesus was "conceived of the Virgin Mary by the power of the Holy Spirit."

St. Luke writes of the virginal conception of Jesus from the standpoint of Mary. To her question, "How can this be since I know not man?" the angel replied by appealing to God's power.

St. Matthew's viewpoint is that of Joseph, who was informed in a dream-vision that Mary's child was of no human father. God accomplishes his saving purposes without dependence on the will of the flesh and the will of man (Jn. 1:13). God shows his favor where he chooses — whether for the barren Sara, wife of Abraham, or aged Elizabeth, the wife of Zechariah, or the Virgin Mary. In the words of the promise to Abraham, repeated by Gabriel to Mary, "Nothing is impossible to God" (Lk. 1:37; Gn. 18:14).

Mary and Joseph accepted as God's will the virginal conception, an unprecedented event, the sign of God sending his Son to be the Savior. Their lives were henceforth totally dedicated to the service of Jesus.

As various forms of Christian witness developed in the Church, the conviction that Mary remains always a virgin came to be held as Catholic doctrine. The Gospels leave undecided the identity of the "brethren" of Jesus. From lived experience, by the fourth century the Church had come to see Mary's life-long virginity as part of her commitment to her Son and his mission. Such "development of doctrine" remains a point of difference between Catholics and Protestants, although the great Reformers — Luther, Calvin and later John Wesley — all held that Mary was ever-Virgin.

St. Luke and St. John on Mary

Along with the role of Mary in the childhood of Jesus, St. Luke sees her as part of the fulfillment of messianic prophecy. The Second Vatican Council spoke of "the exalted daughter of Zion in whom the times are fulfilled after the long waiting for the promise, and the new economy inaugurated when the Son of God takes on human nature from her in order to free men from sin by the mysteries of his flesh." The expectations of Israel for the Messiah reach their peak in Mary of Nazareth: "She stands out among the Lord's lowly and poor who confidently look for salvation from him" (*Constitution on the Church*, No. 55).

The Gospel of St. John introduces Mary at the opening and closing of her Son's ministry, which began with the first of his signs at Cana (Jn. 2:1-11) and ended on Calvary (Jn. 19). Both scenes deal with a "third day," both turn on the "hour," not yet come at Cana but achieved in the decisive event of Calvary. In both, Jesus addresses his Mother with the unaccustomed title, "woman." The request of Mary at Cana is for more than wine to save the wedding feast. She stands for Israel of old, symbolized by the water pots required for religious purifications; Mary stands also for the new Israel, the Church, the bride of Christ, symbolized by the abundant choice wine of the messianic banquet. The marriage feast looks forward to the hour when Christ, the bridegroom, will lay down his life in love for his bride, the Church.

When Jesus spoke from the cross to his Mother and the beloved disciple, "Woman, behold your son," and "Behold your Mother," more was meant than that the disciple should provide for Mary's care (Jn. 19:26-27). In his farewell discourse at the Last Supper, Jesus spoke of the woman in agony because her hour had come. "But when she has borne her child, she no longer remembers her pain for joy that a man has been born into the world" (Jn. 16:21). The longing of Israel for the coming of the Messiah was sometimes compared to labor pains. The "daughter of Zion" had been promised she would become the mother of all races and all nations. The words of Jesus on Calvary announced the fulfillment of that promise; Mary stands for the "woman" who is mother Church, new Israel, new People of God.

In St. John's Gospel, it is only after his words to his Mother and the disciple that Jesus, knowing "that everything was now finished," said, "I am thirsty," and then, "Now it is finished." "Then he bowed his head and delivered over his spirit" (Jn. 19:28-29).

The giving up of the spirit means both the expiring of Jesus and the giving of the Holy Spirit to the Church. The wine Mary requested at Cana was the wine of the Spirit, to be poured out at the messianic banquet. The prayer for the wine of the Spirit is answered through the self-surrender of Jesus on the cross. The triumphant Christ "gives up his spirit," and the Church comes into being. The Acts of the Apostles describe the effects of the outpouring of the Spirit at Pentecost and afterwards. What Mary requested at Cana, what she prayed for in agony at the cross of Jesus, what she sought before Pentecost in union with the Apostles and relatives and the women — all "with one accord devoted to prayer" — is the gift of the Spirit. At Nazareth Mary conceived her Son, and God became man by the power of the Holy Spirit; in the Upper Room she prayed for the Spirit that Jesus be born again in the members of his Church (*Constitution on the Church*, No. 59).

The New Eve

To the titles of Mary already familiar from the Gospels — "the Virgin," "Favored One," "Mother of Jesus," "Mother of my Lord" (Elizabeth's greeting, meaning "Mother of the Messianic King") — the early Church added other descriptions. By the mid-second century Mary was being compared to Eve. Eve was deceived by the word of the evil angel and by disobedience brought death; Mary, the obedient Virgin, heeded the message of the good angel and by her consent brought Life to the world. The title of "New Eve" became common for Mary. By the time of St. Jerome (d. 419), it was proverbial to say, "Death through Eve, life through Mary."

Immaculate Conception

Reflecting on the Blessed Virgin, Christians pondered various aspects of her holiness. The question arose of her freedom from original sin, God's gift of grace that came to be called her Immaculate Conception (not to be confused with the virginal conception of Jesus, for Mary was the child of the father and mother recalled as Joachim and Anne). It took centuries of development before the Immaculate Conception was held to be revealed by God and defined as dogma by Pius IX in 1854. The absence of clear scriptural evidence was one delaying factor, another was lack of clarity about the meaning of original sin, and most cogent was the requirement that Mary be beneficiary of the saving work of Christ. As the English Anglican John deSatgé expresses it, "Mary, who rejoiced in her Savior, was the last person to have no need of one." The Franciscan John Duns Scotus (d. 1308) suggested that Mary was kept free of original sin by a "preservative redemption" — in anticipation of the foreseen merits of Jesus

Christ — the explanation eventually recognized as revealed truth.

The Assumption

The final facet of Mary's holiness is the Assumption, her union body and soul with the risen Christ in the glory of heaven, defined as dogma by Pope Pius XII in 1950. By the sixth century the feast of the Assumption was being celebrated in the East, a development from a still earlier August 15 feast that had been known as the Memory of Mary (like the birthdays into heaven of the martyrs), as the Passing of Mary, and as the Dormition or Falling Asleep of the Mother of God. There is no compelling biblical testimony; the appeal is to the concordant faith of the Church, convinced that the promise of the resurrection of the flesh in union with the risen Savior has already been fulfilled for the Mother of the Lord, who gave him human birth in her pure body and was his loyal disciple unto the end.

Model of the Church

All beliefs about the Blessed Virgin lead to Christ. God kept her free from original sin for the sake of Jesus, that she might give herself wholeheartedly to his life and work (*Constitution on the Church*, No. 56), and in consideration of his redemptive mission. Mary's Assumption is her reunion with her Son in the power of his resurrection. The Marian privileges of the Immaculate Conception and the Assumption enrich also the self-understanding of the Church, for she is the "most excellent fruit of the redemption, the spotless model of the Church," the one in whom Christians admire God's plan for his Church. "In the most holy Virgin the Church has already reached that perfection whereby she exists without spot or wrinkle (Eph. 5:27)" (*Constitution on the Church*, No. 65).

Mary Immaculate is a sign of the love of Christ for his bride, the Church; the bridegroom purifies her by his blood to make her all-holy. The preface for the Solemnity of the Immaculate Conception (December 8) addresses the Father: "You allowed no stain of sin to touch the Virgin Mary. Full of grace, she was to be a worthy Mother of your Son, your sign of favor to the Church at its beginning, and the promise of its perfection as the bride of Christ, radiantly beautiful."

Faithful to his promise, Christ has prepared a place for his bride, the Church. In Mary, daughter of the Church, now joined to Christ body and soul in glory, the pilgrim Church sees the successful completion of its own journey. The resurrection of Jesus is the central truth; the Assumption of Mary is the living sign of the Church's call to glory, to loving union with the victorious Redeemer. The preface at Mass for August 15 reads: "Today the Virgin Mother of God was taken up into heaven to be the beginning and the pattern of the Church in its perfection, and a sign of sure hope and comfort for your pilgrim people. You would not allow decay to touch her body, for she had given birth in the glory of the Incarnation to your Son, the Lord of all life." (Cf. also *Constitution on the Church*, No. 68.)

Mother of God

In 325 the first ecumenical council, at Nicaea, proclaimed that Jesus is truly Son of God. Defenders of the faith there were the first to call Mary "Mother of God." At the third ecumenical council, Ephesus, in 431, it was solemnly established that the Virgin Mary is indeed "Mother of God," for the Son to whom she gave birth is the pre-existent Second Person of the Blessed Trinity. "Mother of God" had already been used as a popular title in some parts of the Church, and after Ephesus it was adopted in the prayers of the Mass, as is still the practice in the Catholic Church and all Eastern Churches. For example, the current third Eucharistic Prayer reads: "May he (the Holy Spirit) make us an everlasting gift to you (the Father) and enable us to share in the inheritance of your saints, with Mary, the Virgin Mother of God."

Mother of the Church

When the Church began to celebrate the Assumption of Mary, it did so in the conviction Mary did not leave the members of the Church orphans when her days on earth were ended. She continues her interest for them in union with her Son, the supreme intercessor. By the time of the Council of Ephesus in 431, authors of both the East and West — like St. Ephrem of Syria (d. 373) and St. Ambrose of Italy (d. 397) — proposed Mary as the model of Christian life, and the practice of asking her to pray for her clients on earth began to appear. The feasts of the Nativity of Mary (September 8), the Annunciation (March 25) and the Presentation of Jesus (February 2, also known as the Purification of Mary or Candlemas) have been kept from the sixth and seventh centuries.

When the words of Gabriel and Elizabeth from St. Luke's infancy narrative became part of prayer, the first part of the Hail Mary, their use led to deeper awareness of Mary's holiness as well as to counting on her heavenly help — well expressed in the second part of the Hail Mary — "Holy Mary, Mother of God, pray for us sinners now and at the hour of our death," which reached its fixed form only in the fifteenth century. Mary's place in liturgical prayer and in private prayer reflected and strengthened the sense of her continuing role as loving friend in heaven of the Church on earth. People asked Mary's prayers on their behalf, recalling Mary's own "pilgrimage of faith" and trusting in her abiding maternal care.

Greek homilists like St. John of Damascus (d. ca. 749), St. Andrew of Crete (d. 740) and St. Germanus of Constantinople (d. ca. 733) sang Mary's praises and urged confidence in her loving intercession with Christ. In the West, after the upsurge of the Carolingian times (about 800), remembered for the origin of the Saturday observance in honor of Mary, came the flowering of medieval piety, as evidenced in the writings of St. Anselm (d. 1109), St. Bernard (d. 1153) and his fellow Cistercians, and the great scholastic doctors like St. Thomas Aquinas (d. 1274) and St. Bonaventure (d. 1274). The medieval authors described Mary as Mediatrix of grace, Dispensatrix of grace, spiritual Mother. Blessed Guerric, the Cistercian abbot of Igny (France, d. 1157), emphasized the maternal role of Mary in the formation of Christ in the faithful: "Like the Church of which she is a figure, Mary is Mother of all who are born to life."

Christian Unity and Mary

At the Reformation, in reaction to abuses, the invocation of the saints was rejected as harmful to confidence in Christ the unique Mediator. Since the sixteenth century Western Christians have been sharply divided in their understanding of the communion of saints and the legitimacy of "praying to Mary." Recent events, however, hold out hope for a meeting of minds and hearts even in this sensitive area. The Second Vatican Council offered a biblical portrait of Mary without neglecting later developments in doctrine and devotion. The council described the place of Mary in words designed to meet Protestant difficulties; e.g., the much misunderstood word, Mediatrix, was used once only and was explained as completely dependent on the unique mediatorship of Christ (*Constitution on the Church,* Nos. 67, 69).

The conciliar Decree on Ecumenism, issued Nov. 21, 1964, spoke of the "order" or "hierarchy of truths" among Catholic doctrines, which differ in their relationship to the foundation of the faith (No. 11). The foundation is Jesus Christ, and here all Christians share a common profession of faith. The document mentioned realistically some differences that still divide Catholics and other Christians, in this "order of truths": the meaning of the Incarnation and Redemption, the mystery and ministry of the Church, and the role of Mary in the work of salvation (No. 20). The decree also said in this context: "We rejoice to see our separated brethren looking to Christ as the source and center of ecclesiastical communion. Inspired by longing for union with Christ, they feel compelled to search for unity ever more ardently, and to bear witness to their faith among all the peoples of the earth."

The formation of the Ecumenical Society of the Blessed Virgin Mary in England in 1967, and of the American branch in 1976, is an encouraging sign. The American bishops' pastoral, *"Behold Your Mother,"* appealed to the "basic reverence" of all Christians for Mary, "a veneration deeper than doctrinal differences and theological disputes" (Nos. 101-112). Pope Paul VI's major document, *Marialis Cultus*, contains an appeal to other Christians (Nos. 32 and 33). With Christians of the East, said Pope Paul, Catholics honor the Mother of God as "hope of Christians." Catholics join with Anglicans and Protestants in common praise of God, using the Virgin's own words (Lk. 1:46-55).

It may well be that the growing interest in the bonds between the Blessed Virgin and the Holy Spirit will help bring Christians together. The Spirit of unity inspired Mary's prophecy: "All generations will call me blessed, because he who is mighty has done great things for me" (Lk. 1:48-49).

APPARITIONS OF THE BLESSED VIRGIN MARY

Only eight of the best known apparitions of the Blessed Virgin Mary are described briefly below.

The sites of the following apparitions have become shrines and centers of pilgrimage. Miracles of the moral and physical orders have been reported as occurring at these places and/or in connection with related practices of prayer and penance.

Banneux, near Liege, Belgium: Mary appeared eight times between Jan. 15 and Mar. 2, 1933, to an 11-year-old peasant girl, Mariette Beco, in a garden behind the family cottage in Banneux, near Liege. She called herself the Virgin of the Poor, and has since been venerated as Our Lady of the Poor, the Sick, and the Indifferent. A small chapel was built by a spring near the site of the apparitions and was blessed Aug. 15, 1933. Approval of devotion to Our Lady of Banneux was given in 1949 by Bishop Louis J. Kerkhofs of Liege, and a statue of that title was solemnly crowned in 1956.

Over 100 sanctuaries throughout the world are dedicated to the honor of Our Lady of Banneux.

The **International Union of Prayer,** for devotion to the Virgin of the Poor, has approximately two million members.

Beauraing, Belgium: Mary appeared 33 times between Nov. 29, 1932, and Jan. 3, 1933, to five children in the garden of a convent school in Beauraing. A chapel, which became a pilgrimage center, was erected on the spot. Reserved approval of devotion to Our Lady of Beauraing was given Feb. 2,

1943, and final approbation July 2, 1949, by Bishop Charue of Namur.

The **Marian Union of Beauraing**, a prayer association for the conversion of sinners, has thousands of members throughout the world (see Pro Maria Committee).

Fatima, Portugal: Mary appeared six times between May 13 and Oct. 13, 1917, to three children in a field called Cova da Iria near Fatima, north of Lisbon. She recommended frequent recitation of the Rosary; urged works of mortification for the conversion of sinners; called for devotion to herself under the title of her Immaculate Heart; asked that the people of Russia be consecrated to her under this title, and that the faithful make a Communion of reparation on the first Saturday of each month.

The apparitions were declared worthy of belief in October, 1930, after a seven-year canonical investigation, and devotion to Our Lady of Fatima was authorized under the title of Our Lady of the Rosary. In October, 1942, Pius XII consecrated the world to Mary under the title of her Immaculate Heart. Ten years later, in the first apostolic letter addressed directly to the peoples of Russia, he consecrated them in a special manner to Mary.

Fatima, with its sanctuary and basilica, ranks with Lourdes as the greatest of modern Marian shrines.

(See First Saturday Devotion.)

Guadalupe, Mexico: Mary appeared four times in 1531 to an Indian, Juan Diego, on Tepeyac hill outside of Mexico City, and instructed him to tell Bishop Zumarraga of her wish that a church be built there. The bishop complied with the request about two years later after being convinced of the genuineness of the apparition by the evidence of a miraculously painted life-size figure of the Virgin on the mantle of the Indian. The mantle bearing the picture has been preserved and is enshrined in the Basilica of Our Lady of Guadalupe, which has a long history as a center of devotion and pilgrimage in Mexico. The shrine church, originally dedicated in 1709 and subsequently enlarged, has the title of basilica.

Benedict XIV, in a decree issued in 1754, authorized a Mass and Office under the title of Our Lady of Guadalupe for celebration on Dec. 12, and named Mary the patroness of New Spain. Our Lady of Guadalupe was designated patroness of Latin America by St. Pius X in 1910 and patroness of the Americas by Pius XII in 1945.

Knock, Ireland: An apparition of Mary, along with the figures of St. Joseph and St. John the Apostle, was witnessed by at least 15 persons in the evening of Aug. 21, 1879, near the parish church of Knock, County Mayo. A commission appointed by the Bishop of Tuam to investigate the matter reported that testimony confirming the apparition was "trustworthy and satisfactory."

La Salette, France: Mary appeared as a sorrowing and weeping figure Sept. 19, 1846, to two peasant children, Melanie Matthieu, 15, and Maximin Giraud, 11, at La Salette in southern France. The message she confided to them, regarding the necessity of penance, was communicated to Pius IX in 1851 and has since been known as the "secret" of La Salette. Bishop de Bruillard of Grenoble declared in 1851 that the apparition was credible, and devotion to Mary under the title of Our Lady of La Salette was authorized. The devotion has been confirmed by popes since the time of Pius IX, and a Mass and Office with this title were authorized in 1942. The shrine church was given the title of minor basilica in 1879.

Lourdes, France: Mary, identifying herself as the Immaculate Conception, appeared 18 times between Feb. 11 and July 16, 1858, to 14-year-old Bernadette Soubirous at the grotto of Massabielle near Lourdes in southern France. Her message concerned the necessity of prayer and penance for the conversion of men. Mary's request that a chapel be built at the grotto and spring was fulfilled in 1862 after four years of rigid examination established the credibility of the apparitions. Devotion under the title of Our Lady of Lourdes was authorized later, and a Feb. 11 feast commemorating the apparitions was instituted by Leo XIII. St. Pius X extended this feast throughout the Church in 1907.

The Church of Notre Dame was made a basilica in 1870, and the Church of the Rosary was built later. The underground Church of St. Pius X, consecrated Mar. 25, 1958, is the second largest church in the world, with a capacity of 20,000 persons.

Our Lady of the Miraculous Medal, France: Mary appeared three times in 1830 to Catherine Laboure in the chapel of the motherhouse of the Daughters of Charity of St. Vincent de Paul, Rue de Bac, Paris. She commissioned Catherine to have made the medal of the Immaculate Conception, now known as the Miraculous Medal, and to spread devotion to her under this title. In 1832, the medal was struck according to the model revealed to Catherine.

Secret of Fatima

Sister Lucy, a Carmelite nun and one of the trio of shepherd children to whom Mary appeared, wrote a three-part account of an apparition which occurred July 13, 1917. The first part concerned a vision of hell. The second dealt with the conversion of the peoples of Russia through devotion to Mary under the title of her Immaculate Heart. The third part was the so-called "secret" which, it was said, was not to be opened until 1960 or the death of Sister Lucy, whichever came first. Presumably, the "secret" was a prophecy of dire events. To date, it has not been disclosed.

Eastern Catholic Churches

The Second Vatican Council, in its *Decree on Eastern Catholic Churches,* stated the following points.

"The Catholic Church holds in high esteem the institutions of the Eastern Churches, their liturgical rites, ecclesiastical traditions, and Christian way of life. For, distinguished as they are by their venerable antiquity, they are bright with that tradition which was handed down from the apostles through the Fathers, and which forms part of the divinely revealed and undivided heritage of the universal Church" (No. 1).

"That Church, Holy and Catholic, which is the Mystical Body of Christ, is made up of the faithful who are organically united in the Holy Spirit through the same faith, the same sacraments, and the same government and who, combining into various groups held together by a hierarchy, form separate Churches or rites. . . . It is the mind of the Catholic Church that each individual Church or rite retain its traditions whole and entire, while adjusting its way of life to the various needs of time and place" (No. 2).

"Such individual Churches, whether of the East or of the West, although they differ somewhat among themselves in what are called rites (that is, in liturgy, ecclesiastical discipline, and spiritual heritage) are, nevertheless, equally entrusted to the pastoral guidance of the Roman Pontiff, the divinely appointed successor of St. Peter in supreme government over the universal Church. They are consequently of equal dignity, so that none of them is superior to the others by reason of rite" (No. 3).

Eastern Heritage: "Each and every Catholic, as also the baptized . . . of every non-Catholic Church or community who enters into the fullness of Catholic communion, should everywhere retain his proper rite, cherish it, and observe it to the best of his ability . . ." (No. 4).

". . . The Churches of the East, as much as those of the West, fully enjoy the right, and are in duty bound, to rule themselves. Each should do so according to its proper and individual procedures . . ." (No. 5).

"All Eastern rite members should know and be convinced that they can and should always preserve their lawful liturgical rites and their established way of life, and that these should not be altered except by way of an appropriate and organic development . . ." (No. 6).

Patriarchs: "The institution of the patriarchate has existed in the Church from the earliest times and was recognized by the first ecumenical Synods.

"By the name Eastern Patriarch is meant the bishop who has jurisdiction over all bishops (including metropolitans), clergy, and people of his own territory or rite, in accordance with the norms of law and without prejudice to the primacy of the Roman Pontiff . . ." (No. 7).

"Though some of the patriarchates of the Eastern Churches are of later origin than others, all are equal in patriarchal dignity. Still the honorary and lawfully established order of precedence among them is to be preserved" (No. 8).

"In keeping with the most ancient tradition of the Church, the Patriarchs of the Eastern Churches are to be accorded exceptional respect, since each presides over his patriarchate as father and head.

"This sacred Synod, therefore, decrees that their rights and privileges should be re-established in accord with the ancient traditions of each Church and the decrees of the ecumenical Synods.

"The rights and privileges in question are those which flourished when East and West were in union, though they should be somewhat adapted to modern conditions.

"The Patriarchs with their synods constitute the superior authority for all affairs of the patriarchate, including the right to establish new eparchies and to nominate bishops of their rite within the territorial bounds of the patriarchate, without prejudice to the inalienable right of the Roman Pontiff to intervene in individual cases" (No. 9).

"What has been said of Patriarchs applies as well, under the norm of law, to major archbishops, who preside over the whole of some individual Church or rite" (No. 10).

Sacraments: "This sacred Ecumenical Synod endorses and lauds the ancient discipline of the sacraments existing in the Eastern Churches, as also the practices connected with their celebration and administration . . ." (No. 12).

"With respect to the minister of holy chrism (confirmation), let that practice be fully restored which existed among Easterners in most ancient times. Priests, therefore, can validly confer this sacrament, provided they use chrism blessed by a Patriarch or bishop."

"In conjunction with baptism or otherwise, all Eastern-Rite priests can confer this sacrament validly on all the faithful of any rite, including the Latin; licitly, however, only if the regulations of both common and particular law are observed. Priests of the Latin rite, to the extent of the faculties they enjoy for administering this sacrament, can confer it also on the faithful of Eastern Churches, without prejudice to rite. They do so licitly if the regulations of both common and particular law are observed" (No. 14).

"The faithful are bound on Sundays and

feast days to attend the divine liturgy or, according to the regulations or custom of their own rite, the celebration of the Divine Praises. That the faithful may be able to satisfy their obligation more easily, it is decreed that this obligation can be fulfilled from the Vespers of the vigil to the end of the Sunday or the feast day . . ." (No. 15).

"Because of the everyday intermingling of the communicants of diverse Eastern Churches in the same Eastern region or territory, the faculty for hearing confession, duly and unrestrictedly granted by his proper bishop to a priest of any rite, is applicable to the entire territory of the grantor, also to the places and the faithful belonging to any other rite in the same territory, unless an Ordinary of the place explicitly decides otherwise with respect to the places pertaining to his rite" (No. 16).

". . . This sacred Synod ardently desires that where it has fallen into disuse the office of the permanent diaconate be restored. The legislative authority of each individual church should decide about the subdiaconate and the minor orders . . ." (No. 17).

"By way of preventing invalid marriages between Eastern Catholics and baptized Eastern non-Catholics, and in the interests of the permanence and sanctity of marriage and of domestic harmony, this sacred Synod decrees that the canonical 'form' for the celebration of such marriages obliges only for lawfulness. For their validity, the presence of a sacred minister suffices, as long as the other requirements of law are honored" (No. 18).

Worship: "Henceforth, it will be the exclusive right of an ecumenical Synod or the Apostolic See to establish, transfer, or suppress feast days common to all the Eastern Churches. To establish, transfer, or suppress feast days for any of the individual Churches is within the competence not only of the Apostolic See but also of a patriarchal or archiepiscopal synod, provided due consideration is given to the entire region and to other individual Churches" (No. 19).

"Until such time as all Christians desirably concur on a fixed day for the celebration of Easter, and with a view meantime to promoting unity among the Christians of a given area or nation, it is left to the Patriarchs or supreme authorities of a place to reach a unanimous agreement, after ascertaining the views of all concerned, on a single Sunday for the observance of Easter" (No. 20).

"With respect to rules concerning sacred seasons, individual faithful dwelling outside the area or territory of their own rite may conform completely to the established custom of the place where they live. When members of a family belong to different rites, they are all permitted to observe sacred seasons according to the rules of any one of these rites" (No. 21).

"From ancient times the Divine Praises have been held in high esteem among all Eastern Churches. Eastern clerics and religious should celebrate these Praises as the laws and customs of their own traditions require. To the extent they can, the faithful too should follow the example of their forbears by assisting devoutly at the Divine Praises" (No. 22).

Origin

The Church had its beginnings in Palestine, whence it spread to other regions of the world. As it spread, certain cities or jurisdictions became key centers of Christian life and missionary endeavor—notably, Jerusalem, Alexandria, Antioch and Constantinople in the East, and Rome in the West — with the result that their practices became diffused throughout their spheres of influence. Various rites originated from these practices which, although rooted in the essentials of Christian faith, were different in significant respects because of their relationships to particular cultural patterns.

Patriarchal Jurisdictions

The main lines of Eastern Church organization and liturgy were drawn before the Roman Empire was separated into Eastern and Western divisions in 292. It was originally co-extensive with the boundaries of the Eastern Empire. Its jurisdictions were those of the patriarchates of Alexandria and Antioch (recognized as such by the Council of Nicaea in 325), and of Jerusalem and Constantinople (given similar recognition by the Council of Chalcedon in 451). These were the major parent bodies of the Eastern Rite Churches which for centuries were identifiable only with limited numbers of nationality and language groups in Eastern Europe, the Middle East and parts of Asia and Africa. Their members are now scattered throughout the world.

RITES AND FAITHFUL OF EASTERN CHURCHES

(Principal source of statistics: *Annuario Pontificio*. The statistics are for Eastern-Rite jurisdictions only, and do not include Eastern-Rite Catholics under the jurisdiction of Roman-Rite bishops. Some of the figures reported are only approximate. Some of the jurisdictions listed may be inactive because of government suppression.)

The Byzantine, Alexandrian, Antiochene, Armenian and Chaldean are the five principal rites used in their entirety or in modified form by the various Eastern churches. The number of Eastern Catholics throughout the world is more than 12 million.

Alexandrian Rite

Called the Liturgy of St. Mark, the Alexandrian Rite was modified by the Copts and

Melkites, and contains elements of the Byzantine Rite of St. Basil and the liturgies of Sts. Mark, Cyril and Gregory of Nazianzen. The liturgy is substantially that of the Coptic Church, which is divided into two branches — the Coptic or Egyptian, and the Ethiopian or Abyssinian.

The faithful of this rite are:

COPTS: Returned to Catholic unity about 1741; situated in Egypt, the Near East; liturgical languages are Coptic, Arabic. Jurisdictions (located in Egypt): patriarchate of Alexandria, three dioceses; 113,525.

ETHIOPIANS: Returned to Catholic unity in 1846: situated in Ethiopia, Eritrea, Jerusalem, Somalia; liturgical language is Geez. Jurisdictions (located in Ethiopia): one archdiocese, two dioceses; 98,800.

Antiochene Rite

This is the source of more derived rites than any of the other parent rites. Its origin can be traced to the Eighth Book of the *Apostolic Constitutions* and to the Liturgy of St. James of Jerusalem, which ultimately spread throughout the whole patriarchate and displaced older forms based on the *Apostolic Constitutions*.

The faithful of this rite are:

MALANKARESE: Returned to Catholic unity in 1930; situated in India; liturgical languages are Syriac, Malayalam. Jurisdictions (located in India): one archdiocese, two dioceses; 235,647.

MARONITES: United to the Holy See since the time of their founder, St. Maron; have no counterparts among the separated Eastern Christians: situated throughout the world: liturgical languages are Syriac, Arabic. Jurisdictions (located in Lebanon, Cyprus, Egypt, Syria, U.S., Brazil, Australia): patriarchate of Antioch, 16 archdioceses and dioceses, one patriarchal vicariate; 1,500,000. Where no special jurisdictions exist, they are under jurisdiction of local Roman-Rite bishops.

SYRIANS: Returned to Catholic unity in 1781; situated in Asia, Africa, the Americas, Australia; liturgical languages are Syriac, Arabic. Jurisdictions (located in Lebanon, Iraq, Egypt, Syria and Turkey): patriarchate of Antioch, seven archdioceses and dioceses, three patriarchal vicariates; 81,266.

Armenian Rite

Substantially, although using a different language, this is the Greek Liturgy of St. Basil; it is considered an older form of the Byzantine Rite, and incorporates some modifications from the Antiochene Rite.

The faithful of this rite are:

ARMENIANS, exclusively: Returned to Catholic unity during the time of the Crusades; situated in the Near East, Europe, Africa, the Americas, Australasia: liturgical language is Classical Armenian. Jurisdictions (located in Lebanon, Iran, Iraq, Egypt, Syria, Turkey, Poland, France, Greece, Rumania): patriarchate of Cilicia, eight archdioceses and dioceses, one exarchate, two ordinariates; 82,480.

Byzantine Rite

Based on the Rite of St. James of Jerusalem and the churches of Antioch, and reformed by Sts. Basil and John Chrysostom, the Byzantine Rite is proper to the Church of Constantinople. (The city was called Byzantium before Constantine changed its name; the modern name is Istanbul.) It is now used by the majority of Eastern Catholics and by the Eastern Orthodox Church (which is not in union with Rome). It is, after the Roman, the most widely used rite.

The faithful of this rite are:

ALBANIANS: Returned to Catholic unity about 1628; situated in Albania; liturgical language is Albanian. Jurisdiction (located in Albania): one apostolic administration.

BULGARIANS: Returned to Catholic unity about 1861; situated in Bulgaria; liturgical language is Old Slavonic. Jurisdiction (located in Bulgaria): one apostolic exarchate.

BYELORUSSIANS, also known as WHITE RUSSIANS: Returned to Catholic unity in the 17th century; situated in Europe, the Americas, Australia; liturgical language is Old Slavonic. They have an apostolic visitor residing at Rome.

GEORGIANS: Returned to Catholic unity in 1861; situated in Georgia (Southern Russia), France; liturgical language is Georgian. They have an apostolic administrator.

GREEKS: Returned to Catholic unity in 1829; situated in Greece, Asia Minor, Europe; liturgical language is Greek. Jurisdictions (located in Greece and Turkey): two exarchates; 2,570.

HUNGARIANS: Descendants of Ruthenians who returned to Catholic unity in 1646; situated in Hungary, the rest of Europe, the Americas; liturgical languages are Greek, Hungarian, English. Jurisdictions (located in Hungary): one diocese and one exarchate; 319,340.

ITALO-ALBANIANS: Have never been separated from Rome; situated in Italy, Sicily, the Americas; liturgical languages are Greek, Italo-Albanian. Jurisdictions (located in Italy): two dioceses, one abbacy; 67,288.

MELKITES (GREEK CATHOLICS-MELKITES): Returned to Catholic unity during the time of the Crusades, but definitive reunion did not take place until early in the 18th century; situated in the Middle East, Asia, Africa, Europe, the Americas, Australia; liturgical languages are Greek, Arabic, English, Portuguese, Spanish. Jurisdictions (located in Syria, Lebanon, Jordan, Israel, U.S., Brazil): patriarchate of Antioch (with patriarchal vicariates in Egypt, Sudan, Jerusalem, Iraq and Kuwait), 16 archdioceses and dioceses; approximately one million.

ROMANIANS: Returned to Catholic unity in 1697; situated in Rumania, the rest of Europe, the Americas; liturgical language is Modern Romanian. Jurisdictions (located in Rumania): one archdiocese, four dioceses. They have an apostolic visitor in the U.S.

RUSSIANS: Returned to Catholic unity about 1905; situated in Europe, the Americas, Australia, China; liturgical language is Old Slavonic. Jurisdictions (located in Russia and China): two exarchates.

RUTHENIANS, or CARPATHO-RUSSIANS (Rusins): Returned to Catholic unity in the Union of Brest-Litovek, 1596, and the Union of Uzhorod, Apr. 24, 1646; situated in Hungary, Czechoslovakia, elsewhere in Europe, the Americas, Australia; liturgical languages are Old Slavonic, English. Jurisdictions (located in Russia and the U.S.): one archdiocese, three dioceses.

SLOVAKS: Jurisdiction (located in Czechoslovakia): one diocese (also has jurisdiction over Byzantine-rite Catholics in Czechoslovakia).

UKRAINIANS, or GALICIAN RUTHENIANS: Returned to Catholic unity about 1595; situated in Europe, the Americas, Australasia; liturgical languages are Old Slavonic and Ukrainian. Jurisdictions (located in Russian Galicia, Poland, the U.S., Canada, England, Australia, Germany, France, Brazil, Argentina): three archdioceses, 10 dioceses, five apostolic exarchates: 4,394,460 (some figures date from 1943).

YUGOSLAVS, SERBS and CROATIANS: Returned to Catholic unity in 1611; situated in Yugoslavia, the Americas; liturgical language is Old Slavonic. Jurisdiction (located in Yugoslavia): one diocese (which also has jurisdiction over all Byzantine-Rite faithful in Yugoslavia); 47,930. They are under the jurisdiction of Ruthenian bishops elsewhere.

Chaldean Rite

This rite, listed as separate and distinct by the Sacred Congregation for the Oriental Churches, was derived from the Antiochene Rite.

The faithful of this rite are:

CHALDEANS: Descendants of the Nestorians, returned to Catholic unity in 1692; situated throughout the Middle East, in Europe, Africa, the Americas; liturgical languages are Syriac, Arabic. Jurisdictions (located in Iraq, Iran, Lebanon, Syria, Turkey): patriarchate of Babylonia, 19 archdioceses and dioceses; 279,450. There are patriarchal vicars for Jordan and Egypt.

SYRO-MALABARESE: Descended from the St. Thomas Christians of India; situated mostly in the Malabar region of India; they use a Westernized and Latinized form of the Chaldean Rite in Syriac and Malayalam. Jurisdictions (located in India): two archdioceses, 16 dioceses; 2,472,979.

EASTERN JURISDICTIONS

For centuries Eastern-Rite Catholics were identifiable with a limited number of nationality and language groups in certain countries of the Middle East, Eastern Europe, Asia and Africa. The persecution of religion in the Soviet Union since 1917 and in Iron Curtain countries since World War II, however — in addition to decimating and destroying the Church in those places—has resulted in the emigration of many Eastern-Rite Catholics from their homelands. This forced emigration, together with voluntary emigration, has led to the spread of Eastern Rites and their faithful to many other countries.

Europe

(Apostolic visitors for Byzantine Rite faithful in western Europe are: Archbishop Miroslav Marusyn, for Ukrainians who have no bishop of their own; Bishop Ceslao Sipovic for Byelorussians).

ALBANIA: Byzantine Rite, apostolic administration.

AUSTRIA: Byzantine Rite, ordinariate.

BULGARIA: Byzantine Rite (Bulgarians), apostolic exarchate.

CZECHOSLOVAKIA: Byzantine Rite (Slovakians and other Byzantine-Rite Catholics), eparchy.

ENGLAND: Byzantine Rite (Ukrainians), apostolic exarchate.

FRANCE: Byzantine Rite (Ukrainians), apostolic exarchate.

Armenian Rite, apostolic exarchate.

Ordinariate for all other Eastern-Rite Catholics.

GERMANY: Byzantine Rite (Ukrainians), apostolic exarchate.

GREECE: Byzantine Rite, apostolic exarchate.

Armenian Rite, ordinariate.

HUNGARY: Byzantine Rite (Hungarians), eparchy, apostolic exarchate.

ITALY: Byzantine Rite (Italo-Albanians), two eparchies, one abbacy.

POLAND: Byzantine Rite (Ukrainian), apostolic exarchate.

Armenian Rite, archeparchy.

RUMANIA: Byzantine Rite (Romanians), metropolitan, four eparchies.

Armenian Rite, ordinariate.

RUSSIA: Byzantine Rite (Russians), apostolic exarchate; (Ruthenians), eparchy; (Ukrainians), major archeparchy, two eparchies.

YUGOSLAVIA: Byzantine Rite (Yugoslav and other Byzantine-Rite Catholics), eparchy.

Asia

CHINA: Byzantine Rite (Russians), apostolic exarchate.

CYPRUS: Antiochene Rite (Maronites), archeparchy.

INDIA: Antiochene Rite (Malankarese), metropolitan see, two eparchies.

Chaldean Rite (Syro-Malabarese), two metropolitan sees, 16 eparchies.

IRAN: Chaldean Rite (Chaldeans), two metropolitan sees, one archeparchy, one eparchy.

Armenian Rite, eparchy.

IRAQ: Antiochene Rite (Syrians), two archeparchies.

Byzantine Rite (Greek-Melkites), patriarchal vicariate.

Chaldean Rite (Chaldeans), patriarchate, two metropolitan sees, eight archeparchies and eparchies.

Armenian Rite, archeparchy.

ISRAEL (includes Jerusalem): Antiochene Rite (Syrians), patriarchal vicariate; (Maronites), patriarchal vicariate.

Byzantine Rite (Greek-Melkites), archeparchy, patriarchal vicariate.

Chaldean Rite (Chaldeans), patriarchal vicariate.

Armenian Rite, patriarchal vicariate.

JORDAN: Byzantine Rite (Greek-Melkites), archeparchy.

KUWAIT: Byzantine Rite (Greek-Melkites), patriarchal vicariate.

LEBANON: Antiochene Rite (Maronites), patriarchate, eight archeparchies and eparchies; (Syrians), patriarchate.

Byzantine Rite (Greek-Melkites), seven metropolitan and archeparchal sees.

Chaldean Rite (Chaldeans), eparchy.

Armenian Rite, patriarchate, eparchy.

SYRIAN ARAB REPUBLIC: Antiochene Rite (Maronites), one archeparchy, two eparchies; (Syrians), four archeparchies.

Byzantine Rite (Greek-Melkites), patriarchate, four metropolitan sees, one archeparchy.

Chaldean Rite (Chaldeans), eparchy.

Armenian Rite, archeparchy, eparchy, patriarchal vicariate.

TURKEY (Europe and Asia): Antiochene Rite (Syrians), patriarchal vicariate.

Byzantine Rite (Greeks), apostolic exarchate.

Chaldean Rite (Chaldeans), one archeparchy, two eparchies.

Armenian Rite, archeparchy.

Oceania

AUSTRALIA: Byzantine Rite (Ukrainians), apostolic exarchate.

Antiochene Rite (Maronites), eparchy.

Africa

EGYPT, ARAB REPUBLIC OF: Alexandrian Rite (Copts), patriarchate, three eparchies.

Antiochene Rite (Maronites), eparchy; (Syrians), eparchy.

Byzantine Rite (Greek-Melkites), patriarchal vicariate.

Chaldean Rite (Chaldeans), patriarchal vicariate.

Armenian Rite, eparchy.

ETHIOPIA: Alexandrian Rite (Ethiopians), metropolitan see, two eparchies.

SUDAN: Byzantine Rite (Greek-Melkites), patriarchal vicariate.

North America

CANADA: Byzantine Rite (Ukrainians), one metropolitan, four eparchies; (Slovaks), apostolic visitor.

UNITED STATES: Antiochene Rite (Maronites), eparchy.

Byzantine Rite (Ukrainians), one metropolitan see, two eparchies; (Ruthenians), one metropolitan see, two eparchies; (Greek-Melkites), eparchy; (Romanians), apostolic visitor.

Other Eastern-Rite Catholics are under the jurisdiction of local Roman-Rite bishops. (See Eastern-Rite Catholics in the United States.)

South America

ARGENTINA: Byzantine Rite (Ukrainians), eparchy.

Ordinariate for all other Eastern-Rite Catholics.

BRAZIL: Antiochene Rite (Maronites), eparchy.

Byzantine Rite (Greek-Melkites), eparchy; (Ukrainians), eparchy.

Ordinariate for all other Eastern-Rite Catholics.

SYNODS, ASSEMBLIES

These assemblies are collegial bodies which have pastoral authority over members of the Eastern Rite Churches.

Patriarchal Synods: Maronites: Antoine Khoraiche, patriarch of Antioch of the Maronites.

Melkites: Maximos V Hakim, patriarch of Antioch of the Greek Catholics-Melkites.

Chaldeans: Paul II Cheikho, patriarch of Babylonia of the Chaldeans.

Copts: Cardinal Stephanos I Sidarouss, C.M., patriarch of Alexandria of the Copts.

Syrians: Ignace Antoine II Hayek, patriarch of Antioch of the Syrians.

Armenians: Hemaiagh Pierre XVII Ghedighian, patriarch of Cilicia of the Armenians.

Assemblies: Assembly of Ordinaries of the Arab Republic of Egypt: Cardinal Stephanos I Sidarouss, C.M., patriarch of Alexandria of the Copts, president.

Assembly of Catholic Patriarchs and Bishops of Lebanon: Antoine Khoraiche, patriarch of Antioch of the Maronites, president.

Assembly of Ordinaries of the Syrian Arab Republic: Maximos V Hakim, patriarch of Antioch of the Greek Catholics-Melkites, president.

Interritual Union of the Bishops of Iraq: Paul II Cheikho, patriarch of Babylonia of the Chaldeans, president.

Conference of the Ukrainian Catholic Hierarchy (Feb. 9, 1962).

Malabarese Episcopal Conference (June 4, 1970): Cardinal Joseph Parecattil, Ernakulam, president.

Iranian Episcopal Conference (Aug. 11, 1977).

Of the collegial bodies listed above, the patriarchal synods have the most authority. In addition to other prerogatives, they have the right to elect bishops and regulate discipline for their respective rites.

EASTERN RITES IN U.S.

(Statistics, from the *Official Catholic Directory*, are membership figures reported by Eastern-Rite jurisdictions. Additional Eastern-Rite Catholics are included in statistics for Roman-Rite dioceses.)

Byzantine Rite

Ukrainians: There are 244,983 in three jurisdictions in the U.S.: the metropolitan see of Philadelphia (1924, metropolitan 1958) and the suffragan sees of Stamford, Conn. (1956), and St. Nicholas of Chicago (1961).

Ruthenians: There are 281,240 in three jurisdictions in the U.S.: the metropolitan see of Pittsburgh (est. 1924 at Pittsburgh; metropolitan and transferred to Munhall, 1969; transferred to Pittsburgh, 1977) and the suffragan sees of Passaic, N.J. (1963), and Parma, Ohio (1969). Hungarian and Croatian Byzantine Catholics in the U.S. are also under the jurisdiction of Ruthenian-Rite bishops.

Melkites (Greek Catholics-Melkites): In 1979, 22,300 (of approximately 55,000) were reported under the jurisdiction of the Melkite eparchy of Newton, Mass. (established as an exarchate, 1965; eparchy, 1976).

Romanians: There are approximately 5,000 in 16 Romanian Catholic Byzantine Rite parishes in the U.S., each under the jurisdiction of the Roman-Rite bishop of the territory in which it is located: Cleveland diocese (4 parishes), Detroit (2), Gary (2), Pittsburgh (1), Rockford (2), Trenton (2), and Youngstown (3). No separate statistics are available. The Association of Romanian Catholics of America (see Index) was established in 1948 to preserve the identity of Romanian Catholics within the general framework of the Catholic Church in America. It has petitioned the Holy See for a bishop of the rite in the U.S. In 1972, the Holy See assigned Msgr. Octavian Barlea as an apostolic visitor to Romanians in the U.S.

Byelorussians: Have one parish in the U.S. — Christ the Redeemer, Chicago, Ill. — and are under the jurisdiction of the local Roman-Rite bishop.

Russians: Have parishes in California (St. Andrew, El Segundo, and Our Lady of Fatima Center, San Francisco); Massachusetts (Our Lady of Kazan, Boston); New York (St. Michael's Chapel, Pope John XXIII Reunion Center). They are under the jurisdiction of local Roman-Rite bishops.

Antiochene Rite

In 1979, 30,600 (of approximately 153,000) Maronites were reported under the jurisdiction of the eparchy of St. Maron, Brooklyn (established at Detroit as an exarchate, 1966; eparchy, 1972; transferred to Brooklyn, 1977).

Armenian Rite

Have parishes in California (Our Lady Queen of Martyrs, Los Angeles); Massachusetts (Holy Cross, Cambridge); Michigan (St. Vartan, Detroit); New Jersey (Sacred Heart, Paterson); New York (Armenian Catholic Community, Forest Hills, Brooklyn). They are under the jurisdiction of local Roman-Rite bishops.

Chaldean Rite

Have parishes in California (St. Thomas the Apostle, Turlock); Illinois (St. Ephram, Chicago); and Michigan (Mother of God, Detroit). They are under the jurisdiction of local Roman-Rite bishops.

BYZANTINE DIVINE LITURGY

The Divine Liturgy in all rites is based on the consecration of bread and wine by the narration-reactualization of the actions of Christ at the Last Supper. Aside from this fundamental usage, there are differences between the Roman (Latin) Rite and Eastern Rites, and among the Eastern Rites themselves. Following is a general description of the Byzantine Divine Liturgy which is in widest use in the Eastern-Rite Churches.

In the Byzantine, as in all Eastern Rites, the bread and wine are prepared at the start of the Liturgy. The priest does this in a little niche or at a table in the sanctuary. Taking a round loaf of leavened bread stamped with religious symbols, he cuts out a square host and other particles while reciting verses expressing the symbolism of the action. When the bread and wine are ready, he says a prayer of offering and incenses the oblations, the altar, the icons and the people.

At the altar a litany for all classes of people is sung by the priest. The congregation answers, "Lord, have mercy."

The Little Entrance comes next. In procession, the priest leaves the sanctuary carrying the Book of the Gospels, and then returns. He sings prayers especially selected for the day and the feast. These are followed by the solemn singing of the prayer, "Holy God, Holy Mighty One, Holy Immortal One."

The Epistle follows. The Gospel is sung or read by the priest facing the people at the middle door of the sanctuary.

An interruption after the Liturgy of the Catechumens, formerly an instructional period for those learning the faith, is clearly marked. Catechumens, if present, are dismissed with a prayer. Following this are a prayer and litany for the faithful.

The Great Entrance or solemn Offertory Procession then takes place. The priest first says a long silent prayer for himself, in preparation for the great act to come. Again he incenses the oblations, the altar, the icons and people. He goes to the table on the gospel side for the veil-covered paten and chalice. When he arrives back at the sanctuary door, he announces the intention of the Mass in the prayer: "May the Lord God remember all of you in his kingdom, now and forever."

After another litany, the congregation recites the Nicene Creed.

Consecration

The most solemn portion of the sacrifice is introduced by the preface, which is very much like the preface of the Roman Rite. At the beginning of the last phrase, the priest raises his voice to introduce the singing of the Sanctus. During the singing he reads the introduction to the words of consecration.

The words of consecration are sung aloud, and the people sing "Amen" to both consecrations. As the priest raises the Sacred Species in solemn offering, he sings: "Thine of Thine Own we offer unto Thee in behalf of all and for all."

A prayer to the Holy Spirit is followed by the commemorations, in which special mention is made of the all-holy, most blessed and glorious Lady, the Mother of God and ever-Virgin Mary. The dead are remembered and then the living.

A final litany for spiritual gifts precedes the Our Father. The Sacred Body and Blood are elevated with the words, "Holy Things for the Holy." The Host is then broken and commingled with the Precious Blood. The priest recites preparatory prayers for Holy Communion, consumes the Sacred Species, and distributes Holy Communion to the people under the forms of both bread and wine. During this time a communion verse is sung by the choir or congregation.

The Liturgy closes quickly after this. The consecrated Species of bread and wine are removed to the side table to be consumed later by the priest. A prayer of thanksgiving is recited, a prayer for all the people is said in front of the icon of Christ, a blessing is invoked upon all, and the people are dismissed.

VESTMENTS, APPURTENANCES

Sticharion: A long white garment of linen or silk with wide sleeves and decorated with embroidery; formerly the vestment for clerics in minor orders, acolytes, lectors, chanters, and subdeacons; symbolic of purity.

Epitrachelion: A stole with ends sewn together, having a loop through which the head is passed; its several crosses symbolize priestly duties.

Zone: A narrow clasped belt made of the same material as the epitrachelion; symbolic of the wisdom of the priest, his strength against enemies of the Church and his willingness to perform holy duties.

Epimanikia: Ornamental cuffs; the right cuff symbolizing strength, the left, patience and good will.

Phelonion: An ample cape, long in the back and sides and cut away in front; symbolic of the higher gifts of the Holy Spirit.

Antimension: A silk or linen cloth laid on the altar for the Liturgy; it may be decorated with a picture of the burial of Christ and the instruments of his passion; the relics of martyrs are sewn into the front border.

Eileton: A linen cloth which corresponds to the Roman-Rite corporal.

Poterion: A chalice or cup which holds the wine and Precious Blood.

Diskos: A shallow plate, which may be elevated on a small stand, corresponding to the Roman-Rite paten.

Asteriskos: Made of two curved bands of gold or silver which cross each other to form a double arch; a star depends from the junction, which forms a cross; it is placed over the diskos holding the consecrated bread and is covered with a veil.

Veils: Three are used, one to cover the poterion, the second to cover the diskos, and the third to cover both.

Spoon: Used in administering Holy Communion by intinction; consecrated leavened bread is dipped into consecrated wine and spooned onto the tongue of the communicant.

Lance: A metal knife used for cutting up the bread to be consecrated during the Liturgy.

BYZANTINE FEATURES

Art: Named for the empire in which it developed, Byzantine art is a unique blend of imperial Roman and classic Hellenic culture with Christian inspiration. The art of the Greek Middle Ages, it reached a peak of development in the 10th or 11th century. Characteristic of its products, particularly in mosaic and painting, are majesty, dignity, refinement and grace. Its sacred paintings, called icons, are reverenced highly in all Eastern Rites.

Church Building: The classical model of Byzantine church architecture is the Church of the Holy Wisdom (Hagia Sophia), built in Constantinople in the first half of the sixth century and still standing. The square structure, extended in some cases in the form of a cross, is topped by a distinctive onion-shaped dome and surmounted by a triple-bar cross. The altar is at the eastern end of building, where the wall bellies out to form an apse. The altar and sanctuary are separated from the body of the church by a fixed or movable screen, the iconostas, to which icons or sacred pictures are attached (see below).

Clergy: The Byzantine Rite has married as well as celibate priests. In places other than the US, where married candidates have not been accepted for ordination since about 1929, men already married can be ordained to the diaconate and priesthood and can continue in marriage after ordination. Celibate deacons and priests cannot marry after ordination; neither can a married priest remarry after the death of his wife. Bishops must be unmarried.

Iconostas: A large screen decorated with sacred pictures or icons which separates the sanctuary from the nave of a church; its equivalent in the Roman Rite, for thus separating the sanctuary from the nave, is an altar rail.

An iconostas has three doors through which the sacred ministers enter the sanctuary during the Divine Liturgy: smaller (north and south) Deacons' Doors and a large central Royal Door.

The Deacons' Doors usually feature the icons of Sts. Gabriel and Michael; the Royal Door, the icons of the Evangelists — Matthew, Mark, Luke and John. To the right and left of the Royal Door are the icons of Christ the Teacher and of the Blessed Virgin Mary with the Infant Jesus. To the extreme right and left are the icons of the patron of the church and St. John the Baptist (or St. Nicholas of Myra).

Immediately above the Royal Door is a picture of the Last Supper. To the right are six icons depicting the major feasts of Christ, and to the left are six icons portraying the major feasts of the Blessed Virgin Mary. Above the picture of the Last Supper is a large icon of Christ the King.

Some icon screens also have pictures of the 12 Apostles and the major Old Testament prophets surmounted by a crucifixion scene.

Liturgical Language: In line with Eastern tradition, Byzantine practice has favored the use of the language of the people in the liturgy. Two great advocates of the practice were Sts. Cyril and Methodius, apostles of the Slavs, who devised the Cyrillic alphabet and pioneered the adoption of Slavonic in the liturgy.

Sacraments: Baptism is administered by immersion, and confirmation is conferred at the same time. The Eucharist is administered by intinction, i.e., by giving the communicant a piece of consecrated leavened bread which has been dipped into the consecrated wine. When giving absolution in the sacrament of penance, the priest holds his stole over the head of the penitent. Distinctive marriage ceremonies include the crowning of the bride and groom. Ceremonies for anointing the sick closely resemble those of the Roman Rite. Holy orders are conferred by a bishop.

Sign of the Cross: Eastern-Rite Catholics have a distinctive way of making it (see entry in the Glossary). The sign of the cross in conjunction with a deep bow, instead of a genuflection, expresses reverence for the presence of Christ in the Blessed Sacrament.

Theology: The theology of Eastern-Rite Churches is highly mystical and speculative, perhaps more so than that of the Western Church — with which it adheres firmly to the bases of Scripture and apostolic tradition.

SEPARATED EASTERN CHURCHES

Orthodox

Orthodox Churches, the largest and most widespread of the separated Eastern Churches, have much in common with their Eastern Catholic counterparts, including many matters of faith and morals, general discipline, valid orders and sacraments, and liturgy. One important difference is their acceptance of only the first seven ecumenical councils. Another is their rejection of any single supreme head of the Church. They do not acknowledge and hold communion with the pope.

Like their Catholic counterparts, Orthodox Churches are organized in jurisdictions under patriarchs. The patriarchs are the heads of approximately 15 autocephalic and several other autonomous jurisdictions organized along lines of nationality and/or language.

The Ecumenical Patriarch of Constantinople, Dimitrios I, has the primacy of honor among his equal patriarchs but his actual jurisdiction is limited to his own patriarchate. As the spiritual head of worldwide Orthodoxy, he keeps the book of the Holy Canons of the Autocephalous Churches, in which recognized Orthodox Churches are registered, and has the right to call Pan-Orthodox assemblies.

The definitive Orthodox break with Rome dates from 1054.

Top-level relations between the Churches have improved in recent years through the efforts of former Ecumenical Patriarch Athenagoras I, John XXIII, Paul VI and Patriarch Dimitrios I. Pope Paul met with Athenagoras three times before the latter's death in 1972. The most significant action of both spiritual leaders was their mutual nullification of excommunications imposed by the two Churches on each other in 1054.

The largest Orthodox body in the western hemisphere is the Greek Orthodox jurisdiction consisting of the Archdiocese of New York, nine dioceses in the U.S., and one diocese each in Canada and South America; it is headed by Archbishop Iakovos and has an estimated membership of 1.5 million. The second largest is the Orthodox Church in America, with approximately 850,000 members; it was given independent status by the Patriarchate of Moscow May 18, 1970, against the will of Athenagoras I who refused to register it in the book of the Holy Canons of Autocephalous Churches. An additional 650,000 or more Orthodox belong to smaller national and language jurisdictions.

Heads of Orthodox jurisdictions in this hemisphere hold membership in the Standing Conference of Canonical Orthodox Bishops in the Americas.

Jurisdictions

The principal jurisdictions of the Greek, Russian and other Orthodox Churches are as follows.

Greek: Patriarchate of Constantinople, with jurisdiction in Turkey, Crete, the Dodecanese, Western Europe, the Americas, Australia; Dimitrios I is Ecumenical Patriarch.

Patriarchate of Alexandria, with jurisdiction in Egypt and the rest of Africa; there is also a native African Orthodox Church in Kenya and Uganda.

Patriarchate of Antioch (Melkites or Syrian Orthodox), with jurisdiction in Syria, Lebanon, Iraq, Australasia, the Americas; Syrian or Arabic, in place of Greek, is the liturgical language.

Patriarchate of Jerusalem, with jurisdiction in Israel and Jordan.

Churches of Greece, Cyprus and Sinai are autocephalic but maintain relations with their fellow Orthodox.

Russian: Patriarchate of Moscow with jurisdiction centered in the Soviet Union.

Other: Patriarchate of Serbia, with jurisdiction in Yugoslavia, Western Europe, the Americas, Australasia.

Patriarchates of Rumania and Bulgaria.

Katholikate of Georgia, the Soviet Union.

Byelorussians and Ukrainian Byzantines.

Churches of Albania, China, Czechoslovakia, Estonia, Finland, Hungary, Japan, Latvia, Lithuania, Poland.

Other minor communities in various places; e.g., Korea, the US, Carpatho-Russia.

The Division of Archives and Statistics of the Eastern Orthodox World Foundation reported a 1970 estimate of more than 200 million Orthodox Church members throughout the world. Other sources estimate the total to be approximately 125 million.

Nestorians, Monophysites

Unlike the majority of Eastern Christian Churches, several bodies do not acknowledge all of the first seven ecumenical councils. Nestorians acknowledge only the first two councils; they do not accept the doctrinal definition of the Council of Ephesus concerning Mary as the Mother of God. Monophysite Armenians, Syrians, Copts, Ethiopians and Jacobites acknowledge only the first three councils; they do not accept the doctrinal definition of the Council of Chalcedon concerning the two natures in Christ.

The Armenian Church has communicants in the Soviet Union, the Middle and Far East, the Americas.

The Coptic Church has communicants in Egypt and elsewhere.

The Ethiopian or Abyssinian Church has communicants in Africa, the Middle East, the Americas, India.

The Jacobite Church (West Syrians) has communicants in the Middle East, the Americas, India.

Nestorians (Assyrians) are scattered throughout the world.

It is estimated that there are approximately 10 million or more members of these other Eastern Churches throughout the world. For various reasons, a more accurate determination is not possible.

Conference of Orthodox Bishops

The Standing Conference of Canonical Orthodox Bishops in the Americas was established in 1960 to achieve cooperation among the various ethnic churches.

Member churches of the conference are the: Albanian Orthodox Diocese of America (Ecumenical Patriarchate), American Carpatho-Russian Greek Catholic Diocese, Antiochian Orthodox Christian Archdiocese of New York and All North America, Bulgarian Eastern Orthodox Church, Greek Orthodox Church of North and South America, Orthodox Church in America, Romanian Orthodox Missionary Episcopate in America, Serbian Orthodox Church in the United States of America and Canada, Ukrainian Orthodox Church of America (Ecumenical Patriarchate), Holy Ukrainian Autocephalic Orthodox Church in Exile.

Patriarchs: High-ranking patriarchs of separated Eastern Churches are Ecumenical Orthodox Patriarch Dimitrios I (Papadopoulos) of Constantinople (Istanbul) and Coptic Orthodox Patriarch Shenouda III (Nazeer Gayed) of Alexandria.

New Orthodox Charter

The Greek Orthodox Archdiocese of North and South America, the largest Orthodox jurisdiction in the western hemisphere, announced a new charter of organization and procedure in June, 1978.

In effect since Sept. 1, the charter provided for one diocese each in Canada and South America, one archdiocese (New York) and seven dioceses in the United States (Boston, Charlotte, Chicago, Denver, Detroit, Pittsburgh and San Francisco). The jurisdictions, formerly districts under auxiliary bishops, are headed by diocesan bishops under the overall supervision of Archbishop Iakovos, presiding prelate of the Archdiocese of New York.

The charter also established a synod of bishops and prescribed norms for the selection of the archbishop and bishops.

EASTERN ECUMENISM

The Second Vatican Council, in the *Decree on Eastern Catholic Churches,* pointed out the special role they have to play "in promoting the unity of all Christians, particularly Easterners." The document also stated in part:

"The Eastern Churches in communion with the Apostolic See of Rome have a special role to play in promoting the unity of all Christians, particularly Easterners, according to the principles of this sacred Synod's *Decree on Ecumenism* first of all by prayer, then by the example of their lives, by religious fidelity to ancient Eastern traditions, by greater mutual knowledge, by collaboration, and by a brotherly regard for objects and attitudes" (No. 24).

"If any separated Eastern Christian should, under the guidance of grace of the Holy Spirit, join himself to Catholic unity, no more should be required of him than what a simple profession of the Catholic faith demands. A valid priesthood is preserved among Eastern clerics. Hence, upon joining themselves to the unity of the Catholic Church, Eastern clerics are permitted to exercise the orders they possess, in accordance with the regulations established by the competent authority" (No. 25).

"Divine Law forbids any common worship (*communicatio in sacris*) which would damage the unity of the Church, or involve formal acceptance of falsehood or the danger of deviation in the faith, of scandal, or of indifferentism. At the same time, pastoral experience clearly shows that with respect to our Eastern brethren there should and can be taken into consideration various circumstances affecting individuals, wherein the unity of the Church is not jeopardized nor are intolerable risks involved, but in which salvation itself and the spiritual profit of souls are urgently at issue.

"Hence, in view of special circumstances of time, place, and personage, the Catholic Church has often adopted and now adopts a milder policy, offering to all the means of salvation and an example of charity among Christians through participation in the sacraments and in other sacred functions and objects. With these considerations in mind, and 'lest because of the harshness of our judgment we prove an obstacle to those seeking salvation,' and in order to promote closer union with the Eastern Churches separated from us, this sacred Synod lays down the following policy:

"In view of the principles recalled above, Eastern Christians who are separated in good faith from the Catholic Church, if they ask of their own accord and have the right dispositions, may be granted the sacraments of penance, the Eucharist, and the anointing of sick. Furthermore, Catholics may ask for these same sacraments from those non-Catholic ministers whose Churches possess valid sacraments, as often as necessity or a genuine spiritual benefit recommends such a course of action, and when access to a Catholic priest is physically or morally impossible" (Nos. 26, 27).

"Again, in view of these very same principles, Catholics may for a just cause join with their separated Eastern brethren in sacred functions, things, and places" (No. 28).

"This more lenient policy with regard to common worship involving Catholics and their brethren of the separated Eastern Churches is entrusted to the care and execution of the local Ordinaries so that, by taking counsel among themselves and, if circumstances warrant, after consultation also with the Ordinaries of the separated Churches, they may govern relations between Christians by timely and effective rules and regulations" (No. 29).

EASTERN ECUMENICAL BRIEFS

Agreed Statement on the Church: Catholic and Orthodox theologians, meeting for their 10th consultation since 1966, issued an "Agreed Statement on the Church" Dec. 10, 1974. One of the central points in the statement was the difference of views regarding the position and status of the Pope and the Patriarch of Constantinople in the hierarchy of their churches.

The statement said:

"The Catholic Church recognizes that the position of Peter in the college of the Apostles finds visible expression in the Bishop of Rome who exercises those prerogatives defined by Vatican Council I within the whole church of Christ in virtue of this primacy.

"The Orthodox Church finds this teaching at variance with its understanding of primacy within the whole church. It appears to destroy the tension between independence and collegiality (in the universal and particular churches). For independence, a basic condition for collegiality, appears to be removed as a consequence of the jurisdictional teaching role attributed to the Patriarch of the West by Vatican Council I. The Orthodox believe that a necessary primacy in the church depends on the consent of the church and is at present exercised by the Patriarch of Constantinople.

"Our two traditions are not easily harmonized. Yet we believe that the Spirit is ever active to show us the way by which we can live together as one and many. We have the hope that we will be open to his promptings wherever they may lead."

The theological consultation was under the joint sponsorship of the U.S. Bishops' Committee for Ecumenical and Interreligious Affairs and the Standing Conference of Canonical Orthodox Bishops in America.

Orthodox Guidelines: A 66-page document entitled "Guidelines for Orthodox Churches in Ecumenical Relations" was published in February, 1974, by the Standing Conference of Canonical Orthodox Bishops in the Americas. Among the subjects of guidelines were:

• Marriage: Normally marriage in the Orthodox Church "takes place only between members of that Church." There are, however, occasions in which an Orthodox priest may perform a "mixed marriage," under certain conditions. Clergy of other churches may give a blessing or exhort a couple, but do not actually "assist" or "participate" in the marriage service.

• Baptism: Orthodox Churches accept baptism in the name of the Trinity in another church if "proof of the fact of baptism" can be authenticated.

• Eucharist: "Holy Communion will not be sought by Orthodox Christians outside the Church, nor will it be offered to those who do not confess the Orthodox Church as their mother."

• Reciprocity: The "principle of reciprocity" governs preaching in ecumenical situations, meaning that Orthodox priests may preach in non-Orthodox churches and non-Orthodox may speak in Orthodox churches.

Bishops and Presbyters: A document published in July, 1976, by the Orthodox-Roman Catholic Consultation in the U.S. Signatories indicated the following points of common understanding: (1) Ordination in apostolic succession is required for pastoral office in the Church. (2) Presiding at the Eucharistic celebration is a task belonging to those ordained to pastoral service. (3) The offices of bishop and presbyter are different realizations of the sacrament of order. (4) Those ordained are claimed permanently for the service of the Church. The statement noted that questions requiring serious study were the possible ordination of women, clerical celibacy, and the compatibility of certain occupations with pastoral office.

Principle of Economy: A statement issued by the same body at the same time, concerning God's plan and activity in human history for salvation. The concept of "economy" was not completely defined. It appeared that Orthodox understanding precludes recognition of the validity of the sacraments of other Christian churches.

Ministry: Ministry, especially that of bishop, was the principal subject under discussion at a meeting of an international group of Catholic and Orthodox theologians held in December, 1977, in Chambesy, Switzerland. In the context of a joint statement on the relationship between the incarnational and spiritual aspects of church life, they said: "There is no church of Christ without ministries of the Spirit, but there are no ministries without the church; hence, (there are) no ministries apart from or above the community" of the church.

Marriage: A statement entitled "The Sanctity of Marriage," issued in December, 1978, by the Eastern Orthodox-Roman Catholic Consultation in the U.S., acknowledged agreement about the sacramental nature and permanence of marriage while noting Orthodox positions regarding divorce (permitted in some circumstances) and validity (the marriage of Orthodox communicants must be blessed by an Orthodox priest).

Meetings

Procedural Questions: Members of the Inter-Orthodox Theological Commission, meeting June 20 to 25, 1977, near Geneva, discussed the possibilities of Catholic-Orthodox union and methods to be followed in future dialogue with a similar commission of Catholic theologians.

Similar discussion of procedural questions concerning official dialogue was the principal business of a meeting of representatives of the Catholic and Orthodox Churches held Mar. 29 to Apr. 1, 1978, at the Vatican.

Oriental Catholic Consultation: Dialogue between representatives of the Catholic Church and the Armenian Orthodox Church, in the planning stage since 1976, was expanded in February, 1978, to include representatives of other Oriental Orthodox Churches in the United States. Participating in the newly formed Oriental Orthodox-Roman Catholic Consultation were members of the Armenian Apostolic, Assyrian, Coptic, Ethiopian and Indian Malabar Churches.

Coptic Dialogue: Representatives of the Vatican Secretariat for Promoting Christian Unity and of the Coptic Orthodox Church met for the fourth time Mar. 13 to 18, 1978, in Cairo. Their discussions concerned the role of councils in the Church, the sacraments in relation to the Church and the economy of salvation, relations between the Churches, and the promotion of local contacts for the improvement of mutual relations.

Basis of Dialogue

Pope John Paul met June 23, 1979, with a delegation of the Coptic Orthodox Church of Alexandria headed by Shenouda III, pope of Alexandria and patriarch of the See of St. Mark. He said, in part:

"The Catholic Church bases its dialogue of truth and charity with the Coptic Orthodox Church on the principles proclaimed by the Second Vatican Council."

Similar views were expressed with respect to relations with the Greek Orthodox June 28, 1979, when the Pope met and exchanged greetings with Greek Orthodox Metropolitan Meliton at the Vatican.

Protestant Churches

Men, Doctrines, Churches of the Reformation

Some of the leading figures, doctrines and churches of the Reformation are covered below. A companion article covers Major Protestant Churches in the United States.

John Wycliff (c. 1320-1384): English priest and scholar who advanced one of the leading Reformation ideas nearly 200 years before Martin Luther — that the Bible alone is the sufficient rule of faith — but had only an indirect influence on the 16th century Reformers. Supporting belief in an inward and practical religion, he denied the divinely commissioned authority of the pope and bishops of the Church; he also denied the Real Presence of Christ in the Holy Eucharist, and wrote against the sacrament of penance and the doctrine of indulgences. Nearly 20 of his propositions were condemned by Gregory XI in 1377; his writings were proscribed more extensively by the Council of Constance in 1415. His influence was strongest in Bohemia and Central Europe.

John Hus (c. 1369-1415): A Bohemian priest and preacher of reform who authored 30 propositions condemned by the Council of Constance. Excommunicated in 1411 or 1412, he was burned at the stake in 1415. His principal errors concerned the nature of the Church and the origin of papal authority. He spread some of the ideas of Wycliff but did not subscribe to his views regarding faith alone as the condition for justification and salvation, the sole sufficiency of Scripture as the rule of faith, the Real Presence of Christ in the Eucharist, and the sacramental system. In 1457 some of his followers founded the Church of the Brotherhood which later became known as the United Brethren or Moravian Church and is considered the earliest independent Protestant body.

Martin Luther (1483-1546): An Augustinian friar, the key figure in the Reformation. In 1517, as a special indulgence was being preached in Germany, and in view of needed reforms within the Church, he published at Wittenberg 95 theses concerning matters of Catholic belief and practice. Leo X condemned 41 statements from Luther's writings in 1520. Luther, refusing to recant, was excommunicated the following year. His teachings strongly influenced subsequent Lutheran theology; its statements of faith are found in the Book of Concord (1580).

Luther's doctrine included the following:

The sin of Adam, which corrupted human nature radically (but not substantially), has affected every aspect of man's being. Justification, understood as the forgiveness of sins and the state of righteousness, is by grace for Christ's sake through faith. Faith involves not merely intellectual assent but an act of confidence by the will. Good works are indispensably necessary concomitants of faith, but do not merit salvation. Of the sacraments, Luther retained baptism, penance and the Holy Communion as effective vehicles of the grace of the Holy Spirit; he held that in the Holy Communion the consecrated bread and wine are the Body and Blood of Christ. The rule of faith is the divine revelation in the Sacred Scriptures. He rejected purgatory, indulgences and the invocation of the saints, and held that prayers for the dead have no efficacy.

Lutheran tenets not in agreement with Catholic doctrine were condemned by the Council of Trent.

Anabaptism: Originated in Saxony in the first quarter of the 16th century and spread rapidly through southern Germany. Its doctrine included several key Lutheran tenets but was not regarded with favor by Luther, Calvin or Zwingli. Anabaptists believed that baptism is for adults only and that infant baptism is invalid. Their doctrine of the Inner Light, concerning the direct influence of the Holy Spirit on the believer, implied rejection of Catholic doctrine concerning the sacraments and the nature of the Church. Eighteen articles of faith were formulated in 1632 in Holland. Mennonites are Anabaptists.

Ulrich Zwingli (1484-1531): A priest who triggered the Reformation in Switzerland with a series of New Testament lectures in 1519, later disputations and by other actions. He held the Gospel to be the only basis of truth; rejected the Mass (which he suppressed in 1525 at Zurich), penance and other sacraments; denied papal primacy and doctrine concerning purgatory and the invocation of saints; rejected celibacy, monasticism and many traditional practices of piety. His symbolic view of the Eucharist, which was at odds with Catholic doctrine, caused an irreconcilable controversy with Luther and his followers. Zwingli was killed in a battle between the forces of Protestant and Catholic cantons in Switzerland.

John Calvin (1509-1564): French leader of the Reformation in Switzerland, whose key tenet was absolute predestination of some persons to heaven and others to hell. He rejected Catholic doctrine in 1533 after becoming convinced of a personal mission to reform the Church. In 1536 he published the first edition of *Institutes of the Christian Religion,* a systematic exposition of his doctrine which became the classic textbook of Reformed — as distinguished from Lutheran — theology. To Luther's principal theses — regarding

Scripture as the sole rule of faith, the radical corruption of human nature, and justification by faith alone — he added absolute predestination, certitude of salvation for the elect, and the incapability of the elect to lose grace. His Eucharistic theory, which failed to mediate the Zwingli-Luther controversy, was at odds with Catholic doctrine. From 1555 until his death Calvin was the virtual dictator of Geneva, the capital of the non-Lutheran Reformation in Europe.

Arminianism: A modification of the rigid predestinationism of Calvin, set forth by acob Arminius (1560-1609) and formally stated in the *Remonstrance* of 1610. Arminianism influenced some Calvinist bodies.

Unitarianism: A 16th century doctrine which rejected the Trinity and the divinity of Christ in favor of a uni-personal God. It claimed scriptural support for a long time but became generally rationalistic with respect to "revealed" doctrine as well as in ethics and its world-view. One of its principal early proponents was Faustus Socinus (1539-1604), a leader of the Polish Brethren.

A variety of communions developed in England in the Reformation and post-Reformation periods.

Anglican Communion: This communion, which regards itself as the same apostolic Church as that which was established by early Christians in England, derived not from Reformation influences but from the renunciation of papal jurisdiction by Henry VIII (1491-1547). His Act of Supremacy in 1534 called Christ's Church an assembly of local churches subject to the prince, who was vested with fullness of authority and jurisdiction. In spite of Henry's denial of papal authority, this Act did not reject substantially other principal articles of faith. Notable changes, proposed and adopted for the reformation of the church, took place in the subsequent reigns of James VI and Elizabeth, with respect to such matters as Scripture as the rule of faith, the sacraments, the nature of the Mass, and the constitution of the hierarchy.

The Anglican Communion is called Episcopal because its prelates have the title and function of bishops. (See Anglican Orders.)

Puritans: Extremists who sought church reform along Calvinist lines in severe simplicity. (Use of the term was generally discontinued after 1660.)

Presbyterians: Basically Calvinistic, called Presbyterian because church polity centers around assemblies of presbyters or elders. John Knox (c. 1513-1572) established the church in Scotland.

Congregationalists: Evangelical in spirit and seeking a return to forms of the primitive church, they uphold individual freedom in religious matters, do not require the acceptance of a creed as a condition for communion, and regard each congregation as autonomous. Robert Browne influenced the beginnings of Congregationalism.

Quakers: Their key belief is in internal divine illumination, the inner light of the living Christ, as the only source of truth and inspiration. George Fox (1624-1691) was one of their leaders in England. Called the Society of Friends, the Quakers are noted for their pacificism.

Baptists: So called because of their doctrine concerning baptism. They reject infant baptism and consider only baptism by immersion as valid. Leaders in the formation of the church were John Smyth (d. 1612) in England and Roger Williams (d. 1683) in America.

Methodists: A group who broke away from the Anglican Communion under the leadership of John Wesley (1703-1791), although some Anglican beliefs were retained. Doctrines include the witness of the Spirit to the individual and personal assurance of salvation. Wesleyan Methodists do not subscribe to some of the more rigid Calvinistic tenets held by other Methodists.

Universalism: A product of 18th-century liberal Protestantism in England. The doctrine is not Trinitarian.

MAJOR PROTESTANT CHURCHES IN THE UNITED STATES

There are more than 250 Protestant church bodies in the United States.

The majority of U.S. Protestants belong to the following denominations: Baptist, Methodist, Lutheran, Presbyterian, Protestant Episcopal, the United Church of Christ, the Christian Church (Disciples of Christ), Holiness Sects.

See Ecumenical Dialogues, Briefs and related entries for coverage of relations between the Catholic Church and other Christian churches.

Baptist Churches
(Courtesy of the Division of Communication, American Baptist Churches in the U.S.A.)

Baptist churches, comprising the largest of all American Protestant denominations, were first established by John Smyth near the beginning of the 17th century in England. The first Baptist church in America was founded at Providence by Roger Williams in 1639.

Largest of the nearly 30 Baptist bodies in the U.S. are:

The Southern Baptist Convention, 460 James Robertson Parkway, Nashville, Tenn. 37219, with 13 million members;

The National Baptist Convention, U.S.A., Inc., 915 Spain St., Baton Rouge, La. 70802, with 6.5 million members;

The National Baptist Convention of

America, 954 Kings Rd., Jacksonville, Fla. 32204, with 2.6 million members.

The American Baptist Churches in the U.S.A., Valley Forge, Pa. 19481, with 1.5 million members.

The total number of U.S. Baptists is more than 29 million. The world total is 33 million.

Proper to Baptists is their doctrine on baptism. Called an "ordinance" rather than a sacrament, baptism by immersion is a sign that one has experienced and decided in favor of the salvation offered by Christ. It is administered only to persons who are capable of the experience of faith, which is the sole criterion of salvation and which involves the obligation to a life of virtue. Baptism is not administered to infants.

Baptists do not have a formal creed but generally subscribe to two professions of faith formulated in 1689 and 1832 and are in general agreement with classical Protestant theology regarding Scripture as the sole rule of faith, original sin, justification through faith in Christ, and the nature of the Church. Their local churches are autonomous.

Worship services differ in form from one congregation to another. Usual elements are the reading of Scripture, a sermon, hymns, vocal and silent prayer. The Lord's Supper, called an "ordinance," is celebrated at various intervals.

Methodist Churches

(Courtesy of Joe Hale, General Secretary of the World Methodist Council.)

John Wesley (1703-1791), an Anglican clergyman, was the founder of Methodism. In 1738, following a period of missionary work in America and strongly influenced by the Moravians, he experienced a new conversion to Christ and shortly thereafter became a leader in a religious awakening in England. By the end of the 18th century, Methodism was strongly rooted also in America.

The United Methodist Church, formed in 1968 by a merger of the Methodist Church and the Evangelical United Brethren Church, is the second largest Protestant denomination in the U.S., with 9.8 million members; its principal agencies are located in New York, Evanston, Ill., Nashville, Tenn., Washington, D.C. (Council of Bishops, 100 Maryland Ave. N.E. 20002), Dayton, O., and Lake Junaluska, N.C. (World Methodist Council, P.O. Box 518. 28745). The second largest body, with more than two million communicants, is the African Methodist Episcopal Church; its headquarters are located at 1724 Villa Place, Nashville. The four other major churches are the African Methodist Episcopal Zion, Christian Methodist Episcopal, Free Methodist Church and the Wesleyan Church. The total Methodist membership in the U.S. is about 14 million.

Worldwide, there are more than 60 autonomous Methodist/Wesleyan churches in 90 countries, with a membership of more than 20 million. All of them participate in the World Methodist Council, which gives global unity to the witness of Methodist communicants.

Methodism, although it has a base in Calvinistic theology, rejects absolute predestination and maintains that Christ offers grace freely to all men, not just to a select elite. Wesley's distinctive doctrine was the "witness of the Spirit" to the individual soul and personal assurance of salvation. He also emphasized the central themes of conversion and holiness. Methodists are in general agreement with classical Protestant theology regarding Scripture as the sole rule of faith, original sin, justification through faith in Christ, the nature of the Church, and the sacraments of baptism and the Lord's Supper. Church polity is structured along episcopal lines in America, with ministers being appointed to local churches by a bishop; churches stemming from British Methodism do not have bishops but vest appointive powers within an appropriate conference. Congregations are free to choose various forms of worship services; typical elements are readings from Scripture, sermons, hymns and prayers.

Lutheran Churches

(Courtesy of Tom Dorris, assistant director of the Lutheran News Bureau, 360 Park Ave. South, New York, N.Y. 10010.)

The origin of Lutheranism is generally traced to Oct. 31, 1517, when Martin Luther tacked "95 Theses" to the door of the castle church in Wittenberg, Germany. This call to debate on the subject of indulgences and related concerns has come to symbolize the beginning of the Reformation. Luther and his supporters intended to reform the Church they knew. Though Lutheranism has come to be visible in separate denominations and national churches, at its heart it professes itself to be a confessional movement within the one, holy, catholic and apostolic Church.

The world's 70 million Lutherans form the third largest grouping of Christians, following Roman Catholics and Eastern Orthodox. About 53 million belong to churches which make up the Lutheran World Federation, headquartered in Geneva; President Josiah Kibira is Bishop of the Northwest Diocese of The Evangelical Lutheran Church in Tanzania. Eight countries count more than one million Lutherans each: West Germany (23.2 million), United States (8.6 million), Sweden (8.0 million), East Germany (6.7 million), Denmark (4.7 million), Finland (4.6 million), Norway (3.8 million), Indonesia (1.7 million).

Numbering about nine million, Lutherans are the fourth largest grouping of North American Christians, exceeded by Roman Catholics, Baptists and Methodists. About 95 per cent of them belong to one of three denominations: Lutheran Church in America, three million members, 231 Madison Avenue, New York, N.Y. 10016; Lutheran Church-Missouri Synod, 2.7 million, 500 N. Broadway, St. Louis, Mo. 63102; American Lutheran Church, 2.4 million, 422 S. Fifth St., Minneapolis, Minn. 55415.

In addition, there are about a dozen other smaller Lutheran denominations in North America. The three largest are: Wisconsin Evangelical Lutheran Synod, 400,000 members, 3512 W. North Ave., Milwaukee, Wis. 53208; the Association of Evangelical Lutheran Churches, 110,000, 12015 Manchester Rd., St. Louis, Mo. 63131; Evangelical Lutheran Church of Canada, 82,000, 247 First Ave. North, Saskatoon, Saskatchewan S7K 4H5. (This is the only independent Canadian denomination; most other Canadian Lutherans belong to the Lutheran Church in America or the Missouri Synod.)

The three large bodies and the Association of Evangelical Lutheran Churches form the Lutheran Council in the U.S.A., a cooperative agency for work in theological studies; communication; research and planning; institutional, military and campus ministry; governmental affairs; higher education; immigration and refugee services; youth agency relations; American Indian concerns; domestic disaster relief and other social ministries. The council's main offices are at 360 Park Ave. South, New York, N.Y. 10010. A similar organization, the Lutheran Council in Canada, is headquartered at 500-365 Hargrave St., Winnipeg, Manitoba R3B 2K3.

The Lutheran Church in America, the American Lutheran Church and the Association of Evangelical Lutheran Churches also form Lutheran World Ministries, the U.S. agency of the Lutheran World Federation, headquartered at 360 Park Ave. South, New York, N.Y. 10010. Its Canadian counterpart is the Canadian National Committee of the Lutheran World Federation, headquartered at 500-365 Hargrave St., Winnipeg, Manitoba R3B 2K3.

The statements of faith which have shaped the confessional life of Lutheranism are found in the *Book of Concord*. This 1580 collection includes the three ancient ecumenical creeds (Apostles', Nicene and Athanasian), Luther's *Large and Small Catechisms* (1529), the *Augsburg Confession* (1530) and the *Apology* in defense of it (1531), the *Smalcald Articles* (including the "Treatise on the Power and Primacy of the Pope") (1537), and the *Formula of Concord* (1577).

The central Lutheran doctrinal proposition is that Christians "receive forgiveness of sins and become righteous before God by grace, for Christ's sake."

Baptism and the Lord's Supper (Holy Communion, the eucharist) are universally celebrated among Lutherans as sacramental means of grace in which the Word and promise of God are made visible by being bound to earthly elements — water, bread and wine. In baptism, a person is reborn and by God's gracious action is made a member of the Church catholic. Likewise, the eucharist celebrates and re-presents God's gracious action. With the body and blood of Christ — "in, with, and under" the bread and wine — come the gifts of life, salvation, forgiveness.

Lutherans also treasure the Word proclaimed in the reading of the Scriptures, preaching from the pulpit, and pronouncement of absolution. The Word read and preached is always part of the celebration of the sacrament of the altar. Absolution is usually imparted generally, but it may also be given individually in connection with private confession.

Although it was not the wish of the early Lutherans to deny the bishop's place as the ordinary minister of ordination, the general unwillingness of 16th century bishops to ordain Lutheran pastors led to the usual Lutheran system of presbyteral rather than episcopal ordination. Lutherans are concerned to preserve apostolic succession in life and doctrine, and generally concede the value, though not the necessity, of ordination by bishops.

Marriage and confirmation continue as non-sacramental rites among Lutherans. Confirmation has been generally connected with first communion, though recent years have seen a tendency to separate the two. In the U.S., the tendency is to have first communion around grade-five age, though infant communion is not unknown. Confirmation, sometimes called affirmation of the baptismal covenant, generally occurs during the junior high school years, slightly younger than in European practice.

Lutheran jurisdictions corresponding to dioceses are called districts or synods in North America. There are more than 100 of them on the continent. Because they relate to different national denominations, more than one of these jurisdictions includes the same geographic area. The head of a district or synod, chosen by lay and clergy delegates to a convention, is known as a bishop or a president, depending on the denomination and jurisdiction. The terms "diocese" and "bishop" are more common among European Lutherans and Asian, African and Latin American Lutherans whose roots derive from European missionary efforts.

A visitor to a North American Lutheran parish would generally find adornments, vestments, church calendars and an order of service similar to that of many Episcopal or Roman Catholic congregations. Though the Reformers continued to celebrate the eucharist every Sunday and on other special days, Lutherans strayed from their confessional norm under various historical and philosophic influences. The North American practice has until recent years been monthly celebration. Weekly celebration is increasingly common and is generally stressed as the desired practice by Lutheran liturgical and sacramental theologians. Lutherans generally like to sing in worship, and successive generations have built up a rich tradition of church music and hymnody. A new North American *Lutheran Book of Worship* was introduced in 1978.

Presbyterian Churches

(Courtesy of Gerald W. Gillette, United Presbyterian Church in the U.S.A.; and Office of the General Assembly, Presbyterian Church in the United States.)

Presbyterians are so called because of their type of church government, by presbyters or elders.

Presbyterianism was founded on Reformed (as distinguished from Lutheran) theological positions laid down by John Calvin. Countries in which it acquired early strength and influence were Switzerland, France, Holland, Scotland and England.

Presbyterianism spread widely in this country in the latter part of the 18th century and afterwards. Presently, it has approximately 4.5 million communicants in nine bodies. The largest of these are:

The United Presbyterian Church in the U.S.A., 475 Riverside Drive, New York, N.Y. 10027, with 2.6 million members. This body was formed May 28, 1958, by a merger of the Presbyterian Church in the U.S.A and the United Presbyterian Church of North America.

The Presbyterian Church in the United States, 341 Ponce de Leon Avenue N.E., Atlanta, Ga. 30308, with about 900,000 members.

In Presbyterian doctrine, baptism and the Lord's Supper, viewed as seals of the covenant of grace, are regarded as sacraments. Baptism, which is not necessary for salvation, is conferred on infants and adults. The Lord's Supper is celebrated as a covenant of the Sacrifice of Christ.

The Church is twofold, being invisible and also visible; it consists of all of the elect and all those Christians who are united in Christ as their immediate head.

Presbyterians are in general agreement with classical Protestant theology regarding Scripture as the sole rule of faith, original sin, and justification through faith in Christ.

Presbyterian congregations are governed by elders and ministers. On higher levels there are presbyteries, synods and a general assembly with various degrees of authority over local bodies.

Worship services, simple and dignified, include sermons, prayer, reading of the Scriptures and hymns. The Lord's Supper is celebrated at intervals.

Doctrinal developments of the past several years included approval in May, 1967, by the General Assembly of the United Presbyterian Church of a contemporary confession of faith to supplement the historic Westminster Confession. The new confession emphasizes the commitment of the Church and its members to reconciliatory and apostolic works in society.

Protestant Episcopal Church

(Courtesy of Charles M. Guilbert, Custodian of the Standard Book of Common Prayer.)

The Protestant Episcopal Church, also officially known as the Episcopal Church, regards itself as the same apostolic church as that which was established by early Christians in England. It was established in this country during the Revolutionary period. Its constitution and Prayer Book were adopted at a general convention held in 1789. It has approximately 3 million members.

Offices of the U.S. executive council are located at 815 Second Ave., New York, N.Y. 10017.

This church, which belongs to the Anglican Communion, subscribes to the branch theory of the Church of Christ, holding that it consists of the Church of Rome, the Eastern Orthodox Church, and the Anglican Communion, and that the heads of these churches are of equal rank in authority.

Worldwide, the Anglican Communion has 26 independent provinces. The chief prelate is the Archbishop of Canterbury.

There is considerable variety in Protestant Episcopal beliefs and practices. Official statements of belief and practice are found in the Apostles' Creed, the Nicene Creed and the Book of Common Prayer, but interpretation is not uniform. Scripture has primary importance with respect to the rule of faith, and some authority is attached to tradition.

All seven sacraments, veneration of the saints, and a great many other Catholic teachings are accepted by some Episcopalians but contested by others.

An episcopal system of church government prevails, but clergymen of lower rank and lay persons also have an active voice in ecclesiastical affairs. The levels of government are the general convention, the executive council, territorial provinces and dioceses, and local parishes. At the parish level, the congregation has the right to select its own rector or pastor.

Liturgical worship is according to the Book of Common Prayer as established (1928) or proposed (1976), but ceremonial practices correspond with the doctrinal positions of the various congregations and range from a ceremony similar to the Roman Mass to services of a less elaborate character.

United Church of Christ

(Courtesy of Joseph H. Evans, secretary of the United Church of Christ.)

The 1,769,104-member United Church of Christ was formed in 1957 by a union of the Congregational Christian and the Evangelical and Reformed Churches. The former was originally established by the Pilgrims and the Puritans of the Massachusetts Bay Colony, while the latter was founded in Pennsylvania in the early 1700's by settlers from Central Europe. The denomination has 6,502 congregations throughout the United States.

It considers itself "a united and uniting church" and keeps itself open to all ecumenical options.

Its headquarters are located at 297 Park Ave., South, New York, N.Y. 10010.

Its statement of faith recognizes Jesus Christ as "our crucified and risen Lord (who) shared our common lot, conquering sin and death and reconciling the world to himself." It believes in the life after death, and the fact that God "judges men and nations by his righteous will declared through prophets and apostles."

The United Church further believes that Christ calls its members to share in his baptism "and eat at his table, to join him in his passion and victory." Ideally, according to its Lord's Day Service, Communion is to be celebrated weekly. Like other Calvinistic bodies, it believes that Christ is spiritually present in the sacrament.

The United Church is governed along congregational lines, and each local church is autonomous. However, the actions of its biennial General Synod are taken with great seriousness by congregations. Between synods, a 43-member executive council oversees the work of the church.

Christian Church (Disciples of Christ)

(Courtesy of Robert L. Friedly, Executive Director, Office of Communication.)

The Christian Church (Disciples of Christ) originated early in the 1800's from two movements against rigid denominationalism led by Presbyterians Thomas and Alexander Campbell in western Pennsylvania and Barton W. Stone in Kentucky. The two movements developed separately for about 25 years before being merged in 1832.

The church, which identifies itself with the Protestant mainstream, now has approximately 1.3 million members in the U.S. and Canada. The greatest concentration of members in the U.S. is located roughly along the old frontier line, in an arc sweeping from Ohio and Kentucky through the Midwest and down into Oklahoma and Texas.

The general offices of the church are located at 222 South Downey Ave., Box 1986, Indianapolis, Ind. 46206.

The church's persistent concern for Christian unity is based on a conviction expressed in a basic document, *Declaration and Address,* dating from its founding. The document states: "The church of Christ upon earth is essentially, intentionally and constitutionally one."

The Disciples have no official doctrine or dogma. Their worship practices vary widely from more common informal services to what could almost be described as "high church" services. Membership is granted after a simple statement of belief in Jesus Christ and baptism by immersion; many congregations admit un-immersed transfers from other denominations. The Lord's Supper, generally called Communion, is always open to Christians of all persuasions. Lay men and women routinely preside over the Lord's Supper, which is celebrated each Sunday; they often preach and perform other pastoral functions as well. Distinction between ordained and non-ordained members is blurred somewhat because of the Disciples' emphasis on all members of the church as ministers.

The Christian Church is oriented to congregational government, and has a unique structure in which three levels of polity (general, regional and congregational) operate as equals rather than in a pyramid of authority. At the national or international level, it is governed by a general assembly which has voting representation direct from congregations and regions as well as all ordained clergy.

The Holiness Sects

Perfectionist, Pentecostal and a variety of Evangelical churches and sects have a large membership in the U.S.

These groups do not form a denomination in the strict sense of the term, since they are separate and have their own particular characteristics. Classification under a common heading is possible, however, because they all share the same general spirit and spring from a common origin. John Wesley's teaching on justification is the doctrinal thread common to all of these churches — personal holiness, realized in the life of each individual, is the key to a full Christian life. Hence the name, "Holiness Movement." Its origin is traceable to the revival movement of the 19th century.

The Perfectionist branch of this large group includes such foundations as the Church of the Nazarene, the Church of God (Anderson, Ind.), and the Pilgrim Holiness Church. On the Pentecostal side are the Assemblies of God, the numerous Churches of God, and many bodies with the word Pentecostal in their titles. There are also many other very small cults which are similar in spirit to the larger churches.

Ecumenism

The modern ecumenical movement, which started about 1910 among Protestants and led to formation of the World Council of Churches in 1948, developed outside the mainstream of Catholic interest for many years. It has now become for Catholics as well one of the great religious facts of our time.

The magna charta of ecumenism for Catholics is a complex of several documents which include, in the first place, the *Decree on Ecumenism* promulgated by the Second Vatican Council Nov. 21, 1964. Other enactments underlying and expanding this decree are the *Dogmatic Constitution on the Church,* the *Decree on Eastern Catholic Churches,* and the *Pastoral Constitution on the Church in the Modern World.*

VATICAN II DECREE

The following excerpts from the *Decree on Ecumenism* cover the broad theological background and principles and indicate the thrust of the Church's commitment to ecumenism.

"... Men who believe in Christ and have been properly baptized are brought into a certain, though imperfect, communion with the Catholic Church. Undoubtedly, the differences that exist in varying degrees between them and the Catholic Church — whether in doctrine and sometimes in discipline, or concerning the structure of the Church — do indeed create many and sometimes serious obstacles to full ecclesiastical communion. These the ecumenical movement is striving to overcome . . ." (No. 3).

Elements Common to Christians

"Moreover some, even very many, of the most significant elements or endowments which together go to build up and give life to the Church herself can exist outside the visible boundaries of the Catholic Church: the written word of God; the life of grace; faith, hope, and charity, along with other interior gifts of the Holy Spirit and visible elements. All of these, which come from Christ and lead back to Him, belong by right to the one Church of Christ" (No. 3).

[In a later passage, the decree singled out a number of elements which the Catholic Church and other churches have in common but not in complete agreement: confession of Christ as Lord and God and as mediator between God and man; belief in the Trinity; reverence for Scripture as the revealed word of God; baptism and the Lord's Supper; Christian life and worship; faith in action; concern with moral questions.]

"The brethren divided from us also carry out many of the sacred actions of the Christian religion. Undoubtedly, in ways that vary according to the condition of each Church or Community, these actions can truly engender a life of grace, and can be rightly described as capable of providing access to the community of salvation.

"It follows that these separated Churches and Communities, though we believe they suffer from defects already mentioned, have by no means been deprived of significance and importance in the mystery of salvation. For the Spirit of Christ has not refrained from using them as means of salvation which derive their efficacy from the very fullness of grace and truth entrusted to the Catholic Church" (No. 3).

Unity Lacking

"Nevertheless, our separated brethren, whether considered as individuals or as Communities and Churches, are not blessed with that unity which Jesus Christ wished to bestow on all those whom He has regenerated and vivified into one body and newness of life — that unity which the holy Scriptures and the revered tradition of the Church proclaim. For it is through Christ's Catholic Church alone, which is the all-embracing means of salvation, that the fullness of the means of salvation can be obtained. It was to the apostolic college alone, of which Peter is the head, that we believe our Lord entrusted all the blessings of the New Covenant, in order to establish on earth the one Body of Christ into which all those should be fully incorporated who already belong in any way to God's People . . ." (No. 3).

What the Movement Involves

"Today, in many parts of the world, under the inspiring grace of the Holy Spirit, multiple efforts are being expended through prayer, word, and action to attain that fullness of unity which Jesus Christ desires. This sacred Synod, therefore, exhorts all the Catholic faithful to recognize the signs of the times and to participate skillfully in the work of ecumenism.

"The 'ecumenical movement' means those activities and enterprises which, according to various needs of the Church and opportune occasions, are started and organized for the fostering of unity among Christians. These are:

- "First, every effort to eliminate words, judgments, and actions which do not respond to the condition of separated brethren with truth and fairness and so make mutual relations between them more difficult.

- "Then, 'dialogue' between competent experts from different Churches and Communities (scholarly ecumenism). . . .

- "In addition, these Communions cooperate more closely in whatever projects a Christian conscience demands for the common good (social ecumenism).

• "They also come together for common prayer, where this is permitted (spiritual ecumenism).

• "Finally, all are led to examine their own faithfulness to Christ's will for the Church and, wherever necessary, undertake with vigor the task of renewal and reform.

"... It is evident that the work of preparing and reconciling those individuals who wish for full Catholic communion is of its nature distinct from ecumenical action. But there is no opposition between the two, since both proceed from the wondrous providence of God" (No. 4).

Primary Duty of Catholics

"In ecumenical work, Catholics must assuredly be concerned for their separated brethren, praying for them, keeping them informed about the Church, making the first approaches towards them. But their primary duty is to make an honest and careful appraisal of whatever needs to be renewed and achieved in the Catholic household itself, in order that its life may bear witness more loyally and luminously to the teachings and ordinances which have been handed down from Christ through the apostles.

"... Every Catholic must ... aim at Christian perfection (cf. Jas. 1:4; Rom. 12:1-2) and, each according to his station, play his part so that the Church ... may daily be more purified and renewed, against the day when Christ will present her to Himself in all her glory, without spot or wrinkle (cf. Eph. 5:27).

"... Catholics must joyfully acknowledge and esteem the truly Christian endowments from our common heritage which are to be found among our separated brethren....

"Nor should we forget that whatever is wrought by the grace of the Holy Spirit in the hearts of our separated brethren can contribute to our own edification. Whatever is truly Christian never conflicts with the genuine interests of the faith; indeed, it can always result in a more ample realization of the very mystery of Christ and the Church ..." (No. 4).

Participation in Worship

Norms concerning participation by Catholics in the worship of other Christian Churches were sketched in this conciliar decree and elaborated in a number of other documents such as: the *Decree on Eastern Catholic Churches,* promulgated by the Second Vatican Council in 1964; *Interim Guidelines for Prayer in Common,* issued June 18, 1965, by the US Bishops' Committee for Ecumenical and Inter-Religious Affairs; a *Directory on Ecumenism,* published in 1967 by the Vatican Secretariat for Promoting Christian Unity; additional communications from the US Bishops' Committee, and numerous sets of guidelines issued locally by and for dioceses throughout the US.

The norms encourage common prayer services for Christian unity and other intentions. Beyond that, they draw a distinction between separated churches of the Reformation tradition and separated Eastern churches, in view of doctrine and practice the Catholic Church has in common with the latter concerning the apostolic succession of bishops, holy orders, liturgy, and other credal matters.

Full participation by Catholics in official Protestant liturgies is prohibited, because it implies profession of the faith expressed in the liturgy. Intercommunion by Catholics at Protestant liturgies is prohibited. Under certain conditions, Protestants may be given Holy Communion in the Catholic Church (see Intercommunion). A Catholic may stand as a witness, but not as a sponsor, in baptism, and as a witness in the marriage of separated Christians. Similarly, a Protestant may stand as a witness, but not as a sponsor, in a Catholic baptism, and as a witness in the marriage of Catholics.

Separated Eastern Churches

The principal norms regarding liturgical participation with separated Eastern Christians are included under Eastern Ecumenism.

ECUMENICAL AGENCIES

Vatican Secretariat

The top-level agency for Catholic ecumenical efforts is the Vatican Secretariat for Promoting Christian Unity, which originated in 1960 as a preparatory commission for the Second Vatican Council. Its purposes are to provide guidance and, where necessary, coordination for ecumenical endeavor by Catholics, and to establish and maintain relations with representatives of other Christian Churches for ecumenical dialogue and action.

The secretariat, first under the direction of Cardinal Augustin Bea, S. J., and now of Cardinal Johannes Willebrands, has established firm working relations with representative agencies of other churches and the World Council of Churches. It has joined in dialogue with Orthodox Churches, the Anglican Communion, the Lutheran World Federation, the World Alliance of Reformed Churches, the World Methodist Council and other religious bodies. In the past several years, staff members and representatives of the secretariat have been involved in one way or another in nearly every significant ecumenical enterprise and meeting held throughout the world, including the Fifth General Assembly of the World Council of Churches.

While the secretariat and its counterparts in other churches have focused primary attention on theological and other related problems of Christian unity, they have also begun, and in increasing measure, to emphasize the responsibilities of the churches for greater unity of witness and effort in areas of humanitarian need.

Bishops' Committee

The U.S. Bishops' Committee for Ecumenical and Interreligious Affairs was established by the American hierarchy in 1964. Its purposes are to maintain relationships with other Christian churches and other religious communities at the national level, to advise and assist dioceses in developing and applying ecumenical policies, and to maintain liaison with corresponding Vatican offices — the Secretariats for Christian Unity and Non-Christian Religions.

This standing committee of the National Conference of Catholic Bishops is chaired by Bishop Bernard F. Law of Springfield-Cape Girardeau. Operationally, the committee is assisted by the Rev. John F. Hotchkin, director; the Rev. J. Peter Sheehan, associate director; Dr. Eguene J. Fisher, executive secretary of the Secretariat for Catholic-Jewish Relations; the Rev. John B. Sheerin, consultant for Catholic-Jewish Relations.

The committee co-sponsors several national consultations with other churches and confessional families. These bring together on a regular basis Catholic representatives and their counterparts from the American Baptist Convention, the Christian Church (Disciples of Christ), the Episcopal Church, the Lutheran World Federation (U.S. Committee), the United Methodist Church, the Orthodox Churches, the Oriental Orthodox Churches, the Alliance of Reformed Churches (North American area), the Interfaith Witness Department of the Home Mission Board of the Southern Baptist Convention. Reports of consultations conducted under committee auspices are published periodically and are available through the Publications Office of the U.S. Catholic Conference. (See Ecumenical Dialogues.)

The committee relates with the National Council of Churches of Christ, through membership in the Faith and Order Commission and through observer relationship with the Commission on Regional and Local Ecumenism, and has sponsored a joint study committee investigating the possibility of Roman Catholic membership in that body.

Advisory and other services are provided by the committee to ecumenical commissions and agencies in dioceses throughout the country.

Through the Secretariat for Catholic-Jewish Relations, the committee is in contact with several national Jewish agencies and bodies. Issues of mutual interest and shared concern are reviewed for the purpose of furthering deeper understanding between the Catholic and Jewish communities.

Through the Secretariat for Non-Christians, moderated by Cardinal William W. Baum of Washington, the committee promotes activity in wider areas of dialogue. The Rev. John F. Hotchkin serves as executive secretary for this secretariat.

Offices of the committee are located at 1312 Massachusetts Ave. N.W., Washington, D.C. 20005.

World Council

The World Council of Churches is a fellowship of churches which acknowledge "Jesus Christ as Lord and Savior." It is a permanent organization providing constituent members — nearly 300 churches with some 450 million communicants in 100 countries — with opportunities for meeting, consultation and cooperative action with respect to doctrine, worship, practice, social mission, evangelism and missionary work, and other matters of mutual concern.

The WCC was formally established Aug. 23, 1948, in Amsterdam with ratification of a constitution by 147 communions. This action merged two previously existing movements — Life and Work (social mission), Faith and Order (doctrine) — which had initiated practical steps toward founding a fellowship of Christian churches at meetings held in Oxford, Edinburgh and Utrecht in 1937 and 1938. A third movement for cooperative missionary work, which originated about 1910 and, remotely, led to formation of the WCC, was incorporated into the council in 1971 under the title of the International Missionary Council (World Mission and Evangelism).

Four additional general assemblies of the council have been held since the charter meeting of 1948: in Evanston, Ill. (1954), New Delhi, India (1961), Uppsala, Sweden (1968) and Nairobi, Kenya (1975).

Between assemblies, the council operates through a central committee which meets every 12 or 18 months, and an executive committee which meets every six months.

The council continues the work of the International Missionary Council, the Commission on Faith and Order, and the Commission on Church and Society. The structure of the council has three program units: Faith and Witness, Justice and Service, Education and Communication.

Liaison between the council and the Vatican has been maintained since 1966 through a joint working group. Roman Catholic membership in the WCC is a question officially on the agenda of this body. The Joint Commission on Society, Development and Peace (SODEPAX) is an agency of the council and the Pontifical Commission for Justice and Peace. Roman Catholics serve individually as full members of the Commission on Faith and Order and in various capacities on other program committees of the council.

WCC headquarters are located in Geneva, Switzerland. The United States Conference for the World Council of Churches at 475 Riverside Drive, New York, N.Y. 10027, provides liaison between the U.S. churches and Geneva. The WCC also maintains fraternal relations with regional, national and local councils of churches throughout the world.

The Rev. Philip A. Potter, a Methodist from the Island of Dominica, West Indies, was elected secretary general of the WCC in August, 1972.

WCC presidents are: Ms. Annie Jiagge, Ghana; the Rev. J. Miguez-Bonino, Argentina; General T. B. Simatupang, Indonesia; Archbishop O. Sundby, Sweden; Dr. Cynthia Wedel, U.S.A.; His Holiness Ilia, patriarch of the Gregorian Orthodox Church, S.S.R.

National Council

The National Council of the Churches of Christ U.S.A., the largest ecumenical organization in the United States, is a cooperative federation of 32 Protestant, Orthodox and Anglican church bodies having about 40 million members.

The NCCC, established by the churches in 1950, was structured through the merger of 12 separate cooperative agencies. Presently, through three main program divisions and five commissions, the NCCC carries on work in behalf of member churches in home and overseas missions, Christian education, communications, disaster relief and rehabilitation, family life, stewardship, regional and local ecumenism, and other areas.

Policies of the NCCC are determined by a governing board of approximately 250 members appointed by the constituent churches. The governing board meets twice a year.

The NCCC's annual budget approximates $29 million, about 75 per cent of which is devoted to compassionate ministries of aid and relief to victims of disasters and endemic poverty in lands overseas.

The president and general secretary, respectively, are Rev. M. William Howard and Dr. Claire Randall.

NCCC headquarters are located at 475 Riverside Drive, New York, N.Y. 10027.

Consultation

The Consultation on Church Union, officially begun in 1962, is a venture of American churches seeking a united church "truly catholic, truly evangelical, and truly reformed." The churches engaged in this process, representing 25 million Christians, are the African Methodist Episcopal Church, the African Methodist Episcopal Zion Church, the Christian Church (Disciples of Christ), the Christian Methodist Episcopal Church, the Episcopal Church, the Presbyterian Church in the United States, the United Church of Christ, the United Methodist Church, and the United Presbyterian Church in the U.S.A. The National Council of Community Churches joined the COCU in 1976.

From 1970 to 1973 the member churches studied the first draft of a plan of union for the proposed Church of Christ Uniting. The responses to this plan, on the one hand, gave evidence of an historic consensus on faith, worship, and ministry; on the other hand, they revealed the need for mature involvement in order to discover the structures of a united church. The 11th plenary at Memphis, April, 1973, called for a future agenda involving the congregations more intimately, explored divisive factors such as racism, and affirmed the doctrinal and liturgical rapprochement already achieved. An affirmation of mutual recognition of membership was accepted and sent to the churches at the 12th plenary held at Cincinnati Nov. 4 to 8, 1974. At the 1976 plenary meeting, six chapters of "an emerging consensus" as a "theological basis for union" were approved for study by COCU members.

Two experimental liturgies, "An Order of Worship for The Proclamation of the Word of God and The Celebration of the Lord's Supper With Commentary" (1968) and "An Order for Holy Baptism" (1973), have been developed. An ecumenical lectionary has also been produced. Another series of eucharistic texts was published in 1978. The 1979 plenary accepted a series of questions to be posed to each church arising out of the mutual recognition of members, and moved ahead on a draft agreement on the ordained ministry.

The general secretary of COCU is the Rev. Gerald F. Moede. The Rev. Rachel Henderlite was elected president in November, 1976.

Offices are located at 228 Alexander St., Princeton, N.J. 08540.

ECUMENICAL DIALOGUES

(Source: Bishops' Committee for Ecumenical and Interreligious Affairs, National Conference of Catholic Bishops.)

Following is a list of principal consultations, from Mar. 16, 1965, involving representatives of the U.S. Catholic Bishops' Committee for Ecumenical and Interreligious Affairs and representatives of other Christian Churches, with names of the churches, places and dates of meetings, and the subject matter of discussions.

Baptist Convention, American (Division of Cooperative Christianity): (1) De Witt, Mich., Apr. 3, 1967 — American Baptist and Roman Catholic dialogue; a Baptist view of areas of theological agreement. (2) Green Lake, Wis., Apr. 29, 1968 — Baptism and confirmation; Christian freedom and ecclesiastical authority. (3) Schiller Park, Ill., Apr. 28, 1969 — Nature and communication of grace; Christian freedom and ecclesiastical authority; baptism and confirmation.

(4) Atchison, Kan., Apr. 17, 1970 — Role of the Church, resume of years past and the future; Roman Catholic-American Baptist dialogues; observations concerning bilateral ecumenical conversations and the future course of American Baptist-Roman Catholic conversations.

(5) Detroit, Mich., Apr. 23 to 24, 1971 — Theological perspective on clergy and lay issues and relations; theology of the local church; growth in understanding. (6) Liberty, Mo., Apr. 14 to 15, 1972 — Relationships between Church and State.

Baptists, Southern (Ecumenical Institute, Wake Forest University): (1) Winston-Salem, N.C., May 8, 1969 — Impact of biblical criticism on Roman Catholicism and contemporary Christianity in general; holy use of the world; creeds and the Faith; liturgy and spontaneity in worship; retreat, revival and monasticism; world view of ecumenism.

(2) St. Benedict, La., Feb. 4, 1970 — Liturgy and spontaneity in worship; perspectives on Baptist views on Scripture and tradition; the priesthood of all Christians; authority of the Old Testament; Baptist concepts of the Church; retreat, revival and monasticism. (3) Louisville, Ky., May 13, 1970 — The priesthood of all Christians; the ecumenical tide — a pastoral perspective; the enduring meaning of the Old Testament; retreat, revival and monasticism.

(4) Daytona Beach, Fla., Feb. 1 to 3, 1971 — Issues and answers, prepared by the Interfaith Witness Department of the Home Mission Board, Southern Baptist Convention. (5) Houston, Tex., Oct. 16 to 18, 1972 — Second regional conference planned in conjunction with the Interfaith Witness Department.

(6) Marriottsville, Md., Feb. 4 to 6, 1974 — Third regional conference, planned in conjunction with the Interfaith and Witness Department, concerning different types of reform and their appropriateness at different levels of church life. (7) Menlo Park, Calif., Oct. 27 to 29, 1975 — Fourth regional conference. The theme: "Conversion to Christ and Life-Long Growth in the Spirit."

(8) Winston-Salem, N.C., Nov. 10-12, 1975 — Fraternal dialogue, planned in conjunction with the Ecumenical Institute of Wake Forest University and Belmont Abbey College, on the abortion issue in Christian perspective, with publication of a statement and proceedings.

(9) Winston-Salem, N.C., Nov. 3-5, 1976 — Dialogue, planned as above, on Church-state issues, with publication of a statement and proceedings.

(10) Kansas City, Mo., Nov. 28 to 30, 1977 — Fifth regional conference on the theme, "The Theology and Experience of Worship."

(11) Cincinnati, O., Apr. 28 to 30, 1978 — Inauguration of a scholars' dialogue, with presentation of papers on the Church in the New Testament and the experience of God in the Church.

(12) Cincinnati, O., Nov. 3 to 5, 1978 — Roman Catholicism in the U.S.A., an historical perspective; Southern Baptist experience in America; overviews of each tradition by the other; the local congregation or church.

(13) St. Louis, Mo., Apr. 20 to 22, 1979 — Salvation as understood and taught in both traditions.

Christian Church, Disciples of Christ (Council on Christian Unity): (1) Indianapolis, Ind., Mar. 16, 1967 — A look at Disciples for Catholics. (2) Kansas City, Mo., Sept. 25, 1967 — Roman Catholic view of the nature of unity being sought; opportunities in the contemporary ecumenical movement. (3) St. Louis, Mo., Apr. 29, 1968 — Eucharistic sharing.

(4) Washington, D.C., Oct. 16, 1968 — Disciple of Christ inquiry regarding the sacramentality of marriage; pastoral reflections on mixed marriage. (5) New York, N.Y., Apr. 25, 1969 — Recognition and reconciliation of ministries; theological presuppositions concerning ministry among the Disciples; role of the priest in the Catholic community.

(6) Columbus, O., Nov. 3 to 5, 1970 — The parish concept in a plan of union (Consultation on Church Union); directions emerging in Catholic parish life. (7) New York, N.Y., June 8 to 10, 1971 — Disciples' theology of baptism; meaning of baptism as liberation, incorporation, empowerment.

(8) Indianapolis, Ind., Mar. 8 to 10, 1972 — Ministry of healing and reconciliation as practiced in the two communities. (9) Madison, Wis., June 26 to 28, 1972 — Review and summary of five years of dialogue; planning for future themes.

(10) Pleasant Hill, Shaker Town, Ky., May 22 to 24, 1973 — The Church in the New Testament.

(11) Indianapolis, Ind., Jan. 5-6, 1977 — Planning session, with the Council on Christian Unity of the Christian Church and the International Disciples Ecumenical Consultative Council, for a five-year consultation on the topic, "Apostolicity and Catholicity in the Visible Unity of the Church."

(12) Indianapolis, Ind., Sept. 22 to 27, 1977 — First session of a new and international consultation on the nature of the Church and elements of unity relating to it from New Testament and historical perspectives.

(13) Rome, Italy, Dec. 9 to 14, 1978 — Baptism, gift and call in the search for unity; study of various modes of baptism.

Episcopal (The Anglican-Roman Catholic Consultation, Joint Commission on Ecumenical Relations): (1) Washington, D.C., June 22, 1965 — Preliminary discussions. (2)

Kansas City, Mo., Feb. 2, 1966 — Eucharist as source or expression of community; Eucharist as sign and cause of unity, and the Church as a Eucharistic fellowship.

(3) Providence, R.I., Oct. 10, 1966 — Function of the minister in Eucharistic celebration; minister of the Eucharist. (4) Milwaukee, Wis., May 2, 1967 — Eucharist. (5) Jackson, Miss., Jan. 5, 1968 — Various aspects of the ministerial priesthood and the priesthood of the faithful in Eucharistic celebration; the priest's place and function in the Church's mission of service; the laity in Episcopal Church government.

(6) Liberty, Mo., Dec. 2, 1968 — Directions of the ecumenical movement; episcopal symbol of unity in the Christian community; collegiality; Citizens for Educational Freedom; a layman's view of jurisdictional and cultural factors in division; Church and society in contemporary America.

(7) Boynton Beach, Fla., Dec. 8, 1969 — All in each place; toward the reconciliation of the Roman Catholic Church and Churches of the Anglican Communion; an approach to designing a Roman Catholic-Episcopal parish; preparation of joint statement on the meeting. (8) Green Bay, Wis., June 17, 1970 — Is the (COCU — Consultation on Church Union) plan of union truly Catholic, with special reference to the priest and the episcopacy?; Anglican-Roman Catholic dialogue — achievement and prognostication.

(9) St. Benedict, La., Jan. 26 to 29, 1971 — The primacy of jurisdiction of the Roman Pontiff according to the First Vatican Council; the teaching of the Second Vatican Council concerning the hierarchy of truths; analysis of the ground of "Church Elements: An Ecclesiological Investigation."

(10) Liberty, Mo., June 20 to 23, 1971 — Gift of infallibility; sharing in the teaching authority of the Church; official view of episcopacy in the Episcopal Church in the USA; symposium on Hans Kung's *Infallibility? An Inquiry*; dogma as an ecumenical problem; Revelation and statement in Anglicanism; revised working paper on theological truth, propositions and Christian unity; reflections on the teaching ministry of the Church.

(11) New York, N.Y., Jan 20 to 24, 1972 — Theological truth, propositions and Christian unity; the Protestant Episcopal Church's view of authority, tradition and the Bible; a comment on the Windsor "Statement of Eucharistic Agreement" issued by the International Anglican-Roman Catholic Consultation.

(12) Cincinnati, O., June 12 to 15, 1972 — The notion of *typos* and *typoi* as applied to the forms of the Christian Church; correspondences and differences in the Anglican and Roman Catholic understanding and exercise of teaching authority.

(13) Cincinnati, O., Mar. 18 to 22, 1973 — Formulation of a preliminary draft on the purpose of the Church. (14) Vicksburg, Miss., Jan. 6 to 10, 1974 — Formulation of a response to the "Canterbury Statement" of the International Anglican-Roman Catholic Consultation on ministry and ordination; discussion and amendment of a draft on the purpose of the Church; other subjects in a continuing dialogue on the mission of the Church.

(15) Cincinnati, O., Nov. 10 to 13, 1974 — Discussion on the nature of authority in Anglicanism and Roman Catholicism. Report prepared on the purpose of the Church. (16) Cincinnati, O., June 22 to 25, 1975 — Special ad hoc consultation on women and orders.

(17) Erlanger, Ky., Oct. 21-24, 1975 — Continuation of discussion on women and orders, with release of joint statement on the ordination of women. (18) Overland Park, Kan., Mar. 10-13, 1976 — Continuation of discussion on authority in the Church.

(19) New Orleans, La., Jan. 19-22, 1977 — Presentation and discussion of a paper entitled "Some Implications of a 'Communio Ecclesiology' for the Authority Question"; formulation of an initial response to the "Venice Statement" (see separate entry); near completion of a 12-year report on the consultation.

(20) Cincinnati, O., Aug. 9 to 12, 1977 — Preparation of a second response to the Venice Statement, "Authority in the Church," and of a 12-year report, "Where We are: A Challenge for the Future" (planned for publication). (21) Savannah, Ga., Mar. 7 to 10, 1978 — Christian anthropology and discussion of issues raised by the topic of the 12-year report in dialogue.

(22) Cincinnati, O., Jan. 3 to 6, 1979 — Christian anthropology in the patristic period and documents of the Second Vatican Council on the subject; New Testament arguments for and against the ordination of women.

Lutheran, U.S.A. (National Committee of the Lutheran World Federation): (1) Baltimore, Md., Mar. 16, 1965 — Exploratory discussion. (2) Baltimore, Md., July 6, 1965 — Nicene Creed as dogma of the Church. (3) Chicago, Ill., Feb. 10, 1966 — Baptism, in the context of the New Testament; Lutheran understanding; teaching of the Council of Trent.

(4) Washington, D.C., Sept. 22, 1966 — Eucharist as sacrifice, in traditional and contemporary Catholic and Lutheran contexts. (5) New York, N.Y., Apr 7, 1967 — Propitiation and five presentations on various aspects of the Eucharist. (6) St. Louis, Mo., Sept. 29, 1967 — Eucharist. (7) New York, Mar. 8, 1968 — Intercommunion, with respect to Catholic discipline, Lutheran practice, and theological reflections.

(8) Williamsburg, Va., Sept. 27, 1968 — Ministry; the competent minister of the Eu-

charist; scriptural foundations of diakonia (ministry of service). (9) San Francisco, Calif., Feb. 21, 1969 — Apostolic succession in the patristic era and in a contemporary view; Lutheran view of the validity of Lutheran orders; Christian priesthood in the light of documents of the Second Vatican Council.

(10) Baltimore, Md., Sept. 26, 1969 — The minister of the Eucharist, according to the Council of Trent; the use of "Church" as applied to Protestant denominations in the documents of Vatican II; Lutheran doctrine of the ministry — Catholic and Reformed; the ordained minister and layman in Lutheranism. (11) St. George, Bermuda, Feb. 19, 1970 — Preparation of joint statement on the ministry.

(12) New York, N.Y., May, 1970. (13) Chicago, Ill., Oct. 30 to Nov. 1, 1970. (14) Miami, Fla., Feb. 19 to 22, 1971 — Peter and the New Testament; the papacy in the late patristic era, Middle Ages, Renaissance; text of the *Dogmatic Constitution on the Church* (Vatican II) with respect to the papacy and infallibility.

(15) Seabury, Conn., Sept. 24 to 27, 1971 — An investigation of the concept of divine right *(jus divinum);* teaching of the First Vatican Council on primacy and infallibility; a Lutheran understanding of what papal primacy in the Church might mean.

(16) New Orleans, La., Feb. 18 to 21, 1972 — Further discussion of the concept of divine right; ecumenical projections concerning the Petrine office; teaching authority in the Lutheran Church. (17) Minneapolis, Minn., Sept. 22 to 25, 1972 — Further investigation of the Petrine function; councils and conciliarism.

(18) San Antonio, Tex., Feb. 16 to 19, 1973 — Discussion of work and papers of the Petrine panel concerning ministry and the Church universal, Catholic and Lutheran interpretive statements; work on papal primacy papers. (19) Allentown, Pa., Sept. 21 to 24, 1973 — Work on a joint statement concerning ministry and the Church universal, the concluding session on this topic; selection of infallibility as the next topic for consideration. (20) Marriottsville, Md., Feb. 15 to 17, 1974 — Start of discussion on infallibility; commissioning of 16 future research papers.

(21) Princeton, N.J., Sept. 19 to 22, 1974 — Scriptural studies re infallibility, inquiries into the teachings of early Lutheranism. (22) St. Louis, Mo., Jan. 30 to Feb. 2, 1975 — Historical and systematic studies of the teaching of infallibility. (23) Washington, D.C., Apr. 2 to 3, 1975 — Special meeting of several Lutheran presidents and Catholic bishops to review the work of the scholars' consultation and propose future directions. Press report issued.

(24) Washington, D.C. Sept. 17 to 21, 1975 — Further historical and case studies re infallibility: ecumenical councils and Marian definitions. (25) Scottsdale, Ariz., Feb. 19 to 22, 1976 — Infallibility discussion continued.

(26) Washington, D.C., Apr. 2-3, 1975 — Meeting of Lutheran presidents and Catholic bishops to evaluate the direction and progress of Lutheran-Catholic dialogue in the U.S., with release of a joint statement. (27) Washington, D.C., Feb. 4-5, 1976 — Continuation of discussion concerning the direction and progress of dialogue.

(28) Gettysburg, Pa., Sept. 15-18, 1976 — Presentation of papers entitled: "Draft I — Authority and Doctrine," "The Roman View of the Petrine Office in the Church 366-461," "The Status of the Nicene Creed as Dogma in the Church," "Ecumenical Methodology — Report of Task Force."

(29) Washington, D.C., Feb. 16-20, 1977 — Discussion of the second draft of a common statement; presentation of a "Note on the Papacy as an Object of Faith."

(30) Columbia, S.C., Sept. 14 to 18, 1977 — Continued discussion of the common statement, "Infallibility and Teaching Authority in the Church." (31) Lantana, Fla., Feb. 15 to 19, 1978 — Discussion on the fourth draft of a comon statement reporting the findings of dialogue on infallibility.

(32) Minneapolis, Minn., Sept. 13 to 17, 1978 — Statement on infallibility produced. (33) Cincinnati, O., Feb. 14 to 18, 1979 — Beginning of study of justification. (34) Princeton, N.J., Sept. 13 to 16, 1979 — Further study of justification.

Methodist (United Methodist Church): (1) Chicago, Ill., June 28, 1966 — Methodists and Roman Catholics: comments for Catholic-Methodist conversation. (2) Chicago, Ill., Dec. 18, 1966 — Salvation, faith and good works; Catholic Church and faith. (3) Lake Junaluska, N.C., June 28, 1967 — Roman Catholic position regarding the Spirit in the Church; mission of the Holy Spirit, in the light of the Second Vatican Council's *Dogmatic Constitution on the Church* and the writings of John Wesley.

(4) New York, N.Y., Dec. 17, 1967 — Three generations of Church-State argumentation. (5) San Antonio, Tex., Sept. 30, 1968 — Shared convictions about education. (6) Delaware, O., Oct. 9, 1969 — Major Methodist ecumenical documents; an appraisal of some documents of Vatican II; racial confrontation in Roman Catholicism, Methodism and the National Council of Churches. (7) Chicago, Ill., Jan. 30, 1970 — Review and planning.

(8) Washington, D.C., Dec. 16, 1970 — Completion of a statement of shared convictions about education. Task force meetings during 1971. (9) Cincinnati, O., Feb. 25 to 26, 1972 — Ministry in the United Methodist Church and the spirituality of the ordained

ministry; problems of ministry. (10) Dayton, O., Oct. 13 to 14, 1972 — Dialogue on the holiness of the Church and Christian holiness.

(11) Washington, D.C., Mar. 9 to 10, 1973 — Spirituality of the ministry. (12) Washington, D.C., Nov. 1 to 2, 1973 — Start of preparatory work on a consensus statement on spirituality of the ministry.

(13) Washington, D.C., Jan. 30 to Feb. 2, 1975 — Report prepared on Catholic and United Methodist understandings of holiness and spirituality in the ordained ministry; statement on holiness and spirituality of the ordained ministry released in January, 1976.

(14) Washington, D.C., May 16, 1977 — Planning session for the next round of dialogue.

(15) Washington, D.C., Dec. 4 to 6, 1977 — New phase of dialogue on the Eucharist in both traditions. (16) Marriottsville, Md., Apr. 16 to 18, 1978 — Continuing research on Eucharistic theology as developed in the two churches.

(17) Washington, D.C., Oct. 12 to 14, 1978 — Eucharistic practice in both traditions. (18) Marriottsville, Md., May 17 to 19, 1979 — The Eucharist; contemporary eucharistic devotional practices of both traditions.

Orthodox (Standing Conference of Canonical Orthodox Bishops of America): Sept. 9, 1965 — Preliminary discussions. (1) New York, N.Y., Sept. 29, 1966 — Consultation led to appointment of task forces to investigate differences in theological methods, questions of sacramental sharing, possible cooperation in theological education and the formation of seminarians. (2) Worcester, Mass., May 5, 1967 — Theological diversity and unity; intercommunion; common witness in theological education. (3) Maryknoll, N.Y., Dec. 7, 1968 — Eucharist and Church; indissolubility of marriage; cooperation in theological education.

(4) Worcester, Mass., Dec. 12, 1969 — Orthodox and Catholic views of the Eucharist and membership in the Church; an agreed statement on the Eucharist. (5) New York, N.Y., May 19, 1970 — New Order of the Mass; membership of schismatics and heretics in the ancient Church; current legislation of the Catholic Church and current practices of the Greek Orthodox Church concerning common worship; current legislation of the Catholic Church concerning mixed marriages; Orthodox view of mixed marriages; an agreed statement on mixed marriages.

(6) Brookline, Mass., Dec. 4, 1970 — Ministers, doctrine and practice of matrimony in Eastern and Western traditions. (7) Barlin Acres, Mass., Nov. 3 to 4, 1971 — Ethical issues relating to marriage; revision of an agreed statement on mixed marriages; the primacy of Rome as seen by the Eastern Church.

(8) New York, N.Y., Dec. 6, 1973 — Study of a draft statement on the sanctity of marriage. (9) Washington, D.C., May 23 to 24, 1974 — Dialogical process; witness of the Church on the American scene; approval of an agreed statement on respect for life; Orthodox and Catholic views of contemporary Orthodoxy and Catholicism.

(10) New York, N.Y., Dec. 9 to 10, 1974 — Prepared and issued an agreed statement on the Church. (11) Washington, D.C., May 19 to 20, 1975 — Dialogue on the local church and on the theology of priesthood. (12) New York, N.Y., Jan. 23 to 24, 1976 — Further dialogue on the theology of priesthood, et al.

(13) Washington, D.C., May 18-19, 1976 — Additional discussion of theology of the priesthood, and ecumenical councils; release of joint statements entitled "The Principle of Economy" and "The Pastoral Office."

(14) Brookline, Mass., Jan. 13-14, 1977 — Presentations on "Orthodox/Roman Catholic Marriages Revisited" and of two reports on the first pre-synodal Pan-Orthodox Conference in preparation for the coming Great and Holy Council.

(15) Washington, D.C., Sept. 28 to 29, 1977 — Presentation and discussion of papers concerning the agenda of the forthcoming Great and Holy Council of the Orthodox Church, the theology of marriage and Orthodox-Roman Catholic marriages.

(16) New York, N.Y., Jan. 24 to 25, 1978 — Preparation of a common statement on the sanctity of marriage, authorization for writing a history of the Orthodox-Roman Catholic Consultation.

(17) Washington, D.C., May 15 to 16, 1978 — Additional work on a common statement on the sanctity of marriage, and initial discussion concerning the religious upbringing of children in Orthodox-Catholic marriages.

(18) New York, N.Y., Dec. 7 to 8, 1978 — Study of the religious formation of children of marriages between Eastern Orthodox and Roman Catholics; release of "An Agreed Statement on the Sanctity of Marriage."

(19) Washington, D.C., Mar. 15 to 16, 1979 — Continued study of a draft entitled "Joint Recommendations on the Spiritual Formation of Children of Marriages between Orthodox and Roman Catholics."

Orthodox, Oriental (Armenian, Coptic, Ethiopian, Indian Malabar and Syrian Orthodox Churches): (1) New York N.Y., Jan. 27, 1978 — Start of a new consultation, with initial consideration of a historical study of Oriental Orthodoxy.

(2) New York, N.Y., May 26 to 27, 1978 — Purpose and method of dialogue; histories of Oriental Orthodox Churches. (3) Washington, D.C., Dec. 1 to 2, 1978 — Presentation of papers on the Council of Chalcedon, Christology and the Church today, concluding that ancient controversy over Christology

does not seem to apply at the present time. (4) New York, N.Y., May 25 to 26, 1979 — Roman Catholic Christology; Eucharistic Liturgy of the Syrian Orthodox Church.

Presbyterian and Reformed (The Roman Catholic-Presbyterian Consultation Group, North American Council of the World Alliance of Reformed Churches): (1) Washington, D.C., July 27, 1965 — Exploratory discussions. (2) Philadelphia, Pa., Nov. 26, 1965 — Role of the Holy Spirit in renewal and reform of the Church. (3) New York, May 12, 1966 — Roman Catholic view of Scripture and tradition; apostolic and ecclesiastical tradition.

(4) Chicago, Ill., Oct. 27, 1966 — Development of doctrine; dialogue, a program of peace, prayer and study for Roman Catholics and Protestants. (5) Collegeville, Minn., Apr. 26, 1967 — Order and ministry in the Reformed tradition; validity of orders; changes in mixed marriage. (6) Lancaster, Pa., Oct. 26, 1967 — Work was begun on a joint statement on ministry. (7) Bristow, Va., May 9, 1968 — Structures and ministries. (8) Allen Park, Mich., Oct. 24, 1968 — Marriage. (9) Charleston, S.C., May 21, 1969 — Validation of ministries and ministry; theological view of marriage.

(10) Macatawa, Mich., Oct. 30, 1969 — Apostles and apostolic succession in the patristic era; report concerning office; divorce and remarriage as understood in the United Presbyterian Church in the USA; the Church and second marriage; recommendations for changes regarding inter-Christian marriages. (11) Morristown, N.J., May 13, 1970 — Joint statements on ministry in the Church and women in Church and society.

(12) Princeton, N.J., Oct. 29 to 30, 1970 — Episcopal/presbyteral polity; episcopacy. (13) Columbus, O., May 13 to 15, 1971 — Ministry in the Church; man-woman relationships; the future of the Church. (14) Richmond, Va., Oct. 28 to 30, 1971 — Reports finalized on women in the Church and ministry in the Church. (15) Oct. 26 to 29, 1972 — The shape of the unity we seek.

(16) Columbus, O., May 30 to June 2, 1973 — Theological and sociological views of the shape of unity we seek. (17) Columbus, O., Oct. 24 to 27, 1973 — Renewed discussion of the previous topic. (18) Columbus, O., May 8 to 11, 1974 — Further discussion of the previous topic in the light of Scripture, tradition, theology and reflection on the total Christian experience; worship and belief; discussion of plans for publication of a book on progress of the dialogue.

(17) Cincinnati, O., Oct. 24 to 26, 1974 — Dialogue on the unity we seek in worship and in structures. (18) Washington, D.C., May 22 to 24, 1975 — Report prepared on the mission and nature of the one Church of Christ, with attention to the unity sought in worship, in structure and in common faith.

(19) Princeton, N.J., Oct. 20-23, 1976 — Presentation of: an overview of the history of the consultation; a paper covering a Roman Catholic summary of the diversity and unity of current Christian responses to moral issues facing the Church; a paper on ethics and ethos in the Reformed/Presbyterian tradition.

(20) Washington, D.C., May 25 to 27, 1977 — Human rights, distributive justice and the abortion issue as faced by the churches. (21) Princeton, N.J., Oct. 6 to 7, 1977 — Discussion of racism in South Africa and continuation of a study on human rights.

(22) Washington, D.C., May 30 to June 1, 1978 — Study of the problem of unwanted pregnancies; preparation of statements on abortion and human rights. (23) Washington, D.C., Mar. 4 to 6, 1979 — Re-drafting of proposed statements on abortion and human rights.

ECUMENICAL BRIEFS

Statements: The ecumenical statements listed below, and others like them, reflect the views of participants in the dialogues which produced them. They have not been formally accepted by the respective churches as formulations of doctrine or points of departure for practical changes in discipline.

• The "Windsor Statement" on Eucharistic doctrine, published Dec. 31, 1971, by the Anglican-Roman Catholic International Commission of theologians. (For text, see pages 132-33 of the 1973 *Catholic Almanac*.)

• The "Canterbury Statement" on ministry and ordination, published Dec. 13, 1973, by the same commission (For excerpts, see pages 127-30 of the 1975 *Catholic Almanac*.)

• "Papal Primacy / Converging Viewpoints," published Mar. 4, 1974, by the dialogue group sanctioned by the U.S.A. National Convention of the World Lutheran Federation and the U.S. Bishops' Committee for Ecumenical and Interreligious Affairs. (For excerpts, see pages 130-31 of the 1975 *Catholic Almanac*.)

• An "Agreed Statement on the Purpose of the Church," published Oct. 31, 1975, by the Anglican-Roman Catholic Consultation in the U.S., in which the signatories agreed on the purpose and mission of the Church "insofar as it faithfully preaches the Gospel of salvation and manifests the love of God in service." It noted that "Roman Catholics and Episcopalians believe that there is but one Church of Christ," and endorsed social action for human liberation.

• "Christian Unity and Women's Ordination," published Nov. 7, 1975, by the same consultation, in which it was said that the ordination of women (approved in principle by the Anglican Communion but not by the

Catholic Church) would "introduce a new element" in dialogue but would not mean the end of consultation nor the abandonment of its declared goal of full communion and organic unity. (A similar view was expressed in an exchange of letters between Pope Paul and Anglican Archbishop Donald Coggan of Canterbury, between July 8, 1975, and Mar. 23, 1976.)

• "Holiness and Spirituality of the Ordained Ministry," issued early in 1976 by theologians of the Catholic Church and the United Methodist Church; the first statement resulting from dialogue begun in 1966.

• "Mixed Marriages," published in the spring of 1976 by the Anglican-Roman Catholic Consultation in the U.S. It was similar in some respects to the statement, "Implementation of the Apostolic Letter on Mixed Marriages," approved by the National Conference of Catholic Bishops Nov. 16, 1970. It differed in softening the statement of a Catholic party's responsibility to do everything possible to raise children in the Catholic faith and favored greater freedom for having the marriage ceremony according to the rite of another Christian church.

• "Bishops and Presbyters," see under Eastern Ecumenical Briefs.

• "The Principle of Economy," see under Eastern Ecumenical Briefs.

• "Venice Statement" on authority in the Church, published Jan. 20, 1977, by the Anglican-Roman Catholic International Commission of theologians. Its major headings were Christian authority, authority of the ordained ministry and of the community, authority in the community of churches, the primacy of the bishop of Rome, authority in matters of faith, conciliar and primatial authority. Differences were cited in Catholic and Anglican views with respect to scriptural passages related to claims of the Roman See to primacy of authority, the divine right of the successors of St. Peter, papal infallibility and universal jurisdiction over the Church.

• "Response to the Venice Statement," issued Jan. 4, 1978, by the Anglican-Roman Catholic Consultation in the U.S.A., citing additional questions regarding the sharing of authority in the Church, the nature of the primacy of Rome, and the relation of indefectibility to infallibility.

• "The Presence of Christ in Church and World," published early in 1978 by representatives of the Vatican Secretariat for Promoting Christian Unity and the World Alliance of Reformed Churches. The wide-ranging statement noted considerable degrees of mutual understanding and some agreement, along with substantial differences of view on several subjects — especially papal infallibility.

• "An Ecumenical Approach to Marriage," published in January, 1978, in the form of a report on five or more years of dialogue among representatives of the Catholic Church, the Lutheran World Federation and the World Alliance of Reformed Churches. Significant agreement was reported on doctrinal and pastoral aspects of marriage. Objections continued from the Lutheran and Reformed sides, however, with respect to the sacramental nature of marriage, and to Catholic requirements in cases of mixed marriages: (1) that the marriage normally take place with a priest as the officiating minister, and (2) that the Catholic party promise to do everything possible to raise children in the Catholic faith.

• "Teaching Authority and Infallibility in the Church," released in October, 1978, by the Catholic-Lutheran dialogue group in the U.S., noting similarities and differences between Lutheran understanding of the indefectibility of the Church and the Catholic doctrine of papal infallibility.

• "The Eucharist," reported early in 1979, in which the Roman Catholic-Lutheran Commission indicated developing convergence of views concerning the nature and sacrificial aspect of the Mass, and the significance of believing, active participation in the Eucharist.

• "The Holy Spirit," issued Feb. 12, 1979, by the International Catholic-Methodist Commission, citing points of common faith in the Holy Spirit.

Models of Unity: Ways of approaching Christian unity were under study at a meeting Mar. 15 to 21, 1976, in Liebfrauenberg, France, of the Joint Working Group of theologians co-sponsored by the Lutheran World Federation and the Vatican Secretariat for Promoting Christian Unity. The models were those keyed to the concepts of: organic union (advocated by church union movements), conciliar fellowship (in the manner of the World Council of Churches), concord (as among Lutherans and Reformed Christians), reconciled diversity (as among world confessional families), and sister churches (as in dialogue among Catholics, Orthodox and Anglicans).

Mutual Christian witness by members of different religious bodies, through pastoral and social service, is also considered a way of moving toward the goal of Christian unity.

Evaluation Wanted: Members of the Vatican Secretariat for Promoting Christian Unity, at a plenary meeting Nov. 13 to 18, 1978, called for "an evaluation, in some official way," of documents produced in recent years by bilateral consultations between representatives of the Catholic Church and other religions. Discussed during the meeting were: documents on the Eucharist, ministry and authority produced by the Anglican-Roman Catholic International Commission (see above); the "Malta Report" on the Church and the Gospel which concluded the first phase of consultations with the Lutheran World Federation; the report, "The Presence of Christ in the Church and in the World" (see above); two reports published in consultations with the World Methodist Council; the final report on the first phase of dialogue with Pentecostal churches; dialogue with the Coptic Orthodox Church of Egypt.

Ecumenical Cooperation: The Committee on Society, Development and Peace, jointly sponsored by the Vatican and the World Council of Churches, announced in February, 1979, that its mandate had been extended for three years, through 1981. During that time, the committee reported it would undertake case studies of ecumenical social cooperation throughout the world. The agency was established in 1968.

Reappraisal Sought: The Anglican-Roman Catholic International Commission issued a statement June 7, 1979, in which it called for a reappraisal by the Catholic Church of the papal bull *Apostolicae Curae*, issued by Leo XIII in 1896, which declared Anglican orders null and void.

CATHOLIC-JEWISH RELATIONS

The Second Vatican Council, in addition to the *Decree on Ecumenism* concerning the movement for unity among Christians, stated the mind of the Church on a similar matter in a *Declaration on the Relationship of the Church to Non-Christian Religions*. This document, as the following excerpts indicate, backgrounds the reasons and directions of the Church's regard for the Jews. (Other portions of the document, not cited here, refer to Hindus, Buddhists and Moslems.)

Spiritual Bond

"As this sacred Synod searches into the mystery of the Church, it recalls the spiritual bond linking the people of the New Covenant with Abraham's stock.

"For the Church of Christ acknowledges that, according to the mystery of God's saving design, the beginnings of her faith and her election are already found among the patriarchs, Moses, and the prophets. She professes that all who believe in Christ, Abraham's sons according to faith (cf. Gal. 3:7), are included in the same patriarch's call, and likewise that the salvation of the Church was mystically foreshadowed by the Chosen People's exodus from the land of bondage.

"The Church, therefore, cannot forget that she received the revelation of the Old Testament through the people with whom God in His inexpressible mercy deigned to establish the Ancient Covenant. Nor can she forget that she draws sustenance from the root of that good olive tree onto which have been grafted the wild olive branches of the Gentiles (cf. Rom.11:17-24). Indeed, the Church believes that by His cross Christ, our Peace, reconciled Jew and Gentile, making them both one in Himself (cf. Eph. 2:14-16).

". . . The Jews still remain most dear to God because of their fathers, for He does not repent of the gifts He makes nor of the calls He issues (cf. Rom. 11:28-29). In company with the prophets and the same Apostle (Paul), the Church awaits that day, known to God alone, on which all peoples will address the Lord in a single voice and 'serve him with one accord' (Zeph. 3:9; Cf. Is. 66:23; Ps. 65:4; Rom. 11:11-32).

No Anti-Semitism

"Since the spiritual patrimony common to Christians and Jews is thus so great, this sacred Synod wishes to foster and recommend that mutual understanding and respect which is the fruit above all of biblical and theological studies, and of brotherly dialogues.

"True, authorities of the Jews and those who followed their lead pressed for the death of Christ (cf. Jn. 19:6); still, what happened in His passion cannot be blamed upon all the Jews then living, without distinction, nor upon the Jews of today. Although the Church is the new People of God, the Jews should not be presented as repudiated or cursed by God, as if such views followed from the holy Scriptures. All should take pains, then, lest in catechetical instruction and in the preaching of God's Word they teach anything out of harmony with the truth of the gospel and the spirit of Christ.

"The Church repudiates all persecutions against any man. Moreover, mindful of her common patrimony with the Jews, and motivated by the gospel's spiritual love and by no political considerations, she deplores the hatred, persecutions, and displays of anti-Semitism directed against the Jews at any time and from any source. . . ." (4).

". . . The Church rejects, as foreign to the mind of Christ, any discrimination against men or harassment of them because of their race, color, condition of life, or religion. . . ." (No. 5).

Bishops' Secretariat

The American hierarchy's first move toward implementation of the Vatican II *Declaration on the Relationship of the Church to Non-Christian Religions* was to establish, in 1965, a Subcommission for Catholic-Jewish Relations in the framework of its Commission for Ecumenical and Interreligious Affairs. This subcommission was reconstituted and given the title of secretariat in September, 1967. Its moderator is Bishop Francis J. Mugavero of Brooklyn. The Secretariat for Catholic-Jewish Relations is located at 1312 Massachusetts Ave. N.W., Washington, D.C. 20005. The executive director is Dr. Eugene J. Fisher.

According to the key norm of a set of guidelines issued by the secretariat Mar. 16, 1967: "The general aim of all Catholic-Jewish meetings (and relations) is to increase our understanding both of Judaism and the Catholic faith, to eliminate sources of tension and misunderstanding, to initiate dialogue or conversations on different levels, to multiply intergroup meetings between Catholics and Jews, and to promote cooperative social action."

Vatican Guidelines

In a document issued Jan. 3, 1975, the Vatican Commission for Religious Relations with the Jews offered a number of suggestions and guidelines for implementing the Christian-Jewish portion of the Second Vatican Council's "Declaration on Relations with Non-Christian Religions."

Among "suggestions from experience" were those concerning dialogue, liturgical links between Christian and Jewish worship, the interpretation of biblical texts, teaching and education for the purpose of increasing mutual understanding, and joint social action.

The document concluded with the statement:

"On Oct. 22, 1974, the Holy Father instituted for the universal Church this Commission for Religious Relations with the Jews, joined to the Secretariat for Promoting Christian Unity. This special commission, created to encourage and foster religious relations between Jews and Catholics — and to do so in collaboration with other Christians — will be, within the limits of its competence, at the service of all interested organizations, providing information for them and helping them to pursue their task in conformity with the instructions of the Holy See.

"The commission wishes to develop this collaboration in order to implement, correctly and effectively, the express intentions of the (Second Vatican) Council."

NCCB Statement

In a statement issued Nov. 20, 1975, in commemoration of the 10th anniversary of the Second Vatican Council's declaration on non-Christian religions, the National Conference of Catholic Bishops welcomed the Vatican guidelines and hailed the "new era in Catholic-Jewish affairs" which "ended a centuries-long silence between Church and Synagogue."

Lamenting the "de-Judaizing process" that set in early in the Church's history — and which "dulled our awareness of our Jewish beginnings," the bishops affirmed that "most essential concepts in the Christian creed grew at first in Judaic soil. Uprooted from that soil, these basic concepts cannot be perfectly understood."

The bishops called on theologians to reconsider the "long-neglected passages" of the Letter to the Romans (Chapters 9 to 11) as a base for "exploring the continuing relationship of the Jewish people with God and their spiritual bonds with the New Covenant" in a positive manner.

Noting also that "an overwhelming majority of Jews see themselves bound in one way or another to the land of Israel," the bishops stated that, "whatever difficulties Christians may experience in sharing this view, they should strive to understand this link between land and people which Jews have expressed in their writings and worship throughout two millenia as a longing for the homeland, holy Zion."

International Liaison Committee

The International Catholic-Jewish Liaison Committee reviewed progress in dialogue at a meeting held Mar. 28 to 30, 1977, in Venice. Participants focused special attention on an address given by Tommaso Federici, a consultor to the Vatican Commission for Religious Relations with the Jews.

Speaking about the mission and witness of the Church, Federici said that the Church clearly rejects "any form of proselytism" which intrudes on the free will and personal decision-making of Jews.

He defined proselytism as "any form of witness and preaching which in any way constitutes a physical, moral, psychological or cultural constraint on Jews, both as individuals and in community, which might in any way destroy or even simply reduce their personal judgments, free will and full autonomy of decision on the personal or community level."

Federici condemned "every sort of judgment or expression of discrimination, contempt or restriction against the Jewish people or individual Jews, or against their faith, worship or general culture, and in particular against their religious culture, their past and present history, their existence and its meaning."

He also encouraged efforts "to get to know the history of Israel through studying the Bible and exploring in depth the spirit, existence, history and mission of Israel, her survival in history, her election, call and privileges as recognized by the New Testament."

The contents of the paper were called "a significant development in the Catholic Church that is bound to contribute to deeper understanding between the two faiths," by Rabbi Henry Siegman, a member of the Synagogue Council of America and of the liaison committee.

Papal View

Pope Jonn Paul, calling attention to the presence of Jewish leaders at Battery Park, New York, Oct. 4, 1979, declared:

"I address a special word of greeting to the leaders of the Jewish community whose presence here honors me greatly. A few months ago, I met with an international group of Jewish representatives in Rome. On that occasion, recalling the initiatives undertaken following the Second Vatican Council under my predecessor, Paul VI, I stated that 'our two communities are connected and closely related at the very level of their respective identities,' and that on this basis 'we recognize with utmost clarity that the path along which we should proceed is one of fraternal dialogue and fruitful collaboration.' "

JUDAISM

Judaism is the religion of the Old Testament and of contemporary Jews. Divinely revealed and with a patriarchal background (Abraham, Isaac, Jacob), it originated with the Mosaic Covenant, was identified with the Israelites, and achieved distinctive form and character as the religion of The Law from this Covenant and reforms initiated by Ezra and Nehemiah after the Babylonian Exile.

Judaism does not have a formal creed but its principal points of belief are clear. Basic is belief in one transcendent God who reveals himself through The Law, the prophets, the life of his people and events of history. The fatherhood of God involves the brotherhood of men. Religious faith and practice are equated with just living according to The Law. Moral conviction and practice are regarded as more important than precise doctrinal formulation and profession. Formal worship, whose principal act was sacrifice from Canaanite times to 70 A. D., is by prayer, reading and meditating upon the sacred writings, and observance of the Sabbath and festivals.

Judaism has messianic expectations of the complete fulfillment of the Covenant, the coming of God's kingdom, the ingathering of his people, final judgment and retribution for all men. Views differ regarding the manner in which these expectations will be realized—through a person, the community of God's people, an evolution of historical events, an eschatological act of God himself. Individual salvation expectations also differ, depending on views about the nature of immortality, punishment and reward, and related matters.

The sacred books are the 24 books of the Masoretic Hebrew Text of The Law, the Prophets and the Writings (see The Bible). Together, they contain the basic instruction or norms for just living. In some contexts, the term Law or Torah refers only to the Pentateuch (Genesis, Exodus, Leviticus, Numbers, Deuteronomy); in others, it denotes all the sacred books and/or the whole complex of written and oral tradition.

Also of great authority are two Talmuds which were composed in Palestine and Babylon in the fourth and fifth centuries A.D., respectively. They consist of the Mishna, a compilation of oral laws, and the Gemara, a collection of rabbinical commentary on the Mishna. Midrash are collections of scriptural comments and moral counsels.

Priests were the principal official ministers during the period of sacrificial and temple worship. Rabbis were, and continue to be, teachers and leaders of prayer. The synagogue is the place of community worship. The family and home are focal points of many aspects of Jewish worship and practice.

Of the various categories of Jews, Orthodox are the most conservative in adherence to strict religious traditions. Others — Reformed, Conservative, Reconstructionist — are liberal in comparison with the Orthodox. They favor greater or less modification of religious practices in accommodation to contemporary culture and living conditions.

Principal events in Jewish life include the circumcision of males, according to prescriptions of the Covenant; the bar mitzvah which marks the coming-of-age of boys in Judaism at the age of 13; marriage; and observance of the Sabbath and festivals.

Sabbath and Festivals

Observances of the Sabbath and festivals begin at sundown of the previous calendar day and continue until the following sundown.

Sabbath: Saturday, the weekly day of rest prescribed in the Decalogue.

Booths (Tabernacles): A seven-to-nine-day festival in the month of Tishri (Sept.-Oct.), marked by some Jews with Covenant-renewal and reading of The Law. It originated as an agricultural feast at the end of the harvest and got its name from the temporary shelters used by workers in the fields.

Hanukkah (The Festival of Lights, the Feast of Consecration and of the Maccabees): Commemorates the dedication of the new altar in the Temple at Jerusalem by Judas Maccabeus in 165 B.C. The eight-day festival, during which candles in an eight-branch candelabra are lighted in succession, one each day, occurs near the winter solstice, close to Christmas time.

Passover: A seven-day festival commemorating the liberation of the Israelites from Egypt. The narrative of the Exodus, the Haggadah, is read at ceremonial Seder meals on the first and second days of the festival, which begins on the 14th day of Nisan (Mar.-Apr.).

Pentecost (Feast of Weeks): Observed 50 days after Passover. Some Jews regard it as commemorative of the anniversary of the revelation of The Law to Moses.

Purim: A joyous festival observed on the 14th day of Adar (Feb.-Mar.), commemorating the rescue of the Israelites from massacre by the Persians through the intervention of Esther. The festival is preceded by a day of fasting. A gift- and alms-giving custom became associated with it in medieval times.

Rosh Hashana (Feast of the Trumpets, New Year): Observed on the first day of Tishri (Sept.-Oct.), the festival focuses attention on the day of judgment and is marked with meditation on the ways of life and the ways of death. It is second in importance only to the most solemn observance of Yom Kippur, which is celebrated 10 days later.

Yom Kippur (Day of Atonement): The highest holy day, observed with strict fasting. It occurs 10 days after Rosh Hashana.

ISLAM

Islam is the religion of Mohammed and his followers, called Moslems, or Muslims. Islam, meaning submission to God, originated with Mohammed (570-632), an Arabian, who taught that he had received divine revelation and was the last and greatest of the prophets.

Moslems believe in one God. There were six great prophets—Adam, Noah, Abraham, Moses, Jesus and Mohammed—and Mohammed was the greatest. The creed states: "There is no God but Allah and Mohammed is the prophet of Allah."

The principal duties of Moslems are to: profess the faith by daily recitation of the creed; pray five times a day facing in the direction of the holy city of Mecca; give alms; fast daily from dawn to dusk during the month of Ramadan; make a pilgrimage to Mecca once if possible.

Moslems believe in a final judgment, heaven and hell. Polygamy is practiced. Some dietary regulations are in effect. The weekly day of worship is Friday, and the principal service is at noon in a mosque. Moslems do not have an ordained ministry. The general themes of their prayer are adoration and thanksgiving.

The basis of Islamic belief is the Koran, the created word of God revealed to Mohammed by the angel Gabriel over a period of 20 years. The contents of this sacred book are complemented by the Sunna, a collection of sacred traditions, and reinforced by Ijma, the consensus of Moslems which guarantees them against error in matters of belief and practice.

There are several sects of Moslems.

Conciliar Statement

The attitude of the Church toward Islam was stated as follows in the Second Vatican Council's *Declaration on the Relationship of the Church to Non-Christian Religions* (No. 3).

"Upon the Moslems, too, the Church looks with esteem. They adore one God, living and enduring, merciful and all-powerful, Maker of heaven and earth and Speaker to men. They strive to submit wholeheartedly even to His inscrutable decrees, just as did Abraham, with whom the Islamic faith is pleased to associate itself. Though they do not acknowledge Jesus as God, they revere Him as a prophet. They also honor Mary, His virgin mother; at times they call on her, too, with devotion. In addition they await the day of judgment when God will give each man his due after raising him up. Consequently, they prize the moral life, and give worship to God especially through prayer, almsgiving and fasting.

"Although in the course of the centuries many quarrels and hostilities have arisen between Christians and Moslems, this most sacred Synod urges all to forget the past and to strive sincerely for mutual understanding. On behalf of all mankind, let them make common cause of safeguarding and fostering social justice, moral values, peace and freedom."

Dialogue

The purposes of Catholic-Moslem dialogue, which has been rather sketchy, were the subject of joint agreement between the Vatican Secretariat for Non-Christians, and a delegation of the Supreme Council of Islamic Affairs, at a Vatican meeting Dec. 16 to 20, 1970.

Their objectives, as stated in a communique, were to:

• hold regular consultations on Moslem-Christian relations, social, cultural and spiritual questions;

• maintain contact through appointed officers and in other ways;

• do everything possible to develop good relations between Christians and Moslems, in order to strengthen the fraternity existing among believers who share respect for all religious values and faith in God;

• continue efforts for justice and peace in the world.

Representatives of the secretariat and the council denounced every type of discrimination in national and international life. They also expressed hope for the success of efforts to establish peace with justice and honor in the Middle East.

A commission for Vatican-Moslem relations was established in 1974 as part of the Secretariat for Non-Christians.

1978 Meeting

One of several meetings of Catholic and Moslem representatives since 1970 took place Apr. 12 and 13, 1978, at the El Azhar Islamic center in Cairo. Conversations centered around the need for mutual efforts toward better understanding among Christians and Moslems, and for the defense and spread of religious values in the world. (These same concerns were the subjects of a message addressed to Moslem leaders by Cardinal Pignedoli in August, 1979.)

NON-REVEALED RELIGIONS

Hinduism: The traditional religion of India with origins dating to about 5,000 B.C. Its history is complex, including original Vedic Hinduism, with a sacred literature (Veda) of hymns, incantations and other elements, and with numerous nature gods; Brahmanism, with emphasis on ceremonialism and its power over the gods; philosophical speculation, reflected in the Upanishads, with development of ideas concerning Karma, reincarnation, Brahman, and the manner of achieving salvation; the cults of Vishnu, Shiva and other deities; reforms in Hinduism and in relation to Islam and Christianity.

The principal tenets of Hinduism are open to various interpretations. Karma is the law of the deed, of sowing and reaping, of retribution. It determines the progress of a person toward liberation from the cycle of rebirths necessary for salvation. Liberation is accomplished in stages, through successive reincarnations which indicate the previous as well as the existing state of a person. The means of liberation are the practice of ceremonialism and asceticism; faith in, devotion to and worship of the gods Vishnu and Shiva in their several incarnations; and/or knowledge attained through disciplined meditation called Yoga. Salvation, according to philosophical Hinduism, consists in absorption in Brahman, the neuter world-soul. Vishnu, the sun-god, and Shiva, the destroyer or generative force of the universe, are the principal popular deities. Ancient belief in nature gods (pantheism) is reflected in sacred respect for some animals. The concept of reincarnation underlies the caste system in Indian society.

There are many sects in Hinduism, which does not have a definite creed. It lends itself easily to syncretism or amalgamation with other beliefs, as evidenced in the 15th century Sikh movement which adopted the monotheism and militancy of Islam. Hindu rituals are various and elaborate, with respect to foods, festivals, pilgrimages, marriage and other life-events.

Buddhism: Originated in the sixth century B.C. in reaction to formalism, pantheism and other trends in Hinduism. The Buddha, the Enlightened One, was Sidartha Gautama, an Indian prince, who sought to explain human suffering and evil and to find a middle way between the extremes of austerity and sensuality.

The four noble truths of Buddhism are: (1) existence involves suffering or pain; (2) suffering comes from craving: (3) craving can be overcome; (4) the way to overcome craving is to follow the "noble eightfold path" of right views, right intention, right speech, right action, right livelihood, right effort, right mindfulness and right concentration.

Karma, the deed-principle of judgment and retribution, and reincarnation are elements of Buddhism. The ultimate objective of life is Nirvana — the absorption of a person into the absolute — which ends the cycles of rebirth.

Buddhism is essentially atheistic and more of a moral philosophy and ethical system than a religion. It has a cultic element in veneration for Buddha. Monasteries, temples and shrines are places of contemplation and ritualistic observance. There are several categories of Buddhist monks and nuns.

Buddhism has many sects. Mahayana Buddhism, with an elaborate ideology, is strong in China, Korea and Japan. Hinayana Buddhism is common in Southeast Asia. Zen Buddhism is highly contemplative. Lamaism in Tibet is a combination of Buddhism and local demonolatry.

Confucianism: An ethical system based on the teachings of Confucius (c. 551-479 B.C.). It is oriented toward the moral perfection of individuals and society, the attainment of the harmony of individual and social life with the harmony of the universe, through conduct governed by the relationships of humanity, justice, ritual and courtesy, wisdom, and fidelity. Originally and basically humanistic, Confucianism was eventually mingled with elements of Chinese religion. It exerted a strong influence on national life in China from 125 to the beginning of the 20th century, despite some periods of decline.

Taoism: Originated in China several centuries before the Christian era and became a fully developed religious system by the fifth century A.D. As a religion of mystery, it developed extreme polytheism, with the Jade Emperor as the highest deity; sought blessings and long life by means of alchemy; fostered superstition and witchcraft; took on organizational and other aspects of Buddhism, with several categories of priests and nuns; exerted strong ethical influence on the lower classes; split into many sects; adopted features from other religions; became the starting point of many secret societies. One of its key tenets — that the way of nature is the guide to human conduct — resulted in a form of quietism opposed to the social concern of Confucianism.

Shinto: The way of the gods, the sum total of the cultic beliefs and practices of the ancestral religion of Japan which originated from nature and ancestor worship. Shinto is pantheistic and has many objects of devotion, the highest being the Ruler of Heaven; is practiced with detailed rituals in public shrines, which are cultic centers; has strong social influence. Sectarian Shinto has about 13 recognized sects and many offshoots. Shinto, with principal concern for this-worldly blessing, has ben affected by Buddhist and Confucian influences.

Glossary

A

Abbess: The female superior of a monastic community of nuns; e.g., Benedictines, Poor Clares, some others. Elected by members of the community, an abbess has general authority over her community but no sacramental jurisdiction. Earliest evidence of the use of the title, a feminine derivative of the Aramaic *abba* (father), dates from early in the sixth century.

Abbey: See Abbot, Monastery.

Abbot: The male superior of a monastic community of men religious; e.g., Benedictines, Cistercians, some others. Elected by members of the community, an abbot has ordinary jurisdiction and general authority over his community. He has some episcopal privileges. The title derives from the Aramaic *abba* (father); first given to the spiritual fathers and guides of hermits in Egypt in the fourth century, it was appropriated in the Rule of St. Benedict to the heads of abbeys and monasteries. Eastern-Rite equivalents of an abbot are a *hegumen* and an *archimandrite*.

A regular abbot is the head of an abbey or monastery. An abbot general or archabbot is the head of a congregation consisting of several monasteries. An abbot primate is the head of the modern Benedictine Confederation.

A few regular abbots have had jurisdiction, similar in some respects to that of a bishop in his diocese, over the residents and institutions of districts (*abbacies nullius*) not belonging to a diocese. Pope Paul stated in a document issued on his own initiative Dec. 29, 1976, that no more such abbacies would be established, except in cases of extraordinary necessity; also, that such abbacies, with the possible exception of ones of historical significance (like Monte Cassino, the cradle of the Benedictine Order) would be phased out of existence. The only *abbacy nullius* ever in the U.S. was Belmont Abbey, N.C.

Abjuration: Renunciation of apostasy, heresy or schism by a solemn oath.

Ablution: A term derived from Latin, meaning washing or cleansing, and referring to the cleansing of the hands of a priest celebrating Mass, after the offering of gifts; and to the cleansing of the chalice with water and wine after Communion.

Abortion: The expulsion of a nonviable human fetus from the womb of the mother, with moral implications stemming from the humanity of the fetus from the moment of conception and its consequent right to life.

Accidental expulsion, as in cases of miscarriage, is without moral fault.

Direct abortion, in which a fetus is intentionally removed from the womb, constitutes a direct attack on an innocent human being, a violation of the Fifth Commandment. It is punished in church law by the penalty of excommunication, which is automatically incurred by all baptized persons involved; i.e., the consenting mother and necessary physical and/or moral cooperators. Direct abortion is not justifiable for any reason, e.g.: therapeutic, for the physical and/or psychological welfare of the mother; preventive, to avoid the birth of a defective or unwanted child; social, in the interests of family and/or community.

Indirect abortion, which occurs when a fetus is expelled during medical or other treatment of the mother for a reason other than procuring expulsion, is permissible under the principle of double effect for a proportionately serious reason; e.g., when a medical or surgical procedure is necessary to save the life of the mother.

Absolution: The act by which an authorized priest, acting as the agent of Christ and minister of the Church, grants forgiveness of sins in the sacrament of penance. The essential formula of absolution is: "I absolve you from your sins; in the name of the Father, and of the Son, and of the Holy Spirit. Amen.

Priests receive the power to absolve in virtue of their ordination and the right to exercise this power in virtue of faculties of jurisdiction given them by their bishop, their religious superior, or by canon law. The faculties of jurisdiction can be limited or restricted regarding certain sins and penalties or censures.

In cases of necessity, and also in cases of the absence of their own confessors, Eastern and Roman Rite Catholics may ask for and receive sacramental absolution from a priest of a separated Eastern Church. Separated Eastern Christians may similarly ask for and receive sacramental absolution from an Eastern or Roman Rite priest.

Any priest can absolve a person in danger of death; in the absence of a priest with the usual faculties, this includes a laicized priest or a priest under censure.

(See additional entry under Sacraments.)

Absolution, General: (1) Sacramental absolution given without confession of sin, when confession is impossible. Persons so absolved are required to confess, in their next confession, the mortal sins from which they were so absolved.

(2) A blessing of the Church to which a plenary indulgence is attached, given at the hour of death, and at stated times to members of religious institutes and third orders.

Accessory to Another's Sin: One who culpably assists another in the performance of an evil action. This may be done by counsel, command, provocation, consent, praise, flat-

**tery, concealment, participation, silence, defense of the evil done.

Adoration: The highest act and purpose of religious worship, which is directed in love and reverence to God alone in acknowledgment of his infinite perfection and goodness, and of his total dominion over creatures. Adoration, which is also called *latria*, consists of internal and external elements, private and social prayer, liturgical acts and ceremonies, and especially sacrifice.

Adultery: (1) Sexual intercourse between a married person and another to whom one is not married; a violation of the obligations of chastity and justice. The Sixth Commandment prohibition against adultery is also regarded as a prohibition against all external sins of a sexual nature.

(2) Any sin of impurity (thought, desire, word, action) involving a married person who is not one's husband or wife has the nature of adultery.

Adventists: Members of several Christian sects whose doctrines are dominated by belief in a more or less imminent second advent or coming of Christ upon earth for a glorious 1,000-year reign of righteousness. This reign, following victory by the forces of good over evil in a final Battle of Armageddon, will begin with the resurrection of the chosen and will end with the resurrection of all other men and the annihilation of the wicked. Thereafter, the just will live forever in a renewed heaven and earth. A sleep of the soul takes place between the time of death and the day of judgment. There is no hell. The Bible, in fundamentalist interpretation, is regarded as the only rule of faith and practice.

About six sects have developed in the course of the Adventist movement which originated with William Miller (1782-1849) in the United States. Miller, on the basis of calculations made from the Book of Daniel, predicted that the second advent of Christ would occur between 1843 and 1844. After the prophecy went unfulfilled, divisions occurred in the movement and the Seventh Day Adventists, whose actual formation dates from 1860, emerged as the largest single body. The observance of Saturday instead of Sunday as the Lord's Day dates from 1844.

Advent Wreath: A wreath of laurel, spruce, or similar foliage with four candles which are lighted successively in the weeks of Advent to symbolize the approaching celebration of the birth of Christ, the Light of the World, at Christmas. The wreath originated among German Protestants.

Agape: A Greek word, meaning love, love feast, designating the meal of fellowship eaten at some gatherings of early Christians. Although held in some places in connection with the Mass, the agape was not part of the Mass, nor was it of universal institution and observance. Legislation against it was passed by the Council of Carthage (397) and other councils because of abuses. It was infrequently observed by the fifth century and disappeared altogether between the sixth and eighth centuries. In recent years, a limited revival has taken place in the course of the liturgical and ecumenical movements.

Age of Reason: (1) The time of life when one begins to distinguish between right and wrong, to understand an obligation and take on moral responsibility; seven years of age is the presumption in church law.

(2) Historically, the 18th century period of Enlightenment in England and France, the age of the Encyclopedists and Deists. According to a basic thesis of the Enlightenment, human experience and reason are the only sources of certain knowledge of truth; consequently, faith and revelation are discounted as valid sources of knowledge, and the reality of supernatural truth is called into doubt and/or denied.

Aggiornamento: An Italian word having the general meaning of bringing up to date, renewal, revitalization, descriptive of the processes of spiritual renewal and institutional reform and change in the Church; fostered by the Second Vatican Council.

Agnosticism: A theory which holds that man cannot have certain knowledge of immaterial reality, especially the existence of God and things pertaining to him. Immanuel Kant, one of the philosophical fathers of agnosticism, stood for the position that God, as well as the human soul, is unknowable on speculative grounds; nevertheless, he found practical imperatives for acknowledging God's existence, a view shared by many agnostics. The First Vatican Council declared that the existence of God and some of his attributes can be known with certainty by human reason, even without divine revelation. The word agnosticism was first used, in the sense given here, by T. H. Huxley in 1869.

Agnus Dei: A Latin phrase, meaning Lamb of God.

(1) A title given to Christ, the Lamb (victim) of the Sacrifice of the New Law (on Calvary and in Mass).

(2) A prayer said at Mass before the reception of Holy Communion.

(3) A sacramental. It is a round paschal-candle fragment blessed by the pope. On one side it bears the impression of a lamb, symbolic of Christ. On the reverse side, there may be any one of a number of impressions; e.g., the figure of a saint, the name and coat of arms of the reigning pope. The *agnus dei* may have originated at Rome in the fifth century. The first definite mention of it dates from about 820.

Alleluia: An exclamation of joy derived from Hebrew, All hail to him who is, praise God. It is used in the liturgy and other prayer on joyful occasions during the church year.

Allocution: A formal type of papal address,

as distinguished from an ordinary sermon or statement of views.

Alms: An act, gift or service of compassion, motivated by love of God and neighbor, for the help of persons in need; an obligation of charity, which is measurable by the ability of one person to give assistance and by the degree of another's need. Almsgiving, along with prayer and fasting, is regarded as a work of penance as well as an exercise of charity. (See Corporal and Spiritual Works of Mercy.)

Alpha and Omega: The first and last letters of the Greek alphabet, used to symbolize the eternity of God (Rv. 1:8) and the divinity and eternity of Christ, the beginning and end of all things (Rv. 21:6; 22:13). Use of the letters as a monogram of Christ originated in the fourth century or earlier.

Amen: A Hebrew word meaning truly, it is true. In the Gospels, Christ used the word to add a note of authority to his statements. In other New Testament writings, as in Hebrew usage, it was the concluding word to doxologies. As the concluding word of prayers, it expresses assent to and acceptance of God's will.

Anathema: A Greek word with the root meaning of cursed or separated and the adapted meaning of excommunication, used in church documents, especially the canons of ecumenical councils, for the condemnation of heretical doctrines and of practices opposed to proper discipline.

Anchorite: A kind of hermit living in complete isolation and devoting himself exclusively to exercises of religion and severe penance according to a rule and way of life of his own devising. In early Christian times, anchorites were the forerunners of the monastic life. The closest contemporary approach to the life of an anchorite is that of Carthusian and Camaldolese hermits.

Angels: Purely spiritual beings with intelligence and free will, whose name indicates their mission as ministers of God and ministering spirits to men. They were created before the creation of the visible universe; the devil and bad angels, who were created good, fell from glory through their own fault. In addition to these essentials of defined doctrine, it is held that angels are personal beings; they can intercede for men; fallen angels were banished from God's glory in heaven to hell; bad angels can tempt men to commit sin. The doctrine of guardian angels, although not explicitly defined as a matter of faith, is rooted in long-standing tradition. No authoritative declaration has ever been issued regarding choirs or various categories of angels: according to theorists, there are nine choirs, consisting of seraphim, cherubim, thrones, dominations, principalities, powers, virtues, archangels and angels. In line with scriptural usage, only three angels can be named—Michael, Raphael and Gabriel.

Angelus: A devotion which commemorates the Incarnation of Christ. It consists of three versicles, three Hail Marys and a special prayer, and recalls the announcement to Mary by the Archangel Gabriel that she was chosen to be the Mother of Christ, her acceptance of the divine will, and the Incarnation (Lk. 1:26-38). The Angelus is recited at 6 a.m., noon and 6 p.m. The practice of reciting the Hail Mary in honor of the Incarnation was introduced by the Franciscans in 1263. The *Regina Caeli,* commemorating the joy of Mary at Christ's Resurrection, replaces the Angelus during the Easter season.

Anger: Passionate displeasure arising from some kind of offense suffered at the hands of another person, frustration or other cause, combined with a tendency to strike back at the cause of the displeasure; a violation of the Fifth Commandment and one of the capital sins if the displeasure is out of proportion to the cause and/or if the retaliation is unjust.

Anglican Orders: Holy orders conferred according to the rite of the Anglican (Episcopal) Church, which Leo XIII declared null and void in the bull *Apostolicae Curae,* Sept. 13, 1896. The orders were declared null because they were conferred according to a rite that was considered substantially defective in form and intent, and because of a break in apostolic succession that occurred when Matthew Parker became head of the Anglican hierarchy in 1559.

In making his declaration, Pope Leo cited earlier arguments against validity made by Julius III in 1553 and 1554 and by Paul IV in 1555. He also noted related directives requiring absolute ordination, according to the Catholic ritual, of convert ministers who had been ordained according to the Anglican Ordinal.

Antichrist: The man of sin, the lawless and wicked antagonist of Christ and the work of God; a mysterious figure of prophecy mentioned in the New Testament. Supported by Satan, submitting to no moral restraints, and armed with tremendous power, Antichrist will set himself up in opposition to God, work false miracles, persecute the People of God, and employ unimaginable means to lead men into error and evil during a period of widespread defection from the Christian faith before the end of time; he will be overcome by Christ. Catholic thinkers have regarded Antichrist as a person, a caricature of Christ, who will lead a final violent struggle against God and His people; they have also applied the title to personal and impersonal forces in history hostile to God and the Church. Official teaching has said little about Antichrist. In 1318, it labeled as partly heretical, senseless, and fanciful the assertions made by the Fraticelli about his coming; in 1415, the Council of Constance condemned the Wycliff thesis that excommunications made by the pope and other prelates were the actions of Antichrist.

Antiphon: (1) A short verse or text, generally from Scripture, recited in the Liturgy of the Hours before and after psalms and canticles.

(2) Any verse sung or recited by one part of a choir or congregation in response to the other part, as in antiphonal or alternate chanting.

Apologetics: The science and art of building and presenting the case for, accounting for, explaining, defending, justifying the reasonableness of the Christian faith, by a wide variety of means including facts of experience, history, science, philosophy. The constant objective of apologetics, as well as of the total process of pre-evangelization, is preparation for response to God in faith; its ways and means, however, are subject to change in accordance with the various needs of people and different sets of circumstances.

Apostasy: (1) The total and obstinate rejection or abandonment of the Christian faith by a baptized person who continues to call himself a Christian. External manifestation of this rejection constitutes the crime of apostasy, and the person, called an *apostate,* automatically incurs a penalty of excommunication.

(2) Apostasy from orders is the unlawful withdrawal from or rejection of the obligations of the clerical state by a man who has received major orders. The canonical penalty for such apostasy is excommunication.

(3) Apostasy from the religious life occurs when a religious with perpetual vows unlawfully leaves the community with the intention of not returning, or actually remains outside the community for 30 days without permission. The canonical penalty for such apostasy is excommunication.

Apostolate: The ministry or work of an apostle. In Catholic usage, the word is an umbrella-like term covering all kinds and areas of work and endeavor for the service of God and the Church and the good of people. Thus, the apostolate of bishops is to carry on the mission of the Apostles as pastors of the People of God: of priests, to carry out the sacramental and pastoral ministry for which they are ordained; of religious, to follow and do the work of Christ in conformity with the evangelical counsels and their rule of life; of lay persons, as individuals and/or in groups, to give witness to Christ and build up the kingdom of God through practice of their faith, professional competence and the performance of good works in the concrete circumstances of daily life. Apostolic works are not limited to those done within the Church or by specifically Catholic groups, although some apostolates are officially assigned to certain persons or groups and are under the direction of church authorities. Apostolate derives from the commitment and obligation of baptism, confirmation, holy orders, matrimony, the duties of one's state in life, etc.

Apostolic Succession: Bishops of the Church, who form a collective body or college, are successors to the Apostles by ordination and divine right; as such they carry on the mission entrusted by Christ to the Apostles as guardians and teachers of the deposit of faith, principal pastors and spiritual authorities of the faithful. The doctrine of apostolic succession is based on New Testament evidence and the constant teaching of the Church, reflected as early as the end of the first century in a letter of Pope St. Clement to the Corinthians. A significant facet of the doctrine is the role of the pope as the successor of St. Peter, the vicar of Christ and head of the college of bishops. The doctrine of apostolic succession means more than continuity of apostolic faith and doctrine; its basic requisite is ordination by the laying on of hands in apostolic succession.

Archangel: An angel who carries out special missions for God in his dealings with men. Three of them are named in the Bible: Michael, leader of the angelic host and protector of the synagogue; Raphael, guide of Tobiah and healer of his father, who is regarded as the patron of travelers; Gabriel, called the angel of the Incarnation because of his announcement to Mary that she was to be the Mother of Christ.

Archdiocese: An ecclesiastical jurisdiction headed by an archbishop. An archdiocese is usually a metropolitan see, i.e., the principal one of a group of dioceses comprising a province; the other dioceses in the province are suffragan sees.

Archives: Documentary records, and the place where they are kept, of the spiritual and temporal government and affairs of the Church, a diocese, church agencies like the departments of the Roman Curia, bodies like religious institutes, and individual parishes. The collection, cataloguing, preserving, and use of these records are governed by norms stated in canon law and particular regulations. The strictest secrecy is always in effect for confidential records concerning matters of conscience, and documents of this kind are destroyed as soon as circumstances permit.

Archpriest: For some time, before and during the Middle Ages, a priest who took the place of a bishop at liturgical worship. In Europe, the term is sometimes used as an honorary title. It is also an honorary title in Eastern-Rite Churches.

Asceticism: The practice of self-discipline. In the spiritual life, asceticism — by personal prayer, meditation, self-denial, works of mortification, and outgoing interpersonal works — is motivated by love of God and contributes to growth in holiness.

Ashes: Religious significance has been associated with their use as symbolic of penance since Old Testament times. Thus, ashes of palm blessed on the previous Sunday of the Passion are placed on the foreheads of the faithful on Ash Wednesday to remind them to do works of penance, especially during the season of Lent, and that they are dust and unto dust will return. Ashes are a sacramental.

Aspergillum: A vessel or device used for sprinkling holy water. The ordinary type is a metallic rod with a bulbous tip which absorbs the water and discharges it at the motion of the user's hand.

Aspersory: A portable metallic vessel, similar to a pail, for carrying holy water.

Aspiration: Short exclamatory prayer; e.g., My Jesus, mercy.

Atheism: Denial of the existence of God, finding expression in a system of thought (speculative atheism) or a manner of acting (practical atheism) as though there were no God.

The Second Vatican Council, in its *Pastoral Constitution on the Church in the Modern World* (Nos. 19 to 21), noted that a profession of atheism may represent an explicit denial of God, the rejection of a wrong notion of God, an affirmation of man rather than of God, an extreme protest against evil. It said that such a profession might result from acceptance of such propositions as: there is no absolute truth; man can assert nothing, absolutely nothing, about God; everything can be explained by scientific reasoning alone; the whole question of God is devoid of meaning.

The constitution also cited two opinions of influence in atheistic thought. One of them regards recognition of dependence on God as incompatible with human freedom and independence. The other views belief in God and religion as a kind of opiate which sedates man on earth, reconciling him to the acceptance of suffering, injustice, shortcomings, etc., because of hope for greater things after death, and thereby hindering him from seeking and working for improvement and change for the better here and now.

All of these views, in one way or another, have been involved in the No-God and Death-of-God schools of thought in recent and remote history.

Atonement: The redemptive activity of Christ, who reconciled man with God through his Incarnation and entire life, and especially by his suffering and Resurrection. The word also applies to prayer and good works by which men join themselves with and take part in Christ's work of reconciliation and reparation for sin.

Attributes of God: Perfections of God. God possesses—and is—all the perfections of being, without limitation. Because he is infinite, all of these perfections are one, perfectly united in him. Man, however, because of the limited power of understanding, views these perfections separately, as distinct characteristics—even though they are not actually distinct in God. God is: almighty, eternal, holy, immortal, immense, immutable, incomprehensible, ineffable, infinite, invisible, just, loving, merciful, most high, most wise, omnipotent, omniscient, omnipresent, patient, perfect, provident, supreme, true.

Avarice (Covetousness): A disorderly and unreasonable attachment to and desire for material things; called a capital sin because it involves preoccupation with material things to the neglect of spiritual goods and obligations of justice and charity.

Ave Maria: See Hail Mary.

B

Baldachino: A canopy over an altar.

Beatification: A preliminary step toward canonization of a saint. It begins with an investigation of the candidate's life, writings and heroic practice of virtue, and the certification of at least two miracles worked by God through his intercession. If the findings of the investigation so indicate, the pope decrees that the Servant of God may be called *Blessed* and may be honored locally or in a limited way in the liturgy. Additional procedures lead to canonization (see separate entry).

Beatific Vision: The intuitive, immediate and direct vision and experience of God enjoyed in the light of glory by all the blessed in heaven. The vision is a supernatural mystery.

Beatitude: A literary form of the Old and New Testaments in which blessings are promised to persons for various reasons. Beatitudes are mentioned 26 times in the Psalms, and in other books of the Old Testament. The best known beatitudes — identifying blessedness with participation in the kingdom of God and his righteousness, and descriptive of the qualities of Christian perfection — are those recounted in Mt. 5:3-11 and Lk. 6:20-22.

In Matthew's account, the beatitudes are:

"How blest are the poor in spirit: the reign of God is theirs.

"Blest too are the sorrowing; they shall be consoled.

"(Blest are the lowly; they shall inherit the land.)

"Blest are they who hunger and thirst for holiness; they shall have their fill.

"Blest are they who show mercy; mercy shall be theirs.

"Blest are the single-hearted for they shall see God.

"Blest too are the peacemakers; they shall be called sons of God.

"Blest are those persecuted for holiness' sake; the reign of God is theirs.

"Blest are you when they insult you and persecute you and utter every kind of slander against you because of me."

In Luke's account, the beatitudes are:

"Blest are you poor; the reign of God is yours.

"Blest are you who hunger; you shall be filled.

"Blest are you who are weeping; you shall laugh.

"Blest shall you be when men hate you, when they ostracize you and insult you and proscribe your name as evil because of the Son of Man."

Benediction of the Blessed Sacrament: A short exposition of the Eucharist for adoration by and blessing of the faithful. Devotional practices include the singing of Eucharistic and other hymns, and recitation of the Divine Praises. Benediction, in its present form, dates from about the 15th century and is a form of liturgical worship.

Benedictus: The canticle or hymn of Zechariah at the circumcision of St. John the Baptist (Lk. 1:68-79). It is an expression of praise and thanks to God for sending John as a precursor of the Messiah. The *Benedictus* is recited in the Liturgy of the Hours as part of the Morning Prayer.

Bible Service: A devotion consisting essentially of common prayer of a biblical or liturgical character, several readings from Scripture, and a homily on the texts.

Biglietto: A papal document of notification of appointment to the cardinalate.

Biretta: A stiff, square hat with three ridges on top worn by clerics in church and on other occasions.

Blasphemy: Any expression of insult or contempt with respect to God, principally, and to holy persons and things, secondarily; a violation of the honor due to God in the context of the First and Second Commandments.

Blasphemy of the Spirit: Deliberate resistance to the Holy Spirit, called the unforgivable sin (Mt. 12:31) because it makes his saving action impossible. Thus, the only unforgivable sin is the one for which a person will not seek pardon from God.

Blessing: Invocation of God's favor, by official ministers of the Church or by private individuals. Blessings are recounted in the Old and New Testaments, and are common in the Christian tradition. The Church, through its ordained ministers (bishops and priests, especially), invokes divine favor in liturgical blessings; e.g., of the people at Mass, of the gifts to be consecrated at Mass, of persons and things on various occasions. Sacramentals — such as crucifixes, crosses, rosaries, scapulars, medals — are blessed by ministers of the Church for the invocation of God's favor on those who use them in the proper manner. Many types of blessings are listed in the *Roman Ritual*. Private blessings, as well as those of an official kind, are efficacious. Blessings are imparted with the Sign of the Cross and appropriate prayer.

Boat: A small vessel used to hold incense which is to be placed in the censer.

Brief, Apostolic: A papal letter, less formal than a bull, signed for the pope by a secretary and impressed with the seal of the Fisherman's Ring. Simple apostolic letters of this kind are issued for beatifications and with respect to other matters.

Bull, Apostolic: The most solemn form of papal document, beginning with the name and title of the pope (e.g., Paul VI, Servant of the Servants of God), dealing with an important subject, and having attached to it either a leaden seal called a bulla or a red ink imprint of the device on the seal. Bulls are known as apostolic letters with the seal. The seal, on one side, has representations of the heads of Sts. Peter and Paul; on the other side, the name of the reigning pope. Bulls are issued to confer the titles of bishops and cardinals, to promulgate canonizations, and for other purposes. A collection of bulls is called a *bullarium*.

Burial, Ecclesiastical: Interment with church rites and in consecrated ground. Catechumens as well as baptized Catholics have a right to ecclesiastical burial. A non-Catholic partner in a mixed marriage may be buried in a Catholic cemetery with the Catholic partner.

C

Calumny: Harming the name and good reputation of a person by lies; a violation of obligations of justice and truth. Restitution is due for calumny.

Calvary: A knoll about 15 feet high just outside the western wall of Jerusalem where Christ was crucified, so called from the Latin *calvaria* (skull) which described its shape.

Canon: A Greek word meaning rule, norm, standard, measure.

(1) The word designates the Canon of Sacred Scripture, which is the list of books recognized by the Church as inspired by the Holy Spirit.

(2) In the sense of regulating norms, the word designates the body or corpus of Canon Law enacted and promulgated by ecclesiastical authority for the orderly administration and government of the Church. The Code of Canon Law now in force in the Roman Church has been in effect since 1918. It consists of 2,414 canons which are divided into five books covering general rules, ecclesiastical persons, sacred things, trials, crimes and punishments. The code is now under review for the purpose of revision. Eastern-Rite Churches have their own canon law.

(3) The term also designates the four canons, (Eucharistic prayers, anaphoras) of the Mass, the core of the liturgy.

(4) Certain dignitaries of the Church have the title of Canon, and some religious are known as Canons.

Canonization: An infallible declaration by the pope that a person, who died as a martyr and/or practiced Christian virtue to a heroic degree, is now in heaven and is worthy of honor and imitation by all the faithful. Such a declaration is preceded by the process of beatification and another detailed investigation concerning the person's reputation for holiness, his writings, and (except in the case of martyrs) miracles ascribed to his intercession after his death. Miracles are not required for martyrs. The pope can dispense from some of the formalities ordinarily required in canonization procedures (equivalent canonization), as Pope John XXIII did in the canonization of St. Gregory Barbarigo on May 26, 1960. A saint is worthy of honor in liturgical worship throughout the universal Church.

From its earliest years the Church has venerated saints. Public official honor always required the approval of the bishop of the place. Martyrs were the first to be honored. St. Martin of Tours, who died in 397, was a early non-martyr venerated as a saint. The first official canonization by a pope for the universal Church was that of St. Ulrich by John XV in 993. Alexander III reserved the process of canonization to the Holy See in 1171. In 1588 Sixtus V established the Sacred Congregation of Rites for the principal purpose of handling causes for beatification and canonization: this function is now the work of the Congregation for the Causes of Saints. The present procedure is outlined in canons 1999-2141 of the Code of Canon Law and in a 1969 enactment by Paul VI.

The essential portion of a canonization decree states:

"For the honor of the holy and undivided Trinity; for the exaltation of the Catholic faith and the increase of Christian life; with the authority of our Lord Jesus Christ, of the blessed Apostles Peter and Paul, and with our own authority; after mature deliberation and with the divine assistance, often implored; with the counsel of many of our brothers.

"We decree and define that (name) is a saint and we inscribe him (her) in the Catalogue of Saints, stating that he (she) shall be venerated in the universal Church with pious devotion.

"In the name of the Father and of the Son and of the Holy Spirit. Amen."

The official listing of saints and blessed is contained in the *Roman Martyrology* and related decrees issued after its last publication. Butler's unofficial *Lives of the Saints* (1956) contains 2,565 entries.

The Church regards all persons in heaven as saints, not just those who have been officially canonized.

(See Beatification, Saints, Canonizations by Leo XIII and His Successors.)

Canticle: A scriptural chant or prayer differing from the psalms. Three of the canticles prescribed for use in the Liturgy of the Hours are: The *Magnificat* (Lk. 1:46-55), the *Benedictus* (Lk. 1:68-79), and the *Nunc Dimittis* (Lk. 2:29-32).

Capital Punishment: Punishment for crime by means of the death penalty. The political community, which has authority to provide for the common good, has the right to defend itself and its members against unjust aggression and may in extreme cases punish with the death penalty persons found guilty before the law of serious crimes against individuals and a just social order. Such punishment is essentially vindictive. Its value as a crime deterrent is a matter of perennial debate. The prudential judgment as to whether or not there should be capital punishment belongs to the civic community. The U.S. Supreme Court, in a series of decisions dating from June 29, 1972, ruled against the constitutionality of statutes on capital punishment except in specific cases and with appropriate consideration, with respect to sentence, of mitigating circumstances of the crime.

Capital punishment was the subject of a statement issued Mar. 1, 1978, by the Committee on Social Development and World Peace, U.S. Catholic Conference. The statement said, in part: "The use of the death penalty involves deep moral and religious questions as well as political and legal issues. In 1974, out of a commitment to the value and dignity of human life, the Catholic bishops of the United States declared their opposition to capital punishment. We continue to support this position, in the belief that a return to the use of the death penalty can only lead to the further erosion of respect for life in our society. Violent crime in our society is a serious matter which should not be ignored. We do not challenge society's right to punish the serious and violent offender, nor do we wish to debate the merits of the arguments concerning this right. Past history, however, shows that the death penalty in its present application has been discriminatory with respect to the disadvantaged, the indigent and the socially impoverished. Furthermore, recent data from correction sources definitely question the effectiveness of the death penalty as a deterrent to crime."

Additional statements against capital punishment have been issued by numerous bishops and other sources.

Capital Sins: Moral faults which, if habitual, give rise to many more sins. They are pride, covetousness, lust, anger, gluttony, envy, sloth.

The opposite virtues are: humility, liberality, chastity, meekness, temperance, brotherly love, diligence.

Cardinal Virtues: The four principal moral virtues are prudence, justice, temperance and fortitude.

Catacombs: Underground Christian cemeteries in various cities of the Roman Empire and Italy, especially in the vicinity of Rome; the burial sites of many martyrs and other Christians. Developed from aboveground cemeteries, their passageways, burial niches and assembly rooms were dug out of tuffa, a soft clay which hardened into rock-like consistency on drying. The earliest ones date from the third century; in the fourth, they became the scene of memorial services as the veneration of martyrs increased in popularity; in the seventh and eighth centuries, they were plundered by the Lombards and other invaders. The relics of many martyrs were removed to safer places in the ninth century; afterwards, the catacombs fell into neglect and oblivion until interest in them revived in the 16th century. The catacombs have been excavated extensively, yielding considerable information about early Christian symbolism and art, dating from the third century on, and other aspects of Christian life and practice.

Catafalque: A small structure like a bier, used at services for the dead in the absence of the corpse.

Catechism: A summary of Christian doctrine in question and answer form, used for purposes of instruction.

Catechumen: A person preparing, in a program of instruction and spiritual formation for baptism and reception into the Church.

Cathedra: A Greek word for chair, designating the chair or seat of a bishop in the principal church of his diocese, which is therefore called a cathedral (see separate entry).

Cathedraticum: The tax paid to a bishop by all churches and benefices subject to him for the support of episcopal administration and for works of charity.

Catholic: A Greek word, meaning universal, first used in the title Catholic Church in a letter written by St. Ignatius of Antioch about 107 to the Christians of Smyrna.

Celebret: A Latin word, meaning Let him celebrate, the name of a document issued by a bishop or other superior stating that a priest is in good standing and therefore should be given opportunity to celebrate Mass or perform other priestly functions.

Celibacy: The unmarried state of life, required in the Roman or Latin Church of candidates for holy orders and of men already ordained to holy orders, for the practice of perfect chastity and total dedication to the service of people in the ministry of the Church. Celibacy is enjoined as a condition for ordination by church discipline and law, not by dogmatic necessity.

In the Roman Church, a consensus in favor of celibacy developed in the early centuries while the clergy included both celibates and men who had been married once. The first local legislation on the subject was enacted by a local council held in Elvira, Spain, about 306; it forbade bishops, priests, deacons and other ministers to have wives. Similar enactments were passed by other local councils from that time on, and by the 12th century particular laws regarded marriage by clerics in major orders to be not only unlawful but also null and void. The latter view was translated by the Second Lateran Council in 1139 into what seems to be the first written universal law making holy orders an invalidating impediment to marriage. In 1563 the Council of Trent ruled definitely on the matter and established the discipline still in force in the Roman Church.

Some exceptions to this discipline have been made in recent years. Several married Protestant ministers who became converts and were subsequently ordained to the priesthood have been permitted to continue in marriage. Married men over the age of 35 can be ordained to the permanent diaconate.

Recent agitation for optional rather than mandatory celibacy for priests has diminished, without change in church law.

Eastern Church discipline on celibacy differs from that of the Roman Church. In line with legislation enacted by the Synod of Trullo in 692 and still in force, candidates for holy orders may marry before becoming deacons and may continue in marriage thereafter, but marriage after ordination is forbidden. Eastern-Rite bishops in the US, however, do not ordain married candidates for the priesthood. Eastern-Rite bishops are unmarried.

Cenacle: The room in Jerusalem where Christ ate the Last Supper with his Apostles.

Censer: A metal vessel with a perforated cover and suspended by chains, in which incense is burned. It is used at some Masses, Benediction of the Blessed Sacrament and other liturgical functions.

Censorship of Books: An exercise of vigilance by the Church for safeguarding authentic religious teaching.

According to a decree issued by the Congregation for the Doctrine of the Faith Apr. 9, 1975, the following regulations are in effect.

(1) Pre-publication clearance is required for: editions of Sacred Scripture, liturgical texts and books of private devotion, catechisms and other writings relating to catechetical instruction. Books dealing with Scripture, theology, canon law, church history and religious or moral disciplines may not be used as basic texts in educational institutions (from elementary to university levels) unless they have been published with the approval of competent church authority.

(2) Pre-publication clearance is recommended for all books on the aforementioned subjects, even though they are not used as basic texts in teaching.

(3) Books or other writings dealing with religion or morals may not be displayed, sold or given out in churches or oratories unless published with the approval of competent ecclesiastical authority.

(4) Except for a just and reasonable cause,

Catholics should not write for newspapers, magazines or periodicals which regularly and openly prove to be inimical to the Catholic religion and good morals. The approval of the local bishop is required before clerics or members of religious institutes (who also need the approval of their superior) may write for such publications.

Permission to publish works of a religious character, together with the apparatus of reviewing them beforehand, falls under the authority of the bishop of the place where the writer lives or where the works are published.

Clearance for publication is usually indicated by the terms *Nihil obstat* (Nothing stands in the way) issued by the censor and *Imprimatur* (Let it be printed) authorized by the bishop. The clearing of works for publication does not necessarily imply approval of an author's viewpoint or his manner of handling a subject.

Censures: Spiritual penalties inflicted by the Church on baptized persons for committing certain serious sins, which are classified as crimes in canon law, and for being or remaining obstinate therein. Excommunication, suspension and interdict have been the censures in force since the time of Innocent III (1214). Their intended purposes are to deter persons from committing sins which, more seriously and openly than others, threaten the common good of the Church and its members; to punish and correct offenders; and to provide for the making of reparation for harm done to the community of the Church. Censures may be incurred automatically (*ipso facto*) on the commission of certain offenses for which fixed penalties have been laid down in church law (*latae sententiae*); or they may be inflicted by sentence of a judge (*ferendae sententiae*). Obstinacy in crime— also called contumacy, disregard of a penalty, defiance of church authority — is presumed by law in the commission of crimes for which automatic censures are decreed. The presence and degree of contumacy in other cases, for which judicial sentence is required, is subject to determination by a judge. Absolution can be obtained from any censure, provided the person repents and desists from obstinacy. Absolution may be reserved to the pope, the bishop of a place, or the major superior of an exempt clerical religious institute. In danger of death, any priest can absolve from all censures; in other cases, faculties to absolve from reserved censures can be exercised by competent authorities or given to other priests.

Ceremonies, Master of: One who directs the proceedings of a rite or ceremony during the function.

Chamberlain: (1) The Chamberlain of the Holy Roman Church is a cardinal who administers the property and revenues of the Holy See. On the death of the pope he becomes head of the College of Cardinals and summons and directs the conclave until a new pope is elected.

(2) The Chamberlain of the Sacred College of Cardinals has charge of the property and revenues of the College and keeps the record of business transacted in consistories.

(3) The Chamberlain of the Roman Clergy is the president of the secular clergy of Rome.

Chancellor: Notary of a diocese, who draws up written documents in the government of the diocese; takes care of, arranges and indexes diocesan archives, records of dispensations and ecclesiastical trials.

Chancery (1) A branch of church administration that handles written documents used in the government of a diocese.

(2) The administrative office of a diocese, a bishop's office.

Chapel: A building or part of another building used for divine worship; a portion of a church set aside for the celebration of Mass or for some special devotion.

Chaplain: A priest appointed for the pastoral service of any division of the armed forces, religious communities, institutions, various groups of the faithful.

Chaplet: A term, meaning little crown, applied to a rosary or, more commonly, to a small string of beads used for devotional purposes; e.g., the Infant of Prague chaplet.

Chapter: A general meeting of delegates of religious orders for elections and the handling of other important affairs of their communities.

Charisms: Gifts or graces given by God to men for the good of others and the Church. Examples are special gifts for apostolic work, prophecy, healing, discernment of spirits, the life of evangelical poverty, here-and-now witness to faith in various circumstances of life.

The Second Vatican Council made the following statement about charisms in the *Dogmatic Constitution on the Church* (No. 12):

"It is not only through the sacraments and Church ministries that the same Holy Spirit sanctifies and leads the People of God and enriches it with virtues. Allotting His gifts 'to everyone according as he will' (I Cor. 12:11), He distributes special graces among the faithful of every rank. By these gifts He makes them fit and ready to undertake the various tasks or offices advantageous for the renewal and upbuilding of the Church, according to the words of the Apostle: 'The manifestation of the Spirit is given to everyone for profit' (1 Cor. 12:7). These charismatic gifts, whether they be the most outstanding or the more simple and widely diffused, are to be received with thanksgiving and consolation, for they are exceedingly suitable and useful for the needs of the Church.

"Still, extraordinary gifts are not to be rashly sought after, nor are the fruits of apostolic labor to be presumptuously expected from them. In any case, judgment as to their genuineness and proper use belongs to those who preside over the Church, and to whose special competence it belongs, not indeed to extinguish the Spirit, but to test all things and hold fast to that which is good" (cf. 1 Thes. 5:12; 19-21).

Charity: Love of God above all things for his own sake, and love of one's neighbor as oneself because and as an expression of one's love for God; the greatest of the three theological virtues. The term is sometimes also used to designate sanctifying grace.

Chastity: Properly ordered behavior with respect to sex. In marriage, the exercise of the procreative power is integrated with the norms and purposes of marriage. Outside of marriage, the rule is self-denial of the voluntary exercise and enjoyment of the procreative faculty in thought, word or action.

The vow of chastity, which reinforces the virtue of chastity with the virtue of religion, is an evangelical counsel and one of the three vows professed by religious.

Chirograph or Autograph Letter: A letter written by a pope himself, in his own handwriting.

Christ: The title of Jesus, derived from the Greek translation *Christos* of the Hebrew term *Messiah*, meaning the Anointed of God, the Savior and Deliverer of his people. Christian use of the title is a confession of belief that Jesus is the Savior.

Christianity: The sum total of things related to belief in Christ — the Christian religion, Christian churches, Christians themselves, society based on and expressive of Christian beliefs, culture reflecting Christian values.

Christians: The name first applied about the year 43 to followers of Christ at Antioch, the capital of Syria. It was used by the pagans as a contemptuous term. The word applies to persons who profess belief in the divinity and teachings of Christ and who give witness to him in life.

Christian Science: A religious doctrine consisting of Mary Baker Eddy's interpretation and formulation of the actions and teachings of Christ. Its basic tenets reflect Mrs. Eddy's ideas regarding the reality of spirit and its control and domination of what is not spirit. The basic statement of the doctrine is contained in *Science and Health, with Key to the Scriptures*, which she first published in 1875, nine years after being saved from death and healed on reading the New Testament.

Mary Baker Eddy (1821-1910) established the church in 1879, and in 1892 founded at Boston the First Church of Christ, Scientist, of which all other Christian Science churches are branches. The individual churches are self-governing and self-supporting under the general supervision of a board of directors. Services consist of readings of portions of Scripture and *Science and Health*. One of the church's publications, *The Christian Science Monitor*, has a worldwide reputation as a journal of news and opinion.

Church: (1) See several entries under Church, Catholic. The universal Church is the Church spread throughout the world. The local Church is the Church in a particular locality; e.g., a diocese. Inasmuch as the members of the Church are on earth, in purgatory, or in glory in heaven, the Church is called militant, suffering, or triumphant.

(2) In general, any religious body.

(3) Place of divine worship.

Churching: A rite of thanksgiving in which a blessing is given to women after childbirth. The rite is reminiscent of the Old Testament ceremony of purification (Lv. 12:2-8).

Circumcision: A ceremonial practice symbolic of initiation and participation in the covenant between God and Abraham.

Circumincession: The indwelling of each divine Person of the Holy Trinity in the others.

Clergy: Men ordained to holy orders and assigned to pastoral and other ministries for the service of the people and the Church.

(1) Diocesan or secular clergy are committed to pastoral ministry in parishes and in other capacities in a local church (diocese) under the direction of their bishop, to whom they are bound by a promise of obedience.

(2) Regular clergy belong to religious institutes (orders, congregations, societies) and are so called because they observe the rule (*regula*, in Latin) of their respective institutes. They are committed to the ways of life and apostolates of their institutes. In ordinary pastoral ministry, they are under the direction of local bishops as well as their own superiors.

Clericalism: A term generally used in a derogatory sense to mean action, influence and interference by the Church and the clergy in matters with which they allegedly should not be concerned. Anticlericalism is a reaction of antipathy, hostility, distrust and opposition to the Church and clergy arising from real and/or alleged faults of the clergy, overextension of the role of the laity, or for other reasons.

Cloister: The enclosure of a convent or monastery, which members of the community may not leave or outsiders enter without due permission. Enclosure is of two kinds: papal, in monasteries of religious with solemn vows; episcopal, in the houses of other religious.

Code: A digest of rules or regulations, such as the Code of Canon Law.

Collegiality: The bishops of the Church, in union with and subordinate to the pope — who has full, supreme and universal power over the Church which he can always exercise independently — have supreme teaching and pastoral authority over the whole Church. In addition to their proper authority of office for the good of the faithful in their respective dioceses or other jurisdictions, the bishops have authority to act for the good of the universal Church. This collegial authority is exercised in a solemn manner in an ecumenical council and can also be exercised in other ways sanctioned by the pope. Doctrine on collegiality was set forth by the Second Vatican Council in the *Dogmatic Constitution on the Church.* (See separate entry.)

By extension, the concept of collegiality is applied to other forms of participation and co-responsibility by members of a community.

Commissariat of the Holy Land: A special jurisdiction within the Order of Friars Minor, whose main purposes are the collecting of alms for support of the Holy Places in Palestine and staffing of the Holy Places and missions in the Middle East with priests and brothers. There are 69 such commissariats in 33 countries. One of them has headquarters at Mt. St. Sepulchre, Washington, D.C. Franciscans have had custody of the Holy Places since 1342.

Communion of Faithful, Saints: The communion of all the People of God — on earth, in heavenly glory, in purgatory — with Christ and each other in faith, grace, prayer and good works.

Concelebration: The liturgical act in which several priests, led by one member of the group, offer Mass together, all consecrating the bread and wine. Concelebration has always been common in churches of Eastern Rite. In the Roman Rite, it was long restricted, taking place only at the ordination of bishops and the ordination of priests. The *Constitution on the Sacred Liturgy* issued by the Second Vatican Council set new norms for concelebration.

Concordance, Biblical: An alphabetical verbal index enabling a user knowing one or more words of a scriptural passage to locate the entire text.

Concordat: A Church-state treaty with the force of law concerning matters of mutual concern — e.g., rights of the Church, appointment of bishops, arrangement of ecclesiastical jurisdictions, marriage laws, education. Approximately 150 agreements of this kind have been negotiated since the Concordat of Worms in 1122.

Concupiscence: Any tendency of the sensitive appetite. The term is most frequently used in reference to desires and tendencies for sinful sense pleasure.

Confession: Sacramental confession is the act by which a person tells or confesses his sins to a priest who is authorized to give absolution in the sacrament of penance.

Confessor: (1) A male saint who lived a life of eminent sanctity and heroic virtue, but who did not suffer martyrdom for his faith.

(2) A priest who administers the sacrament of penance.

Confraternity: An association whose members practice a particular form of religious devotion and/or are engaged in some kind of apostolic work. When a confraternity reaches the stage where affiliations similar to itself are formed and adopt its rules, it takes the name of archconfraternity.

Conscience: Practical judgment concerning the moral goodness or sinfulness of an action. In the Catholic view, this judgment is made by reference of the action, its attendant circumstances and the intentions of the person to the requirements of divine law as expressed in the Ten Commandments, the summary law of love for God and neighbor, the life and teaching of Christ, and the authoritative teaching and practice of the Church with respect to the total demands of divine Revelation.

A person is obliged: (1) to obey a certain and correct conscience; (2) to obey a certain conscience even if it is inculpably erroneous; (3) not to obey, but to correct, a conscience known to be erroneous or lax; (4) to rectify a scrupulous conscience by following the advice of a confessor and by other measures; (5) to resolve doubts of conscience before acting.

It is legitimate to act for solid and probable reasons when a question of moral responsibility admits of argument (see Probabilism). It is also legitimate to resolve doubts in difficult cases by having recourse to a reflex principle (e.g., by following the manner of acting of a well-informed and well-intentioned group of persons in similar circumstances).

Conscience, Examination of: Self-examination to determine one's spiritual state before God, especially regarding one's sins and faults. It is recommended as a regular practice and is practically necessary in preparing for the sacrament of penance. The *particular examen* is a regular examination to assist in overcoming specific faults and imperfections.

Consecration of a Church: See Dedication of a Church.

Consistory: An assembly of cardinals presided over by the pope. Consistories are secret (pope and cardinals only), semi-public (plus other prelates), and public (plus other attendants).

Constitution: (1) An apostolic or papal constitution is a document in which a pope enacts and promulgates law.

(2) A formal and solemn document issued by an ecumenical council on a doctrinal or pastoral subject, with binding force in the whole Church; e.g., the four constitutions issued by the Second Vatican Council on the Church, liturgy, Revelation, and the Church in the modern world.

(3) The constitutions of religious orders spell out details of and norms drawn from the various rules for the guidance and direction of the life and work of members of each institute.

Consubstantiation: A theory which holds that the Body and Blood of Christ coexist with the substance of bread and wine in the Holy Eucharist. This theory, also called *impanation*, is incompatible with the doctrine of transubstantiation.

Contraception: Anything done by positive interference to prevent sexual intercourse from resulting in conception. Direct contraception is against the order of nature. Indirect contraception — as a secondary effect of medical treatment or other action having a necessary, good, non-contraceptive purpose — is permissible under the principle of the double effect. The practice of rhythm is not contraception because it does not involve positive interference with the order of nature.

Contrition: Sorrow for sin coupled with a purpose of amendment. Contrition arising from a supernatural motive is necessary for the forgiveness of sin.

(1) Perfect contrition is total sorrow for and renunciation of attachment to sin, arising from the motive of pure love of God. Perfect contrition, which implies the intention of doing all God wants done for the forgiveness of sin, is sufficient for the forgiveness of serious sin and the remission of all temporal punishment due for sin. Confession is required before the reception of another sacrament. (The intention to receive the sacrament of penance is implicit — even if unrealized, as in the case of some persons — in perfect contrition.)

(2) Imperfect contrition or attrition is sorrow arising from a quasi-selfish supernatural motive; e.g., the fear of losing heaven, suffering the pains of hell, etc. Imperfect contrition is sufficient for the forgiveness of serious sin when joined with absolution in confession, and sufficient for the forgiveness of venial sin even outside of confession.

Contumely: Personal insult, reviling a person in his presence by accusation of moral faults, by refusal of recognition or due respect; a violation of obligations of justice and charity.

Corporal Works of Mercy: Feeding the hungry, giving drink to the thirsty, clothing the naked, visiting the imprisoned, sheltering the homeless, visiting the sick, burying the dead.

Councils: Bodies representative of various categories of members of the Church which participate with bishops and other church authorities in making decisions and carrying out action programs for the good of the Church and the accomplishment of its mission to its own members and society in general. Examples are priests' senates or councils, councils of religious and lay persons, parish councils, diocesan pastoral councils.

Councils, Plenary: National councils or councils of the bishops of several ecclesiastical provinces, assembled under the presidency of a papal legate to take action related to the life and mission of the Church in the area under their jurisdiction. The membership of such councils is fixed by canon law; their decrees, when approved by the Holy See, are binding in the territory (see Index, Plenary Councils of Baltimore).

Councils, Provincial: Meetings of the bishops of a province. The metropolitan, or ranking archbishop, of an ecclesiastical province convenes and presides over such councils in a manner prescribed by canon law to take action related to the life and mission of the Church in the province. Acts and decrees must be approved by the Holy See before being promulgated. Provincial councils should be held at least once every 20 years.

Counsels, Evangelical: Gospel counsels of perfection, especially voluntary poverty, perfect chastity and obedience, which were recommended by Christ to those who would devote themselves exclusively and completely to the immediate service of God. Religious bind themselves by public vows to observe these counsels in a life of total consecration to God and service to people through various kinds of apostolic works.

Counter-Reformation: The period of approximately 100 years following the Council of Trent, which witnessed a reform within the Church to stimulate genuine Catholic life and to counteract effects of the Reformation.

Covenant: A bond of relationship between parties pledged to each other. God-initiated covenants in the Old Testament included those with Abraham, Noah, Moses, Levi, David. The Mosaic (Sinai) covenant made Israel God's Chosen People on terms of fidelity to true faith, true worship, and righteous conduct according to the Decalogue. The New Testament covenant, prefigured in the Old Testament, is the bond men have with God through Christ. All men are called to be parties to this perfect and everlasting covenant, which was mediated and ratified by Christ.

Creation: The production by God of something out of nothing. The biblical account of creation is contained in the first two chapters of Genesis.

Creator: God, the supreme, self-existing Being, the absolute and infinite First Cause of all things.

Creature: Everything in the realm of being is a creature, except God.

Cremation: The reduction of a human corpse to ashes by means of fire. Cremation is not in line with Catholic tradition and practice, even though it is not opposed to any article of faith. It can be permitted for serious reasons. The general practice, however, was forbidden in a decree issued May 19, 1886, by the Sacred Congregation of the Holy Office.

This ruling was incorporated in the Code of Canon Law (Canons 1203, 1240), which generally banned the practice of cremation, forbade following orders for cremation, and deprived of the last rites and ecclesiastical burial those who directed that their bodies be cremated and did not retract the directions.

The principal reason behind the prohibition against cremation was the fact that, historically, the practice had represented an attempt to deny the doctrine of the resurrection of the body. It also appeared to be a form of violence against the body which, as the temple of the Holy Spirit during life, should be treated with reverence.

The Congregation for the Doctrine of the Faith, under date of May 8, 1963, circulated among bishops an instruction which upheld the traditional practices of Christian burial but modified anti-cremation legislation. Cremation may be permitted for serious reasons, of a private as well as public nature, provided it does not involve any contempt of the Church or of religion, or any attempt to deny, question, or belittle the doctrine of the resurrection of the body. The person may receive the last rites and be given ecclesiastical burial. A priest may say prayers for the deceased at the crematorium, but full liturgical ceremonies may not take place there.

Crib: A devotional representation of the birth of Jesus. The custom of erecting cribs is generally attributed to St. Francis of Assisi who in 1223 obtained from Pope Honorius III permission to use a crib and figures of the Christ Child, Mary, St. Joseph, and others, to represent the mystery of the Nativity.

Crosier: The bishop's staff, symbolic of his pastoral office, responsibility and authority.

Crypt: An underground or partly underground chamber; e.g., the lower part of a church used for worship and/or burial.

Cura Animarum: A Latin phrase, meaning care of souls, designating the pastoral ministry and responsibility of bishops and priests.

Curia: The personnel and offices through which (1) the pope administers the affairs of the universal Church, the *Roman Curia* (see separate entry), or (2) a bishop the affairs of a diocese, *diocesan curia*. The principal officials of a diocesan curia are the vicar general of the diocese, the chancellor, officials of the diocesan tribunal or court, examiners, consultors, auditors, notaries.

Custos: A religious superior who presides over a number of convents collectively called a custody. In some religious institutes, a custos may be the deputy of a higher superior.

D

Deaconess — A woman officially appointed and charged by the Church to carry out service-like functions. Phoebe apparently was one (Rom. 16:1-2); a second probable reference to the office is in Tm. 3:11.

The office — for assistance at the baptism of women, for pastoral service to women and for works of charity — had considerable development in the third and also in the fourth century when the actual term came into use (in place of such designations as *diacona, vidua, virgo canonica*). Its importance declined subsequently with the substitution of infusion in place of immersion as the common method of baptism in the West, and with the increase of the practice of infant baptism. There is no record of the ministry of deaconess in the West after the beginning of the 11th century. The office continued, however, for a longer time in the East.

Several Christian churches have had revivals of the office of deaconess since the 1830s. There is a contemporary movement in support of such a revival among some Catholics.

The Vatican's Theological Commission, in a paper prepared in 1971, noted that there had been in the past a form of diaconal ordination for women. With a rite and purpose distinctive to women, it differed essentially from the ordination of deacons, which had sacramental effects.

Dean: (1) A priest with supervisory responsibility over a section of a diocese known as a deanery. The post-Vatican II counterpart of a dean is an episcopal vicar.

(2) The senior or ranking member of a group.

Dean of the Sacred College: The president of the College of Cardinals (the ranking cardinal bishop). He is elected by the cardinals holding title to the suburban sees of Rome.

Decision: A judgment or pronouncement on a cause or suit, given by a church tribunal or official with judicial authority. A decision has the force of law for concerned parties.

Declaration: (1) An ecclesiastical document which presents an interpretation of an existing law.

(2) A position paper on a specific subject; e.g., the three declarations issued by the Second Vatican Council on religious freedom, non-Christian religions, and Christian education.

Decree: An edict or ordinance issued by a pope and/or by an ecumenical council, with binding force in the whole Church; by a department of the Roman Curia, with binding force for concerned parties; by a territorial body of bishops, with binding force for persons in the area; by individual bishops, with binding force for concerned parties until revocation or the death of the bishop.

The nine decrees issued by the Second Vatican Council were combinations of doctrinal and pastoral statements with executive orders for action and movement toward renewal and reform in the Church.

Dedication of a Church: The ceremony whereby a church is solemnly set apart for the worship of God. The custom of dedicating churches had an antecedent in Old Testament ceremonies for the dedication of the Temple, as in the times of Solomon and the Maccabees. The earliest extant record of the dedication of a Christian church dates from early in the fourth century, when it was done simply by the celebration of Mass. Other ceremonies developed later. A church can be dedicated by a simple blessing or a solemn consecration. The rite of consecration is performed by a bishop.

Definitors: Members of the governing council of a religious order, each one having a decisive vote equal to the vote of the general or provincial superior.

Deism: A system of natural religion which acknowledges the existence of God but regards him as so transcendent and remote from man and the universe that divine revelation and the supernatural order of things are irrelevant and unacceptable. It developed from rationalistic principles in England in the 17th and 18th centuries, and had Voltaire, Rousseau and the Encyclopedists among its advocates in France.

Despair: Abandonment of hope for salvation arising from the conviction that God will not provide the necessary means for attaining it, that following God's way of life for salvation is impossible, or that one's sins are unforgivable; a serious sin against the Holy Spirit and the theological virtues of hope and faith, involving distrust in the mercy and goodness of God and a denial of the truths that God wills the salvation of all men and provides sufficient grace for it. Real despair is distinguished from unreasonable fear with respect to the difficulties of attaining salvation, from morbid anxiety over the demands of divine justice, and from feelings of despair.

Detachment: Control of affection for creatures by two principles: (1) supreme love and devotion belong to God; (2) love and service of creatures should be an expression of love for God.

Detraction: Revelation of true but hidden faults of a person without sufficient and justifying reason; a violation of requirements of justice and charity, involving the obligation to make restitution when this is possible without doing more harm to the good name of the offended party. In some cases, e.g., to prevent evil, secret faults may and should be disclosed.

Devil: (1) Lucifer, Satan, chief of the fallen angels who sinned and were banished from heaven. Still possessing angelic powers, he can cause such diabolical phenomena as possession and obsession, and can tempt men to sin.

(2) Any fallen angel.

Devil's Advocate: See Promoter of the Faith.

Devotion: (1) Religious fervor, piety; dedication.

(2) The consolation experienced at times during prayer; a reverent manner of praying.

Devotions: Pious practices of members of the Church include not only participation in various acts of the liturgy but also in other acts of worship generally called popular or private devotions. Concerning these, the Second Vatican Council said in the *Constitution on the Sacred Liturgy* (No. 13): "Popular devotions of the Christian people are warmly commended, provided they accord with the laws and norms of the Church. Such is especially the case with devotions called for by the Apostolic See. Devotions proper to the individual churches also have a special dignity. . . . These devotions should be so drawn up that they harmonize with the liturgical seasons, accord with the sacred liturgy, are in some fashion derived from it, and lead the people to it, since the liturgy by its very nature far surpasses any of them."

Devotions of a liturgical type are Benediction of the Blessed Sacrament, recitation of the Little Office of the Blessed Virgin Mary or of Vespers and Compline. Examples of para-liturgical devotion are a Bible Service or Vigil, and the Angelus, Rosary and Stations of the Cross, which have a strong scriptural basis.

Dies Irae: The opening Latin words, Day of Wrath, of a hymn for requiem Masses, written in the 13th century by the Franciscan Thomas of Celano.

Diocese: A fully organized ecclesiastical jurisdiction under the pastoral direction of a bishop as local ordinary.

Discalced: Of Latin derivation and meaning without shoes, the word is applied to religious orders or congregations whose members go barefoot or wear sandals.

Disciple: A term used sometimes in reference to the Apostles but more often to a larger number of followers (70 or 72) of Christ mentioned in Lk. 10:1.

Disciplina Arcani: A Latin phrase, meaning discipline of the secret and referring to a practice of the early Church, especially during the Roman persecutions, to: (1) conceal Christian truths from those who, it was feared, would misinterpret, ridicule and profane the teachings, and persecute Christians for believing them; (2) instruct catechumens in a gradual manner, withholding the teaching of certain doctrines until the catechumens proved themselves of good faith and sufficient understanding.

Dispensation: The relaxation of a law in a particular case. Laws made for the common good sometimes work undue hardship in particular cases. In such cases, where sufficient reasons are present, dispensations may be granted by proper authorities. Bishops, religious superiors and others may dispense from certain laws; the pope can dispense from all ecclesiastical laws. No one has authority to dispense from obligations of the divine law.

Divination: Attempting to foretell future or hidden things by means of things like dreams, necromancy, spiritism, examination of entrails, astrology, augury, omens, palmistry, drawing straws, dice, cards, etc. Practices like these attribute to creatural things a power which belongs to God alone and are violations of the First Commandment.

Divine Praises: Fourteen praises recited or sung at Benediction of the Blessed Sacrament in reparation for sins of sacrilege, blasphemy and profanity. Some of these praises date from the end of the 18th century.

Blessed be God.
Blessed be his holy Name.
Blessed be Jesus Christ, true God and true Man.
Blessed be the Name of Jesus.
Blessed be his most Sacred Heart.
Blessed be his most Precious Blood.
Blessed be Jesus in the most holy Sacrament of the Altar.
Blessed be the Holy Spirit, the Paraclete.
Blessed be the great Mother of God, Mary most holy.
Blessed be her holy and Immaculate Conception.
Blessed be her glorious Assumption.
Blessed be the name of Mary, Virgin and Mother.
Blessed be St. Joseph, her most chaste Spouse.
Blessed be God in his Angels and in his Saints.

Double Effect Principle: Actions sometimes have two effects closely related to each other, one good and the other bad, and a difficult moral question can arise: Is it permissible to place an action from which two such results follow? It is permissible to place the action, if: the action is good in itself and is directly productive of the good effect; the circumstances are good; the intention of the person is good; the reason for placing the action is proportionately serious to the seriousness of the indirect bad effect. For example: Is it morally permissible for a pregnant woman to undergo medical or surgical treatment for a pathological condition if the indirect and secondary effect of the treatment will be the loss of the child? The reply is affirmative, for these reasons: The action, i.e., the treatment, is good in itself, cannot be deferred until a later time without very serious consequences, and is ordered directly to the cure of critically grave pathology. By means of the treatment, the woman intends to save her life, which she has a right to do. The loss of the child is not directly sought as a means for the cure of the mother but results indirectly and in a secondary manner from the placing of the action, i.e., the treatment, which is good in itself.

The double effect principle does not support the principle that the end justifies the means.

Doxology: (1) The lesser doxology, or ascription of glory to the Trinity, is the Glory be to the Father. The first part dates back to the third or fourth century, and came from the form of baptism. The concluding words, As it was in the beginning, etc., are of later origin.

(2) The greater doxology, Glory to God in the highest, begins with the words of angelic praise at the birth of Christ recounted in the Infancy Narrative (Lk. 2:14). It is often recited at Mass. Of early Eastern origin, it is found in the *Apostolic Constitutions* in a form much like the present.

Dulia: A Greek term meaning the veneration or homage, different in nature and degree from that given to God, paid to the saints. It includes honoring the saints and seeking their intercession with God.

Duty: A moral obligation deriving from the binding force of law, the exigencies of one's state in life, and other sources.

E

Easter Controversy: A three-phase controversy over the time for the celebration of Easter.

Some early Christians in the Near East, called Quartodecimans, favored the observance of Easter on the 14th day of Nisan, the spring month of the Hebrew calendar, whenever it occurred. Against this practice, Pope St. Victor I, about 190, ordered a Sunday observance of the feast.

The Council of Nicaea, in line with usages of the Church at Rome and Alexandria, decreed in 325 that Easter should be observed on the first Sunday following the first full moon of spring.

Uniformity of practice in the West was not achieved until several centuries later, when the British Isles, in delayed compliance with measures enacted by the Synod of Whitby in 664, accepted the Roman date of observance.

Unrelated to the controversy is the fact that some Eastern Christians, in accordance with traditional calendar practices, celebrate Easter at a different time than the Roman and Eastern-Rite churches.

Easter Duty: The serious obligation binding Catholics of Roman Rite, by a precept of the Church, to receive Holy Communion during the Easter time; in the US, from the first Sunday of Lent to Trinity Sunday.

Easter Water: Holy water blessed with special ceremonies and distributed on the Easter Vigil; used during Easter Week for blessing the faithful and homes.

Ecclesiology: Study of the nature, constitution, members, mission, functions, etc., of the Church.

Ecstasy: An extraordinary state of mystical experience in which a person is so absorbed in God that the activity of the exterior senses is suspended.

Ecumenism: The movement of Christians and their churches toward the unity willed by Christ. The Second Vatican Council called the movement "those activities and enterprises which, according to various needs of the Church and opportune occasions, are started and organized for the fostering of unity among Christians" (*Decree on Ecumenism,* No. 4). Spiritual ecumenism, i.e., mutual prayer for unity, is the heart of the movement. The movement also involves scholarly and pew-level efforts for the development of mutual understanding and better interfaith relations in general, and collaboration by the churches and their members in the social area.

Elevation: The raising of the host after consecration at Mass for adoration by the faithful. The custom was introduced in the Diocese of Paris about the close of the 12th century to offset an erroneous teaching of the time which held that transubstantiation of the bread did not take place until after the consecration of the wine in the chalice. The elevation of the chalice following the consecration of the wine was introduced in the 15th century.

End Justifies the Means: An unacceptable ethical principle which states that evil means may be used to produce good effects.

Envy: Sadness over another's good fortune because it is considered a loss to oneself or a detraction from one's own excellence; one of the seven capital sins, a violation of the obligations of charity.

Epikeia: A Greek word meaning reasonableness and designating a moral theory and practice, a mild interpretation of the mind of a legislator who is prudently considered not to wish positive law to bind in certain circumstances. Use of the principle is justified in practice when the lawgiver himself cannot be appealed to and when it can be prudently assumed that in particular cases, e.g., because of special hardship, he would not wish the law to be applied in a strict manner. Epikeia may not be applied with respect to acts that are intrinsically wrong or those covered by laws which automatically make them invalid.

Episcopate: (1) The office, dignity and sacramental powers bestowed upon a bishop at his ordination.

(2) The body of bishops collectively.

Equivocation: (1) The use of words, phrases, or gestures having more than one meaning in order to conceal information which a questioner has no strict right to know. It is permissible to equivocate (have a broad mental reservation) in some circumstances.

(2) A lie, i.e., a statement of untruth. Lying is intrinsically wrong. A lie told in joking, evident as such, is not wrong.

Eschatology: Doctrine concerning the last things: death, judgment, heaven and hell, and the final state of perfection of the People and Kingdom of God at the end of time.

Eternity: The interminable, perfect possession of life in its totality without beginning or end; an attribute of God, who has no past or future but always is. Man's existence has a beginning but no end and is, accordingly, called immortal.

Ethics: Moral philosophy, the science of the morality of human acts deriving from natural law, the natural end of man, and the powers of human reason. It includes all the spheres of human activity — personal, social, economic, political, etc. Ethics is distinct from but can be related to moral theology, whose primary principles are drawn from divine Revelation.

Eucharistic Congresses: Public demonstrations of faith in the Holy Eucharist. Combining liturgical services, other public ceremonies, subsidiary meetings, different kinds of instructional and inspirational elements, they are unified by central themes and serve to increase understanding of and devotion to Christ in the Eucharist, and to relate this liturgy of worship and witness to life.

The first international congress developed from a proposal by Marie Marthe Tamisier of Touraine, organizing efforts of Msgr. Louis Gaston de Segur, and backing by industrialist Philibert Vrau. It was held with the approval of Pope Leo XIII at the University of Lille, France, and was attended by some 800 persons from France, Belgium, Holland, England, Spain and Switzerland.

International congresses are planned and held under the auspices of a permanent committee for international Eucharistic congresses. Participants include clergy, religious and lay persons from many countries, and representatives of national and international Catholic organizations. Popes have usually been represented by legates, but Paul VI attended two congresses personally, the 38th at Bombay and the 39th at Bogota.

Forty-one international congresses were held from 1881 to 1976:

Lille (1881), Avignon (1882), Liege (1883), Freiburg (1885), Toulouse (1886), Paris (1888), Antwerp (1890), Jerusalem (1893), Rheims (1894), Paray-le-Monial (1897), Brussels (1898), Lourdes (1899), Angers (1901), Namur (1902), Angouleme (1904), Rome (1905), Tournai (1906), Metz (1907), London (1908), Cologne (1909), Montreal (1910), Madrid (1911), Vienna (1912), Malta (1913), Lourdes (1914), Rome (1922), Amsterdam (1924), Chicago (1926), Sydney (1928), Carthage (1930), Dublin (1932), Buenos Aires (1934), Manila (1937), Budapest (1938), Barcelona (1952), Rio de Janeiro (1955), Munich, Germany (1960), Bombay, India (1964), Bogota, Colombia (1968), Melbourne, Australia (1973), Philadelphia (1976).

The Vatican announced in June, 1977, that the 42nd international congress would be held in 1981 at Lourdes.

Eugenics: The science of heredity and environment for the physical and mental improvement of offspring. Extreme eugenics is untenable in practice because it advocates immoral means, such as compulsory breeding of the select, sterilization of persons said to be unfit, abortion, and unacceptable methods of birth regulation.

Euthanasia: Mercy killing, the direct causing of death by painless means for the purpose of ending human suffering. Euthanasia is murder and is totally illicit, for the natural law forbids the direct taking of one's own life or that of an innocent person.

The use of drugs to relieve suffering in serious cases, even when this results in a shortening of life as an indirect and secondary effect, is permissible under conditions of the double effect principle. It is also permissible for a seriously ill person to refuse to follow — or for other responsible persons to refuse to permit — extraordinary medical procedures even though the refusal might entail shortening of life.

Evolution: Scientific theory concerning the development of the physical universe from unorganized matter (inorganic evolution) and, especially, the development of existing forms of vegetable, animal and human life from earlier and more primitive organisms (organic evolution). Various ideas about evolution were advanced for some centuries before scientific evidence in support of the main-line theory of organic evolution, which has several formulations, was discovered and verified in the second half of the 19th century and afterwards. This evidence — from the findings of comparative anatomy and other sciences — confirmed evolution within species and cleared the way to further investigation of questions regarding the processes of its accomplishment. While a number of such questions remain open with respect to human evolution, a point of doctrine not open to question is the immediate creation of the human soul by God.

For some time, theologians regarded the theory with hostility, considering it to be in opposition to the account of creation in the early chapters of Genesis and subversive of belief in such doctrines as creation, the early state of man in grace, and the fall of man from grace. This state of affairs and the tension it generated led to considerable controversy regarding an alleged conflict between religion and science. Gradually, however, the tension was diminished with the development of biblical studies from the latter part of the 19th century onwards, with clarification of the distinctive features of religious truth and scientific truth, and with the refinement of evolutionary concepts.

So far as the Genesis account of creation is concerned, the Catholic view is that the writer(s) did not write as a scientist but as the communicator of religious truth in a manner adapted to the understanding of the people of his time. He used anthropomorphic language, the figure of days and other literary devices to state the salvation truths of creation, the fall of man from grace, and the promise of redemption. It was beyond the competency and purpose of the writer(s) to describe creation and related events in a scientific manner.

Excommunication: A penalty or censure by which a baptized person is excluded from the communion of the faithful, for committing and remaining obstinate in certain sins specified in canon law and technically called crimes. As by baptism a person is made a member of the Church in which there is a communication of spiritual goods, so by excommunication he is deprived of the same spiritual goods until he repents and receives absolution. Even though excommunicated, a person is still responsible for the normal obligations of a Catholic.

Existentialism: A philosophy with radical concern for the problems of individual existence and identity viewed in particular here-and-now patterns of thought which presuppose irrationality and absurdity in human life and the whole universe. It is preoccupied with questions about freedom, moral decision and responsibility against a background of denial of objective truth and universal norms of conduct; is characterized by prevailing anguish, dread, fear, pessimism, despair; is generally atheistic, although its modern originator, Soren Kierkegaard (d. 1855), and Gabriel Marcel attempted to give it a Christian orientation. Pius XII called it "the new erroneous philosophy which, opposing itself to idealism, immanentism and pragmatism, has assumed the name of existentialism, since it concerns itself only with the existence of individual things and neglects all consideration of their immutable essences" (Encyclical *Humani Generis*, Aug. 12, 1950).

Exorcism: (1) Driving out evil spirits; a rite in which evil spirits are charged and commanded on the authority of God and with the prayer of the Church to depart from a person or to cease causing harm to a person suffering from diabolical possession or obsession. The sacramental is officially administered by a priest delegated for the purpose by the bishop of the place. Elements of the rite include the Litany of Saints; recitation of the Our Father, one or more creeds, and other prayers; specific prayers of exorcism; the reading of Gospel passages, and use of the Sign of the Cross. Private exorcism for the liberation of a person from the strong influence of evil spirits, through prayer and the use of sacramentals like holy water, can be done by anyone.

(2) Exorcisms which do not imply the conditions of either diabolical possession or obsession form part of the ceremony of baptism, and are also included in formulas for various blessings; e.g., of water.

F

Faculties: Grants of jurisdiction, or authority, granted by the law of the Church or superiors (pope, bishop, religious superior) for exercise of the powers of holy orders; e.g., priests are given faculties to hear confessions, officiate at weddings; bishops are given faculties to grant dispensations, etc.

Faith: In religion, faith has several aspects. Catholic doctrine calls faith the assent of the mind to truths revealed by God, the assent being made with the help of grace and by command of the will on account of the authority and trustworthiness of God revealing. The term faith also refers to the truths that are believed (content of faith) and to the way in which a person, in response to Christ, gives witness to and expresses his belief in daily life (living faith).

All of these elements, and more, are included in the following statement:

" 'The obedience of faith' (Rom. 16:26; cf. 1:5; 2 Cor. 10:5-6) must be given to God who reveals, an obedience by which man entrusts his whole self freely to God, offering 'the full submission of intellect and will to God who reveals' (First Vatican Council, *Dogmatic Constitution on the Catholic Faith,* Chap. 3), and freely assenting to the truth revealed by Him. If this faith is to be shown, the grace of God and the interior help of the Holy Spirit must precede and assist, moving the heart and turning it to God, opening the eyes of the mind, and giving 'joy and ease to everyone in assenting to the truth and believing it' " (Second Council of Orange, Canon 7) (Second Vatican Council, *Constitution on Revelation,* No. 5). Faith is necessary for salvation.

Faith, Rule of: The norm or standard of religious belief. The Catholic doctrine is that belief must be professed in the divinely revealed truths in the Bible and tradition as interpreted and proposed by the infallible teaching authority of the Church.

Fast, Eucharistic: Eating and the drinking of any liquids except water are prohibited for one hour before the reception of Holy Communion. Water never breaks the Eucharistic fast, which is prescribed for reasons of reverence and preparation. By way of exception, the period of fasting is 15 minutes for the sick and aged, even though not confined to bed or a home, and those caring for them who wish to receive Communion with them but cannot fast for an hour without inconvenience (Instruction, *Immensae Caritatis,* Congregation for the Discipline of the Sacraments, Jan. 29, 1973).

Those who are ill, even though not confined to bed, may take nonalcoholic beverages and liquid or solid medicine before Holy Communion without any time limit.

Father: A title of priests, who are regarded as spiritual fathers because they are the ordinary ministers of baptism, by which persons are born to supernatural life, and because of their pastoral service to people.

Fear: A mental state caused by the apprehension of present or future danger. Grave fear does not necessarily remove moral responsibility for an act, but may lessen it.

First Friday: A devotion consisting of the reception of Holy Communion on the first Friday of nine consecutive months in honor of the Sacred Heart of Jesus and in reparation for sin. (See Sacred Heart, Promises.)

First Saturday: A devotion tracing its origin to the apparitions of the Blessed Virgin Mary at Fatima in 1917. Those practicing the devotion go to confession and, on the first Saturday of five consecutive months, receive Holy Communion, recite five decades of the Rosary, and meditate on the mysteries for 15 minutes.

Fisherman's Ring: A signet ring engraved with the image of St. Peter fishing from a boat, and encircled with the name of the reigning pope. It is not worn by the pope. It is used to seal briefs, and is destroyed after each pope's death.

Forgiveness of Sin: Catholics believe that sins are forgiven by God through the mediation of Christ in view of the repentance of the sinner and by means of the sacrament of penance. (See Penance.)

Fortitude: Courage to face dangers or hardships for the sake of what is good; one of the four cardinal virtues and one of the seven gifts of the Holy Spirit.

Fortune Telling: Attempting to predict the future or the occult by means of cards, palm reading, etc.; a form of divination, prohibited by the First Commandment.

Forty Hours Devotion: A Eucharistic observance consisting of solemn exposition of the Blessed Sacrament in commemoration of the time Christ's body lay in the tomb, coupled with special Masses and forms of prayer, for the purposes of making reparation for sin and praying for God's blessings of grace and peace. The devotion was instituted in 1534 in Milan. St. John Neumann of Philadelphia was the first bishop in the U.S. to prescribe its observance in his diocese. For many years in this country, the observance was held annually on a rotating basis in all parishes of a diocese. Simplified and abbreviated Eucharistic observances have taken the place of the devotion in some places.

Forum: The sphere in which ecclesiastical authority or jurisdiction is exercised.

(1) External: Authority is exercised in the external forum to deal with matters affecting the public welfare of the Church and its members. Those who have such authority because of their office (e.g., diocesan bishops) are called ordinaries.

(2) Internal: Authority is exercised in the internal forum to deal with matters affecting the private spiritual good of individuals. The

sacramental forum is the sphere in which the sacrament of penance is administered; other exercises of jurisdiction in the internal forum take place in the non-sacramental forum.

Franciscan Crown: A seven-decade rosary used to commemorate the seven Joys of the Blessed Virgin: the Annunciation, the Visitation, the Nativity of Our Lord, the Adoration of the Magi, the Finding of the Child Jesus in the Temple, the Apparition of the Risen Christ to his Mother, the Assumption and Coronation of the Blessed Virgin. Introduced in 1422, the Crown originally consisted only of seven Our Fathers and 70 Hail Marys. Two Hail Marys were added to complete the number 72 (thought to be the number of years of Mary's life), and one Our Father, Hail Mary and Glory be to the Father are said for the intention of the pope.

Freedom, Religious: The Second Vatican Council declared that the right to religious freedom in civil society "means that all men are to be immune from coercion on the part of individuals or of social groups and of any human power, in such wise that in matters religious no one is to be forced to act in a manner contrary to his own beliefs. Nor is anyone to be restrained from acting in accordance with his own beliefs, whether privately or publicly, whether alone or in association with others, within due limits" of requirements for the common good. The foundation of this right in civil society is the "very dignity of the human person" (*Declaration on Religious Freedom*, No. 2).

The conciliar statement did not deal with the subject of freedom within the Church. It noted the responsibility of the faithful "carefully to attend to the sacred and certain doctrine of the Church" (No. 14).

Freemasons: A fraternal order which originated in London in 1717 with the formation of the first Grand Lodge of Freemasons. From England, the order spread to Europe and elsewhere. Its original deistic and nondenominational ideology was transformed in Latin countries into a compound of atheism, anticlericalism and irreligion. Since 1877, Grand Orient Freemasonry has been denied recognition by the Scottish and York Rites because of its failure to require belief in God and the immortality of the soul as a condition of membership. In some places, Freemasonry has been regarded as subversive of the state; in Catholic quarters, it has been considered hostile to the Church and its doctrine. In the United States, Freemasonry is generally known as a fraternal and philanthropic order.

Catholics have been forbidden to join the Freemasons, under penalty of excommunication, for serious pastoral reasons. Eight different popes in 17 different pronouncements, and at least six different local councils, condemned Freemasonry. The first condemnation was made by Clement XII in 1738. Eastern Orthodox and many Protestant bodies have also opposed the order.

The existing prohibition against membership in the Freemasons by Catholics was modified by the contents of a letter written in 1974 by Cardinal Franjo Seper, prefect of the Congregation for the Doctrine of the Faith. The letter said that Catholic laymen may join Masonic lodges which do not plot against the Church. The letter also said: "Clerics, religious and members of secular institutes are still forbidden in every case to join any Masonic association."

Free Will: The faculty or capability of making a reasonable choice among several alternatives. Freedom of will underlies the possibility and fact of moral responsibility.

Friar: Term applied to members of mendicant orders to distinguish them from members of monastic orders. (See Mendicants.)

Fruits of the Holy Spirit: Charity, joy, peace, patience, benignity, goodness, longanimity, mildness, faith, modesty, continence, chastity.

G

Gambling: The backing of an issue with a sum of money or other valuables, which is permissible if the object is honest, if the two parties have the free disposal of their stakes without prejudice to the rights of others, if the terms are thoroughly understood by both parties, and if the outcome is not known beforehand. Gambling often falls into disrepute and may be forbidden by civil law, as well as by divine law, because of cheating, fraud and other accompanying evils.

Gehenna: Greek form of a Jewish name, *Gehinnom*, for a valley near Jerusalem, the site of Moloch worship; used as a synonym for hell.

Genuflection: Bending of the knee, a natural sign of adoration or reverence, as when persons genuflect with the right knee in passing before the tabernacle to acknowledge the Eucharistic presence of Christ.

Gethsemani: A Hebrew word meaning oil press, designating the place on the Mount of Olives where Christ prayed and suffered in agony the night before he died.

Gifts of the Holy Spirit: Supernatural habits disposing a person to respond promptly to the inspiration of grace; promised by Christ and communicated through the Holy Spirit, especially in the sacrament of confirmation. They are: wisdom, understanding, counsel, fortitude, knowledge, piety, fear of the Lord.

Gluttony: An unreasonable appetite for food and drink; one of the seven capital sins.

God: The infinitely perfect Supreme Being, uncaused and absolutely self-sufficient, eternal, the Creator and final end of all things.

The one God subsists in three equal Persons, the Father and the Son and the Holy Spirit. God, although transcendent and distinct from the universe, is present and active in the world in realization of his plan for the salvation of men, principally through Revelation, the operations of the Holy Spirit, the life and ministry of Christ, and the continuation of Christ's ministry in the Church.

The existence of God is an article of faith, clearly communicated in divine Revelation. Even without this Revelation, however, the Church teaches, in a declaration by the First Vatican Council, that men can acquire certain knowledge of the existence of God and some of his attributes. This can be done on the bases of principles of reason and reflection on human experience.

Non-revealed arguments or demonstrations for the existence of God have been developed from the principle of causality; the contingency of man and the universe; the existence of design, change and movement in the universe; human awareness of moral responsibility; widespread human testimony to the existence of God.

Grace: A free gift of God to men (and angels), grace is a created sharing or participation in the life of God. It is given to men through the merits of Christ and is communicated by the Holy Spirit. It is necessary for salvation. The principal means of grace are the sacraments (especially the Eucharist), prayer and good works.

Sanctifying or habitual grace makes men holy and pleasing to God, adopted children of God, members of Christ, temples of the Holy Spirit, heirs of heaven capable of supernaturally meritorious acts. With grace, God gives men the supernatural virtues and gifts of the Holy Spirit. The sacraments of baptism and penance were instituted to give grace to those who do not have it; the other sacraments, to increase it in those already in the state of grace. The means for growth in holiness, or the increase of grace, are prayer, the sacraments, and good works. Sanctifying grace is lost by the commission of serious sin.

Each sacrament confers sanctifying grace for the special purpose of the sacrament; in this context, grace is called sacramental grace.

Actual grace is a supernatural help of God which enlightens and strengthens a person to do good and to avoid evil. It is not a permanent quality, like sanctifying grace. It is necessary for the performance of supernatural acts. It can be resisted and refused. Persons in the state of serious sin are given actual grace to lead them to repentance.

Grace at Meals: Prayers said before meals, asking a blessing of God, and after meals, giving thanks to God. In addition to traditional prayers for these purposes, many variations suitable for different occasions are possible, at personal option

H

Habit: (1) A disposition to do things easily, given with grace (and therefore supernatural) and/or acquired by repetition of similar acts.
(2) The garb worn by religious.

Hagiography: Writings or documents about saints and other holy persons.

Hail Mary: A prayer addressed to the Blessed Virgin Mary; also called the *Ave Maria* (Latin equivalent of Hail Mary) and the Angelic Salutation. In three parts, it consists of the words addressed to Mary by the Archangel Gabriel on the occasion of the Annunciation, in the Infancy Narrative (Hail full of grace, the Lord is with you, blessed are you among women.); the words addressed to Mary by her cousin Elizabeth on the occasion of the Visitation (Blessed is the fruit of your womb.); a concluding petition (Holy Mary, Mother of God, pray for us sinners now and at the hour of our death. Amen.). The first two salutations were joined in Eastern Rite formulas by the sixth century, and were similarly used at Rome in the seventh century. Insertion of the name of Jesus at the conclusion of the salutations was probably made by Urban IV about 1262. The present form of the petition was incorporated into the breviary in 1514.

Heaven: The state of those who, having achieved salvation, are in glory with God and enjoy the beatific vision.

The phrase, kingdom of heaven, refers to the order or kingdom of God, grace, salvation.

Hell: The state of punishment of the damned — i.e., those who die in mortal sin, in a condition of self-alienation from God and of opposition to the divine plan of salvation. The punishment of hell begins immediately after death and lasts forever.

Hermit: See Anchorite.

Heroic Act of Charity: The completely unselfish offering to God of one's good works and merits for the benefit of the souls in purgatory rather than for oneself. Thus a person may offer to God for the souls in purgatory all the good works he performs during life, all the indulgences he gains, and all the prayers and indulgences that will be offered for him after his death. The act is revocable at will, and is not a vow. Its actual ratification depends on the will of God.

Heterodoxy: False doctrine, teaching or belief; a departure from truth.

Holy See: (1) The diocese of the pope, Rome.
(2) The pope himself and/or the various officials and bodies of the Church's central administration at Vatican City — the Roman Curia — which act in the name and by authority of the pope.

Holy Spirit: God the Holy Spirit, third Person of the Holy Trinity, who proceeds from the Father and the Son and with whom he is equal in every respect; inspirer of the prophets and writers of sacred Scripture; promised by Christ to the Apostles as their advocate and strengthener; appeared in the form of a dove at the baptism of Christ and as tongues of fire at his descent upon the Apostles; soul of the Church and guarantor, by his abiding presence and action, of truth in doctrine; communicator of grace to men, for which reason he is called the sanctifier.

Holy Water: Water blessed by the Church and used as a sacramental, a practice which originated in apostolic times.

Holy Year: A year during which the pope grants the plenary Jubilee Indulgence to the faithful who fulfill certain conditions. For those who make a pilgrimage to Rome during the year, the conditions are reception of the sacraments of penance and the Eucharist, visits and prayer for the intention of the pope in the basilicas of St. Peter, St. John Lateran, St. Paul and St. Mary Major. For those who do not make a pilgrimage to Rome, the conditions are reception of the sacraments and prayer for the pope during a visit or community celebration in a church designated by the bishop of the locality.

Holy Year observances have biblical counterparts in the Years of Jubilee observed at 50-year intervals by the pre-exilic Israelites — when debts were pardoned and slaves freed (Lv. 25:25-54) — and in sabbatical years observed from the end of the Exile to 70 A.D. — in which debts to fellow Jews were remitted.

The practice of Christians from early times to go on pilgrimage to the Holy Land, the shrines of martyrs and the tombs of the Apostles in Rome influenced the institution of Holy Years. There was also a prevailing belief among the people that every 100th year was a year of "Great Pardon." Accordingly, even before Boniface VIII formally proclaimed the first Holy Year Feb. 22, 1300, scores of thousands of pilgrims were already on the way to or in Rome.

Medieval popes embodied in the observance of Holy Years the practice of good works (reception of the sacraments of penance and the Eucharist, pilgrimages and/or visits to the tombs of the Apostles, and related actions) and spiritual benefits (particularly, special indulgences for the souls in purgatory). These and related practices, with suitable changes for celebrations in local churches, remain staple features of Holy Year observances.

The first three Holy Years were observed in 1300, 1350 and 1390. Subsequent ones were celebrated at 25-year intervals except in 1800 and 1850 when, respectively, the French invasion of Italy and political turmoil made observance impossible. Pope Paul II (1464-1471) set the 25-year timetable. In 1500, Pope Alexander VI prescribed the start and finish ceremonies — the opening and closing of the Holy Doors in the major basilicas on successive Christmas Eves. All but a few of the earlier Holy Years were classified as ordinary. Several, like the one held in 1933 to commemorate the 19th centenary of the death and resurrection of Christ, were in the extraordinary category.

Holy Year 1975 coincided with the 10th anniversary of the closing of the Second Vatican Council. Its themes also coincided with the renewal emphasis which dominated the council, and were related to the main topic — the evangelization of the modern world — on the 1974 agenda of the Synod of Bishops.

Homosexuality: The condition of a person whose sexual orientation is toward persons of the same rather than the opposite sex. Some psychologists regard it as an arrested state of emotional development. The condition, usually discovered during adolescence rather than deliberately caused, is not normal but is not sinful in itself. Homosexual acts against nature are objectively wrong; subjective responsibility for such acts, however, may be conditioned and diminished by compulsion and related factors.

Hope: One of the three theological virtues, by which one firmly trusts that God wills his salvation and will give him the means to attain it.

Hosanna: A Hebrew word, meaning O Lord, save, we pray.

Host, The Sacred: The bread under whose appearances Christ is and remains present in a unique manner after the consecration which takes place during Mass. (See Transubstantiation.)

Humility: A virtue which induces a person to evaluate himself at his true worth, to recognize his dependence on God, and to give glory to God for the good he has and can do.

Hyperdulia: The special veneration accorded the Blessed Virgin Mary because of her unique role in the mystery of Redemption, her exceptional gifts of grace from God, and her pre-eminence among the saints. Hyperdulia is not adoration; only God is adored.

Hypnosis: A mental state resembling sleep, induced by suggestion, in which the subject does the bidding of the hypnotist. Hypnotism is permissible under certain conditions: the existence of a serious reason, e.g., for anesthetic or therapeutic purposes, and the competence and integrity of the hypnotist. Hypnotism may not be practiced for the sake of amusement. Experiments indicate that, contrary to popular opinion, hypnotized subjects may be induced to perform immoral acts which, normally, they would not do.

Hypostatic Union: The union of the human and divine natures in the one divine Person of Christ.

I

Icons: Byzantine-style paintings or representations of Christ, the Blessed Virgin and other saints, venerated in the Eastern Churches where they take the place of statues.

Idolatry: Worship of any but the true God; a violation of the First Commandment.

IHS: In Greek, the first three letters of the name of Jesus — Iota, Eta, Sigma.

Immortality: The survival and continuing existence of the human soul after death.

Immunity of the Clergy: Exemption of clerics from military duty and civil service.

Impurity: Unlawful indulgence in sexual pleasure. (See Chastity.)

Incardination: The affiliation of a priest to his diocese. Every secular priest must belong to a certain diocese. Similarly, every priest of a religious community must belong to some jurisdiction of his community; this affiliation, however, is not called incardination.

Incarnation: (1) The coming-into-flesh or taking of human nature by the Second Person of the Trinity. He became human as the Son of Mary, being miraculously conceived by the power of the Holy Spirit, without ceasing to be divine. His divine Person hypostatically unites his divine and human natures.

(2) The supernatural mystery coextensive with Christ from the moment of his human conception and continuing through his life on earth; his sufferings and death; his resurrection from the dead and ascension to glory with the Father; his sending, with the Father, of the Holy Spirit upon the Apostles and the Church; and his unending mediation with the Father for the salvation of men.

Incense: A granulated substance which, when burnt, emits an aromatic smoke. It symbolizes the zeal with which the faithful should be consumed, the good odor of Christian virtue, the ascent of prayer to God.

Incest: Sexual intercourse with relatives by blood or marriage; a sin of impurity and also a grave violation of the natural reverence due to relatives. Other sins of impurity (desire, etc.) concerning relatives have the nature of incest.

Index of Prohibited Books: A list of books which Catholics were formerly forbidden to read, possess or sell, under penalty of excommunication. The books were banned by the Holy See after publication because their treatment of matters of faith and morals and related subjects were judged to be erroneous or serious occasions of doctrinal error. Some books were listed in the Index by name; others were covered under general norms. The Congregation for the Doctrine of the Faith declared June 14, 1966, that the Index and its related penalties of excommunication no longer had the force of law in the Church. Persons are still obliged, however, to take normal precautions against occasions of doctrinal error.

The first *Roman Index of Prohibited Books*, which served the same purposes as earlier lists, was published in 1559 by the Holy Office at the order of Paul IV. The Council of Trent, with the approval of the same pope, authorized another Index in 1564. Seven years later, St. Pius V set up a special Congregation for the Reform of the Index and Correction of Books, and gave it universal jurisdiction. In the course of time, many additions and modifications affecting the Index were made. In 1897, Leo XIII issued complete legislation on the subject, and in 1917 Benedict XV turned over to the Congregation of the Holy Office the function of censoring publications in accordance with the provisions of canon law.

Indifferentism: A theory that any one religion is as true and good — or false — as any other religion, and that it makes no difference, objectively, what religion one professes, if any. The theory is completely subjective, finding its justification entirely in personal choice without reference to or respect for objective validity. It is also self-contradictory, since it regards as equally acceptable — or unacceptable — the beliefs of all religions, which in fact are not only not all the same but are in some cases opposed to each other.

Indulgence: According to *The Doctrine and Practice of Indulgences*, an apostolic constitution issued by Paul VI Jan. 1, 1967, an indulgence is the remission before God of the temporal punishment due for sins already forgiven as far as their guilt is concerned, which a follower of Christ — with the proper dispositions and under certain determined conditions — acquires through the intervention of the Church. The Church grants indulgences in accordance with doctrine concerning the superabundant merits of Christ and the saints, the Power of the Keys, and the sharing of spiritual goods in the Communion of Saints.

An indulgence is partial or plenary, depending on whether it does away with either part or all of the temporal punishment due for sin. Both types of indulgences can always be applied to the dead by way of suffrage; the actual disposition of indulgences applied to the dead rests with God.

(1) Partial indulgence: Properly disposed faithful who perform an action to which a partial indulgence is attached obtain, in addition to the remission of temporal punishment acquired by the action itself, an equal remission of punishment through the intervention of the Church. (This grant was formerly designated in terms of days and years.) The proper dispositions for gaining a partial indulgence are sorrow for sin and freedom from serious sin, performance of the required good work, and the intention (which can be general or immediate) to gain the indulgence.

In addition to customary prayers and other good works to which partial indulgences are attached, the *Enchiridion Indulgentiarum* published in 1968 included general grants of partial indulgences to the faithful who: (a) with some kind of prayer, raise their minds to God with humble confidence while carrying out their duties and bearing the difficulties of everyday life; (b) motivated by the spirit of faith and compassion, give of themselves or their goods for the service of persons in need; (c) in a spirit of penance, spontaneously refrain from the enjoyment of things which are lawful and pleasing to them.

(2) Plenary indulgence: To gain a plenary indulgence, it is necessary for a person to be free of all attachment to sin, to perform the work to which the indulgence is attached, and to fulfill the three conditions of sacramental confession, Eucharistic Communion, and prayer for the intention of the pope. The three conditions may be fulfilled several days before or after the performance of the prescribed work, but it is fitting that Communion be received and prayers for the intentions of the pope be offered on the same day the work is performed. The condition of praying for the pope's intention is fully satisfied by praying one Our Father and one Hail Mary, and sometimes the Creed, but persons are free to choose other prayers.

Four of the several devotional practices for which a plenary indulgence is granted are: (a) adoration of the Blessed Sacrament for at least one-half hour; (b) devout reading of sacred Scripture for at least one-half hour; (c) the Way of the Cross; (d) recitation of the Marian Rosary in a church or public oratory or in a family group, a religious community or pious association. Only one plenary indulgence can be gained in a single day.

Indult: A favor or privilege granted by competent ecclesiastical authority, giving permission to do something not allowed by the common law of the Church.

Infant Jesus of Prague: An 18-inch-high wooden statue of the Child Jesus which has figured in a form of devotion to the Holy Childhood and Kingship of Christ since the 17th century. Of uncertain origin, the statue was presented by Princess Polixena to the Carmelites of Our Lady of Victory Church, Prague, in 1628.

Infused Virtues: The theological virtues of faith, hope, and charity; principles or capabilities of supernatural action, they are given with sanctifying grace by God rather than acquired by repeated acts of a person. They can be increased by practice; they are lost by contrary acts. Natural-acquired moral virtues, like the cardinal virtues of prudence, justice, temperance, and fortitude, can be considered infused in a person whose state of grace gives them supernatural orientation.

Inquisition: A tribunal for dealing with heretics, authorized by Gregory IX in 1231 to search them out, hear and judge them, sentence them to various forms of punishment, and in some cases to hand them over to civil authorities for punishment. The Inquisition was a creature of its time when crimes against faith, which threatened the good of the Christian community, were regarded also as crimes against the state, and when heretical doctrines of such extremists as the Cathari and Albigensians threatened the very fabric of society. The institution, which was responsible for many excesses, was most active in the second half of the 13th century.

Inquisition, Spanish: An institution peculiar to Spain and the colonies in Spanish America. In 1478, at the urging of King Ferdinand, Pope Sixtus IV approved the establishment of the Inquisition for trying charges of heresy brought against Jewish (Marranos) and Moorish (Moriscos) converts. It acquired jurisdiction over other cases as well, however, and fell into disrepute because of irregularities in its functions, cruelty in its sentences, and the manner in which it served the interests of the Spanish crown more than the accused persons and the good of the Church. Protests by the Holy See failed to curb excesses of the Inquisition, which lingered in Spanish history until early in the 19th century.

I N R I: The first letters of words in the Latin inscription atop the cross on which Christ was crucified: (I)esus (N)azaraenus, (R)ex (J)udaeorum — Jesus of Nazareth, King of the Jews.

Insemination, Artificial: The implanting of human semen by some means other than consummation of natural marital intercourse. In view of the principle that procreation should result only from marital intercourse, donor insemination is not permissible. The use of legitimate artificial means to further the fruitfulness of marital intercourse is permissible.

In Sin: The condition of a person called spiritually dead because he does not possess sanctifying grace, the principle of supernatural life, action and merit. Such grace can be regained through repentance.

Instruction: A document containing doctrinal explanations, directive norms, rules, recommendations, admonitions, issued by the pope, a department of the Roman Curia or other competent authority in the Church. To the extent that they so prescribe, instructions have the force of law.

Intercommunion: The common celebration and reception of the Eucharist by members of different Christian churches; a pivotal issue in ecumenical theory and practice. Catholic participation and intercommunion in the Eucharistic liturgy of another church without a valid priesthood and with a variant Eucharistic belief is out of order. Under certain conditions, other Christians may receive the Eucharist in the Catholic Church (see additional Intercommunion entry). Intercommunion is acceptable to some Protestant churches and unacceptable to others.

Interdict: An ecclesiastical penalty imposed on persons and places for certain violations of church law. If the interdict is personal, the interdicted persons may not take part in certain liturgical services, administer or receive certain sacraments. If the interdict is local, persons may not take part in certain liturgical services, administer or receive certain sacraments in the interdicted places.

Interdict is different from excommunication, and does not involve exclusion of a person from the community of the faithful.

Interregnum: The period of time between the death of a pope and the election of his successor. Another term applied to the period is *Sede vacante,* meaning the See (of Rome) being vacant.

The main concerns during an interregnum are matters connected with the death and burial of the pope, the election of his successor, and the maintenance of ordinary routine for the proper functioning of the Roman Curia and the Diocese of Rome.

Interregnum procedures follow norms contained in the apostolic constitution *Romano Pontifici Eligendo* (concerning the vacancy of the Apostolic See and the election of the Roman Pontiff) issued by Paul VI Oct. 1, 1975. This constitution superseded two others previously in force: *Vacantis Apostolicae Sedis,* issued by Pius XII Dec. 8, 1945, and *Summi Pontificis Electione,* issued by John XXIII Sept. 5, 1962.

"During the vacancy of the Apostolic See," the constitution states, "the government of the Church is entrusted to the Sacred College of Cardinals for the sole dispatch of ordinary business and of matters which cannot be postponed, and for the preparation of everything necessary for the election of the new pope."

The general congregation of the whole college, presided over by the dean, sub-dean or senior cardinal, has responsibility for major decisions during an interregnum. Other decisions of a routine nature are left to a particular congregation consisting of the chamberlain of the Holy Roman Church and three assistant cardinals.

The chamberlain of the Holy Roman Church and the dean of the college are the key officials, with directive responsibilities before and during the electoral conclave. The chamberlain is in general charge of ordinary administration. He — or the dean prior to a chamberlain's election by the cardinals — certifies the death of the pope; orders the destruction of the Fisherman's Ring and personal seals of the pope; and sets in motion procedures, carried out in collaboration with the dean, for informing the world about the pope's death, for funeral preparations, and for summoning and supervising the conclave for the election of a new pope.

Cardinals in charge of departments of the Roman Curia relinquish their offices at the death of the pope. Remaining in office, however, are the vicar of Rome, for ordinary jurisdiction over the diocese, and the major penitentiary. The substitute secretary of state or papal secretariat maintains the secretariat in a status quo. Papal representatives, such as nuncios and apostolic delegates, remain in office.

The congregations, offices and tribunals of the Curia retain ordinary jurisdiction for routine affairs but may not initiate new business during an interregnum.

If the pope should die during sessions of an ecumenical council or the Synod of Bishops, they would automatically be suspended.

The deceased pope is buried in St. Peter's Basilica, following prescribed ceremonies and traditional customs during a mourning period of nine days.

The conclave for the election of a new pope begins no sooner than 15 and no later than 20 days after the death of his predecessor. On the election of the new pope, the interregnum comes to an end. (See Papal Election.)

Intinction: A method of administering Holy Communion under the dual appearances of bread and wine, in which the consecrated host is dipped in the consecrated wine before being given to the communicant. The administering of Holy Communion in this manner, which has been traditional in Eastern-Rite liturgies, was authorized in the Roman Rite for various occasions by the *Constitution on the Sacred Liturgy* promulgated by the Second Vatican Council.

Irenicism: Peace-seeking, conciliation, as opposed to polemics; an important element in ecumenism, provided it furthers pursuit of the Christian unity willed by Christ without degenerating into a peace-at-any-price disregard for religious truth.

Irregularity: An impediment to the lawful reception or exercise of holy orders. The Church instituted irregularities — which include apostasy, heresy, homicide, attempted suicide — out of reverence for the dignity of the sacraments.

Itinerarium: Prayers for a spiritually profitable journey.

J

Jansenism: Opinions developed and proposed by Cornelius Jansenius (1585-1638). He held that: human nature was radically and intrinsically corrupted by original sin; some men are predestined to heaven and others to hell; Christ died only for those predestined to heaven; for those who are predestined, the operations of grace are irresistible. Jansenism also advocated an extremely rigorous code of morals and asceticism. The errors were proscribed by Urban VIII in 1642, by Innocent X in 1653, by Clement XI in 1713, and by other popes. Despite these condemnations, the rigoristic spirit of Jansenism lingered for a long time afterwards, particularly in France.

Jehovah's Witnesses: The Witnesses, together with the Watchtower and Bible Tract Society, trace their beginnings to a Bible class organized by Charles Taze Russell in 1872 at Allegheny, Pa. They take their name from a passage in Isaiah (43:12): " 'You are my witnesses,' says Jehovah." They are generally fundamentalist and revivalist with respect to the Bible, and believe that Christ is God's Son but is inferior to God. They place great emphasis on the Battle of Armageddon (as a decisive confrontation of good and evil) that is depicted vividly in Revelation, believing that God will then destroy the existing system of things and that, with the establishment of Jehovah's Kingdom, a small band of 144,000 spiritual sons of God will go to heaven, rule with Christ, and share in some way their happiness with some others.

Each Witness is considered by the society to be an ordained minister charged with the duty of spreading the message of Jehovah, which is accomplished through publications, house-to-house visitations, and other methods. The Witnesses refuse to salute the flag of any nation, regarding this as a form of idolatry, or to sanction blood transfusions even for the saving of life. There are approximately one million Witnesses in more than 22,000 congregations in some 80 countries. The freedom and activities of Witnesses are restricted in some places.

Jesus: The name of Jesus, meaning Savior in Christian usage, derived from the Aramaic and Hebrew *Yeshua* and *Joshua,* meaning *Yahweh* is salvation.

Jesus Prayer: A form of prayer dating back to the fifth century, "Lord Jesus Christ, Son of God, have mercy on me (a sinner)."

Joys of the Blessed Virgin Mary, Seven: (See Franciscan Crown.)

Judgment: (1) Last or final judgment: Final judgment by Christ, at the end of the world and the general resurrection.

(2) Particular judgment: The judgment that takes place immediately after a person's death, followed by entrance into heaven, hell or purgatory.

Jurisdiction: Right, power, authority to rule. Jurisdiction in the Church is of divine institution; has pastoral service for its purpose; includes legislative, judicial and executive authority; can be exercised only by persons with the power of orders.

(1) Ordinary jurisdiction is attached to ecclesiastical offices by law; the officeholders, called ordinaries, have authority over those who are subject to them.

(2) Delegated jurisdiction is that which is granted to persons rather than attached to offices. Its extent depends on the terms of the delegation.

Justice: One of the four cardinal virtues by which a person gives to others what is due to them as a matter of right. (See Cardinal Virtues.)

Justification: The act by which God makes a person just, and the consequent change in the spiritual status of a person, from sin to grace; the remission of sin and the infusion of sanctifying grace through the merits of Christ and the action of the Holy Spirit.

K

Kerygma: Proclaiming the word of God, in the manner of the Apostles, as here and now effective for salvation. This method of preaching or instruction, centered on Christ and geared to the facts and themes of salvation history, is designed to dispose people to faith in Christ and/or to intensify the experience and practice of that faith in those who have it.

Keys, Power of the: Spiritual authority and jurisdiction in the Church, symbolized by the keys of the kingdom of heaven. Christ promised the keys to St. Peter, as head-to-be of the Church (Mt. 16:19), and commissioned him with full pastoral responsibility to feed his lambs and sheep (Jn. 21:15-17), The pope, as the successor of St. Peter, has this power in a primary and supreme manner. The bishops of the Church also have the power, in union with and subordinate to the pope. Priests share in it through holy orders and the delegation of authority.

Examples of the application of the Power of the Keys are the exercise of teaching and pastoral authority by the pope and bishops, the absolving of sins in the sacrament of penance, the granting of indulgences, the imposing of spiritual penalties on persons who commit certain serious sins.

L

Laicization: (1) The process by which a man ordained to holy orders is relieved of the obligations of orders and the ministry and is returned to the status of a lay person. Applications by diocesan clergy are filed with their bishop and forwarded for processing to the congregation of the Roman Curia authorized to grant the indult of laicization.

(2) The process by which a religious is relieved of the obligations of vows and membership in his or her institute. Applications are filed with the proper religious superior and forwarded for processing to the Congregation for Religious which is authorized to grant the appropriate indult.

Languages of the Church: The first language in church use, for divine worship and the conduct of ecclesiastical affairs, was Aramaic, the language of the first Christians in and around Jerusalem. As the Church spread westward, Greek was adopted and prevailed until the third century when it was supplanted by Latin for official use in the West.

According to traditions established very early in churches of the Eastern Rites, many different languages were adopted for use in divine worship and for the conduct of ecclesiastical affairs. The practice was, and still is, to use the vernacular or a language closely related to the common tongue of the people.

In the Western Church, Latin prevailed as the general official language until the promulgation on Dec. 4, 1963, of the *Constitution on the Sacred Liturgy* by the second session of the Second Vatican Council. Since that time, vernacular languages have come into use in the Mass, administration of the sacraments, and the Liturgy of the Hours. The change was introduced in order to make the prayers and ceremonies of divine worship more informative and meaningful to all. Latin, however, remains the official language for administrative and procedural matters.

Law: An ordinance or rule governing the activity of things.

(1) *Natural law:* Moral norms corresponding to man's nature by which he orders his conduct toward God, neighbor, society and himself. This law, which is rooted in human nature, is of divine origin, can be known by the use of reason, and binds all men having the use of reason. The Ten Commandments are declarations and amplifications of natural law. The primary precepts of natural law, to do good and to avoid evil, are universally recognized, despite differences with respect to understanding and application resulting from different philosophies of good and evil.

(2) *Divine positive law:* That which has been revealed by God. Among its essentials are the twin precepts of love of God and love of neighbor, and the Ten Commandments.

(3) *Ecclesiastical law:* That which is established by the Church for the spiritual welfare of the faithful and the orderly conduct of ecclesiastical affairs. (See Canon Law.)

(4) *Civil law:* That which is established by a socio-political community for the common good.

Lector: A reader of scriptural passages and other selections at Mass and other services of worship.

Legitimation: Removal of the status of illegitimacy; e.g., by marriage of the parents.

Liberalism: A multiphased trend of thought and movement favoring liberty, independence and progress in moral, intellectual, religious, social, economic and political life. Traceable to the Renaissance, it developed through the Enlightenment, the rationalism of the 19th century, and modernist- and existentialist-related theories of the 20th century. Evaluations of various kinds of liberalism depend on the validity of their underlying principles. Extremist positions — regarding subjectivism, libertinarianism, naturalist denials of the supernatural, and the alienation of individuals and society from God and the Church were condemned by Gregory XVI in the 1830's, Pius IX in 1864, Leo XIII in 1899, and St. Pius X in 1907. There is, however, nothing objectionable about forms of liberalism patterned according to sound principles of Christian doctrine.

Life in Outer Space: Whether rational life exists on other bodies in the universe besides earth, is a question for scientific investigation to settle. The possibility can be granted, without prejudice to the body of revealed truth.

Limbo: The limbo of the fathers was the state of rest and natural happiness after death enjoyed by the just of pre-Christian times until they were admitted to heaven following the Ascension of Christ. Belief in this matter is stated in the Apostles' Creed. The existence of a limbo for unbaptized persons of infant status — a state of rest and natural happiness — has never been formally defined.

Litany: A prayer in the form of responsive petition; e.g., St. Joseph, pray for us, etc. There are seven litanies approved for liturgical use: Litanies of Loreto (Litany of the Blessed Mother), the Holy Name, All Saints, the Sacred Heart, the Precious Blood, St. Joseph, Litany for the Dying. Others may be used privately.

Little Office of the Blessed Virgin Mary: A shortened version of a Liturgy of the Hours honoring the Blessed Virgin. It dates from about the middle of the eighth century.

Liturgical Languages: (See Languages of the Church.)

Loreto, House of: A Marian shrine in Loreto, Italy, consisting of the home of the Holy Family which, according to an old tradition, was transported in a miraculous manner from Nazareth to Dalmatia and finally to Loreto between 1291 and 1294. Investigations conducted shortly after the appearance of the structure in Loreto revealed that its dimensions matched those of the house of the Holy Family missing from its place of enshrinement in a basilica at Nazareth. Among the many popes who regarded it with high honor was John XXIII, who went there on pilgrimage Oct. 4, 1962. The house of the Holy Family is enshrined in the Basilica of Our Lady.

Lust: A disorderly desire for sexual pleasure; one of the seven capital sins.

M

Magi: In the Infancy Narrative of St. Matthew's Gospel (2:1-12), three wise men from the East whose visit and homage to the Child Jesus at Bethlehem indicated Christ's manifestation of himself to non-Jewish people. The narrative teaches the universality of salvation. The traditional names of the Magi are Caspar, Melchior and Balthasar.

Magnificat: The canticle or hymn of the Virgin Mary on the occasion of her visitation to her cousin Elizabeth (Lk. 1:46-55). It is an expression of praise, thanksgiving and acknowledgment of the great blessings given by God to Mary, the Mother of the Second Person of the Blessed Trinity made Man. The Magnificat is recited in the Liturgy of the

Hours as part of the Evening Prayer.

Martyr: A Greek word, meaning witness, denoting one who voluntarily suffered death for the faith or some Christian virtue.

Martyrology: A catalogue of martyrs and other saints, arranged according to the calendar. The *Roman Martyrology* contains the official list of saints venerated by the Church. Additions to the list are made in beatification and canonization decrees of the Congregation for the Causes of Saints. The Martyrology is being revised to conform with other liturgical books.

Mass for the People: On Sundays and certain feasts throughout the year pastors are required to offer Mass for the faithful committed to their care. If they cannot offer the Mass on these days, they must do so at a later date or provide that another priest offer the Mass.

Master of Novices: The person in charge of the training and formation of candidates for a religious institute during novitiate.

Materialism: Theory which holds that matter is the only reality, and everything in existence is merely a manifestation of matter; there is no such thing as spirit, and the supernatural does not exist. Materialism is incompatible with Christian doctrine.

Meditation: Mental, as distinguished from vocal, prayer, in which thought, affections, and resolutions of the will predominate. There is a meditative element to all forms of prayer, which always involves the raising of the heart and mind to God.

Mendicants: A term derived from Latin and meaning beggars, applied to members of religious orders without property rights; the members, accordingly, worked or begged for their support. The original mendicants were Franciscans and Dominicans in the early 13th century; later, the Carmelites, Augustinians, Servites and others were given the mendicant title and privileges, with respect to exemption from episcopal jurisdiction and wide faculties for preaching and administering the sacrament of penance. The practice of begging is limited at the present time, although it is still allowed with the permission of competent superiors and bishops. Mendicants are supported by free will offerings and income received for spiritual services and other work.

Mercy, Divine: The love and goodness of God, manifested particularly in a time of need.

Merit: In religion, the right to a supernatural reward for good works freely done for a supernatural motive by a person in the state of and with the assistance of grace. The right to such reward is from God, who binds himself to give it. Accordingly, good works, as described above, are meritorious for salvation.

Metempsychosis: Theory of the passage or migration of the human soul after death from one body to another for the purpose of purification from guilt. The theory denies the unity of the soul and human personality, and the doctrine of individual moral responsibility.

Millennium: A thousand-year reign of Christ and the just upon earth before the end of the world. This belief of the Millenarians, Chiliasts, and some sects of modern times is based on an erroneous interpretation of Rv. 20.

Miracles: Observable events or effects in the physical or moral order of things, with reference to salvation, which cannot be explained by the ordinary operation of laws of nature and which, therefore, are attributed to the direct action of God. They make known, in an unusual way, the concern and intervention of God in human affairs for the salvation of men. The most striking examples are the miracles worked by Christ. Numbering about 35, they included his own Resurrection; the raising of three persons to life (Lazarus, the daughter of Jairus, the son of the widow of Naim); the healing of blind, leprous and other persons; nature miracles; and prophecies, or miracles of the intellectual order.

The foregoing notion of miracles, which is based on the concept of a fixed order of nature, was not known by the writers of Sacred Scripture. In the Old Testament, particularly, they called some things miraculous which, according to the definition in contemporary use, may or may not have been miracles. Essentially, however, the occurrences so designated were regarded as exceptional manifestations of God's care and concern for the salvation of his people. The miracles of Christ were miracles in the full sense of the term.

The Church believes it is reasonable to accept miracles as manifestations of divine power for purposes of salvation. God, who created the laws of nature, is their master; hence, without disturbing the ordinary course of things, he can — and has in the course of history before and after Christ — occasionally set aside these laws and has also produced effects beyond their power of operation. The Church does not call miraculous anything which does not admit of easy explanation; on the contrary, miracles are admitted only when the events have a bearing on the order of grace and every possible natural explanation has been tried and found wanting.

(The transubstantiation — i.e., the conversion of the whole substance of bread and wine, their sensible appearances alone remaining, into the Body and Blood of Christ in the act of Consecration at Mass — is not an observable event. Traditionally, however, it has been called a miracle.)

Missal: A liturgical book of Roman Rite also called the *Sacramentary,* containing the celebrant's prayers of the Mass, along with general instructions and ceremonial directives. The Latin text of the new *Roman Missal*, replacing the one authorized by the Council of Trent in the 16th century, was published by the Vatican Polyglot Press in 1970. Its use in English was made mandatory in the U.S. from Dec. 1, 1974. Readings and scriptural responsories formerly in the missal are contained in the *Lectionary*.

Missiology: Study of the missionary nature, constitution and activity of the Church in all aspects: theological reasons for missionary activity, laws and instructions of the Holy See, history of the missions, social and cultural background, methods, norms for carrying on missionary work.

Mission: (1) Strictly, it means being sent to perform a certain work, such as the mission of Christ to redeem mankind, the mission of the Apostles and the Church and its members to perpetuate the prophetic, priestly and royal mission of Christ.

(2) A place where: the Gospel has not been proclaimed; the Church has not been firmly established; the Church, although established, is weak.

(3) An ecclesiastical territory with the simplest kind of canonical organization, under the jurisdiction of the Congregation for the Evangelization of Peoples.

(4) A church or chapel without a resident priest.

(5) A special course of sermons and spiritual exercises conducted in parishes for the purpose of renewing and deepening the spiritual life of the faithful and for the conversion of lapsed Catholics.

Modernism: The "synthesis of all heresies," which appeared near the beginning of the 20th century. It undermines the objective validity of religious beliefs and practices which, it contends, are products of the subconscious developed by mankind under the stimulus of a religious sense. It holds that the existence of a personal God cannot be demonstrated, the Bible is not inspired, Christ is not divine, nor did he establish the Church or institute the sacraments. A special danger lies in modernism, which is still influential, because it uses Catholic terms with perverted meanings. St. Pius X condemned 65 propositions of modernism in 1907 in the decree *Lamentabili* and issued the encyclical *Pascendi* to explain and analyze its errors.

Monastery: The dwelling place, as well as the community thereof, of monks belonging to the Benedictine and Benedictine-related orders like the Cistercians and Carthusians; also, the Augustinians and Canons Regular. Distinctive of monasteries are: their separation from the world; the papal enclosure or strict cloister; the permanence or stability of attachment characteristic of their members; autonomous government in accordance with a monastic rule, like that of St. Benedict in the West or of St. Basil in the East; the special dedication of its members to the community celebration of the liturgy as well as to work that is suitable to the surrounding area and the needs of its people. Monastic superiors of men have such titles as abbot and prior; of women, abbess and prioress. In most essentials, an abbey is the same as a monastery.

Monk: A member of a monastic order — e.g., the Benedictines, the Benedictine-related Cistercians and Carthusians, and the Basilians, who bind themselves by religious profession to stable attachment to a monastery, the contemplative life and the work of their community. In popular use, the title is wrongly applied to many men religious who really are not monks.

Monotheism: Belief in and worship of one God.

Morality: Conformity or difformity of behavior to standards of right conduct. (See Commandments of God, Precepts of the Church, Conscience, Law.)

Mormons: Members of the Church of Jesus Christ of Latter-Day Saints. The church was established by Joseph Smith (1805-1844) at Fayette, N.Y., three years after he said he had received from an angel golden tablets containing the *Book of the Prophet Mormon*. This book, the Bible, *Doctrine and Covenants,* and *The Pearl of Great Price,* are the basic doctrinal texts of the church. Characteristic of the Mormons are strong belief in the revelations of their leaders, among whom was Brigham Young; a strong community of religious-secular concern; a dual secular and spiritual priesthood, and vigorous missionary activity. The headquarters of the church are located at Salt Lake City, Utah, where the Mormons first settled in 1847.

Mortification: Acts of self-discipline, including prayer, hardship, austerities and penances undertaken for the sake of progress in virtue.

Motu Proprio: A Latin phrase designating a document issued by a pope on his own initiative. Documents of this kind often concern administrative matters.

Mysteries of Faith: Supernatural truths whose existence cannot be known without revelation by God and whose intrinsic truth, while not contrary to reason, can never be wholly understood even after revelation. These mysteries are above reason, not against reason. Among them are the divine mysteries of the Trinity, Incarnation and Eucharist.

Some mysteries — e.g., concerning God's attributes — can be known by reason without revelation, although they cannot be fully understood.

N

Necromancy: Supposed communication with the dead; a form of divination.

Non-Expedit: A Latin expression. It is not expedient (fitting, proper), used to state a prohibition or refusal of permission.

Novena: A term designating public or private devotional practices over a period of nine consecutive days; or, by extension, over a period of nine weeks, in which one day a week is set aside for the devotions.

Novice: A person preparing, in a formal period of trial and formation called the *novitiate,* for membership in a religious institute. The novitiate lasts more than a year and ends with the profession of temporary vows or other temporary commitment to the religious life. Current norms require a total 12-month period of seclusion for novices; to this is added other periods of time spent in apostolic work for the sake of experience. A novice, while acquiring experience of the religious life, is not bound by the obligations of professed members of the institute, is free to leave at any time, and may be discharged at the discretion of competent superiors. The immediate superior of a novice is a master or mistress of novices.

Nun (1) Strictly, a member of a religious order of women with solemn vows (moniales).

(2) In general, all women religious, even those in simple vows who are more properly called sisters.

Nunc Dimittis: The canticle or hymn of Simeon at the sight of Jesus at the Temple on the occasion of his presentation (Lk. 2:29-32). It is an expression of joy and thanksgiving for the blessing of having lived to see the Messiah. It is one of the canticles prescribed in the Liturgy of the Hours.

O

Oath: Calling upon God to witness the truth of a statement. Violating an oath, e.g., by perjury in court, or taking an oath without sufficient reason, is a violation of the honor due to God.

Obedience: Submission to one in authority. General obligations of obedience fall under the Fourth Commandment. The vow of obedience professed by religious is one of the evangelical counsels.

Obsession, Diabolical: The extraordinary state of one who is seriously molested by evil spirits in an external manner. Obsession is more than just temptation.

Occultism: Practices involving ceremonies, rituals, chants, incantations, other cult-related activities intended to affect the course of nature, the lives of practitioners and others, through esoteric powers of magic, diabolical or other forces; one of many forms of superstition.

Octave: A period of eight days given over to the celebration of a major feast such as Easter.

Oils, Holy: The oils consecrated by bishops on Holy Thursday or another suitable day, and by priests under certain conditions for use in certain sacraments and consecrations.

(1) The oil of catechumens (olive or vegetable oil), used at baptism and the ordination of priests.

(2) Chrism (olive or vegetable oil mixed with balm), used at baptism, in confirmation, at the ordination of a bishop, in the consecration of churches, altars, altarstones, chalices, patens, and in the blessing of bells.

(3) Oil of the sick (olive or vegetable oil) used in anointing the sick.

Old Catholics — Several sects, including: (1) the Church of Utrecht, which severed relations with Rome in 1724; (2) the National Polish Church in the U.S., which had its origin near the end of the 19th century; (3) German, Austrian and Swiss Old Catholics, who broke away from union with Rome following the First Vatican Council in 1870 because they objected to the dogma of papal infallibility.

The formation of the Old Catholic communion of Germans, Austrians and Swiss began in 1870 at a public meeting held in Nuremberg under the leadership of A. Dollinger. Four years later episcopal succession was established with the ordination of an Old Catholic German bishop by a prelate of the Church of Utrecht. In line with the "Declaration of Utrecht" of 1889, they accept the first seven ecumenical councils and doctrine formulated before 1054, but reject communion with the pope and a number of other Catholic doctrines and practices. They have a valid priesthood and valid sacraments. *The Oxford Dictionary of the Christian Church* notes that they have recognized Anglican ordinations since 1925, that they have had full communion with the Church of England since 1932, and that their bishops, using their own formula, have taken part in the ordination of Anglican bishops.

This communion does not recognize the "Old Catholic" status of several smaller sects calling themselves such. In turn, connection with it is disavowed by the Old Roman Catholic Church headquartered in Chicago, which contends that it has abandoned the traditions of the Church of Utrecht.

The United States is the only English-speaking country with Old Catholic communities.

Oratory: A chapel.

Ordinariate: An ecclesiastical jurisdiction for special purposes and people. Examples are the military ordinariate of the US, for service personnel, and Eastern-Rite ordinariates in places where Eastern-Rite dioceses do not exist.

Ordinary: One who has the jurisdiction of an office: the pope, diocesan bishops, vicars general, prelates of missionary territories, vicars apostolic, prefects apostolic, vicars capitular during the vacancy of a see, superiors general, abbots primate and other major superiors of men religious.

Ordination: The consecration of sacred ministers for divine worship and the service of men in things pertaining to God. The power of ordination comes from Christ and the Church, and must be conferred by a minister capable of communicating it.

Organ Transplants: The transplanting of organs from one person to another is permissible for serious reasons provided it is done with the consent of the concerned parties and does not result in the death or essential mutilation of the donor. Advances in methods and technology have increased the range of transplant possibilities in recent years. Despite such progress, unresolved problems have slowed the pace of some transplant practice, especially with respect to the heart. The first successful heart transplant was performed Dec. 3, 1967, on Louis Washkansky, 56, by a team headed by Dr. Christian Barnard in Cape Town, South Africa.

Original Sin: The sin of Adam (Gn. 2:8—3:24), personal to him and passed on to all men as a state of privation of grace. Despite this privation and the related wounding of human nature and weakening of natural powers, original sin leaves unchanged all that man himself is by nature. The scriptural basis of the doctrine was stated especially by St. Paul in 1 Cor. 15:21, ff., and Romans 5:12-21. Original sin is remitted by baptism and incorporation in Christ, through whom grace is given to persons.

O Salutaris Hostia: The first three Latin words, O Saving Victim, of a Benediction hymn.

Ostpolitik: Policy adopted by Pope Paul VI in an attempt to improve the situation of Eastern European Catholics through diplomatic negotiations with their governments.

Oxford Movement: A movement in the Church of England from 1833 to about 1845 which had for its objective a threefold defense of the church as a divine institution, the apostolic succession of its bishops, and the Book of Common Prayer as the rule of faith. The movement took its name from Oxford University and involved a number of intellectuals who authored a series of influential *Tracts for Our Times*. Some of its leading figures — e.g., F. W. Faber, John Henry Newman and Henry Edward Manning — became converts to the Catholic Church. In the Church of England, the movement affected the liturgy, historical and theological scholarship, the status of the ministry, and other areas of ecclesiastical life.

P

Paganism: A term referring to non-revealed religions, i.e., religions other than Christianity, Judaism and Mohammedanism.

Palms: Blessed palms are a sacramental. They are blessed and distributed on the Sunday of the Passion in commemoration of the triumphant entrance of Christ into Jerusalem. Ashes of the burnt palms are used on Ash Wednesday.

Pange Lingua: First Latin words, Sing, my tongue, of a hymn in honor of the Holy Eucharist, used particularly on Holy Thursday and in Eucharistic processions.

Pantheism: Theory that all things are part of God, divine, in the sense that God realizes himself as the ultimate reality of matter or spirit through being and/or becoming all things that have been, are, and will be. The theory leads to hopeless confusion of the Creator and the created realm of being, identifies evil with good, and involves many inherent contradictions.

Papal Election: The pope is elected by members of the College of Cardinals in a secret conclave or meeting convened ordinarily in secluded quarters of the Vatican Palace between 15 and 20 days after the death of his predecessor. Cardinals under the age of 80, totaling no more than 120, are eligible to participate in a papal election.

Following are some of the principal regulations decreed by Paul VI Oct. 1, 1975, in the apostolic constitution *Romano Pontifici Eligendo* (concerning the vacancy of the Apostolic See and the election of the Roman Pontiff).

The ordinary manner of election is by scrutiny, with two votes each morning and afternoon in the Sistine Chapel until one of the candidates receives a two-thirds plus one vote majority.

Alternative methods, which can be adopted by unanimous agreement of the cardinals in difficult cases, are provided for: (1) by delegation, in which the cardinals designate a limited number (nine to 15) to make the choice; (2) by changing the majority rule from two-thirds plus one vote to an absolute majority plus one; (3) by limiting final choice, if the procedure in force becomes protracted, to one between the two candidates who received the largest numbers of votes, but not a required majority, in the most recent balloting.

An unusual manner of election is by acclamation or inspiration — that is, by spontaneous, unanimous choice without any need for normal voting procedure.

The elected candidate is asked by the dean of the college if he accepts the election. If he does so and is already a bishop, he immediately becomes the bishop of Rome and pope, and signifies the name by which he will be called. The cardinals then pledge their obedience to him before the senior cardinal deacon proclaims his election to the world from the main balcony of the Vatican and the new pope imparts his blessing *Urbi et Orbi*. If the candidate is not a bishop, he is so ordained before receiving the pledge of obedience and being proclaimed pope. The subsequent coronation of the pope is a ceremonial recognition of the fact of his election.

The pope is elected for life. If one should resign, a new pope would be elected in accordance with the foregoing regulations.

Rigid rules govern the conclave — its personnel, freedom from internal and external influence and interference, absolute secrecy (with a ban on recording devices and a prohibition against any disclosures).

Ordinarily, the first indication that a new pope has been elected is a plume of white smoke rising from the Vatican on burning of the last ballots.

(See College of Cardinals, Interregnum.)

Early methods of electing a pope — with various degrees of participation by the clergy and people of Rome and others — were set aside by Pope Nicholas II, who decreed in 1059 that cardinal bishops would be the electors. Further modification of the process was decreed by the Lateran Council in 1179 (that election would take place by a two-thirds majority vote of the cardinals) and by Pope Gregory X in 1274 (regarding a secluded conclave arrangement for elections).

Paraclete: A title of the Holy Spirit meaning, in Greek, Advocate, Consoler.

Parental Duties: All duties related to the obligation of parents to provide for the welfare of their children. These obligations fall under the Fourth Commandment.

Parish: A community of the faithful served by a pastor charged with responsibility for providing them with full pastoral service. Most parishes are territorial, embracing all of the faithful in a certain area of a diocese; some are personal or national, for certain classes of people, without strict regard for their places of residence.

Parousia: The coming, or saving presence, of Christ which will mark the completion of salvation history and the coming to perfection of God's kingdom at the end of the world.

Paschal Candle: A large candle, symbolic of the risen Christ, blessed and lighted on the Easter Vigil and placed at the Gospel side of the altar until Ascension Day. It is ornamented with five large grains of incense, representing the wounds of Christ, inserted in the form of a cross; the Greek letters Alpha and Omega, symbolizing Christ the beginning and end of all things, at the top and bottom of the shaft of the cross; and the figures of the current year of salvation in the quadrants formed by the cross.

Paschal Precept: The church law requiring the faithful to receive Holy Communion during the Easter time.

Passion of Christ: Sufferings of Christ, recorded in the four Gospels.

Pastor: An ordained minister charged with responsibility for the doctrinal, sacramental and related service of people committed to his care; e.g., a bishop for the people in his diocese, a priest for the people of his parish.

Pater Noster: The initial Latin words, Our Father, of the Lord's Prayer.

Peace, Sign of: A gesture of greeting — e.g., a handshake — exchanged by the ministers and participants at Mass.

Pectoral Cross: A cross worn on a chain about the neck and over the breast by bishops and abbots as a mark of their office.

Penance or Penitence: (1) The spiritual change or conversion of mind and heart by which a person turns away from sin, and all that it implies, toward God, through a personal renewal under the influence of the Holy Spirit. In the apostolic constitution *Paenitemini*, Pope Paul VI called it "a religious, personal act which has as its aim love and surrender to God." Penance involves sorrow and contrition for sin, together with other internal and external acts of atonement. It serves the purposes of reestablishing in one's life the order of God's love and commandments, and of making satisfaction to God for sin. A divine precept states the necessity of penance for salvation: "Unless you do penance, you shall all likewise perish" (Lk. 13:3) . . . "Be converted and believe in the Gospel" (Mk. 1:15).

In the penitential discipline of the Church, the various works of penance have been classified under the headings of prayer (interior), fasting and almsgiving (exterior). The Church has established minimum requirements for the common and social observance of the divine precept by Catholics — e.g., by requiring them to fast and/or abstain on certain days of the year. These observances, however, do not exhaust all the demands of the divine precept, whose fulfillment is a matter of personal responsibility; nor do they have any real value unless they proceed from the internal spirit and purpose of penance.

Related to works of penance for sins actually committed are works of mortification. The purpose of the latter is to develop — through prayer, fasting, renunciations and similar actions — self-control and detachment from things which could otherwise become occasions of sin.

(2) Penance is a virtue disposing a person to turn to God in sorrow for sin and to carry out works of amendment and atonement.

(3) The sacrament of penance and sacramental penance.

Perjury: Taking a false oath, lying under oath, a violation of the honor due to God.

Persecution, Religious: A campaign waged against a church or other religious body by persons and governments intent on its destruction. The best known campaigns of this type against the Christian Church were the Roman persecutions which occurred intermittently from about 54 to the promulgation of the Edict of Milan in 313, The most extensive persecutions took place during the reigns of Nero, the first major Roman persecutor, Domitian, Trajan, Marcus Aurelius, and Diocletian. Besides the Roman persecutions, the Catholic Church has been subject to many others, including those of the 20th century in Communist-controlled countries.

Peter's Pence: A collection made each year among Catholics for the maintenance of the pope and his works of charity. It was originally a tax of a penny on each house, and was collected on St. Peter's day, whence the name. It originated in England in the eighth century.

Petition: One of the four purposes of prayer. In prayers of petition, persons ask of God the blessings they and others need.

Pharisees: Influential class among the Jews, referred to in the Gospels, noted for their self-righteousness, legalism, strict interpretation of the Law, acceptance of the traditions of the elders as well as the Law of Moses, and beliefs regarding angels and spirits, the resurrection of the dead and judgment. Most of them were laymen, and they were closely allied with the Scribes; their opposite numbers were the Sadducees. The Pharisaic and rabbinical traditions had a lasting influence on Judaism following the destruction of Jerusalem in 70 A.D.

Pious Fund: Property and money originally accumulated by the Jesuits to finance their missionary work in Lower California. When the Jesuits were expelled from the territory in 1767, the fund was appropriated by the Spanish Crown and used to support Dominican and Franciscan missionary work in Upper and Lower California. In 1842 the Mexican government took over administration of the fund, incorporated most of the revenue into the national treasury, and agreed to pay the Church interest of six per cent a year on the capital so incorporated. From 1848 to 1967 the fund was the subject of lengthy negotiations between the US and Mexican governments because of the latter's failure to make payments as agreed. A lump-sum settlement was made in 1967 with payment by Mexico to the US government of more than $700,000, to be turned over to the Archdiocese of San Francisco.

Polytheism: Belief in and worship of many gods or divinities, especially prevalent in pre-Christian religions.

Poor Box: Alms-box; found in churches from the earliest days of Christianity.

Pope Joan: Alleged name of a woman falsely said to have been pope from 855-858, the years of the reign of Benedict III. The myth was not heard of before the 13th century.

Portiuncula: (1) Meaning little portion (of land), the Portiuncula was the chapel of Our Lady of the Angels near Assisi, Italy, which the Benedictines gave to St. Francis early in the 13th century. He repaired the chapel and made it the first church of the Franciscan Order. It is now enshrined in the Basilica of St. Mary of the Angels in Assisi.

(2) The Portiuncula Indulgence, or Pardon of Assisi, was authorized by Honorius III. Originally, it could be gained for the souls in purgatory only in the chapel of Our Lady of the Angels; by later concessions, it could be gained also in other Franciscan and parish churches. According to legislation now in force, the Portiuncula Indulgence can be gained once on the day of Aug. 2, or on the following Sunday with permission of the bishop of the place. The conditions are, in addition to freedom from attachment to sin: reception of the sacraments of penance and the Eucharist on or near the day; a visit to a parish church on the day, during which the Our Father and Creed are offered for the intentions of the pope.

Possession, Diabolical: The extraordinary state of a person who is tormented from within by evil spirits who exercise strong influence over his powers of mind and body.

Postulant: One of several names used to designate a candidate for membership in a religious institute during the period before novitiate.

Poverty: (1) The quality or state of being poor, in actual destitution and need, or being poor in spirit. In the latter sense, poverty means the state of mind and disposition of persons who regard material things in proper perspective as gifts of God for the support of life and its reasonable enrichment, and for the service of others in need. It means freedom from unreasonable attachment to material things as ends in themselves, even though they may be possessed in small or large measure.

(2) One of the evangelical counsels professed by religious as a vow. It involves the voluntary renunciation of rights of ownership and of independent use and disposal of material goods (solemn vow); or, the right of independent use and disposal, but not of the radical right of ownership (simple vow). Religious institutes provide their members with necessary and useful goods and services from common resources. The manner in which goods are received and/or handled by religious is determined by poverty of spirit and the rule and constitutions of their institute. Practice of the vow of poverty is undergoing some change in the contemporary renewal in religious life.

Pragmatism: Theory that the truth of ideas, concepts and values depends on their utility or capacity to serve a useful purpose rather than on their conformity with objective standards; also called utilitarianism.

Prayer: The raising of the mind and heart to God in adoration, thanksgiving, reparation and petition. Prayer, which is always mental because it involves thought and love of God, may be vocal, meditative, private and personal, social, and official. The official prayer of the Church as a worshipping community is called the liturgy.

Precepts: Commands or orders given to individuals or communities in particular cases; they establish law for concerned parties. Preceptive documents are issued by the pope, departments of the Roman Curia and other competent authority in the Church.

Presence of God: A devotional practice of increasing one's awareness of the presence and action of God in daily life.

Presumption: A violation of the theological virtue of hope, by which a person striving for salvation either relies too much on his own capabilities or expects God to do things which he cannot do, in keeping with his divine attributes, or does not will to do, according to his divine plan. Presumption is the opposite of despair.

Preternatural Gifts: Exceptional gifts, beyond the exigencies and powers of human nature, enjoyed by Adam in the state of original justice: immunity from suffering and death, superior knowledge, integrity or perfect control of the passions. These gifts were lost as the result of original sin; their loss, however, implied no impairment of the integrity of human nature.

Pride: Unreasonable self-esteem; one of the seven capital sins.

Prie-Dieu: A French phrase, meaning pray God, designating a kneeler or bench suitable for kneeling while at prayer.

Priesthood of the Laity: Lay persons share in the priesthood of Christ in virtue of the sacraments of baptism and confirmation. They are not only joined with Christ for a life of union with him but are also deputed by him for participation in his mission, now carried on by the Church, of worship, teaching, witness and apostolic works. St. Peter called Christians "a royal priesthood" (1 Pt. 2:9) in this connection. St. Thomas Aquinas declared: "The sacramental characters (of baptism and confirmation) are nothing else than certain sharings of the priesthood of Christ, derived from Christ himself."

The priesthood of the laity differs from the official ministerial priesthood of ordained priests and bishops — who have the power of holy orders for celebrating the Eucharist, administering the other sacraments, and providing pastoral care. The ministerial priesthood, by divine commission, serves the universal priesthood. (See Role of Sacraments.)

Primary Option: The life-choice of a person for or against God which shapes the basic orientation of moral conduct.

Prior: A superior or an assistant to an abbot in a monastery.

Privilege: A favor, an exemption from the obligation of a law. Privileges of various kinds, with respect to ecclesiastical laws, are granted by the pope, departments of the Roman Curia and other competent authority in the Church.

Probabilism: A moral system for use in cases of conscience which involve the obligation of doubtful laws. There is a general principle that a doubtful law does not bind. Probabilism, therefore, teaches that it is permissible to follow an opinion favoring liberty, provided the opinion is certainly and solidly probable. Probabilism may not be invoked when there is question of: a certain law or the certain obligation of a law; the certain right of another party; the validity of an action; something which is necessary for salvation.

Pro-Cathedral: A church used as a cathedral.

Promoter of the Faith: An official of the Congregation for the Causes of Saints, whose role in beatification and canonization procedures is to establish beyond reasonable doubt the validity of evidence regarding the holiness of prospective saints and miracles attributed to their intercession.

Prophecies of St. Malachy: These so-called prophecies, listing the designations of 102 popes and 10 antipopes, bear the name they have because they have been falsely attributed to St. Malachy, bishop of Armagh, who died in 1148. Actually, they are forgeries by an unknown author and came to light only in the last decade of the 16th century.

The first 75 prophecies cover the 65 popes and 10 antipopes from Celestine II (1143-1144) to Gregory XIV (1590-91), and are exact with respect to names, coats of arms, birthplaces, and other identifying characteristics. This portion of the work, far from being prophetic, is the result of historical knowledge or hindsight. The 37 designations following that of Gregory are vague, fanciful, and subject to wide interpretation. According to the prophecies, John Paul II, from the Labor of the Sun, will have only two successors before the end of the world.

Prophecy: (1) The communication of divine revelation by inspired intermediaries, called prophets, between God and his people. Old Testament prophecy was unique in its origin and because of its ethical and religious content, which included disclosure of the saving will of Yahweh for the people, moral censures of sin and violations of the Law and Covenant, in the form of promises, admonitions, reproaches and threats. Although Moses and other earlier figures are called prophets, the period of prophecy is generally dated from the early years of the monarchy to about 100 years after the Babylonian Exile. From that time on the written Law and its interpreters supplanted the prophets as guides of the people. Old Testament prophets are cited in the New Testament, with awareness that God spoke through them and that some of their oracles were fulfilled in Christ. John the Baptist is the outstanding prophetic figure in the New Testament. Christ never claimed the title of prophet for himself, although some people thought he was one. There were prophets in the early Church, and St. Paul mentioned the charism of prophecy in 1 Cor. 14:1-5. Prophecy disappeared after New Testament times. Revelation is classified as the prophetic book of the New Testament.

(2) In contemporary non-scriptural usage, the term is applied to the witness given by persons to the relevance of their beliefs in everyday life and action.

Province: (1) A territory comprising one archdiocese called the metropolitan see and one or more dioceses called suffragan sees. The head of the archdiocese, an archbishop, has metropolitan rights and responsibilities over the province.

(2) A division of a religious order under the jurisdiction of a provincial superior.

Prudence: Practical wisdom and judgment regarding the choice and use of the best ways and means of doing good; one of the four cardinal virtues.

Punishment Due for Sin: The punishment which is a consequence of sin. It is of two kinds:

(1) Eternal punishment is the punishment of hell, to which one becomes subject by the commission of mortal sin. Such punishment is remitted when mortal sin is forgiven.

(2) Temporal punishment is a consequence of venial sin and/or forgiven mortal sin; it is not everlasting and may be remitted in this life by means of penance. Temporal punishment unremitted during this life is remitted by suffering in purgatory.

Purgatory: The state or condition in which those who have died in the state of grace, but with some attachment to sin, suffer for a time before they are admitted to the glory and happiness of heaven. In this state and period of passive suffering, they are purified of unrepented venial sins, satisfy the demands of divine justice for temporal punishment due for sins, and are thus converted to a state of worthiness of the beatific vision.

R

Racism: A theory which holds that any one or several of the different races of the human family are inherently superior or inferior to any one or several of the others. The teaching denies the essential unity of the human race, the equality and dignity of all men because of their common possession of the same human nature, and the participation of all men in the divine plan of redemption. It is radically opposed to the virtue of justice and the precept of love of neighbor. Differences of superiority and inferiority which do exist are the result of accidental factors operating in a wide variety of circumstances, and are in no way due to essential defects in any one or several of the branches of the one human race. The theory of racism, together with practices related to it, is incompatible with Christian doctrine.

Rash Judgment: Attributing faults to another without sufficient reason; a violation of the obligations of justice and charity.

Rationalism: A theory which makes the mind the measure and arbiter of all things, including religious truth. A product of the Enlightenment, it rejects the supernatural, divine revelation, and authoritative teaching by any church.

Recollection: Meditation, attitude of concentration or awareness of spiritual matters and things pertaining to salvation and the accomplishment of God's will.

Relativism: Theory which holds that all truth, including religious truth, is relative, i.e., not absolute, certain or unchanging; a product of agnosticism, indifferentism, and an unwarranted extension of the notion of truth in positive science. Relativism is based on the tenet that certain knowledge of any and all truth is impossible. Therefore, no religion, philosophy or science can be said to possess the real truth; consequently, all religions, philosophies and sciences may be considered to have as much or as little of truth as any of the others.

Relics: The physical remains and effects of saints, which are considered worthy of veneration inasmuch as they are representative of persons in glory with God. First class relics are parts of the bodies of saints, and instruments of their penance and death; second class relics are objects which had some contact with their persons. Catholic doctrine proscribes the view that relics are not worthy of veneration. In line with norms laid down by the Council of Trent and subsequent enactments, discipline concerning relics is subject to control by the Congregation for the Causes of Saints.

Religion: The adoration and service of God as expressed in divine worship and in daily life. Religion is concerned with all of the relations existing between God and man, and between man and man because of the central significance of God. Objectively considered, religion consists of a body of truth which is believed, a code of morality for the guidance of conduct, and a form of divine worship. Subjectively, it is man's total response, theoretically and practically, to the demands of faith; it is living faith, personal engagement, self-commitment to God. Thus, by creed, code and cult, a person orders and directs his life in reference to God and, through what the love and service of God implies, to his fellow men and all things.

Reliquary: A vessel for the preservation and exposition of a relic; sometimes made like a small monstrance.

Reparation: The making of amends to God for sin committed; one of the four ends of prayer and the purpose of penance.

Rescript: A written reply by an ecclesiastical superior regarding a question or request; its provisions bind concerned parties only. Papal dispensations are issued in the form of rescripts.

Reserved Case: A sin or censure, absolution from which is reserved to religious superiors, bishops, the pope, or confessors having special faculties. Reservations are made because of the serious nature and social effects of certain sins and censures.

Restitution: An act of reparation for an injury done to another. The injury may be caused by taking and/or retaining what belongs to another or by damaging either the property or reputation of another. The intention of making restitution, usually in kind, is required as a condition for the forgiveness of sins of injustice, even though actual restitution is not possible.

Ring: In the Church a ring is worn as part of the insignia of bishops, abbots, et al.; by sisters to denote their consecration to God and the Church. The wedding ring symbolizes the love and union of husband and wife.

Ritual: A book of prayers and ceremonies used in the administration of the sacraments and other ceremonial functions. In the Roman Rite, the standard book of this kind is the Roman Ritual. Revisions have been made — e.g., in the rites of baptism — since the Second Vatican Council.

Rogito: The official notarial act or document testifying to the burial of a pope.

Rosary: A form of mental and vocal prayer centered on mysteries or events in the lives of Jesus and Mary. Its essential elements are meditation on the mysteries and the recitation of a number of decades of Hail Marys, each beginning with the Lord's Prayer. Introductory prayers may include the Apostles' Creed, an initial Our Father, three Hail Marys and a Glory be to the Father; each decade is customarily concluded with a Glory be to the Father; at the end, it is customary to say the Hail, Holy Queen and a prayer from the liturgy for the feast of the Blessed Virgin Mary of the Rosary.

The **Mysteries of the Rosary,** which are the subject of meditation, are: (1) Joyful — the Annunciation to Mary that she was to be the Mother of Christ, her visit to Elizabeth, the birth of Jesus, the presentation of Jesus in the Temple, the finding of Jesus in the Temple. (2) Sorrowful — Christ's agony in the Garden of Gethsemani, scourging at the pillar, crowning with thorns, carrying of the Cross to Calvary, and crucifixion. (3) Glorious — the Resurrection and Ascension of Christ, the descent of the Holy Spirit upon the Apostles, Mary's Assumption into heaven and her crowning as Queen of angels and men.

The complete Rosary, called the Dominican Rosary, consists of 15 decades. In customary practice, only five decades are usually said at one time. Rosary beads are used to aid in counting the prayers without distraction.

The Rosary originated through the coalescence of popular devotions to Jesus and Mary from the 12th century onward. Its present form dates from about the 15th century. Carthusians contributed greatly toward its development; Dominicans have been its greatest promoters.

S

Sabbath: The seventh day of the week, observed by Jews and Sabbatarians as the day for rest and religious observance.

Sacramentary: One of the first liturgical books, containing the celebrant's part of the Mass and rites for administration of the sacraments. The earliest book of this kind, the Leonine Sacramentary, dates from the middle or end of the sixth century.

The sacramentary, incorporating most of the contents of the *Roman Missal,* was reintroduced in the Roman Rite following the promulgation of the *Constitution on the Sacred Liturgy* by the Second Vatican Council.

Sacrarium: A basin with a drain leading directly into the ground; standard equipment of a sacristy.

Sacred Heart, Enthronement: An acknowledgment of the sovereignty of Jesus Christ over the Christian family, expressed by the installation of an image or picture of the Sacred Heart in a place of honor in the home, accompanied by an act of consecration.

Sacred Heart, Promises: Twelve promises to persons having devotion to the Sacred Heart of Jesus, which were communicated by Christ to St. Margaret Mary Alacoque in a private revelation in 1675: (1) I will give them all the graces necessary in their state in life. (2) I will establish peace in their homes. (3) I will comfort them in all their afflictions. (4) I will be their secure refuge during life and, above all, in death. (5) I will bestow abundant blessing upon all their undertakings. (6) Sinners shall find in my Heart the source and the infinite ocean of mercy. (7) By devotion to my Heart tepid souls shall grow fervent. (8) Fervent souls shall quickly mount to high perfection. (9) I will bless every place where a picture of my Heart shall be set up and honored. (10) I will give to priests the gift of touching the most hardened hearts. (11) Those who promote this devotion shall have their names written in my Heart, never to be blotted out. (12) I will grant the grace of final penitence to those who communicate (receive Holy Communion) on the first Friday of nine consecutive months.

Sacrilege: Violation of and irreverence toward a person, place or thing that is sacred because of public dedication to God; a sin against the virtue of religion. Personal sacrilege is violence of some kind against a cleric or religious, or a violation of chastity with a cleric or religious. Local sacrilege is the desecration of sacred places. Real sacrilege is irreverence with respect to sacred things, such as the sacraments and sacred vessels.

Sacristy: A utility room where vestments, church furnishings and sacred vessels are kept and where the clergy vest for sacred functions.

Sadducees: The predominantly priestly party among the Jews in the time of Christ, noted for extreme conservatism, acceptance only of the Law of Moses, and rejection of the traditions of the elders. Their opposite numbers were the Pharisees.

Saints, Cult of: The veneration, called dulia, of holy persons who have died and are in glory with God in heaven; it includes honoring them and petitioning them for their intercession with God. Liturgical veneration is given only to saints officially recognized by the Church; private veneration may be given to anyone thought to be in heaven. The veneration of saints is essentially different from the adoration given to God alone; by its very nature, however, it terminates in the worship of God.

According to the Second Vatican Council's *Dogmatic Constitution on the Church* (No. 50): "It is supremely fitting... that we love those friends and fellow heirs of Jesus Christ, who are also our brothers and extraordinary benefactors, that we render due thanks to God for them and 'suppliantly invoke them and have recourse to their prayers, their power and help in obtaining benefits from God through His Son, Jesus Christ, our Lord, who is our sole Redeemer and Savior.' For by its very nature every genuine testimony of love which we show to those in heaven tends toward and terminates in Christ, who is the 'crown of all saints.' Through Him it tends toward and terminates in God, who is wonderful in His saints and is magnified in them."

Salvation: The liberation of men from sin and its effects, reconciliation with God in and through Christ, the attainment of union with God forever in the glory of heaven as the supreme purpose of life and as the God-given reward for fulfillment of his will on earth. Salvation-in-process begins and continues in this life through union with Christ in faith professed and in action; its final term is union with God and the whole community of the saved in the ultimate perfection of God's kingdom. The Church teaches that: God wills the salvation of all men; men are saved in and through Christ; membership in the Church established by Christ, known and understood as the community of salvation, is necessary for salvation; men with this knowledge and understanding who deliberately reject this Church, cannot be saved. In the context of Catholic belief, the Catholic Church is the Church founded by Christ. (See below, Salvation outside the Church.)

Salvation History: The facts and the record of God's relations with men, in the past, present and future, for the purpose of leading them to live in accordance with his will for the eventual attainment after death of salvation, or everlasting happiness with him in heaven.

The essentials of salvation history are: God's love for all men and will for their salvation; his intervention and action in the world to express this love and bring about their salvation; the revelation he made of himself and the covenant he established with the Israelites in the Old Testament; the perfecting of this revelation and the new covenant of grace through Christ in the New Testament; the continuing action-for-salvation carried on in and through the Mystical Body of Christ, the Church; the communication of saving grace to men through the merits of Christ and the operations of the Holy Spirit in the here-and-now circumstances of daily life and with the cooperation of men themselves.

Salvation outside the Church: The Second Vatican Council covered this subject summarily in the following manner: "Those also can attain to everlasting salvation who through no fault of their own do not know the gospel of Christ or His Church, yet sincerely seek God and, moved by grace, strive by their deeds to do His will as it is known to them through the dictates of conscience. Nor does divine Providence deny the help necessary for salvation to those who, without blame on their part, have not yet arrived at an explicit knowledge of God, but who strive to live a good life, thanks to His grace. Whatever good or truth is found among them is looked upon by the Church as a preparation for the gospel. She regards such qualities as given by Him who enlightens all men so that they may finally have life" *(Dogmatic Constitution on the Church,* No. 16).

Satanism: Worship of the devil, a blasphemous inversion of the order of worship which is due to God alone.

Scandal: Conduct which is the occasion of sin to another person.

Scapular: (1) A part of the habit of some religious orders like the Benedictines and Dominicans; a nearly shoulder-wide strip of cloth worn over the tunic and reaching almost to the feet in front and behind. Originally a kind of apron, it came to symbolize the cross and yoke of Christ.

(2) Scapulars worn by lay persons as a sign of association with religious orders and for devotional purposes are an adaptation of monastic scapulars. Approved by the Church as sacramentals, they consist of two small squares of woolen cloth joined by strings and are worn about the neck. They are given for wearing in a ceremony of investiture or enrollment. There are nearly 20 scapulars for devotional use: the five principal ones are generally understood to include those of Our Lady of Mt. Carmel (the brown Carmelite Scapular), the Holy Trinity, Our Lady of the

Seven Dolors, the Passion, the Immaculate Conception.

Scapular Medal: A medallion with a representation of the Sacred Heart on one side and of the Blessed Virgin Mary on the other. Authorized by St. Pius X in 1910, it may be worn or carried in place of a scapular by persons already invested with a scapular.

Scapular Promise: According to a legend of the Carmelite Order, the Blessed Virgin Mary appeared to St. Simon Stock in 1251 at Cambridge and declared that wearers of the brown Carmelite Scapular would be saved from hell and taken to heaven by her on the first Saturday after death. The validity of the legend has never been the subject of official decision by the Church. Essentially, it expresses belief in the intercession of Mary and the efficacy of sacramentals in the context of truly Christian life.

Schism: Derived from a Greek word meaning separation, the term designates formal and obstinate refusal by a baptized person, called a *schismatic,* to be in communion with the pope and the Church. The canonical penalty is excommunication. One of the most disastrous schisms in history resulted in the definitive separation of the Church in the East from union with Rome about 1054.

Scholasticism: The term usually applied to the Catholic theology and philosophy which developed in the Middle Ages.

Scribes: Hebrew intellectuals noted for their knowledge of the Law of Moses, influential from the time of the Exile to about 70 A.D. Many of them were Pharisees. They were the antecedents of rabbis and their traditions, as well as those of the Pharisees, had a lasting influence on Judaism following the destruction of Jerusalem in 70 A.D.

Scruple: A morbid, unreasonable fear and anxiety that one's actions are sinful when they are not, or more seriously sinful than they actually are. Compulsive scrupulosity is quite different from the transient scrupulosity of persons of tender or highly sensitive conscience, or of persons with faulty moral judgment.

Seal of Confession: The obligation of secrecy which must be observed regarding knowledge of things learned in connection with the confession of sin in the sacrament of penance. The seal covers matters whose revelation would make the sacrament burdensome. Confessors are prohibited, under penalty of excommunication, from making any direct revelation of confessional matter; this prohibition holds, outside of confession, even with respect to the person who made the confession unless the person releases the priest from the obligation. Persons other than confessors are obliged to maintain secrecy, but not under penalty of excommunication. General, non-specific discussion of confessional matter does not violate the seal.

Secularism: A school of thought, a spirit and manner of action which ignores and/or repudiates the validity or influence of supernatural religion with respect to individual and social life. In describing secularism in their annual statement in 1947, the bishops of the United States said in part: " . . . There are many men — and their number is daily increasing — who in practice live their lives without recognizing that this is God's world. For the most part they do not deny God. On formal occasions they may even mention his name. Not all of them would subscribe to the statement that all moral values derive from merely human conventions. But they fail to bring an awareness of their responsibility to God into their thought and action as individuals and members of society. This, in essence, is what we mean by secularism."

See: Another name for diocese or archdiocese.

Seminary: A house of study and formation for men, called seminarians, preparing for the priesthood. Traditional seminaries date from the Council of Trent in the middle of the 16th century; before that time, candidates for the priesthood were variously trained in monastic schools, universities under church auspices, and in less formal ways. At the present time, seminaries are undergoing considerable change for the improvement of academic and formation programs and procedures.

Sermon on the Mount: A compilation of sayings of Our Lord in the form of an extended discourse in Matthew's Gospel (5:1 to 7:27) and, in a shorter discourse, in Luke (6:17-49). The passage in Matthew, called the "Constitution of the New Law," summarizes the living spirit of believers in Christ and members of the kingdom of God. Beginning with the Beatitudes and including the Lord's Prayer, it covers the perfect justice of the New Law, the fulfillment of the Old Law in the New Law of Christ, and the integrity of internal attitude and external conduct with respect to love of God and neighbor, justice, chastity, truth, trust and confidence in God.

Servile Work: Work that is mainly physical and done for the sake of material purposes, in distinction from so-called liberal and artistic work which, although involving physical effort, is of a mental and intellectual nature. Commonly classified as servile are such works as farming, manufacturing, commercial operations, mining, etc. Liberal works are those like studying, teaching, designing, writing, typing, etc. The classification of work as servile or otherwise depends in part on custom and cultural interpretation. The reception of pay for work has nothing to do with its classification. Servile work is prohibited on Sundays and holy days of obligation unless there is sound reason for it.

Seven Last Words of Christ: Words of Christ on the Cross. (1) "Father, forgive them; for they do not know what they are doing." (2) To the penitent thief: "I assure you: today you will be with me in Paradise." (3) To Mary and his Apostle John: "Woman, there is your son . . . There is your mother." (4) "My God, my God, why have you forsaken me?" (5) "I am thirsty." (6) "Now it is finished." (7) "Father, into your hands I commend my spirit."

Shrine, Crowned: A shrine approved by the Holy See as a place of pilgrimage. The approval permits public devotion at the shrine and implies that at least one miracle has resulted from devotion at the shrine. Among the best known crowned shrines are those of the Virgin Mary at Lourdes and Fatima.

Shroud of Turin: A strip of brownish linen cloth, 14 feet, three inches in length and three feet, seven inches in width, bearing the front and back imprint of a human body. A tradition dating from the seventh century, which has not been verified beyond doubt, claims that the shroud is the fine linen in which the body of Christ was wrapped for burial. The early history of the shroud is obscure. It was enshrined at Lirey, France, in 1354 and was transferred in 1578 to Turin, Italy, where it has been kept in the cathedral down to the present time. Scientific investigation, which began in 1898, seems to indicate that the markings on the shroud are those of a human body. The shroud, for the first time since 1933, was placed on public view from Aug. 27 to Oct. 8, 1978, and was seen by an estimated 3.3 million people. Scientists conducted intensive studies of it for several days after the end of public viewing.

Sick Calls: When a person is confined at home by illness or other cause and is unable to go to church for reception of the sacraments, a parish priest should be informed and arrangements made for him to visit the person at home. Such visitations are common in pastoral practice, both for special needs and for providing persons with regular opportunities for receiving the sacraments.

Prepared for the visit should be: a conveniently placed table covered with a white cloth; on it should be a crucifix, two lighted candles, a glass with water, a spoon and napkin.

The priest, carrying the Blessed Sacrament, should be escorted to and from the sick person by someone carrying a lighted candle. Members of the household should be present when the sick person receives Holy Communion and/or anointing of the sick.

Sign of the Cross: A sign, ceremonial gesture or movement in the form of a cross by which a person confesses faith in the Holy Trinity and Christ, and intercedes for the blessing of himself, other persons, and things. In Roman-Rite practice, a person making the sign touches the fingers of the right hand to his forehead, below the breast, left shoulder and right shoulder while saying: "In the name of the Father, and of the Son, and of the Holy Spirit." The sign is also made with the thumb on the forehead, the lips, and the breast. For the blessing of persons and objects, a large sign of the cross is made by movement of the right hand. In Eastern-Rite practice, the sign is made with the thumb and first two fingers of the right hand joined together and touching the forehead, below the breast, the right shoulder and the left shoulder; the formula generally used is the doxology, "O Holy God, O Holy Strong One, O Immortal One." The Eastern manner of making the sign was general until the first half of the 13th century; by the 17th century, Western practice involved the whole right hand and the reversal of direction from shoulder to shoulder.

Signs of the Times: Contemporary events, trends and features in culture and society, the needs and aspirations of people, all the factors that form the context in and through which the Church has to carry on its saving mission. The Second Vatican Council spoke on numerous occasions about these signs and the relationship between them and a kind of manifestation of God's will, positive or negative, and about subjecting them to judgment and action corresponding to the demands of divine revelation through Scripture, Christ, and the experience, tradition and teaching authority of the Church.

Simony: The deliberate intention and act of selling and/or buying spiritual goods or material things so connected with the spiritual that they cannot be separated therefrom; a violation of the virtue of religion, and a sacrilege, because it wrongfully puts a material price on spiritual things, which cannot be either sold or bought. In church law, actual sale or purchase is subject to censure in some cases. The term is derived from the name of Simon Magus, who attempted to buy from Sts. Peter and John the power to confirm people in the Holy Spirit (Acts 8:4-24).

Sin: (1) Actual sin is rejection of God manifested by free and deliberate violation of his law by thought, word or action. (a) Mortal sin — involving serious matter, sufficient reflection and full consent — results in total alienation from God, making a person dead to sanctifying grace, incapable of performing meritorious supernatural acts and subject to everlasting punishment. (b) Venial sin — involving less serious matter, reflection and consent — does not have such serious consequences.

(2) Original sin (See separate entry).

Sins against the Holy Spirit: Despair of salvation, presumption of God's mercy, impugning the known truths of faith, envy at another's spiritual good, obstinacy in sin, final impenitence. Those guilty of such sins stubbornly resist the influence of grace and, as long as they do so, cannot be forgiven.

Sins, Occasions of: Circumstances (persons, places, things, etc.) which easily lead to sin. There is an obligation to avoid voluntary proximate occasions of sin, and to take precautions against the dangers of unavoidable occasions.

Sins That Cry to Heaven for Vengeance: Willful murder, sins against nature, oppression of the poor, widows and orphans, defrauding laborers of their wages.

Sister: Any woman religious, in popular speech; strictly, the title applies only to women religious belonging to institutes whose members never professed solemn vows. Most of the institutes whose members are properly called sisters were established during and since the 19th century. Women religious with solemn vows, or belonging to institutes whose members formerly professed solemn vows, are properly called nuns.

Sisterhood: A generic term referring to the whole institution of the life of women religious in the Church, or to a particular institute of women religious.

Situation Ethics: A subjective, individualistic ethical theory which denies the binding force of ethical principles as universal laws and preceptive norms of moral conduct, and proposes that morality is determined only by situational conditions and considerations and the intention of the person. In an instruction issued on the subject in May, 1956, the Congregation for the Holy Office said:

"It ignores the principles of objective ethics. This 'New Morality,' it is claimed, is not only the equal of objective morality, but is superior to it.

"The authors who follow this system state that the ultimate determining norm for activity is not the objective order as determined by the natural law and known with certainty from this law. It is instead some internal judgment and illumination of the mind of every individual by which the mind comes to know what is to be done in a concrete situation.

"This ultimate decision of man is, therefore, not the application of the objective law to a particular case after the particular circumstances of a 'situation' have been considered and weighed according to the rules of prudence, as the more important authors of objective ethics teach; but it is, according to them, immediate, internal illumination and judgment.

"With regard to its objective truth and correctness, this judgment, at least in many things, is not ultimately measured, is not to be measured or is not measurable by any objective norm found outside man and independent of his subjective persuasion, but it is fully sufficient in itself....

"Much that is stated in this system of 'Situation Ethics' is contrary to the truth of reality and to the dictate of sound reason. It gives evidence of relativism and modernism, and deviates far from the Catholic teaching handed down through the ages."

Slander: Attributing to a person faults which he does not have; a violation of the obligations of justice and charity, for which restitution is due.

Sloth: One of the seven capital sins; spiritual laziness, involving distaste and disgust for spiritual things; spiritual boredom, which saps the vigor of spiritual life. Physical laziness is a counterpart of spiritual sloth.

Sorcery: A kind of black magic in which evil is invoked by means of diabolical intervention; a violation of the virtue of religion.

Soteriology: The division of theology which treats of the mission and work of Christ as Redeemer.

Species, Sacred: The appearances of bread and wine (color, taste, smell, etc.) which remain after the substance has been changed at the Consecration of the Mass into the Body and Blood of Christ. (See Transubstantiation.)

Spiritism: Attempts to communicate with spirits and departed souls by means of seances, table tapping, ouija boards, and other methods; a violation of the virtue of religion. Spiritualistic practices are noted for fakery.

Spiritual Works of Mercy: Works of spiritual assistance, motivated by love of God and neighbor, to persons in need: counseling the doubtful, instructing the ignorant, admonishing sinners, comforting the afflicted, forgiving offenses, bearing wrongs patiently, praying for the living and the dead.

Stational Churches, Days: Churches, especially in Rome, where the clergy and lay people were accustomed to gather with their bishop on certain days for the celebration of the liturgy. The 25 early titular or parish churches of Rome, plus other churches, each had their turn as the site of divine worship in practices which may have started in the third century. The observances were rather well developed toward the latter part of the fourth century, and by the fifth they included a Mass concelebrated by the pope and attendant priests. On some occasions, the stational liturgy was preceded by a procession from another church called a collecta. There were 42 Roman stational churches in the eighth century, and 89 stational services were scheduled annually in connection with the liturgical seasons. Stational observances fell into disuse toward the end of the Middle Ages. Some revival was begun by John XXIII in 1959 and continued by Paul VI.

Stations of the Cross: A series of meditations on the sufferings of Christ: his condemnation to death and taking up of the Cross; the first fall on the way to Calvary; meeting his Mother; being assisted by Simon of Cyrene, and by Veronica who wiped his face; the second fall; meeting the women of Jerusalem; the third fall; being stripped and nailed to the Cross; his death; the removal of his body from the Cross and his burial. Depictions of these scenes are mounted in most churches, chapels and in some other places, beneath small crosses.

A person making the Way of the Cross passes before these Stations, or stopping points, pausing at each for meditation. If the Stations are made by a group of people, only the leader has to pass from Station to Station. Prayer for the intentions of the pope is required for gaining the indulgence granted for the Stations.

Those unable to make the Stations in the ordinary manner, because they are impeded from visiting a church or other place where the Stations are, can still practice the devotion by meditating on the sufferings of Christ; praying the Our Father, Hail Mary and Glory for each Station and five times in commemoration of the wounds of Christ; and praying for the intentions of the pope. This practice has involved the use of a Stations Crucifix.

A recent development in this devotion is toward greater awareness of the relation of the Passion to the Resurrection-Ascension; this trend, in some circles, has led to the erection of a 15th—unofficial—station. The concept amounts to an extension of the whole customary thrust of the devotion.

The Stations originated, remotely, from the practice of Holy Land pilgrims who visited the actual scenes of incidents in the Passion of Christ. Representations elsewhere of at least some of these scenes were known as early as the fifth century. Later, the Stations evolved in connection with and as a consequence of strong devotion to the Passion in the 12th and 13th centuries. Franciscans, who were given custody of the Holy Places in 1342, promoted the devotion widely; one of them, St. Leonard of Port Maurice, became known as the greatest preacher of the Way of the Cross in the 18th century. The general features of the devotion were fixed by Clement XII in 1731.

Statutes: Virtually the same as decrees (see separate entry), they almost always designate laws of a particular council or synod rather than pontifical laws.

Stigmata: Marks of the wounds suffered by Christ in his crucifixion, in hands and feet by nails, and side by the piercing of a lance. Some persons, called stigmatists, have been reported as recipients or sufferers of marks like these. The Church, however, has never issued any infallible declaration about their possession by anyone, even in the case of St. Francis of Assisi whose stigmata seem to be the best substantiated and may be commemorated in the Roman-Rite liturgy. Ninety percent of some 300 reputed stigmatists have been women. Judgment regarding the presence, significance, and manner of causation of stigmata would depend, among other things, on irrefutable experimental evidence.

Stipend, Mass: An offering given to a priest for applying the fruits of the Mass according to the intention of the donor. The offering is a contribution to the support of the priest. The disposition of the fruits of the sacrifice, in line with doctrine concerning the Mass in particular and prayer in general, is subject to the will of God. In the early Christian centuries, when Mass was not offered for the intentions of particular persons, the participants made offerings of bread and wine for the sacrifice and their own Holy Communion, and of other things useful for the support of the clergy and the poor. Some offerings may have been made as early as the fourth century for the celebration of Mass for particular intentions, and there are indications of the existence of this practice from the sixth century when private Masses began to be offered. The earliest certain proof of stipend practice, however, dates from the eighth century. By the 11th century, along with private Mass, it was established custom.

Stole Fee: An offering given on certain occasions; e.g., at a baptism, wedding, funeral, for the support of the clergy who administer the sacraments and perform other sacred rites.

Stoup: A vessel used to contain holy water.

Suffragan See: Any diocese, except the archdiocese, within a province.

Suicide: The taking of one's own life; a violation of God's dominion over human life. Ecclesiastical burial is denied to persons who deliberately commit suicide while in full possession of their faculties; it is permitted in cases of doubt.

Supererogation: Good and virtuous actions which go beyond the obligations of duty and the requirements enjoined by God's law as necessary for salvation. Examples of these works are the profession and observance of the evangelical counsels of poverty, chastity, and obedience, and efforts to practice charity to the highest degree.

Supernatural: Above the natural; that which exceeds and is not due or owed to the essence, exigencies, requirements, powers and merits of created nature. While man has no claim on supernatural things and does not need them in order to exist and act on a natural level, he does need them in order to exist and act in the higher order or economy of grace established by God for his salvation.

God has freely given to man certain things which are beyond the powers and rights of his human nature. Examples of the supernatural are: grace, a kind of participation by man in the divine life, by which man becomes capable of performing acts meritorious for salvation; divine revelation by which God manifests himself to man and makes known truth that is inaccessible to human reason alone; faith, by which man believes divine truth because of the authority of God who reveals it through Sacred Scripture and tradition and the teaching of his Church.

Superstition: A violation of the virtue of religion, by which God is worshipped in an unworthy manner or creatures are given honor which belongs to God alone. False, vain, or futile worship involves elements which are incompatible with the honor and respect due to God, such as error, deception, and bizarre practices. Examples are: false and exaggerated devotions, chain prayers and allegedly unfailing prayers, the mixing of unbecoming practices in worship. The second kind of superstition attributes to persons and things powers and honor which belong to God alone. Examples are: idolatry, divination, magic, spiritism, necromancy.

Suspension: A penalty by which a cleric is forbidden to exercise some or all of his powers of orders and jurisdiction, or to accept the financial support of his benefices.

Swearing: Taking an oath; calling upon God to witness the truth of a statement; a legitimate thing to do for serious reasons and under proper circumstances, as in a court of law. To swear without sufficient reason is to dishonor God's name; to swear falsely in a court of law is perjury.

Swedenborgianism: A doctrine developed in and from the writings of Emmanuel Swedenborg (1688-1772), who claimed that during a number of visions he had in 1745 Christ taught him the spiritual sense of Sacred Scripture and commissioned him to communicate it to others. He held that, just as Christianity succeeded Judaism, so his teaching supplemented Christianity. He rejected belief in the Trinity, original sin, the Resurrection, and all the sacraments except baptism and the Eucharist. His followers are members of the Church of the New Jerusalem or of the New Church.

Syllabus, The: (1) When not qualified, the term refers to the list of 80 errors accompanying Pope Pius IX's encyclical *Quanta Cura,* issued in 1864.

(2) The *Syllabus* of St. Pius X in the decree *Lamentabili,* issued by the Holy Office July 4, 1907, condemning 65 heretical propositions of modernism. This schedule of errors was followed shortly by that pope's encyclical *Pascendi,* the principal ecclesiastical document against modernism, issued Sept. 8, 1907.

Synod, Diocesan: Meeting of representative persons of a diocese — priests, religious, lay persons — with the bishop, called by him for the purpose of considering and taking action on matters affecting the life and mission of the Church in the diocese. Persons taking part in a synod have consultative status; the bishop alone is the legislator, with power to authorize synodal decrees. According to canon law, every diocese should have a synod every 10 years.

T

Te Deum: The opening Latin words, Thee, God, of a hymn of praise and thanksgiving prescribed for use in the Office of Readings (Matins of the Liturgy of the Hours) on many Sundays, solemnities and feasts.

Temperance: Moderation, one of the four cardinal virtues.

Temptation: Any enticement to sin, from any source: the strivings of one's own faculties, the action of the devil, other persons, circumstances of life, etc. Temptation itself is not sin. Temptation can be avoided and overcome with the use of prudence and the help of grace.

Thanksgiving: An expression of gratitude to God for his goodness and the blessings he grants; one of the four ends of prayer.

Theism: A philosophy which admits the existence of God and the possibility of divine revelation; it is generally monotheistic and acknowledges God as transcendent and also active in the world. Because it is a philosophy rather than a system of theology derived from revelation, it does not include specifically Christian doctrines, like those concerning the Trinity, the Incarnation and Redemption.

Theological Virtues: The virtues which have God for their direct object: faith, or belief in God's infallible teaching; hope, or confidence in divine assistance; charity, or love of God. They are given to a person with grace in the first instance, through baptism and incorporation in Christ.

Theology: Knowledge of God and religion, deriving from and based on the data of divine Revelation, organized and systematized according to some kind of scientific method. It involves systematic study and presentation of the truths of divine Revelation in Sacred Scripture, tradition, and the teaching of the Church.

The Second Vatican Council made the following declaration about theology and its relation to divine Revelation: "Sacred theology rests on the written word of God, together with sacred tradition, as its primary and perpetual foundation. By scrutinizing in the light of faith all truth stored up in the mystery of Christ, theology is most powerfully strengthened and constantly rejuvenated by that word. For the sacred Scriptures contain the word of God and, since they are inspired, really are the word of God; and so the study of the sacred page is, as it were, the soul of sacred theology" *(Constitution on Revelation.* No. 24).

Theology has been divided under various subject headings. Some of the major fields have been: dogma, moral, pastoral, ascetics (the practice of virtue and means of attaining holiness and perfection), mysticism (higher states of religious experience). Other subject headings include ecumenism (Christian unity, interfaith relations), ecclesiology (the nature and constitution of the Church), Mariology (doctrine concerning the Blessed Virgin Mary), the sacraments, etc.

Tithing: Contribution of a portion of one's income, originally one-tenth, for purposes of religion and charity. The practice is mentioned 46 times in the Bible. In early Christian times, tithing was adopted in continuance of Old Testament practices of the Jewish people, and the earliest positive church legislation on the subject was enacted in 567. Catholics are bound in conscience to contribute to the support of their church, but the manner in which they do so is not fixed by law. Tithing, which amounts to a pledged contribution of a portion of one's income, has aroused new attention in recent years in the United States.

Titular Sees: Dioceses where the Church once flourished but which later were overrun by pagans or Moslems and now exist only in name or title. Bishops without a territorial or residential diocese of their own; e.g., auxiliary bishops, are given titular sees.

Transfinalization, Transignification: Terms coined to express the sign value of consecrated bread and wine with respect to the presence and action of Christ in the Eucharistic sacrifice and the spiritually vivifying purpose of the Eucharistic banquet in Holy Communion. The theory behind the terms has strong undertones of existential and "sign" philosophy, and has been criticized for its openness to interpretations at variance with the doctrine of transubstantiation and the abiding presence of Christ under the appearances of bread and wine after the sacrifice of the Mass and Communion have been completed. The terms, if used as substitutes for transubstantiation, are unacceptable; if they presuppose transubstantiation, they are acceptable as clarifications of its meaning.

Transubstantiation; "The way Christ is made present in this sacrament (Holy Eucharist) is none other than by the change of the whole substance of the bread into his Body, and of the whole substance of the wine into his Blood (in the Consecration at Mass) . . . this unique and wonderful change the Catholic Church rightly calls transubstantiation" (encyclical *Mysterium Fidei* of Paul VI, Sept. 3, 1965). The first official use of the term was made by the Fourth Council of the Lateran in 1215. Authoritative teaching on the subject was issued by the Council of Trent.

Treasury of the Church: The superabundant merits of Christ and the saints from which the Church draws to confer spiritual benefits, such as indulgences.

Triduum: A three-day series of public or private devotions.

U-Z

Usury: Excessive interest charged for the loan and use of money; a violation of justice.

Veronica: A word resulting from the combination of a Latin word for true, *vera*, and a Greek word for image, *eikon*, designating a likeness of the face of Christ or the name of a woman said to have given him a cloth on which he caused an imprint of his face to appear. The veneration at Rome of a likeness depicted on cloth dates from about the end of the 10th century; it figured in a popular devotion during the Middle Ages, and in the Holy Face devotion practiced since the 19th century. A faint, undiscernible likeness said to be of this kind is preserved in St. Peter's Basilica. The origin of the likeness is uncertain, and the identity of the woman is unknown. Before the 14th century, there were no known artistic representations of an incident concerning a woman who wiped the face of Christ with a piece of cloth while He was carrying the Cross to Calvary.

Viaticum: Holy Communion given to those in danger of death. The word, derived from Latin, means provision for a journey through death to life hereafter.

Vicar General: A prelate appointed by a bishop to help him, as a deputy, in the administration of his diocese. Because of his office, he has the same jurisdictional authority as the bishop except in cases reserved to the bishop by himself or by church law.

Virginity: Observance of perpetual sexual abstinence. The state of virginity, which is embraced for the love of God by religious with a public vow or by others with a private vow, was singled out for high praise by Christ (Mt. 19:10-12) and has always been so regarded by the Church. In the encyclical *Sacra Virginitas*, Pius XII stated: "Holy virginity and that perfect chastity which is consecrated to the service of God is without doubt among the most perfect treasures which the founder of the Church has left in heritage to the society which he established."

Paul VI approved in 1970 a rite in which women can consecrate their virginity "to Christ and their brethren" without becoming members of a religious institute. The *Ordo Consecrationis Virginum*, a revision of a rite promulgated by Clement VII in 1596, is traceable to the Roman liturgy of about 500.

Virtue: A habit or established capability for performing good actions. Virtues are *natural* (acquired and increased by repeating good acts) and/or *supernatural* (given with grace by God).

Vocation: A call to a way of life. Generally, the term applies to the common call of all men, from God, to holiness and salvation. Specifically, it refers to particular states of life, each called a vocation, in which response is made to this universal call; viz., marriage, the religious life and/or priesthood, the single state freely chosen or accepted for the accomplishment of God's will. The term also applies to the various occupations in which persons make a living. The Church supports the freedom of each individual in choosing a particular vocation, and reserves the right to pass on the acceptability of candidates for the priesthood and religious life. Signs or indicators of particular vocations are many, including a person's talents and interests, circumstances and obligations, invitations of grace and willingness to respond thereto.

Vow: A promise made to God with sufficient knowledge and freedom, which has as its object a moral good that is possible and better than its voluntary omission. A person who professes a vow binds himself by the virtue of religion to fulfill his promise. The best known examples of vows are those of poverty, chastity and obedience professed by religious (see Evangelical Counsels, individual entries).

Public vows are made before a competent person, acting as an agent of the Church, who accepts the profession in the name of the Church, thereby giving public recognition to the person's dedication and consecration to God and divine worship. Vows of this kind are either solemn, rendering all contrary acts invalid as well as unlawful; or simple, rendering contrary acts unlawful. Solemn vows are for life; simple vows are for a definite period of time or for life. Vows professed without public recognition by the Church are called private vows. The Church, which has authority to accept and give public recognition to vows, also has authority to dispense persons from their obligations for serious reasons.

Week of Prayer for Christian Unity: Eight days of prayer, from Jan. 18 to 25, for the union of all men in the Church established by Christ. On the initiative of Father Paul James Francis, S.A., of Graymoor, N.Y., it originated in 1908 as the Chair of Unity Octave. In recent years, its observance on an interfaith basis has increased greatly.

Witness, Christian: Practical testimony or evidence given by Christians of their faith in all circumstances of life — by prayer and general conduct, through good example and good works, etc.; being and acting in accordance with Christian belief; actual practice of the Christian faith.

Zucchetto: A skullcap worn by bishops and other prelates.

OUR LADY OF CZESTOCHOWA

The Black Madonna, the icon of Our Lady of Czestochowa, is enshrined on the "Hill of Light," Jasna Gora, above the city of Czestochowa in south central Poland. Long the center and focus of Marian devotion since it was brought there in 1382, it is the primary symbol of Polish religious faith and freedom.

The icon is a portrayal of Mary holding the Child Jesus. Their faces and hands are dark, as though they had been burned or stained by smoke. Three cuts are on one of Mary's cheeks, put there by robbers who desecrated the icon in 1430.

The origin of the icon is not clear. Elements of the legend say it was painted by St. Luke on a panel made by St. Joseph for the home of the Holy Family in Nazareth; that it was transported from the Holy Land to Constantinople; that it was given in 988 to a Ukrainian princess, Anna, the wife of Vladimir of Kiev; and that it eventually was brought to Czestochowa in 1382. The *Catholic Encyclopedia* notes another possibility, that the icon was of Greek-Italian origin in the ninth century.

The location of the icon on the hill above Czestochowa was related to the establishment of a priory of Paulite monks there, also in 1382. A shrine was built some time after 1386. A church was erected in 1644, and a 344-foot tower was raised in 1702.

Our Lady of Czestochowa was declared the Queen of Poland in 1656, and the icon was solemnly crowned in 1717 during the pontificate of Pope Clement XI.

The shrine has a long history as the greatest pilgrimage and religious center in Central Europe.

The shrine has undergone changes, some of them violent, in the years since 1382. Even in this century it has been a target of search and harassment by officials of the Communist government in control of the country since the end of World War II.

One thing has not changed, however; that is the significance of the icon and Czestochowa in the religious and patriotic life of the Polish people.

There are those who claim that Czestochowa is a more important capital of the nation than Warsaw.

THEOLOGICAL UNION

The Washington Theological Union, founded by six religious orders in 1968 and with the title, Washington Theological Coalition, until 1977, is a theological and pastoral institute for the training of candidates for the priesthood and other ministries, and for the continuing education of priests.

About 25 religious communities are represented in the current student body of approximately 275, including women religious, lay women and several non-Catholics. The WTC is the only institute of its kind in the East.

Father Vincent Cushing, O.F.M., is president of the WTU. Father James Coriden is the academic dean. The WTU address is 9001 New Hampshire Ave., Silver Spring, Md.

OLDER VOCATIONS

The number of men in their late 20s, 30s and even older applying for admission to places and courses of study and formation for the priesthood has been significant in recent years. For some of them, the priesthood represents a second career. Their rate of survival — to ordination and subsequently in the priesthood — appears to be good.

Biographies of Catholics

(In addition to the biographical entries below, others are listed in the Index.)

A

Abelard, Peter (1079-1142): French philosopher, theologian; contributed to scholastic method although he had nominalistic tendencies.

Achillini, Alessandro (1463-1512): Italian physicist, astronomer; inaugurated reaction against Ptolemaic astronomy.

Adam, Karl (1876-1966): German theologian, writer; *Spirit of Catholicism*.

Adenauer, Konrad (1876-1967): German statesman; chancellor of West Germany, 1949-63.

Africanus, Sextus Julius (3rd cent.): Christian historian; wrote history of world from creation to 221 A.D.

Agreda, Mary of (1602-1665): Spanish Poor Clare, mystical writer; *Mystical City of God and the Divine History of the Virgin Mother of God*.

Alan of Walsingham (died 1364): English monk, architect.

Alarcon, Pedro Antonio de (1833-1891): Spanish writer, statesman.

Alberione, Giacomo (1884-1971): Italian priest; founder of Pauline Fathers and Daughters of St. Paul for work in communications field.

Albert or Albrecht (died 1229): Founder and first bishop of Riga, apostle of Livonia.

Albornoz, Gil Alvarez Carillo de (1310-1367): Spanish cardinal, general, statesman; negotiated return of the papal states, 1354; his *Egidian Constitutions* for them prevailed until 1816; archbishop of Toledo.

Alcuin, Albinus (735-804): English scholar; abbot of Tours; educator among Franks.

Alexander of Hales (1180-1245): English theologian, philosopher; first Franciscan teacher at Paris; called Doctor Irrefragabilis.

Alfred the Great (849-899): First Saxon king of England; noted for wise laws, spread of religion and learning.

Allen, Frances (1784-1819): American religious; daughter of Ethan Allen; convert, 1807; professed vows in community of Hospital Sisters at Hotel-Dieu, Montreal, 1810.

Allers, Rudolf (1883-1963): Austrian-born psychologist; d. Maryland; taught at Catholic University of America, 1938-48, and Georgetown University, 1948-63.

Allori, Alessandro (1535-1607) and his son **Cristofano** (1577-1621): Italian painters, Florentine school.

Amiot, Jean Marie (1718-1793): French Jesuit, missionary to China, author.

Ammen, Daniel (1820-1898): American naval officer in Civil War; author.

Ampere, Andre Marie (1775-1836): French physicist; pioneer in electrodynamics; term ampere named for him.

Anderson, William H. (1799-1875): American mathematician and astronomer; on US expedition to Dead Sea, 1848; convert, 1849.

Angelico, Fra (Giovanni da Fiesole) (1387-1455): Italian Dominican painter of religious subjects.

Anglin, Timothy (1822-1896): Canadian journalist and legislator. Father of **Margaret Mary Anglin** (1876-1958): actress, Laetare medalist.

Animuccia, Giovanni (1500?-1571): Italian composer of sacred music.

Apponyi, Albert, Count (1846-1933): Hungarian statesman, parliamentary leader for 40 years; head of Hungary's peace delegation in Paris, 1920.

Argenlieu, Georges Thierry d' (1889-1964): French admiral, Carmelite priest; naval officer in World War I; entered Carmelites, 1920, and ordained priest (Father Louis of the Trinity); recalled to active duty during World War II, fought with Free French; governor general of Indo-China after the war; returned to monastery, 1947.

Arnold, Thomas (1823-1900): English educator; convert, 1856.

Avery, Martha (Moore) (1851-1929): American Socialist, political economist, author; convert, 1903; a founder of the Catholic Truth Guild, 1917.

B

Bacon, Roger (1214-1294): English Franciscan, philosopher, experimental scientist; considered optical and astronomical laws, possibilities of scientific invention, gunpowder.

Baegert, Johann Jacob (1717-1777): Jesuit missionary, ethnographer; author of works on Lower California.

Balboa, Vasco Nunez de (1475-1517): Spanish adventurer; discovered Pacific Ocean, 1513.

Baldwin, Charles Sears (1867-1935): American educator, author; convert, 1934.

Baldwin, Geoffrey P. (1892-1951): American military officer in World Wars I and II; convert, 1937; chief of CARE in Italy.

Banim, John (1798-1842) and **Michael** (1796-1874): First national novelists of Ireland; John called the Scott of Ireland.

Barber, Virgil (1787-1847): American Jesuit; prominent New England Episcopal minister before his conversion, 1816, with his wife and five children; all eventually entered religious life; ordained 1822; established first Catholic church and school in New Hampshire at Claremont. His father **Daniel** (1756-1834) was also an Episcopal minister before he followed the rest of his family into the Church in 1818; wrote *Catholic Worships and Piety Explained*.

Biographies

Barbour, John (1316?-1395): Scottish poet, author of the epic romance, *The Bruce*.

Baring, Maurice (1874-1945): English poet, novelist, critic, author of works on Russia; convert, 1909.

Barry, John (1745-1803): American naval officer, b. Ireland; naval hero in Revolution.

Bartholomeus Anglicus (13th cent.): English Franciscan, author of a medieval encyclopedia of science.

Bartolommeo, Fra (1475-1517): Florentine Dominican, religious painter.

Bayley, James Roosevelt (1814-1877): American prelate; convert, 1842; ordained priest, 1844; bishop of Newark, N. J. 1853-72; archbishop of Baltimore 1872-77.

Bayma, Joseph (1816-1892): Italian Jesuit, mathematician, scientist; author of *Molecular Mechanics*.

Bazin, Rene (1853-1932): French novelist, biographer, travel writer; member of French Academy.

Bea, Augustin (1881-1968): German Jesuit, cardinal, Biblical scholar, leader in Christian reunion movement.

Beardsley, Aubrey Vincent (1872-1898): British illustrator; convert, 1895.

Beaton (Bethune), David (1494-1546): Scottish prelate, statesman; cardinal archbishop of St. Andrews; chancellor of Scotland; opposed efforts of Henry VIII to separate Scotland from loyalty to Holy See.

Beauregard, Pierre (1818-1893): American Confederate general; graduate of West Point; superintendent of West Point for five days; resigned to serve with Confederate Army.

Beccaria, Giovanni Battista (1716-1781): Italian physicist; early researcher in electricity.

Becquerel, Antoine Cesar (1788-1878): French physicist, electrochemist; invented the constant cell, a differential galvanometer, an electric thermometer.

Becquerel, Antoine Henri (1852-1908): French physicist; discoverer of radioactivity in uranium; shared 1903 Nobel Prize in physics with the Curies.

Beethoven, Ludwig van (1770-1827): German composer; works include symphonies, concertos and sonatas.

Behaim, Martin (1459-1507): German geographer; constructed a terrestrial globe, 1492.

Bellini, Gentile (1429-1507) and **Giovanni** (1430-1516): Venetian painters.

Belloc, Hilaire (1870-1953): English journalist, essayist, poet, novelist, historian, biographer, critic, apologist.

Benson, Robert Hugh (1871-1914): English author of historical fiction, other works; Anglican clergyman before conversion, 1903; ordained to priesthood, 1904.

Benson, William Shepherd (1855-1932): American naval officer; first chief of naval operations, 1915-19; convert.

Bentley, John Francis (1839-1902): English architect; promoted Gothic revival in England; designed Cathedral of Westminster.

Berengario da Carpi, Jacopo (1470-1530): Italian anatomist; a founder of modern science of anatomy.

Bernanos, Georges (1888-1948): French journalist, novelist; works concerned principally with struggle of the soul against evil.

Bernard, Claude (1813-1878): French physiologist; studied the glycogenic function of the liver, sympathetic nervous system.

Bernini, Giovanni Lorenzo (1598-1680): Italian sculptor of wide influence; architect of St. Peter's.

Bertrand, Louis (1866-1941): French novelist, biographer.

Beschi, Costanzo Giuseppe (1680-1746): Italian Jesuit missionary; famous for linguistic and literary work in the Tamil language.

Besse, Jean Martial Leon (1861-1920): Benedictine monk, historian.

Bianchini, Francesco (1662-1729): Italian astronomer; secretary, under Clement XI, of papal commission for calendar reform.

Bickerstaffe-Drew, Francis (1858-1928): English author (under pseudonym of **John Ayscough**); convert, priest.

Bielski, Marcin (1495-1575): Polish historian, poet.

Bienville, Sieur de (1680-1768): French explorer, governor of Louisiana colony.

Biggs, Richard Keys (1886-1962): American concert organist, composer, choir master; convert.

Billuart, Charles Rene (1685-1757): Belgian Dominican theologian, preacher.

Binet, Jacques Philippe Marie (1786-1856): French mathematician, astronomer; Binet's theorem.

Biondo, Flavio (1388-1463): Italian historian, archaeologist.

Biot, Jean Baptiste (1774-1862): French physicist; studied polarization of light; Biot's law.

Blondel, Maurice (1861-1949): French philosopher; works include *L'Action, La Pensée*.

Blowick, John (1889-1972): Irish priest; founder with Bishop Edward Galvin of the Society of St. Columban, 1916.

Bloy, Leon (1846-1917): French writer, social reformer.

Boccaccio, Giovanni (1313-1375): Italian author; known as father of Italian prose; *Decameron*.

Boethius, Anicius Manlius (480?-524?): Roman statesman and philosopher; author of *The Consolation of Philosophy*.

Boileau-Despreaux, Nicolas (1636-1711): French poet, satirist, critic.

Bolland, John van (1596-1665): Flemish Jesuit; editor of *Acta Sanctorum*, continued by Bollandists.

Bolzano, Bernard (1781-1848): Bohemian mathematician; formulated theory of functions.

Bona, Giovanni (1609-1674): Italian cardinal, author of liturgical encyclopedia.

Bonaparte, Charles J. (1851-1921): American cabinet official; secretary of navy 1905-06; attorney general, 1906-09.

Bordone, Paris (1500-1571): Venetian painter, pupil of Titian.

Borrus, Christopher (1583-1632): Oceanic geographer.

Boscovich, Ruggiero Giuseppe (1711-1787): Italian Jesuit, astronomer, physicist; offered a molecular theory of matter.

Bosio, Antonio (1575-1629): Italian archaeologist, called Columbus of the Catacombs.

Bossuet, Jacques Benigne (1627-1704): French prelate; pulpit orator, author.

Botticelli, Sandro (1444-1510): Florentine painter.

Bourdaloue, Louis (1632-1704): French Jesuit, pulpit orator.

Bourgeois, Louis (1819-1878): French archaeologist; presented and developed problem of the eoliths, 1863.

Bracton, Henry de (died 1268): English jurist; author of treatise *On the Laws and Customs of England*.

Braille, Louis (1809-1852): Blind French teacher of the blind; inventor of Braille system of raised-point printing.

Bramante, Donato (1444-1514): Italian architect; made plan for reconstruction of St. Peter's.

Branly, Edouard (1846-1940): French physicist; discovered coherer, making wireless telegraphy possible.

Brennan, Francis J. (1894-1968): American cardinal, Roman Curia official; ordained priest, 1920; professor at St. Charles Seminary, Overbrook, Pa., 1920-40; judge, 1940-59, and dean, 1959-67, of the Sacred Roman Rota; ord. bishop June 25, 1967; cardinal, June 26, 1967.

Brentano, Klemens (1778-1842): German poet; rejoined Catholic Church, 1818; recorded revelations of Anne Catherine Emmerich.

Breuil, Henri (1877-1961): French priest, archaeologist; authority on prehistoric art.

Broun, Heywood Campbell (1888-1939): American journalist, author; convert, 1939.

Browne, Charles Farrar (pseud. Artemus Ward) (1834-1867): American humorist, journalist, lecturer.

Brownson, Orestes Augustus (1803-1876): American scholar, essayist, philosopher, controversialist; was successively a Presbyterian, Universalist minister and Unitarian minister before his conversion, 1844.

Bruckner, Anton (1824-1896): Austrian composer and organist.

Brumidi, Constantini (1805-1880): American painter, b. Italy; became naturalized citizen; noted for his frescoes in Capitol at Washington, D.C.

Brunelleschi, Filippo (1377-1466): Italian architect; called founder of Renaissance architecture; established theory of perspective.

Brunetiere, Ferdinand (1849-1906): French critic, editor, professor of literature; convert.

Buck, Edward Eugene (Gene) (1885-1957): American popular song lyricist, producer; president of American Society of Composers, Authors and Publishers (ASCAP), 1924-41.

Budenz, Louis (1891-1972): American journalist; prominent member of American Communist Party, 1935 to 1945, when he was received back into the Church; major witness in the McCarthy hearings in the 1950's.

Bullitt, William C. (1891-1967): American diplomat; first ambassador to Russia; convert shortly before his death.

Burke, John (1859-1937): American jurist, politician; governor of North Dakota, 1907-21; treasurer of US, 1913-21; judge, 1924, and later chief justice of North Dakota supreme court. Represents North Dakota in Statuary Hall.

Burke, Thomas Nicholas (1830-1882): Irish Dominican preacher.

Burnand, Sir Francis Crowley (1836-1917): English playwright; editor of *Punch* (1880-1906), and English *Catholic Who's Who;* convert, 1857.

Burnett, Peter Hardemann (1807-1895): American jurist, politician; judge of Oregon supreme court, first governor of California, member of California supreme court; convert, 1846.

Butler, Alban (1711-1773): English author; *Lives of the Saints*.

Butler, Pierce (1866-1939): American attorney, jurist; associate justice United States Supreme Court, 1923-39.

Byrd, William (1540?-1623): English organist, composer; founder of English Madrigal School.

C

Cabeza de Vaca, Alvar Nunez (1490-1557): Spanish explorer; colonial governor in Paraguay.

Cabot, John (1450-1498): Italian navigator; discovered mainland of North America, June 24, 1497.

Cabral, Pedro Alvarez de (1460-1526): Portuguese navigator; discovered Brazil, which he named Vera Cruz.

Caedmon (died 670): First great English Christian poet; lay brother at monastery in Whitby.

Caius (Kees, Keys, Kay, Key), John (1510-1573): English physician; lecturer on anatomy; author.

Cajetan, Tommaso De Vio (1469-1534): Italian cardinal, philosopher, theologian.

Caldani, Leopold Marco Antonio (1725-1813): Italian anatomist, physiologist; furthered anatomical studies on function of spinal cord.

Calderon de La Barca, Pedro (1600-1681): Spanish priest, dramatist; author of over 200 works.

Calvert, Cecil (1605-1675): English proprietor; second Lord Baltimore; responsible for enactment of religious toleration in Maryland colony.

Calvert, George (1580-1632): English proprietor; first Lord Baltimore; held important posts under James I; was granted territory of Baltimore colony but died before grant of charter; convert, 1625.

Camel (Kamel), George Joseph (1661-1706): Moravian Jesuit missionary, botanist; studied plants and natural history of Philippines.

Camoes, Luiz Vaz de (1524-1580): Portuguese poet, dramatist.

Campbell, James (1812-1893): American jurist, cabinet official; US postmaster general, 1853-57.

Cano, Melchior (1509-1560): Spanish Dominican, theologian; called father of fundamental theology.

Canova, Antonio (1757-1822): Italian sculptor of the modern classic school.

Canute (II) the Great (994?-1035): King of Denmark, England, Norway.

Cardano, Girolamo (1501-1576): Italian physician, mathematician.

Cardijn, Joseph (1882-1967): Belgian cardinal, founder of the Young Christian Workers; cardinal, 1965.

Carey, Mathew (1760-1839): American publisher, economist and author, b. Ireland; first extensive US Catholic publisher.

Carnoy, Jean Baptiste (1836-1899): Belgian priest, biologist; pioneer cytologist.

Carpini, Giovanni de Piano (c. 1180-1252): Italian Franciscan, companion of St. Francis; missionary in Germany; papal envoy to Great Khan of the Mongols, 1246; wrote *Liber Tartarorum* recounting in detail the life and customs of the Mongols.

Carrel, Alexis (1873-1944): French surgeon, biologist; developed surgical techniques, experimented on transplantation of organs; author; member Pontifical Academy of Sciences; Nobel Prize for physiology and medicine, 1912.

Carroll, Charles (1737-1832): American statesman; member of Continental Congress, 1776-78; signer of Declaration of Independence; member Maryland Congress and first US Senate, 1789-92. Represents Maryland in Statuary Hall.

Carroll, Daniel (1730-1796): American patriot; brother of Archbishop John Carroll; delegate to Continental Congress, 1780-84, Constitutional Convention, 1787; congressman from Maryland, 1789-91.

Carroll, John (1735-1815): American prelate; ordained priest, 1761; first bishop of the hierarchy of the US (bishop, 1789-1808, and archbishop, 1808-15 of Baltimore); also apostolic administrator of Louisiana and Two Floridas, 1805-15; founder of Georgetown University, 1791.

Carson, Christopher (Kit) (1809-1868): American trapper, scout, Indian agent.

Cartier, Jacques (1491-c. 1557): French explorer of coasts of Labrador and Newfoundland; ascended the St. Lawrence to Montreal.

Caruso, Enrico (1873-1921): Italian operatic tenor.

Cassini, Jean Dominique (1625-1712): French astronomer; first director of Paris observatory; made important discoveries regarding Saturn, parallax of sun.

Cassiodorus, Flavius Aurelius (c. 490-c. 580): Roman statesman, writer, founder of monasteries.

Castelli, Benedetto (c. 1572-1644): Italian Benedictine, mathematician, physicist; authority on hydraulics.

Cauchy, Augustin Louis (1789-1857): French mathematician; did research in calculus, developed wave theory in optics.

Cavalieri, Francesco Bonaventura (1598-1647): Italian religious, mathematician; originated method of indivisibles; forerunner of integral calculus.

Caxton, William (1422-1491): First English printer.

Cellini, Benvenuto (1500-1571): Italian sculptor; worker in gold and bronze.

Cervantes Saavedra, Miguel de (1547-1616): Spanish novelist; *Don Quixote.*

Cesalpino, Andrea (1519-1603): Italian botanist, physician; important contributor to work on plant morphology, physiology; anticipated Linnaean system of classification.

Cezanne, Paul (1839-1906): French painter; a leader of postimpressionism.

Challoner, Richard (1691-1781): English bishop; re-edited Douay Bible.

Champlain, Samuel de (1567-1635): French explorer; Father of New France, founder of Quebec; discovered Lake Champlain.

Champollion, Jean Francois (1790-1832): French Egyptologist; discovered through the Rosetta Stone a system for deciphering hieroglyphics.

Chandler, Joseph Ripley (1792-1880): American journalist, congressman; Grand Master of Free Masons before conversion, 1849; US minister to Naples during administration of Buchanan; US congressman from Pennsylvania, 1849-55.

Charlemagne (742-814): King of the Franks, Emperor of the West, founder of Holy Roman Empire; promoted spread of Christianity, learning; defender of the papacy.

Charles Martel (c. 689-741): Duke of Austrasia; halted Saracen advance on western Europe at Battle of Tours (732), and thereafter was called Martel *(The Hammer);* grandfather of Charlemagne.

Chateaubriand, Francois Rene de (1768-1848): French author; influential in history of Romantic Movement.

Chaucer, Geoffrey (1340-1400): Father of English poetry; *Canterbury Tales.*

Chauliac, Guy de (1300-1370): French surgeon; gave authoritative description of bubonic plague, Black Death of 14th century.

Chavez, Dennis (1888-1962): American legislator; member New Mexico State legislature, 1920-30; US congressman, 1931-35; US senator, 1935-62. Represents New Mexico in Statuary Hall.

Cherubini, Maria Luigi (1760-1842): Italian composer of ecclesiastical and operatic works.

Chesterton, Gilbert K. (1874-1936): English essayist, poet, novelist, biographer, journalist; Prince of Paradox; convert, 1922.

Chevreul, Michel Eugene (1786-1889): French chemist; did research in animal fats; discovered margarine, oleine, stearine.

Cimabue, Giovanni (Cenni di Pepo) (1240-1302): Florentine painter; religious subjects.

Claudel, Paul (1868-1955): French author, diplomat; elected to French Academy, 1946.

Clavius, Christopher (1537-1612): Jesuit astronomer, mathematician; introduced decimal point.

Clerke, Agnes Mary (1842-1907): Irish astronomer.

Coady, Moses Michael (1882-1959): Canadian priest, educator; organizer of cooperatives among Canadian fishermen, known as Antigonish movement.

Cobo, Bernabe (1582-1657): Spanish Jesuit, naturalist; author of *History of the New World*, on Latin America.

Cody, Col. William F. (Buffalo Bill) (1846-1917): American Pony Express rider, army guide and scout, hunter, Indian fighter; entered Church just before death.

Collins, Michael (1890-1922): Irish revolutionary leader and soldier.

Colombo, Matteo Realdo (1516-1559): Italian anatomist; discovered pulmonary circulation.

Columbus, Christopher (1451-1506): Genoese explorer; discovered the Americas in 1492.

Connell, Francis J. (1888-1967): American Redemptorist priest, moral theologian, author.

Connelly, Mother Cornelia (1809-1879): American-born foundress; married to Pierce Connelly, an Episcopalian minister; her conversion, 1835, was followed three months later by her husband's; granted permanent separation by Rome and entered convent so her husband could become a priest; sent to England at request of Cardinal Wiseman and founded Society of the Holy Child Jesus, 1846; her husband renounced the priesthood, 1849; his legal attempt to force her to return to married life was unsuccessful.

Constantine the Great (c. 280-337): Roman emperor; granted liberty of worship to Christians by Edict of Milan, 313; established Constantinople as capital of the Eastern Empire.

Copernicus, Nicolaus (1473-1543): Polish astronomer; founder of modern astronomy; taught the revolution of planets around the sun and the rotation of the earth on its axis.

Coppee, Francois (1842-1908): French poet, dramatist, novelist; member of French Academy, 1884.

Cordoba, Francisco Fernandez de (d. 1518?): Spanish explorer; discovered Yucatan, 1517.

Corneille, Pierre (1606-1684): French dramatist; great influence on French tragedy, *Le Cid*.

Corot, Jean Baptiste Camille (1796-1875): French landscape artist.

Correggio, Antonio Allegri (1494-1534): Lombard painter; noted for mastery of light and shade; religious subjects.

Cortez, Hernando (1485-1547): Spanish explorer, soldier; conquered Mexico.

Cory, Herbert Ellsworth (1883-1947): American educator, social scientist, author; convert, 1933.

Coulomb, Charles Augustine (1736-1806): French physicist; investigated electricity and magnetism; stated coulomb's law; the coulomb named for him.

Couperin, Francois (1668-1733): French composer; first great composer for the harpsichord.

Cousin, Jean (1490-1560), and his son **Jean** (1522-1590): French painters, workers in stained glass.

Crashaw, Richard (1613-1649): English poet of metaphysical school; convert, 1646.

Crawford, Francis Marion (1854-1909): American novelist, b. Italy; convert, 1880.

Credi, Lorenz di (1459-1537): Florentine painter; religious subjects.

Creighton, John (1831-1907) and his brother **Edward** (1802-1874): American philanthropists; benefactors of Creighton University; in 1861 took part in laying first telegraph line linking California to rest of the nation.

Cushing, Richard J. (1895-1970): American cardinal; ordained priest, 1921; auxiliary bishop of Boston, 1939-44; archbishop of Boston, 1944-70; cardinal, 1958; founded Missionary Society of St. James the Apostle to recruit diocesan priests for Latin American missions; promoted charitable works especially among exceptional children.

D

Dablon, Claude (1619-1697): French Jesuit missionary in America; superior of Canadian missions.

Daly, Thomas A. (1871-1948): American journalist and poet.

Damien, Father (Joseph de Veuster) (1840-1889): Belgian missionary; joined Picpus Fathers, 1860; from 1873 to his death, devoted his life to caring for lepers on Molokai, in Hawaiian Islands; contracted the disease three years before his death. Represents Hawaii in National Statuary Hall.

Daniel-Rops, Henri (pseud. of Henri Jules Petiot) (1901-1965): French writer on Church history and other subjects; member of French Academy.

Dante Alighieri (1265-1321): Florentine poet; *Divina Commedia, Vita Nuova, De Monarchia.*

Daumer, Georg Friedrich (1800-1875): German writer; anti-Christian works until conversion, 1858; author of *Meine Konversion.*

Davenport, Sir William (1606-1668): English poet and dramatist.

Dawson, Christopher (1889-1970): English author, scholar; convert from Anglicanism, 1914; principal themes of his works are cultural history and philosophy of religion.

DeGaulle, Charles Andre Joseph Marie (1890-1970): French general, statesman; leader of French forces in World War II; president of France.

Delacroix, Ferdinand Victor Eugene (1799-1863): French painter; romantic school.

Delaroche, Paul (1797-1856): French painter, of the Eclectic school; portrait and historical subjects.

DeRossi, Giovanni Battista (1822-1894): Italian archaeologist; aroused interest in Christian antiquities.

Descartes, Rene (1596-1650): French scientist and philosopher; founder of analytic geometry.

De Soto, Hernando (1500-1542): Spanish explorer; discovered lower course of Mississippi River, 1541.

De Valera, Eamon (1882-1975): Irish independence leader and statesman, b. New York; prime minister and president of Ireland.

De Vaux, Roland (1903-1971): French Dominican; biblical archaeologist and exegete; head of Ecole Biblique, Jerusalem; headed international team of scholars who edited Dead Sea Scrolls.

Devlin, Joseph (1872-1934): Irish politician.

Dias, Bartholomew (1450-1500): Portuguese navigator; discovered Cape of Good Hope, 1488.

Dimnet, Ernest (1869-1954): French priest, lecturer, writer.

Dior, Christian (1905-1957): French fashion designer.

Divisch, Wénceslaus (religious name, **Procopius**) (1698-1765): Moravian Premonstratensian monk; erected a lightning rod in 1754, before Franklin's work was known.

Dolci, Carlo (1616-1686): Florentine painter; religious and portrait subjects.

Donatello or **Donato di Niccolo di Betto Bardi** (1386-1466): Italian sculptor; called the founder of modern sculpture.

Dongon, Thomas (1634-1715): Colonial governor of New York, 1682-88; b. Ireland.

Donizetti, Gaetano (1797-1848): Italian operatic composer.

Dooley, Thomas A. (1927-1961): American physician; co-founder of MEDICO, organized to establish medical services in underdeveloped countries; author.

Doria, Andrea (1468-1560): Genoese admiral, statesman; Father of Peace, Liberator of Genoa.

Drexel, Mary Katherine (1858-1955): American missionary; foundress of Sisters of the Blessed Sacrament for Indians and Colored People, 1891.

Drum, Hugh A. (1879-1951): American army officer in World Wars I and II.

Dryden, John (1631-1700): English poet, playwright; poet laureate, 1670; convert, 1686.

Duffy, Sir Charles Gavan (1816-1903): Irish nationalist, political leader in Australia after he emigrated there (1856), author.

Dulong, Pierre Louis (1785-1838): French chemist, physicist; author with Petit of formula determining the specific heat of solids.

Dumas, Jean Baptiste (1800-1884); French chemist; did important research on vapor densities.

Dunne, Peter Finley (1867-1936): American humorist, journalist; creator of Irish philosophical character "Mr. Dooley."

Duns Scotus, John (1256-1308): Scottish scholastic theologian; Franciscan; advanced best theological arguments for doctrine of the Immaculate Conception; known as Doctor Subtilis.

Durer, Albrecht (1471-1528): German painter of Renaissance school, engraver, wood-cut artist; called inventor of etching.

Durkin, Martin P. (1894-1955): American union leader, cabinet official; secretary of labor, 1953.

Dutton, Ira (Brother Joseph) (1843-1931): American missionary; convert, 1883; assisted Father Damien in work among lepers at Molokai, served there for 42 years, beginning in 1886.

Dwight, Thomas (1843-1911): American surgeon, anatomist; convert, 1855.

E

Eck, Johann (1486-1543): German theologian; outstanding opponent of Luther.

Eckhel, Joseph Hilarius (1737-1798): Austrian Jesuit; founder of modern numismatics.

Eichendorff, Joseph von (1788-1857): German lyric poet, novelist, critic.

Elgar, Edward (1857-1934): English composer. *Pomp and Circumstance.*

Emmerich, Anne Catherine (1774-1824): German Augustinian nun, mystic; her visions were recorded by the poet Klemens Brentano.

Endlicher, Stephen (1804-1849): Hungarian botanist, linguist; elaborated a system of classifying plants.

England, John (1786-1842): American prelate, b. Ireland, bishop of Charleston, S. C., 1820-42; founded *United States Catholic Miscellany,* the first US Catholic weekly newspaper; opponent of trusteeism.

Epee, Charles Michel de L' (1712-1789):

French priest; developed a sign alphabet for deaf-mutes.

Erasmus, Desiderius (1466-1536): Dutch scholar, Renaissance leader.

Escriva de Belaguer, Jose Maria (1902-1975): Spanish priest, author; founder of Opus Dei, 1928. (See Index.)

Estaing, Jean Baptiste d' (1729-1794): French naval commander; aided Americans during Revolution.

Eustachius, Bartolommeo (1524-1574): Italian anatomist; Eustachian tube, valve, named for him.

Ewing, J. Franklin (1905-1968): American Jesuit priest, anthropologist, missiologist, author.

Ewing, Thomas (1789-1871): American lawyer; US senator from Ohio, 1831-37, 1850-51; secretary of the treasury, 1841; secretary of the interior, 1849-50; convert, 1871.

Eyck, Hubert Van (1366-1426) and his brother **Jan** (1370-1440): Painters, founders of Flemish school; developed process of oil painting; religious and portrait subjects.

F

Faber, Frederick William (1814-1863): British author of spiritual works, hymns; convert, 1845; priest.

Fabre, Jean Henri (1823-1915): French entomologist and author.

Fabricius, Hieronymus (Fabricius ab Aquapendente) (1537-1619): Italian anatomist, surgeon; described valvular system of the veins; teacher of Harvey.

Fallopio, Gabriello (1523-1562): Italian anatomist; discovered Fallopian tubes.

Farley, James A. (1892-1976): American political leader; U.S. postmaster general, 1933-1940; elder statesman of Democratic party.

Farley, John (1842-1918): American cardinal, b. Ireland; came to US 1864; ordained priest, 1870; vicar general, 1891, auxiliary, 1895, and archbishop, 1902-18, of New York; cardinal, 1911.

Faye, Herve Auguste Etienne Albans (1814-1902): French astronomer; discovered comet named for him; invented zenithal collimator.

Fenelon, Francois de Salignac de la Mothe (1651-1715): French prelate, theologian.

Ferrari, Ludovico (1522-1565): Italian mathematician; discovered method of resolving equations of the fourth degree.

Fink, Francis A. (1907-1971): American editor, publisher; associated with *Our Sunday Visitor* from 1930 until his death; president of the Catholic Press Association, 1950-52; recipient of 1971 St. Francis de Sales Award of the Catholic Press Association.

Fischer, Max (1893-1954): European and American journalist, b. Germany; teacher, author; convert, while a student.

Fitzgibbon, Catherine (Sister Irene) (1823-1896): American religious, b. England; joined Sisters of Charity, 1850; founder of Foundling Hospital in New York City, 1869.

FitzSimons, Thomas (1741-1811): American merchant and congressman, b. Ireland; signer of the Constitution; member of first Congress of US.

Fizeau, Armand Hippolyte Louis (1819-1896): French physicist; experimentally determined velocity of light.

Flanagan, Edward Joseph (1886-1948): American priest, b. Ireland; founder of Boys' Town, Nebraska, 1917.

Floyd, John P. (1807-1863): American politician, cabinet official, military leader; governor of Virginia, 1850-53; secretary of war, 1857-61; brigadier general of Confederate Army, 1861; convert, about 1852.

Foch, Ferdinand (1851-1929): French soldier; supreme commander of Allied forces, 1918; led 1918 offensive to victory.

Ford, Francis X. (1892-1952): American Maryknoll missioner; sent to China, 1918; bishop of Kaying, 1935; imprisoned by communists in 1950; he died as a result of his treatment.

Fortunatus of Brescia (1701-1754): Italian Franciscan, pioneer morphologist.

Fortunatus, Venantius Honorius Clementianus (530-610): Latin poet; bishop of Poitiers; wrote the hymn *Vexilla Regis*.

Foster, John G. (1823-1874): American army officer; served with Union army in Civil War; convert, 1861.

Foucauld, Charles Eugene de (1858-1916): French hermit; army officer and explorer in Africa before joining Trappists, 1890; set up hermitage in Sahara among Moslem tribes; killed by desert tribesmen revolting against French; produced studies of Tuareg language and literature.

Foucault, Jean Bernard Leon (1819-1868): French physicist; experimented on light and heat; invented gyroscope, 1852; discovered Foucault electric current.

Fowler, Gene (1891-1960): American journalist, playwright, author.

Francis of Vitoria (1480-1546): Spanish Dominican, theologian; a founder of international law.

Franck, Cesar Auguste (1822-1890): Belgian-French composer; pioneer of modern French instrumental school.

Frassen, Claudius (1620-1711): French Franciscan theologian; author of *Scotus Academicus*, a presentation of the theology of Duns Scotus.

Fraunhofer, Joseph von (1787-1826): Bavarian physicist, optician; discovered Fraunhofer lines; initiated spectrum analysis, the basis of spectrography.

Frechette, Louis Honore (1839-1908): Canadian journalist, poet, prose writer.

Freppel, Charles Emile (1827-1891): French prelate, pulpit orator; bishop of Angers; leader of clerical party; founder of Catholic University of the West (Angers), 1875.

Fresnel, Augustin Jean (1788-1827): French physicist; contributor to science of optics, wave theory of light; introduced compound lenses for lighthouse use.

Froissart, Jean (1337-1410): French historian.

Frontenac, Louis de Buade, Count (1620-1698): French soldier, colonial governor of New France; encouraged explorations of Joliet, La Salle, others.

G

Gagarin, Ivan Sergeevich (1814-1882): Russian diplomat, writer; convert, 1843; joined Jesuits.

Galilei, Galileo (1564-1642): Italian astronomer, physicist; discovered moon shines with reflected light, observed milky way, four satellites of Jupiter, phases of Venus, sunspots; discovered laws of projectiles, principles of virtual velocities, gave exposition of principles of flotation. Summoned before Inquisition on two occasions for his defense of the Copernican system, an action which at the time was considered irreconcilable with implications of Christian faith.

Galvani, Luigi (1737-1798): Italian physician, physicist; experimented to determine electrical forces involved in muscular movements; founder of galvanism.

Galvin, Edward J. (1882-1956): Irish bishop, missionary in China; co-founder with Father John Blowick of the Columban Fathers, 1916; held under house arrest for three years following Communist takeover of China in 1949; expelled, 1952.

Gama, Vasco da (1469?-1524): Portuguese explorer; discovered new sea route to India.

Garcia, Moreno Gabriel (1821-1875): Ecuadorian journalist, patriot, president of Ecuador; assassinated.

Garrigou-Lagrange, Reginald (1877-1964): French Dominican theologian, philosopher, author of works in all fields of theology; teacher at the University of St. Thomas (Angelicum), Rome, 1909-58; consultor to congregations of the Roman Curia.

Gasquet, Francis Aidan (1846-1929): English Benedictine, cardinal; head of commission for revision of the Vulgate; historian.

Gassendi, Pierre (1592-1655): French philosopher, called Bacon of France; advocate of empirical method.

Gaston, William (1778-1844): American jurist; first student at Georgetown University; North Carolina congressman, judge, member of North Carolina supreme court; responsible for repeal of law which disenfranchised Catholics in his native state, 1835.

Gay-Lussac, Joseph Louis (1778-1850): French chemist, physicist; conducted important research on gases; improved methods of organic analysis.

Geoffrey of Monmouth (1100-1154): English bishop, chronicler; influential in development of national romance in English literature.

Ghiberti, Lorenzo di Cione di Ser Buonaccorso (1378-1455): Florentine painter, sculptor, goldsmith.

Ghirlandajo, Domenico (Domenico de Tommaso Bigordi) (1449-1498): Florentine painter, mosaic and fresco artist; teacher of Michelangelo.

Gibbons, Floyd (1887-1939): American journalist, war correspondent.

Gibbons, James (1834-1921): American cardinal; ordained priest, 1861; vicar apostolic of North Carolina, 1868-72; bishop of Richmond, 1872-77; archbishop of Baltimore 1877-1921; cardinal, 1886; patriot, controversialist; writer; Apostolic Delegate to Third Plenary Council of Baltimore; championed rights of labor.

Gibson, Hugh S. (1883-1954): American diplomat; minister to Poland, ambassador to Belgium, 1927-33, 1937-38, and Brazil; director, Intergovernmental Committee for European Migration; convert, 1938.

Gigli, Beniamino (1890-1957): Italian operatic tenor.

Gill, Eric (1882-1940): English sculptor, engraver, author; convert, 1913.

Gillis, James Martin (1876-1957): American Paulist priest, author, editor, radio orator; editor of the *Catholic World* for 26 years.

Gilmore, Patrick (1829-1892): American bandmaster and composer, b. Ireland.

Giocondo de Verona (1433-1515): Italian Franciscan architect, engineer, antiquarian; architect of St. Peter's.

Gioja, Flavio (14th c.): Italian mariner; contributed to improvement of compass.

Giorgione, Giorgio (1478-1511): Painter of Venetian school.

Giotto di Bondone (1276-1337): Florentine painter, architect, sculptor, fresco artist.

Glennon, John (1862-1946): American cardinal, b. Ireland; ordained priest, 1884; coadjutor bishop of Kansas City, Mo., 1896-1903; archbishop of St. Louis, 1903-46; cardinal, 1946; one of founders of the National Catholic War Council.

Gluck, Christoph Willibald (1714-1787): German operatic composer.

Gobban Saer (560-645): Irish ecclesiastical architect.

Godfrey of Bouillon (1061-1100): French crusader, duke of Lower Lorraine; elected ruler of Jerusalem after its capture in 1099; defender of the Holy Sepulchre.

Goldstein, David (1870-1958): American apologist, b. England; convert, 1905; pioneer of street preaching and Catholic Evidence Guild work; organized the Catholic Truth Guild of Boston, 1917; author.

Goodyear, William Henry (1846-1923): American author, museum curator in New York and Brooklyn, historian; convert, 1880.

Gordon, Andrew (1712-1751): Scottish Benedictine monk; first to use a cylinder of glass to produce frictional electricity; invented electrical chimes.

Gorres, Joseph von (1776-1848): German journalist, literateur.

Gounod, Charles Francois (1818-1893): French composer of operatic and Church music.

Gower, John (1325-1408): English poet.

Goya y Lucientes, Francisco Jose de (1746-1828): Spanish painter, etcher, lithographer; greatest painter of Spanish national customs.

Greco, El (Kyriakos Theotokopoulos) (1548-1614 or 1625): Greek-born painter of Castillian school.

Gregory of Valencia (1550-1603): Spanish Jesuit, moral theologian; works on usury and lawful rates of interest.

Grijalva, Juan de (1489-1527): Spanish explorer; completed exploration of Yucatan, discovering Mexico.

Grimaldi, Francesco Maria (1618-1663): Italian Jesuit, physicist; discovered diffraction of light.

Guardini, Romano (1885-1968): German priest (b. Italy), theologian, philosopher, author; *The Lord.*

Guido d'Arezzo (995-1050): Benedictine monk, musical theorist; reformer of musical notation.

Guilday, Peter (1884-1947): American priest; leading authority on Church history in US, founder of *Catholic Historical Review.*

Guiney, Louise Imogen (1861-1920): American poet and essayist.

Gurian, Waldemar (1902-1954): American educator and author, b. Russia; convert from Judaism.

Gutenberg, Johann (1400-1468): German printer, inventor of printing from movable type; first to print the Bible, 1452.

H

Haldeman, Samuel Stehman (Felix Aqo, pseud.) (1812-1880): American educator, author; convert, 1843; founder of National Academy of Sciences.

Hannegan, Robert E. (1903-1949): American cabinet official, politician; US postmaster general, 1945-47.

Hardee, William J. (1817-1873): American Confederate general; graduate West Point, 1838; author of *Rifle and Light Infantry Tactics,* used as army textbook at that time.

Harland, Henry (1861-1905): American novelist; used pseudonym **Sidney Luska** in earlier works; convert, 1897.

Harris, Joel Chandler (1848-1908): American journalist, author; creator of Uncle Remus; convert two weeks before his death.

Hassard, John Rose Greene (1836-1888): American journalist, author; convert, 1851; first editor of the *Catholic World.*

Hauy, Rene Just (1743-1822): French priest, mineralogist; a founder of the science of crystallography.

Hawks, Edward F. (1878-1955): American priest, author, b. South Wales; Anglican clergyman before conversion, 1908; ordained priest, 1911.

Haydn, Franz Joseph (1732-1809): Austrian composer; earliest master of symphony and quartet; composer of Austrian national anthem.

Hayes, Carlton J. H. (1882-1964): American historian, educator, diplomat, author; *Political and Social History of Modern Europe;* convert, 1904.

Hayes, Patrick J. (1867-1938): American cardinal; ordained priest, 1892; auxiliary of New York, 1914; ordinary of the armed forces, 1917; archbishop of New York, 1919-38; cardinal, 1924; one of founders of National Catholic Welfare Council.

Healy, George (1813-1894): American portrait painter.

Hebert, Louis Philippe (1850-1917): Canadian sculptor; member of Royal Canadian Academy, 1883.

Hecker, Isaac Thomas (1819-1888): American priest, founder of the Congregation of St. Paul (Paulists); convert, 1844; joined Redemptorists and ordained priest, 1849; founded Paulists 1858 with several companions; first superior, 1858-88; founder of the *Catholic World.*

Heis, Eduard (1806-1877): German astronomer; first ascertained the point of departure of meteors; drew chart of 5,421 stars, with first authentic map of milky way.

Helmont, Jan Baptista van (1577-1644): Flemish physician, chemist; introduced chemical methods in biological studies; introduced word "gas" to designate aeriform fluids.

Hengler, Lawrence (1806-1858): German priest; inventor of horizontal pendulum used in seismographs.

Hennepin, Louis (1640-1701): Belgian Franciscan, explorer; first European to see, describe and depict Niagara Falls; explored Great Lakes region, upper Mississippi.

Henry the Navigator (1394-1460): Portuguese prince; discovered Azores, Madeira, Cape Verde Islands; traced African coast as far as Sierra Leone.

Herdtrich, Christian Wolfgang (1625-1684): Austrian Jesuit missionary; probably wrote first Chinese-Latin dictionary; made Confucius known to Europeans.

Herrera, Francisco de, the Elder (1576-1656): Spanish painter; a founder of the National School of Spain.

Heude, Pierre (1836-1902): French Jesuit missionary, zoologist; authority on land mollusks of China.

Hewit, Augustine Francis (1820-1897): American priest; Congregationalist, Episcopalian minister before conversion, 1846; ordained priest, 1847; assisted Isaac Hecker in founding Paulists.

Heywood, John (1497-1580): English poet, dramatist.

Hill, John Austin (Speakman) (1779-1828): American Dominican, b. England; after conversion joined Dominicans and was ordained priest at Rome; missionary in Ohio.

Holbein, Hans, the Younger (1497-1543): German portrait and historical painter; woodcut artist.

Holland, John Philip (1840-1914): American inventor, b. Ireland; settled at Paterson, N.J.; inventor of first practical submarine.

Hopkins, Gerard Manley (1844-1889): English Jesuit, poet; convert, 1866.

Horner, William Edmonds (1793-1853): American surgeon, anatomist, author; convert, 1839; discovered tensor tarsi, now called Horner's muscle, 1824.

Hubbard, Bernard R. (1889-1962): American Jesuit explorer; called The Glacier Priest; convert, joined Jesuits, 1908; Alaskan explorer; head of Santa Clara Univ. department of geology.

Hugh of St. Victor (1096-1141): Theologian, philosopher, mystic; a founder of scholasticism.

Hughes, John J. (1797-1864): American prelate, b. Ireland; arrived US, 1817; ordained priest, 1826; coadjutor (1837), bishop (1842) and first archbishop (1850-64) of New York; vigorous defender of Catholicism against Know-Nothings and Native Americans; abolished trusteeism; established Catholic school system in his archdiocese; laid cornerstone of St. Patrick's Cathedral (1858).

Hunton, George K. (1888-1967): American lawyer, editor; pioneer in Catholic field for interracial justice.

Hunyady, Janos (1387-1456): Hungarian defender of Christendom against the Turks; assisted at crucial defense of Belgrade, 1456.

Huysmans, Joris Karl (1848-1907): French novelist; convert 1895; Benedictine Oblate.

I

Ingres, Jean (1780-1867): Leading French classical painter; historical subjects.

Innocent III (1161-1216): Pope, 1198-1216; encouraged fourth crusade, promoted efforts against the Albigensians; convoked and presided at the Fourth Lateran Council, 1215; strenuously asserted supremacy of the Church over the state.

Ireland, John (1838-1918): American prelate, b. Ireland; arrived US, 1849; ordained priest, 1861; chaplain in Union army, 1862-63; bishop (1884) and first archbishop (1888-1918) of St. Paul; helped found Catholic University of America (1889); outspoken opponent of national churches.

Ives, Levi Silliman (1797-1867): American Episcopal bishop; convert, 1852; founder of New York Catholic Protectory.

J

Jacopone da Todi (1230-1306): Italian Franciscan poet; *Stabat Mater*.

Jaricot, Pauline (1799-1862): French charitable worker; founded Society for the Propagation of the Faith, 1822, to raise funds for foreign missions.

Jimenez, Juan Ramon (1881-1958): Spanish lyric poet; awarded Nobel Prize for literature, 1956.

John of Austria, Don (1547-1578): Spanish general; commander of fleet that defeated Turks at Lepanto, 1571.

Joliet, Louis (1645-1700): French Canadian explorer of Mississippi with Marquette, 1673.

Jones, Inigo (1573-1652): English architect; designer of stage sets for Ben Jonson and others; introduced Palladian type of architecture in England.

Jorgensen, Johannes (1866-1956): Danish writer; convert, 1896; author of *St. Francis of Assisi*.

Judge, Thomas A. (1868-1933): American priest; founder of Missionary Servants of the Most Blessed Trinity (sisters), 1927, and the Missionary Servants of the Most Holy Trinity (priests and brothers).

Jugan, Jeanne (1792-1879): French foundress; established Little Sisters of the Poor, 1839, to care for aged poor.

Jussieu, Bernard de (1699-1777): French botanist; introduced a natural system for classification of plants.

Justinian I (483-565): Eastern Roman emperor; issued *Corpus Juris Civilis*, code of Roman law.

K

Katona, Stephen (1732-1811): Hungarian Jesuit, historian; author of 40-volume history of Hungary.

Kaye-Smith, Sheila (1887-1956): English author; convert 1929.

Kelly, William (1811-1888): American ironmaster; invented converter for the making of steel; now known as Bessemer's process after Englishman who patented a similar process.

Kenna, John E. (1848-1893): American legislator; private in Confederate Army; US congressman, 1876-80; US senator, 1883-93. Represents West Virginia in Statuary Hall.

Kennedy, John F. (1917-1963): Thirty-fifth president of the United States and first Catholic to hold that office; elected to Congress, 1946, 1948, 1950; to the Senate, 1952, 1958; to the presidency of the US, 1960; assassinated Nov. 22, 1963, at Dallas, Tex.; author; *Why England Slept, Profiles in Courage*.

Kennedy, Joseph P. (1888-1969): American businessman, diplomat; father of John and Robert Kennedy.

Kennedy, Robert F. (1925-1968): American politician, brother of President John F. Kennedy; cabinet official; attorney with justice department, 1951-52; US attorney general, 1961-65; US senator from New York, 1965-68; assassinated while campaigning for Democratic presidential nomination.

Keyes, Edward Lawrence (1843-1924): American physician; convert.

Keyes, Frances Parkinson (1885-1970): American author of popular novels and other works; wrote more than 50 books; convert, 1939.

Kilmer, Alfred Joyce (1886-1918): American poet; convert, 1913, with his wife; killed in action in World War I; works include *Trees and Other Poems*. His wife **Aline Murray Kilmer** (1888-1941): Lecturer, poet; wrote several books of collected verse.

Kir, Felix-Adrien (1876-1968): French priest, politician; mayor of Dijon from 1940.

Kircher, Athanasius (1601-1680): German Jesuit, archaeologist; inventor of magic lantern; stated germ theory of disease.

Knox, Ronald A. (1888-1957): English priest, author; convert, ordained, 1919; translated Vulgate Bible into English.

Kodaly, Zoltan (1882-1967): Hungarian composer; authority on folk music.

Konarski, Stanislaus (1700-1773): Polish priest, educator, author; influential in development of modern Polish literature.

Kosciusko, Tadeusz (1746-1817): Polish patriot; served in Continental Army in American Revolution; headed Polish rebellion, 1794, became dictator; died in Switzerland.

Kreisler, Fritz (1873-1962): American violinist and composer, b. Austria; became US citizen, 1943; convert, 1947.

L

La Bruyere, Jean de (1645-1696): French critic and moralist.

Lacordaire, Jean Baptiste Henri (1802-1861): French Dominican, pulpit orator; member of French Academy.

Laennec, Rene Theophile Hyacinthe (1781-1826): French physician; introduced auscultation, invented stethoscope.

La Farge, John (1835-1910): American artist and author.

La Farge, John (1880-1963): American Jesuit priest, son of artist John La Farge; scholar, author, editor of *America*, 1944-1948; leader in interracial work, a founder and director of the Catholic Interracial Council of New York City, and of the National Catholic Rural Life Conference; author of *The Manner Is Ordinary, The Catholic Viewpoint on Race Relations, An American Amen*.

La Fontaine, Jean de (1621-1695): French poet, known as a fabulist.

Lainez, Diego (1512-1565): Spanish theologian; second general of the Society of Jesus; made important contribution to work of Council of Trent.

Lamarck, Jean Baptiste de Monet, Chevalier de (1744-1829): French botanist, zoologist; originator of evolutionary theory called Lamarckism; divided animals into vertebrates and invertebrates.

Langton, Stephen (d. 1228): English prelate, cardinal archbishop of Canterbury; led English barons against King John; first of the subscribing witnesses to the Magna Charta.

Laplace, Pierre Simon (1749-1827): French astronomer, mathematician; proposed the nebular hypothesis.

LaSalle, Rene Robert Cavelier, Sieur de (1643-1687): French explorer; discovered Ohio River, explored Mississippi River valley.

Lasso, Orlando di (1532-1594): Belgian composer of over 2,000 works.

Lathrop, Rose Hawthorne (Mother Alphonsa) (1851-1926): American foundress, author; daughter of Nathaniel Hawthorne; convert, 1891, with her husband, **George Parsons Lathrop** (1851-1898); founded Dominican Congregation of St. Rose of Lima (Servants of Relief for Incurable Cancer) after her husband's death; established home at Hawthorne, N.Y.

Latreille, Pierre Andre (1762-1833): French entomologist; classified insects and crustaceans.

Laurier, Sir Wilfrid (1841-1919): Canadian statesman; prime minister, 1896-1911.

Lavigerie, Charles Martial Allemand (1825-1892): French prelate; archbishop of Algiers, 1867; cardinal, 1882; leader in abolition of slavery; founded White Fathers, 1874, for mission work in Africa.

Lavoisier, Antoine Laurent (1743-1794): French chemist; called father of modern chemistry.

Le Fort, Gertrud von (1876-1971): German poet and novelist; convert, 1925; works include *The Veil of Veronica* and *The Song on the Scaffold*, which was the source for the opera *Dialogue of the Carmelites*.

Lehar, Ferenc or **Franz** (1870-1948): Hungarian composer of operettas, orchestral works.

Lemaitre, Jules (1853-1914): French writer, literary and dramatic critic.

Lemcke, Henry (1796-1882): American Benedictine, b. Germany; Lutheran preacher; convert, 1824; ordained priest, 1826; came to US as missionary, 1834; instrumental in bringing first Benedictines to the US; joined Benedictines, 1852.

L'Enfant, Pierre Charles (1754-1825): French engineer; drew up plans for national capital, Washington, D.C.

Leo XIII (1810-1903): Pope, 1878-1903; scholar, statesman, Latinist; author of many encyclicals (see Index).

Leverrier, Urbain Jean Joseph (1811-1877): French astronomer; calculated presence of Neptune; founded the International Meteorological Institute.

Linacre, Thomas (1460-1524): English physician, humanist; assisted in founding of College of Physicians.

Lingard, John (1771-1851): English priest, author of historical works on England.

Linton, Moses L. (1808-1878): American physician; convert, 1844; president of first US

Conference of St. Vincent de Paul Society, 1845; organized first medical monthly in US, *The St. Louis Medical and Surgical Journal*, 1848.

Lippi, Fra Filippo (1406-1469): Florentine painter; religious subjects.

Liszt, Franz von (1811-1886): Hungarian piano virtuoso, composer.

Locke, Jesse A. (1859-1952): American educator; Protestant Episcopal minister; convert, 1893.

Lombard, Peter (1100-1160): Italian theologian; bishop of Paris; author of *Sententiarum Libri Quatuor*, a synthesis of theology which exerted wide influence.

Longstreet, James (1821-1904): American army officer; graduate of West Point; resigned commission to serve with Confederate forces; convert, 1877.

Lord, Daniel (1888-1955): American Jesuit; popular writer; associated with editorial staff of *Queen's Work* from 1913 until his death; wrote hundreds of pamphlets; his books include *Played by Ear*, his autobiography.

Lorraine, Claude de (1600-1682): French painter; landscape subjects.

Louis the Great (1326-1382): King of Hungary, 1342-1382, and Poland, 1370-1382.

Loviner, John Forest (1896-1970): American Franciscan priest; founder and director of St. Anthony's Guild; publisher of catechetical materials for the Confraternity of Christian Doctrine; key figure in production of the *New American Bible*.

Lugo, John de (1583-1660): Spanish Jesuit, cardinal, theologian.

M

Mabillon, Jean (1632-1707): French Benedictine, father of science of paleography; author of *Acta Sanctorum Ordinis S. Benedicti*.

McCarran, Patrick A. (1876-1954): American jurist, legislator; chief justice Nevada supreme court, 1917-18; US senator, 1932-54; sponsored Internal Security (McCarran) Act, 1950; co-sponsor of McCarran-Walter Immigration and Nationality Act, 1952. Represents Nevada in Statuary Hall.

McCarthy, Joseph R. (1908-1957): American politician; senator from Wisconsin, 1946 until his death; controversial investigator of Communism in US.

McClellan, William Hildrup (1874-1951): American educator, author; Episcopalian minister; convert, 1908; ordained Jesuit priest, 1918.

McCloskey, John (1810-1885): First American cardinal; ordained priest, 1834; coadjutor bishop of New York 1844-47; first bishop of Albany, 1847-64; archbishop of New York, 1864-85, cardinal, 1875.

McCormack, John (1884-1945): Irish-American tenor; b. Ireland, became American citizen 1919.

McCormick, Anne O'Hare (1882-1954): American journalist, b. England of American parents; awarded Pulitzer prize (1937) for European correspondence.

McGivney, Michael Joseph (1852-1890): American priest; founder of Knights of Columbus, 1882.

McGranery, James P. (1895-1963): American congressman, cabinet official; US attorney general, 1952-53.

McGrath, J. Howard (1903-1966): American politician, cabinet official; governor of Rhode Island, 1940-46; US senator, 1946; US attorney general, 1949-52.

McKay, Claude (1890-1948): American Black poet and novelist, b. Jamaica, B.W.I.; came to US, 1912; author of *A Long Way from Home* (1937), his autobiography; convert, 1944.

McKenna, Joseph (1843-1926): American jurist, cabinet official; US congressman from California, 1885-92; US circuit judge, 1892-97; US attorney general 1897-98; associate justice US Supreme Court, 1898-1925.

McLoughlin, John (1784-1857): Pioneer settler of Oregon, b. Canada; fur trader, physician; encouraged settlement of Oregon Territory; became American citizen; called Father of Oregon. Represents Oregon in National Statuary Hall.

MacMahon, Marie Edme Patrice Maurice de (1808-1893): Marshal of France, 1859, and president, 1873-1897; military leader.

McQuaid, Bernard J. (1823-1909): American prelate; ordained priest, 1848; helped found Seton Hall College; chaplain in Civil War; first bishop of Rochester, N.Y., 1868-1909; promoter of Catholic schools.

Madeleva, Sister M. (Mary Evaline Wolf) (1887-1964): American educator, poet; joined Holy Cross Sisters, 1908.

Magellan, Ferdinand (1480-1521): Portuguese navigator; led expedition which first circumnavigated globe; discovered Strait of Magellan, Ladrones, Philippines, where he was slain.

Magsaysay, Ramon (1907-1957): Philippine statesman; crushed the Communist (Huk) Rebellion in 1948-53; third president of the Philippine Republic.

Mahler, Gustav (1880-1911): Bohemian composer and conductor; convert, 1897.

Malherbe, Francois de (1555-1628): French poet; influenced exact usage of language.

Mallinckrodt, Hermann von (1821-1874); German leader of Center Party against Kulturkampf.

Mallory, Stephen Russell (1813-1873): American Confederate political leader, b. Trinidad; US senator from Florida, 1851-1861; resigned when Florida seceded; naval secretary of the Confederacy.

Malory, Sir Thomas (d. 1470): English author of the *Morte d'Arthur*.

Malpighi, Marcello (1628-1694): Italian anatomist; called father of microscopic anatomy.

Malus, Etienne Louis (1775-1812): French engineer, physicist; discovered polarization of light, invented polariscope.

Mangan, James C. (1803-1849): Irish poet.

Manning, Henry Edward (1808-1892): English cardinal, author; convert, 1851.

Mansard, Nicolas Francois (1598-1666): French architect.

Mantegna, Andrea (1431-1506): Italian painter, muralist, engraver; leader of Paduan school.

Manutius, Aldus (1450-1515): Italian scholar, printer, publisher; founded Aldine press.

Manzoni, Alessandro (1785-1873); Italian poet, novelist; *I Promessi Sposi*.

Marconi, Guglielmo (1874-1937): Italian engineer, inventor; outstanding contributor to development of wireless telegraphy, radio; Nobel Prize for physics, 1909.

Mariotte, Edme (1620-1684): French physicist; researcher in hydrodynamics.

Maritain, Jacques (1882-1973): French philosopher, intellectual, author; foremost exponent of Christian humanism; convert, 1906, with his wife, **Raissa** (1883-1960); both played important part in French Catholic revival.

Martini, Giambattista (1706-1784): Italian Franciscan, composer of Church music, theorist and teacher.

Masaccio, Tommaso (1401-1428): Italian painter, fresco artist of Florentine school; influenced advance to Renaissance painting; called father of modern art.

Massillon, Jean Baptiste (1663-1742): French preacher; bishop of Clermont.

Matthias Corvinus (Hunyady) (1440-1490): One of Hungary's greatest kings, 1458-1490; repelled Turks, fought against Bohemians, Frederick III; patron of arts, literature; introduced Golden Age in Hungary; founded library.

Mauriac, Francois (1885-1970): French writer; awarded Nobel Prize for literature, 1952; works include the novels *The Desert of Love, The Viper's Triangle*.

Mauro, Fra (d. c. 1459): Italian Camaldolese monk, cosmographer; Fra Mauro Highlands, named for him by 17th century astronomers, was the landing site of Apollo 14.

Maxmilian I, the Great (1573-1651): Duke and elector of Bavaria; opposed Protestant cause; founded Catholic League, 1609.

Mazarin, Jules (1602-1661): French cardinal, statesman; prime minister of France under Louis XIII and Louis XIV; concluded Thirty Years' War by Treaty of Westphalia; strengthened France as European power.

Meagher, Thomas F. (1823-1867): American politician and soldier, b. Ireland; came to US, 1852; joined Union forces in Civil War; became brigadier general of Irish Brigade organized by him; territorial secretary of Montana, 1865.

Mendel, Gregor Johann (1822-1884): Austrian Augustinian monk, botanist; formulated Mendelian laws of heredity.

Mercier, Desire Joseph (1851-1926): Belgian prelate, philosopher; cardinal archbishop of Malines; promoter of neo-scholastic philosophy; leader against demands of German invaders in 1914; restored Louvain University after World War I; in 1924 began Malines Conversations, an attempt to unify the Anglican and Roman churches.

Mersenne, Marin (1588-1648): French mathematician.

Merton, Thomas (Father M. Louis) (1915-1968): American Trappist priest and author, b. France; convert, 1939; works include *The Seven Storey Mountain* (his autobiography), *Waters of Siloe, Conjectures of a Guilty Bystander;* articles in opposition to nuclear war.

Mestrovic, Ivan (1883-1962): Yugoslav sculptor; religious and mythological subjects, Slav folklore, portrait busts; works include *Pieta* at Notre Dame Univ., where he was a professor from 1955-62.

Metternich, Klemens Wenzel Nepomuk Lothar von (1773-1859): Austrian statesman and diplomat.

Meynell, Alice Thompson (1847-1922): English poet, essayist, leader in Catholic literary revival in England; convert. Her husband, **Wilfrid Meynell** (1852-1948): Journalist, publisher, biographer; he and his wife discovered Francis Thompson; convert.

Mezzofanti, Giuseppe (1774-1849): Italian cardinal, linguist, custodian-in-chief of Vatican Library.

Michelangelo Buonarroti (1475-1564): Italian architect, sculptor, painter, poet; outstanding figure of the Renaissance.

Mikolajczyk, Stanislaus (1901-1967): Polish politician; leader of Polish Peasant party in exile; settled in US, 1947.

Miller, Nathan L. (1868-1953): American politician; governor of New York; convert shortly before death.

Millet, Jean Francois (1814-1875): French painter; landscape and religious subjects.

Mindszenty, Jozsef (1892-1975): Hungarian cardinal; primate of Hungary, 1946-74; his anti-communism led to his arrest in 1948 and sentencing to life imprisonment after a mock trial; freed for several days in 1956 during short-lived revolt by Hungarian freedom fighters; granted refuge in U.S. Embassy in Budapest from 1956 to 1971 when he left Hungary under orders from the Vatican; died at Vienna; symbol of resistance to Communism.

Minton, Sherman (1890-1965): American jurist; US senator, 1935-40; associate justice US Supreme Court, 1949-56; convert, 1961.

Mistral, Gabriela (pen name of **Lucila Godoy de Alcayaga**) (1889-1957): Chilean poet; Nobel Prize for literature, 1945.

Mitchell, James P. (1902-1964): American cabinet official; labor relations expert; US secretary of labor, 1953-61.

Mitchell, John (1870-1919): American labor leader; president of United Mine Workers; convert, 1907.

Mohler, Johann Adam (1796-1838): German theologian.

Mohr, Josef (1792-1848): Austrian priest, poet; *Silent Night*.

Molina, Luis de (1535-1600): Spanish Jesuit, theologian; author of *Concordia*, expounding a system for the reconciliation of grace and free will, called Molinism.

Mondino (dim. for Raimondo) dei Luicci (1275-c. 1327): Italian anatomist.

Monge, Gaspard (1746-1818): French mathematician; called founder of descriptive geometry.

Montcalm, Marquis Louis Joseph de (1712-1759): French marshal, military commander in Canada; fatally wounded in Battle of Quebec.

Montessori, Maria (1870-1952): Italian physician, educator; originator of Montessori method for education of children.

Monteux, Pierre (1875-1964): American conductor, b. France; US citizen, 1942; led most of the world's greatest orchestras.

Moon, Parker Thomas (1892-1936): American historian, educator, author, editor; convert, 1914.

Moore, Thomas (1779-1852): National lyricist of Ireland.

Moore, Thomas Verner (1877-1969): American priest, psychiatrist, educator, author; joined Carthusians in 1947 — had earlier been a Paulist and Benedictine.

Morgagni, Giovanni Battista (1682-1771): Italian physician; founder of anatomical pathology.

Morley, Sylvanus Griswold (1883-1948): American archeologist; convert.

Moylan, Stephen (1734-1811): American patriot, b. Ireland; immigrated to US 1768; joined Continental Army, 1775; aide-de-camp and secretary to General Washington, 1776; leader of cavalry division.

Mozart, J. C. Wolfgang Amadeus (1756-1791): Austrian composer of more than 600 works in a wide range of forms.

Muench, Aloysius J. (1889-1962): American cardinal; ordained priest, 1913; bishop of Fargo, 1935-59; apostolic visitator and liaison representative between US military government and German hierarchy, 1946; nuncio to Germany, 1951-59; cardinal, 1959.

Muller, Johann (1436-1476): German mathematician, astronomer; assisted in calendar reform.

Muller, Johannes Peter (1801-1858): German physiologist, comparative anatomist.

Murillo, Bartolome Esteban (1617-1682): Spanish artist of the Andalusian school; master of color contrast; religious subjects.

Murphy, Frank (1890-1949): American jurist, cabinet official; mayor of Detroit, 1930-33; US high commissioner to the Philippines, 1935-36; governor of Michigan, 1936-38; US attorney general 1939-40; associate justice of US Supreme Court, 1940-49.

Murphy, John Benjamin (1857-1916): American surgeon; inventor of Murphy button; Laetare Medalist, 1902.

Murray, John C. (1904-1967): American Jesuit priest, educator, theologian, ecumenist, international expert on Church-state relations, author.

Murray, Philip (1886-1952): American labor leader, b. Scotland.

N

Nathan, George Jean (1882-1958): American dramatic critic, editor, author; founder with H. L. Mencken of *The American Mercury*; convert, 1957.

Nelaton, Auguste (1807-1873): French surgeon; inventor of Nelaton probe.

Newman, John Henry (1801-1890): English cardinal, theologian; leader of Oxford Movement; convert, 1845; ordained to priesthood, 1847; founded Oratorians in England; master of prose style; author of historical and apologetical works, poems, novels.

Nicholas of Lyra (1270-1340): Franciscan biblical scholar.

Nieuland, Julius Arthur (1878-1936): American priest of Congregation of Holy Cross, b. Belgium; chemist, botanist; Notre Dame scientist, contributed to invention of Lewisite gas; discovered method for producing synthetic rubber.

Niza, Marcos de (d. 1558): Franciscan missionary, explored parts of Arizona and New Mexico, 1539; accompanied Coronado's expedition.

Nobili, Leopoldo (1784-1835): Italian physicist, inventor of the thermopile.

Noll, John F. (1875-1956): American prelate, author, editor; ordained priest, 1898; bishop of Fort Wayne, Ind., 1925-56; founder and editor of weekly newspaper *Our Sunday Visitor*, 1912; wrote *Father Smith Instructs Jackson*, other books and pamphlets.

Nollet, Jean-Antoine (1700-1770): French priest, physicist; researcher in electricity; invented an electroscope.

Noyes, Alfred (1880-1958): English poet; convert, 1927.

O

O'Callahan, Joseph (1906-1964): American Jesuit priest; Navy chaplain in World War II; awarded the Congressional Medal of Honor, for action aboard the carrier Franklin on Mar. 19, 1945.

Ocampo, Sebastian (1466-1521): Spanish explorer; circumnavigated Cuba, proved its insular character.

O'Connell, Daniel (1775-1847): Irish statesman, nationalist leader; known as the Liberator; responsible for Catholic emancipation, 1829.

O'Connor, (Mary) Flannery (1925-1964): American novelist and short-story writer.

O'Dwyer, Joseph (1841-1898): American physician; developed method of aiding breathing to prevent asphyxia in diphtheria.

Oertel, Abraham (1527-1598): Flemish geographer; publisher of an atlas.

O'Hara, Edwin Vincent (1881-1956): American prelate; ordained priest, 1905; bishop of Great Falls, Mont. 1930-39; bishop of Kansas City, Mo., 1939-56; title of archbishop, 1954; leader in catechetical work in the US; founder of National Catholic Rural Life Conference.

O'Higgins, Bernardo (1778-1842): Chilean soldier, statesman; Liberator of Chile.

Olaf (II) Haraldsson, Saint (995-1030): King of Norway, 1016-1028; attempted conversion of his country; killed in battle; patron of Norway; canonized, 1164.

Orellana, Francisco de (1500-1546): Spanish navigator, explored the Amazon River.

Origen (185-254): Theologian and writer, head of catechetical schools at Alexandria, Caesarea; author of biblical, theological works.

Orosius, Paul (380?-?): Spanish priest; author of book of universal history.

Oursler, Fulton (1893-1952): American author, editor, lecturer; convert 1943; works include *The Greatest Story Ever Told* and *The Greatest Book Ever Written*.

Ozanam, Frederic (1813-1853): French historian; a founder of St. Vincent de Paul Society. (See Index.)

Ozanam, Jacques (1640-1717): French mathematician.

P

Pacioli, Luca (1450?-1520?): Italian Franciscan, mathematician; author of first description of double-entry bookkeeping.

Paderewski, Ignace (1860-1941): Polish pianist, conductor, composer; first premier of Poland after World War I.

Palestrina, Giovanni Pierluigi da (1526-1594): Italian composer of Church music in medieval moods; noted for polyphonic style.

Palladio, Andrea (1518-1580): Italian architect; controlling influence of 17th-century architecture called Palladian.

Palmer, Gretta (1905-1953): American journalist, author; convert, 1946.

Papini, Giovanni (1881-1956): Italian writer; convert, 1918; author of *Life of Christ*.

Pare, Ambroise (1517-1590): French surgeon; called father of modern surgery; introduced artery ligature.

Paris, Bruno Paulin Gaston (1839-1903): French philologist, author.

Parsch, Pius (1884-1954): Austrian Augustinian, theologian, Scripture scholar, liturgist.

Parsons, Wilfrid (1887-1958): American Jesuit priest, editor, author, educator; editor-in-chief of *America*, 1925-36.

Pascal, Blaise (1623-1662): French philosopher, scientist; demonstrated that a column of air has weight; author of *Pensees*.

Pasteur, Louis (1822-1895): French chemist; developed a vaccine against hydrophobia; founded Pasteur Institute; father of bacteriology.

Pastor, Ludwig von (1854-1928): German historian; *The History of the Popes from the Beginning of the Middle Ages*.

Patmore, Coventry (1823-1896): English poet; convert, 1864.

Pazmany, Peter (1570-1637): Hungarian Jesuit, cardinal; leader of Counter Reformation; translated Bible into Hungarian; called founder of modern Hungarian literature.

Peguy, Charles Pierre (1873-1914): French poet and writer; outstanding Catholic defender of Dreyfus; founded the journal *Cahiers de la Quinzaine*; works include *The Mystery of the Charity of Joan of Arc* and religious meditations.

Pelouze, Theophile Jules (1807-1867): French chemist; developed production of guncotton, nitrocellulose.

Pepin the Short (714-768): King of the Franks, son of Charles Martel, father of Charlemagne; first Frank crowned with religious ceremonies; defeated Lombards and restored central Italy to the Holy See.

Perosi, Lorenzo (1872-1956): Italian priest, composer.

Perugino, Il (Pietro Vannucci) (1446-1523): Italian painter; leader of Umbrian school; teacher of Raphael; religious subjects.

Petau (Petavius), Denys (1583-1652): French Jesuit, theologian; called father of the history of dogma.

Petrarch (Francesco Petrarca) (1304-1374): Italian poet.

Piazzi Giuseppe (1746-1826): Italian monk, astronomer; discovered Ceres, first known asteroid.

Picard, Jean (1620-1682): French astronomer; accurately measured degree of a meridian.

Pinturicchio, Bernardino di Betto di Biagio (1454-1513): Italian painter of the Umbrian school; historical and religious subjects.

Pio, Padre (Francesco Forgione) (1887-1968): Italian Capuchin priest; reputed stigmatist.

Pire, Dominique Georges (1910-1969): Belgian priest; awarded Nobel Peace Prize in 1958 for work for displaced persons.

Pisano, Andrea (1270-1348) and his son **Nino** (1315-1368); Italian sculptors.

Pisano, Nicolo (1225-1278): Italian sculptor; works among greatest of Romanesque style. His son, **Giovanni** (1240-1320): Sculptor, architect.

Pitra, Jean Baptiste Francois (1812-1889):

French Benedictine, cardinal, scholar.

Pizarro, Francisco (1470-1541): Spanish explorer, conqueror of Peru.

Plumier, Charles (1646-1704): French botanical explorer of Antilles, Central America.

Pole, Reginald (1500-1558): English prelate, cardinal archbishop of Canterbury; opposed divorce of Henry VIII; papal legate, participant in Council of Trent.

Polo, Marco (1245-1324): Early traveler to China, b. Venice; *Book of Marco Polo*.

Ponce de Leon (1460-1521): Spanish explorer; discovered Florida.

Pope, Alexander (1688-1744): English poet; master of the rimed couplet.

Pouget, Jean Francois Albert du, Marquis de Nadaillac (1817-1904): French anthropologist; authority on cave drawings.

Poulenc, Francis (1899-1963): French composer; noted for religious works.

Poussin, Nicolas (1594-1665): French painter; historical and landscape subjects.

Price, Thomas Frederick (1860-1919): American missionary; co-founder with Bishop Walsh of the Catholic Foreign Mission Society of America (Maryknoll Fathers); called the Tar Heel Apostle.

Pro, Miguel (1891-1927): Mexican Jesuit; fled Mexico during 1914 Revolution; returned to Mexico, 1926, after his ordination in Belgium; arrested, 1927, and shot to death by police in Mexico City.

Prohaszka, Ottokar (1858-1927): Hungarian bishop; preacher, author.

Provancher, Leon Abel (1820-1892): Canadian priest, naturalist; called father of natural history in Canada.

Puccini, Giacomo (1858-1924): Italian operatic composer.

Pugin, Augustus Welby Northmore (1812-1852): English architect.

Pulaski, Casimir (1748-1779): Polish patriot, fought in American Revolution; called Father of the American Cavalry; fatally wounded at Savannah.

Puvis de Chavannes, Pierre (1824-1898): French muralist.

Q

Quinlan, Thomas (1896-1970): Irish Columban missionary bishop; served in China, 1920-34; prefect apostolic of Chun Cheon, Korea, 1934; interned by Japanese during World War II; imprisoned by North Koreans, 1950-53.

Quinones, Francis (1482-1540): Spanish Franciscan, cardinal, liturgist; worked on revision of breviary.

R

Racine, Jean Baptiste (1639-1699): French dramatic poet.

Rameau, Jean-Philippe (1683-1764): French organist, music theorist, operatic composer.

Randall, James Ryder (1839-1908): American journalist, poet, song writer; *Maryland, My Maryland*.

Raphael Santi (1483-1520): Italian painter of religious, portrait, other subjects; architect of St. Peter's; among greatest of Renaissance painters.

Reeve, Arthur Benjamin (1882-1936): American educator, author; convert, 1926.

Regnault, Henri Victor (1810-1878): French chemist, physicist; authority in thermometry.

Reiffenstuel, Anaclete (Johann Georg) (1641-1703): German Franciscan, theologian, canonist.

Reinhold, Hans (1897-1968): American pioneer in liturgical movement, b. Germany; came to US, 1936; naturalized citizen.

Reni, Guido (1575-1642): Italian painter of the Eclectic school; religious and other subjects.

Repplier, Agnes (1858-1950): American author, essayist.

Reymont, Wladislaw (1867-1925): Polish novelist; awarded Nobel Prize for literature in 1924 for *The Peasants*.

Ribera, Jose (1588-1652): Spanish painter of Neapolitan school, etcher; religious subjects.

Ricci, Matteo (1552-1610): Italian Jesuit missionary in India and China; introduced Christianity in China; author.

Riccioli, Giovanni Battista (1598-1671): Italian Jesuit, astronomer; introduced some lunar nomenclature in use today.

Richelieu, Armand Jean du Plessis, Duc de (1585-1642): French cardinal, statesman; founder of the French Academy, 1634.

Ritter, Joseph E. (1892-1967): American cardinal; ordained priest, 1917; auxiliary bishop, 1933, bishop, 1934, and first archbishop, 1944, of Indianapolis; archbishop of St. Louis, 1946-67; cardinal, 1961; ordered desegregation of St. Louis archdiocesan schools, 1957; was outspoken US progressive bishop at Vatican II; first Mass in vernacular in US offered in his diocese.

Robbia, Luca della (1400-1482): Florentine sculptor; developed a glaze for terra cotta ware (Robbia work).

Robinson, William Callyhan (1834-1911): American jurist, author; Episcopalian minister; convert, 1863.

Rochambeau, Jean Baptiste Donatien de Vimeur, Conte de (1725-1807): French general; led French forces sent to aid Americans in Revolution.

Rockne, Knute Kenneth (1888-1931): American football player; coach, b. Norway; immigrated to US, 1893; football coach, Notre Dame University, 1918-31; convert, 1925.

Rodzinski, Artur (1894-1958): American symphony conductor, b. Yugoslavia; became US citizen, 1933.

Rosecrans, William Starke (1819-1898): American army officer; graduate of West

Point; army commander during the Civil War; Federal official; convert, 1845.

Rossini, Gioacchino Antonio (1792-1868): Italian operatic composer and innovator in orchestration.

Roualt, Georges (1871-1958): French painter of modern school; convert.

Rubens, Peter Paul (1577-1640): Flemish painter; great colorist, landscape, portrait, historical, religious subjects.

Rubruck, William (1220-1293): French Franciscan missionary and traveler in the East, especially China.

Ruth, George Herman (Babe) (1894-1948): American baseball player and record holder; convert, 1906.

Ruysbroeck, John, Bl. (1293-1381): Flemish mystical theologian; beatified, 1908.

Ryan, Abram J. (1838-1886): American priest, poet; called Poet of the Confederacy.

S

San Gallo, Giuliano Giamberti da (1445-1516); his brother, **Antonio da San Gallo, the Elder** (1455-1534); their nephew, **Antonio da San Gallo, the Younger** (1483-1546): Italian architects.

San Martin, Jose de (1778-1850): South American soldier, statesman; defeated Spanish in Argentina, established independence of Chile, proclaimed independence and called Protector of Peru.

Santorini, Giovanni Domenico (1681-1737): Italian physician, anatomist; discovered emissary veins leading out of sinuses, risory muscles, fissures in external ear.

Sarbiewki, Mathias Casimir (1595-1640): Polish Jesuit, poet; called Horace of Poland.

Sarto, Andrea del (1486-1531): Florentine painter; great colorist, master of light and shade; religious subjects.

Savage, (Charles) Courtenay (1890-1946): American playwright, author; convert, 1937.

Scanderbeg (George Castriota) (c. 1403-1468): Albanian national hero; leader in Albanian independence movement against Turks.

Scarlatti, Alessandro (1659-1725): Italian operatic composer; called founder of modern opera.

Scheiner, Christoph (1579-1650): German Jesuit, astronomer; made independent discovery of sunspots.

Schlegel, Friedrich von (1772-1829): German Romantic poet, essayist, novelist; convert, 1803.

Schmid, Christoph von (1768-1854): German educator, pioneer writer of children's books.

Schmidt, Wilhelm (1868-1954): German Divine Word priest, ethnologist and historian of religions.

Schubert, Franz Peter (1797-1828): Austrian composer of symphonic and other orchestral works.

Schuman, Robert (1886-1963): French statesman; leader of the Popular Republican Party; Premier of France twice (November, 1947-July, 1948; Aug. 31-Sept. 9, 1948); major figure in post-World War II efforts at European unity; author of Schuman Plan for pooling French and German coal and steel production, a forerunner of the Common Market.

Schuyler, Philippa (1932-1967): American pianist, news correspondent.

Searle, George Mary (1839-1918): American priest and astronomer, b. England of American parents; came to US, 1840; convert, 1866; joined Paulists, 1868; ordained, 1871; director of Vatican Observatory, 1898.

Schwann, Theodor (1810-1882): German anatomist, physiologist; founder of cell theory.

Schwarz, Berthold (13th or 14th c.): German Franciscan; called inventor of gunpowder.

Secchi, Angelo (1818-1878): Italian Jesuit, astronomer; professor at Georgetown University; did spectroscopic work on sun, stars, classification of stars; invented meteorograph.

Segura y Saenz, Pedro (1880-1957): Spanish cardinal, primate of Spain; outspoken critic of Nazism, Fascism and Franco regime.

Seidl, Johann Gabriel (1804-1875): Austrian journalist, poet; author of words for Austrian national anthem.

Semmelweis, Ignaz Philipp (1818-1865): Hungarian physician; pioneer of antiseptic treatment in obstetrics.

Semmes, Raphael (1809-1877): American naval officer, lawyer; commander in US Navy; resigned, 1861, to enter Confederate Navy; commanded the Sumter and the Alabama, commerce destroyers.

Sienkiewicz, Henryk (1846-1916): Polish novelist; awarded Nobel Prize for literature.

Shea, Sir Ambrose (1815-1905): Canadian political leader; member of House of Assembly of Newfoundland; governor of Bahamas.

Shea, John Dawson Gilmary (1824-1892): American historian, author; *History of the Catholic Church in the United States.*

Sheridan, Philip H. (1831-1888): American army officer; graduate of West Point; general cavalry commander during the Civil War.

Shevchenko, Taras (1814-1861): Ukrainian poet, nationalist; founder of the Society of Sts. Cyril and Methodius for Ukrainian independence.

Shields, James (1806-1879): American soldier and statesman, b. Ireland; arrived US, 1823, settled in Kaskaskia, Ill.; army officer, politician; general in Mexican War; governor of Oregon Territory, 1849; US senator from Illinois, 1849-55, from Minnesota, 1858-59; moved to California, 1859; brigadier general in Civil War, resigned commission, 1863;

moved to Missouri; US senator from Missouri, 1879. Represents Illinois in Statuary Hall.

Shipman, Andrew Jackson (1857-1915): American lawyer, author; convert, 1876; authority on Church law.

Sitwell, Edith (1887-1964): English poet, critic, novelist; convert, 1955.

Skinner, Henrietta Channing Dana (1857-1928): American author; convert, 1878.

Smith, Alfred Emanuel (1873-1944): American politician; governor of New York; Democratic presidential candidate, 1928, the first Catholic ever nominated.

Smith, Ignatius (1886-1957): American Dominican priest, orator, teacher, retreat master.

Smith, Matthew (1891-1960): American priest, editor; founder of Register chain of newspapers.

Sobieski, John III (1624-1696): Polish king, soldier; rescued Vienna from Turks, caused their expulsion from Poland and Hungary.

Spalding, John Lancaster (1840-1916): American prelate; nephew of Martin Spalding, below; author of books on religion, philosophy and social issues; advocate of Catholic parochial school system; served on President Roosevelt's Anthracite Coal Strike Commission, 1902; first bishop of Peoria, 1876-1908, when he resigned because of ill health.

Spalding, Martin J. (1810-1872): American prelate; bishop of Louisville, 1848-64; archbishop of Baltimore, 1864-72; author of numerous books; helped establish American College of Louvain; advocate of a North American College in Rome and an American Catholic university.

Spallanzani, Lazzaro (1729-1799): Italian naturalist; experimenter on digestion, other functions; disproved theory of spontaneous generation.

Spearman, Frank Hamilton (1859-1937): American author; convert, 1884; Laetare Medalist, 1935.

Spellman, Francis J. (1889-1967): American cardinal; ordained priest, 1916; served in papal secretariat of state, 1925-32; auxiliary of Boston, 1932; archbishop of New York, 1939-67; cardinal, 1946; military vicar of US; author.

Starr, Eliza Allen (1824-1901): American educator, author; convert, 1856; first woman Laetare Medalist, 1885.

Stensen, Niels (Steno, Nicolaus) (1638-1687): Danish bishop, anatomist; discovered excretory duct of parotid glands, convert, 1667.

Stepinac, Alojzije (1898-1960): Yugoslav cardinal, b. Croatia; condemned Nazism and Communism; sentenced to 16 years' imprisonment 1946; released 1951 and placed under house arrest; considered martyr and symbol of Church under persecution in Yugoslavia.

Stoddard, Charles Warren (1843-1909): American journalist, poet, author; convert, 1867.

Stoddard, John Lawson (1850-1931): American author, lecturer; convert, 1922.

Stone, James Kent (Fr. Fidelis, C.P.) (1840-1921): American missionary priest, author; Episcopalian minister, 1866; convert, 1869; ordained priest, 1872.

Storer, Horatio Robinson (1830-1922): American physician, medical professor, author; convert, 1897.

Stoss, Veit (1440-1533): German sculptor; master wood-carver.

Stradivari, Antonio (1644-1737): Italian violin maker.

Stritch, Samuel (1887-1958): American cardinal; ordained priest, 1910; bishop of Toledo, 1921-30; archbishop of Milwaukee, 1930-39; archbishop of Chicago, 1939-58; cardinal, 1946; first American appointed to the Roman Curia, died before he could take up his post as pro-prefect of the Sacred Congregation for the Propagation of the Faith.

Sturzo, Luigi (1871-1959): Italian priest-statesman.

Suarez, Francisco (1548-1617): Spanish Jesuit, theologian considered a founder of international law; author of many works; *Doctor Eximius*.

T

Tabb, John Banister (1845-1909): American poet, served in Confederate navy, convert, 1872; ordained priest, 1884.

Taggart, Marion Ames (1866-1945): American author, convert, 1880.

Takamine, Jokichi (1854-1922): Japanese-American chemist; developed Takadiastase, isolated adrenalin; convert.

Talbot, Matthew (1856-1925): Irish layman noted for his sanctity; a reformed alcoholic, is considered a model for those with this condition; his cause for beatification is under consideration.

Taney, Roger Brooke (1777-1864): American jurist, cabinet official; US attorney general, 1831-33; secretary of the treasury, 1833-34; chief justice United States Supreme Court, 1836-64; associated with the Dred Scott decision, 1857.

Tasso, Torquato (1544-1595): Italian poet.

Teilhard de Chardin, Pierre (1881-1955): French Jesuit; paleontologist and explorer.

Tekakwitha, Kateri (1656-1680): American Indian maiden; Lily of the Mohawks; instructed by Jesuit missionaries and baptized at age of 20; her cause for beatification is under consideration.

Thayer, John (1755-1815): American priest; Protestant chaplain during Revolutionary War; convert, 1783; first native New England priest; missionary in Kentucky; author.

Thomas, Charles Louis Ambrose (1811-

1896): Alsatian composer of operatic and other works.

Thomas a Kempis (1380-1471): Dutch Augustinian, considered author of the *Imitation of Christ*.

Thomas of Celano (1200-1255): Italian Franciscan; biographer of St. Francis of Assisi.

Thompson, Francis (1859-1907): English poet; *The Hound of Heaven*.

Tieffentaller, Joseph (1710-1785): Jesuit missionary, geographer.

Tintoretto, Jacopo Robusti (1518-1594): Italian painter of Venetian school; religious and portrait subjects.

Tisserant, Eugene (1884-1972): French cardinal, scholar; librarian and archivist of the Vatican; headed Congregation for the Eastern Churches for more than 20 years; dean of the College of Cardinals, 1951-72; specialist in Oriental languages; member of the French Academy.

Titian or **Tiziano Vecelli** (1477-1576): Italian painter, greatest of the Venetian school; frescoes in wide range of subjects; portraits.

Tobin, Maurice J. (1901-1953): American politician, cabinet official; mayor of Boston, 1937, 1941; governor of Massachusetts, 1944; US secretary of labor, 1949-53.

Tocqueville, Alexis Charles de (1805-1859): French writer, statesman; *La Democratie en Amerique*.

Torricelli, Evangelista (1608-1647): Italian mathematician, physicist; improved telescope, invented barometer.

Toscanelli, Paolo dal Pozzo (1397-1482): Italian physician, geographer; probably aided Columbus.

Toscanini, Arturo (1867-1957): Italian operatic and symphony conductor.

Tulasne, Louis Rene (1815-1885): French botanist; called founder of modern mycology.

U

Undset, Sigrid (1882-1949): Norwegian novelist; Nobel Prize for literature, 1928; *Kristen Lavransdatter*; convert, 1924.

V

Valentine, Basil (born 1394): Benedictine monk; founder of analytical chemistry.

Vandyke (Van Dyck), Sir Anthony (1599-1641): Flemish associate of Rubens, English court painter; religious and portrait subjects.

Vasari, Giorgio (1511-1574): Italian painter, architect; founder of modern art history and criticism.

Vasquez, Gabriel (1551-1604): Spanish Jesuit, theologian.

Vegan Lope Felix de (Vega) Carpio (1562-1635): Spanish priest, dramatic poet; founder of Spanish national drama.

Velasquez, Diego Rodriguez de Silva y (1599-1660): Spanish painter; master of naturalism; historical, portrait, religious and other subjects.

Verdi, Giuseppe (1813-1901): Italian composer of operatic and other works.

Verne, Jules (1828-1905): French writer; scientific fiction.

Vernier, Pierre (1580-1637): French mathematician; formulated vernier scale for accurate linear and angular magnitude.

Veronese, Paolo (1528-1588): Italian painter of Venetian school; Painter of Pageants: religious frescoes and paintings.

Verrazano, Giovanni da (1485-1528): Italian navigator; explored coast of North America for Francis I of France; claimed by his countrymen to be discoverer of Hudson River.

Verrocchio, Andrea del (1435-1488): Florentine sculptor and painter of Tuscan school.

Vesalius, Andreas (1514-1564): Belgian anatomist; founder of modern anatomy.

Vespucci, Amerigo (1451-1512): Italian navigator; called discoverer of mainland of America, named after him.

Vico, Francesco de (1805-1848): Italian Jesuit, astronomer; discovered six comets.

Viete (Vieta), Francois, Seigneur de La Bigottiere (1540-1603): French mathematician; founder of modern algebra, which he applied to geometry and trigonometry.

Vignola, Giacomo Barozzi da (1507-1573): Italian architect; architectural theorist.

Vincent of Beauvais (1190-1264): French Dominican; author of comprehensive scientific encyclopedia.

Vinci, Leonardo da (1452-1519): Florentine painter, sculptor, architect, engineer, scientist; paintings mainly of religious subjects; founder of science of hydraulics, researcher in meteorology, anatomy, mathematics.

Vladimir, Saint (956-1015): First Christian ruler of Russia.

Volta, Alessandro, Count (1754-1827): Italian physicist; early researcher in electricity; the volt named for him.

Vorosmarty, Michael (1800-1855): Hungarian poet; his lyric poem "Szozat" became a national anthem.

W-Z

Wagner, Robert F. (1877-1953): American public official and judge, b. Nastatten Hessen, Germany; US senator, 1926-49; sponsor of Wagner National Labor Relations Act; convert, 1946.

Waldseemuller, Martin (1470-1518): German cartographer; made first modern atlas; first to use the name America.

Walker, Frank C. (1886-1959): American politician, cabinet official; US postmaster general, 1940-45.

Walsh, James Joseph (1865-1942): American physician, author; *The Thirteenth, the Greatest of Centuries*.

Walsh, William Thomas (1891-1949): American historian.

Walworth, Clarence Augustus (1820-1900): American priest; convert, 1845; ordained,

1848; assisted Isaac Hecker in founding the Paulists, whom he left because of illness; author.

Ward, Maisie (1889-1975): English-born publisher, writer, lecturer; charter member of Catholic Evidence Guild; cofounder, with her husband, Frank Sheed, of the publishing house of Sheed and Ward in 1926 in London.

Warren, Leonard (1911-1960): American opera star; convert from Judaism 1942; baritone of Metropolitan Opera.

Wattson, Lewis Thomas (Father James Francis Paul) (1863-1940): American founder; as Episcopalian presbyter, founded Friars of the Atonement, 1899; inaugurated Chair of Unity Octave, 1908; founded St. Christopher's Inn, Garrison, N.Y.; convert with members of his community, 1909; ordained priest, 1910.

Waugh, Evelyn (1903-1966): English writer; convert, 1930.

Weber, Karl Maria von (1786-1826): German composer of operatic and other works; a founder of German opera.

Weigel, Gustave (1900-1964): American Jesuit priest, theologian, author; pioneer in Catholic-Protestant dialogue; consultor of the Vatican Secretariat for Promoting Christian Unity.

White, Edward Douglass (1845-1921): American jurist; US senator, 1891-94; associate justice US Supreme Court, 1894-1910; chief justice, 1910-21; wrote decisions for more than 700 of the 4,000 cases decided during his time on the Court. Represents Louisiana in Statuary Hall.

White, Helen C. (1896-1967): American educator, author.

Wilde, Oscar (1856-1900): Irish poet; dramatist; convert shortly before his death.

William of Ockham (Occam) (1300-1349): English Franciscan; philosopher, logician; author of the philosophical axiom, "beings are not to be multiplied without necessity."

William the Conqueror (1027-1087): Duke of Normandy; invaded England, 1066, defeated Harold at Hastings, crowned King of England.

Williams, Michael (1877-1950): American journalist and author, b. Halifax, Nova Scotia; founded *Commonweal*, 1924.

Winckelmann, Johann Joachim (1717-1768): German art historian, classical archaeologist; convert, 1754.

Windle, Sir Bertram (1858-1929): English scientist; professor at Toronto University, Canada, from 1919; author of works intended to explain relations between scientific progress and Church teaching.

Windthorst, Ludwig (1812-1891): German statesman, leader of Center Party.

Wiseman, Nicholas Patrick (1802-1865): English cardinal, archbishop of Westminster; influenced Catholic revival, encouraged Oxford Movement.

Wynne, Robert J. (1851-1922): American cabinet official; US postmaster general, 1904-05.

Ximenez (Jimenez) de Cisneros, Francisco (1437-1517): Spanish Franciscan, cardinal, statesman.

Yoshida, Shigeru (1878-1967): Japanese statesman; prime minister of Japan, 1946-54; convert shortly before his death.

Zrinyi, Nicholas, Count (1620-1664): Hungarian general, poet; author of first Hungarian epic, *The Fall of Szigets*.

Zurbaran, Francisco de (1598-1664): Spanish painter; religious subjects.

MISSIONARIES TO THE AMERICAS

Allouez, Claude Jean (1622-1689): French Jesuit; missionary in Canada and midwestern US; preached to 20 different tribes of Indians and baptized over 10,000; vicar general of Northwest.

Altham, John (1589-1640): English Jesuit; missionary among Indians in Maryland.

Anchieta, Jose (1534-1597): Portuguese Jesuit, b. Canary Islands; missionary in Brazil; writer.

Andreis, Felix de (1778-1820): Italian Vincentian; missionary and educator in western US.

Aparicio, Bl. Sebastian (1502-1600): Franciscan brother, born Spain; settled in Mexico, c. 1533; worked as road builder and farmer before becoming Franciscan at about the age of 70; beatified, 1787; feast, Feb. 25.

Badin, Stephen T. (1768-1853): French missioner; came to US, 1792, when Sulpician seminary in Paris was closed; ordained, 1793, Baltimore, the first priest ordained in US; missionary in Kentucky, Ohio and Michigan; bought land on which Notre Dame University now stands; buried on its campus.

Baraga, Frederic (1797-1868): Slovenian missionary bishop in US; studied at Ljubljana and Vienna, ordained, 1823; came to US, 1830; missionary to Indians of Upper Michigan; first bishop of Marquette, 1857-1868; wrote Chippewa grammar, dictionary, prayer book and other works.

Bertran, St. Louis (1526-1581): Spanish Dominican; missionary in Colombia and Caribbean, 1562-69; canonized, 1671; feast, Oct. 9.

Bourgeoys, Bl. Marguerite (1620-1700): French foundress, missionary; settled in Canada, 1653; founded Congregation of Notre Dame de Montreal, 1658; beatified, 1950; feast, Jan. 19.

Brebeuf, St. John de (1593-1649): French Jesuit; missionary among Huron Indians in Canada; martyred by Iroquois, Mar. 16, 1649; canonized, 1930; one of Jesuit North American martyrs; feast, Oct. 19.

Cancer de Barbastro, Louis (1500-1549): Spanish Dominican; began missionary work in Middle America, 1533; killed at Tampa Bay, Fla.

Castillo, Bl. John de (1596-1628): Spanish Jesuit; worked in Paraguay Indian mission settlements (reductions); martyred; beatified, 1934; feast, Nov. 17.

Catala, Magin (1761-1830): Spanish Franciscan; worked in California mission of Santa Clara for 36 years.

Chabanel, St. Noel (1613-1649): French Jesuit; missionary among Huron Indians in Canada; murdered by renegade Huron, Dec. 3, 1649; canonized, 1930; one of Jesuit North American martyrs; feast, Oct. 19.

Chaumonot, Pierre Joseph (1611-1693): French Jesuit; missionary among Indians in Canada.

Claver, St. Peter (1581-1654): Spanish Jesuit; missionary among Negroes of South America and West Indies; canonized, 1888; patron of Catholic missions among Negroes; feast, Sept. 9.

Daniel, St. Anthony (1601-1648): French Jesuit; missionary among Huron Indians in Canada; martyred by Iroquois, July 4, 1648; canonized, 1930; one of Jesuit North American martyrs; feast, Oct. 19.

De Smet, Pierre Jean (1801-1873): Belgian-born Jesuit; missionary among Indians of northwestern US; served as intermediary between Indians and US government; wrote on Indian culture.

Duchesne, Bl. Rose Philippine (1769-1852): French nun; educator and missionary in the US; established first convent of the Society of the Sacred Heart in the US, at St. Charles, Mo. (later Florissant); founded schools for girls; did missionary work among Indians; beatified, 1940; feast, Nov. 17.

Farmer, Ferdinand (family name, Steinmeyer) (1720-1786): German Jesuit; missionary in Philadelphia, where he died; one of the first missionaries in New Jersey.

Flaget, Benedict J. (1763-1850): French Sulpician bishop; came to US, 1792; missionary and educator in US; first bishop of Bardstown, Ky. (now Louisville), 1810-32; 1833-50.

Gallitzin, Demetrius (1770-1840): Russian prince, born The Hague; convert, 1787; ordained priest at Baltimore, 1795; frontier missionary, known as Father Smith; Gallitzin, Pa., named for him.

Garnier, St. Charles (c. 1606-1649): French Jesuit; missionary among Hurons in Canada; martyred by Iroquois, Dec. 7, 1649; canonized, 1930; one of Jesuit North American martyrs; feast, Oct. 19.

Gibault, Pierre (1737-1804): Canadian missionary in Illinois and Indiana; aided in securing states of Ohio, Indiana, Illinois, Michigan and Wisconsin for the Americans during Revolution.

Gonzalez, Bl. Roch (1576-1628): Paraguayan Jesuit; worked in Paraguay Indian mission settlements (reductions); martyred; beatified, 1934; feast, Nov. 17.

Goupil, St. Rene (1607-1642): French Jesuit brother; missionary companion of St. Isaac Jogues among the Hurons; martyred, Sept. 29, 1642; canonized, 1930; one of Jesuit North American martyrs; feast, Oct. 19.

Gravier, Jacques (1651-1708): French Jesuit; missionary among Indians of Canada and midwestern US.

Jesuit North American Martyrs: Isaac Jogues, Anthony Daniel, John de Brebeuf, Gabriel Lalemant, Charles Garnier, Noel Chabanel (Jesuit priests), and Rene Goupil and John Lalande (lay missionaries) who were martyred between Sept. 29, 1642, and Dec. 9, 1649, in the missions of New France; canonized June 29, 1930; feast, Oct. 19. See separate entries.

Jogues, St. Isaac (1607-1646): French Jesuit; missionary among Indians in Canada; martyred near present site of Auriesville, N.Y., by Mohawks, Oct. 18, 1646; canonized, 1930; one of Jesuit North American martyrs; feast, Oct. 19.

Kino, Eusebio (1645-1711): Italian Jesuit; missionary and explorer in US; arrived Southwest, 1681; established 25 Indian missions, took part in 14 exploring expeditions in northern Mexico, Arizona and southern California; helped develop livestock raising and farming in the area. He was selected in 1965 to represent Arizona in Statuary Hall.

Lalande, St. John (d. 1646): French lay missionary, companion of Isaac Jogues; martyred by Mohawks at Auriesville, N.Y., Oct. 19, 1646; canonized, 1930; one of Jesuit North American martyrs; feast, Oct. 19.

Lalemant, St. Gabriel (1610-1649): French Jesuit; missionary among the Hurons in Canada; martyred by the Iroquois, Mar. 17, 1649; canonized, 1930; one of Jesuit North American martyrs; feast, Oct. 19.

Lamy, Jean Baptiste (1814-1888): French prelate; came to US, 1839; missionary in Ohio and Kentucky; bishop in Southwest from 1850; first bishop (later archbishop) of Santa Fe, 1850-1885. He was nominated in 1951 to represent New Mexico in Statuary Hall.

Las Casas, Bartolome (1474-1566): Spanish Dominican; missionary in Haiti, Jamaica and Venezuela; reformer of abuses against Indians and Negroes; bishop of Chalapas, Mexico, 1544-47; historian.

Manogue, Patrick (1831-1895): Missionary bishop in US, b. Ireland; migrated to US; miner in California; studied for priesthood at St. Mary's of the Lake, Chicago, and St. Sulpice, Paris; ordained, 1861; missionary among Indians of California and Nevada; coadjutor bishop, 1881-84, and bishop, 1884-86, of Grass Valley; first bishop of Sacramento, 1886-1895, when see was transferred there.

Margil, Antonio (1657-1726): Spanish Franciscan; missionary in Middle America; apostle of Guatemala; established missions in Texas.

Marie de l'Incarnation, Ven. (1599-1672): French Ursuline nun; arrived in Canada, 1639; first superior of Ursulines in Quebec; missionary to Indians; writer.

Marquette, Jacques (1637-1675): French Jesuit; missionary and explorer in America; sent to New France, 1666; began missionary work among Ottawa Indians on Lake Superior, 1668; accompanied Joliet down the Mississippi to mouth of the Arkansas, 1673, and returned to Lake Michigan by way of Illinois River; made a second trip over the same route; his diary and map are of historical significance. He was selected in 1895 to represent Wisconsin in Statuary Hall.

Massias, St. John de (1585-1645); Dominican brother, a native of Spain; entered Dominican Friary at Lima, Peru, 1622; served as doorkeeper until his death; beatified, 1837; canonized 1975; feast, Sept. 18.

Mazzuchelli, Samuel C. (1806-1864): Italian Dominican; missionary in midwestern US; called Builder of the West; writer.

Membre, Zenobius (1645-1687): French Franciscan; missionary among Indians of Illinois; accompanied LaSalle expedition down the Mississippi (1681-1682) and Louisiana colonizing expedition (1684) which landed in Texas; murdered by Indians.

Nerinckx, Charles (1761-1824): Belgian priest; missionary in Kentucky; founded Sisters of Loretto at the Foot of the Cross.

Nobrega, Manoel (1517-1570): Portuguese Jesuit; leader of first Jesuit missionaries to Brazil, 1549.

Padilla, Juan de (d. 1542): Spanish Franciscan; missionary among Indians of Mexico and southwestern US; killed by Indians in Kansas; protomartyr of the U.S.

Palou, Francisco (c. 1722-1789): Spanish Franciscan; accompanied Junipero Serra to Mexico, 1749; founded Mission Dolores in San Francisco; wrote history of the Franciscans in California.

Pariseau, Mother Mary Joseph (1833-1902): Canadian Sister of Charity of Providence; missionary in state of Washington from 1856; founded first hospitals in northwest territory; artisan and architect. Represents Washington in National Statuary Hall.

Peter of Ghent (d. 1572): Belgian Franciscan brother; missionary in Mexico for 49 years.

Porres, St. Martin de (1579-1639): Peruvian Dominican oblate; his father was a Spanish soldier and his mother a Negro freedwoman from Panama; called wonder worker of Peru; beatified, 1837; canonized, 1962; feast, Nov. 3.

Quiroga, Vasco de (1470-1565): Spanish missionary in Mexico; founded hospitals; bishop of Michoacan, 1537.

Ravalli, Antonio (1811-1884): Italian Jesuit; missionary in far-western United States, mostly Montana, for 40 years.

Raymbaut, Charles (1602-1643): French Jesuit; missionary among Indians of Canada and northern US.

Richard, Gabriel (1767-1832): French Sulpician; missionary in Illinois and Michigan; a founder of University of Michigan; elected delegate to Congress from Michigan, 1823; first priest to hold seat in the House of Representatives.

Rodriguez, Bl. Alonso (1598-1628): Spanish Jesuit; missionary in Paraguay; martyred; beatified, 1934; feast, Nov. 17.

Rosati, Joseph (1789-1843): Italian Vincentian; missionary bishop in US (vicar apostolic of Mississippi and Alabama, 1822; coadjutor of Louisiana and the Two Floridas, 1823-26; administrator of New Orleans, 1826-29; first bishop of St. Louis, 1826-1843).

Sahagun, Bernardino de (c. 1500-1590): Spanish Franciscan; missionary in Mexico for over 60 years; expert on Aztec archaeology.

Seelos, Francis X. (1819-1867): Redemptorist missionary, born Bavaria; ordained, 1844, at Baltimore; missionary in Pittsburgh and New Orleans.

Serra, Junipero (1713-1784): Spanish Franciscan, b. Majorca; missionary in America; arrived Mexico, 1749, where he did missionary work for 20 years; began work in Upper California in 1769 and established nine of the 21 Franciscan missions along the Pacific coast; baptized some 6,000 Indians and confirmed almost 5,000; a cultural pioneer of California. Represents California in Statuary Hall.

Seghers, Charles J. (1839-1886): Belgian missionary bishop in North America; Apostle of Alaska; archbishop of Oregon City (now Portland), 1880-1884; murdered by berserk companion while on missionary journey.

Solanus, St. Francis (1549-1610): Spanish Franciscan; missionary in Paraguay, Argentina and Peru; Wonder Worker of the New World; canonized, 1726.

Sorin, Edward F. (1814-1893): French priest; member of Congregation of Holy Cross; sent to US in 1841; founder and first president of the University of Notre Dame; missionary in Indiana and Michigan.

Todadilla, Anthony de (1704-1746): Spanish Capuchin; missionary to Indians of Venezuela; killed by Motilones.

Turibius de Mogrovejo, St. (1538-1606): Spanish archbishop of Lima, Peru, c. 1580-1606; canonized 1726; feast, Apr. 27.

Twelve Apostles of Mexico (early 16th century): Franciscan priests; arrived in Mexico, 1524: Fathers Martin de Valencia (leader), Francisco de Soto, Martin de la Coruna, Juan Suares, Antonio de Ciudad Rodrigo, Toribio de Benevente, Garcia de Cisneros, Luis de Fuensalida, Juan de Ribas, Francisco Ximenes; Brothers Andres de Coroboda, Juan de Palos.

Valdivia, Luis de (1561-1641): Spanish Jesuit; defender of Indians in Peru and Chile.

Vasques de Espinosa, Antonio (early 17th century): Spanish Carmelite; missionary and explorer in Mexico, Panama and western coast of South America.

Vieira, Antonio (1608-1687): Portuguese Jesuit; preacher; missionary in Peru and Chile; protector of Indians against exploitation by slave owners and traders; considered foremost prose writer of 17th-century Portugal.

White, Andrew (1579-1656): English Jesuit; missionary among Indians in Maryland.

Wimmer, Boniface (1809-1887): German Benedictine; missionary among German immigrants in the US.

Youville, Bl. Marie Marguerite d' (1701-1771): Canadian widow; foundress of Sisters of Charity (Grey Nuns), 1738, at Montreal; beatified, 1959.

Zumarraga, Juan de (1468-1548): Spanish Franciscan; missionary; first bishop of Mexico; introduced first printing press in New World, published first book in America, a catechism for Aztec Indians; extended missions in Mexico and Central America; vigorous opponent of exploitation of Indians; approved of devotions at Guadalupe; leading figure in early church history in Mexico.

FRANCISCAN MISSIONS OF UPPER CALIFORNIA

The 21 Franciscan missions of Upper California were established during the 54-year period from 1769 to 1822. Located along the old El Camino Real, or King's Highway, they extended from San Diego to San Francisco and were the centers of Indian civilization, Christianity and industry in the early history of the state.

Fray Junipero Serra was the great pioneer of the missions of Upper California. He and his successor as superior of the work, Fray Fermin Lasuen, each directed the establishment of nine missions. One hundred and 46 priests of the Order of Friars Minor, most of them Spaniards, labored in the region from 1769 to 1845; 67 of them died at their posts, two as martyrs. The regular time of mission service was 10 years.

The missions were secularized by the Mexican government in the 1830's but were subsequently restored to the Church by the US government. They are now variously used as the sites of parish churches, a university, houses of study and museums.

The names of the missions and the order of their establishment were as follows:

San Diego de Alcala, San Carlos Borromeo (El Carmelo), San Antonio de Padua, San Gabriel Arcangel, San Luis Obispo de Tolosa, San Francisco de Asis (Dolores), San Juan Capistrano;

Santa Clara de Asis, San Buenaventura, Santa Barbara, La Purisima Concepcion de Maria Santisima, Santa Cruz, Nuestra Senora de la Soledad, San Jose de Guadalupe;

San Juan Bautista, San Miguel Arcangel, San Fernando Rey de Espana, San Luis Rey de Francia, Santa Ines, San Rafael Arcangel, San Francisco Solano de Sonoma (Sonoma).

HUMAN DEVELOPMENT

The Campaign for Human Development was inaugurated by the U.S. Catholic Conference in November, 1969, to combat injustice, oppression, alienation and poverty in this country in three significant ways:

• by making people in this country, especially Catholics, aware of the poverty, oppression and/or injustice afflicting some 35 million persons, through programs of education and public instruction;

• by funding self-help programs begun and carried out by the poor or by the poor and non-poor working together;

• by seeking a re-evaluation of the priorities of individuals, families, the Church and the civic community with respect to the stewardship of God-given goods.

The campaign got under way with a collection taken up in all parishes throughout the country on Nov. 22, 1970. Seventy-five per cent of the money contributed in this and subsequent annual collections was placed in a national fund principally for funding self-help projects and also for educational purposes; 25 per cent remained in the dioceses where it was collected, for similar use on the local levels.

More than $50 million in grants have been allocated by the national office since 1970; grants to 125 projects in 1979 totaled a bit more than $6.3 million. Diocesan allocations since 1970 have amounted to approximately $20 million.

Aid requests are reviewed by a broadly representative committee of 40 members which passes its recommendations for funding on to the 12-member Bishops' Committee for the Campaign for Human Development. Requests for aid from the national office are about 10 times greater than the some 125 programs funded each year.

Father Marvin Mottet is executive director of the campaign; his assistant is Timothy Collins. Bishop Joseph H. Hodges of Wheeling-Charleston is chairman of the bishops' committee.

The national office is located at 1312 Massachusetts Ave. N.W., Washington, D.C. 20005.

The Church in Countries Throughout the World

(Principal sources for statistics: *Annuario Pontificio, 1979; Statistical Yearbook of the Church, 1976* (the latest available edition). Figures are as of Jan. 1, 1978, or Jan. 1 of the year indicated. See Index under names of countries for additional entries on 1979 events.)

Abbreviation code: archd. — archdiocese; dioc. — diocese; ap. ex. — apostolic exarchate; prel. — prelature; abb. — abbacy; v.a. — vicariate apostolic; p.a. — prefecture apostolic; a.a. — apostolic administration; card. — cardinal; abp. — archbishop; nat. — native; bp. — bishop; priests (dioc. — diocesan or secular priests; rel. — those belonging to religious orders; sem. — seminarians (major); p.d. — permanent deacons; bros. — brothers (1977); srs. — sisters; sch. — schools (elementary and secondary); bap. — baptisms; Caths. — Catholic population; tot. pop. — total population.

Afars and Issas: See Djibouti.

Afghanistan: Republic in south-central Asia; capital, Kabul. Christianity antedated Moslem conquest in the seventh century but was overcome by it. All inhabitants are subject to the law of Islam. Christian missionaries are prohibited. The few Catholics in the country are foreign embassy and technical personnel. Population (1977 est.), 20,340,000.

Albania: Communist people's republic in the Balkans, bordering the Adriatic Sea; capital, Tirana. Christianity was introduced before the middle of the fourth century. The Byzantine-Rite Church broke from unity with Rome following the schism of 1054; it has been suppressed. The Latin (Roman) Church, which prevailed in the north, has been wiped out by persecution since 1945, with the expulsion of Italian missionaries; a number of death and prison sentences and other repressive measures against bishops, priests, religious and lay persons; the closing of Catholic schools and a seminary; the cutting of lines of communication with the Holy See. In 1967, the government proclaimed itself the first atheist state in the world.

Archd., 2; dioc., 3; abb., 1; a.a. 1; bp., 3 (impeded). No statistics are available. The Catholic population was estimated at 143,500 in 1969 by the CSMC "World Mission Map"; tot. pop. (1977 est.), 2,620,000.

Algeria: Republic in northwest Africa: capital, Algiers. Christianity, introduced at an early date, succumbed to Vandal devastation in the fifth century and Moslem conquest in 709, but survived for centuries in small communities into the 12th century. Missionary work was unsuccessful except in service to traders, military personnel and captives along the coast. Church organization was established after the French gained control of the territory in the 1830's. A large number of Catholics were among the estimated million Europeans who left the country after it secured independence from France July 5, 1962. Islam is the state religion. Algeria maintains diplomatic relations with Vatican City.

Archd., 1; dioc., 3; card., 1; bp., 3 (1 nat.); parishes, 86; priests, 217 (100 dioc., 117 rel.); sem. 1; p.d., 1; bros., 25; srs., 556; bap., 49; Caths., 56,800 (.3%); tot. pop., 17,910,000.

Andorra: Autonomous principality in the Pyrenees, under the rule of co-princes — the French head of state and the bishop of Urgel, Spain; capital, Andorra la Vella. Christianity was introduced at an early date. Catholicism is the state religion. The principality is under the ecclesiastical jurisdiction of the Spanish diocese of Urgel.

Parishes, 6; priests, 13 (9 dioc., 4 rel.); bros., 6; srs., 29; sch., 2; bap., 435; Caths., 24,000 (1977); tot. pop. (1977 est.), 27,200.

Angola: Independent (Nov. 11, 1975) republic in west Africa; capital, Luanda. Evangelization by Catholic missionaries, dating from about 1570, reached high points in the 17th and 18th centuries. Independence from Portugal in 1975 left the Church with a heavy loss of personnel when about half of the foreign missionaries fled the country. In 1977, two ecclesiastical provinces were established. All but two of the hierarchy are from the native clergy. Angola has an apostolic delegate.

Archd., 3; dioc., 9; abp., 3 (nat.); bp., 9 (7 nat.); parishes, 173; priests, 240 (85 dioc., 155 rel.); sem., 27; bap., 79,440; Caths., 2,932,244 (42.6%); tot. pop., 6,881,650.

Anguilla: Self-governing British island territory in the Caribbean. Under ecclesiastical jurisdiction of St. John's diocese, Antigua. Statistics included in St. Christopher (Kitts)-Nevis.

Antigua: Self-governing British Associated State in the Caribbean; capital, St. John's.

Dioc., 1; bp., 1; parishes, 2; priests, 3 (rel.); sem., 2; bros., 6; srs., 8; sch., 4; studs., 1,358; bap., 150; Caths., 7,000 (9.8%); tot. pop., 71,000 (1977).

Arabian Peninsula: Christianity, introduced in various parts of the peninsula in early Christian centuries, succumbed to Islam in the seventh century. The native population is entirely Moslem. The only Christians are foreigners. Most of the peninsula is under the ecclesiastical jurisdiction of the Vicariate Apostolic of Arabia located in Abu Dhabi, United Arab Emirates. The area has an apostolic delegate (to the Red Sea Region). See individual countries: Bahrain, Oman, Qatar, Saudi Arabia, United Arab Emirates, Yemen, and Peoples Democratic Republic of Yemen.

Argentina: Republic in southeast South America, bordering on the Atlantic; capital, Buenos Aires. Priests were with the Magellan exploration party and the first Mass in the country was celebrated Apr. 1, 1519. Missionary work began in the 1530's, diocesan organization in the late 1540's, and effective evangelization about 1570. Independence from Spain was proclaimed in 1816. Since its establishment in the country, the Church has been influenced by Spanish cultural and institutional forces, antagonistic liberalism, government interference and opposition; the latter reached a climax during the last five years of the first presidency of Juan Peron (1946-1955). Political chaos in recent years has resulted in widespread violations of human rights and increased terrorist violence. Catholicism is the state religion. Argentina maintains diplomatic relations with Vatican City.

Archd., 12; dioc., 42; prel., 2; ord., 1; card., 4; abp., 10; bp., 64; parishes, 2,157; priests, 4,888 (2,228 dioc., 2,660 rel.); sem., 629; p.d., 24; bros., 1,017; srs., 12,005; sch., 2,613; bap., 516,490; Caths. (est.), 23,975,200 (92%); tot. pop., 26,060,000.

Australia: Commonwealth, member of the British Commonwealth, island continent southeast of Asia; capital, Canberra. The first Catholics in the country were Irish under penal sentence, 1795-1804; the first public Mass was celebrated May 15, 1803. Official organization of the Church dates from 1820. The country was officially removed from mission status in March, 1976. Australia established diplomatic relations with Vatican City in 1973.

Archd., 7; dioc., 20; abb., 1; mission "sui juris," 1; ap. ex., 1; card., 2; abp., 7; bp., 34; parishes, 1,405; priests, 3,624 (2,235 dioc., 1,389 rel.); sem., 321; p.d., 6; bros., 2,194; srs., 11,563; sch., 1,831; bap., 72,155; Caths., 3,727,175 (27%); tot. pop. 13,965,285.

Austria: Republic in central Europe; capital, Vienna. Christianity was introduced by the end of the third century, strengthened considerably by conversion of the Bavarians from about 600, and firmly established in the second half of the eighth century. Catholicism survived and grew stronger as the principal religion in the country in the post-Reformation period, but suffered from Josephinism in the 18th century. Although liberated from much government harassment in the aftermath of the Revolution of 1848, it came under pressure again some 20 years later in the Kulturkampf. During this time the Church became involved with a developing social movement. The Church faced strong opposition from Socialists after World War I and suffered persecution from 1938 to 1945 during the Nazi regime. Some Church-state matters are regulated by a concordat originally concluded in 1934. Austria maintains diplomatic relations with Vatican City.

Archd., 2; dioc., 7; abb., 1; ord., 1; card., 1; abp., 2; bp., 14; parishes, 3,047; priests, 6,010 (3,559 dioc., 2,451 rel.); sem., 365; p.d., 88; bros., 712; srs., 12,160; sch., 315; bap., 79,336; Caths., 6,613,400 (88%); tot. pop., 7,520,000.

Azores: North Atlantic island group 750 miles west of Portugal, of which it is part. Christianity was introduced in the second quarter of the 15th century.

Bahamas: Independent (July 10, 1973) island group in the British Commonwealth, consisting of some 700 (30 inhabited) small islands southeast of Florida and north of Cuba; capital, Nassau. On Oct. 12, 1492, Columbus landed on one of these islands, where the first Mass was celebrated in the New World. Organization of the Catholic Church in the Bahamas dates from about the middle of the 19th century. Voted to establish diplomatic relations with Vatican City in 1979.

Dioc., 1; bp., 1; parishes, 32; priests, 47 (10 dioc., 37 rel.); sem., 5; p.d., 4; bros., 4; srs., 66; sch., 18; bap., 1,420; Caths., 26,340 (12%); tot. pop., 226,080.

Bahrain: Island state in Persian Gulf; capital, Manama. Under ecclesiastical jurisdiction of Arabia vicariate apostolic.

Priests, 2 (rel); srs., 12; sch., 2; studs., 1,212; bap., 115; Caths., 4,000 (1.5%) tot. pop., 259,000.

Balearic Islands: Spanish province consisting of an island group in the western Mediterranean. Statistics are included in those for Spain.

Bangladesh: Formerly the eastern portion of Pakistan. Officially constituted as a separate nation Dec. 16, 1971; capital, Dacca. Islam is the principal religion; freedom of religion is granted. There were Jesuit, Dominican and Augustinian missionaries in the area in the 16th century. A vicariate apostolic (of Bengali) was established in 1834; the hierarchy was erected in 1950. Bangladesh established diplomatic relations with Vatican City in 1972.

Archd., 1; dioc., 3; abp., 1 (nat.); bp., 3 (nat.); parishes, 42; priests, 147 (42 dioc., 105 rel.); sem., 38; bros., 48; srs., 455; sch., 331; bap., 7,132; Caths., 147,060 (.18%); tot. pop. 79,614,020.

Barbados: Parliamentary democracy in the British Commonwealth (independent since 1966), easternmost of the Caribbean islands; capital, Bridgetown. About 70 per cent of the people are Anglicans. Voted to establish diplomatic relations with Vatican City in 1979.

Dioc., 1; bp., 1; parishes, 6; priests, 9 (3 dioc., 6 rel.); bros., 5; srs., 66; sch., 5; bap., 261; Caths., 10,000 (4%); tot. pop., 247,000 (1977).

Belgium: Constitutional monarchy in northwestern Europe; capital, Brussels. Christianity was introduced about the first quarter of the fourth century and major evangelization was completed about 730. During the rest of the medieval period the Church had firm diocesan and parochial organization, generally vigorous monastic life, and influential monastic and cathedral schools. Lutherans and Calvinists made some gains during the Reformation period but there was a strong Catholic restoration in the first half of the 17th century, when the country was under Spanish rule. Jansenism disturbed the Church from about 1640 into the 18th century. Josephinism, imposed by an Austrian regime, hampered the Church late in the same century. Repressive and persecutory measures were enforced during the Napoleonic conquest. Freedom came with separation of Church and state in the wake of the Revolution of 1830, which ended the reign of William I. Thereafter, the Church encountered serious problems with philosophical liberalism and political socialism. Catholics have long been engaged in strong educational, social and political movements. Except for one five-year period (1880-1884), Belgium has maintained diplomatic relations with Vatican City since 1835.

Archd., 1; dioc., 7; card., 1; bp., 14; parishes, 3,921; priests, 13,305 (8,443 dioc., 4,862 rel.); sem., 311; p.d., 162; bros., 2,302; srs., 27,589; sch., 4,978; bap., 106,598; Caths., 8,997,980 (90.7%); tot. pop., 9,920,261.

Belize (formerly British Honduras): Self-governing colony in Central America; capital, Belmopan. Its history has points in common with Guatemala, where evangelization began in the 16th century.

Dioc., 1; bp., 1; parishes, 12; priests, 38 (11 dioc., 27 rel.); sem., 4; bros., 9; srs., 79; sch., 111; bap., 3,541; Caths., 87,000 (60%); tot. pop., 145,000.

Benin (formerly Dahomey): Republic in west Africa, bordering on the Atlantic; member of the French Community; capitals, Cotonou, Porto Novo. Missionary work was very limited from the 16th to the 18th centuries. Effective evangelization dates from 1894. The hierarchy was established in 1955. The majority of Christians are Catholics. Benin maintains diplomatic relations with Vatican City.

Archd., 1; dioc., 5; card., 1 (nat.); abp., 1 (nat.); bp., 5 (4 nat.); parishes, 114; priests, 151 (74 dioc., 77 rel.); sem., 28; bros., 19; srs., 333; sch., 6; bap., 12,283; Caths., 500,770 (15.2%); tot. pop., 3,290,000.

Bermuda: British dependency, consisting of 360 islands (20 of them inhabited) nearly 600 miles east of Cape Hatteras; capital, Hamilton. Catholics were not permitted until about 1800. Occasional pastoral care was provided the few Catholics there by visiting priests during the 19th century. Early in the 1900's priests from Halifax began serving the area. A prefecture apostolic was set up in 1953. The first bishop assumed jurisdiction in 1956. The only Catholic school in Bermuda was the first to admit black students, in 1961.

Dioc., 1; bp., 1; parishes, 7; priests, 9 (1 dioc., 8 rel.); p.d., 1; bros., 8; srs., 9; sch., 2; bap., 111; Caths., 9,000 (15.5%); tot. pop., 58,000.

Bhutan: Constitutional monarchy in the Himalayas, northeast of India; capital, Thimphu. Most of the population are Buddhists. Ecclesiastical jurisdiction is under the Darjeeling diocese, India.

Parish, 1; priests, 8 (rel.); bros., 6; srs., 8; sch., 6; bap., 11; Caths., 200; tot. pop., 1,202,000 (1977).

Bolivia: Republic in central South America; capital, Sucre; seat of government, La Paz. Catholicism, the official religion, was introduced in the 1530's and the first bishopric was established in 1552. Effective evangelization among the Indians, slow to start, reached high points in the middle of the 18th and the beginning of the 19th centuries and was resumed about 1840. Independence from Spain was proclaimed in 1825, at the end of a campaign that started in 1809. The republic inherited the Spanish right of nominating candidates for bishoprics. Church-state relations are regulated by a 1951 concordat with the Holy See. Bolivia maintains diplomatic relations with Vatican City.

Archd., 4; dioc., 3; prel., 3; v.a., 6; card., 1; abp., 3; bp., 19; parishes, 425; priests, 805 (220 dioc., 585 rel.); sem., 93; p.d., 15; bros., 191; srs., 1,440; sch., 932; bap., 173,407; Caths., 5,522,590 (93.8%); tot. pop., 5,886,230.

Botswana: Republic (independent since 1966) in southern Africa, member of the British Commonwealth; capital, Gaborone. Botswana has an apostolic delegate (to South Africa).

Dioc., 1; bp., 1; priests, 24 (3 dioc., 21 rel.); bros., 2; srs., 53; sch., 12; bap., 1,814; Caths., 28,200 (3.7%); tot. pop., 750,000.

Brazil: Republic in northeast South America; capital, Brasilia. One of several priests with the discovery party celebrated the first Mass in the country Apr. 26, 1500. Evangelization began some years later and the first diocese was erected in 1551. During the colonial period, which lasted until 1822, evangelization made some notable progress—especially in the Amazon region between 1680 and 1750 — but was seriously hindered by government policy and the attitude of colonists regarding Amazon Indians the missionaries tried to protect from exploitation and slavery. The Jesuits were suppressed in 1782 and other missionaries expelled as well. Liberal anti-Church influence grew in strength. The government gave minimal support but exercised maximum control over the Church. After the proclamation of independence from Portugal in 1822 and throughout the regency, government control was tightened and the Church suffered greatly from dissident actions of ecclesiastical brotherhoods, Masonic anti-clericalism and general decline in religious life. Church and state were separated by the constitution of 1891, proclaimed two years after the end of the empire. The Church carried into the 20th century a load of inherited liabilities and problems amid increasingly difficult political, economic and social conditions affecting the majority of the population. A number of bishops, priests, religious and lay persons have been active in movements for social and religious reform. Brazil maintains diplomatic relations with Vatican City.

Archd., 33; dioc., 146; prel., 42; abb., 2; ord., 1; card., 7; abp., 35; bp., 226; parishes, 6,196; priests, 12,676 (5,026 dioc., 7,650 rel.); sem., 2,761; p.d., 220; bros., 2,744; srs., 35,457; sch., 4,247; bap., 2,612,757, Caths., 98,589,000 (90.3%); tot. pop., 109,181,000 (1977).

Brunei: State under British protection, on the northern coast of Borneo; capital, Brunei. Under ecclesiastical jurisdiction of Miri diocese, Malaysia.

Parishes, 3; priests, 6 (2 dioc., 4 rel.); srs., 4; sch., 7; bap., 166; Caths., 5,000 (2.8%); tot. pop., 177,000 (1977).

Bulgaria: People's republic in southeastern Europe on the eastern part of the Balkan peninsula; capital, Sofia. Christianity was introduced before 343 but disappeared with the migration of Slavs into the territory. The baptism of Boris I about 865 ushered in a new period of Christianity which soon became involved in switches of loyalty between Constantinople and Rome. Through it all the Byzantine, and later Orthodox, element remained stronger and survived under the rule of Ottoman Turks into the 19th century. The few modern Latin Catholics in the country are traceable to 17th century converts from heresy. The Byzantines are products of a reunion movement of the 19th century. In 1947 the constitution of the new republic decreed the separation of Church and state. Catholic schools and institutions were abolished and foreign religious banished in 1948. A year later the apostolic delegate was expelled. Ivan Romanoff, vicar general of Plovdiv, died in prison in 1952. Bishop Eugene Bossilkoff, imprisoned in 1948, was sentenced to death in 1952; his fate remained unknown until 1975 when the Bulgarian government informed the Vatican that he had died in prison shortly after being sentenced. Roman and Bulgarian Rite vicars apostolic were permitted to attend the Second Vatican Council from 1962 to 1965. All church activity is under surveillance and/or control by the government, which professes to be atheistic. Pastoral and related activities are strictly limited. Most of the population is Orthodox. There was some improvement in Bulgarian-Vatican relations in 1975, following a visit of Bulgarian President Todor Zhivkov to Pope Paul VI June 19 and talks between Vatican and Bulgarian representatives at the Helsinki Conference in late July. The needs of the church in Bulgaria were outlined by Pope John Paul II in a private audience with the Bulgarian foreign minister in December, 1978 (see December News Events). In 1979, the Sofia-Plovdiv vicariate apostolic was raised to a diocese and a bishop was appointed for the vacant see of Nicopoli.

Dioc., 2; ap. ex., 1; bp., 3; Caths. (est.), 65,000 (.7%); tot. pop., 8,800,000.

Burma: Union of Burma, a republic in southeast Asia, on the Bay of Bengal; capital, Rangoon. Christianity was introduced about 1500. Small-scale evangelization had limited results from the middle of the 16th century until the 1850's when effective organization of the Church began. The hierarchy was established in 1955. Buddhism was declared the state religion in 1961, but the state is now officially secular. In 1965, church schools and hospitals were nationalized. In 1966, all foreign missionaries who had entered the country after 1948 for the first time were forced to leave when the government refused to renew their work permits. Despite these setbacks, the Church has shown some progress in recent years. Burma has an apostolic delegate (pro-nuncio to Bangladesh).

Archd., 2; dioc., 6; p.a., 1; abp., 2 (nat.); bp., 6 (5 nat.); parishes, 126; priests, 213 (171 dioc., 42 rel.); sem., 80; bros., 48; srs., 627; bap., 20,009; Caths., 350,550 (1.1%); tot. pop., 31,510,000.

Burundi: Republic since 1966, near the equator in east-central Africa; capital, Bujumbura. The first permanent Catholic mission station was established late in the 19th century. Large numbers of persons were received into the Church following the ordination of the first Burundi priests in 1925. The first native bishop was appointed in 1959. Most education takes place in schools under Catholic auspices. In 1972-73, the country was torn by tribal warfare between the Tutsis, the ruling minority, and the Hutus. Burundi maintains diplomatic relations with Vatican City.

Archd., 1; dioc., 5; abp., 1 (nat.); bp., 4 (nat.); parishes, 182; priests, 391 (164 dioc., 227 rel.); sem., 62; p.d., 1; bros., 147; srs., 697; sch., 402; bap., 66,164; Caths., 2,137,140 (53.8%); tot. pop., 3,970,000.

Cambodia: See Kampuchea.

Cameroon: Republic in west Africa, bordering on the Gulf of Guinea; capital, Yaounde. Effective evangelization began in the 1890's, although Catholics had been in the country long before that time. In the 40-year period from 1920 to 1960, the number of Catholics increased from 60,000 to 700,000. The first native priests were ordained in 1935. Twenty years later the first native bishops were ordained and the hierarchy established.

Cameroon maintains diplomatic relations with Vatican City.

Archd., 1; dioc., 12; abp., 1 (nat.); bp., 12 (7 nat.); parishes, 292; priests, 729 (263 dioc., 466 rel.); sem., 205; p.d., 21; bros., 216; srs., 1,191; sch., 993; bap., 64,976; Caths. (est.), 1,734,200 (26%); tot. pop., 6,670,000.

Canada: Independent federation in the British Commonwealth, comprising the northern half of North America; capital, Ottawa. Canada maintains diplomatic relations with Vatican City. (See The Church in Canada.)

Archd., 18; dioc., 51; abb., 1; card., 4; abp., 16; bp., 107 (includes 36 retired); parishes 5,836; priests, 13,050 (7,734 dioc., 5,316 rel.); bros., 4,418; srs., 40,241; Caths., 9,991,243 (42.6%); tot. pop., 23,444,200. (Statistics are from 1979 Directory of Canadian Conference of Catholic Bishops.)

Canary Islands: Two Spanish provinces, consisting of seven islands, off the northwest coast of Africa. Evangelization began about 1400. Almost all of the one million inhabitants are Catholics. Statistics are included in those for Spain.

Cape Verde Islands: Independent (July 5, 1975) island group in the Atlantic 300 miles west of Senegal; formerly a Portuguese overseas province; capital, Praia, San Tiago Island. Evangelization began some years before the estadablishment of the first diocese in 1532. Cape Verde Islands established diplomatic relations with Vatican City in 1976.

Dioc., 1; bp., 1; parishes, 30; priests, 50 (13 dioc., 37 rel.); bros., 4; srs., 32; sch., 7; bap., 5,162; Caths., 283,370 (91%); tot. pop., 310,000.

Caroline and Marshall Islands: U.S. trust territory in the southwest Pacific; scheduled for independence in 1981. Effective evangelization began in the late 1880's.

Dioc., 1; bp., 1; parishes, 22; priests, 34 (2 dioc., 32 rel.); sem., 6; p.d., 22; bros., 7; srs., 39; sch., 12; bap., 1,559; Caths., 47,360 (42%); tot. pop., 111,700.

Cayman Islands: British colony in Caribbean; capital, George Town on Grand Cayman. Under ecclesiastical jurisdiction of Kingston diocese, Jamaica.

Priest, 1 (rel.); sch., 1 (elementary); bap., 15; Caths., 200; tot. pop., 11,000 (1977).

Central African Republic: Former French colony (independent since 1960) in central Africa; capital, Bangui. Effective evangelization dates from 1894. The region was organized as a mission territory in 1909. The first native priest was ordained in 1938. The hierarchy was organized in 1955. The Central African Republic established diplomatic relations with Vatican City in 1975.

Archd., 1; dioc., 5; abp., 1 (nat.); bp., 4; parishes, 68; priests, 196 (28 dioc., 168 rel.); sem., 37; p.d., 1; bros., 55; srs., 285; sch., 18; bap., 13,4084 Caths., 325,870 (15.5%); tot. pop., 2,102,480.

Ceuta: Spanish possession (city) on the northern tip of Africa, south of Gibraltar. Statistics are included in those for Spain.

Ceylon: See Sri Lanka, Republic of.

Chad: Republic (independent since 1960) in north-central Africa, member of the French Community; capital, N'Djamena (Fort Lamy). Evangelization began in 192', leading to firm organization in 1947 and establishment of the hierarchy in 1955. Chad has an apostolic delegate (pro-nuncio, Central African Republic).

Archd., 1; dioc., 3; abp., 1; bp., 3 (1 nat.); parishes, 12; priests, 167 (20 dioc., 147 rel.); sem., 11; bros., 36; srs., 216; sch., 54; bap., 7,925; Caths., 222,310 (5.2%); tot. pop., 4,200,000.

Chile: Republic on the southwestern coast of South America; capital, Santiago. Priests were with the Spanish conquistadores on their entrance into the territory early in the 16th century. The first parish was established in 1547 and the first bishopric in 1561. Overall organization of the Church took place later in the century. By 1650 most of the peaceful Indians in the central and northern areas were evangelized. Missionary work was more difficult in the southern region. Church activity was hampered during the campaign for independence, 1810 to 1818, and through the first years of the new government, to 1830. Later gains were made, into this century, but hindering factors were shortages of native clergy and religious and attempts by the government to control church administration through the patronage system in force while the country was under Spanish control. Separation of Church and state were decreed in the constitution of 1925. Church-state relations were strained during the regine of Marxist president Salvator Allende Gossens (1970-73). He was overthrown in a bloody coup and was reported to have committed suicide Sept. 11, 1973. Conditions remained unsettled under the military government which assumed control after the coup. Since 1974, the Chilean bishops have issued several statements criticizing government policies violating human rights and urging release of political prisoners. The Church-backed Vicariate of Solidarity was established in 1976 to give legal aid to political prisoners and aid eir families. Chile maintains diplomatic relations with Vatican City.

Archd., 5; dioc., 14; prel., 3; v.a., 2; card., 1; abp., 4; bp., 22; parishes, 798; priests, 2,030 (706 dioc., 1,324 rel.); sem., 286; p.d., 169; bros., 364; srs., 4,718; sch., 779; bap., 169,154; Caths., 9,271,874 (86.6%); tot. pop., 10,700,000.

China *(This article concerns mainland China which has been under Communist control since 1949):* People's Republic in eastern part of

Asia; capital, Peking. Christianity was introduced by Nestorians who had some influence on part of the area from 635 to 845 and again from the 11th century until 1368. John of Monte Corvino started a Franciscan mission in 1294; he was ordained an archbishop about 1307. Missionary activity involving more priests increased for a while thereafter but the Franciscan mission ended in 1368. The Jesuit Matteo Ricci initiated a remarkable period of activity in the 1580's. By 1700 the number of Catholics was reported to be 300,000. The Chinese Rites controversy, concerning the adaptation of rituals and other matters to Chinese traditions and practices, ran throughout the 17th century, ending in a negative decision by mission authorities in Rome. Bl. Francis de Capillas, the protomartyr of China, was killed in 1648. Persecution, a feature of Chinese history as recurrent as changes in dynasties, occurred several times in the 18th century and resulted in the departure of most missionaries from the country. The Chinese door swung open again in the 1840's and progress in evangelization increased with an extension of legal and social tolerance. At the turn of the 20th century, however, the Boxer Rebellion took one or the other kind of toll among an estimated 30,000 victims. Missionary work in the 1900's reached a new high in every respect before the disaster of persecution initiated by Communists before and especially since they established the republic in 1949. The Reds began a savage persecution as soon as they came into power. Among its results were the expulsion of over 5,000 foreign missionaries, 510 of whom were American priests, brothers and nuns; the arrest, imprisonment and harassment of all members of the native religious, clergy and hierarchy; the forced closing of 3,932 schools, 216 hospitals, 781 dispensaries, 254 orphanages, 29 printing presses and 55 periodicals; denial of the free exercise of religion to all the faithful; the detention of hundreds of priests, religious and lay persons in jail and their employment in slave labor; the proscription of the Legion of Mary and other Catholic Action groups for "counter-revolutionary activities" and "crimes against the new China"; complete outlawing of missionary work and pastoral activity. The government formally established a Patriotic Association of Chinese Catholics in July, 1957. Relatively few priests and lay persons joined the organization, which was condemned by Pius XII in 1958. The government formed the nucleus of what it hoped might become the hierarchy of a schismatic Chinese church by "electing" 26 bishops and having them consecrated validly but illicitly between Apr. 13, 1958, and Nov. 15, 1959, without the permission or approval of the Holy See. By Jan. 21, 1962, a total of 42 bishops were consecrated in this manner. In March, 1960, Bishop James E. Walsh, M.M., the last American missionary in China, was sentenced and placed in custody for a period of 20 years. He was released in the summer of 1970. There seemed to be an opening to the West by China in 1979. What this might mean for the Church in that country is open to question.

Archd., 20; dioc., 93; p.a., 29. No Catholic statistics are available. In 1949 there were between 3,500,000-4,000,000 Catholics, about .7 per cent of the total population; the 1969 "CSMC World Mission Map" estimated 3,200,000 Catholics, .5 per cent of the population. The latter figure is only an estimate; there is no way of knowing the actual situation. Tot. pop. (1977 est.), 865,680,000.

Colombia: Republic in northwest South America, with Atlantic and Pacific borders; capital, Bogota. Evangelization began in 1508. The first two dioceses were established in 1534. Vigorous development of the Church was reported by the middle of the 17th century despite obstacles posed by the multiplicity of Indian languages, government interference through patronage rights and otherwise, rivalry among religious orders and the small number of native priests among the predominantly Spanish clergy. Some persecution, including the confiscation of property, followed in the wake of the proclamation of independence from Spain in 1819. The Church was affected in many ways by the political and civil unrest of the nation through the 19th century and into the 20th. Various aspects of Church-state relations are regulated by a concordat with the Vatican signed July 12, 1973, and ratified July 2, 1975. The new concordat replaced one which had been in effect with some modifications since 1887. In late 1976, the bishops released a statement reaffirming their concern for social justice but rejecting actions of radical Catholic groups such as Priests for Latin America and Christians for Socialism as Marxist-oriented and destructive of Church unity. Colombia maintains diplomatic relations with Vatican City.

Archd., 11; dioc., 30; prel., 2; v.a., 7; p.a., 7; card., 1; abp., 10; bp., 48; parishes, 2,168; priests, 5,126 (3,117 dioc., 2,009 rel.); sem., 882; p.d., 10; bros., 1,194; srs., 18,072; sch., 2,441; bap., 654,340; Caths., 24,652,800 (96.3%); tot. pop., 25,600,000.

Comoro Islands: Consists of main islands of Grande Comore, Anjouan, Moheli and Mayotte in Indian Ocean off southeast coast of Africa; capital, Moroni, Grande Comore Island. Former French territory; independent (July 6, 1975) except Mayotte which voted to remain part of France. The majority of the population is Moslem. An apostolic administration for Catholics (formerly under administration of the Ambanja diocese, Madagascar) was established June 20, 1975.

A.a., 1; bp., 1; priests, 3 (rel.); srs., 1; bap., 14; Caths., 1,200 (.3%); tot. pop., 370,000.

Congo Republic: Republic in west central Africa, member of the French Community; capital, Brazzaville. Small-scale missionary work with little effect preceded modern evangelization dating from the 1880's. The work of the Church has been affected by political instability, Communist influence, tribalism and hostility to foreigners. The hierarchy was established in 1955. Congo established diplomatic relations with the Vatican in 1977.

Archd., 1; dioc., 2; abp., 1 (nat.); bp., 2 (nat); parishes, 57; priests, 127 (47 dioc., 80 rel.); sem., 34; bros., 17; srs., 101; sch., 9; bap., 10,375; Caths., 492,540 (40.5%); tot. pop., 1,216,800 (some statistics are from 1976).

Cook Islands: Self-governing territory of New Zealand, an archipelago of small islands in Oceania. Evangelization by Protestant missionaries started in 1821, resulting in a predominantly Protestant population. The first Catholic missionary work began in 1894. The hierarchy was established in 1966.

Dioc., 1; bp., 1; parishes, 12; priests, 10 (1 dioc., 9 rel.); bros., 3; srs., 14; sch., 3; bap., 101; Caths., 2,690 (12%); tot. pop., 21,970.

Costa Rica: Republic in Central America; capital, San Jose. Evangelization began about 1520 and proceeded by degrees to real development and organization of the Church in the 17th and 18th centuries. The republic became independent in 1838. Twelve years later church jurisdiction also became independent with the establishment of a bishopric in the present capital. Costa Rica maintains diplomatic relations with Vatican City.

Archd., 1; dioc., 3; v.a., 1; abp., 1; bp., 4; parishes, 155; priests, 390 (255 dioc., 135 rel.); sem., 102; p.d., 10; bros., 36; srs., 830; sch., 55; bap., 52,841; Caths., 1,972,390 (95.5%); tot. pop., 2,063,170.

Cuba: Republic under Communist dictatorship, south of Florida; capital, Havana. Effective evangelization began about 1514, leading eventually to the predominance of Catholicism on the island. Native vocations to the priesthood and religious life were unusually numerous in the 18th century but declined in the 19th. The island became independent of Spain in 1902 following the Spanish-American War. Fidel Castro took control of the government Jan. 1, 1959. In 1961, after Cuba was officially declared a socialist state, the University of Villanueva was closed, 350 Catholic schools were nationalized and 136 priests expelled. A greater number of foreign priests and religious had already left the country. Freedom of worship and religious instruction are limited to church premises and no social action is permitted the Church, which survives under surveillance. A new constitution approved in 1976 guaranteed freedom of conscience but restricted its exercise. Cuba maintains diplomatic relations with Vatican City.

Archd., 2; dioc., 5 (new one erected in 1979); abp., 2; bp., 5; parishes, 220; priests, 213 (115 dioc., 98 rel.); sem., 48; bros., 26; srs., 215; bap., 25,458; Caths. (est.), 3,963,000 (41.6%); tot. pop., 9,460,000.

Cyprus: Republic in the eastern Mediterranean; capital, Nicosia. Christianity was preached on the island in apostolic times and has a continuous history from the fourth century. Latin and Eastern rites were established but the latter prevailed and became Orthodox after the schism of 1054. Roman and Orthodox Christians have suffered under many governments, particularly during the period of Turkish dominion from late in the 16th to late in the 19th centuries, and from differences between the 80 per cent Greek majority and the Turkish minority. About 80 per cent of the population are Orthodox. Cyprus established diplomatic relations with Vatican City in 1973. Maronite Rite Catholics are under the jurisdiction of the archdiocese of Cyprus (of the Maronites), whose archbishop resides in Lebanon. Roman Rite Catholics are under the jurisdiction of the Roman Rite patriarchate of Jerusalem.

Archd., 1 (Maronite); abp., 1 (resides in Lebanon); parishes, 8; priests, 15 (rel.); bros., 1; srs., 97; sch., 12; bap., 26; Caths., 6,000 (.9%); tot. pop., 639,000 (1977).

Czechoslovakia: Federal socialist republic (since 1969) in Central Europe, consisting of the Czech Socialist Republic, capital Prague; and the Slovak Socialist Republic, capital Bratislava. The republics have local autonomy but are subordinate to the Federal Assembly at Prague made up of representatives from both regions. The Czech and Slovak regions of the country have separate religious and cultural backgrounds. Christianity was introduced in Slovakia in the 8th century by Irish and German missionaries and the area was under the jurisdiction of German bishops. In 863, at the invitation of the Slovak ruler Rastislav who wanted to preserve the cultural and liturgical heritage of the people, Sts. Cyril and Methodius began pastoral and missionary work in the region, ministering to the people in their own language. The saints introduced Old Slovak (Old Church Slavonic) into the liturgy and did so much to evangelize the territory that they are venerated as the apostles of Slovakia. A diocese established at Nitra in 880 had a continuous history except for a century ending in 1024. The Church in Slovakia was severely tested by the Reformation and political upheavals. After World War I, when it became part of the Republic of Czechoslovakia, it was 75 per cent Catholic. In the Czech lands, the martyrdom of Prince Wenceslaus in 929 triggered the spread of Christianity. Prague has had a continuous history as a diocese since 973. A parish system was organized about the 13th century in Bohemia and Moravia, the land of the Czechs. Mendicant orders strengthened relations with the Latin Rite in the 13th century. In the next century the teachings of John Hus in Bohemia brought trouble to the Church in the forms of schism and heresy, and initiated a series of religious wars which continued for decades following his death at the stake in 1415. Church property was confiscated, monastic communities were scattered and even murdered, ecclesiastical organization was shattered, and so many of the faithful joined the Bohemian Brethren that Catholics became a minority. The Reformation, with the way prepared by the Hussites and cleared by other factors, affected the Church seriously. A Counter Reformation got underway in the 1560's and led to a gradual restoration through the thickets of Josephinism, the Enlightenment, liberalism and troubled politics. In 1920, two years after the establishment of the Republic of Czechoslovakia, the schismatic Czechoslovak Church was proclaimed at Prague, resulting in numerous defections from the Catholic Church in the Czech region. In Ruthenia, 112,000 became Russian Orthodox between 1918 and 1930. Vigorous persecution of the church began in Slovakia before the end of World War II when Communists mounted a 1944 offensive against bishops, priests and religious. In 1945, church schools were nationalized, youth organizations were disbanded, the Catholic press was curtailed, the training of students for the priesthood was seriously impeded. Msgr. Josef Tiso, president of the Slovak Republic, was tried for "treason" in December, 1947, and was executed the following April. Between 1945 and 1949 approximately 10 per cent of the Slovak population spent some time in jail or a concentration camp. Persecution began later in the Czech part of the country, following the accession of the Gottwald regime to power early in 1948. Hospitals, schools and property were nationalized and Catholic organizations were liquidated. A puppet organization was formed in 1949 to infiltrate the Church and implement an unsuccessful plan for establishing a schismatic church. In the same year Archbishop Josef Beran of Prague was placed under house arrest. (He left the country in 1965, was made a cardinal, and died in 1969 in Rome.) A number of theatrical trials of bishops and priests were staged in 1950. All houses of religious were taken over between March, 1950, and the end of 1951. An Eastern Rite diocese, Presov, in Slovakia, was dissolved in 1950 and pressure was applied on the clergy and faithful to join the Orthodox Church. Diplomatic relations with Vatican City were terminated in 1950. About 3,000 priests were deprived of liberty in 1951 and attempts were made to force "peace priests" on the people. In 1958 it was reported that 450 to 500 priests were in jail; an undisclosed number of religious and Byzantine Rite priests had been deported; two bishops released from prison in 1956 were under house arrest; one bishop was imprisoned at Leopoldov and two at the Mirov reformatory. In Bohemia, Moravia and Silesia, five of six dioceses were without ruling bishops; one archbishop and two bishops were active but subject to "supervision"; most of the clergy refused to join the "peace priests." In 1962 only three bishops were permitted to attend the first session of the Second Vatican Council. From January to October, 1968, Church-state relations improved to some extent under the Dubcek regime: a number of bishops were reinstated; some 3,000 priests were engaged in the pastoral ministry, although 1,500 were still barred from priestly work; the "peace priests" organization was disbanded; the Eastern Rite Church, with 147 parishes, was reestablished. In 1969, an end was ordered to rehabilitation trials for priests and religious, but no wholesale restoration of priests and religious to their proper ways of life and work was in prospect. In 1972 the government ordered the removal of nuns from visible but limited apostolates to farms and mental hospitals where they would be out of sight. In 1973, the government allowed the ordination of four bishops — one in the Czech region and three in the Slovak region. Reports from Slovakia late in the same year stated that authorities there had placed severe restrictions on the education of seminarians and the functioning of priests. Government restrictions continued to hamper the work of priests and nuns in recent years. Talks between Vatican and Czech officials, held since 1974, have had some results.

Archd., 3; dioc., 10; card., 1; bp., 6 (1 impeded); parishes, 4,112; priests, 3,920 (3,452 dioc., 468 rel.); sem., 242; bros., 47; srs., 4,340; bap., 127,758; Caths. (est.), 10,821,600 (72%); tot. pop., 15,030,000.

Dahomey: See Benin.

Danzig (Gdansk): Baltic seaport at the mouth of the Vistula River; incorporated into Poland after World War II. The diocese has a Christian history dating from the 10th century. Statistics are included in those for Poland.

Denmark, including the Faroe Islands and Greenland: Constitutional monarchy in northwestern Europe, north of West Germany; capital, Copenhagen. Christianity was introduced in the ninth century and the first diocese for the area was established in 831. Intensive evangelization and full-scale organization of the Church occurred from the second half of the 10th century and ushered in a period of great development and influence in the 12th and 13th centuries. Decline followed, resulting in almost total loss to the Church during the Reformation when Lutheranism became the national religion. Catholics were considered foreigners until religious freedom was legally assured in 1849. Modern development of the Church dates from the second half of the 19th century. About 95 per cent of the population are Evangelical Lutherans. Denmark has an apostolic delegate (to Scandinavia).

Dioc., 1; bp., 1; parishes, 52; priests, 109 (34 dioc., 75 rel.); sem., 5; bros., 8; srs., 550; sch., 32; bap., 374; Caths., 26,750 (.5%); tot. pop., 5,090,000.

Djibouti (formerly French Territory of Afars and Issas): Independent (1977) republic in east Africa, on the Gulf of Aden; capital, Djibouti. Christianity in the area, formerly part of Ethiopia, antedated but was overcome by the Arab invasion of 1200. Modern evangelization, begun in the latter part of the 19th century, had meager results. The hierarchy was established in 1955. The territory has an apostolic delegate (to the Red Sea Region).

Dioc., 1; bp., 1; parishes, 9 (1 dioc., 8 rel.); p.d., 1; bros., 12; srs., 23; sch., 15; bap., 20; Caths., 12,000; tot. pop., 300,000.

Dominica: Independent (Nov. 3, 1978) state in Caribbean; capital, Roseau. Evangelization began in 1642.

Dioc., 1; bp., 1; parishes, 16; priests, 24 (3 dioc., 21 rel.); sem., 1; p.d., 1; bros., 4; srs., 37; sch., 6; bap., 1,331; Caths., 67,000 (88%); tot. pop., 76,000.

Dominican Republic: Caribbean republic on the eastern two-thirds of the island of Hispaniola, bordering on Haiti; capital, Santo Domingo. Evangelization began shortly after discovery by Columbus in 1492 and church organization, the first in America, was established by 1510. Catholicism is the state religion. The Dominican Republic maintains diplomatic relations with Vatican City.

Archd., 1; dioc., 7; card., 1; abp., 2; bp., 9; parishes, 197; priests, 499 (108 dioc., 391 rel.); sem., 92; p.d., 19; bros., 63; srs., 1,380; sch., 277; bap., 80,680; Caths., 4,730,450 (94.2%); tot. pop., 5,020,640.

Ecuador: Republic on the west coast of South America; capital, Quito. Evangelization began in the 1530's. The first diocese was established in 1545. A synod, one of the first in the Americas, was held in 1570 or 1594. Multiphased missionary work, spreading from the coastal and mountain regions into the Amazon, made the Church highly influential during the colonial period. The Church was practically enslaved by the constitution enacted in 1824, two years after Ecuador, as part of Colombia, gained independence from Spain. Some change for the better took place later in the century, but from 1891 until the 1930's the Church labored under serious liabilities imposed by liberal governments. The concordat of 1866 was violated; foreign missionaries were barred from the country for some time; the property of religious orders was confiscated; education was taken over by the state; traditional state support was refused; legal standing was denied; attempts to control church offices were made through insistence on rights of patronage. A period of harmony and independence for the Church began after agreement was reached on Church-state relations in 1937. Ecuador maintains diplomatic relations with Vatican City.

Archd., 3; dioc., 10; prel., 1; v.a., 5; p.a., 3; card., 1; abp., 2; bp., 21; parishes, 671; priests, 1,354 (611 dioc., 743 rel.); sem., 69; p.d., 8; bros., 371; srs., 3,740; sch., 935; bap., 215,128; Caths., 6,889,420 (92.7%); tot. pop., 7,430,302.

Egypt, Arab Republic of: Republic in northeastern Africa, bordering on the Mediterranean; capital, Cairo. Alexandria was the influential hub of a Christian community established by the end of the second century; it became a patriarchate and the center of the Coptic Church, and had great influence on the spread of Christianity in various parts of Africa; Monasticism developed from desert communities of hermits in the third and fourth centuries. Arianism was first preached in Egypt in the 320's. In the fifth century, the Coptic church went Monophysite through failure to accept doctrine formulated by the Council of Chalcedon in 451 with respect to the two natures of Christ. The country was thoroughly Arabized after 640 and was under the rule of Ottoman Turks from 1517 to 1798. English influence was strong during the 19th century. A monarchy established in 1922 lasted about 30 years, ending with the proclamation of a republic in 1953-54. By that time Egypt had become the leader of pan-Arabism against Israel. It waged two unsuccessful wars against Israel in 1948-49 and 1967. Between 1958 and 1961 it was allied with Syria and Yemen, in the United Arab Republic. Islam, the religion of some 90 percent of the population, is the state religion. Egypt maintains diplomatic relations with Vatican City.

Patriarchate, 2 (Alexandria for the Copts and for the Melkites); dioc., 6; v.a., 3; card., 1; bp., 12; parishes, 212; priests, 353 (167 dioc., 186 rel.); sem., 68; p.d., 1; bros., 75; srs., 1,702; sch., 238; bap., 2,024; Caths., 138,305 (.35%); tot. pop., 38,740,000.

El Salvador: Republic in Central America; capital, San Salvador. Evangelization affecting the whole territory followed Spanish occupation in the 1520's. The country was administered by the captaincy general of Guatemala until 1821 when independence from Spain was declared and it was annexed to Mexico. El Salvador joined the Central American Federation in 1825, decreed its own independence in 1841 and became a republic formally in 1856. In recent years, Church efforts to achieve social justice have resulted in persecution of the Church. (See Index for 1979 events.) El Salvador maintains diplomatic relations with Vatican City.

Archd., 1; dioc., 4; abp., 1; bp., 5; parishes, 229; priests, 373 (173 dioc., 200 rel.); sem., 69;

bros., 70; srs., 735; sch., 161; bap., 120,690; Caths., 3,782,916 (91.1%); tot. pop., 4,150,189.

England: Center of the United Kingdom of Great Britain (England, Scotland, Wales) and Northern Ireland, off the northwestern coast of Europe; capital, London. The arrival of St. Augustine of Canterbury and a band of monks in 597 marked the beginning of evangelization. Real organization of the Church took place some years after the Synod of Whitby, held in 663. Heavy losses were sustained in the wake of the Danish invasion in the 780's, but recovery starting from the time of Alfred the Great and dating especially from the middle of the 10th century led to Christianization of the whole country and close Church-state relations. The Norman Conquest of 1066 opened the Church in England to European influence. The 13th century was climactic, but decline had already set in by 1300 when the country had an all-time high of 17,000 religious. In the 14th century, John Wycliff presaged the Protestant Reformation. Henry VIII, failing in 1529 to gain annulment of his marriage to Catherine of Aragon, refused to acknowledge papal authority over the Church in England, had himself proclaimed its head, suppressed all houses of religious, and persecuted persons — Sts. Thomas More and John Fisher, among others — for not subscribing to the Oath of Supremacy and Act of Succession. He held the line on other-than-papal doctrine, however, until his death in 1547. Doctrinal aberrations were introduced during the reign of Edward VI (1547-53), through the Order of Communion, two books of Common Prayer, and the Articles of the Established Church. Mary Tudor's attempted Catholic restoration (1553-58) was a disaster, resulting in the deaths of more than 300 Protestants. Elizabeth (1558-1603) firmed up the Established Church with formation of a hierarchy, legal enactments and multi-phased persecution. One hundred and 11 priests and 62 lay persons were among the casualties of persecution during the underground Catholic revival which followed the return to England of missionary priests from France and The Lowlands. Several periods of comparative toleration ensued after Elizabeth's death. The first of several apostolic vicariates was established in 1685; this form of church government was maintained until the restoration of the hierarchy and diocesan organization in 1850. The revolution of 1688 and subsequent developments to about 1781 subjected Catholics to a wide variety of penal laws and disabilities in religious, civic and social life. The situation began to improve in 1791, and from 1801 Parliament frequently considered proposals for the repeal of penal laws against Catholics. The Act of Emancipation restored citizenship rights to Catholics in 1829. Restrictions remained in force for some time afterwards, however, on public religious worship and activity. The hierarchy was restored in 1850. Since then the Catholic Church, existing side by side with the Established Churches of England and Scotland, has followed a general pattern of growth and development. England has a diplomatic minister to Vatican City; there is an apostolic delegate in England.

Archd., 4; dioc., 14; ap. ex., 1; card., 1; abp., 3; bp., 32; parishes, 2,511; priests, 6,273 (4,145 dioc., 2,128 rel.); sem., 454; p.d., 32; bros., 671; srs., 11,219; sch., 2,609; bap., 71,058; Caths., 4,061,068 (8.4%); tot. pop., 47,877,200.

Equatorial Guinea: Republic on the west coast of Africa, consisting of Rio Muni on the mainland and the islands of Fernando Po and Annobon in the Gulf of Guinea: capital, Malabo (Santa Isabel). Evangelization began in 1841. Restrictive measures have been enacted against the Church since the country became independent of Spain in 1968. Equatorial Guinea has an apostolic delegate.

Dioc., 2; parishes, 21; priests, 26 (14 dioc., 12 rel.); sem., 15; bros., 5; srs., 42; bap., 1,040; Caths., 240,000 (75%); tot. pop., 320,000.

Ethiopia (Abyssinia): Constitutional monarchy in northeast Africa; capital, Addis Ababa. The country was evangelized by missionaries from Egypt in the fourth century and had a bishop by about 340. Following the lead of its parent body, the Egyptian (Coptic) Church, the Church in the area succumbed to the Monophysite heresy in the sixth century. Catholic influence was negligible for centuries. An ordinariate for the Ethiopian Rite was established in Eritrea in 1930. An apostolic delegation was set up in Addis Ababa in 1937 and several jurisdictions were organized, some under the Congregation for the Oriental Churches and others under the Congregation for the Evangelization of Peoples. Most of the Catholics in the country are in the former Italian colony of Eritrea. Ethiopia maintains diplomatic relations with Vatican City.

Archd., 1; dioc., 2; v.a., 3; p.a., 2; abp., 1; bp., 4; parishes, 163; priests, 457 (155 dioc., 302 rel.); sem. 68; p.d., 1; bros., 112; srs., 795; sch., 221; bap., 10,562; Caths., 195,350 (.6%); tot. pop., 29,058,600.

Falkland Islands: British colony off the southern tip of South America.

P.a., 1; parish, 1; priests, 2 (rel.); Caths., 200; tot. pop., 2,000 (1977).

Faroe Islands: Island group in North Atlantic; Danish possession. Under ecclesiastical jurisdiction of Copenhagen diocese.

Parish, 1; priest, 1 (rel.); srs., 15; sch., 2; Caths., 100; tot. pop., 40,000 (1977).

Fiji: Independent member of the British Commonwealth, 100 inhabited islands in the southwest Pacific; capital, Suva. Marist missionaries began work in 1844 after Methodism had been firmly established. A prefecture apostolic was organized in 1863. The hierarchy was established in 1966. Established diplomatic relations with Vatican City September, 1978.

Archd., 1; abp., 1; parishes, 33; priests, 71 (16 dioc., 55 rel.); sem., 11; bros., 47; srs., 248; sch., 55; bap., 1,883; Caths., 50,340 (8.3%); tot. pop., 599,820.

Finland: Republic in northern Europe; capital, Helsinki. Swedes evangelized the country in the 12th century. The Reformation swept the country, resulting in the prohibition of Catholicism in 1595, general reorganization of ecclesiastical life and affairs, and dominance of the Evangelical Lutheran Church. Catholics were given religious liberty in 1781 but missionaries and conversions were forbidden by law. The first Finnish priest since the Reformation was ordained in 1903 in Paris. A vicariate apostolic for Finland was erected in 1920. A law on religious liberty, enacted in 1923, banned the foundation of monasteries. Finland maintains diplomatic relations with Vatican City.

Dioc., 1; bp., 1; parishes, 5; priests, 18 (3 dioc., 15 rel.); bros., 2; srs., 35; sch., 2; bap., 73; Caths., 3,235 (.06%); tot. pop., 4,700,000.

France: Republic in western Europe; capital, Paris. Christianity was known around Lyons by the middle of the second century. By 250 there were 30 bishoprics. The hierarchy reached a fair degree of organization by the end of the fourth century. Vandals and Franks subsequently invaded the territory and caused barbarian turmoil and doctrinal problems because of their Arianism. The Frankish nation was converted following the baptism of Clovis about 496. Christianization was complete by some time in the seventh century. From then on the Church, its leaders and people, figured in virtually every important development — religious, cultural, political and social — through the periods of the Carolingians, feudalism, the Middle Ages and monarchies to the end of the 18th century. The great University of Paris became one of the intellectual centers of the 13th century. Churchmen and secular rulers were involved with developments surrounding the Avignon residence of the popes and curia from 1309 until near the end of the 14th century and with the disastrous Western Schism that followed. Strong currents of Gallicanism and conciliarism ran through ecclesiastical and secular circles in France; the former was an ideology and movement to restrict papal control of the Church in the country, the latter sought to make the pope subservient to a general council. Calvinism invaded the country about the middle of the 16th century and won a strong body of converts. Jansenism with its rigorous spirit and other aberrations appeared in the next century, to be followed by the highly influential Enlightenment. The Revolution which started in 1789 and was succeeded by the Napoleonic period completely changed the status of the Church, taking a toll of numbers by persecution and defection and disenfranchising the Church in practically every way. Throughout the 19th century the Church was caught up in the whirl of imperial and republican developments and made the victim of official hostility, popular indifference and liberal opposition. In this century, the Church has struggled with problems involving the heritage of the Revolution and its aftermath, the alienation of intellectuals, liberalism, the estrangement of the working classes because of the Church's former identification with the ruling class, and the massive needs of contemporary society. France maintains diplomatic relations with Vatican City.

Archd., 18; dioc., 75; prel., 1; ap. ex., 2; ord., 1; card., 7; abp., 14; bp., 97; parishes, 38,236; priests, 41,163 (33,892 dioc., 7,271 rel.); sem., 1,275; p.d., 47; bros., 5,201; srs., 90,048; sch., 9,554; bap., 539,872; Caths., 45,027,000 (85.1%); tot. pop., 52,915,000 (1977).

Gabon: Republic on the west coast of Equatorial Africa, member of the French Community; capital, Libreville. Sporadic missionary effort took place before 1881 when effective evangelization began. The hierarchy was established in 1955. Gabon maintains diplomatic relations with Vatican City.

Archd., 1; dioc., 3; abp., 1 (nat.); bp., 3 (nat.); parishes, 57; priests, 113 (33 dioc., 80 rel.); sem., 11; bros., 38; srs., 134; sch., 221; bap., 6,704; Caths., 410,870 (56.7%); tot. pop., 724,160 (population figures were compiled from 1979 Annuario Pontificio; other sources report total population of 560,000 with an estimated Catholic percentage of 25-45%).

Gambia, The: Republic (1970) on the northwestern coast of Africa, smallest state in Africa, member of the British Commonwealth; capital, Banjui. The country was under the jurisdiction of a vicariate apostolic until 1931. The hierarchy was established in 1957. Established diplomatic relations with Vatican City, 1978.

Dioc., 1; bp., 1; parishes, 3; priests, 20 (rel.); sem. 10; bros., 2; srs., 21; sch., 39; bap., 626; Caths., 11,970 (2.1%); tot. pop., 553,160.

Germany: Country in northern Europe partitioned in 1949 into the Communist German Democratic Republic in the East (capital, East Berlin) and the German Federal Republic in the West (capital, Bonn). Christianity was introduced in the third century, if not earlier. Trier, which became a center for missionary activity, had a bishop by 400. Visigoth invaders introduced Arianism in the fifth century but were converted in the seventh century by the East Franks, Celtic and other missionaries. St. Boniface, the apostle of Germany, established real ecclesiastical organization in the eighth century. The Church had great influence during the Carolingian period. Bishops from that time onward began to act in dual roles as pastors and rulers, a state of affairs which led inevitably to confusion and conflict in Church-state relations and perplexing problems of investiture. The Church developed strength and vitality through the Middle Ages but succumbed to abuses which antedated and prepared the ground for the Reformation. Luther's actions from 1517 made Germany a confessional battleground. Religious strife continued until conclusion of the Peace of Westphalia at the end of the Thirty Years' War in 1648. Nearly a century earlier the Peace of Augsburg (1555) had been designed, without success, to assure a degree of tranquillity by recognizing the legitimacy of different religious confessions in different states, depending on the decisions of princes. The implicit principle that princes should control the churches emerged in practice into the absolutism and Josephinism of subsequent years. St. Peter Canisius and his fellow Jesuits spearheaded a Counter Reformation in the second half of the 16th century. Before the end of the century, however, 70 per cent of the population of north and central Germany were Lutheran. Calvinism also had established a strong presence. The Church gained internal strength in a defensive position. Through much of the 19th century, however, its influence was eclipsed by Protestant intellectuals and other influences. It suffered some impoverishment also as a result of shifting boundaries and the secularization of property shortly after 1800. It came under direct attack in the Kulturkampf of the 1870's but helped to generate the opposition which resulted in a dampening of the campaign of Bismarck against it. Despite action by Catholics on the social front and other developments, discrimination against the Church spilled over into the 20th century and lasted beyond World War I. Catholics in politics struggled with others to pull the country through numerous postwar crises. The dissolution of the Center Party, agreed to by the bishops in 1933 without awareness of the ultimate consequences, contributed negatively to the rise of Hitler to supreme power. Church officials protested the Nazi anti-Church and anti-Semitic actions, but to no avail. After World War II Christian leadership had much to do with the recovery of Western Germany. East Germany, gone Communist under Russian auspices, initiated a program of control and repression of the Church in 1948 and 1949. With no prospect of success for measures designed to split bishops, priests, religious and lay persons, the regime has concentrated most of its attention on mind control, especially of the younger generation, by the elimination of religious schools, curtailment of freedom for religious instruction and formation, severe restriction of the religious press, and the substitution since the mid-50's of youth initiation and Communist ceremonies for the rites of baptism, confirmation, marriage, and funerals. Bishops are generally forbidden to travel outside the Republic. The number of priests is decreasing, partly because of reduced seminary enrollments ordered by the government since 1958. In 1973, the Vatican appointed three apostolic administrators and one auxiliary (all titular bishops) for the areas of three West German dioceses located in East Germany. West Germany maintains diplomatic relations with Vatican City.

West Germany: Archd., 5; dioc., 17 (includes Berlin which covers part of East Germany); ap., ex., 1; card., 5; abp., 3; bp., 62; parishes, 11,744; priests, 22,576 (16,691 dioc., 5,885 rel.); sem., 2,300; p.d., 403; bros., 2,812; srs., 67,220; sch., 932; bap., 241,054; Caths., 27,860,000 (45.3%); tot. pop., 61,498,000. (1977, except for hierarchy).

East Germany: Dioc., 1 (Meissen); a.a., 1 (Gorlitz; there are also 3 territories with apostolic administrators); bp., 8; parishes, 917; priests, 1,525 (1,276 dioc., 249 rel.); sem., 212; p.d., 22; bros., 59; srs., 3,299; sch., 19; bap., 8,925; Caths., 1,260,000 (7.5%); tot. pop., 16,786,000. (1977, except for hierarchy).

Ghana: Republic on the western coast of Africa, bordering on the Gulf of Guinea, member of the British Commonwealth; capital, Accra. Priests visited the country in 1482, 11 years after discovery by the Portuguese, but missionary effort — hindered by the slave trade and other factors — was slight until 1880 when systematic evangelization began. A prefecture apostolic was set up in 1879. The hierarchy was established in 1950. Ghana maintains diplomatic relations with Vatican City.

Archd., 2; dioc., 7; abp., 2 (nat.); bp., 7 (nat.); parishes, 138; priests, 399 (140 dioc., 259 rel.); sem., 192; bros., 104; srs., 424; sch., 1,773; bap., 37,673; Caths., 1,260,298 (12.1%); tot. pop., 10,400,000.

Gibraltar: British colony on the tip of the Spanish Peninsula on the Mediterranean. Evangelization took place after the Moors were driven out near the end of the 15th century. The Church was hindered by the British who acquired the colony in 1713. Most of the Catholics were, and are, Spanish and Italian immigrants and their descendants. A vicariate apostolic was organized in 1817. The diocese was erected in 1910.

Dioc., 1; bp., 1; parishes, 4; priests, 14 (11 dioc., 3 rel.); p.d., 1; srs., 23; sch., 1; bap., 319; Caths., 21,500 (71.3%); tot. pop., 30,120.

Gilbert Islands: British colony in the southwest Pacific in Oceania. French Missionaries of the Sacred Heart began work in the islands in 1888. A vicariate for the islands was organized in 1897. The hierarchy was established in 1966.

Dioc., *1; bp.*, *1; parishes*, *22; priests*, *20 (2 dioc.*, *18 rel.); sem.*, *2; bros.*, *4; srs.*, *42; sch.*, *3; bap.*, *1,049; Caths.*, *29,300 (41.2%); tot. pop.*, *63,600. (Statistics are for the Tarawa, Nauru and Funafuti diocese which includes the Gilbert Islands, Republic of Nauru and the Tuvalu Islands.)*

Greece, including Crete: Kingdom in southeastern Europe on the Balkan Peninsula; capital, Athens. St. Paul preached the Gospel at Athens and Corinth on his second missionary journey and visited the country again on his third tour. Other Apostles may have passed through also. Two bishops from Greece attended the First Council of Nicaea. After the division of the Roman Empire, the Church remained Eastern in rite and later broke ties with Rome as a result of the schism of 1054. A Latin-Rite jurisdiction was set up during the period of the Latin Empire of Constantinople, 1204-1261, but crumbled afterwards. Unity efforts of the Council of Florence had poor results. The country now has Greek Catholic and Latin jurisdictions. The Greek Orthodox Church is predominant.

Archd., *4; dioc.*, *4; v.a.*, *1; ap. ex.*, *1; ord.*, *1; abp.*, *1; bp.*, *4; parishes*, *48; priests*, *102 (60 dioc.*, *42 rel.); sem.*, *6; bros.*, *43; srs.*, *163; sch.*, *34; bap.*, *367; Caths.*, *45,490 (.5%); tot. pop.*, *9,190,000.*

Greenland: Danish island province northeast of North America; capital, Godthaab. Catholicism was introduced about 1000. The first diocese was established in 1124 and a line of bishops dated from then until 1537. The first known churches in the western hemisphere, dating from about the 11th century, were on Greenland; the remains of 19 have been unearthed. The departure of Scandinavians and spread of the Reformation reduced the Church to nothing. The Moravian Brethren evangelized the Eskimos from the 1720's to 1901. By 1930 the Danish Church — Evangelical Lutheran — was in full possession. Since 1930 priests have been in Greenland, which is part of the Copenhagen diocese. There are about 60 Catholics in the area.

Grenada: Independent island state in the West Indies; capital, St. George's. Established diplomatic relations with Vatican City in 1979.

Dioc., *1; bp.*, *1; parishes*, *20; priests*, *22 (6 dioc.*, *16 rel.); sem.*, *3; p.d.*, *2; bros.*, *7; srs.*, *20; sch.*, *34; bap.*, *1,426; Caths.*, *68,000; tot. pop.*, *111,180.*

Guadeloupe: French overseas department in the Leeward Islands of the West Indies; capital, Basse-Terre. Catholicism was introduced in the islands in the 16th century.

Dioc., *1; bp.*, *1; parishes*, *46; priests*, *85 (45 dioc.*, *40 rel.); sem.*, *6; bros.*, *7; srs.*, *205; sch.*, *22; bap.*, *7,218; Caths.*, *300,000; tot. pop.*, *324,000.*

Guam: U.S. territory in the southwest Pacific; capital, Agana. The first Mass was offered in the Mariana Islands in 1521. The islands were evangelized by the Jesuits, from 1668, and other missionaries. The first native Micronesian bishop was ordained in 1970.

Dioc., *1; bp.*, *1 (nat.); parishes*, *31; priests*, *57 (26 dioc.*, *31 rel.); sem.*, *5; p.d.*, *10; bros.*, *8; srs.*, *141; sch.*, *14; bap.*, *4,272; Caths.*, *115,470; tot. pop.*, *124,050.*

Guatemala: Republic in Central America; capital, Guatemala City. Evangelization dates from the beginning of Spanish occupation in 1524. The first diocese, for all Central American territories administered by the captaincy general of Guatemala, was established in 1534. The country became independent in 1839, following annexation to Mexico in 1821, secession in 1823 and membership in the Central American Federation from 1825. In 1870, a government installed by a liberal revolution repudiated the concordat of 1853 and took active measures against the Church. Separation of Church and state was decreed; religious orders were suppressed and their property seized; priests and religious were exiled; schools were secularized. Full freedom was subsequently granted. Guatemala maintains diplomatic relations with Vatican City.

Archd., *1; dioc.*, *8; prel.*, *2; a.a.*, *2; card.*, *1; bp.*, *15; parishes*, *341; priests*, *641 (173 dioc.*, *468 rel.); sem.*, *86; p.d.*, *3; bros.*, *120; srs.*, *1,104; sch.*, *232; bap.*, *181,985; Caths.* *5,509,000 (88%); tot. pop.* *6,256,000. (Catholic and total population figures are from 1976 Statistical Yearbook of the Church; others are from 1979 Annuario Pontificio.)*

Guiana, French (Cayenne): French overseas department on the northeast coast of South America; capital, Cayenne. Catholicism was introduced in the 17th century. The Cayenne diocese was established in 1956.

Dioc., *1; bp.*, *1; parishes*, *26; priests*, *31 (8 dioc.*, *23 rel.); bros.*, *1; srs.*, *89; sch.*, *7; bap.*, *1,147; Caths.*, *46,000; tot. pop.*, *56,000.*

Guinea: Republic on the west coast of Africa; capital, Conakry. Occasional missionary work followed exploration by the Portuguese about the middle of the 15th century; organized effort dates from 1877. The hierarchy was established in 1955. Following independence from France in 1958, Catholic schools were nationalized, youth organizations banned and missionaries restricted. Foreign missionaries were expelled in 1967. Archbishop Tchidimbo of Conakry, sentenced to life imprisonment in 1971 on a charge of conspiring to overthrow the government, was released in August, 1979; he resigned his see.

Archd., *1; dioc.*, *1; p.a.*, *1; abp.*, *1 (nat.); bp.*, *1 (nat.); parishes*, *28; priests*, *18 (17 dioc.*, *1 rel.); sem.*, *13; bros.*, *1; srs.*, *22; bap.*, *1,752; Caths.*, *43,298 (.1%); tot. pop.*, *4,600,000.*

Guinea-Bissau (formerly Portuguese Guinea): Independent state on the west coast of Africa; capital, Bissau. Catholicism was introduced in the second half of the 15th century but limited missionary work, hampered by the slave trade, had meager results. Missionary work in this century dates from 1933. A prefecture apostolic was established in 1955 (made a diocese in 1977). Guinea-Bissau has an apostolic delegate.

Dioc., 1; bp., 1; parishes, 15; priests, 36 (rel); bros., 11; srs., 16; bap., 759; Caths., 41,000 (6.3%); tot. pop., 650,000 (some figures are from 1975).

Guyana: Republic on the northern coast of South America; capital, Georgetown. In 1899 the Catholic Church and other churches were given equal status with the Church of England and the Church of Scotland, which had sole rights up to that time. Most of the Catholics are Portuguese. The Georgetown diocese was established in 1956, 10 years before Guyana became independent of England. The first native bishop was appointed in 1971. Schools were nationalized in 1976.

Dioc., 1; bp., 1; parishes, 25; priests, 64 (7 dioc., 57 rel.); sem., 2; bros., 5; srs., 54; bap., 2,461; Caths., 94,500 (11.8%); tot. pop., 800,000.

Haiti: Caribbean republic on the western third of Hispaniola adjacent to the Dominican Republic; capital, Port-au-Prince. Evangelization followed discovery by Columbus in 1492. Capuchins and Jesuits did most of the missionary work in the 18th century. From 1804, when independence was declared, until 1860, the country was in schism. Relations were regularized by a concordat concluded in 1860, when an archdiocese and four dioceses were established. Factors hindering the development of the Church have been a shortage of native clergy, inadequate religious instruction and the prevalence of voodoo. Political upheavals in the 1960's had serious effects on the Church. Haiti maintains diplomatic relations with Vatican City.

Archd., 1; dioc., 6; abp., 1; bp., 7; parishes, 185; priests, 398 (196 dioc., 202 rel.); sem., 80; p.d., 2; bros., 201; srs., 660; sch., 694; bap., 107,206; Caths., 4,613,690 (85.9%); tot. pop. 5,368,750.

Honduras: Republic in Central America; capital, Tegucigalpa. Evangelization preceded establishment of the first diocese in the 16th century. Under Spanish rule and after independence from 1823, the Church held a favored position until 1880 when equal legal status was given to all religions. Honduras maintains diplomatic relations with Vatican City.

Archd., 1; dioc., 3; prel., 2; abp., 1; bp., 6; parishes, 121; priests, 229 (75 dioc., 154 rel.); sem., 20; bros., 17; srs., 263; sch., 51; bap., 100,875; Caths., 3,082,000 (92%); tot. pop., 3,350,000.

Hong Kong: British crown colony at the mouth of the Canton River, adjacent to the southeast Chinese province of Kwangtung. A prefecture apostolic was established in 1841. Members of the Pontifical Institute for Foreign Missions began work there in 1858. The Hong Kong diocese was erected in 1946.

Dioc., 1; bp., 1; parishes, 29; priests, 339 (73 dioc., 266 rel.); sem., 18; bros., 83; srs., 781; sch., 309; bap., 5,353; Caths., 256,940 (5.7%); tot. pop., 4,482,000.

Hungary: People's republic in east central Europe; capital, Budapest. The early origins of Christianity in the country, whose territory was subject to a great deal of change, is not known. Magyars accepted Christianity about the end of the 10th century. St. Stephen I (d. 1038) promoted its spread and helped to organize some of its historical dioceses. Bishops early became influential in politics as well as in the Church. For centuries the country served as a buffer for the Christian West against barbarians from the East, notably the Mongols in the 13th century. Religious orders, whose foundations started from the 1130's, provided the most effective missionaries, pastors and teachers. Outstanding for years were the Franciscans and Dominicans; the Jesuits were noted for their work in the Counter-Reformation from the second half of the 16th century onwards. Hussites and Waldensians prepared the way for the Reformation which struck at almost the same time as the Turks. The Reformation made considerable progress after 1526, resulting in the conversion of large numbers to Lutheranism and Calvinism by the end of the century. Most of them or their descendants returned to the Church later, but many Magyars remained staunch Calvinists. Turks repressed the churches, Protestant as well as Catholic, during a reign of 150 years but they managed to survive. Domination of the Church was one of the objectives of government policy during the reigns of Maria Theresa and Joseph II in the second half of the 18th century; their Josephinism affected Church-state relations until the first World War. More than 100,000 Eastern Rite schismatics were reunited with Rome about the turn of the 18th century. Secularization increased in the second half of the 19th century, which also witnessed the birth of many new Catholic organizations and movements to influence life in the nation and the Church. Catholics were involved in the social chaos and anti-religious atmosphere of the years following World War I, struggling with their compatriots for religious as well as political survival. After World War II Communist strength, which had manifested itself with less intensity earlier in the century, was great long before it forced the legally elected president out of office in 1947 and imposed a Soviet type of constitution on the country in 1949. The campaign against the Church started with the disbanding of Catholic organizations in 1946. In 1948, "Caritas," the Catholic charitable organization, was taken over and all Catholic schools, colleges and institutions were suppressed. Interference in church administration and attempts to split the bishops preceded the arrest of Cardinal Mindszenty on Dec. 26, 1948, and his sentence to life imprisonment in 1949. (He was free for a few days during the unsuccessful uprising of 1956. He then took up residence at the U.S. Embassy in Budapest where he remained until September, 1971, when he was permitted to leave the country. He died in 1975 in Vienna.) In 1950, religious orders and congregations were suppressed and 10,000 religious were interned. At least 30 priests and monks were assassinated, jailed or deported. About 4,000 priests and religious were confined in jail or concentration camps. The government sponsored a national "Progressive Catholic" church and captive organizations for priests and "Catholic Action," which attracted only a small minority. Signs were clear in 1965 and 1966 that a 1964 agreement with the Holy See regarding episcopal appointments had settled nothing. Six bishops were appointed by the Holy See and some other posts were filled, but none of the prelates were free from government surveillance and harassment. Four new bishops were appointed by the Holy See in January and ordained in Budapest in February, 1969; three elderly prelates resigned their sees. Shortly thereafter, peace priests complained that the "too Roman" new bishops would not deal with them. Talks between Vatican and Hungarian representatives during the past several years have resulted in the appointment of bishops to fill all of Hungary's 11 residential sees.

Archd., 3; dioc., 8; abb., 1; ap. ex., 1; card 1; abp., 2; bp., 15; parishes, 2,180; priests, 3,319 (3,184 dioc., 135 rel.); sem., 257; bros., 25; srs., 57; sch., 11; bap., 89,327; Caths., 6,496,500 (61%); tot. pop., 10,650,000.

Iceland: Island republic between Norway and Greenland; capital, Reykjavik. Irish hermits were there in the eighth century. Missionaries subsequently evangelized the island and Christianity was officially accepted about 1000. The first bishop was ordained in 1056. The Black Death had dire effects and spiritual decline set in during the 15th century. Lutheranism was introduced from Denmark between 1537 and 1552 and made the official religion. Some Catholic missionary work was done in the 19th century. Religious freedom was granted to the few Catholics in 1874. A vicariate was erected in 1929 (made a diocese in 1968). Iceland maintains diplomatic relations with Vatican City.

Dioc., 1; bp., 1; parishes, 2; priests, 6 (1 dioc., 5 rel.); sem., 3; srs., 54; sch., 3; bap., 21; Caths., 1,433; tot. pop., 222,055.

India: Republic on the subcontinent of south central Asia, member of the British Commonwealth; capital, New Delhi. Longstanding tradition credits the Apostle Thomas with the introduction of Christianity in the Kerala area. Evangelization followed the establishment of Portuguese posts and the conquest of Goa in 1510. Jesuits, Franciscans, Dominicans, Augustinians and members of other religious orders figured in the early missionary history. An archdiocese for Goa, with two suffragan sees, was set up in 1558. Five provincial councils were held between 1567 and 1606. The number of Catholics in 1572 was estimated to be 280,000. This figure rose to 800,000 in 1700 and declined to 500,000 in 1800. Missionaries had some difficulties with the British East India Co. which exercised virtual government control from 1757 to 1858. They also had trouble because of a conflict that developed between policies of the Portuguese government, which pressed its rights of patronage in episcopal and clerical appointments, and the Congregation for the Propagation of the Faith, which sought greater freedom of action in the same appointments. This struggle eventuated in the schism of Goa between 1838 and 1857. In 1886, when the number of Catholics was estimated to be one million, the hierarchy for India and Ceylon was restored. Jesuits contributed greatly to the development of Catholic education from the second half of the 19th century. A large percentage of the Catholic population is located around Goa and Kerala and farther south. The country is predominantly Hindu. India maintains diplomatic relations with Vatican City.

Patriarchate, 1 (titular of East Indies); archd., 19; dioc., 85; p.a., 2; card., 2; abp., 18; bp., 81; parishes, 4,251; priests, 10,364 (6,184 dioc., 4,180 rel.); sem., 4,542; p.d., 19; bros., 2,366; srs., 43,075; sch., 8,674; bap., 282,113; Caths., 9,537,000 (1.6%); tot. pop., 610,077,000 (1977, except for jurisdictions).

Indonesia: Republic southeast of Asia, consisting of some 3,000 islands including Kalimantan (most of Borneo), Sulawesi (Celebes), Java, the Lesser Sundas, Moluccas, Sumatra, Timor and West Irian (Irian Jaya, western part of New Guinea); capital, Jakarta. Evangelization by the Portuguese began about 1511. St. Francis Xavier, greatest of the modern missionaries, spent some 14 months in the area. Christianity was strongly rooted in some parts of the islands by 1600. Islam's rise to dominance began at this time. The Dutch East Indies Co., which gained effective control in the 17th century, banned evangelization by Catholic missionaries for some time but Dutch secular and religious priests managed to resume the work. A vicariate of Batavia for all the Dutch East Indies was set up in 1841. About 90 per cent of the population is Moslem. The hierarchy was established in 1961. Indonesia maintains diplomatic relations with Vatican City.

Archd., 7; dioc., 24; p.a., 2; card., 1; abp., 6;

bp., 22; parishes, 361; priests, 1,522 (162 dioc., 1,360 rel.); sem., 356; p.d., 7; bros., 687; srs., 3,853; sch., 3,990; bap., 135,785; Caths., 3,024,210 (2.1%); tot. pop., 142,000,000. (Statistics for former Portuguese Timor which was annexed by Indonesia in 1976 are listed separately; see Timor, Eastern.)

Iran: Constitutional monarchy in southwestern Asia, between the Caspian Sea and the Persian Gulf; capital, Teheran. Some of the earliest Christian communities were established in this area outside the (then) Roman Empire. They suffered persecution in the fourth century and were then cut off from the outside world. Nestorianism was generally professed in the late fifth century. Islam became dominant after 640. Some later missionary work was attempted but without success. Religious liberty was granted in 1834, but Catholics were the victims of a massacre in 1918. Islam is the religion of perhaps 98 per cent of the population. In 1964 the country had 100,000 Monophysites, the largest group of Christians, and some 20,000 Nestorians. Catholics belong to the Latin, Armenian and Chaldean rites. Iran (Persia until 1935) maintains diplomatic relations with Vatican City.

Archd., 4; dioc., 2; abp., 4; bp., 1; parishes, 24; priests, 58 (16 dioc., 42 rel.); sem., 2; p.d., 1; bros., 6; srs., 65; sch., 27; bap., 381; Caths., 42,000 (.1%); tot. pop., 33,590,000.

Iraq: Republic in southwestern Asia, between Iran and Saudi Arabia; capital, Baghdad. Some of the earliest Christian communities were established in the area, whose history resembles that of Iran. Catholics belong to the Armenian, Chaldean, Latin and Syrian rites; Chaldeans are most numerous. Islam is the religion of some 90 per cent of the population. Iraq maintains diplomatic relations with Vatican City.

Patriarchate, 1; archd., 9; dioc., 5; mission "sui juris," 1; patriarch, 1; abp., 9; bp., 3; parishes, 109; priests, 144 (112 dioc., 32 rel.); sem., 21; bros., 10; srs., 212; bap., 5,298; Caths. (approx.), 297,000 (2.4%); tot. pop., 11,910,000.

Ireland: Republic in the British Isles; capital, Dublin. St. Patrick, who is venerated as the apostle of Ireland, evangelized parts of the island for some years after the middle of the fifth century. Conversion of the island was not accomplished, however, until the seventh century or later. Celtic monks were the principal missionaries. The Church was organized along monastic lines at first, but a movement developed in the 11th century for the establishment of jurisdiction along episcopal lines. By that time many Roman usages had been adopted. The Church gathered strength during the period from the Norman Conquest of England to the reign of Henry VIII despite a wide variety of rivalries, wars, and other disturbances. Henry introduced an age of repression of the faith which continued for many years under several of his successors. The Irish suffered from proscription of the Catholic faith, economic and social disabilities, subjection to absentee landlords and a plantation system designed to keep them from owning property, and actual persecution which took an uncertain toll of lives up until about 1714. Most of those living in the northern part of Ireland became Anglican and Presbyterian in the 1600's but the south remained strong in faith. Some penal laws remained in force until emancipation in 1829. Nearly 100 years later Ireland was divided by two enactments which made Northern Ireland, consisting of six counties, part of the United Kindgom (1920) and gave dominion status to the Irish Free State, made up of the other 26 counties (1922). This state (Eire, in Gaelic) was proclaimed the Republic of Ireland in 1949. The Catholic Church predominates but religious freedom is guaranteed for all. Ireland maintains diplomatic relations with Vatican City.

Archd., 4; dioc., 23; card., 1; abp., 3; bp., 27; parishes, 1,289; priests, 5,892 (3,772 dioc., 2,120 rel.); sem., 628; bros., 1,926; srs., 12,759; sch., 4,267; bap., 79,227 (preceding figures include Northern Ireland); Caths., 2,970,400 (94%); tot. pop., 3,160,000.

Ireland, Northern: Part of the United Kingdom, it consists of six of the nine counties of Ulster in the northeast corner of Ireland; capital, Belfast. History is given under Ireland, above. For recent developments, see Index.

Caths. (approx.), 505,000 (32%); tot. pop. (1975 est.), 1,537,000 (other statistics are included in Ireland).

Israel: Parliamentary democracy in the Middle East, at the eastern end of the Mediterranean; capitals, Jerusalem and Tel Aviv (diplomatic). Israel was the birthplace of Christianity, the site of the first Christian communities. Some persecution was suffered in the early Christian era and again during the several hundred years of Roman control. Moslems conquered the territory in the seventh century and, except for the period of the Kingdom of Jerusalem established by Crusaders, remained in control most of the time up until World War I. The Church survived in the area, sometimes just barely, but it did not prosper greatly or show any notable increase in numbers. The British took over the protectorate of the area after World War I. Partition into Israel for the Jews and Palestine for the Arabs was approved by the United Nations in 1947. War broke out a year later with the proclamation of the Republic of Israel. The Israelis won the war and 50 per cent more territory than they had originally been ceded. War broke out again for six days in June, 1967, and in October, 1973, resulting in a Middle East crisis which persists to the present time. Caught in the middle of the conflict are hundreds of thousands of dispossessed

Palestinian refugees. Judaism is the faith professed by about 85 percent of the inhabitants; approximately one-third of them are considered observants. Most of the Arab minority are Moslems. The Acre archdiocese for Melkites is situated in Israel. Maronites are subject to the bishop of Tyr, Lebanon. Latins are under the jurisdiction of the Roman patriarchate of Jerusalem. Israel has an apostolic delegate.

Caths., 35,671; tot. pop., 3,610,000.

Italy: Republic in southern Europe; capital, Rome. A Christian community was formed early at Rome, probably by the middle of the first century. St. Peter established his see there. He and St. Paul suffered death for the faith there in the 60s. The early Christians were persecuted at various times there, as in other parts of the empire, but the Church developed in numbers and influence, gradually spreading out from towns and cities in the center and south to rural areas and the north. Organization, in the process of formation in the second century, developed greatly between the fifth and eighth centuries. By the latter date the Church had already come to grips with serious problems, including doctrinal and disciplinary disputes that threatened the unity of faith, barbarian invasions, and the need for the pope and bishops to take over civil responsibilities because of imperial default. The Church has been at the center of life on the peninsula throughout the centuries. It emerged from underground in 313, with the Edict of Milan, and rose to a position of prestige and lasting influence. It educated and converted the barbarians, preserved culture through the early Middle Ages and passed it on to later times, suffered periods of decline and gained strength through recurring reforms, engaged in military combat for political reasons and intellectual combat for the preservation and development of doctrine, saw and patronized the development of the arts, experienced all human strengths and weaknesses in its members, knew triumph and the humiliation of failure. For long centuries, from the fourth to the 19th, the Church was a temporal as well as spiritual power. This temporal aspect complicated its history in Italy. Since the 1870's, however, when the Papal States were annexed by the Kingdom of Italy, the history became simpler — but remained complicated — as the Church, shorn of temporal power, began to find new freedom for the fulfillment of its spiritual mission. Italy maintains diplomatic relations with Vatican City.

Patriarchate, 1; archd., 56; dioc., 215; prel., 4; abb., 9; card., 36; abp., 40; bp., 290; parishes, 28,367; priests, 61,784 (40,855 dioc., 20,929 rel.); sem., 5,880; p.d., 100; bros., 6,528; srs., 145,083; sch., 3,858; bap., 789,665; Caths., 54,765,000 (97.5%); tot. pop., 56,189,000 (1977, except for cardinals).

Ivory Coast: Republic in western Africa, member of the French Community; capital, Abidjan. The Holy Ghost Fathers began systematic evangelization in 1895. The first native priests from the area were ordained in 1934. The hierarchy was set up in 1955. Ivory Coast maintains diplomatic relations with Vatican City.

Archd., 1; dioc., 7; abp., 1 (nat.); bp., 8 (nat.); parishes, 150; priests, 382 (104 dioc., 278 rel.); sem., 64; p.d., 1; bros., 86; srs., 500; sch., 331; bap., 17,932; Caths., 720,430 (10.1%); tot. pop., 7,083,470.

Jamaica: Parliamentary democracy in the West Indies, member of the British Commonwealth; capital, Kingston. Franciscans and Dominicans evangelized the island from about 1512 until 1655. Missionary work was interrupted after the English took possession but was resumed by Jesuits about the turn of the 19th century. A vicariate apostolic was organized in 1837. The hierarchy was established in 1967. Established diplomatic relations with Vatican City in 1979.

Archd., 1; dioc., 1; abp., 1; bp., 1; parishes, 18; priests, 105 (21 dioc., 84 rel.); sem., 1; p.d., 2; bros., 9; srs., 215; sch., 85; bap., 3,732; Caths., 187,220 (8.9%); tot. pop., 2,090,000.

Japan: Constitutional monarchy in the northwest Pacific; capital, Tokyo. Jesuits began evangelization in the middle of the 16th century and about 300,000 converts, most of them in Kyushu, were reported at the end of the century. The Nagasaki Martyrs were victims of persecution in 1597. Another persecution took some 4,000 lives between 1614 and 1651. Missionaries, banned for two centuries, returned about the middle of the 19th century and found Christian communities still surviving in Nagasaki and other places in Kyushu. A vicariate was organized in 1846. Religious freedom was guaranteed in 1889. The hierarchy was established in 1891. Japan maintains diplomatic relations with Vatican City.

Archd., 3; dioc., 13; p.a., 1; card., 1; abp., 2; bp., 14; parishes, 721; priests, 1,908 (488 dioc., 1,420 rel.); sem., 192; p.d., 2; bros., 368; srs., 6,789; sch., 303; bap., 10,536; Caths., 390,569 (.34%); tot. pop., 113,860,000.

Jerusalem: The entire city, site of the first Christian community, has been under Israeli control since the Israeli-Arab war of June, 1967. There are two patriarchates in the city, Melkite and Latin. Jerusalem has an apostolic delegate.

Jordan: Constitutional monarchy in the Middle East; capital, Amman. Christianity there dates from apostolic times. Survival of the faith was threatened many times under the rule of Moslems from 636 and Ottoman Turks from 1517 to 1918, and in the Islamic Emirate of Trans-Jordan from 1918 to 1949. Since the creation of Israel, some 500,000 Palestinian refugees, some of them Christians, have been in Jordan. Islam is the state religion but religious freedom is guaranteed for all. Jordan has an apostolic delegate.

The statistics which follow are for the Greek Melkite-Rite Catholics of the Archdiocese of Petra and Philadelphia in Jordan. Separate statistics are not available for the Latin (Roman)-Rite Catholics under the jurisdiction of the Latin patriarchate of Jerusalem.

Archd., 1; abp., 1; parishes, 32; priests, 22 (17 dioc., 5 rel.); sem. 4; srs., 34; sch., 21; Caths., 18,240; tot. pop. (1976), 2,780,000.

Kampuchea (Democratic Kampuchea): Former names — Khmer Republic, Cambodia. Republic (Oct. 9, 1970) in southeast Asia, bordering on the Gulf of Siam, Thailand, Laos and Vietnam; capital Phnom Penh. Evangelization dating from the second half of the 16th century had limited results, more among Vietnamese than Khmers. Thousands of Catholics of Vietnamese origin were forced to flee in 1970 because of Khmer hostility. The status of the Church remained uncertain following the Khmer Rouge takeover in April, 1975. Foreign missionaries were expelled immediately. Local clergy and religious were sent to work the land; whether they would be able to minister to the faithful was not known. Buddhism is the state religion. The country has an apostolic delegate.

V.a., 1; p.a., 2; bp., 1; parishes, 21; priests, 29 (16 dioc., 13 rel.); sem., 3; bros., 16; srs., 61; Caths., 13,835 (.2%); tot. pop., 8,354,000. (Statistics are from 1973, 1974.)

Kashmir and Jammu: Statistics included in India.

Kenya: Republic in eastern Africa bordering on the Indian Ocean, member of the British Commonwealth; capital, Nairobi. Systematic evangelization by the Holy Ghost Fathers began in 1892, nearly 40 years after the start of work by Protestant missionaries. The hierarchy was established in 1953. Kenya maintains diplomatic relations with Vatican City.

Archd., 1; dioc., 13; p.a., 1; card., 1 (nat.); bp., 13 (9 nat.); parishes, 232; priests, 814 (201 dioc., 613 rel.); sem., 240; bros., 171; srs., 1,826; sch., 4,025; bap., 161,916; Caths., 2,500,000 (17.4%); tot. pop., 14,300,000.

Korea: Peninsula in eastern Asia, east of China, divided into the (Communist) Democratic People's Republic in the North, formed May 1, 1948, with Pyongyang as its capital; and the Republic of Korea in the South, with Seoul as the capital. Some Catholics may have been in Korea before it became a "hermit kingdom" toward the end of the 16th century and closed its borders to foreigners. The real introduction to Catholicism came through lay converts in the last quarter of the 18th century. A priest arriving in the country in 1794 found 4,000 Catholics there who had never seen a priest. A vicariate was erected in 1831 but was not manned for several years thereafter. There were 15,000 Catholics by 1857. Four persecutions in the 19th century took a terrible toll; several thousands died in the last one, 1866-69. Freedom of religion was granted in 1883 when Korea opened its borders. Progress was made thereafter. The hierarchy was established in 1962. Since the war of 1950-1953, there have been no signs of Catholic life in the North, which has been blanketed by a news blackout. In July, 1972, both Koreas agreed to seek peaceful means of reunification. The South maintains diplomatic relations with Vatican City. Bishop Tji of Won Ju, South Korea, convicted and sentenced to 15 years' imprisonment in 1974 on a charge of inciting to rebellion, was released in February, 1975.

North Korea: Dioc., 2; abb., 1; bp., 1 (exiled); tot. pop., 16,650,000. No recent Catholic statistics available; there were an estimated 100,000 Catholics reported in 1969.

South Korea: Archd., 3; dioc., 11; card., 1; abp., 2; bp., 13; parishes, 530; priests, 940 (670 dioc., 267 rel.); sem., 475; bros., 150; srs., 2,769; sch., 92; bap., 52,641; Caths. 1,100,320 (3%); tot. pop., 36,161,470.

Kuwait: Constitutional monarchy (sultanate or sheikdom) in southwest Asia bordering on the Persian Gulf. Remote Christian origins probably date to apostolic times. Islam is the predominant and official religion. Kuwait maintains diplomatic relations with Vatican City.

V.a., 1; bp., 1; parishes, 3; priests, 8 (3 dioc., 5 rel.); srs., 26; sch., 7; bap., 361; Caths., 24,000 (2.2%); tot. pop., 1,100,000.

Laos: Constitutional monarchy in southeast Asia, surrounded by China, Vietnam, Kampuchea, Thailand and Burma; capital, Vientiane. Systematic evangelization by French missionaries started about 1881; earlier efforts ended in 1688. A vicariate apostolic was organized in 1899 when there were 8,000 Catholics and 2,000 catechumens in the country. Most of the foreign missionaries were expelled following the communist takeover in 1975. Buddhism is the state religion. Laos has an apostolic delegate.

V.a., 4; bp., 3 (nat.); priests, 23 (8 dioc., 15 rel.); sem., 8; bros., 2; srs., 60; sch., 5; Caths., 35,000 (1%); tot. pop., 3,383,000 (1977).

Lebanon: Republic in the Middle East, north of Israel; capital, Beirut. Christianity, introduced in apostolic times, was firmly established by the end of the fourth century and has remained so despite heavy Moslem influence since early in the seventh century. The country is the center of the Maronite Rite. Lebanon maintains diplomatic relations with Vatican City.

There are 18 ecclesiastical jurisdictions in Lebanon serving the following rites: Armenian (1 diocese); Chaldean (1 diocese); Roman (1 vicariate apostolic); Maronite (3 archdioceses and 5 dioceses); Greek Melkite (1 metropolitan see, 6 archdioceses); the Syrians are served by a patriarchal vicar. The patriarchs of Antioch of the Syrians and Antioch of the Maronites reside in Lebanon. Catholics (est.), 1,000,000; tot. pop., 3,030,000.

Lesotho: Constitutional monarchy, an enclave in the southeastern part of the Republic of South Africa; capital, Maseru. Oblates of Mary Immaculate, the first Catholic missionaries in the area, started evangelization in 1862. A prefecture apostolic was organized in 1894. The hierarchy was established in 1951. Lesotho maintains diplomatic relations with Vatican City.

Archd., 1; dioc., 3; abp., 1 (nat.); bp., 3 (2 nat.); parishes, 71; priests, 131 (19 dioc., 112 rel.); sem., 11; bros., 58; srs., 805; sch., 515; bap., 22,680; Caths., 517,300 (47.7%); tot. pop., 1,083,290.

Liberia: Republic in western Africa, bordering on the Atlantic; capital, Monrovia. Missionary work and influence, dating interruptedly from the 16th century, were slight before the Society of African Missions undertook evangelization in 1906. Liberia maintains diplomatic relations with Vatican City.

V.a., 2; bp., 2 (nat.); parishes, 46; priests, 49 (8 dioc., 41 rel.); sem., 13; p.d., 3; bros., 20; srs., 77; sch., 67; bap., 2,866; Caths., 29,120 (1.6%); tot. pop., 1,800,000.

Libya: Arab republic in northern Africa, on the Mediterranean between Egypt and Tunisia; capitals are Tripoli and Benghasi. Christianity was probably preached in the area at an early date but was overcome by the spread of Islam from the 630's. Islamization was complete by 1067 and there has been no Christian influence since then. The Catholics in the country belong to the foreign colony. Islam is the state religion. Libya has an apostolic delegate (to North Africa).

V.a., 3; p.a., 1; bp., 2; parishes, 3; priests, 9 (6 dioc., 3 rel.); srs., 142; bap., 42; Caths., 10,000 (.4%); tot. pop., 2,500,000.

Liechtenstein: Constitutional monarchy in central Europe, in the Alps and on the Rhine between Switzerland and Austria; capital, Vaduz. Christianity in the country dates from the fourth century; the area has been under the jurisdiction of Chur, Switzerland, since about that time. The Reformation had hardly any influence in the country. Catholicism is the state religion but religious freedom for all is guaranteed by law.

Parishes, 10; priests, 27 (dioc.); srs., 123; sch., 1; bap., 500; Caths., 21,000; tot. pop., 24,000.

Luxembourg: Constitutional monarchy in western Europe, between Belgium, Germany and France; capital, Luxembourg. Christianity, introduced in the fifth and sixth centuries, was firmly established by the end of the eighth century. A full-scale parish system was in existence in the ninth century. Monastic influence was strong until the Reformation, which had minimal influence in the country. The Church experienced some adverse influence from the currents of the French Revolution. Luxembourg maintains diplomatic relations with Vatican City.

Dioc., 1; bp., 1; parishes, 274; priests, 477 (377 dioc., 100 rel.); sem., 16; bros., 28; srs., 1,343; sch., 12; bap., 3,403; Caths. 342,140 (95%); tot. pop., 360,000.

Macao: Portuguese province in southeast Asia across the Pearl River estuary from Hong Kong. Christianity was introduced by the Jesuits in 1557. Diocese was established in 1576. Macao served as a base for missionary work in Japan and China.

Dioc., 1; bp., 1; parishes, 8; priests, 77 (38 dioc., 39 rel.); sem., 6; bros., 15; srs., 203; sch., 51; bap., 638; Caths., 41,000; tot. pop., 280,000.

Madagascar (Malagasy Republic): Member of the French Community, off the eastern coast of Africa; capital, Tananarive. Missionary efforts were generally fruitless from early in the 16th century until the Jesuits were permitted to start open evangelization about 1845. A prefecture apostolic was set up in 1850 and a vicariate apostolic in the north was placed in charge of the Holy Ghost Fathers in 1898. There were 100,000 Catholics by 1900. The first native bishop was ordained in 1936. The hierarchy was established in 1955. Madagascar maintains diplomatic relations with Vatican City.

Archd., 3; dioc., 14; card., 1 (nat.); abp., 2 (nat.); bp., 15 (12 nat.); parishes, 130; priests, 656 (146 dioc., 510 rel.); sem., 100; bros., 316; srs., 1,636; sch., 1,551; bap., 74,771; Caths., 1,814,000 (21.3%); tot. pop. 8,520,000.

Madeira Islands: Portuguese province, an archipelago 340 miles west of the northwestern coast of Africa; capital, Funchal. Catholicism has had a continuous history since the first half of the 15th century. Statistics are included in those for Portugal.

Malawi: Republic in the interior of eastern Africa, member of the British Commonwealth; capital, Lilongwe. Missionary work, begun by Jesuits in the late 16th and early 17th centuries, was generally ineffective until the end of the 19th century. The White Fathers arrived in 1889 and later were joined by others. A vicariate was set up in 1897. The hierarchy was established in 1959. Malawi maintains diplomatic relations with Vatican City.

Archd., 1; dioc., 6; abp., 1 (nat.); bp., 6 (4 nat.); parishes, 115; priests, 309 (89 dioc., 220 rel.); sem., 142; bros., 91; srs., 539; sch., 659; bap., 45,144; Caths., 1,230,175 (20.9%); tot. pop., 5,871,320.

Malaysia: Parliamentary democracy in southeastern Asia, member of the British Commonwealth, federation of former states of Malaya, Sabah (former Br. North Borneo), and Sarawak; capital, Kuala Lumpur. Christianity, introduced by Portuguese colonists about 1511, was confined almost exclusively to Malacca until late in the 18th century. The effectiveness of evangelization increased from then on because of the recruitment and training of native clergy. Singapore (see separate entry), founded in 1819, became a center for missionary work. Seventeen thousand Catholics were in the Malacca diocese in 1888. Effective evangelization in Sabah and Sarawak began in the second half of the 19th century. The hierarchy was established in 1973. Malaysia has an apostolic delegate.

Archd., 2; dioc., 4; abp., 2; bp., 4 (nat.); parishes, 136; priests, 257 (165 dioc., 92 rel.); sem., 44; p.d., 1; bros., 119; srs., 559; sch., 356; bap., 12,690; Caths., 379,310 (3%); tot. pop., 12,500,000.

Maldives: Republic, an archipelago 400 miles southwest of India and Ceylon; capital, Male. No serious attempt was ever made to evangelize the area, which is completely Moslem.

Tot. pop., 122,000.

Mali: Republic, inland in western Africa; capital, Bamako. Catholicism was introduced late in the second half of the 19th century. Missionary work made little progress in the midst of the predominantly Moslem population. A vicariate was set up in 1921. The hierarchy was established in 1955. Mali has an apostolic delegate.

Archd., 1; dioc., 5; abp., 1 (nat.); bp., 5 (3 nat.); parishes, 38; priests, 145 (19 dioc., 126 rel.); sem., 16; bros., 14; srs., 167; sch., 56; bap., 2,121; Caths., 53,000 (.9%); tot. pop., 5,900,000.

Malta: Parliamentary democracy, member of the British Commonwealth, 58 miles south of Sicily; capital, Valletta. Early catacombs and inscriptions are evidence of the early introduction of Christianity. St. Paul was shipwrecked on Malta in 60. Saracens controlled the island(s) from 870 to 1090, a period of difficulty for the Church. The line of bishops extends from 1090 to the present. Malta maintains diplomatic relations with Vatican City.

Archd., 1; dioc., 1; abp., 1; bp., 1; parishes, 79; priests, 1,059 (564 dioc., 495 rel.); sem., 77; bros., 87; srs., 1,676; sch., 41; bap., 56,656; Caths., 305,580 (94.6%); tot. pop., 322,720.

Mariana Islands: U.S. Trust territory in Pacific (scheduled to become a U.S. commonwealth). Under ecclesiastical jurisdiction of Agana diocese, Guam. Statistics included in Guam.

Martinique: French overseas department in the West Indies, about 130 miles south of Guadeloupe; capital, Fort-de-France. Catholicism was introduced in the 16th century. The hierarchy was established in 1967.

Archd., 1; abp., 1; parishes, 47; priests, 97 (44 dioc., 53 rel.); sem., 11; bros., 16; srs., 210; sch., 10; bap., 4,916; Caths., 300,000; tot. pop., 369,000.

Mauritania: Islamic republic on the northwest coast of Africa; capital, Nouakchott. With few exceptions, the Catholics in the country are members of the foreign colony.

Dioc., 1; bp., 1; parishes, 6; priests, 11 (2 dioc., 9 rel.); srs., 22; sch., 2; bap., 34; Caths., 5,000 (.4%); tot. pop., 1,350,000.

Mauritius: Self-governing island state, member of the British Commonwealth, 500 miles east of Madagascar; capital, Port Louis. Catholicism was introduced by Vincentians in 1722. Port Louis, made a vicariate in 1819, was a jumping-off point for missionaries to Australia, Madagascar and South Africa. Mauritius maintains diplomatic relations with Vatican City.

Dioc., 1; bp., 1; parishes, 43; priests, 102 (52 dioc., 50 rel.); sem., 9; srs., 322; sch., 67; bap., 6,414; Caths., 300,000 (33.3%); tot. pop., 900,000.

Melilla: Spanish possession in northern Africa. Statistics are included in those for Spain.

Mexico (United States of Mexico): Republic in Middle America. Christianity was introduced early in the 16th century. Mexico City, made a diocese in 1530, became the missionary and cultural center of the whole country. Missionary work, started in 1524 and forwarded principally by Franciscans, Dominicans, Augustinians and Jesuits, resulted in the baptism of all persons in the central plateau by the end of the century. Progress there and in the rest of the country continued in the following century but tapered off and went into decline in the 18th century, for a variety of reasons ranging from diminishing government support to relaxations of Church discipline. The wars of independence, 1810-21, in which some Catholics participated, created serious problems of adjustment for the Church. Social problems, political unrest and government opposition climaxed in the constitution of 1917 which practically outlawed the Church. Persecution took serious tolls of life and kept the Church underground, under Calles, 1924-1928, again in 1931, and under Cardenas in 1934. President Camacho, 1940-1946, ended persecution and instituted a more lenient policy. The Church, however, still labors under legal and practical disabilities. Mexico has an apostolic delegate.

Archd., 11; dioc., 53; prel., 7; v.a., 2; card., 3 (1979); abp., 12; bp., 66; parishes, 3,615; priests, 9,375 (6,791 dioc., 2,584 rel.); sem., 2,631; p.d., 13; bros., 928; srs., 23,667; sch., 2,579; bap., 1,912,671; Caths., 58,590,000 (94%); tot. pop., 62,329,000 (1977).

Monaco: Constitutional monarchy, an enclave on the Mediterranean coast of France near the Italian border; capital, Monaco-Ville. Christianity was introduced before 1000. Catholicism is the official religion but freedom is guaranteed for all. Monaco has a minister at Vatican City.

Dioc., 1; bp., 1; parishes, 5; priests, 33 (11 dioc., 22 rel.); sem., 5; p.d., 1; bros., 38; srs., 68; sch., 8; bap., 131; Caths., 21,790 (87%); tot. pop., 25,030.

Mongolian Peoples' Republic: Republic in north central Asia; capital Ulan Bator. Christianity was introduced by Nestorians. Some Franciscans were in the country in the 13th and 14th centuries, en route to China. Limited evangelization efforts from the 18th century had little success among the Mongols in Outer Mongolia, where Buddhism has predominated for hundreds of years. No Christians were known to be there in 1953. There may be a few Catholics in Inner Mongolia. No foreign missionaries have been in the country since 1953.

Pop., 1,500,000.

Montserrat: British island possession in Caribbean; capital, Plymouth. Under ecclesiastical jurisdiction of St. John's diocese, Antigua.

Parish, 1; priests, 2 (rel.); srs., 4; sch., 1; bap., 34; Caths., 1,000; tot. pop., 13,000.

Morocco: Constitutional monarchy in northwest Africa with Atlantic and Mediterranean coastlines; capital, Rabat. Christianity was known in the area by the end of the third century. Bishops from Morocco attended a council at Carthage in 484. Catholic life survived under Visigoth and, from 700, Arab rule; later it became subject to influence from the Spanish, Portuguese and French. Islam is the state religion. The hierarchy was established in 1955. Morocco maintains diplomatic relations with Vatican City.

Archd., 2; abp., 2; parishes, 65; priests, 113 (30 dioc., 83 rel.); bros., 18; srs., 455; sch., 62; bap., 284; Caths., 69,790 (.37%); tot. pop., 18,600,000.

Mozambique: Independent (June 25, 1975) republic in southeast Africa, bordering on the Indian Ocean; former Portuguese territory; capital, Maputo (formerly Lourenco Marques). Christianity was introduced by Portuguese Jesuits about the middle of the 16th century. Evangelization continued from then until the 18th century when it went into decline largely because of the Portuguese government's expulsion of the Jesuits. Conditions worsened in the 1830's, improved after 1881, but deteriorated again during the anticlerical period from 1910 to 1925. Conditions improved in 1940, the year Portugal concluded a new concordat with the Holy See and the hierarchy was established. Outspoken criticism by missionaries of Portuguese policies in Mozambique resulted in Church-state tensions in the years immediately preceding independence. The first two native bishops were ordained March 9, 1975. Mozambique has an apostolic delegate.

Archd., 1; dioc., 8; abp., 1 (nat.); bp., 8 (6 nat.); parishes, 257; priests, 321 (30 dioc., 291 rel.); sem., 13; p.d., 1; bros., 107; srs., 583; bap., 25,878; Caths., 1,534,880 (16.2%); tot. pop., 9,443,420.

Namibia (South West Africa): Territory in South Africa in dispute between the Republic of South Africa and the United Nations (scheduled for independence by the end of 1978); capital, Windhoek. The area shares the history of the Republic of South Africa. Namibia has an apostolic delegate (to South Africa).

V.a., 2; bp., 3; parishes, 60; priests, 71 (2 dioc., 69 rel.); p.d., 8; bros., 52; srs., 303; sch., 92; bap., 6,772; Caths., 141,930 (15.7%); tot. pop., 900,000.

Nauru: Independent republic in western Pacific; capital, Yaren District. Under ecclesiastical jurisdiction of Tarawa, Nauru and Funafuti diocese. Statistics included in Gilbert Islands.

Nepal: Constitutional monarchy, the only Hindu kingdom in the world, in central Asia south of the Himalayas between India and Tibet; capital, Katmandu. Little is known of the country before the 15th century. Some Jesuits passed through from 1628 and some sections were evangelized in the 18th century, with minimal results, before the country was closed to foreigners. Conversions from Hinduism, the state religion, are not recognized in law. Christian missionary work is not allowed. Catholics in the country have been under the jurisdiction of the Patna diocese, India, since 1919.

Tot. pop., 13,140,000.

Netherlands: Kingdom in northwestern Europe; capital, Amsterdam (seat of the government, The Hague). Evangelization, begun about the turn of the sixth century by Irish, Anglo-Saxon and Frankish missionaries, resulted in Christianization of the country by 800 and subsequent strong influence on The Lowlands. Invasion by French Calvinists in 1572 brought serious losses to the Catholic Church and made the Reformed Church dominant. Catholics suffered a practical persecution of official repression and social handicap in the 17th century. The schism of Utrecht occurred in 1724. Only one-third of the population was Catholic in 1726. The Church had only a skeleton organization from 1702 to 1853, when the hierarchy was reestablished. Despite this upturn, cultural isolation was the experience of Catholics until about 1914. From then on new vigor came into the life of the Church, and a whole new climate of interfaith relations began to develop. Before and for some years following the Second Vatican Council, the thrust and variety of thought and practice in the Dutch Church moved it to the vanguard position of "progressive" renewal. The Netherlands maintains diplomatic relations with Vatican City.

Archd., 1; dioc., 6; card., 3; bp., 6; parishes, 1,793; priests, 6,092 (2,554 dioc., 3,538 rel.); sem., 248; p.d., 5; bros., 3,458; srs., 22,793; sch., 1,695; bap., 59,412; Caths., 5,663,765 (40.8%); tot. pop., 13,850,000.

Netherlands Antilles (Curacao): Autonomous part of the Kingdom of The Netherlands. Consists of two groups of islands in the Caribbean: Curacao, Aruba and Bonaire, off the northern coast of Venezuela; and St. Eustatius, Saba and the southern part of St. Martaan, southeast of Puerto Rico; capital, Willemstad on Curacao. Christianity was introduced in the 16th century. Apostolic delegation was established in 1975.

Dioc., 1; bp., 1; parishes, 45; priests, 59 (9 dioc., 50 rel.); sem., 3; bros., 69; srs., 189; sch., 192; bap., 3,350; Caths., 212,000; tot. pop., 245,000.

New Caledonia: French territory consisting of several islands in Oceania east of Queensland, Australia; capital, Noumea. Catholicism was introduced in 1843, nine years after Protestant missionaries began evangelization. A vicariate was organized in 1847. The hierarchy was established in 1966.

Archd., 1; abp., 1; parishes, 36; priests, 60 (11 dioc., 49 rel.); sem., 2; bros., 52; srs., 193; sch., 71; bap., 1,998; Caths., 88,750 (65.7%); tot. pop., 135,000.

New Guinea: See Papua New Guinea.

New Hebrides: Islands in the southwest Pacific, about 500 miles west of Fiji, under joint British-French administration; capital, Vila. Effective, though slow, evangelization by Catholic missionaries began about 1887. A vicariate apostolic was set up in 1904. The hierarchy was established in 1966.

Dioc., 1; bp., 1; parishes, 16; priests, 24 (3 dioc., 21 rel.); sem., 4; bros., 15; srs., 77; sch., 32; bap., 663; Caths., 15,950; tot. pop., 101,000.

New Zealand: Dominion in the British Commonwealth, a group of islands in Oceania 1,200 miles southeast of Australia: capital, Wellington. Protestant missionaries were the first evangelizers. On North Island, Catholic missionaries started work before the establishment of two dioceses in 1848; their work among the Maoris was not organized until about 1881. On South Island, whose first resident priest arrived in 1840, a diocese was established in 1869. These three jurisdictions were joined in a province in 1896. The Marists were the outstanding Catholic missionaries in the area. New Zealand established diplomatic relations with Vatican City in 1973.

Archd., 1; dioc., 3; bp., 6; parishes, 284; priests, 802 (448 dioc., 354 rel.); sem., 43; bros., 343; srs., 1,996; sch., 313; bap., 8,230; Caths. (1977), 446,000 (14.2%); tot. pop., 3,138,000.

Nicaragua: Republic in Central America: capital, Managua. Evangelization began shortly after the Spanish conquest about 1524 and eight years later the first bishop took over jurisdiction of the Church in the country. Jesuits were leaders in missionary work during the colonial period, which lasted until the 1820's. Evangelization endeavor increased after establishment of the republic in 1838. In this century it was extended to the Atlantic coastal area where Protestant missionaries had begun work about the middle of the 1900's. Terrorist activity by the National Guard against peasant families and political dissidents was condemned by the bishops in a pastoral letter in 1977. (See News Events for 1979 developments.) Nicaragua maintains diplomatic relations with Vatican City.

Archd., 1; dioc., 4; prel., 1; v.a., 1; abp., 1; bp., 6; parishes, 183; priests, 304 (117 dioc., 187 rel.); sem., 54; p.d., 13; bros., 89; srs., 661; sch., 273; bap., 74,883; Caths., 2,281,387 (93.2%); tot. pop., 2,447,438.

Niger: Republic in west central Africa; capital, Niamey. The first mission was set up in 1831. A prefecture apostolic was organized in 1942 and the first diocese was established in 1961. The country is predominantly Moslem. Niger maintains diplomatic relations with Vatican City.

Dioc., 1; bp., 1; parishes, 14; priests, 24 (3 dioc., 21 rel.); sem., 1; bros., 10; srs., 72; sch., 18; bap., 145; Caths., 12,000 (.2%); tot. pop., 5,000,000.

Nigeria: Republic in western Africa; capital, Lagos. The Portuguese introduced Catholicism in the coastal region in the 15th century. Capuchins did some evangelization in the 17th century but systematic missionary work did not get underway along the coast until about 1840. A vicariate for this area was organized in 1870. A prefecture was set up in 1911 for missions in the northern part of the country where Islam was strongly entrenched. From 1967, when Biafra seceded, until early in 1970 the country was torn by civil war. The hierarchy was established in 1950. Nigeria has an apostolic delegate.

Archd., 3; dioc., 26; card., 1 (nat.); abp., 4 (3 nat.); bp., 26 (19 nat.); parishes, 312; priests, 950 (460 dioc., 490 rel.); sem., 634; p.d., 4; bros., 111; srs., 663; sch., 1,359; bap., 234,648; Caths., 4,279,990 (5.7%); tot. pop., 75,000,000.

Norway: Constitutional monarchy in northern Europe, the western part of the Scandinavian peninsula; capital, Oslo. Evangelization begun in the ninth century by missionaries from England and Ireland put the Church on a firm footing about the turn of the 11th century. The first diocese was set up in 1153 and development of the Church progressed until the Black Death in 1349 inflicted losses from which it never recovered. Lutheranism, introduced from outside in 1537 and furthered cautiously, gained general acceptance by about 1600 and was made the state religion. Legal and other measures crippled the Church, forcing priests to flee the country and completely disrupting normal activity. Changes for the better came in the 19th century, with the granting of religious liberty in 1845 and the repeal of many legal disabilities in 1897. Norway was administered as a single apostolic vicariate from 1892 to 1932, when it was divided into three jurisdictions under the supervision of the Congregation for the Propagation of the Faith, Norway has an apostolic delegate (to Scandinavia).

Dioc., 1; prel., 2; bp., 3; parishes, 27; priests, 62 (17 dioc., 45 rel.); bros., 3; srs., 390; sch., 5; bap., 213; Caths., 12,574 (.3%); tot. pop., 4,031,190.

Oman: Independent monarchy in eastern corner of Arabian Peninsula; capital, wmuscat. Under ecclesiastical jurisdiction of Arabia vicariate apostolic.

Parish, 1 (first Catholic church dedicated in November, 1977); priests, 2 (rel.); bap., 15; Caths., 1,000 (.1%); tot. pop., 791,000 (1977).

Pakistan: Islamic republic in southwestern Asia, member of the British Commonwealth; capital, Islamabad. (Formerly included East Pakistan which became the independent nation of Bangladesh in 1971.) Islam, firmly established in the eighth century, is the state religion. Christian evangelization of the native population began about the middle of the 19th century, years after earlier scattered attempts. The hierarchy was established in 1950. Pakistan maintains diplomatic relations with Vatican City.

Archd., 1; dioc., 5; card., 1 (nat.); bp., 5 (3 nat.); parishes, 51; priests, 229 (90 dioc., 139 rel.); sem., 21; p.d., 2; bros., 52; srs., 645; sch., 224; bap., 18,638; Caths., 393,840 (.5%); tot. pop., 74,000,000.

Panama: Republic in Central America; capital, Panama City. Catholicism was introduced by Franciscan missionaries and evangelization started in 1514. The Panama diocese, oldest in the Americas, was set up at the same time. The Catholic Church has favored status and state aid for missions, charities and parochial schools, but religious freedom is guaranteed to all religions. Panama maintains diplomatic relations with Vatican City.

Archd., 1; dioc., 3; prel., 1; v.a., 1; abp., 1; bp., 6; parishes, 133; priests, 281 (79 dioc., 209 rel.); sem., 23; p.d., 7; bros., 58; srs., 490; sch., 70; bap., 34,456; Caths., 1,543,120 (87%); tot. pop., 1,770,000.

Papua New Guinea: Independent (Sept. 16, 1975) republic (formerly under Australian administration) in southwest Pacific; member of British Commonwealth. Consists of the eastern half of the southwestern Pacific island of New Guinea and the Northern Solomon Islands; capital, Port Moresby. (For statistics on the Indonesian portion of New Guinea, see Indonesia.) Marists began evangelization about 1844 but were handicapped by many factors, including "spheres of influence" laid out for Catholic and Protestant missionaries. A prefecture apostolic was set up in 1896 and placed in charge of the Divine Word Missionaries. The territory suffered greatly during World War II. Hierarchy was established for New Guinea and adjacent islands in 1966. Papua New Guinea established diplomatic relations with the Vatican in 1977.

Archd., 3; dioc., 13; abp., 2; bp., 15; parishes, 243; priests, 479 (51 dioc., 428 rel.); sem., 62; p.d., 2; bros., 280; srs., 927; sch., 830; bap., 29,338; Caths. (1977), 826,000 (29.2%); tot. pop., 2,829,000.

Paraguay: Republic in central South America; capital, Asuncion. Catholicism was introduced in 1542, evangelization began almost immediately. A diocese erected in 1547 was occupied for the first time in 1556. On many occasions thereafter dioceses in the country were left unoccupied because of political and other reasons. Jesuits who came into the country after 1609 devised the reductions system for evangelizing the Indians, teaching them agriculture, husbandry, trades and other useful arts, and giving them experience in property use and community life. The reductions were communes of Indians only, under the direction of the missionaries. About 50 of them were established in southern Brazil, Uruguay and northeastern Argentina as well as in Paraguay. They had an average population of three to four thousand. At their peak, some 30 reductions had a population of 100,000. Political officials regarded the reductions with disfavor because they did not control them and feared that the Indians trained in them might foment revolt and upset the established colonial system under Spanish control. The reductions lasted until about 1768 when their Jesuit founders and directors were expelled from Latin America. Church-state relations following independence from Spain in 1811 were tense as often as not because of government efforts to control the Church through continued exercise of Spanish patronage rights and by other means. The Church as well as the whole country suffered a great deal during the War of the Triple Alliance from 1865-70. After that time, the Church had the same kind of experience in Paraguay as in the rest of Latin America with forces of liberalism, anticlericalism, massive educational needs, poverty, a shortage of priests and other personnel. Most recently church leaders have been challenging the government to initiate long-needed economic and social reforms. Paraguay maintains diplomatic relations with Vatican City.

Archd., 1; dioc., 7; prel., 2; v.a., 2; abp., 1; bp., 12; parishes, 252; priests, 463 (173 dioc., 290 rel.); sem., 58; p.d., 2; bros., 101; srs., 794; sch., 297; bap., 69,491; Caths., 2,532,590 (91.3%); tot. pop., 2,773,890.

Peru: Republic on the western coast of South America; capital, Lima. An effective diocese became operational in 1537, five years after the Spanish conquest. Evangelization, already underway, developed for some time after 1570 but deteriorated before the end of the colonial period in the 1820's. The first native-born saint of the new world was a Peruvian, Rose of Lima, a Dominican tertiary who died in 1617 and was canonized in 1671. In the new republic founded after the wars of independence the Church experienced problems of adjustment and many of the difficulties that cropped up in other South American countries: government efforts to control it through continuation of the patronage rights of the Spanish crown; suppression of houses of religious and expropriation of church property; religious indifference and outright hostility. The Church was given special status but was not made the established religion. Repressive measures by the government against labor protests have been condemned by Church leaders in the past several years. Peru maintains diplomatic relations with Vatican City.

Archd., 7; dioc., 12; prel., 14; v.a., 8; card., 1; abp., 6; bp., 36; parishes, 1,111; priests, 2,200 (852 dioc., 1,348 rel.); sem., 434; p.d., 25; bros., 481; srs., 4,695; sch., 739; bap., 390,102; Caths., 14,915,000 (92.7%); tot. pop., 16,090,000 (1977).

Philippine Islands: Republic, an archipelago of 7,000 islands off the southeast coast of Asia; capital, Quezon City. Systematic evangelization was begun in 1564 and resulted in firm establishment of the Church by the 19th century. During the period of Spanish rule, which lasted from the discovery of the islands by Magellan in 1521 to 1898, the Church experienced difficulties with the patronage system under which the Spanish crown tried to control ecclesiastical affairs through episcopal and other appointments. This system ended in 1898 when the United States gained possession of the islands and instituted a policy of separation of Church and state. Anticlericalism flared late in the 19th century. The Aglipayan schism, an attempt to set up a nationalist church, occurred a few years later, in 1902. The republic maintains diplomatic relations with Vatican City. The martial-law government of Ferdinand Marcos, imposed in 1972, has been under attack for the past several years for violations of human rights. The bishops issued a pastoral letter on government relations in 1977 calling for equal rights for all and protesting government interference in the Church's work of evangelization.

Archd., 13; dioc., 33; prel., 11; v.a., 4; card., 2; abp., 11; bp., 62; parishes, 1,865; priests, 4,487 (2,261 dioc., 2,226 rel.); sem., 3,300; p.d., 18; bros., 537; srs., 7,104; sch., 1,311; bap., 1,223,337; Caths., 36,710,000 (83.9%); tot. pop., 43,751,000 (1977).

Poland: People's republic in eastern Europe; capital, Warsaw. The first traces of Christianity date from the second half of the ninth century. Its spread was accelerated by the union of the Slavs in the 10th century. The first bishopric was set up in 968. The Gniezno archdiocese, with suffragan sees and a mandate to evangelize the borderlands as well as Poland, was established in 1000. Steady growth continued thereafter, with religious orders and their schools playing a major role. Some tensions with the Orthodox were experienced. The Reformation, supported mainly by city dwellers and the upper classes, peaked from about the middle of the 16th century, resulting in numerous conversions to Lutheranism, the Reformed Church and the Bohemian Brethren. A successful Counter-Reformation, with the Jesuits in a position of leadership, was completed by about 1632. The movement served a nationalist as well as religious purpose; in restoring religious unity to a large degree, it united the country against potential invaders, the Swedes, Russians and Turks. The Counter-Reformation had bad side effects, leading to the repression of Protestants long after it was over and to prejudice against Orthodox who returned to allegiance with Rome in 1596 and later. The Church, in the same manner as the entire country, was adversely affected by the partitions of the 18th and 19th centuries. Russification hurt the Orthodox who had reunited with Rome and the Latins who were in the majority. Germans extended their Kulturkampf to the area they controlled. The Austrians exhibited some degree of tolerance. In the republic established after World War I the Church reorganized itself, continued to serve as a vital force in national life, and enjoyed generally harmonious relations with the state. Progressive growth was strong until 1939 when disaster struck in the form of invasion by German and Russian forces and six years of war. In 1945, seven years before the adoption of a Soviet-type of constitution, the Communist-controlled government initiated a policy that included a constant program of atheistic propaganda; a strong campaign against the hierarchy and clergy; the imprisonment in 1948 of 700 priests and even more religious; rigid limitation of the activities of religious; censorship and curtailment of the Catholic press and Catholic Action; interference with church administration and appointments of the clergy; the "deposition" of Cardinal Wyszynski in 1953 and the imprisonment of other members of the hierarchy; the suppression of "Caritas," the Catholic charitable organization; promotion of "Progressive Catholic" activities and a small minority of "patriotic priests." Establishment of the Gomulka regime, the freeing of Cardinal Wyszynski in

October, 1956, and the signing of an agreement two months later by bishops and state officials, led to some improvement of conditions. The underlying fact, however, was that the regime conceded to Catholics only so much as was necessary to secure support of the government as a more tolerable evil than the harsh and real threat of a Russian-imposed puppet government like that in Hungary. This has been the controlling principle in Church-state relations. Auxiliary Bishop Ladislaw Rubin of Gniezno sketched the general state of affairs in March, 1968. He said that there was no sign that the government had any intention of releasing its oppressive grip on the Church. As evidence of the "climate of asphyxiation" in the country he cited: persistent questioning of priests by officials concerning their activities; the prohibition against Catholic schools, hospitals and charitable works; the financial burden of a 60 per cent tax on church income. Cardinal Wyszynski denounced "enforced atheism" in a Lenten pastoral in the same year. In May, 1969, the bishops drafted a list of grievances against the government which, they said, were "only some examples of difficulties which demonstrated the situation of the Church in our homeland." The grievances were: refusal of permits to build new churches and establish new parishes; refusal of permission "for the organization of new religion classes"; pressure on Catholics who attend religious ceremonies; censorship and the lack of an independent Catholic daily newspaper; lack of representation in public life; restriction of "freedom to conduct normal pastoral work" in the western portion of the country. There was a move toward improvement in Church-state relations in 1971-72. In 1973, the Polish bishops issued a pastoral letter urging Catholics to resist the official atheism imposed by the government. In 1974 the Polish bishops expressed approval of renewed Vatican efforts at regularizing Church-state relations but insisted that they (the bishops) be consulted on every step of the negotiations. The bishops have continued their sharp criticism of anti-religious policies and programs of the government. Regular contacts on a working level were established by the Vatican and Poland in 1974.

Archd., 8; dioc., 23; ap. ex., 1; card., 3; abp., 2; bp., 67; parishes, 7058; priests, 18,110 (14,248 dioc., 3,862 rel.); sem., 3,493; bros., 1,192; srs., 25,154; sch., 35; bap., 587,160; Caths., 32,154,400 (92.6%); tot. pop., 34,700,000.

Polynesia, French: French possession in the southern Pacific, including Tahiti and the Marquesas Islands; capital, Papeete. The first phase of evangelization in the Marquesas Islands, begun in 1838, resulted in 216 baptisms in 10 years. A vicariate was organized in 1848 but real progress was not made until after the baptism of native rulers in 1853. Persecution caused missionaries to leave the islands several times. By the 1960's, more than 95 per cent of the population was Catholic. Isolated attempts to evangelize Tahiti were made in the 17th and 18th centuries. Two Picpus Fathers began missionary work in 1831. A vicariate was organized in 1848. By 1908, despite the hindrances of Protestant opposition, disease and other factors, the Church had firm roots.

Archd., 1; dioc., 1; abp., 1 (nat.); bp., 1; parishes, 71; priests, 41 (8 dioc., 33 rel.); sem., 2; bros., 30; srs., 65; sch., 20; bap., 1,200; Caths., 47,160; tot. pop., 137,070.

Portugal: Republic in the western part of the Iberian peninsula; capital, Lisbon. Christianity was introduced before the fourth century. From the fifth century to early in the eighth century the Church experienced difficulties from the physical invasion of barbarians and the intellectual invasion of doctrinal errors in the forms of Arianism, Priscillianism and Pelagianism. The Church survived under the rule of Arabs from about 711 and of the Moors until 1249. Ecclesiastical life was fairly vigorous from 1080 to 1185, and monastic influence became strong. A decline set in about 1450. Several decades later Portugal became the jumping-off place for many missionaries to newly discovered colonies. The Reformation had little effect in the country. Beginning about 1750, Pombal, minister of foreign affairs and prime minister, mounted a frontal attack on the Jesuits whom he succeeded in expelling from Portugal and the colonies. His anti-Jesuit campaign successful Pombal also attempted, and succeeded to some extent, in controlling the Church in Portugal until his fall from power about 1777. Liberal revolutionaries with anti-Church policies made the 19th century a difficult one for the Church. Similar policies prevailed in Church-state relations in this century until the accession of Salazar to power in 1928. In 1940 he concluded a concordat with the Holy See which regularized Church-state relations but still left the Church in a subservient condition. The prevailing spirit of church authorities in Portugal has been conservative. In 1971 several priests were tried for subversion for speaking out against colonialism and for taking part in guerrilla activities in Angola. A military coup of Apr. 25, 1974, triggered a succession of chaotic political developments which led to an attempt by Communists, after receiving only 18 per cent of the votes cast in a national election, to take over the government in the summer of 1975. Portugal maintains diplomatic relations with Vatican City.

Patriarchate, 1; archd., 2; dioc., 16; card., 1; abp., 2; bp., 22; parishes, 4,020; priests, 4,702 (3,731 dioc., 971 rel.); sem., 311; p.d., 2; bros., 571; srs., 7,818; sch., 342; bap., 167,881; Caths., 8,774,880 (95.3%); tot. pop., 9,207,550.

Puerto Rico: A U.S. commonwealth, the smallest of the Greater Antilles, 885 miles southeast of the southern coast of Florida; capital, San Juan. Following its discovery by Columbus in 1493, the island was evangelized by Spanish missionaries and remained under Spanish ecclesiastical as well as political control until 1898 when it became a possession of the United States. The original diocese, San Juan, was erected in 1511. The present hierarchy was established in 1960. Puerto Rico has an apostolic delegate (nuncio to Dominican Republic).

Archd., 1; dioc., 4; card., 1; bp., 8; parishes, 256; priests, 712 (298 dioc., 414 rel.); sem., 84; p.d., 5; bros., 123; srs., 1,490; sch., 193; bap., 17,662; Caths., 2,726,570 (84.6%); tot. pop., 3,222,350.

Qatar: Independent state in the Persian Gulf; capital, Doha. Under ecclesiastical jurisdiction of Arabia vicariate apostolic.

Priest, 1 (rel.); bap., 48; Caths., 2,000; tot. pop., 95,000.

Reunion: French overseas department, 450 miles east of Madagascar; capital, Saint-Denis. Catholicism was introduced in 1667 and some intermittent missionary work was done through the rest of the century. A prefecture apostolic was organized in 1712. Vincentians began work there in 1817 and were joined later by Holy Ghost Fathers. Reunion has an apostolic delegate.

Dioc., 1; bp., 1; parishes, 67; priests, 118 (61 dioc., 57 rel.); sem., 2; bros., 44; srs., 449; sch., 30; bap., 11,901; Caths., 445,000; tot. pop., 485,000.

Rhodes: Greek island in the Aegean Sea, 112 miles from the southwestern coast of Asia Minor. A diocese was established about the end of the third century. A bishop from Rhodes attended the Council of Nicaea in 325. Most of the Christians followed the Eastern Churches into schism in the 11th century and became Orthodox. Turks controlled the island from 1522 to 1912. The small Catholic population, for whom a diocese existed from 1328 to 1546, lived in crossfire between Turks and Orthodox. After 1719 Franciscans provided pastoral care for the Catholics, for whom an archdiocese was erected in 1928. Statistics are included in Greece.

Rhodesia (Zimbabwe): Self-governing state in south central Africa; capital, Salisbury. Earlier unsuccessful missionary ventures preceded the introduction of Catholicism in 1879. Missionaries began to make progress after 1893. The hierarchy was established in 1955; the first black bishop was ordained in 1973. In 1969, four years after the government of Ian Smith made a unilateral declaration of independence from England, a new constitution was enacted for the purpose of assuring continued white supremacy over the black majority. Catholic and Protestant prelates in the country have protested rigorously against the constitution and related enactments as opposed to human rights of the blacks and restrictive of the Church's freedom to carry out its pastoral, educational and social service functions. Irish-born Bishop Donal Lamont, convicted and sentenced to 10 years' imprisonment in 1976 for failing to report the presence of guerrillas, was deprived of his Rhodesian citizenship and deported in 1977. (See News Events for 1979 developments.) Rhodesia has an apostolic delegate (to South Africa).

Archd., 1; dioc., 4; p.a. 1; abp. 1 (nat.); bp., 5 (2 nat.; total includes Bishop Lamont who was exiled); parishes, 69; priests, 339 (58 dioc., 281 rel.); sem., 80; bros., 125; srs., 982; sch., 163; bap., 28,640; Caths., 622,590 (9.3%); tot. pop., 6,640,000.

Rumania: Socialist republic in southeastern Europe; capital, Bucharest. Latin Christianity, introduced in the third century, all but disappeared during the barbarian invasions. The Byzantine Rite was introduced by the Bulgars about the beginning of the eighth century and established firm roots. It eventually became Orthodox, but a large number of its adherents returned later to union with Rome. Attempts to reintroduce the Latin Rite on any large scale have been unsuccessful. Communists took over the government following World War II, forced the abdication of Michael I in 1947, and enacted a Soviet type of constitution in 1952. By that time a campaign against religion was already in progress. In 1948 the government denounced a concordat concluded in 1929, nationalized all schools and passed a law on religions which resulted in the disorganization of Church administration. The 1.5 million-member Rumanian Byzantine Rite Church, by government decree, was incorporated into the Rumanian Orthodox Church, and the Orthodox bishops then seized the cathedrals of Roman Catholic bishops. Five of the six Latin Rite bishops were immediately disposed of by the government, and the last was sentenced to 18 years' imprisonment in 1951, when a great many arrests of priests and laymen were made. Religious orders were suppressed in 1949. Since 1948 more than 50 priests have been executed and 200 have died in prison. One hundred priests were reported in prison at the end of 1958. Some change for the better in Church-state relations was reported after the middle of the summer of 1964, although restrictions were still in effect. About 1,200 priests were engaged in parish work in August, 1965.

Archd., 2; dioc., 8; ord., 1; bp., 2. No recent statistics are available on the number of Catholics. There were an estimated 1,140,000 Catholics (5.9% of the population) in 1969. Tot. pop., 21,533,000.

Rwanda: Republic in east central Africa; capital, Kigali. Catholicism was introduced about the turn of the 20th century. The hierarchy was established in 1959. Intertribal warfare between the ruling Hutus (90 per cent of the population) and the Tutsis (formerly the ruling aristocracy) has plagued the country for several years. Rwanda maintains diplomatic relations with Vatican City.

Archd., 1; dioc., 5; abp., 1 (nat.); bp., 5 (4 nat.); parishes, 105; priests, 380 (206 dioc., 174 rel.); sem., 134; bros., 175; srs., 718; sch., 812; bap., 81,709; Caths., 1,935,000 (43%); tot. pop., 4,500,000.

Ryukyu Islands: Consists of Okinawa and 72 other islands in western Pacific. Statistics included in Japan.

St. Christopher (Kitts)-Nevis: British Associated State in West Indies; capital, Basseterre, on St. Christopher. Under ecclesiastical jurisdiction of St. John's diocese, Antigua.

Parishes, 8; priests, 4 (rel.); srs., 9; sch., 2; bap., 80; Caths., 4,000; tot. pop., 66,000 (statistics include Anguilla).

St. Lucia: British Associated State in West Indies; capital, Castries.

Archd., 1; bp., 1; parishes, 22; priests, 31 (8 dioc., 23 rel.); sem., 2; p.d., 1; bros., 2; srs., 34; sch., 58; bap., 3,405; Caths., 96,000; tot. pop., 110,000.

St. Pierre and Miquelon: French overseas territory, islands near the southwest coast of Newfoundland. Catholicism was introduced about 1689.

V.a., 1; bp., 1; parishes, 3; priests, 6 (1 dioc., 5 rel.); bros., 1; srs., 15; sch., 6; bap., 102; Caths., 6,020; tot. pop., 6,050.

St. Vincent: British Associated State in West Indies; capital, Kingstown. Under ecclesiastical jurisdiction of Bridgetown-Kingstown diocese, Barbados.

Parishes, 6; priests, 6 (rel.); sem., 12; bros., 6; srs., 10; sch., 5; bap., 367; Caths., 13,000; tot. pop., 97,000 (1977).

Samoa: Independent state in the southwestern Pacific; capital, Apia. Catholic missionary work began in 1845. Most of the missions now in operation were established by 1870 when the Catholic population numbered about 5,000. Additional progress was made in missionary work from 1896. The first Samoan priest was ordained in 1892. The hierarchy was established in 1966.

Dioc., 1; card., 1; parishes, 18; priests, 25 (6 dioc., 19 rel.); sem., 21; bros., 21; srs., 130; sch., 16; bap., 1,258; Caths., 31,000 (20.5%); tot. pop., 151,000 (1977).

Samoa, American: Unincorporated U.S. territory in southwestern Pacific, consisting of six small islands; capital, Fagotogo on the Island of Tutuila. Under ecclesiastical jurisdiction of Samoa and Tokelau diocese, Samoa.

Parishes, 5; priests, 5 (1 dioc., 4 rel.); bros., 6; srs., 13; sch., 5; bap., 196; Caths., 4,000; tot. pop., 32,000 (1977).

San Marino: Republic, a 24-square-mile enclave in northeastern Italy; capital, San Marino. The date of initial evangelization is not known, but a diocese was established by the end of the third century. Ecclesiastically, it forms part of the diocese of San Marino-Montefeltro in Italy. San Marino is represented by a minister at Vatican City.

Parishes, 12; priests, 5 (dioc.); srs., 7; bap., 304; Caths., 19,000 (95%); tot. pop., 20,000.

Sao Tome and Principe: Independent republic (July 12, 1975), consisting of two islands off the western coast of Africa in the Gulf of Guinea; former Portuguese territory; capital Sao Tome. Evangelization was begun by the Portuguese who discovered the islands in 1471-72. The Sao Tome diocese was established in 1534.

Dioc., 1; parishes, 12; priests, 4 (1 dioc., 3 rel.); bros., 2; srs., 15; bap., 2,699; Caths., 70,000; tot. pop., 80,000.

Saudi Arabia: Monarchy occupying four-fifths of Arabian peninsula; capital, Riyadh (Taif, summer capital). Under ecclesiastical jurisdiction of Arabia vicariate apostolic.

Priests, 5 (rel.); srs., 2; bap., 19; Caths., 8,000; tot. pop., 9,240,000 (1977).

Scotland: Part of the United Kingdom, in the northern British Isles; capital, Edinburgh. Christianity was introduced by the early years of the fifth century. The arrival of St. Columba and his monks in 563 inaugurated a new era of evangelization which reached into remote areas by the end of the sixth century. He was extremely influential in determining the character of the Celtic Church, which was tribal, monastic, and in union with Rome. Considerable disruption of church activity resulted from Scandinavian invasions in the late eighth and ninth centuries. By 1153 the Scottish Church took a turn away from its insularity and was drawn into closer contact with the European community. Anglo-Saxon religious and political relations, complicated by rivalries between princes and ecclesiastical superiors, were not always the happiest. Religious orders expanded greatly in the 12th century. From shortly after the Norman Conquest of England to 1560 the Church suffered adverse effects from the Hundred Years' War, the Black Death, the Western Schism and other developments. In 1560 parliament abrogated papal supremacy over the Church in Scotland and committed the country to Protestantism in 1567. The Catholic Church was proscribed, to remain that way for more than 200 years, and the hierarchy was disbanded. Defections made the Church a minority religion from that time on. Presbyterian church government was ratified in 1690. Priests launched the Scottish Mission in 1653, incorporating themselves as a mission body under a prefect apostolic and working underground to serve the faithful in much the same way their confreres did in England. About 100 heather priests, trained in clandestine places in the heather country, were ordained by the early 19th century. Catholics got some relief from legal disabilities in 1793 and more later. Many left the country about that time. Some of their numbers were filled subsequently by immigrants from Ireland. The hierarchy was restored in 1878. Scotland, though predominantly Protestant, has a better record for tolerance than Northern Ireland.

Archd., 2; dioc., 6; card., 1; abp., 1; bp., 9; parishes, 467; priests, 1,062 (827 dioc., 235 rel.); sem., 131; p.d., 1; bros., 162; srs., 1,269; sch., 300; Caths., 811,540 (14.7%); tot. pop., 5,520,205 (1977).

Senegal: Republic, member of the French Community, in western Africa; capital, Dakar. The country had its first contact with Catholicism through the Portuguese some time after 1460. Some incidental missionary work was done by Jesuits and Capuchins in the 16th and 17th centuries. A vicariate for the area was placed in charge of the Holy Ghost Fathers in 1779. More effective evangelization efforts were accomplished after the Senegambia vicariate was organized in 1863. The hierarchy was established in 1955. Senegal maintains diplomatic relations with Vatican City.

Archd., 1; dioc., 4; p.a., 1; card., 1 (nat.); bp., 4 (nat.); parishes, 53; priests, 188 (44 dioc., 144 rel.); sem., 54; bros., 118; srs., 494; sch., 148; bap., 7,382; Caths., 209,510 (4%); tot. pop., 5,150,000.

Seychelles Islands: Independent (1976) group of 92 islands in the Indian Ocean 970 miles east of Kenya; capital, Victoria on Mahe. Catholicism was introduced in the 18th century. A vicariate apostolic was organized in 1852. All education in the islands was conducted under Catholic auspices until 1954. The colony has an apostolic delegate (pro-nuncio to Kenya).

Dioc., 1; bp., 1 (nat.); parishes, 17; priests, 21 (3 dioc., 18 rel.); bros., 12; srs., 62; sch., 33; bap., 1,427; Caths., 55,630; tot. pop., 61,900.

Siberia: Republic in the USSR, in northern Asia.

Dioc., 1; v.a. 1.

Sierra Leone: Republic, member of the British Commonwealth, on the western coast of Africa; capital, Freetown. Catholicism was introduced in 1858. Members of the African Missions Society, the first Catholic missionaries in the area, were joined by Holy Ghost Fathers in 1864. Protestant missionaries were active in the area before their Catholic counterparts. Educational work had a major part in Catholic endeavor. The hierarchy was established in 1950. Sierra Leone has an apostolic delegate.

Archd., 1; dioc., 2; abp., 1; bp., 2 (1 nat.); parishes, 26; priests, 107 (8 dioc., 99 rel.); sem., 26; bros., 13; srs., 85; sch., 500; bap., 2,288; Caths., 55,060 (1.7%); tot. pop., 3,200,000.

Sikkim: Associated state of India in the Himalayas south of Tibet; capital, Gangtok. Some evangelization took place after 1848. Buddhism is the state religion. The territory is under the jurisdiction of the diocese of Darjeeling, India.

Singapore: Independent island republic off the southern tip of the Malay Peninsula; member of the British Commonwealth; capital, Singapore. Christianity was introduced in the area by Portuguese colonists about 1511. Singapore was founded in 1819; the first parish church was built in 1846. Singapore has an apostolic delegate.

Archd., 1; abp., 1 (nat.); parishes, 24; priests, 84 (52 dioc., 32 rel.); sem., 5; bros., 46; srs., 224; sch., 55; bap., 2,700; Caths., 80,700 (3.3%); tot. pop., 2,400,000.

Solomon Islands: Independent (July 7, 1978) island group in Oceania; capital, Honiara, on Guadalcanal. Evangelization of the Southern Solomons, begun earlier but interrupted because of violence against them, was resumed by the Marists in 1898. A vicariate apostolic was organized in 1912. A similar jurisdiction was set up for the Western Solomons in 1959. World War II caused a great deal of damage to mission installations. Catholic statistics for the Northern Solomons, where Catholic missionary work started in 1899 and a vicariate was set up in 1930, are included in those reported for Papua New Guinea.

Archd., 1; dioc., 1; abp., 1; bp., 2; parishes, 23; priests, 39 (7 dioc., 32 rel.); sem., 10; bros., 23; srs., 121; bap., 1,861; Caths., 34,420; tot. pop., 248,650.

Somalia: Republic on the eastern coast of Africa; capital, Mogadishu. The country has been Moslem for centuries. Pastoral activity has been confined to immigrants. Schools and hospitals were nationalized in 1972, resulting in the departure of some foreign missionaries. Somalia has an apostolic delegate (to the Red Sea Region).

Dioc., 1; bp., 1; parishes, 2; priests, 6 (rel.); bros., 2; srs., 65; bap., 22; Caths., 2,100; tot. pop., 3,350,000.

South Africa: Republic in the southern part of Africa; capitals, Cape Town (legislative) and Pretoria (administrative). Christianity was introduced by the Portuguese who discovered the Cape of Good Hope in 1498. Boers, who founded Cape Town in 1652, expelled Catholics from the region. There was no Catholic missionary activity from that time until the 19th century. After a period of British opposition, a bishop established residence in 1837 and evangelization got underway thereafter among the Bantus and white immigrants. In recent years church authorities have strongly protested the white supremacy policy of apartheid which seriously infringes the human rights of the native blacks and impedes the Church from carrying out its pastoral, educational and social service functions. The hierarchy was established in 1951. South Africa has an apostolic delegate.

Archd., 4; dioc., 18; abb., 1; p.a., 3; card., 1; abp., 3; bp., 20; parishes, 508; priests, 1,128 (280 dioc., 848 rel.); sem., 100; p.d., 61; bros., 428; srs., 4,087; sch., 477; bap., 72,478; Caths., 1,865,949 (7%); tot. pop., 26,130,000.

South West Africa: See Namibia.

Spain: Nominal monarchy on the Iberian peninsula in southwestern Europe; capital, Madrid. Christians were on the peninsula by 200; some of them suffered martyrdom during persecutions of the third century. A council held in Elvira about 304/6 enacted the first legislation on clerical celibacy in the West. Vandals invaded the peninsula in the fifth century, bringing with them an Arian brand of Christianity which they retained until their conversion following the baptism of their king Reccared, in 589. One of the significant developments of the seventh century was the establishment of Toledo as the primatial see. The Visigoth kingdom lasted to the time of the Arab invasion, 711-14. The Church survived under Moslem rule but experienced some doctrinal and disciplinary irregularities as well as harassment. Reconquest of most of the peninsula was accomplished by 1248; unification was achieved during the reign of Ferdinand and Isabella. The discoveries of Columbus and other explorers ushered in an era of colonial expansion in which Spain became one of the greatest mission-sending countries in history. In 1492, in repetition of anti-Semitic actions of 694, the expulsion of unbaptized Jews was decreed, leading to mass baptisms but a questionable number of real conversions in 1502. (The Jewish minority numbered about 165,000.) Activity by the Inquisition followed. Spain was not seriously affected by the Reformation. Ecclesiastical decline set in about 1650. Anti-Church actions authorized by a constitution enacted in 1812 resulted in the suppression of religious and other encroachments on the leaders, people and goods of the Church. Political, religious and cultural turmoil recurred during the 19th century and into the 20th. A revolutionary republic was proclaimed in 1931, triggering a series of developments which led to civil war from 1936 to 1939. During the conflict, which pitted leftist Loyalists against the forces of Francisco Franco, 6,632 priests and religious and an unknown number of lay persons perished in addition to thousands of victims of combat. One-man, one-party rule, established after the civil war and with rigid control policies with respect to personal liberties and social and economic issues, continued for more than 35 years before giving way after the death of Franco to democratic reforms. The Catholic Church, long the established religion, was disestablished under a new constitution providing guarantees of freedom for other religions as well. Disestablishment was ratified with modifications of a 1976 revision of the earlier concordat of 1953. Spain maintains diplomatic relations with Vatican City.

Archd., 13; dioc., 50; prel., 1; card., 4; abp., 8; bp., 64; parishes, 21,438; priests, 33,363 (22,913 dioc., 10,450 rel.); sem., 3,246; p.d., 3; bros., 7,457; srs., 81,382; sch., 4,732; bap., 655,233; Caths., 35,504,000 (98.7%); tot. pop., 35,971,000 (1977).

Spanish North Africa: Includes the cities of Ceuta and Melilla on the northern coast of Africa, which are considered part of metropolitan Spain.

Spanish Sahara: See Western Sahara.

Sri Lanka (formerly Ceylon): Independent socialist republic, island southeast of India; capital, Colombo. Effective evangelization began in 1543 and made great progress by the middle of the 17th century. The Church was seriously hampered during the Dutch period from about 1650 to 1795. Anti-Catholic laws were repealed by the British in 1806. The hierarchy was established in 1886. Leftist governments and other factors have worked against the Church since the country became independent in 1948. The high percentage of indigenous clergy and religious has been of great advantage to the Church. Sri Lanka maintains diplomatic relations with Vatican City.

Archd., 1; dioc., 6; p.a., 1; card., 1 (nat.); abp., 1 (nat.); bp., 7 (nat.); parishes, 286; priests, 529 (320 dioc., 209 rel.); sem., 160; p.d., 1; bros., 1; srs., 2,329; sch., 49; bap., 28,755; Caths., 980,301 (7%); tot. pop., 14,000,000.

Sudan: Republic in northeastern Africa, the largest country on the continent; capital, Khartoum. Christianity was introduced from Egypt and gained acceptance in the sixth century. Under Arab rule, it was eliminated in the northern region. No Christians were in the country in 1600. Evangelization attempts begun in the 19th century in the south yielded hard-won results. By 1931 there were nearly 40,000 Catholics there, and considerable progress was made by missionaries after that time. In 1957, a year after the republic was established, Catholic schools were nationalized. An act restrictive of religious freedom went into effect in 1962, resulting in the harassment and expulsion of foreign missionaries. By 1964 all but a few Sudanese missionaries had been forced out of the southern region. The northern area, where Islam predominates, is impervious to Christian influence. Late in 1971 some missionaries were allowed to return to work in the South. Southern Sudan was granted regional autonomy within a unified country in March, 1972, thus ending often bitter fighting between the North and

South dating back to 1955. The hierarchy was established in 1974. Sudan maintains diplomatic relations with Vatican City.

Archd., 2; dioc., 5; abp., 2 (1 nat.); bp., 5 (nat.); parishes, 81; priests, 143 (60 dioc., 83 rel.); sem., 31; bros., 35; srs., 194; sch., 40; bap., 18,214; Caths., 693,600 (4%); tot. pop., 17,277,740.

Surinam (formerly Dutch Guiana): Independent (Nov. 25, 1975) state in northern South America; capital, Paramaribo. Catholicism was introduced in 1683. Evangelization began in 1817.

Dioc., 1; bp., 1; parishes, 9; priests, 40 (4 dioc., 36 rel.); sem., 1; bros., 31; srs., 111; sch., 132; bap., 2,197; Caths., 73,800 (16.4%); tot. pop., 450,000.

Swaziland: Constitutional monarchy in southern Africa; almost totally surrounded by the Republic of South Africa; capital, Mbabane. Missionary work was entrusted to the Servites in 1913. A prefecture apostolic was organized in 1923. The hierarchy was established in 1951. Swaziland has an apostolic delegate (to South Africa).

Dioc., 1; bp., 1 (nat.); priests, 36 (4 dioc., 32 rel.); sem., 2; bros., 13; srs., 108; sch., 60; bap., 1,467; Caths., 35,000; tot. pop., 500,000.

Sweden: Kingdom in northwestern Europe; capital, Stockholm. Christianity was introduced by St. Ansgar, a Frankish monk, in 829/30. The Church became well established in the 12th century and was a major influence at the end of the Middle Ages. Political and other factors favored the introduction and spread of the Lutheran Church which became the state religion in 1560. The Augsburg Confession of 1530 was accepted by the government; all relations with Rome, in the country since the 12th century, were severed; monasteries were suppressed; the very presence of Catholics in the country was forbidden in 1617. A decree of tolerance for foreign Catholics was issued about 1781. Two years later a vicariate apostolic was organized for the country. In 1873 Swedes were given the legal right to leave the Lutheran Church and join another Christian church. (Membership in the Lutheran Church is presumed by law unless notice is given of membership in another church.) In 1923 there were only 11 priests and five churches in the country. Since 1952 Catholics have enjoyed almost complete religious freedom. The hierarchy was reestablished in 1953. Hindrances to growth of the Church are the strongly entrenched established church, limited resources, a clergy shortage and the size of the country. Sweden has an apostolic delegate (to Scandinavia).

Dioc., 1; bp., 1; parishes, 29; priests, 95 (30 dioc., 65 rel.); sem., 1; bros., 6; srs., 229; sch., 2; bap., 678; Caths., 81,020 (.9%); tot. pop., 8,300,000.

Switzerland: Republic in central Europe; capital, Bern. Christianity was introduced in the fourth century or earlier and was established on a firm footing before the barbarian invasions of the sixth century. Constance, established as a diocese in the seventh century, was a stronghold of the faith against the pagan Alamanni, in particular, who were not converted until some time in the ninth century. During this period of struggle with the barbarians, a number of monasteries of great influence were established. The Reformation in Switzerland was triggered by Zwingli in 1519 and furthered by him at Zurich until his death in battle against the Catholic cantons in 1531. Calvin set in motion the forces that made Geneva the international capital of the Reformation and transformed it into a theocracy. Catholics mobilized a Counter-Reformation in 1570, six years after Calvin's death. Struggle between Protestant and Catholic cantons was a fact of Swiss life for several hundred years. The Helvetic Constitution enacted at the turn of the 19th century embodied anti-Catholic measures and consequences, among them the dissolution of 130 monasteries. The Church was reorganized later in the century to meet the threats of liberalism, radicalism and the Kulturkampf. In the process, the Church, even though on the defensive, gained the strength and cohesion that characterizes it to the present time. The six dioceses in the country are immediately subject to the Holy See. In 1973, constitutional articles banning Jesuits from the country and prohibiting the establishment of convents and monasteries were repealed. There is a papal nuncio to Switzerland, but Switzerland does not have a diplomatic officer accredited to Vatican City.

Dioc., 6; abb., 2; bp., 8; parishes, 1,694; priests, 4,379 (2,761 dioc., 1,618 rel.); sem., 227; p.d., 2; bros., 336; srs., 10,048; sch., 63; Caths., 3,141,087 (48.5%); tot. pop., 6,476,391.

Syria: Arab republic in southwest Asia; capital, Damascus. Christian communities were formed in apostolic times. It is believed that St. Peter established a see at Antioch before going to Rome. Damascus became a center of influence. The area was the place of great men and great events in the early history of the Church. Monasticism developed there in the fourth century. So did the Monophysite and Monothelite heresies to which portions of the Church succumbed. Byzantine Syrians who remained in communion with Rome were given the name Melkites. Christians of various persuasions — Jacobites, Orthodox and Melkites — were subject to various degrees of harassment from the Arabs who took over in 638 and from the Ottoman Turks who isolated the country and remained in control from 1516 to the end of World War II. Syria maintains diplomatic relations with Vatican City.

There are 19 ecclesiastical jurisdictions in

Syria serving the following rites: Armenian (1 archdiocese, 1 diocese); Chaldean (1 diocese); Roman (1 vicariate apostolic); Maronite (1 patriarchate, whose patriarch resides in Lebanon, 2 archdioceses and 1 diocese); Greek Melkite (1 patriarchate, 5 archdioceses); Syrian (1 patriarchate, whose patriarch resides in Lebanon, 4 archdioceses). Catholics, 204,000; tot. pop., 7,840,000.

Taiwan (Formosa): Location of the Nationalist Government of the Republic of China, an island 100 miles off the southern coast of mainland China; capital, Taipei. Attempts to introduce Christianity in the 17th century were unsuccessful. Evangelization in the 19th century resulted in some 1,300 converts in 1895. Missionary endeavor was hampered by the Japanese who occupied the island following the Sino-Japanese war of 1894-95. Nine thousand Catholics were reported in 1938. Great progress was made in missionary endeavor among the Chinese who emigrated to the island following the Communist take-over of the mainland in 1949. The hierarchy was established in 1952. Nationalist China maintains diplomatic relations with Vatican City.

Archd., 1; dioc., 6; abp., 1; bp., 5; parishes, 514; priests, 739 (218 dioc., 521 rel.); sem., 58; bros., 86; srs., 1,191; sch., 55; bap., 4,823; Caths., 277,320 (1.6%); tot. pop., 16,321,370.

Tanzania: Republic (consisting of former Tanganyika on the eastern coast of Africa and former Zanzibar, an island group off the eastern coast); capital, Dar es Salaam (future capital, Dodoma). The first Catholic mission in the former Tanganyikan portion of the republic was manned by Holy Ghost Fathers in 1868. The hierarchy was established there in 1953. Zanzibar was the landing place of Augustinians with the Portuguese in 1499. Some evangelization was attempted between then and 1698 when the Arabs expelled all priests from the territory. There was no Catholic missionary activity from then until the 1860's. The Holy Ghost Fathers arrived in 1863 and were entrusted with the mission in 1872. Zanzibar was important as a point of departure for missionaries to Tanganyika, Kenya and other places in East Africa. A vicariate for Zanzibar was set up in 1906. Tanzania maintains diplomatic relations with Vatican City.

Archd., 2; dioc., 22; a.a., 1; card., 1 (nat.); abp., 1 (nat.); bp., 22 (20 nat.); parishes, 583; priests, 1,340 (655 dioc., 685 rel.); sem., 337; p.d., 1; bros., 311; srs., 3,305; sch., 155; bap., 129,496; Caths., 3,149,870 (19.6%); tot. pop., 16,000,000.

Thailand (Siam): Constitutional monarchy in southeastern Asia; capital, Bangkok. The first Christians in the region were Portuguese traders who arrived early in the 16th century. A number of missionaries began arriving in 1554 but pastoral care was confined mostly to the Portuguese until the 1660's. Evangelization of the natives got underway from about that time. A seminary was organized in 1665, a vicariate was set up four years later, and a point of departure was established for missionaries to Tonkin, Cochin China and China. Persecution and death for some of the missionaries ended evangelization efforts in 1688. It was resumed, however, and made progress from 1824 onwards. In 1881 missionaries were sent from Siam to neighboring Laos. The hierarchy was established in 1965. Thailand maintains diplomatic relations with Vatican City.

Archd., 2; dioc., 8; abp., 2 (nat.); bp., 8 (7 nat.); parishes, 160; priests, 312 (133 dioc., 179 rel.); sem., 176; bros., 151; srs., 1,142; sch., 236; bap., 6,478; Caths., 179,450 (.4%); tot. pop., 44,000,000.

Tibet: Autonomous region of China in eastern Asia, north of the Himalayas; capital, Lhasa. Christian contact and evangelization attempts have been almost fruitless. Some 1,200 Catholics were reported in Tibet about 1950. Syrians visited the area in the seventh century and evangelization attempts were made by Jesuits, 1624-35 and later, Capuchins, 1707-45, and others afterwards. They all met resistance and some met death. Missionaries do not have access to the country.

Tot. pop., 2,000,000.

Timor, Eastern: Former Portuguese overseas province in the Malay archipelago; annexed by Indonesia in 1976.

Dioc., 1; priests, 32 (25 dioc., 7 rel.); srs., 16 (no other statistics reported).

Togo: Republic on the western coast of Africa; capital, Lome. The first Catholic missionaries in the area, where slave raiders operated for nearly 200 years, were members of the African Missions Society who arrived in 1563. They were followed by Divine Word Missionaries in 1914, when a prefecture apostolic was organized. At that time the Catholic population numbered about 19,000. The African Missionaries returned after their German predecessors were deported following World War I. The first native priest was ordained in 1922. The hierarchy was established in 1955. Togo has an apostolic delegate (to West Africa).

Archd., 1; dioc., 3; abp., 1 (nat.); bp., 3 (2 nat.); parishes, 66; priests, 145 (55 dioc., 90 rel.); sem., 24; bros., 46; srs., 277; sch., 277; bap., 10,176; Caths., 474,210 (20.1%); tot. pop., 2,353,070.

Tokelau Islands: Pacific islands administered by New Zealand. Under ecclesiastical jurisdiction of Samoa and Tokelau diocese, Samoa.

Parish, 1; priest, 1 (rel.); bap., 33; Caths., 1,000.

Tonga: Polynesian monarchy in the southwestern Pacific, consisting of about 150 islands, member of the British Commonwealth; capital Nuku'alofa. Marists started missionary work in 1842, some years after Protestants had begun evangelization. By 1880 the Catholic population numbered about 1,700. A vicariate was organized in 1937. The hierarchy was established in 1966.

Dioc., 1; bp., 1 (nat); parishes, 12; priests, 23 (7 dioc., 16 rel.); sem., 7; bros., 3; srs., 64; sch., 8; bap., 492; Caths., 15,130; tot. pop., 100,000.

Transkei: Independent (Oct. 26, 1976) state carved out of South Africa; capital, Umtata. Statistics included in South Africa.

Trinidad and Tobago: Independent nation, consisting of two islands in the Caribbean, member of the British Commonwealth; capital, Port-of-Spain. The first Catholic church in Trinidad was built in 1591, years after several missionary ventures had been launched and a number of missionaries killed. Capuchins were there from 1618 until about 1802. Missionary work continued after the British gained control early in the 19th century. Cordial relations have existed between the Church and state, both of which have manifested their desire for the development of native clergy. Established diplomatic relations with Vatican City in 1978.

Archd., 1; abp., 1; parishes, 61; priests, 116 (23 dioc., 93 rel.); sem., 9; bros., 24; srs., 177; sch., 154; bap., 7,710; Caths., 370,000 (33%); tot. pop., 1,120,000.

Tunisia: Republic on the northern coast of Africa; capital, Tunis. There were few Christians in the territory until the 19th century. A prefecture apostolic was organized in 1843 and the Carthage archdiocese was established in 1884. The Catholic population in 1892 consisted of most of the approximately 50,000 Europeans in the country. When Tunis became a republic in 1956, most of the Europeans left the country. The Holy See and the Tunisian government concluded an agreement in 1964 which changed the Carthage archdiocese into a prelacy and handed over some ecclesiastical property to the republic. A considerable number of Moslem students are in Catholic schools, but the number of Moslem converts to the Church has been small. Tunisia maintains diplomatic relations with Vatican City.

Prel., 1; abp., 1; parishes, 24; priests, 61 (26 dioc., 35 rel.); p.d., 1; bros., 17; srs., 250; sch., 31; bap., 58; Caths., 18,000 (.3%); tot. pop., 5,870,000.

Turkey: Republic in Asia Minor and southeastern Europe, capital, Ankara. Christian communities were established in apostolic times, as attested in the Acts of the Apostles, some of the Epistles of St. Paul, and Revelation. The territory was the scene of heresies and ecumenical councils, the place of residence of Fathers of the Church, the area in which ecclesiastical organization reached the dimensions of more than 450 sees in the middle of the seventh century. The region remained generally Byzantine except for the period of the Latin occupation of Constantinople from 1204 to 1261, but was conquered by the Ottoman Turks in 1453 and remained under their domination until establishment of the republic in 1923. Christians, always a minority, numbered more Orthodox than Latins; they were all under some restriction during the Ottoman period. They suffered persecution in the 19th and 20th centuries, the Armenians being the most numerous victims. Turkey is overwhelmingly Moslem. Catholics are tolerated to a degree. Turkey maintains diplomatic relations with Vatican City.

Patriarchate, 1 (Cilicia for the Armenians, the patriarch resides in Lebanon); archd., 3; dioc., 2; v.a., 2; mission "sui juris," 1; ap. ex., 1; Caths., 26,000; tot. pop., 42,130,000.

Tuvalu (Ellice Islands): Independent island nation in Oceania. Statistics included in Gilbert Islands.

Turks and Caicos Islands: British possession in West Indies; capital, Grand Turk. Under ecclesiastical jurisdiction of Nassau diocese, Bahamas.

Parish, 1; bap., 3 (inf.); Caths., 400; tot. pop., 6,000.

Uganda: Republic in eastern Africa, member of the British Commonwealth; capital, Kampala. The White Fathers were the first Catholic missionaries, starting in 1879. Persecution broke out from 1885 to 1887, taking a toll of 22 Catholic martyrs, who were canonized in 1964, and a number of Anglican victims. (Pope Paul honored all those who died for the faith during a visit to Kampala in 1969.) By 1888, there were more than 8,000 Catholics. Evangelization was resumed in 1894, after being interrupted by war, and proceeded thereafter. The first native African bishop was ordained in 1939. The hierarchy was established in 1953. The Church was supressed during the erratic regime of Pres. Idi-Amin, who was deposed in the spring of 1979. Uganda maintains diplomatic relations with Vatican City.

Archd., 1; dioc., 11; card., 1 (nat.); bp., 11 (8 nat.); parishes, 297; priests, 747 (390 dioc., 357 rel.); sem., 589; bros., 275; srs., 1,872; sch., 1,613; bap., 211,588; Caths., 4,392,146 (35.5%); tot. pop., 12,350,000.

Union of Soviet Socialist Republics: Union of 15 Soviet Socialist Republics in northern Eurasia, from the Baltic Sea to the Pacific; Russian capital, Moscow. The Orthodox Church has been predominant in Russian history. It developed from the Byzantine Church before 1064. Some of its members subsequently established communion with Rome as the result of reunion movements but most of them remained Orthodox. The government has always retained some kind of general or particular control of this church. Latins, always a minority, had a little more freedom. From the beginning of the Communist government in 1917, all churches of whatever kind — including Jews and Moslems — became the targets of official campaigns designed to negate their influence on society and/or to eliminate them entirely. An accurate assessment of the situation of the Catholic Church in Russia is difficult to make. Its dimensions, however, can be gauged from the findings of a team of research specialists made public by the Judiciary Committee of the U.S. House of Representatives in 1964. It was reported: "The fate of the Catholic Church in the USSR and countries occupied by the Russians from 1917 to 1959 shows the following: (a) the number killed: 55 bishops; 12,800 priests and monks; 2.5 million Catholic believers; (b) imprisoned or deported: 199 bishops; 32,000 priests and 10 million believers; (c) 15,700 priests were forced to abandon their priesthood and accept other jobs; and (d) a large number of seminaries and religious communities were dissolved; 1,600 monasteries were nationalized, 31,779 churches were closed. 400 newspapers were prohibited, and all Catholic organizations were dissolved." Several Latin Rite churches are open; e.g., in Moscow, Leningrad, Odessa and Tiflis. An American chaplain is stationed in Moscow to serve Catholics at the U.S. embassy there. Recent reports indicate that, despite repression and attempts at Sovietization, the strongholds of Catholicism in the USSR are Lithuania (incorporated in the USSR in 1940, together with Estonia and Latvia) and the Ukraine.

Ecclesiastical jurisdictions, 21 (including 7 in Lithuania, 2 in Latvia, 1 in Estonia); card., 1 (Cardinal Slipyi of the Ukraine, living in Rome since his release in 1963 from 18 years' imprisonment); bp., 9 (apostolic administrators or auxiliaries; four are impeded or exiled; 1 bishop was ordained in 1972, Valerians Zondaks, titular bishop of Tabaicara and auxiliary to the apostolic administrator of Riga and Liepaja, Latvia); tot. pop., 258,000,000. No Catholic statistics are available. Some recent reports estimate the Catholic population of Lithuania to be 3 million, in a total population of 3.1 million.

United Arab Emirates: Independent state along Persian Gulf; capital, Abu Dhabi.

V.a., 1; bp., 1; priests, 5 (2 dioc., 3 rel.); srs., 26; sch., 10; bap., 277; Caths., 10,000; tot. pop., 229,000.

United States: See Catholic History in the United States, Statistics of the Church in the United States.

Upper Volta: Republic inland in western Africa; capital, Ouagadougou. White Fathers started the first missions in 1900 and 1901. White Sisters began work in 1911. A minor and a major seminary were established in 1926 and 1942, respectively. The first native bishop in modern times from West Africa was ordained in 1956 and the first cardinal created in 1965. The hierarchy was established in 1955. Upper Volta established diplomatic relations with Vatican City in 1973.

Archd., 1; dioc., 8; card., 1 (nat.); bp., 9 (8 nat.); parishes, 96; priests, 389 (139 dioc., 250 rel.); sem., 68; bros., 152; srs., 587; sch., 20; bap., 20,658; Caths., 440,270 (7%); tot. pop., 6,300,000.

Uruguay: Republic (called the Eastern Republic of Uruguay) on the southeast coast of South America; capital, Montevideo. The Spanish established a settlement in 1624 and evangelization followed. Missionaries followed the reduction pattern to reach the Indians, form them in the faith and train them in agriculture, husbandry, other useful arts, and the experience of managing property and living in community. Montevideo was made a diocese in 1878. The constitution of 1830 made Catholicism the religion of the state and subsidized some of its activities, principally the missions to the Indians. Separation of Church and state was provided for in the constitution of 1917. Uruguay maintains diplomatic relations with Vatican City.

Archd., 1; dioc., 9; abp., 1; bp., 11; parishes, 224; priests, 542 (195 dioc., 347 rel.); sem., 34; p.d., 10; bros., 146; srs., 1,578; bap., 43,415; Caths., 2,263,530 (80.5%); tot. pop., 2,810,000.

Vatican City: See separate entry.

Venezuela: Republic in northern South America; capital, Caracas. Evangelization began in 1513-14 and involved members of a number of religious orders who worked in assigned territories, developing missions into pueblos or towns and villages of Indian converts. Nearly 350 towns originated as missions. Fifty-four missionaries met death by violence from the start of missionary work until 1817. Missionary work was seriously hindered during the wars of independence in the second decade of the 19th century and continued in decline through the rest of the century as dictator followed dictator in a period of political turbulence. Restoration of the missions got underway in 1922. The first diocese was established in 1531. Most of the bishops have been native Venezuelans. The first diocesan synod was held in 1574. Church-state relations are regulated by an agreement concluded with the Holy See in 1964. Venezuela maintains diplomatic relations with Vatican City.

Archd., 6; dioc., 17; v.a., 4; card., 1; abp., 6; bp., 29; parishes, 960; priests, 2,058 (894 dioc., 1,164 rel.); sem., 199; p.d., 11; bros., 323; srs., 3,888; sch., 880; bap., 327,458; Caths., 12,120,980 (95%); tot. pop., 12,740,000.

Vietnam: Country in southeastern Asia, reunited officially July 2, 1976, as the Socialist Republic of Vietnam; capital, Hanoi. Previously, from 1954, partitioned into the Democratic Peoples' Republic of Vietnam in the North (capital, Hanoi) and the Republic of Vietnam in the South (capital, Saigon). Catholicism was introduced in 1533 but missionary work was intermittent until 1615 when Jesuits arrived to stay. One hundred thousand Catholics were reported in 1639. Two vicariates were organized in 1659. A seminary was set up in 1666 and two native priests were ordained two years later. A congregation of native women religious formed in 1670 is still active. Severe persecution broke out in 1698, three times in the 18th century, and again in the 19th. Between 100,000 and 300,000 persons suffered in some way from persecution during the 50 years before 1883 when the French moved in to secure religious liberty for the Catholics. Most of the 117 beatified Martyrs of Vietnam were killed during this 50-year period. After the French were forced out of Vietnam in 1954, the country was partitioned at the 17th parallel. The North went Communist and the Viet Cong, joined by North Vietnamese regular army troops in 1964, fought to gain control of the South. In 1954 there were approximately 1,114,000 Catholics in the North and 480,000 in the South. More than 650,000 fled to the South to avoid the government repression that silenced the Church in the North. In South Vietnam, the Church continued to develop during the war years. Fragmentary reports about the status of the Church since the end of the war in 1975 have been ominous. Freedom of religious belief and practice was promised by the Revolutionary Government in May, 1975, shortly after its capture of Saigon (Ho Chi Min City). The hierarchy was established in 1960. The apostolic delegation, formerly in Saigon, was transferred to Hanoi in 1976; it is presently vacant.

Archd., 3; dioc., 22; card., 1 (1979); abp., 5; bp., 30; parishes, 1,382; priests, 2,392 (1,931 dioc., 461 rel.); sem., 1,457; m. rel., 1,125; w. rel., 7,130; sch., 1,351; inst., 501; Caths., 2,749,475 (6.4%); tot. pop.(UN est.), 42,650,000. (The preceding statistics are from 1974 and earlier.)

Virgin Islands: Organized unincorporated U.S. territory, about 34 miles east of Puerto Rico; capital, Charlotte Amalie on St. Thomas (one of the three principal islands). The islands were discovered by Columbus in 1493 and named for St. Ursula and her virgin companions. Missionaries began evangelization in the 16th century. A church on St. Croix dates from about 1660; another, on St. Thomas, from 1774. The Baltimore archdiocese had jurisdiction over the islands from 1804 to 1820 when it was passed on to the first of several places in the Caribbean area. Some trouble arose over a pastoral appointment in the 19th century, resulting in a small schism. The Redemptorists took over pastoral care in 1858; normal conditions have prevailed since.

Dioc., 1; bp., 1; parishes, 6; priests, 17 (1 dioc., 16 rel.); bros., 1; srs., 28; sch., 5; bap., 756; Caths., 26,000; tot. pop., 110,000.

Wales: Part of the United Kingdom, on the western part of the island of Great Britain. Celtic missionaries completed evangelization by the end of the sixth century, the climax of what has been called the age of saints. Welsh Christianity received its distinctive Celtic character at this time. Some conflict developed when attempts were made — and proved successful later — to place the Welsh Church under the jurisdiction of Canterbury; the Welsh opted for direct contact with Rome. The Church made progress despite the depredations of Norsemen in the eighth and ninth centuries. Norman infiltration occurred near the middle of the 12th century, resulting in a century-long effort to establish territorial dioceses and parishes to replace the Celtic organizational plan of monastic centers and satellite churches. The Western Schism produced split views and allegiances. Actions of Henry VIII in breaking away from Rome had serious repercussions. Proscription and penal laws crippled the Church, resulted in heavy defections and touched off a 150-year period of repression in which more than 91 persons died for the faith. Methodism prevailed by 1750. Modern Catholicism came to Wales with Irish immigrants in the 19th century, when the number of Welsh Catholics was negligible. Catholic emancipation was granted in 1829. The hierarchy was restored in 1850.

Archd., 1; dioc., 1; abp., 1; bp., 2; parishes, 170; priests, 335 (184 dioc., 151 rel.); sem., 24; bros., 36; srs., 740; sch., 130; bap., 2,942; Caths., 143,620 (5.1%); tot. pop., 2,828,210.

Wallis and Futuna Islands: French territory in the southwestern Pacific. Marists, who began evangelizing the islands in 1836-7, were the first Catholic missionaries. The entire populations of the two islands were baptized by the end of 1842 (Wallis) and 1843 (Futuna). The first missionary to the latter island was killed in 1841; he was the first martyr of the Pacific. Most of the priests on the islands are native Polynesians. The hierarchy was established in 1966.

Dioc., 1; bp., 1 (nat.); parishes, 5; priests, 12 (5 dioc., 7 rel.); sem., 2; bros., 3; srs., 46; sch., 9; bap., 328; Caths., 9,700; tot. pop., 9,730.

Western Sahara: Former Spanish overseas province (Spanish Sahara) on the northwestern coast of Africa. Territory is under control of Morocco and Mauritania (1976). Islam is the religion of non-Europeans. A prefecture apostolic was established in 1954 for the European Catholics there.

P.a., 1; parishes, 3; priests, 7 (rel); bros., 1; srs., 19; bap., 197; Caths., 16,000. (Figures are for the area covered by the prefecture apostolic of Western Sahara.)

Yemen: Arab republic in southwestern Arabia; capital, Sana. Christians perished in the first quarter of the sixth century. Moslems have been in control since the seventh century. The state religion is Islam. In 1973, for the first time in 1,400 years, Catholic personnel — priests, religious, lay persons — were invited to work in the country as staff of a government hospital; they were not to engage in proselytizing. Under ecclesiastical jurisdiction of Arabia vicariate apostolic.

Tot. pop., 7,000,000.

Yemen, Peoples Democratic Republic of: Republic in the southern part of the Arabian peninsula; capitals, Aden and Medina as-Shaab. No Christian community has existed there since the Moslem conquest of the seventh century. Under ecclesiastical jurisdiction of Arabia vicariate apostolic.

Tot. pop., 1,800,000.

Yugoslavia: Socialist republic in southeastern Europe; capital, Belgrade. Christianity was introduced from the seventh to ninth centuries in the regions which were combined to form the nation after World War I. Since these regions straddled the original line of demarcation for the Western and Eastern Empires (and churches), and since the Reformation had little lasting effect, the Christians are nearly all either Roman Catholics or Byzantines (some in communion with Rome, the majority Orthodox). Yugoslavia was proclaimed a Socialist republic in 1945. Repression of religion became government policy. Between May, 1945, and December, 1950, persecution took the following toll: almost two-thirds of 22 dioceses lost their bishops; about 348 priests were killed; 200 priests were under arrest and in prison; 12 of 18 seminaries were closed; the Catholic press was confiscated; religious instruction was suppressed in all schools; 300 religious houses and institutions were confiscated, and nuns and other religious driven out; all Church property was expropriated; the ministry of priests was severely restricted and subject to government interference; many thousands of the faithful shared the fate of priests and religious in death, imprisonment and slave labor. Cardinal Stepinac, arrested in 1946 and the symbol of the Church under persecution in Yugoslavia, died Feb. 10, 1960. In an agreement signed June 25, 1966, the government recognized the Holy See's spiritual jurisdiction over the Church in the country and guaranteed to bishops the possibility of maintaining contact with Rome in ecclesiastical and religious matters. The Holy See confirmed the principle that the activity of ecclesiastics, in the exercise of priestly functions, must take place within the religious and ecclesiastical sphere, and that abuse of these functions for political ends would be illegal. Less than two months after the agreement was signed, a group of exiled Croatian priests issued a statement in which they accused the Yugoslav government of failing to abide by it. According to others, an improvement was noticeable. Yugoslavia maintains diplomatic relations with Vatican City.

Archd., 8; dioc., 13; a.a., 1; card., 1; abp., 9; bp., 22; parishes, 2,785; priests, 4,239 (2,875 dioc., 1,364 rel.); p.d., 3; bros., 272; srs., 6,590; sch., 2; bap., 85,534; Caths., 6,856,920 (31.5%); tot. pop., 21,720,000.

Zaire (formerly the Congo): Republic in south central Africa; capital, Kinshasa. Christianity was introduced in 1484 and evangelization began about 1490. The first native bishop in black Africa was ordained in 1518. Subsequent missionary work was hindered by faulty methods of instruction and formation, inroads of the slave trade, wars among the tribes, and Portuguese policy based on the patronage system and having all the trappings of anti-clericalism in the 18th and 19th centuries. Modern evangelization started in the second half of the 19th century. The hierarchy was established in 1959. In the civil disorders which followed independence in 1960, some missions and other church installations were abandoned, thousands of people reverted to tribal religions and many priests and religious were killed. Church-state tensions have developed in recent years because of the Church's criticism of the anti-Christian thrust of Pres. Mobutu's "Africanization" policies. Zaire maintains diplomatic relations with Vatican City.

Archd., 6; dioc., 41; card., 1 (nat.); abp., 5 (nat.); bp., 42 (35 nat.); parishes, 848; priests, 2,381 (639 dioc., 1,742 rel.); sem., 590; p.d., 38; bros., 845; srs., 3,939; sch., 384; bap., 300,223; Caths., 11,094,000 (43.3%); tot. pop., 25,629,000 (1977).

Zambia: Republic in central Africa; capital, Lusaka. Portuguese priests did some evangelizing in the 16th and 17th centuries but no results of their work remained in the 19th century. Jesuits began work in the south in the 1880's and White Fathers in the north and east in 1895. Evangelization of the western region began for the first time in 1831. The number of Catholics doubled in the 20 years following World War II. Zambia maintains diplomatic relations with Vatican City.

Archd., 2; dioc., 7; abp., 2 (nat.); bp., 7 (5 nat.); parishes, 198; priests, 425 (71 dioc., 354 rel.); sem., 79; bros., 164; srs., 654; sch., 47; bap., 47,353; Caths., 1,230,500 (23%); tot. pop., 5,350,000.

COMMUNISM

The substantive principles of modern Communism, a theory and system of economics and social organization, were stated about the middle of the 19th century by Karl Marx, author of *The Communist Manifesto* and, with Friedrich Engels, *Das Kapital*.

The elements of Communist ideology include: radical materialism; dialectical determinism; the inevitability of class struggle, which is to be furthered, for the ultimate establishment of a worldwide classless society; common ownership of productive and other goods; the subordination of all persons and institutions to the dictatorship of the collectivity; denial of the rights, dignity and liberty of persons; militant atheism and hostility to religion; utilitarian morality.

Communism in theory and practice has been the subject of many papal documents and statements. Pius IX condemned it in 1846. Leo XIII dealt with it at length in the encyclicals *Quod Apostolici Muneris* in 1878 and *Rerum Novarum* in 1891. Pius XI wrote on the same subject in the encyclicals *Quadragesimo Anno* in 1931 and *Divini Redemptoris* in 1937.

Pius XII, besides writing and speaking about Communism on many occasions, authorized the June 13, 1949, decree of the Congregation of the Holy Office which contained these as well as other provisions: Catholics are forbidden to join the Communist Party; Catholics who knowingly and willingly profess the doctrines of Communism, or defend its principles, or spread its errors are automatically excommunicated. Catholics who join the Communist Party under the force of hard circumstances (as in Iron Curtain countries, for the sake of work needed to support their families) but do not subscribe to its ideology, are not excommunicated.

John XXIII condemned the errors of Communism as intrinsically evil. In the encyclical *Peace on Earth*, however, without going soft on Communism, he sanctioned prudent and cautious efforts to work with Communists for the solution of social and economic problems.

Virtually all of the papal documents on Communism set forth Christian social teachings and urge action for the establishment of a just social order which should be its own best defense against Communism.

During the pontificate of Paul VI, Vatican diplomats have held talks and conducted negotiations with officials of Communist governments in Eastern Europe in efforts to improve the status of the Church, especially in Hungary, Bulgaria and Poland. Results have been partially to the good, particularly with respect to the appointment of several bishops as heads of long-vacant dioceses. Otherwise, negotiations have not substantially eased government suppression of religion.

This policy of seeking a livable accommodation with Communist regimes has been criticized in some quarters which call for a stronger expression of care and concern for people of the "Church of Silence."

CATHOLIC WORLD STATISTICS

(Principal sources: *Annuario Pontificio, 1979; Statistical Yearbook of the Church, 1976*, the latest available edition.)

Patriarchates: 13. Eastern Rites, 8 (Asia, 6; Africa, 2). Roman Rite, 5 (Asia, 2; Europe, 2; West Indies, 1).

Archdioceses: 491 (Asia, 120; Oceania, 15; Africa, 52; Europe, 145; South America, 83; North and Middle America, 76).

Dioceses: 1,803 (Asia, 341; Oceania, 46; Africa, 290; Europe, 536; South America, 294; North and Middle America, 296).

Prelatures: 106 (Asia, 13; Africa, 1; Europe, 9; South America, 71; North and Middle America, 12).

Abbacies: 20 (Asia, 1; Oceania, 1; Africa, 1; Europe, 14; South America, 2; North and Middle America, 1).

Vicariates Apostolic: 72 (Asia, 15; Africa, 13; Europe, 2; South America, 36; North and Middle America, 6).

Prefectures Apostolic: 60 (Asia, 38; Africa, 11; South America, 11).

Apostolic Administrations: 9 (Asia, 1; Africa, 2; Europe, 4; North and Middle America, 2).

Missions "Sui Juris": 4 (Asia, 3; Oceania, 1).

Apostolic Exarchates, Ordinariates: 19 (Asia, 1; Oceania, 1; Europe, 15; South America, 2).

Cardinals (as of Oct. 10, 1979): **130** (Asia, 10; Oceania, 3; Africa, 12; Europe, 68; South America, 17; North and Middle America, 20).

Archbishops: 407 (Asia, 83; Oceania, 13; Africa, 47; Europe, 93; South America, 78; North and Middle America, 93).

Bishops: 2,447 (Asia, 273; Oceania, 66; Africa, 307; Europe, 787; South America, 490; North and Middle America, 524).

Priests, Total: 404,306 (Asia, 24,997; Oceania, 5,321; Africa, 15,777; Europe, 240,083; South America, 32,279; North and Middle America, 85,849).

Priests, Diocesan: 257,551 (Asia, 13,278; Oceania, 2,828; Africa, 5,195; Europe, 170,437; South America, 14,041; North and Middle America, 51,772).

Priests, Religious: 146,755 (Asia, 11,719; Oceania, 2,493; Africa, 10,582; Europe 69,646; South America, 18,238; North and Middle America, 34,077).

Brothers: 69,300 (Asia, 5,554; Oceania, 3,038; Africa, 4,764; Europe, 33,903; South America, 6,969; North and Middle America, 15,072).

Seminarians: 60,376 (Asia, 10,533; Oceania, 1,026; Africa, 4,812; Europe, 23,199; South America, 6,663; North and Middle America, 14,143).

Permanent Deacons: 4,853 (Asia, 51; Oceania, 40; Africa, 107; Europe, 925; South America, 494; North and Middle America, 3,236).

Sisters: 950,379 (Asia, 80,214; Oceania, 15,666; Africa, 33,396; Europe, 532,512; South America, 87,135; North and Middle America, 201,456).

Baptisms: 16,482,758 (Asia, 1,768,162; Oceania, 126,380; Africa, 1,937,329; Europe, 3,751,323; South America, 5,177,546; North and Middle America, 3,722,018).

Catholic Population: 724,434,000 (18 per cent of total world population of 4,016,330,000). Asia, 55,689,000 (2.4 per cent; total population, 2,350,491,000). Oceania, 5,365,000 (25.1 per cent; total population, 21,363,000). Africa, 50,221,000 (12.2 per cent; total population, 411,894,000). Europe, 263,088,000 (39.5 per cent; total population, 666,839,000. South America, 199,077,000 (91.2 per cent; total population, 218,378,000. North and Middle America, 150,994,000 (43.4 per cent; total population, 347,365,000). (Figures, as of beginning of 1977, are from the *Statistical Yearbook of the Church.*)

EPISCOPAL CONFERENCES

(Principal source: *Annuario Pontificio.*)

Episcopal conferences, organized and operating under general norms and particular statutes approved by the Holy See, are official bodies in and through which the bishops of a given country or territory act together as pastors of the Church.

Listed below according to countries or regions are titles and addresses of conferences and names and sees of presidents (archbishops unless otherwise noted).

Africa, North: Conference Episcopal d'Afrique du Nord, 13 rue Khelifa Boukhalfa, Algiers, Algeria. Card. Leon-Etienne Duval (Algiers).

Africa, South: Southern African Catholic Bishops' Conference (SACBC), P.O. Box 941, Pretoria 0001, S. Africa. Abp.-Bp. Joseph P. Fitzgerald (Johannesburg).

Angola: Conferencia Episcopal de Angola e Sao Tome (CEAST), C.P. 1230, Luanda, Angola. Eduardo Andre Muaca (Luanda).

Antilles: Antilles Episcopal Conference, P.O. Box 43, Kingston 6, Jamaica, W.I. Samuel E. Carter (Jamaica).

Arab Countries: Conference des Eveques Latins dans les Regions Arabes (CELRA), Latin Patriarchate, P.O. Box 14152, Jerusalem (Old City). Patriarch Giacomo Beltritti (Jerusalem).

Argentina: Conferencia Episcopal Argentina (CEA), Calle Paraguay 1867, Buenos Aires. Card. Raul Francisco Primatesta (Cordoba).

Australia: Australian Episcopal Conference, P.O. Box 297, Kingston, A.C.T., 2604. Card. James Darcy Freeman (Sydney).

Austria: Osterreichische Bischofskonferenz, Rotenturmstrasse 2, A1010 Vienna. Card. Franz Koenig (Vienna).

Bangladesh: Catholic Bishops' Conference (CBCB), P.O. Box 3, Dacca-2. Michael Rozario (Dacca).

Belgium: Bisschoppenconferentie van Belgie — Conference Episcopale de Belgique, Wollemarkt 15, Mechelen.

Benin: Conference Episcopale du Benin, B.P. 491, Cotonou. Christophe Adimou (Cotonou).

Bolivia: Conferencia Episcopal de Bolivia (CEB), Casilla 205, Sucre. Card. Jose Clemente Maurer (Sucre).

Brazil: Conferencia Nacional dos Bispos do Brasil (CNBB), C.P. 13-2067, 70000 Brasilia, D.F. Bp. Ivo Lorscheiter (Santa Maria).

Bulgaria: Ulitza Pashovi 10-B, Sofia VI. Bp. Metodio Dimitrow Stratiew (Apostolic Exarch, Sofia).

Burma: Burma Catholic Bishops' Conference (BCBC), 292 Prome Rd., Sanchaung P.O. Alphonse U Than Aung (Mandalay).

Cameroon: Conference Episcopale Nationale du Cameroun, P.O. Box 82, Mankon-Bamenda. Bp. Paul Verdzekov (Bamenda).

Canada: See Index: Canadian Conference of Catholic Bishops.

Central African Republic: Conference Episcopale Centrafricaine (CECA), B.P. 798, Bangui. Joachim N'Dayen (Bangui).

Chad: Conference Episcopale du Tchad, B.P., 456, N'Djamena. Paul Dalmais (N'Djamena).

Chile: Conferencia Episcopal de Chile (CECH), Casilla 13191, Correo 21, Santiago de Chile. Abp.-Bp. Francisco de Borja Valenzuela Rios (San Felipe).

China (Republic of China, Taiwan): Regional Episcopal Conference of China, Lane 32, Kuangfu Rd., Taipeh, Taiwan. Joseph Kuo, pro-pres. (Tit. Abp. Salamina).

Colombia: Conferencia Episcopal de Colombia, Apartado 7448, Bogota D.E. Mario Revollo Bravo (Nueva).

Congo: Conference Episcopale du Congo.

Costa Rica: Conferencia Episcopal de Costa Rica (CECOR), Arzobispado, San Jose, Costa Rica. Roman Arrieta Villalobos (San Jose de Costa Rica).

Cuba: Conferencia Episcopal de Cuba (CEC), Apartado 594, Havana. Francisco Ricardo Oves Fernandez (Havana).

Dominican Republic: Conferencia del Episcopado Dominicano (CED), Apartado 186, Santo Domingo. Card. Octavio Antonio Beras Rojas (Santo Domingo).

Ecuador: Conferencia Episcopal Ecuatoriana, Apartado 1081, Quito. Card. Pablo Munoz Vega (Quito).

El Salvador: Conferencia Episcopal de El Salvador (CEDES). Bp. Pedro Arnoldo Aparicio y Quintanilla (San Vicente).

Ethiopia: Conferenza Episcopale di Etiopia, P.O. Box 21903, Addis Ababa. Paulos Tzadua (Addis Ababa).

France: Conference Episcopale Francaise, 106 rue du Bac, 75341 Paris CEDEX 07. Card. Roger Etchegaray (Marseilles).

Gabon: Conference Episcopale du Gabon,

B.P. 2146, Libreville. Andre Fernand Anguile (Libreville).

Gambia, Liberia and Sierra Leone: Inter-Territorial Episcopal Conference, P.O. Box 893, Freetown, Sierra Leone. Bp. Augustus Azzolini (Makeni, Sierra Leone).

Germany: Deutsche Bischofskonferenz, Kaiserstrasse 163, D-5300 Bonn. Card. Joseph Hoeffner (Cologne). Berliner Bischofskonferenz, Franzosische Strasse 34, DDR-108 Berlin. Card. Alfred Bengsch (Berlin).

Ghana: Ghana Bishops' Conference, P.O. Box 247, Accra. Bp. Dominic Kodwo Andoh (Accra).

Great Britain: Bishops' Conference of England and Wales, Archbishop's House, Westminster, London, S.W. 1. George Patrick Dwyer (Birmingham). Bishops' Conference of Scotland, 42 Greenhill Gardens, Edinburgh 10. Card. Gordon J. Gray (Saint Andrews and Edinburgh).

Greece: Conferenza Episcopale di Grecia, Archeveche Catholique, Corfu. Antonio Varthalitis (Corfu, Zante and Cefalonia.)

Guatemala: Conferencia Episcopal de Guatemala (CEG), 4 Calle 9-45, zona 1, Ciudad de Guatemala. Bp. Angelico Melotto Mazzardo (Solola).

Guinea: Conference Episcopale de la Guinee, B.P. 1006 Bis, Conakry.

Haiti: Conference Episcopale de Haiti (CEH), Archeveche, Port-au-Prince. Bp. Jean-Jacques-Claudius Angenor (Les Cayes).

Honduras: Conferencia Episcopal de Honduras (CEH), Arzobispado, Tegucigalpa. Hector Enrique Santos Hernandez (Tegucigalpa).

Hungary: Magyar Puspoki Kar, Berenyi Zsigmond u. 2, Pf. 25, H-2501 Esztergom. Card. Laszlo Lekai (Esztergom).

India: Catholic Bishops' Conference of India (CBCI). Card. Lawrence Trevor Picachy (Calcutta).

Indonesia: General Conference of the Ordinaries of Indonesia (MAWI), Taman Cut Mutiah 10, Jakarta II/14. Card. Justinus Darmojuwono (Semarang).

Ireland: Episcopal Meetings, "Ara Coeli," Armagh. Card. Tomas O'Fiaich (Armagh).

Italy: Conferenza Episcopale Italiana (CEI), Circonvallazione Aurelia, 50, 00165 Roma. Card. Anastasio Alberto Ballestrero, O.C.D. (Turin).

Ivory Coast: Conference Episcopale de la Cote d'Ivoire, B.P. 1287, Abidjan. Bernard Yago (Abidjan).

Japan: Japan Catholic Bishops' Conference, Catholic Center, 10-34 Uenomachi, Nagasaki-shi. Card. Joseph Asajiro Satowaki (Nagasaki).

Kenya: Kenya Episcopal Conference (KEC), P.O. Box 842, Eldoret. Bp. John Njenga (Eldoret).

Korea: Catholic Conference of Korea, C.P.O. Box 16, Seoul. Victorinus Kong-Hi Youn (Kwang Ju).

Laos and Kampuchea (Cambodia): Conference Episcopale du Laos et de la Rep. Khmere.

Latvia: Pils Jela, 2, Riga. Bp. Giuliano Vaivods (Ap. Admin., Riga and Liepaja).

Lesotho: Lesotho Catholic Bishops' Conference, P.O. Box 267, Maseru. Alfonso Liguori Morapeli (Maseru).

Liberia: See Gambia, Liberia and Sierra Leone.

Lithuania: Vilniaus gatve 4, Kaunas. Bp. Giuseppe Matulaitis-Labukas (Ap. Admin., Kaunas and Vilkaviskis).

Madagascar: Conference Episcopale du Madagascar, 102 bis, Av. Marechal Joffre Antaninena, B. P 667, Tananarive. Card. Victor Razafimahatratra (Tananarive).

Malawi: Episcopal Conference of Malawi, P.O. Box 5368, Limbe. James Chiona (Blantyre).

Malaysia-Singapore: Catholic Bishops' Conference of Malaysia-Singapore, P.O. Box 327, Kuching, Malaysia. Peter Chung Hoan Ting (Kuching).

Mali: Conference Episcopale du Mali, B.P. 298, Bamako. Luc Auguste Sangare (Bamako).

Malta: Conferenza Episcopale Maltese, Archbishop's Curia, Valletta. Joseph Mercieca (Malta).

Mexico: Conferencia del Episcopado Mexicano (CEM), Apartado Postal 1-331, Gaudalajara. Card. Jose Salazar Lopez (Guadalajara).

Mozambique: Conferencia Episcopal de Mocambique (CEM), C.P. 286, Maputo. Bp. Jaime Pedro Goncalves (Beira).

Netherlands: Nederlandse Bisschoppen Konferentie, Postbus 13049, Biltstraat 121, Utrecht. Card. Johannes Willebrands (Utrecht).

New Zealand: New Zealand Episcopal Conference.

Nicaragua: Conferencia Episcopal de Nicaragua, Arzobispado, Managua. Bp. Manuel Salazar Espinosa (Leon).

Nigeria: National Episcopal Conference of Nigeria, P.O. Box 951, Lagos. Card. Dominic Ignatius Ekandem (Bp., Ikot Ekpene).

Pacific: Conference des Eveques du Pacifique (CEPAC), P.O. Box 1200, Suva, Fiji. Bp. Patelisio Punou-Ki-Hihifo Finau (Tonga).

Pakistan: Pakistan Episcopal Conference, St. Patrick's Cathedral, Karachi 3. Card. Joseph Cordeiro (Karachi).

Panama: Conferencia Episcopal de Panama (CEP), Apartado 386, Panama 1. Marcos Gregorio McGrath (Panama).

Papua New Guinea and Solomon Islands: Bishops' Conference of Papua New Guinea and Solomon Islands, P.O. Box 69, Mendi. Bp. Firmin Schmidt, O.F.M. Cap. (Mendi).

Paraguay: Conferencia Episcopal Paraguaya (CEP), Calle Alberdi 782, Casilla Correo 1436, Asuncion. Bp. Felipe Santiago Benitez Avalos (Villarrica).

Peru: Conferencia Episcopal Peruana, Apartado 310, Lima 1. Card. Juan Landazuri Ricketts (Lima).

Philippine Islands: Catholic Bishops' Conference of the Philippines (CBCP), P.O. Box 1160, Manila. Card. Jaime L. Sin (Manila).

Poland: Konferencja Episkopatu Polski, Ul. Miodowa 17, 00-246 Warsaw. Card. Stefan Wyszynski (Gniezno and Warsaw).

Portugal: Conferencia Episcopal Portuguesa, Campo dos martires de Patria, 43-1 Esq., Lisbon 1. Card. Antonio Ribeiro (Patriarch of Lisbon).

Puerto Rico: Conferencia Episcopal Puertorriquena (CEP), Apartado 1967, San Juan de Puerto Rico 00903. Card. Luis Aponte Martinez (San Juan).

Rhodesia: Rhodesia Catholic Bishops' Conference, P.O. Box 8135, Causeway, Salisbury. Patrick Chakaipa (Salisbury).

Rumania: Palatul Episcopiei, Alba Julia. Bp. Aaron Marton (Alba Julia).

Rwanda-Burundi: Conference des Ordinaires du Rwanda et du Burundi (COREB), B.P. 690, Bujumbura, Burundi. Bp. Michel Ntuyahaga (Bujumbura).

Scandinavia: Conferentia Episcopalis Scandiae, Bredgade 69 A, DK 1260 Copenhagen K, Denmark. Bp. John W. Gran (Oslo, Norway).

Senegal-Mauritania: Conference Episcopale du Senegal-Mauritania, B.P. 5082, Dakar, Fann. Senegal. Card. Hyacinthe Thiandoum (Dakar).

Sierra Leone: See Gambia, Liberia and Sierra Leone.

Spain: Conferencia Episcopal Espanola, Alfonso XI, 4, 1°, Madrid 14. Card. Vicente Enrique y Tarancon (Madrid).

Sri Lanka: Catholic Bishops' Conference of Sri Lanka, Archbishop's House, Borella, Colombo 8. Bp. Anthony de Saram (Galle).

Sudan: Sudan Episcopal Conference (SEC), P.O. Box 49, Khartoum. Bp. Gabriel Zubeir (Wau).

Switzerland: Conference des Eveques Suisses, Secretariat, av. Moleson 30, CH-1700 Fribourg 1. Bp. Pierre Mamie (Lausanne, Geneva and Fribourg).

Tanzania: Tanzania Episcopal Conference (TEC), P.O. Box 2133, Dar-es-Salaam. Bp. Mario Epifanio Abdallah Mgulunde (Iringa).

Thailand: Conference des Eveques de Thailand, Assumption Church, Oriental Avenue, Bangkok 5. Bp. Robert Ratna Bamrungtrakul (Chiang Mai).

Togo: Conference Episcopale du Togo, B.P. 348, Lome. Robert Dosseh Anyron (Lome).

Uganda: Uganda Episcopal Conference, P.O. Box 2886, Kampala. Bp. Hadrian Ddungu (Masaka).

United States: See National Conference of Catholic Bishops.

Upper Volta and Niger: Conference des Eveques de la Haute Volta et du Niger, B.P. 90, Ouagadougou, Upper Volta. Bp. Dieudonne Yougbare (Koupela, Upper Volta).

Uruguay: Conferencia Episcopal Uruguaya (CEU), Avenida Uruguay 1319, Montevideo. Bp. Humberto Tonna (Florida).

Venezuela: Conferencia Episcopal de Venezuela (CEV), Apartado Postal 954, Caracas 101. Domingo Roa Perez (Maracaibo).

Vietnam: Conference Episcopale du Vietnam, Phan-Dinh-Ohung, Hochiminhville 180. Paul Nguyen van Binh (Hochiminhville).

Yugoslavia: Biskupska Konferencija Jugoslavije, Kapitol 31, P.B. 02-406, Zagreb. Franjo Kuharic (Zagreb).

Zaire: Conference Pleniere des Ordinaires du Zaire, B.P. 223, Sankuru; or B.P. 3258, Gombe-Kinshasa. Bp. Yungu (Tshumbe).

Zambia: Zambia Episcopal Conference, P.O. Box 1965, Lusaka. Bp. Dennis Harold De Jong (Ndola).

Territorial Conferences

Territorial as well as national episcopal conferences have been established in some places. Some conferences of this kind are still in the planning stage.

Africa: Association of Member Episcopal Conferences in Eastern Africa (AMECEA): Represents Uganda, Kenya, Tanzania, Zambia and Malawi; Ethiopia was accepted as associate member in 1977. Bishop James Odongo, Tororo, Uganda, president. Address: P.O. Box 21191, Nairobi, Kenya.

Symposium of Episcopal Conferences of Africa and Madagascar (Malagasy Republic) (Symposium des Conferences Episcopales d'Afrique et de Madagascar, SCEAM): Cardinal Paul Zoungrana, Ouagadougou, Upper Volta, president. Address: P.O. Box 7530, Accra-North, Ghana.

Regional Episcopal Conference of French-Speaking West Africa (Conference Episcopale Regionale de l'Afrique de l'Ouest Francophone, CERAO): Abp. Robert Dosseh Anyron, Lome, Togo.

Association of Episcopal Conferences of English-Speaking West Africa (AECEWA): Card. Dominic Ignatius Ekandem, Ikot Ekpene, Nigeria, president.

Association of Episcopal Conferences of Congo, Central African Republic and Chad: Abp. Joachim N'Dayen, Bangui, Central African Republic, president.

Asia: Federation of Asian Bishops' Conferences (FABC): Represents 14 Asian episcopal conferences (excluding the Middle East). Headquarters, P.O. Box 2948, Hong Kong. Established in 1970; statutes approved experimentally Dec. 6, 1972. Bishop Mariano Gaviola, Military Vicar, Philippines, president.

Europe: Council of European Bishops' Conferences (Consilium Conferentiarum Episcopalium Europae, CCEE): Card. Roger Etchegaray, Marseilles, France, president. Address of secretariat: Klosterhof 6b, CH-9000 St. Gallen, Switzerland.

Central and South America: Latin American Bishops' Conference (Consejo Episcopal LatinoAmericano, CELAM): Established in 1956; statutes approved Nov. 9, 1974. Represents 22 Latin American national bishops' conferences. Abp. Alfonso Lopez Trujillo, Medellin, Colombia, president. Address of the secretariat: Apartado Aereo 5278, Bogota, D.E., Colombia.

Episcopal Secretariat of Central America and Panama (Secretariado Episcopal de America Central y Panama, SEDAC): Statutes approved experimentally Sept. 26, 1970. Archbishop Miguel Obando Bravo, Managua, Nicaragua, president.

INTERNATIONAL CATHOLIC ORGANIZATIONS

(Principal source: General Secretary, Conference of International Catholic Organizations.)

Guidelines

International organizations wanting to call themselves "Catholic" are required to meet standards set by the Vatican's Council for the Laity and to register with and get the approval of the Papal Secretariat of State, according to guidelines published in *Acta Apostolicae Sedis* under date of Dec. 23, 1971. The guidelines were made public in March, 1972.

Among conditions for the right of organizations to "bear the name Catholic" are:

• leaders "will always be Catholics," and candidates for office will be approved by the Secretariat of State;

• adherence by the organization to the Catholic Church, its teaching authority and teachings of the Gospel;

• evidence that the organization is really international with a universal outlook and that it fulfills its mission through its own management, meetings and accomplishments.

The guidelines also stated that leaders of the organizations "will take care to maintain necessary reserve as regards taking a stand or engaging in public activity in the field of politics or trade unionism. Abstention in these fields will normally be the best attitude for them to adopt during their term of office."

The guidelines were in line with a provision stated by the Second Vatican Council in the *Decree on the Apostolate of the Laity*: "No project may claim the name 'Catholic' unless it has obtained the consent of the lawful church authority."

They made it clear that all organizations are not obliged to apply for recognition, but that the Church "reserves the right to recognize as linked with her mission and her aims those organizations or movements which see fit to ask for such recognition."

Conference

Conference of International Catholic Organizations: A permanent body for collaboration among various organizations which seek to promote the development of international life along the lines of Christian principles. Eleven international Catholic organizations participated in its foundation and first meeting in 1927 at Fribourg, Switzerland. In 1951, the conference established its general secretariat and adopted governing statutes which were approved by the Vatican Secretariat of State in 1953.

The permanent secretariat is located at 1, route du Jura, CH-1700 Fribourg, Switzerland. Address of the general secretary: 186, rue Washington, B-1050 Brussels, Belgium. Other conference addresses are: 1 rue de Varembe, CH-1200 Geneva, Switzerland (Information Center); 9, rue Cler, F-75007 Paris, France (International Catholic Center for UNESCO); ICO Information Center, 323 East 47th St., New York, N.Y. 10017.

International Organizations

International Catholic organizations are listed below. Information includes name, date and place of establishment (when available), address of general secretariat. An asterisk indicates that the organization is a member of the Conference of International Catholic Organizations. Approximately 24 of the organizations have consultative status with other international or regional non-governmental agencies.

Ad Lucem (1932, Lille, France): 12, rue Guy de la Brosse, F-75005, Paris, France. Work for the Third World.

Apostleship of Prayer (1849): Borgo Santo Spirito 5, I-00193 Rome, Italy. National secretariat in most countries. (See Index.)

Apostolatus Maris (Apostleship of the Sea) (1922, Glasgow, Scotland): Pontifical Commission for Migration and Tourism, Piazza San Calisto 16, I-00153 Rome, Italy. (See Index.)

Associationes Juventutis Salesianae (Associations of Salesian Youth) (1847): Via della Pisana, 1111, 00163 Rome, Italy.

Blue Army of Our Lady of Fatima: (See Index.)

Caritas Internationalis* (1951, Rome, Italy): Piazza San Calisto 16, I-00153, Rome, Italy. Coordinates relief aid on an international level.

Catholic Fraternity of the Sick and Infirm (1942, Verdun, France): Foyer des Malades, 49 rue Saint-Sauveur, F-55100 Verdun, France.

Catholic International Education Office* (1952): 60, rue des Eburons, B-1040 Brussels, Belgium.

Catholic International Federation for Physical and Sports Education (1911; present name, 1957): 5, rue Cernuschi, F-75017 Paris, France.

Catholic International Union for Social Service* (1925, Milan, Italy): rue de la Poste 111, B-1030 Brussels, Belgium (general secretariat).

"Focolarini" (1943, Trent, Italy): Via di Frascati, 42, I-00040 Rocca di Papa (Rome), Italy. (See Index: Focolare Movement.)

General Union of Pastoral Work for Youth (1966): Via Palestro 26, I-00185, Rome, Italy.

International Association of Charities of St. Vincent de Paul* (1617, Chatillon les Dombes, France): 38, rue d'Alsace-Lorraine, B-1050 Brussels, Belgium. (See Index: St. Vincent de Paul Society.)

International Association of Children of Mary (1847): 67 rue de Sèvres, F-75006 Paris, France.

International Catholic Auxiliaries (1937, Belgium): 91, rue de la Servette, CH-1202 Geneva, Switzerland.

International Catholic Child Bureau* (1947): 65, rue de Lausanne, CH-1202 Geneva, Switzerland.

International Catholic Conference of Guiding* (1965): Avenida Marechal Camara, 186, 20.000 Rio de Janeiro, Brazil. Founded by member bodies of interdenominational World Association of Guides and Girl Scouts.

International Catholic Film Organization* (1928, The Hague, The Netherlands): 8, rue de l'Orme, B-1040 Brussels, Belgium, (general secretariat). Federation of national Catholic film offices.

International Catholic Association for Service to Young Women and Girls* (1897): 1, route du Jura, CH-1700 Fribourg, Switzerland. Welfare of Catholic girls living away from home.

International Catholic Migration Commission (1951): 65, rue de Lausanne, CH-1202 Geneva, Switzerland. Coordinates Catholic activities to help migrants.

International Catholic Rural Association (1962, Rome): Piazza San Calisto 16, I-00153 Rome, Italy. International body for agricultural and rural organizations.

International Catholic Conference of Scouting* (1948): Calle Reina Victoria, 16, Barcelona 21, Spain.

International Catholic Union of the Press*: Avenue de la Gare des Eaux-Vives, CH-1207 Geneva, Switzerland. Coordinates and represents at the international level the activities of Catholics and Catholic federations or associations in the field of press and information. Has five specialized branches: International Federation of Catholic Dailies and Periodicals (1928); International Federation of Catholic Journalists (1927); International Federation of Catholic Press Agencies (1950); International Catholic Association of Teachers and Scientific or Technical Research Workers on Information (1968); Federation of Church Press Associations (1974).

International Centre for Studies in Religious Education* (1934-35, Louvain, Belgium, under name Catechetical Documentary Centre; present name, 1956): 184, rue Washington, B-1050 Brussels, Belgium. Also referred to as Lumen Vitae Centre; concerned with all aspects of religious formation.

International Christian Union of Business Executives (1931): 49, avenue d' Auderghem, B-1040 Brussels, Belgium.

International Committee of Catholic Nurses* (1933): Square Vergote, 43, B-1040 Brussels, Belgium.

International Cooperation for Socio-Economic Development (1965, Rome, Italy): 104, Avenue Elisabeth, B-1030 Brussels, Belgium.

International Council of Catholic Men* (Unum Omnes) (1948): Piazza San Calisto 16, I-00153 Rome, Italy.

International Crusade for the Blind (1957): 88, Avenue Denfert-Rochereau, F-75014 Paris, France, Coordinates action of Catholic groups and associations for the blind and develops their apostolate.

International Federation of Catholic Parochial Youth Communities (1962, Rome, Italy): Kipdorp 30, B-2000 Antwerp, Belgium.

International Federation of Catholic Rural Movements* (1964, Lisbon, Portugal): 92, rue Africaine, B-1050 Brussels, Belgium.

International Federation of Catholic Medical Associations (1954): Zeedijk 816, B-8300 Knokke, Belgium.

International Federation of Catholic Pharmacists* (1954): 60 avenue des Pages, F-78110 Le Vesinet, France.

International Federation of Catholic Universities* (1949): 77 bis, rue de Grenelle, F-75007 Paris, France.

International Federation of Institutes for Social and Socio-Religious Research (1952): Vlamingenstraat, 116, B-3000 Leuven, Belgium.

International Military Apostolate (1967): Mariahilfestrasse, 20, rue Notre-Dame des Champs, F-75006 Paris, France. Comprised of organizations of military men.

International Movement of Apostolate of Children* (1929, France): 8, rue Duguay-Trouin, F-75006 Paris, France.

International Movement of Apostolate in Middle and Upper Classes* (1963): Piazza San Calisto 16, I-00153 Rome, Italy. Evangelization of adults of the independent milieus (that part of population known as old or recent middle class, aristocracy, bourgeoisie or "white collar").

International Movement of Catholic Agricultural and Rural Youth (1954, Annevoie, Belgium): Diestsevest 24, B-3000 Leuven, Belgium (permanent secretariat).

International Young Catholic Students (1946, Fribourg, Switzerland; present name, 1954): 171 rue de Rennes, F-75006 Paris, France.

International Young Christian Workers* (1925, Belgium): 26, rue Juste Lipse, B-1040 Brussels, Belgium.

Laity and Christian Community (1966, Algiers, Algeria): 80, rue de Tourbillon, CH-1950 Sion, Switzerland. Universal brotherhood.

Legion of Mary* (1921, Dublin, Ireland): De Montfort House, North Brunswick St., Dublin, Ireland. (See Index.)

Liga Catholica Internationalis Sobrietas (International Catholic League against Alcoholism) (1897, Brussels, Belgium): Karlstrasse 40, Lorenz-Werthmannhaus, D-78 Freiburg/Br., Germany.

Medicus Mundi: Mozartstrasse 9, 51 Aachen, Germany. Place medicine at service of poor.

Movement for a Better World (1952): Centro Internationale Pio XII, Via dei Laghi Km. 10, I-00040 Rocca di Papa, Italy. (See Index.)

Our Lady's Teams (Equipes Notre-Dame) (1937, France): 49, rue de la Glacière, F-75013 Paris, France. Movement for spiritual formation of couples.

Pax Christi (1950): Celebesstraat 60, The Hague, The Netherlands. (See Index.)

Pax Romana* (1921, Fribourg, Switzerland, divided into two movements, 1947):

International Movement of Catholic Students* (1921): 171, rue de Rennes, F-75006, Paris, France. For undergraduates.

International Catholic Movement for Intellectual and Cultural Affairs* (1947): 1 route du Jura, CH-1700 Fribourg, Switzerland. For university graduates. Has professional secretariats at: Stradhouderskade 86, Amsterdam, The Netherlands (artists); Biesseltsebaan, 40, Nijmegen, The Netherlands (teachers); 18 rue de Varenne, F-75007 Paris, France (engineers); via della Conciliazione 4d, I-00193 Rome, Italy (lawyers).

St. Joan's International Alliance (1911 in England; present title, 1931): 48, chemin des Coudriers, CH-1121 Geneva, Switzerland.

Salesian Cooperators (1876): Via Maria Ausiliatrice 32, 10100 Turin, Italy. Third Salesian family founded by St. John Bosco; Members commit themselves to an apostolate at the service of the Church, giving particular attention to youth in the Salesian spirit and style.

Secular Franciscan Order (1221, first Rule approved): Via delle Mura Aurelis, 9, I-00165, Rome, Italy. (See Index.)

Serra International (1953, in U.S.): (See Index.)

Society of St. Vincent de Paul* (1933): 5, rue Pré-aux-Clercs, F-75007 Paris, France.

The Grail (1921), Nijmegen, The Netherlands): 5, Sayad Sokkar St. Matareya, Cairo, Egypt (temporary secretariat). (See Index.).

Third Order of St. Dominic (1285): Convento Santa Sabina, Piazza Pietro d'Illiria, Aventino, I-00153 Rome, Italy. (See Index.)

UNDA: International Catholic Association for Radio and Television* (1928, Cologne, Germany): rue de l'Orme, 12, B-1040 Brussels, Belgium. (See Index.)

Unio Internationalis Laicorum in Servitio Ecclesiae (1965, Aachen, Germany): Breite Strasse 106-110, Postfach 102068, D-5 Cologne, Germany. Consists of national and diocesan associations of persons who give professional services to the Church.

Union of Adorers of the Blessed Sacrament (1937): Largo dei Monti Parioli 3, I-00197, Rome, Italy.

World Catholic Federation for the Biblical Apostolate (1969, Rome): Rittelstrasse, 12, D 7000, Stuttgart 1, Germany.

World Federation of Catholic Youth* (1926; present title, 1968, with amalgamation of World Federation of Catholic Young Women and Girls and the International Catholic Youth Federation): 31 avenue de l'Hopital-Francais, B-1080 Brussels, Belgium.

World Federation of Christian Life Communities* (1953): 8, Borgo Santo Spirito, C.P. 6139, I-00100 Rome, Italy. First Sodality of Our Lady founded in 1563.

World Movement of Christian Workers* (1961): 90, rue des Palais, B-1030 Brussels, Belgium.

World Organization of Former Students of Catholic Schools (1967, Rome): 19, Boulevard de Picpus, F-75012 Paris, France.

World Union of Catholic Philosophical Societies (1948, Amsterdam, The Netherlands): The Catholic University of America, Washington, D.C. 20064.

World Union of Catholic Teachers* (1951): Piazza San Calisto 16, I-00153, Rome, Italy.

World Union of Catholic Women's Organizations* (1910): 20, rue Notre Dame des Champs, F-75006 Paris, France.

Regional Organizations

European Association for Catholic Adult Education (1963, Lucerne, Switzerland): Dransdorfer Weg 15/IV, D-53 Bonn, Germany.

European Forum of National Committees of the Laity (1968): Mutsaerstraat 32, B 2000 Antwerp, Belgium.

Movimiento Familiar Cristiano (1949-50, Montevideo and Buenos Aires): 7953, C.P. 480, Belo Horizonte, Brazil. Christian Family Movement of Latin America.

The Catholic Church in Canada

The first date in the remote background of the Catholic history of Canada was July 7, 1534, when a priest in the exploration company of Jacques Cartier celebrated Mass on the Gaspe Peninsula.

Successful colonization and the significant beginnings of the Catholic history of the country date from the foundation of Quebec in 1608 by Samuel Champlain and French settlers. Montreal was established in 1642.

The earliest missionaries were Franciscan Recollects and Jesuits who arrived in 1615 and 1625, respectively. They provided some pastoral care for the settlers but worked mainly among the 100,000 Indians — Algonquins and Huron-Iroquois — in the interior and in the Lake Ontario region. Eight Jesuits, the North American Martyrs, were killed in the 1640's. Sulpician Fathers, who arrived in Canada late in the 1640's, played a part in the great missionary period which ended about 1700.

Kateri Tekakwitha, Lily of the Mohawks, the first North American Indian candidate for canonization, died in 1680.

The communities of women religious with the longest histories in Canada are the Canonesses of St. Augustine, since 1637; the Ursulines, since 1639; and the Hospitallers of St. Joseph, since 1642. Communities of Canadian origin are the Congregation of Notre Dame, founded by Bl. Marguerite Bourgeoys in 1658, and the Grey Nuns, formed by Bl. Marie Marguerite d'Youville in 1738.

Ecclesiastical organization began with the appointment of Francois Montmorency de Laval as vicar apostolic of New France in 1658 — 26 years after France canceled England's claim to possession of the country. In 1674, Quebec became the first diocese in the territory.

In 1713, the French Canadian population numbered 18,000. In the same year, the Treaty of Utrecht ceded Acadia, Newfoundland and the Hudson Bay Territory to England. The Acadians were scattered among the American Colonies in 1755.

The English acquired possession of Canada and its 70,000 French-speaking inhabitants in virtue of the Treaty of Paris in 1763. Anglo-French and Anglican-Catholic differences and tensions developed. The pro-British government at first refused to recognize the titles of church officials, hindered the clergy in their work and tried to install a non-Catholic educational system. Laws were passed which guaranteed religious liberties to Catholics (Quebec Act of 1774, Constitutional Act of 1791, legislation approved by Queen Victoria in 1851), but it took some time before actual respect for these liberties matched the legal enactments. The initial moderation of government antipathy toward the Church was caused partly by the loyalty of Catholics to the Crown during the American Revolution and the War of 1812.

The 15 years following the passage in 1840 of the Act of Union, which joined Upper and Lower Canada, were significant. New communities of men and women religious joined those already in the country. The Oblates of Mary Immaculate, missionaries par excellence in Canada, advanced the penetration of the West which had been started in 1818 by Abbe Provencher. New jurisdictions were established, and Quebec became a metropolitan see in 1844. The first Council of Quebec was held in 1851. The established Catholic school system enjoyed a period of growth.

Laval University was inaugurated in 1854 and canonically established in 1876.

Archbishop Taschereau of Quebec was named Canada's first cardinal in 1886.

The apostolic delegation to Canada was set up in 1899. It became a nunciature October 16, 1969, with the establishment of diplomatic relations with the Vatican.

Early in this century, Canada had eight ecclesiastical provinces, 23 dioceses, three vicariates apostolic, 3,500 priests, 2.4 million Catholics, about 30 communities of men religious, and 70 or more communities of women religious. The Church in Canada was phased out of mission status and removed from the jurisdiction of the Congregation for the Propagation of the Faith in 1908.

The greatest concentration of Catholics is in the eastern portion of the country. In the northern and western portions, outside metropolitan centers, there are some of the most difficult parish and mission areas in the world. Bilingual (English-French) differences in the general population are reflected in the Church; for example, in the parallel structures of the Canadian Conference of Catholic Bishops, which was established in 1943. Quebec is the center of French cultural influence. Many language groups are represented among Catholics, who include about 255,000 members of Eastern Rite in a metropolitan see and four eparchies.

Education, a past source of friction between the Church and the government, is administered by the civil provinces in a variety of arrangements authorized by the Canadian Constitution. Denominational schools have tax support in one way in Quebec and Newfoundland, and in another way in Alberta, Ontario and Saskatchewan. Several provinces provide tax support only for public schools, making private financing necessary for separate church-related schools.

ECCLESIASTICAL JURISDICTIONS OF CANADA

Provinces

Names of ecclesiastical provinces and metropolitan sees in bold face: suffragan sees in parentheses. The Winnipeg archdiocese (Latin) is not a metropolitan see.

Edmonton (Calgary, St. Paul).
Grouard-McLennan (Mackenzie-Ft. Smith, Prince George, Whitehorse).
Halifax (Antigonish, Charlottetown, Yarmouth).
Keewatin-LePas (Churchill-Hudson Bay, Labrador-Schefferville, Moosonee).
Kingston (Alexandria-Cornwall, Peterborough, Sault Ste. Marie).
Moncton (Bathurst, Edmundston, St. John).
Montreal (Joliette, St. Jean-de-Quebec, St. Jerome, Valleyfield).
Ottawa (Hearst, Hull, Mont-Laurier, Pembroke, Rouyn-Noranda, Timmins).
Quebec (Amos, Chicoutimi, Ste.-Anne-de-la-Pocatiere, Trois Rivieres).
Regina (Gravelbourg, Prince Albert, Saskatoon, Abbey of St. Peter).
Rimouski (Gaspe, Hauterive).
St. Boniface (no suffragans).
St. John's (Grand Falls, St. George).
Sherbrooke (Nicolet, St. Hyacinthe).
Toronto (Hamilton, London, St. Catharines, Thunder Bay).
Vancouver (Kamloops, Nelson, Victoria).
Winnipeg — Ukrainian (Edmonton, New Westminster, Saskatoon, Toronto).

Archdioceses, Archbishops

Edmonton, Alta. (St. Albert, 1871; archdiocese, transferred Edmonton, 1912): Joseph N. MacNeil, archbishop, 1973.

Grouard-McLennan, Alta. (v. a. Athabaska-Mackenzie, 1862; Grouard, 1927; archdiocese Grouard-McLennan, 1967); Henri Legare, O.M.I., archbishop, 1972.

Halifax, N. S. (1842; archdiocese, 1852): James M. Hayes, archbishop, 1967.

Keewatin-Le Pas, Man. (v. a., 1910; archdiocese, 1967): Paul Dumouchel, O. M. I., archbishop, 1967.

Kingston, Ont. (1826; archdiocese, 1889): Joseph L. Wilhelm, archbishop, 1966.

Moncton, N.B. (1936): Donat Chiasson, archbishop, 1972.

Montreal, Que. (1836; archdiocese, 1886): Paul Gregoire, archbishop, 1968. Lawrence P. Whelan, Valerien Belanger, Andre Cimichella, O. S. M., Leonard Crowley, Jean-Marie Lafontaine, auxiliaries.

Ottawa, Ont. (Bytown, 1847, name changed, 1854; archdiocese, 1886): Joseph Aurele Plourde, archbishop, 1967. John Beahen, Gilles Belisle, auxiliaries.

Quebec, Que. (v. a., 1658; diocese, 1674; archdiocese, 1819; metropolitan, 1844; primatial see, 1956): Cardinal Maurice Roy, archbishop, 1947. Lionel Audet, Louis Vachon, Jean-Paul Labrie, auxiliaries.

Regina, Sask. (1910; archdiocese, 1915): Charles A. Halpin, archbishop, 1973.

Rimouski, Que. (1867; archdiocese, 1946): Gilles Ouellet, P.M.E., archbishop, 1973.

St. Boniface, Man. (1847; archdiocese, 1871): Antoine Hacault, archbishop, 1974.

St. John's, Nfld. (p. a., 1784; v. a., 1796; diocese, 1847; archdiocese, 1904): Alphonsus Penney, archbishop, 1979.

Sherbrooke, Que. (1874; archdiocese, 1951); J.-M. Fortier, archbishop, 1968.

Toronto, Ont. (1841; archdiocese, 1870): Cardinal G. Emmett Carter, archbishop, 1978. Aloysius M. Ambrozic, Michael Pearse Lacey, Robert B. Clune, Leonard J. Wall, auxiliaries.

Vancouver, B. C. (v. a. British Columbia, 1863; diocese New Westminster, 1890; archdiocese Vancouver, 1908): James F. Carney, archbishop, 1969. Lawrence Sabatini, C.S., auxiliary.

Winnipeg, Man. (1915): Cardinal George B. Flahiff, C.S.B., archbishop, 1961.

Winnipeg, Man. (Ukrainian Byzantine Rite) (Ordinariate of Canada, 1912; ap. ex. Central Canada, 1948; ap. ex. Manitoba, 1951; archdiocese Winnipeg, 1956): Maxim Hermaniuk, C.SS.R., archbishop, 1956.

Dioceses, Bishops

Alexandria-Cornwall, Ont. (1890): Eugene Philippe LaRocque, bishop, 1974.

Amos, Que. (1938): Gerard Drainville, bishop, 1978.

Antigonish, N. S. (Arichat, 1844; transferred, 1886): William E. Power, bishop, 1960.

Bathurst, N. B. (Chatham, 1860; transferred, 1938): Edgar Godin, bishop, 1969.

Calgary, Alta. (1912): Paul J. O'Byrne, bishop, 1968.

Charlottetown, P. E. I. (1829): Francis J. Spence, bishop, 1970.

Chicoutimi, Que. (1878): Jean-Guy Couture, bishop, 1979. Roch Pedneault, auxiliary.

Churchill-Hudson Bay, Man. (p. a., 1925; v. a. Hudson Bay, 1931; diocese Churchill, 1967; Churchill-Hudson Bay, 1968): Omer Robidoux, O. M. I., bishop, 1970.

Edmonton, Alta. (Ukrainian Byzantine Rite) (ap. ex., 1948; diocese, 1956): Nile Nicholas Savaryn, O.S.B.M., bishop, 1948. Martin Greschuk, auxiliary.

Edmundston, N.B. (1944): Fernand Lacroix, C.J.M., bishop, 1970.

Gaspe, Que. (1922): Bertrand Blanchet, bishop, 1973.

Grand Falls, Nfld. (Harbour Grace, 1856; present title, 1964):

Gravelbourg, Sask. (1930): Noel Delaquis, bishop, 1974.

Hamilton, Ont. (1856): Paul F. Reding, bishop, 1973. James H. MacDonald, auxiliary.

Hauterive, Que. (p. a., 1882; v. a., 1905; diocese Gulf of St. Lawrence, 1945; name changed, 1960): Roger Ebacher, bishop, 1979.

Hearst, Ont. (p. a., 1918; v. a., 1920; diocese, 1938): Roger Despatie, bishop, 1973.

Hull, Que. (1963): Adolphe Proulx, bishop, 1974.

Joliette, Que. (1904): Rene Audet, bishop, 1968.

Kamloops, B. C. (1945): Adam Exner, O.M.I., bishop, 1974.

Labrador-Schefferville (v. a. Labrador, 1945; diocese, 1967): Peter A. Sutton, O.M.I., bishop, 1974.

London, Ont. (1855; transferred Sandwich, 1859; London, 1869): John Sherlock, bishop, 1978.

Mackenzie-Fort Smith, N.W.T. (v. a. Mackenzie, 1901; diocese Mackenzie-Fort Smith, 1967): Paul Piché, O.M.I., bishop, 1967.

Mont-Laurier, Que. (1913): Jean Gratton, bishop, 1978.

Moosonee, Ont. (v. a. James Bay, 1938; diocese Moosonee, 1967): Jules Leguerrier, O.M.I., bishop, 1967.

Nelson, B. C. (1936): Wilfred Emmett Doyle, bishop, 1958.

New Westminster, B.C. (Ukrainian Byzantine Rite) (1974): Jerome Chimy, O.S.B.M., bishop, 1974.

Nicolet, Que. (1885): Albertus Martin, bishop, 1950.

Pembroke, Ont. (v.a. 1882; diocese, 1898): Joseph R. Windle, bishop, 1971.

Peterborough, Ont. (1882): James L. Doyle, bishop, 1976.

Prince Albert, Sask. (v.a., 1890; diocese, 1907): Laurent Morin, bishop, 1959.

Prince George, B. C. (p.a., 1908; v. a. Yukon and Prince Rupert, 1944; diocese Prince George, 1967): J. Fergus O'Grady, O.M.I., bishop, 1967.

Rouyn-Noranda, Que. (1973): Jean-Guy Hamelin, bishop, 1974.

Sainte-Anne-de-la-Pocatiere, Que. (1951): C.-H. Levesque, bishop, 1968.

St. Catharines, Ont. (1958): Thomas B. Fulton, bishop, 1978.

St. George's, Nfld. (p. a., 1870; v.a., 1890; diocese, 1904): Richard T. McGrath, bishop, 1970.

St. Hyacinthe, Que. (1852): Louis-de-Gonzague Langevin, bishop, 1979.

Saint-Jean-de-Quebec (1933): Bernard Hubert, bishop, 1978.

St. Jerome, Que. (1951): Charles Valois, bishop, 1977.

Saint John, N.B. (1842): Arthur J. Gilbert, bishop, 1974.

St. Paul in Alberta (1948): Raymond Roy, bishop, 1972.

Saskatoon, Sask. (1933): James P. Mahoney, bishop, 1967.

Saskatoon, Sask. (Ukrainian Byzantine Rite) (ap. ex., 1951; diocese, 1956): Andrew J. Roborecki, bishop, 1951.

Sault Ste. Marie, Ont. (1904): Alexander Carter, bishop, 1958. Bernard F. Pappin, Gerard Dionne, auxiliaries.

Thunder Bay, Ont. (Ft. William, 1952; transferred, 1970): John A. O'Mara, bishop, 1976.

Timmins, Ont. (v.a. Temiskaming, 1908; diocese Haileybury, 1915; present title, 1938): Jacques Landriault, bishop, 1971.

Toronto, Ont. (Ukrainian Byzantine Rite) (ap. ex., 1948; diocese, 1956): Isidore Borecky, bishop, 1948, Michael Rusnak, C.SS.R., auxiliary.

Trois-Rivieres, Que. (1852): Laurent Noel, bishop, 1975.

Valleyfield, Que. (1892): Robert Lebel, bishop, 1976.

Victoria, B.C. (diocese Vancouver Is., 1846; archdiocese, 1903; diocese Victoria, 1908): Remi J. De Roo, bishop, 1962.

Whitehorse, Y. T. (v.a., 1944; diocese 1967): Hubert P. O'Connor, O.M.I., bishop, 1971.

Yarmouth, N.S. (1953): Augustin-Emile Burke, bishop, 1968.

Military Vicariate of Canada (1951): Cardinal Maurice Roy, military vicar.

Abbacy of St. Peter, Muenster, Sask. (1921): Jerome Weber, O.S.B. (blessed, 1960).

BIOGRAPHIES OF CANADIAN BISHOPS

(Sources: Almanac survey; *1979 Directory of Canadian Conference of Catholic Bishops; Annuario Pontificio.* Data as of July 18, 1979.)

Ambrozic, Aloysius M.: b. Jan. 27, 1930; ord. priest June 4, 1955; ord. titular bishop of Valabria and auxiliary bishop of Toronto, May 27, 1976.

Audet, Lionel: b. May 22, 1908, Ste. Marie de Beauce, Que.; ord. priest July 8, 1934; ord. titular bishop of Tibari and auxiliary bishop of Quebec, May 1, 1952.

Audet, Rene: b. Jan. 18, 1920, Montreal, Que.; ord. priest May 30, 1948; ord. titular bishop of Chonochora and auxiliary bishop of Ottawa, July 31, 1963; bishop of Joliette, Jan. 3, 1968.

Baudoux, Maurice: b. July 10, 1902, Louviere, Belgium; ord. priest July 17, 1929; ord. bishop of St. Paul in Alberta, Oct. 28, 1948; titular archbishop of Preslavus and coadjutor archbishop of St. Boniface, Mar. 4, 1952; archbishop of St. Boniface, Sept. 14, 1955; retired Sept. 7, 1974.

Beahen, John: b. Feb. 14, 1922, Ottawa, Ont.; ord. priest June 15, 1946; ord. titular bishop of Ploaghe and auxiliary bishop of Ottawa, June 21, 1977.

Belanger, Valerien: b. Apr. 6, 1902, Valleyfield, Que.; ord. priest May 29, 1926; ord titular bishop of Cyrene and auxiliary bishop of Montreal, May 11, 1956.

Belisle, Gilles: b. Oct. 7, 1923, Clarence Creek, Ont.; ord. priest Feb. 2, 1950; ord. titular bishop of Uccula and auxiliary bishop of Ottawa, June 21, 1977.

Blais, Leo: b. Apr. 28, 1904, Dollar Bay, Mich.; ord. priest June 14, 1930; ord. bishop of Prince Albert, Aug. 28, 1952; titular bishop of Geron and auxiliary bishop of Montreal, Feb. 28, 1959; retired 1959.

Blanchet, Bertrand: b. Sept. 19, 1932, Saint Thomas de Montmagny, Que.; ord. priest May 20, 1956; ord. bishop of Gaspe, Dec. 8, 1973.

Borecky, Isidore: b. Oct. 1, 1911, Ostrovec, Ukraine; ord. priest July 17, 1938; ord. titular bishop of Amathus in Cypro and exarch of Toronto, May 27, 1948; bishop of Toronto (Ukrainians), Nov. 3, 1956.

Brodeur, Rosario L.: b. Oct. 30, 1889, Acton Vale, Que.; ord. priest June 17, 1916; ord. titular bishop of Mideo and coadjutor bishop of Alexandria, June 30, 1941; bishop of Alexandria, July 27, 1941; retired Oct. 15, 1966.

Burke, Augustin-Emile: b. Jan. 22, 1922, Sluice Point, N.S.; ord. priest Mar. 25, 1950; ord. bishop of Yarmouth, May 14, 1968.

Cabana, Georges: b. Oct. 23, 1894, Notre Dame de Granby, Que; ord. priest July 28, 1918; ord. titular archbishop of Anchialo and coadjutor archbishop of St. Boniface, June 30, 1941; coadjutor archbishop of Sherbrooke, Jan. 20, 1952; archbishop of Sherbrooke, May 28, 1952; retired Feb. 7, 1968.

Carew, William A.: b. Oct. 23, 1922, St. John's, Nfld., ord. priest June 15, 1947; ord. titular archbishop of Telde, Jan. 4, 1970; nuncio to Rwanda and Burundi, 1970-74; apostolic delegate to Jerusalem and Palestine and pro-nuncio to Cyprus, 1974.

Carney, James F.: b. June 28, 1915, Vancouver, B.C.; ord. priest Mar. 21, 1942; ord. titular bishop of Obori and auxiliary bishop of Vancouver, Feb. 11, 1966; archbishop of Vancouver, Jan. 8, 1969.

Carter, Alexander: b. Apr. 16, 1909, Montreal, Que.; ord. priest June 6, 1936; ord. titular bishop of Sita and coadjutor bishop of Sault Ste. Marie, Feb. 2, 1957; bishop of Sault Ste. Marie, Nov. 22, 1958.

Carter, G. Emmett: (See Cardinals, Biographies.)

Charbonneau, Paul E.: b. May 4, 1922, Ste. Therese de Blainville, Que.; ord. priest May 31, 1947; ord. titular bishop of Thapsus and auxiliary bishop of Ottawa, Jan. 18, 1961; first bishop of Hull, May 21, 1963; retired Apr. 12, 1973, because of ill health.

Chiasson, Donat: b. Jan. 2, 1930, Paquetville, N.B.; ord. priest May 6, 1956; ord. archbishop of Moncton, June 1, 1972.

Chimy, Jerome I., O.S.B.M.: b. Mar. 12, 1919, Radway, Alta.; ord. priest, June 29, 1944; ord. first bishop of New Westminster, B.C., for the Ukrainians, Sept. 5, 1974.

Cimichella, Andre, O.S.M.: b. Feb. 21, 1921, Grotte Santo Stefano, Italy; ord. priest May 26, 1945; ord. titular bishop of Quiza and auxiliary of Montreal, July 16, 1964.

Clune, Robert B.: b. 1921, Toronto, Ont.; ord. priest May 26, 1945; ord. titular bishop of Lucubaza and auxiliary bishop of Toronto, 1979.

Coderre, Gerard Marie: b. Dec. 19, 1904, St. Jacques de Montcalm, Que.; ord. priest May 30, 1931; ord. titular bishop of Aegae and coadjutor bishop of St.-Jean-de-Quebec, Sept. 12, 1951; bishop of St.-Jean-de-Quebec, Feb. 3, 1955. Retired May 3, 1978.

Couture, Jean-Guy: b. May 6, 1929, St.-Jean-Baptiste de Quebec, Que.; ord. priest May 30, 1953; ord. bishop of Hauterive, Que., Aug. 15, 1975; bishop of Chicoutimi, Apr. 5, 1979.

Couturier, Gerard: b. Jan. 12, 1913, St. Louis du Ha Ha, Que; ord. priest Mar. 25, 1938; ord. bishop of Hauterive, Feb. 28, 1957; resigned see Sept. 7, 1974.

Crowley, Leonard: b. Dec. 28, 1921, Montreal, Que.; ord. priest May 31, 1947; ord. titular bishop of Mons and auxiliary bishop of Montreal, Mar. 24, 1971.

Decosse, Aime: b. June 21, 1903, Somerset, Man.; ord. priest July 4, 1926; ord. bishop of Gravelbourg, Jan. 20, 1954; retired May 12, 1973.

Delaquis, Noel: b. Dec. 25, 1934, Notre-Dame-de-Lourdes, Man.; ord. priest June 5, 1958; ord. bishop of Gravelbourg, Feb. 19, 1974.

De Roo, Remi J.: b. Feb. 24, 1924, Swan Lake, Man.; ord. priest June 8, 1950; ord. bishop of Victoria, Dec. 14, 1962.

Desmarais, Joseph A.: b. Oct. 31, 1891, Upton, Que.; ord. priest July 25, 1914; ord. titular bishop of Ruspe and auxiliary bishop of St. Hyacinthe, Apr. 22, 1931; bishop of Amos, June 20, 1939; retired Oct. 31, 1968.

Despatie, Roger : b. Apr. 12, 1927, Sudbury, Ont.; ord. priest Apr. 12, 1952; ord. titular bishop of Usinaza and auxiliary bishop of Sault Ste. Marie, June 28, 1968; bishop of Hearst, Feb. 8, 1973.

Dionne, Gerard: b. June 19, 1919, Saint-Basile, N.B.; ord. priest May 1, 1948; ord. titular bishop of Garba and auxiliary bishop of Sault Ste. Marie, Apr. 8, 1975.

Douville, Arthur: b. July 22, 1894, St. Casimir de Portneuf, Que.; ord. priest May 25, 1919; ord. titular bishop of Vita and auxiliary bishop of St. Hyacinthe, Jan. 29, 1940; coadjutor bishop of St. Hyacinthe, Mar. 21, 1942; bishop of St. Hyacinthe, Nov. 27, 1942; retired June 13, 1967.

Doyle, James L.: b. June 20, 1929, Chatam, Ont.; ord. priest June 12, 1954; ord. bishop of Peterborough June 28, 1976.

Doyle, W. Emmett: b. Feb. 18, 1913, Calgary, Alta.: ord. priest June 5, 1938; ord. bishop of Nelson, Dec. 3, 1958.

Drainville, Gerard: b. May 20, 1930, L'Isle-du-Pas, Que.; ord. priest May 30, 1953; ord. bishop of Amos, June 12, 1978.

Dumouchel, Paul, O.M.I.: b. Sept. 19, 1911, St. Boniface, Man.; ord. priest June 24, 1936; ord. titular bishop of Sufes and vicar apostolic of Keewatin, May 24, 1955; archbishop of Keewatin-Le Pas, July 13, 1967.

Ebacher, Roger: Vicar general of Amos; appointed bishop of Hauterive, June 30, 1979.

Exner, Adam, O.M.I.: b. Dec. 24, 1928, Killaly, Sask.; ord. priest July 7, 1957; ord. bishop of Kamloops, B.C., Mar. 12, 1974.

Flahiff, George F.: (See Cardinals Biographies.)

Fortier, Jean-Marie: b. July 1, 1920, Quebec, Que.; ord. priest June 16, 1944; ord. titular bishop of Pomaria and auxiliary bishop of Ste. Anne-de-la-Pocatiere, Jan. 23, 1961; bishop of Gaspe, Jan. 19, 1965; archbishop of Sherbrooke, Apr. 20, 1968.

Frenette, Emilien: b. May 6, 1905, Montreal, Que.; ord. priest May 30, 1931; ord. bishop of St. Jerome, Sept. 12, 1951; retired June 11, 1971.

Fulton, Thomas B.: b. Jan. 13, 1918, St. Catharines, Ont.; ord. priest June 7, 1941; ord. titular bishop of Cursola and auxiliary bishop of Toronto, Jan. 6, 1969; bishop of St. Catharines, July 7, 1978.

Gagnon, Edouard, P.S.S.: b. Jan. 15, 1918, Port Daniel, Que.; ord. priest Aug. 15, 1940; ord. bishop Mar. 25, 1969; bishop of St. Paul in Alberta 1969-72; rector of Canadian College in Rome, 1972- ; vice-president and secretary of Vatican Committee for the Family, 1973.

Gilbert, Arthur J.: b. Oct. 26, 1915, Oromocto, N.B.; ord. priest June 3, 1943; ord. bishop of St. John, N.B., June 19, 1974.

Godin, Edgar: b. May 31, 1911, Neguac, N.B.; ord. priest June 15, 1941; ord. bishop of Bathurst, July 25, 1969.

Gratton, Jean: b. Dec. 4, 1924, Wendover, Ont.; ord. priest Apr. 27, 1952; ord. bishop of Mont Laurier, June 29, 1978.

Gregoire, Paul: b. Oct. 24, 1911, Verdun, Que.; ord. priest May 22, 1937; ord. titular bishop of Curubis and auxiliary bishop of Montreal, Dec. 27, 1961; archbishop of Montreal, Apr. 20, 1968.

Greschuk, Martin: b. Nov. 7, 1923, Innisfree, Alta.; ord. priest June 11, 1950; ord. titular bishop of Nazianus and auxiliary bishop of Edmonton of the Ukrainians, Oct. 3, 1974.

Hacault, Antoine: b. Jan. 17, 1926, Bruxelles, Man.; ord. priest May 20, 1951; ord. titular bishop of Media and coadjutor of St. Boniface, Sept. 8, 1964; archbishop of St. Boniface, Sept. 7, 1974.

Hains, Gaston: b. Sept. 10, 1921, Drummondville, Que.; ord. priest June 15, 1946; ord. titular bishop of Belesana and auxiliary bishop of St. Hyacinthe, Oct. 10, 1964; coadjutor bishop of Amos, 1967; bishop of Amos, Oct. 31, 1968; retired 1978.

Halpin, Charles A.: b. Aug. 30, 1930, St. Eustache, Man.; ord. priest May 27, 1956; ord. archbishop of Regina, Nov. 26, 1973.

Hamelin, Jean-Guy: b. Oct. 8, 1925, St. Severin-de-Proulxville, Que.; ord. priest June 11, 1949; ord. first bishop of Rouyn-Noranda, Que., Feb. 9, 1974.

Hayes, James M.: b. May 27, 1924, Halifax, N.S.; ord. priest June 15, 1947; ord. titular bishop of Reperi and apostolic administrator of Halifax, Apr. 20, 1965; archbishop of Halifax, June 22, 1967.

Hermaniuk, Maxim, C.SS.R.: b. Oct. 30, 1911, Nove Selo, Ukraine; ord. priest Sept. 4, 1938; ord. titular bishop of Sinna and exarch of Manitoba (Ukrainians), June 29, 1951; archbishop of Winnipeg (Ukrainians), Nov. 3, 1956.

Hubert, Bernard: b. June 1, 1929, Beloeil, Que.; ord. priest May 30, 1953; ord. bishop of St. Jerome, Sept. 12, 1971; coadjutor bishop of Saint-Jean-de-Quebec, 1977; succeeded as bishop of Saint-Jean-de-Quebec, May 3, 1978.

Jennings, Edward Q.: b. Oct. 4, 1896, Saint John, N.B.; ord. priest Dec. 27, 1925; ord. titular bishop of Sala and auxiliary bishop of Vancouver, June 11, 1941; bishop of Kamloops, Feb. 22, 1946; bishop of Fort William (now Thunder Bay), May 14, 1952; resigned Sept. 18, 1969.

Jette, Edouard: b. Aug. 9, 1898, St. Jacques, Que.; ord. priest May 31, 1923; ord. titular bishop of Tabe and auxiliary of Joliette, Apr. 14, 1948; retired 1968.

Jordan, Anthony, O.M.I.: b. Nov. 10, 1901, Broxburn, Scotland; ord. priest June 23, 1929; ord. titular bishop of Vada and vicar apostolic of Prince Rupert, B.C., Sept. 8, 1945; titular archbishop of Silyum and coadjutor of Edmonton, Apr. 17, 1955; archbishop of Edmonton, Aug. 11, 1964; retired July 2, 1973.

Labrie, Jean-Paul: b. Nov. 4, 1922, Laurieville, Que.; ord. priest May 20, 1951; ord. titular bishop of Urci and auxiliary bishop of Quebec, May 14, 1977.

Lacey, Michael Pearse: b. 1918, Toronto, Ont.; ord. priest May 23, 1943; ord. titular bishop of Diano and auxiliary bishop of Toronto, 1979.

Lacroix, Fernand, C.J.M.: b. Oct. 16, 1919, Quebec; ord. priest Feb. 10, 1946; ord. bishop of Edmundston, Oct. 20, 1970.

Lafontaine, Jean-Marie: b. Apr. 4, 1923, Montreal, Que.; ord. priest May 22, 1948;

ord. titular bishop of Ursona and auxiliary bishop of Montreal, May 27, 1979.

Landriault, Jacques: b. Sept. 23, 1921, Alfred, Ont.; ord. priest Feb. 9, 1947; ord. titular bishop of Cadi and auxiliary bishop of Alexandria, July 25, 1962; bishop of Hearst, May 27, 1964; app. bishop of Timmins, Mar. 24, 1971.

Langevin, Louis-de-Gonzague, P.B.: b. Oct. 31, 1921, Oka, Que.; ord. priest Feb. 2, 1950; ord. titular bishop of Rosemarkie and auxiliary of St. Hyacinthe Sept. 23, 1974; bishop of St. Hyacinthe, July 18, 1979.

LaRocque, Eugene Philippe: b. Mar. 27, 1927, Windsor, Ont.; ord. priest June 7, 1952; ord. bishop of Alexandria, Ont., Sept. 3, 1974; title of see changed to Alexandria-Cornwall, 1976.

Lebel, Robert: b. Nov. 8, 1924, Trois-Pistoles, Que.; ord. priest June 18, 1950; ord. titular bishop of Alinda and auxiliary of St. Jean de Quebec, May 12, 1974; bishop of Valleyfield, May 12, 1976.

Le Blanc, Camille A.: b. Aug. 25, 1898, Barachois, N.B.; ord. priest Apr. 5, 1924; ord. bishop of Bathurst, Sept. 8, 1942; retired Jan. 8, 1969.

Legare, Henri, O.M.I.: b. Feb. 20, 1918, Willow Bunch, Sask.; ord. priest June 29, 1943; ord. first bishop of Labrador-Schefferville, Sept. 9, 1967; archbishop of Grouard-McLennan, Nov. 21, 1972.

Leger, Paul-Emile: (See Cardinals, Biographies).

Leguerrier, Jules, O.M.I.: b. Feb. 18, 1915, Clarence Creek, Ont.; ord. priest June 19, 1943; ord. titular bishop of Bavagaliana and vicar apostolic of James Bay, June 29, 1964; first bishop of Moosonee, July 13, 1967.

Lemieux, Marie Joseph, O.P.: b. May 10, 1902, Quebec, Que.; ord. priest Apr. 15, 1928; ord. bishop of Sendai, Japan, June 29, 1936; titular bishop of Calydon, 1941; apostolic administrator of Gravelbourg, 1942; bishop of Gravelbourg, 1944; archbishop of Ottawa, 1953; retired 1966.

Levesque, Charles Henri: b. Dec. 29, 1921, St. Andre de Kamouraska, Que.; ord. priest June 13, 1948; ord. titular bishop of Guzabeta and auxiliary bishop of Ste.-Anne-de-la-Pocatiere, Dec. 27, 1965; bishop of Ste.-Anne-de-la-Pocatiere, Aug. 17, 1968.

Levesque, Louis: b. May 27, 1908, Amqui, Que.; ord. priest June 26, 1932; ord. bishop of Hearst, Aug. 15, 1952; titular archbishop of Egnatia and coadjutor of Rimouski, Apr. 13, 1964; archbishop of Rimouski, Feb. 25, 1967; retired May 14, 1973.

Lussier, Philippe, C.SS.R.: b. Oct. 3, 1911, Weedon, Que.; ord. priest Sept. 18, 1937; ord. bishop of St. Paul in Alberta, Aug. 17, 1952; retired Aug. 17, 1968.

McCarthy, Thomas J.: b. Oct. 4, 1905, Goderich, Ont.; ord. priest May 25, 1929; ord. bishop of Nelson, Aug. 1, 1955; bishop of St. Catharines, Nov. 9, 1958. Retired 1978.

MacDonald, James H.: b. Apr. 28, 1925, Wycogama, N.S.; ord. priest June 28, 1953; ord. titular bishop of Gibba and auxiliary bishop of Hamilton April 17, 1978.

MacEachern, Malcolm A.: b. Oct. 5, 1901, Broad Cove Chapel, N.S.; ord. priest June 11, 1927; ord. bishop of Charlottetown, Jan. 18, 1955; retired Feb. 24, 1970.

McGrath, Richard T.: b. June 17, 1912, Oderin, Placentia Bay, Nfld.; ord. priest June 24, 1936; ord. bishop of St. George's, Nfld., July 22, 1970.

MacNeil, Joseph N.: b. Apr. 15, 1924, Sydney, N.S.; ord. priest May 23, 1948; ord. bishop of St. John, N.B., June 24, 1969; archbishop of Edmonton, July 6, 1973.

Mahoney, James P.: b. Dec. 7, 1927, Saskatoon, Sask.; ord. priest June 7, 1952; ord. bishop of Saskatoon, Dec. 13, 1967.

Martin, Albertus: b. Oct. 4, 1913, Southbridge, Mass.; ord. priest May 18, 1939; ord. titular bishop of Bassiana and coadjutor bishop of Nicolet, Oct. 7, 1950; bishop of Nicolet, Nov. 8, 1950.

Melancon, Georges: b. Apr. 7, 1886, Saint-Guillaume d'Upton, Que.; ord. priest Sept. 12, 1909; ord. bishop of Chicoutimi, July 23, 1940; retired Feb. 18,1961.

Morin, Laurent: b. Feb. 14, 1908, Montreal, Que.; ord. priest May 27, 1934; ord. titular bishop of Arsamosata and auxiliary bishop of Montreal, Oct. 30, 1955; bishop of Prince Albert, Feb. 28, 1959.

Noel, Laurent: b. Mar. 19, 1920, Saint-Just-de-Bretenieres, Que.; ord. priest June 16, 1944; ord. titular bishop of Agathopolis and auxiliary bishop of Quebec, Aug. 29, 1963; bishop of Trois Rivieres, Nov. 5, 1975.

O'Byrne, Paul J.: b. Dec. 21, 1922, Calgary, Alta.; ord. priest Feb. 21, 1948; ord. bishop of Calgary, Aug. 22, 1968.

O'Connor, Hubert P., O.M.I.: b. Feb. 17, 1928, Huntingdon, Que.; ord. priest June 5, 1955; ord. bishop of Whitehorse, Dec. 8, 1971.

O'Grady, John Fergus, O.M.I.: b. July 27, 1908, Macton, Ont.; ord. priest June 29, 1934; ord. titular bishop of Aspendus and vicar apostolic of Prince Rupert, Mar. 7, 1956; first bishop of Prince George, July 13, 1967.

O'Mara, John A.: b. Nov. 17, 1924, Buffalo, N.Y.; ord. priest June 1, 1951; ord. bishop of Thunder Bay, June 29, 1976.

O'Neill, Michael C.: b. Feb. 15, 1898, Kemptville, Ont.; ord. priest Dec. 21, 1927; ord. archbishop of Regina, Apr. 14, 1948; retired Sept. 26, 1973.

Ouellet, Gilles, P.M.E.: b. Aug. 14, 1922, Bromptonville, Que.; ord. priest June 30, 1946; ord. bishop of Gaspe, Nov. 23, 1968; app. archbishop of Rimouski, Apr. 27, 1973. President Canadian Conference of Catholic Bishops, 1977.

Ouellette, Andre: b. Feb. 4, 1913, Salem, Mass.; ord. priest June 11, 1938; ord. titular bishop of Carre and auxiliary bishop of Mont-Laurier, Feb. 25, 1957; bishop of Mont-Laurier, Mar. 27, 1965; retired Feb. 1978.

Pappin, Bernard F.: b. July 10, 1928, Westmeath, Ont.; ord. priest May 27, 1954; ord. titular bishop of Aradi and auxiliary bishop of Sault Ste. Marie, Apr. 11, 1975.

Pare, Marius: b. May 22, 1903, Montmagny, Que.; ord. priest July 3, 1927; ord. titular bishop of Aegae and auxiliary bishop of Chicoutimi, May 1, 1956; bishop of Chicoutimi, Feb. 18, 1961. Retired Apr. 5, 1979.

Parent, Charles Eugene: b. Apr. 22, 1902, Notre Dame-de-Neiges-des-Trois-Pistoles, Que.; ord. priest Mar. 7, 1925; ord. titular bishop of Diana and auxiliary bishop of Rimouski, May 24, 1944; app. archbishop of Rimouski, Mar. 2, 1951; retired Feb. 25, 1967.

Pedneault, Roch: b. Apr. 10, 1927, Saint Joseph d'Alma, Que.; ord. priest Feb. 8, 1953; ord. titular bishop of Aggersel and auxiliary of Chicoutimi, Que., June 29, 1974.

Pelletier, Georges Leon: b. Aug. 19, 1904, Saint-Epiphane, Que.; ord. priest June 24, 1931; ord. titular bishop of Hephaestus and auxiliary bishop of Quebec, Feb. 24, 1943; bishop of Trois Rivieres, July 26, 1947; retired Oct. 31, 1975.

Penney, Alphonsus L.: b. Sept. 17, 1924, St. John's, Nfld.; ord. priest June 29, 1949; ord. bishop of Grand Falls, Jan. 18, 1973; archbishop of St. John's, Nfld., Apr. 5, 1979.

Piche, Paul, O.M.I.: b. Sept. 14, 1909, Gravelbourg, Sask.; ord. priest Dec. 23, 1934; ord. titular bishop of Orcistus and vicar apostolic of Mackenzie, June 11, 1959; first bishop of Mackenzie-Fort Smith, July 13, 1967.

Plourde, Joseph Aurele: b. Jan. 12, 1915, St. Francois de Madawaska, N.B.; ord. priest May 7, 1944; ord. titular bishop of Lapda and auxiliary bishop of Alexandria, Aug. 26, 1964; archbishop of Ottawa, Jan. 2, 1967.

Pocock, Philip: b. July 2, 1906, St. Thomas, Ont.; ord. priest June 14, 1930; ord. bishop of Saskatoon, June 29, 1944; titular archbishop of Aprus and coadjutor archbishop of Winnipeg, Aug. 6, 1951; archbishop of Winnipeg, Jan. 14, 1952; titular archbishop of Isauropolis and coadjutor archbishop of Toronto, Feb. 18, 1961; archbishop of Toronto, Mar. 30, 1971; retired Apr. 29, 1978.

Power, William E.: b. Sept. 27, 1915; Montreal, Que.; ord. priest June 7, 1941; ord. bishop of Antigonish, July 20, 1960; president Canadian Conference of Catholic Bishops, 1971-73.

Proulx, Adolphe J.: b. Dec. 12, 1927, Hanmer, Ont., Canada; ord. priest Apr. 17, 1954; ord. titular bishop of Missua and auxiliary bishop of Sault Ste. Marie, Feb. 24, 1965; bishop of Alexandria, Apr. 28, 1967; bishop of Hull, Feb. 13, 1974.

Reding, Paul F.: b. Feb. 14, 1925, Hamilton, Ont.; ord. priest June 3, 1950; ord. titular bishop of Liberalia and auxiliary bishop of Hamilton, Sept. 14, 1966; bishop of Hamilton, Sept. 14, 1973.

Robichaud, Norbert: b. Apr. 1, 1905, St. Charles, N.B.; ord. priest May 1, 1931; ord. archbishop of Moncton, Sept. 8, 1942; retired Mar. 23, 1972.

Robidoux, Omer, O.M.I.: b. Nov. 19, 1913 Saint-Pierre-Jolys, Man.; ord. priest June 29, 1939; ord. bishop of Churchill-Hudson Bay, May 20, 1970.

Roborecki, Andrew: b. Dec. 12, 1910, in western Ukraine; arrived Winnipeg, Man., 1912; ord. priest July 18, 1934; ord. titular bishop of Tanais and auxiliary bishop of Ukrainian Catholic Diocese of Central Canada, May 27, 1948; exarch of Saskatchewan, 1951; bishop of Saskatoon (Ukrainians), Nov. 3, 1956.

Routhier, Henri, O.M.I.: b. Feb. 28, 1900, Pincher Creek, Alta.; ord. priest Sept. 7, 1924; ord. titular bishop of Naissus and coadjutor vicar apostolic of Grouard, Sept. 8, 1945; vicar apostolic of Grouard, 1953; archbishop of Grouard-McLennan, July 13, 1967; retired Nov. 21, 1972.

Roy, Maurice: (Cardinals, Biographies.)

Roy, Raymond: b. May 3, 1919, St. Boniface, Man.; ord. priest May 31, 1947; ord. bishop of St. Paul in Alberta, July 18, 1972.

Rusnak, Michael, C.SS.R.: b. Aug. 21, 1921, Beaverdale, Pa.; ord. priest July 3, 1949; ord. titular bishop of Tzernicus and auxiliary bishop of Toronto eparchy and apostolic visitator to Slovak Catholics of Byzantine rite in Canada, Jan. 2, 1965.

Ryan, Joseph F.: b. Mar. 1, 1897, Dundas, Ont.; ord. priest May 21, 1921; ord. bishop of Hamilton, Oct. 19, 1937; retired Mar. 27, 1973.

Sabatini, Lawrence, C.S.: b. May 15, 1930, Chicago, Ill.; ord. priest Mar. 19, 1957; ord. titular bishop of Nasai and auxiliary bishop of Vancouver, Sept. 21, 1978.

Sanschagrin, Albert, O.M.I.: b. Aug. 5, 1911, Saint-Tite, Que.; ord. priest May 24, 1936; ord. titular bishop of Bagi and coadjutor bishop of Amos Sept. 14, 1957; bishop of Saint-Hyacinthe, June 13, 1967. Retired July 18, 1979.

Savaryn, Nile Nicholas, O.S.B.M.: b. May 19, 1905, Stary Sambir, Ukraine; ord. priest Aug. 23, 1931; ord. titular bishop of Jos and auxiliary bishop of the Catholic Ukrainian diocese in Canada, July 1, 1943; bishop of apostolic exarchate for western Canada, 1948; bishop of Edmonton (Ukrainians), Nov. 3, 1956.

Sherlock, John M.: b. Jan. 20, 1926, Regina, Sask.; ord. priest June 3, 1950; ord. titular bishop of Macriana and auxiliary of

London, Ont., Aug. 28, 1974; bishop of London, July 7, 1978.

Skinner, Patrick J., C.J.M.: b. Mar. 9, 1904, St. John's, Nfld.; ord. priest May 30, 1929; ord. titular bishop of Zenobia and auxiliary bishop of St. John's, Mar. 17, 1950; archbishop of St. John's, Mar. 23, 1951. Retired Apr. 5, 1979.

Smith, William J.: b. Jan. 2, 1897, Greenfield, Ont.; ord. priest June 16, 1927; ord. bishop of Pembroke, July 25, 1945; retired Feb. 8, 1971.

Spence, Francis J.: b. June 3, 1926, Perth, Ont.; ord. priest Apr. 16, 1950; ord. titular bishop of Nova and auxiliary bishop of the military vicariate, June 15, 1967; bishop of Charlottetown, Aug. 15, 1970.

Sutton, Peter A., O.M.I.: b. Oct. 18, 1934, Chandler, Que.; ord. priest Oct. 22, 1960; ord. bishop of Labrador-Schefferville, July 18, 1974.

Tessier, Maxime: b. Oct. 9, 1906, St. Sebastien, Que.; ord. priest June 14, 1930; ord. titular bishop of Christopolis and auxiliary bishop of Ottawa, Aug. 2, 1951; coadjutor bishop of Timmins, 1953; bishop of Timmins, May 8, 1955; retired Mar. 24, 1971.

Vachon, Louis-Albert: b. Feb. 4, 1912, Saint-Frederic, Que.; ord. priest June 11, 1938; ord. titular bishop of Mesarfelta and auxiliary bishop of Quebec, May 14, 1977.

Valois, Charles: b. Apr. 24, 1924, Montreal, Que.; ord. priest June 3, 1950; ord. bishop of St. Jerome, June 29, 1977.

Wall, Leonard J.: b. 1925, Windsor, Ont.; ord. priest June 11, 1949; ord. titular bishop of Leptiminus and auxiliary bishop of Toronto, 1979.

Webster, Benjamin I.: b. Mar. 7, 1898, Spofforth, Eng.; ord. priest May 26, 1923; ord. titular bishop of Paphos and auxiliary bishop of Toronto, Nov. 21, 1946; bishop of Peterborough, Apr. 21, 1954; retired Mar. 12, 1968.

Whelan, Lawrence P.: b. Oct. 16, 1899, Montreal, Que.; ord. priest Dec. 19, 1925; ord. titular bishop of Opus and auxiliary bishop of Montreal, Aug. 15, 1941.

Wilhelm, Joseph L.: b. Nov. 16, 1909, Walkerton, Ont.; ord. priest June 9, 1934; ord. titular bishop of Saccaea and auxiliary bishop of Calgary, Aug. 22, 1963; archbishop of Kingston, Dec. 14, 1966.

Windle, Joseph R.: b. Aug. 28, 1917, Ashdad, Ont.; ord. priest May 16, 1943; ord. titular bishop of Uzita and auxiliary bishop of Ottawa, Jan. 18, 1961; coadjutor bishop of Pembroke, 1969; bishop of Pembroke, Feb. 15, 1971.

CANADIAN CONFERENCE OF CATHOLIC BISHOPS

The Canadian Conference of Catholic Bishops was established Oct. 12, 1943, as a permanent voluntary association of the bishops of Canada, was given official approval by the Holy See in 1948, and acquired the status of an episcopal conference after the Second Vatican Council.

The CCCB acts in two ways: (1) as a strictly ecclesiastical body through which the bishops act together with pastoral authority and responsibility for the Church throughout the country; (2) as an operational secretariat through which the bishops act on a wider scale for the good of the Church and society.

At the top of the CCCB organizational table are the president, an executive committee, an administrative board and a plenary assembly. The membership consists of all the bishops of Canada.

Departments and Offices

The CCCB's work is planned and co-ordinated by a Pastoral Team of 14 members — six bishops and six staff members (lay and clergy) and the two general secretaries.

The CCCB has six departments and four offices all of which work in both French and English: (I) Department for Theology, Liturgy and Canon Law; (II) Department for Christian Education and Communications; (III) Department for Missions; (IV) Department for Social Life; (V) Department for Internal Relations; (VI) Department for Extraordinary Affairs and Social Communications. Offices for (1) Christian Education (2) Liturgy (3) Missions (4) Social Affairs.

The general secretariat consists of a French and an English general secretary and their assistants and directors of public relations.

Administrative services for purchasing, archives and library, accounting, personnel, publications, printing and distribution are supervised by directors who relate to the general secretaries.

Various advisory councils and committees with mixed memberships of lay persons, religious, priests and bishops also serve the CCCB on a variety of topics.

Operations

Meetings for the transaction of business are held twice a year by the plenary assembly, every month except July and August by the executive committee, and four times a year by the administrative board.

Archbishop Gilles Ouellet of Rimouski, Que., is president of the CCCB; Archbishop Joseph N. MacNeil of Edmonton, Alta., is vice-president.

Headquarters are located at 90 Parent Ave., Ottawa, K1N 7B1, Canada.

ORGANIZATIONS

The Catholic Church Extension Society of Canada supports home missions. Address: 67 Bond St., Toronto, Ontario M5B 1X6.

The Oblate Indian-Eskimo Council of Canada, 238 Argyle St., Ottawa.

The Canadian Catholic Women's League, with a membership of more than 100,000. Address: 890 St. James St., Winnipeg, Man. R3G 3J7.

STATISTICS OF CATHOLIC CHURCH IN CANADA

(Source: 1979 Directory of the Canadian Conference of Catholic Bishops. Archdioceses are indicated by an asterisk. For dioceses marked +, see Canadian Dioceses with Interprovincial Lines.)

Canada's 10 civil provinces and two territories are divided into 17 ecclesiastical provinces consisting of 17 metropolitan sees (archdioceses) and 52 suffragran sees (51 dioceses and one abbacy); there is also one archdiocese immediately subject to the Holy See. (See listing of Ecclesiastical Provinces elsewhere in this section.)

This table presents a regional breakdown of Catholic statistics. In some cases, the totals are approximate because diocesan boundaries fall within several civil provinces.

Civil Province Diocese	Cath. Pop.	Dioc. Priests	Rel. Priests	Total Priests	Bros.	Srs.	Parishes
Newfoundland	209,376	118	43	161	96	548	176
*St. John's	109,315	55	20	75	62	341	40
Grand Falls	35,140	35	1	36	15	72	45
Labrador-Schefferville+	21,873	—	21	21	9	49	25
St. George's	43,048	28	1	29	10	86	66
Prince Edward Island							
Charlottetown	51,215	81	4	85	—	263	56
Nova Scotia	275,533	305	51	356	14	1,059	241
*Halifax	113,000	77	22	99	1	420	73
Antigonish	126,333	203	11	214	12	573	127
Yarmouth	36,200	25	18	43	1	66	41
New Brunswick	317,724	304	121	425	64	1,329	257
*Moncton	78,000	80	63	143	27	415	64
Bathurst	107,049	90	27	117	22	359	57
Edmundston	52,675	59	16	75	12	250	35
St. John	80,000	75	15	90	3	305	101
Quebec	5,386,209	4,527	2,819	7,346	3,614	27,937	1,917
*Montreal	1,533,777	785	1,210	1,995	1,080	8,421	280
*Quebec	908,011	871	520	1,391	689	7,051	276
*Rimouski	159,844	264	48	312	30	1,150	116
*Sherbrooke	230,876	327	135	462	150	1,563	149
Amos	105,349	100	28	128	23	329	82
Chicoutimi	266,233	301	103	404	133	1,027	106
Gaspe	102,376	110	19	129	11	303	63
Hauterive	99,596	63	35	98	27	297	52
Hull	154,800	93	62	155	27	350	65
Joliette	146,189	156	60	216	145	626	55
Mont Laurier	67,067	77	46	123	58	243	62
Nicolet	164,399	242	38	280	165	1,197	85
Rouyn-Noranda	59,649	41	26	67	23	214	44
Ste-Anne-de-la-Pocatiere	91,027	201	15	216	18	496	54
St. Hyacinth	280,510	263	110	373	345	1,738	112
St. Jean de Quebec	405,000	172	93	265	168	849	88
St. Jerome	212,948	114	108	222	157	343	65
Trois Rivieres	237,453	219	106	325	257	1,334	97
Valleyfield	161,105	128	57	185	108	406	66
Ontario	2,402,118	1,403	1,325	2,728	373	5,321	1,195
*Kingston	59,042	82	7	89	—	311	70
*Ottawa	285,303	166	270	436	125	1,297	107
*Toronto	900,000	293	521	814	110	1,032	210

Canadian Statistics

Civil Province Diocese	Cath. Pop.	Dioc. Priests	Rel. Priests	Total Priests	Bros.	Srs.	Parishes
Ontario							
Alexandria-Cornwall	53,000	52	8	60	11	140	34
Hamilton	277,013	145	161	306	37	460	119
Hearst	34,400	23	9	32	3	81	41
London	308,253	255	121	376	24	800	174
Moosonee+	3,000	—	13	13	14	21	8
Pembroke+	55,348	86	15	101	3	288	72
Peterborough	41,989	58	6	64	1	179	75
St. Catharines	100,000	53	39	92	4	79	47
Sault Ste. Marie	170,000	135	94	229	15	454	115
Thunder Bay	55,000	25	40	65	5	67	86
Timmins	59,770	30	21	51	21	112	37
Manitoba	212,500	161	218	379	66	1,083	292
*Keewatin-LePas+	30,000	—	40	40	13	60	45
*St. Boniface	80,000	98	63	161	36	660	70
*Winnipeg	97,500	63	94	157	12	353	155
Churchill-Hudson Bay+	5,000	—	21	21	5	10	22
Saskatchewan	202,075	205	168	373	30	860	425
*Regina	91,400	91	51	142	6	269	193
Gravelbourg	14,175	30	8	38	4	115	58
Prince Albert	40,000	44	38	82	7	212	86
Saskatoon	44,500	40	42	82	3	174	63
St. Peter Muenster (Abb.)	12,000	—	29	29	10	90	25
Alberta	318,400	237	227	464	52	936	432
*Edmonton	154,000	112	113	225	26	610	173
*Grouard-McLennan	30,000	8	44	52	9	89	60
Calgary	114,000	91	61	152	15	152	125
St. Paul	20,400	26	9	35	2	85	74
British Columbia	308,859	157	172	329	57	676	329
*Vancouver	175,000	76	99	175	31	377	88
Kamloops	27,000	17	12	29	7	55	80
Nelson	37,839	32	13	45	—	59	54
Prince George	25,020	5	25	30	11	50	56
Victoria	44,000	27	23	50	8	135	51
Yukon Territory							
Whitehorse+	6,592	—	17	17	2	14	24
Northwest Territories+							
MacKenzie-Ft. Smith	25,108	2	41	43	25	56	36
Eastern Rites	199,875	179	85	264	25	153	396
*Winnipeg	55,000	36	20	56	2	41	43
Edmonton	52,375	41	21	62	11	35	118
New Westminster	7,000	8	6	14	—	3	20
Saskatoon	25,500	25	18	43	4	42	130
Toronto	60,000	69	20	89	8	32	85
Military Vicariate	75,659	55	25	80	—	6	60
TOTALS 1979	9,991,243	7,734	5,316	13,050	4,418	40,241	5,836
Totals 1978	10,082,341	7,885	5,489	13,374	4,441	40,522	5,880

Dioceses with Interprovincial Lines

The following dioceses, indicated by + in the table, have interprovincial lines.

Labrador-Schefferville includes the Labrador region of Newfoundland and the northern part of Quebec province.

Moosonee, Ont., includes part of Quebec province.

Pembroke, Ont., includes one county of Quebec province.

Keewatin-Le Pas includes part of Manitoba

and Saskatchewan provinces.

Churchill-Hudson Bay includes part of Northwest Territories.

Whitehorse, Y.T., includes part of British Columbia.

Northwest Territories totals do not include an area within the boundaries of the Churchill-Hudson Bay diocese.

PERCENTAGE OF CATHOLICS

Catholic population statistics are from the 1979 Directory of the Canadian Conference of Catholic Bishops; total population figures are 1978 estimates.

The table presents a regional breakdown of Catholic percentage in total population. In some cases, the Catholic totals are approximate because diocesan boundaries fall within several civil provinces. See Index: Canadian Dioceses with Interprovincial Lines.

Civil Province Territory	Cath. Pop.	Total Pop.	Cath. Pct.
Alberta	318,400	1,936,200	16.4
British Columbia	308,859	2,523,400	12.2
Manitoba	212,500	1,034,700	20.5
New Brunswick	317,724	691,900	45.9
Newfoundland	209,376	564,800	37.0
Nova Scotia	275,533	839,600	32.8
Ontario	2,402,118	8,441,100	28.4
Prince Edward Is.	51,215	121,900	42.0
Quebec	5,386,209	6,280,900	85.8
Saskatchewan	202,075	944,000	21.4
Northwest Territories	25,108	43,700	57.4
Yukon	6,592	22,000	29.9
Eastern Rites	199,875	—	—
Military Vicariate	75,659	—	—
TOTALS 1979	9,991,243	23,444,200	42.6
Totals 1978	10,082,341	23,243,000	43.3

CANADIAN SHRINES

Our Lady of the Cape (Cap de la Madeleine), Queen of the Most Holy Rosary: The Three Rivers, Quebec, parish church, built of fieldstone in 1714 and considered the oldest stone church on the North American continent preserved in its original state, was rededicated June 22, 1888, as a shrine of the Queen of the Most Holy Rosary. Thereafter, the site increased in importance as a pilgrimage and devotional center, and in 1904 St. Pius X decreed the crowning of a statue of the Blessed Virgin which had been donated 50 years earlier to commemorate the dogma of the Immaculate Conception. In 1909, the First Plenary Council of Quebec declared the church a shrine of national pilgrimage. In 1964, the church at the shrine was given the status and title of minor basilica.

St. Anne de Beaupre: The devotional history of this shrine in Quebec, which has been called the "Lourdes of the New World," began with the reported cure of a cripple, Louis Grimont, on Mar. 16, 1658, the starting date of construction work on a small chapel of St. Anne. The original building was successively enlarged and replaced by a stone church which was given the rank of minor basilica in 1888. The present structure, a Romanesque-Gothic basilica, houses the shrine proper in its north transept. The centers of attraction are an eight-foot-high oaken statue and the great relic of St. Anne, a portion of her forearm.

St. Joseph's Oratory: The massive oratory basilica standing on the western side of Mount Royal and overlooking the city of Montreal had its origin in a primitive chapel erected there by Brother Andre, C.S.C., in 1904. Eleven years later, a large crypt was built to accommodate an increasing number of pilgrims, and in 1924 construction work was begun on the large church. A belfry, housing a 60-bell carillon and standing on the site of the original chapel, was dedicated May 15, 1955, as the first major event of the jubilee year observed after the oratory was given the rank of minor basilica.

Martyrs' Shrine: A shrine commemorating several of the Jesuit Martyrs of North America who were killed between 1642 and 1649 in the Ontario and northern New York area is located on the former site of old Forte Sainte Marie.

CATHOLIC PUBLICATIONS

(Sources: *Catholic Press Directory,* Canadian Conference of Catholic Bishops.)

Newspapers

British Columbia Catholic, The, w; 150 Robson St., Vancouver, B.C. V6B 2A7.

Catholic New Times (national), biweekly; 80 Sackville St., Toronto, Ont. M5A 3E5.

Catholic Register, The, (national), w; 67 Bond St., Toronto, Ont. M5B 1X6.

Catholic Times, The, 10 times a year; 38 Macaulay Ave., St. Lambert, Que. J4R 2G6.

Diocesan News, m; P.O. Box 1689, Charlottetown, P.E.I. C1A 7N4.

Esprit Vivant, m; 1915 est, Blvd. Gouin, Montreal, Que. H2B 1W7.

Monitor, The, m; P.O. Box 986, St. John's, Nfld..

New Freeman, The, w; Box 6609, Sta. A, St. John, N.B. E2L 4S1.

Our Sunday Visitor (national), w; 200 Noll Plaza, Huntington, Ind. 46750.

Prairie Messenger, w; St. Peter's Press, Muenster, Sask. S0K 2Y0.

Presence, m; 256 King Edward Ave., Ottawa, Ont. K1N 7M1.

Teviskes, Ziburiai (Lithuanian), w; 2185 Stavebank Rd., Mississauga, Ont. L5C 1T3.

Western Catholic Reporter, w; 10562 109th St., Edmonton, Alta. T5H 3B2.

Magazines

Annals of St. Anne de Beaupre, m; Box

1000, St. Anne de Beaupre, Que. GOA 3CO; Basilica of St. Anne.

Apostolat, bm; 460, le Rue, Richelieu, Que. J3L 3W2, Oblates of Mary Immaculate.

Bulletin/Le Bulletin (French-English), m; 324 E. Laurier St., Ottawa, Ont. K1N 6P6. Canadian Religious Conference.

Canadian Layman, The, bm; 88 Plymouth St., Box 5438, Ottawa, Ont. K2C 3J1.

Canadian League, The, 4 times a year; 2375 A Ness Ave., Winnipeg, Man. R3J 1A5.

Centre News, q; 830 Bathurst St., Toronto, Ont.

Christian Communications, 4 times a year; 223 Main St., Ottawa, Ont. K1S 1C4.

Companion of St. Francis and St. Anthony, m; 15 Chestnut Park Rd., Toronto, Ont. M4W 1W5; Conventual Franciscan Fathers.

Field At Home, q; 10 Montcrest Blvd., Toronto Ont. M4K 1J7.

Indian Record, 6 times a year; 1301 Wellington Crescent, Winnipeg, Man. R3N-0A9.

Kateri (English-French), q; P.O. Box 70, Caughnawaga, Que. JO1 1BO.

Logos (Ukrainian, English and French), q; 165 Catherine St., Yorkton, Sask.

Magazine Actualite, m; 2120 Sherbrooke St. E., Montreal 133, Que.

Martyrs' Shrine Message, q; Midland, Ont. L4R 4K3.

Messager de Saint Antoine, 10 times a year; Lac-Bouchette, Que. GOW IVO.

Messenger of the Sacred Heart, m; 833 Broadview Ave., Toronto, Ont. M4K 2P9.

Missions Etrangeres, 6 times a year; 59 Rue Desnoyers, Laval, Que. H7G 14A.

Oblate Missions, q; 17 Graham Ave., Ottawa K1S 0B6 Ont.

Oratory, 5 times a year; 3800 Ch. Reine-Marie, Montreal Que. H3V 1H6.

Our Family, m; P. O. Box 249, Battleford, Sask.; S0M 0E0; Oblates of Mary Immaculate.

Prete et Pasteur, m; 4450 St. Hubert St., Montreal, Que. H2J 2W9.

Redeemer's Voice, m; 165 Catherine St., Yorkton, Sask.

Regard de Foi, 6 times a year; 5875 Est. rue Sherbrooke, Montreal, Que. H1N 1B6.

Relations, m; 8100 Blvd., Saint-Laurent, Montreal Que. H2P 2L9; Jesuit Fathers.

Restoration, m; Combermere, P.O. Ont., KOJ 1LO; Madonna House.

Sainte Anne de Beaupre, m; Basilica of St. Anne, Que. GOA 3CO.

a **Scarboro Missions,** m; 2685 Kingston Rd., Scarboro, Ont. M1M 1M4.

Spiritan News, 4 times a year; 2475 Queen St., Toronto, Ont. M4E 1H8.

Unity, bm; 308 Young St., Montreal, Que. H3C 2G2.

CATHOLIC CHARISMATIC RENEWAL

(Written with the assistance of the National Communications Office Serving the Catholic Charismatic Renewal.)

The movement originated with a handful of Duquesne University students and faculty members in the 1966-67 academic year and spread from there to Notre Dame, Michigan State University, the University of Michigan and to other campuses and cities throughout the country. Ten years later, the findings of a Gallup poll indicated that about three million adult Catholics in the U.S. considered themselves part of the movement. The movement is flourishing in Canada and has an estimated 200,000 participants outside North America.

Large attendance was reported at a series of ecumenical "Jesus '79" rallies on Pentecost weekend in June in more than 20 U.S. cities. Similar rallies were held in Ireland, England and other countries.

Keys to the Movement

Scriptural keys to the renewal are:
• Christ's promise to send the Holy Spirit upon the Apostles;
• the description, in the Acts of the Apostles, of the effects of the coming of the Holy Spirit upon the Apostles on Pentecost;
• St. Paul's explanation, in the Letter to the Romans, of the charismatic gifts (for the good of the Church and persons) the Holy Spirit would bestow on Christians;
• New Testament evidence concerning the effects of charismatic gifts in and through the early Church.

The personal key to the renewal is baptism of the Holy Spirit. This is not a new sacrament but the personally experienced actualization of grace already sacramentally received.

The experience of baptism of the Holy Spirit is often accompanied by the reception of one or more charismatic gifts.

Among the movement's strongest points of emphasis are prayer, openness to the Holy Spirit, community experience and the sharing of spiritual gifts.

The characteristic form of the renewal is the weekly prayer meeting, a gathering which includes periods of spontaneous prayer, singing, sharing of experience and testimony, fellowship and teaching.

Cardinal Leo J. Suenens has a mandate from Pope John Paul to guide the evolution of the Catholic charismatic renewal so that it may fully enter into the heart of the Church.

The movement has an International Communications Office, located at Rue du Vallon, 20, 1040 Bruxelles, Belgium; and a National Communications Office, directed by Kevin M. Ranaghan, at 237 N. Michigan, South Bend, Ind. 46601. Bishop Kenneth Povish of Lansing is chairman of the U.S. Bishops' Ad Hoc Committee for the Charismatic Renewal.

The Catholic Church in the United States

The starting point of the mainstream of Catholic history in the United States was Baltimore at the end of the Revolutionary War, although before that time Catholic explorers had traversed much of the country and missionaries had done considerable work among the Indians in the Southeast, Northeast and Southwest.

Beginning of Organization

Father John Carroll's appointment as superior of the American missions on June 9, 1784, was the first step toward organization of the Church in this country.

At that time, according to a report he made to Rome in 1785, there were approximately 25,000 Catholics in the general population of four million. Many of them had been in the Colonies for several generations. Among them were such outstanding figures as Charles Carroll, a member of the Continental Congress and signer of the Declaration of Independence; Thomas FitzSimons of Philadelphia and Oliver Pollock, the Virginia agent, who raised funds for the militia; Commander John Barry, father of the American Navy, and numerous high-ranking army officers. For the most part, however, Catholics were an unknown minority laboring under legal and social handicaps.

Father Carroll, the brother of Charles Carroll, was named the first American bishop in 1789 and placed in charge of the Diocese of Baltimore, whose boundaries were coextensive with those of the United States. He was consecrated in England Aug. 15, 1790, and installed in his see the following Dec. 12.

Ten years later, Father Leonard Neale became his coadjutor and the first bishop ordained in the United States. Bishop Carroll became an archbishop in 1808 when Baltimore was designated a metropolitan see and the new dioceses of Boston, New York, Philadelphia and Bardstown were established. These jurisdictions were later subdivided, and by 1840 there were, in addition to Baltimore, 15 dioceses, 500 priests and 663,000 Catholics in the general population of 17 million.

Priests and First Seminaries

The number of the 24 original priests was gradually augmented with the arrival of others from France, after the Civil Constitution on the Clergy went into effect there, and other countries. Among the earliest arrivals were several Sulpicians who established the first seminary in the US, St. Mary's, Baltimore, in 1791. By 1815, 30 alumni of the school had been ordained to the priesthood. By that time, two additional seminaries were in operation: Mt. St. Mary's, established in 1809 at Emmitsburg, Md., and St. Thomas, founded two years later, at Bardstown, Ky. These and similar institutions founded later played key roles in the development and growth of the American clergy.

Early Schools

Early educational enterprises included the establishment in 1791 of a school at Georgetown which later became the first Catholic university in the US; the opening of a secondary school for girls, conducted by Visitation Nuns, in 1792 at Georgetown; and the start of a similar school in the first decade of the 19th century at Emmitsburg, Md., by Saint Elizabeth Ann Seton and the Sisters of Charity of St. Joseph, the first religious community of American foundation.

By the 1840's, which saw the beginnings of the present public school system, more than 200 Catholic elementary schools, half of them west of the Alleghenies, were in operation. From this start, the Church subsequently built the greatest private system of education in the world.

Trusteeism

The initial lack of organization in ecclesiastical affairs, nationalistic feeling among Catholics and the independent action of some priests were factors involved in several early crises.

In Philadelphia, some German Catholics withdrew from one parish in 1789 and founded one of their own, Holy Trinity, which they maintained until 1802. Controversy over the affair reached the point of schism in 1796. Philadelphia was also the scene of the Hogan Schism, which developed in the 1820's when Father William Hogan, with the aid of lay trustees, seized control of St. Mary's Cathedral. His movement, for churches and parishes controlled by other than canonical procedures and run in extra-legal ways, was nullified by a decision of the Pennsylvania Supreme Court in 1822.

Similar troubles seriously disturbed the peace of the Church in other places, principally New York, Baltimore, Buffalo, Charleston and New Orleans.

Dangers arising from the exploitation of lay control were gradually diminished with the extension and enforcement of canonical procedures and with changes in civil law about the middle of the century.

Bigotry

Bigotry against Catholics waxed and waned during the 19th century and into the 20th. The first major campaign of this kind, which developed in the wake of the panic of 1819 and lasted for about 25 years, was mounted in 1830 when the number of Catholic immigrants began to increase to a noticeable degree. Nativist anti-Catholicism generated a great deal of violence, represented by climaxes in loss of life and property in Charlestown, Mass., in 1834, and in Philadelphia 10 years later. Later bigotry was fomented by the Know-Nothings, in the 1850's; the Ku Klux Klan, from 1866; the American Protective Association, from 1887; and the Guardians of Liberty. Perhaps the last eruption of overt anti-Catholicism occurred during the campaign of Alfred E. Smith for the presidency in 1928. Observers feel the issue was laid to rest in the political area with the election of John F. Kennedy to the presidency in 1960.

Growth and Immigration

Between 1830 and 1900, the combined factors of natural increase, immigration and conversion raised the Catholic population to 12 million. A large percentage of the growth figure represented immigrants: some 2.7 million, largely from Ireland, Germany and France, between 1830 and 1880; and another 1.25 million during the 80's when eastern and southern Europeans came in increasing numbers. By the 1860's the Catholic Church, with most of its members concentrated in urban areas, was one of the largest religious bodies in the country.

The efforts of progressive bishops to hasten the acculturation of Catholic immigrants occasioned a number of controversies, which generally centered around questions concerning national or foreign-language parishes. One of them, called Cahenslyism, arose from complaints that German Catholic immigrants were not being given adequate pastoral care.

Immigration continued after the turn of the century, but its impact was more easily cushioned through the application of lessons learned earlier in dealing with problems of nationality and language.

Councils of Baltimore

The bishops of the growing US dioceses met at Baltimore for seven provincial councils between 1829 and 1849.

In 1846, they proclaimed the Blessed Virgin Mary patroness of the United States under the title of the Immaculate Conception, eight years before the dogma was proclaimed.

After the establishment of the Archdiocese of Oregon City in 1846 and the elevation to metropolitan status of St. Louis, New Orleans, Cincinnati and New York, the first of the three plenary councils of Baltimore was held.

The first plenary assembly was convoked on May 9, 1852, with Archbishop Francis P. Kenrick of Baltimore as papal legate. The bishops drew up regulations concerning parochial life, matters of church ritual and ceremonies, the administration of church funds and the teaching of Christian doctrine.

The second plenary council, meeting from Oct. 7 to 21, 1866, under the presidency of Archbishop Martin J. Spalding, formulated a condemnation of several current doctrinal errors and established norms affecting the organization of dioceses, the education and conduct of the clergy, the management of ecclesiastical property, parochial duties and general education.

Archbishop (later Cardinal) James Gibbons called into session the third plenary council which lasted from Nov. 9 to Dec. 7, 1884. Among highly significant results of actions taken by this assembly were the preparation of the line of Baltimore catechisms which became a basic means of religious instruction in this country; legislation which fixed the pattern of Catholic education by requiring the building of elementary schools in all parishes; the establishment of the Catholic University of America in Washington, D.C., in 1889; and the determination of six holy days of obligation for observance in this country.

The enactments of the three plenary councils have had the force of particular law for the Church in the United States.

The Holy See established the Apostolic Delegation at Washington, D.C., on Jan. 24, 1893.

Slavery and Negroes

In the Civil War period, as before, Catholics reflected attitudes of the general population with respect to the issue of slavery. Some supported it, some opposed it, but none were prominent in the Abolition Movement. Gregory XVI had condemned the slave trade in 1839, but no contemporary pope or American bishop published an official document on slavery itself. The issue did not split Catholics in schism as it did Baptists, Methodists and Presbyterians.

Catholics fought on both sides in the Civil War. Five hundred members of 20 or more sisterhoods served the wounded of both sides.

One hundred thousand of the four million slaves emancipated in 1863 were Catholics; the highest concentrations were in Louisiana, about 60,000, and Maryland, 16,000. Three years later, their pastoral care was one of the subjects covered in nine decrees issued by the Second Plenary Council of Baltimore. The measures had little practical effect with respect to integration of the total Catholic community, predicated as they were on the proposition that individual bishops should handle questions regarding segregation in churches and related matters as best they could in the pattern of local customs.

Long entrenched segregation practices continued in force through the rest of the 19th century and well into the 20th. The first effective efforts to alter them were initiated by Cardinal Joseph Ritter of St. Louis in 1947, Cardinal (then Archbishop) Patrick O'Boyle of Washington in 1948, and Bishop Vincent Waters of Raleigh in 1953.

Friend of Labor

The Church became known during the 19th century as a friend and ally of labor in seeking justice for the working man. Cardinal Gibbons journeyed to Rome in 1887, for example, to defend and prevent a condemnation of the Knights of Labor by Leo XIII. The encyclical *Rerum Novarum* was hailed by many American bishops as a confirmation, if not vindication, of their own theories. Catholics have always formed a large percentage of union membership, and some have served unions in positions of leadership.

The American Heresy

Near the end of the century some controversy developed over what was characterized as Americanism or the phantom heresy. It was alleged that Americans were discounting the importance of contemplative virtues, exalting the practical virtues, and watering down the purity of Catholic doctrine for the sake of facilitating convert work.

The French translation of Father Walter Elliott's *Life of Isaac Hecker,* which fired the controversy, was one of many factors that led to the issuance of Leo XIII's *Testem Benevolentiae* in January, 1899, in an attempt to end the matter. It was the first time the orthodoxy of the Church in the US was called into question.

Schism

In the 1890's, serious friction developed between Poles and Irish in Scranton, Buffalo and Chicago, resulting in schism and the establishment of the Polish National Church. A central figure in the affair was Father Francis Hodur, who was excommunicated by Bishop William O'Hara of Scranton in 1898. Nine years later, his ordination by the Old Catholic Archbishop of Utrecht gave the new church its first bishop.

Another schism of the period led to formation of the American Carpatho-Russian Orthodox Greek Catholic Church.

Coming of Age

In 1900, there were 12 million Catholics in the total US population of 76 million, 82 dioceses in 14 provinces, and 12,000 priests and members of about 40 communities of men religious. Many sisterhoods, most of them of European origin and some of American foundation, were engaged in Catholic educational and hospital work, of which they have always been the main support.

The Church in the United States was removed from mission status with promulgation of the apostolic constitution *Sapienti Consilio* by Pope St. Pius X on June 29, 1908.

Before that time, and even into the early 20's, the Church in this country received financial assistance from mission-aid societies in France, Bavaria and Austria. Already, however, it was making increasing contributions of its own. At the present time, it is the heaviest national contributor to the worldwide Society for the Propagation of the Faith.

American foreign missionary personnel increased from 14 or less in 1906 to 7,148 by 1975 (197 diocesan priests, 3,692 religious priests and brothers, 2,850 sisters, 65 seminarians, 344 lay persons). The first missionary seminary in the US was in operation at Techny, Ill., in 1909, under the auspices of the Society of the Divine Word. Maryknoll, the first American missionary society, was established in 1911 and sent its first priests to China in 1918. Despite these contributions, the Church in the US has not matched the missionary commitment of some other nations.

Bishops' Conference

A highly important apparatus for mobilizing the Church's resources was established in 1917 under the title of the National Catholic War Council. Its name was changed to National Catholic Welfare Conference several years later, but its objectives remained the same: to serve as an advisory and coordinating agency of the American bishops for advancing works of the Church in fields of social significance and impact — education, communications, immigration, social action, legislation, youth and lay organizations.

The forward thrust of the bishops' social thinking was evidenced in a program of social reconstruction they recommended in 1919. By 1945, all but one of their twelve points had been enacted into legislation.

The NCWC was renamed the United States Catholic Conference (USCC) in November, 1966, when the hierarchy also organized itself as a territorial conference with pastoral-juridical authority under the title, National Conference of Catholic Bishops. The USCC is carrying on the functions of the former NCWC.

Pastoral Concerns

The potential for growth of the Church in this country by immigration was sharply reduced but not entirely curtailed after 1921 with the passage of restrictive federal legislation. As a result, the Catholic population became more stabilized and, to a certain extent and for many reasons, began to acquire an identity of its own.

Some increase-from-outside has taken place in the past 50 years, however; from Canada, from central and eastern European countries, and from Puerto Rico and Latin American countries since World War II. This influx, while not as great as that of the 19th century and early 20th, has enriched the Church here with a sizable body of Eastern-Rite Catholics for whom eight ecclesiastical jurisdictions were established between 1924 and 1969. It has also created a challenge for pastoral care of the Spanish-speaking.

The Church continues to grapple with serious pastoral problems in rural areas, where about 600 counties are no-priest land. The National Catholic Rural Life Conference was established in 1922 in an attempt to make the Catholic presence felt on the land, and the Glenmary Society since its foundation in 1939 has devoted itself to this single apostolate. Religious communities and diocesan priests are similarly engaged.

Other challenges lie in the cities and suburbs where 75 percent of the Catholic population lives. Conditions peculiar to each segment of the metropolitan area have developed in recent years as the flight to the suburbs has not only altered some traditional aspects of parish life but has also, in combination with many other factors, left behind a complex of special problems in the inner city.

Phenomena of Change

The Church in the US is presently in a stage of transition from a relatively stable and long established order of life and action to a new order of things. Some of the phenomena of this period are:

• differences in trends and emphasis in theology, and in interpretation and implementation of directives of the Second Vatican Council, resulting in situations of conflict;

• the changing spiritual formation, professional education, style of life and ministry of priests and religious (men and women), which are altering influential patterns of pastoral and specialized service;

• vocations to the priesthood and religious life, which are generally in decline;

• departures from the priesthood and religious life which, while small percentage-wise, are numerous enough to be a matter of serious concern;

• decline of traditional devotional practices;

• exercise of authority along the lines of collegiality and subsidiarity;

• structure and administration, marked by a trend toward greater participation in the life and work of the Church by its members on all levels, from the parish on up;

• alienation from the Church, leading some persons into the catacombs of an underground church, "anonymous Christianity" and religious indifferentism;

• education, undergoing crisis and change in Catholic schools and seeking new ways of reaching out to the young not in Catholic schools and to adults;

• social witness in ministry to the world, which is being shaped by the form of contemporary needs — e.g., race relations, poverty, the peace movement, the Third World;

• ecumenism, involving the Church in interfaith relations on a wider scale than before.

BACKGROUND DATES IN U.S. CATHOLIC CHRONOLOGY

Dates in this section refer mostly to earlier "firsts" and developments in the background of Catholic history in the United States. For other dates, see various sections of the Almanac.

Alabama

1540: Priests crossed the territory with De Soto's expedition.

1560: Five Dominicans in charge of mission at Santa Cruz des Nanipacna.

1682: La Salle claimed territory for France.

1704: Jesuits established first parish church at Fort Louis de la Mobile.

1722: Mobile, formerly under the Quebec diocese, became part of a vicariate apostolic with Florida. Capuchins, Carmelites and Jesuits working there.

1829: Mobile-Birmingham diocese established; made two separate dioceses, 1969.

1830: Spring Hill College, Mobile, established.

1834: Visitation Nuns established an academy at Summerville.

Alaska

1779: Mass celebrated for first time on shore of Port Santa Cruz on lower Bucareli Bay on May 13 by Franciscan John Riobo.

1868: Alaska placed under jurisdiction of Vancouver Island.

1878: Father John Althoff became first resident missionary.

1886: Archbishop Charles J. Seghers, "Apostle of Alaska," murdered by a guide; had surveyed southern and northwest Alaska in 1873 and 1877, respectively.

Sisters of St. Anne first nuns in Alaska.

1894: Alaska made prefecture apostolic.

1901: Jesuits reorganized their missions, established a church at Nome.

1905: Sisters of Providence opened hospital at Nome.

1916: Alaska made vicariate apostolic.

1917: In first ordination in territory, Rev. G. Edgar Gallant raised to priesthood.

1951: Juneau diocese established.

1962: Fairbanks diocese established.

1966: Anchorage archdiocese established.

Arizona

1539: Franciscan Marcos de Niza explored the state.

1540: Franciscans Juan de Padilla, Juan de la Cruz and Marcos de Niza accompanied Coronado expedition through the territory.

1629: Spanish Franciscans began work among Moqui Indians.

1632: Franciscan Martin de Arvide killed by Indians.

1680: Franciscans Jose de Espeleta, Augustin de Santa Maria, Jose de Figueroa and Jose de Trujillo killed in Pueblo Revolt.

1700: Jesuit Eusebio Kino established mission at San Xavier del Bac, near Tucson.

1767: Jesuits expelled; Franciscans took over 10 missions.
1828: Spanish missionaries expelled by Mexican government.
1863: Jesuits returned to San Xavier.
1869: Sisters of Loretto arrived to conduct schools at Bisbee and Douglas.
1897: Tucson diocese established.
1969: Phoenix diocese established.

Arkansas

1541: Priests accompanied De Soto expedition through the territory.
1673: Marquette visited Indians in east.
1686: Henri de Tonti established trading post, first white settlement in territory.
1702: Fr. Nicholas Foucault working among Indians.
1805: Bishop Carroll of Baltimore appointed Administrator Apostolic of Arkansas.
1838: Sisters of Loretto opened first Catholic school.
1843: Little Rock diocese established. There were about 700 Catholics in state, two churches, one priest.
1853: Sisters of Mercy founded St. Mary's Convent at Fort Smith.

California

1542: Cabrillo discovered Upper (Alta) California; name of priest accompanying expedition unknown.
1602: On Nov. 12 Carmelite Andres de la Ascencion offered first recorded Mass in California on shore of San Diego Bay.
1697: Missionary work in Lower and Upper Californias entrusted to Jesuits.
1767: Jesuits expelled from territory. Spanish Crown confiscated their property, including the Pious Fund for Missions. Upper California missions entrusted to Franciscans.
1769: Franciscan Junipero Serra began establishment of Franciscan missions in California, near present San Diego. (See Franciscan Missions of Upper California.)
1775: Franciscan Luis Jayme killed by Indians at San Diego Mission.
1779: Diocese of Sonora, Mexico, which included Upper California, established.
1781: On Sept. 4 an expedition from San Gabriel Mission founded present city of Los Angeles — Pueblo "de Nuestra Senora la Reina de Los Angeles."
Franciscans Francisco Hermenegildo Garces, Juan Antonio Barreneche, Juan Marcello Diaz and Jose Matias Moreno killed by Indians.
1812: Franciscan Andres Quintana killed at Santa Cruz Mission.
1822: Interference and aggression toward missions initiated by Mexican government.
Dedication on Dec. 8 of Old Plaza Church, "Assistant Mission of Our Lady of the Angels," oldest church in Los Angeles.
1833: Missions secularized, finally confiscated.
1840: Pope Gregory XVI established Diocese of Both Californias.
1846: Peter H. Burnett, first governor of California, received into Catholic Church.
1848: Upper California ceded to the United States.
1850: Monterey diocese erected; title changed to Monterey-Los Angeles, 1859; and to Los Angeles, 1922.
1851: University of Santa Clara chartered.
1852: Lower California detached from Monterey diocese.
1853: San Francisco archdiocese established.
1855: US returned confiscated California missions to Church.
1863: Sisters of Notre Dame de Namur opened women's College of Notre Dame at Belmont.
1868: Grass Valley diocese established; transferred to Sacramento in 1886.
1922: Monterey-Fresno diocese established; became separate dioceses, 1967.
1934: Sesquicentennial of Serra's death observed; Serra Year officially declared by Legislature and Aug. 24 observed as Serra Day.
1936: Los Angeles made archdiocese. San Diego diocese established.
1952: Law exempting non-profit, religious-sponsored elementary and secondary schools from taxation upheld in referendum, Nov. 4.
1953: Archbishop James Francis McIntyre of Los Angeles made cardinal by Pius XII.
1962: Oakland, Santa Rosa and Stockton dioceses established.
1973: Archbishop Timothy Manning of Los Angeles made cardinal by Pope Paul VI.
1976: Orange diocese established.
1978: San Bernardino diocese established.

Colorado

1858: First parish in Colorado established.
1864: Sisters of Loretto at the Foot of the Cross, first nuns in the state, established academy at Denver.
1868: Vicariate Apostolic of Colorado and Utah established.
1887: Denver diocese established.
1888: Regis College founded.
1951: Denver made archdiocese.
Pueblo diocese established.

Connecticut

1651: Probably first priest to enter state was Jesuit Gabriel Druillettes; ambassador of Governor of Canada, he participated in a New England Colonial Council at New Haven.
1755: Catholic Acadians, expelled from Nova Scotia, settled in the state.
1791: Rev. John Thayer, first missionary to visit state's Catholics on regular basis, offered Mass at home of Noah Webster.
1808: Connecticut became part of Boston diocese.
1818: Religious freedom established by

new constitution, although the Congregational Church remained, in practice, the state church.

1828: Father Bernard O'Cavanaugh became first resident priest in state.

1829: First Catholic church in state established at Hartford.

Catholic Press of Hartford established.

1843: Hartford diocese established.

1882: Knights of Columbus founded by Father Michael J. McGivney.

1942: Fairfield University founded.

1953: Norwich and Bridgeport dioceses established. Hartford made archdiocese.

1956: Byzantine Rite Exarchate of Stamford established; made eparchy, 1958.

Delaware

1730: Mount Cuba, New Castle County, the scene of Catholic services.

1750: Jesuit mission at Apoquiniminck administered from Maryland.

1772: First permanent parish established at Coffee Run.

1792: French Catholics from Santo Domingo settled near Wilmington.

1816: St. Peter's Church, later the cathedral of the diocese, erected at Wilmington.

1830: Daughters of Charity opened school and orphanage at Wilmington.

1868: Wilmington diocese established.

1869: Visitation Nuns established residence in Wilmington.

District of Columbia

1641: Jesuit Andrew White evangelized Anacosta Indians.

1774: Father John Carroll ministered to Catholics.

1789: Georgetown, first Catholic college in US, established.

1791: Pierre Charles L'Enfant designed the Federal City of Washington. His plans were not fully implemented until the early 1900's.

1792: James Hoban designed the White House.

1794: Father Anthony Caffrey began St. Patrick's Church, first parish church in the new Federal City.

1801: Poor Clares opened school for girls in Georgetown; first school established by nuns in US.

1802: First mayor of Washington, appointed by President Jefferson, was Judge Robert Brent.

1889: Catholic University of America founded.

1893: Apostolic Delegation established with Archbishop Francesco Satolli as the first delegate.

1919: National Catholic Welfare Conference (now the United States Catholic Conference) organized by American hierarchy to succeed National Catholic War Council.

1920: Cornerstone of National Shrine of Immaculate Conception laid.

1939: Washington made archdiocese of equal rank with Baltimore, under direction of same archbishop.

1947: Washington archdiocese received its own archbishop, was separated from Baltimore; became a metropolitan see in 1965.

1967: Archbishop Patrick A. O'Boyle of Washington made cardinal by Pope Paul VI.

1976: Archbishop William Baum of Washington made a cardinal by Pope Paul VI.

Florida

1513: Ponce de Leon discovered Florida.

1521: Missionaries accompanying Ponce de Leon and other explorers probably said first Masses within present limits of US.

1528: Franciscans landed on western shore.

1539: Twelve missionaries landed with De Soto at Tampa Bay.

1549: Dominican Luis Cancer de Barbastro and two companions slain by Indians near Tampa Bay.

1565: City of St. Augustine, oldest in US, founded by Pedro Menendez de Aviles, who was accompanied by four secular priests.

America's oldest mission, Nombre de Dios, was established.

Father Martin Francisco Lopez de Mendoza Grajales became the first parish priest of St. Augustine, where the first parish in the US was established.

1572: St. Francis Borgia, general of the Society, withdrew Jesuits from Florida.

1606: Bishop Juan de las Cabeyas de Altamirano, O.P., conducted the first episcopal visitation in the US.

1620: The chapel of Nombre de Dios was dedicated to Nuestra Senora de la Leche y Buen Parto (Our Nursing Mother of the Happy Delivery); oldest shrine to the Blessed Mother in the US.

1704: Destruction of Florida's northern missions by English and Indian troops led by Governor James Moore of South Carolina. Franciscans Juan de Parga, Dominic Criodo, Tiburcio de Osorio, Augustine Ponze de Leon, Marcos Delgado and two Indians, Anthony Enixa and Amador Cuipa Feliciano, were slain by the invaders.

1735: Bishop Francis Martinez de Tejadu Diaz de Velasco, auxiliary of Santiago, was the first bishop to take up residence in US, at St. Augustine.

1793: Florida and Louisiana were included in Diocese of New Orleans.

1857: Eastern Florida made a vicariate apostolic.

1870: St. Augustine diocese established.

1917: Convent Inspection Bill passed; repealed 1935.

1958: Miami diocese established.

1968: Miami made metropolitan see; Orlando and St. Petersburg dioceses established.

1976: Pensacola-Tallahassee diocese established.

Georgia

1540: First priests to enter were chaplains with De Soto. They celebrated first Mass within territory of 13 original colonies.

1566: Pedro Martinez, first Jesuit martyr of the New World, was slain by Indians on Cumberland Island.

1569: Jesuit mission was opened at Guale Island by Father Antonio Sedeno.

1572: Jesuits withdrawn from area.

1595: Five Franciscans assigned to Province of Guale.

1597: Five Franciscan missionaries killed in coastal missions.

1606: Bishop Altamirano, O.P., conducted visitation of the Georgia area.

1612: First Franciscan province in US erected under title of Santa Elena; it included Georgia, South Carolina and Florida.

1655: Franciscans had nine flourishing missions among Indians.

1702: Spanish missions ended as result of English conquest.

1796: Augustinian Father Le Mercier was first post-colonial missionary to Georgia.

1798: Catholics granted right of refuge.

1800: First church erected in Savannah on lot given by city council.

1810: First church erected in Augusta on lot given by State Legislature.

1850: Savannah diocese established; became Savannah-Atlanta, 1937; divided into two separate sees, 1956.

1962: Atlanta made metropolitan see.

Hawaii

1825: Pope Leo XII entrusted missionary efforts in Islands to Sacred Hearts Fathers.

1827: The first Catholic missionaries arrived — Fathers Alexis Bachelot, Abraham Armand and Patrick Short, along with three lay brothers. After three years of persecution, the priests were forcibly exiled.

1836: Father Arsenius Walsh, SS. CC., a British subject, was allowed to remain in Islands but was not permitted to proselytize or conduct missions.

1839: Hawaiian government signed treaty with France granting Catholics freedom of worship and same privileges as Protestants.

1844: Vicariate Apostolic of Sandwich Islands (Hawaii) erected.

1873: Father Damien de Veuster of the Sacred Hearts Fathers arrived in Molokai and spent the remainder of his life working among lepers.

1941: Honolulu diocese established, made a suffragan of San Francisco.

Idaho

1840: Jesuit Pierre de Smet preached to the Flathead and Pend d'Oreille Indians; probably offered first Mass in state.

1842: Jesuit Nicholas Point opened a mission among Coeur d'Alene Indians near Maries.

1863: Secular priests sent from Oregon City to administer to incoming miners.

1867: Sisters of Holy Names of Jesus and Mary opened first Catholic school at Idaho City.

1868: Idaho made a vicariate apostolic.

1870: First church in Boise established. Church lost most of missions among Indians of Northwest Territory when Commission on Indian Affairs appointed Protestant missionaries to take over.

1893: Boise diocese established.

Illinois

1673: Jesuit Jacques Marquette, accompanying Joliet, preached to Indians.

1674: Pere Marquette set up a cabin for saying Mass in what later became City of Chicago.

1675: Pere Marquette established Mission of the Immaculate Conception among Kaskaskia Indians.

1679: La Salle brought with him Franciscans Louis Hennepin, Gabriel de la Ribourde, and Zenobius Membre.

1680: Father Ribourde was killed by Kickapoo Indians.

1689: Jesuit Claude Allouez died after 32 years of missionary activity among Indians of Midwest; he had evangelized 100,000 Indians of 20 different tribes and baptized 10,000. Jesuit Jacques Gravier succeeded Allouez as vicar general of Illinois.

1730: Father Gaston, a diocesan priest, was killed at the Cahokia Mission.

1763: British conquest of the territory resulted in banishment of Jesuits.

1778: Father Pierre Gibault championed Colonial cause in the Revolution and aided greatly in securing states of Ohio, Indiana, Illinois, Michigan and Wisconsin for Americans.

1827: The present St. Patrick's Parish at Ruma, oldest English-speaking Catholic congregation in state, was founded.

1833: Visitation Nuns established residence in Kaskaskia.

1843: Chicago diocese established.

1853: Quincy diocese established; transferred to Alton, 1857; Springfield, 1923.

1860: Quincy College founded.

1877: Peoria diocese established.

1880: Chicago made archdiocese.

1887: Belleville diocese established.

1908: Rockford diocese established.

First American Missionary Congress held in Chicago.

1924: Archbishop Mundelein of Chicago made cardinal by Pope Pius XI.

1926: The 28th International Eucharistic Congress, first held in US, convened in Chicago.

1946: Blessed Frances Xavier Cabrini, former resident of Chicago, was canonized;

first US citizen raised to dignity of altar.
Archbishop Samuel A. Stritch of Chicago made cardinal by Pope Pius XII.
1948: Joliet diocese established.
1958: Cardinal Stritch appointed Pro-Prefect of the Sacred Congregation for the Propagation of the Faith — the first US-born prelate to be named to the Roman Curia.
1959: Archbishop Albert G. Meyer of Chicago made cardinal by Pope John XXIII.
1961: Eparchy of St. Nicholas of the Ukrainians established at Chicago.
1967: Archbishop John P. Cody of Chicago made cardinal by Pope Paul VI.

Indiana

1679: Recollects Louis Hennepin and Gabriel de la Ribourde entered state.
1686: Land near present Notre Dame University at South Bend given by French government to Jesuits for mission.
1732: Church of St. Francis Xavier founded at Vincennes.
1778: Father Gibault aided George Rogers Clark in campaign against British in conquest of Northwest Territory.
1793: First school in Indiana built at Vincennes by Father John Francis Rivet.
1834: Vincennes diocese, later Indianapolis, established.
1840: Sisters of Providence founded St. Mary-of-the-Woods College for women.
1842: University of Notre Dame founded by Holy Cross Fathers.
1843: Immigration of German farmers to Indiana swelled Catholic population.
1853: First Benedictine community established in state at St. Meinrad.
1857: Fort Wayne diocese established; changed to Fort Wayne-South Bend, 1960.
1944: Indianapolis made archdiocese. Lafayette and Evansville dioceses established.
1957: Gary diocese established.

Iowa

1673: A Peoria village on Mississippi was visited by Pere Marquette.
1679: Fathers Louis Hennepin and Gabriel de la Ribourde visited Indian villages.
1836: First permanent church, St. Raphael's, founded at Dubuque by Dominican Samuel Mazzuchelli.
1837: Dubuque diocese established.
1838: St. Joseph's Mission founded at Council Bluffs by Jesuit Father De Smet.
1843: Sisters of Charity of the Blessed Virgin Mary were first sisterhood in state.
Sisters of Charity opened Clarke College, Dubuque.
1844: Brothers of St. Joseph opened academy for boys at Dubuque.
1850: First Trappist Monastery in state, Our Lady of New Melleray, was begun.
1881: Davenport diocese established.
1882: St. Ambrose College, Davenport, established.
1893: Dubuque made archdiocese.
1902: Sioux City diocese established.
1911: Des Moines diocese established.

Kansas

1542: Franciscan Juan de Padilla, first martyr of the United States, was killed in central Kansas.
1858: St. Benedict's College founded.
1863: Sisters of Charity opened orphanage at Leavenworth, and St. John's Hospital in following year.
1877: Leavenworth diocese established; transferred to Kansas City in 1947.
1887: Dioceses of Concordia (transferred to Salina in 1944) and Wichita established.
1888: Oblate Sisters of Providence opened an orphanage for Negro boys at Leavenworth, first west of Mississippi.
1951: Dodge City diocese established.
1952: Kansas City made archdiocese.

Kentucky

1775: First settlers in Kentucky were Catholics.
1787: Father Charles Francis Whelan, first resident priest, ministered to settlers of Bardstown.
1806: Dominican Fathers built Priory of St. Rose, later founded St. Thomas Aquinas College.
1808: Bardstown diocese established; transferred to Louisville, 1840.
1811: Rev. Guy L. Chabrat became first priest ordained west of the Allegheny Mountains.
1812: Sisters of Loretto founded, first religious community in US without foreign affiliation.
Sisters of Charity of Nazareth founded, the second native community of women founded in the West.
1814: Nazareth College for women established.
1816: Cornerstone of St. Joseph's Cathedral, Bardstown, laid; called "The Cathedral in the Wilderness."
1817: St. Thomas Seminary founded.
1830: Hon. Benjamin J. Webb founded *Catholic Advocate* first Catholic weekly in Kentucky.
1847: Trappist monks took up residence in Gethsemani.
1849: Cornerstone of Cathedral of the Assumption laid at Louisville.
1852: Know-Nothing troubles in state.
1853: Covington diocese established.
1937: Louisville made archdiocese. Owensboro diocese established.
1956: State Court of Appeals upheld right of Catholic Sisters to teach in state's public schools even though they wore religious habits.

Louisiana

1682: La Salle's expedition, accompanied by two priests, completed discoveries of De Soto at mouth of Mississippi. La Salle named territory Louisiana.

1699: French Catholics founded colony of Louisiana.

First recorded Mass offered Mar. 3, by Franciscan Father Anastase Douay.

1706: Father John Francis Buisson de St. Cosme was killed near Donaldsonville.

1717: Franciscan Anthony Margil established first Indian mission school of San Miguel de Linares.

1718: City of New Orleans founded by Jean Baptiste Le Moyne de Bienville.

1720: First resident priest in New Orleans was the French Recollect Prothais Boyer.

1725: Capuchin Fathers opened school for boys.

1727: Ursuline Nuns founded convent in New Orleans, oldest convent in what is now US; they conducted a school, hospital and orphan asylum.

1793: New Orleans diocese established.

1850: New Orleans made archdiocese.

1853: Natchitoches diocese established; transferred to Alexandria in 1910; became Alexandria-Shreveport in 1976.

1892: Sisters of Holy Family, a Negro congregation, established at New Orleans.

1912: Loyola University of South established.

1918: Lafayette diocese established.

1925: Xavier University established in New Orleans.

1961: Baton Rouge diocese established.

1962: Catholic schools on all levels desegregated in New Orleans archdiocese.

1977: Houma-Thibodaux diocese established.

Maine

1604: First Mass in territory celebrated by Father Nicholas Aubry, accompanying De Monts' expedition which was authorized by King of France to begin colonizing region.

1605: Colony founded on St. Croix Island; two secular priests served as chaplains.

1613: Four Jesuits attempted to establish permanent French settlement near mouth of Kennebec River.

1619: French Franciscans began work among settlers and Indians; driven out by English in 1628.

1630: New England made a prefecture apostolic in charge of French Capuchins.

1633: Capuchin Fathers founded missions on Penobscot River.

1646: Jesuits established Assumption Mission on Kennebec River.

1688: Church of St. Anne, oldest in New England, built at Oldtown.

1704: English soldiers destroyed French missions.

1724: English forces again attacked French settlements, killed Jesuit Sebastian Rale.

1853: Portland diocese established.

1854: Know-Nothing uprising resulted in burning of church in Bath.

1856: Anti-Catholic feeling continued; church at Ellsworth burned.

1864: Sisters of Congregation of Notre Dame from Montreal opened academy at Portland.

1875: James A. Healy, first bishop of Negro blood consecrated in US, became second Bishop of Portland.

Maryland

1634: Maryland established by Lord Calvert. Two Jesuits among first colonists.

First Mass offered on Island of St. Clement in Lower Potomac by Jesuit Father Andrew White.

St. Mary's founded by English and Irish Catholics.

1641: St. Ignatius Parish founded by English Jesuits at Chapel Point, near Port Tobacco.

1649: Religious Toleration Act passed by Maryland Assembly. It was repealed in 1654 by Puritan-controlled government.

1651: Cecil Calvert, second Lord Baltimore, gave Jesuits 10,000 acres for use as Indian mission.

1658: Lord Baltimore restored Toleration Act.

1672: Franciscans came to Maryland under leadership of Father Massius Massey.

1688: Maryland became royal colony as a result of the Revolution in England; Anglican Church became the official religion (1692); Toleration Act repealed; Catholics disenfranchised and persecuted until 1776.

1784: Father John Carroll appointed prefect apostolic for the territory embraced by new Republic.

1789: Baltimore became first diocese established in US, with John Carroll as first bishop.

1790: Carmelite Nuns founded convent at Port Tobacco, the first in the English-speaking Colonies.

1791: First Synod of Baltimore held.

St. Mary's Seminary, first seminary in US, established.

1793: Rev. Stephen T. Badin first priest ordained by Bishop Carroll.

1800: Jesuit Leonard Neale became first bishop consecrated in present limits of US.

1806: Cornerstone of Assumption Cathedral, Baltimore, was laid.

1808: Baltimore made archdiocese.

1809: St. Joseph's College, first women's college in US, founded.

Sisters of Charity of St. Joseph founded by St. Elizabeth Ann Seton; first native American sisterhood.

1821: Assumption Cathedral, Baltimore, formally opened.
1829: Oblate Sisters of Charity, a Negro congregation, established at Baltimore.
First Provincial Council of Baltimore held; six others followed, in 1833, 1837, 1840, 1843, 1846 and 1849.
1836: Roger B. Taney appointed Chief Justice of Supreme Court by President Jackson.
1852: First of the three Plenary Councils of Baltimore convened. Subsequent councils were held in 1866 and 1884.
1855: German Catholic Central Verein founded.
1886: Archbishop Gibbons of Baltimore made cardinal by Pope Leo XIII.
1965: Archbishop Shehan of Baltimore made cardinal by Pope Paul VI.

Massachusetts

1630: New England made a prefecture apostolic in charge of French Capuchins.
1647: Massachusetts Bay Company enacted an anti-priest law.
1732: Although Catholics were not legally admitted to colony, a few Irish families were in Boston; a priest was reported working among them.
1755-56: Acadians landing in Boston were denied services of a Catholic priest.
1775: General Washington discouraged Guy Fawkes Day procession in which pope was carried in effigy, and expressed surprise that there were men in his army "so void of common sense as to insult the religious feelings of the Canadians with whom friendship and an alliance are being sought."
1780: The Massachusetts State Constitution granted religious liberty, but required a religious test to hold public office and provided for tax to support Protestant teachers of piety, religion and morality.
1788: First public Mass said in Boston on Nov. 2 by Abbe de la Poterie, first resident priest.
1803: Church of Holy Cross erected in Boston with financial aid given by Protestants headed by John Adams.
1808: Boston diocese established.
1831: Irish Catholic immigration increased.
1832: St. Vincent's Orphan Asylum, oldest charitable institution in Boston, opened by Sisters of Mercy.
1834: Ursuline Convent in Charlestown burned by a Nationalist mob.
1843: Holy Cross College founded.
1855: Catholic militia companies disbanded; nunneries' inspection bill passed.
1859: St. Mary's, first parochial school in Boston, opened.
1860: Portuguese Catholics from Azores settled in New Bedford.
1870: Springfield diocese established.
1875: Boston made archdiocese.
1904: Fall River diocese established.
1911: Archbishop O'Connell of Boston made cardinal by Pope Pius X.
1950: Worcester diocese established.
1958: Archbishop Richard J. Cushing of Boston made cardinal by Pope John XXIII.
1966: Apostolic Exarchate for Melkites in the US established, with headquarters in Boston; made an eparchy in 1976.
1973: Archbishop Humberto S. Medeiros of Boston made cardinal by Pope Paul VI.

Michigan

1641: Jesuits Isaac Jogues and Charles Raymbaut preached to Chippewas; named Sault-Sainte Marie Rapids.
1660: Jesuit Rene Menard opened first regular mission in Lake Superior region.
1668: Pere Marquette founded Sainte Marie Mission at Sault-Sainte Marie.
1671: Pere Marquette founded St. Ignace Mission at Michilimackinac.
1701: Fort Pontchartrain founded on present site of Detroit and placed in command of Antoine de la Mothe Cadillac. The Chapel of Sainte-Anne-de-Detroit founded.
1706: Franciscan Father Delhalle killed by Indians at Detroit.
1823: Father Gabriel Richard elected delegate to Congress from Michigan territory; he was the first priest chosen for the House of Representatives.
1833: Father Frederic Baraga celebrated first Mass in present Grand Rapids.
Detroit diocese established, embracing whole Northwest Territory.
1843: *Western Catholic Register* founded at Detroit.
1845: St. Vincent's Hospital, Detroit, opened by Sisters of Charity.
1848: Cathedral of Sts. Peter and Paul, Detroit, consecrated.
1853: Vicariate Apostolic of Upper Michigan established.
1857: Sault-Ste. Marie diocese established; later transferred to Marquette.
1877: University of Detroit founded.
1882: Grand Rapids diocese established.
1897: Nazareth College for women founded.
1937: Detroit made archdiocese. Lansing diocese established.
1938: Saginaw diocese established.
1946: Archbishop Edward Mooney of Detroit created cardinal by Pope Pius XII.
1949: Opening of St. John's Theological (major) Seminary at Plymouth; this was first seminary in US serving an entire ecclesiastical province (Detroit).
1966: Apostolic Exarchate for Maronites in US established, with headquarters in Detroit; made an eparchy in 1972; transferred to Brooklyn, 1977.
1969: Archbishop John Dearden of Detroit made cardinal by Pope Paul VI.

1971: Gaylord and Kalamazoo dioceses established.

Minnesota

1680: Falls of St. Anthony discovered by Franciscan Louis Hennepin.

1727: First chapel, St. Michael the Archangel, erected near town of Frontenac and placed in charge of French Jesuits.

1732: Fort Charles built; Jesuits ministered to settlers.

1736: Jesuit Jean Pierre Aulneau killed by Indians.

1739: Swiss Catholics from Canada settled near Fort Snelling; Bishop Loras of Dubuque, accompanied by Father Pellamourgues, visited the Fort and administered sacraments.

1841: Father Lucian Galtier built Church of St. Paul, thus forming nucleus of modern city of same name.

1850: St. Paul diocese established.

1851: Sisters of St. Joseph arrived in state.

1857: University of St. John founded.

1888: St. Paul made archdiocese; name changed to St. Paul-Minneapolis in 1966.

1889: Duluth, St. Cloud and Winona dioceses established.

1909: Crookston diocese established.

1958: New Ulm diocese established.

Mississippi

1540: Chaplains with De Soto expedition entered territory.

1682: Franciscans Zenobius Membre and Anastase Douay preached to Taensa and Natchez Indians. Father Membre offered first recorded Mass in the state on Mar. 29, Easter Sunday.

1698: Priests of Quebec Seminary founded missions near Natchez and Fort Adams.

1702: Father Nicholas Foucault murdered by Indians near Fort Adams.

1721: Missions practically abandoned, with only Father Juif working among Yazoos.

1725: Jesuit Mathurin de Petit carried on mission work in northern Mississippi.

1729: Indians tomahawked Jesuit Paul du Poisson near Fort Rosalie; Father Jean Souel shot by Yazoos.

1736: Jesuit Antoine Senat burned at stake by Chickasaws.

1822: Vicariate Apostolic of Mississippi and Alabama established.

1825: Mississippi made a separate vicariate apostolic.

1837: Natchez diocese established; became Natchez-Jackson in 1956; transferred to Jackson in 1977.

1848: Sisters of Charity opened orphan asylum and school in Natchez.

1977: Biloxi diocese established.

Missouri

1700: Jesuit Gabriel Marest established a mission among Kaskaskia Indians near St. Louis.

1734: French Catholic miners and traders settled Old Mines and Sainte Genevieve.

1750: Jesuits visited French settlers.

1762: Mission established at St. Charles.

1767: Carondelet mission established.

1770: First church founded at St. Louis.

1811: Jesuits established Indian mission school at Florissant.

1818: Bishop Dubourg arrrrived at St. Louis, with Vincentians Joseph Rosati and Felix de Andreis. St. Louis University, the diocesan (Kenrick) seminary and the Vincentian Seminary in Perryville trace their origins to them.

1826: St. Louis diocese established.

1828: Sisters of Charity opened first hospital west of the Mississippi, at St. Louis.

1832: *The Shepherd of the Valley*, first Catholic paper west of the Mississippi.

1845: First conference of Society of St. Vincent de Paul in US founded at St. Louis.

1847: St. Louis made archdiocese.

1865: A Test Oath Law passed by State Legislature (called Drake Convention) to crush Catholicism in Missouri. Law declared unconstitutional by Supreme Court in 1866.

1867: College of St. Teresa for women founded at Kansas City.

1868: St. Joseph diocese established.

1880: Kansas City diocese established.

1946: Archbishop John J. Glennon of St. Louis made cardinal by Pope Pius XII.

1956: Kansas City and St. Joseph dioceses combined into one see. Jefferson City and Springfield-Cape Girardeau dioceses established.

1961: Archbishop Joseph E. Ritter of St. Louis made cardinal by Pope John XXIII.

1969: Archbishop John J. Carberry of St. Louis made cardinal by Pope Paul VI.

Montana

1743: Pierre and Francois Verendrye, accompanied by Jesuit Father Coquart, may have explored territory.

1833: Indian missions handed over to care of Jesuits by Second Provincial Council of Baltimore.

1840: Jesuit Pierre De Smet began missionary work among Flathead and Pend d'Oreille Indians.

1841: St. Mary's Mission established by Father De Smet and two companions on the Bitter Root River in present Stevensville.

1845: Jesuit Antonio Ravalli placed in charge of St. Mary's Mission; Ravalli County named in his honor.

1859: Fathers Point and Hoecken established St. Peter's Mission near the Great Falls.

1869: Sisters of Charity founded a hospital, school and orphanage in Helena.

1877: Vicariate Apostolic of Montana established.
1884: Helena diocese established.
1904: Great Falls diocese established.
1910: Carroll College founded.
1935: Rev. Joseph M. Gilmore became first Montana priest elevated to hierarchy.

Nebraska

1541: Coronado expedition, accompanied by Franciscan Juan de Padilla, reached the Platte River.
1673: Pere Marquette visited Nebraska Indians.
1720: Franciscan Juan Miguel killed by Indians near Columbus.
1855: Father J. F. Tracy administered to Catholic settlement of St. Patrick and to Catholics in Omaha.
1856: Land was donated by Governor Alfred Cumming for a church in Omaha.
1857: Nebraska vicariate apostolic established.
1878: Creighton University established.
1881: Poor Clares, first contemplative group in state, arrived in Omaha.
Duchesne College established.
1885: Omaha diocese established.
1887: Lincoln diocese established.
1912: Kearney diocese established; name changed to Grand Island, 1917.
1917: Father Flanagan founded Boy's Town for homeless boys, an institution which gained national and international recognition in subsequent years.
1945: Omaha made archdiocese.

Nevada

1774: Franciscan missionaries passed through Nevada on way to California missions.
1860: First parish, serving Genoa, Carson City and Virginia City, established.
1862: Rev. Patrick Manogue appointed pastor of Virginia City. He established a school for boys and girls, an orphanage and hospital.
1871: Church erected at Reno.
1931: Reno diocese established; name changed to Reno-Las Vegas, 1977.

New Hampshire

1630: Territory made part of a prefecture apostolic embracing all of New England.
1784: State Constitution included a religious test which barred Catholics from public office; local support was provided for public Protestant teachers of religion.
1818: The Barber family of Claremont was visited by their son Virgil (converted to Catholicism in 1816) accompanied by Father Charles Ffrench, O.P. The visit led to the conversion of the entire Barber family.
1823: Father Virgil Barber, minister who became a Jesuit priest, built first Catholic church and school at Claremont.
1830: Church of St. Aloysius erected at Dover.
1853: New Hampshire made part of the Portland diocese.
1858: Sisters of Mercy began to teach school at St. Anne's, Manchester.
1877: Catholics obtained full civil liberty and rights.
1884: Manchester diocese established.
1893: St. Anselm's College founded; St. Anselm's Abbey canonically erected.
1937: Francis P. Murphy became first Catholic governor of New Hampshire.

New Jersey

1668: William Douglass of Bergen was refused a seat in General Assembly because he was a Catholic.
1672: Fathers Harvey and Gage visited Catholics in Woodbridge and Elizabethtown.
1701: Tolerance granted to all but "papists."
1744: Jesuit Theodore Schneider of Pennsylvania visited German Catholics of New Jersey.
1762: Fathers Ferdinand Farmer and Robert Harding working among Catholics in state.
1776: State Constitution tacitly excluded Catholics from office.
1799: Foundation of first Catholic school in state, St. John's at Trenton.
1803: First parish in northern New Jersey founded at Echo Lake.
1814: First church in Trenton erected.
1844: Catholics obtained full civil liberty and rights.
1853: Newark diocese established.
1856: Seton Hall University established.
1881: Trenton diocese established.
1937: Newark made archdiocese. Paterson and Camden dioceses established.
1947: US Supreme Court ruled on N.J. bus case, permitting children attending non-public schools to ride on buses and be given other health services provided for those in public schools.
1957: Seton Hall College of Medicine and Dentistry established: the first medical school in state; it was run by Seton Hall until 1965.
1963: Byzantine Eparchy of Passaic established.

New Mexico

1539: Territory explored by Franciscan Marcos de Niza.
1544: Franciscans Juan de la Cruz and Louis de Ubedan lay brother, killed by Indians.
1581: Franciscans Augustin Rodriguez, Juan de Santa Maria and Francisco Lopez named the region "New Mexico"; they later died at hands of Indians.

1598: Juan de Onate founded a colony at Chamita, where first chapel in state was built.
1609: Santa Fe founded, future headquarters for missions of New Mexico.
1631: Franciscan Pedro de Miranda was killed by Indians.
1632: Franciscan Francisco Letrado was killed by Indians.
1672: Franciscan Pedro de Avila y Ayala was killed by Indians.
1675: Franciscan Alonso Gil de Avila was killed by Indians.
1680: Indians massacred 21 missionaries; missions destroyed.
1684: Franciscan Manuel Beltran was killed by Indians.
1692: Missions restored.
1696: Indians rebelled, massacred five more missionaries.
1850: Jean Baptiste Lamy appointed head of newly established Vicariate Apostolic of New Mexico.
1852: Sisters of Loretto arrived in Santa Fe.
1853: Santa Fe diocese established.
1859: Christian Brothers arrived, established first school for boys in New Mexico (later St. Michael's College).
1865: Sisters of Charity started first orphanage and hospital in Santa Fe. It was closed in 1966.
1875: Santa Fe made archdiocese.
1939: Gallup diocese established.

New York

1524: Giovanni de Verrazano was first white man to enter New York Bay.
1627: Franciscan Joseph d'Aillon discovered oil at Seneca Springs, near Cuba, N.Y.
1642: Jesuits Isaac Jogues and Rene Goupil were mutilated by Mohawks; Rene Goupil was killed by them shortly afterwards. Dutch Calvinists rescued Father Jogues.
1646: Jesuits Isaac Jogues and John Lalande were martyred by Iroquois at Ossernenon, now Auriesville.
1654: The Onondagas were visited by Jesuits from Canada.
1655: First permanent mission established near Syracuse.
1656: Church of St. Mary erected near Lake Onondaga.
Catherine Tekakwitha, "Lily of the Mohawks, was born at Ossernenon, now Auriesville (d. in Canada, 1680).
1658: Indian uprisings destroyed missions among Cayugas, Senecas and Oneidas.
1664: English took New Amsterdam and replaced French priests with their own missionaries.
Duke of York ordered religious freedom in Province of New York.
1667: Missions were restored under protection of Garaconthie, Onondaga chief.
1678: Franciscan Louis Hennepin, first white man to view Niagara Falls, celebrated Mass there.
1682: Thomas Dongan appointed governor by Duke of York.
1683: English Jesuits came to New York, later opened a school.
1700: Although Assembly enacted a bill calling for religious toleration of all Christians in 1683, other penal laws were now enforced against Catholics; all priests were ordered out of the province.
1709: Jesuit missions were abandoned.
1741: Because of an alleged popish plot to burn city of New York, four whites were hanged and 11 Negroes burned at stake.
1777: A rejected amendment of the State Constitution stated that Catholics ought not to hold lands or participate in civil rights unless they swore that no pope or priests may absolve them from allegiance to the state.
1785: Cornerstone was laid for St. Peter's Church, New York City, first permanent structure of Catholic worship in state.
Trusteeism began to cause trouble at New York.
1806: State Test Oath repealed.
1808: New York diocese established.
1828: New York State Legislature enacted a law upholding sanctity of seal of confession.
1834: First native New Yorker to become a secular priest, Rev. John McCloskey, was ordained.
1841: Fordham University and Manhattanville College established.
1847: Albany and Buffalo dioceses established.
1850: New York made archdiocese.
1853: Brooklyn diocese established.
1856: Present St. Bonaventure University and Christ the King Seminary founded at Allegany.
1858: Cornerstone of St. Patrick's Cathedral, New York City, was laid.
1868: Rochester diocese established.
1872: Ogdensburg diocese established.
1875: Archbishop John McCloskey of New York made first American cardinal by Pope Pius IX.
1878: Franciscan Sisters of Allegany were first native American community to send members to foreign missions.
1880: William R. Grace was first Catholic mayor of New York City.
1886: Syracuse diocese established.
1911: Archbishop John M. Farley of New York made cardinal by Pope Pius X.
Catholic Foreign Mission Society of America (Maryknoll) opened a seminary for foreign missions, the first of its kind in US. The Maryknollers were also unique as the first US-established foreign mission society.
1917: Military Ordinariate established with headquarters at New York.
1919: Alfred E. Smith became first elected Catholic governor.

1924: Archbishop Patrick Hayes of New York made cardinal by Pope Pius XI.
1930: Jesuit Martyrs of New York and Canada were canonized on June 29.
1946: Archbishop Francis J. Spellman of New York made cardinal by Pope Pius XII.
1957: Rockville Centre diocese established.
1969: Archbishop Terence Cooke of New York made cardinal by Pope Paul VI.

North Carolina

1526: The Ayllon expedition attempted to establish a settlement on Carolina coast.
1540: De Soto expedition, accompanied by chaplains, entered state.
1776: State Constitution denied office to "those who denied the truths of the Protestant religion."
1805: The few Catholics in state were served by visiting missionaries.
1821: Bishop John England celebrated Mass in the ballroom of the home of William Gaston at New Bern, marking the start of organization of the first parish, St. Paul's, in the state.
1835: William Gaston, State Supreme Court Justice, succeeded in having repealed the article denying religious freedom.
1852: First Catholic church erected in Charlotte.
1868: North Carolina vicariate apostolic established.
Catholics obtained full civil liberty and rights.
1874: Sisters of Mercy arrived, opened an academy, several schools, hospitals and an orphanage.
1878: Belmont Abbey College founded.
1910: Mary Help of Christians Abbey Nullius established at Belmont; suppressed in 1977.
1924: Raleigh diocese established.
1971: Charlotte diocese established.

North Dakota

1742: Pierre and Francois Verendrye, accompanied by Jesuit Father Coquart, explored territory.
1818: Canadian priests ministered to Catholics in area.
1839: Jesuit Father De Smet made first of five trips among Mandan and Gros Ventre Indians.
1848: Father George Belcourt, first American resident priest in territory, reestablished Pembena Mission.
1874: Grey Nuns invited to conduct a school at Fort Totten.
1889: Fargo diocese established.
1893: Benedictines founded St. Gall Monastery at Devil's Lake. (It became an abbey in 1903.)
1909: Bismarck diocese established.
1959: Archbishop Aloysius J. Muench, bishop of Fargo, made cardinal by Pope John XXIII.

Ohio

1749: Jesuits in expedition of Celeron de Bienville preached to Indians.
First religious services were held within present limits of Ohio. Jesuits Joseph de Bonnecamp and Peter Potier celebrated Mass at mouth of Little Miami River and in vicinity of Sandusky Bay, respectively.
1751: First Catholic settlement founded among Huron Indians near Sandusky by Father de la Richardie.
1790: Benedictine Pierre Didier ministered to French immigrants.
1812: Bishop Flaget of Bardstown visited and baptized Catholics of Lancaster and Somerset Counties.
1818: Dominican Father Fenwick built St. Joseph's Church and established first Dominican convent in Ohio.
1821: Cincinnati diocese established.
1831: Xavier University founded.
1843: Seven members of Congregation of Most Precious Blood arrived in Cincinnati from France.
1845: Cornerstone laid for St. Peter's Cathedral, Cincinnati; this was first cathedral west of Alleghenies.
1847: Cleveland diocese established.
1850: Cincinnati made archdiocese.
Marianists opened St. Mary's Institute, now University of Dayton.
1865: Sisters of Charity opened hospital in Cleveland, first institution of its kind in city.
1868: Columbus diocese established.
1871: Ursuline College for women opened at Cleveland.
1910: Toledo diocese established.
1935: Archbishop John T. McNicholas, O.P., founded the Institutum Divi Thomae in Cincinnati for fundamental research in natural sciences.
1943: Youngstown diocese established.
1944: Steubenville diocese established.
1969: Byzantine Rite Eparchy of Parma established.

Oklahoma

1540: De Soto expedition, accompanied by chaplains, explored territory.
1541: Coronado expedition, accompanied by Franciscan Juan de Padilla, explored state.
1630: Spanish Franciscan Juan de Salas labored among Indians.
1700: Scattered Catholic families were visited by priests from Kansas and Arkansas.
1874: First Catholic church built by Father Smyth at Atoka.
1876: Prefecture Apostolic of Indian Territory established with Benedictine Isidore Robot as its head.
1886: First Catholic day school for Choc-

taw and white children opened by Sisters of Mercy at Kribs.
1891: Vicariate Apostolic of Oklahoma and Indian Territory established.
1905: Oklahoma diocese established; title changed to Oklahoma City and Tulsa, 1930.
1917: Benedictine Heights College for women founded.
Carmelite Sisters of St. Theresa of the Infant Jesus founded at Oklahoma City.
1972: Oklahoma City made archdiocese. Tulsa diocese established.

Oregon

1603: Vizcaino explored northern Oregon coast.
1774: Franciscan missionaries accompanied Juan Perez on his expedition to coast, and Heceta a year later.
1811: Catholic Canadian trappers and traders with John J. Astor expedition founded first American settlement — Astoria.
1834: Indian missions in Northwest entrusted to Jesuits by Holy See.
1838: Abbe Blanchet appointed vicar general to Bishop of Quebec with jurisdiction over area which included Oregon Territory.
1839: First Mass celebrated at present site of St. Paul.
1843: Oregon vicariate apostolic established.
St. Joseph's College for boys opened.
1844: Jesuit Pierre de Smet established Mission of St. Francis Xavier near St. Paul.
Sisters of Notre Dame de Namur, first to enter Oregon, opened an academy for girls.
1846: Vicariate made an ecclesiastical province with Bishop Blanchet as first Archbishop of Oregon City (now Portland).
Walla Walla diocese established; suppressed in 1853.
1847: First priest was ordained in Oregon.
1848: First Provincial Council of Oregon.
1857: Death of Dr. John McLoughlin, "Father of Oregon."
1865: Rev. H. H. Spalding, a Protestant missionary, published the Whitman Myth to hinder work of Catholic missionaries.
1874: Catholic Indian Mission Bureau established.
1875: St. Vincent's Hospital, first in state, opened at Portland.
1903: Baker diocese established.
1922: Anti-private school bill sponsored by Scottish Rite Masons was passed by popular vote, 115,506 to 103,685.
1925: US Supreme Court declared Oregon anti-private school bill unconstitutional.
1953: First Trappist monastery on West Coast established in Willamette Valley north of Lafayette.

Pennsylvania

1673: Priests from Maryland ministered to Catholics in the Colony.
1682: Religious toleration was extended to members of all faiths.
1720: Jesuit Joseph Greaton became first resident l missionary of Philadelphia.
1734: St. Joseph's Church, first Catholic church in Philadelphia, was opened.
1741: Jesuit Fathers Schneider and Wappeler ministered to German immigrants.
Conewego Chapel, a combination chapel and dwelling, was built by Father William Wappeler, S.J., a priest sent to minister to the German Catholic immigrants who settled in the area in the 1730's.
1782: St. Mary's Parochial School opened at Philadelphia.
1788: Holy Trinity Church, Philadelphia, was incorporated; first exclusively national church organized in US.
1797: Augustinian Matthew Carr founded St. Augustine parish, Philadelphia.
1799: Prince Demetrius Gallitzin (Father Augustine Smith) built church in western Pennsylvania, at Loretto.
1808: Philadelphia diocese established.
1814: St. Joseph's Orphanage was opened at Philadelphia; first Catholic institution for children in US.
1842: University of Villanova founded by Augustinians.
1843: Pittsburgh diocese established.
1844: Thirteen persons killed, two churches and a school burned in Know-Nothing riots at Philadelphia.
1846: First Benedictine Abbey in New World founded near Latrobe by Father Boniface Wimmer.
1852: Redemptorist John Nepomucene Neumann became fourth bishop of Philadelphia. He was beatified in 1963 and canonized in 1977.
1853: Erie diocese established.
1868: Scranton and Harrisburg dioceses established.
1871: Chestnut Hill College, first for women in state, founded.
1875: Philadelphia made archdiocese.
1901: Altoona-Johnstown diocese established.
1913: Byzantine Rite Apostolic Exarchate of Philadelphia established; became metropolitan see, 1958.
1921: Archbishop Dennis Dougherty made cardinal by Pope Benedict XV.
1924: Byzantine Rite Apostolic Exarchate of Pittsburgh established; made an eparchy in 1963; raised to metropolitan status and transferred to Munhall, 1969; transferred back to Pittsburgh in 1977.
1951: Greensburg diocese established.
1958: Archbishop John O'Hara, C.S.C., of Philadelphia made cardinal by Pope John.
1961: Allentown diocese established.
1967: Archbishop John J. Krol of Philadelphia made cardinal by Pope Paul VI.
1969: Bishop John J. Wright of Pittsburgh

made cardinal by Pope Paul VI and transferred to Curia post.

1976: The 41st International Eucharistic Congress, the second held in the U.S. convened in Philadelphia, August 1-8.

Rhode Island

1663: Colonial Charter granted freedom of conscience.

1719: Laws denied Catholics the right to hold public office.

1829: St. Mary's Church, Pawtucket, was first Catholic church in state.

1837: Parochial schools inaugurated in state.

First Catholic church in Providence was built.

1851: Sisters of Mercy began work in Rhode Island.

1872: Providence diocese established.

1900: Trappists took up residence in state.

1917: Providence College founded.

South Carolina

1569: Jesuit Juan Rogel was the first resident priest in the territory.

1573: First Franciscans arrived in southeastern section.

1606: Bishop Altamirano conducted visitation of area.

1655: Franciscans had two missions among Indians; later destroyed by English.

1697: Religious liberty granted to all except "papists."

1790: Catholics given right to vote.

1820: Charleston diocese established.

1822: Bishop England founded *U.S. Catholic Miscellany*, first Catholic paper of a strictly religious nature in US.

1830: Sisters of Our Lady of Mercy, first in state, took up residence at Charleston.

1847: Cornerstone of Cathedral of St. John the Baptist, Charleston, was laid.

1861: Cathedral and many institutions destroyed in Charleston fire.

South Dakota

1842: Father Augustine Ravoux began ministrations to French and Indians at Fort Pierre, Vermilion and Prairie du Chien; printed devotional book in Sioux language the following year.

1867: Parish organized among the French at Jefferson.

1878: Benedictines opened school for Sioux children at Fort Yates.

1889: Sioux Falls diocese established.

1902: Lead diocese established; transferred to Rapid City, 1930.

1950: Mount Marty College for women founded.

1952: Blue Cloud Abbey, first Benedictine foundation in state, was dedicated.

Tennessee

1541: Cross planted on shore of Mississippi by De Soto; accompanying the expedition were Fathers John de Gallegos and Louis De Soto.

1682: Franciscan Fathers Membre and Douay accompanied La Salle to present site of Memphis; may have offered the first Masses in the territory.

1800: Catholics were served by priests from Bardstown, Ky.

1822: Non-Catholics assisted in building church in Nashville.

1837: Nashville diocese established.

1843: Sisters of Charity opened a school for girls in Nashville.

1921: Sisters of St. Dominic opened Siena College for women at Memphis.

1940: Christian Brothers College founded at Memphis.

1970: Memphis diocese established.

Texas

1541: Missionaries with De Soto and Coronado entered territory.

1553: Dominicans Diego de la Cruz, Hernando Mendez, Juan Ferrer, Brother Juan de Mina killed by Indians.

1675: Bosque-Larios missionary expedition entered region; Father Juan Larios offered first recorded Mass.

1689: Four Franciscans founded first mission, San Francisco de los Tejas.

1703: Mission San Francisco de Solano founded on Rio Grande.

1717: Franciscan Antonio Margil founded six missions in northeast.

1721: Franciscan Brother Jose Pita killed by Indians at Carnezeria.

1728: Site of San Antonio settled.

1738: Construction of San Fernando Cathedral at San Antonio.

1744: Mission of San Francisco de Solano rebuilt as the Alamo.

1750: Franciscan Francisco Xavier was .iled by Indians; so were Jose Ganzabal in 1752, and Alonzo Ferrares and Jose Esteban in 1758.

1793: Mexico secularized missions.

1825: Government of Texas secularized all Indian missions.

1830: Irish priests ministered to settlements of Refugio and San Patricio.

1841: Vicariate of Texas established.

1847: Ursuline Sisters established their first academy in territory at Galveston.

Galveston diocese established.

1852: Oblate Fathers and Franciscans arrived in Galveston to care for new influx of German Catholics.

St. Mary's College founded at San Antonio.

1854: Know-Nothing Party began to stir up hatred against Catholics.

1858: Texas Legislature passed law entitling all schools granting free scholarships and meeting state requirements to share in school fund.

1874: San Antonio diocese established.
1881: St. Edward's College founded: became first chartered college in state in 1889.
Sisters of Charity founded Incarnate Word College at San Antonio.
1890: Dallas diocese established; changed to Dallas-Ft. Worth, 1953; made two separate dioceses, 1969.
1912: Corpus Christi diocese established.
1914: El Paso diocese established.
1926: San Antonio made archdiocese. Amarillo diocese established.
1947: Austin diocese established.
1961: San Angelo diocese established.
1965: Brownsville diocese established.
1966: Beaumont diocese established.

Utah

1776: Franciscans Silvestre de Escalante and Atanasio Dominguez reached Utah (Salt) Lake; first white men known to enter the territory.
1858: Jesuit Father De Smet accompanied General Harney as chaplain on expedition sent to settle troubles between Mormons and US Government.
1866: On June 29 Father Edward Kelly offered first Mass in Salt Lake City in Mormon Assembly Hall.
1886: Utah vicariate apostolic established.
1891: Salt Lake City diocese established.
1926: College of St. Mary-of-the-Wasatch for women was founded.

Vermont

1609: Champlain expedition passed through territory.
1666: Captain La Motte built fort and shrine of St. Anne on Isle La Motte; Sulpician Father Dollier de Casson celebrated first Mass.
1668: Bishop Laval of Quebec administered confirmation in region; this was the first area in northeastern US to receive an episcopal visit.
1710: Jesuits ministered to Indians near Lake Champlain.
1793: Discriminatory measures against Catholics were repealed.
1830: Father Jeremiah O'Callaghan became first resident priest in state.
1853: Burlington diocese established.
1854: Sisters of Charity arrived to conduct St. Joseph's Orphanage at Burlington.
1904: St. Michael's College founded.
1951: First Carthusian foundation in America established at Whitingham.

Virginia

1526: Dominican Antonio de Montesinos offered first Mass on Virginia soil.
1561: Dominicans visited the coast.
1571: Father John Baptist de Segura and seven Jesuit companions killed by Indians.
1642: Priests outlawed and Catholics denied right to vote.
1689: Capuchin Christopher Plunket was captured and exiled to a coastal island where he died in 1697.
1776: Religious freedom granted.
1791: Father Jean Dubois arrived at Richmond with letters from Lafayette. The House of Delegates was placed at his disposal for celebration of Mass.
1796: A church was built at Alexandria.
1820: Richmond diocese established.
1822: Trusteeism created serious problems in diocese; Bishop Kelly resigned the see.
1848: Sisters of Charity opened an orphan asylum at Norfolk.
1866: School Sisters of Notre Dame and Sisters of Charity opened academies for girls at Richmond.
1974: Arlington diocese established.

Washington

1775: Spaniards explored the region.
1838: Fathers Blanchet and Demers, "Apostles of the Northwest," were sent to territory by archbishop of Quebec.
1840: Log church for Indians was built on Whidby Island, Puget Sound.
1843: Vicariate Apostolic of Oregon, including Washington, was established.
1844: Mission of St. Paul founded at Colville.
Six Sisters of Notre Dame de Namur began work in area.
1850: Nesqually diocese established; transferred to Seattle, 1907.
1856: Providence Academy, the first permanent Catholic school in the Northwest, was built at Fort Vancouver by Mother Joseph Pariseau of the Sisters of Charity of Providence.
1887: Gonzaga University founded.
1913: Spokane diocese established.
1951: Seattle made archdiocese. Yakima diocese established.

West Virginia

1749: Father Joseph de Bonnecamps, accompanying the Bienville expedition, may have offered first Mass in the territory.
1821: First Catholic church in Wheeling.
1838: Sisters of Charity founded school at Martinsburg.
1848: Visitation Nuns established academy for girls at Mt. de Chantal.
1850: Wheeling diocese established; name changed to Wheeling-Charleston, 1974.
Wheeling Hospital incorporated, the oldest Catholic charitable institution in territory.
1955: Wheeling College established.

Wisconsin

1661: Jesuit Rene Menard, first known missionary in the territory, was killed or lost in the Black River district.
1665: Jesuit Claude Allouez founded Mission of the Holy Ghost at La Pointe Chegoi-

megon, now Bayfield; was the first permanent mission in region.

1673: Father Marquette and Louis Joliet traveled from Green Bay down the Wisconsin and Mississippi rivers.

1762: Suppression of Jesuits in French Colonies closed many missions for 30 years.

1843: Milwaukee diocese established.

1853: St. John's Cathedral, Milwaukee, was built.

1864: Marquette University established.

1868: Green Bay and La Crosse dioceses established.

1875: Milwaukee made archdiocese.

1905: Superior diocese established.

1946: Madison diocese established.

Wyoming

1840: Jesuit Pierre de Smet offered first Mass near Green River.

1851: Father De Smet held peace conference with Indians near Fort Laramie.

1867: Father William Kelly, first resident priest, arrived in Cheyenne and built first church a year later.

1873: Father Eugene Cusson became first resident pastor in Laramie.

1875: Sisters of Charity of Leavenworth opened school and orphanage at Laramie.

1884: Jesuits took over pastoral care of Shoshone and Arapaho Indians.

1887: Cheyenne diocese established.

1949: Weston Memorial Hospital opened near Newcastle.

Puerto Rico

1493: Island discovered by Columbus on his second voyage; he named it San Juan de Borinquen (the Indian name for Puerto Rico).

1509: Juan Ponce de Leon, searching for gold, colonized the island and became its first governor; present population descended mainly from early Spanish settlers.

1511: Diocese of Puerto Rico established as suffragan of Seville, Spain; Bishop Alonso, sailing from Spain in 1512, became first bishop to take up residence in New World.

1645: Synod held in Puerto Rico to regulate frequency of Masses according to distances people had to walk.

1898: Puerto Rico ceded to U.S. (became self-governing Commonwealth in 1952); inhabitants granted U.S. citizenship in 1917.

1924: Diocese of Puerto Rico renamed San Juan de Puerto Rico and made immediately subject to the Holy See; Ponce diocese established.

1948: Catholic University of Puerto Rico founded at Ponce through efforts of Bishop James E. McManus, C.SS.R., 1947-63.

1960: San Juan made metropolitan see. Arecibo diocese established.

1964: Caguas diocese established.

1973: Archbishop Luis Aponte Martinez of San Juan made first native Puerto Rican cardinal by Pope Paul VI.

1976: Mayaguez diocese established.

Virgin of Providence officially approved as Patroness of Puerto Rico by Pope Paul VI.

Catholics in Presidents' Cabinets

(For biographical data on some of these entries, see Index.)

Roger B. Taney, Attorney General 1831-33, Secretary of Treasury 1833-34; app. by Andrew Jackson.

James Campbell, Postmaster General 1853-57; app. by Franklin Pierce.

John B. Floyd, Secretary of War 1857-61; app. by James Buchanan.

Joseph McKenna, Attorney General 1897-98; app. by William McKinley.

Robert J. Wynne, Postmaster General 1904-05; app. by Theodore Roosevelt.

Charles Bonaparte, Secretary of Navy 1905-06, Attorney General 1906-09; app. by Theodore Roosevelt.

James A. Farley, Postmaster General 1933-40; app. by Franklin D. Roosevelt.

Frank Murphy, Attorney General 1939-40; app. by Franklin D. Roosevelt.

Frank C. Walker, Postmaster General 1940-45; app. by Franklin D. Roosevelt.

Robert E. Hannegan, Postmaster General 1945-47; app. by Harry S. Truman.

J. Howard McGrath, Attorney General 1949-52; app. by Harry S. Truman.

Maurice J. Tobin, Secretary of Labor; 1949-53; app. by Harry S. Truman.

James P. McGranery, Attorney General 1952-53; app. by Harry S. Truman.

Martin P. Durkin, Secretary of Labor 1953; app. by Dwight D. Eisenhower.

James P. Mitchell, Secretary of Labor 1953-61; app. by Dwight D. Eisenhower.

Robert F. Kennedy, Attorney General 1961-65; app. by John F. Kennedy, reapp. by Lyndon B. Johnson.

Anthony Celebrezze, Secretary of Health, Education and Welfare 1962-65; app. by John F. Kennedy, reapp. by Lyndon B. Johnson.

John S. Gronouski, Postmaster General 1963-65; app. by John F. Kennedy, reapp. by Lyndon B. Johnson.

John T. Connor, Secretary of Commerce 1965-67; app. by Lyndon B. Johnson.

Lawrence O'Brien, Postmaster General 1965-68; app. by Lyndon B. Johnson.

Walter J. Hickel, Secretary of Interior 1969-71; app. by Richard M. Nixon.

John A. Volpe, Secretary of Transportation 1969-72; app. by Richard M. Nixon.

Maurice H. Stans, Secretary of Commerce, 1969-72; app. by Richard M. Nixon.

Peter J. Brennan, Secretary of Labor, 1973-75; app. by Richard M. Nixon, reapp. by Gerald R. Ford.

William E. Simon, Secretary of Treasury,

1974-76; app. by Richard M. Nixon, reapp. by Gerald R. Ford.

Joseph A. Califano, Jr., Secretary of Health, Education and Welfare, 1977-79; app. by Jimmy Carter.

Benjamin Civiletti, Attorney General, 1979- ; app. by Jimmy Carter.

Moon Landrieu, Secretary of Housing and Urban Development, 1979- ; app. by Jimmy Carter.

Men who became Catholics after leaving Cabinet posts: Thomas Ewing, Secretary of Treasury under William A. Harrison, and Secretary of Interior under Zachary Taylor; Luke E. Wright, Secretary of War under Theodore Roosevelt; Albert B. Fall, Secretary of Interior under Warren G. Harding.

Catholic Justices of the Supreme Court

(For biographical data on some of these entries, see Index.)

Roger B. Taney, Chief Justice 1836-64; app. by Andrew Jackson.

Edward D. White, Associate Justice 1894-1910, app. by Grover Cleveland; Chief Justice 1910-21, app. by William H. Taft.

Joseph McKenna, Associate Justice 1898-1925; app. by William McKinley.

Pierce Butler, Associate Jusice 1923-39; app. by Warren G. Harding.

Frank Murphy, Associate Justice 1940-49; app. by Franklin D. Roosevelt.

William Brennan, Associate Justice 1956-; app. by Dwight D. Eisenhower.

Sherman Minton, Associate Justice from 1949 to 1956, became a Catholic several years before his death in 1965.

Catholics Represented in National Statuary Hall

(For biographies, see Index.)

Statues of 12 Catholics deemed worthy of national commemoration by the donating states are among 91 enshrined in National Statuary Hall and other places in the US Capitol. The Hall, formerly the chamber of the House of Representatives, was erected by Act of Congress July 2, 1864.

Donating states, names and years of placement are listed. An asterisk indicates placement of a statue in the Hall itself.

Arizona: Rev. Eusebio Kino, S. J., missionary, 1965.

California: Rev. Junipero Serra, O. F. M.* missionary, 1931.

Hawaii: Father Damien, missionary, 1969.

Illinois: Gen. James Shields, statesman, 1893.

Louisiana: Edward D. White, Justice of the US Supreme Court (1894-1921), 1955.

Maryland: Charles Carroll,* statesman, 1901.

Nevada: Patrick A. McCarran,* statesman, 1960.

New Mexico: Dennis Chavez, statesman, 1966. (Archbishop Jean B. Lamy, pioneer prelate of Santa Fe, was nominated for Hall honor in 1951.)

North Dakota: John Burke,* US treasurer, 1963.

Oregon: Dr. John McLoughlin, pioneer, 1953.

Washington: Mother Mary Joseph Pariseau, pioneer missionary and humanitarian. (Selected in 1977; statue still to be placed.)

West Virginia: John E. Kenna, statesman, 1901.

Wisconsin: Rev. Jacques Marquette, S. J., missionary, explorer, 1895.

CHURCH-STATE DECISIONS

(Among sources of this listing of US Supreme Court decisions was *The Supreme Court on Church and State,* Joseph Tussman, editor; Oxford University Press, New York, 1962.)

Terrett v. Taylor, 9 Cranch 43 (1815): The Court declared unconstitutional an act of the Virginia Legislature which denied property rights to Protestant Episcopal churches in the state. Religious corporations, like other corporations, have rights to their property.

Vidal v. Girard's Executors, 2 Howard 205 (1844): The Court upheld the will of Stephen Girard, which barred ministers of any religion from serving as faculty members or visitors in a school he established for orphans.

Watson v. Jones, 13 Wallace 679 (1872): The Court declared that a member of a religious organization may not appeal to secular courts against a decision made by a church tribunal within the area of its competence.

Reynolds v. United States, 98 US 145 (1879): The Court declared, in reference to the Mormon practice of polygamy, that one may not knowingly violate by external practices the law of the land on religious grounds, since such conduct would make the professed doctrines of belief superior to federal or state law. One must keep the external practice of religion within the framework of laws enacted for the common welfare. This was the first decision rendered on the Free Exercise Clause of the First Amendment.

Davis v. Beason, 133 US 333 (1890): The Court upheld the denial of the right of Mormons to vote in Idaho if they refused to sign a registration oath stating that they were not bigamists or polygamists and would not encourage or preach bigamy or polygamy.

Church of Latter-Day Saints v. United States, 136 US 1 (1890): The Court upheld an Act of Congress which annulled the charter of the Corporation of the Church of Jesus Christ of Latter-Day Saints, and declared "forfeited to the government all its real estate except a small portion used exclusively for public worship" (Tussman, *op. cit.,* p. 33). The Court held that the Corporation continually used its power to violate US laws prohibiting polygamy.

Church of the Holy Trinity v. United States, 143 US 226 (1892): The Court declared it is not "a misdemeanor for a church of this country to contract for the services of a Christian minister residing in another nation" (from the text of the decision).

Bradfield v. Roberts, 175 US 291 (1899): The Court denied that an appropriation of government funds for an institution (Providence Hospital, Washington, D.C.) run by Roman Catholic sisters violated the No Establishment Clause of the First Amendment.

Pierce v. Society of Sisters, 268 US 510 (1925): The Court denied that a state can require children to attend public schools only. The Court held that the liberty of the Constitution forbids standardization by such compulsion, and that the parochial schools involved had claims to protection under the Fourteenth Amendment.

Cochran v. Board of Education, 281 US 370 (1930): The Court upheld a Louisiana statute providing textbooks at public expense for children attending public or parochial schools. The Court held that the children and state were beneficiaries of the appropriations, with incidental secondary benefit going to the schools.

United States v. MacIntosh, 283 US 605 (1931): The Court denied that anyone can place allegiance to the will of God above his allegiance to the government, since such a person could make his own interpretation of God's will the decisive test as to whether he would or would not obey the nation's law. The Court stated that the nation, which has a duty to survive, can require citizens to bear arms in its defense.

Hamilton v. Regents of University of California, 293 US 245 (1934): The Court rejected a "claim to exemption from R.O.T.C. based on conscientious objection to war" (Tussman *op. cit.,* p. 64). If such an exemption were allowed, the liberties of the objector might be extended to the point of refusal to pay taxes in furtherance of a war or any other end condemned by his conscience. This would be an undue exaltation of the right of private judgment.

Cantwell v. Connecticut, 310 US 296 (1940): The Court declared that the right to religious freedom is violated by a statute requiring a person to secure a permit from a government official before soliciting money for alleged religious purposes from someone not of his or her sect. Such a practice would constitute censorship of religion.

Minersville School District v. Gobitis, 310 US 586 (1940): The Court upheld the right of a state to require the salute to the national flag from school children, even from those who refused to do so for sincere religious reasons.

Jones v. City of Opelika, 316 US 584 (1942): The court upheld licensing ordinances in three municipalities against "the claim by Jehovah's Witnesses that they interfere with the free exercise of religion" (Tussman, *op. cit.,* p. 91).

Murdock v. Commonwealth of Pennsylvania, 319 US 105 (1943): In a reversal of the decision handed down in Jones v. City of Opelika, the Court declared the licensing unconstitutional since it violated a freedom guaranteed under the First Amendment. The selling of religious literature by traveling preachers does not make evangelism the equivalent of a commercial enterprise taxable by the State.

Jones v. City of Opelika, 316 US 584 105 (1943): The Court declared that the Constitution denies a city the right to control the expression of men's minds and denies also the right of men to win others to their views through a program of taxes levied against such activity.

Douglas v. City of Jeannette, 319 US 157 (1943): The Court again upheld the proselytizing rights of Jehovah's Witnesses, ruling unconstitutional the action of any public authority in regulating or taxing such activity.

West Virginia State Board of Education v. Barnette, 319 US 624 (1943): In a reversal of the decision handed down in Minersville School District v. Gobitis, the Court declared unconstitutional a state statute requiring of all children a salute to the national flag and a pledge of allegiance which a child may consider contrary to sincere religious beliefs.

Prince v. Commonwealth of Massachusetts, 321 US 158 (1944): The Court upheld a "child-labor regulation against the claim that it prevents a child from performing her religious duty" (Tussman, *op. cit.,* p. 170). The Court asserted a general principle that the state has a wide range of power for limiting parental freedom and authority in things affecting the child's welfare.

United States v. Ballard, 322 US 78 (1944): The Court upheld the general principle that "the truth of religious claims is not for secular authority to determine" (Tussman, *op. cit.,* p. 181).

In Re Summers, 325 US 561 (1945): The Court upheld "the denial, to an otherwise qualified applicant, of admission to the bar on the basis of the applicant's religiously motivated 'conscientious scruples against participation in war' " (Tussman, *op. cit.,* p. 192). The petitioner was barred because he could not in good faith take the prescribed oath to support the Constitution of Illinois which required service in the state militia in times of necessity.

Girouard v. United States, 328 US 61 (1946): In a ruling related to that handed down in United States v. MacIntosh, the Court affirmed the opinion that the refusal of an alien to bear arms does not deny him citizenship.

Everson v. Board of Education, 330 US 1 (1947): The Court upheld the constitutionality of a New Jersey statute authorizing free school bus transportation for parochial as well as public school students. The Court expressed the opinion that the benefits of public welfare legislation, included under such bus transportation, do not run contrary to the concept of separation of Church and State.

McCollum v. Board of Education, 333 US 203 (1948): The Court declared unconstitutional a program for releasing children, with parental consent, from public school classes so they could receive religious instruction on public school premises from representatives of their own faiths.

Zorach v. Clauson, 343 US 306 (1952): The Court upheld the constitutionality of a New York statute permitting, on a voluntary basis, the release during school time of students from public school classes for religious instruction given off public school premises.

Kedroff v. St. Nicholas Cathedral, 344 US 94 (1952): The Court ruled against an action of New York in taking "control of St. Nicholas Cathedral away from the Moscow hierarchy" (Tussman, *op. cit.,* p. 292), on the ground that the controversy involved a matter of church government.

Fowler v. Rhode Island, 345 US 67 (1953): The Court upheld the right of a Jehovah's Witness to preach in a public park against a city ordinance which forbade such preaching. The Court held that the ordinance, as construed and applied, discriminated against the Witness and therefore amounted to preferment by the state of other religious groups.

Torcaso v. Watkins, 367 US 488 (1961): The Court declared unconstitutional a Maryland requirement that one must make a declaration of belief in the existence of God as part of the oath of office for notaries public.

McGowan v. Maryland, 81 Sp Ct 1101; **Two Guys from Harrison v. McGinley,** 81 Sp Ct 1135; **Gallagher v. Crown Kosher Super Market,** 81 Sp Ct 1128; **Braunfeld v. Brown,** 81 Sp Ct 1144 (1961): The Court ruled that Sunday closing laws do not violate the No Establishment of Religion Clause of the First Amendment, even though the laws were religious in their inception and still have some religious overtones. The Court held that, "as presently written and administered, most of them, at least, are of a secular rather than of a religious character, and that presently they bear no relationship to establishment of religion as those words are used in the Constitution of the United States."

Engel v. Vitale, 370 US 42 (1962): The Court declared that the voluntary recitation in public schools of a prayer composed by the New York State Board of Regents is unconstitutional on the ground that it violates the No Establishment of Religion Clause.

Abington Township School District v. Schempp and **Murray v. Curlett,** 83 Sp Ct 1560 (1963): The Court ruled that Bible reading and recitation of the Lord's Prayer in public schools, with voluntary participation by students, are unconstitutional on the ground that they violate the No Establishment of Religion Clause of the First Amendment.

Sherbert v. Verner, 83 A Sp Ct 1790 (1963): The Court ruled that individuals of any religious faith may not, because of their faith or lack of it, be deprived of the benefits of public welfare legislation.

Chamberlin v. Dade County, 83 Sp Ct 1864 (1964): The Court reversed a decision of the Florida Supreme Court concerning the constitutionality of prayer and devotional Bible reading in public schools during the school day, as sanctioned by a state statute which specifically related the practices to a sound public purpose.

Board of Education v. Allen, No. 660 (1968): The Court declared constitutional the New York school book loan law which requires local school boards to purchase books with state funds and lend them to parochial and private school students.

Flast v. Cohen, No. 416 (1968): The Court held that individual taxpayers can bring suits to challenge federal expenditures on grounds that they violate the principle of separation of Church and State even though generally taxpayers cannot challenge federal expenditures in court.

Walz v. Tax Commission of New York (1970): The Court upheld the constitutionality of a New York statute exempting church-owned property from taxation.

Earle v. DiCenso, Robinson v. DiCenso, Lemon v. Kurtzman, Tilton v. Richardson (1971): In Earle v. DiCenso and Robinson v. DiCenso, the Court ruled unconstitutional a 1969 Rhode Island statute which provided salary supplements to teachers of secular subjects in parochial schools; in Lemon v. Kurtzman, the Court ruled unconstitutional a 1968 Pennsylvania statute which authorized the state to purchase services for the teaching of secular subjects in nonpublic schools. The principal argument against constitutionality in these cases was that the statutes and programs at issue entailed excessive entanglement of government with religion. In Tilton v. Richardson, the Court held that this argument did not apply to a prohibitive degree with respect to federal grants, under the Higher Education Facilities Act of 1963, for the construction of facilities for nonreligious purposes by four church-related institutions of higher learning, three of which were Catholic, in Connecticut.

Amish Decision (1972): In a case appealed on behalf of Yoder, Miller and Yutzy, the Court ruled that Amish parents were exempt from a Wisconsin statute requiring them to send their children to school until the age of 16. The Court said in its decision that secondary schooling exposed Amish children to attitudes, goals and values contrary to their beliefs, and substantially hindered "the religious development of the Amish child and his integration into the way of life of the Amish faith-community at the crucial adolescent state of development."

Committee for Public Education and Religious Liberty, et al., v. Nyquist, et al., No. 72-694 (1973): The Court ruled that provisions of a 1972 New York statute were unconstitutional on the grounds that they were violative of the No Establishment Clause of the First Amendment and had the "impermissible effect" of advancing the sectarian activities of church-affiliated schools. The programs ruled unconstitutional concerned: (1) maintenance and repair grants, for facilities and equipment, to ensure the health, welfare and safety of students in nonpublic, non-profit elementary and secondary schools serving a high concentration of students from low income families; (2) tuition reimbursement ($50 per grade school child, $100 per high school student) for parents (with income less than $5,000) of children attending nonpublic elementary or secondary schools; tax deduction from adjusted gross income for parents failing to qualify under the above reimbursement plan, for each child attending a nonpublic school.

Sloan, Treasurer of Pennsylvania, et al., v. Lemon, et al., No. 72-459 (1973): The Court ruled unconstitutional a Pennsylvania Parent Reimbursement Act for Nonpublic Education which provided funds to reimburse parents (to a maximum of $150) for a portion of tuition expenses incurred in sending their children to nonpublic schools. The Court held that there was no significant difference between this and the New York tuition reimbursement program (above), and declared that the Equal Protection Clause of the Fourteenth Amendment cannot be relied upon to sustain a program held to be violative of the No Establishment Clause.

Levitt, et al., v. Committee for Public Education and Religious Liberty, et al., No. 72-269 (1973): The Court ruled unconstitutional the Mandated Services Act of 1970 under which New York provided $28 million ($27 per pupil from first to seventh grade, $45 per pupil from seventh to 12th grade) to reimburse nonpublic schools for testing, recording and reporting services required by the state. The Court declared that the act provided "impermissible aid" to religion in contravention of the No Establishment Clause.

In related decisions handed down June 25, 1973, the Court: (1) affirmed a lower court decision against the constitutionality of an Ohio tax credit law benefiting parents with children in nonpublic schools; (2) reinstated an injunction against a parent reimbursement program in New Jersey; (3) affirmed South Carolina's right to grant construction loans to church-affiliated colleges, and dismissed an appeal contesting its right to provide loans to students attending church-affiliated colleges **(Hunt v. McNair, Durham v. McLeod).**

Wheeler v. Barrera (1974): The Court ruled that nonpublic school students in Missouri must share in federal funds for educationally deprived students on a comparable basis with public school students under Title I of the Elementary and Secondary Education Act of 1965.

Norwood v. Harrison (93 S. Ct. 2804): The Court ruled that public assistance which avoids the prohibitions of the "effect" and "entanglement" tests (and which therefore does not substantially promote the religious mission of sectarian schools) may be confined to the secular functions of such schools.

Wiest v. Mt. Lebanon School District (1974): The Court upheld a lower court ruling that invocation and benediction prayers at public high school commencement ceremonies do not violate the principle of separation of Church and state.

Meek v. Pittenger (1975): The Court ruled unconstitutional portions of a Pennsylvania law providing auxiliary services for students of nonpublic schools; at the same time, it ruled in favor of provisions of the law permitting textbook loans to students of such schools. In denying the constitutionality of auxiliary services, the Court held that they had the "primary effect of establishing religion" and involved "excessive entanglement" of Church and state officials with respect to supervision; objection was also made against providing such services only on the premises of non-public schools and only at the request of such schools.

Roemer v. Board of Public Works of Maryland, 96 S. Ct. 2337 (1976): The Court ruled that a Maryland statute which authorized state funds to any private institution meeting certain minimal criteria was constitutional. The Court said the statute met the test previously outlined in Lemon v. Kurtzman because the colleges were not pervasively sectarian and the aid was in fact intended only for secular purposes.

Serbian Eastern Orthodox Diocese v. Milivojevich, 96 S. Ct. 2372 (1976): The Court held unconstitutional the decision of the Illinois Supreme Court that the Serbian Orthodox Church had arbitrarily removed one of its bishops and that its reorganization of the diocese was beyond the power of the church. The Court declared that the First Amendment does not permit civil courts to make ecclesiastical decisions.

TWA, Inc., v. Hardison, 75-1126; **International Association of Machinists and Aero Space Workers v. Hardison,** 75-1385 (1977): The Court ruled that federal civil rights legislation does not require employers to make more than minimal efforts to accommodate employees who want a particular working day off as their religion's Sabbath Day, and that an employer cannot accommodate such an employee by violating seniority systems determined by a union collective bargaining agreement. The Court noted that its ruling was not a constitutional judgment but an interpretation of existing law.

Wolman v. Walter (1977): The Court ruled constitutional portions of an Ohio statute providing tax-paid textbook loans and some auxiliary services (standardized and diagnostic testing, therapeutic and remedial services, off school premises) for nonpublic school students. It decided that other portions of the law, providing state funds for nonpublic school field trips and instructional materials (audio-visual equipment, maps, tape recorders), were unconstitutional.

THE WALL OF SEPARATION

Thomas Jefferson, in a letter written to the Danbury (Conn.) Baptist Association Jan. 1, 1802, coined the metaphor, "a wall of separation between Church and State," to express a theory concerning interpretation of the religion clauses of the First Amendment: "Congress shall make no law respecting an establishment of religion or prohibiting the free exercise thereof."

The metaphor was cited for the first time in judicial proceedings in 1879, in the opinion by Chief Justice Waite in Reynolds v. United States. It did not, however, figure substantially in the decision.

Accepted as Rule

In 1947 the wall of separation gained acceptance as a constitutional rule, in the decision handed down in Everson v. Board of Education. Associate Justice Black, in describing the principles involved in the No Establishment Clause, wrote:

"Neither a state nor the Federal Government can set up a church. Neither can pass laws which aid one religion, aid all religions, or prefer one religion over another. Neither can force nor influence a person to go to or to remain away from church against his will or force him to profess a belief or disbelief in any religion. No person can be punished for entertaining or professing religious beliefs or disbeliefs, for church attendance or non-attendance. No tax in any amount, large or small, can be levied to support any religious activities or institutions, whatever they may be called, or whatever form they may adopt to teach or practice religion. Neither a state nor the Federal Government can, openly or secretly, participate in the affairs of any religious organizations or groups and vice versa. In the words of Jefferson, the clause against establishment of religion by law was intended to erect 'a wall of separation between Church and State.' "

Mr. Black's associates agreed with his statement of principles, which were framed without reference to the Freedom of Exercise Clause. They disagreed, however, with respect to application of the principles, as the split decision in the case indicated. Five members of the Court held that the benefits of public welfare legislation — in this case, free bus transportation to school for parochial as well as public school students — did not run contrary to the concept of separation of Church and State embodied in the First Amendment.

Different Opinions

Inside and outside the legal profession, opinion is divided concerning the wall of separation and the balance of the religion clauses of the First Amendment.

The view of absolute separationists, carried to the extreme, would make government the adversary of religion. The bishops of the United States, following the McCollum decision in 1948, said that the wall metaphor had become for some persons the "shibboleth of doctrinaire secularism."

Proponents of governmental neutrality toward religion are of the opinion that such neutrality should not be so interpreted as to prohibit incidental aid to religious institutions providing secular services.

In the realm of practice, federal and state legislatures have enacted measures involving incidental benefits to religious bodies. Examples of such measures are the tax exemption of church property; provision of bus rides, book loans and lunch programs to students in church-related as well as public schools; military chaplaincies; loans to church-related hospitals; the financing of studies by military veterans at church-related colleges under GI bills of rights.

CHURCH TAX EXEMPTION

The exemption of church-owned property was ruled constitutional by the US Supreme Court May 4, 1970, in the case of Walz v. The Tax Commission of New York.

Suit in the case was brought by Frederick Walz, who purchased in June, 1967, a 22-by-29-foot plot of ground in Staten Island valued at $100 and taxable at $5.24 a year. Shortly after making the purchase, Walz instituted a suit in New York State, contending that the exemption of church property from taxation authorized by state law increased his own tax rate and forced him indirectly to support churches in violation of his constitutional right to freedom of religion under the First Amendment. Three New York courts dismissed the suit, which had been instituted by mail. The Supreme Court, judging that it had probable jurisdiction, then took the case.

In a 7-1 decision affecting Church-state relations in every state in the nation, the Court upheld the New York law under challenge.

For and Against

Chief Justice Warren E. Burger, who wrote the majority opinion, said that Congress from its earliest days had viewed the religion clauses of the Constitution as authorizing statutory real estate tax exemption to religious bodies. He declared: "Nothing in this national attitude toward religious tolerance and two centuries of uninterrupted freedom from taxation has given the remotest sign of leading to an established church or religion, and on the contrary it has operated affirmatively to help guarantee the free exercise of all forms of religious beliefs."

Justice William O. Douglas wrote in dissent that the involvement of government in religion as typified in tax exemption may seem inconsequential but: "It is, I fear, a long step down the establishment path.... Perhaps I have been misinformed. But, as I read the Constitution and the philosophy, I gathered that independence was the price of liberty."

Burger rejected Douglas' "establishment" fears. If tax exemption is the first step toward establishment, he said, "the second step has been long in coming."

The basic issue centered on the following question: Is there a contradiction between federal constitutional provisions against the establishment of religion, or the use of public funds for religious purposes, and state statutes exempting church property from taxation?

In the Walz' decision, the Supreme Court ruled that there is no contradiction.

Legal Background

The U.S. Constitution makes no reference to tax exemption.

There was no discussion of the issue in the Constitutional Convention nor in debates on the Bill of Rights.

In the Colonial and post-Revolutionary years, some churches had established status and were state-supported. This state of affairs changed with enactment of the First Amendment, which laid down no-establishment as the federal norm. This norm was adopted by the states which, however, exempted churches from tax liabilities.

No establishment, no hindrance, was the early American view of Church-state relationships.

This view, reflected in custom law, was not generally formulated in statute law until the second half of the 19th century, although specific tax exemption was provided for churches in Maryland in 1798, in Virginia in 1800, and in North Carolina in 1806.

The first major challenge to church property exemption was initiated by the Liberal League in the 1870's. It reached the point that President Grant included the recommendation in a State of the Union address in 1875, stating that church property should bear its own proportion of taxes. The plea fell on deaf ears in Congress, but there was some support for the idea at state levels. The exemption, however, continued to survive various challenges.

About 36 state constitutions contain either mandatory or permissive provisions for exemption. Statutes provide for exemption in all other states.

There has been considerable litigation challenging this special exemption, but most of it focused on whether a particular property satisfied statutory requirements. Few cases before Walz focused on the strictly constitutional question, whether directly under the First Amendment or indirectly under the Fourteenth Amendment.

Objections

Objectors to the tax exempt status of churches feel that churches should share, through taxation, in the cost of the ordinary benefits of public services they enjoy, and/or that the amount of "aid" enjoyed through exemption should be proportionate to the amount of social good they do.

According to one opinion, exemption is said to weaken the independence of churches from the political system which benefits them by exemption.

In another view, exemption is said to involve the government in decisions regarding what is and what is not religion.

Unrelated Income

Taxation of the unrelated business income of churches is a different matter. In a joint statement on this subject issued in May, 1969, the U.S. Catholic Conference and the National Council of Churches said they favored "elimination of the specific exemption of churches from taxation on income from regularly conducted commercial business activities which are unrelated to their exempt functions."

The two groups prefaced the statement with the observation:

"Under existing law many types of organizations are granted exemption from the income tax. Certain exempt organizations, including charitable, educational and some religious organizations, labor unions, business leagues, etc., are nevertheless subjected to tax upon their incomes from any unrelated business; and rents derived from debt-financed property (under leases for periods in excess of five years) are included in unrelated business taxable income.

"The tax upon unrelated business taxable income does not apply to churches, or conventions or associations of churches.

"Such exemption makes available to churches a potential advantage over taxpaying organizations engaged in commercial business activities."

U.S. Catholic Jurisdictions, Hierarchy, Statistics

The organizational structure of the Catholic Church in the United States consists of 32 provinces with as many archdioceses (metropolitan sees), 136 suffragan sees (dioceses), two jurisdictions immediately subject to the Holy See — the Eparchy of St. Maron for the Maronites and the Melkite Eparchy of Newton — and the Military Ordinariate. Each of these jurisdictions is under the direction of an archbishop or bishop, called an ordinary, who has apostolic responsibility and authority for the pastoral service of the people in his care.

The structure includes the territorial episcopal conference known as the National Conference of Catholic Bishops. In and through this body, which is strictly ecclesiastical and has defined juridical authority, the bishops exercise their collegiate pastorate over the Church in the entire country (see Index).

Related to the NCCB is the United States Catholic Conference, a civil corporation and operational secretariat through which the bishops, in cooperation with other members of the Church, act on a wider-than-ecclesiastical scale for the good of the Church and society in the United States (see Index).

The representative of the Holy See to the Church in this country is the Apostolic Delegate, Archbishop Jean Jadot (see Index).

ECCLESIASTICAL PROVINCES

(Sources: *The Official Catholic Directory*, NC News Service.)

The 32 ecclesiastical provinces bear the names of archdioceses, i.e., of metropolitan sees.

Anchorage: Archdiocese of Anchorage and suffragan sees of Fairbanks, Juneau. Geographical area: Alaska.

Atlanta: Archdiocese of Atlanta (Ga.) and suffragan sees of Savannah (Ga.), Charlotte and Raleigh (N.C.), Charleston (S.C.). Geographical area: Georgia, North Carolina, South Carolina.

Baltimore: Archdiocese of Baltimore (Md.) and suffragan sees of Wilmington (Del.), Arlington and Richmond (Va.), Wheeling-Charleston (W. Va.). Geographical area: Maryland (except five counties), Delaware, Virginia, West Virginia.

Boston: Archdiocese of Boston (Mass.) and suffragan sees of Fall River, Springfield and Worcester (Mass.), Portland (Me.), Manchester (N.H.), Burlington (Vt.). Geographical area: Massachusetts, Maine, New Hampshire, Vermont.

Chicago: Archdiocese of Chicago and suffragan sees of Belleville, Joliet, Peoria, Rockford, Springfield. Geographical area: Illinois.

Cincinnati: Archdiocese of Cincinnati and suffragan sees of Cleveland, Columbus, Steubenville, Toledo, Youngstown. Geographical area: Ohio.

Denver: Archdiocese of Denver (Colo.) and suffragan sees of Pueblo (Colo.), Cheyenne (Wyo.). Geographical area: Colorado, Wyoming.

Detroit: Archdiocese of Detroit and suffragan sees of Gaylord, Grand Rapids, Kalamazoo, Lansing, Marquette, Saginaw. Geographical area: Michigan.

Dubuque: Archdiocese of Dubuque and suffragan sees of Davenport, Des Moines, Sioux City. Geographical area: Iowa.

Hartford: Archdiocese of Hartford (Conn.) and suffragan sees of Bridgeport and Norwich (Conn.), Providence (R.I.). Geographical area: Connecticut, Rhode Island.

Indianapolis: Archdiocese of Indianapolis and suffragan sees of Evansville, Fort Wayne-South Bend, Gary, Lafayette. Geographical area: Indiana.

Kansas City (Kans.): Archdiocese of Kansas City and suffragan sees of Dodge City, Salina, Wichita. Geographical area: Kansas.

Los Angeles: Archdiocese of Los Angeles and suffragan sees of Fresno, Monterey, Orange, San Bernardino, San Diego. Geographical area: Southern and Central California.

Louisville: Archdiocese of Louisville (Ky.) and suffragan sees of Covington and Owensboro (Ky.), Memphis and Nashville (Tenn.). Geographical area: Kentucky, Tennessee.

Miami: Archdiocese of Miami and suffragan sees of Orlando, Pensacola-Tallahassee, St. Augustine, St. Petersburg. Geographical area: Florida.

Milwaukee: Archdiocese of Milwaukee and suffragan sees of Green Bay, La Crosse, Madison, Superior. Geographical area: Wisconsin.

Newark: Archdiocese of Newark and suffragan sees of Camden, Paterson, Trenton. Geographical area: New Jersey.

New Orleans: Archdiocese of New Orleans (La.) and suffragan sees of Alexandria-Shreveport, Baton Rouge, Houma-Thibodaux, and Lafayette (La.), Birmingham and Mobile (Ala.), Biloxi and Jackson (Miss.). Geographical area; Louisiana, Alabama, Mississippi.

New York: Archdiocese of New York and suffragan sees of Albany, Brooklyn, Buffalo, Ogdensburg, Rochester, Rockville Centre, Syracuse. Geographical area: New York.

Oklahoma City: Archdiocese of Oklahoma City (Okla.) and suffragan sees of Tulsa (Okla.) and Little Rock (Ark.). Geographical area: Oklahoma, Arkansas.

Omaha: Archdiocese of Omaha and suffragan sees of Grand Island, Lincoln. Geographical area: Nebraska.

Philadelphia: Archdiocese of Philadelphia and suffragan sees of Allentown, Altoona-Johnstown, Erie, Greensburg, Harrisburg, Pittsburgh, Scranton. Geographical area: Pennsylvania.

Philadelphia (Byzantine Rite): Metropolitan See of Philadelphia (Byzantine Rite) and Eparchies of St. Nicholas of the Ukrainians in Chicago and Stamford, Conn. The jurisdiction extends to all Ukrainian Catholics in the U.S. from the ecclesiastical province of Galicia in the Ukraine.

Pittsburgh (Byzantine Rite): Metropolitan See of Pittsburgh, Pa. and Eparchies of Passaic (N.J.), Parma (Ohio).

Portland: Archdiocese of Portland (Ore.) and suffragan sees of Baker (Ore.), Boise (Ida.), Great Falls and Helena (Mont.). Geographical area: Oregon, Idaho, Montana.

St. Louis: Archdiocese of St. Louis and suffragan sees of Jefferson City, Kansas City-St. Joseph, Springfield-Cape Girardeau. Geographical area: Missouri.

St. Paul and Minneapolis: Archdiocese of St. Paul and Minneapolis (Minn.) and suffragan sees of Crookston, Duluth, New Ulm, St. Cloud and Winona (Minn.), Bismarck and Fargo (N.D.), Rapid City and Sioux Falls (S.D.). Geographical area: Minnesota, North Dakota, South Dakota.

San Antonio: Archdiocese of San Antonio (Tex.) and suffragan sees of Amarillo, Austin, Beaumont, Brownsville, Corpus Christi, Dallas, Fort Worth, Galveston-Houston and San Angelo (Tex.). Geographical area: Texas (except the Diocese of El Paso).

San Francisco: Archdiocese of San Francisco (Calif.) and suffragan sees of Oakland, Sacramento, Santa Rosa and Stockton (Calif.), Agaña (Guam), Honolulu (Hawaii), Reno-Las Vegas (Nev.), Salt Lake City (Utah). Geographical area: Northern California, Nevada, Utah, Hawaii, Guam, the Marianas Islands and Ryukyus Islands.

Santa Fe: Archdiocese of Santa Fe (N.M.) and suffragan sees of Gallup (N.M.), Phoenix and Tucson (Ariz.), El Paso (Tex.). Geographical area: New Mexico, Arizona, Diocese of El Paso (Tex.).

Seattle: Archdiocese of Seattle and suffragan sees of Spokane, Yakima. Geographical area: Washington.

Washington: Archdiocese of Washington, D.C., and suffragan see of St. Thomas (Virgin Islands). Geographical area: District of Columbia, five counties of Maryland, Virgin Islands.

ARCHDIOCESES, DIOCESES, ARCHBISHOPS, BISHOPS

(Sources: *The Official Catholic Directory;* NC News Service. As of Oct. 15, 1979.)

Archdioceses are indicated by an asterisk.

Albany, N.Y. (1847): Howard J. Hubbard, bishop, 1977.

Former bishops: John McCloskey, 1847-64; John J. Conroy, 1865-77; Francis McNeirny, 1877-94; Thomas M. Burke, 1894-1915; Thomas F. Cusack, 1915-18; Edmund F. Gibbons, 1919-54; William A. Scully, 1954-69; Edwin B. Broderick, 1969-76.

Alexandria-Shreveport, La. (1853): Lawrence P. Graves, bishop, 1973. William B. Friend, auxiliary.

Established at Natchitoches, transferred to Alexandria 1910; present title 1977.

Former bishops: Augustus M. Martin, 1853-75; Francis X. Leray, 1877-79, administrator, 1879-83; Anthony Durier, 1885-1904; Cornelius Van de Ven, 1904-32; D. F. Desmond, 1933-45; Charles P. Greco, 1946-73.

Allentown, Pa. (1961): Joseph McShea, bishop, 1961.

Altoona-Johnstown, Pa. (1901): James J. Hogan, bishop, 1966.

Established as Altoona, name changed, 1957.

Former bishops: Eugene A. Garvey, 1901-20; John J. McCort, 1920-36; Richard T. Guilfoyle, 1936-57; Howard J. Carroll, 1958-60; J. Carroll McCormick, 1960-66.

Amarillo, Tex. (1926): Vacant as of Sept. 10, 1979.

Former bishops; Rudolph A. Gerken, 1927-33; Robert E. Lucey, 1934-41; Laurence J. Fitzsimon, 1941-58; John L. Morkovsky, 1958-63; Lawrence M. De Falco, 1963-79.

Anchorage,* Alaska (1966): Francis T. Hurley, archbishop, 1976.

Former archbishop: Joseph T. Ryan, 1966-75.

Arlington, Va. (1974): Thomas J. Welsh, bishop, 1974.

Atlanta,* Ga. (1956; archdiocese, 1962): Thomas A. Donnellan, archbishop, 1968.

Former ordinaries: Francis E. Hyland, 1956-61; Paul J. Hallinan, first archbishop, 1962-68.

Austin, Tex. (1947): Vincent M. Harris, bishop, 1971.

Former bishop: Louis J. Reicher, 1947-71.

Baker, Ore. (1903): Thomas J. Connolly, bishop, 1971.

Established as Baker City, name changed, 1952.

Former bishops: Charles J. O'Reilly, 1903-18; Joseph F. McGrath, 1919-50; Francis P. Leipzig, 1950-71.

Baltimore,* Md. (1789; archdiocese, 1808): William D. Borders, archbishop, 1974. T. Austin Murphy, P. Francis Murphy, J. Francis Stafford, auxiliaries.

Former ordinaries: John Carroll, 1789-1815, first archbishop; Leonard Neale, 1815-17; Ambrose Marechal, S.S., 1817-28; James Whitfield, 1828-34; Samuel Eccleston, S.S.,

1834-51; Francis P. Kenrick, 1851-63; Martin J. Spalding, 1864-72; James R. Bayley, 1872-77; Cardinal James Gibbons, 1877-1921; Michael J. Curley, 1921-47; Francis P. Keough, 1947-61, Cardinal Lawrence J. Shehan, 1961-74.

Baton Rouge, La. (1961): Joseph V. Sullivan, bishop, 1974.

Former bishop: Robert E. Tracy, 1961-74.

Beaumont, Tex. (1966): Bernard J. Ganter, bishop, 1977.

Former bishops: Vincent M. Harris, 1966-71; Warren L. Boudreaux, 1971-77.

Belleville, Ill. (1887): William M. Cosgrove, bishop, 1976. Stanley G. Schlarman, auxiliary.

Former bishops: John Janssen, 1888-1913; Henry Althoff, 1914-47; Albert R. Zuroweste, 1948-76.

Biloxi, Miss. (1977): (Joseph) Lawson E. Howze, bishop, 1977.

Birmingham, Ala. (1969): Joseph G. Vath, bishop, 1969.

Bismarck, N. Dak. (1909): Hilary B. Hacker, bishop, 1957.

Former bishops: Vincent Wehrle, O.S.B., 1910-39; Vincent J. Ryan, 1940-51; Lambert A. Hoch, 1952-56.

Boise, Ida. (1893): Sylvester Treinen, bishop, 1962.

Former bishops: Alphonse J. Glorieux, 1893-1917; Daniel M. Gorman, 1918-27; Edward J. Kelly, 1928-56; James J. Byrne, 1956-62.

Boston,* Mass. (1808; archdiocese, 1875): Cardinal Humberto S. Medeiros, archbishop, 1970. Lawrence J. Riley, Thomas V. Dailey, John M. D'Arcy, Joseph J. Ruocco, John J. Mulcahy, Daniel A. Hart, auxiliaries.

Former ordinaries: John L. de Cheverus, 1810-23; Benedict J. Fenwick, S.J., 1825-46; John B. Fitzpatrick, 1846-66; John J. Williams, 1866-1907, first archbishop; Cardinal William O'Connell, 1907-44; Cardinal Richard Cushing, 1944-70.

Bridgeport, Conn. (1953): Walter W. Curtis, bishop, 1961.

Former bishop: Lawrence J. Shehan, 1953-61.

Brooklyn, N.Y. (1853): Francis J. Mugavero, bishop, 1968. Charles R. Mulrooney, Joseph P. Denning, auxiliaries.

Former bishops: John Loughlin, 1853-91; Charles E. McDonnell, 1892-1921; Thomas E. Molloy, 1921-56; Bryan J. McEntegart, 1957-68.

Brownsville, Tex. (1965): John J. Fitzpatrick, bishop, 1971.

Former bishops: Adolph Marx, 1965; Humberto S. Medeiros, 1966-70.

Buffalo, N.Y. (1847): Edward D. Head, bishop, 1973. Pius A. Benincasa, Bernard J. McLaughlin, auxiliaries.

Former bishops: John Timon, C.M., 1847-67; Stephen V. Ryan, C.M., 1868-96; James E. Quigley, 1897-1903; Charles H. Colton, 1903-15; Dennis J. Dougherty, 1915-18; William Turner, 1919-36; John A. Duffy, 1937-44; John F. O'Hara, C.S.C., 1945-51; Joseph A. Burke, 1952-62; James McNulty, 1963-72.

Burlington, Vt. (1853): John A. Marshall, bishop, 1972.

Former bishops: Louis De Goesbriand, 1853-99; John S. Michaud, 1899-1908; Joseph J. Rice, 1910-38; Matthew F. Brady, 1938-44; Edward F. Ryan, 1945-56; Robert F. Joyce, 1957-71.

Camden, N.J. (1937): George H. Guilfoyle, bishop, 1968. James L. Schad, auxiliary.

Former bishops: Bartholomew J. Eustace, 1938-56; Justin J. McCarthy, 1957-59; Celestine J. Damiano, 1960-67.

Charleston, S.C. (1820): Ernest L. Unterkoefler, bishop, 1964.

Former bishops: John England, 1820-42; Ignatius W. Reynolds, 1844-55; Patrick N. Lynch, 1858-82; Henry P. Northrop, 1883-1916; William T. Russell, 1917-27; Emmet M. Walsh, 1927-49; John J. Russell, 1950-58; Paul J. Hallinan, 1958-62; Francis F. Reh, 1962-64.

Charlotte, N.C. (1971): Michael J. Begley, bishop, 1972.

Cheyenne, Wyo. (1887): Joseph Hart, bishop, 1978.

Former bishops: Maurice F. Burke, 1887-93; Thomas M. Lenihan, 1897-1901; James J. Keane, 1902-11; Patrick A. McGovern, 1912-51; Hubert M. Newell, 1951-78.

Chicago,* Ill. (1843; archdiocese, 1880): Cardinal John Cody, archbishop, 1965; Alfred L. Abramowicz, Nevin Hayes, O. Carm., auxiliaries.

Former ordinaries: William Quarter, 1844-48; James O. Van de Velde, S.J., 1849-53; Anthony O'Regan, 1854-58; James Duggan, 1859-70; Thomas P. Foley, administrator, 1870-79; Patrick A. Feehan, 1880-1902, first archbishop; James E. Quigley, 1903-15; Cardinal George Mundelein, 1915-39; Cardinal Samuel Stritch, 1939-58; Cardinal Albert Meyer, 1958-65.

Cincinnati,* Ohio (1821; archdiocese, 1850): Joseph L. Bernardin, archbishop, 1972. Nicholas Elko, (titular archbishop), Daniel E. Pilarczyk, auxiliaries.

Former ordinaries: Edward D. Fenwick, O.P., 1822-32; John B. Purcell, 1833-83, first archbishop; William H. Elder, 1883-1904; Henry Moeller, 1904-1925; John T. McNicholas, O.P., 1925-50; Karl J. Alter, 1950-69; Paul F. Leibold, 1969-72.

Cleveland, Ohio (1847): James A. Hickey, bishop, 1974. Gilbert I. Sheldon, James P. Lyke, O.F.M., James A. Griffin, Anthony M. Pilla, auxiliaries.

Former bishops: L. Amadeus Rappe, 1847-70; Richard Gilmour, 1872-91; Ignatius F. Horstmann, 1892-1908; John P. Farrelly, 1909-21; Joseph Schrembs, 1921-45; Edward

F. Hoban, 1945-66; Clarence G. Issenmann, 1966-74.

Columbus, Ohio (1868): Edward J. Herrmann, bishop, 1973. George A. Fulcher, auxiliary.

Former bishops: Sylvester H. Rosecrans, 1868-78; John A. Watterson, 1880-99; Henry Moeller, 1900-03; James J. Hartley, 1904-44; Michael J. Ready, 1944-57; Clarence Issenmann, 1957-64; John J. Carberry, 1965-68; Clarence E. Elwell, 1968-73.

Corpus Christi, Tex. (1912): Thomas J. Drury, bishop, 1965.

Former bishops; Paul J. Nussbaum, C.P., 1913-20; Emmanuel B. Ledvina, 1921-49; Mariano S. Garriga, 1949-65.

Covington, Ky. (1853): William A. Hughes, bishop, 1979.

Former bishops: George A. Carrell, S.J., 1853-68; Augustus M. Toebbe, 1870-84; Camillus P. Maes, 1885-1914; Ferdinand Brossart, 1916-23; Francis W. Howard, 1923-44; William T. Mulloy, 1945-59; Richard Ackerman, C.S.Sp., 1960-79.

Crookston, Minn. (1909): Victor Balke, bishop, 1976.

Former bishops: Timothy Corbett, 1910-38; John H. Peschges, 1938-44; Francis J. Schenk, 1945-60; Laurence A. Glenn, 1960-70; Kenneth J. Povish, 1970-75.

Dallas, Tex. (1890): Thomas Tschoepe, bishop, 1969.

Established 1890, as Dallas, title changed to Dallas-Ft. Worth 1953; redesignated Dallas, 1969, when Ft. Worth was made diocese.

Former bishops: Thomas F. Brennan, 1891-92; Edward J. Dunne, 1893-1910; Joseph P. Lynch, 1911-54; Thomas K. Gorman, 1954-69.

Davenport, Ia. (1881): Gerald F. O'Keefe, bishop, 1966.

Former bishops: John McMullen, 1881-83; Henry Cosgrove, 1884-1906; James Davis, 1906-26; Henry P. Rohlman, 1927-44; Ralph L. Hayes, 1944-66.

Denver,* Colo. (1887; archdiocese, 1941): James V. Casey, archbishop, 1967. George R. Evans, Richard C. Hanifen, auxiliaries.

Former ordinaries: Joseph P. Machebeuf, 1887-89; Nicholas C. Matz, 1889-1917; J. Henry Tihen, 1917-31; Urban J. Vehr, 1931-67, first archbishop.

Des Moines, Ia. (1911): Maurice J. Dingman, bishop, 1968.

Former bishops: Austin Dowling, 1912-19; Thomas W. Drumm, 1919-33; Gerald T. Bergan, 1934-48; Edward C. Daly, O.P., 1948-64; George J. Biskup, 1965-67.

Detroit,* Mich. (1833; archdiocese, 1937): Cardinal John F. Dearden, archbishop, 1958. Thomas J. Gumbleton, Walter J. Schoenherr, Arthur H. Krawczak, auxiliaries.

Former ordinaries: Frederic Rese, 1833-71; Peter P. Lefevere, administrator, 1841-69; Caspar H. Borgess, 1871-88; John S. Foley, 1888-1918; Michael J. Gallagher, 1918-37; Cardinal Edward Mooney, 1937-58, first archbishop.

Dodge City, Kans. (1951): Eugene J. Gerber, bishop, 1977.

Former bishops: John B. Franz, 1951-59; Marion F. Forst, 1960-76.

Dubuque,* Iowa (1837; archdiocese, 1893): James J. Byrne, archbishop, 1962. Francis J. Dunn, auxiliary.

Former ordinaries: Mathias Loras, 1837-58; Clement Smyth, O.C.S.O., 1858-65; John Hennessy, 1866-1900, first archbishop; John J. Keane, 1900-11; James J. Keane, 1911-29; Francis J. Beckman, 1930-46; Henry P. Rohlman, 1946-54; Leo Binz, 1954-61.

Duluth, Minn. (1889): Paul F. Anderson, bishop, 1969.

Former bishops: James McGolrick, 1889-1918; John T. McNicholas, O.P., 1918-25; Thomas A. Welch, 1926-59; Francis J. Schenk, 1960-69.

El Paso, Tex. (1914): Vacant as of Oct. 15, 1979.

Former bishops: Anthony J. Schuler, S.J., 1915-42; Sidney M. Metzger, 1942-78. Patrick F. Flores, 1978-79.

Erie, Pa. (1853): Alfred M. Watson, bishop, 1969. Michael J. Murphy, coadjutor.

Former bishops: Michael O'Connor, 1853-54; Josue M. Young, 1854-66; Tobias Mullen, 1868-99; John E. Fitzmaurice, 1899-1920; John M. Gannon, 1920-66; John F. Whealon, 1966-69.

Evansville, Ind. (1944): Francis Raymond Shea, bishop, 1970.

Former bishops: Henry J. Grimmelsman, 1944-65; Paul F. Leibold, 1966-69.

Fairbanks, Alaska (1962): Robert L. Whelan, S.J., bishop, 1968.

Former bishop: Francis D. Gleeson, S.J., 1948-68.

Fall River, Mass. (1904): Daniel A. Cronin, bishop, 1970.

Former bishops: William Stang, 1904-07; Daniel F. Feehan, 1907-34; James E. Cassidy, 1934-51; James L. Connolly, 1951-70.

Fargo, N. Dak. (1889): Justin A. Driscoll, bishop, 1970.

Established at Jamestown, transferred, 1897.

Former bishops: John Shanley, 1889-1909; James O'Reilly, 1910-34; Aloysius J. Muench, 1935-59; Leo F. Dworschak, 1960-70.

Fort Wayne-South Bend, Ind. (1857): William E. McManus, bishop, 1976. Joseph R. Crowley, auxiliary.

Established as Fort Wayne, name changed, 1960.

Former bishops: John H. Luers, 1858-71; Joseph Dwenger, C.Pp. S., 1872-93; Joseph Rademacher, 1893-1900; Herman J. Alerding, 1900-24; John F. Noll, 1925-56; Leo A. Pursley, 1957-76.

Fort Worth, Tex. (1969): John J. Cassata, bishop, 1969.

Fresno, Calif. (1967): Hugh A. Donohoe, bishop, 1969. Roger M. Mahony, auxiliary.

Formerly Monterey-Fresno, 1922.

Former bishops (Monterey-Fresno): John J. Cantwell, administrator, 1922-24; John B. MacGinley, first bishop, 1924-32; Philip G. Sher, 1933-53; Aloysius J. Willinger, 1953-67.

Former bishop (Fresno): Timothy Manning, 1967-69.

Gallup, N. Mex. (1939): Jerome J. Hastrich, bishop, 1969.

Former bishop: Bernard T. Espelage, O.F.M., 1940-69.

Galveston-Houston, Tex. (1847): John L. Morkovsky, bishop, 1975. John E. McCarthy, auxiliary.

Established as Galveston, name changed, 1959.

Former bishops: John M. Odin, C.M., 1847-61; Claude M. Dubuis, 1862-92; Nicholas A. Gallagher, 1892-1918; Christopher E. Byrne, 1918-50; Wendelin J. Nold, 1950-75.

Gary, Ind. (1957): Andrew G. Grutka, bishop, 1957.

Gaylord, Mich. (1971): Edmund C. Szoka, bishop, 1971.

Grand Island, Neb. (1912): Lawrence McNamara, bishop, 1978.

Established at Kearney, transferred, 1917.

Former bishops: James A. Duffy, 1913-31; Stanislaus V. Bona, 1932-44; Edward J. Hunkeler, 1945-51; John L. Paschang, 1951-72; John J. Sullivan, 1972-77.

Grand Rapids, Mich. (1882): Joseph Breitenbeck, bishop, 1969. Joseph C. McKinney, auxiliary.

Former bishops: Henry J. Richter, 1883-1916; Michael J. Gallagher, 1916-18; Edward D. Kelly, 1919-26; Joseph G. Pinten, 1926-40; Joseph C. Plagens, 1941-43; Francis J. Haas, 1943-53; Allen J. Babcock, 1954-69.

Great Falls, Mont. (1904): Thomas J. Murphy, bishop, 1978.

Former bishops: Mathias C. Lenihan, 1904-30; Edwin V. O'Hara, 1930-39; William J. Condon, 1939-67; Eldon B. Schuster, 1968-77.

Green Bay, Wis. (1868): Aloysius J. Wycislo, bishop, 1968. Robert F. Morneau, auxiliary.

Former bishops: Joseph Melcher, 1868-73; Francis X. Krautbauer, 1875-85; Frederick X. Katzer, 1886-91; Sebastian G. Messmer, 1892-1903; Joseph J. Fox, 1904-14; Paul P. Rhode, 1915-45; Stanislaus V. Bona, 1945-67.

Greensburg, Pa. (1951): William G. Connare, bishop, 1960. Norbert F. Gaughan, auxiliary.

Former bishop: Hugh L. Lamb, 1951-59.

Harrisburg, Pa. (1868): Joseph T. Daley, bishop, 1971. William H. Keeler, auxiliary.

Former bishops: Jeremiah F. Shanahan, 1868-86; Thomas McGovern, 1888-98; John W. Shanahan, 1899-1916; Philip R. McDevitt, 1916-35; George L. Leech, 1935-71.

Hartford,* Conn. (1843; archdiocese, 1953): John F. Whealon, archbishop, 1969. John F. Hackett, Peter A. Rosazza, auxiliaries.

Former ordinaries: William Tyler, 1844-49; Bernard O'Reilly, 1850-56; F. P. MacFarland, 1858-74; Thomas Galberry, O.S.A., 1876-78; Lawrence S. McMahon, 1879-93; Michael Tierney, 1894-1908; John J. Nilan, 1910-34; Maurice F. McAuliffe, 1934-44; Henry J. O'Brien, 1945-68, first archbishop.

Helena, Mont. (1884): Elden F. Curtiss, bishop, 1976.

Former bishops: John B. Brondel, 1884-1903; John P. Carroll, 1904-25; George J. Finnigan, C.S.C., 1927-32; Ralph L. Hayes, 1933-35; Joseph M. Gilmore, 1936-62; Raymond Hunthausen, 1962-75.

Honolulu, Hawaii (1941): John J. Scanlan, bishop, 1968. Joseph A. Ferrario, auxiliary.

Former bishop: James J. Sweeney, 1941-68.

Houma-Thibodaux, La. (1977): Warren L. Boudreaux, bishop, 1977.

Indianapolis,* Ind. (1834; archdiocese, 1944): Vacant as of Sept. 10, 1979.

Established at Vincennes, transferred, 1898.

Former ordinaries: Simon G. Bruté, 1834-39; Celestine de la Hailandiere, 1839-47; John S. Bazin, 1847-48; Maurice de St. Palais, 1849-77; Francis S. Chatard, 1878-1918; Joseph Chartrand, 1918-33; Joseph E. Ritter, 1934-46, first archbishop; Paul C. Schulte, 1946-70; George J. Biskup, 1970-79.

Jackson, Miss. (1837): Joseph B. Brunini, bishop, 1968. William R. Houck, auxiliary.

Established at Natchez; title changed to Natchez-Jackson, 1956; transferred to Jackson, 1977 (Natchez made titular see).

Former bishops: John J. Chanche, S.S., 1841-52; James Van de Velde, S.J., 1853-55; William H. Elder, 1857-80; Francis A. Jansens, 1881-88; Thomas Heslin, 1889-1911; John E. Gunn, S.M., 1911-24; Richard O. Gerow, 1924-67.

Jefferson City, Mo. (1956): Michael F. McAuliffe, bishop, 1969.

Former bishop: Joseph Marling, C.Pp.S., 1956-69.

Joliet, Ill. (1948): Joseph Imesch, bishop, 1979. Raymond J. Vonesh, Daniel Kucera, O.S.B., auxiliaries.

Former bishop: Martin D. McNamara, 1949-66. Romeo Blanchette, 1966-79.

Juneau, Alaska (1951): Michael Kenny, bishop, 1979.

Former bishops: Dermot O'Flanagan, 1951-68; Joseph T. Ryan, administrator, 1968-71; Francis T. Hurley, 1971-76, administrator, 1976-79.

Kalamazoo, Mich. (1971): Paul V. Donovan, bishop, 1971.

Kansas City,* Kans. (1877; archdiocese,

1952); Ignatius J. Strecker, archbishop, 1969. Marion F. Forst, auxiliary.

Established as vicariate apostolic, 1850, became Diocese of Leavenworth, 1877, transferred to Kansas City 1947.

Former ordinaries: J. B. Miege, vicar apostolic, 1851-74; Louis M. Fink, O.S.B., vicar apostolic, 1874-77, first bishop, 1877-1904; Thomas F. Lillis, 1904-10; John Ward, 1910-29; Francis Johannes, 1929-37; Paul C. Schulte, 1937-46; George J. Donnelly, 1946-50; Edward Hunkeler, 1951-69, first archbishop.

Kansas City-St. Joseph, Mo. (Kansas City, 1880; St. Joseph, 1868; united 1956): John J. Sullivan, bishop, 1977. George K. Fitzsimons, auxiliary.

Former bishops (Kansas City): John J. Hogan, 1880-1913; Thomas F. Lillis, 1913-38; Edwin V. O'Hara, 1939-56; John P. Cody, 1956-61; Charles H. Helmsing, 1962-77.

Former bishops (St. Joseph): John J. Hogan, 1868-80, administrator, 1880-93; Maurice F. Burke, 1893-1923; Francis Gilfillan, 1923-33; Charles H. Le Blond, 1933-56.

La Crosse, Wis. (1868): Frederick W. Freking, bishop, 1965. John J. Paul, auxiliary.

Former bishops: Michael Heiss, 1868-80; Kilian C. Flasch, 1881-91; James Schwebach, 1892-1921; Alexander J. McGavick, 1921-48; John P. Treacy, 1948-64.

Lafayette, Ind. (1944): Raymond J. Gallagher, bishop, 1965.

Former bishops: John G. Bennett, 1944-57; John J. Carberry, 1957-65.

Lafayette, La. (1918): Gerard L. Frey, bishop, 1973.

Former bishops: Jules B. Jeanmard, 1918-56; Maurice Schexnayder, 1956-72.

Lansing, Mich. (1937): Kenneth J. Povish, bishop, 1975. James Sullivan, auxiliary.

Former bishops: Joseph H. Albers, 1937-65; Alexander Zaleski, 1965-75.

Lincoln, Neb. (1887): Glennon P. Flavin, bishop, 1967.

Former bishops: Thomas Bonacum, 1887-1911; J. Henry Tihen, 1911-17; Charles J. O'Reilly, 1918-23; Francis J. Beckman, 1924-30; Louis B. Kucera, 1930-57; James V. Casey, 1957-67.

Little Rock, Ark. (1843): Andrew J. McDonald, bishop, 1972.

Former bishops: Andrew Byrne, 1844-62; Edward Fitzgerald, 1867-1907; John Morris, 1907-46; Albert L. Fletcher, 1946-72.

Los Angeles,* Calif. (1840; archdiocese, 1936): Cardinal Timothy Manning, archbishop, 1970. John J. Ward, Juan A. Arzube, Thaddeus A. Shubsda, Manuel D. Moreno, auxiliaries.

Former ordinaries: Francisco Garcia Diego y Moreno, O.F.M., 1840-46; Joseph S. Alemany, O.P., 1850-53; Thaddeus Amat, C.M., 1854-78; Francis Mora, 1878-96; George T. Montgomery, 1896-1903; Thomas J. Conaty, 1903-15; John J. Cantwell, 1917-47, first archbishop; Cardinal James McIntyre, 1948-70.

Louisville,* Ky. (1808; archdiocese, 1937): Thomas J. McDonough, archbishop, 1967. Charles G. Maloney, auxiliary.

Established at Bardstown, transferred, 1841.

Former ordinaries: Benedict J. Flaget, S.S. 1810-32; John B. David, S.S., 1832-33; Benedict J. Flaget, S.S., 1833-50; Martin J. Spalding, 1850-64; Peter J. Lavialle, 1865-67; William G. McCloskey, 1868-1909; Denis O'Donaghue, 1910-24; John A. Floersh, 1924-67, first archbishop.

Madison, Wis. (1946): Cletus F. O'Donnell, bishop, 1967. George O. Wirz, auxiliary.

Former bishop: William P. O'Connor, 1946-67.

Manchester, N.H. (1884): Odore J. Gendron, bishop, 1974. Robert Mulvee, auxiliary.

Former bishops: Denis M. Bradley, 1884-1903; John B. Delany, 1904-06; George A. Guertin, 1907-32; John B. Peterson, 1932-44; Matthew F. Brady, 1944-59; Ernest J. Primeau, 1960-74.

Marquette, Mich. (1857): Mark F. Schmitt, bishop, 1978.

Former bishops: Frederic Baraga, 1857-68; Ignatius Mrak, 1869-78; John Vertin, 1879-99; Frederick Eis, 1899-1922; Paul J. Nussbaum, C.P., 1922-35; Joseph C. Plagens, 1935-40; Francis Magner, 1941-47; Thomas L. Noa, 1947-68; Charles A. Salatka, 1968-77.

Memphis, Tenn. (1970): Carroll T. Dozier, bishop, 1971.

Miami,* Fla. (1958; archdiocese, 1968): Edward McCarthy, archbishop, 1977. John J. Nevins, Agustin A. Roman, auxiliaries.

Former ordinary: Coleman F. Carroll, 1958-77, first archbishop.

Milwaukee,* Wis. (1843; archdiocese, 1875): Rembert G. Weakland, O.S.B., archbishop, 1977. Leo J. Brust, auxiliary.

Former ordinaries: John M. Henni, 1844-81, first archbishop; Michael Heiss, 1881-90; Frederick X. Katzer, 1891-1903; Sebastian G. Messmer, 1903-30; Samuel A. Stritch, 1930-39; Moses E. Kiley, 1940-53; Albert G. Meyer, 1953-58; William E. Cousins, 1959-77.

Mobile, Ala. (1829): John L. May, bishop, 1969.

Former bishops: Michael Portier, 1829-59; John Quinlan, 1859-83; Dominic Manucy, 1884; Jeremiah O'Sullivan, 1885-96; Edward P. Allen, 1897-1926; Thomas J. Toolen, 1927-69.

Monterey in California (1967): Harry A. Clinch, bishop, 1967.

Formerly Monterey-Fresno, 1922.

Former bishops (Monterey-Fresno): John J. Cantwell, administrator, 1922-24; John B. MacGinley, first bishop, 1924-32; Philip G. Sher, 1933-53; Aloysius J. Willinger, 1953-67.

Nashville, Tenn. (1837): James D. Niedergeses, bishop, 1975.

Former bishops: Richard P. Miles, O.P., 1838-60; James Whelan, O.P., 1860-64; Patrick A. Feehan, 1865-80; Joseph Rademacher, 1883-93; Thomas S. Byrne, 1894-1923; Alphonse J. Smith, 1924-35; William L. Adrian, 1936-69; Joseph A. Durick, 1969-75.

Newark,* N.J. (1853; archdiocese, 1937): Peter L. Gerety, archbishop, 1974. John J. Dougherty, Jerome Pechillo, T.O.R., Robert F. Garner, Joseph A. Francis, S.V.D., Dominic A. Marconi, auxiliaries.

Former ordinaries: James R. Bayley, 1853-72; Michael A. Corrigan, 1873-80; Winand M. Wigger, 1881-1901; John J. O'Connor, 1901-27; Thomas J. Walsh, 1928-52, first archbishop; Thomas A. Boland, 1953-74.

New Orleans,* La. (1793; archdiocese, 1850): Philip M. Hannan, archbishop, 1965. Harold R. Perry, S. V. D., Stanley J. Ott, auxiliaries.

Former ordinaries: Luis Penalver y Cardenas, 1793-1801; John Carroll, administrator, 1809-15; W. Louis Dubourg, S.S., 1815-25; Joseph Rosati, C.M., administrator, 1826-29; Leo De Neckere, C.M., 1829-33; Anthony Blanc, 1835-60, first archbishop; Jean Marie Odin, C.M., 1861-70; Napoleon J. Perche, 1870-83; Francis X. Leray, 1883-87; Francis A. Janssens, 1888-97; Placide L. Chapelle, 1897-1905; James H. Blenk, S.M., 1906-17; John W. Shaw, 1918-34; Joseph F. Rummel, 1935-64; John P. Cody, 1964-65.

Newton, Mass. (Melkite Rite) (1966; eparchy, 1976): Archbishop Joseph Tawil, exarch, 1969, first eparch, 1976.

Former ordinary: Justin Najmy, 1966-68.

New Ulm, Minn. (1957): Raymond A. Lucker, bishop, 1975.

Former bishop: Alphonse J. Schladweiler, 1958-76.

New York,* N.Y. (1808; archdiocese, 1850): Cardinal Terence J. Cooke, archbishop, 1968. John J. Maguire, coadjutor archbishop, 1965. Patrick V. Ahern, James P. Mahoney, Anthony F. Mestice, Theodore McCarrick, Austin Vaughan, Francisco Garmendia, auxiliaries.

Former ordinaries: Richard L. Concanen, O.P., 1808-10; John Connolly, O.P., 1814-25; John Dubois, S.S., 1826-42; John J. Hughes, 1842-64, first archbishop; Cardinal John McCloskey, 1864-85; Michael A. Corrigan, 1885-1902; Cardinal John Farley, 1902-18; Cardinal Patrick Hayes, 1919-38; Cardinal Francis Spellman, 1939-67.

Norwich, Conn. (1953): Daniel P. Reilly, bishop, 1975.

Former bishops: Bernard J. Flanagan, 1953-59; Vincent J. Hines, 1960-75.

Oakland, Calif. (1962): John S. Cummins, bishop, 1977.

Former bishop: Floyd L. Begin, 1962-77.

Ogdensburg, N.Y. (1872): Stanislaus Brzana, bishop, 1968.

Former bishops: Edgar P. Wadhams, 1872-91; Henry Gabriels, 1892-1921; Joseph H. Conroy, 1921-39; Francis J. Monaghan, 1939-42; Bryan J. McEntegart, 1943-53; Walter P. Kellenberg, 1954-57; James J. Navagh, 1957-63; Leo R. Smith, 1963; Thomas A. Donnellan, 1964-68.

Oklahoma City,* Okla. (1905; archdiocese, 1972): Charles A. Salatka, archbishop, 1977.

Former ordinaries: Theophile Meerschaert, 1905-24; Francis C. Kelley, 1924-48; Eugene J. McGuinness, 1948-57; Victor J. Reed, 1958-71; John R. Quinn, 1971-77, first archbishop.

Omaha,* Nebr. (1885; archdiocese, 1945): Daniel E. Sheehan, archbishop, 1969.

Former ordinaries: James O'Gorman, O.C.S.O., 1859-74, vicar apostolic; James O'Connor, vicar apostolic, 1876-85, first bishop, 1885-90; Richard Scannell, 1891-1916; Jeremiah J. Harty, 1916-27; Francis Beckman, administrator, 1926-28; Joseph F. Rummel, 1928-35; James H. Ryan, 1935-47, first archbishop; Gerald T. Bergan, 1948-69.

Orange, Calif. (1976): William R. Johnson, bishop, 1976.

Orlando, Fla. (1968): Thomas J. Grady, bishop, 1974.

Former bishop: William Borders, 1968-74.

Owensboro, Ky. (1937): Henry J. Soenneker, bishop, 1961.

Former bishop: Francis R. Cotton, 1938-60.

Parma, Ohio (Byzantine Rite) (1969): Emil Mihalik, eparch, 1969.

Passaic, N.J. (Byzantine Rite) (1963): Michael J. Dudick, eparch, 1968. Thomas V. Dolinay, auxiliary.

Former bishop: Stephen Kocisko, 1963-68.

Paterson, N.J. (1937): Frank J. Rodimer, bishop, 1978.

Former bishops: Thomas H. McLaughlin, 1937-47; Thomas A. Boland, 1947-52; James A. McNulty, 1953-63; James J. Navagh, 1963-65; Lawrence B. Casey, 1966-77.

Pensacola-Tallahassee, Fla. (1975): Rene H. Gracida, bishop, 1975.

Peoria, Ill. (1877): Edward W. O'Rourke, bishop, 1971.

Former bishops: John L. Spalding, 1877-1908; Edmund M. Dunne, 1909-29; Joseph H. Schlarman, 1930-51; William E. Cousins, 1952-58; John B. Franz, 1959-71.

Philadelphia,* Pa. (1808; archdiocese, 1875): Cardinal John Krol, archbishop, 1961. Gerald V. McDevitt, John J. Graham, Martin Lohmuller, Edward T. Hughes, auxiliaries.

Former ordinaries: Michael Egan, O.F.M., 1810-14; Henry Conwell, 1820-42; Francis P. Kenrick, 1842-51; John N. Neumann, C.SS.R., 1852-60; James F. Wood, 1860-83, first archbishop; Patrick J. Ryan, 1884-1911;

Edmond F. Prendergast, 1911-18; Cardinal Dennis Dougherty, 1918-51; Cardinal John O'Hara, C.S.C., 1951-60.

Philadelphia,* Pa. (Byzantine Rite) (1924; metropolitan, 1958): Myroslav J. Lubachivsky, archbishop, 1979.
Former ordinaries: Stephen Ortynsky, O.S.B.M., 1907-16; Constantine Bohachevsky, 1924-61; Ambrose Senyshyn, O.S.B.M., 1961-76; Joseph Schmondiuk, 1977-78.

Phoenix, Ariz. (1969): James S. Rausch, bishop, 1977.
Former bishop: Edward A. McCarthy, 1969-76.

Pittsburgh,* Pa. (Byzantine Rite) (1924; metropolitan, 1969): Stephen J. Kocisko, eparch, 1968, first metropolitan, 1969. John Bilock, auxiliary.
Former ordinaries: Basil Takach 1924-48; Daniel Ivancho, 1948-54; Nicholas T. Elko, 1955-67.

Pittsburgh, Pa. (1843): Vincent M. Leonard, bishop, 1969. John B. McDowell, Anthony G. Bosco, auxiliaries.
Former bishops: Michael O'Connor, 1843-53, 1854-60; Michael Domenec, C.M., 1860-76; J. Tuigg, 1876-89; Richard Phelan, 1889-1904; J.F. Regis Canevin, 1904-20; Hugh C. Boyle, 1921-55; John F. Dearden, 1950-58; John J. Wright, 1959-69.

Portland, Me. (1853): Edward C. O'Leary, bishop, 1974. Amedee W. Proulx, auxiliary.
Former bishops: David W. Bacon, 1855-74; James A. Healy, 1875-1900; William H. O'Connell, 1901-06; Louis S. Walsh, 1906-24; John G. Murray, 1925-31; Joseph E. McCarthy, 1932-55; Daniel J. Feeney, 1955-69; Peter L. Gerety, 1969-74.

Portland,* Ore. (1846): Cornelius M. Power, archbishop, 1974. Paul E. Waldschmidt, C.S.C., Kenneth D. Steiner, auxiliaries.
Established as Oregon City, name changed, 1928.
Former ordinaries: Francis N. Blanchet, 1846-80 vicar apostolic, first archbishop; Charles J. Seghers, 1880-84; William H. Gross, C.SS.R., 1885-98; Alexander Christie, 1899-1925; Edward D. Howard, 1926-66; Robert J. Dwyer, 1966-74.

Providence, R.I. (1872): Louis E. Gelineau, bishop, 1972. Kenneth A. Angell, auxiliary.
Former bishops: Thomas F. Hendricken, 1872-86; Matthew Harkins, 1887-1921; William A. Hickey, 1921-33; Francis P. Keough, 1934-47; Russell J. McVinney, 1948-71.

Pueblo, Colo. (1941): Vacant as of Oct. 15, 1979.
Former bishops: Joseph C. Willging, 1942-59; Charles A. Buswell, 1959-79.

Raleigh, N.C. (1924): F. Joseph Gossman, bishop, 1975. George E. Lynch, auxiliary.
Former bishops: William J. Hafey, 1925-37; Eugene J. McGuinness, 1937-44; Vincent S. Waters, 1945-75.

Rapid City, S. Dak. (1902): Harold J. Dimmerling, bishop, 1969.
Established at Lead, transferred, 1920.
Former bishops: John Stariha, 1902-09; Joseph F. Busch, 1910-15; John J. Lawler, 1916-48; William T. McCarty, C.SS.R., 1948-69.

Reno-Las Vegas, Nev. (1931): Norman McFarland, bishop, 1976.
Established at Reno; title changed to Reno-Las Vegas, 1976.
Former bishops: Thomas K. Gorman, 1931-52; Robert J. Dwyer, 1952-66; Joseph Green, 1967-74.

Richmond, Va. (1820): Walter F. Sullivan, bishop, 1974.
Former bishops: Patrick Kelly, 1820-22; Richard V. Whelan, 1841-50; John McGill, 1850-72; James Gibbons, 1872-77; John J. Keane, 1878-88; Augustine Van de Vyver, 1889-1911; Denis J. O'Connell, 1912-26; Andrew J. Brennan, 1926-45; Peter L. Ireton, 1945-58; John J. Russell, 1958-73.

Rochester, N.Y. (1868): Matthew H. Clark, bishop, 1979. Dennis W. Hickey, John E. McCafferty, auxiliaries.
Former bishops: Bernard J. McQuaid, 1868-1909; Thomas F. Hickey, 1909-28; John F. O'Hern, 1929-33; Edward F. Mooney, 1933-37; James E. Kearney, 1937-66; Fulton J. Sheen, 1966-69; Joseph L. Hogan, 1969-78.

Rockford, Ill. (1908): Arthur J. O'Neill, bishop, 1968.
Former bishops: Peter J. Muldoon, 1908-27; Edward F. Hoban, 1928-42; John J. Boylan, 1943-53; Raymond P. Hillinger, 1953-56; Loras T. Lane, 1956-68.

Rockville Centre, N.Y. (1957): John R. McGann, bishop, 1976. Gerald Ryan, James Daly, auxiliaries.
Former bishop: Walter P. Kellenberg, 1957-76.

Sacramento, Calif. (1886): Vacant as of Sept. 10, 1979.
Former bishops: Patrick Manogue, 1886-95; Thomas Grace, 1896-1921; Patrick J. Keane, 1922-28; Robert J. Armstrong, 1929-57; Joseph T. McGucken, 1957-62; Alden J. Bell, 1962-79.

Saginaw, Mich. (1938): Francis F. Reh, bishop, 1969.
Former bishops: William F. Murphy, 1938-50; Stephen S. Woznicki, 1950-68.

St. Augustine, Fla. (1870): John J. Snyder, bishop, 1979.
Former bishops: Augustin Verot, S.S., 1870-76; John Moore, 1877-1901; William J. Kenny, 1902-13; Michael J. Curley, 1914-21; Patrick J. Barry, 1922-40; Joseph P. Hurley, 1940-67; Paul F. Tanner, 1968-79.

St. Cloud, Minn. (1889): George H. Speltz, bishop, 1968.
Former bishops: Otto Zardetti, 1889-94; Martin Marty, O.S.B., 1895-96; James Trobec, 1897-1914; Joseph F. Busch, 1915-53; Peter Bartholome, 1953-68.

St. Louis,* Mo. (1826; archdiocese, 1847): Vacant as of Sept. 10, 1979. George J. Gottwald, Charles R. Koester, Edward T. O'Meara, John Wurm, auxiliaries.

Former ordinaries: Joseph Rosati, C.M., 1827-43; Peter R. Kenrick, 1843-95, first archbishop; John J. Kain, 1895-1903; Cardinal John Glennon, 1903-46; Cardinal Joseph Ritter, 1946-67; Cardinal John J. Carberry, 1968-79.

St. Maron, Brooklyn, N.Y. (Maronite Rite) (1966; eparchy, 1972): Francis Zayek, exarch, 1966, first eparch, 1972.

Established at Detroit; transferred to Brooklyn, 1977.

St. Nicholas in Chicago (Byzantine Rite Eparchy of St. Nicholas of the Ukrainians) (1961): Jaroslav Gabro, eparch, 1961.

St. Paul and Minneapolis,* Minn. (1850; archdiocese, 1888): John R. Roach, archbishop, 1975. John F. Kinney, auxiliary.

Former ordinaries: Joseph Cretin, 1851-57; Thomas L. Grace, O.P., 1859-84; John Ireland, 1884-1918, first archbishop; Austin Dowling, 1919-30; John G. Murray, 1931-56; William O. Brady, 1956-61; Leo Binz, 1962-75.

St. Petersburg, Fla. (1968): W. Thomas Larkin, bishop, 1979.

Former bishop: Charles McLaughlin, 1968-78.

Salina, Kans. (1887): Vacant as of Oct. 15, 1979.

Established at Concordia, transferred, 1944.

Former bishops: Richard Scannell, 1887-91; John J. Hennessy, administrator, 1891-98; John F. Cunningham, 1898-1919; Francis J. Tief, 1921-38; Frank A. Thill, 1938-57; Frederick W. Freking, 1957-64; Cyril J. Vogel, 1965-79.

Salt Lake City, Utah (1891): J. Lennox Federal, bishop, 1960.

Former bishops: Lawrence Scanlan, 1891-1915; Joseph S. Glass, C.M., 1915-26; John J. Mitty, 1926-32; James E. Kearney, 1932-37; Duane G. Hunt, 1937-60.

San Angelo, Tex. (1961): Joseph A. Fiorenza, bishop, 1979.

Former bishops: Thomas J. Drury, 1962-65; Thomas Tschoepe, 1966-69; Stephen A. Leven, 1969-79.

San Antonio,* Tex. (1874; archdiocese, 1926): Patrick F. Flores, archbishop, 1979. Hugo Gerbermann, M.M., Raymond J. Pena, auxiliaries.

Former ordinaries: Anthony D. Pellicer, 1874-80; John C. Neraz, 1881-94; John A. Forest, 1895-1911; John W. Shaw, 1911-18; Arthur Jerome Drossaerts, 1918-40, first archbishop; Robert E. Lucey, 1941-69; Francis Furey, 1969-79.

San Bernardino, Calif. (1978): Phillip F. Straling, bishop, 1978.

San Diego, Calif. (1936): Leo T. Maher, bishop, 1969. Gilbert Espinoza Chavez, auxiliary.

Former bishops: Charles F. Buddy, 1936-66; Francis J. Furey, 1966-69.

San Francisco,* Calif. (1853): John R. Quinn, archbishop, 1977. Roland Pierre Du Maine, Francis A. Quinn, auxiliaries.

Former ordinaries: Joseph S. Alemany, O.P., 1853-84; Patrick W. Riordan, 1884-1914; Edward J. Hanna, 1915-35; John Mitty, 1935-61; Joseph T. McGucken, 1962-77.

Santa Fe,* N. Mex. (1850; archdiocese, 1875): Robert Sanchez, archbishop, 1974.

Former ordinaries: John B. Lamy, 1850-85, first archbishop; John B. Salpointe, 1885-94; Placide L. Chapelle, 1894-97; Peter Bourgade, 1899-1908; John B. Pitaval, 1909-18; Albert T. Daeger, O.F.M., 1919-32; Rudolph A. Gerken, 1933-43; Edwin V. Byrne, 1943-63; James P. Davis, 1964-74.

Santa Rosa, Calif. (1962): Mark J. Hurley, bishop, 1969.

Former bishop: Leo T. Maher, 1962-69.

Savannah, Ga. (1850): Raymond Lessard, bishop, 1973.

Former bishops: Francis X. Gartland, 1850-54; John Barry, 1857-59; Augustin Verot, S.S., 1861-70; Ignatius Persico, O.F.M. Cap., 1870-72; William H. Gross, C.SS.R., 1873-85; Thomas A. Becker, 1886-99; Benjamin J. Keiley, 1900-22; Michael Keyes, S.M., 1922-35; Gerald P. O'Hara, 1935-59; Thomas J. McDonough, 1960-67; Gerard L. Frey, 1967-72.

Scranton, Pa. (1868): J. Carroll McCormick, bishop, 1966. James C. Timlin, auxiliary.

Former bishops: William O'Hara, 1868-99; Michael J. Hoban, 1899-1926; Thomas C. O'Reilly, 1928-38; William J. Hafey, 1938-54; Jerome D. Hannan, 1954-65.

Seattle,* Wash. (1850; archdiocese, 1951): Raymond Hunthausen, archbishop, 1975. Nicholas E. Walsh, auxiliary.

Established as Nesqually, name changed, 1907.

Former ordinaries: Augustin M. Blanchet, 1850-79; Aegidius Junger, 1879-95; Edward J. O'Dea, 1896-1932; Gerald Shaughnessy, S.M., 1933-50; Thomas A. Connolly, first archbishop, 1950-75.

Sioux City, Ia. (1902): Frank Greteman, bishop, 1970.

Former bishops: Philip J. Garrigan, 1902-19; Edmond Heelan, 1919-48; Joseph M. Mueller, 1948-70.

Sioux Falls, S. Dak. (1889): Paul V. Dudley, bishop, 1978.

Former bishops: Martin Marty, O.S.B., 1889-94; Thomas O'Gorman, 1896-1921; Bernard J. Mahoney, 1922-39; William O. Brady, 1939-56; Lambert A. Hoch, 1956-78.

Spokane, Wash. (1913): Lawrence H. Welsh, bishop, 1978.

Former bishops: Augustine F. Schinner,

1914-25; Charles D. White, 1927-55; Bernard J. Topel, 1955-78.

Springfield-Cape Girardeau, Mo. (1956): Bernard F. Law, bishop, 1973.
Former bishops: Charles Helmsing, 1956-62; Ignatius J. Strecker, 1962-69; William Baum, 1970-73.

Springfield, Ill. (1853): Joseph A. McNicholas, bishop, 1975.
Established at Quincy, transferred to Alton 1857; transferred to Springfield 1923.
Former bishops: Henry D. Juncker, 1857-68; Peter J. Baltes, 1870-86; James Ryan, 1888-1923; James A. Griffin, 1924-48; William A. O'Connor, 1949-75.

Springfield, Mass. (1870): Joseph F. Maguire, bishop, 1977.
Former bishops: Patrick T. O'Reilly, 1870-92; Thomas D. Beaven, 1892-1920; Thomas M. O'Leary, 1921-49; Christopher J. Weldon, 1950-77.

Stamford, Conn. (Byzantine Rite) (1956): Basil Losten, eparch, 1977.
Former eparchs: Ambrose Senyshyn, O.S.B.M., 1956-61; Joseph Schmondiuk, 1961-77.

Steubenville, Ohio (1944): Albert H. Ottenweller, bishop, 1977.
Former bishop: John K. Mussio, 1945-77.

Stockton, Calif. (1962): Vacant as of Sept. 10, 1979.
Former bishops: Hugh A. Donohoe, 1962-69; Merlin J. Guilfoyle, 1969-79.

Superior, Wis. (1905): George A. Hammes, bishop, 1960.
Former bishops: Augustine F. Schinner, 1905-13; Joseph M. Koudelka, 1913-21; Joseph G. Pinten, 1922-26; Theodore M. Reverman, 1926-41; William P. O'Connor, 1942-46; Albert G. Meyer, 1946-53; Joseph Annabring, 1954-59.

Syracuse, N.Y. (1886): Francis J. Harrison, bishop, 1976. Thomas J. Costello, auxiliary.
Former bishops: Patrick A. Ludden, 1887-1912; John Grimes, 1912-22; Daniel J. Curley, 1923-32; John A. Duffy, 1933-37; Walter A. Foery, 1937-70; David F. Cunningham, 1970-76.

Toledo, Ohio (1910): John A. Donovan, bishop, 1967. James R. Hoffman, auxiliary.
Former bishops: Joseph Schrembs, 1911-21; Samuel A. Stritch, 1921-30; Karl J. Alter, 1931-50; George J. Rehring, 1950-67.

Trenton, N.J. (1881): Vacant as of Sept. 10, 1979. John C. Reiss, auxiliary.
Former bishops: Michael J. O'Farrell, 1881-94; James A. McFaul, 1894-1917; Thomas J. Walsh, 1918-28; John J. McMahon, 1928-32; Moses E. Kiley, 1934-40; William A. Griffin, 1940-50; George W. Ahr, 1950-79.

Tucson, Ariz. (1897): Francis J. Green, bishop, 1960.
Former bishops: Peter Bourgade, 1897-99; Henry Granjon, 1900-22; Daniel J. Gercke, 1923-60.

Tulsa, Okla. (1972): Eusebius J. Beltran, bishop, 1978.
Former bishop: Bernard J. Ganter, 1973-77.

Washington,* D.C. (1939): Cardinal William Baum, archbishop, 1973. Thomas W. Lyons, Eugene A. Marino, S.S.J., Thomas Kelly, O.P., auxiliaries.
Former ordinaries: Michael J. Curley, 1939-47; Cardinal Patrick O'Boyle, 1948-73.

Wheeling-Charleston, W. Va. (1850): Joseph H. Hodges, bishop, 1962. James E. Michaels, S.S.C., auxiliary.
Established as Wheeling; name changed, 1974.
Former bishops: Richard V. Whelan, 1850-74; John J. Kain, 1875-93; Patrick J. Donahue, 1894-1922; John J. Swint, 1922-62.

Wichita, Kans. (1887): David M. Maloney, bishop, 1967.
Former bishops: John J. Hennessy, 1888-1920; Augustus J. Schwertner, 1921-39; Christian H. Winkelmann, 1940-46; Mark K. Carroll, 1947-67.

Wilmington, Del. (1868): Thomas Mardaga, bishop, 1968.
Former bishops: Thomas A. Becker, 1868-86; Alfred A. Curtis, 1886-96; John J. Monaghan, 1897-1925; Edmond Fitzmaurice, 1925-60; Michael Hyle, 1960-67.

Winona, Minn. (1889): Loras J. Watters, bishop, 1969.
Former bishops: Joseph B. Cotter, 1889-1909; Patrick R. Heffron, 1910-27; Francis M. Kelly, 1928-49; Edward A. Fitzgerald, 1949-69.

Worcester, Mass. (1950): Bernard J. Flanagan, bishop, 1959. Timothy J. Harrington, auxiliary.
Former bishop: John J. Wright, 1950-59.

Yakima, Wash. (1951): William Skylstad, bishop, 1977.
Former bishops: Joseph P. Dougherty, 1951-69; Cornelius M. Power, 1969-74; Nicholas E. Walsh, 1974-76.

Youngstown, Ohio (1943): James W. Malone, bishop, 1968.
Former bishops: James A. McFadden, 1943-52; Emmet M. Walsh, 1952-68.

Military Ordinariate (1917): Cardinal Terence J. Cooke, military vicar, 1968. Joseph T. Ryan, coadjutor archbishop, 1975. William Moran, John J. O'Connor, military delegates.
Former military vicars: Cardinal Patrick Hayes, 1917-38; Cardinal Francis Spellman, 1939-67.

Military Ordinariate

The Military Ordinariate or Vicariate, is the diocese which serves members of the armed forces of the United States wherever they are. It has jurisdiction over: military and

Veterans Administration hospital chaplains; personnel of the armed forces and members of their families and dependents habitually living with them; members of the Coast Guard, National Guard, Air National Guard and Civil Air Patrol when on active duty; persons living on military installations and/or attached to military offices or VA facilities.

The ordinariate was canonically established on a permanent basis by a decree of the Sacred Consistorial Congregation dated Sept. 8, 1957. Cardinal Terence J. Cooke, Archbishop of New York, is Military Vicar. Offices of the ordinariate are located at 1011 First Ave., New York, N.Y. 10022.

MISSIONARY BISHOPS

Africa

Namibia (South West Africa): Keetmanshoop (vicariate apostolic), Edward F. Schlotterback, O.S.F.S.

Nigeria: Sokoto (diocese), Michael J. Dempsey, O.P.

South Africa: De Aar (diocese), Joseph A. De Palma, S.C.J.

Keimos (diocese), John Minder, O.S.F.S.

Tanzania: Arusha (diocese), Dennis V. Durning, C.S.Sp.

Nachingwea (diocese), Arnold R. Cotey, S.D.S.

Asia

China: Chowtsun (diocese), Henry A. Pinger, O.F.M. Expelled.

Wuchow (diocese), Frederick A. Donaghy, M.M. Expelled.

India: Bhagalpur (diocese), Urban McGarry, T.O.R.

Patna (diocese), Augustine F. Wildermuth, S.J.

Indonesia: Agats (diocese), Alphonse A. Sowada, O.S.C.

Korea: Inchon (diocese), William J. McNaughton, M.M.

Pakistan: Multan (diocese), Ernest B. Boland, O.P.

Philippine Islands: Cotabato (diocese), Philip M. Smith, O.M.I., coadjutor.

Marbel (prelacy), Reginald Arliss, C.P.

Tagum (prelacy), Joseph W. Regan, M.M.

Taiwan: Taichung (diocese), William F. Kupfer, M.M.

Turkey: Izmir (archdiocese), John H. Boccella, T.O.R.

Central America, West Indies

Bahamas: Nassau (diocese), Paul L. Hagarty, O.S.B.

Belize: Belize (diocese), Robert L. Hodapp, S.J.

Dominican Republic: San Juan de la Maguana (diocese), Ronald G. Connors, C.SS.R.,

Guatemala: Guatemala (archdiocese), Richard J. Ham, M.M., auxiliary.

Honduras: Comayagua (diocese), Gerald Scarpone, O.F.M.

Nicaragua: Bluefields (vicariate apostolic), Salvator Schlaefer, O.F.M.Cap.

Virgin Islands: St. Thomas (diocese), Edward Harper, C.SS.R.

Oceania

Caroline and Marshall Islands (diocese), Martin J. Neylon, S.J.

New Hebrides: Port Vila (diocese), Francis Lambert, S.M.

Papua New Guinea: Goroko (diocese), John E. Cohill, S.V.D. Raymond R. Caesar, S.V.D. coadjutor.

Kavieng (diocese), Alfred M. Stemper, M.S.C.

Madang (archdiocese), Leo Arkfeld, S.V.D.

Mendi (diocese), Firmin Schmidt, O.F.M.Cap.

Mount Hagen (diocese), George Bernarding, S.V.D.

Wewak (diocese), Leo Arkfeld, S.V.D., Archbishop of Madang, apostolic administrator.

South America

Bolivia: Coroico (prelacy), Thomas R. Manning, O.F.M.

La Paz (archdiocese), Andrew B. Schierhoff, auxiliary.

Santa Cruz (archdiocese), Charles A. Brown, M.M., auxiliary.

Brazil: Abaete do Tocantins (prelacy), Angelo Frosi, S.X.

Belem do Para (archdiocese), Jude Prost, O.F.M., auxiliary.

Borba (prelacy), Adrian J. M. Veigle, T.O.R.

Cristalandia (prelacy), James A. Schuck, O.F.M.

Jatai (diocese), Benedict D. Coscia, O.F.M. Michael P. Mundo, auxiliary.

Paranagua (diocese), Bernard Nolker, C.SS.R.

Rui Barbosa (diocese), Mathias Schmidt, O.S.B.

Santarem (prelacy), James C. Ryan, O.F.M.

Sao Paulo (archdiocese), Alfred Novak, C.SS.R., auxiliary.

Sao Salvador da Bahia (archdiocese), Thomas W. Murphy, C.SS.R., auxiliary.

Peru: Chulucanas (prelacy), John McNabb, O.S.A.

Pope John Paul's message for the celebration of the 1979 World Mission Day in October emphasized the Church's commitment to promote the dignity and worth of all people. This was also the basic theme of the encyclical "Redemptor Hominis" he issued in March.

CATHOLIC POPULATION OF THE UNITED STATES

(Source: *The Official Catholic Directory, 1979*; figures as of Jan. 1, 1979. Archdioceses are indicated by an asterisk; for dioceses marked +, see Dioceses with Interstate Lines.)

Section, State Diocese	Catholics	Dioc.	Priests Rel.	Total	Perm. Deacons	Bros.	Sisters	Parishes
NEW ENGLAND	5,660,872	4,132	2,555	6,687	275	809	12,836	1,694
Maine, Portland	269,460	228	128	356	2	37	876	144
New Hampshire, Manchester	279,269	285	97	382	—	58	1,192	126
Vermont, Burlington	159,630	167	62	229	—	28	372	100
Massachusetts	3,031,244	2,176	1,713	3,889	92	380	7,294	785
*Boston	2,016,272	1,332	1,160	2,482	71	218	4,820	408
Fall River	332,000	225	196	421	—	47	760	113
Springfield	352,476	271	153	424	—	35	995	136
Worcester	330,496	358	204	562	21	80	719	128
Rhode Island, Providence	597,596	388	223	611	43	181	1,299	157
Connecticut	1,323,673	888	332	1,220	138	125	1,803	382
*Hartford	792,840	522	122	644	120	62	737	223
Bridgeport	336,263	227	131	358	13	8	697	85
Norwich+	194,570	139	79	218	5	55	369	74
MIDDLE ATLANTIC	13,186,212	9,627	5,610	15,237	640	1,921	34,944	3,909
New York	6,571,635	4,500	3,103	7,603	192	1,187	16,257	1,717
*New York	1,825,090	1,068	1,634	2,702	85	471	5,646	410
Albany	408,648	398	190	588	22	107	1,300	203
Brooklyn	1,458,951	937	413	1,350	48	283	2,463	223
Buffalo	914,152	603	362	965	22	78	2,411	298
Ogdensburg	170,659	195	43	238	—	39	397	122
Rochester	369,711	414	170	584	—	38	1,047	161
Rockville Centre	1,038,505	467	151	618	1	140	2,139	129
Syracuse	385,919	418	140	558	14	31	854	171
New Jersey	2,885,940	1,894	916	2,810	377	324	5,258	695
*Newark	1,400,727	833	504	1,337	215	166	2,439	252
Camden	330,662	383	45	428	45	17	420	127
Paterson	316,994	296	244	540	84	63	1,143	103
Trenton	837,557	382	123	505	33	78	1,256	213
Pennsylvania	3,728,637	3,233	1,591	4,824	71	410	13,429	1,497
*Philadelphia	1,377,258	998	693	1,691	1	251	5,919	308
Allentown	263,255	307	107	414	—	29	990	152
Altoona-Johnstown	150,559	168	116	284	1	30	271	120
Erie	218,012	290	65	355	—	10	607	128
Greensburg	234,105	193	111	304	1	12	453	118
Harrisburg	212,600	178	81	259	43	9	902	111
Pittsburgh	912,959	632	290	922	25	59	3,088	320
Scranton	359,889	467	128	595	—	10	1,199	240
SOUTH ATLANTIC	2,898,913	2,165	2,010	4,175	216	563	7,104	1,230
Delaware, Wilmington+	121,070	121	92	213	1	26	432	54
Maryland, *Baltimore	413,321	353	351	704	80	143	2,054	149
District of Columbia								
*Washington+	397,213	351	673	1,024	77	194	981	128
Virginia	269,835	224	174	398	24	26	677	152
Arlington	160,481	79	91	170	23	19	297	54
Richmond	109,354	145	83	228	1	7	380	98
West Virginia								
Wheeling-Charleston	101,502	138	89	227	2	23	457	113
North Carolina	91,931	117	83	200	2	7	359	119
Charlotte	44,683	56	57	113	1	7	221	61
Raleigh	47,248	61	26	87	1	—	138	58
South Carolina, Charleston	58,399	82	56	138	15	21	267	72
Georgia	138,860	150	120	270	7	45	403	95
*Atlanta	93,016	83	87	170	7	36	190	50
Savannah	45,844	67	33	100	—	9	213	45
Florida	1,306,782	629	372	1,001	8	78	1,474	348
*Miami	799,400	295	190	485	4	43	672	129

U.S. Catholic Statistics

Section, State Diocese	Catholics	Dioc.	Priests Rel.	Total	Perm. Deacons	Bros.	Sisters	Parishes
Florida								
Orlando	162,268	131	20	151	—	—	187	61
Pensacola-Tallahassee	38,597	49	8	57	—	—	77	34
St. Augustine	63,509	50	28	78	1	—	114	44
St. Petersburg	243,008	104	126	230	3	35	424	80
EAST NORTH CENTRAL	10,188,405	7,976	4,981	12,957	845	1,930	31,608	4,181
Ohio	2,356,313	2,077	998	3,075	157	506	7,354	958
*Cincinnati	500,000	462	422	884	41	254	2,036	256
Cleveland	951,000	665	291	956	15	144	2,572	253
Columbus	209,285	235	65	300	18	18	750	109
Steubenville	53,500	169	14	183	1	8	162	74
Toledo	345,640	283	130	413	73	34	1,300	150
Youngstown	296,888	263	76	339	9	48	534	116
Indiana	720,081	752	606	1,358	30	265	4,004	447
*Indianapolis	200,010	239	185	424	—	107	1,939	142
Evansville	91,093	131	23	154	14	6	469	74
Ft. Wayne-S. Bend	148,248	127	243	370	15	110	1,088	84
Gary	195,333	143	96	239	1	35	362	86
Lafayette	85,397	112	59	171	—	7	146	61
Illinois	3,567,541	2,277	1,828	4,105	426	686	9,006	1,103
*Chicago	2,415,354	1,295	1,286	2,581	353	323	5,332	445
Belleville	119,539	167	39	206	2	12	472	130
Joliet	401,000	209	173	382	15	279	1,063	111
Peoria	231,395	251	119	370	18	21	748	171
Rockford	216,614	172	105	277	38	19	373	102
Springfield	183,639	183	106	289	—	32	1,018	144
Michigan	1,987,528	1,316	646	1,962	130	171	4,670	815
*Detroit	1,187,382	617	436	1,053	78	130	2,800	344
Gaylord	82,861	59	19	78	—	4	162	59
Grand Rapids	144,515	152	43	195	19	7	681	90
Kalamazoo	91,950	54	33	87	11	8	318	46
Lansing	213,084	158	59	217	8	18	256	83
Marquette	98,431	129	25	154	—	1	175	89
Saginaw	169,305	147	31	178	14	3	278	104
Wisconsin	1,556,942	1,554	903	2,457	102	302	6,574	858
*Milwaukee	707,015	651	539	1,190	73	178	3,727	265
Green Bay	332,673	298	251	549	29	75	1,133	194
La Crosse	217,015	288	42	330	—	29	771	174
Madison	212,639	212	52	264	—	18	699	138
Superior	87,600	105	19	124	—	2	244	87
EAST SOUTH CENTRAL	655,165	962	448	1,410	110	349	4,067	626
Kentucky	359,312	528	171	699	44	143	2,867	287
*Louisville	202,581	258	123	381	44	125	1,504	126
Covington	108,000	189	28	217	—	7	1,087	85
Owensboro	48,731	81	20	101	—	11	276	76
Tennessee	103,656	130	66	196	48	102	335	92
Memphis	40,459	53	29	82	23	82	163	33
Nashville	63,197	77	37	114	25	20	172	59
Alabama	99,597	162	143	305	17	28	445	132
Birmingham	49,139	67	66	133	17	13	198	56
Mobile	50,458	95	77	172	—	15	247	76
Mississippi	92,600	142	68	210	1	76	420	115
Biloxi	50,912	63	29	92	—	64	106	42
Jackson	41,688	79	39	118	1	12	314	73
WEST NORTH CENTRAL	3,319,340	4,109	2,019	6,128	209	774	15,861	2,683
Minnesota	1,019,495	1,001	468	1,469	34	164	4,485	674
*St. Paul and Minneapolis	539,407	392	211	603	29	67	1,748	217
Crookston	44,065	53	25	78	—	3	302	47
Duluth	93,632	104	34	138	—	4	346	77
New Ulm	72,889	118	5	123	1	—	181	74

Section, State Diocese	Catholics	Dioc.	Priests Rel.	Total	Perm. Deacons	Bros.	Sisters	Parishes
Minnesota								
St. Cloud	149,749	160	174	334	4	65	1,134	135
Winona	119,753	174	19	193	—	25	774	124
Iowa	**535,291**	**914**	**140**	**1,054**	**31**	**78**	**2,477**	**512**
*Dubuque	238,064	380	102	482	15	59	1,450	191
Davenport	105,000	199	18	217	—	18	480	119
Des Moines	79,952	127	13	140	14	—	215	84
Sioux City	112,275	208	7	215	2	1	332	118
Missouri	**783,098**	**953**	**762**	**1,715**	**97**	**376**	**4,192**	**497**
*St. Louis	526,398	577	519	1,096	29	213	3,248	248
Jefferson City	74,977	135	13	148	24	16	146	92
Kansas City-St. Joseph	137,812	163	174	337	43	54	599	97
Springfield-Cape Girardeau	43,911	78	56	134	1	93	199	60
North Dakota	**172,979**	**227**	**101**	**328**	**1**	**27**	**668**	**191**
Bismarck	75,131	80	68	148	—	21	317	74
Fargo	97,848	147	33	180	1	6	351	117
South Dakota	**139,705**	**184**	**111**	**295**	**7**	**47**	**602**	**174**
Rapid City	40,138	41	45	86	5	19	103	52
Sioux Falls	99,567	143	66	209	2	28	499	122
Nebraska	**331,824**	**421**	**216**	**637**	**39**	**52**	**1,199**	**274**
*Omaha	213,559	227	184	411	39	37	867	138
Grand Island	51,989	81	4	85	—	—	152	50
Lincoln	66,276	113	28	141	—	15	180	86
Kansas	**336,948**	**409**	**221**	**630**	—	**30**	**2,238**	**361**
*Kansas City	145,000	126	135	261	—	22	1,239	119
Dodge City	36,522	57	13	70	—	—	191	49
Salina	60,339	80	45	125	—	5	351	98
Wichita	95,087	146	28	174	—	3	457	95
WEST SOUTH CENTRAL	**3,793,501**	**2,010**	**1,696**	**3,706**	**493**	**562**	**7,094**	**1,568**
Arkansas, Little Rock	**54,312**	**113**	**63**	**176**	**3**	**52**	**523**	**84**
Louisiana	**1,301,192**	**698**	**568**	**1,266**	**91**	**235**	**2,013**	**474**
*New Orleans	532,878	226	319	545	41	154	1,180	133
Alexandria-Shreveport	80,716	120	46	166	—	12	222	84
Baton Rouge	175,000	96	66	162	2	9	123	67
Houma-Thibodaux	130,000	51	17	68	15	11	73	35
Lafayette	382,598	205	120	325	33	49	415	155
Oklahoma	**113,847**	**177**	**60**	**237**	**17**	**30**	**490**	**127**
*Oklahoma City	68,459	112	35	147	9	20	263	73
Tulsa	45,388	65	25	90	8	10	227	54
Texas	**2,324,150**	**1,022**	**1,005**	**2,027**	**382**	**245**	**4,068**	**883**
*San Antonio	587,330	200	248	448	59	117	1,520	163
Amarillo	82,740	68	23	91	27	—	150	60
Austin	142,550	105	55	160	4	34	190	81
Beaumont	82,273	54	33	87	1	4	111	44
Brownsville	311,794	41	68	109	—	17	167	59
Corpus Christi	171,647	81	86	167	12	19	295	74
Dallas	150,946	102	108	210	91	5	365	61
El Paso+	217,748	85	75	160	33	21	375	78
Fort Worth	86,729	63	39	102	18	16	182	78
Galveston-Houston	425,000	179	241	420	108	12	666	141
San Angelo	65,393	44	29	73	29	—	47	44
MOUNTAIN	**1,642,297**	**1,170**	**796**	**1,966**	**263**	**227**	**3,135**	**788**
Montana	**128,702**	**224**	**64**	**288**	**10**	**13**	**260**	**133**
Great Falls	65,792	89	41	130	4	4	173	73
Helena	62,910	135	23	158	6	9	87	60
Idaho, Boise	**78,866**	**94**	**21**	**115**	—	**4**	**150**	**67**
Wyoming, Cheyenne+	**50,000**	**58**	**11**	**69**	**1**	**2**	**48**	**39**
Colorado	**398,419**	**284**	**265**	**549**	**68**	**43**	**1,166**	**188**
*Denver	298,211	181	204	385	65	30	935	128
Pueblo	100,208	103	61	164	3	13	231	60

U.S. Catholic Statistics

Section, State Diocese	Catholics	Dioc.	Priests Rel.	Total	Perm. Deacons	Bros.	Sisters	Parishes
New Mexico	370,777	207	143	350	40	111	567	151
*Santa Fe	324,821	160	91	251	33	87	406	93
Gallup+	45,956	47	52	99	7	24	161	58
Arizona	449,000	201	205	406	122	26	670	131
Phoenix	258,000	111	122	233	61	20	312	75
Tucson	191,000	90	83	173	61	6	358	56
Utah, Salt Lake City	56,533	51	43	94	21	16	118	38
Nevada, Reno-Las Vegas	110,000	51	44	95	1	12	156	41
PACIFIC	5,828,207	2,780	2,735	5,515	230	818	11,233	1,518
Washington	486,462	383	401	784	64	43	1,353	227
*Seattle	355,279	224	262	486	48	35	890	130
Spokane	74,983	97	119	216	16	8	399	58
Yakima	56,200	62	20	82	—	—	64	39
Oregon	313,713	230	253	483	1	68	971	153
*Portland	288,029	186	241	427	1	68	876	124
Baker	25,684	44	12	56	—	—	95	29
California	4,778,302	2,083	1,921	4,004	143	619	8,464	1,021
*Los Angeles	1,964,000	599	682	1,281	59	152	3,836	278
*San Francisco	620,250	316	590	906	10	156	1,816	153
Fresno	348,296	122	51	173	—	18	180	85
Monterey	95,000	84	24	108	—	25	211	43
Oakland	386,765	146	210	356	28	112	627	85
Orange	332,044	113	117	230	13	16	509	46
Sacramento	249,015	186	83	269	1	49	317	90
San Bernardino	235,665	133	42	175	10	15	220	85
San Diego	344,111	253	67	320	19	24	492	87
Santa Rosa	91,809	81	25	106	2	48	155	38
Stockton	111,347	50	30	80	1	4	101	31
Alaska	39,730	38	54	92	22	8	87	53
*Anchorage	20,430	21	17	38	—	1	30	17
Fairbanks	14,000	6	36	42	16	7	42	27
Juneau	5,300	11	1	12	6	—	15	9
Hawaii, Honolulu	210,000	46	106	152	—	80	358	64
EASTERN RITES	579,123	541	108	649	15	12	496	498
*Philadelphia	166,388	118	14	132	1	1	214	109
St. Nicholas	29,959	34	12	46	1	1	20	36
Stamford	48,636	59	20	79	—	1	41	52
*Pittsburgh	151,395	81	8	89	—	4	143	84
Parma	33,211	60	5	65	—	—	19	54
Passaic	96,634	84	21	105	2	1	38	88
St. Maron	30,600	73	—	73	2	—	10	49
Newton (Melkite)	22,300	32	28	60	9	4	11	26
MILITARY VICARIATE	1,850,000	—	—	—	—	—	—	—
TOTALS 1979	49,602,035	35,472	22,958	58,430	3,296	7,965	128,378	18,695
Totals 1978	49,836,176	35,766	22,719	58,485	2,498	8,460	129,391	18,625
Totals 1969	47,873,238	37,454	22,166	59,620	—	11,755	167,167	18,146

Dioceses with Interstate Lines

Diocesan lines usually fall within a single state and in some cases include a whole state.

The following dioceses, with their statistics as reported in tables throughout the Almanac, are exceptions.

Norwich, Conn., includes Fisher's Island, N.Y.

Wilmington, Del., includes all of Delaware and nine counties of Maryland.

Baltimore, includes all of Maryland except nine counties under the jurisdiction of Wilmington and five under Washington.

Washington, D.C., includes five counties of Maryland.

El Paso, Tex., includes seven counties of New Mexico.

Gallup, N.M., has jurisdiction over several counties of Arizona.

Cheyenne, Wyo., includes all of Yellowstone National Park.

PERCENTAGE OF CATHOLICS IN U.S. POPULATION

(Source: *The Official Catholic Directory, 1979*; figures are as of Jan. 1, 1979. Total general population figures at the end of the table are U.S. Census Bureau estimates for Jan. 1 of the respective years. Archdioceses are indicated by an asterisk; for dioceses marked +, see Dioceses with Interstate Lines.)

Section, State Diocese	Catholic Pop.	Total Pop.	Cath. Pct.
NEW ENGLAND	**5,660,872**	**14,135,003**	**40.04**
Maine, Portland	269,460	1,018,000	26.47
New Hampshire			
Manchester	279,269	784,000	35.62
Vermont, Burlington	159,630	483,300	33.03
Massachusetts	3,031,244	7,750,873	39.11
*Boston	2,016,272	5,789,478	34.83
Fall River	332,000	530,000	66.64
Springfield	352,476	791,642	44.52
Worcester	330,496	639,753	51.66
Rhode Island, Providence	597,596	935,000	63.91
Connecticut	1,323,673	3,163,830	41.84
*Hartford	792,840	1,755,190	45.18
Bridgeport	336,263	832,900	40.37
Norwich+	194,570	575,740	33.79
MIDDLE ATLANTIC	**13,186,212**	**38,276,220**	**34.45**
New York	6,571,635	18,541,142	35.44
*New York	1,825,090	5,044,800	36.18
Albany	408,648	1,472,684	27.75
Brooklyn	1,458,951	4,400,000	33.16
Buffalo	914,152	1,743,500	52.43
Ogdensburg	170,659	404,102	42.23
Rochester	369,711	1,465,500	25.23
Rockville Centre	1,038,505	2,786,846	37.26
Syracuse	385,919	1,223,710	31.54
New Jersey	2,885,940	8,105,065	35.61
*Newark	1,400,727	2,802,000	49.99
Camden	330,662	1,318,792	25.07
Paterson	316,994	1,471,602	21.54
Trenton	837,557	2,512,671	33.33
Pennsylvania	3,728,637	11,630,013	32.06
*Philadelphia	1,377,258	3,616,400	38.08
Allentown	263,255	1,000,000	26.32
Altoona-Johnstown	150,559	624,800	24.10
Erie	218,012	857,037	25.44
Greensburg	234,105	719,084	32.56
Harrisburg	212,600	1,607,000	13.23
Pittsburgh	912,959	2,241,430	40.73
Scranton	359,889	964,262	37.32
SOUTH ATLANTIC	**2,898,913**	**34,545,941**	**8.39**
Delaware, Wilmington+	121,070	860,500	14.07
Maryland, *Baltimore	413,321	2,449,721	16.88
District of Columbia			
*Washington+	397,213	2,098,200	18.93
Virginia	269,835	4,995,129	5.40
Arlington	160,481	1,317,500	12.18
Richmond	109,354	3,677,629	2.97
West Virginia			
Wheeling-Charleston	101,502	1,744,237	5.82
North Carolina	91,931	5,644,000	1.63
Charlotte	44,683	2,850,000	1.57
North Carolina			
Raleigh	47,248	2,794,000	1.69
South Carolina			
Charleston	58,399	2,848,000	2.05
Georgia	138,860	4,825,350	2.88
*Atlanta	93,016	3,225,350	2.88
Savannah	45,844	1,600,000	2.86
Florida	1,306,782	9,080,804	14.39
*Miami	799,400	3,311,700	24.14
Orlando	162,268	1,785,500	9.09
Pensacola-Tallahassee	38,597	819,811	4.71
St. Augustine	63,509	1,027,000	6.18
St. Petersburg	243,008	2,136,793	11.37
EAST NORTH CENTRAL	**10,188,405**	**40,720,528**	**25.02**
Ohio	2,356,313	10,717,777	21.98
*Cincinnati	500,000	2,668,300	18.74
Cleveland	951,000	2,882,600	32.99
Columbus	209,285	1,901,100	11.01
Steubenville	53,500	545,060	9.81
Toledo	345,640	1,438,800	24.02
Youngstown	296,888	1,281,917	23.16
Indiana	720,081	5,220,553	13.79
*Indianapolis	200,010	2,022,366	9.89
Evansville	91,093	435,177	20.93
Ft. Wayne-S. Bend	148,248	973,764	15.22
Gary	195,333	802,366	24.34
Lafayette	85,397	986,880	8.65
Illinois	3,567,541	11,184,644	31.90
*Chicago	2,415,354	5,750,405	42.00
Belleville	119,539	807,682	14.80
Joliet	401,000	1,166,000	34.39
Peoria	231,395	1,434,428	16.13
Rockford	216,614	934,938	23.17
Springfield	183,639	1,091,191	16.83
Michigan	1,987,528	8,961,975	22.18
*Detroit	1,187,382	4,413,100	26.90
Gaylord	82,861	419,700	19.74
Grand Rapids	144,515	899,238	16.08
Kalamazoo	91,950	796,812	11.54
Lansing	213,084	1,532,800	13.90
Marquette	98,431	304,347	32.34
Saginaw	169,305	595,978	28.41
Wisconsin	1,556,942	4,635,579	33.59
*Milwaukee	707,015	2,039,217	34.67
Green Bay	332,673	736,053	45.20
La Crosse	217,015	667,849	32.49
Madison	212,639	850,556	25.00
Superior	87,600	341,904	25.62
EAST SOUTH CENTRAL	**655,165**	**13,375,979**	**4.90**
Kentucky	359,312	3,479,786	10.32
*Louisville	202,581	1,302,017	15.56

U.S. Catholic Statistics

Section, State Diocese	Catholic Pop.	Total Pop.	Cath. Pct.
Kentucky			
Covington	108,000	1,500,000	7.20
Owensboro	48,731	677,769	7.19
Tennessee	103,656	4,066,093	2.55
Memphis	40,459	1,300,000	3.11
Nashville	63,197	2,766,093	2.28
Alabama	99,597	3,550,800	2.80
Birmingham	49,139	2,200,000	2.23
Mobile	50,458	1,350,800	3.73
Mississippi	92,600	2,279,300	4.06
Biloxi	50,912	579,300	8.79
Jackson	41,688	1,700,000	2.45
WEST NORTH CENTRAL	**3,319,340**	**16,279,336**	**20.39**
Minnesota	1,019,495	3,805,292	26.79
*St. Paul and Minneapolis	539,407	2,017,225	26.74
Crookston	44,065	220,132	20.02
Duluth	93,632	421,700	22.20
New Ulm	72,889	280,000	26.03
St. Cloud	149,749	349,853	42.80
Winona	119,753	516,382	23.19
Iowa	535,291	2,780,146	19.25
*Dubuque	238,064	956,078	24.90
Davenport	105,000	687,000	15.28
Des Moines	79,952	624,185	12.81
Sioux City	112,275	512,883	21.89
Missouri	783,098	4,597,754	17.03
*St. Louis	526,398	1,922,400	27.38
Jefferson City	74,977	670,706	11.18
Kansas City- St. Joseph	137,812	1,271,000	10.84
Springfield- Cape Girardeau	43,911	733,648	5.98
North Dakota	172,979	617,737	28.00
Bismarck	75,131	244,777	30.69
Fargo	97,848	372,960	26.23
South Dakota	139,705	660,208	21.16
Rapid City	40,138	178,208	22.52
Sioux Falls	99,567	482,000	20.66
Nebraska	331,824	1,550,336	21.40
*Omaha	213,559	744,940	28.67
Grand Island	51,989	299,012	17.39
Lincoln	66,276	506,384	13.09
Kansas	336,948	2,267,863	14.86
*Kansas City	145,000	882,028	16.44
Dodge City	36,522	215,535	16.94
Salina	60,339	330,405	18.26
Wichita	95,087	839,895	11.32
WEST SOUTH CENTRAL	**3,793,501**	**21,917,002**	**17.31**
Arkansas, Little Rock	54,312	2,186,000	2.48
Louisiana	1,301,192	3,896,707	33.39
*New Orleans	532,878	1,263,200	42.18
Alexandria-Shreveport	80,716	1,083,132	7.45
Baton Rouge	175,000	643,437	27.20
Houma-Thibodaux	130,000	182,000	71.43
Lafayette	382,598	724,938	52.78
Oklahoma	113,847	2,756,000	4.13
*Oklahoma City	68,459	1,596,200	4.29
Tulsa	45,388	1,159,800	3.91
Texas	2,324,150	13,078,295	17.77
*San Antonio	587,330	1,359,086	43.21
Amarillo	82,740	800,000	10.34
Austin	142,550	945,864	15.07
Beaumont	82,273	586,598	14.02
Brownsville	311,794	442,518	70.46
Corpus Christi	171,647	545,000	31.49
Dallas	150,946	2,671,709	5.65
El Paso+	217,748	800,000	27.22
Fort Worth	86,729	1,470,559	5.90
Galveston-Houston	425,000	2,900,000	14.65
San Angelo	65,393	556,961	11.74
MOUNTAIN	**1,642,297**	**9,919,917**	**16.55**
Montana	128,702	728,258	17.67
Great Falls	65,792	351,858	18.70
Helena	62,910	376,400	16.71
Idaho, Boise	78,866	857,000	9.20
Wyoming, Cheyenne+	50,000	400,000	12.50
Colorado	398,419	2,599,929	15.32
*Denver	298,211	2,203,221	13.53
Pueblo	100,208	396,708	25.26
New Mexico	370,777	1,077,130	34.42
*Santa Fe	324,821	779,500	41.67
Gallup+	45,956	297,630	15.44
Arizona	449,000	2,307,600	19.46
Phoenix	258,000	1,497,000	17.23
Tucson	191,000	810,600	23.56
Utah, Salt Lake City	56,533	1,300,000	4.35
Nevada, Reno-Las Vegas	110,000	650,000	16.92
PACIFIC	**5,828,207**	**29,436,929**	**19.80**
Washington	486,462	3,736,028	13.02
*Seattle	355,279	2,738,928	12.97
Spokane	74,983	610,100	12.29
Yakima	56,200	387,000	14.52
Oregon	313,713	2,472,828	12.69
*Portland	288,029	2,172,328	13.26
Baker	25,684	300,500	8.55
California	4,778,302	21,975,073	21.74
*Los Angeles	1,964,000	7,846,231	25.03
*San Francisco	620,250	2,694,200	23.02
Fresno	348,296	1,329,150	26.20
Monterey	95,000	484,363	19.61
Oakland	386,765	1,711,900	22.59
Orange	332,044	1,800,000	18.45
Sacramento	249,015	1,758,500	14.16
San Bernardino	235,665	1,358,844	17.34
San Diego	344,111	1,826,880	18.83
Santa Rosa	91,809	557,850	16.46
Stockton	111,347	607,155	18.34
Alaska	39,730	357,000	11.13
*Anchorage	20,430	195,000	10.48
Fairbanks	14,000	117,000	11.96
Juneau	5,300	45,000	11.78
Hawaii, Honolulu	210,000	896,000	23.44
EASTERN RITES	**579,123**	—	—
MILITARY VICARIATE	**1,850,000**	—	—
TOTALS 1979	**49,602,035**	**219,484,000**	**22.60**
Totals 1978	49,836,176	217,739,000	22.89
Totals 1969	47,873,238	202,237,631	23.67

INFANT BAPTISMS AND CONVERTS IN THE UNITED STATES

(Source: *The Official Catholic Directory, 1979*; figures as of Jan. 1, 1979. Archdioceses are indicated by an asterisk; for dioceses marked +, see Dioceses with Interstate Lines.)

Section, State Diocese	Infant Baptisms	Converts
NEW ENGLAND	**79,301**	**2,415**
Maine, Portland	4,524	427
New Hampshire, Manchester	4,876	241
Vermont, Burlington	2,442	183
Massachusetts	43,015	880
*Boston	27,118	500
Fall River	6,222	108
Springfield	4,826	162
Worcester	4,849	110
Rhode Island, Providence	7,160	173
Connecticut	17,284	511
*Hartford	9,754	281
Bridgeport	4,525	108
Norwich+	3,005	122
MIDDLE ATLANTIC	**208,258**	**11,036**
New York	109,814	4,529
*New York	31,260	1,122
Albany	6,961	518
Brooklyn	26,117	726
Buffalo	9,921	382
Ogdensburg	2,749	249
Rochester	6,742	649
Rockville Centre	19,070	385
Syracuse	6,994	498
New Jersey	44,107	1,605
*Newark	17,435	419
Camden	6,542	482
Paterson	6,653	237
Trenton	13,477	467
Pennsylvania	54,337	4,902
*Philadelphia	20,284	1,664
Allentown	3,916	221
Altoona-Johnstown	2,557	300
Erie	4,146	513
Greensburg	2,990	301
Harrisburg	3,716	743
Pittsburgh	11,340	778
Scranton	5,388	382
SOUTH ATLANTIC	**48,073**	**7,583**
Delaware, Wilmington+	2,563	348
Maryland, *Baltimore	7,470	1,118
District of Columbia		
*Washington+	6,384	716
Virginia	5,707	845
Arlington	3,393	304
Richmond	2,314	541
West Virginia		
Wheeling-Charleston	1,683	518
North Carolina	2,083	572
Charlotte	970	312
Raleigh	1,113	260
South Carolina, Charleston	1,341	339
Georgia	2,661	826
*Atlanta	1,706	428
Savannah	955	398
Florida	18,181	2,301
*Miami	9,945	517
Orlando	2,551	470
Pensacola-Tallahassee	794	438
St. Augustine	1,360	277
St. Petersburg	3,531	599
EAST NORTH CENTRAL	**169,838**	**20,179**
Ohio	37,297	4,820
*Cincinnati	9,046	1,072
Cleveland	12,469	1,275
Columbus	3,554	882
Steubenville	1,041	237
Toledo	6,522	756
Youngstown	4,665	598
Indiana	13,546	2,554
*Indianapolis	4,062	899
Evansville	1,713	276
Ft. Wayne-South Bend	2,901	494
Gary	3,212	404
Lafayette	1,658	481
Illinois	57,186	6,390
*Chicago	34,985	3,454
Belleville	2,125	480
Joliet	7,369	444
Peoria	4,539	802
Rockford	4,554	520
Springfield	3,614	690
Michigan	34,750	4,275
*Detroit	18,800	1,735
Gaylord	1,579	224
Grand Rapids	3,025	648
Kalamazoo	1,700	329
Lansing	4,692	827
Marquette	2,045	215
Saginaw	2,909	297
Wisconsin	27,059	2,140
*Milwaukee	11,961	941
Green Bay	5,493	303
La Crosse	4,116	422
Madison	3,605	331
Superior	1,884	143
EAST SOUTH CENTRAL	**13,415**	**3,027**
Kentucky	7,241	1,060
*Louisville	3,915	521
Covington	2,101	291
Owensboro	1,225	248
Tennessee	2,245	752
Memphis	947	265
Nashville	1,298	487
Alabama	1,944	704
Birmingham	894	384

U.S. Catholic Statistics

Section, State Diocese	Infant Baptisms	Converts
Alabama		
Mobile	1,050	320
Mississippi	1,985	511
Biloxi	1,127	241
Jackson	858	270
WEST NORTH CENTRAL	**69,167**	**9,711**
Minnesota	21,487	1,840
*St. Paul and Minneapolis	10,983	933
Crookston	1,010	116
Duluth	1,850	170
New Ulm	1,673	171
St. Cloud	3,402	220
Winona	2,569	230
Iowa	11,286	1,635
*Dubuque	4,428	752
Davenport	2,529	229
Des Moines	1,793	371
Sioux City	2,536	283
Missouri	14,565	2,836
*St. Louis	9,212	1,488
Jefferson City	1,788	357
Kansas City-St. Joseph	2,648	702
Springfield-Cape Girardeau	917	289
North Dakota	3,916	427
Bismarck	1,741	148
Fargo	2,175	279
South Dakota	3,239	493
Rapid City	1,072	118
Sioux Falls	2,167	375
Nebraska	7,347	1,092
*Omaha	4,557	579
Grand Island	1,229	217
Lincoln	1,561	296
Kansas	7,327	1,388
*Kansas City	2,828	492
Dodge City	931	162
Salina	1,397	250
Wichita	2,171	484
WEST SOUTH CENTRAL	**102,786**	**7,309**
Arkansas, Little Rock	1,217	399
Louisiana	25,462	1,668
*New Orleans	9,265	621
Alexandria-Shreveport	1,910	384
Baton Rouge	3,486	232
Houma-Thibodaux	2,347	72
Lafayette	8,454	359
Oklahoma	2,671	1,082
*Oklahoma City	1,730	496
Tulsa	941	586
Texas	73,436	4,160
*San Antonio	18,920	431
Amarillo	3,176	167
Austin	3,428	367
Beaumont	1,550	276
Brownsville	7,443	82
Corpus Christi	8,107	180
Dallas	4,824	751
El Paso+	8,014	134
Fort Worth	2,566	437
Galveston-Houston	13,127	1,155
Texas		
San Angelo	2,281	180
MOUNTAIN	**40,883**	**3,702**
Montana	3,195	533
Great Falls	1,712	246
Helena	1,483	287
Idaho, Boise	1,849	436
Wyoming, Cheyenne+	1,555	183
Colorado	10,897	811
*Denver	8,559	671
Pueblo	2,338	140
New Mexico	8,677	529
*Santa Fe	7,331	269
Gallup+	1,346	260
Arizona	11,457	692
Phoenix	5,901	466
Tucson	5,556	226
Utah, Salt Lake City	1,537	235
Nevada, Reno-Las Vegas	1,716	283
PACIFIC	**142,883**	**9,567**
Washington	8,270	1,443
*Seattle	5,237	988
Spokane	1,473	301
Yakima	1,560	154
Oregon	4,413	809
*Portland	3,692	655
Baker	721	154
California	124,349	6,864
*Los Angeles	59,527	2,132
*San Francisco	12,731	810
Fresno	10,458	366
Monterey	3,275	132
Oakland	6,497	697
Orange	8,424	541
Sacramento	5,493	623
San Bernardino	4,980	556
San Diego	8,117	684
Santa Rosa	1,809	132
Stockton	3,038	191
Alaska	965	102
*Anchorage	540	56
Fairbanks	297	27
Juneau	128	19
Hawaii, Honolulu	4,886	349
EASTERN RITES	**4,133**	**325**
*Philadelphia	779	23
St. Nicholas	323	32
Stamford	334	5
*Pittsburgh	732	54
Parma	402	60
Passaic	605	33
St. Maron	659	91
Newton (Melkite)	299	27
MILITARY VICARIATE	**17,414**	**2,351**
TOTALS 1979	**896,151**	**77,205**
Totals 1978	890,677	78,598
Totals 1969	1,095,172	102,865

STATISTICAL SUMMARY OF THE CHURCH IN THE U.S.

(Principal source: *The Official Catholic Directory, 1979*. Comparisons are with figures reported in the previous edition.)

Catholic Population: 49,602,035 (22.59 per cent of the total population); decrease, 234,141.

Jurisdictions: 32 archdioceses; 138 dioceses (including Guam); the military vicariate.

Cardinals: 10 (7 head archiepiscopal sees, 3 are retired). As of Sept. 10, 1979.

Archbishops: 55 (29 residential archbishops, including 7 cardinals; 3 titular archbishops; 19 retired, including 3 cardinals; 4 serving outside the U.S.) As of Sept. 10, 1979.

Bishops: 359 (130 residential bishops; 111 titular bishops (109 are auxiliaries); 71 are retired; 47 serving outside the U.S.). As of Sept. 10, 1979.

Abbots: 81.

Priests: 58,430; decrease, 55. Includes: diocesan or secular priests, 35,472 (decrease, 294); religious order priests, 22,958 (increase, 239).

Permanent Deacons: 3,296; increase, 798.

Brothers: 7,965; decrease, 495.

Sisters: 128,378; decrease, 1,013.

Seminarians: 13,960; decrease, 1,038. Includes: diocesan seminarians, 8,694 (decrease, 866); religious order seminarians, 5,266 (decrease, 172).

Infant Baptisms: 896,151; increase, 5,474.

Converts: 77,205; decrease, 1,393.

Marriages: 340,489; decrease, 840.

Deaths: 407,102; increase, 2,939.

Parishes: 18,695; increase, 70.

Seminaries, Diocesan: 92; decrease, 6.

Religious Seminaries, Novitiates, Scholasticates: 258; decrease, 20.

Colleges and Universities: 241; increase, 3. Students, 483,760; increase, 26,262.

High Schools: 1,542; decrease, 30. Students, 853,606; decrease, 15,622.

Elementary Schools: 8,240; decrease, 59. Students, 2,379,816; decrease, 22,962.

Teachers: 169,149; decrease, 1,838. Includes: priests, 5,800 (decrease, 602); scholastics, 162 (decrease, 46); brothers, 3,179 (decrease, 340); sisters, 43,713 (decrease, 2,957); lay teachers, 116,295 (increase, 2,107).

Public School Students in Religious Instruction Programs: 4,786,029; increase, 134,633. Includes: high school students, 1,086,150 (increase, 76,511); elementary school students, 3,699,879 (decrease, 58,122).

Catholic Hospitals: 720; decrease, 8. Patients treated, 34,171,565; increase, 745,717.

Nurses Schools: 121; decrease, 3. Student nurses, 20,136; decrease, 519.

Homes for Aged: 498; increase, 12. Residents, 62,903; increase, 3,128.

Orphanages: 206; children, 14,506; Children in Foster Homes: 15,006.

CATHEDRALS IN THE UNITED STATES

A cathedral is the principal church in a diocese, the one in which the bishop has his seat (*cathedra*). He is the actual rector, although many functions of the church, which usually serves a parish, are the responsibility of a priest serving as the administrator. Because of the dignity of a cathedral, the dates of its dedication and its patronal feast are observed throughout a diocese.

The pope's cathedral, the Basilica of St. John Lateran, is the highest-ranking church in the world.

(Archdioceses are indicated by asterisk.)

Albany, N.Y.: Immaculate Conception.
Alexandria-Shreveport, La.: St. Francis Xavier. (Alexandria); St. John Berchmans (Shreveport Co-Cathedral).
Allentown, Pa.: St. Catherine of Siena.
Altoona-Johnstown, Pa.: Blessed Sacrament (Altoona); St. John Gualbert (Johnstown Co-Cathedral).
Amarillo, Tex.: St. Laurence.
Anchorage,* Alaska: Holy Family.
Arlington, Va: St. Thomas More.
Atlanta,* Ga.: Christ the King.
Austin, Tex.: St. Mary (Immaculate Conception).
Baker, Ore.: St. Francis de Sales.
Baltimore,* Md.: Mary Our Queen; Basilica of the Assumption of the Blessed Virgin Mary (Co-Cathedral).
Baton Rouge, La.: St. Joseph.
Beaumont, Tex.: St. Anthony (of Padua).
Belleville, Ill.: St. Peter.
Biloxi, Miss.: Nativity of the Blessed Virgin Mary.
Birmingham, Ala.: St. Paul.
Bismarck, N.D.: Holy Spirit.
Boise, Ida.: St. John the Evangelist.
Boston,* Mass.: Holy Cross.
Bridgeport, Conn.: St. Augustine.
Brooklyn, N.Y.: St. James.
Brownsville, Tex.: Immaculate Conception.
Buffalo, N.Y.: St. Joseph.
Burlington, Vt.: Immaculate Conception.
Camden, N.J.: Immaculate Conception.
Charleston, S.C.: St. John the Baptist.
Charlotte, N.C.: St. Patrick.
Cheyenne, Wyo.: St. Mary.
Chicago,* Ill.: Holy Name.
Cincinnati,* Ohio: St. Peter in Chains.
Cleveland, Ohio: St. John the Evangelist.
Columbus, Ohio: St. Joseph.
Corpus Christi, Tex.: Corpus Christi.
Covington, Ky.: Basilica of the Assumption.
Crookston, Minn.: Immaculate Conception.

Dallas, Tex.: Cathedral-Santuario de Guadalupe.
Davenport, Ia.: Sacred Heart.
Denver,* Colo.: Immaculate Conception.
Des Moines, Ia.: St. Ambrose.
Detroit,* Mich.: Blessed Sacrament.
Dodge City, Kans.: Sacred Heart.
Dubuque,* Ia.: St. Raphael.
Duluth, Minn.: Holy Rosary.
El Paso, Tex.: St. Patrick.
Erie, Pa.: St. Peter.
Evansville, Ind.: Most Holy Trinity (Pro-Cathedral).
Fairbanks, Alaska: Sacred Heart.
Fall River, Mass.: St. Mary of the Assumption.
Fargo, N.D.: St. Mary.
Fort Wayne-S. Bend, Ind.: Immaculate Conception (Fort Wayne); St. Matthew (South Bend Co-Cathedral).
Fort Worth, Tex.: St. Patrick.
Fresno, Calif.: St. John the Baptist.
Gallup, N.M.: Sacred Heart.
Galveston-Houston, Tex.: St. Mary (Galveston); Sacred Heart (Houston Co-Cathedral).
Gary, Ind.: Holy Angels.
Gaylord, Mich.: St. Mary, Our Lady of Mt. Carmel.
Grand Island, Nebr.: Nativity of Blessed Virgin Mary.
Grand Rapids, Mich.: St. Andrew.
Great Falls, Mont.: St. Ann.
Green Bay, Wis.: St. Francis Xavier.
Greensburg, Pa.: Blessed Sacrament.
Harrisburg, Pa.: St. Patrick.
Hartford,* Conn.: St. Joseph.
Helena, Mont.: St. Helena.
Honolulu, Hawaii: Our Lady of Peace.
Houma-Thibodaux, La.: St. Francis de Sales (Houma); St. Joseph (Thibodaux Co-Cathedral).
Indianapolis,* Ind.: Sts. Peter and Paul.
Jackson, Miss.: St. Peter.
Jefferson City, Mo.: St. Joseph.
Joliet, Ill.: St. Raymond.
Juneau, Alaska: Nativity of the Blessed Virgin Mary.
Kalamazoo, Mich.: St. Augustine.
Kansas City,* Kans.: St. Peter the Apostle.
Kansas City-St. Joseph, Mo.: Immaculate Conception (Kansas City); St. Joseph (St. Joseph Co-Cathedral).
La Crosse, Wis.: St. Joseph.
Lafayette, Ind.: St. Mary.
Lafayette, La.: St. John the Evangelist.
Lansing, Mich.: St. Mary.
Lincoln, Nebr.: Cathedral of the Risen Christ.
Little Rock, Ark.: St. Andrew.
Los Angeles,* Calif.: St. Vibiana.
Louisville,* Ky.: Assumption.
Madison, Wis.: St. Raphael.
Manchester, N.H.: St. Joseph.
Marquette, Mich.: St. Peter.
Memphis, Tenn.: Immaculate Conception.
Miami,* Fla.: St. Mary.
Milwaukee,* Wis.: St. John.
Mobile, Ala.: Immaculate Conception (Minor Basilica).
Monterey, Calif.: San Carlos Borromeo.
Nashville, Tenn.: Incarnation.
Newark,* N.J.: Sacred Heart.
New Orleans,* La.: Cathedral (Basilica) of St. Louis.
Newton, Mass. (Melkite Rite): Our Lady of the Annunciation (Roslindale, Boston).
New Ulm, Minn.: Holy Trinity.
New York,* N.Y.: St. Patrick.
Norwich, Conn.: St. Patrick.
Oakland, Calif.: St. Francis de Sales.
Ogdensburg, N.Y.: St. Mary.
Oklahoma City,* Okla.: Our Lady of Perpetual Help.
Omaha,* Nebr.: St. Cecilia.
Orange, Calif.: Holy Family.
Orlando, Fla.: St. James.
Owensboro, Ky.: St. Stephen.
Parma, Ohio (Byzantine Rite): St. John the Baptist.
Passaic, N.J. (Byzantine Rite): St. Michael.
Paterson, N.J.: St. John the Baptist.
Pensacola-Tallahassee, Fla.: Sacred Heart (Pensacola); St. Thomas More (Tallahassee Co-Cathedral).
Peoria, Ill.: St. Mary.
Philadelphia,* Pa.: Sts. Peter and Paul (Minor Basilica).
Philadelphia,* Pa. (Byzantine Rite): Immaculate Conception.
Phoenix, Ariz.: Sts. Simon and Jude.
Pittsburgh,* Pa. (Byzantine Rite): St. John the Baptist, Munhall.
Pittsburgh, Pa.: St. Paul.
Portland, Me.: Immaculate Conception.
Portland,* Ore.: Immaculate Conception.
Providence, R.I.: Sts. Peter and Paul.
Pueblo, Colo.: Sacred Heart.
Raleigh, N.C.: Sacred Heart.
Rapid City, S.D.: Our Lady of Perpetual Help.
Reno-Las Vegas, Nev.: St. Thomas Aquinas (Reno), Guardian Angel (Las Vegas Co-Cathedral).
Richmond, Va.: Sacred Heart.
Rochester, N.Y.: Sacred Heart.
Rockford, Ill.: St. Peter.
Rockville Centre, N.Y.: St. Agnes.
Sacramento, Calif.: Blessed Sacrament.
Saginaw, Mich.: St. Mary.
St. Augustine, Fla.: St. Augustine (Minor Basilica).
St. Cloud, Minn.: St. Mary.
St. Louis,* Mo.: St. Louis.
St. Maron, Brooklyn, N.Y. (Maronite Rite): Our Lady of Lebanon.
St. Nicholas in Chicago (Byzantine Rite): St. Nicholas.
St. Paul and Minneapolis,* Minn.: St. Paul

(St. Paul); Basilica of St. Mary (Minneapolis Co-Cathedral).
St. Petersburg, Fla.: St. Jude the Apostle.
Salina, Kans.: Sacred Heart.
Salt Lake City, Utah: The Madeleine.
San Angelo, Tex.: Sacred Heart.
San Antonio,* Tex.: San Fernando.
San Bernardino, Calif: Holy Rosary.
San Diego, Calif.: St. Joseph.
San Francisco,* Calif.: St. Mary (Assumption).
Santa Fe,* N.M.: San Francisco de Asis.
Santa Rosa, Calif.: St. Eugene.
Savannah, Ga.: St. John the Baptist.
Scranton, Pa.: St. Peter.
Seattle,* Wash.: St. James.
Sioux City, Ia.: Epiphany.
Sioux Falls, S.D.: St. Joseph.
Spokane, Wash.: Our Lady of Lourdes.
Springfield, Ill.: Immaculate Conception.
Springfield, Mass.: St. Michael.
Springfield-Cape Girardeau, Mo.: St. Agnes (Springfield): St. Mary (Cape Girardeau Co-Cathedral).
Stamford, Conn. (Byzantine Rite): St. Vladimir (Pro-Cathedral).
Steubenville, Ohio: Holy Name.
Stockton, Calif: Annunciation.
Superior, Wis.: Christ the King.
Syracuse, N.Y.: Immaculate Conception.
Toledo, Ohio: Blessed Virgin Mary of the Holy Rosary.
Trenton, N.J.: St. Mary (Assumption).
Tucson, Ariz.: St. Augustine.
Tulsa, Okla.: Holy Family.
Washington,* D.C.: St. Matthew.
Wheeling-Charleston, W. Va.: St. Joseph (Wheeling); Sacred Heart (Charleston Co-Cathedral).
Wichita, Kans.: Immaculate Conception.
Wilmington, Del.: St. Peter.
Winona, Minn.: Sacred Heart.
Worcester, Mass.: St. Paul.
Yakima, Wash.: St. Paul.
Youngstown, Ohio: St. Columba.

BASILICAS IN U.S., CANADA

Basilica is a title assigned to certain churches because of their antiquity, dignity, historical importance or significance as centers of worship. Major basilicas have the papal altar and holy door, which is opened at the beginning of a Jubilee Year; minor basilicas enjoy certain ceremonial privileges.

Among the major basilicas are the patriarchal basilicas of St. John Lateran, St. Peter, St. Paul Outside the Walls and St. Mary Major in Rome; St. Francis and St. Mary of the Angels in Assisi, Italy.

The patriarchal basilica of St. Lawrence, Rome, is a minor basilica.

The dates in the listings below indicate when the churches were designated as basilicas.

Minor Basilicas in U.S., Puerto Rico

Alabama: Mobile, Cathedral of the Immaculate Conception (Mar. 10, 1962).
California: San Francisco, Mission Dolores (Feb. 8, 1952); Carmel, Old Mission of San Carlos (Feb. 5, 1960); Alameda, St. Joseph (Jan. 21, 1972); San Diego, Mission San Diego de Alcala (Nov. 17, 1975).
Florida: St. Augustine, Cathedral of St. Augustine (Dec. 4, 1976).
Illinois: Chicago, Our Lady of Sorrows (May 4, 1956), Queen of All Saints (Mar. 26, 1962).
Indiana: Vincennes, Old Cathedral (Mar. 14, 1970).
Iowa: Dyersville, St. Francis Xavier (May 11, 1956).
Kentucky: Trappist, Our Lady of Gethsemani (May 3, 1949); Covington, Cathedral of Assumption (Dec. 8, 1953).
Louisiana: New Orleans, St. Louis King of France (Dec. 9, 1964).
Maryland: Baltimore, Assumption of the Blessed Virgin Mary (Sept. 1, 1937).
Massachusetts: Roxbury, Perpetual Help ("Mission Church") (Sept. 8, 1954).
Minnesota: Minneapolis. St. Mary (Feb. 1, 1926).
Missouri: Conception, Basilica of Immaculate Conception (Sept. 14, 1940); St. Louis, St. Louis King of France (Jan. 27, 1961).
New York: Brooklyn, Our Lady of Perpetual Help (Sept. 5, 1969); Buffalo, St. Adalbert's (Aug. 11, 1907); Lackawanna, Our Lady of Victory (1926); Youngstown, Blessed Virgin Mary of the Rosary of Fatima (Oct. 7, 1975).
Ohio: Carey, Shrine of Our Lady of Consolation (Oct. 21, 1971).
Pennsylvania: Latrobe, St. Vincent Basilica, Benedictine Archabbey (Aug. 22, 1955); Conewago, Basilica of the Sacred Heart (June 30, 1962); Philadelphia, Sts. Peter and Paul (Sept. 27, 1976).
Wisconsin: Milwaukee, St. Josaphat (Mar. 10, 1929).
Puerto Rico: San Juan, Cathedral of San Juan (Jan. 25, 1978).

Minor Basilicas in Canada

Manitoba: St. Boniface, Cathedral Basilica of St. Boniface (June 10, 1949).
Newfoundland: St. John's, Cathedral Basilica of St. John the Baptist.
Nova Scotia: Halifax, St. Mary's Basilica (June 14, 1950).
Ontario: Ottawa, Basilica of Notre Dame; London, St. Peter's Cathedral (Dec. 13, 1961).
Prince Edward Island: Charlottetown, Basilica of St. Dunstan.
Quebec: Sherbrooke, Cathedral Basilica of St. Michael (July 31, 1959). Montreal, Cathedral Basilica of St. James the Greater; St. Jo-

seph of Mount Royal. Cap-de-la-Madeleine, Basilica of Our Lady of the Cape (Aug. 15, 1964). Quebec, Basilica of Notre Dame; St. Anne de Beaupre, Basilica of St. Anne.

CHANCERY OFFICES OF U.S. ARCHDIOCESES AND DIOCESES

A chancery office, under this or another title, is the central administrative office of an archdiocese or diocese.

(Archdioceses are indicated by asterisk.)

Albany, N.Y.: 465 State St., Box 6297, Quail Station. 12206.

Alexandria-Shreveport, La.: 2315 Texas Ave., P. O. Box 7417, Alexandria. 71306.

Allentown, Pa.: 202 N. 17th St., P.O. Box F. 18105.

Altoona-Johnstown, Pa.: Box 126, Logan Blvd., Hollidaysburg, Pa. 16648.

Amarillo, Tex.: 1800 N. Spring St., P. O. Box 5644. 79107.

Anchorage,* Alaska: P. O. Box 2239. 99510.

Arlington, Va.: 200 N. Glebe Rd. 22203.

Atlanta,* Ga.: 756 W. Peachtree St. N.W. 30308.

Austin, Tex.: N. Congress and 16th, P. O. Box 13327. Capitol Sta. 78711.

Baker, Ore.: Baker and First Sts., P. O. Box 826, 97814.

Baltimore,* Md.: 320 Cathedral St. 21201.

Baton Rouge, La.: P. O. Box 2028. 70821.

Beaumont, Tex.: 703 Archie St., P. O. Box 3948. 77704.

Belleville, Ill.: 5312 W. Main St., Box 896. 62223.

Biloxi, Miss.: P.O. Box 1189. 39533.

Birmingham, Ala.: P. O. Box 2086. 35201.

Bismarck, N.D.: 420 Raymond St., Box 1575. 58501.

Boise, Ida.: Box 769, 420 Idaho St. 83701.

Boston,* Mass.: 2121 Commonwealth Ave., Brighton, Mass. 02135.

Bridgeport, Conn.: The Catholic Center, 238 Jewett Ave. 06606.

Brooklyn, N.Y.: 75 Greene Ave., P.O. Box C. 11202.

Brownsville, Tex.: P. O. Box 2279. 78520.

Buffalo, N.Y.: 35 Lincoln Parkway. 14222.

Burlington, Vt.: 351 North Ave. 05401.

Camden, N.J.: 1845 Haddon Ave., P.O. Box 709, 01801.

Charleston, S.C.: 119 Broad St., P.O. Box 818. 29402.

Charlotte, N.C.: P.O. Box 3776. 28203.

Cheyenne, Wyo.: Box 426. 82001.

Chicago,* Ill.: 155 E. Superior. 60611.

Cincinnati,* O.: 29 E. 8th St. 45202.

Cleveland, O.: Chancery Bldg., 1027 Superior Ave. 44114.

Columbus, O.: 198 E. Broad St. 43215.

Corpus Christi, Tex.: 620 Lipan St. 78401.

Covington, Ky.: 1140 Madison Ave., P.O. Box 192. 41012.

Crookston, Minn.: 1200 Memorial Dr., P.O. Box 610. 56716.

Dallas, Tex.: 3915 Lemmon Ave., P.O. Box 19507. 75219.

Davenport, Ia.: St. Vincent Center, 2706 Gaines St. 52804.

Denver,* Colo.: 200 Josephine St. 80206.

Des Moines, Ia.: 2910 Grand Ave., P.O. Box 1816. 50306.

Detroit,* Mich.: 1234. Washington Blvd. 48226.

Dodge City, Kans.: 910 Central Ave., P.O. Box 849. 67801.

Dubuque,* Ia.: 1229 Mt. Loretta Ave. 52001.

Duluth, Minn.: 215 W. 4th St. 55806.

El Paso, Tex.: 1200 N. Mesa St. 79902.

Erie, Pa.: 205 W. 9th St. 16501.

Evansville, Ind.: P.O. Box 4169. 47711.

Fairbanks, Alaska: 1316 Peger Rd. 99701.

Fall River, Mass.: 47 Underwood St., Box 2577. 02722.

Fargo, N.D.: 1310 Broadway, Box 1750. 58102.

Fort Wayne-South Bend, Ind.: P.O. Box 390, Fort Wayne. 46801.

Fort Worth, Tex.: 1206 Throckmorton St. 76102.

Fresno, Calif.: P.O. Box 1668, 1550 N. Fresno St. 93717.

Gallup, N. Mex.: 711 S. Puerco Dr., P.O. Box 1338. 87301.

Galveston-Houston, Tex.: 1700 San Jacinto St., Houston. 77002.

Gary, Ind.: 975 W. Sixth Ave., P.O. Box M-474. 46401.

Gaylord, Mich.: M-32 West, P.O. Box 700. 49735.

Grand Island, Nebr.: 311 W. 17th St., P.O. Box 996. 68801.

Grand Rapids, Mich.: 265 Sheldon Ave. S. E. 49503.

Great Falls, Mont.: 725 Third Ave. N., P.O. Box 1399. 59403.

Green Bay, Wis.: Box 66. 54305.

Greensburg, Pa.: 723 E. Pittsburgh St. 15601.

Harrisburg, Pa.: P.O. Box 2153. 17105.

Hartford,* Conn.: 134 Farmington Ave. 06105.

Helena, Mont.: 612 Harrison Ave., P.O. Box 1729. 59601.

Honolulu, Hawaii: 1184 Bishop St. 96813.

Houma-Thibodaux, La.: 1220 Aycock St., P.O. Box 9077, Houma, La. 70360.

Indianapolis,* Ind.: 1350 N. Pennsylvania St. 46206.

Jackson, Miss.: 237 E. Amite St., P.O. Box 2248. 39205.

Jefferson City, Mo.: 605 Clark Ave. P.O. Box 417. 65101.

Joliet, Ill.: 425 Summit St. 60435.

Juneau, Alaska: 419 6th St. 99801.

Kalamazoo, Mich.: 215 N. Westnedge. Ave. 49005.

Kansas City,* Kans.: 2220 Central Ave., P.O. Box 2328. 66110.

Kansas City-St. Joseph, Mo.: P.O. Box 1037, Kansas City. 64141.

La Crosse, Wis.: P.O. Box 69. 54601.

Lafayette in Indiana: 610 Lingle Ave. 47902.

Lafayette, La.: P.O. Drawer 3387. 70501.

Lansing, Mich.: 300 W. Ottawa. 48933.

Lincoln, Nebr.: 3400 Sheridan Blvd., P.O. Box 80328. 68501.

Little Rock, Ark.: 2415 N. Tyler St. 72207.

Los Angeles,* Calif.: 1531 W. 9th St. 90015.

Louisville,* Ky.: 212 E. College St., P.O. Box 1073. 40201.

Madison, Wis.: 15 E. Wilson St. 53701.

Manchester, N. H.: 153 Ash St. 03105.

Marquette, Mich.: 444 S. Fourth St., P.O. Box 550. 49855.

Memphis, Tenn.: 1325 Jefferson Ave., 38104.

Miami,* Fla.: 6301 Biscayne Blvd. 33138.

Milwaukee,* Wis.: 345 N. 95th St., P.O. Box 2018. 53201.

Mobile, Ala.: 400 Government St., P.O. Box 1966. 36601.

Monterey, Calif.: 580 Fremont Blvd. 93940.

Nashville, Tenn.: 2400 21st Ave. S. 37219.

Newark,* N.J.: 31 Mulberry St. 07102.

New Orleans,* La.: 7887 Walmsley Ave. 70125.

Newton, Mass. (Melkite Rite): 19 Dartmouth St., W. Newton, Mass. 02165.

New Ulm, Minn.: Chancery Drive. 56073.

New York,* N.Y.: 1011 First Ave. 10022.

Norwich, Conn.: 201 Broadway, P.O. Box 587. 06360.

Oakland, Calif.: 2900 Lakeshore Ave. 94610.

Ogdensburg, N.Y.: 622 Washington St. 13669.

Oklahoma City,* Okla.: P.O. Box 18838. 73118.

Omaha,* Nebr.: 100 N. 62nd St. 68132.

Orange, Calif.: 440 S. Batavia St. 92668.

Orlando, Fla.: P.O. Box 1800. 32802.

Owensboro, Ky.: 4003 Frederica St. 42301.

Parma, Ohio (Byzantine Rite): 1900 Carlton Rd. 44134.

Passaic, N.J. (Byzantine Rite): 101 Market St. 07055.

Paterson, N.J.: 777 Valley Rd., Clifton. 07013.

Pensacola-Tallahassee, Fla.: 11 N. "B" St., Pensacola. 32501.

Peoria, Ill.: 607 N.E. Madison Ave. 61603.

Philadelphia,* Pa.: 222 N. 17th St. 19103.

Philadelphia,* Pa. (Byzantine Rite): 815 N. Franklin St. 19123.

Phoenix, Ariz.: 400 E. Monroe St. 85004.

Pittsburgh,* Pa. (Byzantine Rite): 54 Riverview Ave. 15214.

Pittsburgh, Pa.: 111 Blvd. of the Allies. 15222.

Portland, Me.: 510 Ocean Ave., Woodfords P.O. Box H. 04103.

Portland in Oregon*: 2838 E. Burnside St. 97214.

Providence, R.I.: Cathedral Sq. 02903.

Pueblo, Colo.: 1426 Grand Ave. 81003.

Raleigh, N.C.: 300 Cardinal Gibbons Dr. 27606.

Rapid City, S.D.: 606 Cathedral Dr., P.O. Box 678. 57709.

Reno-Las Vegas, Nev.: 515 Court St., Reno 89509. (Mailing address: P.O. Box 1211, Reno. 89504.)

Richmond, Va.: 807 Cathedral Pl. 23220.

Rochester, N.Y.: 1150 Buffalo Rd. 14624.

Rockford, Ill.: 1245 N. Court St. 61101.

Rockville Centre, N.Y.: 50 N. Park Ave. 11570.

Sacramento, Calif.: 1119 K St., P.O. Box 1706. 95808.

Saginaw, Mich.: 5800 Weiss St. 48603.

St. Augustine, Fla.: Suite 1648, Gulf Life Tower, Jacksonville, Fla. 32207.

St. Cloud, Minn.: P.O. Box 1248. 56301.

St. Louis,* Mo.: 4445 Lindell Blvd. 63108.

St. Maron (Maronite Rite), Brooklyn, N.Y.: 205 82nd St., P.O. Box 333, Ft. Hamilton Sta., Brooklyn. 11209.

St. Nicholas in Chicago (Byzantine Rite): 2245 W. Rice St. 60622.

St. Paul and Minneapolis,* Minn.: 226 Summit Ave., St. Paul. 55102.

St. Petersburg, Fla.: 6363 9th Ave. N. 33710. P.O. Box 13109. 33733.

Salina, Kans.: 421 Country Club Rd., P.O. Box 999. 67401.

Salt Lake City, Utah: 333 E. S. Temple. 84111.

San Angelo, Tex.: 116 S. Oakes. Box 1829. 76902.

San Antonio,* Tex.: 9123 Lorene Lane, P.O. Box 32648. 78284.

San Bernardino, Calif.: 1450 North D St. 92405.

San Diego, Calif.: P.O. Box 80428. 92138.

San Francisco,* Calif.: 445 Church St. 94114.

Santa Fe,* N. Mex.: 202 Morningside Dr. S.E., Albuquerque. 87108.

Santa Rosa, Calif.: 398 10th St., P.O. Box 1297. 95402.

Savannah, Ga.: 225 Abercorn St., P.O. Box 8789. 31412.

Scranton, Pa.: 300 Wyoming Ave. 18503.

Seattle,* Wash.: 907 Terry Ave. 98104.

Sioux City, Ia.: P.O. Box 1530. 51102.

Sioux Falls, S.D.: 423 N. Duluth Ave. 57104.

Spokane, Wash.: 1023 W. Riverside Ave. 99201.

Springfield, Illinois: 524 E. Lawrence Ave. 62705.

Springfield, Mass.: 76 Elliot St. 01105. P.O. Box 1730, 01101.

Springfield-Cape Girardeau, Mo.: 200 McDaniel Bldg., Springfield. 65806.

Stamford, Conn. (Byzantine Rite): 161 Glenbrook Rd. 06902.

Steubenville, Ohio: 422 Washington St., P.O. Box 969. 43952.

Stockton, Calif.: 1105 N. Lincoln St. 95203. P.O. Box 4237. 95204.

Superior, Wis.: 1201 Hughitt Ave. 54880.

Syracuse, N.Y.: 240 E. Onondaga St., 13202.

Toledo, Ohio: 2544 Parkwood Ave. 43610.

Trenton, N.J.: 701 Lawrenceville Rd. 08648.

Tucson, Ariz.: 192 S. Stone Ave., Box 31, 85702.

Tulsa, Okla.: P.O. Box 2009. 74101.

Washington,* D.C.: 1721 Rhode Island Ave. N.W. 20036.

Wheeling-Charleston, W. Va.: 1300 Byron St., Wheeling. 26003.

Wichita, Kans.: 424 N. Broadway. 67202.

Wilmington, Del.: P.O. Box 2030. 19899.

Winona, Minn.: P.O. Box 588. 55987.

Worcester, Mass.: 49 Elm St. 01609.

Yakima, Wash.: 222 Washington Mutual Bldg., P.O. Box 505. 98907.

Youngstown, Ohio: 144 W. Wood St. 44503.

NATIONAL CATHOLIC CONFERENCES

The two conferences described below are related in membership and directive control but distinct in nature, purpose and function.

The National Conference of Catholic Bishops (NCCB) is a strictly ecclesiastical body in and through which the bishops of the United States act together, officially and with authority as pastors of the Church. It is the sponsoring organization of the United States Catholic Conference.

The United States Catholic Conference (USCC) is a civil corporation and operational secretariat in and through which the bishops, together with other members of the Church, act on a wider scale for the good of the Church and society. It is sponsored by the National Conference of Catholic Bishops.

The principal officers of both conferences are: Archbishop John R. Quinn, president; Archbishop John R. Roach, vice president; Archbishop Thomas A. Donnellan, treasurer; Bishop Thomas C. Kelly, O.P., general secretary.

The membership of the Administrative Committee of the NCCB and the Administrative Board of the USCC is identical.

Headquarters of both conferences are located at 1312 Massachusetts Ave. N.W., Washington, D.C. 20005.

NCCB

The National Conference of Catholic Bishops, established by action of the U.S. hierarchy Nov. 14, 1966, is a strictly ecclesiastical body with defined juridical authority over the Church in this country. It was set up with the approval of the Holy See and in line with directives from the Second Vatican Council. Its constitution was formally ratified during the November, 1967, meeting of the U.S. hierarchy.

The NCCB is a development from the Annual Meeting of the Bishops of the United States, whose pastoral character was originally approved by Pope Benedict XV Apr. 10, 1919.

The address of the Conference is 1312 Massachusetts Ave. N.W., Washington, D.C. 20005.

Pastoral Council

The conference, one of many similar territorial conferences envisioned in the conciliar *Decree on the Pastoral Office of Bishops in the Church* (No. 38), is "a council in which the bishops of a given nation or territory (in this case, the United States) jointly exercise their pastoral office to promote the greater good which the Church offers mankind, especially through the forms and methods of the apostolate fittingly adapted to the circumstances of the age."

Its decisions, "provided they have been approved legitimately and by the votes of at least two-thirds of the prelates who have a deliberative vote in the conference, and have been recognized by the Apostolic See, are to have juridically binding force only in those cases prescribed by the common law or determined by a special mandate of the Apostolic See, given either spontaneously or in response to a petition of the conference itself."

All bishops who serve or have served the Church in the U.S., its territories and possessions, have membership and voting rights in the NCCB.

Officers, Committees

The conference operates through a number of bishops' committees with functions in specific areas of work and concern. Their basic assignments are to prepare materials on the basis of which the bishops, assembled as a conference, make decisions, and to put suitable action plans into effect.

The principal officers are: Archbishop John R. Quinn, president; Archbishop John R. Roach, vice president; Archbishop Thomas A. Donnellan, treasurer; Bishop Thomas C. Kelly, O.P., general secretary.

These officers, with several other bishops, hold positions on executive-level committees — Executive Committee, the Committee on Budget and Finance, the Committee on Personnel and Administrative Services, and the Committee on Research, Plans and Programs. They also, with other bishops, serve on the NCCB Administrative Board.

The standing committees and their chairmen (Archbishops and Bishops) are as follows.

American Board of Catholic Missions, John J. Fitzpatrick.

Arbitration, Roger Mahony.

Boundaries of Dioceses and Provinces, John R. Quinn.

Canon Law, Joseph L. Bernardin.

Church in Latin America, Nevin W. Hayes.

Doctrine, Cardinal William Baum.

Ecumenical and Interreligious Affairs, Ernest L. Unterkoefler.

Human Values, Austin B. Vaughan.

Laity, Albert H. Ottenweller.

Liaison with Priests, Religious and Laity, Joseph A. McNicholas.

Liturgy, Rembert Weakland, O.S.B.

Men Religious, John May.

Missions, William G. Connare.

Nomination of Bishops, John R. Quinn.

North American College, Louvain, Edward W. O'Rourke

North American College, Rome, Frank H. Greteman.

Pastoral Research and Practices, Norman F. McFarland.

Permanent Diaconate, Eugene A. Marino.

Priestly Formation, Michael J. Murphy.

Priestly Life and Ministry, Raymond J. Gallagher.

Vocations, Kenneth J. Povish.

Welfare Emergency Relief, John R. Quinn.

Women Religious, John R. McGann.

Ad hoc committees and their chairmen are as follows.

Call to Action Plan, John R. Roach.

Catholic Charismatic Renewal, Kenneth J. Povish.

Diocesan Finances, Cardinal John Dearden.

Evangelization, Francis T. Hurley.

Farm Labor, James S. Rausch.

Hispanic Affairs, Robert Sanchez.

Inter-Rite, William G. Connare.

Liaison with National Office for Black Catholics, William R. Johnson.

Marxism-Communism, Joseph A. McNicholas.

Migration and Tourism, Rene H. Gracida.

National Collections, Thomas J. McDonough.

Parishes, Edward C. O'Leary.

Pro-Life Activities, Cardinal Terence J. Cooke.

Women in Society and Church, Michael F. McAuliffe.

USCC

The United States Catholic Conference, Inc. (USCC), is the operational secretariat and service agency of the National Conference of Catholic Bishops for carrying out the civic-religious work of the Church in this country. It is a civil corporation related to the NCCB in membership and directive control but distinct from it in purpose and function.

The address of the Conference is 1312 Massachusetts Ave. N.W., Washington, D.C. 20005.

Service Secretariat

The USCC, as of Jan. 1, 1967, took over the general organization and operations of the former National Catholic Welfare Conference, Inc., whose origins dated back to the National Catholic War Council of 1917. The council underwent some change after World War I and was established on a permanent basis Sept. 24, 1919, as the National Catholic Welfare Council to serve as a central agency for organizing and coordinating the efforts of U.S. Catholics in carrying out the social mission of the Church in this country. In 1923, its name was changed to National Catholic Welfare Conference, Inc., and clarification was made of its nature as a service agency of the bishops and the Church rather than as a conference of bishops with real juridical authority in ecclesiastical affairs.

The Official Catholic Directory states that the USCC assists "the bishops in their service to the Church in this country by uniting the people of God where voluntary collective action on a broad interdiocesan level is needed. The USCC provides an organizational structure and the resources needed to insure coordination, cooperation, and assistance in the public, educational and social concerns of the Church at the national or interdiocesan level."

Officers, Departments

The principal officers of the USCC are Archbishop John R. Quinn, president; Archbishop John R. Roach, vice president; Archbishop Thomas A. Donnellan, treasurer; Bishop Thomas C. Kelly, O.P., general secretary. These officers, with several other bishops, hold positions on executive-level committees — the Executive Committee; the Committee on Research, Plans and Programs; the Committee on Budget and Finance; the Committee on Personnel and Administrative Services. They also serve on the Administrative Board.

The Executive Committee, organized in 1969, is authorized to handle matters of urgency between meetings of the Administrative Board and the general conference, to coordinate items for the agenda of general meetings, and to speak in the name of the USCC.

The major departments and their chairmen (Archbishops and Bishops) are: Communications, Joseph R. Crowley; Education, Daniel E. Pilarczyk; Social Development and World Peace, Edward D. Head. Each department is supervised by a committee composed of an equal number of episcopal and non-episcopal members, including lay persons.

A national Advisory Council of bishops, priests, men and women religious, lay men and women advises the Administrative Board on overall plans and operations of the USCC.

The administrative general secretariat, in addition to other duties, supervises staff-service offices of Finance and Administration, General Counsel, Government Liaison, and Research, Plans and Programs.

Most of the organizations and associations affiliated with the USCC are covered in separate Almanac entries.

NCCB-USCC REGIONS

For meeting and other operational purposes, the members of the National Conference of Catholic Bishops and the U.S. Catholic Conference are grouped in the following geographical regions.

I. Maine, Vermont, New Hampshire, Massachusetts, Rhode Island, Connecticut.

II. New York.

III. New Jersey, Pennsylvania.

IV. Delaware, District of Columbia, Florida, Georgia, Maryland, North Carolina, South Carolina, Virgin Islands, Virginia, West Virginia.

V. Alabama, Kentucky, Louisiana, Mississippi, Tennessee.

VI. Michigan, Ohio.

VII. Illinois, Indiana, Wisconsin.

VIII. Minnesota, North Dakota, South Dakota, Wyoming, Colorado.

IX. Iowa, Kansas, Missouri, Nebraska.

X. Arizona, Arkansas, New Mexico, Oklahoma, Texas.

XI. California, Hawaii, Nevada, Utah, Caroline-Marshall Islands, Guam.

XII. Idaho, Montana, Alaska, Washington, Oregon.

MEETINGS OF THE CONFERENCES OF BISHOPS

November 13 to 16, 1978

The meeting, held in Washington, D.C., was attended by approximately 250 members of the U.S. hierarchy. The presiding officer was Archbishop John J. Quinn, president of the National Conference of Catholic Bishops and the United States Catholic Conference.

Presidential Address: Archbishop Quinn said in an opening address that the answer of the Church to the crisis of faith in contemporary society is "service."

"The response to unbelief and doubt, the response to the widening secularization of culture, lies — at its highest point — in our own response to the call to holiness and in our search for union with God. It lies, too, in our presence and participation in human affairs, and in our active contribution to solving the anxious human dilemmas of our time, and in our eager collaboration in building up the earthly city for the glory of God. . . . Few societies have had greater need of this unique Christian contribution than ours. Perhaps none has recognized the need less. And here precisely is our challenge."

Papal Message: Pope John Paul II, in a special message transmitted to the meeting by Cardinal Jean Villot, said he confirmed "for the ministry of bishops the absolute priority to be given to guarding and teaching ever more effectively the sacred deposit of Christian doctrine."

Budget: Approved a budget of $16.3 million for NCCB-USCC operations in 1979 (as compared with a budget of $11,480,455 for 1978). Among the largest allocations were those for Migration and Refugee Services ($5.6 million) and the Department of Education ($1.54 million).

Also approved, by a vote of 130 to 16, was a 1979 assessment increase of one cent per Catholic, from seven to eight cents, in each diocese for NCCB-USCC support. A proposal for another increase in 1980 was turned down by a vote of 123 to 23.

By-Law Change: Approved by voice vote a by-law change withdrawing the voting rights of retired bishops in NCCB-USCC affairs. The change was in line with the practice of other episcopal conferences.

Catechetical Directory: Received a letter from the Congregation for the Clergy stating general approval of the text of *Sharing the Light of the Faith,* the National Catechetical Directory. The letter said it was "a generally faithful application of the *General Catechetical Directory,"* but added that there were "certain points of importance that should be reworked before the publication of the first edition." These points concerned the Directory's coverage of revelation, first confession and first Communion, general absolution and the priesthood. (For text of the letter, see National Catechetical Directory.)

Committees: Archbishop Quinn announced the formation of ad hoc committees to review procedures of the Plans and Programs Committee in deciding priorities for funding and to study the structure of general meetings of the conferences.

Communications Collection: A proposal for a nationwide collection to provide funding for the use of radio, television and other media in evangelization was passed by a two-thirds majority vote during the meeting and afterwards by mail. The plan envisioned a possible income of $7 million, with equal shares for national and diocesan use.

Elections: Archbishop Thomas J. Donnellan was elected treasurer, as also were the following (Archbishops, Bishops) chairmen of committees: Joseph L. Bernardin (Canonical Affairs), Ernest L. Unterkoeffler (Ecumenical and Interreligious Affairs), Daniel E.

Pilarczyk (Education), Austin B. Vaughan (Human Values), Albert H. Ottenweller (Laity), Joseph A. McNicholas (Liaison with Priests, Religious and Laity), Rembert Weakland (Liturgy), John J. Fitzpatrick (Missions), Michael J. Murphy (Priestly Formation).

Handicapped: Approved by a vote of 216 to 2 a pastoral letter on the handicapped. The letter noted that "the Church must become an advocate for and with the handicapped," and must "reach out to welcome gratefully those who seek to participate in the ecclesial community." Agenices of the NCCB and the USCC were directed "to address the concerns of handicapped individuals" in their plans and programs. Dioceses, the bishop said, "might make their most valuable contribution in the area of education," and by focusing special attention "on those actually serving handicapped individuals, whether in parishes or some other setting." The letter encouraged efforts at parish levels for contact with the handicapped and action to facilitate their full participation in church life.

The bishops turned down for a second time a proposal for the establishment of a special office for the handicapped because of a lack of funds. The need for such an office was open to question, it was said, given the existence and operation of several organizations and many more diocesan agencies engaged in service to the handicapped.

Liturgy: Three proposals were presented during the meeting.

• Communion More than Once a Day: The bishops voted 200 to 20 to petition the Holy See for permission that would allow "the clergy and faithful to receive the Holy Eucharist on a given day as often as they participate in eucharistic liturgies that are truly distinct celebrations." (Provisions for the reception of Communion twice a day under certain conditions were already in force, in virtue of an instruction, *Immensae Caritatis,* approved by Pope Paul VI Jan. 20, 1973. The Congregation for the Sacraments subsequently declared that the norms of the instruction should not be set aside "merely from motives of devotion." See Holy Communion Twice a Day.)

• Holy Communion under the Forms of Bread and Wine: More than two-thirds of the bishops voted during the meeting or afterwards by mail for allowing the reception of Holy Communion under the forms of bread and wine at Mass on Sundays and holy days — subject to the options of bishops, priests celebrating Mass and persons receiving the Eucharist. (Reception of Communion in this manner on certain occasions was already provided for in directives issued by the Congregation for Divine Worship in 1967 and 1970, and in the General Instruction on the Roman Missal, No. 242.)

Numerous objections were raised against the proposal. It was said that it could lead to irreverence and confusion, would be impractical and unsanitary, would result in a multiplication of special eucharistic ministers, and would entail extra expense and extra time for the administration of Communion.

• Creeds: A motion to allow use of the Apostles' Creed in place of the Nicene Creed at Masses for the people was rejected for want of a two-thirds majority vote. (Such optional use of the Apostles' Creed had been authorized by the Vatican in at least 17 countries, including Canada, France, India, Paraguay and several African nations.

During discussion of this motion, Archbishop Rembert Weakland, new chairman of the Liturgy Committee, mentioned "great dissatisfaction" among bishops with respect to English translations of the Eucharistic Prayers and biblical texts of the Mass authorized by the International Commission for English in the Liturgy. He said the committee would conduct a review of the translations.

Middle East Statement: Approved by a vote of 215 to 8 a statement praising the Camp David accords of the previous summer and expressing support for all efforts toward real peace in the Middle East. The paper, like one issued by the bishops in 1973, focused on five specific points:

• Israel has the right to sovereignty with secure and recognized boundaries.

• Palestinians have the right to participate in negotiations affecting their destiny and to a state of their own.

• Just compensation should be given to Jews and Arabs deprived of property during the past 30 years because of the Middle East conflict.

• Jerusalem's unique religious significance should be recognized and preserved through internationally guaranteed access to the Holy Places and through preservation of the city's religious pluralism.

• The United Nations Resolution 242 is still useful as a basis for peace in the Middle East.

The statement also included an amendment on Lebanon, which declared:

"The dimensions of the Lebanese problems are so great that a grave responsibility for assistance lies not only with a group of nations, but requires the interest, care and action of the international community, especially the continuing involvement of the United Nations. The urgent needs of the nation are that the cease-fire be preserved, that the Lebanese army be rebuilt to provide for the internal security of the country, that discussions among local parties be fostered to establish a new constitution safeguarding the human rights and religious liberty of all inhabitants in Lebanon, and that the sovereignty of Lebanon be securely preserved. The neutrality of Lebanon must be guaranteed and preserved in order to keep the country independent and sovereign."

Reports and Views: The bishops received committee reports and heard views expressed about a number of subjects, including: vocations to the priesthood and religious life; clergy retirement, pastoral ministry to Hispanics and migrant workers; continuing support for criteria already in force for the allocation of funds by the Campaign for Human Development; dialogue with women on ministry; pro-life activities; apostolic succession, a topic of interfaith dialogue; an appeal to President Carter for intervention on behalf of refugees from Southeast Asia. The bishops also considered ways and means of monitoring government actions which some speakers called unwarranted interference in church affairs.

Decisions Reversed: Before the meeting began, the Administrative Board of the USCC overruled earlier decisions of the Committee on Plans and Programs to terminate the Secretariat for Human Values and to phase out, prematurely in 1979, the research and counsultation services of Msgr. George Higgins. The committee decisions, it was reported, were made for budgetary reasons. The board's reversal was made in response to adverse criticism from church and civic leaders.

May 1 to 3, 1979

Two hundred and 75 bishops attended the meeting in Chicago.

Presidential Address: Archbishop John R. Quinn keyed his opening presidential address to the contents of Pope John Paul's encyclical *Redemptor Hominis* and to two objectives stated by the Holy Father the previous January during the Third General Assembly of Latin American Bishops in Puebla, Mexico.

The objectives were: "to affirm the necessity of the social involvement of the Church, and to affirm that the Church always does this precisely as a community of faith living in the light of divine revelation and thus committed to shaping history in light of a transcendent vision of the human person."

The conference president related these objectives to:

• The Priesthood: "The first service of the Church to the world is holiness and fidelity, and . . . we bishops and priests are called to be leaders precisely in the daily search for holiness and the daily witness of fidelity."

• Human Life, with special references: "Abortion certainly, and to some degree the laboratory production of human life, poison the psychological wellspring of reverence for the sovereignty of the human person."

• Middle East: "For steps beyond the (Camp David) peace treaty which will deal with the rights of the Palestinians and broaden the negotiating process in a way that other Arab states will be moved to participate in it."

• Puebla Meeting of Latin American Bishops: The commitment of the bishops at their meeting Jan. 27 to Feb. 13, with respect to the role of the Church in evangelization and human liberation, raises the question of the social responsibility of the Church. This responsibility "must certainly mean, at the minimum, participation in the public debate about U.S. policies and practice toward developing nations and what responsible stewardship means for the Church in the matter of its own corporate investments." Situations and structures of injustice, he said, "call for daring initiatives to produce more appropriate institutions for relations among states and peoples not based on violence and terrorism."

The bishops agreed to a study of the feasibility of a Puebla-like meeting oriented to conditions of the Church in the U.S. (See Third General Assembly of Latin American Bishops.)

Church-State Relations: Bishop William E. McManus of Fort Wayne-South Bend called attention to the need for coping with situations involving the possibility of government encroachment on the freedom and rights of the Church. Examples of such situations were intervention by the National Labor Relations Board in Catholic school teacher negotiations and efforts to require church-related schools to pay unemployment insurance taxes. The Church, he urged, should have its own way of handling these and similar matters.

Conference Meetings: Continuing study was reported by Archbishop Joseph L. Bernardin, of Cincinnati, of questions related to the frequency, structure, agenda and formalities of NCCB-USCC meetings, for the purpose of developing "more opportunities" for effective interaction among the bishops and action by the conferences. These subjects were the principal items on the agenda of the meeting.

Confirmation: Auxiliary Bishop Joseph McKinney of Grand Rapids appealed for the development of confirmation follow-up programs to offset the drift of young persons away from the Church after reception of the sacrament.

Liturgy: Archbishop Rembert Weakland, O.S.B., reported that suggestions had been made for changing the position of some parts of the Mass, including the *Gloria* and the sign of peace. In response, his committee framed the following resolution: "Whereas there are requests and needs to study the place, role and function of the various elements of the present *Ordo Missae;* and whereas it is the belief that no changes should be introduced piecemeal at this time: we have resolved that the Bishops' Committee on the Liturgy initiate at once a vigorous study of the ritual elements of the *Ordo Missae* with a view toward future adaptations apropos to the Catholic Church in the U.S."

Bishop John R. McGann of Rockville Centre, noting a 15-year decline in the practice, recommended that the bishops issue a pastoral statement on frequent and regular reception of the sacrament of reconciliation.

Ordination of Women: Archbishop Quinn announced that a petition from the Women of the Church Coalition, challenging the "Declaration on the Question of the Admission of Women to the Ministerial Priesthood," was being forwarded to the Vatican without endorsement. The petition, signed by 13,000 persons and approved by 13 national organizations, urged the bishops — which they refused to do — to ask for repeal of the argument that only men, because of their sex, could be ordained as priest-representatives of Christ.

Synod Delegates: Delegates elected to attend the 1980 assembly of the Synod of Bishops were: Archbishops Quinn, Bernardin, and Robert F. Sanchez of Santa Fe, and Auxiliary Bishop J. Francis Stafford of Baltimore. Alternates were Bishops Walter W. Curtis of Bridgeport and Lawrence Welsh of Spokane.

Women Religious: The Committee for Liaison with Women Religious reported that some communities were using funds withdrawn from corporate investments for their own needs (retirement programs, past debts, current operating expenses) rather than for assistance to the needy and other ministerial concerns. Also reported was a suggestion for expanded consultation with respect to decisions on divestment and subsequent fund allocations.

STATE CATHOLIC CONFERENCES

These conferences are agencies of bishops and dioceses in the various states. Their general purposes are to develop and sponsor cooperative programs designed to cope with pastoral and common-welfare needs, and to represent the dioceses before governmental bodies, the public, and in private sectors. Their membership consists of representatives from the dioceses in the states — bishops, clergy and lay persons in various capacities.

The **National Association of State Catholic Conference Directors** maintains liaison with the general secretariat of the United States Catholic Conference. Thomas A. Horkan, Jr., of Florida is president.

Alaska Catholic Conference, 419 6th St., Juneau, Alaska 99801; exec. dir., Frank W. Matulich.

Arizona Catholic Conference, 400 E. Monroe St., Phoenix, Ariz. 85004; exec. dir., Thomas F. Allt.

California Catholic Conference, 926 J St., Suite 1100, Sacramento, Calif. 95814; exec. dir., Msgr. John A. Dickie.

Colorado Catholic Conference, 200 Josephine St., Denver, Colo. 80206; exec. dir., Sr. Loretto Anne Madden.

Connecticut Catholic Conference, 134 Farmington Ave., Hartford, Conn. 06105; exec. dir., William Wholean.

Florida Catholic Conference, P.O. Box 1571, Tallahassee, Fla. 32302; exec. dir., Thomas A. Horkan, Jr.

Georgia Catholic Conference, 206 Seventh St., Augusta, Ga. 30902; exec. dir., Cheatham E. Hodges, Jr.

Illinois Catholic Conference, 201 E. Ohio St., Chicago, Ill. 60611; 300 E. Monroe St., Springfield, Ill. 62701; exec. dir., Rev. William J. Lion.

Indiana Catholic Conference, Suite 315, 5435 Emerson Way N., Indianapolis, Ind. 46226; exec. dir., Raymond R. Rufo.

Iowa Catholic Conference, 818 Insurance Exchange Building, Des Moines, Iowa 50309; exec. dir., Timothy McCarthy.

Kansas Catholic Conference, 702 Commercial National Bank Bldg., Kansas City, Kan. 66101; exec. dir., Vincent W. DeCoursey.

Kentucky Catholic Conference, P.O. Box 1073, Louisville, Ky. 40201; chairman, Most Rev. Thomas J. McDonough, Archbishop of Louisville.

Louisiana Catholic Conference, P.O. Box 52948, New Orleans, La. 70152; exec. dir., Emile Comar.

Maryland Catholic Conference, 320 Cathedral St., Baltimore, Md. 21201; exec. dir., Francis X. McIntyre.

Massachusetts Catholic Conference, Parker House, Room 180, Boston, Mass. 02107; exec. dir., Rev. Michael F. Groden.

Michigan Catholic Conference, P.O. Box 10157, Lansing, Mich. 48901; exec. dir., Thomas M. Bergeson.

Minnesota Catholic Conference, 145 University Ave., W., St. Paul, Minn. 55103; exec. dir., John F. Markert.

Missouri Catholic Conference, P.O. Box 1022, Jefferson City, Mo. 65102; exec. dir., Miss Peggy J. Keilholz.

Montana Catholic Conference, P.O. Box 1708, Helena, Mont. 59601; exec. dir., John Frankino.

Nebraska Catholic Conference, 521 S. 14th St., Lincoln, Nebr. 68508; exec. dir., James R. Cunningham.

New Jersey Catholic Conference, 211 N. Warren St., Trenton, N.J. 08618; exec. dir., Edward J. Leadem.

New York State Catholic Conference, 11 N. Pearl St., Albany, N.Y. 12207; exec. dir., Charles J. Tobin, Jr.

North Dakota Catholic Conference, 107 N.

4th St. — Room 11, Bismarck, N. Dak. 58501; exec. dir., Mrs. Kitty Engelstad.

Ohio, Catholic Conference of, 174 E. Long St., Suite 600, Columbus, Ohio 43215; exec. dir., Theodore N. Staudt.

Oregon Catholic Conference was established in 1979 by the bishops of Oregon.

Pennsylvania Catholic Conference, 509 N. Second St., Harrisburg, Pa. 17105; exec. dir., Howard J. Fetterhoff.

Texas Catholic Conference, 3001 S. Congress Ave., Austin, Tex. 78704; exec. dir., Bro. Richard Daly, C.S.C.

Washington State Catholic Conference, 1319 2nd Ave., Seattle, Wash. 98101; exec. dir. Rev. D. Harvey McIntyre.

Wisconsin Catholic Conference, 30 W. Mifflin St., Suite 910, Madison, Wis. 53703; exec. dir., Charles M. Phillips.

Biographies of American Bishops

(Sources: Almanac survey, *The Official Catholic Directory*, NC News Service. As of Oct. 20, 1979.)

A

Abramowicz, Alfred L.: b. Jan. 27, 1919, Chicago, Ill.; educ. St. Mary of the Lake Seminary (Mundelein, Ill.), Gregorian Univ. (Rome); ord. priest May 1, 1943; ord. titular bishop of Paestum and auxiliary bishop of Chicago, June 13, 1968.

Ackerman, Richard Henry, C.S.Sp.: b. Aug. 30, 1903, Pittsburgh, Pa.; educ. Duquesne Univ. (Pittsburgh, Pa.), St. Mary's Scholasticate (Norwalk, Conn.), Univ. of Fribourg (Switzerland); ord. priest Aug. 28, 1926; ord. titular bishop of Lares and auxiliary bishop of San Diego, May 22, 1956; app. bishop of Covington, Apr. 4, 1960; resigned Nov. 28, 1978.

Ahern, Patrick V.: b. Mar. 8, 1919, New York, N.Y.; educ. Manhattan College and Cathedral College (New York City), St. Joseph's Seminary (Yonkers, N.Y.), St. Louis Univ. (St. Louis, Mo.), Notre Dame Univ. (Notre Dame, Ind.); ord. priest Jan. 27, 1945; ord. titular bishop of Naiera and auxiliary bishop of New York, Mar. 19, 1970.

Ahr, George William: b. June 23, 1904, Newark, N.J.; educ. St. Vincent College (Latrobe, Pa.), Seton Hall College (S. Orange, N.J.), North American College (Rome); ord. priest July 29, 1928; ord. bishop of Trenton, Mar. 20, 1950; resigned 1979.

Anderson, Paul F.: b. Apr. 20, 1917, Roslindale, Mass.; educ. Boston College (Chestnut Hill, Mass.), St. John's Seminary (Brighton, Mass.); ord. priest Jan. 6, 1943; ord. titular bishop of Polignando and coadjutor bishop of Duluth, Oct. 17, 1968; bishop of Duluth, Apr. 30, 1969.

Angell, Kenneth A.: b. Aug. 3, 1930, Providence, R.I.; educ. St. Mary's Seminary (Baltimore, Md.); ord. priest May 26, 1956; ord. titular bishop of Septimunicia and auxiliary bishop of Providence, R.I., Oct. 7, 1974.

Arkfeld, Leo, S.V.D.: b. Feb. 4, 1912, Butte, Nebr.; educ. Divine Word Seminary (Techny, Ill.), Sacred Heart College (Girard, Pa.); ord. priest Aug. 15, 1943; ord. titular bishop of Bucellus and vicar apostolic of Central New Guinea, Nov. 30, 1948; name of vicariate changed to Wewak, May 15, 1952; first bishop of Wewak, Nov. 15, 1966; app. archbishop of Madang, Papua New Guinea, Dec. 19, 1975.

Arliss, Reginald, C.P.: b. Sept. 8, 1906, East Orange, N.J.; educ. Immaculate Conception Seminary (Jamaica, N.Y.) and other Passionist houses of study; ord. priest Apr. 28, 1934; missionary in China for 16 years, expelled 1951; missionary in Philippines; rector of the Pontifical Philippine College Seminary in Rome, 1961-69; ord. titular bishop of Cerbali and prelate of Marbel, Philippines, Jan. 30, 1970.

Arzube, Juan: b. June 1, 1918, Guayaquil, Ecuador; educ. Rensselaer Polytechnic Institute (Troy, N.Y.), St. John's Seminary (Camarillo, Calif.); ord. priest May 5, 1954; ord. titular bishop of Civitate and auxiliary bishop of Los Angeles, Mar. 25, 1971.

B

Balke, Victor: b. Sept. 29, 1931, Meppen, Ill.; educ. St. Mary of the Lake Seminary (Mundelein, Ill.), St. Louis Univ. (St. Louis, Mo.); ord. priest May 24, 1958; ord. bishop of Crookston, Sept. 2, 1976.

Bartholome, Peter William: b. Apr. 2, 1893, Bellechester, Minn.; educ. Campion College (Prairie du Chien, Wis.), St. Paul Seminary (St. Paul, Minn.), Apollinare (Rome); ord. priest June 12, 1917; ord. titular bishop of Lete and coadjutor bishop of St. Cloud, Mar. 3, 1942; bishop of St. Cloud, May 31, 1953; resigned 1968.

Baum, William W.: (See Cardinals, Biographies.)

Begley, Michael J.: b. Mar. 12, 1909, Mattineague, Mass.; educ. Mt. St. Mary Seminary (Emmitsburg, Md.); ord. priest May 26, 1934; ord. first bishop of Charlotte, N.C., Jan. 12, 1972.

Bell, Alden J.: b. July 11, 1904, Peterborough, Ont., Canada; educ. St. Joseph's College (Mountain View, Calif.), St. Patrick's Seminary (Menlo Park, Calif.), Catholic Univ. (Washington, D.C.); ord. priest May 14, 1932; ord. titular bishop of Rhodopolis and auxiliary bishop of Los Angeles, June 4, 1956; app. bishop of Sacramento, Mar. 30, 1962; resigned 1979.

Beltran, Eusebius J.: b. Aug. 31, 1934, Ashley, Pa.; educ. St. Charles Seminary (Philadelphia, Pa.); ord. priest May 14, 1960; ord. bishop of Tulsa Apr. 20, 1978.

Benincasa, Pius A.: b. July 8, 1913, Niagara Falls, N.Y.: educ. Propaganda Univ. and Lateran Univ. (Rome); ord. priest Mar. 27, 1937; served in Vatican Secretariat of State, 1954-64; ord. titular bishop of Buruni and auxiliary bishop of Buffalo, June 29, 1964.

Bernardin, Joseph L.: b. Apr. 2, 1928, Columbia, S.C.; educ. St. Mary's Seminary (Baltimore, Md.), Catholic Univ. (Washington, D.C.); ord. priest Apr. 26, 1952; ord. titular bishop of Lugura and auxiliary bishop of Atlanta, Apr. 26, 1966; general secretary of the USCC and NCCB, 1968-72; app. archbishop of Cincinnati, Nov. 21, 1972; installed Dec. 19, 1972; president NCCB/USCC, 1974-77.

Bernarding, George, S.V.D.: b. Feb. 15, 1912, Carrick, Pa.; educ. Divine Word Seminary (Girard, Pa.); ord. priest Aug. 13, 1939; ord. titular bishop of Belabitene and first vicar apostolic of Mount Hagen, New Guinea, Apr. 21, 1960; first bishop of Mount Hagen, Nov. 15, 1966.

Bilock, John M.: b. June 20, 1916, McAdoo, Pa.; educ. St Procopius College and Seminary (Lisle, Ill.); ord. priest Feb. 3, 1946; vicar general of Byzantine archdiocese of Munhall, 1969; ord. titular bishop of Pergamum and auxiliary bishop of Munhall, May 15, 1973; title of see changed to Pittsburgh, 1977.

Binz, Leo: b. Oct. 31, 1900, Stockton, Ill.; educ. Loras College (Dubuque, Ia.), St. Mary's Seminary (Baltimore, Md.), Sulpician Seminary (Washington, D.C.), North American College, Propaganda Univ., Gregorian Univ. (Rome); ord. priest Mar. 15, 1924; ord. titular bishop of Pinara and coadjutor bishop and apostolic administrator of Winona, Dec. 21, 1942; app. titular archbishop of Silyum and coadjutor archbishop of Dubuque, Oct. 15, 1949; app. assistant at the papal throne, June 11, 1954; archbishop of Dubuque, Dec. 2, 1954; app. archbishop of St. Paul, Dec. 16, 1961, installed Feb. 28, 1962; title changed to St. Paul and Minneapolis, 1966; retired May 28, 1975. Died Oct. 8, 1979.

Biskup, George J.: b. Aug. 23, 1911, Cedar Rapids, Ia.; educ. Loras College (Dubuque, Ia). North American College (Rome), State Univ. of Iowa (Iowa City, Ia); ord. priest Mar. 19, 1937; ord. titular bishop of Hemeria and auxiliary bishop of Dubuque, Apr. 24, 1957; app. bishop of Des Moines, Jan. 30, 1965; app. titular archbishop of Tamalluma and coadjutor of Indianapolis, July 26, 1967; archbishop of Indianapolis, Jan. 14, 1970; resigned 1979. Died Oct. 17, 1979.

Blanchette, Romeo: b. Jan. 6, 1913, St. George, Ill.; educ. St. Mary of the Lake Seminary (Mundelein, Ill.), Gregorian Univ. (Rome); ord. priest Apr. 3, 1937; vicar general of Joliet, 1950-66; ord. titular bishop of Maxita and auxiliary of Joliet, Apr. 3, 1965; app. bishop of Joliet, July 19, 1966, installed Aug. 31, 1966; resigned 1979.

Boccella, John H., T.O.R.: b. June 25, 1912, Castelfranci, Italy; came to US at the age of two; educ. St. Francis College and Seminary (Loretto, Pa.), Angelicum Univ. (Rome), Catholic Univ. (Washington, D.C.); ord. priest Mar. 29, 1941; minister general of Third Order Regular, 1947-65; ord. archbishop of Izmir, Turkey, Apr. 17, 1968.

Bokenfohr, John, O.M.I.: b. Jan. 28, 1903, West Point, Nebr.; ord. priest July 11, 1927; ord. bishop of Kimberley, S. Africa, May 3, 1963; resigned July 17, 1974.

Boland, Ernest B., O.P.: b. July 10, 1925, Providence, R.I.; educ. Providence College (Rhode Island), Dominican Houses of Study (Somerset, Ohio; Washington, D.C.); ord. priest June 9, 1955; ord. bishop of Multan, Pakistan, July 25, 1966.

Borders, William D.: b. Oct. 9, 1913, Washington, Ind.; educ. St. Meinrad Seminary (St. Meinrad, Ind.), Notre Dame Seminary (New Orleans, La.), Notre Dame Univ. (Notre Dame, Ind.); ord. priest May 18, 1940; ord. first bishop of Orlando, June 14, 1968; app. archbishop of Baltimore, Apr. 2, 1974, installed June 26, 1974.

Bosco, Anthony G.: b. Aug. 1, 1927, New Castle, Pa.; educ. St. Vincent Seminary (Latrobe, Pa.), Lateran Univ. (Rome); ord. priest June 7, 1952; ord. titular bishop of Labicum and auxiliary of Pittsburgh, June 30, 1970.

Boudreaux, Warren L.: b. Jan. 25, 1918, Berwick, La.; educ. St. Joseph's Seminary (St. Benedict, La.), St. Sulpice Seminary (Paris, France), Notre Dame Seminary (New Orleans, La.), Catholic Univ. (Washington, D.C.); ord. priest May 30, 1942; ord. titular bishop of Calynda and auxiliary bishop of Lafayette, La., July 25, 1962; app. bishop of Beaumont, June 5, 1971; app. first bishop of Houma-Thibodaux, installed June 5, 1977.

Breitenbeck, Joseph M.: b. Aug. 3, 1914, Detroit, Mich.; educ. University of Detroit, Sacred Heart Seminary (Detroit, Mich.), North American College and Lateran Univ. (Rome), Catholic Univ. (Washington, D.C.); ord. priest May 30, 1942; ord. titular bishop of Tepelta and auxiliary bishop of Detroit, Dec. 20, 1965; app. bishop of Grand Rapids, Oct. 15, 1969, installed Dec. 2, 1969.

Brizgys, Vincas: b. Nov. 10, 1903, Plyniai, Lithuania; ord. priest June 5, 1927; ord. titular bishop of Bosano and auxiliary bishop of Kaunas, Lithuania, May 10, 1940; taken into custody and deported to Germany, 1944; liberated by Americans, 1945; U.S. citizen, 1958.

Broderick, Edwin B.: b. Jan. 16, 1917, New York, N.Y.; educ. Cathedral College (New York City), St. Joseph's Seminary (Yonkers, N.Y.), Fordham Univ. (New York City); ord. priest May 30, 1942; ord. titular bishop of

Tizica and auxiliary of New York, Apr. 21, 1967; bishop of Albany, 1969-76; executive director of Catholic Relief Services, 1976.

Brown, Charles, A., M.M.: b. Aug. 20, 1919, New York, N.Y.; educ. Cathedral College (New York City), Maryknoll Seminary (Maryknoll, N.Y.); ord. priest June 9, 1946; ord. titular bishop of Vallis and auxiliary bishop of Santa Cruz, Bolivia, Mar. 27, 1957.

Brunini, Joseph B.: b. July 24, 1909, Vicksburg, Miss.; educ. Georgetown Univ. (Washington, D.C.), North American College (Rome), Catholic Univ. (Washington, D.C.); ord. priest Dec. 5, 1933; ord. titular bishop of Axomis and auxiliary bishop of Natchez-Jackson, Jan. 29, 1957; apostolic administrator of Natchez-Jackson, 1966; app. bishop of Natchez-Jackson, Dec. 2, 1967, installed Jan. 29, 1968; title of see changed to Jackson, 1977.

Brust, Leo J.: b. Jan. 7, 1916, St. Francis, Wis.; educ. St. Francis Seminary (Milwaukee, Wis.), Canisianum (Innsbruck, Austria), Catholic Univ. (Washington, D.C.); ord. priest May 30, 1942; ord. titular bishop of Suelli and auxiliary bishop of Milwaukee, Oct. 16, 1969.

Brzana, Stanislaus J.: b. July 1, 1917, Buffalo, N.Y.; educ. Christ the King Seminary (St. Bonaventure, N.Y.), Gregorian Univ. (Rome); ord. priest June 7, 1941; ord, titular bishop of Cufruta and auxiliary bishop of Buffalo, June 29, 1964; bishop of Ogdensburg, Oct. 22, 1968.

Burke, James C., O.P.: b. Nov. 30, 1926, Philadelphia, Pa.; educ. King's College (Wilkes-Barre, Pa.), Providence College (R.I.); ord. priest June 8, 1956; ord. titular bishop of Lamiggiga and prelate of Chimbote, Peru, May 25, 1967, resigned 1978. Vicar for urban affairs, Wilmington, Del., diocese.

Buswell, Charles A.: b. Oct. 15, 1913, Homestead, Okla.; educ. St. Louis Preparatory Seminary (St. Louis, Mo.), Kenrick Seminary (Webster Groves, Mo.), American College, Univ. of Louvain (Belgium); ord. priest July 9, 1939; ord. bishop of Pueblo, Sept. 30, 1959; resigned Sept. 18, 1979.

Byrne, James J.: b. July 28, 1908, St. Paul, Minn.; educ. Nazareth Hall Preparatory Seminary and St. Paul Seminary (St. Paul, Minn.), Univ. of Minnesota (Minneapolis, Minn.); Louvain Univ. (Belgium); ord. priest June 3, 1933; ord. titular bishop of Etenna and auxiliary bishop of St. Paul, July 2, 1947; app. bishop of Boise, June 16, 1956; app. archbishop of Dubuque, Mar. 19, 1962, installed May 8, 1962.

C

Caesar, Raymond R., S.V.D.: b. Feb. 14, 1932, Eunice, La.; educ. Divine Word Seminary (Bay St. Louis, Miss.); Catholic Univ. (Washington, D.C.); ord. priest June 4, 1961; missionary in New Guinea from 1962; ord. coadjutor bishop of Goroka, Papua New Guinea, Oct. 25, 1978.

Caillouet, L. Abel.: b. Aug. 2, 1900, Thibodaux, La.; educ. St. Joseph's Preparatory Seminary (St. Benedict, La.), St. Mary's Seminary (Baltimore, Md.), North American College (Rome); ord. priest Mar. 7, 1925; ord. titular bishop of Setea and auxiliary bishop of New Orleans, Oct. 28, 1947; retired July 7, 1976.

Carberry, John J.: (See Cardinals, Biographies.)

Carroll, Mark K.: b. Nov. 19, 1896, St. Louis, Mo.; educ. St. Louis Preparatory Seminary and Kenrick Seminary (St. Louis, Mo.); ord. priest June 10, 1922; ord. bishop of Wichita, Apr. 23, 1947; retired, 1963, but retained title; resigned, 1967.

Casey, James V.: b. Sept. 22, 1914, Osage, Ia.; educ. Loras College (Dubuque, Ia.), North American College (Rome), Catholic Univ. (Washington, D.C.); ord. priest Dec. 8, 1939; ord. titular bishop of Citium and auxiliary bishop of Lincoln, Apr. 24, 1957; bishop of Lincoln, June 14, 1957; app. archbishop of Denver, Feb. 22, 1967, installed May 17, 1967.

Cassata, John J.: b. Nov. 8, 1908, Galveston, Tex.; educ. St. Mary's Seminary (La Porte, Tex.), North American College, Urbana Univ. and Gregorian Univ. (Rome); ord. priest Dec. 8, 1932; ord. titular bishop of Bida and auxiliary bishop of Dallas-Fort Worth, June 5, 1968; app. bishop of Fort Worth, Aug. 27, 1969, installed Oct. 21, 1969.

Chavez, Gilbert Espinoza: b. May 9, 1932, Ontario, Calif.; educ. St. Francis Seminary (El Cajon, Calif.), Immaculate Heart Seminary (San Diego), Univ. of California; ord. priest Mar. 19, 1960; ord. titular bishop of Magarmel and auxiliary of San Diego, June 21, 1974.

Clark, Matthew H.: b. July 15, 1937, Troy, N.Y.; educ. St. Bernard's Seminary (Rochester, N.Y.), Gregorian Univ. (Rome); ord. priest Dec. 19, 1962; ord. bishop of Rochester, May 27, 1979; installed June 26, 1979.

Clinch, Harry A.: b. Oct. 27, 1908, San Anselmo, Calif.; educ. St. Joseph's College (Mountain View, Calif.), St. Patrick's Seminary (Menlo Park, Calif.); ord. priest June 6, 1936; ord. titular bishop of Badiae and auxiliary bishop of Monterey-Fresno, Feb. 27, 1957; app. first bishop of Monterey in California, installed Dec. 14, 1967.

Cody, John P.: (See Cardinals, Biographies.)

Cohill, John Edward, S.V.D.: b. Dec. 13, 1907, Elizabeth, N.J.; educ. Divine Word Seminary (Techny, Ill.); ord. priest Mar. 20, 1936; ord. first bishop of Goroko, Papua New Guinea, Mar. 11, 1967.

Comber, John W., M.M.: b. Mar. 12, 1906, Lawrence, Mass.; educ. St. John's Preparatory College (Danvers, Mass.), Boston College (Boston, Mass.), Maryknoll Seminary (Maryknoll, N.Y.); ord. priest Feb. 1, 1931; superior general of Maryknoll, 1956-66; ord. titular bishop of Foratiana, Apr. 9, 1959.

Connare, William G.: b. Dec. 11, 1911, Pittsburgh, Pa.; educ. Duquesne Univ. (Pittsburgh, Pa.), St. Vincent Seminary (Latrobe, Pa.); ord. priest June 14, 1936; ord. bishop of Greensburg, May 4, 1960.

Connolly, James L.: b. Nov. 15, 1894, Fall River, Mass.; educ. St. Charles College (Catonsville, Md.), St. Mary's Seminary (Baltimore, Md.), Catholic Univ. (Washington, D.C.), Louvain Univ. (Belgium); ord. priest Dec. 21, 1923; rector of St. Paul (Minn.) minor seminary 1940-43, major seminary 1943-45; ord. titular bishop of Mylasa and coadjutor of Fall River, May 24, 1945; bishop of Fall River, May 17, 1951; resigned Oct. 30, 1970.

Connolly, Thomas Arthur: b. Oct. 5, 1899, San Francisco, Calif.; educ. St. Patrick's Seminary (Menlo Park, Calif.), Catholic Univ. (Washington, D.C.); ord. priest June 11, 1926; ord. titular bishop of Sila and auxiliary bishop of San Francisco, Aug. 24, 1939; app. coadjutor bishop of Seattle, Feb. 28, 1948; succeeded as bishop of Seattle, May 18, 1950; first archbishop of Seattle, June 23, 1951; retired Feb. 25, 1975.

Connolly, Thomas J.: b. July 18, 1922, Tonopah, Nev.; educ. St. Patrick's Seminary (Menlo Park, Calif.), Catholic Univ. (Washington, D.C.), Lateran Univ. (Rome); ord. priest Apr. 8, 1947; ord. bishop of Baker, June 30, 1971.

Connors, Ronald G., C.SS.R.: b. Nov. 1, 1915, Brooklyn, N.Y.; ord. priest June 22, 1941; ord. titular bishop of Equizetum and coadjutor bishop of San Juan de la Maguana, Dominican Republic, July 20, 1976; succeeded as bishop of San Juan de la Maguana, July 20, 1977.

Cooke, Terence J.: (See Cardinals, Biographies.)

Coscia, Benedict Dominic, O.F.M.: b. Aug. 10, 1922, Brooklyn, N.Y.; educ. St. Francis College (Brooklyn, N.Y.), Holy Name College (Washington, D.C.); ord. priest June 11, 1949; ord. bishop of Jataí, Brazil, Sept. 21, 1961.

Cosgrove, William M.: b. Nov. 26, 1916, Canton, Ohio; educ. John Carroll Univ. (Cleveland, O.); ord. priest Dec. 18, 1943; ord. titular bishop of Trisipa and auxiliary bishop of Cleveland, Sept. 3, 1968; app. bishop of Belleville, installed Oct. 28, 1976.

Costello, Thomas J.: b. Feb. 23, 1929, Camden, N.Y.; educ. Niagara Univ. (Niagara Falls, N.Y.), St. Bernard's Seminary (Rochester, N.Y.), Catholic Univ. (Washington, D.C.); ord. priest June 5, 1954; ord. titular bishop of Perdices and auxiliary bishop of Syracuse Mar. 13, 1978.

Cotey, Arnold R., S.D.S.: b. June 15, 1921, Milwaukee, Wis.; educ. Divine Savior Seminary (Lanham, Md.), Marquette Univ. (Milwaukee, Wis.); ord. priest June 7, 1949; ord. first bishop of Nachingwea, Tanzania, Oct. 20, 1963.

Cousins, William E.: b. Aug. 20, 1902, Chicago, Ill.; educ. Quigley Seminary (Chicago, Ill.), St. Mary of the Lake Seminary (Mundelein, Ill.); ord. priest Apr. 23, 1927; ord. titular bishop of Forma and auxiliary bishop of Chicago, Mar. 7, 1949; app. bishop of Peoria, May 21, 1952; archbishop of Milwaukee, Jan. 27, 1959; retired 1977.

Cronin, Daniel A.: b. Nov. 14, 1927, Newton, Mass.; educ. St. John's Seminary (Boston, Mass.), North American College and Gregorian Univ. (Rome); ord. priest Dec. 20, 1952; attaché apostolic nunciature (Addis Ababa), 1957-61; served in papal Secretariat of State, 1961-68; ord. titular bishop of Egnatia and auxiliary bishop of Boston, Sept. 12, 1968; bishop of Fall River, Dec. 16, 1970.

Crowley, Joseph R.: b. Jan. 12, 1915, Fort Wayne, Ind.; educ. St. Mary's College (St. Mary, Ky.), St. Meinrad Seminary (St. Meinrad, Ind.); served in US Air Force, 1942-46; ord. priest May 1, 1953; editor of *Our Sunday Visitor* 1958-67; ord. titular bishop of Maraguis and auxiliary bishop of Fort Wayne-South Bend, Aug. 24, 1971.

Cummins, John S.: b. Mar. 3, 1928, Oakland, Calif.; educ. St. Patrick's Seminary (Menlo Park, Calif.), Catholic Univ. (Washington, D.C.), Univ. of California; ord. priest Jan. 24, 1953; executive director of the California Catholic Conference 1971-76; ord. titular bishop of Lambaesis and auxiliary bishop of Sacramento, May 16, 1974; app. bishop of Oakland, installed June 30, 1977.

Curtis, Walter W.: b. May 3, 1913, Jersey City, N.J.; educ. Fordham Univ. (New York City), Seton Hall Univ. (South Orange, N.J.), Immaculate Conception Seminary (Darlington, N.J.), North American College and Gregorian Univ. (Rome), Catholic Univ. (Washington, D.C.); ord. priest Dec. 8, 1937; ord. titular bishop of Bisica and auxiliary bishop of Newark, Sept. 24, 1957; app. bishop of Bridgeport, 1961, installed Nov. 21, 1961.

Curtiss, Elden F.: b. June 16, 1932, Baker, Ore.; educ. St. Edward Seminary College and St. Thomas Seminary (Kenmore, Wash.); ord. priest May 24, 1958; ord. bishop of Helena, Mont., Apr. 28, 1976.

D

Daily, Thomas V.: b. Sept. 23, 1927, Belmont, Mass.; educ. Boston College, St. John's Seminary (Brighton, Mass.); ord. priest Jan. 10, 1952; missionary in Peru for five years as a member of the Society of St. James the Apostle; ord. titular bishop of Bladia and auxiliary bishop of Boston, Feb. 11, 1975.

Daley, Joseph T.: b. Dec. 21, 1915, Connerton, Pa.; educ. St. Charles Borromeo Seminary (Philadelphia, Pa.); ord. priest June 7, 1941; ord. titular bishop of Barca and auxiliary bishop of Harrisburg, Pa., Jan. 7, 1964; coadjutor bishop of Harrisburg, Aug. 2, 1967; bishop of Harrisburg, Oct. 19, 1971.

Daly, James: b. Aug. 14, 1921, New York, N.Y.; educ. Cathedral College (Brooklyn, N.Y.), Immaculate Conception Seminary (Huntington, L.I.); ord. priest May 22, 1948; ord. titular bishop of Castra Nova and auxiliary bishop of Rockville Centre, May 9, 1977.

Danglmayr, Augustine: b. Dec. 11, 1898, Muenster, Tex.; educ. Subiaco College (Arkansas), St. Mary's Seminary (La Porte, Tex.), Kenrick Seminary (St. Louis, Mo.); ord. priest June 10, 1922; ord. titular bishop of Olba, Oct. 7, 1942; auxiliary bishop of Dallas-Ft. Worth, 1942-69.

D'Antonio, Nicholas, O.F.M.: b. July 10, 1916, Rochester, N.Y.; educ. St. Anthony's Friary (Catskill, N.Y.); ord. priest June 7, 1942; ord. titular bishop of Giufi Salaria and prelate of Olancho, Honduras, July 25, 1966; resigned 1977; app. vicar general of New Orleans archdiocese and episcopal vicar for Spanish Speaking, August, 1977.

D'Arcy, John M.: b. Aug. 18, 1932, Brighton, Mass.; educ. St. John's Seminary (Brighton, Mass.), Angelicum Univ. (Rome); ord. priest Feb. 2, 1957; spiritual director of St. John's Seminary; ord. titular bishop of Mediana and auxiliary bishop of Boston, Feb. 11, 1975.

Dargin, Edward Vincent: b. Apr. 25, 1898, New York, N.Y.; educ. Fordham Univ. (New York City), St. Joseph Seminary (Dunwoodie, N.Y.), Catholic Univ. (Washington, D.C.); ord. priest Sept. 23, 1922; ord. titular bishop of Amphipolis and auxiliary bishop of New York, Oct. 5, 1953; app. episcopal vicar, 1966. Retired.

Davis, James Peter: b. June 9, 1904, Houghton, Mich.; educ. St. Joseph's College (Mountain View, Calif.), St. Patrick's Seminary (Menlo Park, Calif.); ord. priest May 19, 1929; ord. bishop of San Juan, Puerto Rico, Oct. 6, 1943; app. first archbishop of San Juan, July 30, 1960; app. archbishop of Santa Fe, installed Feb. 25, 1964; resigned June 4, 1974.

Dearden, John Francis: (See Cardinals, Biographies.)

Deksnys, Antanas L.: b. May 9, 1906, Buteniskiai, Lithuania; educ. Metropolitan Seminary and Theological and Philosophical Faculty at Vytautas the Great Univ. (all at Kaunas, Lithuania), Univ. of Fribourg (Switzerland); ord. priest May 30, 1931; served in US parishes at Mt. Carmel, Pa., and East St. Louis, Ill.; ord. titular bishop of Lavellum, June 15, 1969; assigned to pastoral work among Lithuanians in Western Europe.

Dempsey, Michael J., O.P.: b. Feb. 22, 1912, Providence, R.I.; entered Order of Preachers (Dominicans), Chicago province, 1935; ord. priest June 11, 1942; ord. bishop of Sokoto, Nigeria, Aug. 15, 1967.

Denning, Joseph P.: b. Jan. 4, 1907, Flushing, L.I.; educ. Cathedral College (Brooklyn, N.Y.), Immaculate Conception Seminary (Huntington, L.I.), St. Mary's Seminary (Baltimore, Md.); ord. priest May 21, 1932; ord. titular bishop of Mallus and auxiliary bishop of Brooklyn, Apr. 22, 1959.

De Palma, Joseph A., S.C.J.: b. Sept. 4, 1913, Walton, N.Y.; ord. priest May 20, 1944; superior general of Congregation of Priests of the Sacred Heart, 1959-67; ord. first bishop of De Aar, South Africa, July 19, 1967.

Dimmerling, Harold J.: b. Sept. 23, 1914, Braddock, Pa.; educ. St. Fidelis Preparatory Seminary (Herman, Pa.), St. Charles Seminary (Columbus, O.), St. Francis Seminary (Loretto, Pa.); ord. priest May 2, 1940; ord. bishop of Rapid City, Oct. 30, 1969.

Dingman, Maurice J.: b. Jan. 20, 1914, St. Paul, Ia.; educ. St. Ambrose College (Davenport, Ia.), North American College and Gregorian Univ. (Rome), Catholic Univ. (Washington, D.C.); ord. priest Dec. 8, 1939; ord. bishop of Des Moines, June 19, 1968.

Dolinay, Thomas V.: b. July 24, 1923, Uniontown, Pa.; educ. St. Procopius College (Lisle, Ill.); ord. priest May 16, 1948; editor *Eastern Catholic Life*, 1966- ; ord. titular bishop of Tiatira and auxiliary bishop of Byzantine rite diocese of Passaic, Nov. 23, 1976.

Donaghy, Frederick Anthony, M.M.: b. Jan. 13, 1903, New Bedford, Mass.; educ. Holy Cross College (Worcester, Mass.), St. Mary's Seminary (Baltimore, Md.), Maryknoll Seminary (Maryknoll, N.Y.); ord. priest Jan. 29, 1929; ord. titular bishop of Setea and vicar apostolic of Wuchow, China, Sept. 21, 1939; title changed to bishop of Wuchow, Apr. 11, 1946; expelled by Communists.

Donahue, Stephen Joseph: b. Dec. 10, 1893, New York, N. Y.; educ. Cathedral College (New York, N.Y.), St. Joseph's Seminary (Dunwoodie, N.Y.), North American College (Rome); ord. priest May 22, 1918; ord. titular bishop of Medea and auxiliary bishop of New York, May 1, 1934. Retired.

Donnellan, Thomas A.: b. Jan. 24, 1914, New York, N.Y.; educ. Cathedral College and St. Joseph's Seminary (New York, N.Y.), Catholic Univ. (Washington, D.C.); ord. priest June 3, 1939; ord. bishop of Ogdensburg, Apr. 9, 1964; app. archbishop of Atlanta, installed July 16, 1968.

Donohoe, Hugh A.: b. June 28, 1905, San Francisco, Calif.; educ. St. Patrick's Preparatory and Major Seminaries (Menlo Park, Calif.), Catholic Univ. (Washington, D.C.); ord. priest June 14, 1930; ord. titular bishop of Taium and auxiliary bishop of San Francisco, Oct. 7, 1947; app. first bishop of Stockton, Jan. 27, 1962; app. bishop of Fresno, Aug. 27, 1969, installed Oct. 7, 1969.

Donovan, John A.: b. Aug. 5, 1911, Chatham, Ont., Canada; educ. Sacred Heart Seminary (Detroit, Mich.), North American College and Gregorian Univ. (Rome); ord. priest Dec. 8, 1935; ord. titular bishop of Rhasus and auxiliary bishop of Detroit, Oct. 26, 1954; app. bishop of Toledo, installed Apr. 18, 1967.

Donovan, Paul V.: b. Sept. 1, 1924, Bernard, Iowa; educ. St. Gregory's Seminary (Cincinnati, Ohio), Mt. St. Mary's Seminary (Norwood, Ohio), Lateran Univ. (Rome); ord. priest May 20, 1950; ord. first bishop of Kalamazoo, Mich., July 21, 1971.

Dougherty, John J.: b. Sept. 16, 1907, Jersey City, N.J.; educ. Seton Hall Univ. (S. Orange, N.J.), Immaculate Conception Seminary (Darlington, N.J.), North American College, Gregorian Univ., Pontifical Biblical Institute (Rome); ord. priest July 23, 1933; ord. titular bishop of Cotenna and auxiliary bishop of Newark, Jan. 24, 1963.

Dozier, Carroll T.: b. Aug. 18, 1911, Richmond, Va.; educ. Holy Cross College (Worcester, Mass.), Gregorian Univ. (Rome); ord. priest, Mar. 19, 1937, Rome; ord. first bishop of Memphis, Jan. 6, 1971.

Driscoll, Justin A.: b. Sept. 30, 1920, Bernard, Ia.; educ. Loras College (Dubuque, Ia.), Catholic Univ. (Washington, D.C.); ord. priest July 28, 1945; president of Loras College, 1967-70; ord. bishop of Fargo, Oct. 28, 1970.

Drury, Thomas J.: b. Jan. 4, 1908, Co. Sligo, Ireland; educ. St. Benedict's College (Atchison, Kans.), Kenrick Seminary (St. Louis, Mo.); ord. priest June 2, 1935; ord. first bishop of San Angelo, Tex., Jan. 24, 1962; app. bishop of Corpus Christi, installed Sept. 1, 1965.

Dudick, Michael J.: b. Feb. 24, 1916, St. Clair, Pa.; educ. St. Procopius College and Seminary (Lisle, Ill.); ord. priest Nov. 13, 1945; ord. bishop of Byzantine Rite Eparchy of Passaic, Oct. 24, 1968.

Dudley, Paul: b. Nov. 27, 1926, Northfield, Minn.; educ. Nazareth College and St. Paul Seminary (St. Paul, Minn.); ord. priest June 2, 1951; ord. titular bishop of Ursona and auxiliary bishop of St. Paul and Minneapolis, Jan. 25, 1977; app. bishop of Sioux Falls, installed Dec. 13, 1978.

Duhart, Clarence James, C.SS.R.: b. Mar. 23, 1912, New Orleans, La.; ord. priest June 29, 1937; ord. bishop of Udon Thani, Thailand, Apr. 21, 1966; resigned Oct. 2, 1975.

DuMaine, Roland Pierre: b. Aug. 2, 1931, Paducah, Ky.; educ. St. Joseph's College (Mountain View, Calif.), St. Patrick's College and Seminary (Menlo Park, Calif.), Univ. of California (Berkley), Catholic Univ. (Washington, D.C.); ord. priest June 5, 1957; ord. titular bishop of Sarda and auxiliary bishop of San Francisco, June 29, 1978.

Dunn, Francis J.: b. Mar. 22, 1922, Elkader, Ia.; educ. Loras College (Dubuque, Ia.), Kenrick Seminary (St. Louis, Mo.), Angelicum (Rome, Italy); ord. priest Jan. 11, 1948; chancellor of Dubuque, Aug. 27, 1960; ord. titular bishop of Turris Tamallani and auxiliary bishop of Dubuque, Aug. 27, 1969; app. vicar general, Aug. 28, 1969.

Durick, Joseph Aloysius: b. Oct. 13, 1914, Dayton, Tenn.; educ. St. Bernard Minor Seminary (St. Bernard, Ala.), St. Mary's Seminary (Baltimore, Md.), Urban Univ. (Rome); ord. priest May 23, 1940; ord. titular bishop of Cerbal and auxiliary bishop of Mobile-Birmingham, Mar. 24, 1955; app. coadjutor bishop of Nashville, Tenn., installed Mar. 3, 1964; apostolic administrator, 1966; bishop of Nashville, Sept. 10, 1969; resigned Apr. 4, 1975, to work with inmates of Federal correctional institutions and their families.

Durning, Dennis V., C.S.Sp.: b. May 18, 1923, Germantown, Pa.; educ. St. Mary's Seminary (Ferndale, Conn.); ord. priest June 3, 1949; ord. first bishop of Arusha, Tanzania, May 28, 1963.

E

Elko, Nicholas T.: b. Dec. 14, 1909, Donora, Pa.; educ. Duquesne Univ. (Pittsburgh, Pa.), Seminary of Uzhorod (Czechoslovakia) Louvain Univ. (Belgium); ord. priest Sept. 30, 1934; ord. titular bishop of Apollonias and apostolic administrator of Byzantine-Rite exarchy of Pittsburgh, Mar. 6, 1955; succeeded as exarch of Pittsburgh, Sept. 5, 1955; became eparch when Pittsburgh was raised to eparchy, July, 1963; app. titular archbishop of Dara, 1967, and ordaining prelate for Byzantine Rite in Rome; head of Oriental liturgical commission; app. auxiliary bishop of Cincinnati, Aug. 10, 1971.

Etteldorf, Raymond P.: b. Aug. 12, 1911, Ossian, Ia.; educ. Loras College (Dubuque, Ia.), Gregorian Univ. (Rome); ord. priest Dec. 8, 1937; secretary general of Supreme Council for direction of Pontifical Missionary Works, 1964-68; secretary of Pontifical Commission for Economic Affairs, 1968-69; ord. titular archbishop of Tindari, Jan. 6, 1969; papal representative to New Zealand and the Pacific Islands, 1968-74; pro-nuncio to Ethiopia, 1974.

Evans, George R.: b. Sept. 25, 1922, Denver, Colo.; educ. Notre Dame Univ. (Notre Dame, Ind.), St. Thomas Seminary (Denver, Colo.), Apollinare Univ. (Rome, Italy); ord. priest May 31, 1947; ord. titular bishop of Tubyza and auxiliary bishop of Denver, Apr. 23, 1969.

F

Federal, Joseph Lennox: b. Jan. 13, 1910, Greensboro, N.C.; educ. Belmont Abbey

College (Belmont Abbey, N.C.), Niagara Univ. (Niagara Falls, N.Y.), Univ. of Fribourg (Switzerland), North American College and Gregorian Univ. (Rome); ord. priest Dec. 8, 1934; ord. titular bishop of Appiaria and auxiliary bishop of Salt Lake City, Apr. 11, 1951; app. coadjutor with right of succession, May, 1958; bishop of Salt Lake City, Mar. 31, 1960.

Ferrario, Joseph A.: b. Mar. 3, 1926, Scranton, Pa.; educ. St. Charles College (Catonsville, Md.), St. Mary's Seminary (Baltimore, Md.), Catholic Univ. (Washington, D.C.); Univ. of Scranton; ord. priest May 19, 1951; ord. titular bishop of Cuse and auxiliary bishop of Honolulu Jan. 13, 1978.

Fiorenza, Joseph A.: b. Jan. 25, 1931, Beaumont, Tex.; educ. St. Mary's Seminary (LaPorte, Tex.); ord. priest May 29, 1954; ord. bishop of San Angelo, Oct. 25, 1979.

Fitzpatrick, John J.: b. Oct. 12, 1918, Trenton, Ont., Canada; educ. Urban Univ. (Rome), Our Lady of the Angels Seminary (Niagara Falls, N.Y.); ord. priest Dec. 13, 1942; ord. titular bishop of Cenae and auxiliary bishop of Miami, Aug. 28, 1968; bishop of Brownsville, Tex., May 28, 1971.

Fitzsimons, George K.: b. Sept. 4, 1928, Kansas City, Mo.; educ. Rockhurst College (Kansas City, Mo.), Immaculate Conception Seminary (Conception, Mo.); ord. priest Mar. 18, 1961; ord. titular bishop of Pertusa and auxiliary bishop of Kansas City-St. Joseph, July 3, 1975.

Flanagan, Bernard Joseph: b. Mar. 31, 1908, Proctor, Vt.; educ. Holy Cross College (Worcester, Mass.), North American College (Rome), Catholic Univ. (Washington, D.C.); ord. priest Dec. 8, 1931; ord. first bishop of Norwich, Nov. 30, 1953; app. bishop of Worcester, installed, Sept. 24, 1959.

Flavin, Glennon P.: b. Mar. 2, 1916, St. Louis, Mo.; educ. Kenrick Seminary (St. Louis, Mo.); ord. priest Dec. 20, 1941; ord. titular bishop of Joannina and auxiliary bishop of St. Louis, May 30, 1957; app. bishop of Lincoln, installed Aug. 17, 1967.

Fletcher, Albert Lewis: b. Oct. 28, 1896, Little Rock, Ark.; educ. Little Rock College and St. John's Seminary (Little Rock, Ark.); ord. priest June 4, 1920; ord. titular bishop of Samos and auxiliary bishop of Little Rock, Apr. 25, 1940; bishop of Little Rock, Dec. 7, 1946; resigned July 4, 1972.

Flores, Felixberto C.: b. Jan. 13, 1921, Agana, Guam; educ. St. John's Seminary (Brighton, Mass.), Fordham Univ. (New York); ord. priest Apr. 30, 1949; ord. titular bishop of Stonj, May 17, 1970, and apostolic administrator of the diocese of Agana, Guam; installed second residential bishop of Agana, July 12, 1972.

Flores, Patrick F.: b. July 26, 1929, Ganado, Tex.; educ. St. Mary's Seminary (Houston, Tex.); ord. priest May 26, 1956; ord. titular bishop of Itolica and auxiliary bishop of San Antonio, May 5, 1970 (first MexicanAmerican bishop); app. bishop of El Paso, Apr. 4, 1978, installed May 29, 1978; app. archbishop of San Antonio 1979.

Forst, Marion F.: b. Sept. 3, 1910, St. Louis, Mo.; educ. St. Louis Preparatory Seminary (St. Louis, Mo.), Kenrick Seminary (Webster Groves, Mo.); ord. priest June 10, 1934; ord. bishop of Dodge City, Mar. 24, 1960; app. titular bishop of Scala and auxiliary bishop of Kansas City, Kans. Oct. 16, 1976.

Francis Joseph A., S.V.D.: b. Sept. 30, 1923, Lafayette, La.; educ. St. Augustine Seminary (Bay St. Louis, Miss.), St. Mary Seminary (Techny, Ill.), Catholic Univ. (Washington, D.C.); ord. priest Oct. 7, 1950; president Conference of Major Superiors of Men, 1974-76, and the National Black Catholic Clergy Caucus; ord. titular bishop of Valliposita and auxiliary bishop of Newark, June 25, 1976.

Franz, John B.: b. Oct. 29, 1896, Springfield, Ill.; educ. Quincy College (Quincy, Ill.), Kenrick Seminary (Webster Groves, Mo.), Catholic Univ. (Washington, D.C.); ord. priest June 13, 1920; ord. first bishop of Dodge City, Aug. 29, 1951; app. bishop of Peoria, installed Nov. 4, 1959; resigned May 24, 1971.

Freking, Frederick W.: b. Aug. 11, 1913, Heron Lake, Minn.; educ. St. Mary's College (Winona, Minn.), North American College and Gregorian Univ. (Rome), Catholic Univ. (Washington, D.C.); ord. priest July 31, 1938; ord. bishop of Salina, Nov. 30, 1957; app. bishop of La Crosse, Dec. 30, 1964, installed Feb. 24, 1965.

Frey, Gerard L.: b. May 10, 1914, New Orleans, La.; educ. Notre Dame Seminary (New Orleans, La.); ord. priest Apr. 2, 1938; ord. bishop of Savannah, Aug. 8, 1967; app. bishop of Lafayette, La., Nov. 7, 1972, installed Jan, 7, 1973.

Friend, William B.: b. Oct. 22, 1931, Miami, Fla.; educ. St. Mary's College (St. Mary, Ky.), Mt. St. Mary Seminary (Emmitsburg, Md.), Catholic Univ. (Washington, D.C.), Notre Dame Univ. (Notre Dame, Ind.); ord. priest May 7, 1959; app. titular bishop of Pomaria and auxiliary bishop of Alexandria-Shreveport, La., Sept. 8, 1979.

Frosi, Angelo, S. X.: b. Jan. 31, 1924, Baffano Cremona, Italy; ord. priest May 6, 1948; U.S. citizen; ord. titular bishop of Magneto, May 1, 1970, and prelate of Abaete do Tocantins, Brazil.

Fulcher, George A.: b. Jan. 30, 1922, Columbus, Ohio; educ. St. Charles Borromeo Seminary (Columbus, O.), Mt. St. Mary of the West Seminary (Norwood, O.), North American College and Angelicum (Rome); ord. priest Feb. 28, 1948; ord. titular bishop of Morosbisdus and auxiliary bishop of Columbus, July 18, 1976.

Furlong, Philip J.: b. Dec. 8, 1892, New York, N.Y.; educ. Cathedral College (New York, N.Y.), St. Joseph's Seminary (Yonkers, N.Y.); ord. priest May 18, 1918; ord. titular bishop of Araxa and auxiliary to military vicar, Jan. 25, 1956. Retired.

G

Gabro, Jaroslav: b. July 31, 1919, Chicago, Ill.; educ. St. Procopius College (Lisle, Ill.), St. Charles College (Catonsville, Md.), St. Basil's College (Stamford, Conn.), St. Josaphat's Seminary and Catholic Univ. (Washington, D.C.); ord. priest Sept. 27, 1945; ord. first eparch of the eparchy of St. Nicholas of the Ukrainians, in Chicago, Oct. 26, 1961, installed Dec. 12, 1961.

Gallagher, Raymond J.: b. Nov. 19, 1912, Cleveland, Ohio; educ. John Carroll Univ. and Our Lady of the Lake Seminary (Cleveland, O.); ord. priest Mar. 25, 1939; secretary of the National Conference of Catholic Charities 1961-65; ord. bishop of Lafayette in Indiana, Aug. 11, 1965.

Ganter, Bernard J.: b. July 17, 1928, Galveston, Tex.; educ. Texas A & M Univ. (College Sta., Tex.), St. Mary's Seminary (La Porte, Tex.), Catholic Univ. (Washington, D.C.); ord. priest May 22, 1952; chancellor of Galveston-Houston diocese, 1966-73; ord. first bishop of Tulsa, Feb. 7, 1973; app. bishop of Beaumont, Tex., Oct. 18, 1977, installed Dec. 13, 1977.

Garmendia, Francisco: b. Nov. 6, 1924, Lozcano, Spain; ord. priest June 29, 1947, in Spain; came to New York in 1964; became naturalized citizen; ord. titular bishop of Limisa and auxiliary bishop of New York, June 29, 1977. Vicar for Spanish pastoral development in New York archdiocese.

Garner, Robert F.: b. Apr. 27, 1920, Jersey City, N.J.; educ. Seton Hall Univ. (S. Orange, N.J.), Immaculate Conception Seminary (Darlington, N.J.); ord. priest June 15, 1946; ord. titular bishop of Blera and auxiliary bishop of Newark, June 25, 1976.

Gaughan, Norbert F.: b. May 30, 1921, Pittsburgh, Pa.; educ. St. Vincent College (Latrobe, Pa.), Univ. of Pittsburgh; ord. priest Nov. 4, 1945; ord. titular bishop of Taraqua and auxiliary bishop of Greensburg, June 26, 1975.

Gelineau, Louis E.: b. May 3, 1928, Burlington, Vt.; educ. St. Michael's College (Winooski, Vt.), St. Paul's Univ. Seminary (Ottawa, Ont.), Catholic Univ. (Washington, D.C.); ord. priest June 5, 1954; ord. bishop of Providence, R.I., Jan. 26, 1972.

Gendron, Odore: b. Sept. 13, 1921, Manchester, N.H.; educ. St. Charles Borromeo Seminary (Sherbrooke, Que., Canada), Univ. of Ottawa, St. Paul Univ. Seminary (Ottawa, Ont., Canada); ord. priest May 31, 1947; ord. bishop of Manchester, Feb. 3, 1975.

Gerber, Eugene J.: b. Apr. 30, 1931, Kingman, Kans.; educ. St. Thomas Seminary (Denver, Colo.), Wichita State Univ.; Catholic Univ. (Washington, D.C.), Angelicum (Rome); ord. priest May 19, 1959; ord. bishop of Dodge City, Dec. 14, 1976.

Gerbermann, Hugo, M.M.: b. Sept. 11, 1913, Nada, Tex.; educ. St. John's Minor and Major Seminary (San Antonio, Tex.), Maryknoll Seminary (Maryknoll, N.Y.); ord. priest Feb. 7, 1943; missionary work in Ecuador and Guatemala; ord. titular bishop of Amathus and prelate of Huehuetenango, Guatemala, July 22, 1962; first bishop of Huehuetenango, Dec. 23, 1967; app. titular bishop of Pinkel and auxiliary bishop of San Antonio, July 24, 1975.

Gerety, Peter L.: b. July 19, 1912, Shelton, Conn.; educ. Sulpician Seminary (Paris, France); ord. priest June 29, 1939; ord. titular bishop of Crepedula and coadjutor bishop of Portland, Me., with right of succession, June 1, 1966; app. apostolic administrator of Portland, 1967; bishop of Portland, Me., Sept. 15, 1969; app. archbishop of Newark, Apr. 2, 1974; installed June 28, 1974.

Gerrard, James J.: b. June 9, 1897, New Bedford, Mass.; educ. St. Laurent College (Montreal, Que.), St. Bernard's Seminary (Rochester, N.Y.); ord. priest May 26, 1923; ord. titular bishop of Forma and auxiliary bishop of Fall River, Mar. 19, 1959. Retired January, 1976.

Gleeson, Francis D., S.J.: b. Jan. 17, 1895, Carrollton, Mo.; educ. Mount St. Michael's Scholasticate (Spokane, Wash.), St. Francis Xavier College (Ona, Spain); entered the Society of Jesus, 1912; ord. priest July 29, 1926; ord. titular bishop of Cotenna and vicar apostolic of Alaska, Apr. 5, 1948; first bishop of Fairbanks, Aug. 8, 1962; retired Nov. 15, 1968.

Glenn, Laurence A.: b. Aug. 25, 1900, Bellingham, Wash.; educ. St. John's Univ. (Collegeville, Minn.), Catholic Univ. (Washington, D.C.); ord. priest June 11, 1927; ord. titular bishop of Tuscamia and auxiliary bishop of Duluth, Sept. 12, 1956; app. bishop of Crookston, Jan. 27, 1960, installed Apr. 20, 1960; resigned 1970.

Glennie, Ignatius T., S.J.: b. Feb. 5, 1907, Mexico City; educ. Mt. St. Michael's Scholasticate (Spokane, Wash.), Pontifical Seminary (Kandy, Ceylon), St. Mary's College (Kurdeong, India); entered Society of Jesus, 1924; ord. priest Nov. 21, 1938; ord. bishop of Trincomalee, Ceylon, Sept. 21, 1947; title of see changed to Trincomalee-Batticaloa (Sri Lanka), 1967; resigned Feb. 15, 1974.

Gorman, Thomas Kiely: b. Aug. 30, 1892, Pasadena, Calif.; educ. St. Mary's Seminary (Baltimore, Md.), Catholic Univ. (Washington, D.C.), Louvain Univ. (Belgium); ord. priest June 23, 1917; ord. bishop of Reno,

July 22, 1931; installed as titular bishop of Rhasus and coadjutor bishop of Dallas-Fort Worth, with right of succession, May 8, 1952; bishop of Dallas-Fort Worth, Aug. 20, 1954; resigned 1969.

Gossman, F. Joseph: b. Apr. 1, 1930, Baltimore, Md.: educ. St. Charles College (Catonsville, Md.), St. Mary's Seminary (Baltimore, Md.), North American College (Rome), Catholic Univ. (Washington, D.C.); ord. priest Dec. 17, 1955; ord. titular bishop of Agunto and auxiliary bishop of Baltimore, Sept. 11, 1968; named urban vicar, June 13, 1970; app. bishop of Raleigh April 8, 1975.

Gottwald, George J.: b. May 12, 1914, St. Louis, Mo.; educ. Kenrick Seminary (Webster Groves, Mo.); ord. priest June 9, 1940; ord. titular bishop of Cedamusa and auxiliary bishop of St. Louis, Aug. 8, 1961.

Gracida, Rene H.: b. June 9, 1923, New Orleans, La.; educ. Rice Univ. and Univ. of Houston (Houston, Tex.), Univ. of Fribourg (Switzerland); ord. priest May 23, 1959; ord. titular bishop of Masuccaba and auxiliary bishop of Miami, Jan. 25, 1972; app. first bishop of Pensacola-Tallahassee, Oct. 1, 1975, installed Nov. 6, 1975.

Grady, Thomas J.: b. Oct. 9, 1914, Chicago, Ill.; educ. St. Mary of the Lake Seminary (Mundelein, Ill.), Gregorian Univ. (Rome), Loyola Univ. (Chicago, Ill.); ord. priest Apr. 23, 1938; ord. titular bishop of Vamalla and auxiliary bishop of Chicago, Aug. 24, 1967; app. bishop of Orlando, Fla., Nov. 11, 1974, installed Dec. 16, 1974.

Graham, John J.: b. Sept. 11, 1913, Philadelphia, Pa.; educ. St. Charles Borromeo Seminary (Philadelphia, Pa.), Pontifical Roman Seminary (Rome, Italy); ord. priest Feb. 26, 1938; ord. titular bishop of Sabrata and auxiliary bishop of Philadelphia, Jan. 7, 1964.

Graner, Lawrence L., C.S.C.: b. Apr. 3, 1901, Franklin, Pa.; educ. Holy Cross Seminary (Notre Dame, Ind.), Holy Cross Mission Seminary (Washington, D.C.); entered Congregation of the Holy Cross, 1924; ord. priest June 24, 1928; ord. bishop of Dacca, India, Apr. 23, 1947; title changed to archbishop of Dacca, July 15, 1950; retired Nov. 23, 1967.

Graves, Lawrence P.: b. May 4, 1916, Texarkana, Ark.; educ. St. John's Seminary (Little Rock, Ark.), North American College (Rome), Catholic Univ. (Washington, D.C.); ord. priest June 11, 1942; ord. titular bishop of Vina and auxiliary bishop of Little Rock, Apr. 25, 1969; app. bishop of Alexandria, May 22, 1973, installed Sept. 18, 1973; title of see changed to Alexandria-Shreveport, Jan. 12, 1977.

Graziano, Lawrence, O.F.M.: b. Apr. 5, 1921, Mt. Vernon, N.Y.; educ. Mt. Alvernia Seminary (Wappingers Falls, N.Y.); ord. priest Jan. 26, 1947; ord. titular bishop of Limata and auxiliary bishop of Santa Ana, El Salvador, Sept. 21, 1961; app. coadjutor bishop of San Miguel, El Salvador, with right of succession, 1965; bishop of San Miguel, Jan. 10, 1968; resigned June 27, 1969.

Greco, Charles Paschal: b. Oct. 29, 1894, Rodney, Miss.; educ. St. Joseph's Seminary (St. Benedict, La.), Louvain Univ. (Belgium), Dominican Univ. (Fribourg, Switzerland); ord. priest July 25, 1918; ord. bishop of Alexandria Feb. 25, 1946; retired May 22, 1973.

Green, Francis J.: b. July 7, 1906, Corning, N.Y.; educ. St. Patrick's Seminary (Menlo Park, Calif.); ord. priest May 15, 1932; ord. titular bishop of Serra and auxiliary bishop of Tucson, Sept. 17, 1953; named coadjutor of Tucson with right of succession, May 11, 1960; bishop of Tucson, Oct. 26, 1960.

Green, Joseph: b. Oct. 13, 1917, St. Joseph, Mich.; educ. St. Joseph Seminary (Grand Rapids, Mich.). St. Gregory Seminary (Cincinnati, O.), St. Mary's Seminary (Norwood, O.), Lateran Univ. (Rome); ord. priest July 14, 1946; ord. titular bishop of Trisipa and auxiliary bishop of Lansing, Aug. 28, 1962; app. bishop of Reno, installed May 25, 1967; resigned Dec. 6, 1974.

Grellinger, John B.: b. Nov. 5, 1899, Milwaukee, Wis.; educ. Marquette Univ. and St. Francis Seminary (Milwaukee, Wis.), Urban Univ. and Gregorian Univ. (Rome); ord. priest July 14, 1929; ord. titular bishop of Syene and auxiliary bishop of Green Bay, July 14, 1949; retired Sept. 22, 1974.

Greteman, Frank H.: b. Dec. 25, 1907, Willey, Ia.; educ. Loras Academy and Loras College (Dubuque, Ia.), North American College (Rome), Catholic Univ. (Washington, D.C.); ord. priest Dec. 8, 1932; ord. titular bishop of Vissalsa and auxiliary bishop of Sioux City, May 26, 1965; bishop of Sioux City, Dec. 9, 1970.

Griffin, James A.: b. June 13, 1934, Fairview Park, O.; educ. St. Charles College (Baltimore, Md.), Borromeo College (Wicklife, O.); St. Mary Seminary (Cleveland, O.); Lateran Univ. (Rome); Cleveland State Univ.; ord. priest May 28, 1960; ord. titular bishop of Holar and auxiliary bishop of Cleveland, Aug. 1, 1979.

Grutka, Andrew G.: b. Nov. 17, 1908, Joliet, Ill.; educ. St. Procopius College and Seminary (Lisle, Ill.), Urban Univ. and Gregorian Univ. (Rome); ord. priest Dec. 5, 1933; app. moderator of lay activities in Gary diocese, 1955; ord. first bishop of Gary, Feb. 25, 1957; app. member of Pontifical Marian Academy, Jan. 5, 1970; president, 1971-76, and chairman of board 1976-   , of Catholic Communications Foundation.

Guilfoyle, George H.: b. Nov. 13, 1913, New York, N.Y.; educ. Georgetown Univ. (Washington, D.C.), Fordham Univ. (New York City), St. Joseph's Seminary (Dunwoodie, N.Y.), Columbia Univ. Law School (New York City); ord. priest Mar. 25, 1944;

ord. titular bishop of Marazane and auxiliary bishop of New York, Nov. 30, 1964; app. bishop of Camden, installed Mar. 4, 1968.

Guilfoyle, Merlin J.: b. July 15, 1908, San Francisco, Calif.; educ. St. Joseph's College (Mountain View, Calif.), St. Patrick's Seminary (Menlo Park, Calif.), Catholic Univ. (Washington, D.C.); ord. priest June 10, 1933; ord. titular bishop of Bulla and auxiliary bishop of San Francisco, Sept. 21, 1950; app. bishop of Stockton, Nov. 19, 1969, installed Jan. 13, 1970; resigned for reasons of health, 1979.

Gumbleton, Thomas J.: b. Jan. 26, 1930, Detroit, Mich.; educ. St. John Provincial Seminary (Detroit, Mich.), Pontifical Lateran Univ. (Rome); ord. priest June 2, 1956; ord. titular bishop of Ululi and auxiliary bishop of Detroit, May 1, 1968.

H

Hacker, Hilary B.: b. Jan. 10, 1913, New Ulm, Minn.; educ. St. Paul Seminary (St. Paul, Minn.), Gregorian Univ. (Rome); ord. priest June 4, 1938; ord. bishop of Bismarck, N. Dak., Feb. 27, 1957.

Hackett, John F.: b. Dec. 7, 1911, New Haven, Conn.; educ. St. Thomas Seminary (Bloomfield, Conn.), Seminaire Ste. Sulpice (Paris); ord. priest June 29, 1936; ord. titular bishop of Helenopolis in Palaestina and auxiliary bishop of Hartford, Mar. 19, 1953.

Hagarty, Paul Leonard, O.S.B.: b. Mar. 20, 1909, Greene, Ia.; educ. Loras College (Dubuque, Ia.), St. John's Seminary and St. John's Univ. (Collegeville, Minn.); entered Order of St. Benedict, 1931; ord. priest June 6, 1936; ord. titular bishop of Arba and vicar apostolic of the Bahamas, Oct. 19, 1950; first bishop of Nassau, July 5, 1960.

Ham, J. Richard, M.M.: b. July 11, 1921, Chicago, Ill.; educ. Maryknoll Seminary (New York); ord. priest June 12, 1948; missionary to Guatemala, 1958; ord. titular bishop of Puzia di Numidia and auxiliary bishop of Guatemala, Jan. 6, 1968.

Hammes, George A.: b. Sept. 11, 1911, St. Joseph Ridge, Wis.; educ. St. Lawrence Seminary (Mt. Calvary. Wis.), St. Louis Preparatory Seminary (St. Louis, Mo.), Kenrick Seminary (Webster Groves, Mo.), Sulpician Seminary, Catholic Univ. (Washington, D.C.); ord. priest May 22, 1937; ord. bishop of Superior, May 24, 1960.

Hanifen, Richard C.: b. June 15, 1931, Denver, Colo,; educ. Regis College and St. Thomas Seminary (Denver, Colo.), Catholic Univ. (Washington, D.C.), Lateran Univ. (Rome); ord. priest June 6, 1959; ord. titular bishop of Abercorn and auxiliary bishop of Denver, Sept. 20, 1974.

Hannan, Philip M.: b. May 20, 1913, Washington, D.C.; educ. St. Charles College (Catonsville, Md.), Catholic Univ. (Washington, D.C.), North American College (Rome); ord. priest Dec. 8, 1939; ord. titular bishop of Hieropolis and auxiliary bishop of Washington, D.C., Aug. 28, 1956; app. archbishop of New Orleans, installed Oct. 13, 1965.

Harper, Edward, C.SS.R.: b. July 23, 1910, Brooklyn, N.Y.; educ. Redemptorist Houses of Study; ord. priest June 18, 1939; ord. titular bishop of Heraclea Pontica and first prelate of Virgin Islands, Oct. 6, 1960; became first bishop, 1977, when prelacy was made diocese of St. Thomas.

Harrington, Timothy J.: b. Dec. 19, 1918, Holyoke, Mass.; educ. Holy Cross College (Worcester, Mass.), Grand Seminary (Montreal, Que.), Boston College School of Social Work; ord. priest Jan. 19, 1946; ord. titular bishop of Rusuca and auxiliary bishop of Worcester, Mass., July 2, 1968.

Harris, Vincent M.: b. Oct. 14, 1913, Conroe, Tex.; educ. St. Mary's Seminary (La Porte, Tex.), North American College and Gregorian Univ. (Rome), Catholic Univ. (Washington, D.C.); ord. priest Mar. 19, 1938; ord. first bishop of Beaumont, Tex., Sept. 28, 1966; app. titular bishop of Rotaria and coadjutor bishop of Austin, Apr. 27, 1971; bishop of Austin, Nov. 16, 1971.

Harrison, Francis J.: b. Aug. 12, 1912; Syracuse, N.Y.; educ. Notre Dame Univ. (Notre Dame, Ind.), St. Bernard's Seminary (Rochester, N.Y.), ord. priest June 4, 1937; ord. titular bishop of Aquae in Numidia and auxiliary bishop of Syracuse, Apr. 22, 1971; app. bishop of Syracuse, Nov. 9, 1976, installed Feb. 6, 1977.

Hart, Daniel A.: b. Aug. 24, 1927, Lawrence, Mass.; educ. St. John's Seminary (Brighton, Mass.); ord. priest Feb. 2, 1953; ord. titular bishop of Tepelta and auxiliary bishop of Boston, Oct. 18, 1976.

Hart, Joseph: b. Sept. 26, 1931, Kansas City, Missouri; educ. St. John Seminary (Kansas City, Mo.), St. Meinrad Seminary (Indianapolis, Ind.); ord. priest May 1, 1956; ord. titular bishop of Thimida Regia and auxiliary bishop of Cheyenne, Wyo., Aug. 31, 1976; app. bishop of Cheyenne, installed June 12, 1978.

Hastrich, Jerome J.: b. Nov. 13, 1914, Milwaukee, Wis.; educ. Marquette Univ., St. Francis Seminary (Milwaukee, Wis.); ord. priest Feb. 9, 1941; ord. titular bishop of Gurza and auxiliary bishop of Madison, Sept. 3, 1963; app. bishop of Gallup, N.Mex., Sept. 3, 1969.

Hayes, James Thomas Gibbons, S.J.: b. Feb. 11, 1889, New York City; educ. St. Francis Xavier's College (New York City), Jesuit Novitiate (St. Andrew-on-the-Hudson, N.Y.), Jesuit House of Studies (Tronchiennes, Belgium); entered the Society of Jesus, Aug. 14, 1907; ord. priest June 29, 1921; ord. bishop of Cagayan, P.I., June 18, 1933; first archbishop of Cagayan, June 29, 1951; resigned Oct. 13, 1970.

Hayes, Nevin W., O.Carm: b. Feb. 17, 1922, Chicago, Ill.; entered Carmelite novitiate Aug. 15, 1939; educ. Mt. Carmel College (Niagara Falls, Canada), Whitefriars Hall and Catholic Univ. (Washington, D.C.); ord. priest June 8, 1946; prelate nullius of Sicuani, Peru, 1959; ord. titular bishop of Nova Sinna and prelate of Sicuani, Aug. 5, 1965; resigned November 1970; app. auxiliary bishop of Chicago, Feb. 2, 1971.

Head, Edward D.: b. Aug. 5, 1919, White Plains, N.Y.; educ. Cathedral College, St. Joseph's Seminary, Columbia Univ. (New York City); ord. priest Jan. 27, 1945; director of New York Catholic Charities; ord. titular bishop of Ardsratha and auxiliary bishop of New York, Mar. 19, 1970; app. bishop of Buffalo, Jan. 23, 1973, installed Mar. 19, 1973.

Helmsing, Charles H.: b. Mar. 23, 1908, Shrewsbury, Mo.; educ. St. Louis Preparatory Seminary (St. Louis, Mo.), Kenrick Seminary (Webster Groves, Mo.); ord. priest June 10, 1933; ord. titular bishop of Axomis and auxiliary bishop of St. Louis, Apr. 19, 1949; first bishop of Springfield-Cape Girardeau, Aug. 24, 1956; bishop of Kansas City-St. Joseph, 1962, installed Apr. 3, 1962; resigned June 25, 1977.

Herrmann, Edward J.: b. Nov. 6, 1913, Baltimore, Md.; educ. Mt. St. Mary's Seminary (Emmitsburg, Md.), Catholic Univ. (Washington, D.C.); ord. priest June 12, 1947; ord. titular bishop of Lamzella and auxiliary bishop of Washington, D.C., Apr. 26, 1966; app. bishop of Columbus, June 26, 1973.

Hettinger, Edward Gerhard: b. Oct. 14, 1902, Lancaster, O.; educ. St. Vincent's College (Beatty, Pa.); ord. priest June 2, 1928; ord. titular bishop of Teos and auxiliary bishop of Columbus, Feb. 24, 1942; retired October, 1977.

Hickey, Dennis W.: b. Oct. 28, 1914, Dansville, N.Y.; educ. Colgate Univ. and St. Bernard's Seminary (Rochester, N.Y.); ord. priest June 7, 1941; ord. titular bishop of Rusuccuru and auxiliary bishop of Rochester, N.Y., Mar. 14, 1968.

Hickey, James A.: b. Oct. 11, 1920, Midland, Mich.; educ. Sacred Heart Seminary (Detroit, Mich.), Catholic Univ. (Washington, D.C.), Lateran Univ. and Angelicum (Rome), Michigan State Univ.; ord. priest June 15, 1946; ord. titular bishop of Taraqua and auxiliary bishop of Saginaw, Apr. 14, 1967; rector of North American College, Rome, 1969-74; app. bishop of Cleveland, June 5, 1974; installed July 16, 1974.

Hines, Vincent J.: b. Sept. 14, 1912, New Haven, Conn.; educ. St. Thomas Seminary (Bloomfield, Conn.), St. Sulpice Seminary (Paris), Lateran Univ. (Rome); ord. priest May 2, 1937; ord. bishop of Norwich, Conn., Mar. 17, 1960; retired June 17, 1975.

Hoch, Lambert A.: b. Feb. 6, 1903, Elkton, S.D.; educ. Creighton Univ. (Omaha, Nebr.), St. Paul Seminary (St. Paul, Minn.); ord. priest May 30, 1928; ord. bishop of Bismarck, Mar. 25, 1952; app. bishop of Sioux Falls Dec. 5, 1956; retired June 1978.

Hodapp, Robert L., S.J.: b. Oct. 1, 1910. Mankato, Minn.; educ. St. Stanislaus Seminary (Florissant, Mo.), St. Louis Univ. (St. Louis, Mo.); ord. priest June 18, 1941; ord. bishop of Belize, June 26, 1958.

Hodges, Joseph H.: b. Oct. 8, 1911, Harper's Ferry, W.Va.; educ. St. Charles College (Catonsville, Md.), North American College (Rome); ord. priest Dec. 8, 1935; ord. titular bishop of Rusadus and auxiliary bishop of Richmond, Oct. 15, 1952; named coadjutor bishop of Wheeling with right of succession, May 24, 1961; bishop of Wheeling, Nov. 23, 1962; title of see changed to Wheeling-Charleston 1974.

Hoffman, James R.: b. June 12, 1932, Fremont, O.; educ. Our Lady of the Lake Minor Seminary (Wawasee, Ind.), St. Meinrad College (St. Meinrad, Ind.); Mt. St. Mary Seminary (Norwood, O.); Catholic Univ. (Washington, D.C.); ord. priest July 28, 1957; ord. titular bishop of Italica and auxiliary bishop of Toledo, June 23, 1978.

Hogan, James J.: b. Oct. 17, 1911, Philadelphia, Pa.; educ. St. Charles College (Catonsville, Md.), St. Mary's Seminary (Baltimore), Gregorian Univ. (Rome), Catholic Univ. (Washington, D.C.); ord. priest Dec. 8, 1937; ord. titular bishop of Philomelium and auxiliary bishop of Trenton, Feb. 25, 1960; app. bishop of Altoona-Johnstown, installed July 6, 1966.

Hogan, Joseph L.: b. Mar. 11, 1916, Lima, N.Y.; educ. St. Bernard's Seminary (Rochester, N.Y.), Canisius College (Buffalo, N.Y.), Angelicum (Rome); ord. priest June 6, 1942; ord. bishop of Rochester, Nov. 28, 1969; resigned Nov. 28, 1978.

Houck, William Russell: b. June 26, 1926, Mobile Ala.; educ. St. Bernard Junior College (Cullman, Ala.), St. Mary's Seminary College and St. Mary's Seminary (Baltimore, Md.), Catholic Univ. (Washington, D.C.); ord. priest May 19, 1951; ord. titular bishop of Alessano and auxiliary bishop of Jackson, Miss., May 27, 1979, by Pope John Paul II.

Howard, Edward Daniel: b. Nov. 5, 1877, Cresco, Ia.; educ. St. Joseph's College (Dubuque, Ia.), St. Mary's College (St. Mary's, Kans.), St. Paul Seminary (St. Paul, Minn.); ord. priest June 12, 1906; ord. titular bishop of Isaurópolis and auxiliary bishop of Davenport, Apr. 8, 1924; app. archbishop of Oregon City, Apr. 30, 1926; title changed to archbishop of Portland, Sept. 26, 1928; resigned Dec. 14, 1966; assigned titular see of Albule.

Howze, (Joseph) Lawson E.: b. Aug. 30, 1923, Daphne, Ala.; convert to Catholicism, 1948; educ. St. Bonaventure Univ. (St. Bonaventure, N.Y.); ord. priest May 7, 1959; ord.

titular bishop of Massita and auxiliary bishop of Natchez-Jackson, Jan. 28, 1973; app. first bishop of Biloxi, Miss., Mar. 8, 1977; installed June 6, 1977.

Hubbard, Howard J.: b. Oct. 31, 1938, Troy, N.Y.; educ. St. Joseph's Seminary (Dunwoodie, N.Y.); North American College and Gregorian Univ. (Rome), Catholic Univ. (Washington, D.C.); ord. priest Dec. 18, 1963; ord. bishop of Albany, Mar. 27, 1977.

Hughes, Edward T.: b. Nov. 13, 1920, Landowne, Pa.; educ. St. Charles Seminary, Univ. of Pennsylvania (Philadelphia, Pa.); ord. priest May 31, 1947; ord. titular bishop of Segia and auxiliary bishop of Philadelphia, July 21, 1976.

Hughes, William A.: b. Sept. 23, 1921, Youngstown, O.; educ. St. Charles College (Catonsville, Md.), St. Mary's Seminary (Cleveland, O.) Notre Dame Univ. (Notre Dame, Ind.); ord. priest Apr. 6, 1946; ord. titular bishop of Inis Cathaig and auxiliary bishop of Youngstown, Sept. 12, 1974; app. bishop of Covington, installed May 8, 1979.

Hunthausen, Raymond G.: b. Aug. 21, 1921, Anaconda, Mont.; educ. Carroll College (Helena, Mont.), St. Edward's Seminary (Kenmore, Wash.), St. Louis Univ. (St. Louis, Mo.), Catholic Univ. (Washington, D.C.), Fordham Univ. (New York City), Notre Dame Univ. (Notre Dame, Ind.); ord. priest June 1, 1946; ord. bishop of Helena, Aug. 30, 1962; app. archbishop of Seattle, Feb. 25, 1975.

Hurley, Francis T.: b. Jan. 12, 1927, San Francisco, Calif.; educ. St. Patrick's Seminary (Menlo Park, Calif.), Catholic Univ. (Washington, D.C.); ord. priest June 16, 1951; assigned to NCWC in Washington, D.C., 1957; assistant (1958) and later (1968) associate secretary of NCCB and USCC; ord. titular bishop of Daimlaig and auxiliary bishop of Juneau, Alaska, Mar. 19, 1970; app. bishop of Juneau, July 20, 1971, installed Sept. 8, 1971; app. archbishop of Anchorage, May 4, 1976, installed July 8, 1976.

Hurley, Mark J.: b. Dec. 13, 1919, San Francisco, Calif.; educ. St. Patrick's Seminary (Menlo Park, Calif.), Univ. of California (Berkeley), Catholic Univ. (Washington, D.C.), Lateran Univ. (Rome), Univ. of Portland (Portland, Ore.); ord. priest Sept. 23, 1944; ord. titular bishop of Thunusuda and auxiliary bishop of San Francisco, Jan. 4, 1968; app. bishop of Santa Rosa, Nov. 19, 1969.

I-J

Imesch, Joseph L.: b. June 21, 1931, Detroit, Mich.; educ. Sacred Heart Seminary (Detroit, Mich.), North American College, Gregorian Univ. (Rome); ord. priest Dec. 16, 1956; ord. titular bishop of Pomaria and auxiliary bishop of Detroit, Apr. 3, 1973; app. bishop of Joliet, June 30, 1979.

Issenmann, Clarence G.: b. May 30, 1907, Hamilton, O.; educ. St. Joseph's College (Rensselaer, Ind.), St. Gregory's Seminary (Cincinnati, O.), St. Mary of the West Seminary (Norwood, O.); ord. priest June 29, 1932; ord. titular bishop of Phytea and auxiliary bishop of Cincinnati, May 25, 1954; bishop of Columbus, 1957-64; app. titular bishop of Filaca, coadjutor bishop of Cleveland and apostolic administrator *"sede plena,"* 1964; bishop of Cleveland, 1966; resigned June 5, 1974, because of ill health.

Johnson, William R.: b. Nov. 19, 1918, Tonopah, Nev.; educ. Los Angeles College and St. John's Seminary (Camarillo, Calif.), National Catholic School of Social Service, Catholic Univ. (Washington, D.C.); ord. priest May 28, 1944; ord. titular bishop of Blera and auxiliary bishop of Los Angeles, Mar. 25, 1971; app. first bishop of Orange, Calif., Mar. 30, 1976, installed June 18, 1976.

Joyce, Robert F.: b. Oct. 7, 1896, Proctor, Vt.; educ. Univ. of Vermont (Burlington, Vt.), Grand Seminary (Montreal, Canada); ord. priest May 26, 1923; ord. titular bishop of Citium and auxiliary bishop of Burlington, Oct. 28, 1954; installed as bishop of Burlington, Feb. 26, 1957; resigned Dec. 14, 1971.

K

Keeler, William H.: b. Mar. 4, 1931, San Antonio, Tex.; educ. St. Charles Seminary (Overbrook, Pa.), North American College (Rome); ord. priest July 17, 1955; app. titular bishop of Dulcigno and auxiliary bishop of Harrisburg, July, 1979.

Kellenberg, Walter P.: b. June 3, 1901, New York, N.Y.; educ. Cathedral College (New York, City), St. Joseph Seminary (Dunwoodie, N.Y.); ord. priest June 2, 1928; ord. titular bishop of Joannina and auxiliary bishop of New York, Oct. 5, 1953; app. bishop of Ogdensburg, Jan. 19, 1954; app. first bishop of Rockville Centre Apr. 16, 1957, installed May 27, 1957; retired May 4, 1976.

Kelly, Thomas C., O.P.: b. July 14, 1931, Rochester, N.Y.; educ. Providence College (Providence, R.I.), Immaculate Conception College (Washington, D.C.), Angelicum (Rome); professed in Dominicans, Aug. 26, 1952; secretary, apostolic delegation, Washington, D.C., 1965-71; associate general secretary, 1971-77, and general secretary, 1977- , NCCB/USCC; ord. titular bishop of Tusurus and auxiliary bishop of Washington, D.C., Aug. 15, 1977.

Kenny, Michael H.: b. June 26, 1937, Hollywood, Calif.; educ. St. Joseph College (Mountain View, Calif.), St. Patrick's Seminary (Menlo Park, Calif.), Catholic Univ. (Washington, D.C.), ord. priest Mar. 30, 1963; ord. bishop of Juneau, May 27, 1979.

Kinney, John: b. June 11, 1937, Oelwein, Iowa; educ. Nazareth Hall and St. Paul Seminaries (St. Paul, Minn.); Pontifical Lateran University (Rome); ord. priest Feb. 2, 1963; ord. titular bishop of Caorle and auxiliary bishop of St. Paul and Minneapolis, Jan. 25, 1977.

Kocisko, Stephen: b. June 11, 1915, Minneapolis, Minn.; educ. Nazareth Hall Minor Seminary (St. Paul, Minn.), Pontifical Ruthenian College, Urban Univ. (Rome); ord. priest Mar. 30, 1941; ord. titular bishop of Teveste and auxiliary bishop of apostolic exarchate of Pittsburgh, Oct. 23, 1956; installed as first eparch of the eparchy of Passaic, Sept. 10, 1963; app. eparch of Byzantine-Rite diocese of Pittsburgh, installed Mar. 5, 1968; app. first metropolitan of Munhall, installed June 11, 1969; title of see changed to Pittsburgh, 1977.

Koester, Charles R.: b. Sept. 16, 1915, Jefferson City, Mo.; educ. Conception Academy (Conception, Mo.), St. Louis Preparatory Seminary and Kenrick Seminary (St. Louis, Mo.), North American College (Rome); ord. priest Dec. 20, 1941; ord. titular bishop of Suacia and auxiliary bishop of St. Louis, Feb. 11, 1971.

Krawczak, Arthur H.: b. Feb. 2, 1913, Detroit, Mich.; educ. Sacred Heart Seminary, Sts. Cyril and Methodius Seminary (Orchard Lake, Mich.), Catholic Univ. (Washington, D.C.); ord. priest May 18, 1940; ord. titular bishop of Subbar and auxiliary bishop of Detroit, Apr. 3, 1973.

Krol, John J.: (See Cardinals, Biographies.)

Kucera, Daniel, O.S.B.: b. May 7, 1923, Chicago, Ill.; educ. St. Procopius College (Lisle, Ill.), Catholic Univ. (Washington, D.C.); professed in Order of St. Benedict, June 16, 1944; ord. priest May 26, 1949; abbot, St. Procopius Abbey, 1964-71; pres. Illinois Benedictine College, 1959-65 and 1971-76; ord. titular bishop of Natchez and auxiliary bishop of Joliet, July 21, 1977.

Kupfer, William F., M.M.: b. Jan. 28, 1909, Brooklyn, N.Y.; educ. Cathedral College (Brooklyn, N.Y.), Maryknoll Seminary (Maryknoll, N.Y.); ord. priest June 11, 1933; missionary in China; app. prefect apostolic of Taichung, Formosa, 1951; ord. first bishop of Taichung, July 25, 1962.

L

Lambert, Francis, S.M.: b. Feb. 7, 1921, Lawrence, Mass.; educ. Marist Seminary (Framingham, Mass.); ord. priest, June 29, 1946; served in Marist missions in Oceania; provincial of Marist Oceania province, 1971; ord. bishop of Port Vila, New Hebrides, Mar. 20, 1977.

Lardone, Francesco: b. Jan. 12, 1887, Moretta, Italy; educ. Pontifical Schools of Theology and Canon Law and Royal Univ. (Turin); ord. priest June 29, 1910; became an American citizen, 1937; ord. titular archbishop of Rhizaeum and apostolic nuncio to Haiti and the Dominican Republic, June 30, 1949; app. apostolic nuncio to Peru, Nov. 21, 1953; papal representative to Turkey (first apostolic delegate, then internuncio), 1959-66.

Larkin, W. Thomas: b. Mar. 31, 1923, Mt. Morris, N.Y.; educ. St. Andrew Seminary and St. Bernard Seminary (Rochester, N.Y.); Angelicum Univ. (Rome); ord. priest May 15, 1947; ord. bishop of St. Petersburg, May 27, 1979.

Law, Bernard F.: b. Nov. 4, 1931, Torreon, Mexico; educ. Harvard Univ. (Cambridge, Mass.), St. Joseph Seminary (St. Benedict, La.), Pontifical College Josephinum (Worthington, O.); ord. priest May 21, 1961; editor of *Mississippi Register* (now *Mississippi Today*), 1963-68; director of NCCB Committee on Ecumenical and Interreligious Affairs, 1968-71; vicar general of Natchez-Jackson diocese, 1971-73; ord. bishop of Springfield-Cape Girardeau, Mo., Dec. 5, 1973.

Leech, George Leo: b. May 21, 1890, Ashley, Pa.; educ. St. Charles Borromeo Seminary (Overbrook, Pa.), Catholic Univ. (Washington, D.C.); ord. priest May 29, 1920; ord. titular bishop of Mela and auxiliary bishop of Harrisburg, Oct. 17, 1935; bishop of Harrisburg Dec. 19, 1935; resigned Oct. 19, 1971; app. titular bishop of Allegheny.

Leipzig, Francis P.: b. June 29, 1895, Chilton, Wis.; educ. St. Francis Seminary (Milwaukee, Wis.), Mt. Angel Seminary (St. Benedict, Ore.), St. Patrick's Seminary (Menlo Park, Calif.); ord. priest Apr. 14, 1920; ord. bishop of Baker, Sept. 12, 1950; retired June 30, 1971.

Lemay, Leo, S.M.: b. Sept. 23, 1909, Lawrence, Mass.; educ. Marist College (Washington, D.C.), Gregorian Univ. (Rome); ord. priest Apr. 15, 1933; ord. titular bishop of Agbia and vicar apostolic of North Solomon Islands, Sept. 21, 1960; first bishop of Bougainville, Nov. 15, 1966; resigned July 1, 1974.

Leonard, Vincent M.: b. Dec. 11, 1908, Pittsburgh, Pa.; educ. Duquesne Univ. (Pittsburgh, Pa.), St. Vincent Seminary (Latrobe, Pa.); ord. priest June 16, 1935; ord. titular bishop of Arsacal and auxiliary bishop of Pittsburgh, Apr. 21, 1964; app. bishop of Pittsburgh, installed July 2, 1969.

Lessard, Raymond W.: b. Dec. 21, 1930, Grafton, N.D.; educ. St. Paul Seminary (St. Paul, Minn.), North American College (Rome); ord. priest Dec. 16, 1956; served on staff of the Congregation for Bishops in the Roman Curia, 1964-73; ord. bishop of Savannah, Apr. 27, 1973.

Leven, Stephen A.: b. Apr. 30, 1905, Blackwell, Okla.; educ. St. Gregory's College (Shawnee, Okla.), St. Benedict's College (Atchison, Kans.), St. Mary's Seminary (La Porte, Tex.), American College (Louvain, Belgium); ord. priest June 10, 1928; ord. titular bishop of Bure and auxiliary bishop of

San Antonio, Feb. 8, 1956; app. bishop of San Angelo, Tex., installed Nov. 25, 1969; resigned 1979.

Lohmuller, Martin J.: b. Aug. 21, 1919, Philadelphia, Pa.; educ. St. Charles Borromeo Seminary (Philadelphia, Pa.), Catholic Univ. (Washington, D.C.); ord. priest June 3, 1944; ord. titular bishop of Ramsbury and auxiliary bishop of Philadelphia, Apr. 2, 1970.

Losten, Basil: b. May 11, 1930, Chesapeake City, Md.; educ. St. Basil's College (Stamford, Conn.), Catholic University (Washington, D.C.); ord. priest June 10, 1957; ord. titular bishop of Arcadiopolis in Asia and auxiliary bishop of Ukrainian archeparchy of Philadelphia, May 25, 1971; app. apostolic administrator of archeparchy, 1976; app. bishop of Ukrainian eparchy of Stamford, 1977.

Lubachivsky, Myroslav J.: b. June 24, 1914, Dolynian, Ukraine; educ. Innsbruck Univ. (Austria), Gregorian Univ. and Biblicum (Rome); began pastoral work in U.S. in 1947; app. archbishop of Ukrainian rite archeparchy of Philadelphia, September, 1979.

Lucker, Raymond A.: b. Feb. 24, 1927, St. Paul, Minn.; educ. St. Paul Seminary (St. Paul, Minn.); University of Minnesota (Minneapolis), Angelicum (Rome); ord. priest June 7, 1952; director of USCC department of education, 1968-71; ord. titular bishop of Meta and auxiliary bishop of St. Paul and Minneapolis, Sept. 8, 1971; app. bishop of New Ulm, Dec. 23, 1975, installed Feb. 19, 1976.

Lyke, James P., O.F.M.: b. Feb. 18, 1939, Chicago, Ill.; educ. Quincy College (Quincy, Ill.), Antonianum (Rome); professed in Order of Friars Minor, June 21, 1963; ord. priest June 24, 1966; president of National Black Catholic Clergy Caucus; ord. titular bishop of Furnos Minor and auxiliary bishop of Cleveland, Aug. 1, 1979.

Lynch, George E.: b. Mar. 4, 1917, New York, N.Y.; educ. Fordham Univ. (New York), Mt. St. Mary's Seminary (Emmitsburg, Md.), Catholic Univ. (Washington, D.C.); ord. priest May 29, 1943; ord. titular bishop of Satafi and auxiliary bishop of Raleigh Jan. 6, 1970.

Lyons, Thomas W.: b. Sept. 26, 1923, Washington, D.C.; educ. St. Charles College (Catonsville, Md.), St. Mary's Seminary (Baltimore, Md.); ord. priest May 22, 1948; ord. titular bishop of Mortlach and auxiliary bishop of Washington, D.C., Sept. 12, 1974.

M

McAuliffe, Michael F.: b. Nov. 22, 1920, Kansas City, Mo.; educ. St. Louis Preparatory Seminary (St. Louis, Mo.), Catholic Univ. (Washington, D.C.): ord. priest May 31, 1945; ord. bishop of Jefferson City, Aug. 18, 1969.

McCafferty, John E.: b. Jan. 6, 1920, New York, N.Y.; educ. St. Andrew's and St. Bernard's Seminaries (Rochester, N.Y.), Catholic Univ. (Washington, D.C.); ord. priest Mar. 17, 1945; ord. titular bishop of Tanudaia and auxiliary bishop of Rochester, Mar. 14, 1968.

McCarrick, Theodore E.: b. July 7, 1930, New York, N.Y.; educ. Fordham Univ. (Bronx, N.Y.), St. Joseph's Seminary (Dunwoodie, N.Y.), Catholic Univ. (Washington, D.C.); ord. priest May 31, 1958; dean of students Catholic Univ. of America, 1961-63; pres., Catholic Univ. of Puerto Rico, 1965-69; secretary to Cardinal Cooke, 1970; ord. titular bishop of Rusubisir and auxiliary bishop of New York, June 29, 1977.

McCarthy, Edward A.: b. Apr. 10, 1918, Cincinnati, O.; educ. Mt. St. Mary Seminary (Norwood, O.), Catholic Univ. (Washington, D.C.), Lateran and Angelicum (Rome); ord. priest May 29, 1943; ord. titular bishop of Tamascani and auxiliary bishop of Cincinnati, June 15, 1965; first bishop of Phoenix, Ariz., Dec. 2, 1969; app. coadjutor archbishop of Miami, Fla., July 7, 1976; succeeded as archbishop of Miami, July 26, 1977.

McCarthy, John E.: b. June 21, 1930, Houston, Tex.; educ. Univ. of St. Thomas (Houston, Tex.); ord. priest May 26, 1956; assistant director Social Action Dept. USCC, 1967-69; executive director Texas Catholic Conference; ord. titular bishop of Pedena and auxiliary bishop of Galveston-Houston, Mar. 14, 1979.

McCauley, Vincent, C.S.C.: b. Mar. 8, 1906, Council Bluffs, Ia.; educ. Notre Dame Univ. (Notre Dame, Ind.), Holy Cross Seminary (Washington, D.C.); ord. priest June 24, 1943; ord. first bishop of Fort Portal, Uganda, May 18, 1961; resigned to Africanize the diocese Dec. 1, 1972; general secretary of Association of Member Episcopal Conferences in Eastern Africa (AMECEA), Nairobi, Kenya.

McCormick, J. Carroll: b. Dec. 15, 1907, Philadelphia, Pa.; educ. College Ste. Marie (Montreal), St. Charles Seminary (Overbrook, Pa.), Minor and Major Roman Seminary (Rome); ord. priest July 10, 1932; ord. titular bishop of Ruspae and auxiliary bishop of Philadelphia, Apr. 23, 1947; app. bishop of Altoona-Johnstown, installed Sept. 21, 1960; app. bishop of Scranton, installed May 25, 1966.

McDevitt, Gerald V.: b. Feb. 23, 1917, Philadelphia, Pa.; educ. St. Charles Seminary (Philadelphia, Pa.), Pontifical Roman Seminary (Rome), Catholic Univ. (Washington, D.C.); ord. priest May 30, 1942; ord. titular bishop of Tigias and auxiliary bishop of Philadelphia, Aug. 1, 1962.

McDonald, Andrew J.: b. Oct. 24, 1923, Savannah, Ga.; educ. St. Mary's Seminary (Baltimore, Md.), Catholic Univ. (Washington,

D.C.), Lateran Univ. (Rome); ord. priest May 8, 1948; ord. bishop of Little Rock, Sept. 5, 1972.

McDonald, William J.: b. June 17, 1904, Mooncoin, Ireland; educ. St. Kieran's College and Seminary (Kilkenny, Ireland), Catholic Univ. (Washington, D.C.); ord. priest June 10, 1928; rector of Catholic Univ. of America, 1957-67; ord. titular bishop of Aquae Regiae and auxiliary bishop of Washington, May 19, 1964; app. auxiliary bishop of San Francisco, July 26, 1967; retired 1979.

McDonough, Thomas J.: b. Dec. 5, 1911, Philadelphia, Pa.; educ. St. Charles Seminary (Overbrook, Pa.), Catholic Univ. (Washington, D.C.); ord. priest May 26, 1938; ord. titular bishop of Thenae and auxiliary bishop of St. Augustine, Apr. 30, 1947; app. auxiliary bishop of Savannah, Jan. 2, 1957; named bishop of Savannah, installed Apr. 27, 1960; app. archbishop of Louisville, installed May 2, 1967.

McDowell, John B.: b. July 17, 1921, New Castle, Pa.; educ. St. Vincent College, St. Vincent Theological Seminary (Latrobe, Pa.), Catholic Univ. (Washington, D.C.); ord. priest Nov. 4, 1945; superintendent of schools, Pittsburgh diocese, 1955-70; ord. titular bishop of Tamazuca, and auxiliary bishop of Pittsburgh, Sept. 8, 1966.

McEleney, John J., S.J.: b. Nov. 13, 1895, Woburn, Mass.; educ. Boston College (Boston, Mass.), Jesuit Scholasticate (New England Province), entered Society of Jesus, 1918; ord. priest June 18, 1930; app. provincial of New England Province, 1944; ord. titular bishop of Zeugma and vicar apostolic of Jamaica, Apr. 15, 1950; title changed to bishop of Kingston, Feb. 29, 1956; archbishop of Kingston, Sept. 14, 1967; retired Sept. 1, 1970.

McFarland, Norman F.: b. Feb. 21, 1922, Martinez, Calif.; educ. St. Patrick's Seminary (Menlo Park, Calif.), Catholic Univ. (Washington, D.C.); ord. priest June 15, 1946; ord. titular bishop of Bida and auxiliary bishop of San Francisco, Sept. 8, 1970; apostolic adminstrator of Reno, 1974; app. bishop of Reno, Feb. 10, 1976, installed Mar. 31, 1976; title of see changed to Reno-Las Vegas, 1977.

McGann, John R.: b. Dec. 2, 1924, Brooklyn, N.Y.; educ. Cathedral College (Brooklyn, N.Y.), Immaculate Conception Seminary (Huntington, L.I.); ord. priest June 3, 1950; ord. titular bishop of Morosbisdus and auxiliary bishop of Rockville Centre, Jan. 7, 1971; vicar general and episcopal vicar; app. bishop of Rockville Centre May 3, 1976, installed June 24, 1976.

McGarry, Urban, T.O.R.: b. Nov. 11, 1911, Warren, Pa.; ord. priest Oct. 3, 1942, in India; prefect apostolic of Bhagalpur, Aug. 7, 1956; ord. first bishop of Bhagalpur, India, May 10, 1965.

McGucken, Joseph T.: b. Mar. 13, 1902, Los Angeles, Calif.; educ. St. Patrick's Seminary (Menlo Park, Calif.), North American College (Rome); ord. priest Jan. 15, 1928; ord. titular bishop of Sanavus and auxiliary bishop of Los Angeles, Mar. 19, 1941; app. coadjutor bishop of Sacramento with right of succession, Oct. 26, 1955; bishop of Sacramento, Jan. 14, 1957; archbishop of San Francisco, installed Apr. 3, 1962; resigned Feb. 22, 1977.

McGurkin, Edward A., M.M.: b. June 22, 1905, Hartford, Conn.; educ. Maryknoll Seminary (Maryknoll, N.Y.); ord. priest Sept. 14, 1930; ord. first bishop of Maswa, Tanganyika, Oct. 3, 1956; title of see changed to Shinyanga (Tanzania), 1957; resigned Jan. 30, 1975.

McKinney, Joseph C.: b. Sept. 10, 1928, Grand Rapids, Mich.; educ. St. Joseph's Seminary (Grand Rapids, Mich.), Seminaire de Philosophie (Montreal, Canada), Urban Univ. (Rome, Italy); ord. priest Dec. 20, 1953; ord. titular bishop of Lentini and auxiliary bishop of Grand Rapids, Sept. 26, 1968.

McLaughlin, Bernard J.: b. Nov. 19, 1912, Buffalo, N.Y.; educ. Urban Univ. (Rome, Italy); ord. priest Dec. 21, 1935, at Rome; ord. titular bishop of Mottola and auxiliary bishop of Buffalo, Jan. 6, 1969.

McManus, William E.: b. Jan. 27, 1914, Chicago, Ill.; educ. St. Mary of the Lake Seminary (Mundelein, Ill.), Catholic Univ. (Washington, D.C.); ord. priest Apr. 15, 1939; ord. titular bishop of Mesarfelta and auxiliary bishop of Chicago, Aug. 24, 1967; app. bishop of Fort Wayne-South Bend, Aug. 31, 1976, installed Oct. 19, 1976.

McNabb, John C., O.S.A.: b. Dec. 11, 1925, Beloit, Wis.; educ. Villanova Univ. (Villanova, Pa.), Augustinian College and Catholic Univ. (Washington, D.C.), De Paul Univ. (Chicago, Ill.); ord. priest May 24, 1952; ord. titular bishop of Saia Maggiore and prelate of Chulucanas, Peru, June 17, 1967.

McNamara, Lawrence J.: b. Aug. 5, 1928, Chicago, Ill.; educ. St. Paul Seminary (St. Paul, Minn.), Catholic Univ. (Washington, D.C.); ord. priest May 30, 1953; executive director of Campaign for Human Development 1973-77; ord. bishop of Grand Island, Nebr., Mar. 28, 1978.

McNaughton, William J., M.M.: b. Dec. 7, 1926, Lawrence, Mass.; educ. Maryknoll Seminary (Maryknoll, N.Y.); ord. priest June 13, 1953; ord. titular bishop of Thuburbo Minus and vicar apostolic of Inchon, Korea, Aug. 24, 1961; title changed to bishop of Inchon, Mar. 10, 1962.

McNicholas, Joseph A.: b. Jan. 13, 1923, St. Louis, Mo.; educ. Cardinal Glennon College, Kenrick Seminary and St. Louis Univ. (all in St. Louis, Mo.); ord. priest June 7, 1949; ord. titular bishop of Scala and auxiliary bishop of St. Louis, Mar. 25, 1969; app. bishop of

Springfield, Ill., July 22, 1975, installed Sept. 3, 1975.

McShea, Joseph M.: b. Feb. 22, 1907, Latimer, Pa.; educ. St. Charles Seminary (Philadelphia, Pa.), Major Pontifical Roman Seminary (Rome); ord. priest Dec. 6, 1931; ord. titular bishop of Mina and auxiliary bishop of Philadelphia, Mar. 19, 1952; app. first bishop of Allentown, installed Apr. 11, 1961.

Maginn, Edward J.: b. Jan. 4, 1897, Glasgow, Scotland; educ. Holy Cross College (Worcester, Mass.), St. Joseph's Seminary (Yonkers, N.Y.); ord. priest June 10, 1922; ord. titular bishop of Curium and auxiliary bishop of Albany, Sept. 12, 1957; apostolic administrator of Albany, 1966-69; retired July 8, 1972.

Maguire, John J.: b. Dec. 11, 1904, New York, N.Y.; educ. Cathedral College (New York City), St. Joseph's Seminary (Dunwoodie, N.Y.), North American College (Rome); ord. priest Dec. 22, 1928; ord. titular bishop of Antiphrae and auxiliary bishop of New York, June 29, 1959; app. titular archbishop of Tabalta and coadjutor archbishop of New York, Sept. 15, 1965.

Maguire, Joseph F.: b. Sept. 4, 1919, Boston, Mass.; educ. Boston College, St. John's Seminary (Boston, Mass.); ord. priest June 29, 1945; ord. titular bishop of Macteris and auxiliary bishop of Boston, Feb. 2, 1972; app. coadjutor bishop of Springfield, Mass., Apr. 13, 1976; succeeded as bishop of Springfield, Mass., Oct. 15, 1977.

Maher, Leo T.: b. July 1, 1915, Mount Union, Ia.; educ. St. Joseph's College (Mountain View, Calif.); St. Patrick's Seminary (Menlo Park, Calif.); ord. priest Dec. 18, 1943; ord. first bishop of Santa Rosa, April 5, 1962; bishop of San Diego, Oct. 4, 1969.

Mahoney, James P.: b. Aug. 16, 1925, Kingston, N.Y.; educ. St. Joseph's Seminary (Dunwoodie, N.Y.); ord. priest May 19, 1951; ord. titular bishop of Ipagro and auxiliary bishop of New York, Sept. 15, 1972.

Mahony, Roger M.: b. Feb. 27, 1936, Hollywood, Calif.; educ. St. John's Seminary (Camarillo, Calif.), National Catholic School of Social Service (Catholic Univ., Washington, D.C.); ord. priest May 1, 1962; ord. titular bishop of Tamascani and auxiliary bishop of Fresno, Mar. 19, 1975.

Malone, James W.: b. Mar. 8, 1920, Youngstown, O.; educ. St. Charles Preparatory Seminary (Catonsville, Md.), St. Mary's Seminary (Cleveland, O.), Catholic Univ. (Washington, D.C.); ord. priest May 26, 1945; ord. titular bishop of Alabanda and auxiliary bishop of Youngstown, Mar. 24, 1960; apostolic administrator, 1966; bishop of Youngstown, installed June 20, 1968.

Maloney, Charles G.: b. Sept. 9, 1912, Louisville, Ky.; educ. St. Joseph's College (Rensselaer, Ind.), North American College (Rome); ord. priest Dec. 8, 1937; ord. titular bishop of Capsa and auxiliary bishop of Louisville, Feb. 2, 1955.

Maloney, David M.: b. Mar. 15, 1912, Littleton, Colo.; educ. St. Thomas Seminary (Denver, Colo.), Gregorian Univ. and Apollinare Univ. (Rome); ord. priest Dec. 8, 1936; ord. titular bishop of Ruspe and auxiliary bishop of Denver, Jan. 4, 1961; app. bishop of Wichita, Kans., Dec. 6, 1967.

Manning, Thomas R., O.F.M.: b. Aug. 29, 1922, Baltimore, Md.; educ. Duns Scotus College (Southfield, Mich.), Holy Name College (Washington, D.C.); ord. priest June 5, 1948; ord. titular bishop of Arsamosata and prelate of Coroico, Bolivia, July 14, 1959.

Manning, Timothy: (See Cardinals, Biographies.)

Marcinkus, Paul C.: b. Jan. 15, 1922, Cicero, Ill.; ord. priest May 3, 1947; served in Vatican secretariat from 1952; ord. titular bishop of Orta, Jan. 6, 1969; secretary (1968-71) and president (1971-) of Institute for Works of Religion (Vatican Bank).

Marconi, Dominic A.: b. Mar. 13, 1927, Newark, N.J.; educ. Seton Hall Univ. (S. Orange, N.J.), Immaculate Conception Seminary (Darlington, N.J.), Catholic Univ. (Washington, D.C.); ord. priest May 30, 1953; ord. titular bishop of Bure and auxiliary bishop of Newark, June 25, 1976.

Mardaga, Thomas J.: b. May 14, 1913, Baltimore, Md.; educ. St. Charles College (Catonsville, Md.), St. Mary's Seminary (Baltimore, Md.); ord. priest May 14, 1940; ord. titular bishop of Mutugenna and auxiliary bishop of Baltimore, Jan. 25, 1967; app. bishop of Wilmington, installed Apr. 6, 1968.

Marino, Eugene A., S.S.J.: b. May 29, 1934, Biloxi, Miss.; educ. Epiphany Apostolic College and Mary Immaculate Novitiate (Newburgh, N.Y.), St. Joseph's Seminary (Washington, D.C.), Catholic Univ. (Washington, D.C.), Loyola Univ. (New Orleans, La.), Fordham Univ. (New York City); ord. priest June 9, 1962; ord. titular bishop of Walla Walla and auxiliary bishop of Washington, D.C., Sept. 12, 1974.

Marling, Joseph M., C.Pp.S.: b. Aug. 31, 1904, Centralia, W. Va.; educ. St. Joseph's College (Collegeville, Ind.), St. Charles Seminary (Carthagena, O.), Catholic Univ. (Washington, D.C.); ord. priest Feb. 21, 1929; ord. titular bishop of Thasus and auxiliary bishop of Kansas City, Mo., Aug. 6, 1947; app. first bishop of Jefferson City, Aug. 24, 1956; resigned 1969; assigned titular see of Lesina. Died Oct. 2, 1979.

Marshall, John A.: b. Apr. 26, 1928, Worcester, Mass.; educ. Holy Cross College (Worcester, Mass.), Sulpician Seminary (Montreal), North American College and Gregorian Univ. (Rome), Assumption College (Worcester); ord. priest Dec. 19, 1953; ord. bishop of Burlington, Jan. 25, 1972.

May, John L.: b. Mar. 31, 1922, Evanston,

Ill.; educ. St. Mary of the Lake Seminary (Mundelein, Ill.); ord. priest May 3, 1947; general secretary and vice-president of the Catholic Church Extension Society, 1959; ord. titular bishop of Tagarbala and auxiliary bishop of Chicago, Aug. 24, 1967; bishop of Mobile, Ala., Sept. 29, 1969.

Medeiros, Humberto S.: (See Cardinals, Biographies.)

Mendez, Alfred, C.S.C.: b. June 3, 1907, Chicago, Ill.; educ. Notre Dame Univ. (Notre Dame, Ind.), Institute of Holy Cross (Washington, D.C.); ord. priest June 24, 1935; ord. first bishop of Arecibo, Puerto Rico, Oct. 28, 1960; resigned Jan. 24, 1974.

Mestice, Anthony F.: b. Dec. 6, 1923, New York, N.Y.; educ. St. Joseph Seminary (Yonkers, N.Y.); ord. priest June 4, 1949; ord. titular bishop of Villa Nova and auxiliary bishop of New York Apr. 27, 1973.

Metzger, Sidney Matthew: b. July 11, 1902, Fredericksburg, Tex.; educ. St. John's Seminary (San Antonio, Tex.), North American College (Rome); ord. priest Apr. 3, 1926; ord. titular bishop of Birtha and auxiliary bishop of Santa Fe, Apr. 10, 1940; app. coadjutor bishop of El Paso, Dec. 26, 1941; bishop of El Paso, Dec. 1, 1942; retired May 29, 1978.

Michaels, James E., S.S.C.: b. May 30, 1926, Chicago, Ill.; educ. Columban Seminary (St. Columban, Neb.), Gregorian Univ. (Rome); ord. priest Dec. 21, 1951; ord. titular bishop of Verbe and auxiliary bishop of Kwang Ju, Korea, Apr. 14, 1966; app. auxiliary bishop of Wheeling, Apr. 3, 1973; title of see changed to Wheeling-Charleston, 1974.

Mihalik, Emil J.: b. Feb. 6, 1920, Pittsburgh, Pa.; educ. St. Procopius Seminary (Lisle, Ill.), Duquesne Univ. (Pittsburgh, Pa.); ord. priest Sept. 21, 1945; ord. first bishop of Byzantine Rite diocese of Parma, O., June 12, 1969.

Minder, John, O.S.F.S.: b. Nov. 1, 1923, Philadelphia, Pa.; ord. priest June 3, 1950; ord. bishop of Keimos, South Africa, Jan. 10, 1968.

Moran, William J.: b. Jan. 15, 1906, San Francisco, Calif.; educ. St. Patrick's Seminary (Menlo Park, Calif.); ord. priest June 20, 1931; Army chaplain, 1933; ord. titular bishop of Centuria and auxiliary to the military vicar, Dec. 13, 1965.

Moreno, Manuel D.: b. Nov. 27, 1930, Placentia, Calif.; educ. Univ. of California (Los Angeles), Our Lady Queen of Angels (San Fernando, Calif.), St. John's Seminary (Camarillo, Calif.); ord. priest Apr. 25, 1961; ord. titular bishop of Tanagra and auxiliary bishop of Los Angeles, Feb. 19, 1977.

Morkovsky, John Louis: b. Aug. 16, 1909, Praha, Tex.; educ. St. John's Seminary (San Antonio, Tex.), North American College, Urban Univ. and Gregorian Univ. (Rome), Catholic Univ. (Washington, D.C.); ord. priest Dec. 5, 1933; ord titular bishop of Hieron and auxiliary bishop of Amarillo, Feb. 22, 1956; app. bishop of Amarillo, Aug. 27, 1958; titular bishop of Tigava and coadjutor bishop of Galveston-Houston with right of succession, June 11, 1963; apostolic administrator; president Texas Conference of Churches, 1970-72; bishop of Galveston-Houston, Apr. 22, 1975.

Morneau, Robert F.: b. September, 1938, New London, Wis.; educ. St. Norbert's College (De Pere, Wis.), Sacred Heart Seminary (Oneida, Wis.), Catholic Univ. (Washington, D.C.); ord. priest May 28, 1966; ord. titular bishop of Massa Lubrense and auxiliary bishop of Green Bay, Feb. 22, 1979.

Morrow, Louis La Ravoire, S.D.B.: b. Dec. 24, 1892, Weatherford, Tex.; educ. Salesian School and Palafox (Puebla, Mexico); professed in Salesians of St. John Bosco, Sept. 29, 1912; ord. priest May 21, 1921; ord. bishop of Krishnagar, India, Oct. 29, 1939; resigned Oct. 31, 1969.

Mueller, Joseph M.: b. Dec. 1, 1894, St. Louis, Mo.; educ. Pontifical College Josephinum (Worthington, O.); ord. priest June 14, 1919; ord. titular bishop of Sinda and coadjutor bishop of Sioux City, Oct. 16, 1947; bishop of Sioux City, Sept. 20, 1948; resigned Oct. 15, 1970.

Mugavero, Francis John: b. June 8, 1914, Brooklyn, N.Y.; educ. Cathedral College (Brooklyn, N.Y.), Immaculate Conception Seminary (Huntington, N.Y.), Fordham Univ. (New York City); ord. priest May 18, 1940; ord. bishop of Brooklyn, Sept. 12, 1968.

Mulcahy, John J.: b. June 26, 1922, Dorchester, Mass.; educ. St. John's Seminary (Brighton, Mass.); ord. priest May 1, 1947; rector Pope John XXIII Seminary for Delayed Vocations, 1969-73; ord. titular bishop of Penafiel and auxiliary bishop of Boston, Feb. 11, 1975.

Mulrooney, Charles R.: b. Jan. 13, 1906, Brooklyn, N.Y.; educ. Cathedral College (Brooklyn, N.Y.), St. Mary's Seminary (Baltimore, Md.), Sulpician Seminary (Washington, D.C.); ord. priest June 10, 1930; ord. titular bishop of Valentiniana and auxiliary bishop of Brooklyn, Apr. 22, 1959.

Mulvee, Robert E.: b. Feb. 15, 1930, Boston, Mass.; educ. St. Thomas Seminary (Bloomfield, Conn.), University Seminary (Ottawa, Ont., Canada), American College (Louvain, Belgium), Lateran Univ. (Rome); ord. priest June 30, 1957; ord. titular bishop of Summa and auxiliary bishop of Manchester, N.H., Apr. 14, 1977.

Mundo, Michael P.: b. July 25, 1937, New York, N.Y.; educ. Fordham Univ. (Bronx, N.Y.), St. Jerome's College (Kitchener, Ont., Canada), St. Francis Seminary (Loretto, Pa.); ord. May 19, 1962; missionary in Brazil from 1963; ord. titular bishop of Blanda Julia and auxiliary bishop of Jatai, Brazil, June 2, 1978.

Murphy, Michael J.: b. July 1, 1915, Cleveland, O.; educ. Niagara Univ. (Niagara Falls, N.Y.); North American College (Rome), Catholic Univ. (Washington, D.C.); ord. priest Feb. 28, 1942; ord. titular bishop of Ariendela and auxiliary bishop of Cleveland, June 11, 1976; app. coadjutor bishop of Erie, Nov. 20, 1978.

Murphy, Philip Francis: b. Mar. 25, 1933, Cumberland, Md.; educ. St. Mary Seminary (Baltimore, Md.), North American College (Rome); ord. priest Dec. 20, 1958; ord. titular bishop of Tacarata and auxiliary bishop of Baltimore, Feb. 29, 1976.

Murphy, T. Austin: b. May 11, 1911, Baltimore, Md.; educ. St. Charles College (Catonsville, Md.), St. Mary's Seminary (Baltimore, Md.); ord priest June 10, 1937; ord. titular bishop of Appiaria and auxiliary bishop of Baltimore, July 3, 1962.

Murphy, Thomas J.: b. Oct. 3, 1932, Chicago, Ill.; educ. Quigley Preparatory Seminary (Chicago, Ill.), St. Mary of the Lake Seminary (Mundelein, Ill.); ord. priest Apr. 12, 1958; ord. bishop of Great Falls, Mont. Aug. 21, 1978.

Murphy, Thomas W., C.SS.R.: b. Dec. 17, 1917, Omaha, Nebr.; educ. St. Joseph's College (Kirkwood, Mo.); ord. priest June 29, 1943; ord. first bishop of Juazeiro, Brazil, Jan. 2, 1963; resigned Dec. 29, 1973; app. titular bishop of Sululos and auxiliary bishop of Sao Salvador da Bahia, Brazil, Jan. 31, 1974.

N

Nelson, Knute Ansgar, O.S.B.: b. Oct. 1, 1906, Copenhagen, Denmark; educ. Abbey of Maria Laach (Germany), Brown Univ. (Providence, R.I.); professed in the Order of St. Benedict, May 30, 1932; ord. priest May 22, 1937; became an American citizen, Mar. 4, 1941; ord. titular bishop of Bilta and coadjutor bishop of Stockholm, Sweden, Sept. 8, 1947; succeeded as bishop of Stockholm, Oct. 1, 1957; retired; titular bishop of Dura. 1962.

Nevins, John J.: b. Jan. 19, 1932, New Rochelle, N.Y.; educ. Iona College (New Rochelle, N.Y.), Catholic Univ. (Washington, D.C.); ord. priest June 6, 1959; ord. titular bishop of Rusticana and auxiliary bishop of Miami, Mar. 24, 1979.

Newell, Hubert M.: b. Feb. 16, 1904, Denver, Colo.; educ. Regis College and St. Thomas Seminary (Denver, Colo.), Catholic Univ. (Washington, D.C.); ord. priest June 15, 1930; ord. titular bishop of Zapara and coadjutor bishop of Cheyenne, Sept. 24, 1947; bishop of Cheyenne, Nov. 10, 1951; retired Dec. 5, 1977.

Neylon, Martin J., S.J.: b. Feb. 13, 1920, Buffalo, N.Y.; ord. priest June 18, 1950; ord. titular bishop of Libertina and coadjutor vicar apostolic of the Caroline and Marshall Islands, Feb. 2, 1970; vicar apostolic of Caroline and Marshall Is., Sept. 20, 1971; first bishop when vicariate apostolic was raised to diocese, 1979.

Niedergeses, James D.: b. Feb. 2, 1917, Lawrenceburg, Tenn.; educ. St. Bernard College (St. Bernard, Ala.), St. Ambrose College (Davenport, Ia.), Mt. St. Mary Seminary of the West and Athenaeum (Cincinnati, Ohio); ord. priest May 20, 1944; ord. bishop of Nashville May 20, 1975.

Nold, Wendelin J.: b. Jan. 18, 1900, Bonham, Tex.; educ. St. Mary's Seminary (La Porte, Tex.), North American College (Rome); ord. priest Apr. 11, 1925; ord. titular bishop of Sasima and coadjutor bishop of Galveston, Feb. 25, 1948, succeeded as bishop of Galveston, Apr. 1, 1950; title of see changed to Galveston-Houston, 1959; resigned Apr. 22, 1975.

Nolker, Bernard, C.SS.R.: b. Sept. 25, 1912, Baltimore, Md.; educ. St. Mary's College (North East, Pa.), St. Mary's College (Ilchester, Md.), Mt. St. Alphonsus Seminary (Esopus, N.Y.); ord. priest June 18, 1939; ord. first bishop of Paranagua, Brazil, Apr. 25, 1963.

Noser, Adolph A., S.V.D.: b. July 4, 1900, Belleville, Ill.; educ. Quincy College (Quincy, Ill.), St. Mary's Mission House (Techny, Ill.), Angelicum (Rome); received into the Society of the Divine Word, 1921; ord. priest Sept. 27, 1925; ord. titular bishop of Capitolias and vicar apostolic of Accra, Gold Coast, British West Africa, Aug. 22, 1947; title changed to bishop of Accra, Apr. 18, 1950; transferred to titular see of Hierpiniana and vicariate apostolic of Alexishaven, New Guinea, Jan. 8, 1953; first archbishop of Madang, Nov. 15, 1966; retired Dec. 19, 1975.

Novak, Alfred, C.SS.R.: b. June 2, 1930, Dwight, Nebr.; educ. Immaculate Conception Seminary (Oconomowoc, Wis.); ord. priest July 2, 1956; ord. titular bishop of Vardimissa and auxiliary bishop of Sao Paulo, Brazil, May 25, 1979.

O

O'Boyle, Patrick A.: (See Cardinals, Biographies.)

O'Connor, John J.: b. Jan. 15, 1920, Philadelphia, Pa.; educ. St. Charles Borromeo Seminary (Philadelphia, Pa.), Catholic Univ., Georgetown Univ. (Washington, D.C.); ord. priest Dec. 15, 1945; U.S. Navy chief of chaplains, 1975; ord. titular bishop of Cursola and auxiliary to the military vicar, May 27, 1979.

O'Connor, Martin J.: b. May 18, 1900, Scranton, Pa.; educ. St. Thomas College (Scranton, Pa.), St. Mary's Seminary (Baltimore, Md.), North American College, Urban Univ. and Apollinaris (Rome); ord. priest Mar. 15, 1924; ord. titular bishop of Thespia and auxiliary bishop of Scranton, Jan. 27, 1943; rector of North American College 1946-1964; app. titular archbishop of Laodicea in Syria, Sept. 5, 1959; apostolic nuncio to Malta, 1965-69; president emeritus Pontifical Commission for Social Communication.

O'Connor, William A.: b. Dec. 27, 1903, Chicago, Ill.; educ. Quigley Seminary (Chicago, Ill.), St. Mary of the Lake Seminary (Mundelein, Ill.), Urban Univ. (Rome); ord. priest Sept. 24, 1927; ord. bishop of Springfield, Ill., Mar. 7, 1949; retired July 22, 1975.

O'Donnell, Cletus F.: b. Aug. 22, 1917, Waukon, Ia.; educ. St. Mary Seminary (Mundelein, Ill.), Catholic Univ. (Washington, D.C.); ord. priest May 3, 1941; ord. titular bishop of Abritto and auxiliary bishop of Chicago, Dec. 21, 1960; app. bishop of Madison, Feb. 22, 1967, installed Apr. 25, 1967.

O'Keefe, Gerald: b. Mar. 30, 1918, St. Paul, Minn.; educ. College of St. Thomas, St. Paul Seminary (St. Paul, Minn.); ord. priest Jan. 29, 1944; ord. titular bishop of Candyba and auxiliary bishop of St. Paul July 2, 1961; bishop of Davenport, Oct. 20, 1966, installed Jan. 4, 1967.

O'Leary, Edward C.: b. Aug. 21, 1920, Bangor, Me.; educ. Holy Cross College (Worcester, Mass.), St. Paul's Seminary (Ottawa, Canada); ord. priest June 15, 1946; ord. titular bishop of Moglena and auxiliary bishop of Portland, Me., Jan. 25, 1971; app. bishop of Portland, installed Dec. 18, 1974.

O'Meara, Edward T.: b. Aug. 3, 1921, St. Louis, Mo.; educ. Cardinal Glennon College and Kenrick Seminary (St. Louis, Mo.), Angelicum (Rome); ord. priest Dec. 21, 1946; app. national director of Society for the Propagation of the Faith, 1967; ord. titular bishop of Thisiduo and auxiliary bishop of St. Louis, Feb. 13, 1972.

O'Neill, Arthur J.: b. Dec. 14, 1917, East Dubuque, Ill.; educ. Loras College (Dubuque, Ia.), St. Mary's Seminary (Baltimore, Md.); ord. priest Mar. 27, 1943; ord. bishop of Rockford, Oct. 11, 1968.

O'Rourke, Edward W.: b. Oct. 31, 1917, Downs, Ill.; educ. St. Mary's Seminary (Mundelein, Ill.), Aquinas Institute of Philosophy and Theology (River Forest, Ill.); ord. priest May 28, 1944; exec. dir. National Catholic Rural Life Conference, 1960-71; ord. bishop of Peoria, July 15, 1971.

Ott, Stanley J.: b. June 29, 1927, Gretna, La.; educ. Notre Dame Seminary (New Orleans, La.), North American College and Gregorian Univ. (Rome); ord. priest Dec. 8, 1951; ord. titular bishop of Nicives and auxiliary bishop of New Orleans, June 29, 1976.

Ottenweller, Albert H.: b. Apr. 5, 1916, Stanford, Mont.; educ. St. Joseph's Seminary (Rensselaer, Ind.), Catholic Univ. (Washington, D.C.); ord. priest June 19, 1943; ord. titular bishop of Perdices and auxiliary bishop of Toledo, May 29, 1974; app. bishop of Steubenville, Oct. 11, 1977, installed Nov. 22, 1977.

P

Pardy, James V., M.M.: b. Mar. 9, 1898, Brooklyn, N. Y.; educ. St. Francis College (Brooklyn), Fordham Univ. (New York City), Catholic Univ. (Washington, D.C.); ord. priest. Jan. 26, 1930; ord. titular bishop of Irenopolis and first vicar apostolic of Cheong Ju, Korea, Sept. 16, 1958; title changed to bishop of Cheong Ju, Mar. 10, 1962; retired June 17, 1969.

Paschang, John L.: b. Oct. 5, 1895, Hemingford, Nebr.; educ. Conception College (Conception, Mo.), St. John Seminary (Collegeville, Minn.), Catholic Univ. (Washington, D.C.); ord. priest June 12, 1921; ord. bishop of Grand Island, Oct. 9, 1951; resigned July 25, 1972.

Paul, John J.: b. Aug. 17, 1918, La Crosse, Wis.; educ. Loras College (Dubuque, Iowa), St. Mary's Seminary (Baltimore, Md.), Marquette Univ. (Milwaukee, Wis.), ord. priest Jan. 24, 1943; ord. titular bishop of Lambaesis and auxiliary bishop of La Crosse, Aug. 4, 1977.

Pearce, George H., S.M.: b. Jan. 9, 1921, Brighton, Mass.; educ. Marist College and Seminary (Framington, Mass.); ord. priest Feb. 2, 1947; ord. titular bishop of Attalea in Pamphylia and vicar apostolic of the Samoa and Tokelau Islands, June 29, 1956; title changed to bishop of Apia, June 21, 1966; app. archbishop of Suva, Fiji Islands, June 22, 1967; resigned Apr. 10, 1976.

Pechillo, Jerome, T.O.R.: b. May 16, 1919, Brooklyn, N.Y.; educ. Catholic Univ. (Washington, D.C.); ord. priest June 10, 1947; ord. titular bishop of Novasparsa and prelate of Coronel Oviedo, Paraguay, Jan. 25, 1966; app. auxiliary bishop of Newark, N.J., Mar. 6, 1976.

Pena, Raymond: b. Feb. 19, 1934, Robstown, Tex.; educ. Assumption Seminary (San Antonio, Tex.); ord. priest May 25, 1957; ord. titular bishop of Trisipa and auxiliary bishop of San Antonio, Dec. 13, 1976.

Pernicone, Joseph M.: b. Nov. 4, 1903, Regalbuto, Sicily; educ. Cathedral College (New York City), St. Joseph's Seminary (Dunwoodie, N.Y.), Catholic Univ. (Washington, D.C.); ord. priest Dec. 18, 1926; ord. titular bishop of Hadrianapolis and auxiliary bishop of New York, May 5, 1954; app. episcopal vicar, 1966. Retired.

Perry, Harold R., S.V.D.: b. Oct. 9, 1916, Lake Charles, La.; educ. St. Augustine Seminary (Bay St. Louis, Miss.), St. Mary's Seminary (Techny, Ill.); ord. priest Jan. 6, 1944; app. provincial of southern province of Society of the Divine Word, 1964; ord. titular bishop of Mons in Mauretania and auxiliary bishop of New Orleans, Jan. 6, 1966.

Pilarczyk, Daniel E.: b. Aug. 12, 1934, Dayton, Ohio; educ. St. Gregory's Seminary (Cincinnati, O.), Urban Univ. (Rome), Xavier Univ. and Univ. of Cincinnati (Cincinnati, O.); ord. priest Dec. 20, 1959; ord. titular bishop of Hodelm and auxiliary bishop of Cincinnati, Dec. 20, 1974.

Pilla, Anthony M.: b. Nov. 12, 1932, Cleveland, O.; educ. St. Gregory College Seminary (Cincinnati, O.), Borromeo College Seminary (Wickliffe, O.), St. Mary Seminary and John Carroll Univ. (Cleveland, O.); ord. priest May 23, 1959; ord. titular bishop of Scardona and auxiliary bishop of Cleveland, Aug. 1, 1979.

Pinger, Henry A., O.F.M.: b. Aug. 16, 1897, Lindsay, Nebr.; educ. Our Lady of Angels Seminary (Cleveland, O.), St. Anthony's Seminary (St. Louis, Mo.); professed in the Order of Friars Minor, June 18, 1918; ord. priest June 27, 1924; ord. titular bishop of Capitolias and vicar apostolic of Chowtsun, China, Sept. 21, 1937; title changed to bishop of Chowtsun, Apr. 11, 1946; imprisoned by Reds in 1951, released in 1956; expelled.

Povish, Kenneth J.: b. Apr. 19, 1924, Alpena, Mich.; educ. St. Joseph's Seminary (Grand Rapids, Mich.), Sacred Heart Seminary (Detroit, Mich.), Catholic Univ. (Washington, D.C.); ord. priest June 3, 1950; ord. bishop of Crookston, Sept. 29, 1970; app. bishop of Lansing, Oct. 8, 1975, installed Dec. 11, 1975.

Power, Cornelius M.: b. Dec. 18, 1913, Seattle, Wash.; educ. St. Patrick's College (Menlo Park, Calif.), St. Edward's Seminary (Kenmore, Wash.), Catholic Univ. (Washington, D.C.); ord. priest June 3, 1939; ord. bishop of Yakima, May 1, 1969, installed May 20, 1969; app. archbishop of Portland, Ore., Jan. 22, 1974, installed Apr. 17, 1974.

Primeau, Ernest J.: b. Sept. 17, 1909, Chicago, Ill.; educ. Loyola Univ. (Chicago, Ill.), St. Mary of the Lake Seminary (Mundelein, Ill.), Lateran Univ. (Rome); ord. priest Apr. 7, 1934; ord. bishop of Manchester, Feb. 25, 1960; resigned Jan. 30, 1974; app. director of Villa Stritch, Rome, 1974.

Prost, Jude, O.F.M.: b. Dec. 6, 1915, Chicago, Ill.; educ. Our Lady of the Angels Seminary (Cleveland, O.), St. Joseph's Seminary (Teutopolis, Ill.); ord. priest June 24, 1942; ord. titular bishop of Fronta and auxiliary bishop of Belem do Para, Brazil, Nov. 1, 1962.

Proulx, Amedee W.: b. Aug. 31, 1932, Sanford, Me.; educ. St. Hyacinthe Seminary (Quebec), St. Paul Univ. Seminary (Ottawa), Catholic Univ. (Washington, D.C.); ord. priest May 31, 1958; ord. titular bishop of Clipia and auxiliary bishop of Portland, Me., Nov. 12, 1975.

Pursley, Leo A.: b. Mar. 12, 1902, Hartford City, Ind.; educ. Mt. St. Mary's Seminary (Cincinnati, O.); ord. priest June 11, 1927; ord. titular bishop of Hadrianapolis in Pisidia and auxiliary bishop of Fort Wayne, Sept. 19, 1950; app. apostolic administrator of Fort Wayne, Mar. 9, 1955; installed as bishop of Fort Wayne, Feb. 26, 1957; title of see changed to Fort Wayne-South Bend, 1960; resigned Aug. 31, 1976.

Q

Quinn, Francis A.: b. Sept. 11, 1921, Los Angeles, Calif.; educ. St. Joseph's College (Mountain View, Calif.), St. Patrick's Seminary (Menlo Park, Calif.), Catholic Univ. (Washington, D.C.); Univ. of California (Berkley); ord. priest June 15, 1946; ord. titular bishop of Numana and auxiliary bishop of San Francisco, June 29, 1978.

Quinn, John R.: b. Mar. 28, 1929, Riverside, Calif.; educ. St. Francis Seminary (El Cajon, Calif.), North American College (Rome); ord. priest July 19, 1953; ord. titular bishop of Thisiduo and auxiliary bishop of San Diego, Dec. 12, 1967; bishop of Oklahoma City and Tulsa, Nov. 30, 1971; first archbishop of Oklahoma City, Dec. 19, 1972; app. archbishop of San Francisco Feb. 22, 1977, installed Apr. 26, 1977; president NCCB/USCC, 1977-

R

Rausch, James S.: b. Sept. 4, 1928, Albany, Minn.; educ. St. Thomas College (St. Paul, Minn.), Univ. of Minnesota (Minneapolis), Gregorian Univ. (Rome); ord. priest June 2, 1956; associate general secretary of USCC 1970-72; general secretary of NCCB-USCC, 1972-77; ord. titular bishop of Summa an auxiliary bishop of St. Cloud, Apr. 26, 1973; app. bishop of Phoenix Jan. 25, 1977, installed Mar. 22, 1977.

Raya, Joseph M.: b. July 20, 1917, Zahle, Lebanon; educ. St. Louis College (Paris, France), St. Anne's Seminary (Jerusalem); ord. priest July 20, 1941; came to U.S., 1949, became U.S. citizen; ord. archbishop of Acre, Israel, of the Melkites, Oct. 20, 1968; resigned Aug. 20, 1974; assigned titular metropolitan see of Scytopolis.

Regan, Joseph W., M.M.: b. Apr. 5, 1905, Boston, Mass.; educ. Boston College (Boston, Mass.), St. Bernard's Seminary (Rochester, N.Y.), Maryknoll Seminary (Maryknoll, N.Y.); ord. priest Jan. 27, 1929; missionary in China 15 years; in Philippines since 1952; ord. titular bishop of Isinda and prelate of Tagum, Philippine Islands, Apr. 25, 1962.

Reh, Francis F.: b. Jan. 9, 1911, New York, N.Y.; educ. St. Joseph's Seminary (Dunwoodie, N.Y.), North American College and Gregorian Univ. (Rome); ord. priest Dec. 8, 1935; ord. bishop of Charleston, S.C., June 29, 1962; named titular bishop of Macriana in Mauretania, 1964; rector of North American College, 1964-68; bishop of Saginaw, installed Feb. 26, 1969.

Reicher, Louis J.: b. June 14, 1890, Piqua, O.; educ. St. Mary's Seminary (Cincinnati, O.), St. Mary's Seminary (La Porte, Tex.); ord. priest Dec. 6, 1918; ord. first bishop of Austin, Apr. 14, 1948; resigned Nov. 15, 1971.

Reilly, Daniel P.: b. May 12, 1928, Providence, R.I.; educ. Our Lady of Providence Seminary (Warwick, R.I.), St. Brieuc Major Seminary (Cotes du Nord, France); ord. priest May 30, 1953; ord. bishop of Norwich, Aug. 6, 1975.

Reilly, Thomas F., C.SS.R.: b. Dec. 20, 1908, Boston, Mass.; educ. Mt. St. Alphonsus Seminary (Esopus, N.Y.), Catholic Univ. (Washington, D.C.); ord. priest June 10, 1933; ord. titular bishop of Themisonium and prelate of San Juan de la Maguana, Dominican Republic, Nov. 30, 1956; first bishop of San Juan de la Maguana, Nov. 21, 1969; retired 1977.

Reiss, John C.: b. May 13, 1922, Red Bank, N.J.; educ. Catholic Univ. (Washington, D.C.), Immaculate Conception Seminary (Darlington, N.J.); ord. priest May 31, 1947; ord. titular bishop of Simidicca and auxiliary bishop of Trenton, Dec. 12, 1967.

Riley, Lawrence J.: b. Sept. 6, 1914; Boston, Mass.; educ. Boston College and St. John's Seminary (Boston, Mass.), North American College and Gregorian Univ. (Rome), Catholic Univ. (Washington, D.C.); ord. priest Sept. 21, 1940; ord. titular bishop of Daimlaig and auxiliary bishop of Boston, Feb. 2, 1972.

Roach, John R.: b. July 31, 1921, Prior Lake, Minn.; educ. St. Paul Seminary (St. Paul, Minn.), Univ. of Minnesota (Minneapolis); ord. priest June 18, 1946; ord. titular bishop of Cenae and auxiliary bishop of St. Paul and Minneapolis, Sept. 8, 1971; app. archbishop of St. Paul and Minneapolis, May 28, 1975; vice-president NCCB/USCC, 1977.

Rodimer, Frank J.: b. Oct. 25, 1927, Rockaway, N.J.; educ. Seton Hall Prep (South Orange, N.J.), St. Charles College (Catonsville, Md.), St. Mary's Seminary (Baltimore, Md.), Immaculate Conception Seminary (Darlington, N.J.), Catholic Univ. (Washington, D.C.); ord. priest May 19, 1951; ord. bishop of Paterson Feb. 28, 1978.

Rodriguez, Migúel, C.SS.R.: b. Apr. 18, 1931, Mayaguez, P.R.; educ. St. Mary's Minor Seminary (North East, Pa.), Mt. St. Alphonsus Major Seminary (Esopus, N.Y.); ord. priest June 22, 1958; ord. bishop of Arecibo, P.R., Mar. 23, 1974.

Roman, Agustin: b. May 5, 1928, San Antonio de los Banos, Havana, Cuba; educ. San Alberto Magno Seminary (Matanzas, Cuba), Missions Etrangeres (Montreal, Canada), Barry College (Miami, Fla.); ord. priest July 5, 1959, Cuba; vicar for Spanish speaking in Miami archdiocese, 1976; ord. titular bishop of Sertei and auxiliary bishop of Miami, Mar. 24, 1979.

Rosazza, Peter Anthony: b. Feb. 13, 1935, New Haven, Conn.; educ. St. Thomas Seminary (Bloomfield, Conn.), Dartmouth College (Hanover, N.H.), St. Bernard's Seminary (Rochester, N.Y.), St. Sulpice (Issy, France); ord. priest June 29, 1961; ord. titular bishop of Oppido Nuovo and auxiliary bishop of Hartford, June 24, 1978.

Rudin, John J., M.M.: b. Nov. 27, 1916, Pittsfield, Mass.; educ. Maryknoll Seminary (Maryknoll, N.Y.), Gregorian Univ. (Rome); ord. priest June 11, 1944; ord. first bishop of Musoma, Tanzania, Oct. 3, 1957; retired 1979.

Ruocco, Joseph J.: b. Apr. 21, 1922, Boston, Mass.; educ. St. John's Seminary (Brighton, Mass.); ord. priest May 6, 1948; ord. titular bishop of Polignano and auxiliary bishop of Boston, Feb. 11, 1975.

Russell, John J.: b. Dec. 1, 1897, Baltimore, Md.; educ. St. Charles College (Catonsville, Md.), St. Mary's Seminary (Baltimore, Md.), North American College (Rome); ord. priest July 8, 1923; ord. bishop of Charleston, Mar. 14, 1950; bishop of Richmond, July 3, 1958; retired Apr. 30, 1973.

Ryan, Gerald: b. Aug. 24, 1923, Brooklyn, N.Y.; educ. Cathedral College (Brooklyn, N.Y.), Immaculate Conception Seminary (Huntington, L.I.), Fordham Univ. Graduate School of Social Work (Bronx, N.Y.); ord. priest June 3, 1950; ord. titular bishop of Munatiana and auxiliary bishop of Rockville Centre, May 9, 1977.

Ryan, James C., O.F.M.: b. Nov. 17, 1912, Chicago, Ill.; educ. St. Joseph's Seraphic Seminary (Westmont, Ill.), Our Lady of the Angels Seminary (Cleveland, O.); ord. priest June 24, 1938; ord. titular bishop of Margo and prelate of Santarem, Brazil, April 9, 1958.

Ryan, Joseph T.: b. Nov. 1, 1913, Albany, N.Y.; educ. Manhattan College (New York City); ord. priest June 3, 1939; national secretary of Catholic Near East Welfare Assn. 1960-65; ord. first archbishop of Anchorage, Alaska, Mar. 25, 1966; app. titular archbishop of Gabi and coadjutor archbishop of the military ordinariate, Oct. 24, 1975, installed Dec. 13, 1975.

S

Salatka, Charles A.: b. Feb. 26, 1918, Grand Rapids, Mich.; educ. St. Joseph's Seminary (Grand Rapids, Mich.), Catholic Univ. (Washington, D.C.), Lateran Univ. (Rome); ord. priest Feb. 24, 1945; ord. titular bishop of Cariana and auxiliary bishop of Grand Rapids, Mich., Mar. 6, 1962; app. bishop of Marquette, installed Mar. 25, 1968; app. archbishop of Oklahoma City, Sept. 27, 1977; installed Dec. 15, 1977.

Sanchez, Robert: b. Mar. 20, 1934, Socorro, N.M.; educ. Immaculate Heart Seminary (Santa Fe, N.M.), Gregorian Univ. (Rome), Catholic Univ. (Washington, D.C.); ord. priest Dec. 20, 1959; ord. archbishop of Santa Fe, N.M., July 25, 1974.

Scanlan, John J.: b. May 24, 1906, County Cork, Ireland; educ. National Univ. of Ireland (Dublin), All Hallows College (Dublin); ord. priest June 22, 1930; U.S. citizen 1938; ord. titular bishop of Cenae and auxiliary bishop of Honolulu, Sept. 21, 1954; bishop of Honolulu, installed May 1, 1968.

Scarpone, Gerald, O.F.M.: b. Oct. 1, 1928, Watertown, Mass.; ord. priest June 24, 1956; ord. coadjutor bishop of Comayagua, Feb. 21, 1979; succeeded as bishop of Comayagua, May 30, 1979.

Schad, James L.: b. July 20, 1917, Philadelphia, Pa.; educ. St. Mary's Seminary (Baltimore, Md.); ord. priest Apr. 10, 1943; ord. titular bishop of Panatoria and auxiliary bishop of Camden, Dec. 8, 1966.

Schexnayder, Maurice: b. Aug. 13, 1895, Wallace (now Vacherie), La.; educ. Chenet Institute (New Orleans, La.), St. Joseph's Seminary (St. Benedict, La.), St. Mary's Seminary (Baltimore, Md.), North American College (Rome); ord. priest Apr. 11, 1925; ord. titular bishop of Tuscamia and auxiliary bishop of Lafayette, La., Feb. 22, 1951; bishop of Lafayette, La., May 24, 1956; retired Nov. 7, 1972.

Schierhoff, Andrew B.: b. Feb. 10, 1922, St. Louis, Mo.; ord. priest Apr. 14, 1948; missionary in Bolivia from 1956; ord. titular bishop of Cerenza and auxiliary of La Paz, Bolivia, Jan. 6, 1969.

Schladweiler, Alphonse: b. July 18, 1902, Milwaukee, Wis.; educ. St. Joseph College (Teutopolis, Ill.), St. Paul's Seminary (St. Paul, Minn.), Univ. of Minnesota (Minneapolis, Minn.); ord. priest June 9, 1929; ord. first bishop of New Ulm, Jan. 29, 1958; retired Feb. 19, 1976.

Schlaefer, Salvator, O.F.M. Cap.: b. June 27, 1920, Campbellsport, Wis.; ord. priest June 5, 1946; missionary in Bluefields, Nicaragua from 1947; ord. titular bishop of Fiumepiscense and vicar apostolic of Bluefields, Nicaragua, Aug. 12, 1970.

Schlarman, Stanley Gerard: b. July 27, 1933, Belleville, Ill.; educ. St. Henry Prep Seminary (Belleville, Ill.), Gregorian Univ. (Rome), St. Louis Univ. (St. Louis, Mo.); ord. priest July 13, 1958, Rome; ord. titular bishop of Capri and auxiliary bishop of Belleville, May 14, 1979.

Schlotterback, Edward F., O.S.F.S.: b. Mar. 2, 1912, Philadelphia, Pa.; educ. Catholic Univ. (Washington, D.C.); ord. priest Dec. 17, 1938; ord. titular bishop of Balanea and vicar apostolic of Keetmanshoop, Namibia, June 11, 1956.

Schmidt, Firmin M., O.F.M.Cap.: b. Oct. 12, 1918, Catherine, Kans.; educ. Catholic Univ. (Washington, D.C.); ord. priest June 2, 1946; app. prefect apostolic of Mendi, Papua New Guinea, Apr. 3, 1959; ord. titular bishop of Conana and first vicar apostolic of Mendi, Dec. 15, 1965; became first bishop of Mendi when vicariate apostolic was raised to a diocese, Nov. 15, 1966.

Schmidt, Mathias, O.S.B.: b. Apr. 21, 1931, Wortonville, Kans.; ord. priest May 30, 1957; missionary in Brazil; ord. titular bishop of Mutugenna and auxiliary bishop of Jatai, Brazil, Sept. 10, 1972; bishop of Rui Barbosa, Brazil, May 14, 1976.

Schmitt, Mark: b. Feb. 14, 1923, Algoma, Wis., educ. Salvatorian Seminary (St. Nazianz, Wis.), St. John's Seminary (Collegeville, Minn.); ord. priest May 22, 1948; ord. titular bishop of Ceanannus Mor and auxiliary bishop of Green Bay, June 24, 1970; app. bishop of Marquette, Mar. 21, 1978, installed May 8, 1978.

Schoenherr, Walter J.: b. Feb. 28, 1920, Detroit, Mich.; educ. Sacred Heart Seminary (Detroit, Mich.), Mt. St. Mary Seminary (Norwood, O.); ord. priest Oct. 27, 1945; ord. titular bishop of Timidana and auxiliary bishop of Detroit, May 1, 1968.

Schuck, James A., O.F.M.: b. Jan. 17, 1913, Treverton, Pa.; educ. St. Joseph's Seminary (Callicoon, N.Y.), St. Bonaventure's University (St. Bonaventure, N.Y.). Holy Name College (Washington, D.C.); ord. priest June 11, 1940; ord. titular bishop of Avissa and prelate of Cristalandia, Brazil, Feb. 24, 1959.

Schulte, Paul Clarence: b. Mar. 18, 1890, Fredericktown, Mo.; educ. St. Francis Solanus College (Quincy, Ill.), Kenrick Seminary (Webster Groves, Mo.); ord. priest June 11, 1915; ord. bishop of Leavenworth, Sept. 21, 1937; archbishop of Indianapolis, July 27, 1946; resigned Jan. 14, 1970; assigned titular see of Elicrora.

Schuster, Eldon B.: b. Mar. 10, 1911, Calio, N. Dak.; educ. Loras College (Dubuque, Ia.), Catholic Univ. (Washington, D.C.), Oxford Univ. (England), St. Louis Univ. (St. Louis, Mo.); ord. priest May 27, 1937; ord. titular bishop of Amblada and auxiliary bishop of Great Falls, Mont., Dec. 21, 1961; app. bishop of Great Falls, Dec. 2, 1967, installed Jan. 23, 1968; resigned Dec. 28, 1977.

Shea, Francis R.: b. Dec. 4, 1913, Knoxville, Tenn.; educ. St. Mary's Seminary (Baltimore, Md.), North American College (Rome), Peabody College (Nashville, Tenn.); ord. priest Mar. 19, 1939; ord. bishop of Evansville, Ind., Feb. 3, 1970.

Sheehan, Daniel E.: b. May 14, 1917, Emerson, Nebr.; educ. Creighton Univ. (Omaha, Nebr.), Kenrick Seminary (Webster Groves, Mo.), Catholic Univ. (Washington, D.C.); ord. priest May 23, 1942; ord. titular bishop of Capsus and auxiliary bishop of Omaha,

Mar. 19, 1964; app. archbishop of Omaha, installed Aug. 11, 1969.

Sheen, Fulton J.: b. May 8, 1895, El Paso, Ill.; educ. St. Viator College (Kankakee, Ill.), St. Paul Seminary (St. Paul, Minn.), Catholic Univ. (Washington, D.C.), Louvain Univ. (Belgium), Collegium Angelicum (Rome); ord. priest Sept. 20, 1919; app. national director of the Pontifical Society for the Propagation of the Faith, 1950; ord. titular bishop of Caesariana and auxiliary bishop of New York, June 11, 1951; app. bishop of Rochester, installed Dec. 15, 1966; resigned Oct. 15, 1969; titular archbishop of Newport; named assistant to the pontifical throne, July, 1976.

Shehan, Lawrence Joseph: (See Cardinals, Biographies.)

Sheldon, Gilbert I.: b. Sept. 20, 1926, Cleveland, O.; educ. John Carroll Univ. and St. Mary Seminary (Cleveland, O.); ord. priest Feb. 28, 1953; ord. titular bishop of Taparura and auxiliary bishop of Cleveland, June 11, 1976.

Shubsda, Thaddeus A.: b. Apr. 2, 1925, Los Angeles, Calif.; educ. St. John's Seminary (Camarillo, Calif.); ord. priest Apr. 26, 1950; ord. titular bishop of Trau and auxiliary bishop of Los Angeles, Feb. 19, 1977.

Skylstad, William: b. Mar. 2, 1934, Omak, Wash.; educ. Pontifical College Josephinum (Worthington, Ohio), Washington State Univ. (Pullman, Wash.), Gonzaga Univ. (Spokane, Wash.); ord. priest May 21, 1960; ord. bishop of Yakima, May 12, 1977.

Smith, Philip F., O.M.I.: b. Oct. 16, 1924, Lowell, Mass.; ord. priest Oct. 29, 1950; ord. titular bishop of Lamfua and vicar apostolic of Jolo, Philippine Islands, Sept. 8, 1972; app. coadjutor bishop of Cotabato, Philippines, April, 1979.

Snyder, John J.: b. Oct. 25, 1925, New York, N.Y.; educ. Cathedral College (Brooklyn, N.Y.), Immaculate Conception Seminary (Huntington, N.Y.); ord. priest June 9, 1951; ord. titular bishop of Forlimpopli and auxiliary bishop of Brooklyn, Feb. 2, 1973; app. bishop of St. Augustine, October, 1979.

Soenneker, Henry J.: b. May 27, 1907, Melrose, Minn.; educ. Pontifical Josephinum College (Worthington, O.), Catholic Univ. (Washington, D.C.); ord. priest May 26, 1934; ord. bishop of Owensboro, Apr. 26, 1961.

Sowada, Alphonse A., O.S.C.: b. June 23, 1933, Avon, Minn.; educ. Holy Cross Scholasticate (Fort Wayne, Ind.), Catholic Univ. (Washington, D.C.), ord. priest May 31, 1958; missionary in Indonesia from 1958; ord. bishop of Agats, Indonesia, Nov. 23, 1969.

Speltz, George H.: b. May 29, 1912, Altura, Minn.; educ. St. Mary's College, St. Paul's Seminary (St. Paul, Minn.), Catholic Univ. (Washington, D.C.); ord. priest June 2, 1940; ord. titular bishop of Claneus and auxiliary bishop of Winona, Mar. 25, 1963; app. coadjutor bishop of St. Cloud, Apr. 4, 1966; bishop of St. Cloud, Jan. 31, 1968.

Stafford, James Francis: b. July 26, 1932, Baltimore, Md.; educ. St. Mary's Seminary (Baltimore, Md.), North American College and Gregorian Univ. (Rome); ord. priest Dec. 15, 1957; ord. titular bishop of Respecta and auxiliary bishop of Baltimore, Feb. 29, 1976.

Steiner, Kenneth Donald: b. Nov. 25, 1936, David City, Nebr.; educ. Mt. Angel Seminary (St. Benedict, Ore.), St. Thomas Seminary (Seattle, Wash.); ord. priest, May 19, 1962; ord. titular bishop of Avensa and auxiliary bishop of Portland, Ore., Mar. 2, 1978.

Stemper, Alfred M., M.S.C.: b. Jan. 2, 1913, Black Hammer, Minn.; ord. priest June 26, 1940; ord. titular bishop of Eleutheropolis and vicar apostolic of Kavieng, New Guinea, Oct. 28, 1957; first bishop of Kavieng, Nov. 15, 1966.

Straling, Phillip F.: b. Apr. 25, 1933, San Bernardino, Calif.; educ. Immaculate Heart Seminary, St. Francis Seminary, Univ. of San Diego and San Diego State University (San Diego, Calif.), North American College (Rome); ord. priest Mar. 19, 1959; ord. first bishop of San Bernardino, Nov. 6, 1978.

Strecker, Ignatius J.: b. Nov. 23, 1917, Spearville, Kans.; educ. St. Benedict's College (Atchison, Kans.), Kenrick Seminary (Webster Groves, Mo.), Catholic Univ. (Washington, D.C.); ord. priest Dec. 19, 1942; ord. bishop of Springfield-Cape Girardeau, Mo., June 20, 1962; archbishop of Kansas City, Kans., Oct. 28, 1969.

Sullivan, James S.: b. July 23, 1929, Kalamazoo, Mich.; educ. Sacred Heart Seminary (Detroit, Mich.), St. John Provincial Seminary (Plymouth, Mich.); ord. priest June 4, 1955; ord. titular bishop of Siccessi and auxiliary bishop of Lansing, Sept. 21, 1972.

Sullivan, John J.: b. July 5, 1920, Horton, Kans.; educ. Kenrick Seminary (St. Louis, Mo.); ord. priest Sept. 23, 1944; vice-president of Catholic Church Extension Society and national director of Extension Lay Volunteers, 1961-68; ord. bishop of Grand Island, Sept. 19, 1972; app. bishop of Kansas City-St. Joseph, June 27, 1977, installed Aug. 17, 1977.

Sullivan, Joseph V.: b. Aug. 15, 1919, Kansas City, Mo.; educ. Sulpician Seminary (Washington, D.C.), Catholic Univ. (Washington, D.C.); ord. priest June 1, 1946; ord. titular bishop of Tagamuta and auxiliary bishop of Kansas City-St. Joseph, Apr. 3, 1967; app. Bishop of Baton Rouge, Aug. 13, 1974.

Sullivan, Walter F.: b. June 10, 1928, Washington, D.C.; educ. St. Mary's Seminary (Baltimore, Md.), Catholic Univ. (Washington, D.C.); ord. priest May 9, 1953; ord. titular bishop of Selsea and auxiliary bishop of Richmond, Va., Dec. 1, 1970; app. bishop of Richmond, June 4, 1974.

Swanstrom, Edward E.: b. Mar. 20, 1903, New York, N.Y.; educ. Fordham Univ. (New York City), St. John's Seminary (Brooklyn, N.Y.), New York School of Social Work; ord. priest June 2, 1928; director of Catholic Relief Services 1947-76; ord. titular bishop of Arba and auxiliary bishop of New York, Oct. 28, 1960; retired Mar. 20, 1978.

Szoka, Edmund C.: b. Sept. 14, 1927, Grand Rapids, Mich.; educ. Sacred Heart Seminary (Detroit, Mich.), St. John's Provincial Seminary (Plymouth, Mich.), Lateran Univ. (Rome); ord. priest June 5, 1954; ord. first bishop of Gaylord, Mich., July 20, 1971.

T

Tanner, Paul F.: b. Jan. 15, 1905, Peoria, Ill.; educ. Marquette Univ. (Milwaukee, Wis.), Kenrick Seminary (Webster Groves, Mo.), St. Francis Seminary (Milwaukee, Wis.), Catholic Univ. (Washington, D.C.); ord. priest May 30, 1931; assistant director NCWC Youth Department 1940-45; assistant general secretary of NCWC 1945-58; general secretary of NCWC (now USCC) 1958-68; ord. titular bishop of Lamasba, Dec. 21, 1965; bishop of St. Augustine, Mar. 27, 1968; resigned 1979.

Tawil, Joseph: b. Dec. 25, 1913, Damascus, Syria; ord. priest July 20, 1936; ord. titular archbishop of Mira and patriarchal vicar for eparchy of Damascus of the Patriarchate of Antioch for the Melkites, Jan. 1, 1960; apostolic exarch for faithful of the Melkite rite in the U.S., Oct. 31, 1969; app. first eparch when exarchate was raised to eparchy, July 15, 1976; title of see changed to Newton, 1977.

Timlin, James C.: b. Aug. 5, 1927, Scranton, Pa.; educ. St. Charles College (Catonsville, Md.), St. Mary's Seminary (Baltimore, Md.), North American College (Rome); ord. priest July 16, 1951; ord. titular bishop of Gunugo and auxiliary bishop of Scranton, Sept. 21, 1976.

Topel, Bernard J.: b. May 31, 1903, Bozeman, Mont.; educ. Carroll College (Helena, Mont.), Grand Seminary (Montreal), Catholic Univ. (Washington, D.C.), Harvard Univ. (Cambridge, Mass.), Notre Dame Univ. (Notre Dame, Ind.); ord. priest June 7, 1927; ord. titular bishop of Binda and coadjutor bishop of Spokane, Sept. 21, 1955; bishop of Spokane, Sept. 25, 1955; retired Apr. 11, 1978.

Tracy, Robert E.: b. Sept. 14, 1909, New Orleans, La.; educ. St. Joseph's Preparatory Seminary (St. Benedict, La.), Notre Dame Seminary (New Orleans); ord. priest June 12, 1932; national chaplain of Newman Federation; 1954-56; ord. titular bishop of Sergentiza and auxiliary bishop of Lafayette, La., May 19, 1959; app. first bishop of Baton Rouge, Aug. 10, 1961; resigned Mar. 21, 1974.

Treinen, Sylvester: b. Nov. 19, 1917, Donnelly, Minn.; educ. Crosier Seminary (Onamia, Minn.), St. Paul Seminary (St. Paul, Minn.); ord. priest June 11, 1946; ord. bishop of Boise, July 25, 1962.

Tschoepe, Thomas: b. Dec. 17, 1915, Pilot Point, Tex.; educ. Pontifical College Josephinum (Worthington, O.); ord. priest May 30, 1943; ord. bishop of San Angelo, Tex., Mar. 9, 1966; app. bishop of Dallas, Tex., Aug. 27, 1969.

U-V

Unterkoefler, Ernest L.: b. Aug. 17, 1917, Philadelphia, Pa.; educ. Catholic Univ. (Washington, D.C.); ord. priest May 18, 1944; ord. titular bishop of Latopolis and auxiliary bishop of Richmond, Va., Feb. 22, 1962; app. bishop of Charleston, Dec. 12, 1964, installed Feb. 22, 1965.

Vath, Joseph G.: b. Mar. 12, 1918, New Orleans, La.; educ. Notre Dame Seminary (New Orleans, La.), Catholic Univ. (Washington, D.C.); ord. priest June 7, 1941; ord. titular bishop of Novaliciana and auxiliary bishop of Mobile-Birmingham, May 26, 1966; app. first bishop of Birmingham, Oct. 8, 1969.

Vaughan, Austin B.: b. Sept. 27, 1927, New York, N.Y.; educ. North American College and Gregorian Univ. (Rome), ord. priest Dec. 8, 1951; pres. Catholic Theological Society of America, 1967; rector of St. Joseph's Seminary (Dunwoodie, N.Y.), 1973; ord. titular bishop of Cluain Iraird and auxiliary bishop of New York, June 29, 1977.

Veigle, Adrian J.M., T.O.R.: b. Sept. 15, 1912, Lilly, Pa.; educ. St. Francis College (Loretto, Pa.), Pennsylvania State College; ord. priest May 22, 1937; ord. titular bishop of Gigthi and prelate of Borba, Brazil, June 9, 1966.

Vogel, Cyril J.: b. Jan. 15, 1905, Pittsburgh, Pa.; educ. Duquesne Univ. (Pittsburgh, Pa.), St. Vincent's Seminary (Latrobe, Pa.); ord. priest June 7, 1931; ord. bishop of Salina, June 17, 1965. Died Oct. 4, 1979.

Vonesh, Raymond J.: b. Jan. 25, 1916, Chicago, Ill.; educ. St. Mary of the Lake Seminary (Mundelein, Ill.), Gregorian Univ. (Rome); ord. priest May 3, 1941; ord. titular bishop of Vanariona and auxiliary bishop of Joliet, Ill., Apr. 3, 1968.

W

Waldschmidt, Paul E., C.S.C.: b. Jan. 7, 1920, Evansville, Ind.; educ. Notre Dame Univ. (Notre Dame, Ind.), Holy Cross College (Washington, D.C.), Laval Univ. (Quebec), Angelicum (Rome), Louvain (Belgium), Sorbonne (Paris), ord. priest June 24, 1946; president University of Portland, 1962-   ; ord. titular bishop of Citium and auxiliary bishop of Portland, Ore., Mar. 2, 1978.

Walsh, James Edward, M.M.: b. Apr. 30, 1891, Cumberland, Md.; educ. Mt. St. Mary's College (Emmitsburg, Md.), Maryknoll Foreign Mission Seminary (Maryknoll, N.Y.); entered Catholic Foreign Mission Society (Maryknoll, N.Y.), 1912; ord. priest Dec. 7, 1915; ord. titular bishop of Sata and vicar apostolic of Kongmoon, China, May 22, 1927; superior general of Maryknoll, July 21, 1936, until Aug. 7, 1946; gen. general secretary, Catholic Central Bureau, Shanghai, China, Aug. 24, 1948; placed under house arrest in October, 1958, detained in Shanghai hospital; sentenced to 20 years' imprisonment for "espionage," Mar., 1960; released 1970.

Walsh, Nicholas E.: b. Oct. 20, 1916, Burnsville, Minn.; educ. St. Paul Seminary (St. Paul, Minn.), Catholic Univ. (Washington, D.C.), Pontifical Palafoxianum Seminary (Puebla, Mexico), Register College of Journalism (Denver, Colo.); ord. priest June 6, 1942; first editor of *Idaho Register;* diocesan vicar for Mexican Americans; ord. bishop of Yakima, Oct. 28, 1974; app. titular bishop of Bolsena and auxiliary bishop of Seattle, Aug. 10, 1976.

Ward, John J.: b. Sept. 28, 1920, Los Angeles, Calif.; educ. St. John's Seminary (Camarillo, Calif.), Catholic Univ. (Washington, D.C.); ord. priest May 4, 1946; ord. titular bishop of Bria and auxiliary of Los Angeles, Dec. 12, 1963.

Watson, Alfred M.: b. July 11, 1907, Erie, Pa.; educ. St. Mary's Seminary (Baltimore, Md.), Catholic Univ. (Washington, D.C.); ord. priest May 10, 1934; ord. titular bishop of Nationa and auxiliary bishop of Erie, June 29, 1965; app. bishop of Erie, 1969, installed May 13, 1969.

Watters, Loras J.: b. Oct. 14, 1915, Dubuque, Ia.; educ. Loras College (Dubuque, Ia.), Gregorian Univ. (Rome), Catholic Univ. (Washington, D.C.); ord. priest June 7, 1941; ord. titular bishop of Fidoloma and auxiliary bishop of Dubuque, Aug. 26, 1965; bishop of Winona, installed Mar. 13, 1969.

Weakland, Rembert G., O.S.B.: b. Apr. 2, 1927, Patton, Pa.; joined Benedictines, 1945; ord. priest June 24, 1951; abbot-primate of Benedictine Confederation, 1967-77; ord. archbishop of Milwaukee, Nov. 8, 1977.

Weldon, Christopher J.: b. Sept. 6, 1905, New York, N.Y.; educ. Montreal College (Canada), St. Joseph's Seminary (Dunwoodie, N.Y.), Catholic Univ. (Washington, D.C.); ord. priest Sept. 21, 1939; ord. bishop of Springfield, Mass., Mar. 24, 1950; retired Oct. 15, 1977.

Welsh, Lawrence H.: b. Feb. 1, 1935, Winton, Wyo.; educ. Univ. of Wyoming (Laramie, Wyo.), St. John's Seminary (Collegeville, Minn.), Catholic Univ. (Washington, D.C.); ord. priest May 26, 1962; ord. bishop of Spokane, Dec. 14, 1978.

Welsh, Thomas J.: b. Dec. 20, 1921, Weatherly, Pa.; educ. St. Charles Borromeo Seminary (Philadelphia, Pa.), Catholic Univ. (Washington, D.C.); ord. priest May 30, 1946; ord. titular bishop of Scattery Island and auxiliary bishop of Philadelphia, Apr. 2, 1970; app. first bishop of Arlington, Va., June 4, 1974, installed Aug. 13, 1974.

Whealon, John F.: b. Jan. 15, 1921, Barberton, O.; educ. St. Charles College (Catonsville, Md.), St. Mary's Seminary (Cleveland, O.); ord. priest May 26, 1945; ord. titular bishop of Andrapa and auxiliary bishop of Cleveland, July 6, 1961; app. bishop of Erie, Dec. 9, 1966, installed Mar. 7, 1967; archbishop of Hartford, installed Mar. 19, 1969.

Whelan, Robert L., S.J.: b. Apr. 16, 1912, Wallace, Ida.; educ. St. Michael's College (Spokane, Wash.), Alma College (Alma, Calif.); ord. priest June 17, 1944; ord. titular bishop of Sicilibba and coadjutor bishop of Fairbanks, Alaska, with right of succession, Feb. 22, 1968; bishop of Fairbanks, Nov. 30, 1968.

Wildermuth, Augustine F., S.J.: b. Feb. 20, 1904, St. Louis, Mo.; educ. St. Stanislaus Seminary (Florissant, Mo.), St. Michael's Scholasticate (Spokane, Wash.), Sacred Heart College (Shembaganur, S. India), St. Mary's College (Kurseong, India), Gregorian Univ. (Rome); entered Society of Jesus, 1922; ord. priest July 25, 1935; ord. bishop of Patna, India, Oct. 28, 1947.

Wirz, George O.: b. Jan. 17, 1929, Monroe, Wis.; educ. St. Francis Seminary and Marquette Univ. (Milwaukee, Wis.); Cath. Univ. (Washington, D.C.); ord. priest May 31, 1952; ord. titular bishop of Municipa and auxiliary bishop of Madison, Mar. 9, 1978.

Wurm, John N.: b. Dec. 6, 1927, Overland, Mo.; educ. Kenrick Seminary and St. Louis Univ. (St. Louis, Mo.); ord. priest Apr. 3, 1954; ord. titular bishop of Plestia and auxiliary bishop of St. Louis, Aug. 17, 1976.

Wycislo, Aloysius John: b. June 17, 1908, Chicago, Ill.; educ. St. Mary's Seminary (Mundelein, Ill.), Catholic Univ. (Washington, D.C.); ord. priest Apr. 4, 1934; ord. titular bishop of Stadia and auxiliary bishop of Chicago, Dec. 21, 1960; app. bishop of Green Bay, installed Apr. 16, 1968.

Z

Zayek, Francis: b. Oct. 18, 1920, Manzanillo, Cuba; ord. priest Mar. 17, 1946; ord. titular bishop of Callinicum and auxiliary bishop for Maronites in Brazil, Aug. 5, 1962; named apostolic exarch for Maronites in U.S., with headquarters in Detroit; installed June 11, 1966; first eparch of St. Maron of Detroit, Mar. 25, 1972; see transferred to Brooklyn, June 27, 1977.

Zuroweste, Albert R.: b. Apr. 26, 1901, East St. Louis, Ill.; educ. St. Francis College (Quincy, Ill.), Kenrick Seminary (Webster

Groves, Mo.), Catholic Univ. (Washington, D.C.); ord. priest June 8, 1924; ord. bishop of Belleville, Jan. 29, 1948; retired Oct. 29, 1976.

RETIRED U.S. PRELATES

Information, as of Oct. 20, 1979, includes name of the prelate and see held at the time of retirement; archbishops are indicated by an asterisk. Most of the prelates listed below resigned their sees because of age. See Index: Biographies of American Bishops.

The preferred form of address of retired prelates is *Former Archbishop* or *Bishop of* (last see held).

Richard H. Ackerman, C.S.Sp. (Covington), George W. Ahr (Trenton), Peter W. Bartholome (St. Cloud), Alden J. Bell (Sacramento), Romeo Blanchette (Joliet), John Bokenfohr, O.M.I. (Kimberley, S. Africa), James C. Burke, O.P. (Chimbote, Peru, prelate), Charles A. Buswell (Pueblo), L. Abel Caillouet (New Orleans, auxiliary), Cardinal John Carberry* (St. Louis), Mark K. Carroll (Wichita), James L. Connolly (Fall River), Thomas Connolly* (Seattle), William E. Cousins* (Milwaukee), Augustine Danglmayr (Ft. Worth, auxiliary), Nicholas D'Antonio, O.F.M. (Olancha, Honduras).

Edward V. Dargin (New York, auxiliary), James P. Davis* (Santa Fê), Stephen J. Donahue (New York, auxiliary), Clarence J. Duhart, C.SS.R. (Udon Thani, Thailand), Joseph A. Durick (Nashville), Albert L. Fletcher (Little Rock), John B. Franz (Peoria), Philip J. Furlong (Military Vicariate, delegate),

James J. Gerrard (Fall River, auxiliary), Francis D. Gleeson, S.J. (Fairbanks), Laurence A. Glenn (Crookston), Ignatius T. Glennie, S.J. (Trincomalee-Batticaloa, Sri Lanka), Thomas K. Gorman (Dallas-Ft. Worth), Lawrence L. Graner* (Dacca, Bangladesh), Lawrence Graziano, O.F.M. (San Miguel, El Salvador), Charles P. Greco (Alexandria), Joseph Green (Reno), John B. Grellinger, (Green Bay, auxiliary), Merlin J. Guilfoyle (Stockton).

James T. Hayes, S.J.* (Cagayan, Philippines), Charles H. Helmsing (Kansas City-St. Joseph), Edward G. Hettinger (Columbus, auxiliary), Vincent D. Hines (Norwich), Lambert A. Hoch (Sioux Falls), Joseph L. Hogan (Rochester), Edward D. Howard* (Portland, Ore.), Clarence G. Issenmann (Cleveland), Robert F. Joyce (Burlington), Walter P. Kellenberg (Rockville Centre), George L. Leech (Harrisburg), Francis P. Leipzig (Baker), Leo Lemay, S.M. (Bougainville, Solomon Is.), Stephen J. Leven (San Angelo).

William McDonald (San Francisco, auxiliary), John J. McEleney, S.J.* (Kingston, Jamaica), Joseph T. McGucken* (San Francisco), Edward A. McGurkin, M.M. (Shinyanga, Tanzania), Edward J. Maginn (Albany, auxiliary), Alfred Mendez, C.S.C. (Arecibo, P.R.), Sidney M. Metzger (El Paso).

Louis La Ravoire Morrow, S.D.B. (Krishnagar, India), Joseph M. Mueller (Sioux City), Knute Ansgar Nelson, O.S.B. (Stockholm, Sweden), Hubert M. Newell (Cheyenne), Wendelin J. Nold (Galveston-Houston), Adolph A. Noser, S.V.D.* (Madang, Papua New Guinea), Cardinal Patrick O'Boyle* (Washington, D.C.).

Martin J. O'Connor* (Prefect Emeritus, Pontifical Commission for Social Communications), William A. O'Connor (Springfield, Ill.), James V. Pardy, M.M. (Cheong Ju, Korea), John L. Paschang (Grand Island), George H. Pearce, S.M.* (Suva, Fiji Islands), Joseph M. Pernicone (New York, auxiliary), Ernest J. Primeau (Manchester), Leo A. Pursley (Fort Wayne-South Bend), Joseph M. Raya* (Acre).

Louis J. Reicher (Austin), Thomas F. Reilly, C.SS.R. (San Juan de la Maguana, Dominican Republic), John J. Rudin, M.M. (Musoma, Tanzania), John J. Russell (Richmond), Maurice Schexnayder (Lafayette, La.), Alphonse Schladweiler (New Ulm), Paul C. Schulte* (Indianapolis; titular archbishop of Elicora), Eldon B. Schuster (Great Falls).

Fulton J. Sheen* (Rochester; titular archbishop, Newport). Cardinal Lawrence J. Shehan* (Baltimore), Edward E. Swanstrom (New York, auxiliary), Paul F. Tanner (St. Augustine), Bernard J. Topel (Spokane), Robert E. Tracy (Baton Rouge), James E. Walsh, M.M. (Kongmoon, China, vicar apostolic), Christopher J. Weldon (Springfield, Mass.), Albert R. Zuroweste (Belleville).

BISHOP-BROTHERS

(See separate entries for biographical data. The asterisk indicates brothers who were bishops at the same time.)

There have been nine pairs of brother-bishops in the history of the U.S. hierarchy.

Living: Francis T. Hurley,* archbishop of Anchorage and Mark J. Hurley* of Santa Rosa.

Deceased: Francis Blanchet* of Oregon City (Portland) and Augustin Blanchet* of Walla Walla; John S. Foley of Detroit and Thomas P. Foley of Chicago; Francis P. Kenrick,* apostolic administrator of Philadelphia, bishop of Philadelphia and Baltimore, and Peter R. Kenrick* of St. Louis; Matthias C. Lenihan of Great Falls and Thomas M. Lenihan of Cheyenne; James O'Connor, vicar apostolic of Nebraska and bishop of Omaha, and Michael O'Connor of Pittsburgh and Erie; Jeremiah F. and John W. Shanahan, both of Harrisburg; Sylvester J. Espelage, O.F.M.,* of Wuchang, China, who died 10 days after the ordination of his brother, Bernard T. Espelage,* O.F.M., of Gallup; Coleman F. Carroll* of Miami and Howard Carroll* of Altoona-Johnstown.

U.S. BISHOPS OVERSEAS

Archbishop Raymond P. Etteldorf, pro-nuncio to Ethiopia; Bishop Anthony L. Deksnys, pastoral work among Lithuanians in Western Europe; Bishop Paul C. Marcinkus, president of Institute for Works of Religion (Vatican Bank); Bishop Ernest Primeau, former bishop of Manchester, N.H., director of Villa Stritch, Rome.

(See also Missionary Bishops.)

AMERICAN BISHOPS OF THE PAST

Information includes dates, place of birth if outside the US, date of ordination to the priesthood, sees held, and, in the case of non-residential bishops, the name of the titular see in parentheses.

A

Adrian, William L. (1883-1972): ord. Apr. 15, 1911; bp. Nashville, 1936-69 (ret.).

Albers, Joseph (1891-1965): ord. June 17, 1916; aux. bp. Cincinnati (Lunda), 1929-37; first bp. Lansing, 1937-65.

Alemany, Joseph Sadoc, O.P. (1814-1888): b. Spain; ord. Mar. 11, 1837; bp. Monterey (now Los Angeles), 1850-53; first abp. San Francisco, 1853-84 (res.).

Alencastre, Stephen P., SS.CC. (1876-1940): b. Madeira; ord. Apr. 5, 1902; coad. v.a. Sandwich Is. (Arabissus), 1924-36; v.a. Sandwich Is. (now Honolulu), 1936-40.

Alerding, Herman J. (1845-1924): b. Germany; ord. Sept. 22, 1869; bp. Fort Wayne, 1900-24.

Allen, Edward P. (1853-1926): ord. Dec. 17, 1881; bp. Mobile, 1897-1926.

Alter, Karl J. (1885-1977): ord. June 4, 1910; bp. Toledo, 1931-50; abp. Cincinnati, 1950-69 (ret.).

Althoff, Henry (1873-1947): ord. July 26, 1902; bp. Belleville, 1914-47.

Amat, Thaddeus, C.M. (1811-1878): b. Spain; ord. Dec. 23, 1837; bp. Monterey (now Los Angeles), 1854-78.

Anderson, Joseph (1865-1927): ord. May 20, 1892; aux. bp. Boston (Oyrina), 1909-27.

Anglim, Robert, C.SS.R. (1922-1973): ord. Jan. 6, 1948; prelate Coari, Brazil (Gaguari), 1966-73.

Annabring, Joseph (1900-1959): b. Hungary; ord. May 3, 1927; bp. Superior, 1954-59.

Appelhans, Stephen A., S.V.D. (1905-1951): ord. May 5, 1932; v.a. East New Guinea (Catula), 1948-51.

Armstrong, Robert J. (1884-1957): ord. Dec. 10, 1910; bp. Sacramento, 1929-57.

Arnold, William R. (1881-1965): ord. June 13, 1908; delegate of US military vicar (Phocaea), 1945-65.

Atkielski, Roman R. (1898-1969): ord. May 30, 1931; aux. bp. Milwaukee (Stobi), 1947-69.

B

Babcock, Allen J. (1898-1969): ord. Mar. 7, 1925; aux. bp. Detroit (Irenopolis), 1947-54; bp. Grand Rapids, 1954-69.

Bacon, David W. (1815-1874): ord. Dec. 13, 1838; first bp. Portland, Me., 1855-74.

Baldwin, Vincent J. (1907-1979): ord. July 26, 1931; aux. bp. Rockville Centre (Bencenna), 1962-79.

Baltes, Peter J. (1827-1886): b. Germany; ord. May 31, 1852; bp. Alton (now Springfield), Ill., 1870-86.

Baraga, Frederic: See Index.

Barron, Edward (1801-1854): b. Ireland; ord. 1829; v.a. The Two Guineas (Constantina), 1842-44 (res.), missionary in US.

Barry, John (1799-1859): b. Ireland; ord. Sept. 24, 1825; bp. Savannah, 1857-59.

Barry, Patrick J. (1868-1940): b. Ireland; ord. June 9, 1895; bp. St. Augustine, 1922-40.

Baumgartner, Apollinaris, O.F.M. Cap. (1899-1970): ord. May 30, 1926; v.a. Guam (Joppa), 1945-65; first bp. Agana, Guam, 1965-70.

Bayley, James Roosevelt: See Index.

Bazin, John S. (1796-1848): b. France; ord. July 22, 1822; bp. Vincennes (now Indianapolis), 1847-48.

Beaven, Thomas D. (1851-1920): ord. Dec. 18, 1875; bp. Springfield, Mass., 1892-1920.

Becker, Thomas A. (1832-1899): ord. June 18, 1859; first bp. Wilmington, 1868-86; bp. Savannah, 1886-99.

Beckman, Francis J. (1875-1948): ord. June 20, 1902; bp. Lincoln, 1924-30; abp. Dubuque, 1930-46 (res.).

Begin, Floyd L. (1902-1977): ord. July 31, 1927; aux. bp. Cleveland (Sala), 1947-62; first bp. Oakland, 1962-77.

Benjamin, Cletus J. (1909-1961): ord. Dec. 8, 1935; aux. bp. Philadelphia (Binda), 1960-61.

Bennett, John G. (1891-1957): ord. June 27, 1914; first bp. Lafayette, Ind., 1944-57.

Bergan, Gerald T. (1892-1972): ord. Oct. 28, 1915; bp. Des Moines, 1934-48; abp. Omaha, 1948-69 (ret.).

Bidawid, Thomas M. (1910-1971): b. Iraq; ord. May 15, 1935; US citizen; first abp. Ahwaz, Iran (Chaldean Rite), 1968-70; Chaldean patriarchal vicar for United Arab Republic, 1970-71.

Blanc, Anthony (1792-1860): b. France; ord. July 22, 1816; bp. New Orleans, 1835-50; first abp. New Orleans, 1850-60.

Blanchet (brothers): Augustin M. (1797-1887): b. Canada; ord. June 3, 1821; bp. Walla Walla, 1846-50; first bp. Nesqually (now Seattle), 1850-79 (res.). **Francis N.** (1795-1883): b. Canada; ord. July 19, 1819; v.a. Oregon Territory (Philadelphia, Adrasus), 1843-46; first abp. Oregon City (now Portland), 1846-80 (res.).

Blenk, James H., S.M. (1856-1917): b. Germany; ord. Aug. 16, 1885; bp. San Juan, 1899-1906; abp. New Orleans, 1906-17.

Boardman, John J. (1894-1978): ord. May 21, 1921; aux. bp. Brooklyn (Gunela), 1952-77 (ret.).

Boeynaems, Libert H., SS.CC. (1857-1926): b. Belgium; ord. Sept. 11, 1881; v.a. Sandwich Is. (now Honolulu) (Zeugma), 1903-26.

Bohachevsky, Constantine (1884-1961): b. Austrian Galicia; ord. Jan. 31, 1909; ap. ex. Ukrainian Byzantine Catholics in US (Amisus), 1924-58; first metropolitan of Byzantine Rite archeparchy of Philadelphia, 1958-61.

Boileau, George, S.J. (1912-1965): ord. June 13, 1948; coad. bp. Fairbanks (Ausuccura), 1964-65.

Boland, Thomas A. (1896-1979): ord. Dec. 23, 1922; aux. bp. Newark (Irina), 1940-47; bp. Paterson, 1947-52; abp. Newark, 1953-74 (ret.).

Bona, Stanislaus (1888-1967): ord. Nov. 1, 1912; bp. Grand Island, 1932-44; coad. bp. Green Bay (Mela), 1944-45; bp. Green Bay, 1945-67.

Bonacum, Thomas (1847-1911): b. Ireland; ord. June 18, 1870; first bp. Lincoln, 1887-1911.

Borgess, Caspar H. (1826-1890): b. Germany; ord. Dec. 8, 1848; coad. bp. and ap. admin. Detroit (Calydon), 1870-71; bp. Detroit, 1871-87 (res.).

Bourgade, Peter (1845-1908): b. France; ord. Nov. 30, 1869; v.a. Arizona (Thaumacus), 1885-97; first bp. Tucson, 1897-99; abp. Santa Fe, 1899-1908.

Boylan, John J. (1889-1953): ord. July 28, 1915; bp. Rockford, 1943-53.

Boyle, Hugh C. (1873-1950): ord. July 2, 1898; bp. Pittsburgh, 1921-50.

Bradley, Denis (1846-1903): b. Ireland; ord. June 3, 1871; first bp. Manchester, 1884-1903.

Brady, John (1842-1910): b. Ireland; ord. Dec. 4, 1864; aux. bp. Boston (Alabanda), 1891-1910.

Brady, Matthew F. (1893-1959): ord. June 10, 1916; bp. Burlington, 1938-44; bp. Manchester, 1944-59.

Brady, William O. (1899-1961): ord. Dec. 21, 1923; bp. Sioux Falls, 1939-56; coad. abp. St. Paul (Selymbria), June-Oct. 1956; abp. St. Paul, 1956-61.

Brennan, Andrew J. (1877-1956): ord. Dec. 17, 1904; aux. bp. Scranton (Thapsus), 1923-26; bp. Richmond, 1926-45 (res.).

Brennan, Thomas F. (1853-1916): b. Ireland; ord. July 14, 1880; first bp. Dallas, 1891-93; aux. bp. St. John's, Newfoundland (Usula), 1893-1905 (res.).

Broderick, Bonaventure (1868-1943): ord. July 26, 1896; aux. bp. Havana, Cuba (Juliopolis), 1903-05 (res.).

Brondel, John B. (1842-1903): b. Belgium; ord. Dec. 17, 1864; bp. Vancouver Is., 1879-84; first bp. Helena, 1884-1903.

Brossart, Ferdinand (1849-1930): b. Germany; ord. Sept. 1, 1892; bp. Covington, 1916-23 (res.).

Brute, Simon G. (1779-1839): b. France; ord. June 11, 1808; first bp. Vincennes (now Indianapolis), 1834-39.

Buddy, Charles F. (1887-1966): ord. Sept. 19, 1914; first bp. San Diego, 1936-66.

Burke, Joseph A. (1886-1962): ord. Aug. 3, 1912; aux. bp. Buffalo (Vita), 1943-52; bp. Buffalo, 1952-62.

Burke, Maurice F. (1845-1923): b. Ireland; ord. May 22, 1875; first bp. Cheyenne, 1887-93; bp. St. Joseph, 1893-1923.

Burke, Thomas M. (1840-1915): b. Ireland; ord. June 30, 1864; bp. Albany, 1894-1915.

Busch, Joseph F. (1866-1953): ord. July 28, 1889; bp. Lead (now Rapid City), 1910-15; bp. St. Cloud, 1915-53.

Byrne, Andrew (1802-1862): b. Ireland; ord. Nov. 11, 1827; first bp. Little Rock, 1844-62.

Byrne, Christopher E. (1867-1950): ord. Sept. 23, 1891; bp. Galveston, 1918-50.

Byrne, Edwin V. (1891-1963): ord. May 22, 1915; first bp. Ponce, 1925-29; abp. San Juan, 1929-43; abp. Santa Fe, 1943-63.

Byrne, Leo C. (1908-1974): ord. June 10, 1933; aux. bp., St. Louis (Sabadia), 1954-61; coad. bp. Wichita, 1961-67; coad. abp. (Plestra) St. Paul and Minneapolis, 1967-74.

Byrne, Patrick J., M.M. (1888-1950): ord. June 23, 1915; apostolic delegate to Korea (Gazera), 1949-50.

Byrne, Thomas S. (1841-1923): ord. May 22, 1869; bp. Nashville, 1894-1923.

C

Canevin, J. F. Regis (1853-1927): ord. June 4, 1879; coad. bp. Pittsburgh (Sabrata), 1903-04; bp. Pittsburgh, 1904-21 (res.).

Cantwell, John J. (1874-1947): b. Ireland; ord. June 18, 1899; bp. Monterey-Los Angeles, 1917-22; bp. Los Angeles-San Diego, 1922-36; first abp. Los Angeles, 1936-47.

Carrell, George A., S.J. (1803-1868): ord. Dec. 20, 1827; first bp. Covington, 1853-68.

Carroll (brothers): **Coleman F.** (1905-1977): ord. June 15, 1930; aux. bp. Pittsburgh (Pitanae), 1953-58; first bp. Miami, 1958-68 and first abp., 1968-77. **Howard J.** (1902-1960): ord. Apr. 2, 1927; bp. Altoona-Johnstown, 1958-60.

Carroll, James J. (1862-1913): ord. June 15, 1889; bp. Nueva Segovia, P. I., 1908-12 (res.).

Carroll, John: See Index.

Carroll, John P. (1864-1925): ord. July 7, 1886; bp. Helena, 1904-25.

Cartwright, Hubert J. (1900-1958): ord. June 11, 1927; coad. bp. Wilmington (Neve), 1956-58.

Caruana, George (1882-1951): b. Malta; ord. Oct. 28, 1905; bp. Puerto Rico (name changed to San Juan, 1924), 1921-25; ap. del.

Mexico (Sebastea in Armenia), 1925-27; internuncio to Haiti, 1927-35; ap. nuncio to Cuba, 1935-47 (ret.).

Casey, Lawrence B. (1905-1977): ord. June 7, 1930; aux. bp. Rochester (Cea), 1953-66; bp. Paterson, 1966-77.

Cassidy, James E. (1869-1951): ord. Sept. 8, 1898; aux. bp. Fall River (Ibora), 1930-34; bp. Fall River, 1934-51.

Chabrat, Guy Ignatius, S.S. (1787-1868): b. France; ord. Dec. 21, 1811; coad. bp. Bardstown (Bolina), 1834-47 (res.).

Chanche, John J., S.S. (1795-1852): ord. June 5, 1819; bp. Natchez (now Jackson), 1841-52.

Chapelle, Placide L. (1842-1905): b. France; ord. June 28, 1865; coad. abp. Santa Fe (Arabissus), 1891-94; abp. Santa Fe, 1894-97; abp. New Orleans, 1897-1905.

Chartrand, Joseph (1870-1933): ord. Sept. 24, 1892; coad. bp. Indianapolis (Flavias), 1910-18; bp. Indianapolis, 1918-33.

Chatard, Francis S. (1834-1918): ord. June 14, 1862; bp. Vincennes (now Indianapolis—title changed in 1898), 1878-1918.

Cheverus, John Lefebvre de (1768-1836): b. France; ord. Dec. 18, 1790; bp. Boston, 1810-23 (returned to France, made cardinal 1836).

Christie, Alexander (1848-1925): ord. Dec. 22, 1877; bp. Vancouver Is., 1898-99; abp. Oregon City (now Portland), 1899-1925.

Clancy, William (1802-1847): b. Ireland; ord. May 24, 1823; coad. bp. Charleston (Oreus), 1834-37; v.a. British Guiana, 1837-43.

Collins, John J., S.J. (1856-1934): ord. Aug. 29, 1891; v.a. Jamaica (Antiphellus), 1907-18 (res).

Collins, Thomas P., M.M. (1915-1973): ord. June 21, 1942; v.a. Pando, Bolivia (Sufetula), 1961-68 (res.).

Colton, Charles H. (1848-1915): ord. June 10, 1876; bp. Buffalo, 1903-15.

Conaty, Thomas J. (1847-1915): b. Ireland; ord. Dec. 21, 1872; rector of Catholic University, 1896-1903; tit. bp. Samos, 1901-03; bp. Monterey-Los Angeles (now Los Angeles), 1903-15.

Concanen, Richard L., O.P. (1747-1810): b. Ireland; ord. Dec. 22, 1770; first bp. New York. 1808-10 (detained in Italy, never reached his see).

Condon, William J. (1895-1967): ord. Oct. 14, 1917; bp. Great Falls, 1939-67.

Connolly, John, O.P. (1750-1825): b. Ireland; ord. Sept. 24, 1774; bp. New York, 1814-25.

Conroy, John J. (1819-1895): b. Ireland; ord. May 21, 1842; bp. Albany, 1865-77 (res.).

Conroy, Joseph H. (1858-1939): ord. June 11, 1881; aux. bp. Ogdensburg (Arindela), 1912-21; bp. Ogdensburg, 1921-39.

Conwell, Henry (1748-1842): b. Ireland; ord. 1776; bp. Philadelphia, 1820-42.

Corbett, Timothy (1858-1939): ord. June 12, 1886; first bp. Crookston, 1910-38 (res.).

Corrigan, Joseph M. (1879-1942): ord. June 6, 1903; rector of Catholic University, 1936-42; tit. bp. Bilta, 1940-42.

Corrigan, Michael A. (1839-1902): ord. Sept. 19, 1863; bp. Newark, 1873-80; coad. abp. New York (Petra), 1880-85; abp. New York, 1885-1902.

Corrigan, Owen (1849-1929): ord. June 7, 1873; aux. bp. Baltimore (Macri), 1908-29.

Cosgrove, Henry (1834-1906): ord. Aug. 27, 1857; bp. Davenport, 1884-1906.

Costello, Joseph A. (1915-1978): ord. June 7, 1941; aux. bp. Newark (Choma), 1963-78.

Cote, Philip, S.J. (1896-1970): ord. Aug. 14, 1927; v. a. Suchow, China (Polystylus), 1935-46; first bp. Suchow, 1946-70 (imprisoned by Chinese Communists, 1951; expelled from China, 1953; ap. admin. Islands of Quemoy and Matsu, 1969-70).

Cotter, Joseph B. (1844-1909): b. England; ord. May 3, 1871; first bp. Winona, 1889-1909.

Cotton, Francis R. (1895-1960): ord. June 17, 1920; first bp. Owensboro, 1938-60.

Cowley, Leonard P. (1913-1973): ord. June 4, 1938; aux. bp. St. Paul and Minneapolis (Pertusa), 1958-73.

Crane, Michael J. (1863-1928): ord. June 15, 1889; aux. bp. Philadelphia (Curium), 1921-28.

Cretin, Joseph (1799-1857): b. France; ord. Dec. 20, 1823; bp. St. Paul, 1851-57.

Crimont, Joseph R., S.J. (1858-1945): b. France; ord. Aug. 26, 1888; v. a. Alaska (Ammaedara), 1917-45.

Crowley, Timothy J., C.S.C. (1880-1945): b. Ireland; ord. Aug. 2, 1906; coad. bp. Dacca (Epiphania), 1927-29; bp. Dacca, 1929-45.

Cunningham, David F. (1900-1979): ord. June 12, 1926; aux. bp., 1950-67, and coad. bp., 1967-79, Syracuse (Lampsacus); bp. Syracuse, 1970-76 (ret.).

Cunningham, John F. (1842-1919): b. Ireland; ord. Aug. 8, 1865; bp. Concordia, 1898-1919.

Curley, Daniel J. (1869-1932): ord. May 19, 1894; bp. Syracuse, 1923-32.

Curley, Michael J. (1879-1947): b. Ireland; ord. Mar. 19, 1904; bp. St. Augustine, 1914-21; abp. Baltimore, 1921-39; title changed to abp. Baltimore and Washington, 1939-47.

Curtis, Alfred A. (1831-1908): convert, 1872; ord. Dec. 19, 1874; bp. Wilmington, 1886-96 (res.).

Cusack, Thomas F. (1862-1918): ord. May 30, 1885; aux. bp. New York (Temiscyra), 1904-15; bp. Albany, 1915-18.

Cushing, Richard J.: See Index.

D

Daeger, Albert T., O.F.M. (1872-1932): ord. July 25, 1896; abp. Santa Fe, 1919-32.

Daly, Edward C., O.P. (1894-1964): ord. June 12, 1921; bp. Des Moines, 1948-64.

Damiano, Celestine (1911-1967): ord. Dec. 21, 1935; apostolic delegate to South Africa (Nicopolis in Epiro), 1952-60; bp. Camden, 1960-67.

Danehy, Thomas J., M.M. (1914-1959): ord. Sept. 17, 1939; ap. admin. v. a. Pando, Bolivia (Bita), 1953-59.

David, John B., S.S. (1761-1841): b. France; ord. Sept. 24, 1785; coad. bp. Bardstown (Mauricastrum), 1819-32; bp. Bardstown (now Louisville), 1832-33 (res.).

Davis, James (1852-1926): b. Ireland; ord. June 21, 1878; coad. bp. Davenport (Milopotamus), 1904-06; bp. Davenport, 1906-26.

De Cheverus, John L.: See Cheverus, John.

De Goesbriand, Louis (1816-1899): b. France; ord. July 13, 1840; first bp. Burlington, 1853-99.

De la Hailandiere, Celestine (1798-1882): b. France; ord. May 28, 1825; bp. Vincennes (now Indianapolis), 1839-47 (res.).

Delany, John B. (1864-1906): ord. May 23, 1891; bp. Manchester, 1904-06.

Demers, Modeste, (1809-1871): b. Canada; ord. Feb. 7, 1836; bp. Vancouver Is., 1846-71.

Dempsey, Michael R. (1918-1974): ord. May 1, 1943; aux. bp. Chicago (Truentum), 1968-74,

De Neckere, Leo, C.M. (1799-1833): b. Belgium; ord. Oct. 13, 1822; bp. New Orleans, 1829-33.

De Saint Palais, Maurice (1811-1877): b. France; ord. May 28, 1836; bp. Vincennes (now Indianapolis), 1849-77.

Desmond, Daniel F. (1884-1945): ord. June 9, 1911; bp. Alexandria, 1933-45.

Dinand, Joseph N., S.J. (1869-1943): ord. June 25, 1903; v. a. Jamaica (Selinus), 1927-29 (res.).

Dobson, Robert (1867-1942): ord. May 23, 1891; aux. bp. Liverpool, Eng. (Cynopolis), 1922-42.

Domenec, Michael, C.M. (1816-1878): b. Spain; ord. June 30, 1839; bp. Pittsburgh, 1860-76; bp. Allegheny, 1876-77 (res.).

Donahue, Joseph P. (1870-1959): ord. June 8, 1895; aux. bp. New York (Emmaus), 1945-59.

Donahue, Patrick J. (1849-1922): b. England; ord. Dec. 19, 1885; bp. Wheeling, 1894-1922.

Donnelly, George J. (1889-1950): ord. June 12, 1921; aux. bp. St. Louis (Coela), 1940-46; bp. Leavenworth (now Kansas City — title changed in 1947), 1946-50.

Donnelly, Henry E. (1904-1967): ord. Aug. 17, 1930; aux. bp. Detroit (Tymbrias), 1954-67.

Donnelly, Joseph F. (1909-1977): ord. June 29, 1934; aux. bp. Hartford (Nabala), 1965-77.

Doran, Thomas F. (1856-1916): ord. July 4, 1880; aux. bp. Providence (Halicarnassus), 1915-16.

Dougherty, Dennis (1865-1951): ord. May 31, 1890; bp. Nueva Segovia, P.I., 1903-08; bp. Jaro, P.I., 1908-15; bp. Buffalo, 1915-18; abp. Philadelphia, 1918-1951; cardinal, 1921.

Dougherty, Joseph P. (1905-1970): ord. June 14, 1930; first bp. Yakima, 1951-69; aux. bp. Los Angeles (Altino), 1969-70.

Dowling, Austin (1868-1930): ord. June 24, 1891; first bp. Des Moines, 1912-19; abp. St. Paul, 1919-30.

Drossaerts, Arthur J. (1862-1940): b. Holland; ord. June 15, 1889; bp. San Antonio 1918-26; first abp. San Antonio, 1926-40.

Drumm, Thomas W. (1871-1933): b. Ireland; ord. Dec. 21, 1901; bp. Des Moines, 1919-33.

Dubois, John, S.S. (1764-1842): b. France; ord. Sept. 28, 1787; bp. New York, 1826-42.

Dubourg, Louis William, S.S. (1766-1833): b. Santo Domingo; ord. 1788; bp. Louisiana and the Two Floridas (now New Orleans), 1815-25; returned to France; bp. Montauban, 1826-33; abp. Besancon 1833.

Dubuis, Claude M. (1817-1895): b. France; ord. June 1, 1844; bp. Galveston, 1862-92 (res.).

Dufal, Peter, C.S.C. (1822-1898): b. France; ord. Sept. 29, 1852; v.a. Eastern Bengal (Delcon), 1860-78; coad. bp. Galveston, 1878-80 (res.).

Duffy, James A. (1873-1968): ord. May 27, 1899; bp. Kearney (see transferred to Grand Island, 1917), 1913-31 (res.).

Duffy, John A. (1884-1944): ord. June 13, 1908; bp. Syracuse, 1933-37; bp. Buffalo, 1937-44.

Duggan, James (1825-1899): b. Ireland; ord. May 29, 1847; coad. bp. St. Louis (Gabala), 1857-59; bp. Chicago, 1859-80 (res.). Inactive from 1869 because of illness.

Dunn, John J. (1869-1933): ord. May 30, 1896; aux. bp. New York (Camuliana), 1921-33.

Dunne, Edmund M. (1864-1929): ord. June 24, 1887; bp. Peoria, 1909-29.

Dunne, Edward (1848-1910): b. Ireland; ord. June 29, 1871; bp. Dallas, 1893-1910.

Durier, Anthony (1832-1904): b. France; ord. Oct. 28, 1856; bp. Natchitoches (now Alexandria-Shreveport), La., 1885-1904.

Dwenger, Joseph, C.Pp.S. (1837-1893): ord. Sept. 4, 1859; bp. Fort Wayne, 1872-93.

Dworschak, Leo F. (1900-1976): ord. May 29, 1926; coad. bp. Rapid City (Tium), 1946-47; aux. bp. Fargo, 1947-60; bp. Fargo, 1960-70 (ret.).

Dwyer, Robert J. (1908-1976): ord. June 11, 1932; bp. Reno, 1952-66; abp. Portland, Ore., 1966-74 (res.).

E

Eccleston, Samuel, S.S. (1801-1851): ord. Apr. 24, 1825; coad. bp. Baltimore (Thermae), Sept.-Oct., 1834; abp. Baltimore, 1834-51.

Egan, Michael, O.F.M. (1761-1814): b. Ire-

American Bishops of the Past

land; first bp. Philadelphia, 1810-14.

Eis, Frederick (1843-1926): b. Germany; ord. Oct. 30, 1870; bp. Sault Ste. Marie and Marquette (now Marquette), 1899-1922 (res.).

Elder, William (1819-1904): ord. Mar. 29, 1846; bp. Natchez (now Jackson), 1857-80; coad. bp. Cincinnati (Avara), 1880-83; abp. Cincinnati, 1883-1904.

Elwell, Clarence E. (1904-1973): ord. Mar. 17, 1929; aux. bp. Cleveland (Cone) 1962-68; bp. Columbus, 1968-73.

Emmet, Thomas A., S.J. (1873-1950): ord. July 30, 1909; v.a. Jamaica (Tuscamia), 1930-49 (res.).

England, John: See Index.

Escalante, Alonso Manuel, M.M. (1906-1967): b. Mexico; ord. Feb. 1, 1931; v.a. Pando, Bolivia (Sora), 1943-60 (res.).

Espelage (brothers): Bernard T., O.F.M. (1892-1971): ord. May 16, 1918; bp. Gallup, 1940-69 (res.). **Sylvester J., O.F.M.** (1877-1940): ord. Jan. 18, 1900; v.a. Wuchang, China (Oreus), 1930-40.

Eustace, Bartholomew J. (1887-1956): ord. Nov. 1, 1914; bp. Camden, 1938-56.

F

Fahey, Leo F. (1898-1950): ord. May 29, 1926; coad. bp. Baker City (Ipsus), 1948-50.

Farley, John: See Index.

Farrelly, John P. (1856-1921): ord. Mar. 22, 1880; bp. Cleveland, 1909-21.

Fearns, John M. (1897-1977): ord. Feb. 19, 1922; aux. bp. New York (Geras), 1957-72 (ret.).

Fedders, Edward L., M.M. (1913-1973): ord. June 11, 1944; prelate Juli, Peru (Antiochia ad Meadrum), 1963-73.

Feehan, Daniel F. (1855-1934): ord. Dec. 29, 1879; bp. Fall River, 1907-34.

Feehan, Patrick A. (1829-1902): b. Ireland; ord. Nov. 1, 1852; bp. Nashville, 1865-80; first abp. Chicago, 1880-1902.

Feeney, Daniel J. (1894-1969): ord. May 21, 1921; aux. bp. Portland, Me. (Sita), 1946-52; coad. bp. Portland, 1952-55; bp. Portland, 1955-69.

Feeney, Thomas J., S.J. (1894-1955): ord. June 23, 1927; v.a. Caroline and Marshall Is. (Agnus), 1951-55.

Fenwick, Benedict J., S.J. (1782-1846): ord. June 11, 1808; bp. Boston, 1825-46.

Fenwick, Edward D., O.P. (1768-1832): ord. Feb. 23, 1793; first bp. Cincinnati, 1822-32.

Fink, Michael, O.S.B. (1834-1904): b. Germany; ord. May 28, 1857; coad. v.a., 1871-74, and v.a., 1874-77, Kansas and Indian Territory (Eucarpia); first bp. Leavenworth (now Kansas City), 1877-1904.

Finnigan, George, C.S.C. (1885-1932): ord. June 13, 1915; bp. Helena, 1927-32.

Fitzgerald, Edward (1833-1907): b. Ireland; ord. Aug. 22, 1857; bp. Little Rock, 1867-1907.

Fitzgerald, Edward A. (1893-1972): ord. July 25, 1916; aux. bp. Dubuque (Cantanus), 1946-49; bp. Winona, 1949-69 (res.).

Fitzgerald, Walter J., S.J. (1883-1947): ord. May 16, 1918; coad. v.a. Alaska (Tymbrias), 1939-45; v.a. Alaska, 1945-47.

Fitzmaurice, Edmond (1881-1962): b. Ireland; ord. May 28, 1904; bp. Wilmington, 1925-60 (res.).

Fitzmaurice, John E. (1837-1920): b. Ireland; ord. Dec. 21, 1862; coad. bp. Erie (Amisus), 1898-99; bp. Erie, 1899-1920.

Fitzpatrick, John B. (1812-1866): ord. June 13, 1840; aux. bp. Boston (Callipolis), 1843-46; bp. Boston, 1846-66.

Fitzsimon, Laurence J. (1895-1958): ord. May 17, 1921; bp. Amarillo, 1941-58.

Flaget, Benedict, S.S.: See Index.

Flaherty, J. Louis (1910-1975): ord. Dec. 8, 1936; aux. bp. Richmond (Tabudo), 1966-75.

Flannelly, Joseph F. (1894-1973): ord. Sept. 1, 1918; aux. bp. New York (Metelis), 1948-70 (res.).

Flasch, Kilian C. (1831-1891): b. Germany; ord. Dec. 16, 1859; bp. La Crosse, 1881-91.

Floersh, John (1886-1968): ord. June 10, 1911; coad. bp. Louisville (Lycopolis), 1923-24; bp. Louisville, 1924-37; first abp. Louisville, 1937-67 (res.).

Foery, Walter A. (1890-1978): ord. June 10, 1916; bp. Syracuse, 1937-70 (ret.).

Foley (brothers): John S. (1833-1918): ord. Dec. 20, 1856; bp. Detroit, 1888-1918. **Thomas** (1822-1879): ord. Aug. 16, 1846; coad. bp. and ap. admin. Chicago (Pergamum), 1870-79.

Foley, Maurice P. (1867-1919): ord. July 25, 1891; bp. Tuguegarao, P.I., 1910-16; bp. Jaro, P.I., 1916-19.

Ford, Francis X., M.M.: See Index.

Forest, John A. (1838-1911): b. France; ord. Apr. 12, 1863; bp. San Antonio, 1895-1911.

Fox, Joseph X. (1855-1915): ord. June 7, 1879; bp. Green Bay, 1904-14 (res.).

Furey, Francis J. (1905-1979): ord. Mar. 15, 1930; aux. bp. Philadelphia (Temnus), 1960-63; coad bp. San Diego, 1963-66; bp. San Diego, 1966-69; abp. San Antonio, 1969-79.

G

Gabriels, Henry (1838-1921): b. Belgium; ord. Sept. 21, 1861; bp. Ogdensburg, 1892-1921.

Galberry, Thomas, O.S.A. (1833-1878): b. Ireland; ord. Dec. 20, 1856; bp. Hartford, 1876-78.

Gallagher, Michael J. (1866-1937): ord. Mar. 19, 1893; coad. bp. Grand Rapids (Tiposa in Mauretania), 1915-16; bp. Grand Rapids, 1916-18; bp. Detroit, 1918-37.

Gallagher, Nicholas (1846-1918): ord. Dec. 25, 1868; coad. bp. Galveston (Canopus), 1882-92; bp. Galveston, 1892-1918.

Gannon, John M. (1877-1968): ord. Dec. 21, 1901; aux. bp. Erie (Nilopolis), 1918-20; bp. Erie, 1920-66 (res.).

Garcia Diego y Moreno, Francisco, O.F.M. (1785-1846): b. Mexico; ord. Nov. 14, 1808; bp. Two Californias (now Los Angeles), 1840-46.

Garriga, Mariano S. (1886-1965): ord. July 2, 1911; coad. bp. Corpus Christi (Syene), 1936-49; bp. Corpus Christi, 1949-65.

Garrigan, Philip (1840-1919): b. Ireland; ord. June 11, 1870; first bp. Sioux City, 1902-19.

Gartland, Francis X. (1808-1854): b. Ireland; ord. Aug. 5, 1832; first bp. Savannah, 1850-54.

Garvey, Eugene A. (1845-1920): ord. Sept. 22, 1869; first bp. Altoona (now Altoona-Johnstown), 1901-20.

Gercke, Daniel J. (1874-1964): ord. June 1, 1901; bp. Tucson, 1923-60 (res.).

Gerken, Rudolph A. (1887-1943): ord. June 10, 1917; first bp. Amarillo, 1927-33; abp. Santa Fe, 1933-43.

Gerow, Richard O. (1885-1976): ord. June 5, 1909; bp. Natchez-Jackson (now Jackson), 1924-67 (ret).

Gibbons, Edmund F. (1868-1964): ord. May 27, 1893; bp. Albany, 1919-54 (res.).

Gibbons, James: See Index.

Gilfillan, Francis (1872-1933): b. Ireland; ord. June 24, 1895; coad. bp. St. Joseph (Spiga), 1922-23; bp. St. Joseph, 1923-33.

Gill, Thomas E. (1908-1973): ord. June 10, 1933; aux. bp. Seattle (Lambesis) 1956-73.

Gilmore, Joseph M. (1893-1962): ord. July 25, 1915; bp. Helena, 1936-62.

Gilmour, Richard (1824-1891): b. Scotland; ord. Aug. 30, 1852; bp. Cleveland, 1872-91.

Girouard, Paul J., M.S. (1898-1964): ord. July 26, 1927; first bp. Morondava, Madagascar, 1956-64.

Glass, Joseph S., C.M. (1874-1926): ord. Aug. 15, 1897; bp. Salt Lake City, 1915-26.

Glennon, John: See Index.

Glorieux, Alphonse J. (1844-1917): b. Belgium; ord. Aug. 17, 1867; v.a. Idaho (Apollonia), 1885-93; bp. Boise, 1893-1917.

Goesbriand, Louis J. de (1816-1899): b. France; ord. July 13, 1840; first bp. Burlington, 1853-99.

Gorman, Daniel (1861-1927): ord. June 24, 1893; bp. Boise, 1918-27.

Grace Thomas (1841-1921): b. Ireland; ord. June 24, 1876; bp. Sacramento, 1896-1921.

Grace, Thomas L., O.P. (1814-1897): ord. Dec. 21, 1839; bp. St. Paul, 1859-84 (res.).

Granjon, Henry (1863-1922): b. France; ord. Dec. 17, 1887; bp. Tucson, 1900-22.

Griffin, James A. (1883-1948); ord. July 4, 1909; bp. Springfield, Ill., 1924-48.

Griffin, William A. (1885-1950): ord. Aug. 15, 1910; aux. bp. Newark (Sanavus), 1938-40; bp. Trenton, 1940-50.

Griffin, William R. (1883-1944): ord. May 25, 1907; aux. bp. La Crosse (Lydda), 1935-44.

Griffiths, James H. (1903-1964): ord. Mar. 12, 1927; aux. bp. New York and delegate of US military vicar (Gaza), 1950-64.

Grimes, John (1852-1922): b. Ireland; ord. Feb. 19, 1882; coad. bp. Syracuse (Hemeria), 1909-12; bp. Syracuse, 1912-22.

Grimmelsman, Henry J. (1890-1972): ord. Aug. 15, 1915; first bp. Evansville, 1945-65 (res.).

Gross, William H., C.SS.R. (1837-1898): ord. Mar. 21, 1863; bp. Savannah, 1873-85; abp. Oregon City (now Portland), 1885-98.

Guertin, George A. (1869-1932): ord. Dec. 17, 1892; bp. Manchester, 1907-32.

Guilfoyle, Richard T. (1892-1957): ord. June 2, 1917; bp. Altoona (now Altoona-Johnstown), 1936-57.

Gunn, John E., S.M. (1863-1924); b. Ireland; ord. Feb. 2, 1890; bp. Natchez (now Jackson), 1911-24.

H

Haas, Francis J. (1889-1953): ord. June 11, 1913; bp. Grand Rapids, 1943-53.

Hafey, William (1888-1954): ord. June 16, 1914; first bp. Raleigh, 1925-37; coad. bp. Scranton (Appia), 1937-38; bp. Scranton, 1938-54.

Hagan, John R. (1890-1946): ord. Mar. 7, 1914; aux. bp. Cleveland (Limata), 1946.

Haid, Leo M., O.S.B. (1849-1924): ord. Dec. 21, 1872; v.a. N. Carolina (Messene), 1888-1910; abbot Mary Help of Christians abbacy, 1910-24.

Hallinan, Paul J. (1911-1968): ord. Feb. 20, 1937; bp. Charleston, 1958-62; first abp. Atlanta, 1962-68.

Hanna, Edward J. (1860-1944): ord. May 30, 1885; aux. bp. San Francisco (Titiopolis), 1912-15; abp. San Francisco, 1915-35 (res.).

Hannan, Jerome D. (1896-1965): ord. May 22, 1921; bp. Scranton, 1954-65.

Harkins, Matthew (1845-1921): ord. May 22, 1869; bp. Providence, 1887-1921.

Hartley, James J. (1858-1944): ord. July 10, 1882; bp. Columbus, 1904-44.

Harty, Jeremiah J. (1853-1927): ord. Apr. 28, 1878; abp. Manila, 1903-16; abp. Omaha, 1916-27.

Hayes, Patrick J.: See Index.

Hayes, Ralph L. (1884-1970): ord. Sept. 19, 1909; bp. Helena 1933-35; rector North American College, 1935-44; bp. Davenport, 1944-66 (res.).

Healy, James A. (1830-1900): ord. June 10, 1854; bp. Portland 1875-1900.

Heelan, Edmond (1868-1948): b. Ireland; ord. June 24, 1890; aux. bp. Sioux City (Gerasa), 1919-20; bp. Sioux City, 1920-48.

Heffron, Patrick (1860-1927): ord. Dec. 22, 1884; bp. Winona, 1910-27.

Heiss, Michael (1818-1890): b. Germany; ord. Oct. 18, 1840; bp. La Crosse, 1868-80;

coad. abp. Milwaukee (Hadrianopolis), 1880-81; abp. Milwaukee, 1881-90.

Hendrick, Thomas A. (1849-1909): ord. June 7, 1873; bp. Cebu, P.I., 1904-09.

Hendricken, Thomas F. (1827-1886): b. Ireland; ord. Apr. 25, 1853; bp. Providence, 1872-86.

Hennessy, John (1825-1900): b. Ireland; ord. Nov. 1, 1850; bp. Dubuque, 1866-93; first abp. Dubuque, 1893-1900.

Hennessy, John J. (1847-1920): b. Ireland; ord. Nov. 28, 1869; first bp. Wichita, 1888-1920; ap. admin. Concordia (now Salina), 1891-98.

Henni, John M. (1805-1881): b. Switzerland; ord. Feb. 2, 1829; first bp. Milwaukee, 1844-75; first abp. Milwaukee, 1875-81.

Henry, Harold W., S.S.C. (1909-1976): ord. Dec. 21, 1932; v.a. Kwang Ju, Korea (Coridala), 1957-62; first abp. Kwang Ju, 1962-71; ap. admin. p.a. Cheju-Do, Korea (Thubunae), 1971-76.

Heslin, Thomas (1845-1911): b. Ireland; ord. Sept. 8, 1869; bp. Natchez (now Jackson), 1889-1911.

Heston, Edward L. (1907-73): ord. Dec. 22, 1934; sec. Sacred Congregation for Religious and Secular Institutes, 1969-71; pres. Pontifical Commission for Social Communications, 1971-73; tit. abp. Numidea, 1972.

Hickey, David F., S.J. (1882-1973): ord. June 27, 1917; v.a. Belize, Br. Honduras (Bonitza), 1948-56; first bp. Belize, 1956-57 (res.); tit. abp. Cabasa, 1957-73.

Hickey, Thomas F. (1861-1940): ord. Mar. 25, 1884; coad. bp. Rochester (Berenice), 1905-09; bp. Rochester, 1909-28 (res.).

Hickey, William A. (1869-1933): ord. Dec. 22, 1893; coad. bp. Providence (Claudiopolis), 1919-21; bp. Providence, 1921-33.

Hillinger, Raymond P. (1904-1971): ord. Apr. 2, 1932; bp. Rockford, 1953-56; aux. bp. Chicago (Derbe), 1956-71.

Hoban, Edward F. (1878-1966): ord. July 11, 1903; aux. bp. Chicago (Colonia), 1921-28; bp. Rockford, 1928-42; coad. bp. Cleveland (Lystra), 1942-45; bp. Cleveland, 1945-66.

Hoban, Michael J. (1853-1926): ord. May 22, 1880; coad. bp. Scranton (Halius), 1896-99; bp. Scranton, 1899-1926.

Hogan, John J. (1829-1913): b. Ireland; ord. Apr. 10, 1852; first bp. St. Joseph, 1868-80; first bp. Kansas City, 1880-1913.

Horstmann, Ignatius (1840-1908): ord. June 10, 1865; bp. Cleveland, 1892-1908.

Howard, Francis W. (1867-1944): ord. June 16, 1891; bp. Covington, 1923-44.

Hughes, John J.: See Index.

Hunkeler, Edward J. (1894-1970): ord. June 14, 1919; bp. Grand Island, 1945-51; bp. Kansas City, Kans. 1951-52; first abp. Kansas City, 1952-69 (res.).

Hunt, Duane G. (1884-1960): ord. June 27, 1920; bp. Salt Lake City, 1937-60.

Hurley, Joseph P. (1894-1967): ord. May 29, 1919; bp. St. Augustine, 1940-67.

Hyland, Francis E. (1901-1968): ord. June 11, 1927; aux. bp. Savannah-Atlanta (Gomphi), 1949-56; bp. Atlanta, 1956-61 (res.).

Hyle, Michael W. (1901-1967): ord. Mar. 12, 1927; coad bp. Wilmington, 1958-60; bp. Wilmington, 1960-67.

I

Ireland, John: See Index.

Ireton, Peter L. (1882-1958): ord. June 20, 1906; coad. bp. Richmond (Cyme), 1935-45; bp. Richmond, 1945-58.

J

Janssen, John (1835-1913): b. Germany; ord. Nov. 19, 1858; first bp. Belleville, 1888-1913.

Janssens, Francis A. (1843-1897): b. Holland; ord. Dec. 21, 1867; bp. Natchez (now Jackson), 1881-88; abp. New Orleans, 1888-97.

Jeanmard, Jules B. (1879-1957): ord. June 10, 1903; first bp. Lafayette, La., 1918-56 (res.).

Johannes, Francis (1874-1937): b. Germany; ord. Jan. 3, 1897; coad. bp. Leavenworth (Thasus), 1928-29; bp. Leavenworth (now Kansas City), 1929-37.

Jones, William A., O.S.A. (1865-1921): ord. Mar. 15, 1890; bp. San Juan, 1907-21.

Juncker, Henry D. (1809-1868): b. Lorraine (France); ord. Mar. 16, 1834; first bp. Alton (now Springfield), Ill., 1857-68.

Junger, Aegidius (1833-1895): b. Germany; ord. June 27, 1862; bp. Nesqually (now Seattle), 1879-95.

K

Kain, John J. (1841-1903): ord. July 2, 1866; bp. Wheeling, 1875-93; coad. abp. St. Louis (Oxyrynchus), 1893-95; abp. St. Louis, 1895-1903.

Katzer, Frederick X. (1844-1903): b. Austria; ord. Dec. 21, 1866; bp. Green Bay, 1886-91; abp. Milwaukee, 1891-1903.

Keane, James J. (1856-1929): ord. Dec. 23, 1882; bp. Cheyenne, 1902-11; abp. Dubuque, 1911-29.

Keane, John J. (1839-1918): b. Ireland; ord. July 2, 1866; bp. Richmond, 1878-88; rector of Catholic University, 1888-97; consultor of Congregation for Propagation of the Faith, 1897-1900; abp. Dubuque, 1900-11 (res.).

Keane, Patrick J. (1872-1928): b. Ireland; ord. June 20, 1895; aux. bp. Sacramento (Samaria), 1920-22; bp. Sacramento, 1922-28.

Kearney, James E. (1884-1977): ord. Sept. 19, 1908; bp. Salt Lake City, 1932-37; bp. Rochester, 1937-66 (ret.).

Kearney, Raymond A. (1902-1956): ord. Mar. 12, 1927; aux. bp. Brooklyn (Lysinia), 1935-56.

Keiley, Benjamin J. (1847-1925): ord. Dec.

31, 1873; bp. Savannah, 1900-22 (res.).

Kelleher, Louis F. (1889-1946): ord. Apr. 3, 1915; aux. bp. Boston (Thenae), 1945-46.

Kelley, Francis C. (1870-1948): b. Canada; ord. Aug. 23, 1893; bp. Oklahoma, 1924-48.

Kelly, Edward D. (1860-1926): ord. June 16, 1886; aux. bp. Detroit (Cestrus), 1911-19; bp. Grand Rapids, 1919-26.

Kelly, Edward J. (1890-1956): ord. June 2, 1917; bp. Boise, 1928-56.

Kelly, Francis M. (1886-1950): ord. Nov. 1, 1912; aux. bp. Winona (Mylasa), 1926-28; bp. Winona, 1928-49 (res.).

Kelly, Patrick (1779-1829): b. Ireland; ord. July 18, 1802; first bp. Richmond, 1820-22 (returned to Ireland; bp. Waterford and Lismore, 1822-29).

Kennally, Vincent, S.J. (1895-1977): ord. June 20, 1928; v.a. Caroline and Marshall Islands (Sassura), 1957-71 (ret.).

Kennedy, Thomas F. (1858-1917): ord. July 24, 1887; rector North American College, 1901-17; tit. bp. Hadrianapolis, 1907-15; tit. abp. Seleucia, 1915-17.

Kenny, William J. (1853-1913): ord. Jan. 15, 1879; bp. St. Augustine, 1902-13.

Kenrick (brothers): **Francis P.** (1796-1863): b. Ireland; ord. Apr. 7, 1821; coad. bp. Philadelphia (Aratha), 1830-42; bp. Philadelphia, 1842-51; abp. Baltimore, 1851-63. **Peter** (1806-1896): b. Ireland; ord. Mar. 6, 1832; coad. bp. St. Louis (Adrasus), 1841-43; bp., 1843-47, and first abp. 1847-95. St. Louis (res.).

Keough, Francis P. (1890-1961): ord. June 10, 1916; bp. Providence, 1943-47; abp. Baltimore, 1947-61.

Keyes, Michael, S.M. (1876-1959): b. Ireland; ord. June 21, 1907; bp. Savannah, 1922-35 (res.).

Kiley, Moses E. (1876-1953): b. Nova Scotia; ord. June 10, 1911; bp. Trenton, 1934-40; abp. Milwaukee, 1940-53.

Killeen, James (1917-1978): ord. May 30, 1942; aux. bp. Military Vicariate (Valmalla), 1975-78.

Klonowski, Henry T. (1898-1977): ord. Aug. 8, 1920; aux. bp. Scranton (Daldis), 1947-73 (ret.).

Kogy, Lorenz S., O.M. (1895-1963): b. Georgia, Russia; ord. Nov. 15, 1917; U.S. citizen, 1944; patriarchal vicar for Armenian diocese of Beirut (Comana), 1951-63.

Koudelka, Joseph (1852-1921): b. Austria; ord. Oct. 8, 1875; aux. bp. Cleveland (Germanicoplis), 1908-11; aux. bp. Milwaukee, 1911-13; bp. Superior, 1913-21.

Kowalski, Rembert, O.F.M. (1884-1970): ord. June 22, 1911; v.a. Wuchang, China (Ipsus), 1942-46; first bp. Wuchang, 1946-70 (in exile from 1953).

Kozlowski, Edward (1860-1915): b. Poland; ord. June 29, 1887; aux. bp. Milwaukee (Germia), 1914-15.

Krautbauer, Francis X. (1824-1885): b. Germany; ord. July 16, 1850; bp. Green Bay, 1875-85.

Kucera, Louis B. (1888-1957): ord. June 8, 1915; bp. Lincoln, 1930-57.

L

Lamb, Hugh (1890-1959): ord. May 29, 1915; aux. bp. Philadelphia (Helos), 1936-51; first bp. Greensburg, 1951-59.

Lamy, Jean B.: See Index.

Lane, Loras (1910-1968): ord. Mar. 19, 1937; aux. bp. Dubuque (Bencenna), 1951-56; bp. Rockford, 1956-68.

Lane, Raymond A., M.M. (1894-1974): ord. Feb. 8, 1920; v.a. Fushun, Manchukuo (Hypaepa), 1940-46; sup. gen. Maryknoll, 1946-56.

Laval, John M. (1854-1937): b. France; ord. Nov. 10, 1877; aux. bp. New Orleans (Hierocaesarea), 1911-37.

Lavialle, Peter J. (1819-1867): b. France; ord. Feb. 12, 1844; bp. Louisville, 1865-67.

Lawler, John J. (1862-1948): ord. Dec. 19, 1885; aux. bp. St. Paul (Hermopolis), 1910-16; bp. Lead (now Rapid City), 1916-48.

Le Blond, Charles H. (1883-1958): ord. June 29, 1909; bp. St. Joseph, 1933-56 (res.).

Ledvina, Emmanuel (1868-1952): ord. Mar. 18, 1893; bp. Corpus Christi, 1921-49 (res.).

Lefevere, Peter P. (1804-1869): b. Belgium; ord. Nov. 30, 1831; coad. bp. and admin. Detroit (Zela), 1841-69.

Leibold, Paul F. (1914-1972): ord. May 18, 1940; aux. bp. Cincinnati (Trebenna), 1958-66; bp. Evansville, 1966-69; abp. Cincinnati, 1969-72.

Lenihan (brothers): **Mathias C.** (1854-1943): ord. Dec. 20, 1879; first bp. Great Falls, 1904-30 (res.). **Thomas M.** (1844-1901): b. Ireland; ord. Nov. 19, 1868; bp. Cheyenne, 1897-1901.

Leray, Francis X. (1825-1887): b. France; ord. Mar. 19, 1852; bp. Natchitoches (now Alexandria-Shreveport, La.), 1877-79; coad. bp. New Orleans and admin. of Natchitoches (Jonopolis), 1879-83; abp. New Orleans, 1883-87.

Ley, Felix, O.F.M. Cap. (1909-1972): ord. June 14, 1936; ap. admin. Ryukyu Is., (Caporilla), 1968-72.

Lillis, Thomas F. (1861-1938): ord. Aug. 15, 1885; bp. Leavenworth (now Kansas City, Kans.), 1904-10; coad. bp. Kansas City, Mo. (Cibyra), 1910-13; bp. Kansas City, Mo., 1913-38.

Lootens, Louis (1827-1898): b. Belgium; ord. June 14, 1851; v. a. Idaho and Montana (Castabala), 1868-76 (res.).

Loras, Mathias (1792-1858): b. France; ord. Nov. 12, 1815; first bp. Dubuque, 1837-58.

Loughlin, John (1817-1891): b. Ireland; ord. Oct. 18, 1840; first bp. Brooklyn, 1853-91.

Lowney, Denis M. (1863-1918): b. Ireland;

American Bishops of the Past

ord. Dec. 17, 1887; aux. bp. Providence (Hadrianopolis), 1917-18.

Lucey, Robert E. (1891-1977): ord. May 14, 1916; bp. Amarillo, 1934-41; abp. San Antonio, 1941-69 (ret.).

Ludden, Patrick A. (1838-1912): b. Ireland; ord. May 21, 1865; first bp. Syracuse, 1887-1912.

Luers, John (1819-1871): b. Germany; ord. Nov. 11, 1846; first bp. Fort Wayne, 1858-71.

Lynch, Joseph P. (1872-1954): ord. June 9, 1900; bp. Dallas, 1911-54.

Lynch, Patrick N. (1817-1882): b. Ireland; ord. Apr. 5, 1840; bp. Charleston, 1858-82.

M

McAuliffe, Maurice F. (1875-1944): ord. July 29, 1900; aux. bp. Hartford (Dercos), 1925-34; bp. Hartford, 1934-44.

McCarthy, Joseph E. (1876-1955): ord. July 4, 1903; bp. Portland, Me., 1932-55.

McCarthy, Justin J. (1900-1959): ord. Apr. 16, 1927; aux. bp. Newark (Doberus), 1954-57; bp. Camden, 1957-59.

McCarty, William T., C.SS.R. (1889-1972): ord. June 10, 1915; military delegate (Anea), 1943-47; coad. bp. Rapid City, 1947-48; bp. Rapid City, 1948-69 (res.).

McCloskey, James P. (1870-1945): ord. Dec. 17, 1898, bp. Zamboanga, P.I., 1917-20; bp. Jaro, P.I., 1920-45.

McCloskey, John: See Index.

McCloskey, William G. (1823-1909): ord. Oct. 6, 1852; bp. Louisville, 1868-1909.

McCormick, Patrick J. (1880-1953): ord. July 6, 1904; aux. bp. Washington (Atenia), 1950-53.

McCort, John J. (1860-1936): ord. Oct. 14, 1883; aux. bp. Philadelphia (Azotus), 1912-20; bp. Altoona, 1920-36.

McDevitt, Philip R. (1858-1935): ord. July 14, 1885; bp. Harrisburg, 1916-35.

McDonnell, Charles E. (1854-1921): ord. May 19, 1878; bp. Brooklyn, 1892-1921.

McDonnell, Thomas J. (1894-1961): ord. Sept. 20, 1919; aux. bp. New York (Sela), 1947-51; coad. bp. Wheeling, 1951-61.

McEntegart, Bryan (1893-1968): ord. Sept. 8, 1917; bp. Ogdensburg, 1943-53; rector Catholic University (Aradi), 1953-57; bp. Brooklyn, 1957-68.

McFadden, James A. (1880-1952): ord. June 17, 1905; aux. bp. Cleveland (Bida), 1932-43; first bp. Youngstown, 1943-52.

MacFarland, Francis P. (1819-1874): ord. May 1, 1845; bp. Hartford, 1858-74.

McFaul, James A. (1850-1917): b. Ireland; ord. May 26, 1877; bp. Trenton, 1894-1917.

McGavick, Alexander J. (1863-1948): ord. June 11, 1887; aux. bp. Chicago (Marcopolis), 1899-1921; bp. La Crosse, 1921-48.

McGeough, Joseph F. (1903-1970): ord. Dec. 20, 1930; internuncio Ethiopia, 1957-60; apostolic delegate (Hemesa) S. Africa, 1960-67; nuncio Ireland, 1967-69.

McGill, John (1809-1872): ord. June 13, 1835; bp. Richmond, 1850-72.

MacGinley, John B. (1871-1969): b. Ireland; ord. June 8, 1895; bp. Nueva Caceres, 1910-24; first bp. Monterey-Fresno, 1924-32 (res.).

McGolrick, James (1841-1918): b. Ireland; ord. June 11, 1867; first bp. Duluth, 1889-1918.

McGovern, Patrick A. (1872-1951): ord. Aug. 18, 1895; bp. Cheyenne, 1912-51.

McGovern, Thomas (1832-1898): b. Ireland; ord. Dec. 27, 1861; bp. Harrisburg, 1888-98.

McGrath, Joseph F. (1871-1950): b. Ireland; ord. Dec. 21, 1895; bp. Baker City (now Baker), 1919-50.

McGuinness, Eugene (1889-1957): ord. May 22, 1915; bp. Raleigh, 1937-44; coad. bp. Oklahoma City and Tulsa (Ilium), 1944-48; bp. Oklahoma City and Tulsa, 1948-57.

McIntyre, James F. (1886-1979): ord. May 21, 1921; aux. bp. New York (Cirene), 1941-46; coad. abp. New York (Palto), 1946-48; abp. Los Angeles, 1948-70 (ret.); cardinal, 1953.

McLaughlin, Charles B. (1913-1978): ord. June 6, 1941; aux. bp. Raleigh (Risinium), 1964-68; first bp. St. Petersburg, 1968-78.

McLaughlin, Thomas H. (1881-1947): ord. July 26, 1904; aux. bp. Newark (Nisa), 1935-37; first bp. Paterson, 1937-47.

McMahon, John J. (1875-1932): ord. May 20, 1900; bp. Trenton, 1928-32.

McMahon, Lawrence S. (1835-1893): ord. Mar. 24, 1860; bp. Hartford, 1879-93.

McManaman, Edward P. (1900-1964): ord. Mar. 12, 1927; aux. bp. Erie (Floriana), 1948-64.

McManus, James E., C.SS.R. (1900-1976): ord. June 19, 1927; bp. Ponce, P.R., 1947-63; aux. bp. New York (Banda), 1963-70 (ret.).

McMullen, John (1832-1883): b. Ireland; ord. June 20, 1858; first bp. Davenport, 1881-83.

McNamara, John M. (1878-1960): ord. June 21, 1902; aux. bp. Baltimore (Eumenia), 1928-47; aux. bp. Washington, 1947-60.

McNamara, Martin D. (1898-1966): ord. Dec. 23, 1922; first bp. Joliet, 1949-66.

McNeirny, Francis (1828-1894): ord. Aug. 17, 1854; coad. bp. Albany (Rhesaina), 1872-77; bp. Albany, 1877-94.

McNicholas, John T., O.P. (1877-1950): b. Ireland; ord. Oct. 10, 1901; bp. Duluth, 1918-25; abp. Cincinnati, 1925-50.

McNulty, James A. (1900-1972): ord. July 12, 1925; aux. bp. Newark (Methone), 1947-53; bp. Paterson, 1953-63; bp. Buffalo, 1963-72.

McQuaid, Bernard J.: See Index.

McSorley, Francis J., O.M.I. (1913-1971): ord. May 30, 1939; v.a. Jolo, P.I. (Sozusa), 1958-71.

McVinney, Russell J. (1898-1971): ord. July 13, 1924; bp. Providence, 1948-71.

Machebeuf, Joseph P. (1812-1889): b. France; ord. Dec. 17, 1836; v. a. Colorado and Utah (Epiphania), 1868-1887; first bp. Denver, 1887-89.

Maes, Camillus P. (1846-1915): b. Belgium; ord. Dec. 19, 1868; bp. Covington, 1885-1915.

Magner, Francis (1887-1947): ord. May 17, 1913; bp. Marquette, 1941-47.

Mahoney, Bernard (1875-1939): ord. Feb. 27, 1904; bp. Sioux Falls, 1922-39.

Maloney, Thomas F. (1903-1962): ord. July 13, 1930; aux. bp. Providence (Andropolis), 1960-62.

Manogue, Patrick: See Index.

Manucy, Dominic (1823-1885): ord. Aug. 15, 1850; v. a. Brownsville (Dulma), 1874-84; bp. Mobile, Mar.-Sept., 1884 (res.); reappointed v.a. Brownsville (Maronea) (now diocese of Corpus Christi), 1884-85.

Marechal, Ambrose, S.S. (1766-1828): b. France; ord. June 2, 1792; abp. Baltimore, 1817-28.

Markham, Thomas F. (1891-1952): ord. June 2, 1917; aux. bp. Boston (Acalissus), 1950-52.

Martin, Augustus M. (1803-1875): b. France; ord. May 31, 1828; first bp. Natchitoches (now Alexandria), 1853-75.

Marty, Martin, O.S.B. (1834-1896): b. Switzerland; ord. Sept. 14, 1856; v. a. Dakota (Tiberias), 1880-89; first bp. Sioux Falls, 1889-95; bp. St. Cloud, 1895-96.

Marx, Adolph (1915-1965): b. Germany; ord. May 2, 1940; aux. bp. Corpus Christi (Citrus), 1956-65; first bp. Brownsville, 1965.

Matz, Nicholas C. (1850-1917): b. France; ord. May 31, 1874; coad. bp. Denver (Telmissus), 1887-89; bp. Denver, 1889-1917.

Mazzarella, Bernardino N., O.F.M. (1904-1979): ord. June 5, 1931; prelate Olancho, Honduras (Hadrianopolis in Pisidia), 1957-63; first bp. Comayagua, Honduras, 1963-79.

Meerschaert, Theophile (1847-1924): b. Belgium; ord. Dec. 23, 1871; v. a. Oklahoma and Indian Territory (Sidyma), 1891-1905; first bp. Oklahoma, 1905-24.

Melcher, Joseph (1806-1873): b. Austria; ord. Mar. 27, 1830; first bp. Green Bay, 1868-73.

Messmer, Sebastian (1847-1930): b. Switzerland; ord. July 23, 1871; bp. Green Bay, 1892-1903; abp. Milwaukee, 1903-30.

Meyer, Albert (1903-1965): ord. July 11, 1926; bp. Superior, 1946-53; abp. Milwaukee, 1953-58; abp. Chicago, 1958-65; cardinal, 1959.

Michaud, John S. (1843-1908): ord. June 7, 1873; coad. bp. Burlington (Modra), 1892-99; bp. Burlington, 1899-1908.

Miege, John B., S.J. (1815-1884): b. France; ord. Sept. 12, 1844; v. a. Kansas and Indian Territory (now Kansas City) (Messene), 1851-74 (res.).

Miles, Richard P., O.P. (1791-1860): ord. Sept. 21, 1816; first bp. Nashville, 1838-60.

Minihan, Jeremiah F. (1903-1973); ord. Dec. 21, 1929; aux. bp. Boston (Paphus), 1954-73.

Misner, Paul B., C.M. (1891-1938): ord. Feb. 23, 1919; v.a. Yukiang, China (Myrica), 1935-38.

Mitty, John J. (1884-1961): ord. Dec. 22, 1906; bp. Salt Lake, 1926-32; coad. abp. San Francisco (Aegina), 1932-35; abp. San Francisco, 1935-61.

Moeller, Henry (1849-1925): ord. June 10, 1876; bp. Columbus, 1900-03; coad. abp. Cincinnati (Areopolis), 1903-04; abp. Cincinnati, 1904-25.

Molloy, Thomas E. (1884-1956): ord. Sept. 19, 1908; aux. bp. Brooklyn (Lorea), 1920-21; bp. Brooklyn, 1921-56.

Monaghan, Francis J. (1890-1942): ord. May 29, 1915; coad. bp. Ogdensburg (Mela), 1936-39; bp. Ogdensburg, 1939-42.

Monaghan, John J. (1856-1935): ord. Dec. 18, 1880; bp. Wilmington, 1897-1925 (res.).

Montgomery, George T. (1847-1907): ord. Dec. 20, 1879; coad. bp. Monterey-Los-Angeles (Thmuis), 1894-96; bp. Monterey-Los Angeles (now Los Angeles), 1896-1903; coad. abp. San Francisco (Auxum), 1903-07.

Mooney, Edward (1882-1958): ord. Apr. 10, 1909; ap. del. India (Irenopolis), 1926-31; ap. del. Japan, 1931-33; bp. Rochester, 1933-37; first abp. Detroit, 1937-58; cardinal, 1946.

Moore, John (1835-1901): b. Ireland; ord. Apr. 9, 1860; bp. St. Augustine, 1877-1901.

Mora, Francis (1827-1905): b. Spain; ord. Mar. 19, 1856; coad. bp. Monterey-Los Angeles (Mosynopolis), 1873-78; bp. Monterey-Los Angeles (now Los Angeles), 1878-96 (res.).

Morris, John (1866-1946): ord. June 11, 1892; coad. bp. Little Rock (Acmonia), 1906-07; bp. Little Rock, 1907-46.

Mrak, Ignatius (1810-1901): b. Austria; ord. July 31, 1837; bp. Sault Ste. Marie and Marquette (now Marquette), 1869-78 (res.).

Muench, Aloysius: See Index.

Muldoon, Peter J. (1862-1927): ord. Dec. 18, 1886; aux. bp. Chicago (Tamasus), 1901-08; first bp. Rockford, 1908-27.

Mullen, Tobias (1818-1900): b. Ireland; ord. Sept. 1, 1844; bp. Erie, 1868-99 (res.).

Mulloy, William T. (1892-1959): ord. June 7, 1916; bp. Covington, 1945-59.

Mundelein, George (1872-1939): ord. June 8, 1895; aux. bp. Brooklyn (Loryma), 1909-15; abp. Chicago, 1915-39; cardinal, 1924.

Murphy, Joseph A., S.J. (1857-1939): b. Ireland; ord. Aug. 26, 1888; v. a. Belize, Br. Honduras (Birtha), 1923-39.

Murphy, William F. (1885-1950): ord. June 13, 1908; first bp. Saginaw, 1938-50.

Murray, John G. (1877-1956): ord. Apr. 14, 1900; aux. bp. Hartford (Flavias), 1920-25; bp. Portland, 1925-31; abp. St. Paul, 1931-56.

Mussio, John K. (1902-1978): ord. Aug. 15, 1935; bp. Steubenville, 1945-77 (ret.).

N

Najmy, Justin, O.S.B.M. (1898-1968): b. Syria; ord. Dec. 25, 1926; ap. ex. Melkites (Augustopolis in Phrygia), 1966-68.

Navagh, James J. (1901-1965): ord. Dec. 21, 1929; aux. bp. Raleigh (Ombi), 1952-57; bp. Ogdensburg, 1957-63; bp. Paterson, 1963-65.

Neale, Leonard (1746-1817): ord. June 5, 1773; coad. bp. Baltimore (Gortyna), 1800-15; abp. Baltimore, 1815-17.

Neraz, John C. (1828-1894): b. France; ord. Mar. 19, 1853; bp. San Antonio, 1881-1894.

Neumann, John, St.: See Index.

Newman, Thomas A., M.S. (1903-1978) ord. June 29, 1929; first bp. Prome, Burma, 1961-75 (ret.).

Niedhammer, Matthew A., O.F.M. Cap. (1901-1970): ord. June 8, 1927; v. a. Bluefields, Nicaragua (Caloe), 1943-70.

Nilan, John J. (1855-1934): ord. Dec. 2, 1878; bp. Hartford, 1910-34.

Noa, Thomas L. (1892-1977): ord. Dec. 23, 1916; coad. bp. Sioux City (Salona), 1946-47; bp. Marquette, 1947-68 (ret.).

Noll, John F.: See Index.

Northrop, Henry P. (1842-1916): ord. June 25, 1865; v.a. North Carolina (Rosalia), 1881-83; bp. Charleston, 1883-1916.

Nussbaum, Paul J., C.P. (1870-1935): ord. May 20, 1894; first bp. Corpus Christi, 1913-20 (res.); bp. Sault Ste. Marie and Marquette (now Marquette), 1922-35.

O

O'Brien, Henry J. (1896-1976): ord. July 8, 1923; aux. bp. Hartford (Sita), 1940-45; bp. Hartford, 1945-53, and first abp. Hartford, 1953-68 (res.).

O'Brien, William D. (1878-1962): ord. July 11, 1903; aux. bp. Chicago (Calynda), 1934-62.

O'Connell, Denis J. (1849-1927): b. Ireland; ord. May 26, 1877; aux. bp. San Francisco (Sebaste), 1908-12; bp. Richmond, 1912-26 (res.).

O'Connell, Eugene (1815-1891): b. Ireland; ord. May 21, 1842; v. a. Marysville (Flaviopolis), 1861-68; first bp. Grass Valley, 1868-84 (res.).

O'Connell, William H. (1859-1944): ord. June 8, 1884; bp. Portland, 1901-06; coad. bp. Boston (Constantia), 1906-07; abp. Boston, 1907-44; cardinal, 1911.

O'Connor (brothers): **James** (1823-1890): b. Ireland; ord. Mar. 25, 1848; v. a. Nebraska (Dibon), 1876-85; first bp. Omaha, 1885-90. **Michael, S.J.** (1810-1872): b. Ireland; ord. June 1, 1833; first bp. Pittsburgh, 1843-53; first bp. of Erie, 1853-54; bp. Pittsburgh, 1854-60 (resigned, joined Jesuits).

O'Connor, John J. (1855-1927): ord. Dec. 22, 1877; bp. Newark, 1901-27.

O'Connor, William P. (1886-1973): ord. Mar. 10, 1912; bp. Superior, 1942-46; first bp. Madison, 1946-67 (res.).

O'Dea, Edward J. (1856-1932): ord. Dec. 23, 1882; bp. Nesqually (now Seattle — title changed in 1907), 1896-1932.

Odin, John M., C.M. (1800-1870): b. France; ord. May 4, 1823; v. a. Texas (Claudiopolis), 1842-47; first bp. Galveston, 1847-61; abp. New Orleans, 1861-70.

O'Donaghue, Denis (1848-1925): ord. Sept. 6, 1874; aux. bp. Indianapolis (Pomaria), 1900-10; bp. Louisville, 1910-24 (res.).

O'Dowd, James T. (1907-1950): ord. June 4, 1932; aux. bp. San Francisco (Cea), 1948-50.

O'Farrell, Michael J. (1832-1894): b. Ireland; ord. Aug. 18, 1855; first bp. Trenton, 1881-94.

O'Flanagan, Dermot (1901-1973): b. Ireland; ord. Aug. 27, 1929; first bp. Juneau, 1951-68 (res.).

O'Gara, Cuthbert, C.P. (1886-1968): b. Canada; ord. May 26, 1915; v.a. Yuanling, China (Elis), 1934-46; first bp. Yuanling, 1946-68 (imprisoned, 1951, and then expelled, 1953, by Chinese Communists).

O'Gorman, James, O.C.S.O. (1804-1874): b. Ireland; ord. Dec. 23, 1843; v.a. Nebraska (now Omaha) (Raphanea), 1859-74.

O'Gorman, Thomas (1843-1921): ord. Nov. 5, 1865; bp. Sioux Falls, 1896-1921.

O'Hara, Edwin V.: See Index.

O'Hara, Gerald P. (1888-1963): ord. Apr. 3, 1920; aux. bp. Philadelphia (Heliopolis), 1929-35; bp. Savannah (title changed to Savannah-Atlanta in 1937), 1935-59 (res.); regent of Rumania nunciature, 1946-50 (expelled); nuncio to Ireland, 1951-54; ap. del. to Great Britain, 1954-63.

O'Hara, John F., C.S.C. (1886-1960): ord. Sept. 9, 1916; delegate of US military vicar (Mylasa), 1940-45; bp. Buffalo, 1945-51; abp. Philadelphia, 1951-60; cardinal, 1958.

O'Hara, William (1816-1899): b. Ireland; ord. Dec. 21, 1842; first bp. Scranton, 1868-99.

O'Hare, William F., S.J. (1870-1926): ord. June 25, 1903; v.a. Jamaica (Maximianopolis), 1920-26.

O'Hern, John F. (1874-1933): ord. Feb. 17, 1901; bp. Rochester, 1929-33.

O'Leary, Thomas (1875-1949): ord. Dec. 18, 1897; bp. Springfield, Mass., 1921-49.

Olwell, Quentin, C.P. (1898-1972); ord. Feb. 4, 1923; prelate Marbel, P.I. (Thabraca), 1961-69 (ret.).

O'Regan, Anthony (1809-1866): b. Ireland; ord. Nov. 29, 1834; bp. Chicago, 1854-58 (res.).

O'Reilly, Bernard (1803-1856): b. Ireland; ord. Oct. 16, 1831; bp. Hartford, 1850-56.

O'Reilly, Charles J. (1860-1923): b. Canada; ord. June 29, 1890; first bp. Baker City (now Baker), 1903-18; bp. Lincoln, 1918-23.

O'Reilly, James (1855-1934): b. Ireland;

ord. June 24, 1880; bp. Fargo, 1910-34.
O'Reilly, Patrick T. (1833-1892): b. Ireland; ord. Aug. 15, 1857; first bp. Springfield, Mass., 1870-92.
O'Reilly, Peter J. (1850-1924): b. Ireland; ord. June 24, 1877; aux. bp. Peoria (Lebedus), 1900-24.
O'Reilly, Thomas C. (1873-1938): ord. June 4, 1898; bp. Scranton, 1928-38.
Ortynsky, Stephen, O.S.B.M. (1866-1916): b. Poland; ord. July 18, 1891; first Ukrainian Byzantine Rite bishop in US (Daulia), 1907-16.
O'Shea, John A., C.M. (1887-1969): ord. May 30, 1914; v.a. Kanchow, China (Midila), 1928-46; first bp. Kanchow, 1946-69 (expelled by Chinese Communists, 1953).
O'Shea, William F., M.M. (1884-1945): ord. Dec. 5, 1917; v.a. Heijon, Japan (Naissusz), 1939-45; prisoner of Japanese 1941-42.
O'Sullivan, Jeremiah (1842-1896): b. Ireland; ord. June 30, 1868; bp. Mobile, 1885-96.

P

Paschang, Adolph J., M.M. (1895-1968): ord. May 21, 1921; v.a. Kong Moon, China (Sasima), 1937-46; first bp. Kong Moon, 1946-68 (expelled by Communists, 1951).
Pellicer, Anthony (1824-1880): ord. Aug. 15, 1850; first bp. San Antonio, 1874-80.
Penalver y Cardenas, Luis (1749-1810): b. Cuba; ord. Apr. 4, 1772; first bp. Louisiana and the Two Floridas (now New Orleans), 1793-1801; abp. Guatemala, 1801-06 (res.).
Perche, Napoleon J. (1805-1883): b. France; ord. Sept. 19, 1829; abp. New Orleans, 1870-83.
Persico, Ignatius, O.F.M. Cap. (1823-1895): b. Italy; ord. Jan. 24, 1846; bishop from 1854; bp. Savannah-Atlanta, 1870-72; cardinal, 1893.
Peschges, John H. (1881-1944): ord. Apr. 15, 1905; bp. Crookston, 1938-44.
Peterson, John B. (1871-1944): ord. Sept. 15, 1899; aux. bp. Boston (Hippos), 1927-32; bp. Manchester, 1932-44.
Phelan, Richard (1828-1904): b. Ireland; ord. May 4, 1854; coad. bp. Pittsburgh (Cibyra), 1885-89; bp. Pittsburgh, 1889-1904.
Pinten, Joseph G. (1867-1945): ord. Nov. 1, 1890; bp. Superior, 1922-26; bp. Grand Rapids, 1926-40 (ret.).
Pitaval, John B. (1858-1928): b. France; ord. Dec. 24, 1881; aux. bp. Santa Fe (Sora), 1902-09; abp. Santa Fe, 1909-18 (res.).
Plagens, Joseph C. (1880-1943): b. Poland; ord. July 5, 1903; aux. bp. Detroit (Rhodiapolis), 1924-35; bp. Sault Ste. Marie and Marquette (title changed to Marquette, 1937), 1935-40; bp. Grand Rapids, 1941-43.
Portier, Michael (1795-1859): b. France; ord. May 16, 1818; v.a. Two Floridas and Alabama (Olena), 1826-29; first bp. Mobile, 1829-59.
Prendergast, Edmond (1843-1918): b. Ireland; ord. Nov. 17, 1865; aux. bp. Philadelphia (Scilium), 1897-1911; abp. Philadelphia, 1911-18.
Purcell, John B. (1800-1883): b. Ireland; ord. May 20, 1826; bp., 1833-50, and first abp., 1850-83, Cincinnati.

Q

Quarter, William (1806-1848): b. Ireland; ord. Sept. 19, 1829; first bp. Chicago, 1844-48.
Quigley, James E. (1855-1915): b. Canada; ord. Apr. 13, 1879; bp. Buffalo, 1897-1903; abp. Chicago, 1903-15.
Quinlan, John (1826-1883): b. Ireland; ord. Aug. 30, 1852; bp. Mobile, 1859-83.
Quinn, William Charles, C.M. (1905-1960): ord. Oct. 11, 1931; v.a. Yukiang, China (Halicarnassus), 1940-46; first bp. Yukiang, 1946-60 (expelled by Chinese Communists, 1951).

R

Rademacher, Joseph (1840-1900): ord. Aug. 2, 1863; bp. Nashville, 1883-93; bp. Fort Wayne, 1893-1900.
Rappe, Louis Amadeus (1801-1877): b. France; ord. Mar. 14, 1829; first bp. Cleveland, 1847-70 (res).
Ready, Michael J. (1893-1957): ord. Sept. 14, 1918; bp. Columbus, 1944-57.
Reed, Victor J. (1905-1971): ord. Dec. 21, 1929; aux. bp. Oklahoma City and Tulsa (Limasa), 1957-58; bp. Oklahoma City and Tulsa, 1958-71.
Rehring, George J. (1890-1976): ord. Mar. 28, 1914; aux. bp. Cincinnati (Lunda), 1937-50; bp. Toledo, 1950-67 (res.).
Reilly, Edmond J. (1897-1958): ord. Apr. 1, 1922; aux. bp. Brooklyn (Nepte), 1955-58.
Rese, Frederic (1791-1871): b. Germany; ord. Mar. 15, 1823; first bp. Detroit, 1833-71. Inactive from 1841 because of ill health.
Reverman, Theodore (1877-1941): ord. July 26, 1901; bp. Superior, 1926-41.
Reynolds, Ignatius A. (1798-1855): ord. Oct. 24, 1823; bp. Charleston, 1844-55.
Rhode, Paul P. (1871-1945): b. Poland; ord. June 17, 1894; aux. bp. Chicago (Barca), 1908-15; bp. Green Bay, 1915-45.
Rice, Joseph J. (1871-1938): ord. Sept. 29, 1894; bp. Burlington, 1910-38.
Rice, William A., S.J. (1891-1946): ord. Aug. 27, 1925; v.a. Belize, Br. Honduras (Rusicade), 1939-46.
Richter, Henry J. (1838-1916): b. Germany; ord. June 10, 1865; first bp. Grand Rapids, 1883-1916.
Riley, Thomas J. (1900-1977): ord. May 20, 1927; aux. bp. Boston (Regiae), 1959-76 (ret.).
Riordan, Patrick W. (1841-1914): b. Canada; ord. June 10, 1865; coad. abp. San Francisco (Cabasa), 1883-84; abp. San Francisco, 1884-1914.
Ritter, Joseph E.: See Index.
Robinson, Pascal C., O.F.M. (1870-1948):

b. Ireland; ord. Dec. 21, 1901; ap. visitor to Palestine, Egypt, Syria and Cyprus (Tyana), 1927-29; ap. nuncio to Ireland, 1929-48.

Rohlman, Henry P. (1876-1957): b. Germany; ord. Dec. 21, 1901; bp. Davenport, 1927-44; coad. abp. Dubuque (Macra), 1944-46; abp. Dubuque, 1946-54 (res.).

Rooker, Fraderick Z. (1861-1907): ord. July 25, 1888; bp. Jaro, P.I., 1903-07.

Ropert, Gulstan F., SS.CC. (1839-1903): b. France; ord. May 26, 1866; v.a. Sandwich (now Hawaiian) Is. (Panopolis), 1892-1903.

Rosati, Joseph, C. M.: See Index.

Rosecrans, Sylvester (1827-1878): ord. June 5, 1853; aux. bp. Cincinnati (Pompeiopolis), 1862-68; first bp. Columbus, 1868-78.

Rouxel, Gustave A. (1840-1908): b. France; ord. Nov. 4, 1863; aux. bp. New Orleans (Curium), 1899-1908.

Rummel, Joseph (1876-1964): b. Germany; ord. May 24, 1902; bp. Omaha, 1928-35; abp. New Orleans, 1935-64.

Russell, William T. (1863-1927): ord. June 21, 1889; bp. Charleston, 1917-27.

Ryan, Edward F. (1879-1956): ord. Aug. 10, 1905; bp. Burlington, 1945-56.

Ryan, James (1848-1923): b. Ireland; ord. Dec. 24, 1871; bp. Alton (now Springfield), Ill., 1888-1923.

Ryan, James H. (1886-1947): ord. June 5, 1909; rector Catholic University, 1928-35; tit. bp. Modra, 1933-35; bp., 1935-45, and first abp. Omaha, 1945-47.

Ryan, Patrick J. (1831-1911): b. Ireland; ord. Sept. 8, 1853; coad. bp. St. Louis (Tricomia), 1872-84; abp. Philadelphia, 1884-1911.

Ryan, Stephen, C.M. (1826-1896): b. Canada; ord. June 24, 1849; bp. Buffalo, 1868-96.

Ryan, Vincent J. (1884-1951): ord. June 7, 1912; bp. Bismarck, 1940-51.

S

Salpointe, John B. (1825-1898): b. France; ord. Dec. 20, 1851; v.a. Arizona (Dorylaeum), 1869-84; coad. abp. Santa Fe (Anazarbus), 1884-85; abp. Santa Fe, 1885-94 (res.).

Scanlan, Lawrence (1843-1915): b. Ireland; ord. June 28, 1868; v.a. Utah (Laranda), 1887-91; bp. Salt Lake (now Salt Lake City), 1891-1915.

Scannell, Richard (1845-1916): b. Ireland; ord. Feb. 26, 1871; first bp. Concordia (now Salina), 1887-91; bp. Omaha, 1891-1916.

Schenk, Francis J. (1901-1969): ord. June 13, 1926; bp. Crookston, 1945-60; bp. Duluth, 1960-69.

Scher, Philip G. (1880-1953): ord. June 6, 1904; bp. Monterey-Fresno, 1933-53.

Schinner, Augustine (1863-1937): ord. Mar. 7, 1886; first bp. Superior, 1905-13; first bp. Spokane, 1914-25 (res.).

Schlarman, Joseph H. (1879-1951): ord. June 29, 1904; bp. Peoria, 1930-51.

Schmitt, Adolph G., C.M.M. (1905-1976): b. Bavaria; U.S. citizen 1945; v.a. Bulawayo (Nasai), Rhodesia, 1951-55; first bp. Bulawayo, 1955-74 (ret.). Murdered by terrorists.

Schmondiuk, Joseph (1912-1978): ord. Mar. 29, 1936; aux. bp. Philadelphia exarchate (Zeugma in Syria), 1956-61; eparch Stamford, 1961-77; abp. Philadelphia, 1977-78.

Schott, Lawrence F. (1907-1963): ord. July 15, 1935; aux. bp. Harrisburg (Eluza), 1956-63.

Schrembs, Joseph (1866-1945): b. Germany; ord. June 29, 1889; aux. bp. Grand Rapids (Sophene), 1911; first bp. Toledo, 1911-21; bp. Cleveland, 1921-45.

Schuler, Anthony J., S.J. (1869-1944): ord. June 27, 1901; first bp. El Paso, 1915-42 (res.).

Schwebach, James (1847-1921): b. Luxembourg; ord. June 16, 1870; bp. La Crosse, 1892-1921.

Schwertner, August J. (1870-1939): ord. June 12, 1897; bp. Wichita, 1921-39.

Scully, William (1894-1969): ord. Sept. 20, 1919; coad. bp. Albany (Pharsalus), 1945-54; bp. Albany, 1954-69.

Sebastian, Jerome D. (1895-1960): ord. May 25, 1922; aux. bp. Baltimore (Baris in Hellesponto), 1954-60.

Seghers, Charles J.: See Index.

Seidenbusch, Rupert, O.S.B. (1830-1895): b. Germany; ord. June 22, 1853; v.a. Northern Minnesota (Halia), 1875-88 (res.).

Senyshyn, Ambrose, O.S.B.M. (1903-1976): b. Galicia; ord. Aug. 23, 1931; aux. bp. Ukrainian Catholic Diocese of U.S. (Maina), 1942-56; first bp. Stamford (Byzantine Rite), 1958-61; abp. Philadelphia (Byzantine Rite), 1961-76.

Seton, Robert J. (1839-1927): b. Italy; ord. Apr. 15, 1865; tit. abp. Heliopolis, 1903-27. Grandson of St. Elizabeth Seton.

Shahan, Thomas J. (1857-1932): ord. June 3, 1882; rector, Catholic University of America, 1909-27; tit. bp. Germanicopolis, 1914-32.

Shanahan (brothers): **Jeremiah F.** (1834-1886): ord. July 3, 1859; first bp. Harrisburg, 1868-86. **John W.** (1846-1916): ord. Jan. 2, 1869; bp. Harrisburg, 1899-1916.

Shanley, John (1852-1909): ord. May 30, 1874; first bp. Jamestown (see transferred to Fargo in 1897), 1889-1909.

Shanley, Patrick H., O.C.D. (1896-1970): b. Ireland; ord. Dec. 21, 1930; US citizen; prelate Infanta, P.I. (Sophene), 1953-60 (res.).

Shaughnessy, Gerald, S.M. (1887-1950): ord. June 20, 1920; bp. Seattle, 1933-50.

Shaw, John W. (1863-1934): ord. May 26, 1888; coad. bp. San Antonio (Castabala), 1910-11; bp. San Antonio, 1911-18; abp. New Orleans, 1918-34.

Sheehan, Edward T., C.M. (1888-1933): ord. June 7, 1916; v. a. Yukiang, China (Calydon), 1929-33.

Sheil, Bernard J. (1886-1969): ord. May 21, 1910; aux. bp. Chicago (Pegae), 1928-69; tit.

abp. Selge, 1959-69. Founder of Catholic Youth Organization.

Smith, Alphonse (1883-1935): ord. Apr. 18, 1908; bp. Nashville, 1924-35.

Smith, Eustace, O.F.M. (1908-1975): ord. June 12, 1934; v.a. Beirut, Lebanon (Apamea Cibotus), 1958-73.

Smith, Leo R. (1905-1963): ord. Dec. 21, 1929; aux. bp. Buffalo (Marida), 1952-63; bp. Ogdensburg, 1963.

Smyth, Clement, O.C.S.O. (1810-1865):b. Ireland; ord. May 29, 1841; coad. bp. Dubuque (Thennesus), 1857-58; bp. Dubuque, 1858-65.

Spalding, John L.: See Index.
Spalding, Martin J.: See Index.
Spellman, Francis J.: See Index.

Spence, John S. (1909-1973): ord. Dec. 5, 1933; aux. bp. Washington (Aggersel), 1964-73.

Stang, William (1854-1907): b. Germany; ord. June 15, 1878; first bp. Fall River, 1904-07.

Stanton, Martin W. (1897-1977): ord. June 14, 1924; aux. bp. Newark (Citium) 1957-72 (ret.).

Stariha, John (1845-1915): b. Austria; ord. Sept. 19, 1869; first bp. Lead (now Rapid City), 1902-09 (res.).

Steck, Leo J. (1898-1950): ord. June 8, 1924; aux. bp. Salt Lake City (Ilium), 1948-50.

Stock, John (1918-1972): ord. Dec. 4, 1943; aux. bp. Philadelphia (Ukrainian Rite) (Pergamum), 1971-72.

Stritch, Samuel: See Index.

Sullivan, Bernard, S.J. (1889-1970): ord. June 26, 1921; bp. Patna, India, 1929-46 (res.).

Sweeney, James J. (1898-1968): ord. June 20, 1925; first bp. Honolulu, 1941-68.

Swint, John J. (1879-1962): ord. June 23, 1904; aux. bp. Wheeling (Sura), 1922; bp. Wheeling, 1922-62.

T

Takach, Basil (1879-1948): b. Austria-Hungary; ord. Dec. 12, 1902; first ap. ex. Pittsburgh Byzantine Rite exarchy (Zela), 1924-48.

Taylor, John E., O.M.I. (1914-1976): ord. May 25, 1940; bp. Stockholm, Sweden, 1962-76.

Thill, Francis A. (1893-1957): ord. Feb. 28, 1920; bp. Concordia (title changed to Salina in 1944), 1938-57.

Tief, Francis J. (1881-1965): ord. June 11, 1908; bp. Concordia (now Salina), 1921-38 (res.).

Tierney, Michael (1839-1908): b. Ireland; ord. May 26, 1866; bp. Hartford, 1894-1908.

Tihen, J. Henry (1861-1940): ord. Apr. 26, 1886; bp. Lincoln, 1911-17; bp. Denver, 1917-31 (res.).

Timon, John, C.M. (1797-1867): ord. Sept. 23, 1826; first bp. Buffalo, 1847-67.

Toebbe, Augustus M. (1829-1884): b. Germany; ord. Sept. 14, 1854; bp. Covington, 1870-84.

Toolen, Thomas J. (1886-1976): ord. Sept. 27, 1910; bp. (pers. tit. abp., 1954), Mobile, 1927-69 (ret.).

Treacy, John P. (1890-1964): ord. Dec. 8, 1918; coad. bp. La Crosse (Metelis), 1945-48; bp. La Crosse, 1948-64.

Trobec, James (1838-1921): b. Austria; ord. Sept. 8, 1865; bp. St. Cloud, 1897-1914 (res.).

Tuigg, John (1820-1889): b. Ireland; ord. May 14, 1850; bp. Pittsburgh, 1876-89.

Turner, William (1871-1936): b. Ireland; ord. Aug. 13, 1893; bp. Buffalo, 1919-36.

Tyler, William (1806-1849): ord. June 3, 1829; first bp. Hartford, 1844-49.

V

Van de Velde, James O., S.J. (1795-1855): b. Belgium; ord. Sept. 16, 1827; bp. Chicago, 1849-53; bp. Natchez (now Jackson), 1853-55.

Van de Ven, Cornelius (1865-1932): b. Holland; ord. May 31, 1890; bp. Natchitoches (title changed to Alexandria, 1910; now Alexandria-Shreveport), 1904-32.

Van de Vyver, Augustine (1844-1911): b. Belgium; ord. July 24, 1870; bp. Richmond, 1889-1911.

Vehr, Urban J. (1891-1973): ord. May 29, 1915; bp. 1931-41; and first abp. Denver, 1941-67 (res.).

Verdaguer, Peter (1835-1911): b. Spain; ord. Dec. 12, 1862; v. a. Brownsville (Aulon), 1890-1911.

Verot, Augustin, S.S. (1805-1876): b. France; ord. Sept. 20, 1828; v. a. Florida (Danaba), 1858-61; bp. Savannah, 1861-70; bp. St. Augustine, 1870-76.

Vertin, John (1844-1899): b. Austria; ord. Aug. 31, 1866; bp. Sault Ste. Marie and Marquette (now Marquette), 1879-99.

W

Wade, Thomas, S.M. (1893-1969): ord. June 15, 1922; v. a. Northern Solomons (Barbalissus), 1930-69.

Wadhams, Edgar (1817-1891): convert, 1846; ord. Jan. 15, 1850; first bp. Ogdensburg, 1872-91.

Walsh, Emmet (1892-1968): ord. Jan. 15, 1916; bp. Charleston, 1927-49; coad. bp. Youngstown (Rhaedestus), 1949-52; bp. Youngstown, 1952-68.

Walsh, James A., M.M. (1867-1936): ord. May 20, 1892; co-founder with Thomas F. Price of Maryknoll, first US-established foreign mission society and first sponsor of a US foreign mission seminary; superior of Maryknoll, 1911-36; tit. bp. Syene, 1933-36.

Walsh, Louis S. (1858-1924): ord. Dec. 23, 1882; bp. Portland, Me., 1906-24.

Walsh, Thomas J. (1873-1952): ord. Jan.

27, 1900; bp. Trenton, 1918-28; bp., 1928-37, and first abp., 1937-52, Newark.

Ward, John (1857-1929): ord. July 17, 1884; bp. Leavenworth (now Kansas City), 1910-29.

Waters, Vincent S. (1904-1974): ord. Dec. 8, 1931; bp. Raleigh, 1945-74.

Watterson, John A. (1844-1899): ord. Aug. 9, 1868; bp. Columbus, 1880-99.

Wehrle, Vincent, O.S.B. (1855-1941): b. Switzerland; ord. Apr. 23, 1882; first bp. Bismarck, 1910-39 (res.).

Welch, Thomas A. (1884-1959): ord. June 11, 1909; bp. Duluth, 1926-59.

Whelan, James, O.P. (1822-1878): b. Ireland; ord. Aug. 2, 1846; coad. bp. Nashville (Marcopolis), 1859-60; bp. Nashville, 1860-64 (res.).

Whelan, Richard V. (1809-1874): ord. May 1, 1831; bp. Richmond, 1841-50; bp. Wheeling, 1850-74.

White, Charles (1879-1955): ord. Sept. 24, 1910; bp. Spokane, 1927-55.

Whitfield, James (1770-1834): b. England; ord. July 24, 1809; coad. bp. Baltimore (Apollonia), 1828; abp. Baltimore, 1828-34.

Wigger, Winand (1841-1901): ord. June 10, 1865; bp. Newark, 1881-1901.

Willging, Joseph C. (1884-1959): ord. June 20, 1908; first bp. Pueblo, 1942-59.

Williams, John J. (1822-1907); ord. May 17, 1845; bp., 1866-75, and first abp., 1875-1907, Boston.

Willinger, Aloysius J., C.SS.R. (1886-1973): ord. July 2, 1911; bp. Ponce, P.R., 1929-46; coad. bp. Monterey-Fresno, 1946-53; bp. Monterey-Fresno, 1953-67 (res.).

Winkelmann, Christian H. (1883-1946): ord. June 11, 1907; aux. bp. St. Louis (Sita), 1933-39; bp. Wichita, 1939-46.

Wood, James F. (1813-1883): convert, 1836; ord. Mar. 25, 1844; coad. bp. Philadelphia (Antigonea), 1857-60; bp., 1860-75, and first abp., 1875-83, Philadelphia.

Woznicki, Stephen (1894-1968): ord. Dec. 22, 1917; aux. bp. Detroit (Peltae), 1938-50; bp. Saginaw, 1950-68.

Wright, John J. (1909-1979): ord. Dec. 8, 1935; aux. bp. Boston (Egee), 1947-50; bp. Worcester, 1950-59; bp. Pittsburgh, 1959-69; cardinal, 1969; prefect Congregation of the Clergy, 1969-79.

Y-Z

Young, Josue (1808-1866): ord. Apr. 1, 1838; bp. Erie, 1854-66.

Zaleski, Alexander, M. (1906-1975): ord. July 12, 1931; aux. bp. Detroit (Lyrbe), 1950-64; coad. bp. Lansing, 1964-65; bp. Lansing 1965-75.

Zardetti, Otto (1847-1902): b. Switzerland; ord. Aug. 21, 1870; first bp. St. Cloud, 1889-94; abp. Bucharest, Rumania, 1894-95 (res.).

YEAR OF THE CHILD

The observance of an International Year of the Child in 1979 was proposed by Father Joseph Moerman in a letter addressed to the secretary general of the United Nations in January, 1973. The proposal was adopted by the U.N. in December, 1976, and Father Moerman, secretary general of the International Catholic Child Bureau, was named chairman of the Non-Governmental Organizations' Committee for the IYC.

The purposes of the observance were to stimulate international, national and organizational efforts to enhance awareness of the special needs of children and to initiate sustained activities for their benefit.

Planned activities included the expansion of existing programs on behalf of children, seminars and conferences on child-related issues, the preparation of special audio-visual materials for the year, and the promotion of local events through affiliates of international organizations.

A U. S. committee was created in 1978 to promote participation in this country. More than a dozen Catholic groups took part, including Catholic Relief Services, the Holy Childhood Association and the National Conference of Catholic Charities.

FAMILY YEAR, CONFERENCE

The National Conference of Catholic Bishops approved in May, 1978, a pastoral action plan for family ministry involving: diocesan planning for family programs in 1979; putting into effect parish programs and the celebration of Family Year in 1980; a decade of "reflection and research" during the 1980s for the development of quality family life programs; emphasis on the social mission of the family by Catholic participation in the White House Conference on Families.

White House Conference

Plans for programs under the aegis of the White House were approved at a meeting July 19 and 20, 1979, of the National Advisory Committee. They included not a single conference at the White House but hearings in several cities from September on and major meetings in three or four cities during the summer of 1980 — all for the purpose of examining the impact of public policies on families and of formulating appropriate recommendations to be submitted to the President.

The principal officers named for the White House Conference were chairman Jim Guy Tucker, a former Congressman from Arkansas, and executive director John Carr, a staff member of the Campaign for Human Development.

Members of the advisory committee included Auxiliary Bishop Francis Stafford of Baltimore and Rashley Moten, director of Catholic Charities, Kansas City, Mo.

Religious

Religious orders and congregations, collectively called **religious institutes,** are special societies in the Church. Their members, called **religious,** commit themselves to observance of the evangelical counsels of poverty, chastity and obedience in a community kind of life in accordance with rules and constitutions approved by church authority.

Religious Institutes

The particular goal of each institute and the means of realizing it in practice are stated in the rule and constitutions proper to the institute. Local bishops, with permission of the Holy See, can give approval for rules and constitutions of **institutes of diocesan rank. Pontifical rank** belongs to institutes approved by the Holy See. General jurisdiction over all religious is exercised by the Congregation for Religious and Secular Institutes. General legislation concerning religious is contained in Canons 487 to 681 of the Code of Canon Law and in subsequent enactments, especially since the Second Vatican Council.

All religious institutes are commonly called religious orders, despite the fact that there are differences between orders and congregations. The best known **orders** include the Benedictines, Trappists, Franciscans, Dominicans, Carmelites and Augustinians, for men; and the Carmelites, Poor Clares, Dominicans of the Second Order and Visitation Nuns, for women. Members of the orders have solemn vows; their communities have papal enclosure and exemption, and are bound to perform the Liturgy of the Hours (Divine Office) in choir as a common practice. Members of the **congregations** have simple vows. The orders are older than the congregations, which did not appear until the 16th century.

Contemplative institutes are oriented to divine worship and service within the confines of their communities, by prayer, penitential practices, other spiritual activities and self-supporting work; engagement in outside active ministry is subordinate to their contemplative pursuits. Examples are the Trappists and Carthusians, the Carmelite and Poor Clare nuns. **Active institutes** are geared primarily for the ministry and many kinds of apostolic work. **Mixed institutes** combine elements of the contemplative and active ways of life. While most institutes of men and women can be classified as active, all of them have some contemplative aspects.

Historical Development

The basis of the life of religious institutes was the invitation Christ extended to men (Mt. 19:16ff.) to follow him with special dedication in a life like his own, which was that of a poor and chaste man under obedience to the Father.

In the earliest years of Christianity, some men and women dedicated themselves to the service of God in a special manner. Among them were holy women, deaconesses and virgins mentioned in the Acts of the Apostles, and confessors and ascetics like St. Clement of Rome, St. Ignatius of Antioch and St. Polycarp.

In the third and fourth centuries, there were traces of a kind of religious profession, and the root idea of the life began to produce significant results in the solitary and community hermitages of Egypt and Syria under the inspiration of men like St. Paul of Thebes, St. Anthony the Abbot and St. Pachomius.

St. Basil, "Father of Monasticism in the East," exerted a deep and still continuing influence on the development of religious life among men and women. His opposite number in the West was St. Benedict, whose rule or counsels, dating from about 530, set the pattern of monastic life for men and women which prevailed for nearly six centuries and which still endures. Before his time, St. Augustine framed guidelines for community life which are still being followed by some men and women religious.

Mendicant orders, whose members were freer than the monks for works of the active ministry, made their appearance early in the 13th century and began to change some of the established aspects of religious life. Religious women, however, continued to live in the monastic manner.

A significant change in religious life developed in the 16th century when several communities of men with simple rather than solemn vows were approved; among them were **clerics regular** like the Jesuits and Barnabites. Some of these communities are considered to be orders, although they differ in some respects from the older orders.

The Sisters of Charity, in 1633, were the first community of women with simple vows to gain church approval. Since that time, the number and variety of female communities have greatly increased. Women religious, no longer restricted to the hidden life of prayer, became engaged in many kinds of work including education, health and social service, and missionary endeavor.

Clerical communities of men — i. e., those whose membership is predominantly composed of priests — are similarly active in many types of work. Their ditinctive fields are education, home and foreign missions, retreats, special assignments and the communications media, as well as the internal life and conduct of their own communities. They also engage in the ordinary pastoral ministry which is the principal work of diocesan or secular priests. They are generally called **regular clergy** because of the rule of life (*regula* in Latin) they follow.

Non-clerical or lay institutes of men are the various brotherhoods whose non-ordained members (called **lay brothers**, or simply **brothers**) are engaged in educational and hospital work, missionary endeavors, and other special fields.

Some of the institutes of men listed below have a special kind of status because their members, while living a common life like that which is characteristic of religious, do not profess the vows of religious. Examples are the Maryknoll Fathers, the Oratorians of St. Philip Neri, the Paulists and Sulpicians. They are called **societies of the common life without vows.**

RENEWAL OF RELIGIOUS LIFE

Following are key excerpts from the *Decree on the Appropriate Renewal of Religious Life* promulgated by the Second Vatican Council.

"A life consecrated by a profession of the counsels (of poverty, chastity and obedience) is of surpassing value. Such a life has a necessary role to play in the circumstances of the present age. That this kind of life and its contemporary role may achieve greater good for the Church, this sacred Synod issues the following decrees. They concern only the general principles which must underlie an appropriate renewal of the life and rules of religious communities. These principles apply also to societies living a community life without the exercise of vows, and to secular institutes, though the special character of both groups is to be maintained. After the Council, the competent authority will be obliged to enact particular laws opportunely spelling out and applying what is legislated here" (No. 1).

"The appropriate renewal of religious life involves two simultaneous processes: (1) a continuous return to the sources of all Christian life and to the original inspiration behind a given community and (2) an adjustment of the community to the changed conditions of the times. . . .

"(a) Since the fundamental norm of the religious life is a following of Christ as proposed by the gospel, such is to be regarded by all communities as their supreme law.

"(b) It serves the best interests of the Church for communities to have their own special character and purpose. Therefore loyal recognition and safekeeping should be accorded to the spirit of founders, as also to all the particular goals and wholesome traditions which constitute the heritage of each community.

"(c) All communities should participate in the life of the Church. According to its individual character, each should make its own and foster in every possible way the enterprises and objectives of the Church in such fields as these: the scriptural, liturgical, doctrinal, pastoral, ecumenical, missionary, and social.

"(d) Communities should promote among their members a suitable awareness of contemporary human conditions and of the needs of the Church. . . .

"(e) Since the religious life is intended above all else to lead those who embrace it to an imitation of Christ and to union with God through the profession of the evangelical counsels, the fact must be honestly faced that even the most desirable changes made on behalf of contemporary needs will fail of their purpose unless a renewal of spirit gives life to them. Indeed such an interior renewal must always be accorded the leading role even in the promotion of external works" (No. 2).

"The manner of living, praying, and working should be suitably adapted to the physical and psychological conditions of today's religious and also, to the extent required by the nature of each community, to the needs of the apostolate, the requirements of a given culture, the social and economic circumstances anywhere, but especially in missionary territories."

Allowance should be made for prudent experimentation in the direction of renewal and adaptation (No. 3).

". . . The hope of renewal must be lodged in a more diligent observance of rule and of constitution rather than in a multiplication of individual laws" (No. 4).

Various Communities

"The members of each community should recall above everything else that by their profession of the evangelical counsels they have given answer to a divine call to live for God alone not only by dying to sin (cf. Rom. 6:11) but also by renouncing the world. They have handed over their entire lives to God's service in an act of special consecration which is deeply rooted in their baptismal consecration and which provides an ampler manifestation of it.

"Inasmuch as their self-dedication has been accepted by the Church, they should realize that they are committed to her service as well.

". . . The members of each community should combine contemplation with apostolic love. By the former they adhere to God in mind and heart; by the latter they strive to associate themselves with the work of redemption and to spread the Kingdom of God" (No. 5).

"Members of those communities which are totally dedicated to contemplation give themselves to God alone in solitude and silence and through constant prayer and ready penance. No matter how urgent may be the needs of the active apostolate, such communities will always have a distinguished part to play in Christ's Mystical Body. . . . Their manner of living should be revised according to the aforementioned principles and standards of appropriate renewal, though their withdrawal from the world and the practices of their contemplative life should be maintained at their holiest" (No. 7).

Communities geared for apostolic action "should skillfully harmonize their observances and practices with the needs of the apostolate to which they are dedicated," with due regard for diversity (No. 8). This norm applies to monastic institutes, which should preserve their special character; to communities which "closely join the apostolic life with choral prayer and monastic observances"; and to "the lay religious life, for both men and women" (Nos. 9 and 10).

[See Secular Institutes for a quotation from the decree on the subject.]

The Vows, Authority

"That chastity which is practiced 'on behalf of the heavenly Kingdom' (Mt. 19:12), and which religious profess, deserves to be esteemed as a surpassing gift of grace. For it liberates the human heart in a unique way (cf. 1 Cor. 7:32-35) and causes it to burn with greater love for God and all mankind. It is therefore an outstanding token of heavenly riches, and also a most suitable way for religious to spend themselves readily in God's service and in works of the apostolate. . . .

"Since the observance of total continence intimately involves the deeper inclinations of human nature, candidates should not undertake the profession of chastity nor be admitted to its profession except after a truly adequate testing period and only if they have the needed degree of psychological and emotional maturity" (No. 12).

"Poverty voluntarily embraced in imitation of Christ provides a witness which is highly esteemed, especially today. Let religious painstakingly cultivate such poverty, and give it new expressions if need be. . . .

". . . Members of a community ought to be poor in both fact and spirit, and have their treasures in heaven (cf. Mt. 6:20).

". . . Communities as such should aim at giving a kind of corporate witness to their own poverty. . . .

"To the degree that their rules and constitutions permit, religious communities can rightly possess whatever is necessary for their temporal life and their mission. Still, let them avoid every appearance of luxury, of excessive wealth, and accumulation of possessions" (No. 13).

"Through the profession of obedience, religious offer to God a total dedication of their own wills as a sacrifice of themselves; they thereby unite themselves with greater steadiness and security to the saving will of God. . . . Under the influence of the Holy Spirit, religious submit themselves to their superiors, whom faith presents as God's representatives, and through whom they are guided into the service of all their brothers in Christ. . . . In this way . . . religious assume a firmer commitment to the ministry of the Church and labor to achieve the mature measure of the fullness of Christ (cf. Eph. 4:13).

"Therefore, in a spirit of faith and of love for God's will, let religious show humble obedience to their superiors in accord with the norms of the rule and constitution. . . . Let them bring to the execution of commands and to the discharge of assignments entrusted to them the resources of their minds and wills, and their gifts of nature and grace. Lived in this manner, religious obedience will not diminish the dignity of the human person but will rather lead it to maturity in consequence of that enlarged freedom which belongs to the sons of God.

". . . Each superior should himself be docile to God's will in the exercise of his office. Let him use his authority in a spirit of service for the brethren. . . . Governing his subjects as God's own sons, and with regard for their human personality, a superior will make it easier for them to obey gladly. Therefore he must make a special point of leaving them appropriately free with respect to the sacrament of penance and direction of conscience. Let him give the kind of leadership which will encourage religious to bring an active and responsible obedience to the offices they shoulder and the activities they undertake. Therefore a superior should listen willingly to his subjects and encourage them to make a personal contribution to the welfare of the community and of the Church. Not to be weakened, however, is the superior's authority to decide what must be done and to require the doing of it.

"Let chapters and councils faithfully acquit themselves of the governing role given to them; each should express in its own way the fact that all members of the community have a share in the welfare of the whole community and a responsibility for it" (No. 14).

EQUAL RIGHTS AMENDMENT

The Equal Rights Amendment was passed by Congress and submitted to the states Mar. 22, 1972, for ratification by Mar. 22, 1979. The amendment, first proposed in 1923, states: "Equality of rights under the law shall not be denied by the United States or by any state on account of sex."

Indiana was the 35th and last state to ratify the amendment, Jan. 18, 1977. With ratification by three more states necessary for enactment, Congress voted in October, 1978, to extend the ratification period to June 30, 1982, and to turn down a proposal that would have permitted states to rescind ratification already given. Four states — Idaho, Nebraska, South Dakota and Tennessee — have voted for rescission.

RELIGIOUS INSTITUTES OF MEN IN THE UNITED STATES

(Sources: *Official Catholic Directory;* Catholic Almanac survey.)

African Missions, Society of, S.M.A.: Founded 1856, at Lyons, France, by Bishop Melchior de Marion Bressilac. General motherhouse, Rome, Italy; American provincialate, 23 Bliss Ave., Tenafly, N.J. 07670. Missionary work in West Africa, Bahama Islands and inner city parishes.

Assumptionists (Augustinians of the Assumption), AA.: Founded 1845, at Nimes, France, by Rev. Emmanuel d'Alzon; in US, 1946. General motherhouse, Rome, Italy; US province, 329 W. 108th St., New York, N.Y. 10025. Educational, parochial, ecumenical, retreat, foreign mission work.

Atonement, Franciscan Friars of the, S.A.: Founded as an Anglican Franciscan community in 1898 at Garrison, N.Y., by Rev. Paul Wattson. Community corporately received into the Catholic Church in 1909. Motherhouse, St. Paul Friary, Christian Unity Center, Garrison N.Y. 10524. Ecumenical, mission, retreat and charitable works.

Augustinians (Order of St. Augustine), O.S.A.: Established canonically in 1256 by Pope Alexander IV; in US, 1796. General motherhouse, Rome, Italy.

St. Thomas of Villanova Province (1796), Villanova, Pa. 19085.

Our Mother of Good Counsel Province (1941), Tolentine Center, 20300 Governors Hwy., Olympia Fields, Ill. 60461.

St. Augustine Province, 2060 N. Vermont Ave., Los Angeles, Calif. 90027.

Good Counsel Vice-Province, St. Augustine Priory, Richland, N.J. 08350.

Augustinian Recollects, O.A.R.: Founded 1588; in US, 1944. General motherhouse, Rome, Italy; US provincial residence, 29 Ridgeway Ave., West Orange, N.J. 07052. Missionary, parochial, education work.

Barnabites (Clerics Regular of St. Paul), C.R.S.P.: Founded 1530, in Milan, Italy, by St. Anthony M. Zaccaria. Generalate, Rome, Italy; American headquarters, 1023 Swann Rd., Youngstown, N.Y. 14174. Parochial, educational, mission work.

Basil the Great, Order of St. (Ukrainian), O.S.B.M.: General motherhouse, Rome, Italy; US province, 31-12 30th St., Long Island City, N.Y. 11106. Parochial work among Byzantine Ukrainian Rite Catholics.

Basilian Fathers (Congregation of the Priests of St. Basil), C.S.B.: Founded 1822, at Annonay, France. General motherhouse, 20 Humewood Dr., Toronto, Ont. M6C 2W2, Canada. Educational, parochial work.

Basilian Salvatorian Fathers: Founded 1684, at Saida, Lebanon, by Eftimios Saifi; in US, 1953. General motherhouse, Saida, Lebanon; American headquarters, 30 East St., Methuen, Mass. 01844. Educational, parochial work among Eastern Rite peoples.

Benedictines (Order of St. Benedict), O.S.B.: Founded 529, in Italy, by St. Benedict of Nursia; in US, 1846.

• American Cassinese Federation (1855). Rt. Rev. Martin Burne, O.S.B., pres., St. Mary's Abbey, Delbarton, Morristown, N.J. 07960. Abbeys and Priories belonging to the federation:

St. Vincent Archabbey, Latrobe, Pa. 15650; St. John's Abbey, Collegeville, Minn. 56321; St. Benedict's Abbey, Atchison, Kans. 66002; St. Mary's Abbey, Delbarton, Morristown, N.J. 07960; Newark Abbey, 528 High St., Newark, N.J. 07102; Belmont Abbey, Belmont, N.C. 28012; St. Bernard's Abbey, St. Bernard P.O., Ala. 35138; St. Procopius Abbey, 5601 College Rd., Lisle, Ill. 60532; St. Gregory Abbey, Shawnee, Okla. 74801; St. Leo Abbey, St. Leo, Fla. 33574; Assumption Abbey, Richardton, N. Dak. 58652;

St. Bede Abbey, Peru, Ill. 61354; St. Martin's Abbey, Lacey, Wash. 98503; Holy Cross Abbey, P.O. Box 351, Canon City, Colo. 81212; St. Anselm's Abbey, Manchester, N.H. 03102; St. Andrew's Abbey, 2900 East Blvd., Cleveland, O. 44104; St. Maur Monastery, 4615 N. Michigan Rd., Indianapolis, Ind. 46208; St. Mark's Monastery, South Union, Ky. 42283; Holy Trinity Priory, P.O. Box 990, Butler, Pa. 16001; Benedictine Priory, 6502 Seawright Dr., Savannah, Ga. 31406; Woodside Priory, 302 Portola Rd., Portola Valley, Calif. 94025.

• Swiss-American Federation (1870), Rt. Rev. Raphael De Salvo O.S.B., pres., New Subiaco Abbey, New Subiaco, Ark. 72865. Abbeys and priory belonging to the federation:

St. Meinrad Archabbey, St. Meinrad, Ind. 47577; Conception Abbey, Conception, Mo. 64433; St. Michael Abbey, Elkhorn, Nebr. 68022; New Subiaco Abbey, Subiaco, Ark. 72865; St. Joseph's Abbey, St. Benedict, La. 70457; Mt. Angel Abbey, St. Benedict, Ore. 97373; Marmion Abbey, Butterfield Rd., Aurora, Ill. 60504;

St. Benedict's Abbey, Benet Lake, Wis. 53102; Glastonbury Abbey, 16 Hull St., Hingham, Mass. 02043; Westminster Abbey, Mission, B.C., Canada; St. Pius X Abbey, Pevely, Mo. 63070; Blue Cloud Abbey, Marvin, S. Dak. 57251; Corpus Christi Abbey, Star Route, Box A-38-A, Sandia, Tex. 78383; St. Charles Priory, Benet Hill, Oceanside, Calif. 92054.

• English Benedictine Congregation: St. Anselm's Abbey, 4501 S. Dakota Ave. N.E., Washington, D.C. 20017; Abbey of St. Gregory, Cory's Lane, Portsmouth, R.I. 02871; Priory of St. Mary and St. Louis, 500 S. Mason Rd., St. Louis, Mo. 63141.

• Congregation of St. Ottilien for Foreign

Missions, St. Paul's Abbey, Newton, N.J. 07860; Benedictine Mission House, Schuyler, Neb. 68661.

• Congregation of the Annunciation, St. Andrew Priory, Valyermo, Calif. 93563.

• Houses not in Congregations: Mount Saviour Monastery, Pine City, N.Y. 14871; Conventual Priory of St. Gabriel the Archangel, Weston, Vt. 05161.

Benedictines, Olivetan, O.S.B.: General motherhouse, Siena, Italy. US foundation, Our Lady of Mt. Olivet Monastery, 4029 Ave. G, Lake Charles, La. 70601.

Benedictines, Sylvestrine, O.S.B.: Founded 1231, in Italy by Sylvester Gozzolini. General motherhouse, Rome, Italy; US foundations; 17320 Rosemont Rd., Detroit, Mich. 48219; 2711 E. Drahner Rd., Oxford, Mich. 48051; 1697 State Highway S-3, Clifton, N.J. 07012.

Bethlehem Missionaries, Society of, S.M.B.: Founded 1921, at Immensee, Switzerland, by Rt. Rev. Canon Peter Bondolfi. General motherhouse, Immensee, Switzerland; US headquarters, 5630 E. 17th Ave., Denver, Colo. 80220. Foreign mission work.

Blessed Sacrament, Congregation of the, S.S.S.: Founded 1856, at Paris, France, by St. Pierre Julien Eymard; in US, 1900. General motherhouse, Rome, Italy; US address, 5384 Wilson Mills Rd., Cleveland, O. 44143. Perpetual adoration and Eucharistic apostolate.

Camaldolese Congregation, Cam. O.S.B.: Founded 1012, at Camaldoli, near Arezzo, Italy, by St. Romuald; in US. 1958. General motherhouse, Arezzo, Italy; US foundation, Immaculate Heart Hermitage, Big Sur, Calif. 93920.

Camaldolese Hermits of the Congregation of Monte Corona, Er. Cam.: Founded 1520, from Camaldoli, Italy, by Bl. Paul Giustiniani. General motherhouse, Frascati (Rome), Italy; US foundation, Holy Family Hermitage, Bloomingdale, O. 43910.

Camillians (Order of St. Camillus; Clerics Regular, Ministers of the Sick), O.S.Cam.: Founded 1582, at Rome, by St. Camillus de Lellis; in US, 1923. General motherhouse, Rome, Italy; North American province, 10100 W. Blue Mound Rd., Wauwatosa, Wis. 53226.

Carmelites (Order of Our Lady of Mt. Carmel), O. Carm.: General motherhouse, Rome, Italy. Educational, charitable work.

Most Pure Heart of Mary Province (1864), 45 E. Dundee Rd., Barrington, Ill. 60010.

St. Elias Province (1931), 69-34 52nd Ave., Maspeth, N.Y. 11378.

Mt. Carmel Hermitage, Pineland, R.D. 1, Box 36, New Florence, Pa. 15944 (immediately subject to Prior General.)

Carmelites, Order of Discalced, O.C.D.: Established 1562, a Reform Order of Our Lady of Mt. Carmel; in US, 1935. General motherhouse, Rome, Italy. Parochial, foreign mission work.

St. Therese of Oklahoma Province (1935), 1125 S. Walker St., P.O. Box 26127, Oklahoma City, Okla. 73126.

Immaculate Heart of Mary Province (1947), P.O. Box 67, Hubertus, Wis. 53033.

Anglo-Irish Province, 510 N. El Molino St., Alhambra, Calif. 91801.

Polish Province of the Holy Spirit, 1628 Ridge Rd., Munster, Ind. 46321.

Carthusians, Order of, O. Cart.: Founded 1084, in France, by St. Bruno; in US, 1951. General motherhouse, St. Pierre de Chartreuse, France; US charterhouse, Arlington, Vt. 05250. Cloistered, contemplatives.

Charity, Servants of, S.C.: Founded 1908, in Italy, by Bl. Luigi Guanella. General motherhouse, Rome, Italy; U.S. headquarters, Don Guanella School, Sproul Rd., Springfield, Pa. 19064.

Christ, Society of, S.Ch.: Founded 1932, General Motherhouse, Poznan, Poland; US address, 3000 Eighteen Mile Rd., Sterling Heights, Mich. 48078.

Cistercians, Order of, S.O. Cist.: Founded 1098, by St. Robert. Headquarters, Rome, Italy.

Our Lady of Spring Bank Abbey, 34639 W. Fairview Rd., Oconomowoc, Wis. 53066.

Our Lady of Gerowval Monastery, Rose Hill, Miss. 39356.

Our Lady of Dallas Monastery, Rt. 2, Box 1, Irving, Tex. 75062.

Cistercian Monastery of Our Lady of Fatima, P.O. Box 295, Moorestown, N.J. 08057.

Cistercians of the Strict Observance, Order of (Trappists), O.C.S.O.: Founded 1098, in France, by St. Robert; in US, 1848. Generalate, Rome, Italy.

Our Lady of Gethsemani Abbey (1848), Trappist P.O., Ky. 40073.

Our Lady of New Melleray Abbey (1849), Dubuque, Iowa 52001.

St. Joseph's Abbey (1825), Spencer, Mass. 01562.

Holy Spirit Monastery (1944), Conyers, Ga. 30207.

Our Lady of Guadalupe Abbey (1947), Lafayette, Ore. 97127.

Our Lady of the Holy Trinity Abbey (1947), Huntsville, Utah 84317.

Abbey of the Genesee (1951), Piffard, N.Y. 14533.

Our Lady of Mepkin Abbey (1949), Moncks Corner, S. Car. 29461.

Our Lady of the Holy Cross Abbey (1950), Berryville, Va. 22611.

Our Lady of the Assumption Abbey, Rt. 5, Ava, Mo. 65608.

Our Lady of New Clairvaux Abbey (1955), Vina, Calif. 96092.

St. Benedict's Monastery (1956), Snowmass, Colo. 81654.

Claretians (Missionary Sons of the Immaculate Heart of Mary), C.M.F.: Founded 1849, at Vich, Spain, by St. Anthony Mary Claret.

General motherhouse, Rome, Italy. Mission, parochial, educational work.

Western Province, 1119 Westchester Pl., Los Angeles, Calif. 90019.

Eastern Province, 400 N. Euclid Ave. Oak Park, Ill. 60302.

Clerics Regular Minor (Adorno Fathers) C.R.M.: Founded 1589, at Naples, Italy, by Ven. Augustine Adorno and St. Francis Caracciolo. General motherhouse, Rome, Italy; US address, 575 Darlington Ave., Ramsey, N.J. 07446.

Columban, Society of St. (St. Columban Foreign Mission Society): Founded 1918. General motherhouse, Dublin, Ireland. US headquarters, St. Columbans, Nebr. 68056. Foreign mission work.

Consolata Society for Foreign Missions, I.M.C.: Founded 1901, at Turin, Italy, by Father Joseph Allamano. General motherhouse, Rome, Italy; US headquarters, P.O. Box C, Lincoln Hwy., Somerset, N.J. 08873.

Crosier Fathers (Canons Regular of the Order of the Holy Cross), O.S.C.: Founded 1210, in Belgium by Bl. Theodore De Celles. Generalate, Amersfoort, Netherlands; US province, 711 Lincoln Ave., St. Paul, Minn. 55105. Mission, retreat, educational work.

Cross, Priests of the Congregation of Holy, C.S.C.: Founded 1837, in France; in US, 1841. Generalate, Rome, Italy. Educational and pastoral work; home missions and retreats; foreign missions; social services and apostolate of the press.

Indiana Province (1841), 1304 E. Jefferson Blvd., South Bend, Ind. 46617.

Eastern Province (1952), 835 Clinton Ave., Bridgeport, Conn. 06604.

Southern Province (1968), 812 Audubon St., New Orleans, La. 70118.

Divine Word, Society of the, S.V.D.: Founded 1875, in Holland, by Bl. Arnold Janssen; in US, 1897. General motherhouse, Rome, Italy.

Northern Province of the Blessed Virgin (1964), Techny, Ill. 60082.

Sacred Heart Province (Eastern Province) (1940), 1025 Michigan Ave. N.E., Washington, D.C. 20017.

St. Augustine's Province (Southern Province) (1940), 201 Ruella Ave., Bay St. Louis, Miss. 39520.

St. Therese Province (Western Province) (1964), 2181 W. 25th St., Los Angeles, Calif. 90018.

Dominicans (Order of Friars Preachers), O.P.: Founded early 13th century, in France by St. Dominic. General headquarters, Rome, Italy. Preaching, literary, scientific pursuits.

St. Joseph Province (1806), 141 E. 65th St., New York, N.Y. 10021.

Holy Name of Jesus Province (1912), 5877 Birch Ct., Oakland, Calif. 94609.

St. Dominic Province (1873), 5353 Notre Dame de Grace Ave., Montreal, Que. H4A 1L2, Canada.

St. Albert the Great Province (1939), 1909 S. Ashland Ave., Chicago, Ill. 60608.

Spanish Province, US foundation (1926), P.O. Box 277, San Diego, Tex. 78384.

Edmund, Society of St., S.S.E.: Founded 1843, in France, by Fr. Jean Baptiste Muard. General motherhouse, Edmundite Generalate, Fairholt, S. Prospect St., Burlington, Vt. 05401. Educational, missionary work.

Eudists (Congregation of Jesus and Mary), C.J.M.: Founded 1643, in France, by St. John Eudes. General motherhouse, Rome, Italy; Canadian province, 6125 Première Ave., Charlesbourg, Quebec G1H 2V9, Canada. Educational, missionary work.

Francis, Third Order Regular of St., T.O.R.: Founded 1221, in Italy; in US, 1910. General motherhouse, Rome, Italy. Educational, parochial, missionary work.

Most Sacred Heart of Jesus Province (1910), 601 Pitcairn Pl., Pittsburgh, Pa. 15232.

Immaculate Conception Province, 2006 Edgewater Parkway, Silver Springs, Md. 20903.

Commissariat of the Spanish Province (1924), 301 Jefferson Ave., Waco, Tex. 76702.

Francis de Sales, Oblates of St., O.S.F.S.: Founded 1871, by Fr. Louis Brisson. General motherhouse, Rome, Italy. Educational work.

Wilmington-Philadelphia Province (1906), 2200 Kentmere Parkway, Box 1452, Wilmington, Del. 19899.

Toledo-Detroit Province (1966), Box 4683, Toledo, Ohio 43611.

Franciscans (Order of Friars Minor), O.F.M.: Founded 1209 in Italy, by St. Francis of Assisi; in US, 1844. General motherhouse, Rome, Italy. Preaching, missionary, educational, parochial, charitable work.

St. John the Baptist Province (1844), 1615 Vine St., Cincinnati, Ohio 45210.

Sacred Heart Province (1858), 3140 Meramec St., St. Louis, Mo. 63118.

Assumption of the Blessed Virgin Mary Province (1887), Pulaski, Wis. 54162.

Most Holy Name of Jesus Province (1901), 135 W. 31st St., New York, N.Y. 10001.

St. Barbara Province (1915), 1500 34th Ave., Oakland, Calif. 94601.

Immaculate Conception Province, 147 Thompson St., New York, N.Y. 10012.

Holy Cross Custody (1912), 1400 Main St., P.O. Box 608, Lemont, Ill. 60439.

Most Holy Savior Custody, 232 S. Home Ave., Pittsburgh, Pa. 15202.

St. John Capistran Custody (1928), 1290 Hornberger Ave., Roebling, N.J. 08554.

St. Stephen Transylvanian Commissariat (1948), 517 S. Belle Vista Ave., Youngstown, Ohio 44509.

Holy Family Croatian Custody, (1927),

4848 S. Ellis Ave., Chicago, Ill. 60615.

St. Casimir Lithuanian Vicariate, Kennebunkport, Me. 04046.

Holy Gospel Province (Mexico), US foundation, 2400 Marr St., El Paso, Tex. 79903.

Saints Francis and James Province (Jalisco, Mexico), US foundation, 504 E. Santa Clara St., Hebbronville, Tex. 78361.

Eastern District, Commissariat of the Holy Land, Mt. St. Sepulchre, 14th and Quincy Sts. N.E., Washington, D.C. 20017.

St. Mary of the Angels Custody, Byzantine Slavonic Rite, P.O. Box 270, Sybertsville, Pa. 18251.

Academy of American Franciscan History, P.O. Box 34440, Washington, D.C. 20034.

Franciscans (Order of Friars Minor Capuchin), O.F.M. Cap.: Established in 1528 as a separate jurisdiction of the order founded in 1209 by St. Francis of Assisi. General motherhouse, Rome, Italy. Missionary, parochial work, chaplaincies.

St. Joseph Province (1857), 1740 Mt. Elliott Ave., Detroit, Mich. 48207.

St. Augustine Province (1873), 220 37th St., Pittsburgh, Pa. 15201.

St. Mary Province (1952), 30 Gedney Park Dr., White Plains, N.Y. 10605.

Province of the Stigmata (1918), St. Francis Friary, Newton, N.J. 07860.

California Vice-Province (St. Patrick's Province of Ireland), 1721 Hillside Dr., Burlingame, Calif. 94010.

Sts. Adalbert and Stanislaus Province (Warsaw, Poland), Manor Dr., Oak Ridge, N.J. 07438.

Province of Mid-America (1977), St. Conrad Friary, 2 E. 75th St., Kansas City, Mo. 64114.

Texas Capuchin Fraternity (Province of Navarre, Spain), 5605 Bernal Dr., Dallas, Tex. 75212.

Franciscans (Order of Friars Minor Conventual), O.F.M. Conv.: Established in 1517 as a separate jurisdiction of the order founded in 1209 by St. Francis of Assisi; first US foundation, 1852. General curia, Rome, Italy. Missionary, educational, parochial work.

Immaculate Conception Province (1852), P.O. Box 830, Union City, N.J. 07087.

St. Anthony of Padua Province (1903), 1300 Dundalk Ave., Baltimore, Md. 21222.

St. Bonaventure Province (1939), 6107 Kenmore Ave., Chicago, Ill.

Our Lady of Consolation Province (1926), Mt. St. Francis, Ind. 47146.

Our Lady of Guadalupe Custody (vice-province), P.O. Drawer F, Hobbs, N. Mex. 88240.

St. Joseph Cupertino Custody (1978), 4532 Torrance Blvd., Torrance, Calif. 90503.

Glenmary Missioners (The Home Missioners of America): Founded 1939, in US. General headquarters, Fairfield, Ohio; mailing address, P.O. Box 46404, Cincinnati, Ohio 45246. Home mission work.

Holy Family, Congregation of the Missionaries of the, M.S.F.: Founded 1895, in Holland, by Rev. John P. Berthier. General motherhouse, Rome, Italy; US headquarters, 10415 Midland Blvd., St. Louis, Mo. 63114. Belated vocations for the missions.

Holy Family, Sons of the, S.F.: Founded 1864, at Barcelona, Spain, by Joseph Manyanet; in US, 1920. General motherhouse, Barcelona, Spain; US address, 401 Randolph Rd., Silver Spring, Md. 20904.

Holy Ghost Fathers, C.S.Sp.: Founded 1703, in Paris, by Claude Francois Poullart des Places; in US, 1872. General motherhouse, Rome, Italy. Missions, education.

Eastern Province (1872), 852 College Ave., Pittsburgh, Pa. 15232.

Western Province (1964), 919 Briarcliff, San Antonio, Tex. 78213.

Holy Ghost Fathers of Ireland (1971), U.S. delegate (East), 48-49 37th St., Long Island City, N.Y. 11101.

Holy Ghost, Missionaries of the, M.Sp.S.: Founded 1914, at Mexico City, Mexico, by Felix Rougier. General motherhouse, Mexico City; US headquarters, 4433 Santa Fe Ave., Vernon, Calif. 90058. Missionary work.

Immaculate Heart of Mary Mission Society (Missionhurst), C.I.C.M.: Founded 1862, at Scheut, Brussels, Belgium, by Very Rev. Theophile Verbist. General motherhouse, Rome, Italy; US province, 4651 N. 25th St., Arlington, Va. 22207. Home and foreign mission work.

Jesuits (Society of Jesus), S.J.: Founded 1534, in France, by St. Ignatius Loyola; in US, 1833. Generalate, Rome, Italy. Missionary, educational, literary work.

Maryland Province (1833), 5704 Roland Ave., Baltimore, Md. 21210.

New York Province (1943), 501 E. Fordham Rd., Bronx, N.Y. 10458.

Missouri Province (1863), 4511 W. Pine Blvd., St. Louis, Mo. 63108.

New Orleans Province (1907), 6301 Stratford Pl., P.O. Box 6378, New Orleans, La. 70174.

California Province (1909), College at Prospect Aves., P.O. Box 519, Los Gatos, Calif. 95030.

New England Province (1926), 393 Commonwealth Ave., Boston, Mass. 02115.

Chicago Province, 509 N. Oak Park Ave., Oak Park, Ill. 60302.

Oregon Province (1932), 2222 N.W. Hoyt, Portland, Ore. 97210.

Detroit Province (1955), 7303 W. Seven Mile Rd., Detroit, Mich. 48221.

Wisconsin Province (1955), 2120 W. Clybourn St., Suite 200, Milwaukee, Wis. 53233.

Joseph, Congregation of St., C.S.J.: General motherhouse, Rome, Italy; US vice province, 4076 Case Rd., Avon, Ohio 44011. Parochial, missionary, educational work.

Joseph, Oblates of St., O.S.J.: Founded 1878, in Italy, by Bishop Joseph Marello. General motherhouse, Rome, Italy. Parochial, educational work.

Eastern Province, R.D. No. 2, Pittston, Pa. 18640.

Western Province, P.O. Box 82, Tomales, Calif. 94971.

Josephite Fathers, C.J.: General motherhouse, Ghent, Belgium; US foundation, 989 Brookside Ave., Santa Maria, Calif. 93454.

Josephite Fathers (St. Joseph's Society of the Sacred Heart), S.S.J.: Founded 1866, in England, by Cardinal Vaughan; in US, 1871. General motherhouse, 1130 N. Calvert St., Baltimore, Md. 21202. Work in Negro missions.

LaSalette, Missionaries of Our Lady of, M.S.: Founded 1852, by Msgr. de Bruillard; in US, 1892. Motherhouse, Rome, Italy.

Our Lady of Seven Dolors Province (1933), P.O. Box 6127, Hartford, Conn. 06106.

Immaculate Heart of Mary Province (1945), P.O. Box 538, Attleboro, Mass. 02703.

Mary Queen Province (1958), 4650 S. Broadway, St. Louis, Mo. 63111.

Mary Queen of Peace Vice Province (1967), P.O. Box 95, Georgetown, Ill. 61846.

Legionaries of Christ (Missionaries of the Sacred Heart of Jesus and the Sorrowful Virgin), L.C.: Founded 1941, in Mexico, by Rev. Marcial Maciel. General motherhouse, Rome, Italy; US novitiate, 393 Derby Ave., Orange, Conn. 06477.

Marian Fathers, M.I.C.: Founded 1673; US foundation, 1913. General motherhouse, Rome, Italy. Educational, parochial, mission, publication work.

St. Casimir Province (1930), 6336 S. Kilbourn Ave., Chicago, Ill. 60629.

St. Stanislaus Kostka Province (1948), Eden Hill, Stockbridge, Mass. 01262.

Marianists (Society of Mary; Brothers of Mary), S.M.: Founded 1817, at Bordeaux, France, by Rev William-Joseph Chaminade; in US, 1849. General motherhouse, Rome, Italy. Educational work.

Cincinnati Province (1849), 4435 E. Patterson Rd., Dayton, Ohio 45430.

St. Louis Province (1908), 4538 Maryland Ave., St. Louis, Mo. 63156.

Pacific Province (1948), Cupertino, Calif. 95014.

New York Province (1961), 4301 Roland Ave., Baltimore, Md. 21210.

Mariannhill, Congregation of the Missionaries of, C.M.M.: Trappist monastery, begun in 1882 by Abbot Francis Pfanner in Natal, South Africa, became an independent modern congregation in 1909; in US, 1920. Generalate, Rome, Italy; US-Canadian headquarters, 23715 Ann Arbor Trail, Dearborn Heights, Mich. 48127. Foreign mission work.

Marist Fathers (Society of Mary), S.M.: Founded 1816, at Lyons, France, by Jean Claude Colin; in US, 1863. General motherhouse, Rome, Italy. Educational, foreign mission, pastoral work.

Washington Province (1924), 4408 8th St. N.E., Washington D.C. 20017.

Northeastern Province (1924), 72 Beacon St., Chestnut Hill, Mass. 02167.

San Francisco Western Province (1961), 625 Pine St., San Francisco, Calif. 94108.

Mary Immaculate, Oblates of, O.M.I.: Founded 1816, in France, by Bl. Charles Joseph Eugene de Mazenod; in US, 1849. General motherhouse, Rome, Italy. Educational, mission work.

Southern US Province (1904), 7711 Madonna Rd., San Antonio, Tex. 78216.

Our Lady of Hope, Eastern Province (1883), 350 Jamaicaway, Boston, Mass. 02130.

St. John the Baptist Province (1921), 45 Kenwood Ave., Worcester, Mass. 01605.

Central Province (1924), 104 N. Mississippi River Blvd., St. Paul, Minn. 55104.

Western Province (1953), 290 Lenox Ave., Oakland, Calif. 94610.

Italian Province, US foundation, St. Nicholas Church, 442 Brinkerhoff Ave., Palisades Park, N.J. 07650.

Maryknoll Fathers (Catholic Foreign Mission Society of America), M.M.: Founded 1911, in US, by Frs. Thomas F. Price and James A. Walsh. General Center, Maryknoll, N.Y. 10545.

Mekhitarist Order of Vienna, C.M.Vd.: Established 1773. General headquarters, Vienna, Austria; US addresses, Our Lady Queen of Martyrs Church, 1327 Pleasant Ave., Los Angeles, Calif. 90033 and Holy Cross Church, 100 Mt. Auburn St., Cambridge, Mass. 02138. Work among Armenians in US.

Mercedarians (Order of Our Lady of Mercy), O.D.M.: Founded 1218, in Spain, by St. Peter Nolasco. General motherhouse, Rome, Italy; US headquarters, 8692 Lake St., LeRoy, N.Y. 14482.

Mercy, Congregation of Priests of (Fathers of Mercy), C.P.M.: Founded 1808, in France, by Rev. Jean Baptiste Rauzan; in US, 1839. General motherhouse, Cold Spring, N.Y. 10516. Mission work.

Mill Hill Missionaries (St. Joseph's Society for Foreign Missions), M.H.M.: Founded 1866, in England, by Cardinal Vaughan; in US, 1951. General motherhouse, London, England; American headquarters, Albany, N.Y. 12203.

Missionaries of St. Charles, Congregation of the, C.S.: Founded 1887, at Piacenza, Italy, by Bishop John Baptist Scalabrini. General motherhouse, Rome, Italy.

St. Charles Borromeo Province (1888), 27 Carmine St., New York, N.Y. 10014.

St. John Baptist Province (1903), 546 N. East Ave., Oak Park, Ill. 60302.

Missionaries of the Holy Apostles, M.Ss.A.: Founded 1962, Washington, D.C., by Eusebe M. Menard. North American headquarters, Box 695, Moorefield, W. Va. 26836.

Monks of the Brotherhood of St. Francis (Monks of New Skete, Byzantine Rite): Founded 1966, in US. New Skete Monastery, Cambridge, N.Y. 12816.

Montfort Fathers (Missionaries of the Company of Mary), S.M.M.: Founded 1715, by St. Louis Marie Grignon de Montfort; in US, 1948. General motherhouse, Rome, Italy; US headquarters, 101-18 104th St., Ozone Park, N.Y. 11416. Mission work.

Oratorian Fathers (Congregation of the Oratory of St. Philip Neri), C.O.: Founded 1575, at Rome, by St. Philip Neri. Central administration, Rome, Italy; a confederation of autonomous houses. US addresses: P.O. Box 11586, Rock Hill, S.C. 29730; P.O. Box 1688, Monterey, Calif. 93940; 4040 Bigelow Blvd., Pittsburgh, Pa. 15213; P.O. Box 211, Yarnell, Ariz. 85362; P.O. Drawer II, Pharr, Tex. 78577.

Pallottines (Society of the Catholic Apostolate), S.A.C.: Founded 1835, at Rome, by St. Vincent Pallotti. General motherhouse, Rome, Italy. Charitable, educational, parochial, mission work.

Immaculate Conception Province (1952), P.O. Box 573, Pennsauken, N.J. 08810.

Mother of God Province (1946), 5424 W. Blue Mound Rd., Milwaukee, Wis. 53208.

Irish Province, US address: 3352 4th St., Wyandotte, Mich. 48192.

Mercy of God Region, 303 Goundry St., North Tonawanda, N.Y. 14120.

Queen of Apostles Province (1909), 448 E. 116th St., New York, N.Y. 10029.

Christ the King Province, 3452 Niagara Falls, Blvd., No. Tonawanda, NY 14120.

Paraclete, Servants of the, s.P.: Founded 1947, Santa Fe, N.M., archdiocese. General motherhouse, Rome, Italy; US motherhouse, Jemez Springs, N.M. 87025. Devoted to care of priests.

Paris Foreign Missions Society, M.E.P.: Founded 1662, at Paris, France. Headquarters, Paris, France; US establishment, 930 Ashbury St., San Francisco, Calif. 94117. Mission work and training of native clergy.

Passionists (Congregation of the Passion), C.P.: Founded 1720, in Italy, by St. Paul of the Cross. General motherhouse, Rome, Italy.

St. Paul of the Cross Province (1852), 1901 West St., Union City, N.J. 07087.

Holy Cross Province (Western Province), 5700 N. Harlem Ave., Chicago, Ill. 60631.

Patrick's Missionary Society, S.P.S.: Founded 1932, at Wicklow, Ireland, by Msgr. Patrick Whitney; in US, 1953. International headquarters, Kiltegan Co., Wicklow, Ireland. US foundations: 70 Edgewater Rd., Cliffside Park, N.J. 07010; 19536 Eric Dr., Saratoga, Calif. 95070; 1347 W. Granville Ave., Chicago, Ill. 60660.

Pauline Fathers (Order of St. Paul the First Hermit), O.S.P.: Founded 1215; established in US, 1955. General motherhouse, Czestochowa, Jasna Gora, Poland; US headquarters, P.O. Box 151, Doylestown, Pa. 18901.

Pauline Fathers (Society of St. Paul for the Apostolate of Communications), S.S.P.: Founded 1914, by Very Rev. James Alberione; in US, 1932. Motherhouse, Rome, Italy; American province, 6745 Lake Shore Rd., Derby, N.Y. 14047.

Paulists (Missionary Society of St. Paul the Apostle), C.S.P.: Founded 1858, in New York, by Fr. Isaac Thomas Hecker. General offices, 86 Dromore Rd., Scarsdale, N.Y. 10583. Missionary, ecumenical, pastoral work.

Piarists (Order of the Pious Schools), Sch.P.: Founded 1617, at Rome, Italy, by St. Joseph Calasanctius. General motherhouse, Rome, Italy. American headquarters, 1339 Monroe St. N.E., Washington, D.C. 20017. Educational work.

Pontifical Institute for Foreign Missions, P.I.M.E.: Founded 1850, in Italy, at request of Pope Pius IX. General motherhouse, Rome, Italy; US headquarters, 17330 Quincy Ave., Detroit, Mich. 48221. Foreign mission work.

Precious Blood, Society of, C.Pp.S.: Founded 1815, in Italy, by St. Gaspar del Bufalo. General motherhouse, Rome, Italy.

Cincinnati Province, 431 E. Second St., Dayton, O. 45402.

Kansas City Province, Ruth Ewing Rd., Liberty, Mo. 64068.

Pacific Province, 24 Ursuline Rd., Santa Rosa, Calif. 95401.

Atlantic Vicariate, 65 Highland Ave., Rochester, N.Y. 14620.

Premonstratensians (Order of the Canons Regular of Premontre; Norbertines), O. Praem.: Founded 1120, at Premontre, France, by St. Norbert. Generalate, Rome, Italy. Educational, parish work.

St. Norbert Abbey, 1016 N. Broadway, DePere, Wis. 54115.

Daylesford Abbey, 220 S. Valley Rd., Paoli, Pa. 19301.

St. Michael's Priory, 1042 Star Route, Orange, Calif. 92667.

Providence, Sons of Divine, F.D.P.: Founded 1893, at Tortona, Italy, by Don Aloysius Orione; in US, 1933. General motherhouse, Tortona, Italy; US address, 111 Orient Ave., E. Boston, Mass. 02128.

Redemptorists (Congregation of the Most Holy Redeemer), C.SS.R.: Founded 1732, in Italy, by St. Alphonsus Mary Liguori. General motherhouse, Rome, Italy. Mission work.

Men Religious

Baltimore Province (1850), 7509 Shore Rd., Brooklyn, N.Y. 11209.

St. Louis Province (1875), Box 6, Glenview, Ill. 60025.

Oakland Province (1952), 3696 Clay St., San Francisco, Calif. 94118.

New Orleans Vice-Province, 1527 3rd St., New Orleans, La., 70130.

Resurrectionists (Priests of the Congregation of the Resurrection), C.R.: Founded 1836, in France, under direction of Bogdan Janski. Motherhouse, Rome, Italy;

Chicago Province, 2250 N. Latrobe Ave., Chicago, Ill. 60639.

Ontario Kentucky Province, Resurrection College, Westmont Rd., N., Waterlo, Ont. N2L 3G7, Canada.

Rosminians (Institute of Charity), I.C.: Founded 1828, in Italy, by Antonio Rosmini-Serbati. General motherhouse, Rome, Italy; US address, 2327 W. Heading Ave., Peoria, Ill. 61604. Charitable work.

Sacerdotal Fraternity, Congregation of the, C.F.S.: Founded 1901, at Paris, France; US foundation, 1959. General house, 500 Ave. Claremont, Montreal (Westmount), Que. H3Y 2N5 Canada. Care of priests.

Sacred Heart, Missionaries of the, M.S.C.: Founded 1854, by Rev. Jules Chevelier. General motherhouse, Rome, Italy; US province, 305 S. Lake St., P.O. Box 270, Aurora, Ill. 60507.

Sacred Heart of Jesus, Congregation of the (Sacred Heart Priests and Brothers), S.C.J.: Founded 1877, in France. General motherhouse, Rome, Italy; US headquarters, Sacred Heart Monastery, Hales Corners, Wis. 53130. Educational, preaching, mission work.

Sacred Hearts, Fathers of the (Picpus Fathers), SS.CC.: Founded 1805, in France, by Fr. Coudrin. General motherhouse, Rome, Italy. Mission, educational work.

Eastern Province (1946), 3 Adams St. (Box 111), Fairhaven, Mass. 02719.

Western Province (1970), 32418 Stage Rd., Hemet, Calif. 92343.

Hawaiian Province, Box 797, Kaneohe, Oahu, Hawaii 96744.

Sacred Hearts of Jesus and Mary, Missionaries of the, M.SS.CC.: Founded at Naples, Italy, by Ven. Gaetano Errico. General motherhouse, Rome, Italy; US headquarters, 2249 Shore Rd., Linwood, N.J. 08221.

Salesians of St. John Bosco (Society of St. Francis de Sales), S.D.B.: Founded 1859, by St. John (Don) Bosco. General motherhouse, Rome, Italy.

St. Philip the Apostle Province (1902), 148 Main St., New Rochelle, N.Y. 10802.

San Francisco Province (1926), 1100 Franklin St., San Francisco, Calif. 94109.

Salvatorians (Society of the Divine Savior), S.D.S.: Founded 1881, in Rome, by Fr. Francis Jordan; in US, 1896. General motherhouse, Rome, Italy; US province, 1735 Hi-Mount Blvd., Milwaukee, Wis. 53208. Educational, parochial, mission work; campus ministries, chaplaincies.

Scalabrinians: See Missionary Fathers of St. Charles, Congregation of the.

Servites (Order of Friar Servants of Mary), O.S.M.: Founded 1237, at Florence, Italy, by Seven Holy Founders. Generalate, Rome, Italy. General apostolic ministry.

Eastern Province (1967) 3401 S. Home Ave., Berwyn, Ill. 60402.

Western Province (1967), 5210 Somerset St., Buena Park, Calif. 90621.

Somascan Fathers, C.R.S.: Founded 1534, at Somasca, Italy, by St. Jerome Emilian. General motherhouse, Rome, Italy; US addresses: 628 Hanover St., Manchester, N.H. 03104; Pine Haven Boys Center, River Rd., Allenstown, P.O. Suncook, N.H. 03275.

Sons of Mary Missionary Society (Sons of Mary, Health of the Sick), F.M.S.I.: Founded 1952, in the Boston archdiocese, by Rev. Edward F. Garesche, S.J. Headquarters, 567 Salem End Rd., Framingham, Mass. 01701. Dedicated to health of the sick; medical, pastoral and social work in home and foreign missions.

Stigmatine Fathers and Brothers (Congregation of the Sacred Stigmata), C.S.S.: Founded 1816, by Bl. Gaspare Bertoni. General motherhouse, Rome, Italy; US headquarters, 36 Fairmont Ave., Newton, Mass. 02158. Parish work.

Sulpicians (Society of Priests of St. Sulpice), S.S.: Founded 1641, at Paris, by Rev. Jean Jacques Olier. General motherhouse, Paris, France; US province, 5408 Roland Ave., Baltimore, Md. 21210. Education of seminarians and priests.

Theatines (Congregation of Clerics Regular): C.R.: Founded 1524, at Rome, by St. Cajetan. General motherhouse, Rome, Italy; US headquarters, 1050 S. Birch St., Denver, Colo. 80222.

Trappists: See Cistercians of the Strict Observance.

Trinitarians (Order of the Most Holy Trinity), O.SS.T.: Founded 1198, by St. John of Matha. General motherhouse, Rome, Italy; US headquarters, Park Heights Ave., Box 5719, Baltimore, Md. 21208.

Trinity, Missionary Servants of the Most Holy, S.T.: Founded 1929, by Fr. Thomas Augustine Judge. Generalate, 503 Rock Creek Church Rd. N.W., Washington, D.C. 20010. Home mission work.

Verona Fathers (Sons of the Sacred Heart of Jesus), F.S.C.J.: Founded 1885, in Italy. General motherhouse, Rome, Italy; US headquarters, 8108 Beechmont Ave., Cincinnati, Ohio 45230. Mission work.

Viatorian Fathers (Clerics of St. Viator), C.S.V.: Founded 1831, in France, by Fr. Louis Joseph Querbes. General motherhouse,

Rome, Italy: US headquarters, 1212 E. Euclid St., Arlington Hts., Ill. 60004. Educational work.

Vincentians (Congregation of the Mission; Lazarists), C.M.: Founded 1625, in Paris, by St. Vincent de Paul; in US, 1867. General motherhouse, Rome, Italy. Educational work.

Eastern Province (1867), 500 E. Chelten Ave., Philadelphia, Pa. 19144.

Midwestern Province (1888), 1849 Cass Ave., St. Louis, Mo. 63106.

New England Province (1975), 1109 Prospect Ave., W. Hartford, Conn. 06105.

American Italian Branch, Our Lady of Pompei Church, 3600 Claremont St., Baltimore, Md. 21224.

American Spanish Branch (Barcelona, Spain), St. Peter's Rectory, 118 Congress St., Brooklyn, N.Y. 11201.

American Spanish Branch (Zaragoza, Spain), Holy Agony Church, 1834 3rd Ave., New York, N.Y. 10029.

Western Province (1975), 649 W. Adams Blvd., Los Angeles, Calif. 90007.

Southern Province (1975), 1302 Kipling St., Houston, Tex. 77006.

Vocationist Fathers (Society of Divine Vocations), S.D.V.: Founded 1920, in Italy; in US, 1962. General motherhouse, Naples, Italy; US address, 170 Broad St., Newark, N.J. 07104.

White Fathers, W.F.: Founded 1868, at Algiers, by Cardinal C.M.A. Lavigerie. General motherhouse, Rome, Italy; US headquarters, 777 Belvidere Ave., Plainfield, N.J. 07062. Missionary work in Africa.

Xaverian Missionary Fathers, S.X.: Founded 1895, by Archbishop Conforti, at Parma, Italy. General motherhouse, Rome, Italy; U.S. province, 12 Helene Ct., Wayne, N.J. 07470. Foreign mission work.

INSTITUTES OF BROTHERS

Alexian Brothers, C.F.A.: Founded 14th century in western Germany and Belgium during the Black Plague. Motherhouse, Aachen, Germany; generalate, Signal Mountain, Tenn. 37377. Hospital and general health work.

Carmelite Brothers of the Holy Eucharist, C.F.S.E.: Founded 1975 at Fort Wayne, Ind. Motherhouse, 2264 Marshall Ave., Elm Grove, Wheeling, W. Va. 26003.

Charity, Brothers of, F.C.: Founded 1807, in Belgium, by Canon Peter J. Triest. General motherhouse, Rome, Italy: American District, 1008 N. 70th Ave., Philadelphia, Pa. 19126. Charitable, educational work.

Christian Brothers, Congregation of, C.F.C. (formerly Christian Brothers of Ireland): Founded 1802 at Waterford, Ireland, by Edmund Ignatius Rice. General motherhouse, Rome, Italy. Educational work.

American Province, Eastern US (1916), 21 Pryor Terr., New Rochelle, N.Y. 10801. 354.

American Province, Western US (1966), P.O. Box 85R, Romeoville, Ill. 60441.

Christian Instruction, Brothers of (La Mennais Brothers), F.I.C.: Founded 1817, at Ploermel, France, by Abbe Jean Marie de la Mennais and Abbe Gabriel Deshayes. General motherhouse, Rome, Italy; American province, Notre Dame Institute, Alfred, Me. 04002.

Christian Schools, Brothers of the (Christian Brothers), F.S.C.: Founded 1680, at Reims, France, by St. Jean Baptiste de la Salle. General motherhouse, Rome, Italy; US Conference, 100 De La Salle Dr., P.O. Box 356, Romeoville, Ill. 60441. Educational, charitable work.

Baltimore Province (1845), Box 85, Adamstown, Md. 21710.

Central Province (1966), 200 De La Salle Dr., Romeoville, Ill. 60441.

New York Province (1848), 330 Riverside Dr., New York, N.Y. 10025.

Long Island-New England Province (1957), Christian Brothers Center, 635 Ocean Ave., Narragansett, R.I. 02882.

St. Louis Province (1849), 1886 Rue de la Salle, Glencoe, Mo. 63038.

San Francisco Province (1868), P.O. Box A-D, Saint Mary's College, Moraga, Calif. 94575.

New Orleans-Santa Fe (1921), De La Salle, Lafayette, La. 70501.

Winona Province (1963), 807 Summit Ave., St. Paul, Minn. 55105.

Cross, Congregation of Holy, C.S.C.: Founded 1837, in France, by Rev. Basil Moreau; US province, 1841. Generalate, Rome, Italy. Educational work.

Midwest Province (1841), Box 460, Notre Dame, Ind. 46556.

Southwest Province (1956), St. Edward's University, Austin, Tex. 78704.

Eastern Province (1956), 84 Overlook Circle, New Rochelle, N.Y. 10804.

Francis, Brothers of Poor of St., C.F.P.: Founded 1857. Motherhouse, Aachen, Germany; US province, Mt. Alverno, Fayetteville, Ohio. 45118. Educational work, especially with poor and emotionally disturbed youth.

Francis Xavier, Brothers of St. (Xaverian Brothers), C.F.X.: Founded 1839, in Belgium, by Theodore J. Ryken. Generalate, Rome, Italy. Educational work.

Sacred Heart Province, 10516 Summit Ave., Kensington, Md. 20795.

St. Joseph Province, 704 Brush Hill Rd., Milton, Mass. 02186.

Franciscan Brothers of Brooklyn, O.S.F.: Founded in Ireland; established at Brooklyn, 1858. Generalate, 135 Remsen St., Brooklyn, N.Y. 11201. Educational work.

Franciscan Brothers of Christ the King, O.S.F.: Founded 1961. General motherhouse, 1310 W. Pleasant St., Davenport, Ia. 52804.

Franciscan Brothers of the Good News, O.S.F.: Founded 1970 in Archdiocese of New York. Central friary, Mount Road, Cummington, Mass. 01026. Combine volunteer works of mercy with contemplative life of prayer in hermitages.

Franciscan Brothers of the Holy Cross, F.F.S.C.: Founded 1862, in Germany. Generalate, Hausen, Linz Rhein, West Germany; US region, R.R. 1, Springfield, Ill. 62707. Educational work.

Franciscan Missionary Brothers of the Sacred Heart of Jesus, O.S.F.: Founded 1927, in the St. Louis, Mo., archdiocese. Motherhouse, R.R. 3, Box 39, Eureka, Mo. 63025. Care of aged, infirm, homeless men and boys.

Good Shepherd, Society of Brothers of the, B.G.S.: Founded 1951, by Bro. Mathias Barrett. Motherhouse, P.O. Box 389, Albuquerque, N.M. 87102. Operate shelters and refuges for aged and homeless; homes for handicapped men and boys, alcoholic rehabilitation center.

Guadalupe, Brothers of Our Lady of: Founded 1974 in Gallup, N. Mex., by Bishop Jerome Hastrich. Motherhouse, 500 S. Woodrow Dr., Gallup, N. Mex. Team ministry apostolate.

Holy Eucharist, Brothers of the, F.S.E.: Founded in US, 1957. Generalate, P.O. Box 25, Plaucheville, La. 71362. Teaching, social, clerical, nursing work.

Immaculate Heart of Mary, Brothers of the, F.I.C.M.: Founded 1948, at Steubenville, Ohio, by Bishop John K. Mussio. Motherhouse, 609 N. 7th St., Steubenville, Ohio 43952. Educational, charitable work.

Immaculate Heart of Mary, Brothers of Charity: Founded 1957, in US. Motherhouse, 2737 Pleasant St., Riverside, Calif. 92507.

John of God, Brothers of the Hospitaller Order of St., O.H.: Founded 1537, in Spain. General motherhouse, Rome, Italy; US headquarters, 2035 W. Adams Blvd., Los Angeles, Calif. 90018. Nursing work and related fields.

Little Brothers of Jesus: Generalate, Rome, Italy; U.S. foundation, 2833 Cochrane, Detroit, Mich. 48216.

Little Brothers of St. Francis, Fraternity of Peace and Love, O.S.F.: Founded 1970 in Archdiocese of Boston. Address: 789 Parker St., Roxbury, Mass. 02120. Combine contemplative life with street ministry apostolate.

Marist Brothers, F.M.S.: Founded 1817, in France, by Bl. Marcellin Champagnat. General motherhouse, Rome, Italy; US address, 1241 Kennedy Blvd., Bayonne, N.J. 07002. Educational, social, catechetical work.

Mercy, Brothers of, F.M.M.: Founded 1856, in Germany. General motherhouse, Montabaur, Germany. American headquarters, 4520 Ransom Rd., Clarence, N.Y. 14031. Hospital work.

Mercy, Brothers of Our Lady of, C.F.M.M.: Founded 1844, in The Netherlands by Abp. J. Zwijsen. Generalate, Tilburg, The Netherlands; US region, 2336 South "C" St., Oxnard, Calif. 93030.

Patrician Brothers (Brothers of St. Patrick), F.S.P.: Founded 1808, in Ireland, by Bishop Daniel Delaney; US novitiate, 7820 Bolsa Ave., Midway City, Calif. 92655. Educational work.

Pius X, Brothers of St.: Founded 1952, at La Crosse, Wis., by Bishop John P. Treacy. Motherhouse, Box 438, DeSoto, Wis. 54624. Education, health fields, agriculture, religious education, social work.

Presentation Brothers, F.P.M.: Founded 1802, at Waterford, Ireland, by Edmund Ignatius Rice. General motherhouse, Cork, Ireland. U.S. foundation (Canadian Province), 368 S. Ellsworth, Marshall, Mo. 65340.

Rosary, Brothers of the Holy, F.S.R.: Founded 1956, in US. Address, 101 Boynton Lane, Reno, Nev. 89502.

Sacred Heart, Brothers of the, S.C.: Founded 1821, in France, by Rev. Andre Coindre. General motherhouse, Rome, Italy, Educational work.

New Orleans Province (1847), P.O. Box 89, Bay St. Louis, Miss. 39520.

New England Province (1945), Pascoag, R.I. 02859.

New York Province (1960), R.D. 1, Box 215, Belvidere, N.J. 07823.

ORGANIZATIONS OF MEN

Conference of Major Superiors of Men: A consultative body for discussion of the affairs of men religious in this country, and a liaison body for establishing and maintaining contact among religious institutes and with the Holy See, bishops, diocesan clergy, and Catholic and civic associations. The conference, which was formed in 1956, was officially established Mar. 23, 1960, by decree of the Congregation for Religious and Secular Institutes.

The general objective of the conference is to promote the spiritual and apostolic welfare of religious priests and brothers in the U.S.

Conference membership consists of 255 major superiors of institutes with a combined total of approximately 40,000 members.

The Rev. Alan McCoy, O.F.M., is president of the conference. The executive secretary is Brother Thomas More Page, C.F.X.

The national secretariat is located at 1302 Eighteenth St. N.W., Suite 601, Washington, D.C. 20036.

National Assembly of Religious Brothers: Founded in 1972 as a grassroots organization open to members of all-brother institutes as well as mixed institutes of priests and brothers. It is a service organization for its members and those affected by their apostolates.

The primary objectives of the NARB are: to publicize the unique vocations of brothers, to encourage the development of the spiritual life of all brothers; to promote increased awareness among brothers of their ministerial power for good; to provide a corporate voice for brothers in shaping the future of religious life; to heighten their concern with and involvement in the needs of the Church and society; and to further communication among brothers and provide liaison with various organizations of the Church.

Membership in the assembly is open to brothers in the U.S. and Canada.

The address is 9001 New Hampshire Ave., Silver Spring, Md. 20910.

MEMBERSHIP OF RELIGIOUS INSTITUTES OF MEN

Below are world membership statistics from *Annuario Pontificio* of institutes of men of pontifical right with 500 or more members; the number of priests is in parentheses. Also listed are institutes with less than 500 members with houses in the United States.

Most of the institutes reported decreases in membership between 1977 and 1978.

Jesuits (20,132)	27,726
Franciscans (Friars Minor) (14,792)	21,326
Salesians (11,060)	17,306
Franciscans (Capuchins) (8,814)	12,312
Brothers of Christian Schools	11,093
Benedictines (6,492)	10,147
Dominicans (5,673)	7,397
Marist Brothers	7,225
Redemptorists (5,053)	6,821
Oblates of Mary Immaculate (4,785)	6,173
Society of the Divine Word (3,195)	5,274
Vincentians (3,713)	4,186
Franciscans (Conventuals) (2,733)	4,007
Holy Spirit, Congregation (3,192)	3,927
Augustinians (2,763)	3,603
Discalced Carmelites (2,401)	3,367
White Fathers (2,731)	3,161
Passionists (2,416)	3,159
Trappists (1,526)	3,050
Christian Brothers	3,005
Claretians (1,947)	2,884
Priests of the Sacred Heart (1,933)	2,699
Missionaries of the Sacred Heart of Jesus (1,926)	2,593
Marianists (622)	2,209
Holy Cross, Congregation (968)	2,150
Pallottines (1,439)	2,125
Carmelites (Ancient Observance) (1,603)	2,123
Brothers of the Sacred Heart (36)	2,051
Marists (1,569)	1,970
Hospitallers of St. John of God (110)	1,814
Piarists (1,381)	1,768
Picpus Fathers (1,371)	1,661
Verona Fathers (1,124)	1,639
Brothers of Christian Instruction	1,609
Congregation of the Immaculate Heart of Mary (1,347)	1,591
Cistercians (Common Observance) (887)	1,442
Brothers of Christian Instruction of St. Gabriel (22)	1,434
Montfort Fathers (1,084)	1,427
Society of African Missions (1,265)	1,409
Assumptionists (1,125)	1,340
Servants of Mary (976)	1,288
Augustinians (Recollects) (1,030)	1,280
Premonstratensians (1,030)	1,280
Viatorians (470)	1,252
Salvatorians (844)	1,228
Carmelties of BVM (803)	1,213
Blessed Sacrament Fathers (846)	1,212
Pious Society of St. Paul (548)	1,192
Consolata Fathers (863)	1,051
Missionaries of Holy Family (769)	1,045
Little Workers of Divine Providence (748)	1,040
Ministers of Sick (Camillians) (677)	1,018
Mill Hill Missionaries (921)	995
Brothers of Charity	989
Columbans (892)	976
Oblates of St. Francis de Sales (720)	956
Maryknollers (770)	931
LaSalette Missionaries (673)	927
Franciscans (Third Order Regular) (598)	861
Xaverian Missionaries (634)	843
Canons Regular of St. Augustine (730)	842
Mercedarians (579)	818
Missionaries of the Most Precious Blood (607)	771
Congregation of St. Joseph (549)	752
Legionaries of Christ (113)	726
Brothers of the Immaculate Conception (4)	712
Pontifical Institute for Foreign Missions (610)	675
Scalabrinians (606)	667
Paris Foreign Mission Society (645)	647
Brothers of Our Lady of Mercy	634
Crosier Fathers (448)	599
Trinitarians (395)	569
Sulpicians (567)	567
Eudists (469)	557
Mariannhill Missionaries (302)	529
Servants of Charity (382)	511
Barnabites (414)	511
Brothers of Our Lady of Lourdes	505
Xaverian Brothers	504
Congr. of St. Basil (Canada) (428)	495
Oratorians (356)	469
Stigmatine Fathers (360)	447
St. Patrick's Mission Society (391)	440
Rosminians (315)	408
Carthusians (239)	397
Somascan Fathers (279)	395
Missionaries of the Holy Spirit (199)	377
Society of Christ (222)	374
Bethlehem Missionaries (270)	345
Oblates of St. Joseph (253)	339
Marian Fathers (226)	334
Paulists (240)	288
Little Brothers of Jesus (76)	266

Brothers of St. Patrick	246
Order of St. Paul the First Hermit (122)	226
Josephite Fathers (S.S.J.) (190)	219
Atonement Friars (137)	218
Missionary Servants of the Most Holy Trinity (149)	218
Presentation Brothers	212
Alexian Brothers	210
Vocationist Fathers (180)	209
Theatines (105)	158
Josephites (C.J.) (126)	150
Sons of Holy Family (122)	144
Bros. of Poor of St. Francis	137
Brothers of Mercy	131
Priests of St. Edmund (93)	122
Basilian Salvatorian Fathers (84)	121
Glenmary Missioners (74)	117
Congr. of Sacerdotal Fraternity (53)	94
Franciscan Bros. of Holy Cross (3)	81
Camaldolese (26)	73
Servants of Holy Paraclete (38)	46
Mekhitarist Order of Vienna (23)	23

RELIGIOUS INSTITUTES OF WOMEN IN THE UNITED STATES

(Sources: *Official Catholic Directory*; Catholic Almanac survey.)

Africa, Missionary Sisters of Our Lady of (White Sisters), S.A.: Founded 1869, at Algiers, Algeria, by Cardinal Lavigerie; in US, 1929. General motherhouse, Frascati, Italy; US headquarters, 5335 16th St., N.W., Washington, D.C. 20011. Medical, educational, catechetical and social work in Africa.

Agnes, Sisters of St., C.S.A.: Founded 1858, in US, by Caspar Rehrl. General motherhouse, 475 Gillett St., Fond du Lac, Wis. 54935. Educational, hospital, social work.

Ann, Sisters of St., S.S.A.: Founded 1834, in Italy; in US, 1952. General motherhouse, Rome, Italy; US headquarters, Mount St. Ann, Ebensburg, Pa. 15931.

Anne, Sisters of St., S.S.A.: Founded 1850, at Vaudreuil, Que., Canada; in US, 1866. General motherhouse, Lachine, Que., Canada; US address, 720 Boston Post Rd., Marlboro, Mass. 01752. Educational, social work.

Anthony, Missionary Servants of St., M.SS.A.: Founded 1929, in US, by Rev. Peter Baque. General motherhouse, 100 Peter Baque Rd., San Antonio, Tex. 78209. Social work.

Apostolate, Sisters Auxiliaries of the, A.A.: Founded 1903, in Canada; in US, 1911. General motherhouse, 689 Maple Terr., Monongah, W. Va. 26554. Educational, social work.

Assumption, Little Sisters of the, L.S.A.: Founded 1865, in France; in US, 1891. General motherhouse, Paris, France; US motherhouse, 1195 Lexington Ave., New York, N.Y. 10028. Social work.

Assumption, Religious of the, R.A.: Founded 1839, in France; in US, 1919. General motherhouse, Paris, France; US province, 227 N. Bowman Ave., Merion, Pa. 19066. Educational work.

Assumption of the Blessed Virgin, Sisters of the, S.A.S.V.: Founded 1853, in Canada; in US, 1891. General motherhouse, Nicolet, Que., Canada; American province, North Main St., Petersham, Mass. 01366. Educational, mission, social work.

Basil the Great, Sisters of the Order of St. (Pittsburgh Byzantine Rite), O.S.B.M.: Founded fourth century, by St. Basil the Great. Motherhouse, Mount St. Macrina, West National Pike, Uniontown, Pa. 15401. Educational, social work.

Basil the Great, Sisters of the Order of St. (Ukrainian Byzantine Rite), O.S.B.M.: Founded fourth century, in Cappadocia, by St. Basil the Great; in US, 1911. Generalate, Rome, Italy; US motherhouse, 710 Fox Chase Rd., Philadelphia, Pa. 19111. Educational, social work.

Benedictine Nuns of the Primitive Observance, O.S.B.: Founded c. 529, in Italy; in US, 1948. US motherhouse, Regina Laudis Monastery, Bethlehem, Conn. 06751. Cloistered.

Benedictine Sisters, O.S.B.: Founded c. 529, in Italy; in US, 1852. General motherhouse, Eichstatt, Bavaria, Germany. US addresses: St. Vincent's Archabbey, Latrobe, Pa. 15650; St. Emma's Retreat House and Convent, 1001 Harvey St., Greensburg, Pa. 15601; St. Walburga Convent, Boulder, Colo. 80302.

Benedictine Sisters (Bedford, N.H.), O.S.B.: Founded in US, 1957. Regina Pacis, 75 Wallace Rd., Bedford, N.H. 03102.

Benedictine Sisters, Missionary, O.S.B.: Founded 1885. Generalate, Rome, Italy; US motherhouse, 300 N. 18th St., Norfolk, Nebr. 68701.

Benedictine Sisters, Olivetan, O.S.B.: Founded 1887, in US. General motherhouse, Holy Angels Convent, Jonesboro, Ark. 72401. Educational, hospital work.

Benedictine Sisters of Perpetual Adoration of Pontifical Jurisdiction, Congregation of the, O.S.B.: Founded 529, in Italy; in US, 1874. General motherhouse, 8300 Morganford Rd., St. Louis, Mo. 63123.

Benedictine Sisters of Pontifical Jurisdiction, O.S.B.: Founded c. 529, in Italy. No general motherhouse in US. Three federations.

• Federation of St. Scholastica (1922). Pres., Sister Johnette Putnam, O.S.B., St. Scholastica Academy, Box 1210, Covington, La. 70433. Motherhouses belonging to the federation:

Mt. St. Scholastica, Atchison, Kans. 66002; Benedictine Sisters of Elk Co., St. Joseph's Convent, St. Mary's, Pa. 15857; Mt. St. Benedict Motherhouse, 6101 E. Lake Rd., Erie, Pa. 16511; Benedictine Sisters of Chicago, St. Scholastica Priory, 7430 Ridge Blvd.,

Chicago, Ill. 60645; Benedictine Convent of the Sacred Heart, 1910 Maple Ave., Lisle, Ill. 60532; Our Lady of Sorrows Convent, 5900 W. 147th St., Oak Forest, Ill. 60452; St. Walburga Convent, 851 N. Broad St., Elizabeth, N.J. 07208; Benedictine Sisters, Mt. St. Mary Priory, 4530 Perrysville Ave., Pittsburgh, Pa. 15229;

Red Plains Priory, P.O. Box 60165, Oklahoma City, Okla. 73146; St. Joseph's Convent, 2200 S. Lewis, Tulsa, Okla. 74114; St. Gertrude's Motherhouse, Ridgely P.O., Md. 21660; St. Walburga Convent, Villa Madonna, 2500 Amsterdam Rd., Covington, Ky. 41016; Sacred Heart Convent, Cullman, Ala. 35055; St. Scholastica Priory, Stafford Rd., Covington, La. 70433; Holy Family Convent, Benet Lake, Wis. 53102; St. Benedict's Convent, Bristow, Va. 22013; St. Scholastica Convent, P.O. Box 700, Boerne, Tex. 78006; St. Lucy's Priory, Glendora, Calif. 91740; Holy Name Priory, St. Leo, Fla. 33574.

• Federation of St. Gertrude the Great (1937). Sacred Heart Convent, Yankton, S.D. 57078. Motherhouses belonging to the federation:

Mother of God Priory, Watertown, S. Dak. 57201; Sacred Heart Convent, Yankton, S. Dak. 57078; Mt. St. Benedict Convent, Crookston, Minn. 56716; Sacred Heart Priory, Richardton, N. Dak. 58652; St. Martin's Priory of the Black Hills, R.R. 4, Box 253, Rapid City, S. Dak. 57701; Convent of the Immaculate Conception, Ferdinand, Ind. 47532; Priory of St. Gertrude, Cottonwood, Ida. 83522;

St. Benedict Priory, Fox Bluff Box 5070, Madison, Wis. 53705; Queen of Angels Priory, Mt. Angel, Ore. 97362; St. Scholastica's Convent, Albert Pike and Rogers Ave., Fort Smith, Ark. 72913; Our Lady of Peace Convent, 1511 Wilson, Columbia, Mo. 65201; Queen of Peace Priory, 701 Rolla, Belcourt, N. Dak. 58316. Convent of Our Lady of Grace, Beech Grove, Ind. 46107; Holy Spirit Convent, 9725 Pigeon Pass Rd., Sunnymead, Calif. 92388.

• Federation of St. Benedict (1947). Pres., Sister Enid Smith, O.S.B., St. Benedict's Convent, St. Joseph, Minn. 56374. Motherhouses belonging to the federation:

St. Benedict's Convent, St. Joseph, Minn. 56374; St. Scholastica Priory, Kenwood Ave., Duluth, Minn. 55811; St. Bede's Priory, Priory Rd., Eau Claire, Wis. 54701; St. Mary Priory, Nauvoo, Ill. 62354; Annunciation, Priory, Apple Creek Rd., Bismarck, N. Dak. 58501; St. Paul's Priory, 2675 Larpenteur Ave. E., St. Paul, Minn. 55109; St. Placid Priory, 4600 Martin Way, Olympia, Wash. 98506.

Bethany, Congregation of Oblates of, C.O.B.: Founded 1902 in France; in US, 1959. Motherhouse, Canada; US address: Regina Cleri Home, 4538 Lindell Blvd., St. Louis, Mo. 63108.

Bethany, Sisters of, C.V.D.: Founded 1928, in El Salvador; in US 1949. General motherhouse, Santa Tecla, El Salvador. US address: 850 N. Hobart Blvd., Los Angeles, Calif. 90029.

Bethlemita Sisters, Daughters of the Sacred Heart of Jesus, S.C.I.F.: Founded 1861, in Guatemala. Motherhouse, Bogota, Colombia; US address, St. Joseph Residence, 330 W. Pembroke St., Dallas, Tex. 75208.

Blessed Virgin Mary, Institute of the (Loreto Sisters), I.B.V.M.: Founded 17th century in Belgium; in US, 1954. General motherhouse, Dublin, Ireland; US addresses, 6351 N. 27th Ave., Phoenix, Ariz. 85017; 810 Patrick Lane, Prescott, Ariz. 86301; 202 S. Kendrick, Flagstaff, Ariz. 86001.

Blessed Virgin Mary, Institute of the (Sisters of Loretto), I.B.V.M.: Founded 1609, in Belgium; in US, 1880. US address, Box 508, Wheaton, Ill. 60187. Educational work.

Bon Secours, Sisters of, C.B.S.: Founded 1824, in France; in US, 1881. General motherhouse, Rome, Italy; US motherhouse, Marriottsville Rd., Marriottsville, Md. 21104. Hospital work.

Bridgettine Sisters (Order of the Most Holy Savior), O.SS.S.: Founded 1344, at Vadstena, Sweden, by St. Bridget; in US, 1957. General motherhouse, Rome, Italy; US address, Vikingsborg, Darien, Conn. 06820.

Brigid, Congregation of St., C.S.B.: Founded 1807, in Ireland; in US, 1953. US regional house, 5118 Loma Linda Dr., San Antonio, Tex. 78201.

Carmel, Congregation of Our Lady of Mount, O. Carm.: Founded 1825, in France; in US, 1833. General motherhouse, P.O. Box 476, Lacombe, La. 70445. Educational work.

Carmel, Institute of Our Lady of Mount, O. Carm.: Founded 1854, in Italy; in US, 1947. General motherhouse, Rome, Italy; US headquarters, 5 Wheatland St., Peabody, Mass. 01960. Domestic work.

Carmel Community, C.C.: Founded 1975, Columbus, O. Address, 2065 Barton Pl., Columbus, O. 43209. Contemplative.

Carmelite Missionaries of St. Theresa, C.M.S.T.: Founded 1903, in Mexico. General motherhouse, Mexico City, Mexico; US foundation, 9600 Deertrail Rd., Houston, Tex. 77003.

Carmelite Sisters (Corpus Christi), O. Carm.: Founded 1908, in England; in US, 1920. General motherhouse, Tunapuna, Trinidad, W.I. US addresses: St. Teresa Convent, 130 Highland Ave., Middletown, N.Y. 10904; Mt. Carmel Home, 21 Battery St., Newport, R.I. 02840. Home and foreign mission work.

Carmelite Sisters for the Aged and Infirm, O. Carm.: Founded 1929, at New York, by Cardinal Patrick Hayes, Motherhouse, Avila-on-Hudson, Germantown, N.Y. 12526. Social work.

Carmelite Sisters of Charity, C.a.Ch.: Founded 1826 at Vich, Spain, by St. Joaquina de Vedruna. General motherhouse, Rome, Italy; US address, 19950 Anita Ave., Castro Valley, Calif. 94546.

Carmelite Sisters of St. Therese of the Infant Jesus, C.S.T.: Founded 1917, in US. General motherhouse, 1300 Classen Dr., Oklahoma City, Okla. 73103. Educational, social work.

Carmelite Sisters of the Divine Heart of Jesus, D.C.J.: Founded 1891, in Germany; in US, 1912. General motherhouse, Sittard, Holland. US provincial houses: 1230 Kavanaugh Pl., Milwaukee, Wis. 52313 (Northern Province); 10341 Manchester Rd., St. Louis, Mo. 63122 (Central Province); 4130 Alameda St., Corpus Christi, Tex. 78416 (South Western Province). Educational, social, mission work.

Carmelite Sisters of the Sacred Heart, O.C.D.: Founded 1904, in Mexico. General motherhouse, Guadalajara, Mexico; US address, 920 E. Alhambra Rd., Alhambra, Calif. 91801. Educational, hospital work, day nurseries.

Carmelites, Calced (Carmelite Nuns of the Ancient Observance), O. Carm.: Founded 1452, in The Netherlands; in US, 1930, from Naples, Italy, convent. US Monasteries: Carmel of Mary, Wahpeton, N.D. 58075; Carmel of the Sacred Heart, 430 Laurel Ave., Hudson, Wis. 54016. Cloistered.

Carmelites, Discalced, O.C.D.: Founded 1562, Spain. First foundation in US in 1790, at Charles County, Md.; this monastery was moved to Baltimore. Monasteries in US are listed below, according to states.

Alabama: 716 Dauphin Island Pkwy., Mobile 36606. Arkansas: 7201 W. 32nd St., Little Rock 72204. California: 215 E. Alhambra Rd., Alhambra 91801; 27601 Highway 1, Carmel 93923; 68 Rincon Rd., Kensington 94707; 3361 E. Ocean Blvd., Long Beach 90803; 2150 Stockton Blvd., Sacramento 95817; 5158 Hawley Blvd., San Diego 92116; 721 Parker Ave., San Francisco 94118; 530 Blackstone Dr., San Rafael 94903; 1000 Lincoln St., Santa Clara 95050.

Colorado: 6138 S. Gallup St., Littleton 80120. Georgia: Coffee Bluff, 11 W. Back St., Savannah 31406; Illinois: River Rd. and Central, Des Plaines 60016. Indiana: 2500 Cold Springs Rd., Indianapolis 46222; 63 Allendale Pl., Terre Haute 47802. Iowa: R.R. 1, Eldridge 52748; 2901 S. St. Cecilia St., Sioux City 51106. Kansas: 3535 Wood Ave., Kansas City, 66102. Kentucky: 1740 Newburg Rd., Louisville 40205. Louisiana: Carmel Ave., Lafayette 70507; 5212 St. Bernard Ave., New Orleans 70122.

Maryland: 1318 Dulaney Valley Rd., Towson, Baltimore 21204. Massachusetts: 61 Mt. Pleasant Ave., Roxbury, Boston 02119; 15 Mt. Carmel Rd., Danvers 01923; Sol-E-Mar Rd., S. Dartmouth 02748. Michigan: 16630 Wyoming Ave., Detroit 48221; 1036 Valley Ave. N.W., Grand Rapids 49504; U.S. 2 Highway, P.O. Box 397, Iron Mountain 49801; 3501 Silver Lake Rd., Traverse City 49684. Minnesota: 8251 De Montreville Trail N., Lake Elmo 55042. Mississippi: 2155 Terry Rd., Jackson 39204.

Missouri: 2201 W. Main St., Jefferson City 65101; 9150 Clayton Rd., Ladue, St. Louis Co. 63124; 424 E. Republic Rd., Springfield 65807. Nevada: 1950 La Fond Dr., Reno 89509. New Hampshire: 275 Pleasant St., Concord, 03301. New Jersey: P.O. Box 785, Flemington 08822; 189 Madison Ave., Morristown 07960. New Mexico: Mt. Carmel Rd., Santa Fe 87501. New York: 745 St. John's Pl., Brooklyn 11216; 1381 University Ave., Bronx, 10452; 75 Carmel Rd., Buffalo 14214; 1931 W. Jefferson Rd., Pittsford 14534; 68 Franklin Ave., Saranac Lake 12983; 428 Duane Ave., Schenectady 12304.

Ohio: 3176 Fairmount Blvd., Cleveland Heights 44118. Oklahoma: 4200 N. Meridian Ave., Oklahoma City 73112. Oregon: 87609 Green Hill Rd., Eugene 97402. Pennsylvania: Thornbrow, Elysburg 17824; 510 E. Gore Rd., Erie 16509; R.D. 6, Box 28, Center Dr., Latrobe 15650; R.D. 1, Box 75-G, Loretto 15940; 66th Ave. and Old York Rd. (Oak Lane), Philadelphia 19126. Rhode Island: Watson Ave. at Nayatt Rd., Barrington 02806.

Texas: P.O. Box 210, Dallas 75211; 1600 Sunset Terr., Ft. Worth 76102; 1100 Parthenon Pl., Roman Forest, New Caney 77357. 1104 Kentucky Ave., San Antonio 78201. Utah: 5714 Holladay Blvd., Salt Lake City 84121. Vermont: Beckley Hill, Barre, 05641. Washington: 2215 N.E. 147th St., Seattle 98155. Wisconsin: W267 N2517 Meadowbrook Rd., Pewaukee 53072.

Casimir, Sisters of St., S.S.C.: Founded 1907, in US. General motherhouse, 2601 W. Marquette Rd., Chicago, Ill. 60629. Educational, hospital, social work.

Cenacle, Congregation of Our Lady of the Retreat in the, R.C.: Founded 1826, in France; in US, 1892. General motherhouse, Rome, Italy. US provinces: 154-27 Horace Harding Expressway, Flushing, N.Y. 11367; 284 Foster St., Brighton, Mass. 02135; 513 Fullerton Pkwy., Chicago, Ill. 60614.

Charity, Daughters of Divine, F.D.C.: Founded 1868, at Chanty, Austria; in US, 1913. General motherhouse, Rome, Italy. US provinces: 56 Meadowbrook Rd., White Plains, N.Y. 10605; 39 N. Portage Path, Akron, O. 44303; 1315 N. Woodward Ave., Bloomfield Hills, Mich. 48013. Educational, hospital work.

Charity, Religious Sisters of, R.S.C.: Founded 1815, in Ireland; in US, 1953. Motherhouse, Dublin, Ireland; US headquarters, Marycrest Manor, 10664 St. James Dr., Culver City, Calif. 90230.

Charity, Little Missionary Sisters of, P.M.C.: Founded 1915, in Italy; in US, 1949. General motherhouse, Rome, Italy; US headquarters, 201 Washington St., S. Groveland, Mass. 01834.

Charity, Missionaries of, M.C.: Founded 1950, in Calcutta, India, by Mother Teresa. General motherhouse, 54A Acharya Jagadish C. Bose Road, Calcutta 16, India. U.S. address, 335 E. 145th St., Bronx, N.Y. 10451. Service of the poor.

Charity, Sisters of (of Seton Hill), S.C.: Founded 1870, at Altoona, Pa., from Cincinnati foundation. Generalate, Mt. Thor Rd., Greensburg, Pa. 15601. Educational, hospital, social work.

Charity, Sisters of (Grey Nuns of Montreal), S.G.M.: Founded 1738, in Canada by Bl. Marie Marguerite d'Youville; in US, 1855. General motherhouse, Pierrefonds, Roxboro 910, Que., Canada; US motherhouse, 10 Pelham Rd., Lexington, Mass. 02173.

Charity, Sisters of (of Leavenworth), S.C.L.: Founded 1858, in US. General motherhouse, Leavenworth, Kans. 66048.

Charity, Sisters of (of Nazareth), S.C.N.: Founded 1812, in US. General motherhouse, Nazareth P. O., Nelson Co., Ky. 40048.

Charity, Sisters of (of St. Augustine), C.S.A.: Founded 1851, at Cleveland, O. General motherhouse, 5232 Broadview Rd., Richfield, O. 44286.

Charity, Sisters of Christian, S.C.C.: Founded 1849, in Germany; in US, 1873. General motherhouse, Rome, Italy. US provinces: Mallinckrodt Convent, Mendham, N.J. 07945; Maria Immaculata Convent, Ridge Rd. at Walnut, Wilmette, Ill. 60091, Educational, other work.

Charity, Vincentian Sisters of, V.S.C.: Founded 1835, in Austria; in US, 1902. General motherhouse, 8200 McKnight Rd., Pittsburgh, Pa. 15237.

Charity, Vincentian Sisters of, V.S.C.: Founded 1928, at Bedford, O. General motherhouse, 1160 Broadway, Bedford, O. 44146.

Charity of Cincinnati, Ohio, Sisters of, S.C.: Founded 1809. General motherhouse, Mt. St. Joseph, Ohio 45051. Educational, hospital, social work.

Charity of Ottawa, Sisters of (Grey Nuns of the Cross), S.C.O.: Founded 1845, at Ottawa, Canada; in US, 1857. General motherhouse, Ottawa, Canada; US provincial house, 975 Varnum Ave., Lowell, Mass. 01854. Educational, hospital work, extended health care.

Charity of Our Lady, Mother of Mercy, Sisters of, S.C.M.M.: Founded 1832, in Holland; in US, 1874. General motherhouse, Rome, Italy; US provincialate, 80 Taylor Ave., East Haven Conn. 06512.

Charity of Our Lady of Mercy, Sisters of, O.L.M.: Founded 1829, in US. General motherhouse, Charleston, S.C. 29412. Educational, hospital work.

Charity of Quebec, Sisters of (Grey Nuns), S.C.Q.: Founded 1849, at Quebec; in US, 1890. General motherhouse, 265 rue de Le Pelletier, Beauport, Quebec GIC 3X7, Canada. Social work.

Charity of St. Elizabeth, Sisters of (Convent, N.J.), S.C.: Founded 1859, at Newark, N. J. Generalate, Convent, N. J. 07961. Educational, hospital work.

Charity of St. Hyacinthe, Sisters of (Grey Nuns), S.C.S.H.: Founded 1840, at St. Hyacinthe, Canada; in US, 1878. General motherhouse, 665 Avenue Bourdages, SUD, St. Hyacinthe, Quebec J27 4J8, Canada. Regional house, 98 Campus Ave., Lewiston Me. 04240.

Charity of St. Joan Antida, Sisters of, S.C.S.J.A.: Founded 1799, in France; in US, 1932. General motherhouse, Rome, Italy; US motherhouse, 8560 N. 76th Pl., Milwaukee, Wis. 53223.

Charity of St. Louis, Sisters of, S.C.S.L.: Founded 1803, in France; in US, 1910. General motherhouse, Rome, Italy; US provincial house, 422 Robin Ct., Cheshire, Conn. 06410.

Charity of St. Vincent de Paul, Daughters of, D.C.: Founded 1633, in France; in US 1809, at Emmitsburg, Md., by St. Elizabeth Ann Seton. General motherhouse, Paris, France. US provinces: Emmitsburg, Md. 21727; 7800 Natural Bridge Rd., Normandy, St. Louis, Mo. 63121; 9400 New Harmony Rd., Evansville, Ind. 47712; 96 Menands Rd., Albany, N.Y. 12204; 26000 Altamont Rd., Los Altos, Calif. 94022.

Charity of St. Vincent de Paul, Sisters of, Halifax, S.C.H.: Founded 1856, at Halifax, N. S., from Emmitsburg, Md., foundation. Generalate, Mt. St. Vincent, Halifax, N. S. Canada. U.S. addresses: Boston Province, 50 Aspen Ave., Auburndale, Mass. 02166; New York Province, 410 Grant Ave., Brooklyn. N.Y. 11208. Educational, hospital, social work.

Charity of St. Vincent de Paul, Sisters of, New York, S.C.: Founded 1817, from Emmitsburg, Md. General motherhouse, Mt. St. Vincent on Hudson, New York, N.Y. 10471. Educational, hospital work.

Charity of St. Vincent de Paul, Sisters of, S.V.Z.: Founded 1845, in Croatia; in U.S., 1955. General motherhouse, Zagreb, Yugoslavia; U.S. foundation, 171 Knox Ave., West Seneca, N.Y. 14224.

Charity of the Blessed Virgin Mary, Sisters of, B.V.M.: Founded 1833, in US. General motherhouse, Mt. Carmel, Dubuque, Ia. 52001. Educational work.

Charity of the Immaculate Conception of Ivrea, Sisters of, S.C.I.C.: General motherhouse, Rome, Italy; US address, Immaculate

Virgin of Miracles Convent, R.D. 2, Mt. Pleasant, Pa. 15666.

Charity of the Incarnate Word, Congregation of the Sisters of, C.C.V.I.: Founded 1869, at San Antonio, Tex., by Bishop C. M. Dubuis. General motherhouse, 4515 Broadway, San Antonio, Tex. 78209.

Charity of the Incarnate Word, Congregation of the Sisters of (Houston, Tex.), C.C.V.I.: Founded 1866, in US, by Bishop C. M. Dubuis. General motherhouse, 6510 Lawndale Ave., Houston, Tex. 77023. Educational, hospital, social work.

Charity of the Sacred Heart, Daughters of, F.C.S.C.J.: Founded 1823, at La Salle de Vihiers, France; in US, 1905. General motherhouse, La Salle de Vihiers, France; U.S. address, Sacred Heart Province, Littleton, N.H. 03561.

Charles Borromeo, Missionary Sisters of St. (Scalabrini Srs.): Founded 1895, in Italy; in US, 1941. American novitiate, 1414 N. 37th Ave., Melrose Park, Ill. 60601.

Child Jesus, Sisters of the Poor, P.C.J.: Founded 1844, at Aix-la-Chapelle, Germany; in US, 1924. General motherhouse, Simpelveld, Holland; American provincialate, 4567 Olentangy River Rd., Columbus, O. 43214.

Chretienne, Sisters of Ste., S.S.CH.: Founded 1807, in France; in US, 1903. General motherhouse, Metz, France; American provincial house, 297 Arnold St., Wrentham, Mass. 02093. Educational, hospital, mission work.

Christ, Adorers of the Blood of, A.S.C.: Founded 1834, in Italy; in US, 1870. General motherhouse, Rome, Italy. US provinces: Ruma Province, Rt. 1, Box 115, P.O. (P.O. Red Bud), Ill. 62278; 1400 South Sheridan, Wichita, Kans. 67213; Columbia, Pa. 17512. Educational, hospital work.

Christ the King, Sister Servants of, S.S.C.K.: Founded 1936, in US. General motherhouse, Loretto Convent, Mt. Calvary, Wis. 53057

Christian Doctrine, Sisters of Our Lady of, R.C.D.: Founded 1910, at New York. Motherhouse, Marydell, Montebello Rd., Suffern, N.Y. 10901.

Christian Education, Religious of, R.C.E.: Founded 1817, in France; in US, 1905. General motherhouse, Paris, France; US provincial residence, 36 Hillcrest Rd., Belmont, Mass. 02178.

Cistercian Nuns of the Strict Observance, Order of, O.C.S.O.: Founded 1125, in France, by St. Stephen Harding; in US, 1949. General motherhouse, France. US addresses: Mt. St. Mary's Abbey, Arnold St. (R.F.D. Box 500), Wrentham, Mass. 02093; Our Lady of the Santa Rita Abbey, Box 97, Sonoita, Ariz. 85637; Our Lady of the Redwoods Abbey, Whitethorn, Calif. 95489; Abbey of Our Lady of the Mississippi, R.R. 3, Dubuque, Ia. 52001.

Clergy, Congregation of Our Lady, Help of the, C.L.H.C.: Founded 1961, in US. Motherhouse, Maryvale Convent, Maple Ave., Higganum, Conn. 06441.

Clergy, Servants of Our Lady Queen of the, S.R.C.: Founded 1929, in Canada; in US, 1936. General motherhouse, Lac-au-Saumon, Que., GOJ 1MO, Canada.

Colettines: See Franciscan Poor Clare Nuns.

Columban, Missionary Sisters of St., S.S.C.: Founded 1922, in Ireland; in US, 1930. General motherhouse, Wicklow, Ireland; US region, 1250 W. Loyola Ave., Chicago, Ill. 60626.

Consolata Missionary Sisters, M.C.: Founded 1910, in Italy; in US, 1954. General motherhouse, Turin, Italy; US headquarters, 6801 Belmont Rd., Belmont, Mich. 49306.

Cordi-Marian Missionary Sisters, M.C.M.: Founded 1921, in Mexico; in US, 1926. General motherhouse, 2910 Morales St., Morales, Mexico.

Cross, Daughters of the, D.C.: Founded 1640, in France; in US, 1855. General motherhouse, 1000 Fairview St., Shreveport, La. 71104. Educational work.

Cross, Daughters of, of Liege, F.C.: Founded 1883, in Liege, Belgium; in US, 1958. US address, 165 W. Eaton Ave., Tracy, Calif. 95376.

Cross, Sisters of the Holy, C.S.C.: Founded 1841, at Le Mans, France; in US, 1843. General motherhouse, Notre Dame, Ind. 46556. Educational, hospital work.

Cross and of the Seven Dolors, Sisters of the Holy, C.S.C.: Founded 1847, in Canada; in US, 1881. General motherhouse, Montreal, Que., Canada; US provincial house, Fairview Rd., Pittsfield, N.H. 03263. Educational work.

Cross and Passion, Sisters of the (Passionist Sisters), C.P.: Founded 1852; in US, 1924. General motherhouse, Bolton, England; US address: Mt. St. Joseph, Wakefield, R.I. 02878

Cross and Passion of Our Lord Jesus Christ, Nuns of the (Passionist Nuns), C.P.: Founded 1771, in Italy, by St. Paul of the Cross; in US, 1910. US convents: 2715 Churchview Ave., Pittsburgh, Pa. 15227; 631 Griffin Pond Rd., Clarks Summit, Pa. 18411; 1420 Benita Ave., Owensboro, Ky. 42301; 751 Donaldson Hwy., Erlanger, Ky. 41018; 1032 Clayton Rd., Ellisville, Mo. 63011. Contemplatives.

Crucified, Augustinian Daughters of the: Founded 1840, in Italy. General motherhouse, Rome, Italy; US novitiate, 420 Lincoln Hwy., Malvern, Pa. 19355.

Cyril and Methodius, Sisters of Sts., SS.C.M.: Founded 1909, in US, by Rev. Matthew Jankola. General motherhouse,

Danville, Pa. 17821. Educational, hospital work.

Disciples of the Divine Master, Sister, P.D.D.M.: Founded 1924; in US, 1948. General motherhouse, Rome, Italy; US headquarters, 60 Sunset Ave., Staten Island, N.Y. 10314.

Divine Compassion, Sisters of, R.D.C.: Founded 1886, in US. General motherhouse, 52 N. Broadway, White Plains, N.Y. 10603. Educational work.

Divine Love, Oblates to, Sisters, R.O.D.A.: Founded 1923, in Italy; in US, 1947. General motherhouse, Rome, Italy; US novitiate, Beekman Rd., Hopewell Junction, N.Y. 12533.

Divine Spirit, Congregation of the, C.D.S.: Founded 1956, in US, by Archbishop John M. Gannon. Motherhouse, 409 W. 6th St., Erie, Pa. 16507. Educational, social work; care of aged.

Dominicans

Dominican Nuns of the Second Order of Perpetual Adoration, O.P.: Founded 1206, in France; in U.S., 1880. Cloistered. Independent monasteries in US:

St. Dominic, 13th Ave. and S. 10th St., Newark, N.J. 07103; Corpus Christi, 1230 Lafayette Ave., Bronx, N.Y. 10474; Blessed Sacrament, 29575 Middlebelt, Farmington Hills, Mich. 48018; Holy Name, 3020 Erie Ave., Hyde Park, Cincinnati, O. 45208; Monastery of the Angels, 1977 Carmen Ave., Los Angeles, Calif. 90068; Corpus Christi, 215 Oak Grove Ave., Menlo Park, Calif. 94025;

Mother of God, 1430 Riverdale St., W. Springfield, Mass. 01089; Our Lady of the Rosary, 335 Doat St., Buffalo, N.Y. 14211; Our Lady of Grace, North Guilford, Conn. 06437; Infant Jesus, 1501 Lotus Lane, Lufkin, Tex. 75901; Our Lady of the Rosary (Rosary Shrine), Morris and Springfield Aves., Summit, N.J. 07901; Mary the Queen, 1310 W. Church St., Elmira, N.Y. 14905.

Dominican Rural Missionaries, O.P.: Founded 1932, in France; in US, 1951, at Abbeville, La. General motherhouse, Luzarches, France; US motherhouse, 1318 S. Henry St., Abbeville, La. 70510.

Dominican Sisters of Bethany, Congregation, O.P.: Founded 1866, in France. Motherhouse, France; US novitiate, 204 Ridge St., Millis, Mass. 02054.

Dominican Nuns of the Perpetual Rosary, O.P.: Founded 1880, at Calais, France. Contemplative. Independent monasteries in US:

14th and West Sts., Union City, N.J. 07087; 1500 Hadden Ave., Camden, N.J. 08103; 217 N. 68th St., Milwaukee, Wis. 53213; 720 Maiden Choice Lane, Catonsville, Md. 21228; Marbury, Ala. 36051; 3000 South Ave., La Crosse, Wis. 54601; 1834 Lititz Pike, Lancaster, Pa. 17601; 802 Court St., Syracuse, N.Y. 13208.

Dominican Sisters of the Presentation, O.P.: Founded 1684, in France; in US, 1906. General motherhouse, Tours, France; US headquarters, 3012 Elm St., Dighton, Mass. 02715. Hospital work.

Dominican Sisters of the Roman Congregation of St. Dominic, O.P.: Founded 1621, in France; in US, 1904. General motherhouse, Rome, Italy; US province, 510 Westerfield Dr., Davenport, Ia. 52806. Educational work.

Eucharistic Missionaries of St. Dominic, O.P.: Founded 1927, in Louisiana. General motherhouse, 1101 Aline St., New Orleans, La. 70115. Parish mission work.

Maryknoll Sisters of St. Dominic, M.M.: Founded 1912, in New York. Center, Maryknoll, N.Y. 10545.

Religious Missionaries of St. Dominic, O.P.: General motherhouse, Rome, Italy. US foundations: 808 S. Wright St., Alice, Texas 78332; 1123 N. Staples St., Corpus Christi, Tex. 78401; 432 N. Oak St., Santa Paula, Calif. 93060.

Sisters of the Third Order of St. Dominic, O.P.: Thirty congregations in the US. Educational, hospital work. Names of congregations are given below, followed by the date of foundation, and location of motherhouse.

St. Catharine of Siena, 1822. St. Catharine, Ky. 40061.

St. Mary of the Springs, 1830. Columbus Ohio 43219.

Most Holy Rosary, 1849. Sinsinawa, Wis. 53824.

Most Holy Name of Jesus, 1850. San Rafael, Calif. 94901.

Holy Cross, 1853. Albany Ave., Amityville, N.Y. 11701.

Most Holy Rosary, 1859. Mt. St. Mary on Hudson, Newburgh, N.Y. 12550.

St. Cecilia, 1860. Eighth Ave. N. and Clay St., Nashville, Tenn. 37208.

St. Mary, 1860. 4601 Cleveland Ave., New Orleans, La. 70119.

St. Catherine of Siena, 1862. 5635 Erie St., Racine, Wis. 53402.

Our Lady of the Sacred Heart, 1873. 1237 W. Monroe St., Springfield, Ill. 62704.

Our Lady of the Rosary, 1876. Sparkill, N.Y. 10976.

Queen of the Holy Rosary, 1876. Mission San Jose, Calif. 94538.

Most Holy Rosary, 1877. Adrian, Mich. 49221.

Our Lady of the Sacred Heart, 1877. 2025 E. Fulton St., Grand Rapids, Mich. 49503.

St. Dominic, 1878. Blauvelt, N.Y. 10913.

Immaculate Conception (Dominican Sisters of the Sick Poor), 1879. P.O. Box 231, Ossining, N.Y. 10562. Social work.

St. Catherine de Ricci, 1880. 2850 N. Providence Rd., Media, Pa. 19063.

Sacred Heart of Jesus, 1881. Mt. St. Dominic, Caldwell, N.J. 07006.

Sacred Heart, 1882. 6501 Almeda Rd., Houston, Tex. 77021.

St. Thomas Aquinas, 1888. 423 E. 152nd St., Tacoma, Wash. 98445.

Holy Cross, 1890. P.O. Box 280, Edmonds, Wash. 98020.

St. Catherine of Siena, 1891. 37 Park St., Fall River, Mass. 02721.

St. Rose of Lima (Servants of Relief for Incurable Cancer), 1896. Hawthorne, N.Y. 10532.

Immaculate Conception, 1902. 3600 Broadway, Great Bend, Kans. 67530.

St. Catherine of Siena, 1911. 4600 93rd St., Kenosha, Wis. 53140.

St. Rose of Lima, 1923. 775 Drahner Rd., Oxford, Mich. 48051.

Immaculate Conception, 1929. 9000 W. 81st St., Justice, Ill. 60458.

Immaculate Heart of Mary, 1929. Akron, Ohio 44313.

Immaculate Heart of Mary Province (Dominican Sisters of Spokane). W. 3102 Fort George Wright Dr., Spokane, Wash. 99204.

St. Catherine of Siena of Oakford, Republic of South Africa, 1955. General motherhouse, Natal, Republic of South Africa; US motherhouse, 1855 Miramonte Ave., Mountain View, Calif. 94040.

(End, Listing of Dominicans)

Dorothy, Institute of the Sisters of St., S.S.D.: Founded 1834, in Italy; in US, 1911. General motherhouse, Rome, Italy; US motherhouse, Villa Fatima, Taunton, Mass. 02780.

Eucharist, Religious of the, R.E.: Founded 1857, in Belgium; in US, 1900. General motherhouse, Belgium; US foundation, 2907 Ellicott Terr., N.W., Washington, D.C. 20008.

Eucharistic Missionary Sisters, E.M.S.: Founded 1943, in Mexico. Motherhouse, Our Lady of Loretto Convent, 267 N. Belmont Ave., Los Angeles, Calif. 90026.

Family, Congregation of the Sisters of the Holy, S.S.F.: Founded 1842, in US. General motherhouse, 6901 Chef Menteur Hway., New Orleans, La. 70126. Educational, hospital work.

Family, Little Sisters of the Holy, P.S.S.F.: Founded 1880, in Canada; in US, 1900. General motherhouse, Sherbrooke, Que., Canada. Domestic work.

Family, Sisters of the Holy, S.H.F.: Founded 1872, in US. General motherhouse, P.O. Box 3248, Mission San Jose, Calif. 94538. Educational, social work.

Family of Nazareth, Sisters of the Holy, C.S.F.N.: Founded 1875, in Italy; in US, 1885. General motherhouse, Rome, Italy. US provinces: 353 N. River Rd., Des Plaines, Ill. 60016; Grant and Frankford Aves., Torresdale, Philadelphia, Pa. 19114; 285 Bellevue Rd., Pittsburgh, Pa. 15229; Marian Heights, 1428-1, Monroe Turnpike, Monroe, Conn. 06868; 1814 Egyptian Way, Box 757, Grand Prairie, Tex. 75050.

Filippini, Religious Teachers, M.P.F.: Founded 1692, in Italy; in US, 1910. General motherhouse, Rome, Italy; US provinces: Villa Walsh, Morristown, N.J. 07960; 474 East Rd., Bristol, Conn. 06010. Educational work.

Francis de Sales, Oblate Sisters of St., O.S.F.S.: Founded 1866, in France; in US, 1951. General motherhouse, Troyes, France; US headquarters, Villa Aviat Convent, Childs, Md. 21916. Educational, social work.

Franciscans

Bernardine Sisters of the Third Order of St. Francis, O.S.F.: Founded 1457, at Cracow, Poland; in US, 1894. Generalate, 647 Spring Mill Rd., Villanova, Pa. 19085. Educational, hospital, social work.

Congregation of the Servants of the Holy Infancy of Jesus, O.S.F.: Founded 1855, in Germany; in US, 1929. General motherhouse, Wuerzburg, Germany; American motherhouse, P. O. Box 708, Plainfield, N.J. 07061.

Congregation of the Third Order of St. Francis of Mary Immaculate, O.S.F.: Founded 1865, in US, by Fr. Pamphilus da Magliano, O.F.M. General motherhouse, 520 Plainfield Ave., Joliet, Ill. 60435. Educational work.

Conventuals of the Third Order of St. Francis of the Mission of the Immaculate Virgin, O.S.F.: Founded 1893, in New York. General motherhouse, Hastings-on-Hudson, N.Y. 10706. Educational, hospital work.

Daughters of St. Francis of Assisi, D.S.F.: Founded 1890, in Austria-Hungary; in US, 1946. Provincial motherhouse, 507 N. Prairie St., Lacon, Ill. 61540. Nursing, CCD work.

Felician Sisters (Congregation of the Sisters of St. Felix), C.S.S.F.: Founded 1855, in Poland; in US, 1874. General motherhouse, Rome, Italy. US provinces: 36800 Schoolcraft Rd., Livonia, Mich. 48150; 600 Doat St., Buffalo, N.Y. 14211; 3800 Peterson Ave., Chicago, Ill. 60645; 260 South Main St., Lodi, N.J. 07644; 1500 Woodcrest Ave., Coraopolis, Pa. 15108; 1315 Enfield St., Enfield, Conn. 06082; 4210 Meadowlark Lane, S.E., Rio Rancho, N. Mex. 87124.

Franciscan Handmaids of the Most Pure Heart of Mary, F.H.M.: Founded 1917, in US. General motherhouse, 15 W. 124th St., New York, N.Y. 10027. Educational, social work.

Franciscan Hospitaller Sisters of the Immaculate Conception, F.H.I.C.: Founded 1876, in Portugal; in US, 1960. General motherhouse, Oporto, Portugal; US novitiate, 300 S. 17th St., San Jose, Calif. 95112.

Franciscan Missionaries of Mary, F.M.M.:

Founded 1877, in India; in US, 1904. General motherhouse, Rome, Italy; US provincialate, 225 E. 45th St., New York, N.Y. 10017. Foreign mission work.

Franciscan Missionaries of Our Lady, O.S.F.: Founded 1854, at Calais, France; in US, 1913. General motherhouse, Desvres, France; US motherhouse, 4200 Essen Lane, Baton Rouge, La. 70809. Hospital work.

Franciscan Missionaries of St. Joseph (Mill Hill Sisters), F.M.S.J.: Founded 1883, at Rochdale, Lancashire, England; in US, 1952. General motherhouse, Eccleshall, Stafford, England; US headquarters, Franciscan House, 1006 Madison Ave., Albany, N.Y. 12208.

Franciscan Missionaries of the Divine Motherhood, F.M.D.M.: Founded 1935, in England; US foundation, Convent of the Holy Spirit, East Greenbush, N.Y. 12061.

Franciscan Missionary Sisters for Africa, O.S.F.: American foundation, 1953. Generalate, Ireland; US headquarters, 172 Foster St., Brighton, Mass. 02135.

Franciscan Missionary Sisters of Assisi, S.F.M.G.: First foundation in US, 1961. General motherhouse, Assisi, Italy; US address, St. Francis Convent, 1039 Northampton St., Holyoke, Mass. 01040.

Franciscan Missionary Sisters of Our Lady of Sorrows, O.S.F.: Founded 1937, in China, by Bishop R. Palazzi, O.F.M.; in US, 1849. US address, 2385 Laurel Glen Rd., Santa Cruz, Calif. 95060. Educational, social, domestic, retreat and foreign mission work.

Franciscan Missionary Sisters of the Divine Child, F.M.D.C.: Founded 1927, at Buffalo, N.Y., by Bishop William Turner. General motherhouse, 6380 Main St., Williamsville, N.Y. 14221. Educational, social work.

Franciscan Missionary Sisters of the Immaculate Conception, O.S.F.: Founded 1874, in Mexico; in US, 1927. US provincial house, 11306 Laurel Canyon Blvd., San Fernando, Calif. 91340.

Franciscan Missionary Sisters of the Sacred Heart, F.M.S.C.: Founded 1860, in Italy; in US, 1865. Generalate, Rome, Italy; US provincialate, 250 South St., Peekskill, N.Y. 10566. Educational and social welfare apostolates and specialized services.

Franciscan Poor Clare Nuns (Poor Clares, Order of St. Clare, Poor Clares of St. Colette), P.C., O.S.C., P.C.C.: Founded 1212, at Assisi, Italy, by St. Francis of Assisi; in US, 1875. Proto-monastery, Assisi, Italy. Addresses of autonomous motherhouses in US are listed below.

3625 N. 65th Ave., Omaha, Nebr. 68104; 720 Henry Clay Ave., New Orleans, La. 70118; 509 S. Kentucky Ave., Evansville, Ind. 47714; 1310 Dellwood Ave., Memphis Tenn. 38127; 920 Centre St., Jamaica Plain, Mass. 02130; 201 Crosswicks St., Bordentown, N.J. 08505; 1271 Langhorne-Newton Rd., Langhorne, Pa. 19047; 4419 N. Hawthorne St., Spokane, Wash. 99205; 142 Hollywood Ave., Bronx, N.Y. 10465; 421 S. 4th St., Sauk Rapids, Minn. 56379; 8650 Russell Ave., S. Minneapolis, Minn. 55431; 3501 Rocky River Dr., Cleveland, O. 44111;

89th and Kean Ave., Hickory Hills, Ill. 60457; 280 State Park Dr., Aptos, Calif. 95003; 2111 S. Main St., Rockford, Ill. 61102; 215 E. Los Olivos St., Santa Barbara, Calif. 93105; P.O. Box 333, Lowell, Mass. 01853; 809 E. 19th St., Roswell, N. Mex. 88201; 28210 Natoma Rd., Los Altos Hills, Calif. 94022; 1916 N. Pleasantburg Dr., Greenville, S.C. 29609; 28 Harpersville Rd., Newport News, Va. 23601; 805 N. Malfalfa Rd., Kokoma, Ind. 46901; 4000 Sherwood Blvd., Delray Beach, Fla. 33445; 200 Marycrest Dr., St. Louis, Mo. 63129.

Franciscan Sisters, Daughters of the Sacred Hearts of Jesus and Mary, O.S.F.: Founded 1860, in Germany; in US, 1872. Generalate, Rome, Italy; US motherhouse, P.O. Box 667, Wheaton, Ill. 60187. Educational, hospital, social work.

Franciscan Sisters of Allegany, N.Y., O.S.F.: Founded 1859, at Allegany, N.Y., by Fr. Pamphilus da Magliano, O.F.M. General motherhouse Allegany, N.Y. 14706. Educational, hospital, foreign mission work.

Franciscan Sisters of Baltimore, O.S.F.: Founded 1868, in England; in US, 1881. General motherhouse, 3725 Ellerslie Ave., Baltimore, Md. 21218. Educational work.

Franciscan Sisters of Chicago, O.S.F.: Founded 1894, in US. General motherhouse, 1220 Main St., Lemont, Ill. 60439. Educational, hospital, social work.

Franciscan Sisters of Christian Charity, O.S.F.: Founded 1869, in US. Holy Family Convent, 2409 S. Alverno Rd., Manitowoc, Wis. 54220. Educational, hospital work.

Franciscan Sisters of Little Falls, Minn., O.S.F.: Founded 1891, in US. General motherhouse, Little Falls, Minn. 56345. Health, education, social services.

Franciscan Sisters of Mary Immaculate of the Third Order of St. Francis of Assisi, F.M.I.: Founded 16th century, in Switzerland; in US, 1932. General motherhouse, Rome, Italy; US provincial house, 4301 N.E. 18th Ave., Amarillo, Tex. 79107.

Franciscan Sisters of Our Lady of Perpetual Help, O.S.F.: Founded 1901, in US, from Joliet, Ill., foundation. General motherhouse, 201 Brotherton Lane, St. Louis, Mo. 63135. Educational, hospital work.

Franciscan Sisters of the Blessed Virgin Mary of the Holy Angels, B.M.V.A.: Founded 1863, at Neuwied, Germany; in US, 1923. General motherhouse, Rhine, Germany; US motherhouse, 1388 Prior Ave. S., St. Paul,

Minn. 55116. Educational, hospital, social work.

Franciscan Sisters of Ringwood, F.S.R.: Founded 1927, at Passaic, N.J. General motherhouse, Mt. St. Francis, Ringwood, N.J. 07456. Educational work.

Franciscan Sisters of St. Elizabeth, F.S.S.E.: Founded 1866, at Naples, Italy; in US, 1919. General motherhouse, Rome; US address, 449 Park Rd., Parsippany, N.J. 07054.

Franciscan Sisters of St. Joseph, F.S.S.J.: Founded 1897, in US. General motherhouse, 5286 S. Park Ave., Hamburg, N.Y. 14075. Educational, hospital work.

Franciscan Sisters of the Atonement, Third Order Regular of St. Francis (Graymoor Sisters), S.A.: Founded 1898, in US, as Anglican community; entered Church, 1909. General motherhouse, Graymoor, Garrison P.O., N.Y. 10524. Mission work.

Franciscan Sisters of the Immaculate Conception, O.S.F.: Founded in Germany; in US, 1928. General motherhouse, Kloster, Bonlanden, Germany; US province, 291 W. North St., Buffalo, N.Y. 14201.

Franciscan Sisters of the Immaculate Conception, O.S.F.: Founded 1901, in US. General motherhouse, 1000 30th St., Rock Island, Ill. 61201. Hospital work.

Franciscan Sisters of the Immaculate Conception, Missionary, O.S.F.: Founded 1873, in US. General motherhouse, Rome, Italy; US address, 790 Centre St., Newton, Mass. 02158. Educational work.

Franciscan Sisters of the Immaculate Conception and St. Joseph for the Dying, O.S.F.: Founded 1919, in US. General motherhouse, 485 Church St., Monterey, Calif. 93940.

Franciscan Sisters of the Poor, S.F.P.: Founded 1845, at Aix-la-Chapelle, Germany, by Bl. Frances Schervier; in US, 1858. Community service center, 23 Middagh St., Brooklyn, N.Y. 11201. Hospital, social work.

Franciscan Sisters of the Sacred Heart, O.S.F.: Founded 1876, in US. General motherhouse, Mokena, Ill. 60448. Educational, hospital, mission work.

Franciscan Sisters of the Third Order of the Immaculate Conception, F.S.I.C.: Founded 1879, in Spain; in US, 1958. General motherhouse, Madrid, Spain; US foundation, Immaculate Mary Home, Holme Circle and Welsh Rd., Philadelphia, Pa. 19136.

Hospital Sisters of the Third Order of St. Francis, O.S.F.: Founded 1844, in Germany; in US, 1875. General motherhouse, Muenster, Germany; US motherhouse, Box 42, Springfield, Ill. 62705. Hospital work.

Institute of the Franciscan Sisters of the Eucharist, F.S.E.: Founded 1973. Motherhouse, 405 Allen Ave., Meriden, Conn. 06450.

Little Franciscan Sisters of Mary, P.F.M.: Founded 1889, in US. General motherhouse, Baie St. Paul, Que., Canada. US province, 55 Moore Ave., Worcester, Mass. Educational, hospital, social work.

Missionaries of the Third Order of St. Francis of Our Lady of the Prairies, O.L.P.: Founded 1960, in US. General motherhouse, Powers Lake, N.D. 58773.

Missionary Sisters of the Immaculate Conception of the Mother of God, S.M.I.C.: Founded 1910, in Brazil; in US, 1922, Generalate, P.O. Box 204, 779 Broadway, Paterson, N.J. 07514. Mission, educational, hospital work.

Mothers of the Helpless, M.D.: Founded 1873, in Spain; in US, 1916. General motherhouse, Valencia, Spain; US address, 432 W. 20th St., New York, N.Y. 10011.

Philip Neri Missionary Teachers, Sisters of St., R.F.: Founded 1858, in Spain; in US, 1956. Motherhouse, Barcelona, Spain; US address: Convent of St. Philip Neri, 1259 St. Albert St., Reno, Nev. 89506.

Poor Clares of Perpetual Adoration, P.C.P.A.: Founded 1854, at Paris, France; in US, 1921, at Cleveland, Ohio. US monasteries: 4200 N. Market Ave., Canton, O. 44714; 2311 Timlin Rd., Portsmouth, O. 45662; 4108 Euclid Ave., Cleveland, O. 44103; 3900 13th St. N.E., Washington, D.C. 20017; 5817 Old Leeds Rd., Birmingham, Ala. 35210. Contemplative, cloistered, perpetual adoration.

School Sisters of St. Francis, O.S.F.: Founded 1874, in US. General motherhouse, 1501 S. Layton Blvd., Milwaukee, Wis. 53215.

School Sisters of St. Francis (Bethlehem, Pa.), O.S.F.: Founded 1843, in Austria; in US, 1913. General motherhouse, Rome, Italy; US province, 395 Bridle Path Rd., Bethlehem, Pa. 18017. Educational work.

School Sisters of St. Francis (Pittsburgh, Pa.), O.S.F.: Founded 1913, in US. Provincial motherhouse, 934 Forest Ave., Pittsburgh, Pa. 15202. Educational, nursing work.

School Sisters of the Third Order of St. Francis (Savannah, Mo.), O.S.F.: Founded 1842, in Austria; in US, 1924. Provincial house, La Verna Hts., Savannah, Mo. 64485. Educational, hospital work.

School Sisters of the Third Order of St. Francis (Panhandle, Tex.), O.S.F.: Founded 1845, in Austria; in US, 1942. General motherhouse, Vienna, Austria; US center and novitiate, Sancta Maria Convent, Panhandle, Tex. 79068. Educational, social work.

Sisters of Charity of Our Lady, Mother of the Church, S.C.M.C.: Established 1970, in US. Motherhouse, Baltic, Conn. 06330. Teaching, nursing, care of aged, and dependent children.

Sisters of Our Lady of Mercy (Mercedarians), S.O.L.M.: General motherhouse, Rome, Italy; US addresses: 70 Bay 47th St.

Brooklyn, N.Y. 11214; St. Edward School, Pine Hill, N.J. 08021.

Sisters of Mercy of the Holy Cross, S.C.S.C.: Founded 1856, in Switzerland; in US. 1912. General motherhouse, Ingenbohl, Switzerland; US provincial house, Merrill, Wis. 54452.

Sisters of St. Elizabeth, S.S.E.: Founded 1931, at Milwaukee, Wis. General motherhouse, 745 N. Brookfield Rd., Brookfield, Wis. 53005.

Sisters of St. Francis (Clinton, Iowa), O.S.F.: Founded 1868, in US. General motherhouse, Bluff Blvd. and Springdale Dr., Clinton, Ia. 57232. Educational, hospital, social work.

Sisters of St. Francis (Millvale, Pa.), O.S.F.: Founded 1865, Pittsburgh, Pa. General motherhouse, 146 Hawthorne Rd., Millvale P.O., Pittsburgh, Pa. 15209. Educational, hospital work.

Sisters of St. Francis of Christ the King, O.S.F.: Founded 1869, in Austria. General motherhouse, Rome, Italy; US provincial house, Lemont, Ill. 60439. Educational work, home for aged.

Sisters of St. Francis of Penance and Christian Charity, O.S.F.: Founded 1835, in Holland; in US, 1874. General motherhouse, Rome, Italy. US provinces: 4421 Lower River Rd., Stella Niagara, N.Y. 14144; 2851 W. 52nd Ave., Denver, Colo. 80221; 3910 Bret Harte Dr., P.O. Box 1028, Redwood City, Calif. 94064.

Sisters of St. Francis of Philadelphia, O.S.F.: Founded 1855, at Philadelphia, by St. John N. Neumann. General motherhouse, Convent of Our Lady of the Angels, Glen Riddle, Pa. 19037. Educational, hospital work.

Sisters of St. Francis of the Congregation of Our Lady of Lourdes, O.S.F.: Founded 1916, in US. General motherhouse, 6832 Convent Blvd., Sylvania, O. 43560. Educational, hospital work.

Sisters of St. Francis of the Holy Cross, O.S.F.: Founded 1881, in US, by Rev. Edward Daems, O.S.C. General motherhouse, Rt. 1, Green Bay (Bay Settlement), Wis. 54301. Educational, nursing work; home for aged.

Sisters of St. Francis of the Holy Eucharist, O.S.F.: Founded 1424, in Switzerland; in US, 1893. General motherhouse, Ashland and Prewitt Sts., Nevada, Mo. 64772. Educational, social work.

Sisters of St. Francis of the Immaculate Conception, O.S.F.: Founded 1890, in US. General motherhouse, 2408 W. Heading Ave., Peoria, Ill. 61604. Educational, social work.

Sisters of St. Francis of the Immaculate Heart of Mary, O.S.F.: Founded 1241, in Bavaria; in US, 1913. General motherhouse, Rome, Italy; US motherhouse, Hankinson, N.D. 58041. Educational, hospital work.

Sisters of St. Francis of the Martyr St. George, O.S.F.: Founded in 1859, in Germany; in US, 1923. General motherhouse, Thuine, Hanover, Germany; US motherhouse, Alton, Ill. 62002. Social, hospital, foreign mission work.

Sisters of St. Francis of the Perpetual Adoration, O.S.F.: Founded 1863, in Germany; in US, 1875. General motherhouse, Olpe, Germany. US provinces: Box 766, Mishawaka, Ind. 46544; P.O. Box 1060, Colorado Springs, Colo. 80901. Educational, hospital work.

Sisters of St. Francis of the Providence of God, O.S.F.: Founded 1922, in US, by Msgr. M. L. Krusas. General motherhouse, Grove and McRoberts Rds., Pittsburgh, Pa. 15234. Educational, hospital work.

Sisters of St. Joseph of the Third Order of St. Francis, S.S.J.: Founded 1901, in US. General motherhouse, 107 S. Greenlawn Ave., South Bend, Ind. 46617. Educational, hospital work.

Sisters of St. Mary of the Third Order of St. Francis, S.S.M.: Founded 1872, in US. General motherhouse, 1100 Bellevue Ave., St. Louis, Mo. 63117. Hospital, social work.

Sisters of the Holy Infant Jesus, I.J.: Founded 1662, at Rouen, France; in US, 1950. General motherhouse, Paris, France. US addresses: 20 Reiner St., Colma, Calif. 94014; St. John the Baptist School, Healdsburg, Calif. 95448; St. Veronica's School, South San Francisco, Calif. 94015.

Sisters of the Sorrowful Mother (Third Order of St. Francis), S.S.M.: Founded 1883, in Italy; in US, 1889. General motherhouse, Rome, Italy. US provinces: 6618 N. Teutonia Ave., Milwaukee, Wis. 53209; 9 Pocono Rd., Denville, N.J. 07834; Tulsa Provincialate, R.R. Box 167, Broken Arrow, Okla. 74012. Educational, hospital work.

Sisters of the Third Franciscan Order Minor Conventuals, O.S.F.: Founded 1860, at Syracuse, N.Y. General motherhouse, 1024 Court St., Syracuse, N.Y. 13208. Educational, hospital work.

Sisters of the Third Order of St. Francis, O.S.F.: Founded 1877, in US, by Bishop John L. Spalding. Motherhouse, Edgewood Hills, E. Peoria, Ill. 61611. Hospital work.

Sisters of the Third Order of St. Francis, O.S.F.: Founded 1894, in US. Motherhouse, Mt. Alverno Convent, R.R. 3, Box 64, Maryville, Mo. 64468. Hospital work.

Sisters of the Third Order of St. Francis, O.S.F.: Founded 1861, at Buffalo, N.Y., from Philadelphia foundation. General motherhouse, 400 Mill St., Williamsville, N.Y. 14221. Educational, hospital work.

Sisters of the Third Order of St. Francis (Oldenburg, Ind.), O.S.F.: Founded 1851, in US. General motherhouse, Convent of the Immaculate Conception, Oldenburg, Ind. 47036. Educational work.

Sisters of the Third Order of St. Francis of Assisi, O.S.F.: Founded 1849, in US. General motherhouse, 3221 S. Lake Dr., Milwaukee, Wis. 53207. Educational work.

Sisters of the Third Order of St. Francis of Penance and Charity, O.S.F.: Founded 1869, in US, by Rev. Joseph Bihn. Motherhouse, St. Francis Convent, St. Francis Ave., Tiffin, O. 44883. Educational, hospital work.

Sisters of the Third Order of St. Francis of the Holy Family, O.S.F.: Founded 1875, in US. General motherhouse, Mt. St. Francis, Dubuque, Ia. 52001. Education, hospital work.

Sisters of the Third Order of St. Francis of the Perpetual Adoration, F.S.P.A.: Founded 1849, in US. Generalate, 912 Market St., La Crosse, Wis. 54601. Educational, health care.

Sisters of the Third Order Regular of St. Francis of the Congregation of Our Lady of Lourdes, O.S.F.: Founded 1877, in US. General motherhouse, Assisi Heights, Rochester, Minn. 55901. Education, hospitals.

(End, Listing of Franciscans)

Good Shepherd Sisters (Servants of the Immaculate Heart of Mary), S.C.I.M.: Founded 1850, in Canada; in US, 1882. General motherhouse, Quebec, Canada; Provincial House, Bay View, Saco, Maine 04072. Educational, social work.

Good Shepherd, Sisters of Our Lady of Charity of the, R.G.S.: Founded 1641, in France; in US, 1843. Generalate, Rome, Italy. US provinces: 9517 Leebrook Dr., Cincinnati, O. 45231; Mt. St. Florence, Peekskill, N.Y. 10566; 9407 Stateside Ct., Silver Spring, Md. 20903; 7654 Natural Bridge Rd., St. Louis, Mo. 63121; 389 N. Oxford St., St. Paul, Minn. 55104.

Graymoor Sisters: See Franciscan Sisters of the Atonement.

Grey Nuns of the Sacred Heart, G.N.S.H.: Founded 1921, in US. General motherhouse, Quarry Rd., Yardley, Pa. 19067.

Guadalupe, Sisters of, O.L.G.: Founded 1946, in Mexico City. General motherhouse, Mexico City, Mexico; US address, St. Mary's College, Winona, Minn. 55987.

Guardian Angels, Sisters of the Holy, S.A.C.: Founded 1839, in France. General motherhouse, Madrid, Spain; US foundation, 1245 S. Van Ness, Los Angeles, Calif. 90019.

Handmaids of Mary Immaculate, A.M.I.: Founded 1952 in Helena, Mont. Address: Ave Maria Institute, Washington, N.J. 07882.

Handmaids of the Precious Blood, Congregation of, H.P.B.: Founded 1947, at Jemez Springs, N.M. General motherhouse, Villa Cor Jesu, Jemez Springs, N.M. 87025.

Helpers, Society of, H.H.S.: Founded 1856, in France; in US, 1892. General motherhouse, Paris, France; American province, 303 Barry Ave., Chicago, Ill. 60657.

Hermanas Catequistas Guadalupanas, H.C.G.: Founded 1923, in Mexico; in US, 1950. General motherhouse, Mexico; US foundation, 4110 S. Flores, San Antonio, Tex. 78214.

Holy Child Jesus, Society of the, S.H.C.J.: Founded 1846, in England; in US, 1862. General motherhouse, Rome, Italy. US province: 620 Edmonds Ave., Drexel Hill, Pa. 19026.

Holy Faith, Sisters of the, S.H.F.: Founded 1856, in Ireland; in US, 1953. General motherhouse, Dublin, Ireland; US regional superior, 13817 S. Pioneer Blvd., Norwalk, Calif. 90650.

Holy Ghost, Sisters of the, C.H.G.: Founded 1913, in US, by Most Rev. J. F. Regis Canevin. General motherhouse, 5246 Clarwin Ave., West View, Pittsburgh, Pa. 15229. Educational, nursing work; care of aged.

Holy Ghost and Mary Immaculate, Sister Servants of, S.H.G.: Founded 1893, in US. General motherhouse, 301 Yucca St., San Antonio, Tex. 78203. Education, hospital work.

Holy Heart of Mary, Servants of the, S.S.C.M.: Founded 1860, in France; in US, 1889. General motherhouse, Montreal, Que., Canada; US motherhouse, 145 S. 4th St., Kankakee, Ill. 60901. Educational, hospital, social work.

Holy Names of Jesus and Mary, Sisters of the, S.N.J.M.: Founded 1843, in Canada; in US, 1859. General motherhouse, Pierrefonds H9K 1C6, P.Q., Canada. US addresses: Oregon Province, Marylhurst, Ore. 97036; California Province, P.O. Box 907, Los Gatos, Calif. 95030; New York Province, 1061 New Scotland Rd., Albany, N.Y. 12208; Washington Province, W. 2911 Ft. Wright Dr., Spokane, Wash. 99204.

Holy Spirit, Daughters of the, D.H.S.: Founded 1706, in France; in US, 1902. General motherhouse, Bretagne, France; US motherhouse, 72 Church St., Putnam, Conn. 06260. Educational work, district nursing.

Holy Spirit, Mission Sisters of the, M.SS.Sp.: Founded 1932, at Cleveland, O. Motherhouse, 1030 N. River Rd., Saginaw, Mich. 48603.

Holy Spirit, Missionary Sisters, Servants of the: Founded 1889, in Holland; in US, 1901. Generalate, Rome, Italy; US motherhouse, Convent of the Holy Spirit, Techny, Ill. 60082.

Holy Spirit, Sisters of the, C.S.Sp.: Founded 1890, in Rome, Italy; in US, 1929. General motherhouse, 10102 Granger Rd., Garfield Hts., Ohio 44125. Educational, social, nursing work.

Holy Spirit of Perpetual Adoration, Sister Servants of the: Founded 1896, in Holland; in US, 1915. General motherhouse, Steyl, Holland; US motherhouse, 2212 Green St., Philadelphia, Pa. 19130.

Home Mission Sisters of America (Glenmary Sisters): Founded 1952, in US. Motherhouse, 4580 Colerain Ave., Cincinnati, O. 45223.

Home Visitors of Mary, Sisters, H.V.M.: Founded 1949, in Detroit, Mich. Motherhouse, 356 Arden Park, Detroit, Mich. 48002.

Humility of Mary, Congregation of, C.H.M.: Founded 1854, in France; in US, 1864. US address, Convent of Humility of Mary, Ottumwa, Ia. 52501.

Humility of Mary, Sisters of the, H.M.: Founded 1854, in France; in US, 1864. US address, Villa Maria, Pa. 16155.

Immaculate Conception, Little Servant Sisters of the: Founded 1850, in Poland; in US, 1926. General motherhouse, Poland; US provincial house, 184 Amboy Ave., Woodbridge, N.J. 07095.

Immaculate Conception, Sisters of the, R.C.M.: Founded 1892, in Spain; in U.S., 1962. General motherhouse, Madrid, Spain; U.S. foundation, 867 Oxford, Clovis, Calif. 93612.

Immaculate Conception, Sisters of the, C.I.C.: Founded 1874, in US. General motherhouse, 4920 Kent St., Metairie, La. 70002.

Immaculate Conception of the Blessed Virgin Mary, Sisters of the (Lithuanian), M.I.C.: Founded 1918, at Mariampole, Lithuania; in US, 1936. General motherhouse, Mariampole, Lithuania; US headquarters, Immaculate Conception Convent, Putnam, Conn. 06260.

Immaculate Heart of Mary, Daughters of the, I.H.M.: Founded 1952, in US. Diocesan foundation. General motherhouse, Sunset Gardens, Wintersville, Ohio 43952.

Immaculate Heart of Mary, Missionary Sisters, I.C.M.: Founded 1897, in India; in US, 1919. Generalate, Rome, Italy; US address, 1710 N. Glebe Rd., Arlington, Va. 22207. Educational social, foreign mission work.

Immaculate Heart of Mary, Sisters of the, I.M.F.: Founded 1848, in Spain; in US, 1878. General motherhouse, Rome, Italy. US province, 4100 Sabino Canyon Rd., Tucson, Ariz. 85715. Educational work.

Immaculate Heart of Mary, Sisters of the (California Institute of the Most Holy and Immaculate Heart of the B.V.M.), I.H.M.: Founded 1848, in Spain; in US, 1871. Generalate, 3431 Waverly Dr., Los Angeles, Calif. 90027.

Immaculate Heart of Mary, Sisters, Servants of the, I.H.M.: Founded 1845, in US, by Rev. Louis Florent Gillet. Central administration, 610 W. Elm St., Monroe, Mich. 48161.

Independent communities: Villa Maria, Immaculata, Pa. 19345; Immaculate Heart of Mary Generalate, Marywood, Scranton, Pa. 18509.

Incarnate Word and Blessed Sacrament, Congregation of, V.I.: Founded 1625, in France; in US, 1853. U.S. motherhouse: 4600 Bissonnet St., Bellaire, Tex. 77401.

Incarnate Word and Blessed Sacrament, Congregation of the, of the Archdiocese of San Antonio, I.W.B.S.: Motherhouses: 1101 Northeast Water St., Victoria, Tex. 77901; 2930 S. Alameda St., Corpus Christi, Tex. 78404.

Incarnate Word and Blessed Sacrament, Sisters of the, S.I.W.: Founded 1625, in France; in US 1853. Motherhouse, 6618 Pearl Rd., Parma Heights, Cleveland, O. 44130.

Infant Jesus, Sisters of the (Nursing Sisters of the Sick Poor), C.I.J.: Founded 1835, in France; in US, 1905. General motherhouse, 310 Prospect Park W., Brooklyn, N.Y. 11215.

Jeanne d'Arc, Sisters of Ste.: Founded 1914, in America, by Rev. Marie Clement Staub, A.A. General motherhouse, 1681 Chemin St. Louis, Quebec, G1S 1G4, Canada; US novitiate, 29 Whitman Rd., Worcester, Mass. 01609. Spiritual and temporal service of priests.

Jesus, Congregation of Daughters of, F.J.: Founded 1834, in France; in US, 1904. General motherhouse, Kermaria, Locmine, France; American motherhouse, 9040 84th Ave., Edmonton, Alberta T6C 1E4, Canada. Educational, hospital work.

Jesus, Daughters of, F.I.: Founded 1871, in Spain; in US, 1950. General motherhouse, Rome, Italy; US foundation, 410 Grand St., Apt. 24F, New York, N.Y. 10002.

Jesus, Little Sisters of: Founded 1939, in Sahara; in US, 1952. General motherhouse, Rome, Italy; US headquarters, 700 Irving St. N.W., Washington, D.C. 20017.

Jesus, Society of the Sisters, Faithful Companions of, F.C.J.: Founded 1820, in France; in US, 1896. General motherhouse, Kent, England. US convents: 46 Woodland St., Fitchburg, Mass. 01420; 20 Atkins St., N. Providence, R.I. 02908; 6 Lincoln St., Centredale, R.I. 02911; Corys Lane, Portsmouth, R.I. 02871.

Jesus Crucified, Congregation of: Founded 1930, in France; in US, 1955. General motherhouse, Brou, France; US foundations: Regina Mundi Priory, Devon, Pa. 19333; St. Paul's Priory, 61 Narragansett, Newport, R.I. 02840.

Jesus Crucified and the Sorrowful Mother, Poor Sisters of, C.J.C.: Founded 1924, in US, by Rev. Alphonsus, C.P. General motherhouse, Thatcher St., Brockton, Mass. 02402. Educational, home nursing work.

Jesus-Mary, Religious of, R.J.M.: Founded 1818, at Lyons, France; in US, 1877. General motherhouse, Rome, Italy; US province, 8908 Riggs Rd., Hyattsville, Md. 20782. Educational work.

Jesus, Mary and Joseph, Missionaries of, M.J.M.J.: Founded 1942, in Spain; in US, 1956. General motherhouse, Madrid, Spain; US regional house, 12940 Up River Rd., Corpus Christi, Tex. 78410.

Jesus the Priest, Oblate Sisters of, O.J.S.:

Women Religious

Founded 1937, in Mexico City; in US, 1950. Motherhouse, Mexico City, Mexico; US address, La Salle Institute, Glencoe, Mo. 63038.

John the Baptist, Sisters of St., C.S.J.B.: Founded 1878, in Italy; in US, 1906. General motherhouse, Rome, Italy; US provincialate, Anderson Hill Rd., Purchase, N.Y. 10577. Educational work.

Joseph, Missionary Servants of St., M.SS.J.: Founded 1874, in Spain; in US, 1957. General motherhouse, Salamanca, Spain; US address, 203 N. Spring St., Falls Church, Va. 22046.

Joseph, Poor Sisters of St.: Founded 1880, in Argentina. General motherhouse, Muniz, Argentina; US addresses, St. John's Seminary, Rt. 2, Box 389, Richmond, Va. 23229; Casa Belen, Bethlehem, Pa. 78015; St. Gabriel Day Care Center, Alexandria, Va. 22312.

Joseph, Religious Daughters of St., F.S.J.: Founded 1875, in Spain. General motherhouse, Spain; US foundation, 319 N. Humphreys Ave., Los Angeles, Calif. 90022.

Joseph, Religious Hospitallers of St., R.H.S.J.: Founded 1636, in France; in US, 1894. General motherhouse, 5621 Cantenbury Ave., Montreal, Que., Canada. Hospital work.

Joseph, Sisters of St., C.S.J.: Founded 1650, in France; in US, 1836, at St. Louis. US motherhouses:

637 Cambridge St., Brighton, Mass. 02135; 1515 W. Ogden Ave., La Grange Park, Ill., 60525; 480 S. Batavia St., Orange, Calif. 92666; Mt. St. Joseph Convent, Chestnut Hill, Philadelphia, Pa. 19118.

St. Joseph Convent, Brentwood, N.Y. 11717; 23 Agassiz Circle, Buffalo, N.Y. 14214; Avila Hall, Clement Rd., Rutland, Vt. 05701; 3430 Rocky River Dr. N.W., Cleveland, O. 44111; Main St. and Division Rd., Tipton, Ind. 46072; Nazareth, Mich. 49074; 1425 Washington St., Watertown, N.Y. 13601; Mt. Gallitzin Motherhouse, Baden, Pa. 15005; 819 W. 8th St., Erie, Pa. 16502.

4095 East Ave., Rochester, N.Y. 14610; 13th and Washington Sts., Concordia, Kans. 66901; Holyoke, Mass. 01040; 1412 E. 2nd St., Superior, Wis. 54880; Pogue Run Rd., Wheeling, W. Va. 26003; 3700 E. Lincoln St., Wichita, Kans. 67218.

Joseph, Sisters of St. (Lyons, France), C.S.J.: Founded 1650, in France; in US, 1906. General motherhouse, Lyons, France; US motherhouse, 93 Halifax St., Winslow, Me. 04901. Educational, hospital work.

Joseph, Sisters of St., of Peace, C.S.J.: Founded 1884, in England. Generalate, 1302 18th St. N.W., Suite 703, Washington, D.C. 20036. Educational, hospital, social service work.

Joseph of Carondelet, Sisters of St., C.S.J.: Founded 1650, in France; in US, 1836, at St. Louis, Mo. US headquarters, 2307 S. Lindbergh Blvd., St. Louis, Mo. 63131.

Joseph of Chambery, Sisters of St.: Founded 1650, in France; in US, 1885. Generalate, Rome, Italy; US motherhouse, 27 Park Rd., West Hartford, Conn. 06119. Educational, hospital, social work.

Joseph of Cluny, Sisters of St., S.J.C.: Founded 1807, in France. General motherhouse, Paris, France; US provincial house, Cluny Convent, Brenton Rd., Newport, R.I. 02840.

Joseph of Medaille, Sisters of, C.S.J.: Founded 1823, in France; in US, 1855. Became an American congregation Aug. 29, 1977. General motherhouse (temporarily), 5108 Reading Rd., Cincinnati, Ohio 45237.

Joseph of St. Augustine, Fla., Sisters of St., S.S.J.: General motherhouse, 241 St. George St., St. Augustine, Fla. 32084. Educational, hospital, social work.

Joseph of St. Mark, Sisters of St., S.S.J.S.M.: Founded 1845, in France; in US, 1937. General motherhouse, Alsace-Lorraine, France; US motherhouse, 21800 Chardon Rd., Euclid, Cleveland, O. 44117. Social, domestic work.

Joseph the Worker, Sisters of St., S.J.W.: General motherhouse, St. Joseph Convent, 143 S. Main St., Walton, Ky. 41094.

Lamb of God, Sisters of the, A.D.: Founded 1945, in France; in US, 1958. General motherhouse, France; US foundation, 1516 Parrish Ave., Owensboro, Ky. 42301.

Living Word, Sisters of the, S.L.W.: Founded 1975, in US. Motherhouse, The Center, 7200 N. Osceola Ave., Chicago, Ill. 60648. Education, hospital, parish ministry work.

Loretto at the Foot of the Cross, Sisters of, S.L.: Founded 1812 in US, by Rev. Charles Nerinckx. General motherhouse, Nerinx, Ky. 40049. Educational work.

Louis, Congregation of Sisters of St., S.S.L.: Founded 1842, in France; in US, 1949. General motherhouse, Monaghan, Ireland; US novitiate, 22300 Mulholland Dr., Woodland Hills, Calif. 91364. Educational work.

Marian Sisters of the Diocese of Lincoln: Founded 1954. Motherhouse, Marycrest, Waverly, Nebr. 68462.

Marian Society of Dominican Catechists, O.P.: Founded 1954 in Alexandria, La., diocese. General motherhouse, Boyce, La. 71409. Diocesan community.

Marianites of Holy Cross, Congregation of the Sisters, M.S.C.: Founded 1841, in France; in US, 1843. General motherhouse, Sarthe, France; US provinces: 4123 Woodland Dr., New Orleans, La. 70114; Great Rd. and Drakes Corner, Princeton, N.J. 08540.

Marist Sisters, Congregation of Mary, S.M.: Founded 1824, in France. General motherhouse, Rome, Italy; US convents:

Dearborn Hts., Mich. 48125; E. Detroit, Mich.; Wheeling, W. Va. 26002.

Maronite Antonine Sisters: Established in US, 1966. US address, 2961 N. Lipkey Rd., R.D. 2, North Jackson, Ohio 44451.

Martha of Prince Edward Island, Sisters of St., C.S.M.: Founded 1916, in Canada; in US, 1961. General motherhouse, 141 Mt. Edward Rd., Charlottetown, P.E.I., Canada.

Marthe, Sisters of Sainte (of St. Hyacinthe), S.M.S.H.: Founded 1883, in Canada; in US, 1929. General motherhouse 800, rue St. Pierre, St. Joseph de Hyacinthe, Que. J27 1N7, Canada.

Mary, Company of, O.D.N.: Founded 1607, in France; in US, 1926. General motherhouse, Rome, Italy; US motherhouse, 16791 E. Main St., Tustin, Calif. 92680.

Mary, Daughters of the Heart of, D.H.M.: Founded 1790, in France; in US, 1851. Generalate, Paris, France; US provincialate, 1339 Northampton St., Holyoke, Mass. 01040. Educational work.

Mary, Little Company of, Nursing Sisters, L.C.M.: Founded 1877, in England; in US, 1893. General motherhouse, Rome, Italy; US provincial house, 9350 S. California Ave., Evergreen Park, Ill. 60642.

Mary, Missionary Sisters of the Society of (Marist Sisters), S.M.S.M.: Founded 1845, at St. Brieuc, France; in US, 1922. General motherhouse, Rome, Italy; US regional house, 357 Grove St., Waltham, Mass. 02154. Foreign missions.

Mary, Servants of, O.S.M.: Founded 13th century, in Italy; in US, 1893. General motherhouse, Rome, Italy; US provincial motherhouse, 7400 Military Ave., Omaha, Nebr. 68134.

Mary, Servants of (Servite Sisters), O.S.M.: Founded 13th century, in Italy; in US, 1912. General motherhouse, Our Lady of Sorrows Convent, Ladysmith, Wis. 54848.

Mary, Sisters of St., of Oregon, S.S.M.O.: Founded 1886, in Oregon, by Bishop William H. Gross, C.Ss.R. General motherhouse, 4440 S.W. 148th Ave., Beaverton, Ore. 97005. Educational, nursing work.

Mary, Sisters Servants of, O.S.M.: Founded 1861, in Italy; in US, 1916. Generalate, Rome, Italy; US motherhouse, 13811 S. Western Ave., Blue Island, Ill. 60406. Educational, hospital work.

Mary, Sisters Servants of (Trained Nurses), S. de M.: Founded 1851, at Madrid, Spain; in US, 1914. General motherhouse, Rome, Italy; US motherhouse, 800 N. 18th St., Kansas City, Kans. 66102. Home nursing.

Mary and Joseph, Daughters of, D.M.J.: Founded 1817, in Belgium; in US, 1926. Generalate, Rome, Italy; American provincial house, 5300 Crest Rd., Rancho Palos Verdes, Calif. 90274.

Mary Help of Christians, Daughters of (Salesian Sisters of St. John Bosco), F.M.A.: Founded 1872, in Italy, by St. John Bosco and St. Mary Dominic Mazzarello; in US, 1908. General motherhouse, Rome, Italy; US motherhouse, Haledon, N.J. 07508. Education, youth work.

Mary of Namur, Sisters of St., S.S.M.N.: Founded 1819, at Namur, Belgium; in US, 1863. General motherhouse, Namur, Belgium. US provinces: 3756 Delaware Ave., Kenmore, N.Y. 14217; 3300 Hemphill St., Ft. Worth, Tex. 76110.

Mary of Providence, Daughters of St., D.S.M.P.: Founded 1872, at Como, Italy; in US, 1913. General motherhouse, Rome, Italy; US provincial house, 4200 N. Austin Ave., Chicago, Ill. 60634. Educational work.

Mary of the Catholic Apostolate, Sisters of (Schoenstatt Sisters of Mary), S.A.C.: Founded 1926 at Schoenstatt, Germany; in US, 1949. General motherhouse, Schoenstatt, Germany. US addresses: Star Route 1, Box 100, Rockport, Tex. 78382; W. 284-N.698 Cherry Lane, Waukesha, Wis. 53186.

Mary of the Immaculate Conception, Daughters of, D.M.: Founded 1904, in US, by Msgr. Lucian Bojnowski. General motherhouse, 314 Osgood Ave., New Britain, Conn. 06053. Educational, hospital work.

Mary Immaculate, Daughters of (Marianist Sisters), F.M.I.: Founded 1816, in France, by Very Rev. William-Joseph Chaminade. General motherhouse, Rome, Italy; US foundation, 251 W. Ligustrum Dr., San Antonio, Tex. 78228. Educational work.

Mary Immaculate, Religious of, R.M.I.: Founded 1876, in Spain; in US, 1954. General motherhouse, Rome, Italy: US foundation 719 Augusta St., San Antonio, Tex. 78215.

Mary Immaculate, Sisters Servants of, S.M.I: Founded 1892, in Ukraine; in US, 1935. General motherhouse, Rome, Italy; US province, 209 W. Chestnut Hill Ave., Philadelphia, Pa. 19118. Educational, hospital work.

Mary Immaculate of Mariowka, Sister Servants of, S.S.M.I.: Founded 1878 in Poland. General motherhouse, Poland; American provincialate, 1220 Tugwell Dr., Catonsville, Md. 21228.

Mary Reparatrix, Society of, S.M.R.: Founded 1857, in France; in US, 1908. Generalate, Rome, Italy; US province, 14 E. 29th St., New York, N.Y. 10016.

Medical Mission Sisters (Society of Catholic Medical Missionaries, Inc.), S.C.M.M.: Founded 1925, in US. Generalate, Rome, Italy; US headquarters, 8400 Pine Rd., Philadelphia, Pa. 19111. Medical work, especially in mission areas.

Medical Missionaries of Mary, M.M.M.: Founded 1937, in Ireland, by Mother Mary Martin; in US, 1950. General motherhouse, Drogheda, Ireland; US headquarters, 563 Minneford Ave., City Island, Bronx, N.Y. 10464. Medical aid in missions.

Mercedarian Missionaries of Berriz, M.M.B.: Founded 1930, in Spain; in US, 1946. General motherhouse, Berriz, Spain; US headquarters, 918 E. 9th St., Kansas City, Mo. 64106.

Mercy, Daughters of Our Lady of, D.M.: Founded 1837, in Italy, by St. Mary Joseph Rossello; in US, 1919. General motherhouse, Savona, Italy; US motherhouse, Villa Rossello, Catawba Ave., Newfield, N.J. 08344. Educational, hospital work.

Mercy, Missionary Sisters of Our Lady of, M.O.M.: Founded 1938, in Brazil; in US, 1955. General motherhouse, Brazil; US address, 388 Franklin St., Buffalo, N.Y. 14202.

Mercy, Sisters of, R.S.M.: Founded 1831, in Ireland, by Mother Mary Catherine McAuley. US motherhouses:

634 New Scotland Ave., Albany, N.Y. 12208; 273 Willoughby Ave., Brooklyn, N.Y. 11205; S. 5245 Murphy Rd., Orchard Park, N.Y. 14127; 100 Mansfield Ave., Burlington, Vt. 05401; 1125 Prairie Dr., N.E., Cedar Rapids, Ia. 52402; 444 E. Grandview Blvd., Erie, Pa. 16504; 249 Steele Rd., W. Hartford, Conn. 06117.

Windham, N.H. 03087; Merion, Pa. 10966; 3333 Fifth Ave., Pittsburgh, Pa. 15213; 605 Stevens Ave., Portland, Me. 04103; Belmont, N. Car. 28012; 1437 Blossom Rd., Rochester, N.Y. 14610; 535 Sacramento St., Auburn, Calif. 95603.

2300 Adeline Dr., Burlingame, Calif. 94010; US Route 22 at Tirrell Rd., Plainfield, N.J. 07061; 101 Barry Rd., Worcester, Mass. 01609.

Mercy, Sisters of, of the Union in the United States of America, R.S.M.: Founded 1831 in Ireland, by Mother M. Catherine McAuley; union formed in 1929. U.S. provinces:

P.O. Box 10490, Baltimore, Md. 21209; 10024 S. Central Park Ave., Chicago, Ill. 60642; 2301 Grandview Ave., Cincinnati, Ohio 45206; 29000 Eleven Mile Rd., Farmington Hills, Mich. 48018; 541 Broadway, Dobbs Ferry, N.Y. 10522; 1801 S. 72nd St., Omaha, Nebr. 68124; R.D. 3, Cumberland, R.I. 02864; 2039 N. Geyer Rd., St. Louis, Mo. 63131; Dallas, Pa. 18612.

Mercy, Sisters of, Daughters of Christian Charity of St. Vincent de Paul, S.M.D.C.: Founded 1842, in Hungary; US foundation, Rt. 1, Box 353, Hewitt, N.J. 07421.

Mercy of the Blessed Sacrament, Sisters of: Founded 1910 in Mexico. U.S. foundation, 555 E. Mountain View, Barstow, Calif. 92311.

Mill Hill Sisters; See Franciscan Missionaries of St. Joseph.

Minim Sisters of Mary Immaculate, C.F.M.M.: Founded 1886, in Mexico; in U.S. 1926. General motherhouse, Leon, Guanajuato, Mexico; US address, St. Joseph Hospital Convent, Box 1809, Nogales, Ariz. 85621.

Misericorde Sisters, S.M.: Founded 1848, in Canada; in US, 1887. General motherhouse. 12435 Ave. Misericorde, Montreal H4J 2G3, Canada. Hospital work.

Mission Helpers of the Sacred Heart, M.H.S.H.: Founded 1890, in US. General motherhouse, 1001 W. Joppa Rd., Baltimore, Md. 21204. Religious education, social work.

Missionary Catechists of the Sacred Hearts of Jesus and Mary (Violetas), M.C.: Founded 1927, in Mexico; in US, 1943. Motherhouse, Tlalpan, Mexico; US address, 209 W. Murray St., Victoria, Tex. 77901.

Missionary Sisters of the Catholic Apostolate (Pallottine Missionary Sisters), S.A.C.: Founded in Rome, 1843; in US, 1912. Generalate, Rome, Italy; US provincialate, Rt. 2, 15270 Old Halls Ferry Rd., Florissant, Mo. 63034.

Mother of God, Missionary Sisters of the, M.S.M.G.: Byzantine, Ukrainian Rite, Stamford. Motherhouse, 711-719 N. Franklin St., Philadelphia, Pa. 19123.

Mother of God, Sisters Poor Servants of the, S.M.G.: Founded 1869, at London, England; in US, 1947. General motherhouse, Maryfield, Roehampton, London. US addresses: High Point, N.C. 27260; Norton, Va. 24273; 1800 Geary St., Philadelphia, Pa. 19145. Hospital work.

Nazareth, Poor Sisters of: Founded in England; U.S. foundation, 1924. General motherhouse, Hammersmith, London, England; US novitiate, 3333 Manning Ave., Los Angeles, Calif. 90064.

Notre Dame Sisters: Founded 1853, in Czechoslovakia; in US, 1910. General motherhouse, Javornik, Czechoslovakia; US motherhouse, 3501 State St., Omaha, Nebr. 68112. Educational work.

Notre Dame, School Sisters of, S.S.N.D.: Founded 1833, in Germany; in US, 1847. General motherhouse, Rome, Italy. US provinces: 700 W. Highland Rd., Mequon, Wis. 53092; 6401 N. Charles St., Baltimore, Md. 21212; 320 E. Ripa Ave., St. Louis, Mo. 63125; Good Counsel Hill, Mankato, Minn. 56011; Wilton, Conn. 06897; Rt. 2, Box 4, Irving, Tex. 75060; 9515 S. Loomis St., Chicago, Ill. 60643.

Notre Dame, Sisters of, S.N.D.: Founded 1850, at Coesfeld, Germany; in US, 1874. General motherhouse, Rome, Italy. US provinces: 13000 Auburn Rd., Chardon, O. 44024; 1601 Dixie Highway, Covington, Ky. 41011; 3837 Secor Rd., Toledo, O. 43623; 624 W. Potrero Rd., Thousand Oaks, Calif. 91360.

Notre Dame, Sisters of the Congregation of, C.N.D.: Founded 1653, in Canada; in US, 1860. General motherhouse, Montreal, Que., Canada; U.S. province, 223 West Mountain Rd., Ridgefield, Conn. 06877. Education.

Notre Dame de Namur, Sisters of, S.N.D.: Founded 1803, in France; in US, 1840. General motherhouse, Rome, Italy. US provinces: 328 Dartmouth St., Boston, Mass. 02116; Jeffrey's Neck Rd., Ipswich, Mass. 01938; 1561 N. Benson Rd., Fairfield, Conn. 06430; Ilchester, Md. 21083; 701 E. Columbia Ave., Cincinnati, O. 45215; 14800 Bohlman Rd., Saratoga, Calif. 95070. Educational work.

Notre Dame de Sion, Congregation of, N.D.S.: Founded 1843, in France; in US, 1892. Generalate, Rome, Italy; US provincial house, 3823 Locust St., Kansas City, Mo. 64109. Creation of better understanding and relations between Christians and Jews.

Notre Dame des Anges, Missionary Sisters of, M.N.D.A.: Founded 1922, in Canada; in US, 1949. General motherhouse, Lennoxville, Canada; US address, St. Mary's Catechetical School, 320 N. Main St., Union City, Conn. 06770.

Our Lady of Mercy, Sisters of: General motherhouse, Wexford, Ireland; US foundation, Epiphany Convent, Rt. 10, Box 161, Malone Dr., Lake City, Fla. 32055.

Our Lady of Sorrows, Sisters of, O.L.S.: Founded 1839, in Italy; in US, 1947. General motherhouse, Rome, Italy; US headquarters, 10450 Ellerbe Rd., Shreveport, La. 71106.

Our Lady of the Garden, Sisters of, O.L.G.: Founded 1829, in Italy, by St. Anthony Mary Gianelli. Motherhouse, Rome, Italy; U.S. address, Round Hill Rd., Middletown, Conn. 06457.

Pallottine Sisters of the Catholic Apostolate, C.S.A.C.: Founded 1843, at Rome, Italy; in US, 1889. General motherhouse, Rome; US motherhouse, St. Patrick's Villa, Harriman Heights, Harriman, N.Y. 10926. Educational work.

Parish Visitors of Mary Immaculate, P.V.M.I.: Founded 1920, in New York. General motherhouse, Box 658, Monroe, N.Y. 10950. Mission work.

Passionist Sisters: See Cross and Passion, Sisters of the.

Paul, Angelic Sisters of St.: Founded 1535, in Milan, Italy; US address, Fatima Shrine, Swan Rd., Youngstown, N.Y. 14174.

Paul, Daughters of St., Missionary Sisters of the Catholic Editions, D.S.P.: Founded 1915, at Alba, Piedmont, Italy; in US, 1932. General motherhouse, Rome, Italy; US provincial house, 50 St. Paul's Ave., Jamaica Plain, Mass. 02130. Apostolate of the communications arts.

Paul of Chartres, Sisters of St., S.P.C.: Founded 1696, in France. General house, Rome, Italy; US address, County Road 492, Marquette, Mich. 49855.

Peter Claver, Missionary Sisters of St., S.S.P.C.: Founded 1894; in US, 1914. General motherhouse, Rome, Italy; US address, 667 Woods Mill Rd. S., Chesterfield, Mo. 63017.

Pious Schools, Sisters of, Sch. P.: Founded 1829 in Spain; in US, 1954. General motherhouse, Rome, Italy; US headquarters, 9925 Mason Ave., Chatsworth, Calif. 91311.

Poor, Little Sisters of the, L.S.P.: Founded 1839, in France; in US, 1868. General motherhouse, St. Pern, France. US provinces: 110-30 221st St., Queens Village, N.Y. 11429; 601 Maiden Choice Lane, Baltimore, Md. 21228; 80 W. Northwest Hwy., Palatine, Ill. 60067. Social work.

Poor Clare Missionary Sisters (Misionaras Clarisas), M.C.: Founded Mexico. General motherhouse, Rome, Italy; US novitiate, 1019 N. Newhope, Santa Ana, Calif. 92703.

Poor Clare Nuns: See Franciscan Poor Clare Nuns.

Poor Clares (Sisters of St. Clare), P.C.: General motherhouse, Dublin, Ireland; US foundation, 37 E. Emerson, Chula Vista, Calif. 92011.

Poor Handmaids of Jesus Christ (Ancilla Domini Sisters), P.H.J.C.: Founded 1851, in Germany; in US, 1868. General motherhouse, Dernbach, Westerwald, Germany; US motherhouse, Donaldson, Ind. 46513. Educational, hospital work.

Precious Blood, Daughters of Charity of the Most: Founded 1872, at Pagani, Italy; in US, 1908. General motherhouse, Rome, Italy; US convent, 1482 North Ave., Bridgeport, Conn. 06604.

Precious Blood, Missionary Sisters of the, C.P.S.: Founded 1885, at Mariannhill, South Africa; in US, 1925. Generalate, Rome, Italy; US novitiate, New Holland Ave., P.O. Box 97, Shillington, Pa. 19607. Home and foreign mission work.

Precious Blood, Sisters Adorers of the, A.P.B.: Founded 1861, in Canada; in US, 1890. General motherhouses: 2520, rue Girouard, St. Hyacinthe, Que. J2S 7B8, Canada (French); Box 2035, London N6A 4C5, Ont., Canada (English). Contemplatives.

Precious Blood, Sisters of the, C.Pp.S.: Founded 1834, in Switzerland; in US, 1844. Generalate, 4000 Denlinger Rd., Dayton, Ohio 45426. Educational, hospital work.

Precious Blood, Sisters of the Most, C.Pp.S.: Founded 1845, in Steinerberg, Switzerland; in US, 1870. General motherhouse, 204 N. Main St., O'Fallon, Mo. 63366. Educational work.

Presentation, Sisters of St. Mary of the, S.M.P.: Founded 1829, in France; in US, 1903. General motherhouse, Broons, Cotes-du-Nord, France. US address, Maryvale Novitiate, Valley City, N. Dak. 58072. Educational, hospital work.

Presentation of Mary, Sisters of the, P.M.: Founded 1796, in France; in US, 1873. General motherhouse, Rome, Italy. US provincial houses: 495 Mammoth Rd., Manchester, N.H. 03104; 209 Lawrence St., Methuen, Mass. 01844.

Presentation of the B.V.M., Sisters of the, P.B.V.M.: Founded 1777, in Ireland; in US,

1854. US motherhouses: 2360 Carter Rd., Dubuque, Ia. 52001; R.D. 2, Box 101, Newburgh, N.Y. 12550; 8931 Callaghan Rd., San Antonio, Tex. 78230; 2340 Turk St., San Francisco, Calif. 94118; Watervliet, N.Y. 12189.

Route 1, Fargo, N. Dak. 58102; 250 S. Davis Dr., P.O. Box 1113, Warner Robbins, Ga. 31093; Aberdeen, S. Dak. 57401; 1300 E. Cedar, Globe, Ariz. 85501; 1555 E. Dana, Mesa, Ariz. 85201; 366 South St., Fitchburg, Mass. 01420.

Providence, Daughters of Divine, F.D.P.: Founded 1832, Italy; in US, 1964. General motherhouse, Rome, Italy; US foundation, 1029 N. Atlanta St., Metairie, La. 70003.

Providence, Missionary Catechists of Divine, M.C.D.P.: Founded 1930, as a filial society; adjunct branch of Sisters of Divine Providence (San Antonio). Formation house, 2318 Castroville Rd., San Antonio, Tex. 78237.

Providence, Oblate Sisters of, O.S.P.: Founded 1829, in US. General motherhouse, 701 Gun Rd., Baltimore, Md. 21227. Educational work.

Providence, Sisters of, S.P.: Founded 1861, in Canada; in US, 1873. General motherhouse, Our Lady of Victory Convent, Brightside, Holyoke, Mass. 01040.

Providence, Sisters of, S.P.: Founded 1843, in Canada; in US, 1854. General motherhouse, Montreal, Canada. US provinces: 1511 Third Ave., Seattle, Wash. 98101; 9 E. 9th Ave., Spokane, Wash. 99202.

Providence, Sisters of (of St. Mary-of-the-Woods), S.P.: Founded 1806, in France; in US, 1840. Generalate, St. Mary-of-the-Woods, Ind. 47876.

Providence, Sisters of Divine, C.D.P.: Founded 1762, in France; in US, 1866. Generalate, Box 197, Helotes, Tex. 78023. Educational, hospital work.

Providence, Sisters of Divine, C.D.P.: Founded 1851, in Germany; in US, 1876. Generalate, Rome, Italy. US provinces: 9000 Babcock Blvd., Allison Park, Pa. 15101; 8351 Florissant Rd., Normandy, Mo. 63121; Box 2, Rte. 80, Kingston, Mass. 02364. Educational, hospital work.

Providence, Sisters of Divine (of Kentucky), C.D.P.: Founded 1762, in France; in US, 1889. General motherhouse, Moselle, France; US province, Melbourne, Ky. 41059. Educational, hospital work, domestic work.

Redeemer, Oblates of the Most Holy, O.SS.R.: Founded 1864, in Spain. General motherhouse, Spain; US foundation, 60-80 Pond St., Jamaica Plain, Mass. 02130.

Redeemer, Order of the Most Holy, O.SS.R.: Founded 1731, by St. Alphonsus Liguori; in US, 1957. US addresses: Mother of Perpetual Help Monastery, Esopus, N.Y. 12429; St. Alphonsus Monastery, Liguori, Mo. 63057.

Redeemer, Sisters of the Divine, S.D.R.: Founded 1849, in Niederbronn, France; in US, 1912. General motherhouse, Rome, Italy; US motherhouse, 999 Rock Run Road, Elizabeth, Pa. 15037. Educational, hospital work; care of the aged.

Redeemer, Sisters of the Holy, S.H.R.: Founded 1849, in Alsace; in US, 1924. General motherhouse, Wuerzburg, Germany; US regional house, Huntingdon Valley, Pa. 19006. Personalized medical care in hospitals, homes for aged and private homes.

Refuge, Sisters of Our Lady of Charity of the, O.L.C.: Founded 1641, in Caen, France, by St. John Eudes; in U.S., 1855. Autonomous houses were federated in 1944 and in May, 1978, the North American Union of the Sisters of Our Lady of Charity was established. General motherhouse and administrative center, Box 327, Wisconsin Dells, Wis. 53965. Primarily devoted to re-education and rehabilitation of women and girls in residential and non-residential settings.

Reparation of the Congregation of Mary, Sisters of, S.R.C.M.: Founded 1903, in US. Motherhouse, St. Zita's Villa, Monsey, N.Y. 10952.

Resurrection, Sisters of the, C.R.: Founded 1891, in Italy; in US, 1900. General motherhouse, Rome, Italy. US provinces: 7432 Talcott Ave., Chicago, Ill. 60631; Mt. St. Joseph, Castleton-on-Hudson, N.Y. 12033. Educational work.

Rita, Sisters of St., O.S.A.: General motherhouse, Wurzburg, Germany. US foundation, St. Monica's Convent, 3920 Green Bay Rd., Racine, Wis. 53404.

Rosary, Congregation of Our Lady of the Holy, R.S.R.: Founded 1874, in Canada; in US, 1899. General motherhouse, C.P. 2020, Rimouski, Que., Canada. Educational work.

Rosary, Missionary Sisters of Our Lady of the Holy, H.R.S.: Founded 1924, in Ireland; in US, 1954. Motherhouse, Dublin, Ireland. US novitiate, 214 Ashwood Rd., Villanova, Pa. 19085. African missions.

Sacrament, Missionary Sisters of the Most Blessed, M.SS.S.: General motherhouse, Madrid, Spain; US foundation: 1111 Wordin Ave., Bridgeport, Conn. 06605.

Sacrament, Nuns of the Perpetual Adoration of the Blessed, A.P.: Founded 1807, in Rome, Italy; in US, 1925. US monasteries: 145 N. Cotton Ave., El Paso, Tex. 79901; 771 Ashbury St., San Francisco, Calif. 94117.

Sacrament, Oblate Sisters of the Blessed, O.S.B.S.: Founded 1935, in US; motherhouse, St. Sylvester Convent, Marty, S.D. 57361. Care of American Indians.

Sacrament, Religious Mercedarians of the Blessed, R.M.SS.: Founded 1910, in Mexico; in US, 1926. General motherhouse, Mexico City, Mexico; US convent, 222 W. Cevallos St., San Antonio, Tex. 78204.

Sacrament, Servants of the Blessed, S.S.S.:

Founded 1858, in France, by St. Pierre Julien Eymard; in US, 1947. General motherhouse, Rome, Italy; American vice-provincial house, 101 Silver St., Waterville, Me. 04901. Contemplative.

Sacrament, Sisters of the Blessed, for Indians and Colored People, S.B.S.: Founded 1891, in US. General motherhouse, Cornwells Heights, Pa. 19020.

Sacrament, Sisters of the Most Holy, M.H.S.: Founded 1851, in France; in US, 1872. General motherhouse, 409 W. St. Mary Blvd. (P.O. Box 2429), Lafayette, La. 70501.

Sacrament, Sisters Servants of the Blessed, S.S.B.S.: Founded 1904, in Mexico. General motherhouse, Guadalajara, Mexico. US address, 536 Rockwood Ave., Calexico, Calif. 92231.

Sacramentine Nuns (Religious of the Order of the Blessed Sacrament and Our Lady), O.S.S.: Founded 1639, in France; in US, 1912. US monasteries: 23 Park Ave., Yonkers, N.Y. 10703; US 31, Conway, Mich. 49722. Perpetual adoration of the Holy Eucharist.

Sacred Heart, Daughters of Our Lady of the: Founded 1882, in France; in US, 1955. General motherhouse, Rome, Italy; US address, 424 E. Browning Rd., Bellmawr, N.J. 08031. Educational work.

Sacred Heart, Missionary Sisters of the (Cabrini Sisters), M.S.C.: Founded 1880, in Italy, by St. Frances Xavier Cabrini; in US, 1889. General motherhouse, Rome, Italy; US provinces: 223 E. 19th St., New York, N.Y. 10003 (Eastern); 428 St. James Pl., Chicago, Ill. 60614 (Western). Educational, health, social and catechetical work.

Sacred Heart, Religious of the Apostolate of the, R.A.: General motherhouse, Madrid, Spain; US address, 1120 6th St., Miami Beach, Fla., 33139.

Sacred Heart, Society Devoted to the, S.D.S.H.: Founded 1940, in Hungary; in US, 1956. US motherhouse, 728 S. Hudson Ave., Los Angeles, Calif. 90005. Educational work.

Sacred Heart, Society of the, R.SC.J.: Founded 1800, in France; in US, 1818. General motherhouse, Rome, Italy. US provinces: 1177 King St., Greenwich, Conn. 06830; 2047 W. Fargo, Chicago, Ill. 60645; 541 S. Mason Rd., St. Louis, Mo. 63141; 453 Miller Ave., S. San Francisco, Calif. 94080; 842 Commonwealth Ave., Newton, Mass. 02159. Educational work.

Sacred Heart of Jesus, Apostles of, A.S.C.J.: Founded 1894, in Italy; in US, 1902. General motherhouse, Rome, Italy; US motherhouse, 265 Benham St., Hamden, Conn. 06514. Educational, social work.

Sacred Heart of Jesus, Handmaids of the, A.C.J.: Founded 1877, in Spain. General motherhouse, Rome, Italy; US province, 2025 Church Rd., Wyncote, Pa. 19095. Educational, retreat work.

Sacred Heart of Jesus, Missionary Sisters of the Most (Hiltrup), M.S.C.: Founded 1899, in Germany; in US, 1908. General motherhouse, Rome, Italy; US province, Hyde Park, Reading, Pa. 19605. Educational, hospital, social work.

Sacred Heart of Jesus, Oblate Sisters of the, O.S.H.J.: Founded 1894; in US, 1949. General motherhouse, Rome, Italy; US headquarters, 50 Warner Rd., Hubbard, Ohio 44425. Educational, social work.

Sacred Heart of Jesus, Servants of the Most: Founded 1894, in Poland; in US, 1959. General motherhouse, Cracow, Poland; US address, 231 Arch St., Cresson, Pa. 16630.

Sacred Heart of Jesus, Sisters of the, S.S.C.J.: Founded 1816, in France; in US, 1903. General motherhouse, St. Jacut, Brittany, France; US provincial house, 5922 Blanco Rd., San Antonio, Tex. 78216. Educational, hospital, domestic work.

Sacred Heart of Jesus and of the Poor, Servants of the (Mexican), S.S.H.J.P.: Founded 1885, in Mexico; in US, 1907. General motherhouse, Apartado 92, Puebla, Pue., Mexico; US regional house, 237 Tobin Pl., El Paso, Tex. 79905.

Sacred Heart of Jesus for Reparation, Congregation of the Handmaids of the: Founded 1918, in Italy; in US, 1958. US address, Sunshine Park, R.D. 3, Steubenville, Ohio 43952.

Sacred Heart of Mary, Religious of the, R.S.H.M.: Founded 1848, in France; in US, 1877. Generalate, Rome, Italy. US provinces; 15 E. 81st St., New York, N.Y. 10028; 8008 Loyola Blvd., Los Angeles, Calif. 90045.

Sacred Hearts, Religious of the Holy Union of the, S.U.S.C.: Founded 1826, in France; in US, 1886. Generalate, Rome, Italy. US provinces: 550 Rock St., Fall River, Mass. 02720; Main St., Groton, Mass. 01450. Educational work.

Sacred Hearts and of Perpetual Adoration, Sisters of the, SS.CC.: Founded 1797, in France; in US, 1908. General motherhouse, Rome, Italy; US motherhouse, 330 Main St., N. Fairhaven, Mass. 02719. Educational work.

Sacred Hearts of Jesus and Mary, Sisters of the, S.H.J.M.: Established 1953, in US. General motherhouse, Essex, England; US address, 310 San Carlos Ave., El Cerrito, Calif. 94530.

Savior, Company of the, C.S.: Founded 1952, in Spain; in US, 1962. General motherhouse, Madrid, Spain; US foundation, 820 Clinton Ave., Bridgeport, Conn. 06608.

Savior, Sisters of the Divine, S.D.S.: Founded 1888, in Italy; in US, 1895. General motherhouse, Rome, Italy; US motherhouse, 4311 N. 100th St., Milwaukee, Wis. 53222. Educational, hospital work.

Social Service, Sisters of, S.S.S.: Founded 1908, in Hungary; in US, 1926. General motherhouse, 1120 Westchester Pl., Los Angeles, Calif. 90019.

Social Service, Sisters of, S.S.S.: Founded in Hungary, 1923. US address, 440 Linwood Ave., Buffalo, N.Y. 14209. Social work.

Teresa of Jesus, Society of St., S.T.J.: Founded 1876, in Spain; in US, 1910. General motherhouse, Rome, Italy; US provincial house, 154 Fair Ave., San Antonio, Tex. 78223.

Thomas of Villanova, Congregation of Sisters of St., S.S.T.V.: Founded 1661, in France; in US, 1948. General motherhouse, Neuilly-sur-Seine, France; US foundation W. Rocks Rd., Norwalk, Conn. 06851.

Trinity, Missionary Servants of the Most Blessed, M.S.B.T.: Founded 1912, in US, by Very Rev. Thomas A. Judge. General motherhouse, 3501 Solly St., Philadelphia, Pa. 19136. Educational, social work.

Trinity, Sisters of the Most Holy, O.Ss.T.: Founded 1198, in Rome; in US, 1920. General motherhouse, Rome, Italy; US address, Immaculate Conception Province, 21320 Euclid Ave., Euclid, Ohio 44117. Educational work.

Ursula of the Blessed Virgin, Society of the Sisters of St., S.U.: Founded 1606, in France; in US, 1902. General motherhouse, Tours, France; US novitiate, Rhinebeck, N.Y. 12572. Educational work.

Ursuline Nuns (Roman Union), O.S.U.: Founded 1535, in Italy; in US, 1727. Generalate, Rome, Italy. US provinces: 323 E. 198th St., New York, N.Y. 10458; Crystal Heights Rd., Crystal City, Mo. 63019; 639 Angela Dr., Santa Rosa, Calif. 95401; 71 Lowder St., Dedham, Mass. 02026,

Ursuline Nuns of the Congregation of Paris, O.S.U.: Founded 1535, in Italy; in US, 1727. US motherhouses: St. Martin, O. 45170; East and Miami Sts., Paola, Kans. 66071; 3115 Lexington Rd., Louisville, Ky. 40206; 2600 Lander Rd., Cleveland, O. 44124; Maple Mount, Ky. 42356; 2413 Collingwood Blvd., Toledo, O. 43620; 4250 Shields Rd., Canfield, O. 44406; 1339 E. McMillan St., Cincinnati, O. 45206.

Ursuline Nuns of the Congregation of Tildonk, Belgium, R.U.: Founded 1535, in Italy; in US, 1924. Generalate, Tildonk, Belgium; US address, 81-15 Utopia Parkway, Jamaica, N.Y. 11432. Educational, foreign mission work.

Ursuline Sisters (Irish Ursuline Union), O.S.U.: General motherhouse, Blackrock, Cork, Ireland; US address, 1973 Torch Hill Rd., Columbus, Ga. 31903.

Ursuline Sisters of Mount Calvary, O.S.U.: Founded 1535, in Italy; in US, 1910. General motherhouse, Mount Calvary, Germany; US motherhouse, 1026 N. Douglas Ave., Belleville, Ill. 62221. Educational work.

Venerini Sisters, Religious, M.P.V.: Founded 1685, in Italy; in US, 1909. General motherhouse, Rome, Italy; US provincialate; 23 Edward St., Worcester, Mass. 01605.

Verona, Missionary Sisters of, M.S.V.: Founded 1875, in Italy; in US, 1950. US address, 1307 Lakeside Ave., Richmond, Va. 23228. Hospital, social, educational work.

Victory Missionary Sisters, Our Lady of, O.L.V.M.: Founded 1922, in US. Motherhouse, Victory Noll, Box 109, Huntington, Ind. 46750. Educational, social work.

Vincent de Paul, Sisters: See Charity of St. Vincent de Paul, Sisters of.

Visitation Nuns, V.H.M.: Founded 1610, in France; in U.S. (Georgetown, D.C.), 1799. Contemplative, educational work. Two federations in U.S.

First Federation of North America. Major pontifical enclosure. Pres., Mother Mary Gabriella Muth, Monastery of the Visitation, 2002 Bancroft Pkwy., Wilmington, Del. 19806. Addresses of monasteries belonging to the federation: 2300 Springhill Ave., Mobile, Ala. 36607; 9001 Old Georgetown Rd., Bethesda, Md. 20014; 2002 Bancroft Pkwy., Wilmington, Del. 19806; 256th St. and Arlington Ave., Bronx, N.Y. 10471; 2209 E. Grace St., Richmond, Va. 23223; 5820 City Ave., Philadelphia, Pa. 19131; 1745 Parkside Blvd., Toledo, O. 43607; 2055 Ridgedale Dr., Snellville, Ga. 30278.

Second Federation of North America. Constitutional enclosure. Pres., Rev. Mother Anne Madeline Ernstmann, Visitation Monastery, 3200 S.W. Dash Point Rd., Federal Way, Wash. 98003. Addresses of monasteries belonging to the federation: 1500 35th St., Washington, D.C. 20007; 3020 N. Ballas Rd., St. Louis, Mo. 63131; 200 E. Second St., Frederick, Md. 21701; Mt. St. Chantal Monastery of the Visitation, Wheeling, W. Va. 26003; 700 Academy Rd., Baltimore, Md. 21228; Ridge Blvd. and 89th St., Brooklyn, N.Y. 11209; 1600 Murdock Ave., Parkersburg, W. Va. 26101; 2000 Sixteenth Ave., Rock Island, Ill. 61201; 2475 Dodd Rd., Mendota Heights, St. Paul, Minn. 55120; Visitation Monastery, Georgetown, Ky. 40324; 3200 S.W. Dash Point Rd., Federal Way, Wash. 98003.

Visitation of the Congregation of the Immaculate Heart of Mary, Sisters of the, S.V.M.: Founded 1952, in US. Motherhouse, 900 Alta Vista St., Dubuque, Ia. 52201. Educational work.

Vocationist Sisters (Sisters of the Divine Vocations): Founded 1921, in Italy. General motherhouse, Naples, Italy; US foundation, Perpetual Help Nursery, 172 Broad St., Newark, N.J. 07104.

White Sisters: See Africa, Missionary Sisters of Our Lady of.

Wisdom, Daughters of, D.W.: Founded 1703, in France, by St. Louis Marie Grignon de Montfort; in US, 1904. General motherhouse, Vendee, France; US province, 385 S.

Ocean Ave., Islip, N.Y. Educational, hospital work.

Xaverian Missionary Society of Mary, Inc., x.m.m.: Founded 1945, in Italy; in US, 1954. General motherhouse, Parma, Italy; US address, 242 Salisbury St., Worcester, Mass. 01609.

Xavier Mission Sisters (Catholic Mission Sisters of St. Francis Xavier), X.M.S.: Founded 1946, at Warren, Mich., by Cardinal Edward Mooney. General motherhouse, 37179 Moravian Dr., Mount Clemens, Mich. 48043. Educational, hospital, social work in missions.

ORGANIZATIONS OF WOMEN RELIGIOUS

Association of Contemplative Sisters: Founded by nearly 140 representatives of 57 communities in the U.S. and Canada in August, 1969. Its principal purpose is development of the contemplative life-style for effective service to the Church. It has a membership of approximately 700. Sister Lilla Marie Hull, M.M., is president. The central office is located at 920 Centre St., Jamaica Plain, Mass. 02130.

Consortium Perfectae Caritatis: Named Association of Perfect Love after the Latin title of the Second Vatican Council's *Decree on the Appropriate Renewal of Religious Life,* and organized in March, 1971, at a meeting of nearly 150 sisters from 48 communities in the U.S. and Canada. Its purposes are to encourage the development of religious life in line with Vatican II guidelines and related directives, and to share experiences in the renewal of religious life. Sister Mary Elise, S.N.D., is executive director of the national council. The mailing address is 13000 Auburn Rd., Chardon, Ohio 44024. Rev. James A. Viall is coordinator.

Las Hermanas: A national organization of women religious of Hispanic origin formed in 1971 for the purpose of being "actively present to the ever-changing needs" of the Spanish-speaking — through programs of cultural awareness and training for persons in ministry to the Spanish-speaking. The organization, with sister associates and lay affiliates, is directed by a national coordinating team headed by Sisters Teresita Basso, Consuelo Covarrubias and Ramona Jean Corrales. The national office is located at 187 Clayton Ave., San Jose, Calif. 95110.

Leadership Conference of Women Religious: An association of major superiors of religious communities of women, with the purpose of promoting the spiritual and apostolic calling and works of sisterhoods in the U.S. Organized in the late 50s and approved by the Congregation for Religious and Secular Institutes June 13, 1962, it has a membership of approximately 600. Its original name, changed in 1971, was the Conference of Major Superiors of Women. With its formerly affiliated Sister Formation Conference, it inaugurated measures for the religious and professional development of sisters and has contributed to the renewal of religious life in this country. Sister Theresa Kane, R.S.M., is president; Sister Lora Ann Quinone, C.D.P., is executive director. The national secretariat is located at 1302 Eighteenth St. N.W., Washington, D.C. 20036.

National Assembly of Women Religious: Formed in 1970, the assembly is a movement and organization of women and men associates of the Church. Its objectives are the promotion of a ministry of justice particularly, but not exclusively, for women in the Church and in economic systems, and the reconciliation of differences between laywomen and sisters and between men and women in the Church. The 1979 membership consisted of 73 diocesan councils and 2,000 individuals. Sister Mary O'Keefe and Sister Merle Nolde are co-directors. Offices are located at 1307 S. Wabash Ave., Chicago, Ill. 60605.

National Black Sisters' Conference: Organized in August, 1968, for the purposes of determining priorities in service to black people, of promoting black vocations and the development of religious life in the unique black life-style, and to influence the formational and recruitment practices of white religious communities. Its members include 150 black sisters belonging to 123 religious communities. Sister Cora Marie Billings, R.S.M., is coordinator. The mailing address of the conference is P.O. Box 28216, Philadelphia, Pa. 19131.

National Coalition of American Nuns: Organized under the leadership of Sister Margaret Traxler, S.S.N.D., in July, 1969, for efforts to secure recognition and development of the role of women in the Church and society, along with advocacy for social activism. Sister Andrea Lee is president. Offices are located at 1307 S. Wabash Ave., Chicago, Ill 60605.

National Sisters' Vocation Conference: Formed in September, 1970, as a national organization dedicated to promoting understanding of the role of women, especially religious, in the Church through work in the vocation apostolate. It coordinates and provides informational and other services to persons and organizations in the vocation apostolate, and assists prospective candidates for religious life. Its membership includes approximately 2,000 women and men. Sister Gertrude Wemhoff, O.S.B., is executive director. The national office is located at 1307 S. Wabash Ave., Chicago, Ill. 60605.

Religious Formation Conference: Originally organized with the title of the Sister Formation Conference in 1952, for the purpose of promoting the spiritual and professional formation of sisters in the U.S. With a current membership of both men and women religious, the conference focuses on initial and on-going formation work in religious communities and secular institutes. Sister Carla Przybilla, O.S.F., is executive director. The national office is located at 1234 Massachusetts Ave. N.W., Washington, D.C. 20005.

Sisters Uniting: Formed in March, 1971, as a council of representatives of national organizations of women religious seeking to promote and express solidarity in defense of Gospel values. Participating bodies included the Association of Contemplative Sisters, Las Hermanas, the Religious Formation Conference, the National Sisters' Vocation Conference, the National Coalition of American Nuns, the Leadership Conference of Women Religious and the National Assembly of Women Religious. Sister Maria Iglesias, S.C., is president. The mailing address is 1234 Massachusetts Ave. N.W., Washington, D.C. 20005.

Other Conferences

International Union of Superiors General (Women): Established in 1965, with approval of its statutes by the Congregation for Religious and Secular Institutes in 1967. Sister Regina Casey of the Missionaries of the Sacred Heart "St. Frances Xavier Cabrini" is president.

Latin American Confederation of Religious: Established in 1959, with approval of its statutes by the Congregation for Religious and Secular Institutes in 1967. Father Carlos Palmes, S.J., is president.

National Conference of Vicars for Religious: Established in 1967 as a national organization of diocesan officials concerned with relations between their respective dioceses and religious communities engaged therein. A service and informational agency for vicars, it also carries on liaison with the Congregation for Religious and Secular Institutes, the National Conference of Catholic Bishops and other organizations concerned with religious. The president is Father Joseph A. Galante, 222 N. 17th St., Philadelphia, Pa. 19103.

National Conferences: Conferences of religious superiors, generally separate for men and women, have been established in 19 countries in Europe, 14 in North and Central America, 10 in South America, 20 in Africa, and 19 in Asia and Oceania.

Union of Superiors General (Men): Established in 1957, with approval of its statutes by the Congregation for Religious and Secular Institutes in 1967. Father Pedro Arrupe, S.J., is president.

World Conference of Secular Institutes: Established in 1974.

Vocation Council

Formation of the National Catholic Vocation Council was announced early in January, 1977, replacing the National Center for Church Vocations. Its purpose is to service efforts of mutual concern and benefit to member organizations in the recruitment and development of vocations to the priesthood and religious life.

Member organizations with representatives on the board of directors are: the National Sisters Vocation Conference, the National Conference of Diocesan Vocation Directors, the National Conference of Religious Vocation Directors of Men, Serra International, the Bishops' Committee on Vocations (National Conference of Catholic Bishops), the Leadership Conference of Women Religious and the Conference of Major Superiors of Men.

Brother James Gaffney, C.F.C., is president; Father Dennis H. Hoffmann is chairman of the administrative committee.

Offices are located at 1307 S. Wabash Ave., Chicago, Ill. 60605

SECULAR INSTITUTES

(Sources: Almanac survey; *Directory of Secular Institutes with Foundations in the U.S.A.*, published by the Publications Office, U.S. Catholic Conference; *Annuario Pontificio*.)

Secular institutes are societies of men and women living in the world who dedicate themselves by vow or promise to observe the evangelical counsels and to carry on apostolic works suitable to their talents and opportunities in the areas of their everyday life.

"Secular institutes are not religious communities but they carry with them in the world a profession of evangelical counsels which is genuine and complete, and recognized as such by the Church. This profession confers a consecration on men and women, laity and clergy, who reside in the world. For this reason they should chiefly strive for total self-dedication to God, one inspired by perfect charity. These institutes should preserve their proper and particular character, a secular one, so that they may everywhere measure up successfully to that apostolate which they were designed to exercise, and which is both in the world and, in a sense, of the world" (*Decree on the Appropriate Renewal of Religious Life*, No. 11; Second Vatican Council).

A secular institute reaches maturity in several stages. It begins as an association of the faithful, technically called a pious union, with the approval of a local bishop. Once it has proved its viability, he can give it the status of an institute of diocesan right, in accordance with norms and permission emanating from the Congregation for Religious and Secular Institutes. On issuance of a separate decree from this congregation, an institute of diocesan right becomes an institute of pontifical right.

Secular institutes, which originated in the latter part of the 18th century, were given full recognition and approval by Pius XII Feb. 2, 1947, in the apostolic constitution *Provida Mater Ecclesia.* On Mar. 25 of the same year a special commission for secular institutes was set up within the Congregation for Religious. Institutes were commended and confirmed by Pius XII in a motu proprio of Mar. 12, 1948, and were the subject of a special instruction issued a week later, Mar. 19, 1948.

The **United States Conference of Secular Institutes (CSI)** was established in October, 1972, following the organization of the World Conference of Secular Institutes in Rome. Its membership is open to all canonically erected secular institutes with members living in the United States. The conference was organized to offer secular institutes an opportunity to exchange experiences, to do research in order to help the Church carry out its mission, and to search for ways and means to make known the existence of secular institutes in the U.S. Address: 7007 Bradley Blvd., Bethesda, Md. 20034.

Institutes in the U.S.

Caritas Christi: Originated in Marseilles, 1937; for women. Established as a secular institute of pontifical right Mar. 19, 1955. Address: P.O. Box 162, River Forest, Ill. 60305.

Company of St. Paul: Originated in Milan, Italy, 1920; for lay people and priests. Approved as a secular institute of pontifical right June 30, 1950. Address: 8 Carman Rd., Scarsdale, N.Y. 10583.

Company of St. Ursula, Daughters of St. Angela Merici ("The Angelines"): Founded in Brescia, Italy, 1535; for women. Approved as a secular institute of pontifical right 1958. Address: Lina Moser, President, Via Rosmini 128, 38100 Trento, Italy.

DeSales Secular Institute: Founded in Vienna, Austria, 1940; for women. Pontifical right, 1964. Address: Rev. John Conmy, O.S.F.S., DeChantal National Center, 2019 Delaware Ave., Wilmington, Del. 19806.

Diocesan Laborer Priests: Approved as a secular institute of pontifical right, 1952. The specific aim of the institute is the promotion, sustenance and cultivation of apostolic, religious and priestly vocations. Address: 3706 15th St. N.E., Washington, D.C. 20017.

Handmaids of Divine Mercy: Founded in Bari, Italy, 1951; for women. Approved as an institute of pontifical right 1972. Address: Mary I. DiFonzo, 2410 Hughes Ave., Bronx, N.Y. 10458. International membership of 980.

Institute of Secular Missionaries: Founded in Vitoria, Spain, 1939; for women. Approved as a secular institute, 1955. Address: 2710 Ruberg Ave., Cincinnati, O. 45211, Att. E. Dilger.

Institute of the Heart of Jesus: Originated in France Feb. 2, 1791; restored Oct. 29, 1918; for diocesan priests and lay people. Received final approval from the Holy See as a secular institute of pontifical right Feb. 2, 1952. Rev. Jean Grebouval, superior general. Addresses: Central House, 202 Avenue du Maine, Paris 14me, France; U.S. address, Rev. John Lorenz, P.O. Box 4692, Des Moines, Iowa 50306. International membership of approximately 1,900.

Mission of Our Lady of Bethany: Founded in Plessis-Chevet, France, 1948; for women. Approved as an institute of diocesan right 1965. Address: Rev. Michael J. Rooney, Good Shepherd Church, Box 336, Glenville, W. Va. 26351.

Missionaries of the Kingship of Christ the King: Under this title are included three distinct and juridically separate institutes founded by Agostino Gemelli, O.F.M. (1878-1959).

(1) Women Missionaries of the Kingship of Christ — Founded in 1919, in Italy; definitively approved as an institute of pontifical rite 1953. Established in 15 countries. U.S. branch established 1950. Age at time of entrance, 21 to 40.

(2) Men Missionaries of the Kingship of Christ — Founded 1928, in Italy, as an institute of diocesan right. U.S. branch established 1962.

(3) Priest Missionaries of the Kingship of Christ — Established in U.S., 1954; approved as institute of pontifical right July 15, 1978. For diocesan priests.

Address: Rev. Stephen Hartdegen, O.F.M., Holy Name College, 14th and Shepherd Sts. N.E., Washington, D.C. 20017.

Oblate Missionaries of Mary Immaculate: Founded, 1952, and approved as a secular institute Feb. 2, 1962; for women. Dedicated to living and bearing witness to the charity of Christ. Addresses: Oblate Missionaries of Mary Immaculate, 91 Brookfield St., Lawrence, Mass. 01843. 7535 Boulevard Parent, Trois Rivieres, P. Q., Canada. International membership of approximately 800.

Rural Parish Workers of Christ the King: Originated in Cottleville, Mo., 1942; for women. An approved secular institute of the Archdiocese of St. Louis. Dedicated to the service of neighbor, especially in rural areas. Address: Box 300, Rt. 1, Cadet, Mo. 63630.

Schoenstatt Sisters of Mary: Originated in Schoenstatt, Germany, 1926; for women. Established as a secular institute of diocesan right May 20, 1948; of pontifical right Oct. 18, 1948. Addresses: Schoenstatt Sisters of Mary, W. 284 N. 698 Cherry Lane, Waukesha, Wis. 53186; House Schoenstatt, Star Rt. 1, Box 100, Rockport, Tex. 78382. International membership of more than 2,700.

Secular Institute of Gospel Missionaries:

Founded in Sicily, 1951; for women. Approved as an institute of diocesan right Nov. 29, 1968. Address: Lia Cerrito, Piazza Busacca 2, 90145 Palermo, Sicily.

Secular Institute of Pius X: Originated in Manchester, N.H., 1940; for priests and laymen. Approved as a secular institute, 1959 (first secular institute of diocesan right founded in the U.S. to be approved by the Holy See). Also admits married and unmarried men as associate members. Addresses: Lynchville Park, Goffstown, N.H. 03045. C.P. 1815, Quebec City, P.Q., Canada.

Society of Our Lady of the Way: Originated, 1936; for women. Approved as a secular institute of pontifical right Jan. 3, 1953. Address: Society of Our Lady of the Way, 707 Stockton, San Francisco, Calif. 94108. International membership, 300.

Teresian Institute: Founded in Spain 1911 by Pedro Poveda. Approved as an institute of pontifical right Jan. 11, 1924. Address: 235 Cypress St., Newton Centre, Mass. 02159.

Voluntas Dei: Originated in Canada, 1958; for secular priests, laymen and couples. Approved as a secular institute May 6, 1965. Addresses: Institute Voluntas Dei, 7385, Blvd. Parent, Trois-Rivieres, Que., Canada G9A 5E1. Rev. Maurice Roy, St. William's Mission, Navajo Star Route 2, Box 64, W. Gallup, N. Mex. 87301. International membership of approximately 150.

The *Annuario Pontificio* lists the following **secular institutes of pontifical right which are not established in the U.S.:**

For men: Christ the King; Institute of Our Lady of Life; Institute of Prado; Opus Dei; Priests of the Sacred Heart of Jesus.

For women: Alliance in Jesus through Mary; Apostles of the Sacred Heart; Catechists of the Sacred Heart of Jesus (Ukrainian); Cordimarian Filiation; Daughters of the Nativity of Mary; Daughters of the Queen of the Apostles; Daughters of the Sacred Heart; Evangelical Crusade; Faithful Servants of Jesus; Institute of the Blessed Virgin Mary (della Strada); Institute of Notre Dame du Travail; Institute of Our Lady of Life; Little Apostles of Charity; Love and Peace in Christ Jesus; Missionaries of Royal Priesthood; Missionaries of the Sick; Oblates of Christ the King; Oblates of the Sacred Heart of Jesus; Opus Dei; Servants of Jesus the Priest; Union of the Daughters of God; Workers of Divine Love; Workers of the Cross.

Associations

Association of Mary Immaculate: Founded in Hartford, Conn., 1963, by Mary Matthew; separate sections for men and women. Received diocesan approval Jan. 28, 1977. Address: 2923 Lauderdale Dr. E., Jacksonville, Fla. 32211.

Caritas: Originated in New Orleans, 1950; for women. Address: Box 308, Abita Springs, La. 70420.

Daughters of Our Lady of Fatima: Originated in Lansdowne, Pa., 1949; for women. Received diocesan approval, Jan., 1952. Address: Fatima House, Rolling Hills Rd., Ottsville, Pa. 18942.

Don Bosco Volunteers: For women who love Don Bosco's spirit and choose to follow in his footsteps. Take temporary vows for six years, then for life. Address: Don Bosco Volunteers, Don Bosco College, Newton, N.J. 07860.

Focolare Movement: Inaugurated in Trent, Italy, in 1943, by Chiara Lubich and a small group of companions; for men and women. Approved as an association of the faithful, 1962. It is not a secular institute by statute; however, vows are observed by its totally dedicated core membership of 3,000 who live in small communities called Focolare (Italian word for "hearth") centers. There are 13 resident centers in the U.S. and two in Canada. GEN (New Generation) is the youth organization of the movement. An estimated 70,000 are affiliated with the movement in the U.S. and Canada; 3,000,000, worldwide. Publications include *Living City*, monthly; *GEN II* and *GEN III* for young people and children. Three week-long summer conventions, called "Mariapolis" ("City of Mary"), are held annually. National headquarters: 250 E. 73rd St., New York, N.Y. 10021 (women); 206 Skillman Ave., Brooklyn, N.Y. 11211 (men).

Institute of Apostolic Oblates: Founded in Rome, Italy, 1947; for women. Address: 2125 W. Walnut Ave., Fullerton, Calif. 92633 (provincial house).

Jesus Caritas Fraternity of Fr. Charles de Foucauld: Originated in Ars, France, 1952; for women. Established as an association of perfection May 31, 1962. Address: Miss Patricia M. Collins, 3843 N. Spaulding, Chicago, Ill. 60018. International membership of approximately 550.

Jesus Caritas Priest Fraternities of Charles de Foucauld: An open and loose structure of small groups of priests who meet each month to pray together and share their faith experiences. U.S. address: Rev. Thomas McCormick, John XXIII University Center, 1220 University Ave., Fort Collins, Colo. 80521.

Madonna House Apostolate: Originated in Toronto, Canada, 1930; for priests and lay persons. Diocesan pious union. Address: Madonna House, Combermere, Ontario, Canada KOJ 1LO — Catherine Doherty (women), Jim Guinan (men), Rev. J. Callahan (priests). International membership and missions.

Pax Christi: Lay institute of men and women dedicated to witnessing to Christ, with special emphasis on service to the poor in Mississippi. Addresses: St. Francis Center, 708 Ave. I, Greenwood, Miss. 38930; LaVerna House, 2108 Altawoods Blvd., Jackson, Miss. 39204.

SECULAR ORDERS

Secular orders (commonly called third orders) are societies of the faithful living in the world who seek to deepen their Christian life and apostolic commitment in association with and according to the spirit of various religious institutes. The orders are called "third" because their foundation followed the establishment of the first (for men) and second (for women) religious orders with which they are associated.

Augustine, Third Order Secular of St.: Founded, 13th century; approved Nov. 7, 1400.

Carmel (The Lay Carmelite Order) (Calced): Founded, 13th century; approved by Pope Nicholas V, Oct. 7, 1452. Address: Aylesford, National Scapular Center, I-55 and Cass Ave. N. Darien, Ill. 60559. Approximately 16,000 members in U.S.

Carmel, Third Order Secular of Our Blessed Lady of Mt., and St. Teresa of Jesus (Discalced): Rule based on the Carmelite reform established by St. Teresa and St. John of the Cross, 16th century; approved Mar. 23, 1594. Office of National Secretariat, U.S.A.; P.O. Box 3079, San Jose, Calif. 95116. Approximately 3,500 members in U.S.

Dominic, Third Order Secular of St. (The Dominican Laity): Founded in the 13th century. Addresses of provincial directors: 487 Michigan Ave. N.E., Washington, D.C. 20017; 1909 S. Ashland Ave., Chicago, Ill. 60608; St. Peter Martyr Priory, 241 S. Detroit St., Los Angeles, Calif. 90036.

Franciscan Order, Secular (SFO): Founded, 1209 by St. Francis of Assisi; approved Aug. 30, 1221. Executive Secretary, Mrs. Mary R. Teoli, 1901 Prior Rd., Wilmington, Del. 19809. Approximately 1.5 million in the world, 45,000 in U.S. in 28 provinces.

Mary, Third Order of: Founded, Dec. 8, 1850; rule approved by the Holy See, 1857. Addresses of provincial directors: Marist College, 220 Taylor St. N.E., Washington, D.C. 20017; 7 Harvard St., P. O. Box 66, Charlestown, Mass. 02129; 320 N. 20th Dr. W., Phoenix, Ariz. 85009. Approximately 14,000 in the world, 5,600 in U.S.

Mary, Third Order Secular of Servants of (Servite): Founded, 1233; approved, 1304. Address: Director of Third Order, 6741 Rock Hill Rd., St. Louis, Mo. 63121.

Mercy, Secular Third Order of Our Lady of (Mercedarian): Founded, 1219 by St. Peter Nolasco; approved the same year.

Norbert, Third Order of St.: Founded, 1122 by St. Norbert; approved by Pope Honorius II, 1126. Address: St. Norbert Abbey, De Pere, Wis.

Trinity, Third Order Secular of the Most Holy: Founded, about 1198; approved, 1219. Address: Trinitarian Provincial Offices, P.O. Box 5719, Baltimore, Md. 21208.

Oblates of St. Benedict are lay persons affiliated with a Benedictine abbey or monastery who strive to direct their lives, as circumstances permit, according to the spirit and Rule of St. Benedict.

REFUGEES

Malaysia's threat in the middle of June, 1979, to force 75,000 refugees crowding its shores out to sea and almost certain death probably did more than anything else to alert the world at large to the sad plight of some 400,000 displaced persons languishing, starving, suffering from illness and dying in transit camps and on inhospitable islands in Southeast Asia. The threat was not carried out, but the conditions of the refugees remain critical.

Later in the summer, three international conferences — in Bali, Tokyo and Geneva — produced pledges from a number of countries including the United States (to increase aid funding and double monthly admissions to 14,000), Britain and France (to admit 10,000 more), Canada (to take 3,000), Japan (funding) and the Philippines (to provide a transit campsite). The pledges promised some relief, but not enough.

The U.N. High Commissioner for Refugees reported that between 1975 and the early part of 1979 permanent residency was granted to Indochinese refugees by the U.S. (200,000), France (50,000), Australia (21,000), Canada (13,000), West Germany (3,438), the United Kingdom (1,470), Japan (3).

About half of the refugees admitted to the United States have been resettled here through the agency of Migration and Refugee Services, U.S. Catholic Conference, with the cooperation of many diocesan and parish organizations and individuals.

UNDOCUMENTED ALIENS

Leonel Castillo, former commissioner of the Immigration and Naturalization Service, is authority for the estimate of approximately four million undocumented aliens in the United States. Their principal countries of origin are in Latin America and the Caribbean area. More than 75 per cent of them are Hispanic. Most are baptized Catholics, a fact of considerable concern to the Church. They are subject in various ways to victimization by employers, legal disabilities, prejudice and misconceptions.

Douglas S. Massey, a research assistant in the Office of Population Research at Princeton University, wrote in the May 31, 1979, edition of *The New York Times*: "The United States is not being inundated by an out-of-control 'invasion' of illegal immigrants; nor is it likely that illegal aliens represent a burden to taxpayers; nor is there any clear evidence that, on balance, illegal aliens displace American workers."

Missionary Activity of the Church

UNITED STATES FOREIGN MISSIONARIES

(Data on U.S. foreign missionary personnel in the following tables were gathered by, and are reproduced with permission of, the United States Catholic Mission Council, 1302 Eighteenth St. N.W., Washington, D.C. 20036.

(For additional information about the Church in mission areas, see News Events and other Almanac entries.)

Field Distribution, 1979

(Under this and following headings, Alaska, Hawaii, etc., are considered abroad because they are outside the 48 contiguous states.)

Africa: 923 (513 men; 410 women). Largest numbers in Tanzania, 166; Kenya, 147; Ghana, 115; Zambia, 70; Nigeria, 69.

Near East: 65 (44 men; 21 women). Largest numbers in Israel, 28; Egypt, 18; Lebanon, 11.

Far East: 1,562 (1,093 men; 469 women). Largest numbers in Philippines, 430; Japan, 355; Taiwan, 169; Korea, 153; India, 135; Hong Kong, 80.

Oceania: 743 (357 men; 386 women). Largest groups in Hawaii, 269; Papua New Guinea, 214; Australia, 55; Caroline Islands, 38; Samoa, 36.

Europe: 37 (20 men; 17 women). Largest groups in Finland, 12; Sweden, 10; Denmark, 7.

North America: 332 (121 men; 211 women). Largest group in Alaska, 200.

Caribbean Islands: 562 (309 men; 253 women). Largest groups in Puerto Rico, 265; Jamaica, 127; Haiti, 51.

Central America: 686 (420 men; 266 women). Largest groups in Guatemala, 197; Mexico, 193.

South America: 1,545 (846 men; 699 women). Largest groups in Brazil, 477; Peru, 444; Bolivia, 247; Chile, 181.

TOTAL: 6,455 (3,723 men; 2,732 women).

Men Religious, 1979

Sixty-six mission-sending groups had 3,442 priests and brothers in overseas assignments.

Maryknoll Fathers: 621 in 25 countries; largest group, 60 in Tanzania.
Jesuits: 572 in 37 countries; largest group, 98 in the Philippines.
Franciscans (O.F.M.): 214 in 21 countries; largest group, 65 in Brazil.
Divine Word Missionaries: 175 in 13 countries; largest group, 60 in Papua New Guinea.
Redemptorists: 159 in 7 countries; largest group, 65 in Brazil.
Oblates of Mary Immaculate: 153 in 18 countries; largest group, 36 in Mexico.
Capuchins (O.F.M. Cap.): 142 in 10 countries; largest group, 32 in Papua New Guinea.
Marianists: 140 in 13 countries; largest group, 47 in Hawaii.
Benedictines: 92 in 14 countries; largest group, 18 in Guatemala.
Columbans: 81 in 10 countries; largest group, 31 in the Philippines.
Dominicans: 67 in 9 countries; largest group, 20 in Nigeria.
Brothers of the Christian Schools: 66 in 11 countries; largest group, 25 in the Philippines.
Holy Cross Fathers: 66 in 11 countries; largest group, 23 in Bangladesh.
Holy Ghost Fathers: 63 in 6 countries; largest group, 27 in Tanzania.
Holy Cross Brothers: 55 in 9 countries; largest group, 19 in Brazil.
Passionists: 54 in 5 countries; largest group, 26 in the Philippines.
Conventual Franciscans (O.F.M. Conv.): 45 in 8 countries; largest group, 16 in Zambia.
La Salette Fathers: 43 in 5 countries; largest group, 14 in the Philippines.
Marist Fathers: 38 in 8 countries; largest group, 13 in Papua New Guinea.
Vincentians: 38 in 6 countries; largest group, 23 in Panama.
Augustinians: 32 in 3 countries; largest group, 20 in Peru.
Missionaries of the Sacred Heart: 30 in 3 countries; largest group, 23 in Papua New Guinea.
White Fathers: 26 in 10 countries; largest group, 6 in Tanzania.
Marist Brothers: 25 in 8 countries; largest groups, 11 each in Japan and the Philippines.
Sacred Heart Brothers: 23 in 4 countries; largest group, 11 in Zambia.
Verona Fathers: 23 in 7 countries; largest group, 7 in Uganda.
Franciscan Friars of the Atonement (Graymoor): 23 in 2 countries; larger group, 12 in Japan.
Missionhurst: 22 in 5 countries; largest group, 11 in the Dominican Republic.

Thirty-eight other mission-sending institutes had 19 or less members in overseas assignments.

Diocesan Priests, 1979

One hundred and 87 diocesan priests from

82 dioceses were in overseas assignments in 1979.

The largest groups were from Boston (23 in 4 countries) and St. Louis (14 in 2 countries).

Fifty-three of the diocesan priests in overseas assignments were members of the **Missionary Society of St. James the Apostle**, founded by Cardinal Richard J. Cushing of Boston in 1958. Its director is Reverend George F. Emerson, 24 Clark Street, Boston, Mass. 02109.

Sisters, 1979

One hundred and 90 mission-sending groups had 2,568 sisters in overseas assignments.

Maryknoll Sisters: 409 in 23 countries; largest group, 66 in Hawaii.

Marists: 103 in 14 countries; largest group, 19 in Papua New Guinea.

School Sisters of Notre Dame: 98 in 17 countries; largest group, 16 in Puerto Rico.

Sisters of St. Joseph (Carondelet): 69 in 3 countries; largest group, 39 in Hawaii.

Medical Mission Sisters: 66 in 16 countries; largest group, 19 in Ghana.

Daughters of Charity: 61 in 11 countries; largest group, 33 in Bolivia.

Sisters of Notre Dame de Namur: 58 in 6 countries; largest groups, 13 each in Hawaii and Brazil.

Franciscan Missionaries of Mary: 57 in 17 countries; largest group, 8 each in Ghana and Australia.

Ursulines of the Roman Union: 45 in 14 countries; largest group, 8 in Thailand.

Benedictines: 42 in 8 countries; largest group, 13 in Colombia.

Servants of the Immaculate Heart of Mary (Philadelphia): 40 in 2 countries; larger group, 29 in Peru.

Sisters of the Third Franciscan Order, Minor Conventuals (Syracuse): 37 in 3 countries; largest group, 24 in Hawaii.

Sisters of the Holy Cross: 35 in 4 countries; largest group, 16 in Brazil.

Franciscan Sisters of Allegany: 35 in 3 countries; largest group, 21 in Jamaica.

Servants of the Holy Spirit: 31 in 7 countries; largest group, 11 in Ghana.

Servants of the Immaculate Heart of Mary (Monroe): 28 in 7 countries; largest group, 9 in Puerto Rico.

Society of the Sacred Heart: 27 in 8 countries; largest group, 16 in Japan.

Sisters of St. Joseph (Brentwood, N.Y.): 26 in 3 countries; largest group, 23 in Puerto Rico.

Sisters of Notre Dame: 25 in 2 countries; larger group, 14 in India.

Adorers of the Blood of Christ: 25 in 5 countries; largest group, 8 in Liberia.

Sisters of the Most Precious Blood (O'Fallon): 24 in 3 countries; largest group, 12 in Finland.

Sisters of St. Joseph of Peace: 23 in 5 countries; largest group, 10 in Alaska.

Religious Sisters of Mercy of the Union in the U.S.A.: 23 in 6 countries; largest group, 10 in Honduras.

Sisters of the Holy Child Jesus: 23 in 5 countries; largest group, 10 in Nigeria.

Franciscan Sisters of Christian Charity: 23 in 2 countries; larger group, 19 in Hawaii.

Little Sisters of the Poor: 22 in 12 countries; largest groups, 3 each in Algeria, Hong Kong, and India.

Missionary Sisters of the Immaculate Conception: 22 in 6 countries; largest group, 14 in Canada.

Sisters of the Holy Names of Jesus and Mary: 21 in 5 countries; largest group, 9 in Peru.

Sisters of the Assumption of the B.V.M.: 21 in 3 countries; largest group, 16 in Canada.

School Sisters of St. Francis: 20 in 6 countries; largest group, 7 in Costa Rica.

One hundred and 60 other mission-sending institutes had 19 or less members in overseas assignments.

Lay Volunteers, 1979

Two hundred and 58 lay volunteers of 26 sponsoring organizations were in overseas assignments in 1979.

Jesuit Volunteer Corps: 70 in Alaska.

Maryknoll Lay Missioners: 42 in 11 countries; largest group, 6 in Guatemala.

Lay Mission Helpers: 40 in 13 countries; largest group, 8 in Papua New Guinea.

Frontier Apostolate: 29 in Canada.

Catholic Medical Mission Board: 14* in 6 countries; largest groups, 4 each in Ghana and Haiti. (*This figure represents only those whose term of service is for at least one year. In addition, 52 short-term volunteers served in 11 countries during the past year.)

Davenport Diocese: 11 in 14 countries; largest group, 4 in Puerto Rico.

Erie Diocese: 7 in 2 countries; larger group, 6 in Mexico.

Milwaukee Latin American Office: 7 in 6 countries; largest group, 2 in Grenada.

Holy Cross Volunteers: 6 in Brazil.

The 17 other sponsoring organizations had 5 members or less in overseas assignments.

U.S. Mission Council

The United States Catholic Mission Council, which took over and expanded functions of the former Mission Secretariat, started operations Sept. 1, 1970, "to provide a forum and organ for the evaluation, coordination and fostering, in the United States, of the worldwide missionary effort of the Church."

Structurally, the council is made up of five seven-member committees representing the National Conference of Catholic Bishops, the Conference of Major Superiors of Men, the

Leadership Conference of Women Religious, the National Council of Catholic Laity and mission agencies. Heads of the committees form the executive board which meets at least quarterly to oversee the implementation of policies and programs determined at annual meetings of the whole committee.

Typical activities of the council are educational efforts related to the Church's teaching about its missionary nature, the sponsorship of conferences on theological and pastoral foundations of missionary endeavor, liaison and cooperation with missionary bodies of other Christian churches.

U.S. FOREIGN MISSIONARIES, 1960-1979

Year	Diocesan Priests	Religious Priests	Religious Brothers	Religious Sisters	Seminarians	Lay Persons	Total
1960	14	3018	575	2827	170	178	6782
1962	31	3172	720	2764	152	307	7146
1964	80	3438	782	3137	157	532	8126
1966	215	3731	901	3706	201	549	9303
1968	282	3727	869	4150	208	419	9655
1970	373	3117	666	3824	90	303	8373
1972+	246	3182	634	3121	97	376	7656
1973	237	3913*		3012		529	7691
1974	220	3084	639	2916	101	458	7418
1975	197	3023	669	2850	65	344	7148
1976	193	2961	691	2840	68	257	7010
1977	182	2882	630	2781	42	243	6760
1978	166	2830	610	2673	43	279	6601
1979	187	2800	592	2568	50	258	6455

*Includes religious brothers and seminarians.
+A corrected total for 1972 should read 7937, indicating losses of 436 from 1970 to 1972 and 246 from 1972 to 1973.

FIELD DISTRIBUTION BY AREAS, 1960-1979

Year	Africa	Far East	Near East	Oceania	Europe	N. Amer.	Carib. Is.	Cent. Amer.	S. Amer.	Total
1960	781	1959	111	986	203	337	991	433	981	6782
1962	901	2110	75	992	93	224	967	537	1247	7146
1964	1025	2332	122	846	69	220	1056	660	1796	8126
1966	1184	2453	142	953	38	211	1079	857	2386	9303
1968	1157	2470	128	1027	33	251	1198	936	2455	9655
1970	1141	2137	59	900	38	233	1067	738	2080	8373
1972	1107	1955	59	826	39	234	819	728	1889	7656
1973	1229	1962	54	811	40	253	796	763	1783	7691
1974	1121	1845	60	883	43	241	757	752	1716	7418
1975	1065	1814	71	808	37	252	698	734	1669	7148
1976	1042	1757	68	795	34	313	671	712	1618	7010
1977	1003	1659	62	784	34	296	629	702	1591	6760
1978	966	1601	57	769	34	339	593	705	1537	6601
1979	923	1562	65	743	37	332	562	686	1545	6455

HOME MISSIONS

The expression "home missions" is applied to places in the U.S. where the local church does not have its own resources, human and otherwise, which are needed to begin or, if begun, to survive and grow. These areas share the name "missions" with their counterparts in foreign lands because they too need outside help to provide the personnel and means for making the Church present and active there in carrying out its mission for the salvation of people.

Dioceses in the Southeast, the Southwest, and the Far West are most urgently in need of outside help to carry on the work of the Church. Millions of persons live in counties in which there are no resident priests. Many others live in rural areas beyond the reach and influence of a Catholic center. According to recent statistics compiled by the Glenmary Research Center, there are nearly 600 priestless counties in the United States. Many states generally thought to be well off from a pastoral standpoint include areas in which the Catholic Church and the ministry of priests are virtually unknown.

About 20 per cent of the total U.S. population and less than three per cent of the Catholic population live within the boundaries of the 17 "most missionary" dioceses of the country. A "Survey of the Catholic Weakness" conducted by the National Catholic Rural Life Conference disclosed that the Catholic Church ranked near the bottom of about 40 religious bodies in percentage of rural membership.

A number of forces are at work to meet the pastoral needs of these missionary areas and to establish permanent churches and operating institutions where they are required. In many dioceses, one or more missions and stations are attended from established parishes and are gradually growing to independent status. Priests, brothers and sisters belonging to scores of religious institutes are engaged full-time in the home missions. Lay persons, some of them in affiliation with special groups and movements, are also involved.

The Society for the Propagation of the Faith, which conducts an annual collection for mission support in all parishes of the U.S., allocates 40 per cent of this sum for disbursement to home missions through the American Board of Catholic Missions.

The Catholic Church Extension Society provides one million dollars or more a year for the building of mission installations and related needs.

Special mission support is the purpose of the Commission for the Catholic Missions among the Colored People and the Indians.

Diocesan, parochial and high school mission societies frequently undertake projects in behalf of the home missions.

Glenmary Missioners

The Glenmary Home Missioners, founded by Father W. Howard Bishop in 1939, is the only home mission society established for the sole purpose of carrying out the pastoral ministry in small towns and the rural districts of the United States. With 74 priests and 29 professed brothers as of Mar. 31, 1979, the Glenmary Missioners had 39 mission bases and 50 satellite missions in the archdioceses of Atlanta and Cincinnati, and in the dioceses of Birmingham, Charlotte, Covington, Dallas, Little Rock, Nashville, Jackson, Tulsa, Owensboro, Savannah, Richmond and Wheeling-Charleston.

The Rev. Robert C. Berson is president.

National headquarters are located in Fairfield, O. The mailing address is P.O. Box 46404, Cincinnati, O. 45246.

Sisters

The Glenmary Home Mission Sisters of America, founded July 16, 1952, had 19 professed members engaged in work in six social and catechetical centers, one house of study and one promotional center, in the archdioceses of Cincinnati and St. Louis, and the dioceses of Covington, Dallas, Little Rock, Owensboro, Savannah. Much of their work was concentrated in rural areas where poverty was prevalent. The community also conducts an associate program for laywomen interested in work in home mission areas for two or more years.

Sister Michelle Teff is president. The community has headquarters at 3636 Semloh Ave., Cincinnati, Ohio 45239.

Black Missions

The Commission for Catholic Missions among the Colored People and the Indians reported the following (January, 1976, latest available) statistics for 73 dioceses in which it supplied financial assistance: 862,216 Catholics, 680 churches, 998 priests, 23,849 infant baptisms, 6,597 adults received into the Church, 402 schools, 110,292 students. The total number of black Catholics was estimated to be more than 900,000.

Dioceses reporting the largest numbers of black Catholics were: Lafayette, La., 82,014; Chicago, Ill., 80,000; New Orleans, La., 75,000; Washington, D.C., 72,295; New York, N.Y., 50,000; Los Angeles, Calif., 45,000; Philadelphia, Pa., 41,577; Detroit, Mich., 36,000; Galveston-Houston, Tex., 33,710; Brooklyn, N.Y., 30,000; St. Louis, Mo., 29,050; and Baltimore, Md., 21,500. The total black Catholic population of these 12 mainly urban dioceses numbered 596,146; they comprised more than 69% of the total black Catholic population of the 73 dioceses covered in the report.

The report, noting that it was impossible to determine "whether, or to what extent, lapsed Catholics are included in a parish or diocesan report," stated that the number of black Catholics had increased 450 per cent during the past half-century.

The commission report, which was limited in scope, did not cover all aspects of the Church's ministry to the black population, which was estimated to number more than 22 million. (See Index: Black Catholics.)

Indian Missions

The Commission for Catholic Missions among the Colored People and the Indians reported the following statistics (May, 1979) for 46 dioceses and one religious community to whom it supplied financial assistance: 192,220 Catholics, 454 churches, 339 priests, 3,665 infant baptisms, 492 adults received into the Church, 56 elementary schools, seven high schools.

The states with the largest number of missions and Catholic Indians are Arizona, New Mexico, South Dakota and Montana, where almost two-thirds of the reservation Indians now live. Seventy-one churches and chapels and four schools were maintained with 43 priests engaged in serving more than 29,760 Catholic Indians in these areas. Fifty-four missions and one school are located in the states of California, North Dakota, Minnesota, Wisconsin and Wyoming where 39 priests are serving the estimated 44,568 Catholic Indians there. Alaska has 45 mission churches and chapels and 32 priests to minister to approximately 27,000 Indians. In other states, the Commission reported, reservations were small; consequently only several schools and from one to five missions were maintained in most of them.

According to the most recent census reports, it was estimated that 300,000 Indians were living on federal reservations and 307,000 in urban areas. An estimated 25,000 Catholic Indians were not on reservations.

Support Bodies

The Catholic Church Extension Society: This society was established for the purpose of preserving and extending the Church in the U.S. and its dependencies principally through the collection and disbursement of funds for missions. Since the time of its founding in 1905, approximately $73 million have been received and expended for this purpose. Disbursements in fiscal year 1978 amounted to $4 million.

Works of the society are supervised by a board of governors consisting of twelve members: Cardinal John Cody, archbishop of Chicago, chancellor; Rev. Edward J. Slattery, acting president; five bishops or priests, and five laymen. Society headquarters are located at 35 E. Wacker Drive, Chicago, Ill. 60601.

Commission for Catholic Missions among the Colored People and the Indians: Organized in 1886, this commission provides financial support ($3.075 million allocated in 1977-78 year to 127 dioceses) for religious works among Blacks and Indians in the United States. Funds are raised by an annual collection in all parishes of the country.

Cardinal John J. Krol is head of the board of directors. Msgr. Paul A. Lenz is secretary. Commission headquarters are located at 2021 H St. N.W., Washington, D.C. 20006.

Bureau of Catholic Indian Missions: Established in 1874 as the representative of Catholic Indian missions before the federal government and the public; made permanent organization in 1883 by Third Plenary Council of Baltimore. After a remarkable history of rendering important services to the Indian people, the bureau continues to represent the Catholic Church in the U.S. in her apostolate to the American Indian. Concerns are evangelization, catechesis, liturgy, family life, education, advocacy. Cardinal John Krol is president of the board; Msgr. Paul A. Lenz is secretary. Address: 2021 H St., Washington, D.C. 20006.

Tekakwitha Conference: Established in 1939, the Conference includes active and former Catholic missionaries among Native American people and Native American people recognized as leaders in their respective churches. The primary focus is evangelization in eight areas of concern: development of Native American ministry, catechesis, liturgy, family life, evangelical liberation, ecumenical cooperation and urban ministry. The annual Conference serves as an opportunity for exchange of ideas, approaches and mutual support. Publications include annual Proceedings and 40th Anniversary Edition of Tekakwitha Conference. President is Rev. Gilbert F. Hemauer, O.F.M. Cap. Address: P.O. Box 165, Medicine Lake, Mont. 59247.

APPALACHIA COMMITTEE

The 600-member Catholic Committee of Appalachia consists of bishops, priests, religious and lay persons engaged in pastoral and social justice ministry in the 13-state region. Appalachia has been defined by Congress as including all of West Virginia and parts of Alabama, Georgia, Kentucky, Maryland, Mississippi, New York, North Carolina, Ohio, Pennsylvania, South Carolina, Tennessee and Virginia.

In 1975, "This Land Is Home to Me: A Pastoral Letter on Powerlessness in Appalachia," was issued by the Catholic bishops of the region. Implementation of the document — through personal presence and assistance in circumstances of need experienced by its members and community groups — is the primary purpose of the committee. Members are involved with community groups in cooperative efforts on such matters of concern as flood prevention, housing, land ownership, health care, labor rights at J. P. Stevens and the Stearns and Jericol mines, nuclear disarmament, and the improvement of schools.

The committee belongs to the Commission on Religion in Appalachia, an interfaith group with members from 15 communions and 13 ecumenical units.

Sister Honor Murphy, O.P., is executive director. Address: 31-A S. Third Ave., Prestonburg, Ky. 41653.

AGRIMISSIO

Agrimissio is a service office established for the purpose of assisting missionaries in rural development work. Founded in 1970 by Msgr. Luigi Ligutti, its honorary president, it is sponsored by the Union of Superiors General (of male religious), the International Union of Superiors General (of female religious), and the National Catholic Rural Life Conference in the U.S. It promotes cooperation among missionaries, the Rome headquarters of religious orders, governmental and non-governmental organizations, especially the international Food and Agriculture Organization.

Msgr. John F. McDonald is executive secretary. Headquarters are located at the Palazzo S. Calisto, 00120, Vatican City.

The bishops of the United States, in a statement issued in 1977, urged Catholics to increase their "understanding of the present needs, aspirations and values of the American Indian peoples."

Education

LEGAL STATUS OF CATHOLIC EDUCATION

The right of private schools to exist and operate in the United States is recognized in law. It was confirmed by the U.S. Supreme Court in 1925 when the tribunal ruled (Pierce v. Society of Sisters, see Church-State Decisions of the Supreme Court) that an Oregon state law requiring all children to attend public schools was unconstitutional.

Private schools are obliged to comply with the education laws in force in the various states regarding such matters as required basic curricula, periods of attendance, and standards for proper accreditation.

The special curricula and standards of private schools are determined by the schools themselves. Thus, in Catholic schools, the curricula include not only the subject matter required by state educational laws but also other fields of study, principally, education in the Catholic faith.

The Supreme Court has ruled that the First Amendment to the U.S. Constitution, in accordance with the No Establishment of Religion Clause of the First Amendment, prohibits direct federal and state aid from public funds to church-affiliated schools. (See several cases in Church-State Decisions of the Supreme Court.)

Public Aid

This prohibition does not extend to all child-benefit and public-purpose programs of aid to students of non-public elementary and secondary schools.

Statutes authorizing such programs have been ruled constitutional on the grounds that they:
- have a "secular legislative purpose";
- neither inhibit nor advance religion as a "principal or primary effect";
- do not foster "excessive government entanglement with religion."

Aid programs considered constitutional have provided bus transportation, textbook loans, school lunches and health services, and "secular, neutral or non-ideological services, facilities and materials provided in common to all school children," public and non-public.

Aid is provided most commonly in the form of auxiliary services such as transportation of students to and from school, textbook loans, instructional materials, health services, guidance and counseling, testing, special education, vocational education. A number of states offer free lunch programs and even cooperative central purchasing arrangements.

With respect to college and university education in church-affiliated institutions, the Supreme Court has upheld the constitutionality of statutes providing student loans and, under the Federal Higher Education Facilities Act of 1963, construction loans and grants for secular-purpose facilities.

Catholic schools are exempt from real estate taxation in all of the states. Since Jan. 1, 1959, nonprofit parochial and private schools have also been exempt from several federal excise taxes.

Shared Time

In a shared time program of education, students enrolled in Catholic or other church-related schools take some courses (e.g., religion, social studies, fine arts) in their own schools and others (e.g., science, mathematics, industrial arts) in public schools. Such a program, outlined in 1956 by Dr. Erwin L. Shaver of the Massachusetts Council of Churches, has been given serious consideration in recent years by Catholic and other educators. Its constitutionality has not been seriously challenged, but practical problems — relating to teacher and student schedules, transpgrtation, adjustment to new programs, and other factors — are knotty.

Limited shared time programs involving Catholic school students have been in operation since 1927 in Caledonia, Minn., since 1945 in Rutland, Vt., and for a number of years in several communities in Connecticut, Illinois, Michigan, Minnesota, Pennsylvania and Ohio. Since 1964, programs have also been reported operative in Iowa, New Jersey, Oregon, Washington and Wisconsin.

Released Time

Several million children of elementary and high school age of all denominations have the opportunity of receiving religious instruction on released time. Under released time programs they are permitted to leave their public schools during school hours to attend religious instruction classes held off the public school premises. They are released at the request of their parents. Public school authorities merely provide for their dismissal, and take no part in the program.

The first released time program was set up at Gary, Ind., in 1914. In 1905 a proposal had been made by Dr. George U. Wenner, to the Interfaith Conference on Federation, that public school pupils be given a day off a week for religious instruction in their churches. In 1876 a court decision in Vermont left to the discretion of local school boards whether they would release public school students for religious instruction.

In New York, where released time began in 1917, a law was passed in 1940 which authorized school boards to permit the release of public school pupils from class, at the request of their parents, to attend religious instruction off public school premises. The U.S. Supreme Court upheld the constitutionality of the measure in the case of Zorach v. Clauson in 1952.

Released time programs are operative in many states at this time.

ESEA

The first major federal aid to education program in U.S. history containing provisions benefitting parochial school students was enacted by the first session of the 89th Congress and signed into law by President Lyndon B. Johnson on Apr. 11, 1965. The 1965 Elementary and Secondary School Aid Law was passed by the House of Representatives (263 to 153) on Mar. 26 and by the Senate (73 to 18) on Apr. 9.

Provisions

The principal provisions of the $1.3 billion program were stated in three of the eight titles of the law.

• 1. One billion dollars was allocated to public school districts under a formula based chiefly on the number of children in schools who came from families earning less than $2,000 a year. The grant was intended to cover half of the cost of education for each eligible pupil.

Parochial and other private school pupils in the same low-income bracket were to benefit by extensions to them by local public school districts of shared services or facilities. Public school districts were required to take these children into account when making plans to aid needy students.

• 2. About $100 million was provided to buy textbooks for pupils, materials and volumes for school libraries, and some instructional equipment. All were to be owned by a public agency, such as a local school district or library, but they could be loaned to children attending nonpublic schools.

• 3. Another $100 million was to be used to establish educational centers to benefit both public and private school pupils with cultural enrichment programs and other special services. Public agencies would operate these centers, but the legislation required that private school educators and others from outside the public schools take part in planning for them.

Avoids Impasse

President Johnson presented his program to the Congress on Jan. 12, 1965, in a special message which indicated his intention of avoiding the separation of Church and State impasse which had blocked all earlier aid proposals pertaining to nonpublic, and especially church-affiliated, schools. The aim of the program, under public control, is to serve the public purpose by aiding disadvantaged pupils in public and nonpublic schools.

Program Regulations

Regulations for the administration of programs under the new law were issued Sept. 15, 1965, by the U.S. Office of Education. The leading norms were as follows.

• Participation of Nonpublic School Children: Must be "substantially comparable" to that of public school children.

• Special Projects: Can include "broadened health services, school breakfasts for poor children, and guidance and counseling services" in addition to strictly educational offerings. Public school teachers can go to private schools to offer special services, and mobile or portable equipment can be placed on private school premises temporarily.

• Aid for Textbooks and Library Resources: Materials are to be loaned by public agencies to private school teachers and pupils, not to the schools themselves.

To be distributed to private school pupils on an equal basis with public school student numbers, the materials must be approved for use in public schools and can include books, periodicals, documents, pamphlets, photographic works, musical scores, maps, charts, globes, sound recordings, films and video tapes.

If constitutional restrictions prevent a state from allowing its agencies to act as channels for aid to teachers and pupils in nonpublic schools, the U.S. Commissioner of Education can use a bypass procedure to provide for the distribution of authorized materials and services.

ESEA, since its passage, has been refunded in several stages and amended in some respects but has remained substantially the same as enacted.

The findings of a study reported in February, 1978, indicated that nonpublic school students were being short-changed in the quantity and quality of their participation in ESEA programs. Thomas Vitullo Martin, who conducted the study with a grant from the National Institute of Education, reported that only 43 per cent of public school districts (with nonpublic schools within their boundaries) provided ESEA services to nonpublic school students.

The 95th Congress enacted the Education Amendments of 1978 which extended for five years nearly all federal categorical-aid programs for elementary and secondary schools except vocational education and programs for the handicapped. Many new programs were authorized, and requirements were extended for the equitable participation of nonpublic school students in practically all of them.

SCHOOL AID DECISIONS

(See several decisions of this type in listing, Church-State Decisions of the Supreme Court.)

The U.S. Supreme Court handed down landmark decisions June 25, 1973, against the constitutionality of programs of aid to nonpublic school education on the elementary and secondary levels in New York and Pennsylvania. Grounds for the decisions were that the programs violated the No Establishment Clause of the First Amendment, that they had the "impermissible effect" of advancing sectarian activities, and that they were generative of religious divisiveness.

New York, Pennsylvania Cases

The decisions struck down provisions in New York statutes for maintenance and repair grants for certain nonpublic school facilities (9 to 0), tuition reimbursement (6 to 3) or tax credits (6 to 3) for parents with children in nonpublic schools, and payment to nonpublic schools for specified services mandated by the state (8 to 1). A Pennsylvania reimbursement program shared the same fate as its New York counterpart (6 to 3).

Rhode Island Ruling

In different decisions with the same thrust, the Court had ruled on June 28, 1971, against the constitutionality of a Rhode Island statute providing salary supplements for teachers of secular subjects in parochial schools in the state, and of a purchase-of-services program for instruction in secular subjects in nonpublic schools in Pennsylvania.

Analysis of Decisions

The New York and Pennsylvania decisions indicated that the Court would strike down any program containing the potential for massive subsidies, either direct or indirect, for education in church-affiliated elementary and secondary schools. So commented Father Charles M. Whelan, S.J., constitutional lawyer and professor of law at Fordham University.

In an analysis of the rulings, Father Whelan said that it seemed "reasonably clear" that all five programs at issue suffered from "three fatal defects":

• "Roman Catholic schools got the lion's share of the benefits."
• The total amount of money involved in the programs, although small, "could easily be expanded to provide massive subsidies for education in parochial schools."
• "There was no way for public schools, parents and students to benefit as well as nonpublic schools, parents and students."

The primary argument against the programs was the "effect" argument. Father Whelan called this a development parallel with the "excessive entanglement" argument in the Lemon decision. He said that the "narrow channel between the Scylla and Charybdis of effect and entanglement" spoken of by Justice Powell (who delivered the majority opinion) will probably "prove too narrow in the immediate future for any new programs specially designed to insure the survival, much less the well-being, of nonpublic elementary and secondary schools."

Meek v. Pittenger

The Supreme Court by a vote of 6 to 3 May 19, 1975, ruled unconstitutional portions of a Pennsylvania law that provided auxiliary services for students of nonpublic schools. The services, budgeted at $12 million, included counseling, testing and psychological services, speech and hearing therapy, teaching and related services for exceptional, handicapped and educationally deprived children.

At the same time, the Court ruled in favor of provisions of the law permitting textbook loans to students of nonpublic schools.

Wolman v. Walter

The U.S. Supreme Court ruled June 24, 1977, constitutional portions of an Ohio law providing for textbook loans and some auxiliary services (standardized and diagnostic testing, therapeutic and remedial services, off school premises) for nonpublic school students, while holding unconstitutional other portions providing state funds for nonpublic school field trips and instructional materials (audio-visual equipment, maps, tape recorders).

NCEA

The National Catholic Educational Association, founded in 1904, is a voluntary organization of educational institutions and individuals concerned with Catholic education in the U.S. Its objectives are to promote and encourage the principles and ideals of Christian education and formation by suitable service and other activities.

The NCEA has 14,000 institutional and individual members. Its official publication is *Momentum*. Numerous service publications are issued to members.

Archbishop Joseph Bernardin of Cincinnati, Ohio, is chairman of the association. The Rev. John F. Meyers is president.

Headquarters are located at: Suite 350, One Dupont Circle, Washington, D.C. 20036.

Other Educational Associations

National Association of Boards of Education: Founded in 1971 and made a department of the National Catholic Educational Association in 1973, to develop and promote policy-making boards for the advancement of Catholic education. Has a national membership of 1,982. Publishes *PolicyMaker* four times a year. The executive director is Dr.

Mary-Angela Harper. Office: One Dupont Circle, Suite 350, Washington, D.C. 20036.

National Forum of Catholic Parent Organizations: Founded in 1976 as a commission of the National Catholic Educational Association, to support and promote the role of parents as primary educators of their children. Has a national membership of 625 affiliates. Publishes *Parentcator* 5 five times a year. The president is Vincent Post of Yonkers, N.Y. Office: One Dupont Circle, Suite 350, Washington, D.C. 20036.

CATHOLIC SCHOOLS AND STUDENTS IN THE UNITED STATES

(Source: *The Official Catholic Directory, 1979*; figures as of Jan. 1, 1979. Archdioceses are indicated by an asterisk.)

Section, State Diocese	Univs. Colleges	Students	High Schools	Students	Elem. Schools	Students
NEW ENGLAND	28	53,266	132	66,659	541	147,786
Maine, Portland	1	550	4	1,300	23	6,055
New Hampshire, Manchester	6	3,488	6	2,470	32	7,122
Vermont, Burlington	3	2,267	3	1,329	13	2,898
Massachusetts	9	29,408	75	34,669	239	71,166
*Boston	4	20,761	58	24,431	155	47,585
Fall River	1	2,535	6	2,840	22	6,504
Springfield	1	450	4	3,292	36	10,029
Worcester	3	5,662	7	4,106	26	7,048
Rhode Island, Providence	2	7,527	13	6,696	64	18,399
Connecticut	7	10,026	31	20,195	170	42,146
*Hartford	3	1,793	15	10,996	98	24,082
Bridgeport	2	7,797	11	5,968	51	13,223
Norwich	2	436	5	3,231	21	4,841
MIDDLE ATLANTIC	65	156,275	391	257,156	2,201	723,669
New York	31	80,670	168	111,704	945	333,099
*New York	15	39,588	69	40,415	283	104,190
Albany	3	5,747	13	5,916	64	16,509
Brooklyn	2	17,802	24	25,314	178	96,785
Buffalo	6	13,020	25	10,847	157	35,460
Ogdensburg	1	277	3	1,291	28	5,796
Rochester	—	—	9	7,488	78	21,006
Rockville Centre	2	1,896	16	14,738	90	36,903
Syracuse	2	2,340	9	5,695	67	16,450
New Jersey	8	17,739	99	52,726	468	146,410
*Newark	4	15,730	49	23,428	216	65,335
Camden	—	—	12	7,580	70	21,488
Paterson	3	765	15	6,653	64	18,383
Trenton	1	1,244	23	15,065	118	41,204
Pennsylvania	26	57,866	124	92,726	788	244,160
*Philadelphia	10	26,618	47	54,595	289	123,875
Allentown	2	1,570	10	5,697	77	15,300
Altoona-Johnstown	2	2,165	3	2,081	41	8,512
Erie	3	5,899	10	4,935	55	16,392
Greensburg	2	1,824	2	1,512	50	9,885
Harrisburg	—	—	10	5,207	59	13,380
Pittsburgh	3	9,347	30	12,388	157	43,048
Scranton	4	10,443	12	6,311	60	13,768
SOUTH ATLANTIC	14	36,060	127	65,678	545	165,420
Delaware, Wilmington	—	—	8	5,105	30	10,822
Maryland, *Baltimore	4	7,250	25	13,419	91	27,426
District of Columbia, *Washington	3	20,204	26	11,754	83	25,640
Virginia	1	850	14	5,623	55	17,523
Arlington	1	850	4	2,641	27	9,393
Richmond	—	—	10	2,982	28	8,130
West Virginia, Wheeling-Charleston	1	1,144	9	2,489	36	6,417
North Carolina	2	1,008	3	1,158	38	9,309
Charlotte	2	1,008	2	940	19	4,751
Raleigh	—	—	1	218	19	4,558

Section, State Diocese	Univs. Colleges	Students	High Schools	Students	Elem. Schools	Students
South Carolina, Charleston	—	—	4	1,503	31	6,428
Georgia	—	—	7	3,828	30	9,466
Atlanta	—	—	2	1,646	13	4,435
Savannah	—	—	5	2,182	17	5,031
Florida	3	5,604	31	20,799	151	52,389
*Miami	2	4,610	16	11,126	61	24,006
Orlando	—	—	5	2,781	27	8,613
Pensacola-Tallahassee	—	—	1	815	10	2,703
St. Augustine	—	—	2	1,488	15	5,323
St. Petersburg	1	994	7	4,589	38	11,744
EAST NORTH CENTRAL	**50**	**109,510**	**330**	**207,990**	**2,184**	**629,522**
Ohio	12	26,680	94	61,368	527	171,051
*Cincinnati	5	18,522	24	18,825	127	43,600
Cleveland	3	5,295	28	20,742	165	63,281
Columbus	1	860	15	6,145	56	15,397
Steubenville	1	837	4	1,527	20	3,550
Toledo	1	476	17	9,016	94	26,867
Youngstown	1	690	6	5,113	65	18,356
Indiana	9	16,567	26	14,968	214	49,908
*Indianapolis	2	1,408	9	5,610	78	17,134
Evansville	—	—	5	2,212	30	5,434
Ft. Wayne-South Bend	5	12,591	5	3,678	44	11,519
Gary	1	1,592	5	3,006	43	12,246
Lafayette	1	976	2	462	19	3,575
Illinois	13	41,947	107	79,575	682	208,026
*Chicago	7	33,508	69	56,347	392	139,527
Belleville	1	825	4	2,745	57	9,841
Joliet	3	5,442	9	6,586	65	19,054
Peoria	—	—	8	4,374	58	13,033
Rockford	—	—	8	4,808	48	12,075
Springfield	2	2,172	9	4,715	62	14,496
Michigan	8	17,092	69	32,279	334	101,961
*Detroit	5	13,363	45	21,481	163	64,284
Gaylord	—	—	5	1,173	20	4,027
Grand Rapids	1	1,918	4	2,873	41	8,753
Kalamazoo	1	629	3	1,189	22	3,924
Lansing	1	1,182	6	3,308	40	10,917
Marquette	—	—	1	123	12	2,935
Saginaw	—	—	5	2,132	36	7,121
Wisconsin	8	7,224	34	19,800	427	98,576
*Milwaukee	4	3,882	15	11,245	180	47,317
Green Bay	2	1,900	9	3,672	100	22,873
La Crosse	1	1,012	7	3,492	77	15,068
Madison	1	430	3	1,391	48	9,421
Superior	—	—	—	—	22	3,897
EAST SOUTH CENTRAL	**9**	**7,871**	**57**	**25,743**	**295**	**68,655**
Kentucky	5	5,101	30	14,425	163	37,670
*Louisville	3	2,997	11	8,219	81	21,356
Covington	1	1,272	14	4,432	54	11,032
Owensboro	1	832	5	1,774	28	5,282
Tennessee	2	1,449	10	5,231	42	10,415
Memphis	1	1,126	5	2,843	16	4,861
Nashville	1	323	5	2,388	26	5,554
Alabama	2	1,321	5	3,000	53	12,182
Birmingham	1	417	2	1,048	26	4,979
Mobile	1	904	3	1,952	27	7,203
Mississippi	—	—	12	3,087	37	8,388
Biloxi	—	—	6	2,019	17	3,375
Jackson	—	—	6	1,068	20	5,013

School Statistics

Section, State Diocese	Univs. Colleges	Students	High Schools	Students	Elem. Schools	Students
WEST NORTH CENTRAL	35	48,639	174	74,090	940	208,399
Minnesota	9	14,701	27	11,667	230	53,697
*St. Paul and Minneapolis	3	7,423	14	9,275	111	32,890
Crookston	—	—	2	344	12	1,910
Duluth	1	1,212	—	—	15	2,279
New Ulm	—	—	3	849	29	4,525
St. Cloud	3	3,908	3	1,015	38	7,143
Winona	2	2,158	5	184	25	4,950
Iowa	8	8,035	31	13,868	173	34,408
*Dubuque	3	3,386	11	5,623	75	16,446
Davenport	4	3,663	8	2,213	37	5,192
Des Moines	—	—	2	2,140	21	4,646
Sioux City	1	986	10	3,892	40	8,124
Missouri	7	18,577	49	26,734	282	70,031
*St. Louis	5	13,163	34	19,859	178	48,762
Jefferson City	—	—	2	986	36	6,286
Kansas City-St. Joseph	2	5,414	10	5,166	46	12,178
Springfield-Cape Girardeau	—	—	3	723	22	2,805
North Dakota	2	1,128	9	2,497	35	6,270
Bismarck	1	922	7	1,792	20	3,701
Fargo	1	206	2	705	15	2,569
South Dakota	2	866	4	1,772	28	5,182
Rapid City	—	—	1	478	4	871
Sioux Falls	2	866	3	1,294	24	4,311
Nebraska	1	563	36	10,977	101	19,930
*Omaha	1	563	23	8,145	68	15,211
Grand Island	—	—	7	1,222	9	1,156
Lincoln	—	—	6	1,610	24	3,563
Kansas	6	4,769	18	6,575	91	18,881
*Kansas City	3	2,737	7	3,548	41	9,624
Dodge City	1	605	—	—	11	1,582
Salina	1	775	7	1,210	12	2,065
Wichita	1	652	4	1,817	27	5,610
WEST SOUTH CENTRAL	12	20,530	121	51,090	505	152,832
Arkansas, Little Rock	—	—	6	2,154	32	5,450
Louisiana	4	7,965	62	28,814	200	79,611
*New Orleans	4	7,965	28	17,678	94	43,133
Alexandria-Shreveport	—	—	7	2,203	25	6,543
Baton Rouge	—	—	7	2,914	24	11,249
Houma-Thibodaux	—	—	3	1,257	15	4,852
Lafayette	—	—	17	4,762	42	13,834
Oklahoma	1	282	5	2,179	29	5,279
*Oklahoma City	1	282	2	943	17	3,019
Tulsa	—	—	3	1,236	12	2,260
Texas	7	12,283	48	17,943	244	62,492
*San Antonio	4	6,398	15	4,284	56	15,248
Amarillo	—	—	2	422	12	2,036
Austin	1	2,119	1	282	15	3,219
Beaumont	—	—	2	691	10	2,199
Brownsville	—	—	2	792	8	2,315
Corpus Christi	—	—	3	1,147	25	5,243
Dallas	1	2,030	7	3,316	32	9,315
El Paso	—	—	3	1,167	18	4,103
Fort Worth	—	—	4	1,515	15	4,052
Galveston-Houston	1	1,736	9	4,327	48	13,841
San Angelo	—	—	—	—	5	921
MOUNTAIN	6	7,230	37	14,175	198	46,810
Montana	2	2,636	6	1,771	22	3,664
Great Falls	1	1,252	4	926	17	2,740
Helena	1	1,384	2	845	5	924

School Statistics

Section, State Diocese	Univs. Colleges	Students	High Schools	Students	Elem. Schools	Students
Idaho, Boise	1	48	1	487	12	1,809
Wyoming, Cheyenne	—	—	1	154	7	1,451
Colorado	1	1,055	12	3,864	59	13,939
*Denver	1	1,055	9	3,437	48	12,282
Pueblo	—	—	3	427	11	1,657
New Mexico	2	3,491	4	1,667	31	7,287
*Santa Fe	2	3,491	3	1,563	22	5,467
Gallup	—	—	1	104	9	1,820
Arizona	—	—	8	4,042	44	13,504
Phoenix	—	—	6	2,986	26	8,471
Tucson	—	—	2	1,056	18	5,033
Utah, Salt Lake City	—	—	3	879	8	2,164
Nevada, Reno-Las Vegas	—	—	2	1,311	15	2,992
PACIFIC	20	44,056	168	90,232	780	228,415
Washington	4	8,554	13	7,212	84	19,782
*Seattle	2	4,749	9	5,562	59	14,834
Spokane	2	3,805	3	1,371	18	3,371
Yakima	—	—	1	279	7	1,577
Oregon	2	3,448	11	4,140	54	10,881
*Portland	2	3,448	10	3,997	51	10,330
Baker	—	—	1	143	3	551
California	13	29,879	134	74,406	607	185,929
*Los Angeles	4	7,619	61	34,749	230	76,299
*San Francisco	4	15,828	27	15,012	106	32,031
Fresno	—	—	2	1,277	24	6,102
Monterey	—	—	4	828	18	3,342
Oakland	4	2,660	11	6,432	55	15,377
Orange	—	—	6	4,282	35	13,791
Sacramento	—	—	9	3,885	42	10,681
San Bernardino	—	—	2	1,572	29	8,459
San Diego	1	3,772	5	3,056	43	13,456
Santa Rosa	—	—	5	1,926	13	3,257
Stockton	—	—	2	1,387	12	3,134
Alaska	—	—	2	225	3	470
*Anchorage	—	—	—	—	1	109
Fairbanks	—	—	2	225	1	234
Juneau	—	—	—	—	1	127
Hawaii, Honolulu	1	2,175	8	4,249	32	11,353
EASTERN RITES	2	323	5	793	51	8,308
*Philadelphia	1	313	1	356	18	3,294
St. Nicholas	—	—	1	138	3	804
Stamford	1	10	3	299	10	1,248
*Pittsburgh	—	—	—	—	6	924
Parma	—	—	—	—	6	980
Passaic	—	—	—	—	8	1,058
St. Maron	—	—	—	—	—	—
Newton (Melkite)	—	—	—	—	—	—
TOTALS 1979	241	483,760	1,542	853,606	8,240	2,379,816
Totals 1978	238	457,498	1,572	869,268	8,299	2,402,778
Totals 1969	297	435,716	2,181	515,351	10,406	3,917,919

Pope John Paul, addressing a gathering of Catholic university and college presidents and other personnel Oct. 7, 1979, in Washington, D.C., said: "A Catholic university or college must make a specific contribution to the Church and to society through high-quality scientific research, in-depth study of problems and a just sense of history, together with concern to show the full meaning of the human person regenerated in Christ, thus favoring the complete development of the person.... The goals of Catholic higher education go beyond education for production, professional competence . . .; they aim at the ultimate destiny of the human person, at the full justice and holiness born of truth."

REPORT ON CATHOLIC EDUCATION

The status of Catholic educational institutions in the United States at the beginning of 1979, 1978 and 1969 were reflected in figures (as of Jan. 1) reported by *The Official Catholic Directory, 1979.*

Colleges and Universities: 241 (3 more than in 1978 and 56 less than in 1969).

College and University Students: 483,760 (26,262 more than in 1978 and 48,044 more than in 1969).

High Schools: 1,542 (30 less than in 1978 and 639 less than in 1969).

High School Students: 853,606 (15,662 less than in 1978 and 261,745 less than in 1969).

Public High School Students Receiving Religious Instruction: 1,086,150 (76,511 more than in 1978 and 376,591 less than in 1969).

Elementary Schools: 8,240 (59 less than in 1978 and 2,166 less than in 1969).

Elementary School Students: 2,379,816 (22,962 less than in 1978 and 1,538,103 less than in 1969).

Public Elementary School Students Receiving Religious Instruction: 3,699,879 (58,122 more than in 1978 and 295,813 less than in 1969).

Teachers, Full-Time: 169,149 (1,838 less than in 1978 and 35,808 less than in 1969).

Lay Teachers: 116,295 (2,107 more than in 1978 and 20,932 more than in 1969).

Sisters: 43,713 (2,957 less than in 1978 and 49,005 less than in 1969).

Priests: 5,800 (602 less than in 1978 and 5,180 less than in 1969).

Brothers: 3,179 (340 less than in 1978 and 2,112 less than in 1969).

Scholastics: 162 (46 less than in 1978 and 443 less than in 1968).

Enrollment Trend: Catholic elementary and secondary school enrollment remained in decline as of Jan. 1, 1979, but the rate of decrease was less than in several previous years.

Enrollment losses in recent years have been attributed to a combination of factors, including: changes in the schools; rising costs of tuition — related, among other things, to the declining number of priests and religious in teaching and administrative positions; the declining birth rate; the exodus of many families from city parishes with formerly large schools to the suburbs where there are relatively few available Catholic schools.

One effect of the exodus to the suburbs has been an increase in the size of black, other minority and non-Catholic enrollment in inner-city schools. The National Catholic Educational Association reported in March, 1979, that the number of black students in Catholic elementary and secondary schools was 39,000 higher in 1978-79 than in 1970-71. Hispanic enrollment increased by 29,100 during the same period.

Teachers: The number of lay teachers increased again, widening the ratio of lay to religious teachers to more than two to one.

1979 Decisions of the U.S. Supreme Court:

• Ruled in March that the National Labor Relations Act of 1935 does not give the National Labor Relations Board jurisdiction in the labor disputes of teachers in Catholic schools.

• Refused early in April to extend a temporary injunction against the reimbursement (provided for in a New York statute) of church-related schools for mandated testing and services.

• Declared unconstitutional late in May a New Jersey law providing a tax credit to parents for tuition paid to church-related schools attended by their children.

Unemployment Insurance Tax: The legal counsel of the U.S. Catholic Conference advised Catholic school administrators to comply, under protest, with an administrative ruling of Labor Secretary Ray Marshall that they pay unemployment insurance taxes for their teachers. The protest proviso envisioned the possible unconstitutionality of the ruling, in view of excessive entanglement of the government with religion. Courts in Alabama and Louisiana ruled in 1979 that church-related schools in those states are not bound to pay the taxes.

Department of Education: A bill passed by the House and Senate and signed into law by President Carter in the fall of 1979 created a new Cabinet post and removed virtually all responsibility for federal education concerns from the Department of Health, Education and Welfare (to be called henceforth the Department of Health and Human Services). The new department was authorized to take over the functions of the U.S. Office of Education; one of its components is an Office of Non-Public Education whose deputy commissioner is responsible for service in the named area.

Tuition Tax Credits: The first major floor action on federal assistance to nonpublic, especially church-related, schools took place during the second session of the 95th Congress in the context of debate about tuition tax credits for parents with students in nonpublic schools. Considerable support but not enough votes were in favor of such credits.

U.S. Private Schools

These 1977-78 figures on generally church-affiliated elementary and secondary schools and their estimated enrollments (in parentheses) were reported by Catherine M. Anthony in *Our Sunday Visitor*, July 9, 1978.

Catholic, 9,822 (3,289,000); Lutheran, 2,200 (235,000); National Association of Independent Schools, 760 (285,000); Seventh Day Adventists, 1,095 (75,589); Orthodox

Hebrew Day Schools, 456 (83,200); Baptist (1976-77 statistics), 310 (87,917); Calvinist, 322 (62,269); Episcopal, 800 (150,000).

CATHOLIC TEACHER UNIONS

Many dioceses, parishes and private institutions have sound working agreements with teachers, reached in the course of negotiations with them as individuals and in groups variously called unions, associations or federations. In numerous cases procedures formerly in vogue when priests and religious formed the staff majority have been altered to accommodate the concerns of the larger number of lay teachers (about 65 per cent), regarding pay scales, working conditions, tenure, benefits, grievance procedures and their role in administration.

Pressure, however, has been mounting for larger-scale unionizations, to protect teacher rights against authoritarian administration and unfair practices, and to give teachers a more responsible share in running schools.

In a response to this demand, the U.S. Catholic Conference set up a subcommittee on teacher unions which met Feb. 15 to 17, 1977, with representative school administrators and union advocates. One of the products of the meeting was a statement describing the distinctive nature and purpose of Catholic schools and subscribing to accepted principles regarding the rights of teachers to organize and bargain collectively with school administrators.

Opinions

During the meeting with the subcommittee, Harold Isenberg, president of New York Local 2092 of the American Federation of Teachers, noted that old lines of school administration needed improvement to suit the conditions of a lay majority staff. He objected to the refusal of some administrators to deal realistically and openly with teachers, individually and through unions, and of all of them to accept intervention by the NLRB in cases of union elections, bargaining and the settlement of disputes arising from real or alleged unfair practices in labor relations.

Advocates of unionization argue with justification that teachers have a right to collective bargaining, that they deserve salaries and other contract provisions commensurate with their needs and the quality of their work, and that they need collective protection against authoritative and arbitrary actions by some administrators.

Bishops and school administrators have shown considerable reluctance to deal with unions, especially those which are affiliated with the 450,000-member American Federation of Teachers. Behind the objection is the AFT's record of opposition to public aid for students in nonpublic schools. Also regarded as objectionable is its advocacy of the dissemination of information on birth control and abortion in sex education. Affiliates claim, however, that they are not in sympathy with or bound by these commitments of the federation.

Fears have also been expressed that union demands, financial and otherwise, might drive schools out of existence, change their character, or diminish control over them by the Church.

National Association

The purpose of the National Association of Catholic School Teachers, as stated by the executive board in mid-January, 1979, is "to work with diocesan officials in an attempt to draw up acceptable guidelines that can be used by all parties to insure that the teachings of the Church are as applicable to the employer-employee relationship within the institutional Church as the Church has taught for so many years they are in the public and private sectors of industry."

The association was formed by several groups of teachers formerly affiliated with the National Federation of Teachers, AFL-CIO. Members are locals in Philadelphia, Pittsburgh, Youngstown and Brooklyn, along with individuals in Louisville and Honolulu. Groups loosely linked with the association are in Scranton, San Francisco, Los Angeles, Altoona-Johnstown, Kansas City, Mo., and Cleveland. The president is John J. Reilly, head of the Philadelphia Association of Catholic Teachers.

Supreme Court Decision

The U.S. Supreme Court handed down a significant decision Mar. 21, 1979, in which it ruled that the National Labor Relations Act of 1935 does not give jurisdiction to the National Labor Relations Board over teachers and their organizations in Catholic schools. The ground of the decision was that the NLRA does not provide for such intervention. The Court did not address the question: Would NLRB intervention amount to unconstitutional entanglement of government with religion? The case originated in representational disputes in Catholic schools in the Archdiocese of Chicago and the Diocese of Fort Wayne-South Bend.

Msgr. George G. Higgins, commenting in a 1979 Labor Day statement on the decision and the prevailing condition of teacher-administration relations in Catholic schools, pointed out the responsibility of those in charge of Catholic schools to develop agencies and procedures analogous to those of the NLRB to deal with union negotiations.

One such agency is the Board of Equity in Baltimore, established more than a year earlier for the settlement of differences between persons and institutions in the archdiocese.

UNIVERSITIES AND COLLEGES IN THE UNITED STATES

(Sources: Almanac survey; *The Official Catholic Directory*.)

Listed below are institutions of higher learning established under Catholic auspices. Some of them are now independent.

Information includes: name of each institution; indication of male (m), female (w), coeducational (c) student body; name of founding group or group with which the institution is affiliated; year of foundation; number of students, in parentheses.

Albertus Magnus College (w): 700 Prospect St., New Haven, Conn. 06511. Dominican Sisters; 1925 (560).

Albuquerque, University of (c): St. Joseph Pl. N.W., Albuquerque, N.M. 87140. Sisters of St. Francis; 1940 (3,000).

Allentown College of St. Francis de Sales (c): Center Valley, Pa. 18034. Oblates of St. Francis de Sales; 1965 (757).

Alvernia College (c): Reading, Pa. 19607. Bernardine Sisters; 1958 (848).

Alverno College (w): 3401 S. 39th St. Milwaukee, Wis. 53215. School Sisters of St. Francis; 1936; independent (1,165).

Anna Maria College (c): Sunset Lane, Paxton, Mass. 01612. Sisters of St. Anne; 1946 (1,178).

Annhurst College (c): Woodstock, Conn. 06281. Daughters of the Holy Spirit; 1941 (345).

Aquinas College (c): 1607 Robinson Rd. S. E., Grand Rapids, Mich. 49506. Sisters of St. Dominic; 1922 (1,684).

Assumption College (c): 50 Old English Rd., Worcester, Mass. 01609. Assumptionist Fathers; 1904 (1,914).

Avila College (c): 11901 Wornall Rd., Kansas City, Mo. 64145. Sisters of St. Joseph of Carondelet; 1916 (2,000).

Barat College (w): 700 Westleigh Rd., Lake Forest, Ill. 60045. Society of the Sacred Heart; 1919; independent (736).

Barry College (c): 11300 N.E. 2nd Ave., Miami, Fla. 33161. Dominican Sisters; 1940 (2,003).

Bellarmine College (c): 2000 Norris Pl., Louisville, Ky. 40205; Louisville archdiocese, 1950 (1,801).

Belmont Abbey College (c): Belmont, N.C. 28012. Benedictine Fathers; 1876 (699).

Benedictine College (c): Atchison, Kans. 66002. Benedictines, 1971 (936).

Biscayne College (c): 16400 N.W. 32nd Ave., Miami, Fla. 33054. Augustinian Fathers; 1962 (2,277).

Boston College (University Status) (c): Chestnut Hill, Mass. 02167. Jesuit Fathers; 1863 (16,571).

Brescia College (c): 120 W. 7th St., Owensboro, Ky. 42301. Ursuline Sisters; 1925 (832).

Briar Cliff College (c): W. 3303 Rebecca St., Sioux City, Ia. 51104. Sisters of St. Francis of the Holy Family; 1930 (1,055).

Cabrini College (c): Radnor, Pa. 19087. Missionary Srs. of Sacred Heart; 1957 (570, day and evening).

Caldwell College (w): Caldwell, N.J. 07006. Dominican Sisters; 1939 (673).

Calumet College (c): 2400 New York Ave., Whiting, Ind. 46394. Society of the Precious Blood, 1951 (1,592).

Canisius College (c): 2001 Main St., Buffalo, N.Y. 14208. Jesuit Fathers; 1870; independent (4,089).

Cardinal Newman College (c): 7701 Florissant Rd., St. Louis, Mo. 63121. Catholic college with autonomous board of trustees; 1976.

Cardinal Stritch College (c): 6801 N. Yates Rd., Milwaukee, Wis. 53217. Sisters of St. Francis of Assisi; 1932; independent (1,123).

Carlow College (w): 3333 5th Ave., Pittsburgh, Pa. 15213. Sisters of Mercy; 1929 (921).

Carroll College (c): Helena, Mont. 59601. Diocesan Clergy; 1909 (1,384).

Catholic University of America, The (c): Fourth St. and Michigan Ave. N.E., Washington, D.C. 20064. Hierarchy of the United States; 1887. Pontifical University (7,800).

Catholic University of Puerto Rico (c): Ponce, P.R. Hierarchy of Puerto Rico; Pontifical University (9,079).

Chaminade University (c): 3140 Waialae Ave., Honolulu, Hawaii 96816. Marianists; 1955 (2,175).

Chestnut Hill College (w): Philadelphia, Pa. 19118. Sisters of St. Joseph; 1871 (710).

Christian Brothers College (c): 650 E. Parkway S., Memphis, Tenn. 38104. Brothers of the Christian Schools; 1871 (940).

Clarke College (w): 1550 Clarke Dr., Dubuque, Iowa 52001. Sisters of Charity, BVM; 1843 (650).

Creighton University (c): 2500 California St., Omaha, Neb. 68178. Jesuit Fathers; 1878 (5,027).

Dallas, University of (c): Irving, Tex. 75061. Private; 1956; independent (2,030).

Dayton, University of (c): 300 College Park Ave., Dayton, Ohio 45409. Marianists; 1850 (8,319).

De Paul University (c): 2323 N. Seminary Ave., Chicago, Ill. 60614. Vincentians; 1898 (12,149).

Detroit, University of (c): McNicholas Rd. at Livernois, Detroit, Mich. 48221. Jesuit Fathers; 1877 (8,300).

Dominican College of Blauvelt (c): Blauvelt, N.Y. 10913. Dominican Sisters; 1952 (1,135).

Dominican College of San Rafael (c): San Rafael, Calif. 94901. Dominican Sisters; 1890; independent (688).

Duquesne University (c): 801 Bluff St.,

N.W., Pittsburgh, Pa. 15219. Holy Ghost Fathers; 1878 (7,124).

D'Youville College (c): 320 Porter Ave., Buffalo, N.Y. 14201. Grey Nuns of the Sacred Heart; 1908; independent (1,569).

Edgecliff College (c): 2220 Victory Pkwy., Cincinnati, Ohio 45206. Sisters of Mercy; 1935 (868).

Edgewood College (c): 855 Woodrow St., Madison, Wi . 53711. Dominican Sisters; 1927 (540).

Emmanuel College (w): 400 The Fenway, Boston, Mass. 02115. Sisters of Notre Dame of Namur; independent (1,039).

Fairfield University (c): Fairfield, Conn. 06430. Jesuit Fathers; 1942 (4,791).

Felician College (w): S. Main St., Lodi, N.J. 07644. Felician Sisters; 1942 (659).

Fontbonne College (c): 6800 Wydown Blvd., St. Louis, Mo. 63105. Sisters of St. Joseph of Carondelet; 1917 (878).

Fordham University (c): Fordham Rd. and Third Ave., New York, N.Y. 10458. Society of Jesus (Jesuits); 1841; independent (14,964).

Fort Wright College (c): W. 4000 Randolph Rd., Spokane, Wash. 99204. Sisters of the Holy Names of Jesus and Mary; 1939 (405).

Gannon College (c): 109 W. 6th St., Erie, Pa. 16541. Diocese of Erie; 1944 (3,500).

Georgetown University (c): 37th and O Sts. N.W., Washington, D.C. 20057. Jesuit Fathers; 1789 (12,000).

Georgian Court College (w): Lakewood, N.J. 08701. Sisters of Mercy; 1908 (1,123). Coed in evening and graduate divisions.

Gonzaga University (c): Spokane, Wash. 99258. Jesuit Fathers; 1887 (3,390).

Great Falls, College of (c): 1301 20th St. S., Great Falls, Mont. 59405. Sisters of Providence; 1932 (1,179).

Gwynedd-Mercy College (c): Gwynedd Valley, Pa. 19437. Sisters of Mercy; 1948; independent (936).

Holy Cross, College of the (c): Worcester, Mass. 01610. Jesuit Fathers; 1843 (2,570).

Holy Family College (c): Grant and Frankford Aves., Philadelphia, Pa. 19114. Sisters of Holy Family of Nazareth; 1954 (1,142).

Holy Names College (c): 3500 Mountain Blvd., Oakland, Calif. 94619. Sisters of the Holy Names of Jesus and Mary; 1868 (611).

Illinois Benedictine College (c): Lisle, Ill. 60532. Benedictine Fathers; 1887 (1,431).

Immaculata College (w): Immaculata, Pa. 19345. Sisters, Servants of the Immaculate Heart of Mary; 1920 (763).

Incarnate Word College (c): 4301 Broadway, San Antonio, Tex. 78209. Sisters of Charity of the Incarnate Word; 1881 (1,553).

Iona College (c): 715 North Ave., New Rochelle, N.Y. 10801. Congregation of Christian Brothers; 1940; independent (5,400).

John Carroll University (c): North Park and Miramar Blvds., Cleveland, Ohio. 44118. Jesuit Fathers; 1886 (3,800).

Kansas Newman College (formerly Sacred Heart College) (c): 3100 McCormick Ave., Wichita, Kans. 67213. Sisters Adorers of the Blood of Christ; 1933 (652).

King's College (c): Wilkes-Barre, Pa. 18711. Holy Cross Fathers; 1946 (2,115).

Ladycliff College (w): Highland Falls, N.Y. 10928. Franciscan Sisters; 1933; independent (501).

La Roche College (c): 9000 Babcock Blvd., Pittsburgh, Pa. 15237. Sisters of Divine Providence; 1963 (1,260)

La Salle College (c): 20th St. and Olney Ave., Philadelphia, Pa. 19141. Brothers of the Christian Schools; 1863 (6,587)

Le Moyne College (c): Syracuse, N.Y. 13214. Jesuit Fathers; 1946; independent (1,800).

Lewis University (c): Romeoville, Ill. 60441. Christian Brothers; 1930 (3,500).

Loras College (c): 1450 Alta Vista St., Dubuque, Ia. 52001. Archdiocese of Dubuque; 1839 (1,721).

Loretto Heights College (c): 3001 S. Federal Blvd., Denver, Colo. 80236. Sisters of Loretto; 1918; independent (746).

Loyola College (c): 4501 N. Charles St., Baltimore, Md. 21210, Jesuits; 1852; combined with Mt. St. Agnes College, 1971 (4,774).

Loyola Marymount University (c): 7101 W. 80th St., Los Angeles, Calif. 90045. Society of Jesus; Religious of Sacred Heart of Mary, Sisters of St. Joseph of Orange; 1911 (5,879).

Loyola University (c): 6363 St. Charles Ave., New Orleans, La. 70118. Jesuit Fathers; 1904 (4,212).

Loyola University of Chicago (c): 820 N. Michigan Ave., Chicago, Ill. 60611. Jesuit Fathers; 1870 (15,155).

Madonna College (c): 36600 Schoolcraft Rd., Livonia, Mich. 48150. Felician Sisters; 1937 (3,000).

Manhattan College (c): 4513 Manhattan College Pkwy., New York, N.Y. 10471. Brothers of the Christian Schools; 1853; independent (4,600). Cooperative program with College of Mt. St. Vincent.

Marian College (c): Fond du Lac, Wis. 54935. Sisters of St. Agnes; 1936 (517).

Marian College (c): 3200 Cold Spring Rd., Indianapolis, Ind. 46222. Sisters of St. Francis (Oldenburg, Ind.); 1937 (801).

Marist College (c): Poughkeepsie, N.Y. 12601. Marist Brothers of the Schools; 1946; independent (1,899).

Marquette University (c): 615 N. 11th St., Milwaukee, Wis. 53233. Jesuit Fathers; 1881; independent (13,638).

Mary College (c): Bismarck, N.D. 58501. Benedictine Sisters; 1959 (911).

Marycrest College (c): 1607 W. 12th St., Davenport, Iowa 52804. Sisters of the Humility of Mary; 1939 (1,568).

Marygrove College (c): 8425 W. Mc-

Nicholas Rd., Detroit, Mich. 48221. Sisters, Servants of the Immaculate Heart of Mary; 1910 (871).

Marymount College (w): Tarrytown, N.Y. 10591. Religious of the Sacred Heart of Mary; 1907; independent (828).

Marymount College of Kansas (c): Salina, Kans. 67401. Sisters of St. Joseph of Concordia; 1922 (775).

Marymount College of Virginia (w): 2807 N. Glebe Rd., Arlington, Va. 22007. Religious of the Sacred Heart of Mary; 1950 (710).

Marymount Manhattan College (w): 221 E. 71st St., New York, N.Y. 10021. Religious of the Sacred Heart of Mary; 1948; independent (2,300).

Maryville College (c): 13550 Conway Rd., St. Louis, Mo. 63141. Religious of the Sacred Heart; 1872; independent (1,380).

Marywood College (w): Scranton, Pa. 18509. Sisters, Servants of the Immaculate Heart of Mary; 1915 (3,123). Coed in graduate division.

Mater Dei College (c): Riverside Dr., Ogdensburg, N.Y. 13669. Sisters of St. Joseph; 1960 (300).

Mercy College (c): 8200 W. Outer Dr., Detroit, Mich. 48219. Sisters of Mercy; 1941 (2,339).

Mercyhurst College (c): 501 E. 38th St., Erie, Pa. 16501. Sisters of Mercy; 1926 (1,587).

Merrimack College (c): North Andover, Mass. 01845. Augustinians; 1947 (2,050).

Misericordia (College Misericordia) (w): Dallas, Pa. 18612. Religious Sisters of Mercy of the Union; 1924 (750).

Molloy College (w): 1000 Hempstead Ave., Rockville Centre, N.Y. 11570. Dominican Sisters; 1955 (1,500).

Mount Marty College (c): Yankton, S.D. 57078. Benedictine Sisters; 1936 (580).

Mount Mary College (w): 2900 W. Menomonee River Pkwy., Milwaukee, Wis. 53222. School Sisters of Notre Dame; 1913 (1,115).

Mt. Mercy College (c): Elmhurst Dr., Cedar Rapids, Ia. 52402. Sisters of Mercy; 1928 (1,015).

Mt. St. Joseph on the Ohio, College of (w): Mt. St. Joseph, Ohio 45051. Sisters of Charity; 1920 (1,224).

Mt. St. Mary College (w): Hooksett, N.H. 03106. Sisters of Mercy; 1934; independent (201).

Mt. St. Mary College (c): Newburgh, N.Y. 12550. Dominican Sisters; 1959; independent (1,046).

Mt. St. Mary College (c): Emmitsburg, Md. 21727. Diocesan Clergy; 1808; independent (1,340).

Mt. St. Mary's College (w): 12001 Chalon Rd., Los Angeles, Calif. 90049. Sisters of St. Joseph of Carondelet; 1925 (1,080). Coed in music, nursing and graduate programs.

Mt. St. Vincent, College of (c): Mt. St. Vincent-on-Hudson, New York, N.Y. 10471. Sisters of Charity; 1847; independent (1,200). Cooperative program with Manhattan College.

Mundelein College (w): 6363 N. Sheridan Rd., Chicago, Ill. 60660. Sisters of Charity of the Blessed Virgin Mary; 1929 (1,662).

Nazareth College (c): Nazareth, Mich. 49074. Sisters of St. Joseph; 1924 (640).

Nazareth College (c): East Ave., Rochester, N.Y. 14610. Sisters of St. Joseph of Rochester; 1924; independent (2,772).

New Rochelle, College of (w): 29 Castle Pl., New Rochelle, N.Y. 10801 (main campus). Ursuline Nuns; 1904; independent (4,066). Coed in nursing, graduate, new resources divisions.

Niagara University (c): Niagara Univ., N.Y. 14109. Vincentian Fathers; 1856 (4,500).

Notre Dame, College of (c): Belmont, Calif. 94002. Sisters of Notre Dame de Namur; 1868; independent (1,195).

Notre Dame, University of (c): Notre Dame, Ind. 46556. Congregation of Holy Cross; 1842 (8,731).

Notre Dame College (w): 4545 College Rd., Cleveland, Ohio 44121. Sisters of Notre Dame; 1922 (585).

Notre Dame College (w): Manchester, N.H. 03104. Sisters of the Holy Cross; 1950 (629).

Notre Dame of Maryland, College of (w): 4701 N. Charles St., Baltimore, Md. 21210. School Sisters of Notre Dame; 1873 (639).

Ohio Dominican College (c): Columbus, Ohio 43219. Dominican Srs.; 1911 (860).

Our Lady of Angels College (w): Aston, Pa. 19014. Sisters of St. Francis; 1965 (674).

Our Lady of Holy Cross College (c): 4123 Woodland Dr., New Orleans, La. 70114. Congregation of Sisters Marianites of Holy Cross (788).

Our Lady of the Elms, College of (w): Chicopee, Mass. 01013. Sisters of St. Joseph; 1928 (500).

Our Lady of the Lake University of San Antonio (c): 411 S.W. 24th St., San Antonio, Tex. 78285. Sisters of Divine Providence; 1911 (1,709).

Portland, University of (c): 5000 N. Willamette Blvd., Portland, Ore. 97203. Holy Cross Fathers; 1901; independent (2,708).

Providence College (c): River Ave. and Eaton St., Providence, R.I. 02918. Dominican Friars; 1917 (4,186).

Quincy College (c): 1831 College Ave., Quincy, Ill. 62301. Franciscan Fathers; 1860 (1,646).

Regis College (c): W. 50th Ave. and Lowell Blvd. Denver, Colo. 80221. Jesuit Fathers; 1887 (1,030).

Regis College (w): Weston, Mass. 02193. Sisters of St. Joseph; 1927; independent (1,070).

Rivier College (w): Nashua, N.H. 03060.

Sisters of the Presentation of Mary; 1933; independent (1,650). Coed continuing education and graduate divisions.

Rockhurst College (c): 5225 Troost Ave., Kansas City, Mo. 64110. Jesuit Fathers; 1910 (3,515).

Rosary College (c): 7900 Division St., River Forest, Ill. 60305. Dominican Sisters; 1901 (1,641).

Rosemont College (w): Rosemont, Pa. 19010. Society of the Holy Child Jesus; 1921 (679).

Sacred Heart College (w): Belmont, N.C. 28012. Sisters of Mercy; 1935 (394).

Sacred Heart University (c): Fairfield (P.O. Bridgeport), Conn. 06604. Diocese of Bridgeport; 1963; independent (3,278).

St. Ambrose College (c): Davenport, Ia. 52803. Diocese of Davenport; 1882 (1,818).

St. Anselm's College (c): Manchester N.H. 03102. Benedictine Monks; 1889 (1,932).

St. Basil's College (m): 195 Glenbrook Rd., Stamford, Conn. 06902. Byzantine-Ukrainian Rite Diocese of Stamford; 1939.

Saint Benedict, College of (w): St. Joseph, Minn. 56374. Benedictine Sisters; 1913 (1,921).

St. Bonaventure University (c): St. Bonaventure, N.Y. 14778. Franciscan Friars; 1856; independent (2,600).

St. Catherine, College of (w): 2004 Randolph St., St. Paul, Minn. 55105. Sisters of St. Joseph of Carondelet; 1905 (2,201).

St. Edward's University (c): Austin, Tex. 78704. Holy Cross Brothers; 1885 (2,119).

St. Elizabeth, College of (w): Convent Station, N.J. 07961. Sisters of Charity; 1899; independent (675).

St. Francis, College of (c): 500 Wilcox St., Joliet, Ill. 60435. Sisters of St. Francis of Mary Immaculate; 1925; independent (600).

St. Francis College (c): 180 Remsen St., Brooklyn, N.Y. 11201. Franciscan Brothers; 1884; private, independent in the Franciscsan tradition (3,100).

St. Francis College (c): 2701 Spring St., Fort Wayne, Ind. 46808. Sisters of St. Francis; 1890 (1,372).

St. Francis College (c): Loretto, Pa. 15940. Franciscan Fathers; 1847 (1,654).

St. John Fisher College (c): 3690 East Ave., Rochester, N.Y. 14618. Basilian Fathers; 1951; independent (1,700).

St. John's University (c): Grand Central and Utopia Pkwys., Jamaica, N.Y. 11439 (Queens Campus); 300 Howard Ave., Grymes Hill, Staten Island, N.Y. 10301 (Staten Island Campus). Vincentian Fathers; 1870 (17,029).

St. John's University (m): Collegeville, Minn. 56321. Benedictine Fathers; 1857 (1,971). Coed in graduate school.

St. Joseph College (w): 1678 Asylum Ave., West Hartford, Conn. 06117. Sisters of Mercy; 1932 (1,200). Coed in graduate school.

St. Joseph's College (c): Standish (P.O. N. Windham), Me. 04062. Sisters of Mercy; 1915 (461).

Saint Joseph's College (c): Rensselaer, Ind. 47978. Society of the Precious Blood; 1889 (976).

St. Joseph's University (c): City Ave. at 54th St., Philadelphia, Pa. 19131. Jesuit Fathers; 1851 (5,587).

St. Joseph's College (c): 245 Clinton Ave., Brooklyn, N.Y. 11205 and Roe Blvd., Patchogue, N.Y. 11772. Sisters of St. Joseph; 1916; independent.

St. Joseph the Provider, College of (c): Clement Rd., Rutland, Vt. 05701. Sisters of St. Joseph; 1954; independent (230).

Saint Leo College (c): Saint Leo, Fla. 33574. Order of St. Benedict; 1889; independent (994).

St. Louis University (c): 221 N. Grand Blvd., St. Louis, Mo. 63103. Jesuit Fathers; 1818 (10,364).

Saint Martin's College (c): Lacey, Wash. 98503. Benedictine Monks; 1895 (751).

St. Mary, College of (w): 1901 S. 72nd St., Omaha, Neb. 68124. Sisters of Mercy; 1923; independent (563).

St. Mary College (w): Leavenworth, Kans. 66048. Sisters of Charity of Leavenworth; 1923 (770).

St. Mary of the Plains College (c): Dodge City, Kans. 67801. Sisters of St. Joseph of Wichita; 1952 (585).

St. Mary-of-the-Woods College (w): St. Mary-of-the-Woods, Ind. 47876. Sisters of Providence; 1840 (632).

St. Mary's College (w): Notre Dame, Ind. 46556. Sisters of the Holy Cross; 1844 (1,819).

St. Mary's College (c): Orchard Lake, Mich. 48033. Secular Clergy; 1885 (218).

St. Mary's College (c): Moraga, Calif. 94575. Brothers of the Christian Schools; 1863 (1,445).

St. Mary's College (c): Winona, Minn. 55987. Brothers of the Christian Schools; 1913 (1,258).

St. Mary's Dominican College (w): 7214 St. Charles Ave., New Orleans, La. 70118. Dominican Sisters; 1910 (754).

St. Mary's University (c): One Camino Santa Maria, San Antonio, Tex. 78284. Society of Mary (Marianists); 1852 (3,286).

St. Michael's College (c): Winooski Park, Vt. 05404. Society of St. Edmund; 1904 (1,551).

St. Norbert College (c): De Pere, Wis. 54115. Norbertine Fathers; 1898; independent (1,559).

St. Peter's College (c): 2641 Kennedy Blvd., Jersey City, N.J. 07306. Jesuit Fathers; 1872 (4,295).

St. Rose, College of (c): 432 Western Ave., Albany, N.Y. 12203. Sisters of St. Joseph of Carondelet; 1920; independent (2,442).

St. Scholastica, College of (c): 1200 Kenwood Ave., Duluth, Minn. 55811. Benedictine Sisters; 1912 (1,162).

Saint Teresa, College of (w): Winona, Minn. 55987. Sisters of St. Francis; 1907 (900).

St. Thomas, College of (c): St. Paul, Minn. 55101. Archdiocese of St. Paul; 1885 (4,482).

St. Thomas, University of (c): 3812 Montrose Blvd., Houston, Tex. 77006. Basilian Fathers; 1947 (1,751).

St. Thomas Aquinas College (c): Sparkill, N.Y. 10976. Dominican Sisters of Sparkill; 1952; independent, corporate board of trustees (1,200).

St. Vincent College (m): Latrobe, Pa. 15650. Benedictine Fathers; 1846 (946).

St. Xavier College (c): 3700 W. 103rd St., Chicago, Ill. 60655. Sisters of Mercy; chartered 1847 (1,900).

Salve Regina — The Newport College (c): Ochre Point Ave., Newport, R.I. 02840. Sisters of Mercy; 1934 (1,600).

San Diego, University of (c): Alcala Park, San Diego, Calif. 92110. San Diego diocese and Religious of the Sacred Heart; 1949; independent (4,000).

San Francisco, University of (c): 2130 Fulton St., San Francisco, Calif. 94117. Jesuit Fathers; 1855 (6,392).

Santa Clara, University of (c): Santa Clara, Calif. 95053. Jesuit Fathers; 1851 (7,295).

Santa Fe, College of (c): Santa Fe, N. Mex. 87501. Brothers of the Christian Schools; 1947 (1,272).

Scranton, University of (c): Scranton, Pa. 18510. Jesuit Fathers; 1888 (4,437).

Seattle University (c): Broadway and Madison, Seattle, Wash. 98122. Jesuit Fathers; 1891 (3,966).

Seton Hall University (c): South Orange, N.J. 07079. Diocesan Clergy; 1856 (9,991).

Seton Hill College (w): Greensburg, Pa. 15601. Sisters of Charity of Seton Hill; 1883 (790).

Siena College (c): Loudonville, N.Y. 12211. Franciscan Friars; 1937 (2,300).

Siena Heights College (c): Adrian, Mich. 49221. Dominican Sisters; 1919; independent (1,182).

Silver Lake College of Holy Family (c): 2406 S. Alverno Rd., Manitowoc, Wis. 54220. Franciscan Sisters of Christian Charity; 1935 (341).

Southern Benedictine College (c): St. Bernard, Ala. 35138. Benedictine Monks and Sisters; 1976; independent. Formed by merger of Cullman (junior) and St. Bernard (senior) colleges (450).

Spalding College (c): 851 S. 4th St., Louisville, Ky. 40203. Sisters of Charity of Nazareth; 1814 (as Nazareth Academy); independent (988).

Spring Hill College (c): Mobile, Ala. 36608. Jesuit Fathers; 1830 (904).

Steubenville, College of (c): Steubenville, Ohio 43952. Franciscan Fathers; 1946 (847).

Stonehill College (c): North Easton, Mass. 02356. Holy Cross Fathers; 1948; independent (2,535).

Thomas More College (c): Turkey Foot Rd., Box 85, Fort Mitchell, Covington, Ky. 41017. Diocese of Covington; 1921 (1,423).

Trinity College (w): Colchester Ave., Burlington, Vt. 05401. Sisters of Mercy; 1925 (532).

Trinity College (w): Michigan Ave. and Franklin St. N.E., Washington, D.C. 20017. Sisters of Notre Dame de Namur; 1897 (808). Coed in graduate school.

Ursuline College (w): Lander Rd. and Fairmont Blvd., Cleveland, Ohio 44124. Ursuline Nuns; 1871 (860).

Villa Maria College (w): 2551 W. Lake Rd., Erie, Pa. 16505. Sisters of St. Joseph; 1925 (617).

Villanova University (c): Villanova, Pa. 19085. Augustinian Fathers; 1842 (9,422).

Viterbo College (c): La Crosse, Wis. 54601. Franciscan Sisters; 1890 (1,012).

Walsh College (c): 2020 Easton St. N.W., Canton, Ohio 44720. Brothers of Christian Instruction; 1958 (690).

Wheeling College (c): 316 Washington Ave., Wheeling, W. Va. 26003. Jesuit Fathers; 1954 (703).

Xavier University (c): Victory Pkwy. and Dana Ave., Cincinnati, Ohio 45207. Jesuit Fathers; 1831 (6,382).

Xavier University of Louisiana (c): 7325 Palmetto St., New Orleans, La. 70125. Sisters of Blessed Sacrament; 1925; lay/religious administration board (1,934).

Catholic Junior Colleges

Ancilla Domini College (c): Donaldson, Ind. 46513. Ancilla Domini Sisters; 1937 (330).

Aquinas Junior College (c): Harding Rd., Nashville, Tenn. 37205. Dominican Sisters; 1961 (323).

Donnelly College (c): 1236 Sandusky Ave., Kansas City, Kans. 66102. Archdiocesan College; 1949 (961).

Elizabeth Seton College (c): 1061 N. Broadway, Yonkers, N.Y. 10701. Sisters of Charity; 1960; independent (1,259).

Harriman College (c): Harriman Heights Rd., Harriman, N.Y. 10926. Sisters of the Catholic Apostolate; 1956; independent (367).

Hilbert College (c): 5200 S. Park Ave., Hamburg, N.Y. 14075. Franciscan Sisters of St. Joseph; 1957; independent (636).

Holy Cross Junior College (c): Notre Dame, Ind. 46556. Brothers of Holy Cross; 1966 (225).

Lourdes College (c): Sylvania, Ohio 43560. Franciscan Srs.; 1958 (525).

Manor Junior College (w): Fox Chase

Manor, Jenkintown, Pa. 19046. Sisters of St. Basil the Great; 1947 (312).

Maria College (c): 700 New Scotland Ave., Albany, N.Y. 12208. Sisters of Mercy; 1963 (420).

Maria Regina College (w): 1024 Court St., Syracuse, N.Y. 13208. Franciscan Sisters; 1963; independent (399).

Marymount Palos Verdes College (c): Rancho Palos Verdes, Calif. 90274. Religious of the Sacred Heart of Mary (348).

Mt. Aloysius Junior College (c): Cresson, Pa. 16630. Sisters of Mercy; 1939 (533).

Mt. St. Clare College (c): Bluff Blvd., and Springdale Dr., Clinton, Ia. 52732. Clinton Franciscans; 1928 (232).

Ottumwa Heights College (c): Grandview Ave., Ottumwa, Ia. 52501. Sisters of the Humility of Mary; 1925 (323).

Presentation College (c): Aberdeen, S.D. 57401. Sisters of the Presentation; 1951 (390).

St. Catharine College (c); St. Catharine, Ky. 40061. Dominican Sisters; 1931 (159).

St. Gertrude, College of (c): Cottonwood, Ida. 83522. Benedictine Sisters.

St. Gregory's College (c): Shawnee, Okla. 74801. Benedictine Fathers; 1876 (282).

St. Mary's College of O'Fallon (c): 200 N. Main St., O'Fallon, Mo. 63366. Sisters of the Most Precious Blood; 1921 (487).

St. Mary's Junior College (c): 2500 S. 6th St., Minneapolis, Minn. 55454. Sisters of St. Joseph of Carondelet. (815).

Springfield College in Illinois (c): 1500 N. Fifth St., Springfield, Ill. 62702. Ursuline Nuns; 1929 (503).

Trocaire College (c): 110 Red Jackett Pkwy., Buffalo, N.Y. 14220. Sisters of Mercy; 1958; independent (734).

Villa Julie College (c): Green Spring Valley Rd., Stevenson, Md. 21153. Sisters of Notre Dame de Namur; 1952; independent (566).

Villa Maria College of Buffalo (c): 240 Pine Ridge Rd., Buffalo, N.Y. 14225. Felician Srs.; 1960 (513).

CAMPUS MINISTRY

"Campus ministry is a pastoral apostolate of service to the members of the entire college community (Catholic and secular) through concern and care for persons, the proclamation of the Gospel, and the celebration of the liturgy," according to a set of guidelines drawn up by an eight-member commission of the National Catholic Educational Association. The general purpose of the ministry is to make the Church present and active in the academic community.

Ideally, according to the guidelines, elements of the ministry — carried on by teams of priests, men and women religious, and lay persons — include liturgical leadership; pastoral counseling; coordination of expressions and energies for religious life on campus; Christian witness on social and moral issues; objective and independent mediation between various groups on campus; participation in religious aspects of the work of the administration, faculty and students.

Status, Agencies

The dimensions and challenge of the campus ministry are evident from estimates that approximately 75 to 80 per cent of 1.8 million Catholics in colleges and universities are on secular or non-Catholic private campuses. Serving them are about 1,500 full-time and 1,000 part-time campus ministry personnel.

The Office of Campus and Young Adult Ministries, under the Department of Education of the U.S. Catholic Conference, has responsibility for continuing support of ministry in this field. Rev. Patrick H. O'Neill, O.S.A., is director, with offices at 1312 Massachusetts Ave. N.W., Washington, D.C. 20005.

Information and services are furnished by the National Committee of Diocesan Directors of Campus Ministry. This is a committee of members elected from each of the 12 ecclesiastical regions of the U.S., and is an advisory body to the office.

The autonomous Catholic Campus Ministry Association, whose former equivalent was the National Newman Chaplain's Association, is headquartered at 780 Student Center Building, Wayne State University, Detroit, Mich. 48202. Sister Margaret M. Ivers, I.B.V.M., is executive director.

DIOCESAN AND INTERDIOCESAN SEMINARIES

(Sources: Almanac survey; *Official Catholic Directory;* NC News Service.)

Information, according to states, includes names of archdioceses and dioceses, and names and addresses of seminaries. Types of seminaries, when not clear from titles, are indicated in most cases. Interdiocesan seminaries are generally conducted by religious orders for candidates for the priesthood from several dioceses. The list does not include houses of study only for members of religious communities. Archdioceses are indicated by an asterisk.

California: Los Angeles* — St. John's Seminary (major), 5012 E. Seminary Rd., Camarillo. 93010; St. John's College Seminary, 5118 E. Seminary Rd., Camarillo. 93010.

San Diego — St. Francis Seminary (college residence), 1667 Santa Paula Dr., San Diego 92111.

San Francisco* — St. Patrick's Seminary (major), 320 Middlefield Rd., Menlo Park. 94025; St. Patrick's College, P.O. Box 151, Mountain View 94042. St. Joseph High School (preparatory), Mountain View 94042.

Colorado: Denver* — St. Thomas Theological Seminary (major), 1300 S. Steele St., Denver 80210.

Connecticut: Hartford* — St. Thomas Seminary (minor), 467 Bloomfield Ave., Bloomfield. 06002.

Norwich — Holy Apostles College (Delayed vocation seminary), 33 Prospect Hill Rd., Cromwell 06416.

Stamford Byzantine Rite — Ukrainian Catholic Seminary: St. Basil College (major), 195 Glenbrook Rd., Stamford 06902; St. Basil's Preparatory School, (minor), 39 Clovelly Rd., Stamford 06902.

District of Columbia: Washington* — Theological College, The Catholic University of America, 401 Michigan Ave., N.E. 20064.

Florida: Miami* — St. John Vianney College Seminary, 2900 S.W. 87th Ave., Miami 33165; St. Vincent de Paul Seminary (major), Military Trail, P.O. Box 460, Boynton Beach. 33435.

Hawaii: Honolulu — St. Stephen's Seminary (college level), P.O. Box 699, Kaneohe. 96744.

Illinois: Belleville — St. Henry's Preparatory Seminary, 5901 W. Main St., Belleville 62223.

Chicago* — Quigley Preparatory Seminary (North), 103 East Chestnut St., Chicago 60611; Quigley Preparatory Seminary (South), 7740 South Western Ave., Chicago 60620; Niles College of Loyola University, 7135 N. Harlem Ave., Chicago 60631; St. Mary of the Lake Seminary, Mundelein. 60060.

Joliet — St. Charles Borromeo Seminary, High School, Rt. 53A and Airport Rd., Lockport. 60441.

Springfield — Immaculate Conception Seminary, 1903 E. Lakeshore Dr., Springfield 62708.

Indiana: Indianapolis* — St. Meinrad Seminary, College and School of Theology (interdiocesan), St. Meinrad. 47577.

Iowa: Davenport — St. Ambrose Seminary, 518 W. Locust St., Davenport 52803.

Dubuque* — Seminary of St. Pius X, Loras College, Dubuque 52001.

Kansas: Kansas City* — Savior of the World Seminary (minor), 12601 Parallel Ave., Kansas City 66109.

Kentucky: Covington — Seminary of St. Pius X, Erlanger. 41018.

Owensboro — St. Mark's School of Theology Seminary for Belated Vocations, South Union 42283.

Louisiana: Baton Rouge — St. Joseph Diocesan Preparatory Seminary, 3300 Hundred Oaks Ave., Baton Rouge 70821.

Lafayette — Immaculata Seminary (high school), 1408 Carmel Ave., Lafayette (70501

New Orleans* — Notre Dame Seminary Graduate School of Theology, 2901 S. Carrollton Ave., New Orleans 70118; St. John Vianney Preparatory School, 3810 Monroe St., New Orleans 70118; St. Joseph Seminary College (interdiocesan), St. Benedict 70457.

Maryland: Baltimore* — St. Mary's Seminary and University, 5400 Roland Ave., Baltimore 21210; Mt. St. Mary's Seminary, Emmitsburg. 21727.

Massachusetts: Boston* — St. John's Seminary, 127 Lake St., Brighton. 02135; St. John's Seminary, College of Liberal Arts, 197 Foster St., Brighton 02135; Pope John XXIII National Seminary, 558 South Ave., Weston. 02193.

Melkite Eparchy of Newton — St. Gregory the Theologian Seminary, 233 Grant Ave., Newton 02159.

Michigan: Detroit* — Sacred Heart Seminary College, Inc., 2701 Chicago Blvd., Detroit 48206; St. Mary's Preparatory, St. Mary's College and Sts. Cyril and Methodius Seminary (independent institution primarily serving Polish-American community), Orchard Lake 48033; St. John's Provincial Seminary (major for dioceses in Detroit province), 44011 Five Mile Rd., Plymouth. 48170.

Grand Rapids — St. Joseph's Minor Seminary, 600 Burton St., S.E., Grand Rapids 49507.

Minnesota: St. Cloud — School of Theology (St. John's Seminary), Collegeville. 56321.

St. Paul and Minneapolis* — St. Paul Seminary, 2260 Summit Ave., St. Paul. 55105; St. John Vianney Seminary, 2115 Summit Ave., St. Paul. 55105.

Winona — Immaculate Heart of Mary Seminary, St. Mary's College, Winona 55987.

Missouri: Jefferson City — St. Thomas Aquinas Preparatory Seminary, 245 N. Levering Ave. Hannibal. 63401.

Kansas City-St. Joseph — St. John's Diocesan Seminary (high school), 2015 E. 72nd St. Kansas City. 64132.

St. Louis* — St. Louis Roman Catholic Theological Seminary (Kenrick Seminary), 7800 Kenrick Rd., St. Louis 63119; Cardinal Glennon College, 5200 Glennon Dr., St. Louis 63119; St. Louis Preparatory Seminary, 5200 Shrewsbury Ave., St. Louis 63119 (South), 3500 St. Catherine St., Florissant 63033 (North).

Montana: Helena — Diocesan Pre-Seminary Program, Carroll College, Helena 59601.

New Jersey: Newark* — Immaculate Conception Seminary (major), Darlington, Mahwah. 07430; College Seminary of the Immaculate Conception, Seton Hall Divinity School, South Orange. 07079.

New Mexico: Gallup — Cristo Rey College Seminary, 205 E. Wilson, Gallup 87301.

Santa Fe* — Immaculate Heart of Mary Seminary, Mt. Carmel Rd., Santa Fe 87501

New York: Brooklyn — Cathedral Preparatory Seminary of the Immaculate Conception, 555 Washington Ave., Brooklyn 11238; Cathedral Preparatory Seminary of the Immaculate Conception, 56-25 92nd St., Elmhurst. 11373; Cathedral College of the Immaculate Conception, 7200 Douglaston Parkway, Douglaston. 11362.

Buffalo — Christ the King Seminary (interdiocesan), 711 Knox Rd., East Aurora. 14052.

New York* — St. Joseph's Seminary (major), Dunwoodie, Yonkers. 10704: Cathedral Preparatory Seminary, 555 West End Ave., New York 10024.

Ogdensburg — Wadhams Hall, Riverside Dr., Ogdensburg 13669.

Rochester — Becket Hall College Seminary, 75 Fairport Rd., E. Rochester. 14445; St. Bernard's Seminary, 2260 Lake Ave., Rochester 14612.

Rockville Centre — Immaculate Conception Diocesan Seminary, Lloyd Harbor, Huntington, L.I. 11743; St. Pius X Preparatory Seminary, 1220 Front St., Uniondale, L.I. 11553.

St. Maron Eparchy, Brooklyn — Our Lady of Lebanon Maronite Seminary, 7164 Alaska Ave. N.W., Washington, D.C. 20012.

Syracuse — Aquinas House, 702 Danforth St., Syracuse 13208.

North Dakota: Fargo — Cardinal Muench Seminary, 100 35th Ave. N.E., Fargo 58102.

Ohio: Cincinnati* — Mt. St. Mary's Seminary of the West, 5440 Moeller Ave., Norwood. 45212; The Athenaeum of Ohio, St. Gregory's Seminary College, 6616 Beechmont Ave., Cincinnati. 45230.

Cleveland — St. Mary's Seminary, 1227 Ansel Rd., Cleveland 44108; Borromeo College of Ohio, 28700 Euclid Ave. Wickliffe. 44092.

Columbus — Pontifical College Josephinum (interdiocesan), Worthington. 43085.

Toledo — Holy Spirit Seminary, 5201 Airport Highway, Toledo 43615.

Oregon: Portland* — Mt. Angel Seminary (major) and Mt. Angel Preparatory High School, St. Benedict 97373; St. John Vianney House of Studies, 1538 Southwest Montgomery St., Portland 97201.

Pennsylvania: Erie — St. Mark's Seminary, 429 E. Grandview Blvd., Erie 16504.

Philadelphia* — Theological Seminary of St. Charles Borromeo, Overbrook. 19151.

Philadelphia Byzantine Rite (Ukrainians)* — St. Josaphat's Seminary, 201 Taylor St. N.E., Washington, D.C. 20017.

Pittsburgh Byzantine Rite (Ruthenians)* — Byzantine Catholic Seminary of Sts. Cyril and Methodius, 3605 Perrysville Ave., Pittsburgh. 15214.

Pittsburgh — St. Paul Seminary, 2900 Noblestown Rd. 15205; St. Fidelis Seminary High School (interdiocesan), Herman. 16039.

Scranton — St. Pius X Seminary (college division), Dalton. 18414.

Rhode Island: Providence — Our Lady of Providence Seminary (major), Warwick Neck Ave., Warwick. 02889.

South Dakota: Sioux Falls — Diocesan Minor Seminary, 3100 W. 41st St., Sioux Falls 57105.

Texas: Corpus Christi — Corpus Christi Minor Seminary, Rt. 1, Box 500. 78415.

Dallas — Holy Trinity Seminary (major), P.O. Box 3068, Irving. 75061.

El Paso — St. Charles Seminary High School, P.O. Box 17548, El Paso 79917.

Galveston-Houston — St. Mary's Seminary (major), 9845 Memorial Dr. Houston. 77024.

San Antonio* — The Assumption-St. John's Seminary, 2600 W. Woodlawn Ave., San Antonio 78284.

Washington: Seattle* — St. Edward Hall, 204 S. 140th, Seattle 98168.

Spokane — Bishop White Seminary, E. 429 Sharp Ave., Spokane 99202.

West Virginia: Wheeling-Charleston — St. Joseph Preparatory Seminary, Rt. 6, Vienna. 26101; Seminary House of Studies, 1252 National Rd., Wheeling. 26003.

Wisconsin: Madison — Holy Name Seminary (High School), 3577 High Point Rd., Madison 53711.

Milwaukee* — St. Francis Seminary School of Pastoral Ministry, 3257 S. Lake Dr., Milwaukee 53207; St. Francis de Sales College, De Sales Seminary High School, 3501 S. Lake Dr., Milwaukee 53207.

NFPC

The National Federation of Priests' Councils was organized by 233 delegates from 127 priests' organizations at a charter meeting held in Chicago May 20 and 21, 1968.

Its stated purpose is to give priests' councils, official or unofficial, a representative voice in matters of presbyteral, pastoral and ministerial concern to the U.S. and the universal Church.

The NFPC has a membership of 113 senates, councils and associations.

The president is Father James E. Ratigan of Joliet, Ill. Headquarters are located at 1307 S. Wabash Ave., Chicago, Ill. 60605.

JOHN XXIII CENTER

The John XXIII Center for Eastern Christian Studies was established in 1951 by Father Feodor Wilcock and a group of other Eastern-Rite Jesuits. It operates a wide variety of ecumenical activities related to Eastern Christian studies. One of its projects is the John XXIII Institute, believed to be the only academic institution outside of Rome offering a degree in the theology of the Eastern tradition of Christianity.

Father John C. Geary, S.J., is acting head of the center, located at 2502 Belmont Ave., Bronx, N.Y. 10458.

U.S. SEMINARIES AND STUDENTS, 1962-1979
(Source: *The Official Catholic Directory.*)

Year	Dioc. Seminaries	Total Dioc. Students	Religious Seminaries Scholasticates	Total Rel. Students	Total Seminarians
1962	98	23,662	447	22,657	46,319
1963	107	25,247	454	22,327	47,574
1964	112	26,701	459	22,049	48,750
1965	117	26,762	479	22,230	48,992
1966	126	26,252	481	21,862	48,114
1967	123	24,293	452	21,086	45,379
1968	124	22,232	437	17,604	39,836
1969	122	19,573	407	14,417	33,990
1970	118	17,317	383	11,589	28,906
1971	110	14,987	340	10,723	25,710
1972	106	13,554	326	9,409	22,963
1973	107	12,925	304	8,855	21,780
1974	109	11,765	293	7,583	19,348
1975	104	11,223	269	6,579	17,802
1976	102	11,015	269	6,232	17,247
1977	100	10,344	287	5,599	15,943
1978	98	9,560	278	5,438	14,998
1979	92	8,694	258	5,266	13,960

PONTIFICAL UNIVERSITIES

(Principal source: *Annuario Pontificio.*)

These universities, listed according to country of location, have been canonically erected and authorized by the Sacred Congregation for Catholic Education to award degrees in stated fields of study.

New laws and norms governing ecclesiastical universities and faculties were promulgated in the apostolic constitution *Sapientia Christiana*, issued Apr. 15, 1979, and scheduled to go into effect in the 1980-81 academic year or the 1981 academic year, according to the scholastic calendar in use in various places.

Argentina: Catholic University of S. Maria of Buenos Aires (June 16, 1960): Juncal 1912, Buenos Aires.

Belgium: Catholic University of Louvain (Dec. 9, 1425; 1834), with autonomous institutions for French- (Louvain) and Flemish- (Leuven) speaking: Place de l'Universite I, 1348 Louvain-La-Neuve (French); Naamsestraat 22B, 3000 Leuven (Flemish).

Brazil: Pontifical Catholic University of Rio de Janeiro (Jan. 20, 1947): Rua Marques de Sao Vicente 209, Rio de Janeiro, Est. de Guanabara.

Pontifical Catholic University of Rio Grande do Sul (Nov. 1, 1950): Praca Dom. Sebastiao 2, Porto Alegre, Estado do Rio Grande do Sul.

Pontifical Catholic University of Sao Paulo (Jan. 25, 1947): Rua Monte Alegre 984, Sao Paulo.

Pontifical University of Campinas (Sept. 8, 1956): Rua Marechal Deodoro 1099, Campinas, Sao Paulo, Brazil.

Canada: Laval University (Mar. 15, 1876): Case Postale 460, Quebec GIK 7P4.

St. Paul University (formerly University of Ottawa) (Feb. 5, 1889): 223, Rue Main, Ottawa, KIS IC4, Ontario.

University of Sherbrooke (Nov. 21, 1957): Chemin Ste.-Catherine, Cite Universitaire, Sherbrooke, Que. JIK 2RI.

Chile: Catholic University of Chile (June 21, 1888): Avenida Bernardo O'Higgins 340, Casilla 114D, Santiago de Chile.

Catholic University of Valparaiso (Nov. 1, 1961): Avenida Brasil 2950, Casilla 4059, Valparaiso.

Colombia: Bolivarian Pontifical Catholic University (Aug. 16, 1945): Calle 52, N. 43-53, Medellin.

Pontifical Xaverian University (July 31, 1937): Carrera 7, N. 40-62, Bogota D.E.

Cuba: Catholic University of St. Thomas of Villanueva (May 4, 1957): Avenida Quenta 16,660, Marianao, Havana. Taken over by the Castro government in May, 1961.

Ecuador: Catholic University of Ecuador (July 16, 1954): Doce de Octubre, N. 1076, Apartado 2184, Quito.

El Salvador: José Simeón Cañas University (Sept. 15, 1965): San Salvador.

Ethiopia: University of Asmara (Sept. 8, 1960): Via Menelik II, 45, Post Office Box 1220, Asmara.

France: Catholic Faculties of Lille (Nov. 18, 1875): Boulevard Vauban 60, 59046 Lille.

Catholic Faculties of Lyons (Nov. 22, 1875): 25, Rue du Plat, 69288 Lyons.

Catholic Institute of Paris (Aug. 11, 1875): 21, Rue d'Assas, 75270 Paris.

Catholic Institute of Toulouse (Nov. 15,1877): Rue de la Fonderie 31, 31068 Toulouse.

Catholic University of the West (Sept. 16, 1875): 3, Place Andre Leroy, B.P. 808, 49004 Angers.

Germany: Gesamthochschule Eichstatt

(Jan. 25, 1975): Ostenstrasse 26, D-8833 Eichstatt.

Guatemala: Rafael Landivar University (Oct. 18, 1961): 17 Calle 8-64, Z 10 Guatemala.

Ireland: St. Patrick's College (Mar. 29, 1896): Maynooth, Co. Kildare.

Italy: Catholic University of the Sacred Heart (Dec. 25, 1920): Largo Gemelli 1, 20123 Milan.

Japan: *Jochi Daigaku* (Sophia University) (Mar. 29, 1913): Chiyoda-Ku, Kioi-cho 7, Tokyo.

Lebanon: St. Joseph University of Beirut (Mar. 25, 1881).: Rue de l'Universite St.-Joseph, Boite Postale 293, Beyrouth.

Netherlands: Roman Catholic University (June 29, 1923): Wilhelminasingel 13, Nijmegen.

Nicaragua: Central American University (1961): Apartado 69, Managua D.N.

Panama: University of S. Maria la Antigua (May 27, 1965): Apartado 2143, Panama 1.

Paraguay: Catholic University of Our Lady of the Assumption (Feb. 2, 1965): Comuneros e Independencia Nacional, Asuncion.

Peru: Catholic University of Peru (Sept. 30, 1942): Apartado 1761, Lima.

Philippine Islands: Pontifical University of Santo Tomas (Nov. 20, 1645): Espana Street, Manila.

Poland: Catholic University of Lublin (July 25, 1920): Aleje Raclawickie 14, Skr. Poczt. 279, 20-950, Lublin.

Portugal: Portuguese Catholic University (Nov. 1, 1967): Palma de Cima, Lisbon 4.

Puerto Rico: Catholic University of Puerto Rico (Aug. 15, 1972): Ponce, Puerto Rico 00731.

Spain: Catholic University of Navarra (Aug. 6, 1960): Ciudad Universitaria, Pamplona.

Pontifical University "Comillas" (Mar. 29, 1904): Canto Blanco, Apartado Postal 3082, Madrid.

Pontifical University of Salamanca (Sept. 25, 1940): Compania 1, Apartado 23, Salamanca.

University of Deusto (Aug. 10, 1963): Avenida de las Universidades, 28, Apartado 1, Bilbao.

Taiwan (China): Fu Jen Catholic University (Nov. 15, 1923, at Peking; reconstituted at Taipeh, Sept. 8, 1961): Hsinchuang, Taipeh Hsien.

United States: Catholic University of America (Mar. 7, 1889): Washington, D.C. 20064.

Georgetown University (Mar. 30, 1833): 37th and O Sts. N.W., Washington, D.C. 20057.

Niagara University (June 21, 1956): Niagara University, N.Y. 14109.

Venezuela: Catholic University "Andres Bello" (Sept. 29, 1963): Esquina Jesuitas, Apartado 422, Caracas.

Ecclesiastical Faculties

(Source: *Annuario Pontificio*)

These faculties in Catholic seminaries and universities, listed according to country of location, have been canonically erected and authorized by the Sacred Congregation for Catholic Education to award degrees in stated fields of study. In addition to those listed here, there are other faculties of theology or philosophy in state universities and for members of certain religious orders only.

Australia: Faculty of Theology, Sydney (Feb. 2, 1954).

Austria: Theological Faculty, Linz (Oct. 15, 1977).

Brazil: Faculty of Philosophy at the Aloysius Institute, Rio de Janeiro (July 15, 1941; Mar. 12, 1977).

Canada: Pontifical Institute of Medieval Studies, Toronto (Oct. 18, 1939).

Dominican Faculty of Theology of Canada, Ottawa (1965; Nov. 15, 1975).

Regis College — Toronto Section of the Jesuit Faculty of Theology in Canada, Toronto (Feb. 17, 1956; Dec. 25, 1977).

Germany: Theological Faculty, Paderborn (June 11, 1966).

Theological Faculty of the Major Episcopal Seminary, Trier (Sept. 8, 1955)

Philosophical Faculty, Munich (1932; Oct. 25, 1971).

Theological-Philosophical Faculty, Frankfurt (1932; June 7, 1971).

Great Britain: Heythrop College, University of London, London (Nov. 1, 1964). Theology, philosophy.

India: Institute of Philosophy and Theology, Poona (July 27, 1926).

Institute of Theology, Alwaye, Kerala (Feb. 24, 1972).

"Vidyajyoti," Institute of Religious Studies, Faculty of Theology, Delhi (1932; Dec. 9, 1974).

Dharmaran Pontifical Institute of Theology and Philosophy, Bangalore (Jan. 6, 1976).

St. Peter's Pontifical Institute of Theology, Bangalore (Jan. 6, 1976).

"Satya Nilayam," Institute of Philosophy and Culture. Faculty of Philosophy, Shembaganur (Sept. 8, 1932; Dec. 15, 1976).

Italy: Interregional Theological Faculty, Milan (Aug. 8, 1935).

Pontifical Theological Faculty of the Most Sacred Heart of Jesus, Cagliari, of the Pontifical Regional Seminary of Sardinia (July 5, 1927).

Pontifical Ambrosian Institute of Sacred Music, Milan (Mar. 12, 1940).

Theological Faculty of Southern Italy, Naples. Two sections: St. Thomas Aquinas Capodimonte (Oct. 31, 1941) and St. Louis

Posillipo (Mar. 16, 1918). Pastoral Ignatian Institute, Messina (July 31, 1972).
Faculty of Philosophy "Aloisianum," Gallarate (1937; Mar. 20, 1974).

Ivory Coast: Catholic Institute of West Africa, Abidjan (Aug. 12, 1975).

Lebanon: University Centre for Religious and Ecclesiastical Sciences, Kaslik (Oct. 20, 1974).

Madagascar: Superior Institute of Theology, at the Regional Seminary of Tananarive, Ambatoroka (Apr. 21, 1960).

Peru: Pontifical and Civil Faculty of Theology, Lima (July 25, 1571).

Poland: Theological Faculty, Poznan (1969; pontifical designation, June 2, 1974).

Spain: Theological Faculty of Barcelona, of the Major Seminary of Barcelona and the College of St. Francis Borgia of San Cugat del Valles (Mar. 7, 1968).

Theological Faculty, Granada (1940; July 31, 1973).

Theological Faculty of the North, of the Metropolitan Seminary of Burgos and the Diocesan Seminary of Vitoria (Feb. 6, 1967).

Theological Faculty "San Vicente Ferrer," Valencia (Jan. 23, 1974).

Switzerland: Theological Faculty, Chur (Jan. 1, 1974).

Theological Faculty, Luzerne (Dec. 25, 1973).

United States: St. Mary's Seminary and University. School of Theology, Baltimore (May 1, 1822).

St. Mary of the Lake Faculty of Theology, Chicago (Sept. 30, 1929).

The Jesuit School of Theology, Berkeley, Calif. (Feb. 2, 1934, as "Alma College," Los Gatos, Calif.).

Vietnam: Theological Faculty of the Pontifical National Seminary of St. Pius X, Dalat (July 31, 1965). Activities suppressed.

The Pontifical College Josephinum (Theological Seminary and Preparatory Department) at Worthington, Ohio, is a regional pontifical seminary. Established Sept. 1, 1888, it is immediately subject to the Holy See.

Institutes of Higher Studies in Rome

(Source: *Annuario Pontificio.*)

Pontifical Gregorian University (1552). Theology, canon law, philosophy, psychology, science of religion, church history, missiology, social sciences. Associated with the university are:

The **Pontifical Biblical Institute** (May 7, 1909), with faculties of Scripture and ancient Oriental studies.

The **Pontifical Institute of Oriental Studies** (Oct. 15, 1917), with faculties of Oriental ecclesiastical studies and Oriental canon law.

Pontifical Lateran University (1773). Theology, canon law, civil law, philosophy, moral theology, literature.

Pontifical Urban University (1627). Theology, philosophy, missiology.

Pontifical University of St. Thomas Aquinas (Angelicum) (1580), of the Order of Preachers. Theology, canon law, philosophy, social sciences, spirituality.

Pontifical University Salesianum (May 3, 1940; university designation May 24, 1973), of the Salesians of Don Bosco. Canon law, theology, philosophy, pedagogy, and the **Pontifical Institute of Higher Latin Studies** (Feb. 22, 1964).

Pontifical Athenaeum of St. Anselm (1687), of the Benedictines. Theology, philosophy, liturgy, monastic studies.

Pontifical Athenaeum Antonianum (of St. Anthony) (May 17, 1933), of the Order of Friars Minor. Theology, canon law, philosophy, and the affiliated School of Biblical Studies in Jerusalem.

Pontifical Institute of Sacred Music (1911); May 24, 1931).

Pontifical Institute of Christian Archeology (Dec. 11, 1925).

Pontifical Theological Faculty "St. Bonaventure" (Dec. 18, 1587), of the Order of Friars Minor Conventual.

Pontifical Theological Faculty of Sts. Teresa of Jesus and John of the Cross (Teresianum) July 16, 1935), of the Carmelites. Theology, spirituality.

Pontifical Theological Faculty "Marianum" (1398), of the Servants of Mary.

Pontifical Institute of Arabic Studies (1926), of the White Fathers.

PONTIFICAL ACADEMY

(Sources: *Annuario Pontificio,* NC News Service.)

The Pontifical Academy of Sciences was constituted in its present form by Pius XI Oct. 28, 1936, in virtue of *In Multis Solaciis,* a document issued on his own initiative.

The academy is the only supranational body of its kind in the world, with a pope-selected, life-long membership of outstanding mathematicians and experimental scientists from many countries. The normal complement of members is 70; the total number, however, includes additional honorary and supernumerary members. Non-Catholics as well as Catholics belong to the academy.

Purposes of the academy are to honor pure science and its practitioners, to promote the freedom of pure science and to foster research.

The academy originated as the Accademia Linceorum (lynxes) in Rome Aug. 17, 1603. Pius IX reorganized this body and gave it a new name — Pontificia Accademia dei Nuovi Lincei — in 1847. It was taken over by the Italian state in 1870 and called the Accademia

Nationale dei Lincei, Leo XIII reconstituted it with a new charter in 1887. Pius XI designated the Vatican Gardens as the site of academy headquarters in 1922 and gave it its present title and status in 1936. Four years later he gave the title of Excellency to its members.

Scientists in the U.S. who presently hold membership in the Academy are: Edward Adalbert-Doisy, professor emeritus of biochemistry at St. Louis University School of Medicine (May 29, 1948); Franco Rasetti, professor emeritus of physics at John Hopkins University, Baltimore, Md. (Oct. 28, 1936); George Speri Sperti, director of the Institutum Divi Thomae in the Athanaeum of Ohio (Oct. 28, 1936); William Wilson Morgan, professor emeritus of astronomy at the University of Chicago (Sept. 24, 1964); Albert Szent-Gyorgyi, director of muscle research at the Marine Biological Laboratory, Woods Hole, Mass. (Apr. 10, 1970), Rita Levi-Montalcini, professor of biology at St. Louis University and director of the Cellular Biology Laboratory of the CNR, Rome (June 24, 1974); Severo Ochoa, professor emeritus, of the Roche Institute of Molecular Biology, Nutley, N.J. (June 24, 1974); Marshall Warren Nierenberg, professor of biochemistry at the National Institutes of Health, Bethesda, Md. (June 24, 1974); George Palade, professor of cellular biology at Yale University, New Haven, Conn. (Dec. 2, 1975); Victor Weisskopf, professor of physics at the Massachusetts Institute of Technology, Cambridge, Mass. (Dec. 2, 1975).

Appointed Apr. 17, 1978, were: David Baltimore, professor of biology, Har Gobind Khorana, professor of biochemistry, and Alexandar Rich, professor of biophysicis — all at the Massachusetts Institute of Technology, Cambridge, Mass.; Roger Walcott Sperry, professor of psychobiology, California Institute of Technology, Pasadena, Calif.

Deceased U.S. members of the Academy were: George D. Birkhoff, Alexis Carrel, Herbert Sidney Langfeld, Robert A. Millikan, Thomas H. Morgan, Theodore von Karman, Victor F. Hess, Peter Debye, Hugh Stott Taylor.

Other members of the Academy are listed below according to country of location; dates of their selection are given in parentheses.

Argentina: Luis F. Leloir (Apr. 22, 1968).

Austria: Hans Tuppy (Apr. 10, 1970).

Belgium: Christian de Duve (Apr. 16, 1970).

Brazil: Carlos Chagas (Aug. 18, 1961); Johanna Dobereiner (Apr. 17, 1978); Crodowaldo Pavan (Apr. 17, 1978).

Canada: Gerhard Herzberg (Sept. 24, 1964); Karel Wiesner (Apr. 17, 1978).

Chile: Hector Croxatto Rezzio (Dec. 2, 1975).

Denmark: Bengt Georg Stromgren (Dec. 2, 1975); Aage Bohr (Apr. 17, 1978).

England: Hermann Alexander Bruck (Apr. 5, 1955); Paul Adrien Dirac (Aug. 18, 1961); Alan Lloyd Hodgkin (Apr. 22, 1968); Alfred R. Ubbelohde (Apr. 22, 1968); Percy C. C. Garnham (Apr. 10, 1970); George Porter (June 24, 1974); Martin Ryle (Dec. 2, 1975).

France: Louis de Broglie (Apr. 5, 1955); Jean Lecomte (Sept. 24, 1964); Pierre Raphael Lepine (Sept. 24, 1964); Louis Leprince-Ringuet (Aug. 18, 1961); Jerome Lejeune (June 24, 1974); Andre Blanc-LaPierre (Apr. 17, 1978).

Germany: Wolfgang Gentner (Apr. 10, 1970); Rudolf L. Mossbauer (Apr. 10, 1970); Feodor Lynen (Apr. 17, 1978).

Greece: George Joachimoglu (Apr. 10, 1970).

Israel: Michael Sela (Dec. 2, 1975).

Italy: Giovanni Battista Bonino (May 23, 1942); Bettolo Giovanni Battista Marini (Apr. 22, 1968); Giuseppe Colombo (Apr. 17, 1978); Giuseppe Moruzzi (Apr. 17, 1978); Giampietro Puppi (Apr. 17, 1978).

Japan: Paul Sanichiro Mizushima (Aug. 18, 1961); Hideki Yukawa (Apr. 8, 1961).

Netherlands: Jan Hendrik Oort (Aug. 18, 1961).

New Zealand: Albert William Liley (Apr. 17, 1978).

Pakistan: Salimuzzaman Siddiqui (Sept. 24, 1964).

Peru: Alberto Hurtado (Aug. 18, 1961).

Portugal: Antonio De Almeida (Apr. 8, 1961).

Spain: Manuel Lora Tomayo (Sept. 24, 1964).

Sweden: Sven Horstadius (Aug. 18, 1961).

Switzerland: John Carew Eccles (Apr. 8, 1961), Thomas Lambo (June 24, 1974).

Vatican City: Daniel J. Kelly O'Connell, S.J. (Sept. 24, 1964).

Venezuela: Marcel Roche (Apr. 10, 1970).

Supernumerary members are: Alfons Stickler, S.D.B., prefect of the Vatican Library; Msgr. Martino Giusti, prefect of the Secret Vatican Archives.

President of the Academy is Carlos Chagas (Nov. 5, 1972).

NORTH AMERICAN COLLEGE

The North American College was founded by the bishops of the United States in 1859 as a residence and house of formation for U.S. seminarians and graduate students in Rome. The first ordination of an alumnus took place June 14, 1862. Pontifical status was granted the college by Leo XIII Oct. 25, 1884.

Students living at the college study theology and related subjects in the various pontifical universities and institutes in Rome, principally at the Pontifical Gregorian University.

The college is directed by an American rector and staff, and operates under the auspices of a U.S. bishops' committee which was set up in 1924.

Social Services

The National Conference of Catholic Charities: Established in 1910 to help advance and promote the charitable programs and activities of Catholic community and social service agencies in the United States. As the central and national organization for this purpose, it services member agencies and institutions by consultation, information and assistance in planning and evaluating social service programs under Catholic auspices.

The principal fields of service in which Catholic Charities agencies are engaged are family counseling, child welfare, services for unmarried mothers, community services, day care centers, neighborhood center programs, and care of the aged. Community organization and social action are also functions of Catholic Charities.

The NCCC conducts research with respect to service to the aging, community self-help programs, the institutional care of children, and other social service projects. It represents the Catholic philosophy of social service to government agencies and personnel, and to professional organizations in the field. Its publications include *Charities USA*, a monthly membership magazine, and *Social Thought*, a quarterly produced jointly with the National School of Social Service of the Catholic University of America.

The NCCC membership includes approximately 545 diocesan agencies, more than 300 institutions and 3,000 individuals.

Msgr. Lawrence Corcoran is executive director of the conference, with offices at 1346 Connecticut Ave. N.W., Washington, D.C. 20036.

The Society of St. Vincent de Paul, originally called the Conference of Charity: An association of Catholic laity devoted to personal service of the poor through the spiritual and corporal works of mercy. The first conference was formed at Paris in 1833 by Frederic Ozanam and his associates.

The first conference in the U.S. was organized in 1845 at St. Louis. There are now approximately 4,000 units of the society in this country, with a membership of about 34,000.

In the past 50 years, members of the society in this country have distributed among poor persons financial and other forms of assistance valued at approximately $225 million.

U.S. Vincentian councils and conferences participating in "twinning" programs assist their poorer counterparts abroad by sending them correspondence, information and financial aid on a continuing basis.

Under the society's revised regulations, women are being admitted to membership. Increasing emphasis is being given to stores and rehabilitation workshops of the society through which persons with marginal income can purchase refurbished goods at minimal cost. Handicapped persons are employed in renovating goods and store operations.

Joseph Rouast of Paris, France, is president of the Council General, the governing body of the society. There are approximately 700,000 members in the world.

The office of the U.S. Superior Council is located at 4140 Lindell Blvd., St. Louis, Mo. 63108.

Catholic Health Association of the United States, formerly Catholic Hospital Association: Founded in 1915, is a service organization for about 900 Catholic-sponsored health care facilities located throughout the United States.

The association is dedicated to the healing mission of the Church by promoting health of those who are sick or infirm because of age or disability; by respecting human dignity in the experience of sickness and death; and by fostering physical, psychological, emotional, spiritual and social well-being of people.

John Curley is president. Executive offices are located at 1438 S. Grand Boulevard, St. Louis, Mo. 63104.

The Official Catholic Directory, 1979, reported 643 Catholic general hospitals with 164,967 beds treating 33,632,403 patients annually; 86 special hospitals with 6,818 beds treating 539,162; and 121 nurses' schools with 20,136 students.

National Association of Catholic Chaplains: Founded in 1965, it is affiliated with the U.S. Catholic Conference. Membership is approximately 3,000.

The association conducts workshops, seminars and institutes for persons engaged in institutional pastoral ministry.

The office of the association is located at 1312 Massachusetts Ave. N.W., Washington, D.C. 20005.

HUMAN LIFE FOUNDATION

The Human Life Foundation came into being in 1968 as the bishops of the United States responded to the appeal of Pope Paul VI for the initiation of scientific research to improve methods of child spacing in keeping with the tenets of his encyclical, *Humanae Vitae.*

Edward B. Hanify, Esq., is chairman of the board of directors. Dr. William A. Lynch is chairman of the foundation's science committee. Lawrence J. Kane is executive director. Offices are located at 425 Investment Building, 1151 K St. N.W., Washington, D.C. 20005.

FACILITIES FOR RETIRED AND AGED PERSONS

(Sources: Almanac survey, *The Official Catholic Directory*.)

This list covers residence, health care and other facilities for the retired and aged under Catholic auspices. Information includes name, type of facility if not evident from the title, address, and total capacity (in parentheses); unless noted otherwise, facilities are for both men and women. Many facilities for the aged offer intermediate nursing care.

Alabama: Allen Memorial Home (Nursing Home), 735 S. Washington Ave., Mobile 36603 (94).

Good Samaritan Hospital Nursing Home, 1107 Voeglin St., Selma 36701 (26).

Sacred Heart Residence (Nursing Home), Little Sisters of the Poor, 1655 McGill Ave., Mobile 36604 (145).

Villa Mercy (Nursing Care Facility), Daphne 36526 (137).

Arizona: Sacred Heart Home for the Aged, Little Sisters of the Poor, 1110 N. 16th St., Phoenix 85006 (170).

Villa Maria Geriatric Center (Skilled Nursing Facility and Apartments), 2310 N. Columbus Blvd., Tucson 85712 (87 beds, 50 apartments).

Arkansas: Benedictine Manor (Retirement Home), 2nd and Grand Sts., Hot Springs 71901 (100).

California: Casa Manana Inn, 3700 N. Sutter St., Stockton 95204 (175).

Cathedral Plaza, 1551 Third Ave., San Diego 92101 (221 apartments).

Catholic Women's Center (Residence for Retired Senior Women), 195 E. San Fernando St., San Jose 95112 (48).

Ellis Seniors Residence, 3263 First Ave., Sacramento 95817.

Little Flower Haven (Residential Care Facility for Retired), 8585 La Mesa Blvd., La Mesa 92041 (93).

Little Sisters of the Poor, 2700 E. First St., Los Angeles 90033 (140).

Little Sisters of the Poor, 2647 E. 14th St., Oakland 94601 (100).

Little Sisters of the Poor, 300 Lake St., San Francisco 94118 (140).

Madonna Residence (Retirement Home for Women over 60), 1055 Pine St., San Francisco 94109 (46).

Marian Residence (Retirement Home), 124 S. College Dr., Santa Maria 93454 (46).

Nazareth House, 2121 N. 1st St., Fresno 93703 (80).

Nazareth House, 3333 Manning Ave., Los Angeles 90064 (100).

Nazareth House, 245 Nova Albion Way, Terra Linda, San Rafael 94903 (120).

Nazareth House Retirement Home, 6333 Rancho Mission Rd., San Diego 92108.

Our Lady of Fatima Villa (Nursing Home, Women), 20400 Saratoga-Los Gatos Rd., Saratoga 95070 (85).

Our Lady's Home, 3431 Foothill Blvd., Oakland 94601 (200).

St. Francis Home (Elderly and Retired Women), 1718 W. 6th St., Santa Ana 92703 (87).

St. Francis Manor, Inc., 2515 J St., Sacramento 95816.

Villa Siena (Residence), 1855 Miramonte, Mountain View 94040 (48).

Colorado: Little Sisters of the Poor, 3630 W. 30th Ave., Denver 80211 (118).

St. Elizabeth Center (Retirement Home), 2825 W. 32nd Ave., Denver 80211 (147).

Connecticut: Augustana Homes, Simeon Rd., Bethel 06801.

Notre Dame Convalescent Home, 76 West Rocks Rd., Norwalk 06851 (60).

Regina Pacis Villa (Residence), RFD No. 1, Pomfret Center 06259 (16).

St. Joseph Guest Home (Women, Employed and Retired), 311 Greene St., New Haven 06511 (86).

St. Joseph's Home for the Aged, 88 Jackson St., Willimantic 06226 (37).

St. Joseph's Manor, Carmelite Srs. for Aged and Infirm, 6448 Main St., Trumbull 06611 (285).

St. Joseph's Residence, Little Sisters of the Poor, 1365 Enfield St., Enfield, Conn. 06082 (94).

St. Lucian's Home for the Aged, 532 Burritt St., New Britain 06053 (65).

St. Mary's Home (Residence and Health Care Facility), 291 Steele Rd., W. Hartford 06117 (177).

Villa Maria Rest Home for the Aged, West St., Thompson 06277 (30).

Delaware: Jeanne Jugan Residence, Little Sisters of the Poor, 185 Salem Church Rd., Newark 19713.

Florida: All Saints Home for the Aged, 2040 Riverside Ave., Jacksonville 32204 (59).

Carroll Manor, 3665 S. Miami Ave., Miami 33133

Casa Calderon, Inc., P.O. Box 2395, Tallahassee 32304. Apartments.

Cor Jesu Retirement Center, 4918 N. Habana Ave., Tampa 33614 (78).

Florida Manor Nursing Home, P.O. Box 5577, Orlando 32805.

Haven of Our Lady of Peace (Residence and Health Care Facility), 5203 9th Ave., Pensacola 32504 (88).

Maria Manor Health Care Center, 10300

Facilities for Retired, Aged 633

4th St. N., St. Petersburg 33702 (274).
Marian Towers, Inc. (Retirement Apartments), 17505 North Bay Rd., Miami Beach 33160.
Pennsylvania Retirement Residence, 208 Evernia St., W. Palm Beach 33401 (176).
St. Andrew Towers (Retirement Apartments), 2700 N.W. 99th Ave., Coral Springs 33065.
St. Elizabeth Gardens, Inc. (Retirement Apartments), 801 N.E. 33rd St., Pompano Beach 33064.
St. Joseph's Residence, 3485 N.W. 30th St., Ft. Lauderdale 33311.
Villa Maria Retirement Home, 1055 N.E. 123rd St., North Miami 33161.

Illinois: Addolorato Villa (Residence), Highway 83, McHenry Rd., Wheeling 60090 (103).
Alvernia Manor (Residence), 1598 Main St., Lemont 60439 (56).
Carlyle Healthcare Center, 501 Clinton St., Carlyle 62231 (128).
Carmelite Retirement Village, Cass Ave. N., at I-55 (Stevenson), Darien 60559 (96 units, 150 residents).
Holy Family Villa (Residence and Health Care,), Lemont 60439 (106).
Huber Memorial Home (Women), 1000 30th St., Rock Island 61201 (22).
Maryhaven, Inc. (Intermediate Care Facility), 1700 E. Lake Ave., Glenview 60025 (147).
Mayslake Village (Retirement Apartments), 1801 35th St., Oak Brook 60521 (481 Apartments).
Meredith Memorial Home, Public Square, Belleville 62220 (88).
Merkle-Knipprath Nursing Home, Rt. 1, Clifton 60927.
Mother Theresa Home, 1270 Main St., Lemont 60439 (58).
Our Lady of Angels Retirement Home, 1201 Wyoming, Joliet 60435 (100).
Our Lady of the Snows Apartment Community (Retirement Apartment Community; Health Care Program), 9500 W. Ill., Rt. 15, Belleville 62223 (200).
Rosary Hill Convalescent Home, 9000 W. 81st St., Justice 60458 (60).
St. Andrew Home, 7000 N. Newark Ave., Chicago 60648 (198).
St. Ann's Health Care Center, 770 State St., Chester 62233 (92).
St. Ann's Home and Infirmary, Waukegan and Techny Rds., Techny 60082 (175).
St. Augustine's Home, Little Sisters of the Poor, 2358 Sheffield Ave., Chicago 60614 (110).
St. Benedict Home, 6930 W. Touhy Ave., Niles 60648 (52).
St. Joseph's Home, S. 6th St. Rd., Springfield 62703 (76).
St. Joseph's Home, 2223 W. Heading Ave., Peoria 61604 (200).
St. Joseph's Home for the Aged, 649 E. Jefferson St., Freeport 61032 (109).
St. Joseph's Home for the Elderly, 80 W. Baldwin Rd., Palatine 60067 (208).
St. Joseph's Home for the Aged, 2650 N. Ridgeway Ave., Chicago 60647 (173).
St. Patrick's Residence (Sheltered and Intermediate Care; Skilled Nursing Facility), 22 E. Clinton St., Joliet 60431 (202).
Villa Saint Cyril (Residence), 1111 St. John's Ave., Highland Park 60035 (80).
Villa Scalabrini (Residence), Northlake 60164 (155).

Indiana: Providence Home, 502 W. 9th St., Jasper 47546 (58).
Providence Retirement Home, 703 E. Spring St., New Albany 47150 (73).
Regina Pacis Home (Skilled Nursing and Intermediate Care Facility), 3900 Washington Ave., Evansville 47715 (154).
Sacred Heart Home (Residence and Comprehensive Nursing), R.R. 2, Avilla 46710 (130).
St. Anne Home (Residence and Comprehensive Nursing), 1900 Randalia Dr., Ft. Wayne 46805 (140).
St. Anthony's Medical Center, Nursing Home, Main and Franciscan Rd., Crown Point 46307 (211).
St. Augustine Home, Little Sisters of the Poor, 2345 W. 86th St., Indianapolis 46260 (186).
St. John's Home for the Aged, Little Sisters of the Poor, 1236 Lincoln Ave., Evansville 47714 (130).
St. Paul Hermitage (Residence and Comprehensive Nursing), 501 N. 17th St., Beech Grove 46107 (104).

Iowa: The Alverno Health Care Facility, Clinton 42732 (136).
Bishop Drumm Home for the Aged, 1409 Clark St., Des Moines 50314 (138).
Holy Spirit Retirement Home (Nursing Home), 1701 W. 25th St., Sioux City 51103 (94).
Kahl Home for the Aged and Infirm (Health Facility), 1101 W. 9th St., Davenport 52804 (125).
The Marian Home, 2400 6th Ave. North, Fort Dodge 50501 (97).
Mary of the Angels Home (Women, Employed and Retired), 605 Bluff St., Dubuque 52001 (85).
Padre Pio Health Care Center, Inc. (Residence, Nursing Home), 3325 Windsor, Dubuque 52001 (250).
Ritter Home for Retired Women, 1837 Sunnyside Ave., Burlington 52601 (6).
St. Anthony Nursing Home, 406 E. Anthony St., Carroll 51401 (78).
St. Francis Continuation Care and Nursing Home, Burlington 52601 (74)

Kansas: Mt. Joseph (Intermediate Care Facility), 1110 W. 11, R.R. 1, Concordia 66901 (100).

St. John's Rest Home (Intermediate Care Facility), 701 Seventh St., Victoria 67671 (45).

St. Joseph's Home, 759 Vermont Ave., Kansas City 66101.

Villa Maria, Inc. (Intermediate Care Facility), 116 S. Central, Mulvane 67110 (66).

Kentucky: Carmel Home (Residence and Nursing Home), Old Hartford Rd., Owensboro 42301 (82).

Cardome Residence for Women, Georgetown 40324 (30).

Carmel Manor (Personal Care Home), Carmel Manor Rd., Ft. Thomas, 41075 (99).

Home for Senior Citizens, P.O. Box R. 1, Philpot 42366 (68).

Madonna Manor Nursing Home, 2344 Amsterdam Rd., Covington 41016 (Cottages for Senior Citizens: 9, with 48 apartments).

St. Charles Nursing Home, 500 Farrell Dr., Covington 41011 (147).

St. Margaret of Cortona Home (Women), 1310 Leestown Pike, Lexington 40508 (24).

Taylor Manor Nursing Home, Versailles 40383 (89).

Louisiana: Bethany M.H.S. Nursing Home (Women), P.O. Box 2308, Lafayette 70501 (38).

Chateau de Notre Dame (Residence and Nursing Home), 2832 Burdette St., New Orleans 70125 (110 residential units, 180 nursing beds).

Christopher Inn Apartments, 2110 Royal St., New Orleans 70116.

Consolata Home (Nursing and Extended Care), 2319 E. Main St., New Iberia 70560.

Lafon Nursing Home of the Holy Family, 6900 Chef Menteur Hwy., New Orleans 70126.

Mary-Joseph Residence for the Elderly, 4201 Woodland Dr., New Orleans 70114 (180).

Mater Dolorosa Adult Group Home, 1215 Dublin St., New Orleans 70118.

Ollie Steele Burden Manor (Retirement Home and Skilled Nursing Care), 4220 Essen Lane, Baton Rouge 70809 (46).

Our Lady of Prompt Succor Home (Nursing and Extended Care Facility), 751 E. Prudhomme Lane, Opelousas 70570.

St. Charles Nursing Home, P.O. Box 508, Newellton 71357.

St. Joseph's Home (Nursing Home), 2301 Sterlington Rd., Monroe 71201 (119).

St. Margaret's Home (Nursing Home, Women), 504 Tricou St., New Orleans 70117 (82).

Wynhoven Apartments (Residence for Senior Citizens), 4600 - 10th St., Marrero 70072 (200).

Maine: Deering Pavilion (Apartments for Senior Citizens), 800 Forest Ave., Portland 04103 (200 units).

Marcotte Nursing Home, 100 Campus Ave., Lewiston 04240 (377).

Mt. St. Joseph (Nursing Home), Highwood St., Waterville 04901 (77).

St. Andre Health Care Facility, Inc. (Nursing Home), 407 Pool Rd., Biddeford 04005 (96).

St. John Valley Security Home (Boarding-Nursing Home), 40 Riverview St., Madawaska 04756 (87). Elderly Home, Inc., 9-1st Ave., Madawaska 04756 (48 apartments).

St. Joseph Manor, 1137 Washington Ave., Portland 04103.

Seton Village, Inc., 1 Carver St., Waterville 04901.

Villa Muir, Home for Women, Bay View, Saco 04072 (15).

Maryland: Carroll Manor (Residence and Nursing Home), 4922 La Salle Rd., Hyattsville 20782 (210).

Little Sisters of the Poor, St. Martin's Home (for the Aged), 601 Maiden Choice Lane, Baltimore 21228 (236).

Sacred Heart Home, 5805 Queens Chapel Rd., Hyattsville 20782 (102).

St. Joseph Nursing Home, 1222 Tugwell Dr., Baltimore 21228.

Stella Maris Hospice (Long-term Geriatrics), 2300 Dulaney Valley Rd., Towson 21204 (399).

Villa Rosa (Nursing Home), Lottsford Vista Rd., Mitchellville 20716 (59).

Massachusetts: Beaven-Kelly Home for Aged Men (Rest Home), 1245 Main St., Brightside, Holyoke 01040 (55).

Catholic Memorial Home (Nursing Home), 2446 Highland Ave., Fall River 02720 (293).

Don Orione Nursing Home, 111 Orient Ave., East Boston 02128 (200). Adult day care center (30).

D'Youville Manor (Nursing Home), 981 Varnum St., Lowell 01854 (197). Day care program (20).

Jeanne Jugan Residence, Little Sisters of the Poor (Nursing Home), 186 Highland Ave., Somerville 02143 (120).

Madonna Manor (Nursing Home), Washington St., N. Attleboro 02760 (83).

Marian Manor (Nursing Home), 130 Dorchester St., S. Boston, 02127 (376).

Marian Manor (Nursing Home), 33 Summer St., Taunton 02780 (129).

Maristhill Nursing Home, 66 Newton St., Waltham 02154 (120).

Mary Immaculate Nursing Home, Bennington St., Lawrence 01841 (250).

Mt. St. Vincent Nursing Home, Holy Family Rd., Holyoke 01040 (115).

Our Lady's Haven (Nursing Home), 71 Center St., Fairhaven 02719 (130).

The Protectory, Inc., 133 Maple St.,

Facilities for Retired, Aged

Lawrence 01854 (Congregate Housing).
Sacred Heart Home (Nursing Home), 359 Summer St., New Bedford 02740 (213).
St. Francis Home for Aged, 37 Thorne St., Worcester 01604 (85).
St. Joseph Manor Nursing Home, 215 Thatcher St., Brockton 02402 (56).
St. Joseph's Manor (Rest Home, Women), 321 Centre St., Dorchester, Boston 02122 (95).
St. Luke's Home (Rest Home, Women), 85 Spring St., Springfield 01105 (92).
St. Patrick's Manor (Nursing Home), 863 Central St., Framingham 01701 (292).

Michigan: Bishop Noa Home for Senior Citizens, Escanaba 49829 (109).
Burtha M. Fisher Home, Little Sisters of the Poor (Residence and Nursing Home), 17550 Southfield Rd., Detroit 48235 (183).
Carmel Hall (Residence and Nursing Home), Woodward Ave., Detroit 48201 (500).
Casa Maria, 600 Maple Vista, Imlay City 48444 (48).
Kundig Center (Residence), 3300 Jefferies Freeway, Detroit 48208 (180). Rooms and apartments.
Lourdes Nursing Home, 2300 Watkins Lake Rd., Pontiac 48054 (108).
Madonna Villa, 17825 Fifteen Mile Rd., Fraser, Clinton Township 48026.
Marian Hall (Residence), 529 Detroit St., Flint 48502 (115).
Marian-Oakland West, 29250 W. Ten Mile Rd., Farmington Hills 48024.
Marian Place (Residence), 408 W. Front St., Monroe 48161. (42).
Marycrest Manor (Skilled Nursing Facility), 15475 Middlebelt Rd., Livonia 48154 (55).
Marydale Center for Senior Citizens (Board and Apartments), 3147 Tenth Ave., Port Huron 48060 (66).
Maryhaven, 11350 Reeck Rd., Southgate 48195.
St. Ann's Home, (Residence and Nursing Home), 2161 Leonard St. N.W., Grand Rapids 49304 (112).
St. Catherine Cooperative House for Elderly Women, 1641 Webb Ave., Detroit 48206.
St. Elizabeth Briarbank (Residence), 1315 N. Woodward Ave., Bloomfield Hills 48013 (56).
St. Francis Home (Nursing Home), 915 N. River Rd., Saginaw 48603 (100).
St. John Vianney Cooperative House for Men, 4806 Mt. Elliot, Detroit 48207 (30).
St. Joseph's Home for the Aged, 4800 Cadieux Rd., Detroit 48224 (100).
Stapleton Center (Residence), 9341 Agnes St., Detroit 48214 (65).
Villa Elizabeth (Nursing Home), 2100 Leonard St. N.E., Grand Rapids 49505 (136).
Villa Francisca (Residence, Women), 565 W. Long Lake Rd., Bloomfield Hills 48013 (18).
Villa Marie, 15131 Newburgh Rd., Livonia 48154.

Minnesota: Assumption Nursing Home, Cold Spring 56320 (68).
Bethany Home, Onamia 56359 (40).
Divine Providence Community Home, Sleepy Eye 56085 (58).
Divine Providence Home (Skilled Nursing Home), Ivanhoe 56142 (51).
Little Sisters of the Poor (Skilled Nursing and Intermediate Care), 90 Wilkin St., St. Paul 55102 (153).
Loretto Hospital Geriatric Unit, 1324-5th North St., New Ulm 56073 (31).
Madonna Towers (Retirement Apartments), 4001 19th Ave. N.W., Rochester 55901 (145).
Mary Rondorf Retirement Home, 222 5th St. N., Staples 56479 (84).
Mother of Mercy Nursing Home, Albany 56307 (62).
Regina Nursing Home and Retirement Residence, Hastings 55033 (61, nursing home; 74, retirement home).
Sacred Heart Hospice (Nursing Home), 1200 Twelfth St. S.W., Austin 55912 (59).
St. Ann's Residence, 330 E. 3rd St., Duluth 55805 (200).
St. Anne Hospice (Residence and Nursing Care), 1347 W. Broadway, Winona 55987 (118).
St. Benedict Center (Nursing Home), 1810 Minnesota Blvd. S.E., St. Cloud 56301 (220).
St. Elizabeth's Hospital and Nursing Home, 1200-5th Grant Blvd., Wabasha 55981 (53).
St. Francis Home, Breckenridge 56520 (124).
St. Francis Residence, 516 Walsh St., Crookston 56716.
St. Mary's Rehabilitation Center, 2512 S. 7th St., Minneapolis 55454 (240).
St. Mary's Hospital and Nursing Home, Winsted 55395 (95).
St. Mary's Home, 1925 Norfolk Ave., St. Paul 55116 (140).
St. Mary's Villa (Nursing Home), Pierz 56364 (66).
St. Otto's Home (Nursing Home), Little Falls 56345 (159).
St. Therese Home (Residence and Health Care Facility) (302) and St. Therese Retirement Apartments (226), 8000 Bass Lake Rd., New Hope 55428.
St. Vincent's Rest Home (Nursing Home), Summit Ave., Crookston 56716 (80).
St. William's Nursing Home, Parkers Prairie 56361 (61).
Villa of St. Francis Nursing Home, Morris 56267 (112).

Mississippi: Santa Maria Retirement

Apartments, 305 E. Beach St., Biloxi, 39530.
Villa Maria Retirement Apartments, 921 Porter Ave., Ocean Springs 39564.

Missouri: The Alverne (Retirement Home), 1014 Locust St., St. Louis 63101 (251).
Cathedral Square Towers, 444 W. 12th St., Kansas City 64105. Apartments.
Chariton Apartments (Retirement Apartments), 4249 Michigan Ave., St. Louis 63117 (122 units; 132 residents).
DePaul Community Health Center — St. Anne's Division (Nursing Home), 12349 DePaul Dr., Bridgeton 63044 (114).
LaVerna Heights Retirement Home (Women), 104 E. Park Ave., Savannah 64485 (40).
LaVerna Village Nursing Home, 904 Hall Ave., Savannah 64485 (120).
Little Sisters of the Poor, St. Alexis Home, 5331 Highland Ave., Kansas City 64110 (160).
Little Sisters of the Poor (Home for Aged), 3225 N. Florissant Ave., St. Louis 63107 (264).
Mother of Good Counsel Home, 6825 Natural Bridge Rd., Normandy, 63121.
Our Lady of Mercy Home (Residence and Nursing Home), 918-24 E. 9th St., Kansas City 64106 (153).
Our Lady of Mercy Country House, Box 451, R.R. No. 4, Liberty 64038 (39).
Our Lady of Perpetual Help Nursing Home, 3419 Gasconade St., St. Louis 63118 (112).
St. Agnes Home for the Aged, 10341 Manchester Rd., Kirkwood 63122 (130).
St. John's Hospital — Mercy Villa Division (Nursing Home), 1845 S. Rogers, Springfield 65804 (150).
St. Joseph Hill Nursing Care Facility (Men), Highway FF, Eureka 63025 (130).
St. Joseph's Home, 723 First Capitol Dr., St. Charles 63301 (101).
St. Joseph's Home for the Aged, 1550 W. Main St., Jefferson City 65101 (75).

Nebraska: Bergen Mercy Care Center (residence), 1870 S. 75th St., Omaha 68124 (193)
Madonna Professional Care Center, 2200 S. 52nd St., Lincoln 68506 (182).
Mercy Fontenelle Center, 4500 Ames Ave., Omaha 68104 (37).
Mt. Carmel Home, Keens' Memorial (Nursing Home), 412 W. 18th St., Kearney 68847 (76).
New Cassel Retirement Center, 900 N. 90th St., Omaha 68114. (75).
St. Joseph's Home (Custodial Foster Home), 320 E. Decatur St., West Point 68788 (51).
St. Joseph's Nursing Home, 401 N. 18th St., Norfolk 68701.
St. Joseph's Villa, David City 68632. (65).

New Hampshire: Mount Carmel Nursing Home, 235 Myrtle St., Manchester 03104 (120).
St. Ann Home, 195 Dover Point Rd., Dover 03820 (52).
St. Francis Home for Aged, Court St., Laconia 03246 (51).
St. Teresa Manor (Nursing Home), 519 Bridge St., Manchester 03104 (49).
St. Vincent de Paul Nursing Home, Providence Ave., Berlin 03570 (72).

New Jersey: Holy Family Residence (Women), 44 Rifle Camp Rd., P.O. Box 536, W. Paterson 07424 (62).
Little Sisters of the Poor, St. Joseph Home, 140 Shepherd Lane, Totowa 07512 (250).
Mater Dei Nursing Home, RD 3, Box 164, Rt. 40, P.O. Newfield 08344 (64).
Morris Hall, Home for the Aged (Residence and Skilled Nursing Home), 2361 Lawrenceville Rd., Lawrenceville 08648 (125).
Mount St. Andrew Villa (Residence), 55 W. Midland Ave., Paramus 07652 (59).
Our Lady's Residence (Nursing Home), Glendale and Clematis Aves., Pleasantville 08232 (104).
St. Ann's Home for the Aged (Residence and Nursing Care, Women), 198 Old Bergen Rd., Jersey City 07305 (105).
St. Joseph's Home (women), 240 Longhouse Dr., Hewitt 07421.
St. Joseph's Rest Home for Aged Women, 46 Preakness Ave., Paterson 07502 (30).
St. Joseph's Villa, Peapack 07977 (12).
St. Mary's Catholic Home (Skilled Nursing Home), 1730 Kresson Rd., Cherry Hill 08003 (94).
Villa Maria (Residence), 641 Somerset St., N. Plainfield 07061 (79).

New Mexico: Good Shepherd Manor (Shelter Care Home for Aged), Little Brothers of the Good Shepherd, P.O. Box 10248, Albuquerque 87114 (45).

New York: Bernardine Apartments, 417 Churchill Ave., Syracuse 13205.
Consolation Nursing Home Inc., 111 Beach Dr., West Islip 11795 (250).
Ferncliff Nursing Home, P.O. Box 386, River Rd., Rhinebeck 12572 (320).
Frances Schervier Home and Hospital, 2975 Independence Ave., New York 10463 (364).
The Heritage (Residence), 1450 Portland Ave., Rochester 14621.
Holy Family Home, 410 Mill St., Williamsville 14221 (85).
Little Sisters of the Poor, Notre Dame Home, 660 E. 183rd St., Bronx 10458 (175).
Little Sisters of the Poor, Holy Family Home, 1740-84th St., Brooklyn 11214 (175).
Little Sisters of the Poor, Queen of Peace

Facilities for Retired, Aged

Residence (Skilled Nursing and Health-Related Facility), 110-30 221st St., Queens Village 11429 (202).

Loretto Rest, Inc., 700 Brighton Ave., Syracuse 13205.

Madonna Home of Mercy Hospital (Nursing Home and Extended Care Facility) (140), and Mercy Hospital Health Related Facility (Residence) (58), Watertown 13601.

Madonna Residence, 1 Prospect Park W., Brooklyn, 11215 (290).

Marillac House (Apartments for Active or Retired Senior Citizens), 301 Orchard, Fayettville 13066 (52 units).

Mary Manning Walsh Home (Nursing Home), 1339 York Ave., New York 10021 (347).

Mercy General Hospital Nursing Home Unit, Tupper Lake 12986 (26).

Mt. Carmel Home (Nursing Home, Women), 539 W. 54th St., New York 10019 (92).

Mt. Loretto Convalescent and Rest Home, (Skilled Nursing Facility), Sisters of the Resurrection, R.D., 3, Amsterdam 12010 (81).

Nazareth Nursing Home, and Health Related Facility, 291 W. North St., Buffalo 14201 (122).

Our Lady of Hope Residence (Home for the Aged), Little Sisters of the Poor, 1 Jeanne Jugan Lane, Latham 12210 (250).

Ozanam Hall for the Elderly, 42-41 201st St., Bayside 11361 (432).

Providence Rest Home (Women), 3304 Waterbury Ave., Bronx 10465 (154).

Resurrection Rest Home (Nursing Home and Health Related Facility, Women), Castleton 12033 (51).

Sacred Heart Home (Residence) 4520 Ransom Rd., Clarence 10431. Brothers of Mercy Health Facilities, 10570 Bergtold Rd., Clarence 14031. Brothers of Mercy Housing Co., Inc. (Apartments), 10500 Bergtold Rd., Clarence 14031.

Sacred Heart Nursing Home, 8 Mickle St., Plattsburgh 12901 (89).

St. Ann's Home (Nursing Home and Extended Care Facility), 1500 Portland Ave., Rochester 14621 (354).

St. Anthony's Home for the Aged, 5285 S. Park Ave., Hamburg 14075 (68).

St. Columban's on the Lake (Retirement Home), Silver Creek 14136 (50).

St. Elizabeth Home, 5539 Broadway, Lancaster 14086 (102).

St. Francis Home (Nursing and Intermediate Care Facility), 147 Reist St., Williamsville 14221 (98).

St. Joseph's Guest Home, 350 Cuba Hill Rd., Huntington 11743 (60).

St. Joseph's Home (Nursing Home), 420 Lafayette St., Ogdensburg 13669 (82).

St. Joseph's Nursing Home, 2535 Genesee St., Utica 13501 (120).

St. Joseph's Villa, 38 Prospect Ave., Catskill 12414. (New facility is under construction.)

St. Luke Manor for Chronically Ill, 17 Wiard St., Batavia 14020 (20).

St. Mary's Manor and Bishop McNulty Hall, 515 Sixth St. Niagara Falls 14301 (119).

St. Patrick's Home for the Aged and Infirm, 66 Van Cortland Park S., Bronx 10463 (214).

St. Teresa's Nursing Home, 120 Highland Ave., Middletown 10940 (92).

St. Vincent's Home for the Aged, 319 Washington Ave., Dunkirk 14048 (36).

St. Zita's Home (Women), 143 W. 14th St., New York 10011.

Teresian House, Washington Ave. Extension, Albany 12203 (300).

Uihlein Mercy Center (Nursing Home), Lake Placid 12946 (96).

North Carolina: Maryfield Nursing Home, Greensboro Rd., High Point 27260 (115).

North Dakota: Holy Family Guest Home (Nursing Home), Carrington 58421 (38).

Manor St. Joseph (Residence), Edgeley 58533 (50).

Marillac Manor (Retirement Apartments), 1016 N. 28th St., Bismarck 58501. (54 apartments).

St. Anne's Guest Home, 813 Lewis Blvd., Grand Forks 58201 (100).

St. Olav Guest (Retirement) Home, Powers Lake 58773 (20).

St. Vincent's Nursing Home, 1021 N. 26th St., Bismarck 58501 (94).

Ohio: Alvernia Rest Home (Residence and Nursing Care for Aged), 6765 State Rd., Cleveland 44134 (143).

Archbishop Leibold Home for the Aged, Little Sisters of the Poor, 476 Riddle Rd., Cincinnati 45220 (208).

Assumption Nursing Home, 550 W. Chalmers Ave., Youngstown 44511 (126).

Francesca Residence, 39 N. Portage Path, Akron 44303 (50).

Franciscan Terrace (Residence and Nursing Care), 60 Compton Rd., Cincinnati 45215.

House of Loreto (Nursing Home), 2812 Harvard Ave. N.W., Canton 44709 (98).

Jennings Hall (Intermediate Care Facility), 10204 Granger Rd., Garfield Heights 44125 (107).

Kirby Manor (Retirement Apartments), 11500 Detroit Ave., Cleveland 44102 (202 suites).

Little Sisters of the Poor, St. Joseph and Mary Home for Aged, 4291 Richmond Rd., Cleveland 44122 (196).

Maria-Joseph Home for the Aging and Lourdes Hall Nursing Home, 4950 Salem Ave., Dayton 45416 (144).

Mt. St. Joseph (Nursing Home), 21800 Chardon Rd., Cleveland 44117 (100).

Nazareth Towers, 300 E. Rich St., Columbus 43215.
Sacred Heart Home, 4900 Navarre Ave., Oregon 43616 (200).
St. Augustine Manor (Nursing Home), 7818 Detroit Ave., Cleveland 44102 (194).
St. Edward Nursing Home, 3131 Smith Rd., Akron 44313 (143).
St. Francis Home for the Aged, 182 St. Francis Ave., Tiffin 44883 (106).
St. Joseph's Hospice (Nursing Home), 2308 Reno Dr., Louisville 44641 (100).
St. Margaret's Hall (Residence and Nursing Facility), 1960 Madison Rd., Cincinnati 45206 (145).
St. Raphael Home (Nursing Home), 1550 Roxbury Rd., Columbus 43212 (80).
St. Rita's Home, 880 Greenlawn Ave., Columbus 43223 (100).
St. Theresa Home for the Aged, 6760 Belkenton Pl., Cincinnati 45236 (120).
Schroder Manor (Residence and Skilled Nursing Care), 1302 Millville Ave., Hamilton 45013 (85).
The Siena Home (Skilled Nursing Home), 235 W. Orchard Spring Dr., Dayton 45415 (99).
Villa Maria Skilled Nursing Home, Green Springs 44836 (150).
Villa Sancta Anna Home for Aged, 25000 Chagrin Blvd., Beachwood 44122 (68).

Oklahoma: Franciscan Villa, 51st and Lynn Lane, Broken Arrow 74012.
St. Ann's Nursing Home, 3825 N.W. 19th St., Oklahoma City 73107 (82).

Oregon: Benedictine Nursing Center, S. Main St., Mt. Angel 97362 (105).
Maryville Nursing Home, 14645 S.W. Farmington, Beaverton 97005 (120).
Mt. St. Joseph's Residence and Extended Care Center, 3060 S.E. Stark St., Portland 97214 (317).
St. Anthony's Hospital Extended Care Facility, Pendleton 97801 (65).
St. Catherine's Residence and Nursing Center, 3959 Sheridan Ave., North Bend 97459 (166).
St. Elizabeth's Nursing Home, Baker 97814 (100).

Pennsylvania: Ascension Manor I (Senior Citizen Housing), 911 N. Franklin St., Philadelphia 19123 (140 units).
Ascension Manor II (Senior Citizen Housing), 970 N. 7th St., Philadelphia 19123 (140 units).
Christ the King Manor, 1100 W. Long Ave., Du Bois 15801 (100).
Corpus Christi Residence (Women), 7165 Churchland St., Pittsburgh 15206.
Drueding Infirmary, Master and Lawrence Sts., Philadelphia 19122 (50).
Garvey Manor (Nursing Home), Logan Blvd., Hollidaysburg, 16648 (150).
Holy Family Home, Little Sisters of the Poor, 5300 Chester Ave., Philadelphia 19143 (220).
Holy Family Manor (Skilled Nursing Facility), 1200 Spring St., Bethlehem 18018 (200).
Holy Ghost Guest Home (Women), 4537 Wm. Flynn Hwy., Allison Park 15101 (17).
Immaculate Mary Home, (Skilled Nursing Facility), Holme Circle and Welsh Rd., Philadelphia 19136 (300).
John XXIII Home, 2250 Shenango Freeway, Sharon 16146 (100).
Little Flower Manor Nursing Home, 1201 Springfield Rd., Darby 19023 (122).
Little Flower Manor of Diocese of Scranton, (Long-Term Skilled Nursing and Intermediate Care Facility), 200 S. Meade St., Wilkes-Barre 18702.
Little Sisters of the Poor, 1028 Benton Ave. N.S., Pittsburgh 15212 (184).
Little Sisters of the Poor, Holy Family Residence, 2500 Adams Ave., Scranton 18509 (82).
Maria Joseph Manor, Danville 17821 (94).
Marian Manor (Residence and Nursing Care), 2695 Winchester Dr., Pittsburgh 15220 (172).
Mt. Trexler Skilled Nursing Unit of Sacred Heart Hospital, Limeport 18060 (65).
Our Lady Help of Christians Home (Nursing Home, Women), 56th St. and City Line Ave., Philadelphia 19131 (17).
Redeemer Village, Huntingdon Pike, Meadowbrook 19046 (150 apartments).
Sacred Heart Manor (Nursing Home), 6445 Germantown Ave., Philadelphia 19119 (144).
St. Anne Home (Residence and Nursing Care), R.D. 2, Columbia 17512 (120).
St. Anne Home for the Elderly (Skilled Nursing Facility), 685 Angela Dr., Greensburg 15601 (125).
St. Basil's Home for Women, Uniontown 15401 (18).
St. Ignatius Nursing Home, 4401 Haverford Ave., Philadelphia 19104 (176).
St. John Neumann Nursing Home, 10400 Roosevelt Blvd. Philadelphia 19116 (196).
St. Joseph Home for the Aged, 1182 Holland Rd., Holland 18966 (92).
St. Joseph Home for the Aged (Skilled Nursing Facility), 5324 Penn Ave., Pittsburgh 15224 (150).
St. Joseph's House of Hospitality (Low Income Senior Citizen Residence for Men and Women), 1635 Bedford Ave., Pittsburgh 15219 (65). Under sponsorship of St. Vincent de Paul Society.
St. Joseph Manor (Skilled Nursing Facility), 1616 Huntingdon Pike, Meadowbrook 19046 (250).
St. Joseph's Residence for Men, 1111 S. Cascade St., New Castle 16101.
St. Leonard's Guest Home, 601 N. Mont-

gomery St., Hollidaysburg 16648 (22).
St. Mary's Home of Erie, 607 E. 26th St., Erie 16504 (110).
St. Mary's Manor for Sighted and Unsighted, 701 Lansdale Ave., Lansdale 19446 (160).
St. Mary's Villa (Nursing Home), Elmhurst 18416 (121).
Villa de Marillac Nursing Home (Women), 5300 Stanton Ave., Pittsburgh 15206 (50).
Villa St. Teresa (Residence), 1215 Springfield Rd., Darby 19023 (46).
Villa Teresa (Nursing Home), 1051 Avila Rd., Harrisburg 17109 (178).
Vincentian Home for the Chronically Ill., Perrymont Rd., Pittsburgh 15237 (153).

Rhode Island: Holy Trinity Home for Aged of the Little Sisters of the Poor, 964 Main St., Pawtucket 02860 (132).
L'Hospice St. Antoine (Home for Aged), 400 Mendon Rd., North Smithfield 02895 (245).
St. Clare Home for the Aged, 309 Spring St., Newport 02840 (44).
Scalabrini Villa (Convalescent, Rest — Nursing Home). 860 N. Quidnessett Rd., North Kingstown 02852 (70).

South Carolina: Carter-May Home, 1660 Ingram Rd., Charleston 29407 (12).

South Dakota: Brady Memorial Home (Skilled Nursing Facility), 500 S. Ohlman St., Mitchell 57301 (60).
Maryhouse, Inc. (Skilled Nursing Facility), 717 E. Dakota, Pierre 57501 (82).
Mother Joseph Manor (Skilled Nursing Facility), 1002 North Jay St., Aberdeen 57401 (60).Apartment units (7).
St. William's Home for the Aged (55), Angela Hall (Supervised Living) (20), 901 E. Virgil, Box 432, Milbank 57252.
Tekakwitha Nursing Home, Sisseton 57262 (102).

Tennessee: Alexian Brothers Rest Home (Retired Men and Women), Signal Mountain 37377 (150).
Ave Maria Guild Home (Nursing Home), 2805 Charles Bryan Rd., Memphis 38134 (73).

Texas: Home for Aged Women, 920 S. Oregon St., El Paso 79901 (24).
Laurelwood Medical Complex (Home for Aged and Convalescants), 2717 N. Flores St., San Antonio 78212.
Mother of Perpetual Help Home (Intermediate Care Facility), 519 E. Madison Ave., Brownsville 78520 (39).
Mt. Carmel Home (Custodial Care Home), 4130 S. Alameda St., Corpus Christi 78411 (92).
The Regis (Retirement Home and Nursing Care), 400 Austin Ave., Waco 76701 (420).
The Retirement Residence, Inc., 2819 Rio Grande, Austin 78705 (100).
St. Ann's Home for the Aged (Nursing Home), P.O. Box 1179, Panhandle 79068 (52).
St. Anthony's Center (Skilled Nursing, Rehabilitation), 6301 Almeda Rd., Houston 77021 (272).
St. Benedict's Nursing Home, Alamo and Johnson Sts., San Antonio 78204 (197).
St. Dominic Residence Hall, 2401 E. Holcombe Blvd., Houston 77021.
St. Francis Village, Inc. (Retired and Elderly), Crowley. Mailing address — P.O. Box 16310, Ft. Worth 76133 (400).
St. Joseph Residence, 330 W. Pembroke St., Dallas 75208 (49).
San Juan Nursing Home, San Juan 78589 (52).

Utah: St. Joseph Villa (Skilled Nursing Home), 474 Westminster Ave., Salt Lake City 84115 (98).

Vermont: Loretto Home for Aged, 59 Meadow St., Rutland 05701 (54).
Michaud Memorial Manor (Residence), Derby Line 05830 (24).
St. Joseph's Home for Aged, 243 N. Prospect St., Burlington 05401 (53).

Virginia: St. Francis Home, 2511 Wise St., Richmond 23225 (25).
St. Joseph's Home for the Aged, Little Sisters of the Poor, 1503 Michael Rd., Richmond 23229.

Washington: Cathedral Plaza Apartments (Retirement Apartments), W. 1120 Sprague Ave., Spokane 99204 (150).
The Delaney, W. 242 Riverside Ave., Spokane 99201 (84).
The De Paul Retirement Apartments, 4831 35th Ave. S.W., Seattle 98126 (105 units).
Fahy Garden Apartments, W. 1403 Dean Ave., Spokane 99201 (31).
Fahy West Apartments, W. 1523 Dean Ave., Spokane 99201 (55).
The Josephinum (Retirement Home), 1902 2nd Ave., Seattle 98101 (228).
Mt. St. Vincent Nursing Center, 4831 35th Ave., S.W., Seattle 98126 (198).
The O'Malley, E. 707 Mission, Spokane 99202 (100).
St. Joseph Nursing Home, 1006 North H St., Aberdeen 98520 (33).
St. Joseph Care Center (Nursing Home), West 20 — 90th Ave., Spokane 99204 (103).

West Virginia: Knights of St. George Home, Wellsburg 26070 (44).
Welty Home for the Aged (Women), 21 Washington Ave., Wheeling 26003 (44).

Wisconsin: Bethany-St. Joseph Health Care Center, 2507 Shelby Rd., La Crosse 54601 (226).
Divine Savior Nursing Home, 715 W.

Pleasant St., Portage 53901 (111).

Franciscan Villa of South Milwaukee, Inc. 3601 S. Chicago Ave., S. Milwaukee 53172 (150).

Hope Nursing Home, 439 Ashford Ave., Lomira 53048 (40).

McCormick Memorial Home for the Aged, 212 Iroquois St., Green Bay 54301 (70).

Marian Catholic Home, 3333 W. Highland Blvd., Milwaukee 53208 (340).

Marycrest (Residence, Women), 600 Third Ave., Durand 54736 (16).

Maryhill Manor Nursing and Retirement Home, 973 Main St., Niagara 54151 (49).

Milwaukee Catholic Home, Inc., 2462 N. Prospect Ave., Milwaukee 53211 (160).

Nazareth House (Skilled Nursing Facility), Stoughton 53589 (100).

Sacred Heart Hospital Nursing Home, Tomahawk 54487 (31).

St. Ann Rest Home (Intermediate Care Facility, Women), 2020 S. Muskego Ave., Milwaukee 53204 (54).

St. Anne's Home for the Elderly (Aged Poor), 3800 N. 92nd St., Milwaukee 53222 (210).

St. Camillus Health Center (Skilled Nursing Home), 10100 W. Bluemound Rd., Wauwatosa 53226 (188).

St. Catherine Infirmary (Nursing Home), 5635 Erie St., Racine 53402 (39).

St. Elizabeth Home, 502 St. Lawrence Ave., Janesville 53545.

St. Elizabeth's Nursing Home (Women), 745 N. Brookfield Rd., Brookfield 53005 (18).

St. Francis Home, 709 S. 10th St., La Crosse 54601 (93).

St. Francis Home (Skilled Nursing Facility), 2325 E. 3rd St., Superior 54880 (52).

St. Francis Home (Skilled Nursing), 365 Gillett St., Fond du Lac 54935 (70).

St. Francis Manor (Retirement Residence), 3553 S. 41st St., Milwaukee (5).

St. Joan Antida Nursing Home (Women), 6640 W. Beloit Rd., W. Allis 53219 (76).

St. Joseph's Home, 705 Clyman St., Watertown 53094 (88).

St. Joseph's Home, 9244 29th Ave., Kenosha 53140 (89).

St. Joseph's Home, 5301 W. Lincoln Ave., W. Allis 53219 (124).

St. Joseph's Nursing Home, Arcadia 54612 (72).

St. Joseph's Nursing Home, 2415 Cass St., La Crosse 54601 (62).

St. Joseph's Nursing Home, 400 Water Ave., Hillsboro 54634 (75).

St. Joseph Residence, Inc. (Nursing Home), 1925 Division St., New London 54961 (107).

St. Mary's Home for the Aged (Residence and Nursing Care), 2005 Division St., Manitowoc 54220 (157).

St. Mary's Nursing Home (Women), 3516 W. Center St., Milwaukee 53210 (121).

St. Monica's Senior Citizens Home, 3920 N. Green Bay Rd., Racine 53404 (90).

St. Paul Home (Residence and Skilled Nursing Home), 509 W. Wisconsin Ave., Kaukauna 54130 (54).

Villa Clement (Nursing and Convalescent Center), 9047 W. Greenfield Ave., W. Allis 53214 (190).

Villa Loretto Nursing Home, Mount Calvary 53057 (52).

Villa Madonna, 1170 W. Windlake Ave., Milwaukee 53215 (45).

FACILITIES FOR HANDICAPPED CHILDREN AND ADULTS

Sources: Almanac survey; *1979 Directory of Catholic Special Facilities and Programs for Handicapped Children and Adults,* published by the National Catholic Educational Association; *1979 Official Catholic Directory.*

This listing covers facilities and programs with educational and training orientation. Information about other services for the handicapped can generally be obtained from the Catholic Charities Office or its equivalent (c/o Chancery Office) in any diocese. (See Index for listing of addresses of chancery offices in the U.S.)

Abbreviation code: b, boys; c, coeducational; d, day; g, girls; r, residential. Other information includes chronological age for admission. The number in parentheses at the end of an entry indicates total capacity or enrollment.

Deaf and Hard of Hearing

California: St. Joseph's School for Deaf and Hard of Hearing (d,c; 3-14 yrs.), 1 Santa Maria Way, Orinda 94563.

Illinois: Department of Vision and Hearing, Catholic Charities, 721 N. LaSalle St., Chicago 60610. Special classes (d,c) for hearing-impaired children in Chicago archdiocese, pre-school and elementary level. Marian School for Hearing Impaired (at Most Holy Redeemer School), 9536 S. Millard Ave., Evergreen Park 60642. Itinerant services for children fully mainstreamed in regular Catholic schools. Services for hearing-impaired children under age 3 and their parents.

Holy Trinity Day Classes for the Deaf (c; 3-14 yrs.) 1910 Taylor, Chicago 60612 (35).

Louisiana: Chinchuba Institute (r,d,c; 2-16 yrs.), P.O. Box 187, Marrero 70072 (123).

Massachusetts: Boston School for the Deaf (r,d,c; 3-17 yrs.), 800 N. Main St., Randolph. 02368 (304).

Missouri: St. Joseph Institute for the Deaf (r,d,c; 3½-15 yrs.), 1483 82nd Blvd., University City, 63132 (150).

New Jersey: Mt. Carmel Guild Pre-School

Deaf Program (d,c), 17 Mulberry St., Newark. 07102 (80).

New York: Cleary School for the Deaf (d,c; 2½-14 yrs.), 301 Smithtown Blvd., Lake Ronkonkoma, L.I. 11779 (105).

St. Francis de Sales School for the Deaf (d,c; pre-school through 8th grade), 260 Eastern Parkway, Brooklyn 11225.

St. Joseph's School for the Deaf (d,c; 3-13 yrs.), 1000 Hutchinson River Pkwy, Bronx. 10465 (250).

St. Mary's School for the Deaf (r,d,c; 3-21 yrs.), 2253 Main St., Buffalo. 14214 (260).

Ohio: St. Rita School for the Deaf (r,c; 4 yrs. and older), 1720 Glendale-Milford Rd., Cincinnati. 45215 (150).

Pennsylvania: Abp. Ryan Memorial Institute for Deaf (d,c; parent-infant programs through 8th grade), 3509 Spring Garden St., Philadelphia. 19104 (80).

De Paul Institute (d,c; birth-21 yrs.), Castlegate Ave., Pittsburgh. 15226 (173).

Wisconsin: St. John's School for the Deaf (r,d,c; 3-20 yrs.), 3680 S. Kinnickinnic Ave., Milwaukee. 53207 (160).

Emotionally And/Or Socially Maladjusted

This listing includes facilities for homeless, neglected, emotionally disturbed children and youth.

Arizona: Patterdell, 1820 W. Northern Ave., Phoenix. 85021.

Arkansas: St. Michael School, Monastery of Our Lady of Charity (d,c; 6 yrs. and up), 1125 Malvern Ave., Hot Springs 71901.

California: American Boys Ranch (r; 12-16 yrs.), 14700 Manzanita Park Rd., Beaumont. 92223 (109).

Gracenter, Convent of the Good Shepherd (r, women), 501 Cambridge, San Francisco 94134 (9).

Hanna Boys Center (r; 10-15 yrs.), Box 100, Sonoma. 95476 (80).

Rancho San Antonio (r,b; 12-16 yrs.), 21000 Plummer St., Chatsworth. 91311 (118).

Stanford Lathrop Memorial Home and Group Homes, Sisters of Social Service, 800 N. Street, Sacramento 95814. Conduct six homes for boys and girls.

Colorado: Excelsior Youth Centers (r,g; 12-21 yrs.), 15151 E. Quincy Ave., Denver 80232 (74).

Mt. St. Vincent Home (r,c; 5-13 yrs.), 4159 Lowell Blvd., Denver. 80211 (45).

Connecticut: Highland Heights — St. Francis Home for Children (r,d,c; 8-12 yrs.), 651 Prospect St., New Haven. 06505 (38).

Mt. St. John (r,b; 11-16 yrs.), Kirtland St., Deep River. 06417 (75).

Delaware: Our Lady of Grace Home for Children (r,c; 6-12 yrs.), 487 Chestnut Hill Rd., Newark 19713 (28).

Florida: Boystown of Florida (r; 13-17 yrs.), 11400 SW 137th Ave., Miami 33186 (45).

Georgia: Village of St. Joseph (r,d,c; 6-16 yrs.), 2969 Butner Rd. S.W., Atlanta 30331.

Hawaii: Child Development Center (c; 3-6 yrs; therapeutic day treatment center), 2345 Nuuanu Ave., Honolulu. 96817 (12).

Illinois: Group Home — Virginia Residence (r,g; 14-18 yrs.), 1434 W. Estes Ave., Chicago. 60626 (8).

Group Home, Marcella Residence (g; 14-18 yrs.), 3636 N. Janssen, Chicago. 60657 (8).

Guardian Angel Home (r,d,c; 5-15 yrs.), Plainfield at Theodore St., Joliet 60435.

House of the Good Shepherd, Heart of Mary High School (r,g; 13-18 yrs.), 1126 W. Grace St., Chicago. 60613 (90).

Loyola Univ. of Chicago Child Guidance Center and Day School (c; pre-school to adolescence), 1043 W. Loyola Ave., Chicago 60626 (37).

St. Joseph Carondelet Child Center (r,b; 5-14 yrs.), 739 E. 35th St., Chicago. 60616 (45).

Indiana: Father Gibault School for Boys (r; 10-16 yrs.), 5901 Dixie Bee Rd., Terre Haute. 47802 (108).

Hoosier "Boys" Town (r; 10-15 yrs.), Schererville. 46375 (80).

Kentucky: Boys' Haven (r; 13 18 yrs.), 3201 Bardstown Rd., Louisville. 40205 (51).

Maryhurst School (r,g; 13-17 yrs.), 1015 Dorsey Lane, Louisville 40223.

Our Lady of the Highlands (r,g; teen-age high school age), 938 Highland Ave., Ft. Thomas. 41075 (50).

Louisiana: Hope Haven — Madonna Manor School and Home (r,b; 6-17 yrs.), 1101 Barataria Blvd., Marrero 70072 (158).

Maison Marie Group Home (r,g; 13-18 yrs.), 3020 Independence St., Metairie 70002 (12).

Maryland: Christ Child Institute for Children (r,d,c; 3-10½ yrs.), Edson Lane, Rockville. 20852 (28r, 15d). Also conducts group home.

Good Shepherd Center (r,d,g; 14-18 yrs.), 4100 Maple Ave., Baltimore. 21227 (90r, 30d).

Massachusetts: Cushing Hall (r,b; 11-14½ yrs.), 279 Tilden Rd., Scituate. 02066 (40). Diagnostic treatment center.

McAuley Nazareth Home (r,c; 10-21 yrs.), 77 Mulberry St., Leicester 01524. Program for autistic.

McAuley Nazareth Home for Boys (r; 6-10 yrs.), 77 Mulberry St., Leicester. 01524 (30).

Madonna Hall (r,g; 13-17 yrs.), Cushing Hill Dr., Marlboro 01752 (55).

Nazareth Child Care Center (r,d,c; 2-12 yrs.), 420 Pond St., Jamaica Plain, Mass. 02130 (112).

Our Lady of Providence Children's Center (r,d,c; 6-12 yrs.), 2112 Riverdale St., W. Springfield. 01089 (50).

St. Vincent Home (r,c), 2425 Highland Ave., Fall River 02720 (85).

Michigan: Barat House, Barat Human Services, League of Catholic Women (r,g; 12-16 yrs.), 5250 John R. St., Detroit. 48202 (24).

Boysville of Michigan, Inc. (r; 13-18 yrs.), 8744 Clinton-Macon Rd., Clinton. 49236 (180).

Don Bosco Hall (r,b; 13-17 years.), 10001 Petoskey Ave., Detroit. 48204 (38).

Jordan House (r,g; 16-21 yrs.), 17487 Alwyne, Detroit 48203 (6). Group home.

St. John's Home (r,c; 9-16 yrs.), 385 E. Leonard N.E., Grand Rapids 49503 (40).

St. Vincent Home for Children (r,c; 5-15 yrs.), 2800 W. Willow St., Lansing 48917 (38).

Villa Maria, Sisters of the Good Shepherd (r,g; 13-17 yrs.), 1315 Walker St. N.W., Grand Rapids. 49504 (40).

Vista Maria School (r,g; 13-17 yrs.), 20651 W. Warren Ave., Dearborn Heights. 48127 (90).

Minnesota: Busch Center (r,c; 8-16 yrs.), 1726 7th Ave. S., St. Cloud 56301 (20). Temporary emergency shelter care facility.

Home of the Good Shepherd, (r,g; 14-17 yrs.), 5100 Hodgson Rd., St. Paul. 55112 (60).

St. Cloud Children's Home (r,c; 12-16 yrs.), 1726 7th Ave. S., St. Cloud. 56301 (72).

St. James Children's Home (r,c), Woodland Hills, Duluth 55803 (120).

Tiffany House Group Home (c), 374 4th Ave. S., St. Cloud 56301 (11).

Missouri: Child Center of Our Lady of Grace (r,d,c; 4-12 yrs.), 7900 Natural Bridge Rd., St. Louis. 63121 (72).

Marillac School (r,d,c; 7-11 yrs.), 310 W. 106th St., Kansas City. 64114 (100 day, 25 boarders).

Marygrove (r,g; 13-17 yrs.), 2705 Mullanphy Lane, Florissant. 63031 (70).

Nebraska: Father Flanagan's Boys' Home (r; 10-18 yrs.), Boys Town, Nebr. 68010 (r, 390; d, 307).

Nevada: St. Yves High School (r,g; 13-17 yrs.), 7000 North Jones Blvd., Las Vegas, 89106 (60).

New Jersey: Catholic Community Services, Mt. Carmel Guild Children's CMHC (d,c; 3-18 yrs.), 17 Mulberry St., Newark 07102 (58).

Christopher House (c), 55 N. Clinton Ave., Trenton 08607. After care day center.

Collier School (d,c; 13-17 yrs.), Wickatunk 07765.

Guidance Clinic (c), 39 N. Clinton Ave., Trenton 08607. After care day center.

Mt. St. Joseph Children's Center (c), Shepherd Lane, Totowa 07512 (17).

Pelletier Day School (c; 13-17 yrs.), 939 Parkside Ave., Trenton 08618 (32).

New York: The Astor Home for Children (r,c; 5-12 yrs.), 36 Mill St., Rhinebeck 12572 (70). The Astor Group Home Program (adolescents), 662 E. 231st St., Bronx 10466 (50). Also has out-patient programs.

Baker Hall (r,d,b; 10-18 yrs.), 150 Martin Rd., Lackawanna. 14218 (90).

Immaculate Heart of Mary Children's Home and School (r,c; 6-12 yrs.), William and Kennedy Sts., Buffalo 14206 (50).

LaSalle School (r,d; 12-18 yrs.), 391 Western Ave., Albany. 12203 (145). Also conducts group homes.

Lincoln Hall (r,b; 12-16 yrs.), Lincolndale. 10540 (250).

Madonna Heights School for Girls (r; 11-17 yrs.), Burrs Lane, Huntington. 11743 (110). Also conducts group homes on Long Island.

Our Lady of Charity School (r,g; 12-18 yrs.), Hamburg. 14075 (50).

Saint Anne Institute (r,d,g; 12-18 yrs.), 25 W. Lawrence St., Albany. 12206 (190).

St. Helena's Residence (r,g; 12-17 yrs.), 120 W. 60th St., New York. 10011 (20).

St. John's of Rockaway Beach (r,b; 10-18 yrs.), 144 Beach 111th St., Rockaway Park. 11694 (112). Also conducts group homes in Rockaway and Richmond Hill.

North Dakota: Home on the Range for Boys (r; 12-18 yrs.), Sentinel Butte. 58654 (36).

Ohio: Children's Village of St. Vincent de Paul (Parmadale) (r,c; 3-21 yrs.), 6753 State Rd., Parma. 44134 (200).

Diocesan Child Guidance Center, Inc. (d,c; preschool), 840 W. State St., Columbus 43222.

Marycrest School for Girls (r,g; 13-18 yrs.), 7800 Brookside Rd., Independence. 44131 (70).

Rosemont School (r,g;d,c; 12-18 yrs.), 2440 Dawnlight Ave., Columbus. 43211 (150).

St. Anthony Home for Boys (r; 14-19 yrs.), 6753 State Rd., Parma. 44134.

Oregon: Christie School (r,g; 9-16 yrs.), Marylhurst 97036 (26).

St. Mary's Home for Boys (r; 9-17 yrs.), 16535 S.W. Tualatin Valley Highway, Beaverton. 97005 (43).

Villa St. Rose School for Girls (r; 12-18 yrs.), 597 N. Dekum St., Portland. 97217 (51).

Pennsylvania: De LaSalle in Towne (d,b; 13-17 yrs.), 25 S. Van Pelt St., Philadelphia 19103 (100).

De LaSalle Vocational Day Treatment (b; 15-18 yrs.), P.O. Box 344 — Street Rd. and Bristol Pike, Cornwells Hts. 19020 (125).

Gannondale School for Girls (r; 12-17 yrs.), 4635 E. Lake Rd., Erie. 16511 (57).

Good Shepherd Services of Germantown (r,g; 14-18 yrs.), 5301 Chew Ave., Philadelphia 19138 (20). Two group homes.

Harborcreek School for Boys (r; 10-17 yrs.), 5712 Iroquois Ave., Harborcreek. 16421 (135). Also conducts group homes.

Lourdesmont School (r,g; 14-17 yrs.), 537 Venard Rd., Clarks Summit. 18411 (50). Also conducts day school (c).

Pauline Auberle Foundation, The Auberle

Home for Boys (r,b; 13-18 yrs.), 1101 Hartman St., McKeesport. 15132 (50).

St. Gabriel Hall (r,d,b; 10-17 yrs.), P.O. Box 390, Phoenixville. 19460 (177). Group homes.

St. Michael's School for Boys (r,b; 12-16 yrs.), Hoban Heights, Tunkhannock 18657 (120).

Toner Institute (r,b; 9-13 yrs.), Castlegate Ave., Pittsburgh. 15226 (52).

Tennessee: DeNeuville Heights School for Girls (r; 12-18 yrs.), 3060 Baskin St., Memphis. 38127 (52).

Texas: Mt. St. Michael Home and School for Girls (r,g; 12-18 yrs.), 4500 W. Davis St., Dallas. 75211 (120).

St. Joseph Youth Center (r,c; 12-17 yrs.), 901 S. Madison St., Dallas. 75208 (48).

Washington: Marian Heights High School (r,g; 13-18 yrs.), 3754 W. Indian Trail Rd., Spokane. 99208 (50).

Morning Star Boys Ranch (Spokane Boys' Ranch, Inc.), (r,b; 11-14 yrs.), Box 781-A Route 3, Spokane. 99203 (56).

Wisconsin: Mary Hill Center (r,g; 13-19 yrs.), 3310 N. Dousman St., Milwaukee 53212 (22).

Our Lady of Charity High School (r,g; 13-18 yrs.), 2640 West Point Rd., Green Bay 54303 (76).

St. Aemilian Child Care Center, Inc. (r&d,b; 6-12 yrs.), 8901 W. Capitol Dr., Milwaukee. 53222 (47).

St. Charles Boys Home (r; 12-18 yrs.), 151 S. 84th St., Milwaukee. 53214 (56).

St. Michael's Home for Children (r,c; 9-18 yrs.), 2902 East Ave. S., La Crosse. 54601 (42).

Wyoming: St. Joseph's Children's Home (r,c; 6-18 yrs.), P.O. Box 1117, Torrington 82240 (60). Also conducts group home.

Developmentally Handicapped

This listing includes facilities for children and youth with learning disabilities and/or mental retardation.

Alabama: Father Walter Memorial Child Care Center (r,c; birth-12 yrs.), 2815 Forbes Dr., Montgomery 36110 (34). Skilled nursing facility.

California: Catholic Charities "Empower" Services to Developmentally Disabled Persons, 433 Jefferson St., Oakland 94607. Services include (in various locations): Tap Center (d; adults); Concord House (r; adults); C.O.R.E. (d; adults outreach program for homebound); Case Management (d; adults, children — social workers); Religious Nurture Program (d; adults, children).

Helpers of the Mentally Retarded, Inc., 2626 Fulton St., San Francisco. 94118. Conducts three homes: Helpers Home for Girls (18 years and older), 2608 Fulton St. and 2626 Fulton St., San Francisco. 94118; Helpers Home for Men (18 years and older), 2750 Fulton St., San Francisco, 94118.

Kennedy Child Study Center (d,c; 5-13 yrs.), 1339 - 20th St., Santa Monica. 90404 (80). Also conducts a developmental nursery (18 mos.-3 yrs.) and a preschool for children from culturally deprived areas (3-5 yrs.).

St. Madeleine Sophie's Training Center (d,c; 18 yrs. and older), 2111 E. Madison Ave., El Cajon. 92021 (80).

St. Vincent School (r,d,c; 8-14 yrs.), P.O. Drawer V, 4300 Calle Real, Santa Barbara. 93102 (135).

Tierra del Sol (d,c; 18 yrs. and older), 9919 Sunland Blvd., Sunland. 91040 (100).

Connecticut: Gengras Center (d,c; 6-21 yrs.), St. Joseph College, 1678 Asylum Ave., W. Hartford 06117 (60).

Special Education Department, Diocese of Bridgeport, 238 Jewett Ave., Bridgeport 06606.

District of Columbia: Lt. Joseph P. Kennedy Jr. Institute (d,c; 5-20 yrs.), 801 Buchanan St. N.E., Washington. 20017 (120). Also conducts group home and sheltered workshop.

St. Gertrude's School of Arts and Crafts (r,d,g; 6-18 yrs.), 4801 Sargent Rd. N.E., Washington. 20017 (48).

Florida: Marian Center Services for Developmentally Handicapped and Mentally Retarded (r,d,c), 15701 Northwest 37th Ave., Opa Locka. 33054. Offers variety of services.

Marian School for Exceptional Children (d,c; 6 mos.-5 yrs.), 326 Pine Terr., W. Palm Beach 33401.

Morning Star School (d,c; 4-12 yrs.), 725 Mickler Rd., Jacksonville. 32211 (70).

Morning Star School (d,c; 3-12 yrs.), 954 Leigh Ave., Orlando. 32804 (45).

Morning Star School (d,c; 4-16 yrs.), 4661 - 80th Ave., N., Pinellas Park. 33565 (50).

Morning Star School (d,c; 6-13 yrs.), 302 E. Linebaugh Ave., Tampa. 33612 (70).

Hawaii: Special Education Center of Oahu (SECO) (d,c; 3-20 yrs.), 708 Palekaua St., Honolulu 96816.

Illinois: Bartlett Learning Center (c;r, 5-12 yrs.; d, 3-12 yrs.), 801 W. Bartlett Rd., Bartlett. 60103 (138).

Good Shepherd Manor (permanent home for men; 18 yrs.), P.O. Box 260, Momence. 60954 (120).

Lt. Joseph P. Kennedy, Jr., School (r,b;d,c; 6-21 yrs.) and Job Training Center (c; 16 yrs. and older), 123rd and Wolf Rd., Palos Park. 60464 (110).

Misericordia Home South (r,c; 1 mo.-6 yrs.), 2916 W. 47th St., Chicago. 60632 (125).

Misericordia Home North (r,c; 4-21 yrs.), 6300 North Ridge, Chicago (60).

Mt. St. Joseph (mentally handicapped women; 20-45 yrs.), Route 3, Box 365, Lake Zurich. 60047 (160).

St. Francis School for Exceptional Children (r,c; 4-12 yrs.), 1209 S. Walnut Ave., Freeport. 61032 (32).

St. Jude School (d,c; 6-16 yrs.), 2nd and Spring Ave., Aviston. 62216 (30).

St. Mary of Providence (r,d,g; 4-21 yrs.), 4200 N. Austin Ave., Chicago. 60634 (190).

St. Rose Center (d,c; 3-15 yrs.), 4911 S. Hoyne Ave., Chicago. 60609 (60).

St. Vincent Residential School (c; 12 yrs. and older), and St. Vincent Community Living Facility (adults), 659 E. Jefferson St., Freeport. 61032.

Special Education Program of the East St. Louis Deanery (d,c; 5-16 yrs.), 8213 Church Lane, East St. Louis. 62203 (48).

Indiana: Marian Day School (d,c; 6-18 yrs.), 625 Bellemeade Ave., Evansville. 47713 (45).

Providence House (r, men; 18 yrs. and up), 520 W. 9th St., Jasper 47546 (66).

St. Bavo Special Class (d,c; 6-15 yrs.), 512 W. 8th St., Mishawaka. 46544 (12).

St. Mary Child Center School (d,c; 3-16 yrs.), 311 N. New Jersey St., Indianapolis. 46204 (32). Developmentally Disabled.

Iowa: Special Services — Office of Education (r,c), P.O. Box 1180, 1229 Mt. Loretto, Dubuque 52001. Conducts several homes which provide training and work experience, organizes and coordinates religion classes for retarded.

Kansas: Holy Family Center (d,c; 6-18 yrs.), 619 S. Maize Rd., Wichita. 67209 (65).

Lakemary Center, Inc. (r,d,c; 3-16 yrs.), 100 Lakemary Dr., Paola. 66071 (72r,35d).

Kentucky: Msgr. Pitt Learning Center (d,c; 5 yrs. and older), 10715 Ward Ave., Louisville 40223 (74).

Ursuline Special Education Learning Center (d,c; 3½-14 yrs.), 3105 Lexington Rd., Louisville. 40206 (50-56).

Louisiana: Department of Special Education, Archdiocese of New Orleans, 1522 Chippewa St., New Orleans. 70130. Conducts day classes, a special day school, and a vocational rehabilitation center for the mentally retarded (300).

Department of Special Education, Diocese of Baton Rouge, P.O. Box 53326, Baton Rouge. 70805. Conducts 10 classes for elementary and junior high special students and one vocational evaluation and training center for young men and women 16 years and older.

Holy Angels Institute (r,c; teen-age, 14 yrs. and older; nursery, 2 mo. to kindergarten age), 10450 Ellerbe Rd., Shreveport. 71106 (140).

Padua House (r,c; birth-18 yrs.), 200 Beta St., Belle Chase 70037 (44).

Regina Caeli Center (d,c; 6-16 yrs.), 3903 Kingston, Lake Charles. 70605 (45).

St. Francis de Sales Interparochial Special Education School (d,c; 6-16 yrs.), 300 Verret St., Houma 70361 (30).

St. Mary Learning Center, St. Mary's Home (d,c; 6-18 yrs.), 601 W. St. Mary, Lafayette 70506 (50).

St. Mary's Training School (r,c; 3-22 yrs.), P.O. Drawer 7768, Alexandria 71306. (150).

St. Michael Vocational Training Center (d,c; 16-21 yrs.), 1522 Chippewa St., New Orleans 70130.

Maryland: The Benedictine School for Exceptional Children (r,c; 6-16 yrs.), Ridgely. 21660 (100). Also conducts Habilitation Center (r,c; 17 yrs. and older).

St. Elizabeth School for Special Education (d,c; 12 yrs. and older), 801 Argonne Dr., Baltimore. 21218 (145).

St. Francis School for Special Education (d,c; 3-13 yrs.), 2226 Maryland Ave., Baltimore. 21218 (60).

Villa St. Louise, (r), 2520 Pot Spring Rd., Timonium 21093 (30).

Massachusetts: Cardinal Cushing School and Training Center (r,d,c; 6-22 yrs.), Hanover. 02339 (165).

Mercy Centre for Developmental Disabilities (d,c; 3-22 yrs.), 25 West Chester St., Worcester. 01605 (108).

Nazareth Hall on the Cape (d,c; 6-15 yrs.), 261 South St., Hyannis. 02601 (25).

Nazareth Hall for Exceptional Children (d,c; 7-14 yrs.), 887 Highland Ave., Fall River, 02720 (70).

Nazareth Vocational Center (d,c; 18-21 yrs.), 707 Highland Ave., Fall River. 02720 (24).

St. Coletta Day School (d,c; 7-12 yrs., admission age), 85 Washington St., Braintree. 02184 (150).

Michigan: Our Lady of Providence Center (r,d,g; 5-17 yrs., child caring; 18-26, adult foster care), 16115 Beck Rd., Northville. 48167 (100).

St. Louis School (r,b; 8-18 yrs.), 16195 Old U.S. 12, Chelsea. 48118 (90).

Missouri: Department of Special Education, Archdiocese of St. Louis, 4472 Lindell Blvd., St. Louis. 63108. Conducts 27 special day classes (c; 5-16 yrs.) and 2 day classes for pre-school children (c; 2-6 yrs.).

Good Shepherd Manor (residential for developmentally disabled men; 16 yrs. and up), Little Brothers of the Good Shepherd, 3220 E. 23rd St., Kansas City. 64127 (43).

St. Joseph's Vocational Center (c; 15-21 yrs.), 5341 Emerson Ave., St. Louis. 63120 (135).

St. Mary's Special School (r,c; 5-16 yrs.), 5341 Emerson Ave., St. Louis. 63120 (138).

St. Peter's Special Classes (d,c; 5-21 yrs.), 314 W. High St., Jefferson City. 65101 (38).

Universal Sheltered Workshop (c, adults), 6912 W. Florissant Ave., St. Louis 63136. Sheltered employment.

Nebraska: Villa Marie School (r,d,c; 7-16 yrs.), Rt. 1, Box 109, Waverly. 68462 (25).

Madonna School for Exceptional Children

Facilities for Handicapped

(d,c; 5-21 yrs.), 2537 N. 62nd St., Omaha 68104 (65).

New Jersey: Alhambra Pavilion Child Study Center (c; 5-10 yrs.), 31 Centre St., Newark. 07102 (50).

Archbishop Damiano School (d,c), 532 Delsea Dr., Westville Grove 08093.

Catholic Community Services, Archbishop Boland Rehabilitation and Training Center (d,c; 16-55 yrs.), 450 Market St., Newark 07105.

Child Study Center (d,c; 4-8 yrs.), 272 Main St., Ridgefield Park. 07660 (17).

Department of Special Education, Diocese of Camden, 1845 Haddon Ave., Camden 08108. Services include: Archbishop Damiano School (above), and full time programs at 6 Catholic Schools; adult evening classes (18-65 yrs.); religious education programs.

Department of Special Education, Diocese of Paterson. Murray House (r; adults), 391 Main St., Paterson. 07501. Also conducts two other group homes, an Adult Opportunity Center, a farm and a summer camp.

Felician School for Exceptional Children (r,d,c; 2½-14 yrs.), 260 S. Main St., Lodi 07644.

McAuley School for Exceptional Children (d,c; 5-9 yrs.), Rt. 22 and Terrill Rd., N. Plainfield. 07061 (30).

Marian Center (d,c; 7-14 yrs.), Delsea Dr. and Chestnut St., Vineland. 08360 (30).

Mount Carmel Guild — Department of Special Education and Psychological Services, Archdiocese of Newark, 1180 Raymond Blvd., Newark. 07102. Conducts day classes for the mentally retarded. Also conducts work training programs.

Sr. Georgine Learning Center (d,c; 6-17 yrs.), 544 Chestnut Ave., Trenton. 08611 (30).

New Mexico: Notre Dame on the Rio Grande (r; custodial facility for males, 8 yrs. and older; no maximum age), 1301-15 Mountain Rd., Albuquerque. 87104 (15).

St. Joseph's Manor (r,b; 14-29 yrs.), P.O. Box 610, Bernalillo. 87004. Little Brothers of the Good Shepherd, P.O. Box 610, Bernalillo 87004. Twenty-four-hour child care center for mentally and physically handicapped.

New York: Cantalician Center for Learning (d,c; birth-21 yrs.), 3233 Main St., Buffalo. 14214 (250).

Cantalician Center Workshop (d,c; 18 yrs. and older), 2101 Kenmore Ave., Buffalo. 14207. Also conducts a vocational evaluation and rehabilitation training program.

Cobb Memorial School (r,c; 6-10 yrs.), Altamont. 12009 (50).

Friends of L'Arche of Greater Syracuse, Inc. (r, adults), 1611 Court St., Syracuse 13208. Long-term facility following philosophy of Jean Vanier and L'Arche movement.

Maryhaven Vocational Rehabilitation Center (d,c; 16 yrs. and older), 450 Myrtle Ave., Port Jefferson. 11777 (90).

St. Catherine Center for Children (r,c; birth to 12 yrs. and d,c; 3-12 yrs.), 30 N. Main St., Albany. 12203 (140). Also conducts group home and specialized foster care programs.

St. Joseph School for Exceptional Children (r,d,c; 5-21 yrs.), 10807 Bennett Rd., Dunkirk. 14048 (30).

School of the Holy Childhood (d,c; 7-18 yrs.), 1150 Buffalo Rd., Rochester. 14624 (85). Adult program, 18-50 yrs.

Special Education Department, Diocese of Brooklyn (d,c; 3-18 yrs.), Office of Education, 345 Adams St., Brooklyn, 11201 (235).

Special Education Department, Archdiocese of New York, 1011 First Ave., New York. 10022. Conducts 13 special day classes in 9 parish schools.

North Carolina: Holy Angels Nursery (r,c; birth to 12 yrs.), Belmont. 28012 (66).

Ohio: Good Shepherd Manor (permanent care of men 18 years and older), P.O. Box 387, Wakefield 45687 (104).

Mary Immaculate School for Exceptional Children (d,c; 7-14 yrs.), 3837 Secor Rd., Toledo. 43623 (80). For children with learning disabilities.

Marymount Rehabilitation Services (vocational rehabilitation; 16 yrs. and older), 12215 Granger Rd., Cleveland. 44125.

MRS Industries (c; sheltered workshop), 4765 E. 131st St., Garfield Heights 44105.

Mt. Aloysius (r, men; 21 yrs. and over), Tile Plant Rd., New Lexington. 43764 (100).

Our Lady of Angels Special School (d,c; 7-16 yrs.), 3570 Rocky River Dr., Cleveland. 44111 (30).

Our Lady of the Elms Special School (d,c; 6-15 yrs.), 1230 W. Market St., Akron. 44313 (74).

Rose Mary, The Johanna Graselli Rehabilitation and Education Center (r,c; 3-12 yrs.), 19350 Euclid Ave., Cleveland. 44117 (40).

St. John's Villa (r,c,b, 4-14 yrs; g, 4-18 yrs., continued care, g, 18 yrs. and over), 620 Roswell Rd. N.W., Carrollton. 44615 (221).

St. Joseph Center (d,c; 6-16 yrs.), 2346 W. 14th St., Cleveland. 44113 (70).

Sheltered Workshop and Training Center (c; 16 yrs. and older), 1890 W. 22nd St., Cleveland. 44113 (35).

Oregon: Emily School for Multi-Handicapped Children (d,c; 2½-5 yrs.), 830 N.E. 47th Ave., Portland. 97213 (12).

Providence Children's Nursing Center (r; nursing care), 830 N. E. 47th Ave., Portland. 97213 (54).

Pennsylvania: Clelian Heights School for Exceptional Children (r,d,c; 6-16 yrs.), R.D. 9, Box 607, Greensburg. 15601 (100). Also conducts re-socialization program (r,d,c; 16-20 yrs.).

Department of Special Education, Diocese of Pittsburgh, 162 Steuben St., Pittsburgh.

15220. Conducts a program consisting of five special day classes.

Don Guanella School (r,d,b; 6-15 yrs.) and C. K. Center (r,c; adults, post-school age), Sproul Rd., Springfield. 19064.

McGuire Memorial (r,d,c; infancy to 7 yrs.), 2119 Mercer Rd., New Brighton. 15066 (99).

Mercy Day School: Center for Special Learning (d,c; 6-18 yrs.), 830 S. Woodward St., Allentown. 18103 (80).

Our Lady of Confidence Day School (c; 5-18 yrs.), 1099 W. Luzerne St., Philadelphia. 19140 (68b, 56g).

St. Anthony School for Exceptional Children (r,d,c; 6-16 yrs.), 13th St. and Hulton Rd., Oakmont. 15139 (150).

St. Joseph Day School (c; 6-18 yrs.), 619 Mahantongo St., Pottsville. 17901 (40).

St. Joseph's Children and Maternity Hospital (r,c; birth-20 yrs.), 2010 Adams Ave., Scranton. 18509 (88).

St. Katherine School (d,c; 4-18 yrs.), William Rd. and Bowman Ave., Philadelphia. 19151 (95 b, 95 g).

St. Mary of Providence Center (r,d,g; 6-14 yrs.), Elverson. 19520 (120).

Tennessee: Madonna Day School for Retarded Children (d,c; 5-16), 4189 Leroy, Memphis. 38108 (50).

St. Bernard School for Exceptional Children, 2021 21st Ave. S., Nashville 37212 (25).

Texas: Notre Dame of Dallas Special School (d,c; 6-12 yrs.), Rt. 2, Box 4, Irving. 75062. (108). Notre Dame Vocational School, at same address, provides work-study program for exceptional young people over 16.

Virginia: St. Coletta School (d,c; 4-21 yrs.), 1305 N. Jackson St., Arlington. 22201 (45).

St. Mary's Infant Home (r,c; 3 days-9 yrs.), 317 Chapel St., Norfolk. 23504 (50).

Wisconsin: St. Coletta School (r,c), Jefferson. 53549 (372). Offers the following programs:

a complete program of special education from kindergarten through elementary and advanced levels (r,d,c);

a work training center in preparation for job placement (r,c; 17-20 yrs.);

a residential care center (r,c; 45-85 yrs.);

a half-way house to give guidance and assist with problems (r,c; 18-24 yrs.);

a sheltered workshop to provide employment for the mentally retarded in a sheltered environment (r,c; 25-45 yrs.).

St. Coletta Day School (c; 8-16 yrs.), 1725 N. 54th St., Milwaukee. 53208 (16).

Orthopedically Handicapped

Alabama: Father Purcell Memorial (r,c; birth to 14 yrs.), 2048 W. Fairview Ave., Montgomery. 36108 (52). Skilled nursing home.

Kentucky: United Cerebral Palsy Center (d,c; birth and up), 71 Orphanage Rd., Fort Mitchell, 41017 (131).

Pennsylvania: St. Edmond's Home for Crippled Children (r,c; 2-10 yrs.)., 320 S. Roberts Rd., Rosemont. 19010 (50).

Visually Handicapped

Illinois: Department of Vision and Hearing, Catholic Charities, 721 N. LaSalle St., Chicago, 60610. Itinerant education services for visually impaired students attending regular Catholic elementary and high schools in Chicago archdiocese.

Maine: The Visual Education Center, Inc. (d,c; 3-20 yrs.), 14 Locust St., Portland. 04111 (18).

Diocesan Human Relations Services, Inc., 41 Birch St., Biddeford 04005; 15 Vaughn St., Caribou 04736. Itinerant services.

New Jersey: St. Joseph's School for the Multiple Handicapped Blind (r,d,c; 3-21 yrs.), 253 Baldwin Ave., Jersey City. 07306 (25).

New York: Catholic Charities Services for Visually Impaired, 272 Merrick Rd., Lynbrook. 11563.

Catholic Guild for the Blind (itinerant teaching program, c; 5-17 yrs.), 345 Adams St., Brooklyn. 11201.

Lavelle School for the Blind (r,d,c; 3-20 yrs.), 221st St. and Paulding Ave., Bronx. 10469 (120).

Pennsylvania: Vision Program, Archdiocese of Philadelphia. St. Lucy Day School (d,c; 5-14 yrs.), 929 S. Farragut St., Philadelphia. 19143 (80). Also provides vision consultant services to parish schools and high schools.

OTHER SOCIAL SERVICES

Cancer Hospitals or Homes: The following homes or hospitals specialize in the care of cancer patients. They are listed according to state.

Penrose Cancer Hospital, Sisters of Charity of Cincinnati, 2215 N. Cascade Ave., Colorado Springs, Colo. 80907.

Our Lady of Perpetual Help Home, Servants of Relief for Incurable Cancer, 760 Washington St., S.W., Atlanta, Ga. 30315 (54).

Rose Hawthorne Lathrop Home, Servants of Relief for Incurable Cancer, 1600 Bay St., Fall River, Mass. 02724 (35).

Our Lady of Good Counsel Free Cancer Home, Servants of Relief for Incurable Cancer, 2076 St. Anthony Ave., St. Paul, Minn. 55104 (49).

Calvary Hospital, Little Company of Mary Sisters, 1740-70 Eastchester Rd., Bronx, N.Y. 10461 (200).

St. Rose's Free Home for Incurable Cancer, Servants of Relief for Incurable Cancer, 71 Jackson St., New York, N.Y. 10002 (45).

Rosary Hill Home, Servants of Relief for

Incurable Cancer, Hawthorne, N.Y. 10532 (82).

Holy Family Home, Servants of Relief for Incurable Cancer, 6707 State Rd., Cleveland, O. 44134 (100).

Sacred Heart Free Home for Incurable Cancer, Servants of Relief for Incurable Cancer, 1315 W. Hunting Park Ave., Philadelphia, Pa. 19140 (59).

Drug Abuse: Rehabilitation centers and outpatient clinics have been established in several dioceses. Facilities include:

Dismas House for Drug Rehabilitation (men), 396 Straight St., Paterson, N.J. 07501.

St. Joseph's Hospital, L. E. Phillips Center for the Chemically Dependent, 2661 County Trunk I, Chippewa Falls, Wis. 54729 (46).

New Hope Manor (live in therapeutic community for rehabilitation of female drug addicts), Graymoor, Garrison, N.Y. 10524.

St. Luke Center (clinic), 3290 N.W. 7th St., Miami, Fla. 33125.

Alcoholics: Some priests and religious throughout the U.S. are committed in a special way to the personal rehabilitation and pastoral care of alcoholics through participation in Alcoholics Anonymous and other programs. Facilities for the rehabilitation of alcoholics include:

St. Christopher's Inn, Atonement Friars, Graymoor, Garrison, N.Y. 10524 (capacity, 180). Simple detoxification and recovery; 21 days; ages 18-70.

Matt Talbot Inn, 2270 Professor St., Cleveland, Ohio 44113 (capacity 27 men; Halfway House; residential treatment for male alcoholics).

Mt. Carmel Hospital for Alcoholism (20 beds), and Mt. Carmel Rehabilitation Center for Male Alcoholics (50 beds), 396 Straight St., Paterson, N.J. 07501. McNulty House for Male Alcoholics (10 beds), 101 Cedar St., Paterson, N.J. 07501. Straight and Narrow Alcohol Abuse Services (outpatient services), 896 E. 19th St., Paterson, N.J. 07501.

Sacred Heart Rehabilitation Center: 569 Elizabeth St., Detroit, Mich. 48201 (130 beds, early treatment); 400 Stoddard Rd., Memphis, Mich. 48041 (125 beds, advance treatment). Both facilities serve male and female live-in clients. Three Halfway Houses for employed residents who complete full program.

The National Clergy Conference on Alcoholism was established to conduct workshops in various dioceses to instruct priests on ways of dealing with problem drinkers.

Convicts: Priests serve as full- or part-time chaplains in penal and correctional institutions throughout the country. Limited efforts have been made to assist in the rehabilitation of released prisoners in Halfway House establishments.

Dining Rooms; Facilities for Homeless: Representative of places where meals are provided, and in some cases lodging and other services as well, are:

St. Anthony's Dining Room, 121 Golden Gate Ave., San Francisco, Calif. 94102, where more than 13 million free meals have been served since 1950. Founded by Rev. Alfred Boeddeker, O.F.M.

St. Vincent de Paul Dining Room, 23rd and Grove Sts., Oakland, Calif. 94604. Administered by Little Brothers of the Good Shepherd.

Ozanam Inn, Little Brothers of the Good Shepherd, 843 Camp St., New Orleans, La. 70130. Under sponsorship of the St. Vincent de Paul Society.

St. Vincent's Dining Room, 505 W. 3rd St., Reno, Nev. 89503.

St. Vincent's Dining Room, 650 S. Main St., Las Vegas, Nev. 89101.

Good Shepherd Refuge, Little Brothers of the Good Shepherd, 601 2nd St. S.W., Albuquerque, N.M. 87102.

Holy Name Centre for Homeless Men, Inc., 18 Bleeker St., New York, N.Y. 10012. A day shelter for alcoholic, homeless men. Provides social services and aid to transients and those in need. Affiliated with New York Catholic Charities.

Mercy Hospice, Sisters of Mercy, 334 S. 13th St., Philadelphia, Pa. 19107. Temporary shelter and relocation assistance for homeless women.

St. Christopher Inn, Graymoor, Garrison, N.Y. 10524. Temporary shelter (21 days for homeless and needy men). A.A. program, referral, counseling.

St. John's Hospice for Men, Little Brothers of the Good Shepherd, 1221 Race St., Philadelphia, Pa. 19107. Founded in 1963. Hot breakfast and dinner served to all in need; accommodations for 35 men for night shelter; clothing distributed daily to needy.

Camillus House, Little Brothers of the Good Shepherd, 726 N.E. First Ave., Miami, Fla. 33132.

Temporary Shelters: Facilities for runaways, the abused and exploited include:

Convent of the Good Shepherd, 1500 S. Arlington Ave., Los Angeles, Calif. 90019. For battered women with children.

Covenant House, 260 W. 44th St., New York, N.Y. 10036. Non-sectarian. Executive director, Rev. Bruce Ritter, O.F.M. Conv. For homeless and exploited children.

Crescent House, 2929 S. Carrollton Ave., New Orleans, La. 70118. Temporary residence for abused women and their children.

Unwed Mothers: Residential and care services for unwed mothers are available in many dioceses.

Unclassified social services are rendered to many people in the normal operations of parishes and other institutions.

Organizations for Handicapped

(See separate article for a listing of facilities for the handicapped.)

Blind

The Carroll Center for the Blind (formerly the Catholic Guild for All the Blind): Located at 770 Centre St., Newton, Mass. 02158, the center conducts diagnostic evaluation and rehabilitation programs for blind people over 16 years of age, and maintains programs in community services for all ages, volunteer and special services, casework and counseling, low-vision training and professional training. It offers a large range of services for blind people who are not in residence, and maintains an office of public education and information. The executive director is Rachel Rosenbaum.

Xavier Society for the Blind: The Society is located at 154 E. 23rd St., New York, 10010. Founded in 1900 by Rev. Joseph Stadelman, S.J., it is a center for publications for the blind and maintains a circulating library of approximately 7,000 volumes in Braille, large type and on tape. Its many publications include *The Catholic Review,* a monthly selection of articles of current interest from the Catholic press presented for the visually handicapped in Braille, on tape, and in large print. The director of Xavier is Rev. Anthony F. La Bau, S.J.

The Deaf

According to the National Catholic Office for the Deaf, there are approximately 95,000 Catholics among the total deaf population of 410,522. (The deaf were defined by the 1974 National Census of the Deaf Population as "those persons who could not hear and understand speech and who had lost — or never had — that ability prior to 19 years of age.) Reported statistics indicated: Students in Catholic schools for the deaf, 1,969; teachers, 570 (147 were religious). Personnel involved in out-of-school pastoral ministry to the deaf included: priests, 97 (35 full-time, 62 part-time); permanent deacons, 6 (part-time); sisters, 72 (27 full-time, 45 part-time); brothers, 3 (1 full-time, 2 part-time); lay people, 69 (4 full-time, 65 part-time).

Organizations involved in work for the deaf include the following.

International Catholic Deaf Association: Established by deaf adults in Toronto, Canada, in 1949, the association has more than 5,000 members in 115 chapters, mostly in the U.S. It is the only international lay association founded and controlled by deaf Catholic adults. It is affiliated with the World Federation of the Deaf. Home office address: 814 Thayer Ave., Silver Spring, Md. 20910. The ICDA publishes *The Deaf Catholic,* a quarterly, and sponsors an annual convention.

National Catholic Office for the Deaf: Formally established in 1976, at Washington, D.C., to provide pastoral service to those who teach deaf children and adults, to the parents of deaf children, to pastors of deaf persons, and to organizations of the deaf. The office develops liturgical and religious education materials; organizes workshops, pastoral weeks, community weeks, leadership programs, cursillos; and serves as a clearinghouse for information concerning ministry to the deaf. It publishes *Listening,* a pastoral service for the hearing impaired, five times a year. The executive director is Rev. David Walsh, C.SS.R. Address: Trinity College, Washington, D.C. 20017.

Mentally Retarded

National Apostolate with Mentally Retarded Persons: Established in 1968, the apostolate has headquarters at Trinity College, P.O. Box 4588, Washington, D.C. 20017. It publishes the quarterly *NAMPR Journal* and a monthly newsletter, and has available a bibliography on the religious education of the retarded. Sr. Bernadette S. Downes, C.I.J., is president of the apostolate; the executive director is Bro. Joseph Moloney, O.S.F.

Service Agency

Special Education Department, National Catholic Educational Association: Established in 1954 to coordinate under one agency information and service functions for all areas of special education under Catholic auspices. The executive director is Sr. Suzanne Hall, S.N.D. de N. Address: One Dupont Circle N.W., Suite 350, Washington, D.C. 20036.

BIRTHRIGHT

Birthright is a nondenominational guidance and referral service organization offering pregnant women alternatives to abortion, in line with the motto, "It is the right of every pregnant woman to give birth and the right of every child to be born."

Started by Mrs. Louise Summerhill of Toronto, Canada, in 1968, it has chapters in Canada, the United States, the United Kingdom, New Zealand, Australia and South Africa. Each of these units, manned by volunteers, operates a crisis center where women can come to discuss their problems privately.

The executive director of Birthright, U.S.A., is Mrs. D. Cocciolone, 62 Hunter St., Woodbury, N.J. 08096.

Birthright, although it has Catholics among its volunteers and draws some support from Catholic sources, insists on its original independent and nondenominational character. Its operations have been adopted by other pro-life groups. Birthright telephone numbers are listed in scores of local directories.

Retreats

There is great variety in retreat and renewal programs, with orientations ranging from the traditional to teen encounters. Central to all of them are celebration of the liturgy and deepening of a person's commitment to faith and witness in life.

Features of many of the forms are as follows.

Traditional Retreats: Centered around conferences and the direction of a retreat master; oriented to the personal needs of the retreatants; including such standard practices as participation in Mass, reception of the sacraments, private and group prayer, silence and meditation, discussions.

Team Retreat: Conducted by a team of several leaders or directors (priests, religious, lay persons) with division of subject matter and activities according to their special skills and the nature and needs of the group.

Closed Retreat: Involving withdrawal for a period of time — overnight, several days, a weekend — from everyday occupations and activities.

Open Retreat: Made without total disengagement from everyday involvements, on a part-time basis.

Private Retreat: By one person, on a kind of do-it-yourself basis with the one-to-one assistance of a director.

Special Groups: With formats and activities geared to particular groups; e.g., members of Alcoholics Anonymous, vocational groups and apostolic groups.

Marriage Encounters: Usually weekend periods of husband-wife reflection and dialogue; introduced into the U.S. from Spain in 1967.

Charismatic Renewal: Featuring elements of the movement of the same name; "Spirit-oriented"; communitarian and flexible, with spontaneous and shared prayer, personal testimonies of faith and witness.

Christian Community: Characterized by strong community thrust.

Teen Encounters, SEARCH: Formats adapted to the mentality and needs of youth, involving experience of Christian faith and commitment in a community setting.

Christian Maturity Seminars: Similar to teen encounters in basic concept but different to suit persons of greater maturity.

Cursillo: see separate entry.

Movement for a Better World: see separate entry.

Conference

Retreats International Inc.: The first organization for promoting retreats in the U.S. was started in 1904 in California. Its initial efforts and the gradual growth of the movement led to the formation in 1927 of the National Catholic Laymen's Retreat Conference, the forerunner of the men's division of Retreats International. The women's division developed from the National Laywomen's Retreat Movement which was founded in Chicago in 1936. The men's and women's divisions merged July 9, 1977. The services of the organization include the bimonthly *Retreat World* newsletter, the preparation of promotional material for retreat recruiting, the organization of regional retreat groups and sponsorship of a national triennial convention. The officers are: Bishop Albert H. Ottenweller of Steubenville, episcopal advisor; Henry J. Balling, Jr., president; Rev. Thomas W. Gedeon, S.J., executive director. National office: Memorial Library — Room 1112, Notre Dame, Ind. 46556.

HOUSES OF RETREAT AND RENEWAL

(Sources: Almanac survey; *1979 Directory of Retreat Houses in the United States and Canada*, compiled by Retreats International; *The Official Catholic Directory*.)

Abbreviation code: m, men; w, women; mc, married couples; y, youth. Houses and centers without code generally offer facilities to all groups. An asterisk after an abbreviation indicates that the facility is primarily for the group designated but that special groups are also accommodated. Houses furnish information concerning the types of programs they offer.

Alabama: Blessed Trinity Shrine Retreat, Holy Trinity 36859.

Visitation Sacred Heart Retreat House, 2300 Spring Hill Ave., Mobile 36607.

Alaska: Holy Spirit Retreat House, Star Route A, Box 388, Anchorage 99502.

Arizona: Franciscan Renewal Center, Casa de Paz y Bien, 5802 E. Lincoln Dr., Box 220, Scottsdale 85252.

Mount Claret Cursillo Center (ecumenical), 4633 N. 54th St., Phoenix 85018.

Picture Rocks Retreat — A Christian Renewal Center, 7101 W. Picture Rocks Rd., Cortaro 85230. Mailing address, Box 569, Cortaro 85230.

Spiritual Life Institute (individuals only), Nada Contemplative Center, Sedona 86336.

Arkansas: The Abbey Retreat (Coury House), Subiaco 72865.

California: Angela Center (ecumenical), 535 Angela Dr., Santa Rosa 95401.

Camp Mariastella (y*, families, ecumenical), Wrightwood 92397. Office, 1120 Westchester Pl., Los Angeles 90019.

Cenacle Retreat House 5340 Fair Oaks Blvd., Carmichael 95608.
Christ the King Retreat Center, Box 156, Citrus Heights 95610.
Christian Brothers Retreat House (students), 2233 Sulphur Springs Ave., St. Helena 94574.
El Carmelo Christian Renewal Center, 926 E. Highland Ave., Redlands 92373.
El Retiro, Jesuit Retreat House, P.O. Box 128, Los Altos 94022.
Holy Spirit Retreat House, 4316 Lanai Rd., Encino 91316.
Immaculate Heart Retreat House (w, mc), 3431 Waverly Dr., Los Angeles 90027.
La Casa de Maria, 800 El Bosque Rd., Santa Barbara 93108.
Manresa Retreat House (m*), P.O. Box K, Azusa 91702.
Mary and Joseph Retreat House, 5300 Crest Rd., Palos Verdes 90274.
Mater Dolorosa Retreat House (m*), 700 N. Sunnyside Ave., Sierra Madre 91024.
Mission San Miguel, San Miguel 93451.
Mount Mary Immaculate, 3254 Gloria Terr., Lafayette 94549.
Mt. Tabor Monastery, 17001 Tomki Rd., Redwood Valley 95470.
New Camaldoli Immaculate Heart Hermitage (m*, private), Big Sur 93920.
Old Mission San Luis Rey Retreat, 4050 Mission Ave., San Luis Rey 92068.
Poverello of Assisi Retreat House, 1519 Woodworth St., San Fernando 91340.
Sacred Heart Retreat House (w*), 920 E. Alhambra Rd., Alhambra 91801.
St. Andrew's Priory Retreat House, Valyermo 93563.
St. Anthony's Retreat House, P.O. Box 248, Three Rivers 93271.
St. Charles Priory, Benet Hill, Oceanside 92054.
St. Clare's Retreat (w*), 2381 Laurel Glen Rd. Santa Cruz 95065.
St. Francis Retreat, P.O. Box 1070, San Juan Bautista 95045.
St. Joseph's Salesian Youth Center (St. Dominic Savio Retreat House) (y), 8301 Arroyo Dr., Rosemead 91770.
San Damiano Retreat, P.O. Box 767, Danville 94526.
Santa Sabina Center, 1520 Grand Ave., San Rafael 94901.
Serra Retreat (m*), P.O. Box 127, Malibu 90265.
Vallombrosa Center (w*), 250 Oak Grove Ave., Menlo Park 94025.
Villa Maria del Mar, Santa Cruz. Mailing address, 2-1918 E. Cliff Dr., Santa Cruz 95062.

Colorado: Bethlehem Center, RR 1, Box 192, Broomfield 80020.
Convent of St. Walburga (w*), 6717 S. Boulder Rd., Boulder 80303.
El Pomar Renewal Center, 1661 Mesa Ave., Colorado Springs 80906.
Sacred Heart Retreat House, Box 185, Sedalia 80135.

Connecticut: Cenacle Center for Meditation and Spiritual Renewal (w*), Wadsworth St., Box 550, Middletown 06457.
Edmundite Apostolate Center, Enders Island, Mystic 06355.
Holy Family Retreat (m, mc*), 303 Tunxis Rd., West Hartford 06107.
Immaculata Retreat House, Route 32, Windham Rd., Willimantic 06226.
Mercy Center, 167 Neck Rd., Madison 06443.
Our Lady of Calvary Retreat House, Colton Rd., Farmington 06032.
Villa Maria Retreat House (w), 159 Sky Meadow Dr., Stamford 06903.

Delaware: St. Francis Renewal Center, 1901 Prior Rd., Wilmington 19809.

District of Columbia: Washington Retreat House (w*), 4000 Harewood Rd. N.E., Washington 20017.

Florida: Cenacle Retreat House, 1400 S. Dixie Highway, Lantana 33462.
Dominican Retreat House (Mary Queen of Apostles), 7275 S.W. 124th St., Kendall 33156.
Franciscan Center (ecumenical), 3010 Perry Ave., Tampa 33603.
Holy Name Priory, P.O. Drawer H, St. Leo 33574.
Our Lady of Florida Retreat House, 1300 US Hwy. No. 1, North Palm Beach 33408.
St. Leo's Abbey (m), St. Leo 33574.

Georgia: Ignatius House, 6700 Riverside Dr. N.W., Atlanta 30328.
Monastery of the Holy Spirit (m), Conyers 30207.

Idaho: Nazareth, 4450 N. Five Mile Rd., Boise 83702.

Illinois: Aylesford Carmelite Spiritual Center, I-55 at Cass Ave., N, Darien 60559.
Bellarmine Hall (m*), Box 268, Barrington 60010.
Bishop Lane Retreat House, R.R. 2, Box 214 A, Rockford 61102.
Cabrini Contact Center, 9430 Golf Rd., Des Plaines 60016.
Cenacle Retreat House, 513 Fullerton Parkway, Chicago 60614.
Cenacle Retreat and Conference Center, P.O. Box 340, Warrenville 60555.
Childerley Retreat House (university students), 506 McHenry Rd., Wheeling 60090.
Christian Life Center, 1209 W. Ogden Ave., La Grange Park 60525.

Franciscan Apostolic Center, P.O. Box 42, Sangamon Ave., Springfield 67205.

King's House, N. 66th St., Belleville 62223.

King's House of Retreats, Box 165, Henry 61537.

La Salle Manor, Christian Brothers Retreat House (y*), Plano 60545.

Longwood Cenacle, 11600 Longwood Dr., Chicago 60643.

National Shrine of Our Lady of the Snows, 9500 W. Illinois Route 15, Belleville 62223.

Our Lady of Angels Retreat and Renewal Center, 1901 E. 18th St., Quincy 62301.

Resurrection Center, 2710 S. Country Club Rd., Woodstock 60098.

St. Francis Retreat, Mayslake, 1717 31st St., Oak Brook 60521.

St. Joseph Retreat House, 353 N. River Rd., Des Plaines 60016.

St. Mary's Retreat House, P.O. Box 608, 1400 W. Main St., Lemont 60439.

Techny Towers, International Mission Center, Techny 60082.

Tolentine Center, 20300 Governors Highway, Olympia Fields 60461.

Viatorian Villa, 3015 N. Bayview Lane, McHenry 60050.

Villa Redeemer, Box 6, Glenview 60025.

Indiana: Alverna Center, 8140 Spring Mill Rd., Indianapolis 46260.

Crosier Ministry Center, 2620 E. Wallen Rd., Ft. Wayne 46825.

John XXIII Center, 407 W. McDonald St., Hartford City 47348.

Kordes Enrichment Center, R.R. 1, Box 215 C, Ferdinand 47532.

Lourdes Retreat House (m*), Box 156, Cedar Lake 46303.

Mount Saint Francis Retreat Center, Mount Saint Francis 47146.

Our Lady of Fatima Retreat House, 5353 E. 56th St., Indianapolis 46226.

Our Lady of Fatima Retreat House, Box O, Notre Dame 46556.

St. Jude Guest House, St. Meinrad 47577.

St. Maur Theological Center, 4545 Northwestern Ave., Indianapolis 46208.

Sarto Retreat House, 4200 N. Kentucky Ave., Evansville 47711.

Iowa: American Martyrs Retreat House, P.O. Box 605, Cedar Falls 50613.

Colfax Interfaith Spiritual Center, Box 37, Colfax, 50054.

Kansas: St. Augustine Retreat Center, A 3301 Parallel Parkway, Kansas City 66104.

St. Benedict's Abbey (m, mc*), Atchison 66002.

Villa Christi Retreat House, 3033 W. Second St., Wichita 67203.

Kentucky: Marydale Center, Donaldson Rd., Erlanger 41018.

Our Lady of Gethsemani (m, private), The Guestmaster, Abbey of Gethsemani, Trappist 40073.

Placid House, St. Mark's Priory, South Union 42283.

Saint Thomas Center, 170 Crabbs Lane, Louisville 40206.

Louisiana: Abbey Christian Life Center, St. Joseph's Abbey, St. Benedict 70457.

Ave Maria Retreat House, Route 1, Box 0368 AB, Marrero 70072.

Cenacle Retreat House (w*), 5500 St. Mary St., Metairie 70011.

Manresa House of Retreats (m), P.O. Box 89, Convent 70723.

Maryhill Retreat House (Christian Life Center), 600 Maryhill Rd., Pineville 71360.

Our Lady of the Oaks Retreat House, P.O. Box D, Grand Coteau 70541.

Maine: St. Paul's Center, Oblate Fathers Retreat House (French-English), 136 State St., Augusta 04330.

Maryland: CYO Retreat Center, P.O. Box 4235, 401 Randolph Rd., Silver Spring 20904.

CYO Retreat House (y*), 15523 York Rd.,Sparks 21152.

Christian Brothers Retreat House (y*), Rt. 15 South, Adamstown 21710.

Loyola Retreat House-on-Potomac, Faulkner 20632.

Manresa-on-Severn, P.O. Box 9, Annapolis 21404.

Marriottsville Spiritual Center, Marriottsville 21104.

St. Joseph Spiritual Center, 3800 Frederick Ave., Baltimore 21229.

Massachusetts: Calvary Retreat Center, Passionist Community, 59 South St., Shrewsbury 01545.

Campion Renewal Center, 319 Concord Rd., Weston 02193.

Cenacle Retreat House, 200 Lake St., Brighton, Boston 02135.

Christian Formation Center, River Rd., Andover 01810

Eastern Point Retreat House, Gonzaga Hall, Gloucester 01930.

Espousal Center, 554 Lexington St., Waltham 02154.

Esther House of Spiritual Renewal, Sisters of St. Anne, 783 Grove St., Worcester 01605.

Genesis Spiritual Life Center, 53 Mill St., Westfield 01085.

Glastonbury Abbey (Benedictine Monks), 16 Hull St., Hingham 02043.

Guest Retreat House, St. Joseph's Abbey, Spencer 01562.

Holy Cross Fathers Retreat House, Washington St., N. Easton 02356.

Jesuit Center, Sullivan Square, Charlestown, Boston 02129.

La Salette Center for Christian Living, 947 Park St., Attleboro 02703.
Loretto Retreat House, Jeffrey's Neck Rd., Ipswich 01938.
Marian Center (w*), 1365 Northampton St., Holyoke 01040.
Miramar Retreat House, Duxbury, 02332.
Mother of God Retreat House (boys), Old Groveland Rd., Bradford 01830.
Mother of Sorrows Retreat House (m*), 110 Monastery Ave., W. Springfield 01089.
Mt. Carmel Christian Life Center, Oblong Rd., Williamstown 01267.
Sacred Heart Center for Youth Ministry, Salesians of St. John Bosco, P.O. Box 271, Ipswich 01938.
St. Stephen Priory (Dominican), 20 Glen St., Dover, Mass. 02030.
Salvatorian Center, 30 East St., Methuen 01844.

Michigan: Blessed Sacrament Retreat House, Sacramentine Sisters, Conway 49722.
Capuchin Retreat, Box 188, Washington 48094.
Christian Friendship House (y*), 1975 N. River Rd., St. Clair 48079.
Manresa Jesuit Retreat House, 1390 Quarton Rd., Bloomfield Hills 48013.
Mary Reparatrix Retreat Center (w*), 13600 Virgil, Detroit 48223.
Marygrove Center, Garden 49835.
Portiuncula in the Pines, 703 E. Main St., De Witt 48820.
Queen of Angels Retreat, Box 2026, 3400 S. Washington Blvd., Saginaw 48605.
St. Basil's Center, 3990 Giddings Rd., Pontiac 48057.
St. Lazare Retreat House, W. Spring Lake Rd., Spring Lake 49456.
St. Mary's Retreat House (w*), 775 W. Drahner Rd., Oxford 48051.
St. Paul of the Cross Retreat House, 23333 Schoolcraft, Detroit 48223.

Minnesota: The Cenacle, 1221 Wayzata Blvd., Wayzata 55391.
Center for Spiritual Development, 301 S. 10th St., Olivia 56277.
Christian Brothers Retreat Center, Rt. 2, Box 18, Marine-on-St. Croix 55047.
Christian Community Center, Assisi Heights, Rochester 55901.
Epiphany House of Prayer, 266 Summit Ave., St. Paul 55102.
Fitzgerald Center, Immaculate Heart of Mary Seminary, Terrace Heights, Winona 55987.
Franciscan Retreats, Conventual Franciscan Friars, Prior Lake 55372.
Jesuit Retreat House (m), 8243 N. Demontreville Trail North, Lake Elmo 55109.
King's House of Retreats, 621 S. First Ave., Buffalo 55313.
Maryhill Retreat House, Society of Daughters of the Heart of Mary, 260 Summit Ave., St. Paul 55102.
Minneapolis Catholic Youth Center (y), 2120 Park Ave. S., Minneapolis 55404.
Welch Center (y), 605 N. Central Ave., Duluth 55807.

Mississippi: St. Augustine's (m*), Divine Word Missionaries, Bay St. Louis 39520.

Missouri: Cenacle Retreat House (w*), 900 S. Spoede Rd., St. Louis 63131.
Family Life Center (mc*), St. Pius X Abbey, Abbey Rd., Pevely 63070.
Jesuit Retreat House of the Immacolata, RFD 4, Box 450, Liberty 64068. Office, 300 E. 36th St., P.O. Box 1037, Kansas City 64141.
Maria Fonte Solitude (private), P.O. Box 322, High Ridge 63049.
Marian Hall Retreat Center, Conception Seminary College, Conception 64433.
Marianist Apostolic Center, Glencoe 63038.
Our Lady of Assumption Abbey (m, w), Trappists, Rt. 5, Box 193, Ava 65608.
Our Lady of the Ozarks, P.O. Box 424, Carthage 64836.
Pallottine Renewal Center, R.R. 2, 15270, Old Halls Ferry Rd., Florissant 63034.
Passionist Retreat of Our Lady, Retreat House, Passionist Fathers and Brothers, 3036 Bellerive Dr., St. Louis 63121.
Queen of Heaven Solitude (private), Rt. 1, Box 107A, Marionville 65705.
The White House Retreat (m), 7400 Christopher Dr., St. Louis 63129.

Montana: Ursuline Retreat Center, 2300 Central Ave., Great Falls 59401.

Nebraska: Crosier Renewal Center, 223 E. 14th St., P.O. Box 789, Hastings 68901.
Good Counsel, R.R. 1, Box 110, Waverly 68462.
The Mary J. O'Donnell Center (y*), c/o University Chaplains, Creighton Univ., 2500 California St., Omaha 68178.
St. Columbans Foreign Mission Society, St. Columbans 68056.

New Hampshire: The Common - St. Joseph Monastery, Discalced Carmelite Friars, Peterborough 03458.
New Hampshire Monastery, Hundred Acres, New Boston 03070.
Oblate Fathers Retreat House, Hudson 03051.
St. Francis Friary and Retreat House, 860 Central Rd., Rye Beach 03871.

New Jersey: Bethlehem Center for Prayer and Spiritual Growth (hermitage experience), Pleasant Hill Rd., Box 315, Chester 07930.

Blackwood Center, St. Pius X House, Box 216, Blackwood 08012.
Blessed Trinity Missionary Retreat Cenacle (w*), 1190 Long Hill Rd., Stirling 07980.
Carmel Retreat House, 1071 Ramapo Valley Rd., Mahwah 07430.
Cenacle Retreat House, River Rd., Highland Park 08904.
Good Shepherd Center, 74 Kahdena Rd., Morristown 07960.
Loyola House of Retreats, 161 James St., Morristown 07960.
Marianist Christian Family Living Center (families), Cape and Yale Ave., Cape May Point 08212.
Mt. St. John Academy, Gladstone, N.J. 07934.
Queen of Peace Retreat House, Route 206, Newton 07860.
St. Bonaventure Retreat House (m), 174 Ramsey St., Paterson 07501.
St. Joseph's Villa (w), Srs. of St. John the Baptist, Peapack 07977.
San Alfonso Retreat House, 755 Ocean Ave., Long Branch 07740.
Villa Pauline Retreat and Guest House (w*), Hilltop Rd., Mendham 07945.
Xavier Center, Convent Station 07961.

New Mexico: Dominican Retreat House, Our Lady Queen of Peace, 5825 Coors Rd. S.W., Albuquerque 87105.
Holy Cross Retreat House, P.O. Box 158, Mesilla Park 88047.
Our Lady of Guadalupe Monastery (families - pentecostal), Pecos 87552.

New York: Bergamo East Conference Center, Chaminade Rd., Marcy 13403.
Bethany Retreat House, Route 208, Highland Mills 10930.
Bethlehem Retreat House (m*), Abbey of the Genesee, Piffard 14533.
Bishop Molloy Retreat House (m), 86-45 178th St., Jamaica, L.I. 11432.
Cabrini-on-the Hudson, West Park, N.Y. 12493.
Cardinal Spellman Retreat House, Passionist Fathers, 5801 Palisade Ave., Bronx (Riverdale) 10471.
Cenacle Center for Spiritual Renewal, Cenacle Rd., Lake Ronkonkoma 11779.
Cenacle Center for Spiritual Renewal, Cross Rd., Ardsley 10502.
The Cenacle: Center for Spiritual Renewal, 693 East Ave., Rochester 14607.
Christ the King Retreat House, 500 Brookford Rd., Syracuse 13224.
Cormaria Retreat House (w*), Sag Harbor, L.I. 11963.
Diocesan Cursillo Center (Spanish), 118 Congress St., Brooklyn 11201.
Dominican Retreat House, 1945 Union St., Schenectady 12309.
Don Bosco Retreat House, Filor's Lane, West Haverstraw 10993.
Graymoor Christian Unity Center, Graymoor, Garrison 10524.
Jesuit Retreat House, North American Martyrs Shrine, Auriesville 12016.
Mary Reparatrix Retreat Center, 14 E. 29th St., New York 10016.
Monastery of the Precious Blood (w), Ft. Hamilton Parkway and 54th St., Brooklyn 11219.
Mount Alvernia Retreat House, Wappingers Falls 12590.
Mount Augustine Retreat House and Apostolic Center, 144 Campus Rd., Staten Island 10301.
Mount Manresa Retreat House, 239 Fingerboard Rd., Staten Island 10305.
Notre Dame Retreat House, Box 342, Foster Rd., Canandaigua 14424.
Queen of Apostles Retreat House, North Haven, Sag Harbor 11963.
Regina Maria Retreat House (w*), 77 Brinkerhoff St., Plattsburgh 12901.
Renewal Center, Diocese of Buffalo, 6969 Strickler Rd., Clarence Center 14032. Poustinia available.
St. Andrew's House, 89 A St. Andrew's Rd., Walden 12586.
St. Columban's Retreat House, P.O. Box 816, Derby 14047.
St. Gabriel Passionist Retreat House, 64 Burns Rd., P.O. Box P, Shelter Island 11965.
St. Ignatius Retreat House, Searington Rd., Manhasset, L.I. 11030.
St. Josaphat's Retreat House, East Beach Rd., Glen Cove 11542.
St. Joseph Center (Spanish Center), 523 W. 142nd St., New York 10031.
Stella Maris Retreat House and Center for Renewal, 130 E. Genesee St., Skaneateles 13152.
Tagaste Monastery Retreat House (m, y), Suffern 10901.

North Carolina: Maryhurst Retreat House, P.O. Box 38, Pinehurst 28374.

North Dakota: Queen of Peace Retreat, Redemptorist Fathers, 1310 N. Broadway, Fargo 58102.
Sacred Heart Priory, Richardton 58652.

Ohio: Bergamo Conference Center, 4435 E. Patterson Rd., Dayton 45430.
Franciscan Renewal Center, 320 West St., Carey 43316.
Friarhurst Retreat House, 8136 Wooster Pike, Cincinnati 45227.
Holy Trinity Oratory, 6832 Convent Blvd., Sylvania 43560.
Jesuit Renewal Center, P.O. Box 289, Milford 45150.
Jesuit Retreat House, 5629 State Rd., Cleveland 44134.

Loyola of the Lakes, 700 Killinger Rd., Clinton 44216.
Maria Stein Center, 2365 St. Johns Rd., Maria Stein 45860.
Mary Reparatrix Retreat Center (w*), 3350 Ruther Ave., Cincinnati 45220.
Men of Milford Retreat House (m, mc), Box 348, Milford 45150.
MSC Center, Rt. 4, Shelby 44875.
Our Lady of the Pines, 1250 Tiffin St., Fremont 43420.
Sacred Heart, 3128 Logan Ave., Box 6074, Youngstown 44501.
St. Anthony Pilgrim House, 321 Clay St., Carey 43316.
St. Joseph Christian Life Center, 18485 Lake Shore Blvd., Cleveland 44119.
Shrine Center for Renewal, Diocese of Columbus, 5277 E. Broad St., Columbus 43213.

Oklahoma: St. Gregory's Abbey, Shawnee 74801.

Oregon: Loyola Retreat House (Jesuit Center for Spiritual Renewal), 3220 S.E. 43rd St., Portland 97206.
Mt. Angel Abbey Guest-Retreat Center, St. Benedict 97373.
Our Lady of Peace Retreat (w*), 3600 S. W. 170th Ave., Beaverton 97005.
St. Benedict Lodge, 56630 N. Bank Rd., McKenzie Bridge 97401.
Trappist Abbey Retreat (m*, private), P.O. Box 97, Lafayette 97127.

Pennsylvania: Byzantine Catholic Seminary (m), 3605 Perrysville Ave., Pittsburgh 15214.
Cenacle Retreat House (w*), 4721 Fifth Ave., Pittsburgh 15213.
Dominican Retreat House (w*), Ashbourne Rd. and Juniper Ave., Elkins Park 19117.
Fatima House, Rolling Hills Rd., Ottsville 18942.
Jesuit Center for Spiritual Growth, Church Rd., Wernersville 19565.
Marian Hall, St. Joseph Convent/Academy, R.D. 2, Columbia 17512.
Marie Wald Retreat House, Convent of the Precious Blood, New Holland Ave., Shillington 19607.
Mercy Center, Box 370, Dallas 18612.
Our Lady of Fatima Center, Griffin Rd., Box 143, Elmhurst 18416.
Retreat Center, Mt. St. Macrina, Box 878, Uniontown 15401.
St. Alphonsus Retreat House (m), Box 218, Tobyhanna 18466 (1,200).
St. Ann's Retreat House, Carrolltown Rd., Ebensburg 15931.
St. Emma Retreat House, 1001 Harvey St., Greensburg 15601.
St. Fidelis Seminary (summer only), Herman 16039.

St. Francis Retreat House, 3918 Chipman Rd., Easton 18042.
St. Francis Retreat House (w), Monocacy Manor, Bethlehem 18017.
St. Gabriel's Retreat House (w), 631 Griffin Pond Rd., Clarks Summit 18411.
St. Joseph's-in-the-Hills (m*), Malvern 19355.
St. Paul of the Cross Retreat House, 148 Monastery Ave., Pittsburgh 15203.
Saint Raphaela Mary Retreat House, 616 Coopertown Rd., Haverford 19041.
St. Vincent Retreat House (m*, summer), Latrobe 15650.
Villa Maria Retreat House, Box 218, Wernersville 19585.
Villa of Our Lady of the Poconos (w), Mt. Pocono 18344.

Rhode Island: Carmel Spiritual Center, 21 Battery St., Newport 02840.
Ephpheta House — A Center for Renewal, 10 Manville Hill Rd; mailing address, P.O. Box 1, Manville 02838.
Our Lady of Peace Retreat House, Ocean Rd., Narragansett 02882.
St. Dominic Savio Youth Center (y*), Broad Rock Rd., Box 67, Peace Dale 02883.

South Carolina: Springbank Christian Center, Dominican Retreat House, Kingstree 29556.

South Dakota: St. Martin's Community Center, R.R. 4, Box 253, Rapid City 57701.

Tennessee: Nazareth, House of the Lord, 1306 Dellwood Ave., Memphis 88127.

Texas: Catholic Renewal Center of North Texas, 4503 Bridge St., Ft. Worth 76103.
Cenacle Retreat House, 420 N. Kirkwood, Houston 77079.
Christian Holiday House and Renewal Center, Oblate Fathers, P.O. Box 635, Dickinson 77539.
Holy Name Retreat House (m*), 430 Bunker Hill Rd., Houston 77024.
Montserrat Jesuit Retreat House, P.O. Box 398, Lake Dallas 75065.
Mt. Tabor Retreat House, 12940 Up River Rd., Corpus Christi 78410.
Our Lady of the Pillar Christian Renewal Center, 2507 N.W. 36th St., San Antonio 78228.
Saint Joseph Retreat House (Casa San Jose), 127 Oblate Dr., San Antonio 78216.
San Juan Retreat House, ("El Rancho Alegre"), Diocese of Brownsville, P.O. Box 998, San Juan 78589.

Utah: Our Lady of the Holy Trinity Retreat House (m), Huntsville 84317.
Our Lady of the Mountains, 1794 Lake St., Ogden 84401.

Virginia: Dominican Retreat (w*), 7103 Old Dominion Dr., McLean 22101.
Franciscan Center for Spiritual Renewal, Rt. 642, Box 825, Winchester 22601..
Holy Family Retreat House, Redemptorist Fathers, Box 3151, Hampton 23363.
Missionhurst Retreat Center, 4651 N. 25th St., Arlington 22207.
Spiritual Renewal Center (Genesis House), Rt. 2, Box 388 B, Richmond 23233.
St. Francis de Sales Retreat, Powhaten 23139.

Washington: Camp Field Retreat Center, P.O. Box 128, Leavenworth 98826.
Immaculate Heart Retreat House, Route 3, Box 653, Spokane 99203.
Redemptorist Palisades Retreat, P.O. Box 3739, Federal Way 98003.
St. Peter the Apostle Diocesan Retreat Center, P.O. Box 86, Cowiche 98923.
Visitation Retreat Center (w), 3200 S.W. Dash Point Rd., Federal Way 98003.

Wisconsin: Cardoner Retreat Center, 1501 S. Layton Blvd., Milwaukee 53215.
Holy Name Retreat House (m), Chambers Island; mailing address, 1825 Riverside Drive, P.O. Box 337, Green Bay 54305.
Jesuit Retreat House, 4800 Fahrnwald Rd., Oshkosh 54901.
Marynook — House of the Lord, 500 S. 12th St., Galesville 54630.
Monte Alverno Retreat House, 1000 N. Ballard Rd., Appleton 54911.
Mother of Perpetual Help, 1800 N. Timber Trail Lane, Oconomowoc 53066.
Retreat/Renewal Center, Notre Dame of the Lake, 700 W. Highland Rd., Mequon 53092.
Retreat Programs, St. Benedict's Abbey, Benet Lake 53102.
St. Anthony Retreat Center, Marathon 54448.
St. Benedict Center (ecumenical retreat and conference center), Fox Bluff, P.O. Box 5070, Madison 53705.
St. Francis Friary and Retreat Center, 503 S. Browns Lake Dr., Burlington 53105.
St. Vincent Pallotti Center, Rt. 3, Box 47, Elkhorn 53121.
Schoenstatt Center, W. 284 N. 698 Cherry Lane, Waukesha 53186.
Siena Center, 5635 Erie St., Racine 53402.

HOUSE OF PRAYER EXPERIENCE

(Source: Sister Ann E. Chester, I.H.M., 70 W. Boston Blvd., Detroit, Mich. 48202.)

The purpose of the House of Prayer Experience (HOPE) movement is to help active religious and priests and lay persons to acquire a contemporary style of contemplative life for renewal, inner growth and a more joyful personal and communal life in the light of the Gospel.

The starting point of participation in the movement is an extended period, from several weeks to several years, of concentration on intensive prayer with a community — a house of prayer experience. The result sought is the development of a style of prayer and contemplation with a carry-over that integrates and permeates religion and life.

Programs

The communities of houses of prayer consist of a relatively stable core of members with an authentic call to a deeper prayer life and of guests who come and go for shorter or longer periods of participation. The stability of the core group, while not a now-and-forever type of commitment, is such as to guarantee continuity in programs and the resources of experienced personnel in conducting them.

Program elements include the liturgy, meditation, scriptural reading and dialogue, shared prayer in the shared life of community, silence and solitude, search for new forms of prayer and for new adaptations of traditional forms — all against the background of existential conditions. The elements are oriented toward individual and personal needs and to various types of ministry, such as contemplative prayer itself and ministries concerned with a parish, the family, youth, inner-city pastoral work, spiritual development, the charismatic movement.

Two hundred and four listings were reported in the third *Annual Directory, Houses of Prayer*, released in the spring of 1979 by Clarity Publishing, Inc. (75 Champlain St., Albany, N.Y. 12204). Eighty-two of the houses were sponsored by more than 50 religious congregations of men and women, and 16 by dioceses. The 204 figure represented a 46 per cent increase in listings over those reported in 1978. Fifty-nine of the houses had programs focusing on the spiritual traditions of major religious orders. Houses of prayer or prayer study/experience centers were located in 36 of the 50 states. There were also 13 Canadian listings.

PARISHES PRAISED

Pope John Paul, during a visit Oct. 28, 1979, to the Rome parish of St. Pius V, called parishes the "scene of evangelization" and called on priests and religious to join him in combatting the "great spiritual crisis" of our times.

He told more than 5,000 people attending an outdoor Mass that he made the visit primarily because he wanted "to be among you to feel the heartbeat and the life of your community." He also said the parish is the scene of great and varied work similar to agricultural work, in reference to the responsorial psalm of the day: "Going they went and wept, casting their seeds. . . . Those who sow in tears shall reap in joy."

Lay Persons and Their Apostolate

SPECIAL AGENCIES

Some of the following agencies are engaged in carrying out programs of the United States Catholic Conference. Additional agencies are reported in other Almanac entries.

Religious Education/CCD (Confraternity of Christian Doctrine): Its objective is the religious education of persons from early childhood through adult life.

The modern expansion of Religious Education/CCD dates from publication of the encyclical letter *Acerbo Nimis* by Pope St. Pius X in 1905. His directive, that CCD programs be established in every parish, was incorporated in the Code of Canon Law and was reaffirmed by the Second Vatican Council in the *Decree on the Bishops' Pastoral Office in the Church.*

Religious Education/CCD programs are parish-based. Policies are developed by parish boards or commissions, and responsibility for administering programs rests ideally with a coordinator or director who is a trained professional in religious education.

On the diocesan level, Religious Education is coordinated by a director with a staff operating under the title of an office of religious education or a similar title. The diocesan office coordinates and acts as consultant to the work of local parish and regional programs; it conducts teacher-training courses, issues guidelines for unified programs, provides overall in-service aid and resources for local staffs and programs.

On the national level, Religious Education/CCD (formerly called the National Center for the Confraternity of Christian Doctrine, and since 1969 under the Department of Education, U.S. Catholic Conference) provides field and informational services along with representation for local diocesan programs and staffs. On the international level, it participates in programs which find their roots with the Vatican congregations that deal with religious education or catechesis.

Publications under the direction of Religious Education/CCD include *Living Light,* Catechetical Sunday materials and numerous other publications developed in conjunction with the National Conference of Diocesan Directors of Religious Education.

The Rev. David Beebe is representative for Religious Education/CCD in the Department of Education, U.S. Catholic Conference.

Offices are located at 1312 Massachusetts Ave. N.W. 20005.

National Council of Catholic Men: A federation of Catholic organizations through which Catholic men may be heard nationally on matters of common interest. NCCM is a constituent of the National Council of Catholic Laity.

The president is William H. Sandweg.

Offices are located at 4712 Randolph Dr., Annandale, Va. 22003.

National Council of Catholic Women: A federation of some 10,000 organizations of Catholic women in the U.S.; founded in 1920. NCCW unites Catholic organizations and individual Catholic women of the U.S., develops their leadership potential, assists them to act upon current issues in the Church and society, provides a medium through which Catholic women may speak and act upon matters of common interest, and relates to other national and international organizations in the solution of present-day problems. It is an affiliate of the World Union of Catholic Women's Organizations.

Mary Helen Madden is the executive director. The official publication is *Catholic Women,* issued 6 times a year.

National office: 1312 Massachusetts Ave. N.W., Washington, D.C. 20005.

National Council of Catholic Laity: Formed in 1971 by the National Council of Catholic Men and the National Council of Catholic Women to provide direction and guidance to existing and new lay organizations. It sponsors conferences and is a contact agency for information about specialized groups in the Church. The publication is *NCCL News.*

The principal officers are Thomas Simmons, president; Isabelle Collora and David Bartkus, vice presidents.

The mailing address is P.O. Box 14525, Cincinnati, Ohio 45214.

National Catholic Rural Life Conference: Founded in 1923 through the efforts of Bishop Edwin V. O'Hara for the purpose of promoting the general welfare of rural people by a program of extensive services, publications and rural-related activities. Publications include the monthly *Catholic Rural Life.*

The conference has approximately 5,000 members among rural pastors, farmers, teachers, sociologists, economists, agricultural agents and officials. There are 110 officially appointed diocesan rural life directors.

Most Rev. Maurice J. Dingman, bishop of Des Moines, Ia., is president. William J. Schaefer, Jr., is the executive director.

National headquarters are located at 4625 N.W. Beaver Dr., Des Moines, Ia. 50322.

Catholic Relief Services—USCC: The official overseas aid and development agency of American Catholics; it is a separately incorporated organization of the U.S. Catholic Conference.

CRS was founded in 1943 by the bishops of the United States to help civilians in Europe and North Africa caught in the disruption and devastation of World War II.

Initially, CRS collected, purchased and shipped to war-torn countries huge quantities of food, clothing, medicines and other relief supplies which were distributed to hundreds of thousands of displaced persons, prisoners of war, bombed-out families, widows, orphans and other war victims.

As conditions in Europe improved in the late 1940s and early 1950s, the works conducted by CRS spread to other continents and areas — Asia, Africa and Latin America.

CRS maintains branch offices in 52 countries around the world and, because of its global network of strategically located warehouse facilities, is able to respond instantaneously to meet the needs of those afflicted by disaster or emergencies. Help is given to all those in need regardless of race, creed, color or political affiliation.

In addition to its highly acclaimed disaster relief work, CRS carries on day-to-day development programs in 86 of the poorest countries of the world. These programs, such as "food for work" projects, nutrition-health projects, school-feeding programs, etc., are designed to help people help themselves and to raise the standards of living not only of the individual but of families and entire communities.

CRS operations are funded, for the most part, from the proceeds of an annual collection — Catholic Relief Services Annual Aid Appeal — held during the Lenten season in more than 18,000 Catholic churches in the U.S. Support is also received from private philanthropic foundations in the U.S., Europe and Australasia. Assistance from the federal government takes three forms: (a) food availabilities under Title II of Public Law 480; (b) defrayment of ocean freight costs on U.S. government-donated foods and all accredited relief supplies generated by CRS itself; and (c) grants for refugee relief and resettlement.

Each year, CRS also sponsors a nationwide clothing collection during the month of November that yields more than 15 million pounds of used clothing, blankets and material remnants.

In the year ending Dec. 31, 1978, the CRS global program in 86 countries had a total value in excess of $280 million.

Most Rev. Edwin B. Broderick, former bishop of Albany, is the executive director.

CRS headquarters are located at 1011 First Ave., New York, N.Y. 10022.

Family Life, USCC Department of Education: Established in 1931 as a central service agency for assisting, developing and coordinating family life programs throughout the United States. It provides information, program models, services and materials for marriage and family life education. It also provides assistance to dioceses in implementing the Plan of Pastoral Action for Family Ministry.

Rev. Donald Conroy is representative for family life in the Department of Education, USCC. Cecilia M. Bennett is staff assistant for the family plan project.

Headquarters are located at 1312 Massachusetts Ave. N.W., Washington, D.C.

SPECIAL APOSTOLATES AND GROUPS

Apostleship of the Sea: An international Catholic organization for the moral, social and spiritual welfare of seafarers and those involved in the maritime industry. It was founded in 1920 in Glasgow, Scotland, and formally approved by the Holy See in 1922. It is promoted and directed by the Pontifical Commission for Migrants and Tourism, Piazza San Calisto 16, Rome, Italy 00153. The U.S. unit is the Apostleship of the Sea in the United States, an affiliate of the NCCB-USCC, established in 1947. It serves 80 port chaplains in 73 U.S. ports on the seacoasts and the Great Lakes. Operations include a hospitality and welcoming program as well as counseling and spiritual services carried on by individual port chaplains through Catholic maritime clubs in New York, N.Y.; Mobile, Ala.; Oakland, San Francisco, and Wilmington, Calif.; Seattle, Wash.; and interfaith clubs located in Chicago, Ill.; Milwaukee, and Green Bay, Wis.; Duluth, Minn.; Cleveland, O.; Newark and Port Elizabeth, N.J.; Norfolk, Va.; Jacksonville and Tampa, Fla.; Houston, Galveston, Corpus Christi and Brownsville, Tex. Recent developments have emphasized the interfaith cooperation on the port level in seamen's ministry. The episcopal promoter of the conference is Most Rev. Rene Gracida, P.O. Drawer 6068, Tallahassee, Fla. 32301. Rev. James P. Keating, port chaplain of Chicago, is national director. The national office is located at 9501 S. Ewing Ave., Chicago, Ill. 60617. Also affiliated with the Apostleship of the Sea in the United States is the **National Catholic Conference for Seafarers.** The president is Rev. Rivers Patout, All Saints Church, 215 E. 10th St., Houston, Tex. 77008.

Auxiliaries of Our Lady of the Cenacle (1878, France): An association of Catholic laywomen, under the direction of the Congregation of Our Lady of the Cenacle, who serve God through their own professions and life styles by means of vows. Members live a fully secular life consecrated according to the spirituality of the Cenacle and pursue individual apostolates. They number approximately 150 throughout the world. U.S. regional director: Sister Agnes Sauer, r.c., P.O. Box 494, Carmichael, Calif. 95608.

Catholic Central Union of America (1855): One of the oldest Catholic lay organizations in the U.S., the Union is devoted to the development and vigor of Christian principles in personal, social, cultural, economic and civic life. It was the first society ever given an official mandate for Catholic Action by a committee of the American bishops, in 1936. A bureau in St. Louis is the center for the separate but coordinated direction of the National Catholic Women's Union. The headquarters is also a publishing house (*Social Justice Review, The Catholic Woman's Journal,* other publications), a library of German-Americana and Catholic Americana, a clearinghouse for information, and a center for works of charity. Aid is given to the missions, and maintenance and direction are provided for St. Elizabeth's Settlement and Day Nursery in St. Louis. Union membership is approximately 15,000. Harvey J. Johnson is director of the Central Bureau located at 3835 Westminster Place, St. Louis, Mo. 63108. (See also: National Catholic Women's Union.)

Catholic Medical Mission Board (1928): Founded by Dr. Paluel Flagg and the Rev. Edward Garesche, S.J. Its purposes are to gather and ship medical supplies, and to recruit and assign medical and paramedical personnel to overseas mission hospitals and dispensaries. Since its foundation, it has shipped approximately 40 million pounds of supplies. In 1978, more than $9 million in medicines were shipped to 1,736 mission distribution centers in 55 countries. Also in 1978, 68 medical volunteers were placed in 14 countries; 17 additional volunteers were similarly assigned during the first three months of 1979. The Rev. Joseph J. Walter, S.J., is the director. Office: 10 W. 17th Street, New York, N.Y. 10011.

Center for Applied Research in the Apostolate (CARA Research Conference Center): A research and development agency in the field of the Church's worldwide religious and social mission. Its purpose is to gather information for the use of decision-makers in evaluating the present status of the Church's mission of service and in planning programs of development toward greater effectiveness of its multiphased ministry in the future. CARA has research and planning programs focused on: church personnel (recruitment, selection training, utilization, effectiveness), overseas areas, diocesan planning, religious life, health care ministry, and other subjects. CARA was incorporated as a non-profit corporation in the District of Columbia Aug. 5, 1964. John V. O'Connor, S.J., is executive director. Offices are located at 3700 Oakview Terrace, N.E., Washington, D.C. 20017.

Christian Family Movement (CFM) (1947): Originating in Chicago and having a membership of married couples and individuals, its purpose is to Christianize family life and create communities conducive to Christian family life. Since 1968, CFM in the U.S. has included couples from all Christian churches. The International Confederation of Christian Family Movements embraces a worldwide membership. National and international headquarters: 2500 New York Ave., P.O. Box 792, Whiting, Ind. 46394. Spanish-speaking, CFM was organized in 1969 under the title **Movimiento Familiar Cristiano (MFC).** Headquarters: 2401 E. Holcombe Blvd., Room 102, Houston, Tex. 77021.

Christian Life Communities: Formerly known as Sodalities of Our Lady, they are groups of men and women, adults and youth, joined with other people involved in living their full Christian vocation and commitment in the world. The governing principles and operating norms of Sodalities, revised in the spirit of documents of the Second Vatican Council, were promulgated and approved by Pope Paul VI in 1971. The Spiritual Exercises of St. Ignatius remain a specific source and characteristic of the spirituality of the movement. Christian Life Communities are located in 42 countries; the U.S. Federation is comprised of approximately 150 communities. Most Rev. Louis Gelineau, bishop of Providence, R.I., is episcopal moderator. National office: 3721 Westminster Blvd., St. Louis, Mo. 63108. The World Federation office is located in Rome.

Cursillo Movement: An instrument of Christian renewal designed to form and stimulate persons to engage in apostolic action individually and in the organized apostolate, in accordance with the mission which individuals have to transform the environments in which they live into Christian environments. The movement originated in Spain, where the first cursillo was held near Palma, Mallorca, in 1949. It was introduced in the U.S. in 1957 and is functioning in more than 120 dioceses. The method of the movement involves a three-day weekend called a cursillo and a follow-up program known as the post-cursillo.

The weekend is an intensive experience in Christian community living centered on Christ and built around 15 talks (10 by laymen, five by priests), active participation in discussions and related activities, the celebration of the liturgy. The follow-up program focuses on small weekly reunions of three to five persons and larger group reunions, called ultreyas, in which participants share experiences and insights derived from their prayer life, study and apostolic action. The movement operates within the framework of diocesan and parish pastoral plans, and functions autonomously in each diocese under the direction of the bishop. Responsibility for growth and effectiveness rests with a diocesan leaders' school, a diocesan secretariat, or both. Most Rev. Joseph Green, former bishop of Reno, is episcopal advisor to the movement. Gerald P. Hughes is coordinator of the National Cursillo Center, P.O. Box 210226, Dallas, Tex. 75211.

Frontier Apostolate (1956): Volunteers for a minimum of two years' service in their professional line (teachers, secretaries, catechists, etc.) in the Diocese of Prince George, British Columbia, Canada. More than 2,000 have served since the start of the corps by Bishop Fergus O'Grady. There are about 160 men and women from 8 different countries actively engaged in works throughout the diocese. Address: Bishop O'Grady, College Rd., P.O. Box 7000, Prince George, B.C., Canada V2N 3Z2.

Grail, The (1921): An international movement of women concerned about the full development of all peoples, working in education, religious, social and cultural areas. Founded by Rev. Jacques van Ginneken, S.J., in The Netherlands, it was introduced in the U.S. in 1940. Grail participants include women from Australia, Belgium, Brazil, Canada, Egypt, France, Germany, Ghana, India, Indonesia, Italy, Japan, The Netherlands, Nigeria, Philippines, Portugal, Scotland, South Africa, Switzerland, Tanzania, Uganda, United States. U.S. headquarters: Grailville, Loveland, Ohio 45140. International Secretariat: 5, Sayed Sokkar St., Matareya, Cairo, Egypt.

Group Seven (1971): Started by the Glenmary Home Missioners to recruit Catholic men and women (married, single, religious, permanent deacon), 21 years of age and older for periods of two years or more in the U.S. home mission apostolate, particularly in the 17-state area of Appalachia, the South and Southeast. Members support themselves in their own profession or trade. They are given orientation and opportunity for ongoing mission training. Address: P.O. Box 1376, Wise, Va. 24293.

International Liaison (1963): A referral, placement and liaison agency for the volunteer lay ministry; an affiliate of the USCC. It was founded by Rev. George Mader in the Archdiocese of Newark and in 1975 was incorporated as the U.S. Catholic Coordinating Center for Lay Volunteer Ministries. It coordinates efforts of laity seeking placement in U.S. or overseas missions. It issues a Newsletter periodically listing personnel needs in mission areas. Matthew Paratore is the executive director. Office: 1234 Massachusetts Ave. N.W., Washington, D.C. 20005.

Jesuit Volunteer Corps: Northwest (1956): Established by the Oregon Province of the Jesuits, for service to the underprivileged. There are 160 volunteers working among Eskimos and Indians in Alaska, on Indian reservations and in inner-city areas in the Northwest. Rev. Lawrence L. Gooley, S.J., is the director. Headquarters: P.O. Box 3928, Portland Ore. 97208.

Lay Mission-Helpers Association (1955): It trains and assigns men and women for work in overseas apostolates for periods of three years. Approximately 550 members of the association have served in overseas assignments since 1955. The Rev. Msgr. Lawrence O'Leary is director of the association. Headquarters: 1531 West Ninth St., Los Angeles, Calif. 90015.

The **Mission Doctors Association** recruits, trains and sends Catholic physicians and their families to mission hospitals and clinics throughout the world for tours of two to three years. Address: 1531 W. Ninth St., Los Angeles, Calif. 90015.

Legion of Mary (1921): Founded in Dublin, its purposes are exclusively spiritual, viz., the sanctification of its members and service to others. It is one of the largest lay organizations in the Church. U.S. address for information: The Legion of Mary, St. Louis Regional Senatus, Box 1313, St. Louis, Mo. 63188. The supreme governing body has offices at De Montfort House, North Brunswick St., Dublin 7, Ireland.

Movement for a Better World (1952): An international movement founded by Rev. Riccardo Lombardi, S.J. Its U.S. contingent of some 20 persons conducts renewal programs with a distinctive communitarian thrust for the purpose of motivating Christian witness and action for making a better world. U.S. and eastern regional office, P.O. Box H, Far Rockaway, N.Y. 11691; western regional office, St. Thomas Seminary, Kenmore, Wash. 98028.

Opus Dei: An association of Catholic faithful who strive to practice the Christian virtues, in their own states in life and through the exercise of their own professions or occupations in order to carry on an apostolate of witness to Christ. Since the purpose is strictly spiritual, members are free to hold the most diverse views on temporal matters, thus assuring a real pluralism of opinions in all cultural, economic, political and similar areas. Founded in Madrid in 1928 by Msgr. Josemaria Escriva de Balaguer (1902-1975), it received full approval from the Holy See June 16, 1950. Membership: more than 70,000 of 80 nationalities from all continents in separate branches for men and women. In the U.S., Opus Dei conducts corporate works in the East, Midwest and on the West Coast. An information office is located at 330 Riverside Dr., New York, N.Y. 10025. Elsewhere, the association conducts universities, training schools for farmers and workers, and numerous educational and charitable centers. The legal names of the association in the U.S. are: Opus Dei; The Work of God, Inc.

Pax Christi (1948): International Catholic

peace movement. Originated in Lourdes, France, as a union of French and German Catholics to symbolize a mutual effort to heal wounds inflicted by World War II, spread to Poland and Italy, and acquired its international title when it merged with the English organization Pax. A general secretariat is located at Antwerp, Belgium. **Pax Christi-USA**, was founded in 1973 to establish peacemaking as a priority for the American Catholic Church, to work for disarmament, amnesty, selective conscientious objection, and to support the United Nations. A newsletter is published quarterly; membership, 2,000. Sr. Mary Evelyn Jegen, S.N.D., is national coordinator. Address: 3000 N. Mango Ave., Chicago, Ill. 60634.

Pax Romana — American Graduate and Professional Commission: The U.S. affiliate of Pax Romana, an international Catholic movement for intellectual and cultural affairs (see Catholic International Organizations). The president is Professor Thomas E. Bird, Queens College, CUNY, Flushing, N.Y. 11367. The Pax Romana representative to the United Nations is the Rev. John A. Radano, Seton Hall University, South Orange, N.J. 07079.

Regis College Lay Apostolate (1950): Founded by Sister Mary John Sullivan, C.S.J., it enlists college graduates for a year of teaching service in home and overseas missions. More than 450 lay apostles from Regis College and more than 400 from other colleges have served since the beginning of the program. Headquarters: Regis College, Weston, Mass. 02193

Southwest Volunteer Apostolate: Recruits and places volunteers for work among the Indians and Spanish-speaking of the Diocese of Gallup. Mailing address: P. O. Box 1338, Gallup, N.M. 87301.

Center of Concern (1972): An independent, public-interest group engaged in analysis, education and advocacy relating to issues of global concern. Discussion is carried on within the framework of social justice. A newsletter, *Center Focus*, is published bimonthly. Peter J. Henriot, S.J., is director. Address: 3700 13th St. N.E., Washington, D.C. 20017.

CATHOLIC YOUTH ORGANIZATIONS

Angelic Warfare Confraternity (Cord of St. Thomas Confraternity) (1649), 141 E. 65th St., New York, N.Y. 10021. Apostolate for preservation of personal chastity; St. Thomas Aquinas is its patron.

Boy Savior Youth Movement (1874): 30 W. 16th St., New York, N.Y. 10011; 18,000 in 35 schools.

Boy Scouts in the Catholic Church: The National Catholic Committee on Scouting works in cooperation with the Boy Scouts of America in promoting the basic principles of Catholicism among one million Catholics among the BSA membership of 4 million. *Boy's Life*. Committee Chairman, Ben M. Hauserman, 5711 Grant Ave., Cleveland, Ohio 44105.

Camp Fire Girls, Inc. (1910): 4601 Madison Ave., Kansas City, Mo. 64112. The Youth Activities representative of the USCC acts as advisor in matters pertaining to Catholic participation in the Camp Fire program. To help young people learn and grow in their individual ways through participation in enjoyable activities. Open to youth up to 21 years of age. Membership: approximately 500,000 (no exact statistics available on number of Catholics participating).

Catholic Youth Organization (CYO): Name of official, parish-centered diocesan Catholic youth programs throughout the country. The National CYO Federation is a constituent member of the Youth Activities section, USCC; 1312 Massachusetts Ave. N.W., Washington, D.C. 20005. CYO promotes a program of spiritual, social and physical activities. The original CYO was organized by Bishop Bernard Sheil of Chicago in 1930.

Columbian Squires (1925): P.O. Drawer 1670, New Haven, Conn. 06507. Junior organization of the Knights of Columbus. To train and develop leadership through active participation in a well-organized program of activities. Membership: 12- to 18-year-old Catholic boys. More than 18,000 in 900 circles (local units) active in the U.S., Canada, Puerto Rico, Mexico and the Philippines. *Squires Newsletter*, monthly.

Forest Rangers and Rangerettes, Catholic Order of Foresters: 305 W. Madison St., Chicago, Ill. 60606. To develop physical, mental and moral lives of members. *Catholic Forester*. Membership: youth up to 16 years of age —approximately 29,860 in 850 subordinate courts in U.S. High Chief Ranger, Louis E. Caron.

Girl Scouts of the U.S.A.: 830 Third Ave., New York, N.Y. 10022. Girls from most archdioceses and dioceses in the U.S. and its possessions participate in Girl Scouting. The Youth Activities section, USCC, cooperates with Girl Scouts of the U.S.A. *Girl Scout Leader; The American Girl; Daisy*. Membership: more than three million (no exact statistics available on number of Catholic girls participating).

Holy Childhood Association (Pontifical Association of the Holy Childhood) (1843): 1234 Massachusetts Ave. N.W., Washington, D.C. 20005 (national office); 800 Allegheny Ave., Pittsburgh, Pa. 15233 (program distribution center). The official children's mission-aid society of the Church; provides assistance to children in 94 mission countries. Furnishes mission education programs and materials to pupils in Catholic elementary schools and religious education programs. *It's Our World*, four times a year. National Director, Rev. Francis W. Wright, C.S.Sp.

Junior Catholic Daughters of the Americas: 10 W. 71st St., New York, N.Y. 10023. A major department of the Catholic Daughters of the Americas. To promote development of the whole person, service to others, spiritual growth. Membership: Teens (15 to 18 years old); Juniors (11 to 14 years old); Juniorettes (6 to 10 years old).

League of Tarcisians of the Sacred Heart (1917): 3 Adams St., Fairhaven, Mass. 02719. Organize children as junior apostles of the Sacred Heart. Director, Rev. Francis Larkin, SS.CC.

National Catholic Forensic League (1952): To develop articulate Catholic leaders through an inter-diocesan program of speech and debate activities. *Newsletter*, quarterly. Membership: 600 schools; membership open to Catholic, private and public schools through the local diocesan league. President (1978-80), Miss Annetterose Callahan, 4159 Canal St., New Orleans, La. 70119.

National Christ Child Society Inc. (1887): 5151 Wisconsin Ave. N.W., Washington, D.C. 20016. Founder, Mary V. Merrick. A welfare organization for the care of underprivileged adults and children. Membership: approximately 10,000 adult and junior members in 29 cities in U.S. President, Mrs. Alfred Walsh.

St. Dominic Savio Club: Don Bosco, Filor's Lane, West Haverstraw, N.Y. 10993. To promote a program of spiritual, intellectual and recreational activities. *Savio Notes*, monthly. Membership: students in grades three through ten — 12,000 members, 375 unit clubs, 62 foreign country units and more than one million in Lay Savio Movement (past Savios) throughout the world.

Young Christian Students: 7436 W. Harrison, Forest Park, Ill. 60130. A student movement for Christian personal and social change. Membership: 500 in high schools and parishes.

Fraternities and Sororities

Alpha Delta Gamma (1924): P.O. Box 54321, Los Angeles, Calif. 90054. Fraternity. *Alphadetity*. Membership: 7,260 in 12 college chapters and 11 alumni associations.

Delta Epsilon Sigma (1939): Belmont Abbey College, Belmont, N.C. 28012. National scholastic honor society for students, faculty and alumni of colleges and universities with a Catholic tradition. Membership: 21,000 in 100 chapters. Secretary, Rev. Dr. Neil W. Tobin.

Kappa Gamma Pi (1926): A national Catholic college women's honor society for graduates who, in addition to academic excellence, have shown outstanding leadership in extra-curricular activities. *Kappa Gamma Pi News*, quarterly. Membership: approximately 16,000 in 123 colleges; 40 alumnae chapters in metropolitan areas. National Moderator, Rev. Cyril F. Meyer, C.M., St. John's Univ., Jamaica, N.Y. 11432. President, Dr. Sally Ann Vonderbrink, 5747 Colerain Ave., Cincinnati, O. 45239.

Phi Kappa Theta: 332 Main St., Worcester, Mass. 01608. National collegiate fraternity with a Catholic heritage. Merger (1959) of Phi Kappa Fraternity, founded at Brown Univ. in 1889, and Theta Kappa Phi Fraternity, founded at Lehigh Univ. in 1919. *The Temple Magazine* quarterly, and newsletter, *The Sun*. Membership: 4,000 undergraduate and 33,000 alumni in 65 collegiate and 25 alumni chapters. Executive Director, Robert L. Wilcox.

Youth Activities, USCC

The Youth Activities section of the Department of Education of the United States Catholic Conference, established in 1940, is a coordinating and service agency for Catholic youth work throughout the country.

The National CYO Federation is the organization within the section which serves diocesan organizations.

USCC Youth Activities maintains liaison with the U.S. Youth Council, the World Assembly of Youth, the World Federation of Catholic Youth and other groups.

Marisa Guerin is the representative for Youth Activities and director of the National Catholic Youth Organization Federation.

Offices are at 1312 Massachusetts Ave. N.W., Washington, D.C. 20005.

PAPAL COUNSEL

Pope John Paul, at Mass Oct. 1, 1979, on the Boston Common, urged young people to exercise an option of love for Christ.

"Do I, then, make a mistake when I tell you, Catholic youth, that it is part of your task in the world and the Church to reveal the true meaning of life where hatred, neglect or selfishness threaten to take over the world? Faced with problems and disappointments, many people will try to escape from their responsibility: escape in selfishness, escape in sexual pleasure, escape in drugs, escape in violence, escape in indifference and cynical attitudes. But today I propose to you the option of love which is the opposite of escape. If you really accept that love from Christ, it will lead you to God. Perhaps in the priesthood or religious life; perhaps in some special service to your brothers and sisters: especially to the needy, the poor, the lonely, the abandoned, those whose rights have been trampled upon, or those whose basic needs have not been provided for. Whatever you make of your life, let it be something that reflects the love of Christ.

ASSOCIATIONS, MOVEMENTS, SOCIETIES IN THE U.S.

(Principal source: Almanac survey.)
See Index for other associations, movements and societies covered elsewhere.

A

Academy of American Franciscan History (1944), Box 34440, Washington, D.C. 20034. Dir., Rev. Alexander Wyse, O.F.M.

Academy of California Church History (1946), P.O. Box 1668, Fresno, Calif. 93717. Pres., Msgr. Denis J. Doherty.

Albertus Magnus Guild (1953). Society of Christian scientists. Pres., Rev. William D. Sullivan, S.J., Boston College, Chestnut Hill, Mass. 02167.

American Benedictine Academy (1947). Scholarly Benedictine society. Pres., Rev. Colman Grabert, O.S.B., St. Meinrad Archabbey, St. Meinrad, Ind. 47577.

American Catholic Correctional Chaplains Association (1952), 275 in 475 institutions. Pres., Rev. Leo F. Trimbur; Sec., Rev. Dismas Boeff, O.S.B., 2900 East Blvd., Cleveland, O. 44104.

American Catholic Historical Association (1919), Catholic University of America, Washington, D.C. 20064. *The Catholic Historical Review*, quarterly. Sec., Rev. Robert Trisco.

American Catholic Philosophical Association (1926), Catholic University of America, Washington, D.C. 20064; 1,400. *New Scholasticism*, quarterly, *Proceedings*, annually. Nat. Sec., George F. McLean, O.M.I.

American Committee on Italian Migration (1952), 373 Fifth Ave., New York, N.Y. 10016; 6,000. *ACIM Newsletter*, 6 times a year. Sec., Rev. Joseph A. Cogo, C.S.

American Society of Mature Catholics (1962), 1100 W. Wells St., Milwaukee, Wis. 53223; 6,100 members. Organization for economic advantage, social activities and apostolic work for retired persons. Pres., Merlin Victora.

Ancient Order of Hibernians in America, Inc. (1836); 120,000. *National Hibernian Digest*, bimonthly. Nat. Pres., Thomas D. McNabb; Nat. Sec., John W. Duffy, c/o P.O. Box 700, Riverdale Station, Bronx, N.Y. 10471.

Apostleship of Prayer (1849-France; 1861-U.S.): 114 E. 13th St., New York, N.Y. 10003. *Monthly Leaflet*, 1,200,000. Promotes Daily Offering and Sacred Heart devotion.

Apostolate for Family Consecration (1975), The House of St. Joseph, Box 220, Kenosha, Wis. 53141; 4,800 members. Family reinforcement by transforming neighborhoods into God-centered communities.

Apostolate of Christian Action, P.O. Box 24, Fresno, Calif. 93707. *Divine Love*, quarterly.

Archconfraternity of Christian Mothers (Christian Mothers) (1881), 220 37th St., Pittsburgh, Pa. 15201; over 3,400 branches. Monthly newsletter and quarterly bulletin. Dir., Rev. Bertin Roll, O.F.M. Cap.

Archconfraternity of Our Lady of Perpetual Help and St. Alphonsus (1871), 526 59th St., Brooklyn, N.Y. 11220. 1,250 branches.

Archconfraternity of Perpetual Adoration (1893), St. John's Abbey, Collegeville, Minn. 56321. Dir. Gen., Rt. Rev. John Eidenschink, O.S.B.

Archconfraternity of the Holy Ghost (1912), Holy Ghost Preparatory School, Cornwells Heights, Pa. 19020 (U.S. headquarters). Nat. Dir., Very Rev. Henry J. Brown, C.S.Sp.

Association for Religious and Value Issues in Counseling (1962), division of American Personnel and Guidance Association, 1607 New Hampshire Ave., N.W., Washington, D.C. 20009. 868 members; *Counseling and Values*, and *Newsletter*, quarterlies. Pres., Sr. Therese M. Roberts, 308 14th Ave. N.E., Ft. Lauderdale, Fla. 33301.

Association for Social Economics (formerly the Catholic Economic Association) (1941), De Paul University, 25 E. Jackson Blvd., Chicago, Ill. 60604; 1,200. *Review of Social Economy*, triannually.

Association for the Sociology of Religion (formerly the American Catholic Sociological Society) (1938), Loyola University of Chicago, 6525 N. Sheridan Rd., Chicago, Ill. 60626. *Sociological Analysis*, quarterly. Exec. Sec., Robert McNamara.

Association of Catholic Trade Unionists (1937), 58 Washington Square South, New York, N.Y. 10012. Exec. Sec., John C. Donohue.

Association of Marian Helpers (1946), Stockbridge, Mass. 01262; 695,000, mostly in U.S. *The Marian Helpers Bulletin*, quarterly.

Association of Romanian Catholics of America (1948), 4309 Olcott Ave., E. Chicago, Ind. 46312.

B

Blue Army of Our Lady of Fatima (1946), Ave Maria Institute, Washington, N.J. 07882; worldwide membership. *Soul*, bimonthly. Pres., Most Rev. Joao Pereira Venancio, former bishop of Leiria (Fatima), Portugal. U.S. Pres., Msgr. Charles B. Murphy.

C

Calix Society (1947), 7601 Wayzata Blvd., Minneapolis, Minn. 55426; 2,000 members in U.S. and Canada; *Chalice*, monthly. Association of Catholic alcoholics maintaining their sobriety through affiliation with and participation in Alcoholics Anonymous. Dir., R. D. Dickinson.

Campaign for Surplus Rosaries and the **Mid-America Rosary Museum** (1948), 1821

W. Short 17th St., North Little Rock, Ark. 72114. Collect rosaries and religious articles for free distribution to the poor throughout the world. Lay Internatl. Chairman, P. Marion Chudy, S.F.O.

Canon Law Society of America (1939), 1933 Spielbusch Ave., Toledo, O. 43624. To further research and study in canon law; 1,500. Exec. Coord., Rev. Donald E. Heintschel.

Cardinal Mindszenty Foundation (CMF) (1958), P.O. Box 11321, St. Louis, Mo. 63105. To combat communism with knowledge and facts. Exec. Sec., Eleanor Schlafly.

Catholic Aid Association (1878), 49 W. Ninth St., St. Paul, Minn. 55102; 78,000. *Catholic Aid News*, monthly. Fraternal life insurance society. Pres., F. L. Spanner.

Catholic Alliance for Communications (formerly Catholic Institute of the Press, 1944), 1011 First Ave., New York, N.Y. 10022. To foster Christian principles and action among working members of the communications fields. Pres., Thomas A. Brennan.

Catholic Alumni Clubs International (1957), To advance social, cultural and spiritual well-being of members. Membership limited to single Catholics with professional education; 7,000 in 50 clubs in U.S. and Canada. International Pres., Frances M. McDonald. Chaplain, Rev. David Sauter, S.J., Georgetown Preparatory School, Rockville, Md. 20852.

Catholic Apostolate of Radio, Television and Advertising (1954), 1011 First Ave., New York, N.Y. 10022; 1,700 in New York City. Pres., John Curran.

Catholic Audio-Visual Educators Association (CAVE) (1953), Pres., Rev. Joseph Breslin, Cardinal O'Hara High School, Eagle and Spoul Rds., Springfield, Pa. 19064.

Catholic Bible Society of America, Inc. (1957), P.O. Box 2296, Dallas, Tex. 75221. Place Bibles in hospitals of Diocese of Dallas and elsewhere. Pres. Mrs. James S. Adams.

Catholic Biblical Association of America (1936), Catholic University of America, Washington, D.C. 20064; 915. *The Catholic Biblical Quarterly*. Pres., Rev. Carroll Stuhlmueller, C.P.

Catholic Big Brothers, Inc. (of Archdiocese of New York) (1918), 1011 First Ave., New York, N.Y. 10022; Newsletter, quarterly. To provide opportunities for male identification to fatherless boys, 8-15 years of age, through services of qualified adult male volunteers.

Catholic Big Sisters, Inc. (of the Archdiocese of New York), 60 Lafayette St., New York, N.Y. 10013. Voluntary organization providing adjunctive services to Family Court, for girls up to 16 and boys up to 10 years of age. Dir., Hortense Baffa.

Catholic Business Education Association (1945). 2,001. Vice-Pres., Sister Mary Matthew McCloskey, R.S.M., Box 1169, Vicksburg, Miss. 39180.

Catholic Commission on Intellectual and Cultural Affairs (CCICA) (1946), 620 Michigan Ave. N.E., Washington, D.C. 20064; 290. Exec. Dir., Rev. William J. Rooney.

Catholic Committee on Urban Ministry (1967), Notre Dame, Ind. 46556. To support social ministry throughout the country. Dir., Sr. Helen C. Volkomener, S.P.

Catholic Conference on Ethnic and Neighborhood Affairs (1974): 1521 16th St. N.W., Washington, D.C. 20036. Network of Catholic priests, religious and laity working for cultural justice within the church and society. Dir., Bro. Ronald Pasquariello, F.M.S.

Catholic Daughters of the Americas (1903), 10 W. 71st St., New York, N.Y. 10023; 180,000. *Share Magazine*. Nat. Regent, Miss Mary Murray.

Catholic Evidence Guild (1918, in England; 1931, in US), c/o 127 W. 31st St., New York, N.Y. 10001. Lay movement for spread of Catholic truth by means of outdoor speaking.

Catholic Family Life Insurance (1868), 1572 E. Capitol Dr., Milwaukee, Wis. 53211; 45,000. *The Family Friend*, quarterly. Pres., David L. Springob.

Catholic Family Missionary Alliance (1977), Our Lady of the Angels Monastery, 5817 Old Leeds Rd., Birmingham, Ala. 35210. Dir., Mother M. Angelica, P.C.P.A.

Catholic Golden Age: Scranton Life Bldg., Scranton, Pa. 18503; 500,000. *CGA Newsletter*, bimonthly. Assist Catholics over 50 years of age in their religious and secular needs.

Catholic Guardian Society (1913), 1011 First Ave., New York, N.Y. 10022. Exec. Dir., James P. O'Neill.

Catholic Home Bureau for Dependent Children (1898), 1011 First Ave., New York, N.Y. 10022. Exec. Dir., Sr. M. Una McCormack.

Catholic Interracial Council of New York, Inc. (1934), 225 E. 52nd St., New York, N.Y. 10022. Sponsors educational programs and publications on Christian principles in intergroup relations; Newsletter, quarterly. Exec. Dir., John J. Garra.

Catholic Interracial Councils: See National Catholic Conference for Interracial Justice.

Catholic Knights of America (1877), 217 E. 8th St., Cincinnati, O. 45202; 19,560. *Catholic Knights of America Journal*, monthly. Fraternal insurance society.

Catholic Knights of St. George (1881), 709 Brighton Rd., Pittsburgh, Pa. 15233; 67,000. *Knight of St. George*, bimonthly. Fraternal insurance society. Pres., Joseph J. Miller.

Catholic Kolping Society (1923), 2003 Wintergreen Ave., Mt. Prospect, Ill. 60056. *Kolping Banner*, monthly. Fraternal society.

Catholic Lawyers' Guild. Organization usually on a diocesan basis, under different titles.

Catholic League (1943), 1200 N. Ashland Ave., Chicago, Ill. 60622. Exec. Dir., Most Rev. Alfred Abramowicz.

Catholic Library Association (1921), 461

W. Lancaster Avenue, Haverford, Pa., 19041; 3,640. *Catholic Library World,* monthly (Sept.-April), bimonthly (May-June, July-Aug.); *Catholic Periodical and Literature Index.* Pres., Sr. Franz Lang, O.P., Exec. Dir., Matthew R. Wilt.

Catholic Near East Welfare Association (Near East Missions) (1926), 1011 First Ave., New York, N.Y. 10022. *Near East Missions,* weekly column in 132 diocesan and four national newspapers. Aids missionary activity in 18 countries (under jurisdiction of the Sacred Congregation for the Oriental Church) in Europe, Africa and Asia, including the Holy Land. Nat. Sec., Rev. Msgr. John G. Nolan.

Catholic Negro-American Mission Board (1907), 335 Broadway, Room 1102, New York, N.Y. 10013; 15,000. *Educating in Faith,* bimonthly. Dir., Rev. Benjamin M. Horton, S.S.J.

Catholic One Parent Organization (COPO): To give widows and widowers an opportunity to meet others in the same situation, blending social and spiritual programs. Organized in various dioceses.

Catholic Order of Foresters (1883), 305 W. Madison St., Chicago, Ill. 60606; 170,535 in 28 states. *The Catholic Forester,* bimonthly. Fraternal insurance society. High Chief Ranger, Louis E. Caron.

Catholic Pamphlet Society (1938), 2171 Fillmore Ave., Buffalo, N.Y. 14214. Parish pamphlet rack distributors. Dir., Rev. Msgr. Paul T. Cronin.

Catholic Peace Fellowship (1964), North Broadway, Upper Nyack, N.Y. 10960; 6,500, *CPF Bulletin.* Peace education and action, development of the pacifist tradition within the Catholic Church. Nat. Sec., Thomas C. Cornell.

Catholic Press Association of the U.S., Inc. (1911), 119 N. Park Ave., Rockville Centre, N.Y. 11570. *The Catholic Journalist* monthly; *Catholic Press Directory,* annually. Pres., Ethel M. Gintoft, Exec. Dir., James A. Doyle.

Catholic Theological Society of America (1946), Office of Secretary, St. Mary of the Lake Seminary, Mundelein, Ill. 60060; 1,150. *Proceedings,* annually. Pres., Rev. William J. Hill, O.P. (1979-80).

Catholic Traditionalist Movement (1964), 210 Maple Ave., Westbury, N.Y. 11590.

Catholic Truth Society (1922), 2816 E. Burnside St., Portland, Ore. 97214.

Catholic Union of the Sick in America, Inc. (CUSA) (1947), 63 Wall St., New York, N.Y. 10005 (legal office); 1,200. Admin. Leader, Miss Anna Marie Sopko, 176 W. 8th St., Bayonne, N.J. 07002 (national central office).

Catholic War Veterans (1935), 2 Massachusetts Ave. N.W., Washington, D.C. 20001; 1,500 posts, *Catholic War Veteran,* bimonthly.

Catholic Worker Movement (1933), 36 E. First St., New York, N.Y. 10003. *The Catholic Worker,* 9 times a year. Lay apostolate founded by Peter Maurin and Dorothy Day; has Houses of Hospitality in 29 U.S. cities and several communal farms in various parts of the country. Promotes pacifism and anarchism in that it is decentralist, and believes in what the popes have termed the principle of subsidiarity, urging decentralization in the school system, community control, and in the economic field credit unions, cooperatives and unions of workers and mutual aid.

Catholic Workman (Katolicky Delnik) (1891), New Prague, Minn. 56071; 18,023. *Catholic Workman,* monthly. Fraternal and insurance society. Pres. Rudy G. Faimon.

Catholic Writers' Guild of America (1919), 65 East 89th St., New York, N.Y. 10028. Exec. Sec., Rev. Bernard J. McMahon.

Catholics United for the Faith (1968), 222 North Ave., New Rochelle, N.Y. 10801; 13,000 in U.S. and Canada; *CUF Newsletter,* monthly. Lay apostolate founded in response to Vatican II's call to the laity. Pres., H. Lyman Stebbins.

Center for Pastoral Liturgy (1975), Catholic University of America, Washington, D.C. 20064. Concerned with promotion of pastoral-liturgical action in the U.S.; sponsors programs, publications, conferences, and workshops oriented toward the service of local churches. Dir., Rev. G. Thomas Ryan.

Central Association of the Miraculous Medal (1915), 475 E. Chelten Ave., Philadelphia, Pa. 19144. *Miraculous Medal,* quarterly. Dir., Rev. Robert P. Cawley.

Chaplains' Aid Association, Inc. (1917), 1011 First Ave., New York, N.Y. 10022. Pres., Most Rev. Philip J. Furlong.

Christopher Movement (1945), 12 E. 48th St., New York, N.Y. 10017. Without formal organization or meetings, the movement stimulates personal initiative and responsible action in line with Christian principles, particularly in the fields of education, government, industrial relations and communications. Christopher radio and TV programs are broadcast by 2,000 stations; 700,000 copies of *Christopher News Notes* are distributed seven times a year without subscription fee; 360 weekly and 19 daily newspapers carry Christopher columns. Dir., Rev. John Catoir.

Citizens for Educational Freedom (1959): Nonsectarian group concerned with non-public education. National office: Suite 854 Washington Bldg., 15th St. and New York Ave. N.W., Washington, D.C. 20005.

Confraternity of the Immaculate Conception of Our Lady of Lourdes (1874), Box 561, Notre Dame, Ind. 46556. Distributors of Lourdes water.

Confraternity of the Most Holy Rosary: See Rosary Altar Society.

Convert Movement Our Apostolate

(CMOA) (1945), formerly Convert Makers of America, c/o Our Lady of Grace Rectory, 430 Avenue W, Brooklyn, N.Y. 11223. *Bulletin* quarterly. To train and assist lay persons on a parish level to discuss and present the Faith to interested persons on a one-to-one basis.

Crusade for a More Fruitful Preaching and Hearing of the Word of God, Inc. (1937), Allendale, N.J. 07401; *Voices from the Pew*, 2 times a year for seminarians. Pres., Mrs. Barbara Durbin.

Czech Catholic Union of Texas (K.J.T.) (1889), 214 Colorado St., La Grange, Tex. 78945; 15,833. *Nasinec*, weekly, and *K. J. T. News*, monthly. Fraternal and insurance society. Pres., Amos Pavlik.

D

Damien-Dutton Society for Leprosy Aid, Inc. (1944), 616 Bedford Ave., Bellmore, N.Y. 11710; 25,000. *Damien Dutton Call*, quarterly. Provides medicine, rehabilitation and research for conquest of leprosy. Pres., Howard E. Crouch, Dir., Sr. Mary Augustine, S.M.S.M.

Daughters of Isabella (1897), 375 Whitney Ave., New Haven, Conn. 06511; 120,000. International Regent, Mrs. Martine O. Ward.

E

Edith Stein Guild, Inc. (1955), Promotes Judaeo-Christian understanding and assists Jewish converts; 860. ESG *Newsletter*. Address, Church of Our Lady of Victory, 60 William St., New York, N.Y. 10006.

Enthronement of the Sacred Heart in the Home (1907), 3 Adams St., Fairhaven, Mass. 02719; over 2,500,000. Nat. Dir., Rev. Francis Larkin, SS.CC.

Eucharistic Guard for Nocturnal Adoration (1938), 800 North Country Club Rd., Tucson, Ariz. 85716.

Eymard League (1948), 194 E. 76 St., New York, N.Y. 10021; approximately 26,000. *Eymard League Bulletin*, quarterly. Nat. Dir., Rev. Ralph A. Lavigne, S.S.S.

F

Families for Christ (1977), 6026 W. Harwood Ave., Orlando, Fla., 32811; 7,500. Promote social reign of Christ. Pres., Albert Barone.

Family Communion Crusade, Inc. (1950), 194 E. 76th St., New York, N.Y. 10021. Exec. Dir., Rev. Hector C. Lemieux, S.S.S.

Family Rosary Crusade (1942), **Crusade for Family Prayer**, and **Families for Prayer** 773 Madison Ave., Albany, N.Y. 12208. Dir., Rev. Patrick Peyton, C.S.C.

Federation of Diocesan Liturgical Commissions (FDLC) (1969), 1307 S. Wabash, Chicago, Ill. 60605. Association of liturgical commission personnel for assisting and coordinating efforts in liturgical renewal. *FDLC Newsletter*. Administrator, Rev. Carl A. Last.

Fellowship of Catholic Scholars (1977), St. John's University, Jamaica, N.Y. 11439; 400 members. Interdisciplinary research and publications of Catholic scholars in accord with the magisterium of the Catholic Church. Pres., Prof. J. Hitchcock; Exec. Sec., Msgr. George A. Kelly.

First Catholic Slovak Ladies' Association, USA (1892), 24950 Chagrin Blvd., Beachwood, Ohio 44122; 105,000. *Fraternally Yours*, monthly. Fraternal insurance society. Pres., Louise M. Yash.

First Catholic Slovak Union (Jednota) (1890), 3289 E. 55th St., Cleveland, Ohio 44127; 115,097. *Jednota*, weekly. Exec. Sec., Stephen F. Ungvarsky.

First Friday Clubs (1936). Organized on local basis; about 90 clubs in US, others elsewhere. Objectives are to spread devotion to the Sacred Heart, encourage members to receive Holy Communion on First Fridays and to meet at breakfast, luncheon or dinner for discussions of Catholic interest.

Franciscan Apostolate of the Way of the Cross (1949), 174 Ramsey St., Paterson, N.J. 07501. Stations Crucifix available on request. Dir., Rev. Cassian J. Kirk, O.F.M.

Friendship House (1938), 343 S. Dearborn, Room 317, Chicago, Ill. 60604. *Community*, quarterly. Work for social justice through nonviolence. Assist prisoners; locate daily employment for day labor workers; promote educational activities related to nonviolence and simple living. Co-directors, Pat Caraher and Kevin Reed.

G

Gabriel Richard Institute (1949), 2315 Orleans Ave., Detroit, Mich. 48207. Conducts leadership technique courses in 18 dioceses.

Gelasian Guild (1976), Association of Catholic attorneys working with the USCC; concerned with scholarly study of legal questions affecting Church-state relations. Pres., Rev. Charles Whelan, S.J. Mailing address: James A. Serritella, Secretary-Treasurer, P.O. Box 4993, Chicago, Ill. 60680.

Gregorian Institute of America (1942), 7404 S. Mason Ave., Chicago, Ill. 60638. Pres., Edward J. Harris.

Guard of Honor of the Immaculate Heart of Mary (1932), 135 West 31st St., New York, N.Y. 10001. An archconfraternity approved by the Holy See whose members cultivate devotion to the Blessed Virgin Mary, particularly through a daily Guard Hour of Prayer.

Guild of Catholic Lawyers (1928), Empire State Bldg., 350 Fifth Ave., Room 316, New York, N.Y. 10001; 600. Pres., Joseph T. Gatti.

Guild of Our Lady of Ransom (1948), c/o St. Timothy's Rectory, 650 Nichols St., Norwood, Mass. 02062. For aid to inmates, former inmates and families of inmates of prisons in the Boston archdiocese. Exec. Dir. and Treas., Rev. Joseph P. McDermott.

Guild of St. Paul (1937), 601 Hill'n Dale, Lexington, Ky. 40503; 13,542; Nat. Spir. Dir., Rev. Msgr. Leonard Nienaber; Pres., Robert Parks.

H

Holy Name Society (in US) (1909), 141 E. 65th St., New York, N.Y. 10021; 5,000,000. Promote reverence for and devotion to the Holy Name of Jesus and develop lay apostolate programs in line with renewal aims of the Second Vatican Council, Nat. Dir., Rev. Brendan Larnen, O.P.

Holy Name Society, National Association (NAHNS) (1970), 516 N. Front St., Minersville, Pa. 17954. Association of diocesan and parochial Holy Name Societies. Exec. Sec., Stephen Andrusisian.

Hungarian Catholic League of America, Inc. (1945), 32 E. 30th St., New York, N.Y. 10016. Member of the National Catholic Resettlement Council. *Catholic Hungarian Sunday*, weekly. Pres., Rev. Msgr. John S. Sabo.

I

Illinois Club for Catholic Women (1920), 720 North Michigan, Chicago, Ill., 60611. *Triune-News*, monthly. Pres., Mrs. Lydon Wild.

Institute on Religious Life (1974), 4200 N. Austin Ave., Chicago, Ill. 60634; 350 members. *Consecrated Life*, irregularly; *Religious Life*, quarterly. To foster more effective understanding and implementation of teachings of the magisterium on religious life. Pres., Most Rev. James J. Hogan.

International Institute of the Heart of Jesus (1972), 7700 Blue Mound Rd., Milwaukee Wis. 53213 (corporate headquarters); 14 Borgo Angelico, 00193 Rome, Italy (executive offices). Promote awareness and appreciation of the mystery of the Heart of Christ and establish an international forum for the apostolate. Pres., Harry G. John.

Italian Catholic Federation of California, Central Council (1924), 1801 Van Ness Ave., San Francisco, Calif. 94109; 30,000; *Bollettino*, monthly. Sec., Armand De Martini.

J

John Carroll Society, The (1951), 1666 K St. N.W., Washington, D.C. 20006. Pres. Martin J. McNamara, Esq., Sec., Hon. Howard T. Markey.

Judean Society, Inc., The (1966), 1075 Space Park Way No. 336, Mt. View, Calif. 94043; over 800. International organization for divorced Catholic women. Self-help, mutual-help counseling groups. Foundress/Internatl., Dir., Frances A. Miller.

K

Knights of Peter Claver (1909), 1825 Orleans Ave., New Orleans, La. 70116; 17,000. *The Claverite*, bimonthly. Fraternal and aid society. Sup. Knight, M. J. Frank.

Knights of St. John, Supreme Commandery (1886), 6517 Charles Ave., Parma, O. 44129; Sup. Sec., Brig. Gen. Salvatore La Bianca.

Knights of St. John, Supreme Ladies' Auxiliary (1900), Cheektowaga, N.Y. 14225; 15,000.

Knights of the Immaculata (Militia Immaculatae, M.I.) (1917), National Center, 1600 W. Park Ave., Libertyville, Ill. 60048; canonically established with international headquarters in Rome. A pious association for evangelization and catechesis beginning with members' own inner renewal, under the patronage of the Blessed Virgin Mary.

L

Ladies of Charity of the United States, Association of (1960), 7806 Natural Bridge Rd., P.O. Box 5730, St. Louis, Mo. 63121; 40,000. International Association founded by St. Vincent de Paul in 1617. Pres., Mrs. A. J. Mayer, 5339 N. Santa Monica Blvd., Milwaukee, Wis. 53217.

League of St. Dymphna, National Shrine of St. Dymphna, 3000 Erie St. S., Box 4, Massillon, Ohio 44646. Director, Rev. M. M. Herttna.

Lithuanian Groups: Ateitininkai (1907), 1443 S. 50th Ave., Cicero, Ill. 60658; to promote Lithuanian Catholic action; Pres., Dr. Petras Kisielius. Lithuanian Catholic Alliance (1889), 73 S. Washington St., Wilkes-Barre, Pa. 18701; 147 branches; *Garsas*, monthly; fraternal insurance organization; Pres., Thomas E. Mack. Lithuanian Roman Catholic Federation of America (1906), 8761 W. Outer Dr., Detroit, Mich. 48219; umbrella organization for Lithuanian parishes and organizations; Pres., Prof Justinas Pikunas. Four organizations with offices at 351 Highland Blvd., Brooklyn, N.Y. 11207 — Knights of Lithuania (1913), educational-fraternal association; Pres., Philip Skabeikis. Lithuanian American Catholic Services (1975); religious, educational, research and service association; Exec. Dir., Rev. Casimir Pugevicius. Lithuanian Catholic Religious Aid, Inc. (1961); to assist persecuted Catholics in Lithuania; Pres., Most Rev. Vincent Brizgys. Lithuanian Roman Catholic Priests' League (1909); religious-professional association; Pres., Rev. Zenonas Smilga.

Little Flower Mission League (1957), P.O. Box 25, Plaucheville, La. 71362. Sponsored by the Brothers of the Holy Eucharist.

Little Flower Society (1923), 11343 S. Michigan Ave., Chicago, Ill. 60628; 40,000, *Little Flower News*, monthly. Nat. Dir., Rev. Quentin Duncan, O. Carm.

Liturgical Conference, The, 810 Rhode Island Ave. N.E., Washington, D.C. 20018. *Liturgy, Living Worship, Homily Service.* Education, research and publication programs for renewing and enriching Christian liturgical life. Pres., Sr. Mary Collins, O.S.B.

Loyal Christian Benefit Association (1890), 305 W. 6th St., Erie, Pa. 16512; 56,623. *The Fraternal Leader,* bimonthly. Pres., Miss Bertha M. Leavy.

M

Marian Movement of Priests, Nat. Dir., Rev. Albert G. Roux, P.O. Box 8, St. Francis, Me. 04774.

Mariological Society of America (1949), Marian Library, University of Dayton, Dayton, O. 45469: 350. *Marian Studies,* annually.

Markham Prayer Card Apostolate (Apostolate To Aid the Dying) (1931), Franciscan Sisters of the Poor, 60 Compton Rd., Cincinnati, Ohio 45215. Dir., Rev. Herman H. Kenning.

Maryheart Crusaders, The (1964), 22 Button St., Meriden, Conn. 06450; 1,500. *The Maryheart Crusader,* 4 times a year. To reunite fallen-away Catholics and promote religious education for adults. Pres., Louise D'Angelo.

Men of the Sacred Hearts (1964), Shrine of the Sacred Heart, Harleigh, Pa. 18225; 2,500. *From the Hearts* (newsletter), quarterly. Promote enthronement of Sacred Heart.

Missionary Association of Catholic Women (1916), 1425 N. Prospect Ave., Milwaukee, Wis. 53202. Pres., Mrs. Joseph Gockel.

Missionary Cenacle Apostolate (M.C.A.) (1909), 3501 Solly Ave., Philadelphia, Pa. 19136; 1,500. Lay prayer and action community affiliated with Cenacle.

Missionary Vehicle Association, Inc. (MIVA), 514 Allegheny River Blvd., P.O. Box 63, Oakmont, Pa. 15139. To raise funds to provide vehicles of all types to missionaries in need. Nat. Dir., Rev. Leonard J. Tuozzolo, S.S.Sp.

Morality in Media, Inc. (1962), 475 Riverside Dr., New York, N.Y. 10027; 50,000 members. Newsletter, 8 times a year. To stop traffic in pornography constitutionally and effectively, and promote principles of love, truth and taste in the media. Pres., Rev. Morton A. Hill, S.J.

N

National Alliance of Czech Catholics (1917), 2657-59 S. Lawndale Ave., Chicago, Ill. 60623; 450 parishes. Pres., Mrs. Mildred R. Janda.

National Association of Church Personnel Administrators (1973), 426 E. 5th St., Cincinnati, O. 45202. Pres., Rev. Philip Seher. Exec. Dir., Sr. Sheila McEvoy, S.N.J.M.

National Association of Diocesan Ecumenical Officers, Pres., Rev. Alex J. Brunett, 17500 Farmington Rd., Livonia, Mich. 48152.

National Association of Pastoral Musicians (1976), 1029 Vermont Ave. N.W., Washington, D.C. 20005; 7,000. *Pastoral Music,* six times a year. For clergy and musicians. Pres. and Exec. Dir., Rev. Virgil C. Funk.

National Association of Priest Pilots (1964), Pres., Rev. John Hemann, 1701 Mulberry St., Waterloo, Iowa 50703.

National Catholic Bandmasters' Association (1953), Box 523, Notre Dame University, Notre Dame, Ind. 46556. *The School Musician Magazine.*

National Catholic Cemetery Conference (1949), 710 N. River Rd., Des Plaines, Ill. 60016. *The Catholic Cemetery,* monthly. Pres., Rev. Msgr. Joseph F. Rebman.

National Catholic Conference for Interracial Justice (1960), 1200 Varnum St. N.E., Washington, D.C. 20017. *Commitment,* bimonthly. Serves 150 Catholic human relations and urban affairs groups; sponsors education and action programs on societal problems. Exec. Dir., Msgr. Aloysius Welsh.

National Catholic Development Conference (1968), 119 N. Park Ave., Rockville Centre, N.Y. 11570. Professional association of organizations and individuals engaged in raising funds for Catholic charitable activities. Pres., Rev. James J. Close; Exec. Dir., George T. Holloway.

National Catholic Disaster Relief Committee, 1346 Connecticut Ave. N.W., Suite 307, Washington, D.C. 20036.

National Catholic Pharmacists Guild of the United States (1962), 400 members; *The Catholic Pharmacist.* Exec. Dir., John P. Winkelmann, 1012 Surrey Hills Dr., St. Louis, Mo. 63117.

National Catholic Society of Foresters (1891), 35 E. Wacker, Chicago, Ill. 60601; 76,693; *National Catholic Forester,* bimonthly. A fraternal insurance society. Pres., Mrs. Dolores M. Johnson.

National Catholic Stewardship Council (1962), 1234 Massachusetts Ave. N.W., Washington, D.C. 20005. To promote the biblical concept of total Christian stewardship in the contemporary Church. Exec. Dir. Rev. James M. Mackey.

National Catholic Women's Union (1916), 3835 Westminster Pl., St. Louis, Mo. 63108; 16,000. *The Catholic Woman's Journal,* 10 times a year.

National Center for Urban Ethnic Affairs (1971): 1521 16th St. N.W., Washington, D.C. 20036. To continue the expression of the Church's concern for problems of urban society. An affiliate of the USCC. Pres., Dr. John A. Kromkowski.

National Church Goods Association, 1114 Greenfield Lane, Mt. Prospect. 60056. Pres., Jack Carmody.

National Clergy Conference on Alcoholism, 3112-7th St. N.E., Washington, D.C. 20017. Exec. Dir., Rev. James J. Powderly.

National Conference of Religious Vocations

Directors of Men (NCRVDM), 22 W. Monroe St., Chicago, Ill. 60603.

National Federation of Catholic Physicians' Guilds (1927), 850 Elm Grove, Suite 11, Elm Grove, Wis. 53122; 6,700 in 88 autonomous guilds in U.S. and Canada, *Linacre Quarterly*. Pres., Eugene Diamond, M.D.

National Federation of Spiritual Directors (1970). Pres., Rev. Robert B. Sidner, St. Meinrad Seminary College, St. Meinrad, Ind. 47577.

National Guild of Catholic Psychiatrists, Inc. (1949). Integration of psychiatry and Roman Catholic theology. *The Bulletin*. Pres. (1976-1979), Sr. Anna Polcino, M.D., 120 Hill St., Whitinsville, Mass. 01588.

National Organization for Continuing Education of Roman Catholic Clergy, Inc. (1973). Membership, 107 dioceses, 62 religious provinces, 27 affiliated institutions. Pres., Rev. Robert M. Schwartz, 212 N. Moore, St. Paul, Minn. 55104.

Network (1971), 1029 Vermont Ave. N.W., Washington, D.C. 20005. Religious legislative lobby group on social justice.

Nocturnal Adoration Society of the United States (1882), 194 E. 76th St., New York, N.Y. 10021; 57,000 in 528 units. Nat. Dir., Rev. Hector C. Lemieux, S.S.S.

O

Order of the Alhambra (1904), 4200 Leeds Ave., Baltimore, Md. 21229. 11,000 in U.S. and Canada. Fraternal society dedicated to assisting retarded children. Supreme Commander, Robert T. Pastel.

P

Paulist League (1924), 415 W. 59th St., New York, N.Y. 10019; 23,700. Dir., Rev. Donald C. Campbell.

Philangeli (Friends of the Angels) (1949 in England; 1956 in U.S.), Viatorian Fathers, 1115 E. Euclid St., Arlington Heights, Ill. 60004; approximately 750,000 in 60 countries. To encourage devotion to the angels.

Pious Union of Prayer (1898), St. Joseph's Home, P.O. Box 288, Jersey City, N.J. 07303; 65,000. *St. Joseph's Messenger and Advocate of the Blind*, quarterly.

Pious Union of the Holy Spirit (1900), 30 Gedney Park Dr., White Plains, N.Y. 10605. Pres., Rev. Jerome McHugh, O.F.M. Cap.

Pontifical Mission for Palestine (1949), c/o Catholic Near East Welfare Association, 1011 First Ave., New York, N.Y. 10022. Field offices in Beirut, Lebanon, Jerusalem and Amman, Jordan. The papal relief agency for 1.5 million Palestinian refugees in Lebanon, Syria, Jordan, and the Gaza Strip. Distributes food, clothing, other essentials; maintains medical clinics, orphanages, libraries, refugee camp schools and chapels, the Pontifical Mission Center for the Blind (Gaza), the Pontifical Mission Libraries (Jerusalem, Bethlehem, Nazareth), the Epheta Institute for Deaf-Mutes (Bethlehem). Pres., Rev. Msgr. John G. Nolan.

Pontifical Missionary Union in the USA (1936), 366 Fifth Ave., New York, N.Y. 10001; *Worldmission*, quarterly. Nat. Dir., Most Rev. Edward T. O'Meara.

Priests' Eucharistic League (1887), 194 E. 76th St., New York, N.Y. 10021; 17,500. *Emmanuel*, monthly. Nat. Dir., Rev. Paul J. Bernier, S.S.S.

Pro Ecclesia Foundation (1970), 663 Fifth Ave., New York, N.Y. 10022. To answer attacks against Church and promote Church teachings. *Pro Ecclesia*, monthly; *Talks of Pope John Paul II*, semimonthly; *The Common Good*, quarterly. Pres., Timothy A. Mitchell.

Pro Maria Committee (1952), 22 Second Ave., Lowell, Mass. 01854. Promote devotion to Our Lady of Beauraing (See Index).

The Providence Association of the Ukrainian Catholics in America (Ukrainian Catholic Fraternal Benefit Society) (1912), 817 N. Franklin St., Philadelphia, Pa. 19123. *America* (Ukrainian-English).

R

Raskob Foundation for Catholic Activities, Inc. (1945), Kennett Pike and Montchanin Rd., P.O. Box 4019, Wilmington, Del. 19807. Exec. Vice Pres., Gerard S. Garey.

Reparation Society of the Immaculate Heart of Mary, Inc. (1946), 100 E. 20th St., Baltimore, Md. 21218. *Fatima Findings*, monthly. Dir. Rev. John Ryan, S.J.

Rosary Altar Society (Confraternity of the Most Holy Rosary) (1891, in US), 141 E. 65th St., New York, N.Y. 10021; 3,000,000. Prov. Dir., Rev. Frederick M. Jelly, O.P.

Rosary League (1901), Franciscan Sisters of the Atonement, Graymoor, Garrison, N.Y. 10524. 1,600.

S

Sacred Heart League, Walls, Miss. 38680; 500,000. Promote devotion to the Sacred Heart; through the Auto League it promotes careful, prayerful driving. Dir., Rev. Gregory Bezy, S.C.J.

St. Ansgar's Scandinavian Catholic League (1910), 40 W. 13th St., New York, N.Y. 10011; 1,000. *St. Ansgar's Bulletin*, annually.

St. Anthony's Guild (1924), Paterson, N.J. 07509. *Anthonian*, quarterly. Dir., Rev. Salvator Fink, O.F.M.

St. Apollonia Guild (1958), 2186 Draper Ave., St. Paul, Minn. 55113. For Catholic dentists. Pres., Dr. Terrance L. Tri.

St. Jude League (1929), 221 W. Madison St., Chicago, Ill. 60606. *St. Jude Journal*, bimonthly. Dir., Rev. Mark J. Brummel, C.M.F.

St. Margaret of Scotland Guild, Inc. (1938), Graymoor, Garrison, N.Y. 10524; 2,200.

Moderator, Bro. Gerard Hand, S.A.

St. Martin de Porres Guild (1935), 141 E. 65th St., New York, N.Y. 10021. Gen. Dir., Rev. Timothy Shea, O.P.

St. Thomas Aquinas Foundation of the Dominican Fathers of the United States (STAF). Mod., Very Rev. Thomas H. McBrien, O.P., Providence College, Providence, R.I. 02918

Serra International (1938), 22 W. Monroe St., Chicago, Ill. 60603; 13,000 members in 418 clubs in more than 31 countries. *Serran*, bimonthly. Fosters vocations to the priesthood, and religious life, trains Catholic lay leadership. Formally aggregated to the Pontifical Society for Priestly Vocations, 1951. Pres., William P. Cashman.

Slovak Catholic Federation of America (1911), Pres., Rev. Joseph V. Adamec, 1515 Cass Ave., Bay City, Mich. 48706. *Good Shepherd (Dobry Pastier)*, quarterly. The following fraternal organizations hold continuous membership: First Catholic Slovak Union, First Catholic Slovak Ladies Assn.; Slovak Catholic Sokol; Penna. Slovak Catholic Union; Ladies Penna. Slovak Catholic Union; First Slovak Wreath of the Free Eagle.

Slovak Catholic Sokol (1905), 205 Madison St., Passaic, N.J. 07055; 51,965. *Katolicky Sokol*, weekly; *Priatel Dietok*, monthly.

Society for the Propagation of the Faith (1822), 366 Fifth Ave., New York, N.Y. 10001. *Mission, Worldmission*, quarterlies. Is subject to direction of Sacred Congregation for the Evangelization of Peoples. Nat. Dir., Most Rev. Edward T. O'Meara.

Society of St. Peter the Apostle for Native Clergy (1898), 366 Fifth Ave., New York, N.Y. 10001; 160 branches. Organized as the Pope's own mission aid society for the maintenance of diocesan seminaries and diocesan seminarians in mission countries. Nat. Dir., Most Rev. Edward T. O'Meara.

Spiritual Life Institute of America (1961), R.R. 3, Sedona, Arizona 86336. *Desert Call*, seasonal. An eremetical movement to foster the contemplative spirit in America. Founder, Rev. William McNamara, O.C.D. Second foundation: Primitive Wilderness Hermitage, Kemptville, Yarmouth Co., Nova Scotia, Canada.

Stewardship Services, Inc., Suite 913, 1234 Massachusetts Ave. N.W., Washington, D.C. 20005. Non-profit membership organization that provides financial management consulting services for Catholic dioceses, congregations and institutions. Exec. Dir., Thomas J. Jenkins, Jr.

T

Te Deum International (1940), 611 S. 6th St., Springfield, Ill. 62701; 27 chapters. For Catholic adult education on current and international affairs.

Theresians of America (1961), 5326 E. Pershing Ave., Scottsdale, Ariz. 85254; 6,000. Spiritual, intellectual and apostolic organization concerned with the vocation to Christian womanhood in both religious and lay states. Nat. Dir. and founder, Very Rev. Msgr. Elwood C. Voss.

U

United Societies of U.S.A. (1903), 613 Sinclair St., McKeesport, Pa. 15132; 4,375 members. *Prosvita-Enlightenment*, monthly newspaper.

United States Catholic Historical Society (1884). 300. *Journal*, quarterly; and *Monograph Series*, annually. Exec. Sec., James J. Mahoney, St. Joseph's Seminary, Yonkers, N.Y. 10704.

V

Veneration Society of Sanctity, Inc. (1975), 1322 Cranwood Square S., Columbus, O. 43229.

Vernacular Society (1946), P.O. Box 207, Passaic, N.J. 07055; 500. *Vernacular*, newsletter. Pres., Reinhold Kissner.

W-Y

Western Catholic Union (1877), W.C.U. Bldg., 506-510 Maine St., Quincy, Ill. 62301; 27,351 members. *Western Catholic Union Record*, monthly.

William J. Kerby Foundation (1941), Exec. Dir., Rev. Robert F. Grewen, S.J., Syracuse-Kemper Bldg., Room 814, Syracuse, N.Y. 13202.

Wisconsin Council of Catholic Women (1915), 810 Farwell Dr., Madison, Wis. 53704. Pres., Mrs. Patrick McCormick.

Word of God Institute (1972), 487 Michigan Ave. N.E., Washington, D.C. 20017. For renewed biblical preaching and evangelization. Dir., Rev. John Burke, O.P.

Young Ladies' Institute (1887), 50 Oak St., San Francisco, Calif. 94102. Grand Sec. Mrs. Sylvia Sharman.

Young Men's Institute (1883), 50 Oak St., San Francisco, Calif. 94102; 4,500. *Institute Journal*, bimonthly. Grand Sec., B. G. Merdinger.

Knights of Columbus

The Knights of Columbus, which originated as a fraternal benefit society of Catholic men, was founded by Father Michael J. McGivney and chartered by the General Assembly of Connecticut Mar. 29, 1882.

In line with their general purpose to be of service to the Church, the Knights are active in many apostolic works and community programs.

Since January, 1947, the Knights have sponsored a program of Catholic advertising in secular publications with national circulation. This has brought some 6 million inquiries and led to more than 600,000 enrollments in courses in the Catholic faith. In recent years the Knights have broadened this program to include other media for spreading Christian and religious ideals. As a result substantial contributions have been made to support the work of the John LaFarge Institute in New York, the Catholic Communications Foundation in New York, and the Center for Applied Research in the Apostolate (CARA) in Washington. In 1975 the Knights also undertook funding of the link-up costs for telecasting papal ceremonies throughout the world via satellite.

K. of C. scholarship funds — two at the Catholic University of America, another for disbursement at other Catholic colleges in the U.S., one at Canadian colleges and others for the Philippines and Mexico — have provided college educations for some 1,500 students since 1914.

The order promotes youth activity through sponsorship of the Columbian Squires and through cooperation with other organized youth groups.

Recent programs undertaken by the Knights include: promotion of vocations to the priesthood and religious life; promotion of rosary devotion with free distribution of more than 100,000 rosaries a year; efforts to halt the increased killing of the unborn; assistance to the retarded and other disadvantaged people.

In 1978, local units of the Knights contributed more than $20.5 million to charitable and benevolent causes, and gave more than seven million hours of community service.

K. of C. membership, as of Mar. 1, 1979, was 1,297,114 in 6,458 councils in the U.S., Canada, the Philippines, Cuba, Mexico, Puerto Rico, Panama, Guatemala, Guam and the Virgin Islands. Insurance assets, as of Dec. 31, 1978, amounted to $780,805,005 and total insurance in force, $4,473,962,025.

The Knights' publication, *Columbia,* has the greatest circulation (over 1.2 million) of any Catholic monthly in North America.

Virgil C. Dechant is Supreme Knight. Richard B. Scheiber is Supreme Secretary.

International headquarters are located at One Columbus Plaza, New Haven, Conn. 06507.

CPA AWARDS

Catholic Press Association Awards for material published in 1978 were presented during the CPA convention held Apr. 24 to 27, 1979, in Fort Lauderdale, Fla. A number of first-place awards are listed below.

Newspapers

General excellence, national newspapers; *National Catholic Reporter,* Kansas City, Mo.

General excellence, diocesan newspapers: *The Church World,* Portland, Me. (1-13,000 circ.); *The Beacon,* Paterson, N.J. (13,001-34,000 circ.); *The Chicago Catholic* (over 34,001 circ.).

Best front page: *The Church World* (tabloid), Portland, Me., *The Tennessee Register* (standard), Nashville, Tenn. (1-13,000); *The Beacon* (tabloid), Paterson, N.J., *The Morning Star* (standard), Lafayette, La. (13,001-34,000); *The Tablet* (tabloid), Brooklyn, N.Y., *Our Sunday Visitor* (standard), Huntington, Ind. (over 34,001).

Best campaign in the public interest: *The Church World,* Portland, Me., for "The Maine Indian Land Claims" (1-13,000); *Mississippi Today,* Jackson, Miss., for coverage of 1978 Mississippi Legislature, (13,001-34,000); *The Michigan Catholic,* Detroit, Mich., for series on community attitudes toward mentally retarded (over 34,000).

Best news report orginating with a newspaper: *The Evangelist,* Albany, N.Y., for "Local Catholics Demonstrate Compassion's Reach," by Sr. Mary Ann Walsh.

Best background, in-depth or interpretive reporting: *The Church World,* Portland Me., for "The Plight of the Aroostook Potato Farmer," by Henry Gosselin.

Best editorial: *Our Sunday Visitor,* Huntington, Ind., for "Pro-Life Hit List" (unsigned).

Best editorial page or section: *The Catholic Standard and Times,* Philadelphia, Pa.

Best human interest feature story: *The Tennessee Register,* Nashville, Tenn., for "The Pines Were Beautiful, the Strawberries Sweet ... But Few People Came to Church," by Eleanor C. McGrorty.

Best spiritual life column: *The Tennessee Register,* Nashville, Tenn., for "The Bible," columns by Rev. James A. Black.

Best general commentary column: *National Catholic Reporter,* Kansas City, Mo., for columns by Rick Casey.

Best culture, arts and leisure column: *The Catholic Post,* Peoria, Ill., for columns by Albina Aspell.

Best syndicated column: Alt Publishing Co., Green Bay, Wis., for columns by Dolores Curran.

Best youth coverage: *Courier-Journal,* Rochester, N.Y.

Best photo story originating with a newspaper: *National Catholic Reporter,* Kansas City, Mo., for "Neighbors ... An Appalachian Portfolio," photos by Gordon Baer.

Best photograph originating with a newspaper: *The Denver Catholic Register,* Denver, Colo., for photo of an Indian woman by Dave Vaughn.

Best coverage of the death of a pope: *Pittsburgh Catholic,* Aug. 11, 1978.

Best coverage of the election of a pope: *The Long Island Catholic,* Rockville Centre, N.Y., Sept. 7, 1978.

Best example of circulation promotion: *The Chicago Catholic.*

Communications

CATHOLIC PRESS STATISTICS

The *1979 Catholic Press Directory*, published by the Catholic Press Association, reported 500 newspapers and magazines in North America with a total circulation of 26,758,236. The figures reflected an increase in the number of periodicals (newspapers +8; magazines, +21) but a decrease in circulation (newspapers, -52,641; magazines, -157,908).

Newspapers

United States: 157; circulation, 5,462,313.
National newspapers, 9; circulation, 666,458.
(Weeklies: *National Catholic Register*, 77,000; *National Catholic Reporter*, 43,985; *Our Sunday Visitor*, 344,150; *Twin Circle*, 58,993; *The Wanderer*, 43,865; *El Visitante Dominical*, 21,030. Monthlies: *Bolletino*, 28,435; *Impact*, 44,000; *PADRES*, 5,000.)
Diocesan newspapers, 148; circulation, 4,795,855 (includes 7 diocesan editions of *Our Sunday Visitor* with a circulation of 103,340).

Canada: 12; circulation, 177,328.
National newspapers, 3; circulation, 73,420.
(Weeklies: *Catholic Register*, 55,570; *Our Sunday Visitor*, 10,850. Biweekly: *Catholic New Times*, 7,000.)
Diocesan newspapers, 9; circulation, 103,908.

West Indies, Others: 3 (diocesan); circulation, 19,700.

Diocesan newspapers in the U.S. with large circulations include: *Long Island Catholic*, Rockville Centre (158,241); *Chicago Catholic* (155,710); *Catholic Herald Citizen*, Milwaukee (139,150); *Pittsburgh Catholic* (114,000); *Clarion Herald*, New Orleans and Houma-Thibodaux (100,049); *The Tablet*, Brooklyn (99,451); *Catholic Universe Bulletin*, Cleveland (85,950); *The Catholic Standard and Times*, Philadelphia (85,272); The Evangelist, Albany (84,201); *The Catholic Voice*, Oakland (82,917); *The Texas Catholic Herald*, Galveston-Houston (79,745); *St. Louis Review* (75,002); *The Monitor*, Trenton (73,242); *Denver Catholic Register* (69,900); *The Pilot*, Boston (69,700); *The Michigan Catholic*, Detroit (67,500).

The oldest Catholic weekly newspaper in the U.S. is *The Pilot* of Boston, established in 1829 (under a different title).

Magazines

United States and Canada: 328; circulation, 21,098,895.
English-language magazines, 300; circulation, 20,528,979.
Other-language magazines, 28; circulation, 569,916.

America (circulation, 38,186) and *Commonweal* (circulation, 20,000) are the only weekly and biweekly magazines, respectively, of general interest.

The monthly magazine with the largest circulation (1,219,991) is *Columbia*, the official organ of the Knights of Columbus.

General-interest monthly magazines with large circulations include: *Catholic Digest* (559,800); *Liguorian* (470,000); *St. Anthony Messenger* (283,862); *Sign* (133,161); *U.S. Catholic* (58,749).

CATHOLIC NEWSPAPERS AND MAGAZINES IN THE U.S.

(Sources: *Catholic Press Directory, 1979*; Almanac survey; NC News Service.)

Abbreviation code: a, annual; bm, bimonthly; m, monthly; q, quarterly; w, weekly.

Circulation figures for some of these newspapers and magazines are given in the article, Catholic Press Statistics.

Newspapers

Advocate, The, w; 37 Evergreen Pl., E. Orange, N.J. 07018; Newark archdiocese.

Alive, m; 400 East Monroe, Phoenix, Ariz. 85004; Phoenix diocese.

Anchor, The w; 410 Highland Ave., Fall River, Mass. 02722; Fall River diocese.

Arizona Catholic Lifetime, biweekly; 64 W. Ochoa St., Tucson, Ariz. 85701.

Arlington Catholic Herald, w; 200 N. Glebe Rd., Suite 614, Arlington, Va. 22203; Arlington diocese.

Beacon, The, w; Box A, Pequannock, N.J. 07440; Paterson diocese.

Bishop's Bulletin, bm; 423 N. Duluth Ave., Sioux Falls, S. Dak. 57104.

Bolletino, m; 1801 Van Ness Ave., San Francisco, Calif. 94109; Central Council of Italian Catholic Federation.

Byzantine Catholic World, w; 3643 Perrysville Ave., Pittsburgh, Pa. 15214; Pittsburgh Byzantine archdiocese.

Catholic Accent, w; P.O. Box 850, Greensburg, Pa. 15601; Greensburg diocese.

Catholic Advance, The, w; 424 N. Broadway, Wichita, Kans. 67202; Wichita diocese.

Catholic Banner, w; P.O. Box 818, Charleston, S.C. 29401; Charleston diocese.

Catholic Bulletin, w; 244 Dayton Ave., St. Paul, Minn. 55102; St. Paul and Minneapolis archdiocese, New Ulm diocese.

Catholic Chronicle, w; P.O. Box 1866, Toledo, O. 43603; Toledo diocese.
Catholic Commentator, The, w; P.O. Box 14746, Baton Rouge, La. 70808; Baton Rouge diocese.
Catholic Communicator, w; 202 Morningside Dr. S.E., Albuquerque, N.M. 87108. Santa Fe archdiocese.
Catholic Crosswinds, semi-monthly; 1001 N. Grand Ave., Pueblo, Colo. 81003; Pueblo diocese.
Catholic Exponent, w; 320 Ohio One Bldg., 25 E. Boardman St., Youngstown, O. 44503; Youngstown diocese.
Catholic Free Press, w; 47 Elm St., Worcester, Mass. 01609; Worcester diocese.
Catholic Herald, The, w; 5890 Newman Ct., Sacramento, Calif. 95819; Sacramento diocese.
Catholic Herald Citizen, w; P.O. Box 736, Milwaukee, Wis. 53201; Milwaukee archdiocese.
Catholic Herald Citizen — Madison Edition, w; P.O. Box 1176, Madison, Wis. 53701.
Catholic Herald Citizen — Superior Edition, w; 1512 N. 12th St., Superior, Wis. 54880.
Catholic Hungarian's Sunday, w; 1739 Mahoning Ave., Youngstown, O. 44509.
Catholic Key to the News, The, w; P.O. Box 1037, Kansas City, Mo. 64141; Kansas City-St. Joseph diocese.
Catholic Light, biweekly; 300 Wyoming Ave., Scranton, Pa. 18503; Scranton diocese.
Catholic Messenger, w; 407 Brady St., Davenport, Ia. 52805; Davenport diocese.
Catholic Mirror, w; 200 Jewett Bldg., Des Moines, Ia. 50309.
Catholic Missourian, w; P.O. Box 1107, Jefferson City, Mo. 65101; Jefferson City diocese.
Catholic News, The, w; 68 W. Broad St., Mt. Vernon, N.Y. 10552; New York archdiocese.
Catholic Northwest Progress, w; 907 Terry Ave., Seattle, Wash. 98104; Seattle archdiocese, Yakima diocese.
Catholic Observer, biweekly; 57 Observer St., Springfield, Mass. 01101; Springfield diocese.
Catholic Post, The, w; P.O. Box 1722, Peoria, Ill. 61656; Peoria diocese.
Catholic Register, w; Box 126-C, Logan Blvd., Hollidaysburg, Pa. 16648; Altoona-Johnstown diocese.
Catholic Review, w; 320 Cathedral St., Baltimore, Md. 21203; Baltimore archdiocese.
Catholic Sentinel, w; 2816 E. Burnside St., Portland, Ore. 97214; Portland archdiocese, Baker diocese.
Catholic Spirit, The, w; 161 Edgington Lane, Wheeling, W. Va. 26003; Wheeling-Charleston diocese.
Catholic Standard, w; 1711 N. St., N.W., Washington, D.C. 20036; Washington archdiocese.
Catholic Standard and Times, w; 222 N. 17th St., Philadelphia, Pa. 19103; Philadelphia archdiocese; Allentown diocese.
Catholic Star Herald, w; 1845 Haddon Ave., Camden, N.J. 08103; Camden diocese.
Catholic Sun, The, w; 257 E. Onondaga St., Syracuse, N.Y. 13202; Syracuse diocese.
Catholic Telegraph, w; 326 W. 7th St., Cincinnati, O. 45202; Cincinnati archdiocese.
Catholic Times, w; P.O. Box 636, Columbus, O. 43216; Columbus diocese.
Catholic Transcript, w; 785 Asylum Ave., Hartford, Conn. 06105; Hartford archdiocese, Bridgeport and Norwich dioceses.
Catholic Universe Bulletin, w; 1027 Superior Ave. N.E., Cleveland, O. 44114; Cleveland diocese.
Catholic Virginian, w; 14 N. Laurel St., Richmond, Va. 23220; Richmond diocese.
Catholic Voice, The, w; 2918 Lakeshore Ave., Oakland, Calif. 94610; Oakland diocese.
Catholic Voice, The, w; 6060 N.W. Radial, Omaha, Nebr. 68104; Omaha archdiocese.
Catholic Week, w; P.O. Box 349, Mobile, Ala. 36601; Mobile diocese.
Catholic Weekly, The, w; P.O. Box 1405, Saginaw, Mich. 48605; Saginaw diocese.
Catholic Weekly, The, w; 1628 Lambden Rd., Flint, Mich. 48501; Lansing diocese.
Catholic Witness, The, w; P.O. Box 2555, Harrisburg, Pa. 17105; Harrisburg diocese.
Central California Register, biweekly; P.O. Box 1668, 1550 N. Fresno St., Fresno, Calif. 93717; Fresno diocese.
Central Washington Catholic, m; P.O. Box 505, Yakima, Wash. 98907. Yakima diocese.
Challenge, The, semimonthly; P.O. Box 14082, Jefferson Sta., Detroit, Mich. 48214. St. Maron diocese.
Chicago Catholic, The w; 155 E. Superior St., Chicago, Ill. 60611; Chicago archdiocese.
Church Today, every 3 weeks; P.O. Box 7417, Alexandria, La. 71306; Alexandria-Shreveport diocese.
Church World, w; Industry Rd., Brunswick, Me. 04011; Portland diocese.
Clarion Herald, w; 523 Natchez St., New Orleans, La. 70130; New Orleans archdiocese; Houma-Thibodaux diocese.
Common Sense, w; 1325 Jefferson Ave., Memphis, Tenn. 38104; Memphis diocese.
Compass, The, w; P.O. Box 909, Green Bay, Wis. 54305; Green Bay diocese.
Concern, m (exc. Aug.); 153 Ash St., Manchester, N.H. 03105; Manchester diocese.
Courier, The, biweekly; P.O. Box 588, Winona, Minn. 55987; Winona diocese.
Courier-Journal, w; 67 Chestnut St., Rochester, N.Y. 14604; Rochester diocese.
Criterion, The, w; P.O. Box 174, Indianapolis, Ind. 46206; Indianapolis archdiocese.

Dakota Catholic Action, 9 times a year; P.O. Box 128, Wilton, N.D. 58579; Bismarck diocese.
Darbininkas (Lithuanian), w; 341 Highland Blvd., Brooklyn, N.Y. 11207; Lithuanian Franciscan Fathers.
Denver Catholic Register, w; P.O. Box 1620, Denver, Colo. 80201; Denver archdiocese.
Dialog, The, w; 1925 Delaware Ave., Wilmington, Del. 19899; Wilmington diocese.
Diocese of Orange Bulletin, m; 440 S. Batavia, Orange, Calif. 92668.
Draugas (Lithuanian), daily; 4545 W. 63rd St., Chicago, Ill. 60629; Lithuanian Catholic Press Society.

Eastern Catholic Life, w; 101 Market St., Passaic, N.J. 07055; Passaic Byzantine eparchy.
Eastern Kansas Register, The, w; 2220 Central, Kansas City, Kans. 66110; Kansas City archdiocese.
Eastern Montana Catholic Register, w; 725 Third Ave. N., Great Falls, Mont. 59403; Great Falls diocese.
Eastern Oklahoma Catholic, bm; Box 520, Tulsa, Okla. 74101; Tulsa diocese.
El Visitante de Puerto Rico, w; Box 1967, San Juan, P.R. 00903.
El Visitante Dominical (Spanish), Oblates of Mary Immaculate, P.O. Box 96, San Antonio, Tex. 78291.
Evangelist, The, w; 39 Philip St., Albany, N.Y. 12207; Albany diocese.

Florida Catholic, The, w; 620 N. Magnolia Ave., Orlando, Fla. 32802; Orlando and St. Petersburg dioceses.

Gary Sunday Visitor, w; P.O. Box M-356, Gary, Ind. 46401.
Georgia Bulletin, w; 756 W. Peachtree St. N.W., Atlanta, Ga. 30308; Atlanta archdiocese.
Globe, The, w; 1821 Jackson St., Sioux City, Ia. 51105; Sioux City diocese.
Good News Visitor, of Northwest Florida, w; 209 S. Calhoun St., Tallahassee, Fla. 32301; Pensacola-Tallahassee diocese.
Guardian, The, w; P.O. Box 7417, Little Rock, Ark. 72217; Little Rock diocese.

Harmonizer, The, (Edition O.S.V.), w; P.O. Box 390, Fort Wayne, Ind. 46801; Fort Wayne-S. Bend diocese.
Hawaii Catholic Herald, w; 1184 Bishop St., Honolulu, H.I. 96813; Honolulu diocese.
Hlas Naroda (Voice of the Nation) (Czech-English), w; 2657-59 S. Lawndale Ave., Chicago. 60623.
Horizons, semimonthly; 1900 Carlton Rd., Parma, O. 44134; Parma diocese.

Idaho Register, w; P.O. Box 2835, Boise, Idaho 83701; Boise diocese.
Impact, 12 times a year; 1234 Massachusetts Ave. N.W., Washington, D.C. 20005; National Office for Black Catholics.
Inland Register, w; P.O. Box 48, Spokane, Wash. 99210; Spokane diocese.
Inside Passage, w; 419 6th St., Juneau, Alaska 99801; Juneau and Fairbanks dioceses.
Intermountain Catholic Register, The, w; P.O. Box 2489, Salt Lake City, Utah 84110; Salt Lake City diocese.

Jednota (Slovak-Eng.), w; Jednota and Rosedale Aves.; Middletown, Pa. 17057; First Catholic Slovak Union.
Joliet Catholic Explorer, w; 425 Summit St., Joliet, Ill. 60435; Joliet diocese.

Lafayette Sunday Visitor, w; P.O. Box 1603, Lafayette, Ind. 47902; Lafayette diocese.
Lake Shore Visitor, w; 2-M Commerce Bldg., Erie, Pa. 16512; Erie diocese.
Long Island Catholic, The, w; P.O. Box 700, Hempstead, N.Y. 11551; Rockville Centre diocese.

Message, The, w; P.O. Box 4169, Evansville, Ind. 47711; Evansville diocese.
Messenger, The, w; 224 W. Washington St., Belleville, Ill. 62222; Belleville diocese.
Messenger, The, w; 1044 Scott St., Covington, Ky. 41012; Covington diocese.
Michigan Catholic, The, w; 644 Selden St., Detroit, Mich. 48201; Detroit archdiocese.
Mirror, The, biweekly; M.P.O. Box 847, Springfield, Mo. 65801; Springfield-Cape Girardeau diocese.
Mississippi Today, w; P.O. Box 2130, Jackson, Miss. 39205; Jackson and Biloxi dioceses.
Monitor, The, w; 441 Church St., San Francisco, Calif. 94114; San Francisco archdiocese, Stockton and Santa Rosa dioceses, Calif.; Reno-Las Vegas diocese, Nev.
Monitor, The, w; 139 N. Warren St., Trenton, N.J. 08607; Trenton diocese.
Morning Star, The, w; P.O. Box 3223, Lafayette, La. 70502; Lafayette diocese.

Narod Polski (Polish-Eng.) semi-monthly; 984 Milwaukee Ave., Chicago, Ill. 60622.
Nasa Nada (Eng.-Croatian), biweekly; 1414 W. 119th St., Crown Point, Ind. 46307.
National Catholic Register, w; 1901 Avenue of the Stars, Suite 1511, Los Angeles, Calif. 90067.
National Catholic Reporter, The, w; P.O. Box 281, Kansas City, Mo. 64141; published by laymen.
New Star, The, w; 2208 W. Chicago Ave., Chicago, Ill. 60622; St. Nicholas of Chicago Ukrainian diocese.

North Carolina Catholic, w; 300 Cardinal Gibbons Dr., Raleigh, N.C. 27606; Raleigh and Charlotte dioceses.

North Country Catholic, w; P.O. Box 326, Ogdensburg, N.Y. 13669; Ogdensburg diocese.

Northwestern Kansas Register, w; P.O. Box 958, Salina, Kans. 67401; Salina diocese.

Observer, The, w; P.O. Box 2079, Monterey, Calif. 93940; Monterey diocese.

Observer, The, w; 921 W. State St., Rockford, Ill. 61103; Rockford diocese.

One Voice, w; P.O. Box 10822, Birmingham, Ala. 35202; Birmingham diocese.

Our Northland Diocese, m; 319 S. Ash, Crookston, Minn. 56716; Crookston diocese.

Our Sunday Visitor, w; 200 Noll Plaza, Huntington, Ind. 46750; national edition and official publication for 7 dioceses; Our Sunday Visitor, Inc..

Outlook, m (Sept.-June); 215 W. 4th St., Duluth, Minn. 55806; Duluth diocese.

PADRES, m; 3112 W. Ashby, San Antonio, Tex. 78228.

Pilot, The, w; 49 Franklin St., Boston, Mass. 02110; Boston archdiocese.

Pittsburgh Catholic, The, w; 110 Third Ave., Pittsburgh, Pa. 15222; Pittsburgh diocese.

Polish American Journal, m; 413 Cedar Ave., Scranton, Pa. 18505.

Proclaimer, w; P.O. Box 2824, Kalamazoo, Mich. 49003; Kalamazoo diocese.

Providence Visitor, w; 184 Broad St., Providence, R.I. 02903; Providence diocese.

Record, The, w; 433 S. 5th St., Louisville, Ky. 40202; Louisville archdiocese.

St. Cloud Visitor, w; 810 Germain St., St. Cloud, Minn. 56301; St. Cloud diocese.

St. Joseph's-Blatt (German-Eng.), m; St. Benedict, Ore. 97373; Manfred F. Ellenberger.

St. Louis Review, w; 462 N. Taylor Ave., St. Louis, Mo. 63108; St. Louis archdiocese.

Shlakh — The Way, w; 805 N. Franklin St., Philadelphia, Pa. 19123; Philadelphia archeparchy. Stamford and Chicago eparchies.

Sooner Catholic, The, biweekly; P.O. Box 32180, Oklahoma City, Okla. 73132; Oklahoma City archdiocese.

Southern Cross, The, w; P.O. Box 81869, San Diego, Calif. 92138; San Diego diocese.

Southern Cross, The, w; 601 E. 6th St., Waynesboro, Ga. 30830; Savannah diocese.

Southern Nebraska Register, w; P.O. Box 80329, Lincoln, Nebr. 68501; Lincoln diocese.

Southwest Kansas Register, w; P.O. Box 1317, Dodge City, Kans. 67801; Dodge City diocese.

Steubenville Register, w; 419 S. 4th St., Steubenville, O. 43952; Steubenville diocese.

Tablet, w; 1 Hanson Pl., Brooklyn, N.Y. 11243; Brooklyn diocese.

Tennessee Register, The, w; 2400 21st Ave. S., Nashville, Tenn. 37212; Nashville diocese.

Texas Catholic, w; 3915 Lemmon Ave., Dallas, Tex. 75219; Dallas and Fort Worth dioceses.

Texas Catholic Herald, The, w; 1700 San Jacinto St., Houston, Tex. 77002; Galveston-Houston diocese.

Texas Catholic Herald — Austin Edition, w; 1401 Washington Ave., Waco, Tex. 76702; Austin diocese.

Texas Catholic Herald — Beaumont, w; P.O. Box 3944, Beaumont, Tex. 77704; Beaumont diocese.

Texas Concho Register, biweekly; 116 S. Oakes, San Angelo, Tex. 76901; San Angelo diocese.

Texas Gulf Coast Catholic, w; P.O. Box 2584, Corpus Christi, Tex. 78403; Corpus Christi diocese.

Tidings, The, w; 1530 W. 9th St., Los Angeles, Calif. 90015; Los Angeles archdiocese.

Time and Eternity, w; 514 E. Lawrence St., Springfield, Ill. 62703; Springfield diocese.

Times-Review, The, w; P.O. Box 937, La Crosse, Wis. 54601; La Crosse diocese.

Today's Catholic, w; P.O. Box 12429, San Antonio, Tex. 78212; San Antonio archdiocese.

Twin Circle, w; 1901 Avenue of the Stars, Suite 1511, Los Angeles, Calif. 90067.

Upper Peninsula Catholic, w; P.O. Box 548, Marquette, Mich. 49855; Marquette diocese.

Vermont Catholic Tribune, w; Bishop Brady Center, 351 North Ave., Burlington, Vt. 05401; Burlington diocese.

Voice, The, w; 6201 Biscayne Blvd., Miami, Fla. 33138; Miami archdiocese.

Voice of the Southwest, w; P.O. Box 68, Lumberton, N. Mex. 87547; Gallup diocese.

Wanderer, The, w; 201 Ohio St., St. Paul, Minn. 55107.

WestMont Word, biweekly; P.O. Box 1729, Helena, Mont. 59601; Helena diocese.

West Nebraska Register, w; P.O. Box 608, Grand Island, Nebr. 68801; Grand Island diocese.

West River Catholic, m; 606 Cathedral Dr., Rapid City, S. Dak. 57709; Rapid City diocese.

West Texas Catholic, w; 1800 N. Spring, Amarillo, Tex. 79107; Amarillo diocese.

Western Michigan Catholic, w; 650 Burton S.E., Grand Rapids, Mich. 49507; Grand Rapids diocese.

Western New York Catholic Visitor, w; 100 S. Elmwood Ave., Buffalo, N.Y. 14202; Buffalo diocese.

Witness, The, w; 1229 Mt. Loretta, Dubuque, Ia. 52001; Dubuque archdiocese.

Wyoming Register, w; P.O. Box 1308, Cheyenne, Wyo. 82001.

Magazines, Other Periodicals

A.D. Correspondence, 26 times a year; Notre Dame, Ind. 46556.

ADRIS Newsletter, q; Department of Theology, Fordham University, Bronx, N.Y. 10458. Association for the Development of Religious Information Services.

AGAPE, 12 times a year; 4012 Monterey, Edina, Minn. 55416; CFM and Marriage Encounter.

AIM (Aids in Ministry), q; 1800 W. Winnemac Ave., Chicago, Ill. 60640.

Alaskan Shepherd, 6 times a year; 1312 Peger Rd., Fairbanks, Alaska 99701.

America, w; 106 W. 56th St., New York, N.Y. 10019.

American Benedictine Review, q; 2nd and Division Sts., Atchison, Kans. 66002.

American Midland Naturalist, q; Notre Dame, Ind. 46556.

Americas, The, q; Box 34440, Washington, D.C. 20034; Academy of American Franciscan History.

Amerikanski Slovenec (Slovenian), w; 6117 St. Clair Ave., Cleveland, O. 44103; Slovenian Catholic Union.

Annunciation, The, q; 2 Forest Ave., Cohoes, N.Y. 12044.

Anthonian, q; Paterson, N.J. 07509; St. Anthony's Guild.

Anthropological Quarterly, q; 620 Michigan Ave. N.E., Washington, D.C. 20064.

Apostolate of Our Lady, m; Carey, O. 43316; Our Lady of Consolation National Shrine.

Apostolate of the Little Flower, bm; P.O. Box 5280, 906 Kentucky Ave., San Antonio, Tex. 78201; Discalced Carmelite Fathers.

Ateitis (Lithuanian), m; 7235 S. Sacramento Ave., Chicago, Ill. 60629; Ateitis Federation.

Ave Maria (Polish), 6 times a year; 600 Doat St., Buffalo, N.Y. 14211; Felician Srs.

Bells of St. Ann, 3 times a year; Belcourt, N.D. 58316; St. Ann's Indian Mission.

Benedictine Orient, bm; 2400 Maple Ave., Lisle, Ill. 60532.

Benedictines, semiannually; Mt. St. Scholastica, Atchison, Kans. 66002.

Bernardine Bulletin, The, semiannually; 647 Spring Mill Rd., Villanova, Pa. 19085; Bernardine Srs..

Best Sellers, m; Univ. of Scranton, Scranton, Pa. 18510.

Better World, q; Belford, N.J. 07718; Mary Productions Guild.

Bible Today, The, 6 times a year; Liturgical Press, Collegeville, Minn. 56321.

Brothers' Newsletter, q; Passionist Monastery, P.O. Box 150, West Springfield, Mass. 01089; National Assembly of Religious Brothers.

Call Board, The, 5 times a year; 227 W. 45th St., New York, N.Y. 10036; Catholic Actors' Guild.

Camillian: Journal of the National Association of Catholic Chaplains, q; 1312 Massachusetts Ave. N.W., Washington, D.C. 20005; National Association of Catholic Chaplains.

CHD Newsletter, q; 1312 Massachusetts Ave. N.W. Washington, D.C.; Campaign for Human Development.

Catechist, The, m (exc. Dec., June-Aug.); 2451 E. River Rd., Dayton, O. 45439.

Catholic Action News, m (Sept.-May); P.O. Box 1750, Fargo, N. Dak. 58102; Fargo diocese.

Catholic Aid News, m; 49 W. 9th St., St. Paul, Minn. 55102.

Catholic Apostolate Newsletter, bm; 5424 Blue Mound Rd., Milwaukee, Wis. 53208; Pallottine Fathers.

Catholic Biblical Quarterly, q; Catholic University of America, Washington, D.C. 20064; Catholic Biblical Assn.

Catholic Cemetery, The, m; 710 N. River Rd., Des Plaines, Ill. 60016.

Catholic Charismatic, 6 times a year; Paulist Press, 545 Island Rd., Ramsey, N.J. 07446.

CCH Echoes, q; P.O. Box 481, Alton, Ill. 62002; Catholic Children's Home.

Catholic Digest, The, m; P.O. Box 3090, St. Paul, Minn. 55165.

Catholic Forester Magazine, bm; 305 W. Madison St., Chicago, Ill. 60606; Catholic Order of Foresters.

Catholic Golden Age Newsletter, q; Scranton Life Bldg., Scranton, Pa. 18503.

Catholic Historical Review, q; Catholic University of America, Washington, D.C. 20064; American Catholic Historical Assn.

Catholic Journalist, The, m; 119 N. Park Ave. Rockville Centre, N.Y. 11570; Catholic Press Association.

C.K. of A. Journal, m; 217 E. 8th St., Cincinnati, O. 45202; Catholic Knights of America.

C.L. of C. Index, m; 2770 E. Main St., Columbus, O. 43209.

Catholic Lawyer, q; St. John's University, Jamaica, N.Y. 11432; St. Thomas More Institute for Legal Research.

Catholic League Newsletter, m; 1100 W. Wells St., Milwaukee, Wis. 53233; Catholic League for Religious and Civil Rights.

Catholic Library World, 10 times a year; 461 W. Lancaster Ave., Haverford, Pa. 19041; Catholic Library Association.

Catholic Life Magazine, m (exc. July-Aug.); 35750 Moravian Dr., Fraser, Mich. 48026; PIME Missionaries.

Catholic Mind, The, m (exc. July-Aug.); 106 W. 56th St., New York, N.Y. 10019.

Catholic Near East Magazine, q; 1011 First Ave., New York, N.Y. 10022.

Catholic Periodical and Literature Index,

bm; 461 W. Lancaster Ave., Haverford, Pa. 19041; Catholic Library Association.

Catholic Pharmacist, q; 1012 Surrey Hills Dr., St. Louis, Mo. 63117; National Catholic Pharmacists Guild.

Catholic Press Directory, a; 119 N. Park Ave. Rockville Centre, N.Y. 11570; Catholic Press Assn.

Catholic Quote, m; Valparaiso, Nebr. 68065; Rev. Jerome Pokorny.

Catholic Review (Braille), m; 154 E. 23rd St., New York, N.Y. 10010; Xavier Society for the Blind.

Catholic Rural Life, m; 3801 Grand Ave., Des Moines, Ia. 50312; National Catholic Rural Life Conference.

Catholic Trends, biweekly; 1312 Massachusetts Ave. N.W. Washington, D.C. 20005; NC News Service.

Catholic University of America Law Review, q; Washington, D.C. 20064.

Catholic War Veteran, bm; 2 Massachusetts Ave. N.W., Washington, D.C. 20001.

Catholic Woman, bm; 1312 Massachusetts Ave. N.W., Washington, D.C. 20005. National Council of Catholic Women.

Catholic Woman's Journal, m; 3835 Westminster Pl., St. Louis, Mo. 63108.

Catholic Worker, 9 times a year; 36 E. First St., New York, N.Y. 10003; Dorothy Day.

Catholic Workman, m; 112½ E. Main, New Prague, Minn. 56071.

Charities USA, m; 1346 Connecticut Ave. N.W., Washington, D.C. 20036; National Conference of Catholic Charities.

Chicago Studies, 3 times a year; P.O. Box 665, Mundelein, Ill. 60060.

Christian Life Communicator, m; 3721 Westminster Pl., St. Louis, Mo. 63108; National Federation of Christian Life Communities.

Christian Renewal News, 890 Hillcrest Dr., Pomona, Calif. 91768; Apostolate of Christian Renewal.

Christopher News Notes, 7 times a year; 12 E. 48th St., New York, N.Y. 10017; The Christophers, Inc.

Classical Bulletin, 6 times a year; 221 N. Grand Blvd., St. Louis, Mo. 63103.

Classical Folia, biennial; College of Holy Cross, Worcester, Mass. 01610; Institute for Early Christian Iberian Studies (history of Spain and Portugal from 50-711 A.D.).

Claverite, The, bm; 1821 Orleans Ave., New Orleans, La. 70116; Knights of Peter Claver.

Columban Mission, m (exc. June, Aug.); St. Columbans, Nebr. 68056; Columban Fathers.

Columbia, m; One Columbus Plaza, New Haven, Conn. 06507; Knights of Columbus.

Columbian, The, w; 188 W. Randolph St., Chicago, Ill. 60601.

Commitment, 6 times a year; 1200 Varnum St. N.E., Washington, D.C. 20017; National Catholic Conference for Interracial Justice.

Commonweal, biweekly; 232 Madison Ave., New York, N.Y. 10016.

Communio — International Catholic Review, q; Gonzaga University, Spokane, Wash. 99202.

Communique, 3 times a year; 1307 S. Wabash Ave., Chicago, Ill. 60605; National Assembly of Women Religious.

Community, q; 343 S. Dearborn St., Chicago, Ill. 60604; Friendship House.

Consecrated Life, up to 4 times a year; 4200 N. Austin Ave., Chicago, Ill. 60634; Institute on Religious Life. English edition of *Informationes,* official publication of Sacred Congregation for Religious and Secular Institutes.

Consolata, 6 times a year; P.O. Box C, Somerset, N.J. 08873.

Contact, 10 times a year; 123-15 14 Ave., College Point, N.Y. 11356; Sisters of St. Dominic.

Contemplative Review, q; Beckley Hill, Barre, Vt. 05647; Association of Contemplative Sisters.

Continuum, q; St. Xavier College, Chicago, Ill. 60655.

Cord, The, m; St. Bonaventure University, St. Bonaventure, N.Y. 14778.

Counseling and Values, q; 1607 New Hampshire Ave. N.W., Washington, D.C. 20009; Association for Religious and Value Issues in Counseling.

Critic, The (Newsletter), 22 times a year; 180 N. Wabash Ave., Chicago, Ill. 60601; Thomas More Association.

Cross Currents, q; 103 Van Houten Fields, W. Nyack, N.Y. 10994.

Crossroads Radio, bm; 1089 Elm St., W. Springfield, Mass. 01089.

Crusader's Almanac, The, q; 1400 Quincy St. N.E., Washington, D.C. 20017; Commissariat of the Holy Land.

CRUX of Prayer, m; 75 Champlain St., Albany, N.Y. 12204.

CRUX of the News, w; 75 Champlain St., Albany, N.Y. 12204.

Damien-Dutton Call, q; 616 Bedford Ave., Bellmore, N.Y. 11710.

Daystar, a; 172 Foster St., Brighton, Mass. 02135; Franciscan Missionary Sisters for Africa.

Deaf Blind Weekly, The (Braille), w; 154 E. 23rd St., New York, N.Y. 10010; Xavier Society for the Blind.

Desert Call, q; SLIA-Nada, Star Rt. 1, Sedona, Ariz. 86336; Spiritual Life Institute of America.

Diakonia, 3 times a year; Fordham Univ., Bronx, N.Y. 10458; John XXIII Center for Eastern Christian Studies.

Dimensions, m; 119 N. Park Ave., Rockville Centre, N.Y. 11570; National Catholic Development Conference.

Divine Love, q; P.O. Box 24, Fresno, Calif. 93707.

Divine Word Messenger, q; Bay St. Louis, Miss. 39520.

Divine Word Missionaries, q; Techny, Ill. 60082.

Ecumenical Trends, m (exc. July-Aug.); Graymoor Ecumenical Institute, Garrison, N.Y. 10524.

Ecumenist, The, 6 times a year; Paulist Press, 1865 Broadway, New York, N.Y. 10023.

Educating in Faith, bm; 335 Broadway, New York, N.Y. 10013; Catholic Negro-American Mission Board.

Emmanuel, m (bm July-Aug.); 194 E. 76th St., New York, N.Y. 10021; Blessed Sacrament Fathers.

Emmaus Letter, q; 1312 Massachusetts Ave. N.W., Washington, D.C. 20005. National CYO Federation.

Encounter, 2 times a year; 200 Lake St., Boston, Mass. 02135; Religious of the Cenacle.

Envoy, 5 times a year; Office of Public Relations, Catholic University of America, Washington, D.C. 20064.

Eucharist, bm; 194 E. 76th St., New York, N.Y. 10021.

Extension, m; 35 E. Wacker Dr., Chicago, Ill. 60605; Catholic Church Extension Society.

Family, m; 50 St. Paul's Ave., Boston, Mass. 02130; Daughters of St. Paul.

Family Friend, q; P.O. Box 11563, Milwaukee, Wis. 53211; Catholic Family Life Insurance.

Fatima Findings, m; 100 E. 20th St., Baltimore, Md. 21218; Reparation Society of the Immaculate Heart of Mary.

Fellowship of Catholic Scholars Newsletter, q; St. John's University, Jamaica, N.Y. 11439.

Filipino Catholic Newsmagazine, semimonthly; 114 E. 2nd St., Los Angeles, Calif. 90012; Filipino Catholic Publications, Inc.

Franciscan Herald, m; 1434 W. 51st St., Chicago, Ill. 60609.

F.M.A. Focus, q; 276 W. Lincoln Ave., Mt. Vernon, N.Y. 10550; Franciscan Mission Associates.

Franciscan Reporter, q; 3140 Meramec St., St. Louis, Mo. 63138.

Franciscan Studies, a; St. Bonaventure, N.Y. 14778; Franciscan Institute.

Fraternal Leader, bm; 305 W. 6th St., Erie, Pa. 16512; Loyal Christian Benefit Association.

Fund Raising Forum, m; 119 N. Park Ave., Rockville Centre, N.Y. 11570; National Catholic Development Conference.

Glenmary's Challenge, q; P.O. Box 46404, Cincinnati, O. 45246; Glenmary Home Missioners.

Good Shepherd (Slovak and English), q; 205 Madison St., Passaic, N.J. 07055; Slovak Catholic Federation of America.

Grain and Fire, q; P.O. Box 25, Plaucheville, La. 71360; Brothers of the Holy Eucharist.

Harmony, 4 or 5 times a year; 8300 Morganford Rd., St. Louis, Mo. 63123; Benedictine Srs. of Perpetual Adoration.

Holy Name Newsletter, m (exc. July-Aug.); P.O. Box 4033, Rocky Mount, N.C. 27801; National Association of the Holy Name Society.

Homiletic and Pastoral Review, m; 86 Riverside Dr., New York, N.Y. 10024.

Hospital Progress, m; 1438 S. Grand Blvd., St. Louis, Mo. 63104; Catholic Hospital Association.

I.C. Good News, q; P.O. Box 24811, Philadelphia, Pa. 19130; North City Catholic Conference, Inc.

Immaculata, m; 8000 39th Ave., Kenosha, Wis. 53142; Franciscan Fathers.

In-Formation, 8 times a year; 1234 Massachusetts Ave., N.W., Washington, D.C. 20005; Religious Formation Conference.

Institute Journal, bm; 50 Oak St., San Francisco, Calif. 94102; Young Men's Institute.

Integrity, m; 6243 S. Fairfield Ave., Chicago, Ill. 60629; Rev. L. Dudley Day, O.S.A.

International Review of Natural Family Planning, q; St. John's University, Collegeville, Minn. 56321; Human Life Center.

It's Our World, 4 times a year; 800 Allegheny Ave., Pittsburgh, Pa. 15233; Pontifical Assn. of the Holy Childhood.

Jesuit, The, q; 39 E. 83rd St., New York, N.Y. 10028.

Jesuit, The (New Orleans Edition), q; 1607 Pere Marquette Bldg., New Orleans, La. 70112.

Jesuit Blackrobe, q; 3601 W. Fond du Lac Ave., Milwaukee, Wis. 53216.

Jesuit Bulletin, 4 times a year; 4511 W. Pine Blvd., St. Louis, Mo. 63108; Jesuit Seminary Aid Association.

Josephite Harvest, The, q; 1130 N. Calvert St., Baltimore, Md. 21202; Josephite Missionaries.

Jurist, The, q; Catholic University of America, Washington, D.C. 20064; School of Canon Law.

Katolicky Sokol (Catholic Falcon) (Slovak-English), w; 205 Madison St., Passaic, N.J. 07055; Slovak Catholic Sokol.

Kinship, q; P.O. Box 23072, Cincinnati, O. 45223; Glenmary Sisters.

KIT — Keeping in Touch, m; 1820 Mt. Elliott Ave., Detroit, Mich. 48207; Capuchin Province of St. Joseph.

Knights of St. John, q; 6517 Charles Ave., Cleveland, O. 44129.

Kolping Banner, m; 115-14 227th St., Cambria Hghts., N.Y. 11411; Catholic Kolping Society.

Laiskai Lietuviams (Letters to Lithuanians) (Lithuanian), m (exc. Aug.), 2345 W. 56th St., Chicago, Ill. 60636.

Laivas (Lithuanian), m; 4545 W. 63rd St., Chicago, Ill. 60629.

Land of Cotton, q; 2048 W. Fairview Ave., Montgomery, Ala. 36108.

Law Briefs, m; 1312 Massachusetts Ave. N.W., Washington, D.C. 20005; Office of General Counsel, USCC.

Leaves, bm; 23715 Ann Arbor Trail, Dearborn Heights, Mich. 48127; Mariannhill Fathers.

Letter from St. Paul Newsletter, 8-10 times a year; 955 Lake Dr., St. Paul, Minn. 55120; National Marriage Encounter.

Liguorian, m; 1 Liguori Rd., Liguori, Mo. 63057; Redemptorist Fathers.

Linacre Quarterly, q; 850 Elm Grove Rd., Elm Grove, Wis. 53122; Federation of Catholic Physicians Guilds.

Listening, 5 times a year; Trinity Colege, Washington, D.C. 20017; National Catholic Office for the Deaf.

Little Bronzed Angel, bm; St. Paul's Indian Mission, Marty, S.D. 53761; Benedictine Fathers.

Little Flower Magazine, bm; 1125 S. Walker, Oklahoma City, Okla. 73126; Discalced Carmelite Fathers.

Liturgy, bm; 810 Rhode Island Ave. N.E. Washington, D.C. 20018.

Living Light, The, q; Our Sunday Visitor, Inc., 200 Noll Plaza, Huntington, Ind. 46750, publisher; official magazine of National Center of Religious Education — CCD.

Love/Life/Death Issues, q; St. John's University, Collegeville, Minn. 56321; Human Life Center.

Marian Helpers Bulletin, q; Stockbridge, Mass. 01262; Association of Marian Helpers and of the Congregation of Marian Fathers.

Marquette Today, q; 1212 W. Wisconsin Ave., Milwaukee, Wis. 53233.

Marriage and Family Living, m; Abbey Press, St. Meinrad, Ind. 47577.

Marriage Encounter, m; 955 Lake Dr., St. Paul, Minn. 55120; National Marriage Encounter.

Mary Magazine and Aylesford News, bm; Cass Ave. N. at I-55, Westmont, Ill. 60559; Carmelite Fathers.

Maryknoll Magazine, m; Maryknoll, N.Y. 10545; Catholic Foreign Mission Society.

Master's Work, q; Convent of Holy Spirit, Techny, Ill. 60082; Holy Spirit Missionary Sisters.

Mature Catholic, bm; 1100 W. Wells St., Milwaukee, Wis. 53233; American Society of Mature Catholics.

Media and Values, q; 1962 S. Shenandoah, Los Angeles, Calif. 90034; National Sisters Communication Service.

Media-Mix, 221 W. Madison St., Chicago, Ill. 60606; Claretian Publications.

Mediatrix, q; 6301 12th Ave., Brooklyn, N.Y. 11219.

Medical Mission News, bm; 10 W. 17th St., New York, N.Y. 10011; Catholic Medical Mission Board, Inc.

Medical Mission Sisters News, 4 times a year; 8400 Pine Road, Philadelphia, Pa. 19111.

Men of Malvern, bm; Malvern, Pa. 19355; Laymen's Retreat League of Philadelphia.

Mercy Profile, q; 2303 Grandview Ave., Cincinnati, O. 45206; Sisters of Mercy.

Messenger, The, m; 16010 Detroit Ave., Lakewood, O. 44107.

MHS Review (Franciscanews), q; 232 S. Home Ave., Pittsburgh, Pa. 15202.

Miesiecznik Franciszkanski (Polish), m; Franciscan Printery, Pulaski, Wis. 54162; Franciscan Fathers.

Migration Today, 5 times a year; 209 Flagg Pl., Staten Island, N.Y. 10304; Center for Migration Studies.

Miraculous Medal, The, q; 475 E. Chelten Ave., Philadelphia, Pa. 19144; Central Association of the Miraculous Medal.

Mission, bm; 366 Fifth Ave., New York, N.Y. 10001; Society for Propagation of the Faith.

Mission, bm; 1663 Bristol Pike, Cornwell Heights, Pa. 19020; Sisters of the Blessed Sacrament.

Mission Helper, The, q; 1001 W. Joppa Rd., Baltimore, Md. 21204; Mission Helpers of the Sacred Heart.

Missionhurst, 6 times a year; 4651 N. 25th St., Arlington, Va. 22207; Immaculate Heart of Mary Mission Society, Inc.

Mission Intercom, 10 times a year; 1302 18th St. N.W., Suite 702, Washington, D.C. 20036; U.S. Catholic Mission Council.

Missionaries of Africa Report, bm; 1622 21st St. N.W., Washington, D.C. 20009; Society of Missionaries of Africa (White Fathers).

Modern Liturgy, 8 times a year; Resource Publications, 7291 Coronado Dr., San Jose, Calif. 95129.

Modern Schoolman, The, q; 3700 W. Pine Blvd., St. Louis, Mo. 63108; St. Louis University.

Momentum, 4 times a year; Suite 350, One Dupont Circle, Washington, D.C. 20036; National Catholic Educational Asssociation.

Mother Cabrini Messenger, bm; Mother Cabrini Contact Center, Des Plaines, Ill. 60016. Mother Cabrini League.

Mount Loretto Review, a; 108 Bedell St., Staten Island, N.Y. 10309.

MSC Spotlite, bm; 305 S. Lake St., Aurora, Ill. 60507; Missionaries of the Sacred Heart.

Mwangaza, 3 times a year; 172 Foster St., Brighton, Mass. 02135; Franciscan Missionary Sisters for Africa.

My Daily Visitor, bm; 200 Noll Plaza, Huntington, Ind. 46750; Our Sunday Visitor, Inc.

NAWR Trends, m (Sept.-June); 1307 S. Wabash Ave., Chicago, Ill. 60605.

National Catholic Forester, bm; 35 E. Wacker Dr., Chicago, Ill. 60601.

National Communications Office Newsletter, 8-12 times a year; 237 N. Michigan St., South Bend, Ind. 46601; Catholic Charismatic Renewal.

National Jesuit News, m; St. Joseph's College, Philadelphia, Pa. 19131.

Network Quarterly, 1029 Vermont Ave. N.W., No. 650, Washington, D.C. 20005.

New Catholic World, bm; 1865 Broadway, New York, N.Y. 10023.

New Covenant, m; P.O. Box 8617, Main St. Station, Ann Arbor, Mich. 48107; Charismatic Renewal Services.

New Scholasticism, q; Notre Dame, Ind. 46556; American Catholic Philosophical Association.

News/Views, 5 times a year; 1307 S. Wabash Ave., Chicago, Ill. 60605; National Sisters Vocation Conference.

News and Views, q; 3900 Westminster Pl.; St. Louis, Mo. 63108; Sacred Heart Program.

Newsletter, The, 3 times a year; 1234 Massachusetts Ave. N.W., Washington, D.C. 20005; International Liaison for Lay Volunteer Service.

Newsletter of the Bureau of Catholic Indian Missions, 10 times a year; 2021 H St. N.W., Washington, D.C. 20006.

North American Voice of Fatima, biweekly; 1023 Swann Rd., Youngstown, N.Y. 14174.

Notre Dame Magazine, 5 times a year; Notre Dame Univ., Notre Dame, Ind. 46556.

Nova et Vetera, m; 37 Evergreen Pl., E. Orange, N.J. 07018.

Nursing Sisters Today, q; 310 Prospect Park W., Brooklyn, N.Y. 11215; Congregation of Infant Jesus.

Oblate World and Voice of Hope, bm; 350 Jamaica Way, Boston, Mass. 02130; Oblates of Mary Immaculate.

On Comm, m; 1511 Third Ave., Seattle, Wash. 98101; Catholic Communications Northwest.

Origins, 48 times a year; 1312 Massachusetts Ave., N.W., Washington, D.C. 20005; NC News Service.

Our Lady of the Snows, bm; 15 S. 59th St., Belleville, Ill. 62223; Shrine of Our Lady of the Snows.

Our Lady's Digest, bm; Box 777, Twin Lakes, Wis. 53181; La Salette Fathers.

Our Lady's Missionary, m; Topsfield Rd., Ipswich, Mass. 01938; La Salette Fathers.

Our Sunday Visitor Magazine, w; Noll Plaza, Huntington, Ind. 46750.

Pacer, bm; 500 17th Ave., Seattle, Wash. 98124; Providence Medical Center.

Padres' Trail, 6 times a year; St. Michael's Mission, St. Michael, Ariz. 86511; Franciscan Fathers.

Paraclete, 4 times a year; P.O. Box 2000, Wheaton, Md. 20902; Holy Ghost Fathers.

Parish Visitor, q; 25 Elm St., Oneonta, N.Y. 13820; Parish Visitors of Mary Immaculate.

Passionist Orbit, q; 5700 N. Harlem Ave., Chicago, Ill. 60631; Passionist Fathers.

Pastoral Life, m; Route 224, Canfield, Ohio 44406; Society of St. Paul.

Pastoral Music, 6 times a year; 1029 Vermont Ave. N.W. Washington, D.C. 20005; National Association of Pastoral Musicians.

Paulist Fathers News, 4 times a year; 1865 Broadway, New York, N.Y. 10023.

Perpetual Help World, q; 294 E. 150th St., Bronx, N.Y. 10451; Redemptorists.

Philosophy Today, q; Carthagena Station, Celina, Ohio 45822.

Pilgrim, q; Jesuit Fathers, Auriesville, N.Y. 12016; Shrine of North American Martyrs.

Pope Speaks, The, q; Our Sunday Visitor, Inc., 200 Noll Plaza, Huntington, Ind. 46750.

Priatel Dietok (Children's Friend) (Slovak), m; 205 Madison St., Passaic, N.J. 07055; Slovak Catholic Sokol.

Priest, The, 11 times a year; 200 Noll Plaza, Huntington, Ind. 46750; Our Sunday Visitor, Inc.

Probe, m (Oct.-June); 1307 S. Wabash Ave., Chicago, Ill. 60605; NAWR.

Professional Placement Newsnotes, bm; 10 W. 17th St., New York, N.Y. 10011; Catholic Medical Mission Board, Inc.

Program Supplement, 18 times a year; Columbus Plaza, New Haven, Conn. 06507; Knights of Columbus.

Quarterly, The, 2021 H St. N.W., Washington, D.C. 20006; Commission for Catholic Missions Among the Colored People and the Indians.

Queen; bm; 40 S. Saxon Ave., Bay Shore, N.Y. 11706; Montfort Fathers.

Reign of the Sacred Heart, m; Hales Corners, Wis. 53130.

Religion Teacher's Journal, m (Sept.-May); W. Mystic, Conn. 06388.

Religious Book Review, q; 125 Mineola Ave., Roslyn Heights, N.Y. 11577

Religious Life, q; 4200 N. Austin Ave., Chicago, Ill. 60634; Institute on Religious Life.

Religious Media Today, q; 432 Park Ave. S., New York, N.Y. 10016.

Renascence, q; Marquette University, Milwaukee, Wis. 53233.
Respect Life Report, m; 1312 Massachusetts Ave. N.W., Washington, D.C. 20005; Committee for Pro-Life Activities, NCCB.
Review for Religious, bm; Suite 428, 3601 Lindell Blvd., St. Louis, Mo. 63108.
Review of Politics, q; Box B, Notre Dame, Ind. 46556.
Review of Social Economy, 3 times a year; 25 E. Jackson Blvd., Chicago, Ill. 60604; Association for Social Economics.
Roses and Gold from Our Lady of the Ozarks, m; 1740 Grand Ave., Carthage, Mo. 64836.
Roze Maryi (Polish); m; Eden Hill, Stockbridge, Mass. 01262.

Sacred Music, q; 548 Lafond Ave., St. Paul, Minn. 55103.
St. Anthony Messenger, m; 1615 Republic St., Cincinnati, O. 45210; Franciscan Fathers.
St. Anthony's Newsletter, m; Mt. St. Francis, Ind. 47146.
St. Joseph's Advocate, q; Mill Hill Missionaries, Albany, N.Y. 12203.
St. Joseph's Messenger and Advocate of the Blind, q; St. Joseph Home, P.O. Box 288, Jersey City, N.J. 07303.
Salesian Bulletin, bm; 148 Main St., New Rochelle, N.Y. 10802; Salesian Fathers.
Salesian Missions, q; 148 Main St., New Rochelle, N.Y. 10802; Salesians of St. John Bosco.
Salvatorian Newsletter, The, q; Society of the Divine Savior, Salvatorian Center, New Holstein, Wis. 53062.
Sandal Prints, bm; 1820 Mt. Elliott Ave., Detroit, Mich. 48207; Capuchin Fathers.
School Guide, a; 68 W. Broad St., Mt. Vernon, N.Y. 10552.
School Sister, The, q; Notre Dame of the Lake, Mequon, Wis. 53092.
Science Studies, a; St. Bonaventure University, St. Bonaventure, N.Y. 14778.
Scripture in Church, 4 times a year; P.O. Box 9, Northport, N.Y. 11768.
Second Spring, bm; 121 Golden Gate Ave., San Francisco, Calif. 94102; Adult Benevolent Association.
Serenity, q; 601 Maiden Choice Lane, Baltimore, Md. 21228; Little Sisters of the Poor.
Serran, The, bm; 22 W. Monroe St., Chicago, Ill. 60603; Serra International.
Share, 1312 Massachusetts Ave. N.W., Washington, D.C. 20005; Dept. of Communications, USCC.
Share, q; P.O. Box 589, Plaquemine, La. 70764; Catholic Daughters of the Americas.
Shepherd's Call, The, q; 901 Thirteenth St., N.W., Albuquerque, N.M. 87103; Brothers of Good Shepherd.
Sign, The, 10 times a year; Monastery Place, Union City, N.J. 07087; Passionist Fathers.
Silent Advocate, bm; St. Rita School for the Deaf, 1720 Glendale-Milford Rd., Cincinnati, O. 45215.
Sister Miriam Teresa League of Prayer Bulletin, q; League Headquarters, Convent Station, N.J. 07961.
Sistersharing, bm; 1962 Shenandoah, Los Angeles, Calif. 90034; National Sisters Communications Service.
SC News, m (Sept.-May); 4400 Churchman Ave., Louisville, Ky. 40215; Sisters of Charity of Nazareth.
Sisters Today, m (exc. July-Aug.); St. John's Abbey, Collegeville, Minn. 56321.
Social Justice Review, bm; 3835 Westminster Pl., St. Louis, Mo. 63108; Catholic Central Union of America.
Social Thought, q; 1346 Connecticut Ave. N.W., Washington, D.C. 20036; National Conference of Catholic Charities.
Sodalis Polonia, 9 times a year; St. Mary's College, Orchard Lake, Mich. 48033; Sts. Cyril and Methodius Seminary.
Sons of Mary Missionary Society, q; 567 Salem End Rd., Framingham, Mass. 01701.
Sophia, m; 719 Washington St., Steubenville, O. 43952; Newton Melkite eparchy.
Soul, bm; Ave Maria Institute, Washington, N.J. 07882; Blue Army.
Spirit, biannually; Seton Hall University, South Orange, N.J. 08824; poetry magazine.
Spirit and Life, 6 times a year; 8300 Morganford Rd., St. Louis, Mo. 63123; Benedictine Srs. of Perpetual Adoration.
Spiritual Book News, 8 times a year; Notre Dame, Ind. 46556.
Spiritual Life, q; 2131 Lincoln Rd. N.E., Washington, D.C. 20002; Discalced Carmelites.
Spirituality Today (formerly Cross and Crown), q; 1909 S. Ashland Ave., Chicago, Ill. 60608, Dominican Fathers.
Squires Newsletter, m; Columbus Plaza, New Haven, Conn. 06507; Columbian Squires.
Studies in the Spirituality of Jesuits, 5 times a year; 3700 W. Pine Blvd., St. Louis, Mo. 63108.
Sword, 3 times a year; 29 N. Broadway, Joliet, Ill. 60435.

Theological Studies, q; Georgetown Univ., 37th and O Sts., N.W., Washington, D.C. 20057.
Theology Digest, q; 3634 Lindell Blvd., St. Louis, Mo. 63108.
Theresian, News, The, 6 times a year; 5326 E. Pershing Ave., Scottsdale, Ariz. 85254.
Thomist, The, q; 487 Michigan Ave. N.E., Washington, D.C. 20017; Dominican Fathers.
Thought, q; Fordham University Press, Box L, Bronx, N.Y. 10458; Fordham University.

Today's Catholic Teacher, m (Sept.-May); 2451 E. River Rd., Suite 200, Dayton, O. 45439.

Today's Parish, m (Sept.-May); P.O. Box 180, West Mystic, Conn. 06340.

Topic, semi-annually; 151 Thompson St., New York, N.Y. 10012. Secular Franciscan Order, Province of Immaculate Conception.

Trinity Missions, q; P.O. Box 30, Silver Springs, Md. 20910.

Ultreya Magazine, m; 4500 W. Davis St., Dallas, Tex. 75211. Cursillo Movement.

L'Union (French), q; 1 Social St., Woonsocket, R.I. 02895.

UNIREA, The Union (Romanian and English), m; 4309 Olcott Ave., East Chicago, Ind. 46312.

U.S. Catholic, m; 221 W. Madison St., Chicago, Ill. 60606; Claretian Fathers.

Verona Fathers Missions, 6 times a year; 2104 St. Michael's St., Cincinnati, O. 45205.

Venture, 27 times during school year; 200 Noll Plaza, Hungtinton, Indiana 46750; Our Sunday Visitor, Grades 4-6.

Visions, 27 times during school year; 200 Noll Plaza, Huntington, Ind. 46750; Our Sunday Visitor, Grades 7-8.

Vox Regis Alumni Newsletter, 3 times a year; 711 Knox Rd., East Aurora, N.Y. 14052; Christ the King Seminary.

Waif's Messenger, m; Drawer X, Chicago, Ill. 60690; Mission of Our Lady of Mercy.

Way — of St. Francis, 10 times a year; 109 Golden Gate Ave., San Francisco, Calif. 94102; Franciscan Fathers of California, Inc.

Western Catholic Union Record, m; 906 W.C.U. Bldg., Quincy, Ill. 62301; Western Catholic Union.

Wheeling College Chronicle, 4 times a year; 316 Washington Ave., Wheeling, W. Va. 26003.

Word of God, w; 2187 Victory Blvd., Staten Island, N.Y. 10314; Society of St. Paul.

Working for Boys, q; Box A, Danvers, Mass. 01923; Xaverian Brothers.

Worldmission, q; 366 5th Ave., New York, N.Y. 10001; Society for the Propagation of the Faith.

Worldwide Family Spirit, m; 233-26 Mariano St., Woodland Hills, Calif. 91364, Worldwide Marriage Encounter.

Worship, 6 times a year; St. John's Abbey, Collegeville, Minn. 56321. North American Academy of Liturgy.

Worship Times, q; 7291 Coronado Dr. No. 3, San Jose, Calif. 95129.

Xaverian Missions Newsletter, 9 times a year; 101 Summer St., Holliston, Mass. 01746; Xaverian Missionary Fathers.

Your Edmundite Missions Newsletter, bm; 1428 Broad St., Selma, Ala. 36701; Southern Missions of Society of St. Edmund.

Zeal, q; St. Elizabeth Mission Society of the Sisters of St. Francis, Allegany, N.Y. 14706.

Books

The Official Catholic Directory, annual, P. J. Kenedy and Sons, 866 Third Ave., New York, N.Y. 10022. First edition, 1817.

The Catholic Almanac, annual; Our Sunday Visitor, Inc., 200 Noll Plaza, Huntington, Ind. 46750, publisher; editorial offices, 620 Route 3, Clifton, N.J. 07013. First edition, 1904.

The American Catholic Who's Who, biennial; NC News Service, 1312 Massachusetts Ave., N.W., Washington, D.C. 20005. First volume, 1934-35.

BOOK CLUBS

Catholic Book Club (1928), 106 W. 56th St., New York, N.Y. 10019. Sponsors the Campion Award.

Catholic Digest Book Club (1954), Catholic Digest Magazine, P.O. Box 43090, St. Paul, Minn. 55164.

Herald Book Club (1958), Franciscan Herald Press, 1434 W. 51st St., Chicago, Ill. 60609.

Thomas More Book Club (1939), Thomas More Association, 180 N. Wabash Ave., Chicago, Ill. 60601.

International Periodicals

African Ecclesiastical Review, bm; Gaba Publications, P.O. Box 908, Eldoret, Kenya.

Australasian Catholic Record, q; St. Patrick's Seminary, Manly, New South Wales, Australia.

Biblical Theology, biannual; 44 Old Manse Rd., Newtownabbey, Co. Antrim, N. Ireland BT37 ORX.

Christ to the World, bm; Via G, Nicoterra 31, 00195, Rome, Italy.

Clergy Review, m; 48 Great Peter St., London, SW1P 2HB, England.

Communio-International Catholic Review, q; Gonzaga Univ., Spokane, Wash. 99258.

Doctrine and Life, m and **Supplement to Doctrine and Life,** bm; Dominican Publications, St. Saviour's, Dublin 1, Ireland.

Downside Review, q; Newman Bookshop, 87 St. Aldates, Oxford, England.

Dublin Review, q; 14 Howick Place, London, S.W. 1, England.

Eastern Churches Review, semi-annual; 9 Alfred St., Oxford, England.

Faith Today, 10 times a year; Dominican Publications, St. Saviour's, Dublin 1, Ireland.

Furrow, m; St. Patrick's College, Maynooth, Ireland.

Heythrop Journal q; Heythrop College, 11 Cavendish Sq., London W1M, OAN, England.

Horizons: Journal of the College Theology Society, semi-annual; Waterloo, Ont., Canada (Editorial Office: Villanova Univ., Villanova, Pa. 19085.)

International Philosophical Quarterly, q; Fordham University, Bronx, N.Y. 10458.

Irish Theological Quarterly, q; St. Patrick's College, Maynooth, Ireland.

L'Osservatore Romano, w; Vatican City.

Louvain Studies, semi-annual; Naamsestraat 100 B-3000, Louvain, Belgium.

Lumen Vitae, q; International Center for Studies in Religious Education, 184, rue Washington, 1050 Brussels, Belgium.

Mediaeval Studies, annual; Pontifical Institute of Mediaeval Studies, 59 Queen's Park Crescent East, Toronto, Ont., Canada M5S 2C4.

Month, m; 114 Mount St., London, W1Y, 6AH, England.

Music and Liturgy, q; Fowler Wright Books, Ltd., Tenbury Wells, Worcs., England.

New Blackfriars, m; edited by English Dominicans, Blackfriars, Oxford, England.

One in Christ, q; Benedictine Priory, Priory Close — Southgate, London N14 4AT, Eng. (U.S. agency, Grailville, Loveland, O. 45140).

Philosophical Studies, annual; St. Patrick's College, Maynooth, Ireland.

Recusant History, biannual; Catholic Record Society, 114 Mount St., London, W1Y 6AH, England.

Religion and Society, q; Christian Institute for the Study of Religion and Society, 17 Miller Rd., P.O. Box 4600, Bangalore 560 046, India.

Scripture in Church, q; Dominican Publications, St. Saviour's, Dublin 1, Ireland. (U.S. publisher, Costello Publishing, 88 Nautilus Ave., Northport, L.I., N.Y. 11768.)

Studies in Religion/Sciences Religieuses (bilingual); q; Wilfrid Laurier Press, Waterloo, Ont. N2L 3C5.

Sursum Corda—Lift Up Your Hearts, bm; Box 79, Box Hill, Victoria, Australia 3128.

Tablet, The w; 48 Great Peter St., SW1P 2HB, London, England.

Teaching All Nations, q; East Asian Pastoral Institute, Box 1815, Manila, Philippines.

Teilhard Review, The, 3 times a year; The Teilhard Centre for the Future of Man, 81 Cromwell Rd., London SW7 5BW, England.

Theology, bm; S.P.C.K. Holy Trinity Church, Marylebone Rd., London, N.W. 1, England.

Way, The, q; 39 Fitzjohn Ave., London NW3 5JT, England.

Catholic News Agencies

(Sources: International Catholic Union of the Press, Geneva; Catholic Press Association, U.S.)

Argentina: Agencia Informativa Catolica Argentina (AICA), Rodriguez Pena 846, Casilla de Correo Central 2886, Buenos Aires.

Austria: Katholische Presse-Agentur (Kathpress), Wollzeile 1010 Vienna 1.

Belgium: Centre d'Information de Presse (CIP), 38 avenue des Arts, 1040 Bruxelles (Brussels).

Germany: Katholische Nachrichten Agentur (KN), Adenauer Allee 134, 5300 Bonn 1.

Great Britain: Catholic Information Office of England and Wales (CIOEW), 74, Gallows Hill Lane, Abbots Langley, Herts WD5 OB2.

Hungary: Magyar Kurir, Karolyi w 4-8, Postafiok 41, Budapest V.

India: News Bureau India, 13/16, School Marg, Rajinder Nagar, New Delhi 110060

Italy: Agenzia Stampa Catholica Associata (ASCA), v. uffici del Vicario 30, I-00186 Rome.

Japan: TO-SEI, 10-1 Rokubancho, Chiyodaku, Tokyo 102.

Spain: Prensa Asociada (PA), Alfonso XI, 4—Apartado 14530, Madrid 14.

LOGOS, Mateo Inurria 15, Apartado 466, Madrid — 16.

Switzerland: Katholische Internationale Presse-Agentur (KIPA), Case Postale 1054 CH 1701, Fribourg.

Centre International de Reportages et d'Information Culturelle (CIRIC), 10, av. de la Gare-des-Eaux Vives, CH-1207 Geneva.

United States of America: NC News Service (NC), 1312 Massachusetts Ave. N.W., Washington, D.C. 20005.

Yugoslavia: Aktusinosti Krscanska Sadasnjost (AKSA), Marulicev TRG 14, Zagreb p.p. 02-748.

Zaire: Documentation et Information Africaine (DIA), B.P. 2598, Kinshasa I.

U.S. Press Services

NC News Service (NC), established in 1920, provides a worldwide daily news report by wire throughout the continental U.S. and to Europe, and by mail to Canadian and most overseas subscribers, serving more than 400 Catholic periodicals, foreign news agencies, broadcasters including Vatican Radio, and institutional subscribers. It also provides feature and photo services; "Origins," a documentary and text service; "Catholic Trends," a fortnightly newsletter; "Know Your Faith," a weekly religious education package; *The American Catholic Who's Who,* a biennial directory. NC is represented in all U.S. dioceses and 40 foreign countries. It has a two-member bureau in Rome. It is a division of the United States Catholic Conference, with offices at 1312 Massachusetts Ave. N.W., Washington, D.C. 20005. The director and editor-in-chief is Richard W. Daw.

Religious News Service (RNS) provides domestic and foreign Catholic and other religious news in daily photos and features; "The

Religious News Reporter," a weekly 15-minute radio and/or TV package; "The Week in Religion," a feature. RNS was inaugurated in 1933 by the National Conference of Christians and Jews as an independent news agency. Its offices are located at 43 W. 57th St., New York, N.Y. 10019.

Eastern Rite Information Service (ER), for Eastern Church news; 2208 W. Chicago Ave., Chicago, Ill. 60622.

Spanish-Language Service: A weekly news summary, *Resumen Semanal de Noticias*, issued by NC News Service, is used by a number of diocesan newspapers. Some papers carry features of their own in Spanish.

CATHOLIC WRITERS' MARKET
(Source: Almanac survey.)

Editors call the following suggestions to the attention of writers:

Manuscripts should be typewritten, double-spaced, on one side of the page.

Writers should know the editorial policy, purpose and style of the publication to which they submit manuscripts. Sample copies may easily be obtained, often for the mere cost of postage. Some editors suggest that writers send outlines of proposed material, in order to facilitate editorial decision and direction. "Timely" copy should be submitted considerably in advance of the date of proposed publication; some editors advise a period of three months. Authors are urged to avoid sermonizing. Writers should not expect extensive criticism of their work, although they should profit from advice and direction when these are given. Editors are not required to state their reasons for rejecting manuscripts. Replies regarding the acceptance or rejection of copy are usually made within a few weeks.

All writers should send to editors stamped, self-addressed envelopes for the return of material. Those who write to Canadian editors may use international reply coupons, not U.S. stamps.

Payment is made on acceptance or publication. Rates are sometimes variable because of the reputation of the writer, the quality and length of the manuscript, the amount of editorial work required for its final preparation.

America: 106 W. 56th St., New York, N.Y. 10019. Ed., Rev. Joseph A O'Hare, S.J. Weekly, circulation 37,000; $14 per year.

ARTICLES on important public issues evaluated scientifically and morally; serious and authenticated articles on family life, education, religion, and social and political issues with ethical or religious implications; occasionally, "thought" pieces; 1,000-2,000 words—3¢ a word. VERSE, short and modern, befitting a Catholic publication but not necessarily religious—$7.50 and up. No fiction.

Annals of St. Anne de Beaupre, The: P.O. Box 1000, St. Anne de Beaupre, Que., Canada G0A 3C0. Ed., Rev. Francois Plourde, C.SS.R. Monthly, circulation 70,000; $3.50 per year.

FICTION: Stories of general Catholic interest, preferably with slant on devotion to St. Anne; 1,500-1,600 words — 1½-2¢ a word. ARTICLES of solid general interest to Catholics: on aspects of devotion to St. Anne, relative to history of the devotion in North America or elsewhere: on educational or social problems, or situations that should be of concern to all — especially Christians: 1,200-1,700 words — 2¢ a word, Payment on acceptance: report within a month.

Catechist: 2451 E. River Rd., Dayton, O. 45439. Ed., Patricia Fischer. Monthly Sept. through May (exc. Dec.), circulation 46,000; $8.50 per year.

ARTICLES of interest to teachers of religion in parochial schools and CCD programs: 1,200-1,800 words — rate varies. PHOTOGRAPHS, black and white — rate varies. Payment on publication.

Catholic Digest: P.O. Box 43090, St. Paul, Minn. 55164. Ed., Henry Lexau. Monthly, circulation 560,000; $6.97 per year.

ARTICLES of close-to-home interest for average Catholic — rates vary; most frequent payments are $200 for originals, $100 for reprints; payment on acceptance. FILLERS, short features and jokes — rates vary; payment on publication. Cover pictures — $150. No fiction or verse. No queries necessary.

Columban Mission: St. Columbans, Nebr. 68056. Ed., Rev. Peter McPartland. Monthly (exc. June, Aug.); circulation 241,929; $2 per year.

ARTICLES mostly from missions or staff written: occasionally accept feature or factual articles on social and religious aspects of Asian and Latin American life: 2,000 words — $100 and up. PHOTOGRAPHS of Asian and Latin American subjects and photo stories — $10 each.

Columbia: Columbus Plaza, New Haven, Conn. 06507. Ed., Elmer Von Feldt. Monthly, circulation 1,250,000; $3 per year. Official organ of the Knights of Columbus.

ARTICLES dealing with current events, social problems, Catholic apostolic activities: 1,000-3,000 words (must be accompanied by glossy photos) — $100 to $300. FICTION, Christian viewpoint: up to 3,000 words — up to $300. SATIRE: 1,000 words — $100. CARTOONS, pungent, wordless humor — $25. COVERS — $650.

Commonweal: 232 Madison Ave., New York, N.Y. 10016. Ed., James O'Gara. Biweekly, circulation 20,000; $20 per year.

ARTICLES, political, religious and literary subjects: 1,000-3,000 words — 2¢ a word. VERSE, serious poetry of high literary merit — about 40¢ a line.

Crusader's Almanac: Franciscan Monastery, 1400 Quincy St. N.E., Washington, D.C.

20017. Ed., Rev. Bartholomew Bengisser, O.F.M. Quarterly, circulation 85,000; $1 per year.

ARTICLES about the Holy Land, Bible and Crusades given preference — 1¢ a word.

Emmanuel: 194 E. 76th Street, New York, N.Y. 10021. Editor-in-Chief, Rev. Paul J. Bernier, S.S.S. Monthly, bimonthly July-Aug., circulation 15,000; $8 per year.

ARTICLES, spirituality for those in Church ministry, Eucharistic, pastoral, theological, Scriptural: 2,000-3,000 words — $40-$50.

Eucharist: 194 E. 76th St., New York, N.Y. 10021. Ed., Rev. William J. O'Halloran, S.S.S. Bimonthly, circulation 6,378; $4 per year.

ARTICLES, presenting meaning of Eucharist in Catholic spirituality: average length 1,500 words — 2-3¢ a word. Payment on publication.

Hospital Progress: 1438 S. Grand Blvd., St. Louis, Mo. 63104. Ed., R. J. Stephens. Monthly, circulation 14,000; $14 per year.

Official journal of the Catholic Hospital Association.

ARTICLES, hospital-oriented; administrative procedures and theories; hospital departmental services: 1,500-3,000 words — $1 per column inch. BOOK REVIEWS, hospital oriented — payment by agreement.

Institute Journal: 50 Oak St., San Francisco, Calif. 94102. Ed., James R. Mullen. Bimonthly, $1 per year.

FICTION — no fixed rate. PHOTOGRAPHS — $15.

It's Our World: 800 Allegheny Ave., Pittsburgh, Pa. 15233. Ed., Thomas F. Haas. Four times a year (three issues: Grades 1-3, 4-6, 7-8); circulation 3,100,000.

Official publication of Pontifical Association of the Holy Childhood.

ARTICLES, with mission themes suitable for children: 600-800 words — usual rates.

Josephite Harvest, The: 1130 N. Calvert St., Baltimore, Md. 21202. Ed., Rev. Earle A. Newman, S.S.J. Quarterly; circulation 40,000; $2 per year.

ARTICLES concerning apostolate of Catholic Church in U.S. to the black community.

Living Light, The, An Interdisciplinary Review of Christian Education: Editorial offices, Department of Education, 1312 Massachusetts Ave. N.W., Washington D.C. 20005. Quarterly, circulation 4,630; $10 per year.

ARTICLES on religious education, catechetics, Scripture: under 3,000 words — 2¢ per word.

Marian Helpers Bulletin: Eden Hill, Stockbridge, Mass. 01262. Ed., Rev. Walter F. Pelczynski, M.I.C. Quarterly, circulation over 695,000; $1 per year. Overstocked at present.

Marriage and Family Living: St. Meinrad, Ind. 47577. Ed., Ila M. Stabile. Monthly, circulation 52,000; $9 per year.

ARTICLES: (1) aimed at enriching the husband-wife and parent-child relationship by expanding religious and psychological insights or sensitivity: 1,000-2,000 words; (2) informative, aimed at helping couple cope, in practical ways, with problems of modern living: maximum 2,000 words; (3) personal essays relating amusing and/or heartwarming incidents that point up the human side of marriage and family life: maximum 1,500 words — 5¢ a word. PHOTOS: purchased with ms.; 3x11 b & w glossies, color transparencies — $10 minimum. 4-color cover photo — $125; b & w cover photo — $50; 2-page spread in contents — $35; 1-page in contents — $30. Photos of couples especially desired. Model releases required.

Buys North American serial rights only. Report on submissions in 3 to 4 weeks. Sample copy available for 25¢. Payment on acceptance.

Maryknoll: Maryknoll, N.Y. 10545. Ed., Rev. Darryl L. Hunt, M.M. Monthly, circulation more than 300,000; $1.00 per year.

ARTICLES must apply in some way to the hopes and aspirations, the culture, the problems and challenges of peoples in Asia, Africa and Latin America: 1,000-1,500 words — average payment, $100. Outline wanted before submission of material. PHOTOS: More interested in photo stories than in individual black and whites and color transparencies. Photo stories — up to $150, black and white; up to $200, color. Individual photos — $15, black and white; $25, color. Transparencies returned after use. Query to be made before sending photos.

Messenger of the Sacred Heart, The: 833 Broadview Ave., Toronto, Ont., Canada, M4K 2P9. Ed., Rev. F. J. Power, S.J. Monthly, circulation 23,000; $3 per year.

FICTION: stories which appeal to men, written with humor—good family reading: maximum, 2,000 words — 2¢ a word. ARTICLES of Catholic interest: 2,500 words — 2¢ a word. Payment upon acceptance.

Miraculous Medal, The: 475 E. Chelten Ave., Philadelphia, Pa. 19144. Ed., Rev. Robert P. Cawley, C.M. Quarterly, circulation 100,000.

FICTION, of general interest. Catholic in principle: 1,500-2,000 words — 2¢ a word and up. VERSE, religious in theme or turn; preferably about Our Lady: maximum 20 lines — 50¢ a line and up. Payment on acceptance. No articles.

My Daily Visitor: Noll Plaza, Huntington, Ind. 46750. Mng. Ed., Patrick R Moran. Bimonthly, circulation 21,255; $6 per year.

A pocket-sized booklet of reflections for each day of the month.
MATERIAL: Daily reflections based on spiritual meditation, the feast of the day or the liturgical season: maximum 165 words per page (each day's reflection is printed on a separate page) — $100 for series of reflections.

New Catholic World: 1865 Broadway, New York, N.Y. 10023. Mng. Ed., Robert Heyer. Bimonthly, circulation 14,000; $7 per year. Thematic issues.
ARTICLES, related to themes of issue (query editor): about 1,800-2,000 words. Rates of payment supplied.

Our Family: Box 249, Dept. C, Battleford, Sask., Canada SOM OEO. Ed., Rev. Reb Materi, O.M.I. Monthly, circulation 13,049; $5 per year.
FICTION, adult only; stories that reflect lives, problems and concerns of audience; anything true to human nature; no sentimentality or blatant moralizing; stories with "woven in" Christian message: 1,000-3,000 words — 3¢ a word. ARTICLES related to family living; religion, education, social, biographical, marriage, courtship, domestic, institutional: 1,000-3,000 words — 3¢ a word. POETRY, in the market for many more poems; should deal with man in search for himself, for God, for others, for love, for meaning in life, for commitment: 8-30 lines — $3-$10. PHOTOS — purchased with manuscript as package (extra payment for photos); also in search of individual photos for editorial use. FILLERS — anecdotes of inspirational value, straight exposition, short humor. Writers' guide and photo specification sheet available on request (free). A sample copy is available for 50¢. Usually buys first North American serial rights; will consider purchasing second or reprint rights.

Our Sunday Visitor Magazine: Noll Plaza, Huntington, Ind. 46750. Ed., Robert Lockwood. Weekly, circulation 350,000; $9.50 per year.
ARTICLES, no limitation on subjects other than those imposed by good taste and orthodoxy. Picture and text stories, profiles of individuals and organizations; articles that reflect moral, cultural, historical, social, economic and certain political concerns about the U.S. and the world; articles on current problems. Practical, factual and anecdotal material is sought: 750-1,000 words—$75-$100, usual payment. Queries are preferred to unsolicited completed manuscripts. PHOTOGRAPHS, picture stories preferred rather than individual photos. Picture stories (color) — $100 and up. No fiction or poetry.

Parish Family Digest: Noll Plaza, Huntington, Ind. 46750. Ed., Patrick R. Moran. Bimonthly, circulation 140,000.
ARTICLES of timely interest to the young and growing Catholic family as a unit of the Catholic parish — personality profiles, interviews, social concerns, education, humor, inspiration and family and parish-family interrelationships; 1,000 words or less — 5¢ a word. REPRINTS — $25. CARTOONS — $10 each for exclusives. FILLERS — $5 each for exclusives based on personal experience.

Priest, The: 200 Noll Plaza, Huntington, Ind. 46750. Ed., Rev. Albert J. Nevins, M.M. Monthly (exc. Aug.), circulation 11,228; $13 per year.
ARTICLES of benefit to priests and seminarians in any of the following areas: priestly spirituality, contemporary theology, liturgy, apostolate and ministry, pastoral notes, Scripture. Controversial subject matter acceptable provided it does not go beyond the realm of orthodoxy or respect for authority or demands of fraternal charity: 6-15 double-spaced pages — $25 to $100 (about $5 per manuscript page).

Queen of All Hearts: 40 S. Saxon Ave., Bay Shore, N.Y. 11706. Ed., Rev. James McMillan, S.M.M.; Mng. Ed., Rev. Roger M. Charest S.M.M. Bimonthly; circulation 8,500; $5 per year.
FICTION: short stories, preferably with a Marian theme: 1,000-2,000 words. ARTICLES that bring out the importance of devotion to Mary. Payment varies. VERSE with Marian theme — payment, two years' subscription. No artwork or fillers.

Review for Religious: Suite 428, 3601 Lindell Blvd., St. Louis, Mo. 63108. Ed., D.F.X. Meenan, S.J. Bimonthly, circulation 19,476; $8 per year.
ARTICLES, of interest to religious: 3,000-6,000 words — $6 per printed page.

St. Anthony Messenger: 1615 Republic St., Cincinnati, O. 45210. Ed., Rev. Jeremy Harrington, O.F.M. Monthly, circulation 300,000; $8 per year.
FICTION: Written out of a totally Christian background, illuminating the truth of human nature for adults. No preachiness, sentimentality. FACT ARTICLES: 3,000-3,500 words. Outstanding personalities (must be based on personal interview). Information and comment on major movements in the Church: application of Christian faith to daily life; real-life solutions in the areas of a) family life, education; b) personal living (labor, leisure, art, psychology, spirituality). Human interest narrative. Humor. Photos and picture stories. Query letters welcome.

St. Joseph's Messenger and Advocate of the Blind: St. Joseph's Home, P.O. Box 288, Jersey City, N.J. 07303. Ed., Sr. Ursula Maphet, C.S.J. Quarterly, circulation 68,000; $2 per year.
FICTION, and ARTICLES, contemporary, mainstream themes, 500-1,500 words — 1¢ to 3¢ a word.

Salesian Missions: 148 Main St., New Rochelle, New York 10802. Ed., Rev. Edward J.

Cappelletti, S.D.B. Quarterly, circulation 1,000,000; $1 per year.
ARTICLES: mission interest; pertaining to Salesian Society, life, spirit and educational system of St. John Bosco; adolescent interest and education — 5¢ a word and up. PHOTOGRAPHS — $6. Suggest queries before submitting material. Payment on acceptance. Early report.

Sign: Monastery Pl., Union City, N.J. 07087. Ed., Rev. Patrick McDonough, C.P. Monthly, circulation 150,000; $8 per year.
ARTICLES on prayer, sacraments, social concerns, and other topics of Catholic interest: 1,000-3,000 words. Payment varies according to length and quality of article. Photos and drawings welcomed with article submissions. FICTION, religious or providing some insight into the human condition. Payment varies.

Social Justice Review: 3835 Westminster Pl., St. Louis, Mo. 63108. Ed., Harvey J. Johnson, Bimonthly, circulation 1,325; $8 per year.
ARTICLES: research, editorial and review: 2,000-4,000 words—$3 per column. No fiction.

Spiritual Life: 2131 Lincoln Rd., N.E., Washington, D.C. 20002. Ed., Rev. Christopher Latimer, O.C.D. Quarterly, circulation 17,000; $5 per year.
ARTICLES, must follow scope of magazine: 3,000-5,000 words — rate varies. Sample copy and instructions for writers sent upon request.

Spirituality Today: Aquinas Institute, Dubuque, Ia. 52001 (Editorial Office). Ed., Rev. Christopher Kiesling, O.P. Quarterly, circulation 3,500; $5 per year.
ARTICLES concerning any phase of the spiritual life: minimum 3,000-4,000 words — 1¢ a word. No fiction or poetry.

Today's Catholic Teacher: 2451 E. River Rd., Suite 200, Dayton, O. 45439. Ed., Ruth A. Matheny. Monthly Sept. through May (exc. Dec.), circulation 60,000; $7.95 per year.
ARTICLES of professional and personal interest to teachers, administrators, pastors, parish councils and school board members concerning Catholic schools and CCD programs: 600-800 words, 1,500-3,000 words—$15-$75. Premium payment for superior content and writing presentation. Black and white photos helpful. Payment on publication.

WAY — of St. Francis: 109 Golden Gate Ave. San Francisco, Calif. 94102. Ed., Simon Scanlon, O.F.M. Ten times a year, circulation 8,404; $5 per year.
ARTICLES, in keeping with the purpose of the magazine, to bear effective witness to the ideals and aims of the Order of St. Francis: to view the world through Christian eyes; to point up the relationship between abstract belief and concrete action in the modern world: 1,500-2,200 words—$30 to $50. PHOTOGRAPHS: bought with articles.

Working for Boys: Box A, Danvers, Mass. 01223. Ed., Brother Alphonsus Dwyer, C.F.X. (Mss. to Bro. Alois, C.F.X., Assoc. Ed., St. John's High School, Shrewsbury, Mass, 01545.) Quarterly, circulation 20,000; $1 per year.
FICTION, preferably seasonal: 800-1,000 words—3¢ a word. ARTICLES, preferably seasonal: All Souls, Christmas, Easter, Summer: 800-1,000 words—3¢ a word. VERSE, seasonal, 4-16 lines—25¢-50¢ a line.

Worship: St. John's Abbey, Collegeville, Minn. 56321. Ed., Rev. Aelred Tegels, O.S.B. Bimonthly, circulation 6,784; $8 per year.
ARTICLES related to the engagement of the magazine in ongoing study of both the theoretical and pastoral dimensions of liturgy; examines historical traditions of worship in their doctrinal context, the experience of worship in Christian churches, the findings of contemporary theology, psychology, communications, cultural anthropology, and sociology insofar as they have a bearing on public worship: 3,000-5,000 words—2¢ a word for commissioned articles. No fiction or poetry.

RADIO, TELEVISION, THEATRE

Radio

Christopher Radio Program: 15-minute interview-discussion series, "Christopher Closeup," weekly, on 300 stations; a one-minute "Christopher Thought for Today," daily, on more than 1,500 stations. Address: 12 E. 48th St., New York, N.Y. 10017.

Crossroads: Originated in 1954 as the Hour of the Crucified, produced by the Passionist Fathers and Brothers. Weekly, on nearly 700 stations. Director: Rev. Cyril Schweinberg, C.P.; Associate Director: Bro. Damian Carroll, C.P. Address: 1089 Elm St., West Springfield, Mass. 01089.

Encuentro (Spanish-language version of Crossroads): Originated in October, 1972. Weekly, on over 30 Spanish-language stations in U.S. and Latin America. Address: 1089 Elm St., W. Springfield, Mass. 01089.

Guideline: Produced in cooperation with the Office for Film and Broadcasting, NCCB/USCC. Weekly program designed to set forth the teachings of the Catholic Church and to discuss issues the Church faces in the contemporary world; heard on approximately 90 stations (NBC).

On This Rock: Originated in 1941, produced in cooperation with the Office for Film and Broadcasting, NCCB/USCC. A 15-minute weekly program currently employing a youth-oriented music and commentary format; heard on more than 100 stations (ABC).

Radio, TV, Theatre — Communications Services

Sacred Heart Program: Originated in 1939, produced by the Jesuit Fathers. Features five 15-minute programs, one five-minute program and one half-hour program weekly on radio, and one 15-minute TV program weekly. Director, Rev. Denis E. Daly, S.J. Address: 3900 Westminster Place, St. Louis, Mo. 63108.

Television

Directions: Originated in 1960, this weekly half-hour program sustains a news-oriented approach to reporting social, moral and religious issues within a Catholic context. The Office for Film and Broadcasting, NCCB/USCC, cooperates in the production of some 15 segments a year, in addition to interfaith and seasonal specials; carried at variable dates on more than 100 stations (ABC).

For Our Times: Originated in April 1979, this weekly half-hour series produced by CBS in a unique joint cooperative consultation with the Office for Film and Broadcasting, USCC, the National Council of Churches and the New York Board of Rabbis focuses on the ethical and social challenges confronting American society today. Format: documentary and studio discussion (CBS).

Religious Specials: The Office for Film and Broadcasting, NCCB/USCC, cooperates in the production of four one-hour Catholic specials a year and occasional seasonal or trifaith presentations. These programs offer a varied format: film, dramatizations, panel discussions, music and commentary, etc. Catholic portions are telecast on approximately 140 stations (NBC).

Theatre

Catholic University Drama Department: Established in 1937. Offers degree courses in theatre arts, produces five plays a year in The Hartke Theatre, has touring company of graduates (see National Players). Chairman of the department, William H. Graham. Address: Catholic University of America, Washington, D.C. 20064.

National Players: An operation of University Players, a non-profit organization affiliated with the Drama Department of the Catholic University. It originated in 1949 and is the oldest classical touring company in the U.S. Olney Theatre, Olney, Md., an Equity theatre operation of University Players since 1953, was designated the State Summer Theatre of Maryland in 1978.

Catholic Actors' Guild of America, Inc.: Established in 1914 to provide varied services to people in the theatre. Has more than 600 members, publishes *The Call Board* bimonthly. Address: Piccadilly Hotel, 227 W. 45th St., New York, N.Y. 10036.

Communications Services

Centro Video: Mexican-American TV programming. Oblate College of the Southwest, 285 Oblate Dr., San Antonio, Tex. 78216.

Christopher TV Series, "Christopher Closeup": Originated in 1951. Half-hour and quarter-hour interviews in color, weekly, on 80 commercial stations, 130 American Forces Network outlets and 720 cable systems. Address: 12 E. 48th St., New York, N.Y. 10017.

Father Peyton's Family Theater Productions: Films for TV, for sale and rental. Address: 7201 Sunset Blvd., Hollywood, Calif. 90046.

Franciscan Communications Center: An audio-visual media center dedicated to the production of public service broadcasting material and audio-visual media for religious education. Creators and producers of TeleSPOTS and AudioSPOTS, 10- to 60-second public service messages for radio and TV; TeleKETICS films and media kits, filmstrips, slide programs and phonograph records and tapes, for religious, moral and value education; StorySCAPE, a religious education program for the family. Address: 1229 South Santee St., Los Angeles, Calif. 90015.

Mary Productions "Airtime": Originated in 1950. Offers royalty-free scripts for stage, film, radio and tape production. Audio and video tapes of lives of the saints and historical characters. Address: Mary Productions Guild, 58 Lenison Ave., Belford, N.J. 07718.

Paulist Communications: Contracts with dioceses and parishes to provide public service programs free to radio stations and scripts to priest-broadcasters; contacts stations for dioceses. Address: P.O. Box 1057, Pacific Palisades, Calif. 90272.

Paulist Productions: Producers and distributors of the INSIGHT Film Series (available for TV at no charge), and educational film series. Purchase and rental information available. Address: P.O. Box 1057, Pacific Palisades, Calif. 90272.

Sacred Heart Program — TV: Originated in 1954, produced by the Jesuit Fathers. Director, Rev. Denis E. Daly, S.J. Address: 3900 Westminster Pl., St. Louis, Mo. 63108.

Tele-Vue I Productions: Films for TV, mostly educational, for sale and rental. Also available for rental to Catholic schools. Address: Rev. Paul W. Stauder, Old St. Henry's Church, 525 E. Broadway, E. St. Louis, Ill. 62201.

Catholic Television Network (CTN): Instructional TV operations have been established in the following archdioceses and dioceses. Archdioceses are indicated by an asterisk.

Boston,* Mass.: Rev. James Hawker, Director, 468 Beacon St. 02115.

Brooklyn, N.Y.: Rev. Michael J. Dempsey, Director, 1712 10th Ave., 11215.

Chicago,* Ill.: Mr. Charles E. Hinds, Executive Director, One N. Wacker Dr. 60606.

Los Angeles,* Calif.: Mr. Steven J. Gorski, 1520 W. Ninth St. 90015.

New York,* N.Y.: Sr. M. Irene Fugazy, Director, Seminary Ave., Yonkers, N.Y. 10704.

Rockville Centre, N.Y.: Rev. William Ayres, Director, 1345 Admiral Lane, Uniondale, N.Y. 11553.

San Francisco,* Calif.: Most Rev. Pierre Du Maine, 443 Church St. 94114.

UNDA-USA: A national professional Catholic association for broadcasters and allied communicators organized in 1972. It succeeded the Catholic Broadcasters Association of America which in 1948 had replaced the Catholic Forum of the Air organized in 1938. It is a member of the international Catholic association for radio and television known as UNDA (the Latin word for "wave," symbolic of air waves of communication). Subgroups include Catholic Television Network, the Association of Catholic Radio and Television Syndicators, and the Association of Diocesan Directors. UNDA-USA publishes a newsletter six times a year for members, sponsors an annual general assembly and presents the Gabriel Awards annually for excellence in broadcasting. President, Rev. John Geaney, C.S.P., 320 Cathedral St., Baltimore, Md. 21201. National office: 3015 Fourth St. N.E., Washington, D.C. 20017.

Office for Film and Broadcasting (OFB): A unit of the Department of Communication of the United States Catholic Conference.

OFB serves as the principal instrument of the USCC for the exercise of a national pastoral ministry which aims (a) generally, at developing the unique potential that these media possess for contributing to mutual understanding and progress among men, and (b) specifically, at the utilization of these media for communicating the Gospel to the men of our day.

OFB provides a national service of information and cooperation for diocesan communications offices throughout the country. SHARE, a packet of film and broadcasting information, is published monthly.

For parents, educators, parish and other organizations, OFB publishes the twice-monthly *Film and Broadcasting Review*. The subscription publication presents critical reviews and moral classifications for all current theatrical motion pictures in national release; reviews outstanding commercial and public broadcasting television programs; provides educators with a regular service of information and recommendations on resources for film and audiovisual utilization; reports on media issues and developments that call for consumer response. Once a month, the *Review* includes a complete list of current motion pictures with both the OFB classification and the motion picture industry rating noted next to each title.

The office maintains a 16mm film library of Catholic program material and a consultation service for educational and religious film program directors.

For the broadcast media, OFB is responsible for cooperating with the three major networks (ABC, CBS and NBC) in the production of all regularly scheduled network radio and television programs involving Catholic participation (see Radio and Television).

For the Catholic press, OFB publishes a weekly film/broadcast service consisting of reviews, information, articles and photos. Special projects are undertaken with individual publications, religious and general.

OFB also plays a liaison role for the NCCB/USCC with the film and broadcasting industries, national media associations, and religious agencies and organizations. It is a member of OCIC and UNDA, the international Catholic organizations for film and broadcasting, respectively. Consultations and information services are also provided for the Pontifical Commission for Social Communications and the communications offices of national episcopal conferences throughout the world.

Rev. Patrick J. Sullivan, S.J., is the director.

Address: 1011 First Ave., New York, N.Y. 10022.

Foundation

The Catholic Communications Foundation (CCF) was established by the Catholic Fraternal Benefit Societies in 1968 in New York to lend support and assistance to development of the broadcasting apostolate of the Church.

The CCF, in addition to making financial grants (more than $800,000 from 1966 to 1979) for religious programs and programming services, has promoted the development of diocesan communications capabilities and has funded scholarship programs at the Institute for Religious Communications at Loyola University, New Orleans.

CCF officers include Bishop Andrew A. Grutka, chairman of the board and treasurer; Bishop Anthony G. Bosco, president.

Address: Suite 907, 222 N. 17th St., Philadelphia, Pa. 19103.

O'HARA INSTITUTE

The (Archbishop) Edwin V. O'Hara Institute for Rural Ministry Education was founded May 1, 1978, to provide training and other resource services for priests, seminarians, religious and lay persons beginning or already involved in rural ministry.

Msgr. Charles Fortier is director of the institute. Address: P.O. Box M, Des Moines, Iowa 50312.

DIOCESAN COMMUNICATIONS OFFICES, DIRECTORS

(Sources: *1979 Directory of Catholic Communications Personnel*, published by the Office of Public Affairs, USCC; *Official Catholic Directory;* NC News Service. Archdioceses are designated by an asterisk.)

Alabama: Birmingham — Rev. Martin Muller (Communications), Box 6147, Birmingham 35209.

Mobile — Rev. Robert L. Anderson, S.J. (Ed., *The Catholic Week)*, 400 Government St., Mobile 36601.

Alaska: Anchorage* — Chancery Office, P.O. Box 2239, Anchorage 99510.

Fairbanks — Rev. Louis McKernan, C.S.P. (Radio-TV), Pouch 100, North Pole 99705. Rev. James Poole, S.J., Box 988, Nome 99762.

Juneau — Ms. Carol Crater (Ed., *Inside Passage*), 534 Harris St., Juneau 99801; Director (Radio-TV), 419 6th St., Juneau 99801.

Arizona: Phoenix — Mr. James Jennings (Communications), Rev. Msgr. Robert J. Donohoe (Community Relations), 400 E. Monroe St., Phoenix 85004.

Tucson — Ms. Patricia Benton (Mng. Ed., *Arizona Catholic Lifetime*), 64 W. Ochoa St., Tucson 85701.

Arkansas: Little Rock — Msgr. B. Francis McDevitt (Communications, Radio-TV), 617 Louisiana St., Little Rock 72201.

California: Fresno — Mr. Joseph Jasmin (Information), Box 4273, Fresno 93744.

Los Angeles* — Msgr. Joseph Pollard (Communications), 1531 W. 9th St., Los Angeles 90015.

Monterey — Rev. Scott McCarthy (Communications Commission), 126 High St., Santa Cruz 95060; Rev. Felix Migliazzo (Ed., *The Observer*), Box 2079, Monterey 93940.

Oakland — Mrs. Reggie Finney (Public Relations), Rev. Richard Mangini (Ed., *The Catholic Voice*), 2900 Lakeshore Ave., Oakland 94610.

Orange — Rev. Michael P. Driscoll (Communications), 440 S. Batavia St., Orange 92668.

Sacramento — Rev. James T. Murphy (Information), Box 19312, Sacramento 95819; Msgr. James F. Church (Radio-TV), 1121 K St., Sacramento 95814.

San Diego — Mr. James Bastis (Communications), Box 80428, San Diego 92138; Mr. Michael Newman (Ed., *The Southern Cross)*, Box 81869, San Diego 92138.

San Francisco* — Rev. Harry Schlitt (Executive Director, Communications Center), 50 Oak St., San Francisco 94102; Rev. John Penebsky (Director, Information), 441 Church St., San Francisco 94114.

Santa Rosa — Msgr. Walter J. Tappe (Communications), 398 10th St., Santa Rosa 95401.

Stockton — Rev. Lawrence J. McGovern (Information), Box 4237, Stockton 95204.

Colorado: Denver* — Rev. C. B. Woodrich (Information), 200 Josephine St., Denver 80206; Rev. Maurice McInerney (Radio-TV), 29 W. Kiowa St., Colorado Springs 80902.

Pueblo — Ms. Geraldine Carrigan (Communications; Ed., *Catholic Crosswinds*), 1001 N. Grand Ave., Pueblo 81003.

Connecticut: Bridgeport — Rev. Nicholas V. Grieco (Communications), 238 Jewett Ave., Bridgeport 06606; Rev. Alfred J. Sienkiewicz (Radio-TV), 385 Scofieldtown Rd., Stamford 06903.

Hartford* — Rev. Edmund S. Nadolny (Radio-TV), 785 Asylum Ave., Hartford 06105.

Norwich — Sr. Roberta McGrath (Communications), 201 Hickory St., Norwich 06360.

Stamford (Ukrainian Diocese) — Rev. Charles Mezzomo, 161 Glenbrook Rd. Stamford 06902.

Delaware: Wilmington — Mr. F. Eugene Donnelly (Secretary, Communications), Box 2030, Wilmington 19899.

District of Columbia: Washington* — Rev. Maurice T. Fox (Communications), 1721 Rhode Island Ave. N.W., Washington 20036.

Florida: Miami* — Mr. Francis Nolan (Public Relations), 6301 Biscayne Blvd., Miami 33138. Rev. Jose P. Nickse (Radio-TV), 6200 N.E. 4th Ct., Miami 33138.

Orlando — Rev. Joseph B. McGoldrick, O.S.A. (Communications), Box 865, Maitland 32751.

Pensacola-Tallahassee — Mr. Gerald Butterfield (Communications), 217 S. Adams, Tallahassee 32301.

St. Augustine — Rev. Msgr. R. Joseph James (Radio-TV), 1649 Kingsley Ave., Orange Park 32073.

St. Petersburg — Rev. Desmond Daly, P.O. Box 5465, Sun City Center 33570.

Georgia: Atlanta* — Rev. Noel C. Burtenshaw (Ed., *The Georgia Bulletin*), 756 W. Peachtree St. N.W., Atlanta 30308.

Savannah — Rev. Joseph Stranc (Communications), St. John's Center, Grimball Pt. Rd., Savannah 31406.

Hawaii: Honolulu — Msgr. Francis A. Marzen, 1184 Bishop St., Honolulu 96813.

Idaho: Boise — Rev. David L. Riffle (Communications Center), 6003 Overland, Boise 83705.

Illinois: Belleville — Rev. Richard G. Mohr (Communications), 5312 W. Main St. P.O. Box 896, Belleville 62223.

Chicago* — Communications Office, 155 E. Superior St., Chicago 60611.

Joliet — Communications Office, 425 Summit St., Joliet 60435.

Peoria — Vacant.

Rockford — Rev. Richard Kramer (Communications), 126 N. Church St., Rockford 61101.

St. Nicholas in Chicago for Ukrainians — Msgr. Jaroslav Swyschuk (Eastern Rite Information Bureau), 2208 W. Chicago Ave., Chicago 60622.

Springfield — Rev. Richard L. Paynic (Information), Box 15, Springfield 62705.

Indiana: Evansville — Rev. Joseph F. Ziliak (Information), Rev. Jean F. Vogler (Communications), P.O. Box 4169, Evansville 47711.

Fort Wayne-South Bend — Rev. Vincent J. Giese (Ed., *The Harmonizer*), P.O. Box 390, Ft. Wayne 46801.

Gary — Rev. John F. Morales (Communications), P.O. Box M474, Gary 46401.

Indianapolis* — Mr. Charles J. Schisla (Communications), 136 W. Georgia St., Indianapolis 46225.

Lafayette — Rev. Paul Dehner (Information), 3810 W. Jefferson Rd., Kokomo 46901.

Iowa: Davenport — Rev. Francis C. Henricksen (Communications), Box 939, Davenport 52805.

Des Moines — Sister Janet M. Hudspeth, O.P. (Communications), 2910 Grand Ave., Box 1816, Des Moines 50306.

Dubuque* — Rev. Paul L. Weis, 1229 Mt. Loretta Ave. Dubuque 52001.

Sioux City — Mr. Lewis E. Heifner (Ed., *The Globe*), 1821 Jackson St., Sioux City 51105; Msgr. Frank Brady (Radio-TV), 1212 Morningside Ave., Sioux City 51106.

Kansas: Dodge City — Msgr. Norbert C. Temaat, Box 849, Dodge City 67801.

Kansas City* — William Maher (Ed., *The Leaven*), Box 2329, Kansas City 66110; Sr. Shirley Koritnik, S.C.L. (Modern Media), 2220 Central, Kansas City 66110.

Salina — Msgr. Raymond Menard (Information), Box 958, Salina 67401.

Wichita — Rev. Arthur A. Busch, 424 N. Broadway, Wichita 67202.

Kentucky: Covington — Mr. Richard J. Nare (Ed., *The Messenger*), Box 268, Covington 41012.

Louisville* — Rev. John H. Morgan, 1305 W. Market St., Louisville 40203.

Owensboro — Msgr. George Hancock (Information), 4003 Frederica St., Owensboro 42301; Rev. Leonard Reisz (Radio-TV), 1001 W. 7th St., Owensboro 42301.

Louisiana: Alexandria-Shreveport — Mr. Al Nassif (Information), Box 7417, Alexandria 71301.

Baton Rouge — Rev. Gerald Lefebvre (Information), P.O. Drawer 14746, Baton Rouge 70808.

Houma-Thibodaux — Louis Aguirre (Communications), Rev. Richard Hemenway (Radio-TV), P.O. Box 9077, Houma 70360.

Lafayette — Rev. Richard Greene (Communications), Glenn Norwood (Radio-TV), Box 3223, Lafayette 70502.

New Orleans* — Mr. Thomas M. Finney (Communications, Public Relations), Rev. Brian Highfill (Radio-TV), 7887 Walmsley Ave., New Orleans 70125.

Maine: Portland — Mr. Clarence F. McKay (Communications), 510 Ocean Ave., Portland 04103.

Maryland: Baltimore* — Rev. John Geaney, C.S.P. (Communications), 320 Cathedral St., Baltimore 21201.

Massachusetts: Boston* — Mr. George E. Ryan (News Bureau), 49 Franklin St., Boston 02110; Rev. Francis T. McFarland (Radio-TV), 55 Chapel St., Newton 02160.

Fall River — Rev. John F. Moore (Communications), 410 Highland Ave., Fall River 02722; Rev. John F. Hogan, (TV), 494 Slocum Rd., N. Dartmouth 02747.

Springfield — Msgr. David P. Welch (Ed., *Catholic Observer*), Box 1570, Springfield 01101; Rev. Cyril Schweinberg, C.P. (Radio-TV), 1089 Elm St., W. Springfield 01089.

Worcester — Rev. John W. Barrett (Communications), 49 Elm St., Worcester 01609.

Melkite Eparchy of Newton — Rev. James E. King, 19 Dartmouth St., W. Newton 02165.

Michigan: Detroit* — Sister Maureen Rodgers, O.P. (Communications), 305 Michigan Ave., Detroit 48226.

Gaylord — Sr. Nadine Donnelly, O.P. (Communications), 202 W. Mitchell Ave., Gaylord 49735.

Grand Rapids — Msgr. Hugh M. Beahan (Communicatons), 267 Sheldon Ave. S.E., Grand Rapids 49503.

Kalamazoo — Daniel B. Rebant (Communications), 215 N. Westnedge Ave., Kalamazoo 49005.

Lansing — Rev. Donald L. Eder (Communications), 300 W. Ottawa St., Lansing 48933.

Marquette — Rev. Vincent L. Ouellette (Information), Box 548, Marquette 49855.

Saginaw — Rev. Donald Eder (Communications), 2555 Wieneke Rd., Saginaw 48603.

Minnesota: Crookston — Rev. Gerald Noesen (Communications), St. Joseph Church, Red Lake Falls 56750.

Duluth — Mr. Donald St. Dennis, (Information), 215 W. 4th St., Duluth 55806.

New Ulm — Rev. Donald J. Eichinger (Communications), 1400 Chancery Dr., New Ulm 56073.

St. Cloud — Ms. Rosemary Borgert (Information), 810 St. Germain St., Box 1068, St. Cloud 56301.

St. Paul and Minneapolis* — Ms. Joan Bernet (Communications), 226 Summit Ave., St. Paul 55102.

Winona — Ms. Ann DeZell (Communications), Box 949, Winona 55987.

Mississippi: Biloxi — Rev. Michael Treacey, (Assoc. Ed., *Mississippi Today*), P.O. Box 367, Biloxi 39533. Rev. William Vollor (Media Communications), Sacred Heart Church, Rt. 1, Box 618, Pass Christian 39571.

Jackson — Mrs. Janna Avalon, Box 2130, Jackson 39205.

Missouri: Jefferson City — Rev. Hugh Behan (Information), Box 1107, Jefferson City 65102; Mr. Mark Saucier (Communications), Box 417, Jefferson City 65101.

Kansas City-St. Joseph — Ms. Beverly Raynor (Communications Consultant), Box 1037, Kansas City 64141.

St. Louis* — Msgr. Edward O'Donnell (Information), 462 N. Taylor Ave., St. Louis 63108; Mr. Ronald Coleman (Public Relations), 2249 S. Brentwood Blvd., St. Louis 63144. Rev. Joseph M. O'Brien (Radio-TV), 4140 Lindell Blvd., St. Louis 63108.

Springfield-Cape Girardeau — Sister Emile Morgan, D.C. (Communications), McDaniel Bldg., Springfield 65806.

Montana: Great Falls — Rev. Dale McFarlane, 725 3rd Ave. N., Box 2107, Great Falls 59403.

Helena — Sr. Mary Hopkins (Director, Religious Education), Box 1175, Helena 59601.

Nebraska: Grand Island — Rev. Bernard M. Berger (Communications), P.O. Box 608, Grand Island 68801.

Lincoln — Rev. James D. Dawson (Information), Box 80328, Lincoln 68501.

Omaha* — Sister Patricia Kowalski, O.S.M. (Communications), 100 N. 62nd St., Omaha 68132.

Nevada: Reno-Las Vegas — Rev. Thomas Meger, Chancellor, P.O. Box 1211, Reno 89504.

New Hampshire: Manchester — Mr. Jay Cormier (Communications), 153 Ash St., Manchester 03105.

New Jersey: Camden — Msgr. Charles Giglio (Information), Box 709, Camden 08101.

Newark* — Rev. Michael Russo (Communications), 31 Mulberry St., Newark 07102.

Passaic (Byzantine Rite Eparchy) — Most Rev. Thomas Dolinay, 101 Market St., Passaic 07055.

Paterson — Mr. Gerald M. Costello (Communications Secretariat), 163-65 Newark Pompton Turnpike (Box A), Pequannock 07440; Mr. William A. Durbin, Jr. (Communications Center), Rev. Bruce Welch (Radio Programming), 74 Kahdena Rd., Morristown 07960.

Trenton — Sr. Rosemary Jeffries, R.S.M. (Communications), 701 Lawrenceville Rd., Trenton 08648.

New Mexico: Gallup — Rev. Cormac Antram, O.F.M. (Radio-TV), P.O. Box 39, Tohatchi 87325.

Santa Fe* — Mrs. Eileen Stanton (Communications), 2501 San Pedro N.E., Suite E, Albuquerque 87110.

New York: Albany — Rev. Michael Farano (Information), 465 State St., Albany 12206.

Brooklyn — Mr. Frank DeRosa (Information), Box C, Brooklyn 11202.

Buffalo — Rev. Msgr. Robert E. Nesslin (Communications), Msgr. John McMahon (Radio-TV), 100 S. Elmwood Dr., Buffalo 14202.

New York* — Msgr. Eugene V. Clark (Communications), Rev. Jose Alvarez (Spanish Media), 1011 First Ave., New York, N.Y. 10022.

Ogdensburg — Rev. David W. Stinebrickner (Information), 622 Washington St., Ogdensburg 13669; Rev. John L. Downs (Radio-TV), St. Cecilia's Rectory, 23 Grove St., Adams 13605.

Rochester — Rev. Charles J. Latus (Information), 1150 Buffalo Rd., Rochester 14624.

Rockville Centre — Rev. Daniel S. Hamilton (Information), Box 700, Rockville Centre 11551; Rev. William J. Ayres (Radio-TV), 1345 Admiral Lane, Uniondale 11553.

St. Maron Diocese (Maronite Rite) — Mr. John Hayes (Information), 191 Joralemon St., Brooklyn 11201.

Syracuse — Msgr. Robert F. Lavin, 240 E. Onondaga St., Syracuse 13202.

North Carolina: Charlotte — Mr. Harry Wiebler, 1524 E. Moorehead St., Charlotte 28207.

Raleigh — Rev. Joseph G. Vetter (Ed., *North Carolina Catholic*), 300 Cardinal Gibbons Dr., Raleigh 27606.

North Dakota: Bismarck — Rev. John J. Owens, Box 128, Wilton 58579.

Fargo — Sister Mary Ethel Paulus (Ed., *Catholic Action News*), Box 1750, Fargo 58102

Ohio: Cincinnati* — Mr. Daniel J. Kane (Communications), Rev. Theodore Kosse (Radio-TV), 426 E. 5th St., Cincinnati 45202.

Cleveland — Mr. J. Jerome Lackamp (Communications), 1027 Superior Ave., Cleveland 44114.

Columbus — Rev. James P. Hanley (Communications), Rev. Michael Reis (Radio-TV), 197 E. Gay St., Columbus 43215.

Parma (Byzantine Rite Eparchy) — Rev. Thomas Chalina, 5390 W. 220th St., Fairview Park 44126.

Steubenville — Msgr. James C. Marshall, 422 Washington St., Box 969, Steubenville 43952.

Toledo — Mr. Jim Richards (Communications), 2544 Parkwood Ave., Toledo 43610.

Youngstown — Mr. John Lencyk (Communications), 225 Elm St., Youngstown 44503.

Oklahoma: Oklahoma City* — Rev. David F. Monahan (Communications), Box 32180, Oklahoma City 73123.

Tulsa — Rev. William K. Skeehan (Communications), 1324 Madison Blvd., Bartlesville 74003.

Oregon: Baker — Rev. Joseph B. Hayes, Sacred Heart Church, 815 High St., Klameth Falls 97601.

Portland* — Rev. Leo Remington (Radio-TV), 2838 E. Burnside St., Portland 97214.

Pennsylvania: Allentown — Rev. Msgr. Vincent E. Lewellis (Information), 202 N. 17th St., Allentown 18105.

Altoona-Johnstown — Rev. Msgr. Philip Saylor (Information), 126C Logan Blvd., Hollidaysburg 16648.

Erie — Rev. Henry Kriegel (Publicity and Information), Box 4047, Erie 16512.

Greensburg — Mr. John Quigley (Communications), Box 850, Greensburg 15601.

Harrisburg — Ronnie G. Shaeffer (Communications), 4800 Union Deposit Rd., Harrisburg 17105.

Philadelphia* — Communications Office, 222 North 17th St., Philadelphia 19103.

Philadelphia* (Ukrainian) — Rev. Ronald Popkivchak, 519 Union Ave., Bridgeport 19405.

Pittsburgh* (Byzantine Rite) — Msgr. Edward V. Rosack (Information), 624 Park Rd., Ambridge 15003; Most Rev. John M. Bilock (Radio-TV), 54 Riverview Ave., Pittsburgh 15214.

Pittsburgh — Rev. Ronald P. Lengwin (Communications), Mr. Joseph Williams (Information and Public Relations), 111 Boulevard of the Allies, Pittsburgh 15222.

Scranton — Rev. Joseph P. Gilgallon, 300 Wyoming Ave., Box 708, Scranton 18503.

Rhode Island: Providence — Mr. Brian L. Wallin (Communications), One Cathedral Square, Providence 02903.

South Carolina: Charleston — Rev. Robert J. Millard (Communications), P.O. Box 394, Georgetown 29440.

South Dakota: Rapid City — Mr. Brian T. Olszewski, Box 678, Rapid City 57709.

Sioux Falls — Msgr. Louis J. Delahoyde, 423 N. Duluth Ave., Sioux Falls 57104.

Tennessee: Memphis — Msgr. Paul W. Clunan (Communications), 203 S. White Station Rd., Memphis 38117.

Nashville — Mr. Joseph A. Sweat (Public Affairs), 2400 21st Ave. S., Nashville 37212.

Texas: Amarillo — Msgr. Leroy T. Matthiesen (Information), Box 5644, Amarillo 79107; Msgr. Richard F. Vaughan (Radio-TV), 4122 Bonham St., Amarillo 79110.

Austin — Rev. Victor Goertz (Ed., *Texas Catholic Herald*), 1401 Washington Ave., Waco 76702.

Beaumont — Mrs. Edythe Capreol (Communications and Information), P.O. Box 3948, Beaumont 77704.

Brownsville — Sr. Michelle Marie Kuntscher (Communications), Box 2279, Brownsville 78520.

Corpus Christi — Mr. John J. Foley (Public Information), 1424 Baldwin St., Corpus Christi 78404. Rev. Robert E. Freeman (Radio-TV), 1201 Leopard St., Corpus Christi 78401.

Dallas — Mr. Steve Landregan (Information), Box 19507, Dallas 75219; Mr. Ed Hallack (Radio-TV), 4168 Willow Grove Rd., Dallas 75220.

El Paso — Mr. Andrew Sparke (Communications Media), P.O. Box 838, El Paso 79945.

Fort Worth — Rev. Eugene Witkowski, 1206 Throckmorton St., Ft. Worth 76102; Mr. Jerry Thomas (Radio-TV), 4801 W. Freeway, Ft. Worth 76107.

Galveston-Houston — Msgr. John L. Fos, 1700 San Jacinto St., Houston 77002; Rev. William L. Young (Radio-TV), 10330 Hillcroft, Houston 77096.

San Angelo — Mr. Frank Trudo (Communications), Box 1829, San Angelo 76902.

San Antonio* — Rev. Brian Wallace, O.M.I. (Communications), P.O. Box 12429, San Antonio 78212.

Utah: Salt Lake City — Msgr. W. H. McDougall (Information), 331 E. S. Temple St., Salt Lake City 84111; Rev. Thomas J. Meersman (Radio-TV), 1327 E.S. Second St., Salt Lake City 84102.

Vermont: Burlington — Rev. Joseph T. Sullivan (Communications), 351 North Ave., Burlington 05401.

Virginia: Arlington — Ms. Ellen McCloskey (Communications), 200 N. Glebe Rd., Arlington 22203.

Richmond — Mr. Bob Edwards (Communications), 811 Cathedral Pl., Richmond 23220.

Washington: Seattle* — Dr. Maury R. Sheridan (Communications), 1511 3rd Ave., Melbourne House, Seattle 98101.

Spokane — Mr. Dan Morris, W. 1023 Riverside Ave., P.O. Box 48, Spokane 99210.

Yakima — Rev. Robert J. Shields, Box 567, Zillah 98953.

West Virginia: Wheeling-Charleston — Rev. Victor Seidel, S.T., Box 230, Wheeling 26003.

Wisconsin: Green Bay — Rev. Steven Halbach (Ed., *The Compass*), 1825 Riverside Dr., Green Bay 54301; Mr. Tony Kuick (Radio-TV), Box 66, Green Bay 54305.

La Crosse — Rev. Robert McKillip (Communications), Box 937, La Crosse 54601.

Madison — Rev. Stephen Umhoefer (Communications), High Point Rd. Rt. 2, Madison 53711.

Milwaukee* — Sr. Mary Luke (Radio-TV), 4063 N. 64th St., Milwaukee 53216.

Superior — Rev. Robert Urban (Information), 1512 N. 12th St., Superior 54880.

Wyoming: Cheyenne — Rev. Philip Colibraro (Information), Box 940, Douglass 82633.

Catholic Communications Northwest: Regional communications center serving dioceses in Alaska, Idaho, Montana, Oregon and Washington. Executive Director, Dr. Maury Sheridan, 1511 3rd Ave., Seattle, Wash. 98101.

Delaware Valley Catholic Office for Television and Radio: Interdiocesan agency of the Archdiocese of Philadelphia and the dioceses of Camden and Trenton, N.J.; and Wilmington, Del. Address: 222 North 17th St., Philadelphia, Pa. 19103.

Other Communications Offices

International Mission Radio Association: Rev. Jude Bradley, O.S.B., treasurer-administrator, St. Paul's Abbey, Newton, N.J. 07860.

Jesuits in Communication in North America (JESCOM): Rev. Donald R. Campion, S.J., acting director, Suite 402, 1717 Massachusetts Ave., N.W., Washington, D.C. 20005.

Maryknoll Media Relations: Rev. Ronald Saucci, M.M., director, Maryknoll Fathers, Walsh Building, Maryknoll, N.Y. 10545.

National Franciscan Communications Conference: Rev. James J. Gardiner, S.A., president, Graymoor, Garrison, N.Y. 10524.

National Sisters Communications Service: Sister Elizabeth Thoman, executive director, 1962 S. Shenandoah St., Los Angeles, Calif. 90034.

National Office

The National Catholic Office for Information (NCOI), successor to the NCWC Bureau of Information, serves as the official spokesman for both the United States Catholic Conference and the National Conference of Catholic Bishops in relating to the news media. The NCOI is part of the NCCB/USCC Office for Public Affairs.

The office prepares and distributes news releases; handles inquiries from the press; arranges news media coverage of bishops' meetings; offers public information and public relations counsel on a day-to-day basis to the office of the general secretary of the USCC and the NCCB, and to other agencies and staff members; performs a number of special research and writing functions on behalf of the conferences and their staffs.

The office also provides services and coordination for diocesan information offices.

William Ryan is director of the office, which is located at 1312 Massachusetts Ave. N.W., Washington, D.C. 20005.

CHRISTOPHER AWARDS

Christopher Awards were presented Feb. 22, 1979, in New York City to 73 writers, directors and producers for their work in television, films and books.

Award winners were selected on the basis of works which embodied artistic and technical excellence and which had received a significant degree of public acceptance as well as affirming the highest value of the human spirit. Below is a partial list.

The award is a bronze medallion which bears the Christopher motto: "Better to light one candle than to curse the darkness."

Television Specials

"ABC News Closeup: The Class That Went to War," ABC; Richard Gerdau.

"Bing Crosby: His Life and Legend," ABC; Franklin Konigsberg, Marshall Flaum.

"CBS Reports: Any Place But Here," CBS; Howard Stringer, Tom Spain, Maurice Murad.

"Damien," PBS/KHET; Nino J. Martin, Aldyth Morris.

"The Defection of Simas Kudirka, CBS; Gerald I. Isenberg, Gerald W. Abrams, Richard Briggs, David Lowell Rich, Bruce Feldman.

"Les Miserables," CBS; Norman Rosemont, Glenn Jordan, John Gay.

"Little Women," NBC; David Victor, David Lowell Rich, Suzanne Clauser.

"Long Journey Back," ABC; Lee Rich, Philip Capice, Robert Lovenheim, Mel Damski, Audrey Davis Levin.

"Lovey: A Circle of Children, Part II," CBS; David Susskind, Frederick Brogger, Diana Kerew, Jud Taylor, Josh Greenfeld.

"Mom and Dad Can't Hear Me: An ABC Afterschool Special," ABC; Daniel Wilson, Fran Sears, Larry Elikann, Irma Reichert, Daryl Warner.

"One in a Million: The Ron LeFlore Story," CBS; Roger Gimbel, Tony Converse, William S. Gilmore Jr., William A. Graham, Stanford Whitmore.

"Rodeo Red and the Runaway: An NCB Special Treat," NBC; Linda Gottlieb, Doro Bachrach, Bert Salzman.

"A Woman Called Moses," NBC; Ike Jones, Michael Jaffe, Paul Wendkos, Lonne Elder III.

Motion Pictures

"Bread and Chocolate," World Northal; Mauricio Lodi-Sè, Franco Brusati, Iaia Fiastri, Nino Manfredi.

"Madam Rosa," Atlantic Releasing; Moshe Mizrahi.

"Movie Movie," Warner Brothers; Stanley Donen, Larry Gelbart, Sheldon Keller.

Special Awards were given to Milton Berle; Archbishop Fulton J. Sheen; The "Lou Grant" Show.

Honors and Awards

Pontifical Orders

The Pontifical Orders of Knighthood are secular orders of merit whose membership depends directly on the pope. Details regarding the various orders are handled by a special agency in the Secretariat of Briefs, an office in the Papal Secretariat of State.

Supreme Order of Christ (Militia of Our Lord Jesus Christ): The highest of the five pontifical orders of knighthood, the Supreme Order of Christ was approved Mar. 14, 1319, by John XXII as a continuation in Portugal of the suppressed Order of Templars. Members were religious with vows and a rule of life until the order lost its religious character toward the end of the 15th century. Since that time it has existed as an order of merit. Paul VI, in 1966, restricted awards of the order to Christian heads of state.

Order of the Golden Spur (Golden Militia): Although the original founder is not certainly known, this order is one of the oldest knighthoods. Indiscriminate bestowal and inheritance diminished its prestige, however, and in 1841 Gregory XVI replaced it with the Order of St. Sylvester and gave it the title of Golden Militia. In 1905 St. Pius X restored the Order of the Golden Spur in its own right, separating it from the Order of St. Sylvester. Paul VI, in 1966, restricted awards of the order to Christian heads of state.

Order of Pius IX: Founded by Pius IX June 17, 1847, the order is awarded for outstanding services for the Church and society, and may be given to non-Catholics as well as Catholics. The title to nobility formerly attached to membership was abolished by Pius XII in 1939. In 1957 Pius XII instituted the Class of the Grand Collar as the highest category of the order; in 1966, Paul VI restricted this award to heads of state "in solemn circumstances." The other three classes are of Knights of the Grand Cross, Knight Commanders with and without emblem, and Knights. The new class was created to avoid difficulties in presenting papal honors to Christian or non-Christian leaders of high merit.

Order of St. Gregory the Great: First established by Gregory XVI in 1831 to honor citizens of the Papal States, the order is conferred on persons who are distinguished for personal character and reputation, and for notable accomplishment. The order has civil and military divisions, and three classes of knights.

Order of St. Sylvester: Instituted Oct. 31, 1841, by Gregory XVI to absorb the Order of the Golden Spur, this order was divided into two by St. Pius X in 1905, one retaining the name of St. Sylvester and the other assuming the title of Golden Militia. Membership consists of three degrees: Knights of the Grand Cross, Knight Commanders with and without emblem, and Knights.

Ecclesiastical Order

Order of the Holy Sepulchre: Critical opinion is divided regarding various details of the history of the order. It is certain, however, that these knights first appeared in the Holy Land and were in existence at the end of the 11th century. Some assign earlier dates or origin, claiming as founders St. James the Apostle, first bishop of Jerusalem, and St. Helena, builder of the Basilica of the Holy Sepulchre. Others hold that Godfrey of Bouillon instituted the order in 1099 and that it took its name from the Holy Sepulchre where its members were knighted.

The order lost a great deal of prestige after the fall of the Latin Kingdom of Jerusalem and the consequent departure of the knights from the Holy Land. It was united with the Knights of St. John in 1489, came under the grand mastership of Alexander VI in 1496 and shortly thereafter was split into three national divisions, German, French and Spanish. Pius IX re-established the Latin patriarchate of Jerusalem in 1847 and gave the patriarch the faculty of conferring the order of knighthood. This right had been held by the Franciscan custos following the appointment of the Friars as guardians of the Holy Land in 1342. Three classes of membership were designated in 1868. Leo XIII later instituted the Cross of Honor (which does not confer knighthood) in three classes — gold, silver and bronze — and also the Dames of the Holy Sepulchre. From 1907 to 1928 the pope was grand master, an office now held by a cardinal. Revised statutes for the order went into effect in 1949, 1962 and 1967. The 1949 constitution enjoined the knights "to revive in modern form the spirit and ideal of the Crusades with the weapons of faith, the apostolate, and Christian charity."

The Order of the Holy Sepulchre now has five classes: 12 Knights of the Collar and four degrees, with separate divisions of each for men and women — Grand Cross, Commanders with Plaque, Commanders and Knights. Three honorary decorations are awarded, vis., Palm of the Order, Cross of Merit (which may be bestowed on non-Catholics), and the Pilgrim's Shell.

Investiture ceremonies combine a profession of faith with the ancient ritual of knighthood dubbing. Candidates do not take monastic vows but pledge an upright Christian life and loyalty to the pope.

The grand master of the order is Cardinal Maximilien de Furstenberg.

There are four lieutenancies of the order in the United States.

Order of Malta

The Sovereign Military Hospitaller Order of St. John of Jerusalem of Rhodes and of Malta traces its origin to a group of men who maintained a Christian hospital in the Holy Land in the 11th century. The group was approved as a religious order — the Hospitallers of St. John — by Paschal II in 1113.

The order, while continuing its service to the poor, principally in hospital work, assumed military duties in the following century and included knights, chaplains and sergeants-at-arms among its members. All the knights were professed monks with the vows of poverty, chastity and obedience. Headquarters were located in the Holy Land until the last decade of the 13th century and on Rhodes after 1308 (whence the title, Knights of Rhodes).

After establishing itself on Rhodes, the order became a sovereign power like the sea republics of Italy and the Hanseatic cities of Germany, flying its own flag, coining its own money, floating its own navy, and maintaining diplomatic relations with many nations.

The order was forced to abandon Rhodes in 1522 after the third siege of the island by the Turks under Sultan Suliman I. Eight years later, the Knights were given the island of Malta, where they remained as a bastion of Christianity until near the end of the 18th century. Headquarters have been located in Rome since 1834.

The title of Grand Master of the Order, in abeyance for some time, was restored by Leo XIII in 1879. A more precise definition of both the religious and the sovereign status of the order was embodied in a new constitution of 1961 and a code issued in 1966.

Religious aspects of the order are subject to regulation by the Holy See. At the same time the sovereignty of the order, which is based on international law, is recognized by the Holy See and by 40 countries with which full diplomatic relations are maintained.

The four main classifications of members are: Knights of Justice, who are religious with the vows of poverty, chastity and obedience; Knights of Obedience, who make a solemn promise to strive for Christian perfection; Knights of Honor and Devotion and of Grace and Devotion, of noble lineage; and Knights of Magistral Grace. There are also chaplains, Dames and Donats of the order.

The order, with five grand priories, three sub-priories and 36 national associations, is devoted to hospital and charitable work of all kinds in some 68 countries.

The Grand Master, who is the sovereign head of the order, has the title of Most Eminent Highness with the rank of Cardinal. He must be of noble lineage and under solemn vows for a minimum period of 10 years.

The present Grand Master is Fra' Angelo de Mojana di Cologna, a lawyer of Milan, who was elected for life May 8, 1962, by the Council of State.

The address of headquarters of the order is Via Condotti, Palazzo Malta, 00187 Roma, Italia.

Papal Medals

Pro Ecclesia et Pontifice: This decoration ("For the Church and the Pontiff") had its origin in 1888 as a token of the golden sacerdotal jubilee of Leo XIII; he bestowed it on those who had assisted in the observance of his jubilee and on persons responsible for the success of the Vatican Exposition. The medal bears the likeness of Leo XIII on one side; on the other, the tiara, the papal keys, and the words *Pro Ecclesia et Pontifice.* Originally, the medal was issued in gold, silver or bronze. St. Pius X ordered that it be of gold only. It is awarded in recognition of service to the Church and the papacy.

Benemerenti: Several medals ("To a well-deserving person") have been conferred by popes for exceptional accomplishment and service. The medals, which are made of gold, silver or bronze, bear the likeness and name of the reigning pope on one side; on the other, a laurel crown and the letter "B."

These two medals may be given by the pope to both men and women. Their bestowal does not convey any title or honor of knighthood.

AMERICAN CATHOLIC AWARDS

Aquinas Medal, by the American Catholic Philosophical Association for outstanding contributions to the field of Catholic philosophy.

Jacques Maritain (1951), Etienne Gilson (1952), Gerald Smith, S.J. (1955), Gerald B. Phelan (1959), Rudolf Allers (1960), James A. McWilliams, S.J. (1961) Charles De Koninck (1964), James Collins (1965).

Martin C. D'Arcy (1967), Dr. Josef Pieper (1968), Leo R. Ward (1969), Bernard Lonergan, S.J. (1970), Henry B. Veatch (1971), Joseph Owens, C.SS.R. (1972), A. Hilary Armstrong (1973), Cornelio Fabro (1974), Anton Pegis (1975), Mortimer J. Adler (1976), Frederick C. Copleston (1977), Fernand Van Steenberghen (1978).

Bellarmine Medal (1955), by Bellarmine College (Louisville, Ky.), to persons in national or international affairs who, in controversial matters, exemplify the characteristics of St. Robert Bellarmine in charity, justice and temperateness.

Jefferson Caffery (1955), Gen. Carlos Romulo (1956), U.S. Rep. John W. McCormack (1957), Frank M. Folsom (1958), Robert D. Murphy (1959), James P. Mitchell (1960), Frederick H. Boland (1961);

Gen. Alfred M. Gruenther (1962), Henry Cabot Lodge (1963), R. Sargent Shriver (1964), Irene Dunne (1965), Sen. Everett M. Dirksen (1966), Nicholas Katzenbach (1967), Danny Thomas (1968), J. Irwin Miller (1969), Theodore M. Hesburgh, C.S.C. (1970), Sen. John Sherman Cooper (1971), (no award, 1972), Dr. William B. Walsh (1973), Most Rev. Fulton J. Sheen (1974), William F. Buckley, Jr. (1977), Rev. Jesse L. Jackson (1979).

Borromeo Award (1960), by Carroll College (Helena, Mont.), for zeal, courage and devotion in the spirit of St. Charles Borromeo.

William D. Murray (1960), Robert E. Sullivan (1961), Vincent H. Walsh (1962), Leo V. Kelly (1963), Joseph A. Kimmet (1964), Dr. W. E. Long (1965), Frank E. Blair (1968), Gough, Booth, Shanahan and Johnson (1971), Egon E. Mallman, S.J. (1973), Christian Brothers of Ireland (1974), Most Rev. Raymond Hunthausen (1975), Dominican Sisters of Spokane, Wash., of the Province of the Immaculate Heart of Mary (1976), Rev. Emmett Shea (1977), Most Rev. Eldon B. Schuster (1978), Rev. Paul B. Kirchen (1979).

Brent Award (1976), by the Diocese of Arlington, Va., for distinguished service to fellowman.

Dr. Mildred F. Jefferson (1976), Most Rev. John J. Russell (1977), U.S. Rep. Henry J. Hyde and William B. Ball, Esq. (1978), Mrs. Hazel Hagarty (1979).

Campion Award (1955), by the Catholic Book Club for distinguished service in Catholic letters.

Jacques Maritain (1955), Helen C. White (1956), Paul Horgan (1957), James Brodrick, S.J. (1958), Sister M. Madeleva (1959), Frank J. Sheed and Maisie Ward (1960), John La Farge, S.J. (1961), Harold C. Gardiner, S.J. (1962);

T. S. Eliot (1963), Barbara Ward (1964), Msgr. John T. Ellis (1965), John Courtney Murray, S.J. (1966), Phyllis McGinley (1967), Dr. George N. Shuster (1968), G. B. Harrison (1970), Walter and Jean Kerr (1971), Karl Rahner, S.J. (1974), John J. Delaney (1976).

Cardinal Gibbons Medal (1949) by the Alumni Association of the Catholic University of America for distinguished and meritorious service to the Church, the United States or the Catholic University.

Carlton J. H. Hayes (1949), Gen. Carlos P. Romulo (1950), Fulton Oursler (1951), Most Rev. Fulton J. Sheen (1953), J. Edgar Hoover (1954), Gen. J. Lawton Collins (1955), U.S. Sen. John F. Kennedy and Ignatius Smith, O.P. (1956), Most Rev. Bryan J. McEntegart (1957), Thomas E. Murray (1958);

Gen. Alfred M. Gruenther (1959), Karl F. Herzfeld (1960), Charles G. Fenwick (1961), Luke E. Hart (1962), John W. McCormack (1963), John A. McCone (1964), R. Sargent Shriver (1965), James J. Norris (1967), Danny Thomas (1968), Theodore Hesburgh, C.S.C. (1969), Dr. Carroll Hochwalt (1970), Danny Thomas (1971), Cardinal Patrick O'Boyle (1972), Helen Hayes (1973), Sen. Mike Mansfield (1974), Judge John J. Sirica (1975), Cardinal Lawrence Shehan (1976), Benjamin T. Rome (1977), Dr. Clarence C. Walton (1978).

Cardinal Spellman Award (1947), by the Catholic Theological Society for outstanding achievement in the field of theology.

Revs. Francis J. Connell, C.SS.R., Emmanuel Doronzo, O.M.I., Gerald Yelle, S.S., William R. O'Connor, John C. Murray, S.J. (1947); Eugene Burke, C.S.P. (1948), Bernard J. J. Lonergan, S.J. (1949), John C. Murray, S.J. (1950), Msgr. William R. O'Connor (1951), Emmanuel Doronzo, O.M.I. (1952), Gerald Kelly, S.J. (1953), Francis J. Connell, C.SS.R. (1954), Edmond D. Benard (1955), John C. Ford, S.J. (1956);

Gerard Yelle, S.S. (1957), Msgr. Joseph C. Fenton (1958), Juniper Carol, O.F.M. (1959), Rev. John Quasten (1960), Cyril C. Vollert, S.J. (1961), Walter J. Burghardt, S.J. (1962), Rev. Francis Dvornik (1963), Barnabas Ahern, C.P. (1964), Godfrey Diekmann, O.S.B. (1965), Paul K. Meagher, O.P. (1966), John L. McKenzie, S.J. (1967), Dr. Martin R. P. McGuire (1968), Richard A. McCormick, S.J. (1969), Avery Dulles, S.J. (1970), Raymond E. Brown, S.S. (1971).

For recipients after 1971, see John Courtney Murray Award.

Catholic Action Medal (1934), by St. Bonaventure University (St. Bonaventure, N.Y.).

Alfred E. Smith (1934), Michael Williams (1935), Joseph Scott (1936), Patrick Scanlan (1937), George J. Gillespie (1938), William F. Montavon (1939), John J. Craig (1940), John S. Burke (1941), Dr. George Speri Sperti (1942), Francis P. Matthews (1943);

Jefferson Caffery (1944), John A. Coleman (1945), David Goldstein (1946), Clement Lane (1947), Paul W. Weber (1948), Bruce M. Mohler (1949), Edward M. O'Connor (1950), Richard F. Pattee (1951), James M. O'Neill (1952), John E. Swift (1953);

Frank M. Folsom (1954), Walter L. McGuiness (1955), Carlton J. H. Hayes (1956), Thomas E. Murray (1957), Paul V. Murray (1958), Dr. John L. Madden (1959), Christopher H. Dawson (1960), Stephen Kuttner (1961), Charles De Koninck (1962), Lt. Gen. G. Trudeau (1963), Frank J. Sheed (1964), Danny Thomas (1965), Walter and Jean Kerr (1966), Sir Hugh Stott Taylor (1967), Maurice Lavanoux (1968).

The Catholic University of America Patronal Medal (1974), by the University for outstanding contributions to the Catholic Church and in promoting interest and devotion to Mary, patroness of the University.

Most Rev. Fulton J. Sheen (1974), Sister M. Claudia Honsberger, I.H.M. (1975), Rev. Theodore A. Koehler (1976), Rev. Ross

MacKenzie, Presbyterian clergyman (1977).

Cecilia Medal (1952), by the Music Department of Boys Town (Nebr.) for outstanding work in liturgical music.

Winifred T. Flanagan (1952), Dom Francis Missia (1953), Omer Westendorf (1954), Dom Ermin Vitry (1955), William A. Reilly (1956), Flor Peeters (1957), Roger Wagner (1958), Most Rev. Gerald T. Bergan (1959), Francis T. Brunner, C.SS.R. (1960), Jean Langlois (1961);

James B. Welch (1962), W. Ripley Dorr (1963), C. Alexander Peloquin (1964), Dr. Louise Cuyler (1965), Dr. Eugene Selhorst (1966), Dr. Paul Manz (1967), Myron J. Roberts (1968), Norman T. Letter (1969), Rev. Elmer Pfeil (1969), Rev. Richard Schuler (1970).

Christian Culture Award (1941), by Assumption University (Canada) to outstanding exponents of Christian ideals.

Sigrid Undset (1941), Jacques Maritain (1942), Philip Murray (1943), Frank J. Sheed (1944), Arnold M. Walter (1945), Henry Ford II (1946), George S. Sperti (1947), Richard Pattee (1948), Étienne Gilson (1949), Paul Doyon (1950), Christopher Dawson (1951), John C.H. Wu (1952);

Charles Malik (1953), Ivan Mestrovic (1954), F. W. Foerster (1955), Paul Martin (1956), Robert Speaight (1947), Allen Tate (1958), Barbara Ward (1959), John Cogley (1960), Peter Drucker (1961), Benjamin E. Mays (1962), John Quincy Adams (1963);

William Foxwell Albright (1964), Dr. Karl Stern (1965), John Howard Griffin (1966), Edith K. Peterkin (1967), Dr. Mircea Eliade (1968), Dr. James D. Collins (1969), Dorothy Day (1970), Dr. Marshall McLuhan (1971), James M. Cameron (1972), Jean Vanier (1973), Robert J. Kreyche (1974), John T. Noonan, Jr. (1975), Dorothy Donnelly (1976), William Kurelek (1977), Anthony Walsh (1978), Malcolm Muggeridge (1979).

Collegian Award (1949), by "The Collegian," weekly student newspaper of La Salle College (Phila.), for public service in the field of communications.

Ed Sullivan (1949), Morley Cassidy (1950), Bob Considine (1951), Red Smith (1952), George Sokolsky (1953), Edward R. Murrow (1954), David Lawrence (1955), Jim Bishop (1956), Richard W. Slocum (1957), Chet Huntley (1958);

John C. O'Brien (1959), Walter Cronkite (1960), David Brinkley (1961), James Reston (1962), Charles Collingwood (1963), Art Buchwald (1964), Nancy Dickerson (1965), Charles Schulz (1966), Sandy Grady (1967), Harrison E. Salisbury (1968), Ralph W. Howard (1969), (not awarded 1970-77), Lawrence M. O'Rourke (1978).

Damien-Dutton Award (1953), by the Damien-Dutton Society for service toward conquest of leprosy or for the promotion of better understanding of social problems connected with the disease.

Stanley Stein (1953), Joseph Sweeney, M.M. (1954), Sister Marie Suzanne (1955), Dr. Perry Burgess (1956), John Farrow (1957), Dr. H. Windsor Wade (1958), Sister Hilary Ross (1959), Msgr. Louis J. Mendelis (1960), Dr. Kensuke Mitsuda (1961), Pierre d'Orgeval, SS.CC. (1962);

Eunice Weaver (1963), Dr. Robert Cochrane (1964), John F. Kennedy, posthumously (1965), The Peace Corps (1966), Dr. Howard A. Rusk (1967), Dr. Frans Hemerijckx (1968), Dr. Victor G. Heiser (1969), Dr. Dharmendra (1970), Dr. Chapman H. Binford (1971), Dr. Patricia Smith (1972), Dr. Jacinto Convit (1973), Dr. Jose N. Rodriguez (1974), Dr. Oliver Hasselblad (1975), Dr. Yoshio Yoshie (1976), Drs. Paul and Margaret Brand (1977), Dr. Fernando Latapi (1978).

Edith Stein Award (1955), by the Edith Stein Guild for service toward better understanding between Christians and Jews.

Sister Noemi de Sion (1956), Authur B. Klyber, C.SS.R. (1957), Rev. John M. Oesterreicher (1958), John J. O'Connor (1959), Victor J. Donovan, C.P. (1960), Jacques and Raissa Maritain (1961), Gerard E. Sherry (1962), Mother Kathryn Sullivan, R.S.C.J. (1963), Paulist Press (1964), Rev. Edward N. Flannery (1965), Mother Katherine Hargrove, R.S.C.J. (1966), Gregory Baum, O.S.A. (1967), Sr. Rose Albert Thering (1968), Msgr. Vincent O. Genova (1969), Dr. Joseph Lichten (1970), Philip Scharper (1971), Rabbi Marc Tanenbaum (1972), Leon Paul (1973).

Emmanuel D'Alzon Medal (1954), by Assumptionists to persons exemplifying the ideals of their founder.

Jacques Maritain (1954), Michael F. Doyle (1955), Cardinal Richard J. Cushing (1956), Mother Mary St. Elizabeth (1956), Most Rev. John J. Wright (1959), Paolino Gerli (1960), Most Rev. Honoré van Waeyenbergh (1961), J. Peter Grace (1963), Danny Thomas (1967), Miss Mary Dowd, posthumously (1970), Most Rev. Bernard J. Flanagan (1974).

Father McKenna Award (1950), by the national headquarters of the Holy Name Society, for outstanding service to the society's ideals.

Msgr. John J. Murphy, Msgr. Henry J. Watterson, Msgr. Frederic J. Allchin (1950), Eustace Struckhoff, O.F.M., Msgr. Joseph A. McCaffrey, Msgr. Francis P. Connelly, Rev. Raymond E. Jones, Msgr. Joseph E. Maguire, Msgr. Edward J. Kelly, Msgr. J. Frederick Kriebs, Rev. Thomas E. O'Connell, Very Rev. Charles L. Elslander, Rev. Joseph J. Heim, Msgr. F. Borgias Lehr (1951);

Rev. Francis J. Hannegan (1954), Rev. Charles A. Hoot, Rev. Louis A. Hinnebusch, O.P., Rev. John O. Purcell, Rev. Paul M. Lackner (1955), Msgr. F. J. Timoney (1958),

Rev. Thomas F. McNicholas (1960), James A. Quinn, O.P., and Rev. John C. Griffith (1961), Msgr. Joseph A. Aughney (1962), Msgr. Cornelius P. Higgins (1963), Msgr. Charles P. Mynaugh (1964), Msgr. Charles P. Muth, Rev. Patrick J. Foley (1971), Rev. Msgr. Robert T. Kickham (1973), Rev. John D. Malone, O.P. (1975), Rev. John Bendix (1977).

Franciscan International Award (1958), by the Conventual Franciscans (Prior Lake, Minn.) for outstanding contributions to the American way of life.

Mr. and Mrs. Ignatius A. O'Shaughnessy (1959), Archbishop William O. Brady (1960), Lawrence Welk (1961), Charles Kellstad (1962), Dr. Finn J. Larsen (1963), Dr. Charles W. Mayo (1964), Ara Parseghian (1965), F. K. Weyerhaueser (1966);

Alcoholics Anonymous (1967), James T. Griffin (1968), George S. Harris (1969), Baroness Catherine DeHueck Doherty (1970), Harry Reasoner (1971), Dr. Billy Graham (1972), Dr. and Mrs. John C. Willke (1973), Gov. Patrick J. Lucey (1974), Joe and Jan Rigert (1975), Dr. B. F. Pearson (1976), Francis S. MacNutt, O.P. (1977), Dr. Mildred F. Jefferson (1978), Bruce Ritter, O.F.M. Conv. (1979).

Good Samaritan Award (1968), by the National Catholic Development Conference to recognize the concern for one's fellowman exemplified by the Good Samaritan.

Bishop Edward E. Swanstrom (1968), Berard Scarborough, O.F.M. (1969), Bishop Joseph B. Whelan, C.S.Sp. (1970), Mother Teresa (1971), Bishop Michael R. Dempsey (1972), Msgr. Ralph W. Beiting (1973), Rev. Daniel Egan, S.A. (1974), Dr. Isabel S. Dumont and Joan Mulder (1975), Msgr. Clement H. Kern (1976), Sister Maria Rosa Leggol, S.S.S.F. (1977), Bruce Ritter, O.F.M. Conv. (1978).

Hoey Awards (1942), by the Catholic Interracial Council of New York (225 E. 52nd St., New York, N.Y. 10022) for the promotion of interracial justice. Presented annually to two persons who have worked to promote social and interracial justice.

Frank A. Hall and Edward La Salle (1942), Philip Murray and Ralph H. Metcalfe (1943), Mrs. Edward V. Morrell and John L. Yancey (1944), Paul D. Williams and Richard Barthe (1945), Richard Reid and Charles L. Rawlings (1946), Julian J. Reiss and Clarence T. Hunter (1947), Mrs. Anna McGarry and Ferdinand L. Rousseve (1948), John J. O'Connor and M. C. Clarke (1949), J. Howard McGrath and Lou Montgomery (1950), Mrs. Roger L. Putnam and Francis M. Hammond (1951);

Charles F. Vatterot, Jr., and Joseph J. Yancey (1952), Joseph J. Morrow and John B. King (1953), Mrs. Gladys D. Woods and Collins J. Seitz (1954), Millard F. Everett and Dr. James W. Hose (1955), Frank M. Folsom and Paul G. King (1956), George Meany and James W. Dorsey (1957), James T. Harris and Robert S. Shriver, Jr. (1958), Percy H. Steele, Jr., and John P. Nelson (1959);

William Duffy, Jr., and George A. Moore (1960), Ralph Fenton and Mrs. Osma Spurlock (1961), Benjamin Muse and Dr. Eugene T. Reed (1962), James T. Carey and Percy H. Williams (1963), Arthur J. Holland and Frederick O'Neal (1964), Gerard E. Sherry and James R. Dumpson (1965), Jane M. Hoey and Mrs. Roy Wilkins (1966), Dr. Frank Horne and Lt. Gov. Malcolm Wilson (1967), E. H. Molisani and John Strachan (1968);

Harold E. McGannon and Hulan E. Jack (1969), George P. McManus, Alfred B. Del Bello, Maceo A. Thomas and Cleo Joseph L. Froix, M.D. (1970), Most Rev. Francis J. Mugavero and Most Rev. Harold R. Perry (1971), Joseph F. Crangle and Alen E. Pinado (1972), Meade H. Esposito and Robert B. Boyd (1973), Hon. Harold A. Stevens and Thomas Van Arsdale (1974), Hon. Kenneth E. Sherwood, Joseph Trerotola (1975), William M. Ellinghaus and Hon. Lucille Rose (1976), Hon. Carlos Romero Barcelo and Lena Horne (1977), J. Peter Grace and Hon. Basil A. Paterson (1978).

Honor et Veritas Award (1959), by the Catholic War Veterans to outstanding Americans.

Cardinal Francis J. Spellman (1960), Gen. Douglas MacArthur (1961), U. S. Sen. Thomas J. Dodd (1962), Gen. William Westmoreland (1966), Dean Rusk (1967), Col. Martin T. Riley (1968), Theodore M. Hesburgh, C.S.C. (1969), Kenneth D. Wells (1970), Danny Thomas (1971), Thomas V. Cuite (1972), Lawrence Welk (1973), Congressman Melvin Price (1975).

Howard R. Marraro Prize (1973), by the American Catholic Historical Association for a book on Italian history or Italo-American history or relations.

Eric W. Cochrane (1974), Silvano Tomasi (1975), Sarah Rubin Blanshei (1977), Paul F. Grendler (1978).

Insignis Medal (1951), by Fordham University for extraordinary distinction in the service of God and humanity.

Dr. Carlos Espinosa Davila, Arthur H. Hayes (1955), Pierre Harmel, Victor Andres Belaunde (1956), M. E. Michelet (1957), Daniel Linehan, S.J., Dr. Victor F. Hess (1958), Dr. George N. Shuster, John H. Tully, Albert Conway (1959), Charles F. Vatterot, Cardinal Agagianian, Charles Norman and Lucy W. Shaffer, David C. Cronin, S.J. (1960);

Cardinal Spellman (1961), Edward P. Gilleran (1962), Joseph A. Martino, William J. Tracy (1963), Brother James M. Kenny, S.J., and Austin Ripley (1966), Vincent T. Lombardi (1967), Melkite Patriarch Maximos V Hakim of Antioch (1968), Joseph and Marian

Kaiser (1970), Joseph P. Routh (1973), Edgar Debany and Cardinal Sergio Pignedoli (1975).

John Courtney Murray Award (1972), by the Catholic Theological Society for distinguished achievement in theology. Originated in 1947 as the Cardinal Spellman Award.

Rev. Charles E. Curran (1972), Bernard Lonergan, S.J. (1973), George A. Tavard, A.A. (1974), Rev. Carl Peter (1975), Rev. Richard P. McBrien (1976), Frederick E. Crowe (1977), Edward J. Kilmartin, S.J. (1978), Bernard Cooke (1979).

John Gilmary Shea Prize (1944), by the American Catholic Historical Association for scholarly works on the history of the Catholic Church broadly considered.

Carlton J. H. Hayes (1946), John H. Kennedy (1950), George W. Pare (1951), Rev. Philip Hughes (1954), Annabelle M. Melville (1955), Rev. John Tracy Ellis (1956), Rev. Thomas J. McAvoy, C.S.C. (1957), Rev. John M. Daley, S.J. (1958), Rev. Robert A. Graham, S.J. (1959);

Rev. Maynard Geiger, O.F.M. (1960), Rev. John C. Murray, S.J. (1961), Francis Dvornik (1962), Oscar Halecki (1963), Helen C. White (1964), John T. Noonan (1965), Rev. Robert I. Burns, S.J. (1966 and 1967), Rev. Edward S. Surtz, S.J. (1968), Robert Brentano (1969), David M. Kennedy (1970), Jaroslav Pelikan (1971), John T. Noonan (1972), Robert E. Quirk (1973), Bro. Thomas W. Spalding, C.F.X. (1974), Jay P. Dolan (1975), Emmet Larkin (1976), Timothy Tackett (1977), Charles W. Jones (1978).

John La Farge Memorial Award for Interracial Justice (1965), by the Catholic Interracial Council of New York. Presented annually to a leading citizen of the community regardless of race, color or creed for promoting social and interracial justice.

Cardinal Francis J. Spellman (1965), U.S. Sen. Jacob K. Javits (1966), Gov. Nelson Rockefeller (1967), George F. Meany (1968), Whitney M. Young, Jr. (1969), Harry Van Arsdale, Jr. (1970), John V. Lindsay (1971), Earl W. Brydges (1972), Louis K. Lefkowitz (1973), Arthur Levitt (1974), Robert F. Wagner (1975), Gustave L. Levy (1976), Cardinal Terence Cooke (1977), E. Howard Molisani (1978), Gov. Hugh L. Carey (1979).

King Award (1971), by the U.S. Catholic Historical Society for significant contribution in the study of the history of the Catholic Church in the U.S.

Jeremiah F. O'Sullivan (1971), Oskar Halecki (1972), Ross J. S. Hoffman (1973), Joseph G. E. Hopkins (1974), Victor L. Ridder (1975), Elisa A. Carrillo (1976).

Laetare Medal (1883), by the University of Notre Dame for distinguished accomplishment for Church or nation by an American Catholic.

John Gilmary Shea (1883), Patrick J. Keeley (1884), Eliza Allen Starr (1885), Gen. John Newton (1886), Edward Preuss (1887), Patrick V. Hickey (1888), Mrs. A. H. Dorsey (1889), William J. Onahan (1890), Daniel Dougherty (1891), Henry F. Brownson (1892);

Patrick Donahoe (1893), Augustin Daly (1894), Mrs. James Sadlier (1895), Gen. William S. Rosecrans (1896), Dr. Thomas A. Emmet (1897), Timothy E. Howard (1898), Mary G. Caldwell (1899), John Creighton (1900), William B. Cochran (1901), Dr. J. B. Murphy (1902);

Charles J. Bonaparte (1903), Richard C. Kerens (1904), Thomas B. Fitzpatrick (1905), Dr. Francis Quinlan (1906), Katherine E. Conway (1907), James C. Monaghan (1908), Frances Tiernan (Christian Reid) (1909), Maurice F. Egan (1910), Agnes Repplier (1911), Thomas M. Mulry (1912);

Charles G. Hebermann (1913), Edward Douglass White (1914), Mary V. Merrick (1915), Dr. James J. Walsh (1916), Admiral William S. Benson (1917), Joseph Scott (1918), George Duval (1919), Dr. Lawrence F. Flick (1920), Elizabeth Nourse (1921), Charles P. Neil (1922);

Walter G. Smith (1923), Charles D. Maginnis (1924), Dr. Edward F. Zahm (1925), Edward N. Hurley (1926), Margaret Anglin (1927), Jack J. Spalding (1928), Alfred E. Smith (1929), Frederick P. Kenkel (1930), James J. Phelan (1931), Dr. Stephen J. Maher (1932);

John McCormack (1933), Mrs. Nicholas F. Brady (1934), Frank Spearman (1935), Richard Reid (1936), Jeremiah Ford (1937), Dr. Irvin Abell (1938), Josephine Brownson (1939), Gen. Hugh A. Drum (1940), William T. Walsh (1941), Helen C. White (1942);

Thomas F. Woodlock (1943), Anne O'Hare McCormick (1944), G. Howland Shaw (1945), Carlton J. H. Hayes (1946), William G. Bruce (1947), Frank C. Walker (1948), Irene Dunne (Mrs. Francis Griffin) (1949), Gen. Joseph L. Collins (1950), John H. Phelan (1951), Thomas E. Murray (1952)·

I. A. O'Shaughnessy (1953), Jefferson Caffery (1954), George Meany (1955), Gen. Alfred M. Gruenther (1956), Clare Boothe Luce (1957), Frank M. Folsom (1958), Robert D. Murphy (1959), George N. Shuster (1960), Pres. John F. Kennedy (1961), Dr. Francis J. Braceland (1962);

Adm. George W. Anderson, Jr. (1963), Phyllis McGinley (1964), Frederick D. Rossini (1965), Mr. and Mrs. Patrick F. Crowley (1966), J. Peter Grace (1967), R. Sargent Shriver (1968), Justice William J. Brennan, Jr. (1969), Dr. William D. Walsh (1970), Walter and Jean Kerr (1971), Dorothy Day (1972), Rev. John A. O'Brien (1973), James A. Farley (1974), Sister Ann Ida Gannon, B.V.M. (1975), Paul Horgan (1976), Mike Mansfield

(1977), Msgr. John Tracy Ellis (1978), Helen Hayes (1979).

Marianist Award (1949), by the University of Dayton for outstanding service in America to the Mother of God (until 1966); for outstanding contributions to mankind (from 1967).

Juniper Carol, O.F.M. (1950), Daniel A. Lord, S.J. (1951), Patrick J. Peyton, C.S.C. (1952), Roger Brien, S.G.G. (1953), Emil Neubert, S.M. (1954), Joseph A. Skelly, C.M. (1955), Frank Duff (1956), Eugene F. Kennedy and John McShain (1957), Winifred A. Feely (1958), Abp. John F. Noll (1959), Eamon R. Carroll, O. Carm. (1960), Coley Taylor (1961), Abbe Rene Laurentin (1963), Philip C. Hoelle, S.M. (1964), Cyril O. Vollert, S.J. (1965), Eduardo Frei Montalvo (1967).

Marian Library Medal (1953), by the Marian Library of the University of Dayton for books in English on the Blessed Virgin Mary. Awarded every four years (from 1971), at the time of an International Mariological Congress, to a scholar for Mariological studies.

Most Rev. Fulton J. Sheen (1953), Msgr. John S. Kennedy (1954), Rev. William G. Most (1955), Ruth Cranston (1956), Juniper Carol, O.F.M. (1957), Donald C. Sharkey and Joseph Debergh, O.M.I. (1958); Edward O'Connor, C.S.C. (1959), John J. Delaney (1960), Sister Mary Pierre, S.M. (1961), Marion A. Habig, O.F.M. (1962), Titus F. Cranny, S.A. (1963), Hilda C. Graef (1964), Edward Schillebeeckx, O.P. (1965), Cyril Vollert, S.J. (1966), Thomas O'Meara, O.P. (1967), Charles Balic, O. F. M. (1971), Giuseppe M. Besutti (1975).

Mater et Magistra Award (1963), by the College of Mt. St. Joseph on the Ohio to women for social action in the pattern and spirit of the encyclical *Mater et Magistra.*

Jane Hoey (1964), Mary Dolan (1965), Mrs. Anne Fremantle (1966), Margaret Mealey (1967), Mrs. Arthur L. Zepf, Sr. (1968), Alice R. May (1969), Mother Teresa (1974).

Mendel Medal (1928), by Villanova University for scientists.

Dr. John A. Kolmer (1929), Dr. Albert F. Zahm (1930), Dr. Karl F. Herzfeld (1931), Dr. Francis P. Garvan (1932), Dr. Hugh Stott Taylor (1933), Abbe Georges Lemaitre (1934), Dr. Francis Owen Rice (1935), Rev. Julius A. Nieuwland, C.S.C. (1936), Pierre Teilhard de Chardin, S.J. (1937), Dr. Thomas Parran (1938);

Rev. John M. Cooper (1939), Dr. Peter J W. Debye (1940), Dr. Eugene M. K. Geiling (1941), Dr. Joseph A. Becker (1942), Dr. George Speri Sperti (1943), Dr. John C. Hubbard (1946), Frank N. Piasecki (1954), James B. Macelwane, S.J. (1955), Dr. William J. Thaler (1960), Dr. James A. Shannon (1961), Maj. Robert M. White (1963), D- Charles A. Hufnagel (1965), Dr. Alfred M. Bongiovanni (1968).

Msgr. John P. Monaghan Social Action Award by the Assn. of Catholic Trade Unionists; originally (1948), the Quadragesimo Anno Medal.

John Quincy Adams (1948), Brother Justin, F.S.C. (1949), Joseph Bierne (1950), Rev. Raymond A. McGowan (1951), Philip Murray (1952), Charles M. Halloran (1953), U.S. Sen. Robert F. Wagner, Sr. (1954), Rev. John P. Monaghan (1955), John C. Cort (1956), Msgr. Joseph F. Connolly (1957);

George Meany (1958), Robert F. Kennedy (1959), Thomas Carey (1960), James B. Carey (1961), Rev. Joseph Hammond (1966), Paul Jennings (1967), Matthew Guinan (1968), David Sullivan (1969), Vincent McDonnell (1970).

The O'Neill D'Amour Award (1976), by the National Association of Boards of Education/NCEA, for outstanding contribution of statewide, regional, national or international significance to the Catholic board movement.

Rev. Msgr. Olin J. Murdick (1977).

Peace Award (1950), by the Secular Franciscan Order.

Myron C. Taylor (1950), John Foster Dulles (1951), John W. McCormack (1952), John C. Wu (1953), Ralph Bunche (1954), John R. Gariepy (1956), Most Rev. Richard J. Cushing (1957), Patrick McGeehan, Sr. (1958), Victor Andres Belaunde (1959), J. Edgar Hoover (1960), George K. Hunton (1961);

Mrs. Lester Auberlin (1962), Rev. Martin Luther King (1963), Most Rev. John J. Wright (1964), Pope Paul VI (1965), Cardinal Wyszynski (1966), Bishop Fred Pierce Corson (1967), Robert F. Kennedy, posthumously (1968), Msgr. Robert Fox (1969), Bishop James Walsh, M.M. (1970), Jean Vanier (1972), Mother Teresa of Calcutta (1974), Dom Helder Camara (1975), Archbishop Joseph L. Bernardin (1976), Jose Francisco Garcia Bauer (1977), Manuella Mattioli (1978).

Peter Guilday Prize (1972), by the American Catholic Historical Association for articles accepted by the editors of the *Catholic Historical Review* which are the first scholarly publications of their authors.

James P. Gaffey (1972), B. Robert Kreiser (1974), J. Dean O'Donnell, Jr. (1976), Mark A. Gabbert (1977), Virginia W. Leonard (1978).

Pius XII Marian Award (1955), by the Montfort Missionaries for promotion of the devotion of consecration to the Immaculate Heart of Mary.

Denis M. McAuliffe, O.P. (1955), James M. Keane, O.S.M. (1956), Rev. John Cantwell (1957), Marie Delicia Unson (1958), Rev. Herman J. Vincent of St. Henry's Parish, Bridge City, Tex., and parishioners of

Awards

St. Helen's Mission, Orangefield, Tex. (1959), Leo Dillon (1960), De Montfort Groups of Detroit, Mich., and Rev. Thomas Kerwin, their spiritual director (1961), Frank Duff (1965), Mr. and Mrs. Thomas F. Larkin, Jr. (1973).

Poverello Medal (1949), by The College of Steubenville (Ohio), "in recognition of great benefactions to humanity, exemplifying in our age the Christ-like spirit of charity which filled the life of St. Francis of Assisi."

Alcoholics Anonymous Fellowship (1949), Edward F. Hutton (1950), the Court of Last Resort, New York, N.Y. (1951), The Lions International (1952), Variety Clubs International (1953), Llewellyn J. Scott (1954), Dr. Jonas E. Salk and Associates (1955), Mother Anna Dengel (1956), Catherine de Hueck Doherty (1957), D. M. Hamill (1958);

Daniel W. Egan, T.O.R. (1959, posthumously), Mrs. Emma C. Zeis (1960), Donald H. McGannon (1961), Jane Wyatt (1962), Birgit Nilsson (1963), Arthur Joseph Rooney (1964), Joe E. Brown (1965), Project Hope (1966), Lena F. Edwards, M.D. (1967), VISTA (1968), Jack Twyman (1969), The Salvation Army (1970), Most Rev. John K. Mussio (1971). Bro. George J. Hungerman, F.M.S.I., M.D. (1972), The Dismas Committee of the St. Vincent de Paul Society (1973) U.S. Sen Mark O. Hatfield (1974), Sr. Mary Agatha, O.S.F., and Rev Kevin R. Keelan, T.O.R. (1975), Mother Teresa of Calcutta (1976), Dorothy Day (1977), Leon Jaworski (1978).

Regina Medal (1959), by the Catholic Library Association for outstanding contributions to children's literature.

Eleanor Farjeon (1959), Anne Carroll Moore (1960), Padraic Colum (1961), Frederick G. Melcher (1962), Ann Nolan Clark (1963), May Hill Arbuthnot (1964), Ruth Sawyer Durand (1965), Leo Politi (1966), Bertha Mahoney Miller (1967), Marguerite de Angeli (1968), Lois Lenski (1969), Ingri and Edgar Parin d'Aulaire (1970), Tasha Tudor (1971) Miendert DeJong (1972); Frances Clarke Sayers (1973), Robert McCloskey (1974), Lynd Ward and May McNeer (1975), Virginia Haviland (1976), Marcia Brown (1977), Scott O'Dell (1978), Morton Schindel (1979).

Rerum Novarum Award (1949), by St. Peter's College (Jersey City, N. J.) for outstanding work in the interests of industrial peace.

Raymond Reiss (1949), Justin McAghon (1950), Frederick W. Mansfield (1951), Most Rev. Karl J. Alter (1952), Martin P. Durkin (1953), Christopher W. Hoey (1954), James P. Mitchell (1955), George Meany (1956), Henry Ford II (1957), Hugh E. Sheridan (1958);

Joseph F. Finnegan (1959), Cardinal Richard Cushing (1960), Joseph D. Keenan (1961), (no award 1962), Louis C. Seaton (1963).

Richard Reid Memorial Award (1963), by the Catholic Institute of the Press (now the Catholic Alliance for Communications) in memory of its cofounder.

Thomas A. Brennan (1963), James A. Connolly (1964), John J. Sheehan (1965), Arthur Hull Hays (1966), Victor L. Ridder (1968), Bob Considine (1969).

The Saint De La Salle Medal, by Manhattan College, for significant contribution to the moral, cultural or educational life of the nation.

John F. Brosnan (1951), Cardinal Francis Spellman (1952), Most Rev. Joseph P. Donahue (1953), Most Rev. Edwin V. O'Hara, posthumously (1950), Sr. Mary Emil, I.H.M. (1957), Msgr. Joseph E. Schieder (1958), Very Rev. Bro. Bertrand, O.S.F. (1959), Dr. Roy J. Deferrari (1960).

John Courtney Murray, S.J. (1961), Bro. Clair Stanislaus, F.S.C. (1962), Most Rev. Bryan J. McEntegart (1963), Sr. M. Rose Eileen, C.S.C. (1964), Mother Kathryn Sullivan, R.S.C.J. (1965), Bro. Bernard Peter, F.S.C. (1966), Dr. William Hughes Mulligan (1967), C. Alfred Koob, O. Praem. (1968), Theodore M. Hesburgh, C.S.C. (1970), Most Rev. Edwin B. Broderick (1971), Very Rev. Bro. Charles Henry, F.S.C. (1972), Mary Shea Giordano (1973), Dorothy Day (1974), Henry Viscardi, Jr. (1975), Sister Elinor R. Ford, O.P. (1976), John D. de Butts (1977), Thomas A. Murphy (1978), Gabriel Hauge (1979).

St. Francis de Sales Award (1959), by the Catholic Press Association for distinguished contribution to Catholic journalism.

Dale Francis (1959), Frank A. Hall (1960), John C. Murray, S.J. (1961), Albert J. Nevins, M.M. (1962), Floyd Anderson (1963), Rev. Patrick O'Connor (1964), John Cogley (1965), Joseph Breig (1966), John Reedy, C.S.C. (1967), Bishop James P. Shannon (1968), no award (1969), Msgr. Robert G. Peters (1970), Francis A. Fink (1971), Jeremy Harrington, O.F.M. (1972), Robert E. Burns (1973), Gerard E. Sherry (1974), John B. Sheerin, C.S.P. (1975), Lillian R. Block (1976), A.E.P. Wall (1977), Donald Thorman, posthumously (1978), Walter J. Burghardt, S.J. (1979).

St. Francis Xavier Medal (1954), by Xavier University (Cincinnati) to persons exemplifying the spirit of St. Francis Xavier.

Most Rev. Fulton J. Sheen, Rev. Leo Kampsen, Msgr. Frederick G. Hochwalt (1954), James Keller, M.M. (1955), Gen. Carlos P. Romulo (1956), Stan Musial, Aloysius A. Breen, S.J., Edwin G. Becker (1957), Msgr. (Maj. Gen.) Patrick J. Ryan, Msgr. (Maj. Gen.) Terrence P. Finnegan, Msgr. (Rear Adm.) George A. Rosso (1958);

T. L. Bouscaren, S.J. and Dr. Thomas A. Dooley (1959), Neal Ahern and Celestine J. Steiner, S.J. (1960), Philip J. Scharper (1961), Charles Dismas Clark, S.J. (1962), Pres. John F. Kennedy (posthumously) and J. Paul Spaeth (1963), James B. Donovan (1964), Charles H. Keating, Jr. (1965), Frank Blair (1967), Martin H. Work (1968), Lt. Col. William A. Anders and Archbishop Karl J. Alter (1969), Bishop James E. Walsh, M.M. (1970), Lawrence Welk, Rev. Msgr. Ralph W. Beiting (1971), Paul L. O'Connor, S.J. (1972), James F. Maguire, S.J., Edward P. VonderHaar (posthumously) (1973), G. Milton Wurzelbacher (1974), D. J. O'Conor (posthumously) (1975), Bishop John K. Mussio (1977), C. Robert Beirne and George H. Brueggeman (1978).

St. Vincent de Paul Medal (1948), by St. John's University (Jamaica, N.Y.), for outstanding service to Catholic charities.

Francis D. McGarey (1948), John A. Coleman (1949), Aloysius L. Fitzpatrick (1950), Frank J. Lewis (1951), Howard W. Fitzpatrick (1952), Richard F. Mulroy (1953), Harry J. Kirk (1954), Bernard J. Keating (1955), John M. Nolan (1956), John R. Gariepy (1957);

Charles E. McCarthy (1958), Frederick V. Goess (1959), Maurice J. Costello, M.D. (1960), Thomas F. Hanley (1961), John J. Lynch (1962), William H. Walters (1963), George E. Heneghan (1964), James A. Quigney (1965), Henry J. Shields (1966);

Eugene McGovern (1967), George J. Krygier (1968), James A. Cousins (1969), Edward T. Reilly (1970), T. Raber Taylor (1971), Luke J. Smith (1972), William C. Rohrkemper (1973), Edward V. Murtaugh (1974), Frank V. Buckley (1975), Martin J. Loftus (1976), John F. Coppinger (1977).

Serra Award of the Americas (1947), by the Academy of American Franciscan History for service to Inter-American good will.

Sumner Welles (1947), Pablo Martinez del Rio (1948), Dr. Herbert E. Bolton (1949), Gabriela Mistral (1950), Carlos E. Castaneda (1951), Victor A. Belaunde (1952), Clarence Haring (1953), Alceu Amoroso Lima (1954), France V. Scholes (1956);

Silvio Zavala (1957), John Tate Lanning (1958), John Basadre (1959), Arthur Preston Whitaker (1960), Marcel Bataillon (1961), Javier Malagon y Barcelo (1962), Dr. George P. Hammond (1964), Augustin Millares Carlo (1970), Max Savelle (1976), Miguel Leon-Portilla (1978).

Signum Fidei Medal (1942), by the Alumni Association of La Salle College (Phila.) for noteworthy contributions to the advancement of humanitarian principles in keeping with Christian tradition.

Brother E. Anselm, F.S.C. (1942), Karl H. Rogers (1943), Very Rev. Edward V. Stanford, O.S.A. (1944), Mrs. Edward V. Morrell (1945), Cardinal Dennis Dougherty (1946), Max Jordan (1947), John J. Sullivan (1948), Dr. Louis H. Clerf (1949), Most Rev. Gerald P. O'Hara (1950), Most Rev. Fulton J. Sheen (1951);

John H. Harris (1952), James Keller, M.M. (1953), John M. Haffert (1954), Dr. Francis J. Braceland (1955), Matthew H. McCloskey (1956), Henry Viscardi, Jr. (1957), no award (1958), Dr. Joseph J. Toland, Jr. (1959), Luke E. Hart (1960), Joseph E. McCafferty (1961);

Martin H. Work (1962), R. Sargent Shriver (1963), Mother M. Benedict, M.D. (1964), Sen. Eugene McCarthy (1965), William B. Ball (1966), Frank Folsom (1967), Rev. Leon H. Sullivan (1968), Rev. William J. Finley (1969);

Dr. James W. Turpin (1970), Lisa A. Richette, Esq. (1971), Rev. Melvin Floyd (1972), Elwood E. Kieser, C.S.P. (1973), Msgr. Philip J. Dowling (1974), James C. Giuffre, M.D. (1975), Most Rev. Bernard J. Topel (1976), Mildred Jefferson, M.D. (1977), Judge Genevieve Blatt (1978), Rita Ungaro Schiavone (1979).

Soteriological Award (1967), by the Confraternity of the Passion (Third Order of the Passionists, St. Michael's Monastery, Union City, N.J.) for outstanding exemplification of sharing in the Passion of Christ in contemporary society.

Most Rev. Cuthbert M. O'Gara, C.P. (1967), Mrs. Martin Luther King, Jr. (1968), Veronica's Veil Players (1969), Mother Mary Teresa Benedetti, C.P. (1970), Dr. Billy Graham (1971), Mrs. Flo Kuhn (1972), Rev. Martin J. Tooker, C.P. (1973), Mrs. Mary Sloan (1974), Aileen Leary (1975), Marie Gallagher (1976), Grete Faber and Georgianna Wendt (1977), Regina Adamecz (1978).

Stella Maris Medal (1960), by Mary Manse College (Toledo, O.) for service.

Alice R. May (1960), Emma Endres Kountz (1961), Elizabeth M. Zepf (1962), Judge Geraldine F. Macelwane (1963), Ven. Mother Mary Adelaide, O.S.F. (1964), Marian Rejent, M.D. (1966), Mrs. Irene Hubbard McCarthy (1967), Sr. Ruth Hickey, S.G.M. (1969), Mrs. Ella Phillips Stewart (1970), Sr. M. Lawrence Wilson (1971), Mrs. Carol Pietrykowski (1972), Miss Rita O'Grady (1973), Mildred L. Bayer, R.N. (1975).

Sword of Loyola (1964), by Loyola University of Chicago to person or persons exemplifying Ignatius of Loyola's courage, dedication and service.

J. Edgar Hoover (1964), Col. James McDivitt and Maxime A. Faget (1965), Lt. Dieter Dengler (1966), Brig. Gen. David Sarnoff (1967), Capt. Edward V. Rickenbacker (1968), Dr. Thomas O. Paine and William A. Anders (1969), Most Rev. Fulton I Sheen (1970), Helen Hayes (1971), James F. Maguire, S.J. (1972), Mr. and Mrs Foster G.

McGaw (1973), John F. Smith, Jr. (1974), Bob Newhart (1975), Arthur Fiedler (1976), Mildred F. Jefferson, M.D. (1977), Rev. Vincent T. O'Keefe, S.J. (1978).

Thomas More Association Medal (1954), by the Thomas More Association for distinguished contribution to Catholic literature during the year.

Doubleday and Co., Inc. (1954), Alfred A. Knopf, Inc. (1955), P. J. Kenedy and Sons, Inc. (1956), Farrar, Straus and Cudahy, Inc. (1957), Hawthorn Books (1958), Sheed and Ward, Inc. (1959), J. B. Lippincott Co. (1960), Doubleday and Co., Inc. (1961), Random House, Inc. (1962);

William Morrow and Co., Inc. (1963), Harper and Row (1964), Farrar, Straus and Giroux (1965), Doubleday and Co., Inc. (1966), Herder and Herder (1967), Hans Kueng (1968), John L. McKenzie, S.J. (1969), Daniel Callahan (1970). Daniel Berrigan, S.J. (1971), Andrew Greeley and Eugene Kennedy, M.M. (1972), Graham Greene (1973), Piers Paul Read (1974), John J. Delaney (1975), Tom McHale (1976), Andrew Greeley (1977), Eugene Kennedy (1978).

U.S. Catholic Award (1978), by editors of *U.S. Catholic* magazine for furthering the cause of women in the Church.

Sr. Agnes Cunningham, S.S.C.M. (1978), Sr. Marjorie Tuite, O.P. (1979).

Vercelli Medal (1947), by the Holy Name Society for distinguished service to ideals of the society.

William Bruce, Paul M. Brennan, Joseph Scott, Stephen Barry, Patrick Kennedy (1947), R. W. Hoogstraet (1948), William H. Collins (1949), Ward D. Hopkins (1950), Charles A. Burkholder, James C. Connell, James T. Vocelle, Edwin J. Allen, Fred A. Muth, Austin J. Roche, Michael Lawlor (1951), Michael L. Roche (1953), Maurice J. O'Sullivan, Lucien T. Vivien, Jr. (1954);

John A. Lee, Sr., Daniel M. Hamill, Clarence F. Boggan, Louis J. Euler, Henry J. McGreevy, Ralph F. Nunlist (1955), James J. McDonnell (1957), Joseph J. Wilson (1958), William J. Meehan (1959), Paul Meade (1960), William T. Tavares (1961), David M. Martin (1962), Bert M. Walz (1963), Herbert Michelbrook (1964), Alfred A. McGarraghy (1965), Frank J. Beuerlein (1968), Humbert J. Campana (1970), Richard Asmus (1971), Charles J. Little (1973), William J. Burke, Jr. (1974), Stephen Andrusisian (1975), James P. Bailey (1976), Lanaux Marston (1977).

DEATHS OCTOBER 1, 1978 TO OCTOBER 1, 1979

Baldwin, Bishop Vincent J., 72, Sept. 16, West Islip, N.Y.; auxiliary bishop of Rockville Centre from 1962.

Barbieri, Cardinal Antonio Maria, O.F.M. Cap., 86, July 6, Montevideo, Uruguay; retired archbishop (1940-76) of Montevideo; first Uruguayan cardinal, 1958.

Bartlett, Dewey, 59, Mar. 1, Tulsa, Okla.; Republican senator from Oklahoma, 1972-78; supported and initiated pro-life, energy, national defense measures.

Boland, Paschal, O.S.B., 67, Apr. 1, St. Meinrad, Ind.; general manager of Abbey Press, 1944-55, 1968-76; editor; syndicated columnist.

Boland, Archbishop Thomas A., 83, Mar. 16, Orange, N.J.; archbishop of Newark from 1953 to 1974, when he retired.

Bruening, Rev. Paul, 50, Dec. 23, 1978, Nashville, Ill.; pastor, prison chaplain, teacher; killed in automobile accident while on Christmas rounds to shut-ins.

Callan, Josephine McGarry, 95, November, 1978, Washington, D.C.; a founder of drama department at Catholic Univeristy of America; noted speech coach.

Catich, Rev. Edward M., 73, Apr. 14, Davenport, Iowa; award-winning graphic artist; calligrapher.

Childs, Frederick R., 70, Dec. 25, 1978, Stamford, Conn.; post-impressionist artist.

Connolly, Msgr. Matthew, 64, Apr. 10, San Francisco, Calif.; San Francisco port chaplain.

Coury, George, 73, Jan. 4, Miami, Fla.; investment broker and civic leader; philanthropist.

Cunningham, Bishop David F., 78, Feb. 22, Syracuse, N.Y.; bishop of Syracuse from 1970 to 1976, when he retired.

Daly, Mary Tinley, 75, Mar. 13, Washington, D.C.; author; wrote syndicated column on family life; 1951 recipient of Magnificat Medal.

DeFalco, Bishop Lawrence M., 64, Sept. 22, Amarillo, Tex.; bishop of Amarillo from 1963 to Aug. 28, 1979, when he retired.

Delargey, Cardinal Reginald, 64, Jan. 29, Wellington, New Zealand; archbishop of Wellington from 1974; cardinal from 1976.

De Riedmatten, Rev. Henri, O.P., 60, Apr. 9, Rome, Italy; Swiss-born secretary of *Cor Unum,* Vatican coordinating agency for Catholic relief organizations.

Dhanis, Rev. Edouard, S.J., 76, Dec. 17, 1978, Rome, Italy; Belgian theologian; important figure at Second Vatican Council.

DiJorio, Cardinal Alberto, 95, Sept. 5, Rome, Italy; oldest member of college of cardinals; Roman Curia official from 1918 to 1968, when he retired; cardinal from 1958.

Donovan, Rev. John F., M.M., 73, Nov. 28, 1978, Hong Kong; missionary; former vicar general of Maryknoll.

DuVigneaud, Dr. Vincent, 77, Dec. 11, 1978, White Plains, N.Y.; biochemist; awarded 1955 Nobel Prize for chemistry for his work on hormones.

Empie, Rev. Paul, 70, Sept. 1, Zionsville, Pa.; leading Lutheran ecumenist, co-chair-

Filipiak, Cardinal Boleslaw, 77, Oct. 12, 1978, Poznan, Poland; dean of the Sacred Roman Rota, 1967-76; cardinal from 1976.

Fontana, Dr. Mario, 75, Aug. 7, Rome, Italy; personal physician to Popes John XXIII, Paul VI and John Paul I.

Frings, Cardinal Joseph, 91, Dec. 17, 1978, Cologne, Germany; archbishop of Cologne from 1942 to 1969, when he retired; cardinal from 1946.

Furey, Archbishop Francis J., 74, Apr. 23, San Antonio, Tex.; archbishop of San Antonio from 1969.

Gomez Marijuan, Bishop Francisco, C.M.F., 70, January; Salamanca, Spain; missionary in Equatorial Guinea from 1931 to 1971, when he was expelled; bishop of Malabo, Equatorial Guinea, 1958 to 1974, when he resigned.

Granahan, Kathryn O'Hay, 83, July 10, Norristown, Pa.; Democratic congresswoman from Pennsylvania, 1956-62; U.S. treasurer, 1963-66.

Hellegers, Dr. Andre, 52, May 8, Uithoorn, Netherlands; Dutch-born gynecologist; bioethicist; founder and director of Kennedy Institute of Ethics at Georgetown University.

Loeven, Rev. Paul C., C.M., 62, Aug. 23, Cape May, N.J.; chaplain at Seton Shrine, Emmitsburg, Md.

McCarthy, Rev. Raphael, S.J., 92, September, St. Louis, Mo.; former college president; psychology professor emeritus, St. Louis Univ.

McDade, Sister Mary Teresa Francis, S.C., 75, Dec. 11, 1978, Dubuque, Iowa; education professor emeritus, Clark College, Dubuque.

McIntyre, Cardinal James Francis, 83, July 16, Los Angeles, Calif.; archbishop of Los Angeles from 1948 to 1970, when he retired; cardinal from 1953.

McLaughlin, Bishop Charles B., 65, Dec. 14, 1978, St. Petersburg, Fla.; first bishop of St. Petersburg, 1968.

Manion, Clarence E., 83, July 28, South Bend, Ind.; dean of University of Notre Dame Law School 1925-52; author.

Marique, Rev. Joseph, S.J., 79, Apr. 9, Worcester, Mass.; editor and founder of *Classical Folia*; founder of Institute for Early Christian Iberian Studies, Holy Cross College.

Mazzarella, Bishop Bernardino, O.F.M., 75, May 30, Comayagua, Honduras; missionary in Central America; bishop of Comayagua from 1963.

Metcalfe, Rep. Ralph H., 68, October, 1978, Chicago, Ill.; Democratic congressman from Illinois; a founding member of Congressional Black Caucus; silver and gold medalist in 1936 Olympics.

Meyer, Rev. Cyril F., C.M., 78, Feb. 4, Germantown, Pa.; provincial director of education of eastern province of Vincentian Fathers.

Meir, Golda, 80, Dec. 8, 1978, Jerusalem, Jewish leader; Israeli prime minister, and head of Labor Party, 1969-74.

Miller, Don, 77, July 29, Cleveland, Ohio; U.S. attorney; retired Bankruptcy Court judge; one of legendary "Four Horsemen" of Notre Dame.

Murphy, Rev. Patrick, S.V.D., 51, Dec. 12, 1978, Port Moresby, New Guinea; Australian theologian, ecumenical adviser to Catholic Bishops' Conference of Papua New Guinea.

Morgan, Neville J., 55, May 1, Washington, D.C.; general manager and co-founder of *Catholic Standard*, Washington archdiocesan paper.

Nervi, Pier Luigi, 87, Jan. 9, Rome, Italy; architect; designed Vatican audience hall, San Francisco Cathedral.

Nevins, Rev. Joseph V., S.S., 95, July 22, Baltimore, Md.; oldest Supician priest in U.S.

O'Malley, Walter, 75, Aug. 9, Los Angeles, Calif., less than a month after the death of his wife, Kay O'Malley, who died July 12 at 72; board chairman of Los Angeles Dodgers.

Ottaviani, Cardinal Alfredo, 88, Aug. 3, Vatican City; prefect emeritus of Congregation for the Doctrine of Faith which he headed, 1959-68; cardinal from 1953.

Randolph, A. Philip, 90, May 16, Washington, D.C.; Methodist; black civil rights leader; organized first black labor union in U.S.

Sands, Rev. John D., 46, May, Littletown, N.H. director of Alpha House, a home for delinquent boys; killed by former mental patient and wife who took over St. Rose of Lima rectory.

Schmondiuk, Archbishop Joseph, 66, Dec. 25, 1978, Philadelphia, Pa.; Ukrainian-Rite archbishop of Philadelphia from 1977.

Tarpey, Mother Mary Columba, 87, Aug. 27, Ossining, N.Y.; head of Maryknoll Sisters, 1946-58; subject of *Time* cover story Apr. 11, 1975.

Trin-Nhu-Khue, Cardinal Joseph-Marie, 78, Nov. 27, 1978, Hanoi, Vietnam; archbishop of Hanoi from 1960; cardinal from 1976.

Tunney, Gene, 80, Nov. 7, 1978, Greenwich, Conn.; businessman; former boxer, retired as undefeated world heavyweight champion, 1929.

Villot, Cardinal Jean, 73, Mar. 9, Rome, Italy; French cardinal; Vatican secretary of state under three popes; handled operations of Church during interim periods between papal reigns in 1978 and presided over conclaves; cardinal from 1965.

Walen, Msgr. Joseph C., 66, March, Grand Rapids, Mich.; founding editor of *The Western Michigan Catholic*.

Wright, Cardinal John, 70, Aug. 10, Cambridge, Mass.; prefect of Congregation for the clergy; highest ranking American in Roman Curia; cardinal from 1969.